Microsoft®
ENCARTA®
DICTIONARY

St. Martin's Paperbacks

A BLOOMSBURY REFERENCE BOOK

Created from the Bloomsbury Database of World English

First published in the United States of America in 2002 by
St. Martin's Press
175 Fifth Avenue
New York, NY 10010

Library of Congress Cataloging-in-Publication Data is available on request.

ISBN 0-312-98362-X

Typeset by Selwood Systems, Midsomer Norton, Radstock, United Kingdom
Printed in the United States of America

US General Editor
Anne H. Soukhanov

Executive Editor
Susan Jellis

Senior Lexicographer
Lesley Brown

Senior Editor
Rosalind Fergusson

Editors
David Barnett
Carol Braham
Bob Clevenger
Scott Forbes
David Hallworth
Stephen Handorf
Ruth Hein
Ann-Marie Imbornoni
Julie Plier
Howard Sargeant
Ian Spackman
Donald Watt
Pamela White

Science and Technical Editors
Alan D. Levy
James E. Shea

Word Histories
Lesley Brown

Phonetics
Dinah Jackson

Usage Notes
Rosalind Fergusson
Anne H. Soukhanov

Special Contributors
Andrew Harnack,
Foundation Professor,
Department of English,
Eastern Kentucky
University

Gene Kleppinger,
Information Technology
and Delivery Services,
Eastern Kentucky
University

Project Manager
Katy McAdam

Project Assistants
Charlotte Regan
Joel Adams

Design
Nigel Partridge
Nathan Burton

Proofreaders
Sandra Anderson
Pat Bulhosen
Josephine M. P. Curtis
Isabel Griffiths
Ruth Hillmore
Irene Lakhani
Jill Leatherbarrow
Adèle Linderholm
Susan Turner

Keyboarders
Simon Arnold
Dan Cosserat
Katherine Hill
Rebecca McKee
Lisa Milford

BLOOMSBURY REFERENCE

Editor-in-Chief
Dr. Kathy Rooney

Publisher
Nigel Newton

Dictionaries Publisher
Faye Carney

Production Director
Penny Edwards

Database Manager
Edmund Wright

Production Editor
Nicky Thompson

Using Your Dictionary

Entry word

ab·bot /ábbət/ *n* the head of a monastery
—**ab·bot·ship** *n*

Biographical entry

Ab·bott /ábbət/, **Berenice** (1898–1991) US
photographer

Cross-reference to more common spelling

ABC *n UK* = ABCs *npl* ◊ **as easy as ABC**
extremely easy

Regional label   Set phrase

Inflected form   Style label

a·bide /ə bíd/ (**a·bode** /ə bṓd/ *or* **a·bid·ed**,
a·bid·ing) *v* **1** *vt* tolerate ○ *I can't abide disobedient children.* **2** *vi* dwell *(archaic)*
—□ **abide by** *vt* follow or accept a rule or decision

Phrasal (two-word) verb

Geographical entry

Ab·i·lene /ábbə leèn/ city in central Texas.
Pop. 108,257 (1998).

Definition number   Definition

a·bil·i·ty /ə bíllətee/ *n* **1** the state of being able
to do something **2** skill, talent, or intelligence

SYNONYMS **ability, skill, competence, aptitude, talent, capacity, capability** CORE
MEANING: the necessary skill, knowledge, or
experience to do something

Synonyms note

Example of use   Derived word

ab·ject /áb jèkt, ab jékt/ *adj* **1** extremely bad
or unpleasant ○ *abject poverty* **2** despicable
○ *abject cruelty* —**ab·jec·tion** /ab jéksh'n/ *n*
—**ab·ject·ly** *adv*

Inflected form

a·ble /áyb'l/ (**a·bler**, **a·blest**) *adj* **1** in a position
to do something **2** capable or talented
—**a·bly** *adv* ◊ See note at **intelligent**

Cross-reference to boxed note

Triangle warning of disputed usage

ab·o·rig·i·ne /ábbə ríjjənee/ *n* **1** ⚠ an original
inhabitant of a place *(often offensive)* **2** an
animal or plant that has existed in a place
since the earliest times **3** **Aborigine** an original inhabitant of Australia

USAGE Avoid the use of **aborigine** without a
capital letter to refer to a person who has
lived in an area from the earliest known times.

Usage note   Usage label

Word origins note

a·bove·board /ə bùv báwrd/ *adj* honest and
legal —**a·bove·board** *adv*

ORIGIN Aboveboard was originally a gambling
term indicating that a player's hands were
above the gaming table, or "board," and concealed nothing.

Incorrect spelling

~~abreviation~~ incorrect spelling of **abbreviation**

Pronunciation

ac·a·de·mi·a /ákə deèmee ə/, **ac·a·de·me** /ákə
deèm/ *n* academic life

Alternate form of entry word

Symbol for hi-tech term

⚡**ac·cess** /ák sèss/ *n* **1** a means of entry or
approach ○ *gained access via an upstairs
window* **2** the right or opportunity to use
something or meet somebody ■ *vt* **1** enter
a place **2** retrieve data from a computer

SPELLCHECK Do not confuse the spelling of
access and **excess** ("a surplus"), which
sound similar.

Spellcheck note   New part of speech

Symbols in this Dictionary

□ marks phrasal (two- or three-word) verbs
■ marks new part of speech
○ marks examples of use
◇ marks set phrases
= cross-refers to more common spelling

◊ cross-refers to related entry or boxed note
♦ cross-refers to name of person or place
⚡ marks high-tech terms
⚠ marks a disputed usage

Introduction to the Internet

Andrew Harnack and Gene Kleppinger

THE WORLD WIDE WEB (WWW) emerged in the 1990s as the most popular interface used to gather Internet information. Its availability through personal computers has brought the realm of information out of library reference rooms to every home and office. This article provides some basic guidelines to finding and evaluating online information, and observing accepted standards of online communication, or "netiquette."

Conducting effective online searches

When you conduct a search, the terms you enter are called *keywords*, and the results you obtain are called *hits*. Most search tools permit you to specify relations between keywords in the following ways:

- Enclose your keywords in quotation marks when you want to search for an entire phrase.
- Use an asterisk to denote words having a common stem so that your hits contain occurrences of various forms of that keyword. For example, searching for *millenni** will produce hits that contain *millennia, millennium, millennial,* etc.
- Use lowercase unless you want to restrict your hits to contain a specific capitalized form.
- Use connecting words or symbols, called Boolean operators, to restrict your search. Common Boolean operators are the words AND, OR, NOT, and NEAR. For example, when you submit the expression *"piano sonata" and beethoven,* you tell the search tool that you want pages containing both of these terms. But when you type *"piano sonata" and not beethoven,* you can expect hits that contain the first term but exclude the second. Some search tools substitute symbols for these operators, such as the plus sign for AND and the minus sign for NOT. See the Help screen for your search tool to find the format you should use.

Evaluating the reliability of an Internet source

Once you have accessed your chosen sites, you need to be ready to judge the quality of their content. Elizabeth Kirk summarizes this evaluation process in "Evaluating Information Found on the Internet" at <http://www.library.jhu.edu/elp/useit/evaluate/ >. She identifies six major criteria for evaluating all forms of information: authorship, publishing body, point of view or bias, referral to other sources, accuracy and verifiability, and up-to-dateness.

The following sites also offer cogent advice on how best to evaluate the information on websites:

- **Evaluating Web Resources**
  <http://www2.widener.edu/Wolfgram-Memorial-Library/webevaluation/webeval.htm>
- **Evaluating Websites: Criteria and Tools**
  <http://www.library.cornell.edu/okuref/research/webeval.html>
- **Thinking Critically about World Wide Web Resources**
  <http://www.library.ucla.edu/libraries/college/help/critical/index.htm>

Basic online "netiquette" and ethical codes

When writing or communicating within online environments, you are encouraged to observe commonly accepted standards of behavior, known generally as netiquette:

When composing web documents

1. Avoid plagiarism by acknowledging your web sources. Be aware of legal issues. Writers who misuse copyrighted materials or publish obscene, harassing, or threatening materials on the Internet can violate local, state, national, or international laws and be subject to litigation. As a writer and publisher of electronic documents, you are responsible for what you allow users worldwide to access.
2. Notify website owners when you make links to their web pages.
3. Indicate the last date of revision (preferably at the end of the document) so readers can gauge the currency of your publication.
4. Keep URLs as simple as possible.
5. Include your document's URL in the document itself, preferably after the date of publication or last revision.
6. Near the end of your publication, give readers the opportunity to send you an e-mail message.

When communicating by e-mail

1. Provide subject lines that give a short description of your message's content or main point.
2. When replying to or forwarding a message, change the subject line if necessary, especially if the content of your message moves in a new direction.
3. Write crisp, clear messages. Avoid overly long sentences. In general, make your online paragraphs shorter than those you would write for an offline medium. Skip a line between paragraphs (rather than indenting them) to make your messages easier to read. Use numbered lists when possible. When quoting from a previous message, quote only what is necessary.
4. Use normal capitalization. Don't send messages using all capital letters (capitalized text is harder to read than lowercase or mixed-case text). In addition, messages composed in capital letters are said to "shout" rather than make their point through effective language.
5. If you cannot italicize text, use underscore marks or asterisks to indicate titles or emphasis. For example: Has anyone read _Moby-Dick_ lately? I have, and it took me a *long* time!
6. When responding, delete e-mail headers. Trim routing information so that your correspondent doesn't have to read it.
7. When sending attachments, always tell the recipient what software you used to create the file. If appropriate, indicate how big the file is so that he or she can download it at a convenient time.
8. Compose useful signature files. Most e-mail programs let you create a signature (sig) file that automatically appears at the end of each message you send. It might, for example, contain your full name, your e-mail address, your homepage URL, your affiliation, and information about contacting you offline.
9. Edit and proofread your text before you send it.

When participating in discussion forums and mailing lists

1. Read introductory Frequently Asked/Answered Questions (FAQs) and subscription confirmation notices.
2. Read messages for a while and get a feel for the tone of the conversations before posting
3. Ask for private responses when appropriate.
4. Delete extraneous text when responding to previous postings.
5. Respect other people. Offensive behavior and language are generally not welcome.

Using copyrighted sources in your work

To avoid embarrassment and more serious consequences of plagiarism, make a habit of providing accurate and complete citations for information you find on the web.

Be aware that anyone can use today's fast search tools to detect plagiarism by searching the web for texts containing identifiable strings of words from the document in question. In addition, many graphics now contain digital watermarks that enable web managers to trace the unauthorized use of copyrighted images.

If you want to publish a large part or all of the content of a copyrighted source on the Internet, for example as part of a website, write to the copyright holder and request permission to use the desired text, image, or file. If permission is denied, you must respect the denial. You may, of course, create a hyperlink to the source itself, refer to the source, or paraphrase or summarize its contents, citing the source appropriately.

Recommended websites

For an extensive list of Internet sources related to numerous academic disciplines and areas of professional specialization, visit Andrew Harnack and Eugene Kleppinger, *Online! A Reference Guide to Using Internet Sources* at <http://www.bedfordstmartins.com/online/ires.html>.

A

a¹ (*pl* **a's**), **A** (*pl* **A's** *or* **As**) *n* the 1st letter of the English alphabet

a² *abbr* are²

a³ (*stressed*) /ay/ (*unstressed*) /ə/ *indef art* **1** refers to one person or thing not previously specified **2** indicates a type of person or thing o *He's a genius.* **3** one o *a thousand people* **4** per o *twice a day* **5** indicates somebody not known personally o *There's a Mr. O'Flynn here to see you.* ◊ See note at **an**

A¹ *symbol* ampere

A² *abbr* **1** adult **2** answer

A³ /ay/ *n* **1** the 6th note in the musical scale of C major **2** the highest grade of a student's work **3** a human blood type containing a specific antigen ◊ **from A to Z** extremely thoroughly

A., Å *symbol* angstrom

AA *abbr* Alcoholics Anonymous

A.A. *abbr* **1** antiaircraft **2** Associate of Arts

AAA /ˈtrɪpl ˈay/ American Automobile Association

aard·vark /ˈaʌrd vaʌrk/ *n* a burrowing African mammal with a long snout

> **ORIGIN Aardvark** comes from an Afrikaans word that literally means "earth pig."

Aar·hus ♦ Århus

Aar·on /ˈairən/, **Hank** (*b.* 1934) US baseball player

AARP *abbr* American Association of Retired Persons

Ab *n* JUDAISM = **Av**

AB¹ *abbr* Alberta

AB² *n* a human blood type containing two specific antigens

a.b. *abbr* at bat

A.B. *abbr* Bachelor of Arts

ABA *abbr* **1** *also* **A.B.A.** American Bar Association **2** American Basketball Association **3** American Booksellers Association

a·back /ə bák/ ◊ **taken aback** surprised and upset or shocked

ab·a·cus /ˈábbəkəss/ (*pl* **-cus·es** *or* **-ci** /-sī, -kī/) *n* a counting device consisting of a frame with beads or balls on rods

> **ORIGIN Abacus** ultimately comes from a Hebrew word meaning "dust." It was used in Greek for a sand-covered board for drawing and writing on, and later meant "table for arithmetical calculations." The exact form **abacus** came into English via Latin. The first recorded use of it in English to mean "counting device" was in the late 17C.

ab·a·lo·ne /ˈábbə lốnee/ *n* a shellfish that has a shell with a line of holes and a pearly interior

a·ban·don /ə bándən/ *v* **1** *vt* leave a person or animal behind for others to take care of **2** *vt* leave a place because of danger **3** *vt* renounce something previously done **4** *vt* give up control of something o *As troops closed in the town was abandoned to its fate.* **5** *vt* halt something in progress **6** *vr* give in to emotion ■ *n* lack of inhibition or self-restraint —**a·ban·doned** *adj* —**a·ban·don·ment** *n*

a·base /ə báyss/ (**a·based**, **a·bas·ing**) *v* **1** *vt* belittle or degrade **2** *vr* behave in a way that lowers your sense of dignity —**a·base·ment** *n*

a·bash /ə básh/ *vt* make ashamed —**a·bash·ed·ly** /-ədlee/ *adv*

a·bate /ə báyt/ (**a·bat·ed**, **a·bat·ing**) *vti* gradually make or become less (*fml or literary*) —**a·bate·ment** *n*

ab·at·toir /ˈábbə twaːr, -twaʌr/ *n* a place for killing animals for meat

Ab·bas /ˈábbəss/ (566?–653) Arabian merchant

~~abbatoir~~ incorrect spelling of **abattoir**

ab·bess /ˈábbəss/ *n* the head of a convent

ab·bey /ˈábbee/ (*pl* **-beys**) *n* **1** a monastery or convent **2** a church used by monks or nuns

ab·bot /ˈábbət/ *n* the head of a monastery —**ab·bot·ship** *n*

Ab·bott /ˈábbət/, **Berenice** (1898–1991) US photographer

abbr., abbrev. *abbr* abbreviation

ab·bre·vi·ate /ə bréevee ayt/ (**-at·ed, -at·ing**) *vt* shorten a word or text

ab·bre·vi·a·tion /ə bréevee áysh'n/ *n* **1** a reduced form of a word or phrase **2** the reduction of the full form of a word or phrase

ABC *n UK* = **ABCs** *npl* **2** ◊ **as easy as ABC** extremely easy

ABCs *npl* **1** the alphabet o *learned her ABCs* **2** the essentials o *the ABCs of carpentry*

ab·di·cate /ˈábdi kàyt/ (**-cat·ed, -cat·ing**) *v* **1** *vti* resign a position, especially the throne **2** *vt* neglect a duty or responsibility —**ab·di·ca·tion** /ˈábdi káysh'n/ *n*

ab·do·men /ˈábdəmən/ *n* **1** the part of the body containing the stomach and intestines **2** the rear part of an insect —**ab·dom·i·nal** /ab dómmin'l/ *adj*

ab·duct /ab dúkt/ *vt* take somebody away by force —**ab·duc·tion** *n* —**ab·duc·tor** *n*

Ab·dul-Jab·bar /ab dōōl jə baʌr/, **Kareem** (*b.* 1947) US basketball player

Ab·dul·lah II /ab dōōllə/ (*b.* 1962) king of Jordan (1999–)

Ab·e·lard /ˈábbə laːrd, àbbə laʌr/, **Peter** (1079–1142) French philosopher and theologian

Ab·e·na·ki /ˈábbə naːakee, àbbə nákee/ (*pl same or* **-kis**), **Ab·na·ki** /àab naːakee, áb nákee/ *n* a member of a Native North American people who now live in Maine and S Quebec —**Ab·e·na·ki** *adj*

⚡**ABEND** /áb ènd/ *n* **1** *also* **ab·end** a sudden computer program failure. Full form **abnormal end 2** warns e-mail correspondents of an imminent loss of Internet access. Full form **absent by enforced Net deprivation**

Ab·er·deen /ábbər deèn, àbbər deèn/ port and industrial center in NE Scotland. Pop. 227,430 (1996). —**Ab·er·don·i·an** /àbbər dóneə ən/ *n, adj*

Ab·er·nath·y /ábbər nàthee/, **Ralph David** (1926–90) US civil rights leader

ab·er·rant /ə bérrənt/ *adj* not typical —**ab·er·rance** *n*

ab·er·ra·tion /àbbə ráysh'n/ *n* **1** a deviation from what is usual **2** a lapse

a·bet /ə bét/ (**a·bet·ted, a·bet·ting**) *vt* give help, especially in committing a crime —**a·bet·tor** *n*

a·bey·ance /ə báy ənss/ *n* suspension of activity or operation ○ *travel plans now in abeyance because of bad weather* —**a·bey·ant** *adj*

ab·hor /ab háwr/ (**-horred, -hor·ring**) *vt* detest

ab·hor·rent /ab háwrənt/ *adj* arousing feelings of repugnance —**ab·hor·rence** *n*

a·bide /ə bíd/ (**a·bode** /ə bód/ *or* **a·bid·ed, a·bid·ing**) *v* **1** *vt* tolerate ○ *can't abide disobedient children.* **2** *vi* dwell (*archaic*)
☐ **abide by** *vt* follow or accept a rule or decision

a·bid·ing /ə bíding/ *adj* enduring

Ab·i·djan /àbbi jaàn/ cultural and commercial capital of the Côte d'Ivoire. Pop. 1,929,079 (1988).

Ab·i·lene /ábbə leèn/ city in central Texas. Pop. 108,257 (1998).

a·bil·i·ty /ə bíllətee/ *n* **1** the state of being able to do something **2** skill, talent, or intelligence

---

SYNONYMS ability, skill, competence, aptitude, talent, capacity, capability CORE MEANING: the necessary skill, knowledge, or experience to do something

---

ab·ject /áb jèkt, ab jékt/ *adj* **1** extremely bad or unpleasant ○ *abject poverty* **2** despicable ○ *abject cruelty* —**ab·jec·tion** /ab jéksh'n/ *n* —**ab·ject·ly** *adv*

ab·jure /ab joòr/ (**-jured, -jur·ing**) *vt* **1** formally renounce a belief **2** abstain from something (*literary*) —**ab·ju·ra·tion** /àbjə ráysh'n/ *n*

Ab·kha·zi·a /ab káyzhə, -zhee ə/ autonomous republic in the Republic of Georgia. Pop. 537,500 (1990).

ab·la·tive /ábblətiv/ *n* a grammatical case identifying the source, agent, or instrument of the action of the verb —**ab·la·tive** *adj*

a·blaze /ə bláyz/ *adj* **1** on fire **2** brightly lit

a·ble /áyb'l/ (**a·bler, a·blest**) *adj* **1** in a position to do something **2** capable or talented —**a·bly** *adv* ◊ See note at **intelligent**

-able *suffix* **1** capable of or fit for ○ *readable* **2** tending to ○ *changeable* —**ability** *suffix*

a·ble-bod·ied /áyb'l bóddeed/ *adj* healthy

a·ble-bod·ied sea·man, a·ble sea·man *n* a sailor with basic training

a·ble·ism /áyb'l ìzzəm/ *n* discrimination in favor of people who are not physically or mentally challenged —**a·ble·ist** *adj, n*

ab·lu·tion /ə bloósh'n/ *n* ritual washing or cleansing of the body ■ **ab·lu·tions** *npl* washing yourself (*fml or humorous*)

ab·ne·gate /ábnə gàyt/ (**-gat·ed, -gat·ing**) *vt* renounce (*fml*) —**ab·ne·ga·tion** /àbnə gáysh'n/ *n*

ab·nor·mal /ab náwrm'l, əb-/ *adj* unusual or not as expected —**ab·nor·mal·i·ty** /àb nawr mállətee/ *n* —**ab·nor·mal·ly** *adv*

a·board /ə báwrd/ *adv, prep* onto a ship or vehicle

a·bode[1] /ə bód/ *n* somebody's home (*literary*)

a·bode[2] /ə bód/ past participle, past tense of **abide**

a·bol·ish /ə bóllish/ *vt* put an end to

ab·o·li·tion /àbbə lísh'n/ *n* **1** the process of abolishing something **2** *also* **Abo·li·tion** the ending of slavery in the United States

ab·o·li·tion·ist /àbbə lísh'nist/ *n* **1** *also* **Abo·li·tion·ist** an opponent of slavery **2** somebody who seeks to ban something —**ab·o·li·tion·ism** *n*

A-bomb *n* an atomic bomb

a·bom·i·na·ble /ə bómminəb'l, -bómnəb'l/ *adj* loathsome or extremely unpleasant —**a·bom·i·na·bly** *adv*

A·bom·i·na·ble Snow·man *n* a yeti

a·bom·i·nate /ə bómmi nàyt/ (**-nat·ed, -nat·ing**) *vt* loathe (*literary*)

a·bom·i·na·tion /ə bòmmi náysh'n/ *n* **1** something horrible, disgusting, or shameful **2** intense dislike (*literary*)

ab·o·rig·i·nal /àbbə ríjjənəl/ *adj* **1** existing in a place from the earliest known times **2 Aboriginal** of the earliest inhabitants of Australia ■ *n* **1** an original inhabitant **2 Aboriginal** an original inhabitant of Australia ◊ See note at **native**

ab·o·rig·i·ne /àbbə ríjjənee/ *n* **1** △ an original inhabitant of a place (*often offensive*) **2** an animal or plant that has existed in a place since the earliest times **3 Aborigine** an original inhabitant of Australia

---

USAGE Avoid the use of **aborigine** without a capital letter to refer to a person who has lived in an area from the earliest known times.

---

a·bort /ə báwrt/ *v* **1** *vti* remove a fetus to end a pregnancy **2** *vi* have a miscarriage (*technical*) **3** *vti* end something, or come to an end, prematurely

a·bor·ti·fa·cient /ə bàwrtə fáysh'nt/ *adj* causing a fetal abortion —**a·bor·ti·fa·cient** *n*

a·bor·tion /ə báwrsh'n/ *n* **1** an operation to end a pregnancy **2** a miscarriage *(technical)* —**a·bor·tion·ist** *n*

a·bor·tive /ə báwrtiv/ *adj* **1** not successfully completed **2** disrupted in development —**a·bor·tive·ly** *adv*

ABO sys·tem *n* a system that classifies human blood by dividing it into the four groups A, B, AB, and O

a·bound /ə bównd/ *vi* **1** be plentiful **2** be well supplied

a·bout /ə bówt/ *prep* **1** in connection with **2** approximately ■ *adv, prep* **1** in various places **2** in different directions ■ *adv* **1** in circulation **2** into a reversed position ◇ **what something** *or* **somebody is (all) about** what something or somebody involves or has as a purpose *(infml)*

a·bout-face *vi* turn around *(usually a command)* ■ *n* **1** a reversal of an opinion or policy **2** a turn to face in the opposite direction

a·bove /ə búv/ *prep* over, higher than, or on top of ■ *prep, adv* **1** more than **2** superior to ■ *prep* **1** beyond ◇ *above criticism* **2** in a position of higher respect or importance than ■ *adv, adj* in a previous place in writing *(often in combination)* ◇ *using the information from the table above* ◇ *the above-cited graph* ■ *adv* overhead, in a higher position, or on top ◇ **above all** as the most important thing

a·bove-board /ə bùv báwrd/ *adj* honest and legal —**a·bove-board** *adv*

ORIGIN Aboveboard was originally a gambling term indicating that a player's hands were above the gaming table, or "board," and concealed nothing.

ab·ra·ca·dab·ra /àbbrəkə dábbrə/ *interj* supposedly ensures the success of a magic trick

a·brade /ə bráyd/ (**a-brad·ed, a·brad·ing**) *vti* wear away

A·bra·ham /áybrə hàm/, **A·bram** /áybrəm/ *n* in the Bible, the first Hebrew leader

ab·ra·sion /ə bráyzh'n/ *n* **1** the process of wearing away **2** a scraped area of skin

ab·ra·sive /ə bráyssiv, -ziv/ *adj* **1** using friction and roughness to smooth or clean **2** harsh in manner ■ *n* a smoothing substance —**ab·ra·sive·ly** *adv* —**ab·ra·sive·ness** *n*

a·breast /ə brést/ *adv* side by side ■ *adj* well-informed

~~abreviation~~ incorrect spelling of **abbreviation**

a·bridge /ə bríj/ (**a-bridged, a·bridg·ing**) *vt* shorten something such as text —**a·bridged** *adj* —**a·bridg·ment** *n*

a·broad /ə bráwd/ *adv* **1** away from your own country **2** in circulation **3** everywhere

ab·ro·gate /ábbrə gàyt/ (**-gat·ed, -gat·ing**) *vt* repeal or abolish formally *(fml)* —**ab·ro·ga·tion** /àbbrə gáysh'n/ *n* ◇ See note at **nullify**

a·brupt /ə brúpt/ *adj* **1** sudden **2** brusque **3** steep —**a·brupt·ly** *adv* —**a·brupt·ness** *n*

ABS *n* a system of electronically controlled brakes that prevents a vehicle's wheels locking if the driver brakes suddenly. Full form **anti-lock braking system**

ab·scess /ab sèss/ *n* a pus-filled cavity —**ab·scessed** *adj*

ab·scond /ab skónd, əb-/ *vi* **1** run away secretly **2** escape from a place of detention

ab·sence /ábs'nss/ *n* **1** the state of not being present **2** time spent away

~~absense~~ incorrect spelling of **absence**

ab·sent[1] /ábs'nt/ *adj* **1** not present ◇ *absent from school* **2** inattentive ■ *prep* without —**ab·sent·ly** *adv*

ab·sent[2] /ab sént/ *vr* leave or stay away ◇ *absented themselves from the meeting*

ab·sen·tee /àbs'n teé/ *n* somebody not present

ab·sen·tee bal·lot *n* a vote cast away from a voting place

ab·sen·tee·ism /àbs'n teè ìzzəm/ *n* frequent absence, especially from work

ab·sent-mind·ed *adj* habitually inattentive or forgetful —**ab·sent-mind·ed·ly** *adv* —**ab·sent-mind·ed·ness** *n*

ab·sinthe /ábsinth/, **ab·sinth** *n* an alcoholic drink made from wormwood

ab·so·lute /ábsə lòot, àbsə lóot/ *adj* **1** complete and unmitigated ◇ *an absolute fool* **2** having total power or authority **3** not dependent on or qualified by anything else **4** measured relative to absolute zero ■ *n* *also* **Ab·so·lute** in philosophy, ultimate reality —**ab·so·lute·ly** *adv*

ab·so·lute ma·jor·i·ty *n* a winning number of votes that is more than half of the total

ab·so·lute ze·ro *n* the lowest possible temperature

ab·so·lu·tion /àbsə lóosh'n/ *n* forgiveness for sin

ab·so·lut·ism /ábsə lòot ìzzəm/ *n* **1** a political system in which a ruler's power is absolute **2** a philosophical theory regarding values as objective —**ab·so·lut·ist** *n, adj*

ab·solve /əb zólv, -sólv/ (**-solved, -solv·ing**) *vt* **1** state publicly or officially that somebody is blameless **2** relieve of obligation **3** forgive

ab·sorb /əb sáwrb, -záwrb/ *vt* **1** soak up or take in something such as a liquid or nutrients **2** not transmit or pass on light, noise, or energy **3** engross somebody **4** incorporate something into a larger entity **5** use up or require something in quantity —**ab·sorbed** *adj* —**ab·sorb·er** /əb sáwrbər, -záwrbər/ *n* —**ab·sorb·ing** *adj*

ab·sorb·ent /əb sáwrbənt, -záwrb-/ *adj* able to absorb liquid —**ab·sorb·en·cy** *n*

~~absorbtion~~ incorrect spelling of **absorption**

ab·sorp·tion /əb sáwrpsh'n, -záwrp-/ *n* **1** total mental concentration **2** the soaking up of a liquid **3** incorporation into something larger —**ab·sorp·tive** adj

ab·stain /əb stáyn/ vi **1** not vote **2** choose not to do something

ab·ste·mi·ous /əb steémee əss/ adj moderate or restrained in eating and drinking

ab·sten·tion /əb sténsh'n/ n **1** a vote neither for nor against **2** the process of abstaining

ab·sti·nence /ábstənənss/ n self-denial —**ab·sti·nent** adj —**ab·sti·nent·ly** adv

ab·stract adj /áb stràkt, ab strákt/ **1** not physical or concrete **2** theoretical rather than applied **3** describes art that emphasizes form over realism ■ n /áb stràkt, ab strákt/ **1** a printed summary **2** an intellectual concept **3** an abstract artwork ■ vt /əb strákt/ summarize —**ab·stract·ly** adv —**ab·stract·ness** n

ab·stract·ed /ab stráktəd/ adj preoccupied

ab·strac·tion /ab stráksh'n/ n **1** a generalized concept **2** the process of abstracting **3** preoccupation

ab·stract noun n a noun that signifies a concept or quality, e.g., "truth"

ab·struse /ab strooss/ adj difficult to understand —**ab·struse·ly** adv ◊ See note at **obscure**

ab·surd /əb súrd, -zúrd/ adj **1** ludicrous **2** meaningless ■ n also **Ab·surd** the state of living in a meaningless universe —**ab·surd·i·ty** n —**ab·surd·ly** adv

A·bu Dha·bi /aà boo daàbee/ capital of the United Arab Emirates, on an island in the Persian Gulf. Pop. 605,000 (1990).

A·bu·ja /aà boò jaà/ official capital of Nigeria. Pop. 339,100 (1995).

a·bun·dant /ə búndənt/ adj **1** plentiful **2** well-supplied ○ *abundant in natural resources* —**a·bun·dance** n —**a·bun·dant·ly** adv

~~abundent~~ incorrect spelling of **abundant**

a·buse n /ə byóoss/ **1** maltreatment **2** improper use **3** insulting or offensive language ■ vt /ə byóoz/ (**a·bused, a·bus·ing**) **1** misuse something **2** treat somebody badly **3** insult somebody ◊ See note at **misuse**

a·bu·sive /ə byóossiv/ adj **1** insulting or offensive **2** involving illegal, improper, or harmful activities —**a·bu·sive·ly** adv

a·but /ə bút/ (**a·but·ted, a·but·ting**) vti be adjacent to something

a·but·ment /ə bútmənt/ n **1** the state of being adjacent **2** the point at which two things abut **3** a structure that supports or bears the thrust of something

a·bys·mal /ə bízm'l/ adj **1** appallingly bad **2** very deep —**a·bys·mal·ly** adv

a·byss /ə bíss/ n **1** a very deep chasm **2** endless space

Ab·ys·sin·i·a /ábbə sínnee ə/ n former name for Ethiopia —**Ab·ys·sin·i·an** adj, n

Ab·zug /áb tsoòg/, **Bella** (1920–98) US feminist, lawyer, and politician

---

✦ **ac** abbr academic organization (in Internet addresses)

Ac symbol actinium

AC abbr **1** air conditioning **2** alternating current

ac. abbr acre

a/c abbr account

A/C abbr **1** account **2** air conditioning

a·ca·cia /ə káyshə/ (pl -**cias** or same) n **1** a bush or tree with small fluffy yellow flowers **2** gum arabic

ac·a·de·mi·a /ákə deèmee ə/, **ac·a·de·me** /ákə deèm/ n academic life

ac·a·dem·ic /ákə démmik/ adj **1** of education **2** scholarly and intellectual **3** irrelevant in practice ■ n **1** a university teacher **2** a scholarly person —**ac·a·dem·i·cal·ly** adv

ac·a·de·mi·cian /ákədə mísh'n, ə kàddə-/ n **1** an academic **2** a member of a scholarly society

a·cad·e·my /ə káddəmee/ (pl -**mies**) n **1** a society promoting knowledge or culture **2** a specialized educational institution **3** a private preparatory school (usually in school names) **4** the academic world

---

ORIGIN The original **Academy** was the school that the Greek philosopher Plato founded in the 4C BC. It was named for a park on the outskirts of Athens, where he taught his philosophy. The word came into English via Latin and French.

A·cad·e·my A·ward n a movie award given by the Academy of Motion Picture Arts and Sciences

A·ca·di·a /ə káydee ə/ n former French colony in NE North America —**A·ca·di·an** n, adj

a cap·pel·la /aà kə péllə, àkə péllə/ adv, adj by singers without instrumental accompaniment

Ac·a·pul·co /àkə poólkō, àakə pool-/ seaport and resort in S Mexico. Pop. 687,292 (1995).

acc. abbr **1** account **2** accusative

~~academic~~ incorrect spelling of **academic**

ac·cede /ak seéd/ (**-ced·ed, -ced·ing**) vi **1** agree to something, especially unwillingly **2** come to power

---

SPELLCHECK Do not confuse the spelling of **accede** and **exceed** ("be greater than"), which sound similar.

---

ac·cel·er·ate /ak séllə ràyt/ (**-at·ed, -at·ing**) vti **1** go or cause to go faster **2** happen or cause to happen sooner than planned or expected —**ac·cel·er·a·tion** /ak sèllə ráysh'n/ n

✦ **ac·cel·er·at·ed graph·ics port** n a computer interface that allows the display of three-dimensional graphics

ac·cel·er·a·tor /ak séllə ràytər/ n **1** a control mechanism that makes a vehicle go faster **2** a chemical that speeds up a reaction

✦ **ac·cel·er·a·tor card, ac·cel·er·a·tor board** n a circuit board added to a computer to make it operate faster

ac·cent *n* /ák sènt/ **1** a manner of pronunciation **2** a stress on a syllable or musical note **3** a mark on a letter indicating stress or pronunciation **4** the main emphasis o *The accent is on safety.* ■ *vt* /ák sènt, ak sént/ emphasize or stress

ac·cen·tu·ate /ak sénchoo àyt/ (**-at·ed**, **-at·ing**) *vt* **1** draw attention to something **2** stress a syllable or musical note —**ac·cen·tu·a·tion** /ak sènchoo áysh'n/ *n*

ac·cept /ak sépt/ *v* **1** *vt* take something offered **2** *vti* say yes to something such as an invitation **3** *vt* believe something **4** *vt* endure or tolerate something **5** *vt* acknowledge and come to terms with something **6** *vt* take the blame for something **7** *vt* allow somebody to become a member **8** *vt* regard somebody or something with approval —**ac·cep·tance** *n* —**ac·cept·ed** *adj*

ac·cept·a·ble /ak séptəb'l/ *adj* **1** adequate **2** approved of —**ac·cept·a·bil·i·ty** /ak séptə bíllətee/ *n* —**ac·cept·a·bly** *adv*

✦**ac·cess** /ák sèss/ *n* **1** a means of entry or approach o *gained access via an upstairs window* **2** the right or opportunity to use something or meet somebody ■ *vt* **1** enter a place **2** retrieve data from a computer

> **SPELLCHECK** Do not confuse the spelling of **access** and **excess** ("a surplus"), which sound similar.

~~accessable~~ incorrect spelling of **accessible**

ac·ces·si·ble /ak séssəb'l/ *adj* **1** easy to enter or reach physically **2** easily understood **3** readily available —**ac·ces·si·bil·i·ty** /ak sèssə billətee/ *n* —**ac·ces·si·bly** *adv*

ac·ces·sion /ak sésh'n/ *n* **1** the process of coming to power **2** the acceptance by a state of a treaty **3** agreement, especially when given unwillingly **4** an addition to a collection

ac·ces·sor·ize /ak séssə rìz/ (**-ized**, **-iz·ing**) *v* **1** *vti* complete an outfit with accessories **2** *vt* provide something with accessories

ac·ces·so·ry /ak séssəree/ *n* (*pl* **-ries**) **1** an optional part **2** a fashion item such as a hat or handbag **3** somebody who helps a criminal ■ *adj* additional

✦**ac·cess pro·file** *n* a description of the pattern of Internet use of a specific user

✦**ac·cess time** *n* the speed of a computer in accessing data

ac·ci·dent /áksidənt, áksi dènt/ *n* **1** chance o *I met him by accident.* **2** a collision involving a moving vehicle **3** a mishap, or an unplanned, unfortunate event **4** a chance happening

ac·ci·den·tal /àksə dént'l/ *adj* **1** happening by chance **2** incidental ■ *n* a musical note marked with a sharp, flat, or natural sign that is not in the key signature —**ac·ci·den·tal·ly** *adv*

~~accidently~~ incorrect spelling of **accidentally**

ac·claim /ə kláym/ *vt* **1** praise publicly and enthusiastically **2** pronounce to be something deserving praise o *was acclaimed as the winner* ■ *n* public and enthusiastic praise —**ac·cla·ma·tion** /àklə máysh'n/ *n*

ac·cli·ma·tize /ə klímə tìz/ (**-tized**, **-tiz·ing**), **ac·cli·mate** /ə klímət, áklə màyt/ (**-mat·ed**, **-mat·ing**) *vti* adapt or become adapted to a new environment —**ac·cli·ma·ti·za·tion** /ə klímətə záysh'n/ *n*

ac·co·lade /áko làyd, -làad/ *n* **1** a sign or expression of praise **2** public recognition

> **ORIGIN** The root of **accolade** is Latin *collum* "neck," which is also the source of English *collar*. The underlying idea is of putting your arm around somebody's neck as a sign of congratulations.

ac·com·mo·date /ə kómmə dàyt/ (**-dat·ed**, **-dat·ing**) *v* **1** *vt* adjust actions in response to the needs of **2** *vt* allow for **3** *vt* have room for **4** *vt* provide lodging for **5** *vi* adapt to a new situation

ac·com·mo·dat·ing /ə kómmə dàyting/ *adj* obliging somebody's wishes —**ac·com·mo·dat·ing·ly** *adv*

ac·com·mo·da·tion /ə kòmmə dáysh'n/ *n* **1** willingness to oblige **2** an agreement or compromise **3** adjustment or adaptation ■ **ac·com·mo·da·tions** *npl* **1** lodging **2** room or space

~~accomodate~~ incorrect spelling of **accommodate**

~~accomodation~~ incorrect spelling of **accommodation**

ac·com·pa·ni·ment /ə kúmpənimənt, -pni-/ *n* **1** a musical part that supports a soloist or more prominent performers **2** an item that goes with another

ac·com·pa·nist /ə kúmpənist, -pnist/ *n* a musician who plays an accompaniment

ac·com·pa·ny /ə kúmpənee, -pnee/ (**-nied**, **-nies**) *v* **1** *vt* escort **2** *vt* be present or occur with **3** *vt* supplement **4** *vti* provide the musical accompaniment for

ac·com·plice /ə kómpliss/ *n* somebody who helps a wrongdoer or criminal

ac·com·plish /ə kómplish/ *vt* succeed in doing

> **SYNONYMS accomplish, achieve, attain, realize, carry out, pull off** CORE MEANING: bring to a successful conclusion

ac·com·plished /ə kómplisht/ *adj* **1** talented or skilled **2** complete and definite o *an accomplished fact*

ac·com·plish·ment /ə kómplishmənt/ *n* **1** the achieving of something **2** something achieved **3** a talent or skill

ac·cord /ə káwrd/ *v* **1** *vt* give or grant o *was accorded the same privileges as her predecessor* **2** *vi* agree o *accords with my own view* ■ *n* **1** an agreement **2** consensus or harmony

ac·cor·dance /ə káwrd'nss/ *n* conformity with

what is required ○ *in accordance with official guidelines*

ac·cord·ing·ly /ə káwrdinglee/ *adv* **1** correspondingly **2** in consequence

ac·cord·ing to *prep* **1** in proportion to **2** as stated or determined by

ac·cor·di·on /ə káwrdee ən/ *n* a musical instrument with a bellows in the middle that forces air through metal reeds

ac·cost /ə káwst/ *vt* approach and stop somebody aggressively or suggestively

⨍ **ac·count** /ə kównt/ *n* **1** a report **2** an explanation **3** an arrangement for keeping money in a bank **4** an arrangement for obtaining goods or services on credit **5** a contract providing Internet access **6** a customer ■ **ac·counts** *npl* the financial records of a person or organization ■ *vt* consider or regard as *(fml)* ○ *We would account it a privilege to serve you.* ◇ **call somebody to account** demand an explanation of somebody's actions ◇ **on account of** because of ◇ **on no account** not ever ◇ **on somebody's account** out of concern for somebody's well-being ◇ **take account of, take into account** consider when making a decision
□ **account for** *vt* explain

ac·count·a·ble /ə kówntəb'l/ *adj* **1** responsible for something **2** responsible to somebody —**ac·count·a·bil·i·ty** /ə kòwntə bíllətee/ *n*

ac·count·ant /ə kówntənt/ *n* somebody who maintains and checks financial accounts —**ac·count·an·cy** *n*

ac·count·ing /ə kównting/ *n* maintenance and checking of financial records

ac·counts pay·a·ble *npl* a record of money owed by a company

ac·counts re·ceiv·a·ble *npl* a record of money owed to a company

~~accoustic~~ incorrect spelling of **acoustic**

ac·cou·ter /ə kóotər/, **ac·cou·tre** (-**tred**, -**tring**) *vt* equip

ac·cou·ter·ment /ə kóotərmənt/, **ac·cou·tre·ment** /ə kóotrə-/ *n* **1** an accessory or associated piece of equipment **2** a piece of military equipment

Ac·cra /ə kráa, ákrə/ capital of Ghana. Pop. 953,500 (1990 estimate).

ac·cred·it /ə kréddət/ *vt* **1** give authority to **2** give official recognition to —**ac·cred·i·ta·tion** /ə krèddə táysh'n/ *n*

ac·cre·tion /ə kréesh'n/ *n* an increase resulting from accumulation or addition

~~accross~~ incorrect spelling of **across**

ac·crue /ə króo/ (-**crued**, -**cru·ing**) *vi* **1** *vi* come into somebody's possession **2** *vi* increase **3** *vt* gather over a period of time ○ *investments accruing interest* —**ac·cru·al** *n*

ac·cul·tur·ate /ə kúlchə ràyt/ (-**at·ed**, -**at·ing**) *v* **1** *vi* take on another culture **2** *vt* change the culture of —**ac·cul·tur·a·tion** /ə kùlchə ráysh'n/ *n*

ac·cu·mu·late /ə kyóomyə làyt/ (-**lat·ed**, -**lat·ing**) *vti* collect over a period of time —**ac·cu·mu·la·tion** /ə kyòomyə láysh'n/ *n* —**ac·cu·mu·la·tive** /-lətiv, -làytiv/ *adj* ◇ See note at **collect**

⨍ **ac·cu·mu·la·tor** /ə kyóomyə làytər/ *n* a section of computer memory for short-term storage

ac·cu·rate /ákyərət/ *adj* **1** representing the truth **2** free from errors —**ac·cu·ra·cy** /-rəsee/ *n* —**ac·cu·rate·ly** *adv*

ac·curs·ed /ə kúrst, -səd/, **ac·curst** /ə kúrst/ *adj* *(literary)* **1** doomed **2** horrible —**ac·curs·ed·ly** /-sədlee/ *adv*

ac·cu·sa·tion /àkyə záysh'n/ *n* **1** an allegation of wrongdoing **2** the accusing of somebody, or the state of being accused

ac·cu·sa·tive /ə kyóozətiv/ *n* a grammatical case identifying the direct object of a verb or the object of a preposition —**ac·cu·sa·tive** *adj*

ac·cuse /ə kyóoz/ (-**cused**, -**cus·ing**) *v* **1** *vti* confront and blame somebody **2** *vt* charge with a crime —**ac·cused** *n*

ac·cus·tom /ə kústəm/ *vt* make used to something

ac·cus·tomed /ə kústəmd/ *adj* habitual

AC/DC *adj* powered by a battery or electrical outlet. Full form **alternating current/direct current**

ace *n* **1** a playing card with a single mark **2** in tennis, a serve that the opponent cannot return **3** in golf, a hole in one **4** a successful fighter pilot **5** somebody with an exceptional skill *(infml)* ■ *vt* (**aced**, **ac·ing**) **1** in tennis, serve an ace **2** in golf, play a hole in a single stroke **3** defeat soundly *(slang)*

a·cer·bic /ə súrbik/ *adj* bitter —*an acerbic remark* —**a·cer·bi·cal·ly** *adv* —**a·cer·bi·ty** *n*

~~acessory~~ incorrect spelling of **accessory**

ac·e·tate /ássə tàyt/ *n* **1** a derivative of acetic acid **2** cellulose acetate

a·ce·tic ac·id /ə séetik-/ *n* CH_3COOH the main component of vinegar. Use: manufacture of drugs, dyes, plastics, fibers.

ac·e·tone /ássə tòn/ *n* C_3H_6O a colorless flammable liquid. Use: paint and nail polish solvent.

a·cet·y·lene /ə sétt'lən, -l èen/ *n* C_2H_2 a flammable gas. Use: in welding.

⨍ **ACH** *n* an interbank payment network. Full form **automated clearinghouse**

ache /ayk/ *n* a dull constant pain ■ *vi* (**ached**, **ach·ing**) **1** feel or be the site of a dull constant pain **2** yearn for the presence of somebody or something **3** want something badly *(infml)* —**ach·ing·ly** *adv* —**ach·y** *adj*

A·che·be /ə cháy bay, aa-/, **Chinua** (b. 1930) Nigerian novelist

~~acheive~~ incorrect spelling of **achieve**

a·chene /ə kéen/, **a·kene** *n* a dry single-seeded fruit that does not open to release its seed

Ach·e·son /áchəss'n/, **Dean** (1893–1971) US secretary of state (1949–52)

a·chieve /ə cheev/ (**a·chieved, a·chiev·ing**) *vt* succeed in doing or gaining —**a·chiev·a·ble** *adj* —**a·chieve·ment** *n* ◊ See note at **accomplish**

A·chil·les /ə kílleez/ *n* in Greek mythology, a hero of the Trojan War

A·chil·les' heel *n* a small but fatal weakness

ORIGIN In Greek mythology, Achilles' mother dipped him in the river Styx as a baby to make him invulnerable, but the heel she held him by remained dry and became his only point of weakness. He died when struck in the heel by an arrow.

A·chil·les ten·don *n* the tendon that connects the heel to the calf muscles

ach·ro·mat·ic /ákrə máttik/ *adj* 1 white, gray, or black 2 able to reflect or refract light without spectral color separation —**ach·ro·mat·i·cal·ly** *adv* —**a·chro·ma·tism** /-mə tízzəm/ *n*

ac·id /ássid/ *n* 1 a corrosive chemical compound with a sour taste 2 LSD (*slang*) ■ *adj* 1 of an acid 2 sharp, bitter, or sarcastic —**a·cid·ic** /ə síddik/ *adj* —**a·cid·i·ty** /ə síddətee/ *n*

a·cid·i·fy /ə síddə fī/ (**-fied, -fies**) *vti* make or become acid

ac·id rain *n* polluted rain containing dilute acid

ac·id re·flux *n* the return of stomach contents to the esophagus

ac·id rock *n* rock music suggesting the influence of psychedelic drugs

ac·id test *n* a decisive test

ac·knowl·edge /ək nóllij/ (**-edged, -edg·ing**) *v* 1 *vt* admit the truth or validity of 2 *vti* respond to a greeting or message 3 *vt* show appreciation of —**ac·knowl·edged** *adj* —**ac·knowl·edg·ment** *n*

~~acclaim~~ incorrect spelling of **acclaim**

ACLU *abbr* American Civil Liberties Union

ac·me /ákmee/ *n* the highest point

ac·ne /áknee/ *n* a skin disease causing pimples

ORIGIN Acne has its origin in a mistake. The Greek word meaning "highest point," from which English *acme* comes, could also mean "pimple." It was wrongly copied in this sense with *n* rather than *m*.

ac·o·lyte /ákə līt/ *n* 1 a cleric's assistant in performing liturgical rites 2 a follower or assistant

~~accommodate~~ incorrect spelling of **accommodate**

~~accommodation~~ incorrect spelling of **accommodation**

~~acompany~~ incorrect spelling of **accompany**

A·con·ca·gua /ákən kaàgwə, aàkən-/ highest mountain in the Andes and in the western hemisphere, in W Argentina. Height 22,834 ft./6,960 m.

ac·o·nite /ákə nīt/ *n* 1 an extract from a dried poisonous root. Use: homeopathic remedy. 2 a plant with purple, blue, or white hooded flowers and poisonous roots

~~according~~ incorrect spelling of **according**

a·corn /áy kàwrn/ *n* an oval-shaped fruit of an oak tree, in a cup-shaped base

a·corn squash *n* an acorn-shaped squash

a·cous·tic /ə kóostik/, **a·cous·ti·cal** /-stik'l/ *adj* 1 of sound 2 designed to control or carry sound 3 not amplified o *an acoustic guitar* —**a·cous·ti·cal·ly** *adv*

a·cous·tics /ə kóostiks/ *n* the study of sound (*+ sing verb*) ■ *npl* the sound-carrying ability of a room (*+ pl verb*) —**ac·ous·ti·cian** /ákoo stísh'n/ *n*

ac·quaint /ə kwáynt/ *vt* make aware —**ac·quaint·ed** *adj*

ac·quain·tance /ə kwáyntənss/ *n* 1 somebody slightly known 2 slight knowledge o *only a basic acquaintance with French theater*

ac·qui·esce /ákwee éss/ (**-esced, -esc·ing**) *vi* agree to something passively —**ac·qui·es·cence** *n* —**ac·qui·es·cent** *adj* ◊ See note at **agree**

ac·quire /ə kwír/ (**-quired, -quir·ing**) *vt* 1 obtain 2 learn or develop o *a habit I acquired in the army* —**ac·quired** *adj* ◊ See note at **get**

ac·quired im·mune de·fi·cien·cy syn·drome, ac·quired im·mu·no·de·fi·cien·cy syn·drome *n* full form of **AIDS**

ac·quired taste *n* a liking for something that only develops gradually

ac·qui·si·tion /ákwi zísh'n/ *n* 1 the acquiring of something 2 a new possession

ac·qui·si·tions /ákwi zísh'nz/ *n* a company department responsible for taking over other businesses (*+ sing verb*)

ac·quis·i·tive /ə kwízzətiv/ *adj* eager to acquire things —**ac·quis·i·tive·ly** *adv* —**ac·quis·i·tive·ness** *n*

ac·quit /ə kwít/ (**-quit·ted, -quit·ting**) *v* 1 *vt* declare innocent 2 *vr* behave or perform (*fml*) o *acquitted themselves admirably*

ac·quit·tal /ə kwítt'l/ *n* a not-guilty verdict

a·cre /áykər/ *n* a unit of area equal to 4,840 sq. yd./4,046.86 sq. m ■ **a·cres** *npl* land

a·cre·age /áykərij, áykrij/ *n* land measured in acres

ac·rid /ákrəd/ *adj* 1 unpleasantly pungent 2 bitter in tone or character —**a·crid·i·ty** /ə kríddətee/ *n* —**ac·rid·ly** *adv*

~~acrilic~~ incorrect spelling of **acrylic**

ac·ri·mo·ni·ous /ákrə mōnee əss/ *adj* resentful and angry —**ac·ri·mo·ni·ous·ly** *adv* —**ac·ri·mo·ny** /ákrə mōnee/ *n*

ac·ro·bat /ákrə bàt/ *n* a gymnastic entertainer —**ac·ro·bat·ic** /ákrə báttik/ *adj*

ac·ro·bat·ics /ákrə báttiks/ *n* (*+ sing or pl verb*) 1 gymnastic feats performed as entertainment **2** great skill or complexity ○ *verbal acrobatics*

ac·ro·nym /ákrə nĭm/ *n* a word formed from the initials of other words, e.g., "NAFTA"

a·crop·o·lis /ə króppəliss/ *n* **1** the fortified citadel of a city in ancient Greece **2 A·crop·o·lis** the ancient citadel of Athens in Greece that was the religious focus of the city

a·cross /ə kráws, -króss/ *prep* **1** on the opposite side of **2** from one side to the other of **3** throughout ■ *adj, adv* so as to cross ■ *adv* **1** at or to the other side **2** measured in width

a·cross-the-board *adj, adv* affecting everyone or everything equally

a·cros·tic /ə króstik/ *n* a set of written lines containing letters that form a word when read downward

a·cryl·ic /ə kríllik, a-/ *n* **1** a synthetic fiber **2** a type of paint containing resin made from acrylic acid —**a·cryl·ic** *adj*

a·cryl·ic ac·id *n* $C_3H_4O_2$ a corrosive liquid. Use: manufacture of resins.

act *n* **1** something done **2** the process of doing something **3** a main part of a play **4** a performance in a show **5** a performer **6** a pretense **7** a record of a decision of a lawmaking body ■ *v* **1** *vi* take action ○ *need to act at once* **2** *vti* behave in a particular way **3** *vi* behave in a way intended to impress or deceive **4** *vi* function ○ *acts as a barrier* **5** *vi* be a substitute ○ *acting for the manager in her absence* **6** *vi* have an effect ○ *The painkiller starts to act immediately.* **7** *vti* play a role **8** *vi* be an actor ◇ **get your act together** become more organized (*slang*)

□ **act out** *vt* express a feeling

□ **act up** be troublesome

act·ing /ákting/ *n* the art, profession, or performance of an actor ■ *adj* carrying out particular duties or doing somebody else's job temporarily

ac·tin·ide /áktə nĭd/ *n* any element in the series of radioactive elements beginning with actinium and ending with lawrencium

ac·tin·i·um /ak tínnee əm/ *n* (*symbol* **Ac**) a radioactive metallic chemical element

ac·tion /ákshən/ *n* **1** the process of doing something **2** something done **3** a movement ○ *the action of a piston* **4** energetic activity **5** legal proceedings **6** the main events of a movie or novel **7** function or influence ○ *the action of water on stone* **8** fighting during a war **9** an operating mechanism ■ *interj* tells movie actors to start performing

ac·tion·a·ble /ákshənəb'l/ *adj* giving cause for legal action

ac·ti·vate /áktə vàyt/ (-**vat·ed**, -**vat·ing**) *v* **1** *vt* make or become active **2** *vt* make radioactive —**ac·ti·va·tion** /áktə váysh'n/ *n*

ac·tive /áktiv/ *adj* **1** moving around **2** busy ○ *an active life* **3** having a chemical effect ○ *an active ingredient* **4** showing involvement ○ *an active role* **5** needing and using energy **6** describes a volcano that is not extinct **7** describes a verb or the voice of a verb in which the subject performs the action described by the verb ■ *n* the active voice of a verb —**ac·tive·ly** *adv*

⚡**ac·tive cell** *n* an open spreadsheet cell

ac·tive du·ty, ac·tive ser·vice *n* full military duty

⚡**ac·tive-ma·trix dis·play** *n* a flat liquid-crystal screen with high color resolution

⚡**ac·tive ser·ver page** *n* an HTML page processed on a server

ac·tiv·ism /áktə vìzzəm/ *n* vigorous organized action in pursuing a political or social end —**ac·tiv·ist** *n, adj*

ac·tiv·i·ty /ak tívvətee/ (*pl* -**ties**) *n* **1** something that somebody does (*often pl*) ○ *leisure activities* **2** physical exercise **3** the state of being active

act of God *n* an event beyond human control

ac·tor /áktər/ *n* a performer in plays or movies

ac·tress /áktrəss, -triss, -tress/ *n* a female performer in plays or movies

USAGE Many actresses now prefer to refer to themselves as actors.

Acts of the A·pos·tles *n* a book of the Bible in which the early history of the Christian church is described (+ *sing verb*)

ac·tu·al /ákchoo əl/ *adj* **1** real **2** existing now

ac·tu·al·i·ty /àkchoo állətee/ (*pl* -**ties**) *n* **1** something that is real **2** everything that really exists or happens

ac·tu·al·ize /ákchoo ə lìz/ (-**ized**, -**iz·ing**) *vt* **1** make real or actual **2** portray or represent realistically —**ac·tu·al·i·za·tion** /àkchoo ələ záysh'n/ *n*

ac·tu·al·ly /ákchoo əlee/ *adv* **1** in fact ○ *I've never actually been there.* **2** expresses a contradictory opinion or fact ○ *Actually, she's my sister.*

ac·tu·ar·y /ákchoo èrree, àkshoo-/ (*pl* -**ies**) *n* a statistician who calculates insurance risks —**ac·tu·ar·i·al** /àkchoo áiree əl, àkshoo-/ *adj*

ac·tu·ate /ákchoo àyt/ (-**at·ed**, -**at·ing**) *vt* **1** cause somebody to act in a particular way **2** cause a mechanism to start working (*fml*)

a·cu·i·ty /ə kyóo ətee/ *n* keenness of hearing, sight, or intellect

a·cu·men /ə kyóomən, ákyə-/ *n* sharpness of mind

~~acumulate~~ incorrect spelling of **accumulate**

ac·u·pres·sure /ákyoo prèshər/ *n* a therapeutic treatment using manual pressure on specific parts of the body

ac·u·punc·ture /ákyoo pùngkchər/ *n* a therapeutic treatment using needles inserted in the skin at specific points —**ac·u·punc·tur·ist** *n*

~~acurate~~ incorrect spelling of **accurate**

a·cute /ə kyoot/ *adj* **1** very great or bad ○ *an acute financial crisis* **2** perceptive ○ *an acute grasp of foreign affairs* **3** powerful and sensitive ○ *acute eyesight* **4** describes an angle of less than 90 degrees **5** describes a disease that is severe and of short duration ■ *n also* **a·cute ac·cent** a specific mark above a letter, as in "á" or "ó" —**a·cute·ly** *adv* —**a·cute·ness** *n*

ad *n* an advertisement (*infml*)

AD, A.D. *adv* indicates a date after the birth of Jesus Christ. Full form **anno Domini**

> **USAGE** AD is traditionally put before the numeral to which it relates (AD *1453*), but after if the century is spelled out: *the 5th century* AD. Some writers use PE (Present Era) or CE (Common Era) to avoid the association with Christianity.

⚡**A·da** /áydə/ *n* a high-level computer language that is easy to read

> **ORIGIN Ada** is named for the English mathematician Augusta Ada Byron, Countess of Lovelace (1815–52).

ad·age /áddij/ *n* a saying

a·da·gio /ə daájee ō, -zhee ō, -jō/ *adv* slowly (*musical direction*) —**a·da·gio** *n, adj*

Ad·am /áddəm/ *n* in the Bible, the first man ◇ **not know from Adam** have never met or seen before

ad·a·mant /áddəmənt, -mant/ *adj* firmly set in your opinion —**ad·a·mant·ly** *adv*

Abigail Adams

Ad·ams /áddəmz/, **Abigail** (1744–1818) US first lady and early feminist

Ad·ams, Ansel (1902–84) US photographer

Ad·ams, Gerry (b. 1948) Northern Ireland politician

Ad·ams, Henry (1838–1918) US historian

John Adams

Ad·ams, John (1735–1826) 2nd president of the United States (1797–1801)

John Quincy Adams

Ad·ams, John Quincy (1767–1848) 6th president of the United States (1825–29)

Ad·ams, Samuel (1722–1803) American Revolutionary leader

Ad·am's ap·ple *n* the lump at the front of the throat, visible in men

a·dapt /ə dápt/ *vti* change to meet different requirements —**ad·ap·ta·tion** /à dap táysh'n, àddəp-/

a·dapt·a·ble /ə dáptəb'l/ *adj* **1** changing easily **2** adjustable —**a·dapt·a·bil·i·ty** /ə dàptə bíllətee/ *n* —**a·dapt·a·bly** *adv*

a·dapt·er /ə dáptər/, **a·dapt·or** *n* a device for connecting otherwise incompatible parts

a·dap·tive /ə dáptiv/ *adj* usable in different conditions —**a·dap·tive·ly** *adv*

A·dar /ə daár/ *n* the 12th month of the year in the Jewish calendar

A·dar Rish·on /-ríshon/ *n* the name given to the month of Adar during a leap year in the Jewish calendar

A·dar She·ni /-sháynee/ *n* a 13th month added to the Jewish calendar after Adar in leap years

⚡**ADC** *abbr* **1** Aid to Dependent Children **2** Air Defense Command **3** analog-to-digital converter

add *v* **1** *vt* put something into or join something onto something else **2** *vti* calculate a total **3** *vi* increase the effect of something ○ *This adds to our problems.*

□ **add up** *v* **1** *vti* calculate or reach a total **2** *vi* make sense

□ **add up to** *vt* amount to or result in

ADD *abbr* attention deficit disorder

Ad·dams /áddəmz/, **Jane** (1860–1935) US reformer and feminist

ad·den·dum /ə déndəm/ (*pl* **-da** /-də/) *n* **1** something added **2** a supplement to a book

add·er[1] /áddər/ *n* somebody or something that adds

ad·der[2] /áddər/ *n* a small venomous European snake

> **ORIGIN** An **adder** was originally *a nadder*: the *n* was lost when this common combination of words was misinterpreted.

ad·dict /áddikt/ *n* **1** somebody dependent on something such as a drug **2** an enthusiast

ad·dic·tion /ə díksh'n/ *n* **1** dependence on something such as a drug **2** great interest or devotion —**ad·dict·ed** *adj*

ad·dic·tive /ə dĭktiv/ *adj* causing addiction

⚡**add-in** *n* COMPUT = **add-on**

Ad·dis Ab·a·ba /áddiss ábbəbə/ capital of Ethiopia. Pop. 1,047,300 (1994).

Ad·di·son /áddiss'n/, **Joseph** (1672–1719) English essayist and politician

ad·di·tion /ə dísh'n/ *n* **1** the process of adding **2** something added **3** the calculation of a total **4** a building annex

ad·di·tion·al /ə dísh'n'l, -dísh'n'l/ *adj* extra —**ad·di·tion·al·ly** *adv*

ad·di·tive /áddətiv/ *n* something added, e.g., to food ■ *adj* involving adding something (*fml*)

ad·dle /ádd'l/ (-dled, -dling) *vti* **1** confuse **2** rot or spoil

⚡**add-on, add·in** *n* a piece of extra equipment for a computer

⚡**ad·dress** *n* /ə dréss, á dréss/ **1** the words or numbers identifying the location of a building, organization, or person **2** /ə dréss/ a formal talk **3** a number specifying a location in a computer's memory ■ *vt* /ə dréss/ **1** write an address on an item of mail **2** speak or make a speech to somebody **3** deal with a problem or issue

ad·dress·ee /á dre seé, ə dréss eé/ *n* somebody to whom an item of mail is addressed

⚡**ad·dress har·vest·er** *n* a computer program that collects e-mail addresses from the Internet

ad·duce /ə doóss, ə dyoóss/ (-duced, -duc·ing) *vt* offer as evidence (*fml*) —**ad·duc·i·ble** *adj*

Ad·e·laide /ádd'l àyd/ state capital and main port of South Australia. Pop. 1,088,400 (1998).

A·den /áad'n, áyd'n/ **1** port and second largest city in Yemen. Pop. 400,783 (1993 estimate). **2** former British protectorate that is now part of Yemen

Ad·en·au·er /ádd'n òw ər/, **Konrad** (1876–1967) German chancellor of West Germany (1949–63)

ad·e·noids /ádd'n oydz/ *npl* a mass of tissue at the back of the throat —**ad·e·noi·dal** /áddə nóyd'l/ *adj*

a·dept *adj* /ə dépt/ skillful ■ *n* /ádd ept/ a skilled person —**a·dept·ly** *adv* —**a·dept·ness** *n*

ad·e·quate /áddəkwət/ *adj* **1** sufficient to meet a need **2** just barely sufficient to meet a need —**ad·e·qua·cy** *n* —**ad·e·quate·ly** *adv*

adequately incorrect spelling of **adequately**

ADHD *abbr* attention deficit hyperactivity disorder

ad·here /əd heér, ad-/ (-hered, -her·ing) *vi* **1** act in accordance with o *adhere to the rules* **2** stick or hold firmly o *adhering to their beliefs* —**ad·her·ence** *n*

ad·her·ent /əd heérənt, ad-, əd hérrənt/ *n* a supporter ■ *adj* sticky (*fml*)

ad·he·sion /əd heézh'n, ad-/ *n* **1** the ability to stick or hold firmly **2** support for a cause

or leader **3** the joining of normally unconnected body parts by bands of fibrous tissue

ad·he·sive /əd heéssiv, ad-, -heéziv/ *n* a substance used to stick things together ■ *adj* sticky

ad hoc /ad hók, -hók/ *adj, adv* just for a specific purpose

adiet incorrect spelling of **addict**

a·dieu /ə dyoó, ə doó/ *interj, n* (*pl* **a·dieux** /ə dyoóz, ə doóz/ *or* **a·dieus** /ə dyoóz, ə doóz/) goodbye, or an utterance of this (*literary*)

ad in·fi·ni·tum /ad ìnfə nítəm/ *adv* endlessly

ad·i·os /áddee áws, àadee-/ *interj* goodbye (*infml*)

ad·i·pose /áddə pòss/ *adj* fatty ■ *n* fat —**ad·i·pos·i·ty** /áddə póssətee/ *n*

Ad·i·ron·dack Moun·tains /áddə rón dak-/, **Ad·i·ron·dacks** /-daks/ mountain chain in NE New York State. Highest peak Mt. Marcy 5,344 ft./1,629 m.

adj. *abbr* **1** adjective **2** adjunct

Adj. *abbr* adjutant

ad·ja·cent /ə jáyss'nt/ *adj* neighboring or adjoining —**ad·ja·cen·cy** *n*

ad·jec·tive /ájjəktiv/ *n* a word qualifying or describing a noun, e.g., "blue" in "blue eyes" —**ad·jec·ti·val** /ájjək tív'l/ *adj*

ad·join /ə jóyn/ *vti* be next to or share a border with something —**ad·join·ing** *adj*

ad·journ /ə júrn/ *v* **1** *vti* postpone or defer **2** *vi* move as a group o *We adjourned to the lounge.* —**ad·journ·ment** *n*

ad·judge /ə júj/ (-judged, -judg·ing) *vt* make a judgment or declaration about

ad·ju·di·cate /ə joódi kàyt/ (-cat·ed, -cat·ing) *vti* **1** make an official or judicial decision about something **2** judge a competition —**ad·ju·di·ca·tion** /ə joódi káysh'n/ *n* —**ad·ju·di·ca·tor** *n*

ad·junct /áj ùngkt/ *n* **1** something extra added on **2** an assistant ■ *adj* attached temporarily to a staff o *an adjunct professor* —**ad·junc·tion** /ə júngksh'n/ *n* —**ad·junc·tive** *adj*

ad·jure /ə joór/ (-jured, -jur·ing) *vt* **1** command solemnly **2** make an appeal to —**ad·ju·ra·tion** /àjjə ráysh'n/ *n*

ad·just /ə júst/ *v* **1** *vt* change something slightly to make it fit or function better **2** *vti* adapt yourself to new circumstances —**ad·just·a·ble** *adj* —**ad·just·ment** *n*

ad·just·er /ə jústər/, **ad·jus·tor** *n* an insurance claim assessor

ad·ju·tant /ájjətənt/ *n* a commanding officer's administrative assistant

Ad·ler /áddlər/, **Alfred** (1870–1937) Austrian psychiatrist

ad lib /ád líb/ *adv* without advance preparation

ad-lib /ád líb/ *vti* (ad-libbed, ad-lib·bing) improvise a speech or performance ■ *adj* unplanned ■ *n* an improvised remark in a performance —**ad·lib·ber** *n*

ad·min /ád mln/ *n* an administrative assistant

ad·min·is·ter /əd mínnəstər/ *vt* 1 be in charge of 2 dispense o *administer justice* 3 give as medication —**ad·min·is·tra·ble** *adj*

ad·min·is·tra·tion /əd mìnnə stráysh'n/ *n* 1 the management of business or government 2 management or government staff 3 a term of office 4 the executive branch of a government 5 the process of administering something —**ad·min·is·tra·tive** /əd mínnə stràytiv/ —**ad·min·is·tra·tor** /əd mínnə stràytər/ *n*

ad·mi·ra·ble /ádmərəb'l/ *adj* deserving approval —**ad·mi·ra·bly** *adv*

ad·mi·ral /ádmərəl/ *n* 1 a naval commander 2 a brightly colored butterfly —**ad·mi·ral·ty** *n*

> **ORIGIN** The Arabic word from which **admiral** comes meant "commander" – in fact it is the same word that gave us *emir*. The *-al* ending comes from an Arabic element meaning "of," and it was the familiarity of titles like "commander of the sea" and "commander of the faithful" that led Europeans to misunderstand the two Arabic forms, *amir-al*, as one. The word meant "commander, emir" when first adopted into English, but as naval power became significant throughout Europe in the 15C **admiral** became firmly associated with the sea.

ad·mire /əd mír/ (-mired, -mir·ing) *vt* 1 be impressed by 2 respect —**ad·mi·ra·tion** /àdmə ráysh'n/ *n* —**ad·mir·er** *n*

admirine incorrect spelling of **admission**

admissable incorrect spelling of **admissible**

ad·mis·si·ble /əd míssəb'l/ *adj* 1 allowable 2 allowed to enter 3 describes evidence acceptable in court —**ad·mis·si·bil·i·ty** /əd míssə bíllətee/ *n*

ad·mis·sion /əd mísh'n/ *n* 1 right of entry 2 the fee for entry 3 a confession or declaration

ad·mit /əd mít/ (-mit·ted, -mit·ting) *v* 1 *vti* acknowledge that something is true or possible 2 *vt* allow somebody to enter 3 *vti* confess to a fault or error

ad·mit·tance /əd mítt'nss/ *n* 1 permission to enter 2 entry to a place

ad·mit·ted·ly /əd míttədlee/ *adv* as must be acknowledged

ad·mix·ture /əd míkschər, ad-/ *n* 1 a product of mixing 2 an ingredient 3 the process of mixing ingredients

ad·mon·ish /əd mónnish/ *vt* 1 rebuke or reprimand 2 advise or warn —**ad·mon·ish·ment** *n* —**ad·mo·ni·tion** /àdmə nísh'n/ *n*

ad nau·se·am /ad náwzee əm/ *adv* to an extreme or annoying degree

ad nauseum incorrect spelling of **ad nauseam**

a·do /ə dóo/ *n* bustle

a·do·be /ə dóbee/ *n* 1 earthen brick 2 a building made of adobe

> **ORIGIN Adobe** was adopted from the Spanish speakers of North America. The Spanish word comes from an Arabic form meaning "the brick," which is itself probably of Egyptian origin.

ad·o·les·cent /àddə léss'nt/ *n* somebody between childhood and adulthood —**ad·o·les·cence** *n* —**ad·o·les·cent** *adj*

adolesent incorrect spelling of **adolescent**

A·do·nis /ə dónniss, -dô-/ *n* a handsome young man

> **ORIGIN** The original **Adonis** was a handsome young man in Greek mythology.

a·dopt /ə dópt/ *vt* 1 legally raise another's child 2 choose to act in accordance with an idea, belief, or plan 3 assume a position or attitude 4 start using a new name or title 5 vote in favor of something —**a·dopt·a·ble** *adj* —**a·dopt·ed** *adj* —**a·dop·tee** /ə dòp teé/ *n* —**a·dop·tion** *n*

a·dop·tive /ə dóptiv/ *adj* related by adoption o *her adoptive parents*

a·dor·a·ble /ə dáwrəb'l/ *adj* delightful or lovable —**a·dor·a·bly** *adv*

a·dore /ə dáwr/ (a·dored, a·dor·ing) *vt* 1 love deeply 2 worship 3 like very much (*infml*) —**ad·o·ra·tion** /àddə ráysh'n/ *n* —**a·dor·er** *n*

a·dorn /ə dáwrn/ *vt* 1 add decoration to 2 enhance —**a·dorn·ment** *n*

⚡ **ADP** *abbr* automatic data processing

ad·re·nal /ə dreen'l/ *adj* 1 of or on the kidneys 2 of the adrenal glands ■ *n* ANAT = adrenal gland

ad·re·nal gland *n* an organ secreting hormones, situated above each kidney

a·dren·a·line /ə drénn'lən/ *n* a hormone that increases blood pressure and heart rate at times of stress or danger

adress incorrect spelling of **address**

A·dri·at·ic Sea /àydree áttik-/ arm of the Mediterranean Sea, between Italy and the Balkan Peninsula

a·drift /ə dríft/ *adj*, *adv* 1 floating without control or direction 2 living without a goal or purpose

a·droit /ə dróyt/ *adj* skillful —**a·droit·ly** *adv* —**a·droit·ness** *n*

⚡ **ADSL** *abbr* asymmetrical digital subscriber line

ad·sorb /əd sáwrb, -záwrb/ *vti* undergo or cause to undergo adsorption

ad·sorp·tion /əd sáwrpsh'n, -záwrp-/ *n* the adhesion of a thin layer of molecules of a substance to the surface of a solid or liquid —**ad·sorp·tive** *adj*

a·du·ki bean *n* PLANTS, FOOD = adzuki bean

ad·u·la·tion /àjjə láysh'n/ *n* excessive admiration —**ad·u·late** /àjjə làyt/ *vt*

a·dult /ə dúlt, á dùlt/ adj 1 fully developed and mature o *an adult male* o *adult life* 2 unsuitable for children ■ n an adult person or other organism —**a·dult·hood** n

a·dul·ter·ate /ə dúltə ràyt/ (-at·ed, -at·ing) vt make impure —**a·dul·ter·a·tion** /ə dùltə ráysh'n/ n —**a·dul·ter·a·tor** n

a·dul·ter·y /ə dúltəree/ n extramarital sex —**a·dul·ter·er** n —**a·dul·ter·ous** adj

~~adultry~~ incorrect spelling of **adultery**

ad·um·brate /áddəm bràyt, ə dúm-/ (-brat·ed, -brat·ing) vt 1 indicate sketchily 2 foreshadow

adv. abbr adverb

ad·vance /əd vánss/ v (-vanced, -vanc·ing) 1 vti move ahead 2 vt put forward as a proposal 3 vt lend or give beforehand 4 vti raise or rise in status 5 vt bring forward in time 6 vti further the progress or improvement of, or undergo progress or improvement ■ n 1 a development or improvement 2 a payment ahead of time 3 a movement ahead 4 a friendly, sometimes suggestive, approach made to somebody *(often pl)* ■ adj 1 ahead of time 2 going in front —**ad·vance·ment** n —**ad·vanc·er** n

ad·vanced /əd vánst/ adj 1 more highly developed 2 far along in progress

ad·vanced de·gree n a master's degree or doctorate

ad·vance poll n a vote before election day

ad·van·tage /əd vántij/ n 1 a superior position 2 a favorable factor 3 a benefit or gain 4 in tennis, the point after deuce ■ vt (-taged, -tag·ing) benefit ◊ **take advantage of** 1 make use of 2 use in a selfish way

ad·van·ta·geous /àdvən táyjəss/ adj 1 giving an advantage 2 useful

ad·vent /ád vènt/ n 1 the arrival of something important 2 **Ad·vent** the four weeks before Christmas

ad·ven·ti·tious /àdvən tíshəss/ adj 1 from an outside or unexpected source 2 developing in an unusual position o *adventitious roots*

ad·ven·ture /əd vénchər/ n 1 an exciting, often risky, experience 2 a bold undertaking 3 involvement in adventures ■ vi (-tured, -tur·ing) engage in a risky activity

ad·ven·tur·er /əd vénchərər/ n 1 somebody in search of adventure 2 somebody pursuing money or status *(disapproving)*

ad·ven·ture·some /əd vénchərsəm/ adj daring

ad·ven·tur·ous /əd vénchərəss/ adj 1 daring 2 risky —**ad·ven·tur·ous·ly** adv —**ad·ven·tur·ous·ness** n

ad·verb /ád vùrb/ n a word modifying a verb or adjective, e.g., "slowly" in "walked slowly" —**ad·ver·bi·al** /ad vúrbee əl/ adj

ad·ver·sar·y /ádvər sèrree/ (pl -ies) n an opponent —**ad·ver·sar·i·al** /ádvər sáiree əl/ adj

ad·verse /ad vúrs, ád vùrs/ adj unfavorable or difficult —**ad·verse·ly** /ad vúrslee/ adv

ad·ver·si·ty /ad vúrsətee/ n misfortune

ad·ver·tise /ádvər tìz/ (-tised, -tis·ing) v 1 vti publicize a commercial product or service 2 vti publicly announce something such as a job vacancy 3 vt tell others about something —**ad·ver·tis·er** n —**ad·ver·tis·ing** n

ad·ver·tise·ment /àdvər tízmənt, ádvər tìz-, əd vúrtəss-/ n 1 a public announcement advertising something 2 advertising

~~advertisement~~ incorrect spelling of **advertisement**

ad·ver·tor·i·al /àdvər táwree əl/ n an advertisement presented as editorial comment

ad·vice /əd víss/ n 1 recommendation about a course of action 2 official information

ad·vis·a·ble /əd vízəb'l/ adj worth doing and sensible —**ad·vis·a·bil·i·ty** /əd vìzə bíllətee/ n

ad·vise /əd víz/ (-vised, -vis·ing) v 1 vti offer advice to somebody 2 vt recommend something 3 vt inform somebody ◊ See note at **recommend**

ad·vis·ed·ly /əd vízədlee/ adv after consideration

ad·vise·ment /əd vízmənt/ n 1 careful consideration or deliberation ◊ *take something under advisement* 2 the act of giving advice

ad·vis·er /əd vízər/, **ad·vi·sor** n somebody who gives advice

ad·vi·so·ry /əd vízəree/ adj giving advice ■ n (pl -ries) 1 an informational bulletin 2 a warning of something to come

ad·vo·cate vt /ádvə kàyt/ (-cat·ed, -cat·ing) recommend or support ■ n /ádvəkət, -kàyt/ 1 a supporter who speaks in favor of something 2 a legal representative 3 a Scottish barrister —**ad·vo·ca·cy** /-kəssee/ n ◊ See note at **recommend**

adz, **adze** n a tool with an arched blade set at right angles to the handle. Use: trimming and shaping wood.

ad·zu·ki bean /ad zóokee-/, **a·du·ki bean** /ə dóokee-/, **a·zu·ki bean** /ə zóokee-/ n 1 a bean used in vegetarian or sweet dishes 2 a plant that produces adzuki beans

Ae·ge·an Sea /i jèe ən-/ arm of the Mediterranean Sea, between Greece and Turkey

ae·gis /éejiss/, **e·gis** ◊ **under the aegis of** with the support or protection of *(fml)*

ORIGIN The Greek word from which **aegis** comes was used for the goatskin shield of the god Zeus, a symbol of his traditional function as a protector. The English form comes from Latin.

Ae·ne·as /i nèe əss/ n in Greek and Roman mythology, a Trojan who spent many years traveling after the fall of Troy

Ae·o·lis /èe ə liss/, **Ae·o·li·a** /ee ólee ə/ ancient region on the northwestern coast of Asia Minor —**Ae·o·li·an** adj

ae·on n TIME = **eon**

aer·ate /áir ràyt/ (-at·ed, -at·ing) vt introduce air into —**aer·a·tion** /air ráysh'n/ n

aer·i·al /áiree əl/ adj 1 of or in the air 2 involving aircraft 3 light and insubstantial ■ n UK a radio antenna

aer·ie /áiree, eer-/, **eyr·ie**, **aer·y** (pl -ies), **eyr·y** n a bird of prey's nest

⚡**aero** abbr aviation industry (in Internet addresses)

aero-, aeri-, aer- prefix 1 air, atmosphere, gas ○ aerodynamic 2 aviation ○ aerospace

aer·o·bat·ics /àirō báttiks/ n stunt flying (+ sing or pl verb) —**aer·o·bat·ic** adj

aer·o·bic /air róbik, ə-/ adj 1 of aerobics 2 needing oxygen 3 giving oxygen 4 increasing respiration —**aer·o·bic·al·ly** adv

aer·o·bics /ai róbiks, ə-/ n (+ sing or pl verb) 1 fitness exercises done to music 2 activities that increase respiration

aer·o·dy·nam·ic /àirō dī námmik/ adj 1 designed to reduce air resistance 2 of aerodynamics —**aero·dy·nam·i·cal·ly** adv

aer·o·dy·nam·ics /àirō dī námmiks/ n the study of objects moving through air (+ sing verb) ■ npl aerodynamic properties (+ pl verb) —**aer·o·dy·nam·i·cist** /-əssist/ n

aer·o·gram /áirō gràm/, **aer·o·gramme** n an airmail letter

aer·o·li·za·tion /àirəli záysh'n/ n the airborne transmission of a substance in a vaporized form

aer·o·nau·tics /àirə náwtiks/ n the science of flight (+ sing verb)

aer·o·sol /áirə sòl/ n 1 a container holding a substance that can be dispensed under pressure as a spray 2 a substance sprayed from an aerosol 3 a suspension of particles in a gas

aer·o·sol·ize /áirəsə līz/ (-ized, -iz·ing) vt convert a substance into a spray

aer·o·space /áirō spàyss/ n the atmosphere and outer space ■ adj of aircraft and spacecraft

aer·y n BIRDS = aerie

Aes·chy·lus /éskələss, ées-/ (525?–426 BC) Greek dramatist

Ae·sop /éessəp, ēë sòp/ (620?–560? BC) Greek writer of fables

aes·thete /és theèt/, **es·thete** n a lover of beauty

aes·thet·ic /es théttik/, **es·thet·ic** adj 1 of aesthetics 2 appreciating beauty 3 pleasing in appearance ■ n a set of principles about art —**aes·thet·i·cal·ly** adv

aes·thet·i·cism /es thétti sìzzəm/, **es·thet·i·cism** n 1 the philosophical doctrine that all moral principles are derived from beauty 2 devotion to beauty

aes·thet·ics /es théttiks/, **es·thet·ics** n the philosophical study of beauty (+ sing verb) —**aes·the·ti·cian** /èsthə tísh'n/ n

ae·ti·ol·o·gy n MED, PHILOSOPHY = etiology

a·far /ə faàr/ adv far away (literary)

AFB abbr Air Force Base

AFDC abbr Aid to Families with Dependent Children

af·fa·ble /áffəb'l/ adj friendly and good-natured —**af·fa·bil·i·ty** /àffə bíllətee/ n —**af·fa·bly** adv

af·fair /ə fáir/ n 1 a business matter 2 an incident, especially a scandalous one ○ that odd affair at work last year 3 a responsibility or concern ○ What he does with the information is his own affair. 4 a social event 5 an object of a particular kind ○ The house is a ramshackle affair. 6 a sexual relationship between two people who are not married to each other ■ **af·fairs** npl 1 business matters 2 matters of public interest ○ foreign affairs

af·fect[1] /ə fékt/ vt 1 cause a change in or influence 2 move emotionally

USAGE affect or effect? The verb **affect** means "cause a change in": The floods affected the whole region. The noun **effect** describes the changes that result from this: The effects of the flooding were widespread. The verb **effect**, used in formal contexts, means "make something happen": He effected a cure/a withdrawal/major changes.

af·fect[2] /ə fékt/ vt 1 pretend to have or be something 2 adopt a style or manner

af·fec·ta·tion /à fek táysh'n/ n behavior intended to impress

af·fect·ed /ə féktəd/ adj unnatural and intending or intended to impress —**af·fect·ed·ly** adv —**af·fect·ed·ness** n

af·fect·ing /ə fékting/ adj emotionally moving

af·fec·tion /ə fékshən/ n fondness or liking ■ **af·fect·ions** npl feelings of fondness ◊ See note at **love**

af·fec·tion·ate /ə fékshənət/ adj loving —**af·fec·tion·ate·ly** adv

af·fec·tive /ə féktiv/ adj 1 of emotional expression 2 emotionally moving —**af·fec·tive·ly** adv

af·fi·da·vit /àffi dáyvit/ n a written version of a sworn statement

af·fil·i·ate vti /ə fillee àyt/ (-at·ed, -at·ing) combine with another person or organization ■ n /ə fillee ət, -àyt/ an affiliated member —**af·fil·i·a·tion** /ə fillee áysh'n/ n

af·fin·i·ty /ə fínnitee/ (pl -ties) n 1 a natural liking or identification 2 a similarity or connection 3 relationship by marriage

af·firm /ə fúrm/ vt 1 declare positively and publicly 2 declare support or admiration for —**af·fir·ma·tion** /àffər máysh'n/ n

af·fir·ma·tive /ə fúrmətiv/ adj indicating agreement ■ n 1 a positive assertion 2 a word or statement conveying agreement 3 the side in a debate that supports a proposition ■ interj yes —**af·fir·ma·tive·ly** adv

af·fir·ma·tive ac·tion *n* a social and legal program to stop discrimination

af·fix *vt* /ə fĭks/ 1 fasten or attach 2 add on ■ *n* /ắffĭks/ 1 a part added to a word to modify its meaning or part of speech or to form an inflection 2 something attached

af·flict /ə flĭkt/ *vt* cause distress to

af·flic·tion /ə flĭkshən/ *n* 1 distress 2 a cause of distress

af·flu·ent /ắffloo ənt,. aff loõ–/ *adj* wealthy —**af·flu·ence** *n* —**af·flu·ent·ly** *adv*

ORIGIN Affluent originally meant "flowing," and later "flowing freely" or "abundant." The association with wealth did not develop until the 18C.

af·ford /ə fáwrd/ *vt* 1 be able to buy 2 be able to do or provide without bad consequences ○ We can't afford to be late. 3 be able to spare 4 provide *(fml)* —**af·ford·a·ble** *adj*

af·for·est /ə fáwrəst/ *vt* plant trees on —**af·for·es·ta·tion** /ə fàwrə stáysh'n/ *n*

af·fray /ə fráy/ *n* a fight in a public place

af·front /ə frúnt/ *n* an open insult —**af·front** *vt*

Af·ghan /ắf gàn/ *n* 1 somebody from Afghanistan 2 *also* **Af·ghan hound** a tall dog with a long silky coat —**Af·ghan** *adj*

af·ghan·i /af gánnee, -gáanee/ *(pl* **-is)** *n* the main unit of Afghan currency

Af·ghan·i·stan /af gánni stàn/ landlocked country in SW Asia. Cap. Kabul. Pop. 26,813,057 (2001).

a·fi·cio·na·do /ə fìshə naàdō, ə fīshee ə–/ *(pl* **-dos)** *n* a knowledgeable enthusiast

a·field /ə feeld/ *adv, adj* away from home or customary surroundings ○ wandered far afield

AFL *abbr* 1 American Federation of Labor 2 American Football League

a·flame /ə fláym/ *adj* 1 on fire 2 impassioned

AFL-CIO *abbr* American Federation of Labor and Congress of Industrial Organizations

a·float /ə flṓt/ *adj, adv* 1 floating on water 2 on board a ship 3 financially solvent

a·foot /ə fŏŏt/ *adj, adv* 1 happening, often secretly or subtly 2 on foot

a·fore·men·tioned /ə fáwr mènshənd/ *(fml) adj* mentioned earlier ■ *n* the person or thing previously mentioned

a·fore·said /ə fáwr sèd/ *adj* named earlier *(fml)*

a for·ti·o·ri /aa fàwrtee áwree, ay fàwrtee ṓ rī/ *adv* with more reason

Afr. *abbr* 1 Africa 2 African

a·fraid /ə fráyd/ *adj* 1 frightened 2 reluctant 3 regretful

a·fresh /ə frésh/ *adv* again

Af·ri·ca /ắffrikə/ second largest continent, lying south of Europe with the Atlantic Ocean to the west and the Indian Ocean to ˙the east. Pop. 797,148,044 (2000).

Af·ri·can /ắffrikən/ *adj* of Africa ■ *n* 1 somebody from Africa 2 somebody of African descent

Af·ri·can A·mer·i·can, **Af·ro-A·mer·i·can** *n* an American of African descent —**Af·ri·can A·mer·i·can** *adj* —**Af·ro-A·mer·i·can** *adj*

USAGE African American is now used more commonly than Afro-American to describe Black Americans. Black is a broader term referring to Black people with Caribbean or Hispanic backgrounds as well as to those who are not American. People of color refers to people of whatever origin and nationality who are not Caucasian.

Af·ri·can Car·ib·be·an *n* a Caribbean of African descent —**Af·ri·can Car·ib·be·an** *adj*

Af·ri·kaans /àffri kaáns, -kaánz/ *n* a South African language descended from Dutch ■ *adj* of Afrikaans or Afrikaners

Af·ri·ka·ner /àffri kaánər/ *n* an Afrikaans-speaking South African —**Af·ri·ka·ner** *adj*

Af·ro /ắffrō/ *n (pl* **-ros)** a hairstyle with tight curls ■ *adj* of Africa

aft *adv, adj* at the back of a ship or aircraft

AFT *abbr* American Federation of Teachers

af·ter /ắftər/ *prep* 1 later than 2 behind 3 in pursuit of 4 regarding 5 following from 6 similar to or imitating 7 in conformity to 8 past the hour of ■ *adv* 1 later 2 farther back ■ *conj* following a time when ■ *adj* subsequent ◇ **after all** 1 in spite of other appearances or considerations ○ After all, she's only a beginner. 2 in the end ○ She decided to stay after all.

af·ter·birth /ắftər bùrth/ *n* the placenta expelled after delivery of a fetus

af·ter·care /ắftər kàir/ *n* 1 care provided after leaving a hospital, prison, or other institution 2 counseling of bereaved clients by funeral home staff after a death and the funeral

af·ter·ef·fect /ắftər i fèkt/ *n* a delayed result, effect, or reaction

af·ter·glow /ắftər glṓ/ *n* 1 a glow from a light no longer directly visible 2 a good feeling after something

af·ter·hours *adj* occurring after closing time

af·ter·life /ắftər līf/ *n* 1 life after death 2 a later stage of life

af·ter·mar·ket /ắftər maàrkət/ *n* a market for replacement parts

af·ter·math /ắftər màth/ *n* the consequences of or period following a bad event

ORIGIN Math was a word meaning "mowing," now obsolete. The aftermath was the grass that springs up after mowing, as a second crop.

af·ter·noon /ắftər noṓn/ *n* the time between midday and evening

af·ter·shave /ắftər shàyv/ *n* a soothing scented liquid for men's faces after shaving

af·ter·shock /áftər shòk/ n 1 a small earthquake following a larger one 2 a delayed reaction

af·ter·taste /áftər tàyst/ n 1 a persisting taste 2 an unpleasant feeling after something

af·ter·thought /áftər thàwt/ n something added later

af·ter·ward /áftərwərd/, **af·ter·wards** /-wərdz/ adv at a later time

af·ter·world /áftər wùrld/ n the world of the dead

Ag symbol silver

a·ga /áàgə, ággə/ n in an Islamic country, a military commander

a·gain /ə gén/ adv 1 once more at another time 2 as before 3 in addition 4 on the other hand

a·gainst /ə génst/ prep 1 in competition with 2 in contact with by leaning 3 in collision with 4 in the opposite direction to 5 in contrast with 6 as protection from 7 compared with 8 contrary to

A·ga Khan IV /àagə kaán/ (b. 1936) Swiss-born Muslim leader

Ag·a·mem·non /ággə mém nòn, -nən/ n in Greek mythology, the leader of the Greek army in the Trojan War

a·gape[1] /ə gáyp/ adv, adj (literary) 1 wide open 2 open-mouthed

a·ga·pe[2] /aa gaà pay/ n 1 nonsexual love 2 Christian love

a·gar /áàgər, áy-/, **a·gar-a·gar** n a powdered seaweed extract. Use: gelling agent, thickener, culture medium for microorganisms.

Ag·as·si /ággəssee/, **Andre** (b. 1970) US tennis player

Ag·as·siz /ággəssee/, **Louis** (1807–73) Swiss-born US naturalist and glaciologist

ag·ate /ággət/ n a typically striped form of chalcedony. Use: gems.

a·ga·ve /ə gáavee, -gáy-/ (pl -ves or same) n a spiny-leaved plant. Use: fiber, alcoholic drinks, especially tequila.

age n 1 how old somebody or something is 2 a stage of life 3 legal adulthood 4 the state of being old 5 also **Age** a historical era 6 also **Age** a relatively short division of recent geologic time ■ **ag·es** npl a long time (infml) ■ vti (**aged**, **ag·ing** or **age·ing**) 1 grow or cause somebody to grow old 2 improve or cause something to improve over time

-age suffix 1 action, or result of an action o coinage 2 housing o orphanage 3 condition, office o peerage 4 charge o postage

ag·ed adj 1 /áyjəd/ old or elderly 2 /ayjd/ of a particular age 3 /ayjd/ improved with time ■ /áyjəd/ npl senior citizens

A·gee /áyjee/, **James** (1909–55) US poet, novelist, screenwriter, and movie critic

age group n people of a similar age

age·ism /áyj ìzzəm/, **ag·ism** n discrimination based on age —**age·ist** adj

age·less /áyjləss/ adj 1 never seeming to grow older 2 of all generations —**age·less·ness** n

a·gen·cy /áyjənssee/ (pl -cies) n 1 a company acting as an agent 2 a government organization 3 the office of an agency 4 action or operation

a·gen·da /ə jéndə/ n 1 a list of business matters to be discussed 2 somebody's underlying motive

a·gent /áyjənt/ n 1 somebody representing another 2 somebody providing a particular service for another o a travel agent 3 a government employee 4 something, e.g., a chemical substance, organism, or natural force, that causes an effect 5 a means effecting a result 6 a spy (infml)

a·gent pro·vo·ca·teur /a zhaàN praw váwkə tùr/ (pl **a·gents pro·vo·ca·teurs** /pronunc. same/) n an undercover agent

age of con·sent n the legal age for marriage or sex

age-old adj having existed for a long time

ag·glom·er·ate /ə glómmə ràyt/ (-at·ed, -at·ing) vti collect together in a mass, or form something into a mass —**ag·glom·er·a·tion** /ə glòmmə ráysh'n/ n

ag·glu·ti·nate /ə glòott'n àyt/ (-nat·ed, -nat·ing) vti adhere or cause something to adhere —**ag·glu·ti·na·tion** /ə glòott'n áysh'n/ n

~~aggragate~~ incorrect spelling of aggregate

ag·gra·vate /ággrə vàyt/ (-vat·ed, -vat·ing) vt 1 irritate or anger (infml) 2 make worse —**ag·gra·vat·ing** adj —**ag·gra·vat·ing·ly** adv —**ag·gra·va·tion** /ággrə váysh'n/ n

ag·gre·gate adj /ággrəgət, -gàyt/ forming a total or whole (fml) ■ n /ággrəgət, -gàyt/ 1 a total or whole (fml) 2 mixed stone, gravel, and sand ■ vti /ággrə gàyt/ (-gat·ed, -gat·ing) unite to form a total or whole —**ag·gre·ga·tion** /ággrə gáysh'n/ n

ag·gres·sion /ə grésh'n/ n hostile actions, attitudes, or behavior

ag·gres·sive /ə gréssiv/ adj 1 showing aggression 2 assertive or forceful o aggressive sales tactics —**ag·gres·sive·ly** adv

ag·gres·sor /ə gréssər/ n a person or country that starts a war, fight, or argument

ag·grieve /ə greév/ (-grieved, -griev·ing) vt cause distress to (fml) —**ag·grieved** adj —**ag·griev·ed·ly** /-ədlee/ adv

a·ghast /ə gást/ adj horrified

ag·ile /áj'l/ adj 1 nimble 2 mentally quick —**ag·ile·ly** adv —**a·gil·i·ty** /ə jílláee/ n

ag·i·tate /ájji tàyt/ (-tat·ed, -tat·ing) v 1 vt make anxious 2 vi arouse public feeling or support 3 vt cause to move vigorously or violently —**ag·i·tat·ed** adj —**ag·i·tat·ed·ly** adv —**ag·i·ta·tion** /ájji táysh'n/ n —**ag·i·ta·tor** n

a·glow /ə glṓ/ adj glowing

Ag·new /ág noò/, **Spiro T.** (1918–96) vice president of the United States (1969–73)

ag·nos·tic /ag nóstik/ *n* 1 somebody who denies that God's existence is provable 2 somebody who doubts something o *I'm an agnostic concerning space aliens.* —**ag·nos·tic** *adj*—**ag·nos·ti·cism** /-sizzəm/ *n*

a·go /ə gó/ *adv, adj* before now

a·gog /ə góg/ *adj* very interested

ORIGIN Agog probably comes from the old French phrase *en gogues* meaning "enjoying yourself" (*en* was replaced with *a-*, as in *asleep*). The origin of the old French word *gogue,* "merriment," is not known.

ag·o·nize /ággə nîz/ (-nized, -niz·ing) *v* 1 *vi* spend much time worrying 2 *vti* suffer, or cause somebody to suffer —**ag·o·niz·ing** *adj* —**ag·o·niz·ing·ly** *adv*

ag·o·ny /ággənee/ (*pl* -nies) *n* 1 great physical pain or mental anguish 2 an intense emotion o *an agony of indecision*

ag·o·ra /ággərə, ə gáwrə/ (*pl* **a·go·ras** *or* **a·go·rae** /-ree/) *n* a marketplace, especially in ancient Greece

ag·o·ra·pho·bi·a /àggərə fóbee ə/ *n* fear of open spaces or public places —**ag·o·ra·pho·bic** *adj, n*

🗲 **AGP** *abbr* accelerated graphics port

Ag·ra /aagrə/ city in N India, site of the Taj Mahal. Pop. 891,790 (1991).

~~agragate~~ incorrect spelling of **aggregate**

Ag·ra·hay·a·na /àggrəhī aanə/ *n* HINDUISM, CALENDAR = **Margasirsa**

a·grar·i·an /ə gráiree ən/ *adj* 1 of rural life 2 of land 3 promoting farmers' interests ■ *n* a land reformer —**a·grar·i·an·ism** *n*

a·gree /ə grée/ (**a·greed**) *v* 1 *vi* be in accord 2 *vi* consent to something 3 *vti* reach consensus or a decision about something o *agree on a plan* 4 *vi* be consistent o *The witnesses' stories don't agree.* 5 *vi* be suitable or good for somebody o *The climate doesn't agree with me.* 6 *vi* match grammatically

SYNONYMS agree, concur, acquiesce, consent, assent CORE MEANING: accept an idea, plan, or course of action that has been put forward

a·gree·a·ble /ə grée əb'l/ *adj* 1 pleasing 2 friendly 3 willing to comply —**a·gree·a·ble·ness** *n*—**a·gree·a·bly** *adv*

a·gree·ment /ə gréemənt/ *n* 1 a formal contract 2 consensus 3 grammatical correspondence

~~agression~~ incorrect spelling of **aggression**

~~agressive~~ incorrect spelling of **aggressive**

~~agressor~~ incorrect spelling of **aggressor**

ag·ri·busi·ness /ággri bíznəss/ *n* farming as an industry

ag·ri·cul·ture /ággri kùlchər/ *n* farming —**ag·ri·cul·tur·al** *adj* —**a·gri·cul·tur·al·ist** *n* —**agri·cul·tur·ist** /àggri kúlchərist/ *n*

ag·ro·chem·i·cal /àggrō kémmik'l/, **ag·ri·chem·i·cal** /àggri-/ *n* a chemical used in farming

a·gron·o·my /ə grónnəmee/ *n* the science of soils and plants —**a·gron·o·mist** *n*

a·ground /ə grównd/ *adj, adv* on ground, especially on the bottom of shallow water

AH, A.H. *adv* indicates a date in the Islamic calendar. Full form **anno Hegirae**

a·head /ə héd/ *adv, adj* 1 in front 2 forward 3 to the future 4 earlier 5 in the lead ◊ **get ahead** succeed or advance financially (*infml*)

A·hern /ə húrn/, **Bertie** (*b.* 1951) Irish prime minister (1997–)

AHL *abbr* American Hockey League

a·hold /ə hóld/ ◊ **get ahold of** regain emotional control after a shock or state of anxiety or excitement (*infml*)

-aholic *suffix* dependent on or having an extreme fondness for o *workaholic*

a·hoy /ə hóy/ *interj* attracts the attention of other sailors

🗲 **AI** *abbr* 1 artificial insemination 2 artificial intelligence

aid *vti* give help ■ *n* 1 money or supplies given to those in need 2 assistance o *A passer-by came to my aid.* 3 somebody or something helpful o *visual aids such as maps*

aide *n* 1 an assistant 2 an aide-de-camp ◊ See note at **assistant**

aide-de-camp /àyd də kámp/ (*pl* **aides-de-camp** /àydz-/) *n* a military officer acting as a confidential assistant to a general or senior officer

aide-mé-moire /àyd mem waar/ (*pl* **aide-mé-moires** /*pronunc. same*/ *or* **aides-mé-moire** /*pronunc. same*/) *n* (*fml*) 1 a brief written summary of decisions made in a meeting 2 a memory aid

AIDS /aydz/ *n* a serious disease of the immune system. Full form **acquired immune deficiency syndrome**

ai·ki·do /ī kee dô, ī kée-/ *n* a martial art that uses blows made with the hands and feet

ail /ayl/ *vt* cause to suffer or have problems (*literary*)

SPELLCHECK Do not confuse the spelling of **ail** and **ale** ("beer"), which sound similar.

ai·le·ron /áylə ròn/ *n* a flap on an aircraft wing

Ai·ley /áylee/, **Alvin** (1931–89) US dancer and choreographer

ail·ing /áyling/ *adj* in poor condition o *the nation's ailing steel industry*

ail·ment /áylmənt/ *n* an illness

aim *v* 1 *vi* plan to do something 2 *vt* direct a message, product, action, or blow 3 *vti* point a weapon ■ *n* 1 an intention 2 the aiming of a weapon o *Take aim and fire.* 3 skill in aiming

aim·less /áymləss/ *adj* without purpose —**aim·less·ly** *adv*

ain't *contr* ⚠ a contraction of "am not," "is not," "are not," "have not," or "has not" (*nonstandard*)

USAGE Ain't is one of the most informal verb contractions in English, and its use in formal contexts will undoubtedly be criticized. It is, however, accepted in folk and popular song lyrics, show titles, direct quotations, fictional dialogue, and jocular set phrases such as "You ain't seen nothin' yet."

air /air/ *n* **1** the gases forming the atmosphere **2** the atmosphere of an open space **3** the sky **4** transportation in an aircraft ◊ *send it by air* ◊ *an air terminal* **5** a distinctive quality ◊ *an air of indifference* **6** a melody **7** air conditioning ■ **airs** *npl* affected manners or conduct meant to impress others ■ **v 1** *vti* broadcast, or be broadcast **2** *vt* make known **3** *vti* expose or be exposed to a fresh or warm atmosphere ◊ **clear the air** remove the tension or misunderstanding from a situation ◊ **on (the) air** being broadcast on radio or television ◊ **up in the air** undecided or uncertain ◊ **walk on air** be extremely happy

SPELLCHECK Do not confuse the spelling of **air**, **ere** ("before"), **err** ("make a mistake"), or **heir** ("legal inheritor"), which sound similar.

air bag *n* a bag that inflates as a safety device in a car

air base *n* a military airport

air·borne /áir bàwrn/ *adj* **1** carried by air **2** in flight

air brake *n* **1** an air-operated brake **2** an aircraft brake

air·brush /áir brúsh/ *n* a paint-spraying device —**air·brush** *vt*

air con·di·tion·ing *n* an air-cooling system in a building or vehicle —**air con·di·tioned** *adj* —**air con·di·tion·er** *n*

air·craft /áir kràft/ (*pl same*) *n* a flying vehicle

air·craft car·ri·er *n* a large warship with a deck designed to allow aircraft to take off and land

air·crew /áir kròo/ *n* the crew of an aircraft

air·field /áir feèld/ *n* **1** an area where aircraft can take off and land **2** an airport

air·flow /áir flò/ *n* a flow of air

air·foil /áir fòyl/ *n* a part of an aircraft that moves to provide lift or control

air force *n* a branch of the armed services using aircraft

Air Force One *n* the US President's official airplane

air gun *n* a gun fired by compressed air

air·head /áir hèd/ *n* a person regarded as unintelligent and superficial (*slang insult*)

air·less /áirləss/ *adj* without air, fresh air, or movement of air ◊ *an airless room* ◊ *an airless night* —**air·less·ness** *n*

air·lift /áir lìft/ *n* the transport of people, supplies, or equipment by air, especially in an emergency —**air·lift** *vt*

air·line /áir lìn/ *n* a company operating commercial flights

air·lin·er /áir lìnər/ *n* a large passenger aircraft

air·lock /áir lòk/ *n* **1** an airtight chamber **2** an obstruction in the flow of a liquid caused by an air bubble

air·mail /áir màyl/ *n* **1** the sending of mail by air **2** mail sent by air —**air·mail** *adj*, *vt*

air·man /áirmən/ (*pl* -**men** /-mən/) *n* **1** an enlisted person in the US Air Force **2** a pilot, especially of a military aircraft

air mar·shal *n* a sky marshal

air·plane /áir plàyn/ *n* a flying vehicle with wings and an engine

air·play /áir plày/ *n* the broadcasting of a recording

air·port /áir pàwrt/ *n* an area where civil aircraft may take off and land

air pump *n* a device for compressing or moving air

air rage *n* disruptive or aggressive behavior by passengers aboard an aircraft

air raid *n* an attack by aircraft on a ground target

air ri·fle *n* a rifle fired by compressed air

air·ship /áir shìp/ *n* a powered lighter-than-air aircraft

air·space /áir spàyss/ *n* **1** the space above an area of land claimed by a government **2** the space occupied by a flying aircraft

air speed *n* an aircraft's speed in relation to the air

air·strip /áir strìp/ *n* a runway with no airport facilities

air·tight /áir tìt/ *adj* **1** preventing the passage of air **2** without weak points ◊ *an airtight alibi*

air·time /áir tìm/ *n* the time during which a program or subject is broadcast

air·waves /áir wàyvz/ *npl* radio waves used in broadcasting

air·way /áir wày/ *n* **1** a passage for air from the nose or mouth to the lungs **2** a tube to assist breathing **3** a route for aircraft (*often pl*)

air·wor·thy /áir wùrthee/ *adj* in good enough condition to be safe to fly —**air·wor·thi·ness** *n*

air·y /áiree/ (-**i·er**, -**i·est**) *adj* **1** roomy **2** well ventilated **3** carefree or unconcerned ◊ *an airy wave of her hand* **4** ethereal —**air·i·ly** *adv*

A·i·sha /aàa ee shàà/, **A·ye·shah** (614?–678) wife of the prophet Muhammad

aisle /īl/ *n* a passageway between seating areas or displays of goods

SPELLCHECK Do not confuse the spelling of

aisle and **isle** ("an island"), which sound similar.

aitch /aych/ *n* the letter "h"

Aix-en-Pro·vence /àyk saaN prō vaàNs, èk-/ city in SE France. Pop. 134,222 (1999).

A·jac·cio /aa yaáchō/ capital and main port of Corse-du-Sud Department, W Corsica, France. Pop. 52,880 (1999).

a·jar /ə jaàr/ *adj, adv* partially open

AK *abbr* Alaska

a.k.a., aka *abbr* also known as

Ak·bar /ák baar/ (1542–1605) emperor of India (1556–1605)

AKC *abbr* American Kennel Club

A·khe·na·ton /aàkə naát'n, aàk-/, **Ikh·na·ton** /ik-/ (fl 14C BC) Egyptian pharaoh

Akh·ma·to·va /ak maátəvə, àkmə tōvə/, **Anna** (1889–1966) Russian poet

Ak·i·hi·to /aàkee heétō/ (b. 1933) emperor of Japan (1989–)

a·kim·bo /ə kímbō/ *adj, adv* with the hands on the hips and elbows outward

a·kin /ə kín/ *adj* **1** similar **2** related by blood

~~acknowledge~~ incorrect spelling of **acknowledge**

Ak·ron /ákrən/ city in NE Ohio. Pop. 215,712 (1998).

Al *symbol* aluminum

AL *abbr* **1** Alabama **2** American League

-al *suffix* **1** of or characterized by o *delusional* **2** action, process o *disposal*

à la /aà laa, állə/, **a la** *prep* in the style of

Ala. *abbr* Alabama

Al·a·bam·a /àllə bámmə/ state of the SE United States. Cap. Montgomery. Pop. 4,447,100 (2000). —**Al·a·bam·an** *adj, n* —**Al·a·ba·mi·an** /-báymee ən/ *adj, n*

al·a·bas·ter /állə bástər/ *n* a white or translucent gypsum. Use: decorative carving. ■ *adj* of or like alabaster

à la carte /aà laa kaàrt, àllə-/, **a la carte** *adj, adv* with each dish separately priced

a·lac·ri·ty /ə lákrətee/ *n* eager readiness

al·a·mo /állə mō/ *n Southwest US* a poplar tree

Al·a·mo /állə mō/ chapel in San Antonio, Texas, besieged by Mexican forces in 1836 when all 187 Texan defenders were killed

Al·a·mo·gor·do /àlləmə gáwrdō/ city in S New Mexico, northeast of White Sands Missile Range, site of the first atomic bomb explosion, on July 16, 1945. Pop. 28,312 (1998).

a·larm /ə laárm/ *n* **1** a warning sound, signal, or device **2** a security device attached to property, or the sound it makes **3** an alarm clock **4** fear ■ *vt* **1** frighten **2** warn **3** equip with a security device —**a·larmed** *adj* —**a·larm·ing** *adj* —**a·larm·ing·ly** *adv*

a·larm clock *n* a clock that can be set to sound an alarm to wake somebody

a·larm·ist /ə laármist/ *n* somebody who

spreads unnecessary fear —**a·larm·ism** *n* —**a·larm·ist** *adj*

a·las /ə láss/ *interj* expresses sorrow or regret ■ *adv* unfortunately

Alas. *abbr* Alaska

A·las·ka /ə láskə/ US state in NW North America. Cap. Juneau. Pop. 626,932 (2000). —**A·las·kan** *adj, n*

A·las·ka Na·tive *n* a member of any of the original peoples of Alaska

A·las·ka Range mountain range in S Alaska. Highest peak Mt. McKinley 20,320 ft./6,194 m.

A·las·ka Stan·dard Time, A·las·ka Time *n* the local standard time in Alaska

Al·ba·ni·a /al báynee ə/ country in SE Europe, bordering the Adriatic Sea. Cap. Tirana. Pop. 3,510,484 (2001).

Al·ba·ni·an /al báynee ən/ *n* **1** the official language of Albania **2** somebody from Albania —**Al·ba·ni·an** *adj*

Al·ba·ny /áwlbənee/ **1** capital of New York State. Pop. 94,305 (1998). **2** river in Ontario, Canada. Length 610 mi./982 km.

al·ba·tross /álbə tròss/ (*pl* -**tross·es** *or same*) *n* a large seabird

Al·bee /áwlbee, ál-/, **Edward** (b. 1928) US playwright

al·be·it /àwl beé it/ *conj* even though

Al·be·marle Sound /álbər maàrl-/ inlet of the Atlantic Ocean, in NE North Carolina. Length 50 mi./80 km.

Al·bert /álbərt/, **Prince** (1819–61) German-born prince consort to Queen Victoria

Al·ber·ta /al búrtə/ province in W Canada. Cap. Edmonton. Pop. 2,997,236 (2000).

al·bi·no /al bínō/ (*pl* -**nos**) *n* a person, animal, or plant lacking the usual pigmentation —**al·bi·nism** /álbi nìzzəm/ *n*

al·bum /álbəm/ *n* **1** a book with blank pages for keeping photographs, stamps, or other collected items **2** a music recording

ORIGIN The Latin word *album* means "blank tablet," and comes from *albus* "white." It came into English through a German use of *album amicorum*, "album of friends," an autograph book in which scholars collected signatures and greetings from colleagues.

al·bu·men /al byóomən/ *n* **1** the white of an egg (*technical*) **2** the protein component of egg white

al·bu·min /al byóomin/ *n* a water-soluble protein coagulated by heat —**al·bu·mi·nous** *adj*

Al·bu·quer·que /álbə kùrkee/ largest city in New Mexico. Pop. 419,311 (1998).

Al·ca·traz /álkə tràz/ island in San Francisco Bay, California, site of a federal prison from 1933 to 1963

al·che·my /álkəmee/ *n* **1** an early form of chemistry that sought to change base metals into gold **2** a transforming or enchanting power —**al·chem·i·cal** /al kémmik'l/ *adj* —**al·che·mist** *n*

~~alchol~~ incorrect spelling of **alcohol**

al·co·hol /álkə háwl/ *n* **1** C_2H_5OH a liquid found in intoxicating drinks or used as a solvent **2** drinks containing alcohol

al·co·hol·ic /álkə háwlik/ *adj* **1** of or containing alcohol **2** addicted to alcohol ■ *n* somebody addicted to alcohol

Al·co·hol·ics A·non·y·mous *n* an organization for alcoholics

al·co·hol·ism /álkə haw lìzzəm/ *n* **1** addiction to alcohol **2** alcohol poisoning

Al·cott /áwlkət, ál-/, **Louisa May** (1832–88) US novelist

al·cove /ál kòv/ *n* a recess in a wall

Al·den /áwldən/, **John** (1599?–1687) English-born American colonist

al den·te /àl dén tay, àl déntee/ *adj* cooked just long enough to be still firm and not too soft

al·der /áwldər/ *n* a deciduous tree of northern temperate regions

al·der·man /áwldərmən/ (*pl* **-men** /-mən/) *n* a member of a local council or legislative body

Al·drin /áwldrin/, **Buzz** (*b.* 1930) US astronaut

ale /ayl/ *n* a type of beer ◊ See note at **ail**

~~alein~~ incorrect spelling of **alien**

A·lep·po /ə léppō/ *city* in NW Syria. Pop. 1,582,930 (1994).

a·lert /ə lúrt/ *adj* **1** watchful **2** mentally sharp and responsive ■ *n* **1** a warning of danger **2** a time during which an alert is in effect ■ *vt* warn of danger or difficulties —**a·lert·ly** *adv* —**a·lert·ness** *n*

A·leu·tian Is·lands /ə loósh'n-/ island chain off SW Alaska

A·lex·an·der II /állig zándər/ (1818–81) tsar of Russia (1855–81)

A·lex·an·der tech·nique *n* a method of improving posture by developing awareness of it

> **ORIGIN** The technique is named for the Australian physiotherapist Frederick Alexander (1869–1955), who developed it.

A·lex·an·der the Great (356–323 BC) king of Macedonia (336–323 BC)

A·lex·an·dria /állig zándree ə/ **1** city in E Virginia. Pop. 118,300 (1998). **2** port in N Egypt. Pop. 3,328,000 (1998). —**Al·ex·an·dri·an** *adj*

~~alfabet~~ incorrect spelling of **alphabet**

al·fal·fa /al fálfə/ *n* a plant grown for hay and forage

Al·fred (the Great) /álfrəd/ (849–901) king of Wessex (871–901)

al·fres·co /al fréskō/ *adv, adj* outdoors

al·ga /álgə/ (*pl* **-gae** /-jee/ *or* **-gas**) *n* a photosynthesizing water organism such as seaweed

al·ge·bra /áljəbrə/ *n* the branch of mathematics using letters to represent unknown numbers —**al·ge·bra·ic** /àljə bráyik/ *adj* —**al·ge·bra·i·cal·ly** *adv*

> **ORIGIN Algebra** came via Italian and medieval Latin from an Arabic form meaning literally "the reuniting of broken parts." It was used in the title of a seminal work, "The Science of Reunion and Equation," by the Arab mathematician al-Khwarizmi (780?-850?), whose translated works introduced Arabic numerals to Europe.

Al·ger /áljər/, **Horatio** (1834–99) US writer

Al·ge·ri·a /al jéeree ə/ country in NW Africa. Cap. Algiers. Pop. 31,736,053 (2001). —**Al·ge·ri·an** *adj, n*

Al·giers /al jéerz/ capital of Algeria. Pop. 2,561,992 (1998).

⨍ ALGOL /ál gòl/, **Al·gol** *n* a high-level computer language. Full form **algorithm-oriented language**

Al·gon·qui·an /al góngkee ən, -kwee-/ (*pl same or* **-ans**), **Al·gon·ki·an** /-kee-/ *n* **1** a group of Native North American languages of central and E Canada and parts of the central and E United States **2** a member of an Algonquian-speaking people —**Al·gon·qui·an** *adj*

Al·gon·quin /al góngkin, -kwin/ (*pl same or* **-quins**), **Al·gon·kin** /-kin/ (*pl same or* **-kins**) *n* **1** a member of a group of Native North American peoples living along the Ottawa and St. Lawrence rivers in E Canada. **2** the Algonquian language of the Algonquin people —**Al·gon·quin** *adj*

al·go·rithm /álgə rìthəm/ *n* a problem-solving mathematical procedure or computer program —**al·go·rith·mic** /àlgə ríthmik/ *adj*

Al·ham·bra /al hámbrə/ *n* a citadel and palace in Granada, Spain, built for Moorish kings in the 12C and 13C

Muhammad Ali

A·li /aa leé/, **Muhammad** (*b.* 1942) US boxer

⨍ a·li·as /áylee əss, áylyəss/ *n* **1** an assumed name **2** a name assigned to a computer file or directory ■ *adv* also known as

al·i·bi /állə bì/ (*pl* **-bis**) *n* **1** an accused person's claim of having been somewhere other than at the scene of a crime **2** an excuse (*infml*)

a·li·en /áylyən, -lee ən/ *n* **1** an extraterrestrial being **2** a foreign resident of a country **3** an outsider ■ *adj* **1** outside somebody's pre-

vious experience, or not part of somebody's usual behavior o *an alien practice*
2 foreign **3** extraterrestrial o *an alien spacecraft*

al·ien·ate /áylyə nàyt, áylee ə-/ **(-at·ed, -at·ing)**
vt **1** make somebody unsympathetic or
hostile **2** cause somebody to feel dissatisfied **3** cause something, especially
somebody's affection, to be directed elsewhere —**al·ien·a·tion** /áylyə náysh'n, àylee
ə-/ *n*

a·light¹ /ə lít/ *vi* **1** get
out of a vehicle **2** land after a flight

a·light² /ə lít/ *adj* **1** full of light **2** on fire

a·lign /ə lín/, **a·line (a·lined, a·lin·ing)** *vti*
1 bring or come into line or a correct position **2** ally yourself with a particular side
o *The issue has aligned many citizens behind
the candidate.* —**a·lign·ment** *n*

a·like /ə lík/ *adj* similar in appearance or character ■ *adv* **1** in a similar or the same way
2 both —**a·like·ness** *n*

al·i·men·ta·ry ca·nal /àllə méntəree-/ *n* the
tubular passage between the mouth and
the anus through which food passes for
digestion and elimination as waste

al·i·mo·ny /állə mònee/ *n* financial support to
a former spouse

a·lit past tense and past participle of **alight**¹

a·live /ə lív/ *adj* **1** living **2** still in existence
o *keeping their hopes alive* **3** swarming o *alive
with ants* **4** full of energy or activity o *The
town came alive at midnight.* **5** aware o *alive
to the danger* —**a·live·ness** *n* ◊ See note at
living

al·ka·li /álkə lì/ *(pl* **-lis** *or same)* *n* **1** a chemical
substance that neutralizes acids **2** a soluble
salt harmful to crops —**al·ka·line** /-lìn, -lín/
adj —**al·ka·lin·i·ty** /àlkə línnətee/ *n*

al·ka·loid /álkə lòyd/ *n* a chemical compound
containing nitrogen, found in many plants

all /awl/ *adj* **1** *also* **all of** the whole of o *All
Europe was cold this winter.* o *All of the nation
is affected.* **2** *also* **all of** every one of o *all
employees over 30* o *All of the children were
tired.* **3** any *(after an implicit negative word)*
o *She denied all knowledge of it.* ■ *adv* very
or totally *(infml)* o *I'm all confused.* ■ *pron*
1 the whole number or amount *(+ pl verb)*
o *All of us are going to the game.* **2** everything
or everyone o *All that glitters is not gold.* ■ *n*
somebody's best effort o *I gave it my all.*
◊ **all along** for the whole time ◊ **all but**
almost ◊ **(all) in all** when everything has
been taken into account ◊ **all the same**
1 nevertheless **2** a matter of indifference
o *I'd rather go by train, if it's all the same to
you.*

SPELLCHECK Do not confuse the spelling of
all and **awl** ("a sharp-pointed tool"), which
sound similar.

Al·lah /álə, aálə/ *n* in Islam, the name of God

Al·la·ha·bad /áaləhə bàd, álləhə bàd/ city in N
India. Pop. 858,213 (1991).

al·la·man·da /àllə mándə/ *(pl* **-das** *or same)* *n*
a flowering shrub

all-A·mer·i·can *adj* **1** of the United States
2 chosen as the best US amateur player or
athlete in a specific position or event
3 made of US components ■ *n* **1** an
amateur US player or athlete chosen as the
best **2** a team of the best US players

all-a·round *adj* **1** versatile **2** all-inclusive

al·lay /ə láy/ *vt* **1** calm an emotion or worry
2 relieve pain

all clear *n* **1** a signal that danger is over **2** a
signal to proceed

~~**alledged**~~ incorrect spelling of **alleged**

al·lege /ə léj/ **(-leged, -leg·ing)** *vt* assert
without proof —**al·le·ga·tion** /àllə gáysh'n/ *n*

al·leged /ə léjd/ *adj* claimed but not proved
—**al·leg·ed·ly** /ə léjjədlee/ *adv*

Al·le·ghe·ny /àllə gáynee/ river in Pennsylvania and New York. Length 325
mi./523 km.

Al·le·ghe·ny Moun·tains, Al·le·ghe·nies
range of the Appalachian Mountains in
Pennsylvania, Maryland, West Virginia,
and Virginia. Highest peak Spruce Knob
4,861 ft./1,482 m.

al·le·giance /ə léejənss/ *n* loyalty or devoted
support

~~**allegience**~~ incorrect spelling of **allegiance**

al·le·go·ry /állə gàwree/ *(pl* **-ries)** *n* **1** a work
of literature or art that uses symbolism to
express meaning **2** the use of symbolism
to express meaning —**al·le·gor·i·cal** /àllə
gáwrik'l/ *adj* —**al·le·go·rist** *n*

al·le·gro /ə léggrõ/ *adv* quickly *(musical
direction)* —**al·le·gro** *adj, n*

al·le·lu·ia *interj, n* = **hallelujah**

Al·len /állən/ ◊ **Van Al·len, James**

Al·len, Ethan (1738–89) American Revolutionary soldier

Al·len, Woody (b. 1935) US movie director,
actor, screenwriter, playwright, and humorous essayist

A·llen·de Gos·sens /aa yèn day gáw senss/,
Salvador (1908–73) president of Chile
(1970–73)

Al·len·town /állən tòwn/ city in east central
Pennsylvania. Pop. 100,757 (1998).

al·ler·gen /állərjən/ *n* a substance that causes
an allergic reaction —**al·ler·gen·ic** /àllər
jénnik/ *adj*

al·ler·gic /ə lúrjik/ *adj* **1** having an allergy **2**
or caused by an allergy

al·ler·gy /állərjee/ *(pl* **-gies)** *n* a hyper-
sensitivity to a substance —**al·ler·gist** *n*

al·le·vi·ate /ə léevee àyt/ **(-at·ed, -at·ing)** *vt*
lessen something unpleasant —**al·le·vi·a·
tion** /ə lèevee áysh'n/ *n*

al·ley /állee/ *(pl* **-leys)** *n* **1** *also* **al·ley·way**
/állee wày/ a narrow passage between build-

ings **2** a bowling alley **3** a small street **4** in baseball, an outfield zone

al·ley cat n **1** a homeless cat **2** a disreputable person *(disapproving)*

all fours ◊ **on all fours** crawling along or crouched down on the hands and knees

al·li·ance /ə líˈ ənss/ n **1** an association of people or groups with a common goal **2** the formation of a close relationship

al·lied /ə líd, ál íd/ adj **1** joined in an alliance **2** similar or related o *sociology and allied studies*

al·li·ga·tor /áli gàytər/ n **1** (pl **al·li·ga·tors** or same) a large reptile with powerful jaws **2** leather made from alligator skin

ORIGIN Alligator is an alteration of Spanish *el lagarto*, literally "the lizard." Spanish explorers gave this name to the animal when they encountered it in the Americas.

all in adj extremely tired *(infml)*

all-in-one adj combining two or more things or functions —**all-in-one** n

al·lit·er·a·tion /ə littə ráysh'n/ n the repetition of the same consonants at the beginning of words

~~allmost~~ incorrect spelling of **almost**

al·lo·cate /álə kàyt/ (-cat·ed, -cat·ing) vt give to or set aside for a specific person or purpose —**al·lo·ca·ble** adj —**al·lo·ca·tion** /álə káysh'n/ n

al·lot /ə lót/ (-lot·ted, -lot·ting) vt **1** give as a share **2** earmark or reserve

al·lot·ment /ə lótmənt/ n **1** something allotted **2** the allotting of something

all out adv with maximum effort

all-out adj greatest possible

all o·ver adv *(infml)* **1** everywhere **2** stresses that something is characteristic of somebody o *That's Jackie all over.*

al·low /ə lów/ v **1** vt let somebody do something **2** vt let something happen **3** vt let somebody or yourself have something, especially a benefit or pleasure o *Allow her time to recover.* **4** vi make provision for something **5** vt accept something to be true or valid *(fml)* **6** vi present something as possible or reasonable o *allow of only one interpretation.* —**al·low·a·ble** adj —**al·lowed** adj

□ **allow for** vt allocate an amount for

al·low·ance /ə lów ənss/ n **1** money given regularly by parents to a child **2** an amount of money given for a particular purpose **3** a discount **4** a handicap given in a sport or race **5** an amount allowed **6** the allowing of something ■ vt (-anced, -anc·ing) restrict somebody's allowance to a fixed regular amount

al·loy n /á lòy/ **1** a mixture of metals **2** something that debases what it is added to ■ vt /ə lóy, á lòy/ **1** mix metals **2** debase some-

thing pure by adding ingredients ◊ See note at **mixture**

all-points bul·le·tin n an urgent police broadcast

~~allready~~ incorrect spelling of **already**

all right adj **1** generally good, satisfactory, or pleasant **2** just adequate **3** uninjured ■ interj yes ■ adv **1** in a satisfactory way **2** without any doubt o *It's raining all right.*

USAGE all right or **alright**? **Alright** is regarded as nonstandard. Use **all right** instead.

all·spice /áwl spìss/ n a spice made from the ground dried berries of a tropical tree

all-ter·rain ve·hi·cle n a vehicle designed mainly for off-road use

~~allthough~~ incorrect spelling of **although**

all-time adj best ever *(infml)*

al·lude /ə loʻod/ (-lud·ed, -lud·ing) vi refer indirectly

SPELLCHECK Do not confuse the spelling of **allude** and **elude** ("escape from," "avoid"), which sound similar.

al·lure /ə loʻor/ n a highly attractive and tempting quality o *the allure of the big city* ■ vti (-lured, -lur·ing) attract powerfully —**al·lure·ment** n —**al·lur·ing** adj

al·lu·sion /ə loʻozh'n/ n **1** an indirect reference **2** the process of alluding to somebody or something —**al·lu·sive** adj

al·lu·vi·um /ə loʻovee əm/ (pl **-ums** or **-a** /-ə/) n soil deposited by water —**al·lu·vi·al** adj

~~allways~~ incorrect spelling of **always**

al·ly n /á lìˈ, á líˈ/ vti (-lied, -lies) **1** join in mutually supportive association **2** connect or be connected through marriage ■ n (pl **-lies**) a member of an alliance

al·ma ma·ter /áalmə máatər, àl-/, **Al·ma Ma·ter** n **1** the institution where somebody was educated **2** a college or school song

al·ma·nac /áwlmə nàk, álmə-/ n **1** an annual publication that includes a calendar, astronomical information, and details of anniversaries and events **2** a book of data published annually about a particular subject

al·might·y /awl mítee/ adj all-powerful ■ n **Al·might·y** God

al·mond /áamənd, aál-, ám-, ál-/ n **1** an edible oval-shaped nut **2** a small tree that produces almonds

al·most /áwl mòst, awl mòst/ adv nearly

alms /aamz, aálmz/ npl charitable donations

al·oe /álló/ n a plant with fleshy toothed leaves

al·oe ve·ra /-veéra/ n **1** a soothing plant extract. Use: cosmetics, drugs. **2** a species of aloe with leaves that yield aloe vera

a·loft /ə láwft/ adv high up in the air

a·lo·ha /ə lṓ aa, -haa, aa-/ *interj* Hawaii used as a greeting or farewell

ORIGIN **Aloha** in Hawaiian literally means "love, affection."

a·lo·ha par·ty *n* Hawaii a welcoming or farewell party

a·lone /ə lṓn/ *adj* without help from others ■ *adj* unique in some respect o *Am I alone in thinking this?* ■ *adv, adj* without company o *She returned alone.* —**a·lone·ness** *n*

a·long /ə láwng/ *prep* 1 over the length of o *walked along the path* 2 parallel with o *sailed along the coast* ■ *adv* 1 with somebody o *brought her friends along* 2 forward o *Move along, please.* 3 at or to a place o *There'll be a bus along in a minute.*

a·long·side /ə láwng sīd, ə làwng sīd/ *prep* by the side of o *drew up alongside their car* ■ *adv* by the side o *anchored alongside*

a·loof /ə lóōf/ *adj* 1 remote in manner 2 physically distant or apart —**a·loof·ly** *adv*

a·loud /ə lówd/ *adv* 1 audibly 2 loudly

alp *n* a high mountain

al·pac·a /al pákə/ *n* 1 (*pl* **al·pac·as** *or* same) a mammal related to the llama 2 wool cloth made from alpaca hair

ai·pha /álfə/ *n* 1 the 1st letter of the Greek alphabet 2 **Alpha** a communications code word for the letter "A" ■ *adj* alphabetical

al·pha·bet /álfə bèt/ *n* a set of letters used to represent language

ORIGIN **Alphabet** comes from the names of the first two letters of the Greek alphabet, *alpha* and *beta*.

al·pha·bet·i·cal /àlfə béttik'l/, **al·pha·bet·ic** /-béttik/ *adj* 1 in the order of the letters of the alphabet 2 of an alphabet —**al·pha·bet·i·cal·ly** *adv*

al·pha·bet·ize /álfəbət īz/ (**-ized, -iz·ing**) *vt* put in alphabetical order —**al·pha·bet·i·za·tion** /àlfə bet ə záysh'n/ *n*

al·pha male *n* a dominant male animal

al·pha·nu·mer·ic /àlfənoo mérrik/, **al·pha·mer·ic** /àlfə mérrik/ *adj* combining letters and numbers —**al·pha·nu·mer·i·cal·ly** *adv*

✚ al·pha test *n* a first test of computer software or hardware by its publisher or manufacturer —**al·pha-test** *vt*

al·pine /ál pīn/ *adj* 1 of high mountains 2 **Alpine** of the Alps 3 used in or involving mountain climbing 4 of downhill or slalom skiing ■ *n* a mountain plant

Alps mountain range in S Europe, stretching from SE France to Austria. Highest peak Mont Blanc 15,771 ft./4,807 m.

al·Qae·da /al kídə/, **al·Qai·da** /an international Islamic organization associated with several terrorist incidents, including the attack on the World Trade Center, New York (2001)

al·Quds /al kōōdz/ *n* Arabic name for Jerusalem

al·read·y /awl réddee, áwl redee/ *adv* 1 unexpectedly early o *Have you finished already?* 2 before now, or before a particular time in the past o *She had already left when I arrived.*

al·right /awl rít, áwl rīt/ *adj* generally good, satisfactory, or pleasant *(nonstandard)* ◊ See note at **all right**

Al·sa·tian /al sáysh'n/ *n* somebody from Alsace ■ *adj* from Alsace

al·so /áwlsṓ/ *adv* 1 in addition 2 likewise or similarly 3 moreover *(modifies a whole sentence or clause)*

al·so-ran *n* 1 a losing competitor, especially in a race 2 somebody regarded as unimportant *(disapproving)*

Alta. *abbr* Alberta

Al·tai Moun·tains /ál tī-/ mountain range in central Asia, on the Kazakhstan-Mongolia border. Highest peak Mt. Belukha 15,157 ft./4,620 m.

al·tar /áwltər/ *n* a raised surface in front of or on which religious ceremonies are performed

SPELLCHECK Do not confuse the spelling of **altar** and **alter** ("change"), which sound similar.

al·ter /áwltər/ *v* 1 *vti* change 2 *vt* adjust a garment to fit —**al·ter·a·ble** *adj* —**al·ter·a·tion** /àwltə ráysh'n/ *n* ◊ See note at **altar, change**

al·ter·ca·tion /àwltər káysh'n/ *n* a heated argument —**al·ter·cate** /áwltər kàyt/ *vi*

al·ter e·go /àwltər éegō/ (*pl* **al·ter e·gos**) *n* 1 a second side to somebody's personality 2 a very close friend

al·ter·nate *vi* (**-nat·ed, -nat·ing**) 1 follow in an interchanging pattern o *as night alternates with day* 2 fluctuate ■ *adj* /áwltərnət/ 1 arranged in an alternating pattern 2 every other 3 serving as a backup ■ *n* /áwltərnət/ 1 somebody or something able to serve as a substitute 2 another possibility —**al·ter·nate·ly** /àwltərnətlee/ *adv* —**al·ter·na·tion** /àwltər náysh'n/ *n*

al·ter·nat·ing cur·rent *n* an electric current that regularly reverses direction

al·ter·na·tive /awl túrnətiv/ *n* 1 another possibility 2 the possibility of choosing 3 an option o *I can't decide which of the two alternatives is worse.* ■ *adj* 1 mutually exclusive 2 unconventional o *alternative methods of painting* —**al·ter·na·tive·ly** *adv*

al·ter·na·tive med·i·cine *n* nonorthodox medical treatment or remedies

al·ter·na·tor /áwltər nàytər/ *n* a generator of alternating current

~~alternitive~~ incorrect spelling of **alternative**

al·though /awl thṓ/ *conj* in spite of the fact that

al·tim·e·ter /al tímmətər, álte mèetər/ n an instrument indicating altitude —**al·ti·met·ric** /àltə méttrik/ adj —**al·tim·e·try** /al tímmətree/ n

al·ti·tude /áltə tòod/ n 1 height above sea level 2 a high place (often pl) 3 the angle of an astronomical object above the horizon —**al·ti·tu·di·nal** /àltə tòod'nəl/ adj

⚡ Alt key /áwlt-/ n a function-changing computer key

Alt·man /áwltmən/, **Robert** (b. 1925) US movie director and screenwriter

al·to /áltō/ (pl -tos) n 1 a contralto voice 2 the highest singing voice for a man 3 an alto singer

al·to·geth·er /àwltə géthər, áwltə gèthər/ adv 1 with everything included 2 totally o I'm not altogether satisfied. 3 on the whole o Altogether, it's been a success.

al·tru·ism /áltroo ìzzəm/ n selflessness —**al·tru·ist** n —**al·tru·is·tic** /àltroo ístik/ adj —**al·tru·is·ti·cal·ly** adv

⚡ ALU abbr arithmetic logic unit

a·lum[1] /álləm/ n a colorless or white solid. Use: dyes, water purification, leather dressing.

al·um[2] /ə lúm/ n an alumnus or alumna (infml)

al·u·min·i·um /àlə mínnee əm/ n UK = aluminum

a·lu·mi·num /ə loomənəm/ n (symbol Al) a metallic chemical element. Use: lightweight construction, corrosion-resistant materials

a·lum·na /ə lúmnə/ (pl -nae /-nī, -nèe/) n a woman graduate of a particular institution ◊ See note at **alumnus**

a·lum·nus /ə lúmnəss/ (pl -ni /-nī, -nèe/) n a man graduate of a particular institution

USAGE The plural of the masculine noun **alumnus** is alumni (not alumnuses). The plural of the feminine noun **alumna** is alumnae (not alumnas).

al·ways /áwl wayz, -wiz/ adv 1 every time or continuously 2 through all past or future time 3 if necessary o You can always catch a later train.

⚡ al·ways-on adj 1 describes a home or business where Internet access is not restricted to a specific time 2 continuously connected

Alz·heim·er's dis·ease /áalts hīmərz-/, **Alz·heimer's** n a degenerative medical disorder of the brain causing dementia

ORIGIN The disease is named for the German neurologist Alois Alzheimer (1864–1915), who described it in 1907.

am 1st person present singular of **be**

Am symbol americium

Am. abbr American

a.m., A.M. adj, adv before noon. Full form **ante meridiem**

A.M. abbr Master of Arts

AMA abbr American Medical Association

a·mal·gam /ə málgəm/ n 1 a mixture of elements or characteristics 2 a substance used as filling for tooth cavities ◊ See note at **mixture**

a·mal·ga·mate /ə málgə màyt/ (-mat·ed, -mat·ing) vti combine into a unified whole —**a·mal·ga·ma·tion** /ə màlgə máysh'n/ n

a·man·u·en·sis /ə mànnyoo énsiss/ (pl -ses /-sèez/) n (literary) 1 a scribe 2 a writer's assistant

ORIGIN Amanuensis goes back to a Latin phrase a manu, literally "by hand." It was used in servus a manu, a slave (servus) with secretarial duties.

Am·a·ril·lo /àmmə ríllō/ city in NW Texas. Pop. 171,207 (1998).

am·a·ryl·lis /àmmə rílləss/ (pl -lis·es or same) n a plant with large trumpet-shaped flowers on a single stalk

a·mass /ə máss/ vti gather together or collect over time o amassed a fortune in the 1950s ◊ See note at **collect**

am·a·teur /ámmə tùr, -tər, -chòor/ n 1 somebody doing something for pleasure rather than for pay 2 somebody considered unskilled ■ adj 1 for or by amateurs 2 unskillful or unprofessional —**am·a·teur·ism** n

am·a·teur·ish /ámmə túrish, -chòor-/ adj unskilled or unskillfully done —**am·a·teur·ish·ly** adv —**am·a·teur·ish·ness** n

A·ma·ti /ə máatee/ family of Italian violin makers including **Andrea** (d. 1578), his son **Girolamo** (1556?–1630?), and grandson **Nicolò** (1596–1684)

am·a·to·ry /ámmə tàwree/, **am·a·to·ri·al** /àmmə táwree əl/ adj of love, especially physical love (fml)

~~amateur~~ incorrect spelling of **amateur**

a·maze /ə máyz/ (a·mazed, a·maz·ing) vt fill with wonder or astonishment —**a·mazed** adj —**a·maze·ment** n —**a·maz·ing** adj —**a·maz·ing·ly** adv

Am·a·zon[1] /ámmə zòn, -əzən/ n 1 a mythological woman warrior 2 also **am·a·zon** a strong woman —**Am·a·zo·ni·an** /àmmə zōnee ən/ adj

Am·a·zon[2] /ámmə zòn, -əzən/ world's second longest river. It flows east from N Peru, through N South America and into the Atlantic Ocean in Brazil. Length 4,000 mi./6,400 km. —**Am·a·zo·ni·an** /àmmə zōnee ən/ adj

am·bas·sa·dor /am bássədər, -dàwr/ n 1 a diplomatic representative sent to a foreign country 2 a representative o a goodwill ambassador for the charity —**am·bas·sa·do·ri·al** /am bàssə dáwree əl/ adj —**am·bas·sa·dor·ship** n

am·ber /ámbər/ n 1 a yellow fossil resin. Use: jewelry, ornaments. 2 a brownish yellow color —**am·ber** adj

am·bi·ance /ámbee ənss/, **am·bi·ence** n the atmosphere or mood of a place

am·bi·dex·trous /àmbi dékstrəss/ adj 1 using either hand with equal skill 2 skilled in many ways —**am·bi·dex·trous·ly** adv

---

ORIGIN Ambidextrous, literally "right-handed on both sides," comes from the Latin prefix *ambi-* "both" and the adjective *dexter* "right-handed." The right hand has traditionally been associated with skill.

---

am·bi·ent /ámbee ənt/ adj in the surrounding area o *ambient temperature*

am·bi·ent music n background music

am·big·u·ous /am bíggyoo əss/ adj 1 having more than one meaning 2 causing uncertainty —**am·bi·gu·i·ty** /àmbi gyóoətee/ n —**am·big·u·ous·ly** adv —**am·big·u·ous·ness** n

am·bit /ámbit/ n the scope, extent, or limits of something or somebody

am·bi·tion /am bísh'n/ n 1 desire for success in life o *She lacks ambition.* 2 an objective or goal

am·bi·tious /am bíshəss/ adj 1 having ambition 2 impressive but difficult to achieve o *an ambitious plan* —**am·bi·tious·ly** adv

am·biv·a·lence /am bívvələnss/ n 1 the presence of conflicting ideas or feelings 2 uncertainty —**am·biv·a·lent** adj

am·ble /ámb'l/ vi (-bled, -bling) walk slowly ■ n a slow walk

am·bro·sia /am brṓzhə/ n 1 the food of the mythological deities 2 something delicious (literary)

am·bu·lance /ámbyələnss/ n a vehicle for carrying people to the hospital

---

ORIGIN Ambulance was adopted in the early 19C from French, with the meaning "field hospital," a movable hospital facility set up near a battle site. The French word was formed from *hôpital ambulant*, literally "walking hospital." English **ambulance** later began to be used for a vehicle transporting the wounded and sick.

---

am·bu·la·to·ry /ámbyələ tàwree/ adj of walking or moving (fml) ■ n (pl -ries) a walkway in a church or cloister

am·bush /ámbŏŏsh/ n 1 a surprise attack 2 concealment before attacking o *waiting in ambush* ■ vt attack from a concealed position —**am·bush·er** n

a·me·ba n MICROBIOL = amoeba

a·me·lio·rate /ə méelee ə ràyt/ (-rat·ed, -rat·ing) vti improve (fml) —**a·me·lio·ra·tion** /ə mèelee ə ráysh'n/ n —**a·me·lio·ra·tive** adj

a·men /ay mén, aa-/ interj 1 affirms the content of a prayer or hymn 2 expresses strong agreement

a·me·na·ble /ə mèenəb'l/ adj 1 responsive to suggestion and willing to cooperate 2 susceptible to being affected in a particular way o *The tumor is not amenable to treatment.* —**a·me·na·bil·i·ty** /ə mèenə bíllətee/ n —**a·me·na·bly** adv

a·mend /ə ménd/ vt change something in order to improve or correct it

a·mend·ment /ə méndmənt/ n 1 a change, correction, or improvement to something 2 a change to a motion, bill, or constitution

a·mends /ə méndz/ n restitution of a wrong (+ sing or pl verb) o *a desire to make amends*

A·men·ho·tep III /àa men hṓ tep, àa mən-/ (1411–1379 BC) king of Egypt (1417–1379 BC)

A·men·ho·tep IV ♦ **Akhenaton**

a·men·i·ty /ə ménnə tee, -méen-/ (pl -ties) n 1 an attractive feature, service, or facility (often pl) o *the amenities of a luxury hotel* 2 pleasantness or attractiveness

a·men·or·rhe·a /ay mènnə rée ə/, **a·men·or·rhoe·a** n the unusual absence of menstruation —**a·men·or·rhe·ic** adj

Am·er·a·sian /àmmə ráyzh'n/ n somebody of American and Asian parentage —**Am·er·a·sian** adj

A·mer·i·ca /ə mérrikə/ 1 the United States 2 also **A·mer·i·cas** North, South, and Central America 3 △ North America (infml)

ORIGIN America is first recorded in English in the early 16C. It comes from a Latinized form of the first name of the Italian navigator Amerigo Vespucci (1454–1512).

USAGE The use of **America** to mean the United States may cause offense to people from Canada and Central and South America, and should be avoided. Use *North America* to refer to the United States and Canada together.

A·mer·i·can /ə mérrikən/ n somebody from the United States ■ adj of America

A·mer·i·ca·na /ə mèrri kaánə/ n collectible items from the United States (+ sing or pl verb)

A·mer·i·can cheese n a mild cheese product

A·mer·i·can dream, A·mer·i·can Dream n the idea that everyone in the United States can succeed and prosper

A·mer·i·can In·di·an n a Native American (sometimes offensive) —**A·mer·i·can In·di·an** adj ♦ See note at **Indian**

A·mer·i·can·ism /ə mérrikə nìzzəm/ n a US expression or custom

A·mer·i·can·ize /ə mérrikə nìz/ (-ized, -iz·ing) vti take on or give the qualities associated with the United States —**A·mer·i·can·i·za·tion** /ə mèrrikənə záysh'n/ n

A·mer·i·can plan n a single charge for meals and board

A·mer·i·can Sa·mo·a US territory consisting of a group of islands in the South Pacific. Pop. 67,084 (2001).

A·mer·i·cas /ə mérrikəz/ ♦ **America** 2

am·er·i·ci·um /ˌamməˈrĭshee əm/ *n* (*symbol* **Am**) a radioactive metallic chemical element.

A·mer·ind /ˈammə rĭnd/ *n* the proposed grouping of American languages spoken before Europeans arrived

Am·er·in·di·an /ˌammə rĭndee ən/ *n* a member of an indigenous people of North, South, or Central America (*sometimes offensive*) —**Am·er·in·di·an** *adj* ◊ See note at **Indian**

am·e·thyst /ˈammithəst/ *n* a violet form of quartz. Use: gems.

Amex /ˈammeks/, **AMEX** *abbr* American Stock Exchange

A·mex·i·ca /ə méhee kà/ *n* the US-Mexican border from the Pacific Coast to the Gulf Coast and the cities adjacent to it

ORIGIN The term **Amexica**, a blend of *America* and *Mexico*, was in use as early as 1994 but came to prominence in a July 11, 2001, *Time* article. It designates 26 US and Mexican border communities from San Diego (California) and Tijuana (Mexico) on the Pacific Coast to Brownsville (Texas) and Matamoros (Mexico) on the Gulf Coast, whose populations are essentially bilingual and bi-cultural.

a·mi·a·ble /ˈaymee əbˈl/ *adj* friendly and pleasant —**a·mi·a·bil·i·ty** /ˈaymee ə bíllətee/ *n* —**a·mi·a·bly** *adv*

am·i·ca·ble /ˈammikəbˈl/ *adj* friendly and without bad feelings —**am·i·ca·bil·i·ty** /ˌammikə bíllətee/ *n* —**am·i·ca·bly** *adv*

a·mid /ə míd/, **a·midst** /ə mídst/ *prep* 1 within or among 2 while something is happening

a·mid·ships /ə mídships/, **a·mid·ship** *adv*, *adj* near the center of a vessel

A·min /aa meén/, **Idi** (*b.* 1925) Ugandan head of state (1971–79)

a·mi·no ac·id /ə meènō-/ *n* a constituent of protein

A·mish /ˈaamish/ *npl* the members of a US Protestant group of Mennonite origin —**A·mish** *adj*

a·miss /ə míss/ *adv* incorrectly ◊ *Things began to go amiss.* ■ *adj* wrong ◊ *Something is amiss.*

am·i·ty /ˈammətee/ *n* friendliness (*fml*)

Am·man /aa maàn/ capital of the Kingdom of Jordan. Pop. 1,187,000 (1995).

~~ammendment~~ incorrect spelling of **amendment**

am·me·ter /ˈam meètər/ *n* an instrument measuring electric current

am·mo /ˈammō/ *n* ammunition (*infml*)

am·mo·nia /ə mōnyə/ *n* 1 a pungent gas. Use: fertilizers, explosives, plastics. 2 a solution of ammonia. Use: household cleaners.

am·mo·nite /ˈammə nīt/ *n* the fossilized flat spiral shell of an extinct marine organism —**am·mo·nit·ic** /ˌammə níttik/ *adj*

am·mu·ni·tion /ˌammyə níshˈn/ *n* 1 bullets and missiles 2 explosive material 3 facts used to support an argument

am·ne·sia /am neèzhə/ *n* memory loss —**am·ne·si·ac** *n*, *adj*

am·nes·ty /ˈamnəstee/ (*pl* **-ties**) *n* 1 a pardon 2 a prosecution-free period

Am·nes·ty In·ter·na·tion·al *n* a human rights organization

am·ni·o·cen·te·sis /ˌamnee ō sen teèssiss/ (*pl* **-ses** /-seèz/) *n* a test to determine the genetic constitution of a fetus

a·moe·ba /ə meèbə/ (*pl* **-bas** *or* **-bae** /-bee/), **a·me·ba** (*pl* **-bas** *or* **-bae**) *n* a single-celled organism —**a·moe·bic** *adj* —**a·moe·boid** *adj*

a·mok /ə múk, ə mók/, **a·muck** /ə múk/ *adv* out of control —**a·muck** *adj*

a·mong /ə múng/, **a·mongst** /-múngst/ *prep* 1 surrounded by o *among friends* 2 of or in a group o *among the world's finest* 3 between group members o *divided among six of us*

a·mor·al /ay máwrəl/ *adj* 1 outside the scope of morality 2 without moral standards (*disapproving*) —**a·mor·al·i·ty** /ˌay mə rálitee/ *n* —**a·mor·al·ly** *adv*

am·o·rous /ˈammərəss/ *adj* showing or feeling sexual desire —**am·or·ous·ly** *adv* —**am·or·ous·ness** *n*

a·mor·phous /ə máwrfəss/ *adj* 1 without any clear shape 2 not classifiable as a particular category or type 3 without a crystalline structure —**a·mor·phous·ness** *n*

am·or·tize /ˈammər tīz/ (**-tized**, **-tiz·ing**) *vt* 1 reduce a debt by installments 2 write off the cost of an asset —**am·or·ti·za·tion** /ˌammərtə záysh'n/ *n*

A·mos /ˈayməss/ *n* a book of the Bible that contains the prophecies of Amos, a Hebrew prophet

a·mount /ə mównt/ *n* a quantity □ **amount to** *vt* 1 add up to 2 be equivalent to o *Their action amounts to fraud.*

a·mour-pro·pre /ˌammoor próprə/ *n* self-esteem (*fml*)

amp *n* 1 an ampere 2 an amplifier (*infml*)

am·per·age /ˈampərij/ *n* the number of amperes measured in an electric current

am·pere /ˈam peèr/ *n* (*symbol* **A**) the SI unit of electric current

ORIGIN The **ampere** is named for the French physicist André-Marie Ampère (1775–1836), who was the first person to distinguish between electric current and voltage.

am·per·sand /ˈampər sànd/ *n* the symbol "&," meaning "and"

ORIGIN Ampersand is a contraction of *& per se and*, literally "& by itself (means) and," an old name for the character whose significance is not entirely clear. The character itself is a printed version of a manuscript abbreviation for Latin *et* "and."

am·phet·a·mine /am fétts mèen/ n a stimulant drug

am·phib·i·an /am fíbbee ən/ n 1 a land organism that breeds in water 2 an aircraft or vehicle operating on land and in water —**am·phib·i·an** adj

am·phib·i·ous /am fíbbee əss/ adj 1 living on land and in water 2 operating on land and in water

am·phi·the·a·ter /àmfə theè ətər/ n a circular building, room, or arena with tiered seats for spectators

am·pho·ra /ámfərə/ (pl **-rae** /-ree/ or **-ras**) n a narrow-necked jar with two handles used in the ancient world

am·ple /ámp'l/ (**-pler**, **-plest**) adj 1 more than enough 2 large in body size (often euphemistic) —**am·ple·ness** n —**am·ply** adv

am·pli·fi·er /ámplə fî'r/ n 1 a device that makes sounds louder 2 a device that increases the magnitude of a signal, voltage, or current

am·pli·fy /ámplə fî/ (**-fied**, **-fies**) v 1 vti increase in magnitude 2 vti make or become louder 3 vti add detail to something 4 vt exaggerate —**am·pli·fi·ca·tion** /àmpləfi káysh'n/ n ◊ See note at **increase**

am·pli·tude /ámplə tòod/ n 1 largeness in size, volume, or extent 2 breadth of range

am·poule /am pyoòl/, **am·pule** n a sealed container of medication

am·pu·tate /ámpyə tàyt/ (**-tat·ed**, **-tat·ing**) vti cut off part of the body surgically —**am·pu·ta·tion** /àmpyə táysh'n/ n

am·pu·tee /ámpyə teè/ n somebody who has had a limb amputated

am·ri·ta /am reètə/, **am·ree·ta** n 1 in Hindu mythology, a drink bestowing immortality 2 in Hindu mythology, immortality gained by drinking amrita

Am·rit·sar /əm rítsər/ city in NW India, site of the Sikh Golden Temple. Pop. 708,835 (1991).

Am·ster·dam /ámstər dàm/ capital of and commercial center in the Netherlands. Pop. 731,200 (2000).

a·muck adv, adj = **amok**

A·mu Dar·ya /àà moo daáryə/ longest river in Central Asia. Length 879 mi./1,415 km.

am·u·let /ámmyələt/ n an object or a piece of jewelry considered lucky

A·mund·sen /ámmøndsən/, **Roald** (1872–1928) Norwegian explorer

A·mur /aa moòr/ river in east central Asia. Length 2,700 mi./4,345 km (total river system).

a·muse /ə myoòz/ (**a·mused**, **a·mus·ing**) vt 1 make smile or laugh 2 keep happily occupied —**a·mused** adj —**a·mus·ing** adj —**a·mus·ing·ly** adv

a·muse·ment /ə myoòzmənt/ n 1 the feeling that something is funny 2 a recreational activity 3 a ride, game, or similar attraction

Am·vets /ám vets/, **AMVETS** n a private US organization of chiefly Korean and Vietnam war veterans

an (stressed) /an/ (unstressed) /ən/ adj the form of "a" used before an initial vowel sound

USAGE The practice of using **an** before words beginning with h and an unstressed syllable (e.g., an hotel) is falling out of use, and it is much more usual now to hear a hotel, with the h sounded.

-an, -ian suffix 1 of or relating to o American o European o Christian 2 a person with a particular expertise o librarian

-ana, -iana suffix a collection of objects or information about a topic, person, or place o Americana

An·a·bap·tist /ànnə báptist/ n a member of a 16C Protestant movement advocating adult baptism —**An·a·bap·tist** adj

an·a·bol·ic ster·oid /ànnə bòllik-/ n a synthetic hormone. Use: developing muscle mass and strength.

a·nach·ro·nism /ə nákrə nìzzəm/ n 1 something from an earlier or later historical period than other things in the same context 2 somebody or something that seems to belong to a different historical period —**a·nach·ro·nis·tic** /ə nàkrə nístik/ adj —**a·nach·ro·nis·ti·cal·ly** adv —**a·nach·ro·nous** /ə nákrənəss/ adj —**a·nach·ro·nous·ly** adv

an·a·con·da /ànnə kóndə/ n a nonpoisonous snake, the largest in the boa family

a·nae·mi·a n MED = **anemia**

an·aer·o·bic /ànnə rôbik/ adj 1 not needing oxygen 2 lacking oxygen —**an·aer·o·bic·al·ly** adv

an·aes·the·sia, etc. = **anesthesia**, etc.

an·a·gram /ánnə gràm/ n a word or phrase containing all the letters of another o The word "carthorse" is an anagram of "orchestra." —**an·a·gram·mat·ic** /ànnəgrə máttik/ adj —**an·a·gram·mat·i·cal·ly** adv

An·a·heim /ánnə hìm/ city in SW California. Pop. 295,153 (1998).

a·nal /áyn'l/ adj 1 of the anus 2 obsessively methodical or self-controlled —**a·nal·ly** adv

an·al·ge·si·a /ànn'l jeèzee ə, -jeèzhə/ n 1 insensitivity to pain 2 pain control or relief —**an·al·ge·sic** adj, n

⚡**an·a·log** /ánnə làwg/ adj representing data using a measurable variable physical quantity

⚡**an·a·log com·put·er** n a computer that uses a variable physical quantity to represent data

a·nal·o·gous /ə nálləgəss/ adj similar in some respects —**a·nal·o·gous·ly** adv

an·a·logue /ánnə làwg/ n a corresponding thing

a·nal·o·gy /ə nálləjee/ (*pl* -**gies**) *n* 1 a comparison between similar things 2 a similarity in some respects

a·nal·y·sis /ə nálləssiss/ (*pl* -**ses** /-sèez/) *n* 1 separation into components for examination 2 an examination of something in detail 3 an assessment based on examination 4 psychoanalysis

~~analysys~~ incorrect spelling of **analysis**

an·a·lyt·ic /ànnə líttik/, **an·a·lyt·i·cal** /-líttik'l/ *adj* of or using analysis —**an·a·lyt·i·cal·ly** *adv*

an·a·lyze /ánn'l ìz/ (-**lyzed**, -**lyz·ing**) *vt* 1 break down into components 2 examine in detail 3 treat a patient using psychoanalysis —**an·a·lyz·a·ble** *adj* —**an·a·lyst** /ánn'list/ *n*

an·a·phy·lac·tic shock /ànnəfi làktik-/ *n* a sudden severe allergic reaction

an·ar·chism /ánnər kìzzəm/ *n* 1 ideology rejecting all forms of government 2 the actions of anarchists

an·ar·chist /ánnərkist/ *n* 1 a supporter of anarchism 2 a lawless person

an·ar·chy /ánnərkee/ *n* 1 lack of government 2 a state of chaos —**an·ar·chic** /a naárkik, ə-/ *adj* —**an·ar·chi·cal·ly** *adv*

a·nath·e·ma /ə náthəmə/ *n* 1 an object of loathing 2 a curse

An·a·to·li·a /ànnə tṓlee ə/ Asian part of Turkey —**An·a·to·li·an** *n*, *adj*

a·nat·o·my /ə náttəmee/ (*pl* -**mies**) *n* 1 the physical structure of an organism 2 the study of the structure of the human body 3 the shape of somebody's body (*infml*) —**an·a·tom·i·cal** /ànnə tómmik'l/ *adj* —**a·nat·o·mist** *n*

-ance *suffix* 1 action ○ *utterance* 2 *also* **-ancy** state or condition ○ *elegance*

an·ces·tor /án sèstər, ánsəstər/ *n* 1 a person from a distant generation whom somebody is descended from 2 a forerunner 3 an earlier species from which a plant or animal evolved

an·ces·try /án sèstree, ánsès-/ *n* the family or group that makes up somebody's ancestors —**an·ces·tral** /an séstrəl/ *adj*

an·chor /ángkər/ *n* 1 a device that holds a ship in place 2 any device that keeps somebody or something in place 3 *also* **an·chor·man** /-màn/, **an·chor·per·son** /-pùrs'n/, **an·chor·wo·man** /-wòomman/ an announcer on a news program 4 somebody or something that provides a sense of stability (*literary*) ■ *v* 1 *vt* hold something securely in place 2 *vti* put down a ship's anchor 3 *vt* be an announcer on a news program

an·chor·age /ángkərij/ *n* 1 a place where a ship is anchored 2 something holding somebody or something in place

an·cho·vy /án chōvee, an chōvee/ (*pl* -**vies** *or same*) *n* a small fish usually salted and canned

an·cien ré·gime /aaN syàaN ray zheèm/ (*pl* **an·ciens ré·gimes** /*pronunc. same*/) *n* 1 French society before the Revolution 2 a former system of government or management

an·cient /áynshənt/ *adj* 1 of the distant past 2 very old ■ *n* 1 somebody from a civilization in the distant past 2 somebody of advanced years ■ **an·cients** *npl* 1 the people of ancient Western civilizations 2 the ancient Greek and Roman authors

an·cient his·to·ry *n* the study of old cultures

an·cil·la·ry /ánssə lèrree/ *adj* 1 subordinate 2 providing support ■ *n* (*pl* -**ries**) 1 a subordinate part 2 a nontechnical support employee

and *conj* 1 introduces something additional 2 links two verbs or statements and shows that the second follows the first ○ *Just add water and stir.* 3 introduces a result of something just mentioned ○ *Their work was excellent and won several awards.* 4 stresses repetition or continuity ○ *better and better* 5 plus ○ *One and one are two.* 6 but ○ *Eat a lot of fruit and avoid refined sugar.* 7 moreover ○ *The kids needed clothes, and I hadn't been paid in weeks.* 8 connects ideas and add emphasis ○ *We are courageous. And we will win this battle.* 9 used instead of "to" with infinitives following some verbs (*infml*) ○ *I try and visit her once a week.*

USAGE Using **and** at the beginning of a sentence is not incorrect, and can often be an effective way of drawing attention to what follows: *"You can't get away with this,"* he threatened. *And we knew he meant it.*

⚡ AND /and/ *n* 1 in computing, an operator that links items that must occur together for a specific result to be achieved 2 *also* **AND cir·cuit** a logic circuit used in computers that gives an output value of 1 if the values of all inputs are 1 and an output value of 0 otherwise

An·da·lu·sia /àndə lōozhə, -shee ə/ autonomous region of S Spain. Pop. 7,236,459 (1998). Spanish **Andalucía** —**An·da·lu·si·an** *adj, n*

An·da·man Is·lands /ándəmən-/ island group of E India, between the Bay of Bengal and the **Andaman Sea**. Pop. 240,089 (1991).

an·dan·te /an dántee, aan daán tay, -tee/ *adj, adv* to be played slowly (*musical direction*) —**an·dan·te** *n*

An·der·sen /ándərsən/, **Hans Christian** (1805–75) Danish writer

Marian Anderson

An·der·son /ándərsən/, **Marian** (1897–1993) US contralto

An·der·son, Maxwell (1888–1959) US playwright and screenwriter

An·der·son, Sherwood (1876–1941) US writer

An·des /ándeez/ South American mountain system extending along the western coast from Panama to Tierra del Fuego. Highest peak Aconcagua 22,835 ft./6,960 m. —**An·de·an** /ándee ən/ adj, n

and·i·ron /ánd ìrn/ n a metal holder for logs in a fireplace

An·dor·ra /an dáwrə/ principality in SW Europe between France and Spain. Cap. Andorra la Vella. Pop. 67,627 (2001). —**An·dor·ran** adj, n

An·dor·ra la Vel·la /-lə véllə/ capital of Andorra. Pop. 21,513 (1998).

An·dre·a del Sar·to /àan drày ə del saártō/ (1486–1530) Italian painter

An·drees·sen /an dráyss'n/, **Marc** (b. 1971) US computer scientist and technology executive

An·drew /án drooˈ/, **St.** (d. AD 60) one of the 12 apostles of Jesus Christ

an·drog·y·nous /an drójjənəss/ adj **1** giving an impression of ambiguous sexual identity o *androgynous looks* **2** having both male and female physical characteristics —**an·drog·y·ny** n

an·droid /án dròyd/ n a human-looking robot

an·ec·dote /ánnək dòt/ n a short account of something interesting or amusing —**an·ec·dot·al** /ànnək dôt'l/ adj

a·ne·mi·a /ə neémee ə/, **a·nae·mi·a** n a deficiency of red blood cells —**a·ne·mic** adj

a·ne·mic /ə neémik/, **a·nae·mic** adj having anemia —**a·ne·mic·al·ly** adv

a·nem·o·ne /ə némmənee/ (pl **-nes** or same) n a perennial flowering plant of the buttercup family with wild and cultivated types

~~anenome~~ incorrect spelling of **anemone**

an·es·the·sia /ànnəss theézhə/, **an·aes·the·sia** n medically induced loss of sensation or unconsciousness

an·es·the·si·ol·o·gist /ànnəss theezee óllə jist/, **an·aes·the·si·ol·o·gist** n a doctor who is qualified to administer anesthetics —**an·es·the·si·ol·o·gy** n

an·es·thet·ic /ànnəss théttik/, **an·aes·thet·ic** n a substance that causes anesthesia

—**an·es·thet·ic** adj —**a·nes·the·tist** /ə nésthətist/

a·nes·the·tize /ə nésthə tìz/ (**-tized, -tiz·ing**), **a·naes·the·tize** vt administer an anesthetic to —**an·es·the·ti·za·tion** /ə nèsthətə záysh'n/ n

an·eu·rysm /ánnyə rìzzəm/, **an·eu·rism** n a fluid-filled bulge in an artery that can weaken the wall —**an·eu·rys·mal** /ànnyə rìzm'l/ adj

a·new /ə nooˈ/ adv **1** again **2** in a new way

an·gel /áynjəl/ n **1** in some religions, a heavenly being who acts as God's messenger **2** a kind person **3** a spirit that is believed to protect and guide somebody **4** a financial backer (infml) ◊ See note at **backer**

An·gel Falls world's highest waterfall, in SE Venezuela. Height 3,212 ft./979 m.

an·gel food cake, an·gel cake n a light cake made without egg yolks

an·gel·ic /an jéllik/ adj **1** kind or beautiful **2** well behaved **3** of angels —**an·gel·i·cal·ly** adv

an·gel·i·ca /an jéllikə/ (pl **-cas** or same) n **1** candied plant stems used for decorating cakes and cookies **2** a tall hollow-stemmed flowering plant whose stems are used fo angelica

An·gel·i·co /an jélli kò/, **Fra** (1400?–55) Italian painter

Maya Angelou

An·ge·lou /ánjə lòo/, **Maya** (b. 1928) US writer

An·ge·lus /ánjələss/, **an·ge·lus** n **1** a set of Roman Catholic prayers commemorating the Annunciation and Incarnation **2** a bell announcing the Angelus

an·ger /áng gər/ n a feeling of strong displeasure ■ vti become or make greatly displeased

---

SYNONYMS **anger, annoyance, irritation, indignation, fury, rage, ire, wrath** CORE MEANING: a feeling of strong displeasure in response to an assumed injury

---

an·gi·na /an jínə, ánjənə/, **an·gi·na pec·to·ris** /-péktəriss/ n severe chest pains caused by a lack of blood flowing to the heart

an·gi·o·plas·ty /ánjee ə plàstee/ (pl **-ties**) n surgery to clear a narrowed artery using an inflatable instrument

an·gi·o·sperm /ánjee ə spùrm/ n a plant in which the sex organs are within flowers and the seeds are in a fruit

Ang·kor /áng kàwr/ ancient capital of the early Khmer civilization in NW Cambodia, noted for its temples and monuments

an·gle[1] /áng g'l/ *n* 1 a space between diverging lines or surfaces, or a measure of the space 2 a figure formed by diverging lines 3 a projecting part 4 a position for viewing something o *seen from various angles* 5 a way of considering something o *Look at the problem from another angle.* ■ *v* (-**gled**, -**gling**) 1 *vi* change direction sharply 2 *vt* direct or place something at an angle 3 *vt* present an idea, topic, or opinion with a particular audience in mind or in a biased way

an·gle[2] /áng g'l/ (-**gled**, -**gling**) *vi* 1 fish with a rod 2 attempt to get something for yourself (*infml*) —**an·gler** *n* —**an·gling** *n*

An·gle /áng g'l/ *n* a member of a Germanic people who settled in England in the 5C —**An·gli·an** /áng glee ən/ *adj*, *n*

An·gli·can /áng gləkən/ *adj* of the Anglican Church ■ *n* a member of the Anglican Church

An·gli·can Church, An·gli·can Com·mun·ion *n* a group of Christian churches including the Churches of England and Ireland, as well as the Protestant Episcopal Church

An·gli·cism /áng glə sìzzəm/, **an·gli·cism** *n* 1 a word used in British English 2 an English word used in a foreign language

An·gli·cize /áng glə sìz/, **an·gli·cize** (-**cized**, -**ciz·ing**) *vt* make or become more English —**An·gli·ci·za·tion** /áng gləssə záysh'n/ *n*

An·glo /áng glő/ (*pl* -**glos**), **an·glo** *n* (*infml*) 1 a non-Hispanic white person 2 *Can* a Canadian with British ancestry

USAGE Anglo is the counterpart of *Latino* or *Hispanic.* In one sense it refers to any Caucasian person whose first language is English and whose descent is not Latin American or Hispanic. In another sense **Anglo** refers to any Canadian person whose first language is English and whose descent is British, not French.

Anglo- *prefix* England, English, British o *Anglophile* o *Anglo-American*

An·glo-A·mer·i·can *n* a US or Canadian citizen with British ancestry

An·glo-In·di·an *adj* introduced into English from a South Asian language ■ *n* 1 somebody with British and South Asian ancestry 2 a British person residing in South Asia, especially during colonial times

An·glo-I·rish *npl* Irish people with English ancestry —**An·glo-I·rish** *adj*

An·glo·phile /áng glə fīl/ *n* somebody who likes England and English people —**An·glo·phil·i·a** /áng glə fílllee ə/ *n* —**An·glo·phil·ic** *adj*

An·glo·phobe /áng glə főb/ *n* somebody who dislikes England and English people

—**An·glo·pho·bi·a** /áng glə főbee ə/ *n*
—**An·glo·pho·bic** /-főbik/ *adj*

an·glo·phone /áng glə főn/ *n* a speaker of English ■ *adj* describes a country where English is the native language of most people

An·glo-Sax·on *n* 1 a member of any of the Germanic peoples who settled in England in the 5C 2 the Old English language —**An·glo-Sax·on** *adj*

An·go·la /ang gőlə/ country in west central Africa. Cap. Luanda. Pop. 10,548,000 (1997). —**An·go·lan** *adj*, *n*

an·go·ra /ang gáwrə/ *n* 1 silky wool from a goat 2 a silky-haired goat, cat, or rabbit

an·gos·tu·ra /ang gə stoorə/, **an·gos·tu·ra bark** *n* the bark of a South American tree. Use: flavoring in bitters.

ORIGIN Angostura is named for a city in Venezuela whose modern name is Ciudad Bolívar.

an·gry /áng gree/ (-**gri·er**, -**gri·est**) *adj* 1 feeling very annoyed 2 expressing annoyance 3 stormy-looking 4 inflamed and painful-looking o *an angry bruise* —**an·gri·ly** *adv*

angst *n* 1 in existentialist philosophy, the feeling of dread that comes from an awareness of free will 2 anxiety about personal shortcomings or circumstances ◊ See note at **worry**

ang·strom /ángstrəm/ **ang·strom u·nit** *n* (*symbol* Å) a unit used to measure electromagnetic radiation

An·guil·la /ang gwíllə/ one of the Leeward Islands, in the E Caribbean. Pop. 7,300 (1990).

an·guish /áng gwish/ *n* extreme anxiety ■ *vti* feel or cause to feel anguish —**an·guished** *adj*

an·gu·lar /áng gyələr/ *adj* 1 with sharp edges and corners 2 thin and bony —**an·gu·lar·ly** *adv*

an·hy·drous /an hī drəss/ *adj* with no water in its composition

an·ic·ca /ə nīkə/ *n* in Buddhism, the cycle of birth, life, and death

~~annihilation~~ incorrect spelling of **annihilation**

an·i·line /ánn'lən/ *n* a colorless poisonous liquid. Use: manufacture of dyes, resins, pharmaceuticals, explosives.

an·i·mal /ánnəm'l/ *n* 1 a living organism with independent movement 2 a mammal 3 a person regarded as brutish 4 a person or thing (*infml*) o *The laser printer is a completely different animal.* ■ *adj* 1 derived from animals o *animal fats* 2 instinctive o *animal urges*

an·i·mal hus·band·ry *n* the breeding and care of farm animals

an·i·mal·i·ty /ánnə mállətee/ *n* animal characteristics

an·i·mal rights *npl* rights for animals that are similar to human rights

an·i·mate *vt* /ánnə màyt/ (-**mat·ed**, -**mat·ing**) 1 make lively 2 inspire action or feelings in 3 create using animation techniques ■ *adj* /ánnəmət/ physically alive —**an·i·mat·ed** *adj* —**an·i·mat·ed·ly** *adv* —**a·ni·ma·tor** *n* ◊ See note at **living**

an·i·ma·tion /ànnə máysh'n/ *n* 1 movies made by photographing a sequence of slightly varying pictures or models so that they appear to move 2 liveliness or activity

an·i·ma·tron·ics /ànnəmə trónniks/ *n* the electronic manipulation of puppets or other models (+ *sing verb*) —**an·i·ma·tron·ic** *adj*

an·i·me /ánni mày, -mə/ *n* a Japanese style of animated cartoon, often with violent or sexually explicit content

an·i·mism /ánnə mìzzəm/ *n* the belief that things in nature have souls —**an·i·mist** *adj*, *n* —**an·i·mis·tic** /ànnə místik/ *adj*

an·i·mos·i·ty /ànnə móssətee/ (*pl* -**ties**) *n* hostility or resentment ◊ See note at **dislike**

an·i·mus /ánnəməss/ *n* 1 hostility 2 a feeling that motivates somebody's actions

an·i·on /án ìən/ *n* a negative ion —**an·i·on·ic** /àn ī ónnik/ *adj*

an·ise /ánniss/ *n* 1 aniseed 2 the plant from which aniseed comes

an·i·seed /ánni sèed/ *n* the licorice-flavored seeds of the anise plant. Use: flavoring.

An·ka·ra /ángkərə/ capital of Turkey. Pop. 2,937,524 (1997).

an·kle /ángk'l/ *n* 1 the joint that connects the foot and the leg 2 the slim part of the leg above the ankle

an·klet /ángklət/ *n* 1 a chain or band worn around the ankle 2 a short sock coming just above the ankle

Ann, Cape /an/ peninsula in NE Massachusetts

an·nals /ánn'lz/ *npl* 1 recorded history 2 a historical record arranged chronologically

annalysis incorrect spelling of **analysis**

An·nam /ə nám, á nàm/ region in east central Vietnam —**An·na·mese** /ànnə meéz, -meéss/ *adj*, *n*

An·nan /a naàn, ánnən/, **Kofi** (*b.* 1938) Ghanaian secretary-general of the United Nations (1996–), awarded the Nobel Peace Prize (2001)

An·nap·o·lis /ə náppəliss/ capital of Maryland. Pop. 33,585 (1998).

An·na·pur·na /ànnə poórnə, -púr-/ mountain in the Himalaya range, in Nepal. Height 26,504 ft./8,078 m.

Ann Ar·bor /a aàrbər/ city in SE Michigan. Pop. 109,967 (1998).

Anne /an/ (1665–1714) queen of Great Britain and Ireland (1702–14)

Anne (of Cleves) /-kleevz/ (1515–57) German-born queen of England (1540) as the fourth wife of Henry VIII

an·neal /ə neél/ *vti* make material stronger through heating

an·nex *vt* /ə néks, a-, á nèks/ 1 attach one thing to another 2 take over a territory and make it part of another country 3 attach a quality or condition to something else ■ *n* /á nèks/ a building attached to another —**an·nex·a·tion** /à nek sáysh'n/ *n*

an·ni·hi·late /ə nī́ ə làyt/ (-**lat·ed**, -**lat·ing**) *vt* destroy completely

an·ni·hi·la·tion /ə nī́ ə láysh'n/ *n* complete destruction

an·ni·ver·sa·ry /ànnə vúrsəree/ (*pl* -**ries**) *n* 1 the date of an important past event 2 a celebration or commemoration of an important past event

an·no Dom·i·ni /ánnō dómmi nì, -dómminee/ *adv* full form of **AD**

anno He·gi·rae /ánnō hə jī́ree, ànnō héjjəree/ *adv* full form of **AH**

annoint incorrect spelling of **anoint**

annonymous incorrect spelling of **anonymous**

an·no·tate /ánnə tàyt/ (-**tat·ed**, -**tat·ing**) *vt* add explanatory notes to

an·nounce /ə nównss/ (-**nounced**, -**nounc·ing**) *v* 1 *vt* tell or report publicly 2 *vt* tell people formally of the arrival of 3 *vti* be the announcer on a television or radio program 4 *vti* declare candidacy —**an·nounce·ment** *n*

an·nounc·er /ə nównssər/ *n* 1 somebody who makes public announcements 2 a TV or radio commentator

an·noy /ə nóy/ *vt* 1 make somebody feel impatient or mildly angry 2 harass or bother somebody repeatedly —**an·noy·ance** *n* —**an·noy·ing** *adj* —**an·noy·ing·ly** *adv*

SYNONYMS annoy, irritate, exasperate, vex, irk CORE MEANING: cause a mild degree of anger in somebody

---

an·nu·al /ánnyoo əl/ *adj* 1 happening once a year 2 for a period of one year 3 describes a plant that dies after one season ■ *n* 1 an annual plant 2 a book or magazine published once a year —**an·nu·al·ly** /ánnyoo əlee/ *adv*

an·nu·al meet·ing *n* a yearly meeting of stockholders

an·nu·i·ty /ə noó ətee/ (*pl* -**ties**) *n* 1 a sum of money paid at regular intervals 2 an investment paying a fixed annual sum

an·nul /ə núl/ (-**nulled**, -**nul·ling**) *vt* 1 make a document or agreement invalid 2 declare a marriage invalid —**an·nul·ment** *n* ◊ See note at **nullify**

an·nu·lar /ánnyələr/ *adj* shaped like a ring

An·nun·ci·a·tion /ə nùnssee áysh'n/ *n* 1 in Christianity, the archangel Gabriel's visit to Mary to tell her that she would be the mother of Jesus Christ 2 the Christian festival that commemorates this visit. Date: March 25.

an·ode /á nòd/ *n* 1 the negative terminal of a

battery **2** the positive electrode in an electrolytic cell

an·o·dize /ánnə dìz/ (-dized, -diz·ing) *vt* coat metal with an oxide —**an·o·di·za·tion** /ànnədi záysh'n/ *n*

an·o·dyne /ánnə dìn/ *n* **1** a painkiller **2** a comforting thing (*literary*) ■ *adj* **1** giving relief from pain **2** bland ○ *an anodyne speech* **3** soothing (*literary*)

a·noint /ə nóynt/ *vt* **1** bless somebody with oil **2** ordain a cleric

a·no·le /ə nṓlee/ *n* a tree-climbing lizard that can change color

a·nom·a·ly /ə nómmələe/ (*pl* -lies) *n* **1** an irregularity ○ *looking for anomalies in the blood tests* **2** a strange object or quality —**a·nom·a·lous** *adj*

anon. /ə nón/ *abbr* anonymous

⚡**a·non·y·mi·zer** /ə nónnə mìzər/ *n* a website enabling a user to browse the Internet without leaving any identity traces

a·non·y·mous /ə nónnəməss/ *adj* **1** unnamed or unknown ○ *the anonymous author* **2** with the writer's or creator's name withheld ○ *an anonymous letter* **3** lacking distinctive features ○ *an anonymous shopping mall* —**an·o·nym·i·ty** /ànnə nímmətee/ *n*

⚡**a·non·y·mous FTP** *n* an Internet file transfer in which no password is needed

an·o·rak /ánnə ràk/ *n* **1** a hooded waterproof parka **2** a boring unfashionable person (*humorous*)

an·o·rex·i·a /ànnə réksee ə/ *n* **1** *also* **an·o·rex·i·a ner·vo·sa** an eating disorder deriving from an extreme fear of becoming overweight and marked by excessive dieting to the point of ill health **2** persistent loss of appetite —**an·o·rex·ic** *n, adj*

an·oth·er /ə núthər/ *adj, pron* **1** one more ○ *need another person to help* ○ *May I have another?* **2** one that is different from some other ○ *another way of approaching the problem* ○ *This towel's wet: will you pass me another?*

A·nou·ilh /aa noo ee/, **Jean** (1910–87) French dramatist

ANSI *abbr* American National Standards Institute

an·swer /ánsər/ *n* **1** a response to a question **2** a way of solving something **3** a response to something that somebody says or does ■ *vti* **1** reply or respond to something **2** match or correspond to something ○ *nobody who answers to that description* **3** fulfill a need, wish, or purpose

---

SYNONYMS answer, reply, response, rejoinder, retort, riposte CORE MEANING: something said, written, or done in acknowledgment of a question or remark, or in reaction to a situation

---

☐ **answer back** *vti* reply to somebody impudently

☐ **answer for** *vt* explain a mistake or fault

☐ **answer to** *vt* be accountable to somebody

an·swer·a·ble /ánsərəb'l/ *adj* **1** solvable **2** obliged to explain your actions to somebody

an·swer·ing ma·chine *n* a device that records incoming phone messages

an·swer·ing ser·vice *n* a business that takes phone messages on behalf of customers

ant *n* an insect that lives in complex colonies

-ant *suffix* **1** performing a particular action ○ *coolant* **2** being in a particular condition ○ *hesitant*

ant·ac·id /ant ássid/ *adj* neutralizing acidity in the stomach ■ *n* an antacid drug

an·tag·o·nism /an tággə nìzzəm/ *n* **1** hostility **2** opposition between forces or substances

an·tag·o·nist /an tággənist/ *n* **1** an opponent **2** a character in conflict with the hero in a story —**an·tag·o·nis·tic** /an tággə nístik/ *adj* —**an·tag·o·nis·ti·cal·ly** *adv*

an·tag·o·nize /an tággə nìz/ (-nized, -niz·ing) *vt* arouse hostility in

An·ta·na·na·ri·vo /àntə nànnə reévó, àäntə naä-/ capital of Madagascar. Pop. 1,052,835 (1993).

Ant·arc·tic /an taárktik, -taártik/ region south of the Antarctic Circle —**Ant·arc·tic** *adj*

Ant·arc·ti·ca /an taárktikə, -taártik-/ uninhabited continent surrounding the South Pole

Ant·arc·tic Cir·cle *n* the parallel of latitude at 66°30'S, encircling Antarctica and its surrounding seas

Ant·arc·tic O·cean area of the S Atlantic, Indian, and Pacific oceans that surrounds Antarctica

~~Antartic~~ incorrect spelling of **Antarctic**

an·te /ántee/ *n* **1** a gambler's stake in a card game **2** an amount paid (*infml*) —**an·te** *vti* ◇ **up the ante** demand more in a situation (*infml*)

ante- *prefix* before, in front ○ *anteroom*

ant·eat·er /ánt èetər/ *n* **1** a tropical mammal with a long nose and tongue that feeds on ants **2** a pangolin **3** an echidna **4** an aardvark

an·te·bel·lum /àntee bélləm/ *adj* **1** before any war **2** before the Civil War

an·te·ce·dent /ànti seéd'nt/ *n* **1** something that existed or happened before something else **2** a word that a subsequent word refers back to ■ **an·te·ce·dents** *npl* ancestors ■ *adj* occurring earlier in time (*fml*) —**an·te·ce·dence** *n*

an·te·cham·ber /àntee chàymbər/ *n* a room leading to a larger room

an·te·date /ànti dàyt/ (-dat·ed, -dat·ing) *vt* **1** occur earlier than **2** put an earlier date on

an·te·di·lu·vi·an /ànti də lóóvee ən/ *adj* **1** from a time before the biblical Flood **2** outdated

an·te·lope /ántə lòp/ (*pl* -lopes *or* same) *n* a horned mammal of a large family that includes gazelles and impalas

an·te·na·tal /ántee náyt'l/ *adj* prenatal —**an·te·na·tal·ly** *adv*

an·ten·na /an ténnə/ (*pl* **-nae** /-nee/ *or* **-nas**) *n* **1** a thin sensor on the head of insects and some other organisms **2** a device for sending and receiving radio waves

an·te·pe·nul·ti·mate /ántee pi núltəmət/ *adj* third from last

an·te·ri·or /an teeree ər/ *adj* (*fml*) **1** at the front of something **2** earlier than something else

an·te·room /ántee ròom, -ròom/ *n* a room that leads onto a larger room

an·them /ánthəm/ *n* **1** a song of allegiance and national identity **2** a short hymn sung by the choir during a religious service **3** a rousing popular song ○ *rock anthems*

an·ther /ánthər/ *n* a male flower part containing pollen

ant·hill /ánt hìl/ *n* a mound of earth made by ants during the construction of their nest

an·thol·o·gy /an thólləjee/ (*pl* **-gies**) *n* a collection of different writers' works —**an·thol·o·gist** *n*

ORIGIN The Greek word from which **anthology** derives literally means "a collection of flowers." The original anthologies contained epigrams and short poems by various authors, chosen as being especially fine.

Library of Congress

Susan B. Anthony

An·tho·ny /ánthənee/**, Susan B.** (1820–1906) US social reformer

an·thra·cite /ánthrə sìt/ *n* a hard slow-burning coal

an·thra·co·sis /ànthrə kóssiss/ *n* a lung disease caused by coal dust

an·thrax /án thràks/ *n* an infectious disease of sheep and cattle transmittable to humans, causing skin ulcers (**cutaneous anthrax**) or a form of pneumonia (**pulmonary anthrax**)

anthropo- *prefix* human being ○ *anthropomorphism*

an·thro·poid /ánthrə pòyd/ *adj* **1** of apes **2** like human beings ■ *n* **1** a primate **2** an ape of the family that includes chimpanzees and gorillas —**an·thro·poid·al** /ánthrə póyd'l/ *adj*

an·thro·pol·o·gy /ànthrə pólləjee/ *n* the study of human culture and development —**an·thro·pol·o·gist** *n*

an·thro·po·mor·phism /ànthrəpə máwr fìzzəm/ *n* the attribution of human characteristics to animals —**an·thro·po·mor·phic** *adj* —**an·thro·po·mor·phi·cal·ly** *adv*

an·ti /án tī, -tee/ (*infml*) *adj* opposed to ■ *n* (*pl* **-tis**) somebody who opposes something

anti- *prefix* **1** against or preventing ○ *anticlerical* ○ *anticoagulant* ○ *anti-Communism* **2** opposite ○ *anticlimax* ○ *antiparticle*

an·ti·a·bor·tion /ántī ə báwrsh'n, àntee-/ *adj* opposed to abortion —**an·ti·a·bor·tion·ist** *n*

an·ti·air·craft /án tī áir kràft, àntee-/ *adj* for attacking airplanes

⨍**an·ti·a·li·as·ing** /án tī áylee əssing, àntee-/ *n* the smoothing of the jagged edges of diagonal lines in computer images

an·ti·bac·ter·i·al /ántī bak téeree əl, àntee-/ *adj* preventing, killing, or reducing the growth of bacteria

an·ti·bal·lis·tic mis·sile /ántī bə lístik-, àntee-/ *n* a missile used to destroy a ballistic missile in flight

an·ti·bi·ot·ic /án tī bī óttik, ànti-/ *n* a medication that destroys bacteria —**an·ti·bi·ot·ic** *adj*

an·ti·bod·y /án tī bòddee, ánti-/ (*pl* **-ies**) *n* a protein produced in the body in response to the presence of an antigen, e.g., a bacterium or virus

an·ti·choice *adj* opposed to abortion

An·ti·christ /ántī krìst, àntee-/ *n* **1** an antagonist of Jesus Christ expected by the early Christian Church **2** *also* **an·ti·christ** any opponent of Jesus Christ

an·tic·i·pate /an tíssi pàyt/ (**-pat·ed, -pat·ing**) *vt* **1** act beforehand to prepare for or prevent something **2** expect something ○ *We're anticipating trouble.* —**an·tic·i·pa·tion** /an tìssi páysh'n/ *n*

an·ti·cler·i·cal /án tī klérrik'l, àntee-/ *adj* opposed to the involvement of the clergy in political affairs

an·ti·cli·max /án tī klī̀ màks, àntee-/ *n* **1** a disappointing end after a big buildup **2** a sudden change of tone from the serious to the trivial or dull —**an·ti·cli·mac·tic** /án tī klī̀ máktik, àntee-/ *adj* —**an·ti·cli·mac·ti·cal·ly** *adv*

an·ti·clock·wise /ántī klók wìz, àntee-/ *adj, adv* *UK* counterclockwise

an·ti·co·ag·u·lant /án tī kō ággyələnt, àntee-/ *adj* preventing normal blood clotting —**an·ti·co·ag·u·lant** *n*

an·ti·com·pet·i·tive /án tī kəm péttitiv, àntee-/ *adj* likely or certain to discourage competition

an·ti·con·vul·sant /ántī kən vúlsənt, àntee-/ *adj* controlling convulsions —**an·ti·con·vul·sant** *n* —**an·ti·con·vul·sive** *n, adj*

an·ti·cor·ro·sive /ántī kə róssiv, àntee-/ *adj* controlling corrosion

an·ti·crime /ántī krī́m, àntee-/ *adj* designed to prevent or reduce crime

an·tics /ántiks/ *npl* silly pranks

an·ti·cy·clone /án tī sī́ klòn, àntee-/ *n* an area of atmospheric high pressure that brings generally settled weather

—an·ti·cy·clon·ic /àn tï sï klónnik, àntee-/ adj

an·ti·dem·o·crat·ic /àntï dèmmə kráttik, àntee-/ adj opposed to democracy

an·ti·de·pres·sant /àn tï di préss'nt, àntee-/ n a drug that controls depression —an·ti·de·pres·sant adj —an·ti·de·pres·sive adj

an·ti·dote /ánti dōt/ n 1 a substance that counteracts a poison 2 something that brings welcome relief from something unpleasant o an antidote to boredom

An·tie·tam /an teétəm/ creek near Sharpsburg, Maryland, site of one of the bloodiest battles of the Civil War in September 1862

an·ti·freeze /ánti freez/ n a liquid that lowers the freezing point of another liquid, especially the water in a vehicle's radiator

an·ti·fun·gal /àntï fúng'l, àntee-/ adj preventing or reducing the growth of fungi

an·ti·gen /ántijən/ n a protein that stimulates the production of an antibody —an·ti·gen·ic /ànti jénnik/ adj —an·ti·gen·i·cal·ly adv

An·ti·gua and Bar·bu·da /an teègə ənd baar bóodə/ island nation in the Leeward Islands in the Caribbean Sea. Cap. St. John's. Pop. 66,970 (2001). —An·ti·guan adj, n

an·ti·he·ro /án tï heèrō, àntee-/ (pl -roes) n an unheroic central character —an·ti·her·o·ic /àn tï hi rō ik, àntee-/ adj —an·ti·her·o·ism /àn tï hérrō ïzzəm, àntee-/ n

an·ti·his·ta·mine /àn tï hístəmin, àntee-, -mèen/ n a drug that controls allergies

an·ti·knock /ánti nòk/ n a chemical added to gasoline. Use: prevents engine knock.

An·til·les ◊ Greater Antilles, Lesser Antilles

an·ti·lock brake /àntï lók-, àntee-/ n an electronically controlled brake or braking system to prevent a vehicle's wheels from locking under sudden braking

an·ti·ma·cas·sar /àntee mə kássər/ n a small cloth cover put on the back of a chair to protect the upholstery

an·ti·mat·ter /án tï màttər, ánti-/ n hypothetical matter composed of particles of the same mass as ordinary particles but having opposite properties

an·ti·mo·ny /ánta mōnee/ n (symbol Sb) a brittle metallic chemical element. Use: alloys, electronics

an·ti·nu·cle·ar /àntï noòklee ər, àntee-/ adj opposed to nuclear weapons or power

an·ti·ox·i·dant /àntï óksid'nt, àntee-/ n a substance that inhibits oxidation

an·ti·par·ti·cle /àntï paártik'l, àntee-/ n an elementary particle with the same mass as the corresponding particle but other properties opposite to it

an·ti·pas·to /àntee paàstō, -pás-/ (pl -ti /-tee/) n an appetizer

an·tip·a·thy /an típpəthee/ n a strongly negative feeling —an·tip·a·thet·ic /àntipə théttik, an típpə-/ adj —an·tip·a·thet·i·cal·ly adv ◊ See note at dislike

an·ti·per·spi·rant /àn tï púrspərənt, àntee-/ n a substance that controls sweating —an·ti·per·spi·rant adj

an·tip·o·des /an típpə deèz/ npl 1 places at opposite sides of the Earth 2 opposites of any kind —an·tip·o·dal adj

an·ti·psy·chot·ic /àntï sï kóttik, àntee-/ adj relieving the symptoms of psychosis

an·ti·quar·i·an /àntï kwáiree ən/ adj of or dealing in antiques or rare books ■ n also an·ti·quar·y a collector of or dealer in antiques or antiquities —an·ti·quar·i·an·ism n

an·ti·quat·ed /ánti kwàytəd/ adj ancient or old-fashioned ◊ See note at old-fashioned

an·tique /an teék/ n an old item collected or highly valued because of its age ■ adj 1 old and valuable or collectible 2 from classical times (fml) 3 very old or old-fashioned (infml) ■ vt (-tiqued, -tiqu·ing) give an old and worn appearance to

an·tiq·ui·ty /an tíkwətee/ (pl -ties) n 1 ancient history 2 the state of being very old 3 an ancient object

an·ti·ra·cism /àntï ráy sïzzəm, àntee-/ n opposition to racial discrimination —an·ti·ra·cist adj, n

an·ti·re·jec·tion /àntï ri jéksh'n, àntee-/ adj preventing rejection of a transplanted organ or tissue

an·ti·sat·el·lite /àntï sátt'l īt, àntee-/ adj for use against enemy satellites

an·ti·Sem·i·tism /àn tï sémmi tïzzəm, àntee-/ n hatred of or discrimination against Jews (disapproving) —an·ti·Sem·ite /àn tï sé mīt, àntee-/ n —an·ti·Se·mit·ic /àntï sə mittik, àntee sə míttik/ adj

an·ti·sep·tic /àntï séptik/ adj 1 controlling infection 2 unexciting and unimaginative ■ n a substance that controls infection

an·ti·se·rum /ánti seèrəm/ (pl -rums or -ra /-sīrrə/) n serum containing specific antibodies providing immunity against a disease or venom

an·ti·smok·ing /àntï smóking, àntee-/ adj opposed to tobacco smoking, or designed to stop people from smoking

an·ti·so·cial /àn tï sósh'l, àntee-/ adj 1 not conforming to a society's accepted standards of behavior 2 not sociable —an·ti·so·cial·ly adv

an·ti·stat·ic /àntï státtik, àntee-/, an·ti·stat /ántï stàt, àntee-/ adj controlling static electricity

an·ti·sub·ma·rine /àntï súbmə rèen, àntee-/ adj for use against enemy submarines

an·ti·theft /àntï théft, àntee-/ adj preventing theft

an·tith·e·sis /an títhəssiss/ (pl -ses /-seèz/) n 1 the direct opposite of something 2 use of words or phrases that contrast with each other —an·ti·thet·i·cal /àntï théttik'l/ adj

an·ti·tox·in /àntee tóksin/ n an antibody produced in response to a poison

an·ti·trust /àn tī trúst, àntee-/ *adj* intended to oppose business monopolies

an·ti·vi·ral /àn tī vírəl, antee-/ *adj* describes medication for use against viruses

⨍ **an·ti·vi·rus** /àn tī vírəss, àntee-/ *adj* describes software that identifies and removes computer viruses

ant·ler /ántlər/ *n* one of a pair of branched horns that grow on a deer's head

An·to·ni·o·ni /an tốnee ốnee/, **Michelangelo** (*b.* 1912) Italian movie director

An·to·ny /ántənee/, **Mark** (83?–30 BC) Roman politician and general

an·to·nym /ántə nìm/ *n* a word that means the opposite of another word —**an·ton·y·mous** /an tónnəməss/ *adj* —**an·ton·y·my** /an tónnə mee/ *n*

ant·sy /ántsee/ (**-si·er**, **-si·est**) *adj* (*infml*) 1 nervous 2 fidgety

Ant·werp /ántwərp/ city in Belgium. Pop. 447,632 (1999).

a·ñu /àa noò, -nyoò, á-/, **an·yu** /àa nyoò, á-/ *n* a tropical twining plant with edible tubers

~~anual~~ incorrect spelling of **annual**

A·nu·bis /ə noōbiss/ *n* an ancient Egyptian god of the dead, represented with the head of a jackal

a·nus /áynəss/ *n* the opening at the end of the alimentary canal through which the body's solid waste matter is released

an·vil /ánvil/ *n* 1 a metalworker's hammering block 2 ANAT = **incus**

anx·i·e·ty /ang zī ətee/ *n* 1 a feeling or cause of worry 2 a strong wish to do something o *his anxiety to please* 3 a medical condition marked by extreme apprehension ◊ See note at **worry**

anx·ious /ángkshəss/ *adj* 1 nervous or worried 2 eager 3 producing anxiety o *a few anxious moments* —**anx·ious·ly** *adv* —**anx·ious·ness** *n*

an·y /énnee/ *adj, pron* 1 even one or a little o *I don't want any dessert.* o *I didn't see any.* 2 every o *Any financial adviser would agree.* ■ *adj* without limit o *any number of foods* ■ *adv* 1 to some degree (*before adjectives and adverbs*) o *Are you feeling any better?* 2 at all (*infml*) o *Her manners haven't improved any.*

an·y·bod·y /énnee bòddee, -bùddee/ *pron* anyone

an·y·how /énnee hòw/ *adv* 1 in any case 2 in a careless way o *ideas produced anyhow* 3 in any manner 4 nevertheless

an·y·more /ènnee máwr/, **an·y more** *adv* 1 now (*in negative statements and questions*) o *They sure don't make them like this anymore!* 2 from now on (*in negative statements and questions*) o *I'm not tolerating this anymore.* 3 nowadays (*nonstandard or regional; in positive sentences*)

an·y·one /énnee wùn/ *pron* 1 every person 2 even one person 3 an unimportant person

an·y·place /énnee plàyss/ *adv* anywhere (*infml*)

an·y·thing /énnee thìng/ *pron* something unspecified or unknown ■ *adv* at all (*in negative statements and questions*) o *He isn't anything like his brother.* ◊ **anything but** not at all

an·y·time /énnee tìm/ *adv* at any time (*infml*)

an·yu *n* PLANTS = **añu**

an·y·way /énnee wày/ *adv* 1 in any case 2 regardless of something 3 in a careless way 4 *also* **an·y way** by any means (*infml*)

an·y·ways /énnee wàyz/ *adv* anyway (*nonstandard*)

an·y·where /énnee wàir, - hwàir/ *pron* an unidentified place ■ *adv* 1 to any place 2 at or in any place

a·or·ta /ay áwrtə/ (*pl* **-tas** *or* **-tae** /-tee/) *n* the main artery leaving the heart —**a·or·tic** *adj*

A·oui·ta /ow éetə/, **Said** (*b.* 1960) Moroccan runner

a·pace /ə páyss/ *adv* 1 quickly 2 abreast

A·pach·e /ə páchee/ (*pl same or* **-es**) *n* 1 a member of a Native North American people who now live in Arizona, New Mexico, and Oklahoma 2 the language of the Apache people —**A·pach·e** *adj* —**A·pach·e·an** *adj*

~~apalling~~ incorrect spelling of **appalling**

~~aparatus~~ incorrect spelling of **apparatus**

~~aparent~~ incorrect spelling of **apparent**

~~aparently~~ incorrect spelling of **apparently**

a·part /ə paárt/ *adv* 1 not together o *scheduled appointments a month apart* 2 into pieces 3 moving away after being together 4 removed from consideration o *The bad food apart, it was a pleasant party.* 5 into a poor state or difficult situation o *ripped the peace process apart* ◊ **apart from** 1 with the exception of 2 in addition to

a·part·heid /ə paárt hìt, -hàyt/ *n* a political system that segregates peoples and favors one group over the others

a·part·ment /ə paártmənt/ *n* 1 a home in a larger building 2 *also* **a·part·ment build·ing, a·part·ment block,** *and* **a·part·ment house** a building of residential apartments

ap·a·thy /áppəthee/ *n* 1 lack of enthusiasm or energy 2 emotional emptiness —**ap·a·thet·ic** /àppə théttik/ *adj* —**ap·a·thet·i·cal·ly** *adv*

a·pa·to·saur·us /ə pàttə sáwrəss/, **a·pa·to·saur** /ə pàttə sàwr/ *n* a large plant-eating dinosaur

ape *n* 1 a tailless primate 2 a person regarded as clumsy (*infml insult*) ■ *vt* (**aped, ap·ing**) imitate ◊ See note at **imitate**

~~apear~~ incorrect spelling of **appear**

Ap·en·nines /áppə nīnz/ mountain range that forms the backbone of peninsular Italy. Highest peak Monte Corno 9,554 ft./2,912 m.

a·pe·ri·tif /aa pèrrə téef, ə-/ *n* a drink before a meal

ap·er·ture /áppər chŏŏr/ n 1 a narrow opening 2 an opening that lets light in, e.g., into a camera

~~apetite~~ incorrect spelling of **appetite**

a·pex /áy pèks/ (pl **a·pex·es** or **a·pi·ces** /áppə seez, áy-/) n 1 the highest point or tip 2 the most successful point o *at the apex of his career*

a·pha·sia /-zhə, ə fázhee ə/ n loss of language abilities caused by brain damage —**a·pha·sic** adj

a·phid /áy fid/ n an insect that feeds on plants

aph·o·rism /áffə rìzzəm/ n a short statement expressing a general truth —**aph·o·ris·tic** /áffə rístik/ adj —**aph·o·ris·ti·cal·ly** adv

aph·ro·dis·i·ac /áffrə dízzee àk, -deéz-/ n something that arouses sexual desire —**aph·ro·dis·i·ac** adj

> ORIGIN The Greek word from which **aph-rodisiac** comes is formed from the name of Aphrodite, the goddess of love and beauty in Greek mythology.

Aph·ro·di·te /àffrə dítee/ n in Greek mythology, the goddess of love and beauty. Roman equivalent **Venus**

a·pi·ar·y /áypee èrree/ (pl **-ies**) n a place where bees are raised for their honey

a·piece /ə peéss/ adv for each

a·plomb /ə plóm, -plúm/ n confident poise

> ORIGIN **Aplomb** derives from the French phrase *à plomb* "perpendicular," literally "according to the plumb line," and originally had the meaning "the state of being perpendicular."

a·poc·a·lypse /ə pókə lìps/ n 1 total destruction 2 a revelation of the future

a·poc·a·lyp·tic /ə pòkə líptik/ adj 1 predicting disaster 2 involving destruction

A·poc·ry·pha /ə pókrəfə/ n 1 early Christian writings of disputed authenticity that are included in only some versions of the Bible (+ sing or pl verb) 2 **a·poc·ry·pha** writings or reports that are not regarded as authentic

a·poc·ry·phal /ə pókrəf'l/ adj widely believed or retold but probably not true

ap·o·gee /áppə jeè/ n 1 the best point of something 2 the point in its orbit when the Moon or a satellite is farthest from Earth —**ap·o·ge·an** /áppə jeè ən/ adj

a·po·lit·i·cal /áypə líttək'l/ adj uninterested in politics —**a·po·lit·i·cal·ly** adv

A·pol·lo /ə póllō/ n 1 in Greek mythology, the god of prophecy 2 also **a·pol·lo** a handsome man (literary) —**A·pol·lo·ni·an** /áppə lónee ən/ adj

a·pol·o·get·ic /ə pòllə jéttik/ adj 1 expressing an apology 2 defending something in speech or writing —**a·pol·o·get·i·cal·ly** adv

ap·o·lo·gi·a /áppə lójee ə/ n a formal written defense of a belief or theory (fml)

a·pol·o·gist /ə pólləjist/ n somebody who defends a belief or theory

a·pol·o·gize /ə póllə jíz/ (**-gized**, **-giz·ing**) vi express remorse or regret

a·pol·o·gy /ə pólləjee/ (pl **-gies**) n 1 a statement expressing remorse or regret 2 an inferior example (humorous) o *an apology for a hotel* 3 a formal defense of a belief or theory

ap·o·phthegm n = **apothegm**

ap·o·plec·tic /áppə pléktik/ adj 1 furiously angry 2 exhibiting symptoms of a stroke (archaic)

ap·o·plex·y /áppə plèksee/ n 1 a fit of anger 2 a stroke caused by a brain hemorrhage (archaic)

a·pos·ta·sy /ə póstəssee/ n renunciation of a religious or political belief

a·pos·tate /ə pós tàyt/ n somebody who renounces a belief

a pos·te·ri·o·ri /aà posteeree áw ree, ày-rī/ adj, adv reasoning from observed facts back to causes or from details back to generalities

a·pos·tle /ə póss'l/ n 1 a strong promoter of an idea or cause 2 also **A·pos·tle** one of Jesus Christ's disciples —**a·pos·tle·ship** n

ap·os·tol·ic /áppə stóllik/ adj 1 of the pope 2 of the Apostles

a·pos·tro·phe[1] /ə póstrəfee/ n the punctuation symbol (')

> USAGE The **apostrophe** is used in contractions (e.g., *we've*, *it's*, *hadn't*, *'em*) and some literary words (e.g., *e'en*, *ne'er*) to show that a letter or letters have been omitted. When used to mark the possessive form of nouns, the apostrophe is followed by *s* unless the noun is plural and already ends in *s*: *the cat's tail; my children's computer; the companies' accounts*. For singular nouns ending in *s* it is often acceptable to use either *'* or *'s*: *Dickens' best-loved novel* or *Dickens's best-loved novel*. An apostrophe may also be used to indicate relationships of description (*a summer's day*) or measurement (*ten days' absence*).

a·pos·tro·phe[2] /ə póstrəfee/ n a speech addressing an absent or imaginary person —**ap·os·troph·ic** /áppə stróffik/ adj

a·poth·e·car·y /ə póthə kèrree/ (pl **-ies**) n a pharmacist (archaic)

ap·o·thegm /áppə thèm/, **ap·o·phthegm** n a maxim —**ap·o·theg·mat·ic** /áppə theg máttik/ adj

a·poth·e·o·sis /ə pòthee óssəss/ n 1 the highest level of glory or power 2 the best example o *the apotheosis of Romantic music*

⨍ app n a computer application (infml)

Ap·pa·la·chi·a /áppə láychee ə, -láchə/ n mountainous region of the E United States that includes the Appalachian Mountains

Ap·pa·la·chi·an Moun·tains /áppə láychee ən-/, **Ap·pal·a·chi·ans** North American mountain system, stretching from SE

Canada to central Alabama. Highest peak Mt. Mitchell 6,684 ft./2,037 m.

Ap·pa·la·chi·an Trail *n* a hiking path in the E United States from Maine to Georgia

ap·pall /ə páwl/ *vt* cause shock or disgust —**ap·pall·ing** *adj*

ap·pall·ing /ə páwling/ *adj* 1 shocking or horrifying 2 very bad —**ap·pall·ing·ly** *adv*

Ap·pa·loo·sa /áppə loossə/, **ap·pa·loo·sa** *n* a US saddle horse with a spotted rump

~~apparently~~ incorrect spelling of **apparently**

ap·pa·ra·tus /áppə ráttəss, -ráy-/ (*pl* **-tus·es** or *same*) *n* 1 a piece of equipment 2 a system that allows something to function

ap·par·el /ə párrəl/ *n* clothing

ap·par·ent /ə párrənt/ *adj* 1 obvious 2 seeming ○ *her apparent indifference* —**ap·par·ent·ly** *adv*

ap·pa·ri·tion /áppə rísh'n/ *n* 1 an appearance of something ghostly 2 an appearance of something unexpected or strange (*humorous*)

~~appartment~~ incorrect spelling of **apartment**

ap·peal /ə peél/ *n* 1 an earnest or urgent request ○ *an emotional appeal for forgiveness* 2 attractive qualities 3 a formal request to a higher authority requesting a review of a decision 4 the hearing of a case by a superior court ■ *v* 1 *vi* make an earnest request 2 *vi* make a formal request to a higher authority for a review of a decision 3 *vi* be interesting or attractive 4 *vti* apply to a superior court for a hearing

ap·peal·ing /ə peéling/ *adj* 1 attractive or pleasing 2 requesting help or sympathy ○ *an appealing glance* —**ap·peal·ing·ly** *adv*

ap·pear /ə peér/ *v* 1 *vi* come into view 2 *vi* begin to exist 3 *vti* seem likely 4 *vi* come before the public, especially to perform a duty or to act 5 *vi* be present in a law court and involved in legal proceedings

ap·pear·ance /ə peérənss/ *n* 1 the fact of appearing ○ *the appearance of the first spring flowers* 2 the way somebody or something looks ○ *a youthful appearance* 3 an outward aspect that creates a particular impression (*often pl*) 4 a performance or attendance at a public occasion

~~appearence~~ incorrect spelling of **appearance**

ap·pease /ə peéz/ (**-peased, -peas·ing**) *vt* 1 pacify somebody by agreeing to demands 2 satisfy a need —**ap·pease·ment** *n*

ap·pel·lant /ə péllənt/ *n* somebody who appeals against a court's decision

ap·pel·late /ə péllət/ *adj* describes a court empowered to review decisions made by lower courts

ap·pel·la·tion /áppə láysh'n/ *n* a name or title (*fml*)

ap·pend /ə pénd/ *vt* add or attach something to the end of a document

ap·pend·age /ə péndij/ *n* 1 something small

or secondary attached to something else 2 a projecting body part

ap·pen·dec·to·my /áppən déktəmee/ (*pl* **-mies**) *n* a surgical operation to remove an inflamed or burst appendix

ap·pen·di·ci·tis /ə pèndə sítiss/ *n* inflammation of the appendix

ap·pen·dix /ə péndiks/ (*pl* **-dix·es** or **-di·ces** /-di seèz/) *n* 1 a tube with a closed end leading from the large intestine, near its junction with the small intestine 2 a collection of additional information at the end of a book

ap·per·tain /áppər táyn/ *vi* belong or relate to (*fml*)

ap·pe·tite /áppə tit/ *n* 1 a desire for food 2 a craving

ap·pe·tiz·er /áppə tìzər/ *n* 1 a small dish of food served before the main course of a meal 2 a sample of something designed to stimulate interest

ap·pe·tiz·ing /áppə tizing/ *adj* stimulating the appetite —**ap·pe·tiz·ing·ly** *adv*

ap·plaud /ə pláwd/ *v* 1 *vti* clap hands in approval of 2 *vt* express approval of —**ap·plaud·a·ble** *adj*

ap·plause /ə pláwz/ *n* the clapping of hands in approval

ap·ple /ápp'l/ *n* 1 a firm round fruit with a central core 2 a fruit tree that produces apples

ap·ple·jack /ápp'l jàk/ *n* a brandy distilled from cider

ap·ple pie *n* a dessert consisting of apples in pastry

ap·ple-pie ◊ **in apple-pie order** neat and tidy

ap·ple·sauce /ápp'l sàwss/ *n* sauce made from sweetened apples

⚡**ap·plet** /ápplət/ *n* 1 a simple computer program that performs a single task within a larger application 2 a computer program that is transferred over the Internet and executed by the recipient's computer

ap·pli·ance /ə plí ənss/ *n* 1 a domestic electrical device 2 a device for straightening teeth

ap·pli·ca·ble /ápplikəb'l, ə plíkəb'l/ *adj* relevant or appropriate —**ap·pli·ca·bil·i·ty** /ápplikə bíllətee/ *n* —**ap·pli·ca·bly** *adv*

ap·pli·cant /ápplikənt/ *n* somebody who formally applies for something ◊ See note at **candidate**

⚡**ap·pli·ca·tion** /áppli káysh'n/ *n* 1 a formal request for something 2 the use of something or the process of putting something to use 3 a use or value for a specific purpose 4 hard work 5 a computer program or piece of software designed to enable the end user to perform a specific task

⚡**ap·pli·ca·tion ser·vice pro·vid·er** *n* a company that provides one or more program functions, e.g., accounting, on behalf of another enterprise

ap·pli·ca·tor /áppl> kàytər/ n a device for applying a substance

ap·plied /ə plíd/ adj put to practical use

ap·pli·qué /àppli káy/ n fabric pieces sewn on fabric to form a design —**ap·pli·qué** vt

ap·ply /ə plí/ (**-plied, -plies**) v 1 vi make a formal request 2 vt make use of something to achieve a result o *apply pressure to stop the bleeding* 3 vi be relevant 4 vt spread something over a surface 5 vr give more effort to something o *I could have applied myself more.*

ap·point /ə póynt/ vt select for a position or job —**ap·point·ee** /ə pòyn teé, ə póyntee/ n

ap·point·ed /ə póyntəd/ adj 1 previously agreed on o *met at the appointed time* 2 decorated and furnished *(usually in combination)* o *a well-appointed apartment*

ap·point·ment /ə póyntmənt/ n 1 an arrangement to meet somebody 2 selection of somebody for a job or position 3 a job or position ■ **appointments** npl furniture and fittings

~~appologize~~ incorrect spelling of **apologize**

~~appology~~ incorrect spelling of **apology**

Ap·po·mat·tox /àppə máttəks/ town in central Virginia, site of the 1865 Confederate surrender that ended the Civil War. Pop. 1,772 (1998).

ap·por·tion /ə páwrsh'n/ vt divide among several people

ap·por·tion·ment /ə páwrsh'nmənt/ n 1 the division and allocation of something 2 proportional distribution of US House of Representatives members, based on their states' populations

ap·po·site /áppəzit/ adj particularly appropriate —**ap·po·site·ly** adv —**ap·po·site·ness** n

ap·po·si·tion /àppə zísh'n/ n 1 the positioning of one thing next to another 2 the relationship between adjacent noun phrases that refer to the same person or thing, as in "my son, the actor" —**ap·po·si·tion·al** adj

ap·praise /ə práyz/ (**-praised, -prais·ing**) vt 1 estimate the monetary value of 2 assess the merits or quality of —**ap·prais·al** n

ap·pre·cia·ble /ə preéshəb'l/ adj large enough to be noticed —**ap·pre·cia·bly** adv

ap·pre·ci·ate /ə preéshee àyt/ (**-at·ed, -at·ing**) v 1 vt be grateful for 2 vi gain in value —**ap·pre·ci·a·tion** /ə preéshee áysh'n/ n

ap·pre·cia·tive /ə preéshətiv/ adj grateful or approving —**ap·pre·cia·tive·ly** adv

ap·pre·hend /àppri hénd/ vt 1 put under arrest 2 understand or perceive the importance or existence of

ap·pre·hen·sion /àppri hénsh'n/ n 1 dread 2 the arrest of somebody *(fml)* 3 an idea formed by observation 4 the fact of grasping the importance or existence of something *(fml)*

ap·pre·hen·sive /àppri hénsiv/ adj worried that something bad will happen —**ap·pre·hen·sive·ly** adv —**ap·pre·hen·sive·ness** n

ap·pren·tice /ə préntiss/ n 1 somebody who is learning a trade or craft by working with a skilled professional 2 a novice ■ vt (**-ticed, -tic·ing**) give or take work as an apprentice o *apprenticed himself to a licensed electrician* —**ap·pren·tice·ship** n ◊ See note at **beginner**

ap·prise /ə príz/ (**-prised, -pris·ing**) vt inform *(fml)*

ap·proach /ə próch/ v 1 vti move closer to somebody or something 2 vt speak to in order to ask for something 3 vt deal with in a particular way o *approached the problem carefully* 4 vt come close to being o *statements approaching libel* 5 vti come closer to something in time 6 vi in golf, hit a ball from the fairway toward the green ■ n 1 a coming nearer in space or time 2 a method 3 an informal request or proposal *(often pl)* 4 something that is almost or close to being something else o *an approach to an apology* 5 a path or course leading to something 6 in golf, a shot from the fairway toward the green

ap·proach·a·ble /ə próchəb'l/ adj 1 invitingly friendly 2 easily accessible —**ap·proach·a·bil·i·ty** /ə pròchə bíllətee/ n —**ap·proach·a·bly** adv

ap·pro·ba·tion /àpprə báysh'n/ n approval or consent —**ap·pro·ba·to·ry** /ə pròbə tàwree/ adj

~~approch~~ incorrect spelling of **approach**

ap·pro·pri·ate adj /ə própree ət/ suitable for the occasion or circumstances ■ vt /ə própree àyt/ (**-at·ed, -at·ing**) 1 take something for your own use 2 set money aside for a particular purpose —**ap·pro·pri·ate·ly** adv —**ap·pro·pri·ate·ness** n

ap·pro·pri·a·tion /ə pròpree áysh'n/ n 1 the taking of something for your own use 2 a sum of money set aside for a particular purpose *(often pl)*

ap·prov·al /ə proóv'l/ n 1 a favorable opinion 2 official agreement or permission

ap·prove /ə proóv/ (**-proved, -prov·ing**) v 1 vi consider to be satisfactory or good 2 vt officially agree to or accept as satisfactory —**ap·proved** adj —**ap·prov·ing** adj —**ap·prov·ing·ly** adv

approx. abbr 1 approximate 2 approximately

ap·prox·i·mate adj /ə próksəmət/ 1 nearly exact in number or quantity 2 similar ■ vti /ə próksə màyt/ (**-mat·ed, -mat·ing**) be similar to something else —**ap·prox·i·mate·ly** adv —**ap·prox·i·ma·tion** /ə pròksə máysh'n/ n

~~approximatly~~ incorrect spelling of **approximately**

ap·pur·te·nance /ə púrt'nənss/ *(fml)* n an accessory *(often pl)* ■ **ap·pur·te·nan·ces** npl equipment —**ap·pur·te·nant** adj

APR *abbr* annual percentage rate

Apr. *abbr* April

~~apreciate~~ incorrect spelling of **appreciate**

a·près-ski /àà pray skeé/ *n* social activities after skiing —**a·près-ski** *adj*

a·pri·cot /áppri kòt, áy-/ *n* **1** a small round fruit with a furry yellowish orange skin **2** a fruit tree that produces apricots

A·pril /áyprəl/ *n* the 4th month of the year in the Gregorian calendar

> **ORIGIN** The Latin word from which **April** comes probably goes back to the name of the Greek goddess Aphrodite. It came into Latin by way of Etruscan, an extinct language spoken in parts of Italy before Roman times.

A·pril Fools' Day *n* traditionally, a day on which practical jokes are played. Date: April 1.

a pri·o·ri /àà pree áwree, àmy prī áwrī/ *adj* **1** based on something that is already known **2** assumed or conceived beforehand —**a pri·o·ri** *adv*

a·pron /áyprən/ *n* **1** a protective garment tied over clothes **2** a projecting edge of a platform **3** the paved area at an airport

> **ORIGIN** "An apron" was originally "a napron": the *n* was lost when this common combination of words was misinterpreted. The earlier form *napron* comes from an old French word related to English *napkin*.

ap·ro·pos /àppro pố/ *adj* just right ■ *prep* in regard to ■ *adv* incidentally

~~apropriate~~ incorrect spelling of **appropriate**

~~aproximately~~ incorrect spelling of **approximately**

apse *n* a rounded projecting part of a building, especially the end of a church where the altar is

apt *adj* **1** very appropriate **2** having a tendency to do something ◊ *apt to get angry* **3** quick to learn —**apt·ly** *adv* —**apt·ness** *n*

apt. *abbr* apartment

ap·ti·tude /ápti tòod/ *n* **1** a natural ability **2** quickness in learning ◊ See note at **ability**, **talent**

A·qa·ba, Gulf of /ààkəbə/ northeastern arm of the Red Sea, bordered by Egypt, Israel, Jordan, and Saudi Arabia. Length 99 mi./160 km.

aq·ua /ààkwə, ák-/ *n* water used as a solvent (*technical*)

aqua- *prefix* water ◊ *aquatint*

~~aquaduct~~ incorrect spelling of **aqueduct**

~~aquaint~~ incorrect spelling of **acquaint**

~~aquaintance~~ incorrect spelling of **acquaintance**

Aq·ua-Lung *tdmk* a trademark for an underwater breathing apparatus used by divers

aq·ua·ma·rine /àakwə mə reén, àk-/ *n* **1** a greenish blue form of beryl. Use: gems. **2** a greenish blue color —**aq·ua·ma·rine** *adj*

aq·ua·plane /áàkwə plàyn, ák-/ *n* a board on which a rider stands while being pulled by a motorboat ■ *vi* (**-planed**, **-plan·ing**) ride on an aquaplane

a·quar·i·um /ə kwáiree əm/ (*pl* **-ums** *or* **-a** /-ə/) *n* **1** a container for fish **2** a building containing fish and other water organisms for study and display

A·quar·i·us /ə kwáiree əss/ *n* **1** a zodiacal constellation in the southern hemisphere **2** the 11th sign of the zodiac —**A·quar·i·us** *adj*

a·quat·ic /ə kwáatik/ *adj* **1** of, in, or on water **2** living in water —**a·quat·i·cal·ly** *adv*

aq·ua·tint /àakwə tìnt, ák-/ *n* **1** an etching method producing colors like watercolors **2** an etched picture made using the aquatint method

Aqueduct: ancient Roman aqueduct in Tarragona, Spain

aq·ue·duct /àakwə dùkt, ák-/ *n* **1** a pipe or channel for moving water to a lower level, often across a great distance **2** a bridge carrying a canal across a valley

a·que·ous /áykwee əss, àkwee-/ *adj* watery

aq·ui·line /ákwi lìn/ *adj* **1** thin and curved like an eagle's beak **2** of eagles

A·qui·nas /ə kwínəss/, **Thomas, St.** (1225–74) Italian philosopher and theologian

~~aquire~~ incorrect spelling of **acquire**

~~aquit~~ incorrect spelling of **acquit**

Aq·ui·taine /ákwi tàyn/ region of SW France. Pop. 2,908,359 (1999).

~~aquittal~~ incorrect spelling of **acquittal**

Ar *symbol* argon

AR *abbr* Arkansas

Ar·ab /árrəb/ *n* a member of an Arabic-speaking Semitic people who live throughout SW Asia and North Africa —**Ar·ab** *adj*

ar·a·besque /àrrə bésk/ *n* **1** a ballet position in which the dancer stands on one leg and has the other raised and stretched out behind **2** an ornate design that combines curves and natural shapes such as leaves and flowers **3** a piece of classical music with an ornate melody

A·ra·bi·a /ə ráybee ə/, **A·ra·bi·an Pen·in·su·la** peninsula of SW Asia, bordering the Persian Gulf, the Arabian Sea, and the Red Sea

A·ra·bi·an /ə ráybee ən/ *adj* of Arabia ■ *n* somebody from Arabia

A·ra·bi·an Sea arm of the Indian Ocean

between the Arabian Peninsula and South Asia

Ar·a·bic /árrəbik/ n a Semitic language that is the official language of several countries of SW Asia and North Africa ■ adj 1 of Arabia 2 of Arabic

Ar·a·bic nu·mer·al n any of the standard numbers 0, 1, 2, 3, 4, 5, 6, 7, 8, and 9

ar·a·ble /árrab'l/ adj describes land suitable for growing crops

a·rach·nid /ə ráknid/ n an eight-legged organism of the class that includes spiders and scorpions

a·rach·no·pho·bi·a /ə ràknə fóbee ə/ n fear of spiders —**a·rach·no·phobe** /ə ráknə fõb/ n —**a·rach·no·pho·bic** adj

Yasir Arafat

Ar·a·fat /árrə fàt/, **Yasir** (b. 1929) chairman of the Palestinian Liberation Organization (1968–) and president of the Palestinian National Authority (1996–)

Ar·al Sea /árrəl-/ inland sea in SW Kazakhstan and NW Uzbekistan

Ar·a·ma·ic /àrrə máy ik/ n a Semitic language of the ancient Near East, still spoken in the region —**Ar·a·ma·ic** adj

A·rap·a·ho /ə ráppə hõ/ (pl same or -hos), **A·rap·a·hoe** (pl same or -hoes) n 1 a member of a Native North American people who formerly lived on the Great Plains, and now live in Colorado, Wyoming, and Montana 2 an Algonquian language of W North America. Native speakers: 1,500. —**A·rap·a·ho** adj

Ar·a·rat, Mt. /árrə ràt/ mountain in E Turkey, the landing place of Noah's Ark according to the Bible. Height 16,854 ft./5,137 m.

ar·bi·ter /áarbətər/ n 1 somebody with the authority to settle a dispute 2 somebody with influence over what people say, think, or do

ar·bi·trage /áarbə traazh/ n the simultaneous buying and selling of the same securities or commodities in different markets in order to make a quick profit —**ar·bi·tra·geur** /àarbi traa zhúr/ n

ar·bi·trar·y /áarbə tràiree/ adj 1 based on wishes or feelings, not on facts or observations 2 randomly chosen —**ar·bi·trar·i·ly** /àarbə tráirrəlee/ adv —**ar·bi·trar·i·ness** n

ar·bi·trate /áarbi tràyt/ (-trat·ed, -trat·ing) v 1 vti settle a dispute between others 2 vt submit a dispute to a third party for settlement

—**ar·bi·tra·tion** /àarbi tráysh'n/ n —**ar·bi·tra·tor** n

ar·bor[1] /áarbər/ n 1 a place in a garden where plants are trained to give shade 2 a three-sided trellis for training plants, often incorporating a seat

ar·bor[2] /áarbər/ n an axle on a machine or power tool

Ar·bor Day n a day for planting and appreciating trees. Date: typically the last Friday in April.

ar·bo·re·al /aar báwree əl/ adj 1 living in trees 2 of trees

ar·bo·re·tum /àarbə reétəm/ (pl -tums or -ta /-tə/) n a place where trees are planted for study and display

arc n 1 a curved line or direction of movement 2 a section of a circle 3 an electrical discharge that flows across a gap ■ vi form or move in an arc

ARC abbr AIDS-related complex

ar·cade /aar káyd/ n 1 an avenue of stores 2 an enclosed area with game machines 3 a passageway with arches 4 a series of arches

Ar·ca·di·a[1] /aar káydee ə/, **ar·ca·di·a** n an imagined place of rural bliss —**Ar·ca·di·an** adj

Ar·ca·di·a[2] /aar káydee ə/ mountainous region in the central Peloponnesus, SW Greece —**Ar·ca·di·an** adj, n

ar·cane /aar káyn/ adj 1 mysteriously obscure 2 difficult or impossible to understand —**ar·cane·ly** adv —**ar·cane·ness** n ◊ See note at **obscure**

arch[1] n 1 a curved structure forming the top of a window, doorway, or other space 2 something shaped like an arch o the arch of his eyebrows ■ v 1 vt form into an arch shape 2 vi move in a curving line —**arched** adj

arch[2] adj 1 knowingly playful or mischievous 2 greatest, especially most hostile —**arch·ly** adv —**arch·ness** n

arch- prefix 1 chief, most important o archbishop 2 extreme or very great o archenemy

-arch suffix leader, ruler o matriarch —**-archic** suffix —**archy** suffix

ar·chae·o·lo·gy /àarkee óllajee/, **ar·che·o·lo·gy** n the study of ancient cultures through the remains of their buildings and artifacts —**ar·chae·o·log·i·cal** adj —**ar·chae·ol·o·gist** n

ar·chae·op·ter·yx /àarkee óptəriks/ n a prehistoric bird

ar·cha·ic /aar káy ik/ adj 1 belonging to a much earlier time 2 describes a word that is no longer used in ordinary language 3 outmoded —**ar·cha·i·cal·ly** adv

ar·cha·ism /áarkee ìzzəm/ n a word, expression, practice, or method from an earlier time that is no longer used —**ar·cha·ist** n

arch·an·gel /áark àynjəl/ n a chief or principal angel —**arch·an·gel·ic** adj

arch·bish·op /aarch bíshəp/ *n* a bishop of the highest rank

arch·bish·op·ric /aarch bíshəprik/ *n* **1** an archdiocese **2** the status or term of office of an archbishop

arch·dea·con /aarch deékən/ *n* a member of the clergy of a rank below bishop who acts as a bishop's assistant —**arch·dea·con·ate** *n* —**arch·dea·con·ship** *n*

arch·di·o·cese /aarch dí óssəss/ *n* the area under an archbishop's control —**arch·di·oc·e·san** /aarch dī óssəss'n/ *adj*

arch·duch·ess /aarch dúchəss/ *n* **1** an archduke's wife **2** a princess, especially in imperial Austria

arch·duke /aarch doók/ *n* a prince, especially in imperial Austria

Ar·che·an /aar keé ən/, **Ar·chae·an** *n* an eon of geologic time 3,800–2,500 million years ago —**Ar·che·an** *adj*

arch·en·e·my /aarch énnəmee/ *n* (*pl* **-mies**) *n* **1** a worst enemy **2** *also* **Arch·en·e·my** Satan

ar·che·ol·o·gy, etc. = archaeology etc.

arch·er /aárchər/ *n* somebody who uses a bow and arrow —**arch·er·y** *n*

ar·che·type /aárki típ/ *n* **1** a typical example **2** something that all other things of the type are based on **3** a recurring symbol in art or literature —**ar·che·typ·al** /aárki típ'l/ *adj*

Ar·chi·me·des /aárkə meé deéz/ (287–212 BC) Greek mathematician

ar·chi·pel·a·go /aárkə péllə gō/ (*pl* **-gos** *or* **-goes**) *n* **1** a group of islands (*often in place names*) **2** an area of sea with many islands —**ar·chi·pe·lag·ic** /aárkəpə lájjik/ *adj*

⨍**ar·chi·tect** /aárkə tèkt/ *n* **1** somebody who designs buildings and advises on their construction **2** a creator of something ○ *the architect of economic reform* **3** a developer of the structure of a computer system or program

ar·chi·tec·ton·ic /aárkə tek tónnik/ *adj* **1** of architecture or architectural qualities **2** of the classification of knowledge —**ar·chi·tec·ton·i·cal·ly** *adv*

ar·chi·tec·ture /aárki tèkchər/ *n* **1** the art and science of designing buildings **2** a particular building style —**ar·chi·tec·tur·al** /aárki tékchərəl/ *adj*

ar·chi·trave /aárki tràyv/ *n* **1** the part of a classical building that sits directly on top of the columns **2** a decorative molding around a door or window frame

⨍**ar·chive** /aár kīv/ *n* **1** a collection of documents (*often pl*) **2** a place where archives are held **3** a copy of computer files stored, often in compressed form, on tape or disk **4** a computer file containing other compressed files **5** a directory of files that Internet users can access using anonymous FTP ■ *vt* (**-chived, -chiv·ing**) **1** put a document in an archive **2** transfer computer data from a hard disk to an external storage medium

3 combine and compress computer files for storage —**ar·chi·val** /aar kīv'l/ *adj*

ar·chi·vist /aárkəvist, aár kīvist/ *n* somebody in charge of a document archive

arch·way /aárch wày/ *n* an arched entrance

arc light, arc lamp *n* a bright electric light

arc·tic /aárktik, aártik/ *adj* very cold (*infml*) ■ *n* a warm waterproof overshoe

Arc·tic /aárktik/ *region* north of the Arctic Circle —**Arc·tic** *adj*

Arc·tic Cir·cle *n* the parallel of latitude at 66°30′N that marks the boundary of the Arctic

Arc·tic O·cean world's smallest ocean, mostly ice-covered, situated north of the Arctic Circle. Depth 17,880 ft./5,500 m.

Ar·dennes /aar dén/ forested plateau in SE Belgium, Luxembourg, and NE France, site of the Battle of the Bulge in 1944

ar·dent /aárd'nt/ *adj* passionate —**ar·dent·ly** *adv*

ar·dor /aárdər/ *n* intense emotion

ar·du·ous /aárjoo əss/ *adj* **1** difficult to achieve or endure **2** difficult to climb or cross —**ar·du·ous·ly** *adv* —**ar·du·ous·ness** *n* ◊ See note at **hard**

are[1] (*stressed*) /aar/ (*unstressed*) /ər/ *v* the plural and 2nd person present singular tense of "be"

are[2] /air, aar/ *n* a metric unit of area equal to 100 sq. m

ar·e·a /áiree ə/ *n* **1** the extent of part of a surface enclosed within a boundary **2** a part of a whole ○ *this area of the brain* **3** a region or district **4** a subject, field of knowledge, or sphere of activity

A·re·ci·bo /aárə seèbō/ port in N Puerto Rico. Pop. 93,385 (1990).

a·re·na /ə reé nə/ *n* **1** a stadium **2** a place or situation where there is intense activity

A·rendt /árrənt, aár-/, **Hannah** (1906–75) German-born US philosopher and political theorist

aren't /aarnt/ *contr* (*infml*) **1** am not (*in questions*) **2** are not

A·re·qui·pa /árrə keépə, aà-/ city in S Peru. Pop. 710,103 (1998).

A·res /áireez/ *n* the Greek god of war. Roman equivalent **Mars**

Ar·gen·ti·na /aárjən teénə/ country in S South America. Cap. Buenos Aires. Pop. 37,384,816 (2001). —**Ar·gen·tine** /aárjən tīn, -teèn/ *adj, n* —**Ar·gen·tin·e·an** /aàrjən tínnee ən/ *adj, n*

ar·gon /aár gòn/ *n* (*symbol* **Ar**) a chemical element that is an inert gas. Use: electric lights, gas shield in welding

ar·got /aárgət, -gō/ *n* jargon

ar·gu·a·ble /aárgyoo əb'l/ *adj* **1** plausible or possible **2** open to dispute —**ar·gu·a·bly** *adv*

ar·gue /áargyoo/ (-gued, -gu·ing) v 1 vi have a disagreement or quarrel 2 vti give reasons for something o *argued that they should stay* o *argued for more days off* 3 vti provide evidence for something o *The decrease in crime may argue for a happier society.* ◊ See note at **disagree**

~~argueing~~ incorrect spelling of **arguing**

~~arguement~~ incorrect spelling of **argument**

ar·gu·ment /áargyəmənt/ n 1 a disagreement or quarrel 2 a reason put forward 3 the main point of view expressed in a book, report, or speech 4 a debate about whether something is correct

ar·gu·men·ta·tion /áargyəmən táysh'n, -men-/ n 1 a debate 2 logical reasoning

ar·gu·men·ta·tive /áargyə méntətiv/ adj 1 inclined to disagree 2 characterized by disagreement —**ar·gu·men·ta·tive·ly** adv —**ar·gu·men·ta·tive·ness** n

ar·gyle /áar gīl, aar gíl/, **ar·gyll** adj knitted with a pattern of colored diamonds ■ n a sock or sweater with an argyle diamond pattern

---

ORIGIN The **argyle** pattern is based on the tartan of the branch of the Campbell clan who lived in Argyll in Scotland.

År·hus /áwr hòoss, aàr-/, **Aar·hus** port in Denmark. Pop. 216,564 (1999).

a·ri·a /áaree ə/ n a song in an opera sung solo or as a duet

A·ri·as Sán·chez /áaree aass saàn chez/, **Oscar** (b. 1941) president of Costa Rica (1986–90)

ar·id /árrid/ adj 1 describes a region with an annual rainfall of less than 10 in./25 cm 2 completely lacking in interest or excitement —**a·rid·i·ty** /ə ríddətee/ n —**ar·id·ness** n ◊ See note at **dry**

Ar·ies /áir rèez, -ree èez/ n 1 a zodiacal constellation in the northern hemisphere 2 the 1st sign of the zodiac —**Ar·ies** adj

a·rise /ə ríz/ (a·rose /ə róz/, a·ris·en /ə rízz'n/, a·ris·ing) vi occur or come to notice

Ar·is·tide /áari stéed/, **Jean-Bertrand** (b. 1953) president of Haiti (1991, 1994–96, 2001–)

ar·is·toc·ra·cy /árriss tókrəssee/ (pl -cies) n 1 people of a hereditary nobility or of the highest social class 2 any group regarded as superior to all others 3 government by an elite group, especially a hereditary nobility

a·ris·to·crat /ə rístə kràt/ n a member of an aristocracy —**a·ris·to·crat·ic** /ə rìstə kráttik/ adj

Ar·is·toph·a·nes /árri stóffə nèez/ (448?–385 BC) Greek dramatist

Ar·is·tot·le /árri stòtt'l/ (384–322 BC) Greek philosopher and scientist

a·rith·me·tic /ə ríthmə tìk/ n 1 the branch of mathematics that deals with addition, subtraction, multiplication, and division 2 calculations using basic mathematics ■ adj /árrith méttik/ of arithmetic —**ar·ith·met·i·cal** /árrith méttik'l/ adj —**ar·ith·met·i·cal·ly** adv —**a·rith·me·ti·cian** /ə ríthmə tísh'n/ n

✦**ar·ith·met·ic log·ic u·nit** n the circuit in a computer's central processing unit that makes decisions based on the results of calculations

ar·ith·met·ic pro·gres·sion n a sequence of numbers in which a constant figure is added to each term to give the next

Ariz. abbr Arizona

Ar·i·zo·na /árri zónə/ state in the SW United States. Cap. Phoenix. Pop. 5,130,632 (2000). —**Ar·i·zo·nan** adj, n —**Ar·i·zo·ni·an** adj, n

Ar·ju·na /áarjənə/ n in Hindu mythology, a prince to whom Krishna explains Hindu doctrine

ark n 1 in the Bible, Noah's ship in the story of the Flood 2 also **Ark, Ark of the Covenant** the chest into which, in biblical accounts, Moses placed the Ten Commandments 3 also **Ark** a cabinet in a synagogue containing the Torah scrolls

Ark. abbr Arkansas

Ar·kan·sas /áarkən sàw/ 1 state of the south central United States. Cap. Little Rock. Pop. 2,673,400 (2000). 2 river of the central United States. Length 1,460 mi./2,350 km. —**Ar·kan·san** /aar kánz'n/ n, adj

Ark·wright /áark rìt/, **Sir Richard** (1732–92) British inventor of the cotton spinning frame (1768)

Ar·ling·ton /áarlingtən/ 1 city in NE Virginia. Pop. 177,275 (1998). 2 city in NE Texas. Pop. 306,497 (1998).

arm[1] n 1 a limb attached to the shoulder of the human body 2 a part of a chair that supports the human arm 3 a division of a larger group o *infantry as a combat arm* —**arm·ful** n

arm[2] v 1 vti equip somebody or something with weapons 2 vt activate a bomb or other weapon 3 vt provide somebody with something useful, e.g., information ■ n a weapon (often pl) ■ **arms** npl 1 warfare 2 a coat of arms

ARM abbr adjustable rate mortgage

ar·ma·da /aar maàdə/ n a large fleet of ships

ar·ma·dil·lo /áarmə díllō/ (pl -los or same) n a burrowing mammal with a hard-plated body

Ar·ma·ged·don /áarmə gédd'n/ n an all-destroying war

ORIGIN The original **Armageddon**, in the Bible, is a battle between the forces of good and evil that is predicted to mark the end of the world and precede the Day of Judgment (Revelation 16:16).

---

ar·ma·ture /áarməchər, -tòor, -chòor/ n 1 the moving part in an electromagnetic device 2 a keeper for a magnet 3 a framework for a sculpture

arm·chair /aˈarm chàir/ *n* a chair with rests for the arms ■ *adj* with no first-hand experience ○ *an armchair tourist*

armed forc·es *npl* the troops of a country who fight on land, at sea, or in the air, taken as a whole

Ar·me·ni·a /aar meˈenee ə/ country in W Asia, between the Black and Caspian seas. Cap. Yerevan. Pop. 3,336,100 (2001). —**Ar·me·ni·an** *n, adj*

arm·hole /aˈarm hòl/ *n* a hole in a garment for the arm to fit through

ar·mi·stice /aˈarmistiss/ *n* a truce in a war

Ar·mi·stice Day *n* the anniversary of the end of World War I. Date: November 11.

ar·mor /aˈarmər/ *n* **1** protective clothing of metal or leather worn by soldiers in the past **2** *also* **ar·mor plate** a protective layer of metal covering a military vehicle

ar·mored /aˈarmərd/ *adj* **1** with protective armor **2** equipped with armored vehicles

ar·mor·er /aˈarmərər/ *n* **1** a maker of weapons and armor **2** a person who repairs small arms

ar·mor·y /aˈarməree/ (*pl* **-ies**) *n* **1** a building for storing weapons **2** a building for military training **3** a collection of weapons **4** an arms factory **5** resources of any kind

arm·pit /aˈarm pìt/ *n* a hollow under the arm where it joins the body

arm's-length *adj* without a close relationship ○ *an arms-length business transaction*

Arm·strong /aˈarm stràwng/, **Louis** (1901–71) US jazz trumpeter, singer, and bandleader

Neil Armstrong

Arm·strong, Neil (*b.* 1930) US astronaut

ar·my /aˈarmee/ (*pl* **-mies**) *n* **1** the branch of the armed forces trained to fight on land **2** any trained or armed fighting force **3** a large organized group ○ *an army of volunteers*

Ar·no /aˈarnō/ river in Tuscany, central Italy. Length 150 mi./240 km.

Ar·nold /aˈarn'ld/, **Benedict** (1741–1801) American Revolutionary general and traitor

Ar·nold, Matthew (1822–88) British poet and critic

a·ro·ma /ə rṓmə/ *n* **1** a smell or odor **2** a subtle quality ○ *an aroma of scandal* ◊ See note at **smell**

a·ro·ma·ther·a·py /ə rṓmə thérrəpee/ *n* treatment of physical and psychological dis-

orders using plant oils —**a·ro·ma·ther·a·pist** *n*

ar·o·mat·ic /àrrō máttik/ *adj* having a pleasant smell ■ *n* a fragrant substance or plant —**ar·o·mat·i·cal·ly** *adv*

a·rose past tense of **arise**

a·round /ə równd/ *prep* **1** to or on another side of ○ *around the corner* **2** surrounding or on all sides of **3** regarding ○ *felt anxiety around the process of globalization* ■ *adv* **1** on all sides **2** in an opposite direction ○ *turned around* **3** present or existing ○ *since computers have been around* ■ *adv, prep* **1** from place to place **2** in the vicinity **3** approximately ◊ **have been around** have had enough experience of life not to be easily deceived (*infml*)

a·rouse /ə rówz/ (**a·roused, a·rous·ing**) *vt* **1** stimulate a response ○ *aroused their interest* **2** stimulate sexual desire in somebody —**a·rous·al** *n*

Arp /aarp/, **Jean** (1887–1966) French sculptor

ar·peg·gi·o /aar péjjee ō, -péjjō/ (*pl* **-os**) *n* a series of musical notes in a chord

arr. *abbr* **1** arranged **2** arrival **3** arrives

ar·raign /ə ráyn/ *vt* **1** charge with an offense in court **2** accuse —**ar·raign·ment** *n*

ar·range /ə ráynj/ (**-ranged, -rang·ing**) *v* **1** *vt* plan or prepare for something **2** *vt* put somebody or something in order or position **3** *vt* make an agreement for an event to happen **4** *vti* adapt music —**ar·range·ment** *n* —**ar·rang·er** *n*

ar·rant /árrənt/ *adj* utter or extreme (*disapproving*) ○ *arrant nonsense* —**ar·rant·ly** *adv*

ar·ray /ə ráy/ *n* **1** a collection **2** a striking or orderly arrangement **3** fine clothes (*literary*) **4** an ordered arrangement of numbers or data ■ *vt* **1** arrange in an orderly way (*fml*) **2** put clothes or ornaments on somebody (*literary*) ○ *was arrayed in ermine and diamonds*

ar·rears /ə reˈerz/ *npl* unpaid debts

ar·rest /ə rést/ *vt* **1** take into custody **2** stop or slow (*fml*) **3** capture or hold (*fml*) ○ *arrested our attention* ■ *n* **1** the taking of somebody into custody **2** legal custody ○ *under arrest* **3** a sudden stopping of the movement or operation of something —**ar·rest·ing** *adj* —**ar·rest·ing·ly** *adv*

Ar·rhe·ni·us /ə reˈenee əss/, **Svante August** (1859–1927) Swedish chemist. He developed a theory of ions carrying electrical charges.

ar·ri·val /ə rív'l/ *n* **1** the process, result, or time of arriving **2** somebody or something that arrives

ar·rive /ə rív/ (**-rived, -riv·ing**) *vi* **1** reach a place **2** come, begin, or happen ○ *The moment of departure had arrived.* **3** reach after consideration or discussion ○ *arrive at a decision* **4** become successful or famous (*infml*)

ar·ro·gant /árrəgənt/ *adj* proudly contemptuous or self-important —**ar·ro·gance** *n* —**ar·ro·gant·ly** *adv* ◊ See note at **proud**

ar·ro·gate /árrə gàyt/ (-**gat·ed**, -**gat·ing**) *vt* claim or take without right *(fml)* —**ar·ro·ga·tion** /àrrə gáysh'n/ *n*

ar·row /árrō/ *n* **1** a pointed missile shot from a bow **2** an arrow-shaped direction sign

ar·row·head /árrō hèd/ *n* the point of an arrow

⚡**ar·row key** *n* a computer key that moves the cursor

ar·row·root /árrō ròot/ *n* a starch derived from the rhizome of a tropical plant. Use: cooking.

ORIGIN **Arrowroot** is altered from *aru-aru*, the name for the plant in a Native South American language of Guyana and neighboring countries. It literally means "meal of meals," but because the root of the plant was used to treat wounds caused by poisoned arrows, English-speakers changed it to **arrowroot**.

ar·roy·o /ə róy ō/ (*pl* -**os**) *n* Southwest US **1** a dry gulch **2** a small stream

Ar·roy·o /ə róy ō/, **Gloria** (*b.* 1947) president of the Philippines (2001–)

ar·se·nal /áarsən'l, -nəl/ *n* **1** a place where weapons are stored **2** a stockpile of weapons **3** a supply of resources

ar·se·nic /áarsnik, áarsənik/ *n* **1** (*symbol* **As**) a poisonous solid chemical element. Use: alloys **2** a compound of arsenic. Use: pesticide.

ar·son /áars'n/ *n* the crime of setting fire to property —**ar·son·ist** *n*

art *n* **1** the creation of beautiful or thought-provoking things **2** the works produced by art **3** a branch of art, such as painting or sculpture **4** creation by human beings rather than nature **5** technique or craft **6** skill or ability **7** cunning *(literary)* ■ **arts** *npl* **1** creative activities such as painting, music, and literature **2** nonscientific subjects

art. *abbr* **1** article **2** artillery

Art deco: Chrysler Building, New York City (1930), designed by William van Alen

art dec·o /-dékō/, **Art Dec·o** *n* a 1930s design style using geometric shapes and bold colors

ar·te·fact *n* = artifact

Ar·te·mis /áartəmiss/ *n* in Greek mythology,

the goddess of hunting. Roman equivalent **Diana**

ar·te·ri·o·scle·ro·sis /aar tèeree ō sklə róssiss/ *n* the arterial disease atherosclerosis

ar·ter·y /áartəree/ (*pl* -**ies**) *n* **1** a major blood vessel carrying blood away from the heart **2** a main route —**ar·te·ri·al** /aar tèeree əl/ *adj*

ar·te·sian well /aar téezh'n-/ *n* a well supplying water by natural pressure

ORIGIN The **artesian well** is named for the region of Artois (formerly *Arteis*) in NE France. The first artesian wells were drilled in Artois in the 18C.

art·ful /áartf'l/ *adj* **1** cunning and subtle **2** skillful and adroit —**art·ful·ly** *adv* —**art·ful·ness** *n*

ar·thri·tis /aar thrítəss/ *n* a condition causing stiff and painful joints —**ar·thrit·ic** /aar thríttik/ *adj, n* —**ar·thrit·i·cal·ly** *adv*

ar·thro·pod /áarthrə pòd/ *n* an invertebrate animal such as an insect, arachnid, centipede, or crustacean —**ar·thro·pod** *adj*

Ar·thur /áarthər/ *n* in medieval legend, a king of the Britons whose court was based at Camelot —**Ar·thu·ri·an** /aar thóoree ən/ *adj*

Ar·thur /áarthər/, **Chester A.** (1829–86) 21st president of the United States (1881–85)

Ar·thur, Owen (*b.* 1949) prime minister of Barbados (1994–)

~~artic~~ incorrect spelling of **arctic**

~~artical~~ incorrect spelling of **article**

ar·ti·choke /áartə chòk/ (*pl* -**chokes** or same) *n* **1** a large scaly flower bud eaten as a vegetable **2** a plant that produces artichokes **3** a Jerusalem artichoke

ar·ti·cle /áartik'l/ *n* **1** a piece of nonfiction writing such as one in a newspaper **2** an object or item **3** the word "a," "an," or "the" used before a noun

ar·tic·u·late *adj* /aar tíkyələt/ **1** able to express thoughts, ideas, and feelings coherently in speech **2** expressed coherently ■ *v* /aar tíkyə làyt/ (-**lat·ed**, -**lat·ing**) **1** *vt* express or communicate **2** *vti* speak or say distinctly **3** *vti* join in a way that allows movement —**ar·tic·u·la·cy** *n* —**ar·tic·u·lat·ed** /-làytəd/ *adj* —**ar·tic·u·late·ly** *adv* —**ar·tic·u·late·ness** *n* —**ar·tic·u·la·tion** /-láysh'n/ *n*

ar·ti·fact /áarti fàkt/, **ar·te·fact** *n* an object made by a human being

ar·ti·fice /áartəfəss/ *n* (*fml*) **1** a clever trick **2** insincere behavior

ar·ti·fi·cial /áartə físh'l/ *adj* **1** made by human beings **2** made in imitation of something natural **3** insincere —**ar·ti·fi·ci·al·i·ty** /àart-əfishee állətee/ *n* —**ar·ti·fi·cial·ly** *adv*

ar·ti·fi·cial in·sem·i·na·tion *n* a method of inducing pregnancy without sexual intercourse

⚡**ar·ti·fi·cial in·tel·li·gence** *n* the ability of computers to perform functions that normally require human intelligence

⚡ar·ti·fi·cial life *n* the use of computer systems to simulate various aspects of natural human behavior, such as learning and reproduction

ar·ti·fi·cial res·pi·ra·tion *n* any method of forcing air into the lungs of somebody who has stopped breathing

ar·til·ler·y /aar tílləree/ *n* **1** powerful guns used by armed forces **2** soldiers using powerful guns

ar·ti·san /áartəz'n/ *n* a skilled craftsperson —**ar·ti·san·ship** *n*

art·ist /áartist/ *n* **1** a creator of art, especially a painter or sculptor **2** a skilled person **3** a performer or entertainer

ar·tiste /aar teést/ *n* a performer or entertainer

ar·tis·tic /aar tístik/ *adj* **1** good at or appreciative of art **2** of art —**ar·tis·ti·cal·ly** *adv*

art·ist·ry /áartəstree/ *n* **1** artistic ability **2** great skill

art·less /áartləss/ *adj* **1** without deception **2** totally natural **3** lacking skill, knowledge, or elegance —**art·less·ly** *adv* —**art·less·ness** *n*

art nou·veau /áart noo vṓ, àar-/, **Art Nou·veau** *n* a late 19C design style using flowing lines

arts and crafts *n* the creative design of everyday objects (*+ sing or pl verb*)

art·sy /áartsee/ (**-si·er, -si·est**), **art·y** /áartee/ (**-i·er, -i·est**) *adj* affectedly artistic (*infml*)

art·work /áart wùrk/ *n* **1** a work of art **2** illustrative material for use in a publication

A·ru·ba /ə róobə/ island off the N Venezuelan coast, a self-governing part of the Netherlands. Pop. 70,007 (2001).

a·ru·gu·la /ə róogyələ/ (*pl* **-las** *or* **same**) *n* a plant with peppery leaves used in salads

Ar·y·an /áiree ən/ *n* **1** an Indo-European ancestor or descendant (*dated*) **2** in Nazi ideology, a person regarded as racially superior —**Ar·y·an** *adj*

as (*stressed*) /az/ (*unstressed*) /əz/ *conj* **1** at the time that ○ *fell down as I was running downstairs* **2** what ○ *Do as you like!* **3** because ○ *As we are very late we must hurry up.* **4** introduces a comparison ○ *as white as snow* **5** introduces a clause referring to a previous statement ○ *As I said, it's not easy.* **6** in the way that ○ *Everything went as planned.* **7** in the same way that ○ *She plays the violin well, as her mother once did.* ■ *prep* **1** at the time when ○ *As a child I was very mischievous.* **2** in the capacity of ○ *As a manager I am supposed to think strategically.* ◇ **as far as** the extent to which a situation holds or is relevant ○ *As far as I know, they are still living in Australia.* ◇ **as of** on and after a given date or time ○ *As of yesterday, we hadn't heard from them.* ◇ **as is** in the present condition ◇ **as it were** in a way ○ *We were in clover, as it were.* ◇ **as long as 1** provided that **2** because or seeing that ◇ **as such** in the precise sense (*often with a negative*) ○ *She*

had no experience as such. ◇ **as to** with reference to ◇ **as yet** up to the present time

USAGE Avoid false linkages when using **as** to mean "in the capacity of": *As a judge, you know I do not like being asked such questions* (which one is the judge?).

As *symbol* arsenic

As·ad·ha /áash adə/ *n* the 4th month of the year in the Hindu calendar

as·a·fet·i·da /àssə féttədə, -feét-/ *n* a strong-smelling plant extract. Use: South Asian cooking.

ASAP, asap *abbr* as soon as possible

as·bes·tos /ass béstəss, az-/ *n* a fibrous carcinogenic mineral. Use: formerly, heat-resistant materials.

as·cend /ə sénd/ *v* **1** *vi* move upward **2** *vti* climb something **3** *vt* succeed to an important position ○ *ascend the throne*

as·cen·dant /ə séndənt/, **as·cen·dent** *adj* **1** moving upward (*literary*) **2** dominant (*fml*) —**as·cen·dan·cy** *n*

as·cen·sion /ə sénsh'n/ *n* **1** the process of ascending (*fml*) **2** **As·cen·sion** in Christianity, Jesus Christ's rising to heaven

as·cent /ə sént/ *n* **1** a climb **2** an upward movement **3** a rise to importance

SPELLCHECK Do not confuse the spelling of **ascent** and **assent** ("agree to something"), which sound similar.

as·cer·tain /àssər táyn/ *vt* find out with certainty (*fml*) —**as·cer·tain·a·ble** *adj* —**as·cer·tain·ment** *n*

as·cet·ic /ə séttik/ *adj* of or choosing an austere life of self-denial —**as·cet·ic** *n* —**as·cet·i·cal·ly** *adv* —**as·cet·i·cism** /ə séttə sìzzəm/ *n*

⚡ASCII /áskee/ *n* a computer data exchange standard. Full form **American Standard Code for Information Interchange**

⚡ASCII file *n* a computer text file

a·scor·bic ac·id /ə skàwrbik-/ *n* vitamin C

as·cribe /ə skríb/ (**-cribed, -crib·ing**) *vt* (*fml*) **1** give something as the cause of ○ *ascribed his success to good luck* **2** name somebody as the author of ○ *a poem ascribed to Robert Frost* —**as·crib·a·ble** *adj* —**as·crip·tion** /ə skrípsh'n/ *n*

a·sep·tic /ay séptik/ *adj* **1** without disease-causing microorganisms **2** preventing infection ○ *aseptic techniques* —**a·sep·ti·cal·ly** *adv*

a·sex·u·al /ay sékshoo əl, -sh'l/ *adj* without sex, sex organs, or sexual desire —**a·sex·u·al·i·ty** /ay sèkshoo állətee/ *n* —**a·sex·u·al·ly** *adv*

ash¹ *n* **1** the remains of something burned (*often pl*) ○ *fireplace ashes* **2** volcanic dust

ash² (*pl* **ash·es** *or* **same**) *n* **1** a deciduous tree with winged fruits **2** the hard wood of an ash tree. Use: furniture, tool handles.

a·shamed /ə sháymd/ *adj* full of shame and often embarrassment **—a·sha·med·ly** /-mədlee/ *adv*

A·shan·ti /ə shántee, -shaˈan-/ administrative area and former kingdom in central Ghana

Ashe /ash/, **Arthur** (1943–93) US tennis player

ash·en /ásh'n/ *adj* **1** very pale **2** like ashes

Ash·ga·bat /áashgə báat/ capital of Turkmenistan. Pop. 462,000 (1995).

Ash·or·a /ə shōrə/, **Ash·ur·a** /ə shoorə/ *n* an Islamic festival associated by Sunni Muslims with the death of Muhammad's grandson Husain. Date: 10th day of Muharram.

a·shore /ə sháwr/ *adv* to or on land

~~ashphalt~~ incorrect spelling of **asphalt**

ash·ram /áashrəm/ *n* **1** in Hinduism, a retreat for the practice of yoga and other disciplines **2** a spiritual community

ash·tray /ásh trày/ *n* a container for cigarette, cigar, or pipe ash

A·shur·ba·ni·pal /áshoor báanə páal/ (668–627 BC) king of Assyria

Ash Wednes·day *n* in Christianity, the first day of Lent

ash·y /áshee/ **(-i·er, -i·est)** *adj* **1** extremely pale (*literary*) **2** like ash

A·sia /áyzhə, áyshə/ the world's largest continent, bordered by the Ural and Caucasus mountains and the Arctic, Pacific, and Indian oceans. Pop. estimated 3.46 billion (1995).

A·sia Mi·nor historic region in W Asia, roughly corresponding to Asian Turkey

A·sian /áyzh'n, -sh'n/ *adj* of Asia ■ *n* somebody from Asia

A·sian A·mer·i·can *n* an American of Asian descent **—A·sian A·mer·i·can** *adj*◊ See note at **African American**

A·si·at·ic /àyzhee áttik, àyzee-/ *adj* describes things in or from Asia ○ *a semitropical Asiatic shrub* ○ *an Asiatic port*

a·side /ə síd/ *adv* **1** away or to one side **2** not under consideration ○ *Budget constraints aside, is it feasible?* **3** for future use ■ *n* an actor's comment to the audience

As·i·mov /ázzi mòf, -máwf/, **Isaac** (1920–92) Russian-born US scientist and writer

as·i·nine /áss'n ìn/ *adj* ridiculous **—as·i·nine·ly** *adv* **—as·i·nin·i·ty** /àss'n ínnətee/ *n*

ask *v* **1** *vti* put a question to somebody **2** *vti* request something **3** *vt* invite **4** *vt* require **5** *vt* name as a price
□ **ask after** *vt* inquire about the welfare of

a·skance /ə skánss/ *adv* with suspicion

a·skew /ə skyoó/ *adj, adv* at an angle or off center

ask·ing price *n* the price quoted

ASL *abbr* American Sign Language

a·slant /ə slánt/ *adv* slanting

a·sleep /ə sleép/ *adj* **1** not awake or alert **2** numb through poor blood circulation

As·ma·ra /aaz máarə/ capital of Eritrea. Pop. 431,000 (1995).

a·so·cial /ay sṓsh'l/ *adj* **1** unwilling or unable to interact socially **2** inconsiderate or indifferent to other members of society

~~association~~ incorrect spelling of **association**

asp *n* **1** a snake that killed Cleopatra **2** a S European viper

⚡ **ASP** *abbr* **1** active server page **2** application service provider

as·par·a·gus /ə spárrəgəss/ *n* **1** spear-shaped plant shoots eaten as a vegetable **2** a plant cultivated for its edible shoots

A.S.P.C.A. *abbr* American Society for the Prevention of Cruelty to Animals

as·pect /á spèkt/ *n* **1** one side or part of something **2** appearance **3** the direction toward which something faces **4** a grammatical category of verbs that is independent of tense

as·pen /áspən/ **(***pl* **-pens** *or* **same)** *n* a poplar tree with leaves that flutter in the breeze

As·per·ger's syn·drome /áss pùrjərz-/, **As·per·ger syn·drome** /áss pùrjər-/ *n* a severe developmental disorder akin to autism. Also called **little professor syndrome**

as·per·i·ty /a spérrətee/ *n* **1** harshness or severity (*fml*) **2** roughness (*literary*)

as·per·sion /ə spúrzh'n, -sh'n/ *n* a defamatory remark (*often pl*)

as·phalt /ás fàwlt/ *n* a semisolid bituminous substance. Use: road surfacing, waterproofing, fungicides. ■ *vt* cover with asphalt

as·phyx·i·a /as fíksee ə, əs-/ *n* suffocation

as·phyx·i·ate /as fíksee àyt, əs-/ **(-at·ed, -at·ing)** *vti* suffocate **—as·phyx·i·a·tion** /as fìksee áysh'n, əs-/ *n*

as·pic /áspik/ *n* a salty or tart-tasting jelly

as·pi·dis·tra /àspi dístrə/ *n* a leafy houseplant

as·pi·rate /-rat·ed, -rat·ing/ *vt* /áspə ràyt/ **1** pronounce a sound, such as the letter "h," while breathing out **2** remove liquid or gas by suction, especially from a body cavity (*technical*) **—as·pi·rate** /áspərət, áspə ràyt/ *adj*

as·pi·ra·tion /àspə ráysh'n/ *n* **1** an ambition **2** the process of aspirating

as·pi·ra·tion·al /àspi ráyshən'l, -shnəl/ *adj* ambitious for material success or self-improvement

as·pire /ə spír/ **(-pired, -pir·ing)** *vi* have a particular ambition **—as·pi·rant** /áspərənt, ə spírənt/ *n* **—as·pir·ing** *adj*

as·pi·rin /áspirin, -prin/ **(***pl* **-rins** *or* **same)** *n* **1** a pain-relieving drug **2** a tablet containing aspirin

---

ORIGIN The word **aspirin** was originally coined in German, where it was a contraction of *acetylierte Spirsäure*. This translates as "acetylated spiraeic acid," a former name for salicylic acid, from which aspirin is derived.

~~asprin~~ incorrect spelling of **aspirin**

ass *n* a mammal like a small horse with long ears

As·sad /aa saád/, **Bashar al-** (*b.* 1965) president of Syria (2000–)

As·sad, Hafez al- (1928–2000) president of Syria (1971–2000)

as·sail /ə sáyl/ *vt* 1 attack somebody with words or actions 2 overwhelm somebody's senses —**as·sail·ant** *n*

~~assasin~~ incorrect spelling of **assassin**

as·sas·sin /ə sáss'n/ *n* a murderer, especially one with a political motive

---

ORIGIN Assassin comes from an Arabic word that literally means "users of hashish (cannabis)." The name originally applied to a group of 11C Muslims who took hashish before going on assassination missions.

---

as·sas·si·nate /ə sáss'n àyt/ (**-nat·ed, -nat·ing**) *vt* 1 murder somebody, especially a public figure, for political reasons 2 ruin or destroy something such as somebody's reputation —**as·sas·si·na·tion** /ə sàss'n áysh'n/ *n* ◊ See note at **kill**

as·sault /ə sáwlt/ *n* 1 a physical or verbal attack 2 a sexual attack or rape ■ *vt* attack

as·sault and bat·ter·y *n* physical attack causing bodily harm

as·say /á sày, ə sáy/ *n* 1 examination and analysis 2 the chemical analysis of a substance ■ *vt* 1 examine or analyze 2 attempt *(fml)* —**as·say·er** *n*

as·sem·blage /ə sémblij/ *n* 1 the process of gathering people or things together 2 a collection 3 a work of art made from a collection of different objects

as·sem·ble /ə sémb'l/ (**-bled, -bling**) *v* 1 *vt* put components together to make something 2 *vti* gather together ◊ See note at **collect**

⚡ **as·sem·bler** /ə sémblər/ *n* 1 somebody who puts components together 2 a computer program that converts assembly language into machine language 3 *also* **as·sem·bly lan·guage** a low-level computer language

⚡ **as·sem·bly** /ə sémblee/ (*pl* **-blies**) *n* 1 the putting together of components 2 a gathering together of people 3 a school meeting before classes 4 *also* **As·sem·bly** a consultative or legislative body 5 the translation of assembly language into machine language

as·sem·bly line *n* a series of work stations in a manufacturing system

as·sent /ə sént/ *vi* agree to something ■ *n* an expression of agreement —**as·sent·er** *n* ◊ See note at **agree**

as·sert /ə súrt/ *v* 1 *vt* claim or state something emphatically 2 *vt* insist on or exercise a right 3 *vr* behave forcefully —**as·ser·ter** *n* —**as·ser·tion** /ə súrsh'n/ *n*

as·ser·tive /ə súrtiv/ *adj* 1 acting confidently 2 strong and pronounced —**as·ser·tive·ly** *adv* —**as·ser·tive·ness** *n*

as·sess /ə séss/ *vt* 1 judge or evaluate 2 determine the amount or value of 3 charge as an amount —**as·sess·a·ble** *adj* —**as·sess·ment** *n* —**as·ses·sor** *n*

as·set /á sèt/ *n* somebody or something useful or valuable ■ **as·sets** *npl* 1 the property of a person or organization 2 items constituting the value of an organization

---

ORIGIN Asset derives from the French word for "enough" (modern French *assez*). In the French formerly used in English law courts, "having enough" meant "having enough money or property to settle your debts," and from there **assets** came to mean property or financial resources. For 400 years only the form **assets** was used, as a singular noun ("my assets is..."). Later the -s was interpreted as the English plural ending, and the singular form **asset** appeared in the 19C.

---

as·set-strip·ping *n* the selling of company assets individually for profit —**as·set-strip·per** *n*

as·sid·u·ous /ə síjjoo əss/ *adj* very careful and diligent —**as·sid·u·ous·ly** *adv* ◊ See note at **careful**

as·sign /ə sín/ *vt* 1 give somebody a task or duty 2 send somebody to work somewhere 3 transfer property or rights 4 designate something for a particular use —**as·sign·a·ble** *adj* —**as·sign·er** *n* —**as·sign·or** *n*

as·sig·na·tion /àssig náysh'n/ *n* a lovers' secret meeting

as·sign·ment /ə sínmənt/ *n* 1 a task 2 an appointment 3 a legal transfer

as·sim·i·late /ə símmi làyt/ (**-lat·ed, -lat·ing**) *v* 1 *vti* integrate 2 *vt* absorb nutrients into the tissues of the body —**as·sim·i·la·ble** *adj* —**as·sim·i·la·tion** /ə símmi láysh'n/ *n*

As·sin·i·boin /ə sínnə bòyn/ (*pl* same or **-boins**), **As·sin·i·boine** (*pl* same or **-boines**) *n* 1 a member of a Native North American people who once lived in the N Great Plains, and who now live mainly in Saskatchewan, Alberta, and Montana 2 a Siouan language spoken in S and W Canada and in Montana by the Assiniboin —**As·sin·i·boin** *adj*

As·sin·i·boine /ə sínni bòyn/ river in SE Saskatchewan and S Manitoba, Canada. Length 665 mi./1,070 km.

as·sist /ə síst/ *vti* help ■ *n* a helpful act by a team player

as·sis·tance /ə sístənss/ *n* help made available

as·sis·tant /ə sístənt/ *n* a helper ■ *adj* serving as a deputy ○ *an assistant operating room supervisor*

SYNONYMS assistant, helper, deputy, aide
CORE MEANING: somebody who helps another person in carrying out a task

as·sis·tant pro·fes·sor *n* a university faculty member

as·sist·ed liv·ing *n* 1 residential care for seniors 2 a residential facility offering special care for seniors

assn., assoc. *abbr* association

as·so·ci·ate *v* /ə sóshee àyt, ə sóssee-/ (**-at·ed, -at·ing**) 1 *vt* connect one thing with another in the mind 2 *vi* spend time with somebody ■ *n* /ə sóshee ət, ə sóssee-/ 1 a person with whom somebody has a social or business relationship ○ *couldn't identify any of his associates* ■ *adj* /ə sóshee ət, -àyt, ə sóssee-/ 1 allied 2 without full status as a member **—as·so·ci·a·ble** *adj* **—as·so·ci·ated** *adj* **—as·so·ci·ate·ship** *n*

as·so·ci·ate de·gree *n* a two-year college degree

as·so·ci·ate pro·fes·sor *n* a university teacher

as·so·ci·a·tion /ə sòssee áysh'n, ə sòshee-/ *n* 1 a group of people or organizations 2 a linking or joining of people or things ○ *hasn't profited from her association with him* 3 social interaction ○ *freedom of association* 4 a linked idea

as·so·ci·a·tive /ə sóshee àytiv, ə sóssee-, -ətiv/ *adj* of psychological connections **—as·so·ci·a·tive·ly** *adv*

ϯ **as·so·ci·a·tive mem·o·ry** *n* computer memory accessed by content

as·so·nance /ássɒnɒnss/ *n* similarity of sound **—as·so·nant** *adj*

as·sort·ed /ə sáwrtəd/ *adj* 1 various 2 arranged in groups

as·sort·ment /ə sáwrtmɒnt/ *n* a collection of various similar things

asst. *abbr* assistant

as·suage /ə swáyj/ (**-suaged, -suag·ing**) *vt* relieve something unpleasant (*fml*)

as·sume /ə sóom/ (**-sumed, -sum·ing**) *vt* 1 suppose something to be true 2 take responsibility for something 3 take on a quality ○ *The task assumed Herculean proportions.* **—as·sum·a·ble** *adj* **—as·sumed** *adj* ◊ See note at **deduce**

as·sum·ing /ə sóoming/ *conj* if it is assumed that **—as·sum·ing·ly** *adv*

as·sump·tion /ə súmpshən/ *n* 1 something assumed or taken for granted 2 the assuming of something 3 **As·sump·tion** a Christian festival marking the Virgin Mary's ascent to heaven. Date: August 15.

as·sur·ance /ə shóorənss/ *n* 1 a pledge or promise 2 self-confidence 3 certainty 4 *UK* insurance against a certainty such as death

as·sure /ə shóor/ (**-sured, -sur·ing**) *vt* 1 make confident 2 convince 3 make certain **—as·sur·a·ble** *adj*

as·sured /ə shóord/ *adj* 1 guaranteed 2 self-confident **—as·sur·ed·ly** /ə shóorədlee/ *adv* **—as·sur·ed·ness** /ə shóorədnəss/ *n*

As·syr·i·a /ə sírree ə/ ancient kingdom in present-day N Iraq **—As·syr·i·an** *n, adj*

AST *abbr* 1 Alaska Standard Time 2 Atlantic Standard Time

A·staire /ə stáir/, **Fred** (1899–1987) US dancer and actor

As·ta·na /ə staánə/ capital of Kazakhstan. Pop. 270,400 (1997).

as·ta·tine /ástə tèen/ *n* (*symbol* **At**) a radioactive chemical element. Use: in medicine as a tracer element.

as·ter /ástər/ *n* a garden plant with flowers like daisies

~~asterick~~ incorrect spelling of **asterisk**

as·ter·isk /ástərisk/ *n* a star-shaped symbol used in printing ■ *vt* mark with an asterisk

USAGE The **asterisk** is usually placed at the end or beginning of a word. One or more asterisks may be used to mark a word or phrase in running text that is explained or expanded on elsewhere, usually in a footnote. A string of asterisks is sometimes used when part of a word is omitted, usually part of a swearword: *She was obviously p***ed off.*

a·stern /ə stúrn/ *adv* in or to the stern of a ship or boat

as·ter·oid /ástə ròyd/ *n* a rocky object orbiting the Sun

asth·ma /ázmə/ *n* a respiratory disease, sometimes caused by allergies **—asth·mat·ic** /az máttik/ *adj, n*

a·stig·ma·tism /ə stígmə tìzzəm/ *n* 1 an unequal curving of the eye surface, producing blurred vision 2 a defect in a lens or mirror that prevents light rays from meeting at a single point **—as·tig·mat·ic** /ástig máttik/ *adj*

a·stir /ə stúr/ *adj* 1 up and about 2 moving

a·ston·ish /ə stónnish/ *vt* amaze greatly **—a·ston·ish·ing** *adj* **—a·ston·ish·ing·ly** *adv* **—a·ston·ish·ment** *n*

As·tor /ástər/, **John Jacob** (1763–1848) German-born US fur trader and millionaire

a·stound /ə stównd/ *vt* surprise greatly **—a·stound·ing** *adj* **—a·stound·ing·ly** *adv*

as·tra·khan /ástrə kaan, -kàn/ *n* a fur fabric with a curly black or gray pile. Use: hats, trimming coats.

as·tral /ástrəl/ *adj* 1 of stars 2 in theosophical belief, above the material world **—as·tral·ly** *adv*

a·stray /ə stráy/ *adv* 1 off the right path 2 into error or sin ○ *led astray by questionable companions*

a·stride /ə stríd/ *prep* with one leg on each side of ■ *adv* with the legs apart

as·trin·gent /ə strínjənt/ *n* a substance that draws skin tissues together ■ *adj* sharp and acidic in tone **—as·trin·gen·cy** *n* **—as·trin·gent·ly** *adv*

astro-, astr- *prefix* star, the stars, outer space ○ *astronomy*

as·trol·o·gy /ə ströllɔjee/ *n* the study of the way planets are thought to affect human affairs —**as·trol·o·ger** *n* —**as·tro·log·i·cal** /àstrə lójjik'l/ *adj* —**as·tro·log·i·cal·ly** *adv*

as·tro·naut /ástrə nàwt/ *n* **1** somebody trained to travel in space **2** *US, Can, ANZ* an Asian immigrant frequently traveling back to work in Asia *(infml)*

ORIGIN The sense "Asian immigrant" has its origins in a play on Cantonese words meaning literally "empty wife" and "spaceman." It was coined toward the end of the 20C by Hong Kong migrants to refer to somebody who was still working in Hong Kong but had based his family (the "empty wife" and children) in North America (especially Canada) or Australasia.

as·tro·nom·i·cal /àstrə nómmik'l/, **as·tre·nom·ic** /-nómmik/ *adj* **1** of astronomy **2** immeasurably great *(infml)*

as·tro·nom·i·cal u·nit *n* a distance in space equal to the mean distance between the Earth and the Sun

as·tron·o·my /ə strónnəmee/ *n* the scientific study of the universe —**as·tron·o·mer** *n*

as·tro·phys·ics /àstrə fizziks/ *n* the physics of astronomical objects (+ *sing verb*) —**as·tro·phys·i·cal** *adj* —**as·tro·phys·i·cist** *n*

As·tro·Turf /ástrō tùrf/ *tdmk* a trademark for synthetic turf resembling grass

as·tute /ə stoōt/ *adj* shrewd and perceptive —**as·tute·ly** *adv* —**as·tute·ness** *n*

A·sun·ción /aa sòon syáwn/ capital of Paraguay. Pop. 550,060 (1997).

a·sun·der /ə súndər/ *adv* into separate parts or pieces *(literary)*

As·vi·na /ásh vinə/ *n* the 7th month of the year in the Hindu calendar

As·wan /a swaàn, á swaàn/ city in S Egypt. Pop. 220,000 (1992).

a·sy·lum /ə sīləm/ *n* **1** shelter and protection from danger **2** protection and immunity from extradition **3** an offensive term for a hospital for people with psychiatric disorders *(dated)*

a·sym·met·ri·cal /ày si méttrik'l/, **a·sym·met·ric** /-méttrik/ *adj* not symmetrical or equal ○ *an asymmetrical flower arrangement* —**a·sym·met·ri·cal·ly** *adv* —**a·sym·me·try** /a símmətree/ *n*

⚡**a·sym·met·ri·cal dig·i·tal sub·scrib·er line** *n* a high-speed telephone line

a·sym·met·ric war·fare *n* highly decentralized, unconventional warfare and attacks perpetrated on nation-states and civilians by paramilitaries, guerrillas, and terrorists

a·symp·to·mat·ic /ay slmtə .máttik/ *adj* showing or producing no obvious symptoms —**a·symp·to·mat·i·cal·ly** *adv*

⚡**a·syn·chron·ous com·mu·ni·ca·tion** /ày slngkrənəss-/ *n* the sending of electronic data in one direction one character at a time

at *prep* **1** on or near a specific location or position ○ *a face at the window* **2** attending ○ *at school* **3** indicates when something happens ○ *at midnight* **4** indicates a rate or price ○ *at 60 miles per hour* **5** toward ○ *She glanced at me.* **6** as a reaction to ○ *was amazed at that* **7** in a particular activity or state ○ *an expert at windsurfing* ○ *at risk* **8** in a particular condition or state ○ *at risk of infection* ◊ **at all** in any way, to any extent, or under any conditions

At *symbol* astatine

at. *abbr* **1** atmosphere **2** atomic

A·ta·ca·ma De·sert /àatə kàamə-/ dry plateau in N Chile

A·ta·hual·pa /àatə waàlpə/ (1500?–33) last ruler of the Inca Empire (1532–33)

A·tan·a·soff /ə tánnə sòf/, **John V.** (1903–95) US mathematical physicist. He developed many of the basic techniques later used in the design of the first electronic digital computer.

Mustafa Kemal Atatürk

A·ta·türk /áttə tùrk/, **Mustafa Kemal** (1881–1938) founder and first president of the republic of Turkey (1923–38)

at·a·vis·tic /àttə vístik/ *adj* **1** of the recurrence of a genetic feature after an absence lasting generations **2** primitive and instinctive —**at·a·vism** *n* —**at·a·vis·ti·cal·ly** *adv*

ate past tense of **eat**

-ate *suffix* **1** having, characterized by ○ *duplicate* **2** office, rank ○ *archdeaconate* **3** act on in a particular way ○ *fluoridate* **4** a chemical compound derived from a particular element or compound ○ *nitrate*

atempt incorrect spelling of **attempt**

ATF *abbr* (Bureau of) Alcohol, Tobacco, and Firearms

Ath·a·bas·ca /àthə báskə/ river in Alberta, Canada. Length 765 mi./1,231 km.

Ath·a·bas·ca, Lake lake in N Alberta and N Saskatchewan, Canada

a·the·ist /áytheeist/ *n* somebody who does not believe in God or deities —**a·the·ism** *n* —**a·the·is·tic** /àythee ístik/ *adj*

athelete incorrect spelling of **athlete**

A·the·na /ə theénə/, **A·the·ne** /ə theénee/ *n* in Greek mythology, the goddess of wisdom. Roman equivalent **Minerva**

Ath·ens /áthənz/ capital of Greece. Pop. 772,072 (1991). —**A·the·ni·an** /ə theénee ən/ *adj, n*

ath·er·o·scle·ro·sis /áthərōsklə rṓssis/ *n* an arterial disease obstructing blood flow —**ath·er·o·scle·rot·ic** /áthərōsklə róttik/ *adj*

~~athiest~~ incorrect spelling of **atheist**

ath·lete /áth lèet/ *n* somebody with ability in athletics

> **ORIGIN** The root of **athlete** is the Greek word for "prize." A Greek athlete could in theory be competing for any prize, but the word came to refer only to the physical exercises performed at public games, such as running, discus-throwing, or boxing.

> **USAGE Athlete** is pronounced with two syllables, not three: ath-leet, not ath-uh-leet.

ath·lete's foot *n* a fungal infection of the feet

ath·let·ic /áth léttik/ *adj* 1 of athletes or athletics 2 muscular and strong —**ath·let·i·cal·ly** *adv* —**ath·let·i·cism** /áth léttissiz'm/ *n*

ath·let·ics /áth léttiks/ *n* sports activities (+ *sing or pl verb*)

-ation *suffix* an action or process, or the result of it ○ *alienation* ○ *presentation*

~~atitude~~ incorrect spelling of **attitude**

At·lan·ta /at lántə, ət-/ capital of Georgia, United States. Pop. 403,819 (1998).

At·lan·tic /ət lántik/ *adj* of the Atlantic Ocean ■ *n also* **At·lan·tic O·cean** world's second largest ocean, separating Europe and Africa from North and South America

At·lan·tic Cit·y city in SE New Jersey, noted for its beaches and gambling casinos. Pop. 38,063 (1998).

At·lan·tic Rim *n* the regions bordering the Atlantic Ocean

At·lan·tic Stan·dard Time, At·lan·tic Time *n* the local standard time in Puerto Rico and the Canadian Maritime Provinces

At·lan·tis /at lántiss, ət-/ *n* in Greek mythology, an island that sank into the sea

at·las /áttləss/ *n* a book of maps

> **ORIGIN** Collections of maps were published in the 17C with a picture of the mythological Titan, Atlas, at the front, holding up the world, so they came to be known as **atlases**. In the mythological story, Atlas held up the heavens, not the world.

At·las Moun·tains /áttləss-/ system of mountain ranges in Morocco, Algeria, and Tunisia. Highest peak Jebel Toubkal 13,665 ft./4,165 m.

~~atlass~~ incorrect spelling of **atlas**

ATM *n* an electronic cash machine. Full form **automated teller machine**

at·mos·phere /átmə sfèer/ *n* 1 the gases around an astronomical object 2 the air or climate of a place 3 a mood or tone 4 a unit of pressure —**at·mos·pher·ic** /átməs férrik, -féerik/ *adj* —**at·mos·pher·i·cal** *adj*

at·mos·pher·ic pres·sure *n* the downward pressure exerted by the weight of the overlying atmosphere

at·mos·pher·ics /átmə sférriks, -sféeriks/ *n* 1 the study of electromagnetic radiation in the atmosphere (+ *sing verb*) 2 interference with electronic signals caused by electromagnetic radiation in the atmosphere (+ *sing verb*) 3 the prevailing mood of a situation (+ *pl verb*)

at. no. *abbr* atomic number

a·toll /á tòl/ *n* a coral island surrounding a lagoon

> **ORIGIN Atoll** derives from the language of the Maldives in South Asia.

at·om /áttəm/ *n* 1 the smallest portion into which an element can be divided and still retain its properties 2 a very small amount ○ *not an atom of truth*

a·tom·ic /ə tómmik/ *adj* 1 based on nuclear energy 2 of an atom or atoms —**a·tom·i·cal·ly** *adv*

a·tom·ic en·er·gy *n* nuclear energy

at·om·ize /áttə mìz/ (**-ized, -iz·ing**) *v* 1 *vt* separate into atoms 2 *vt* destroy 3 *vti* change into spray

at·om·iz·er /áttə mìzər/ *n* a spray device

a·ton·al /ay tṓn'l/ *adj* without a musical key —**a·to·nal·i·ty** /àytō nálləteē/ *n* —**a·ton·al·ly** *adv*

a·tone /ə tṓn/ (**a·toned, a·ton·ing**) *vi* make amends (*fml*) ○ *atoned for his misdeeds* —**a·tone·ment** *n*

a·top /ə tóp/ *prep, adv* on or to the top of something

a·tri·um /áytree əm/ (*pl* **-ums** *or* **-a** /-ə/) *n* 1 a central hall with a glass roof 2 a Roman courtyard

a·tro·cious /ə trṓshəss/ *adj* 1 very bad 2 very cruel —**a·tro·cious·ly** *adv*

a·troc·i·ty /ə tróssətee/ (*pl* **-ties**) *n* 1 a shockingly cruel act 2 extreme cruelty ○ *an act of atrocity*

at·ro·phy /áttrəfee/ *n* 1 a wasting away in size or strength ○ *muscle atrophy* 2 a lessening of an ability ■ *vi* (**-phied, -phy·ing, -phies**) weaken —**a·troph·ic** /ə tróffik/ *adj*

at·tach /ə tách/ *v* 1 *vt* fasten or secure to something else 2 *vt* add or append to something else 3 *vi* be associated with 4 *vt* ascribe or assign 5 *vt* place on temporary duty —**at·tach·a·ble** *adj*

at·ta·ché /áttə sháy, a tà-/ *n* a diplomat with a particular role ○ *a military attaché*

at·ta·ché case *n* a slender rigid briefcase

at·tached /ə tácht/ *adj* 1 fastened to or enclosed with something else 2 devoted to or fond of somebody or something

~~attachement~~ incorrect spelling of **attachment**

at·tach·ment /ə táchmənt/ *n* 1 an emotional bond 2 the process of attaching 3 something attached 4 a means of attaching

at·tack /ə ták/ v 1 vti try to harm somebody or something 2 vt criticize somebody 3 vti cause damage to somebody or something ○ *The disease can attack at any age.* 4 vt make a vigorous start on 5 vti try to score against an opposing team ■ n 1 an act of attacking 2 a bout of an illness —**at·tack·er** n

at·tain /ə táyn/ vt 1 accomplish 2 reach a particular state —**at·tain·a·ble** adj ◊ See note at **accomplish**

at·tain·ment /ə táynmənt/ n 1 the accomplishment of a goal 2 something achieved through effort (*often pl*)

at·tempt /ə témpt/ vti try to do ■ n 1 a try or effort 2 an attack ○ *an attempt on her life* ◊ See note at **try**

at·tend /ə ténd/ v 1 vti be present at an event 2 vti regularly go to a particular place 3 vi listen or watch carefully 4 vt accompany or be associated with —**at·ten·dee** /ə tèn dée, à ten-/ n —**at·tend·er** n

□ **attend to** vti deal with

at·ten·dance /ə téndənss/ n 1 presence at an event or place 2 the number of people attending an event

at·ten·dant /ə téndənt/ n somebody serving in a public place 2 a servant or escort ■ adj accompanying or associated ○ *drought and attendant forest fires*

~~attendence~~ incorrect spelling of **attendance**

at·ten·tion /ə ténsh'n/ n 1 mental concentration ○ *pay attention* 2 notice or interest ○ *media attention* 3 appropriate or affectionate treatment 4 a formal military posture ■ interj orders military personnel to stand up straight —**at·ten·tive** adj —**at·ten·tive·ly** adv —**at·ten·tive·ness** n

at·ten·tion def·i·cit dis·or·der, at·ten·tion def·i·cit hy·per·ac·tiv·i·ty dis·or·der n in children, a condition marked by hyperactivity and inability to concentrate

at·ten·u·ate (-at·ed, -at·ing) vti /ə ténnyoo àyt/ make or become weaker or thinner —**at·ten·u·a·tion** /ə ténnyoo áysh'n/ n

at·test /ə tést/ vti 1 be evidence of 2 confirm the validity of —**at·tes·ta·tion** /à te stáysh'n, àttə-/ n —**at·tes·tor** n

at·tic /áttik/ n a room or an area immediately under a roof

ORIGIN Attic was originally an adjective, adopted from French, describing an upper part of a façade that had a row of smaller columns above a main row below. This was the "Attic" style, named for Attica in ancient Greece. The name *attic story* was easily interpreted as meaning "upper story under the beams of a roof," and from there **attic** came to be used as a noun for a story like this, or a room in one.

At·tic /áttik/ adj of Attica ■ n an ancient Greek dialect

At·ti·ca /áttikə/ region of ancient Greece around Athens

At·ti·la /áttˈlə, ə tíllə/ (406?–453?) Hunnish warrior king

at·tire /ə tír/ (fml) n clothing ■ vt (-tired, -tir·ing) put clothes on somebody

at·ti·tude /áttə tòod/ n 1 a personal feeling about something 2 body posture 3 an aggressive and challenging manner (*infml*) ○ *teenagers with attitude* 4 the orientation of an aircraft or spacecraft

at·ti·tu·di·nal /àttə tòod'nəl/ adj insisting on your rights

attn. abbr attention

at·tor·ney /ə túrnee/ (pl -neys) n 1 a lawyer 2 somebody given legal power —**at·tor·ney·ship** n

at·tor·ney gen·er·al (pl **at·tor·neys gen·er·al** or **at·tor·neys gen·er·al**) n the chief legal officer of a country or state

~~attornies~~ incorrect spelling of **attorneys**

at·tract /ə trákt/ vt 1 cause somebody or something to come closer, e.g., by magnetism or temptation 2 elicit a response such as support, interest, or attention 3 appeal or be attractive to somebody

at·trac·tion /ə tráksh'n/ n 1 the power of attracting 2 a quality, feature, or site that attracts people

at·trac·tive /ə tráktiv/ adj 1 pleasant in appearance or manner 2 good-looking 3 interesting or appealing ○ *an attractive proposition* —**at·trac·tive·ly** adv —**at·trac·tive·ness** n

at·trib·ute vt /ə tríbbyoot/ (-ut·ed, -ut·ing) 1 say or think that something was caused or produced by somebody or something 2 assign a particular quality to something ■ n /áttri byòot/ a quality or property —**at·trib·ut·a·ble** adj —**at·tri·bu·tion** /àttrə byòosh'n/ n

at·trib·u·tive /ə tríbbyətiv/ adj preceding the noun in a noun phrase —**at·trib·u·tive·ly** adv

at·tri·tion /ə trísh'n/ n 1 the wearing away of a surface 2 a weakening caused by persistent attack 3 gradual reduction of personnel

At·tu /á tòo/ westernmost of the Aleutian Islands, SW Alaska

At·tucks /áttəks/, **Crispus** (1723?–70) American patriot

ATV abbr all-terrain vehicle

Margaret Atwood

At·wood /át wòod/, **Margaret** (b. 1939) Canadian writer

at. wt. *abbr* atomic weight

a·typ·i·cal /ay típpik'l/ *adj* not typical —**a·typ·i·cal·ly** *adv*

Au *symbol* gold

au·burn /áwbərn/ *adj* reddish brown —**au·burn** *n*

Auck·land /áwkland/ largest city and port in New Zealand. Pop. 1,076,100 (1998).

auc·tion /áwksh'n/ *n* a sale by bidding, or this method of selling ■ *vti* sell goods by inviting bids —**auc·tion·a·ble** *adj*

auc·tion·eer /awksha neŕer/ *n* somebody conducting an auction

au·da·cious /aw dáyshass/ *adj* bold or daring —**au·da·cious·ly** *adv* —**au·dac·i·ty** /aw dássəti/ *n*

W. H. Auden

Au·den /áwd'n/, **W. H.** (1907–73) British-born US poet and dramatist

~~audience~~ incorrect spelling of **audience**

au·di·ble /áwdəb'l/ *adj* capable of being heard —**au·di·bil·i·ty** /àwdə bíllətee/ *n* —**au·di·bly** *adv*

au·di·ence /áwdee anss/ *n* **1** the people watching or listening to a performance or broadcast **2** the readership of a particular author or publication **3** a formal interview

au·di·o /áwdee ò/ *n* the recording and reproduction of sound

audio-, audi- *prefix* sound, hearing o *audiovisual*

au·di·o book *n* a recorded book

au·di·ol·o·gy /àwdee óllajee/ *n* the diagnosis and treatment of hearing loss —**au·di·o·log·i·cal** /àwdee ə lójjik'l/ *adj* —**au·di·ol·o·gist** *n*

au·di·o·tape /áwdee ō tàyp/ *n* **1** magnetic tape for recording sound **2** a sound recording on tape

au·di·o·vis·u·al /àwdee ō vízhoo əl/ *adj* **1** of sound and vision **2** of hearing and sight ■ *n* a teaching aid using sound and vision

au·dit /áwdət/ *n* **1** a check of financial accounts **2** an efficiency check ■ *vt* **1** attend a college class without being graded on work done **2** carry out an audit of something

au·di·tion /aw dísh'n/ *n* **1** a test performance by an actor or musician for a job **2** the sense or process of hearing ■ *vti* do or give somebody an audition

au·di·tor /áwdətər/ *n* **1** somebody who conducts an audit **2** somebody who attends a class but is not graded

au·di·to·ri·um /àwdi táwree əm/ (*pl* **-ums** *or* **-a** /-ə/) *n* **1** a hall or lecture room **2** the part of a theater where the audience sits

au·di·to·ry /áwdə tàwree/ *adj* of hearing

au·dit trail *n* a record of operations or transactions

Au·du·bon /áwdə bòn/, **John James** (1785–1851) Haitian-born US ornithologist, naturalist, and artist

Aug. *abbr* August

au·ger /áwgər/ *n* a hand tool for boring holes

> **SPELLCHECK** Do not confuse the spelling of **auger** and **augur** ("a foreteller of the future," "predict the future"), which sound similar.

aug·ment /awg mént/ *vti* increase or add to something *(fml)* —**aug·men·ta·tion** /àwgmən táysh'n, -men-/ *n* ◊ See note at **increase**

au gra·tin /ō graát'n, ō grátt'n, ō graa taàN/ *adj* with a browned cooked crust

Augs·burg /ówgz bùrg/ city in S Germany. Pop. 262,110 (1997).

au·gur /áwgər/ *n* **1** in ancient Rome, an interpreter of messages from deities **2** a foreteller of the future ■ *vti* indicate what will happen in the future ◊ See note at **auger**

au·gu·ry /áwgyəree, -gə-/ (*pl* **-ries**) *n* **1** divination **2** a portent or omen

au·gust /aw gúst/ *adj* dignified and splendid *(fml)*

Au·gust /áwgəst/ *n* the 8th month of the year in the Gregorian calendar

> **ORIGIN** August is named for the Roman emperor Augustus.

Au·gus·ta /aw gústə, ə-/ **1** city in Georgia, United States. Pop. 187,689 (1998). **2** capital of Maine. Pop. 19,978 (1998).

Au·gus·tine /àwgə steèn, aw gústin/, **St.** (AD 354–430) Roman priest and theologian

Au·gus·tus /aw gústəss/ (63 BC–AD 14) Roman emperor (27 BC–AD 14)

auk /awk/ *n* a black-and-white sea bird

Aung San Suu Kyi /àwng san soo cheé/, **Daw** (*b.* 1945) Burmese human rights activist

aunt /ant, aant/ *n* somebody's father's or mother's sister or sister-in-law —**aunt·hood** *n*

au pair /ō páir/ *n* an international student working as a domestic helper

au·ra /áwrə/ (*pl* **-ras** *or* **-rae** /-reè/) *n* **1** a distinctive quality **2** a force emanating from somebody or something

au·ral /áwrəl/ *adj* of hearing or sound —**au·ral·ly** *adv*

> **USAGE aural** or **oral**? **Aural** has to do with hearing whereas **oral** has to do with speaking or the mouth. An *aural test* is an examination testing comprehension by listening, whereas in an *oral test* the answers are spoken rather than written.

Au·re·li·an /aw reélyən, -lee ən/ (AD 215?–275) Roman emperor (AD 270–275)

Au·re·li·us /aw reéli əs/, **Marcus** (AD 121–180) Roman emperor (AD 161–180) and philosopher

au·re·ole /áwree òl/, or **au·re·o·la** /aw reé ələ/ n 1 a halo 2 the corona of the Sun

au re·voir /āw rəv waár, ö-/ interj goodbye

au·ri·cle /áwrək'l/ n 1 the visible part of the ear 2 an ear-shaped part of the heart

au·ro·ra /aw ráwrə, ə-/ n (pl **-ras** or **-rae** /-ree/) 1 colored lights in the skies around the North or South poles 2 also **Au·ro·ra** dawn 3 **Au·ro·ra** in Roman mythology, the goddess of the dawn —**au·ro·ral** adj

Au·ro·ra /aw ráwrə, ə-/ city in NE Colorado. Pop. 250,604 (1998).

au·ro·ra aus·tra·lis /aw ráwrə aw stráyliss/ n colored lights in the skies around the South Pole

au·ro·ra bo·re·al·is /-bawree álliss/ n colored lights in the skies around the North Pole

Aus. abbr 1 Australia 2 Australian

aus·pice /áwspəss/ ◊ **under the auspices of** with the help or support of a person or organization

aus·pi·cious /aw spíshəss/ adj promising well for the future —**aus·pi·cious·ly** adv —**aus·pi·cious·ness** n

Aust. abbr 1 Australia 2 Australian

Aus·ten /áwstən/, **Jane** (1775–1817) British novelist

aus·tere /aw steér/ adj 1 involving physical hardship 2 strict and severe 3 plain and without luxury or adornment —**aus·tere·ly** adv —**aus·tere·ness** n

aus·ter·i·ty /aw stérrətee/ n (pl **-ties**) 1 severity or plainness 2 an economy measure, or such measures imposed as government policy

Aus·ter·litz /áwstər lìts, ów-/ town in the present-day E Czech Republic, near the site of a major battle in 1805 when Napoleon defeated Russian and Austrian forces

Aus·tin /áwstin/ capital of Texas. Pop. 552,434 (1998).

Aus·tin, Stephen Fuller (1793–1836) US political leader

Austral. abbr 1 Australasia 2 Australia 3 Australian

Aus·tral·a·sia /àwstrəl áyzhə/ Australia, New Zealand, New Guinea, and neighboring islands of the S Pacific Ocean —**Aus·tral·a·sian** adj, n

Aus·tra·lia /aw stráylyə/ country southeast of Asia comprising the continent of Australia and the island of Tasmania. Cap. Canberra. Pop. 19,357,594 (2001).

Aus·tra·lian /aw stráylyən/ adj 1 of Australia 2 of the Aboriginal languages of Australia ■ n 1 somebody from Australia 2 English as it is used in Australia

Aus·tral·ian Alps mountain range in SE Australia. Highest peak Mt. Kosciuszko 7,310 ft./2,228 m.

Aus·tri·a /áwstree ə/ country in central Europe. Cap. Vienna. Pop. 8,150,835 (2001). —**Aus·tri·an** adj, n

Au·stro·ne·sia /àwstrō neézhə, -neésha/ region consisting of Indonesia, Melanesia, Micronesia, Polynesia, and neighboring islands in the Pacific Ocean

au·then·tic /aw théntik, ə-/ adj 1 genuine and original 2 true and trustworthy —**au·then·ti·cal·ly** adv —**au·then·tic·i·ty** /àw then tíssətee, àwthən-/ n

au·then·ti·cate /aw théntə kàyt, ə-/ (-**cat·ed**, -**cat·ing**) vt confirm the genuineness or truth of

au·then·ti·ca·tion /aw thèntə káysh'n/ n 1 the process of authenticating 2 a computer user's identification

au·thor /áwthər/ n 1 a writer 2 the creator or source of something ■ vt 1 be the author of 2 cause —**au·thor·i·al** /aw tháwree əl/ adj —**au·thor·ship** n

au·thor·ing /áwthəring/ n the creation of content for viewing on a computer

au·thor·i·tar·i·an /aw thàwrə táiree ən/ adj strict and demanding obedience to authority —**au·thor·i·tar·i·an** n —**au·thor·i·tar·i·an·ism** n

au·thor·i·ta·tive /ə tháwrə tàytiv/ adj 1 backed by evidence, knowledge, or authority 2 showing authority —**au·thor·i·ta·tive·ly** adv —**au·thor·i·ta·tive·ness** n

au·thor·i·ty /ə tháwrətee/ n (pl **-ties**) 1 the right to command 2 a holder of power 3 power given to somebody 4 a source of reliable information 5 an administrative body o *the local port authority* 6 the ability to command respect

au·thor·ize /áwthə rìz/ (-**ized**, -**iz·ing**) vt give power or permission to somebody or for something —**au·thor·i·za·tion** /àwthərə záysh'n/ n

au·tism /áw tìzzəm/ n a psychological condition that disturbs perceptions and relationships —**au·tis·tic** /aw tístik/ adj —**au·tis·ti·cal·ly** adv

au·to /áwtō/ (pl **-tos**) n a car (infml)

auto- prefix 1 self o *autobiography* 2 automatic o *autopilot*

au·to·bi·og·ra·phy /àwtō bī óggrəfee/ (pl -**phies**) n somebody's life story written by that person —**au·to·bi·og·ra·pher** n —**au·to·bi·o·graph·i·cal** /-bī ə gráffik'l/ adj

au·toch·tho·nous /aw tókthənəss/ adj originating in the same area in which it is now found ◊ See note at **native**

au·toc·ra·cy /aw tókrəssee/ (pl -**cies**) n 1 rule by one person 2 a place ruled by one person

au·to·crat /áwtə kràt/ n 1 a ruler with absolute authority 2 a bossy person —**au·to·crat·ic** /àwtə kráttik/ adj —**au·to·crat·i·cal·ly** adv

au·to·cross /áwtō kràwss/ *n* car racing on rough ground

au·to·graph /áwtə gràf/ *n* somebody's signature, especially a famous person's ■ *vt* write your signature on o *autographing pictures of the band*

au·to·im·mune /àwtō i myóon/ *adj* caused by an allergy to substances occurring naturally in the body o *autoimmune diseases* —**au·to·im·mun·i·ty** *n*

au·to·mak·er /áwtō màykər/ *n* a maker of motor vehicles

au·to·mate /áwtə màyt/ (**-mat·ed, -mat·ing**) *vti* make automatic

au·to·mat·ed tel·ler ma·chine *n* full form of **ATM**

au·to·mat·ic /àwtə máttik/ *adj* **1** functioning without human intervention **2** done by prior arrangement **3** done without thought ■ *n* **1** a gun that fires automatically **2** a motor vehicle with an automatic transmission —**au·to·mat·i·cal·ly** *adv*

au·to·mat·ic pi·lot *n* **1** an automatic steering system **2** autopilot *(slang)*

au·to·mat·ic trans·mis·sion *n* an automatic gear-switching system in a motor vehicle

au·to·ma·tion /àwtə máysh'n/ *n* replacement of human workers by machines

au·tom·a·ton /aw tómmətən, -tòn/ (*pl* **-tons** or **-ta** /-tə/) *n* **1** an independent and complex machine **2** somebody who acts like a machine —**au·tom·a·tous** *adj*

au·to·mo·bile /àwtə mō bèel, -mố bèel/ *n* a passenger-carrying motor vehicle with an engine

au·to·mo·tive /àwtə mốtiv/ *adj* **1** of motor vehicles **2** self-propelled

au·ton·o·mous /aw tónnəməss/ *adj* **1** self-governing **2** free to choose and act —**au·ton·o·my** /aw tónnəmee/ *n*

au·ton·o·mous re·pub·lic *n* a division of the Russian Federation

au·to·pi·lot /áwtō pìlət/ *n* **1** an automatic pilot **2** unthinking or instinctive behavior *(slang)* o *spent the day on autopilot handing out brochures*

au·top·sy /áw tòpsee/ *n* (*pl* **-sies**) **1** a medical examination to find a cause of death **2** an exhaustive critical examination ■ *vt* (**-sied, -sy·ing, -sies**) perform an autopsy on

au·to rac·ing *n* the racing of fast cars

⚡ **au·to·save** /áwtō sàyv/ *n* the automatic saving of computer data

au·to·sug·ges·tion /àwtō sə jéschən/ *n* the influencing of somebody by that person's own power of suggestion

~~autum~~ incorrect spelling of **autumn**

au·tumn /áwtəm/ *n* **1** = **fall s 2** a period between success and decline o *in the autumn of his career as a cellist* —**au·tum·nal** /aw túmn'l/ *adj*

aux·il·ia·ry /awg zíllyəree, -zílləree/ *adj* **1** supporting or supplementary **2** held in reserve

3 secondary ■ *n* (*pl* **-ries**) **1** a supporting or reserve person or thing **2** *also* **aux·il·ia·ry verb** a verb used with another verb, e.g., "have" in "we have met" **3** a member of a supporting military troop o *the Coast Guard Auxiliary*

~~auxillary~~ incorrect spelling of **auxiliary**

Av, Ab *n* the 5th month of the year in the Jewish calendar

AV *abbr* audiovisual

av. *abbr* **1** avenue **2** average

Av. *abbr* avenue

a·vail /ə váyl/ *v* **1** *vr* make use of o *avail yourself of the facilities* **2** *vti* be helpful to somebody else, or help somebody to do something *(fml)* o *Negotiation could not avail the dead-locked diplomats.* ■ *n* help or usefulness o *His protests were to no avail.*

a·vail·a·ble /ə váyləb'l/ *adj* able to be used, obtained, or spoken to —**a·vail·a·bil·i·ty** /ə vàylə bíllətee/ *n*

~~availible~~ incorrect spelling of **available**

av·a·lanche /ávvə lànch/ *n* **1** a rapid fall of dislodged snow down a mountainside **2** an overwhelming quantity

a·vant-garde /àavaant gaárd/ *n* artists with new and experimental ideas and methods ■ *adj* artistically new, experimental, or unconventional

av·a·rice /ávvərəss/ *n* greed for wealth —**av·a·ri·cious** /àvvə ríshəss/ *adj*

⚡ **av·a·tar** /ávvə tàar/ *n* **1** an incarnation of a Hindu deity in human or animal form **2** an embodiment of an idea or concept **3** an image of somebody in virtual reality

Ave. *abbr* avenue

A·ve·don /ávvə dòn/, **Richard** (*b.* 1923) US photographer

a·venge /ə vénj/ (**a·venged, a·veng·ing**) *vt* act in retaliation for or on behalf of

av·e·nue /ávvə nòo/ *n* **1** a wide street **2** a means of approach

a·ver /ə vúr/ (**a·verred, a·ver·ring**) *vt* assert confidently *(fml)* —**a·ver·ment** *n*

av·er·age /ávvərij, ávvrij/ *n* **1** a typical level or amount **2** a figure calculated by dividing a total by the number of items ■ *adj* **1** typical **2** calculated as an average **3** not very good ■ *vt* (**-aged, -ag·ing**) **1** calculate the average of **2** have or do as an average

a·verse /ə vúrss/ *adj* opposed to or disliking something *(fml)* —**a·verse·ly** *adv*

a·ver·sion /ə vúrzh'n/ *n* **1** a strong dislike **2** somebody or something disliked ◊ See note at **dislike**

a·ver·sion ther·a·py *n* **1** therapy to eliminate undesirable behavior by associating it with unpleasant consequences **2** therapy to overcome fears or dislikes

a·vert /ə vúrt/ *vt* **1** prevent something from happening **2** turn your eyes away —**a·vert·i·ble** *adj*

A·ver·y /áyvəree/, **Oswald** (1877–1955) Canadian-born US bacteriologist and geneticist. He discovered that genetic information was transferred through DNA.

a·vi·ar·y /áyvee èrree/ (pl **-ies**) n a large enclosure for birds

a·vi·a·tion /áyvee áysh'n/ n the development and use of aircraft

a·vi·a·tor /áyvee àytər/ n an aircraft pilot

av·id /ávvid/ adj enthusiastic or eager —**av·id·ly** adv

A·vi·gnon /áavee nyóN/ city in SE France. Pop. 85,935 (1999).

a·vi·on·ics /áyvee ónniks/ n 1 technology applied to aircraft and spacecraft (+ sing verb) 2 the technological devices of aircraft and spacecraft (+ pl verb)—**a·vi·on·ic** adj

av·o·ca·do /ávvə kaàdō, àavə-/ (pl **-dos**) n 1 also **av·o·ca·do pear** a green-fleshed edible fruit 2 a tree that produces avocados

> **ORIGIN Avocado** came through Spanish from a Native South American word meaning literally "testicle" (because of the shape of the fruit). The original Spanish form was altered under the influence of the more familiar word avocado "advocate."

av·o·ca·tion /àvvə káysh'n/ n (fml) 1 an occupation 2 a hobby—**av·o·ca·tion·al** adj

A·vo·ga·dro /áavə gaàdrō/, **Amedeo, Conte di Quaregna e Ceretto** (1776–1856) Italian physicist and chemist

a·void /ə vóyd/ v 1 vt keep away from 2 vti not do or prevent from happening —**a·void·a·ble** adj—**a·void·ance** n

av·oir·du·pois /ávvər də póyz/, **a·voir·du·pois weight** n a system for measuring weights based on the pound

A·von /áy vòn, -vən/ river in central England, flowing into the River Severn. Length 96 mi./154 km.

a·vow /ə vów/ vt affirm (fml) —**a·vow·al** n —**a·vow·ed·ly** /ə vówədlee/ adv

a·vun·cu·lar /ə vúngkyələr/ adj of or like an uncle—**a·vun·cu·lar·i·ty** /ə vúngkyə lárrətee/ n —**a·vun·cu·lar·ly** adv

AWACS /áy wàks/ n an airborne military surveillance system. Full form **Airborne Warning and Control System**

a·wait /ə wáyt/ v 1 vti wait for somebody or something 2 vt be going to happen or be given to somebody

a·wake /ə wáyk/ adj 1 not asleep 2 alert or aware ■ vti (**a·woke** /ə wōk/ or **a·waked**, **a·waked** or **a·wok·en** /ə wōkən/, **a·wak·ing**) 1 rouse or emerge from sleep 2 make or become alert or aware

a·wak·en /ə wáykən/ vti wake up —**a·wak·en·ing** n

a·ward /ə wáwrd/ n 1 something given for merit or achievement 2 something granted by a law court or by arbitration ■ vt 1 give

for merit or achievement o awarded the prize to the whole class 2 bestow by judicial decision or by arbitration

a·ware /ə wáir/ adj 1 having knowledge 2 noticing or realizing —**a·ware·ness** n

> **SYNONYMS** aware, **conscious, mindful, cognizant, sensible** CORE MEANING: having knowledge of the existence of something

a·wash /ə wósh/ adj 1 covered in water 2 oversupplied

a·way /ə wáy/ adv 1 uninvolved o stays away from trouble 2 in a different direction o turning his face away 3 into or in the distance o clouds away over there o walked away 4 in the future o only a week away 5 into storage or safekeeping o put the winter clothes away 6 off (follows a verb) o chipped the paint away 7 to or from somebody's possession o gave the old car away 8 until something is used up o frittered away his inheritance 9 gradually o The thunder died away. 10 so as to show a change o a gradual shift away from fossil fuels 11 without stopping o hammered away on the nails ■ adv, adj 1 in another place o will be away until next week o works away from the office 2 in distance or time o is located about 10 minutes away o works in a place not far away ■ adj in golf, farthest from the hole

awe n great respect or wonder mixed with fear ■ vt (**awed, aw·ing**) cause to feel awe

~~awful~~ incorrect spelling of **awful**

awe·some /áwsəm/ adj 1 impressive and frightening 2 excellent (slang) —**awe·some·ly** adv—**awe·some·ness** n

awe·struck /áw strùk/, **awe·strick·en** /-strìkən/ adj full of awe

aw·ful /áwf'l/ adj 1 extremely bad, unpleasant, or distressing 2 ill 3 very great (infml) —**aw·ful·ness** n

aw·ful·ly /áwflee, -fəlee/ adv 1 very 2 badly or unpleasantly

a·while /ə wíl, ə hwíl/ adv for a brief period

awk·ward /áwkwərd/ adj 1 embarrassing or inconvenient 2 difficult or uncomfortable to use 3 without grace or coordination —**awk·ward·ly** adv—**awk·ward·ness** n

> **ORIGIN Awkward** was originally an adverb meaning "in the wrong direction," used in Scotland and N England. The adjective **awkward** meant "back-handed" and "perverse" before it developed its modern senses.

awl /awl/ n a sharp-pointed tool for punching small holes ◊ See note at **all**

awn·ing /áwning/ n an extendable canvas or metal roof

a·woke past tense of **awake**

a·wok·en past participle of **awake**

AWOL /áy wàwl/, **a.w.o.l.** adj away from a position without permission. Full form **absent without leave**

a·wry /ə rī/ *adj* **1** crooked **2** amiss

ax, axe *n* (*pl* **ax·es**) **1** a tool with a flat heavy blade for cutting wood **2** dismissal from a job *(slang)* **3** closure or discontinuation *(slang)* ■ *vt* (**axed, ax·ing**) terminate *(slang)* ◊ **an ax to grind** a personal consideration or motivation

ax·i·om /áksee əm/ *n* **1** a generally accepted truth **2** a basic proposition assumed to be true in a logical system —**ax·i·o·mat·ic** /áksee ə máttik/ *adj*

ax·is /áksiss/ (*pl* **-es** /ák seèz/) *n* **1** a line around which something rotates or is symmetrical **2** a line at the edge of a graph **3** an alliance

ax·le /áks'l/ *n* a shaft or spindle on which a wheel turns

a·ya·tol·lah /ì ə tōlə/ *n* a Shiite religious leader

aye /ī/, **ay** *adv, interj* yes ■ *n* (*pl* **ayes**; *pl* **ayes**) a vote or voter in favor of a motion

A·ye·shah ♦ Aisha

A·yur·ved·ic med·i·cine /àa yoor váydik-, -veèdik-/ *n* an ancient Hindu system of healing

AZ *abbr* Arizona

a·zal·ea /ə záylyə/ (*pl* **-eas** *or* **same**) *n* a flowering bush

a·zan /aa zaàn/ *n* the Islamic call to prayer

A·zer·bai·jan /àzzər bī jaàn, -zhaàn/ country in W Asia. Cap. Baku. Pop. 7,771,092 (2001). —**A·zer·bai·ja·ni** *n, adj*

az·i·muth /ázzəməth/ *n* **1** the eastward angle from north **2** the angular distance along the horizon between a point of reference and another object

Az·nar /àth naàr, àss naàr/, **José María** (*b.* 1953) prime minister of Spain (1996–)

A·zores /áy zàwrz/ archipelago in the N Atlantic Ocean, an autonomous region of Portugal. Pop. 237,800 (1993).

A·zov, Sea of /á zàwf/ shallow inland sea in SW Russia

Az·tec /áz tèk/ *n* **1** a member of a Native Central American people whose empire dominated central Mexico during the 14C and 15C **2** the Nahuatl language —**Az·tec** *adj*

a·zu·ki bean *n* COOK = **adzuki bean**

az·ure /ázhər/ (*literary*) *adj* deep blue ■ *n* **1** the blue sky **2** a deep blue color

B

b (*pl* **b's**), **B** (*pl* **B's** *or* **Bs**) *n* the 2nd letter of the English alphabet

B[1] (*pl* **B's** *or* **Bs**) *n* **1** the 7th note in the musical key of C major **2** the 2nd highest grade of a student's work **3** a human blood type containing a specific antigen

B[2] *symbol* boron

b. *abbr* born

B. *abbr* bay[1] (*on maps*)

ƒ B2B *abbr* business-to-business

ƒ B2C *abbr* business-to-consumer

ƒ B4 *abbr* before (*in e-mails*)

Ba *symbol* barium

BA, B.A. *abbr* **1** Bachelor of Arts **2** batting average

baa (**baaed, baa·ing, baas**) *vi* make the bleat of a sheep —**baa** *n*

ba·ba /báabə/ *n* a rum-flavored cake

Bab·bage, Charles (1791–1871) British mathematician and inventor of mechanical calculating machines that were forerunners of the computer

bab·ble /bább'l/ (**-bled, -bling**) *v* **1** *vti* speak or say something incoherently **2** *vi* talk at length about irrelevant things **3** *vi* make a continuous murmuring sound (*refers to flowing water*) —**bab·ble** *n*

babe *n* **1** a sexually attractive young woman or man *(slang)* **2** a baby

ba·bel /báyb'l, bább'l/ *n* a confused noise (*literary*)

ORIGIN Babel derives from the Tower of Babel, where, according to the Bible, God showed his anger at its construction by causing the people to speak different languages and become unintelligible to one another.

ba·boon /ba boón/ *n* **1** a large monkey with a prominent snout and bare pink patches on its buttocks **2** a person regarded as rude and clumsy (*insult*)

ba·by /báybee/ *n* (*pl* **-bies**) **1** a very young or unborn child or animal **2** a person who behaves childishly (*disapproving*) **3** the youngest member of a family or group **4** used as a term of endearment (*slang; sometimes offensive*) **5** an object of somebody's affection or pride (*slang*) ■ *adj* describes small young vegetables ◊ *baby carrots* ■ *vt* (**-bied, -bies**) treat with excessive care —**ba·by·hood** *n* —**ba·by·ish** *adj*

ORIGIN Before the 11C, the term for what we now call a **baby** was *child*, and it was only after the 11C that *child* began to extend to the slightly more mature age that it now covers. **Baby** appeared in the 14C. It appears to be imitative of sounds made by infants before they can talk.

ba·by bond *n* **1** a bond with a value of less than $1,000 **2** a tax-free savings scheme for children and young people

ba·by boom *n* a large increase in birthrate

ba·by boom·er *n* somebody born in a baby boom such as the one following World War II

ba·by car·riage *n* a wheeled device in which an infant sits or lies, pushed by an adult

ba·by fat *n* childhood plumpness

ba·by grand *n* a small grand piano

Bab·y·lon /bábbələn, -lòn/ capital of ancient Babylonia

Bab·y·lo·ni·a /bàbbə lṓnee ə, -lṓnyə/ ancient empire in Mesopotamia, in present-day Iraq

ba·by's breath (*pl* same *or* **ba·by's breaths**) *n* a plant with small white flowers

ba·by·sit, ba·by·sit /báybi sìt/ (**-sat** /-sàt/, **-sit·ting**) *vti* take care of a child while the parents are away —**ba·by·sit·ter** *n*

ba·by talk *n* the simplified language often used by adults when talking to small children

ba·by tooth *n* a milk tooth

bac·ca·lau·re·ate /bàkə láwree ət/ *n* a bachelor's degree (*fml*)

bac·ca·rat /bàakə raã, bàkə-/ *n* a card game in which players bet against the bank

Bac·chus /bákəss, báakəss/ *n* in classical mythology, the god of wine

Bach /baakh, baak/, **Johann Sebastian** (1685–1750) German composer and organist

bach·e·lor /báchələr, báchlər/ *n* an unmarried man —**bach·e·lor·hood** *n*

Bach·e·lor of Arts *n* a college degree in a humanities subject

Bach·e·lor of Sci·ence *n* a college degree in a science subject

bach·e·lor par·ty *n* a party for a man who is about to get married

Bach flow·er rem·e·dies /bách-/ *npl* a healing method using flower extracts

ORIGIN The remedies are named for their inventor, the British physician Edward Bach (1886–1936).

ba·cil·lus /bə sílləss/ (*pl* **-li** /-síl ì/) *n* a rod-shaped bacterium

back *n* **1** the part of the human body nearest the spine, between the neck and the pelvis **2** the spine, or the area around an organism's spine **3** the rear of an object **4** the part of a seat that supports your back **5** a defensive player on a team **6** a player behind a defensive or offensive line ■ *adv* **1** in a reverse direction in space or time **2** at a distance ○ *Stay back.* **3** into a reclining position ○ *sit back* **4** to the original owner ○ *handed it back* **5** in response ○ *hit him back* **6** to a former condition or topic ○ *get back to the point* ■ *adj* **1** located at the back **2** situated in a remote location, e.g., away from main roads ■ *v* **1** *vti* move backward **2** *vt* support a person, cause, or statement **3** *vt* bet on a person, team, or horse to win a race **4** *vt* reinforce by adding a physical support ○ *back it with cardboard* **5** *vt* provide musical accompaniment for —**back·less** *adj* ◇ **get off somebody's back** stop criticizing or pressuring somebody (*slang*) ◇ **have your back to the wall** be in a difficult situation with no obvious means of escape ◇ **put somebody's back up** annoy or antagonize somebody (*infml*)

USAGE Back can refer either to a change to an earlier time or to a later time. This possibility becomes particularly confusing when the subject is, for example, a decision, now in the past, about what was at the time the future: *Last month she told me she wanted to move my appointment back.* In a context like this, *make earlier* or *make later* is clearer.

□ **back down** *or* **off** *vi* abandon a claim, commitment, or position

□ **back out** *vi* withdraw from a prior commitment

□ **back up** *v* **1** *vt* support somebody or something **2** *vt* copy computer files **3** *vi* form a long line along a road

back·ache /bák àyk/ *n* pain in the back

back-and-forth *n* a repeated exchange of ideas or information

back bench *n* Can, UK, ANZ in a parliament, a seating area for MPs who are junior members of Parliament, or this group of MPs (*usually pl*)

back-bench·er /bák bènchər/ *n* US, Can, ANZ a member of a legislative body who has low seniority

back·bite /bák bìt/ (**-bit** /-bìt/, **-bit·ten** /-bìtt'n/, **-bit·ing**) *vti* make spiteful remarks about somebody —**back·bit·er** *n*

back·board /bák bàwrd, -bòrd/ *n* a board behind the basket in basketball

back·bone /bák bòn/ *n* **1** an animal's spinal column **2** something similar in shape or position to a spinal column **3** any central supporting part **4** strength of character

back·break·ing /bák bràyking/ *adj* physically exhausting

back burn·er *n* one of the heating elements at the rear of a stove

back·cloth /bák klàwth, -klòth/ *n* a theater backdrop

back coun·try *n* US, Can, ANZ a remote rural area

back·date /bák dàyt/ (**-dat·ed, -dat·ing**) *vt* put an earlier date on

back door *n* **1** a rear door **2** an underhand opportunity that gives somebody a dishonest advantage

back-door /bák dàwr/ *adj* indirect or underhand

back·drop /bák dròp/ *n* **1** a painted cloth at the back of a theater stage **2** a setting for something

⚡ **back end** *n* **1** a main computer **2** a piece of software controlling routine tasks

back·er /bákər/ *n* **1** somebody who gives moral or financial support **2** somebody who lays bets

SYNONYMS backer, angel, guarantor,

patron, sponsor CORE MEANING: somebody who provides financial support

back·field /bák fèeld/ n 1 in football, the area of the field behind the line of scrimmage 2 the players behind the line of scrimmage, or their positions

back·fire /bák fīr/ (-fired, -fir·ing) vi 1 have the opposite effect to the one intended 2 produce an explosion of unburned exhaust gases in the exhaust pipe of a motor vehicle —**back·fire** n

back-for·ma·tion n 1 the process of forming a new word by removing a real or imagined affix 2 a new word formed by removing an affix, e.g., "televise" from "television"

back·gam·mon /bák gàmmən/ n 1 a board game in which counters are moved on the throw of a pair of dice 2 in backgammon, a complete victory

back·ground /bák grównd/ n 1 personal circumstances and experiences 2 the circumstances that cause an event 3 the scenery behind something 4 information that explains something 5 a position of inconspicuousness 6 constant low-level radiation ■ adj 1 forming part of the background 2 accompanying

back·ground·er /bák gròwndər/ n an unattributed press briefing

back·ground mu·sic n music to create atmosphere

⚡**back·ground pro·cess·ing** n execution of a subsidiary operation by a computer while the user works with another application

back·hand /bák hànd/ n 1 in racket games, a stroke played with the back of the hand toward the ball 2 a style of handwriting in which the characters slope leftward

back·hand·ed /bák hàndəd/ adj 1 backhand 2 describes a comment with a double meaning, especially an apparent compliment that can also be understood as an insult —**back·hand·ed·ly** adv —**back·hand·ed·ness** n

back·ing /báking/ n 1 support or help 2 the rear surface of something, providing support or protection 3 musical accompaniment

back·lash /bák làsh/ n 1 a strong widespread adverse reaction 2 a violent backward movement

back·list /bák lìst/ n a publisher's range of earlier books that are still in print

back·log /bák lòg, -làwg/ n a number of things still to be done before progress can be made —**back·log** vti

⚡**back of·fice** n a secure area of software ■ adj of internal matters

back·pack /bák pàk/ n 1 a rucksack 2 a set of equipment carried on a person's or an animal's back ■ vi hike or travel with a backpack —**back·pack·er** n

back pay n pay owed for work done earlier

back·ped·al /bák pèdd'l/ v 1 vi pedal backward 2 retract or tone down an earlier statement

back seat n a seat in the back of a vehicle

back·side /bák sīd/ n the buttocks (infml)

⚡**back·slash** /bák slàsh/ n a keyboard character in the form of a left-leaning diagonal line

back·slide /bák slīd/ (-slid /-slìd/, -slid·ing) vi relapse into a former bad or immoral condition —**back·slid·er** n

back·spin /bák spìn/ n the backward spinning motion of a ball that is moving forward

back·stage /bàk stáyj/ adv 1 behind the scenes in a theater 2 in private —**back·stage** /bák stàyj/ adj

back·stop /bák stòp/ n 1 a screen to stop a ball 2 in baseball, a catcher

back·street /bák strèet/ n a minor street ■ adj 1 in a minor street 2 illicit

back·stroke /bák stròk/ n 1 a method of swimming on the back 2 a return stroke or movement in a mechanical system 3 in racket games, a backhand stroke —**back·stroke** vi

back talk n insolent replies

back-to-back adj 1 with backs facing or touching each other 2 consecutive —**back to back** adv

back·track /bák tràk/ vi 1 go back 2 distance yourself from a previous action, opinion, or statement

⚡**back·up** /bák ùp/ n 1 support or assistance 2 a substitute or reserve used when something fails 3 a copy of computer data made for safekeeping 4 the process of copying computer data 5 a traffic holdup 6 musical accompaniment 7 an excess quantity of something that builds up when the normal flow is obstructed —**back·up** adj

back·ward /bákwərd/ adj 1 to or toward the rear 2 positioned the opposite way around or in the opposite order 3 not progressing or developing in the usual way (sometimes offensive) 4 retrograde ○ a backward step 5 toward the past ■ adv also **back·wards** 1 so as to have the back first 2 toward the rear 3 the wrong way around 4 toward the past 5 into a worse condition —**back·ward·ness** n ◇ **bend or lean over backward** make an exceptional effort

back·wash /bák wòsh/ n unpleasant consequences

back·wa·ter /bák wàwtər/ n 1 a small stagnant branch of a river 2 a remote, uneventful place

back·woods /bák wòodz/ n (+ sing or pl verb) 1 remote wooded areas 2 a remote unsophisticated area —**back·woods** adj —**back·woods·man** n

back·yard n 1 a yard behind a house 2 somebody's neighborhood —**back·yard** adj

ba·con /báykən/ n salted and dried meat from the back and sides of a hog ◇ **save some-**

body's bacon save somebody from serious trouble or harm *(infml)*

Ba·con /báykən/, **Sir Francis, 1st Baron Verulam and Viscount St. Albans** (1561–1626) English philosopher, lawyer, and politician

Ba·con, Francis (1909–92) Irish-born British painter

Ba·con, Nathaniel (1647–76) English-born American colonist who led a rebellion against the government of Virginia in 1676

bac·te·ri·a plural of **bacterium**

bac·te·ri·al /bak teéree əl/ *adj* of or caused by bacteria

bac·te·ri·ol·o·gy /bak teéree óllajee/ *n* the scientific study of bacteria —**bac·te·ri·o·log·i·cal** /bak teéree ə lójjik'l/ *adj* —**bac·te·ri·ol·o·gist** *n*

bac·te·ri·o·phage /bak teéree ə fàyj/ *n* a virus that infects bacteria

bac·te·ri·um /bak teéree əm/ *(pl* -**a** /-ə/) *n* a single-celled microorganism without distinct nuclei or organized cell structures, sometimes a cause of disease —**bac·te·roid** /báktə ròyd/ *adj*

Bac·tri·an cam·el /bàktree ən-/ *n* a two-humped camel

bad *adj* (**worse** /wurss/, **worst** /wurst/) **1** of unacceptably poor quality **2** unskilled or incompetent ∘ *a bad rendition of the piano solo* **3** wicked **4** misbehaving and disobedient **5** angry and unpleasant ∘ *in a bad mood* **6** offensive ∘ *bad language* **7** harmful ∘ *a bad influence* **8** rotten ∘ *a bad peach* **9** injured or diseased ∘ *a bad tooth* **10** unwell **11** ashamed, sorrowful, or disappointed ∘ *feel bad about it* **12** more severe or unpleasant than usual ∘ *a bad headache* **13** distressing ∘ *bad news* **14** unfavorable ∘ *a bad report* **15** (*comparative* **bad·der**, *superlative* **bad·dest**) very good *(slang)* ■ *n* unsatisfactory or unpleasant things ∘ *take the bad with the good* ■ *adv* badly *(infml)* —**bad·ness** *n*

SYNONYMS bad, criminal, delinquent, mischievous, naughty CORE MEANING: indicating wrongdoing

bad blood *n* ill feeling

bad debt *n* an amount of money owed but not paid

bade past tense of **bid**

bad faith *n* insincerity, especially as shown in a failure to carry out a stated intention

badge *n* **1** an object worn as a sign of rank, membership, or support **2** an identifying feature ■ *vt* (**badged, badg·ing**) put a badge or identifying mark on

badg·er /bájjər/ *n* a black-and-white nocturnal burrowing mammal ■ *vt* pester

bad·i·nage /bàdd'n aázh/ *n* playful talk *(fml)*

bad·lands /bád làndz/ *npl* a barren area with peaks and gullies formed by erosion

bad·ly /báddlee/ (**worse, worst**) *adv* **1** in an unsatisfactory or incompetent way **2** in a way that causes disappointment or suffering **3** to a severe degree **4** very much **5** in an annoying or immoral way

bad·ly off (**worse off, worst off**) *adj* lacking in what is needed or required

bad·min·ton /bád mìntən/ *n* a game in which players hit a shuttlecock with rackets over a high net

ORIGIN The game of **badminton** takes its name from Badminton House, the country seat of the dukes of Beaufort in Avon, SW England. It was apparently first played there in its modern form, being developed from earlier informal games with a bat and shuttlecock.

bad·mouth /bád mòwth, -mòwth/ *vt* criticize *(slang)*

bad-tem·pered *adj* irritable —**bad-tem·pered·ly** *adv* —**bad-tem·pered·ness** *n*

Baf·fin /báffin/, **William** (1584–1622) English navigator

Baf·fin Bay /báffin-/ *n* large bay separating Greenland and Canada

Baff·in Is·land large island in Nunavut Territory, NE Canada

baf·fle /báff'l/ *vt* (-**fled, -fling**) **1** puzzle somebody **2** control a flow ■ *n* **1** a device that prevents or controls a flow **2** a partition in a loudspeaker that separates sounds of different frequencies —**baf·fle·ment** *n* —**baf·fling** *adj* —**baf·fling·ly** *adv*

bag *n* **1** a container made of a nonrigid material **2** the amount contained in a bag **3** a portable container for equipment or belongings **4** an item of baggage *(often pl)* **5** a purse **6** a number of animals shot by a hunter **7** an offensive term deliberately insulting a woman's age and appearance *(slang insult)* **8** something that somebody is especially interested in or good at *(slang)* **9** in baseball, a base ■ **bags** *npl* loose skin under the eyes ■ *v* (**bagged, bag·ging**) **1** *vt* put something into a bag **2** *vti* bulge or make something bulge —**bag·ful** *n* ◇ **in the bag** certain to be achieved or obtained *(infml)*

bag·a·telle /bàggə tél/ *n* **1** a short playful piece of music **2** a board game in which balls are rolled past obstacles into numbered holes **3** something unimportant *(fml)*

ba·gel /báyg'l/ *n* a ring-shaped bread roll with a chewy texture

bag·gage /bággij/ *n* **1** suitcases and bags carried by travelers **2** ideas, opinions, or feelings derived from past experiences, especially when regarded as an emotional encumbrance *(infml)*

bag·gage car *n* a car on a train holding baggage only

bag·gy /bággee/ (-**gi·er, -gi·est**) *adj* hanging loose on the body —**bag·gi·ly** *adv* —**bag·gi·ness** *n*

Bagh·dad /bág dàd/, **Bag·dad** capital of Iraq. Pop. 4,336,000 (1995).

bag la·dy n a homeless woman who carries her possessions around in bags (infml)

ƒ**bag·pipe** /bág pìp/ n a pair of bagpipes ■ **bag·pipes** npl a wind instrument consisting of an inflatable bag with several pipes through which air is forced to produce the notes —**bag·pip·er** n

ba·guette /ba gét/ n 1 a stick-shaped loaf of bread 2 a rectangular gemstone

Bag·ui·o /baàgee ò/ summer capital of the Philippines. Pop. 268,772 (1999).

bah interj expresses disgust

Ba·ha·mas /ba haàmaz, -háymaz/ island nation in the Atlantic Ocean southeast of Florida. Cap. Nassau. Pop. 297,852 (2001). —**Ba·ha·mi·an** /ba háymee ən, ba haà-/ n, adj

Bah·rain /baa ráyn/, **Bah·rein** island state in the Persian Gulf off the coast of Saudi Arabia. Cap. Manama. Pop. 645,361 (2001). —**Bah·rain·i** n, adj

baht /baat/ (pl **bahts** or **same**) n the main unit of Thai currency

Bai·kal, Lake /bī kaàl/ world's deepest lake, in S Siberia, Russia. Depth 5,371 ft./1,637 m.

bail[1] /bayl/ n 1 money paid to secure somebody's temporary release from legal custody and guarantee the person's future appearance in court 2 temporary release from custody ■ vt free somebody by paying bail
□ **bail out** vt help somebody out of trouble (slang)

bail[2] /bayl/ vti empty water from a boat
□ **bail out** vi (infml) 1 parachute from a plane 2 escape from a difficult situation

bail[3] /bayl/ n a semicircular handle or support

bai·ley /báylee/ n 1 the outer wall of a castle 2 a courtyard inside a castle wall

Bai·ley bridge /báylee-/ n a temporary bridge made of prefabricated parts

ORIGIN The bridge is named for the British engineer Sir D. Coleman Bailey (1901–85), who designed it.

bail·iff /báylif/ n a court official who supervises prisoners and keeps order in the courtroom

bail·i·wick /báyli wìk/ n somebody's sphere of specialized knowledge

Bai·ram /bī raàm/ n each of two Islamic festivals, the Lesser Bairam, marking the end of Ramadan, or the Greater Bairam, marking the end of the Islamic year

Baird /baird/, **John Logie** (1888–1946) British inventor. He demonstrated an electromechanical television system in 1926.

bait /bayt/ n 1 a piece of food to lure an animal 2 an enticement of any kind ■ vt 1 put food on a hook to catch a fish 2 tease or taunt 3 attack an animal with dogs

baize /bayz/ n green woolen cloth. Use: to cover pool and card tables.

Ba·ja Cal·i·for·nia /baà haa-/ peninsula in NW Mexico. Length 760 mi./1,200 km.

ƒ**bak** abbr a file extension indicating a backup file

bake vti (**baked**, **bak·ing**) 1 cook food in an oven without fat or oil 2 harden something by heating ■ n 1 a batch of baked food 2 a party with baked food (infml; often in combination)

baked beans npl navy beans in a spiced tomato sauce

bak·er /báykər/ n somebody who makes bread and cakes

bak·er's doz·en n thirteen

ORIGIN Retailers of bread formerly received an extra loaf with each dozen from the baker, which they were entitled to keep as profit. This is why the **baker's dozen** is 13 rather than 12.

Ba·kers·field /báykərz feeld/ city in California. Pop. 210,284 (1998).

bak·er·y /báykəree/ (pl **-ies**) n 1 a place where food is baked 2 a store selling baked food

bak·ing pow·der n a mixture containing sodium bicarbonate, starch, and acids. Use: making cakes rise.

bak·ing so·da n sodium bicarbonate. Use: making cakes rise.

ba·kla·va /baàklə vaà, baàklə vaà/ n a dessert made with thin layers of phyllo pastry, nuts, and syrup or honey

bak·sheesh /bák sheesh, bak sheesh/ n a tip or bribe

Ba·ku /baa koó/ capital of Azerbaijan. Pop. 1,708,000 (1999).

Ba·ku·nin /bə koónin, -koónyin/, **Mikhail** (1814–76) Russian anarchist

bal·a·lai·ka /bàllə líka/ n a Russian stringed instrument with a triangular body

bal·ance /bállənss/ n 1 the condition of remaining steady on a relatively small base 2 the stability that results when opposite forces have equal strength 3 a state in which various elements form a harmonious whole 4 emotional stability 5 a weighing machine 6 a counterweight 7 the remainder 8 a position of equal debit and credit 9 a difference between debit and credit ■ v (**-anced, -anc·ing**) 1 vti remain in or give something equilibrium 2 vti be or place something in a precarious position 3 vt assess something 4 vt weigh something 5 vti be equal or cancel something out 6 vt bring elements into harmony 7 vt make the elements of a chemical or mathematical equation equal 8 vt equalize the debit and credit sides of a financial account ◊ **hang in the balance** be in a situation in which success and failure seem equally likely ◊ **on balance** taking all the relevant factors into consideration

bal·ance beam *n* an elevated horizontal bar on which women gymnasts perform, or the event in which this is used

bal·anced /bállənst/ *adj* **1** even-handed **2** combining elements in a healthy way **3** mentally stable

bal·ance of pay·ments *n* a nation's debits and credits

bal·ance of pow·er *n* **1** equilibrium of power between nations **2** the power to affect a situation decisively

bal·ance of trade *n* the difference between a nation's imports and exports

bal·ance sheet *n* a statement of debits and credits

Bal·an·chine /bállən chee̅n, bàllən chée̅n/, **George** (1904–83) Russian-born US dancer and choreographer

bal·bo·a /bal bố ə/ *n* the main unit of Panamanian currency

Bal·bo·a /bal bố ə/, **Vasco Núñez de** (1475?–1519) Spanish explorer

bal·co·ny /bálkənee/ (*pl* **-nies**) *n* **1** a platform on the wall of a building, usually enclosed by a rail or parapet **2** in a theater, a raised area of seating

bald /bawld/ *adj* **1** with little or no hair on the head **2** with no fur, grass, trees, or other natural covering **3** worn in texture ○ *bald tires* **4** not explained or elaborated on ○ *the bald truth* **5** describes a bird or mammal with white markings on the head —**bald·ness** *n*

bald ea·gle *n* a North American bird of prey with a white head and tail

bal·der·dash /báwldər dàsh/ *n* nonsense

bald-faced *adj* shamelessly undisguised —**bald-faced·ly** *adv* —**bald-faced·ness** *n*

bald·ing /báwlding/ *adj* going bald

Bob Adelman

James Baldwin

Bald·win /báwldwin/, **James** (1924–87) US writer

bale *n* a large bundle of hay or other raw material ■ *vti* (**baled, bal·ing**) make something into bales

Bal·e·ar·ic Is·lands /bàllee árrik-/ island group in the W Mediterranean including Majorca, Menorca, and Ibiza. It is an autonomous region of Spain. Pop. 736,865 (1991).

bale·ful /báylfəl/ *adj* **1** threatening **2** harmful —**bale·ful·ly** *adv* —**bale·ful·ness** *n*

balence incorrect spelling of **balance**

Ba·li /baalee/ island east of Java, S Indonesia. Pop. 2,895,600 (1995).

balk /bawk/, **baulk** *v* **1** *vi* stop short **2** *vi* turn away **3** *vti* refuse to deal with **4** *vi* in baseball, make an illegal pitching move ■ *n* **1** a large piece of wood **2** an unplowed ridge **3** in baseball, an illegal pitching move **4** in billiards, an area behind the balkline

Bal·kan Moun·tains /báwlkən-/ mountain range in Yugoslavia and Bulgaria. Highest peak Botev Peak 7,795 ft./2,376 m.

Bal·kan Pen·in·su·la peninsula in SE Europe

Bal·kan States, Bal·kans /báwlkənz/ the countries on the Balkan Peninsula —**Bal·kan** *adj*

balk·line /báwk lìn/ *n* a dividing line on a billiard table

balk·y /báwkee/ (**-i·er, -i·est**) *adj* stubbornly uncooperative —**balk·i·ly** *adv* —**balk·i·ness** *n*

ball¹ *n* **1** a round object that is thrown, hit, or kicked in many games and sports **2** a rounded object or mass **3** any game played with a ball **4** a ball played in a particular way ○ *a long ball into the end zone* **5** in baseball, a pitch that is not a strike **6** a round solid projectile **7** a rounded body part, e.g., at the base of the thumb or just behind the toes ○ *the ball of the foot* ■ *vti* make into or form a ball ◇ **on the ball** aware of what is going on and quick to respond *(infml)*

ball² *n* a formal dance

Ball, Lucille (1911–89) US actor

bal·lad /bálləd/ *n* **1** a narrative song **2** a slow romantic song —**bal·lad·ist** *n* —**bal·lad·ry** *n*

bal·last /bálləst/ *n* **1** heavy material carried in a ship's hold to give stability **2** anything that gives extra bulk or stability **3** gravel used as the foundation for a road or railroad track, or in making concrete ■ *vt* load with ballast

ball bear·ing *n* a bearing that uses small metal balls to reduce friction between moving metal parts

ball boy *n* in tennis, a boy who retrieves balls during a game

ball cock *n* a rod with a floating ball at one end that regulates the level of water in a tank

bal·le·ri·na /bàllə reénə/ *n* a principal woman dancer in a ballet company

bal·let /ba láy, bá làyl/ *n* **1** a form of dramatic dance characterized by conventional steps and movements **2** a story performed by ballet dancers **3** a group of ballet dancers —**bal·let·ic** /ba léttik, bə-/ *adj*

ball game, ball·game /báwl gàym/ *n* a baseball game

ball girl *n* in tennis, a girl who retrieves balls during a game

bal·lis·tic /bə lístik/ *adj* of projectiles

bal·lis·tic mis·sile *n* a large missile that has no guidance system on board

bal·lis·tics /bə lístiks/ *n* (+ *sing verb*) **1** the study of projectiles **2** the study of firearms

bal·loon /bə lóon/ *n* **1** a toy consisting of a small rubber bag filled with air **2** a large gas-filled bag with a gondola, used as a form of air transport **3** a rounded device encircling a character's speech in a cartoon ◼ *vi* **1** form a large rounded shape **2** increase in amount ◇ **go over like a lead balloon** be completely unsuccessful *(slang)*

bal·loon·ing /bə lóoning/ *n* traveling in a balloon

bal·loon mort·gage *n* a mortgage with a large final payment

bal·lot /bállət/ *n* **1** a voting system in which votes are cast in secret **2** *also* **bal·lot pa·per** a paper or other device by which to cast a vote **3** the total number of votes cast in a ballot ◼ *v* **1** *vt* cast ballots or a ballot in voting **2** *vi* ask for a vote

bal·lot box *n* **1** a box for completed ballots **2** election by ballot

ball·park /báwl paark/ *n* **1** a park for playing baseball **2** a touchdown area for spacecraft ◼ *adj* approximate *(infml)*

ball·point /báwl pòynt/, **ball·point pen** *n* a pen with a rotating ball at its tip

ball·room /báwl ròom, -rồom/ *n* a room used for dancing

ball·room danc·ing *n* a style of formal dancing with set patterns of steps for couples

bal·ly·hoo /bállee hồo/ *n* **1** sensational advertising **2** an uproar ◼ *vt* (-hooed, -hoo·ing) publicize something loudly

balm /baam, baalm/ *n* **1** an oily plant extract used in soothing ointments **2** something that soothes

balm·y /báamee, baálmee/ *adj* (-i·er, -i·est) *adj* describes pleasantly mild weather —**balm·i·ness** *n*

ba·lo·ney /bə lónee/ *n* (*pl* -neys) *n* **1** a bologna sausage **2** nonsense *(infml)*

~~baloon~~ incorrect spelling of **balloon**

bal·sa /báwlsə, baàl-/, **bal·sa wood** *n* a lightweight wood. Use: insulation, making models.

bal·sam /báwlsəm, baál-/ *n* **1** an oily resinous plant substance. Use: in perfumes, medicines. **2** a preparation containing balsam **3** any flowering plant of the jewelweed family that includes impatiens —**bal·sam·ic** /bawl sámmik, baal-/ *adj*

bal·sam·ic vin·e·gar *n* a dark-colored, sweet Italian vinegar

Bal·tic Sea /báwltik-/ sea in N Europe between Sweden, Finland, Russia, Estonia, Latvia, Lithuania, Poland, Germany, and Denmark

Bal·tic States Estonia, Latvia, and Lithuania, considered as a group

Bal·ti·more /báwltə màwr/ port and largest city in Maryland. Pop. 645,593 (1998).

Ba·lu·chi·stan /bə lòochi stán/ mountainous dry region in SW Pakistan and SE Iran

bal·us·ter /bálləstər/ *n* a post supporting a handrail

bal·us·trade /bállə stràyd/ *n* a decorative railing along the edge of a balcony or bridge

Bal·zac /báwl zàk, bál-, baal zaàk/, **Honoré de** (1799–1850) French novelist —**Bal·zac·i·an** /bal zákee ən, -záysh'n/ *adj*

Ba·ma·ko /baàmə kố/ capital of Mali. Pop. 1,016,167 (1998).

bam·boo /bam bóo/ (*pl* -boos) *n* **1** the strong hollow stems of a tropical plant. Use: furniture, cane supports. **2** a tropical plant with tall, stiff, woody stems that produces bamboo

---

ORIGIN Bamboo comes ultimately from Malay. The earliest English forms ended in *-s*, because the direct source was Dutch *bamboes*, but this was later taken to be the English plural ending and a new singular form came into use.

---

bam·boo shoot *n* a vegetable used in East Asian cooking

bam·boo·zle /bam bóoz'l/ *vt* trick or deceive somebody *(infml)*

ban *vt* (**banned, ban·ning**) **1** forbid something officially or legally **2** stop somebody from doing something ◼ *n* an official or legal order forbidding something

ba·nal /bə nál, báyn'l, bə naál/ *adj* dull and unoriginal —**ba·nal·i·ty** *n* —**ba·nal·ly** *adv*

ba·nan·a /bə nánnə/ *n* **1** a long curved yellow fruit **2** the tropical plant that produces bananas

ba·nan·a re·pub·lic *n* a small dictatorship with an economy dependent on the export of a single product *(disapproving)*

ba·nan·a split *n* a sundae made of a banana, ice cream, and toppings

~~banerupcy~~ incorrect spelling of **bankruptcy**

band[1] *n* **1** a group of musicians playing together, e.g., a group playing pop music **2** a group of people with the same beliefs or purpose ◇ *a growing band of supporters* ◻ **band together** *vi* unite as a group

band[2] *n* **1** a strip or loop of fabric, elastic, or other material **2** a strip of material whose color or texture contrasts with the other material it is attached to **3** a plain ring worn on a finger **4** a range or group within a larger one

band·age /bándij/ *n* a cloth strip for covering an injury —**band·age** *vt*

Band-Aid *tdmk* a trademark for an adhesive bandage with a central gauze pad

ban·dan·na /ban dánnə/, **ban·dan·a** n a bright cotton scarf worn around the head or neck

Ban·dar Se·ri Be·ga·wan /bùndər sèrree bə gaàwən/ capital of Brunei. Pop. 50,000 (1995 estimate).

B & B abbr bed and breakfast (infml)

ban·deau /bàn dó/ (pl **-deaux** /-dóz/ or **-deaus**) n **1** a ribbon or band for the hair **2** a band of material worn over the breasts

ban·di·coot /bándi koòt/ n an Australasian marsupial with a long pointed nose

ban·dit /bándit/ n an armed robber **—ban·dit·ry** n

band·stand /bánd stànd/ n a public platform for a brass band to play on

Ban·dung /baàn doòng/ city in W Java, Indonesia. Pop. 3,557,665 (1997).

band·wag·on /bánd wàggən/ n **1** an increasingly popular movement or cause **2** a wagon for musicians during a parade

⚡ **band·width** /bánd wìdth/ n **1** a range of radio frequencies **2** the capacity of an Internet connection or other communication channel

ban·dy /bándee/ vt (**-died, -dies**) casually exchange words ■ adj (**-di·er, -di·est**) describes legs that curve outward so the knees cannot meet

bane n **1** a cause of continual misery **2** a cause of death, destruction, or ruin (literary) **—bane·ful —bane·ful·ly —bane·ful·ness**

bang n **1** a sudden loud noise **2** a sharp hit ◇ **bangs** npl hair cut short and worn across the forehead ■ v **1** vti hit hard or noisily **2** vti hit accidentally ○ bang into the furniture **3** vti close hard and noisily **4** vi make a loud noise ■ adv suddenly ◇ **bang for your buck** value for money spent or effort expended (slang) ◇ **go out with a bang** end or finish something in a dramatic way (infml)

Ban·ga·lore /báng gə làwr/ capital of Karnataka State, India. Pop. 2,660,088 (1991).

Bang·kok /báng kòk/ capital and main port of Thailand. Pop. 5,882,000 (1990).

Bang·la·desh /baàng glə désh/ country in South Asia, on the Bay of Bengal, east of India. Cap. Dhaka. Pop. 131,269,860 (2001). **—Bang·la·desh·i** n, adj

ban·gle /báng g'l/ n **1** a rigid bracelet **2** a disk or other decoration that hangs from a bracelet

Ban·gor /báng gawr, -gər/ port in south central Maine. Pop. 30,508 (1998).

Ban·gui /baàng geè/ capital of the Central African Republic. Pop. 524,000 (1996).

ban·ish /bánnish/ vt **1** send away from a place as a punishment **2** get rid of **—ban·ish·ment** n

ban·is·ter /bánnəstər/, **ban·nis·ter** n **1** a handrail on a staircase **2** a post supporting a handrail

ban·jo /bánjò/ (pl **-jos** or **-joes**) n a five-stringed instrument with a flat circular body

Ban·jul /baàn joòl/ capital of the Gambia. Pop. 44,200 (1994).

bank[1] n **1** a financial institution offering checking accounts and other financial services, or its local office **2** a fund of money or tokens for use in gambling games **3** a source of resources, e.g., of blood ■ v **1** vt deposit money in a bank **2** vi have an account with a particular financial institution

---

ORIGIN The three English words **bank** all come ultimately from the same ancient Germanic root, which is also the source of bench. The "bank of a river" form arrived in the 12C from a Scandinavian language. The "bank of oars" form was adopted in the 13C from a French word meaning "bench." The financial institution form came in the 15C from Italian, possibly via French; the sense developed in Italian from the table (or "bench") on which banking was transacted.

□ **bank on** vt rely on

bank[2] n **1** the side of a waterway **2** a ridge of sand below the surface of water **3** a pile of earth or snow with sloping sides **4** a mass of clouds **5** a slope at a bend in a racetrack **6** the angle of an aircraft as it turns in the sky ■ v **1** vti pile up, or form something into a pile **2** vt cover a fire with coal to make it burn slowly **3** vti tilt an aircraft in the air or a motorcycle on a bend, or become tilted

bank[3] n **1** a row of similar things **2** a bench on which rowers sit, or a row of oars in a galley ■ vt put into rows

bank·a·ble /bángkəb'l/ adj **1** likely to bring in money **2** acceptable to a bank

bank ac·count n an arrangement with a bank by which a customer can deposit and withdraw money

bank bal·ance n the amount of money in a bank account

bank·book /bángk boòk/ n a passbook for a savings account

bank·er /bángkər/ n **1** somebody who owns or manages a bank **2** in a gambling game, the player in charge of the bank

bank·note /bángk nòt/ n a piece of paper money

bank rate n an interest rate set by a central bank

bank·roll /bángk ròl/ n **1** a roll of paper money **2** a fund of money ■ vt provide financing for (slang)

bank·rupt /bángk rùpt/ adj **1** judged legally unable to pay debts **2** completely lacking in a particular good quality **—bank·rupt** n, vt **—bank·rupt·cy** n

bank state·ment n a statement showing the transactions in a bank account over a specific period

Ban·ne·ker /bánnəkər/, **Benjamin** (1731–1806) American mathematician and astronomer

♪ban·ner /bánnər/ *n* 1 a cloth with a design or message on it, usually carried on two poles 2 a guiding principle 3 a website advertisement 4 a flag 5 *also* **ban·ner head·line** a newspaper headline in large letters that runs the entire width of a page ■ *adj* especially good

ban·nis·ter *n* ARCHIT = banister

Ban·nis·ter /bánnistər/, **Sir Roger** (b. 1929) British athlete. He was the first person to run the mile in under four minutes (1954).

banns *npl* the announcement of a forthcoming marriage in a church *(fml)*

ba·ño /báanyō/ (*pl* **-ños** /báanyōs/) *n Hispanic* a bathroom

ban·quet /bángkwit/ *n* an elaborate ceremonial meal —**ban·quet** *vi*

ban·shee /bán shee/ *n* a supposed female spirit who wails to warn of impending death

---

ORIGIN Banshee comes from Irish, and means literally "woman from the fairy world."

---

ban·tam /bántəm/ *n* a small domestic fowl ■ *adj* 1 miniature 2 too confident and slightly aggressive

ban·tam·weight /bántəm wàyt/ *n* 1 the weight category for boxers between flyweight and featherweight 2 a boxer who competes at bantamweight

ban·ter /bántər/ *n* lighthearted teasing remarks ■ *vi* exchange teasing remarks

Ban·ting /bánting/, **Sir Frederick Grant** (1891–1941) Canadian physician

Ban·tu /bántoo/ (*pl* same *or* **-tus**) *n (sometimes offensive)* 1 the group of African languages that includes Xhosa and Zulu 2 a member of a large group of peoples from equatorial and southern Africa —**Ban·tu** *adj*

ban·yan /bányən, -yàn/ *n* a tropical tree with roots that grow down from the branches to form secondary trunks

ba·o·bab /báy ō bàb, báa-/ *n* a tropical tree with a thick short trunk and edible fruit

bap·tism /báp tìzzəm/ *n* 1 a religious ceremony symbolizing purification or marking acceptance into a religious faith 2 an initiation —**bap·tis·mal** /bap tízməl/ *adj*

bap·tism of fire *n* 1 a difficult or dangerous first experience in a new situation 2 a soldier's first battle

Bap·tist /báptəst/ *n* a member of a Protestant denomination that baptizes people by total immersion when they are old enough to understand and declare their faith —**Bap·tist** *adj*

bap·tize /bap tíz, báp tìz/ (**-tized, -tiz·ing**) *v* 1 *vti* perform the ceremony of baptism on 2 *vt* name during a baptism 3 *vt* initiate into a new experience or situation

bar¹ *n* 1 a relatively long straight piece of a solid material 2 a small block of a solid substance ○ *a gold bar* 3 something that blocks or hinders progress 4 a place where alcoholic drinks can be bought and drunk 5 a counter where drinks are served 6 a place providing a particular product or service ○ *a heel bar* 7 in a law court, the railing that separates the area for the judge, jury, and lawyers from the rest of the court 8 *also* **Bar** lawyers or their profession ○ *the federal and state Bars* 9 in music, a unit of time 10 a vertical line separating musical units 11 a metal strip showing rank 12 a ridge of sand on the seabed or a riverbed ■ *vt* (**barred, bar·ring**) 1 fasten with a bar 2 block 3 refuse entry to ■ *prep* excluding ○ *It was our team's finest hour, bar none.*

bar² *n* a unit of pressure equal to 14.5 lb per sq. in.

Ba·rak /bə rák/, **Ehud** (b. 1942) Israeli prime minister (1999–2001)

barb *n* 1 a reverse point on an arrow or hook that makes it difficult to remove 2 a wounding remark 3 a thick filament of a feather that sticks out from the main shaft 4 a bristle on a plant ■ *vt* put a reverse point on an arrow or hook —**barbed** *adj*

Bar·ba·dos /baar báydəss, -báydōss/ island nation of the Windward Islands in the E Caribbean. Cap. Bridgetown. Pop. 275,330 (2001). —**Bar·ba·di·an** *n, adj*

bar·bar·i·an /baar báiree ən/ *n* 1 a member of a people regarded as uncivilized *(sometimes offensive)* 2 a person regarded as uncultured or highly aggressive —**bar·bar·i·an·ism** *n*

bar·bar·ic /baar bárrik/ *adj* 1 cruel 2 uncivilized or unsophisticated *(sometimes offensive)* —**bar·bar·i·cal·ly** *adv*

bar·ba·rism /báarbə rìzzəm/ *n* 1 a cruel act 2 the nature of a civilization when regarded as primitive *(sometimes offensive)* 3 an ungrammatical word or expression

bar·bar·i·ty /baar bárrətee/ (*pl* **-ties**) *n* 1 a cruel act 2 an uncivilized condition

bar·ba·rous /báarbərəss/ *adj* 1 extremely cruel 2 uncivilized *(sometimes offensive)* 3 ungrammatical —**bar·ba·rous·ly** *adv* —**bar·ba·rous·ness** *n*

Bar·ba·ry ape /báarbəree-/ *n* a tailless monkey with greenish brown hair

bar·be·cue /báarbə kyòo/ *n* 1 an apparatus for cooking outdoors 2 an outdoor party with food cooked outdoors 3 food cooked on a grill —**bar·be·cue** *vt*

ORIGIN Barbecue came through Spanish into English in the 17C, from a Native South American language. It originally meant simply "wooden framework," but the use of a framework for outdoor cooking gave rise to the sense "an animal or meat cooked outdoors." Later the word came also to refer to a gathering at which such meat was eaten. The original "framework" sense died out in the 17C, but **barbecue** came again to refer to an apparatus for cooking outdoors in the late 19C.

barbed wire *n* wire with spikes along its length, used for keeping out intruders or attackers

bar·bel /baárb'l/ *n* a slender feeler like a whisker on the mouth of a fish

bar·bell /baár bèl/ *n* a long metal bar with weights at each end, used in weightlifting

bar·ber /baárbər/ *n* somebody who cuts men's hair ■ *vti* cut a man's hair

bar·ber·shop /baárbər shòp/ *n* 1 a barber's place of business 2 music for men singing in harmony

bar·bi·can /baárbikən/ *n* a strong defensive tower at the entrance to a town or fortress

bar·bie /baárbee/ *n* UK, Aus a barbecue (infml)

bar·bi·tu·rate /baar bíchərət, -ràyt/ *n* a sedative drug

Bar·bu·da /baar boódə/ ♦ Antigua and Barbuda —**Bar·bu·dan** *n, adj*

Bar·ce·lo·na /baárssə lónə/ city and port in NE Spain. Pop. 1,505,581 (1998).

bar chart *n* a bar graph

⚡ **bar code** *n* a computer code on merchandise sold in stores, read by an optical scanner at the checkout

bard *n* 1 an ancient Celtic poet 2 any poet (literary or humorous) —**bard·ic** *adj*

Bar·deen /baar deén/, **John** (1908–91) US physicist

bare /bair/ *adj* (**bar·er**, **bar·est**) 1 not covered by clothing 2 without plants 3 without the usual furnishings or decorations 4 basic ○ *the bare facts* 5 only just sufficient ○ *the bare essentials* ■ *vt* (**bared, bar·ing**) expose ○ *an investigative report that bared the details of the conspiracy* —**bare·ness** *n* ◊ See note at **naked**

SPELLCHECK Do not confuse the spelling of **bare** and **bear** (the animal), which sound similar.

bare·back /báir bàk/ *adv, adj* on an unsaddled horse

bare·bones /bàir bónz/ *adj* basic

bare·faced /bàir fáyst/ *adj* 1 shamelessly undisguised 2 with an uncovered or clean-shaven face —**bare·fac·ed·ly** /-fáystlee, -fáyssəd-/ *adv* —**bare·fac·ed·ness** /-fáystnəs, -fáysədnəs/ *n*

bare·foot /báir fòot/ *adj, adv* without shoes

bare·hand·ed /bàir hándəd/ *adj, adv* without weapons or gloves

bare·head·ed /bàir héddəd/ *adj, adv* with the head uncovered

bare·ly /báirlee/ *adv* 1 to a very limited extent ○ *barely conscious* 2 simply and without decoration ○ *a barely furnished office*

Ba·rents Sea /bàrrənts-/ part of the Arctic Ocean, north of Norway, Finland, and Russia and south of Franz Josef Land

barf (infml) *vti* produce vomit ■ *n* something vomited

bar·fly /baár flî/ (*pl* -**flies**) *n* a person who frequents bars (slang)

bar·gain /baárgən/ *n* 1 something offered or bought at less than the normal price 2 an agreement that gives each side obligations 3 property or merchandise acquired as a result of a transaction ■ *v* 1 *vi* negotiate with somebody 2 *vt* exchange something —**bar·gain·er** *n*

□ **bargain for** *vt* be prepared for

bar·gain·ing chip *n* something that can be used as an asset in negotiations

barge *n* 1 a long narrow flat-bottomed boat used for transporting freight 2 an open boat used on ceremonial occasions or for parties 3 a small motorboat used by a high-ranking naval officer ■ *vti* (**barged, barg·ing**) move or push people roughly

□ **barge in** *vi* intrude

~~bargin~~ incorrect spelling of **bargain**

bar graph *n* a graph with bars representing values

ba·ris·ta /bə rístə/ *n* somebody employed to make coffee

bar·i·tone /bárri tòn/ *n* a man's singing voice between bass and tenor in range, or a man with this voice

bar·i·um /báiree əm/ *n* (symbol **Ba**) a silver-white chemical element. Use: alloys

bark[1] *n* the abrupt sound made by a dog ■ *v* 1 *vi* make a dog's sound 2 *vti* speak or say abruptly and aggressively

bark[2] *n* the outer layer of a tree ■ *vt* 1 graze the skin on a part of your body 2 strip the bark from a tree

bark[3], **barque** *n* 1 a small ship with sails set breadthways 2 a small boat

bar·keep·er /baár keèpər/ *n* 1 somebody who runs or owns a bar 2 a server in a bar

Bar·kley /baárklee/, **Alben W.** (1877–1956) vice president of the United States (1949–53)

bar·ley /baárlee/ *n* 1 the edible seeds of a cereal plant. Use: foods, malt production, livestock feed. 2 the cereal crop from which the grain barley comes

bar·maid /baár màyd/ *n* a woman serving in a bar

bar·man /baármən/ (*pl* -**men** /-mən/) *n* UK a man serving in a bar

bar mitz·vah /baar mítsvə/ *n* 1 the ceremony that marks a Jewish boy's 13th birthday 2 a Jewish boy as he reaches the age of 13

barn *n* 1 a large farm outbuilding used as a grain store or livestock shelter 2 any large plain functional building

bar·na·cle /baárnək'l/ *n* a hard-shelled organism that clings to rocks and ships

bar·na·cle goose *n* a European wild goose with gray wings and a black-and-white head and body

Bar·nard /báar naàrd/, **Christiaan** (1922–2001) South African surgeon. He performed the world's first successful human heart transplant operation (1967).

barn dance *n* a party with square dancing

barn owl *n* a whitish owl that nests in barns

barn·storm /báarn stàwrm/ *vti* (*infml*) **1** travel from place to place giving performances **2** tour rural areas making political speeches —**barn·storm·er** *n* —**barn·storm·ing** *adj*

Bar·num /báarnəm/, **P.T.** (1810–91) US showman

barn·yard /báarn yaàrd/ *n* the area of a farm around a barn

bar·o·graph /bárrə gràf/ *n* a barometer supplying a continuous printed record —**bar·o·graph·ic** /bàrrə gráffik/ *adj*

ba·rom·e·ter /bə rómmətər/ *n* **1** an instrument that measures changes in atmospheric pressure for weather forecasting **2** an indicator of the public mood —**bar·o·met·ric** /bàrrə méttrik/ *adj* —**bar·o·met·ri·cal·ly** *adv* —**ba·rom·e·try** *n*

bar·on /bárrən/ *n* **1** a nobleman of low rank **2** a powerful person ○ *an oil baron* **3** a medieval nobleman

---

SPELLCHECK Do not confuse the spelling of **baron** and **barren** ("not productive"), which sound similar.

---

bar·on·ess /bárrənəss, bárrə nèss/ *n* **1** a noblewoman of low rank **2** a baron's wife or widow

bar·on·et /bárrənət, bárrə nèt/ *n* a British nobleman of the lowest hereditary rank —**bar·on·et·cy** /bárrənətsee/ *n*

ba·ro·ni·al /bə rốnee əl/ *adj* **1** of barons **2** large and impressive

ba·roque /bə rốk, -rók/, **Ba·roque** *n* **1** a flamboyant style of European architecture and art popular from the 16C to the 18C **2** 17C classical music —**ba·roque** *adj*

barque *n* NAUT = **bark³**

bar·rack /bárrək/ *n* a barracks ▪ *vt* put soldiers in barracks

bar·racks /bárrəks/ *n* soldiers' quarters (+ *sing or pl verb*)

bar·ra·cu·da /bàrrə kóodə/ (*pl* -**das** *or same*) *n* a predatory ocean fish with a long body and protruding teeth

bar·rage /bə raázh/ *n* **1** a military bombardment **2** an overwhelming amount ○ *a barrage of criticism* ▪ *vt* (-**raged**, -**rag·ing**) **1** fire continuously on an enemy **2** direct something continuously, e.g., with complaints

barre /baar/ *n* a hip-high rod on a dance studio's wall, used for support by dancers while exercising

bar·rel /bárrəl/ *n* **1** a cylindrical container with a flat top and bottom for storing liquids **2** the amount held by a barrel **3** in the oil industry, a unit of volume equal to approximately 42 US gal. or 159 liters **4** in the brewing industry, a unit of volume equal to approximately 31 US gal. or 164 liters **5** the tube-shaped part of a gun ▪ *vti* (-**reled** *or* -**relled**, -**rel·ing** *or* -**rel·ling**) travel fast (*infml*) —**bar·rel·ful** *n* ◊ **over a barrel** in a situation of powerlessness ◊ **scrape the bottom of the barrel** use something of very poor quality

bar·rel or·gan *n* a mechanical organ operated by hand

bar·ren /bárrən/ *adj* **1** without trees or plants **2** not producing fruit **3** unable to have children (*literary*) **4** not yielding useful results ▪ *n* flat scrubby land (*often pl*) —**bar·ren·ly** *adv* —**bar·ren·ness** *n* ◊ See note at **baron**

bar·ri·cade /bárri kàyd, bàrri káyd/ *n* a defensive barrier ▪ *vt* (-**cad·ed**, -**cad·ing**) obstruct something or protect yourself with barricades

bar·ri·er /bárree ər/ *n* **1** a structure that blocks access to or demarcates an area **2** an obstruction **3** a limit or threshold ○ *the sound barrier*

bar·ri·er reef *n* a ridge of coral running parallel to a coastline

bar·ring /báaring/ *prep* except for

bar·ri·o /báaree ò/ (*pl* -**os**) *n* **1** a Spanish-speaking part of a US city **2** a district of a Spanish town

bar·ris·ter /bárrəstər/ *n* **1** *Can* a lawyer in a Canadian court **2** *UK* in England and Wales, a lawyer qualified to represent clients in the higher courts

bar·row¹ /bárrō/ *n* a wheelbarrow

bar·row² /bárrō/ *n* an ancient burial mound

Bar·row /bárrō/, **Clyde** (1909–34) US outlaw. He and Bonnie Parker robbed banks and killed 12 people before being killed by police.

Bar·ry·more /bárri màwr/ family of US actors including **Lionel** (1878–1954), his sister **Ethel** (1879–1959), and his brother **John** (1882–1942)

bar·tend·er /báar tèndər/ *n* somebody serving in a bar

bar·ter /báartər/ *v* **1** *vti* exchange goods or services **2** *vi* negotiate the terms of an agreement ▪ *n* **1** the process of bartering **2** things bartered

Barth /baarth/, **John** (*b.* 1930) US writer

Bar·thol·di /baar tóldee, -thóldee/, **Frédéric-Auguste** (1834–1904) French sculptor. He created the Statue of Liberty (1886).

Bar·tho·lo·mew /baar thóllə myòo/, **St.** (*fl* AD 1C) one of the 12 apostles of Jesus Christ

Bart·lett /báartlət/, **John** (1820–1905) US publisher and reference-book compiler

Bar·tók /baár tòk, -tàwk/, **Béla** (1881–1945) Hungarian composer

Bar·ton /baárt'n/, **Clara** (1821–1912) US philanthropist, founder of the American Red Cross

Bar·uch /bə roók/ n a book in the Roman Catholic Bible and the Protestant Apocrypha traditionally ascribed to Baruch, a disciple of the prophet Jeremiah

Bar·uch /bə roók/, **Bernard** (1870–1965) US financier and economist

bar·y·on /bárree òn/ n a subatomic particle belonging to a group that undergoes strong interactions —**bar·y·on·ic** /bàrree ónnik/ adj

Mikhail Baryshnikov

Ba·rysh·ni·kov /bə ríshni kàwf/, **Mikhail** (b. 1948) Russian-born US ballet dancer and choreographer

ba·salt /bə sáwlt, báy sàwlt/ n 1 a black shiny volcanic rock 2 black unglazed pottery —**ba·sal·tic** /bə sáwltik/ adj

bas·cule /báskyool/ n 1 a counterbalanced device that pivots on a central axis 2 also **bas·cule bridge** a bridge with a lifting roadway

base[1] /bayss/ n 1 the lowest, bottom, or supporting part 2 a fundamental principle 3 a place from which activities start or are coordinated 4 a main ingredient to which others are added 5 the part of a body organ by which it is attached to another structure 6 the number on which a counting system is founded 7 a number that is multiplied a particular number of times 8 a baseline for a calculation 9 a chemical compound that reacts with an acid to form a salt 10 in baseball, any of the corners of the infield that a batter must touch while running ■ vt (**based, bas·ing**) 1 make a base for 2 station in or assign to a base ◊ **have all bases covered** have made preparations to deal with whatever happens ◊ **off base** wrong ◊ **touch base (with somebody)** communicate briefly

SPELLCHECK Do not confuse the spelling of **base** and **bass** ("low in musical pitch"), which sound similar.

base[2] /bayss/ (**bas·er, bas·est**) adj 1 lacking morals 2 of poor quality 3 describes a coin that contains a higher proportion of inexpensive metals than usual —**base·ly** adv —**base·ness** n

base·ball /báyss bàwl/ n 1 a bat-and-ball game in which the batter runs around a diamond-shaped infield to score a run 2 a ball used in baseball

base·ball cap n a close-fitting cap with a long visor

base·board /báyss bàwrd/ n 1 a board serving as the base of something 2 a board covering a wall and floor joint

base hit n in baseball, a hit allowing a batter to reach base

base jump·ing n parachuting from tall buildings and cliffs

Ba·sel /baáz'l/, **Bas·le** /baal/ city in NW Switzerland. Pop. 168,735 (1998).

base·less /báyssləss/ adj 1 not based on fact or supported by evidence 2 without a base or foundation —**base·less·ly** adv —**base·less·ness** n

base·line /báyss lìn/ n 1 a line used as the basis for a calculation, e.g., in navigation 2 in tennis, badminton, or basketball, a boundary line at the end of a court 3 in baseball, a line between bases, or the area within which a runner must stay while running between bases

base·ment /báyssmənt/ n 1 an underground story of a building 2 the foundation of a wall or building

base met·al n any common inexpensive metal

ba·ses plural of basis

bash (infml) vt 1 strike with a heavy blow 2 criticize harshly ■ n 1 a big party 2 a heavy blow

bash·ful /báshfəl/ adj shy —**bash·ful·ly** adv —**bash·ful·ness** n

ba·sic /báyssik/ adj 1 most important 2 elementary 3 without extra parts o a basic salary 4 containing or consisting of a chemical base 5 alkaline 6 describes a chemical salt that contains hydroxide or oxide groups ■ **ba·sics** npl the most important or elementary things relating to a sphere of activity —**ba·sic·i·ty** /bay síssətee/ n

⚡**BA·SIC** /báyssik/, **Ba·sic** n a computer programming language that uses common English terms and algebra. Full form **Beginners All-purpose Symbolic Instruction Code**

ba·si·cal·ly /báysikəlee/ adv 1 introduces the most important reason or a simplified explanation 2 in general

~~basicly~~ incorrect spelling of **basically**

Ba·sie /báyssee/, **Count** (1904–84) US composer and bandleader

bas·il /báyz'l, bázz'l/ n 1 the aromatic leaves of a herb. Use: flavoring. 2 a plant with aromatic leaves

ba·sil·i·ca /bə síllikə, -zíllikə/ n 1 a Roman Catholic church given special privileges by the Pope 2 an ancient Roman building with

a long central nave and a semicircular apse
—**ba·sil·i·can** adj

bas·i·lisk /básselisk, bázz-/ n 1 a mythical reptile whose breath or look was fatal 2 a small lizard that can run on its long hind legs

ba·sin /báyss'n/ n 1 an open container for washing 2 the contents of a basin 3 an area of land draining into a river or lake 4 a bowl-shaped depression in the Earth 5 a circular formation of sloping rock strata

ba·sis /báyssiss/ (pl **-ses** /-seèz/) n 1 the foundation of an argument or idea 2 a way of proceeding o work on a part-time basis 3 a main component or ingredient

bask vi 1 lie in the pleasurable warmth of the sun 2 get pleasure from something

bas·ket /báskat/ n 1 a woven container, often with a handle 2 the contents of a basket 3 in basketball, a net or a goal scored —**bas·ket·ful** n

bas·ket·ball /báskat bàwl/ n 1 a ball game played by two teams of five players who pass the ball by hand on an indoor court 2 a ball used in basketball

bas·ket·ry /báskatree/, **bas·ket·work** /-wùrk/ n 1 the craft of making baskets 2 baskets collectively

Basle ◊ Basel

bas mitz·vah n JUDAISM = bat mitzvah

basque /bask/ n a woman's tight-fitting corset

Basque /bask/ n 1 a member of a European people of N Spain and SW France 2 the language of the Basque people —**Basque** adj

Basque Coun·try autonomous region of N Spain. Pop. 2,098,628 (1998).

Bas·ra /báazra/ port in SE Iraq. Pop. 406,296 (1987).

bas·re·lief /bàa-/ n 1 flat sculpture in which the design projects only slightly from the background surface 2 a piece of bas-relief

bass¹ /bayss/ n 1 a man's singing voice of the lowest range, or a man with that voice 2 the lowest musical or singing part in a harmony 3 the low-frequency element of audio reproduction ■ adj 1 deep in tone 2 low in pitch ◊ See note at base¹

bass² /bass/ (pl same or **bass·es**) n 1 a spiny-finned fish 2 bass as food

bass clef n a musical symbol indicating that the top line of the music represents the A below middle C

Basse·terre /bass táir, baass-/ capital of St. Kitts and Nevis, on the southwestern coast of St. Kitts island. Pop. 12,220 (1994).

bass gui·tar n a low-pitched guitar

bas·si·net /bàssa nét, bássa nèt/ n a baby's bed shaped like a basket

bass·ist /báyssist/ n the player of a bass guitar or double bass

bas·soon /ba soòn, ba-/ n a low-pitched wood-

wind instrument of the oboe family —**bas·soon·ist** n

Bass Strait /báss-/ channel between mainland Australia and Tasmania, approximately 140 mi./225 km wide

bas·tard /bástard/ n 1 an offensive term for somebody regarded as obnoxious and disagreeable (slang insult) 2 an offensive term for somebody born to unmarried parents (archaic or offensive) ■ adj 1 not genuine and of lesser value o bastard quartz 2 an offensive term meaning born to unmarried parents

baste¹ (bast·ed, bast·ing) vt moisten during cooking

baste² (bast·ed, bast·ing) vt 1 sew loosely 2 sew with rows of diagonal stitches

baste³ (bast·ed, bast·ing) vt 1 beat somebody severely 2 scold

bas·tion /báschan, bástee an/ n 1 a strong supporter or defender of something 2 a fortified place 3 a projecting part of a wall or fortification

bat¹ n 1 a club used in sports 2 a heavy stick or club 3 in baseball, a batter 4 a blow from a stick ■ v (bat·ted, bat·ting) 1 in baseball or cricket, have a turn at batting 2 vt strike with a bat ◊ **go to bat for** support or assist somebody (infml) ◊ **(right) off the bat** immediately (infml)

bat² n a small nocturnal flying mammal with leathery wings

ORIGIN The noun **bat** referring to an animal has a different origin from the verb **bat** as in "batting your eyelids," and neither is related to the **bat** used in games. The original name of the flying mammal ended in a /k/ sound, not /t/, and came from a Scandinavian language. The verb **bat** "blink" derives from the French verb that gave us batter "hit repeatedly." The sports **bat** is the oldest of all these words, and its origin is not known for certain.

---

bat³ (bat·ted, bat·ting) vt blink an eye

~~batalion~~ incorrect spelling of **battalion**

bat·boy /bát bòy/ n in baseball, a person who looks after the team's equipment

batch n 1 a quantity regarded as a group or unit 2 an amount of food baked at one time ■ vt arrange into batches, or process as a batch

~~batchelor~~ incorrect spelling of **bachelor**

ⅴ **batch file** n a computer file containing a series of consecutive commands

ⅴ **batch proc·ess·ing** n a method of processing data in which a computer gathers jobs and processes them when time becomes available

Bates, Katherine Lee (1859–1929) US educator and writer

bath /bath/ n (pl **baths** /baths, bathz/) 1 an occasion when somebody washes the body with soap and water in a large tub 2 a bathtub **3** a bathroom **4** a treatment that involves immersing the body in a substance, e.g., mud **5** a liquid used for a particular purpose, e.g., developing photographs ■ **baths** *npl* **1** a building with facilities for people to have baths **2** a spa where patrons avail themselves of the water from natural mineral springs ◊ **take a bath** suffer a severe financial setback *(slang)*

Bath /bath/ city in SW England, a spa since Roman times. Pop. 84,100 (1994).

bathe /bayth/ (**bathed, bath·ing**) *v* **1** *vti* wash somebody or yourself in a bath **2** *vt* cleanse a wound **3** *vt* dip something in a liquid **4** *vt* cover something, e.g., with light or color **5** *vi* swim or paddle in open water

bath·er /báythər/ *n* a swimmer

ba·thet·ic /bə thétik/ *adj* **1** showing bathos **2** trite or absurdly sentimental —**ba·thet·ic·al·ly** *adv*

bath·house /báth hòws/ (*pl* **-houses** /-hòwzəz/) *n* **1** a building equipped with baths **2** a building for changing before swimming

bath·ing suit /báything-/ *n* a swimsuit

bath mitz·vah *n* JUDAISM = **bat mitzvah**

ba·thos /báy thòss, -tháwss/ *n* **1** insincere, excessively sentimental pathos **2** a sudden ludicrous change in speech or writing from an important or elevated subject to something commonplace

bath·robe /báth ròb/ *n* a loose-fitting garment worn after or before bathing

bath·room /báth ròom, -ròom/ *n* **1** a room with a toilet **2** a room containing a bathtub

bath·tub /báth tùb/ *n* a container in which you sit to wash your body

bath·y·sphere /bátha sfèer/ *n* a diving sphere that can be lowered to great depths

ba·tik /bə téek, báttik/ *n* **1** a fabric printing technique that involves blanking out areas with wax **2** fabric dyed using this technique

Ba·tis·ta y Zal·dí·var /bə téestə ee zaal dèe vàar/, **Fulgencio** (1901–73) Cuban soldier and head of state (1940–44, 1952–59)

bat mitz·vah /baat mítsvə/, **bath mitz·vah, bas mitz·vah** /baass-/ *n* **1** the ceremony that marks a Jewish girl's 13th birthday **2** a Jewish girl as she reaches the age of 13

ba·ton /bə tón, báttn/ *n* **1** a stick for conducting music **2** a police officer's stick used as a weapon **3** a relay runner's stick **4** a drum major's stick

Bat·on Rouge /báttn ròozh/ capital of Louisiana. Pop. 211,551 (1998).

bats·man /bátsmən/ (*pl* **-men** /-mən/) *n* in cricket, a player who is batting or who specializes in batting

bat·tal·ion /bə tállyən/ *n* **1** a military unit consisting of three or more companies **2** a large group of soldiers acting together **3** a large number of people or organisms *(often pl)*

~~battalion~~ incorrect spelling of **battalion**

bat·ten /báttn/ *n* **1** a strip of wood or plastic used, e.g., to keep the edge of a sail in shape **2** a wooden slat used for fastening down the hatches on a ship ■ *vt* support or fasten with battens

bat·ter[1] /báttər/ *vt* **1** hit repeatedly **2** subject to persistent attack —**bat·tered** *adj*

bat·ter[2] /báttər/ *n* a mixture of flour, milk, and eggs used for making cakes and pancakes or for coating food before frying ■ *vt* coat food in batter

bat·ter[3] /báttər/ *n* a player who is batting, especially in baseball

bat·ter·ing ram *n* **1** formerly, a heavy beam used to break down fortifications **2** a heavy implement used to break down doors

bat·ter·y /báttəree/ (*pl* **-ies**) *n* **1** a portable source of electricity consisting of a number of electric cells **2** the unlawful use of physical force on somebody **3** in baseball, a pitcher and catcher **4** a grouping of artillery pieces or machine guns **5** a gun or artillery emplacement **6** an army artillery unit **7** a grouping of similar things used or considered together **8** the percussion section of an orchestra

bat·ting /bátting/ *n* padding or stuffing used in the textile industry

bat·tle /báttl/ *n* **1** a large-scale fight between armed forces **2** a struggle ■ *v* (**-tled, -tling**) **1** *vi* fight an enemy **2** *vi* strive **3** *vt* struggle against ◊ See note at **fight**

bat·tle·ax /báttl àks/ *n* **1** a broad-headed ax **2** a woman who is regarded as fearsomely aggressive *(insult)*

bat·tle cruis·er *n* an armed warship lighter and faster than a battleship

bat·tle cry *n* **1** a shout made by soldiers when going into battle **2** a supporters' slogan

bat·tle·field /báttl fèeld/, **bat·tle·ground** /-grównd/ *n* **1** the site of a battle **2** an area of conflict

bat·tle line *n* the area along which a battle is fought

bat·tle·ments /báttl mənts/ *npl* indentations on a parapet

bat·tle·ship /báttl shìp/ *n* a large, heavily armed and armored warship, smaller than an aircraft carrier

bat·ty /báttee/ (**-ti·er, -ti·est**) *adj* slightly eccentric *(infml)* —**bat·ti·ness** *n*

bau·ble /báwb'l/ *n* a trinket

⨍ **baud** /bawd/ *n* a unit of data transmission speed equal to one unit element per second

ORIGIN The **baud** is named for the French engineer J. M. E. Baudot (1845–1903), who invented a method of transmitting information using binary digits.

Baude·laire /bōd láir/, **Charles** (1821–67) French poet and critic

Bau·haus /bów hòwss/ *n* an early 20C German school of architecture and design

baulk *v, n* = **balk**

baux·ite /báwk sìt/ *n* an ore that is the principal source of aluminum

Ba·var·i·a /bə váiree ə/ state in SE Germany. Cap. Munich. Pop. 12,086,548 (1998). —**Ba·var·i·an** *n, adj*

bawd·y /báwdee/ (-i·er, -i·est) *adj* with a sexual content that is humorous or obscene —**bawd·i·ly** *adv* —**bawd·i·ness** *n*

bawl *vti* 1 shout loudly 2 cry noisily (*infml*) ■ *n* a loud shout
□ **bawl out** *vt* scold loudly (*infml*)

bay¹ *n* a wide curved inlet of the sea

bay² *n* 1 a special area or compartment 2 a recessed part of a floor or room 3 a bay window

bay³ *n* a small evergreen tree of the laurel family with aromatic leaves

bay⁴ *n* 1 an animal of reddish brown color 2 a reddish brown color —**bay** *adj*

bay⁵ *vi* 1 howl plaintively 2 call noisily and aggressively for something to happen ■ *n* a position of no escape ◊ **keep somebody** or **something at bay** keep somebody or something unpleasant at a distance

Ba·ya·món /bì aa món/ city in NE Puerto Rico. Pop. 220,262 (1990).

bay leaf *n* an aromatic leaf of a bay tree. Use: seasoning.

bay·o·net /báy ənət, bày ə nét/ *n* a blade attached to a rifle ■ *vt* (-net·ed or -net·ted, -net·ing or -net·ting) stab with a bayonet

bay·ou /bí òo, -ò̀/ (*pl* -ous) *n* 1 a sluggish meandering stream through lowland swamps 2 a tributary to a larger body of water

Bay·reuth /bī róyt/ city in S Germany, site of an annual Wagner opera festival. Pop. 72,840 (1997).

bay win·dow *n* a rounded or three-sided window that projects from an outside wall

ba·zaar /bə záar/ *n* 1 a sale of goods to raise money for charity 2 a street market in North Africa and Southwest Asia

~~bazaar~~ incorrect spelling of **bazaar**

ba·zoo·ka /bə zóoka/ *n* a portable antitank weapon fired from the shoulder

BBC *abbr* British Broadcasting Corporation

BB gun *n* an air rifle

ORIGIN *BB* is the official designation of shot that is 0.18 in.

BBQ *abbr* barbecue

⚡**BBS** *abbr* bulletin board system

BC, B.C. *adv* indicates a date before the birth of Jesus Christ (*after dates*) Full form **before Christ**

B.C. *abbr* British Columbia

bcc, b.c.c. *abbr* blind carbon copy

⚡**BCD** *abbr* binary coded decimal

BCE, B.C.E. *adv* used as a non-Christian equivalent of BC in dates. Full form **before the Common Era**

be (*stressed*) /bee/ (*unstressed*) /bi/ (*1st person sing past indicative* **was** (*stressed*) /woz, wuz/ (*unstressed*) /wəz/, *2nd person sing past indicative* **were** (*stressed*) /wur/ (*unstressed*) /wər/, *3rd person sing past indicative* **was**, *1st person pl past indicative* **were**, *2nd person pl past indicative* **were**, *3rd person pl past indicative* **were**, *past subjunctive* **were**, *past participle* **been** /bin/, *present subjunctive* **be**, *1st person present sing* **am** (*stressed*) /am/ (*unstressed*) /əm/, *2nd person present sing* **are** (*stressed*) /aar/ (*unstressed*) /ər/, *3rd person present sing* **is** /iz/, *1st person present pl* **are**, *2nd person present pl* **are**, *3rd person present pl* **are**) *vi* 1 used after "it" to give a description or judgment of something ○ *It is a good thing that we left early.* 2 used after "there" to indicate that something exists or is true ○ *There are many problems with her essay.* 3 exist ○ *I think, therefore I am.* 4 happen or take place ○ *The meeting was at four o'clock.* 5 make a visit ○ *I was in Italy during the summer.* 6 have a particular quality ○ *This sentence is concise.* 7 remain as a fact or situation ○ *The facts are these: it is cold and unhealthy here.* ■ *aux v* 8 expresses continuation or future intention ○ *My legs are getting tired.* ○ *I am leaving on the next train.* 9 forms the passive ○ *She was sent on the mission.* 10 used with an infinitive to express the future ○ *The meeting is to take place tomorrow.*

Be *symbol* beryllium

be- *prefix* make ○ *belittle*

beach /beech/ *n* a strip of sand or pebbles on a coast ■ *vti* 1 haul a boat ashore 2 strand or become stranded on shore ○ *a whale that had been beached during a storm*

SPELLCHECK Do not confuse the spelling of **beach** and **beech** (the tree), which sound similar.

beach·comb·er /beech kòmər/ *n* somebody who salvages things from a beach

beach·head /beech hèd/ *n* a captured enemy beach

bea·con /beekən/ *n* 1 a flashing light as a warning and guide 2 a radio transmitter that broadcasts navigation signals 3 a signal fire formerly lit on a hill as a warning

bead /beed/ *n* 1 a small ball or round gemstone strung on a necklace 2 a drop of moisture 3 a decorative raised edge or rim, e.g., on furniture 4 a knob that forms the front part of the sight of a gun ■ **beads** *npl* 1 a rosary 2 a necklace ■ *v* 1 *vt* decorate with beads 2 *vi* form into beads —**bead·ed** *adj*

bead·ing /beeding/ *n* material used for making a decorative trim, e.g., on furniture

bea·dle /beéd'l/ n 1 the caretaker of a synagogue 2 a minor church official with varying duties, including ushering

bead·y /beédee/ (-i·er, -i·est) adj like beads —**bead·i·ness** n

bea·gle /beég'l/ n a small smooth-haired dog

beak /beek/ n 1 a bird's mouth 2 the protruding part of the mouth of organisms other than birds 3 a projecting part —**beaked** adj —**beak·less** adj

beak·er /beékər/ n 1 a laboratory container 2 a wide-mouthed cup without a handle

be-all ◊ **the be-all and end-all** the thing or person regarded as the most important

beam /beem/ n 1 a horizontal structural support 2 a line of light 3 a narrow stream of radiation 4 a radar signal that guides ships or aircraft 5 a broad smile 6 a ship's breadth 7 a side of a ship 8 a pivoted horizontal part of a balance 9 a main supporting shaft, e.g., of a plow ■ v 1 vti smile broadly 2 vt send as a radio or TV signal 3 vti shine brightly

bean /been/ n 1 a long, thin, usually green seed pod eaten cooked whole as a vegetable 2 a small, rounded, often kidney-shaped seed eaten as a vegetable and often dried for preserving 3 a plant with edible pods and seeds 4 the human head (slang) ■ vt hit on the head (slang) ◊ **spill the beans** reveal secret information (infml)

bean·bag /beén bàg/ n 1 a bean-filled bag used in games 2 a large cushion used as a seat

bean count·er n an accountant (slang; sometimes offensive)

bean curd n tofu

bean·ie /beénee/ n a tight-fitting hat like a skullcap

bean·pole /beén pòl/ n a stick supporting a bean plant

bean sprouts npl young crisp shoots of sprouted bean seeds eaten as food

bear[1] /bair/ n 1 a large strong mammal with thick shaggy fur and long claws 2 a medium-sized furry mammal similar but unrelated to true bears ○ a koala bear 3 a bad-tempered person (infml) 4 somebody who anticipates a downturn in the economy and stock prices ◊ See note at **bare**

bear[2] /bair/ (**bore** /bawrn/ or **born** /bawrn/) v 1 vti tolerate something ○ Can you bear this heat? No, I can't bear it. 2 vt support the weight of something 3 vti withstand being subjected to something ○ Will her theories bear scrutiny? 4 vt merit something ○ bear further investigation 5 vt accept something as a responsibility 6 vt be characterized by something ○ bears no relation to reality 7 vt show physical signs of something ○ bears a likeness to his uncle 8 vt carry something 9 vt produce something 10 vt give birth to a child 11 vt have a particular thought or

feeling ○ I bore him no ill will. 12 vi head in a particular direction 13 vt behave in a particular way ○ bore himself well

☐ **bear on** or **upon** vt be relevant to

☐ **bear out** vt confirm as correct

☐ **bear up** vi stay cheerful in difficulties

bear·a·ble /báirəb'l/ adj tolerable

beard /beerd/ n 1 the hair growing on a man's chin 2 a growth of long hair on a plant or animal ■ vt oppose or confront confidently —**beard·ed** adj —**beard·less** adj

bear·er /báirər/ n 1 somebody who brings, carries, or holds something 2 the holder of a note redeemable for payment

bear hug n 1 a tight embrace 2 a squeezing hold in wrestling

bear·ing /báiring/ n 1 relevance to something else ○ This has no bearing on the matter under discussion. 2 a way of moving or standing 3 a calculation of direction or geographic position 4 a support for a moving machine part

bear·ish /báirish/ adj 1 clumsy 2 bad-tempered 3 anticipating a bad economy and falling stock prices

bear mar·ket n a stock market characterized by bearish activity

bé·ar·naise sauce /bàir nayz-, bày aar-/ n a sauce thickened with egg yolk and flavored with tarragon

bear·skin /báir skìn/ n 1 a bear's pelt 2 a soldier's tall fur hat

beast /beest/ n 1 a large animal 2 the instinctive or aggressive side of somebody's personality 3 a brutal person

beast·ly /beéstlee/ adj nasty or horrible —**beast·li·ness** n

beat /beet/ v (**beat**, **beat·en** /beét'n/) 1 vt defeat somebody 2 vt hit somebody or something repeatedly 3 vi knock against something repeatedly ○ waves beating against the rocks 4 vi pulsate (refers to the heart or pulse) 5 vt set a musical rhythm ○ beating time with her baton 6 vt stir a liquid mixture, cream, or eggs vigorously 7 vt arrive or finish ahead of somebody else or of a time limit 8 vt surpass something ○ beat the long jump record 9 vt make or shape something by hitting or trampling ○ a beaten path 10 vti flap so as to fly (refers to wings) 11 vti drive game animals from cover ■ n 1 a steady throbbing (often in combination) ○ a heartbeat 2 a striking of one thing against another 3 a set or dominant rhythm 4 the usual route, especially of a police officer ■ adj tired out (slang) —**beat·ing** n ◊ See note at **defeat**

SPELLCHECK Do not confuse the spelling of **beat** and **beet** (the plant), which sound similar.

☐ **beat down** vi come down strongly (refers to sun or rain)

□ **beat up** *vt* injure with blows *(infml)*

be·a·tif·ic /beè ə tíffik/ *adj* blissfully happy *(literary)* —**be·a·tif·i·cal·ly** *adv*

~~beatiful~~ incorrect spelling of **beautiful**

be·a·ti·fy /beé àtti fi/ (**-fied, -fies**) *vt* **1** in the Roman Catholic Church, state officially that a dead person lived a holy life **2** make somebody extremely happy *(literary)* —**be·at·i·fi·ca·tion** /bee àttəfi káysh'n/ *n*

be·at·i·tude /bee àttə tood/ *n (literary)* **1** the perfect happiness and inner peace supposed to be enjoyed by the soul in heaven **2** great happiness and serenity

Beat·les /beét'lz/ (1959–70) British pop music group including **Paul McCartney** (*b.* 1942), **John Lennon** (1940–80), **George Harrison** (1943–2001), and **Ringo Starr** (*b.* 1940)

beat·nik /beétnik/ *n* a member of a group rejecting traditional values in the 1950s

beat·up *adj* dilapidated *(infml)*

beau /bō/ (*pl* **beaus** or **beaux** /bōz/) *n* a boy-friend *(dated)*

Beau·fort scale /bōfərt-/ *n* a scale indicating wind speed

ORIGIN The scale is named for the Irish admiral Sir Francis Beaufort (1774–1857).

Beau·fort Sea /bōfərt-/ section of the Arctic Ocean northwest of Canada and north of Alaska. Depth 15,360 ft. / 4,682 m.

Beau·har·nais /bō aar náy/, **Joséphine de** ♦ **Joséphine**

Beau·jo·lais /bōzhə láy/ *n* a light French wine from the Beaujolais district of Burgundy

beau monde /bō mónd, -máwnd/ *n* high society

Beau·mont /bō mònt/ port in SE Texas. Pop. 109,841 (1998).

Beau·re·gard /bōrə gaàrd/, **Pierre Gustave Toutant** (1818–93) US Confederate general

~~beaurocracy~~ incorrect spelling of **bur·eaucracy**

beau·te·ous /byoótee əss/ *adj* beautiful *(literary)* —**beau·te·ous·ness** *n*

beau·ti·cian /byoo tísh'n/ *n* somebody giving beauty treatments

beau·ti·ful /byoótəf'l/ *adj* very pleasing, especially to look at —**beau·ti·ful·ly** *adv*

beau·ti·fy /byoóti fi/ (**-fied, -fies**) *vt* make something beautiful —**beau·ti·fi·ca·tion** /byoótəfi káysh'n/ *n* —**beau·ti·fi·er** *n*

beau·ty /byoótee/ (*pl* **-ties**) *n* **1** a pleasing and impressive quality, especially of appearance **2** a beautiful woman **3** a fine thing

beau·ty par·lor *n* a place for beauty treatments

beau·ty queen *n* the winner of a contest for beautiful women

beau·ty spot *n* **1** a popular scenic place **2** *also* **beau·ty mark** a small natural mark on the face

Simone de Beauvoir

Beau·voir /bō vwaàr/, **Simone de** (1908–86) French writer

beaux plural of **beau**

bea·ver /beévər/ *n* **1** (*pl* **bea·vers** or *same*) a furry flat-tailed water mammal **2** fur from a beaver

bea·ver·board /beévər bàwrd/ *n* wood-fiber building board. Use: ceilings, inner walls.

Bea·ver·brook /beévər brŏŏk/, **Max Aitken, 1st Baron** (1879–1964) Canadian-born British newspaper owner and politician

be·bop /beé bòp/ *n* fast complex jazz music originating in the 1940s

be·calm /bi kaám/ *vt* stop a sailboat through lack of wind

be·came past tense of **become**

be·cause /bi káwz, -kúz/ *conj* **1** for the reason that **2** seeing that ○ *It must have been raining because the sidewalk is wet.* ◊ See note at **reason**

bé·cha·mel sauce /bàyshə mel-/ *n* a sauce made with milk, flour, and butter

ORIGIN The sauce is named for its inventor, Louis, Marquis de Béchamel (1630–1703), steward to Louis XIV of France.

beck *n* a nod *(literary)*

Beck·er /békər/, **Boris** (*b.* 1967) German tennis player

Beck·et /békət/, **Thomas à, St.** (1118?–70) English saint and martyr

Samuel Beckett

Beck·ett /békət/, **Samuel** (1906–89) Irish-born writer

beck·on /békən/ *vti* **1** gesture to somebody to come **2** attract or tempt somebody *(literary)*

be·come /bi kúm/ (**-came** /-káym/, **-come, -com·ing**) *v* **1** *vi* come to be **2** *vt* suit the appearance or status of —**be·com·ing** *adj*

□ **become of** *vt* happen to

~~becouse~~ incorrect spelling of **because**

bec·que·rel /be krél, béko rèl/ *n* (*symbol* **Bq**) an SI unit of radioactivity

ORIGIN The unit is named for the French physicist Antoine Henri Becquerel (1852–1908).

bed *n* **1** a piece of furniture on which to sleep **2** a place for sleeping **3** sleep or rest in a bed *o time for bed* **4** a patch of soil for growing plants **5** the ground under a body of water **6** a surface on which something is built or laid **7** a layer of rock ■ *vt* (**bed·ded, bed·ding**) set firmly into a surrounding mass or surface

□ **bed down** *vi* settle down for sleep, usually in a makeshift bed *o I'll bed down on the sofa.*

B.Ed. *abbr* Bachelor of Education

bed and break·fast *n* **1** overnight accommodations and breakfast in a guest house or private dwelling **2** a guesthouse

be·daub /bi dáwb/ *vt* smear thickly or carelessly (*literary*)

be·daz·zle /bi dázz'l/ (**-zled, -zling**) *vt* astonish and impress greatly (*literary*)

bed·bug /béd bùg/ *n* a small insect found in bedding that sucks blood

bed·clothes /béd klòthz, -klòz/ *npl* bed coverings

bed·ding /bédding/ *n* **1** the mattress, pillows, and coverings of a bed **2** material for animals to sleep on **3** a foundation layer

bed·ding plant *n* an annual plant for a flower bed

be·deck /bi dék/ *vt* make pretty by decorating *o trees bedecked with colored lights*

be·dev·il /bi dévv'l/ *vt* cause continual problems to **—be·dev·il·ment** *n*

bed·fel·low /béd fèllò/ *n* an associate

bed·lam /bédləm/ *n* uproar and chaos

ORIGIN Bedlam is a contraction of *Bethlehem*. The original bedlam was the Hospital of St. Mary of Bethlehem in London, England, which housed people with psychiatric disorders.

Bed·ou·in /béddoo ən, bédwin/ (*pl* **-ins** *or same*), **Bed·u·in** *n* a nomadic Arab **—Bed·ou·in** *adj*

bed·pan /béd pàn/ *n* a shallow container for urination or defecation in bed

bed·post /béd pòst/ *n* a post at the corner of a bed

be·drag·gled /bi drágg'ld/ *adj* wet, dirty, and messy

bed·rid·den /béd rìdd'n/ *adj* confined to bed

bed·rock /béd ròk/ *n* **1** underlying rock **2** underlying facts or principles

bed·roll /béd ròl/ *n* a traveler's rolled-up bedding

bed·room /béd ròòm, -ròom/ *n* a room for sleeping

bed·room com·mu·ni·ty *n* a commuters' suburb

bed·side /béd sìd/ *n* the space beside a bed **—bed·side** *adj*

bed·side man·ner *n* a doctor's manner when dealing with patients

bed·sore /béd sàwr/ *n* a skin ulcer resulting from long confinement to bed

bed·spread /béd sprèd/ *n* a top cover for a bed

bed·stead /béd stèd/ *n* the frame of a bed

bed·time /béd tìm/ *n* time for bed

Bed·u·in *n, adj* PEOPLES = **Bedouin**

bee *n* **1** a flying insect that makes honey **2** a gathering for activity and socializing

beech /beech/ *n* **1** a deciduous tree with smooth gray bark **2** the wood of a beech tree. Use: See note at **beach**. ◊ See note at **beach**

Bee·cher /béechər/, **Henry Ward** (1813–87) US cleric and orator

Bee·cher, Lyman (1775–63) US cleric

beef *n* **1** meat from cattle **2** (*pl* **beeves** *or same*) an animal giving beef **3** a complaint (*slang*) ■ *vi* complain (*slang*)

□ **beef up** *vt* make stronger or more effective (*infml*) *o beef up the article with some statistics*

beef·a·lo /béefə lò/ (*pl same or* **-loes**) *n* a bison–cattle hybrid

beef·burg·er /béef bùrgər/ *n* a burger made with beef

beef·cake /béef kàyk/ *n* muscular men (*infml*)

beef·eat·er /béef èetər/ *n* a guard at the Tower of London wearing a Tudor-style uniform

beef·steak fun·gus /béef stàyk-/ *n* an edible fungus with a large reddish cap

beef·steak to·ma·to /béef stàyk-/ *n* a large tomato

beef·y /béefee/ (**-i·er, -i·est**) *adj* **1** muscular **2** powerful (*infml*) **—beef·i·ness** *n*

bee·hive /bée hìv/ *n* a structure housing a colony of bees

bee·keep·er /bée kèepər/ *n* somebody who keeps bees **—bee·keep·ing** *n*

bee·line /bée lìn/ *n* a direct path or course *o We made a beeline for the comfortable seats.*

Be·el·ze·bub /bee élzə bùb/ *n* the devil

been past participle of **be**

beep *n* a short high noise made by a car horn or electronic device ■ *v* **1** *vti* make or cause to make a beep **2** *vt* page somebody using a beeper

beep·er /béepər/ *n* a pager that emits beeps (*infml*)

beer /beer/ *n* **1** an alcoholic drink brewed from malt and hops **2** a carbonated or fermented nonalcoholic drink *o root beer*

SPELLCHECK Do not confuse the spelling of **beer** and **bier** ("a stand for a casket"), which sound similar.

bees·wax /bée'z wàks/ *n* wax produced by bees or commercially processed. Use: polish, candles, crayons.

beet /beet/ *n* a plant with an edible swollen

root. Use: cooking, animal feed, sugar production ◊ See note at **beat**

Bee·tho·ven /báy tòvən/, **Ludwig van** (1770–1827) German composer

bee·tle[1] /beét'l/ *n* an insect with a pair of outer wings that form a hard covering for the inner wings

bee·tle[2] /beét'l/ (**-tled, -tling**) *vi* overhang or jut out (*literary*)

be·fall /bi fáwl/ (**-fell** /-fél/, **-fall·en** /-fáwlən/) *vti* happen, or happen to (*literary*)

be·fit /bi fít/ (**-fit·ted, -fit·ting**) *vt* be appropriate for —**be·fit·ting** *adj* —**be·fit·ting·ly** *adv*

be·fore /bi fáwr/ *prep, conj, adv* **1** earlier than **2** preceding in sequence ■ *prep* **1** in the presence of ◊ *spoke before a huge crowd* **2** with more importance than **3** ahead of ■ *adv* previously ■ *conj* rather than ◊ *I'll die before I'll tell you anything about it.*

be·fore·hand /bi fáwr hànd/ *adv* in advance

be·friend /bi frénd/ *vt* make friends with

be·fud·dle /bi fúdd'l/ (**-dled, -dling**) *vt* make confused or perplexed —**be·fud·dled** *adj* —**be·fud·dle·ment** *n*

beg (**begged, beg·ging**) *vti* **1** ask earnestly for something **2** ask for charity
□ **beg off** *vi* ask to be excused from doing something

be·gan past tense of **begin**

be·get /bi gét/ (**-got** /-gót/, **-got·ten** /-gótt'n/ or **-got, -get·ting**) *vt* **1** cause something to happen **2** father a child (*archaic*)

beg·gar /béggər/ *n* somebody who begs for charity ■ *vt* be beyond description or belief ◊ *a catastrophe that beggars understanding*

beg·gar·ly /béggərlee/ *adj* paltry —**beg·gar·li·ness** *n*

~~begger~~ incorrect spelling of **beggar**

be·gin /bi gín/ (**-gan** /-gán/, **-gun** /-gún/, **-gin·ning**) *vti* **1** do something that was not being done before **2** come or bring into being

Be·gin /báygin/, **Menachem** (1913–92) Russian-born Israeli prime minister (1977–83)

~~begining~~ incorrect spelling of **beginning**

be·gin·ner /bi gínnər/ *n* somebody who has just started learning or doing something

SYNONYMS beginner, apprentice, greenhorn, novice, tyro CORE MEANING: a person who has not acquired the necessary experience or skills to do something

be·gin·ning /bi gínning/ *n* the start or first part of something ■ **be·gin·nings** *npl* early conditions ■ *adj* new to a job or activity ◊ *beginning teachers*

be·gone /bi gáwn, -gón/ *interj* go away (*archaic*)

be·go·nia /bi gónyə/ *n* an ornamental flowering plant

be·got past tense of **beget**

be·got·ten past participle of **beget**

be·grime /bi grím/ (**-grimed, -grim·ing**) *vt* cover with grime

be·grudge /bi grúj/ (**-grudged, -grudg·ing**) *vt* **1** resent something that somebody else has ◊ *He's always begrudged me my success.* **2** not want to give something ◊ *She begrudged every dime she paid me.*

be·guile /bi gíl/ (**-guiled, -guil·ing**) *vt* charm —**be·guile·ment** *n* —**be·guil·ing** *adj*

be·gum /báygəm, beé-/ *n* **1** in some Muslim communities, a title of respect for a woman **2** a high-ranking Muslim woman

be·gun past participle of **begin**

be·half /bi háf, -haáf/ ◊ **on behalf of, in behalf of 1** as somebody's representative **2** for somebody's benefit or support

be·have /bi háyv/ (**-haved, -hav·ing**) *vi* **1** act or function in a particular way ◊ *He's been behaving oddly.* **2** conduct yourself politely toward others ◊ *children who won't behave*

ORIGIN The second part of **behave** is the ordinary English verb *have*, with an old stressed pronunciation. It was used in the sense "hold," so that "behaving yourself" was holding or conducting yourself in a particular way. The prefix *be-* added emphasis.

---

be·hav·ior /bi háyvyər/ *n* the way somebody or something behaves —**be·hav·ior·al** *adj*

be·hav·ior·ism /bi háyvyə rìzzəm/ *n* psychology concentrating on observation and modification of behavior —**be·hav·ior·ist** *adj, n* —**be·hav·ior·is·tic** /bi háyvyə rístik/ *adj*

be·head /bi héd/ *vt* cut off the head of

be·he·moth /bi heé məth, beé əməth/ *n* something huge or powerful

---

ORIGIN The original **Behemoth** is a huge beast referred to in the Bible, usually thought to be a hippopotamus (Job 40:15).

---

be·hest /bi hést/ *n* order or request (*fml*) ◊ *at her behest*

be·hind /bi hínd/ *prep, adv* **1** at the back of or following **2** later than ◊ *behind schedule* ■ *adv* **1** in arrears ◊ *She's behind on her payments.* **2** remaining ◊ *was left behind* ■ *prep* **1** causing ◊ *The criminals are behind the robbery.* **2** supporting ◊ *I'm behind you all the way!* ■ *n* somebody's buttocks (*infml*)

be·hold /bi hóld/ (**-held** /-héld/) *vt* look at or see (*fml; often in commands*) —**be·hold·er** *n*

be·hold·en /bi hóld'n/ *adj* under an obligation

be·hoove /bi hoóv, bə-/ (**-hooved, -hoov·ing**) *vt* be fitting for somebody (*fml*)

Bei·der·becke /bídər bèk/, **Bix** (1903–31) US jazz cornet player, pianist, and composer

beige /bayzh/ *n* a very pale brown color —**beige** *adj*

Bei·jing /bày jíng/ capital of China. Pop. 11,300,000 (1995).

be·ing /beé ing/ present participle of **be** ■ *n* **1** existence **2** somebody's essential nature ◊ *loved the child with all her being* **3** a living thing regarded as supernatural or alien **4** a person

Bei·rut /bay rōōt/ capital of Lebanon. Pop. 1,500,000 (1998 estimate).

be·jew·el /bi jŏŏ əl/ vt decorate with jewels —**be·jew·eled** adj

be·la·bor /bi láybər/ vt harp on

Be·la·rus /bèllə rōŏss/ country in E Europe. Cap. Minsk. Pop. 10,350,194 (2001).

be·lat·ed /bi láytid/ adj overdue —**be·lat·ed·ly** adv

be·lay /bi láy/ vti **1** fasten a line to a ship **2** secure a rope attached to a climber

belch vti **1** release stomach gas from the mouth noisily **2** send or come out visibly ○ *chimneys belching smoke* —**belch** n

be·lea·guer /bi lēĕgər/ vt **1** harass or pressurize **2** surround with an army —**be·lea·guer·ment** n

~~beleif~~ incorrect spelling of **belief**

~~beleive~~ incorrect spelling of **believe**

Be·lém /bə lém/ port and capital of Pará State, N Brazil. Pop. 1,144,312 (1996).

Bel·fast /bél fàst, bel fást/ capital of Northern Ireland. Pop. 297,300 (1996).

bel·fry /bélfree/ (pl -**fries**) n **1** the part of a church where bells are hung **2** a bell tower

---

ORIGIN Belfry originally had no connection with bells. The earliest forms had r not l, just like the French word from which the English derives, and meant "movable tower used as a siege engine." The phonetic change from r to l was reinforced by popular association with the word *bell*, which brought about the restriction in meaning to a bell tower or a space where bells are hung.

Bel·gian /bélj'n/ n somebody from Belgium ■ adj **1** of Belgium

Bel·gium /béljəm/ country in NW Europe, bordering the North Sea. Cap. Brussels. Pop. 10,258,762 (2001).

Bel·grade /bél gràyd/ capital of the Federal Republic of Yugoslavia. Pop. 1,594,483 (1998).

be·lie /bi lí/ (-**lied**, -**ly·ing**) vt **1** give a false impression of **2** show to be false

be·lief /bi lééf/ n **1** acceptance that something is true or real **2** confidence that something is good **3** something accepted as true **4** a firm opinion

be·lieve /bi léév/ (-**lieved**, -**liev·ing**) v **1** vt accept as true **2** vt accept as truthful ○ *I don't believe you.* **3** vi think that something exists ○ *believe in ghosts* **4** vi have faith in somebody or something ○ *You have to believe in yourself.* **5** vi have religious faith —**be·liev·a·ble** adj —**be·liev·er** n

~~belligerent~~ incorrect spelling of **belligerent**

be·lit·tle /bi lítt'l/ (-**tled**, -**tling**) vt make something seem less good or important ○ *I don't want to belittle her achievement.* —**be·lit·tle·ment** n

Be·lize /bə léėz/ country in Central America, on the Caribbean Sea. Cap. Belmopan. Pop. 256,062 (2001). —**Be·li·ze·an** n, adj

Be·lize Cit·y main port of Belize, on the Caribbean Sea. Pop. 53,915 (1997).

Bel·kic /bél klch/, **Beriz** (b. 1946) Bosniac representative of the presidency of Bosnia and Herzegovina (2001–) which rotates between a Serb, a Bosnian Muslim, and a Croat

bell n **1** an object or device that makes a ringing sound **2** something with the curved flared shape of a bell ◇ **ring a bell** evoke a vague memory (infml)

Bell, Alexander Graham (1847–1922) Scottish-born US inventor and educator. He made the first intelligible telephonic transmission (1876).

Bel·la Coo·la /bèllə kōōlə/ n a member of a Native North American people living in British Columbia

bel·la·don·na /bèllə dónnə/ n **1** a drug made from poisonous black berries **2** a bush with poisonous black berries

bell-bot·tom pants, bell-bot·toms npl pants with flared legs

belle /bel/ n a beautiful woman

belles-let·tres /bel léttrə/ n literature valued for elegance rather than content (+ sing or pl verb)

bell·hop /bél hòp/, **bell·boy** /-bòy/ n a hotel porter

bel·li·cose /bélli kòss/ adj warlike or ready to quarrel —**bel·li·cos·i·ty** /bèlli kóssətee/ n

bel·lig·er·ent /bə líjjərənt/ adj **1** hostile or aggressive **2** engaged in war ■ n a participant in a war —**bel·lig·er·ence** n —**bel·lig·er·ent·ly** adv

Bel·li·ni /bə léénee/ family of Italian painters including **Jacopo** (1400?–70?) and his sons **Gentile** (1429?–1507) and **Giovanni** (1430?–1516)

Bel·li·ni, Vincenzo (1801–35) Italian composer

bell jar n a bell-shaped glass cover for protecting or containing something

bel·low /béllō/ v **1** vi make the roaring sound of a bull **2** vti shout loudly —**bel·low** n

Bel·low /béllō/, **Saul** (b. 1915) Canadian-born US writer

bel·lows /béllōz/ (pl same) n a device with a compressible chamber for pumping air

bell pep·per n a sweet pepper

bel·ly /béllee/ n (pl -**lies**) **1** the abdomen **2** the stomach (infml) **3** a bulging part ■ vti (-**lied**, -**lies**) bulge ◇ **go** or **turn belly up** go bankrupt or fail

bel·ly·ache /béllee àyk/ (infml) n stomach ache ■ vi (-**ached**, -**ach·ing**) complain

bel·ly·but·ton /béllee bùtt'n/ n the navel (infml)

bel·ly dance n a dance using movements of

the hips and abdomen —**bel·ly danc·er** n —**bel·ly danc·ing** n

bel·ly flop n a dive in which the front of the body hits the water —**bel·ly-flop** vi

bel·ly·ful /béllee fool/ n an excess (infml) ○ I've had a bellyful of his complaining.

bel·ly laugh n a deep unrestrained laugh

Bel·mo·pan /bèlmō pán/ capital of Belize. Pop. 6,785 (1997).

Be·lo Ho·ri·zon·te /bèllō hàwri záwntee/ capital of Minas Gerais State, Brazil. Pop. 2,091,448 (1996).

be·long /bi láwng, -lóng/ vi 1 be somebody's property ○ The car belongs to her sister. 2 be a member or part of something ○ plants belonging to the daisy family 3 be in the right or usual place ○ Where does this chair belong?

be·long·ing /bi láwnging, -lóng-/ n the state of feeling comfortable or accepted in a place ■ **be·long·ings** npl personal possessions

be·lov·ed /bi lúvvid/ (predicatively) /-lúvd/ adj adored ■ n /bi lúvvid/ a loved person ○ a letter from his beloved

be·low /bi lō/ adv 1 under or beneath 2 further on in a text ■ prep, adv at or to a lower level, standard, or grade

belt n 1 a strip of leather or other material worn around the waist 2 a moving band of flexible material used in machinery ○ a fan belt 3 a seat belt or safety belt 4 a drink (slang) 5 an area associated with a particular industry, product, or characteristic ○ the heavy-industry belt 6 a strip of something different ■ vt 1 fasten with a belt 2 hit hard (infml) 3 hit with a belt ◇ **below the belt** unfair ◇ **have something under your belt** have done something that will benefit you in the future ◇ **tighten your belt** reduce your spending

□ **belt out** vt sing or play loudly (infml)

belt-tight·en·ing n a reduction in spending

belt·way /bélt wày/ n a highway skirting an urban area

be·lu·ga /bə loōgə/ (pl **-gas** or same) n 1 a large white sturgeon whose eggs are eaten as caviar 2 a white whale

bel·ve·dere /bélvi dèer/ n a building with a fine view

be·moan /bi mốn/ vt lament or complain about

be·mused /bi myoōzd/ adj bewildered —**be·mus·ed·ly** /-ədlee/ adv —**be·muse·ment** n

Be·na·res /bə naárəz, -eez/ former name for Varanasi

bench n 1 a long backless seat 2 a long worktable 3 a judge's seat in court 4 **Bench** a presiding judge or magistrate 5 **Bench** the judges of a court system 6 the office or position of a judge 7 a seat for sports officials or nonplaying team members, or the people occupying it 8 substitute players on a sports team ■ vt 1 remove a team

member from play 2 provide a place with benches

bench mark n a surveyor's reference marker

✦**bench·mark** /bénch maàrk/ n 1 a standard for measurement or assessment 2 a test of computer performance —**bench·mark** adj, vt

bend v (bent) 1 vti make or become curved or angled 2 vi stoop down 3 vti yield, or force to yield 4 vti change or cause to change direction 5 vt distort for somebody's benefit ○ bend the rules ■ n 1 a curve 2 an act of bending or being bent —**bend·a·ble** adj —**bend·y** adj

bend·er /béndər/ n a drinking spree (slang)

bends n decompression sickness (infml; + sing or pl verb)

be·neath /bi neeth/ prep underneath ○ beneath the bed ○ Beneath his veneer of politeness lay hostility. ■ prep, adv at a lower level ○ officials beneath Cabinet level ○ hills and the village beneath ■ prep too low in character for ○ Gossiping is beneath you.

Ben·e·dic·tine /bènni díktin, -tèen/ n a member of an order founded by St. Benedict of Nursia. —**Ben·e·dic·tine** adj

ben·e·dic·tion /bènni díksh'n/ n 1 an expression of approval 2 a prayer asking for God's blessing

Ben·e·dict of Nur·si·a /bènnədikt əv núrssee ə, -núrshə/, **St.** (480–547) Italian monk considered to be the founder of Western monastic tradition

ben·e·fac·tion /bènnə fáksh'n, bènnə fáksh'n/ n a good deed or charitable gift

ben·e·fac·tor /bènnə fàktər/ n a financial supporter

ben·e·fice /bénnəfiss/ n a church office providing a living through an endowment

be·nef·i·cent /bə néffissənt/ adj (fml) 1 doing good deeds 2 producing benefit —**be·nef·i·cence** n

ben·e·fi·cial /bènnə físh'l/ adj having a good effect —**ben·e·fi·cial·ly** adv

ben·e·fi·ci·ar·y /bènnə físhee èrree, -físhəree/ (pl **-ies**) n somebody who gives or receives a benefit

ben·e·fit /bénnəfit/ n 1 something good or advantageous 2 a payment made to a claimant or person needing assistance by a government, employer, or insurance company 3 a performance for charity ■ vti give or receive help, an advantage, or some other benefit ◇ **give somebody the benefit of the doubt** assume that somebody is innocent or truthful

Be·ne·lux /bénnə lùks/ n Belgium, the Netherlands, and Luxembourg

Be·nét /bi náy/, **Stephen Vincent** (1898–1943) US author and poet

be·nev·o·lent /bə névvələnt/ adj 1 kind 2 charitable —**be·nev·o·lence** n —**be·nev·o·lent·ly** adv

Ben·gal /ben gáwl, beng-/ former province of NE India, now divided into Bangladesh and the Indian state of Bangla —**Ben·ga·lese** /béng'leéz, bèng gǝl-/ n

Ben·gal, Bay of northeastern arm of the Indian Ocean between India, Myanmar, and the Malay peninsula

Ben·ga·li /ben gáwlee, beng-/ n 1 somebody from Bangladesh or Bangla 2 the language of Bangladesh or Bangla —**Ben·ga·li** adj

Ben·gha·zi /ben gáazee, beng-/, **Ben·ga·si** port in NE Libya. Pop. 804,000 (1995).

AKG London

David Ben-Gurion

Ben·Gur·i·on /ben goŏree ǝn/, **David** (1886–1973) Polish-born Israeli prime minister (1948–53, 1955–63)

~~beneficial~~ incorrect spelling of **beneficial**

~~benefit~~ incorrect spelling of **benefit**

be·night·ed /bi nítǝd/ adj unenlightened (fml) —**be·night·ed·ness** n

be·nign /bi nín/ adj 1 kindly 2 not malignant or life-threatening o a benign tumor 3 harmless 4 favorable —**be·nign·ly** adv

Be·nin /bǝ nín, be neén/ country in West Africa between Togo and Nigeria. Cap. Porto-Novo. Pop. 6,590,782 (2001). —**Be·nin·ese** /bènnǝ neéz/ adj, n

Ben·nett /bénnit/, **Richard Bedford, 1st Viscount** (1870–1947) prime minister of Canada (1930–35)

Ben Ne·vis /bèn néviss/ highest mountain in the British Isles, in W Scotland. Height 4,406 ft./1,343 m.

bent past tense, past participle of **bend** ■ adj 1 curved 2 determined o bent on revenge ■ n a natural inclination or talent ◊ See note at **talent**

Ben·tham /bénthǝm/, **Jeremy** (1748–1832) British philosopher, jurist, and social reformer

Ben·ton /béntǝn/, **Thomas Hart** (1889–1975) US artist

ben·zene /bén zèen, ben zeén/ n C_6H_6 a toxic liquid derived from petroleum. Use: manufacture of dyes, polymers, and industrial chemicals.

ben·zine /bén zèen, ben zeén/, **ben·zin** /bén zin/ n a mixture of liquids derived from crude oil. Use: industrial solvent.

be·queath /bi kweéth, -kweéth/ vt 1 leave something to somebody in a will 2 hand something down to posterity —**be·queath·al** n —**be·queath·ment** n

be·quest /bi kwést/ n 1 something bequeathed 2 the bequeathing of something

be·rate /bi ráyt/ (-rat·ed, -rat·ing) vt scold vigorously and at length

Ber·ber /búrbǝr/ (pl -bers or same) n 1 a member of a North African people 2 a group of languages spoken across North Africa, especially in Algeria and Morocco —**Ber·ber** adj

Berch·tes·ga·den /báirkhtǝss gaàd'n/ town in SE Bavaria, Germany, near the site of Adolf Hitler's fortified retreat. Pop. 7,966 (1997).

be·reaved /bi réevd/ adj deprived of a loved one by death ■ n (pl same) somebody bereaved —**be·reave** vt —**be·reave·ment** n

be·reft /bi réft/ adj 1 lacking or deprived of something o bereft of new ideas 2 feeling a sense of loss 3 bereaved

be·ret /bǝ ráy, bér rày/ n a flat round soft hat

Berg /bairg/, **Alban** (1885–1935) Austrian composer

Berg /burg/, **Paul** (b. 1926) US molecular biologist. He identified transfer RNA (1956).

Berg·man /búrgmǝn/, **Ingmar** (b. 1918) Swedish movie director

Berg·man, Ingrid (1915–82) Swedish-born US movie actor

Berg·son /búrgs'n/, **Henri** (1859–1941) French philosopher —**Berg·so·ni·an** /bùrg sőnee ǝn/ n, adj

ber·i·ber·i /bèrree bérree/ n a disease caused by thiamine deficiency

Ber·ing Sea /beéring-, bàir-/ arm of the North Pacific Ocean between the Aleutian Islands, Siberia, and Alaska. Depth 15,659 ft./4,773 m.

Be·ring Strait narrow stretch of sea between Russia and Alaska. At its narrowest point it is 51 mi./82 km wide.

Berke·ley /búrklee/ city in W California. Pop. 108,101 (1998).

ber·ke·li·um /bǝr keélee ǝm, búrklee-/ n (symbol **Bk**) a synthetic radioactive element.

ORIGIN **Berkelium** is named for Berkeley, California, where it was first made.

Berk·shire Hills /búrk sheer-/, **Berk·shires** /búrk sheèrz, -shǝrz/ forested mountains in W Massachusetts. Highest peak Mt. Greylock, 3,491 ft./1,064 m.

Ber·lin /bur lín/ capital of Germany. Pop. 3,472,009 (1997). —**Ber·lin·er** n

Ber·lin, Irving (1888–1989) Russian-born US songwriter

Ber·li·oz /báirlee òz, -òss/, **Hector** (1803–69) French composer

Ber·lus·co·ni /bàirloo skőnee/, **Silvio** (b. 1936) prime minister of Italy (1994, 2001–)

Ber·mu·da /bǝr myoŏdǝ/ group of islands in the W North Atlantic Ocean, a self-governing British dependency. Cap. Hamilton. Pop. 63,503 (2001). —**Ber·mu·dan** n, adj

Ber·mu·da shorts, Ber·mu·das /bər myŏŏdəz/ *npl* knee-length shorts

Bern /burn, bairn/, **Berne** capital of Switzerland. Pop. 123,254 (1998).

Ber·na·dette of Lourdes /bûrnə dét-/, **St.** (1844–79) French nun and visionary

Ber·ners-Lee /bûrnərz leé/, **Tim** (*b*. 1955) British computer scientist who designed and introduced the World Wide Web (1989)

Barnaby's

Sarah Bernhardt

Bern·hardt /búrn hàart/, **Sarah** (1844–1923) French actor

Ber·ni·ni /bər neénee, bair-/, **Gianlorenzo** (1598–1680) Italian sculptor and architect

Ber·noul·li /bər nóolee/ family of Swiss mathematicians including **Johann** or **Jean** (1667–1748), his brother **Jakob** (1654–1705), and his Dutch-born son **Daniel** (1700–82), who was also a physicist

Bern·stein /búrn stīn, -steén/, **Leonard** (1918–90) US conductor, composer, and pianist

ber·ry /bérree/ (*pl* **-ries**) *n* a small juicy or fleshy fruit

---

SPELLCHECK Do not confuse the spelling of **berry** and **bury** ("put in a hole"), which sound similar.

Ber·ry·man /bérreemən/, **John** (1914–72) US poet, writer, and critic

ber·serk /bər súrk, -zúrk/ *adj* extremely angry or violent ○ *She'll go berserk if she finds out.*

ORIGIN Berserk was originally a name for a Viking warrior who fought with unrestrained aggression. The word is Scandinavian, and probably literally means "bear shirt," either because these warriors wore bearskins or because they were fierce.

---

berth *n* **1** a bed on a ship or train **2** a place to moor a ship in dock **3** room to maneuver at sea **4** a parking place ■ *vti* dock or moor a ship

ber·yl /bérrəl/ *n* a mineral occurring in many colors. Use: gems.

be·ryl·li·um /bə rílleé əm/ *n* (*symbol* Be) a lightweight metallic chemical element. Use: alloys

Ber·ze·li·us /bər zeélee əss/, **Jöns Jakob, Baron** (1799–1848) Swedish chemist. He drew up the table of atomic weights.

be·seech /bi seéch/ (**-sought** /-sáwt/ or **-seeched**) *vt* (*literary*) **1** beg somebody to do something **2** beg for something —**be·seech·ing** *adj*

be·set /bi sét/ (**-set, -set·ting**) *vt* **1** harass or trouble continually ○ *was beset with fears* **2** attack on all sides (*fml*)

be·side /bi sīd/ *prep* **1** at the side of **2** compared with **3** in addition to

be·sides /bi sīdz/ *prep, adv* in addition to something or somebody ■ *adv* moreover

be·siege /bi seéj/ (**-sieged, -sieg·ing**) *vt* **1** surround with an army **2** crowd around **3** harass

be·smear /bi smeér/ *vt* smear with mud, dirt, or a greasy or sticky substance

be·smirch /bi smúrch/ *vt* **1** sully somebody's reputation **2** make something dirty (*literary*)

be·sot·ted /bi sóttəd/ *adj* infatuated

be·sought past tense, past participle of **beseech**

be·spat·ter /bi spáttər/ *vt* splash with mud, paint, or a dirty substance

be·speak /bi speék/ (**-spoke** /-spók/, **-spo·ken** /-spókən/) *vt* be a sign of (*fml*) ○ *actions that bespeak complicity*

best *adj* **1** better than all others ○ *the best player* ○ *the best solution* **2** most intimate ○ *my best friends* ■ *adv* **1** more than all others **2** most successfully ○ *It works best in cold weather.* ■ *n* **1** what is best ○ *want the best for their family* **2** somebody or something better than all others ○ *is the best at hockey* **3** the highest possible quality or standard ○ *do your best*

Best, Charles H. (1899–1978) US-born Canadian physiologist

bes·tial /béschəl, beés-/ *adj* inhuman or depraved ○ *bestial cruelty* —**bes·ti·al·i·ty** /bèschee ál/ətee, beés-/ *n*

be·stir /bi stúr/ (**-stirred, -stir·ring**) *vr* start doing something (*fml*) ○ *bestirred themselves*

best man *n* the bridegroom's attendant at a wedding

be·stow /bi stó/ *vt* give or present (*fml*) —**be·stow·al** *n* ◊ See note at **give**

be·stride /bi strīd/ (**-strode** /-stród/, **-strid·den** /-strídd'n/, **-strid·ing**) *vt* stand across with one foot on each side of something (*fml* or *literary*)

best·sell·er /bèst séllər/ *n* a product that is commercially very successful —**best·sell·ing** *adj*

bet *n* **1** an agreement, prediction, or challenge made in relation to a prediction **2** what somebody expects or thinks ○ *My bet is that they'll drop the idea.* **3** somebody or something likely to succeed ○ *a safe bet for the presidency* ■ *vti* (**bet** or **bet·ted, bet·ting**) **1** agree with somebody to give or receive something of value in predicting a result or making a challenge ○ *I bet you $10 you can't lift that rock.* **2** express certainty that something is true (*infml*) ○ *I bet he's forgotten.* —**bet·ting** *n*

⨍ **be·ta** /báytə, beétə/ *n* the 2nd letter of the Greek alphabet ■ *adj* **1** of electrons produced by splitting of neutrons during radioactive decay o *beta particles* o *beta rays* **2** describes software ready for beta tests o *beta version*

be·ta·block·er /n/ a drug regulating heart activity. Use: treatment of high blood pressure.

⚡ **be·ta test** /n/ a test of new computer software by customers —**be·ta-test** *vt*

⚡ **be·ta·ware** /báytə wàir, beétə-/ *n* software ready for beta tests

be·tel /beét'l/ (*pl* -**tels** *or same*) *n* the leaves of an Asian climbing plant chewed as a digestive aid

bete noire /bèt nwáar/ (*pl* **betes noires** /*pronunc. same*/), **bête noire** (*pl* **bêtes noires**) *n* somebody or something you particularly dislike

Beth·le·hem /béthlə hèm, -lee əm/ **1** town in the West Bank near Jerusalem, the traditional birthplace of King David and Jesus Christ. Part of Israel since 1967, it has been administered by the Palestinian Authority since 1995. Pop. 21,947 (1997). **2** city in E Pennsylvania. Pop. 69,383 (1998).

Corbis
Library of Congress

Mary McLeod Bethune

Be·thune /bə thoón, -thyoón/, **Mary McLeod** (1875–1955) US educator and activist

be·tide /bi tíd/ *vti* happen (*literary*)

be·to·ken /bi tókən/ *vt* be a sign of (*literary*)

be·tray /bi tráy/ *vt* **1** harm a person or country by helping or giving information to an enemy **2** reveal an emotion or quality, often unintentionally —**be·tray·al** *n*

be·troth·al /bi tróthəl, -tráwthəl/ *n* engagement to marry somebody (*fml*)

be·trothed /bi tróthd, -tráwtht/ (*pl* -**trotheds** *or same*) *n* the person somebody is engaged to marry (*fml*) —**be·trothed** *adj*

Bet·tel·heim /bétt'l hìm/, **Bruno** (1903–90) Austrian-born US psychologist

bet·ter /béttər/ *adj* **1** more pleasing or acceptable than others of the same class, set, or kind **2** of higher quality or greater usefulness than others **3** improved in health ■ *adv* **1** to a greater degree or higher standard than others or than before **2** preferably ◊ *Such things are better left unsaid.* ■ *vt* **1** surpass **2** improve (*fml*) ■ *n* a superior person (*often pl*) ◊ **get the better of** defeat ◊ **go˙ one better** surpass something or somebody ◊ **had better** ought to

bet·ter·ment /béttərmənt/ *n* improvement, especially affecting somebody's financial or social standing (*fml*)

be·tween /bi tweén/ *prep*, *adv* in an intermediate position with respect to somebody or something o *between the wars* o *houses with fields between* ■ *prep* **1** to and from o *traveling between Seattle and San Francisco* **2** by the joint action of o *We managed to solve it between us.* **3** indicates comparison, choice, or relationship o *the difference between them* o *arguing between themselves* **4** by or to each in a group ◊ **(just) between you and me, (just) between ourselves** in confidence

be·twixt /bi twíkst/ *adv*, *prep* between (*literary*)

~~beutiful~~ incorrect spelling of **beautiful**

bev·el /bév'l/ *n* **1** a slanting edge **2** a tool used to mark or measure angles ■ *vt* make a slanting edge on o *a mirror with edges that had been beveled*

bev·er·age /bévvərij, bévvrij/ *n* a drink other than water

bev·y /bévvee/ (*pl* -**ies**) *n* a group of people or animals

be·wail /bi wáyl/ *vt* lament (*fml*)

be·ware /bi wáir/ *vti* be on guard against somebody or something (*only as a command and in the infinitive*)

be·whis·kered /bi wískərd/ *adj* with whiskers or a beard

be·wil·der /bi wíldər/ *vt* confuse —**be·wil·der·ment** *n*

be·witch /bi wich/ *vt* **1** enchant or captivate o *was bewitched by his charm* **2** cast a magic spell on —**be·witch·ing** *adj* —**be·witch·ment** *n*

be·yond /bee ónd, bi yónd/ *prep*, *adv* on the other side of something ■ *prep* **1** past o *lived beyond their means* **2** except o *no information beyond what we know* ■ *prep*, *adv* after a particular time o *in the next decade and beyond* ■ *prep* impossible for o *tasks that are beyond them*

Be·zos /báyzōwss/, **Jeff** (*b.* 1964) US Internet entrepreneur

BG, B.G. *abbr* Brigadier General

Bha·dra·pa·da /baádrə paádə/, **Bha·dra** *n* the 6th month of the year in the Hindu calendar

bhang /bang/, **bang** *n* cannabis

Bho·pal /bō paál/ capital of Madhya Pradesh State, India. Pop. 1,062,771 (1991).

Bhu·tan /boo tán, -taán/ country in the eastern part of the Himalayan range between India and the Tibet region of China. Cap. Thimphu. Pop. 2,049,412 (2001). —**Bhu·tan·ese** /bóotə neéz/ *n*, *adj*

Bhut·to /bóotō/, **Benazir** (*b.* 1953) prime minister of Pakistan (1988–90, 1993–96)

bi /bī/ *adj* bisexual (*slang*)

Bi *symbol* bismuth

bi- *prefix* two, twice, both ○ *bisexual* ◊ See note at **buy**

Bi·a·fra /bee áffrə, -áəfrə/ region of E Nigeria that was declared a secessionist state between 1967 and 1970 —**Bi·a·fran** *n*, *adj*

bi·an·nu·al /bī ánnyoo əl/ *adj* twice-yearly ◊ See note at **biweekly**

USAGE **biannual** or **biennial**? **Biannual** means "twice a year," whereas **biennial** means "every two years." To avoid confusion use the expressions *twice-yearly* and *two-yearly*.

bi·as /bī əss/ *n* (*pl* **-as·es** *or* **-as·ses**) 1 an unfair preference 2 a diagonal line across the weave of a fabric ○ *a fabric cut on the bias* ■ *vt* (**-ased** *or* **-assed, -as·ing** *or* **-as·sing, -as·es** *or* **-as·ses**) cause to have a bias ■ *adj* diagonal —**bi·ased** *adj*

bi·ath·lon /bī áthlən, -lòn/ *n* a competition that combines cross-country skiing with rifle shooting at targets along the course —**bi·ath·lete** *n*

bib *n* a piece of material protecting a child's clothing under the chin

Bi·ble /bīb'l/ *n* 1 the Christian holy book 2 the Jewish holy book 3 *also* **bí·ble** an authoritative or essential book on a subject

ORIGIN **Bible** comes from a Greek word that means simply "book" and was originally a diminutive of the word for "papyrus, scroll." It reached English through ecclesiastical Latin and French.

bib·li·cal /bíbblik'l/, **Bib·li·cal** *adj* of or like the Bible —**bib·li·cal·ly** *adv*

bib·li·og·ra·phy /bìbblee óggrəfee/ (*pl* **-phies**) *n* 1 a list of books or articles used as sources 2 a list of publications by a particular author, on a particular subject, or issued by a particular publisher 3 the history, classification, or description of books —**bib·li·og·ra·pher** *n* —**bib·li·o·graph·ic** /bìbblee ə gráffik/ *adj* —**bib·li·o·graph·i·cal** *adj*

bib·li·o·phile /bíbblee ə fīl/ *n* a collector of books

bib·u·lous /bíbbyələss/ *adj* tending to drink too much alcohol (*fml*)

bi·cam·er·al /bī kámmərəl/ *adj* with two legislative chambers

bi·cen·ten·ni·al /bì sen ténnee əl/, **bi·cen·ten·a·ry** /bī sen ténnəree, bī séntənèrree/ (*pl* **-ries**) *n* a 200th anniversary —**bi·cen·ten·ni·al** *adj*

bi·ceps /bí sèps/ (*pl same or* **-ceps·es**) *n* a large muscle of the upper arm

bick·er /bíkər/ *vi* argue about something unimportant

bi·coas·tal /bī kóst'l/ *adj* of two coasts, especially the East and West coasts of North America ■ *n* an East-West coast resident or traveler

bi·cus·pid /bī kúspid/ *adj* with two points ■ *n* a premolar tooth

bi·cy·cle /bī sík'l, -sìk'l/ *n* a two-wheeled vehicle moved by pedaling ■ *vi* (**-cled, -cling**) ride a bicycle —**bi·cy·clist** *n*

bid *v* (**bade** /bad, bayd/ *or* **bid, bid·den** /bídd'n/ *or* **bade, bid·ding**) 1 (*past and past participle* **bid**) *vti* offer money for something at an auction 2 (*past and past participle* **bid**) *vi* offer to do work for a specific price ○ *bidding for the contract* 3 *vt* say something to somebody ○ *bade her farewell* ■ *n* 1 an amount of money or a price offered 2 an attempt 3 in cards, a statement of the number of tricks to be taken —**bid·der** *n*

bid·da·ble /bíddəb'l/ *adj* obedient

bid·ding /bídding/ *n* 1 the making of bids 2 somebody's orders ○ *They were eager to do our bidding.*

bide (**bode** *or* **bid·ed, bid·ed, bid·ing**) *vi* stay or remain (*archaic*)

bi·det /bee dáy/ *n* a low basin for washing the genital and anal areas

bi·en·ni·al /bī énnee əl/ *adj* 1 happening every two years 2 describes a plant that flowers in its second year —**bi·en·ni·al** *n* —**bi·en·ni·al·ly** *adv* ◊ See note at **biannual**

bier /beer/ *n* 1 a stand for a casket 2 a frame for carrying a coffin (*literary*) ◊ See note at **beer**

Bierce /beerss/, **Ambrose** (1842–1914?) US writer

bi·fo·cal /bī fók'l, bí fòk'l/ *adj* describes lenses with two focal lengths ■ **bi·fo·cals** *npl* a pair of glasses with bifocal lenses

bi·fur·cate /bīfər kàyt, bī fúr-/ (**-cat·ed, -cat·ing**) *vti* divide or branch into two parts —**bi·fur·ca·tion** /bìfər káysh'n/ *n*

big *adj* (**big·ger, big·gest**) 1 of great size 2 powerful 3 significant 4 older ○ *my big sister* 5 magnanimous ○ *She's a woman with a big heart.* 6 unrealistically ambitious ○ *big ideas* ■ *adv* 1 ambitiously ○ *think big* 2 successfully (*infml*) ○ *went over big at the convention* —**big·ness** *n* ◊ **make it big** be extremely successful (*infml*)

big·a·my /bíggəmee/ *n* the crime of being simultaneously married to two people —**big·a·mist** *n* —**big·a·mous** *adj*

Big Ap·ple *n* New York City (*infml*)

big bang *n* the explosion that is said to have started the universe

Big Broth·er *n* an authority exerting dictatorial control and maintaining a constant watch

ORIGIN The original **Big Brother** featured in George Orwell's novel *Nineteen Eighty-Four* (1949).

big busi·ness *n* large commercial organizations collectively

big cat *n* a large member of the cat family

Big Dip·per *n* a group of stars in the constellation Ursa Major

~~biger~~ incorrect spelling of **bigger**

Big·foot /bíg fŏot/, **big·foot** *n* a legendary humanoid creature of NW North America

big game *n* large animals hunted for sport

big gov·ern·ment *n* an interventionist style of government

big-head·ed /big héddəd/ *adj* conceited *(infml)*

big-heart·ed *adj* kind and generous —**big-heart·ed·ly** *adv* —**big-heart·ed·ness** *n*

Big·horn Moun·tains /bíg hawrn-/ mountain range in N Wyoming and S Montana. Highest peak Cloud Peak, 13,187 ft./4,019 m.

bight /bīt/ *n* **1** a curve of the coastline forming a wide bay **2** a loop in a rope

big-mouth /bíg mòwth/ *(pl* -**mouths** /-mòwths, -mówth z/) *n* a person regarded as indiscreet or boastful *(infml)*

big name *n* somebody or something famous —**big-name** *adj*

big·ot /bíggət/ *n* a person regarded as intolerant, opinionated, and, typically, racist —**big·ot·ed** *adj* —**big·ot·ry** *n*

big screen *n* the movies

big shot *n* an important person *(infml)*

Big Sur /-súr/ coastal region of W California

big-tick·et *adj* expensive *(infml)*

big time *(slang) n* the highest level of success in a profession or other activity ■ *adv* on a grand scale or at the highest level —**big tim·er** *n*

big top *n* **1** a circus tent **2** the circus

big-wig /bíg wìg/ *n* an important person *(slang)*

bi·jou /beé zhoò/ *(pl* -**jous** /-zhoòz/ *or* -**joux** /-zhoò/) *n* a delicate jewel or ornament

bike *(infml) n* a bicycle or motorcycle ■ *vi* (**biked, bik·ing**) go by bike

bik·er /bíkər/ *n* a motorcyclist or bicycle rider

bi·ki·ni /bi keénee/ *n* a woman's two-piece bathing suit

ORIGIN The **bikini** appeared on beaches not long after the United States had tested an atomic bomb on Bikini in 1946. The impact of the swimwear was presumably considered to be equally explosive.

Bi·ki·ni /bə keénee/ atoll consisting of 36 islets in the Marshall Islands, W Pacific Ocean, used as a nuclear testing site by the United States between 1946 and 1958

bi·lat·er·al /bī láttərəl/ *adj* involving two groups of people **2** of or on both sides ○ *bilateral symmetry* —**bi·lat·er·al·ly** *adv*

Bil·ba·o /bil baà ò, -bów/ port in N Spain. Pop. 358,467 (1998).

bile *n* **1** digestive fluid produced in the liver and stored in the gallbladder **2** feelings of bitterness and irritability *(literary)*

bilge *n* **1** the lower part of a boat's hull, or the area inside it **2** dirty water that collects in the bilge **3** nonsense *(infml)*

bi·lin·gual /bī líng gwəl, -gyoò əl/ *adj* **1** speaking two languages **2** in two languages

bil·ious /bíllyəss/ *adj* **1** nauseated **2** nauseatingly unpleasant **3** bad-tempered or irritable —**bil·ious·ly** *adv* —**bil·ious·ness** *n*

bilk *vt* cheat or defraud *(infml)*

bill[1] *n* **1** a statement of money owed **2** an amount to be paid **3** a legislative proposal **4** an advertising poster **5** a list of items, especially a program of entertainment **6** a piece of paper money ■ *vt* **1** send a request for payment to **2** advertise —**bill·a·ble** *adj* ◊ **fill** *or* **fit the bill** be appropriate for a specific purpose

bill[2] *n* **1** a bird's beak **2** the mouthparts of an animal such as a platypus, which resemble a beak

bill·board /bíl bàwrd/ *n* a large board, typically along a highway, for displaying advertisements

bil·let /bíllit/ *n* temporary accommodations for members of the armed forces ■ *v* **1** *vti* assign to or have temporary accommodations **2** *vt* provide temporary accommodations for

bill·fold /bíl fòld/ *n* a wallet

bill·hook /bíl hŏok/ *n* a tool with a broad curved blade. Use: pruning branches off trees.

bil·liards /bíllyərdz/ *n* a game that involves hitting balls on a table with a cue (+ *sing verb*)

bill·ing /bílling/ *n* a position on an entertainment program or advertisement ○ *top billing*

Bil·lings /bíllingz/ city in S Montana. Pop. 91,750 (1998).

bil·lion /bíllyən/ *(pl* -**lions** *or same) n* one thousand million —**bil·lionth** *n*, *adj*

bil·lion·aire /bíllyə naír/ *n* somebody who has money and property worth more than a billion dollars

bill of ex·change *n* a written instruction to pay a sum of money

bill of fare *n* a menu

bill of rights *n* **1** a list of human rights guaranteed by law **2 Bill of Rights** the first ten amendments to the US Constitution

bil·low /bíllō/ *v* **1** *vti* swell or fill with air ○ *billowing sails* **2** *vi* flow in a curling mass ○ *smoke that billowed from the room* —**bil·low** *n* —**bil·low·y** *adj*

bil·ly club /bíllee-/, **bil·ly** *n* a nightstick

bil·ly goat /bíllee-/, **bil·ly** *n* a male goat

Bil·ly the Kid /bíllee-/ (1859–81) US outlaw

bi·me·tal·lic /bī mə tállik/ *adj* made up of two metals

bi·month·ly /bī múnthlee/ *adj* **1** happening or issued every two months **2** happening or issued twice a month ■ *n* *(pl* -**lies**) a bimonthly publication —**bi·month·ly** *adv* ◊ See note at **biweekly**

bin *n* **1** a large storage container **2** a set of shelves for storing wine

bi·na·ry /bínaree/ *adj* 1 consisting of two parts or elements 2 describes a number system with two rather than ten as its base ○ *binary notation*

⚡ **bi·na·ry code** *n* a computer code using the binary number system

⚡ **bi·na·ry cod·ed dec·i·mal** *n* a system using binary numbers for decimals

⚡ **bi·na·ry dig·it** *n* either of the digits 0 and 1

⚡ **bi·na·ry file** *n* a computer file containing characters that only a computer can read

bi·na·ry star *n* a pair of stars with mutual gravitational attraction

bind /bīnd/ *v* (**bound** /bownd/, **bound**) 1 *vt* fasten something firmly to something else by winding a cord around both 2 *vt* wrap a bandage, tape, or cord around something, especially for protection 3 *vt* tie somebody's hands or feet together 4 *vt* protect or decorate the edge of fabric with tape, ribbon, or stitching 5 *vti* cause feelings of loyalty or closeness between people 6 *vt* oblige somebody to do something 7 *vt* fix the pages and cover of a book together, or cause surfaces to stick together ■ *n* something annoying or inconvenient (*infml*) ◊ **in a bind** in a difficult or unpleasant situation

bind·er /bíndər/ *n* 1 a hard cover for holding loose papers or magazines 2 a person or machine that binds something

bind·er·y /bíndəree/ (*pl* -ies) *n* a bookbinding workshop

bind·ing /bínding/ *n* 1 a book cover 2 something holding a book's pages together 3 tape used to bind the edge of fabric 4 a ski fastening ■ *adj* obliging somebody to do something ○ *a binding agreement*

bind·weed /bínd weed/ *n* a weed with twining stems

binge *n* 1 a heavy drinking or eating session 2 a session of self-indulgent activity ■ *vi* (**binged**, **binge·ing** or **bing·ing**) eat or drink too much

Bing·ham /bíngəm/, **George Caleb** (1811–79) US artist

bin·go /bíng gō/ *n* a lottery game played with numbered cards ■ *interj* 1 indicates a win in bingo 2 expresses triumph at success

Bin La·den /bin laádən/, **Osama** (b. 1957) Saudi-born leader of the militant Islamic al-Qaeda organization

bin·na·cle /bínnəkəl/ *n* a housing for a ship's compass

bin·oc·u·lar /bə nókyələr, bī-/ *adj* of or using both eyes

bin·oc·u·lars /bə nókyələrz, bī-/ *npl* a pair of small telescopes linked by one focusing device

bi·no·mi·al /bī nómee əl/ *n* 1 a mathematical expression with two terms 2 a two-part name for an organism, giving its genus and species —**bi·no·mi·al** *adj*

bi·o /bī ō/ (*pl* -os) *n* a biography (*infml*)

bio- *prefix* 1 life, biology ○ *biography* ○ *biochemistry* 2 biological warfare ○ *bioweapon* 3 involving the use of biological or chemical weapons ○ *bioterrorism*

bi·o·chem·is·try /bī ō kémmistree/ *n* 1 the chemistry of living organisms 2 the chemical nature of an organism or system —**bi·o·chem·i·cal** *adj* —**bi·o·chem·ist** *n*

⚡ **bi·o·com·put·er** /bī ō kəm pyootər/ *n* a very fast computer whose calculations are made using biological processes

bi·o·de·grad·a·ble /bī ō di gráydəb'l/ *adj* able to decompose naturally —**bi·o·de·gra·da·tion** /bī ō dèggrə dáysh'n/ *n* —**bi·o·de·grade** *vti*

bi·o·di·ver·si·ty /bī ō dī vúrssətee/ *n* the range of organisms present in an environment

bi·o·eth·ics /bī ō éthiks/ *n* the ethics of medical research and treatment (+ *sing verb*) —**bi·o·eth·i·cal** *adj* —**bi·o·eth·i·cist** *n*

bi·o·gas /bī ō gàs/ *n* a mixture of carbon dioxide and methane. Use: fuel.

bi·og·ra·phy /bī óggrəfee, bee-/ (*pl* -phies) *n* 1 an account of somebody's life 2 biographies in general —**bi·o·graph·er** *n* —**bi·o·graph·i·cal** /bī ə gráffik'l/ *adj*

bi·o·haz·ard /bī ō hàzzərd/ *n* a toxic or infectious agent, or the potential harm such an agent can do to an organism —**bi·o·haz·ard·ous** /bī ō házzərdəss/ *adj*

bi·o·log·i·cal /bī ə lójjik'l/ *adj* 1 of living things 2 of biology 3 genetically related ○ *her biological parents* —**bi·o·log·i·cal·ly** *adv*

bi·o·log·i·cal clock *n* the set of mechanisms that link physiological processes with periodic cycles or with stages of development and aging

bi·o·log·i·cal con·trol *n* pest control by introducing predators

bi·o·log·i·cal war·fare *n* the use of microorganisms to cause disease or death in war

bi·ol·o·gy /bī ólləjee/ *n* 1 the science of life 2 the life forms found in a particular place —**bi·ol·o·gist** *n*

bi·o·mass /bī ō màss/ *n* plant and animal material used as fuel

bi·o·med·i·cine /bī ō méddəssin/ *n* biological science applied to medicine —**bi·o·med·i·cal** /bī ō méddik'l/ *adj*

bi·on·ic /bī ónnik/ *adj* 1 of or having electronically operated replacement body parts 2 of bionics

bi·on·ics /bī ónniks/ *n* (+ *sing verb*) 1 the application of biological information to machine design 2 the use of bionic body parts

bi·o·phys·ics /bī ō fízziks/ *n* the application of physics to biological studies (+ *sing verb*) —**bi·o·phys·i·cal** *adj* —**bi·o·phys·i·cist** *n*

bi·op·sy /bī ópsee/ (*pl* -sies) *n* the removal of living tissue for examination

bi·o·re·me·di·a·tion /bǐ ō ri mèèdee áysh'n/ *n* the use of biological agents such as bacteria to clean up contaminated land

bi·o·rhythm /bǐ ō ríthəm/ *n* a natural cyclical physiological change *(often pl)* —**bi·o·rhyth·mic** /bǐ ō ríthmik/ *adj*

⚡**BIOS** /bǐ òss/ *abbr* basic input-output system

bi·o·sat·el·lite /bǐ ō sàtt'l īt/ *n* a satellite that can be lived in

bi·o·sci·ence /bǐ ō sī ənss/ *n* a science that studies living organisms

bi·o·sphere /bǐ ō sfèer/ *n* the whole area of the Earth's surface, atmosphere, and sea that is inhabited by living organisms

bi·o·tech /bǐ ō tèk/ *n* biotechnology *(infml)*

bi·o·tech·nol·o·gy /bǐ ō tek nóllǝjee/ *n* the use of biological processes in industrial production —**bi·o·tech·no·log·i·cal** /bǐ ō teknə lójjik'l/ *adj*—**bi·o·tech·nol·o·gist** *n*

bi·o·ter·ror·ism /bǐ ō térrə rìzzəm/, **bi·o·ter·ror** /bǐ ō tèrrər/ *n* terrorist acts involving the use of biological or chemical weapons —**bi·o·ter·ror·ist** *adj, n*

bio·threat /bǐ ō thrèt/ *n* a real or perceived threat of the use of biological or chemical weapons

bi·o·tin /bǐ ətin/ *n* a B vitamin found in egg yolk and liver

bio·weap·on /bǐ ō wèppən/ *n* a biological or chemical weapon

bi·par·ti·san /bī paártiz'n, -tiss'n/ *adj* involving two political parties —**bi·par·ti·san·ism** *n*

bi·par·tite /bī paár tìt/ *adj* involving two groups of people

bi·ped /bǐ pèd/ *n* a two-legged animal

bi·plane /bǐ plàyn/ *n* an airplane with two sets of wings, one above the other

bi·po·lar /bī pṓlər/ *adj* 1 of or having two poles 2 having two opposite opinions, attitudes, or natures —**bi·po·lar·i·ty** /bī pō lárrətee/ *n*

bi·po·lar dis·or·der *n* a psychiatric disorder characterized by extreme mood swings

birch /n 1 a tall tree with light colored peeling bark 2 the wood of a birch tree

bird *n* 1 a two-legged feathered winged animal 2 a person of a particular type *(slang)* ○ *He's a wise old bird.* —**bird-like** *adj*

ORIGIN Originally *bird* was applied only to a young bird or nestling. The general word was *fowl*, and this use continued alongside *bird* long after the latter word had lost its restriction. *Fowl* is ultimately from the same ancient root as the verb *fly*, and related forms appear in other languages, but *bird* is unique to English and its origins are completely unknown.

bird·bath /búrd bàth/ *(pl* **-baths** /-bàthz/) *n* a shallow basin for garden birds to bathe in

bird·brain /búrd bràyn/ *n* a person regarded as unintelligent *(infml insult)* —**bird·brained** *adj*

bird dog *n* a hunting dog

bird·er /búrdər/ *n* a birdwatcher

bird·ie /búrdee/ *n* 1 a golf score of one under par 2 a shuttlecock

bird of par·a·dise *n* a plant with flowers like a bird's crested head

bird of pas·sage *n* a migratory bird

bird of prey *n* a bird that kills for food

bird's-eye view *n* 1 a view from high up 2 a general impression

bird·song /búrd sòng/ *n* the sounds made by birds

bird·watch·er /búrd wòchər/ *n* somebody who watches birds as a hobby —**bird·watch·ing** *n*

bi·ret·ta /bə réttə/ *n* a cleric's stiff hat

Bir·ming·ham /búrming hàm, -əm/ 1 largest city in Alabama. Pop. 252,997 (1998). 2 city and industrial center in central England. Pop. 1,020,589 (1996).

birr /beer/ *n* the main unit of Ethiopian currency

birth *n* 1 the time, event, or process of being born or begun 2 somebody's social or national heritage ○ *of noble birth* ■ *adj* biologically related as a parent ○ *his birth mother* ■ *vt Can, Southern US* have or deliver a baby ◊ **give birth** produce a child or young from the womb

birth ca·nal *n* the passageway including the cervix and vagina through which a fetus emerges from the womb

birth cer·tif·i·cate *n* a document recording somebody's birth

birth con·trol *n* the deliberate prevention of pregnancy

birth·day /búrth dày, -dee/ *n* 1 the anniversary of the day of somebody's birth 2 the day of somebody's birth

birth·ing /búrthing/ *n* the process of giving birth ■ *adj* facilitating childbirth

birth·mark /búrth màark/ *n* a permanent blemish on the skin, present from birth

birth pang *n* a contraction of the womb before childbirth ■ **birth pangs** *npl* initial difficulties

birth·place /búrth plàyss/ *n* the place where somebody was born or where something originated

birth·rate /búrth ràyt/ *n* the number of children born per year ○ *a declining birthrate*

birth·right /búrth rìt/ *n* 1 a basic entitlement 2 property or money somebody expects to inherit

birth·stone /búrth stòn/ *n* a stone popularly associated with the month in which somebody was born

Bis·cay, Bay of /bís kày/ arm of the North Atlantic Ocean between W France and N Spain

Bis·cayne Bay /bis káyn, bís kàyn-/ inlet of the Atlantic Ocean in S Florida. Length 40 mi./60 km.

bis·cuit /bískit/ n 1 a small round piece of baked bread 2 unglazed pottery

bise /beez/ n a northerly wind that blows in Switzerland and neighboring parts of Italy and France

bi·sect /bī́ sèkt, bī sékt/ vt 1 split into two 2 halve —**bi·sec·tion** /bī́ séksh'n/ n

bi·sex·u·al /bī́ sékshoo əl, -sékshəl/ adj 1 attracted to both sexes 2 having both male and female characteristics —**bi·sex·u·al** n —**bi·sex·u·al·i·ty** /bī́ sekshoo álltee/ n —**bi·sex·u·al·ly** adv

Bish·kek /bish kék/ capital of Kyrgyzstan. Pop. 585,800 (1996).

bish·op /bíshəp/ n 1 a senior Christian cleric 2 a chess piece that moves diagonally

ORIGIN The Greek word from which *bishop* derives meant "overseer," and had no particular religious connection. It later developed the more specific sense of "church official," which was adopted into ecclesiastical Latin. The Greek form is the direct ancestor of *episcopal* and similar words. The initial *b* in *bishop* comes from a popular Latin variant that had lost the *e-*.

bish·op·ric /bíshəprik/ n 1 a bishop's diocese 2 the rank of a bishop

Bis·marck /bíz màark/ capital of North Dakota. Pop. 54,040 (1998).

Bis·marck, Otto Edward Leopold von, Prince (1815–98) chancellor of the new German Empire (1871–90)

Bis·marck Ar·chi·pel·a·go island group in the W Pacific Ocean, part of Papua New Guinea

Bis·marck Sea arm of the SW Pacific Ocean northeast of New Guinea

bis·muth /bízməth/ n (symbol Bi) a metallic chemical element. Use: alloys, medicines.

bi·son /bíss'n/ n (pl same) a large humped animal resembling an ox

bisque /bisk/ n shellfish soup

Bis·sau /bi sów/ capital and main port of Guinea-Bissau. Pop. 233,000 (1995).

bis·tro /beéstrō, bís-/ n (pl -tros) n a small informal restaurant

bit[1] n 1 a piece or part ◇ *bits of paper* 2 a short time ◇ *wait a bit* ◇ **a bit** somewhat (infml) ◇ **bit by bit** gradually ◇ **bits and pieces** miscellaneous small objects (infml) ◇ **do your bit** contribute your share of work ◇ **every bit** in every way

bit[2] n 1 the mouthpiece of a horse's bridle 2 a detachable cutting part of a drill

⚡ **bit**[3] n 1 a digit in binary notation 2 the smallest unit of information that can be stored in a computer

ORIGIN Bit here is a blend of *binary* and *digit*.

bit[4] past tense, past participle of **bite**

bitch n 1 a female dog 2 a taboo term for a woman regarded as spiteful or bad-tempered (taboo offensive) 3 a complaint (slang; often offensive) 4 something difficult (slang; often offensive) ■ vi complain continually (often offensive)

bitch·y /bíchee/ (-i·er, -i·est) adj malicious or unpleasant in speech or actions (slang; often offensive) —**bitch·i·ly** adv —**bitch·i·ness** n

bite v (bit, bit·ten /bítt'n/ or bit, bit·ing) 1 vti grip or cut something with the teeth 2 vt injure with the fangs or mouthparts 3 vti make firm contact with something 4 vi corrode something ◇ *The acid bites into the metal.* 5 vi take or rise to bait ◇ *no fish biting today* ■ n 1 an act of biting 2 a mouthful 3 an injury produced by biting 4 a pleasantly sharp taste

bit·ing /bíting/ adj 1 very cold 2 cleverly sarcastic —**bit·ing·ly** adv

⚡ **bit map** n a computer image represented as a pattern of dots corresponding to pixels

⚡ **bit-map** (bit-mapped, bit-map·ping) vt represent as a bit map ◇ *a bit-mapped font*

⚡ **bit stream** n a simple unstructured sequence of bits transmitting data

bit·ten past participle of **bite**

bit·ter /bíttər/ adj 1 strong and sharp in taste 2 angry and resentful 3 difficult to accept ◇ *a bitter blow* 4 extremely hostile ◇ *bitter enemies* 5 very cold —**bit·ter·ly** adv —**bit·ter·ness** n

bit·ter end n the very end, however unpleasant ◇ *They held out to the bitter end.*

bit·tern /bíttərn/ n a wading bird with a booming call

bit·ter pill n something unavoidable and unpleasant

bit·ters /bíttərz/ n a flavored alcoholic ingredient in some cocktails (+ sing verb)

bit·ter·sweet /bíttər swèet/ adj 1 both bitter and sweet in taste 2 both happy and sad ■ n 1 a climbing plant with orange capsules and red seeds 2 a poisonous flowering plant

bi·tu·men /bi toóman, -tyoóman, bī́-/ n a road-surfacing material —**bi·tu·mi·nous** adj

~~biulding~~ incorrect spelling of **building**

bi·valve /bī́ vàlv/ n a mollusk with a hinged shell

biv·ou·ac /bívvoo àk, bív wàk/ n 1 a military or mountaineering camp 2 a brief overnight stay ■ vi (-acked, -ack·ing) make a simple temporary camp

bi·week·ly /bī́ weéklee/ adj 1 happening or issued every two weeks 2 happening or issued twice a week ■ n (pl -lies) a biweekly publication —**bi·week·ly** adv

USAGE Confusion is caused by the fact that **biweekly** and **bimonthly** can mean either "once every two weeks or months" or "twice a week or month." To avoid possible confusion, reword the sentence: *The talks are held twice a week at the local school. The talks are held every two weeks at the local school.*

⚡biz *abbr* business *(in Internet addresses)*

~~bizare~~ incorrect spelling of **bizarre**

bi·zarre /bi zaár/ *adj* grotesquely odd —**bi·zarre·ly** *adv* —**bi·zarre·ness** *n*

Bi·zet /bee záy/, **Georges** (1838–75) French composer

Bk *symbol* berkelium

blab (**blabbed, blab·bing**) *vi* (*infml*) **1** tell secrets **2** chatter

blab·ber /blábbər/ *vi* chatter incoherently about something ■ *n* **1** somebody who cannot keep a secret **2** chatter

blab·ber·mouth /blábbər mòwth/ (*pl* **-mouths** /-mòwthz/) *n* somebody who cannot keep a secret (*infml*)

black *adj* **1** of the color of coal **2** without any light **3** *also* **Black** dark-skinned **4** *also* **Black** of African American people **5** served without milk o *black coffee* **6** funny and macabre o *black humor* **7** hopeless o *The future is looking black.* **8** dirty **9** very bad or unfortunate o *a black day for the industry* **10** evil ■ *n* **1** the color of coal **2** *also* **Black** an African American person **3** total darkness **4** a black object or area, e.g., part of a roulette wheel ■ *vt* **1** make something black **2** use black polish on footwear **3** bruise somebody's eye —**black·ly** *adv* —**black·ness** *n* ◇ **in the black** not in debt

USAGE Black is the standard term for a dark-skinned person of African origin or descent. However, many Americans of African descent prefer the more formal term *African American*, used both as noun and adjective. See also **African American**.

□ **black out** *v* **1** *vi* lose consciousness **2** *vt* cause a place to lose its electrical supply

Black, Shirley Temple (*b.* 1928) US actor and ambassador

black-and-blue *adj* bruised

black-and-white *adj* **1** representing or re-producing images not in color **2** clear-cut and straightforward

black·ball /blák bàwl/ *vt* **1** prevent from be-coming a member **2** exclude or ostracize ■ *n* a vote against somebody wanting to become a member

black bean *n* **1** a small dried black seed used in cooking **2** a fermented soybean

black bear *n* **1** a bear that lives in North American forests **2** an Asian bear with black or dark brown fur marked with white

black belt *n* somebody who has achieved the highest level of skill in a martial art, or the belt symbolizing this achievement

black·ber·ry /blák bèrree/ (*pl* **-ries**) *n* **1** a small purple fruit composed of a cluster of parts **2** a thorny bush that produces blackberries

black·bird /blák bùrd/ *n* a common bird with predominantly black feathers

black·board /blák bàwrd/ *n* a board on which teachers write in classrooms

⚡black box *n* **1** an aircraft's flight recorder **2** an electronic component of unknown construction

black bread *n* dark rye bread

black·cap /blák kàp/ *n* **1** a small songbird with a black-topped head **2** a North American raspberry plant

black com·e·dy *n* comedy dealing with un-pleasant subjects

black cur·rant *n* **1** a small edible dark-purple berry **2** a bush that produces black currants

Black Death *n* a 14C epidemic of bubonic plague affecting Europe and Asia

black e·con·o·my *n* the part of an economy consisting of unofficial or illegal earnings

black·en /blákən/ *v* **1** *vti* make or become black **2** *vt* harm somebody's reputation by slander (*fml*)

black eye *n* a bruised area around the eye

black-eyed pea *n* **1** a small bean with a black spot **2** a plant that produces black-eyed peas

black-eyed Su·san /-sóoz'n/ *n* **1** a yellow-orange flower with a dark center **2** a climb-ing plant with yellow-orange flowers

black·fly /blák flì/ (*pl* **-flies** *or same*) *n* a black aphid that infests plants

Black·foot /blák fòot/ (*pl* **-feet** /-fèet/ *or same*) *n* **1** a member of a group of Native North American peoples living in Alberta, Sas-katchewan, and Montana **2** the Al-gonquian language of the Blackfoot people —**Black·foot** *adj*

Black For·est wooded highland region in SW Germany

Black For·est cake, Black For·est ga·teau *n* a rich chocolate cake topped and filled with cherries and whipped cream

black·guard /blággərd, blá gàard/ *n* a dishonest or unprincipled person (*dated*)

⚡black hat hack·er *n* a hacker who accesses a computer system for malicious purposes

Black Hawk /blák hàwk/ (1767–1838) Sauk leader

black·head /blák hèd/ *n* a small plug of dark fatty matter blocking a pore

Black Hills mountainous region in W South Dakota and NE Wyoming, including the Mount Rushmore National Memorial. Highest peak Harney Peak 7,242 ft./2,207 m.

black hole *n* **1** an object in space that pulls all surrounding matter into itself, thought to be formed when a star collapses **2** an imaginary place where things get lost (*humorous*)

black ice *n* thin ice on roads that is difficult to see

black·jack /blák jàk/ n 1 a card game in which the winner is the player holding cards of a total value closest to, but not more than, 21 points 2 in the game of blackjack, a winning combination of cards 3 a weapon in the form of a short leather-covered club ■ vt 1 hit somebody with a blackjack 2 force somebody to do something

Black Ket·tle /blák kèttˈl/ (1803?–68) Cheyenne leader

black knight n a company that makes a hostile takeover bid

black·list /blák lìst/ n a list of people who are excluded or disapproved of ■ vt put on a blacklist

black lung n MED = anthracosis

black mag·ic n magic that invokes evil forces

black·mail /blák màyl/ n 1 the act of forcing somebody to do something by threatening to reveal secret information about them 2 coercion of any kind —**black·mail** vt

black mark n something that gives people a bad opinion of somebody or something

black mar·ket n illegal trading —**black mar·ket·eer** n

black mass n a service of devil-worship that imitates the Christian Mass

Black·mun /blákmən/, **Harry** (1908–99) associate justice of the US Supreme Court (1970–94)

Black Mus·lim n a member of the Nation of Islam, an African American Islamic group based in the United States

black·out /blák òwt/ n 1 a loss of electric power, e.g., because of strikes or fuel shortages 2 a temporary loss of consciousness 3 a refusal to broadcast radio or television programs during a strike 4 the withholding of information, especially by official sources 5 a period of extinguishing or hiding lights during a raid by enemy aircraft 6 a loss of radio communication

black pep·per n pepper made by grinding peppercorns with their dark husks still attached

Black Pow·er n a US political movement formed to engender social and economic equality for Black people

Black Sea inland sea between SE Europe and Asia

black sheep n somebody regarded with shame by other members of a group

Black·shirt /blák shùrt/, **black·shirt** n a European fascist in World War II, especially a member of the Italian Fascist Party

black·smith /blák smìth/ n somebody who makes and repairs objects made of metal

black·snake /blák snàyk/ n a dark nonvenomous snake

black·thorn /blák thàwrn/ n 1 a thorny bush with blue-black berries 2 a walking stick made from the hard wood of a blackthorn

black tie n 1 a black bow tie 2 a formal style of dress for men that includes a black dinner jacket —**black-tie** adj

black·top /blák tòp/ n 1 road-surfacing material 2 a road or other area with a blacktop surface —**black·top** vti

Black·well /blák wèl/, **Elizabeth** (1821–1910) British-born US physician

black wid·ow n a highly poisonous black spider

ORIGIN The name **black widow** comes from the female's habit of eating her mate.

blad·der /bláddər/ n a body organ that stores liquid or gas, especially the organ that stores urine

blad·der wrack n a brown seaweed with bulbous air bladders on its fronds

blade n 1 the cutting part of a tool or weapon 2 a long thin flat part, e.g., of a propeller 3 a thin leaf 4 a dashing man (dated infml) ■ vi (blad·ed, blad·ing) skate on in-line roller skates (infml)

Tony Blair

Blair /blair/, **Tony** (b. 1953) British prime minister (1997–)

Blake /blayk/, **Edward** (1833–1912) Canadian politician

Blake, William (1757–1827) British poet, painter, and engraver —**Blake·i·an** adj

Bla·key /bláykee/, **Art** (1919–90) US jazz drummer and band leader

blame vt (blamed, blam·ing) consider somebody responsible for something bad that happens ■ n responsibility —**blame·less** adj —**blame·wor·thy** adj

blanch, blench v 1 vt put food briefly in boiling water 2 vi turn pale 3 vti remove color from, or lose color

blanc·mange /blə máanj, -máanzh/ n a cold milk-based dessert with a texture similar to that of pudding

bland adj 1 lacking flavor, character, or interest 2 free from anything annoying or upsetting —**bland·ly** adv —**bland·ness** n

blan·dish·ment /blándishmənt/ n 1 the use of flattery 2 a piece of flattery (fml; often pl)

blank adj 1 not written on, drawn on, recorded on, or printed on 2 without any images o a blank screen 3 showing no interest, understanding, or awareness o a blank expression 4 uneventful or unproductive 5 complete o in blank amazement ■ n 1 a complete absence of awareness or memory ○ *My mind was a complete blank.* **2** a period about which nothing is known **3** a space in which to write something on a form or other document **4** a mark indicating a missing word **5** *also* **blank cart·ridge** a gun cartridge without a bullet **6** a piece of a substance from which something is made ■ **v 1** *vt* delete or block out **2** *vi* forget something suddenly and temporarily ○ *I just blanked.* **3** *vt* prevent from scoring —**blank·ly** *adv* —**blank·ness** *n* ◊ **draw a blank** be unable to think of or remember

blank check *n* **1** a check without a stated amount **2** complete freedom to act or decide *(infml)*

blan·ket /bláng·kət/ *n* **1** a large piece of thick cloth used as a cover for a bed **2** a covering layer of a substance ■ *adj* applying to all areas or situations ○ *a blanket instruction* ■ *vt* cover something completely

blank verse *n* unrhymed poetry with a regular rhythm and line length

Blan·tyre-Lim·be /blàn tír lím bày/ largest city in Malawi. Pop. 2,000,000 (1998).

blare /blair/ **(blared, blar·ing)** *v* **1** *vti* make a loud harsh sound **2** *vt* announce —**blare** *n*

blar·ney /bláarnee/ *n* nonsense *(infml)*

> **ORIGIN Blarney** derives from the Blarney Stone, a stone in Blarney Castle near Cork, Ireland, that is said to give the power of persuasive talk to those who kiss it.

bla·sé /blaa záy/ *adj* not impressed or concerned

blas·pheme /blass feém, bláss feèrn/ **(-phemed, -phem·ing)** *v* swear or behave in a way that insults God or a religion —**blas·phem·er** /blass feémar, blásfamar/ *n*

blas·phe·my /blásfomee/ *n* disrespect for God or a religion, or an action that shows such disrespect —**blas·phe·mous** *adj*

blast *n* **1** an explosion, or a sudden rush of air caused by an explosion **2** a sudden strong current of air or gas **3** the loud sound of an explosion **4** the short loud sound of a whistle, horn, or instrument **5** a loud or angry outburst **6** an enjoyable experience *(slang)* ■ **v 1** *vti* blow up with explosives **2** *vt* hit hard *(infml)* **3** *vti* come out or push out with great force and noise *(infml)* **4** *vt* criticize *(infml)* —**blast·er** *n* ◊ **(at) full blast** at maximum volume or speed ◊ See note at **criticize**

☐ **blast off** *vi* be launched into space

blast fur·nace *n* a metal-smelting furnace that uses a current of air to raise the temperature

blast-off /blást àwf, -òf/ *n* the launch of a spacecraft

bla·tant /bláyt'nt/ *adj* obtrusive and conspicuous —**bla·tant·ly** *adv*

> **USAGE blatant** or **flagrant?** A **blatant** lie is one so bare-faced that no one can miss it, whereas

flagrant disregard for human life is unforgivably shameless or outrageous. Avoid using **blatant** to mean merely "obvious" in such sentences as *There seems to be a blatant contradiction.* Here, substitute *obvious, clear,* or *glaring* for **blatant**.

blath·er /bláthər/, **blith·er** /blíthər/ *vi* talk in a boring or unintelligent way *(infml)* —**blath·er** *n*

blaze[1] *vi* **(blazed, blaz·ing)** burn or shine brightly ■ *n* **1** a large bright fire **2** an impressive display ○ *a blaze of publicity* ■ **blaz·es** *npl* adds emphasis *(infml)*

blaze[2] *n* a white mark on an animal's face ■ *vt* **(blazed, blaz·ing) 1** mark a new path **2** lead the way in doing something new

blaze[3] **(blazed, blaz·ing)** *vt* spread news or information loudly and clearly ○ *blazed the scandal all over the front page*

> **ORIGIN Blaze** "spread news" comes from an early Dutch or German verb meaning "blow," and is unrelated to the other **blaze** words.

blaz·er /bláyzər/ *n* a jacket, especially one bearing the badge of a club or institution

bla·zon /bláyz'n/ *vt* **1** announce widely or ostentatiously **2** create or describe a coat of arms ■ *n* a coat of arms

bleach *n* a chemical solution. Use: removing color, cleansing, disinfecting. ■ **v 1** *vt* use bleach on **2** *vti* lighten, or become light, in color

bleach·ers /bleéchərz/ *npl* **1** stadium seats **2** indoor seats in a sports arena

bleak *adj* **1** providing little comfort or shelter **2** without hope or expectation of success **3** cold and cloudy —**bleak·ly** *adv* —**bleak·ness** *n*

blear·y /bleéree/ **(-i·er, -i·est)** *adj* not seeing clearly, usually because of sleepiness —**blear·i·ly** *adv* —**blear·i·ness** *n*

bleat *vi* make the typical noise of a sheep or goat —**bleat** *n*

bleed **(bled)** **v 1** *vi* lose blood from the body through a wound **2** *vt* take blood from somebody as a way of treating illness **3** *vi* feel sadness or pity *(often ironic)* ○ *My heart bleeds for you.* **4** *vi* exude sap **5** *vi* release color **6** *vt* take money or resources from somebody, especially dishonestly *(infml)* **7** *vt* draw off a liquid or gas

bleep *n* a short high-pitched electronic signal ■ **v 1** *vi* make a short high-pitched electronic sound **2** *vt* substitute a bleep for offensive language

blem·ish /blémmish/ *n* **1** a mark or flaw that spoils the appearance of something **2** something that spoils somebody's reputation —**blem·ish** *vt* ◊ See note at **flaw**

blench *vi* flinch or recoil in fear

blend **v 1** *vti* mix one substance thoroughly with another **2** *vt* create by mixing together different types ○ *blended tea* **3** *vti* mix with other people or things so as not to be conspicuous **4** *vti* make a pleasing combination ■ *n* **1** a mixture or combination **2** a food or drink created from different types of the same substance ○ *a coffee blend* ◊ See note at **mixture**

blend·er /bléndər/ *n* **1** an electrical appliance used for mixing or liquidizing food **2** somebody or something that blends foods or drinks

bless (**blessed** *or* **blest**) *vt* **1** make holy in a religious ceremony **2** invoke divine protection on ○ *bless this family* **3** declare approval and support for **4** give a desirable quality to ○ *was blessed with good looks*

ORIGIN Bless derives from the same ancient root as *blood*, and probably originally meant "mark with blood as a religious rite."

bless·ed /blésad/ *adj* **1** holy **2** declared holy by the pope as the first stage toward being declared a saint ■ *adj, adv* adds emphasis (*infml*) —**bless·ed·ly** *adv* —**bless·ed·ness** *n*

bless·ing /blésing/ *n* **1** help from God or another deity **2** a priest's act of invoking divine help or protection **3** a prayer said before a meal **4** something fortunate ○ *It's a blessing that you came so quickly.*

blew 1 past tense of **blow**[1] **2** past tense of **blow**[3]

Bligh /blī/, **William** (1754–1817) British naval officer

blight /blīt/ *n* **1** a destructive force or influence **2** a ruined state **3** a plant disease ■ *vt* **1** ruin **2** affect a plant with blight

blimp *n* a small airship used in World War II

blind /blīnd/ *adj* **1** unable to see, permanently or temporarily **2** unable to recognize or understand something ○ *blind to the consequences* **3** uncontrollable and irrational ○ *blind rage* **4** unquestioning ○ *blind prejudice* **5** marked by lack of awareness ○ *a blind stupor* **6** not giving a clear view ○ *a blind corner* **7** closed at one end ○ *a blind tunnel* **8** done without looking ○ *a blind tasting* ■ *adv* **1** without prior examination or preparation ○ *You shouldn't buy livestock blind.* **2** using an aircraft's instruments only ○ *flying blind* **3** totally (*infml*) ○ *robbed his partner blind* ■ *vt* **1** make permanently blind **2** make unable to judge properly ■ *n* **1** a window covering that can be raised or lowered **2** something that conceals the true nature of somebody's activities **3** a hiding place for hunters —**blind·ly** *adv* —**blind·ness** *n*

blind al·ley *n* **1** a passage that is closed off at one end **2** something that will not produce worthwhile results

blind date *n* **1** a date with somebody you have not met before **2** somebody met on a blind date

blind·er /blīndər/ *n* something that obscures

vision ■ **blind·ers** *npl* eye covers for a horse to keep it looking straight ahead

blind·fold /blīnd fōld/ *n* a bandage tied over somebody's eyes ■ *vt* **1** put a blindfold on **2** prevent from understanding

blind·ing /blīnding/ *adj* impairing vision —**blind·ing·ly** *adv*

blind·man's buff /blīnd manz-/ *n* a children's game in which a blindfolded player tries to catch and identify others

blind side *n* the area that is out of your field of vision

blind-side, blind·side /blīnd sīd/ *vt* **1** attack from the blind side **2** attack when vulnerable

blind spot *n* **1** a small area on the retina that lacks visual receptors **2** an area of knowledge about which somebody is ignorant **3** a direction in which vision is obscured

bli·ni /blínnee, bleénee/ (*pl* **bli·nis** *or* **blin** *or* **same**) *n* a small buckwheat pancake

blink *v* **1** *vti* close and reopen both eyes rapidly **2** *vt* remove something by blinking ○ *blinked away his tears* **3** *vi* flash on and off —**blink** *n* ◊ **on the blink** not working properly (*infml*)

blink·er /blíngkər/ *n* a flashing light

blink·ered /blíngkərd/ *adj* narrow-minded ○ *took a very blinkered attitude*

blip *n* **1** a spot of light that indicates the position of something on a display screen **2** a bleep **3** a sudden temporary problem —**blip** *vi*

bliss *n* **1** perfect happiness **2** spiritual joy —**bliss·ful** /blísf'l/ *adj* —**bliss·ful·ly** *adv*

blis·ter /blístər/ *n* **1** a painful, fluid-filled swelling on the skin **2** a bubble, e.g., on paintwork —**blis·ter** *vti*

blis·ter·ing /blístəring/ *adj* **1** very hot **2** scornful —**blis·ter·ing·ly** *adv*

blis·ter pack *n* a type of package in which a manufactured item is covered in a clear dome of plastic stuck to a cardboard backing

blithe /blīth, blīth/ *adj* cheerful and carefree —**blithe·ly** *adv* —**blithe·ness** *n*

blith·er /blíthər/ *vi* = **blather** (*infml*)

B.Litt. *abbr* Bachelor of Literature

blitz /blits/ *n* **1** a sustained aerial attack **2** a blitzkrieg **3** a concerted effort to get something done (*infml*) ■ *vt* **1** destroy by aerial bombing **2** subject somebody to an overwhelming amount of something (*infml*)

blitz·krieg /blíts kreeg/ *n* a swift military offensive

Blix·en /blíksən/, **Karen** ⧫ **Dinesen, Isak**

~~blizzard~~ incorrect spelling of **blizzard**

bliz·zard /blízzərd/ *n* a heavy snowstorm

bloat·ed /blōtid/ *adj* **1** swollen with liquid, air, or gas **2** too full after overeating —**bloat** *vti* —**bloat·ed·ness** *n*

bloat·er /blṓtər/ n a large herring that has been soaked in brine and smoked

blob n 1 a soft mass of a liquid or semiliquid substance 2 a small spot of color ■ vt (**blobbed, blob·bing**) put on in blobs

bloc /blok/ n 1 a united group of countries 2 a loose coalition in a legislature

SPELLCHECK Do not confuse the spelling of **bloc** and **block** ("square object," "obstruction"), which sound similar.

⚡ **block** /blok/ n 1 a piece of solid material, e.g., concrete 2 a stand for displaying items at an auction 3 the section of a street between two parallel streets 4 a group of buildings bounded on each side by a street 5 a unit of data ○ a block of text 6 something that obstructs or prevents progress 7 a deliberate physical obstruction of play, or the obstructing players 8 a psychological inability to deal with something ■ v 1 vt obstruct or hinder 2 vti physically obstruct a player or ball 3 vti fail to remember something for psychological reasons 4 vt make into a block 5 vt support with a block ◇ **on the block** for sale at an auction ◇ See note at **bloc, hinder**

□ **block out** vt 1 put something out of your mind 2 describe something in a general way

block·ade /blo káyd/ n 1 an organized attempt to prevent the movement of people or goods 2 the people or vehicles forming a blockade ■ vt (**-ad·ed, -ad·ing**) subject a place to a blockade

block·age /blókij/ n something that obstructs movement through a pipe or channel

block and tack·le (pl **blocks and tack·les**) n a system of pulleys through which rope is threaded, used for lifting or pulling things

block·bust·er /blók bùstər/ n something such as a book or movie that achieves widespread popular success (infml)

block·bust·ing /blók bùsting/ n the practice of persuading homeowners to sell low for fear of declining property values (infml) ■ adj commercially successful

block di·a·gram n a diagram of a process or system in which parts are represented by labeled rectangles connected by lines

block·head /blók hèd/ n somebody considered unintelligent (insult)

Block Is·land /blók-/ island of S Rhode Island, in the Atlantic Ocean. Pop. 836 (1990).

Bloem·fon·tein /blóom faan tàyn/ capital of Free State Province, South Africa. Pop. 126,867 (1991).

bloke n UK, ANZ a man (infml) —**bloke·ish** adj

blond, blonde adj 1 describes hair that is yellowish or golden 2 fair-haired and light-skinned 3 light colored ○ blond wood ■ n a fair-haired person —**blond·ness** n

USAGE blond or **blonde**? When describing hair,

blond is normally used of a person of either sex: Jane has blond hair. When describing somebody directly, **blond** is often used of a man or boy and **blonde** of a woman or girl: He is blond. Jane is blonde/is a blonde.

blood /blud/ n 1 the red fluid that circulates in the bodies of humans and other vertebrates 2 the body fluid of invertebrates 3 bloodshed or killing 4 blood considered as a vital life force 5 family or ancestry 6 pure breeding in animals, especially horses ■ vt subject troops to their first experience of battle ◇ **in cold blood** in a way that shows a complete lack of emotion

blood bank n a supply of blood or blood plasma for use in hospitals

blood-bath /blúd bàth/ (pl **-baths** /-bàthz/) n indiscriminate killing

blood broth·er n either one of two men or boys who are sworn friends

blood count n the number of cells and platelets in a given volume of blood, or the act of counting them

blood-cur·dling /blúd kùrdling/ adj arousing extreme fear

blood do·nor n somebody who gives their own blood for use in transfusions

blood group n any class into which human blood is divided for transfusion purposes

blood·hound /blúd hòwnd/ n a large tracking dog with drooping ears and sagging jowls

blood·less /blúdləss/ adj 1 without killing or violence 2 pale and anemic-looking

blood-let·ting /blúd lètting/ n 1 the removal of blood from the body as a treatment for disease or a method of diagnosis 2 bitter quarreling 3 the large-scale laying off of workers

blood·line /blúd līn/ n a line of descent from a particular human or animal ancestor

blood mon·ey n 1 compensation paid to the relatives of somebody who has been killed 2 a fee paid to a hired killer

blood or·ange n an orange with red flesh

blood poi·son·ing n an infection of the blood

blood pres·sure n the pressure exerted by blood against the walls of the blood vessels

blood re·la·tion, blood rel·a·tive n a relative by birth

blood·shed /blúd shèd/ n killings or injuries

blood·shot /blúd shòt/ adj describes an eye that is inflamed and red

blood·stain /blúd stàyn/ n a stain made by blood —**blood-stained** adj

blood·stock /blúd stòk/ n horses bred for racing

blood·stone /blúd stōn/ n a green variety of chalcedony with small red spots or streaks. Use: gems.

blood·stream /blúd strèem/ n the flow of blood around the body

blood·suck·er /blúd sùkər/ n 1 a parasite that sucks blood 2 somebody who exploits somebody else, especially by demanding money

blood sug·ar n the level of glucose in the blood

blood·thirst·y /blúd thùrstee/ (-i·er, -i·est) adj 1 eager for violence 2 full of violence or killing

blood type n a blood group

blood ves·sel n an artery, capillary, or vein

blood·y /blúddee/ adj (-i·er, -i·est) 1 bloodstained 2 involving a great deal of violence or killing 3 adds emphasis to a noun (slang; sometimes offensive) ■ adv adds emphasis to an adjective (slang; sometimes offensive) ■ vt (-ied, -ies) stain with blood

blood·y mar·y, Blood·y Mar·y n a cocktail consisting of vodka, tomato juice, and spices

bloom n 1 a flower 2 the mass of flowers on a single plant 3 the condition of being in flower ○ in full bloom 4 the condition of greatest freshness or health (literary) ○ in the bloom of youth 5 a fresh, healthy appearance or complexion ■ vi 1 come into flower 2 produce plants 3 prosper or flourish (literary) 4 appear healthy (literary)

bloom·ers /bloomərz/ npl loose pants for women, gathered at the ankle and worn under a shorter skirt (dated)

ORIGIN Bloomers are named for the US feminist Amelia Jenks Bloomer (1818–94), who advocated them as sensible and liberated dress for women.

bloop·er /bloopər/ n 1 an embarrassing mistake (infml humorous) 2 in baseball, a weak hit

blos·som /blóssəm/ n 1 a flower or mass of flowers 2 the condition of being in flower ○ in blossom ■ vi 1 come into flower 2 develop well 3 also blos·som out stop being shy

blot n 1 a stain caused by a drop of liquid 2 an eyesore ○ a blot on the landscape 3 a blemish, e.g., on somebody's reputation ■ vt (blot·ted, blot·ting) 1 bring dishonor on the reputation of 2 dry with absorbent material

□ **blot out** vt 1 cover and obscure 2 obliterate from memory

blotch n an irregular spot or mark, especially on skin —**blotch** vti —**blotch·y** adj

blot·ter /blóttər/ n 1 a piece of blotting paper 2 a logbook

blot·ting pa·per n paper that is used to absorb ink

blouse /blowss, blowz/ n a woman's shirt

blow¹ /blō/ v (blew /bloo/, blown /blōn/) 1 vi move as or with a current of air 2 vti send a stream of air out through the mouth 3 vt make something, e.g., glass or bubbles, by blowing 4 vt clear the nose by forcing air

out through it 5 vti make a sound by blowing air through a musical instrument 6 vi expel moist air through a blowhole (refers to whales and other marine mammals) 7 vi breathe hard 8 vti destroy, open, or move something by the force of an explosion 9 vti cause or experience a blowout in a tire (infml) 10 vti burn out or cause a fuse to burn out 11 vt squander money (slang) 12 vti leave suddenly (slang) ■ n 1 an act of blowing 2 a strong wind (infml) ◊ **blow it** spoil your chances of success (slang)

□ **blow out** v 1 vti extinguish with a blast of air 2 vi puncture (refers to tires)

□ **blow over** vi 1 die down (refers to storms) 2 be forgotten (infml)

□ **blow up** v 1 vti destroy or be destroyed by an explosion 2 vti explode or detonate 3 vti inflate 4 vt enlarge using photographic techniques 5 vi become angry (infml)

blow² /blō/ n 1 a hard hit 2 an important action that helps a cause 3 a setback

blow³ /blō/ (blew /bloo/, blown /blōn/) vti be in flower (literary)

blow·back /blō bàk/ n 1 the powdery residue from a fired weapon 2 a reaction, often negative, to a situation (infml) ○ the blowback from the press revelations

blow-dry vt style hair with a hair dryer —**blow-dry** n

blow·er /blō ər/ n any machine that produces a current of air

blow·fly /blō flì/ (pl -flies) n a fly that lays its eggs in rotting meat or in wounds

blow·hard /blō hàard/ n somebody who boasts

blow·hole /blō hòl/ n 1 a nostril in the top of the head of a whale or similar mammal 2 a hole in ice where marine mammals come to the surface to breathe

blown 1 past participle of **blow¹** 2 past participle of **blow³**

blow·out /blō òwt/ n 1 a puncture in a tire 2 a big party (slang)

blow·torch /blō tàwrch/ n a small portable gas burner

blow-up /blō ùp/ n 1 a photographic enlargement 2 an outburst of temper (infml) 3 an explosion

blow·zy /blówzee/ (-zi·er, -zi·est), **blow·sy** (-si·er, -si·est) adj 1 with a red face and a coarse complexion 2 disheveled and unkempt in appearance

BLT n a bacon, lettuce, and tomato sandwich

blub·ber /blúbbər/ vi sob loudly (infml) ■ n 1 the fat that insulates the body of whales and other marine mammals 2 unsightly fat (infml; sometimes offensive) —**blub·ber·er** n

bludg·eon /blújjən/ n a short club ■ vt 1 hit repeatedly with a heavy object 2 coerce or bully

blue adj (blu·er, blu·est) 1 of the color of the sky on a cloudless day 2 slightly purple in skin color 3 depressed (infml) 4 referring to sex in an explicit or offensive way *(infml)* ◊ **blue jokes** ■ *n* **1** the color of the sky **2** a blue pigment **3** a blue ring on an archery target ■ *vti* (**blued, blue·ing** *or* **blu·ing, blues**) make or become blue —**blue·ish** *adj* —**blue·ness** *n* —**blu·ish** *adj* ◊ **out of the blue** unexpectedly

blue ba·by *n* a baby with bluish skin color caused by insufficient oxygen in the blood as a result of a congenital heart defect

blue·bell /blóo bèl/ *n* a woodland plant with small blue bell-shaped flowers

blue·ber·ry /blóo bèrree/ (*pl* **-ries**) *n* **1** an edible dark blue berry **2** the bush that produces blueberries

blue·bird /blóo bùrd/ *n* a songbird with bright blue plumage

blue blood *n* noble descent —**blue-blood·ed** *adj*

blue·bot·tle /blóo bòtt'l/ *n* a large buzzing fly with a metallic blue body

blue cheese *n* any whitish cheese with veins of blue mold

blue chip *n* **1** a valuable stock in a reliable company **2** a valuable asset or company —**blue-chip** *adj*

blue-chip·per *n* a blue-chip company

blue-col·lar *adj* of manual workers

blue·grass /blóo gràss/ *n* **1** a style of country music that features close harmony **2** a blue-green grass. Use: fodder, lawns.

blue jay *n* a bird with blue feathers

blue jeans *npl* jeans of blue denim

Blue Nile river in Ethiopia and Sudan that joins the White Nile to form the Nile at Khartoum. Length 850 mi./1,370 km.

blue pag·es *npl* a section of the telephone book listing government agencies and departments

blue·print /blóo prìnt/ *n* **1** a print of a technical drawing, used as a reference during construction **2** a plan or an action that serves as a model

blue rib·bon *n* a badge made of blue ribbon, awarded for first prize —**blue-rib·bon** *adj*

Blue Ridge, Blue Ridge Moun·tains mountain range in N Georgia, W North Carolina, and W Virginia, the easternmost range of the Appalachian Mountains. Highest peak Mt. Mitchell 6,684 ft./2,037 m.

blues *n* **1** a style of music marked by slow sad songs with a repetitive rhythm (*+sing or pl verb*) **2** (*pl same*) a song or instrumental piece in the style of the blues **3** a feeling of sadness *(infml; + pl verb)*

blue-sky *adj* purely theoretical *(infml)* —**blue-sky** *vi*

blue-stock·ing /blóo stòking/ *n* an offensive term for a highly educated woman with scholarly interests

ORIGIN At the literary gatherings held at the houses of fashionable mid-18C hostesses, it became the custom to wear casual rather than formal dress. In the case of gentlemen's stockings, this meant gray worsted (called "blue" at that time) rather than black silk. This lack of decorum was disapproved of in some quarters, and the participants were dubbed the "Blue Stocking Society." Women who attended the gatherings thus became known as "Blue Stocking Ladies" (even though it was men who had worn the stockings).

bluff[1] *vti* **1** pretend to be confident or knowledgeable **2** deceive other players in a card game about the value of your hand —**bluff** *n*

bluff[2] *n* a cliff with a broad face ■ *adj* blunt but kind in manner —**bluff·ly** *adv* —**bluff·ness** *n*

Blume /blóom/, **Judy** (*b.* 1938) US writer

blun·der /blúndər/ *n* a stupid mistake ■ *vi* **1** make a serious mistake **2** move or act clumsily —**blun·der·ing·ly** *adv* ◊ See note at **mistake**

blun·der·buss /blúndər bùss/ *n* a 17C wide-mouthed gun

ORIGIN **Blunderbuss** is an alteration of Dutch *donderbus*, literally "thunder gun," by association with *blunder*.

blunt *adj* **1** with a cutting edge that is not sharp **2** frank or honest but without sensitivity ■ *v* **1** *vti* become or make something less sharp **2** *vt* lessen or weaken a sense or emotion —**blunt·ly** *adv* —**blunt·ness** *n*

blur *n* **1** a fuzzy or indistinct image **2** a smear or smeared area ■ *vti* (**blurred, blur·ring**) **1** make or become vague ◦ *blurred the line between right and wrong* **2** make or become indistinct in shape or detail —**blur·ry** *adj*

blurb *n* a paragraph promoting a product, especially on a book jacket *(slang)* —**blurb** *vt*

ORIGIN The word **blurb** was coined by the US humorist Gelett Burgess. The noun, first found in print in 1914, is said to have been foreshadowed by a drawing of a young woman on a comic-book jacket of 1907, whose name was given as Miss Blinda Blurb.

blurt *vti* say something impulsively

blush *vi* **1** become red in the face because of embarrassment **2** feel embarrassed *(fml)* ■ *n* **1** a reddening of the face through embarrassment **2** a red or pink glow **3** *also* **blush·er** pink makeup for cheeks

blus·ter /blústər/ *v* **1** *vti* speak or say something loudly or arrogantly **2** *vti* behave in a bullying way toward somebody **3** *vi* blow loudly in gusts *(refers to wind)* —**blus·ter** *n* —**blus·ter·ing·ly** *adv* —**blus·ter·y** *adj*

Blvd. *abbr* Boulevard

B mov·ie *n* a low-budget movie formerly shown before the main feature —**B-mov·ie** *adj*

⌁**bmp, BMP** *abbr* a file extension indicating a bit map file

BMX *n* the riding of bicycles over rough terrain. Full form **bicycle motocross**

b.o. *abbr* 1 broker's order 2 buyer's option

bo·a /bóə/ *n* 1 a tropical snake belonging to the family that kills by winding around its prey 2 a long fluffy scarf of feathers

bo·a con·stric·tor *n* a large boa that kills by winding around its prey

boar /bawr/ (*pl* **boars** *or same*) *n* 1 an uncastrated hog 2 the male of various mammals

> **SPELLCHECK** Do not confuse the spelling of **boar** and **bore** ("make somebody uninterested," "make a hole"), which sound similar.

⌁**board** /bawrd/ *n* 1 a plank of wood 2 a flat sheet of wood or plastic or other hard material 3 a flat surface on which to play a game, usually marked with colored areas 4 a panel on which the controls of items of electrical equipment are mounted 5 a circuit board 6 a group of people chosen to make administrative decisions 7 daily meals provided at the place where somebody lives ■ **boards** *npl* 1 the stage in a theater 2 the wooden wall that encloses an ice hockey rink ■ *v* 1 *vti* get onto a vehicle as a passenger 2 *vti* take passengers on for a journey 3 *vt* go onto a ship in order to attack or inspect it 4 *also* **board up** *vti* cover something with boards 5 *vti* be provided with room and meals ◇ **go by the board** be neglected, no longer used, or cast aside ◇ **on board** 1 into or on a vehicle 2 into or in an existing group or project (*infml*)

> **SPELLCHECK** Do not confuse the spelling of **board** and **bored** ("tired and impatient"), which sound similar.

board·er /báwrdər/ *n* somebody paying for food and a room in a private home or boarding house

board game *n* any game played on a board

board·ing house /báwrding-/ *n* a private house providing rooms and meals to long-term paying guests

board·ing pass, board·ing card *n* an additional ticket that passengers need to show before they are allowed to board a vehicle

board·ing school *n* a school that provides accommodations for students during term time

board·walk /báwrd wàwk/ *n* a raised walkway made of boards, often built along beaches at beach resorts

boast /bōst/ *v* 1 *vti* speak proudly about possessions or accomplishments 2 *vt* possess something desirable ◇ *Our town boasts the world's biggest roller coaster.* ■ *n* 1 an excessively proud statement 2 a desirable possession —**boast·ful** *adj* —**boast·ful·ness** *n*

boat /bōt/ *n* 1 a small vessel for traveling on water 2 any vessel used on water, e.g., a ship or submarine 3 a container shaped like a boat ■ *vti* travel or transport by boat ◇ **in the same boat** in the same situation (*infml*) ◇ **miss the boat** fail to take advantage of an opportunity (*infml*) ◇ **rock the boat** cause trouble (*infml*)

boat·er /bótər/ *n* a straw hat with a flat top

boat hook *n* a pole for pulling or pushing small boats

boat·swain /bóss'n/, **bo's'n** *n* a bosun

boat train *n* a train that takes people to and from a dock

bob[1] (**bobbed, bob·bing**) *vi* 1 bounce quickly, especially on the surface of water 2 make a curtsy, bow, or nod —**bob** *n*

bob[2] *n* a woman's short haircut ■ *vt* (**bobbed, bob·bing**) cut hair short

bob·bin /bóbbin/ *n* a cylinder or spool onto which thread or wire is wound

bob·ble /bóbb'l/ (**-bled, -bling**) *v* 1 *vti* move up and down 2 *vt* handle clumsily (*infml*) —**bob·ble** *n*

bob·by /bóbbee/ (*pl* **-bies**) *n* UK a police officer (*infml dated*)

bob·by pin *n* US, Can, ANZ a thin hair clip

bob·by socks /-sòks/, **bob·by sox** *npl* girls' ankle socks

bob·cat /bób kàt/ *n* a short-tailed wild cat

bob·sled /bób slèd/ *n* 1 a racing sled 2 a sled made of two short sleds ■ *vi* (**-sled·ded, -sled·ding**) ride in a bobsled

bob·white /bób wìt, -hwìt/ (*pl* **-whites** *or same*) *n* a North American quail

Boc·cac·cio /bō kaáchee ò, -chō/, **Giovanni** (1313–75) Italian writer and humanist

bod *n* somebody's body (*slang*)

bode[1] /bōd/ (**bod·ed, bod·ing**) *vti* be a sign that something is about to happen

bode[2] past tense of **bide**

bo·de·ga /bō dáygə/ *n* 1 a small food store 2 a wine store in a Spanish-speaking country

bod·ice /bóddiss/ *n* the upper part of a dress

> **ORIGIN Bodice** was originally *bodies*, the plural of *body*. It represents *body* in the sense "upper part of a garment." The plural form was used because the upper part of women's dresses was often in two parts, fastening down the middle.

bod·i·ly /bóddʼlee/ *adj* of the body ■ *adv* 1 physically 2 using physical force

bod·kin /bódkin/ *n* 1 a large blunt needle 2 a hole-punching tool

bod·y /bóddee/ (*pl* **-ies**) *n* 1 the physical form of a human being or organism 2 the physical remains of a dead human being or organism 3 a torso 4 somebody's figure with regard to shape and muscle tone 5 a group of people **6** a collection o *a body of evidence* **7** a mass o *a body of water* **8** the outer shell of a vehicle **9** the main part of something **10** fullness of flavor in wine **11** the thickness of a liquid **12** fullness of texture, e.g., of hair **13** a person *(infml)*

bod·y blow *n* a serious setback or disappointment

bod·y·build·ing /bóddee bílding/ *n* the practice of muscle-developing —**bod·y·build·er** *n*

bod·y clock *n* somebody's physiological timing mechanism

bod·y dou·ble *n* somebody whose body is filmed instead of that of an actor, especially in a nude scene

bod·y·guard /bóddee gaàrd/ *n* somebody hired to protect somebody from physical attack

bod·y lan·guage *n* bodily mannerisms, postures, and facial expressions regarded as communicating unspoken feelings

bod·y pol·i·tic *n* the people of a nation regarded as a political whole

bod·y search *n* a thorough search of the body of a person suspected of hiding something such as weapons or illegal drugs

bod·y snatch·er *n* formerly, somebody who stole corpses, usually in order to sell them for medical research —**bod·y·snatch·ing** *n*

bod·y stock·ing *n* a close-fitting one-piece garment that covers the body from the neck to the toes

bod·y·work /bóddee wùrk/ *n* **1** the outer shell of a vehicle **2** the repair of vehicle bodies

Boer /bawr, boŏr/ *n* somebody of Dutch descent who settled in South Africa —**Boer** *adj*

bog *n* an area of marshy ground —**bog·gy** *adj*
□ **bog down** *vt* slow the progress of *(infml)* o *got bogged down in unimportant details*

Bo·gart /bő gaàrt/, **Humphrey** (1899–1957) US movie actor

bo·gey /bőgee/ *n* **1** a cause of trouble, annoyance, or fear **2** in golf, a score of one over par ■ *vt* in golf, score one over par for a hole

bog·ey·man /boŏggee màn, bőgee-/ (*pl* **bog·ey·men** /-mèn/), **boog·ey·man** *n* an imaginary person or monster that frightens children

bog·gle /bógg'l/ (**-gling**) *vi* become baffled *(infml)*

Bo·go·tá /bőgə taá/ capital of Colombia. Pop. 6,276,000 (1999).

bo·gus /bőgəss/ *adj* **1** fake or deceitful **2** bad or useless *(slang)*

ORIGIN Bogus is first recorded in American usage in the 1820s, referring to a machine for producing counterfeit money. Its ultimate origins remain unclear.

Bo·he·mi·a /bō heémee ə/ historic region in the present-day W Czech Republic —**Bo·he·mi·an** *adj*, *n*

bo·he·mi·an /bō heémee ən/ *n* somebody with an unconventional lifestyle, especially somebody involved in the arts —**bo·he·mi·an** *adj* —**bo·he·mi·an·ism** *n*

Bohr /bawr/, **Niels** (1885–1962) Danish physicist. He participated in US atomic bomb development during World War II.

bohr·i·um /báwree əm/ *n* (*symbol* **Bh**) a synthetic radioactive chemical element

boil[1] *v* **1** *vti* reach or cause to reach the point at which liquid turns into gas **2** *vti* contain or cause to contain boiling liquid **3** *vti* cook in boiling water or at the temperature at which surface bubbles form o *Boil the spaghetti for about eight minutes.* **4** *vt* clean or sterilize in boiling water **5** *vi* bubble on the surface **6** *vi* get very angry ■ *n* the state of bubbling at a high temperature
□ **boil down** *v* **1** *vti* make or become a thicker liquid by boiling to remove water **2** *vt* summarize *(infml)*
□ **boil down to** *vt* amount to in essence *(infml)*
□ **boil over** *v* **1** *vti* froth up and overflow **2** *vi* overflow with an emotion

boil[2] *n* a pus-filled abscess on skin

boil·er /bóylər/ *n* a water-heating tank used as a source of heat or power

✶ **boil·er·plate** /bóylər plàyt/ *n* **1** formulaic language, especially in official documents **2** a reusable unit of computer code

boil·ing point /bóyling-/ *n* **1** the temperature at which liquid boils **2** the point at which a situation becomes critical

Boi·se /bóyssee, bóyzee/ capital of Idaho. Pop. 157,452 (1998).

bois·ter·ous /bóystərəss, -strəss/ *adj* noisy, energetic, and rowdy —**bois·ter·ous·ly** *adv* —**bois·ter·ous·ness** *n* ◊ See note at **unruly**

~~boistrous~~ incorrect spelling of **boisterous**

bok choy /bòk chóy/ *n* a Chinese cabbage with long white stalks and narrow green leaves

bold /bōld/ *adj* **1** fearless and adventurous **2** requiring a daring personality **3** impudent or presumptuous **4** clear and conspicuous **5** *also* **bold·face** with thicker or darker lines than standard print ■ *n* *also* **bold·face** /bőld fàyss/ bold printing type —**bold·ly** *adv* —**bold·ness** *n*

bole /bōl/ *n* a tree trunk

SPELLCHECK Do not confuse the spelling of **bole** and **bowl** ("a container"), which sound similar.

bo·le·ro /bō láirō, bə-/ (*pl* **-ros**) *n* **1** a Spanish dance that involves stamping and posturing **2** the music for a bolero **3** a short open jacket

Bol·eyn /boŏlin, boŏ lín/, **Anne** (1507?–36) queen of England (1533–36) as the second wife of Henry VIII

bo·li·var /bō leévaar, bólla vər/, **bo·li·var·es** /bō leevaáress/ *n* the main unit of Venezuelan currency

Bo·lí·var /bólə vaàr, bóllə-, bō lée vaar/, **Simón** (1783–1830) South American revolutionary

Bo·liv·i·a /bə lívvee ə, bō-/ landlocked country in west central South America. Cap. La Paz. Pop. 8,300,463 (2001). —**Bo·liv·i·an** n, adj

bo·li·vi·a·no /bə lívwee aànō, bō-/ (pl **-nos**) n the main unit of Bolivian currency

boll /bōl/ n a rounded seed pod, especially of cotton

bol·lard /bóllard/ n a post on a quay for mooring ships

boll wee·vil n a weevil that infests cotton plants

Bol·ly·wood /bóllee woòd/ n a nickname for the Indian film industry

bo·lo·gna /bə lónee, -nə, -nyə/ n smoked sausage made of mixed meats

Bol·she·vik /bólshə vìk, ból-/ n 1 a member of the radical wing of the Russian Socialist party that became the Communist Party in 1918 2 also **bol·she·vik** a Communist or somebody sympathetic to Communism

ORIGIN The Russian form of **Bolshevik** is a derivative of a word meaning "bigger" or "more." The members of the Russian Social Democratic Party, to whom the term was first applied, wanted "big" reforms and were also in the majority, so the name was doubly apt.

bol·ster /bólstər/ vt encourage through support ■ n a long cylindrical pillow

bolt /bōlt/ n 1 a sliding metal bar for fastening a door 2 a metal bar with a screw thread and a flat end, used with a nut for fastening things 3 a lightning flash 4 a large roll of fabric 5 an arrow for a crossbow 6 a sliding part of a gun that ejects a used cartridge ■ v 1 vt lock something with a bolt 2 vi rush away, especially out of fear 3 vt devour food hurriedly 4 vt refuse to support a political party

bolt·hole /bólt hòl/ n a place of refuge

bomb /bom/ n 1 an explosive device or projectile, often timed to explode at a specific time 2 also **Bomb** an atomic bomb regarded as the absolute weapon of mass destruction 3 an artistic failure (infml) 4 a container for an aerosol ■ v 1 vti attack people and places with bombs 2 vi be poor as a performance (infml)

bom·bard /bom baàrd/ vt 1 attack an enemy with missiles 2 overwhelm with something, e.g., questions 3 hit with high-energy particles —**bom·bard·ment** n

bom·bar·dier /bómbər deèr/ n somebody who releases bombs

bom·bast /bóm bàst/ n pompous language —**bom·bas·tic** /bom bástik/ adj —**bom·bas·ti·cal·ly** adv

Bom·bay former name for **Mumbai**

bomb·er /bómmər/ n 1 an aircraft that drops bombs 2 somebody who plants bombs

bomb·er jack·et n a short jacket with an elastic waist

bomb·shell /bóm shèl/ n 1 an artillery shell or bomb 2 a surprising piece of news (infml)

bomb site n an area destroyed by bombs

bo·na fide /bónə fìd, bònə fídee, bónnə fìd, bònnə fídee/ adj 1 authentic 2 sincere and honest

bo·nan·za /bə nánzə/ n 1 a source of great wealth 2 a valuable mineral deposit

Bo·na·parte /bónə paàrt/ ♦ **Napoleon I**

bon·bon /bón bòn/ n a candy

bond n 1 the way in which one surface sticks to another 2 an adhesive substance 3 a link between people, especially an emotional link 4 something that limits behavior 5 a certificate issued by a government or company promising to repay borrowed money at a fixed rate of interest on a specified date 6 a document that legally obliges somebody to pay money 7 a payment securing bail 8 an object such as a rope, band, or chain that binds things together 9 an insurance policy against financial loss 10 a force that binds atoms and ions in a molecule 11 secure storage of goods before payment of duty 12 a technique for overlapping bricks ■ v 1 vt store securely 2 vti adhere or make surfaces adhere 3 vi become linked emotionally 4 vi link atoms or ions with a chemical bond 5 vti convert or be converted into a debt with a bond as security

bond·age /bóndij/ n 1 slavery 2 the practice of being tied up during sex

bond·ed ware·house n a warehouse for storing goods before duty has been paid on them

bond·hold·er /bónd hòldər/ n somebody who owns bonds

bone /bōn/ n 1 any one of the hard parts that form the skeleton in vertebrates 2 the material of which a vertebrate skeleton consists 3 any substance resembling bone, e.g., ivory ■ vt (**boned**, **bon·ing**) remove the bones from ■ adv very ◊ bone idle —**bone·less** adj ◊ **have a bone to pick with somebody** have a cause for disagreement with somebody ◊ **make no bones about** say something frankly

☐ **bone up** vi study intensely (infml)

bone chi·na n 1 fine white porcelain 2 articles made of bone china

bone dry adj extremely dry

bone mar·row n a soft substance inside bones that is involved in the production of red blood cells

bone meal n ground bones used as a fertilizer or animal feed

bon·er /bónər/ n an embarrassing mistake (infml)

bon·fire /bón fìr/ n a large outdoor fire

ORIGIN A **bonfire** was originally a bone fire,

a large outdoor fire on which bones were burned.

Bon·hoef·fer /bón hőfər/, **Dietrich** (1906–45) German pastor and theologian

bon·ho·mie /bònnə meé/ n good-humored friendliness

Bo·nin Is·lands /bónin-/ Japanese island group in the W Pacific Ocean. Pop. 2,303 (1985).

bon mot /bàwN mő/ (pl **bons mots** /bàwN mő, -mőz/) n a witty remark

Bonn /bon, bawn/ city in west central Germany. Pop. 293,072 (1997).

Bon·nard /bŏ naàr/, **Pierre** (1867–1947) French painter

bon·net /bónnət/ n a woman's hat that frames the face and ties under the chin

Bon·ne·ville Salt Flats /bònnəvil-/ barren salt plain in NW Utah, used for setting world land speed records

bon·ny /bónnee/ (**-ni·er, -ni·est**), **bon·nie** adj N England, Scotland attractive

Bo·no /bónō/, **Edward Dе** (b. 1933) Maltese-born British psychologist

bon·sai /bón sĭ, bon sĭ, -zĭ/ (pl same or **-sais**) n 1 the art of growing miniature trees by rigorous pruning of roots and branches 2 a miniaturized tree

bo·nus /bőnəss/ n 1 an unexpected extra 2 an extra amount of money

bon vi·vant /bòN vee vaàN/ (pl **bons vi·vants** /pronunc. same/), **bon vi·veur** /-vee vŭr/ (pl **bons vi·veurs** /-vúrz/) n somebody who enjoys good food, wine, and other luxuries

bon voy·age /bòN vwaa yaàzh/ interj expresses a wish for a good trip

bon·y /bőnee/ (**-i·er, -i·est**) adj 1 very thin and with prominent bones 2 containing many bones 3 of or like bone —**bon·i·ness** n

boo interj 1 expresses disapproval 2 used to startle somebody ■ vti express disapproval of somebody ◊ booed the speaker —**boo** n

boob n somebody considered unintelligent

boo·by /bőobee/ (pl **-bies**) n 1 a person regarded as unintelligent (infml dated) 2 a large tropical seabird

boo·by prize n the loser's prize

boo·by trap n 1 a hidden explosive device 2 a trap set as a practical joke —**boo·by-trap** vt

boog·er /bŏoggər/ n a piece of nasal mucus (slang)

boog·ey·man n = bogeyman

boog·ie /bŏoggee/ (**-ied, -ie·ing**) vi dance to pop music (infml)

boog·ie-woog·ie /bŏoggee wŏoggee/ n a jazz piano style derived from the blues

boo-hoo /boo hŏő/ n, interj the sound of copious weeping

book /bŏok/ n 1 a collection of pages bound together 2 a published work of literature or reference 3 a set of things bound to-

gether, e.g., matches or fabric samples 4 a division of a long literary work 5 a set of rules 6 a bookmaker's record 7 in card games, a number of tricks needed in scoring ■ **books** npl financial accounts ■ v 1 vti make a reservation 2 vt engage as a performer 3 vt charge with a criminal offense —**book·a·ble** adj ◊ **in somebody's book** in somebody's opinion ◊ **throw the book at** impose the maximum penalty on

book·bind·er /bŏok bíndər/ n somebody who binds books professionally —**book·bind·ing** n

book·case /bŏok kàyss/ n a cabinet with shelves for storing books

book club n 1 a firm selling books through the mail at reduced prices 2 a discussion group about books

~~bookeeping~~ incorrect spelling of **bookkeeping**

book·end /bŏok ènd/ n a support for a row of books

book·ie /bŏokee/ n a bookmaker (infml)

book·ing /bŏoking/ n 1 an arrangement by which something such as a hotel room is kept for somebody's future use 2 an arrangement to perform somewhere

book·ish /bŏokish/ adj fond of reading and studying to the exclusion of other activities —**book·ish·ly** adv —**book·ish·ness** n

book·keep·ing /bŏok keèping/ n the process of recording financial transactions —**book·keep·er** n

book·let /bŏoklət/ n a small paper-covered book

book·mak·er /bŏok màykər/ n somebody who receives bets and pays out money to people who win —**book·mak·ing** n

⚡**book·mark** /bŏok maàrk/ n 1 a marker put in a book to show the place where you stopped reading 2 the address of an Internet site, stored for easy access —**book·mark** vt

book·mo·bile /bŏok mō beèl/ n a mobile lending library

Book of Com·mon Prayer n the official book giving the order and content of Episcopal church services

book·plate /bŏok plàyt/ n a label in a book on which the owner's name is listed

book·store /bŏok stàwr/, **book·shop** /bŏok shòp/ n a store selling books

book val·ue n 1 the value of something according to the accounting records of the owner 2 the net value of a business

book·worm /bŏok wùrm/ n 1 an enthusiastic reader (infml) 2 any insect whose larvae eat books

Boole /bool/, **George** (1815–64) British mathematician and logician. His system of algebra is of importance in designing and programming computers. —**Bool·e·an** /bŏolee ən/ adj

⚡**Bool·e·an op·er·a·tor** n a connecting word

or symbol that allows a computer user to include or exclude items in a text search

boom[1] *v* **1** *vi* make a loud deep sound **2** *vt* say with a loud deep sound ■ *n* **1** a loud deep sound **2** a significant increase *o a boom in sales*

boom[2] *n* **1** an extendable overhead pole, especially one carrying the microphone on a movie set **2** a pivoting beam attached to the bottom edge of a sail **3** a floating barrier

boom and bust, **boom or bust** *n* a period of alternate economic growth and recession

boom box *n* a portable CD player with built-in speakers

boom·er /bóomər/ *n* somebody who moves to a place experiencing an economic boom

boo·mer·ang /bóomə ràng/ *n* **1** a curved piece of wood that returns to the thrower **2** something that harms the person who does it ■ *vi* backfire and cause harm to the initiator

boom town *n* a town that quickly becomes prosperous on the back of a new and profitable industry

boon *n* a great benefit

boon com·pan·ion *n* an inseparable friend

boon·docks /bóon dòks/, **boonies** /bóoneez/ *npl* a place that is remote from civilization (*infml*)

boon·dog·gle /bóon dàwg'l, -dògg'l/ *n* a wasteful pursuit (*infml*)

Boone /boon/, **Daniel** (1734–1820) American frontiersman

boor /boor/ *n* an ill-mannered person —**boor·ish** *adj*

boost *vt* **1** improve, strengthen, or increase something **2** assist somebody by pushing or lifting from below **3** vigorously promote —**boost** *n*

boost·er /bóostər/ *n* **1** a vigorous promoter of something or somebody **2** a radio-frequency amplifier **3** somebody or something that encourages something (*usually in combination*) **4** a supplementary dose of a vaccine given to maintain immunity

boost·er seat *n* an extra seat for a child fixed over a car seat or a chair

boot[1] *n* **1** a strong shoe that covers part of the lower leg (*often in combination*) **2** a hard kick **3** dismissal from a job (*infml*) *o was given the boot* **4** a protective covering for a horse's lower leg **5** a military recruit (*infml*) ■ *vt* **1** kick somebody or something hard **2** put a Denver boot on a car

□ **boot out** *vt* force somebody to leave (*infml*)

⚡ **boot**[2] *n* the process of starting or restarting a computer

> **ORIGIN Boot** is a shortening of *bootstrap* in *bootstrap loader*, a simple program that enables a computer to start up and load its operating system.

□ **boot up** *vt* start a computer

boot[3] ◇ **to boot** in addition or also

boot camp *n* a camp for military recruits (*infml*)

boo·tee /bóotee/, **boo·tie** *n* **1** a baby's knitted boot **2** a woman's boot that extends as far as the ankle

booth /booth/ (*pl* **booths** /boothz, booths/) *n* **1** a tent or stall **2** a small enclosed or partitioned compartment

Booth /booth/, **John Wilkes** (1838–65) US actor and assassin of Abraham Lincoln

Booth, William (1829–1912) British religious leader

Boo·thi·a Pen·in·su·la /bóothee ə-/ northernmost tip of mainland North America, in the Northwest Territories, Canada

boot·leg /bóot lèg/ (**-legged, -leg·ging**) *vti* deal in illegal goods —**boot·leg** *adj* —**boot·leg·ger** *n*

boot·strap /bóot stràp/ ◇ **pull yourself up by your (own) bootstraps** improve your situation in life by your own efforts

boo·ty /bóotee/ *n* seized or stolen valuables

booze (*slang*) *n* alcohol ■ *vi* (**boozed, booz·ing**) overindulge in alcohol —**booz·er** *n* —**booz·i·ly** *adv* —**booz·y** *adj*

bop[1] *vi* (**bopped, bop·ping**) (*infml*) **1** go on the spur of the moment **2** dance to pop music ■ *n* bebop

bop[2] (**bopped, bop·ping**) *vt* hit, especially in the face (*infml*)

~~boquet~~ incorrect spelling of **bouquet**

bor·age /báwrij, bórrij/ *n* a plant with blue flowers and thick hairy leaves

bo·rax /báw ràks, báwrəks/ *n* a white crystalline solid. Use: cleaning agent, water softener, preservative.

Bor·deaux[1] /bawr dố/ capital of Gironde Department, SW France. Pop. 215,363 (1999).

Bor·deaux[2] /bawr dố/ *n* wine from the Bordeaux region of France

Bor·den /báwrd'n/, **Lizzie** (1860–1927) US accused murderer

bor·der /báwrdər/ *n* **1** a strip around the edge of something **2** a line dividing two areas of land, or the area around the line **3** a narrow flowerbed ■ *vti* **1** form the boundary between two places **2** be next to

□ **border on** *vt* come close to being *o a policy bordering on the ridiculous*

bor·der·land /báwrdər lànd/ *n* the area at a territory's edge

bor·der·line /báwrdər lìn/ *n* the unclear line between similar states or qualities ■ *adj* **1** not clearly belonging to one category or another **2** describes a physiologically unstable condition **3** describes a medical condition that will develop if no preventive measures are taken

bore[1] /bawr/ *vt* (**bored, bor·ing**) make somebody uninterested, tired, or annoyed ■ *n* somebody or something that bores —**bor·ing** *adj* ◊ See note at **boar**

bore² /bawr/ *vti* (**bored, bor·ing**) **1** make a deep hole in something **2** penetrate ■ *n* the internal diameter of a pipe or similar object

bore³ /bawr/ *n* a tidal wave in a river

bore⁴ /bawr/ past participle of **bear**²

bore·dom /báwrdəm/ *n* the condition of feeling bored

bore·hole /báwr hòl/ *n* a hole drilled in the ground, often to extract water or oil

~~boreing~~ incorrect spelling of **boring**

Borg /bawrg/, **Björn** (*b.* 1956) Swedish tennis player

Bor·ges /báwr hèss/, **Jorge Luis** (1899–1986) Argentine writer

Bor·gia /báwrjə, -zhə/, **Cesare, Duke of the Romagna** (1476?–1507) Italian soldier

Bor·gia, Lucrezia (1480–1519) Italian art patron

Bor·glum /báwrgləm/, **Gutzon** (1867–1941) US sculptor. He carved the monumental heads of four US presidents on Mount Rushmore (1927–41).

Bor·mann /báwr màan/, **Martin** (1900–45?) German Nazi official

born past participle of **bear**² ■ *adj* **1** brought into life **2** developed from a particular source or root cause *o a realization born of long experience* **3** naturally predisposed *o a born leader*

born-a·gain *adj* **1** describes a Christian who has made a commitment as an adult to Jesus Christ **2** of evangelical Christianity **3** enthusiastic and committed

borne past participle of **bear**²

Bor·ne·o /báwrnee ò/ island of the Malay Archipelago in the W Pacific Ocean, divided between Malaysia, Brunei, and Indonesia. Pop. 10,470,800 (1995). —**Bor·ne·an** *n, adj*

bo·ron /báw ròn/ *n* (*symbol* B) a yellow-brown element. Use: alloys, glass, ceramics, in nuclear reactors to absorb radiation.

bor·ough /búr ō, búrrō/ *n* **1** an administrative division of a city **2** a self-governing town

bor·row /báwrō, bórrō/ *v* **1** *vti* receive money as a loan **2** *vt* use somebody else's property **3** *vt* take a book from a library **4** *vt* adopt a word from another language —**bor·row·er** *n* —**bor·row·ing** *n*

borscht /bawrsht/ *n* beet soup

Bosch /bosh, bawsh/, **Hieronymus** (1450?–1516) Dutch painter

Bos·ni·a and Her·ze·go·vi·na /bòznee ə ənd háirtsəgō véenə/ country in SE Europe, between Croatia and the Federal Republic of Yugoslavia. Cap. Sarajevo. Pop. 3,922,205 (2001). —**Bos·ni·an** *adj, n*

Bos·ni·ac /bóznee ak/ *n* a Muslim inhabitant of Bosnia and Herzegovina —**Bos·ni·ac** *adj*

bos·om /bóozzəm, bóozəm/ *n* **1** a woman's breasts **2** a protective place (*literary*) *o back in the bosom of her family* ■ *adj* close in friendship (*infml*) *o a bosom buddy*

Bos·po·rus /bóspərəss/, **Bos·pho·rus** /bósfərəss/ strait linking the Black Sea and the Sea of Marmara that separates European and Asian Turkey. Length 19 mi./31 km.

boss¹ *n* somebody in charge of others, especially at work ■ *vt also* **boss a·round** give orders to others *o The big kids try to boss the little ones.*

boss² *n* **1** a round raised part on a surface, e.g., in the center of a shield **2** a ceiling decoration

bos·sa no·va /bòssə nóvə, bàwssə-/ *n* **1** a lively ballroom dance that originated in Brazil **2** the music for the bossa nova

boss·y /báwssee, bóssee/ (**-i·er, -i·est**) *adj* fond of giving people orders —**boss·i·ly** *adv* —**boss·i·ness** *n*

Bos·ton /báwstən, bós-/ capital of Massachusetts. Pop. 555,447 (1998). —**Bos·to·ni·an** /baw stónee ən, bo-/ *n, adj*

bo·sun /bóss'n/ *n* a ship's officer responsible for maintaining equipment

Bos·well /bóz wèl, -wəl/, **James** (1740–95) Scottish lawyer and biographer

⚡bot *n* a computer program performing routine or time-consuming tasks (*usually in combination*)

bo·tan·i·cal /bə tánnik'l/, **bo·tan·ic** /bə tánnik/ *adj* of plants

bo·tan·i·cal gar·den, bo·tan·ic gar·den *n* a garden where plants are grown and studied (*often pl*)

bot·a·nist /bótt'nist/ *n* a scientist who studies plants

bot·a·ny /bótt'nee/ *n* the scientific study of plants

botch (*infml*) *vt also* **botch up** do something badly because of clumsiness or carelessness ■ *n* a badly done job —**botch·y** *adj*

both /bōth/ *adj* describes two people or things together *o I liked both candidates.* ■ *conj* not just one *o Truancy is both a law-enforcement and an educational issue.*

both·er /bóthər/ *v* **1** *vi* make the effort to do something **2** *vti* make somebody feel worried **3** *vt* make somebody annoyed ■ *n* **1** the effort of doing something **2** a source of annoyance

---

SYNONYMS bother, annoy, bug, disturb, trouble, worry CORE MEANING: interfere with somebody's composure

---

both·er·some /bóthərsəm/ *adj* annoying

Both·ni·a, Gulf of /bóthnee ə/ northern arm of the Baltic Sea, between Finland and Sweden

Bo·tox /bố tòks/ *tdmk* a trademark for an anti-wrinkle beauty treatment in which botulinum toxin is injected into the skin

Bot·swa·na /bot swáanə/ landlocked country in central southern Africa. Cap. Gaborone. Pop. 1,586,119 (2001). —**Bot·swa·nan** *n, adj*

Barnaby's

Sandro Botticelli: *The Birth of Venus* (after 1482)

Bot·ti·cel·li /bòtti chéllee/, **Sandro** (1445–1510) Italian painter

bot·tle /bótt'l/ *n* 1 a container for liquids with a narrow neck and without a handle 2 the amount of liquid contained in a bottle 3 a container for a baby's milk 4 alcoholic drink *(infml)* ◇ *hit the bottle* ■ *vt* (-**tled, -tling**) put in a bottle

□ **bottle up** *vt* contain feelings, especially feelings that would be better expressed

bot·tle-feed *vt* feed a baby or animal with milk from a bottle

bot·tle·neck /bótt'l nèk/ *n* 1 a narrow section of road that slows down traffic 2 something that causes a delay in progress

bot·tom /bóttəm/ *n* 1 the lowest or deepest part of something 2 the underside of something 3 the farthest point of something ◇ *at the bottom of the road* 4 the ground under water 5 the end of a list 6 the root cause of something 7 the lowest level in a hierarchy 8 somebody's buttocks *(infml)* ■ *adj* 1 lowest ◇ *the bottom shelf* 2 in the position of least excellence ◇ *the bottom five teams* —**bot·tom·most** *adj* ◇ **at bottom** in reality

□ **bottom out** *vi* reach the end of a period of decline

bot·tom·land /bóttəm lànd/ *n* fertile land near a river

bot·tom·less /bóttəmləss/ *adj* 1 very deep 2 plentiful ◇ *a bottomless fund*

bot·tom line *n* 1 a company's final profit or loss at the end of an accounting period 2 the most important factor that must be accepted, however unpleasant 3 the lowest acceptable amount, especially of money

bot·u·lism /bóchə lìzzəm/ *n* a type of food poisoning caused by eating contaminated preserved food

Bou·cher /boo sháy/, **François** (1703–70) French painter

bou·doir /boŏ dwàawr, -dwàwr/ *n* a woman's bedroom or private dressing room

bouf·fant /boo faànt/ *adj* describes hair that is teased into a full shape —**bouf·fant** *n*

bou·gain·vil·le·a /bòogən vílleə ə, -víllyə/, **bou·gain·vil·lae·a** *n* a brightly colored ornamental climbing plant

bough /bow/ *n* a large main branch of a tree

SPELLCHECK Do not confuse the spelling of **bough**, **bow** ("bend over"), or **bow** ("front part of a vessel"), which sound similar.

bought past tense, past participle of **buy**

bouil·la·baisse /bóoyə báyss, bóolyə bàyss/ *n* a rich soup made from fish and shellfish

bouil·lon /boŏl yòn, -yən, boŏ yòn/ *n* cooking stock

bouil·lon cube *n* a concentrated stock in solid form

boul·der /bṓldər/ *n* a large round rock

boules /boolz/ *n* an outdoor game of French origin similar to bowling (+ *sing verb*)

boul·e·vard /boõlə vaàrd, boõlə-/ *n* 1 *also* **Boul·e·vard** a wide street *(often in place names)* 2 Can, Midwest a median strip

ORIGIN Boulevard is adopted from French, where its original meaning was "rampart." It later also came to refer to a promenade or walkway built on the top of a disused fortification. The French word comes from the same German and Dutch forms that gave us *bulwark* in English.

Bou·lez /boo léz/, **Pierre** (*b.* 1925) French composer and conductor

~~boullion~~ incorrect spelling of **bouillon**

bounce *v* (**bounced, bounc·ing**) 1 *vti* spring or make something spring away from a surface 2 *vi* jump up and down 3 *vti* reflect or make something reflect from a surface 4 *vi* move in an up-and-down motion 5 *vti* return a check because of insufficient funds, or be returned for this reason ■ *n* 1 the act of rebounding from a surface 2 springiness 3 energy —**bounc·i·ly** *adv* —**bounc·i·ness** *n* —**bounc·y** *adj*

□ **bounce back** *vi* recover quickly

bounc·er /bównssər/ *n* a guard at the door of a bar or nightclub who ejects troublemakers

bounc·ing /bównssing/ *adj* describes a healthy and active baby

bound[1] past participle, past tense of **bind** ■ *adj* 1 certain to do something 2 obligated

bound[2] *vi* go somewhere energetically with long strides —**bound** *n*

bound[3] *adj* 1 on the way somewhere *(often in combination)* 2 destined to achieve something

bound[4] *vt* 1 form the boundary of 2 impose limits on

bound·a·ry /bówndəree, -dree/ (*pl* -**ries**) *n* 1 a border dividing territories 2 a limit 3 in cricket, a shot that crosses the boundary

bound·en /bównd'n/ *v* past participle of **bind** *(literary)* ■ *adj* obligatory

bound·er /bówndər/ *n* a dishonorable person (insult)

bound·less /bówndləss/ *adj* seeming to have no limit —**bound·less·ly** *adv* —**bound·less·ness** *n*

~~boundry~~ incorrect spelling of **boundary**

bounds ◇ **know no bounds** be very great, strong, or intense ◇ **out of bounds** 1 outside the area where somebody is allowed to go 2 beyond what is acceptable

boun·te·ous /bówntee əss/ *adj* generous (*literary*)

boun·ti·ful /bówntəf'l/ *adj* (*literary*) 1 generous 2 in plentiful supply ◊ See note at **generous**

boun·ty /bówntee/ *n* (*pl* **-ties**) 1 a reward of money offered for finding a criminal 2 generosity (*literary*)

bou·quet /bō káy, boo-/ *n* 1 a bunch of flowers 2 the scent of wine ◊ See note at **smell**

bou·quet gar·ni /boo kày gaar neé/ (*pl* **bou·quets gar·nis** /*pronunc. same*/) *n* a bunch or bag of mixed herbs used to flavor food

bour·bon /búrbən/ *n* a type of American whiskey made from corn

Bour·bon /búrbən/ *adj* of the former French royal family —**Bour·bon** *n*

bour·geois /boor zhwáa, bóor zhwáa/ *adj* 1 politically conservative and socially conventional, as the affluent middle classes are often depicted 2 in Marxist political theory, of the capitalist middle class, regarded as exploiters of the working class —**bour·geois** *n* —**bour·geoi·sie** /bóor zhwaa zeé/ *n*

Bourke-White /bùrk wít, -whít/, **Margaret** (1906–71) US photographer and writer

bout /bowt/ *n* 1 an attack of an illness 2 a short period of activity 3 a boxing or wrestling match

bou·tique /boo teék/ *n* 1 a small clothes store 2 a small specialist store

bou·tique brew·er·y *n* a microbrewery

bou·tique ho·tel *n* an upscale, often stylish hotel with an individual character and decor

bou·ton·niere /boòt'n éer, -yáir/ *n* a flower worn in a buttonhole

Bou·tros-Gha·li /boòtròss gaálee/, **Boutros** (b. 1922) Egyptian diplomat and secretary-general of the United Nations (1992–96)

~~bouy~~ incorrect spelling of **buoy**

~~bouyant~~ incorrect spelling of **buoyant**

bo·vine /bó vìn, -vèen/ *adj* 1 of cattle 2 slow (*literary*)

bo·vine spon·gi·form en·ceph·a·lop·a·thy /-spùnjə fawrm en sèffə lóppə thee/ *n* full form of **BSE**

bow¹ /bō/ *n* 1 a knot in which the loops remain visible 2 a weapon for firing arrows 3 a rod for playing stringed instruments 4 a curved shape or part, e.g., a bend in a river ■ *vti* 1 bend, or bend something, into a bow shape 2 draw a bow across the strings of an instrument

bow² /bow/ *v* 1 *vti* bend the head or body forward as a greeting or submission 2 *vt* bend because of heaviness 3 *vi* yield or submit —**bow** *n*

bow³ /bow/ *n* the front part of a vessel ◊ See note at **bough**

bowd·ler·ize /bódlə rìz, bówd-/ (**-ized**, **-iz·ing**) *vti* remove parts of a literary work regarded as indecent —**bowd·ler·ism** *n*

ORIGIN Bowdlerize comes from the name of the British editor Dr. Thomas Bowdler (1754–1825), who in 1818 published an expurgated edition of the works of Shakespeare, omitting words, expressions, and scenes that he considered unsuitable for family reading.

bow·el /bów əl, bowl/ *n* 1 the intestine (*often pl*) 2 the part of the intestine that connects to the anus ■ **bow·els** *npl* the innermost parts of something ◊ *the bowels of the ship*

bow·er /bów ər/ *n* a shady area of a garden

Bow·ie /boò ee, bó ee/, **Jim** (1796?–1836) US pioneer

bowl¹ /bōl/ *n* 1 a round container typically used for food or liquid 2 the amount contained in a bowl 3 a part shaped like a bowl 4 *also* **Bowl** a stadium —**bowl·ful** *n* ◊ See note at **bole**

bowl² /bōl/ *v* 1 *vti* roll a ball 2 *vi* take part in a game of bowling 3 *vti* in cricket, send a ball to a person batting 4 *vt* score a given number of points in bowling 5 *vi* move quickly ■ *n* 1 a wooden ball used in lawn bowling 2 a ball used in tenpin bowling 3 a roll of the ball in bowling or lawn bowling 4 a revolving drum

□ **bowl over** *vt* 1 astonish 2 knock down accidentally

bow·leg·ged /bō léggəd, -légd/ *adj* with outward-curving legs

bowl·er /bólər/ *n* a player in bowling

Bowles /bōlz/, **Paul** (1910–99) US writer and composer

bowl·ing /bóling/ *n* 1 the sport of rolling a ball at pins 2 lawn bowling 3 in cricket, the throwing of the ball to the person batting

bowl·ing al·ley *n* 1 a building for bowling 2 any of the smooth lanes used in bowling

bowl·ing green *n* an area of grass where lawn bowling is played

bow·sprit /bów sprit, bó-/ *n* a spar projecting from the front of a ship

bow tie /bō-/ *n* a tie tied in a bow at the front of the neck

bow win·dow /bó-/ *n* a window that curves out from a wall

bow-wow /bów wòw/ *interj* an imitation of a dog's barking

box¹ *n* 1 a container, usually rectangular and with a lid 2 the amount that a box holds 3 a rectangular shape marked on a surface 4 a separated area of a theater, courtroom, or stadium 5 a small building used as a shelter ◊ *a sentry box* ■ *vt* 1 pack in boxes 2 draw a box around —**box·ful** *n*

□ **box in** *vt* surround and restrict in movement ◊ *a small car boxed in by trucks*

box² *vti* fight somebody using fists and the techniques of boxing

box 99 braggart

box³ (*pl same* or **box·es**) *n* a dense evergreen bush. Use: hedging.

box can·yon *n* a canyon with only one entrance

box-car /bóks kaär/ *n* an enclosed railroad car

box·er¹ /bóksər/ *n* a fighter in the sport of boxing

box·er² /bóksər/ *n* **1** a medium-sized smooth-haired dog with a flat face **2 Box·er** a member of an early-20C Chinese secret society dedicated to removing all foreign influences from Chinese life

box·er shorts, box·ers *npl* loose-fitting underpants

box·ing /bóksing/ *n* the sport of fighting with fists wearing large padded gloves

box lunch *n* a lunch packed in a small box

box num·ber *n* a number assigned to an anonymous address for mail

box of·fice *n* a place where tickets are bought for entertainments such as plays and concerts

box·wood /bóks wòod/ (*pl same* or **-woods**) *n* the box bush

boy *n* **1** a young male person **2** a son ■ **boys** *npl* a group of male friends ■ *interj* expresses pleasure or annoyance —**boy·hood** *n*

boy·cott /bóy kòt/ *vt* refuse to buy or deal with something as a way of protesting against it —**boy·cott** *n*

ORIGIN **Boycotting** began in 1880 when Captain Charles Cunningham Boycott (1832–97), a British estate manager in County Mayo, Ireland, refused to reduce rents, with the result that workers and traders stopped dealing with him.

Boy·er /bóy ər/, **Herbert W.** (b. 1936) US biochemist. He codeveloped the recombinant DNA techniques that became the basis of genetic engineering.

boy·friend /bóy frènd/ *n* a boy or man with whom somebody has a romantic or sexual relationship

boy·ish /bóy ish/ *adj* with youthful male looks or behavior —**boy·ish·ly** *adv* —**boy·ish·ness** *n*

Boyle /boyl/, **Robert** (1627–91) Irish-born English scientist, regarded as one of the founders of modern scientific method and the science of chemistry

Boy Scout *n* a male member of the US Scouts organization

Boze·man /bózmən/ city in SW Montana. Pop. 29,936 (1998).

B.Phil. *abbr* Bachelor of Philosophy

⌀ bps *n* a measurement of computer data transfer speed. Full form **bits per second**

Bq *symbol* becquerel

Br *symbol* bromine

Br. *abbr* **1** Britain **2** British

bra *n* an undergarment supporting a woman's breasts

brace *n* **1** a support for an injured part of the body **2** a clamp **3** a support for a part of a building under construction **4** DENT = **braces** *npl* **5** (*pl same*) a pair of similar things **6** a hand-operated tool for holding a drill bit **7** either of the symbols {} ■ **brac·es** *npl* a dental appliance tightened to straighten teeth ■ *v* (**braced, brac·ing**) **1** *vt* support or strengthen something **2** *vi* prepare for something

brace·let /bráysslit/ *n* a piece of jewelry worn around the wrist or arm

brac·ing /bráyssing/ *adj* refreshingly invigorating

brack·en /brákən/ (*pl same* or **-ens**) *n* a large species of fern

brack·et /brákit/ *n* **1** an L-shaped structure fixed to a wall as a support for something, e.g., a shelf **2** either of the symbols [ ], used in pairs for enclosing and separating text **3** a section of a population or group that falls within particular limits ○ *in a higher tax bracket* ■ *vt* **1** support with brackets **2** put inside brackets **3** group together because of similarities

brack·ish /brákish/ *adj* describes water that is slightly salty

brad *n* a thin nail with a small head

brad·awl /brád àwl/ *n* a hand tool for making holes in wood to prepare for nails or screws to be inserted

Brad·bury /brádbəree/, **Ray Douglas** (b. 1920) US science-fiction writer

Brad·dock /bráddək/, **Edward** (1695–1755) British general

Brad·ford /brádfərd/ city in N England. Pop. 289,376 (1992).

Brad·ford, William (1590–1657) English-born Puritan leader and New England colonial administrator

Brad·ford, William (1663–1752) English-born American printer

Brad·ley /bráddlee/, **Omar** (1893–1981) US general

Brad·street /brád strèet/, **Anne** (1612?–72) English-born New England poet

Bra·dy /bráydee/, **Mathew B.** (1823?–96) US photographer

brag (**bragged, brag·ging**) *vi* talk with too much pride —**brag** *n* —**brag·ging** *n, adj* —**brag·ging·ly** *adv*

brag·ga·do·ci·o /bràggə dósee ò, -shee ò, -shō/ (*pl* **-os**) *n* **1** empty boasting and swaggering self-aggrandizement **2** a braggart

ORIGIN **Braggadocio** is an alteration of the name *Braggadochio*, the personification of boastfulness in *The Faerie Queene* (1590–96) by Edmund Spenser.

brag·gart /bràggərt/ *n* a boastful person

Brahe /braa, braàhee, braà ə/, **Tycho** (1546–1601) Danish astronomer

Brah·ma /braàmə/ n 1 the Hindu god of knowledge and understanding, later called the Creator 2 *also* **Brah·man** in Hinduism, the ultimate impersonal reality underlying everything in the universe

Brah·ma·pu·tra /braàmə poōtrə/ river in Tibet and NE India, emptying into the Ganges delta in Bangladesh. Length 1,800 mi./2,900 km.

Brah·min /braàmin/ (*pl* **-mins** *or* same), **brah·min** n a member of the highest Hindu caste —**Brah·min·ic** /braa mínnik/ *adj*

Johannes Brahms

Brahms /braamz/, **Johannes** (1833–97) German composer

braid n 1 silky cord or interwoven thread used for decorative edging 2 strands of hair interwoven ■ vt 1 interweave strands of something, e.g., hair 2 create something by braiding 3 decorate with braid

Braille /brayl/ n a writing system for visually impaired people consisting of patterns of raised dots that are read by touch

> **ORIGIN Braille** is named for Louis Braille (1809–52), a French educator who invented it in 1828.

brain n 1 in vertebrates, the organ of thought and feeling that controls the nervous system 2 in invertebrates, a similar center for controlling the nervous system 3 intellect or intellectual abilities 4 somebody regarded as very intelligent (*infml*) ■ vt hit on the head (*slang*) ◊ **pick somebody's brain** ask somebody questions in order to get information or ideas ◊ **rack your brains** try very hard to remember something or solve a problem

brain·child /bráyn chīld/ n an original idea that is attributed to somebody

brain death n the end of all brain function —**brain-dead** *adj*

brain drain n the emigration of highly skilled personnel such as scientists to a country offering better opportunities

brain·less /bráynləss/ *adj* regarded as unintelligent —**brain·less·ness** n

brain·pow·er /bráyn pòwər/ n intellectual ability

brain·storm /bráyn stàwrm/ n a brilliant idea (*infml*) ■ vti produce new ideas or solutions

to problems quickly and spontaneously in a group discussion —**brain·storm·ing** n

brain-teas·er /bráyn teèzər/ n a difficult problem or puzzle

brain trust n a group of high-level advisers —**brain trust·er** n

brain·wash /bráyn wòsh/ vt induce to believe or do something by constant repetition

brain wave n a wave of voltage resulting from electrical activity in the brain

brain·y /bráynee/ (**-i·er, -i·est**) *adj* extremely intelligent (*infml*) —**brain·i·ness** n

braise /brayz/ (**braised, brais·ing**) vt cook by browning in fat, adding a little liquid, and simmering in a covered pot

> **SPELLCHECK** Do not confuse the spelling of **braise** and **braze** ("solder"), which sound similar.

brake[1] /brayk/ n 1 a device in a machine or vehicle that slows it down or stops it (*often pl*) 2 something that slows or halts something such as expenditure or development ■ v (**braked, brak·ing**) 1 vti reduce the speed of a vehicle, or slow down or stop 2 vt slow down or halt the progress or development of ◊ See note at **break**

brake[2] /brayk/ n an area of dense bushes

brake pad n a block of material that presses against a disk brake

brake shoe n a curved block that presses against a wheel to slow it down

bram·ble /brámb'l/ n a prickly bush, especially one that produces blackberries or raspberries

bram·bling /brámbling/ n a finch with a speckled head and back and a rusty brown breast

Bramp·ton /brámptən/ city in SE Ontario, Canada. Pop. 268,251 (1996).

bran n the husks of cereal grain removed during milling. Use: supplementary source of dietary fiber.

branch n 1 a part of a tree growing from the trunk 2 a part of a plant stem, root, or flower cluster 3 something that is like a tree branch in structure 4 a store, bank, or another organization belonging to a larger group o *branches in every major city* 5 a subdivision of a large organization with a specific function or purpose 6 a part of a larger area of study o *a branch of medicine* 7 one line of a family descended from a common ancestor 8 a tributary of a river or stream o *a branch of the Colorado River* 9 *Southern US* a creek ■ v 1 vti divide into smaller parts o *The path branches off toward the river.* 2 vi grow branches —**branched** *adj*

□ **branch out** vi expand activities or interests into a new or different area

Bran·cu·si /bran koōzee, braang koōsh/, **Constantin** (1876–1957) Romanian sculptor

brand n 1 a product made by a company and identified by a specific name 2 a particular type or kind o *his brand of humor* 3 an owner's mark burned on an animal's hide ■ *vt* **1** burn an owner's mark on the hide of **2** describe as bad or undesirable ○ *was branded as a cheat* —**brand·ed** *adj*

Bran·deis /brán dĭss/, **Louis** (1856–1941) associate justice of the US Supreme Court (1916–39)

bran·dish /brándĭsh/ *vt* wave about menacingly, theatrically, or triumphantly

brand lead·er *n* the best-selling product in a specific category

brand loy·al·ty *n* the tendency to buy a specific brand of goods repeatedly

brand name *n* a trade name for a product made by a specific company —**brand-named** *adj*

brand-new *adj* completely new

Bran·do /brándō/, **Marlon** (*b.* 1924) US actor

Brandt /brant, braant/, **Willy** (1913–92) chancellor of West Germany (1969–74)

bran·dy /brándee/ *n* an alcoholic spirit distilled from the fermented juice of grapes or other fruit

> **ORIGIN** The earlier form of **brandy** was *brandy wine*, which came from a Dutch word meaning "distilled (literally, burned) wine."

Bran·dy·wine Creek /brándee wīn-/ site of a Revolutionary War battle, near Philadelphia

Brant, Joseph (1742–1807) Mohawk leader

Braque /braak, brak/, **Georges** (1882–1963) French painter

brash *adj* **1** aggressively self-assertive **2** hasty —**brash·ly** *adv* —**brash·ness** *n*

Bra·sí·lia /brə zĭlyə/ capital of Brazil. Pop. 1,821,946 (1996).

brass *n* **1** a yellow alloy of zinc and copper **2** items made of brass ○ *clean the brass* **3** brass musical instruments collectively **4** the players of brass instruments as a section of an orchestra **5** high-ranking military or police officers (*infml*) **6** excessive self-assurance (*infml*) ○ *had the brass to lie about it* —**brass** *adj* —**brass·y** *adj*

brass band *n* a band consisting of brass instruments

bras·se·rie /brássə rée, bràss rée/ *n* a bar serving food and drink

bras·si·ca /brássikə/ *n* a plant of the family that includes cabbage, broccoli, and cauliflower

bras·siere /brə zéer/ *n* a bra

brat *n* an annoyingly demanding and selfish child or young person —**brat·tish** *adj* —**brat·ty** *adj*

Bra·ti·sla·va /bràtti sláavə, braàti-/ capital of Slovakia. Pop. 449,547 (1999).

Brat·tain /brátt'n/, **Walter H.** (1902–87) Chinese-born US physicist. He shared a Nobel Prize in physics (1956) for his research on transistors and semiconductors.

Braun /brown/ ◆ **von Braun, Wernher**

bra·va·do /brə vaàdō/ *n* real or pretended boldness or courage

brave /brayv/ *adj* (**brav·er, brav·est**) having or showing courage ■ *n* a Native North American warrior ■ *vt* (**braved, brav·ing**) **1** face something dangerous or unpleasant with courage and resolution **2** defy something against the odds —**brave·ly** *adv* —**brave·ness** *n* —**brav·er·y** *n*

bra·vo /braávō, braa vṓ/ *interj* expresses approval of a performer or performance ■ *n* (*pl* -**vos**) **1** a cry of "bravo" **2** **Bra·vo** a communications code word for the letter "B"

bra·vu·ra /brə vóorə, -vyóorə/ *n* **1** dazzling artistic flair **2** showy style or behavior

brawl *n* a rough and noisy fight ■ *vi* fight noisily —**brawl·ing** *n*

brawn *n* **1** strong muscles **2** physical strength

brawn·y /bráwnee/ (-**i·er, -i·est**) *adj* muscular and strong-looking —**brawn·i·ly** *adv* —**brawni·ness** *n*

bray *v* **1** *vi* make the characteristic sound of a donkey **2** *vti* speak or say with a harsh rasping voice —**bray** *n*

braze /brayz/ (**brazed, braz·ing**) *vt* join metal with solder ◊ See note at **braise**

bra·zen /bráyz'n/ *adj* **1** bold and unashamed **2** harsh-sounding —**bra·zen·ly** *adv* —**bra·zen·ness** *n*

bra·zier /bráyzhər/ *n* a metal container used outdoors for burning coal or charcoal

Bra·zil /brə zĭl/ country in E South America. Cap. Brasília. Pop. 174,468,580 (2001). —**Bra·zil·i·an** *n, adj*

Bra·zil nut *n* **1** an edible seed with a hard triangular shell **2** an evergreen tree that produces Brazil nuts

Braz·os /brázzōss/ river flowing from E New Mexico through Texas and into the Gulf of Mexico. Length 923 mi./1,490 km.

Braz·za·ville /brázzə vĭl/ capital of the Republic of the Congo. Pop. 1,009,000 (1995 estimate).

breach /breech/ *v* **1** *vt* break through an obstruction **2** *vt* break a law or promise **3** *vti* rise above the surface of the water (*refers to whales*) ■ *n* **1** an opening produced by force **2** a failure to keep or preserve something, e.g., a law or friendship ○ *a breach of confidentiality*

> **SPELLCHECK** Do not confuse the spelling of **breach** and **breech** ("rear part of a gun barrel"), which sound similar.

bread /bred/ *n* **1** a food made by baking a mixture of flour, water, and yeast **2** a means of sustenance or survival **3** money (*slang dated*)

> **SPELLCHECK** Do not confuse the spelling of

bread and bred (past tense of *breed*), which sound similar.

bread and but·ter *n* 1 a dependable source of income 2 the mainstay of something

bread-and-but·ter *adj* 1 involving the basics 2 generating somebody's main income

bread·board /bréd bàwrd/ *n* 1 a board on which to cut bread 2 a test version of an electrical or electronic circuit

bread·fruit /bréd fròòt/ (*pl same or -fruits*) *n* 1 a large round seedless tropical fruit 2 an evergreen tree that produces breadfruit

bread·line /bréd lìn/ *n* a line of people waiting for free food

breadth /bredth/ *n* 1 the distance from one side of something to the other 2 the extent of something ○ *the breadth of her knowledge* 3 broad-mindedness ○ *breadth of vision* —**breadth·ways** *adj, adv* —**breadth·wise** *adj, adv*

bread·win·ner /bréd wìnnər/ *n* somebody whose earnings are a family's main income

break /brayk/ *v* (**broke** /brōk/, **bro·ken** /brṓkən/) 1 vt separate into pieces because of damage 2 vti fracture a bone in part of the body, or sustain a fracture 3 vti damage a part of a machine so that it stops working, or is damaged 4 vti make or develop a tear or hole, e.g., in a surface 5 vt disobey a rule or law 6 vt go back on a promise or agreement ○ *broke his word* 7 vt end a situation, relationship, or association ○ *break the deadlock* 8 vt stop or interrupt an activity or practice 9 vt destroy the career, resolve, or hope of somebody ○ *a role that could make or break her* 10 vti escape from a restraint ○ *break free* 11 vi take a rest period 12 vt reduce the effect or force of something ○ *break a fall* 13 vt beat a record 14 vt exceed a limit 15 vti reveal or be revealed ○ *broke it to me gently* 16 vi become deeper at puberty (*refers to a boy's voice*) 17 vi become unsteady because of emotion (*refers to voices*) 18 vi become light at sunrise 19 vi change after a settled period (*refers to the weather*) 20 vi suddenly start to rain, snow, or hail ○ *before the storm broke* 21 vi turn into surf upon reaching the shore (*refers to waves*) 22 vt decipher a code 23 vt forcibly open a safe 24 vt train a horse to accept a rider 25 vt exchange a bill for coins or smaller bills 26 vi flow out during the first stage of labor (*refers to amniotic fluid*) ○ *Her waters have broken.* 27 vt impoverish or bankrupt somebody 28 vti emerge above the surface of the water 29 vi in boxing or wrestling, separate after being in a clinch ■ *n* 1 a rest period 2 a brief vacation ○ *a temporary period away from a usual activity* ○ *a career break* 4 an end to a relationship, activity, practice, or association 5 a commercial broadcasting pause for, e.g., advertising 6 an interval in a sports game 7 a pause in speech ○ *a break in the conversation* 8 a bone

fracture 9 a weather change 10 an unexpected opportunity to achieve success (*infml*) ○ *his big break* 11 a piece of good or bad luck 12 an advantageous financial situation in which somebody is repaid or makes a reduced payment ○ *a tax break* 13 a sudden escape attempt ○ *make a break for it* 14 sunrise (*literary*) ○ *at the break of day* —**break·a·ble** *adj* ◊ **break even** make neither a profit nor a loss ◊ **give somebody a break** stop nagging or criticizing somebody (*infml*)

SPELLCHECK Do not confuse the spelling of **break** and **brake** ("of a vehicle"), which sound similar.

☐ **break down** *v* 1 vti become upset emotionally 2 vt experience a physical or psychological collapse 3 vi stop functioning properly 4 vti weaken 5 vt divide into component parts

☐ **break in** *vi* 1 enter a place forcibly or illegally 2 interrupt a conversation

☐ **break off** *vti* end a relationship or association

☐ **break out** *vi* 1 develop a skin rash 2 escape from something such as a prison

☐ **break up** *v* 1 vt divide up or interrupt the continuity of 2 vi disperse 3 vti end something such as a romantic or professional relationship

break·age /bráykij/ *n* something broken by accident (*usually pl*) ○ *All breakages must be paid for.*

break·a·way /bráykə wày/ *n* somebody or something that has broken away from a person or group —**break·a·way** *adj*

break·danc·ing /bráyk dànsing/ *n* acrobatic dancing to rap music —**break·dance** *n, vi* —**break·danc·er** *n*

break·down /bráyk dòwn/ *n* 1 a failure to function properly 2 a disruption in communications between people or groups 3 a sudden physical or psychological collapse 4 a summary, explanation, or analysis of data

break·er /bráykər/ *n* 1 a large white-capped wave 2 a device that automatically stops the flow of electricity in a circuit

break·e·ven /bràyk éevən/, **break·e·ven point** *n* the point at which expenditure is equaled by income

break·fast /brékfəst/ *n* the first meal of the day —**break·fast** *vi*

ORIGIN Breakfast is literally the meal with which you "break your fast" after the night. It is first recorded in the 15C.

break·front /bráyk frùnt/ *adj* describes furniture with a middle section that juts out slightly —**break·front** *n*

break-in *n* a forcible or illegal entry

break·ing and en·ter·ing *n* the crime of forcibly entering property

break·ing point n the point at which somebody can no longer cope with a situation or at which a situation reaches a crisis

break·neck /bráyk nèk/ adj dangerously fast ○ at breakneck speed

break·out /bráyk òwt/ n an escape from imprisonment

break point n in tennis, a point that, if won, results in the player who is not serving winning the game

⚡ break·point /bráyk pòynt/ n 1 a pause inserted in a computer program to enable correction of errors 2 a point where something stops, changes, or breaks apart

break·through /bráyk thròo/ n 1 an important discovery with far-reaching consequences 2 the removal of a barrier to progress —**break·through** adj

break·up /bráyk ùp/ n 1 the separation of something such as a company or country into separate units ○ the breakup of the Soviet Union 2 the end of a relationship

break·wa·ter /bráyk wàwtər/ n a barrier protecting the shore from waves

breast /brest/ n 1 one of the two organs on either side of the human chest, which in women are especially prominent and produce milk after childbirth 2 a milk-producing gland in mammals corresponding to the human breast 3 somebody's chest 4 the chest regarded as the seat of emotions (literary) ○ with pride filling my breast 5 a bird or mammal's chest 6 meat from a bird or mammal's chest 7 a projecting point ○ the breast of a hill ■ vt 1 reach the top of a hill 2 push something with the chest

breast·bone /brést bòn/ n a long bone running down the center of the chest

breast-feed (breast-fed) vti feed a baby by holding it so that it can suck milk from the breast

breast·plate /brést plàyt/ n a piece of armor covering the chest

breast·stroke /brést stròk/ n a swimming stroke in which both arms are extended and pulled back in a circular motion while both legs are thrust back and pulled back together —**breast·stroke** vi

breath /breth/ n 1 air that is inhaled and exhaled ○ an inhalation or exhalation of air ○ take a deep breath 3 a slight hint of something ○ a breath of scandal 4 a slight movement of air ○ not a breath of wind —**breath·y** adj ◊ **in the same breath** at almost the same moment ◊ **under your breath** in a whispering or muttering voice

USAGE breath or **breathe**? The noun is **breath** (not a breath of air moving), and the verb is **breathe** (hard to breathe in the sultry air).

breath·a·lyze /bréthə līz/ (-lyzed, -lyz·ing) vt test a driver for drunkenness with a BreathalyzerTM

Breath·a·lyz·er /bréthə līzər/ tdmk a trademark for an apparatus that measures a driver's blood alcohol level

breathe /breeth/ (breathed, breath·ing) v 1 vti take in and blow out air repeatedly in order to stay alive 2 vt exhale something ○ a dragon breathing fire 3 vi allow air in and moisture out (refers to fabrics) 4 vt say something quietly or secretively 5 vi be alive 6 vti allow a person or animal a pause to rest —**breath·a·ble** adj ◊ See note at **breath**

breath·er /breethər/ n 1 somebody who breathes in a particular way (in combination) ○ a heavy breather 2 a pause for a rest (infml)

breath·ing space, breath·ing room n time to rest or think

breath·less /bréthləss/ adj unable to breathe properly because of exertion, illness, or emotion —**breath·less·ly** adv —**breath·less·ness** n

breath·tak·ing /bréth tàyking/ adj extremely exciting or shocking

breath test n a test for measuring a driver's blood alcohol level

Brecht /brekt, brekht/, **Bertolt** (1898–1956) German playwright and director

Breck·in·ridge /brékən rìj/, **John C.** (1821–75) vice president of the United States (1857–61)

bred /bred/ past tense, past participle of **breed** ◊ See note at **breed**

breech /breech/ n 1 the rear part of the barrel of a rifle or shotgun 2 a part of a pulley, to which the rope or chain is attached 3 the buttocks ◊ See note at **breach**

breech birth n a delivery of a baby in which its buttocks or feet emerge first

breech·es /bríchəz, bree-/, **britch·es** /bríchiz/ npl 1 trousers (infml) 2 knee-length pants

breed n 1 a distinct strain of an animal or plant within a species 2 a particular type of person or thing ○ a new breed of managers ■ v (bred) 1 vti mate and produce young 2 vt raise domestic animals or plants for commercial purposes or for competitions 3 vti produce or create something ○ Experience breeds confidence.

breed·er /breedər/ n 1 somebody who breeds animals or plants 2 also **bree·der re·ac·tor** a nuclear reactor that produces more fuel than it consumes

breed·ing /breeding/ n 1 somebody's upbringing and training in manners and social skills 2 somebody's ancestry 3 the mating and producing of young ○ prime breeding stock 4 the development of improved types of animals and plants

breed·ing ground n 1 an area where animals go to mate and produce young 2 an environment that encourages the development of something ○ a breeding ground for new talent

breeze n 1 a light to moderate wind 2 something easily achieved (infml) ■ vi (breezed, breez·ing) move briskly ◊ **shoot the breeze** spend time chatting (slang)
□ **breeze through** vti accomplish a task easily

breez·y /bréezee/ (-i-er, -i-est) adj 1 with a light to moderate wind 2 relaxed and confident —**breez·i·ly** adv —**breez·i·ness** n

Bre·men /bráymən, brémmən/ port in NW Germany. Pop. 549,182 (1997).

Bren·nan /brénnən/, **William J., Jr.** (1906–97) associate justice of the US Supreme Court (1956–90)

Bren·ner Pass /brénnər-/ mountain pass between SW Austria and NE Italy

Bre·scia /brésha/ capital of Brescia Province, N Italy. Pop. 190,909 (1999).

breth·ren /bréthrən/ plural of **brother** n 2 ■ npl members of a group, family, or community (literary or humorous)

Bre·ton /brə tóN/, **André** (1896–1966) French poet and essayist

Bret·ton Woods /brétt'n-/ resort in N New Hampshire, site of the 1944 conference that created the International Monetary Fund and the International Bank for Reconstruction and Development

Breu·ghel ◊ **Brueghel**

breve /brev, breev/ n 1 a mark, ˘, over a short vowel or short or unstressed syllable 2 a musical note equal in length to two whole notes

bre·vi·ar·y /bréevee èrree/ (pl -ies) n in the Roman Catholic Church, a book containing the hymns, psalms, and prayers prescribed for each day

brev·i·ty /brévvətee/ n 1 briefness in time 2 economical use of words

brew /broo/ vti 1 make beer 2 make tea or coffee 3 develop threateningly ○ A scandal was brewing. —**brew** n —**brew·er** n —**brew·ing** n

brew·er·y /bróŏ əree, bróŏree/ (pl -ies) n a building or company that brews beer

Brey·er /brí ər/, **Stephen** (b. 1938) associate justice of the US Supreme Court (1994–)

Brezh·nev /bréźh nef, -nyif/, **Leonid Ilyich** (1906–82) leader of the Communist Party (1964–82) and president (1977–82) of the former Soviet Union

bri·ar¹ /brí ər/ (pl -ars or same), **bri·er** (pl -ers or same) n 1 a tobacco pipe 2 a bush of the heather family with hard woody roots. Use: tobacco pipes.

bri·ar² /brí ər/, **bri·er** n a thorny wild plant, especially a trailing rose

bribe vti (bribed, brib·ing) give somebody money or another incentive to do you a favor, especially an illegal or dishonest one ■ n money or another incentive given to persuade somebody to do something, especially something illegal or dishonest —**brib·a·ble** adj —**brib·er·y** n

bric-a-brac /bríkə bràk/ n small inexpensive ornaments

> **ORIGIN** Bric-a-brac was adopted in the mid-19C, formed from an obsolete French phrase à bric et à brac, meaning "at random."

brick n 1 a small hard block of clay. Use: building or paving material. 2 a rectangular block of something, e.g., ice cream ■ vt make with bricks

brick·bat /brík bàt/ n a harsh criticism

brick·lay·er /brík lày ər/ n a skilled worker who constructs buildings and other permanent structures with bricks —**brick·lay·ing** n

⚡ **bricks-and-mor·tar, brick-and-mor·tar** adj of physical business premises

brick·work /brík wùrk/ n 1 a structure built from bricks 2 the technique or skill of laying bricks

bri·dal /bríd'l/ adj of brides or weddings

> **SPELLCHECK** Do not confuse the spelling of **bridal** and **bridle** ("a harness for a horse's head"), which sound similar.

bride n a woman who is about to marry or has just married

bride·groom /bríd gròom, -gròŏm/ n a man who is about to marry or has just married

brides·maid /brídz màyd/ n a bride's attendant at a wedding

bridge¹ n 1 a structure allowing passage over an obstacle such as a river or road 2 a link or means of approach to something 3 a ship's control room or platform 4 a set of one or more false teeth attached to adjoining teeth 5 the top bony part of the nose 6 the part of a stringed instrument that keeps the strings away from its body ■ vt (bridged, bridg·ing) 1 build a bridge over an obstacle 2 create understanding between people ◊ **burn your bridges** do something that makes it impossible to return to your former position

bridge² n a card game for two pairs of players

bridge·head /bríj hèd/ n a forward position seized in enemy territory and used as a base for further advances

bridge loan n a short-term loan to finance the purchase of one property while another is being sold

Bridge·port /bríj pàwrt/ coastal city in SW Connecticut. Pop. 137,425 (1998).

bridge town n one of a pair of cities or towns on the US-Mexican border separated by the Rio Grande, e.g., Laredo (Texas) and Nuevo Laredo (Mexico)

Bridge·town /bríj tòwn/ capital of Barbados. Pop. 123,000 (1995).

bri·dle /bríd'l/ n 1 a harness for a horse's head 2 a restraint ■ v (-dled, -dling) 1 vt put a bridle on 2 vi react angrily or indignantly

3 *vt* restrain, control, or curb ◊ See note at bridal

bri·dle path *n* a track for horseback riding

Brie /bree/ *n* soft cheese with a whitish rind

brief /breef/ *adj* **1** lasting only a short time **2** concise ■ *n* **1** a synopsis of a document or documents **2** a briefing **3** an attorney's arguments and evidence in a case submitted to a court beforehand ■ **briefs** *npl* a piece of close-fitting underwear for the lower body ■ *vt* give a briefing to —**brief·ly** *adv* —**brief·ness** *n*

brief·case /breef kàyss/ *n* a case with a handle for carrying books and papers

brief·ing /breefing/ *n* a meeting held to provide information, or the information provided

bri·er *n* = briar

brig *n* **1** a square-rigged two-masted sailing ship **2** a military prison, especially on a ship

bri·gade /bri gáyd/ *n* **1** a military unit consisting of two or more battalions or regiments **2** a group with a shared goal or characteristic

brig·a·dier gen·er·al /brìggə deèr-/ (*pl* **brig·a·diers gen·er·al**), **brig·a·dier** *n* an officer in the US or Royal Canadian Army of a rank above colonel

brig·and /bríggənd/ *n* a bandit (*literary*)

brig·an·tine /bríggən teèn/ *n* a two-masted sailing ship with square-rigged sails on the foremast and fore-and-aft sails on the mainmast

bright /brīt/ *adj* **1** reflecting or emitting light ○ *a bright moonlit night* **2** intensely colored ○ *bright blue* **3** intelligent **4** cheerful and lively **5** likely to be successful ○ *a bright future for the company* —**bright** *adv* —**bright·ly** *adv* —**bright·ness** *n* ◊ See note at intelligent

bright·en /brīt'n/ *v* **1** *vi* become cheerful or lively **2** *vt* add color or interest to **3** *vi* become less overcast or rainy **4** *vti* fill or become filled with more light **5** *vti* make or become more promising

Brigh·ton /brīt'n/ coastal city in S England. Pop. 156,124 (1996).

~~brilliant~~ incorrect spelling of brilliant

brill (*pl* same or **brills**) *n* a flatfish closely related to a turbot

bril·liant /brílyənt/ *adj* **1** extremely bright or radiant ○ *brilliant sunshine* **2** intelligent or talented **3** excellent —**bril·liance** *n* —**bril·liant·ly** *adv*

brim *n* **1** the projecting rim around the edge of a hat **2** the top edge of a container ■ *v* (**brimmed**, **brim·ming**) **1** *vti* fill or be full to the top ○ *a cup brimming with hot coffee* **2** *vi* overflow ○ *eyes brimming with tears* —**brim·less** *adj*

brim·ful /brím fŏol/ *adj* **1** full to the top **2** richly supplied with something ○ *brimful of ideas*

brim·stone /brím stòn/ *n* sulfur (*archaic*)

brin·dled /brínd'ld/ *adj* brown or gray with darker streaks or patches

brine *n* **1** salt water for curing, preserving, or developing flavor in food **2** the sea (*literary*)

bring (**brought** /brawt/) *v* **1** *vt* have somebody or something with you when you come to a place ○ *Please bring me a glass of water.* **2** *vt* attract something ○ *a charm supposed to bring luck* **3** *vt* make something happen ○ *Heavy rain brought flooding.* **4** *vt* cause somebody or something to be in a particular state ○ *brought the meeting to a close* **5** *vt* cause something to enter the mind ○ *brought memories of good times* **6** *vr* make yourself do something ○ *She can't bring herself to think about it.* **7** *vt* be sold for a particular price —**bring·er** *n*

□ **bring about** *vt* make happen

□ **bring around** *vt* **1** revive somebody from unconsciousness **2** alter somebody's opinion ○ *We eventually brought him around to our view.*

□ **bring down** *vt* **1** overthrow **2** kill or wound

□ **bring forth** *vt* **1** give birth to young **2** produce fruit or flowers

□ **bring in** *vt* earn money ○ *barely bringing in enough to live on*

□ **bring off** *vt* succeed in doing something difficult

□ **bring on** *vt* cause ○ *exhaustion brought on by overwork*

□ **bring out** *vt* **1** make known **2** emphasize a quality in ○ *That outfit brings out the red in your hair.* **3** produce something for sale ○ *brought out a new version of the software*

□ **bring up** *vt* **1** raise a subject **2** rear a child

brink *n* **1** the very edge **2** the onset of an action, event, or situation, especially an unpleasant one

brink·man·ship /bríngkmən shìp/, **brinks·man·ship** /bríngksmən-/ *n* the practice of taking a dispute to dangerous limits in order to force concessions

brin·y /brínee/ (-i-er, -i-est) *adj* of sea water

bri·o /bree ö/ *n* vigor

bri·oche /bree ósh/ *n* a sweet French bread

bri·quette /bri két/, **bri·quet** *n* a small block of compressed material used as fuel

Bris·bane /brízbən, bríz bàyn/ capital and main port of Queensland. Pop. 1,574,600 (1998).

brisk *adj* **1** quick and energetic ○ *a brisk walk* **2** busy ○ *Business was brisk.* **3** refreshingly cool ○ *brisk autumn days* —**brisk·ly** *adv* —**brisk·ness** *n*

bris·tle /bríss'l/ *n* one of a number of short stiff hairs on a mammal, plant, or a man's face ■ *v* (-tled, -tling) **1** *vti* make hair or fur stiffen because of fear or anger, or show such a response **2** *vi* take offense ○ *bristled at the suggestion* **3** *vi* be thickly covered ○ *a battleship bristling with guns* —**bris·tly** *adj*

Bris·tol /bríst'l/ port in SW England. Pop. 399,633 (1996).

Bris·tol Chan·nel arm of the Atlantic Ocean between S Wales and SW England. Length 85 mi./140 km.

Brit *n* a British person *(infml)*

Brit. *abbr* 1 Britain 2 British

Brit·ain /brítt'n/ ♦ **Great Britain**

Bri·tan·nia /bri tánnyə/ *n* the symbol of Britain, shown as a seated helmeted woman holding a trident

britch·es *npl* CLOTHING = **breeches**

~~Britian~~ incorrect spelling of **Britain**

Brit·ish /bríttish/ *npl* the people of the United Kingdom —**Brit·ish** *adj*

Brit·ish Co·lum·bi·a westernmost province of Canada, on the Pacific coast. Cap. Victoria. Pop. 4,063,760 (2000).

Brit·ish Em·pire *n* a former empire controlled by Great Britain

Brit·ish Eng·lish *n* English as used in the United Kingdom

Brit·ish Isles group of islands in the Atlantic Ocean off NW Europe, including Britain, Ireland, and many smaller islands

Brit·ish ther·mal u·nit *n* a unit of heat measurement

Brit·ish West In·dies British dependent territories in the Caribbean, including Anguilla, the British Virgin Islands, the Cayman Islands, Montserrat, and the Turks and Caicos

Brit·on /brítt'n/ *n* 1 a British person 2 a member of an ancient Celtic people of S Britain

Brit·ta·ny /brítt'nee/ peninsular region in NW France. Pop. 2,906,197 (1999).

Brit·ten /brítt'n/, **Benjamin, Lord Britten of Aldeburgh** (1913–76) British composer

brit·tle /brítt'l/ *adj* hard and easily broken ■ *n* a crunchy candy made from caramel and nuts —**brit·tle·ness** *n*

Br·no /búrnō/ city in the Czech Republic. Pop. 384,727 (1999).

broach /brōch/ *vt* 1 bring up an awkward subject 2 pierce a cask to draw off liquid ■ *n* a tool for piercing casks

---

SPELLCHECK Do not confuse the spelling of **broach** and **brooch** ("a dress ornament"), which sound similar.

---

broad /brawd/ *adj* 1 wide ○ *a broad forehead* ○ *six inches broad* 2 large and spacious ○ *the broad steppes* 3 full and clear to see ○ *a broad grin* 4 covering a wide range ○ *has broad interests* 5 not detailed ○ *a broad outline of the project* 6 meant to be easily understood ○ *a broad hint* 7 describes a strongly regional accent —**broad·ly** *adv* —**broad·ness** *n*

♪ **broad·band** /brawd bànd/ *adj* 1 using many electromagnetic frequencies 2 able to transfer large amounts of data quickly

broad bean *n* 1 a large flat green seed eaten as a vegetable 2 a plant that produces broad beans

broad-brush *adj* attempting to cover all conditions and instances

broad·cast /brawd kàst/ *v* (**-cast** *or* **-cast·ed**) 1 *vti* transmit a program or information on television or radio 2 *vi* perform on television or radio 3 *vt* make something widely known ■ *n* 1 a television or radio program 2 a transmission of television or radio signals —**broad·cast** *adj* —**broad·cast·er** *n* —**broad·cast·ing** *n*

broad·en /brawd'n/ *vti* 1 widen 2 enlarge the range of, or become more wide-ranging

broad gauge *n* railroad track that is wider than the standard gauge

broad jump *n* a long jump in track-and-field sports *(dated)*

broad-leaved, broad-leaf /brawd leef/ **broad-leafed** *adj* describes trees that are not conifers and have broad rather than needle-shaped leaves

broad·loom /brawd loòm/ *adj* describes a carpet woven on a wide loom —**broad·loom** *n*

broad-mind·ed *adj* tolerating a wide range of views and behavior —**broad-mind·ed·ly** *adv* —**broad-mind·ed·ness** *n*

broad·side /brawd sìd/ *n* 1 all the guns on one side of a ship, or the simultaneous firing of them 2 a strong verbal or written attack ■ *adv* 1 with the side facing toward something ○ *hit the rocks broadside* 2 generally and indiscriminately ○ *Her proposals were attacked broadside.*

broad-spec·trum *adj* describes antibiotics effective against a wide range of harmful organisms

Broad·way /brawd wày/ *n* 1 a long avenue in New York City that runs through the theater district 2 the US commercial theater business

bro·cade /brō káyd/ *n* a heavy fabric with a raised design —**bro·cade** *vt* —**bro·cad·ed** *adj*

broc·co·li /brókəlee/ *n* 1 heads of tight green, purple, or white flower buds eaten as a vegetable 2 a plant that produces broccoli

bro·chure /brō shoòr/ *n* a booklet containing information or advertising

♪ **bro·chure site** *n* a simple website advertising a company's products and giving contact details

~~brocoli~~ incorrect spelling of **broccoli**

Brod·sky /bródskee/, **Joseph** (1940–96) Soviet-born US poet and essayist

brogue /brōg/ *n* a regional accent, especially an Irish one

broil *v* 1 *vt* cook using direct heat 2 *vti* be or make very hot ■ *n* 1 use of direct heat to cook something 2 a broiled food

broil·er /bróylər/ *n* 1 a roasting chicken 2 a grate for broiling food

broke[1] past tense of **break**

broke² adj having no money (infml) ◊ **go for broke** risk everything to achieve a goal (infml)

bro·ken /brṓkən/ past participle of **break** ■ adj **1** having been broken **2** out of order o *The CD player is broken.* **3** not continuous **4** split apart by divorce, separation, or desertion o *from a broken home* **5** imperfectly spoken o *in broken English* —**bro·ken·ly** adv —**bro·ken·ness** n

bro·ken-down adj **1** damaged or not working **2** dilapidated

bro·ken-heart·ed /brṓkən haártəd/ adj grief-stricken —**bro·ken-heart·ed·ly** adv

bro·ker /brṓkər/ n **1** a commercial agent or negotiator or a stockbroker ■ vt arrange a deal, sale, or other agreement

bro·ker·age /brṓkərij/ n **1** a payment to a broker **2** the business of a broker

bro·mide /brṓ mìd/ n **1** a bromine compound **2** potassium bromide. Use: sedative.

bro·mine /brṓ meèn/ n (symbol Br) a liquid nonmetallic element. Use: sedatives, photographic materials, drugs.

bron·chi·al /bróngkee əl/ adj of the tubes that carry air from the windpipe to the lungs

bron·chi·tis /brong kítiss/ n inflammation of the membrane lining the airways to the lungs —**bron·chit·ic** /brong kíttik/ adj

bron·chus /bróngkəss/ n (pl -chi /-kì, -keè/) n an air passage to the lungs

bron·co /bróng kò/, **bron·cho** n a wild horse of the W United States

bron·co-bust·er /bróngkō bùstər/ n a horse tamer (infml)

Charlotte Brontë

Bron·të /bróntee/ family of British writers including **Charlotte** (1816–55) and her sisters **Emily** (1818–48) and **Anne** (1820–49)

bron·to·sau·rus /bròntə sáwrəss/, **bron·to·saur** /bróntə sàwr/ n an apatosaurus (dated)

Bronx /brongks/ borough of New York City. Pop. 1,203,789 (1990).

bronze n **1** a yellowish brown alloy of copper and tin or another substance **2** a bronze object, especially a work of art **3** a deep yellowish brown color ■ vt (bronzed, bronz·ing) make something look like bronze —**bronze** adj —**bronzed** adj

Bronze Age n the historical period characterized by the use of bronze tools, between 3500 and 1500 BC

bronze med·al n a medal for third place in a competition —**bronze med·al·ist** n

brooch /brōch, brooch/ n an ornament pinned to clothing ◊ See note at **broach**

brood n the young of a bird or other animal ■ adj kept for breeding o *a brood mare* ■ v **1** vi worry **2** vi think resentful or dark thoughts **3** vti sit on eggs, or cover chicks —**brood·er** n —**brood·ing** adj

brood·y /bróodee/ (-i·er, -i·est) adj ready to incubate eggs —**brood·i·ly** adv —**brood·i·ness** n

brook¹ n a small stream

brook² vt tolerate (literary)

Brooke, Rupert (1887–1915) British poet

Brook·lyn /brǒoklin/ borough of New York City. Pop. 2,300,664 (1990).

Brooks, Gwendolyn (b. 1917) US poet

broom n **1** a long-handled brush with a head of twigs or bristles **2** a bush with bright yellow flowers

broom·stick /brǒom stik/ n the long handle of a broom

bros., Bros. abbr brothers

broth n **1** a liquid made by cooking meat, seafood, vegetables, or poultry in water, used as a base for soups and sauces **2** a clear soup made by cooking meat, poultry, seafood, or vegetables in water and then removing them

broth·el /bróth'l/ n a house where prostitutes work

broth·er /brúthər/ n **1** a male sibling **2** (pl **broth·ers** or **breth·ren**) a member of the same group as another **3** a close male friend

broth·er·hood /brúthər hòod/ n **1** a group or organization of men with a common purpose **2** all the members of a specific profession or trade **3** a feeling of fellowship **4** the relationship or feeling of brothers

broth·er-in-law (pl **broth·ers-in-law**) n **1** a sister's or spouse's sister's husband **2** a spouse's brother

broth·er·ly /brúthərlee/ adj showing the affection of a brother —**broth·er·li·ness** n

brougham /broom, broó əm, brṓm/ n a one-horse carriage with an open driver's seat and a closed passenger compartment

ORIGIN The **brougham** is named for the British politician Henry Peter Brougham, first Baron Brougham and Vaux (1778–1867), who designed it in 1838.

brought past tense, past participle of **bring**

brou·ha·ha /brǒo haa hàa/ n a noisy commotion (infml)

brow n **1** somebody's forehead **2** an eyebrow **3** the top of a hill

brow·beat /brów bèet/ (-beat, -beat·en /-bèet'n/) vt bully or intimidate

brown /brown/ n a color between red and yellow, e.g., the color of wood or soil ■ adj

Barnaby's

1 brown in color 2 suntanned ■ *vti* make
or become brown —**brown·ness** *n*

Brown /brown/, **John** (1800–59) US abolitionist

Brown, Olympia (1835–1926) US suffragist
and cleric

brown-bag *vti* bring a lunch to work from
home

brown·field /brówn feeld/ *n* an urban development site, often industrial, that has
been previously built on but is currently
unused

brown·ie /brównee/ *n* 1 a piece of rich flat
chocolate cake 2 a helpful elf or goblin
3 **Brown·ie** a Girl Scout aged between six
and eight

Brown·ing /brówning/, **Elizabeth Barrett**
(1806–61) British poet

Brown·ing, Robert (1812–89) British poet

brown·out /brówn òwt/ *n* a temporary electric
power reduction

brown sauce *n* a sauce made from meat
stock and flour browned in fat

brown·stone /brówn stòn/ *n* 1 sandstone 2 a
sandstone building

Browns·ville /brównz vìll/ city and port in S
Texas. Pop. 137,883 (1998).

⚡ **browse** (browsed, brows·ing) *v* 1 *vti* read
through casually 2 *vi* look through or over
a collection of something casually 3 *vti* scan
and view computer files, especially on the
World Wide Web 4 *vti* feed on tender vegetation *(refers to animals)* —**browse** *n*

⚡ **brows·er** /brówzər/ *n* 1 a piece of software for
searching the World Wide Web 2 a person
or animal that browses

⚡ **BRS** *n* the on-off switch on a personal computer when used to power down after a
sudden program failure. Full form **big red
switch**

Bru·beck /broò bèk/, **Dave** (*b.* 1920) US jazz
pianist and composer

Bruch /broòk, broòkh/, **Max** (1838–1920)
German composer

Bruck·ner /broòknər/, **Anton** (1824–96) Austrian composer

Brue·ghel /broygəl, broo-/, **Brue·gel, Breu·ghel**
family of Flemish painters including **Pieter**
(1520–69) and his son **Jan** (1568–1625)

Bruges /broozh/ capital of West Flanders Province, W Belgium. Pop. 115,991 (1999).

bruise /brooz/ *n* a discoloration of skin or
tissue caused by pressure or impact ■ *v*
1 *vti* cause a bruise to develop on somebody
or something, or develop a bruise 2 *vt* hurt
somebody emotionally

bruis·er /broózər/ *n* a big strong man *(infml)*

brunch *n* a mid-morning meal combining
breakfast and lunch

Bru·nei /broo ní/ country in NW Borneo. Cap.
Bandar Seri Begawan. Pop. 343,653 (2001).

Bru·nel·les·chi /broònə léskee/, **Filippo** (1377–
1446) Italian architect and sculptor

bru·net /broo nét/ *n* somebody with dark hair
—**bru·net** *adj*

bru·nette /broo nét/ *n* a woman with dark
brown hair —**bru·nette** *adj*

brunt *n* the main impact of something ○ *had
to bear the brunt of her anger*

bru·schet·ta /broo skéttə, -shéttə/ *n* Italian
bread toasted and drizzled with olive oil

brush[1] *n* 1 a tool consisting of bristles or hair
2 an act of brushing 3 a light stroke or
contact 4 a short unpleasant encounter ○ *a
brush with danger* 5 a bushy tail, especially
a fox's kept as a hunting trophy 6 an electrical conductor in a generator or motor ■
v 1 *vti* use a brush on somebody or something 2 *vt* apply something with a brush to
a surface 3 *vt* remove something with a
brush or a brushing motion 4 *vt* reject
somebody or something ○ *brushed aside the
suggestion* 5 *vti* move lightly against something

□ **brush up** *vt* refresh your knowledge of or
skill in

brush[2] *n* 1 thick undergrowth 2 land covered
with thick undergrowth 3 brushwood

brushed *adj* 1 describes a fabric with a soft
raised surface produced by brushing 2 describes a metallic surface with a non-
reflective sheen

brush-off /brúsh àwf/ *n* an abrupt dismissal
(infml)

brush·wood /brúsh woòd/ *n* 1 cut or broken
twigs and branches 2 thick undergrowth

brusque /brusk/ *adj* abrupt in speech or
manner —**brusque·ly** *adv* —**brusque·ness** *n*

Brus·sels /brúss'lz/ capital of Belgium. Pop.
954,460 (1999).

Brus·sels sprout *n* 1 a green vegetable like a
miniature cabbage 2 a plant that produces
Brussels sprouts

bru·tal /broòt'l/ *adj* 1 cruel and violent 2 harsh
and severe —**bru·tal·i·ty** /broo tállətee/ *n*
—**bru·tal·ly** *adv*

bru·tal·ism /broòt'l ìzzəm/ *n* a harsh massive
modern architectural style —**bru·tal·ist** *n,
adj*

bru·tal·ize /broòt'l ìz/ (-ized, -iz·ing) *vt* 1 make
brutal 2 treat brutally —**bru·tal·i·za·tion**
/broòt'li záysh'n/ *n*

brute *n* somebody brutal ■ *adj* 1 purely
physical or instinctive 2 cruel or savage
—**brut·ish** *adj*

Bru·tus /broótəss/, **Marcus Junius** (85?–42 BC)
Roman general

Bry·an /brí ən/, **William Jennings** (1860–1925)
US reformer, orator, and lawyer

Bry·ant /brí ənt/, **William Cullen** (1794–1878)
US poet, critic, and editor

B.S. *abbr* Bachelor of Science

BSA *abbr* Boy Scouts of America

BSE *n* a disease affecting the nervous system
of cattle. Full form **bovine spongiform en-
cephalopathy**

⚡BTW, btw _abbr_ by the way _(in e-mails)_

bub·ba /búbbə/ _n_ 1 _Can, Southern US_ a white working-class Southerner with traditional views 2 _Southern US_ a brother _(often a term of address between man friends or brothers)_

bub·ble /búbbl/ _n_ 1 a thin spherical film containing air or a gas 2 a globule of air or a gas within a liquid or solid 3 a transparent glass or plastic dome ■ _vi_ (-bled, -bling) 1 effervesce or boil up 2 be full of a lively emotion or enthusiasm ○ _bubbling with mirth_

bub·ble bath _n_ 1 a bath preparation that produces foam 2 a bath containing a foamy preparation

bub·ble gum _n_ chewing gum that can be blown into bubbles

⚡bub·ble-jet print·er _n_ a printer in which heated ink forms bubbles that burst on the paper

⚡bub·ble mem·o·ry _n_ computer memory in which data are stored as binary digits represented by the presence or absence of minute areas of magnetization in a semiconductor

bub·bly /búbblee/ (-bli·er, -bli·est) _adj_ foamy or effervescent —**bub·bli·ness** _n_

Bu·ber /bóobər/, **Martin** (1878–1965) Austrian-born Israeli theologian and philosopher

bu·bon·ic plague /boo bónnik-/ _n_ an infectious fatal epidemic disease transmitted by fleas

buc·ca·neer /bùkə néer/ _n_ 1 a pirate on the high seas 2 an unscrupulous businessperson or politician —**buc·ca·neer·ing** _adj, n_

> **ORIGIN Buccaneer** was adopted from a French word that means "somebody who cooks or dries meat on a wooden frame over an open fire." It is formed from a Native South American term for the frame. The hunters who regularly prepared meat in this way were independent and lawless, and became identified with the pirates of the Spanish-American coasts.

Buch·an /búkən/, **John, 1st Baron Tweedsmuir** (1875–1940) British writer and administrator

Bu·chan·an /byoo kánnən, bə-/, **James** (1791–1868) 15th president of the United States (1857–61)

Bu·cha·rest /bóokə rèst/ capital of Romania. Pop. 2,037,000 (1997).

buck[1] _n_ a male animal of some species such as deer, goats, rabbits, and kangaroos ■ _adj_ of the lowest grade within a particular military enlisted rank

□ **buck up** _vti_ make or become more cheerful _(infml)_

buck[2] _v_ 1 _vi_ jump with the back arched and the legs stiff _(refers to horses)_ 2 _vt_ throw a rider by bucking 3 _vi_ move jerkily 4 _vti_ oppose or resist something obstinately

(infml) 5 _vi_ strive with determination _(infml)_ ○ _buck for a promotion_ 6 _vt_ take a risk against something ○ _buck the odds_ —**buck** _n_

buck[3] _n US, Can, ANZ_ a dollar _(infml)_

> **ORIGIN Buck** meaning "dollar" is a shortening of _buckskin_. Buckskins were used as a unit of exchange with Native Americans in early frontier days.

buck[4] _n_ a marker formerly used in poker to indicate somebody's turn to deal ◇ **pass the buck** shift responsibility to somebody else _(infml)_

Buck, Pearl S. (1892–1973) US writer

buck·board /búk bàwrd/ _n_ a horse-drawn carriage with seats mounted on a flexible board

buck·et /búkit/ _n_ 1 a cylindrical container with an open top and a curved handle 2 _also_ **buck·et·ful** the contents of a bucket, or the amount it holds 3 a bucket-shaped object, especially a scoop on a mechanical shovel ◇ **kick the bucket** die _(slang)_

Buck·ing·ham Pal·ace /búkingəm-, -ham-/ _n_ the official London residence of the British monarch

buck·le /búk'l/ _n_ a fastener for a belt, shoe, or strap consisting of a metal frame with a hinged prong ■ _v_ (-led, -ling) 1 _vti_ fasten with a buckle 2 _vti_ bend out of shape 3 _vi_ collapse

□ **buckle down** _vi_ start to work hard _(infml)_
□ **buckle up** _vti_ fasten a seat belt

buck·ram /búkrəm/ _n_ a stiff cotton or linen fabric. Use: bookbinding, stiffening clothes. —**buck·ram** _adj_

buck·shot /búk shòt/ _n_ lead shot for hunting game

buck·skin /búk skìn/ _n_ 1 deerskin 2 soft grayish yellow leather ■ **buck·skins** _npl_ buckskin garments

buck·tooth /búk tòoth/ (_pl_ **-teeth** /-téeth/) _n_ a protruding upper front tooth _(infml)_ —**buck·toothed** _adj_

buck·wheat /búk wèet, -hwèet/ _n_ 1 an edible triangular seed. Use: cereal, flour, animal fodder. 2 a plant that produces buckwheat

bu·col·ic /byoo kóllik/ _adj_ 1 of the countryside 2 of shepherds —**bu·col·i·cal·ly** _adv_

bud _n_ 1 an outgrowth on a plant stem or branch consisting of a shortened stem and immature leaves or flowers 2 an unopened flower 3 an asexual reproductive outgrowth of a simple organism that separates and develops independently ■ _vi_ (**bud·ded, bud·ding**) 1 produce plant buds 2 start to grow from a plant bud 3 begin to develop and increase ◇ **nip something in the bud** stop something at the very beginning _(infml)_

Bu·da·pest /bóodə pèst, -pèsht/ capital of Hungary. Pop. 1,838,753 (1999).

Buddha: Daibutsu (Great Buddha), Kamakura, Japan

bud·dha /bóodda/, **Bud·dha** n 1 in Buddhism, somebody who has attained enlightenment 2 an image of Buddha

Bud·dha /bóodda/ (563?–483? BC) Nepalese-born Indian philosopher

Bud·dhism /bóod ìzzəm/ n a world religion based on the teachings of Buddha —**Bud·dhist** n, adj

bud·ding /búdding/ adj promising o a budding actor

bud·dy /búddee/ (pl -dies) n a friend (infml) —**bud·dy** vi

budge (**budged, budg·ing**) vti 1 move or change the position of something 2 change your opinion or the opinion of somebody else

budg·er·i·gar /bùjjəree gaàr/ n a small parrot often kept in a cage

ORIGIN **Budgerigar** comes from an Aboriginal language of SE Australia, where it meant literally "good cockatoo."

budg·et /búijjət/ n 1 a summary of income and spending 2 a plan for allocating resources 3 an amount of money allocated or needed for a specific purpose or period ■ adj cheap or economical ■ v 1 vti plan the use of money or time o budget $40 a head o budget for growth 2 vi live according to a budget —**budg·et·ar·y** adj

ORIGIN **Budget** comes from a French word that originally referred to a pouch or wallet. It began to refer to a statement or estimate of revenue and expenditure in the mid-18C.

Bue·nos Ai·res /bwàynoss í reez, -aà reez/ capital of Argentina. Pop. 2,965,403 (1991).

buff¹ vt polish ■ n 1 a pale yellowish brown color 2 a soft pale yellow leather made from buffalo, elk, or ox skin 3 a soft cloth for polishing ■ adj 1 pale yellowish brown in color 2 made of buff leather

buff² n an enthusiast or fan

buff³ adj physically fit and strong (infml)

buf·fa·lo /búffə lò/ (pl -loes or -los or same) n 1 a type of horned cattle 2 a North American bison

Buf·fa·lo /búffə lò/ port in W New York. Pop. 300,717 (1998).

Buf·fa·lo Bill ↓ Cody, William Frederick

⚡ **buff·er** /búffər/ n 1 a protection against impact or harm 2 a substance that maintains the pH of a solution 3 a temporary storage area for data being transmitted between two devices that function at different speeds —**buff·er** vt

buff·er zone n a neutral area that lies between hostile groups or territories

buf·fet¹ /bə fáy, boo-/ n 1 a self-service meal 2 a counter or table on which food and drink is displayed 3 a piece of dining-room furniture for storing tableware

buf·fet² /búffət/ n 1 a blow or battering 2 a heavy or repeated blow —**buf·fet** vt

Buf·fett /búffət/, **Warren** (b. 1930) US financier

buf·foon /bə fóon/ n a person regarded as foolish or bumbling —**buf·foon·er·y** n

bug n 1 an insect with thickened forewings and mouthparts adapted for piercing or sucking 2 any insect or similar organism considered to be a pest 3 an infectious microorganism, or an illness caused by one (infml) 4 a defect or error in something (infml) 5 a hidden listening device (infml) ■ v (**bugged, bug·ging**) 1 vt pester (infml) 2 vt hide a listening device in order to hear 3 vi bulge outward (infml; refers to eyes) ◊ See note at **bother**

bug·a·boo /búggə bòo/ (pl -boos) n a source of unreasonable fear or annoyance

bug·bear /búg bàir/ n 1 a continuing nuisance or problem 2 a source of unreasonable fear

bug-eyed adj with bulging eyes (infml)

bug·gy /búggee/ (pl -gies) n 1 a lightweight horse-drawn vehicle 2 a small battery-powered vehicle o a dune buggy 3 a light baby carriage

bu·gle /byoog'l/ n a brass instrument like a short valveless trumpet, used for military signals —**bu·gle** vi —**bu·gler** n

ORIGIN The fuller form **buglehorn** gives a clue to the original meaning of **bugle**, which was "buffalo, wild ox." The word came via French from Latin, and is related to **bucolic**.

build /bild/ v (**built** /bilt/, **built**) 1 vt make a structure by joining its parts together o built a wall 2 vt have something built o The emperor built these pavilions. 3 vti form or develop something o building a solid business reputation 4 vi increase o Tension was building. ■ n the physical structure of somebody's body o his heavy build —**build·er** n

□ **build in** vt 1 incorporate in something's structure 2 include

□ **build up** v 1 vti develop 2 vt praise excessively 3 vt make stronger and healthier

build·ing /bílding/ n 1 a walled roofed structure 2 the business or job of constructing houses or other large structures (often before a noun) o building materials

build·ing block n 1 a large block of concrete or similar material used in the construction industry 2 a component regarded as contributing to the growth of something

build·up /bíld ùp/ n 1 an accumulation of something 2 an impressive description of somebody or something

built-in adj 1 designed or fitted as an integral part 2 forming a natural feature or characteristic

built-up adj 1 containing many buildings 2 made higher or thicker ○ built-up heels

~~buisness~~ incorrect spelling of **business**

Bu·jum·bu·ra /bòojəm bóorrə/ capital of Burundi. Pop. 634,479 (1991 estimate).

Bu·kha·rin /boo kaárin, -khaárin/, Nicolay Ivanovich (1888–1938) Russian revolutionary and political theorist

bulb n 1 an underground plant storage organ from which a new plant grows annually 2 a plant that grows from a bulb 3 a light bulb 4 a rounded part

bul·bous /búlbəss/ adj 1 rounded and swollen-looking 2 growing from a bulb

Bul·finch /bóol finch/, Charles (1763–1844) US architect

Bul·gar·i·a /bul gáiree ə/ country in SE Europe, on the Black Sea. Cap. Sofia. Pop. 7,707,495 (2001). —**Bul·gar·i·an** n, adj

bulge vi (bulged, bulg·ing) swell up or out ■ n 1 a part that has expanded outward 2 a sudden temporary increase —**bulg·ing** adj

bul·gur /búlgər, bóol-/ n dried cracked wheat

bu·lim·i·a /bul límmee ə, byoo-/ n an eating disorder in which bouts of overeating are followed by self-induced vomiting —**bu·lim·ic** adj, n

bulk n 1 large size 2 a large or overweight person's body ○ eased his bulk through the narrow passageway 3 fiber in food 4 the greater part of something ■ adj in or of a large quantity

bulk·head /búlk hèd/ n a partition inside a ship, aircraft, or large vehicle

bulk·y /búlkee/ (-i·er, -i·est) adj 1 awkwardly large 2 heavily built —**bulk·i·ly** adv —**bulk·i·ness** n

bull[1] n 1 an uncastrated adult male of dairy or beef cattle 2 an adult male of large mammals including whales and elephants 3 an investor who buys securities in anticipation of rising prices

bull[2] n a pope's formal written statement

bull[3] n an offensive term for something regarded as nonsensical or untrue (slang)

bull·dog /bóol dàwg, -dòg/ n a smooth-haired muscular dog ■ vt (-dogged, -dog·ging) force a steer to the ground

bull·doze /bóol dòz/ (-doz·ing) vt 1 demolish or remove with a bulldozer 2 force into action (infml)

bull·doz·er /bóol dòzər/ n a construction vehicle used for moving earth or debris

bul·let /bóollət/ n 1 a piece of ammunition used in a firearm 2 also **bul·let point** a large dot highlighting items in a list ◊ **bite the bullet** deal with an unpleasant but unavoidable situation (infml)

bul·le·tin /bóollətən, -t'n/ n 1 a news broadcast of a single news item 2 an official announcement 3 a newsletter

✦ **bul·le·tin board** n 1 a board on which notices are pinned 2 an online forum for exchanging e-mails or information, or for accessing software

bul·let·proof /bóollət pròof/ adj able to resist bullets

~~bullettin~~ incorrect spelling of **bulletin**

bull·fight /bóol fìt/ n a public entertainment in which a bull is baited and usually killed —**bull·fight·er** n —**bull·fight·ing** n

bull·finch /bóol finch/ n a small European bird with a stubby beak, black head, and pink breast

bull·frog /bóol fràwg, -fròg/ n a large frog with a deep croak

bull·head·ed /bóol héddəd/ adj stubborn and uncooperative (infml) —**bull·head·ed·ly** adv —**bull·head·ed·ness** n

bull·horn /bóol hàwrn/ n a hand-held amplifying device for the voice

bul·lion /bóollyən/ n bars of gold or silver

bull·ish /bóollish/ adj 1 expecting rising stock market prices 2 optimistic (infml) —**bull·ish·ness** n

bull mar·ket n a stock market in which prices are rising

bul·lock /bóollək/ n 1 a young bull 2 a castrated bull

bull·pen /bóol pèn/ n 1 a baseball warm-up area for relief pitchers 2 a baseball team's relief pitchers

bull·ring /bóol rìng/ n an arena for bullfights

Bull Run /búll rùn/ stream in NE Virginia, site of two important Confederate victories during the Civil War, on July 21, 1861, and August 29–30, 1862

bull ses·sion n an informal discussion (infml)

bull's eye n 1 the center of a target, which usually carries the highest score 2 a shot that hits the bull's eye 3 a successful maneuver (infml)

bull ter·ri·er n a smooth-haired dog that is a cross between a bulldog and a terrier

bull·whip /bóol wìp, -hwìp/ n a long heavy braided hide whip, knotted at the end

bul·ly /bóollee/ (pl -lies) n somebody who intimidates or mistreats weaker people —**bul·ly** n

bul·ly pul·pit n a position of authority that gives the holder a wide audience

bul·rush /bóol rùsh/ n 1 a plant that grows in wet conditions with leaves resembling grass 2 in the Bible, a papyrus plant

bul·wark /bóolwork/ n 1 a wall built to keep out attackers 2 somebody or something that gives protection or support —**bul·wark** vt

bum (infml) n 1 a good-for-nothing 2 a hobo (sometimes offensive) ■ vt (**bummed**, **bum·ming**) get by begging ■ adj useless

bum·ble /búmb'l/ (-**bled**, -**bling**) v 1 vti speak in a hesitant or muddled way 2 vt move or proceed clumsily —**bum·bling** adj

bum·ble·bee /búmb'l beè/ n a large hairy bee

bump vti 1 hit or knock something 2 move in a jolting or bouncing way o bumped along the dirt road ■ n 1 an accidental knock 2 a lump on a surface o a bump in the road 3 a swelling on the body caused by an impact
□ **bump into** vt meet by chance
□ **bump off** vt murder (slang)

bump·er /búmpər/ n a protective projecting rim on the front or back of a vehicle ■ adj unusually large or successful o a bumper year for apples

bump·er car n a small electric fairground car

bump·kin /búmpkin, búmkin/ n a country person seen as unsophisticated (infml)

bump·tious /búmpshəss/ adj self-important

bump·y /búmpee/ (-**i·er**, -**i·est**) adj 1 having an uneven surface o a bumpy road 2 uncomfortably bouncy o a bumpy ride —**bump·i·ly** adv —**bump·i·ness** n

bun n 1 a small round bread roll, sometimes sweetened 2 a hairstyle in which the hair is coiled at the back of the head

bunch n 1 a collection or group 2 a cluster of fruits on a stem 3 a group of people (infml) ■ vti gather into a close group

Bunche /bunch/, **Ralph** (1904–71) US diplomat

⚡ **bun·dle** /búnd'l/ n 1 a collection of things held together 2 a lot of money (slang) ■ vt (-**dled**, -**dling**) 1 tie things together 2 package computer hardware and software at an inclusive price
□ **bundle up** vti dress warmly (infml)

bung n a plug or stopper ■ vt plug a hole in

bun·ga·low /búng gəlò/ n a small one-story house, sometimes with an attic story

ORIGIN **Bungalow** comes from a Hindi word that means simply "of Bengal" (the region that is now Bangladesh and the Indian state of Bangla).

bun·gee jump /bún jèè-/ n a dive from a high place using an elastic cord tied to the ankles —**bun·gee jump·ing** n

bun·gle /búng g'l/ (-**gled**, -**gling**) vt make fail through carelessness or clumsiness (infml) o bungled the job —**bun·gle** n —**bun·gling** adj —**bun·gling·ly** adv

bun·ion /búnnyən/ n a swelling of the joint of the big toe

bunk¹ n 1 a simple bed built on a shelf or in a recess 2 also **bunk bed** one of a pair of single beds positioned one on top of the other

bunk² n nonsense (slang)

bun·ker /búngkər/ n 1 an underground shelter 2 a sand hazard on a golf course 3 a fuel-storage container on a ship

bun·ker bust·er n a powerful laser-guided bomb designed to penetrate a reinforced target and explode

Bun·ker Hill /búngkər-/ hill in Boston, Massachusetts, near the site of the first battle of the American Revolution in 1775. Height 110 ft./34 m.

bunk·house /búnk hòws/ (pl -**hous·es** /-hòwzəz/) n a dormitory

bun·kum /búngkəm/ n nonsense (infml)

ORIGIN **Bunkum** derives from the name of Buncombe County, North Carolina. In a debate in the US Congress in about 1820 its representative made a long, dull, and irrelevant speech that he refused to cut short because he had to speak "for Buncombe." Buncombe quickly became a byword for long-windedness and nonsense.

bun·ny /búnnee/ (pl -**nies**) n a child's word for a rabbit

Bun·sen /búnsən/, **Robert Wilhelm** (1811–99) German chemist and physicist. He popularized a safe laboratory gas burner.

Bun·sen burn·er n a laboratory gas burner

bunt vt 1 hit a ball gently 2 hit or push somebody with the head or horns

bunt·ing¹ /búnting/ n a small brown or gray songbird

bunt·ing² /búnting/ n strings of cloth or paper used as outdoor decorations

Bu·ñu·el /boonyoo él/, **Luis** (1900–83) Spanish movie director

Bun·yan /búnnyən/, **John** (1628–88) English preacher and writer

Buo·nar·ro·ti /bwàw naa rôtee/, **Michelangelo** ♦ Michelangelo

buoy /boó ee, boy/ n 1 an anchored float that acts as a guide or warning for ships 2 a life buoy ■ vt 1 mark with a buoy 2 keep from falling or sinking

buoy·ant /bóy ənt/ adj 1 causing objects to float 2 tending to float 3 quick to recover emotionally 4 cheerful —**buoy·an·cy** n —**buoy·ant·ly** adv

bur n 1 a prickly seed husk 2 ENG = **burr¹** 1

Bur·bank /búr bàngk/ city in SW California. Pop. 97,430 (1998).

Bur·bank, Luther (1849–1926) US horticulturalist and botanist

bur·ble /búrb'l/ (-**bled**, -**bling**) vi make a bubbling sound —**bur·ble** n

bur·den¹ /búrd'n/ n 1 a load being carried 2 a worrying responsibility ■ vt give a difficult or worrying responsibility

bur·den² /búrd'n/ n 1 a chorus in a song 2 a main or recurring theme in music or literature (literary) ◊ See note at **subject**

bur·den of proof n legal responsibility to prove a charge or allegation

bur·dock /búr dòk/ *n* a tall wild plant with prickly flowers

bu·reau /byoórō/ (*pl* **-reaus** *or* **-reaux** /-rōz/) *n* 1 an organization, or a branch of an organization 2 a government department 3 a chest of drawers, especially a low one

bu·reauc·ra·cy /byoo rókrəsee/ (*pl* **-cies**) *n* 1 administrative officials considered collectively 2 a state or organization operated by officials 3 complex, rigidly applied rules within an organization

bu·reau·crat /byoŏrə kràt/ *n* 1 an administrative or government official 2 an inflexible official

bu·reau·crat·ic /byoòrə kráttik/ *adj* 1 administrative 2 rigidly applying complex rules —**bu·reau·crat·i·cal·ly** *adv*

Bu·ren /búrrən/ ♦ **Van Buren, Martin**

bur·geon /búrjən/ *vi* (*literary*) 1 produce new growth (*refers to plants*) 2 develop rapidly

burg·er /búrgər/ *n* 1 a hamburger 2 a round flat patty made of chicken, fish, vegetables, or nuts, usually served in a bun

Bur·ger /búrgər/, **Warren** (1907–95) chief justice of the US Supreme Court (1969–86)

burgh /burg, búrrō, búrrə/ *n* in *Scotland* a town incorporated by royal charter

burgh·er /búrgər/ *n* a medieval European merchant

bur·glar /búrglər/ *n* an illegal intruder and thief

bur·glar·ize /búrglə rīz/ (**-ized**, **-iz·ing**) *vt* commit burglary

bur·gla·ry /búrgləree/ (*pl* **-ries**) *n* 1 the crime of entering a building to commit a felony, usually theft 2 an act of entering a building illegally to commit theft

~~burgler~~ incorrect spelling of **burglar**

Bur·goyne /bur góyn, búr gòyn/, **John** (1722–92) British army general

bur·gun·dy /búrgəndee/ *n* 1 *also* **Bur·gun·dy** a red or white wine from the Burgundy region of France 2 a deep red color —**bur·gun·dy** *adj*

bur·i·al /bérree əl/ *n* interment of a corpse

Burke /burk/, **Edmund** (1729–97) Irish-born British writer, political philosopher, and politician

Bur·ki·na Fa·so /bər kèenə faásō/ landlocked country in W Africa. Cap. Ouagadougou. Pop. 12,272,289 (2001).

burl *n* a knot on a tree

bur·lap /búr làp/ *n* coarse cloth woven from jute or hemp

bur·lesque /bur lésk/ *n* 1 mockery of a serious matter by ludicrous imitation 2 a variety show that often includes striptease ■ *vt* (**-lesqued**, **-lesq·uing**) mock by ludicrous imitation

Bur·ling·ton /búrlingtən/ 1 city in north central North Carolina. Pop. 44,900 (2000). 2 city in NW Vermont. Pop. 38,453 (1998).

bur·ly /búrlee/ (**-li·er**, **-li·est**) *adj* sturdy and strong —**bur·li·ness** *n*

Bur·ma /búrmə/ former name for **Myanmar**

Bur·mese /bur meéz/ (*pl* same) *n* 1 somebody from Myanmar 2 the official language of Myanmar —**Bur·mese** *adj*

burn *v* (**burned** *or* **burnt**) 1 *vti* be or set something on fire 2 *vti* destroy something, or be destroyed by fire o *The house was burned to the ground.* 3 *vt* damage something by fire or heat o *burned his hand on the iron* 4 *vti* overcook something, or be overcooked 5 *vt* use something up o *burn calories* 6 *vi* feel or look feverish o *Her cheeks were burning.* 7 *vti* cause or experience a hot stinging sensation o *That hot coffee will burn your throat.* 8 *vt* make a mark or hole as a result of intense heat o *burned a hole in my shirt* 9 *vti* become sunburned, or make somebody or a part of the body sunburned 10 *vt* use something as fuel 11 *vi* emit heat or light o *a light burning outside the front porch* 12 *vi* feel a strong emotion o *burning with shame* 13 *vti* electrocute somebody, or be electrocuted (*infml*) ■ *n* 1 a firing of a rocket engine 2 an injury caused by fire, heat, radiation, a chemical, electricity, or friction 3 a mark or hole produced by burning 4 sunburn or windburn 5 a strong physical sensation produced by strenuous exercise, especially aerobics o *go for the burn*

□ **burn off** *vti* dissipate as a result of the sun's heat

□ **burn out** *vti* 1 wear out through heat or friction 2 make or become exhausted through overwork or stress (*infml*)

□ **burn up** *vt* annoy (*infml*)

Burne-Jones /bùrn jónz/, **Sir Edward** (1833–98) British painter and designer

burn·er /búrnər/ *n* 1 a ring or plate on a range that heats up 2 the part of a stove that produces a flame when lit 3 an incinerator or furnace

ƒ **burn-in** *n* a test of an electronic device or piece of software in which it is run continuously for a period of time

burn·ing /búrning/ *adj* 1 ardent o *a burning passion* 2 of urgent importance o *a burning issue*

bur·nish /búrnish/ *vt* 1 polish metal 2 make something shiny

burn·out /búrn òwt/ *n* 1 psychological exhaustion resulting from overwork or stress 2 somebody affected by overwork and stress (*infml*) 3 a mechanical failure caused by overuse, excessive heat or friction, or failure of fuel supply

Burns, Robert (1759–96) Scottish poet

Burn·side /búrn sìd/, **Ambrose** (1824–81) US army general

burnt past tense, past participle of **burn**

burp *n* a belch ■ *v* 1 *vi* bring up gas 2 *vt* make a baby bring up gas

bur·qa /búrkə/, **bur·ka** n a garment with veiled eye holes covering the entire body, worn in public by some Muslim women

burr[1] n 1 a rough edge on cut or drilled metal 2 a woody outgrowth on a tree

burr[2] n 1 a whirring sound 2 a rolled "r" in some regional accents of English —**burr** vti

Burr, Aaron (1756–1836) vice president of the United States (1801–05) who mortally wounded his political rival Alexander Hamilton on July 11, 1804, in a duel

bur·ri·to /bə réetó/ (pl **-tos**) n a filled tortilla

bur·ro /búrō, bóorō/ (pl **-ros**) n a donkey

Bur·roughs /búrrōz/, **William S.** (1914–97) US writer

bur·row /búrrō/ n a hole or tunnel dug for use as a home by a small animal ■ v 1 vti dig or live in a burrow 2 vi force a way into something by creating a hole ○ burrowed deeper into the bedclothes

Bur·sa /búr saà/ city in NW Turkey. Pop. 1,095,842 (1997).

bur·sar /búrsər/ n a treasurer in an educational or religious institution —**bur·sar·ship** n

bur·sa·ry /búrsəree/ (pl **-ries**) n 1 a grant or scholarship awarded to a student 2 a bursar's office

burst v (**burst**) 1 vi split apart because of internal pressure ○ The suitcase had burst open. 2 vt pierce, rupture, or split something open 3 vi be extremely full 4 vi overflow ○ The river burst its banks. 5 vi move, start, or appear suddenly and energetically ○ burst in on the meeting 6 vi be overwhelmed emotionally ○ bursting with excitement 7 vi suddenly start to express an emotion ○ burst into tears ■ n 1 a rupture or explosion 2 a short intense period of something ○ a burst of activity 3 a short sudden volley of gunfire

⚡ **burst·y** /búrstee/ adj moving, transferred, or transmitted in spurts, as data is in a computer network

Bur·ton /búrt'n/, **Harold** (1888–1964) associate justice of the US Supreme Court (1945–58)

Bur·ton, Sir Richard Francis (1821–90) British explorer and linguist

Bu·run·di /boo roondee/ country in east central Africa. Cap. Bujumbura. Pop. 6,223,897 (2001). —**Bu·run·di·an** n, adj

bur·y /bérree/ (**-ied, -ies**) v 1 vt put something in a hole and cover it 2 vt put a corpse in a grave 3 vt cover somebody or something up completely ○ was buried under the rubble 4 vt make something hard to find ○ The apology was buried in fine print. 5 vr concentrate intensely on something ○ buried herself in her family 6 vt suppress or forget something ○ an attempt to bury the past ◊ See note at **berry**

⚡ **bus** /buss/ n (pl **bus·es** or **bus·ses**) 1 a motor vehicle that carries passengers on one or two decks 2 a channel for transferring computer data ■ vti (**bused** or **bussed, bus·ing**

or **bus·sing, bus·es** or **bus·ses**) travel or carry passengers by bus

ORIGIN Bus is a shortening of *omnibus*. It is recorded within a few years of the adoption of *omnibus* from French in the early 19C. The *omnibus* is a vehicle "for everybody," which is what the word means in Latin.

bus·boy /búss bòy/ n somebody employed to clear dirty dishes from tables in a restaurant and assist the server

bus·by /búzbee/ (pl **-bies**) n a soldier's tall fur hat

bush /boosh/ n 1 a woody plant with many branches that is smaller than a tree 2 a dense group of bushes 3 uncultivated and unsettled land 4 a dense mass of something such as hair or a beard ■ vi branch out, spread, or grow thick like a bush ◊ **beat around** or **about the bush** discuss a subject without coming to the point

George Bush

Bush /boosh/, **George** (b. 1924) 41st president of the United States (1989–93)

George W. Bush

Bush, George W. (b. 1946) 43rd president of the United States (2001–)

bush ba·by n a small tree-dwelling nocturnal primate with large eyes and a long tail

bushed /boosht/ adj exhausted from overwork or lack of sleep (infml)

bush·el /boosh'l/ n a unit of dry measure in the US Customary system, equal to 64 US pints/35.24 liters

bush·whack /boosh wàk, -hwàk/ v 1 vt ambush somebody (infml) 2 vi US, Can, Aus cut through or travel through woods —**bush·whack·er** n

bush·y /booshee/ (**-i·er, -i·est**) adj 1 describes hair that is thick and full ○ bushy eyebrows 2 describes a plant that is dense and woody —**bush·i·ness** n

~~busines~~ incorrect spelling of **business**

busi·ness /bíznəss/ n 1 a line of work 2 a commercial organization 3 commercial activity or practice o *It's bad business to neglect smaller clients.* o *I threatened to take my business elsewhere.* 4 personal or private matters o *other people's business* 5 a difficult or unpleasant affair o *that business about the tickets* 6 unspecified activities ■ adj of commerce

busi·ness card n a card with a person's name and business details on it

busi·ness·like /bíznəss līk/ adj 1 efficient and practical 2 unemotional

busi·ness·man /bíznəss mán/ (pl -men /-mèn/) n a man who works in business, especially at a senior level

busi·ness park n an area of businesses and light industry

busi·ness·per·son /bíznəss pùrs'n/ (pl -peo·ple /-peèp'l/) n somebody who works in business

busi·ness plan n a plan of the future strategy and development of a business

busi·ness·wom·an /bíznəss woòmmən/ (pl -wom·en /-wimmin/) n a woman who works in business, especially at a senior level

busk vi UK entertain in the street —**busk·er** n

bus·man's hol·i·day /bùsmanz-/ n a vacation spent doing something similar to your normal work (infml)

⚡ **bus mouse** n a mouse attached to a computer bus

⚡ **bus net·work** n a computer network in which all nodes are connected to a single bus

bust¹ n 1 a woman's breasts 2 a sculpture of the head and shoulders of a person

bust² v (bust·ed or bust) 1 vti burst something 2 vt raid a place, or arrest a person (slang) 3 vti make or become bankrupt (infml) 4 vt demote somebody (infml) 5 vt break up an organization (infml) ■ n 1 economic failure or difficulty (infml) o *boom and bust* 2 a police raid (slang) —**bust** adj —**bust·ed** adj

bust·er /bústər/ n a term of address for a man or a boy (infml)

bus·tier /booss tyáy/ n a woman's strapless bodice

bus·tle¹ /búss'l/ vi (-tled, -tling) work or go hurriedly or busily ■ n energetic activity

bus·tle² /búss'l/ n a pad formerly worn under the back of a woman's skirt

bust·y /bústee/ (-i·er, -i·est) adj with large breasts

bus·y /bízzee/ adj (-i·er, -i·est) 1 engaged in work or other activity 2 full of activity 3 describes a telephone line that is in use 4 too elaborate o *a very busy painting* ■ vr (-ied, -ies) occupy or make busy o *busied himself with the wedding arrangements* —**bus·i·ly** adv —**bus·y·ness** n

bus·y·bod·y /bízzee bòddee/ (pl -ies) n a person regarded as prying or interfering (infml)

but conj 1 introduces an apparent contradiction o *It looks difficult, but it's actually quite easy.* 2 introduces a protest or expression of surprise o *"It's time to leave." "But we just got here!"* 3 introduces further information o *I've forgotten the map, but we probably won't need it.* 4 except that o *I should have phoned, but I don't have your number.* 5 without something else happening (fml) o *It never rains but it pours.* ■ conj, prep except o *nothing but water to drink* ■ adv only (fml) o *We can but try.* ■

buts npl objections (infml)

bu·tane /byoô táyn/ n a colorless flammable gas. Use: lighter fluid, fuel.

butch /boōch/ adj masculine and strong in appearance ■ n a crew cut

butch·er /boōchər/ n 1 a seller of meat 2 somebody who slaughters animals for meat 3 a brutal killer ■ vt 1 slaughter an animal for food 2 kill people brutally 3 botch something (infml) —**butch·er·y** n

but·ler /bútlər/ n the chief manservant of a household

butt¹ v 1 vt hit with the head or horns 2 vi jut out —**butt** n

□ **butt in** vi interrupt

butt² n an object of ridicule or contempt ■ vti abut

butt³ n 1 the thicker or larger end of something, e.g., a rifle 2 the remains of a smoked cigarette 3 the buttocks (infml; sometimes offensive)

butt⁴ n a cask

butte /byoot/ n a flat-topped hill

Butte /byoot/ city in SW Montana. Pop. 33,994 (1998).

but·ter /búttər/ n a soft pale yellow dairy product ■ vt spread butter on —**but·ter·y** adj

□ **butter up** vt flatter (infml)

but·ter bean n a dried lima bean (regional)

but·ter·cup /búttər kùp/ n a wild plant with yellow flowers

but·ter·fat /búttər fàt/ n the fat in dairy products

but·ter·fin·gers /búttər fìnggərz/ (pl same) n somebody who tends to drop things (infml) —**but·ter·fin·gered** adj

but·ter·fly /búttər flì/ n (pl -flies) 1 an insect with large colorful wings 2 also **but·ter·fly stroke** a swimming stroke in which both arms are lifted simultaneously 3 a person lacking concentration ■ **but·ter·flies** npl a nervous feeling in the stomach

but·ter·milk /búttər mìlk/ n a sour-tasting liquid remaining after butter·making

but·ter·nut squash /búttər nut-/ n a club-shaped squash with yellow-orange flesh

but·ter·scotch /búttər skòch/ n a brittle candy or flavoring made from butter and brown sugar

but·tock /búttək/ *n* each of the fleshy mounds above a person's legs and below the hollow of the back *(often pl)*

⚡ **but·ton** /bútt'n/ *n* 1 a small disk put through a hole or loop to fasten clothing 2 a switch that is pressed to activate an electrical device 3 an image on a computer screen that is clicked to activate a task 4 a part of a computer mouse that is pressed or clicked ■ *vti* fasten with buttons ◇ **push somebody's buttons** provoke a reaction in somebody deliberately

but·ton-down *adj* fastened down at the ends with buttons

but·ton·hole /bútt'n hōl/ *n* a hole for a button in clothing

but·ton mush·room *n* a mushroom with a small unopened cap

but·tress /búttrəss/ *n* 1 a supporting structure built against a wall 2 somebody or something that gives support ■ *vt* 1 support a wall with a buttress 2 support or reinforce an argument or opinion

bux·om /búksəm/ *adj* describes a woman with large breasts *(humorous)* —**bux·om·ness** *n*

Bux·te·hude /bóokstə hóodə/, **Dietrich** (1637?–1707) Danish-born German organist and composer

buy /bī/ *v* (**bought** /bawt/) 1 *vti* acquire something by payment 2 *vt* believe in or accept something *(infml)* ○ *I don't buy his excuses.* 3 *vt* bribe somebody 4 *vt* gain time by strategic action 5 *vt* obtain something by sacrifice ■ *n* something bought

> **SPELLCHECK** Do not confuse the spelling of **buy, bi-** ("two"), **by** ("beside, past, through," etc.), or **bye** ("automatic advance in a competition," "goodbye"), which sound similar.

□ **buy off** *vt* bribe

□ **buy out** *vt* 1 pay somebody to relinquish part-ownership ○ *She was bought out by her partners.* 2 purchase all the stock of a company

□ **buy up** *vt* buy all of

buy-back *n* the purchase of shares or goods that you previously sold, according to a contract

buy·er /bī ər/ *n* 1 somebody who buys something 2 somebody whose job is buying goods for a company

buy·out /bī òwt/ *n* the purchase of a controlling interest in a company

buzz *n* 1 a low humming or vibrating sound made by an insect or an electronic device 2 a hum of talk 3 a feeling of excitement or intoxication *(infml)* 4 a telephone call *(infml)* ■ *v* 1 *vi* make a low humming or vibrating sound 2 *vi* be full of activity 3 *vti* activate a buzzer 4 *vt* fly low over *(infml)*

□ **buzz off** *vi* go away *(infml)*

buz·zard /búzzərd/ *n* (*pl* **-zards** *or same*) a vulture

buzz cut *n* a very short, razor-cut hairstyle

buzz·er /búzzər/ *n* an electronic device that buzzes

buzz saw *n* a circular saw

buzz·word /búz wùrd/ *n* a fashionable word *(infml)*

BW *abbr* 1 bacteriological warfare 2 biological warfare 3 *also* **B/W, bw** black-and-white

B.W.I. *abbr* British West Indies

by /bī/ *prep, adv* 1 past in space *(after a verb of movement)* 2 at a place for a short visit ○ *Drop by any time.* ■ *prep* 1 next to or along 2 through 3 no later than ○ *get there by midnight* 4 during ○ *By day he worked in a canning factory.* 5 in measures of ○ *sold by weight* 6 indicates a quantity in multiplication or division ○ *What is 144 divided by 12?* 7 indicates a dimension ○ *2 feet by 3* 8 indicates an amount of difference ○ *increased by 10%* 9 in amounts of a particular size 10 indicates progression ○ *One by one we told our stories.* 11 indicates the person or thing that does or causes something *(after a passive verb)* ○ *was loved by her parents* ○ *got melted by the sun* 12 indicates a creator ○ *a play by Shakespeare* 13 indicates a method, medium, or means ○ *by pressing this button* ○ *traveling by train* ■ *adv* 1 indicates the passage of time ○ *as the weeks go by* 2 away or aside ○ *put some of the money by* ◇ **by and by** after a while *(literary)* ◇ **by the by, by the bye** incidentally ◇ See note at **buy**

by- *prefix* 1 secondary, subsidiary, extra ○ *by-product* 2 past ○ *bygone*

~~bycicle~~ incorrect spelling of **bicycle**

bye[1] /bī/ *n* an automatic advance to the next round of a competition without playing ◇ See note at **buy**

bye[2] /bī/, **bye-bye** *interj* goodbye *(infml)* ◇ See note at **buy**

by·gone /bī gàwn, -gòn/ *adj* of long ago

by·law /bī làw/ *n* 1 a rule governing the internal affairs of an organization 2 a secondary law

> **ORIGIN** The first part of **bylaw** probably comes from an old Scandinavian word for "town, village," and is not the *by-* meaning "subsidiary" or "extra" that is found in such words as *byproduct*.

by-line /bī lìn/ *n* a reporter's name printed at the head of an article

by-pass /bī pàss/ *n* 1 a road around a town 2 an operation to redirect the blood ○ *a heart bypass* ■ *vt* avoid an obstacle or problem by using an alternative route or method

by-prod·uct /bī pròddəkt/ *n* 1 an incidental product in the manufacture of something else 2 a secondary result

Byrd /burd/, **Richard** (1888–1957) US naval officer and explorer

By·ron /bīrən/, **George Gordon Noel, 6th Baron Byron** (1788–1824) British poet

by·stand·er /bí stàndər/ *n* somebody who observes but is not involved in something

⚡ **byte** /bít/ *n* 1 a unit of computer information comprising eight bits 2 a unit of computer memory for storing a single character

ORIGIN Although it is a fairly recent word, the exact origin of **byte** is not certain. It may be an alteration of *bit* as a unit of computer information, influenced by *bite* (of food); or it may be based on "binary digit eight."

by·way /bí wày/ *n* 1 a side road 2 a minor aspect

by·word /bí wùrd/ *n* 1 somebody or something well-known for embodying a particular quality 2 a word or phrase in common use

Byz·an·tine /bízz'n tèen, -tîn, bi zántin/ *adj* 1 of Byzantium 2 of the Eastern Orthodox Church 3 **byz·an·tine** very complex ■ *n* somebody from Byzantium

By·zan·ti·um /bi zánshee əm, -zántee-/ ancient Greek city on the site of modern Istanbul

C

c[1] (*pl* **c's**), **C** (*pl* **C's** *or* **Cs**) *n* 1 the 3rd letter of the English alphabet 2 the Roman numeral for 100

c[2] *abbr* 1 candle 2 carat 3 cubic

C[1] (*pl* **C's** *or* **Cs**) *n* 1 the 1st note in the musical scale of C major 2 the 3rd highest grade of a student's work

C[2] *symbol* 1 capacitance 2 carbon

C[3] *abbr* 1 Celsius 2 century

c., C. *abbr* 1 cent 2 circa (*before dates*) 3 copyright 4 cup

C2B /sèe tə bèe/ *abbr* consumer-to-business

C2C *abbr* consumer-to-consumer

Ca *symbol* calcium

⚡ **CA** *abbr* 1 California 2 Central America 3 certificate authority (*in e-mails*)

ca. *abbr* circa (*before dates*)

cab *n* 1 a taxi 2 the driver's compartment in a large vehicle or machine ■ *vi* (**cabbed**, **cab·bing**) 1 drive a taxi as a job 2 ride in a taxi

ca·bal /kə bál/ *n* 1 a group of conspirators 2 a secret plot

ca·ban·a /kə bánnə, kə bánnyə/ *n* a structure used as a changing room at a beach or pool

cab·a·ret /kàbbə ráy/ *n* a floor show performed in a restaurant, club, or bar

cab·bage /kábbij/ *n* 1 a large round head of green or purple leaves eaten as a vegetable 2 a plant that produces cabbages

Ca·be·za de Va·ca /kə bàyzə də vaàkə/, **Álvar Núñez** (1490?–1557?) Spanish explorer

cab·in /kábbin/ *n* 1 a wooden hut 2 a room on a ship 3 the part of an aircraft or spacecraft for the crew or passengers

cab·in class *n* an intermediate class on passenger ships —**cab·in class** *adj, adv*

cab·in crew *n* the staff of an aircraft who attend to the passengers

cab·in cruis·er *n* a luxurious motor boat

cab·i·net /kábbinət/ *n* 1 a piece of furniture used for storage or display 2 *also* **Cab·i·net** a government leader's advisers

cab·i·net·mak·er /kábbinət màykər/ *n* a woodworker who makes fine furniture —**cab·i·net·mak·ing** *n*

cab·in fe·ver *n* stress from confinement or isolation (*infml*)

ca·ble /káyb'l/ *n* 1 a strong rope or wire 2 a bundle of electrical wires enclosed in a casing 3 *also* **ca·ble·gram** an overseas telegram 4 *also* **ca·ble tel·e·vi·sion** a television system in which signals are transmitted by cable ■ *v* (**-bled, -bling**) 1 *vti* send a telegram 2 *vt* supply a place with cable TV

ca·ble car *n* a compartment suspended or moved by a cable, used for transportation up and down steep hills

ca·ble·cast /káyb'l kàst/ *n* a cable TV broadcast

ca·ble rail·road, ca·ble rail·way *n* a hillside railroad using a moving cable

ca·boo·dle /kə bóod'l/ ◊ **the whole (kit and) caboodle** the whole lot (*infml*)

ca·boose /kə bóoss/ *n* the last car on a freight train

Cab·ot /kábbət/, **John** (1450?–99?) Italian explorer

Cab·ot, Sebastian (1476?–1557) Italian-born English navigator and cartographer

Ca·bri·ni /kə breénee/, **Frances Xavier, St.** (1850–1917) Italian-born US social-welfare worker

cab·ri·o·let /kàbbree ə láy/ *n* a two-door convertible automobile

ca·ca·o /kə káy ō, -kaà ō/ (*pl* **-os** *or same*) *n* 1 a seed from which cocoa products are derived 2 a tree that produces cacao seeds

⚡ **cache** /kash/ *n* 1 a hidden store, e.g., of weapons 2 a secret place for hiding things 3 an area of computer memory for temporary storage

SPELLCHECK Do not confuse the spelling of **cache** and **cash** ("coins and bills"), which sound similar.

ca·chet /ka sháy/ *n* prestige or respect

cack·le /kák'l/ *v* (**-led, -ling**) *vi* 1 laugh harshly and shrilly 2 make a squawking noise (*refers to hens*) —**cack·le** *n*

ca·coph·o·ny /kə kóffənee/ (*pl* **-nies**) *n* an unpleasant combination of loud or jarring sounds —**ca·coph·o·nous** *adj*

cac·tus /káktəss/ (*pl* **-ti** /-tī/ *or* **-tus·es** *or same*) *n* a spiny fleshy desert plant

cad *n* a man who behaves dishonorably *(dated)* —**cad·dish** *adj*

ca·dav·er /kə dávvər/ *n* a corpse

ca·dav·er·ous /kə dávvərəss/ *adj* like a corpse in being extremely thin or pale

⚡ **CAD/CAM** /kád kàm/ *abbr* computer-aided design and manufacturing

cad·die /káddee/, **cad·dy** *(pl* **-dies)** *n* a golfer's assistant —**cad·die** *vi*

⚡ **cad·dy** /káddee/ *(pl* **-dies)** *n* **1** a small container for tea **2** a CD-ROM case

---

ORIGIN Caddy comes from a Malay word that referred to a standard measure for tea set by the East India Company. A tea **caddy** was therefore a container for one "caddy" of tea. A golfer's *caddie* or **caddy** is from a different source. It is an alteration of *cadet*.

---

ca·dence /káyd'nss/ *n* **1** rhythm or rhythmic flow **2** the rise and fall of the voice **3** a closing sequence of musical notes

ca·den·za /kə dénzə/ *n* a virtuoso solo passage near the end of a section or piece of music

ca·det /kə dét/ *n* **1** a trainee in the armed forces or police **2** a member of a military organization for young people —**ca·det·ship** *n*

cadge *(*cadged, cadg·ing*) vti* scrounge or beg something from somebody *(infml)*

Cá·diz /kə díz, káydiz/ capital of **Cádiz** Province, SW Spain. Pop. 143,129 (1998).

cad·mi·um /kádmee əm/ *n (symbol* **Cd)** a soft metallic chemical element. Use: alloys, electroplating, nuclear reactors, pigments, electronics.

cad·re /káddree, kaà dràye/ *n* **1** a group of experienced military professionals **2** a tightly knit or highly trained group **3** a member of a cadre

⚡ **CAE** *abbr* computer-aided engineering

cae·cum *n* ANAT = cecum

Caen /kaaN/ capital of Calvados Department, NW France. Pop. 113,987 (1999).

Cae·sar /seèzər/ *n* **1** a title of Roman emperors **2** *also* **cae·sar** a tyrant

Cae·sar /seèzər/, **Gaius Julius** (100–44 BC) Roman general and political leader —**Cae·sar·e·an** /si záiree ən/ *adj* —**Cae·sar·i·an** /si záiree ən/ *adj*

Cae·sa·re·a /seèzə reè ə/ ancient port in present-day NW Israel

cae·si·um *n* CHEM = cesium

ca·fé /ka fáy, kə fáy/ *n* an informal restaurant serving drinks and light meals

caf·fè lat·te /kaà fe laá te, kà fay-/ *n* an espresso coffee with steamed milk

caf·e·te·ri·a /kàffə teèree ə/ *n* a self-service restaurant

caf·e·to·ri·um /kàffə táwree əm/ *n (pl* **-ri·ums** *or* **-ria** /-ree ə/) *n* a cafeteria and auditorium

caf·feine /ka feèn/ *n* a stimulant found in coffee and tea. Use: in soft drinks and medicine.

~~caffiene~~ incorrect spelling of **caffeine**

caf·tan /káf tàn, kaf tán/, **kaf·tan** *n* a full-length men's tunic worn chiefly in E Mediterranean countries

cage *n* a wire or barred enclosure ■ *vt (*caged, cag·ing*)* put or keep in a cage or confined conditions —**caged** *adj*

Cage, John (1912–92) US composer

ca·gey /káyjee/ *(*-gi·er, -gi·est*)*, **ca·gy** *adj* cautious and secretive *(infml)* —**ca·gi·ly** *adv* —**ca·gi·ness** *n*

Cag·ney /kágnee/, **James** (1899–1986) US movie actor

Ca·guas /kaà gwaàss/ city in E Puerto Rico. Pop. 92,429 (1990).

ca·hoots /kə hoòts/ ◇ **in cahoots (with)** secretly agreeing with somebody to do something, especially something dishonest or illegal *(infml)*

⚡ **CAI** *abbr* computer-aided instruction

Cain /kayn/ ◇ **raise Cain** cause a noisy disturbance *(infml)*

ORIGIN In the Bible, **Cain** was the elder son of Adam and Eve, who killed his brother Abel (Genesis 4).

---

cairn /kairn/ *n* a pile of stones used as a marker

Cairn /kairn/, **Cairn ter·ri·er** *n* a small Scottish terrier with a shaggy coat

Cai·ro /kî rò/ capital of Egypt and Africa's largest city. Pop. 6,789,000 (1998).

Cait·ra /káy trə/ *n* the 1st month of the year in the Hindu calendar

ca·jole /kə jốl/ *(*-joled, -jol·ing*) vti* persuade somebody gently —**ca·jol·er·y** *n*

Ca·jun /káyjən/ *n* **1** in Louisiana, a descendant of French colonists exiled in the 18C from Canada **2** a dialect of French spoken in Louisiana —**Ca·jun** *adj*

ORIGIN Cajun is an alteration of *Acadian*. Acadia was a French colony in Canada (now New Brunswick, Nova Scotia, and Prince Edward Island), whose inhabitants, the original **Cajuns**, moved to the S United States in the 18C, driven out by the British.

---

cake *n* **1** a baked sweet food containing flour and eggs **2** a shaped portion of ground or chopped food **3** a block of something such as soap or ice ■ *vti (*caked, cak·ing*)* form a thick layer or crust on something

cake·walk /káyk wàwk/ *n* a strutting dance

⚡ **CAL** /kal/ *abbr* computer-assisted learning

Cal. *abbr* California

cal·a·bash /kálla bàsh/ *n* **1** a large round fruit or gourd **2** a plant that produces calabashes

cal·a·bre·se /kàlla bráyzee/ *n* a type of broccoli

Ca·lais /ká làye, ka láy/ port in N France, on the English Channel. Pop. 77,333 (1999).

ca·lam·i·ty /kə lámmətee/ (*pl* -ties) *n* a disaster —**ca·lam·i·tous** *adj*

Library of Congress

Calamity Jane

Ca·lam·i·ty Jane /kə làmmətee jáyn/ (1852?–1903) US frontierswoman

cal·ci·fy /kálssə fĭ/ (-fied, -fies) *vti* 1 turn into a calcium compound 2 become hard as a result of calcium deposition (*refers to a body part*) —**cal·ci·fi·ca·tion** /kàlssəfi káysh'n/ *n*

cal·ci·um /kálssee əm/ *n* (*symbol* Ca) a silver-white metallic chemical element found in bone and limestone

cal·cu·late /kálkyə làyt/ (-lat·ed, -lat·ing) *v* 1 *vti* work something out mathematically 2 *vti* consider and decide ○ *calculating how to tackle the problem* 3 *vt US regional, Can* think or suppose —**cal·cu·la·ble** *adj*

ORIGIN The root of **calculate** is Latin *calculus* "pebble" (pebbles were used in counting with an abacus). *Calculus* itself is thought to come from the Latin word for "limestone" from which English *chalk* developed. Sir Humphry Davy also used it as a basis for the word *calcium*, which he coined in 1808.

cal·cu·lat·ing /kálkyə làyting/ *adj* shrewd or scheming —**cal·cu·lat·ing·ly** *adv*

cal·cu·la·tion /kàlkyə láysh'n/ *n* 1 the process of calculating 2 something calculated 3 consideration of something, especially when thinking of personal advantage

cal·cu·la·tor /kálkyə làytər/ *n* an electronic device for arithmetic operations

cal·cu·lus /kálkyələss/ (*pl* -li /-lī/ *or* -lus·es) *n* 1 a branch of mathematics dealing with relationships affected by changing variables 2 a kidney or bladder stone (*technical*)

Cal·cut·ta /kal kúttə/ former name for **Kolkata**

Cal·der /káwldər/, **Alexander** (1898–1976) US painter and sculptor

cal·dron /káwldrən/, **caul·dron** *n* a large pot in which liquids are boiled

cal·en·dar /kálləndər/ *n* 1 a system of calculating the days and months of the year 2 a chart showing the days of a year, often with a separate page for each month 3 a timetable of events during a year

cal·en·dar month *n* any of the 12 named divisions of the year

cal·en·dar year *n* the period from January 1 to December 31

calf¹ /kaf/ (*pl* calves /kavz/) *n* 1 a young cow or bull 2 a young elephant, giraffe, or whale

calf² /kaf/ (*pl* calves /kavz/) *n* the fleshy part of the lower leg

Cal·ga·ry /kálgəree/ city in S Alberta, Canada. Pop. 768,082 (1996).

Cal·houn /kal hoŏn/, **John Caldwell** (1782–1850) vice president of the United States (1825–32)

Ca·li /kaálee/ capital of Valle de Cauca Department, W Colombia. Pop. 2,111,000 (1999).

cal·i·ber /kállibər/ *n* 1 ability, intelligence, or character 2 the diameter of a gun barrel or bullet

cal·i·brate /kálli bràyt/ (-brat·ed, -brat·ing) *vt* 1 mark the scale on a measuring instrument 2 test and adjust the accuracy of a measuring instrument —**cal·i·bra·tion** /kàlli bráysh'n/ *n*

cal·i·co /kállikō/ *n* a brightly printed cotton cloth

ORIGIN Calico is named for the port of Calicut (now called Kozhikode) in SE India, from which the cloth was exported.

Calif. *abbr* California

Cal·i·for·nia /kàlli fáwrnyə/ state in the W United States, on the Pacific Ocean. Cap. Sacramento. Pop. 33,871,648 (2000). —**Cal·i·for·nian** *n, adj*

Cal·i·for·nia, Gulf of arm of the Pacific Ocean between mainland Mexico and Baja California

cal·i·for·ni·um /kàlli fáwrnee əm/ *n* (*symbol* Cf) a synthetic metallic element. Use: neutron source.

Ca·lig·u·la /kə líggyələ/ (AD 12–41) Roman emperor (AD 37–41)

cal·i·pers /kállipərz/ *npl* a device with two hinged legs for measuring diameters

ca·liph /káylif, kállif/ *n* a title taken by Islamic rulers —**ca·liph·ate** /káyli fàyt, kálli-/ *n*

cal·is·then·ics /kàlliss thénniks/ *npl* physical exercises for improving fitness and muscle tone (*+ pl verb*) ■ *n* the performance of calisthenics (*+ sing verb*) —**cal·is·then·ic** *adj*

calk *vt* = **caulk**

call /kawl/ *v* 1 *vti* shout or say loudly ○ *calling for help* 2 *vt* describe or refer to in a particular way 3 *vt* summon 4 *vti* telephone 5 *vt* give a name to 6 *vi* visit 7 *vti* request or arrange for something to happen ○ *call a meeting* 8 *vt* predict, especially in politics ○ *a hard election to call* 9 *vt* demand repayment of ○ *call a loan* 10 *vt* in a sport, declare as an official decision 11 *vt* postpone a game ■ *n* 1 a shout 2 a bird or animal cry 3 a telephone communication 4 a demand ○ *There have been calls for him to resign.* 5 the strong appeal of a place or lifestyle 6 a short visit ○ *make calls on the way home* 7 a declared choice or decision 8 a prediction ○ *a difficult call to make* —**call·er** *n* ◇ **be on call** be available to be summoned for work

□ **call down** *vt* reprimand

□ **call for** *vt* **1** ask for or require **2** stop briefly somewhere to pick up somebody or something

□ **call in** *vt* **1** summon for help or advice **2** request repayment or the return of

□ **call off** *vt* **1** cancel an event **2** stop an animal from attacking

□ **call on** *vt* **1** ask somebody to do something **2** pay somebody a brief visit

□ **call up** *vt* **1** order to active duty in the armed forces **2** evoke

□ **call upon** *vt* **1** ask formally **2** make demands on

Cal·lao /kaa yów/ chief port of Peru. Pop. 424,294 (1998).

Maria Callas

Cal·las /kálləss, kál ass/, **Maria** (1923–77) US-born operatic soprano

call cen·ter *n* a business dealing with customer phone calls

call·er /káwlər/ *n* **1** somebody who telephones or visits **2** an announcer, e.g., of square dance moves

call·er ID *n* a device or service for identifying telephone callers

call girl *n* a prostitute contacted by telephone

cal·lig·ra·phy /kə líggrəfee/ *n* **1** the art of beautiful handwriting **2** beautiful handwriting —**cal·lig·ra·pher** *n* —**cal·li·graph·ic** /kálli gráffik/ *adj*

call-in *adj* describes a radio or television show in which listeners or viewers phone in their opinions

call·ing /káwling/ *n* **1** a strong urge to follow a particular career **2** a job or profession

call·ing card *n* a name card presented by a visitor

cal·lous /kálləss/ *adj* hardhearted —**cal·lous·ly** *adv* —**cal·lous·ness** *n*

SPELLCHECK Do not confuse the spelling of **callous** and **callus** ("thickened skin"), which sound similar.

cal·loused /kálləst/ *adj* having hard thickened skin

cal·low /kállō/ *adj* young and inexperienced

cal·lus /kálləss/ *n* a patch of hard thickened skin ◊ See note at **callous**

calm /kaam/ *adj* **1** not anxious **2** not windy, stormy, or rough ■ *n* **1** peace and quiet **2** an absence of wind ■ *vt* make less anxious

or upset —**calm·a·tive** *adj* —**calm·ly** *adv* —**calm·ness** *n*

cal·o·rie /kállree/ *n* **1** a unit of energy equal to 4.1855 joules **2** a unit of energy often used to measure the energy-producing potential of food

cal·o·rif·ic /kàllə ríffik/ *adj* of heat

cal·um·ny /kálləmnee/ (*pl* **-nies**) *n* (*fml*) **1** defamation **2** a defamatory statement

Cal·va·ry /kálvəree/ hill outside ancient Jerusalem where the Crucifixion of Jesus Christ took place, according to the Bible

calve /kav, kaav/ (**calved, calv·ing**) *vti* give birth to a calf

Cal·vert /kálvərt/ family of English-born American colonial administrators including **George, 1st Baron Baltimore** (1580?–1632), his sons **Cecilius, 2nd Baron Baltimore** (1605–75) and **Leonard** (1606–47), and his grandson **Charles, 3rd Baron Baltimore** (1637–1715)

calves 1 plural of **calf**[1] **2** plural of **calf**[2]

Cal·vin /kálvin/, **John** (1509–64) French-born Swiss Protestant theologian and reformer

Cal·vin·ism /kálvi nìzzəm/ *n* John Calvin's religious doctrine of predestination and of salvation through faith —**Cal·vin·ist** *n, adj*

Cal·vi·no /kal veénō/, **Italo** (1923–85) Cuban-born Italian novelist

ca·lyp·so /kə lípsō/ (*pl* **-sos**) *n* **1** a Caribbean song **2** Caribbean dance music

ca·lyx /káyliks, kálliks/ (*pl* **ca·lyx·es** or **cal·y·ces** /-li seez/) *n* the sepals enclosing a flower bud

cam *n* a machine part that transfers motion

⚡ **CAM** *abbr* computer-aided manufacturing

ca·ma·ra·der·ie /kàamə ráadəree, kàmmə ráddəree/ *n* friendship and trust among a group of people

cam·ber /kámbər/ *n* **1** a convex curve across a road surface **2** the slant of a vehicle's wheels —**cam·ber** *vti*

Cam·bo·di·a /kam bṓdee ə/ country in Southeast Asia. Cap. Phnom Penh. Pop. 12,491,501 (2001). —**Cam·bo·di·an** *n, adj*

Cam·bri·an /kámbree ən/ *n* a period of geologic time 545–495 million years ago —**Cam·bri·an** *adj*

cam·bric /kámbrik/ *n* a thin cotton fabric

ORIGIN **Cambric** is named for the town of Cambrai (*Kamerijk* in Flemish) in N France, where the fabric was originally made.

Cam·bridge /káym brìj/ **1** city in E England. Pop. 116,701 (1996). **2** city in E Massachusetts. Pop. 93,352 (1998).

cam·cord·er /kám kàwrdər/ *n* a portable video camera and recorder

Cam·den /kámdən/ port in SW New Jersey. Pop. 83,546 (1998).

came past tense of **come**

cam·el /kámm'l/ n (pl **cam·els** or same) a large desert animal with one or two humps

cam·el hair, cam·el's hair n 1 the hair of a camel. Use: clothing, rugs. 2 a fabric containing camel hair. Use: coats.

~~camelia~~ incorrect spelling of **camellia**

ca·mel·lia /kə méelyə, kə méelee ə/ n (pl **-lias** or same) n an evergreen shrub with rose-shaped flowers

Cam·e·lot /kámmə lòt/ n the legendary city of King Arthur

Cam·em·bert /kámməm bàir/ n a soft French cheese with an edible rind

cam·e·o /kámmee ò/ n 1 a stone carved in a raised design against a contrasting background 2 a brief appearance by a famous actor in a film or play

cam·er·a /kámmərə, kámmrə/ n 1 a device for taking photographs 2 a device used in producing film, video, or television images

ORIGIN The Latin word *camera* meant "room," originally "vaulted room"; it traveled through French to become English *chamber*. From the early 18C, a mid-17C invention, a small closed box with an aperture through which light from outside could be focused by a lens to produce images of external objects, came to be known as a *camera obscura*, literally "dark room," because the box, or the room it was used in, had to be dark for the image to be seen clearly. By the mid-18C this was shortened to **camera**, and when similar devices began to be used for fixing photographic images in the 19C it was natural that they too should be called **cameras**.

~~cameraderie~~ incorrect spelling of **camaraderie**

cam·er·a-shy adj with a dislike of being photographed or filmed

Cam·e·roon /kámmə róon/ country in west central Africa. Cap. Yaoundé. Pop. 15,803,220 (2001).

cam·i·sole /kámmi sòl/ n a woman's sleeveless undergarment covering the upper torso

~~camoflage~~ incorrect spelling of **camouflage**

cam·o·mile n PLANTS = **chamomile**

cam·ou·flage /kámmə flaàzh, -flaàj/ n protective concealment by resembling the surrounding environment ■ vt (**-flaged, -flag·ing**) 1 conceal by camouflage 2 disguise o *camouflaged his true intentions*

camp[1] n 1 a place with removable accommodations such as tents 2 a place with permanent buildings for a temporary stay o *a prison camp* 3 regional a rustic shack 4 a group of people with the same ideas or aims ■ vi stay temporarily in a tent or similar accommodation

camp[2] adj 1 exaggeratedly or affectedly feminine, especially in a man 2 deliberately and exaggeratedly brash or vulgar —**camp** n —**camp** vi —**camp·y** adj

cam·paign /kam páyn/ n 1 an organized series of actions or events to achieve a particular goal o *an advertising campaign* o *an electoral campaign* 2 a series of military operations ■ vi engage in a campaign —**cam·paign·er** n

~~campain~~ incorrect spelling of **campaign**

cam·pa·ni·le /kàmpə néelee/ (pl **-les** or **-li** /-lee/) n a bell tower, especially a free-standing one

cam·pa·nol·o·gy /kàmpə nólləjee/ n bell-ringing —**cam·pa·nol·o·gist** n

camp bed n a collapsible lightweight bed

Camp·bell /kámbəl/, **Keith** (b. 1954) British microbiologist. With Ian Wilmut he was responsible for the first successful cloning of a mammal from adult cells.

Camp·bell, Kim (b. 1947) first woman prime minister of Canada (1993)

Camp Da·vid /-dáyvid/ presidential retreat in Catoctin Mountain Park, central Maryland

camp·er /kámpər/ n 1 somebody who camps 2 a motor vehicle equipped as a traveling home

camp fol·low·er n 1 somebody unofficially selling products or services, especially prostitution, to the military 2 an uncommitted or temporary supporter of a group

camp·ground /kámp gròwnd/ n an outdoor area designed for camping, usually with facilities such as showers and toilets

cam·phor /kámfər/ n a strong-smelling chemical compound. Use: in medicinal creams, manufacture of celluloid, plastics, and explosives.

camp·site /kámp sìt/ n a unit of land within a campground for a camper to pitch a tent or park a camper

cam·pus /kámpəss/ n the site of an organization or institution, especially a university or college, containing its main buildings and grounds

cam·shaft /kám shàft/ n a shaft with cams attached, especially in an internal combustion engine

AKG London

Albert Camus

Ca·mus /kaa móo/, **Albert** (1913–60) Algerian-born French novelist, essayist, and dramatist

can[1] n 1 a sealed metal container holding food or drink 2 a metal container for liquids such as oil or paint 3 the contents of a can 4 a pressurized container holding liquid to be sprayed 5 prison (slang) 6 a toilet *(slang)* ■ *vt* **(canned, can·ning) 1** seal food or drink in a can **2** dismiss somebody from a job *(slang)* **3** stop behavior regarded as inappropriate under the circumstances *(slang)* —**can·ful** *n*

can[2] *modal v* **1** be able to ○ *Can you swim?* **2** indicates possibility or likelihood ○ *It can be dangerous.* **3** be allowed to ○ *Can I go?* **4** introduces a polite request or offer ○ *Can I make a suggestion?*

USAGE can or **may?** Many people draw a distinction between **can**, meaning "be able to," and **may**, meaning "be allowed to," but in everyday conversation *Can I go?* is as likely to be used as *May I go?* In more formal situations, it is wise to maintain the distinction.

Can. *abbr* **1** Canada **2** Canadian

Can·a·da /kánnədə/ federation occupying the northern half of North America and the second largest country in the world. Cap. Ottawa. Pop. 31,592,805 (2001). —**Ca·na·di·an** /kə náydee ən/ *adj, n*

Can·a·da Day *n* a Canadian holiday. Date: July 1.

Ca·na·di·an /kə náydee ən/ river in Colorado, New Mexico, Texas, and Oklahoma. Length 906 mi./1,460 km.

Ca·na·di·an Shield plateau region of E Canada extending southward and eastward from Hudson Bay

ca·nal /kə nál/ *n* **1** an artificial waterway for ships or boats **2** a tube-shaped passage in the body

Ca·na·let·to /kánnə léttō/, **Antonio** (1697–1768) Italian artist

can·a·lize /kánn'l īz/ (**-lized, -liz·ing**) *v* **1** *vt* build canals in **2** *vi* flow into or form a channel

can·a·pé /kánnə pày, kánnəpee/ *n* a bite-sized piece of bread, cracker, or pastry with a topping, served as an appetizer

ca·nard /kə naárd/ *n* a false report or rumor *(literary)*

ca·nar·y /kə náiree/ (*pl* **-ies**) *n* a yellow finch often kept in cages

ORIGIN The **canary** is named for the Canary Islands, the native habitat of the green finch from which the modern yellow pet bird developed. The name of the islands themselves derives from the Latin word for "dog" that gave us *canine*, because one of them was famous for its large dogs in Roman times.

Ca·nar·y Is·lands /kə náiree-/, **Ca·nar·ies** /kə náireez/ island group in the Atlantic Ocean, off NW Africa, an autonomous region of Spain. Pop. 1,631,498 (1995).

ca·nas·ta /kə nástə/ *n* a variation of rummy played with two packs of cards

Ca·nav·er·al, Cape /kə návvərəl/ cape in east central Florida, the launching site of US crewed space flights

Can·ber·ra /kán bèrrə, -bərə/ capital of Australia, in Australian Capital Territory, SE Australia. Pop. 308,100 (1998).

can-can /kán kàn/ *n* a high-kicking dance performed by women

can·cel /kánss'l/ *v* **1** *vti* stop something previously arranged from happening **2** *vti* end a contract **3** *vt* mark a postage stamp as used **4** *vt* reverse an instruction to a machine **5** *vt* delete something by crossing it out **6** *vti* remove a common factor or term from both parts of a fraction or equation —**can·cel·a·ble** *adj* —**can·cel·la·tion** /kànss'l áysh'n/ *n*

□ **cancel out** *vt* neutralize the effect of something equal or opposite

⚡ **can·cel·bot** /kánss'l bòt/ *n* a computer program that cancels unwanted Internet articles

can·cer /kánssər/ *n* **1** a malignant tumor **2** an illness caused by a malignant tumor **3** something that is fast-spreading and undesirable or destructive **4 Can·cer** a constellation in the northern hemisphere **5 Can·cer** the 4th sign of the zodiac —**Can·cer·i·an** /kan sáiree ən/ *n, adj* —**can·cer·ous** *adj*

ORIGIN Cancer is adopted from a Latin word that literally means "crab." The ancient Greek physician Galen applied the equivalent Greek term to the disease, because the blood vessels around a cancer suggested a crab. Until the 17C the usual English term was *canker*, which came from Latin *cancer* via northern French. Before that **Cancer** usually referred to the constellation, so called because of its sideways movement across the sky.

Can·cún /kàn koón/ island on the NE Yucatán peninsula, SE Mexico. Pop. 311,696 (1995).

can·de·la·brum /kànd'l áabrəm, -ábbrəm/ (*pl* **-bra** /-brə/ *or* **-brums**) a branched candlestick or light fixture

can·did /kándid/ *adj* **1** honest and direct **2** filmed or photographed informally or without the subject's knowledge —**can·did·ly** *adv* —**can·did·ness** *n*

ORIGIN Candid comes from the Latin word for "white," and this was its first English meaning. Later senses "innocent," "pure," and "fair," suggested by associations with whiteness, developed into the modern meaning "honest and direct." The Latin root of *candid* is also the source of *candidate*. Candidates for office in ancient Rome wore white togas.

can·di·date /kándi dàyt, -dət/ *n* a seeker of or suitable person for a political office, job, or prize —**can·di·da·cy** /kándidəssee/ *n*

SYNONYMS candidate, contender, contestant, aspirant, applicant, entrant CORE MEANING: somebody who is seeking to be chosen for something or to win something

can·dle /kánd'l/ n a wax shape, usually cylindrical, with a central wick that can be lit

can·dle·light /kánd'l lìt/ n light from candles —**can·dle·lit** adj

can·dle·stick /kánd'l stìk/ n a tall thin holder for a candle

can·dle·wick /kánd'l wìk/ n tufted cotton fabric. Use: bedcovers, dressing gowns.

can·dor /kándər/ n candidness

can·dy /kándee/ n a small piece or small pieces of sweet food made with sugar and other flavors ■ vt (**-died, -dies**) impregnate or coat with sugar

can·dy ap·ple n an apple coated with a candy substance

can·dy-striped adj with thin colored stripes on a white background

can·dy strip·er /-strìpər/ n a young volunteer hospital worker

cane n 1 a walking stick 2 a stick for beating somebody as a punishment 3 a woody stem of a plant such as bamboo 4 flexible plant stems used to make baskets or furniture

Ca·net·ti /kə néttee/, **Elias** (1905–94) Bulgarian-born British writer

ca·nine /káy nìn/ adj of dogs ■ n also **ca·nine tooth** a pointed tooth between the incisor and the bicuspid

can·is·ter /kánnistər/ n 1 a pressurized or sealed container 2 a metal container with a lid for storing dry foods

can·ker /kángkər/ n 1 a disease of trees affecting the trunk and branches 2 a spreading evil influence —**can·ker·ous** adj

can·na·bis /kánnəbiss/ n 1 a drug derived from the hemp plant 2 the hemp plant

canned adj 1 preserved in a can 2 prerecorded o canned laughter

can·nel·lo·ni /kànn'l ốnee/ n pasta tubes that are stuffed with a filling

can·ner·y /kánnəree/ (pl **-ies**) n a food-canning factory

Cannes /kan, kanz/ n city in SE France. Pop. 67,304 (1999).

can·ni·bal /kánnib'l/ n 1 somebody who eats human flesh 2 an animal that eats its own species —**can·ni·bal·ism** n

can·ni·bal·ize /kánnib'l ìz/ (**-ized, -iz·ing**) vt take parts from something for use elsewhere —**can·ni·bal·i·za·tion** /kànnib'li záysh'n/ n

can·non /kánnən/ n 1 (pl **can·nons** or same) n a historical weapon that fired large iron balls 2 a modern heavy artillery weapon ■ vi collide with or bounce off something

SPELLCHECK Do not confuse the spelling of **cannon** and **canon** ("a rule," "a decree," "a collection," "a musical technique," "one of a cathedral's clergy"), which sound similar.

can·non·ball /kánnən bàwl/ n a ball fired from a cannon in former times

can·not /ká nòt, kə nót/ contr can not

can·ny /kánnee/ (**-ni·er, -ni·est**) adj shrewd —**can·ni·ly** adv —**can·ni·ness** n

ca·noe /kə noó/ n a light narrow boat with pointed ends —**ca·noe** vi

can·on¹ /kánnən/ n 1 a general rule 2 a religious decree 3 a body of religious writings 4 a set of artistic works such as the writings of a particular author 5 a musical technique in which different parts of the same piece are simultaneously sung or played ◊ See note at **cannon**

can·on² /kánnən/ n a member of the Christian clergy attached to a cathedral

cañ·on n GEOG = **canyon**

ca·non·i·cal /kə nónnik'l/, **ca·non·i·c** /kə nónnik/ adj 1 following canon law 2 conforming to general principles —**ca·non·i·cal·ly** adv

can·on·ize /kánnə nìz/ (**-ized, -iz·ing**) vt 1 declare as a saint 2 glorify —**can·on·i·za·tion** /kànnən záysh'n/ n

can·on law n Christian religious law

ca·noo·dle /kə noód'l/ (**-noo·dled, -nood·ling**) vti kiss and cuddle (infml)

can o·pen·er n a device for opening cans

can·o·py /kánnəpee/ (pl **-pies**) n 1 a covering above something for shelter or decoration 2 the layer formed by the treetops in a forest 3 the part of a parachute that opens

~~canot~~ incorrect spelling of **cannot**

cant¹ n 1 talk filled with platitudes 2 hypocritical talk 3 jargon —**cant** vi

cant² n 1 slope, or a sloping surface 2 a jolt that makes something slope ■ vti put or be at an angle

can't /kant/ contr cannot

can·ta·loupe /kánt'l òp/, **can·ta·loup** /n an orange-fleshed melon

can·tan·ker·ous /kan tángkərəss/ adj grouchy —**can·tan·ker·ous·ly** adv —**can·tan·ker·ous·ness** n

can·ta·ta /kən taátə/ n a musical work for voices and instruments, usually on a religious theme

can·teen /kan teén/ n 1 a place where food is served, especially on a military base 2 a portable drinking flask

~~canteloupe~~ incorrect spelling of **cantaloupe**

can·ter /kántər/ n a horse's pace between a gallop and a trot —**can·ter** vi

ORIGIN A **canter** was originally a Canterbury gallop, the pace at which medieval pilgrims rode to the shrine of St. Thomas à Becket at Canterbury in SE England.

Can·ter·bur·y /kántər bèrree/ city in SE England. Pop. 136,481 (1996).

can·ti·le·ver /kánt'l èevər/ n a projecting load-bearing structure supported at only one end

can·ti·na /kan teénǝ/ *n* a bar in a Spanish-speaking country or region

can·to /kántō/ (*pl* -tos) *n* a part of a long poem

can·ton /kántǝn, kán tòn/ *n* a division or sub-division of a country such as Switzerland or France —**can·ton·al** /kántǝn'l, kan tónn'l/ *adj*

Can·ton /kántǝn, kán tòn/ ◊ **Guangzhou**

Can·ton·ese /kàntǝ neèz, -neèss/ (*pl same*) *n* 1 a Chinese language spoken in Guangdong in S China and widely elsewhere 2 somebody from Guangdong —**Can·ton·ese** *adj*

can·ton·ment /kan tónmǝnt, kan tónmǝnt/ *n* 1 temporary accommodation for troops 2 assignment to temporary quarters

Ca·nute /kǝ nyoót, kǝ noót/ (994?–1035) king of England (1016–35), Denmark (1018–35), and Norway (1028–35)

can·vas /kánvǝss/ *n* 1 a strong heavy fabric. Use: sails, tents. 2 a piece of fabric for painting on 3 the floor of a boxing or wrestling ring

SPELLCHECK Do not confuse the spelling of **canvas** and **canvass** ("solicit orders, opinions, or votes"), which sound similar.

can·vass /kánvǝss/, **can·vas** *v* 1 *vti* visit people or a place to solicit orders, opinions, or votes 2 *vt* discuss a proposal or issue thoroughly ■ *n* an opinion poll —**can·vass·er** *n* ◊ See note at **canvas**

can·yon /kánnyǝn/, **ca·ñon** *n* a deep narrow valley

cap *n* 1 a close-fitting hat 2 a cover for the end of something such as a pen or bottle 3 a covering at the top of something 4 the top or upper part of something 5 an upper limit 6 a detonator that explodes when struck 7 an explosive paper disk for a toy gun 8 a covering for a tooth 9 a patch on a bird's head 10 a new surface for a tire ■ *vt* (**capped**, **cap·ping**) 1 cover with a cap 2 lie on top of 3 surpass 4 add the finishing touch to 5 impose an upper limit on —**cap·ful** *n*

⚡**CAP** *abbr* /kap/ computer-aided production

cap. *abbr* capital

ca·pa·bil·i·ty /kàypǝ bíllǝteé/ (*pl* -ties) *n* 1 the ability necessary to do something 2 an ability or characteristic that has potential for development ◊ See note at **ability**

ca·pa·ble /káypǝb'l/ *adj* 1 competent or skilled 2 able to do a particular thing ○ *not capable of murder* 3 susceptible to or permitting something ○ *a remark capable of mis-interpretation* —**ca·pa·bly** *adv*

ca·pa·cious /kǝ páyshǝss/ *adj* big enough to contain a large quantity (*fml*)

ca·pac·i·tance /kǝ pássitǝnss/ *n* 1 the ability to store an electric charge 2 a measure of capacitance equal to the surface charge divided by the electrical potential

ca·pac·i·tor /kǝ pássitǝr/ *n* an electrical component used to store a charge

⚡**ca·pac·i·ty** /kǝ pássǝteé/ (*pl* -ties) *n* 1 mental or physical ability 2 the maximum amount that something can contain ○ *was filled to capacity* ○ *a capacity crowd* 3 maximum productivity ○ *The factory is working to capacity.* 4 an official role ○ *in my capacity as team captain* 5 a measure of electrical output 6 the storage space of a computer device ◊ See note at **ability**

cape¹ *n* a long sleeveless outer garment that is shorter than a cloak

cape² *n* a large headland

Cape Bret·on Is·land /-brétt'n-/ island in NE Nova Scotia, Canada

Cape Cod, Cape Cod cot·tage *n* a style of house, typically one-and-a-half stories, with a rectangular floor plan and a steep gable roof

ca·per¹ /káypǝr/ *n* 1 a playful jump 2 a playful act or trick 3 a dangerous or illegal activity (*infml*) ■ *vi* prance happily

ca·per² /káypǝr/ *n* 1 a small pickled flower bud used for flavoring (*often pl*) 2 a bush that produces capers

Ca·per·na·um /kǝ púrnee ǝm/ city of ancient Palestine, on the northwestern shore of the Sea of Galilee

Cape Town legislative capital of South Africa and capital of **Western Cape Province**. Pop. 2,727,000 (1995).

Cape Verde /-vúrd/ island country in the Atlantic Ocean, west of Senegal. Cap. Praia. Pop. 405,163 (2001).

Cape York Pe·nin·su·la peninsula in N Queensland, Australia, the most northerly point on the Australian mainland

cap·il·lar·y /káppǝ lèrree/ *n* (*pl* -ies) a thin blood vessel ■ *adj* 1 of a phenomenon in which the surface of a liquid rises, falls, or distorts when in contact with a solid ○ *capillary action* 2 of or like blood capillaries¹

cap·i·tal¹ /káppit'l/ *n* 1 a city that is a seat of government 2 a center of a particular activity 3 material wealth 4 cash for investment 5 advantage derived from or useful in a particular situation 6 a letter in its larger form, e.g., A, B, or C (*often pl*) ■ *adj* 1 describes a letter in its larger form ○ *a capital D* 2 of or involving the death penalty 3 functioning as a seat of government ○ *a capital city* 4 of financial capital 5 very serious 6 principal

SPELLCHECK Do not confuse the spelling of **capital** and **capitol** ("legislative building"), which sound similar.

cap·i·tal² /káppit'l/ *n* the upper part of an architectural column

cap·i·tal as·set *n* a fixed asset of a business

cap·i·tal ex·pen·di·ture *n* expenditure on fixed assets

cap·i·tal gain *n* a profit from selling assets (often pl)

cap·i·tal gains tax *n* a tax on the sale of assets

cap·i·tal goods *npl* goods used in the production of other goods

cap·i·tal-in·ten·sive *adj* having high financial cost relative to labor

cap·i·tal·ism /káppit'l ìzzəm/ *n* an economic system based on private ownership of profit-making companies in a free market

cap·i·tal·ist /káppit'list/ *n* 1 an investor of money in business for profit 2 a supporter of capitalism ■ *adj* of capitalism

cap·i·tal·ize /káppit'l ìz/ (-ized, -iz·ing) *v* 1 *vti* write or key in capital letters or with an initial capital letter 2 *vi* take advantage of something ○ *to capitalize on an opponent's mistake* 3 *vt* use debt or budgeted expenditure as financial capital 4 *vt* finance 5 *vt* treat an expenditure as an asset rather than an expense —**cap·i·tal·i·za·tion** /kàppit'li záysh'n/ *n*

cap·i·tal pun·ish·ment *n* the death penalty

cap·i·tal stock *n* the amount of stock issued by a company

cap·i·ta·tion /kàppi táysh'n/ *n* a fixed tax or payment per person

cap·i·tol /káppit'l/ *n* 1 a building for a lawmaking body 2 **Cap·i·tol** the US Congress building ◊ See note at **capital**

ca·pit·u·late /kə píchə làyt/ (-lat·ed, -lat·ing) *vi* 1 surrender 2 consent or yield —**cap·it·u·la·tion** /kə pichə láysh'n/ *n* ◊ See note at **yield**

ca·pon /káy pòn, -pən/ *n* a male chicken castrated to improve its flesh for eating

Al Capone

Ca·pone /kə pṓn/, **Al** (1899–1947) Italian-born US gangster and racketeer

Ca·po·te /kə pṓtee/, **Truman** (1924–84) US writer

cap·puc·ci·no /kàppə chee nṑ, kàapə-/ (pl -nos) *n* frothy milky coffee

ORIGIN The coffee was so called in Italian because it suggested the color of the habit of a *Cappuccino*, a member of an order of friars who wore a cloak with a sharp-pointed hood or *cappuccio*.

~~cappucino~~ incorrect spelling of **cappuccino**

Cap·ra /kápprə/, **Frank** (1897–1991) US movie director and producer

Ca·pri /kə preé, ká preé, kàa preé/ island in the Bay of Naples, S Italy. Pop. 7,075 (1996).

ca·price /kə preéss/ *n* 1 an impulsive tendency 2 a sudden change or action 3 a whim

ca·pri·cious /kə príshəss, kə preéshəss/ *adj* given to sudden changes —**ca·pri·cious·ly** *adv* —**ca·pri·cious·ness** *n*

Cap·ri·corn /kápprri kàwrn/ *n* 1 the 10th sign of the zodiac 2 *also* **Cap·ri·corn·us** a zodiacal constellation in the southern hemisphere

ca·pri pants /kə preé-/, **Ca·pri pants** *npl* women's pants ending just below the knee

cap·si·cum /kápsikəm/ *n* 1 a hot red pepper fruit 2 a plant that produces capsicums

cap·size /káp sìz, kap síz/ (-sized, -siz·ing) *vti* overturn in water (refers to boats)

ƒ caps lock *n* a computer key that capitalizes all letters subsequently typed

cap·stan /kápstən/ *n* 1 a vertical rotating cylinder. Use: moving heavy weights, hauling in ropes. 2 a rotating shaft in a tape recorder

cap·sule /káps'l, káp sòol/ *n* 1 a small soluble container of medicine to be swallowed like a pill 2 a seed case 3 a membrane or sac enclosing an organ or body part 4 a vehicle or cabin for space travel 5 a seal on a container 6 a short summary ■ *adj* 1 very brief 2 compact ■ *vt* (-suled, -sul·ing) 1 put in a capsule 2 summarize —**cap·su·lar** *adj*

cap·sule ho·tel *n* in Japan, a hotel in which the rooms are lockable cubicles

cap·sul·ize /kápsə lìz, kápsəy lìz/ (-ized, -iz·ing) *vt* express concisely

Capt. *abbr* Captain

cap·tain /káptən/ *n* 1 somebody in command of a ship or airplane 2 an officer in the US Navy or Coast Guard of a rank above commander 3 an officer in the US Army, Air Force, or Marine Corps of a rank above first lieutenant 4 *also* **Cap·tain** an officer in the British Army or Royal Marines, or in the Royal Canadian Army or Air Force, of a rank above lieutenant 5 a senior police or fire officer 6 a team leader 7 an important or influential person ○ *captains of industry* ■ *vt* be the captain of —**cap·tain·cy** *n*

cap·tion /kápshən/ *n* 1 a description of an illustration 2 a heading or subheading 3 a movie or television subtitle —**cap·tion** *vt*

cap·tious /kápshəss/ *adj* (literary) 1 excessively critical 2 intended to confuse or entrap an opponent in an argument

cap·ti·vate /káptə vàyt/ (-vat·ed, -vat·ing) *vt* enchant with pleasing or irresistible features —**cap·ti·vat·ing** *adj* —**cap·ti·va·tion** /kàptə váysh'n/ *n*

cap·tive /káptiv/ *n* 1 a prisoner 2 somebody dominated by an emotion ■ *adj* 1 unable to escape 2 irresistibly attracted 3 forced to buy, accept, or pay attention to something ○ *a captive audience* —**cap·tiv·i·ty** /kap tívvətee/ *n*

cap·tor /káptər, káp tàwr/ *n* somebody who holds another person prisoner

✦ **cap·ture** /kápchər/ *vt* (**-tured, -tur·ing**) **1** take a person or animal into captivity **2** seize or take control of something **3** dominate somebody's mind o *captured her imagination* **4** represent something accurately o *a picture capturing the innocence of childhood* **5** record and store data on a computer ◼ *n* **1** an act of capturing or being captured **2** somebody or something captured **3** the recording of data on a computer

~~capuccino~~ incorrect spelling of **cappuccino**

cap·y·ba·ra /kåppi baàra, -bérra/ (*pl* **-ras** or *same*) *n* a large rodent of Central and South America

car *n* **1** a small passenger-carrying road vehicle **2** a compartment for passengers or cargo, e.g., in an airship **3** an elevator

car. *abbr* carat

Ca·ra·cas /kə rákəss/ capital of Venezuela. Pop. 1,964,846 (1992).

ca·rafe /kə ráf/ *n* **1** a container like a bottle with a flared open top for serving cold drinks such as wine or water **2** a container for coffee

car·a·mel /kárrəməl, -mèl, kaàrməl/ *n* **1** melted or dissolved sugar heated until it turns brown **2** a chewy candy

car·a·mel·ize /kárrəmə lìz, kaàrmə-/ (**-ized, -iz·ing**) *vti* change into caramel —**car·a·mel·i·za·tion** /kàrrəməli záysh'n, kaàrməli-/ *n*

car·a·pace /kárrə pàyss/ *n* an animal shell such as that on a turtle's back

car·at /kárrət/ *n* **1** a unit of mass used for gems **2** METALL = **karat**

SPELLCHECK Do not confuse the spelling of **carat** and **carrot** (the vegetable), which sound similar.

Ca·ra·vag·gi·o /kàrrə vaàjee ō, kàrrə vaàjō/, **Michelangelo Merisi da** (1573–1610) Italian painter

car·a·van /kárrə vàn/ *n* **1** a group of desert merchants with camels **2** a group of travelers ◼ *vi* (**-vanned** or **-vaned, -van·ning** or **-van·ing**) travel in a group —**car·a·van·ner** *n*

car·a·van·se·rai /kàrrə vánsə rì/, **car·a·van·sa·ry** /-ree/ *n* **1** a large inn, especially for desert travelers **2** a group of travelers

car·a·way /kárrə wày/ *n* **1** *also* **car·a·way seed** the dried seeds of a flowering plant, used as a spice **2** the plant that produces caraway

car·bine /kaàr beèn, -bìn/ *n* a short lightweight rifle

car·bo·hy·drate /kaàrbō hí dràyt/ *n* **1** a naturally occurring compound that is an important source of energy in food **2** a food containing carbohydrates

car·bol·ic ac·id /kaar bòllik-/ *n* CHEM = **phenol**

car·bon /kaàrbən/ *n* (*symbol* **C**) a nonmetallic chemical element that forms large numbers of organic compounds —**car·bon·ous** *adj*

car·bon 14 /-fawr teèn/ *n* a naturally radioactive carbon isotope. Use: in carbon dating.

car·bon·ate /kaàrbə nàyt/ (**-at·ed, -at·ing**) *vt* add carbon dioxide to a liquid

car·bon cop·y *n* **1** a duplicate made with waxy paper **2** somebody or something identical to somebody or something else (*infml*)

car·bon dat·ing *n* a method of dating organic remains based on their content of carbon 14

car·bon di·ox·ide *n* a colorless odorless atmospheric gas. Use: in refrigeration, carbonated drinks, fire extinguishers.

Car·bon·if·er·ous /kàarbə nìfferəss/ *n* a period of geologic time 354–290 million years ago —**Car·bon·if·er·ous** *adj*

car·bon·ize /kaàrbə nìz/ (**-ized, -iz·ing**) *v* **1** *vti* turn into carbon **2** *vt* cover or coat with carbon —**car·bon·i·za·tion** /kaàrbəni záysh'n/ *n*

car·bon mon·ox·ide *n* a colorless odorless toxic gas released when carbon-based fuels are burned

car·bon pa·per *n* waxy paper formerly used for making copies of documents

car·bun·cle /kaàr bùngk'l/ *n* **1** an inflamed swelling **2** a red gemstone

car·bu·re·tor /kaàrbə ràytər/ *n* a device in an internal combustion engine that mixes the air and fuel

car·cass /kaàrkəss/ *n* **1** the dead body of an animal **2** all that is left of something decayed or destroyed

car·cin·o·gen /kaar sínnəjən, kaàrs'nə jèn/ *n* a cancer-causing substance or agent —**car·cin·o·gen·ic** /kàars'nə jénnik/ *adj*

car·ci·no·ma /kàars'n ṓmə/ *n* a malignant tumor —**car·ci·nom·a·tous** /-ṓmmətəss/ *adj*

card¹ *n* **1** a folded piece of stiff paper, used to send greetings **2** a small piece of stiff paper printed with symbols or figures, used as part of a set for playing games **3** a piece of stiff paper, cardboard, or plastic showing something such as somebody's identity, business affiliation, or membership of a club **4** a small piece of plastic used for buying goods on credit or getting cash **5** a postcard **6** an amusing person (*dated infml*) **7** a piece of colored stiff paper shown to a soccer player who has violated a rule **8** a wine list ◼ *vt* ask to see somebody's identification card (*infml*) ◊ **a card up your sleeve** a secret plan ready to be used if necessary (*infml*) ◊ **in the cards** likely to happen (*infml*) ◊ **play your cards close to your chest** or **vest** be secretive (*infml*) ◊ **put** or **lay your cards on the table** openly reveal your plans (*infml*)

card² /ka:rd/ *vt* comb and clean wool, cotton, or other fibers ■ *n* a tool or machine for carding fiber —**card·er** *n*

car·da·mom /ka:rdəməm/, **car·da·mon** /-mən/ *n* 1 the aromatic seeds and pods of a tropical plant, used as a spice 2 the plant that produces cardamom

card·board /ka:rd bàwrd/ *n* lightweight paper board ■ *adj* two-dimensional or lacking in depth ○ *a cardboard portrayal of the hero*

card-car·ry·ing *adj* 1 officially listed as a member of an organization 2 deeply committed to a cause (*infml*)

card cat·a·log *n* an alphabetical listing on separate cards

card·hold·er /ka:rd hòldər/ *n* an owner of a credit, debit, or other card

car·di·ac /ka:rdee àk/ *adj* of the heart

car·di·ac ar·rest *n* the sudden stopping of the heartbeat

Car·diff /ka:rdif/ capital and largest city of Wales. Pop. 315,040 (1996). Welsh **Caerdydd**

car·di·gan /ka:rdigən/ *n* a long-sleeved sweater that fastens at the front

ORIGIN The **cardigan** is named for James Thomas Brudenell, 7th earl of Cardigan (1797–1868), who was one of the first to wear it.

car·di·nal /ka:rd'nəl/ *n* 1 a high-ranking member of the Roman Catholic clergy who is one of those from whom the next pope is elected 2 a deep red color 3 a bright red bird 4 *also* **car·di·nal num·ber** a number denoting a quantity, not an order, e.g., 2 or 8 ■ *adj* 1 fundamentally important 2 bright red in color

car·di·nal point *n* any of the four principal points of the compass

car·di·nal vir·tue *n* a traditionally important virtue

cardio- *prefix* heart ○ *cardiovascular*

car·di·ol·o·gy /ka:rdee òllajee/ *n* the branch of medicine dealing with disorders of the heart —**car·di·o·log·i·cal** /ka:rdee ə lójjik'l/ *adj* —**car·di·ol·o·gist** *n*

car·di·o·pul·mo·nar·y /ka:rdee ō pòolmə nèrree, -púlmə-/ *adj* of the heart and lungs

car·di·o·vas·cu·lar /ka:rdee ō váskyələr/ *adj* of the heart and blood vessels

Car·do·so /ka:r dóssō/, **Fernando Henrique** (*b.* 1931) president of Brazil (1995–)

Car·do·zo /kaar dózō/, **Benjamin Nathan** (1870–1938) associate justice of the US Supreme Court (1932–38)

cards *n* a game using a set of cards (+ *sing verb*)

card·sharp /ka:rd shaarp/, **card·sharp·er** /-shaarpər/ *n* somebody who cheats regularly at cards

card ta·ble *n* a lightweight table for playing cards on

care /kair/ *v* (**cared, car·ing**) 1 *vti* be interested in or concerned about something ○ *I don't care whether you come or not.* 2 *vi* feel affection ■ *n* 1 the keeping of something in good condition ○ *skin care* 2 careful attention to avoid damage or error 3 a worry 4 attention to somebody's well-being 5 *UK* a local authority's custody and maintenance of a child 6 legal oversight of somebody ◊ See note at **worry**

CARE /kair/ *abbr* Cooperative for American Relief Everywhere

ca·reen /kə reen/ *v* 1 *vi* to move forward at high speed, swaying or swerving 2 *vt* turn a boat on its side for cleaning or repair

ca·reer /kə reer/ *n* 1 a long-term or lifelong job 2 somebody's progress in their chosen profession 3 the general progress of something ■ *adj* 1 expecting to work in a profession for life 2 committing illegal acts throughout a lifetime ■ *vi* lurch rapidly onward

care-free /kair free/ *adj* without worries or responsibilities —**care-free·ness** *n*

care·ful /kairf'l/ *adj* 1 acting with caution 2 showing close attention to detail —**care·ful·ly** *adv* —**care·ful·ness** *n*

SYNONYMS careful, conscientious, scrupulous, thorough, meticulous, painstaking, assiduous, punctilious, finicky, fussy CORE MEANING: exercising care and attention in doing something

~~carefull~~ incorrect spelling of **careful**

care·giv·er /kair givvər/ *n* 1 somebody responsible for caring for a child or dependent adult 2 somebody assisting in the management of somebody's illness —**care·giv·ing** *n*

~~careing~~ incorrect spelling of **caring**

care·less /kairləss/ *adj* 1 not attentive enough to details 2 showing no concern or consideration 3 done or displayed naturally and without effort ○ *a careless charm* —**care·less·ly** *adv* —**care·less·ness** *n*

ca·ress /kə réss/ *vt* 1 touch or stroke affectionately 2 touch or affect in a soothing way ■ *n* a gentle touch

care·tak·er /kair tàykər/ *n* 1 a temporary holder of an office or position 2 somebody offering emotional support

care·tak·er gov·ern·ment *n* a government established temporarily until the next election

care-worn /kair wàwrn/ *adj* exhausted from worry

car·fare /ka:r fàir/ *n* the fare for a bus or taxicab

car·go /ka:rgō/ (*pl* -**goes** *or* -**gos**) *n* 1 goods carried as freight 2 a load

~~carriage~~ incorrect spelling of **carriage**

Car·ib /kárrib/ (*pl* -**ibs** *or same*) *n* 1 a member of a group of Native American people who live in Central America, NE South America, and the Lesser Antilles **2** the language of the Carib people —**Car·ib** adj

Car·ib·be·an /kárrə beé ən, kə ríbbee ən/ region of island groups from the southeastern tip of Florida to the coast of Venezuela, separating the Caribbean Sea from the Atlantic Ocean —**Car·ib·be·an** adj, n

Ca·rib·be·an Sea arm of the Atlantic Ocean, surrounded by the Greater and Lesser Antilles, N South America, and E Central America. Depth (Cayman Trench) 24,720 ft./7,535 m.

car·i·bou /kárrə boo/ (pl same or **-bous**) n a large deer with branched antlers

car·i·ca·ture /kárrəkə choŏr, -chər/ n **1** a drawing, description, or performance that exaggerates characteristics for comic effect **2** a ridiculously inappropriate or poor version of something —**car·i·ca·ture** vt —**car·i·ca·tur·ist** n

car·ies /káireez/ n tooth decay —**car·i·ous** adj

car·il·lon /kárrə lòn, -lən/ n **1** a set of stationary bells hung in a tower and played from a keyboard **2** a tune played on a carillon —**car·il·lon** vi

car·ing /káiring/ adj **1** showing concern **2** of a profession such as nursing that involves looking after people ■ n the provision of medical or other care —**car·ing·ly** adv

car·jack·ing /kaár jàking/ n the hijacking of a car —**car·jack** vti —**car·jack·er** n

Car·lyle /kaar líl, kaár líl/, **Thomas** (1795–1881) Scottish historian and essayist

car·mine /kaármin, -mīn/ n **1** a deep purplish red color **2** a bright red pigment made from cochineal —**car·mine** adj

car·nage /kaárnij/ n **1** the widespread slaughter of people **2** serious injury to a great many people, e.g., in a major accident

car·nal /kaárn'l/ adj **1** of physical needs, not spiritual needs (fml) **2** sensual or sexual —**car·nal·i·ty** /kaar nállətee/ n —**car·nal·ly** adv

car·na·tion /kaar náysh'n/ n a perennial plant of the pink family, with white, pink, or red clove-scented flowers

car·nau·ba /kaar náwbə, -nówbə/ n wax from a palm tree. Use: polish, candles.

Car·ne·gie /kaárnəgee, kaar náygee, -néggee, -néegee/, **Andrew** (1835–1919) Scottish-born US industrialist and philanthropist

Car·ne·gie, Dale (1888–1955) US writer

car·net /kaar náy/ n **1** a book of tickets for use on public transportation **2** a customs document for a car

car·ni·val /kaárnəvəl/ n **1** a large public festival **2** a traveling outdoor amusement show **3** an entertainment with games and prizes **4** the period before Lent celebrated with a carnival in many countries **5 Car·ni·val** in Grenada, an August folk festival with

dancing, music, drinking, and costumed parades

> **ORIGIN Carnival** comes from Italian, and is based on Latin words meaning "meat, flesh" and "raise, lift." It refers to the Christian practice of giving up meat-eating for Lent, the 40 days before Easter. The **carnival** was originally a period of feasting and merry-making before the self-denial and abstinence of Lent.

car·ni·vore /kaárnə vàwr/ n **1** a flesh-eating animal **2** a carnivorous plant

car·niv·o·rous /kaar nívvərəss/ adj **1** meat-eating **2** describes a plant that can digest insects and small invertebrates

car·ob /kárrəb/ (pl **-obs** or same) n **1** an edible powder with a taste like chocolate, made from pods **2** the evergreen Mediterranean tree that produces the pods from which carob is made

car·ol /kárrəl/ n a joyful song, especially one sung by Christians celebrating Christmas ■ vi sing Christmas songs

Ca·ro·li·na /kàrrə línə/ city in NE Puerto Rico. Pop. 188,427 (1996).

Car·o·line Is·lands /kárrə līn-/ archipelago in the W Pacific Ocean, east of the Philippines, comprising the Federated States of Micronesia and the Republic of Palau

ca·rouse /kə rówz/ (**-roused, -rous·ing**) vi drink alcohol and become noisy (literary) —**ca·rous·er** n

car·ou·sel /kàrrə sél, kárrə sèl/ n **1** a merry-go-round at an amusement park or fairground **2** a circular conveyer belt for baggage at an airport **3** a rotating holder that loads photographic slides into a projector

carp[1] vi keep complaining or finding fault ◊ See note at **complain**

carp[2] (pl same or **carps**) n **1** a large freshwater fish with a single fin on its back **2** any fish of the family that includes carp, goldfish, and koi

Car·pa·thi·an Moun·tains /kaar pàythee ən-/ mountain system in E Europe between Slovakia and Poland, extending southward into E Romania. Highest peak Gerlachovka 8,711 ft./2,655 m.

car·pel /kaárp'l/ n a female reproductive organ in a flower

car·pen·ter /kaárpəntər/ n a builder and repairer of wooden structures or objects

car·pen·try /kaárpəntree/ n **1** the work or occupation of a carpenter **2** structures or objects produced by a carpenter

car·pet /kaárpət/ n thick heavy fabric for covering a floor ■ vt cover a floor with a carpet

car·pet·bag·ger /kaárpət bàggər/ n after the Civil War, a Northerner who moved to the South seeking political or commercial advantage

car·pet-bomb *vt* destroy an area with intensive aerial bombing

car·pet·ing /ka'arpɒting/ *n* 1 thick heavy fabric used for carpets 2 carpets collectively

car·pet-sweep·er /ka'arpɒt swe'epər/ *n* a hand-operated carpet-cleaning device

car phone *n* a mobile phone for a car

car pool *n* 1 a group of people who use their own cars in turn to transport the group 2 an arrangement to share cars

car-pool *vi* share driving responsibilities with other people in a group

car·port /ka'ar pàwrt/ *n* an open-sided shelter for a car, attached to a building

car·pus /ka'arpɒss/ (*pl* **-pi** /-pĩ/) *n* any of the eight bones in the wrist joint —**car·pal** *adj*

car·ra·geen·an /kàrrə ge'enən, kárrə ge'enən/, **car·ra·geen·in** *n* a complex carbohydrate obtained from seaweed. Use: commercial preparation of food and drink.

~~carraige~~ incorrect spelling of **carriage**

~~carreer~~ incorrect spelling of **career**

car·rel /kə rél, kárrəl/, **car·rell** *n* a cubicle or small room for individual study

Car·rer·as /kə ráirəss/, **José** (*b.* 1946) Spanish operatic tenor

~~carress~~ incorrect spelling of **caress**

car·riage /kárrij/ *n* 1 a large four-wheeled horse-drawn vehicle 2 a wheeled platform for carrying or supporting something 3 somebody's posture while walking (*fml*) 4 the transporting and delivering of goods 5 a charge for transporting and delivering goods 6 a moving part of a machine, especially the sliding cylinder on a typewriter 7 a baby carriage

~~Carribean~~ incorrect spelling of **Caribbean**

car·ri·er /kárree ər/ *n* 1 a person or organization that transports people or goods 2 a person or organism infected with a disease or carrying a particular gene and able to spread it without showing symptoms of being affected by it 3 an aircraft carrier 4 somebody who delivers mail

car·ri·er pi·geon *n* a domestic pigeon trained to deliver messages and then return home

car·ri·on /kárree ən/ *n* 1 the rotting flesh of a dead animal 2 something decaying or disgusting (*literary*)

Car·roll /kárrəl/, **Lewis** (1832–98) British writer

car·rot /kárrət/ *n* 1 a thin tapering orange root used as a vegetable 2 the biennial plant that produces carrots 3 something offered as an inducement or incentive ◊ See note at **carat**

car·rot-and-stick *adj* combining reward and punishment

car·rot·y /kárrətee/ *adj* describes hair that is a reddish color

car·ry /kárree/ *v* (**-ried**, **-ries**) 1 *vt* hold, move, and take somebody or something along or to another place 2 *vt* be a channel or route ◊ *pipelines carrying oil* 3 *vt* have a transmissible disease 4 *vt* have something with you, e.g., in a pocket 5 *vt* publish or broadcast something 6 *vt* have something as a factor, consequence, or penalty 7 *vt* develop an idea ◊ *carry an argument to its conclusion* 8 *vt* move or behave in a particular way 9 *vt* stock something as merchandise 10 *vti* accept a proposal by voting for it, or be so accepted 11 *vt* keep somebody on the accounts as a debtor ■ *n* (*pl* **-ries**) in football, a run with the ball

□ **carry forward** *vt* transfer an item to the next column in an account or calculation

□ **carry off** *vt* do successfully or well

□ **carry on** *v* 1 *vti* continue doing something ◊ *She carried on after we left.* 2 *vt* be involved in

□ **carry out** *vt* 1 perform or accomplish an idea ◊ *carry out research* 2 do what is ordered, planned, or instructed ◊ See note at **accomplish, perform**

□ **carry over** *v* 1 *vt* transfer an item to the next column in an account or calculation 2 *vt* defer something to the next tax year 3 *vi* continue to produce an effect in changed circumstances

□ **carry through** *vt* 1 do what was planned 2 help somebody survive a difficult experience

car·ry·all /kárree àwl/ *n* 1 a large soft travel bag 2 a passenger vehicle with facing benches

car·ry·ing charge *n* 1 the cost to a business of holding assets that produce no income 2 interest on an unpaid balance

car·ry·on /kárree òn/ *n* an airline passenger's hand luggage —**car·ry·on** *adj*

car·ry·o·ver /kárree òvər/ *n* 1 something deferred or continued with at a later time 2 an item transferred to the next column in an account or calculation

car·sick /ka'ar sìk/ *adj* feeling sick because of the motion of a vehicle —**car·sick·ness** *n*

Car·son /ka'arss'n/, **Kit** (1809–68) US hunter and scout

UPI/Corbis-Bettmann

Rachel Carson

Car·son, Rachel (1907–64) US ecologist

Car·son Cit·y capital of Nevada. Pop. 49,301 (1998).

cart *n* 1 an open horse-drawn vehicle for carrying goods 2 a light vehicle or barrow pushed by hand 3 a trolley for shopping or baggage 4 a lightweight horse-drawn carriage with two wheels **5** a small motorized vehicle **6** a small wheeled table for food or drinks ■ *vt* **1** carry roughly or with difficulty *(infml)* **2** transport from one location to another

Car·ta·ge·na /kaàrtə gáyna, -jeèna, -háyna/ port in NW Colombia. Pop. 877,000 (1999).

carte blanche /kaart blàanch, -blaàNsh/ *n* complete freedom to act

car·tel /kaar tél/ *n* **1** a group of businesses formed to control the course of their industry **2** an alliance of like-minded political groups

The White House

Jimmy Carter

Car·ter /kaártər/, **Jimmy** (*b.* 1924) 39th president of the United States (1977–81)

Car·thage /kaárthij/ ancient city on the coast of N Africa, near present-day Tunis —**Car·tha·gin·i·an** /kaàrthə jínnee ən/ *n*, *adj*

cart·horse /kaárt hàwrss/ *n UK* a large strong horse used for heavy farm work

Car·tier /kaar tyáy, kaàrtee ày/, **Jacques** (1491–1557) French navigator

Car·tier-Bres·son /kaar tyày brə sőn, -brə sáwN/, **Henri** (*b.* 1908) French photographer

car·ti·lage /kaárt'lij/ *n* strong elastic tissue around the joints in the body

car·tog·ra·phy /kaar tóggrəfee/ *n* the science or activity of making maps —**car·tog·ra·pher** *n*

car·ton /kaárt'n/ *n* **1** a cardboard box **2** a plastic or cardboard container for food or drinks **3** the contents of a food or drink carton

car·toon /kaar toón/ *n* **1** an animated movie, especially a humorous movie for children **2** a comic strip **3** a humorous or satirical drawing published in a newspaper or magazine **4** a preliminary drawing of a work of art —**car·toon·ist** *n*

car·tridge /kaártrij/ *n* **1** a cylindrical case holding a bullet or shot and an explosive charge **2** a container of liquid or powder used in a device such as a computer printer **3** a sealed plastic case containing film or tape

cart·wheel /kaárt hweèl/ *n* an acrobatic movement in which the body is turned sideways onto the hands and then onto the feet again ■ *vi* do a cartwheel

Ca·ru·so /kə roósső/, **Enrico** (1873–1921) Italian operatic tenor

carve (**carved, carv·ing**) *vti* cut cooked meat into slices

□ **carve out** *vt* make or achieve through hard work

□ **carve up** *vt* divide among several people *(infml)*

carv·er /kaárvər/ *n* a knife for slicing cooked meats

Car·ver /kaárvər/, **George Washington** (1864–1943) US botanist

carv·ing /kaárving/ *n* **1** an object or design made by cutting wood **2** an act of carving

carv·ing knife *n* a large knife for slicing cooked meat

car wash *n* a place for washing vehicles automatically with revolving brushes and jets of water

car·y·at·id /kèrree áttid, kérree ə tìd/ (*pl* **-ids** or **-i·des** /-i deèz/) *n* in classical architecture, a column in the shape of a female figure

CASA *abbr* Court-Appointed Special Advocate

Cas·a·blan·ca /kàssə bláNgkə, kaàssə blaàngkə/ largest city in Morocco, on the Atlantic coast. Pop. 2,940,623 (1994).

Ca·sals /kə sálz/, **Pablo** (1876–1973) Spanish cellist and composer

Ca·sa·no·va /kàssə nővə/ *n* a promiscuous seducer of women

Ca·sa·no·va /kàssə nővə/, **Giovanni Jacopo, Chevalier de Seingalt** (1725–98) Italian adventurer and author

Ca·sas ♦ **Las Casas, Bartolomé de**

✦ **cas·cade** /ka skáyd/ *n* **1** a small waterfall or series of waterfalls **2** a downward flow of something **3** a succession of things, each affecting the next ■ *v* (**-cad·ed, -cad·ing**) **1** *vti* flow, or make something flow, fast and in large amounts **2** *vi* hang or lie in a flowing mass *(literary)* **3** *vt* arrange the windows on a computer screen so that they overlap, with the title bar of each visible

Cas·cade Range /ka skáyd-/ range of mountains in the NW United States and SW Canada. Highest peak Mt. Rainier, 14,410 ft./4,392 m.

✦ **cas·cad·ing men·u** *n* a menu in a computer program that opens when you select an option from an earlier menu

case[1] *n* **1** a situation or set of circumstances ○ *a case of mistaken identity* **2** an instance of something **3** a subject of investigation or scrutiny **4** a matter or issue in question **5** something examined in a law court **6** an argument for or against something ○ *make a good case for selling the business* **7** a grammatical form of a word that indicates its relationship to other words in a sentence **8** a particular kind of person *(infml)* ○ *a hopeless case* ■ *vt* (**cased, cas·ing**) inspect a place, especially with a view to robbing it *(slang)* ◇ **be on somebody's case** persist in pestering somebody to do something *(slang)* ◇ **in any case** no matter what may happen ◇ **in case of** if something happens

case[2] *n* **1** a holder, container, or outer covering **2** the function of a printed character as either a capital or small letter ■ *vt* (**cased, cas·ing**) put a covering around

⚡**CASE** *abbr* **1** computer-aided software engineering **2** computer-aided systems engineering

case·book /káyss bòok/ *n* a record of legal or medical cases

case his·to·ry *n* a record of somebody's treatment kept by a doctor or social worker

case law *n* law established by precedent, rather than by legislation

case·load /káyss lòd/ *n* the number of cases being handled at a particular time

case·ment /káyssmənt/ *n* a hinged window

case stud·y *n* an analysis of a particular situation used for drawing conclusions in similar situations

case·work /káyss wùrk/ *n* the system of assigning clients to social workers —**case·work·er** *n*

cash /kash/ *n* **1** coins and bills **2** money in any form (*infml*) ○ *earn some cash* ■ *vt* exchange a check for currency —**cash·a·ble** *adj* ◊ See note at **cache**

□ **cash in** *vt* convert something such as an insurance policy into cash

cash-and-car·ry *n* (*pl* **cash-and-car·ries**) **1** a store without a delivery service that sells inexpensive goods for cash **2** the policy of selling goods without a delivery service ■ *adj* cash-only and without delivery

cash·book /kásh bòok/ *n* a record of money spent and received

cash card *n* a plastic card for accessing a bank account

cash cow *n* a source of steady profit (*slang*)

cash crop *n* a crop grown for sale

cash·ew /ká shòo/ *n* **1** *also* **cash·ew nut** a kidney-shaped edible nut **2** the tropical tree that produces cashews

cash flow *n* **1** the movement of money received and spent and its influence on the amount of money available **2** an assessment of a company's income and expenditure

cash·ier[1] /ka shéer/ *n* **1** a bank worker who deals with customers' routine transactions **2** somebody responsible for an organization's financial transactions

ca·shier[2] /ka shéer/ *vt* dismiss from the armed forces for misconduct

cash·ier's check *n* a cleared check issued by a bank

cash·less /káshləss/ *adj* using an electronic method of payment

cash ma·chine *n* an ATM

cash·mere /kázh mèer, kásh-/ *n* **1** a soft luxurious wool fabric **2** a Himalayan goat from whose coat cashmere is made

cash on de·liv·er·y *adv* requiring payment on delivery of merchandise

cash reg·is·ter *n* a machine in a store for recording sales and holding money

cas·ing /káyssing/ *n* an outer covering or frame

ca·si·no /ka seénō/ (*pl* **-nos**) *n* **1** a gambling establishment **2** a point-scoring card game in which the player's hand and an exposed hand can be combined

cask *n* **1** a barrel, especially one containing alcohol **2** the contents of a barrel

cas·ket /káskət/ *n* **1** a coffin **2** a decorative box for valuables

Cas·per /káspər/ city in east central Wyoming. Pop. 48,283 (1998).

Cas·pi·an Sea /káspee ən-/ world's largest inland body of water, between SE Europe and Asia

Cas·san·dra /ka sándrə/ *n* somebody whose warnings of impending disaster are ignored

---

ORIGIN The original **Cassandra** in Greek mythology was the daughter of Priam, king of Troy.

Cas·satt /ka sát/, **Mary** (1845–1926) US artist

cas·sa·va /ka saàvə/ *n* **1** an edible tuber of a tropical plant. Use: as a vegetable, source of tapioca. **2** the plant that produces cassava tubers

cas·se·role /kássə ròl/ *n* **1** a heavy cooking pot for use in an oven **2** a dish of food cooked in liquid in a heavy pot in an oven

cas·sette /ka sét/ *n* a sealed plastic case containing tape or film

cas·sette deck *n* a tape deck that plays or records audio cassettes

cas·sette play·er *n* a machine that plays but does not record audio cassettes

cas·sette re·cord·er *n* a machine that plays and records audio cassettes

Cas·sius /káshəss, kássee əss/ (*fl* 53–42 BC) Roman general and conspirator

cas·sock /kássək/ *n* a priest's full-length robe

cast *v* (**cast**) **1** *vt* throw or fling **2** *vt* register or deposit a vote **3** *vt* cause the appearance of ○ *cast a shadow* **4** *vt* introduce a negative effect ○ *cast doubt on his capability* **5** *vt* direct a look toward **6** *vti* select for a performance or role **7** *vt* form using a mold **8** *vt* shed ○ *a snake that had cast its skin* ■ *n* **1** a throw, or the process of throwing **2** the performers in a production **3** a mold for an object or the object molded **4** a plaster cast **5** the nature of somebody's appearance ○ *a sly cast to his face* **6** a tinge of color **7** skin or horns shed by an animal ◊ See note at **throw**

□ **cast off** *vti* untie mooring lines

□ **cast on** *vti* begin knitting

□ **cast out** *vt* eject, reject, or abandon (*fml*)

cas·ta·net /kàstə nét/ *n* a rhythm instrument consisting of two small concave pieces of hard material clicked together by the fingers

cast·a·way /kástə wày/ *n* a survivor of a ship-wreck —**cast·a·way** *adj*

caste /kast/ *n* **1** a Hindu hereditary social class **2** a group of people identified according to their rank, wealth, descent, or profession **3** somebody's social rank or class

cas·tel·lat·ed /kástə làytəd/ *adj* with battlements or a serrated top edge

cast·er /kástər/, **cas·tor** *n* **1** a small wheel under furniture **2** a small condiment container or stand

cas·ti·gate /kásti gàyt/ (**-gat·ed**, **-gat·ing**) *vt* criticize or punish *(fml)* —**cas·ti·ga·tion** /kàsti gáysh'n/ *n ◊* See note at **criticize**

Cas·tile /ka steél/ central region of Spain

cast·ing /kásting/ *n* an object made with a mold

cast·ing vote *n* a deciding vote to break a tie

cast i·ron *n* hard brittle iron that is shaped in a mold

cast-i·ron *adj* **1** made of cast iron **2** very strong

cas·tle /káss'l/ *n* **1** a large fortified building with tall solid walls, built during the Middle Ages **2** a large country house built to resemble a castle **3** in chess, a rook

cast-off /kást òf, kást àwf/ *n* something or somebody rejected as no longer useful *(often pl)*

cas·tor[1] *n* FURNITURE, HOUSEHOLD= **caster**

cas·tor[2] /kástər/ *n* an aromatic oil secreted by beavers. Use: in medicine, perfumes.

Cas·tor /kástər/ *n* a bright star in the constellation Gemini

cas·tor oil *n* yellowish oil extracted from the seeds of a tropical plant. Use: laxative, lubricant.

cas·trate /ká stràyt/ (**-trat·ed**, **-trat·ing**) *vt* **1** remove the testicles of **2** take away the strength or power of —**cas·tra·tion** /ka stráysh'n/ *n*

Cas·tries /kaà streèz, -streèss/ capital of St. Lucia. Pop. 60,934 (1998).

Fidel Castro

Cas·tro /kástrō/, **Fidel** (*b.* 1927) Cuban prime minister (1959–76) and president (1976–)

ca·su·al /kázhoo əl/ *adj* **1** done by chance or without a plan **2** of or taking on seasonal or temporary work **3** known only slightly *◊ a casual acquaintance* **4** not serious, rigorous, or emotionally committed **5** calm or nonchalant **6** informal or suitable for

informal occasions —**ca·su·al·ly** *adv* —**ca·su·al·ness** *n*

ca·su·al·ty /kázhoo əltee/ (*pl* **-ties**) *n* **1** a victim, especially of an accident or military action **2** *UK* a hospital emergency room

ca·su·ist /kázhoo ist/ *n* **1** somebody who deals with moral and ethical questions **2** somebody using misleadingly subtle reasoning *(disapproving)* —**ca·su·is·tic** /kàzhoo ístik/ *adj* —**ca·su·ist·ry** *n*

ca·sus bel·li /kàssəss béllî, kàyssəss bé lî/ (*pl same*) *n* a situation or event that leads to war *(fml)*

cat *n* **1** a small furry domestic animal that purrs and meows **2** a large wild animal related to the domestic cat, e.g., a lion or tiger **3** a man *(slang dated) ◊* **let the cat out of the bag** disclose a secret or confidential information

CAT *abbr* **1** clear-air turbulence **2** /kat/ computerized axial tomography

cat·a·clysm /káttə klìzzəm/ *n* **1** a disaster causing great changes in society **2** a devastating flood —**cat·a·clys·mic** *adj* —**cat·a·clys·mi·cal·ly** *adv*

cat·a·comb /káttə kòm/ *n* an underground cemetery consisting of passages with burial chambers leading off them *(often pl)*

cat·a·falque /káttə fàlk, -fàwlk/ *n* a decorated platform on which a coffin rests in a public place

~~catagory~~ incorrect spelling of **category**

Cat·a·lan /kátt'l àn, kàtt'l án/ *n* **1** a Romance language spoken in Catalonia, the Balearic Islands, and parts of S France **2** somebody from Catalonia —**Cat·a·lan** *adj*

cat·a·lep·sy /kátt'l èpsee/ *n* a state of unconsciousness resembling a trance —**cat·a·lep·tic** /kàtt'l éptik/ *adj*

cat·a·log /kátt'l òg/, **cat·a·logue** *n* **1** a list of items for sale or on exhibition **2** a list of the holdings in a library **3** a list of related things or events *◊ a catalog of disasters* **4** an alphabetical card file ■ *v* (**-loged**, **-log·ing**; **-logued**, **-logu·ing**) **1** *vti* make a catalog of something **2** *vt* enter an item in a catalog —**cat·a·log·er** *n*

Cat·a·lo·nia /kàtt'l ṓnyə/ autonomous region in NE Spain. Cap. Barcelona. Pop. 6,147,610 (1998). —**Cat·a·lo·nian** *adj, n*

ca·tal·pa /kə tálpə/ *n* a tree with large heart-shaped leaves

cat·a·lyst /kátt'l ìst/ *n* **1** a chemical substance that accelerates a chemical reaction without undergoing change **2** a stimulus to a change or event —**cat·a·lyt·ic** /kàtt'l íttik/ *adj*

cat·a·lyt·ic con·vert·er *n* a chamber in the exhaust system of a vehicle that oxidizes exhaust fumes

cat·a·ma·ran /kàttəmə rán/ *n* a double-hulled boat

ORIGIN Catamaran comes from a language of

S India and N Sri Lanka, and literally means "tied wood."

cat-and-mouse *adj* cruelly exploiting or compounding somebody else's fear

cat·a·pult /kátta pùlt, -pòolt/ *n* **1** a medieval weapon used for hurling stones **2** a mechanism for launching planes or missiles ■ *v* **1** *vti* throw or be thrown with great force **2** *vt* abruptly change the circumstances of o *was catapulted to fame*

cat·a·ract /kátta ràkt/ *n* **1** an opaque eye lens, or a disease causing it **2** a waterfall *(literary)*

ca·tarrh /kə taár/ *n* inflammation of a mucous membrane, especially of the nose or throat —**ca·tarrh·al** *adj* —**ca·tarrh·ous** *adj*

ca·tas·tro·phe /kə tástrəfee/ *n* a disaster

cat·a·stroph·ic /kàttə stróffik/ *adj* **1** causing widespread damage or death **2** very bad or unsuccessful **3** describes an illness that is life-threatening and requires expensive treatment —**cat·a·stroph·i·cal·ly** *adv*

cat·a·ton·ic /kàttə tónnik/ *adj* in a state of inertia or apparent stupor characterized by rigid muscles

Ca·taw·ba /kə táwbə/ (*pl same or* **-bas**) *n* a member of a Native North American people whose surviving members now live mainly in South Carolina

cat bur·glar *n* a stealthy agile burglar

cat·call /kát kàwl/ *n* a jeer

catch /kach, kech/ *v* (**caught** /kawt/) **1** *vti* stop something with the hands or a container **2** *vt* grasp somebody or something suddenly **3** *vt* capture an animal or criminal **4** *vt* reach or get alongside somebody moving ahead **5** *vti* arrive in time to board, e.g., a plane **6** *vti* become infected with a disease **7** *vt* surprise somebody while engaged in an act or in a particular situation o *caught me reading her diary* o *was caught in the rain* **8** *vt* attract somebody's attention **9** *vt* manage to see, e.g., a performance *(infml)* **10** *vti* entangle or trap, or become entangled or trapped **11** *vt* record something on film **12** *vi* begin to burn ■ *n* **1** an instance of catching something **2** somebody who can catch **3** a number of fish or other things caught at one time **4** an ideal romantic partner *(infml)* **5** a device that closes or fastens something **6** a hidden or unexpected disadvantage *(infml)* —**catch·a·ble** *adj*

□ **catch on** *vi* *(infml)* **1** become popular **2** understand something

□ **catch up** *v* **1** *vti* reach somebody or something traveling ahead **2** *vi* get or be brought up to date **3** *vt* engross somebody

□ **catch up with** *vt* **1** find a criminal or wrongdoer **2** finally affect somebody

Catch-22 /-twentee tóo/ (*pl* **Catch-22's** *or* **Catch-22s**), **catch-22** *n* a situation that is impossible to deal with or escape from because of illogical rules

ORIGIN Catch-22 is taken from the title (and

central idea) of a 1961 novel by the US writer Joseph Heller.

catch·all /kách àwl, kéch-/ *n* **1** something encompassing a range of possibilities **2** a storage container for miscellaneous items

catch·er /káchər, kéchər/ *n* **1** in baseball, a player positioned behind the batter **2** something or somebody that catches

catch·ing /káching, kéch-/ *adj* infectious or contagious

catch·ment ar·e·a /káchmənt-/ *n* **1** an area from which rainwater drains into a reservoir **2** the area in a community from which a particular school or hospital accepts pupils or patients

catch phrase *n* a phrase that becomes identified with a specific person

catch-up *n* FOOD = **ketchup**

catch-up *n* an increase in amount or quality

catch·word /kách wùrd, kéch-/ *n* a word that becomes identified with a specific person, period, or activity

catch·y /káchee, kéchee/ (**-i·er**, **-i·est**) *adj* **1** easy to remember **2** attracting interest or attention —**catch·i·ness** *n*

cat·e·chism /kátta kìzzəm/ *n* a set of questions and answers used to test Christian religious knowledge —**cat·e·chis·mal** /kàttə kízm'l/ *adj*

cat·e·gor·i·cal /kàttə gáwrik'l/, **cat·e·gor·ic** /kàttə gáwrik/ *adj* **1** absolute and explicit **2** involving categories —**cat·e·gor·i·cal·ly** *adv*

cat·e·go·rize /káttəgə rìz/ (**-rized**, **-riz·ing**) *vt* put into a category —**cat·e·go·ri·za·tion** /kàttəgəri záysh'n/ *n*

cat·e·go·ry /kátta gàwree/ (*pl* **-ries**) *n* a set of people or things classified together ◊ See note at **type**

ca·ter /káytər/ *vi* **1** provide what is wanted **2** prepare and supply food and drink —**ca·ter·er** *n* —**ca·ter·ing** *n*

cat·er-cor·nered /káttər kàwrnərd/, **cat·ty-cor·nered** /káttee-/, **cat·ty-cor·ner** *adj* diagonal ■ *adv* diagonally

cat·er·pil·lar /káttər pìllər/ *n* a butterfly larva with a long soft body and many legs

ORIGIN Caterpillar probably goes back to Latin words that literally mean "hairy cat."

Cat·er·pil·lar /káttər pìllər/ *tdmk* a trademark for tractors that have continuous treads composed of chain

~~caterpiller~~ incorrect spelling of **caterpillar**

cat·er·waul /káttər wàwl/ *vi* **1** make a loud howling noise **2** argue loudly —**cat·er·waul** *n*

cat·fish /kát fìsh/ (*pl same or* **-fish·es**) *n* a fish with sensitive organs like whiskers around its mouth

cat·gut /kát gùt/ *n* tough thin cord made from

animal intestines. Use: stringing musical instruments, surgical thread.

ca·thar·sis /kə tha̱arsiss/ (*pl* **-ses** /-sēez/) *n* an emotional release brought about by an intense experience

ca·thar·tic /kə tha̱artik/ *adj* inducing catharsis —**ca·thar·ti·cal·ly** *adv*

ca·the·dral /kə the̱edr'l/ *n* the most important church in a diocese

---

ORIGIN A **cathedral** was originally a *cathedral church*, with **cathedral** an adjective derived from Latin *cathedra* "chair, bishop's seat." A **cathedral** is thus a church that houses the bishop's throne. The English word *chair* also comes from Latin *cathedra*, via French.

Cath·er /ka̱thər/, **Willa** (1873–1947) US writer

Cath·er·ine (of Ar·a·gon) /ka̱thrin əv a̱rrə gòn/ (1485–1536) Spanish-born queen of England (1509–33) as the first wife of Henry VIII

Catherine the Great

Cath·er·ine (the Great) (1729–96) empress of Russia (1762–96)

Cath·er·ine wheel *n* a firework that forms a multicolored spinning wheel

cath·e·ter /ka̱thətər/ *n* a thin tube inserted into the body to drain off liquid or keep a passage open

cath·e·ter·ize /ka̱thətə rìz/ (**-ized, -iz·ing**) *vt* put a catheter into —**cath·e·ter·i·za·tion** /kàthətəri za̱ysh'n/ *n*

cath·ode /ka̱ thòd/ *n* **1** the negative electrode in an electrolytic cell or electronic valve **2** the positive terminal in a battery

cath·ode-ray tube *n* a vacuum tube in which a stream of electrons is directed onto a screen to produce an image, e.g., inside a television set

Cath·o·lic /ka̱thlik, ka̱thəlik/ *adj* **1** of the Roman Catholic Church **2** belonging to the community of all Christian churches **3 cath·o·lic** all-inclusive or all-embracing ■ *n* a member of the Roman Catholic Church

Ca·thol·i·cism /kə tho̱llə sìzzəm/ *n* the beliefs and practices of the Roman Catholic Church

Cat·i·line /ka̱ttə lìn/ (108?–62 BC) Roman conspirator

cat·kin /ka̱tkən/ *n* the hanging furry flower clusters on trees such as the willow and birch

---

Cat·lin /ka̱tlin/, **George** (1796–1872) US artist and writer

cat lit·ter *n* absorbent material in which a cat can urinate and defecate indoors

cat·nap /ka̱t nàp/ *n* a short sleep —**cat·nap** *vi*

cat·nip /ka̱tnip/ *n* a plant whose smell attracts cats

cat-o'-nine-tails (*pl same*) *n* a whip made of strands of knotted rope, formerly used for giving beatings

CAT scan /ka̱t-/ *n* a diagnostic radiological scan of parts of the body using computerized axial tomography

cat's cra·dle /-/ *n* a game in which a loop of string is threaded between the fingers in elaborate patterns

cat's-eye *n* **1** a gemstone cut to reflect a narrow band of light **2** a reflective road marker

Cats·kill Moun·tains /ka̱tskil-/ group of mountains in the Appalachian system in SE New York. Highest peak Slide Mountain, 4,204 ft./1,281 m.

cat·suit /ka̱t sòot/ *n* a woman's tight one-piece pantsuit

cat·sup *n* FOOD = ketchup

Catt /kat/, **Carrie Chapman** (1859–1947) US suffragist

cat·ter·y /ka̱ttəree/ (*pl* **-ies**) *n* a place where cats are raised or boarded

cat·tle /ka̱tt'l/ *npl* **1** cows and other farm animals of the ox family **2** people regarded as lacking individuality

---

ORIGIN Originally **cattle** meant "property, goods, wealth." It comes from a northern variant of the French word that gave us *chattel*. Since wealth often derived from livestock, it commonly referred to domestic animals regarded as property, and after 1500 this was practically its sole meaning. From the 16C it has primarily implied cows and oxen.

---

cat·tle guard *n* a barrier for cattle

cat·tle·man /ka̱tt'lmən, -màn/ (*pl* **-men** /-mən, -mèn/) *n* somebody who owns, raises, or works with cattle

cat·tle prod *n* an electrified rod used for driving cattle

cat·ty /ka̱ttee/ (**-ti·er, -ti·est**) *adj* spiteful or malicious —**cat·ti·ly** *adv* —**cat·ti·ness** *n*

cat·ty-corn·ered, cat·ty-corn·er *adj* = cater-cornered

Ca·tul·lus /kə tu̱lləss/, **Gaius Valerius** (84?–54? BC) Roman poet —**Ca·tul·lan** *adj*

cat·walk /ka̱t wàwk/ *n* **1** a raised walkway along which models walk at a fashion show **2** a high walkway

Cau·ca·sia /kaw ka̱yzhə/ region of SE Europe and SW Asia between the Black Sea and the Caspian Sea, comprising Georgia, Armenia, Azerbaijan, and S Russia

Cau·ca·sian /kaw káyzh'n/ *adj* **1** describes people who are white-skinned **2** of Caucasia —**Cau·ca·sian** *n*

Cau·ca·sus Moun·tains /káwkəssəss-/ mountain range extending through Georgia, Armenia, Azerbaijan, and SW Russia, considered a boundary between Europe and Asia. Highest peak El'brus 18,510 ft./5,642 m.

cau·cus /káwkəss/ *n* **1** a closed political meeting **2** a special-interest group ■ *vi* form or hold a caucus

ORIGIN *Caucus* probably comes from a Native North American language. It was first recorded in the United States in the mid-18C.

caught past tense, past participle of **catch**

caul·dron *n* = **caldron**

cau·li·flow·er /káwli flòwr/ *n* **1** a large hard white flower head eaten as a vegetable **2** a plant related to the cabbage that produces cauliflower

cau·li·flow·er ear *n* an ear that has been permanently deformed by being hit repeatedly

caulk /kawk/, **calk** *vt* **1** make a boat watertight by sealing the seams between the planks **2** fill in a gap or crack ■ *n also* **caulk·ing** a substance used to caulk

caus·al /káwz'l/ *adj* **1** being or involving the cause of something **2** expressing a relationship of cause and effect —**caus·al·ly** *adv*

cau·sal·i·ty /kaw zállətee/ *n* the principle that everything has a cause

cau·sa·tion /kaw záysh'n/ *n* **1** the process or fact of causing an effect **2** a cause-and-effect relationship

caus·a·tive /káwzətiv/ *adj* involving a cause and its effect

cause /kawz/ *n* **1** something that makes something else happen or be so **2** a principle or aim that people believe in **3** a lawsuit, or the reason for a lawsuit ■ *vt* (**caused, caus·ing**) be the reason for

cause cé·lè·bre /kàwz sə lébbrə/ (*pl* **causes cé·lè·bres** /*pronunc. same*/) *n* a famous legal case or public controversy

cause·way /káwz wày/ *n* a raised road across marshy land

ORIGIN *Causeway* has no connection with *cause*. It is formed from an earlier word, *causey*, that had the same meaning. Its ultimate root is the Latin word for "limestone."

caus·tic /káwstik/ *adj* **1** corrosive **2** sarcastic ■ *n* a corrosive substance —**caus·ti·cal·ly** *adv* —**caus·tic·i·ty** /kaw stíssətee/ *n* ◊ See note at **sarcastic**

cau·ter·ize /káwtə rìz/ (**-ized, -iz·ing**) *vt* seal a wound with heat, a laser, or an electric current —**cau·ter·i·za·tion** /kàwtəri záysh'n/ *n*

cau·tion /káwsh'n/ *n* **1** carefulness and lack of haste **2** a warning ■ *vt* warn

cau·tion·ar·y /káwsh'n èrree/ *adj* giving or involving a warning

cau·tious /káwshəss/ *adj* showing care and lack of haste —**cau·tious·ly** *adv* —**cau·tious·ness** *n*

SYNONYMS **cautious, careful, chary, circumspect, prudent, vigilant, wary, guarded, cagey** CORE MEANING: showing care or awareness of possibilities

cav·al·cade /kàv'l káyd, káv'l kàyd/ *n* **1** a procession of people on horses or in cars **2** a spectacular or dramatic series of people or things

cav·a·lier /kàv'l éèr/ *adj* showing an arrogant or careless disregard for something or somebody ■ *n* **1** a gentleman (*fml*) **2** **Cav·a·lier** a supporter of King Charles I —**cav·a·lier·ly** *adv*

cav·al·ry /káv'lree/ (*pl* **-ries**) *n* **1** formerly, soldiers on horseback **2** soldiers equipped with tanks and other vehicles —**cav·al·ry·man** *n*

cave *n* a large natural hollow in a rock face or under the ground

□ **cave in** *v* **1** *vti* collapse **2** *vi* yield to persuasion or threats

ca·ve·at /kávee àt, ka'avee-, káyvee-/ *n* a warning or proviso

ca·ve·at emp·tor /-émp tawr/ *n* the principle that the buyer is responsible for making sure purchases are of good quality

ORIGIN The origin is a Latin phrase, "let the buyer beware."

cave-in *n* the collapse of something, or the place where something collapses

cave·man /káyv màn/ (*pl* **-men** /-mèn/) *n* **1** a Stone Age man **2** a brutish or uncivilized man (*infml*)

cav·ern /kávvərn/ *n* a large cave

cav·ern·ous /kávvərnəss/ *adj* **1** large, dark, or deep **2** hollow-sounding

cav·i·ar /kávvee àar, ka'avee-/, **cav·i·are** *n* the salted roe of a large fish, especially the sturgeon

cav·il /káv'l/ *vi* (**-iled** *or* **-illed, -il·ing** *or* **-il·ling**) object for no good reason ■ *n* a trivial and carping criticism

cav·ing /káyving/ *n* the activity of exploring underground caves —**cav·er** *n*

cav·i·ty /kávvətee/ (*pl* **-ties**) *n* **1** a hollow space in something **2** a hole in a tooth

ca·vort /kə váwrt/ *vi* behave in a lively or uninhibited way

Ca·vour /kə vo'or/, **Camillo Benso, Conte di** (1810–61) Italian politician and chief architect of the unification of Italy (1861)

caw *vi* make the cry of a crow

Cax·ton /kákstən/, **William** (1422?–91) English printer

cay /kee, kay/ *n* a small low island or reef

cay·enne /kī én, kay-/, **cay·enne pep·per** *n* a red hot-tasting powder made from the dried ground fruit and seeds of various chilies

Cay·enne /kī én, kay én/ capital of French Guiana. Pop. 41,000 (1990).

Cay·man Is·lands /káymən-/ group of three islands in the NW Caribbean Sea, south of Cuba, a British dependency. Cap. George Town. Pop. 35,527 (2001).

CB *abbr* citizens band

CBA *abbr* cost-benefit analysis

CBC *abbr* Canadian Broadcasting Corporation

⌁**CBT** *abbr* computer-based training

CBW *abbr* **1** chemical and biological warfare **2** chemical and biological weapon

cc, c.c. *abbr* **1** (carbon) copy **2** cubic centimeter

CCTV *abbr* closed-circuit television

CCU *abbr* coronary care unit

Cd *symbol* cadmium

⌁**CD** *abbr* **1** Civil Defense **2** compact disk

cd. *abbr* cord

CDC *abbr* Centers for Disease Control and Prevention

⌁**CDE** *n* a reusable compact disk. Full form **compact disk erasable**

⌁**CDI, CD-I** *n* an interactive compact disk containing text, video, and audio. Full form **compact disk interactive**

⌁**CDR**[1] *n* a compact disk that can be recorded on once but not erased. Full form **compact disk recordable**

CDR[2] *abbr* Commander

⌁**CD-ROM** /sèe dee róm/ *n* a compact disk with a content that can be viewed on a computer but not changed. Full form **compact disk read-only memory**

⌁**CD-RW** *abbr* CD rewritable

CDT *abbr* Central Daylight Time

⌁**CDV** *abbr* CD-video

⌁**CD-vid·e·o** *n* **1** a compact disk with video images **2** a player for CD-videos

Ce *symbol* cerium

CE[1] *adv* used as a non-Christian equivalent of AD in dates. Full form **Common Era**

CE[2] *abbr* civil engineer

~~Ceasar~~ incorrect spelling of **Caesar**

cease /seess/ (**ceased, ceas·ing**) *vti* come or bring to an end

cease·fire /séess fìr/ *n* **1** an agreement to stop fighting **2** an order to stop firing

cease·less /séesslòss/ *adj* continuous or unending —**cease·less·ly** *adv*

Ceau·şes·cu /chow shéskoo/, **Nicolae** (1918–89) Romanian head of state (1967–89)

ce·cum /séekəm/ (*pl* **-ca** /-kə/), **cae·cum** *n* the first part of the large intestine —**ce·cal** *adj*

ce·dar /séedər/ *n* **1** a tall evergreen tree with needles and rounded cones **2** wood from a cedar

Ce·dar Rap·ids city in E Iowa. Pop. 114,563 (1998).

cede /seed/ (**ced·ed, ced·ing**) *vt* surrender or give up something to another country, group, or person

SPELLCHECK Do not confuse the spelling of **cede** and **seed** (of a plant), which sound similar.

ce·di /sáydee/ (*pl* same) *n* the main unit of Ghanaian currency

ce·dil·la /sə díllə/ (*pl* **-las**) *n* a mark placed beneath the letters c (ç) and s (ş) in some languages

ceil·ing /séeling/ *n* **1** the overhead surface of a room **2** an upper limit **3** the level of the lowest clouds in the sky ◊ **hit the ceiling** become very angry

Cel·e·bes /séllə beèz, sə leè beèz/ ▶ Sulawesi

Cel·e·bes Sea arm of the W Pacific Ocean surrounded by the Philippines, Borneo, and Sulawesi

cel·e·brant /sélləbrənt/ *n* **1** a participant in a religious ceremony **2** in some Christian churches, an officiating priest at Communion

cel·e·brate /séllə bràyt/ (**-brat·ed, -brat·ing**) *v* **1** *vt* mark an occasion with festivities **2** *vti* perform a religious ceremony **3** *vt* praise somebody or something publicly —**cel·e·bra·tion** /sèllə bráysh'n/ *n* —**cel·e·bra·to·ry** /séllèbrə tàwree, sə lébbrə-/ *adj*

cel·e·brat·ed /séllə bràytəd/ *adj* famous

ce·leb·ri·ty /sə lébbrətee/ (*pl* **-ties**) *n* **1** a famous person **2** fame

ce·ler·i·ty /sə lérrətee/ *n* quickness (*literary*)

cel·er·y /sélləree/ *n* **1** long greenish white plant stems eaten as a vegetable **2** the plant that produces celery **3** the seeds of the celery plant. Use: as seasoning.

ce·les·tial /sə léschəl/ *adj* **1** of heaven **2** of the sky —**ce·les·tial·ly** *adv*

ce·li·ac dis·ease /séelee àk-/ *n* a disease caused by sensitivity to gluten that makes the digestive system unable to absorb fat

cel·i·bate /sélləbət/ *adj* **1** abstaining from sex **2** unmarried because of a religious vow —**cel·i·ba·cy** *n* —**cel·i·bate** *n* —**cel·i·bate·ly** *adv*

⌁**cell** /sel/ *n* **1** a room for holding a prisoner **2** a small simple room, e.g., in a monastery **3** the smallest unit in the structure of an organism **4** a small enclosed structure, e.g., a compartment in a honeycomb **5** a device that produces electricity by chemical action **6** a small group of activists within a larger organization who work together secretly **7** an area covered by one radio transmitter in a mobile telephone system **8** a space for information in a table

cel·lar /séllər/ *n* **1** an underground room used for storage **2** a storm cellar **3** a stock of wine

cel·lar·age /séllərij/ *n* **1** a fee charged for storing something in a cellar **2** cellar space

cel·lar·ette /sèllə rét/, **cel·lar·et** *n* a wine cabinet

cell-block /sél blòk/ *n* a group of prison cells forming a unit

Cel·li·ni /che leénee/, **Benvenuto** (1500–71) Italian sculptor and goldsmith

cel·list /chéllist/ *n* a cello player

cel·lo /chéllō/ (*pl* **-los**) *n* a large stringed instrument held upright between a seated player's knees

> **ORIGIN** Cello is shortened from *violoncello*, an Italian diminutive of *violone* "double-bass viol."

cel·lo·phane /séllə fàyn/ *n* wrapping material. Use: wrapping, covering.

cell-phone /sél fòn/, **cel·lu·lar phone** *n* a mobile phone operated through a network of radio transmitters

cel·lu·lar /séllyələr/ *adj* **1** involving living cells **2** consisting of small parts or groups **3** organized into cells for radio communication **4** porous or open in texture

cel·lu·lite /séllyə lìt/ *n* fatty deposits beneath the skin that give a lumpy appearance

cel·lu·loid /séllyə lòyd/ *n* a type of transparent plastic. Use: photographic film. —**cel·lu·loid** *adj*

cel·lu·lose /séllyə lòss, -lōz/ *n* the main component of plant cell walls. Use: plastics, lacquers, explosives, synthetic fibers. —**cel·lu·lo·sic** /séllyə lóssik/ *adj*

cel·lu·lose ac·e·tate *n* a chemical compound produced by the action of acid on cellulose. Use: photographic film, plastics, textile fibers, varnishes.

Cel·si·us /sélsee əss, sélshəss/ *adj* measured on a metric temperature scale in which water freezes at 0° and boils at 100° (*generally not in scientific contexts apart from meteorology*)

> **ORIGIN** The scale is named for the Swedish astronomer Anders Celsius (1701–44), who devised it.

celt /selt/ *n* a prehistoric cutting tool

Celt /kelt, selt/ *n* **1** somebody who speaks a Celtic language **2** a member of an ancient people who lived in central and W Europe

Celt·ic /kéltik, séltik/ *adj* of the Celts or their language or culture ■ *n* a language group that includes Scottish Gaelic, Irish, and Breton —**Celt·i·cist** /séltissist, kélt-/ *n*

ce·ment mix·er *n* **1** a portable machine for making concrete **2** a truck with a large rotating drum for making concrete

~~cemetary, cemetry~~ incorrect spelling of **cemetery**

cem·e·ter·y /sémmə tèrree/ (*pl* **-ies**) *n* a burial place

cen·o·taph /sénnə tàf/ *n* a monument to people killed during a war

Ce·no·zo·ic /seènə zō ik, sènnə-/ *n* the present era of geologic time, which began 65 million years ago —**Ce·no·zo·ic** *adj*

cen·sor /sénsər/ *n* **1** an official who examines films, plays, and other works with a view to removing objectionable material **2** somebody or something exercising a suppressing control ■ *vt* **1** remove offensive parts from **2** exercise control over —**cen·so·ri·al** /sen sáwree əl/ *adj*

cen·so·ri·ous /sen sáwree əss/ *adj* tending to be highly critical

cen·sor·ship /sénsər shìp/ *n* **1** the suppression of published or broadcast material **2** any form of suppression

cen·sure /sénshər/ *n* **1** disapproval **2** official condemnation ■ *vt* (**-sured, -sur·ing**) **1** criticize **2** condemn officially —**cen·sur·a·ble** *adj* —**cen·sur·er** *n* ◊ See note at **criticize, disapprove**

cen·sus /sénsəss/ (*pl* **-sus·es**) *n* **1** an official count or survey of a population **2** any systematic count

cent /sent/ *n* a subunit of currency in the United States, Canada, Australia, New Zealand, South Africa, the European Union, and several other countries

cent. *abbr* centigrade

Centaur

cen·taur /sén tàwr/ *n* in Greek mythology, a creature that is half man, half horse

cen·te·nar·i·an /sènt'n áiree ən/ *n* a 100-year-old person ■ *adj* 100 years old

cen·ten·a·ry /sen ténnəree, sént'n èrree/ *adj* **1** happening once a century **2** of a 100th anniversary ■ *n* (*pl* **-ries**) a 100th anniversary

cen·ten·ni·al /sen ténnee əl/ *adj* **1** involving a period of 100 years **2** happening once a century ■ *n* a 100th anniversary —**cen·ten·ni·al·ly** *adv*

cen·ter /séntər/ *n* **1** the middle point, part, or area of something **2** a place for a particular activity ○ *a sports center* **3** the focus of attention, activity, or influence ○ *the issue at the center of the controversy* **4** a place or part where something is concentrated ○ *a population center* **5** also **Cen·ter** politicians or political parties that are neither left-wing nor right-wing **6** in some sports, an attacking player in the middle of the field **7** a pivotal point or axis ■ **v 1** *vt* put something in or send something into the center **2** *vti* focus or be focused on a particular theme

cen·ter back *n* in some sports, a defensive player in the middle of the back line

cen·ter·board /séntər bàwrd/ *n* a retractable keel in a sailboat

cen·tered /séntərd/ *adj* **1** placed in the middle **2** psychologically or emotionally well-balanced —**cen·tered·ness** *n*

cen·ter field *n* **1** in baseball, the part of the outfield behind second base **2** the position of the baseball player responsible for fielding balls hit to center field —**cen·ter field·er** *n*

cen·ter·fold /séntər fòld/ *n* **1** a picture or feature that covers the middle two pages of a magazine **2** somebody posing naked or nearly naked in a centerfold

cen·ter for·ward *n* in some sports, a player in the middle of the attacking line

cen·ter of grav·i·ty *n* **1** the focus of gravitational forces **2** *also* **center of mass** the point at which the total mass of a body is assumed to be centered

cen·ter stage *n* **1** the middle of a theater stage **2** the focus of people's interest —**cen·ter stage** *adv*

centi- *prefix* **1** hundredth ○ *centiliter* **2** hundred ○ *centipede*

cen·ti·grade /sénti gràyd/ *adj* Celsius

cen·ti·li·ter *(symbol* **cl)** a unit of volume equal to 1/100th of a liter

cen·ti·me·ter /sénti mèetər/ *n* *(symbol* **cm)** a metric unit of length equal to 1/100th of a meter

cen·ti·pede /séntə pèed/ *n* an invertebrate organism with a segmented body and many legs

Cen·tral Af·ri·can Re·pub·lic landlocked country in central Africa. Cap. Bangui. Pop. 3,576,884 (2001).

Cen·tral A·mer·i·ca southern part of North America, comprising Guatemala, Belize, Honduras, El Salvador, Nicaragua, Costa Rica, and Panama. Pop. 31,300,000 (1993).

Cen·tral A·sia region comprising the countries of Kazakhstan, Kyrgyzstan, Tajikistan, Turkmenistan, and Uzbekistan

cen·tral bank *n* the main bank of a nation

Cen·tral Day·light Time *n* the summer time variation in central North America

cen·tral gov·ern·ment *n* the part of government that is concerned with national issues

cen·tral heat·ing *n* a system for heating a whole building from one source —**cen·tral·ly heat·ed** *adj*

cen·tral·ism /séntrə lìzzəm/ *n* the concentration of political power in a single authority —**cen·tral·ist** *n, adj*

cen·tral·ize /séntrə lìz/ *(-ized, -iz·ing)* *vti* **1** concentrate political power in a single authority **2** group things in a single place —**cen·tral·i·za·tion** /sèntrəli záysh'n/ *n*

cen·tral nerv·ous sys·tem *n* the brain and the spinal cord

⚡ **cen·tral pro·cess·ing u·nit** *n* the part of a computer that performs operations and executes software commands

Cen·tral Stan·dard Time, Cen·tral Time *n* the local standard time in central North America

cen·tre /séntər/ *n, vti* (-tred, -tring) UK = center

cen·trif·u·gal force /sen trìffyəg'l-/ *n* the force that pulls a rotating object away from the center of rotation

cen·tri·fuge /séntrə fyòoj/ *n* **1** a device that rotates rapidly to separate substances of different densities **2** a device that simulates the effects of gravity or acceleration —**cen·tri·fuge** *vt*

cen·trip·e·tal force /sen trìppət'l-/ *n* the force that pulls a rotating object toward the center of rotation

cen·trism /sén trìzzəm/ *n* the holding of moderate views —**cen·trist** *n, adj*

~~**cen·try**~~ incorrect spelling of **century**

cen·tu·ri·on /sen tóoree ən, -chòoree-/ *n* in ancient Rome, an army officer in charge of a unit of foot soldiers —**cen·tu·ri·al** *adj*

cen·tu·ry /sénchəree/ *(pl* -ries) *n* **1** a period of 100 years **2** a 100-year period in a dating system, counted from year 00 or year 01 **3** in ancient Rome, a unit of soldiers originally comprising 100 men

CEO, C.E.O. *abbr* chief executive officer

ce·ram·ic /sə rámmik/ *n* **1** a hard brittle heat-resistant material made from clay fired at a high temperature **2** a ceramic object —**ce·ram·ic** *adj*

ce·ram·ics /sə rámmiks/ *n* the art or industry of making ceramic objects *(+ sing verb)*

ce·re·al /séeree əl/ *n* **1** a grain used as food **2** a grass cultivated for its edible grain **3** a breakfast food made from cereal grain

---

ORIGIN Cereal came through French from Latin, where it was based on the name of Ceres, the Roman goddess of agriculture.

SPELLCHECK Do not confuse the spelling of **cereal** and **serial** ("a story in parts"), which sound similar.

---

cer·e·bral /sə reébrəl, sérrə-/ *adj* of the brain or intellect

cer·e·bral pal·sy *n* a brain disorder that results in loss of muscle control —**cer·e·bral·pal·sied** *adj*

cer·e·bro·vas·cu·lar ac·ci·dent /sèrrəbrō và-skyələr-, sə reébrə-/, **cer·e·bral vas·cu·lar ac·ci·dent** *n* any physical event, e.g., a cerebral hemorrhage, that may lead to a stroke *(technical)*

cer·e·brum /sə re'ebrəm, sérrə-/ (pl **-brums** or **-bra** /-brə/) n the front part of the brain

cer·e·mo·ni·al /sèrrə mṓnee əl/ adj 1 of formal occasions 2 involving a ceremony ■ n 1 formal etiquette 2 a ritual or ceremony —**cer·e·mo·ni·al·ism** n —**cer·e·mo·ni·al·ly** adv

cer·e·mo·ni·ous /sèrrə mṓnee əss/ adj 1 formal and careful to observe the rules of correct behavior 2 involving ceremony

cer·e·mo·ny /sérrə mṓnee/ (pl **-nies**) n 1 a ritual marking a formal occasion 2 formal etiquette

Cer·es /sér eez/ n in Roman mythology, the goddess of agriculture. Greek equivalent **Demeter**

ce·rise /sə re'ess, -re'ez/ n a vivid pinkish red color —**ce·rise** adj

ce·ri·um /se'eree əm/ n (symbol **Ce**) a gray metallic element. Use: glassmaking, ceramics, cigarette-lighter flints.

⚡CERT /surt/ abbr computer emergency response team (in e-mails)

cert. abbr certificate

cer·tain /súrt'n/ adj 1 having no doubts ○ I'm certain he's the man I saw. 2 known or set 3 inevitable ○ It's certain they'll lose. 4 reliable 5 undeniably present but difficult to define ○ a certain hesitation in his voice 6 not named

cer·tain·ly /súrt'nlee/ adv 1 definitely or without doubt 2 yes

cer·tain·ty /súrt'ntee/ (pl **-ties**) n 1 complete confidence in the truth of something 2 something inevitable 3 somebody or something that is certain of success

cer·ti·fi·a·ble /súrtə fī əb'l/ adj 1 good enough to be given a certificate 2 requiring psychiatric treatment (dated) —**cer·ti·fi·a·bly** adv

⚡cer·tif·i·cate n /sər tíffikət/ 1 a document providing official evidence, information, or approval 2 an electronic identification document used in e-commerce ■ vt /sər tíffi kàyt/ (**-cat·ed, -cat·ing**) 1 award a certificate 2 authorize or prove with a certificate —**cer·ti·fi·ca·tion** /sùrtəfi kásh'n, sər tíffi-/ n

cer·ti·fied mail n mail with proof of delivery

cer·ti·fied pub·lic ac·count·ant n an accountant allowed to practice in a particular state

cer·ti·fy /súrtə fī/ (**-fied, -fies**) v 1 vti confirm the truth or accuracy of 2 vt prove the quality of 3 vt guarantee payment of a check 4 vt issue a certificate to 5 vt declare somebody to have a psychiatric disorder (dated)

~~certin~~ incorrect spelling of **certain**

cer·ti·tude /súrti tòod/ n a feeling of certainty

Cer·van·tes /sur ván te'ez/, **Miguel de** (1547–1616) Spanish novelist and dramatist

cer·vi·cal /súrvik'l/ adj of a cervix

cer·vix /súrviks/ (pl **-vix·es** or **-vi·ces** /-vi se'ez/) n the neck of the womb

ce·sar·e·an /si záiree ən/, **ce·sar·e·an sec·tion** n a delivery of a baby by cutting through the mother's abdomen and womb —**ce·sar·e·an** adj

---

ORIGIN A **Cesarean** is named after Julius Caesar, who is reputed to have been born in this way.

---

ce·si·um /se'ezee əm/ n (symbol **Cs**) a silver-white metallic element. Use: photoelectric cells.

ces·sa·tion /se sáysh'n/ n a stop, pause, or interruption in something

cess·pool /séss pòol/ n 1 an underground container for sewage or other waste matter 2 a filthy or immoral place or situation

Cey·lon /sə lón, say-/ former name for **Sri Lanka** —**Cey·lo·nese** /sə lòn e'ez, sày lon-/ adj, n

Cé·zanne /say zán, -zaán/, **Paul** (1839–1906) French painter

Cf symbol californium

CF abbr 1 center field 2 center fielder 3 cystic fibrosis

cf. abbr compare

c.f., C.F. abbr cost and freight

CFC n a gas used in refrigerators and aerosols. Full form **chlorofluorocarbon**

CFO, C.F.O. abbr chief financial officer

⚡CGI abbr computer-generated imagery

Cha·blis /sha blèe, shə-, shábblee/, **cha·blis** n a dry white wine from central France

cha-cha /chaá chaà/, **cha-cha-cha** /chaá chaa chaá/ n 1 a rhythmic Latin American dance 2 the music for a cha-cha

chad n a fragment of paper such as that punched from a ballot to register a vote

Chad landlocked country in north central Africa. Cap. Ndjamena. Pop. 8,707,078 (2001). —**Chad·i·an** adj, n

Chad, Lake lake in central Africa, at the junction of Nigeria, Niger, and Chad

cha·dor /chúddər/, **cha·dar, chud·dar** n a dark cloak worn by Muslim women in public that covers the head and most of the body

chafe vti (**chafed, chaf·ing**) 1 make or become worn 2 rub something, causing friction or warmth 3 annoy, or become annoyed ■ n 1 soreness or wear 2 a feeling of irritation

chaff[1] n 1 seed coverings removed by threshing 2 glass or nylon filaments dispersed into the air to obstruct radar 3 something worthless

chaff[2] v 1 vt tease lightheartedly 2 vi banter ■ n joking or teasing behavior

chaf·finch /chá fìnch/ n a small European songbird

Cha·gall /shaa gaál/, **Marc** (1887–1985) Russian-born French painter and designer

cha·grin /shə grín/ n a feeling of irritation or humiliation —**cha·grin** vt

chain n 1 a series of joined metal rings used like a rope or as a decorative accessory 2 a number of businesses under one management or ownership 3 a series of geographic formations, e.g., mountains 4 a series of connected things resembling a chain 5 a sequence of related events or facts 6 a series of atoms within a molecule 7 a chain worn as a badge of office 8 a unit of length equal to 66 ft. ■ **chains** npl restraining circumstances (literary) ■ vt 1 fasten with a chain 2 restrict the mobility or independence of —**chained** adj

chain gang n a number of prisoners who work shackled together

chain let·ter n a letter requesting that copies be forwarded to others

chain-link fence /chàyn lingk-/ n a fence made of strong interwoven wire —**chain-link fenc·ing** n

chain mail n armor for a knight made of interlinked rings of metal

chain of com·mand n a hierarchy of authority

chain re·ac·tion n 1 a connected sequence of events 2 a self-sustaining nuclear reaction 3 a series of chemical reactions in which the product of one helps to create the next

chain saw n a portable motor-driven saw with teeth that form a circular chain

chain-smoke vti smoke cigarettes continuously —**chain-smok·er** n

chain stitch n a looped stitch resembling a chain —**chain-stitch** vti

chain store n one of a series of stores owned by the same company

chair n 1 a seat with a back and sometimes arms for one person 2 the electric chair (infml) 3 a chairperson, or the position of a chairperson 4 somebody who holds an endowed professorship ■ vt preside over a committee or meeting

chair lift n a series of seats suspended from a moving cable, used for carrying people up or down a mountain

chair·man /cháirmən/ (pl -men /-mən/) n 1 somebody who presides over a committee or meeting 2 the chief presiding officer of a company —**chair·man·ship** n

chair·per·son /cháir pùrs'n/ (pl -sons) n somebody who presides over a committee or meeting

chair·wom·an /cháir wŏomman/ (pl -en /-wĭmman/) n a woman who presides over a committee or meeting

chaise /shayz/ (pl **chaises** /pronunc. same/) n 1 a chaise longue 2 a light two-wheeled carriage with a hood drawn by one horse

chaise longue /shayz láwng/ (pl **chaise longues** or **chaises longues** /pronunc. same/) n a long low foldable chair with an adjustable back, used on a patio or beach

~~chaise-lounge~~ incorrect spelling of **chaise longue**

chal·ced·o·ny /kal sédd'nee/ n a form of quartz. Use: gems, ornaments. —**chal·ce·don·ic** /kàlsə dónnik/ adj

Chal·de·a /kal dée ə/ ancient region of Mesopotamia, between the Euphrates and the Persian Gulf, in modern-day S Iraq

~~chalenge~~ incorrect spelling of **challenge**

cha·let /sha láy, shá lày/ n a house or cottage traditionally made of wood with wide overhanging eaves

chal·ice /chálliss/ n 1 a metal cup (literary) 2 a cup used at Communion or Mass

chalk /chawk/ n 1 a soft white rock consisting of calcium carbonate 2 a piece of chalk used for writing or drawing, especially on a chalkboard ■ vti draw, write, or mark something with chalk —**chalk·y** adj

□ **chalk up** vt (infml) 1 achieve something significant 2 attribute something to a person or thing

chalk·board /cháwk bàwrd/ n a board on which to write with chalk

chal·lenge /chállənj/ vt (-lenged, -leng·ing) 1 invite somebody to take part in a fight or contest 2 dare somebody to do something 3 call something into question 4 stimulate somebody by making demands on his or her intellect or abilities 5 order somebody to produce identification 6 object to the inclusion of a prospective juror ■ n a claim against voting eligibility

chal·lenged /chállənjd/ adj 1 having a particular impairment ○ physically challenged 2 lacking in a particular quality (humorous; sometimes offensive) ◊ See note at **disabled**

chal·leng·er /chállənjər/ n 1 somebody who seeks a fight 2 somebody who opposes a champion

chal·leng·ing /chállənjing/ adj demanding physical or psychological effort of a stimulating kind —**chal·leng·ing·ly** adv

cham·ber /cháymbər/ n 1 a room with a particular function ○ in the council chamber 2 a compartment for ammunition in a weapon 3 an official assembly, or the place where it meets 4 a body of people organized into a group for a specific purpose 5 a compartment or cavity 6 a bedroom or other room (literary) 7 an official reception room ■ **cham·bers** npl a judge's private office ■ adj of chamber music —**cham·bered** adj

cham·ber·lain /cháymbərlən/ n the manager of a royal or noble household

Cham·ber·lain /cháymbərlən/, **Neville** (1869–1940) British prime minister (1937–40)

Cham·ber·lain, **Wilt** (1936–99) US basketball player

cham·ber·maid /cháymbər màyd/ n a woman who cleans hotel rooms

cham·ber mu·sic n classical instrumental music performed by a small group

cham·ber of com·merce *n* an association of local business people who work together to promote their common interests

cham·ber or·ches·tra *n* a small orchestra that performs classical music

cham·ber pot *n* a large bowl formerly kept in a bedroom and used as a toilet

cha·me·leon /kə mḗelyən, -lee ən/ *n* 1 a lizard that can change color 2 an anole 3 somebody who often changes his or her appearance, opinions, or personality

ORIGIN According to the Greek elements from which it is formed, a **chameleon** is a "ground lion." The name came into English from Greek via Latin, and is first recorded in the 14C.

cham·ois /shámmee/ (*pl* **-ois** /-meez/ *or* **-oix** /-meez/) *n* 1 a mountain-dwelling goat antelope 2 *also* **cham·ois leath·er** soft pliable leather. Use: cleaning, polishing. 3 a chamois leather cloth

cham·o·mile /kámmə mīl, -mèel/, **cam·o·mile** *n* 1 the leaves and flowers of an aromatic plant. Use: medicine, herbal tea. 2 a plant from which chamomile is obtained

champ[1] *n* the process or sound of biting or chewing something vigorously ■ *vti* bite or chew something vigorously

champ[2] *n* a champion (*infml*)

cham·pagne /sham páyn/ *n* a white sparkling wine, properly from the Champagne region of NE France

cham·pi·on /chámpee ən/ *n* 1 the winner of a contest or show 2 a defender of a person or cause ■ *vt* defend a person or cause

ORIGIN A **champion** was originally just a "fighting man." The word entered English from French in this sense in the 13C. A more specific sense, "somebody who fights on behalf of another, or for a cause," co-existed with it from the 14C, as did the figurative extension involving defense by argument rather than physical combat. The meaning "winner" appeared in the early 18C. The French word from which **champion** derives goes back to Latin *campus* "field, arena," which is also the source of English *camp*.

cham·pi·on·ship /chámpee ən shìp/ *n* 1 a contest to decide a champion 2 the title or time of being a champion

Cham·plain, Lake /sham pláyn/ lake on the Vermont-New York border, extending into Quebec, Canada. Depth 399 ft./122 m.

Cham·plain /sham pláyn, shaaN pláN/, **Samuel de** (1567?–1635) French explorer

chance *n* 1 the likelihood that something will happen (*often pl*) ○ *There's a good chance we'll win.* 2 an opportunity or opportune time for doing something ○ *I was given no chance to explain.* 3 the supposed force that makes things happen with no apparent cause 4 a raffle or lottery ticket 5 an un-

expected happening 6 something caused by luck ■ *v* (**chanced, chanc·ing**) 1 *vt* do something risky 2 *vi* do something or happen without a cause or plan

□ **chance on** *or* **upon** *vt* come across unexpectedly

chan·cel /chánss'l/ *n* an area of a church near the altar

chan·cel·ler·y /chánsələree, chánsləree/ (*pl* **-ies**), **chan·cel·lor·y** *n* 1 a chancellor's residence 2 an office attached to an embassy or consulate

chan·cel·lor /chánsələr, chánslər/, **Chan·cel·lor** *n* 1 the head of the government in some parliamentary democracies 2 the chief administrative officer of a university 3 a judge —**chan·cel·lor·ship** *n*

Chan·cel·lors·ville /chánsələrz vil, chánslərz-/ crossroads in NE Virginia, site of a major Confederate victory in the Civil War in 1863

chan·cer·y /chánsəree/ (*pl* **-ies**), **Chan·cer·y** *n* 1 a chancellery 2 a court of equity ruling on matters not covered by common law

chan·cy /chánsee/ (**-i·er, -i·est**) *adj* 1 risky 2 random or haphazard —**chanc·i·ly** *adv* —**chanc·i·ness** *n*

chan·de·lier /shànd'l éer/ *n* a decorative hanging light with several branched parts

chan·dler /chándlər/ *n* a seller of particular goods ○ *a ship's chandler*

Chan·dler /chándlər/, **Raymond** (1888–1959) US writer

Cha·nel /shə nél/, **Coco** (1883–1971) French couturier

Cha·ney /cháynee/, **Lon** (1883–1930) US silent movie actor

~~changable~~ incorrect spelling of **changeable**

change /chaynj/ *v* (**changed, chang·ing**) 1 *vti* become or make somebody or something different 2 *vt* exchange, substitute, or replace somebody or something 3 *vti* pass, or make something pass, from one state to another ○ *Water changes to ice on freezing.* 4 *vti* remove clothes and put on others 5 *vt* exchange money for smaller units of money 6 *vti* move from one vehicle to another on a trip 7 *vt* remove and replace something dirty or used 8 *vt* convert one currency into another ■ *n* 1 an alteration, variation, or modification 2 coins 3 the balance of money given back to a customer paying for something with a larger coin or banknote than the marked price 4 a fresh set of something, especially clothes 5 a sum of money exchanged for a coin or bill of a higher denomination 6 a variation from a routine ○ *I could do with a change.* 7 a transition from one state to another ○ *a change in attitude* 8 menopause (*infml dated*) 9 an exchange, substitution, or replacement of somebody or something

SYNONYMS change, alter, modify, convert,

vary, shift, transform, transmute CORE
MEANING: make or become different

change·a·ble /cháynjəb'l/ *adj* liable to change
or vary —**change·a·bil·i·ty** /chàynjə
bíllətee/ *n* —**change·a·bly** *adv*

~~changeing~~ incorrect spelling of **changing**

change·less /cháynjləss/ *adj* unchanging
—**change·less·ly** *adv* —**change·less·
ness** *n*

change·ling /cháynjling/ *n* in folklore, a child
believed to have been exchanged for
another by fairies

change of life *n* menopause *(infml)*

change·o·ver /cháynj òvər/ *n* a complete
change from one thing to another

change purse *n* a small receptacle for coins

change-up /cháynj ùp/ *n* in baseball, a pitch
that changes speed

Chang Ji·ang /cháàng jee aàng/ ♦ **Yangtze**

Chang·sha /cháàng shàà/ capital of **Hunan**
Province, SE China. Pop. 1,520,000 (1995).

chan·nel /chánn'l/ *n* 1 the part of a frequency
spectrum used in TV or radio transmission
2 a TV or radio station 3 a strip of water
separating an island from a mainland 4 a
navigable passage in a river or harbor 5 a
means of communication *(often pl)* ○ *go
through the proper channels* 6 the course of a
river or canal 7 a supposed spirit medium
8 a tube or passage for a liquid to flow
along ○ *a drainage channel* 9 a groove or
furrow ■ *v* 1 *vt* direct something along a
specific route 2 *vti* act as a medium for a
supposed spirit 3 *vt* make a channel in land
or water 4 *vt* make a groove or furrow in a
surface

Chan·nel Is·lands group of islands in the
English Channel near the French coast, de-
pendencies of the British crown. Pop.
143,534 (1991).

chan·nel-surf *vi* switch rapidly between TV
channels *(infml)* —**chan·nel-surf·er** *n*

Chan·nel Tun·nel *n* a railroad tunnel under
the English Channel

chant *n* 1 a slogan spoken repeatedly by a
crowd in a singsong intonation 2 a musical
passage or text sung on the same note or
series of notes —**chant** *vti*

chan·teuse /shaan tớz/ *(pl* **-teuses** /pronunc.
same/) *n* a woman singer

Cha·nu·kah, Cha·nuk·kah *n* JUDAISM = **Ha·
nukkah**

cha·os /káy òss/ *n* 1 disorder 2 *also* **Cha·os** the
condition supposed to have existed before
the creation of the universe

cha·os the·o·ry *n* the theory that natural
systems are so sensitive that small changes
have far-reaching effects that appear
random

cha·ot·ic /kay óttik/ *adj* 1 disordered 2 apparently random —**cha·ot·i·cal·ly** *adv*

chap[1] *vti* (**chapped, chap·ping**) become or
make sore and cracked by exposure to

wind or cold *(refers to skin)* ■ *n* an area of
sore cracked skin caused by exposure to
wind or cold —**chapped** *adj*

chap[2] *n* the lower half of the jaw

chap. *abbr* chapter

chap·ar·ral /sháppə rál/ *n* a dense thicket of
evergreen oaks in S California

cha·pa·ti /chə paàtee/ *(pl* **-tis** *or* **-ties**),
cha·pat·ti *n* a South Asian flat unleavened
bread

chap·el /cháPP'l/ *n* 1 a room for religious
worship in an institution or large house
2 a separate area of a Christian church for
private prayer 3 a service in a chapel 4 a
funeral home or an area in one for conducting funerals

ORIGIN The original **chapel** was the shrine in
which the cloak of the 4C Roman monk St.
Martin of Tours was kept. *Cappella*, a diminutive of the Latin word for "cloak," is the
source of the French word that was adopted
as **chapel**. The meaning moved from the
cloak, to the building housing it, to any similar
place of worship.

Chap·el Hill town in north central North
Carolina. Pop. 42,865 (1998).

chap·er·on /sháppə ròn/, **chap·er·one** *n* 1 an
older or married woman who supervises a
young single woman at social events 2 a
supervisor accompanying a group of
young people —**chap·er·on** *vti*

chap·lain /chápplin/ *n* a cleric employed by
an institution or a branch of the military to
give religious guidance —**chap·lain·cy** *n*

chap·let /chápplət/ *n* 1 a circle of beads or
flowers worn on the head 2 a string of
Roman Catholic prayer beads

Chap·lin /chápplin/, **Charlie** (1889–1977)
British-born US movie actor, director, and
producer

Chap·man /chápmən/, **John, "Johnny Apple-
seed"** (1774?–1845) US pioneer who
planted apple seeds and tended orchards
throughout the Ohio River valley

chaps *npl* protective leather leggings

chap·ter /cháptər/ *n* 1 a section of a book
with a number or title 2 a period in the
development of something 3 a group of
canons in a cathedral or knights in an order
4 a branch of an organization

Chap·ter 11 /-i lév'n/ *n* a law dealing with
company bankruptcies

chap·ter house *n* 1 a college fraternity or
sorority meeting place 2 a building where
a religious chapter meets

char[1] (**charred, char·ring**) *v* 1 *vti* blacken by
burning 2 *vt* make into charcoal

char[2] *(pl same or* **chars**), **charr** *(pl same or*
charrs) *n* a trout with light-colored spots

char·ac·ter /kérrəktər/ *n* 1 the set of qualities
that make somebody or something dis-
tinctive 2 positive qualities 3 somebody's

reputation **4** somebody in a book, play, or movie **5** an unusual person **6** somebody considered in terms of personality, behavior, or appearance **7** a letter, number, or symbol —**char·ac·ter·ful** *adj*

char·ac·ter ac·tor *n* an actor who plays unusual or distinctive roles

char·ac·ter as·sas·si·na·tion *n* an attack on somebody's reputation

char·ac·ter·is·tic /kèrrəktə rístik/ *n* **1** a defining feature **2** the whole number in a logarithm ■ *adj* typical —**char·ac·ter·is·ti·cal·ly** *adv*

char·ac·ter·i·za·tion /kèrrəktəri záysh'n/ *n* **1** the portrayal of fictional characters in a book, play, or movie **2** a description

char·ac·ter·ize /kérrəktə rìz/ (**-ized, -iz·ing**) *vt* **1** describe **2** be representative of —**char·ac·ter·iz·a·ble** *adj*

char·ac·ter·less /kérrəktərləss/ *adj* not interesting

cha·rade /shə ráyd/ *n* **1** a ridiculous pretense **2** a clue in charades

cha·rades /shə ráydz/ *n* a guessing game involving visual or acted clues for a word or phrase *(+ sing verb)*

char·broil /chaàr bròyl/ *vt* barbecue food —**char·broil·er** *n*

char·coal /chaàr kòl/ *n* a form of carbon. Use: fuel, absorbent in extractors, drawing medium.

chard *n* a plant with large edible leaves and stems eaten as a vegetable

~~chareeter~~ incorrect spelling of **character**

charge *v* (**charged, charg·ing**) **1** *vti* ask somebody for money for goods or services **2** *vti* allow and record a deferred payment for something **3** *vt* formally accuse somebody of a crime **4** *vt* criticize somebody **5** *vt* order somebody to do something **6** *vti* attack somebody or something by rushing forward **7** *vti* restore the power in a battery using electricity **8** *vt* load or fill something (*fml*) ■ *n* **1** the price or fee asked **2** the responsibility for taking care of somebody or something **3** a person for whom somebody else is responsible **4** an accusation or indictment **5** a rush forward to attack **6** the power in an electric battery **7** the positive and negative electric property of matter **8** an amount needed to cause detonation, fill a container, or operate a mechanism **9** an order or command **10** a sudden burst of excitement

charge·a·ble /chaàrjəb'l/ *adj* **1** liable to be reimbursed **2** *UK* liable to result in a criminal charge

charge ac·count *n* an account giving credit

charge card *n* a deferred payment card

⚡charge-coup·led de·vice *n* a semiconductor device that converts light patterns into digital signals for a computer

char·gé d'af·faires /shaàr zhay də fáir/ (*pl* **char·gés d'af·faires** /*pronunc. same*/) *n* a diplomat ranking below an ambassador or heading a minor diplomatic mission

charge nurse *n* a nurse in charge of a ward

charg·er[1] /chaàrjər/ *n* **1** a device for restoring power to electrical batteries **2** a large cavalry horse

charg·er[2] /chaàrjər/ *n* a large flat serving dish, or a dish that is placed below a diner's plate

~~charicature~~ incorrect spelling of **caricature**

char·i·ot /chérree ət/ *n* **1** an ancient two-wheeled horse-drawn vehicle **2** a four-wheeled horse-drawn ceremonial carriage —**char·i·o·teer** /chèrree ə teér/ *n*

cha·ris·ma /kə rízmə/ *n* **1** personal magnetism **2** (*pl* **cha·ris·ma·ta** /-mətə/) a gift or power believed to be divinely bestowed

char·is·mat·ic /kèrriz máttik/ *adj* **1** having charisma **2** describes Christians who seek direct spiritual experiences in worship —**char·is·mat·ic** *n* —**char·is·mat·ic·al·ly** *adv*

char·i·ta·ble /chérritəb'l/ *adj* **1** generous to people in need **2** sympathetic or tolerant in judging **3** of or providing charity —**char·i·ta·bly** *adv*

char·i·ty /chérritee/ (*pl* **-ties**) *n* **1** voluntary provision of help to people in need, or the help provided **2** an organization providing charity **3** sympathy or tolerance in judging **4** impartial love of other people

char·la·tan /shaàrlət'n/ *n* a false claimant of special skill or expertise —**char·la·tan·ism** *n* —**char·la·tan·ry** *n*

Char·le·magne /shaàrlə màyn/ (742–814) Frankish king and emperor of the West (800–814)

Charles /chaarlz/, **Prince of Wales** (*b.* 1948) British heir apparent

Charles I (1600–49) king of England, Scotland, and Ireland (1625–49)

Charles II (1630–85) king of England, Scotland, and Ireland (1660–85)

Charles V (1500–58) Holy Roman Emperor (1519–58) and, as Charles I, king of Spain (1516–56)

Charles, Pierre (*b.* 1954) prime minister of Dominica (2000–)

Charles·ton[1] /chaàrlstən/ *n* a vigorous 1920s dance

Charles·ton[2] /chaàrlstən/ **1** port in SE South Carolina. Pop. 87,044 (1998). **2** capital and largest city of West Virginia. Pop. 55,056 (1998).

char·ley horse /chaàrlee-/ *n* a muscular cramp (*infml*)

Char·lie /chaàrlee/ *n* a communications code word for the letter "C"

Char·lotte /shaàrlət/ city in S North Carolina. Pop. 504,637 (1998).

Char·lotte A·ma·lie /-ɔ məáalyə/ capital and main port of the US Virgin Islands, on S St. Thomas. Pop. 12,000 (1990).

Char·lottes·ville /sháárləts víl/ city in central Virginia. Pop. 38,223 (1998).

Char·lotte·town /sháàrlət tòwn/ capital of Prince Edward Island, Canada. Pop. 32,531 (1996).

charm n 1 the power to delight or attract people 2 a feature that delights or attracts people (often pl) 3 something carried or worn because it is supposed to bring luck 4 a trinket worn on a bracelet or necklace 5 a magic spell ■ v 1 vti delight or attract somebody 2 vt influence somebody by charm or a charm —**charm·er** n —**charm·less** adj

charmed adj extremely lucky

charm·ing /chaárming/ adj able to delight or attract people —**charm·ing·ly** adv

char·nel house /chaàrn'l-/ n a building for bones or dead bodies

charr n FISH = char²

chart n 1 a diagram or table of information 2 a map ■ **charts** npl a list of the best-selling musical recordings in a specific period ■ vt 1 make a chart of something 2 record or describe a plan or progress

char·ter /chaártər/ n 1 a formal document incorporating an organization 2 the written constitution of an organization 3 a document authorizing the setting up of a new branch of an organization 4 the rent or lease of a vehicle 5 a rented or leased vehicle ■ vt rent or lease a vehicle —**char·tered** adj

char·ter flight n a nonscheduled flight

char·ter mem·ber n a founding member of an organization

Char·ter School n a privately run, publicly financed school

Char·tres /shaart, shaártrə/ capital of Eure-et-Loire Department, north central France. Pop. 40,361 (1999).

chart-top·ping adj reaching the top of the music charts —**chart-top·per** n

char·wom·an /chaár wòommən/ (pl -wom·en /-wimmin/) n a woman employed to clean a house or office

char·y /chérree/ (-i·er, -i·est) adj 1 wary 2 reluctant to share, give, or use something —**char·i·ly** adv —**char·i·ness** n ◊ See note at **cautious**

Cha·ryb·dis /kə ríbdiss/ n in Greek mythology, a monster in the form of a dangerous whirlpool at the mouth of the cave of the sea monster Scylla

chase¹ v (chased, chas·ing) 1 vti try to catch or overtake somebody or something 2 vt make a person or animal run away o chased the cat out of the garden 3 vi rush around o I chased around all day. 4 vti try persistently to start a sexual or romantic relationship

with somebody ■ n 1 an attempt to catch or overtake somebody or something 2 a steeplechase 3 a jazz duet ◊ **cut to the chase** address immediately what needs to be dealt with (infml) ◊ See note at **follow**

chase² n 1 the external part of a gun barrel behind the muzzle 2 a groove into which something fits ■ vt (chased, chas·ing) 1 decorate metal or glass by engraving or embossing 2 cut a thread in a screw

Chase, Salmon Portland (1808–73) chief justice of the US Supreme Court (1864–73)

Chase, Samuel (1741–1811) associate justice of the US Supreme Court (1796–1811)

chas·er /cháyssər/ n 1 somebody or something that chases 2 a second drink taken with or after one of a different kind (infml)

chasm /kázzəm/ n 1 a deep hole in the ground 2 a wide break or difference

chas·sis /shássee, chássee/ (pl -sis /-eez, -eez/) n 1 the main frame and the wheels of a vehicle 2 a mounting for an electric or electronic device 3 the landing gear of an aircraft

chaste adj 1 abstaining from sex on moral grounds 2 pure in thought and deed 3 plain in style —**chaste·ly** adv —**chaste·ness** n

chas·ten /cháyss'n/ vt 1 discipline somebody 2 make somebody less self-satisfied and more subdued —**chas·tened** adj —**chas·ten·ing** adj

chas·tise /chá stíz/ (-tised, -tis·ing) vt punish or scold —**chas·tise·ment** n

chas·ti·ty /chástətee/ n 1 sexual abstinence 2 plainness of style

chas·ti·ty belt n a medieval device worn by a woman to prevent her from having sexual intercourse

chas·u·ble /cházzəb'l, chássəb'l/ n a Christian priest's loose outer garment

ꝭ **chat** vi (chat·ted, chat·ting) 1 converse informally 2 exchange messages in real time by computer ■ n 1 an act or period of chatting 2 a songbird with a chattering cry

cha·teau /sha tố/ (pl -teaux /-tố, -tố/ or -teaus /-tố, -tố/), **châ·teau** (pl -teaux /-tố, -tố/) n a French castle

chat·e·laine /shátt'l àyn/ n 1 a lady who is the head of a large fashionable household 2 formerly, the woman in charge of a castle or large house 3 formerly, a chain to which keys were attached, worn by a woman around her waist

ꝭ **chat group** n a group that exchanges messages in real time by computer

ꝭ **chat room** n a facility in a computer network for exchanging messages in real time

Chat·ta·hoo·chee /cháttə hoóchee/ river flowing across N Georgia and forming part of the Georgia-Alabama border. Length 436 mi./702 km.

Chat·ta·noo·ga /chàttə nóogə, chàtt'n oogə/ n a port in SE Tennessee. Pop. 147,790 (1998).

chat·tel /chátt'l/ n an item of movable property

chat·ter /cháttər/ vi 1 talk rapidly and informally about trivial matters 2 make high-pitched sounds resembling speech (refers to animals or machinery) 3 click together because of fear or cold (refers to teeth) —**chat·ter** n

chat·ter·box /cháttər bòks/ n a talkative person (infml)

chat·ty /cháttee/ (-ti·er, -ti·est) adj 1 fond of chatting 2 friendly and informal in tone —**chat·ti·ly** adv —**chat·ti·ness** n ◊ See note at **talkative**

Chau·cer /cháwssər/, **Geoffrey** (1343?–1400) English poet —**Chau·cer·i·an** /chaw seĕree ən/ n, adj

chauf·feur /shṓfər, shō fúr/ n a hired driver ■ vti drive somebody from place to place, especially as a job

ORIGIN **Chauffeur** dates from the late 19C. It comes from French, where it meant "stoker, fireman" and was used also for the stoker, and sometimes the driver, of a steam car. In English it was first used simply for "motorist," but the modern meaning took over at the beginning of the 20C.

chau·vin·ism /shṓvə nìzzəm/ n 1 aggressive patriotism 2 aggressive loyalty to a particular gender, group, or cause —**chau·vin·ist** n —**chau·vin·is·tic** /shṓvə nístik/ adj

ORIGIN **Chauvinism** comes from a Nicholas Chauvin of Rochefort, a veteran of the Napoleonic wars noted for blind patriotism. The name and character became widely known through a popular play of 1831.

Chá·vez /chaả vèz, shaả-/, **César Estrada** (1927–93) US labor leader

Chá·vez, Hugo (b. 1954) president of Venezuela (1999–)

cheap /cheep/ adj 1 costing or charging little 2 poor in quality or low in value 3 undeserving of respect 4 unfair ○ a cheap shot 5 stingy —**cheap** adv —**cheap·ly** adv —**cheap·ness** n

SPELLCHECK Do not confuse the spelling of **cheap** and **cheep** (of a bird), which sound similar.

cheap·en /cheépən/ vti 1 make or become less expensive 2 degrade, or become degraded

cheap·jack /cheép jàk/ n a seller of inferior goods ■ adj inferior in value or quality

cheap·skate /cheép skàyt/ n a stingy person (infml)

cheat /cheet/ v 1 vt deceive somebody to gain an advantage 2 vi break rules to gain an advantage 3 vi be sexually unfaithful 4 vt escape harm or injury by luck or cunning ■ n 1 somebody who cheats 2 a dishonest trick —**cheat·er** n

Che·chen /chéchən/ n 1 somebody from Chechnya 2 the majority language in Chechnya —**Che·chen** adj

Chech·nya /chech nyaả, chéchnee ə/ autonomous republic in SW Russia. Cap. Grozny. Pop. 862,000 (1997).

check v 1 vti examine something to establish its state ○ checked the door to make sure it was locked 2 vti confirm the truth or accuracy of something ○ checking with the insurance company to find out whether he's covered 3 vt halt or slow something ○ efforts to check inflation 4 vt make somebody or something stop suddenly ○ He checked himself in mid-sentence. 5 vt mark something with a check mark 6 vt in sports such as ice hockey, block an opponent 7 vt hand over something such as a coat or baggage for temporary keeping ■ n 1 an examination of something to establish its state 2 something that tests the truth or accuracy of something else 3 a means of control or restraint 4 a small printed form that is filled in and signed to instruct a bank to pay money to the person or firm named on it 5 a restaurant or bar bill 6 a numbered ticket for an item deposited in a cloakroom 7 a symbol shaped like a "V" with a short left side and a long right side 8 a pattern of squares in different colors 9 in chess, a move putting an opponent's king in checkmate 10 in sports such as ice hockey, a blocking move ■ interj in chess, warns that an opponent's king is in check —**check·a·ble** adj

☐ **check in** vti register at a hotel or airport

☐ **check off** vt mark items on a list to show that they have been dealt with

☐ **check out** v 1 vi pay the bill and leave a hotel 2 vi be proved true 3 vt withdraw an item and register its withdrawal ○ checked out three books from the library 4 vti pay or take payment from a customer

check·book /chék bòòk/ n a book of detachable bank checks

⌁ **check box** n a square on a computer screen that is clicked on to select an option

⌁ **check dig·it** n in computing, an extra digit used for validation

checked adj patterned with squares

check·er /chékər/ n 1 a check pattern 2 a piece used in the game of checkers ■ vt 1 mark with a check pattern 2 affect adversely from time to time ○ regrettable incidents that checker his career

check·er·board /chékər bàwrd/ n a game board for playing games such as checkers

check·ered /chékərd/ adj 1 checked 2 characterized by periods of trouble or controversy ○ her checkered past

check·ers /chékərz/ n a board game played by two people, each using 12 pieces (+ sing verb)

check-in *n* **1** registration at a hotel or airport **2** a registration desk **3** somebody checking in at a hotel or airport

check·ing ac·count *n* a bank account that enables you to make withdrawals or payments using checks

check·list /chék list/ *n* a list of items for consideration or action

check·mate /chék màyt/ *n* **1** in chess, a winning position or move in which an opponent's king is in check **2** in chess, a move that produces checkmate ■ *vt* (-mat·ed, -mat·ing) **1** in chess, put an opponent's king in checkmate **2** thwart somebody

ORIGIN **Checkmate** comes ultimately from a Persian phrase meaning "the king is defeated or left helpless." It entered English through French in the Middle Ages.

check-off /chék àwf/ *n* a system of direct authorized deduction of union dues from wages.

check-out /chék òwt/ *n* **1** a departure from a hotel **2** a supermarket point of purchase **3** somebody checking out of a hotel

check·point /chék pòynt/ *n* a place where police or soldiers stop and check vehicles

check·room /chék ròom, -ròom/ *n* a place for depositing belongings

⚡ **check·sum** /chék sùm/ *n* a value used to check for transmission errors in data

check-up /chék ùp/ *n* a medical or dental examination

ched·dar /chéddər/ *n* a hard yellow cheese

cheek *n* **1** the soft side area of the face between the nose and the ear **2** the side of a buttock (*infml*) **3** impertinence (*infml*)

cheek·bone /cheék bòn/ *n* a bone in the face below the eye and above the cheeks

cheek·y /cheékee/ (-i·er, -i·est) *adj* impertinent (*infml*) —**cheek·i·ly** *adv* —**cheek·i·ness** *n*

cheep /cheep/ *n* a shrill sound made by young bird —**cheep** *vi* ◊ See note at **chirp**

cheer *n* **1** a shout of encouragement or support **2** a sense of well-being and optimism ■ *v* **1** *vti* shout encouragement or support to somebody ◊ *cheered them on* **2** *also* **cheer up** *vt* make somebody feel cheerful —**cheer·ing·ly** *adv*

cheer·ful /cheérf'l/ *adj* **1** happy and optimistic **2** bright and pleasant —**cheer·ful·ly** *adv* —**cheer·ful·ness** *n*

cheer·lead·er /cheér lèedər/ *n* a performer who exhorts a crowd to cheer at a sports event

cheer·less /cheérləss/ *adj* depressing —**cheer·less·ly** *adv* —**cheer·less·ness** *n*

cheers *interj* expresses good wishes before drinking an alcoholic drink (*infml*)

cheer·y /cheéree/ (-i·er, -i·est) *adj* cheerful —**cheer·i·ly** *adv* —**cheer·i·ness** *n*

cheese /cheez/ *n* a solid food made from milk curds

cheese·burg·er /cheéz bùrgər/ *n* a hamburger covered with melted cheese, served in a bun

cheese·cake /cheéz kàyk/ *n* **1** a dessert of sweetened soft cheese on a cracker-crumb or pastry base **2** photographs of attractive women (*slang*)

cheese·cloth /cheéz klàwth, -klòth/ *n* a light woven cotton material. Use: lightweight clothes, straining cheese.

chees·y /cheézee/ (-i·er, -i·est) *adj* **1** like cheese **2** cheap and tawdry (*infml*) —**chees·i·ness** *n*

chee·tah /cheéta/ (*pl* **-tahs** *or* **same**) *n* a large wild cat with a yellowish brown blackspotted coat that is the fastest land mammal

Chee·ver /cheévər/, **John** (1912–82) US writer

chef /shef/ *n* a professional cook

chef-d'oeu·vre /shày dóvra, shay dúvr/ (*pl* **chefs-d'oeu·vre** /*pronunc. same*/) *n* a masterpiece

~~cheif~~ incorrect spelling of **chief**

Che·khov /ché kawf, -kawv/, **Anton Pavlovich** (1860–1904) Russian writer —**Chek·ho·vi·an** /che kóvee ən/ *n, adj*

Che·lya·binsk /chel yaábinsk/ city in W Russia. Pop. 1,393,608 (1995).

chem·i·cal /kémmik'l/ *adj* **1** of chemistry **2** composed of chemical substances ■ *n* a substance used in or made by chemistry —**chem·i·cal·ly** *adv*

chem·i·cal a·buse *n* DRUGS = substance abuse

chem·i·cal de·pend·en·cy *n* drug addiction

chem·i·cal en·gi·neer·ing *n* a branch of engineering dealing with the industrial applications of chemistry —**chem·i·cal en·gi·neer** *n*

chem·i·cal re·ac·tion *n* a process that changes the molecular composition of a substance

chem·i·cal war·fare *n* warfare using chemical weapons

chem·i·cal weap·on *n* a weapon containing a life-threatening or disabling chemical

che·mise /sha meéz/ *n* **1** a long loose dress **2** a long loose undergarment

chem·ist /kémmist/ *n* a scientist specializing in chemistry

chem·is·try /kémmistree/ *n* **1** the study of the structure, composition, properties, and reactive characteristics of substances **2** the chemical structure, composition, and properties of a substance **3** the spontaneous reaction of two people to each other

chemo- *prefix* chemical, chemistry ◊ *chemotherapy*

che·mo·re·cep·tor /keèmō ri séptər/ *n* an organ responsive to chemical stimulus

che·mo·ther·a·py /keèmō thérrəpee/, **che·mo** *n* the treatment of diseases, especially cancer, with drugs **—che·mo·ther·a·peu·tic** /-therrə pyóotik/ *adj* **—che·mo·ther·a·pist** *n*

Che·ney /cháynee/, **Dick** (*b.* 1941) vice president of the United States (2001–)

Cheng·du /chùng dóo/ capital of Sichuan Province, south central China. Pop. 4,320,000 (1995).

che·nille /shə néel/ *n* **1** a soft thick cotton or silk fabric with a raised pile. Use: furnishings, clothes. **2** a thick silk, cotton, or worsted cord. Use: embroidery, fringe, trimmings.

Chen·nai /chə ní/ capital of Tamil Nadu State, SE India. Pop. 3,841,396 (1991).

Chen Shui-Bi·an /chən shwày bee án/ (*b.* 1951) president of Taiwan (2000–)

Che·ops /kee òps/ (2549?–2526 BC) Egyptian pharaoh

cheque *n* UK FIN = **check 4**

cher·ish /chérrish/ *vt* **1** love and care for **2** retain in mind fondly or hopefully **—cher·ish·ing·ly** *adv*

Cher·no·byl /chər nób'l/ *n* the site of a nuclear power plant disaster in 1986 near Kiev, Ukraine

Cher·o·kee /chérrəkee/ (*pl* same *or* **-kees**) *n* **1** a member of a Native North American people who now live mainly in Oklahoma and North Carolina **2** the language of the Cherokee people **—Cher·o·kee** *adj*

che·root /shə róot/ *n* a cigar with square-cut ends

cher·ry /chérree/ (*pl* **-ries**) *n* **1** a small round fruit with a hard pit **2** a tree that produces cherries **3** the wood of the tree that produces cherries. Use: furniture-making. **4** *also* **cher·ry red** a deep red color **—cher·ry** *adj*

cher·ry-pick *vti* select only the best of something

cher·ry pick·er *n* a mobile crane with a platform for working off the ground

cher·ry to·ma·to *n* a small tomato

cher·ub /chérrəb/ *n* a depiction of an angel as a chubby child with wings **—che·ru·bic** /chə róobik/ *adj*

Ches·a·peake /chéssə pèek/ city in SE Virginia. Pop. 199,564 (1998).

Ches·a·peake Bay inlet of the Atlantic Ocean separating Virginia and Maryland

Chesh·ire cat /chèshər kát/ *n* the cat from Lewis Carroll's *Alice's Adventures in Wonderland*, whose broad grin remained after it disappeared

chess[1] *n* a game played on a checkered board by two players, each with 16 pieces, whose object is to capture the opponent's king

chess[2] *n* a deck board or floorboard of a pontoon bridge

chess·board /chéss bàwrd/ *n* a checkered board used for playing chess

chess·man /chéss màn/ (*pl* **-men** /-mèn/), **chess·piece** /chéss peèss/ *n* a piece used in playing chess

chest *n* **1** the upper part or front of the human body below the neck and above the stomach **2** a strong rectangular box

ches·ter·field /chéstər feèld/ *n* **1** *Northwest US* a large leather sofa **2** *Can, UK* a sofa with a high back and arms

> **ORIGIN Chesterfields** are named for a 19C earl of Chesterfield (in Derbyshire, England).

chest·nut /chés nùt/ *n* **1** an edible glossy brown nut **2** (*pl* **chest·nuts** *or* same) a tree that bears chestnuts **3** a reddish brown horse **4** a deep reddish brown color **5** an overused joke or story (*infml*) **—chest·nut** *adj*

chest of draw·ers *n* a cabinet containing drawers for storing clothes

che·val glass /shə vál-/ *n* a long mirror that tilts on a frame

chev·a·lier /shə vállee ày/ *n* **1** a French title of honor **2** a French knight or nobleman of the lowest rank

chev·ron /shévvrən/ *n* a V-shaped symbol indicating rank on uniforms

chew *v* **1** *vti* bite food repeatedly in the mouth before swallowing **2** *vti* damage something by gnawing ○ *chewing her nails* **3** *vi* chew tobacco ■ *n* a piece of tobacco for chewing **—chew·a·ble** *adj*

☐ **chew out** *vt* reprimand (*infml*)

☐ **chew over** *vt* think about or discuss

chew·ing gum *n* a sweet flavored substance that is chewed but not swallowed

chew·y /chóo ee/ (**-i·er**, **-i·est**) *adj* requiring chewing **—chew·i·ness** *n*

Chey·enne[1] /shī án/ (*pl* same *or* **-ennes**) *n* **1** a member of a Native North American people who once lived in the W Great Plains **2** the Algonquian language of the Cheyenne people **—Chey·enne** *adj*

Chey·enne[2] /shī án/ **1** river in E Wyoming and South Dakota. Length 527 mi. / 848 km. **2** capital of Wyoming. Pop. 53,640 (1998).

chi /kī/ (*pl* **chis**), **khi** (*pl* **khis**) *n* the 22nd letter of the Greek alphabet

Chiang Kai-shek

Chiang Kai-shek /chàng kī shék/ (1887–1975) Chinese military leader and president of Taiwan (1949–75)

Chi·an·ti /kee aàntee/, **chi·an·ti** *n* a light Italian red wine

Chi·a·pas /chee áapəss/ state in SE Mexico. Cap. Tuxtla Gutiérrez. Pop. 3,637,142 (1997).

chi·a·ro·scu·ro /kee àarə skoórō/ n the artistic use of light and shade —**chi·a·ro·scu·rism** n —**chi·a·ro·scu·rist** n

Chi·ba /chee baà/ capital of Chiba Prefecture, E Honshu, Japan. Pop. 867,289 (2000).

chic /sheek/ adj stylish ■ n style and elegance —**chic·ness** n

Chi·ca·go /shi kaágō/ city in NE Illinois. Pop. 2,802,079 (1998).

Chi·ca·na /chi kaánə/ n a Mexican American woman or girl

USAGE See Chicano.

chi·cane /shi káyn/ n 1 a sharp double bend on a car racing circuit 2 in bridge or whist, a hand with no trumps or no cards of one suit ■ vi (-caned, -can·ing) engage in cheating

chi·can·er·y /shi káynəree/ n trickery or deception

Chi·ca·no /chi kaánō/ n (pl -nos) a Mexican American man or boy

USAGE Chicano and Chicana refer only to Mexican Americans. They do not refer to Mexican residents of Mexico. Historically, Chicano is a dialectal variant of the Mexican Spanish word *mexicano*, "a Mexican," and Chicana is its feminine form. Since opinions about these words can and do differ among the various US Mexican American communities, *Mexican American* is a preferred substitute.

chi·chi /sheéshee/ adj self-consciously stylish (disapproving) —**chi·chi** n

chick n 1 a baby bird 2 a young woman (slang; sometimes offensive)

chick·a·dee /chíkə dèe/ n (pl -dees or same) n a North American gray titmouse with a dark crown on its head and a distinctive call

Chick·a·saw /chíkə sàw/ (pl same or -saws) n 1 a member of a Native North American people who now live mainly in central and S Oklahoma 2 the language of the Chickasaw people —**Chick·a·saw** adj

chick·en /chíkən/ n 1 a common domestic fowl raised for its meat and eggs 2 the meat from a chicken as food 3 a person regarded as cowardly (infml) ■ adj cowardly (infml) ◊ See note at **cowardly**

□ **chicken out** vi lack the nerve to continue (slang)

chick·en-and-egg sit·u·a·tion n a situation in which it is impossible to know which of two related circumstances occurred first and caused the other

chick·en feed n an insignificant amount of money (slang)

chick·en-fried steak n a piece of steak that has been tenderized, dredged in seasoned flour, and fried

chick·en-heart·ed, chick·en-liv·ered adj cowardly

Chick·en Lit·tle n an alarmist

ORIGIN The original **Chicken Little** was a fictional hen that was hit on the head by an acorn and said the sky was falling.

chick·en·pox /chíkən pòks/ n a viral disease usually affecting children and characterized by a rash and fever

chick·en wire n wire fencing

chick·pea /chík peè/ n 1 a yellow edible seed 2 a plant that produces chickpeas

chick·weed /chík weèd/ n a common weed with small white flowers

chic·le /chík'l/ n a gummy substance from the latex of a tropical evergreen tree. Use: making chewing gum.

chic·o·ry /chíkəree/ n (pl -ries) n 1 a ground roasted root used as a coffee additive or substitute 2 a plant that produces chicory leaves and roots

chide (chid or chid·ed, chid or chid·den /chídd'n/ or chid·ed, chid·ing) vti reproach —**chid·ing·ly** adv

chief /cheef/ n 1 the leader of a group or organization 2 a chieftain 3 a ship's principal engineer ■ adj 1 most important, basic, or common 2 highest in authority or rank —**chief·ship** n

chief ex·ec·u·tive n 1 the head of an executive body 2 also **chief ex·ec·u·tive of·fi·cer** the highest-ranking executive of a business or organization 3 the US president

chief jus·tice n 1 the presiding judge in a court with several judges 2 the presiding justice of the US Supreme Court

chief·ly /cheéflee/ adv 1 above all 2 in the main ■ adj of chiefs

chief mas·ter ser·geant n a noncommissioned officer in the US Air Force of a rank above senior master sergeant

chief min·is·ter n the leader of a national or provincial government in various countries with a parliamentary system, or a ruler's chief executive official

chief of staff n 1 a high-ranking officer in the US Army, Air Force, or Marine Corps who is a member of the Joint Chiefs of Staff 2 the person in charge of a military or administrative staff

chief of state n the head of a nation

chief pet·ty of·fi·cer n 1 a noncommissioned officer in the US Navy or Coast Guard of a rank above petty officer 2 the highest-ranking noncommissioned officer in the Royal Canadian Navy

Chief Rab·bi n the senior religious leader in some Jewish communities

chief·tain /cheéftən/ n a leader of a people or similar ethnic group —**chief·tain·cy** n —**chief·tain·ship** n

chif·fon /shĭ fón, shĭ fòn/ n a very light sheer nylon, rayon, or silk fabric ■ adj 1 made of chiffon 2 fluffy because of added whipped egg whites or gelatin

chig·ger /chíggər/ n 1 a parasitic mite larva that feeds on the skin, causing irritation and swelling 2 also **chig·oe** a tropical flea, the female of which burrows under the skin, causing painful itching sores

chi·gnon /shéen yòn, sheen yón/ n a knot of hair worn at the nape of the neck

chi·hua·hua /chə waä waä, chə waáwa/ n a very small dog originating in Mexico

Chi·hua·hua /chə waä waa, shə-/ n capital of Chihuahua State, N Mexico. Pop. 627,662 (1995).

chil·blain /chíl blàyn/ n a red itchy swelling on the fingers or toes caused by the cold (often pl)

child /chīld/ (pl **chil·dren** /chíldrən/) n 1 a young human being between birth and puberty 2 a son or daughter of human parents 3 a baby or an infant 4 an immature person 5 a product or result of a particular environment, period, or influence o a child of the 1960s ◊ **with child** pregnant (literary) ◊ See note at **youth**

Child /chīld/, **Julia** (b. 1912) US cookery expert and author

child a·buse n mistreatment of a child —**child a·bus·er** n

child·bear·ing /chīld bàiring/ n the process of carrying a child in the womb and giving birth to it o Her years of childbearing are over.

child·birth /chīld bûrth/ n the process of giving birth to a child

child·care /chīld kàir/ n the paid care and supervision of children by an adult

child·free /chīld free/ adj describes people who have no children, or a place in which children are not allowed o childfree dining areas

child·hood /chīld hood/ n 1 the state of being a child, or the time when somebody is a child 2 an early stage

child·ish /chíldish/ adj 1 immature 2 like a child —**child·ish·ly** adv —**child·ish·ness** n

child·less /chíldləss/ adj having no children

child·like /chīld līk/ adj having the positive qualities of a child o childlike innocence

child prod·i·gy n an exceptionally talented child

child·proof /chīld proof/ adj 1 hard for a child to open or operate 2 made safe for children ■ vt make safe for children or hard for children to open or operate

child re·straint n a child's safety seat

child's play n a straightforward task

child sup·port n money paid by a divorced parent to support his or her children

Chil·e /chíllee, cheé lày/ country in SW South America. Cap. Santiago. Pop. 15,328,467 (2001). —**Chil·e·an** n, adj

chil·i /chíllee/ (pl **-ies**) n 1 a red or green capsicum pepper pod with a strong flavor 2 also **chili powder** a hot-tasting spice made from ground chilies 3 also **chili con carne** a spicy dish of meat and beans

SPELLCHECK Do not confuse the spelling of **chili** and **chilly** ("cold"), which sound similar.

chill n 1 a moderate coldness 2 a coldness caused by fever or fear 3 a depressing effect ■ adj moderately cold ■ v 1 vt make cold 2 vti refrigerate, or be refrigerated 3 also **chill out** vi calm down or relax (infml) —**chill·ness** n

chill·er /chíllər/ n a refrigerated compartment

chill·ing /chílling/ adj frightening —**chill·ing·ly** adv

chil·lum /chíləm/ n 1 a short straight pipe for smoking marijuana, hashish, or tobacco 2 a quantity of marijuana, hashish, or tobacco

chill·y /chíllee/ (**-i·er**, **-i·est**) adj 1 moderately cold 2 feeling cold 3 unfriendly —**chill·i·ly** adv —**chill·i·ness** n ◊ See note at **chili**

chi·mae·ra /kī meérə, ki-/ n 1 (pl **chi·mae·ras** or same) a deep-sea fish with a skeleton of cartilage and a long thin tail 2 = **chimera**

Chim·bo·ra·zo /chímbə raázô/ mountain peak in central Ecuador. Height 20,702 ft./6,310 m.

chime[1] /chīm/ n 1 the sound of a bell 2 a device for striking a bell (often pl) 3 a percussion instrument consisting of hanging bells, metal bars, or tubes 4 a series of notes sounded by a clock before striking 5 a decoration that moves and makes a pleasant sound in the wind ■ v (**chimed, chim·ing**) 1 vi ring harmoniously 2 vt indicate something by chiming 3 vt produce musical sound by striking a bell 4 vti say something or speak in a musical way

□ **chime in** vi interrupt other people's conversation

chime[2] /chīm/ n a rim of a barrel

chi·me·ra /kī meérə, ki-/, **chi·mae·ra** n something totally unrealistic or impractical

ORIGIN In Greek mythology, Chimera was a monster with a lion's head, goat's body, and serpent's tail.

chi·mer·i·cal /kī meérik'l, ki-/ adj imaginary

chim·ney /chímnee/ (pl **-neys**) n 1 a structure for venting smoke, gas, or steam 2 the part of a chimney rising above a roof 3 a passage inside a chimney for venting smoke, gas, or steam 4 a glass tube protecting a lantern flame 5 a cleft in a rock face through which a climber can ascend

chim·ney pot n a pipe placed on the top of a chimney to increase the draft

chim·ney sweep n somebody whose job is to remove soot from chimneys

chim·pan·zee /chìmpan zeè, chim pánzee/, **chimp** n a medium-sized ape

chin n the part of the face below the lips ■ vti (**chinned, chin·ning**) pull yourself up until your chin is level with a bar you are holding

chi·na /chínə/ n 1 porcelain 2 articles made of china

Chi·na /chínə/ country in East Asia. Cap. Beijing. Pop. 1,273,111,300 (2001).

Chi·na Sea part of the Pacific Ocean extending from Japan to the southern end of the Malay Peninsula. Depth 8,913 ft. /2,717 m.

Chi·na·town /chínə tòwn/ n an area of a city where many Chinese people live

chinch, chinch bug, cinch bug n 1 a small insect that destroys grain 2 Southern US a bedbug

chin·chil·la /chin chíllə/ n 1 (pl chin·chil·las or same) a bushy-tailed rodent raised for its fur 2 chinchilla fur

Chi·nese /chī néez, -néess/ (pl same) n 1 somebody from China 2 the group of languages spoken in China 3 the official language of China —**Chi·nese** adj

Chi·nese cab·bage n 1 a vegetable with wrinkled leaves 2 bok choy

Chi·nese cal·en·dar n the traditional calendar used in China that divides the year into 24 fifteen-day periods and is based on both the lunar and solar cycles

Chi·nese check·ers n a board game played with marbles (+ sing verb)

Chi·nese lan·tern n a paper covering for a light

Chi·nese New Year n a festival day marking the new year. Date: between January 21 and February 19.

chink[1] n a narrow opening ■ vt 1 fill cracks or holes in something with caulk or another substance 2 make cracks in something

chink[2] n a sharp ringing sound ■ vti make or cause to make a sharp ringing sound

chin·less /chínləss/ adj 1 having a receding chin 2 weak and ineffectual

chi·no /cheenō/ n cotton twill fabric. Use: military uniforms, casual pants. ■ **chi·nos** npl clothing made of chino

chi·nook /shi nŏŏk, chi-/ n 1 a warm moist sea wind blowing onto the NE US coast 2 a dry warm wind blowing off the Rocky Mountains

Chi·nook /shi nŏŏk, chi-/ (pl same or -nooks) n 1 a member of a Native North American people who now live in W Washington 2 the extinct language of the Chinook people —**Chi·nook** adj

chin·strap /chín stràp/ n a hat or helmet strap passing under the chin

chintz n patterned glazed cotton fabric

chintz·y /chíntsee/ (-i·er, -i·est) adj 1 miserly 2 cheap and gaudy

~~chior~~ incorrect spelling of **choir**

⨍ **chip** n 1 a small piece that has been broken or cut off something hard 2 a space left in

something hard after a small piece has been broken off or out of it 3 a piece of a thin crisp snack food o corn chips 4 a wafer of semiconductor material 5 a token used as money in gambling 6 a piece of dried dung ■ v(**chipped, chip·ping**) 1 vt break off a small piece from something 2 vi lose small pieces o paint that will not chip easily 3 vt produce a short hit or kick of a ball over an obstacle or opponent o chipped the ball over the water and onto the green 4 vt carve something by removing small pieces 5 vt chop something into chips ◇ **a chip off the old block** a person resembling his or her parents (infml) ◇ **have a chip on your shoulder** behave in a resentful manner (infml) ◇ **when the chips are down** at a time of crisis (infml)

□ **chip in** vti contribute something (infml)

chip·board /chíp bàwrd/ n board made of wood chips

Chip·e·wy·an /chíppə wí ən/ (pl same or -ans) n 1 a member of a Native North American people who live in N Saskatchewan, Manitoba, and the Northwest Territories 2 the language of the Chipewyan people —**Chip·e·wy·an** adj

chip·munk /chíp mùngk/ (pl -munks or same) n a small striped rodent of the squirrel family

chipped beef n dried beef slices

Chip·pen·dale /chíppən dàyl/ adj made in an 18C English furniture style —**Chip·pen·dale** n

chip·per /chíppər/ adj cheerful (infml)

Chip·pe·wa /chíppə wàa, chíppəwə/ n (pl -was or same), adj PEOPLES, LANG = **Ojibwa**

⨍ **chip·set** /chíp sèt/ n a group of microchips functioning as a unit

Chi·rac /sheer ak/, **Jacques** (b. 1932) prime minister (1974–76, 1986–88) and president (1995–) of France

Chir·i·ca·hua /chèeri kaáwə/ (pl same or -huas) n member of a formerly nomadic Apache people —**Chir·i·ca·hua** adj

Chi·ri·co /kírri kò/, **Giorgio de** (1888–1978) Greek-born Italian painter

chi·ro·man·cy /kírə mànsee/ n palmistry —**chi·ro·man·cer** n

chi·rop·o·dy /ki róppədee/ n podiatry —**chi·rop·o·dist** n

chi·ro·prac·tic /kírə práktik, kírə pràktik/ n a medical system in which disease and disorders are considered to be caused by misalignment of the bones —**chi·ro·prac·tor** n

chirp n a short high-pitched sound made by a bird ■ v 1 vi make a chirp 2 vti say or speak in a cheerful manner

chis·el /chízz'l/ n a tool with a flat beveled blade for cutting and shaping wood or stone ■ vti 1 carve with a chisel 2 swindle (infml) o was caught chiseling customers

chis·eled /chízz'ld/ adj sharply-defined in shape or profile o a finely chiseled face

Chis·holm /chízzəm/, **Shirley Anita** (b. 1924) US politician

Chi·și·nău /kèeshi nów/ capital of Moldova. Pop. 770,000 (1995).

chit n a girl regarded as saucily impudent (dated)

chit-chat /chít chàt/ n small talk (infml) —**chit-chat** vi

chi·tin /kítin/ n a protective outer covering on some insects and arthropods and in cell walls —**chi·tin·ous** adj

Chit·ta·gong /chíttə gòng/ port in SE Bangladesh. Pop. 1,566,070 (1991).

chit·ter·lings /chíttlinz/, **chit·lins**, **chit·lings** npl hog intestines cooked and eaten as food

chi·val·ric /shi vállrik, shívv'lrik/ adj of knights and the knights' code

chiv·al·ry /shívv'lree/ n 1 considerate behavior, especially toward women 2 the medieval concept of knighthood —**chiv·al·rous** adj

ORIGIN Chivalry was originally a collective noun for knights or horseman equipped for battle. It was adopted from French, and derives from the Latin word for "horse," which is also the source (via Italian) of **cavalry**. **Chivalry** was also used from the 13C for the status and character of a knight. It began to refer specifically to the qualities of an ideal knight only in the late 18C.

chive /chiv/ n 1 a long narrow tubular leaf with an onion flavor. Use: seasoning food. (usually pl) 2 a plant that produces chives

chiv·vy /chívvee/ (-vied, -vies), **chiv·y**, **chev·y** /chévvee/ vt urge or harass

chla·myd·i·a /klə míddee ə/ (pl -as or same or -ae /-èe/) n 1 a pathogenic bacterium 2 a sexually transmitted disease caused by chlamydia

chlo·ride /kláw rìd/ n a compound containing chlorine and one other element

chlo·ri·nate /kláwri nàyt/ (-nat·ed, -nat·ing) vt combine or treat with chlorine —**chlo·ri·nat·ed** adj —**chlo·ri·na·tion** /klàwri náysh'n/ n

chlo·rine /kláw rèen/ n (symbol Cl) a gaseous poisonous greenish yellow chemical element. Use: water purification, disinfectant.

ORIGIN Chlorine was coined by the British chemist Sir Humphry Davy in 1810. He formed it from a Greek word meaning "green," with reference to the greenish yellow color of the gas. The same Greek word appears in chloroform and chlorophyll.

chlo·ro·form /kláwrə fàwrm/ n a colorless sweet-smelling toxic liquid that rapidly becomes a gas, causing unconsciousness if inhaled. Use: solvent, cleaning agent, formerly, anesthetic. ■ vt render unconscious with chloroform

chlo·ro·phyll /kláwrəfil/, **chlo·ro·phyl** n the green plant pigment involved in photosynthesis

chlo·ro·plast /kláwrə plàst/ n a component of a plant cell containing chlorophyll and involved in photosynthesis —**chlo·ro·plas·tic** /klàwrə plástik/ adj

~~choealate~~ incorrect spelling of **chocolate**

chock n 1 a block to stop something from moving 2 a metal anchor used in climbing ■ vt stop something from moving by securing it with a chock

chock-a-block adj packed full (infml)

chock-full adj completely full (infml)

choc·o·hol·ic /chòkə hóllik/, **choc·a·hol·ic** n a lover of chocolate (humorous)

choc·o·late /chóklət/ n 1 a smooth sweet brown food made from cacao seeds, cocoa butter, milk, and sugar 2 a candy covered in chocolate 3 a drink made from sweetened powdered chocolate and milk —**choc·o·lat·ey** adj

ORIGIN In its earliest use **chocolate** meant only a drink, not the solid food. It came via Spanish from a Native South American word meaning literally "bitter water."

Choc·taw /chók tàw/ (pl same or -taws) n 1 a member of a Native North American people who now live mainly in Oklahoma and S Mississippi 2 the language of the Choctaw people —**Choc·taw** adj

choice /choyss/ n 1 a decision to choose somebody or something 2 the power or freedom to choose ○ They gave us no choice. 3 a selection to choose from ○ a wide choice of styles 4 a selected person or thing ■ adj (choic·er, choic·est) 1 high-quality 2 rude or emphatic (euphemistic) ○ a few choice words ◇ **of choice** the best or most appropriate

choir /kwír/ n 1 a group of singers performing together 2 the area in a church where a choir sings

choir-boy /kwír bòy/ n a boy singer in a church choir

choir-girl /kwír gùrl/ n a girl singer in a church choir

choir·mas·ter /kwír màstər/ n the trainer and conductor of a choir

choke[1] v (choked, chok·ing) 1 vi stop breathing because of a blockage in the throat 2 vt prevent somebody from breathing by squeezing his or her throat 3 vt block a road, passage, or channel 4 vt prevent plants from growing by growing around and over them 5 vi lose your nerve and falter (infml) ■ n 1 a noise of somebody choking 2 a fuel mixture regulator for an engine —**chok·ing** adj

□ **choke back** vt not let an emotion out

choke[2] n the inedible central part of an artichoke

choke chain, choke col·lar *n* a chain collar that tightens easily, used for training a dog

choked up *adj* very distressed or disappointed *(infml)*

choke·point /chók pòynt/ *n* 1 a narrow strait through which shipping must go 2 an obstruction of any kind

chok·er /chókər/ *n* a close-fitting necklace or similar ornament

chol·er·a /kóllərə/ *n* an acute intestinal disease

chol·er·ic /kóllərik, kə lérrik/ *adj* bad-tempered *(literary)* —**chol·er** /kóllər/ *n*

cho·les·ter·ol /kə léstə ràwl/ *n* a steroid alcohol produced in the liver and present in all animal cells but considered a health risk if found in high levels in the blood

chol·la /chóy ə/ *(pl* **-las** *or same) n* a cylindrical cactus

chomp, chump *vti* bite or chew noisily *(infml)* —**chomp** *n*

Chom·sky /chómskee/, **Noam** (*b.* 1928) US linguist

Chong·qing /chòong kíng/, **Chung·king, Ch'ung-ch'ing** city in SW China. Pop. 3,470,000 (1995).

choose /chooz/ (**chose** /chōz/, **cho·sen** /chōz'n/, **choos·ing**) *vti* 1 select ◇ *choose a partner* 2 make a deliberate decision to do something

> **SPELLCHECK** Do not confuse the spelling of **choose** and **chose** (past tense of *choose*).

choos·y /choozee/ (**-i·er, -i·est), choos·ey** *adj* fussy in making choices *(infml)* —**choos·i·ly** *adv* —**choos·i·ness** *n*

Cho O·yu /chò ó yoo/ mountain in the Himalaya range. Height 26,906 ft./8,201 m.

chop[1] *v* (**chopped, chop·ping**) 1 *vt* cut something up with downward strokes of a sharp tool 2 *vt* sever or fell something 3 *vi* make chopping movements 4 *vt* form a hole or passage by chopping ◇ *chopped his way through the undergrowth* 5 *vt* hit somebody or something with a sharp downward movement ■ *n* 1 a small piece of red meat with the bone attached 2 a sharp downward stroke or hit 3 irregular wave motions ◇ *a lot of chop on the bay this morning*

chop[2] *n* a trademark, official stamp, or mark of quality, especially in East Asia

chop-chop *interj, adv* quickly *(infml)*

Cho·pin /shò pàn, -páN/, **Frédéric François** (1810–49) Polish composer and pianist

chop·per /chóppər/ *n* 1 a helicopter *(infml)* 2 a motorcycle or bicycle with high handlebars and a long front fork 3 a cleaver 4 a device for producing a pulsing flow or beam of electricity, light, or radiation ■ **chop·pers** *npl* teeth *(slang)*

chop·py /chóppee/ (**-pi·er, -pi·est**) *adj* rough, with many small waves —**chop·pi·ly** *adv* —**chop·pi·ness** *n*

chops *npl* the jaws *(infml)*

chop·stick /chóp stìk/ *n* one of a pair of narrow sticks used for eating or preparing East Asian food

> **ORIGIN** The first part of **chopstick** meant "quick" in the pidgin English formerly used between Chinese people and Europeans in conducting trade and business. It is an alteration of a Cantonese word meaning "urgent."

chop su·ey /chòp soò ee/ *n* a dish of shredded meat and mixed vegetables

cho·ral /káwrəl/ *adj* 1 performed by a choir 2 of a chorus or choir —**cho·ral·ly** *adv*

cho·rale /kə rál, kaw ráal/ *n* 1 a group of singers specializing in church music 2 a Lutheran hymn tune 3 a piece of music based on a chorale

chord[1] /kawrd/ *n* a group of notes played or sung together —**chord·al** *adj* ◇ **strike** *or* **touch a chord** produce an emotional response

> **USAGE** chord or cord? In musical contexts the spelling is **chord,** in anatomical contexts (*spinal cord, umbilical cord, vocal cords*), **cord** is more usual. **Cord** is also used for a thick, strong string, and as a measurement of cut wood.

chord[2] /kawrd/ *n* 1 a straight line connecting two points on an arc or circle 2 the horizontal part of a truss designed to absorb tension in a roof 3 a cord of the body

chore /chawr/ *n* 1 a routine task *(often pl)* 2 an unenjoyable task

cho·re·o·graph /káwree ə gràf/ *v* 1 *vti* devise dance movements for a piece of music 2 *vt* organize and coordinate —**cho·re·og·ra·pher** /kàwree ógrəfər/ *n*

cho·re·og·ra·phy /kàwree ógrəfee/ *(pl* **-phies**) *n* 1 the devising of dance movements for a piece of music 2 the dance movements for a piece of music —**cho·re·o·graph·ic** /kàwree ə gráffik/ *adj* —**cho·re·o·graph·i·cal·ly** *adv*

cho·ris·ter /káwristər/ *n* a singer in a chorus or choir

cho·ri·zo /chə reèzō/ *(pl* **-zos**) *n* a spicy sausage

chor·tle /cháwrt'l/ *n* a gleeful laugh —**chor·tle** *vi*

> **ORIGIN Chortle** is a blend of *chuckle* and *snort,* coined by Lewis Carroll in *Through the Looking-Glass* (1872).

cho·rus /káwrəss/ *n* 1 a part of a song repeated after each verse 2 a large group of singers performing choral or operatic music together 3 a group of performers singing and dancing together in a musical or variety show 4 a group of actors in a Greek drama speaking or singing together 5 a piece of music for a large group of singers 6 an expression of feeling by many people together o *a chorus of disapproval* ■ *vt* say together

cho·rus girl *n* a woman who sings and dances in a group in a stage or movie production

cho·rus line *n* a chorus of singers and dancers in a musical or variety show

chose past tense of **choose** ◊ see note at **choose**

cho·sen /chōz'n/ past participle of **choose** ■ *adj* select o *one of the chosen few*

chow[1] /chow/ *n* food (*slang*)
□ **chow down** *vi* eat enthusiastically (*infml*)

chow[2] /chow/, **chow chow** *n* a stocky thick-coated dog of a breed originating in China

chow·der /chówdər/ *n* a thick seafood or fish soup

chow mein /chòw máyn/ *n* a dish of noodles, chopped meat, and vegetables

Chré·tien /kràⁿ tyáⁿ/, **Jean** (*b.* 1934) prime minister (1993–) of Canada

Christ /krīst/ *n* 1 Jesus Christ 2 the Messiah in Jewish belief —**Christ·ly** *adj*

ORIGIN Christ came through Latin from Greek, and literally meant "anointed." The Greek was a direct translation of the Hebrew word that came separately into English as *Messiah*.

---

chris·ten /kríss'n/ *vt* 1 baptize and name 2 give a name to 3 use for the first time (*infml*)

Chris·ten·dom /kríss'ndəm/ *n* 1 Christian countries 2 Christians as a group (*fml*)

chris·ten·ing /kríss'ning/ *n* a Christian church ceremony to baptize and name a baby

Chris·tian /kríschən/ *n* a believer in the teachings of Jesus Christ ■ *adj* 1 of the teachings of Jesus Christ 2 of Christianity

Chris·tian E·ra *n* the period of history dating from the year Jesus Christ is believed to have been born

Chris·ti·an·i·ty /krìschee ánnətee, krìstee-/ *n* 1 the religion that follows Christ's teachings 2 the holding of Christian beliefs

Chris·tian name *n* a first name, especially one given at a christening

Chris·tian Sci·ence *n* a religious denomination whose members believe that faith can overcome illness —**Chris·tian Sci·en·tist** *n*

Dame Agatha Christie

Chris·tie /krístee/, **Dame Agatha** (1890–1976) British novelist and playwright

Christ·mas /krísməss/, **Christ·mas Day** *n* a festival celebrating the birth of Jesus Christ. Date: December 25. —**Christ·mas·y** *adj*

Christ·mas car·ol *n* a song celebrating Christmas

Christ·mas Eve *n* the day or evening before Christmas

Christ·mas·time /krísməss tìm/ *n* the period around Christmas

Chris·toph·er /krístəfər/, **St.** (*fl* 3C) patron saint of travelers

chro·mat·ic /krō máttik/ *adj* of color —**chro·mat·i·cal·ly** *adv*

chrome /krōm/ *n* 1 a shiny chromium-plated metal. Use: formerly, car trim. 2 a compound containing chromium 3 chromium ■ *vt* (**chromed, chrom·ing**) 1 coat with chromium 2 treat with a chromium compound

---

ORIGIN Chrome comes from a Greek word meaning "color." It was coined in French as a name for chromium, the compounds of which are brightly colored.

-chrome *suffix* color, pigment o *monochrome*

chrome yel·low *n* a yellow pigment

chro·mi·um /krōmee əm/ *n* (*symbol* **Cr**) a hard bluish white metallic element. Use: alloys, electroplating.

chro·mo·some /krōmə sòm/ *n* a rod-shaped structure in a cell nucleus that carries genes controlling inherited characteristics —**chro·mo·so·mal** /krōmə sóm'l/ *adj*

chron·ic /krónnik/ *adj* 1 describes a long-lasting illness or condition 2 always present o *chronic inflation* 3 habitual o *a chronic liar* —**chron·i·cal·ly** *adv* —**chro·nic·i·ty** /krə níssətee/ *n*

chron·ic fa·tigue syn·drome *n* an illness characterized by exhaustion and weakness

chron·i·cle /krónnik'l/ *n* 1 a chronological account 2 a fictional narrative ■ *vt* (**-cled, -cling**) make a chronological record of —**chron·i·cler** *n*

Chron·i·cles /krónnik'lz/ *n* each of two books of the Bible that tell the story of the Israelites from the creation of Adam to the middle of the 6C (+ *sing verb*)

chrono- *prefix* time o *chronology*

chron·o·log·i·cal /krònnə lójjik'l, krònə-/, **chron·o·log·ic** /-lójjik/ *adj* 1 arranged in the order in which events occur 2 of chronology —**chron·o·log·i·cal·ly** *adv*

chro·nol·o·gy /krə nóllajee/ (*pl* **-gies**) *n* 1 the order in which events occur 2 a list of events in the order they occur —**chro·nol·o·gist** *n*

chro·nom·e·ter /krə nómmətər/ *n* a precision time-measuring instrument

chrys·a·lis /kríss'liss/ *n* an insect in a cocoon at the stage between larva and adult

chry·san·the·mum /kri sánthəməm, -zánthəməm/ *n* a garden plant whose large flowers have dense petal clusters

chub (*pl* **chubs** or **same**) *n* a minnow with a thick rounded body

chub·by /chúbbee/ (**-bi·er**, **-bi·est**) *adj* plump in physique —**chub·bi·ly** *adv* —**chub·bi·ness** *n*

chuck[1] *vt* **1** throw carelessly (*infml*) **2** get rid of (*infml*) **3** tickle affectionately under the chin —**chuck** *n* ◊ See note at **throw**

chuck[2] *n* **1** a clamp on a lathe or drill **2** a cut of beef from the neck or shoulder

chuck·le /chúk'l/ (**-led**, **-ling**) *vti* laugh quietly —**chuck·le** *n*

chug (**chugged**, **chug·ging**) *vi* make or move with a repeated thudding sound like that of a small engine —**chug** *n*

chug·a·lug /chúggə lùg/ (**-lugged**, **-lug·ging**) *vt* drink something such as beer greedily and quickly (*slang*)

chum[1] *n* a friend (*infml*) ■ *vi* (**chummed**, **chum·ming**) be friends

chum[2] *n* fish bait scattered on the water ■ *vti* (**chummed**, **chum·ming**) engage in fishing using chum as bait

chum[3] (*pl* **chums** or **same**), **chum salmon** *n* a salmon with wavy green streaks and blotches

chum·my /chúmmee/ (**-mi·er**, **-mi·est**) *adj* friendly or intimate (*infml*) —**chum·mi·ly** *adv* —**chum·mi·ness** *n*

chump[1] *n* a person regarded as unwise (*infml*)

chump[2] *vti*, *n* = chomp

Chung·king, **Ch'ung-ch'ing** ◊ Chongqing

chunk[1] *n* **1** a thick square-shaped piece **2** a large amount or portion

chunk[2] *vi* clunk

chunk·y /chúngkee/ (**-i·er**, **-i·est**) *adj* solid and square-shaped —**chunk·i·ness** *n*

church *n* **1** a building for public worship, especially in the Christian religion **2** *also* **Church** the followers of a religion, especially Christianity, considered as group **3** a religious service ○ *go to church* **4** *also* **Church** religious leadership, especially when contrasted with state leadership **5** *also* **Church** a branch of the Christian religion —**church·y** *adj*

church·go·er /chúrch gò ər/ *n* a church service attendee —**church·go·ing** *n*, *adj*

Sir Winston Churchill

Chur·chill /chúrchil/, **Sir Winston** (1874–1965) British prime minister (1940–45, 1951–55)

Church of Christ, Sci·en·tist *n* the official name of the Christian Scientist Church

Church of Eng·land *n* the established Christian church in England, governed by bishops with the monarch as its titular head

Church of Je·sus Christ of Lat·ter-Day Saints *n* a church founded in 1830 and based on the Book of Mormon

church·war·den /chúrch wàwrd'n/ *n* an Episcopal or Anglican layperson with church-related, usually business duties

church·yard /chúrch yàard/ *n* a church cemetery

churl·ish /chúrlish/ *adj* **1** crass **2** unkind and grumpy —**churl·ish·ly** *adv* —**churl·ish·ness** *n*

churn *n* a container for making butter ■ *v* **1** *vt* stir milk to make butter **2** *vt* make butter **3** *vti* splash violently **4** *vi* feel unsettled ○ *My stomach was churning.*
□ **churn out** *vt* rapidly produce large quantities of

chute /shoot/ *n* **1** a sloping channel or passage to slide things down **2** a children's slide **3** a parachute (*infml*)

SPELLCHECK Do not confuse the spelling of **chute** and **shoot** ("fire a weapon," "move fast," "take a photograph," "attempt to score a goal"), which sound similar.

---

chut·ney /chútnee/ (*pl* **-neys**) *n* **1** a sweet and spicy fruit relish **2** *Carib* a Caribbean song similar to a calypso

chutz·pah /hóotspə, kh-/, **hutz·pah**, **chutz·pa** *n* self-confidence (*infml*)

CIA *n* a US intelligence and counterintelligence organization operating outside the United States. Full form **Central Intelligence Agency**

cia·bat·ta /chə báttə/ *n* a flat Italian bread made with olive oil

ciao /chow/ *interj* expresses a greeting (*infml*)

ci·ca·da /si káydə, -kaadə/ (*pl* **-das** or **-dae** /-dee/) *n* a large winged insect living in trees and grass, the male of which makes a shrill sound

cic·a·trix /síkətriks/ (*pl* **-tri·ces** /-trĭ seez/) *n* a scar (*technical*)

Cic·e·ro /síssə rò/, **Marcus Tullius** (106–43 BC) Roman philosopher, writer, and politician —**Cic·e·ro·ni·an** /sìssə rṓnee ən/ *adj*

Cid /sid/, **El** (1040?–99) Spanish military leader

CID *n* the detective branch of the UK police. Full form **Criminal Investigation Department**

ci·der /sídər/ *n* **1** a nonalcoholic fresh apple drink **2** an alcoholic drink made from apples

---

ORIGIN In English **cider** has always been made from apples. However, it goes back to a Hebrew word that meant strong drink in general.

---

cieling incorrect spelling of **ceiling**

Cien·fue·gos /syèn fwáy gòss/ capital of **Cienfuegos Province**, central Cuba. Pop. 132,000 (1996).

ci·gar /si gaár/ *n* a roll of tobacco leaves for smoking

~~cigaret~~ incorrect spelling of **cigarette**

cig·a·rette /síggə rèt/ *n* **1** a roll of shredded tobacco with a thin white paper cover **2** a roll of shredded leaves for smoking o *a marijuana cigarette*

~~cigarette~~ incorrect spelling of **cigarette**

ci·lan·tro /si laántrō, -lántrō/ *n* coriander leaves

~~cilinder~~ incorrect spelling of **cylinder**

~~cinamon~~ incorrect spelling of **cinnamon**

CINC, C in C *abbr* Commander in Chief

cinch *n* **1** something easily done (*infml*) **2** something certain to happen (*infml*) **3** a girth for a saddle ■ *vt* **1** tighten something **2** put a cinch on a horse **3** make certain of something (*infml*)

cinch bug *n* INSECTS = **chinch**

Cin·cin·na·ti /sìnsə náttee, -náttə/ city in SW Ohio. Pop. 336,400 (1998).

cin·der /síndər/ *n* a small piece of charred wood or coal ■ **cin·ders** *npl* **1** ashes **2** fragments of solidified lava

cin·der block *n* a concrete building block

Cin·der·el·la /sìndə réllə/ *n* a neglected person or thing ■ *adj* rags-to-riches

---

ORIGIN The original **Cinderella** is a fairy-tale character who is neglected by her sisters and set to drudge in the kitchen but is enabled by her fairy godmother to attend a ball and meet a prince. The story was popularized by a 1697 collection of traditional tales set down by Charles Perrault.

---

cin·e·ma /sínnəmə/ *n* **1** movies collectively (*fml*) **2** a movie theater

---

ORIGIN Cinema derives from a Greek word meaning "movement," which was the basis of French *cinématographe*, the name given to the first film projector by its inventors, Auguste and Louis Lumière, in 1896. This was quickly shortened to *cinéma*, and borrowed into English.

---

cin·e·mat·ic /sìnnə máttik/ *adj* **1** appropriate to movies **2** of movies —**cin·e·mat·i·cal·ly** *adv*

cin·e·ma·tog·ra·phy /sìnnəmə tóggrəfee/ *n* the photographing of motion pictures —**cin·e·ma·tog·ra·pher** *n* —**cin·e·mat·o·graph·ic** /sìnnə mattə gráffik/ *adj*

ci·né·ma vé·ri·té /see nay màa verree táy/ *n* a documentary style of filmmaking

cin·e·phile /sínnə fīl/ *n* a movie enthusiast

cin·na·mon /sínnəmən/ *n* **1** a spice obtained from tree bark **2** a tree with bark from which cinnamon is obtained —**cin·na·mon** *adj*

ci·pher /sífər/, **cy·pher** *n* **1** a written code **2** the key to a cipher **3** a text in cipher ■ *vt* write in code

Cip·ro /sípprō/ *tdmk* a trademark for the antibiotic ciprofloxacin

cip·ro·flox·a·cin /sìpprō flóksə sìn/ *n* a powerful antibiotic used, e.g., in treating anthrax in humans

cir·ca /súrkə/ *prep* on or in approximately a particular date

cir·ca·di·an /sər káydee ən/ *adj* occurring in a 24-hour cycle

~~circiut~~ incorrect spelling of **circuit**

cir·cle /súrk'l/ *n* **1** a continuous round line, every point of which is equidistant from the center **2** the area inside a circle **3** a circle-shaped area, object, or arrangement **4** a group of people with a common interest **5** a section of tiered seating in an upper level of a theater ■ *v* (**-cled, -cling**) **1** *vti* move or move around something along a curving route **2** *vt* mark a ring around something

cir·cuit /súrkit/ *n* **1** a circular path finishing where it began **2** an area bounded by a circular path **3** a single journey around a circular path **4** a regular journey around an area **5** a round of regularly attended or visited events or places **6** a route around which an electrical current can flow ■ *vti* move along a circular path (*fml*)

⨁ **cir·cuit board** *n* a board constituting a printed circuit

cir·cuit break·er *n* a safety shutoff in an electrical circuit

cir·cuit court *n* a court that moves from place to place within a judicial district

cir·cu·i·tous /sər kyōō itəss/ *adj* indirect and lengthy —**cir·cu·i·tous·ly** *adv*

cir·cuit·ry /súrkətree/ *n* **1** the components of an electric circuit **2** the system of circuits in an electric device

cir·cuit train·ing *n* sports training in which different exercises are performed in rotation

cir·cu·lar /súrkyələr/ *adj* **1** like a circle **2** following a curved path that ends where it began **3** not logical because of assuming as true something that needs to be proved **4** circuitous ■ *n* a widely distributed leaflet or notice —**cir·cu·lar·i·ty** /sùrkyə lérrətee/ *n* —**cir·cu·lar·ly** *adv*

cir·cu·lar·ize /súrkyələ rìz/ (**-ized, -iz·ing**) *vt* **1** publicize with leaflets or notices **2** canvass or poll

cir·cu·lar saw *n* a power saw with a rotating blade

cir·cu·late /súrkyə làyt/ (**-lat·ed, -lat·ing**) *v* **1** *vi* move around a circular system **2** *vti* pass or be passed around **3** *vi* flow freely in an enclosed space **4** *vi* mingle at a social event (*infml*) —**cir·cu·la·tor·y** *adv*

cir·cu·la·tion /sùrkyə láysh'n/ n 1 the movement of blood around the body 2 free flow, e.g., of air or water 3 the distribution or communication of something 4 the number of copies of something sold or distributed 5 valid use as money

circum- prefix around ○ circumnavigate

cir·cum·cise /súrkəm sīz/ (-cised, -cis·ing) vt 1 remove the foreskin of the penis of 2 remove the clitoris or the skin of the clitoris of —**cir·cum·ci·sion** /sùrkəm sízh'n/ n

cir·cum·fer·ence /sər kúmfərənss, -kúmfrənss/ n 1 the distance around the edge of a circle or a circular object 2 the edge of a circle or a circular object

cir·cum·flex /súrkəm fléks/, **cir·cum·flex ac·cent** n the pronunciation mark ^ placed above some vowels in some languages

cir·cum·lo·cu·tion /sùrkəm lō kyoosh'n/ n the use of more words than necessary to avoid saying something directly —**cir·cum·loc·u·to·ry** /-lókyə tàwree/ adj

cir·cum·nav·i·gate /sùrkəm návvi gàyt/ (-gat·ed, -gat·ing) vt travel all the way around ○ circumnavigate the globe —**cir·cum·nav·i·ga·tion** /-navi gáysh'n/ n

cir·cum·po·lar /sùrkəm pólər/ adj in or near the polar regions (technical)

cir·cum·scribe /súrkəm skríb/ (-scribed, -scrib·ing) v 1 vt restrict the power or independence of somebody. or something (fml) 2 draw one geometric figure around another so that points touch

cir·cum·spect /súrkəm spèkt/ adj careful to weigh risks or consequences before acting. —**cir·cum·spec·tion** /sùrkəm spéksh'n/ n —**cir·cum·spect·ly** adv ◊ See note at **cau·tious**

cir·cum·stance /súrkəm stàns/ n 1 a condition that affects a situation (usually pl) 2 events or conditions beyond somebody's control ■ **cir·cum·stanc·es** npl prevailing financial, social, or material conditions ◊ **under** or **in the circumstances** taking everything into account

cir·cum·stan·tial /sùrkəm stánsh'l/ adj 1 based on inference, not proof 2 of or contingent on particular circumstances

cir·cum·vent /sùrkəm vént, súrkəm vènt/ vt 1 avoid the restrictions of a law without breaking it 2 outwit somebody —**cir·cum·ven·tion** /sùrkəm vénsh'n/ n

cir·cus /súrkəss/ n 1 a group of traveling entertainers 2 a show performed by traveling entertainers 3 a noisy and confused scene or event (infml) ○ a media circus 4 a Roman stadium where gladiator fights and chariot races were held 5 a show in a Roman circus —**cir·cus·y** adj

cirque /surk/ n a semicircular hollow with steep walls formed by glacial erosion on mountains

cir·rho·sis /si róssiss/ n a chronic liver disease —**cir·rhot·ic** /si róttik/ adj

cir·ro·cu·mu·lus /seerō kyoómyələss/ (pl -li /-lī/) n a high-altitude cloud forming a broken layer

cir·rus /seérəss/ (pl -ri /-ī/) n a high-altitude wispy cloud —**cir·rate** /seér àyt, seérət/ adj

cis /siss/ adj having two atoms on the same side of a double bond

CIS abbr Commonwealth of Independent States

⚡**CISC** abbr complex instruction set computer

cis·tern /sístərn/ n 1 a water tank, especially one providing water for a toilet 2 an underground tank for storing rainwater

cit·a·del /síttəd'l, síttə dèl/ n 1 a fortified building used as a refuge 2 a defender of a principle

ci·ta·tion /sī táysh'n/ n 1 an official document or speech praising a person or group 2 a quotation from an authoritative source used as corroboration 3 an act or the process of citing something 4 an order to appear in court —**ci·ta·tion·al** adj

cite /sīt/ (cit·ed, cit·ing) vt 1 quote as an authority (fml) 2 name officially in a court case 3 officially praise

---

SPELLCHECK Do not confuse the spelling of **cite**, **site** ("a place," "locate something"), and **sight** ("seeing," "see something"), which sound similar.

---

cit·i·fy /sítti fī/ (-fied, -fies) vt (disapproving) 1 turn into a city, or make more urban 2 make too like a city dweller —**cit·i·fi·ca·tion** /sìttifi káysh'n/ n

cit·i·zen /síttiz'n/ n 1 somebody who has the legal right to live in a country either by birth or naturalization 2 a permanent resident of a city or town —**cit·i·zen·ly** adj

cit·i·zen·ry /síttiz'nree/ (pl -ries) n citizens collectively

cit·i·zen's ar·rest n an arrest made by an ordinary citizen

cit·i·zens band n radio frequencies used by the public

cit·i·zen·ship /síttiz'n shìp/ n 1 the legal status of being a citizen of a country 2 the rights and duties of a citizen

cit·ric ac·id /síttrik ássid/ n acid from citrus fruits. Use: flavorings.

cit·ron /síttrən/ n 1 a citrus fruit like a large lemon, whose rind is often candied 2 the small thorny tree that produces citrons

cit·ro·nel·la /sìttrə néllə/ n 1 also **cit·ro·nel·la oil** a pale aromatic oil. Use: perfumery, soap-making, insect repellents. 2 also **cit·ro·nel·la grass** a lemon-scented grass of tropical Asia

cit·rus /síttrəss/ n fruits such as oranges and lemons collectively

cit·y /síttee/ (pl -ies) n 1 a very large municipality 2 the people living in a very large municipality **3** a municipality of specified size

SYNONYMS **city, conurbation, metropolis, town, municipality** CORE MEANING: an urban area where a large number of people live

cit·y coun·cil *n* the governing body of a city

cit·y hall *n* **1** the officials and administrators who run a city **2** a local bureaucracy **3** *also* **City Hall** a city council building

cit·y·scape /síttee skàyp/ *n* **1** a view of a city, especially of its skyline **2** a photograph or painting of a city

cit·y-state *n* an independent state consisting of a sovereign city and its surrounding territory

cit·y·wide /síttee wíd/ *adj* involving an entire city ■ *adv* all over a city

Ciu·dad de Nau·cal·pan de Juá·rez /sèe oo dàad də nō kàal paan də hwaä rèss/ suburban city in south central Mexico near Mexico City. Pop. 723,723.

Ciu·dad Juá·rez /-hwaä rèss, -waä-/ city in N Mexico, across the Rio Grande from El Paso, Texas. Pop. 1,011,786 (1995).

Ciu·dad Ma·de·ro /-mə dérrō/ suburban city in E Mexico on the Gulf of Mexico near Tampico. Pop. 132,444.

Ciu·dad O·bre·gón /-óbrə gòn/ city in NW Mexico SE of Hermosillo. Pop. 165,572.

Ciu·dad Vic·to·ri·a /-vik táwree ə/ capital of Tamaulipas State, NE Mexico. Pop. 243,960 (1995).

civ·et /sívvət/ *n* **1** a musky greasy substance. Use: perfume. **2** *also* **civ·et cat** a wild animal that looks like a cat and secretes civet

civ·ic /sívvik/ *adj* **1** of a city's government **2** of the duties and responsibilities expected of a community member —**civ·i·cal·ly** *adv*

civ·ic cen·ter *n* a municipal entertainment center

civ·ics /sívviks/ *n* the study of citizenship *(+ sing verb)*

civ·il /sívv'l/ *adj* **1** of citizens **2** not military **3** performed by a state or city official o *a civil marriage* **4** describes a legal action that does not involve criminal proceedings **5** polite **6** of a community —**civ·il·ly** *adv*

civ·il de·fense *n* **1** the organizing and training of civilian volunteers to help in times of war or emergency **2** civilian volunteers who participate in civil defense

civ·il dis·o·be·di·ence *n* the refusal to obey a law as a form of nonviolent protest

civ·il en·gi·neer·ing *n* the building of roads, bridges, and other large structures —**civ·il en·gi·neer** *n*

ci·vil·ian /si víllyən/ *n* somebody who is not a member of the armed forces or of a police or fire and rescue department —**ci·vil·ian** *adj*

ci·vil·i·ty /si víllətee/ *(pl* **-ties)** *n* **1** politeness **2** a polite act

civ·i·li·za·tion /sívv'li záysh'n/ *n* **1** a society with a high level of culture and social organization **2** an advanced level of development in society **3** advanced societies in general **4** populated areas

civ·i·lize /sívv'l ìz/ *(-lized, -liz·ing) vt* **1** create a high level of culture and social organization in a place **2** make somebody more socially and culturally refined

civ·i·lized /sívv'l ìzd/ *adj* **1** having advanced cultural and social development **2** refined in tastes or morality

civ·il law *n* the branch of law that deals with the rights of citizens

civ·il lib·er·ties *npl* an individual's basic rights, guaranteed by law —**civ·il lib·er·tar·i·an** *n*

civ·il rights *npl* the basic rights that all citizens in a free nation are supposed to have

civ·il ser·vant *n* a government employee

civ·il serv·ice *n* all the government departments and the people who work in them

civ·il war *n* **1** a war between opposing groups within a country **2** **Civ·il War** the 19C US war between the North and the South **3** **Civ·il War** the 17C English war between the Royalists and the Parliamentarians

civ·vies /sívviz/ *npl* ordinary clothes, as opposed to a military uniform *(infml)*

cl *symbol* centiliter

Cl *symbol* chlorine

clack *vti* make or cause to make a short loud noise —**clack** *n*

clad[1] past tense, past participle of **clothe** ■ *adj* **1** dressed o *clad in blue* **2** covered *(literary; often in combination)* o *ivy-clad walls*

clad[2] **(clad, clad·ding)** *vt* **1** cover a wall with cladding **2** cover metal with a protective layer of material

clad·ding /kládding/ *n* **1** an outer layer of stone, tiles, or wood on an outer wall **2** a protective metal coating bonded to another metal

claim *vt* **1** say that something is true without providing evidence **2** demand something you are entitled to **3** require or demand attention ■ *n* **1** an assertion that something is true **2** the basis for demanding or getting something **3** a demand or request for something you are or feel entitled to **4** a piece of land to which somebody claims a legal right

claim·ant /kláymənt/ *n* somebody making a claim

clair·voy·ant /klair vóy ənt/ *n* somebody who is supposedly psychic —**clair·voy·ance** *n* —**clair·voy·ant** *adj*

clam *n* **1** a burrowing shellfish **2** the soft

edible flesh of a clam **3** a dollar *(slang)* ■ *vi* (**clammed, clam·ming**) collect clams

□ **clam up** *vi* refuse to talk *(infml)*

clam·bake /klám bàyk/ *n* **1** a picnic at which seafood such as clams is cooked and served **2** a relaxed party or gathering *(infml)*

clam·ber /klámbər/ *vi* climb awkwardly —**clam·ber** *n*

clam·my /klámmee/ (**-mi·er, -mi·est**) *adj* unpleasantly cold and damp —**clam·mi·ness** *n*

clam·or /klámmər/ *vi* **1** make desperate and noisy demands **2** shout loudly ■ *n* **1** a persistent demand **2** a loud noise —**clam·or·ous** *adj*

clamp *n* a device with jaws for holding things firmly ■ *vt* fasten or immobilize with a clamp

□ **clamp down** *vi* take firm action to control or stop something

clamp·down /klámp dòwn/ *n* firm action taken to control or stop something

clan *n* **1** a group of related families **2** a group of related Scottish families with a common surname and a single chief **3** a group with a shared aim *(infml)*

clan·des·tine /klan déstín/ *adj* secret or furtive —**clan·des·tine·ly** *adv* ◊ See note at **secret**

clang *vti* make or cause to make a loud ringing noise —**clang** *n*

clank *vti* make or cause to make a short loud metallic noise —**clank** *n*

clan·nish /klánnish/ *adj* inclined to stick together and exclude others —**clan·nish·ly** *adv* —**clan·nish·ness** *n*

clap *v* (**clapped, clap·ping**) **1** *vti* hit your hands together loudly **2** *vt* put something or somebody somewhere quickly ○ *clapped him into jail* ■ *n* **1** a sudden loud sound made by hitting the hands together **2** an expression of approval through applause

clap·board /kláp bàwrd, klábbərd/ *n* a long narrow wooden board. Use: surface siding of buildings.

clap·per /kláppər/ *n* a moving part that strikes the inside of a bell to make it ring

clap·per·board /kláppər bàwrd/ *n* a pair of hinged boards clapped together at the start of each take in a movie to help synchronize picture and sound

clap·trap /kláp tràp/ *n* nonsense *(infml)*

claque /klak/ *n* **1** a group of people hired to applaud or jeer a performance **2** a person's entourage *(disapproving)*

clar·et /klárrət/ *n* a red wine from the Bordeaux region of France

clar·i·fy /klárrə fì/ (**-fied, -fies**) *v* **1** *vt* make easier to understand by explanation **2** *vti* make or become clear or pure by heating or filtering —**clar·i·fi·ca·tion** /klàrrəfi káysh'n/ *n*

clar·i·net /klárrə nèt/ *n* a woodwind instrument with a single reed

clar·i·on call /klárree ən-/ *n* a call to action

clar·i·ty /klárrətee/ *n* the quality of being clear

Clark, George Rogers (1752–1818) American Revolutionary soldier

Clark, Tom Campbell (1899–1977) associate justice of the US Supreme Court (1949–67)

Clark, William (1770–1838) US explorer

clash *v* **1** *vi* fight or argue **2** *vi* be incompatible ○ *Her testimony clashes with the evidence.* **3** *vti* make or cause to make a loud harsh metallic noise **4** *vi* look unpleasant together ○ *His shirt and tie clash.* —**clash** *n* ◊ See note at **fight**

clasp *vt* **1** hold tightly with your hands or arms **2** fasten with a device ■ *n* **1** a small buckle or fastening **2** a tight arm or hand hold

clasp knife *n* a pocket knife with a blade that folds into the handle

class *n* **1** a group of students taught together **2** a period during which students meet and are taught **3** a specific subject taught **4** a number of students who graduate together **5** a group within a society who share the same social or economic status **6** the structure of a society into classes **7** elegance and refinement *(infml)* **8** a categorization according to quality **9** a group of similar items or related organisms ■ *vt* assign to a group ◊ See note at **type**

class ac·tion *n* a legal action brought by several plaintiffs together

class-con·scious *adj* aware of your own social class —**class-con·scious·ness** *n*

clas·sic /klássik/ *adj* **1** of the highest quality or lasting value, especially in the arts **2** definitive as an example of its kind **3** extremely and usually comically typical or fitting *(infml)* ■ *n* **1** a work or created object of lasting value and high quality ○ *a design classic* **2** something that is an outstanding or typical example of its kind ○ *Last night's show was a classic.*

clas·si·cal /klássik'l/ *adj* **1** of ancient Greece or Rome **2** in the ancient Greek or Roman style **3** describes music considered to be serious or intellectual **4** of 18C and 19C European music **5** orthodox or conservative —**clas·si·cal·i·ty** /klàssi kállətee/ *n* —**clas·si·cal·ly** *adv* —**clas·si·cal·ness** *n*

clas·si·cism /klássi sìzzəm/, **clas·si·cal·ism** /klássik'l lìzzəm/ *n* **1** a restrained style in art and architecture based on that of ancient Greece and Rome **2** the study of Greek and Roman culture

clas·si·cist /klássissist/ *n* **1** a scholar of ancient Greek and Latin **2** an advocate of artistic classicism

clas·sics /klássiks/ *n* also **Clas·sics** the study of the language, literature, and history of ancient Greece and Rome *(+ sing verb)* ■ *npl* the literature of ancient Greece or Rome *(+ pl verb)*

clas·si·fi·ca·tion /klàssifi káysh'n/ *n* **1** the organization of things into groups **2** a category within an organized system —**clas·si·fi·ca·to·ry** *adj*

clas·si·fied /klássi fĩd/ *adj* **1** available only to authorized people for reasons of national security **2** grouped by type

clas·si·fied ad·ver·tise·ment, clas·si·fied ad *n* a small advertisement in a newspaper

clas·si·fy /klássi fĩ/ (-fied, -fies) *vt* **1** categorize things or people **2** designate information as being classified for security

class·ism /klá sìzzəm/ *n* discrimination based on social class —**class·ist** *adj, n*

class·less /klássləss/ *adj* **1** not organized into social classes **2** not belonging to a social class

class·mate /klàss màyt/ *n* somebody in the same class at school

class·room /klàss ròom, -room/ *n* a room in a school where people are taught

class strug·gle *n* a struggle for power between social classes

class·y /klássee/ (-i-er, -i-est) *adj* very stylish and elegant (*infml*) —**class·i·ly** *adv* —**class·i·ness** *n*

clat·ter /kláttər/ *vti* make or cause to make a harsh rattling or banging noise

Clau·di·us I /kláwdee əss/ (10 BC–AD 54) Roman emperor (AD 41–54)

clause *n* **1** a group of words that contains a subject and predicate and can sometimes stand as a sentence **2** a section of a legal document —**claus·al** *adj*

claus·tro·pho·bi·a /kláwstrə fṓbee ə/ *n* fear of being in a confined space

claus·tro·pho·bic /kláwstrə fṓbik/ *adj* **1** confined or cramped **2** of or affected by claustrophobia ■ *n* somebody who is affected by claustrophobia —**claus·tro·pho·bi·cal·ly** *adv*

clave past tense of **cleave**²

clav·i·chord /klávvi kàwrd/ *n* an early keyboard instrument like a piano —**clav·i·chord·ist** *n*

clav·i·cle /klávvik'l/ *n* a collarbone —**cla·vic·u·lar** /klə vǐkyələr, klá-/ *adj*

claw *n* **1** an animal's sharp nail **2** each of the pincers on a crab or similar organism **3** something resembling a claw ■ *v* **1** *vti* scratch or dig with claws or fingernails **2** *vt* make by scratching or digging with claws or fingernails —**clawed** *adj*

claw ham·mer *n* a hammer with two prongs at one end of its head for removing nails

clay *n* **1** a fine-grained material that occurs naturally in soil, can be molded when wet, and is hard when baked. Use: making bricks, ceramics, and cement. **2** heavy sticky soil **3** *also* **clay pig·eon** a target launched into the air for shooting —**clay·ey** *adj*

Clay, Cassius ♦ Ali, Muhammad

Clay, Henry (1777–1852) US politician

clay·more /kláy màwr/ *n* a large double-edged sword formerly used by Scottish Highlanders

clean /kleen/ *adj* **1** free of dirt **2** not polluted or adulterated **3** free of infection **4** freshly washed **5** morally upright **6** not obscene **7** blank ○ *a clean chalkboard* **8** with no record of crime or infection **9** streamlined **10** complete ○ *a clean break with the past* **11** producing the least possible pollution ■ *vti* make or become clean ■ *adv* **1** so as to make something clean **2** in a clean way —**clean·ly** *adv* —**clean·ness** *n*

☐ **clean out** *vt* take all the money or belongings of (*slang*)

clean-cut *adj* **1** neat-looking **2** with a sharp outline **3** unambiguously clear

clean·er /kleénər/ *n* **1** somebody employed to clean the interior of a building **2** a substance or machine used in cleaning

clean·ers /kleénorz/ *n* a shop providing a dry-cleaning service ◇ **take to the cleaners** deprive of money or possessions (*slang*)

clean·li·ness /klénlinəss/ *n* the degree to which somebody or something is clean

clean-liv·ing *adj* living a morally upright life

clean room *n* a dirt-free room for special purposes

cleanse /klenz/ (cleansed, cleans·ing) *vt* **1** make thoroughly clean **2** make free from corruption, sin, or guilt —**cleans·ing** *n*

cleans·er /klénzər/ *n* **1** a cleaning substance **2** a cosmetic product for cleaning the face

clean-shav·en *adj* with facial hair shaved off

clean·up /kleén ùp/ *n* **1** a thorough cleaning **2** the elimination of something bad **3** a large gain of assets (*slang*)

⚡ **clear** /kleer/ *adj* **1** free from anything that darkens or obscures **2** transparent ○ *clear glass* **3** free from clouds **4** pure in hue **5** perfect and unblemished **6** easily heard or seen **7** unambiguous, obvious, and allowing no doubt ○ *clear evidence of guilt* ○ *clear instructions* **8** mentally sharp and discerning **9** free from feelings of guilt ○ *a clear conscience* **10** unobstructed ○ *keep the aisles clear* **11** with all contents removed **12** not connected or touching **13** net of deductions or charges **14** debt-free ■ *adv* out of the way ■ *v* **1** *vi* dissipate and disperse ○ *when the mist had cleared* **2** *vi* brighten and become free of clouds or fog **3** *vti* make or become transparent **4** *vt* rid something of extraneous or obstructive matter **5** *vt* remove confusion from the mind **6** *vti* make the mind free, or become free of the dulling effects of, e.g., sleep **7** *vt* prove somebody innocent **8** *vt* open a route by removing obstacles **9** *vt* remove people from a place **10** *vt* disentangle something, e.g., an anchor **11** *vt* move past something without touching it **12** *vti* authorize somebody or something, or be authorized ○ *The plane has been cleared for landing.* **13** vt acquire money as a profit (*infml*) **14** vt pay off a debt **15** vi be authorized and credited to the payee's account ○ *Checks take three days to clear.* **16** vti settle banking accounts through a clearinghouse **17** vt in some sports, get the ball or puck out of your own defense area **18** vt delete computer data —**clear·ly** adv —**clear·ness** n ◇ **in the clear** free from suspicion or blame

□ **clear out** vi leave fast (*infml*)

□ **clear up** v **1** vi become less cloudy **2** vti get or make better **3** vt solve a mystery or explain a misunderstanding

clear·ance /kleéranss/ n **1** the removal of obstructions or unwanted objects **2** permission for something to happen **3** the width or height of an opening **4** a sale of goods at reduced prices to get rid of stock **5** the passage of commercial documents through a clearing house **6** in some sports, the process of clearing the ball or puck from the defense area **7** the forcible removal of people from land

clear-cut adj **1** unambiguous **2** distinctly outlined ■ vt cut all the trees from an area of land ■ n land from which all the trees have been cut

clear-head·ed adj able to think clearly, especially in difficult situations —**clear-head·ed·ly** adv —**clear-head·ed·ness** n

clear·ing /kleéring/ n an open space in a forest

clear·ing·house /kleéring hòwss/ (*pl* -**hous·es** /-hòwzziz/) n **1** an institution that coordinates transactions between banks **2** an agency that collects and distributes information

clear-sight·ed adj **1** having good perception or judgment **2** with keen eyesight

cleat /kleet/ n a piece of metal or hard plastic attached to the sole of a shoe ■ **cleats** npl a pair of sports shoes with metal projections on the soles

cleav·age /kleévij/ n **1** the division or splitting of something **2** a split, division, or separation **3** the hollow visible between the breasts of a woman wearing a low-cut garment

cleave¹ /kleev/ (**cleaved** or **cleft** or **clove** /klōv/, **cleaved** or **cleft** or **clo·ven** /klōv′n/, **cleav·ing**) vti split along a line of natural weakness

cleave² /kleev/ (**cleaved** or **clove** /klōv/ or **clave** /klayv/, **cleaved**, **cleav·ing**) vi cling faithfully to somebody or something (*fml*) ○ *an instructor who cleaves to the curriculum guides*

cleav·er /kleévor/ n a heavy knife used by butchers

clef n in written or printed music, a symbol indicating pitch

cleft /kleft/ vti past tense, past participle of **cleave¹** ■ n **1** a small indentation **2** a gap or split (*fml*) ■ adj split in half or fissured

cleft pal·ate n a congenital fissure in the roof of the mouth

clem·a·tis /klémmətiss, klə máttiss/ (*pl* -**tis·es** or *same*) n a climbing plant with large flowers

Cle·men·ceau /klè maan sṓ, -maaN sáw/, **Georges** (1841–1929) prime minister of France (1906–09, 1917–20)

clem·en·cy /klémmənsee/ n **1** mercy, or an act of mercy **2** mildness in weather

Clem·ens /klémmənz/, **Samuel Langhorne** ▶ **Twain, Mark**

clem·ent /klémmənt/ adj **1** describes weather that is mild or not extreme **2** merciful —**clem·ent·ly** adv

clench vt **1** close your teeth or fist tightly **2** clutch something —**clench** n —**clenched** adj

Cle·o·pat·ra /klèe ə páttrə/ (69–30 BC) Egyptian queen (51–30 BC)

clere·sto·ry /kleér stàwree/ (*pl* -**ries**) n the upper part of a wall that contains windows

cler·gy /klúrjee/ n people ordained for service in an organized religion (+ *sing* or *pl verb*)

cler·ic /klérrik/ n a member of the clergy

cler·i·cal /klérrik′l/ adj **1** of office work **2** of the clergy —**cler·i·cal·ly** adv

clerk n **1** a general office worker **2** a salesclerk **3** a service desk worker **4** a government worker who keeps records **5** an administrator in a court of law —**clerk** vi

ORIGIN Clerk is essentially an older form of *cleric*. It derives from ecclesiastical Latin *clericus* "of the Christian ministry." **Clerks** were originally members of the clergy who, as literate members of medieval society, took on many of the administrative and secretarial functions that later fell to laypeople. From the early 16C **clerk** began to be used for various officials, recordkeepers, copyists, and the like. *Cleric* was introduced from Latin in the early 17C and replaced **clerk** in its original sense.

Cleve·land /kleévlənd/ port in NE Ohio. Pop. 495,817 (1998).

Cleve·land, Grover (1837–1908) 22nd and 24th president of the United States (1885–89, 1893–97)

clev·er /klévvər/ adj **1** creatively intelligent **2** pretentiously or superficially intelligent **3** highly skilled in using the hands **4** *Southern US* having a pleasant disposition —**clev·er·ly** adv —**clev·er·ness** n◊ See note at **intelligent**

cli·ché /klee sháy/ n **1** an overused expression that has lost its original force **2** an overused idea —**cli·chéd** adj

ʄ click n **1** a short sharp sound **2** a press and release of a computer mouse button **3** a speech sound produced by sucking in air ■ v **1** make or cause to make a short sharp sound **2** vti press and release a computer mouse button **3** vi suddenly become clearly understood (*infml*) ○ *It finally clicked where I'd seen him before.* **4** vi communicate or work together easily *(infml)* ○ *The partners never clicked.*

SPELLCHECK Do not confuse the spelling of **click** and **clique** ("a close group"), which sound similar.

✦ **click art** *n* computer clip art

✦ **click rate** *n* the number of times an Internet site in an advertisement is visited, as a percentage of the number of times the advertisement itself is viewed

✦ **clicks-and-mor·tar, click-and-mor·tar** *adj* combining online and traditional sales

✦ **click·stream** /klík streem/ *n* the path of mouse clicks that somebody makes in navigating the World Wide Web

✦ **click·through** /klík thróo/ *n* the measure of the effectiveness of an Internet advertisement based on the number of times it is viewed

✦ **cli·ent** /klí ənt/ *n* **1** somebody using a professional service **2** a customer **3** a computer program that obtains data from another computer in a network

cli·en·tele /klí ən tél, klèe-/ *n* clients or customers as a group

✦ **cli·ent-serv·er, cli·ent/serv·er** *adj* used on a computer network in which processing is divided between a client program on a user's machine and a network server program

cliff *n* a high steep rock face —**cliff·y** *adj*

cliff dwell·er *n* a member of a people who constructed dwellings on ledges of cliffs in the SW United States

cliff·hang·er /klíf hàngər/ *n* **1** an unresolved ending in a serialized drama **2** a tense situation —**cliff·hang·ing** *adj*

cli·mac·ter·ic /klī máktərik, klī mak térrik/ *n* a period of important change —**cli·mac·ter·ic** *adj*

cli·mac·tic /klī máktik/ *adj* **1** exciting **2** of a climax —**cli·mac·ti·cal·ly** *adv*

cli·mate /klímət/ *n* **1** the typical weather in a region **2** a place with weather of a particular type **3** a situation or atmosphere that prevails at a particular time or place —**cli·mat·ic** /klī máttik/ *adj* —**cli·mat·i·cal·ly** *adv*

cli·ma·tol·o·gy /klìmə tólləjee/ *n* the study of climates —**cli·ma·tol·o·gist** *n*

cli·max /klí màks/ *n* **1** the most exciting or important point **2** an orgasm **3** an ever-intensifying sequence of phrases, or the conclusion of such a sequence ■ *v* **1** *vti* reach or bring to the most exciting or important point **2** *vi* have an orgasm

---

ORIGIN Climax derives from a Greek word literally meaning "ladder." From its first use in English in the mid-18C it applied, as in Greek and Latin, to a rhetorical device in which ideas are expressed in order of increasing importance. The sense jumped from the steps

toward the high point to the high point itself in the late 18C.

climb /klīm/ *v* **1** *vti* move toward the top of something, especially using the hands and feet **2** *vi* move with some effort ○ *climbed out of bed* **3** *vi* rise steeply in amount **4** *vi* engage in mountaineering **5** *vti* grow upward, clinging to other plants or a support ■ *n* **1** the process or an act of climbing **2** a hill, mountain, or rock, or the route used to climb it **3** a rise in value or amount

---

SPELLCHECK Do not confuse the spelling of **climb** and **clime** ("place with a particular climate"), which sound similar.

---

climb·er /klímər/ *n* **1** somebody who climbs **2** a plant that clings to another plant or support

climb·ing /klíming/ *n* the activity of climbing mountains

clime /klīm/ *n* a place with a particular type of climate *(fml; often pl)* ◊ See note at **climb**

~~climing~~ incorrect spelling of **climbing**

clinch *v* **1** *vt* resolve something decisively **2** *vi* in boxing or wrestling, put your arms around your opponent **3** *vt* flatten the protruding end of a nail ■ *n* **1** a passionate embrace **2** in boxing or wrestling, a tactic of pinning an opponent's arms down to the side of the body

clinch·er /klínchər/ *n* a deciding factor *(infml)*

cling (**clung**) *vi* **1** hold onto somebody or something tightly **2** stick to something **3** refuse to give up an idea, belief, or custom **4** need somebody emotionally —**cling·ing** *adj*

cling·stone /klíng stòn/ *n* a fruit with flesh that sticks to its pit

cling·y /klíngee/ (-**i·er, -i·est**) *adj (infml)* **1** emotionally dependent **2** sticking to the body —**cling·i·ness** *n*

clin·ic /klínnik/ *n* **1** a medical department for outpatients, often attached to a hospital **2** a specialized medical department or office **3** a group medical practice **4** a teaching session for medical students, interns, and residents at the patients' bedsides

---

ORIGIN Clinic derives ultimately from the Greek word for "bed." It was at first an adjective, acquired through Latin and referring especially to the sickbed. The modern noun came through French or German.

---

clin·i·cal /klínnik'l/ *adj* **1** based on medical treatment or observation **2** unemotional —**clin·i·cal·ly** *adv*

cli·ni·cian /kli níshʹn/ *n* a doctor who works directly with patients

clink[1] *vti* make or cause to make a light ringing sound —**clink** *n*

clink[2] *n* a prison *(slang dated)*

ORIGIN "The Clink" was a prison in South-wark, London, England. The use of **clink** for a prison generally appears to have been extended from this. The name is recorded from the early 16C, but its origin is unknown.

clink·er[1] *n* **1** a hard mass of coal residue in a fire **2** a brick that has been fired too long

clink·er[2] /klíngkər/ *n* a failure, or something of poor quality *(infml)*

The White House

Hillary Rodham Clinton and Bill Clinton

Clin·ton /klíntən, klínt'n/, **Bill** (*b.* 1946) 42nd president of the United States (1993–2001)

Clin·ton, Hillary Rodham (*b.* 1947) US lawyer, first lady (1993–2001), and senator

clip[1] *vt* (**clipped, clipping**) **1** cut or trim something **2** remove something by cutting **3** shorten the time taken for something **4** hit somebody with a glancing blow *(infml)* **5** shorten a speech sound **6** abbreviate a word **7** reduce power or influence ■ *n* **1** a film or TV extract **2** an extract from a newspaper or magazine **3** a glancing blow **4** a particular rate of speed *(infml)*

clip[2] *n* **1** a gripping device *(often in combination)* **2** a piece of jewelry that attaches to clothing **3** a bullet holder for an automatic weapon ■ *v* (**clipped, clip·ping**) **1** *vti* hold or be held with a clip **2** *vt* block a football player illegally

⚡ **clip art** *n* prepared artwork for use in computer documents

⚡ **clip·board** /klíp bàwrd/ *n* **1** a board with a clip for securing papers **2** a part of computer memory where cut or copied data are stored temporarily

clip-clop *n* the sound of horses' hooves on a hard surface ■ *vi* (**clip-clopped, clip-clop·ping**) go clip-clop

clip-on *adj* attaching by means of a clip ■ *n* an accessory that attaches with a clip

clipped *adj* **1** neatly trimmed **2** with each word spoken clearly

clip·per /klípər/ *n* a fast sailing ship ■ **clip·pers** *npl* a tool similar to scissors, used for cutting or clipping something

clip·ping /klípping/ *n* **1** an article cut from a newspaper **2** in football, the illegal blocking of a player from behind ■ **clip·pings** *npl* pieces of hair or grass that have been cut off

clique /kleek, klik/ *n* an exclusive group

—**cliqu·ey** *adj* —**cliqu·ish** *adj* —**cliqu·ish·ness** *n* ◊ See note at **click**

clit·o·ris /klíttəriss/ *n* a sensitive female sex organ at the top of the vulva —**clit·o·ral** *adj*

clo·a·ca /klō áykə/ (*pl* **-cae** /-see/) *n* the terminal part of the gut in reptiles, amphibians, birds, many fishes, and some invertebrates —**clo·a·cal** *adj*

cloak *n* **1** a long sleeveless outer garment that fastens at the neck **2** something that conceals *(fml)* ◦ *left under a cloak of secrecy* ■ *vt* conceal something

cloak-and-dag·ger *adj* full of secrecy

cloak·room /klōk ròom, -ròom/ *n* **1** a coat check **2** a legislators' lounge

clob·ber /klóbbər/ *vt* *(infml)* **1** hit with great force **2** defeat utterly

cloche /klōsh/ *n* **1** a protective glass or clear plastic cover for plants **2** a woman's close-fitting hat with a narrow brim

clock *n* a device for displaying the time ■ *vt* measure the time or speed of *(infml)* ◦ *a car that was clocked at 95 mph*

clock ra·di·o *n* a combination clock and radio

clock·wise /klók wìz/ *adv, adj* in the direction that a clock's hands move

clock·work /klók wùrk/ *n* a system of cogs and springs used to drive a clock or moving toy

clod *n* **1** a lump of earth **2** a person regarded as unintelligent *(insult)* —**clod·dish** *adj*

clod·hop·per /klód hòppər/ *n* a person regarded as awkward and unsophisticated *(infml insult)* ■ **clod·hop·pers** *npl* big heavy shoes or boots *(infml)*

clog *v* (**clogged, clog·ging**) **1** *vti* block or become blocked gradually **2** *vt* hinder movement on or in ■ *n* **1** a heavy shoe made of wood or with a wooden sole **2** an obstruction

cloi·son·né /klòyz'n áy/ *adj* decorated with a pattern of enamel pieces —**cloi·son·né** *n*

clois·ter /klóystər/ *n* **1** a monastery or convent **2** a covered walkway around a courtyard ■ *vr* find a quiet secluded place to go —**clois·tral** *adj*

clois·tered /klóystərd/ *adj* **1** secluded **2** in a monastery

clomp *n, vti* = **clump**[2]

⚡ **clone** /klōn/ *n* **1** a genetically identical organism produced asexually **2** a piece of hardware or software that is a functional copy of a more expensive product ■ *vt* (**cloned, clon·ing**) **1** produce a genetically identical copy of an organism asexually **2** make a copy of an object or product —**clon·al** *adj* ◊ See note at **copy**

ORIGIN Clone is from a Greek word meaning "twig."

---

clop *n* the sound of horses' hooves on a hard surface —**clop** *vi*

close[1] /klōss/ *adj* (**clos·er**, **clos·est**) **1** near in space, time, or relationship **2** about to happen **3** in a very friendly or affectionate relationship o *a close friend* **4** thorough o *a close inspection* **5** decided by a small margin o *a close contest* **6** allowing little space between parts **7** very similar o *a close copy* **8** nearly correct or exact, but not quite **9** secretively silent o *was close about the cause of the disaster* **10** cut very short **11** stingy **12** stuffy and airless ■ *adv* (**clos·er**, **clos·est**) so as to be close —**close·ly** *adv* —**close·ness** *n*

⌁ **close**[2] /klōz/ *v* (**closed**, **clos·ing**) **1** *vti* move to cover an opening **2** *vti* bring together the edges of something **3** *vti* stop operating, or shut down a business temporarily or permanently **4** *vti* block access to something such as a road **5** *vti* come or bring to an end **6** *vti* reduce the distance between two people or things **7** *vt* bring a deal to closure **8** *vt* deactivate and store a computer file or program ■ *n* the end of an activity or period of time

☐ **close in** *vi* approach and surround somebody or something

☐ **close out** *vt* sell off merchandise

☐ **close up** *vti* **1** lock a building at the end of a working day **2** come or bring things closer together

closed *adj* **1** no longer doing business **2** denying access **3** no longer to be discussed or investigated **4** rigidly excluding the ideas of others **5** not admitting outsiders

closed-cap·tioned *adj* broadcast with subtitles

closed-cir·cuit tel·e·vi·sion, **closed-cir·cuit TV** *n* a television transmission system in which cameras transmit pictures by cable to connected monitors

closed-door *adj* not open to the public or the media

closed-end fund *n* an investment company with a fixed number of shares

closed-mind·ed, **close-mind·ed** *adj* not open to new ideas or opinions —**closed-mind·ed·ness** *n*

close·down /klōz dòwn/ *n* a temporary or permanent stopping of work or operations

closed sea·son *n* **1** the period of the year when no hunting is allowed **2** the period between seasonal sports competitions

closed shop *n* a workplace that employs union members only

close-fist·ed *adj* reluctant to spend money —**close-fist·ed·ness** *n*

close-grained *adj* describes wood with a dense texture and a smooth surface

close-in *adj* **1** near the hub of activity **2** taking place at close range

close-knit *adj* mutually supportive

close-mind·ed *adj* = closed-minded

close-mouthed /klōz mówthd/ *adj* reticent

close-out /klōz òwt/ *n* a sale of remaining merchandise

close-run *adj* decided by a small margin

clos·et /klózzət/ *n* an area in which clothes or linens are stored ■ *adj* imagined but not actual or real ■ *vt* put in a room with privacy o *He closeted himself in the study all morning.* ◊ **come out of the closet** acknowledge openly something previously kept secret

close-up /klōss ùp/ *n* **1** a photograph or a movie or television shot taken at close range **2** a detailed look at something ■ *adj* /klōss úp/ at close range

clos·ing /klōzing/ *adj* final o *the closing stages* ■ *n* **1** a fastening **2** a transfer of property ownership **3** an attorney's final summation of a case before a court

clos·ing time *n* the time when a business closes for the day

clo·sure /klózhər/ *n* **1** the permanent ending of a business activity **2** an act or the process of blocking access to something **3** something that closes an opening **4** cloture **5** a sense of finality

clot *n* a thick sticky mass, especially of blood ■ *vti* (**clot·ted**, **clot·ting**) thicken into a mass

cloth /klawth, kloth/ *n* **1** fabric made from thread or fibers **2** a piece of fabric used for a specific purpose (*often in combination*)

clothe /klōth/ (**clothed** *or* **clad**, **cloth·ing**) *vt* **1** put clothes on **2** provide with clothing **3** cover o *a field that was clothed in leaves* **4** conceal or obscure

clothes /klōthz, klōz/ *npl* garments for covering the body

clothes·horse /klōthz hàwrss, klōz-/ *n* **1** somebody who dresses fashionably (*infml*) **2** an indoor drying frame for wet laundry

clothes·line /klōthz lìn, klōz-/ *n* a line on which to hang laundry to dry

cloth·ier /klōthyər/ *n* a retailer of clothes or cloth

cloth·ing /klōthing/ *n* **1** clothes **2** a covering for something

clo·ture /klōchər/ *n* the closing of debate in a legislative body such as the US Senate

cloud *n* **1** a visible mass of water or ice particles in the sky **2** a mass of particles in the air, e.g., dust or smoke **3** a flying mass of insects or birds **4** something that causes worry or gloom ■ *v* **1** *vti* make or become cloudy **2** *vt* make more confused o *cloud the issue* **3** *vt* make appear less good o *It will cloud her reputation.* **4** *vti* make or become troubled or gloomy o *His face clouded with disappointment.* ◊ **on cloud nine** extremely happy (*infml*) ◊ **under a cloud** in disgrace

ORIGIN Cloud originally meant "a mass of earth, a hill." A resemblance between cumulus clouds and hills presumably accounts for the transferred meaning. **Cloud** replaced the earlier word for massed water vapor in the 13C, though that word continued as *welkin*, a poetic name for the sky.

cloud·burst /klówd bùrst/ *n* a sudden heavy rain shower

cloud·ed /klówdəd/ *adj* **1** troubled **2** opaque

cloud·less /klówdləss/ *adj* **1** bright and clear **2** without problems —**cloud·less·ness** *n*

cloud·y /klówdee/ (-i·er, -i·est) *adj* **1** with clouds **2** opaque —**cloud·i·ness** *n*

clout (*infml*) *n* **1** power and influence **2** a blow with the hand or fist ■ *vt* hit with the hand or fist

clove[1] /klōv/ *n* **1** a dried aromatic flower bud used as a spice **2** a tree that produces cloves

ORIGIN The name of the spice **clove** comes ultimately from the Latin word for "nail" (the type that is hammered), from the appearance of the single clove-tree bud and its stalk. The garlic **clove** is from an ancient root that also gave rise to *cleave* "split."

clove[2] /klōv/ *n* a segment of a compound plant bulb, e.g., garlic

clove[3] /klōv/ past tense of **cleave**[1]

clove[4] /klōv/ past tense of **cleave**[2]

clo·ven /klóv'n/ past participle of **cleave**[1] ■ *adj* split in two (*literary*)

clo·ven hoof *n* **1** the divided hoof of a sheep, hog, or similar mammal **2** in Christianity, a mark traditionally indicating the presence of the devil —**clo·ven-hoofed** *adj*

clo·ver /klóvər/ *n* a low-growing plant with rounded three-part leaves. Use: forage. ◇ **in clover** financially well off (*infml*)

clo·ver·leaf /klóvər lèef/ (*pl* **clover·leaves** /-lèevz/) *n* **1** a three-lobed leaf of a clover **2** a highway interchange with a layout that resembles a four-leafed clover

clown /klown/ *n* **1** a comic circus performer **2** somebody who is funny **3** a prankster **4** somebody regarded as ill-mannered or ineffectual (*infml*) ■ *vi* perform as a clown —**clown·ish** *adj*

□ **clown around** *vi* behave comically (*infml*)

cloy *vti* sicken or disgust somebody with too much of something initially thought pleasant —**cloy·ing** *adj*

club *n* **1** a thick stick used as a weapon **2** in golf, a long thin implement for hitting the ball **3** an association of people with a common interest **4** an organization for the pursuit of a sport **5** the premises of an association of people **6** a building providing recreational facilities for its members **7** an organization giving discounts to members in return for regular purchases **8** a nightclub **9** a black symbol like a three-leafed clover on a playing card ■ *vt* (**clubbed, club·bing**) hit with a club

club·bing /klúbbing/ *n* **1** the activity of going to nightclubs **2** a medical condition in which the base of the fingers and toes become thickened

club·foot /klúb fòot/ *n* **1** a congenital condition in which one foot is twisted inward **2** a foot affected by clubfoot —**club·foot·ed** *adj*

club·house /klúb hòwss/ *n* **1** the premises of a sports club **2** a locker room

clubs *n* the suit of cards with a club as its symbol (+ *sing or pl verb*)

club sand·wich *n* a sandwich with two layers of fillings between three slices of bread

club so·da *n* carbonated water drunk alone or mixed with alcohol

cluck *v* **1** *vi* make short low clicking sounds (*refers to hens*) **2** *vti* express disapproval or concern with a clicking sound ■ *n* **1** a hen's low clicking sound **2** a person regarded as unintelligent (*slang*)

clue *n* **1** an aid in solving a mystery or crime **2** a piece of information used in solving a crossword puzzle

□ **clue in** *vt* give necessary information to

clued-in *adj* well-informed (*infml*)

clue·less /klóoləss/ *adj* uninformed and incompetent (*slang*) —**clue·less·ness** *n*

clump[1] *n* **1** a cluster of growing things **2** a mass of similar things ■ *vti* combine into a mass

clump[2], **clomp** *n* a thumping sound ■ *vi* move with a clump

clum·sy /klúmzee/ (-si·er, -si·est) *adj* awkward or badly coordinated —**clum·si·ly** *adv* —**clum·si·ness** *n*

clung past tense, past participle of **cling**

clunk *n* a dull metallic sound —**clunk** *vti*

clunk·y /klúngkee/ (-i·er, -i·est) *adj* awkwardly designed (*infml*)

clus·ter /klústər/ *n* **1** a dense bunch or group **2** a metal design indicating that a military award has been won before ■ *vti* form into a cluster

clus·ter bomb *n* an aerial bomb dispersing smaller bombs as it falls

⚡ **clus·ter con·trol·ler** *n* a central computer in a network

clutch[1] *v* **1** *vt* grip tightly **2** *vi* make a grabbing movement **3** *vi* operate the clutch of a motor vehicle ■ *n* **1** a mechanism that connects rotating shafts in a motor vehicle **2** the pedal activating the clutch in a motor vehicle **3** controlling power (*often pl*) ◇ *was caught in the clutches of terror* **4** a crucial moment (*infml*) **5** a grip on something

clutch[2] *n* a group of eggs or chickens hatched together

clut·ter /klúttər/ *n* **1** a messy collection of objects **2** a disorganized mess ■ *vt* fill with clutter

Clyde /klīd/ river in SW Scotland, flowing through Glasgow to the **Firth of Clyde**. Length 106 mi./171 km.

cm *symbol* centimeter

Cm *symbol* curium

Co *symbol* cobalt

CO¹ *abbr* Colorado

CO², C.O. *abbr* **1** commanding officer **2** conscientious objector

Co. *abbr* **1** Colorado **2** Company (*in names of businesses*) **3** County (*in place names*)

co- *prefix* **1** together, jointly ◦ *coeducation* **2** associate, alternate ◦ *copilot* **3** to the same degree ◦ *coextensive* **4** the complement of an angle ◦ *cotangent*

c/o *abbr* care of

coach *n* **1** a horse-drawn carriage **2** an inexpensive class of travel **3** somebody who trains sports players or performers **4** a railroad car **5** a long-distance bus **6** a tutor ■ *vt* **1** train an athlete or performer **2** give a student private instruction ◊ See note at **teach**

> **ORIGIN Coach** came through French and German from Hungarian, where it was formed from the name of Kocs, a village where carriages and carts were built. The "training" uses arose in 19C British university slang, from a tutor carrying a student through an examination as though in a coach.

coach·ing /kóching/ *n* **1** the profession of training and guiding sports teams **2** training in overcoming emotional problems

coach·man /kóchmən/ (*pl* **-men** /-mən/) *n* the driver of a horse-drawn coach

coach·work /kóch wùrk/ *n* the painted bodywork of a road vehicle or railroad car

co·ag·u·late /kō ággyə làyt/ (**-lat·ed, -lat·ing**) *vti* turn into a semisolid mass —**co·ag·u·la·tion** /kō àggyə láysh'n/ *n*

coal *n* a black rock formed by the decomposition of plant material. Use: fuel.

co·a·lesce /kō ə léss/ (**-lesced, -lesc·ing**) *vti* merge into a single group —**co·a·les·cence** *n*

coal·face /kól fàyss/ *n* a seam of coal being worked

coal·field /kól fèeld/ *n* an area with coal deposits

coal gas *n* **1** a methane and hydrogen mixture. Use: fuel. **2** the gas produced when coal is burned

co·a·li·tion /kō ə lísh'n/ *n* a temporary political or military alliance —**co·a·li·tion·ist** *n*

coal·mine /kól mìn/ *n* a mine where coal is dug —**coal·min·er** *n* —**coal·min·ing** *n*

coal scut·tle *n* a metal container for holding coal for a domestic fire

coal tar *n* a thick black liquid that is a byproduct of coke production. Use: making dyes, drugs, and soap.

coarse /kawrss/ (**coars·er, coars·est**) *adj* **1** rough to the touch **2** consisting of large grains or thick strands **3** lacking good taste, refinement, or propriety —**coarse·ly** *adv* —**coars·en** *vti* —**coarse·ness** *n*

> **SPELLCHECK** Do not confuse the spelling of **coarse** and **course** ("a sequence of events," "a route," "a program of study"), which sound similar.

coast *n* **1** the land next to an ocean or a sea **2** a slide down a slope on a sled ■ *vi* **1** move by momentum alone, without applying power **2** succeed effortlessly —**coast·al** *adj*

coast·er /kóstər/ *n* **1** a small mat for a glass **2** a roller coaster at an amusement park

coast guard *n* **1** an emergency service that rescues people in trouble at sea **2** a member of a coast guard

coast·line /kóst lìn/ *n* the outline of a coast as viewed from the sea or on a map

Coast Moun·tains mountain range in W British Columbia, Canada. Highest peak Mt. Waddington, 13,104 ft./3,994 m.

Coast Rang·es long narrow mountain ranges on the coast of W North America from S Alaska to NW Mexico. Highest peak Mt. Logan 19,551 ft./5,959 m.

coast-to-coast *adj* across a whole island or continent

coat *n* **1** a warm long outer garment with sleeves **2** the fur, wool, or hair covering a mammal **3** a thin covering, e.g., of paint ■ *vt* cover a surface with a thin layer of something

coat check, coat·room /kót ròom, -ròòm/ *n* a place for people to leave their belongings while they are in a public building

coat hang·er *n* a frame on which to hang an article of clothing

coat·ing /kóting/ *n* a thin layer covering something

coat of arms *n* a design on a shield that signifies a specific institution or family

coax /kōks/ *v* **1** *vti* persuade gently, or use gentle persuasion **2** *vt* obtain by gentle persuasion —**coax·ing·ly** *adv*

co·ax·i·al ca·ble /kō àksee əl-/ *n* a two-layer cable used for high-speed transmission, e.g., of television or telephone signals

cob *n* **1** the core to which individual corn kernels are attached **2** a male swan

co·balt /kó bàwlt/ *n* (*symbol* **Co**) a silvery white chemical element. Use: coloring ceramics, alloys.

> **ORIGIN Cobalt** comes from a German word meaning "goblin, demon." The element often occurs as an impurity in silver ore, and German silver miners attributed its presence to goblins' mischief.

Cobb, Ty (1886–1961) US baseball player

cob·ble¹ /kóbb'l/ *n* **1** a cobblestone **2** a naturally rounded rock fragment ■ *vt* (**-bled,**

-bling) pave a road with cobblestones
—**cob·bled** *adj*

□ **cobble together** *vt* make roughly from
what is available

cob·ble[2] /kóbb'l/ (-**bled**, -**bling**) *vt* make or
repair shoes

cob·bler[1] /kóbblər/ *n* a maker or repairer of
shoes

cob·bler[2] /kóbblər/ *n* a baked fruit dessert
with a soft thick crust

cob·ble·stone /kóbb'l stòn/ *n* a small rounded
paving stone —**cob·ble·stoned** *adj*

⚡ **COBOL** /kố bawl/, **Co·bol** *n* a computer programming language designed for business
applications

co·bra /kóbrə/ *n* a venomous snake with a flap
of skin resembling a hood on its head

cob·web /kób wèb/ *n* a spider's dusty web ■
cob·webs *npl* a sluggish mental state

co·ca /kókə/ (*pl* same) *n* **1** the dried leaves of
a South American bush. Use: stimulants,
cocaine, other alkaloids. **2** a bush whose
leaves yield coca

co·caine /kō káyn, kố kàyn/ *n* an addictive
drug processed from coca leaves

coc·cus /kókəss/ (*pl* -**ci** /kók sĩ, kó kĩ/) *n* a
rounded bacterium

coc·cyx /kóksiks/ (*pl* -**cy·ges** /-si jèez/ *or*
-**cy·xes**) *n* a small bone at the base of the
human spine —**coc·cyg·e·al** /kok síjjee əl/
adj

Co·cha·bam·ba /kòchə baàmbə/ capital of
Cochabamba Department, central Bolivia.
Pop. 560,284 (1997).

coch·i·neal /kòchə neèl, kóchə neèl/ *n* a red
dye and food coloring obtained from dried
insect bodies

Co·chise /kố cheèss, -cheèz/ (1815?-74) Chi-
ricahua Apache leader

coch·le·a /kóklee ə, kốklee ə/ (*pl* -**ae** /-èe, -ĩ/ *or*
-**as**) *n* a spiral structure in the inner ear
—**coch·le·ar** *adj*

cock *n* **1** an adult male chicken **2** any adult
male bird **3** the hammer of a gun **4** the
raised position of the hammer of gun **5** a
stopcock **6** the tilted position of a hat ■ *vt*
1 prepare a gun for firing **2** turn your ears
or eyes to listen or look **3** tilt something at
an angle

cock·ade /ko káyd/ *n* an ornamental ribbon
on a hat or livery

cock-a-doo·dle-doo /-doò/ *n* a rooster's call
—**cock-a-doo·dle-doo** *vi*

cock·a·ma·mie /kòkə máymee/, **cock·a·ma·
my** *adj* ridiculous (*infml*)

cock-and-bull sto·ry, **cock-and-bull** *n* an
absurd tale or excuse

cock·a·too /kòkə toò/ (*pl* -**toos**) *n* a parrot with
a prominent crest

ORIGIN Cockatoo came through Dutch from a
Malay word. Its actual form has been influenced by English *cock*.

cock·crow /kók krò/ *n* daybreak (*literary*)

cocked hat *n* a two- or three-cornered hat
worn in the 18C

cock·er·el /kókərəl/ *n* a young domestic
rooster

cock·er span·iel *n* a medium-sized spaniel
with long ears

cock·eyed /kók ìd/ *adj* **1** foolish (*infml*) **2** not
aligned

cock·fight /kók fìt/ *n* an illegal fight between
roosters —**cock·fight·ing** *n*

cock·le[1] /kók'l/ *n* **1** a mollusk with a heart-
shaped two-part shell **2** *also* **cock·le·shell**
the shell of a cockle

cock·le[2] /kók'l/ *n* a weed of the pink family

cock·ney /kóknee/ (*pl* -**neys**), **Cock·ney** *n*
1 somebody born in the East End of
London, England **2** the dialect of native
Londoners from the East End
—**cock·ney·ism** *n*

ORIGIN Cockney comes from old forms that
literally mean "cock's (rooster's) egg." This
was a small misshapen egg, in medieval times
popularly said to be laid by a rooster. The
term came to be used for a "pampered child,"
and then for a "town dweller," considered
less hardy than somebody from the country.
From around 1600 it referred specifically to
"a person born in the city of London, England."

cock·pit /kók pìt/ *n* **1** the part of an aircraft
where the pilot sits **2** a space for the driver
in a racecar **3** an enclosed area containing
the wheel or tiller of a small ship

cock·roach /kók ròch/ *n* a nocturnal oval-
bodied insect that is a household pest

ORIGIN Cockroach came in the early 17C from
Spanish *cucaracha*. A variety of early spellings reflect this, but by the 19C it had been
assimilated to the English forms *cock* and
roach.

cocks·comb /kóks kòm/ *n* **1** a fleshy crest on
the head of a rooster **2** a plant with a crest
of red flowers

cock·sure /kok shoòr, kók shoòr/ *adj* overconfidently certain —**cock·sure·ness** *n*

cock·tail /kók tàyl/ *n* **1** a drink consisting of a
mixture of other drinks, usually alcohol
and a soft drink **2** a light food served as an
appetizer (*usually in combination*) ○ *a shrimp
cocktail*

cock·tail lounge *n* a bar serving cocktails,
especially in a hotel or restaurant

cock·tail party *n* an early evening party

cock·y /kókee/ (-**i·er**, -**i·est**) *adj* arrogantly overconfident (*infml*) —**cock·i·ly** *adv*
—**cock·i·ness** *n*

co·coa /kókō/ *n* **1** a brown powder made from
ground roasted cocoa beans. Use: chocolate, cooking, hot drink. **2** a hot drink
made with cocoa powder

co·coa bean *n* a bean-shaped seed of the cacao tree

co·coa but·ter *n* a fatty substance obtained from cocoa beans. Use: chocolate, cosmetics, suntan oils.

co·co·nut /kốkə nùt/ (*pl same or* -**nuts**) *n* 1 a fruit with a hard fibrous shell, firm white flesh, and sweet juice 2 the edible white flesh of a coconut fruit 3 *also* **co·co·nut palm** a tropical palm tree that produces coconuts

co·co·nut oil *n* oil obtained from the flesh of the coconut. Use: in foods, cosmetics.

co·coon /kə koõn/ *n* 1 the silky cover for a caterpillar or other larva during its pupal stage 2 something that resembles a cocoon in the way that it provides protection or a sense of safety —**co·cooned** *adj*

Coc·teau /kok tố, kawk-/, **Jean** (1889–1963) French writer and movie director

cod (*pl same or* **cods**) *n* 1 a large ocean fish with three dorsal fins 2 cod as food

Cod, Cape peninsula in SE Massachusetts

COD, C.O.D. *abbr* cash on delivery

co·da /kốdə/ *n* 1 the final section of a musical piece 2 a section at the end of a text giving added information

cod·dle /kódd'l/ (-**dled**, -**dling**) *vt* 1 be overprotective of somebody 2 cook an egg gently in water

⌁ **code** *n* 1 a system of letters, numbers, or symbols into which ordinary language is converted for secret transmission 2 a system of letters or numbers that gives information, e.g., a postal area 3 a system of symbols, numbers, or signals that conveys information to a computer 4 a set of rules and regulations ○ *the penal code* 5 standards concerning acceptable behavior ○ *her moral code* ■ *vt* (**cod·ed**, **cod·ing**) put in code —**cod·er** *n*

co·deine /kố dèen/ *n* a derivative of morphine used as a painkiller

code name *n* a name used to disguise the identity of somebody or something —**code-name** *vt*

co·dex /kố dèks/ (*pl* -**di·ces** /-di seèz/) *n* a collection of old manuscript texts in book form

cod·fish /kód fìsh/ (*pl same or* -**fish·es**) *n* a cod

codg·er /kójjər/ *n* a man, especially a man of advanced years regarded as eccentric (*infml insult*)

cod·i·cil /kóddəssil/ *n* 1 an addition to a will that modifies it 2 an appendix to a text (*fml*)

cod·i·fy /kóddi fī/ (-**fied**, -**fies**) *vt* arrange into an organized system —**cod·i·fi·ca·tion** /kòddifi káysh'n/ *n*

cod-liv·er oil *n* a vitamin-rich oil from the liver of a cod. Use: food supplement.

Co·dy /kốdee/, **William Frederick, "Buffalo Bill"** (1846–1917) US scout and entertainer

co·ed /kố èd/, **co·ed** *n* a woman at a college for both men and women (*dated*) ■ *adj* educating men and women together (*infml*)

co·ed·u·ca·tion /kố ejə káysh'n/ *n* the education of both sexes together —**co·ed·u·ca·tion·al** *adj*

co·ef·fi·cient /kố i físh'nt/ *n* 1 the numerical part of an algebraic term 2 a constant that is a measure of a property of a substance

co·erce /kố úrss/ (-**erced**, -**erc·ing**) *vt* force to do something —**co·erc·i·ble** *adj* —**co·er·cion** *n*

co·er·cive /kố úrssiv/ *adj* using force —**co·er·cive·ly** *adv*

Coeur d'A·lene /kàwrd'l áyn/ city in NE Idaho. Pop. 32,565 (1998).

co·e·val /kố eèv'l/ *adj* equal in age or duration (*fml*)

co·ex·ist /kố ig zíst/ *vi* 1 exist at the same time and in the same place 2 live together peacefully —**co·ex·is·tence** *n* —**co·ex·is·tent** *adj*

co·ex·ten·sive /kố ik sténsiv/ *adj* with the same range or limits —**co·ex·ten·sive·ly** *adv*

cof·fee /káwfee, kóffee/ *n* 1 a drink made from ground or processed beans 2 beans for making coffee 3 the bush that produces coffee beans 4 a pale brown color —**cof·fee** *adj*

cof·fee bean *n* a bean-shaped seed of the coffee bush

cof·fee-cake /káwfee kàyk, kóffee-/ *n* a cake eaten with coffee

cof·fee-house /káwfee hòwss, kóffee-/ (*pl* -**hous·es** /-hòwzəz/) *n* a café

cof·fee klatch /-klàch/, **cof·fee klatsch** *n* an informal social gathering

cof·fee-pot /káwfee pòt, kóffee-/ *n* a pot for serving coffee

cof·fee shop *n* an informal restaurant or café

cof·fee ta·ble *n* a low living-room table

cof·fee-ta·ble book *n* a large illustrated book for display or casual perusal

cof·fer /kóffər/ *n* a strongbox ■ **cof·fers** *npl* funds

cof·fin /kóffin/ *n* a box in which a corpse is buried or cremated

cog *n* 1 a tooth on a cogwheel 2 a cogwheel —**cogged** *adj*

co·gent /kốjənt/ *adj* rational and convincing —**co·gen·cy** *n* —**co·gent·ly** *adv* ◊ See note at **valid**

cog·i·tate /kójji tàyt/ (-**tat·ed**, -**tat·ing**) *vti* think deeply and carefully about something (*fml*) —**cog·i·ta·tion** /kòjji táysh'n/ *n* —**cog·i·ta·tive** *adj*

co·gnac /kốn yàk/ *n* high-quality French brandy

cog·nate /kóg nàyt/ *adj* related in some way (*fml*)

~~cognative~~ incorrect spelling of **cognitive**

cog·ni·tion /kog nísh'n/ n 1 acquisition of knowledge through reasoning or perception 2 knowledge acquired via reasoning or perception

cog·ni·tive /kógnitiv/ adj 1 of the acquisition of knowledge by cognition 2 of thought processes —**cog·ni·tive·ly** adv

cog·ni·zance /kógnizənss/ n (fml) 1 a state or degree of awareness 2 the extent of somebody's knowledge

cog·ni·zant /kógnizənt/ adj aware of something (fml) ◊ See note at **aware**

cog·no·men /kog nṓmən/ (pl **-no·mens** or **-nom·i·na** /-nómmənə/) n 1 a nickname (fml) 2 a family name given as the third name to a citizen of ancient Rome —**cog·nom·i·nal** /kog nómmin'l/ adj

cog·no·scen·ti /kógnə shéntee, kònnyə-/ (sing **-te** /-tay/) npl connoisseurs or experts

cog·wheel /kóg weèl, -hweèl/ n a toothed wheel that fits into another to transmit motion

co·hab·it /kō hábbit/ vi 1 live together in a relationship 2 coexist —**co·hab·i·ta·tion** /kō hàbbi táysh'n/ n

Co·han /kṓ hàn/, **George M.** (1878–1942) US actor, songwriter, and playwright

Co·hen /kṓ ən/, **Stanley** (b. 1935) US biochemist. He jointly developed the recombinant DNA techniques that became the basis of genetic engineering.

co·here /kō heér/ (**-hered, -her·ing**) vi (fml) 1 stick together 2 be logically consistent

co·her·ent /kō heérənt/ adj 1 logically or aesthetically consistent 2 able to speak clearly and logically —**co·her·ence** n —**co·her·ent·ly** adv

co·he·sion /kō heézh'n/ n the state of joining or working together —**co·he·sive** /kō heéssiv/ adj —**co·he·sive·ly** adv

co·hort /kṓ hàwrt/ n 1 a group of people 2 a supporter or associate (disapproving) 3 a group of people with statistical similarities 4 in ancient Rome, a unit of the army that was one tenth of a legion 5 a group of soldiers

ORIGIN Cohort derives from a Latin word that literally means "enclosed space." It was then used of "people within an enclosed space," and specifically "an infantry unit of the Roman army." After its adoption into English, it began to be used generally for "a group of people" in the early 18C, and for an "associate" in the United States in the mid-20C.

Coi·ba Is·land /ko eébə-/ island in the Pacific Ocean off the coast of Panama, site of a national park and penal colony. Pop. 850.

coif·fure /kwaa fyoòr/ n a person's hairstyle, especially a woman's (fml) —**coif·fure** vt —**coif·fured** adj

coil n 1 a series of connected loops 2 a single loop in a series 3 a spiral 4 a wire spiral through which an electric current is passed, e.g., to create magnetism ■ v 1 vti curl or wind into loops 2 vi curve or bend

coin n 1 a piece of metal money 2 metal money in general ■ vt 1 mint coins 2 invent a new word or phrase

coin·age /kóynij/ n a new word or phrase

co·in·cide /kō in síd/ (**-cid·ed, -cid·ing**) vi 1 happen at the same time 2 be in the same position or form

co·in·ci·dence /kō ínsidənss/ n 1 a chance happening 2 the fact of happening by chance or at the same time —**co·in·ci·den·tal** /kō insi dént'l/ adj —**co·in·ci·den·tal·ly** adv

co·i·tus /kṓ itəss/ n sexual intercourse (fml or technical) —**co·i·tal** adj

coke[1] n a solid carbon residue produced from coal. Use: fuel.

coke[2] n cocaine (slang)

Coke tdmk a trademark for a cola-flavored soft drink

col n 1 a low point in a mountain ridge 2 a region of low atmospheric pressure

ǂCOL /kol/ abbr computer-oriented language

col. abbr color

Col., Col abbr 1 Colonel 2 Colorado

co·la[1] /kṓlə/ n 1 a sweet soda flavored with cola nuts 2 a tropical evergreen tree that produces cola nuts

co·la[2] plural of **colon**[2]

~~colaborate~~ incorrect spelling of **collaborate**

col·an·der /kúlləndər, kóllən-/ n a strainer for draining water from food

co·la nut n a seed of the cola tree. Use: carbonated drinks, medicines.

~~colateral~~ incorrect spelling of **collateral**

Col·bert /kawl báir/, **Jean-Baptiste** (1619–83) French politician

cold adj 1 at a low temperature 2 making a place seem cooler 3 cooked hot then cooled 4 taciturn and emotionless 5 unfriendly and uncaring 6 no longer recent or fresh and therefore hard to follow o a cold trail ■ n 1 a viral infection of the nose and throat 2 cold weather or conditions ■ adv 1 without any preparation o sang the part cold 2 completely o turned the proposal down cold —**cold·ly** adv —**cold·ness** n ◊ **blow hot and cold** be alternately enthusiastic and indifferent ◊ **out cold** unconscious or in a deep sleep (infml)

cold-blood·ed /-blúddəd/ adj 1 with a body temperature that varies according to the temperature of the surroundings 2 lacking pity or friendliness —**cold-blood·ed·ly** adv —**cold-blood·ed·ness** n

ǂcold-boot /kṓld boòt/ vt restart a computer by turning it off and on again

cold call n a telephone call or visit made to an unknown prospective customer —**cold-call** vt

cold com·fort *n* something that does not help

cold cream *n* a thick cream used for cleansing and softening the skin on the face

cold cuts *npl* slices of cold cooked meat

cold duck *n* sparkling burgundy mixed with champagne

cold feet *npl* a loss of nerve

cold frame *n* a glass structure for protecting young plants

cold-heart·ed /-háartəd/ *adj* lacking sympathy —**cold-heart·ed·ly** *adv* —**cold-heart·ed·ness** *n*

cold shoul·der *n* an instance of unfriendliness —**cold-shoul·der** /kőld shőldər/ *vt*

cold snap *n* a sudden short period of cold weather

cold sore *n* a blister near the lips caused by a virus

cold stor·age *n* chilled conditions in which food is preserved

cold sweat *n* a nervous or frightened state

cold turk·ey *n* 1 the abrupt withdrawal of addictive drugs with no other treatment to ease the symptoms 2 withdrawal symptoms

cold war *n* 1 a state of enmity between nations without open hostilities 2 **Cold War** the hostile but nonviolent Communist-Western relations that existed between 1946 and 1989

Cole, Thomas (1801–48) British-born US artist

Col·e·ridge /kőlərij/, **Samuel Taylor** (1772–1834) British poet

cole·slaw /kől sław/ *n* a cabbage and carrot salad in a mayonnaise dressing

AKG London

Colette

Co·lette /ko lét, kaw lét/ (1873–1954) French novelist

col·ic /kóllik/ *n* 1 a pain in the abdomen, often caused by inflammation or an obstruction 2 crying in babies caused by intestinal discomfort —**col·ic** *adj*

co·li·tis /kə lítiss/ *n* inflammation of the colon —**co·lit·ic** /kə líttik/ *adj*

col·lab·o·rate /kə lábbə ràyt/ (-rat·ed, -rat·ing) *vi* 1 work with another person or group 2 betray others by working with an enemy —**col·lab·o·ra·tion** /kə làbbə ráysh'n/ *n* —**col·lab·o·ra·tive** /-ràytiv, -rətiv/ *adj* —**col·lab·o·ra·tor** *n*

col·lage /kə laázh/ *n* 1 a picture made by sticking pieces of things on a surface 2 the art of making collages —**col·lage** *vti*

col·la·gen /kóllajən/ *n* a protein found in skin and other connective tissue —**col·lag·e·nous** /kə lájjənəss/ *adj*

col·lapse /kə láps/ *v* (-lapsed, -laps·ing) 1 *vi* fall down as a result of structural weakness or a lack of support 2 *vi* fail abruptly 3 *vi* fall, sit, or lie down suddenly 4 *vti* fold for easy storage ■ *n* 1 an abrupt failure or end 2 an act of falling down suddenly 3 a sudden decrease in value —**col·laps·i·ble** *adj*

col·lar /kóllər/ *n* 1 the part of a garment around the neck 2 a band around the neck of an animal to identify it or tie it to a leash 3 a band of color around a mammal's or bird's neck 4 a ring-shaped device or part 5 a police arrest (*slang*) —**col·lared** *adj* ◇ **hot under the collar** angry, irritated, or agitated (*infml*)

col·lar·bone /kóllər bôn/ *n* each of the two curved bones that connect the human breastbone to the shoulder

col·lard /kóllərd/ *n* a kale ■ **col·lards, col·lard greens** *npl* the cooked leaves of a variety of kale

col·late /kó làyt, kə láyt/ (-lat·ed, -lat·ing) *vt* 1 put pages in the correct order 2 bring pieces of information together and compare them —**col·la·tor** *n*

col·lat·er·al /kə láttərəl/ *n* property or goods used as security against a loan ■ *adj* 1 parallel or corresponding 2 descended from the same ancestor but through a different line 3 additional to and in support of something 4 accompanying but secondary 5 obtained by giving property or goods as security

col·lat·er·al dam·age *n* unintended damage to civilian life or property during a military operation

col·la·tion /kə láysh'n, kō-/ *n* 1 the collating of something 2 a light meal

col·league /kó lèeg/ *n* a person somebody works with —**col·league·ship** *n*

col·lect /kə lékt/ *v* 1 *vt* gather and bring things together 2 *vt* obtain and keep objects of the same type 3 *vt* fetch people or things and take them somewhere 4 *vt* take the money or a prize you are entitled to 5 *vti* gather and accumulate in a place 6 *vi* gradually assemble in a place 7 *vt* get control of yourself ■ *adv* charged by the telephone caller to the person receiving the call ■ *adj* describes a telephone call payable by the person receiving it

SYNONYMS collect, accumulate, gather, amass, assemble, stockpile, hoard CORE MEANING: bring dispersed things together

col·lect·ed /kə léktəd/ *adj* 1 calm and composed 2 brought together as a whole

col·lect·i·ble /kə léktəb'l/, **col·lect·a·ble** *n* an object valued by collectors ■ *adj* of interest to collectors

col·lec·tion /kə léksh'n/ *n* 1 a group of people or things 2 the objects owned by a particular collector or held in a museum 3 the process or an act of collecting something

col·lec·tive /kə léktiv/ *adj* 1 shared by or applying to everyone in a group 2 collected to form a whole 3 run by workers, sometimes under state supervision ■ *n* a collective enterprise run by workers —**col·lec·tive·ly** *adv* —**col·lec·tive·ness** *n*

col·lec·tive bar·gain·ing *n* negotiations between a union and management

col·lec·tive farm *n* a state-supervised labor-run farm

col·lec·tive noun *n* a noun that refers to a group of people or things as a unit

col·lec·tiv·ism /kə léktə vìzzəm/ *n* the ownership and management of factories and farms by the people of a nation —**col·lec·tiv·ist** *n*

col·lec·tiv·ize /kə léktə vìz/ (-ized, -iz·ing) *vt* organize an enterprise on collective principles —**col·lec·tiv·i·za·tion** /kə lèktəvi záysh'n/ *n*

col·lec·tor /kə léktər/ *n* 1 somebody who collects objects as a hobby 2 somebody whose job is collecting things, e.g., taxes 3 a container where things collect

col·lec·tor's i·tem *n* an object desired by collectors

col·leen /kə leén, kólleen/ *n* an Irish girl

col·lege /kóllij/ *n* 1 an institution of higher learning that awards bachelor's and sometimes master's degrees 2 a school or division of a university where a particular subject is taught 3 the faculty and students of a college 4 a group of people of the same profession

col·lege cred·it *n* credit for study that can be used toward a college degree

col·le·gi·al /kə leéjee əl, -leéjəl/ *adj* 1 with power shared equally between colleagues 2 of a college or university

col·le·giate /kə leéjət, kə leéjee ət/ *adj* 1 of a college 2 describes a university consisting of separate colleges

~~collegue~~ incorrect spelling of **colleague**

col·lide /kə lĩd/ (-lid·ed, -lid·ing) *vi* 1 crash into somebody or something 2 come into conflict with somebody

col·lie /kóllee/ *n* a dog bred to herd sheep

~~colliflour, colliflower~~ incorrect spelling of **cauliflower**

Col·lins /kóllinz/, **Michael** (1890–1922) Irish politician

col·li·sion /kə lízh'n/ *n* 1 a crash between two moving vehicles, objects, or people 2 a conflict

col·lo·cate /kóllə kàyt/ *v* (-cat·ed, -cat·ing) 1 *vi* occur frequently with another word 2 *vt* put something next to something else *(fml)* ■ *n* a word that frequently occurs with another —**col·lo·ca·tion** /kòllə káysh'n/ *n* —**col·lo·ca·tion·al** *adj*

col·loid /kó lòyd/ *n* a suspension of small particles dispersed in another substance —**col·loid** *adj* —**col·loid·al** /kə lóyd'l, ko-/ *adj*

~~colloquail~~ incorrect spelling of **colloquial**

col·lo·qui·al /kə lókwee əl/ *adj* describes language used in informal speech, rather than in writing —**col·lo·qui·al·ly** *adv*

col·lo·qui·al·ism /kə lókwee ə lìzzəm/ *n* an informal word or phrase

col·lo·qui·um /kə lókwee əm/ (*pl* -ums *or* -a /-ə/) *n* 1 an academic seminar 2 a meeting to discuss something

col·lo·quy /kólləkwee/ (*pl* -quies) *n* 1 a discussion *(fml)* 2 a written dialogue

~~collosal~~ incorrect spelling of **colossal**

col·lude /kə loód/ (-lud·ed, -lud·ing) *vi* work secretly with somebody to do something wrong or illegal

col·lu·sion /kə loózh'n/ *n* secret cooperation between people who do something wrong or illegal —**col·lu·sive** *adj*

Colo. *abbr* Colorado

⌥ **co·lo·ca·tion** /kó lō káysh'n/ *n* the sharing of the facilities of a hosting center with other Internet clients

co·logne /kə lṓn/ *n* a scented liquid that is lighter than perfume

Co·logne /kə lṓn/ port in W Germany. Pop. 963,817 (1997).

Co·lom·bi·a /kə lúmbee ə/ country in NW South America. Cap. Bogotá. Pop. 40,349,388 (2001). —**Co·lom·bi·an** *n, adj*

Co·lom·bo /kə lúmbō/ commercial capital, largest city, and port of Sri Lanka. Pop. 615,000 (1995).

co·lon[1] /kṓlən/ *n* 1 the punctuation mark (:) used to divide distinct but related elements of a sentence 2 a mark (:) used in phonetics after a vowel to show that it is long ◊ See note at **semicolon**

> **USAGE** The **colon** is used to divide a sentence on what the second part explains or elaborates on what has gone before: *They have put forward a different theory: the phenomenon may be caused by global warming.* It is also used to introduce a list or a quotation: *You will need the following equipment: waterproof clothing, strong walking boots, and a map. Martin Luther King wrote in Chaos or Community (1967): "A riot is at bottom the language of the unheard."*

co·lon[2] /kṓlən/ (*pl* -lons *or* -la /-lə/) *n* the part of the large intestine between the cecum and the rectum

co·lón /kə lṓn/ (*pl* -lóns *or* -lo·nes /-ló nàyss/) *n* the main unit of currency in Costa Rica and El Salvador

colo·nel /kúrn'l/, **Colo·nel** *n* a military rank in the US Army, Marine Corps, or Air Force above lieutenant colonel —**colo·nel·cy** *n* —**colo·nel·ship** *n*

SPELLCHECK Do not confuse the spelling of **colonel** and **kernel** ("the edible part of a nut"), which sound similar.

colo·ni·a /kòlla néè ə/ *n* a desert slum near the US-Mexican border

co·lo·ni·al /kə lónee əl/ *adj* 1 of a colony 2 *also* **Co·lo·ni·al** of the British Empire or the British colonies in North America before independence 3 in the style of buildings of the North American colonies 4 living in colonies ■ *n* 1 somebody who lives in a colony 2 a colonial-style house

co·lo·ni·al·ism /kə lónee ə lìzzəm/ *n* the policy of ruling nations as colonies —**co·lo·ni·al·ist** *n* —**co·lo·ni·al·is·tic** /kə lónee ə lístik/ *adj*

co·lon·ic /kō lónnik, kə-/ *adj* of the colon

co·lon·ic ir·ri·ga·tion, co·lon·ic hy·dro·ther·a·py *n* the cleansing of the colon by injecting water into the anus

col·o·nist /kóllənist/ *n* 1 somebody living in a new colony 2 *also* **Col·o·nist** an early European settler in North America

col·o·nize /kóllə nìz/ (-nized, -niz·ing) *vti* 1 establish a colony in another country or place 2 establish an organism in a new ecosystem, or become established as part of a new ecosystem —**col·o·ni·za·tion** /kòlləni záysh'n/ *n*

col·on·nade /kóllə náyd, kóllə nàyd/ *n* a row of columns supporting a roof or arches

col·o·ny /kóllənee/ (*pl* -nies) *n* 1 a country or region ruled by another distant power 2 one of the early British settlements in North America that subsequently formed the United States (*often pl*) 3 a group of organisms living together

col·o·phon /kóllə fòn/ *n* 1 a publisher's emblem on a book 2 the publication details given at the end of a book

col·or /kúllər/ *n* 1 the property of objects that depends on reflected light and is perceived as red, blue, green, or other shades 2 a pigment or dye 3 a hue other than black or white ◦ *printed in color* 4 the shade of somebody's skin 5 a healthy look to the skin 6 brightness and variety in hues 7 a quality that adds interest ◦ *The story lacks color.* ■ **col·ors** *npl* the flag of a national, state, or military unit ■ *v* 1 *vt* change the color of or add color to 2 *vi* take on or change hue 3 *vi* blush 4 *vt* skew an opinion or judgment ◊ **with flying colors** to an excellent standard ◊ See note at **African American**

Col·o·ra·do /kòllə ráddō, -ráadō/ 1 state in the W United States. Cap. Denver. Pop. 4,301,261 (2000). 2 major North American river, rising in N Colorado and flowing southwest through the Grand Canyon. Length 1,450 mi./2,330 km. 3 river in Texas. Length 862 mi./1,390 km.

Col·o·ra·do Des·ert desert area of SE California

Col·o·ra·do Springs city in central Colorado. Pop. 344,987 (1998).

col·or·ant /kúllərənt/ *n* a coloring agent such as a dye

col·or·a·tion /kùllə ráysh'n/ *n* the pattern of color on an object or an organism

col·or·a·tu·ra /kùllərə tóorə, kòllər-/ *n* a demanding and florid passage or piece of vocal music

col·or bar *n* = **color line**

col·or·blind /kúllər blīnd/ *adj* 1 unable to distinguish between some colors 2 not discriminating on the grounds of ethnic group or skin color —**col·or·blind·ness** *n*

col·or·code *vt* identify or distinguish between using colors

col·ored /kúllərd/ *adj* 1 having a particular color or colors (*often in combination*) 2 an offensive term for a member of an ethnic group whose members are dark-skinned (*dated*)

col·or·fast /kúllər fàst/ *adj* containing a dye that will not wash out

col·or·ful /kúllərf'l/ *adj* 1 brightly colored ◦ *colorful costumes* 2 interesting and exciting ◦ *a colorful period of history* —**col·or·ful·ly** *adv* —**col·or·ful·ness** *n*

col·or·ing /kúlləring/ *n* 1 a substance that gives a hue to something 2 appearance with regard to color 3 the characteristic colors of a bird or animal

col·or·ize /kúllə rìz/ (-ized, -iz·ing) *vt* add color to a black-and-white movie

col·or·less /kúllərləss/ *adj* 1 lacking color 2 characterless ◦ *a colorless personality* —**col·or·less·ly** *adv* —**col·or·less·ness** *n*

col·or line, col·or bar *n* a barrier between ethnic groups

co·los·sal /kə lóss'l/ *adj* enormous in size or extent ◦ *a colossal high-rise office building* —**co·los·sal·ly** *adv*

Co·los·sians /kə lósh'nz/ *n* a book of the Bible, originally a letter from St. Paul to the church in the city of Colossae, in Phrygia, Asia Minor (+ *sing verb*)

co·los·sus /kə lóssəss/ (*pl* -si /-ī/) *n* 1 a huge statue 2 an enormously large or powerful person or thing

co·los·to·my /kə lóstəmee/ (*pl* -mies) *n* an operation to create an artificial anus in the abdomen

col·our *n, vti* UK = **color**

colt *n* a young male horse

colt·ish /kóltish/ *adj* lively and energetic —**colt·ish·ly** *adv* —**colt·ish·ness** *n*

Col·trane /kól tràyn/, **John** (1926–67) US jazz saxophonist and composer

Co·lum·bi·a /kə lúmbee ə/ n **1** river that flows through SW Canada and the NW United States into the Pacific Ocean. Length 1,240 mi./2,000 km. **2** city in central Missouri. Pop. 78,915 (1998). **3** capital of South Carolina. Pop. 110,840 (1998).

col·um·bine /kólləm bìn/ (pl **-bines** or same) n a plant with five-petaled flowers with long spurs

Co·lum·bus /kə lúmbəss/ **1** capital and largest city of Ohio. Pop. 670,234 (1998). **2** city in W Georgia. Pop. 182,219 (1998).

Co·lum·bus, Christopher (1451–1506) Italian explorer

Co·lum·bus Day n a US holiday. Date: 2nd Monday in October.

col·umn /kólləm/ n **1** a long cylindrical upright support **2** something with a long cylindrical upright shape o a column of smoke **3** a regularly appearing article in a newspaper or magazine **4** a vertical arrangement of numbers **5** a vertical section of print on a page **6** a line of people or things —**col·um·nar** /kə lúmnər/ adj

col·um·nist /kólləmnist/ n somebody who writes a newspaper or magazine column

⚡com abbr commercial organization (in Internet addresses)

⚡COM n the conversion of computer output to microfilm. Full form **computer output microfilm**

Com. abbr **1** Commander **2** Commodore

co·ma[1] /kómə/ n a long period of unconsciousness

co·ma[2] /kómə/ (pl **-mae** /-mee/) n a cloud around the head of a comet

Co·man·che /kə mánchee/ (pl same or **-ches**) n **1** a member of a Native North American people who now live mainly in Oklahoma **2** the language of the Comanche people —**Co·man·che** adj

~~comand~~ incorrect spelling of **command**

co·ma·tose /kómə tòss/ adj in a coma

comb /kōm/ n **1** a toothed instrument for straightening out or arranging the hair **2** a tool for cleaning wool **3** a rooster's fleshy crest **4** a honeycomb ■ vt **1** arrange the hair or clean wool with a comb **2** search a place thoroughly

com·bat n /kóm bàt/ **1** the process of fighting o unarmed combat **2** a struggle for or against something, or between two forces o combat between good and evil ■ vt /kəm bát, kóm bàt/ (-**bat·ed** or **-bat·ted**, **-bat·ing** or **-bat·ting**) **1** try to destroy or control something dangerous or undesirable o measures to combat pollution **2** resist somebody or something

com·bat·ant /kəm bátt'nt/ n somebody taking part in a war, fight, struggle, or argument

com·bat fa·tigue n a psychological disorder resulting from the stress of battle

com·bat·ive /kəm báttiv/ adj eager to fight or argue —**com·bat·ive·ness** n

com·bi·na·tion /kòmbi náysh'n/ n **1** a mixture or combined set **2** the process or result of combining **3** a set of numbers that open a lock ◊ See note at **mixture**

com·bine vti /kəm bín/ (-**bined**, -**bin·ing**) **1** join or mix together **2** unite chemically to form a single substance ■ n /kóm' bìn/ **1** an association of business or political organizations **2** also **com·bine har·vest·er** a machine that reaps and threshes grain

com·bo /kómbō/ (pl **-bos**) n a jazz group

com·bust /kəm búst/ vti burn with a flame

com·bus·ti·ble /kəm bústəb'l/ adj able or likely to catch fire and burn —**com·bus·ti·bil·i·ty** /kəm bùstə bíllətee/ n —**com·bus·ti·bly** adv

com·bus·tion /kəm búschən/ n **1** the burning of fuel in an engine **2** a chemical reaction producing heat and light —**com·bus·tive** adj

come /kum/ vi (**came** /kaym/, **come**) **1** originate o comes from China **2** happen or exist **3** result o comes from eating too much chocolate **4** approach or reach a place **5** occur in the mind o The idea came to me in the shower. **6** reach a state o came to pieces in my hands **7** amount or add up to o comes to $14.50 ■ prep by a particular time in the future o It should be finished come Wednesday. ◊ **come what may** whatever happens ◊ **have it coming (to you)** deserve punishment or retribution

☐ **come about** vi happen

☐ **come across** v **1** vt find **2** vi be communicated

☐ **come around** vi **1** change your opinion **2** regain consciousness

☐ **come before** vt be judged or considered by

☐ **come by** vt obtain

☐ **come down** vi **1** decrease, e.g., in cost or altitude **2** reach a decision o came down on the side of common sense **3** be handed down

☐ **come in** vi prove to have a particular quality o come in handy

☐ **come in for** vt be subjected to

☐ **come into** vt inherit money

☐ **come of** vt result from o This situation comes of greed.

☐ **come off** vi (infml) **1** happen as planned **2** succeed

☐ **come on** vi **1** automatically start to operate **2** hurry up (usually as a command) **3** begin at a particular time (refers to radio or television programs)

☐ **come out** vi **1** be revealed **2** be published **3** reveal something secret about yourself, especially your sexual preferences **4** become visible in the sky o if the sun comes out

☐ **come out with** vt say

☐ **come through** v **1** vi perform well when most needed (infml) **2** vti survive something unpleasant or dangerous

☐ **come to** vi regain consciousness

□ **come up** vi 1 be mentioned 2 occur unexpectedly

□ **come upon** vt find accidentally

□ **come up to** vt match or equal

□ **come up with** vt produce or devise

come·back /kúm bàk/ n 1 a return to success, fame, or popularity 2 a sharp reply

co·me·di·an /kə meédee ən/ n an entertainer who tells jokes or performs comic acts

co·me·di·enne /kə meèdee én/ n 1 a female comedian 2 a comic actress

come·down /kúm dòwn/ n a decline in status (infml)

com·e·dy /kómmədee/ (pl -dies) n 1 a funny play, movie, or book 2 comedies as a genre 3 humorous entertainment —**co·me·dic** /kə meédik/ adj

~~comeing~~ incorrect spelling of **coming**

come·ly /kúmmlee/ (-li·er, -li·est) adj good-looking (literary) —**come·li·ness** n

ORIGIN **Comely** is probably a shortening of obsolete *becomely* "fitting," formed from *become* in the sense surviving in *becoming*.

come-on n 1 an enticement or inducement (infml) 2 an indication of sexual interest

com·er /kúmmər/ n a potential success (infml)

co·mes·ti·ble /kə méstəb'l/ (fml) n an item of food ■ adj edible

com·et /kómmət/ n an astronomical object composed of a mass of ice and dust with a long luminous tail

ORIGIN **Comet** comes from a Greek word that literally means "long-haired." The tail of a comet was seen as hair streaming in the wind. The word arrived in English in the 12C, via Latin and French.

come-up·pance /kum úppənss/ n something unpleasant regarded as fair punishment (infml) ○ He got his comeuppance in the end.

~~comfortable~~ incorrect spelling of **comfortable**

com·fort /kúmfərt/ n 1 conditions in which somebody feels physically relaxed ○ in the comfort of your own home 2 a source of comfort ○ It's a comfort to know that she's safe. 3 relief from pain or anxiety ■ vt bring comfort to somebody in pain or distress

com·fort·a·ble /kúmftəb'l/, -fərtəb'l/ adj 1 feeling comfort or ease 2 providing comfort 3 adequate or large ○ won by a comfortable majority —**com·for·ta·bly** adv

com·fort·er /kúmfərtər/ n 1 a quilt 2 somebody who gives comfort

com·frey /kúmfree/ n a plant with hairy leaves and stems. Use: in herbal medicine.

com·fy /kúmfee/ (-fi·er, -fi·est) adj comfortable (infml)

com·ic /kómmik/ adj 1 funny 2 of comedy ○ a great comic routine ■ n a comedian ○ worked as a nightclub comic ■ **com·ics** npl the comic strip section of a newspaper

com·i·cal /kómmik'l/ adj causing smiles or laughter —**com·i·cal·ly** adv

comic book n a magazine of cartoons

comic strip n a series of cartoons telling a story or joke

com·ing /kúmming/ adj 1 happening or starting soon 2 likely to be successful ○ She's the coming power in this company. ■ n the arrival of a person or event

coming of age n the reaching of the official age of adulthood

com·ings and go·ings npl busy activity involving frequent arrivals and departures

~~comission~~ incorrect spelling of **commission**

~~comitee~~ incorrect spelling of **committee**

com·ma /kómmə/ n a punctuation mark (,) that represents a pause or separates items in a list

⚡ **com·mand** /kə mánd/ n 1 an order to do something ○ obey their every command 2 control or authority ○ take command ○ in command 3 a thorough knowledge of something ○ a command of French 4 an operating instruction to a computer ■ v 1 vt give a command to 2 vti have authority or control over 3 vt deserve or be entitled to ○ command respect 4 vt be in a position that has a wide view over ○ The balcony commands a view of the bay.

com·man·dant /kòmmən dánt, -daánt/ n an officer in charge of a military establishment

com·mand e·con·o·my n a government-controlled economy

com·man·deer /kòmmən deér/ vt 1 seize for official or military purposes 2 take and use, often by force

com·man·der /kə mándər/ n 1 somebody who commands, especially a military officer 2 an officer in the US, Royal Canadian, British Royal navy or the US Coast Guard of a rank above lieutenant commander

com·man·der in chief (pl com·mand·ers in chief) n a supreme commander

com·mand·ing /kə mánding/ adj 1 impressive or authoritative ○ a commanding presence 2 showing clear superiority ○ a commanding lead —**com·mand·ing·ly** adv

com·mand·ing of·fi·cer n an officer in command

⚡ **com·mand key** n a key that gives an instruction to a computer

com·mand·ment /kə mándmənt/ n a divine command

com·mand mod·ule n the part of a spacecraft where the crew live and operate the controls

com·man·do /kə mándō/ (pl -dos or -does) n a soldier specially trained for dangerous raids

com·mem·o·rate /kə mémmə ràyt/ (-rat·ed, -rat·ing) vt 1 honor the memory of in a ceremony 2 be a memorial to —**com-**

mem·o·ra·tion /kə mèmmə ráysh'n/ n —**com·mem·o·ra·tive** /-rətiv, -ràytiv/ adj, n

com·mence /kə méns/ (-menced, -menc·ing) vti begin

com·mence·ment /kə ménsmənt/ n 1 the beginning of something (fml) ○ the commencement of open hostilities 2 a graduation ceremony

com·mend /kə ménd/ vt 1 praise formally or officially ○ was commended for bravery 2 cause to be accepted ○ The plan has little to commend it. —**com·mend·a·ble** adj —**com·mend·a·bly** adv —**com·mend·a·tion** /kómmen dáysh'n/ n

com·men·su·rate /kə ménsərət, -mènshərət/ adj 1 equal in size 2 proportionate ○ rewards commensurate with the efforts made —**com·men·su·rate·ly** adv —**com·men·su·ra·tion** /kə mènsə ráysh'n, -mènshə-/ n

com·ment /kó mènt/ n 1 a remark or observation 2 an explanatory note ■ vti make a comment about somebody or something

com·men·tar·y /kómmən tèrree/ (pl -ies) n a series of explanatory notes or an explanatory essay

com·men·ta·tor /kómmən tàyter/ n a reporter who analyzes events —**com·men·tate** vi

com·merce /kómmərs/ n trade in goods and services

com·mer·cial /kə múrsh'l/ adj 1 of or for commerce 2 done primarily for profit ■ n a radio or television advertisement —**com·mer·cial·ly** adv

com·mer·cial bank n a bank dealing with businesses

com·mer·cial break n an interruption of a program for commercials

com·mer·cial·ism /kə múrsh'l ìzzəm/ n 1 the principles and methods of commerce 2 excessive emphasis on profit —**com·mer·cial·ist** n —**com·mer·cial·is·tic** /kə mùrsh'l ístik/ adj

com·mer·cial·ize /kə múrsh'l ìz/ (-ized, -iz·ing) vt 1 apply commercial principles or methods to 2 exploit for profit —**com·mer·cial·i·za·tion** /kə mùrsh'li záysh'n/ n

com·min·gle /kə míng g'l/ (-gled, -gling) vti mix (literary)

com·mis·er·ate /kə mízzə ràyt/ (-at·ed, -at·ing) vi express sympathy

com·mis·er·a·tion /kə mìzzə ráysh'n/ n sympathy ■ **com·mis·er·a·tions** npl expressions of sympathy

com·mis·sar·i·at /kòmmi sáiree ət/ n 1 an army supply department 2 a government department in the former Soviet Union before 1946

com·mis·sar·y /kómmi sèrree/ (pl -ies) n 1 a supermarket on a military base 2 a restaurant or cafeteria in a movie or television studio

com·mis·sion /kə mísh'n/ n 1 a fee paid to an agent 2 a task, especially an order to produce a piece of work 3 a government agency 4 a group with a specific task 5 an appointment as a military officer 6 the authority to act as an agent 7 an act of doing or perpetrating ○ the commission of a crime ■ vt 1 assign a task to somebody 2 order something to be produced by somebody 3 make somebody a military officer ◇ **on commission** receiving a percentage of the value of sales made ◇ **out of commission** not in operational use or working order

com·mis·sioned of·fi·cer n a military officer appointed by commission

com·mis·sion·er /kə mísh'nər/ n 1 somebody belonging to or working for a commission 2 a government representative in an administrative area 3 a department head of a public service in a town or city 4 the administrative head of a professional sport —**com·mis·sion·er·ship** n

com·mit /kə mít/ (-mit·ted, -mit·ting) v 1 vi promise devotion or dedication 2 vt promise or devote resources, time, or money 3 vt do something wrong or illegal 4 vt entrust something for protection 5 vt consign or record something ○ committed the numbers to memory 6 vt confine somebody to an institution —**com·mit·ta·ble** adj

~~committee~~ incorrect spelling of **committee**

com·mit·ment /kə mítmənt/ n 1 a responsibility or obligation ○ family commitments 2 dedication to a cause, person, or relationship 3 a previously planned engagement

com·mit·tee /kə míttee/ n a group appointed to perform a function on behalf of a larger group

~~committment~~ incorrect spelling of **commitment**

com·mode /kə mṓd/ n 1 a toilet 2 a decorated cabinet

com·mo·di·ous /kə mṓdee əss/ adj roomy

com·mod·i·ty /kə móddətee/ (pl -ties) n 1 an item bought and sold 2 a useful thing

com·mo·dore /kómmə dàwr/ n a US naval officer of a rank above captain

com·mon /kómmən/ adj 1 shared ○ a common goal 2 of or for all ○ for the common good 3 often occurring or seen 4 used or done by most people ○ in common parlance 5 without special privilege, rank, or status ○ the common people 6 ill-bred or vulgar ■ n 1 a piece of public land 2 common stock —**com·mon·ly** adv —**com·mon·ness** n

com·mon car·ri·er n 1 a transportation company 2 a telecommunications company

com·mon de·nom·i·na·tor n 1 a number divisible by the lower numbers of two or more fractions 2 a shared belief or characteristic

com·mon·er /kómmənər/ *n* an ordinary person who does not belong to the nobility

Com·mon E·ra *n* the Christian Era, especially as used in reckoning dates

com·mon ground *n* an area of agreement between people or groups

com·mon knowl·edge *n* something generally known

com·mon law *n* law that has evolved, as distinct from law established by legislation

com·mon-law *adj* 1 describes an unofficial marriage or a partner in such a marriage 2 of common law

com·mon noun *n* a noun designating any member of a class, e.g. "city," as distinct from a proper noun such as "Paris"

com·mon·place /kómmən plàyss/ *adj* 1 often occurring or encountered 2 unoriginal and uninteresting ■ *n* something commonplace, especially an unoriginal remark —**com·mon·place·ness** *n*

com·mon room *n* a room where residents, staff, or students can relax

com·mons /kómmənz/ *n* 1 a college or university dining hall (+ *sing verb*) 2 **Com·mons** the British House of Commons (+ *sing or pl verb*)

com·mon sense *n* sound practical judgment derived from experience —**com·mon-sense** /kòmmən séns/ *adj* —**com·mon-sen·si·cal** *adj*

com·mon stock *n* stock entitling a holder to a dividend after holders of preferred stock have been paid

com·mon·wealth /kómmən wèlth/ *n* 1 a nation or its people 2 **Com·mon·wealth** an official title of several US states, Massachusetts, Pennsylvania, Kentucky, and Virginia 3 **Com·mon·wealth** a self-governing political unit such as Puerto Rico voluntarily associated with the United States 4 *also* **Com·mon·wealth** an association of states 5 **Com·mon·wealth, Com·mon·wealth of Na·tions** an association of sovereign states with the British monarch as its head

Com·mon·wealth of In·de·pen·dent States *n* an association of former Soviet republics

com·mo·tion /kə mṓsh'n/ *n* a scene of noisy confusion or activity

com·mu·nal /kə myōōn'l/ *adj* 1 shared 2 of or belonging to a community or commune —**com·mu·nal·ly** *adv*

com·mune¹ /kóm yòon/ *n* 1 a community with shared possessions and responsibilities 2 the smallest administrative district in some countries

com·mune² /kə myōōn/ (-muned, -mun·ing) *vi* relate spiritually to something o *communing with nature*

com·mu·ni·ca·ble /kə myōōnikəb'l/ *adj* able to be transmitted or communicated o *a com-*

municable disease —**com·mu·ni·ca·bil·i·ty** /kə myòonikə bíllətee/ *n*

com·mu·ni·cant /kə myōonikənt/ *n* a recipient of the Christian sacrament of Communion

com·mu·ni·cate /kə myōoni kàyt/ (-cat·ed, -cat·ing) *v* 1 *vti* give or exchange information 2 *vi* be connected or have common access 3 *vi* give or receive Communion —**com·mu·ni·ca·tor** *n*

com·mu·ni·ca·tion /kə myòoni káysh'n/ *n* 1 giving or exchange of information 2 a written or spoken message 3 rapport ■ **com·mu·ni·ca·tions** *npl* the technology used for sending and receiving messages (+ *pl verb*) —**com·mu·ni·ca·tion·al** *adj*

com·mu·ni·ca·tions /kə myòoni káysh'nz/ *npl* (+ *pl verb*) 1 the technology used for sending and receiving messages 2 the routes used for sending messages or moving troops and supplies ■ *n* (+ *sing or pl verb*) 1 effective use of words 2 the study of methods of communicating

com·mu·ni·ca·tive /kə myòoni kàytiv/ *adj* 1 talkative 2 of communication

com·mun·ion /kə myóonyən/ *n* 1 a feeling of intimacy 2 a religious group with its own set of beliefs 3 a sense of fellowship between religious groups 4 **Com·mun·ion** a Christian sacrament commemorating Jesus Christ's last meal with his disciples 5 **Com·mun·ion** the consecrated bread and wine consumed at Communion

com·mu·ni·qué /kə myòoni káy, kə myòoni kày/ *n* an official announcement

com·mu·nism /kómmyə nìzzəm/ *n* 1 a classless political system in which all property and wealth are owned by everybody 2 *also* **Com·mu·nism** the Marxist-Leninist version of communism 3 *also* **Com·mu·nism** a totalitarian system of government with a state-controlled economy —**com·mu·nist** *n, adj* —**Com·mu·nist** *n, adj* —**com·mu·nist·ic** /kòmmyə nístik/ *adj*

com·mu·ni·ty /kə myōonátee/ *n* (*pl* -ties) *n* 1 a group of people living in the same area 2 a particular group of people within a society o *the financial community* 3 a group of nations 4 the plants and animals living together in an area

com·mu·ni·ty cen·ter *n* a building used for community activities

com·mu·ni·ty col·lege *n* a nonresidential college offering two-year or three-year courses and awarding diplomas or associate degrees

com·mu·ni·ty ser·vice *n* work beneficial to the community, required of an offender as punishment

com·mute /kə myōot/ (-mut·ed, -mut·ing) *v* 1 *vi* travel regularly between places, especially between home and work 2 *vt* reduce the severity of a penalty 3 *vti* replace something with something else, or be a replacement —**com·mu·ta·tion** /kòmmyə táysh'n/ *n*

com·mut·er /kə myóotər/ n 1 a regular traveler between home and work 2 an airline that provides flights between nearby cities

Co·mo /kó mō/ capital of **Como Province,** N Italy, on the southwestern shore of **Lake Como.** Pop. 83,871 (1997).

Com·o·ros /kómmə rōz, kə máw rōz/ independent state consisting of a group of islands in the Indian Ocean, off the coast of Mozambique. Cap. Moroni. Pop. 596,202 (2001). —**Com·o·ri·an** /kə máwree ən/ n, adj

comp. abbr 1 comparative 2 compensation

com·pact[1] /əd /kəm pákt, kóm pàkt/ adj 1 closely packed together 2 small and efficiently arranged ■ vti /kəm pákt/ make or become more dense or firmly packed ■ n /kóm pàkt/ a case for makeup, especially face powder —**com·pact·ly** adv —**com·pact·ness** n

com·pact[2] /kóm pàkt/ n an agreement

com·pact disk, com·pact disc n a plastic disk on which music or computer data is digitally recorded

com·pan·ion /kəm pánnyən/ n 1 a friend who accompanies or spends time with another 2 a matching article —**com·pan·ion** vt

com·pan·ion·a·ble /kəm pánnyənəb'l/ adj providing or enjoying pleasant company ○ a companionable silence

com·pan·ion·ship /kəm pánnyən shĭp/ n the company of friends, or the relationship between friends

com·pa·ny /kúmpənee/ (pl -nies) n 1 a business enterprise 2 the state or fact of being with other people ○ feel at ease in company 3 a group of people, e.g., actors or soldiers 4 somebody's companions 5 a guest or guests ○ having company for dinner

com·pa·ra·ble /kómpərəb'l, kəm párrəb'l/ adj 1 capable of being compared 2 similar —**com·pa·ra·bil·i·ty** /kòmpərə bíllətee/ n —**com·pa·ra·bly** adv

com·par·a·tive /kəm párrətiv/ adj 1 of or expressing comparison 2 relative ○ He passed with comparative ease. 3 describes an adjective or adverb in a form expressing increase, e.g., "slower" or "more importantly" ■ n the comparative degree, or a comparative form of a word —**com·par·a·tive·ly** adv

com·pare /kəm páir/ vt (-pared, -par·ing) 1 examine for similarities and differences 2 consider or represent as similar ■ n comparison (literary) ○ beautiful beyond compare

com·par·i·son /kəm párriss'n/ n 1 the process or result of comparing 2 similarity

~~comparitive~~ incorrect spelling of **comparative**

com·part·ment /kəm páartmənt/ n 1 a partitioned space 2 a section of a railroad passenger car —**com·part·ment·al** /kəm paart mént'l/ adj

com·part·men·tal·ize /kəm paart mént'l ìz/ (-ized, -iz·ing) vt divide into separate areas or categories —**com·part·men·tal·i·za·tion** /kəm paart ment'li záyish'n/ n

com·pass /kúmpəss, kómpəss/ n a device for finding or indicating direction relative to magnetic north ■ vt 1 surround or encircle 2 understand (fml) ■ n the scope of something such as a subject ■ **com·pass·es** npl a hinged device for drawing circles ■ vt achieve (literary)

com·pas·sion /kəm pásh'n/ n sympathy for the suffering of others

com·pas·sion·ate /kəm pásh'nət/ adj showing compassion —**com·pas·sion·ate·ly** adv

com·pas·sion·ate leave n emergency leave granted for personal reasons, e.g., the death of a close relative

~~compatable~~ incorrect spelling of **compatible**

⌁ **com·pat·i·ble** /kəm páttəb'l/ adj 1 able to exist, live, or work together without conflict 2 consistent ○ not compatible with the facts 3 in computing, able to be used with or substituted for something else —**com·pat·i·bil·i·ty** /kəm pàttə bíllətee/ n —**com·pat·i·bly** adv

com·pa·tri·ot /kəm páytree ət/ n 1 a fellow citizen 2 a comrade, e.g., in the military

com·pel /kəm pél/ (-pelled, -pel·ling) vt force

com·pel·ling /kəm pélling/ adj 1 holding the attention or interest ○ a compelling account 2 making somebody do something ○ a compelling need

com·pen·di·um /kəm péndee əm/ (pl -ums or -a /-ə/) n a short but comprehensive account

com·pen·sate /kómpən sàyt/ (-sat·ed, -sat·ing) v 1 vt pay compensation to 2 vti counterbalance or make up for something —**com·pen·sa·to·ry** /kəm pénsə tàwree/ adj

com·pen·sa·tion /kòmpən sáyish'n/ n 1 money paid to make up for loss or damage, or in return for work done 2 payment of compensation 3 something that makes up for something else ○ excellent rail service as one of the compensations of living abroad

~~competant~~ incorrect spelling of **competent**

com·pete /kəm péet/ (-pet·ed, -pet·ing) vi try to win or do better than others

com·pe·tence /kómpət'ns/, **com·pe·ten·cy** /-tənsee/ n 1 the quality of being competent 2 a specific skill or ability ◊ See note at **ability**

com·pe·tent /kómpət'nt/ adj 1 having enough skill or ability 2 good enough 3 legally capable or qualified —**com·pe·tent·ly** adv

com·pe·ti·tion /kòmpə tísh'n/ n 1 the process of trying to win something or do better than others 2 an activity in which people try to win something 3 the opposition in a competitive situation ○ keep one step ahead of the competition

com·pet·i·tive /kəm péttitiv/ adj 1 involving an attempt to win something or to do better than others 2 inclined to want to achieve more than others 3 as good as or slightly better than that offered by others ○ a highly competitive salary —**com·pet·i·tive·ly** adv —**com·pet·i·tive·ness** n

com·pet·i·tor /kəm péttitər/ n 1 a participant in a competition 2 a rival or opponent in a competitive situation

⚡ **com·pile** /kəm píl/ (-piled, -pil·ing) vt 1 gather together or create from various sources 2 convert from a high-level computer language into an intermediate one —**com·pil·a·tion** /kómpi láysh'n/ n

⚡ **com·pil·er** /kəm pílər/ n 1 somebody who compiles something, e.g., lists or other items 2 a computer program that converts another program from a high-level language into an intermediate language

com·pla·cent /kəm pláyss'nt/ adj self-satisfied and unaware of possible dangers —**com·pla·cen·cy** n —**com·pla·cent·ly** adv

com·plain /kəm pláyn/ vi 1 express unhappiness or dissatisfaction 2 describe symptoms that are being experienced ○ complained of chest pains —**com·plain·er** n

---

SYNONYMS complain, object, protest, grumble, grouse, carp, gripe, whine, nag
CORE MEANING: indicate dissatisfaction with something

---

com·plain·ant /kəm pláynənt/ n somebody who makes a legal complaint

com·plaint /kəm pláynt/ n 1 a statement or cause of unhappiness or dissatisfaction 2 an ailment 3 a formal charge of the commission of a crime

com·plai·sant /kəm pláyss'nt, -pláyz'nt/ adj seeking to please —**com·plai·sance** n —**com·plai·sant·ly** adv

com·ple·ment n /kómpləmənt/ 1 something that completes or perfects something else 2 the quantity required for completeness ○ a full complement of crew members ■ vt /kómplə mènt/ complete or perfect something

---

USAGE complement or compliment? A complement is something added to make a thing complete, whereas a compliment is an expression of praise: This wine is the perfect complement to the meal. My compliments to the chef. A complimentary copy of a book is one given without charge, whereas a complementary copy is one that completes a set of books.

---

com·ple·men·ta·ry /kòmplə méntəree, -méntree/ adj 1 completing or perfecting 2 describes each of two angles that together make a right angle ◊ See note at complement

com·ple·men·ta·ry med·i·cine n medical treatment that addresses the causes rather than the symptoms of disease

com·plete /kəm pleet/ adj 1 whole 2 finished 3 utter or unmitigated ○ a complete waste of time ■ vt (-plet·ed, -plet·ing) 1 make whole 2 finish 3 accomplish —**com·plete·ly** adv —**com·plete·ness** n —**com·ple·tion** n

com·plex adj /kəm pléks, kóm pléks/ 1 difficult to analyze, understand, or solve 2 having many parts ■ n /kóm pléks/ 1 a set of interconnected buildings 2 an unreasonable or obsessive set of feelings that influence behavior —**com·plex·i·ty** /kəm pléksətee/ n

com·plex·ion /kəm plékshən/ n 1 the quality and color of somebody's skin 2 the character or appearance of something ○ puts an entirely new complexion on the matter

com·pli·ant /kəm plí ənt/ adj 1 ready to obey and conform 2 conforming to requirements (often in combination) ○ industry-compliant —**com·pli·ance** n

com·pli·cate /kómpli kàyt/ (-cat·ed, -cat·ing) vt make more complex

com·pli·cat·ed /kómpli kàytəd/ adj having many interrelated parts or elements and therefore difficult to understand or deal with

com·pli·ca·tion /kòmpli káysh'n/ n 1 a difficult or confused state 2 something that increases difficulty or complexity

com·plic·i·ty /kəm plíssətee/ n involvement in wrongdoing —**com·plic·it** adj

com·pli·ment n /kómpləmənt/ 1 an expression of praise 2 a gesture of respect ■ **com·pli·ments** npl expressions of respect and good wishes ■ vt /kómplə mènt/ praise or congratulate ◊ See note at complement

com·pli·men·ta·ry /kòmplə méntəree, -méntree/ adj 1 expressing praise 2 given free as a courtesy or favor ○ complimentary tickets —**com·pli·men·ta·ri·ly** adv ◊ See note at complement

com·ply /kəm plí/ (-plied, -plies) vi obey or conform

com·po·nent /kəm pónənt/ n 1 a part, element, or constituent 2 an electrical or mechanical part ■ adj forming part of a whole —**com·po·nen·tial** /kòmpə nénsh'l/ adj

com·port /kəm páwrt/ v (fml) 1 vr behave 2 vi agree or be consistent ○ an assertion that comports with the established facts —**com·port·ment** n

com·pose /kəm póz/ (-posed, -pos·ing) v 1 make by combining parts 2 vt put together to form a whole 3 vti create a piece of music or writing 4 vt make calm in manner 5 vti set type for printing —**com·pos·er** n

com·posed /kəm pózd/ adj calm and self-possessed —**com·pos·ed·ly** /-pózədlee/ adv

com·pos·ite /kəm pózzit/ adj 1 made up of different parts 2 with flower heads made up of many small flowers —**com·pos·ite** n

com·po·si·tion /kòmpə zísh'n/ n 1 the way in which something is made or in which its parts are arranged 2 the process of composing 3 a piece of music 4 a short essay —**com·po·si·tion·al** adj

com·pos·i·tor /kəm pózzitər/ n a typesetter

com·pos men·tis /kòmpəss méntiss/ adj sane

com·post /kóm pòst/ n decayed organic matter used to enrich soil ■ v 1 vti turn into compost 2 vt treat with compost

com·po·sure /kəm pózhər/ n calmness and self-possession

com·pote /kóm pòt/ n 1 a long-stemmed glass dish 2 a stewed fruit dessert

com·pound[1] n /kóm pównd/ 1 a combination or mixture 2 a substance formed by the chemical combination of elements in fixed proportions ■ adj /kóm pównd, kom pównd, kəm-/ having two or more different parts ■ v /kóm pównd, kəm pównd/ 1 vti combine 2 vt make by combining parts 3 vt intensify ◊ See note at **mixture**

com·pound[2] /kóm pòwnd/ n an enclosed group of buildings

com·pound frac·ture n a fracture in which a broken bone pierces the skin

com·pound in·ter·est n interest calculated on the total of the original sum and interest already accrued

com·pre·hend /kòmprə hénd/ v 1 vti understand 2 vt include (fml) —**com·pre·hend·i·ble** adj

com·pre·hen·si·ble /kòmprə hénsəb'l/ adj intelligible —**com·pre·hen·si·bil·i·ty** /kòmprə hensə bíllətee/ n —**com·pre·hen·si·bly** adv

com·pre·hen·sion /kòmprə hénsh'n/ n 1 the understanding of something 2 the ability to understand ◊ beyond my comprehension

com·pre·hen·sive /kòmprə hénsiv/ adj 1 including or covering many things 2 including or covering everything —**com·pre·hen·sive·ly** adv —**com·pre·hen·sive·ness** n

com·press v /kəm préss/ 1 vti make or become smaller or shorter 2 vt press things together ■ n /kóm préss/ a pad pressed firmly against a part of the body, e.g., to stop bleeding —**com·press·i·ble** adj —**com·pres·sion** /kəm présh'n/ n

com·pres·sor /kəm préssər/ n a machine that compresses gas

~~**comprimise**~~ incorrect spelling of **compromise**

com·prise /kəm príz/ (-prised, -pris·ing) vt 1 include 2 consist of 3 △ constitute

USAGE Comprise is concerned with a whole having a number of parts: The house comprises three bedrooms, a bathroom, a kitchen, and a living room. Use of **comprise** in the sense "constitute" is controversial. Avoid constructions like this if you wish to steer clear of criticism: The house is comprised of three bedrooms, a bathroom, a kitchen, and a living room; Three bedrooms, a bathroom, a kitchen, and a living room comprise the house.

com·pro·mise /kómprə mìz/ n 1 an agreement involving concessions on both sides 2 something accepted when what is wanted is unattainable ■ v (-mised, -mis·ing) 1 vi agree by conceding 2 vt under-

mine or devalue ◊ compromised his integrity 3 vt put at risk ◊ compromising our chances of success

comp·trol·ler /kən trólər/ n a financial supervisor —**comp·trol·ler·ship** n

com·pul·sion /kəm púlshən/ n 1 an act of compelling, or the state of being compelled 2 an impulse or urge

com·pul·sive /kəm púlsiv/ adj 1 unable to resist doing something ◊ a compulsive liar 2 powerfully interesting —**com·pul·sive·ly** adv —**com·pul·sive·ness** n

com·pul·so·ry /kəm púlsəree/ adj 1 required by authority 2 caused by force —**com·pul·so·ri·ly** adv

com·punc·tion /kəm púngkshən/ n shame and regret about wrongdoing

✦ **com·pu·ta·tion** /kòmpyə táysh'n/ n 1 the use of a computer or computers 2 mathematic or arithmetic calculation —**com·pu·ta·tion·al** adj

✦ **com·pute** /kəm pyóot/ (-put·ed, -put·ing) v 1 vt calculate, using numbers 2 vi use a computer

com·put·ed to·mog·ra·phy, com·put·er·ized to·mog·ra·phy n a technique for producing images of cross sections of the body

✦ **com·put·er** /kəm pyóotər/ n an electronic device for processing and storing data

✦ **com·put·er-aid·ed de·sign** n the use of computer software for design

✦ **com·put·er-aid·ed en·gi·neer·ing** n automated engineering analysis using computer simulations

✦ **com·put·er con·fer·enc·ing** n the use of computers to exchange information as if at a meeting

✦ **com·put·er dat·ing** n the business of matching apparently compatible couples by computer

✦ **com·put·er·ese** /kəm pyóotə reéz, -reéss/ n computer jargon (humorous)

✦ **com·put·er game** n a game played on a computer

✦ **com·put·er graph·ics** n generation of pictures on a computer (+ sing verb) ■ npl computer-generated images (+ pl verb)

✦ **com·put·er·ize** /kəm pyóotə rìz/ (-ized, -iz·ing) vt 1 convert to a computer-based system 2 store on a computer —**com·put·er·i·za·tion** /kəm pyóotəri záysh'n/ n

com·put·er·ized to·mog·ra·phy n MED = **computed tomography**

✦ **com·put·er lan·guage** n a language used for writing computer programs

✦ **com·put·er-lit·er·ate** adj able to use computers —**com·put·er lit·er·a·cy** n

✦ **com·put·er·phobe** /kəm pyóotər fòb/ n somebody who dislikes or fears computers (infml) —**com·put·er·pho·bi·a** /kəm pyóotər fóbee ə/ n —**com·put·er·pho·bic** /-fóbik/ adj

✦ **com·put·er sci·ence** n the study of comput-

✦ **com·put·er vi·rus** n a computer program that copies itself into other programs, often causing damage

✦ **com·put·ing** /kəm pyōoting/ n the use of computers

com·rade /kóm ràd, -rəd/ n 1 a friend or companion 2 another member of the same group, especially a soldier —**com·rade·ly** adj —**com·rade·ship** n

con[1] vt (**conned, con·ning**) trick by lying ■ n a dishonest trick or a swindle

con[2] n an argument against doing something ◇ the pros and cons

con[3] n a convict (slang)

Con·a·kry /kónnə krèe, kònnə krèe/ capital and main port of Guinea. Pop. 705,280 (1983 estimate).

✦ **con·cat·e·nate** /kon kátt'n àyt, kən-/ (-nat·ed, -nat·ing) 1 connect into a linked system 2 in computing, link together to form a single unit ■ adj /kon kátt'nət, -kátt'n àyt, kən-/ linked together —**con·cat·e·na·tion** /kon kàtt'n àysh'n, kən-/ n

con·cave /kon káyv, kón kayv/ adj curved inward —**con·cav·i·ty** /kon kávvətee/ n

con·ceal /kən séel/ vt hide something or somebody —**con·ceal·a·ble** adj —**con·ceal·ment** n

con·cede /kən séed/ (-ced·ed, -ced·ing) v 1 vt reluctantly accept something to be true 2 vt grant or yield a right or privilege 3 vti acknowledge defeat in a contest or debate, often before the end

~~conceed~~ incorrect spelling of **concede**

con·ceit /kən séet/ n 1 excessive pride in yourself 2 an exaggerated comparison in literature

con·ceit·ed /kən séetəd/ adj having an excessively high opinion of yourself —**con·ceit·ed·ly** adv —**con·ceit·ed·ness** n ◊ See note at **proud**

con·ceive /kən séev/ (-ceived, -ceiv·ing) v 1 vti think of or imagine something 2 vt invent, devise, or originate 3 vti become pregnant with a child or with young —**con·ceiv·a·ble** adj —**con·ceiv·a·bly** adv

con·cen·trate /kóns'n tràyt/ v (-trat·ed, -trat·ing) 1 vti silently focus your thoughts and attention on something 2 vti devote all efforts and resources to one thing 3 vti cluster together 4 vt make a substance purer, thicker, or stronger, especially by removing water ■ n a concentrated substance

con·cen·tra·tion /kòns'n tráysh'n/ n 1 the devotion of all thoughts or efforts and resources to one thing 2 a cluster of things in a single area 3 the strength of a solution

con·cen·tra·tion camp n 1 a Nazi prison camp in World War II 2 a prison camp for civilians in war

✦ **con·cen·tra·tor** /kóns'n tràytər/ n a telecommunications device that combines outgoing messages

con·cen·tric /kən séntrik, kon-/ adj describes circles and spheres of different sizes with the same center —**con·cen·tri·cal·ly** adv —**con·cen·tric·i·ty** /kòns'n tríssətee/ n

Con·cep·ción /kən sèpsi ón, kàwn sep syáwn/ capital of Bío-Bío Region, central Chile. Pop. 372,252 (1998).

con·cept /kón sèpt/ n 1 something thought or imagined 2 a broad abstract idea or principle ◇ the concept of time 3 the most basic understanding of something ◇ has little concept of what is involved —**con·cep·tu·al** /kən sépchoo əl/ adj —**con·cep·tu·al·ly** adv

con·cep·tion /kən sépshən/ n 1 fertilization of an egg by a sperm 2 a broad understanding of something 3 formulation of an idea 4 the origin or beginnings of something 5 something conceived in the mind —**con·cep·tion·al** adj

con·cept prod·uct n an innovative commercial product not yet in production

con·cep·tu·al art, concept art n art designed to present ideas

con·cep·tu·al·ize /kən sépchoo ə lìz/ (-ized, -iz·ing) vti form a concept of something —**con·cep·tu·al·i·za·tion** /kən sèpchoo əli záysh'n/ n

con·cern /kən súrn/ n 1 worry or a cause of worry 2 caring feelings 3 a matter that affects somebody ◇ It's not my concern. 4 a business enterprise ■ vt 1 make worried 2 be of interest or importance to 3 involve 4 relate to or be about

con·cerned /kən súrnd/ adj 1 anxious or worried 2 interested 3 involved —**con·cern·ed·ly** /-nədlee/ adv

con·cern·ing /kən súrning/ prep about or to do with ◇ information concerning her disappearance

con·cert n /kón sùrt, kónsərt/ 1 a public musical performance 2 concerted action ◇ a concert of criticism ■ vti /kən súrt/ do or plan cooperatively

con·cert·ed /kən súrtəd/ adj planned or done together —**con·cert·ed·ly** adv —**con·cert·ed·ness** n

con·cer·ti·na /kònsər teénə/ n a musical instrument resembling a small accordion —**con·cer·tin·ist** n

---

ORIGIN Concertina looks as though it ought to be from Italian, like so many other musical terms, but in fact it was formed in English from concert. (If it had been an Italian adoption it would have been pronounced with /ch/ like concerto rather than with /s/.) The first **concertina** was patented in Britain in 1829 by its inventor, Sir Charles Wheatstone.

---

con·cert·mas·ter /kónsərt màstər/ n a symphony orchestra's first violinist

con·cer·to /kən cháirtō/ (pl -tos or -ti /-tee/) n

an instrumental musical composition for soloist and orchestra

con·ces·sion /kən sésh'n/ n 1 the process or an instance of yielding reluctantly 2 a special privilege 3 something unwillingly admitted or acknowledged 4 a small business outlet inside another establishment 5 a license to use land for a specific purpose 6 *Can* a land subdivision —**con·ces·sion·ar·y** adj

con·ces·sion·aire /kən sésh'n áir/, **con·ces·sion·er** /kən sésh'nər/ n a holder or operator of a concession

conch /kongk, konch/ (*pl* **conchs** /kongks/ *or* **conch·es** /kóncheez/) n 1 a tropical sea animal with a large spiral shell 2 the shell of a conch. Use: horn or trumpet, ornament, jewelry.

con·cierge /kōn syáirzh/ (*pl* **-cierges** /*pronunc. same*/) n a hotel or apartment building employee who helps guests or residents

~~conceive~~ incorrect spelling of **conceive**

con·cil·i·ate /kən sílee àyt/ (**-at·ed, -at·ing**) vti 1 bring opposing parties together 2 regain the support or friendship of —**con·cil·i·a·tion** /kən sílee áysh'n/ n —**con·cil·i·a·to·ry** /-ə táwree/ adj

con·cise /kən síss/ adj short and clearly written or stated —**con·cise·ly** adv —**con·cise·ness** n

con·clave /kón klàyv, kóng klàyv/ n 1 a secret meeting 2 in the Roman Catholic Church, a meeting to elect a pope

con·clude /kən klóod/ (**-clud·ed, -clud·ing**) v 1 vt come to a conclusion about something 2 vti end or finish o *concluded the discussion* 3 vt settle a deal ◊ See note at **deduce**

con·clu·sion /kən klóozh'n/ n 1 a decision or opinion based on reasoning 2 the final part of something (*fml*) 3 the settlement of a deal

con·clu·sive /kən klóossiv/ adj proving something beyond doubt —**con·clu·sive·ly** adv —**con·clu·sive·ness** n

con·coct /kən kókt/ vt 1 create a new dish by mixing ingredients 2 think up a story, excuse, lie, or plan (*disapproving*) —**con·coc·tion** n

con·com·i·tant /kən kómmitənt/ adj happening at the same time —**con·com·i·tance** n —**con·com·i·tant** n

con·cord /kón kàwrd, kóng kàwrd/ n 1 peaceful coexistence or agreement 2 a peace treaty

Con·cord /kóng kàwrd/ 1 city in W California. Pop. 117,708 (1998). 2 town in NE Massachusetts. Pop. 17,076 (1990). 3 capital of New Hampshire. Pop. 37,444 (1998).

con·cor·dance /kən káwrd'nss/ n 1 similarity or agreement 2 an index of all the words used by an author or in a text

con·cor·dant /kən káwrd'nt/ adj showing harmony or agreement (*fml*) —**con·cor·dant·ly** adv

con·course /kón kàwrs, kóng kàwrs/ n a large space where people gather and move about, e.g., in an airport terminal

con·crete n /kón krèet, kóng-, kon krèet, kong-/ a hard construction material containing cement ■ adj /kon krèet, kong-/ 1 solid and real 2 definite o *concrete proposals for reform* ■ vt /kón krèet, kóng-, kon krèet, kong-/ (**-cret·ed, -cret·ing**) cover with concrete —**con·crete·ly** adv —**con·crete·ness** n

con·crete jun·gle n a place full of featureless buildings perceived as hostile

con·crete noun n a word denoting a physical thing, e.g., "clock" or "elephant"

con·cu·bine /kóngkyə bìn, kónkyə-/ n 1 a female lover with the status of a subordinate wife 2 a woman cohabiting with her lover (*dated*) —**con·cu·bi·nage** /kon kyóobinij, kən-/ n

con·cur /kən kúr/ (**-curred, -cur·ring**) vti agree ◊ See note at **agree**

con·cur·rent /kən kúrənt/ adj happening together —**con·cur·rence** n —**con·cur·rent·ly** adv

con·cus·sion /kən kúsh'n/ n 1 a brain injury caused by a blow that can result in temporary disorientation, memory loss, or unconsciousness 2 a sudden jolting or shaking —**con·cus·sive** /-kússiv/ adj

~~condem~~ incorrect spelling of **condemn**

con·demn /kən dém/ vt 1 sentence to a severe punishment 2 state to be bad or unacceptable 3 force to experience something unpleasant 4 ban the use or consumption of —**con·dem·na·tion** /kòn dem náysh'n, -dəm-/ n —**con·dem·na·to·ry** /-démnə tàwree/ adj ◊ See note at **criticize, disapprove**

con·den·sa·tion /kòn den sáysh'n, kòndən sáysh'n/ n 1 a film of water droplets on a cold surface 2 the process of condensing

con·dense /kən déns/ (**-densed, -dens·ing**) v 1 vti change from gas to liquid 2 vt make a text shorter by removing unnecessary words 3 vti thicken by removing water —**con·dens·a·bil·i·ty** /kən dènsə bíllətee/ n

con·densed milk n thickened sweetened milk

con·dens·er /kən dénsər/ n 1 a device that converts gas to liquid 2 a capacitor

con·de·scend /kòndə sénd/ vi 1 behave in a superior way toward others 2 do something that would normally be beneath your dignity o *She condescended to travel with us.* —**con·de·scen·sion** /-sénshən/ n

con·de·scend·ing /kòndə sénding/ adj arrogantly superior —**con·de·scend·ing·ly** adv

~~condesending~~ incorrect spelling of **condescending**

con·di·ment /kóndimənt/ n a seasoning such as salt or pepper used at the table

con·di·tion /kən dísh'n/ n 1 a particular state of repair or ability to function o *a car in good* *condition* **2** a state of fitness or health o *out of condition* **3** a physical disorder **4** a general state or way of being **5** position, rank, or social status *(fml)* **6** one thing necessary for something else to happen o *a condition of the agreement* ■ **con·di·tions** *npl* influential factors or circumstances o *better working conditions* o *poor flying conditions* ■ *vt* **1** train to react in a particular way **2** improve the quality or condition of by special treatment **3** adapt

con·di·tion·al /kən díshən'l, -díshnəl/ *adj* **1** dependent on something else **2** describes a verb form, word, or clause that states a condition or limitation o *a conditional verb form, word, or clause* —**con·di·tion·al·ly** *adv*

con·di·tion·er /kən dísh'nər/ *n* a substance for improving the condition or texture of hair or fabric

con·do /kóndō/ *(pl* -**dos***) n* a condominium *(infml)*

con·dole /kən dól/ *(*-**doled, -dol·ing***) vi* express sympathy

con·do·lence /kən dólənss/ *n* a sympathetic word or message *(often pl)* —**con·do·lent** *adj*

con·dom /kóndəm, kúndəm/ *n* a contraceptive worn on the penis

con·do·min·i·um /kòndə mínnee əm/ *n* **1** an individually owned apartment **2** a building containing condominiums **3** joint government of a country by two or more other countries

con·done /kən dón/ *(*-**doned, -don·ing***) vt* consider wrongdoing acceptable o *condoning violence* —**con·don·a·ble** *adj*

con·dor /kón dàwr, kóndər/ *n* a large Andean vulture

con·duce /kən dóoss/ *(*-**duced, -duc·ing***) vi* contribute to bringing something about *(fml)*

con·du·cive /kən dóossiv/ *adj* tending to bring about a good or intended result o *not conducive to a good working relationship*

con·duct *v* /kən dúkt/ **1** *vti* direct the playing or singing of an instrumental or vocal group **2** *vti* transmit heat, light, sound, or electricity **3** *vt* accompany and guide somebody **4** *vt* carry out, manage, or control something o *conduct business* **5** *vt* behave in a particular manner ■ *n* /kón dúkt/ **1** behavior **2** the management or execution of something o *the conduct of the campaign* —**con·duc·tion** *n* —**con·duc·tive** *adj* —**con·duc·tiv·i·ty** *n* See note at **guide**

con·duc·tor /kən dúktər/ *n* **1** a railroad employee in charge of passengers **2** the director of an orchestra or choir **3** a substance, body, or medium that conducts energy

con·duit /kón dòo it, kóndwit/ *n* **1** a pipe or channel for liquid **2** a protective cover for a cable **3** a means of conveying information

cone *n* **1** an object with a round base that tapers to a point **2** a cone-shaped wafer

for ice cream **3** a seed-bearing structure of pines and firs **4** a light-sensitive cell in the eye

~~conection~~ incorrect spelling of **connection**

cone·flow·er /kón flòwr/ *n* a plant of the daisy family with a cone-shaped center

co·ney /kónee/ *(pl* -**neys***)*, **co·ny** *(pl* -**nies***) n* **1** a rabbit, especially a European rabbit **2** rabbit fur

Co·ney Is·land /kónee-/ amusement area in S Brooklyn, New York City

con·fab·u·late /kən fábbyə làyt/ *(*-**lat·ed, -lat·ing***) vi* have a chat or discussion *(fml)* —**con·fab·u·la·tion** /kən fábbyə láysh'n/ *n*

con·fec·tion /kən fékshən/ *n* a sweet food made from sugar and other ingredients

con·fec·tion·er /kən fékshənər/ *n* a maker of candies

con·fec·tion·ers' sug·ar *n* finely powdered sugar

con·fec·tion·er·y /kən fékshə nèrree/ *n* **1** candies considered collectively **2** the making of candy

con·fed·er·a·cy /kən féddərassee/ *n* **1** a political alliance **2** **Con·fed·er·a·cy** the confederation of the 11 states that seceded from the United States in 1861, starting the Civil War

con·fed·er·ate *n* /kən féddərət/ **1** an ally **2** an accomplice **3** **Con·fed·er·ate** a supporter or soldier of the Confederacy ■ *adj* /kən féddərət/ allied ■ *vti* /kən féddə ràyt/ *(*-**at·ed, -at·ing***)* unite in a confederacy

con·fed·er·a·tion /kən féddə ráysh'n/ *n* **1** a group of loosely allied states **2** the formation of or state of being a confederation **3** **Con·fed·er·a·tion** the original United States **4** **Con·fed·er·a·tion** Canada in 1867

con·fer /kən fúr/ *(*-**ferred, -fer·ring***) v* **1** *vi* discuss something with somebody **2** *vt* give an honor or title to *(fml)* o *conferred an honorary degree on the president* —**con·fer·ment** *n* —**con·fer·ral** *n* ◊ See note at **give**

~~confered~~ incorrect spelling of **conferred**

con·fer·ence /kónfərənss/ *n* **1** a meeting for lectures or discussions **2** a sports league

con·fer·ence call *n* a group telephone conversation

⨏ **con·fer·enc·ing** /kónfərənssing/ *n* the holding of a meeting with participants linked by telephone, video, or computer

con·fess /kən féss/ *v* **1** *vti* admit wrongdoing **2** *vt* reluctantly acknowledge something to be true **3** *vti* admit sins and ask for God's forgiveness

con·fes·sion /kən fésh'n/ *n* **1** an admission of wrongdoing or guilt **2** an open acknowledgment of feelings or beliefs **3** a formal declaration of sins

con·fes·sion·al /kən féshən'l, -féshnəl/ *adj* of an intimate nature ■ *n* a place for confession in a Roman Catholic church

con·fes·sor /kən féssər/ n 1 a priest who hears confessions 2 somebody who confesses

con·fet·ti /kən féttee/ n pieces of colored paper thrown during festive occasions

ORIGIN Confetti is from an Italian plural meaning "small sweets." Small sweets were traditionally thrown at carnivals. English took the word but substituted pieces of paper, and started throwing them at weddings. **Confetti** is from the same Latin source as *confection*.

con·fi·dant /kónfi dànt, kònfi daànt/ n somebody to whom secrets are told

con·fi·dante /kónfi dànt, kònfi daànt/ n a woman to whom secrets are told

con·fide /kən fíd/ (-fid·ed, -fid·ing) vti tell somebody something secret o *She confided the secret to her brother.* o *He confided in his sister.*

con·fi·dence /kónfidənss/ n 1 belief in your own abilities 2 faith in the ability of somebody or something to perform satisfactorily 3 a secret told to somebody 4 a relationship grounded in trust o *told her in confidence*

con·fi·dence game n a fraud using somebody's trust to obtain something of value

con·fi·dent /kónfidənt/ adj 1 self-assured or certain of success 2 convinced o *confident of her opponent's skill* —**con·fi·dent·ly** adv

con·fi·den·tial /kònfi dénsh'l/ adj private and secret —**con·fi·den·ti·al·i·ty** /-denshee állətee/ n —**con·fi·den·tial·ly** adv

⚡**con·fig·u·ra·tion** /kən fìggyə ráysh'n/ n 1 the way in which parts are arranged 2 a shape or outline 3 the setup of the components of a computer system —**con·fig·u·ra·tion·al** adj —**con·fig·u·ra·tive** /kən fíggyə ràytiv/ adj

⚡**con·fig·ure** /kən fíggyər/ (-ured, -ur·ing) vt set up or arrange parts, e.g., of a computer, for a specific purpose

con·fine vt /kən fín/ (-fined, -fin·ing) 1 keep within limits 2 keep from leaving a place o *was confined to her room* ■ **con·fines** /kón fìnz/ npl boundaries

con·fined /kən fínd/ adj cramped, restricted, or completely enclosed o *a confined space*

con·fine·ment /kən fínmənt/ n 1 restriction or limitation within boundaries 2 the process or time of giving birth (dated)

con·firm /kən fúrm/ v 1 vt prove to be true 2 vti make an arrangement definite o *confirm your booking* 3 vt ratify 4 vt in Judaism and Christianity, admit into a religious body —**con·fir·ma·tion** /kònfər máysh'n/ n

con·firmed /kən fúrmd/ adj settled in a habit and unlikely to change

con·fis·cate /kónfi skàyt/ (-cat·ed, -cat·ing) vt take away by authority or as a penalty —**con·fis·ca·tion** /kònfi skáysh'n/ n

con·fla·gra·tion /kònflə gráysh'n/ n a large destructive fire

con·flate /kən fláyt/ (-flat·ed, -flat·ing) vti merge into a unified whole —**con·fla·tion** n

con·flict n /kón flìkt/ 1 a continued battle 2 a disagreement or clash, e.g., between ideas or people ■ vi /kən flíkt/ differ or be incompatible o *opinions that conflicted* ◊ See note at **fight**

con·flu·ence /kón floo ənss/ n 1 a meeting of streams 2 a meeting of two or more things —**con·flu·ent** adj, n

con·form /kən fáwrm/ v 1 vi behave acceptably 2 vi comply with a standard 3 vti be or make similar —**con·form·er** n

con·for·ma·tion /kòn fawr máysh'n/ n 1 the structure or form of something 2 symmetry of parts

con·form·ist /kən fáwrmist/ n somebody who conforms —**con·form·ism** n —**con·form·ist** adj

con·form·i·ty /kən fáwrmətee/ n 1 the following of the behavior or thinking of the majority of people 2 compliance, agreement, or similarity

con·found /kən fównd/ vt 1 bewilder 2 fail to distinguish between 3 prove to be wrong

con·found·ed /kən fówndəd/ adj in a state of bewilderment —**con·found·ed·ly** adv

con·frère /kón fràir/ n a colleague (fml)

con·front /kən frúnt/ vt 1 challenge or defy somebody or something face to face 2 bring somebody face to face with something o *confronted her with the evidence* 3 encounter a difficulty

con·fron·ta·tion /kònfrən táysh'n/ n 1 a face-to-face encounter, especially a hostile one 2 hostility or conflict 3 the process of confronting a difficulty —**con·fron·ta·tion·al** adj

Con·fu·cius /kən fyóoshəss/ (551?–479? BC) Chinese philosopher, administrator, and moralist

con·fuse /kən fyóoz/ (-fused, -fus·ing) vt 1 make somebody unable to think clearly 2 mistake one person or thing for another 3 cause disorder in something —**con·fus·a·ble** adj —**con·fused** adj —**con·fus·ed·ly** /-fyóozədlee/ adv —**con·fus·ing** adj —**con·fus·ing·ly** adv —**con·fu·sion** /-fyóozh'n/ n

con·fute /kən fyóot/ (-fut·ed, -fut·ing) vt prove wrong (fml) —**con·fu·ta·tion** /kònfyə táysh'n/ n

con game n a confidence game (infml)

con·geal /kən jeél/ vti thicken or solidify a liquid, or become thickened or solidified —**con·geal·ment** n

con·gen·ial /kən jeényəl/ adj 1 pleasant and suited to somebody's character and tastes o *a congenial atmosphere* 2 compatible in tastes or interests o *congenial companions* 3 friendly —**con·ge·ni·al·i·ty** /kən jeènee állətee/ n —**con·gen·ial·ly** adv

con·gen·i·tal /kən jénnit'l/ adj 1 existing at somebody's birth o *a congenital disorder* 2 ingrained in somebody's character —**con·gen·i·tal·ly** adv

con·ger eel /kóng gər-/, **con·ger** n a large sea eel

con·ges·tion /kən jéschən/ n 1 excessive traffic or people, making movement difficult 2 excessive fluid in a body part such as the lungs —**con·ges·ted** adj

con·glom·er·ate n /kən glómmərət/ 1 a business organization composed of a number of companies involved in different activities 2 something formed from different things gathered together 3 rock containing pieces of other rocks ■ vti /kən glómmə ràyt/ (-at·ed, -at·ing) gather together to form a mass —**con·glom·er·ate** adj —**con·glom·er·a·tion** /kən glòmmə ráysh'n/ n

Con·go /kóng gō/ Africa's second longest river, rising in the south of the Democratic Republic of the Congo and emptying into the Atlantic Ocean. Length 2,718 mi./4,374 km. ■ 1 also **Con·go, Dem·o·crat·ic Re·pub·lic of the** large equatorial country of Central Africa with a coastline on the Atlantic Ocean. Cap. Kinshasa. Pop. 53,624,718 (2001). 2 also **Con·go, Re·pub·lic of the** country in west central Africa, on the Atlantic coast. Cap. Brazzaville. Pop. 2,894,336 (2001). —**Con·go·lese** /kòng gə leéz, -leéss/ adj, n

Con·go franc n the main unit of currency in the Democratic Republic of the Congo

con·grat·u·late /kən gráchə làyt/ (-lat·ed, -lat·ing) v 1 vt express pleasure to somebody for an achievement or good fortune 2 vr feel self-satisfied ○ She congratulated herself upon winning. —**con·grat·u·la·to·ry** adj

con·grat·u·la·tion /kən gràchə láysh'n/ n the act of congratulating somebody ■ npl, interj **con·grat·u·la·tions** an expression of pleasure at somebody's achievement or good fortune

con·gre·gate /kóng grə gàyt/ (-gat·ed, -gat·ing) vti assemble or gather together, or gather people or animals together

con·gre·ga·tion /kòng grə gáysh'n/ n 1 the worshipers at a religious service 2 the members of a church 3 a gathering of people or animals ○ a congregation of geese

con·gress /kóng grəss/ n 1 a conference or meeting of delegates or representatives 2 **Con·gress** the US federal legislature 3 **Con·gress** the governing and lawmaking body of some other countries —**con·gres·sion·al** /kən gréshən'l, -gréshnəl/ adj —**con·gres·sion·al·ly** adv —**con·gress·man** n —**con·gress·per·son** n —**con·gress·wo·man** n

con·gru·ent /kóng groo ənt, kən groó-/ adj 1 corresponding or consistent (fml) 2 with identical geometric shapes —**con·gru·ence** n —**con·gru·en·cy** n —**con·gru·ent·ly** adv

con·gru·ous /kóng groo əss/ adj 1 appropriate (fml) 2 corresponding or consistent

con·i·cal /kónnik'l/ adj 1 cone-shaped 2 of a cone

con·i·fer /kónnəfər/ n a cone-bearing tree —**co·nif·er·ous** /kə níffərəss/ adj

conj. abbr 1 conjugation 2 conjunction

con·jec·ture /kən jékchər/ n 1 guesswork 2 a guess —**con·jec·tur·al** adj —**con·jec·ture** vti

con·join /kən jóyn/ vti join together (fml)

con·joint /kən jóynt/ adj 1 involving two or more combined entities 2 joined together —**con·joint·ly** adv

con·ju·gal /kónjəg'l/ adj of marriage

con·ju·gal rights npl the rights of a spouse to sexual intercourse

con·ju·gate v /kónjə gàyt/ (-gat·ed, -gat·ing) 1 vt state the forms of a verb 2 vi have different grammatical forms (refers to verbs) ■ adj /kónjəgət, -gàyt/ joined together in pairs (fml) —**con·jug·a·ble** adj —**con·ju·ga·tive** adj

con·ju·ga·tion /kònjə gáysh'n/ n 1 the inflections of a verb 2 reproduction in single-celled organisms —**con·ju·ga·tion·al** adj

con·junc·tion /kən júngkshən/ n 1 the combining of two or more things 2 a simultaneous occurrence 3 a connecting word such as "and" or "if" —**con·junc·tion·al** adj

con·junc·ti·va /kòn jungk tívə/ (pl -vas or -vae /-vee/) n a membrane under the eyelid —**con·junc·ti·val** adj

con·junc·tive /kən júngktiv/ adj 1 serving to connect 2 having been combined —**con·junc·tive·ly** adv

con·junc·ti·vi·tis /kən jùngkti vítiss/ n inflammation of the conjunctiva

con·jure /kónjər/ (-jured, -jur·ing) v 1 vi perform magic tricks 2 vti invoke supposed supernatural forces —**con·ju·ra·tion** /kònjə ráysh'n/ n —**con·jur·er** n —**con·jur·or** n

□ **conjure up** vt 1 create something in the mind 2 produce something as if by magic

conk[1] n a hairstyle in which curly hair has been straightened

conk[2] □ **conk out** vi (infml) 1 fail or break down 2 collapse or fall asleep

con man n a swindler (infml)

con·nect /kə nékt/ v 1 vti link or join together 2 vt associate in the mind with somebody or something 3 vt link to a source of electricity, gas, or water 4 vi allow passengers to transfer from one vehicle to another ○ Does this train connect with the one to Baltimore? —**con·nect·i·ble** adj —**con·nect·or** n

Con·nect·i·cut /kə néttikət/ 1 southernmost state in New England. Pop. 3,405,565 (2000). 2 longest river of New England, flowing through New Hampshire, Vermont, Massachusetts, and Connecticut. Length 407 mi./655 km.

con·nec·tion /kə nékshən/ n 1 the linking or joining of parts, things, or people 2 something that links things ○ check for a loose connection 3 an association ○ denied any *connection with the organization* **4** a transportation link, or a vehicle scheduled to provide such a link **5** a telecommunications link **6** a context ◊ *in this connection* **7** an influential contact *(often pl)* ◊ *has connections in the publishing world* **8** a relative *(often pl)*

con·nec·tive /kə néktiv/ *adj* linking ■ *n* a linking word such as a conjunction —**con·nec·tive·ly** *adv*

con·nec·tive tis·sue *n* tissue that supports and connects body parts

⚡ **con·nec·tiv·i·ty** /kò nek tívvətee/ *n* the ability to communicate with another piece of computer hardware or software

⚡ **con·nect time** *n* the period of time a computer user is logged on to a remote computer

con·nive /kə nîv/ (**-nived, -niv·ing**) *vi* **1** plot or scheme **2** give tacit consent or encouragement to wrongdoing —**con·niv·ance** *n* —**con·niv·ing** *adj*

~~connoiseur~~ incorrect spelling of **connoisseur**

con·nois·seur /kònnə súr/ *n* somebody with expert knowledge or discriminating taste —**con·nois·seur·ship** *n*

Con·nol·ly /kónn'lee/, **Maureen** (1934–69) US tennis player

Con·nors /kónnərs/, **Jimmy** (*b.* 1952) US tennis player

con·no·ta·tion /kònnə táysh'n/ *n* an implied additional meaning —**con·no·ta·tive** /kónnə tàytiv/ *adj*

con·note /kə nốt/ (**-not·ed, -not·ing**) *vt* **1** have an implied additional meaning ◊ *The word "hearth" connotes coziness and warmth.* **2** imply something else ◊ *His reluctance connotes cowardice.*

con·nu·bi·al /kə nóobee əl/ *adj* of marriage *(literary)* —**con·nu·bi·al·ly** *adv*

con·quer /kóngkər/ *vt* **1** seize an area or defeat a people by military force **2** overcome a difficulty or problem **3** make a difficult mountain ascent —**con·quer·or** *n* ◊ See note at **defeat**

con·quest /kón kwèst, kóng-/ *n* **1** the act of conquering **2** something acquired by conquering

con·quis·ta·dor /kon keéstə dàwr, kəng-, -kweéstə-/ (*pl* **-dors** *or* **-dor·es** /-dáw ràyz/) *n* a 16C Spanish conqueror in Mexico, Peru, or Central America

Con·rad /kón ràd/, **Joseph** (1857–1924) Polish-born British writer

con·science /kónshənss/ *n* **1** the sense of right and wrong that governs somebody's conduct **2** compliance with your conscience

con·science-strick·en *adj* feeling guilty

~~conscienscious~~ incorrect spelling of **conscientious**

con·sci·en·tious /kònshee énshəss/ *adj* **1** painstaking and diligent **2** in accordance with

somebody's conscience —**con·sci·en·tious·ly** *adv* —**con·sci·en·tious·ness** *n* ◊ See note at **careful**

con·sci·en·tious ob·jec·tor *n* somebody whose religious or moral beliefs forbid military service

con·scious /kónshəss/ *adj* **1** awake **2** aware **3** considered and deliberate ◊ *a conscious effort not to lose her temper* **4** fully informed, concerned, or interested *(often in combination)* ◊ *safety-conscious* **5** of the part of the mind that thinks and perceives —**con·scious·ly** *adv* ◊ See note at **aware**

con·scious·ness /kónshəssnəss/ *n* **1** the state of being conscious **2** somebody's mind and thoughts **3** the feelings and beliefs shared by a group

con·scious·ness-rais·ing *n* **1** improving people's awareness and understanding of issues **2** the increasing of self-awareness —**con·scious·ness-rais·er** *n*

con·script *vt* /kən skrípt/ compel to do military service ■ *n* /kón skrìpt/ a conscripted military recruit —**con·scrip·tion** /kən skrípsh'n/ *n*

con·se·crate /kónsə kràyt/ (**-crat·ed, -crat·ing**) *vt* **1** declare a place holy **2** dedicate something to a specific purpose **3** bless bread and wine for the Christian sacrament of Communion **4** ordain a Christian priest as a bishop —**con·se·cra·tion** /kònsə kráysh'n/ *n*

con·sec·u·tive /kən sékyətiv/ *adj* successive —**con·sec·u·tive·ly** *adv*

con·sen·su·al /kən sénshoo əl/ *adj* by mutual consent —**con·sen·su·al·ly** *adv*

con·sen·sus /kən sénsəss/ *n* general agreement among all or most members of a group

USAGE The word **consensus** is often misspelled *concensus*, probably from the erroneous influence of the word *census*.

con·sent /kən sént/ *vi* **1** give permission for something **2** agree to do something ■ *n* **1** permission **2** general agreement ◊ See note at **agree**

con·sent·ing a·dult *n* an adult willing to participate in something, especially sexual activity

~~consentrate~~ incorrect spelling of **concentrate**

con·se·quence /kónsəkwənss/ *n* **1** something that follows as a result **2** importance *(fml)*

con·se·quent /kónsəkwənt/ *adj* following as a consequence

con·se·quen·tial /kònsə kwénsh'l/ *adj* **1** arising as an indirect cost **2** important —**con·se·quen·tial·ly** *adv*

con·se·quent·ly /kónsəkwəntlee/ *adv* as a result

~~consern~~ incorrect spelling of **concern**

con·ser·van·cy /kən súrvənsee/ (*pl* **-cies**) *n* an area where land and wildlife are protected

con·ser·va·tion /kònsər váysh'n/ *n* **1** the preservation and care of natural and cultural resources **2** protection from loss, change, or damage —**con·ser·va·tion·al** *adj* —**con·ser·va·tion·ist** *n, adj*

con·ser·va·tism /kən súrvə tìzzəm/ *n* **1** reluctance to accept change **2** a right-wing political viewpoint

con·ser·va·tive /kən súrvətiv/ *adj* **1** reluctant to accept change **2** having a right-wing political viewpoint **3** cautiously moderate o *a conservative estimate* **4** conventional in appearance ■ *n* **1** a traditionalist **2** somebody with a right-wing political viewpoint —**con·ser·va·tive·ly** *adv* —**con·ser·va·tive·ness** *n*

Con·ser·va·tive Par·ty *n* the main British right-wing political party

con·ser·va·tor /kən súrvətər/ *n* **1** a restorer of works of art **2** a protector of the interests of a legally incompetent person

con·ser·va·to·ry /kən súrvə tàwree/ *(pl* **-ries***) n* **1** an advanced music or drama school **2** a glass-walled room for growing plants or relaxing

con·serve *vt* /kən súrv/ (**-served, -serv·ing**) **1** protect something from harm or decay **2** use resources sparingly ■ *n* /kón sùrv, kən súrv/ a fruit preparation resembling jam

~~con·ces·sion~~ incorrect spelling of **concession**

con·sid·er /kən síddər/ *v* **1** *vti* think carefully about something o *time to consider whether this is what you really want* **2** *vt* have as an opinion **3** *vt* show respect for **4** *vt* discuss formally

con·sid·er·a·ble /kən síddərəb'l/ *adj* **1** large **2** significant —**con·sid·er·a·bly** *adv*

con·sid·er·ate /kən síddərət/ *adj* mindful of the needs of others —**con·sid·er·ate·ly** *adv* —**con·sid·er·ate·ness** *n*

con·sid·er·a·tion /kən sìddə ráysh'n/ *n* **1** careful thought or deliberation **2** thoughtfulness or sensitivity toward others **3** a relevant factor in assessing something **4** a payment (*fml*)

con·sid·er·ing /kən síddəring/ *prep, conj* taking something into account ■ *adv* taking everything into account (*usually at the end of a phrase or sentence*) o *We've done a good job, considering.*

~~con·sience~~ incorrect spelling of **conscience**

con·sign /kən sín/ *vt* **1** entrust to the care of another **2** deliver for sale

con·sign·ment /kən sínmənt/ *n* **1** a quantity or package delivered or to be delivered **2** the entrusting of somebody to another's care

~~con·sious~~ incorrect spelling of **conscious**

con·sist /kən síst/ *vi* **1** be made up of diverse parts or things o *The dressing consists of olive oil and vinegar.* **2** be based on or defined by something o *Its attractiveness consists in its simplicity.*

~~con·sis·tent~~ incorrect spelling of **consistent**

con·sis·ten·cy /kən sístənssee/, **con·sis·tence** /-ənss/ *n* **1** the ability to be reliable, constant, or uniform **2** reasonable or logical harmony between parts **3** the degree of thickness or smoothness of a mixture

con·sis·tent /kən sístənt/ *adj* **1** logically harmonious o *consistent with the evidence* **2** reliable, constant, or uniform —**con·sis·tent·ly** *adv*

con·so·la·tion /kònsə láysh'n/ *n* **1** a source of comfort to somebody upset or disappointed **2** comfort given to somebody in distress o *words of consolation*

con·so·la·tion prize *n* a prize for the loser in a game or competition

con·sole[1] /kən sṓl/ (**-soled, -sol·ing**) *vt* comfort somebody in grief —**con·so·la·to·ry** /-sṓlə tàwree/ *adj* —**con·sol·ing·ly** *adv*

con·sole[2] /kón sòl/ *n* **1** a cabinet for a television or musical sound system **2** a control panel **3** a storage compartment between seats in an automobile **4** the part of an organ that houses the keyboards or manuals, pedals, and stops

con·sol·i·date /kən sólli dàyt/ (**-dat·ed, -dat·ing**) *vti* **1** unite, or be united **2** strengthen your position —**con·sol·i·da·tion** /kən sòlli dáysh'n/ *n*

con·som·mé /kònsə máy/ *n* a thin clear soup

con·so·nant /kónsənənt/ *n* a speech sound produced by partly or totally blocking the path of air through the mouth, or the corresponding letter of the alphabet ■ *adj* **1** in agreement (*fml*) **2** containing pleasant chords or harmonies —**con·so·nance** *n* —**con·so·nan·tal** /kònsə nánt'l/ *adj*

con·sort *vi* /kən sáwrt/ associate with undesirable people (*fml*) ■ *n* /kón sàwrt/ **1** *also* **Con·sort** the spouse of a monarch **2** a partner (*fml*)

con·sor·ti·um /kən sáwrtee əm, -sáwrshee əm/ *(pl* **-a** /-ə/*) n* an association of organizations set up for a common purpose

con·spic·u·ous /kən spíkyoo əss/ *adj* **1** easily visible **2** attracting attention —**con·spic·u·ous·ly** *adv*

con·spic·u·ous con·sump·tion *n* extravagant spending to impress others

con·spir·a·cy /kən spírrəssee/ *(pl* **-cies***) n* **1** a secret plan or agreement between two or more people to commit an illegal act **2** a group of conspirators

con·spir·a·cy of si·lence *n* an agreement to keep silent about a matter of public interest

con·spir·a·cy the·o·ry *n* a belief that a particular event is the result of a secret plot —**con·spir·a·cy the·o·rist** *n*

con·spir·a·tor /kən spírrətər/ *n* a member of a group secretly planning an illegal act

con·spir·a·to·ri·al /kən spírrə táwree əl/ *adj* indicating or suggesting involvement in a secret plot ○ *a conspiratorial whisper* —**con·spir·a·to·ri·al·ly** *adv*

con·spire /kən spîr/ (**-spired, -spir·ing**) *vi* 1 plan secretly to act illegally together 2 combine with an unpleasant result ○ *Bad weather and transportation strikes conspired to ruin our trip.*

con·sta·ble /kónstəb'l, kún-/ *n* a police officer of the lowest rank

Con·sta·ble /kónstəb'l, kún-/, **John** (1776–1837) British painter

con·stab·u·lar·y /kən stábbyə lèrree/ (*pl* **-ies**) *n* a military-style police force

con·stant /kónstənt/ *adj* 1 always present 2 happening or done repeatedly 3 not changing or varying 4 faithful ■ *n* 1 an unvarying thing or quality 2 a quantity with a fixed value —**con·stan·cy** *n* —**con·stant·ly** *adv*

Con·stan·tine (the Great) /kónstən tèen, -tìn/ (274–337) Roman emperor (306–37)

Con·stan·ti·no·ple /kòn stant'n óp'l/ former name for **Istanbul**

con·stel·la·tion /kònstə láysh'n/ *n* 1 a group of stars forming a distinctive pattern 2 a gathering of celebrities 3 a group of related things

con·ster·na·tion /kònstər náysh'n/ *n* shocked dismay

con·sti·pa·tion /kònsti páysh'n/ *n* difficulty in defecation —**con·sti·pat·ed** /kónsti pàytəd/ *adj*

con·stit·u·en·cy /kən stíchoo ənsee/ (*pl* **-cies**) *n* 1 an election district 2 the voters in a district

con·stit·u·ent /kən stíchoo ənt/ *n* 1 a resident of an election district 2 a part of a whole ■ *adj* forming a part (*fml*)

con·sti·tute /kónsti tòot/ (**-tut·ed, -tut·ing**) *vt* 1 be or amount to ○ *This letter does not constitute an offer of employment.* 2 be all or a particular part of 3 formally establish (*fml*)

con·sti·tu·tion /kònstə tóosh'n/ *n* 1 a statement of the laws of a country or organization 2 the constitution of the United States 3 somebody's general health and physical resilience 4 the parts, ingredients, or members of something 5 the formal creation or establishment of something

con·sti·tu·tion·al /kònstə tóoshən'l, -tóoshnəl/ *adj* of, involving, or in accordance with a constitution ■ *n* a walk taken for health reasons —**con·sti·tu·tion·al·i·ty** /kònstə toosh'n állətee/ *n* —**con·sti·tu·tion·al·ly** *adv*

con·strain /kən stráyn/ *vt* 1 force to do something 2 limit or restrict —**con·strain·a·ble** *adj*

con·strained /kən stráynd/ *adj* reserved or inhibited

con·straint /kən stráynt/ *n* 1 a limiting factor 2 a lack of warmth or spontaneity 3 restriction of freedom of action

con·strict /kən stríkt/ *v* 1 *vti* make or become narrower 2 *vt* limit or restrict —**con·stric·tion** /kən stríkshən/ *n* —**con·stric·tive** *adj* —**con·stric·tor** *n*

con·struct *vt* /kən strúkt/ 1 build or assemble 2 create in the mind ■ *n* /kón strúkt/ something created in the mind —**con·struct·i·ble** *adj* —**con·struc·tor** *n*

con·struc·tion /kən strúkshən/ *n* 1 the building of something such as a large structure 2 a structure or other thing built 3 the way something is built 4 an interpretation (*fml*) 5 a grammatical arrangement of words —**con·struc·tion·al** *adj*

con·struc·tion pa·per *n* thick colored paper for school artwork

con·struc·tive /kən strúktiv/ *adj* 1 useful or helpful ○ *constructive criticism* 2 structural —**con·struc·tive·ly** *adv* —**con·struc·tive·ness** *n*

con·strue /kən stróo/ (**-strued, -stru·ing**) *v* 1 *vt* interpret 2 *vti* analyze the grammar of a piece of text —**con·stru·al** *n*

con·sul /kóns'l/ *n* 1 a government official living in a foreign city as a diplomat 2 either of the chief magistrates in ancient Rome —**con·su·lar** *adj*

con·su·late /kónsələt/ *n* 1 a consul's office or residence 2 the position or jurisdiction of a consul

con·sult /kən súlt/ *v* 1 *vti* ask somebody for specialist advice or information, or for permission 2 *vt* look at something such as a book or watch for information —**con·sul·ta·tion** /kòns'l táysh'n/ *n* —**con·sul·ta·tive** *adj*

con·sult·ant /kən súltənt/ *n* an expert or professional adviser —**con·sul·tan·cy** *n* —**con·sult·ant·ship** *n*

con·sum·a·bles /kən sóoməb'lz/ *npl* goods that have to be bought regularly because they are used up or wear out —**con·sum·a·ble** *adj*

~~consumate~~ incorrect spelling of **consummate**

con·sume /kən sóom/ (**-sumed, -sum·ing**) *vt* 1 eat or drink 2 use up 3 absorb totally ○ *felt consumed by jealousy* 4 destroy completely ○ *was consumed by fire*

con·sum·er /kən sóomər/ *n* 1 a buyer of goods or services 2 somebody or something that consumes something —**con·sum·er·ship** *n*

con·sum·er du·ra·bles *npl* long-lasting household items

con·sum·er goods *npl* items bought by consumers rather than used to produce other goods

con·sum·er·ism /kən sóomə rìzzəm/ *n* 1 the protection of consumers' rights 2 a materialistic attitude (*disapproving*) 3 the belief that trade in consumer goods is good for the economy —**con·sum·er·ist** *n, adj*

con·sum·ing /kən sóoming/ *adj* extremely intense or absorbing

con·sum·mate v /kónsə màyt/ (**-mat·ed,** **-mat·ing**) **1** vt complete a marriage or relationship by having sexual intercourse **2** vti conclude (fml) ■ adj /kən súmmət, kónsəmət/ **1** supreme or perfect **2** utter or total —**con·sum·mate·ly** adv —**con·sum·ma·tion** /kòn sə máysh'n/ n

con·sump·tion /kən súmpsh'n/ n **1** the eating or drinking of something, or the amount eaten or drunk **2** the use of natural resources or fuels, or the amount used **3** consumer use of goods and services **4** a wasting disease such as tuberculosis (dated)

con·sump·tive /kən súmptiv/ adj **1** engaged in or encouraging consumption, especially in a wasteful or destructive way **2** affected by tuberculosis (dated)

cont. abbr **1** containing **2** contents **3** continental **4** continued **5** continuous

con·tact /kón tàkt/ n **1** communication o in contact with his family **2** physical connection by touch **3** interaction o came into contact with some interesting people and new ideas **4** a useful acquaintance **5** a possible carrier of a disease **6** a contact lens (infml) ■ vt communicate with by telephone, letter, or email ■ adj **1** used for communicating with somebody o a contact address **2** caused by touch —**con·tact·a·ble** /kən táktəb'l/ adj

con·tact lens n a glass or plastic lens worn in the eye

con·ta·gion /kən táyjən/ n **1** the spread of disease by physical contact **2** a disease spread by physical contact **3** a harmful influence that spreads

con·ta·gious /kən táyjəss/ adj **1** describes a disease that can be transmitted by contact **2** having a disease that can be transmitted by contact **3** quickly spread from one person to another o Laughter is contagious. —**con·ta·gious·ly** adv —**con·ta·gious·ness** n

con·tain /kən táyn/ vt **1** have or hold inside **2** include or consist of **3** control or hold back o contained the riot o couldn't contain my excitement —**con·tain·a·ble** adj

con·tain·er /kən táynər/ n an object used to hold something, especially for storage or transport

con·tain·er·ize /kən táynə rìz/ (**-ized, -iz·ing**) vt **1** pack cargo in large containers for transporting **2** modernize a port, system, or industry to handle standard cargo containers —**con·tain·er·i·za·tion** /kən táynəri záysh'n/ n

con·tain·ment /kən táynmənt/ n action to stop the spread of something undesirable

con·tam·i·nate /kən támmi nàyt/ (**-nat·ed, -nat·ing**) vt make impure or polluted —**con·tam·i·nant** n —**con·tam·i·na·tion** /kən támmi náysh'n/ n —**con·tam·i·na·tive** adj

con·tan·go /kən táng gō/ (pl **-gos**) n a basic pricing system in futures trading

con·tem·plate /kóntəm plàyt/ (**-plat·ed, -plat·ing**) vt **1** look at thoughtfully **2** consider seriously **3** have as a possible intention —**con·tem·pla·tion** /kòntəm pláysh'n/ n

con·tem·pla·tive /kən témplətiv/ adj calm and thoughtful —**con·tem·pla·tive·ly** adv —**con·tem·pla·tive·ness** n

con·tem·po·ra·ne·ous /kən tèmpə ráynee əss/ adj happening or existing at the same time —**con·tem·po·ra·ne·i·ty** /kən tèmpərə née ətee, -náy ətee/ n —**con·tem·po·ra·ne·ous·ly** adv

con·tem·po·rar·y /kən témpə rérree/ adj **1** existing or dating from the same period **2** existing now **3** modern in style ■ n (pl **-ies**) **1** somebody or something from the same period **2** somebody of the same age as another

~~contempory~~ incorrect spelling of **contemporary**

con·tempt /kən témpt/ n **1** an attitude of utter disgust or hatred **2** also **con·tempt of court** the crime of willfully disobeying the rules or decisions of a court of law

con·tempt·i·ble /kən témptəb'l/ adj deserving contempt —**con·tempt·i·bil·i·ty** /kən tèmptə bíllətee/ n —**con·tempt·i·ble·ness** n —**con·tempt·i·bly** adv

con·temp·tu·ous /kən témpchoo əss/ adj showing or feeling contempt —**con·temp·tu·ous·ly** adv —**con·temp·tu·ous·ness** n

con·tend /kən ténd/ v **1** vi state or argue that something is true **2** vti compete for something **3** vi deal with something difficult —**con·tend·er** n

✦ **con·tent**[1] /kón tènt/ n **1** the amount of material contained in a whole **2** subject matter **3** the meaning or message of a creative work **4** information available electronically ■ **con·tents** npl **1** everything in a container **2** a list of subject or chapter headings

con·tent[2] /kən tént/ adj **1** also **con·tent·ed** quietly satisfied and happy **2** ready to accept something ■ v **1** vt cause to feel content **2** vr accept or make do with something o We contented ourselves with a light supper. —**con·tent·ed·ly** adv —**con·tent·ed·ness** n —**con·tent·ly** adv —**con·tent·ment** n

con·ten·tion /kən ténshən/ n **1** an assertion in an argument **2** disagreement

con·ten·tious /kən ténshəss/ adj **1** creating disagreement **2** argumentative

con·test /kón tèst/ **1** a competition to find the best **2** a struggle for control ■ vt /kən tést/ **1** challenge or question something **2** take part in a contest to win something —**con·test·a·ble** adj

---

ORIGIN Contest has its origins in legal language. It derives from a Latin verb that meant "call to witness, begin a lawsuit by calling witnesses." That meaning is based on the same word that gave testify and testimony to

English. The element of competition involved in legal battles formed the basis for the more general senses that later developed.

con·tes·tant /kən téstənt/ n somebody competing in a contest ◊ See note at **candidate**

con·text /kón tèkst/ n 1 the text surrounding a word or passage 2 a set of surrounding conditions —**con·tex·tu·al** /kən tékschoo əl/ adj

con·tex·tu·al·ize /kən tékschoo ə líz/ (-ized, -iz·ing) vt place in its context —**con·tex·tu·al·i·za·tion** /kən tèkschoo əli záysh'n/ n

con·tig·u·ous /kən tíggyoo əss/ adj (fml) 1 adjoining something else 2 neighboring another property —**con·tig·u·i·ty** /kòntig gyoo ətee/ n —**con·tig·u·ous·ly** adv —**con·tig·u·ous·ness** n

con·ti·nent[1] /kóntinənt/ n 1 any of the seven large land masses that constitute most of the Earth's dry surfaces 2 **Con·ti·nent** mainland Europe ◊ traveled on the Continent

con·ti·nent[2] /kóntinənt/ adj able to control urination and bowel movements —**con·ti·nence** n

con·ti·nen·tal /kònti nént'l/ adj 1 of the Earth's continents 2 **Con·ti·nen·tal** of mainland Europe 3 **Con·ti·nen·tal** of the original 13 American colonies ■ n **Con·ti·nen·tal** an American soldier during the American Revolution —**con·ti·nen·tal·ism** n —**con·ti·nen·tal·ist** n

con·ti·nen·tal break·fast n a breakfast of bread and coffee

Con·ti·nen·tal Di·vide series of mountain ridges, running from Alaska to Mexico and including the Rocky Mountains, that forms the main watershed of North America

con·ti·nen·tal drift n the theory explaining the movement of continents across the Earth's crust

con·ti·nen·tal shelf n the ocean floor around a continent

con·tin·gen·cy /kən tínjənsee/ (pl -cies) n 1 also **con·tin·gence** something that may happen 2 something set aside for unforeseen emergencies

con·tin·gen·cy fee n a payment for professional services that is conditional upon success

con·tin·gen·cy plan n a plan to deal with a possible problem

con·tin·gent /kən tínjənt/ adj 1 dependent on what may happen or be the case 2 possible but not certain ■ n 1 a group of people 2 a group of military personnel —**con·tin·gent·ly** adv

~~continuous~~ incorrect spelling of **continuous**

con·tin·u·al /kən tínnyoo əl/ adj recurring very frequently —**con·tin·u·al·ly** adv —**con·tin·u·al·ness** n

---

USAGE continual or **continuous**? A **continual** noise is one that is constantly repeated, like a dog's barking, and a **continuous** noise is one that continues without stopping, like the roar of a waterfall. The same distinction applies to the adverbs **continually** and **continuously**: Hecklers continually interrupted the speaker. She drove continuously for two hours. In popular usage, however, **continual** and **continuously** are now frequently used to mean "without stopping."

---

con·tin·u·ance /kən tínnyoo ənss/ n 1 the continuation of something 2 the length of time that something lasts 3 a postponement of legal proceedings

con·tin·u·a·tion /kən tìnnyoo áysh'n/ n 1 the process of continuing 2 an addition or extension

con·tin·ue /kən tínnyoo/ (-ued, -u·ing, -ues) v 1 vti keep going 2 vti last, or cause to last, throughout a particular period 3 vti start again after a break 4 vti say something else 5 vti extend beyond a particular point 6 vi move further 7 vt US, Can, Scotland postpone legal proceedings —**con·tin·ued** adj

con·tin·u·ing /kən tínnyoo ing/ adj existing and likely to continue existing

con·tin·u·ing ed·u·ca·tion n 1 classes for adult students 2 specialist courses designed to update professionals

con·ti·nu·i·ty /kònti noo ətee/ (pl -ties) n 1 the fact of being the same or of not stopping 2 a consistent whole 3 consistency between scenes or shots in a film or broadcast

con·tin·u·ous /kən tínnyoo əss/ adj 1 unchanged or uninterrupted 2 without gaps or breaks 3 describes the progressive aspect of a verb —**con·tin·u·ous·ly** adv —**con·tin·u·ous·ness** n ◊ See note at **continual**

con·tin·u·um /kən tínnyoo əm/ (pl -a /-ə/ or -ums) n a continuous series of things that blend into one another

con·tort /kən táwrt/ v 1 vti twist or be twisted out of its natural shape 2 vt make unrecognizable —**con·tort·ed** adj —**con·tort·ed·ly** adv —**con·tort·ed·ness** n —**con·tor·tive** adj

con·tor·tion /kən táwrsh'n/ n 1 a twisted shape or position 2 a complex maneuver

con·tor·tion·ist /kən táwrsh'nist/ n 1 an acrobat who performs bending feats with the body 2 a skillful manipulator or maneuverer

con·tour /kón tòor/ n an outline (often pl) ■ adj shaped to fit something ■ vt 1 shape to fit 2 put contour lines on

con·tour line n a line on a map connecting points on a land surface that are the same height above sea level

Con·tra /kóntrə/ (pl -tras) n a member of a US-sponsored rebel force that tried to overthrow the Nicaraguan government in the 1980s

contra- *prefix* against, opposite, contrasting ○ *contraband* ○ *contradistinction*

con·tra·band /kóntrə bànd/ *n* goods traded or supplied illegally —**con·tra·band** *adj* —**con·tra·band·age** *n* —**con·tra·band·ist** *n*

con·tra·cep·tion /kòntrə sépsh'n/ *n* 1 prevention of pregnancy 2 methods or devices used to prevent pregnancy

con·tra·cep·tive /kòntrə séptiv/ *n* a device or drug designed to prevent pregnancy —**con·tra·cep·tive** *adj*

con·tra·cep·tive ring *n* a plastic ring inserted into the vagina that releases a constant flow of a contraceptive drug

con·tract *n* /kón tràkt/ a formal or legally binding agreement, or the document that records it ■ *v* /kən trákt/ 1 *vti* shrink or lessen 2 *vti* tighten or draw together 3 *vt* formally or legally agree to do something 4 *vt* get an illness 5 *vt* shorten a word or phrase —**con·tract·i·ble** *adj*
□ **contract out** /kón tràkt-/ *vti* give work to outsiders

con·tract bridge *n* the most common version of bridge, in which points are awarded only for tricks bid and won

con·trac·tion /kən tráksh'n/ *n* 1 reduction in size 2 a tightening or narrowing of a muscle, organ, or other body part 3 a tightening of the womb muscles that occurs before childbirth 4 a shortened word —**con·trac·tion·al** *adj* —**con·trac·tive** *adj*

con·trac·tor /kón tràktər/ *n* a company or person under contract to do a particular job, especially a builder

con·trac·tu·al /kən trákchoo əl/ *adj* involving a formal agreement —**con·trac·tu·al·ly** *adv*

con·tra·dict /kòntrə díkt/ *vt* 1 disagree with 2 show to be not true —**con·tra·dic·tive** *adj* —**con·tra·dic·tive·ly** *adv* —**con·tra·dic·tive·ness** *n* ◊ See note at **disagree**

con·tra·dic·tion /kòntrə díksh'n/ *n* 1 something with illogical or inconsistent parts 2 a statement that opposes somebody or something

con·tra·dic·to·ry /kòntrə díktəree/ *adj* 1 illogical or inconsistent 2 opposing something —**con·tra·dic·to·ri·ly** *adv* —**con·tra·dic·to·ri·ness** *n*

con·tra·dis·tinc·tion /kòntrə di stínkshən/ *n* a distinction made by pointing out contrasting qualities —**con·tra·dis·tinc·tive** *adj*

con·trail /kón tràyl/ *n* a vapor trail made by a high-flying aircraft

con·tral·to /kən trálto/ (*pl* **-tos**) *n* 1 the lowest female vocal range 2 somebody with a contralto voice

con·trap·tion /kən trápshən/ *n* a device or machine (*infml*)

con·tra·pun·tal /kòntrə púnt'l/ *adj* of counterpoint —**con·tra·pun·tal·ly** *adv*

con·trar·i·an /kən tráiree ən/ *n* 1 somebody who always takes an opposing position in a discussion 2 a maverick investor

con·trar·i·wise /kón treree wìz, kən tráiree wìz/ *adv* 1 in the opposite way 2 on the other hand

con·trar·y /kón trèrree/ *adj* 1 conflicting with something ○ *orders that are contrary to ethics* 2 opposite in direction ○ *flew in a direction contrary to the rest of the airplanes* 3 obstructing or hindering progress ○ *slowed by contrary winds* 4 /kón trèrree, kən tráiree/ deliberately disobedient ■ *n* the opposite ○ *argued the contrary instead of agreeing* —**con·trar·i·ly** *adv* —**con·trar·i·ness** *n*

con·trast *n* /kón tràst/ 1 a marked difference 2 a juxtaposition of different things 3 the degree of lightness and darkness in something such as a painting or television image ■ *vti* /kən trást, kón tràst/ be or show to be different —**con·trast·a·ble** *adj* —**con·trast·ing** /kən trásting/ *adj*

con·tra·vene /kòntrə veen/ (**-vened, -ven·ing**) *vt* 1 violate a rule or law 2 contradict somebody —**con·tra·ven·tion** /-vénsh'n/ *n*

~~contraversial~~ incorrect spelling of **controversial**

con·tre·temps /kóntrə taaN, kàwntrə táaN/ *n* a mishap (*fml*)

con·trib·ute /kən tríbbyoot/ (**-ut·ed, -ut·ing**) *v* 1 *vti* give money for a specific purpose 2 *vti* be a partial cause of something 3 *vti* offer an opinion or remark —**con·trib·u·tive** *adj* —**con·trib·u·tor** *n*

con·tri·bu·tion /kòntri byóosh'n/ *n* 1 something given for a specific purpose 2 a role played in achieving something

con·trib·u·to·ry /kən tríbbyə tàwree/ *adj* 1 helping something to happen 2 given along with other things

con·trib·u·to·ry neg·li·gence *n* a victim's partial responsibility for an accident

con·trite /kən trít/ *adj* 1 deeply sorry for a wrong 2 arising from a sense of guilt —**con·trite·ly** *adv* —**con·trite·ness** *n* —**con·tri·tion** /kən trísh'n/ *n*

con·tri·vance /kən trívənss/ *n* a gadget (*fml*)

con·trive /kən trív/ (**-trived, -triv·ing**) *v* 1 *vt* do something by being clever and creative 2 make something ingenious 3 manage to do something

con·trived /kən trívd/ *adj* 1 not natural and spontaneous 2 unlike reality

⚡ **con·trol** /kən tról/ *vt* (**-trolled, -trol·ling**) 1 operate a machine 2 restrain or limit something 3 manage something such as a business ■ *n* 1 the ability or authority to manage something 2 a set of limits and restrictions 3 a place where something is checked or inspected (*usually in combination*) ○ *passport control* 4 a subject used as a comparative standard in an experiment or survey 5 a supervising person or group 6 *also* **con·trol key** a special computer keyboard key pressed with others to

perform specific functions ■ **con·trols** *npl*
1 the system used for controlling something such as a machine or vehicle **2** regulations —**con·trol·la·ble** *adj*

~~controll~~ incorrect spelling of **control**

con·trolled sub·stance *n* a substance, usually a drug, whose use is regulated by law

con·trol·ler /kən trṓlər/ *n* **1** somebody who controls or organizes something **2** a financial supervisor

con·trol·ling in·ter·est *n* ownership of enough of a business to allow ultimate control

con·trol tow·er *n* a building from which aircraft are directed

con·tro·ver·sial /kòntrə vŭrsh'l/ *adj* causing strong argument —**con·tro·ver·sial·ly** *adv*

con·tro·ver·sy /kòntrə vŭrsee/ (*pl* **-sies**) *n* a dispute about a contentious topic

con·tu·ma·cious /kòn too máyshəss/ *adj* flagrantly insubordinate or rebellious

con·tume·ly /kən toõmələe, kón toõmələe, kóntəmələe/ *n* contempt (*literary*)

con·tu·sion /kən toõzh'n/ *n* a bruise (*technical*) —**con·tuse** *vt*

co·nun·drum /kə nŭndrəm/ *n* **1** a word puzzle **2** something confusing or puzzling ◊ See note at **problem**

con·ur·ba·tion /kònnər báysh'n/ *n* a large urban area created when neighboring towns merge into each other. ◊ See note at **city**

con·va·lesce /kònvə léss/ (**-lesced, -lesc·ing**) *vi* undergo a period of recovery from an illness

con·va·les·cent /kònvə léss'nt/ *n* a patient recovering from an illness —**con·va·les·cence** *n* —**con·val·es·cent** *adj*

con·vec·tion /kən véksh'n/ *n* **1** a circulatory motion in a liquid or gas **2** the upward movement of hot air in the atmosphere that leads to cloud formation —**con·vec·tion·al** *adj* —**con·vec·tive** *adj*

con·vec·tor /kən véktər/ *n* a heater that releases heat from a heating element by means of convection

con·vene /kən veen/ (**-vened, -ven·ing**) *vti* gather for a meeting

~~conveniant~~ incorrect spelling of **convenient**

con·ven·ience /kən veenyənss/ *n* **1** the quality of being convenient **2** personal comfort **3** something providing ease or comfort

con·ven·ience food *n* quickly prepared food

con·ven·ience store *n* a small general store

con·ven·ient /kən veenyənt/ *adj* involving little trouble or effort —**con·ven·ient·ly** *adv*

con·vent /kónvənt, kón vènt/ *n* **1** a religious community of women **2** the buildings occupied by a convent

con·ven·tion /kən vénshən/ *n* **1** a gathering of people with a common interest **2** the people attending a formal meeting **3** a

meeting to select candidates **4** a formal agreement **5** the usual way of doing things **6** a familiar device or method

con·ven·tion·al /kən vénshən'l/ *adj* **1** socially accepted **2** usual, established, or traditional **3** not using nuclear weapons or nuclear energy —**con·ven·tion·al·ism** *n* —**con·ven·tion·al·ist** *n* —**con·ven·tion·al·i·ty** /kən vènshə nállətee/ *n* —**con·ven·tion·al·ize** *vt* —**con·ven·tion·al·ly** *adv*

con·verge /kən vŭrj/ (**-verged, -verg·ing**) *vi* **1** reach the same point from different directions ◦ *roads that converged at an intersection* **2** become the same ◦ *rapidly converging political parties* **3** arrive in a large group at the same destination —**con·ver·gence** *n* —**con·ver·gen·cy** *n* —**con·ver·gent** *adj*

con·ver·sant /kən vŭrss'nt/ *adj* having knowledge or experience ◦ *conversant with politics* —**con·ver·sance** *n* —**con·ver·sant·ly** *adv*

con·ver·sa·tion /kònvər sáysh'n/ *n* **1** a casual talk **2** the activity of talking, especially informally

con·ver·sa·tion·al /kònvər sáyshən'l, kònvər sáyshnəl/ *adj* **1** of a conversation **2** informal in language —**con·ver·sa·tion·al·ly** *adv*

con·ver·sa·tion·al·ist /kònvər sáysh'nəlist/, **con·ver·sa·tion·ist** /-sáysh'nist/ *n* somebody who talks with ease

con·ver·sa·tion piece *n* **1** an object that interests people and gets them talking **2** a group portrait

ϟ**con·verse**[1] (**-versed, -vers·ing**) *vi* /kən vŭrs/ **1** talk with another or others **2** interact with a computer

con·verse[2] /kón vŭrs, kən vŭrs/ *n* the opposite of something —**con·verse** *adj* —**con·verse·ly** *adv*

con·ver·sion /kən vŭrzh'n/ *n* **1** a change in nature, form, or function **2** something altered **3** a change from one measuring or calculating system to another **4** adoption of new beliefs **5** in football and rugby, a successful kick of the ball over the crossbar following an attempt or a touchdown —**con·ver·sion·al** *adj*

con·vert *v* /kən vŭrt/ **1** *vti* change something, or be changed, in character, form, or function **2** *vt* change an amount or quantity from one measuring or calculating system to another **3** *vti* change your own or somebody else's beliefs ■ *n* /kón vŭrt/ somebody with changed beliefs ◊ See note at **change**

con·vert·er /kən vŭrtər/, **con·ver·tor** *n* a device that converts one thing into another

con·vert·i·ble /kən vŭrtəb'l/ *adj* **1** capable of being converted **2** exchangeable for gold or another currency ■ *n* a car with a removable roof

con·vex *adj* /kón vèks/ curving outward —**con·vex·i·ty** /kon véksətee/ *n*

con·vey /kən váy/ (**-veyed, -vey·ing, -veys**) vt
1 take a person, people, or things somewhere (fml) 2 communicate something
3 have something as a meaning
—**con·vey·a·ble** adj

con·vey·ance /kən váy ənss/ n 1 the conveying
of people or things 2 a vehicle (fml) 3 a
transfer of ownership

con·vey·or /kən váyr/, **con·vey·er** n 1 also
con·vey·or belt a moving belt that transports objects from one point to another
within a building 2 a means of transmitting
something

con·vict vt /kən víkt/ 1 declare a person
charged of a crime guilty 2 show somebody
to be at fault ■ n /kón víkt/ somebody in
prison —**con·vict·a·ble** adj

con·vic·tion /kən víksh'n/ n 1 a firmly held
belief 2 firmness of belief 3 a guilty verdict

con·vince /kən vínss/ (**-vinced, -vinc·ing**) vt
1 make somebody certain 2 persuade
somebody to do something —**con·vinc·**
i·ble adj

con·vinc·ing /kən vínsing/ adj 1 persuasive
2 beyond doubt —**con·vinc·ing·ly** adv
—**con·vinc·ing·ness** n◊ See note at **valid**

con·viv·i·al /kən vívvee əl/ adj 1 pleasant
because of its friendliness 2 enjoying the
company of others —**con·viv·i·al·i·ty** /kən
vìvvee állətee/ n —**con·viv·i·al·ly** adv

con·vo·ca·tion /kònvə káysh'n/ n 1 a formal
assembly 2 the act of calling a meeting

con·voke /kən vók/ (**-voked, -vok·ing**) vt call a
formal meeting

con·vo·lut·ed /kónvə lootəd/ adj 1 extremely
intricate 2 having many twists or whorls
—**con·vo·lut·ed·ly** adv —**con·vo·lut·ed·**
ness n

con·vo·lu·tion /kònvə loosh'n/ n a curve, coil,
or twist —**con·vo·lu·tion·al** adj

con·vol·vu·lus /kən vólvyələss/ (pl **-lus·es** or
-li /-lī/) n a climbing plant with a twining
growth pattern

con·voy /kón vòy/ n 1 a group of vehicles or
ships traveling together 2 an escort for vehicles or ships —**con·voy** vt

con·vulse /kən vúls/ (**-vulsed, -vuls·ing**) v 1 vti
shake uncontrollably 2 vt disrupt or disturb
—**con·vul·sive** adj —**con·vul·sive·ly** adv
—**con·vul·sive·ness** n

con·vul·sion /kən vúlshən/ n an uncontrollable
shaking of the body (often pl)

co·ny n = coney

coo v (**cooed, coo·ing, coos**) 1 vi make the
soft warbling sound of a pigeon 2 vti say
something very tenderly ■ n a pigeon's
soft warbling sound

cook v 1 vti prepare food 2 vi make or become
hot 3 vt tamper with information in order
to deceive people (slang) ■ n somebody
who prepares food —**cook·a·ble** adj
—**cook·er·y** n /koókəree/

□ **cook up** vt invent something, e.g., an excuse
(infml)

Cook, James, Captain (1728–79) British explorer and cartographer

cook·book /koók boòk/ n a book of recipes for
food preparation

ϟ **cook·ie** /koókee/, **cook·y** (pl **-ies**) n 1 a small
flat sweet cake 2 a person regarded as being
of a particular type or disposition (infml)
o a tough cookie 3 a computer file containing
user information, automatically sent to a
central computer when the user logs on

cook·ie-cut·ter adj identical

cook·ing /koóking/ n 1 the preparation of food
2 prepared food ■ adj used in cooking

Cook Is·lands self-governing island group
in free association with New Zealand, in
the South Pacific Ocean. Pop. 20,611 (2001).

cook-off n a cooking contest

cook·out /koók òwt/ n an outdoor party with
food

cook·top /koók tòp/ n the top part of a stove
where the burners are

cook·ware /koók wàir/ n utensils used in
cooking

ϟ **cook·y** n = cookie

cool adj 1 fairly cold, usually pleasantly so
2 also **cool-head·ed** staying calm under
pressure 3 fashionable (infml) 4 unfriendly
5 describes a style of jazz with a relaxed
rhythm 6 indicates approval or admiration
(slang) 7 indicates agreement or acceptance
(slang) 8 giving an impression of coldness
o television as a cool medium ■ vti 1 make or
become less warm o Wait until the mixture
cools. 2 make or become less intense ■ n
1 calmness under pressure (infml) 2 comparative coldness, especially pleasant coldness —**cool·ness** n ◊ **keep your cool**
remain calm (infml) ◊ **lose your cool**
become angry and excitable (infml)

□ **cool off** vi become cool again

cool·ant /koólənt/ n a substance that prevents
overheating, especially in vehicle engines

cool·er /koólər/ n 1 an insulated food or drink
container 2 a cold drink 3 a large cool room
for food storage

Coo·lidge /koólij/, **Calvin** (1872–1933) 30th
president of the United States (1923–29)

coo·lie /koólee/ n an offensive term for a local
man hired cheaply to do manual labor in
parts of Southeast Asia

cool·ing-off pe·ri·od n 1 a negotiated break
in a dispute 2 a time to reconsider before
making a legally binding agreement

cool·ing tow·er n a chimney for condensing
the steam produced by an industrial
process

cool·ly /koól lee/ adv 1 in a calm manner 2 in
an unfriendly manner

coon n a raccoon (infml)

coon·skin /koón skin/ n raccoon's pelt

coop *n* an enclosure for poultry
□ **coop up** *vt* keep in a small place

co-op /kô òp, kô óp/, **coop** *n* a cooperative *(infml)*

coop·er /koópər/ *n* a barrel-maker
—**coop·er·age** *n*

Coo·per /koópər/, **Gary** (1901–61) US movie actor

Coo·per, James Fenimore (1789–1851) US writer

co·op·er·ate /kô òppə ràyt/ (**-at·ed, -at·ing**), **co-op·er·ate** *v* **1** *vi* work together **2** do what is asked —**co·op·er·a·tion** /kô òppə ráysh'n/ *n*

co·op·er·a·tive /kô òpparàtiv/, **co-op·er·a·tive** *adj* **1** willing to help **2** working together **3** of jointly owned apartment building **4** operated collectively ■ *n* **1** a jointly owned apartment building **2** a business owned by the workers, with profits shared equally —**co·op·er·a·tive·ly** *adv* —**co·op·er·a·tive·ness** *n*

co-opt /kô ópt/ *vt* **1** adopt or appropriate something **2** neutralize the power of a faction by inviting and taking it into a larger group —**co·op·ta·tion** /kô op táysh'n/ *n*

co·or·di·nate /kô áwrdə nàyt/ (**-nat·ed, -nat·ing**) **1** *vt* organize and bring together the parts of a complex enterprise **2** *vti* move or work together smoothly **3** *vt* put or class things together **4** *vti* combine to make a pleasing set or match ■ *n* /kô áwrdənət/ **1** a number specifying the exact position of something **2** somebody or something equal in importance ■ **co·or·di·nates** *npl* matching clothes ■ *adj* /kô áwrdənət/ **1** equal in rank or importance **2** having the same or equal grammatical function **3** involving the use of coordinates —**co·or·di·nat·ed** *adj* —**co·or·di·na·tion** /kô àwrdə náysh'n/ *n* —**co·or·di·na·tive** *adj* —**co·or·di·na·tor** *n*

Co·or·di·nat·ed U·ni·ver·sal Time *n* = Universal Time

coot (*pl* **coots** or same) *n* a darkish water bird with a white beak and long toes

coo·tie /koótee/ *n* US, Can, NZ a louse *(infml)*

cop *n* a police officer *(infml)* ■ *vt* (**copped, cop·ping**) grab something *(slang)* ◊ **cop a plea** negotiate with a prosecutor in order to avoid prosecution *(slang)*
□ **cop out** *vi* avoid doing something out of fear *(slang)*

co·pa·cet·ic /kòpə séttik/, **co·pa·set·ic** *adj* excellent *(slang)*

cope[1] (**coped, cop·ing**) *vi* handle something successfully

cope[2] *n* a priest's cloak

cope[3] (**coped, cop·ing**) *vt* provide a wall with a coping

Co·pen·ha·gen /kôpən hàygən, kòpən haágən/ capital and largest city of Denmark. Pop. 491,082 (1999).

Nicolaus Copernicus

Co·per·ni·cus /kô púrnikəss, kə-/, **Nicolaus** (1473–1543) Polish astronomer —**Co·per·ni·can** *adj*

cop·i·er /kóppee ər/ *n* a photocopier

co·pi·lot /kô pîlət/ *n* an assistant pilot

cop·ing /kôping/ *n* the top course of brick or stone that caps a wall

co·pi·ous /kôpee əss/ *adj* abundant —**co·pi·ous·ly** *adv* —**co·pi·ous·ness** *n*

Aaron Copland

Cop·land /kôpland/, **Aaron** (1900–90) US composer

Cop·ley /kópplee/, **John Singleton** (1738–1815) US painter

cop-out *n* an evasion of responsibility *(slang)*

⚡ **COPPA** /kóppə/ *n* an Act of Congress regulating the collection of data by website operators from children under the age of 13. Full form **Children's Online Privacy Protection Act**

cop·per /kóppər/ *n* **1** (*symbol* **Cu**) a reddish brown metal. Use: wiring, coatings, alloys. **2** a reddish brown color —**cop·per** *adj* —**cop·per·y** *adj*

cop·per·head /kóppər hèd/ (*pl* **-heads** or same) *n* a poisonous reddish brown North American snake

Cop·po·la /kóppələ/, **Francis Ford** (*b.* 1939) US movie director

co·pra /kôprə, kóp-/ *n* dried coconut meat

⚡ **co·pro·ces·sor** /kô pró sèssər/ *n* a second processor in a computer that improves performance

copse *n* an area of densely growing small trees, especially one in which the trees are cut regularly to encourage young growth

cop·ter /kóptər/ *n* a helicopter *(infml)*

cop·u·late /kóppyə làyt/ (**-lat·ed, -lat·ing**) *vi* have sex —**cop·u·la·tion** /kòppyə láysh'n/ *n*

cop·y /kóppee/ *n* (*pl* **-ies**) **1** something that is made exactly like something else **2** one of many identical specimens of something, e.g., a book **3** the written text of something such as a book or newspaper, as distinct from the graphics ■ *vt* (**-ied**, **-ies**) **1** make an identical version of **2** do the same as **3** send a copy of a document to somebody —**cop·y·a·ble** *adj* —**cop·y·ist** *n*

SYNONYMS copy, reproduce, duplicate, clone, replicate, re-create CORE MEANING: make something that resembles something else to a greater or lesser degree

cop·y·cat /kóppee kàt/ (*infml*) *n* somebody who imitates somebody else ■ *adj* done in imitation

cop·y ed·i·tor, cop·y·ed·i·tor /kóppee èddətər/ *n* somebody who corrects written material before its publication

⚡**cop·y pro·tec·tion** *n* a way to prevent software from unauthorized copying —**cop·y-pro·tect·ed** *adj*

cop·y·right /kóppee rìt/ *n* a creative artist's legal right to control the use and re-production of his or her original work —**cop·y·right** *vt*

~~copywrite~~ incorrect spelling of **copyright**

cop·y·writ·er /kóppee rìtər/ *n* a writer of advertisements —**cop·y·writ·ing** *n*

coq au vin /kòk ō váN, -váN/ *n* a French dish of chicken cooked in red wine

co·quette /kō két/ *n* a woman who flirts —**co·quet·tish** *adj*

cor·a·cle /kárrək'l/ *n* a small round boat made of animal skins stretched across a wooden frame

ORIGIN **Coracle** was adopted from Welsh.

Barnaby's

Coral

cor·al /kárrəl/ *n* **1** a marine organism that lives in colonies and has an external skeleton **2** a hard deposit consisting of the skeletons of corals, often forming marine reefs **3** a deep reddish orange color —**cor·al** *adj*

cor·al reef *n* a marine ridge of coral skeletons

Cor·al Sea arm of the SW Pacific Ocean bounded by Australia, New Guinea, the Solomon Islands, and Vanuatu

Cor·bu·sier ♦ **Le Corbusier**

cord *n* **1** thick strong string or rope **2** an electrical cable **3** a body part resembling rope, e.g., the spinal cord **4** a length of material used as a fastening or belt **5** ribbed fabric, especially corduroy ■ *vt* tie with a cord ◊ See note at **chord**

cord·age /káwrdij/ *n* ropes or cords collectively

Cor·day /kawr dáy/, **Charlotte** (1768–93) French assassin of Jean-Paul Marat during the French Revolution

cor·dial /káwrjəl/ *adj* **1** friendly and hospitable **2** deeply felt (*literary*) ○ *has a cordial dislike for dogs* ■ *n* any liqueur —**cor·di·al·i·ty** /kàwr jállətee, -jee állətee/ *n* —**cor·dial·ly** *adv*

cord·ite /káwr dìt/ *n* a smokeless explosive made using gun cotton

cord·less /káwrdləss/ *adj* not needing electricity from a wall outlet

cór·do·ba /káwrdəbə/ *n* the main unit of Nicaraguan currency

Cor·do·ba /káwrdəbə/, **Cór·do·ba** capital of **Córdoba Province**, S Spain. Pop. 309,961 (1998).

cor·don /káwrd'n, -dòn/ *n* **1** a line of people or vehicles or a temporary crowd-control fence encircling an area **2** a ribbon worn as a decoration or as a sign of rank

□ **cordon off** *vt* seal off an area with people, vehicles, or barriers

cor·don bleu /kàwr dawn blóō, -doN-/ *adj* describes cooking of the highest class

cor·do·van /káwrdəvən/ *n* a soft leather

cor·du·roy /káwrdə ròy/ *n* ribbed cotton fabric ■ **cor·du·roys** *npl* pants made of corduroy

ORIGIN **Corduroy** is probably a compound made up of *cord* and *duroy*, which was a lightweight worsted material formerly used for men's clothing. The origins of this name are unknown. A popular explanation of **corduroy** is that it comes from French *corde du roi* "cord of the king," but there is no real evidence for this.

⚡**core** *n* **1** the essential part of something ○ *the core of the argument* **2** the central hard part of a piece of fruit **3** the center of the Earth **4** a sample obtained by drilling **5** the central part of a nuclear reactor **6** formerly, the main memory in a computer before the introduction of semiconductors ■ *adj* essential ■ *vt* (**cored, cor·ing**) take the core out of a piece of fruit

CORE *abbr* Congress of Racial Equality

core cur·ric·u·lum *n* a set of compulsory school subjects

⚡**core dump** *n* a transfer of data from a computer's main memory to an external source

~~corelate~~ incorrect spelling of **correlate**

co·re·lig·ion·ist /kō ri líjjənist/ *n* an offensive term for somebody of the same religion as another person whose beliefs are disapproved of

~~corespondence~~ incorrect spelling of **correspondence**

co·re·spon·dent /kō ri spóndənt/, **co·re·spon·dent** *n* an alleged adulterous sexual partner in divorce proceedings —co-re·spon·den·cy n

core time n the part of the working day during which flextime workers must be at work

Cor·fu /kawr fòò, kàwr fòò/ most northerly of the Ionian Islands, west of Greece. Pop. 107,592 (1991).

cor·gi /káwrgee/ (pl -gis) n a small dog with smooth hair and short legs

co·ri·an·der /kàwree ándar/ n 1 leaves or seeds used as a food flavoring 2 the aromatic plant from which coriander is taken

Cor·inth /káwrinth/ ancient city and modern town in S Greece. Pop. 27,412 (1991).

Co·rin·thi·an /kə rínthee ən/ adj of Corinth, Greece —**Co·rin·thi·an** n

Co·rin·thi·ans /kə rínthee ənz/ n either of two books of the Bible, originally written as letters by St. Paul to the church in Corinth (+ sing verb)

cork n 1 the outer bark of a Mediterranean evergreen oak. Use: bottle stoppers, insulation. 2 a bottle stopper made of cork or plastic ■ vt seal a container with a top —**cork·y** adj

Cork port in SW Ireland. Pop. 180,000 (1996).

cork·age /káwrkij/ n a fee charged in some restaurants for serving the wine that customers bring for themselves

corked adj 1 sealed with a cork 2 describes wine given an unpleasant flavor by a tainted cork

cork·screw /káwrk skròò/ n a device for removing corks from bottles ■ vi move in a spiral path ■ adj shaped like a spiral

cor·mo·rant /káwrmərənt/ n a large diving sea bird with a long neck

corn[1] n 1 grains of the corn plant 2 a tall cereal crop 3 UK, Ireland any cereal crop, especially wheat, barley, or oats 4 corny material or sentiments (infml)

corn[2] n a hard thick patch of skin on the foot

corn·ball /káwrn bàwl/ n an overly sentimental person —**corn·ball** adj

Corn Belt n a corn-growing area

corn bread, corn·bread /káwrn brèd/ n bread made from cornmeal

corn chip n a piece of fried cornmeal batter eaten as a snack

corn·cob /káwrn kòb/ n the core of an ear of corn

corn·crake /káwrn kràyk/ n a speckled bird with a harsh call

corn dog n a hot dog fried in cornmeal batter

cor·ne·a /káwrnee ə/ (pl -as or -ae /-èe/) n a transparent membrane covering the front of the eye —**cor·ne·al** adj

corned beef n cooked and salted beef

cor·ner /káwrnər/ n 1 the angle formed where two lines, boundaries, or surfaces meet 2 an area enclosed by converging lines or boundaries 3 a projecting part 4 a place where two roads meet 5 a difficult situation 6 a quiet or remote place 7 a monopoly of a particular market ■ adj 1 located on a corner 2 intended for a corner ■ v 1 vt force into a difficult position 2 vt acquire a monopoly of 3 vi turn a corner (refers to vehicles or their drivers) ◊ **in somebody's corner** providing somebody with support ◊ **turn the corner** get past the worst part of a difficult situation

cor·ner·stone /káwrnər stòn/ n 1 a fundamentally important person or thing 2 a stone at the corner of two walls

cor·ner store n a store on a street corner

cor·net /kawr nét/ n a brass instrument like a small trumpet

corn-fed adj fed on corn

corn·flakes /káwrn flàyks/ npl a breakfast cereal made from corn

corn·flow·er /káwrn flòwr/ n a blue-flowered plant found in cultivated fields

cor·nice /káwrniss/ n 1 a projecting molding along the top of an external wall 2 a decorative plaster molding around a room where the walls and ceiling meet 3 the part of a classical building that is supported by columns

Cor·nish /káwrnish/ adj of Cornwall, England ■ npl the people of Cornwall, England ■ n an extinct Celtic language of Cornwall, England

corn·meal /káwrn mèel/ n flour made from corn

corn on the cob n an ear of corn cooked whole

corn·pone /káwrn pòn/, **corn pone** n Southern US fried or baked bread made from cornmeal

corn·row /káwrn rò/ n a braided row of hair lying flat against the scalp —**corn·row** vt

corn snow n grainy snow that has thawed and refrozen

corn·starch /káwrn staàrch/ n flour from corn

corn syr·up n syrup from cornstarch

cor·nu·co·pi·a /káwrnə kópee ə/ n 1 an abundance 2 a goat's horn overflowing with produce, symbolizing prosperity —**cor·nu·co·pi·an** adj

Corn·wall /káwrn wàwl, -wəl/ county in the extreme southwest of England. Pop. 482,000 (1995).

Corn·wal·lis /kawrn wólliss/, **Charles, 1st Marquis and 2nd Earl Cornwallis** (1738–1805) British army general who surrendered at Yorktown in 1781

corn·y /káwrnee/ (-i·er, -i·est) adj sentimental in an annoying, unsophisticated way —**corn·i·ly** adv —**corn·i·ness** n

cor·ol·lar·y /káwrə lèrree/ (pl -ies) n 1 a natural consequence of something 2 a fact that must be true when another related statement is proved true

co·ro·na /kə rṓnə/ (*pl* **-nas** *or* **-nae** /-neè/) *n* 1 a ring of light around the Moon 2 the outermost part of the Sun's atmosphere —**co·ro·nal** /káwrən'l, kə rṓn'l/ *adj*

Co·ro·na·do /káwrə naáadṓ/, **Francisco Vásquez de** (1510–54) Spanish explorer

cor·o·nar·y /káwrə nèrree/ *n* (*pl* **-ies**) a heart attack (*infml*) ■ *adj* 1 supplying or draining blood from the heart 2 of the coronary arteries and veins

cor·o·nar·y throm·bo·sis *n* blockage of an artery by a blood clot, often resulting in a heart attack

cor·o·na·tion /káwrə náysh'n/ *n* the ceremony or act of crowning a monarch

cor·o·ner /káwrənər/ *n* an official who investigates suspicious deaths —**cor·o·ner·ship** *n*

cor·o·net /káwrə nét, kórrə nèt/ *n* 1 a small crown 2 a woman's head decoration shaped like a slender crown

Co·rot /kaw rṓ/, **Jean-Baptiste Camille** (1796–1875) French painter

corp. *abbr* corporation

corporation incorrect spelling of **corporation**

cor·po·ra plural of **corpus**

cor·po·ral[1] /káwrpərəl, -prəl/ *adj* of the body —**cor·po·ral·i·ty** /káwrpə rállətee/ *n* —**cor·po·ral·ly** *adv*

cor·po·ral[2] /káwrpərəl, -prəl/ *n* a non-commissioned officer in various armed forces, ranking above a private —**cor·po·ral·cy** *n* —**cor·po·ral·ship** *n*

cor·po·ral[3] /káwrpərəl, káwrprəl/ *n* a white cloth on which the bread and wine are placed during the Christian service of Communion

cor·po·ral pun·ish·ment *n* the act of striking somebody as a punishment

cor·po·rate /káwrpərət, -prət/ *adj* 1 involving businesses or their employees, often as distinct from private individuals 2 having been incorporated 3 of a group as a whole (*fml*) —**cor·po·rate·ly** *adv*

⚡ **cor·po·rate dis·as·ter re·cov·er·y** *n* computer data recovery operations for businesses

cor·po·rate wel·fare *n* laws overtly favoring business interests

cor·po·ra·tion /káwrpə ráysh'n/ *n* 1 a group regarded as an individual by law 2 the governing authority of a municipality

cor·po·rat·ism /káwrpərə tìzzəm, káwrprə-/ *n* the running of a state by large organizations —**cor·po·ra·tist** *adj*, *n*

cor·po·re·al /kawr páwree əl/ *adj* 1 of the physical body 2 material or physical, rather than spiritual —**cor·po·re·al·i·ty** /kawr páwree állətee/ *n* —**cor·po·re·al·ly** *adv*

corps /kawr/ (*pl* **corps** /kawrz/) *n* 1 a specialized military force 2 a tactical military unit made up of two or more divisions 3 a group of associated people o *the press corps*

corps de bal·let /kàwr də ba láy/ (*pl* same) *n* the dancers in a ballet company who do not perform individually

corpse *n* a dead body

corps·man /káwrmən, káwrz-/ (*pl* **-men** /káwr men, kàwrz-/) *n* a soldier trained to give first aid

cor·pu·lent /káwrpyələnt/ *adj* overweight —**cor·pu·lence** *n*

cor·pus /káwrpəss/ (*pl* **-po·ra** /-pərə/) *n* 1 a body of writings 2 the main part

Cor·pus Chris·ti /kàwrpəss krístee/ city and port in SE Texas. Pop. 281,453 (1998).

cor·pus·cle /káwrpəss'l, -pùss'l/ *n* a cell in blood or lymph —**cor·pus·cu·lar** /kawr púskyələr/ *adj*

cor·ral /kə rál/ *n* a fenced area for keeping livestock in ■ *vt* (**-ralled, -ral·ling**) 1 drive animals into a corral 2 gather and control people or things (*infml*)

cor·rect /kə rékt/ *vt* 1 remove errors from something 2 point out errors in something 3 rectify an imperfection in something, e.g., eyesight ■ *adj* 1 accurate or without errors 2 acceptable or meeting a required standard —**cor·rec·tive** *adj* —**cor·rect·ly** *adv* —**cor·rect·ness** *n*

cor·rec·tion /kə rékshən/ *n* 1 an alteration that removes errors 2 a written comment correcting an error in a text 3 removal of errors 4 a fall in stock prices ■ **cor·rec·tions** *npl* the system, buildings, personnel, and protocols used in housing convicted offenders

cor·rec·tion·al /kə rékshən'l/ *adj* 1 of correction 2 of corrections

cor·rec·tion·al fa·cil·i·ty *n* a prison

Cor·reg·i·dor /kə réggi dàwr/ island at the entrance to Manila Bay in the Philippines. In World War II, the scene of intense fighting between US and Filipino forces against Japanese troops. It was recaptured by US forces in 1945.

cor·re·late *v* /káwrə làyt/ (**-lat·ed, -lat·ing**) 1 *vi* have a mutual or complementary relationship, or show things to have one 2 *vt* gather and compare things ■ *adj* /káwrə lət, -làyt/ having a mutual or complementary relationship ■ *n* /káwrə lət, -làyt/ 1 a thing having a mutual or complementary relationship with another 2 one variable related to another variable

cor·re·la·tion /káwrə láysh'n/ *n* 1 a mutual or complementary relationship 2 the act of correlating things —**cor·re·la·tion·al** *adj*

cor·rel·a·tive /kə réllətiv/ *adj* 1 in a mutual or complementary relationship 2 describes words used together in a grammatical construction but not adjacent —**cor·rel·a·tive** *n* —**cor·rel·a·tive·ly** *adv* —**cor·rel·a·tive·ness** *n* —**cor·rel·a·tiv·i·ty** /kə réllə tívvətee/ *n*

cor·re·spond /káwrə spónd/ *vi* 1 conform or be consistent 2 be similar or equivalent

3 write to one another —**cor·re·spond·ing** *adj* —**cor·re·spond·ing·ly** *adv*

cor·re·spon·dence /kàwrə spóndənss/ *n* **1** communication by writing **2** letters or other written messages **3** the state or fact of corresponding to something

cor·re·spon·dence course *n* an educational course taken by mail

cor·re·spon·dent /kàwrə spóndənt/ *n* **1** somebody communicating by writing **2** somebody providing news reports on a particular place or subject ■ *adj* corresponding

cor·ri·dor /káwridər/ *n* **1** a passage inside a building **2** a passageway in a railroad car or ship **3** a strip of land belonging to one country and extending through another **4** a populated strip between urban areas **5** a specific region of airspace for air traffic

cor·rob·o·rate /kə róbbə ràyt/ (**-rat·ed, -rat·ing**) *vt* show or confirm the truth of —**cor·rob·o·ra·tion** /kə ròbbə ráysh'n/ *n* —**cor·rob·o·ra·tive** *adj* —**cor·rob·o·ra·tive·ly** *adv* —**cor·rob·o·ra·tor** *n*

cor·rode /kə ród/ (**-rod·ed, -rod·ing**) *v* **1** *vti* destroy or be destroyed progressively by chemical action **2** *vt* undermine gradually —**cor·rod·i·ble** *adj*

~~**corrolary**~~ incorrect spelling of **corollary**

cor·ro·sion /kə rózh'n/ *n* **1** gradual destruction by chemical action, or the resulting damage **2** rust or other material produced by corrosion —**cor·ro·si·ble** /kə róssəb'l/ *adj*

cor·ro·sive /kə róssiv/ *adj* **1** progressively destructive owing to chemical action **2** destroying something gradually ■ *n* a destructive substance —**cor·ro·sive·ly** *adv* —**cor·ro·sive·ness** *n*

cor·ru·gat·ed /káwrə gàytəd/ *adj* having ridges and troughs —**cor·ru·gate** *vti*

⚡**cor·rupt** /kə rúpt/ *adj* **1** immoral or dishonest **2** depraved **3** describes computer data or software containing errors ■ *v* **1** *vti* make or become dishonest, immoral, or depraved **2** *vt* introduce errors into computer data —**cor·rupt·i·ble** *adj* —**cor·rupt·ly** *adv* —**cor·rupt·ness** *n*

cor·rup·tion /kə rúpsh'n/ *n* **1** dishonest behavior engaged in for personal gain **2** depravity

cor·sage /kawr saázh/ *n* a small bouquet of flowers worn on a dress

cor·sair /káwr sàir/ *n* **1** a pirate, especially on the North African coast between the 16C and 19C **2** a pirate ship or its owner

cor·set /káwrssət/ *n* a stiff undergarment formerly worn by women to shape the waist and breasts or by men to pull in the waist

Cor·si·ca /káwrssikə/ island in the Mediterranean Sea, an administrative region of France. Pop. 249,737 (1990). —**Cor·si·can** *adj, n*

cor·tege /kawr tézh/, **cor·tège** *n* **1** a funeral procession **2** a retinue of attendants

Cor·tés /kawr téz/, **Hernán** (1485–1547) Spanish explorer

cor·tex /káwr tèks/ (*pl* **-ti·ces** /-ti seèz/ *or* **-tex·es**) *n* **1** the outer layer of a body part **2** a layer of plant tissue beneath the epidermis —**cor·ti·cal** /káwrtik'l/ *adj*

cor·ti·sone /káwrti zòn/ *n* a hormone secreted by the adrenal cortex

co·run·dum /kə rúndəm/ *n* a hard mineral form of aluminum oxide. Use: gemstones, abrasives.

cor·vette /kawr vét/ *n* **1** a naval escort ship **2** a small wooden sailing ship with one tier of guns

cos *abbr* cosine

Cos /koss, kawss/ second largest of the Greek Dodecanese Islands, off the coast of Turkey. Pop. 20,350 (1981).

Co·sa Nos·tra /kòssə nóstrə/ *n* an organized crime group in the United States with links to the Sicilian Mafia

ORIGIN **Cosa Nostra** literally means "our concern" in Italian.

co·sign /kó sìn, kō sín/ *vt* **1** sign something jointly **2** sign something as guarantor —**co·sig·na·to·ry** /kō sígnə tàwree/ *n*

co·sine /kó sìn/ *n* a ratio of the length of the adjacent side of a right-angled triangle to the length of the hypotenuse

cos·me·ceut·i·cal /kòzmə soòtik'l/ *n* a cosmetic product claiming pharmaceutical properties, e.g., an anti-aging cream

cos·met·ic /koz méttik/ *n* (*often pl*) **1** a substance applied to the face or body to make it more attractive **2** a superficially attractive aspect ■ *adj* **1** intended to improve appearance **2** done only for appearances —**cos·met·i·cal·ly** *adv*

cos·met·ic sur·ger·y *n* plastic surgery to improve appearance

cos·mic /kózmik/ *adj* **1** of the whole universe **2** great or enormous —**cos·mi·cal·ly** *adv*

cos·mic ra·di·a·tion *n* cosmic rays

cos·mic ray *n* a stream of high-energy radiation from space

cosmo- *prefix* the universe, space ○ *cosmology*

cos·mog·o·ny /koz móggənee/ *n* the study of the origin of the universe —**cos·mog·o·nist** *n*

cos·mol·o·gy /koz mólləjee/ *n* **1** the study of the nature of the universe **2** the scientific study of the structure of the universe —**cos·mo·log·i·cal** /kòzmə lójjik'l/ *adj* —**cos·mol·o·gist** *n*

cos·mo·naut /kózmə nàwt/ *n* a Russian astronaut

cos·mo·pol·i·tan /kòzmə póllit'n/ *adj* **1** containing features of or people from different countries **2** well traveled **3** sophisticated and well educated ■ *n* a well-traveled person —**cos·mo·pol·i·tan·ism** *n*

cos·mos[1] /kóz mòss, -məss/ n 1 the whole universe 2 an ordered system

cos·mos[2] /kóz mòss, -məss/ (pl **-mos·es** or same) n a plant with flowers like daisies

cos·set /kóssət/ vt give excessive care and protection to

cost vt (cost) 1 be priced at 2 cause the loss of ■ n 1 the amount of money paid for or spent doing something 2 the loss of something, or the effort involved in doing something ■ **costs** npl 1 legal expenses 2 the calculated amount of money needed for something ◇ housing costs

cost ac·count·ing n accounting concerned with a business's production costs

co·star /kó staàr/, **co-star** n a performer who shares equal prominence with another ■ v (-starred, -star·ring) 1 vi star jointly with another performer 2 vt feature as a joint star

Cos·ta Ri·ca /kóstə reékə, kòstə-/ country in S Central America between the Caribbean Sea and the Pacific Ocean. Cap. San José. Pop. 3,773,057 (2001). —**Cos·ta Ri·can** n, adj

cost-ef·fec·tive adj economically worthwhile —**cost-ef·fec·tive·ly** adv —**cost-ef·fect·ive·ness** n

cost·ly /káwstlee/ (-li·er, -li·est) adj 1 expensive 2 luxurious 3 involving great time or effort —**cost·li·ness** n

cost of liv·ing n living expenses

cost-plus n a pricing system that calculates the selling price of something by adding a fixed percentage as profit

cost price n the price that a seller has paid for something

cost-push, cost-push in·fla·tion n inflation caused by rising production costs

cos·tume /kós tòom/ n 1 special clothes worn by a performer 2 the clothes traditionally worn during a particular period in the past 3 the clothes worn for a particular activity ■ vt (-tumed, -tum·ing) dress in a costume

---

ORIGIN Costume comes from the same Latin word as custom, which has remained closer to the original meaning. Custom entered English through French in the early Middle Ages. Costume came from French via Italian in the early 18C. At first costume was a term of art criticism and referred to the fashion, furniture, and other features of a painting in relation to their historical accuracy. Current senses did not develop until the 19C.

---

cos·tume jew·el·ry n decorative but cheap jewels

co·sy adj, n UK = cozy

cot[1] n 1 a collapsible lightweight bed 2 UK = crib 1

cot[2] abbr cotangent

co·tan·gent /kó tánjənt/ n a ratio of the length of the side of a right-angled triangle that is adjacent to the angle divided by the opposite side —**co·tan·gen·tial** /kò tan jénsh'l/ adj

Côte d'A·zur /kòt də zoór/ part of the French Riviera near the Italian border

Côte d'I·voire /-dee vwaàr/ country in West Africa, situated north of the Gulf of Guinea. Cap. Yamoussoukro. Pop. 16,393,221 (2001).

co·ter·ie /kótəree, kòtə reé/ n a small exclusive group

co·til·lion /kə tíllyən, kō-/ n 1 a formal ball 2 a complex 18C French dance 3 a dance like a quadrille 4 the music for a cotillion

Co·to·pa·xi /kòtə pàksee/ volcano in the Andes, in central Ecuador. It is the highest active volcano in the world. Height 19,347 ft./5,897 m.

Cots·wolds /kóts wòldz/ range of limestone hills in SW England

cot·tage /kóttij/ n 1 a small house, especially in the country 2 a vacation home 3 a small residential unit, e.g., in a camp —**cot·tag·er** n —**cot·tag·ey** adj

cot·tage cheese n a soft white semisolid cheese with a lumpy texture

cot·tage in·dus·try n a small home-based business

cot·ton /kótt'n/ n 1 a soft white fiber that grows in the seed pods of a bush. Use: textiles. 2 fabric made from cotton 3 something made of cotton fabric (often pl) 4 the tropical and subtropical bush that produces cotton fiber —**cot·ton·y** adj
□ **cotton on** vi begin to understand (infml)
□ **cotton to** vt start liking

Cot·ton Belt n the cotton-growing region of the United States

cot·ton can·dy n candy made with spun sugar threads

cot·ton swab n a cotton-tipped stick used, e.g., for cleaning ears

cot·ton·tail /kótt'n tàyl/ n a North American rabbit

cot·ton·wood /kótt'n wòod/ (pl **-woods** or same) n a poplar tree with seeds that have cottony tufts

cot·ton wool n unprocessed cotton

couch /kowch/ n 1 a long comfortable seat for two or more people 2 a psychiatrist's long seat on which a patient may lie ■ vt phrase in a certain way

cou·chette /koo shét/ n a seat on a train that is convertible to a bed

couch po·ta·to n an inactive person who watches television constantly (slang disapproving)

cou·gar /koógər, -aarl/ (pl **-gars** or same) n a mountain lion

cough /kawf/ v 1 vi expel air from the lungs noisily 2 vt expel something by coughing ■ n 1 an act or sound of coughing 2 an illness causing coughing

cough drop *n* candy that soothes a cough

cough syrup *n* a syrup for soothing coughs

~~cought~~ incorrect spelling of **caught**

could /kŏŏd/ *modal v* **1** past tense of **can** **2** expresses possibility ◊ *You could go tomorrow.* ◊ *We could have gone.* **3** expresses a request ◊ *Could you close the window please?* **4** expresses a polite offer ◊ *You could stay at my place.* ◊ See note at **would**

could·n't /kŏŏdd'nt/ *contr* could not

cou·lis /kŏŏlee/ *(pl same)* *n* a thin purée of fruit or vegetables used as a garnish

cou·lomb /kŏŏ lŏm/ *n* (symbol **C**) a unit of electric charge equal to the amount of charge transported by a current of one ampere in one second

ORIGIN The **coulomb** is named for the French physicist Charles-Augustin de Coulomb (1736–1806), who pioneered research into electricity.

~~counselor~~ incorrect spelling of **counselor**

coun·cil /kŏwns'l/ *n* **1** a group of people who run the administrative affairs of a town or district **2** any committee of appointed people —**coun·cil·man** *n* —**coun·cil·wo·man** *n*

USAGE council or **counsel**? **Council** means a body of people, especially in an advisory or administrative context. **Counsel** most often means a lawyer or lawyers, whereas a *counselor* gives some other kind of professional advice. The verb **counsel** describes the activity of such advisers: *Financial analysts counseled caution.*

coun·cil of war *n* a meeting of senior military officers to discuss strategy in wartime

coun·cil·or /kŏwns'lər/, **coun·cil·lor** *n* **1** a member of an advisory council **2** an elected member of a local council —**coun·cil·or·ship** *n*

coun·sel /kŏwns'l/ *n* **1** a lawyer conducting a case in court **2** somebody who gives advice (+ *sing or pl verb*) **3** advice *(fml; often pl)* ■ *vt* **1** advise to do something *(fml)* **2** advise on personal problems ◊ See note at **council**

coun·sel·ing /kŏwns'ling/, **coun·sel·ling** *n* professional help with personal problems

coun·sel·or /kŏwns'lər/, **coun·sel·lor** *n* **1** somebody who gives advice **2** a professional adviser **3** **coun·sel·or·at·law** *(pl* **coun·sel·ors·at·law)** an attorney **4** a supervisor at a youth camp —**coun·se·lor·ship** *n*

count¹ /kŏwnt/ *v* **1** *vti* say numbers in order **2** *vti* add things up to see how many there are **3** *vt* include in a calculation ◊ *Did you count time as well as expenses?* **4** *vti* consider or be considered **5** *vi* be of importance **6** *vi* have a particular value ■ *n* **1** an act of saying numbers in order **2** an act of adding things up to find a total **3** a total **4** a charge against a defendant on trial **5** in boxing and wrestling, a referee's count after which

a fight or point is decided ◊ **out** *or* **down for the count** unconscious or deeply asleep *(slang)*

☐ **count in** *vt* include

☐ **count on** *vt* **1** rely on **2** be sure of

☐ **count out** *vt* **1** count things one by one **2** exclude somebody or something

count² /kŏwnt/ *n* a nobleman in some European countries

count·a·ble /kŏwntəb'l/ *adj* **1** able to be counted **2** describes a noun that is able to form a plural —**count·a·bly** *adv*

count·down /kŏwnt dŏwn/ *n* **1** a backward count that signals the approach of a major event, e.g., a rocket launch **2** the activities or period immediately before an event

coun·te·nance /kŏwntənənss/ *(fml)* *n* **1** a face or expression **2** composure ■ *vt* (-nanced, -nanc·ing) tolerate or approve of

count·er¹ /kŏwntər/ *n* **1** a flat surface in a store or other business where goods are displayed, served, or paid for **2** a flat surface in a kitchen **3** a small marker in games, usually a disk

coun·ter² /kŏwntər/ *vti* **1** contradict or oppose somebody **2** do something in opposition ■ *adj* contradicting ■ *n* **1** a response in retaliation **2** something done that is the opposite of something else

count·er³ /kŏwntər/ *n* **1** a device that counts or measures something **2** somebody whose job is counting something

counter- *prefix* **1** contrary, opposing ◊ *counterclockwise* **2** complementary, corresponding ◊ *counterpart*

coun·ter·act /kŏwntər ákt/ *vt* lessen the effect of —**coun·ter·ac·tion** *n* —**coun·ter·ac·tive** *adj*

coun·ter·at·tack /kŏwntər ə tàk/ *n* a response to an attack

coun·ter·bal·ance /kŏwntər bàllənss/ *vt* (-anced, -anc·ing) **1** have an equal and opposing effect on **2** balance with an equal weight ■ *n* **1** a counterbalancing person or thing **2** a weight that balances another

coun·ter·claim *n* /kŏwntər klàym/ a claim entered by the defendant in a court case against the plaintiff —**coun·ter·claim·ant** /kŏwntər kláymənt/ *n*

coun·ter·clock·wise /kŏwntər klók wìz/ *adv, adj* in the direction opposite to clockwise ■ *adj* moving opposite to clockwise

coun·ter·cul·ture /kŏwntər kúlchər/ *n* a culture with values that are deliberately in opposition to those of mainstream society —**coun·ter·cul·tur·al** /kŏwntər kúlchərəl/ *adj*

coun·ter·feit /kŏwntər féet/ *adj* **1** forged and therefore not real or legal **2** insincere ■ *v* **1** *vti* forge something, e.g., a signature or money **2** *vt* pretend to feel an emotion ■ *n* a forgery —**coun·ter·feit·er** *n*

~~counterfit~~ incorrect spelling of **counterfeit**

coun·ter·foil /kŏwntər fóyl/ *n* the part of a check kept by the issuer

coun·ter·in·sur·gen·cy /kòwntər in súrjənsee/ *n* action taken by a government to quash a rebellion —**coun·ter·in·sur·gent** *n*

coun·ter·in·tel·li·gence /kòwntər in téllijənss/ *n* activities designed to thwart the activities of enemy spies

coun·ter·in·tu·i·tive /kòwntər in toö itiv/ *adj* contrary to natural expectations —**coun·ter·in·tu·i·tive·ly** *adv*

coun·ter·mand /kówntər mánd, kòwntər mánd/ *vt* 1 cancel a command 2 recall somebody or something previously sent somewhere ■ *n* an order canceling another

coun·ter·mea·sure /kówntər mèzhər/ *n* a defensive reaction

coun·ter·of·fen·sive /kòwntər ə fénsiv/ *n* an offensive launched in response to an enemy offensive

coun·ter·part /kówntər pàart/ *n* 1 a person or thing that corresponds to another 2 a complementary part or thing

coun·ter·point /kówntər pòynt/ *n* 1 the combination of two or more separate melodies so that each remains distinct 2 a contrasting element ■ *vt* 1 contrast with something else 2 arrange music in counterpoint

coun·ter·pro·duc·tive /kòwntər prə dúktiv/ *adj* producing problems —**coun·ter·pro·duc·tive·ly** *adv*

coun·ter·rev·o·lu·tion /kòwntər revə loösh'n/ *n* a revolution that attempts to reverse a previous revolution —**coun·ter·rev·o·lu·tion·ar·y** *n, adj* —**coun·ter·rev·o·lu·tion·ist** *n*

coun·ter·sign /kówntər sìn/ *vt* sign a document already signed, e.g., as a witness to the earlier signature ■ *n* a secret password

coun·ter·ten·or /kówntər tènnər/ *n* 1 a high male singing voice 2 a man with a high singing voice

coun·ter·top /kówntər tòp/ *n* the upper surface of a counter

coun·ter·weight /kówntər wàyt/ *n* 1 a counterbalancing weight 2 something with a compensatory effect —**coun·ter·weight·ed** *adj*

count·ess /kówntəss/ *n* 1 the wife of a count or earl 2 a European noblewoman with the rank of count in her own right

count·less /kówntləss/ *adj* too many to count —**count·less·ly** *adv*

count noun *n* a noun that has a plural form and can be used with "a" or "an"

coun·tri·fied /kúntri fìd/, **coun·try·fied** *adj* 1 in a style appropriate to the countryside 2 unsophisticated

coun·try /kúntree/ *n* (*pl* -tries) 1 a separate nation 2 somebody's homeland 3 a geographically distinct area 4 areas that are farmed and remain relatively undeveloped 5 a region with a special character ○ *mountainous country* 6 a nation's people ○ *the support of the whole country* 7 country music

■ *adj* 1 characteristic of rural areas 2 of country music

coun·try club *n* a private sports and social club

coun·try house *n* a large house in the countryside

coun·try·man /kúntreemən/ (*pl* -men /-mən/) *n* 1 somebody from the same nation as you 2 somebody from the countryside

coun·try mile *n* a considerable distance

coun·try mu·sic, coun·try and west·ern *n* a style of popular music based on the folk music of the US South and the cowboy music of the US West —**coun·try mu·si·cian** *n*

coun·try·side /kúntree sìd/ *n* 1 rural land, usually farmed 2 inhabitants of such a rural area

coun·try·wide /kúntree wìd/ *adj, adv* throughout a nation

coun·try·wom·an /kúntree wòomman/ (*pl* -en /-wìmmin/) *n* 1 a woman from the same nation as you 2 a woman from the countryside

coun·ty /kówntee/ (*pl* -ties) *n* 1 a unit of local government in some states or nations 2 the people of a county

coun·ty coun·cil *n* a local government body administering a county in some parts of the United States

coun·ty seat *n* the capital of a county

coup *n* 1 a seizure of political power, especially by an army 2 a skillful and successful action

coup de grâce /koò də graàss/ (*pl* **coups de grâce** /koò-/), **coup de grace** (*pl* **coups de grace**) *n* 1 the final blow or shot that kills a person or animal 2 an act that assures victory

coup d'é·tat /koò day taà/ (*pl* **coups d'é·tat** *or* **coup d'é·tats** /pronunc. same/) *n* a political coup

coupe /koop/, **cou·pé** /koo páy, koop/ *n* a car with two doors, a sloping back, and a fixed roof

Cou·pe·rin /koòpə rán/, **François** (1668–1733) French composer and organist

cou·ple /kúpp'l/ *n* 1 two similar things considered together 2 a few things of the same kind 3 two people who are romantic, sexual, or married partners 4 two people doing something together 5 something that joins two parts ■ *vt* (-pled, -pling) 1 associate or combine two things 2 join two things

cou·plet /kúpplət/ *n* two lines of verse that form a unit

cou·pling /kúppling/ *n* 1 something that joins two things 2 the act of joining two things together

cou·pon /koò pòn, kyoò-/ *n* 1 a voucher redeemed by a store or company 2 an order form 3 a certificate of interest on a bond

cour·age /kúrrij/ *n* the quality of being brave —**cou·ra·geous** /kə ráyjəss/ *adj* —**cou·ra·geous·ly** *adv*

SYNONYMS **courage, bravery, fearlessness, nerve, guts, pluck, mettle** CORE MEANING: personal resoluteness in the face of danger or difficulties

courageous incorrect spelling of **courageous**

Cour·bet /koor báy/, **Gustave** (1819–77) French painter

cou·ri·er /koôree ər, kúrri-/ *n* 1 an official messenger 2 a secret messenger 3 a person or firm providing a delivery service ■ *vt* send by courier

course *n* 1 the way events develop or progress 2 the progression of a period of time ○ *in the course of the afternoon* 3 a direction traveled 4 an action chosen 5 a class taught at an educational institution 6 a program of study 7 a part of a meal served at one time 8 the path of a river 9 a swift onward movement 10 an established sequence of medical treatment 11 a place where a particular sporting activity is carried on ○ *a golf course* 12 a layer of bricks ■ *v* (coursed, cours·ing) 1 *vi* run fast 2 *vti* hunt animals with greyhounds ◊ **in due course** after an appropriate period of time ◊ See note at **coarse**

⚡ **course·ware** /káwrs wàir/ *n* educational software

course·work /káwrs wùrk/ *n* work assigned to students during an academic course

court[1] *n* 1 a session of an official body with the authority to decide legal cases 2 the room or building where a court is constituted 3 an open space within a walled area 4 an area on which a particular ball game is played 5 a monarch's attendants 6 an important person's followers 7 a short street ◊ **be laughed out of court** be ridiculed severely (*infml*) ◊ **pay court to** try to win influence with or the favor of somebody through flattery or attentiveness

court[2] *v* 1 *vt* be attentive to somebody in order to win favor or influence 2 *vt* try to gain something, e.g., somebody's attention 3 *vt* behave in a way that makes a bad experience likely ○ *courted disaster* 4 *vt* try to win somebody's love (*dated*) 5 *vi* be sweethearts (*dated*)

cour·te·san /káwrtəzən/ *n* a high-class prostitute

cour·te·sy /kúrtəssee/ *n* (*pl* -sies) 1 polite or considerate behavior 2 a polite or considerate action ■ *adj* 1 done for the sake of politeness 2 provided free —**cour·te·ous** /kúrtee əss/ *adj* —**cour·te·ous·ly** *adv* —**cour·te·ous·ness** *n*

court·house /káwrt hòwss/ *n* 1 a building where a law court is based 2 a building where county government is housed

court·i·er /káwrtyər/ *n* 1 a member of a royal court 2 somebody who flatters an important person

courteous incorrect spelling of **courteous**

court·ly /káwrtlee/ (-li·er, -li·est) *adj* having refined manners —**court·li·ness** *n*

court-mar·tial /káwrt már-tial *or* court-mar·tials) 1 a military court 2 a military trial ■ *vt* try an accused person in a military court

court of in·quir·y *n* a military investigating body

court of law *n* a court that hears legal cases

court or·der *n* an order issued by a judge

court·room /káwrt ròom, -ròom/ *n* a hall or room in which a court of law is held

court·ship /káwrt shìp/ *n* 1 the process of trying to gain somebody's love 2 a romantic relationship that is a prelude to marriage 3 ingratiating behavior

court·yard /káwrt yàard/ *n* an open space surrounded by walls

cous·cous /kóoss kòoss/ *n* 1 a food made of small grains of semolina 2 a dish of stew and couscous

cous·in /kúzz'n/ *n* 1 an uncle's or aunt's child 2 a relative descended from a common ancestor 3 somebody with whom you have something in common —**cous·in·ly** *adj*

ORIGIN **Cousin** derives from a Latin word that applied only to a cousin on your mother's side. It meant literally "mother's sister's child." By the time it entered English from French, a father's nephews and nieces were included in its scope. Early English use became wider still, allowing any relative outside the immediate family to be referred to as a **cousin**.

cou·ture /koo toŏr/ *n* 1 fashion design 2 high-fashion clothing

cou·tu·rier /koo toŏree ər, koo toŏree ày/ *n* a fashion designer

cove /kōv/ *n* a small bay enclosed by cliffs

cov·en /kúvv'n, kōv'n/ *n* a group of witches

cov·e·nant /kúvvənənt/ *n* 1 a contract, especially one making payments to a charity 2 **Cov·e·nant** a 17C Scottish pact to defend Presbyterianism 3 a legally binding agreement ■ *vt* promise solemnly or legally to do something —**cov·e·nant·al** /kùvvə nánt'l/ *adj*

Cov·en·try /kóvvəntree, kúvvən-/ city in central England. Pop. 306,503 (1996).

co·ven·ture /kō vénchər/ *vti* undertake a business venture in partnership with another person or firm ■ *n* a business partnership

cov·er /kúvvər/ *v* 1 *vt* put one thing over the whole or top of something else 2 *vt* be all over something 3 *vt* be wrapped around something 4 *vt* put clothing on a part of the body 5 *vt* be worn on a part of the body 6 *vt* put a lid on something 7 *vt* talk or write about, e.g., an event 8 *vt* provide news of something 9 *vt* take something into account

10 vt extend over an area **11** vt hide something **12** vt insure something or insure against something **13** vt be enough to pay for a purchase **14** vt protect somebody from attack, e.g., by aiming a weapon at an enemy **15** vi do somebody else's job **16** vi tell lies for somebody **17** vt copulate with a female (refers to male animals, especially stallions) **18** vt in card games, to play a card of a higher value than another card already played **19** vt in sports, defend an area against an opponent **20** vt sit on eggs (refers to female birds) ■ n **1** something that covers **2** a lid **3** a book or magazine binding **4** a cloth that covers furniture **5** a shelter from the weather **6** a hiding place **7** plants that cover an area of ground **8** defense against attack **9** an assumed identity or pretext that protects, e.g., a spy, from detection **10** a cover charge **11** an understudy **12** an envelope ■ **covers** npl coverings on a bed —**cov·er·a·ble** adj ◊ **blow somebody's cover** expose somebody's disguise, lie, or pretense

☐ **cover up** vt **1** cover something completely **2** conceal something bad

cov·er·age /kúvvərij/ n **1** media attention **2** insurance protection **3** the audience for a television or radio program or the readership of a newspaper or magazine **4** the degree to which something is covered by something else

cov·er·alls /kúvər àwlz/ npl a one-piece protective garment worn over other clothing

cov·er charge n an extra charge for service in a restaurant or nightclub, added to the cost of food or drinks

cov·ered wag·on n a North American pioneer wagon

cov·er girl n a woman model who appears on the front cover of a magazine

cov·er·ing /kúvvəring/ n something that covers

cov·er·let /kúvvərlət/ n a decorative cover for a bed

cov·er let·ter n an accompanying, explanatory letter

cov·er page, cov·er sheet n the top sheet of a fax transmission that bears the sender's name and other details

cov·er sto·ry n **1** the main feature in a magazine, illustrated on the front cover **2** a false story, e.g., to protect a spy's identity

cov·ert /kúvvərt, kô-, kô vúrt/ adj secret ■ n **1** a mass of undergrowth providing cover for game birds **2** a shelter —**cov·ert·ly** adv —**cov·ert·ness** n ◊ See note at **secret**

cov·er-up /kúvvər ùp/, **cov·er·up** n the concealment of something illegal or immoral

cov·et /kúvvət/ v **1** vti greedily desire to have somebody else's property **2** vt desire something very much —**cov·et·er** n —**cov·et·ous** adj ◊ See note at **want**

cov·ey /kúvvee/ (pl -eys) n a group of game birds

cow[1] n **1** a large female mammal kept for its milk and meat **2** a male or female of any breed of domestic cattle **3** a large female mammal, e.g., a female whale

cow[2] vt make submissive

cow·ard /ków ərd/ n somebody who lacks courage

Cow·ard /ków ərd/, **Sir Noel** (1899–1973) British dramatist, actor, and songwriter

cow·ard·ice /ków ərdiss/ n lack of courage

cow·ard·ly /ków ərdlee/ adj lacking courage —**cow·ard·li·ness** n —**cow·ard·ly** adv

---

SYNONYMS cowardly, faint-hearted, spineless, gutless, pusillanimous, craven, chicken CORE MEANING: lacking in courage

---

cow·boy /ków bòy/ n **1** a man who tends cattle in the W United States **2** a male character in Westerns

cow·boy hat n a hat with a high crown and a wide brim

cow·er /ków ər/ vi cringe in fear

cow·girl /ków gùrl/ n **1** a woman who tends cattle in the W United States **2** a woman character in Westerns who rides with cowboys **3** a female rodeo performer

cow·hand /ków hànd/ n a cowboy or cowgirl in the W United States

cow·hide /ków hìd/ n **1** the processed skin of a cow **2** leather made from cowhide

cowl /kowl/ n **1** a monk's hood **2** a hood for a chimney or air vent

cow·lick /ków lìk/ n a tuft of hair on somebody's head that habitually sticks up

cowl·ing /kówling/ n a removable covering for an aircraft engine or fuselage

co·work·er /kô wùrkər/ n a fellow worker

cow·poke /ków pòk/ n a cowboy (infml)

cow·pox /ków pòks/ n a viral skin disease of cattle

cow·rie /kówree/, **cow·ry** (pl -ries) n **1** a brightly colored mollusk **2** a cowrie shell, formerly used as money in some parts of Africa and Asia

cow·shed /ków shèd/ n a building for cattle

cow·slip /ków slìp/ n a small flowering plant of the primrose family

cow town n **1** a cattle-marketing center **2** a small rural town (disapproving)

cox·comb /kóks kòm/ n a fashionable, conceited man (archaic) —**cox·comb·ry** n

cox·swain /kóks'n, -swàyn/ n **1** somebody in charge of the crew in a rowboat **2** somebody in charge of a ship's boat

coy adj **1** pretending in a teasing or flirtatious way to be shy **2** annoyingly uncommunicative —**coy·ly** adv —**coy·ness** n

---

ORIGIN Coy comes from the same Latin word as quiet, and originally meant "quiet, still." This quickly developed to "shy." Both **coy** and quiet entered English directly from French.

coy·o·te /kī ṓtee, kī òt/ (pl **-tes** or same) n a North American mammal like a small wolf

coy·pu /kóy poò/ (pl **-pus** or same) n a very large South American rodent

co·zy /kṓzee/ adj (-zi·er, -zi·est) 1 snug 2 friendly and intimate ■ n (pl -zi·es) a knitted or padded covering to keep something warm —**co·zi·ly** adv —**co·zi·ness** n
◇ **cozy up** 1 cuddle up 2 ingratiate yourself (slang)

CPA, C.P.A. abbr certified public accountant

⚡**cps** abbr characters per second

⚡**CPU** abbr central processing unit

Cr symbol chromium

cr. abbr credit

crab[1] n 1 a crustacean with a broad flat shell and a pair of large pincers at the front 2 the flesh of a crab as food 3 **Crab** the constellation and zodiacal sign Cancer ■ v (**crabbed, crab·bing**) 1 vti scurry sideways 2 vi catch crabs

crab[2] n somebody regarded as bad tempered (infml insult) ■ vi (**crabbed, crab·bing**) criticize (infml)

crab ap·ple, crab-ap·ple /kráb àpp'l/ n 1 a small sour apple. Use: jellies. 2 the tree on which crab apples grow

crab·bed /krábbəd/ adj bad-tempered

crab·by /krábbee/ adj (-bi·er, -bi·est) adj bad-tempered —**crab·bi·ly** adv —**crab·bi·ness** n

crab·grass /kráb gràss/ n a coarse grass with creeping stems

crab·meat /kráb mèet/ n edible crab flesh

crab·wise /kráb wìz/ adv, adj 1 sideways 2 by indirect means

crack v 1 vti break without coming or making something come fully apart 2 vti break with a sharp noise 3 vti make or cause something to make a loud sharp noise 4 vti hit something or somebody hard 5 vti fail or break down, or make something fail or break down 6 vti break down psychologically 7 vi become hoarse or change in pitch (refers to voices) 8 vt decode or solve a code or puzzle 9 vt force your way into something, especially a safe (infml) 10 vt break a molecule into smaller molecules or radicals ■ n 1 a thin break ◦ cracks in the ice 2 a long narrow opening 3 a sharp noise 4 a sharp blow (infml) ◦ a crack over the head 5 an attempt (infml) 6 a purified form of cocaine (slang) ■ adj excellent ◦ She's a crack shot. ◇ **be not all he's** or **she's** or **it's cracked up to be** be not as good as promised or reputed ◇ **fall between** or **through the cracks** be overlooked or forgotten ◇ **crack it** achieve something or be successful (infml) ◇ **get cracking** start moving or doing something quickly or more quickly (infml)

☐ **crack down** vi take strong action against something or somebody undesirable (infml)

☐ **crack up** v (infml) 1 vi have a nervous breakdown 2 vti laugh or cause to laugh uncontrollably

crack·brained /krák bràynd/ adj irrational ◦ a crackbrained idea

crack·down /krák dòwn/ n firm action taken to control something

cracked adj 1 having cracks 2 irrational (infml) 3 coarsely crushed ◦ cracked wheat

⚡**crack·er** /krákər/ n 1 a flat crisp unsweetened wafer 2 somebody who accesses a computer system illicitly 3 UK a cardboard tube holding party favors

crack·le /krák'l/ vi (-led, -ling) 1 make a series of snapping noises like the noises that wood makes when it burns 2 be lively, energetic, or scintillating ■ n 1 a series of snapping noises 2 fine decorative cracks in pottery

crack·ling /krákling/ n snapping or popping noises ■ **crack·lings** npl crisp pieces of fatty meat

crack·ly /kráklee/ adj (-li·er, -li·est) adj 1 brittle in texture 2 making a series of snapping noises

crack·pot /krák pòt/ adj unrealistically imaginative or bizarre (infml) ◦ a crackpot scheme —**crack·pot** n

crack-up n (infml) 1 a nervous breakdown 2 a crash

cra·dle /kráyd'l/ n 1 a baby's bed with rockers 2 the place from which something starts or develops 3 a support for a telephone handset 4 a supporting framework for something being built ■ vt (-dled, -dling) 1 hold carefully and closely 2 put into a cradle

craft n 1 the creation of things by hand 2 an object produced by skillful handwork (often pl) 3 a skilled profession or activity (often in combination) ◦ the craft of filmmaking 4 resourceful devious cunning 5 (pl same) a boat, ship, airplane, or space vehicle (often in combination) ■ vt create something with skill, especially using the hands

crafts·man /kráftsmən/ (pl **-men** /-mən/) n 1 somebody who makes things by hand 2 a skillful person —**crafts·man·like** adj —**crafts·man·ship** n

crafts·per·son /kráfts pùrs'n/ n somebody skilled in making things by hand

crafts·wom·an /kráfts wòomman/ (pl **-en** /-wìmmin/) n a woman who makes things by hand

craft·y /kráftee/ adj (-i·er, -i·est) adj using cunning to deceive people —**craft·i·ly** adv —**craft·i·ness** n

crag n a protruding rocky part of a mountainside

crag·gy /krággee/ adj (-gi·er, -gi·est) adj 1 rocky and steep 2 with rugged facial features —**crag·gi·ness** n

cram (crammed, cram·ming) v 1 vt force something into a small space 2 vt eat food greedily 3 vti study intensively (infml)

cramp[1] n 1 a painful involuntary muscle contraction 2 temporary muscle paralysis ■ **cramps** npl abdominal pain ■ vi be affected with cramp

cramp[2] vt turn sharply ■ n 1 a confined place or situation 2 a device for holding things together

cramped adj 1 lacking space 2 packed into too small a space

cram·pon /krám pòn/ n a set of spikes attached to a climbing boot (usually pl)

Cra·nach /kráa naakh/, **Lucas, the Elder** (1472–1553) German painter and engraver

cran·ber·ry /krán bèrree/ (pl -ries) n 1 a sour red berry. Use: juice, sauces. 2 the evergreen plant that yields cranberries

crane n 1 a machine that lifts heavy objects by means of a movable beam 2 a moving support for a movie or television camera 3 a long-necked, long-legged bird that lives near water ■ v (craned, cran·ing) 1 vti stretch your neck in order to get a better view 2 vt move something by use of a crane

Crane, Hart (1899–1932) US poet

Crane, Stephen (1871–1900) US writer

crane fly n a long-legged fly

cra·ni·um /kráynee əm/ (pl -ums or -a /-ə/) n the skull —**cra·ni·al** adj

crank n 1 a mechanical device for transmitting motion 2 a person regarded as eccentric (infml insult) 3 somebody considered to be bad tempered (infml) 4 powdered methamphetamine used as an illegal drug (slang) ■ vti use a crank on ■ adj from somebody malicious

□ **crank out** vt produce in large quantities (infml)

crank·shaft /krángk shàft/ n a shaft driving or driven by a crank

crank·y /krángkee/ (-i·er, -i·est) adj 1 easily irritated (infml) 2 working unpredictably —**crank·i·ly** adv —**crank·i·ness** n

Cran·mer /kránmər/, **Thomas** (1489–1556) English archbishop

cran·ny /kránnee/ (pl -nies) n a narrow hole —**cran·nied** adj

crap[1] n an offensive term for junk or something worthless or annoying (slang)

crap[2] n a losing throw at craps

crape n 1 light crinkled crepe fabric 2 a black band worn when in mourning

craps n a gambling game played with dice (+ sing or pl verb)

crap·shoot /kráp shòot/ n 1 a craps game 2 a matter of chance (infml)

⚡ **crash** n 1 a vehicle collision 2 a loud noise 3 a computer breakdown 4 a stock market collapse ■ v 1 vti collide or make something collide violently 2 vti make or cause something to make a loud noise 3 vti break into pieces noisily 4 vti move noisily 5 vti have or cause a complete computer failure 6 vi collapse financially 7 vi drop sharply in value 8 vti attend uninvited (infml) 9 vti sleep in a different place from usual (slang) ■ adj rapid and intensive

crash bar·ri·er n a safety barrier along a road

crash course n a rapid and intensive study program

crash di·et n a severe diet in order to lose weight quickly

crash dive n a rapid dive by a submarine

crash-dive (crash-dived or crash-dove) vti 1 descend or make an aircraft descend rapidly and crash 2 make or cause a submarine to make a rapid dive

crash hel·met n a safety helmet for a bicyclist, motorcyclist, or racing driver

crash land·ing n an emergency aircraft landing —**crash-land** /krásh lànd/ vti

crass adj 1 thoughtless and vulgar 2 extreme —**crass·ly** adv —**crass·ness** n

crate n a large box ■ vti (crat·ed, crat·ing) put in a crate

cra·ter /kráytər/ n 1 a circular hole at a volcano summit 2 a hole left by a meteorite or an explosion 3 **Cra·ter** a constellation of the southern hemisphere ■ vti form or make something form craters —**cra·ter·like** adj

cra·vat /krə vát/ n a man's neckerchief tied in front

> **ORIGIN Cravat** is an adoption of a French word meaning literally "Croatian." Croatian mercenaries in French military service wore linen scarfs or neckbands tied at the front. In the 1650s this style became fashionable and the name **cravat** was born.

crave /krayv/ (craved, crav·ing) v 1 vti desire something strongly 2 vt beg somebody for something (archaic) —**crav·ing·ly** adv ◊ See note at **want**

cra·ven /kráyvən/ adj cowardly —**cra·ven·ly** adv —**cra·ven·ness** n ◊ See note at **cowardly**

crav·ing /kráyving/ n a strong desire for something

craw n a bird or insect's crop

craw·dad /kráw dàd/ n Southern US a crayfish

crawl vi 1 move along on the hands and knees 2 move slowly with the body close to the surface 3 move forward very slowly 4 be servile (infml) 5 be overrun 6 have a feeling of being covered by moving insects ◦ made his skin crawl ■ n 1 a very slow speed 2 an overarm swimming stroke

⚡ **crawl·er** /kráwlər/ n 1 an insect or animal that crawls 2 a vehicle with tracks instead of wheels 3 a computer program collecting online documents

crawl space n a horizontal access space in or under a building

cray·fish /kráy fìsh/ (pl same or -fish·es), **craw·fish** /kráw fìsh/ n 1 a freshwater crustacean resembling a lobster **2** crayfish as food

cray·on /kráy òn/ n **1** a colored wax stick for drawing **2** a drawing done using crayons —**cray·on** vti

craze n a fad ■ vti (**crazed, craz·ing**) make or become irrational (often offensive) —**crazed** adj

cra·zy /kráyzee/ (**-zi·er, -zi·est**) adj (infml) **1** an offensive term meaning affected by a psychiatric disorder **2** ridiculous **3** excessively fond of o crazy about tennis —**cra·zi·ly** adv —**cra·zi·ness** n

Cra·zy Horse (1849?–77) Oglala Sioux leader

cra·zy quilt n **1** a quilt of irregular patchwork **2** a hodgepodge

creak /kreek/ vi make or move with a prolonged squeaking sound —**creak** n —**creak·ing** adj

SPELLCHECK Do not confuse the spelling of **creak** and **creek** ("a stream"), which sound similar.

creak·y /kréekee/ (**-i·er, -i·est**) adj making a prolonged squeaking noise —**creak·i·ly** adv —**creak·i·ness** n

cream /kreem/ n **1** the fatty part of milk **2** a creamy lotion **3** a food with a soft texture **4** the best part of something **5** a yellowish-white color **6** a chocolate with a soft center ■ vt **1** mix something until creamy **2** prepare food with cream **3** defeat thoroughly (slang) —**cream** adj

cream cheese n soft white unmatured cheese

cream·er /kréemər/ n **1** a small pitcher for cream **2** a substitute for cream, used in coffee or tea

cream·er·y /kréemaree/ (pl **-ies**) n a business selling dairy products

cream of tar·tar n an ingredient of baking powder

cream puff n a cream-filled pastry

cream so·da n a vanilla-flavored carbonated soft drink

cream·y /kréemee/ (**-i·er, -i·est**) adj **1** smooth or tasting like cream **2** containing cream —**cream·i·ly** adv —**cream·i·ness** n

crease /kreess/ n **1** a fold put in fabric by pressing or crushing **2** a wrinkle in the skin —**creased** adj —**creas·y** adj

cre·ate /kree áyt/ (**-at·ed, -at·ing**) v **1** vt make exist **2** vt give rise to something **3** vti produce a work of art or invent something

cre·a·tion /kree áysh'n/ n **1** the process of making somebody or something exist **2** the Earth and its inhabitants **3** something created by human imagination or invention **4** **Cre·a·tion** the making of the universe by God according to the Bible **5** **Cre·a·tion** the universe as made by God according to the Bible —**cre·a·tion·al** adj

cre·a·tion·ism /kree áysh'n ìzzəm/ n the belief that God created the universe as described in the Bible —**cre·a·tion·ist** adj, n

cre·a·tive /kree áytiv/ adj **1** able to create things **2** new and original in conception **3** using resources imaginatively —**cre·a·tive·ly** adv —**cre·a·tive·ness** n —**cre·a·tiv·i·ty** /kree ay tívvitee/ n

cre·a·tive writ·ing n the writing of stories, poems, and other works of the imagination

cre·a·tor /kree áytər/ n **1** somebody who creates something **2** also **Cre·a·tor** God

crea·ture /kréechər/ n **1** a living being **2** an unpleasant living being **3** somebody or something created o a creature of your imagination **4** a particular type of person o He's a creature of habit.

crea·ture com·forts npl necessities for a comfortable life

crèche /kresh, kraysh/ n a Nativity scene

cre·dence /kréed'nss/ n **1** belief in the truth of something **2** trustworthiness

cre·den·tial /krə dénshəl/ n **1** proof of ability or trustworthiness **2** authentication ■ **cre·dentials** npl official identification ■ vt give credentials —**cre·den·tialed** adj

USAGE **credentialed** or **licensed**? In professional contexts such as diplomacy, medicine, and academe where certification is an issue, **credentialed** is entirely appropriate: a graduate school of arts and sciences having a fully **credentialed** faculty. Avoid using this word in other occupational settings, such as a **credentialed** electrician, where licensed is the appropriate choice.

cre·den·tial·ism /krə dénsh'l ìzzəm/ n too much reliance on credentials

cred·i·bil·i·ty /krèddə bíllətee/ n **1** believableness **2** a willingness to believe something

cred·i·ble /kréddəb'l/ adj **1** believable **2** trustworthy —**cred·i·bly** adv

cred·it /kréddit/ n **1** recognition or an acknowledgment for something **2** a source of pride **3** good reputation **4** a system to pay at a later time **5** somebody's financial status **6** money a customer is owed by a store and can spend there **7** the balance in an account **8** an amount of money paid into an account or against an amount owed **9** the column in which account payments are recorded **10** a completed unit of an educational course **11** recognition of the completion of an educational course unit ■ **cred·its** npl a list of everyone involved in a movie or TV program ■ vt **1** believe **2** recognize as responsible for an achievement **3** attribute **4** add or record as a credit to a bank account ◇ **to somebody's credit** a source of commendation for somebody

cred·it·a·ble /krédditab'l/ adj praiseworthy —**cred·it·a·bil·i·ty** /krèddita bíllatee/ n

cred·it bu·reau *n* an organization that keeps track of people's and organizations' credit rating

cred·it card *n* a bank card for buying goods or services on credit

cred·it line *n* **1** available credit **2** written recognition, e.g., in a book

cred·i·tor /krédditem/ *n* somebody who is owed money

cred·it rat·ing *n* an estimate of somebody's financial creditworthiness

cred·it un·ion *n* a cooperative lending association

cred·it·wor·thy /kréddit wùrthee/ *adj* sufficiently reliable to be given financial credit —**cred·it·wor·thi·ness** *n*

cre·do /kreédō/ (*pl* -**dos**) *n* **1** a statement of beliefs **2** **Cre·do** the statement of Christian beliefs

cre·du·li·ty /krə doolətee/ *n* willingness to believe things too readily

cred·u·lous /krějjələss/ *adj* ready to believe anything —**cred·u·lous·ly** *adv* —**cred·u·lous·ness** *n*

Cree (*pl* same *or* **Crees**) *n* **1** a member of a Native North American people who live in central Canada and Montana **2** the Algonquian language of the Cree people —**Cree** *adj*

creed *n* a statement of beliefs

creek /kreek/ *n* a stream ◊ See note at **creak**

Creek (*pl* same *or* **Creeks**) *n* **1** a member of a Native North American people who now live mainly in central Oklahoma and S Alabama **2** the language of the Creek people —**Creek** *adj*

creel *n* a wicker basket for fish

creep *vi* (**crept** *or* **creeped**) **1** move slowly and quietly **2** move near the ground **3** proceed or develop slowly **4** shiver with disgust **5** spread over a surface by sending out tendrils, suckers, or roots **6** be displaced slightly ■ *n* **1** a slow quiet movement **2** a person regarded as repellent or obsequious (*infml*) **3** a slight displacement ■ **creeps** *npl* an uneasy feeling of fear or disgust (*infml*) —**creep·ing** *adj*

creep·er /kreéper/ *n* **1** a plant that spreads over a surface by sending out tendrils, suckers, or roots **2** a small climbing bird

creep·y /kreépee/ (-**i·er**, -**i·est**) *adj* (*infml*) **1** frighteningly or disgustingly unnerving **2** repellent —**creep·i·ly** *adv* —**creep·i·ness** *n*

cre·mains /kri máynz/ *npl* ashes that remain after cremation

cre·mate /kreé màyt/ (-**mat·ed**, -**mat·ing**) *vt* incinerate a corpse —**cre·ma·tion** *n*

cre·ma·to·ri·um /kreémə táwree əm/ (*pl* -**ums** *or* -**a** /-ə/) *n* a place used for cremation

crème car·a·mel /krèm kaarə mél, -kerr-/ (*pl* **crème car·a·mels** /krèm kaarə mélz, -kerr-/ *or*

crèmes car·a·mel /krèm-, krèmz-/) *n* a cold custard dessert with a caramel sauce

crème de la crème /krèm də laa krém/ *n* the elite of a group

crème de menthe /krèm də mént, -maáNt/ (*pl* **crème de menthes** *or* **crèmes de menthe** /pronunc. same/) *n* a mint-flavored liqueur

crème fraîche /krèm frésh/ *n* thickened sour cream

cre·ole /kreé ōl/ *n* **1** a language of mixed origin **2** **Cre·ole** somebody of French ancestry in the S United States **3** **Cre·ole** the French-based language of Louisiana **4** **Cre·ole** a group of languages spoken in some Caribbean islands **5** **Cre·ole** a Caribbean person of European ancestry **6** **Cre·ole** a Creole speaker ■ *adj* **1** cooked New Orleans style **2** *also* **Cre·ole** of a creole

cre·o·sote /kreé ə sōt/ *n* a wood preservative made from coal tar —**cre·o·sote** *vt*

crepe /krayp/ *n* **1** a light crinkled fabric **2** a thin pancake **3** *also* **crepe pa·per** crinkly decorative paper **4** *also* **crepe rub·ber** rubber in the form of thin crinkled sheets, used for making the soles of shoes

crept past tense, past participle of **creep**

cres·cen·do /krə shéndō/ (*pl* -**dos** *or* -**does** *or* -**di** /-deè/) *n* **1** an increase in loudness in music **2** an intensification of something —**cres·cen·do** *adj*, *adv*

cres·cent /kréss'nt/ *n* **1** an arc shape **2** an arc-shaped object **3** *also* **Cres·cent** the symbol of Islam or Turkey —**cres·cent** *adj*

cress (*pl* same *or* **cress·es**) *n* a plant with pungent-tasting leaves used in salads and as a garnish

crest *n* **1** the top of a curve or slope **2** a culmination **3** a tuft on a bird or animal's head **4** an ornament on the top of a helmet **5** a heraldic symbol of a family or office ■ *v* **1** *vi* rise to a crest **2** *vt* reach or be at the top of —**crest·ed** *adj*

crest·fall·en /krést fáwlən/ *adj* downcast

Cre·ta·ceous /krə táyshəss/ *n* a period of geologic time 142–65 million years ago —**Cre·ta·ceous** *adj*

Crete /kreet/ largest Greek island, in the S Aegean Sea. Pop. 540,054 (1991). —**Cre·tan** *adj*, *n*

Creutz·feldt-Ja·kob dis·ease /króyts felt yaá kawb-/ *n* a slow developing fatal brain disease

cre·vasse /krə váss/ *n* **1** a deep crack, especially in a glacier **2** a crack in a levee ■ *vti* (-**vassed**, -**vass·ing**) form or cause to form crevasses

crev·ice /krévviss/ *n* a fissure, especially in a rock —**crev·iced** *adj*

crew *n* **1** the staff of a ship, aircraft, or spacecraft **2** a group working together on a task **3** a group of friends or associates (*infml*) **4** the rowers and coxswain of a racing boat

5 the sport of rowing ■ *v* **1** *vi* be a crew member **2** *vt* help to operate

crew cut *n* a very short hairstyle

crew neck *n* a round neckline —**crew-neck** *adj*

crib *n* **1** a baby's bed **2** a grain store **3** a horse or cattle stall **4** a container for hay from which livestock feed **5** an act of plagiarism **6** somebody's home *(slang)* ■ *v* (**cribbed, crib-bing**) **1** *vti* plagiarize **2** *vt* put in a crib —**crib-ber** *n*

crib-bage /kríbbij/ *n* a card game with a board and pegs for keeping score

crib-bage board *n* a board with pegs for keeping score in cribbage

crib death *n* the sudden death of infants in their sleep

crick[1] *n* a painful stiffness in the neck or back —**crick** *vt*

crick[2] *n regional* a creek

Crick, Francis H. C. (*b.* 1916) British biophysicist. With James D. Watson and Maurice Wilkins he discovered the structure of DNA (1953).

crick-et[1] /kríkət/ *n* **1** a leaping chirping insect **2** a small toy that clicks

crick-et[2] /kríkət/ *n* an outdoor game for two teams of 11 players using a flat bat, a small hard ball, and wickets —**crick-et** *vi* —**crick-et-er** *n*

cri-er /kríˌr/ *n* **1** somebody or something that cries **2** a town crier

crime *n* **1** an illegal act **2** any act considered morally wrong **3** an undesirable act *(infml)*

Cri-me-a /krī mēˈə/ peninsula in SE Ukraine between the Black Sea and the Sea of Azov —**Crim-e-an** *n, adj*

crime wave *n* a period when an unusually high number of crimes occur

crim-i-nal /krímmin'l/ *n* somebody acting illegally ■ *adj* **1** punishable as a crime **2** of criminals **3** wrong or unacceptable —**crim-i-nal-ly** *adv*

crim-i-nal-ize /krímmin'l īz/ (**-ized, -iz-ing**) *vt* **1** make illegal **2** make into a criminal —**crim-i-nal-i-za-tion** /krímmin'l ī záysh'n/ *n*

crim-i-nol-o-gy /krímmi nólləjee/ *n* the study of crime and criminals —**crim-i-no-log-i-cal** /krímminə lójjik'l/ *adj* —**crim-i-nol-o-gist** *n*

crimp *vt* **1** fold or press the ends or edges of something together **2** interfere with something **3** curl somebody's hair ■ *n* **1** a crimping action **2** a hindrance **3** a tight artificial hair wave **4** a crease formed by crimping

crim-son /krímz'n/ *n* a deep, rich red color ■ *v* **1** *vti* make or become crimson **2** *vi* blush —**crim-son** *adj*

ORIGIN Crimson derives from the name of a small plant-sucking insect (the "kermes"). The bodies of the female adults are dried to be the source of a red dye. The name comes

from Arabic, via Spanish, French, and other Romance forms.

cringe (**cringed, cring-ing**) *vi* **1** retract the head and body in a frightened or servile way **2** react in an embarrassed or uncomfortable way *(infml)* —**cringe** *n* —**cring-er** *n*

crin-kle /kríngk'l/ *vti* **1** crease or wrinkle all over **2** make or cause to make a rustling sound ■ *n* a tiny crease or wave —**crin-kly** *adv*

crin-o-line /krínnlin/ *n* a stiff or hooped petticoat worn to expand a skirt —**crin-o-lined** *adj*

crip-ple /krípp'l/ *n* an offensive term for a person with physical disabilities ■ *vt* (**-pled, -pling**) **1** an offensive term meaning to cause to have a physical disability **2** an offensive term meaning to damage —**crip-pled** *adj* —**crip-pling** *adj*

cri-sis /krísiss/ (*pl* **-ses** /-séez/) *n* **1** a dangerous or worrying time **2** a critical moment or turning point

cri-sis man-age-ment *n* the process of dealing with problems as they arise

crisp *adj* **1** hard but easily broken **2** fresh and crunchy *o a crisp apple* **3** smooth, firm, and clean *o crisp fabric* **4** distinct and clear *o crisp lines* **5** sharp and concise *o a crisp reply* **6** invigorating —**crisp** *vti* —**crisp-ly** *adv* —**crisp-ness** *n*

crisp-y /kríspee/ (**-i-er, -i-est**) *adj* light and crunchy —**crisp-i-ness** *n*

criss-cross /kríss kràwss/ *n* a pattern of lines that cross each other ■ *adj* with crossed vertical and horizontal lines ■ *adv* back and forth ■ *v* **1** *vti* make a pattern of crossed lines on something **2** *vt* go to and fro across something

ORIGIN Crisscross was originally *Christ's cross*. In early use this referred not to a crucifix, but to any mark or figure of a cross.

cri-te-ri-on /krī téeree ən/ (*pl* **-a** /-téeree ə/ or **-ons**) *n* a standard by which to judge things *(often pl)*

USAGE criterion or **criteria? Criterion** is singular, and **criteria** is plural; it is generally regarded as incorrect to use **criteria** as a singular noun (with **criterias** as a bogus plural).

crit-ic /kríttik/ *n* **1** a reviewer of movies, plays, publications, or arts events **2** a fault-finder

crit-i-cal /kríttik'l/ *adj* **1** finding fault **2** giving comments, analyses, or judgments **3** crucial **4** essential **5** life-threatening —**crit-i-cal-ly** *adv* —**crit-i-cal-ness** *n*

crit-i-cal mass *n* **1** the amount of fissionable material required for a nuclear chain reaction **2** a point of change

crit-i-cism /kríttɪ sɪzzəm/ *n* **1** an opinion criticizing somebody or something **2** disapproval **3** assessment of a creative work

crit·i·cize /krítti sīz/ (**-cized**, **-ciz·ing**) vti **1** express disapproval of the faults of somebody or something **2** give a considered assessment of something

---

SYNONYMS criticize, censure, castigate, blast, condemn, nitpick CORE MEANING: express disapproval or dissatisfaction with somebody or something

---

cri·tique /kri teék/ n **1** a review of somebody's work **2** criticism of a creative work —**cri·tique** vt

~~critisism~~ incorrect spelling of **criticism**

crit·ter /kríttər/ n a living thing, often a child or an animal (infml or regional)

croak /krōk/ n a rough low vibrating sound made by a frog, crow, or a person with a sore throat ■ v **1** vi produce a croak **2** vti say or speak in a croak **3** vi die (slang) —**croak·y** adj

Cro·a·tia /krō áyshə, -shee ə/ country in SE Europe, on the Balkan Peninsula, bordering the Adriatic Sea. Cap. Zagreb. Pop. 4,334,142 (2001). —**Cro·a·tian** n, adj

cro·chet /krō sháy/ n needlework using a hook to loop wool or thread ■ vti (**-cheted** /-sháyd/, **-chet·ing** /-sháy ing/) make using crochet —**cro·chet·er** n

crock n **1** a clay pot **2** a lie (slang disapproving)

crocked adj drunk (slang)

crock·er·y /krókəree/ n pottery dishes

Crock·ett /krókət/, **Davy** (1786–1836) US frontiersman

croc·o·dile /krókə dīl/ (pl **-diles** or same) n a large reptile with a long thick-skinned body and strong jaws that lives near water

croc·o·dile tears npl pretended or hypocritical tears

cro·cus /krókəss/ (pl **-cus·es** or **-ci** /-sī, -kee/) n a spring flower with white, purple, or yellow petals

Croe·sus /kreéssəss/ n a very wealthy man

Croe·sus /kreéssəss/ (fl 6C BC) king of Lydia (560–546 BC) who was proverbially wealthy

croft n a small Scottish farm —**croft·er** n —**croft·ing** n

crois·sant /krwaa saánt, -saán, -saàN/ n a crescent-shaped roll

Crom·well /króm wèl, krómmwəl/, **Oliver** (1599–1658) English soldier and Lord Protector of England (1653–58)

crone n an offensive term for a woman of advanced years who is regarded as bad-tempered or malicious (insult)

~~cronic~~ incorrect spelling of **chronic**

~~cronology~~ incorrect spelling of **chronology**

Cro·nus /krónəss/ n in Greek mythology, the god of the sky. Roman equivalent **Saturn**

cro·ny /krónee/ (pl **-nies**) n a close friend

cro·ny·ism /króneeìzzəm/ n the practice of doing favors for friends (disapproving)

crook /krŏŏk/ n **1** a hook-shaped device **2** a shepherd's hooked stick **3** a bend in something **4** a criminal or dishonest person (infml) ■ vti form into a bend

---

ORIGIN A crook "criminal" is literally a "bent person." The use is first recorded in the late 19C, but the word itself dates from the early medieval period and derives from an old Scandinavian form meaning "hook."

---

crook·ed /krŏŏkəd/ adj **1** bent or twisted **2** set at an angle **3** illegal or dishonest (infml) —**crook·ed·ly** adv —**crook·ed·ness** n

croon vti **1** sing or murmur gently **2** sing smoothly and sentimentally —**croon** n —**croon·er** n

crop n **1** a plant grown for food or other use **2** an amount produced by a plant or area in a particular period **3** a group of people or things in relation to a particular period of time **4** a whip handle **5** a short hairstyle **6** a storage pouch in the gullet of many birds ■ vt (**cropped**, **crop·ping**) **1** cut something very short **2** cut off part of a photo

☐ **crop up** vi happen or appear unexpectedly (infml)

crop cir·cle n a mysterious flat circle in a field planted with crops

crop-dust·ing n the spraying of crops with chemicals from the air

crop ro·ta·tion n the growing of different crops in succession on a piece of land

crop top n a women's top exposing the midriff

cro·quet /krō káy/ n **1** a lawn game with balls and mallets **2** a stroke in croquet ■ vti (**-queted**, **-quet·ing**) knock somebody's croquet ball away

cro·quette /krō két/ n a small fried patty or ball of meat, fish, or vegetables

cro·sier /krózhər/, **cro·zier** n a hooked rod carried by bishop

cross n **1** a mark (X) consisting of two lines that bisect each other, used to mark or cancel something, or in place of a signature by somebody who cannot write **2** a Christian symbol consisting of a vertical line intersected at right angles by a shorter line **3** also **Cross** the wooden structure on which, according to the Bible, Jesus Christ died **4** a cross-shaped object or structure **5** a difficulty that has to be borne **6** a hybrid ■ v **1** vti move across **2** vt place things one across the other **3** vti meet at one point **4** vt interbreed plants or animals **5** vt make the Christian sign of the cross over somebody or something **6** vt go against somebody ■ adj annoyed or angry —**cross·a·ble** adj —**cross·ly** adv —**cross·ness** n

☐ **cross off** vt no longer include in a list

☐ **cross out** vt delete with a line

cross- prefix **1** crossing ○ crosspiece **2** opposing, opposite ○ crosscurrent **3** reciprocal, mutual ○ cross-fertilization

cross·bar /kráwss bàar/ n **1** a horizontal pole between two verticals **2** the horizontal bar connecting the handlebars to the saddle in a bicycle frame

cross·bones /kráwss bònz/ npl a symbol of two crossed bones. ▶ skull and crossbones

cross·bow /kráwss bò/ n a weapon that fires bolts —**cross·bow·man** n

cross·breed /kráwss breéd/ vti (-bred /-brèd/) breed new strains from genetically different individuals ■ n a product of crossbreeding —**cross·bred** adj, n

cross·check /kráwss chèk/ vt **1** verify something in another way **2** in hockey, field hockey, or lacrosse, obstruct an opponent by using your stick —**cross·check** n

cross·coun·try adj **1** done over fields or hills, or through woods **2** from one side of a country to the other ■ n races or racing over fields or hills, or through woods

cross·coun·try ski·ing n skiing on flat ground

cross·cul·tur·al adj including or comparing different cultures —**cross·cul·tur·al·ly** adv

cross·cur·rent /kráwss kùrrənt/ n **1** a contrary flow **2** an opposite tendency

cross·ex·am·ine vt **1** question a witness for the opposing side in a law court **2** question somebody relentlessly (infml) —**cross·ex·am·i·na·tion** n —**cross·ex·am·in·er** n

cross·eyed adj an offensive term meaning with both eyes turned toward the nose

cross·fer·til·i·za·tion n **1** the fertilization of a female sex cell by a male sex cell from a different individual, usually of the same species **2** a mutually beneficial exchange of ideas —**cross·fer·til·ize** vti

cross·fire /kráwss fìr/ n **1** gunfire from different directions **2** a fierce clash of opinions

cross·grained adj with the grain running across the length

cross·ing /kráwssing/ n **1** a point where somebody can cross a barrier such as a road, water, or a border **2** a point where routes cross **3** a trip across water

cross·leg·ged /kráwss lèggəd, -lègd/ adj with knees apart and ankles crossed

cross·o·ver /kráwss òvər/ n **1** a crossing place or transfer point **2** the extension of the popularity of an artistic work to a different audience **3** somebody or something whose popularity now extends to a different audience

cross·piece /kráwss peéss/ n a part that crosses a structure

⚡ **cross·plat·form** adj available for different computer systems

cross·pur·pose n a conflicting purpose ◇ at **cross-purposes** acting or speaking in a way that conflicts with what somebody else is

trying to do or say, especially without realizing this

cross·ref·er·ence n a direction to a reader to look elsewhere for information ■ v **1** vt put cross-references into a text **2** also **cross·re·fer** vti direct a reader to look elsewhere for information

cross·roads /kráwss ròdz/ n (+ sing verb) **1** an intersection **2** a decisive moment

cross sec·tion, cross-sec·tion n **1** a plane formed by cutting through an object at right angles to an axis **2** something cut in cross section **3** a representative sample —**cross-sec·tion·al** adj

cross·stitch n **1** a cross-shaped embroidery stitch **2** embroidery using cross-stitches —**cross·stitch** vti

cross·town adj going across town —**cross·town** /kráwss tòwn/ adv

cross·train·er /kráwss tràynər/ n **1** somebody training for different sports **2** a sneaker for use in different sports —**cross·train** vi

cross·walk /kráwss wàwk/ n a designated place for crossing a street

cross·wind /kráwss wìnd/ n a wind blowing across a route

cross·wise /kráwss wìz/ adv so as to cross or be positioned across —**cross·wise** adj

cross·word /kráwss wùrd/, **cross·word puz·zle** n a word puzzle on a square grid, with clues for filling in lines

crotch n **1** the place where the legs join the body **2** a place where a tree divides into two branches —**crotched** adj

crouch vi **1** squat **2** bend in preparation to pounce (refers to animals) —**crouch** n

croup[1] /kroop/ n a childhood throat inflammation producing breathing difficulties —**croup·y** adj

croup[2] /kroop/, **croupe** n the hindquarters of a four-legged animal

crou·pi·er /kroópee ày, -ər/ n somebody in charge of a gambling table in a casino

crou·ton /kroo tòn/ n a crunchy cube of fried bread used as a garnish (usually pl)

crow[1] /krō/ n a large black bird related to the rook and raven ◇ **as the crow flies** in a straight line

crow[2] /krō/ vi **1** cry like a rooster **2** cry out happily (refers to babies) **3** boast —**crow** n

Crow /krō/ (pl same or **Crows**) n **1** a member of a Native North American people who now live in S Montana and Wyoming **2** the language of the Crow people —**Crow** adj

crow·bar /krō bàar/ n a strong metal bar used as a lever —**crow·bar** vt

crowd n **1** a large group of people gathered together **2** a set of people with something in common **3** the mass or majority of people ■ v **1** vi throng together **2** vt fill or pack something **3** vti press near to somebody or something **4** vti herd or cram a group into a place **5** vti advance or pass somebody or something by shoving —**crowd·ed** adj

crown n 1 a headdress symbolizing royalty 2 a headdress or title symbolizing achievement or victory 3 a reigning monarch 4 also **Crown** a monarch's power 5 an emblem resembling a crown 6 the top part of something 7 the top of the head 8 the visible part of a tooth 9 an artificial tooth ■ vt 1 confer royal status on somebody 2 reward somebody with a crown 3 be the summit of something 4 put the finishing touch to something 5 fit a crown on a tooth 6 top one thing with something else

Crown Col·o·ny n a British colony governed by the Crown

crown cor·po·ra·tion n Can a Canadian government-owned company

Crown Court n a criminal court in England and Wales

crowned head n a monarch

crown·ing /krówning/ n 1 a coronation 2 a stage in labor when the baby's head appears ■ adj 1 representing supreme achievement 2 forming a summit

crown prince n a male heir to a throne

crown prin·cess n a female heir to a throne, or the wife of a crown prince

crow's feet npl wrinkles near the eyes

crow's-nest n 1 a lookout point at the top of a ship's mast 2 a high lookout point on land

cro·zier n CHR = crosier

⚡ **CRT** n a computer monitor containing a cathode ray tube

cru·cial /kroosh'l/ adj 1 vital in determining an outcome 2 very important (infml) —**cru·cial·ly** adv

cru·ci·ble /kroossab'l/ n 1 a container for melting ores or metals 2 a set of testing circumstances

~~crucifiction~~ incorrect spelling of **crucifixion**

cru·ci·fix /króossa fiks/ n a representation of the crucified Jesus Christ

cru·ci·fix·ion /króossa fíksh'n/ n 1 a form of execution in which somebody is fixed on an upright cross to die 2 an execution by crucifixion 3 **Cru·ci·fix·ion** the crucifixion of Jesus Christ, according to the Bible

cru·ci·form /króossi fàwrm/ adj cross-shaped

cru·ci·fy /króossi fī/ (-fied, -fies) vt 1 execute somebody by crucifixion 2 treat somebody cruelly

crude adj (crud·er, crud·est) 1 unprocessed o crude ore 2 vulgar o a crude gesture ■ n unrefined petroleum —**crude·ly** adv —**crude·ness** n —**cru·di·ty** n

cru·di·tés /króodi táy/ npl raw vegetable pieces eaten as an appetizer

cru·el /kroo əl/ adj 1 deliberately causing pain or distress 2 painful or distressing —**cru·el·ly** adv —**cru·el·ness** n

cru·el·ty /kroo əltee/ (pl -ties) n 1 a deliberately cruel act 2 the condition of being cruel

cru·et /kroo ət/ n a container for a condiment

cruise /krooz/ v (cruised, cruis·ing) 1 vti travel over an ocean 2 vi move at a steady fast rate 3 vti go out to seek a sexual partner (slang) 4 vi proceed in a casual way ■ n a trip by sea

cruise con·trol n a device in a vehicle for maintaining a uniform speed

cruise mis·sile n a long-range low-flying guided missile

cruis·er /króozar/ n 1 a small warship 2 a cabin cruiser 3 a police car

crul·ler /krúllar/ n a small ring-shaped or twisted piece of deep-fried sweet dough

crumb /krum/ n 1 a small fragment of bread, cake, or cookie 2 a small amount ■ v 1 vt put crumbs on or in food 2 vti crumble

crum·ble /krúmb'l/ v (-bled, -bling) 1 vti reduce or be reduced to tiny bits 2 vi disintegrate ■ n UK a dessert crisp

crum·bly /krúmblee/ (-bli·er, -bli·est) adj 1 tending to crumble 2 containing or covered with many crumbs —**crum·bli·ness** n

crum·my /krúmmee/ (-mi·er, -mi·est) adj (infml) 1 of little value 2 unwell or unhappy

crum·pet /krúmpət/ n a flat cake with an elastic texture and small holes, eaten toasted

crum·ple /krúmp'l/ (-pled, -pling) vti 1 crease and wrinkle 2 collapse, or make collapse —**crum·ple** n —**crum·ply** adj

⚡ **crunch** v 1 vt munch noisily 2 vti make or cause something to make a scrunching sound 3 vt rapidly process numbers or data (infml) ■ n 1 a scrunching sound 2 also **crunch time** a decisive moment 3 a crisis

crunch·y /krúnchee/ (-i·er, -i·est) adj crisp and making a crunching sound when eaten or walked on —**crunch·i·ly** adv —**crunch·i·ness** n

cru·sade /kroo sáyd/ n 1 also **Cru·sade** a medieval military expedition by European Christians to take back areas of the Holy Land from Muslim control 2 a religiously motivated war or campaign 3 a vigorous concerted effort to achieve or stop something ■ vi (-sad·ed, -sad·ing) 1 campaign vigorously 2 fight in a medieval crusade

cru·sad·er /kroo sáydar/ n 1 also **Cru·sad·er** a soldier in one of the medieval crusades 2 a vigorous campaigner for or against something

cruse n a small earthenware container for holding liquids (archaic)

crush v 1 vti compress so as to cause injury or damage 2 vti crease 3 vti grind 4 vt quell a protest by force 5 vt overwhelm somebody or something 6 vt pulp fruit or vegetables 7 vt squash somebody 8 vt humiliate somebody with a remark 9 vi

crowd together ■ *n* 1 a crowd of people 2 a crowded situation 3 a fruit drink 4 an infatuation *(infml)* —**crush·ing** *adj* ◊ See note at **love**

crushed *adj* describes fabric made to look crumpled

crust *n* 1 the hard outer part of a loaf of bread 2 a piece of crust or hard bread 3 the pastry cover or case for a pie 4 a hard outer layer on something 5 the solid outer layer of the Earth 6 a scab ■ *vti* 1 form a crust on something 2 make or become encrusted

crus·ta·cean /kru stáysh'n/ *n* a hard-shelled invertebrate animal with several pairs of legs, antennae, and eyes on stalks —**crus·ta·cean** *adj*

crust·y /krústee/ (-i-er, -i-est) *adj* 1 with a crust 2 curt —**crust·i·ly** *adv* —**crust·i·ness** *n*

crutch *n* 1 a walking aid consisting of a stick with a forearm or armpit rest 2 something providing help or support ■ *vt* support with a crutch

crux (*pl* **crux·es** or **cru·ces** /kroõ seèz/) *n* 1 a crucial point 2 a puzzling problem

Crux *n* the Southern Cross

cry /krī/ *v* (**cried**, **cries**) 1 *vti* weep 2 *vti* shout 3 *vi* make a distinctive sound *(refers to birds or mammals)* 4 *vt* plead something as a reason ◊ *cry hardship* ■ *n* (*pl* **cries**) 1 a loud inarticulate expression of rage, pain, or surprise 2 the distinctive call of a bird or animal 3 a period of weeping 4 a public demand for something 5 a baying of hounds

□ **cry out** *v* 1 *vt* shout loudly 2 *vi* be in need

cry·ba·by /krī bàybee/ (*pl* **-bies**) *n* a person regarded as easily made to cry *(insult)*

cry·ing /krī ing/ *adj* desperate or deplorable and demanding a remedy

cry·o·gen·ics /krī ə jénniks/ *n* the study of extremely low temperatures (+ *sing verb*) —**cry·o·gen·ic** *adj*

crypt *n* an underground chamber

cryp·tic /kríptik/ *adj* ambiguous or obscure. —**cryp·ti·cal·ly** *adv* —**cryp·tic·ness** *n* ◊ See note at **obscure**

crypto- *prefix* secret, hidden ◊ *cryptogram*

cryp·to·gram /kríptə gràm/ *n* 1 a coded message 2 a symbol with a secret meaning

⚡ **cryp·to·graph·ic key** *n* a parameter that determines the transformation of data to encrypted format

cryp·tog·ra·phy /krip tóggrəfee/ *n* 1 the study of codes 2 coded writing —**cryp·tog·ra·pher** *n* —**cryp·to·graph·ic** /krìptə gráffik/ *adj* —**cryp·to·graph·i·cal** *adj*

crys·tal /kríst'l/ *n* 1 a solid with a patterned internal structure 2 a piece of crystal 3 a clear colorless mineral, especially quartz 4 something like a crystal ◊ *snow crystals* ◊ *crystals of salt* 5 heavy sparkling glass 6 crystal glass objects 7 a glass over a watch face ■ *adj* very clear and sparkling

crys·tal ball *n* 1 a fortune teller's globe 2 a means of predicting the future

crys·tal clear *adj* 1 very clear and sparkling 2 obvious or easily understood

crys·tal·line /krístə līn, krístəlin/ *adj* 1 of or like crystal 2 very clear and sparkling

crys·tal·lize /krístə līz/ (-lized, -liz·ing), **crys·tal·ize** (-ized, -iz·ing) *vti* 1 make or become well defined 2 form crystals 3 coat or be coated with sugar crystals —**crys·tal·li·za·tion** /krìstəli záysh'n/ *n*

Cs *symbol* cesium

C.S.A. *abbr* Confederate States of America

CS gas *n* a powerful tear gas

ORIGIN *CS* is from the initial letters of the surnames of the US chemists who developed the gas, B. B. Corson (1896–?) and R. W. Stoughton (1906–57).

C-span *n* a public-affairs cable TV channel

CST *abbr* Central Standard Time

CT *abbr* 1 Central Time 2 computed tomography 3 Connecticut

ct. *abbr* certificate

Ct. *abbr* Connecticut

⚡ **C to C** /sèe tə sée/, **C. to C.**, **C2C** *adj* of an Internet transaction between two consumers. Full form **consumer-to-consumer**

⚡ **CTRL, Ctrl.** *abbr* control (key)

⚡ **CTRL-ALT-DEL** *n* the keystroke combination for rebooting a computer

CT scan *n* MED = **CAT scan**

Cu *symbol* copper

cu. *abbr* cubic

cub *n* 1 an offspring of a carnivorous mammal such as a bear or lion 2 **Cub** a Cub Scout ■ *vi* (**cubbed, cub·bing**) produce cubs

Cu·ba /kyoõbə/ country in the Caribbean Sea composed of two main islands and over 1,000 islets. Cap. Havana. Pop. 11,184,023 (2001). —**Cu·ban** *adj, n*

cub·by·hole /kúbbee hòl/, **cub·by** (*pl* **-bies**) *n* 1 a small space or room 2 a small storage compartment

cube¹ /kyoõb/ *n* 1 a solid figure of six equal sides 2 a cube-shaped object 3 the product of a number multiplied by itself twice ■ *vt* (**cubed, cub·ing**) 1 multiply a number by itself twice 2 dice food 3 tenderize meat

cu·be² /kyoõ bày, kyoõ báy/, **cu·bé** *n* a plant with poisonous roots

cube root *n* a number that, when multiplied by itself twice, equals a given number

cu·bic /kyoõbik/, **cu·bi·cal** *adj* 1 three-dimensional 2 with a volume equal to that of a particular cube 3 cube-shaped 4 of or containing a cubed variable 5 (*symbol* **c**) with three equal axes ■ *n* a cubic expression, equation, or curve

cu·bi·cle /kyoõbik'l/ *n* a partitioned area of a room

cub·ism /kyoŏ bĭzzəm/ *n* an artistic style based on geometric shapes —**cub·ist** *n* —**cu·bis·tic** /kyoo bĭstĭk/ *adj*

cu·bit /kyoŏbĭt/ *n* an ancient unit of length based on the distance from the elbow to the tip of the middle finger

cub re·port·er *n* a novice reporter

Cub Scout *n* a member of the junior branch of the Boy Scouts

cuck·old /kúk'ld/ *n* a man whose wife is unfaithful ■ *vt* make a cuckold of —**cuck·old·ry** *n*

ORIGIN **Cuckold** is related to *cuckoo*. The underlying idea is probably of a man taking over another man's wife in the same way as a cuckoo uses another bird's nest. The word was adopted from French.

cuck·oo /koŏ koŏ, koŏ-/ *n* (*pl* -**oos**) 1 a songbird that lays its eggs in other birds' nests 2 a cuckoo's call ■ *adj* bizarre *(infml)* ■ *vi* (-**ooed**, -**oos**) give the call of the cuckoo

cuck·oo clock *n* a clock with a mechanical cuckoo that indicates the hour

cu·cum·ber /kyoŏ kùmbər/ *n* 1 a long green fruit with white flesh used as a vegetable chiefly in salads 2 a plant that produces cucumbers

Cú·cu·ta /koŏka taá/ capital of Norte de Santander Department, NE Colombia. Pop. 624,000 (1999).

cud *n* partly digested food chewed a second time by a ruminant such as a cow

cud·dle /kúdd'l/ (-**dled**, -**dling**) *v* 1 *vti* tenderly hug 2 *vi* assume a comfortable position —**cud·dle** *n*

cud·dly /kúddlee/ (-**dli·er**, -**dli·est**) *adj* pleasant to hold because of being soft, warm, or endearingly attractive

cudg·el /kújjəl/ *n* a short heavy club —**cudg·el** *vt*

cue¹ /kyoo/ *n* 1 a signal to somebody to do something, especially to a performer to come on stage or start performing 2 a prompt or reminder ■ *vt* (**cued**, **cu·ing**) give a signal or prompt to
☐ **cue in** *vt* instruct or remind

cue² /kyoo/ *n* 1 a stick used to strike the cue ball in pool, billiards, or snooker 2 a long stick used in shuffleboard ■ *vt* (**cued**, **cu·ing**) strike with a cue

cue ball *n* the white ball struck in order to hit another ball in pool or billiards

cue card *n* a large card from which somebody speaking on television reads

Cuen·ca /kwéng kaà, -kə/ capital of Azuay Province, S Ecuador. Pop. 255,028 (1997).

Cuer·na·va·ca /kwàìrnə vaáka/ capital city of Morelos State, south central Mexico. Pop. 316,782 (1995).

cuff¹ /kuf/ *n* 1 the part of a sleeve at the wrist 2 *US, Can, ANZ* the fold at the bottom of a pant leg —**cuff·less** *adj*

cuff² *vt* hit with an open hand —**cuff** *n*

cuff link *n* a fastener for a shirt cuff *(often pl)*

cui·rass /kwi ráss/ *n* a piece of armor for the upper body

cui·sine /kwi zeén/ *n* 1 a cooking style 2 a range of food

cul-de-sac /kùl də sák/ (*pl* **culs-de-sac** /pronunc. same/ or **cul-de-sacs**) *n* 1 a street closed at one end 2 an impasse

Cu·le·bra, Is·la de /koo lébbrə/ island off the eastern coast of Puerto Rico. Pop. 1,542.

Cu·lia·cán /koŏlyə kaàn/ capital of Sinaloa State, W Mexico. Pop. 696,262 (1995).

cu·li·nar·y /kúllə nèrree, kyoŏ-/ *adj* of cooking

cull *vt* 1 remove somebody or something from a group as worthless 2 select somebody or something 3 remove an animal from a herd or flock 4 reduce a herd or group by killing members of it —**cull** *n* —**cull·er** *n*

Cul·len /kúllən/, **Countee** (1903–46) US poet

cul·mi·nate /kúlmə nàyt/ (-**nat·ed**, -**nat·ing**) *vti* 1 come or bring to the highest point 2 finish spectacularly

cul·mi·na·tion /kùlmə náysh'n/ *n* 1 the highest point of something 2 an act of reaching or bringing something to a climax

cu·lottes /koo lóts, koŏ lòts/ *npl* women's shorts resembling a skirt

cul·pa·ble /kúlpəb'l/ *adj* guilty —**cul·pa·bil·i·ty** /kùlpə bíllətee/ *n*

cul·prit /kúlprit/ *n* 1 a wrongdoer 2 an accused person

ORIGIN **Culprit** is thought to derive from a misinterpretation of a written abbreviation used in law courts. The earliest recorded examples, in the late 17C, are all of the formula "Culprit, how will you be tried?", said by the clerk of a court to a person who has pleaded not guilty. It is surmised that this is a misunderstanding of a legal French abbreviation *cul. prist*, representing a longer expression meaning "You are guilty; we are ready to prove it." In 1700 **culprit** is recorded outside the legal formula and court records, meaning "prisoner at the bar, the accused." The modern sense of "wrongdoer" is recorded in the middle of the 18C, and may be influenced by Latin *culpa* "fault, blame."

cult *n* 1 a minority religion regarded with disapproval by the majority 2 a group of adherents to a cult 3 idolization 4 an object of idolization 5 a fad —**cult·ish** *adj* —**cult·ist** *n*

cul·ti·vate /kúltə vàyt/ (-**vat·ed**, -**vat·ing**) *vt* 1 prepare land for crops 2 grow plants 3 improve or develop something through study 4 become friends with somebody for personal advantage —**cul·ti·va·ble** *adj* —**cul·ti·vat·ed** *adj*

cul·ti·va·tion /kùltə váysh'n/ *n* 1 the preparation of land for crops, or the growing of plants **2** improvement or development through education

cul·ti·va·tor /kúltə vàytər/ *n* a soil-breaking device

cul·tur·al /kúlchərəl/ *adj* **1** of a specific culture **2** of the arts —**cul·tur·al·ly** *adv*

cul·ture /kúlchər/ *n* **1** the arts **2** knowledge and sophistication **3** the shared beliefs and values of a group **4** a people with shared beliefs and values **5** the development of artifacts and symbols in the advancement of a society **6** the growing of biological material for scientific purposes **7** a biological material grown for scientific purposes **8** the cultivation of land **9** the development of a skill through training or education ■ *vt* (**-tured, -tur·ing**) grow biological material for scientific purposes

cul·tured /kúlchərd/ *adj* **1** educated and sophisticated **2** grown in a nutrient substance for scientific purposes **3** artificially produced

cul·tured pearl *n* an artificially created pearl

cul·ture shock *n* a feeling of confusion resulting from sudden exposure to an unfamiliar culture

cul·vert /kúlvərt/ *n* **1** an underground duct **2** a structure covering a culvert

Cum·ber·land Gap /kúmbərlənd gàp/ pass through the Cumberland Mountains near the meeting point of Tennessee, Virginia, and Kentucky. Height 1,650 ft./503 m.

cum·ber·some /kúmbərsəm/ *adj* **1** heavy or bulky **2** complicated or problematic —**cum·ber·some·ly** *adv* —**cum·ber·some·ness** *n*

cum·in /kúmmin/ *n* **1** aromatic seeds used as a spice **2** a plant that produces cumin

cum lau·de /kum lów dày, -dee/ *adv, adj* with an academic distinction

ORIGIN The phrase is Latin, and literally means "with praise."

cum·mer·bund /kúmmər bùnd/ *n* a broad band worn around the waist as part of a man's formal dress

cum·mings /kúmmingz/, **e. e.** (1894–1962) US poet

cu·mu·la·tive /kyoómyə làytiv, -lət-/ *adj* gradually building up in strength or effect **2** resulting from successive additions —**cu·mu·la·tive·ly** *adv*

cu·mu·la·tive trau·ma dis·or·der *n* a painful muscle condition

cu·mu·lo·nim·bus /kyoómyə lō nímbəss/ (*pl* **-bi** /-bī/ *or* **-bus·es**) *n* a tall dark thunder cloud

cu·mu·lus /kyoómyələss/ (*pl* **-li** /-lī/) *n* a large fluffy cloud —**cu·mu·lous** *adj*

Cuneiform: Sumerian clay tablet (18C BC)

cu·ne·i·form /kyoóni fàwrm, kyoo neè ə-/ *adj* **1** wedge-shaped **2** of an ancient writing system of SW Asia with wedge-shaped characters **3** of wedge-shaped ankle bones ■ *n* cuneiform script

cun·ni·lin·gus /kùnni líng gəss/ *n* oral stimulation of a woman's genitals

cun·ning /kúnning/ *adj* **1** crafty and deceitful **2** cleverly thought out **3** cute (*infml dated*) ■ *n* **1** craftiness and deceitfulness **2** skillful ingenuity or grace —**cun·ning·ly** *adv* —**cun·ning·ness** *n*

Cun·ning·ham /kúnning hàm/, **Merce** (*b.* 1919) US dancer and choreographer

cup *n* **1** a small drinking container with a handle **2** the contents of a cup **3** a volume measure used in cooking, equal to 8 fl. oz/237 ml **4** an ornamental trophy awarded as a winner's prize **5** a sports competition to win a cup **6** a bowl-shaped object or part ■ *vt* (**cupped, cup·ping**) **1** form a hand or the hands into a cup shape **2** hold something in cupped hands —**cup·ful** *n*

cup·bear·er /kúp bàirər/ *n* somebody who serves wine to royalty

cup·board /kúbbərd/ *n* a storage unit or recess with a door

cup·cake /kúp kàyk/ *n* a small cake baked in a cup-shaped mold and usually frosted

cu·pid /kyoópid/ *n* **1** a representation of a young boy with wings and a bow and arrow, as a symbol of love **2** **Cu·pid** in Roman mythology, the god of love. Greek equivalent **Eros**

cu·pid·i·ty /kyoo píddətee/ *n* greed (*fml*)

cu·po·la /kyoópələ/ *n* **1** a dome-shaped roof **2** a dome on a roof

cu·pric /koóprik/ *adj* containing copper with a valence of 2

cur *n* a mongrel dog

cur·a·ble /kyoórəb'l/ *adj* able to be cured

cu·ra·çao /koòrə sów, -ső/ *n* an orange-flavored liqueur

Cu·ra·çao /koòrə sów, -ső, kyóorə-/ largest island of the Netherlands Antilles, in the Caribbean Sea

cu·ra·cy /kyoórəssee/ (*pl* **-cies**) *n* the position of a curate

cu·ra·re /kyoo raàree/, **cu·ra·ri** *n* **1** a dark resin from certain South American plants. Use: traditional arrow poison, muscle relaxant in medicine. **2** a vine from which curare is obtained

cu·rate[1] /kyóorət/ *n* **1** a priest's assistant **2** a cleric in charge of a parish

cu·rate[2] /kyoór àyt/ (**-rat·ed, -rat·ing**) *v* **1** *vti* look after a museum or gallery **2** *vt* organize an exhibition

cu·ra·tive /kyóorətiv/ *adj* capable of curing ■ *n* a medicine or medical treatment

cu·ra·tor /kyə ráytər, kyóo ràytər/ *n* the head of a museum or gallery —**cu·ra·to·ri·al** /kyóorə táwree əl/ *adj* —**cu·ra·tor·ship** *n*

curb /kurb/ *n* **1** the edge of a sidewalk **2** a line of stones forming the edge of a lawn **3** an imposed limitation **4** a raised part surrounding a skylight or well **5** a horse's bit and attached chain ■ *vt* **1** restrain something **2** provide something with a curb **3** lead a dog off the sidewalk to defecate

curd /kurd/ *n* **1** the solid part of sour milk used for making cheese **2** a substance resembling milk curd ■ *vti* curdle —**curd·y** *adj*

cur·dle /kúrd'l/ (**-dled, -dling**) *vti* separate into curds and whey

cure /kyoor/ *v* (**cured, cur·ing**) **1** *vti* heal a person or animal **2** *vt* treat an illness successfully **3** *vt* resolve a problem **4** *vt* preserve food by drying, smoking, or salting **5** *vt* preserve or treat a substance or material by drying or adding chemicals ■ *n* **1** something that restores health **2** a recovery from ill health **3** a solution to a problem

cure-all *n* a universal remedy

~~curency~~ incorrect spelling of **currency**

cu·ret·tage /kyóorə taázh/, **cu·rette·ment** /kyoo rétmənt/ *n* the process of scraping inside a body cavity to remove unwanted tissue

cur·few /kúr fyoo/ *n* **1** an official order for people to remain indoors after a specified time **2** a time or signal for a curfew **3** the length of a curfew

~~curiculum~~ incorrect spelling of **curriculum**

AKG London

Marie Curie

Cu·rie /kyoóree/, **Marie** (1867–1934) Polish-born French chemist and physicist. She pioneered research into radioactivity.

Cu·rie, Pierre (1859–1906) French physicist. He shared the Nobel Prize in physics in 1903 with his wife, Marie Curie.

cu·ri·o /kyoóree ò/ (*pl* **-os**) *n* an unusual artifact

cu·ri·os·i·ty /kyóoree óssətee/ (*pl* **-ties**) *n* **1** eagerness to know about something **2** inquisitiveness **3** somebody or something interesting and unusual

cu·ri·ous /kyoóree əss/ *adj* **1** eager to know **2** too inquisitive **3** odd —**cu·ri·ous·ly** *adv* —**cu·ri·ous·ness** *n*

~~curiousity~~ incorrect spelling of **curiosity**

Cur·i·ti·ba /kòori teébə/ capital of Paraná State, S Brazil. Pop. 1,476,253 (1996).

cu·ri·um /kyoóree əm/ *n* (*symbol* **Cm**) a silvery-white metallic radioactive element

curl *v* **1** *vti* put hair into waves, coils, or spirals, or be naturally like this **2** *vti* make or become curved or coiled **3** *vi* move in a curve or spiral ■ *n* **1** a lock of hair with a curved or coiled shape (*often pl*) **2** the tendency of hair to curl naturally **3** something curved or coiled **4** the adoption of a curved shape

Curl, Robert Floyd (*b.* 1933) US chemist. He jointly discovered the molecular family of carbon called fullerenes.

curl·er /kúrlər/ *n* **1** a roller or device for curling hair **2** a player of the game of curling

cur·lew /kúr loo/ *n* a large brown shore bird with a curved bill

curl·i·cue /kúrli kyoo/ *n* a curved decorative flourish —**curl·i·cued** *adj*

curl·ing /kúrling/ *n* a sport involving sliding stones on ice

curl·y /kúrlee/ (**-i·er, -i·est**) *adj* **1** with curls **2** curved or coiled —**curl·i·ness** *n*

cur·mudg·eon /kur mújjən/ *n* somebody irritable or stubborn —**cur·mudg·eon·ly** *adj*

cur·rant /kúrrənt/ *n* **1** a small dried grape. Use: in cooking. **2** a small round fruit of a deciduous bush **3** a bush bearing currants

---

ORIGIN The **currant** originates in Corinth in Greece. Small dried grapes of high quality were exported from there in the Middle Ages, and were known in French, and then in English, as "raisins of Corinth." The actual early English form was *raisins of Corauntz,* abbreviated to *Corauntz* by the early 16C and **currant** by the end of the 16C. The term **currant** also came to be applied to northern fruits in the late 16C in the mistaken popular belief that these were the source of the E Mediterranean dried fruit.

SPELLCHECK Do not confuse the spelling of **currant** and **current** ("existing now"), which sound similar.

---

cur·ren·cy /kúrrənsee/ (*pl* **-cies**) *n* **1** a country's money **2** the acceptance of an idea or term

cur·rent /kúrrənt, kúr ənt/ *adj* **1** existing now **2** valid **3** accepted at the present time ■ *n* **1** a flow or stream of water or air **2** a flow of electricity **3** the rate of flow of electricity —**cur·rent·ly** *adv* —**cur·rent·ness** *n* ◊ See note at **currant**

cur·rent e·vents *npl* topical news items

cur·ric·u·lum /kə ríkyələm/ (*pl* **-la** /-lə/ or **-lums**) *n* the subjects taught in an educational institution, or the elements taught in a subject —**cur·ric·u·lar** *adj*

cur·ric·u·lum vi·tae /kə rīkyələm veé tì, -vítee/ (*pl* **cur·ric·u·la vi·tae** /kə rīkyələ-/) *n* a summary of somebody's qualifications and experience

cur·ry[1] /kúrree/ *n* (*pl* **-ries**) **1** a dish of meat, fish, or vegetables in a highly spiced sauce **2** seasoning for curry ■ *vt* (**-ried, -ries**) cook in a highly spiced sauce

> **ORIGIN Curry** comes from a language of S India and N Sri Lanka, and means literally "sauce."

cur·ry[2] /kúrree/ (**-ried, -ries**) *vt* **1** groom a horse **2** give leather a flexible and waterproof finish

cur·ry pow·der *n* a mixture of spices for making curry

curse *n* **1** a swearword **2** an appeal to a supernatural being for evil to happen **3** a source of harm ■ *v* (**cursed, curs·ing**) **1** *vi* use a swearword **2** *vt* swear at **3** *vt* wish evil on

curs·ed /kúrsəd, kurst/ *adj* **1** supposedly made the victim of a curse **2** wicked or hateful **3** annoying or frustrating (*infml*) —**curs·ed·ly** *adv* —**curs·ed·ness** /-nəss/ *n*

cur·sive /kúrsiv/ *adj* written with the letters of a word joined together ■ *n* cursive writing —**cur·sive·ly** *adv*

⨍ **cur·sor** /kúrsər/ *n* a moving marker on a computer screen indicating where a keystroke will appear ■ *vi* move a cursor

cur·so·ry /kúrsəree/ *adj* quick and superficial —**cur·so·ri·ly** *adv* —**cur·so·ri·ness** *n*

curt /kurt/ *adj* **1** rudely brief **2** using few words —**curt·ly** *adv* —**curt·ness** *n*

cur·tail /kur táyl/ *vt* cut short —**cur·tail·ment** *n*

cur·tain /kúrt'n/ *n* **1** a piece of cloth hung to cover a window or door, or around a bed **2** a hanging cloth at the front of a stage in a theater **3** the beginning or end of a performance, act, or scene in a theater **4** a barrier or screen **5** something resembling a curtain ◇ *a curtain of water* ■ *vt* **1** cover or divide with a curtain **2** fit with curtains ◇ **bring down the curtain on** bring to an end (*infml*)

cur·tain call *n* an appearance by a performer to receive applause at the end of a performance

cur·tain rais·er *n* **1** a short performance before the main one **2** a minor event before a major one

~~curtesy~~ incorrect spelling of **courtesy**

~~curtious~~ incorrect spelling of **courteous**

curt·sy /kúrtsee/ (**-sied, -sies**), **curt·sey** *vi* bend the knees with one foot behind the other in respect (*refers to women*) —**curt·sy** *n*

> **ORIGIN Curtsy** is a contracted form of *courtesy*,

used from the beginning of the 16C. It is found in a variety of *courtesy*'s meanings until the mid-17C, but in the late 16C began to specialize as a "respectful gesture," and now is further restricted to a woman's bending of the knees.

cur·va·ceous /kur váyshəss/ *adj* describes a woman with shapely curves —**cur·va·ceous·ness** *n*

cur·va·ture /kúrvə chŏŏr, -chər/ *n* **1** the quality of being curved **2** degree of curve

curve /kurv/ *n* **1** a line with a regular smooth bend **2** something shaped in a curve **3** a statistical method of grading **4** *also* **curve ball** in baseball, a pitched ball that curves to the side ■ *v* (**curved, curv·ing**) **1** *vi* form or cause to form a curve **2** *vti* move in a curve **3** *vt* throw a curve ball **4** *vt* grade students relative to one another —**curved** *adj* —**curv·i·ness** *n* —**curv·y** *adj* ◇ **ahead of the curve** ahead of a trend or trends ◇ **pitch** or **throw somebody a curve** surprise somebody (*infml*)

cush·ion /kŏŏsh'n/ *n* **1** a soft filled bag for sitting on **2** a soft supportive or protective pad **3** something limiting the unpleasant effect of a situation ■ *vt* **1** protect against impact **2** reduce the unpleasant effect of **3** support or place on a cushion —**cush·ion·y** *adj*

cush·y /kŏŏshee/ (**-i·er, -i·est**) *adj* (*infml*) **1** well-paid and easy **2** luxurious —**cush·i·ly** *adv* —**cush·i·ness** *n*

> **ORIGIN Cushy** comes from a Hindi word meaning "pleasant." It is recorded from the 1st decade of the 20C.

cusp *n* **1** a ridge on a molar tooth **2** a point of intersection of two arcs **3** the border between two signs of the zodiac **4** either of the pointed ends of a crescent moon

cuss (*infml*) *vti* swear at somebody or something ■ *n* **1** somebody regarded as annoying **2** a swearword

cus·tard /kústərd/ *n* a dessert of eggs, milk, and sugar —**cus·tard·y** *adj*

> **ORIGIN** A **custard** was originally an open pie of meat or fruit (the name referred to the pie's pastry shell or crust). The filling included stock or milk, often thickened with eggs. By around 1600 the term indicated a dish in its own right made of eggs beaten into milk and cooked.

cus·tard pie *n* a pie thrown in slapstick comedy

Cus·ter /kústər/, **George Armstrong** (1839–76) US soldier

cus·to·di·al /ku stŏdee əl/ *adj* **1** of legal custody of a child **2** janitorial **3** involving detention in prison

cus·to·di·an /ku stŏdee ən/ *n* **1** somebody responsible for taking care of something valuable for somebody else **2** a building janitor **3** a protector or upholder of something valuable —**cus·to·di·an·ship** n

cus·to·dy /kústədee/ n **1** the legal right to take care of a child **2** detention by the police or the authorities **3** the state of being under somebody's protection

cus·tom /kústəm/ n **1** a tradition **2** a habit or practice **3** patronage of a store ■ adj **1** made or changed to order **2** making goods to order ◊ See note at **habit**

cus·tom·ar·y /kústə mèrree/ adj usual or characteristic —**cus·tom·ar·i·ly** /kùstə mérrəlee/ adv ◊ See note at **usual**

cus·tom-built, cus·tom-made adj built specifically for one customer —**cus·tom-build** n

cus·tom·er /kústəmər/ n **1** a buyer of goods or services **2** a particular type of person (infml) o a cool customer

cus·tom·ize /kústə mìz/ (-ized, -iz·ing) vt change according to a specific requirement —**cus·tom·i·za·tion** /kùstəmi záysh'n/ n

cus·toms /kústəmz/ n (+ sing or pl verb) **1** also **Cus·toms** a place where goods entering a country are examined to see what duty is payable on them **2** also **Cus·toms** the government agency responsible for collecting duties on imported goods **3** duties payable on imports and exports

ϟ **cut** /kut/ v (cut, cut·ting) **1** vti divide or separate something into pieces with a sharp tool **2** vti pierce or make a hole in something with a sharp tool **3** vi be sharp enough to cut something **4** vi yield to a blade o bread that cuts easily **5** vt injure somebody with a sharp object and cause bleeding **6** vt shorten something with a sharp tool **7** vt fashion a garment by cutting **8** vi take or be a short cut o This path cuts through the woods. **9** vt reduce or remove a quantity o cut a budget **10** vt shorten something by editing **11** vti delete computer data ♦ **paste 12** vti edit a movie, video, or TV program **13** vi stop filming (usually a command) **14** vt change a scene suddenly when filming **15** vt stop providing something o cut the supply of food to the refugee camps **16** vti turn off a device o cut the engine **17** vti divide a deck of cards in two after shuffling them **18** vt make a recording of a song or songs (infml) **19** vt not attend a class or meeting (infml) **20** vt dilute a liquid **21** vti remove grime from something in cleaning it **22** vti intersect **23** vi change direction sharply o cut to the right **24** vt grow a tooth through the gums **25** vt negotiate an agreement (infml) o cut a deal **26** vt snub somebody **27** vti hurt somebody's feelings ■ n **1** a wound in the skin made by a sharp instrument **2** an incision **3** a reduction **4** a haircut **5** a garment style **6** a removal of a section of text or movie, or a section removed **7** an edited version of a movie o the director's cut **8** a share of money (infml) **9** a stopping of a supply **10** an act of non-

attendance **11** a specific segment of meat **12** a track on a musical recording **13** a block with a design cut in it used for printing (often in combination) **14** hurtful words or behavior **15** a dividing of a deck of cards in two after shuffling them ■ adj **1** injured with something sharp **2** separated with a knife —**cut·ta·ble** adj ◊ **cut and run** leave a place quickly to avoid being caught or detained ◊ **cut both ways** have both advantages and disadvantages ◊ **cut loose** behave in an unrestrained way (infml)

□ **cut back** v **1** vti reduce something **2** vt remove the top of a plant to encourage new growth

□ **cut down** v **1** vti reduce something **2** vt fell a tree **3** vt kill somebody

□ **cut in** v **1** vi interrupt somebody or something **2** vti join the middle of a line **3** vi join traffic dangerously

□ **cut off** vt **1** stop supplying something **2** isolate somebody or something **3** stop somebody from talking

□ **cut out** vi stop functioning o The engine cut out. ■ adj naturally suited for something

□ **cut up** vi behave in a naughty or disruptive way (slang)

cut-and-dried adj **1** decided and fixed **2** predictable

ϟ **cut-and-paste** n a computer facility for deleting data from one place and inserting it in another —**cut-and-paste** vt

cut·a·way /kútə wày/ n a model from which a part is removed to show the inside

cut·back /kút bàk/ n a reduction

cute /kyoot/ (cut·er, cut·est) adj **1** attractive in a childlike or endearing way **2** physically attractive **3** shrewd —**cute·ly** adv —**cute·ness** n

---

ORIGIN Cute is a shortened from of **acute**. It is first recorded in the early 18C, in the sense "shrewd"; "attractive" followed in the early 19C.

---

cute·sy /kyóotsee/ (-si·er, -si·est) adj trying too hard to be charming —**cute·si·ness** n

cut glass n glass with a pattern cut in its surface

cu·ti·cle /kyóotik'l/ n **1** an edge of hard skin at the base of a fingernail or toenail **2** the epidermis **3** the protective outer layer of a plant or animal —**cu·tic·u·lar** /kyoo tíkyələr/ adj

cu·tin /kyóot'n/ n a waxy mixture forming the cuticle of a plant

cut-in n a camera shot that focuses on a smaller portion of a scene already established

cut·lass /kúttləss/ n a short sword formerly used by sailors

cut·ler·y /kúttləree/ n **1** flatware **2** knives and other instruments with blades

cut·let /kúttlət/ n **1** a flat, boneless piece of

meat **2** a flat cake of chopped food covered in breadcrumbs and fried

cut·off /kút àwf/ n **1** the limit or date when something stops **2** an end to the supply of something **3** a valve controlling the flow of fluid or gas **4** a shortcut ■ **cut-offs** npl shorts made by cutting off the legs of pants

cut·out /kút òwt/ n **1** a silhouette shape **2** something cut out **3** a safety device for turning off an electric circuit

ƒ**cut·o·ver** /kút ōvər/ n the transfer from one computer system to a new system ■ adj describes land where the trees have been cut down

cut·ter /kúttər/ n **1** a sharp tool (often pl) **2** somebody who cuts something **3** a small armed patrol boat **4** a single-masted sailboat **5** a ship's boat for transporting passengers or cargo

cut·throat /kút thrōt/ adj aggressive and merciless ■ n a murderer or other dangerous person

cut·ting /kútting/ n **1** a part of a plant removed for propagation **2** a newspaper or magazine clipping ■ adj **1** abrasive and hurtful **2** very cold —**cut·ting·ly** adv

cutting board n a board for cutting food

cutting edge n the most advanced stage of something —**cut·ting-edge** adj

cutting room n a room where film is edited

cut·tle·fish /kútt'l fish/ (pl same or **-fish·es**) n an invertebrate animal with ten arms and an internal shell that lives on the seabed

cut·up /kút ùp/ n somebody funny (infml)

Cuz·co /kooss kò/ capital of Cuzco Department, S Peru. Pop. 278,590 (1998).

CV abbr curriculum vitae

CWO abbr **1** Chief Warrant Officer **2** chief Web officer

cwt., cwt abbr hundredweight

cy·an /sí ən, -àn/ n a greenish-blue color —**cy·an** adj

cy·a·nide /sí ə nīd/ n a poisonous inorganic salt

ƒ**cyber-** prefix **1** computers and information systems o cybernetics **2** virtual reality o cyberspace **3** the Internet o cybercafé

ƒ**cy·ber·ca·fé** /síbər ka fày, -kə fày/ n a coffee shop offering Internet access

ƒ**cy·ber·cast** /síbər kàst/ n a broadcast of an event transmitted on the Internet —**cy·ber·cast** vti

ƒ**cy·ber·med·i·ar·y** /síbər meèdee èrree/ (pl **-ies**) n an organization that facilitates or collects fees for online transactions without owning the products or services

ƒ**cy·ber·nate** /síbər nàyt/ (**-nat·ed, -nat·ing**) vt control a manufacturing process by computer —**cy·ber·na·tion** /síbər náysh'n/ n

ƒ**cy·ber·net·ics** /síbər néttiks/ n (+ sing verb) **1** the study of communication in organisms, organic processes, and mechanical or electronic systems **2** the replication of biological control systems using technology —**cy·ber·net·ic** adj —**cy·ber·ne·ti·cian** /sìbərnə tísh'n/ n

ƒ**cy·ber·self** /síbər sèlf/ (pl **-selves** /-sèlvz/) n a false identity taken on by an Internet user

ƒ**cy·ber·sex** /síbər sèks/ n sexual stimulation involving virtual reality or the Internet

ƒ**cy·ber·space** /síbər spàyss/ n **1** the imagined place where electronic data goes **2** virtual reality

ƒ**cy·ber·squat·ting** /síbər skwòtting/ n the registration of a trademarked domain name in order to sell it to the trademark owner —**cy·ber·squat·ter** n

ƒ**cy·ber·stalk·er** /síbər stàwkər/ n a stalker using the Internet —**cy·ber·stalk·ing** n

ƒ**cy·ber·ter·ror·ism** /síbər térrə rìzzəm/ n the sabotage of computer systems by using the Internet —**cy·ber·ter·ror·ist** n, adj

ƒ**cy·ber·thrill·er** /síbər thrìllər/ n an action entertainment using computers

ƒ**cy·ber·war** /síbər wàwr/ n warfare conducted with and against computer systems

ƒ**cy·borg** /sí bàwrg/ n a part-human, part-robot fictional being

ƒ**cy·brar·y** /sí brèrree/ (pl **-ies**) n an Internet library —**cy·bra·ri·an** /sí bráiree ən/ n

Cyc·la·des /síklə deèz/ large group of Greek islands in the S Aegean Sea. Pop. 88,485 (1981).

cy·cla·men /síkləmən/ n a flowering plant with heart-shaped leaves

cy·cle /sík'l/ n **1** a repeated sequence of events **2** a period of time between repeated events **3** a complete mechanical or electronic process **4** a series of linked literary or musical works **5** a bicycle **6** a motorcycle ■ v (**-cled, -cling**) **1** vti put or go through a cycle **2** vi ride a bicycle

cy·clic /síklik, sík-/, **cy·cli·cal** /síklik'l, sík-/ adj occurring in cycles —**cy·cli·cal·ly** adv —**cy·cli·ci·ty** /sí klíssətee, si-/ n

cy·clist /síklist/ n a rider of a bicycle or motorcycle

cy·clone /sí klōn/ n **1** a large-scale storm system with rotating winds **2** a violent rotating storm —**cy·clon·ic** /sí klónnik/ adj

cy·clops /sí klòps/ (pl **-clop·es** /sí klō peèz/ or same) n **1** a one-eyed crustacean **2** **Cy·clops** in Greek mythology, a one-eyed giant

cyg·net /sígnət/ n a young swan

cyl·in·der /síllindər/ n **1** a tube shape **2** a chamber for a piston in an engine **3** a rotating part of a revolver containing cartridge chambers **4** a tube-shaped geometric solid or surface **5** a tube-shaped object —**cyl·in·dered** adj

cyl·in·der head n the closed detachable end of an engine cylinder

cy·lin·dri·cal /sə líndrik'l/, **cy·lin·dric** /sə líndrik/ adj cylinder-shaped —**cy·lin·dri·cal·ly** adv

cym·bal /símb'l/ *n* a circular brass percussion instrument

SPELLCHECK Do not confuse the spelling of **cymbal** and **symbol** ("a representation"), which sound similar.

---

cyn·ic /sínnik/ *n* **1** somebody believing that people are insincere and motivated by self-interest **2** somebody sarcastic **3 Cyn·ic** an ancient Greek philosopher who believed in virtue through self-control —**Cyn·ic** *adj* —**cyn·i·cism** /sínni sìzzəm/ *n*

cyn·i·cal /sínnik'l/ *adj* **1** distrustful of human nature **2** sarcastic **3** ignoring accepted standards of behavior o *a cynical disregard for the welfare of employees* —**cyn·i·cal·ly** *adv* —**cyn·i·cism** /sínnissizəm/ *n*

cy·no·sure /sínə shòor/ *n* the center of attention *(fml)* —**cy·no·sur·al** /sìnə shòorəl/ *adj*

cy·pher *n* = **cipher**

cy·press /síprəss/ *n* **1** a conifer with hard wood and leaves like scales **2** the hard wood of the cypress tree

Cyp·ri·ot /síppree ət/, **Cyp·ri·ote** *n* somebody from Cyprus ■ *adj* of Cyprus

Cy·prus /síprəss/ island country in the E Mediterranean Sea, partitioned between the Greek Cypriot south and the officially unrecognized Turkish Republic of Northern Cyprus. Cap. Nicosia. Pop. 762,887 (2001).

Cy·ra·no de Ber·ge·rac /sìrrənò də búrzhə ràk/, **Savinien** (1619–55) French poet and dramatist

Cy·ril·lic /sə ríllik/ *adj* of the alphabet used in the Slavic languages ■ *n* the Slavic alphabet

cyst /sist/ *n* **1** a spherical swelling containing fluid in human or animal tissue **2** a cavity or thin-walled sac in an organism —**cys·toid** /sís tòyd/ *adj, n*

cys·tic /sístik/ *adj* **1** of a cyst **2** containing a cyst

cys·tic fi·bro·sis /-fī bróssiss/ *n* a hereditary glandular disease affecting respiratory function

cys·ti·tis /si stítiss/ *n* inflammation of the bladder

cy·tol·o·gy /sī tólləjee/ *n* **1** the scientific study of cell structures and functions **2** the testing of cells from body tissue, especially for cancer diagnosis —**cy·to·log·i·cal** *adj* —**cy·tol·o·gist** *n*

cy·to·plasm /sítō plàzzəm/ *n* the contents of a cell excluding the nucleus —**cy·to·plas·mic** /sítō plázmik/ *adj* —**cy·to·plas·mi·cal·ly** *adv*

czar *n* = **tsar**

cza·ri·na *n* = **tsarina**

Czech /chek/ *n* **1** somebody from the Czech Republic **2** somebody from Czechoslovakia **3** the official language of the Czech Republic —**Czech** *adj*

Czech·o·slo·va·ki·a /chèkəsslə vaakee ə, chèkò slò-/ former country in central Europe, now divided into the Czech Republic and Slovakia

Czech Re·pub·lic country in central Europe. Cap. Prague. Pop. 10,264,212 (2001).

D

d (*pl* **d's**), **D** (*pl* **D's** *or* **Ds**) *n* **1** the 4th letter of the English alphabet **2** the Roman numeral for 500

'd *contr* **1** did **2** had **3** would

d', D' see also under surname

D[1] (*pl* **D's** *or* **Ds**) *n* **1** the second note in the musical scale of C major **2** the 4th highest grade of a student's work

D[2] *symbol* **1** dispersion **2** drag

d. *abbr* **1** daughter **2** day **3** departs **4** depth **5** died

DA *abbr also* **D.A.** district attorney

⚡ **D/A** *abbr* digital-to-analog

dab *vt* (**dabbed, dab·bing**) **1** tap gently **2** apply gently to a surface ■ *n* **1** a small quantity **2** a gentle tap

dab·ble /dáb'l/ (-bled, -bling) *v* **1** *vi* become involved superficially **2** *vti* splash in water, or dip something in water **3** *vi* move under water for food *(refers to ducks)* —**dab·bler** *n*

Dac·ca ♦ **Dhaka**

dace (*pl same or* **dac·es**) *n* a small freshwater fish

da·cha /daachə/ *n* a Russian country home

dachs·hund /daaks hòond, daaksənt/ *n* a short long-bodied dog

---

ORIGIN Dachshund is an adoption of a German word that means literally "badger dog." The breed was originally used to hunt badgers by burrowing into their setts.

~~dachshund~~ incorrect spelling of **dachshund**

dac·tyl /dákt'l/ *n* **1** a metrical foot of three syllables, one long followed by two short **2** a finger or toe

dad, dad·dy /dáddee/ *n* a father *(infml)*

Da·da /daa daa/, **da·da, Da·da·ism** /-ìzzəm/, **da·da·ism** *n* a European movement in literature and art of the early and mid-20C

dad·dy long·legs /-láwng lègz/ (*pl same*) *n* a long-legged arachnid

da·do /dáy dò/ *n* (*pl* **-does** *or* **-dos**) **1** the lower part of an interior wall, decorated differently from the upper part **2** a rectangular groove cut in a board to form part of a joint ■ *vt* (**-doed, -do·ing, -does**) **1** cut a dado in **2** insert into a dado

da·do rail *n* a decorative rail fitted around an interior wall, usually at middle height

Dae·da·lus /dédd'ləss/ *n* in Greek mythology,

a craftsman who built the Labyrinth to house the Minotaur and made wings to escape with his son Icarus

⚡ **dae·mon** /deémən/, **dai·mon** /df mŏn/ *n* **1** a guardian spirit **2** a piece of software that carries out background tasks —**dae·mon·ic** /di mónnik/ *adj*

daf·fo·dil /dáffə dĭl/ *n* a plant with yellow trumpet-shaped flowers

daf·fy /dáffee/ (**-fi·er**, **-fi·est**) *adj* silly (*infml*)

da Ga·ma /də gaámə/ ⬥ Gama, Vasco da

dag·ger /dággər/ *n* **1** a short pointed knife used as a weapon **2** a sign resembling the shape of a dagger, used as a reference mark in a text ■ *vt* mark text with a dagger

Da·guerre /də gáir, daa-/, **Louis Jacques** (1789–1851) French painter and pioneer photographer

dahl /daal/, **dal** *n* a South Asian stew made from pulses

dahl·ia /dáalyə, dál-/ *n* a perennial plant with showy flowers

ORIGIN The **dahlia** is named for the Swedish botanist Andreas Dahl (1751–89), who discovered the plant in Mexico in 1788.

dai·kon /df kŏn, díkən/ *n* a long white radish

dai·ly /dáylee/ *adj* **1** done every day **2** for each day ■ *adv* on every day ■ *n* (*pl* **-lies**) a newspaper published every day (*often pl*)

dai·mon *n* = daemon

dain·ty /dáyntee/ *adj* (**-ti·er**, **-ti·est**) **1** delicate and pretty **2** tasty **3** refined in taste ■ *n* (*pl* **-ties**) a delicacy or tidbit —**dain·ti·ly** *adv* —**dain·ti·ness** *n*

ORIGIN **Dainty** first appears in English as a noun. It comes from a Latin word that is also the source of *dignity*. Both words entered English from French. The French word from which **dainty** derives showed the natural low development of the Latin word, but the French source of *dignity* had been consciously altered to conform to its Latin original. The adjective **dainty** developed from the noun. The idea of a delicacy or tidbit, already present in French, gave rise to the sense "choice, tasty" and then "delicate and pretty."

dai·qui·ri /dákəree/ (*pl* **-ris**) *n* a cocktail made with rum and lemon or lime juice

dair·y /dáiree/ (*pl* **-ies**) *n* an establishment that sells, processes, or produces milk —**dair·y** *adj* —**dair·y·man** *n* —**dair·y·wom·an** *n*

SPELLCHECK Do not confuse the spelling of **dairy** and **diary** ("a personal record of events").

dair·y cat·tle *npl* milk cows

da·is /dáy iss, dí-/ *n* a raised platform in a hall

dai·sy /dáyzee/ (*pl* **-sies**) *n* **1** a tall plant with large petals **2** a low-growing wild flowering plant

ORIGIN **Daisy** is a contraction of *day's eye.*

The flowers open and reveal a yellow disk in the morning, and close again at night.

dai·sy chain *n* a garland of daisies

dai·sy-cut·ter /dáyzee kúttər/ *n* **1** a bomb that detonates just above ground level to clear an area **2** in baseball, a ball that skims the ground (*dated*)

Da·kar /dá kaàr, də kaàr/ capital of Senegal. Pop. 1,708,000 (1995).

Da·ko·ta /də kṓtə/ (*pl* **-tas** *or same*), **Da·ko·tan** /-t'n/ *n* **1** a member of the Sioux people **2** the language of the Dakota people —**Da·ko·ta** *adj*

Da·lai La·ma /daà II laàmə/ *n* the traditional secular and spiritual ruler of Tibet

da·la·si /daa laàssee/ (*pl* **-sis**) *n* the main unit of Gambian currency

dale *n* a lowland valley

AKG London

Salvador Dali

Da·li /daàlee/, **Da·lí, Salvador** (1904–89) Spanish painter —**Da·li·esque** /daàlee ésk/ *adj*

~~dahlia~~ incorrect spelling of **dahlia**

Dal·ian /daa lyaán/ port in NE China. Pop. 2,560,000 (1995).

Dal·las /dálləss/ city in NE Texas. Pop. 1,075,894 (1998).

dal·ly /dállee/ (**-lied, -lies**) *vi* **1** act in a flirtatious manner **2** dawdle or waste time —**dal·li·ance** *n*

Dal·ma·tia /dal máyshə/ coastal region of Croatia bordering the Adriatic Sea

Dal·ma·tian /dal máysh'n/ *n* **1** *also* **dal·ma·tian** a spotted dog **2** somebody from Dalmatia —**Dal·ma·tian** *adj*

Dal·ton /dáwlt'n/, **John** (1766–1844) British physicist and meteorologist. He laid the foundations for modern atomic theory and also first described color blindness.

dam[1] *n* **1** a concrete barrier built across a river or lake to control the flow of water **2** a reservoir confined by a dam ■ *vt* (**dammed, dam·ming**) **1** confine or restrain with a dam **2** obstruct

dam[2] *n* the female parent of an animal, especially of four-legged domestic livestock

dam·age /dámmij/ *n* **1** harm or injury **2** adverse effect **3** cost (*infml*) ■ **dam·ag·es** *npl* money paid as compensation ■ *vt* (**-aged, -ag·ing**) cause harm or injury to —**dam·ag·ing** *adj*

Da·mas·cus /də máskəss/ capital of Syria. Pop.

2,036,000 (1995). —**Da·mas·cene** /dámmə seèn, dàmmə seén/ n, adj

dam·ask /dámməsk/ n fabric into which a pattern has been woven. Use: table linen.

dam·ask rose n a rose with grayish pink flowers. Use: essential oil.

dame n 1 a woman or girl (often offensive) 2 a married woman, especially one in charge of a household (archaic) 3 **Dame** a title given to a woman awarded an order of chivalry 4 **Dame** the wife of a baronet or knight

damn /dam/ interj, adj, adv expresses annoyance (infml; sometimes offensive) ■ vt 1 declare to be bad 2 doom to failure 3 condemn to hell

dam·na·ble /dámnəb'l/ adj detestable (infml) —**dam·na·bly** adv

dam·na·tion /dam náysh'n/ n 1 condemnation to hell or eternal punishment in hell 2 a sin ■ interj expresses anger (dated)

damned /damd/ adj 1 condemned to hell 2 expresses annoyance (infml) ■ adv very (infml) ■ npl people who have been condemned to hell

damned·est /dámdəst/ n (slang) everything somebody can possibly do ■ adj (slang) most amazing

damn·ing /dámming/ adj 1 proving that somebody or something is guilty, wrong, or bad 2 highly critical —**damn·ing·ly** adv

damp adj 1 moist 2 half-hearted ■ n 1 slight wetness 2 a harmful gas found in coalmines ■ vt 1 dampen 2 also **damp down** extinguish or make burn slowly —**damp·ness** n

damp course n a waterproof layer in a brick wall designed to stop damp rising

damp·en /dámpən/ vt 1 moisten 2 deaden or stifle —**damp·en·er** n

damp·er /dámpər/ n 1 a discouraging person or thing 2 a metal plate in a chimney that controls a fire 3 a device to control or stop vibration

dam·sel /dámz'l/ n a girl or young woman (literary)

dam·son /dámz'n/ n 1 a small purple plum 2 a fruit tree that produces damsons

dan, Dan n 1 any of the numbered black-belt proficiency levels in martial arts 2 somebody proficient in a martial art

dance v (danced, danc·ing) 1 vti move rhythmically to music 2 vi jump up and down in an emotional manner 3 vi move quickly or nimbly ■ n 1 a set of rhythmical body movements performed to music 2 a period of dancing 3 an occasion for dancing 4 the art of dancing 5 a piece of music for dancing —**dance·a·ble** adj —**danc·er** n —**danc·ing** n

dance band n a band that plays music for dancing

dance floor n an area of a room for dancing

dance hall n 1 a place where dances are held

2 dance music accompanied by rapping from a DJ

D and C n a gynecological procedure in which some of the lining of the uterus is removed. Full form **dilation and curettage**

dan·de·li·on /dánd'l ì ən/ n a weed with yellow flowers

ORIGIN Dandelion was adopted from a French word meaning literally "lion's tooth." The name probably refers to the tooth-shaped edges of its leaves.

---

dan·der /dándər/ n particles shed from the hair or feathers of an animal

dan·dle /dánd'l/ (**-dled, -dling**) vt 1 move gently up and down 2 fondle or pet

dan·druff /dándrəf/ n scales of dead skin on the scalp —**dan·druff·y** adj

dan·dy /dándee/ adj (**-di·er, -di·est**) excellent (infml dated) ■ n (pl **-dies**) a fashionable man who is too concerned with his appearance (dated) —**dan·di·fy** vt —**dan·di·ly** adv —**dan·dy·ish** adj

Dane n somebody from Denmark

dang interj, adj, adv, vt damn (infml; euphemistic)

dan·ger /dáynjər/ n 1 exposure to harm 2 somebody or something that causes harm (often pl) o the dangers of smoking

dan·ger·ous /dáynjərəss/ adj 1 likely to cause harm 2 involving risk —**dan·ger·ous·ly** adv —**dan·ger·ous·ness** n

dan·gle /dáng g'l/ (**-gled, -gling**) v 1 vti hang or cause to hang loosely 2 vt offer as an inducement —**dan·gly** adj

dan·gling par·ti·ci·ple n a participle not grammatically linked to the word it modifies

---

USAGE Dangling participles typically occur at the beginning of sentences and modify either the wrong thing or nothing in particular: Startled by the noise, her book fell to the floor (but it was she, not her book, who was startled). Lying in the sun, it was hard to think of home (who was lying in the sun?). Correct such mismatches by changing the wording: Startled by the noise, she dropped her book and Lying in the sun, he found it hard to think of home.

Dan·iel /dánnyəl/ n the book of the Bible that tells the story of Daniel, a biblical prophet whose faith in God protected him in a lion's den

Dan·ish /dáynish/ adj of Denmark ■ n 1 the official language of Denmark 2 also **dan·ish** a Danish pastry ■ npl people from Denmark

Dan·ish blue n a blue-veined cheese with a strong taste

Dan·ish pas·try n a puff pastry with a sweet filling

dank adj damp and cold —**dank·ly** adv —**dank·ness** n

Dan·te A·li·ghie·ri /dàan tay alli gyérree/ (1265–1321) Italian poet —**Dan·te·an** /dántee ən, daántee-/ adj, n

Dan·ton /daan tóN/, **Georges Jacques** (1759–94) French lawyer and revolutionary

Dan·ube /dán yòob/ longest river in W Europe, flowing southeastward from SW Germany into the Black Sea. Length 1,770 mi./2,850 km.

Dan·zig /dánsig, daànt sik/ ◆ **Gdansk**

dap·per /dáppər/ adj describes a man who is neat and elegant —**dap·per·ly** adv —**dap·per·ness** n

dap·pled /dáppʹld/, **dap·ple** adj spotted with a different color

dap·ple-gray adj describes a horse of a light gray color with darker spots —**dap·ple-gray** n

DAR abbr 1 damage assessment routine 2 Daughters of the American Revolution

Dar·dan·elles /daàrd'n élz/ strait in NW Turkey linking the Aegean Sea with the Sea of Marmara. Length 43 mi./70 km.

dare /dair/ modal v (**dared**, **dar·ing**) 1 have enough courage for o I dared not ask. ■ vt 2 have the audacity to do 3 issue a challenge to ■ n a challenge

Dare /dair/, **Virginia** (1587–?) American colonist, the first child born to English parents in North America

dare·dev·il /dáir dèvv'l/ n a risk-taker ■ adj 1 with carefree disregard of danger 2 dangerous

Dar es Sa·laam /daàr ess sə laám/ largest city in Tanzania. Pop. 1,747,000 (1995).

dar·ing /dáiring/ adj 1 brave and adventurous 2 risky ■ n boldness —**dar·ing·ly** adv —**dar·ing·ness** n

Da·ri·us I /də rí əss/ (558–486 BC) king of Persia (521–486 BC)

dark adj 1 not light or lit 2 not light in color 3 brownish or blackish 4 miserable o the dark days of the war 5 suggesting anger 6 nasty 7 mysterious 8 unenlightened or unsophisticated (fml) ■ n 1 a place or situation where there is little light 2 night or nightfall —**dark·ness** n ◇ **in the dark** unaware of something

Dark Ag·es npl the period before the Middle Ages

dark choc·o·late n chocolate to which milk has not been added

dark·en /daàrkən/ vti 1 get darker, or make something darker 2 become unhappy, or make somebody unhappy

⚡**dark fib·er** n fiber optic cable that is not transmitting a signal

dark glass·es npl sunglasses

dark horse n 1 a little-known person 2 an unexpectedly successful contestant or candidate

dark·ly /daàrklee/ adv 1 threateningly 2 in black or a dark color

dark mat·ter n matter that astronomers claim makes up most of the universe

dark·room /daàrk room, -ròòm/ n a room for developing photographs

dar·ling /daàrling/ n 1 used as an affectionate term of address 2 a considerate person 3 a favorite ■ adj 1 dearly loved 2 shows approval (infml)

darn[1] vti repair fabric with a network of thread —**darn·ing** n

darn[2] interj, adj, adv, vt damn (infml; euphemistic)

Dar·row /dárrō/, **Clarence** (1857–1938) US lawyer

dart n 1 a short weighted arrow used in the game of darts 2 a short arrow used as a weapon 3 a sudden fast movement 4 a stitched tapering fold in clothing ■ vti move or send swiftly

dart·board /daàrt bàwrd/ n a round target used in the game of darts

darts n an indoor game in which small weighted arrows are thrown at a target (+ sing verb)

Dar·win /daàrwən/, **Charles** (1809–82) British naturalist. He laid the foundation for modern evolutionary theory.

Dar·win·i·an /daar wínnee ən/ adj of Darwin c his evolutionary theories —**Dar·win·i·an** n.

Dar·win·ism /daàrwi nìzzəm/ n the theory that living things originate, evolve, and survive in response to environmental forces —**Dar·win·ist** n, adj

dash n 1 a short horizontal line used as a punctuation mark, often in place of a comma or colon 2 a horizontal line representing a long sound or flash of light in Morse code 3 a rush 4 a sprint race 5 a small quantity of one thing added to another 6 vigor and verve ■ v 1 vi hurry 2 vti knock or throw something violently, or be knocked or violently thrown (fml) 3 vt ruin something 4 vt discourage somebody □ **dash off** vt create quickly (infml)

dash·board /dásh bàwrd/ n a panel of controls and dials in front of the driver of a vehicle

dash·ing /dáshing/ adj 1 stylish 2 spirited (dated) —**dash·ing·ly** adv

das·tard·ly /dástərdlee/ adj treacherous or cowardly —**das·tard·li·ness** n

⚡**da·ta** /dáytə, dáttə/ n (+ sing or pl verb) 1 factual information 2 information processed by a computer ■ plural of **datum**

USAGE Data is, strictly speaking, the plural of the noun datum. Its use as a singular noun is, however, extremely common, especially in computing contexts, and few perceive it as wrong these days.

⚡**da·ta bank** n 1 a store of information, especially when kept on a computer 2 a database

⚡**da·ta·base** /dáytə bàyss/ n a large and structured collection of data on computer that can be accessed quickly

⚡**da·ta cap·ture** *n* the collecting and entering of computer data

⚡**da·ta cen·ter** *n* a place at which large amounts of data or information relating to a particular field of knowledge are stored

⚡**da·ta el·e·ment** *n* the smallest piece of information in an electronic business transaction

⚡**da·ta·glove** /dáytə glùv, dátta-/ *n* a glove used in a virtual reality system to allow the user to explore and feed information into the virtual environment

⚡**da·ta min·ing** *n* the search for hidden information in a database

⚡**da·ta·port** /dáytə pàwrt, dátta-/ *n* a socket for connecting a laptop to the Internet

⚡**da·ta proc·ess·ing** *n* operations performed on computer data

⚡**da·ta pro·tec·tion** *n* 1 the prevention of the misuse of computer data 2 the installation of safeguards for computer data

⚡**da·ta ware·house** *n* a database for commercial analysis

date[1] *n* 1 a string of numbers denoting a particular day, month, and year 2 a time that locates a past or future event 3 a period during which something was made 4 an appointment to meet somebody ○ *a dinner date* 5 a romantic appointment ○ *go out on a date* 6 a partner on a romantic date ■ *v* (**dat·ed, dat·ing**) 1 *vt* put a date on a document 2 *vt* assign a date to something 3 *vi* originate 4 *vi* go out of style 5 *vti* go on romantic dates with somebody ◇ **to date** up to the present time

date[2] *n* 1 a small oval fruit with a single hard narrow seed 2 *also* **date palm** a tall palm tree that produces dates

date·book /dáyt bòok/ *n* an engagement book

dat·ed /dáytəd/ *adj* 1 old-fashioned 2 showing a date

date·line /dáyt lìn/ *n* a line at the head of a newspaper article giving the date and place of writing

date rape *n* rape committed during or after a romantic engagement —**date-rape** *vt*

date stamp *n* a stamp used for marking the date on documents —**date-stamp** *vt*

da·tive /dáytiv/ *n* 1 in some languages, a grammatical word form that expresses an indirect object 2 a word in the dative form —**da·tive** *adj*

da·tum /dáytəm, dáttəm/ (*pl* **-ta** /dáytə, dáttə/) *n* an item of information ◊ See note at **data**

daub /dawb/ *v* 1 *vt* apply blotchily 2 *vti* paint pictures crudely ■ *n* 1 a blotch 2 a bad painting

daugh·ter /dáwtər/ *n* 1 a female child 2 a woman who is the product of something (*literary*) ○ *a true daughter of the revolution*

⚡**daugh·ter·board** /dáwtər bàwrd/ *n* an auxiliary printed circuit board that connects to a computer's motherboard

daugh·ter-in-law (*pl* **daugh·ters-in-law**) *n* a son's wife

Daugh·ters of the A·mer·i·can Rev·o·lu·tion *npl* a women's patriotic society

Dau·mier /dō myáy/, **Honoré** (1808–79) French painter and caricaturist

daunt *vt* frighten or intimidate

daunt·less /dáwntləss/ *adj* not usually frightened —**daunt·less·ly** *adv* —**daunt·less·ness** *n*

dau·phin /dáwfin, dố-/ *n* formerly, a crown prince of France

---

ORIGIN Dauphin is essentially the same word as *dolphin*. Both come from Latin via French, but *dolphin* represents an earlier French form than **dauphin**. The title **dauphin** originally belonged to the lords of the Viennois, an area in SE France, whose coat of arms incorporated three dolphins. After the Viennois province of Dauphiné was sold to the French crown in 1343, the king gave it to his eldest son. From then on all eldest sons of the French monarch inherited it, along with the title **dauphin**.

Da·vao /də vów/ city on Mindanao island in the S Philippines. Pop. 1,191,000 (1995).

dav·en·port /dávvən pàwrt/ *n* 1 a large sofa 2 a writing desk

Dav·en·port /dávvən pàwrt/ city in E Iowa. Pop. 96,842 (1998).

Da·vid /dáyvid/ (*d.* 962 BC) king of Judah (1000–962 BC)

Da·vid /da veéd/, **Jacques-Louis** (1748–1825) French painter

Da·vid-and-Go·li·ath *adj* describes a situation in which a much smaller and apparently weaker person or organization is pitted against one that is very large and powerful

---

ORIGIN The reference is to the biblical story of the killing of the Philistine giant Goliath by the young David using just a sling and a stone (1 Samuel 17).

Da·vies /dáyviss/, **Robertson** (1913–95) Canadian novelist, essayist, and playwright

da Vin·ci ◊ **Leonardo da Vinci**

Da·vis /dáyviss/, **Bette** (1908–89) US movie actor

Da·vis, Jefferson (1808–89) 1st and only president of the Confederate States of America (1861–65)

Da·vis, Miles (1926–91) US jazz trumpeter and composer

Da·vis Cup *n* 1 an international men's tennis competition 2 the trophy awarded in the Davis Cup

Da·vy /dáyvee/, **Sir Humphry** (1778–1829) British chemist. He invented the miner's safety lamp.

daw·dle /dáwd'l/ (**-dled, -dling**) *vi* 1 move annoyingly slowly 2 waste time —**daw·dler** *n* —**daw·dling** *n*, *adj*

Dawes /dawz/, **Charles Gates** (1865–1951) vice president of the United States (1925–29)

dawn n 1 the first appearance of light in the sky as the Sun rises 2 the beginning of something ■ vi 1 begin (refers to a new day) ○ *The day dawned cloudy and wet.* 2 become apparent ○ *It finally dawned on me that few would survive.* 3 start to exist (literary)

dawn·ing /dáwning/ n the beginning of a day or period of time ■ adj developing

dawn raid n 1 a surprise military attack carried out at dawn 2 a corporate takeover strategy that involves buying up shares at the start of a day's financial trading

day n 1 a period of 24 hours 2 the period from sunrise to sunset 3 the part of a 24-hour period when somebody is working or active 4 an indefinite period or point in time 5 a period of fame or popularity 6 the period in somebody's life when he or she is active or involved in something ◇ **carry** or **win the day** gain a victory ◇ **make somebody's day** make somebody very happy ◇ **save the day** prevent defeat or disaster

Da·yan /daa yaán/, **Moshe** (1915–81) Israeli general and politician

day·book /dáy bòok/ n 1 an accounts book for daily records 2 a diary or journal

day·break /dáy bràyk/ n dawn

day·care /dáy kàir/ n supervision or treatment given during the day to dependent people

day·dream /dáy drèem/ n 1 a dream experienced while awake 2 an unrealizable hope or fantasy ■ vi (-dreamed or -dreamt /-drèmt/) think distracting thoughts —**day·dream·er** n —**day·dream·ing** n

Day-Glo /dáy glò/ tdmk a trademark for fluorescent dyes and coloring agents

day job n the job somebody does to earn an income while trying to be successful in another field

day·light /dáy lìt/ n 1 sunlight 2 daytime 3 dawn 4 public awareness or scrutiny

day·light-sav·ing time, day·light time n an adjustment of clock time to allow more hours of daylight at a particular time of year

day·long /dáy làwng/ adj, adv all day

day nurs·er·y n a nursery for preschool children

Day of A·tone·ment n Yom Kippur

day room n a communal recreation room in an institution

day school n 1 a private school without boarding facilities 2 a school with daytime classes only

day·time /dáy tìm/ n the sunlit part of the day ■ adj of or for daytime

day-to-day adj 1 everyday 2 one day at a time

Day·ton /dáyt'n/ city in SW Ohio. Pop. 167,475 (1998).

Day·to·na Beach /day tónə-/ coastal city in NE Florida. Pop. 65,136 (1998).

day trad·ing n the quick buying and subsequent selling of securities on the same day to make a profit on price movements —**day trad·er** n

day trip n a trip completed within a day —**day trip·per** n

daze n a confused state ■ vt (dazed, daz·ing) 1 stun 2 bewilder —**dazed** adj —**daz·ed·ly** /dáyzədlee/ adv

daz·zle /dázz'l/ vti (-zled, -zling) 1 greatly amaze and impress somebody 2 make somebody temporarily unable to see ■ n light that dazzles

daz·zling /dázling/ adj 1 spectacularly impressive 2 very bright —**daz·zling·ly** adv

dB symbol decibel

Db symbol dubnium

✷ **DBA** abbr doing business as (in e-mails)

✷ **DBMS** abbr database management system

DBS abbr direct broadcasting by satellite

DC abbr 1 direct current 2 also **D.C.** District of Columbia

D-day n 1 the beginning of the Allied military operation to liberate Europe from Nazi occupation during World War II 2 the day when any activity is to begin

D.D.S. abbr 1 Doctor of Dental Science 2 Doctor of Dental Surgery

DDT n a powerful insecticide that has been widely banned since 1974. Full form **dichlorodiphenyltrichloroethane**

de, De see also under surname

DE abbr Delaware[2] 1

de- prefix 1 opposite, reverse ○ *deactivate* 2 remove ○ *decaffeinate* 3 reduce ○ *degrade* 4 get off ○ *deplane*

DEA abbr Drug Enforcement Administration

dea·con /deékən/ n 1 in some Christian churches, an ordained person ranking below a priest 2 in some Protestant churches, a layperson assisting a minister

dea·con·ess /deékənəss/ n in some Christian churches, an ordained woman who ranks below a priest

de·ac·ti·vate /dee ákti vàyt/ vt 1 make something inactive 2 remove a military unit from active service —**de·ac·ti·va·tion** /dee ákti váysh'n/ n

dead /ded/ adj 1 no longer alive 2 inanimate 3 without living things 4 without physical sensation 5 unwilling or unable to respond 6 lacking any signs of life 7 lacking activity or interest 8 no longer current or relevant 9 no longer operating 10 not burning 11 not resonant 12 totally quiet 13 sudden, abrupt, and complete 14 exact 15 exhausted (infml) ■ npl dead people ■ adv 1 precisely 2 entirely 3 abruptly or immediately —**dead·ness** n

SYNONYMS dead, deceased, departed, late,

lifeless, defunct, extinct CORE MEANING: no longer living, functioning, or in existence

dead·beat /déd beet/ n 1 somebody who does not pay debts (slang) 2 somebody regarded as irresponsible and lazy (slang insult)

dead bolt, dead·bolt /déd bōlt/ n a bolt without a spring, operated by a key or knob

dead duck n something or somebody with no chance of success or survival (slang)

dead·en /dédd'n/ vt 1 make something less intense or resonant 2 desensitize somebody or something

dead end n 1 a point at which something ends abruptly 2 a passage that ends abruptly 3 a situation that leads nowhere

dead-end adj 1 with a closed end 2 without any prospect of progress or improvement ■ vi come to a dead end

dead hand n an oppressive influence

dead·head /déd hèd/ n a vehicle without passengers (infml) ■ vti drive an empty vehicle

dead heat n a race or other contest in which two or more contestants are at exactly the same point or have the same score —**dead-heat** vi

dead let·ter n 1 a letter that a postal service cannot deliver, e.g., because the address is incomplete 2 an unenforced or ineffective rule

dead·line /déd līn/ n the time by which something must be done or completed

ORIGIN A **deadline** was originally a line marked around the boundary of a prison, beyond which prisoners were forbidden to stray on pain of death.

dead·lock /déd lòk/ n 1 a situation in which a negotiation is stalled because of an unwillingness to compromise 2 in sports, a tied score —**dead·lock** vti

dead loss n a complete loss for which no compensation is available

dead·ly /déddlee/ adj (-li·er, -li·est) 1 causing death 2 very precise ○ deadly aim 3 extremely hostile ○ deadly enemies 4 dull (infml) ■ adv 1 like a dead person ○ deadly pale 2 completely

SYNONYMS **deadly, fatal, mortal, lethal, terminal** CORE MEANING: causing death

dead·ly night·shade /-nīt shàyd/ n the plant belladonna

dead·pan /déd pàn/ adj purposely impassive ■ adv without expression ■ n an expressionless face or performer —**dead·pan** vi

dead reck·on·ing n a method of determining the position of a ship or aircraft by charting its course and speed from a known position

Dead Sea salt lake on the Israel-Jordan border that is 1,312 ft./400 m below sea level, the lowest point on Earth

dead shot n an expert shot

⚡ **dead·start** /déd staàrt/ vti coldboot a computer

dead time n a time lapse between the responses of an electrical component

dead weight n 1 a heavy weight 2 an oppressive burden

dead·wood /déd woòd/ n 1 dead trees and branches 2 a person or thing regarded as useless or superfluous

deaf /def/ adj 1 completely or partially unable to hear 2 unresponsive or indifferent ○ deaf to our plea ■ npl people who are deaf —**deaf·ness** n

USAGE The adjective and noun **Deaf**, when capitalized, refer to the community of hearing-impaired people who use American Sign Language to communicate, and who use **Deaf** to refer to themselves. Avoid using **deaf** in lowercase in such contexts because it is taken to be offensive. A preferred substitute is hearing-impaired.

deaf·en /déff'n/ vt 1 make somebody unable to hear 2 soundproof a room or building

deaf·en·ing /déff'ning/ adj very loud —**deaf·en·ing·ly** adv

deaf-mute adj ⚠ an offensive term meaning unable to hear or speak (dated) —**deaf-mute** n

USAGE **Deaf-mute** and **mute** in reference to people who are unable to hear or speak are highly offensive and should be avoided. Preferred substitutes are hearing-impaired or hearing-and-speech-impaired.

deal[1] /deel/ n 1 a business transaction 2 a bargain (infml) 3 a particular kind of treatment received from somebody (infml) ○ a raw deal 4 in a card game, a distribution of the cards ■ v (dealt /delt/) 1 vti in a card game, distribute the cards 2 vti sell illegal drugs 3 vt make somebody experience or suffer something ◇ cut a deal negotiate an agreement ◇ make a big deal out of treat something as more important than it is (infml)

☐ **deal in** vt trade in something
☐ **deal out** vt distribute
☐ **deal with** vt 1 take action to achieve or solve 2 have as a subject

deal[2] /deel/ n 1 softwood lumber 2 a board of softwood

deal·er /déelər/ n 1 a seller or trader 2 somebody who deals cards 3 a seller of illegal drugs

deal·er·ship /déelər ship/ n 1 a franchise to sell a particular product 2 a dealer's premises

deal·ing /déeling/ n conduct or treatment, especially in business ■ **deal·ings** npl transactions and relations

deal·mak·er /déel màykər/ n a negotiator of business or political deals —**deal·mak·ing** n

dealt past tense, past participle of **deal**[1]

dean /deen/ n 1 a senior academic administrator who manages a faculty 2 a member of the academic staff of a college or university who advises students and is responsible for enforcing rules **3** a senior member of the clergy in some churches —**dean·ship** *n*

ORIGIN Dean derives ultimately from Latin *decem* "ten." From this a compound meaning "person in charge of ten others" was formed and developed into the French form that was the immediate source of **dean**. A variant of that French word was separately adopted into English as *doyen*.

dean·er·y /déeˈnəree/ (*pl* **-ies**) *n* **1** the position or residence of an academic dean **2** a group of parishes administered by a dean

dean's list *n* a list of top students

dear /deer/ *adj* **1** beloved **2** costly **3** charging a lot **4 Dear** used before a name to begin a letter ■ *n* a person who is regarded fondly ■ *interj* expresses shock or regret ○ *Oh dear!* ■ *adv* dearly —**dear·ness** *n*

SPELLCHECK Do not confuse the spelling of **dear** and **deer** (the animal), which sound similar.

Dear·born /déer báwrn/ city in SE Michigan. Pop. 91,691 (1998).

Dear John let·ter, Dear John *n* a letter from a woman terminating a relationship with a man

dear·ly /déerlee/ *adv* **1** with strong feelings **2** at great cost

dearth /durth/ *n* a scarcity or lack ◊ See note at lack

death /deth/ *n* **1** the end of being alive **2** a way of dying **3** the fact that a particular person dies **4** the end of something —**death·less** *adj* —**deathlike** *adj* ◊ **to death** very much ○ *bored to death*

death·bed /déth bèd/ *n* a bed where somebody dies ■ *adj* while dying

death·blow /déth blò/ *n* **1** an action or event that destroys something **2** a killing blow

death camp *n* a camp where prisoners are systematically killed

death cer·tif·i·cate *n* a document recording somebody's death

death-deal·ing *adj* fatal

death knell *n* **1** a signal that something is at an end **2** a bell announcing a death

death·ly /déthlee/ *adj* **1** like death **2** extreme ■ *adv* extremely —**death·li·ness** *n*

death mask *n* a cast of a dead person's face

death pen·al·ty *n* capital punishment

death rate *n* the proportion of deaths to the population of a particular area

death rat·tle *n* a sound made in the throat while dying

death row /-rò/ *n* a set of cells for prisoners awaiting execution

death sen·tence *n* **1** the punishment of death, received in a court of law **2** something that has a fatal result

death's head *n* a human skull or its image

death squad *n* an organized group of people who murder their enemies or political opponents

death-trap /déth tràp/ *n* a dangerous building or vehicle (*infml*)

death war·rant *n* **1** a legal order to execute somebody **2** something that is fatal

death wish *n* a desire to die

deb. *abbr* debit

de·ba·cle /də bák'l, -baàk'l/ *n* **1** a chaotic failure **2** a sudden breakup of river ice in spring

de·bar /di baàr/ (**-barred, -bar·ring**) *vti* exclude somebody from taking part in or belonging to something —**de·bar·ment** *n*

de·bark /di baàrk/ *v* **1** *vi* disembark **2** *vt* unload (*fml*) —**de·bar·ka·tion** /dèe baar káysh'n/ *n*

de·base /di báyss/ (**-based, -bas·ing**) *vt* **1** reduce the quality or purity of **2** reduce the value or importance of —**de·base·ment** *n*

de·bate /di báyt/ *vti* (**-bat·ed, -bat·ing**) **1** talk or argue about something **2** think about opposing aspects of something ■ *n* **1** an organized discussion of an issue **2** argument or prolonged discussion —**de·bat·a·ble** *adj* —**de·bat·a·bly** *adv* —**de·bat·er** *n*

de·bauch /di báwch/ (*fml*) *vt* **1** lead into immoral behavior **2** seduce sexually ■ *n* an episode of immoral behavior —**de·bauch·er** *n* —**de·bauch·er·y** *n*

de Beau·voir, Simone ♦ Beauvoir, Simone de

de·ben·ture /də bénchər/ *n* **1** *also* **de·ben·ture bond** a bond backed only by the credit rating of the issuer **2** a certificate of debt —**de·ben·tured** *adj*

de·bil·i·tate /di bílli tàyt/ (**-tat·ed, -tat·ing**) *vt* sap the strength of —**de·bil·i·tat·ing** *adj* —**de·bil·i·ta·tion** /di bílli táysh'n/ *n* —**de·bil·i·ta·tive** *adj*

de·bil·i·ty /di bíllətee/ *n* general lack of energy or strength

deb·it /débbit/ *n* **1** a recorded debt or expense in accounts **2** a sum of money taken out of a bank account **3** a column for recording debts or expenses in an account ■ *vt* **1** record a debit in an account **2** take money from somebody's account as payment for something

deb·it card *n* a card used for shopping without cash, with the money transferred directly from the buyer's account to the seller's

deb·o·nair /dèbbə náir, débbə nàir/ *adj* sophisticated and elegant —**deb·o·nair·ly** *adv*

de·bouch /di bówch, -boosh/ *vi* **1** move into more open terrain **2** emerge into a wider place (*refers to a valley or a flow of water*)

de·brief /dee breéf/ *vt* question somebody after an event in order to find out information about it —**de·brief·ing** *n*

de·bris /d∂ bree, day–, dáy brèe/, **dé·bris** n fragments of something destroyed

debt /det/ n 1 something that is owed 2 the state of owing something

debt·or /détt∂r/ n somebody who owes another person something

⚡ de·bug /dee búg/ (-bugged, -bug·ging) vt 1 find and remove errors in something, especially a computer program 2 remove secret listening devices from a place —**de·bug·ger** n

de·bunk /dee búngk/ vt show to be wrong or false

De·bus·sy /d∂ byóossee, dèbbyoo sée/, **Claude** (1862–1918) French composer

de·but /day byóo, dáy byòo/ n 1 the first public appearance of a player or performer 2 a young woman's first formal social engagement, marking her entry into fashionable society ■ vti make, or cause to make, a first formal public appearance

deb·u·tante /débbyo tàant/ n a young woman being introduced into fashionable society

dec. abbr 1 declension 2 decrease

Dec. abbr December

dec·ade /dé kàyd, de káyd, d∂ káyd/ n a period of ten years

dec·a·dence /dékəd'nss/ n 1 a process or state of moral decline in society 2 uninhibited self-indulgence

dec·a·dent /dékəd'nt/ adj 1 in decline, especially morally 2 uninhibitedly self-indulgent —**dec·a·dent** n —**dec·a·dent·ly** adv

de·caf /dée kàf/ (infml) n a decaffeinated drink ■ adj decaffeinated

de·caf·fein·at·ed /dee káffə nàytəd/ adj with the caffeine removed ■ n a drink from which the caffeine has been removed —**de·caf·fein·ate** vt

de·cal /dée kàl, di kál/ n a decorative sticker or transfer paper

de·camp /di kámp/ vi 1 suddenly or secretly leave 2 leave a camp —**de·camp·ment** n

de·cant /di kánt/ vt pour a liquid gently into another container so as not to disturb the sediment

de·cant·er /di kántər/ n a decorative bottle for serving drinks

de·cap·i·tate /di káppi tàyt/ (-tat·ed, -tat·ing) vt behead —**de·cap·i·ta·tion** /di kàppi táysh'n/ n

dec·ath·lon /di káthlən, -lòn/ n a contest involving ten athletic events —**dec·ath·lete** n

De·ca·tur /di káytər/, **Stephen** (1779–1820) US naval officer

de·cay /di káy/ v 1 vti decompose, or cause to decompose 2 vti decline, or cause to decline 3 vi undergo radioactive disintegration ■ n 1 a state or process of decline or decomposition 2 a rotten or spoiled part 3 the disintegration of radioactive material 4 a gradual decrease in something

de·cease /di seéss/ n death (literary) ■ vi (-ceased, -ceas·ing) die (fml)

de·ceased /di seést/ (fml) adj recently dead ■ n a person who has recently died ◊ See note at **dead**

de·ceit /di seét/ n 1 the act or practice of misleading somebody 2 something done to mislead

de·ceit·ful /di seétf'l/ adj deliberately misleading —**de·ceit·ful·ly** adv —**de·ceit·ful·ness** n

de·ceive /di seév/ (-ceived, -ceiv·ing) v 1 vt intentionally mislead somebody 2 vr fool yourself

de·cel·er·ate /dee séllə ràyt/ (-at·ed, -at·ing) vi slow down —**de·cel·er·a·tion** /dee sèllə ráysh'n/ n

De·cem·ber /di sémbər/ n the 12th month of the year in the Gregorian calendar

ORIGIN December derives from the name of the tenth month of the Roman year, formed from Latin decem "ten."

de·cen·cy /deéss'nsee/ n 1 conformity with moral standards 2 modesty or propriety ■ **de·cen·cies** npl the commonly accepted standards of good behavior (fml)

de·cent /deéss'nt/ adj 1 conforming to accepted standards of moral behavior 2 above average 3 satisfactory 4 wearing enough clothes to avoid embarrassment (infml) 5 kind —**de·cent·ly** adv —**de·cent·ness** n

de·cen·tral·ize /dee séntrə lìz/ (-ized, -iz·ing) vti reorganize something in order to distribute power more widely —**de·cen·tral·i·za·tion** /dee sèntrəli záysh'n/ n

de·cep·tion /di sépsh'n/ n 1 the practice of misleading somebody 2 something intended to mislead

de·cep·tive /di séptiv/ adj 1 intended to mislead 2 able to be mistaken for something else —**de·cep·tive·ness** n

de·cep·tive·ly /di séptivlee/ adv misleadingly

USAGE Is a **deceptively** large house surprisingly large or surprisingly small? Unless the context makes the meaning clear, **deceptively** is best avoided.

de·ci·bel /déssəb'l, dèssə bèl/ n (symbol dB) a unit of relative loudness

de·cide /di síd/ (-cid·ed, -cid·ing) v 1 vti make a choice or come to a conclusion about something 2 vt end something in a definite way —**de·cid·a·ble** adj

de·cid·ed /di sídəd/ adj 1 obvious ○ a decided slant 2 firm or certain

de·cid·ed·ly /di sídədlee/ adv unmistakably —**de·cid·ed·ness** n

de·cid·er /di sídər/ n something that settles a contest or argument

de·cid·u·ous /di slíjoo əss/ adj 1 describes a plant or tree that sheds its leaves in fall 2 consisting of deciduous trees

~~decieve~~ incorrect spelling of **deceive**

dec·i·mal /déssəm'l/ adj using the number 10

as a base ■ *n* a number in the decimal system —**dec·i·mal·ly** *adv*

dec·i·mal·ize /déssəmə lìz/ (-ized, -iz·ing) *vti* convert a country's currency or measuring system to a decimal system —**dec·i·mal·i·za·tion** /dèssəməli záysh'n/ *n*

dec·i·mal place *n* a position after the decimal point

dec·i·mal point *n* a dot in a decimal number that divides the whole numbers from the smaller divisions

dec·i·mate /déssə màyt/ (-mat·ed, -mat·ing) *vt* 1 kill or remove a large proportion of 2 almost destroy completely —**dec·i·ma·tion** /dèssə máysh'n/ *n*

de·ci·pher /di sífər/ *vt* 1 make out what a piece of writing says 2 work out the meaning of something —**de·ci·pher·a·ble** *adj* —**de·ci·pher·ment** *n*

de·ci·sion /di sízh'n/ *n* 1 a choice or conclusion arrived at after thinking 2 firmness in choosing 3 the process of choosing

de·ci·sive /di síssiv/ *adj* 1 settling something 2 able to make definite decisions —**de·ci·sive·ly** *adv* —**de·ci·sive·ness** *n*

deck *n* 1 a floor on a ship 2 a section of a passenger vehicle on one level 3 an audio unit for playing a particular type of recording 4 a level of a building or other structure 5 a pack of cards 6 an uncovered platform attached to a house ■ *vt* decorate or adorn something or somebody *(literary)* ○ all *decked out for the party* —**decked** *adj* ◇ **hit the deck** fall on the floor or ground *(infml)*

deck chair *n* a folding wood and canvas chair

deck·ing /déking/ *n* waterproof building material

de·claim /di kláym/ *vti* speak, or say formally and dramatically

dec·la·ma·tion /dèklə máysh'n/ *n* 1 a formal dramatic speech 2 the process of declaiming

de·clam·a·to·ry /di klámmə tàwree/ *adj* 1 formal and dramatic in speech 2 loud and impressive but with little meaning —**de·clam·a·to·ri·ly** *adv*

dec·la·ra·tion /dèklə ráysh'n/ *n* 1 a formal statement 2 an official proclamation 3 the process of making a declaration

dec·la·ra·tion of in·de·pen·dence *n* 1 a formal statement asserting freedom 2 **Dec·la·ra·tion of In·de·pen·dence** the document declaring the United States to be free from British rule

de·clar·a·tive /di kláirətiv, -klárətiv/ *adj* in the form of a statement —**de·clar·a·tive·ly** *adv*

de·clare /di kláir/ (-clared, -clar·ing) *v* 1 *vti* announce something clearly or loudly 2 *vt* state something formally or officially 3 *vt* reveal goods to customs officials as dutiable or taxable 4 *vt* announce that a particular condition exists

dé·clas·sé /dày klaa sáy/ *adj* reduced to or having a low class or status in society

de·clas·si·fy /dee klássi fì/ (-fied, -fies) *vt* remove from an official list of confidential or top-secret material —**de·clas·si·fi·ca·tion** /dee klàssi fi káysh'n/ *n*

de·clen·sion /di klénsh'n/ *n* 1 a set of nouns, adjectives, or pronouns that take the same inflections 2 the process by which sets of nouns, adjectives, or pronouns form inflections 3 the process of worsening or falling away *(fml)* —**de·clen·sion·al** *adj*

de·cline /di klín/ *v* (-clined, -clin·ing) 1 *vti* refuse an invitation 2 *vt* refuse to participate in something 3 *vi* diminish 4 *vi* get weaker 5 *vti* form inflections, or list all the inflections of a noun, adjective, or pronoun ■ *n* 1 deterioration 2 a period near the end of something —**dec·li·na·tion** /dèklə náysh'n/ *n*

de·cliv·i·ty /di klívvətee/ (*pl* -ties) *n* 1 a sloping surface 2 the fact that something slopes downward

de·coc·tion /di kóksh'n/ *n* 1 the process of extracting something by boiling a substance 2 a concentrated substance extracted by boiling

de·code /dee kód/ (-cod·ed, -cod·ing) *vt* 1 decipher a coded message 2 establish the meaning of something expressed indirectly —**de·cod·a·ble** *adj* —**de·cod·er** *n*

dé·colle·tage /dày kawl taázh, dày kollə-/ *n* a low neckline

dé·colle·té /dày kawl táy, -kollə táy/ *adj* 1 with a low neckline 2 wearing a low-cut garment ■ *n* a woman's upper chest, visible above a low neckline

de·col·o·nize /dee kóllə nìz/ (-nized, -niz·ing) *vt* grant independence to a colony —**de·col·o·ni·za·tion** /dee kòlləni záysh'n/ *n*

de·com·mis·sion /dèè kə mísh'n/ *vt* remove from service

⨍ **de·com·pil·er** /dèè kəm pílər/ *n* a computer program that translates basic machine code into high-level code

de·com·pose /dèè kəm póz/ (-posed, -pos·ing) *vti* 1 rot, or cause organic matter to rot 2 break down, or cause something to break down, into smaller or simpler pieces —**de·com·pos·a·ble** *adj* —**de·com·po·si·tion** /dèè kompə zísh'n/ *n*

⨍ **de·com·press** /dèè kəm préss/ *vt* 1 reduce the atmospheric pressure in an enclosed space 2 expand computer data stored in a compressed form —**de·com·pres·sion** *n*

de·com·pres·sion cham·ber *n* a sealed room where decompression is carried out

de·com·pres·sion sick·ness, de·com·pres·sion ill·ness *n* a condition experienced by divers who come to the surface of water too quickly, causing nitrogen to form in the blood and tissues

de·con·ges·tant /dèè kən jéstənt/ *n* a medicine that relieves nasal congestion —**de·con·ges·tant** *adj* —**de·con·ges·tive** *adj*

de·con·struct /dèe kən strúkt/ *vt* analyze a text using the theories of deconstruction

de·con·struc·tion /dèe kən strúksh'n/ *n* critical analysis in which no single meaning is assumed and the apparent unity of a symbol, text, or movie is questioned —**de·con·struc·tion·ist** *n*, *adj*

de·con·tam·i·nate /dèe kən támmə nàyt/ (-nat·ed, -nat·ing) *vt* remove contamination from —**de·con·tam·i·na·tion** /dèekən tàmmə náysh'n/ *n* —**de·con·tam·i·na·tive** *adj*

de·con·trol /dèe kən trṓl/ (-trolled, -trol·ling) *vt* remove official restraints or regulations from

de·cor /dáy kawr, day káwr/, **dé·cor** *n* 1 the style of interior furnishings 2 stage scenery

dec·o·rate /dékə ràyt/ (-rat·ed, -rat·ing) *v* 1 *vt* make something attractive by adding ornamental elements 2 *vti* paint or wallpaper a building or room 3 *vt* award somebody a medal

dec·o·ra·tion /dèkə ráysh'n/ *n* 1 ornamentation 2 an attractive item 3 an award or honor 4 the painting and wallpapering in a room

dec·o·ra·tive /dékərətiv, -ràytiv/ *adj* 1 ornamental 2 of the decoration in a room 3 attractive but not functional —**dec·o·ra·tive·ly** *adv* —**dec·o·ra·tive·ness** *n*

dec·o·ra·tor /dékə ràytər/ *n* somebody whose job is decorating rooms ■ *adj* for home decor

dec·o·rous /dékərəss, di káwrəss/ *adj* 1 socially acceptable in a formal or solemn setting 2 dignified —**dec·o·rous·ly** *adv* —**dec·o·rous·ness** *n*

de·co·rum /di káwrəm/ *n* 1 dignity or decorous behavior 2 the appropriateness of an artistic element to the work as a whole

de·cou·ple /dee kúpp'l/ (-pled, -pling) *vt* separate or disengage one thing from another

de·coy /dèe kòy, di kóy/ *n* 1 something used by hunters to attract the animal they are hunting, often a model of the animal itself 2 anything that lures somebody into a trap ■ *vt* deceive by a decoy

ORIGIN Decoy probably represents Dutch *de kooi*, where *de* is the definite article, "the," and *kooi* is the word for "decoy."

de·crease *vti* /di krée̊ss/ (-creased, -creas·ing) lessen, or cause something to lessen, in size or degree ■ *n* /dèe krée̊ss/ 1 a process of decreasing 2 a reduction —**de·creas·ing** *adj* —**de·creas·ing·ly** *adv*

de·cree /di krée̊/ *n* 1 an official order 2 a court ruling —**de·cree** *vt*

de·cree ni·si /-nî̊ sī̊/ (*pl* **de·crees ni·si**) *n* an interim divorce ruling

de·crep·it /di kréppit/ *adj* 1 old and in poor condition 2 not young or strong (*infml*) —**de·crep·it·ly** *adv* —**de·crep·i·tude** *n* ◊ See note at **weak**

de·cre·scen·do /dày krə shéndō, dèe-/ *adv* with decreasing loudness (*musical direction*) ■ *n*

(*pl* **-dos**) a piece of music, or a section of a piece, played decrescendo —**de·cre·scen·do**

de·crim·i·nal·ize /dee krímmənə lī̊z/ (-ized, -iz·ing) *vt* legalize something that was formerly illegal —**de·crim·i·nal·i·za·tion** /dee krímmənəli záysh'n/ *n*

de·cry /di krī̊/ (-cried, -cries) *vt* criticize strongly —**de·cri·al** *n* —**de·cri·er** *n*

de·crypt /dee krípt/ *vt* decode —**de·cryp·tion** *n*

ded·i·cate /déddi kàyt/ (-cat·ed, -cat·ing) *vt* 1 set something aside as special 2 address a work of art to somebody 3 play a piece of music to somebody on the radio, as a tribute 4 devote attention or energy to something 5 set something apart as holy —**ded·i·ca·tive** *adj*

ded·i·cat·ed /déddi kàytəd/ *adj* 1 devoted to a particular cause or job 2 intended only for one purpose

ded·i·ca·tion /dèddi káysh'n/ *n* 1 the quality of being dedicated 2 an inscription in a book 3 a piece of music played on the radio as a tribute to somebody 4 the setting aside of something for a particular purpose —**ded·i·ca·tion·al** *adj*

de·duce /di dóoss/ (-duced, -duc·ing) *vt* 1 reach a particular conclusion by using information logically 2 infer something from a general principle —**de·duc·i·ble** *adj*

SYNONYMS deduce, infer, assume, reason, conclude, work out, figure out CORE MEANING: reach a logical conclusion on the basis of information

de·duct /di dúkt/ *vt* subtract an amount

de·duct·i·ble /di dúktəb'l/ *n* an uninsured amount ■ *adj* 1 allowable against tax 2 liable to be deducted —**de·duct·i·bil·i·ty** /di dùktə billətee/ *n*

de·duc·tion /di dúksh'n/ *n* 1 an amount deducted 2 the subtraction of an amount 3 a conclusion drawn from available information 4 the drawing of a conclusion 5 the process of reasoning logically

de·duc·tive /di dúktiv/ *adj* of deduction —**de·duc·tive·ly** *adv*

deed *n* 1 something done 2 a legal document, especially one enshrining ownership ■ *vt* transfer property to

deem *vt* consider to be (*fml*)

deep *adj* 1 extending down from a surface 2 far from top to bottom or front to back 3 far from the edge or top 4 made up of a particular number of rows 5 coming from or reaching inside the body 6 low in pitch 7 dark in color 8 extreme or intense 9 intellectually profound ■ *adj*, *adv* relatively near your own goal ■ *adv* far ■ *n* the sea —**deep·ly** *adv* —**deep·ness** *n* ◇ **in deep** very involved

deep-dish *adj* describes food baked in a deep container

deep·en /dèepən/ *vti* 1 make or become deep or deeper 2 make or become more intense

deep end *n* the part of a swimming pool where the water is deepest ◊ **go off the deep end** fly into a rage

deep-freeze *vt* 1 freeze something quickly 2 keep something very cold —**deep-fro·zen** *adj*

deep-fry *vt* cook food in deep oil —**deep-fried** *adj*

deep-root·ed, deep-seat·ed *adj* firmly held or believed in

deep-sea *adj* of the deep waters far from the coast

deep-set *adj* describes eyes having deep sockets

Deep South region in the SE United States, usually considered to consist of Alabama, Georgia, Louisiana, Mississippi, and South Carolina, and regarded as the heartland of traditional Southern culture

deer /deer/ (*pl same*) *n* any of various ruminant mammals the males of which have antlers ◊ See note at **dear**

ORIGIN The original meaning of **deer** was simply "animal." It goes back to an ancient root that apparently signified "breathing creature." The modern more restricted sense had superseded "animal" by the 15C.

deer·skin /deer skin/ *n* a deer's hide

de·es·ca·late /dee éskə làyt/ (**de·es·ca·la·ted, de·es·ca·la·ting**) *vt* reduce the level or intensity of a difficult or dangerous situation —**de·es·ca·la·tion** /dee èskə láysh'n/ *n*

de·face /di fáyss/ (**-faced, -fac·ing**) *vt* spoil the appearance of —**de·face·ment** *n*

de fac·to /di fáktō, day fáktō/ *adv* in fact ■ *adj* existing in fact but without legal sanctions

de·fal·cate /di fál kàyt, -fáwl-, déff'l-/ (**-cat·ed, -cat·ing**) *vt* embezzle assets —**de·fal·ca·tion** /dèe fal káysh'n/ *n*

de·fame /di fáym/ (**-famed, -fam·ing**) *vt* harm the reputation of —**def·a·ma·tion** /dèffə máysh'n/ *n* —**de·fam·a·to·ry** /di fámmə tàwree/ *adj* ◊ See note at **malign**

⚡ **de·fault** /di fáwlt/ *n* 1 an option that will be automatically selected by a computer if the user chooses no other 2 a failure to do something, especially to meet a financial obligation, appear in court, or take part in a competition ■ *vi* 1 fail to pay a debt, appear in court, or take part in a competition 2 use a computer's preset option

de·feat /di féet/ *vt* 1 win a victory over an enemy or competitor 2 cause the failure of something 3 baffle somebody ■ *n* 1 an instance of losing to an opponent 2 failure

SYNONYMS **defeat, beat, conquer, vanquish, overcome, triumph over, thrash, trounce** CORE MEANING: win a victory

de·feat·ist /di féetist/ *adj* expecting failure ■ *n* somebody who expects failure —**de·feat·ism** *n*

def·e·cate /déffə kàyt/ (**-cat·ed, -cat·ing**) *v* 1 *vi* expel feces (*fml or technical*) 2 *vt* remove

impurities from a solution —**def·e·ca·tion** /dèffə káysh'n/ *n*

de·fect *n* /dée fèkt, di fékt/ 1 a personal failing or weakness 2 a feature that prevents something from being perfect ■ *vi* /di fékt/ 1 leave your native country for political reasons 2 abandon an allegiance —**de·fec·tion** /di fékshən/ *n* —**de·fec·tor** /di féktər/ *n* ◊ See note at **flaw**

de·fec·tive /di féktiv/ *adj* 1 faulty 2 incomplete —**de·fec·tive·ly** *adv* —**de·fec·tive·ness** *n*

de·fence *n* UK = **defense**

de·fend /di fénd/ *v* 1 *vt* protect somebody or something from attack by an enemy 2 *vti* represent an accused person in court 3 *vt* support a position or belief 4 *vi* in sports, resist an opponent 5 *vt* try to keep a title, especially in sports 6 *vt* in sports, protect your goal —**de·fend·a·ble** *adj* ◊ See note at **safeguard**

de·fen·dant /di féndənt/ *n* the accused person in legal proceedings

~~defendent~~ incorrect spelling of **defendant**

de·fend·er /di féndər/ *n* 1 a supporter 2 a protector 3 in sports, a defensive player 4 the holder of a title that is challenged

de·fense /di fénss/ *n* 1 protection, especially from enemy attack 2 something that gives protection 3 justification 4 a defendant and his or her counsel in court 5 /dèe fènss/ in sports, defensive play or players —**de·fense·less** *adj* —**de·fense·less·ness** *n*

de·fense·man /dèe fènss màn/ (*pl* -**men** /-mèn/) *n* in sports, a defensive player

de·fense mech·a·nism *n* 1 a frame of mind that avoids emotional distress 2 a natural protective response

de·fen·si·ble /di fénsəb'l/ *adj* 1 able to be protected 2 justifiable —**de·fen·si·bly** *adv*

de·fen·sive /di fénsiv/ *adj* 1 quick to deflect perceived criticism 2 designed to give protection 3 in sports, favoring defense as a playing strategy 4 in sports, relating to a defense team —**de·fen·sive·ly** *adv* —**de·fen·sive·ness** *n*

de·fer[1] /di fúr/ (**-ferred, -fer·ring**) *vti* postpone something —**de·fer·ment** *n* —**de·fer·ral** *n*

de·fer[2] /di fúr/ (**-ferred, -fer·ring**) *vi* submit to somebody else's judgment or wishes

~~defered~~ incorrect spelling of **deferred**

def·er·ence /déffərənss/ *n* 1 respect, especially in putting another person's interests first 2 submission

def·er·en·tial /dèffə rénsh'l/ *adj* showing respect, often to the point of obsequiousness —**def·er·en·tial·ly** *adv*

de·ferred an·nu·i·ty *n* an investment that pays out some time after the final premium has been paid

~~deferred~~ incorrect spelling of **deferred**

de·fi·ance /di fí ənss/ *n* open disobedience

de·fi·ant /di fí ənt/ *adj* 1 challenging somebody or something aggressively 2 openly disobedient —**de·fi·ant·ly** *adv*

de·fi·cien·cy /di físh'nsee/ (*pl* **-cies**) *n* **1** a shortage, especially of a nutrient **2** an amount by which something falls short ◊ See note at **lack**

de·fi·cien·cy dis·ease *n* a disease resulting from a lack of required nutrients

de·fi·cient /di físh'nt/ *adj* **1** lacking in something, especially something necessary **2** inadequate —**de·fi·cient·ly** *adv*

def·i·cit /déffissit/ *n* a shortfall ◊ See note at **lack**

def·i·cit spend·ing *n* government spending financed by borrowing

de·file[1] /di fíl/ (**-filed, -fil·ing**) *vt* **1** damage the reputation of **2** destroy the sanctity of —**de·file·ment** *n* —**de·fil·er** *n*

de·file[2] /di fíl/ *n* **1** a narrow mountain pass **2** a narrow passage ■ *vi* (**-filed, -fil·ing**) march in single file

~~definate~~ incorrect spelling of **definite**

~~definately~~ incorrect spelling of **definitely**

de·fine /di fín/ (**-fined, -fin·ing**) *v* **1** *vti* give the meaning of a word **2** *vt* state something exactly **3** *vt* characterize somebody or something **4** *vt* show something clearly —**de·fin·a·ble** *adj* —**de·fin·a·bly** *adv*

def·i·nite /déffinit/ *adj* **1** with clear limits or set *a definite age range for membership* **2** fixed and not to be altered ◦ *Is there a definite date for the meeting?* **3** certain and unlikely to have a change of mind ◦ *I'm definite about this.* **4** obvious or unquestionable ◦ *a definite turn for the better* —**def·i·nite·ness** *n*

USAGE **definite** or **definitive**? **Definite** describes something as being clearly defined or precise without making any strong judgment about it: *He has definite ideas on the subject.* **Definitive** means conclusive, decisive, or authoritative and is a more evaluative word: *It's the definitive book on the subject.*

def·i·nite ar·ti·cle *n* the word "the" in English, or a word with a similar function in another language

def·i·nite·ly /déffanitlee/ *adv* **1** certainly **2** finally and unchangeably ◦ *Has she definitely decided to go?* **3** clearly and unmistakably

def·i·ni·tion /dèffa nísh'n/ *n* **1** a statement of the meaning of a word, e.g., in a dictionary **2** the act of defining an image or sound **3** clarification **4** the clarity of an image or sound, or the sharpness of an edge —**def·i·ni·tion·al** *adj*

de·fin·i·tive /di fínnitiv/ *adj* **1** conclusive and final **2** most authoritative —**de·fin·i·tive·ly** *adv* —**de·fin·i·tive·ness** *n* ◊ See note at **definite**

~~definitly~~ incorrect spelling of **definitely**

de·flate /di fláyt/ (**-flat·ed, -flat·ing**) *v* **1** *vti* let the air out of something, or lose the air inside and become flat **2** *vt* make somebody less confident or hopeful **3** *vt* cause deflation in an economy —**de·flat·ed** *adj*

de·fla·tion /di fláysh'n/ *n* **1** collapse because of air loss **2** loss of confidence or hope

3 reduced economic activity —**de·fla·tion·ar·y** *adj*

de·flect /di flékt/ *v* **1** *vti* change course as a result of hitting something, or cause to change course **2** *vt* direct attention away from —**de·flec·tive** *adj* —**de·flec·tor** *n*

de·flec·tion /di fléksh'n/ *n* **1** a change of course **2** the amount by which something is deflected **3** the act of diverting attention from something

de·flow·er /dee flówr/ *vt* have sex with a virgin (*literary*)

De·foe /də fó/, **Daniel** (1660?–1731) English novelist and journalist

de·fog·ger /dee fáwgər, -fóggər/ *n* **1** a device that removes condensation **2** a liquid for removing condensation

de·fo·li·ant /dee fólee ənt/ *n* a chemical that removes leaves

de·fo·li·ate /dee fólee àyt/ (**-at·ed, -at·ing**) *vt* strip the leaves from —**de·fo·li·a·tion** /dee fólee áysh'n/ *n*

de·for·est /dee fáwrəst/ *vt* remove all or most of the trees from —**de·for·es·ta·tion** /dee fàwrə stáysh'n/ *n*

de·form /di fáwrm/ *v* **1** *vt* make distorted or twisted **2** *vti* spoil —**de·for·ma·tion** /di fàwr máysh'n, dèffar-/ *n* —**de·formed** *adj*

de·for·mi·ty /di fáwrmətee/ (*pl* **-ties**) *n* **1** the condition of being badly formed or disfigured **2** something with a shape that is far from the norm

⚡ **de·frag·ment** /dee frág ment/, **de·frag** /dee frág/ (**-fragged, -frag·ging**) *vt* reorganize the storage space on a computer's hard disk

de·fraud /di fráwd/ *vt* cheat somebody out of money

de·fray /di fráy/ *vt* pay some or all of the cost of —**de·fray·al** *n* —**de·fray·ment** *n*

de·frock /dee frók/ *vt* remove a priest from the clergy

de·frost /dee fráwst/ *v* **1** *vt* remove ice from something **2** *vti* thaw frozen food, or become thawed ■ *n* a product or device that defrosts something —**de·frost·er** *n*

deft *adj* **1** quick and skillful **2** clever —**deft·ly** *adv* —**deft·ness** *n*

de·funct /di fúngkt/ *adj* **1** no longer operating **2** dead (*humorous*) —**de·funct·ness** *n* ◊ See note at **dead**

de·fuse /dee fyóoz/ (**-fused, -fus·ing**) *vt* **1** make a bomb harmless **2** ease a tense or violent situation

SPELLCHECK Do not confuse the spelling of **defuse** and **diffuse** ("spread widely"), which sound similar.

de·fy /di fí/ (**-fied, -fies**) *vt* **1** openly resist the authority of **2** challenge to do something **3** not be explained or clarified by ◦ *defies all logic*

De·gas /də gaá/, **Edgar** (1834–1917) French painter and sculptor

Charles De Gaulle

de Gaulle /də gáwl/, **Charles, General** (1890–1970) president of France (1959–69)

de·gen·er·ate vi /di jénnə ràyt/ (-at·ed, -at·ing) become worse ■ adj /di jénnərət/ **1** in a worsened condition **2** inferior ■ n /di jénnərət/ a person regarded as immoral or corrupt —**de·gen·er·a·cy** n —**de·gen·er·ate·ly** adv —**de·gen·er·a·tion** /di jènnə ráysh'n/ n

de·gen·er·a·tive /di jénnərətiv/ adj gradually worsening

deg·ra·da·tion /dèggrə dáysh'n/ n **1** great humiliation brought about by loss of status or self-esteem **2** the act of humiliating somebody **3** a decline in quality **4** the process of decline or breakdown —**de·grade** /di gráyd/ vti —**de·grad·ed** adj —**de·grad·ing** adj

de·gree /di gree/ n **1** extent or amount **2** an educational qualification awarded by colleges and universities **3** (symbol °) a unit of temperature measurement ○ degrees Celsius **4** (symbol °) a unit for measuring angles **5** (symbol °) a unit of latitude or longitude **6** a classification of murder according to its seriousness **7** a classification of the severity of burns on a body **8** (symbol °) a unit of measurement on some scales, e.g., alcohol content of spirits **9** in grammar the state of an adjective or adverb in the positive, comparative, or superlative form **10** an indication of the closeness of a family relationship

de·gres·sion /di grésh'n/ n a gradual decrease (fml) —**de·gres·sive** adj

de·hu·man·ize /dee hyoómə nìz, -yoómə-/ (-ized, -iz·ing) vt **1** make somebody less human **2** take away the people-friendly features of something —**de·hu·man·i·za·tion** /dee hyoòmani záysh'n/ n —**de·hu·man·iz·ing** adj

de·hu·mid·i·fi·er /dee hyoo míddə fìr,ʹ-yoo-/ n a device for removing moisture from the air in a room or building —**de·hu·mid·i·fi·ca·tion** /dèè hyoo mìddəfi káysh'n/ n —**de·hu·mid·i·fy** vt

de·hy·drate /dee hí dràyt/ (-drat·ed, -drat·ing) v **1** vt remove water from **2** vti lose, or cause somebody to lose, body fluids —**de·hy·drat·ed** adj —**de·hy·dra·tion** /dèè hī dráysh'n, dee hī-/ n

de·ice /dee íss/ (-iced, -ic·ing) vt remove or keep ice from

de·i·fy /dee i fì/ (-fied, -fies) vt **1** make into a god **2** honor or adore —**de·i·fi·ca·tion** /dèè ifi káysh'n/ n

deign /dayn/ vi do something in a manner that shows you think it is beneath you

de·ism /dee ìzzəm/ n belief in God that argues a basis in reason and that holds that God made the world but does not interfere in it —**de·ist** n —**de·is·tic** /dee ístik/ adj

de·i·ty /dee itee/ (pl -ties) n **1** a god or goddess **2** divine status

dé·jà vu /dày zhaa voó/ n **1** the feeling of having experienced something before when you know that this is not true **2** boring familiarity

de·ject·ed /di jéktəd/ adj very unhappy or unhopeful —**de·ject·ed·ly** adv

de·jec·tion /di jéksh'n/ n great unhappiness or lack of hope

de ju·re /dee jooree, day yoo rày/ adv, adj by law

de Klerk /də klúrk/, **F. W.** (b. 1936) president of South Africa (1989–94)

de Koo·ning /də koóning/, **Willem** (1904–97) Dutch-born US artist

del. abbr delete

Del. abbr Delaware[2] 1

de la see also under surname

De·la·croix /də laa krwaá, dèllə-/, **Eugène** (1798–1863) French painter and lithographer

de la Mare /dèllə máir/, **Walter** (1873–1956) British poet, anthologist, and novelist

~~de·lap·i·dat·ed~~ incorrect spelling of **dilapidated**

Del·a·ware[1] /déllə wàir/ (pl same or -wares) n a member of a group of Native North American peoples who now live mostly in Oklahoma, Wisconsin, Kansas, Ontario, and in Canada —**Del·a·ware** adj

Del·a·ware[2] /déllə wàir/ **1** state of the E United States. Cap. Dover. Pop. 783,600 (2000). **2** major river of the E United States, flowing from S New York southward into **Delaware Bay**. Length 390 mi./630 km. —**Del·a·war·e·an** /dèllə wáiree ən/ n, adj

De la Warr /déllə wàir/, **Thomas West, 3rd Baron** (1577–1618) English-born colonial governor

de·lay /di láy/ v **1** vti put something off until later **2** vt make somebody or something late ○ I was delayed at the office. ■ n **1** lateness **2** the extent of lateness

de·layed ac·tion n the activation of a mechanism a short time after it has been set

de·lec·ta·ble /di léktəb'l/ adj **1** good to eat **2** delightful ○ n something very tasty —**de·lec·ta·bil·i·ty** /di lèktə bíllətee/ n —**de·lec·ta·bly** adv

de·lec·ta·tion /dèe lek táysh'n/ n delight (fml)

del·e·gate n /délləgət, déllə gàyt/ somebody chosen to represent or given the authority to act on behalf of another ■ vti /déllə gàyt/ (-gat·ed, -gat·ing) **1** give a task to **2** give

power or authority to somebody
—**del·e·ga·tor** n

del·e·ga·tion /dèllə gáysh'n/ n 1 a group representing others at a meeting or conference 2 the act of giving responsibility to somebody else

~~delemma~~ incorrect spelling of **dilemma**

⚡ **de·lete** /di leet/ vt (-let·ed, -let·ing) remove or erase something printed, written, or stored in a computer ■ n also **de·lete key** a computer key that is pressed to remove data

del·e·te·ri·ous /dèllə téeree əss/ adj harmful
—**del·e·te·ri·ous·ly** adv —**del·e·te·ri·ous·ness** n

⚡ **de·le·tion** /di leesh'n/ n 1 the removal of something written, printed, or stored in a computer 2 something removed or crossed out

de·lev·er·age /dee lévvərij/ (-aged, -ag·ing) vti reduce the debt owed by a business

delft, Delft n white pottery with blue designs

ORIGIN The pottery takes its name from Delft, a city in the W Netherlands.

Del·hi /déllee/ city in N India and capital of the Union Territory of Delhi. Pop. 7,206,704 (1991).

del·i /déllee/ (pl -is) n a delicatessen (infml)

de·lib·er·ate adj /di líbbərət/ 1 intentional 2 careful ■ vti /di líbbə ráyt/ (-at·ed, -at·ing) think about something carefully —**de·lib·er·ate·ly** adv —**de·lib·er·ate·ness** n —**de·lib·er·a·tive** adj

de·lib·er·a·tion /di líbbə ráysh'n/ n (fml) 1 careful thought 2 discussion

del·i·ca·cy /déllikəssee/ (pl -cies) n 1 a delicious or highly prized food 2 sensitivity to the feelings of others 3 the need for tact 4 subtlety and refinement 5 fragility 6 lack of strength

del·i·cate /déllikət/ adj 1 having a fine structure that is easily damaged or broken 2 physically weak or unwell 3 subtle o a delicate shade of blue 4 with fine details 5 skillful 6 needing tact 7 with a refined and sensitive taste 8 easily offended —**del·i·cate·ly** adv —**del·i·cate·ness** n ◊ See note at **fragile**

del·i·ca·tes·sen /dèllikə téss'n/ n 1 a specialized food store 2 prepared food sold in a delicatessen

de·li·cious /di líshəss/ adj 1 good to eat 2 delightful —**de·li·cious·ly** adv —**de·li·cious·ness** n

de·light /di līt/ n 1 joy or pleasure 2 somebody or something that brings joy or pleasure ■ v 1 vti give joy or pleasure to somebody 2 vi gain enjoyment from o delights in outwitting her brother —**de·light·ed** adj —**de·light·ed·ly** adv

de·light·ful /di líttf'l/ adj very pleasing —**de·light·ful·ly** adv —**de·light·ful·ness** n

de·lim·it /di límmit/ vt establish or mark the limits of something —**de·lim·i·ta·tion** /di límmə táysh'n/ n

⚡ **de·lim·it·er** /di límmitər/ n in computing, a character marking the end or beginning of a data element

de·lin·e·ate /di línnee àyt/ (-at·ed, -at·ing) vt 1 describe or explain in detail (fml) 2 draw or portray 3 demarcate —**de·lin·e·a·ble** adj —**de·lin·e·a·tion** /di línnee áysh'n/ —**de·lin·e·a·tive** adj

de·lin·quent /di língkwənt/ n a lawbreaker, especially a young offender ■ adj 1 antisocial or unlawful 2 ignoring a duty (fml) 3 with unpaid sums of money due —**de·lin·quen·cy** n

del·i·quesce /dèlli kwéss/ (-quesced, -quesc·ing) vi dissolve gradually by absorbing moisture from the air —**del·i·ques·cent** adj

de·lir·i·ous /di leéree əss/ adj affected by delirium —**de·lir·i·ous·ly** adv —**de·lir·i·ous·ness** n

de·lir·i·um /di leéree əm/ n 1 a temporary mental disturbance marked by extreme confusion and sometimes hallucinations, caused by fever, poisoning, or brain injury 2 great excitement

de·lir·i·um tre·mens /-treémənz/ n a condition caused by alcoholism, marked by agitation, tremors, and hallucinations

de·liv·er /di lívvər/ v 1 carry something to a person or address 2 vt assist during the birth of a baby 3 vt give birth to a baby 4 vt make a speech or announcement 5 vt throw a ball or punch 6 vi do as you promised 7 vt provide or produce something —**de·liv·er·ance** n

de·liv·er·y /di lívvəree/ (pl -ies) n 1 the act of delivering something 2 a regular visit by a mail service or vendor's vehicle 3 an item brought to a person or address 4 the act of giving birth 5 a manner of speaking

dell n a small valley (literary)

Del·mar·va Pen·in·su·la /del máarvə-/ peninsula in Delaware, Maryland, and Virginia. Length 180 mi./290 km.

de·louse /dee lówss/ (-loused, -lous·ing) vt remove the lice from the skin of a person or animal

Del·phi /dél fī/ ancient Greek town in central Greece, the site of the Temple of Apollo and an oracle

del·phin·i·um /del fínnee əm/ n a tall plant with flowers that grow on spikes

ORIGIN Delphinium derives from a Greek word for "larkspur" that literally means "little dolphin." The name refers to the shape of the flowers.

del·ta /déltə/ n 1 a triangular area of land at the mouth of a river 2 **Del·ta** a communications code word for the letter "D" 3 also **Del·ta** the area around a river delta 4 the 4th letter of the Greek alphabet

del·toid /dél tòyd/ n a thick triangular muscle that covers the shoulder joint ■ adj triangular (technical)

delts *npl* the deltoid muscles *(infml)*

de·lude /di loód/ (**-lud·ed, -lud·ing**) *vt* lead into a false belief —**de·lud·ed** *adj*

del·uge /déllyooj/ *n* **1** a sudden heavy downpour **2** a vast quantity **3 Del·uge** the biblical Flood ■ *vt* (**-uged, -ug·ing**) **1** overwhelm somebody with something **2** flood a place

de·lu·sion /di loózh'n/ *n* **1** a false belief **2** a mistaken notion —**de·lu·sion·al** *adj* —**de·lu·sive** *adj*

de·luxe /di lúks/, **de luxe** *adj* of a luxurious standard

delve (**delved, delv·ing**) *vi* search for information

Dem. *abbr* **1** Democrat **2** Democratic

de·mag·net·ize /dee mágnə tīz/ (**-ized, -iz·ing**) *vt* stop something from being magnetic —**de·mag·net·i·za·tion** /dee màgnəti záysh'n/ *n*

dem·a·gog·ic /dèmmə gójjik, -góggik/, **dem·a·gog·i·cal** /-ik'l/ *adj* appealing to emotions in a way considered politically dangerous —**dem·a·gog·i·cal·ly** *adv*

dem·a·gogue /démmə gòg/, **dem·a·gog** *n* **1** an emotive dictator **2** a popular leader in ancient times —**dem·a·gogu·er·y** *n*

ORIGIN **Demagogue** comes from a Greek word that means literally "leader of the people." The original **demagogues** were unofficial leaders in ancient Athens in the 4C BC who exerted influence in the name of the ordinary people.

de·mand /di mánd/ *n* **1** a forceful request **2** customer interest in buying particular goods or services **3** a need for resources or action ■ *v* **1** *vt* request or ask something forcefully **2** *vti* require resources in order to function or succeed ◊ **on demand** whenever a request is received

de·mand de·pos·it *n* an immediately withdrawable deposit of money

de·mand·ing /di mánding/ *adj* requiring a lot of time or effort

de·mar·cate /di maár kàyt, deè maar kàyt/ (**-cat·ed, -cat·ing**) *vt* **1** determine and set the official borders of a territory **2** set down clearly the bounds of an activity or situation —**de·mar·ca·tion** /dèè maar káysh'n/ *n*

De Ma·ri·a /də ma reè ə/, **Walter** (*b.* 1935) US artist

de·ma·te·ri·al·ize /dèemə teèree ə līz/ (**-ized, -iz·ing**) *vti* disappear or cause to disappear physically or apparently —**de·ma·te·ri·al·i·za·tion** /dèemə teeree əli záysh'n/ *n*

de·mean /di meén/ *vt* humiliate and degrade —**de·mean·ing** *adj*

de·mean·or /di meénər/ *n* outward behavior

de·ment·ed /di méntəd/ *adj* **1** regarded as entirely irrational *(infml)* **2** affected by dementia —**de·ment·ed·ly** *adv* —**de·ment·ed·ness** *n*

de·men·tia /di ménshə/ *n* a progressive deterioration of intellectual functions such as memory

de·mer·it /di mérrit/ *n* **1** a mark against somebody for deficiency or misconduct **2** a negative feature *(often pl)* —**de·mer·i·to·ri·ous** /di mèrrə táwree əss/ *adj*

de·mesne /di máyn/ *n* the lands attached to a large house *(archaic)*

De·me·ter /də meétər/ *n* in Greek mythology, the goddess of corn. Roman equivalent **Ceres**

demi- *prefix* half, partly ◦ *demigod*

dem·i·god /démmee gòd/ *n* **1** somebody treated like a god **2** in mythology, a human being with the powers of a god **3** a minor god

dem·i·john /démmee jòn/ *n* a large bottle with a short narrow neck

ORIGIN **Demijohn** is an alteration of French *dame-jeanne*, literally "Lady Jane," the popular name of the bottle in France. When the word was adopted into English in the mid-18C, its form was closer to the original French. By the 19C it had been assimilated to the more familiar *demi-* "half" and the man's name *John*.

de·mil·i·ta·rize /dee millitə rīz/ (**-rized, -riz·ing**) *vt* remove troops and military equipment from —**de·mil·i·ta·ri·za·tion** /dee millitəri záysh'n/ *n*

de Mille /də mil/, **Agnes** (1909–93) US dancer and choreographer

De Mille, Cecil B. (1881–1959) US movie director and producer

de·mise /di mīz/ *n* *(fml)* **1** somebody's death **2** the end of something

⌿ dem·o /démmō/ (*pl* **dem·os**) *n* **1** something demonstrating features **2** a demonstration of a product *(infml)* **3** a trial version of a piece of software *(infml)* **4** a music sample sent to a recording company *(infml)*

de·mo·bil·ize /dee mṓbə līz/ (**-ized, -iz·ing**) *vti* release members of the armed forces from active duty, or be released from such duty —**de·mo·bil·i·za·tion** /dee mōbəli záysh'n/ *n*

de·moc·ra·cy /di mókrəssee/ (*pl* **-cies**) *n* **1** free and equal representation of people **2** a nation that operates a democracy **3** the control of any organization or institution by its members

dem·o·crat /démmə kràt/ *n* **1** a supporter of democracy **2 Dem·o·crat** a member of the US Democratic Party

dem·o·crat·ic /dèmmə kráttik/ *adj* **1** of or characterized by democracy **2 Dem·o·crat·ic** of the Democratic Party —**dem·o·crat·i·cal·ly** *adv*

Dem·o·crat·ic Par·ty *n* a major US political party

de·moc·ra·tize /di mókrə tīz/ (**-tized, -tiz·ing**) *vt* **1** make a country into a democracy **2** introduce democracy to —**de·moc·ra·ti·za·tion** /di mòkrəti záysh'n/ *n*

De·moc·ri·tus /di mókritəss/ (460?–370? BC) Greek philosopher

dé·mo·dé /dày mō dáy/ *adj* out of style

de·mod·u·late /dee mójjə làyt/ (**-lat·ed, -lat·ing**) *vt* extract a signal carrying information from a radio wave —**de·mod·u·la·tion** /dee mòjjə láysh'n/ *n* —**de·mod·u·la·tor** *n*

dem·o·graph·ic /dèmmə gráffik/ *adj* of human populations —**dem·o·graph·i·cal·ly** *adv*

dem·o·graph·ics /dèmmə gráffiks/ *npl* the characteristics and statistics of a human population

de·mog·ra·phy /di móggrəfee/ *n* **1** the study of human populations **2** the makeup of a particular human population —**de·mog·ra·pher** *n*

de·mol·ish /di móllish/ *vt* **1** destroy a building or structure completely **2** damage something irreparably **3** eat food fast and greedily (*infml*)

dem·o·li·tion /dèmmə lísh'n/ *n* **1** the deliberate destruction of a building or other structure **2** the destruction or annihilation of something ■ **dem·o·li·tions** *npl* explosives

de·mon /déemən/ *n* **1** an evil spirit **2** a personal fear or anxiety **3** an expert at something (*infml*)

de·mon·ic /di mónnik/ *adj* **1** of or resembling a demon **2** intense or frantic —**de·mon·i·cal·ly** *adv*

de·mon·ize /déemə nìz/ (**-ized, -iz·ing**) *vt* cause to appear evil in the eyes of others —**de·mon·i·za·tion** /dèemənī záysh'n/ *n*

de·mon·ol·o·gy /dèemə nólləjee/ *n* the study of demons in folklore —**de·mon·o·log·i·cal** /dèemənə lójjik'l/ *adj* —**de·mon·ol·o·gist** *n*

de·mon·stra·ble /di mónstrəb'l/ *adj* **1** so obvious as to be readily provable **2** capable of being shown to exist or be true —**de·mon·stra·bly** *adv*

dem·on·strate /démmən stràyt/ (**-strat·ed, -strat·ing**) *v* **1** *vt* explain or show how something works **2** *vt* show something convincingly **3** *vi* protest or express support publicly —**dem·on·stra·tor** *n*

dem·on·stra·tion /dèmmən stráysh'n/ *n* **1** a display showing how to do something **2** conclusive proof **3** a public protest or show of support —**dem·on·stra·tion·al** *adj*

de·mon·stra·tive /di mónstrətiv/ *adj* **1** obviously affectionate **2** proving something **3** in grammar, describes a word such as "this" or "those" specifying which person or thing is being referred to —**de·mon·stra·tive·ly** *adv* —**de·mon·stra·tive·ness** *n*

de·mor·al·ize /di máwrə lìz/ (**-ized, -iz·ing**) *vt* erode the morale of —**de·mor·al·i·za·tion** /di màwrəli záysh'n/ *n* —**de·mor·al·iz·ing·ly** *adv*

de·mote /dee mṓt/ (**-mot·ed, -mot·ing**) *vt* reduce the rank or status of —**de·mo·tion** /di mṓsh'n/ *n*

de·mot·ic /di móttik/ *adj* **1** of ordinary people (*fml*) **2** **De·mot·ic** of modern spoken Greek ■ **De·mot·ic** modern spoken Greek

de·mo·ti·vate /dee mṓti vàyt/ (**-vat·ed, -v·at·ing**) *vt* make feel less enthusiastic about doing something —**de·mo·ti·va·tion** /dee mṓti váysh'n/ *n*

Demp·sey /démpsee/, **Jack** (1895–1983) US boxer

de·mur /di múr/ (**-murred, -mur·ring**) *vi* **1** express reluctance **2** object mildly —**de·mur·ral** *n* ◊ See note at **object**

de·mure /di myōōr/ (**-mur·er, -mur·est**) *adj* **1** looking shyly modest **2** affectedly shy or modest —**de·mure·ly** *adv* —**de·mure·ness** *n*

de·mu·tu·al·ize /dee myóōchoo ə lìz/ (**-ized, -iz·ing**) *vti* convert from a mutual organization to a public corporation —**de·mu·tu·al·i·za·tion** /dee myóōchoo əli záysh'n/ *n*

de·mys·ti·fy /dee místə fì/ (**-fied, -fies**) *vt* make less mysterious —**de·mys·ti·fi·ca·tion** /dee mìstəfi káysh'n/ *n*

den *n* **1** a wild animal's lair **2** a room for relaxing **3** a place where illegal activities take place **4** a Cub Scout group **5** a children's hideout

de·nar /déenaar/ *n* the main unit of currency in the Former Yugoslav Republic of Macedonia

de·na·tion·al·ize /dee náshən'l ìz, -náshnə lìz/ (**-ized, -iz·ing**) *vt* **1** sell a state-owned industry or company to private owners **2** deprive a people of national rights or characteristics —**de·na·tion·al·i·za·tion** /dee nàshən'li záysh'n, -nəli-/ *n*

Deng Xiao·ping /dèng show píng, dùng-/ (1904–97) Chinese political leader and national leader of China (1976–97)

de·ni·a·ble /di nì əb'l/ *adj* able to be denied —**de·ni·a·bil·i·ty** /di nì ə bíllətee/ *n* —**de·ni·a·bly** *adv*

de·ni·al /di nì əl/ *n* **1** a statement saying that something is not true **2** refusal to grant something **3** refusal to acknowledge or face something

den·i·er¹ /dénnyər/ *n* a measure of the fineness of a fiber

de·ni·er² /di nír/ *n* somebody who disbelieves

den·i·grate /dénni gràyt/ (**-grat·ed, -grat·ing**) *vt* **1** defame the character or reputation of **2** disparage and belittle —**den·i·gra·tion** /dènni gráysh'n/ *n* —**den·i·gra·tor** *n*

den·im /dénnim/ *n* hard-wearing cotton cloth. Use: clothing, especially jeans. ■ **den·ims** *npl* denim garments

ORIGIN Denim is named for the city of Nîmes in S France where the original cloth, *serge denim*, from French *serge de Nîmes*, was primarily manufactured. It is first recorded in English in the late 17C. The modern word and fabric belong to the 19C.

den·i·zen /dénnizən/ *n* a resident of a place

Den·mark /dén maark/ southernmost country in Scandinavia. Cap. Copenhagen. Pop. 5,352,815 (2001).

den moth·er *n* **1** a woman Cub Scout leader **2** a woman in charge of group

de·nom·i·nate /di nómmə nàyt/ (**-nat·ed, -nat·ing**) vt give a name to (fml)

de·nom·i·na·tion /di nòmmə náysh'n/ n 1 a religious grouping within a faith 2 a unit of value or measure, especially of currency —**de·nom·i·na·tion·al** adj

de·nom·i·na·tor /di nómmə nàytər/ n 1 the number below the line in a fraction 2 a common characteristic

de·note /di nót/ (**-not·ed, -not·ing**) vt 1 have as a particular meaning 2 refer to —**de·no·ta·tion** /dèenò táysh'n/ n —**de·no·ta·tive** /dèe nò tàytiv, di nótətiv/ adj

de·noue·ment /dàynoo maaN/ n 1 the final stage of a story, when everything is revealed or solved 2 the final stage or climax of a series of events

ORIGIN Denouement comes from a French word that means literally "the untying of a knot." It is first recorded in the mid-18C.

de·nounce /di nównss/ (**-nounced, -nounc·ing**) vt criticize or accuse publicly and harshly —**de·nounce·ment** n —**de·nounc·er** n ◊ See note at **disapprove**

dense (**dens·er, dens·est**) adj 1 with parts tightly packed together 2 very thick and difficult to see through or get through 3 regarded as slow to learn or understand (infml disapproving) 4 hard to penetrate intellectually 5 with a high mass —**dense·ly** adv —**dense·ness** n

den·si·ty /dénsətee/ (pl **-ties**) n 1 how full an area is 2 (symbol ρ) relative mass

dent v 1 vti make or suffer a depression in the surface by hitting 2 vt harm or spoil ■ n 1 a depression in a surface 2 damage, e.g., to somebody's reputation

den·tal /dént'l/ adj of dentistry or teeth

den·tal floss n thread for cleaning between the teeth

den·tal hy·gien·ist n somebody whose job is to clean teeth

den·tal sur·geon n a dentist who practices oral surgery

den·tine /dén tèen/, **den·tin** /-tin/ n the calcium-containing part of a tooth, beneath the enamel —**den·tin·al** /den tèen'l, déntən'l/ adj

den·tist /déntist/ n somebody whose job is treating and preventing tooth and gum disorders —**den·tist·ry** n

den·ture /dénchər/ n a partial or complete set of false teeth

de·nude /di nóod/ (**-nud·ed, -nud·ing**) vt remove all covering from somebody or something —**de·nu·da·tion** /dèe noò dáysh'n, dènnyə-/ n

de·nun·ci·a·tion /di nùnsee áysh'n/ n a public condemnation

Den·ver /dénvər/ capital of Colorado. Pop. 499,055 (1998).

Den·ver boot n a device fastened to one of the wheel of a vehicle to immobilize it

de·ny /di nī/ (**-nied, -nies**) vt 1 say that something is not true 2 refuse to let somebody have something 3 refuse to acknowledge something

de·o·dor·ant /dee ódərənt/ n 1 a substance applied to the body, especially under the arms, to mask or prevent body odor 2 any substance that disguises smells

de·o·dor·ize /dee ódə rìz/ (**-ized, -iz·ing**) vt disguise and eliminate the unpleasant smells of —**de·o·dor·iz·er** n

dep. abbr 1 department 2 departs

de·part /di paárt/ vi 1 leave a place, especially at the start of a trip 2 be different

de·part·ed /di paártəd/ adj dead (literary) ■ n the person who has died (fml or literary) ◊ See note at **dead**

de·part·ment /di paártmənt/ n 1 a section of a large organization 2 a major division of a government 3 somebody's specialty (infml) —**de·part·men·tal** /di paàrt mént'l/ adj

de·part·men·tal·ize /dèe paart mént'l ìz/ (**-ized, -iz·ing**) vt divide into departments —**de·part·men·tal·i·za·tion** /dèe paart mént'li záysh'n/ n

de·part·ment store n a large store that sells a wide range of goods

de·par·ture /di paárchər/ n 1 the action of setting off on a trip 2 a change from what is usual

de·par·ture lounge n a waiting area for passengers in an airport

de·pend /di pénd/ vi 1 be affected or decided by other factors 2 vary according to circumstances

☐ **depend on** or **up·on** vt 1 require something in order to exist 2 rely on somebody

de·pend·a·ble /di péndəb'l/ adj reliable —**de·pend·a·bil·i·ty** /di pèndə bíllətee/ n

de·pend·ence /di péndənss/, **de·pend·ance** n 1 a need for something in order to survive 2 a physical or psychological need

de·pend·en·cy /di péndənsee/ (pl **-cies**), **de·pend·an·cy** n 1 a territory under the jurisdiction of another country 2 dependence

de·pend·ent /di péndənt/ n also **de·pend·ant** a family member who is supported financially by another ■ adj 1 needing a particular thing (usually in combination) 2 not able to live without support from others 3 affected or decided by other factors (often in combination) ◊ age-dependent —**de·pend·ent·ly** adv

de·per·son·al·ize /dee púrsən'l ìz, -snəl-/ (**-ized, -iz·ing**) vt make impersonal —**de·per·son·al·i·za·tion** /dee pùrsən'li záysh'n, -snəli-/ n

de·pict /di píkt/ vt 1 describe in words 2 show in an art form —**de·pic·tion** n —**de·pic·tive** adj

de·pil·a·to·ry /di píllə tàwree/ adj removing hair —**de·pil·a·to·ry** n

de·plane /dee plǽyn/ (**-planed, -plan·ing**) *vi* disembark from an airplane

de·plete /di pleét/ (**-plet·ed, -plet·ing**) *vt* **1** use up or reduce **2** empty out —**de·ple·tion** *n*

de·plor·a·ble /di pláwrɔb'l/ *adj* deserving strong condemnation —**de·plor·a·bil·i·ty** /di plàwrɔ bíllɔteé/ *n* —**de·plor·a·bly** *adv*

de·plore /di pláwr/ (**-plored, -plor·ing**) *vt* **1** condemn as unacceptable **2** regret —**de·plor·ing·ly** *adv* ◊ See note at **disapprove**

de·ploy /di plóy/ *v* **1** *vti* position forces in preparation for military action **2** *vt* use something —**de·ploy·ment** *n*

de·pop·u·late /dee póppɔ làyt/ (**-lat·ed, -lat·ing**) *vt* reduce the population of —**de·pop·u·la·tion** /dee pòppɔ láysh'n/ *n*

de·port[1] /di páwrt/ *vt* **1** forcibly repatriate a foreign national **2** banish somebody from his or her country —**de·por·ta·tion** /dèe pawr táysh'n/ *n*

de·port[2] /di páwrt/ *vr* behave ◊ *how she deports herself*

de·port·ee /dèe pawr teé/ *n* a deported person

de·port·ment /di páwrtmɔnt/ *n* the way in which somebody stands, sits, or moves

de·pose /di póz/ (**-posed, -pos·ing**) *v* **1** *vt* remove somebody from office or power **2** *vti* give evidence to a court —**de·pos·al** *n*

de·pos·it /di pózzit/ *v* **1** *vt* put money in a bank **2** *vt* give a sum of money as security **3** *vt* put or leave something somewhere **4** *vti* leave a substance somewhere as part of a natural process ■ *n* **1** an act of putting money in a bank **2** an amount of money paid as security or partial payment **3** something put or left somewhere **4** an accumulation of a substance **5** a coating —**de·pos·i·tor** *n*

de·pos·it ac·count *n* an interest-earning bank account

dep·o·si·tion /dèppɔ zísh'n/ *n* **1** a witness's testimony given under oath, especially a written statement read out in court **2** the ousting of somebody from office or power **3** a building-up of deposits —**dep·o·si·tion·al** *adj*

de·pos·i·to·ry /di pózzi tàwree/ (*pl* **-ries**) *n* a storehouse

de·pos·it slip *n* a form for depositing money

de·pot /deépō, déppō/ *n* **1** a warehouse **2** a railroad or bus station **3** a military storage facility

de·prave /di práyv/ (**-praved, -prav·ing**) *vt* make morally corrupt —**de·praved** *adj* —**de·prav·ed·ly** /-práyvɔdlee, -práyvd-/ *adv* —**de·prav·i·ty** /di práyvɔteé/ *n*

dep·re·cate /dépprɔ kàyt/ (**-cat·ed, -cat·ing**) *vt* **1** condemn as unacceptable **2** belittle —**dep·re·cat·ing** *adj* —**dep·re·ca·tion** /dèpprɔ káysh'n/ *n* —**dep·re·ca·to·ry** /-kɔ tàwree/ *adj*

de·pre·ci·ate /di preéshee àyt/ (**-at·ed, -at·ing**) *v* **1** *vi* lose value, or cause to lose value **2** *vt* belittle —**de·pre·ci·a·tion** /di preèshee áysh'n/ *n* —**de·pre·cia·to·ry** /-ɔ tàwree/ *adj*

dep·re·da·tion /dèpprɔ dáysh'n/ *n* a plundering attack

de·press /di préss/ *vt* **1** make to feel sad or hopeless **2** press down —**de·press·i·ble** *adj* —**de·press·ing** *adj* —**de·press·ing·ly** *adv*

de·pres·sant /di préss'nt/ *n* a drug or agent that slows the body's vital functions —**de·pres·sant** *adj*

de·pressed /di prést/ *adj* **1** feeling very unhappy or hopeless **2** affected by clinical depression **3** lacking economic resources ◊ *a depressed area* **4** not active ◊ *the depressed dollar* ◊ *depressed markets* **5** lower than the surrounding area

de·pres·sion /di présh'n/ *n* **1** unhappiness **2** a psychiatric disorder with symptoms possibly including feelings of acute hopelessness, lack of energy, and suicidal tendencies **3** an economic slump **4** a hollow **5** a mass of low atmospheric pressure

de·pres·sive /di préssiv/ *adj* **1** causing depression **2** affected by depression ■ *n* a habitually depressed person —**de·pres·sive·ly** *adv* —**de·pres·sive·ness** *n*

dep·ri·va·tion /dèpprɔ váysh'n/ *n* **1** a state of poverty **2** the act of taking something away

de·prive /di prív/ (**-prived, -priv·ing**) *vt* **1** not allow somebody to have something **2** take something away from something

de·prived /di prívd/ *adj* lacking the things needed for a comfortable or successful life

de·pro·gram /dee prṓ gràm/ (**-grammed** *or* **-gramed, -gram·ming** *or* **-gram·ing**) *vt* remove the effect of indoctrination from

dept. *abbr* department

depth *n* **1** how deep something is **2** the fact of being deep **3** intensity of color **4** complexity of character **5** breadth of scope ■ **depths** *npl* **1** the lowest point or moment **2** the deep part of something ◊ *the ocean depths* ◊ *She wandered into the depths of the forest.* **3** the middle part of a long process ◊ *in the depths of tedious research*

depth charge *n* an underwater bomb

dep·u·ta·tion /dèppyɔ táysh'n/ *n* **1** a group of representatives **2** the appointment of a deputy

de·pute /di pyoót/ (**-put·ed, -put·ing**) *vt* choose somebody as a representative (*fml*)

dep·u·tize /déppyɔ tìz/ (**-tized, -tiz·ing**) *vt* select as a deputy —**dep·u·ti·za·tion** /dèppyɔti záysh'n/ *n*

dep·u·ty /déppyɔteé/ (*pl* **-ties**) *n* **1** somebody's representative **2** a second-in-command **3** a member of parliament in some countries, e.g., France and Germany **4** a deputy sheriff

de·rail /dee ráyl/ *vti* **1** cause a train to come off the rails **2** cause something to go off course or fail —**de·rail·ment** *n*

de·rail·leur /di ráylɔr/ *n* a device for changing gears on a bicycle that lifts the chain from one sprocket wheel to another

de·range /di ráynj/ (-ranged, -rang·ing) vt
1 make irrational 2 throw into disorder
—de·ranged adj —de·range·ment n

der·by /dúrbee/ (pl -bies) n 1 a race open to
all qualified competitors 2 a round felt hat
3 **Der·by** one of two classic horseraces for
three-year-olds, one run at Epsom,
England, the other in Kentucky

ORIGIN All the uses of **derby** derive from the
classic English horse race known as the
Derby, named for Edward Stanley, 12th earl
of Derby (1752–1834), who founded the race
in 1780. The "hat" sense is said to be from
the wearing of such hats at the Derby race in
Kentucky.

de·reg·u·late /dee réggyə layt/ (-lat·ed, -lat·ing)
vt free an organization or industry from
regulation —de·reg·u·la·tion /dee règgyə
láysh'n/ n —de·reg·u·la·tor n —de·reg·u·
la·to·ry adj

der·e·lict /dérrə lìkt/ adj 1 no longer lived
in 2 in poor condition because of neglect
3 neglectful of duty ■ n 1 a homeless
person (fml) 2 a piece of abandoned property, especially a ship

der·e·lic·tion /dèrrə líkshən/ n 1 neglect of
duty 2 the act of abandoning something

de·ride /di ríd/ (-rid·ed, -rid·ing) vt ridicule

~~de·rigeur~~ incorrect spelling of **de rigueur**

de ri·gueur /də ree gúr/ adj required by etiquette or current fashion

de·ri·sion /di rízh'n/ n mocking scorn
—de·ris·i·ble /di rízəb'l/ adj

de·ri·sive /di ríssiv, -ziv/ adj mockingly scornful —de·ri·sive·ly adv

USAGE **derisive** or **derisory**? **Derisive** means
"showing contempt or ridicule": *a derisive
laugh.* **Derisory** means "deserving contempt
or ridicule": *a derisory offer.*

de·ri·so·ry /di ríssəree, -rízə-/ adj deserving
contempt or ridicule

der·i·va·tion /dèrri váysh'n/ n 1 the source of
something, e.g., a word 2 the formation or
development of a word —der·i·va·tion·al
adj ◊ See note at **origin**

de·riv·a·tive /di rívvətiv/ adj based on something else and therefore unoriginal ■ n
1 a thing derived from another 2 a word
formed from another 3 a chemical product
produced from a related substance ○ *an
opium derivative*

de·rive /di rív/ (-rived, -riv·ing) v 1 vti form
one word from another, or be formed from
another word 2 vti get something from a
source, or come from a source 3 vt deduce
something 4 vt make a chemical compound
from another —de·riv·a·ble adj

der·ma·ti·tis /dùrmə títiss/ n skin inflammation

der·ma·tol·o·gy /dùrmə tólləjee/ n the branch
of medicine dealing with the skin
—der·ma·to·log·i·cal /dùrmətə lójjik'l/ adj
—der·ma·tol·o·gist n

der·mis /dúrmiss/ n a thick layer of skin
beneath the epidermis —der·mal adj

der·o·gate /dérrə gàyt/ (-gat·ed, -gat·ing) v 1 vi
deviate from a norm, rule, or set conditions
2 vi detract (fml) 3 vt criticize or disparage
—der·o·ga·tion /dèrrə gáysh'n/ n —de·rog·
a·tive adj

de·rog·a·to·ry /di róggə tàwree/ adj disparaging —de·rog·a·to·ri·ly /di ròggə
táwrəlee/ adv

der·rick /dérrik/ n 1 a crane for loading things
onto a ship 2 a platform that holds the
drilling equipment over an oil well

ORIGIN A **derrick** was originally a "gallows."
The name comes from the surname of a noted
hangman active in London, England around
1600. However, from the middle of the 18C
derrick referred to various types of hoisting
apparatus.

Der·ri·da /dèrri dàá/, **Jacques** (b. 1930) Algerian-born French philosopher

der·ri·ère /dèrree áir/ n somebody's buttocks
(humorous)

der·ring-do /dérring doò, dèrring dòò/ n brave
adventurous behavior (dated)

ORIGIN **Derring-do** derives from various mis-
understandings and misuses. The phrase
dorring do "daring to do" occurs in the late
14C in a poem by Geoffrey Chaucer, and was
copied in the 15C by the poet John Lydgate
(1370?–1450?). 16C editions of Lydgate mis-
printed this as *derring do*. The poet Edmund
Spenser took this up, but misunderstood the
grammatical construction and treated it as a
noun meaning "brave adventurous behavior."
Spenser's use was revived in the early 19C by
Sir Walter Scott.

der·rin·ger /dérrinjər/ n a pocket-sized short-
barreled pistol

ORIGIN The **derringer** is named for the US
gunsmith Henry Deringer (1786–1868), who
designed it.

der·vish /dúrvish/ n a member of any of
various Muslim religious groups, especially one known for energetic dancing

⚡ **DES** abbr data encryption standard

de·sal·i·nate /dee sálla nàyt/ (-nat·ed, -nat·ing)
vt remove salt from —de·sal·i·na·tion /dee
sàllə náysh'n/ n

des·cant /dés kànt, dís-/ n a high melody
played or sung above the basic melody

Des·cartes /day kaárt/, **René** (1596–1650)
French philosopher and mathematician

de·scend /di sénd/ v 1 vti go down a staircase,
hill, or other downward incline 2 vi come
nearer the ground 3 vi slope downward
4 vti be related to an ancestor 5 vi be inherited from parents or ancestors 6 vi
behave in a way that is below your normal
standards 7 vi arrive suddenly and in
numbers

de·scen·dant /di séndənt/ *n* somebody related to a particular person who lived in the past

de·scent /di sént/ *n* **1** the act of descending **2** a way down **3** a change from better to worse **4** ancestral background **5** a sudden arrival or attack

SPELLCHECK Do not confuse the spelling of **descent** and **dissent** ("disagree"), which sound similar.

de·scribe /di skríb/ (-scribed, -scrib·ing) *vt* **1** give an account of what somebody or something is like **2** label or typify something —**de·scrib·a·ble** *adj*

de·scrip·tion /di skrípshən/ *n* **1** an account of what somebody or something is like **2** the process of describing **3** a variety or type o *cakes of every description*

de·scrip·tive /di skríptiv/ *adj* describing what somebody or something is like —**de·scrip·tive·ly** *adv* —**de·scrip·tive·ness** *n*

⚡**de·scrip·tor** /di skríptər/ *n* in a database, a word used to categorize records of a particular type

de·scry /di skrí/ (-scried, -scries) *vt* catch sight of (*literary*) —**de·scri·er** *n*

~~desease~~ incorrect spelling of **disease**

des·e·crate /déssə kràyt/ (-crat·ed, -crat·ing) *vt* damage or insult something holy —**des·e·cra·tion** /dèssə kráysh'n/ *n*

de·seg·re·gate /dee séggrə gàyt/ (-gat·ed, -gat·ing) *vti* end the enforced separation of racial or social groups —**de·seg·re·ga·tion** /dee sèggrə gáysh'n/ *n* —**de·seg·re·ga·tion·ist** *n*

⚡**de·se·lect** /dèè sə lékt/ *vt* in computing, remove an option from a menu or list —**de·se·lec·tion** *n*

~~desend~~ incorrect spelling of **descend**

de·sen·si·tize /dee sénsə tìz/ (-tized, -tiz·ing) *vt* **1** make somebody or something less sensitive **2** make somebody less allergic —**de·sen·si·ti·za·tion** /dee sènsəti záysh'n/ *n*

~~desent~~ incorrect spelling of **decent**

des·ert[1] /dézzərt/ *n* **1** an area of land with no permanent bodies of water and erratic rainfall **2** a deprived place

de·sert[2] /di zúrt/ *v* **1** *vt* abandon a place or person **2** *vti* leave a branch of the armed forces without permission —**de·sert·ed** *adj* —**de·sert·er** *n* —**de·ser·tion** /di zúrsh'n/ *n*

USAGE desert or dessert? Dessert, pronounced with the stress on the second syllable, means "a sweet course eaten at the end of a meal." **Desert**, pronounced with the stress on the first syllable, means "an area with little rainfall," and with the stress on the second syllable means "something deserved," as in *just deserts*, or is a verb meaning "abandon" or "leave without permission."

de·sert[3] /di zúrt/ *n* a deserved punishment or reward (*usually pl*)

de·sert·i·fi·ca·tion /di zùrtəfi káysh'n/ *n* the process of becoming a desert

des·ert is·land *n* an isolated tropical island

de·serve /di zúrv/ (-served, -serv·ing) *vt* have earned or be worthy of —**de·served** *adj* —**de·serv·ed·ly** /di zúrvədlee/ *adv*

de·serv·ing /di zúrving/ *adj* worthy of receiving something —**de·serv·ing·ly** *adv*

de·sex·u·al·ize /dee sékshoo ə līz/ (-ized, -iz·ing) *vt* **1** suppress the sexual characteristics of **2** remove sexist material —**de·sex·u·al·i·za·tion** /dee sèkshoo əli záysh'n/ *n*

des·ic·cate /déssi kàyt/ (-cat·ed, -cat·ing) *vt* remove the moisture from —**des·ic·cat·ed** *adj* —**des·ic·ca·tion** /dèssi káysh'n/ *n* —**des·ic·ca·tive** *adj*

de·sid·er·a·tum /di sìddə raàtəm, -ráytəm/ (*pl* **-ta** /-tə/) *n* something desired or necessary (*fml*)

de·sign /di zín/ *v* **1** *vti* create a detailed plan of the form and structure of something **2** *vti* plan and make something skillfully **3** *vt* intend something for a particular use ■ *n* **1** a picture of the form and structure of an object **2** the way something is made **3** a decorative pattern **4** the process of designing ■ **de·signs** *npl* a selfish or dishonest plan

des·ig·nate *vt* /dézzig nàyt/ (-nat·ed, -nat·ing) **1** give a name or descriptive label to **2** choose for a particular purpose or position **3** mark or indicate ■ *adj* /dézzignət/ chosen for a future post —**des·ig·na·tive** *adj* —**des·ig·na·to·ry** *adj*

des·ig·nat·ed driv·er *n* a member of a group who agrees not to drink alcohol in order to drive the others home

des·ig·nat·ed hit·ter *n* in baseball, a batter who substitutes for a pitcher

des·ig·na·tion /dèzzig náysh'n/ *n* **1** a name, label, or description **2** the fact of being designated

de·sign·er /di zínər/ *n* somebody who designs things, especially clothes ■ *adj* **1** fashionable **2** designed by somebody famous

de·sign·er drug *n* a drug with effects similar to those of an illegal drug but made legally

de·sign·ing /di zíning/ *adj* scheming

de·sir·a·ble /di zírəb'l/ *adj* **1** worth having **2** sexually attractive —**de·sir·a·bil·i·ty** /di zírə bíllətee/ *n* —**de·sir·a·ble** *n* —**de·sir·a·bly** *adv*

de·sire /di zír/ *vt* (-sired, -sir·ing) **1** wish for **2** find sexually attractive **3** request (*fml*) ■ *n* **1** a craving **2** something wished for (*fml*) ◊ See note at **want**

~~desireable~~ incorrect spelling of **desirable**

de·sir·ous /di zírəss/ *adj* wanting to have something (*fml*)

de·sist /di síst, -zíst/ *vi* cease doing something —**de·sis·tance** *n*

desk *n* **1** a table used for writing or other work **2** a counter where a service is provided

ORIGIN Desk derives from the same Latin and

Greek words as *dish*, *disk*, and *discus*. The key point in the development of **desk** seems to be when the round dish or tray was set on legs and became a table, then a writing table, a sense already acquired in medieval Latin, from which English adopted the word in the 14C.

de·skill /dee skíl/ *vt* automate a job further and remove the need for human skill or initiative

⚡ **desk·top** /désk tòp/ *n* 1 the surface of a desk 2 a display on a computer screen that shows icons representing equipment, programs, and files ■ *adj* usable on top of a desk

⚡ **desk·top pub·lish·ing** *n* the production of professional-looking publications using personal computers

Des Moines /di móyn/ capital of Iowa. Pop. 191,293 (1998).

des·o·late *adj* /déssələt/ 1 uninhabited and bleak 2 sad and without hope 3 dismal ■ *vt* /déssə làyt/ (-**lat·ed**, -**lat·ing**) make desolate —**des·o·late·ly** *adv* —**des·o·la·tion** /déssə láysh'n/ *n*

de So·to /də sōtō/, **Hernando** (1500?–42?) Spanish explorer

de·spair /di spáir/ *n* 1 a feeling of hopelessness 2 a cause of hopelessness ■ *vi* lose hope

de·spair·ing /di spáiring/ *adj* feeling or showing loss of hope —**de·spair·ing·ly** *adv*

~~desparate~~ incorrect spelling of **desperate**

des·patch *vti*, *n* = **dispatch**

des·per·a·do /dèspə raàdō/ (*pl* -**does** *or* -**dos**) *n* a bold violent criminal

des·per·ate /déspərət/ *adj* 1 feeling or expressing a complete lack of hope 2 as a last resort ○ *desperate measures* 3 very serious or bad ○ *desperate hunger* 4 in great need ○ *desperate for money* —**des·per·ate·ly** *adv* —**des·per·a·tion** /dèspə ráysh'n/ *n*

~~desperatly~~ incorrect spelling of **desperately**

des·pi·ca·ble /di spíkab'l/ *adj* worthy of contempt —**des·pi·ca·bly** *adv*

de·spise /di spíz/ (-**spised**, -**spis·ing**) *vt* regard with loathing and contempt

de·spite /di spít/ *prep* 1 regardless of 2 contrary to

de·spoil /di spóyl/ *vt* plunder —**de·spoil·er** *n* —**de·spoil·ment** *n* —**de·spo·li·a·tion** /di spòlee áysh'n/ *n*

de·spon·dent /di spóndənt/ *adj* completely lacking in hope or confidence —**de·spon·dence** *n* —**de·spon·den·cy** *n* —**de·spon·dent·ly** *adv*

des·pot /dés pòt, déspət/ *n* 1 a ruler with absolute power 2 a tyrannical person —**des·pot·ic** /di spóttik/ *adj* —**des·pot·ism** /déspə tìzzəm/ *n*

des·sert /di zúrt/ *n* a sweet dish concluding a meal. ◊ See note at **desert**[2]

des·sert·spoon /di zúrt spòon/ *n* 1 a medium-sized spoon for eating a dessert 2 *also*

des·sert·spoon·ful an amount held by a dessertspoon

des·sert wine *n* a sweet wine served with a dessert

~~dessicated~~ incorrect spelling of **desiccated**

de·sta·bi·lize /dee stáybə lìz/ (-**lized**, -**liz·ing**) *vt* undermine and make unstable —**de·sta·bi·li·za·tion** /dee stàybəli záysh'n/ *n*

des·ti·na·tion /dèsti náysh'n/ *n* 1 the place to which somebody is traveling 2 an intended or destined purpose or end

des·tined /déstind/ *adj* 1 sure to achieve or have something 2 heading toward a place

des·ti·ny /déstinee/ (*pl* -**nies**) *n* 1 somebody's future regarded as preordained 2 *also* **Des·ti·ny** a force that supposedly predetermines events

des·ti·tute /désti tòot/ *adj* 1 lacking the necessities of life 2 completely lacking something ○ *destitute of ideas* —**des·ti·tu·tion** /dèsti tóosh'n/ *n*

de·stroy /di stróy/ *v* 1 *vti* demolish, ruin, or abolish something 2 *vt* defeat somebody convincingly 3 *vt* kill an animal mercifully

de·stroy·er /di stróy ər/ *n* 1 a small fast warship 2 somebody or something that causes destruction

de·struc·tion /di strúksh'n/ *n* 1 the process of destroying something or somebody 2 severe damage caused by something

de·struc·tive /di strúktiv/ *adj* 1 destroying 2 meant to cause damage —**de·struc·tive·ly** *adv* —**de·struc·tive·ness** *n*

des·ul·to·ry /déss'l tàwree/ *adj* 1 aimlessly passing from one thing to another 2 random —**des·ul·to·ri·ly** *adv*

ORIGIN Desultory comes from a Latin word meaning literally "leaping from one thing to another." It referred particularly to the circus trick of jumping between galloping horses.

de·tach /di tách/ *v* 1 *vti* separate or disconnect 2 *vt* send on a separate assignment —**de·tach·a·ble** *adj*

de·tached /di tácht/ *adj* 1 not attached 2 free from emotional involvement —**de·tach·ed·ly** /di táchadlee, di táchtlee/ *adv*

de·tach·ment /di táchmənt/ *n* 1 aloofness 2 lack of bias or personal involvement 3 separation or disconnection 4 a military unit chosen for special duties 5 any specialized group 6 *Can* a Canadian police unit

de·tail *n* /di táyl, dee tàyl/ 1 an individual part, especially one of several items of information 2 the inclusion or description of all elements ○ *attention to detail* 3 an insignificant part 4 a group, especially a military unit, with a special task ■ **de·tails** *npl* personal items ■ *vt* /di táyl/ 1 list items 2 add refinements to something 3 give a specialized assignment to military personnel

de·tailed /di táyld, dee tàyld/ *adj* containing or emphasizing details

de·tain /di táyn/ vt 1 delay the progress of 2 hold in custody —**de·tain·ee** /deè tay neé, di-/ n —**de·tain·ment** n

de·tect /di tékt/ v 1 vt perceive the existence of 2 vti work on crimes —**de·tect·a·ble** adj —**de·tect·a·bly** adv

de·tec·tion /di téksh'n/ n 1 the act of noticing or discovering the existence of something 2 detective work

de·tec·tive /di téktiv/ n somebody who investigates and gathers evidence about possible crimes or wrongdoing —**de·tec·tive** adj

de·tec·tor /di téktər/ n 1 a sensing device 2 somebody or something that detects

dé·tente /day taànt, -taáNt/, **de·tente** n an easing of tension between nations

de·ten·tion /di ténshən/ n 1 the process or state of being held in custody 2 punishment by being detained after school

de·ten·tion home n a place of detention for young people

de·ter /di túr/ (-terred, -ter·ring) vti discourage from taking action —**de·ter·ment** n

de·ter·gent /di túrjənt/ n a chemical cleansing substance —**de·ter·gent** adj

de·te·ri·o·rate /di teèree ə ràyt/ (-rat·ed, -rat·ing) vti become or make worse —**de·te·ri·o·ra·tion** /-teèree ə ráysh'n/ n

de·ter·mi·nant /di túrminənt/ n a cause or determining factor —**de·ter·mi·nant** adj

de·ter·mi·nate /di túrminət/ adj with exact and definite limits —**de·ter·mi·na·cy** n

de·ter·mi·na·tion /di túrmi náysh'n/ n 1 firmness of purpose 2 a fixed purpose 3 the act of discovering or ascertaining something (fml) 4 a decision on a course of action (fml) 5 the settlement of a dispute or contest

de·ter·mine /di túrmin/ (-mined, -min·ing) v 1 vt find out 2 vt decide or settle conclusively 3 vt influence or give form to 4 vt fix the limits of 5 vti adopt or cause to adopt a purpose —**de·ter·min·ing** adj

de·ter·mined /di túrmind/ adj with a firmness of purpose —**de·ter·mined·ly** adv —**de·ter·mined·ness** n

de·ter·min·er /di túrminər/ n 1 a word that comes before a noun and specifies or identifies what it refers to 2 somebody or something that determines

de·ter·min·ism /di túrmi nĭzzəm/ n the belief that everything has a cause and that there is no free will —**de·ter·min·ist** n

de·ter·min·is·tic /di túrmi nístik/ adj 1 of determinism 2 of a knowable outcome —**de·ter·min·is·ti·cal·ly** adv

de·ter·rent /di túrənt, di túrrənt/ n something that deters or is intended to deter ■ adj acting to deter —**de·ter·rence** n

de·test /di tést/ vt hate —**de·tes·ta·tion** /deè te stáysh'n/ n

de·test·a·ble /di téstəb'l/ adj deserving hatred —**de·test·a·bly** adv

de·throne /dee thrón/ (-throned, -thron·ing) vt remove from a throne or position of power —**de·throne·ment** n

det·o·nate /détt'n àyt/ (-nat·ed, -nat·ing) vti explode —**det·o·na·tion** /dètt'n áysh'n/ n —**det·o·na·tor** n

de·tour /deè toòr, di toòr/ n 1 a deviation from a chosen or more direct route 2 an alternative route —**de·tour** vti

de·tox·i·fy /dee tóksi fī/ (-fied, -fies), **de·tox** /deè tòks/ v 1 vti rid somebody or yourself of toxic, especially addictive, substances 2 vt remove or transform a toxic substance —**de·tox** n —**de·tox·i·fi·ca·tion** /dee tòksəfi káysh'n/ n

de·tract /di trákt/ vi take away something that gives quality or value —**de·trac·tion** n —**de·trac·tive** adj —**de·trac·tor** n

de·train /dee tráyn/ vi disembark from a train —**de·train·ment** n

det·ri·ment /déttrimənt/ n damage or disadvantage —**det·ri·men·tal** /dèttri mént'l/ adj —**det·ri·men·tal·ly** adv

de·tri·tus /di trítəss/ n 1 debris 2 rock fragments —**de·tri·tal** adj

De·troit /də tróyt/ city in SE Michigan. Pop. 970,196 (1998).

de trop /də tró/ adj superfluous or excessive (literary)

deuce /dooss/ n 1 a playing card with the value of two 2 in racket games, a tied score requiring an extra margin to win

Deu·ter·on·o·my /dòotə rónnəmee/ n the 5th book of the Bible

deut·sche mark /dóychə maàrk/, **deut·sche mark** n the main unit of the former German currency

De Va·le·ra /dèvvə lérrə/, Eamon (1882–1975) US-born prime minister (1932–48, 1951–54, and 1957–59) and president (1959–73) of Ireland

de·val·ue /dee vállyoo/ (-ued, -u·ing) vti 1 lower a currency's value 2 make or become less valuable —**de·val·u·a·tion** /dee vàllyoo áysh'n/ n —**de·val·u·a·tion·ist** n

dev·as·tate /dévvə stàyt/ (-tat·ed, -tat·ing) vt 1 damage severely 2 upset enormously —**dev·as·ta·tion** /dèvvə stáysh'n/ n

dev·as·tat·ing /dévvə stàyting/ adj 1 severely damaging 2 very upsetting 3 sharply critical —**dev·as·tat·ing·ly** adv

de·vel·op /di vélləp/ v 1 vti change and grow, increase, or become more advanced, or cause to do this 2 vi arise and increase o *tension was developing* 3 vt acquire a feature, habit, or illness 4 vt enlarge on a plan or idea 5 vt turn photographic film into negatives or prints

~~develope~~ incorrect spelling of **develop**

de·vel·oped /di vélləpt/ adj wealthy and industrialized

~~developement~~ incorrect spelling of **development**

de·vel·op·er /di vélləpər/ n 1 somebody who develops something 2 a buyer of land for building 3 chemical for making exposed film into negatives or prints

de·vel·op·ing /di vélləping/ adj describes a country or society that is not industrialized

de·vel·op·ment /di vélləpmənt/ n 1 an event causing or reflecting change (often pl) 2 the act of developing something 3 the fact of being developed 4 a group of houses or other buildings built as a single construction project —**de·vel·op·men·tal** /-vèlləp mént'l/ adj —**de·vel·op·men·tal·ly** adv

De·vi /dáyvee/ n the supreme Hindu goddess, wife of Shiva, manifested in the forms Durga, Kali, Parvati, and Sati

de·vi·ant /déevee ənt/ adj different from the norm or from an accepted standard ■ n somebody regarded as behaving differently or unacceptably —**de·vi·ance** n

de·vi·ate /déevee àyt/ (-at·ed, -at·ing) vi 1 be different 2 turn from a course

de·vi·a·tion /déevee áysh'n/ n 1 a change or difference from what is usual or planned 2 unacceptable behavior or attitudes

de·vice /di víss/ n 1 a tool or machine 2 a ploy or trick 3 a bomb or other explosive 4 a literary or dramatic technique to produce an effect 5 an emblem or motto

~~**devide**~~ incorrect spelling of **divide**

dev·il /dév'l/ n 1 also **Dev·il** in some religions, the personification of the spirit of evil 2 a subordinate evil spirit 3 an evil person 4 a mischievous person or animal 5 a person of a particular kind o a lucky devil ■ vt make food spicy

dev·il·ish /dév'lish/ adj 1 sinister or cruel 2 mischievous ■ adv very (infml dated) —**dev·il·ish·ly** adv

dev·il-may-care adj 1 reckless 2 cheerfully unconcerned

dev·il·ment /dév'lmənt/ n mischievous behavior

dev·il's ad·vo·cate n 1 somebody who argues for the sake of provoking discussion or conflict 2 formerly, a Roman Catholic official opposing canonization

dev·il's food cake n a dark chocolate cake

Dev·il's Is·land rocky islet in the Atlantic Ocean off the coast of French Guiana, formerly the site of a penal colony

dev·il·try /dév'ltree/, **dev·il·ry** /dév'lree/ n 1 evil behavior 2 acts supposedly performed with the help of spirits

de·vi·ous /déevee əss/ adj 1 unfair or underhand 2 roundabout o a devious route —**de·vi·ous·ly** adv —**de·vi·ous·ness** n

de·vise /di víz/ vt (-vised, -vis·ing) think up a plan ■ n an item of property bequeathed —**de·vis·a·ble** adj

de·void /di vóyd/ adj lacking in or without something

dev·o·lu·tion /dèvvə loosh'n/ n 1 the act of delegating responsibilities 2 the delegating of power from a central to a regional or local level —**dev·o·lu·tion·ar·y** adj

dev·o·lu·tion·ist /dèvvə loosh'nist/ n somebody supporting a decentralizing of political power —**dev·o·lu·tion·ist** adj

de·volve /di vólv/ (-volved, -volv·ing) vti transfer or be transferred to another person or organization —**de·volve·ment** n

De·vo·ni·an /də vónee ən/ n a period of geologic time 417–354 million years ago —**De·vo·ni·an** adj

de·vote /di vót/ (-vot·ed, -vot·ing) vt commit or allot to a particular purpose

de·vot·ed /di vótəd/ adj 1 loving and committed 2 dedicated —**de·vot·ed·ly** adv —**de·vot·ed·ness** n

dev·o·tee /dèvvə teé, dèv vō teé/ n 1 an ardent enthusiast 2 a religious person

de·vo·tion /di vósh'n/ n 1 committed love 2 dedication 3 religious fervor (fml) ■ **de·vo·tions** npl prayers —**de·vo·tion·al** adj

de·vour /di vówr/ vt 1 eat quickly 2 take in eagerly 3 destroy (literary) —**de·vour·ing** adj

de·vout /di vówt/ adj 1 very religious 2 very sincere (fml) —**de·vout·ly** adv —**de·vout·ness** n

dew /doo/ n moisture from the air condensed as water droplets on cool outdoor surfaces during the night —**dew·y** adj

SPELLCHECK Do not confuse the spelling of **dew**, **do** ("perform an action"), and **due** ("expected," "ready," "appropriate"), which sound similar.

dew·drop /doo dròp/ n a drop of dew

Dew·ey /doo ee/, **George** (1837–1917) US naval officer

Dew·ey, John (1859–1952) US philosopher, psychologist, and educator

dew·fall /doo fàwl/ n 1 the time at which dew forms 2 the amount of dew that forms

dew·lap /doo làp/ n a hanging flap of skin on an animal's neck —**dew·lapped** adj

dew point n the air temperature at which dew begins to form

dew·y-eyed adj naive and innocent

dex·ter·ous /dékstərəss, dékstrəss/, **dex·trous** /dékstrəss/ adj 1 physically skillful, especially with the hands 2 quick-witted —**dex·ter·i·ty** /dek stérrətee/ n —**dex·ter·ous·ly** adv

ORIGIN Dexterous comes from a Latin word that means literally "right-handed."

dex·trose /dék stróss/ n a form of glucose found in tissue and also manufactured from starch

Dha·ka /daákə, dákə/, **Dac·ca** capital of Bangladesh. Pop. 3,368,940 (1991).

dhar·ma /daármə/ n 1 in Hinduism, somebody's duty to behave according to religious codes 2 in Buddhism, the eternal

truths about life and the universe
—**dhar·mic** *adj*

Dhau·la·gi·ri /dòwlə gèeree/ one of the world's highest mountains, in the Himalayan range in N Nepal. Height 26,811 ft./8,172 m.

dhow /dow/ *n* an Arab sailing ship with low sides, one or two masts, and triangular curving sails

Dhu al-Hij·jah /dool hĭl jàa/ *n* the 12th month of the year in the Islamic calendar

Dhu al-Qa'·dah /dool kăa dàa/ *n* the 11th month of the year in the Islamic calendar

di- *prefix* **1** two, twice, double o *dilemma* **2** containing two atoms, radicals, or groups o *dioxide*

di·a·be·tes /dǐ ə bèe teez, -bèetiss/ *n* a medical disorder causing high levels of sugar in the blood —**di·a·bet·ic** /dǐ ə bèttik/ *adj*, *n*

di·a·bol·i·cal /dǐ ə bóllik'l/, **di·a·bol·ic** /-bóllik/ *adj* **1** relating to the devil **2** evil —**di·a·bol·i·cal·ly** *adv*

di·a·chron·ic /dǐ ə krónnik/ *adj* relating to or showing development through time —**di·a·chron·i·cal·ly** *adv*

di·a·crit·ic /dǐ ə kríttik/ *adj* marking a change ■ *n also* **di·a·crit·i·cal mark** a mark added above or below a letter to show a change from the normal pronunciation

Dí·a de la Ra·za /dèe ə də laa ráa saa/ *n* a holiday in Spanish-speaking regions in commemoration of Christopher Columbus. Date: October 12.

di·a·dem /dǐ ə dèm, dǐ ədəm/ *n* a jeweled headband or crown

ORIGIN **Diadem** came via French and Latin from Greek, where it referred to the regal headband of the Persian kings, which was adopted by Alexander the Great. It was formed from a verb meaning "bind."

di·aer·e·sis *n* LING = **dieresis**

Di·a·ghi·lev /dee àagə lèf/, **Sergei** (1872–1929) Russian ballet impresario

di·ag·no·sis /dǐ əg nóssiss/ (*pl* **-ses** /-sèez/) *n* **1** the identification of an illness **2** the identification of a problem or fault **3** decision reached by diagnosis —**di·ag·nose** /dǐ əg nòz/ *vt* —**di·ag·nos·tic** /dǐ əg nóstik/ *adj* —**di·ag·nos·ti·cian** /dǐ əg nos tísh'n/ *n*

SPELLCHECK Do not confuse the spelling of **diagnosis** and **diagnoses** (plural of *diagnosis*), which sound similar.

di·ag·o·nal /dǐ ággən'l, dǐ ággn'l/ *adj* **1** slanting or oblique **2** with slanting lines or markings ■ *n* **1** a slanting line **2** a line joining angles —**di·ag·o·nal·ly** *adv*

di·a·gram /dǐ ə gràm/ *n* **1** a simple explanatory drawing **2** a chart presenting information graphically —**di·a·gram·mat·ic** /dǐ əgrə máttik/ *adj* —**di·a·gram·mat·i·cal·ly** *adv*

di·al /dǐ əl/ *n* **1** an indicator with a movable pointer **2** a control knob **3** a station in-

dicator on a radio **4** a clock face **5** on some telephones, a disk with holes in it used for calling a number ■ *vti* call a number on a telephone —**di·al·er** *n*

di·a·lect /dǐ ə lèkt/ *n* **1** a regional variety of a language **2** a language regarded as a member of a family of related languages —**di·a·lec·tal** /dǐ ə lékt'l/ *adj*

di·a·lec·tic /dǐ ə léktik/ *n* **1** a tension that exists between conflicting ideas **2** the investigation of truth through discussion **3** *also* **di·a·lec·tics** a method of resolving apparent conflict between ideas by establishing truths on both sides —**di·a·lec·ti·cal** *adj* —**di·a·lec·ti·cian** /dǐ ə lek tísh'n/ *n*

⚡**di·a·log box** *n* a small box on a computer screen that presents the user with a choice

di·a·logue /dǐ ə lòg/, **di·a·log** *n* **1** the characters' words in a play, movie, or book **2** a formal discussion or negotiation **3** a conversation *(fml)* ■ *vi* (**-logued, -logu·ing; -loged, -log·ing**) take part in a dialog

di·al tone *n* the continuous sound that is heard when a telephone receiver is lifted

⚡**di·al-up** *adj* describes a connection between computers that is achieved by means of a modem and a telephone line

di·al·y·sis /dǐ ălləssiss/ *n* **1** the process of filtering waste from the blood of a patient with malfunctioning kidneys **2** the separation of substances from a solution —**di·a·lyt·ic** /dǐ ə líttik/ *adj*

di·a·man·té /dèe ə maǎn tày/ *adj* decorated with imitation diamonds ■ *n* imitation diamonds

di·am·e·ter /dǐ ámmətər/ *n* **1** a line through the center of a circle **2** the width of a circle or of something circular —**di·am·e·tral** /-ətrəl/ *adj* —**di·am·e·tral·ly** *adv*

di·a·met·ri·cal /dǐ ə méttrik'l/ *adj* completely opposite or different —**di·a·met·ri·cal·ly** *adv*

di·a·mond /dǐ əmənd, dímənd/ *n* **1** a hard colorless mineral that is a form of carbon. Use: gems, abrasives, cutting tools. **2** a shape like a square resting on a corner **3** a playing card with a diamond-shaped symbol ■ *adj* 60th ■ *vt* decorate with diamonds

ORIGIN **Diamond** comes ultimately from the Greek word that is also the source of *adamant*. It meant "diamond, hardest iron or steel." The Greek word passed into Latin, after which it took two separate courses. Largely unchanged, it came via French into English as *adamant*. In medieval Latin it was also altered to a *dia-* form, and came via French into English as *diamond*.

di·a·mond an·ni·ver·sa·ry *n* a 60th anniversary, especially a wedding anniversary

Di·a·mond Head promontory and extinct volcano in SE Oahu Island, Hawaii. Height 761 ft./232 m.

di·a·mond ju·bi·lee *n* a 60th anniversary, especially of a monarch's rule

Di·an·a /dī ánnə/ *n* in Roman mythology, the goddess of hunting. Greek equivalent **Artemis**

Diana, Princess of Wales

Di·an·a /dī ánnə/, **Princess of Wales** (1961–97) British princess

di·a·per /dī əpər, dīpər/ *n* a piece of cloth or absorbent paper fabric wrapped around a baby's legs ■ *vt* put a diaper on a baby

ORIGIN Babies' **diapers** were originally made of the fabric **diaper**, a linen or cotton material woven with a pattern of diamonds. The ultimate root is a Greek word meaning "white."

di·aph·a·nous /dī áffənəss/ *adj* 1 transparent 2 insubstantial *(literary)* —**di·a·pha·ne·i·ty** /dī àffə neé itee/ *n*

di·a·phragm /dī ə fràm/ *n* 1 a muscular wall below the rib cage 2 a dome-shaped contraceptive placed inside the vagina 3 a camera's mechanism controlling the opening for light 4 a vibrating disk in sound equipment —**di·a·phrag·mat·ic** /dī ə frag máttik, -frə máttik/ *adj*

~~diaphram~~ incorrect spelling of **diaphragm**

~~diarhea, diarrea~~ incorrect spelling of **diarrhea**

di·a·rist /dī ərist/ *n* a diary writer

di·ar·rhe·a /dī ə reé ə/ *n* 1 frequent and excessive bowel movements 2 watery feces

di·a·ry /dī əree/ *n (pl* **-ries)** 1 a personal record of events in somebody's life, written daily or regularly 2 a blank book for recording personal events ◊ See note at **dairy**

Di·as /deé àss/, **Di·az, Bartolomeu** (1450?–1500) Portuguese navigator and explorer

di·as·po·ra /dī áspərə/ *n* 1 a dispersion of a language, culture, or people 2 **Di·as·po·ra** the exile of the Jews from Israel 3 **Di·as·po·ra** all Jews living outside Israel

di·a·ton·ic /dī ə tónnik/ *adj* of a simple musical scale with seven tones ■ *n* an interval in a diatonic scale —**di·a·ton·i·cal·ly** *adv* —**di·a·ton·i·cism** /-tónni sìzzəm/ *n*

di·a·tribe /dī ə trìb/ *n* a bitter verbal criticism

dibs *npl* a claim to something *(infml)*

dice /dīss/ plural of **die**[2] 1 ■ *n* a gambling game played with dice *(+ sing or pl verb)* ■ *npl* small cubes of food *(+ pl verb)* ■ *v* (**diced, dic·ing**) 1 *vt* cut food into small cubes 2 *vti* gamble with dice 3 *vi* take risks ◊ **load the dice** manipulate a situation unfairly in order to obtain a desired result ◊ **no dice** no

dic·ey /dīssee/ *(*-i-er, -i-est*)*, **dic·y** *adj* risky *(infml)*

di·chot·o·my /dī kóttəmee/ *(pl* **-mies)** *n* a separation into different or contradictory things —**di·chot·o·mous** *adj*

~~dicision~~ incorrect spelling of **decision**

dick *n* a detective *(slang dated)*

dick·ens /díkənz/ *n* adds emphasis *(infml)* ○ *What the dickens are you doing?*

Dick·ens /díkənz/, **Charles** (1812–70) British novelist

Dick·en·si·an /di kénzee ən/ *adj* 1 of or reminiscent of Charles Dickens or his books and their characters or settings 2 full of twists and amazing coincidences

dick·er /díkər/ *vi* haggle *(infml)*

dick·ey /díkee/ *(pl* -eys *or* -ies**), dick·y** *(pl* -ies**), dick·ie** *n* a false shirt front or neck

Dick·in·son /díkinssən/, **Emily** (1830–86) US poet

di·cot·y·le·don /dī kott'l eéd'n/ *n* a plant belonging to the group that has two leaves in the seed —**di·cot·y·le·don·ous** *adj*

dic·ta plural of **dictum**

Dic·ta·phone /díktə fòn/ *tdmk* a trademark for a small hand-held tape recorder used for dictation

dic·tate /dík tàyt, dik táyt/ *v* (**-tat·ed, -tat·ing**) 1 *vti* speak aloud words that are to be written down 2 *vti* give orders or make decisions authoritatively 3 *vt* control or influence ○ *action dictated by the weather conditions* ■ *n* 1 a command given 2 a governing principle

dic·ta·tion /dik táysh'n/ *n* 1 the act of speaking aloud words that are written down or of writing down what is said 2 words written down

dic·ta·tor /dík tàytər/ *n* 1 an absolute ruler 2 an autocratic or domineering person

dic·ta·to·ri·al /dìktə táwree əl/ *adj* 1 tending to give orders or make decisions for others 2 of dictators —**dic·ta·to·ri·al·ly** *adv*

dic·ta·tor·ship /dik táytər shìp/ *n* 1 a dictator's power or rule 2 government by a dictator 3 a country ruled by a dictator

dic·tion /díksh'n/ *n* 1 clarity of speech 2 the choice of words to fit a specific context —**dic·tion·al** *adj*

⚡**dic·tion·ar·y** /díkshə nèrree/ *(pl* -ies**)** *n* 1 a book giving meanings or translations of words 2 an alphabetical list of computer codes used in a program 3 a word-processing tool for checking correct spelling

dic·tum /díktəm/ *(pl* -tums *or* -ta /-tə/**)** *n* a pronouncement *(fml)*

dic·y *adj* = dicey

did past tense of **do**[1]

di·dac·tic /dī dáktik/ *adj* 1 containing a moral or political message 2 fond of instructing or advising others —**di·dac·ti·cal·ly** *adv*

did·dle[1] /dĭdd'l/ (**-dled, -dling**) *vt* cheat somebody *(slang)* —**did·dler** *n*

did·dle[2] /dĭdd'l/ (**-dled, -dling**) *vi (slang)* **1** touch or play with something repeatedly **2** spend time idly

~~dident~~ incorrect spelling of **didn't**

did·ger·i·doo /dĭjjaree dōō/ (*pl* **-doos**), **did·jer·i·doo** *n* an Aboriginal wind instrument with a long thick wooden pipe

did·n't /dĭd'nt/ *contr* did not

Di·do /dī'dō/ *n* in Roman mythology, queen of Carthage

Did·rik·son, Babe /dĭdrikssən/ ⊅ **Zaharias**

die[1] /dī/ (**died, dy·ing, dies**) *v* **1** *vi* stop living **2** *vi* stop existing, especially gradually ○ *feelings I thought had died long ago* **3** *vi* stop functioning ○ *The engine suddenly died.* **4** *vt* die in a particular way ○ *died a gruesome death* **5** *vi* be very eager for something ○ *dying to see them* ◇ **die hard** give up only after sustained resistance ◇ **to die for** highly desirable

---

SPELLCHECK Do not confuse the spelling of **die** and **dye** ("cause to change color," "a coloring agent"), which sound similar.

□ **die away** *vi* grow faint
□ **die down** *vi* fade in strength or intensity
□ **die off** *vi* die one by one
□ **die out** *vi* **1** cease gradually to exist **2** disappear gradually

die[2] /dī/ *n* **1** (*pl* **dice** /dīss/) a numbered cube used in games **2** a cutting, stamping, or pressing tool **3** a molding tool

die·back /dī' băk/ *n* the gradual death of a plant

Die·fen·ba·ker /deéfən bàykər/, **John George** (1895–1979) prime minister of Canada (1957–63)

~~diegn~~ incorrect spelling of **deign**

die·hard /dī' hàard/ *adj* stubbornly resistant to change —**die·hard** *n* —**die·hard·ism** *n*

~~dieing~~ incorrect spelling of **dying**

di·er·e·sis /dī érrssiss/ (*pl* **-ses** /-seèz/), **di·aer·e·sis** (*pl* **-ses**) *n* the mark (¨) added above a vowel to show that it is pronounced as a separate syllable or has a particular pronunciation

die·sel /deèz'l, deèss'l/ *n* **1** *also* **die·sel en·gine** an engine that heats diesel fuel by compression alone **2** a vehicle with a diesel engine **3** *also* **die·sel fuel** a thick oily fuel distilled from petroleum

di·et[1] /dī' ət/ *n* **1** what a person or animal eats **2** a controlled intake of food ■ *adj* designed or promoted for weight loss ■ *vi* eat less in order to lose weight —**di·e·tar·y** *adj* —**di·et·er** *n*

di·et[2] /dī' ət/ *n* a legislative assembly in some countries

di·e·tet·ic /dī ə téttik/ *adj* **1** of people's diets **2** prepared with special diets in mind

di·e·tet·ics /dī ə téttiks/ *n* the study of food and nutrition (+ *sing verb*)

~~dieties~~ incorrect spelling of **deities**

di·e·ti·tian /dī ə tísh'n/, **di·e·ti·cian** *n* a nutrition specialist

~~diferent~~ incorrect spelling of **different**

dif·fer /dĭffər/ *vi* **1** be unlike **2** disagree ◊ See note at **disagree**

dif·fer·ence /dĭffərənss, dĭffrənss/ *n* **1** the state of being unlike somebody or something **2** a distinguishing feature **3** a significant change **4** a disagreement **5** an answer to a subtraction equation

dif·fer·ent /dĭffərənt, dĭffrənt/ *adj* **1** unlike somebody or something else **2** distinct —**dif·fer·ent·ly** *adv*

dif·fer·en·tial /dĭffə rénshəl/ *n* a difference between points on a scale ■ *adj* of differences

dif·fer·en·ti·ate /dĭffə rénshee àyt/ (**-at·ed, -at·ing**) *vti* see or establish differences between things —**dif·fer·en·ti·a·ble** *adj* —**dif·fer·en·ti·a·tion** /dĭffə renshee áysh'n/ *n*

dif·fi·cult /dĭffikəlt/ *adj* **1** hard to do, understand, or deal with **2** full of problems **3** hard to please or persuade —**dif·fi·cult·ness** *n* ◊ See note at **hard**

dif·fi·cul·ty /dĭffikəltee/ *n* (*pl* **-ties**) **1** the quality of being difficult **2** something difficult **3** effort ■ **difficulties** *npl* **1** trouble **2** objections

dif·fi·dent /dĭffid'nt/ *adj* **1** lacking self-confidence **2** reserved or restrained —**dif·fi·dence** *n* —**dif·fi·dent·ly** *adv*

dif·frac·tion /di frăksh'n/ *n* the bending or spreading out of waves, e.g., of light or sound

~~diffrent~~ incorrect spelling of **different**

dif·fuse[1] /di fyóoz/ (**-fused, -fus·ing**) *vti* **1** spread through something **2** scatter or become scattered **3** undergo or subject to diffusion —**dif·fus·i·ble** *adj* ◊ See note at **defuse**

dif·fuse[2] /di fyóoss/ *adj* **1** spread throughout an area **2** lacking organization and conciseness —**dif·fuse·ly** *adv* —**dif·fuse·ness** *n* ◊ See note at **wordy**

dif·fu·sion /də fyóozh'n/ *n* **1** the process or result of diffusing **2** the spread of cultural features **3** the scattering of light as a result of reflection **4** the random movement of atoms, molecules, or ions —**dif·fu·sion·al** *adj*

~~dificult~~ incorrect spelling of **difficult**

dig /dĭg/ (**dug, dig·ging**) *v* **1** *vti* break up or remove earth **2** *vt* create by digging **3** *vti* obtain, uncover, or free by digging **4** *vt* discover by research **5** *vi* search carefully **6** *vti* prod or poke **7** *vt* like or enjoy *(slang dated)* ■ *n* **1** a prod or poke **2** a cutting remark **3** an archeological excavation

□ **dig in** *v* **1** *vi* take up military positions **2** *vi* fight stubbornly **3** *vi* start eating *(infml)*
□ **dig out** *vt* retrieve *(infml)*
□ **dig up** *vt* **1** take out of the ground **2** find out through investigation *(infml)*

⚡ **di·ge·ra·ti** /díjjə ráátee/ *npl* computer experts (*infml*)

di·gest *vt* /dī jést, di-/ **1** process food in the body **2** absorb something mentally **3** organize something systematically to extract essential information **4** abridge something ▪ *n* /dī jèst/ **1** a summary **2** a collection of abridged pieces of writing

di·gest·i·ble /dī jéstəb'l, di-/ *adj* easily digested —**di·gest·i·bil·i·ty** /dī jèstə bíllətee, di-/ *n*

di·ges·tion /dī jéschən, di-/ *n* **1** the processing of food in the body **2** the ability to digest food **3** the ability to absorb ideas —**di·ges·tion·al** *adj*

di·ges·tive /dī jéstiv, di-/ *adj* of digestion ▪ *n* something that aids digestion

dig·ger /díggər/ *n* **1** somebody or something that digs **2** a tool or machine for digging

dig·gings /díggingz/ *n* a place where something is mined **2** material excavated

dig·it /díjjit/ *n* **1** a finger or toe **2** a numeral

⚡ **dig·i·tal** /díjjit'l/ *adj* **1** like a finger or toe **2** done with or operated by the fingers or toes **3** representing data as numbers **4** representing sound or light waves as numbers —**dig·i·tal·ly** *adv*

⚡ **dig·i·tal au·di·o·tape** *n* tape used for recording sound digitally

⚡ **dig·i·tal cash** *n* credits used to buy things online

⚡ **dig·i·tal coins** *npl* small denominations of online currency

⚡ **dig·i·tal com·put·er** *n* a computer processing data in binary form

⚡ **dig·i·tal di·vide** *n* the inequality of access to information technology

⚡ **dig·i·tal en·cryp·tion stan·dard** *n* a standard for data encryption

⚡ **dig·i·tal im·age·ry, dig·i·tal im·ag·ing** *n* the transformation of a digital image by a computer

⚡ **dig·i·tal sig·na·ture** *n* a digital signal that identifies a user

⚡ **Dig·i·tal Sub·scrib·er Line** *n* full form of DSL

dig·i·tal tel·e·vi·sion *n* a television system or set using digital transmission

⚡ **dig·i·tal vid·e·o disk, dig·i·tal ver·sa·tile disk** *n* full form of DVD

⚡ **dig·i·tize** /díjjī tīz/ (-tized, -tiz·ing *or* -tal·iz·ing) *vt* convert to digital form —**dig·i·ti·za·tion** /díjjiti záysh'n/ *n* —**dig·i·tiz·er** *n*

dig·ni·fied /dígnə fīd/ *adj* calm and serious

dig·ni·fy /dígnə fī/ (-fied, -fies) *vt* **1** give distinction to **2** give undeserved attention to

dig·ni·tar·y /dígnə tèrree/ (*pl* -ies) *n* a person of high rank

dig·ni·ty /dígnətee/ *n* **1** pride and self-respect **2** seriousness in behavior **3** worthiness **4** due respect

di·gress /dī gréss/ *vi* move off a central topic —**di·gres·sion** *n*

Di·jon /dee zhóN/ capital of Côte d'Or De-partment, east central France. Pop. 149,867 (1999).

dike /dīk/, **dyke** *n* **1** an embankment built to prevent floods **2** a barrier **3** a ditch —**dike** *vt*

dik·tat /dik táat/ *n* **1** a dictatorial statement **2** a harsh settlement imposed on a defeated enemy

di·lap·i·dat·ed /di láppi dàytəd/ *adj* in disrepair —**di·lap·i·da·tion** /di làppə dáysh'n/ *n*

di·late /dī láyt, dī-, dī láyt/ (-lat·ed, -lat·ing) *v* **1** *vti* become or make larger or wider **2** *vi* talk or write at length —**di·la·ta·tion** /dílə táysh'n, dī-/ *n* —**di·la·tion** /dī láysh'n, di-/ *n*

di·la·to·ry /dílla tàwree/ *adj* **1** slow to do something **2** intended to delay

dil·do /díldō/ (*pl* -dos), **dil·doe** (*pl* -does) *n* a sexual aid shaped like a penis

~~dilema~~ incorrect spelling of **dilemma**

di·lem·ma /di lémmə/ *n* a situation with unsatisfactory choices

dil·et·tante /díllə táant/ (*pl* -tantes *or* -tan·ti /-táantee/) *n* somebody whose interest is only superficial —**dil·et·tan·te** *adj* —**dil·et·tan·tism** *n*

dil·i·gent /díllajənt/ *adj* persistent and hardworking —**dil·i·gence** *n* —**dil·i·gent·ly** *adv*

dill *n* **1** the feathery leaves or the seeds of an aromatic plant. Use: flavoring, garnish. **2** the plant that produces dill

dill pick·le *n* a pickled cucumber flavored with dill

dil·ly /díllee/ (*pl* -lies) *n* a remarkable person or thing (*slang*)

dil·ly-dal·ly /díllee dàllee/ (dil·ly-dal·lied, dil·ly-dal·lies) *vi* waste time in indecision

di·lute /dī lóot, di-/ *v* (-lut·ed, -lut·ing) **1** *vt* make thinner or weaker by adding water or another liquid **2** *vti* lessen in the strength or effect ▪ *adj* thinned by liquid —**di·lute·ness** *n* —**di·lu·tion** *n* —**di·lu·tive** *adj*

dim *adj* (dim·mer, dim·mest) **1** not well lit **2** producing little light **3** dull in color **4** not clearly visible **5** not easy to perceive or understand **6** not clearly remembered **7** not seeing clearly **8** unlikely to be successful **9** regarded as unintelligent (*infml insult*) ▪ *v* (dimmed, dim·ming) **1** *vti* make or become dim **2** *vt* switch headlights to low beams ▪ **dims** *npl* low beams —**dim·ly** *adv* —**dim·ness** *n*

Di·Mag·gio /də máazhee ṑ, də májjee ṑ/, **Joe** (1914–99) US baseball player

dime *n* a coin worth ten cents

> **ORIGIN Dime** originally meant "tenth part, tithe." It was adopted from French in this sense in the 14C. The use of a coin worth ten cents dates from the late 18C.

dime nov·el *n* a cheap melodramatic novel

di·men·sion /di ménshən, dī-/ *n* **1** a measurement of the extent of something in one or more directions **2** an aspect or feature

3 a coordinate used with others to locate something in space and time ■ **di·men·sions** *npl* size or scope ■ *vt* **1** make to required dimensions **2** indicate the dimensions of —**di·men·sion·al** *adj* —**di·men·sion·al·ly** *adv*

dime store *n* a store selling inexpensive goods

dime-store *adj* **1** inexpensive **2** second-rate

di·min·ish /di mínnish/ *vti* **1** make or become smaller **2** appear or cause to appear smaller —**di·min·ished** *adj* —**di·min·ish·ing·ly** *adv* —**di·min·ish·ment** *n*

di·min·ished re·spon·si·bil·i·ty *n* the legal defense that a psychiatric disorder partially reduces culpability for a crime

di·min·u·en·do /di mìnnyoo éndō/ *adv* = decrescendo ■ *n* (*pl* **-dos**) = decrescendo ■ **di·min·u·en·do** *adj*

dim·i·nu·tion /dímmə nóosh'n/ *n* reduction

di·min·u·tive /di mínnyətiv/ *adj* **1** very small **2** describes a word or suffix indicating smallness or fondness —**di·min·u·tive** *n* —**di·min·u·tive·ly** *adv* —**di·min·u·tive·ness** *n*

⚡**DIMM** /dim/ *n* a module adding RAM to a computer. Full form **dual in-line memory module**

dim·mer /dímmər/ *n* **1** *also* **dim·mer switch** a device for varying a light's brightness **2** a switch for dimming car headlights ■ **dim·mers** *npl* low headlight beams

dim·ple /dímpəl/ *n* an indented area in the skin or another surface ■ *v* (**-pled, -pling**) **1** *vi* form a dimple **2** *vt* produce dimples in —**dim·ply** *adj*

dim sum /dím sóom/ *n* dumplings and other Chinese dishes served in small portions as part of a meal

dim·wit /dím wit/ *n* a person regarded as unintelligent (*infml insult*) —**dim·wit·ted** *adj*

din *n* a loud persistent noise ■ *v* (**dinned, din·ning**) **1** *vi* make a loud noise **2** *vt* fix something in somebody's mind through repetition

di·nar /di naár, dée naár/ *n* a currency unit in some North African, SW Asian, and SE European countries

Di·nar·ic Alps /di nèrrik-/ range of the Eastern Alps, extending from NE Italy southeastward along the Adriatic coast of the Balkan Peninsula. Highest peak Bobotov Kuk 8,274 ft./2,522 m.

dine (**dined, din·ing**) *v* **1** *vi* eat dinner **2** *vi* eat a meal **3** *vt* provide dinner for (*infml*)

din·er /dínər/ *n* **1** a person who eats **2** an inexpensive restaurant

Di·nes·en /déenəss'n/, **Isak** (1885–1962) Danish writer

di·nette /di nét/ *n* **1** a small dining area in or near a kitchen **2** a kitchen table and chairs

ding[1] /vti/ ring with a high-pitched sound —**ding** *n*

ding[2] (*infml*) *vt* US, Can, Aus make a dent in ■ *n* US, Can, Aus a dent

ding-a-ling *n* a tinkle of a bell

ding·bat /díng bàt/ *n* **1** a printer's symbol **2** an object used as a missile

ding-dong *n* the sound of a bell

din·ghy /díngee/ (*pl* **-ghies**) *n* a small boat

din·go /díng gō/ (*pl* **-goes**) *n* an Australian wild dog

din·gy /dínjee/ (**-gi·er, -gi·est**) *adj* **1** dirty or faded **2** shabby —**din·gi·ly** *adv* —**din·gi·ness** *n*

din·ing room *n* a room where meals are served

din·ky /díngkee/ (**-ki·er, -ki·est**) *adj* small or unimportant (*infml*)

din·ner /dínnər/ *n* **1** a main meal **2** a banquet

din·ner jack·et *n* a tuxedo

din·ner par·ty *n* a party at which a dinner is served

din·ner the·a·ter *n* a restaurant that also presents plays

din·ner·time /dínnər tìm/ *n* the time when dinner is eaten

din·ner·ware /dínnər wàir/ *n* plates and bowls used to serve and eat a meal

di·no·saur /dínə sàwr/ *n* **1** an extinct reptile that lived in the Mesozoic era **2** an outmoded person or thing —**di·no·sau·ri·an** /dìnə sáwree ən/ *adj*

ORIGIN The scientific name of the **dinosaur** was formed in modern Latin in the mid-19C from Greek words that mean literally "terrible lizard."

dint *n* a dent

di·o·cese /dí əssiss, -ə seèz/ *n* all the churches or the district under a bishop's authority —**di·oc·e·san** /dī óssəss'n/ *adj*

di·ode /dí ōd/ *n* a device that converts alternating electrical current to direct current

Di·og·e·nes /dī ójjə neèz/ (412?–323 BC) Greek philosopher

Di·o·ny·sus /dí ə níssəss/ *n* in Greek mythology, Bacchus

di·o·ram·a /dí ə ráamə, -rámmə/ *n* a miniature three-dimensional replica of a scene —**di·o·ram·ic** /-rámmik/ *adj*

di·ox·ide /dī ók sìd/ *n* a chemical compound with two oxygen atoms

di·ox·in /dī óksin/ *n* any derivative of dibenzo-p-dioxin, a carcinogen and toxic environmental pollutant

dip *v* (**dipped, dip·ping**) **1** *vt* put something briefly in liquid **2** *vi* suddenly move downward ○ *The plane dipped and then flew on.* **3** *vt* lower something ○ *The horse dipped its head.* **4** *vi* become less ○ *Prices dipped sharply.* **5** *vti* put your hand into something in order to remove something **6** *vt* disinfect an animal by total immersion **7** *vi* slope downward ○ *The road dipped toward the river.* ■ *n* **1** an act or instance of dipping **2** a short swim **3** a hollow in the ground **4** a mixture for dipping something into **5** a person regarded as unintelligent *(slang insult)*

□ **dip into** *vt* **1** read only parts of a book **2** use money from savings

diph·the·ri·a /dif théeree ə, díp-/ *n* an infectious bacterial disease that attacks the membranes of the throat and releases a dangerous toxin —**diph·the·ri·al** *adj* —**diph·the·rit·ic** /dífthə ríttik, díptha-/ *adj*

diph·thong /díf tháwng, díp-/ *n* **1** a speech sound consisting of two vowels pronounced as one syllable **2** a character formed by joining two letters —**diph·thon·gal** /dif tháwng g'l, dip-/ *adj*

di·plo·ma /di plṓmə/ *n* **1** an educational certificate **2** an official paper describing rights and privileges

ORIGIN Diploma came via Latin from a Greek word that means literally "folded paper." Because official papers were often folded, the Latin word came to mean "official document, state paper." This sense is recorded in English alongside "document conferring an honor or privilege" from the mid-17C. By the early 18C it referred also to an educational certificate.

di·plo·ma·cy /di plṓmassee/ *n* **1** international relations **2** skill in international dealings **3** tact

dip·lo·mat /dípplə màt/ *n* **1** a government representative abroad **2** a tactful person

dip·lo·mat·ic /dípplə máttik/ *adj* **1** involving diplomacy **2** tactful —**dip·lo·mat·i·cal·ly** *adv*

dip·lo·mat·ic bag *n* a bag in which diplomats' mail is sent

dip·lo·mat·ic corps *n* all the foreign diplomats of a country

dip·lo·mat·ic im·mu·ni·ty *n* a diplomat's freedom from taxation, customs inspections, and other legal restraints

di·plo·ma·tist /di plṓmatist/ *n* a professional diplomat

dip·per /díppər/ *n* **1** a scoop or ladle **2** a small water bird

dip·so·ma·ni·ac /dípsə máynee àk/ *n* an alcoholic *(dated)*

dip·stick /díp stik/ *n* a measuring rod for liquid

~~diptheria~~ incorrect spelling of **diphtheria**

~~dipthong~~ incorrect spelling of **diphthong**

dip·tych /díptik/ *n* a painting consisting of two parts joined together

dire (dir·er, dir·est) *adj* **1** very bad **2** threatening disaster —**dire·ly** *adv* —**dire·ness** *n*

di·rect /di rékt, dī-/ *v* **1** *vt* supervise or manage something **2** *vt* instruct somebody *(fml)* **3** *vt* focus attention or concentrate activities **4** *vt* aim or address something **5** *vt* tell somebody how to get somewhere **6** *vti* provide instructions or guidance to actors or the makers of a movie or play **7** *vt* conduct music or an orchestra ■ *adj* **1** not stopping or deviating o *a direct flight* **2** without intervention o *a direct contact* **3** straightforward

o *a direct appeal to our emotions* **4** precise or exact o *a direct quotation* **5** related in an unbroken line o *a direct descendant* **6** complete or utter o *in direct contradiction to our conclusions* ■ *adv* **1** straight, without diversion **2** with nothing or nobody intervening —**di·rect·ness** *n*

di·rect ac·tion *n* strikes or boycotts intended to influence a government or employer at first hand

di·rect cur·rent *n* electrical current that flows in only one direction

di·rect deb·it *n* payment of a creditor from a bank account by prior arrangement

di·rect dis·course *n* the writing of the exact words used in speech in quotation marks

di·rec·tion /di rékshən, dī-/ *n* **1** the management or supervision of something **2** the way in which something moves, travels, or develops o *takes a new direction* **3** the art or practice of directing a movie or play **4** a sense of purpose **5** an instruction in music ■ **di·rec·tions** *npl* instructions —**di·rec·tion·less** *adj*

di·rec·tion·al /di rékshən'l, dī-/ *adj* **1** of direction **2** more efficient in one direction o *a directional antenna* **3** indicating a trend —**di·rec·tion·al·i·ty** /di rèkshə nállətee, dī-/ *n*

di·rec·tive /di réktiv, dī-/ *n* an order or official instruction ■ *adj* **1** providing guidance **2** showing direction

di·rect·ly /di réktlee, dī-/ *adv* **1** straight, with no deviations **2** with nothing or nobody intervening **3** completely **4** clearly **5** without delay *(fml)*

di·rect mail *n* advertising by mail addressed to individual customers

di·rect mar·ket·ing, di·rect sell·ing *n* a way of selling in which a company deals with individual customers, e.g., through mail order catalogs

di·rect ob·ject *n* a word or phrase representing the person or thing affected directly by the action of the verb in a sentence

di·rec·tor /di réktər, dī-/ *n* **1** a manager of an organized group or activity **2** a member of the board that runs a business **3** somebody who directs a movie or play —**di·rec·to·ri·al** /di rèk táwree əl, dī-/ *adj* —**di·rec·tor·ship** *n*

di·rec·tor·ate /di réktərət, dī-/ *n* a group of directors, e.g., in a business or a government

ϟ **di·rec·to·ry** /di réktəree, dī-/ *(pl* **-ries)** *n* **1** a book listing names, addresses, and telephone numbers **2** an index of computer files

di·rec·to·ry as·sis·tance *n* a telephone company information service that provides telephone numbers

di·rect sell·ing *n* MARKETING = **direct marketing**

di·rect tax *n* a tax on income

dirge *n* **1** a funeral hymn **2** a piece of mournful music

ORIGIN Dirge is a contraction of Latin *dirige*

"guide, direct." *Dirige, Domine, Deus meus,
in conspectu tuo viam meam* "Direct, Lord,
my God, my way in thy sight" (Psalm 5:8)
was formerly part of the funeral service in the
Roman Catholic Church.

dir·ham /də rám, dər hám/ *n* a unit of currency
in some North African and Middle Eastern
countries

dir·i·gi·ble /dírrijəb'l, di ríjjəb'l/ *n* an airship ■
adj steerable

dirk *n* a dagger with a long straight handle

dirn·dl /dúrnd'l/, **dirn·dl skirt** *n* a full skirt
gathered at the waist

dirt *n* **1** a substance that soils or stains **2** earth,
soil, or mud **3** scandalous information
about somebody or something

dirt bike *n* an off-road motorcycle

dirt-cheap *adj, adv* very cheap (*infml*)

dirt farm·er *n* a subsistence farmer —**dirt
farm·ing** *n*

dirt-poor *adj* very poor

dirt·y /dúrtee/ *adj* (-i·er, -i·est) **1** soiled or
stained **2** causing pollution o *a dirty engine*
3 making somebody grimy o *a dirty job*
4 not honest or legal **5** malicious **6** sexually
suggestive **7** expressing anger o *a dirty look*
8 despicable (*infml*) o *a dirty trick* **9** lacking
brightness or clarity **10** stormy o *dirty
weather* ■ *adv* (-i·er, -i·est) **1** unfairly **2** suggestively ■ *vti* (-ied, -ies) make or become
dirty —**dirt·i·ly** *adv* —**dirt·i·ness** *n*

> SYNONYMS **dirty, filthy, grubby, grimy,
> soiled, squalid, unclean** CORE MEANING: not
> clean

dirt·y bomb *n* a bomb containing radioactive
nuclear waste dispersed by means of conventional explosives

dis /diss/ (**dissed, diss·ing, diss·es**), **diss** *vt*
treat disrespectfully (*slang*)

Dis /diss/ *n* **1** in Roman mythology, Pluto **2** in
Roman mythology, the underworld. Greek
equivalent **Hades**

dis- *prefix* **1** undo, do the opposite o *disapprove* **2** the opposite or absence of
o *discourtesy* **3** deprive of, remove from
o *dishonor* **4** not o *disobedient*

dis·a·bil·i·ty /dissə bíllətee/ (*pl* -ties) *n* **1** a
condition that restricts somebody's ability
to perform some or all of the tasks of daily
life **2** payment to persons with a disability
who cannot work **3** a factor that prevents
or disqualifies somebody from doing
something

dis·a·ble /diss áyb'l/ (-**bled, -bling**) *vt* **1** restrict
somebody in everyday activities **2** stop
something from functioning —**dis·a·ble·
ment** *n*

dis·a·bled /diss áyb'ld/ *adj* **1** affected by a
disability **2** unable to operate or function
■ *npl* physically challenged people

> USAGE Though *physically challenged* or
> *people with disabilities* are preferred over the
> adjectival and noun forms of **disabled**, the

adjective **disabled** has a long history of use
by those so affected, as in the name of the
organization *Disabled American Veterans*.

dis·a·buse /dissə byo͞oz/ (-**bused, -bus·ing**) *vt*
make somebody realize that something is
untrue

dis·ad·van·tage /dissəd vántij/ *n* **1** a factor
that makes something less good or valu-
able **2** an unfavorable situation ■ *vt*
(-**taged, -tag·ing**) put in an unfavorable situation

dis·ad·van·taged /dissəd vántijd/ *adj* **1** in a
worse position than other people **2** in an
unfair position competitively

dis·ad·van·ta·geous /diss àdvən táyjəss, diss
advən táyjəss/ *adj* unhelpful or unfavorable
—**dis·ad·van·ta·geous·ly** *adv* —**dis·ad·van·
ta·geous·ness** *n*

dis·a·gree /dissə gree/ *vi* **1** not agree **2** not
correspond **3** have a bad effect

> SYNONYMS **disagree, differ, argue, dispute,
> take issue with, contradict, agree to differ,
> be at odds** CORE MEANING: have or express a
> difference of opinion with somebody

dis·a·gree·a·ble /dissə gree əb'l/ *adj* **1** unpleasant **2** rude or quarrelsome
—**dis·a·gree·a·ble·ness** *n* —**dis·a·gree·
a·bly** *adv*

dis·a·gree·ment /dissə greemənt/ *n* **1** failure
to agree **2** a minor argument

dis·al·low /dissə lów/ *vt* **1** reject something
(*fml*) **2** cancel something previously
allowed —**dis·al·low·ance** *n*

~~**disallusion**~~ incorrect spelling of **disillusion**

dis·am·big·u·ate /diss am bíggyoo àyt/ (-**at·ed,
-at·ing**) *vt* make unambiguous —**dis·am·
big·u·a·tion** /diss am bíggyoo áysh'n/ *n*

~~**disapear**~~ incorrect spelling of **disappear**
~~**disapoint**~~ incorrect spelling of **disappoint**

dis·ap·pear /dissə peer/ *vi* **1** vanish from sight
2 no longer be in a place **3** cease to exist
—**dis·ap·pear·ance** *n*

dis·ap·point /dissə póynt/ *v* **1** *vi* be less good
than expected **2** *vt* fail somebody by not
doing as expected —**dis·ap·point·ed** *adj*
—**dis·ap·point·ed·ly** *adv* —**dis·ap·point·ing**
adj —**dis·ap·point·ing·ly** *adv*

dis·ap·point·ment /dissə póyntmənt/ *n* **1** the
feeling of being let down **2** something disappointing

dis·ap·pro·ba·tion /diss àpprə báysh'n/ *n* condemnation (*fml*)

dis·ap·prov·al /dissə pro͞ov'l/ *n* an attitude of
dislike or condemnation

dis·ap·prove /dissə pro͞ov/ (-**proved, -prov·ing**)
v **1** *vi* judge somebody or something nega-
tively **2** *vt* refuse to sanction (*fml*)
—**dis·ap·prov·ing** *adj* —**dis·ap·prov·ing·ly**
adv

> SYNONYMS **disapprove, frown on, object,**

criticize, condemn, deplore, denounce, censure CORE MEANING: have an unfavorable opinion of

dis·arm /diss aárm/ v 1 vti give up or force to give up weapons 2 vt defuse a bomb 3 vt make somebody feel less hostile —**dis·arm·ing** adj —**dis·arm·ing·ly** adv

dis·ar·ma·ment /diss aárməmənt/ n 1 a reduction in arms 2 the state of having given up arms

dis·ar·range /dissə ráynj/ (-ranged, -rang·ing) vt make untidy —**dis·ar·range·ment** n

dis·ar·ray /dissə ráy/ n 1 a disorganized state 2 untidiness ■ vt 1 make disorganized 2 make somebody feel less hostile (archaic)

dis·as·sem·ble /dissə sémb'l/ (-bled, -bling) vt take apart —**dis·as·sem·bly** n

dis·as·so·ci·ate /dissə sóshee àyt/ (-at·ed, -at·ing) v 1 vt end somebody's association with something 2 vr distance yourself from somebody or something

dis·as·ter /di zástər/ n a very damaging or destructive event

ORIGIN Disasters get their name from astrology. The word was adopted in the late 16C from an Italian word that means literally "ill-starred." In astrology disasters are attributed to the adverse influence of the stars. The Italian word derives from the Latin for "star," the source of astrology itself, as well as astral, astronomy, and other words beginning astro-.

dis·as·ter ar·e·a n a place that is in a state of emergency after a natural disaster

dis·as·ter mov·ie n a movie about a disastrous event

~~disasterous~~ incorrect spelling of **disastrous**

dis·as·trous /di zástrəss/ adj 1 having very damaging or destructive results 2 completely unsuccessful —**dis·as·trous·ly** adv —**dis·as·trous·ness** n

~~disatisfied~~ incorrect spelling of **dissatisfied**

dis·a·vow /dissə vów/ vt deny any knowledge of or association with —**dis·a·vow·al** n —**dis·a·vow·ed·ly** /-ədlee/ adv

dis·band /diss bánd/ vti break up as a group, or break up a group —**dis·band·ment** n

dis·bar /diss baár/ (-barred, -bar·ring) vt bar an attorney from practicing law —**dis·bar·ment** n

dis·be·lief /diss bi leéf/ n a feeling of not believing

dis·be·lieve /diss bi leév/ (-lieved, -liev·ing) v 1 vt not believe 2 vi have no religious faith —**dis·be·liev·er** n —**dis·be·liev·ing** adj —**dis·be·liev·ing·ly** adv

dis·burse /diss búrss/ (-bursed, -burs·ing) vt pay out —**dis·burse·ment** n

SPELLCHECK Do not confuse the spelling of **disburse** and **disperse** ("scatter"), which sound similar.

disc n 1 a disk 2 a phonograph record (infml dated)

dis·card vt /diss kaárd/ 1 throw something away 2 in card games, reject a card from a hand ■ n /diss kaárd/ 1 the act of discarding a playing card 2 something discarded

dis·cern /di súrn/ vt 1 see or notice something that is not obvious 2 understand something —**dis·cern·i·ble** adj —**dis·cern·i·bly** adv —**dis·cern·ment** n

dis·cern·ing /di súrning/ adj showing good judgment and taste —**dis·cern·ing·ly** adv

dis·charge v /diss chaárj/ (-charged, -charg·ing) 1 vti emit or dispose of a liquid or gas 2 vt dismiss or release somebody from something such as a hospital or other institution, employment, or the armed forces 3 vt carry out a duty (fml) 4 vt pay a debt (fml) 5 vti shoot a bullet, or be shot from a gun (fml) 6 vti offload a cargo or empty something of its contents 7 vti lose an electric charge 8 vti drain electricity from a device, or be drained ■ n /diss chaárj/ 1 an act of discharging somebody 2 a flow of liquid, especially mucus, from the body 3 emission or rate of emission 4 the performance of a duty (fml) 5 the payment of a debt (fml) 6 the firing of a gun (fml) 7 a continuous flow of electricity through the air 8 the discharging of cargo or contents

dis·ci·ple /di síp'l/ n 1 a follower of a person or idea 2 also **Dis·ci·ple** one of the 12 original followers of Jesus Christ —**dis·ci·ple·ship** n

dis·ci·pli·nar·i·an /dissəplə náiree ən/ n an enforcer of discipline

dis·ci·pli·nar·y /dissəplə nèrree/ adj 1 of enforcement and punishment 2 of an academic subject

dis·ci·pline /dissəplin/ n 1 the act of making people obey rules 2 a controlled and orderly state, especially among school students 3 calm controlled behavior 4 a field of activity or subject of study 5 punishment ■ v (-plined, -plin·ing) 1 vr make yourself do something regularly 2 vt punish somebody 3 vt teach obedience or order to somebody —**dis·ci·plined** adj

disc jock·ey n a DJ

dis·claim /diss kláym/ vt 1 deny a connection with 2 deny the validity of

dis·claim·er /diss kláymər/ n 1 a refusal to accept responsibility 2 a statement renouncing a legal right

dis·close /diss klóz/ (-closed, -clos·ing) vt 1 tell something previously secret 2 show something previously covered (fml) —**dis·clos·a·ble** adj

dis·clo·sure /diss klózhər/ n the revealing of information that was previously secret

dis·co /dískō/ (pl -cos) n 1 a club or party with dancing to pop music 2 pop music with a steady beat for dancing to 3 a style of dancing to disco music

dis·cog·ra·phy /diss kógrəfee/ (pl -phies) n a list of musical recordings —**dis·cog·ra·pher** n —**dis·co·graph·ic** /dískə gráffik/ adj

dis·col·or /diss kúllar/ *vti* make something take on a faded, darkened, or dirty appearance —**dis·col·or·a·tion** /diss kùllə ráysh'n/ *n* —**dis·col·ored** *adj*

dis·com·fit /diss kúmfit/ *vt (fml)* **1** make somebody unsettled or confused **2** thwart plans —**dís·com·fi·ture** /diss kúmfichər/ *n*

dis·com·fort /diss kúmfərt/ *n* **1** a state of physical unease **2** embarrassment **3** a cause of unease ■ *vt* make uncomfortable *(fml)* —**dis·com·fort·ing** *adj*

dis·com·po·sure /dìskəm pốzhər/ *n* loss of mental or physical composure —**dis·com·pose** *vt*

dis·con·cert /dìskən súrt/ *vt* make somebody feel uneasy —**dis·con·cert·ed** *adj* —**dis·con·cert·ing** *adj*

dis·con·nect /dìskə nékt/ *v* **1** *vti* detach an appliance from a power source **2** *vt* shut off the supply of a public utility **3** *vt* break a telephone connection between two people **4** *vt* detach one part from another —**dis·con·nec·tion** *n*

dis·con·nect·ed /dìskə néktəd/ *adj* lacking any logical connection —**dis·con·nect·ed·ly** *adv* —**dis·con·nect·ed·ness** *n*

dis·con·so·late /diss kónsələt/ *adj* extremely sad and disappointed —**dis·con·so·late·ly** *adv*

dis·con·tent /dìskən tént/ *n* dissatisfied unhappiness

dis·con·tent·ed /dìskən téntəd/ *adj* dissatisfied and unhappy about something —**dis·con·tent·ed·ly** *adv* —**dis·con·tent·ed·ness** *n*

dis·con·tin·ue /dìskən tínnyoo/ (-ued, -u·ing) *v* **1** *vti* stop doing something **2** *vt* stop manufacturing a product —**dis·con·tin·u·ance** *n* —**dis·con·tin·u·a·tion** /dìskən tínyoo áysh'n/ *n* —**dis·con·tin·ued** *adj*

dis·con·ti·nu·i·ty /diss kòntə noŏ ətee/ (*pl* -ties) *n* a break in an otherwise continuous process

dis·con·tin·u·ous /dìskən tínnyoo əss/ *adj* having gaps or breaks

dis·cord /diss káwrd/ *n* **1** a lack of agreement **2** an inharmonious combination of musical sounds

dis·cor·dant /diss káwrd'nt/ *adj* **1** disagreeing **2** lacking in musical harmony —**dis·cor·dance** *n* —**dis·cor·dant·ly** *adv*

dis·co·theque /dískə tèk/ *n* a disco

dis·count *n* /díss kòwnt/ **1** a reduction in the usual price **2** *also* **dis·count rate** the rate at which expected cash returns from a security are converted into its market price **3** the interest deducted from the value of a promissory note before a sale or loan is completed ■ *v* /diss kównt, díss kòwnt/ **1** *vt* reject something as untrue or trivial **2** *vt* reduce a product in price **3** *vti* make a loan at a reduced rate ■ *adj* reduced in price —**dis·count·a·ble** /díss kòwntəb'l, diss kówntəb'l/ *adj*

dis·coun·te·nance /diss kówntənənss/ (-nanced, -nanc·ing) *vt* embarrass *(fml)*

dis·count store, dis·count·er /díss kòwntər, diss kówntər/, **dis·count house** *n* a store selling discounted goods

dis·cour·age /diss kúr ij/ (-aged, -ag·ing) *vt* **1** tend to stop something by making it difficult or unpleasant **2** try to stop somebody from doing something **3** make somebody lose hope or enthusiasm —**dis·cour·age·ment** *n* —**dis·cour·ag·ing** *adj*

dis·course *n* /diss káwrss/ **1** a serious speech or piece of writing **2** a serious conversation **3** the language used in a particular context ○ *political discourse* ■ *vi* /diss káwrs/ (-coursed, -cours·ing) speak or write seriously on a topic

dis·cour·te·sy /diss kúrtəssee/ (*pl* -sies) *n* a rude action or rude behavior —**dis·cour·te·ous** *adj* —**dis·cour·te·ous·ly** *adv*

dis·cov·er /diss kúvvər/ *vt* **1** find something out ○ *soon discovered my mistake* **2** be the first to find or learn something **3** find somebody or something by chance or by searching ○ *was discovered living in Florida* **4** first notice an interest in or a talent for something —**dis·cov·er·er** *n*

dis·cov·er·y /diss kúvvəree/ (*pl* -ies) *n* **1** something learned or found **2** the process of finding out something previously unknown **3** the process of finding somebody or something by chance or by searching

dis·cred·it /diss kréddit/ *vt* **1** damage the reputation or standing of **2** cast doubt on **3** not believe ■ *n* loss of reputation or standing ○ *brought the game into discredit* —**dis·cred·it·a·ble** *adj*

dis·creet /di skréet/ *adj* **1** careful to avoid causing upset or embarrassment to others **2** good at keeping secrets **3** subtle and tasteful ○ *wearing discreet makeup* **4** not ostentatious —**dis·creet·ly** *adv* —**dis·creet·ness** *n*

SPELLCHECK Do not confuse the spelling of **discreet** and **discrete** ("completely separate"), which sound similar.

dis·crep·an·cy /di skréppənsee/ (*pl* -cies) *n* a difference between two things that should match or correspond ○ *found a discrepancy in the figures* —**dis·crep·ant** *adj*

dis·crete /di skréet/ *adj* completely separate —**dis·crete·ly** *adv* —**dis·crete·ness** *n* ◊ See note at **discreet**

dis·cre·tion /di skrésh'n/ *n* **1** the ability to avoid causing upset or embarrassment to others **2** the freedom to decide about something **3** the ability to keep secrets

dis·cre·tion·ar·y /di skrésh'n èrree/ *adj* **1** giving somebody the freedom to decide about something **2** given or refused according to circumstances

dis·crim·i·nate /di skrímmə nàyt/ (-nat·ed, -nat·ing) *v* **1** *vi* treat somebody unfairly because of prejudice 2 *vti* discern differences between things

dis·crim·i·nat·ing /di skrímmə nàyting/ *adj* showing an ability to recognize superior quality —**dis·crim·i·nat·ing·ly** *adv*

dis·crim·i·na·tion /di skrìmmə náysh'n/ *n* 1 unfair treatment of people, e.g., on grounds of race, ethnicity, or gender 2 the ability to recognize superior quality

dis·crim·i·na·to·ry /di skrímmənə tàwree/ *adj* treating somebody unfairly, e.g., on grounds of race, ethnicity, or gender —**dis·crim·i·na·to·ri·ly** *adv*

~~discription~~ incorrect spelling of **description**

dis·cur·sive /di skúrsiv/ *adj* lengthy and containing digressions

dis·cus /dískəss/ (*pl* **-cus·es** or **-ci** /dí skì/) *n* 1 a disk thrown in track-and-field 2 the sporting event of throwing the discus

dis·cuss /di skúss/ *vt* 1 talk about a subject with somebody in order to explore it or reach a decision 2 write or speak about a topic formally —**dis·cus·sant** *n*

dis·cus·sion /di skúsh'n/ *n* 1 a talk among people about a topic or an issue 2 a spoken or written examination of a topic

dis·dain /diss dáyn/ *n* complete lack of respect ■ *vt* regard with contempt —**dis·dain·ful** *adj* —**dis·dain·ful·ly** *adv*

dis·ease /di zeéz/ *n* 1 a condition with pathological symptoms in humans, plants, or animals 2 a disorder with recognizable signs —**dis·eased** *adj*

dis·em·bark /díssəm baárk/ *vi* get off a passenger vehicle —**dis·em·bar·ka·tion** /diss èm baar káysh'n/ *n*

dis·em·bod·ied /díssəm bóddeed/ *adj* lacking physical presence o *the eerie sound of a disembodied voice in the passageway*

dis·em·bow·el /díssəm bówəl/ *vt* remove the internal organs of —**dis·em·bow·el·ment** *n*

dis·em·pow·er /díssəm pówr/ *vt* remove authority or confidence from —**dis·em·pow·er·ment** *n*

dis·en·chant /díssən chánt/ *vt* create dissatisfaction with somebody or something previously regarded as good —**dis·en·chant·ed** *adj* —**dis·en·chant·ment** *n*

dis·en·fran·chise /díssən fránn chìz/ *vt* (**-chised**, **-chis·ing**) *vt* deprive of a right, especially the right to vote —**dis·en·fran·chise·ment** /díssən fránn chìzmənt, -fránchizmənt/ *n*

dis·en·gage /díssən gáyj/ *v* (**-gaged**, **-gag·ing**) *v* 1 *vti* disconnect one thing from another, or become disconnected 2 *vt* detach yourself mentally 3 *vti* end involvement in a war or combat —**dis·en·gage·ment** *n*

dis·en·tan·gle /díssən táng g'l/ (**-gled**, **-gling**) *vt* 1 untangle things that are tied or knotted together 2 clarify something confusing 3 free somebody else or yourself from a complicated situation —**dis·en·tan·gle·ment** *n*

dis·e·qui·lib·ri·um /díss eekwə líbbree əm/ *n* a lack of stability or balance

dis·es·tab·lish /díssə stábblish/ *vt* 1 stop an established custom 2 end the connection between a state and its official church —**dis·es·tab·lish·ment** *n*

dis·fa·vor /diss fáyvər/ *n* 1 the state of being disapproved of 2 a feeling of disapproval

dis·fig·ure /diss fíggyər/ (**-ured**, **-ur·ing**) *vt* spoil the appearance of —**dis·fig·ure·ment** *n*

dis·fran·chise /diss frán chìz/ (**-chised**, **-chis·ing**) *vt* disenfranchise somebody —**dis·fran·chise·ment** /diss frán chìzmənt/ *n*

dis·gorge /diss gáwrj/ (**-gorged**, **-gorg·ing**) *vt* 1 pour out in a stream o *disgorged the contents of her purse* 2 let out in large numbers o *the factory disgorging workers* 3 regurgitate or vomit

dis·grace /diss gráyss/ *n* 1 shame or loss of the respect of others 2 something shameful or unacceptable ■ *vt* (**-graced**, **-grac·ing**) bring shame or loss of respect or status to

dis·grace·ful /diss gráyssfəl/ *adj* shamefully bad or unacceptable —**dis·grace·ful·ly** *adv*

dis·grun·tled /diss grúntl'd/ *adj* dissatisfied and irritated

dis·guise /diss gíz/ *vt* (**-guised**, **-guis·ing**) 1 change somebody's appearance to prevent recognition 2 hide feelings or facts o *could barely disguise her delight* ■ *n* 1 a change of appearance made to prevent recognition 2 the state of being changed in appearance o *went to the ball in disguise* —**dis·guised** *adj*

dis·gust /diss gúst/ *n* 1 strong disapproval or distaste 2 impatient irritation ■ *vt* make somebody feel revolted —**dis·gust·ed** *adj* —**dis·gust·ing** *adj* ◊ See note at **dislike**

dish *n* 1 a single serving of food 2 food prepared according to a particular recipe or style 3 a radio or television receiver ■ **dish·es** *npl* dirty plates, cutlery, and pans o *do the dishes*

□ **dish out** *vt* 1 hand out freely (*infml*) 2 serve food

dis·ha·bille /díssə beél, -beé/, **des·ha·bille** /dèssə beél, -beé/ *n* a state in which somebody is partially or casually dressed (*fml*)

dis·har·mo·ny /diss haármənee/ *n* 1 conflict between people 2 lack of musical harmony —**dis·har·mo·ni·ous** /diss haar mõnee əss/ *adj*

dish·cloth /dísh klàwth/ *n* a cloth for washing or drying dishes

dis·heart·en /diss haárt'n/ *vt* make somebody lose confidence or enthusiasm —**dis·heart·en·ing** *adj*

di·shev·el /di shévv'l/ (**-eled** or **-elled**, **-el·ing** or **-el·ling**) *vt* cause somebody's hair or clothes to look messy —**di·shev·el·ment** *n*

dis·hon·est /diss ónnəst/ *adj* deceitful or lying —**dis·hon·est·ly** *adv*

dis·hon·es·ty /diss ónnəstee/ *n* deceitful behavior

dis·hon·or /diss ónnər/ *n* 1 loss of other people's respect 2 failure or refusal by a bank to pay a check (*fml*) ■ *vt* 1 bring shame on somebody or something **2** break a promise or agreement **3** fail or refuse to pay a check *(fml)*

dis·hon·or·a·ble /diss ónnərəb'l/ *adj* shameful and bringing a loss of respect or reputation —**dis·hon·or·a·bly** *adv*

dis·hon·or·a·ble dis·charge *n* dismissal from the armed forces for misconduct

dish·pan /dísh pàn/ *n* a pan or basin for washing dishes

dish·rag /dísh ràg/ *n* a cloth for washing dishes

dish·tow·el /dísh tòw əl/ *n* a cloth for drying dishes

dish·wash·er /dísh wòshər/ *n* **1** a machine for washing dishes **2** somebody employed to wash dishes

dish·wa·ter /dísh wàwtər/ *n* water used for washing dishes

~~disign~~ incorrect spelling of **design**

dis·il·lu·sion /díssi lóozh'n/ *vt* show somebody that an ideal or belief is mistaken ■ *n also* **dis·il·lu·sion·ment** disappointment caused by realizing that an ideal or belief is mistaken —**dis·il·lu·sioned** *adj*

dis·in·cen·tive /díssin séntiv/ *n* a deterrent or discouragement

dis·in·cli·na·tion /díssinklə náysh'n/ *n* a reluctance to do something —**dis·in·clined** /díssin klínd/ *adj*

dis·in·fect /díssin fékt/ *vt* rid of bacteria using a chemical liquid —**dis·in·fec·tion** *n*

dis·in·fec·tant /díssin féktənt/ *n* a chemical for killing bacteria

dis·in·gen·u·ous /díssin jénnyoo əss/ *adj* slyly insincere —**dis·in·gen·u·ous·ly** *adv*

dis·in·her·it /díssin hérrit/ *vt* deprive of an inheritance —**dis·in·her·i·tance** *n*

dis·in·te·grate /diss íntə gràyt/ *(-grat·ed, -grat·ing) vti* **1** break into fragments **2** lose or cause to lose unity **3** undergo or cause to undergo atomic fission —**dis·in·te·gra·tion** /diss ìntə gráysh'n/ *n*

dis·in·ter /díssin túr/ *(-terred, -ter·ring) vt* **1** dig up a buried corpse **2** expose something hidden *(fml)* —**dis·in·ter·ment** *n*

dis·in·ter·est /diss íntərəst, diss íntrəst/ *vt* cause to lose interest or partiality ■ *n* **1** impartiality **2** a lack of interest ◊ See note at **disinterested**

dis·in·ter·est·ed /diss íntərəstəd, diss íntrəstəd/ *adj* **1** impartial **2** ⚠ not interested —**dis·in·ter·est·ed·ly** *adv*

USAGE disinterested or **uninterested**? **Disinterested** means "impartial" and also has a widely used but much criticized meaning, "not interested."

dis·in·ter·me·di·a·tion /díssintər meedee áysh'n/ *n* the reinvesting of invested money

dis·in·vest /díssin vést/ *vti* withdraw investment in something —**dis·in·vest·ment** *n*

~~disipline~~ incorrect spelling of **discipline**

dis·joint·ed /diss jóyntəd/ *adj* not connected in an easily understandable way —**dis·joint·ed·ly** *adv*

dis·junc·tion /diss júngkshən/ *n* a disconnection of joined parts

dis·junc·tive /diss júngktiv/ *adj* dividing or separating *(technical)* —**dis·junc·tive·ly** *adv*

⚡ **disk, disc** *n* **1** a round flat object **2** a computer storage device **3** a flat round part between the bones of the spine **4** a circular piece of metal on a vehicle's wheel that a pad presses against **5** a circular blade on a plow **6** the center of a flower head

⚡ **disk drive** *n* a device for reading data from and writing data to computer disks

⚡ **disk·ette** /di skét/ *n* COMPUT = **floppy disk**

⚡ **disk op·er·at·ing sys·tem** *n* a computer operating system

dis·like /diss lík/ *vt* (-liked, -lik·ing) have no liking for somebody or something ■ *n* **1** a feeling of disapproval or distaste **2** something considered disagreeable —**dis·lik·a·ble** *adj*

SYNONYMS dislike, distaste, hatred, hate, disgust, loathing, repugnance, abhorrence, animosity, antipathy, aversion, revulsion CORE MEANING: a feeling of not liking somebody or something

⚡ **dis·lo·cate** /díssló kàyt/ *(-cat·ed, -cat·ing) vt* **1** put something out of its usual place **2** move a body part from its normal position —**dis·lo·ca·tion** /diss lò káysh'n/ *n*

dis·lodge /diss lój/ *(-lodged, -lodg·ing) v* remove from a fixed position —**dis·lodg·ment** *n*

dis·loy·al /diss lóy əl/ *adj* failing to support or be true to somebody or something —**dis·loy·al·ly** *adv*—**dis·loy·al·ty** *n*

dis·mal /dízməl/ *adj* **1** depressing **2** of a poor standard or quality —**dis·mal·ly** *adv*

ORIGIN **Dismal** comes ultimately from Latin *dies mali*, literally "evil days," referring to the 24 days in the year that were unlucky according to ancient and medieval belief. The word is first recorded in English as a noun in the early medieval period, in the *dismal*, meaning these days. As an adjective it occurs earliest in *dismal day*, but from the late 16C begins to be associated with things other than "day."

dis·man·tle /diss mánt'l/ *(-tled, -tling) v* **1** *vti* take or come apart **2** *vt* destroy by removing key elements **3** *vt* remove equipment or furniture from —**dis·man·tle·ment** *n*

dis·may /diss máy/ *vt* discourage or alarm ■ *n* a feeling of anxious discouragement —**dis·may·ing·ly** *adv*

dis·mem·ber /diss mémbər/ *vt* **1** remove the limbs from a body **2** divide something up —**dis·mem·ber·ment** *n*

dis·miss /diss míss/ vt 1 end somebody's employment 2 send somebody away 3 refuse to give a legal case further hearing in court 4 refuse to consider something —**dis·miss·al** n —**dis·miss·i·ble** adj

dis·mis·sive /diss míssiv/ adj contemptuously ignoring or refusing to consider something —**dis·mis·sive·ly** adv

dis·mount /diss mównt/ vi 1 get off an animal's back 2 get off a bicycle or motorcycle —**dis·mount** n

CORBIS/Bettmann

Walt Disney

Dis·ney /díznee/, **Walt** (1901–66) US animator and producer

dis·o·be·di·ent /díssə beédee ənt/ adj refusing to obey —**dis·o·be·di·ence** n —**dis·o·be·di·ent·ly** adv

dis·o·bey /díssə báy/ (**-beyed**, **-bey·ing**, **-beys**) vti refuse to obey

dis·o·blig·ing /díssə blíjing/ adj unwilling to help

~~disolve~~ incorrect spelling of **dissolve**

dis·or·der /diss áwrdər/ n 1 an illness 2 a lack of order or organization 3 public violence or rioting

dis·or·dered /diss áwrdərd/ adj 1 messy or confused 2 not functioning normally —**dis·or·dered·ness** n

dis·or·der·ly /diss áwrdərlee/ adj 1 lacking order 2 unruly 3 disturbing the public order —**dis·or·der·li·ness** n

dis·or·der·ly con·duct n behavior likely to cause a breach of the peace

dis·or·gan·i·za·tion /diss àwrgəni záysh'n/ n lack of organization or method —**dis·or·gan·ize** vt

dis·o·ri·ent /diss áwree ènt/ vt make somebody lose his or her bearings —**dis·o·ri·en·ta·tion** /diss àwree ən táysh'n/ n —**dis·o·ri·ent·ed** adj

dis·own /diss ṓn/ vt deny a relationship with —**dis·own·ment** n

~~dispair~~ incorrect spelling of **despair**

dis·par·age /di spérrij/ (**-aged**, **-ag·ing**) vt express contempt or disapproval for —**dis·par·age·ment** n —**dis·par·ag·ing** adj —**dis·par·ag·ing·ly** adv

dis·pa·rate /díspərət, di spérrət/ adj very different —**dis·pa·rate·ly** adv —**dis·pa·rate·ness** n

~~disparirty~~ incorrect spelling of **disparity**

dis·par·i·ty /di spérrətee/ (pl **-ties**) n 1 a lack of equality 2 a lack of similarity

dis·pas·sion·ate /diss pásh'nət/ adj calmly objective —**dis·pas·sion·ate·ly** adv

dis·patch /di spách/ vt 1 send something off 2 deal with quickly 3 kill a person or an animal ■ n 1 an act of dispatching somebody or something 2 speed in doing or going 3 an official message 4 a news report —**dis·patch·er** n

dis·pel /di spél/ (**-pelled**, **-pel·ling**) vt rid somebody's mind of something, e.g., a mistaken idea

dis·pen·sa·ble /di spénsəb'l/ adj not essential

dis·pen·sa·ry /di spénsəree/ (pl **-ries**) n 1 a place where a pharmacist prepares and supplies medicines to patients 2 a medical center on a naval vessel or a military installation

dis·pen·sa·tion /díspən sáysh'n/ n 1 an exemption 2 a document giving an exemption 3 in Christian belief, a divinely ordained system —**dis·pen·sa·tion·al** adj

dis·pense /di spéns/ (**-pensed**, **-pens·ing**) vt 1 distribute something to a number of people 2 supply a product 3 prepare and supply medicines

□ **dispense with** vt manage without

dis·pens·er /di spénsər/ n 1 a device for dispensing goods (usually in combination) 2 a distributor of something

~~dispensible~~ incorrect spelling of **dispensable**

dis·per·sal /di spúrs'l/ n distribution of people or things over an area

dis·perse /di spúrs/ (**-persed**, **-pers·ing**) vti 1 scatter in different directions 2 distribute over a wide area 3 disappear or cause to disappear

dis·per·sion /di spúrsh'n/ n 1 the scattering or distribution of something over an area 2 the state of being scattered or distributed over an area

dis·pir·it·ed /di spírrətəd/ adj discouraged —**dis·pir·it·ed·ly** adv

dis·pir·it·ing /di spírriting/ adj causing discouragement —**dis·pir·it·ing·ly** adv

dis·place /diss pláyss/ (**-placed**, **-plac·ing**) vt 1 move from the usual place 2 force to leave home because of war 3 replace —**dis·place·a·ble** adj

dis·placed per·son n a refugee

dis·place·ment /diss pláyssmənt/ n 1 movement of something from its usual place 2 the fluid displaced by an object such as a ship 3 the amount of movement of an object in a particular direction

dis·play /di spláy/ v 1 vt make visible or evident 2 vti show data or appear on a monitor ■ n 1 a set of things arranged or done for others to see (often in combination) 2 the state of being visible or arranged for viewing 3 an act of showing a feeling or quality o a display of courage 4 an electronic device presenting visual information

dis·please /diss pleéz/ (**-pleased**, **-pleas·ing**) vti annoy —**dis·pleased** adj —**dis·pleas·ure** /diss plézhər/ n

dis·port /dɪ spáwrt/ *vi* behave playfully *(archaic or humorous)*

dis·pos·a·ble /dɪ spóʒəb'l/ *adj* 1 throwaway 2 available for use —**dis·pos·a·bil·i·ty** /dɪ spòʒə bíllətee/ *n* —**dis·pos·a·ble·ness** *n*

dis·pos·a·ble in·come *n* income after obligations have been met

dis·pos·al /dɪ spóz'l/ *n* 1 the process of getting rid of something 2 the orderly arrangement of something 3 the transfer of something to somebody else's ownership 4 a garbage disposal *(infml)* ◊ **at somebody's disposal** available for somebody's use or to do somebody's bidding

dis·pose /dɪ spóz/ (**-posed, -pos·ing**) *v* 1 *vt* put people or things into a particular order or place *(fml)* ○ *a commander who disposed his forces along the coast* 2 *vti* settle something *(fml)* ○ *an outcome to be disposed by the court* 3 *vt* incline somebody to do something
□ **dispose of** *vt* 1 get rid of 2 transfer to somebody else's ownership

dis·posed /dɪ spózd/ *adj* 1 inclined or tending to something 2 with a particular attitude toward ○ *favorably disposed to us*

dis·po·si·tion /dɪspə zísh'n/ *n* 1 temperament 2 a behavioral tendency 3 the settlement of something *(fml)* —**dis·po·si·tion·al** *adj*

dis·pos·sess /dɪspə zéss/ *vt* take away property from *(fml)* —**dis·pos·ses·sion** *n* —**dis·pos·ses·sor** *n*

dis·pos·sessed /dɪspə zést/ *adj* deprived of property or rights ■ *npl* dispossessed people

dis·pro·por·tion /dɪsprə páwrsh'n/ *n* a state of being out of proportion

dis·pro·por·tion·ate /dɪsprə páwrsh'nət/, **dis·pro·por·tion·al** /dɪsprə páwrsh'nəl/ *adj* out of proportion —**dis·pro·por·tion·ate·ly** *adv*

dis·prove /diss proóv/ (**-proved, -prov·ing**) *vt* prove something wrong —**dis·proof** /diss proóf/ *n* —**dis·prov·a·ble** *adj* —**dis·prov·al** *n*

dis·put·a·ble /dɪ spyoótəb'l/ *adj* open to argument —**dis·put·a·bly** *adv*

dis·pu·ta·tion /dɪspyə táysh'n/ *n* *(fml)* 1 argument 2 a formal academic debate

dis·pu·ta·tious /dɪspyə táyshəss/ *adj* argumentative

dis·pute /dɪ spyoót/ *v* (**-put·ed, -put·ing**) 1 *vti* question the truth of 2 *vi* disagree or argue 3 *vt* contest or fight for *(fml)* ○ *disputed territory* ■ *n* 1 an argument 2 a disagreement between workers and management ○ *a labor dispute* ◊ See note at **disagree**

dis·qual·i·fy /diss kwóllə fì/ (**-fied, -fies**) *vt* 1 make ineligible 2 take away a legal right from —**dis·qual·i·fi·ca·tion** /diss kwòlləfi káysh'n/ *n* —**dis·qual·i·fied** *adj*

dis·qui·et /diss kwī ət/ *n* a state of inner unease ■ *vt* make anxious *(literary)* —**dis·qui·et·ing** /diss kw‑əting/ *adj*

dis·qui·si·tion /dɪskwi zísh'n/ *n* a long essay or speech —**dis·qui·si·tion·al** *adj*

Dis·rae·li /diz ráylee/, **Benjamin, 1st Earl of Beaconsfield** (1804–81) British prime minister (1868, 1874–80)

dis·re·gard /dɪssri gaárd/ *vt* ignore ■ *n* lack of attention or respect —**dis·re·gard·ful** *adj*

dis·re·pair /dɪssri páir/ *n* poor condition

dis·rep·u·ta·ble /diss réppyətəb'l/ *adj* not respectable —**dis·rep·u·ta·ble·ness** *n* —**dis·rep·u·ta·bly** *adv*

dis·re·pute /dɪssri pyoót/ *n* lack of a good reputation

dis·re·spect /dɪssri spékt/ *n* a lack of respect ■ *vt* show no respect for —**dis·re·spect·ful** *adj* —**dis·re·spect·ful·ly** *adv*

dis·robe /diss rób/ (**-robed, -rob·ing**) *vti* undress —**dis·robe·ment** *n*

dis·rupt /diss rúpt/ *vt* interrupt the normal course or functioning of —**dis·rup·tion** /diss rúpshən/ *n* —**dis·rup·tive** *adj* —**dis·rup·tive·ly** *adv* —**dis·rup·tive·ness** *n*

~~dissapear~~ incorrect spelling of **disappear**

~~dissapoint~~ incorrect spelling of **disappoint**

dis·sat·is·fac·tion /diss sàttəs fáksh'n/ *n* discontent

dis·sat·is·fy /diss sáttəss fī/ (**-fied, -fies**) *vt* fail to satisfy —**dis·sat·is·fied** *adj*

dis·sect /di sékt/ *v* 1 *vti* cut up a dead organism and examine it scientifically 2 *vt* examine something in detail ○ *dissected the speech* —**dis·sec·tion** /di sékshən/ *n*

dis·sem·ble /di sémb'l/ (**-bled, -bling**) *vi* pretend in order to conceal information or feelings —**dis·sem·blance** *n*

dis·sem·i·nate /di sémmi nàyt/ (**-nat·ed, -nat·ing**) *vti* spread something far and wide —**dis·sem·i·na·tion** /di sèmmi náysh'n/ *n* ◊ See note at **scatter**

dis·sen·sion /di sénshən/ *n* disagreement

dis·sent /di sént/ *vi* 1 disagree with a majority or official view 2 reject the doctrine of an established church 3 withhold assent ■ *n* 1 disagreement from a generally held opinion 2 rejection of the doctrine of an established church 3 a minority judicial opinion 4 refusal to accept a political regime —**dis·sent·er** *n* —**dis·sent·ing** *adj* ◊ See note at **descent**

dis·ser·ta·tion /dɪssər táysh'n/ *n* a long essay, especially one written for a university degree —**dis·ser·ta·tion·al** *adj*

dis·serv·ice /di sùrviss/ *n* an action that causes harm

dis·si·dent /díssidənt/ *n* somebody who disagrees publicly with a political or religious system —**dis·si·dence** *n* —**dis·si·dent** *adj*

dis·sim·i·lar /di símmələr/ *adj* different —**dis·sim·i·lar·i·ty** /díssimə lérrətee/ *n* —**dis·sim·i·lar·ly** *adv*

dis·sim·u·late /di símmyə làyt/ (**-lat·ed, -lat·ing**) *vti* hide your true feelings —**dis·sim·u·la·tion** /di sìmmyə láysh'n/ *n*

dis·si·pate /díssə pàyt/ (**-pat·ed, -pat·ing**) *v* 1 *vti* disappear or cause to disappear gradually ○ *storm clouds dissipating* 2 *vt* spend wastefully —**dis·si·pa·tion** /díssə páysh'n/ *n*

dis·si·pat·ed /díssə pàytəd/ *adj* overindulging in physical pleasure

dis·so·ci·ate /di sṓshee àyt/ (**-at·ed, -at·ing**) *vt* 1 regard as distinct 2 = disassociate —**dis·so·cia·ble** *adj* —**dis·so·ci·a·tive** *adj*

dis·so·lu·tion /díssə lóosh'n/ *n* 1 the breakdown of something into parts 2 the dissolving of an organization, assembly, or relationship 3 the formal closing of an assembly or parliament 4 the ending of a legal relationship

dis·solve /di zólv/ *v* (**-solved, -solv·ing**) 1 *vti* become or make something become absorbed in a liquid 2 *vti* break up an organization 3 *vi* suddenly express an emotion such as laughter or tears o *He dissolved into tears.* 4 *vt* formally close an assembly or parliament 5 *vt* end a legal relationship such as a marriage ■ *n* the fading out of one movie scene and the fading in of the next —**dis·solv·a·ble** *adj*

dis·so·nance /díssənənss/ *n* 1 an unpleasant combination of sounds or musical notes 2 inconsistency between ideas —**dis·so·nant** *adj*

dis·suade /di swáyd/ (**-suad·ed, -suad·ing**) *vt* talk somebody out of doing something —**dis·suad·a·ble** *adj* —**dis·sua·sion** /di swáyzh'n/ *n* —**dis·sua·sive** *adj*

dis·taff /di stàf/ *n* a rod on which wool is wound for use in spinning ◊ **on the distaff side** regarding the women or the female side of a family

dis·tance /dístənss/ *n* 1 length in space, time, or attitude, especially between two things o *the distance between Paris and New York* 2 a place or position at a distinct remove o *seen from a distance* 3 closeness allowing an activity o *within hailing distance* 4 the state of being aloof 5 an interval of time o *at a distance of 20 years* ■ *v* (**-tanced, -tanc·ing**) 1 *vt* put at a distance from o *distanced herself from the family argument* 2 *vt* say or show that you do not support somebody or something o *distanced himself from the disgraced politician* ◊ **go the distance** continue to the end of a task or project

dis·tance learn·ing *n* study by mail or electronic means

dis·tant /dístənt/ *adj* far away in space, time, or attitude —**dis·tant·ly** *adv*

dis·taste /diss táyst/ *n* disapproval or dislike ◊ See note at **dislike**

dis·taste·ful /diss táystf'l/ *adj* unpleasant and eliciting dislike or disapproval —**dis·taste·ful·ly** *adv* —**dis·taste·ful·ness** *n*

dis·tem·per[1] /diss témpər/ *n* a viral disease of domestic animals

dis·tem·per[2] /diss témpər/ *n* paint containing glue or size instead of oil —**dis·tem·per** *vt*

dis·tend /di sténd/ *vti* swell or inflate —**dis·ten·si·ble** /-sténsəb'l/ *adj* —**dis·ten·sion** /-sténsh'n/ *n*

dis·till /di stíl/, **dis·til** /-tílled, -till·ing/ *v* 1 *vt* make alcoholic spirits 2 *vti* purify liquid by heating it and then condensing its vapor 3 *vt* create something from essential elements —**dis·till·a·tion** /díst'l áysh'n/ *n*

dis·til·late /díst'l àyt, díst'lət/ *n* liquid produced by distillation

dis·till·er /di stíllər/ *n* a manufacturer of hard liquor —**dis·till·er·y** *n*

dis·tinct /di stíngkt/ *adj* 1 clearly separate 2 apparent to the senses 3 certain or definite o *a distinct possibility* —**dis·tinct·ly** *adv* —**dis·tinct·ness** *n*

dis·tinc·tion /di stíngkshən/ *n* 1 a difference 2 high quality o *research of distinction* 3 something to be proud of 4 a mark of high achievement

dis·tinc·tive /di stíngktiv/ *adj* uniquely characteristic of somebody or something —**dis·tinc·tive·ly** *adv* —**dis·tinc·tive·ness** *n*

dis·tin·guish /di stíng gwish/ *v* 1 *vti* recognize differences between people or things o *distinguish between virtue and vice* 2 *vt* be the difference between people or things o *What distinguishes dogs from wolves?* 3 *vt* recognize or identify something o *distinguished a flaw in the crystal* 4 *vr* do something well and achieve recognition —**dis·tin·guish·a·ble** *adj* —**dis·tin·guish·ing** *adj*

dis·tin·guished /di stíng gwisht/ *adj* 1 recognized for excellence 2 authoritative and dignified

dis·tort /di stáwrt/ *v* 1 *vti* alter or cause to alter in shape, form, or appearance 2 *vt* describe inaccurately —**dis·tort·ed** *adj* —**dis·tort·ed·ness** *n* —**dis·tor·tion** *n*

dis·tract /di strákt/ *vt* 1 divert somebody's attention from something 2 amuse or entertain somebody —**dis·tract·ed** *adj* —**dis·tract·ing** *adj* —**dis·tract·ing·ly** *adv* —**dis·trac·tor** *n*

dis·trac·tion /di strákshən/ *n* 1 a thing that diverts attention from something else 2 an amusement 3 a state of emotional upset

dis·trait /di stráy/ *adj* distracted and inattentive *(literary)*

dis·traught /di stráwt/ *adj* extremely upset

dis·tress /di stréss/ *n* 1 mental suffering 2 hardship or difficulty 3 severe physical pain ■ *vt* upset somebody —**dis·tress·ful** *adj* —**dis·tress·ing** *adj* —**dis·tress·ing·ly** *adv*

dis·tressed /di strést/ *adj* 1 very upset 2 describes furniture or fabric made to look old 3 repossessed from a bad debtor

dis·tress sig·nal *n* a signal requesting help sent by a ship or aircraft in trouble

dis·trib·ute /di strí byoot/ (**-ut·ed, -ut·ing**) *vt* 1 give or share things out 2 spread or scatter things about 3 sell and deliver goods —**dis·trib·ut·a·ble** *adj* —**dis·tri·bu·tion** /dístrə byóosh'n/ *n* —**dis·tri·bu·tion·al** *adj* ◊ See note at **scatter**

dis·trib·u·tive /di stríbbyətiv/ *adj* 1 involving distribution 2 producing equal results —**dis·trib·u·tive·ly** *adv*

dis·trib·u·tor /di strííbbyətər/, **dis·trib·ut·er** n **1** a person, group, or firm that distributes something **2** a wholesaler **3** a device in an engine for conveying electricity to the spark plugs

dis·trict /dístrikt/ n an area of a town or country

dis·trict at·tor·ney n the official prosecutor for a specific urban jurisdiction

Dis·trict of Co·lum·bi·a federal district of the E United States, coextensive with the city of Washington, D.C.

~~distroy~~ incorrect spelling of **destroy**

dis·trust /diss trúst/ n a lack of trust —**dis·trust** vt —**dis·trust·ful** adj —**dis·trust·ful·ly** adv

dis·turb /di stúrb/ vt **1** interrupt somebody busy **2** make somebody feel anxious or uneasy **3** change the shape or position of something **4** spoil the peace and quiet of something —**dis·turb·ing** adj —**dis·turb·ing·ly** adv◊ See note at **bother**

dis·tur·bance /di stúrbənss/ n **1** disruption **2** a commotion **3** psychological or emotional difficulties

dis·turbed /di stúrbd/ adj **1** anxious or uneasy **2** affected by a psychological disorder

dis·u·ni·ty /diss yoonətee/ n lack of unity

dis·use /diss yooss/ n the state of not being in use —**dis·used** /-yoozd/ adj

ditch n a narrow drainage or irrigation channel ■ v **1** vt abandon or throw away (slang) **2** vti make or cause to make an emergency landing on water (infml)

dith·er /díthər/ vi be agitated and indecisive ■ n an agitated or indecisive state

⫽dith·er·ing /díthəring/ n **1** nervous indecisiveness **2** the mixing of pixels of different colors on a computer screen to create new colors

dit·sy /dítsee/ (**-si·er**, **-si·est**), **dit·zy** (**-zi·er**, **-zi·est**) adj seeming silly or scatterbrained (slang)

dit·to /díttō/ interj indicates that the same thing applies to you (infml) ■ adv indicates that the same thing applies ■ n (pl **-tos**) a pair of symbols (") representing text repeated exactly from what appears above

ORIGIN **Ditto** derives from a northern form of Italian *detto*, literally "said," used in much the same way as English *said* meaning "previously mentioned" (*The said car was later found abandoned*). In Italian, and originally in English in the 17C, it referred only to the month just mentioned. After the 17C, however, it extended its range to mean "the same, similar(ly)."

dit·ty /díttee/ (pl **-ties**) n a short simple song

di·u·ret·ic /dī ə réttik/ adj causing increased urine output —**di·u·ret·ic** n —**di·u·ret·i·cal·ly** adv

di·ur·nal /dī úrn'l/ adj **1** happening or active in the daytime **2** happening every day —**di·ur·nal·ly** adv

div. abbr division

di·va /déevə/ (pl **-vas** or **-ve** /-vay/) n **1** a well-known woman opera singer **2** a successful woman performer

di·van /dī vàn, di ván/ n a backless sofa

ORIGIN **Divan** came into English via French and Italian from Turkish and Persian. It was first adopted in the late 16C as the Ottoman council of state and the room in which it was held. The long seats against the wall that were characteristic of Eastern courts and council chambers had also come to have the Persian name for **divan**, and this appears in English in the early 18C. The modern "sofa" developed from there.

dive /dīv/ vi (**dived** or **dove** /dōv/, **dived**, **div·ing**) **1** jump into water **2** swim or submerge under water **3** descend or make an aircraft descend steeply and rapidly **4** move suddenly and rapidly ○ *dive for the door* **5** drop in value ■ n **1** an act or instance of diving **2** a disreputable bar or club (slang) —**div·er** n —**div·ing** n

dive-bomb vt descend steeply and drop bombs on —**dive-bomb·er** n —**dive-bomb·ing** n

di·verge /di vúrj, dī-/ (**-verged**, **-verg·ing**) vi **1** move apart **2** differ —**di·verg·ing** adj

di·ver·gence /di vúrjənss, dī-/, **di·ver·gen·cy** /-jənsee, -jənsee/ (pl **-cies**) n **1** a difference or disparity **2** the process of moving apart **3** the amount by which one thing differs from something else —**di·ver·gent** adj

di·vers /dívərz/ adj several or many (literary)

di·verse /di vúrss, dī vùrss/ adj **1** consisting of different things ○ *culturally diverse* **2** differing from one other

di·ver·si·fy /di vúrssə fī, dī-/ (**-fied**, **-fies**) vti **1** make or become varied **2** expand into new areas of business —**di·ver·si·fi·ca·tion** /di vùrssəfi káysh'n, dī-/ n —**di·ver·si·fied** n

di·ver·sion /di vúrzh'n, dī-/ n **1** an enjoyable activity **2** a change in the purpose or direction of something **3** a mock attack —**di·ver·sion·ar·y** adj

di·ver·si·ty /di vúrssətee, dī-/ n **1** variety **2** social inclusiveness

di·vert /di vúrt, dī-/ vt **1** change the route of **2** draw attention from **3** change the purpose or use of **4** amuse —**di·vert·ing** adj —**di·vert·ing·ly** adv

di·ver·tic·u·li·tis /dī vərtikyə lítiss/ n inflammation of pockets in the intestine

di·ver·ti·men·to /di vùrtə mén tō/ (pl **-ti** /-tee/ or **-tos**) n a piece of light classical instrumental music

di·vest /di vést, dī-/ vt **1** take something away from somebody or something **2** take something off somebody (fml or humorous) **3** get rid of something —**di·vest·ment** n

di·ves·ti·ture /di vésti chōor, dī-, -véstichər/ n the sale by a company of one or more of its assets

di·vide /di víd/ v (-vid·ed, -vid·ing) 1 vti split into parts, or be split 2 vi move apart in different directions 3 vti share o *divide the spoils of war* 4 vi be a boundary between two places 5 vt cause disagreement between 6 vt mark off in sections 7 vti calculate how many times one number contains another ■ n 1 a boundary or gap 2 a ridge separating watersheds

di·vid·ed high·way n a highway separated into two parts by a center barrier

div·i·dend /dívvi dènd, -dvnd/ n 1 a bonus 2 a stockholder's share of a company's profits 3 a number to be divided by another

di·vid·er /di vídər/ n a device separating something into sections ■ **di·vid·ers** npl a measuring instrument with two hinged legs

di·vid·ing line n something acting as a boundary

div·i·na·tion /dìvvi náysh'n/ n 1 a search for knowledge of the future by supernatural means 2 a prophecy —**di·vin·a·to·ry** /di vínnə tàwree/ adj

di·vine /di vín/ adj 1 being God or a deity 2 of God or a deity 3 relating to worship 4 expresses approval (infml) ■ v (-vined, -vin·ing) discover by guesswork or intuition ■ n 1 a theologian 2 also **Di·vine** God —**di·vin·a·ble** adj —**di·vine·ly** adv

di·vine right n a monarch's supposed God-given right to rule

div·ing bell n a bell-shaped diving apparatus

div·ing board n a raised board beside a swimming pool for diving

div·ing suit n a waterproof suit worn for diving

di·vin·ing rod n a forked stick for detecting water or minerals

di·vin·i·ty /di vínnətee/ (pl -ties) n 1 the quality of being God or a deity 2 theology 3 also **Di·vin·i·ty** God or a deity 4 a kind of fudge

di·vis·i·ble /di vízzəb'l/ adj 1 able to be divided 2 able to be separated —**di·vis·i·bil·i·ty** /di vìzzə bíllatee/ n

di·vi·sion /di vízh'n/ n 1 the splitting of something into parts 2 the sharing of something 3 the dividing of one number by another 4 a disagreement 5 a separate part, section, or unit of something 6 a self-contained unit of an army —**di·vi·sion·al** adj

di·vi·sion sign n a mathematical sign indicating division

di·vi·sive /di víssiv/ adj causing disagreement —**di·vi·sive·ly** adv —**di·vi·sive·ness** n

di·vi·sor /di vízər/ n a number divided into another number

di·vorce /di váwrs/ n 1 the legal ending of a marriage 2 a separation or split o *a divorce between theory and practice* ■ v (-vorced, -vorc·ing) 1 vti legally end a marriage to somebody 2 vt separate o *divorced truth from speculation* —**di·vorced** adj

di·vor·cé /di vàwr sáy/ n a divorced man

di·vor·cée /di vàwr sáy/ n a divorced woman

div·ot /dívvət/ n in golf, a lump of grass and earth dug out accidentally

di·vulge /di vúlj/ (-vulged, -vulg·ing) vt reveal information —**di·vul·gence** n

ORIGIN **Divulge** comes from a Latin word formed from the word meaning "common people" that is also the source of *vulgar*. When first adopted in the 15C it meant simply "make publicly known." It was not until the 17C that it began to imply publishing what had previously been secret.

div·vy /dívvee/ (-vied, -vies) vt divide something up (infml)

Di·wa·li, **Di·va·li** /di wáalee/, /di vaalee/ n a Hindu festival in honor of Lakshmi. Date: autumn.

Dix, Dorothea (1802–87) US philanthropist and reformer

Dix·ie /díksee/ n the southern Confederate states in the US Civil War (infml) ◊ **whistle Dixie** engage in rosy fantasies (infml) o *If you think winning an Olympic gold medal will be a snap, you're whistling Dixie.*

ORIGIN The origin of **Dixie** is not known for certain. It first appears in the late 1850s in the words of the famous song "Dixie," where the actual form is *Dixie's land*. It has been speculated that it is an alteration of *Dixon* in *Mason-Dixon Line*, the boundary between the northern and Confederate states.

Dix·ie·land /díksee lànd/, **dix·ie·land** n jazz originating in New Orleans, with a two-beat rhythm and improvisation

ORIGIN **Dixieland** takes its name from the *Original Dixieland Jazz Band*, the first jazz band to record commercially.

diz·zy /dízzee/ (-zi·er, -zi·est) adj 1 unsteady and giddy 2 causing an unsteady and giddy feeling o *the dizzy height of the tower* 3 considered foolish or thoughtless (infml) —**diz·zi·ly** adv —**diz·zi·ness** n —**diz·zy** vt

DJ n somebody whose job is to play recorded music

D.J. abbr district judge

Dji·bou·ti /ji bōotee/ 1 country in NE Africa, on the Gulf of Aden. Cap. Djibouti. Pop. 460,700 (2001). 2 capital of the Republic of Djibouti. Pop. 383,000 (1995 estimate).

DMV abbr Department of Motor Vehicles

DMZ abbr demilitarized zone

DNA n a nucleic acid molecule that is the major component of chromosomes and carries genetic information. Full form **deoxyribonucleic acid**

DNA fin·ger·print·ing n identification of somebody from his or her DNA

Dnie·per /néepar/ river flowing through W Russia, Belarus, and Ukraine into the Black Sea. Length 1,420 mi./2,290 km.

Dnies·ter /néestar/ river flowing through Ukraine and Moldova into the Black Sea. Length 870 mi./1,400 km.

⚡DNS *abbr* domain name system

do[1] /doo/ (**did** /did/, **done** /dun/, **do·ing**, **does** /duz/) *v* **1** *vt* perform an action, activity, or task ○ *did the cleaning* **2** *vt* use something in a particular way ○ *did nothing with the money* **3** *vt* have an effect or result ○ *These disputes do little to help the peace process.* **4** *vti* work at something ○ *What do you do for a living?* **5** *vt* behave in a particular way ○ *always does what he wants* **6** *vi* progress or get along ○ *The firm is doing well.* **7** *vt* provide something ○ *We don't do lunches.* **8** *vt* achieve a speed or rate ○ *doing 100 mph* **9** *vt* put on a performance of something ○ *going to do "Macbeth"* **10** *vti* be adequate ○ *$10 will do.* **11** *vt* serve time in prison (*slang*) ○ *do 10 to 20 years* **12** *vt* cheat somebody (*infml*) ○ *did her out of her inheritance* **13** *vt* take an illegal drug (*slang*) ■ *aux v* **14** forms questions and negatives ○ *What did she want?* ○ *Do not sit here.* **15** gives emphasis ○ *Do be quiet!* **16** replaces a verb to avoid repetition ○ *I ate less than you did.*
◊ See note at **dew**

□ **do away with** *vt* **1** abolish **2** kill (*infml*)
□ **do in** *vt* (*infml*) **1** kill **2** tire out
□ **do up** *vt* **1** cover with a decorative wrapping **2** dress fashionably (*infml*) **3** fasten ○ *did up the buttons* **4** repair or redecorate
□ **do without** *vt* manage without

do[2] /dō/, **doh** *n* a syllable used in singing the 1st note of a scale

D.O. *abbr* **1** Doctor of Optometry **2** Doctor of Osteopathy

DOA *abbr* dead on arrival

do·a·ble /dóō əb'l/ *adj* able to be done

DOB, d.o.b. *abbr* date of birth

do·bra /dóbrə/ *n* the main unit of currency in São Tomé and Príncipe

⚡doc *abbr* a file extension indicating a document file

do·cent /dóss'nt, dō sént/ *n* **1** a lecturer in some US universities **2** a tourist guide, e.g., at a cathedral or museum

doc·ile /dóss'l/ *adj* quiet and easy to control —**doc·ile·ly** *adv* —**do·cil·i·ty** /do sílletee/ *n*

dock[1] *n* **1** a place for ships to moor **2** a group of piers for ships **3** a pier or wharf **4** a dry dock **5** a loading platform for trains or trucks ■ *vti* **1** moor a vessel **2** link one spacecraft up with another

dock[2] *vt* **1** reduce the wages of somebody as a punishment **2** remove the tail of an animal

dock[3] *n* the place in a courtroom where an accused person sits

dock[4] (*pl* **docks** *or same*) *n* **1** a broad-leafed plant with a long taproot **2** a broad-leafed weed

dock·er /dókər/ *n* SHIPPING = **longshoreman**

dock·et /dókət/ *n* **1** a list of future court cases **2** a book of upcoming court cases **3** a list of things to do ■ *vt* **1** put a legal case on a court calendar **2** list the contents of a package

⚡dock·ing sta·tion *n* a piece of hardware for recharging a portable computer

dock·work·er /dók wùrkər/ *n* SHIPPING = **longshoreman**

dock·yard /dók yaàrd/ *n* a place for building and repairing ships

doc·tor /dóktər/ *n* **1** somebody qualified and licensed to give medical treatment **2** a dentist, veterinarian, or osteopath **3** somebody with the highest university degree (*infml*) ■ *v* **1** *vt* change something in order to deceive **2** *vt* add a drug, alcohol, or poison to food or drink **3** *vti* treat people who are ill —**doc·tor·al** *adj*

ORIGIN Doctor came via French from Latin, where it meant "teacher." In English it was first used for any learned person. Its use in regard to the medical profession was at first just one of many applications of the general sense, and did not become firmly established until the later part of the 16C.

---

doc·tor·ate /dóktərət/ *n* the highest university degree

Doc·tor of Phi·los·o·phy *n* **1** the highest university degree **2** somebody with a Doctor of Philosophy degree

doc·tri·naire /dòktrə náir/ *adj* rigidly adhering to a specified theory —**doc·tri·naire** *n* —**doc·tri·nair·ism** *n* —**doc·tri·nar·i·an** *n*

doc·trine /dóktrin/ *n* **1** a rule or principle forming the basis of a belief or theory **2** a set of religious ideas taught as being truthful or correct —**doc·tri·nal** *adj* —**doc·tri·nal·ly** *adv*

doc·u·dra·ma /dòkyə draàmə/ *n* a dramatization of a true story

⚡doc·u·ment *n* /dókyəmənt/ **1** a formal piece of writing providing information or a record **2** a movie, photograph, or other recording containing information and usable as evidence **3** a computer file such as a database, spreadsheet, or text file ■ *vt* /dókyə mènt/ **1** record in a document **2** support with evidence —**doc·u·ment·a·ble** /dòkyə méntəb'l/ *adj* —**doc·u·ment·al** /dòkyə mént'l/ *adj*

doc·u·men·ta·ry /dòkyə méntəree/ *n* (*pl* **-ries**) a factual movie or TV program on a specific subject ■ *adj* consisting of documents

⚡doc·u·men·ta·tion /dòkyəmən táysh'n/ *n* **1** documents used as evidence or for reference **2** information and instructions for using a piece of computer software

DOD *abbr* Department of Defense

dod·der /dóddər/ *vi* tremble or walk unsteadily —**dod·der·ing** *adj*

do·dec·a·he·dron /dō dekə heédrən/ (*pl* **-drons** *or* **-dra** /-drə/) *n* a solid figure with 12 faces

Do·de·ca·nese /dō dèkkə neéz, -neéss/ group of islands in the SE Aegean Sea that form a department of Greece. Cap. Rhodes. Pop. 145,071 (1981).

dodge *v* (**dodged**, **dodg·ing**) **1** *vti* move quickly to avoid somebody or something **2** *vt* avoid doing something unpleasant ■ n 1 a trick to avoid doing something unpleasant 2 a quick movement to avoid somebody or something

dodge ball n a children's game in which players try to avoid being hit by a large ball

Dodge Ci·ty city in S Kansas, formerly famous as a lawless frontier town. Pop. 22,456 (1998).

dodg·er /dójjər/ n 1 somebody who avoids a duty or responsibility 2 somebody dishonest and untrustworthy

do·do /dó dō/ (pl -dos or -does) n an extinct flightless bird

ORIGIN Dodo was adopted in the early 17C from Portuguese. Its literal meaning was "simpleton, fool." The phrase *as dead as a dodo* is first recorded in the first decade of the 20C, over 200 years after the bird's extinction.

Do·do·ma /dódō màa, dódəma/ capital of Tanzania. Pop. 189,000 (1995).

doe /dō/ n a female mammal such as a deer, rabbit, or goat

SPELLCHECK Do not confuse the spelling of **doe** and **dough** ("of bread"), which sound similar.

DOE abbr Department of Energy

do·er /dóō ər/ n 1 somebody who does a particular thing (often in combination) o a wrong-doer 2 somebody who takes action rather than just thinking or talking about it

does 3rd person present singular of do

does·n't /dúzz'nt/ contr does not

~~does·nt~~ incorrect spelling of **doesn't**

doff vt take off your hat

ORIGIN Doff is a contraction of *do off* in its archaic sense "put or take off." The verb *don* is similarly formed.

dog n 1 a domestic carnivorous animal whose characteristic call is a bark 2 a male dog 3 a wild animal such as a wolf or fox that is related to domestic dogs 4 a woman regarded as not good-looking (insult) 5 a person of a particular type (infml) o You lucky dog! 6 something useless or inferior (infml) ■ **dogs** npl somebody's feet (infml dated) ■ vt (**dog·ged, dog·ging**) 1 bother somebody persistently 2 follow somebody closely ◊ **dog in the manger** preventing others from having what you cannot use yourself ◊ **a dog's life** a wretched existence ◊ **go to the dogs** deteriorate (infml)

dog-and-po·ny show n an elaborate presentation (infml)

dog bis·cuit n a hard cracker for dogs

dog·catch·er /dáwg kàchər, dóg-/ n a person whose job is to catch stray dogs

dog col·lar n a collar for a dog

dog days npl 1 the hottest period of the summer 2 a lazy or unsuccessful period

ORIGIN The name **dog days** is an allusion to

the "Dog Star" or Sirius, the brightest star in the sky. In ancient times it was noted that the hottest period of the year began when Sirius and the Sun rose at the same time.

doge /dōj/ n the chief magistrate in Renaissance Venice and Genoa

dog-eared adj with worn and well-thumbed pages

dog·fight /dáwg fìt, dóg-/ n aerial combat between fighter planes —**dog·fight·ing** n

dog·fish /dáwg fìsh, dóg-/ (pl -fish·es or same) n a small long-tailed shark

dog·ged /dáwgəd, dóggəd/ adj obstinately determined —**dog·ged·ly** adv —**dog·ged·ness** n

dog·ger·el /dáwgərəl, dóggərəl/ n humorous poetry with an irregular rhythm

dog·gy /dáwgee, dóggee/ (pl -gies), **dog·gie** n a dog (babytalk)

dog·gy bag n a bag in which a restaurant customer takes home leftover food (infml)

dog han·dler n a police officer working with a trained dog

dog·house /dáwg hòwss, dóg-/ (pl -hous·es /-hòwzəz, -/) n a dog's shelter ◊ **in the doghouse** in disgrace (infml)

do·gie /dógee/, **do·gy** (pl -gies), **do·gey** (pl -geys) n a motherless calf

dog·leg /dáwg lèg, dóg-/ n 1 a sharp bend in a road 2 in golf, a sharp bend in a fairway —**dog·leg** vi —**dog·leg·ged** /dàwg léggəd, -légd, dòg-/ adj

dog·ma /dáwgma, dógma/ (pl -mas or -ma·ta /-tə, -tə/) n a set of firmly held religious, political, or philosophical beliefs

dog·mat·ic /dawg máttik, dog-/ adj expressing or adhering to strong beliefs —**dog·mat·i·cal·ly** adv —**dog·ma·tism** /dáwgma tìzzəm, dógmə-/ n —**dog·ma·tist** n

dog of·fi·cer n a person whose job is to catch stray dogs

do-good·er /-gòodər/ n somebody who tries to help others, but whose actions may be unwelcome (infml; disapproving)

dog pad·dle n a stroke used by untrained or poor swimmers by which the arms remain submerged while they and the feet kick

dog·sled /dáwg slèd, dóg-/ n a sled pulled by dogs —**dog·sled** vi

dog tag n 1 an identification disk for a member of the military (infml) 2 an identification disk for a dog

dog-tired adj exhausted (infml)

dog·wood /dáwg wòod, dóg-/ (pl -woods or same) n a tree or bush with white flowers and red stems

do·gy n ZOOL = dogie

doh¹ n MUSIC = do²

doh² /dō/ interj humorously acknowledges having done or said something stupid (slang)

Do·ha /dóhə, -háa/ capital and largest city of

Qatar, on the Persian Gulf. Pop. 392,384 (1995).

doi·ly /dóylee/ (*pl* **-lies**) *n* a lacy mat for a plate

ORIGIN The **doily** is named for a 17C fabric seller of London, England. The word originally signified a woolen material. Short for *doily napkin*, it is recorded from the early 18C.

do·ing /dóo ing/ *present participle of* do[1] ■ *n* the performing or carrying out of something ■ **do·ings** *npl* somebody's achievements or social activities

do-it-your·self *n* the activity of making or repairing things yourself in your home —**do-it-your·self·er** *n*

dol·drums /dóldrəmz, dóldrəmz/ *npl* 1 stagnation 2 gloominess 3 an area without wind north of the equator

dole *n* charitable giving to people in need

dole (**dol·ing**, **doled**) □ **dole out** *vt* distribute (*infml*)

dole·ful /dólfəl/ *adj* sad —**dole·ful·ly** *adv* —**dole·ful·ness** *n*

doll /dol/ *n* 1 a child's toy in the shape of a person 2 a woman regarded as goodlooking (*infml; sometimes offensive*)

ORIGIN Doll is from a familiar form of the woman's name *Dorothy*. It is first recorded in the mid-16C, as a term for a man's mistress or lover, but this use died out during the 17C. As a toy it is found from the late 17C. From the early 18C it was used again for a woman, though this time one regarded as pretty if unintelligent or frivolous, a use that later extended to include any attractive woman.

□ **doll up** *vt* dress stylishly (*infml*)

dol·lar /dóllər/ *n* a unit of currency used in the United States, Canada, Australia, New Zealand, and several other countries

ORIGIN Dollar represents a northern form of German *taler*, a former silver coin. This was a shortening of *Joachimstaler*, literally "of Joachim's valley," named for Joachimstal (now Jáchymov in the Czech Republic), where the silver used for the coins was mined. The name **dollar** was formally adopted for the currency of the United States in 1785.

dol·lars-and-cents *adj* purely financial

dol·lar sign *n* the symbol ($) that represents a dollar

doll·house /dól hòwss/ (*pl* **-hous·es** /-hòwzəz/) *n* a toy house

dol·lop /dólləp/ *n* a spoon-sized amount of something soft, especially food (*infml*)

dol·ly /dóllee/ (*pl* **-lies**) *n* 1 a toy doll (*babytalk*) 2 a moving platform for filming moving shots

dol·men /dólmən, dól-/ *n* a prehistoric stone structure believed to have been a tomb

Do·lo·mi·tes /dólə mìts, dòllə-/ mountain group in the NE Italian Alps. Highest peak Marmolada, 10,964 ft./3,342 km.

do·lor /dólər/ *n* sadness (*literary*) —**do·lor·ous** /dólərəss, dóll-/ *adj*

dol·phin /dólfin/ (*pl* **-phins** *or* same) *n* 1 an intelligent sea mammal resembling a large fish, with a beak-shaped snout 2 a large sea game fish

dolt *n* a person regarded as unintelligent (*infml insult*)

↯ do·main /dō máyn, də-/ *n* 1 a sphere of influence 2 somebody's territory 3 the set of possible values specified for a given mathematical function 4 *also* **do·main name** an Internet address

↯ do·main name, **do·main** *n* the Internet address of a computer or network

dome /dōm/ *n* 1 a hemispheric-shaped roof or other structure 2 the hemispheric-shaped top of something —**domed** *adj*

do·mes·tic /də méstik/ *adj* 1 of or used in the home 2 of a family 3 kept as a farm animal or pet 4 not foreign 5 of a nation's internal affairs 6 enjoying home and family life ■ *n* a household servant —**do·mes·ti·cal·ly** *adv*

do·mes·ti·cate /də mésti kàyt/ (**-cat·ed**, **-cat·ing**) *vt* 1 tame a wild animal 2 accustom somebody to home life or housework (*humorous*) —**do·mes·ti·cat·ed** *adj* —**do·mes·ti·ca·tion** /də mèsti káysh'n/ *n*

do·mes·tic·i·ty /dō me stíssətee/ *n* 1 home life 2 a fondness for home life

do·mes·tic part·ner *n* a person with whom somebody cohabits who is not a spouse

dom·i·cile /dómmi sìl, dómmiss'l/ *n* somebody's home (*fml*)

dom·i·ciled /dómmi sìld, dómmiss'ld/ *adj* resident in a particular place

dom·i·nant /dómmanant/ *adj* 1 exerting power over others 2 more important, effective, or prominent than others 3 describes a gene that causes a parental characteristic to occur in any offspring 4 describes a characteristic determined by a dominant gene 5 describes the 5th note of a musical scale —**dom·i·nance** *n* —**dom·i·nant·ly** *adv*

dom·i·nate /dómma nàyt/ (**-nat·ed**, **-nat·ing**) *vti* 1 exert power over 2 be the most important aspect of 3 have a prevailing influence on —**dom·i·na·tion** /dómma náysh'n/ *n*

dom·i·neer·ing /dòmma néering, dómma néering/ *adj* tyrannical or overbearing

~~dominent~~ incorrect spelling of **dominant**

Do·min·go /də míng gō/, **Plácido** (*b.* 1941) Spanish-born operatic tenor

Dom·i·nic /dómminik/, **St.** (1170?–1221) Spanish priest and theologian

Dom·i·ni·ca /dòmmə néekə, də mínnikə/ island country in the Windward Islands, in the E Caribbean Sea. Cap. Roseau. Pop. 70,786 (2001). Length 29 mi./47 km. —**Dom·i·ni·can** *n, adj*

Do·min·i·can /də mínnikən/ *n* a member of the religious order founded by St Dominic —**Do·min·i·can** *adj*

Dom·i·ni·can Re·pub·lic /də mínnikən-/ country on Hispaniola Island in the N

Caribbean Sea. Cap. Santo Domingo. Pop. 8,581,477 (2001). Length 235 mi./380 km. —**Do·min·i·can** n, adj

do·min·ion /də mínnyən/ n 1 ruling power 2 a sphere of influence 3 a land governed by a ruler (often pl) 4 also **Do·min·ion** a self-governing part of the British Commonwealth

Do·min·ion Day n former name for **Canada Day**

dom·i·no /dómmə nõ̀/ (pl **-noes**) n a small playing tile, one of 28 that are covered with up to six dots

dom·i·no ef·fect n a succession of related events, each caused by the preceding one

dom·i·noes /dómmə nõ̀z/ n a game played using dominoes (+ sing verb)

Do·mi·tian /də míshən/, **Marcus** (AD 51–96) Roman emperor (AD 81–96)

don[1] n 1 a leader of an organized crime family 2 a Spanish gentleman or aristocrat 3 **Don** a title used before a man's name in a Spanish-speaking country

don[2] (**donned, don·ning**) vt put on a garment

ORIGIN Don is a contraction of do on in its archaic sense "put on." The verb **doff** is similarly formed.

Don river in W Russia, flowing into the Sea of Azov. Length 1,160 mi./1,870 km.

Do·ña /dónyə/ n a title used before a married woman's name in a Spanish-speaking country

do·nate /dṍ nàyt, dõ nãyt/ (**-nat·ed, -nat·ing**) vt 1 give or present something, especially to a charity 2 give blood, reproductive material, or a body part for another person —**do·na·tion** /dõ náysh'n/ n ◊ See note at **give**

Don·a·tel·lo /dònnə téllõ/ (1386?–1466) Italian sculptor

done /dun/ past participle of **do**[1] ■ adj 1 completed or finished 2 cooked through 3 socially acceptable ○ It's just not done. ■ interj confirms acceptance of a deal

done for adj facing ruin or destruction (infml)

Do·nets /də néts, -nyéts/ river in SW Russia and SE Ukraine. Length 631 mi./1,020 km.

Do·nets'k /də nyétsk/ city in SE Ukraine. Pop. 1,065,000 (1998).

dong[1] n a deep toll of a bell —**dong** vi

dong[2] n the main unit of Vietnamese currency

⚡**don·gle** /dóng g'l, dawng-/ n a device plugged into a computer to allow protected software to be used

Don·i·zet·ti /dònni zéttee/, **Gaetano** (1797–1848) Italian composer

Don Juan /dòn waán, -hwaán/ n a man who has casual sex with many women

don·key /dáwngkee, dóng-/ (pl **-keys**) n a domesticated gray or brown mammal resembling a small long-eared horse

Donne /dun/, **John** (1572–1631) English poet, prose writer, and cleric

Don·ner Pass /dònnər-/ pass in the Sierra Nevada, NE California, named for a group of migrants believed to have resorted to cannibalism when they were snowed in there in 1846–47

do·nor /dónər/ n 1 somebody who gives something, especially money 2 somebody who gives blood, reproductive material, or a body part for another person —**do·nor·ship** n

do·nor card n a card authorizing medical use of the carrier's body parts after death

Don Qui·xo·te /dòn kee hṍtee, -kwíksət/ n an impractical idealist who champions hopeless causes

ORIGIN The original **Don Quixote** was the hero of a romance (1605–15) by the Spanish writer Miguel de Cervantes.

don't /dõnt/ contr do not

do·nut /dṍ nùt/ n FOOD = **doughnut**

doo·dad /dṍo dàd/ n a small object (infml)

doo·dle /dṍod'l/ (**-dled, -dling**) vti scribble drawings or designs absent-mindedly —**doo·dle** n

doo·dle·bug /dṍod'l bùg/ n an ant-lion larva

doom n 1 a dreadful fate 2 an official judgment on somebody (fml) ■ vt condemn to a dreadful fate —**doomed** adj

doom·say·er /dṍom sàyr/ n a predictor of disaster

dooms·day /dṍomz dày/ n 1 also **Dooms·day** the day of the Last Judgment 2 the end of the world

door /dawr/ n 1 a movable panel for opening or closing an entrance 2 a gap forming an entrance ◊ **out of doors** in the open air

door·bell /dáwr bèl/ n an electric bell on or beside a door for the convenience of visitors

do-or-die adj performed or done in utter recklessness

door·jamb /dáwr jàm/, **door·post** /dáwr põst/ n a vertical side piece of the frame of a door

door·keep·er /dáwr kèepər/ n 1 somebody on duty at a door 2 also **Door·keep·er** a legislative officer

door·knob /dáwr nòb/ n a round handle on a door used to open and close it

door·man /dáwr màn, -mən/ (pl **-men** /-mèn, -mən/) n an attendant at the entrance to a building

door·mat /dáwr màt/ n 1 a mat on which to wipe your shoes 2 somebody who submits to inconsiderate treatment (infml; disapproving)

~~doormouse~~ incorrect spelling of **dormouse**

door·nail /dáwr nàyl/ n a stud formerly used on doors

door·plate /dáwr plàyt/ n a sign attached to a door

door·post *n* = doorjamb

door prize *n* a prize for the holder of the winning ticket at an event

door·sill /dáwr sìl/ *n* the bottom part of the frame of a door

door·step /dáwr stèp/ *n* a step in front of a door

door·stop /dáwr stòp/ *n* **1** something used to keep a door open **2** a rubber projection that prevents damage to a wall when a door is opened

door to door *adv* **1** going from one house to the next, usually to solicit or sell something **2** from the start to the finish of a trip —**door-to-door** *adj*

door·way /dáwr wày/ *n* **1** an entrance to a building **2** an opportunity to achieve or escape from something

doo-wop /doò wòp/ *n* harmonized rhythm-and-blues singing of nonsense words

doo·zy /dóozee/ (*pl* **-zies**) *n* something wonderful or awful *(slang)*

do·pa·mine /dópə mèen/ *n* a chemical compound occurring in the brain

dope *n* **1** an illegal drug, especially marijuana *(slang)* **2** an illegal drug affecting the performance of an athlete or racehorse **3** inside information *(slang)* **4** a person regarded as unintelligent *(infml insult)* ■ *vt* (**doped, dop·ing**) add an illegal drug to food or drink

dop·ey /dópee/ (**-i·er, -i·est**), **dop·y** (**-i·er, -i·est**) *adj* **1** half-asleep or drowsy **2** considered unintelligent *(infml)*

dop·pel·gäng·er /dópp'l gàngər/, **dop·pel·gang·er** *n* **1** somebody similar to another person **2** a ghost identical to a living person

Dop·pler ef·fect /dópplər-/, **Dop·pler shift** *n* an apparent change in the frequency of a sound or light wave because of motion

Dor·ic /dáwrik/ *n* an ancient Greek dialect ■ *adj* **1** in a simple classical Greek architectural style **2** of Doric

dork *n* a person regarded as unintelligent or unfashionable *(slang insult)* —**dork·y** *adj*

dorm *n* a dormitory *(infml)*

dor·mant /dáwrmənt/ *adj* **1** not actively growing in order to survive adverse environmental conditions **2** temporarily inactive or not in use **3** not erupting, but not extinct *(refers to volcanoes)* —**dor·man·cy** *n*

dor·mer /dáwrmər/, **dor·mer win·dow** *n* a window projecting from a roof

dor·mi·to·ry /dáwrmi tàwree/ (*pl* **-ries**) *n* **1** a large room with many beds **2** a building where students live

dor·mouse /dáwr mòwss/ (*pl* **-mice** /-mìss/) *n* a small nocturnal reddish brown rodent

dor·sal /dáwrs'l/ *adj* of or on the back —**dor·sal·ly** *adv*

Dort·mund /dáwrtmənd, -mòònt/ inland port in NW Germany. Pop. 600,918 (1997).

do·ry[1] /dáwree/ (*pl* **-ries**) *n* a narrow flat-bottomed high-sided fishing boat

do·ry[2] /dáwree/ (*pl* **-ries**) *n* a bottom-dwelling ocean fish with an extendable mouth

⚡**DOS** *abbr* **1** denial-of-service **2** disk operating system

dos·age /dóssij/ *n* the amount and frequency prescribed for a medication

dose /dōss/ *n* **1** a prescribed amount of medication **2** an amount of radiation to which somebody has been exposed ■ *vt* (**dosed, dos·ing**) give medicine to somebody

Dos Pas·sos /dōss pássōss/, **John** (1896–1970) US writer

dos·si·er /dóssee ày/ *n* a set of papers containing information on somebody or something

Fyodor Dostoyevsky

Dos·toy·ev·sky /dòstə yéfskee/, **Fyodor** (1821–81) Russian novelist

⚡**dot** *n* **1** a written or printed point, especially one above an "i" or "j" or used as a punctuation mark **2** a punctuation mark in an Internet address **3** a spot or speck ○ *The ship was a dot on the horizon.* **4** a small amount of ○ *a dot of butter* **5** the shorter of the two symbols used in Morse code **6** a symbol placed after a musical note to increase its value by half ■ *vt* (**dot·ted, dot·ting**) **1** mark something with a dot **2** sprinkle something with small amounts of something ○ *Dot the surface with butter.* ○ **on the dot (of)** exactly at a particular time

DOT *abbr* Department of Transportation

dot·age /dótij/ *n* physical and mental weakening sometimes experienced in old age *(offensive)*

⚡**dot-com, dot com** *n* an Internet business —**dot-com** *adj* —**dot-com·er** /dot kómmər/ *n*

dote /dōt/ (**dot·ed, dot·ing**) *vi* show extreme fondness for somebody —**dot·ing** *adj* —**dot·ing·ly** *adv*

⚡**dot ma·trix** *n* an array of dots displaying information

⚡**dot pitch** *n* a measure of the clarity of a computer image

dot·ted /dóttəd/ *adj* **1** marked with dots **2** describes musical notes increased in value by a half **3** covered with specks ○ *a sky dotted with stars* **4** spread randomly over an area

dotted line *n* a printed line of dots or dashes

dot·ty /dóttee/ (**-ti·er, -ti·est**) *adj* endearingly irrational or impractical *(infml)* —**dot·ti·ness** *n*

Dou·a·la /doo aálá/, **Du·a·la** largest port in Cameroon. Pop. 1,500,000 (1997).

dou·ble /dúbb'l/ adj **1** being twice as much or many **2** having two equal or similar parts **3** meant for two people **4** folded in two **5** having a double flower petals ■ adv **1** twice as much **2** so as to form two layers or folds ■ n **1** twice the usual amount **2** a person or thing identical to somebody else or something else **3** a hotel room for two people **4** a stand-in for a movie actor **5** in the game of bridge, a call that increases the score for success or failure in a contract **6** in baseball, a hit that enables a batter to reach second base ■ v (-bled, -bling) **1** vti increase twofold **2** vt fold something in two **3** vi have a second function or role **4** vi act as a stand-in **5** vi in the game of bridge, announce a double **6** vi in baseball, make a double —**dou·bly** adv ◊ **on the double** right away and as quickly as possible (infml)

□ **double back** vi go back along the same route

□ **double over** vi bend deeply from the waist

□ **double up** vi **1** share with somebody else **2** bend the body sharply

dou·ble a·gent n a spy working for two nations simultaneously

dou·ble-bar·reled adj describes guns with two barrels

dou·ble bass n the largest instrument in the violin family

dou·ble bed n a bed wide enough for two sleepers

dou·ble bind n **1** a dilemma with two undesirable alternative courses **2** a dilemma caused by contradictory demands

dou·ble-blind adj describes experiments where neither the scientists nor the subjects know which treatment is genuine and which is a control procedure

dou·ble boil·er n a pan that heats the contents of another pan fitted on top of it

dou·ble-book vti promise the same reservation to two people

dou·ble-breast·ed adj describes coats or jackets with a large overlap at the front and two rows of buttons

dou·ble-check vti verify by checking twice

dou·ble chin n a fold of loose flesh under the chin —**dou·ble-chinned** adj

⚡ **dou·ble-click** vti press a mouse button twice quickly, e.g., to activate a command

dou·ble-cross vt betray an associate —**dou·ble-cross·ing** adj

dou·ble date n a situation in which two couples go out socially together —**dou·ble-date** vti

dou·ble-deal·ing n deceit involving betrayal of an associate —**dou·ble-deal·er** n —**dou·ble-deal·ing** adj

dou·ble-deck·er n **1** something with two layers **2** a bus or train with two levels

⚡ **dou·ble den·si·ty** adj with double the storage capacity of a standard computer disk

dou·ble-dig·it adj between 10 and 99

dou·ble-du·ty adj having two functions

dou·ble ea·gle n in golf, three strokes under par

dou·ble-edged adj **1** ambiguous **2** having two purposes or effects

dou·ble en·ten·dre /-aan taándrə, dòò bb'l aaN taàNdrə/ (pl **dou·ble en·ten·dres** /pronunc. same/) n an ambiguous remark with a sexually suggestive meaning

dou·ble fault n in tennis, two consecutive incorrect serves —**dou·ble-fault** vi

dou·ble fea·ture n two movies shown consecutively

dou·ble-head·er n two consecutive games

dou·ble he·lix n the double-spiral molecular structure of DNA

dou·ble in·dem·ni·ty n an insurance payout for accidental death that is double the value of the policy

dou·ble jeop·ard·y n a second prosecution of somebody for the same crime

dou·ble-joint·ed adj able to bend in the opposite direction to that in which joints normally bend —**dou·ble-joint·ed·ness** n

dou·ble life n a life in which somebody has two identities

dou·ble neg·a·tive n a phrase containing two negatives

dou·ble-park vti park alongside another parked vehicle —**dou·ble-park·ing** n

dou·bles /dúbb'lz/ (pl same) n a racket game between pairs of players

dou·ble-sid·ed adj having two usable sides

dou·ble stan·dard n a standard applied unfairly to different groups

dou·blet /dúbblət/ n a man's close-fitting jacket popular between the 15C and 17C

dou·ble take n a delayed reaction of surprise (infml)

dou·ble talk, dou·ble-speak /dúbb'l speèk/ n talk intended to confuse or deceive

dou·ble-think /dúbb'l thingk/ n acceptance of opposing beliefs and falsehoods as a way of deceiving yourself

dou·ble time n **1** double the usual rate of pay **2** a musical tempo twice as fast as the basic tempo **3** a fast marching pace

dou·ble-time (dou·ble-timed, dou·ble-tim·ing) vi march at a fast pace

dou·ble vi·sion n a condition in which the eyes see two of everything

dou·ble wham·my n a pair of unpleasant things happening together (slang)

dou·ble-wide /dúbb'l wīd/ n two mobile homes joined together

dou·bloon /də blóon/ n a former Spanish coin

doubt /dowt/ vt **1** think something unlikely ○ I doubt if he'll come. **2** mistrust ○ no reason to doubt her ■ n mistrustful uncertainty —**doubt·er** n ◊ **beyond (the shadow of a) doubt** completely certain ◊ **in doubt**

1 feeling uncertain **2** unlikely or improbable ◊ See note at **doubtful**

doubt·ful /dówtfəl/ *adj* **1** unsure **2** unlikely —**doubt·ful·ly** *adv* —**doubt·ful·ness** *n*

SYNONYMS **doubtful, uncertain, unsure,** in **doubt, dubious, skeptical** CORE MEANING: feeling doubt or uncertainty

---

doubt·ing Thom·as *n* somebody insisting on proof

ORIGIN The original **doubting Thomas** was the apostle of Jesus Christ in the Bible who would not accept the Resurrection until he had seen and touched Jesus Christ's wounds (John 14:1–7, 20:19–29).

---

doubt·less /dówtləss/ *adv* **1** for sure or certain **2** in all probability

douche /doosh/ *n* **1** the cleaning of a body part with a water jet **2** a piece of equipment producing a cleansing water jet ■ *vti* (**douched, douch·ing**) clean a body part with a water jet

dough /dō/ *n* **1** a mixture of flour and water, often with other ingredients such as yeast, for baking bread or pastry **2** money *(slang)* ◊ See note at **doe**

dough·boy /dó bòy/, **Dough·boy** *n* a US infantryman in World War I

dough·nut /dó nùt/, **do·nut** *n* **1** a sugar-coated cake of deep-fried dough, either ring-shaped or round **2** a 360-degree turn in motor vehicle or watercraft

~~daughter~~ incorrect spelling of **daughter**

dough·ty /dówtee/ (**-ti·er, -ti·est**) *adj* resolute *(dated)* —**dough·ti·ly** *adv* —**dough·ti·ness** *n*

dough·y /dó ee/ (**-i·er, -i·est**) *adj* **1** resembling dough in consistency **2** pale and flabby

Doug·las /dúggləss/, **Stephen A.** (1813–61) US politician

Doug·las, William O. (1898–1980) associate justice of the US Supreme Court (1939–75)

Doug·lass /dúggləss/, **Frederick** (1817–95) US abolitionist, orator, and writer

dou·la /doolə/ *n* a woman who assists in childbirth

dour /dowr, door/ *adj* severe, morose, or unfriendly —**dour·ly** *adv* —**dour·ness** *n*

Dou·ro /dó ròo, dów ròo/, **Due·ro** /dwáirō/ river in N Spain and N Portugal. Length 556 mi./895 km.

douse /dowss, dowz/ (**doused, dous·ing**), **dowse** (**dowsed, dows·ing**) *vt* **1** immerse in water **2** put water or other liquid on —**douse** *n* —**dous·er** *n*

dove[1] /duv/ *n* **1** a heavy-bodied small-headed bird with a cooing call **2** *also* **Dove** a supporter of peace

dove[2] /dōv/ past tense of **dive**

dove·cote /dúv kòt/, **dove·cot** /dúv kòt/ *n* a home for domestic pigeons

Do·ver /dóvər/ **1** capital of Delaware. Pop. 30,369 (1998). **2** city in SE New Hampshire. Pop. 25,953 (1998).

Do·ver, Strait of narrowest part of the English Channel, between Dover, England, and Calais, France. Length 21 mi./34 km.

dove·tail /dúv tàyl/ *v* **1** *vti* fit neatly together **2** *vt* fasten pieces of wood with interlocking V-shaped joints ■ *n also* **dove·tail joint** a joint made using V-shaped projecting pieces of wood

dow·dy /dówdee/ (**-di·er, -di·est**) *adj* plain and unfashionable —**dow·di·ly** *adv* —**dow·di·ness** *n*

dow·el /dów əl/ *n also* **dow·el pin** a peg for joining pieces of wood or metal ■ *vt* join pieces of wood or metal with dowels

dow·er /dowr/ *n* a dowry *(archaic)*

Dow Jones Av·er·age *tdmk* a trademark for an index of the prices of selected stocks, based on a formula developed and revised periodically by Dow Jones & Company, Inc.

⚡ **down**[1] /down/ *prep* **1** to or at a lower level on or in something ○ *ran down the stairs* **2** to or at a position farther along ○ *halfway down the street* ■ *adv* **1** at or to a lower level or position ○ *down in the basement* ○ *get interest rates down* **2** away from the present or a more important location ○ *go down to the beach* **3** to a more southerly place ○ *drive down to Atlanta* **4** short or losing by a particular amount ○ *two goals down at halftime* **5** in part payment or as a deposit ○ *put 5% down* **6** from an earlier to a later period or person ○ *jewels that had been handed down to him* **7** on paper as a record ○ *wrote it down* **8** chosen or scheduled for something ○ *We're down for both sessions.* ■ *adj* **1** unhappy **2** not in operation *(refers to computer systems)* **3** given in part payment or as a deposit ○ *a down payment on the car* ■ *vt* **1** eat or drink quickly **2** make fall to the ground **3** declare a ball out of play ■ *n* in football, one of four consecutive plays in which a team must score or advance ten yards ◊ **be down on** show dislike or hostility toward *(slang)*

ORIGIN The adverb **down** is a very early shortening of archaic *adown*, literally "of a hill," used in the same sense. The noun **down** "hill" now mainly occurs in place names and in the *Downs*, chalk uplands in S England. It may be of Celtic origin, and ultimately related to *town*.

---

down[2] /down/ *n* **1** soft fluffy feathers or hairs **2** a covering of soft hairs

down[3] /down/ *n UK* a grassy treeless hill *(often in place names)* ■ **downs** *npl* rolling grassland

down-and-out *adj* jobless and poor *(infml)*

down-at-heel, down-at-the-heel *adj* shabbily dressed

down·beat /dówn bèet/ *adj* pessimistic ■ *n* **1** the first beat in a bar of music **2** a conductor's downward gesture indicating a downbeat

down·burst /dówn bùrst/ *n* a powerful downward wind associated with thunderstorms, of special danger to aircraft

down·cast /dówn kàst/ *adj* 1 sad 2 looking down

down·draft /dówn dràft/ *n* a downward movement of air

Down East *n* Maine and the other New England States (*infml*) —**Down East·er** *n* —**Down East·ern** *adj*

down·er /dównər/ *n* (*slang*) 1 a sedative drug 2 somebody or something regarded as depressing

down·fall /dówn fàwl/ *n* failure or ruin negating prior success, or a cause of this

down·grade /dówn gràyd/ *vt* (**-grad·ed, -grad·ing**) 1 lower the status or value of 2 move to a less important job ■ *n* a downward slope

down·heart·ed /dòwn haártəd/ *adj* discouraged

down·hill *adv* /down híl/ toward the bottom of a hill ■ *adj* /dówn híl/ sloping down ■ *n* /dówn híl/ a skiing race down a long mountain slope ◊ **go downhill** decline or deteriorate

down·home /dówn hóm/ *adj* unpretentious and simple (*infml*)

Down·ing Street /dówning-/ *n* the London street containing the official residence of the British prime minister

⚡**down·load** /dówn lòd/ *vti* transfer data between computers or be transferred by computer ■ *n* 1 a downloading of data 2 downloaded data

down·mar·ket /dówn maàrkət/ *adj* cheap and of low quality

down pay·ment *n* a partial payment made on a purchase

down·play /dówn plày/ *vt* make something seem less important or serious

down·pour /dówn pàwr/ *n* a heavy fall of rain

down·right /dówn rìt/ *adj* complete and utter ■ *adv* completely and utterly

down·riv·er /dówn rívvər/ *adv, adj* toward the mouth of a river

down·scale /dówn skàyl/ *adj* cheap and of low quality ■ *vti* (**-scaled, -scal·ing**) make or become smaller

down·shift /dówn shìft/ *vi* change a highly paid but stressful job for a lower paid but less stressful one —**down·shift** *n*

down·side /dówn sìd/ *n* a negative side to something positive

down·size /dówn sìz/ (**-sized, -siz·ing**) *v* 1 *vti* make a business smaller by cutting employees' jobs 2 *vt* make something smaller

down·spout /dówn spòwt/ *n* a pipe carrying rainwater from a roof

down·stage /dówn stàyj/ *adv, adj* to or at the front of a stage

down·stairs /dówn stáirz/ *adv* to a lower floor ■ *adj* on a lower floor ■ *n* the lower floor of a building

down·state /dówn stáyt/ *adj, adv* 1 in or to the south of a state 2 away from the main cities of a state —**down·state** *n* —**down·stat·er** *n*

down·stream /dówn strèem/ *adj* 1 situated toward the mouth of a river 2 occurring in the later stages of production ■ *adv* toward the mouth of a river

down·swing /dówn swìng/ *n* 1 a downward trend 2 the downward part of a golfer's swing

Down syn·drome /dówn-/, **Down's syn·drome** /dównz-/ *n* a genetic disorder characterized by unique facial features and some learning disabilities

down-the-line *adj* unwavering

down·time /dówn tìm/ *n* the time when work or production is stopped, e.g., because machinery is not working

down-to-earth *adj* practical and realistic

down·town /down tówn, dówn tòwn/ *adj, adv* US, Can, NZ in or to the center of a city, especially its business center ■ *n* 1 a city center 2 lower Manhattan —**down·town·er** *n*

down·trend /dówn trènd/ *n* a downward trend

down·trod·den /dówn tròdd'n/ *adj* oppressed

down·turn /dówn tùrn/ *n* a reduction in economic activity

down·ward¹ /dównwərd/, **down·wards** /-wərdz/ *adv* 1 toward a lower place, level, or condition 2 to a later time or generation —**down·ward·ly** *adv*

down·ward² /dównwərd/ *adj* 1 moving to a lower place, level, or condition 2 coming from an origin or source

down·ward·ly mo·bile *adj* moving to a lower status, social class, or income bracket —**down·ward mo·bil·i·ty** *n*

down·wind /dówn wínd/ *adv, adj* in the direction of the wind

down·y /dównee/ (**-i·er, -i·est**) *adj* 1 soft and fluffy 2 covered with soft hairs

dow·ry /dówree/ (*pl* **-ries**) *n* a bride's family's gift to her bridegroom

dowse¹ /dowz/ (**dowsed, dows·ing**) *vi* use a divining rod —**dows·er** *n*

dowse² /dowss, dowz/ *vt, n* = **douse**

dows·ing rod *n* a divining rod

doy·en /dóy ən, doy én/ *n* the most senior and respected man in a sphere of activity

doy·enne /doy én/ *n* the most senior and respected woman in a sphere of activity

Doyle /doyl/, **Sir Arthur Conan** (1859–1930) Scottish-born British writer and physician

doz. *abbr* dozen

doze /dóz/ (**dozed, doz·ing**) *vi* 1 have a short light sleep 2 laze or daydream —**doze** *n*
□ **doze off** *vi* fall into a light sleep

doz·en /dúzz'n/ *n* (*pl* same), *det* a group of 12 objects or people ■ *npl*, *adv* **doz·ens** a large number (*infml*) ◊ **has dozens of friends** ◊ **gave away dozens more**

ORIGIN Dozen comes through French from

Latin *duodecim* "twelve," which was formed from *duo* "two" and *decem* "ten."

do·zy /dṓzee/ (**-zi·er, -zi·est**) *adj* **1** drowsy **2** *US, ANZ* rotten —**do·zi·ly** *adv* —**do·zi·ness** *n*

dp *abbr* double play

DP *abbr also* **D.P.** displaced person

⚡ **dpi** /dée pée ī/ *n* a measure of the density of a computer or printer image. Full form **dots per inch**

DPT *abbr* diphtheria, pertussis, tetanus (vaccine)

dr *abbr* dram[1]

dr. *abbr* dram[1]

Dr. *abbr* **1** doctor **2** Drive (*in addresses*)

drab *adj* (**drab·ber, drab·best**) **1** lacking color or brightness **2** boring **3** pale grayish brown in color ■ *n* a pale grayish brown color —**drab·ly** *adv* —**drab·ness** *n*

drach·ma /drákmə/ (*pl* **-mas** *or* **-mae** /-mee/) *n* the main unit of the former Greek currency

Dra·co /dráykō/ (*fl* 7C BC) Athenian political leader and legislator

dra·co·ni·an /drə kṓnee ən/ *adj* excessively harsh

ORIGIN The first person to introduce **draconian** laws was the Athenian statesman Draco in the 7C BC.

draft *n* **1** a current of air **2** a preliminary version of a text, picture, or plan **3** military conscription **4** a system of recruiting players for professional sports teams **5** a bank check **6** the act of pulling something along or drawing something in **7** a mouthful of air, liquid, or smoke **8** beer in barrels **9** the depth needed by a ship to float ■ *vt* **1** call up somebody for military service **2** transfer somebody somewhere for duty **3** make a draft of something ■ *adj* **1** served from the barrel **2** used to pull heavy loads —**draft·ee** *n* —**draft·er** *n* ◇ **on draft** available for serving from the barrel (*refers to beer*)

drafts·man /dráftsmən/ (*pl* **-men** /-mən/) *n* **1** a technical designer **2** a man with a particular skill in drawing ○ *He's an excellent draftsman.* —**drafts·man·ship** *n*

drafts·per·son /dráfts pùrs'n/ *n* a technical designer

draft·y /dráftee/ (**-i·er, -i·est**) *adj* windy and cold —**draft·i·ness** *n*

⚡ **drag** *v* (**dragged, drag·ging**) **1** *vt* pull something heavy along with effort **2** *vt* move or remove somebody or something by pulling with force **3** *vti* trail along the ground **4** *vi* pass or proceed in a slow and boring way **5** *vt* move a computer icon with a mouse **6** *vt* search a body of water with a net or hook **7** *vi* puff on a cigarette, pipe, or cigar (*infml*) ■ *n* **1** a hindrance **2** (*symbol* D) the resistance experienced by a moving object **3** somebody or something boring (*infml*) **4** clothing characteristic of one sex worn by somebody of the other sex (*slang*) **5** a

street or road (*slang*) ◇ **drag your feet** *or* **heels** do something slowly and reluctantly ◇ See note at **pull**

□ **drag down** *vt* **1** bring to a lower level or status **2** make listless or tired

□ **drag in** *vt* involve inappropriately

□ **drag on** *vi* go on too long

□ **drag out** *vt* prolong

⚡ **drag and drop** *vt* move a computer icon somewhere with a mouse

drag·net /drág nèt/ *n* **1** a police hunt for a criminal **2** a weighted net for fishing or for dragging a body of water

drag·on /drággən/ *n* **1** a large fire-breathing mythical monster with wings and a long tail **2** a large lizard

drag·on·fly /drággən flī/ (*pl* **-flies**) *n* a long thin flying insect with transparent wings and a shimmering body

dra·goon /drə goon/ *n* **1** a 17–18C mounted infantryman **2** an 18–19C cavalryman ■ *vt* **1** force into doing something **2** subjugate using military troops

drag race *n* a short race between cars to discover which has the fastest acceleration —**drag rac·er** *n* —**drag rac·ing** *n*

drag·ster /drágstər/ *n* **1** a car specially designed for drag racing **2** the driver of a dragster

drain *n* **1** a pipe that takes sewage or waste water away from a building **2** something that uses up resources **3** the gradual loss or diminishing of an important resource ■ *v* **1** *vti* flow out or away, or allow to flow out or away **2** *vti* empty or become empty by causing a liquid to flow out **3** *vt* make land drier by leading water away from it **4** *vt* drink all the contents of a container **5** *vt* use something up gradually ○ *draining the company's financial resources* **6** *vi* disappear gradually ○ *The color drained from her face.* **7** *vt* leave somebody feeling exhausted ◇ **down the drain** wasted or squandered (*infml*)

drain·age /dráynij/ *n* **1** the process of draining something **2** a sewage system

drain·board /dráyn bàwrd/ *n* a sloping surface next to a sink for drying dishes

drain·er /dráynər/ *n* a rack or container for draining things

drain·pipe /dráyn pīp/ *n* a pipe for draining rainwater away from a roof

drake *n* a male duck

dram[1] *n* **1** a unit of weight equal to 1/16 of an ounce **2** a US unit of weight equal to 1/8 of an ounce

ORIGIN **Dram** derives through Latin from a Greek word that is thought to have originally signified the number of coins that can be held in one hand. The same Greek word is also the source of **drachma**, a unit of Greek currency.

dram[2] *n* the main unit of Armenian currency

⚡ **DRAM** /dée ràm/ *abbr* dynamic random access memory

dra·ma /dráamə, drámmə/ n 1 a serious play written for the stage, television, or radio 2 plays as a genre or subject of study

dra·mat·ic /drə máttik/ adj 1 of or for the theater 2 exciting and intense 3 sudden and marked 4 very impressive in appearance, color, or effect —**dra·mat·i·cal·ly** adv

dra·mat·ic i·ro·ny n a situation in which a character in a play is unaware of something that the audience knows

dra·mat·ics /drə máttiks/ n the production of plays (+ sing or pl verb) ■ npl melodramatic behavior (+ pl verb)

dra·ma·tis per·so·nae /dro máatiss pər sōnee, -nī, dràamətiss-/ npl 1 a list of the characters in a play 2 the characters in a play (fml)

dram·a·tist /drámmətist, draàamətist/ n a playwright

dram·a·tize /drámmə tīz, draàamə-/ (-tized, -tiz·ing) v 1 vt adapt material for the stage 2 vti exaggerate the importance or seriousness of a situation —**dram·a·ti·za·tion** /drammatí záysh'n, draàamə-/ n —**dram·a·tiz·er** n

drank past tense of **drink**

drape v (draped, drap·ing) 1 vt place fabric over something so that it falls in loose folds 2 vi hang in loose folds 3 vt rest part of the body casually on or over something ■ n 1 a curtain hung, e.g., at a window (usually pl) 2 a piece of fabric draped over something 3 the way fabric hangs

drap·er·y /dráypəree/ (pl -ies) n 1 cloth or a piece of cloth arranged to hang in folds 2 a curtain hung, e.g., at a window (usually pl)

dras·tic /drástik/ adj having a powerful effect or far-reaching consequences —**dras·ti·cal·ly** adv

draught n, adj UK = **draft**

Dra·vid·i·an /drə víddee ən/ n 1 a family of languages spoken in S India and NE Sri Lanka 2 a member of an aboriginal Indian people —**Dra·vid·i·an** adj

draw v (drew /droo/ drawn) 1 vti make a picture using, e.g., a pencil 2 vi move in a particular direction with a smooth motion ○ Another car drew alongside ours. 3 vi approach a particular point in time 4 vt pull something toward or away from something else 5 vt pull a vehicle ○ a carriage drawn by six horses 6 vt open or close a curtain 7 vt pull on a string, rope, or cord 8 vt pull back the string of an archery bow 9 vt take something out of its packaging or enclosure ○ drew the letter out of the envelope 10 vti pull a weapon from, e.g., a holster 11 vt remove liquid from a container using a tap 12 vt elicit a response 13 vt find a physical or a moral resource in, e.g., a person ○ drew courage from her example 14 vt obtain information from somebody 15 vt cause attention to be directed in a particular direction ○ draw admiring glances 16 vt attract people wanting to see something ○ The performance always drew crowds. 17 vti suck something such as air or smoke in 18 vi allow a current

of air through a place 19 vt receive money 20 vt write out a check or a legal document 21 vt arrive at a conclusion or inference 22 vt formulate a distinction or parallel ○ drew a distinction between the causes of the two events 23 vt choose something at random 24 vt in card games, take a card or make a player play a certain suit 25 vti finish equal in a sport or game 26 vt disembowel a victim 27 vt in cue games, give backspin to a ball 28 vt in golf, make the ball curve in the direction of the swing ■ n 1 the act of pulling 2 a lottery or raffle, or the selection of a lottery winner 3 a usually random selection of contestants 4 a random choice 5 a popular attraction 6 a contest that neither side wins 7 a pulling of a gun ◊ See note at **pull**

ORIGIN The picture-making sense of **draw** arose from the idea of "drawing" or "pulling" a pen or brush across a surface.

□ **draw back** vi pull back suddenly, e.g., in fear

□ **draw in** vt entice an unwilling participant into an act

□ **draw on** v 1 vt make use of a resource 2 vi move to or enter a later stage ○ as the day drew on

□ **draw out** v 1 vt prolong 2 vi grow longer (refers to days in spring) 3 vt encourage to talk freely

□ **draw up** v 1 vt write out a legal document 2 vti come or bring something to a stop ○ saw the bus draw up

draw·back /dráw bàk/ n a disadvantage

draw·bridge /dráw brij/ n a bridge that can be raised

draw·down /dráw dòwn/ n 1 depletion 2 a lowering of the water level in a reservoir

draw·er /drawr/ n 1 a box-shaped storage compartment that slides in and out of a piece of furniture 2 somebody who writes a check 3 somebody or something that draws

draw·ing /dráw ing/ n 1 a picture made with a pencil, pen, or similar instrument 2 the art of making pictures while not using paint 3 a selection of a lottery winner

draw·ing board n a board on which to draw ◇ back to the drawing board indicates a need to redesign a failed operation or project (infml)

draw·ing card n somebody or something that attracts many of visitors, spectators, or customers

draw·ing room n a formal room in a house used for entertaining guests

ORIGIN A **drawing room** was originally a withdrawing room. It referred to a private room off a more public one, and later to a room to which guests could withdraw after dinner.

drawl vti speak or say slowly ■ n a slow way of speaking —**drawl·er** n —**drawl·ing·ly** adv

drawn past tense of **draw** ■ *adj* tired-looking and haggard

drawn-out *adj* continuing longer than necessary or desirable

draw-string /dráw strìng/ *n* a cord that can be drawn tight to close an opening around a bag or in a garment

dread /dred/ *vti* **1** feel extremely frightened by the prospect of something **2** be reluctant to deal with something ■ *n* **1** terror **2** a source of fear ■ *adj* causing fear or awe (*literary*)

dread-ed /dréddəd/ *adj* feared

dread-ful /drédfəl/ *adj* **1** extremely bad **2** extreme —**dread-ful-ly** *adv* —**dread-ful-ness** *n*

dread-locks /dréd lòks/ *npl* a hairstyle in which long strands are twisted from the scalp to the tips

dread-nought /dréd nàwt/ *n* a battleship with guns all of the same caliber

dream /dreem/ *n* **1** a sequence of images that appear in the mind during sleep **2** a daydream **3** something hoped or wished for **4** an unrealizable hope **5** a state of inattention o *in a dream* **6** something beautiful ■ *v* (**dreamed** *or* **dreamt** /dremt/) **1** *vti* have a dream while sleeping **2** *vi* engage in daydreaming **3** *vi* wish for something o *dreamed of living abroad* **4** *vi* consider o *How could you even dream of doing such a thing?* ■ *adj* ideal o *dream vacation* —**dream-er** *n* —**dream-less** *adj* —**dream-like** *adj*

☐ **dream up** *vt* devise or invent

dream-catch-er /dreém kàchər/ *n* a small hoop-shaped hanging ornament of beads and feathers worn by Native North Americans

dream-land /dreém lànd/ *n* **1** a fantasy world **2** a state of sleep (*infml*)

dream team *n* the ideal combination of people for something (*infml*)

dream tick-et *n* an ideal joint candidacy (*infml*)

dream world *n* a fantasy world

dream-y /dreémee/ (**-i-er**, **-i-est**) *adj* **1** strange, vague, or ethereal **2** given to daydreaming —**dream-i-ly** *adv* —**dream-i-ness** *n*

drea-ry /dreéree/ (**-ri-er**, **-ri-est**) *adj* dull and gloomy —**drea-ri-ly** *adv* —**drea-ri-ness** *n*

dreck *n* worthless nonsense or trash —**dreck-y** *adj*

dredge[1] *n* also **dredg-er** a machine for digging underwater **2** a boat or barge with a dredge on it ■ *v* (**dredged, dredg-ing**) **1** *vt* remove material with a dredge **2** *vti* clear a channel with a dredge

☐ **dredge up** *vt* find hidden information or mention forgotten incidents

dredge[2] (**dredged, dredg-ing**) *vt* sprinkle with a coating of flour or sugar —**dredg-er** *n*

dregs *npl* **1** gritty particles at the bottom of a container of liquid **2** the least valuable part of something

Drei-ser /drísser, -zər/, **Theodore** (1871–1945) US novelist and journalist

drench *vt* make somebody or something completely wet

Dres-den /drézdən/ capital of the state of Saxony, Germany. Pop. 474,443 (1997).

dress *v* **1** *vti* put clothes on yourself or somebody else **2** *vi* wear particular clothing o *usually dresses in black* **3** *vt* decorate a room or object **4** *vt* arrange goods in a window display **5** *vt* bandage or cover a wound **6** *vt* put a sauce on a salad **7** *vt* clean and prepare fish and game for cooking or selling **8** *vt* arrange hair ■ *n* **1** a woman's one-piece garment combining a top and skirt **2** the type of clothes somebody is wearing **3** clothes ■ *adj* formal, or requiring formal attire ◇ **dressed to kill** dressed in very glamorous clothes (*slang*)

☐ **dress down** *v* **1** *vi* wear casual clothes (*infml*) **2** *vt* reprimand somebody

☐ **dress up** *v* **1** *vi* dress formally **2** *vi* put on costumes **3** *vt* disguise something to make it look more pleasant

dres-sage /drə saázh/ *n* **1** the process of training a horse to execute precise movements **2** an event in which horses and riders execute precise movements

dress cir-cle *n* the second-floor gallery in an auditorium

dress code *n* an obligatory or recommended way to dress for something

dress-er /dréssər/ *n* **1** a bedroom chest of drawers **2** a piece of furniture combining shelves and a cupboard **3** somebody who dresses in a specific way **4** an actor's assistant who deals with costumes **5** a personal grooming assistant

dress-ing /dréssing/ *n* **1** a bandage or covering for a wound **2** a sauce for a salad **3** stuffing for a piece of meat

dress-ing-down *n* a severe reprimand

dress-ing gown *n* a coat of soft light material worn indoors

dress-ing room *n* **1** a room in which an actor puts on makeup and costumes **2** a room in which to change clothes

dress-ing ta-ble *n* a bedroom table with drawers and a mirror

dress-mak-er /dréss màykər/ *n* somebody who makes dresses —**dress-mak-ing** *n*

dress re-hears-al *n* **1** a final rehearsal in costume **2** a full-scale practice before an event

dress sense *n* good taste in clothes

dress shirt *n* a man's formal shirt

dress u-ni-form *n* a ceremonial military uniform

dress-y /dréssee/ (**-i-er**, **-i-est**) *adj* **1** elegant in dress **2** requiring guests to dress in style —**dress-i-ly** *adv* —**dress-i-ness** *n*

drew past tense of **draw**

Drey-fus /drífəss, dráy-/, **Alfred** (1859–1935)

French soldier falsely accused of treason by anti-Semites

drib *n* a small, negligible amount of something

drib·ble /dríbb'l/ *v* (**-bled**, **-bling**) 1 *vi* let saliva spill from the mouth 2 *vti* spill or be spilled in drops 3 *vti* in soccer and other ball games, move the ball around skillfully to keep possession 4 *vti* in basketball, move the ball around the court by bouncing it with the hands ■ *n* 1 a tiny amount of liquid 2 an act of dribbling a ball —**drib·bler** *n* —**drib·bly** *adj*

dri·er[1] /dríɔr/ comparative of **dry**

dri·er[2] /dríɔr/, **dry·er** *n* a drying device or machine, especially one for laundry

dri·est /dríɪst/ superlative of **dry**

drift *v* 1 *vi* be carried along by the flow of water or air 2 *vi* move or wander aimlessly 3 *vi* deviate from a set course or position 4 *vti* form or cause to form heaps as a result of wind or water currents ■ *n* 1 a heap or bank of something such as snow or leaves 2 a drifting movement 3 a gradual change 4 the general meaning of something —**drift·y** *adj*

drift·er /dríftɔr/ *n* somebody who never settles in one place for long

drift ice *n* floating ice

drift net *n* a large fishing net supported by floats

drift·wood /dríft wòod/ *n* broken pieces of wood found washed ashore or floating in water

drill[1] *n* 1 an implement that rotates at high speed to bore holes 2 training by repetition 3 a repeated exercise 4 a routine for doing something (*infml*) ■ *v* 1 *vti* bore a hole with a drill 2 *vti* practice marching, or instruct soldiers in marching 3 *vt* teach somebody by rote —**drill·er** *n* ◊ See note at **teach**

drill[2] *n* 1 a furrow for seeds 2 a seed-planting machine 3 a planted row of seeds —**drill** *vt*

drill[3] *n* thick cotton fabric. Use: work clothes, uniforms.

drill[4] *n* a baboon with brown fur and a black face

drill·ing plat·form *n* a structure supporting an oil rig

drill ser·geant *n* a noncommissioned officer who drills soldiers

dri·ly /dríleè/, **dry·ly** *adv* with subtle irony or humor

drink *vti* (**drank**, **drunk**) 1 swallow a liquid 2 imbibe alcohol ■ *n* 1 drinkable liquid 2 an amount of liquid that somebody drinks 3 an alcoholic beverage 4 excessive consumption of alcohol

□ **drink in** *vt* 1 absorb liquid 2 absorb something with the mind and senses

drink·a·ble /dríngkəb'l/ *adj* 1 safe to drink 2 pleasant or enjoyable to drink

drink·er /dríngkɔr/ *n* 1 somebody who drinks a particular beverage (*in combination*)

2 somebody who drinks alcoholic beverages

drink·ing foun·tain *n* a device supplying a jet of drinkable water

drink·ing song *n* a song sung by people drinking alcohol

drink·ing wa·ter *n* water that is safe for human consumption

drip *v* (**dripped**, **drip·ping**) 1 *vti* fall or let fall in drops 2 *vt* let out in a great quantity ○ *a voice dripping malice* ■ *n* 1 a small amount of liquid 2 an instance of a liquid falling in drops 3 the sound of falling drops 4 a person regarded as socially inept (*slang insult*)

drip-dry *adj* requiring no ironing after washing ■ *vti* (**drip-dried**, **drip-dries**) dry naturally without using a drier

drip feed *n* 1 a medical procedure for administering fluid into a patient's vein 2 a fluid used in a drip feed

drip-feed (**drip-fed**) *vt* 1 administer a drip feed to somebody 2 provide plants with a continuous water supply

drip·ping /drípping/ *adj* thoroughly wet

⚡ **drive** /drív/ *v* (**drove** /dróv/, **driv·en** /drív'n/, **driv·ing**) 1 *vti* operate, travel in, or take somebody in a vehicle 2 *vt* provide the power or momentum for 3 *vt* force to do, experience, or be something ○ *was driven to despair* ○ *Fear drove the elephants to stampede.* 4 *vti* move or propel with force ■ *n* 1 a ride taken in a vehicle 2 a driveway 3 *also* **Drive** a wide road (*often in place names*) 4 the means of converting power into motion in a machine (*often in combination*) 5 a computer device with data on a spinning disk 6 a hard hit of a ball 7 a fast direct movement 8 focused energy and determination 9 a powerful motivating force 10 a major organized effort 11 a sustained military attack 12 a roundup of livestock

drive-by, drive-by shoot·ing *n* the firing of a gun at somebody from a moving vehicle (*infml*)

drive-in *n* a business serving customers who stay in their parked cars

driv·el /drív'l/ *n* 1 silly talk 2 drooled saliva ■ *vi* 1 talk nonsense 2 drool —**driv·el·ing** *n*

driv·en /drív'n/ past participle of **drive** ■ *adj* 1 compelled by need or ambition 2 caused by a particular thing (*in combination*) ○ *a demand-driven economy*

driv·er /drívɔr/ *n* 1 somebody who drives or is able to drive a vehicle 2 a golf club used for hitting the ball a long way 3 a tool that applies pressure 4 a strong force, e.g., in an organization

driv·er's seat *n* the seat in a motor vehicle in which the operator sits

dri·ver's test *n* a test to determine driving skill that people must pass in order to drive without supervision on public roads

drive shaft *n* a rotating shaft transmitting

power from the engine to wheels or a pro-peller

drive-through, drive-up *n* a business that serves people who wait by a special window in their cars

drive time *n* 1 weekday commuting hours 2 a time taken to drive from one place to another

drive·way /dr**í**v wày/ *n* a private road connecting to a public road

driv·ing /dr**í**ving/ *adj* 1 falling or being blown hard o *a driving rain* 2 having the ability or influence to make something happen ■ *n* the operating of a vehicle by somebody —**driv·ing·ly** *adv*

driz·zle /dr**í**zz'l/ *n* light rain ■ *v* (-zled, -zling) 1 *vi* rain lightly 2 *vt* dribble liquid over food —**driz·zly** *adj*

drogue par·a·chute /dr**ó**g-/ *n* a small parachute released before a larger one

droll /dr**ó**l/ *adj* oddly amusing —**droll·ness** *n* —**drol·ly** *adv*

droll·er·y /dr**ó**ləree/ *n* 1 quirky humor 2 amusing talk or behavior

drom·e·dar·y /dr**ó**mmə dèrree, drúmmə-/ (*pl* **-ies**) *n* a one-humped camel

drone[1] /dr**ó**n/ (droned, dron·ing) *v* 1 *vi* make a low humming sound 2 *vti* talk or say in a slow boring voice —**drone** *n* —**dron·ing·ly** *adv*

drone[2] /dr**ó**n/ *n* 1 a male bee whose only function is mating 2 a person regarded as lazy (*insult*) 3 an aircraft without a pilot, controlled from the ground

drool *v* 1 *vi* show exaggerated appreciation 2 *vi* dribble saliva 3 *vti* talk nonsense ■ *n* saliva dribbling from the mouth —**drool·ing·ly** *adv*

droop *v* 1 *vti* hang or bend down limply 2 *vi* be dispirited ■ *n* a sagging position —**droop·i·ly** *adv* —**droop·ing·ly** *adv* —**droop·y** *adj*

drop *v* (dropped, drop·ping) 1 *vt* let go of something and cause it to fall 2 *vi* fall from a higher to a lower place 3 *vti* move or decrease to a lower position or level 4 *vti* fall or cause to fall in small round portions of liquid 5 *vi* slope down 6 *vti* lower the voice 7 *vt* stop doing, planning, or talking about something 8 *vt* remove somebody from membership in an organization 9 *vt* omit something, e.g., a word 10 *vi* collapse from exhaustion ■ *n* 1 a small amount or round portion of liquid 2 a very small amount o *not a drop of sympathy* 3 a decrease 4 the distance between a high point and the ground 5 a steep slope or incline 6 a descent or delivery of goods by parachute 7 a maildrop ■ **drops** *npl* liquid medicine applied to the ear, nose, or eye in small quantities ◇ **at the drop of a hat** without needing persuasion or prompting

☐ **drop behind** *vi* gradually get farther behind

☐ **drop by** *or* **in** *or* **over** *vi* visit somebody casually

☐ **drop off** *v* 1 *vi* doze off (*infml*) 2 *vi* undergo a gradual decrease (*infml*) o *Sales have dropped off.* 3 *vt* take and leave somewhere

☐ **drop out** *vi* 1 leave without finishing an activity 2 reject society (*infml*)

drop cloth *n* a large cloth for protecting surfaces from paint or dust

drop cur·tain *n* 1 in a theater, a cloth with scenery painted on it, lowered from the flies 2 a theater curtain that is lowered and raised from above, not opened and closed from the sides

~~draped~~ incorrect spelling of **dropped**

drop-in *n* 1 a casual visitor 2 an informal party without invitations issued

drop kick *n* 1 in football, a way of kicking the ball by dropping it and kicking it just after it bounces 2 in amateur wrestling, an illegal move in which a wrestler leaps into the air and strikes an opponent with both feet —**drop-kick** *vti*

drop leaf *n* a folding extension on a table

drop·let /dr**ó**pplət/ *n* a tiny drop

drop-off *n* 1 a slope in the ground 2 a gradual decrease 3 a point where people, e.g., passengers, are let out of motor vehicles o *an airport taxi drop-off*

drop·out /dr**ó**p òwt/ *n* 1 a student who leaves school or college without graduating 2 somebody who chooses an unconventional lifestyle (*infml*)

drop·per /dr**ó**ppər/ *n* a tube for dispensing drops (*often in combination*)

drop·pings /dr**ó**ppingz/ *npl* animal dung

drop shot *n* in racket games, a soft shot intended to bounce so low that the opponent cannot hit it back

drop·sy /dr**ó**psee/ *n* the medical condition edema (*dated*) —**drop·sied** *adj*

dross *n* something worthless —**dross·y** *adj*

drought /dr**ó**wt/ *n* 1 a long period of extremely dry weather producing a water shortage 2 a serious lack of something necessary —**drought·y** *adj*

drove[1] /dr**ó**v/ past tense of **drive**

drove[2] /dr**ó**v/ *n* a group of animals moving together ■ **droves** *npl* crowds of people ■ *vti* (droved, drov·ing) move animals along —**drov·er** *n*

drown *v* 1 *vti* die or kill by immersion in water 2 *also* **drown out** *vt* prevent from being heard by making a louder sound 3 *vt* cover with too much liquid —**drowned** *adj*

drowse /dr**ó**wz/ (drowsed, drows·ing) *vi* be partway between sleeping and waking —**drowse** *n*

drows·y /dr**ó**wzee/ (-i·er, -i·est) *adj* 1 almost asleep 2 causing sleepiness —**drows·i·ly** *adv* —**drows·i·ness** *n*

drub *vt* (drubbed, drub·bing) 1 beat with a heavy stick 2 defeat comprehensively ■ *n* a blow with a stick —**drub·bing** *n*

drudge *n* somebody who does menial work —**drudge** *vi* —**drudg·ing·ly** *adv*

drudg·er·y /drúdjəree/ n boring or exhausting work

drug n 1 a substance given as a medicine 2 an illegal substance taken for the pleasurable effects it produces ■ vt (**drugged, drug·ging**) 1 give a drug to 2 add a drug to

drugged adj 1 affected by drugs 2 tired and stupefied

drug·gist /drúggist/ n a pharmacist

drug run·ner n somebody who transports illegal drugs

drug·store /drúg stàwr/ n store selling medicines and general merchandise

Dru·id /dróo id/, **dru·id** n 1 a priest of an ancient Celtic religion 2 a modern follower of an ancient Celtic religion —**dru·id·ic** /droo iddik/ adj —**dru·id·i·cal** adj

drum n 1 a percussion instrument consisting of a membrane stretched over a frame 2 a tapping sound 3 a large cylindrical container, spool, or part 4 an eardrum ■ vi (**drummed, drum·ming**) 1 play a drum 2 tap repeatedly on a surface ◊ **bang** or **beat the drum (for)** try to attract favorable attention for (infml)

□ **drum into** vt tell somebody something repeatedly

□ **drum up** vt try to elicit support

drum·beat /drúm beét/ n 1 a tap or rhythmic series of taps on a drum 2 a passionately supported cause —**drum·beat·ing** n

drum ma·jor n the leader of a marching band

drum ma·jor·ette n a young woman marching with a band and twirling a baton

drum·mer /drúmmər/ n a drum player

drum·roll /drúm ròl/ n a continuous drumming, often heralding an important arrival or event

drum·stick /drúm stìk/ n 1 a stick for beating a drum 2 the lower half of the leg of a bird such as a chicken when prepared for eating

drunk past participle of **drink** ■ adj 1 intoxicated with alcohol 2 emotionally carried away ■ n somebody who is habitually drunk

drunk·ard /drúngkərd/ n somebody who is habitually drunk

drunk-driv·ing n driving after having drunk too much alcohol —**drunk-driv·er** n

drunk·en /drúngkən/ adj 1 intoxicated by or as if by alcohol 2 drunk or frequently drunk 3 involving alcohol —**drunk·en·ly** adv —**drunk·en·ness** n

~~drunkeness~~ incorrect spelling of **drunkenness**

drupe n a fruit with a pit inside

dry adj (**dri·er** or **dry·er, dri·est** or **dry·est**) 1 not wet or moist 2 lacking rain or moisture in the air 3 lacking in desired levels of moisture or moistness o dry skin 4 without flesh attached o dry bones 5 thirsty 6 lacking sweetness o dry sherry 7 shrewdly amusing 8 boring and academic 9 matter-of-fact 10 not allowing alcohol sales ■ v (**dried,**

dries) 1 vti make or become dry 2 vt preserve food by extracting moisture —**dry·ness** n

SYNONYMS dry, dehydrated, desiccated, arid, parched, shriveled, sere CORE MEANING: lacking moisture

□ **dry out** vti make or become completely dry

□ **dry up** v 1 vti lose or cause to lose moisture 2 vi stop being available as a resource

dry·ad /drí əd, -àd/ (pl -ads or -ad·es /-ə deéz/) n in Greek mythology, a wood nymph

dry-clean vt clean with chemicals, not with water —**dry-clean·er** n —**dry-clean·ing** n

Dry·den /dríd'n/, **John** (1631–1700) English poet, dramatist, and critic

dry dock n a waterless area for ship repairs —**dry-dock** vti

dry·er[1] comparative of **dry**

dry·er[2] n = drier[2]

dry·est superlative of **dry**

dry-eyed adj not crying or weeping

dry goods npl fabrics, clothing, and notions

dry ice n a solid form of carbon dioxide. Use: refrigeration, production of artificial fog.

dry land n land, not the sea

dry·land /drí lànd/ n areas of little rainfall, collectively (often pl) —**dry·land** adj

dry·ly adv = drily

dry rot n crumbling decay in wood, caused by various fungi

dry run n a rehearsal of a future planned action

dry·wall /drí wàwl/, **dry wall** n 1 plasterboard 2 a wall made of plasterboard —**dry·wall** vt

DSS abbr 1 Department of Social Services 2 Director of Social Services

DST abbr daylight-saving time

⚡ **DTP** abbr desktop publishing

D.T.'s, d.t.'s npl delirium tremens (infml)

DTV abbr digital television

du, Du see also under surname

du·al /dóo əl/ adj having two parts, functions, aspects, or items o dual citizenship o serving a dual purpose —**du·al·ly** adv

SPELLCHECK Do not confuse the spelling of **dual** and **duel** ("a contest"), which sound similar.

du·al·ism /dóo ə lìzzəm/ n 1 a state in which something has two distinct parts or aspects 2 the philosophical theory that human beings are made up of independent constituents, the body and the mind or soul 3 the religious doctrine that the antagonistic forces of good and evil determine the course of events —**du·al·ist** n —**du·al·is·tic** /dóo ə lístik/ adj

du·al·i·ty /doo állətee/ (pl -ties) n a situation or nature with two complementary or opposing parts

dub[1] (**dubbed, dub·bing**) vt give a descriptive nickname to

dub[2] (dubbed, dub·bing) vt 1 add a soundtrack in a different language to a movie or television show 2 copy a recording onto a different recording medium 3 add sounds to a movie —**dub** n

ORIGIN Dub in sound recording is a shortening of *double*.

Du·bai /doo bi´/, **Du·bayy** capital of Dubai state in the NE United Arab Emirates. Pop. 674,100 (1995).

Du Bar·ry /doo bárree/, **Marie Jeanne Bécu, Comtesse** (1743?–93) French courtier and mistress of Louis XV

Dub·ček /dóobb chèk, dóop-/, **Alexander** (1921–92) Czech political leader (1968)

du·bi·e·ty /doo bí ətee/ (pl -ties) n (fml) 1 uncertainty about something 2 something doubtful

du·bi·ous /dóobee əss/ adj 1 unsure about an outcome 2 of doubtful character or quality —**du·bi·ous·ly** adv —**du·bi·ous·ness** n ◊ See note at **doubtful**

Dub·lin /dúbblin/ capital of the Republic of Ireland. Pop. 953,000 (1996). —**Dub·lin·er** n

dub·ni·um /dúbnee əm/ n (symbol Db) a rare unstable chemical element

ORIGIN Dubnium was named in 1967 for Dubna in Russia, site of the Joint Nuclear Institute.

Du Bois /doo bóyss/, **W. E. B.** (1868–1963) US historian, sociologist, and civil rights leader

du·cal /dóok'l/ adj of a duke or dukedom

duc·at /dúkət/ n a coin formerly used in some European countries

Du·champ /doo shaaN/, **Marcel** (1887–1968) French-born US artist

duch·ess /dúchəss/ n 1 a high-ranking noblewoman 2 the wife or widow of a duke

duch·y /dúchee/ (pl -ies) n a duke or duchess's territory

duck[1] (pl ducks or same) n 1 a common water bird with webbed feet and a broad flat bill 2 a female duck 3 a duck as food

ORIGIN Although the verb *duck* is recorded later than the noun *duck* referring to the bird, it is assumed that it comes from an ancient root and that a **duck** is literally a "bird that ducks." No related language uses its form of the word as a name for a bird.

duck[2] v 1 vti move your head down quickly 2 vi move somewhere quickly to avoid being seen 3 vti plunge under water 4 vt avoid dealing with something that ought to be dealt with —**duck** n

duck[3] n strong cotton or canvas cloth. Use: clothing, furnishings. ■ **ducks** npl white pants

duck-billed plat·y·pus n a platypus

duck·ling /dúkling/ n a young duck

ducks and drakes n the activity of skipping stones across water (+ sing verb)

duck·weed /dúk weèd/ n a floating aquatic plant

duct n 1 a tube, pipe, or channel for something such as electrical cables or heated air 2 a tube in a body organ 3 a tube containing electrical cables —**duct·less** adj

duc·tile /dúkt'l/ adj 1 malleable enough to be worked 2 easily influenced —**duc·til·i·ty** /duk tíllətee/ n ◊ See note at **pliable**

duct tape n strong repair and construction tape

dud n 1 a shell that does not explode 2 a failure (infml) ■ adj useless (infml)

dude n (slang) 1 a man 2 a city dweller vacationing on a dude ranch 3 a flashily dressed man

dude ranch n a vacation complex in the W United States offering outdoor activities

dudg·eon /dújjən/ n a fit of pique

duds npl clothes (infml)

due adj 1 expected to arrive 2 awaiting something that is part of a normal progression of events 3 proper and appropriate 4 owed as a debt 5 payable at once or on demand 6 attributable ○ *a delay due to weather* ■ n somebody's right ■ **dues** npl membership fees ■ adv directly and exactly ○ *due west* ◊ **pay your dues** go through a necessary period of suffering or hardship before achieving success ◊ See note at **dew**

du·el /dóo əl/ n 1 a formal fight over a matter of honor 2 a struggle between two parties —**du·el** vi —**du·el·er** n —**du·el·ist** n ◊ See note at **dual**

du·el·ist /dóo əlist/ n 1 a fighter of duels 2 a party to a conflict

~~**du·ely**~~ incorrect spelling of **duly**

Due·ro ◆ Douro

du·et /doo ét/ n 1 a composition for two performers 2 a pair —**du·et·tist** n

duf·fel /dúff'l/, **duf·fle** n 1 thick woolen fabric with a nap on both sides 2 camping and hiking gear

ORIGIN The fabric **duffel** is named for the Belgian town of Duffel, where it was first made.

duf·fel bag n a cylindrical bag with a drawstring

duf·fle coat, duf·fel coat n a thick woolen coat with a hood and toggles

Du·fy /doo feé/, **Raoul** (1877–53) French painter, illustrator, and designer

dug[1] past participle, past tense of **dig**

dug[2] n an animal's milk-producing gland

dug·out /dúg òwt/ n 1 a canoe made from a hollowed log 2 a soldiers' shelter dug into the ground 3 a shelter at the side of a sports field for players who are not on the field

duh interj expresses an ironic response to being told something obvious (slang)

DUI *abbr* driving under the influence

Duis·burg /dóoss burg, dyóoss-/ inland port in NW Germany. Pop. 536,106 (1997).

du jour /doo zhóor/ *adj* 1 offered or served on the current day 2 latest

duke *n* 1 a high-ranking nobleman 2 the ruler of a principality or a duchy 3 a fist (*slang; often pl*) —**duke·dom** *n*

dul·cet /dúlsst/ *adj* pleasant to hear (*fml*)

dul·ci·mer /dúlsəmər/ *n* a zither

dull *adj* 1 boring 2 overcast 3 not bright or vivid 4 not intensely felt 5 muffled in sound 6 blunt and not sharp 7 regarded as unintelligent 8 slow to respond o *dull reflexes* 9 listless ■ *vti* 1 make or become less acute 2 reduce in loudness 3 make or become blunt 4 make or become less bright or intense —**dull·ness** *n* —**dul·ly** *adv*

dull·ard /dúllərd/ *n* somebody regarded as unintelligent or slow to learn (*literary*)

Dull Knife (1810?–83) Cheyenne leader

Du·luth /də lóoth/ major port in NE Minnesota. Pop. 81,228 (1998).

du·ly /dóolee/ *adv* 1 properly and suitably o *duly grateful* 2 at the proper or expected time o *At the signal the train duly departed.*

Du·ma /dóomə, dŏo maá/ *n* 1 modern Russian parliament 2 a tsarist Russian parliament

Du·mas /doo maá, dyoo-/, **Alexandre** (1802–70) and his son **Alexandre** (1824–95) French novelists and dramatists

du Mau·ri·er /doo máwree ày/, **Dame Daphne** (1907–89) British novelist

✦**dumb** /dum/ *adj* 1 regarded as unintelligent (*infml insult*) 2 an offensive term meaning unable to speak 3 temporarily speechless 4 done without speech 5 intentionally silent 6 not able to process data 7 producing no sound 8 lacking human speech —**dumb·ly** *adv* —**dumb·ness** *n*

□ **dumb down** *vti* make something condescendingly simplistic (*infml*)

dumb·bell /dúm bèl/ *n* 1 a piece of exercise equipment consisting of a short metal bar with a weight at each end 2 somebody regarded as lacking in intelligence or common sense (*slang insult*)

dumb bomb *n* an unguided bomb or missile

dumbell *incorrect spelling of* **dumbbell**

dumb·found /dùm fównd, dúm fòwnd/, **dum·found** *vti* make somebody speechless with astonishment

dumb·struck /dúm strùk/ *adj* speechless with shock or astonishment

dumb·wait·er /dúm wàytər/ *n* 1 a small elevator for moving kitchen items between the floors of a building 2 a lazy Susan

dum·my /dúmmee/ *n* (*pl* -mies) 1 a mannequin in a store 2 a model used by a ventriloquist 3 somebody regarded as unintelligent or naive (*infml insult*) 4 a stuffed bag used in football blocking and tackling practice 5 an imitation of something 6 in team games such as soccer or rugby, a feigned pass 7 a person or organization acting as a front for somebody else 8 a nonexplosive form of munition 9 in the game of bridge, an exposed hand 10 a facsimile page or book showing what the final product will look like ■ *vt* (-mied, -mies) make into a facsimile page or book

✦**dump** *vt* 1 deposit something on a surface carelessly 2 throw something out as unwanted 3 get rid of waste at a waste disposal site 4 end a relationship with somebody (*slang*) 5 flood a market with cheap merchandise 6 get rid of stocks 7 relegate somebody to custodial care (*slang disapproving*) 8 transfer unprocessed computer data from one place to another ■ *n* 1 a munitions and supply area 2 a waste disposal site 3 an unpleasant or dirty place (*slang*) 4 an act of discarding something 5 a transfer of unprocessed computer data from one place to another

dump·ling /dúmpling/ *n* a small ball of dough cooked and served with soup or stew

dumps *npl* a gloomy state of mind (*infml*)

Dump·ster /dúmpstər/ *tdmk* a trademark for large trash-and-garbage containers and hoisting units

dump truck *n* a heavy truck with an open bed that can be tilted to unload cargo

dump·y /dúmpee/ (-i-er, -i-est) *adj* regarded as being short and plump (*infml disapproving*) —**dump·i·ness** *n*

dun[1] *n* 1 a brownish gray color 2 a brownish gray horse ■ *adj* (dun·ner, dun·nest) brownish gray

dun[2] (dunned, dun·ning) *vt* harass for the payment of a debt —**dun** *n*

Dun·bar /dún bàar/, **Paul Laurence** (1872–1906) US poet

AKG London

Isadora Duncan

Dun·can /dúngkən/, **Isadora** (1877–1927) US dancer

dunce *n* somebody regarded as unintelligent or slow-witted (*insult*)

ORIGIN Dunce is from the middle name of the Scottish philosopher and theologian John Duns Scotus (?1266–1308). His system of learning was highly influential in the late Middle Ages, but in the 16C his ideas were discredited and ridiculed, so that eventually his name became an insult.

dunce cap *n* a pointed hat formerly worn as a punishment by a pupil regarded as unintelligent

Dun·dee /dun deé/ city in E Scotland. Pop. 150,250 (1996). —**Dun·do·ni·an** /dun dṓnee ən/ n, adj

dune n a hill of sand

dune bug·gy n a motorized beach vehicle

dung n animal excrement or manure —**dung·y** adj

dun·ga·rees /dúng gə reéz, dúng gə reèz/ npl pants made from strong material

dun·geon /dúnjən/ n a prison cell, especially one underground

dunk v 1 vt dip food in a liquid 2 vt quickly submerge something in a liquid 3 vi briefly immerse yourself in water (infml) 4 vt shove somebody's head under water 5 vt in basketball, slam the ball through the hoop from above ■ n also **dunk shot** in basketball, a shot in which the ball is slammed through the hoop from above —**dunk·er** n

Dun·kirk /dún kùrk, dun kúrk/ port in NE France. In World War II over 330,000 Allied troops were evacuated from the town by sea, under constant enemy fire. Pop. 70,850 (1999).

du·o /dóò ō/ (pl -os) n 1 a pair of closely associated people 2 a composition for two performers 3 a pair of musicians who play together 4 a set of two closely related things

duo- prefix two ◇ duopoly

du·o·dec·i·mal /dóò ə déssəm'l/ adj based on the number 12 ■ n 1 a duodecimal number 2 a 12th part —**du·o·dec·i·mal·ly** adv

du·o·de·num /dóò ə deénəm, doo ódd'nəm/ (pl -na /-ə deénə, -ódd'nə/ or -nums) n the first section of the small intestine immediately beyond the stomach —**du·o·de·nal** adj

du·op·o·ly /doo óppəlee/ (pl -lies) n a concentration of economic power in two or-ganizations or companies —**du·op·o·lis·tic** /dóò oppə lístik/ adj

dupe /doop/ vt (**duped, dup·ing**) trick ■ n a victim of deceit

du·ple /dóòp'l/ adj having two beats to the musical bar

du·plex /dóò plèks, dyóó-/ n 1 US, Can, Aus a house divided into two separate apart-ments 2 the transmission of signals over a communications channel in both directions at the same time ■ adj 1 twofold 2 having two parts performing the same function independently

du·pli·cate vt /dóòpli kàyt, dyóópli-/ (**-cat·ed, -cat·ing**) 1 make an exact copy of 2 repeat ■ n /dóòplikət, dyóó-/ 1 an exact copy 2 a spare object of the same kind 3 a repeat of an earlier action or achievement ■ adj /dóòplikət, dyóó-/ 1 copied exactly 2 having two corresponding parts —**du·pli·ca·ble** adj —**du·pli·ca·tive** adj ◇ See note at copy

du·pli·ca·tion /dóòpli káysh'n, dyóópli-/ n 1 the act of repeating or copying something 2 an exact copy

du·pli·ca·tor /dóòpli kàytər, dyóópli-/ n a machine for copying printed matter

du·plic·i·ty /doo plíssətee, dyoo-/ n 1 de-ceitfulness 2 the state of being double (fml) —**du·plic·i·tous** adj

du Pont /doo pónt/, **Pierre S.** (1870–1954) US industrialist

du·ra·ble /dóòrəb'l/ adj lasting for a long time without sustaining damage or wear —**du·ra·bil·i·ty** /dóòrə bíllətee/ n —**du·ra·bly** adv

Du·ran·go /doo ráng gō/ capital of Durango State, central Mexico. Pop. 464,566 (1995).

du·ra·tion /də ráysh'n/ n the time that some-thing lasts —**du·ra·tion·al** adj

Dur·ban /dúrbən/ port in E South Africa. Pop. 1,264,000 (1995).

Dür·er /dóòrər, dyóórər/, **Albrecht** (1471–1528) German painter and engraver

du·ress /dòò réss/ n 1 the use of force or threats 2 illegal force or coercion, e.g., against a criminal suspect

Dur·ham /dúrrəm/ city in central North Caro-lina. Pop. 153,513 (1998).

dur·ing /dóòring/ prep 1 throughout the period of 2 at some point in the period of

Durk·heim /dúrk hìm/, **Émile** (1858–1917) French social theorist

Du·shan·be /doo shámbə, -shaàm-/ capital of Tajikistan. Pop. 664,000 (1995).

dusk n 1 the period after the Sun goes below the horizon but before the sky is dark 2 partial or almost complete darkness (literary)

dusk·y /dúskee/ (-i·er, -i·est) adj 1 dark-colored 2 having little or insufficient light —**dusk·i·ly** adv —**dusk·i·ness** n

Düs·sel·dorf /dóòss'l dàwrf/ capital of North Rhine-Westphalia, west central Germany. Pop. 572,638 (1997).

dust n 1 small dry particles of matter 2 the small particles that something, especially a human body, is reduced to by decay ■ v 1 vti remove household dust from a surface 2 vt sprinkle a powdery substance over something ◇ **bite the dust** 1 die (infml) 2 suffer a total failure (slang) ◇ **gather dust** remain unused

dust bowl n 1 an area in which the dry topsoil is exposed and dust storms occur 2 **Dust Bowl** a large area in the south-central United States that suffered badly from wind erosion during the 1930s

dust cov·er n 1 a cover for protecting equip-ment or furniture 2 also **dust jac·ket** a paper cover that protects a hardback book

dust dev·il n a small dust-laden whirlwind

dust·er /dústər/ n 1 a woman's long loose coat 2 a device for spreading agrochemicals

dust·pan /dúst pàn/ n a container into which dirt can be swept

dust storm n a dust-carrying windstorm

dust·y /dústee/ (-i·er, -i·est) adj 1 full of dust 2 boring

Dutch n the official language of the Neth-erlands ■ npl the people of the Netherlands —**Dutch** *adj* ◇ **go Dutch** pay for your own part of a meal or entertainment

Dutch auc·tion *n* an auction with gradually decreasing prices

Dutch elm dis·ease *n* a serious fungal disease of elm trees

ORIGIN The disease is "Dutch" because it was identified by Dutch scientists.

Dutch·man /dúchmən/ (*pl* -men /-mən/) *n* a man from the Netherlands

Dutch ov·en *n* 1 a heavy cooking pot 2 an open-fronted metal box for cooking food on an open fire

Dutch·wom·an /dúch woommən/ (*pl* -wom·en /-wimmin/) *n* a woman from the Netherlands

du·te·ous /doŏtee əss, dyoŏ-/ *adj* obediently dutiful (*archaic*) —**du·te·ous·ly** *adv* —**du·te·ous·ness** *n*

du·ti·a·ble /doŏtee əbᵊl, dyoŏ-/ *adj* subject to import taxation

du·ti·ful /doŏtif'l, dyoŏ-/ *adj* 1 done to fulfill obligations 2 careful to fulfill obligations —**du·ti·ful·ly** *adv* —**du·ti·ful·ness** *n*

du·ty /doŏtee, dyoŏ-/ (*pl* -ties) *n* 1 an obligation 2 the urge to fulfill obligations 3 a task allocated to somebody 4 an import or export tax 5 suitability for a particular grade of use (*usually in combination*) ○ *heavy-duty carpet*

du·ty-free *adj* exempted from customs or excise duties —**du·ty-free** *adv*

du·ty of·fi·cer *n* an officer on duty at a specific time

Du·va·lier /doŏ vaal yáy/, **François** (1907–71) Haitian national leader (1957–71)

du·vet /doo váy, doŏ vày/ *n* a thick warm quilt for a bed

du·vet day *n* any one of an agreed number of days that some employees can take as leave at short notice in addition to their official vacation entitlement

⚡**DVD** *n* a large-capacity CD used for storing video and audio data. Full form **digital video disk**

⚡**DVD-A** *n* an audio DVD

⚡**DVD-ROM** *n* a video CD-ROM

⚡**DVI** *abbr* digital video imaging

D.V.M. *abbr* Doctor of Veterinary Medicine

Dvo·řák /dváwr zhàak, -zhàk/, **Antonín** (1841–1904) Bohemian Czech composer

⚡**Dvo·rak key·board** /dváwr zhàak-/ *n* a keyboard arranged for quicker typing

---

ORIGIN The keyboard is named for August Dvorak, who devised it in the first part of the 20C.

DVT *abbr* deep-vein thrombosis

dwarf *n* (*pl* **dwarves** or **dwarfs**) 1 a person who is atypically small for medical reasons 2 a plant or animal that is smaller than others of its species 3 an imaginary being resembling a small human ■ *vt* 1 cause to

seem small by comparison 2 stunt the growth of —**dwarf·ish** *adj* —**dwarf·ism** *n*

dwell (**dwelt** or **dwelled**) *vi* reside in a particular place (*literary*) —**dwell·er** *n*

□ **dwell on** or **upon** *vt* think, write, or talk about at length

dwell·ing /dwélling/ *n* a home (*fml*)

DWI *abbr* driving while intoxicated

dwin·dle /dwínd'l/ (-**dled**, -**dling**) *vti* decrease gradually in size, number, or intensity

Dy *symbol* dysprosium

Dyck /dīk/, **Sir Anthony van** (1599–1641) Flemish painter

dye /dī/ *v* 1 *vt* color by soaking in a solution 2 *vi* respond to coloring in a particular way ■ *n* 1 a coloring agent or solution 2 the color produced by a dye —**dy·a·ble** *adj* —**dy·er** *n* ◊ See note at **die**

dyed-in-the-wool *adj* 1 wholeheartedly and stubbornly attached to a viewpoint 2 dyed before weaving

Dy·er /dī ər/, **Mary** (1610?–60) English-born American colonial Quaker martyr

dy·ing /dī ing/ *adj* 1 about to die 2 occurring just before death 3 occurring as something is about to end

Bob Dylan

Dy·lan /díllən/, **Bob** (*b.* 1941) US singer and songwriter

dy·nam·ic /dī námmik/ *adj* 1 full of energy and enthusiasm 2 characterized by vigorous activity and change 3 of energy 4 of dynamics ■ *n* a driving force —**dy·nam·i·cal·ly** *adv*

dy·nam·ics /dī námmiks/ *npl* the forces that produce activity and change in any situation or sphere of existence (+ *pl verb*) ■ *n* the study of motion (+ *sing verb*)

dy·na·mism /dínə mìzzəm/ *n* 1 vigorousness and forcefulness 2 the philosophical or scientific theory that explains an event as the expression of forces residing in the object or person involved —**dy·na·mist** *n*

dy·na·mite /dínə mīt/ *n* 1 a powerful explosive. Use: blasting. 2 a very exciting or dangerous person or thing (*slang*) ■ *vt* (-**mit·ed**, -**mit·ing**) blast with dynamite

---

ORIGIN Dynamite was given its name by its inventor, Alfred Nobel, in 1867. It comes from the Greek word for "strength, force" that is also the base of *dynamism*, *dynamo*, and similar words.

---

dy·na·mo /dínəmō/ (pl **-mos**) n 1 a generator of electricity from mechanical energy 2 an energetic person

dy·nas·ty /dínəstee/ (pl **-ties**) n 1 a succession of hereditary rulers 2 a prominent, powerful family —**dy·nas·tic** /dɪ năstik, dɪ-/ adj

dys·en·ter·y /díss'n tèrree/ n a disease of the lower intestine that causes severe diarrhea and the passage of blood and mucus —**dys·en·ter·ic** /díss'n térrik/ adj

~~dysentry~~ incorrect spelling of **dysentery**

dys·func·tion /diss fúngkshən/ n a medical problem in the functioning of a part of the body

dys·func·tion·al /diss fúngkshən'l/ adj 1 failing to function properly 2 unable to relate emotionally and socially

dys·lex·i·a /diss léksee ə/ n a learning disability marked by difficulty in recognizing and understanding written language —**dys·lex·ic** adj, n

dys·pep·sia /diss pépshə, -pépsee ə/ n indigestion (technical)

dys·pep·tic /diss péptik/ adj 1 having indigestion 2 bad-tempered —**dys·pep·tic** n

dys·pro·si·um /diss prózee əm/ n (symbol **Dy**) a soft silvery chemical element. Use: laser materials, nuclear research.

dys·to·pi·a /diss tópee ə/ n an imaginary place where everything is very bad —**dys·to·pi·an** adj

dys·tro·phy /dístrəfee/ (pl **-phies**), **dys·tro·phi·a** /də stráfee ə/ n a progressive degeneration of body tissue

E

e[1] (pl **e's**), **E** (pl **E's** or **Es**) n the 5th letter of the English alphabet

e[2] symbol 1 electron 2 the transcendental number 2.718 282...

E[1] (pl **E's** or **Es**) n the 3rd note in the musical scale of C major

E[2] abbr 1 east 2 eastern

e. abbr error

e- prefix 1 electronic o e-mail 2 electronic data transfer via the Internet o e-commerce

each /eech/ adj, pron every one of two or more people or things o Each person was given a gift. o Each of them is to receive a gift. ■ adv to or for every one of two or more people or things o Give them two each.

each oth·er pron each of two or more people in a group, having the same relationship

ea·ger /eegər/ adj enthusiastic and excited about doing something o eager to set out o eager faces —**ea·ger·ly** adv —**ea·ger·ness** n

ea·gle /eeg'l/ n 1 a large bird of prey with a soaring flight 2 a golf score of two under par —**ea·glet** n

ea·gle eye n keen eyesight or attention —**ea·gle-eyed** adj

Ea·gle Scout n a Boy Scout who has reached the highest level of attainment

Ea·kins /áykinz/, **Thomas** (1844–1916) US artist

Eames /eemz/, **Charles** (1907–78) US designer and architect

ear[1] /eer/ n 1 the organ of hearing in mammals and other vertebrates 2 the external part of a vertebrate's ear 3 an ability to tell sounds apart o has a good ear ◊ **all ears** listening attentively or enthusiastically (infml) ◊ **have somebody's ear** have frequent access to somebody ◊ **have** or **keep your ear to the ground** pay attention to new developments or information ◊ **out on your ear** unceremoniously thrown out or dismissed (infml) ◊ **wet behind the ears** very inexperienced or naive

ORIGIN The **ear** that you hear with comes from an ancient word that probably meant "perception"; an **ear** of corn comes from a word that meant "be pointed or sharp."

ear[2] /eer/ n a plant part containing grain

ear·ache /eer àyk/ n a pain in the ear

ear·drum /eer drùm/ n a sound-transmitting membrane in the ear

ear·ful /eer fòòl/ n a scolding or tirade of abuse (infml)

Amelia Earhart

Ear·hart /áir hàart/, **Amelia** (1898–1937) US aviator

ear·hole /eer hòl/ n UK the opening leading into the ear (infml)

earl /url/ n a middle-ranking British nobleman —**earl·dom** n

ear·lobe /eer lòb/ n the lower part of the outer ear

ear·ly /úrlee/ adv (**-li·er**, **-li·est**) 1 before the expected time 2 near the beginning o started talking early 3 promptly or soon ■ adj (**-li·er**, **-li·est**) 1 occurring near the beginning 2 occurring before the expected time 3 expected in the near future —**ear·li·ness** n

ear·mark /eer màark/ vt 1 designate something for a particular purpose o funds earmarked for research 2 put an identification mark on an animal's ear ■ n 1 an identifying characteristic (often pl) o all the ear-

marks of success **2** an identification mark on an animal's ear

earn /urn/ *v* **1** *vti* make money by working **2** *vt* acquire something as a reward or result

earn·er /úrnər/ *n* **1** somebody who earns an income o *earners of wages* **2** a source of profit o *a major revenue earner.*

ear·nest /úrnəst/ *adj* intensely serious and sincere —**ear·nest·ly** *adv* —**ear·nest·ness** *n*

earn·ings /úrningz/ *npl* money earned

⚡**EAROM** /ée ròm/ *abbr* electrically alterable read-only memory

ear·phone /éer fòn/ *n* a device that converts electricity to sound and is held to the ear *(often pl)*

ear·piece /éer peèss/ *n* **1** the part of a device that people hear through **2** the part of a glasses frame that goes around the ear

ear·plug /éer plùg/ *n* a soft plug inserted in the ear to keep out noise, water, or cold *(often pl)*

ear·ring /éer ring/ *n* a piece of jewelry worn on the ear *(often pl)*

ear·set /éer sèt/ *n* a piece of equipment attached to a computer or cellphone that enables the user to make telephone calls without using the hands

ear·shot /éer shòt/ *n* the distance in which sound is audible o *out of earshot*

ear·split·ting /éer splìtting/, **ear·pierc·ing** *adj* very loud

earth /urth/ *n* **1** *also* **Earth** the 3rd planet from the Sun, on which human beings live **2** dry land **3** soil in which plants grow —**earth·ward** *adj, adv* —**earth·wards** *adv* ◊ **come back (down) to earth** come back to reality

earth·bound /úrth bòwnd/ *adj* **1** heading toward Earth **2** mundane and unimaginative

earth·en /úrthən/ *adj* made of earth

earth·en·ware /úrthən wàir/ *n* pottery made of baked clay

earth·ling /úrthling/ *n* a human being as contrasted with an extraterrestrial or supernatural being

earth·ly /úrthlee/ *adj* (**-li·er, -li·est**) *adj* **1** characteristic of this world **2** possible or imaginable o *no earthly use*

earth moth·er *n* a sensual and motherly woman

earth·mov·er /úrth mòovər/ *n* a bulldozer or mechanical digger —**earth·mov·ing** *adj*

earth·quake /úrth kwàyk/ *n* **1** a shaking of the Earth's crust resulting from release of stress along a fault line or from volcanic activity **2** a severely disruptive event

earth sci·ence *n* geology or a similar Earth-related science

earth·shak·ing /úrth shàyking/, **earth·shat·ter·ing** /-shàttəring/ *adj* extremely great or important

earth·work /úrth wùrk/ *n* an earth fortification *(often pl)*

earth·worm /úrth wùrm/ *n* a worm that burrows in the soil

earth·y /úrthee/ (**-i·er, -i·est**) *adj* **1** like soil **2** not squeamish or pretentious **3** rather indecent —**earth·i·ly** *adv* —**earth·i·ness** *n*

ear·wax /éer wàks/ *n* a waxy substance secreted by glands in the ear

ear·wig /éer wìg/ *n* a slender insect with pincers at the end of its abdomen

ORIGIN The *wig* of **earwig** is an ancient word that meant "insect," and is probably related to *wiggle*. There is a common myth that earwigs crawl into people's ears.

ease /eez/ *n* **1** lack of difficulty **2** lack of awkwardness **3** comfort and affluence **4** relaxation ■ *v* (**eased, eas·ing**) **1** *vt* make less unpleasant **2** *vt* relieve from pain **3** *also* **ease off** *vi* become less strong or intense **4** *vti* maneuver gently

ea·sel /éez'l/ *n* a support for an artist's canvas or blackboard

ORIGIN The Dutch word that **easel** derives from meant "donkey" (because the easel, like the donkey, carries a load), and is related to English *ass.*

ease·ment /éezmənt/ *n* a limited legal right to use something

eas·i·ly /éezilee, éezlee/ *adv* **1** without difficulty **2** by far o *easily the best* **3** at least o *easily 200 guests*

east /eest/ *n* **1** the direction in which the sun rises **2** the compass point opposite west **3** *also* **East** the part of an area or country that is in the east, or the part of the world to the east of Europe and the west of America ■ *adj* **1** in the east **2** describes a wind that blows from the east ■ *adv* toward the east —**east·bound** *adj*

East Af·ri·ca region in east central Africa, usually including Burundi, Kenya, Rwanda, Somalia, Tanzania, and Uganda —**East Af·ri·can** *n, adj*

East An·gli·a /-áng glee ə/ mainly agricultural region in E England —**East An·gli·an** *n, adj*

East A·sia the countries, territories, and regions of China, Hong Kong, Japan, North Korea, South Korea, Macau, Mongolia, parts of Russia, and Taiwan —**East A·sian** *adj*

East·er /éestər/ *n* **1** a Christian festival marking the resurrection of Jesus Christ. Date: the Sunday following the full moon on or after March 21. **2** the period from Good Friday to Easter Monday

ORIGIN **Easter** comes from the name of a Germanic goddess of the dawn, and is related to *east.* Both come from an ancient word meaning "shine."

⚡Eas·ter egg *n* **1** a colored hen's egg for Easter **2** a hidden element of a computer program

Easter Island

Eas·ter Is·land /éestər-/ island in the South Pacific Ocean belonging to Chile. Pop. 2,095 (1989). —**East·er Is·land·er** *n*

east·er·ly /éestərlee/ *adj* **1** in the east **2** describes a wind that blows from the east ■ *n* a wind from the east —**east·er·ly** *adv*

East·er Mon·day *n* the Monday after the Christian festival of Easter

east·ern /éestərn/ *adj* **1** in the east **2** facing east **3** blowing from the east —**east·ern·most** *adj*

east·ern·er /éestərnər/ *n* somebody from the east of a country or region

East·ern Eu·rope region comprising the countries of east and central Europe that had close ties with the former Soviet Union, including Poland, the Czech Republic, Slovakia, Hungary, Romania, Bulgaria, Albania, and the former Yugoslavia

east·ern hem·i·sphere *n* the part of the Earth that contains Asia, Australasia, and most of Europe and Africa

East·ern Or·tho·dox Church *n* the Orthodox Christian churches of E Europe

East·ern Stan·dard Time, East·ern Time *n* the local standard time in E North America

East Ger·ma·ny former republic of central Europe, now the eastern part of Germany —**East Ger·man** *n, adj*

East In·dies /-índeez/ formerly, India, Southeast Asia, and the Malay Archipelago, especially Indonesia —**East In·di·an** *adj, n*

East·man /éestmən/, **George** (1854–1932) US inventor and philanthropist

east-north·east *n* the compass point between east and northeast —**east-north·east** *adj, adv*

east-south·east *n* the compass point between east and southeast —**east-south·east** *adj, adv*

East Ti·mor disputed territory on the eastern half of the island of Timor in Southeast Asia. Cap. Dili. Pop. 839,700 (1995).

east·ward /éestwərd/ *adj* in the east ■ *n* a direction toward or point in the east ■ *adv also* **east·wards** toward the east —**east·ward·ly** *adj, adv*

eas·y /éezee/ (**-i·er, -i·est**) *adj* **1** not difficult **2** inappropriately effortless ○ *always taking the easy way out* **3** relaxed and informal ○ *had an easy manner* **4** not severe **5** unhurried ○ *an easy pace* **6** not steep ○ *an easy climb* **7** pleasant to experience ○ *easy on the eyes* **8** lacking preferences (*slang*) ○ *You decide. I'm easy.* —**eas·i·ness** *n* ◇ **go easy on** treat gently or leniently (*infml*) ◇ **take it easy 1** relax or not work too hard **2** avoid becoming upset

~~easyer~~ incorrect spelling of **easier**

eas·y·go·ing /éezee gṓ ing/ *adj* **1** relaxed, informal, and tolerant **2** unhurried

eas·y lis·ten·ing *n* soothing popular music

~~easyly~~ incorrect spelling of **easily**

eat /eet/ (**ate** /ayt/, **eat·en** /éet'n/) *v* **1** *vti* consume food as sustenance **2** *vi* have a meal **3** *vt* have as a usual food **4** *vt* cause anxiety to (*slang*) **5** *vt* use a lot of (*slang*) **6** *vt* absorb the cost of (*slang*) **7** *vti* penetrate a surface by corrosive or mechanical action —**eat·er** *n*

☐ **eat into** *vt* use up part of

☐ **eat up** *vt* consume quickly (*infml*) ○ *a job that eats up my time*

eat·a·ble /éetəb'l/ *adj* usable or enjoyable as food

eat·er·y /éetəree/ (*pl* **-ies**) *n* a restaurant (*infml*)

eat·ing dis·or·der *n* an emotional disorder manifesting as an obsessive attitude to food

eau de co·logne /ō də kə lṓn/ *n* scented liquid that is lighter than perfume

eaves /eevz/ *npl* the part of a roof that projects beyond the supporting wall

eaves·drop /éevz dròp/ (**-dropped, -drop·ping**) *vi* listen secretly —**eaves·drop·per** *n*

ORIGIN The obsolete noun **eavesdrop** referred to the ground below the roof of a building onto which rainwater fell from the eaves. It was a place where somebody could stand close enough to hear conversations going on inside.

E·ban /éebən/, **Abba** (*b.* 1915) South African-born Israeli politician and diplomat

ebb *vi* **1** recede from the shore (*refers to the sea or tide*) **2** diminish ■ *n* **1** a tidal movement away from the land **2** a diminution

Eb·o·la /i bṓlə/, **Eb·o·la vi·rus** *n* a usually lethal virus transmitted by blood and body fluids

eb·on·y /ébbənee/ *n* **1** a dark, very hard wood **2** an Asian tree that produces ebony

⚡e-book *n* a handheld electronic device for reading text, or the text itself

e·bul·lient /i búllyənt, i bóollyənt/ *adj* lively and enthusiastic —**e·bul·lience** *n*

⚡e-busi·ness *n* **1** business conducted on the Internet **2** a company using Internet technology

ec·cen·tric /ik séntrik, ek-/ *adj* **1** unconventional **2** off-center **3** not concentric ■ *n* a person regarded as unconventional —**ec·cen·tri·cal·ly** *adv* —**ec·cen·tric·i·ty** /èk sen tríssətee/ *n*

Ec·cle·si·as·tes /ĭ klēèzee ás teèz/ *n* a book of the Bible that discusses the futility of life and how to be a God-fearing person

ec·cle·si·as·tic /ĭ klēèzee ástik/ *n* a member of the Christian clergy

ec·cle·si·as·ti·cal /ĭ klēèzee ástik'l/ *adj* of the Christian Church

Ec·cle·si·as·ti·cus /ĭ klēèzee ástikəss/ *n* a book in some versions of the Bible

E·ce·vit /éjjəvit, èjjə vít/, **Bülent** (*b.* 1925) prime minister of Turkey (1974, 1978–79, 1999–)

ECG *abbr* electrocardiogram

ech·e·lon /éshə lòn/ *n* 1 a level in a hierarchy 2 a formation with each position to the side of the one in front

> **ORIGIN** Echelon derives from French, and comes from the same Latin word as English *scale.*

e·chid·na /ĭ kídnə/ *n* a spiny insect-eating mammal with a long snout

ech·i·na·ce·a /èkə náyssee ə/ *n* 1 an herbal remedy prepared from coneflowers 2 a coneflower

e·chi·no·derm /ĭ kínə dùrm/ *n* a sea animal with a symmetrical body, e.g., a starfish

ech·o /ékō/ *n* (*pl* **-oes**) 1 a repetition of a sound caused by the reflection of the sound waves from a surface 2 a repetition of another person's opinion 3 something that reminds you of something earlier ■ *v* (**-oed, -o·ing**) 1 *vt* repeat something by the reflection of sound waves 2 *vt* repeat another person's opinion 3 *vt* imitate or have elements of something earlier 4 *vi* resound by the reflection of sound waves —**e·cho·ic** /e kō ik/ *adj*

> **ORIGIN** Echo derives from a Greek word relating to sound. In Greek mythology, Echo was a nymph who pined away for love of a youth, Narcissus, until only her voice could be heard.

ech·o cham·ber *n* a room with walls that reflect sound

ech·o·lo·ca·tion /èkō lō káysh'n/ *n* the location of objects using reflection of emitted sounds

Eck·ert /ékərt/, **John Presper** (1919–95) US electronics engineer. He worked with John Mauchly on the ENIAC project (1943–46) that developed the first general-purpose electronic digital computer.

é·clair /ay kláir, áy klàir/ *n* a finger-shaped cake of light pastry filled with cream and usually iced

e·clamp·si·a /ĭ klámpsee ə/ *n* high blood pressure and convulsions in late pregnancy

é·clat /ay klàa, áy klàa/ *n* 1 great success 2 ostentatious display (*literary*)

e·clec·tic /ĭ kléktik/ *adj* 1 made up of elements from various sources 2 choosing from various sources —**e·clec·ti·cal·ly** *adv* —**e·clec·ti·cism** /-slzzəm/ *n*

e·clipse /ĭ klíps/ *n* 1 an obscuring of one astronomical object by another 2 a decline in status or power ■ *vt* (**e·clipsed, e·clips·ing**) 1 obscure another astronomical object 2 outdo or overshadow somebody or something

e·clip·tic /ĭ klíptik/ *n* the circular path of the Sun's annual motion relative to the stars

Ec·o /ékō/, **Umberto** (*b.* 1932) Italian novelist and academic

eco- *prefix* environment, ecology ○ *eco-friendly*

e·co·cide /ékō sĭd, eèkō-/ *n* destruction of the environment

e·co·friend·ly /eèkō frèndlee/ *adj* not harmful to the environment

E. co·li /èè kō lī/ *n* a bacterium in the colon, *Escherichia coli*, that causes food poisoning

e·col·o·gy /ĭ kóllajee/ *n* the study of the relationship between organisms and their environment —**ec·o·log·i·cal** /èkə lójjik'l, eèkə-/ *adj* —**ec·o·log·i·cal·ly** *adv* —**e·col·o·gist** *n*

> **ORIGIN** Ecology was coined by the German scientist Ernst Haeckel from a Greek word meaning "house." The same Greek word gave rise to *economy.*

ƒ e·com·merce *n* business transacted online, especially over the Internet

ec·o·nom·ic /èkə nómmik, eèkə-/ *adj* 1 of economics or a country's economy 2 of material goods and resources 3 = **economical 3**

ec·o·nom·i·cal /èkə nómmik'l, eèkə-/ *adj* 1 resourcefully frugal 2 inexpensive 3 efficient and not wasteful of time or energy —**ec·o·nom·i·cal·ly** *adv*

ec·o·nom·ic mi·grant *n* a traveling worker, especially one who goes to another country for better prospects

ec·o·nom·ics /èkə nómmiks, eèkə-/ *n* the study of the production, distribution, and consumption of goods and services (+ *sing verb*) ■ *npl* financial aspects (+ *pl verb*) —**e·con·o·mist** /ĭ kónnəmist/ *n*

e·con·o·mize /ĭ kónnə mĭz/ *vi* (**-mized, -miz·ing**) reduce expenditures

e·con·o·my /ĭ kónnəmee/ *n* (*pl* **-mies**) 1 a way of organizing the financial affairs of a country or community 2 thrift and cost-consciousness 3 a sparing use of something 4 a saving 5 *also* **e·con·o·my class** a cheaper category of travel, especially on airlines ■ *adj* cheaper

e·con·o·my drive *n* an organized attempt to make savings

ec·o·sphere /ékō sfeèr, eèkō-/ *n* the biosphere

ec·o·sys·tem /ékō slstəm, eèkō-/ *n* a group of interdependent organisms and their environment

ec·o·ter·ror·ism /ěkō térrə rìzzəm, eěkō-/ *n*
1 sabotage carried out in the name of protecting the environment 2 deliberate destruction of the environment —**ec·o·ter·ror·ist** *n*

ec·o·tour·ism /ěkō toór ìzzəm, eěkō-/ *n* tourism that seeks to avoid ecological damage to places visited —**ec·o·tour·ist** *n*

ec·o·war·ri·or /ěkō wàwree ər, eěkō-/ *n* an environmental activist

ec·ru /é kròo, áy-/ *adj* of a pale yellowish brown color —**ec·ru** *n*

~~ecstacy~~ incorrect spelling of **ecstasy**

ec·sta·sy /ěkstəssee/ (*pl.* **-sies**) *n* 1 intense delight 2 *also* **Ec·sta·sy** an illegal synthetic drug used as a stimulant and to relax inhibitions 3 loss of self-control during an intense experience

ec·stat·ic /ik státtik, ek-/ *adj* 1 greatly delighted 2 dominated by an intense emotion —**ec·stat·i·cal·ly** *adv*

ec·to·morph /ěktə màwrf/ *n* a person with long lean limbs

-ectomy *suffix* surgical removal of a body part ○ *appendectomy*

ec·top·ic preg·nan·cy /ek tóppik-/ *n* an egg developing outside the womb

Ec·ua·dor /ěkwə dàwr/ country in NW South America bordering the Pacific Ocean. Cap. Quito. Pop. 13,183,978 (2001). —**E·cua·dor·i·an** /ěkwə dáwree ən/ *n, adj*

ec·u·men·i·cal /ěkyə ménnik'l/, **ec·u·men·ic** /ěkyə ménnik/ *adj* of Christian Church unity —**ec·u·me·nism** /ěkyəmə nìzzəm/ *n*

ec·ze·ma /ěksəmə, égzəmə, ig zeěmə/ *n* a skin condition with reddening, itching, and scaly patches

ed. *abbr* 1 edited 2 edition 3 editor

-ed *suffix* 1 forms the past participle and past tense of regular verbs ○ *passed* 2 having, characterized by, like ○ *redheaded* ○ *bigoted* ○ *hinged*

E·dam /eědəm, eě dàm/ *n* a Dutch cheese usually sold covered with red wax

ed·dy /éddee/ *n* (*pl* **-dies**) a small whirl in flowing liquid or gas ■ *vi* (**-died, -dies**) flow contrary to the main current

Ed·dy /éddee/, **Mary Baker** (1821–1910) US religious leader, founder of Christian Science

e·del·weiss /áyd'l vìss, -wìss/ *n* a small alpine plant with white wooly leaves

e·de·ma /i deěmə/ (*pl* **e·de·mas** *or* **e·de·ma·ta** /-mətə/) *n* 1 excess fluid in the tissues of the body 2 excess fluid in plants

E·den /eéd'n/ *n* 1 in the Bible, the garden where the first man and woman lived 2 a perfect place —**E·den·ic** /ee dénnik/ *adj*

edge *n* 1 a border forming the outermost part of something 2 an area or position above a steep drop 3 a point just before a marked change or event ○ *on the edge of tears* 4 a line where two surfaces meet

5 the cutting side of a blade 6 a sharp quality ○ *an edge to her remarks* 7 an advantage (*infml*) ■ *v* (**edged, edg·ing**) 1 *vt* add a border to 2 *vi* move gradually sideways ◊ **live on the edge** be habitually in highly stressful situations ◊ **on edge** irritated or nervous ◊ **take the edge off** reduce the intensity of

edg·ing /éjjing/ *n* a decorative or protective border

edg·y /éjjee/ (**-i·er, -i·est**) *adj* 1 nervous 2 trend-setting —**edg·i·ly** *adv* —**edg·i·ness** *n*

ed·i·ble /éddəb'l/ *adj* able to be eaten by human beings, or enjoyable to eat

e·dict /eé dìkt/ *n* an authoritative decree or command

ed·i·fice /éddəfiss/ *n* a large building

ed·i·fy /éddə fì/ (**-fied, -fies**) *vt* give useful or improving information to —**ed·i·fi·ca·tion** /éddəfi káysh'n/ *n*

Ed·in·burgh /éd'nbərə, éd'n bùrə/ capital of Scotland. Pop. 448,850 (1996).

Thomas Alva Edison

Ed·i·son /éddiss'n/, **Thomas Alva** (1847–1931) US inventor

ed·it /éddit/ *vt* 1 prepare a text for publication 2 decide the content of a newspaper, magazine, or broadcast program 3 cut a movie or tape to give it its final order and content

e·di·tion /i dísh'n/ *n* 1 a particular version or installment of a publication or program 2 a batch of copies of a publication printed at the same time

ed·i·tor /édditər/ *n* 1 the person in overall charge of a publication 2 a journalist in charge of a specific part of a newspaper or magazine 3 a person who prepares a text for publication 4 somebody who edits movies or tape —**ed·i·tor·ship** *n*

ed·i·to·ri·al /éddi tàwree əl/ *adj* of editing ■ *n* a newspaper article expressing the editor's opinion

ed·i·to·ri·al·ize /éddi tàwree ə lìz/ (**-ized, -iz·ing**) *vi* 1 write editorials 2 write subjectively, especially when inappropriate

Ed·mon·ton /édməntən/ capital of Alberta, Canada. Pop. 616,306 (1996).

⚡ EDP *abbr* electronic data processing

EDT *abbr* Eastern Daylight Time

⚡ edu *abbr* US educational organization (*in Internet addresses*)

ed·u·cate /éjjə kàyt/ (**-cat·ed, -cat·ing**) v 1 vti impart knowledge to somebody by classroom or electronic instruction 2 vt arrange schooling for somebody —**ed·u·ca·ble** /-kəb'l/ adj —**ed·u·ca·tive** adj See note at **teach**

ed·u·cat·ed /éjjə kàytəd/ adj 1 well taught 2 showing good taste, knowledge, or cultivation 3 based on knowledge o *an educated guess*

ed·u·ca·tion /éjjə káysh'n/ n 1 the process of teaching or learning 2 knowledge acquired through teaching 3 a learning experience 4 the study of teaching and learning 5 the system for educating people —**ed·u·ca·tion·al** adj

ed·u·ca·tion·ist /éjjə káysh'nist/, **ed·u·ca·tion·al·ist** /-káyshən'list, -shnəlist/ n an expert in theories of education (disapproving)

ed·u·ca·tor /éjjə kàytər/ n a person whose profession is to instruct students, e.g., on the secondary-school or college level

⨍ **ed·u·tain·ment** /éjjə táynmənt/ n material, e.g., software, that educates and entertains at the same time

Ed·ward I /éddwərd/ (1239–1307) king of England (1272–1307)

Ed·ward II (1284–1327) king of England (1307–27)

Ed·ward III (1312–77) king of England (1327–77)

Ed·ward IV (1442–83) king of England (1461–83)

Ed·ward V (1470–83?) king of England (1483)

Ed·ward VI (1537–53) king of England (1547–53)

Ed·ward VII (1841–1910) king of the United Kingdom (1901–10)

Ed·ward VIII (1894–1972) king of the United Kingdom (January–December 1936), later Duke of Windsor after he abdicated

Ed·ward (the Black Prince) (1330–76) prince of Wales and father of Richard II

Ed·ward (the Con·fes·sor) (1002?–66) saint and king of the English (1042–66)

Ed·ward·i·an /ed wáwrdee ən, ð waárdee-/ adj of the reign of Edward VII of the United Kingdom ■ n somebody who lived in the era of Edward VII

Ed·wards /éddwərdz/, **Jonathan** (1703–58) American colonial theologian and cleric

EEG abbr electroencephalogram

eel (pl **eels** or same) n a long thin fish with a smooth skin and reduced fins

EEOC abbr Equal Employment Opportunity Commission

-eer suffix 1 a contemptible person or act o *profiteer* 2 a person engaged in or concerned with o *charioteer*

ee·rie /éeree/ adj unnerving and suggesting the supernatural —**ee·ri·ly** adv —**ee·ri·ness** n

ORIGIN Eerie was originally a Scottish and N English word meaning "fearful." The focus shifted toward the end of the 18C to the supposedly supernatural cause of the uneasy feeling.

eery incorrect spelling of **eerie**

ef·face /i fáyss/ (**-faced, -fac·ing**) vt rub out or erase —**ef·face·ment** n

ef·fect /i fékt/ n 1 a change resulting from an action 2 success in bringing about change o *I pleaded with them, but to no effect.* 3 the state of being in force or operation o *come into effect* 4 a feeling or impression in the mind o *The overall effect was light and spacious.* 5 a device that adds to the perceived realism of a movie, play, or broadcast (often pl) 6 the essential meaning of a statement o *or words to that effect* ■ **ef·fects** npl belongings (fml) ■ vt achieve or make o *effected a new health care plan* ◊ **in effect** actually ◊ See note at **affect**

ef·fec·tive /i féktiv/ adj 1 producing a result 2 producing a favorable impression o *effective use of imagery* 3 officially in force —**ef·fec·tive·ly** adv —**ef·fec·tive·ness** n

SYNONYMS effective, efficient, effectual, efficacious CORE MEANING: producing a result

ef·fec·tu·al /i fékchoo əl/ adj potentially successful in producing a desired or intended result (fml) —**ef·fec·tu·al·ly** adv ◊ See note at **effective**

ef·fem·i·nate /i fémmənət/ adj describes a man considered to be like a girl or woman (disapproving) —**ef·fem·i·na·cy** n —**ef·fem·i·nate·ly** adv

ef·fer·vesce /èffər véss/ (**-vesced, -vesc·ing**) vi produce tiny gas bubbles (refers to liquids) —**ef·fer·ves·cence** n —**ef·fer·ves·cent** adj

ef·fete /i féet/ adj decadent and lacking vitality —**ef·fete·ly** adv —**ef·fete·ness** n

ef·fi·ca·cious /èffi káyshəss/ adj able to produce a desired result (fml) —**ef·fi·ca·cy** /éffikəssee/ n ◊ See note at **effective**

ef·fi·cient /i físh'nt/ adj 1 well-organized 2 able to function without waste —**ef·fi·cien·cy** n —**ef·fi·cient·ly** adv ◊ See note at **effective**

ef·fi·gy /éffəjee/ (pl **-gies**) n a model or carving of a person

ef·flo·res·cence /èfflə réss'nss/ n a process or time of developing and flourishing (literary) —**ef·flo·res·cent** adj

ef·flu·ence /éffloo ənss/ n a flowing out, e.g., from a sewer

ef·flu·ent /éffloo ənt/ n 1 liquid waste 2 a stream or river that flows out of a larger body of water

ef·flu·vi·um /i flóovee əm, e-/ (pl **-a** /-ə/) n an outflow of something unpleasant or harmful (often pl)

ef·fort /éffərt/ n 1 energy exerted to achieve a purpose 2 activity directed toward a specific end o *the peacekeeping effort* 3 a serious attempt o *made an effort to listen* 4 the result of an attempt o *not a bad effort*

ef·fort·less /éffərtləss/ adj done with no effort —**ef·fort·less·ly** adv —**ef·fort·less·ness** n

ef·front·er·y /ə frúntəree/ n shameless nerve

ef·fu·sion /i fyóo̱zh'n/ n 1 an unrestrained outpouring of feelings 2 a pouring out of something such as liquid or light

ef·fu·sive /i fyóossiv/ adj unrestrained in expressing feelings —**ef·fu·sive·ly** adv

~~eficient~~ incorrect spelling of **efficient**

E-FIT tdmk a trademark for a computer program that creates a likeness of the face of a police suspect, based on a witness's description

⚡**EFRA** /éffrə/ abbr electronic forms routing and approval

⚡**EFTS** /efts/ abbr electronic funds transfer system

e.g. abbr for or as an example

USAGE e.g. or **i.e.**? Use **e.g.**, "for or as an example" (from Latin *exempli gratia*), to list a few items out of many: *I have the laboratory equipment, e.g., [not i.e.] beakers, thermometers, and test tubes.* Use **i.e.**, "that is, that is to say" (from Latin *id est*), to specify one thing only: *The tribunal, i.e., [not e.g.] the military tribunal, is set for noon on Friday.*

⚡**EGA** abbr enhanced graphics adapter

e·gal·i·tar·i·an /i gàllə táiree ən/ adj believing in equality —**e·gal·i·tar·i·an** n —**e·gal·i·tar·i·an·ism** n

egg¹ n 1 a reproductive structure in a protective covering that allows embryo development outside the mother's body 2 a hard-shelled object laid by a hen 3 a female reproductive cell —**egg·y** adj

ORIGIN Egg came into English from an early Scandinavian language. It was used side by side for 200 years with the older native English word, which had a soft *-y-* sound rather than a hard *-g-*. **Egg** took over completely during the 16C. **Egging somebody on**, also from a Scandinavian language, is related to English *edge*.

egg² vt incite o *was egged into making rash promises*

□ **egg on** vt encourage, especially to do something foolish or wrong

egg·cup /ég kùp/ n a small cup for a boiled egg

egg·head /ég hèd/ n an intellectual (infml)

egg·plant /ég plànt/ n US, Can, ANZ 1 a large oval fleshy fruit with a purple skin 2 a plant that produces eggplants

egg roll n a deep-fried cylinder of thin dough filled with a mixture of minced vegetables, often with meat or seafood

egg·shell /ég shèl/ n the hard covering of an egg

e·go /ee̱gō, éggō/ (pl e·gos) n 1 a person's sense of self-esteem o *fragile egos* 2 an inflated sense of self-importance 3 in psychoanalysis, the part of the mind containing consciousness

e·go·cen·tric /èegō séntrik, èggō-/ adj self-centered —**e·go·cen·trism** n

e·go·ism /ee̱gō ìzzəm, éggō-/ n 1 the condition of being self-centered 2 morality derived from self-interest —**e·go·ist** n —**e·go·is·tic** /èegō ístik, éggō-/ adj —**e·go·is·ti·cal** adj

e·go·tism /ee̱gə tìzzəm, éggə-/ n 1 an inflated sense of self-importance 2 the condition of being self-centered —**e·go·tist** n —**e·go·tis·tic** /èegə tístik, èggə-/ adj —**e·go·tis·ti·cal** adj

e·go trip n an action or experience boosting somebody's own ego (slang)

e·gre·gious /i grée̱jəss, -jee əss/ adj outrageously bad (fml) —**e·gre·gious·ly** adv —**e·gre·gious·ness** n

e·gress /ee̱ gréss/ n (fml) 1 a coming or going out 2 an exit

e·gret /ee̱grət, éggrət/ n a heron with long ornamental feathers

E·gypt /ee̱jipt/ country in NE Africa bordering the Mediterranean and the Red seas. Cap. Cairo. Pop. 69,536,644 (2001).

E·gyp·tian /i jípsh'n/ n 1 somebody from Egypt 2 the language of ancient Egypt —**E·gyp·tian** adj

eh /ay, e/ interj Can are you with me? (infml)

Eich·mann /íkmən, íkh màan/, **Adolf** (1906–62) German Nazi official

Eid al-Ad·ha /ee̱d ool áada/, **Eid ul-Ad·ha**, **Eid** n an Islamic festival to end a Mecca pilgrimage

Eid al-Fitr /ee̱d ool fee̱tər/, **Eid ul-Fitr**, **Eid** n an Islamic festival at the end of Ramadan

ei·der /ídər/ (pl **-ders** or same), **ei·der duck** n a large sea duck

ei·der·down /ídər dòwn/ n 1 eider ducks' feathers. Use: stuffing pillows and bed coverings. 2 a bed covering stuffed with soft material

Eif·fel /íf'l/, **Gustave** (1832–1923) French engineer, best known as the designer of the Eiffel Tower (1889)

eight /ayt/ n the number 8 —**eight** adj, pron —**eighth** n, adj, adv

eight ball n a black ball in pool, with the number 8 on it

eight·een /ay tée̱n/ n the number 18 —**eight·een** adj, pron —**eight·eenth** n, adj, adv

eighth note n in music, a note with a time value of one-eighth of a whole note

eight·y /áytee/ n the number 80 ■ **eight·ies** npl 1 the numbers 80 to 89, especially as a range of temperatures 2 the years from 80 to 89 in a century or somebody's life **—eight·i·eth** *n, adj, adv* **—eight·y** *adj, pron*

eigth incorrect spelling of **eight**

Ein·stein /ín stīn/, **Albert** (1879–1955) German-born US physicist. His theory of general relativity revolutionized scientific thought.

ein·stein·i·um /īn stīnee əm/ *n* (*symbol* **Es**) a synthetic radioactive chemical element.

Ei·re /áirə, írə/ Ireland

US Military Academy

Dwight D. Eisenhower

Ei·sen·how·er /ízn hówr/, **Dwight D.** (1890–1969) 34th president of the United States (1953–61)

ei·ther /eéthər, íthər/ *adj, pron* **1** one or the other of two ○ *with either hand* ○ *either of them* **2** indicates a negative ○ *cannot send e-mails to either address* ■ *adj* both ○ *either side of the street* ■ *conj* indicates alternatives ○ *Either you go or you stay.* ■ *adv* indicates connection or partial agreement ○ *You won't find poverty but you won't find luxury either.*

e·jac·u·late *v*/i jákyə làyt/ (**-lat·ed, -lat·ing**) **1** *vti* eject semen during orgasm **2** *vt* exclaim suddenly (*literary*) ■ *n* /i jákyələt/ ejaculated semen **—e·jac·u·la·tion** /i jàkyə láysh'n/ *n*

e·ject /i jékt/ *vt* **1** push out with force **2** remove from a place or position ○ *was ejected from the meeting* **—e·jec·tion** *n*

e·jec·tion seat *n* a seat in a combat fighter aircraft that can be ejected with its occupant in an in-flight emergency

eke /eek/ (**eked, ek·ing**) □ **eke out** *vt* **1** make something last with sparing use **2** supplement something insufficient or inadequate **3** achieve something with effort ○ *eked out a bare existence*

EKG *abbr* electrocardiogram

e·lab·o·rate *adj* /i lábbərət/ **1** finely or richly decorated **2** detailed and thorough ○ *made elaborate preparations* ■ *v* /i lábbə ràyt/ (**-rat·ed, -rat·ing**) **1** *vi* give more detail **2** *vt* work out in detail **—e·lab·o·rate·ly** *adv* **—e·lab·o·rate·ness** *n* **—e·lab·o·ra·tion** /i làbbə ráysh'n/ *n*

é·lan /ay laán, -laáN/, **e·lan** *n* vigor and enthusiasm

e·land /eélənd/ (*pl* **e·lands** *or same*) *n* a large African antelope with humped shoulders and spiraling horns

e·lapse /i láps/ (**e·lapsed, e·laps·ing**) *vi* go by gradually in time

e·las·tic /i lástik/ *n* **1** a stretchy material **2** a rubber band ■ *adj* **1** of or like elastic **2** easily changed **—e·las·ti·ci·ty** /i làss tíssətee, ee-/ *n* **—e·las·ti·cize** *vt* ◊ See note at **pliable**

e·las·tic band *n* a rubber band

e·la·tion /i láysh'n/ *n* great happiness and excitement **—e·late** *vt* **—e·la·ted** *adj*

El·ba /élbə/ island off the coast of W Italy, the place of Napoleon's first period of exile (1814–15)

El·be /élbə, elb/ river in central Europe. Length 724 mi./1,170 km.

El·bert, Mt. /él bùrt/ highest peak in Colorado, and the highest of the Rocky Mountains. Height 14,433 ft./4,399 m.

el·bow /élbō/ *n* the joint in the arm ■ *vti* push somebody with the elbow

el·bow grease *n* hard physical effort (*infml*)

el·bow·room /élbō ròom, -ròòm/ *n* space to move around in comfortably (*infml*)

El·burz Moun·tains /el boorz-/ mountain range in N Iran. Highest peak Damavand 18,386 ft./5,604 m.

eld·er[1] /éldər/ *adj* **1** born earlier **2** superior in rank or experience ■ *n* **1** a person born earlier **2** a senior member of a church or community

el·der[2] /éldər/ *n* a tree with purplish-black berries

el·der·ber·ry /éldər bèrree/ (*pl* **-ries**) *n* **1** a fruit of the elder tree **2** an elder tree

eld·er·ly /éldərlee/ *adj* past middle age (*sometimes offensive*) **—el·der·li·ness** *n*

eld·er states·man *n* a respected senior official

eld·est /éldəst/ *adj* born first

El Do·ra·do /èldə raáدō, -ráydō/ *n* **1** a legendary place of fabulous wealth **2** a place of riches

El·ea·nor of Aq·ui·taine /éllənər əv ákwi tàyn/ (1122?–1204) French-born queen of France (1137–52) and England (1154–89)

e·lect /i lékt/ *v* **1** *vt* choose by vote **2** *vt* decide to do **3** *vti* choose ■ *adj* chosen but not yet in office (*used in combination*) ○ *president-elect*

e·lec·tion /i léksh'n/ *n* **1** an event for choosing a winning candidate by vote **2** a choosing or being chosen by vote ○ *ran for election*

e·lec·tion·eer /i lèkshə neér/ *vi* engage in an election campaign

e·lec·tive /i léktiv/ *adj* **1** requiring election ○ *elective office* **2** not compulsory ○ *elective surgery* ■ *n* an optional subject of study

e·lec·tor /i léktər/ *n* **1** somebody who votes **2** *also* **E·lec·tor** a member of an electoral college **3** *also* **E·lec·tor** a German ruler who elected the Holy Roman Emperor (*often as a title*)

e·lec·tor·al /i léktərəl/ *adj* of elections

E·lec·tor·al Col·lege *n* the formal electing body of the President and Vice President of the United States

e·lec·tor·ate /i léktərət/ *n* a complete body of voters

e·lec·tric /i léktrik/ *adj* 1 involving, using, conveying, or caused by electricity 2 tense or excited o *an electric atmosphere*

e·lec·tri·cal /i léktrik'l/ *adj* 1 involving the application of electricity in technology 2 of electric cables, circuits, or functioning o *You'll need an electrician for the electrical work.* —**e·lec·tri·cal·ly** *adv*

e·lec·tri·cal storm *n* a storm with thunder and lightning

e·lec·tric blan·ket *n* a blanket heated by electricity

e·lec·tric chair *n* a chair for executing criminals by electricity

e·lec·tric eel *n* a fish producing an electric charge

e·lec·tric eye *n* an electric control device using light

e·lec·tric field *n* an area of electric forces

e·lec·tri·cian /i lèk trísh'n, èe lek-/ *n* somebody who works with electrical wiring or apparatus

e·lec·tric·i·ty /i lèk tríssətee, èe lek-/ *n* 1 energy created by moving charged particles 2 electric current, especially as a source of power

e·lec·tric shock *n* a sudden painful reaction caused by an electric current flowing through the body

e·lec·tri·fy /i léktrə fĩ/ (**-fied, -fies**) *vt* 1 convert to the use of electricity 2 charge with electricity 3 be thrilling to —**e·lec·tri·fi·ca·tion** /i lèktrəfi káysh'n/ *n*

e·lec·tro·car·di·o·graph /i lèktrō kaárdee ə gràf/ *n* a device to record heart activity via electrodes placed on the chest —**e·lec·tro·car·di·o·gram** *n* —**e·lec·tro·car·di·og·ra·phy** /-kàardee óggrəfee/ *n*

e·lec·tro·con·vul·sive ther·a·py /i lèktrō kən vúlssiv-/ *n* a treatment for severe psychiatric disorders involving electric shocks

e·lec·tro·cute /i léktrə kyòot/ (**-cut·ed, -cut·ing**) *vt* 1 injure or kill with an electric shock 2 execute in an electric chair —**e·lec·tro·cu·tion** /i lèktrə kyóosh'n/ *n*

e·lec·trode /i lék trōd/ *n* a conductor through which electricity flows

e·lec·tro·en·ceph·a·lo·graph /i lèktrō en séffələ gràf/ *n* a device producing a record of brain activity via electrodes placed on the scalp —**e·lec·tro·en·ceph·a·lo·gram** *n* —**e·lec·tro·en·ceph·a·log·ra·phy** /-sefə lóggrəfee/ *n*

e·lec·trol·y·sis /i lèk tróllisiss, èe lek-/ *n* 1 chemical separation into components using electricity 2 a technique of removing body hair or a growth by applying electricity through a needle

e·lec·tro·lyte /i léktrə lĩt/ *n* 1 a compound that is able to conduct electricity 2 an ion in an

electrolyte 3 an ion in cells, blood, or other organic material

e·lec·tro·lyt·ic /i lèktrə líttik/ *adj* 1 of electrolysis 2 of electrolytes

e·lec·tro·mag·net /i lèktrō mágnət/ *n* a magnetized iron core

e·lec·tro·mag·net·ism /i lèktrō mágnət ìzzəm/ *n* magnetism from electric currents —**e·lec·tro·mag·net·ic** /i lèktrō mag néttik/ *adj* —**e·lec·tro·mag·net·i·cal·ly** *adv*

e·lec·tro·mo·tive force /i lèktrō mōtiv-/ *n* 1 a force that causes the flow of electricity from one point to another 2 (*symbol* **E**) energy in a source such as a battery that is convertible into electricity

e·lec·tron /i lék tròn/ *n* an elementary particle that orbits the nucleus of an atom

⚡**e·lec·tron·ic** /i lèk trónnik, èe lek-/ *adj* 1 involving a controlled flow of electrons 2 using valves, transistors, or silicon chips 3 using or controlled by computer —**e·lec·tron·i·cal·ly** *adv*

⚡**e·lec·tron·ic da·ta proc·ess·ing** *n* computer-based tasks involving the input and manipulation of data

⚡**e·lec·tron·ic mail** *n* full form of **e-mail**

⚡**e·lec·tron·ic point of sale** *n* a computerized checkout system in stores

⚡**e·lec·tron·ic pub·lish·ing** *n* publishing on computer network or CD-ROM

⚡**e·lec·tron·ic purse** *n* a method of prepayment used in e-commerce, in which cash is stored electronically on a microchip

e·lec·tron·ics /i lèk trónniks, èe lek-/ *n* the technology of electronic devices (+ *sing verb*) ■ *npl* electronic parts (+ *pl verb*)

⚡**e·lec·tron·ic sig·na·ture** *n* an encoded attachment to an electronic message, verifying the identity of its sender

e·lec·tron mi·cro·scope /i lèktrō-/ *n* a powerful microscope that uses electron beams —**e·lec·tron mi·cros·co·py** *n*

e·lec·tro·plate /i léktrə plàyt/ (**-plat·ed, -plat·ing**) *vt* coat a surface with metal by electrolysis

e·lec·tro·shock ther·a·py /i lèktrō shok-/ *n* PSYCHIAT = **electroconvulsive therapy**

el·e·gant /élləgənt/ *adj* 1 stylish and graceful 2 pleasingly concise —**el·e·gance** *n* —**el·e·gant·ly** *adv*

el·e·gi·ac /èllə jĩ ək/, **el·e·gi·a·cal** /-ək'l/ *adj* expressing sorrow or regret (*fml*) —**el·e·gi·a·cal·ly** *adv*

~~eligible~~ incorrect spelling of **eligible**

el·e·gy /élləjee/ (*pl* **-gies**) *n* an elegiac poem

ORIGIN The Greek word from which **elegy** derives was originally applied to any song, but by the time it passed from Latin and French into English, it always had overtones of sadness.

el·e·ment /élləmənt/ *n* 1 a separate part or group within a larger whole o *criminal* *elements* **2** a small amount o *an element of risk* **3** a factor leading to something o *a key element in its success* **4 chem·i·cal el·e·ment** a substance that cannot be broken down into a simpler one by chemical reaction ■ **el·e·ments** *npl* **1** the forces of the weather, especially when harsh or damaging **2** basic principles

el·e·men·tal /èllə mént'l/ *adj* **1** fundamental **2** of natural forces —**el·e·men·tal·ly** *adv*

el·e·men·ta·ry /èllə méntəree, -méntree/ *adj* **1** involving only the most basic facts or principles **2** simple to do or understand

el·e·men·ta·ry par·ti·cle *n* a basic indivisible constituent of matter

el·e·men·ta·ry school *n* a school for early education

el·e·phant /éllofənt/ (*pl* -**phants** or same) *n* a large grayish animal with a long trunk and pointed tusks

el·e·phan·ti·a·sis /èllofən tí əssiss/ *n* a disfiguring illness causing swelling

ele·phan·tine /èllə fán tèen, -tìn, éllofən-/ *adj* **1** slow and heavy **2** enormous

el·e·vate /éllə vàyt/ (-**vat·ed**, -**vat·ing**) *vt* **1** raise to a higher level or place **2** raise to a higher rank

el·e·va·tion /èllə váysh'n/ *n* **1** a height above a reference point, especially sea level **2** a raising of something, or the fact of being raised **3** a degree or amount by which something is raised —**el·e·va·tion·al** *adj*

el·e·va·tor /éllə vàytər/ *n* **1** *US, Can, ANZ* a platform or compartment for moving things or people to a higher or lower level in a building **2** a grain storehouse with a mechanism for moving the grain

e·lev·en /i lévv'n/ *n* **1** the number 11 **2** a team of 11, e.g., a soccer team —**e·lev·en** *adj, pron* —**e·lev·enth** *n, adj, adv*

elf (*pl* **elves**) *n* a small imaginary being often considered to be a mischief-maker

elf·in /élfin/ *adj* **1** of or like an elf **2** delicate o *elfin features*

El·gar /él gàar, élgər/, **Sir Edward** (1857–1934) British composer

El Gre·co ♦ Greco, El

e·lic·it /i líssit/ *vt* provoke by way of reaction o *elicited a smile*

> **SPELLCHECK** Do not confuse the spelling of **elicit** and **illicit** ("illegal"), which sound similar.

e·lide /i líd/ (-**e·lid·ed**, **e·lid·ing**) *vt* omit an element of a word or phrase

el·i·gi·ble /éllijəb'l/ *adj* **1** qualified to do, be, or get something **2** marriageable —**el·i·gi·bil·i·ty** /èllijə bíllətee/ *n*

e·lim·i·nate /i límmə nàyt/ (-**nat·ed**, -**nat·ing**) *vt* **1** take away from a list or group, or from consideration **2** put an end to o *seek to eliminate poverty* **3** put out of a competition —**e·lim·i·na·tion** /i lìmmə náysh'n/ *n*

⚡**ELINT** /éllint/, **e·lint** *n* the gathering of information by electronic means. Full form **electronic intelligence**

George Eliot

El·i·ot /éllee ət/, **George** (1819–80) British novelist

El·i·ot, T. S. (1888–1965) US-born British poet, critic, and dramatist

e·li·sion /i lízh'n/ *n* omission of an element of a word or phrase

e·lite /i lèet, ay-/ *n* **1** a privileged minority (+ *sing or pl verb*) **2** a size of printing type, 12 characters per inch —**e·lite** *adj*

e·lit·ism /i lèe tìzzəm, ay-/ *n* belief in the existence of or domination by an elite group —**e·lit·ist** *n, adj*

e·lix·ir /i líksər/ *n* **1** a sweetened liquid drug **2** a remedy to cure all ills

> **ORIGIN** An **elixir** is thought of as a liquid, but it seems to come from a Greek word meaning "dry," and probably referred to a powder for treating wounds.

E·liz·a·beth /i lízzəbəth/ city in NE New Jersey. Pop. 110,661 (1998).

E·liz·a·beth I /i lízzəbəth/ (1533–1603) queen of England and Ireland (1558–1603)

E·liz·a·beth II (*b.* 1926) queen of the United Kingdom (1952–)

E·liz·a·be·than /i lìzzə béethən, -béthən/ *adj* of the reign of Elizabeth I

elk (*pl* same or **elks**) *n* ZOOL = **wapiti**

ell *n* **1** a building extension **2** something L-shaped

Duke Ellington

El·ling·ton /éllingtən/, **Duke** (1899–1974) US jazz pianist, composer, and band leader.

el·lipse /i líps/ *n* a shape resembling an oval

el·lip·sis /i lípsiss/ (*pl* -**ses** /-sèez/) *n* **1** omission of an implied word **2** a mark indicating omitted text, usually in the form of three dots

USAGE The **ellipsis** in the form of three dots is

used when text is omitted from the beginning, middle, or end of a quotation: *Shakespeare wrote, "When sorrows come, they come...in battalions."* (The full quotation is *When sorrows come, they come not single spies, But in battalions.*) When the ellipsis comes at the end of a sentence, it is usually followed by a period.

el·lip·ti·cal /ɪ lɪptɪk'l/, **el·lip·tic** /ɪ lɪptɪk/ *adj* 1 of or like an ellipse 2 highly economical in speech or writing —**el·lip·ti·cal·ly** *adv*

El·lis Is·land /éllɪss-/ island in upper New York Bay near Manhattan, from 1892 to 1954 the chief entry point for immigrants to the United States

El·li·son /élliss'n/, **Larry** (*b.* 1944) US entrepreneur

El·li·son, Ralph (1914–94) US writer

Ells·worth /élz wùrth/, **Oliver** (1745–1807) chief justice of the US Supreme Court (1796–99)

elm *n* 1 a large deciduous tree 2 the wood of the elm tree. Use: fuel, furniture, boats, construction.

El Mis·ti ◊ **Misti**

El Ni·ño /el neéenyō/ *n* a periodic change in Pacific currents, causing weather disruption

el·o·cu·tion /èllə kyoósh'n/ *n* the art of clear speaking —**el·o·cu·tion·ar·y** *adj*

e·lon·gate /ɪ táwng gàyt/ (**-gat·ed, -gat·ing**) *vti* lengthen or become longer —**e·lon·gat·ed** *adj*

e·lope /ɪ lōp/ (**e·loped, e·lop·ing**) *vi* leave secretly to get married —**e·lope·ment** *n*

el·o·quent /éllakwənt/ *adj* 1 speaking or spoken forcefully and with grace 2 expressing emotion clearly —**el·o·quence** *n* —**el·o·quent·ly** *adv*

El Pas·o /el pássō/ city in W Texas on the Rio Grande. Pop. 615,032 (1998).

El Sal·va·dor /el sálva dàwr/ country on the Pacific coast of Central America. Cap. San Salvador. Pop. 6,237,662 (2001).

else /elss/ *adj, adv* 1 in addition ○ *There's something else I'd like to say.* 2 different ○ *go somewhere else*

else·where /élss wàir, -hwàir/ *adv* to or at an unnamed other place

ELT *n* the teaching of English to nonnative speakers. Full form **English language teaching**

e·lu·ci·date /ɪ loóssə dàyt/ (**-dat·ed, -dat·ing**) *vti* explain or clarify —**e·lu·ci·da·tion** /ɪ loóssə dáysh'n/ *n*

e·lude /ɪ loód/ (**e·lud·ed, e·lud·ing**) *vt* 1 escape from or avoid 2 be beyond the understanding or memory of ○ *Her name eludes me.* ◊ See note at **allude**

E·lul /é lùl/ *n* the 6th month of the year in the Jewish calendar

e·lu·sive /ə loóssiv, i-/ *adj* 1 hard to find or catch 2 hard to define, identify, or remember —**e·lu·sive·ly** *adv* —**e·lu·sive·ness** *n*

SPELLCHECK Do not confuse the spelling of **elusive** and **allusive** ("making an allusion"), which sound similar.

elves plural of **elf**

E·ly·si·an Fields *npl* Elysium

E·ly·si·um /ɪ lízhee əm, ə lízzee-/ *n* 1 in Greek mythology, heaven 2 an ideal place or condition —**E·ly·si·an** *adj*

em /em/ *n* a variable measure of printing width, equal to the point size of the type and corresponding to the width of the letter M

'em /əm/ *contr* them (*infml*)

em- *prefix* = **en-** (*before m, b, or p*) ○ *embark*

e·ma·ci·at·ed /ɪ máyshee àytəd/ *adj* very thin because of starvation or illness —**e·ma·ci·a·tion** /ɪ màyshee áysh'n/ *n* ◊ See note at **thin**

⚡**e-mail** /eé màyl/, **e·mail** *n* 1 a system that allows text-based messages to be exchanged electronically, e.g., between computers or cellphones 2 an e-mail message ■ *vt* communicate with or send by e-mail —**e·mail·a·ble** *adj*

em·a·lan·ge·ni plural of **lilangeni**

em·a·nate /émmə nàyt/ (**-nat·ed, -nat·ing**) *v* 1 *vi* come out from a source 2 *vt* send out (*fml*) —**em·a·na·tion** /èmmə náysh'n/ *n*

e·man·ci·pate /ɪ mánssə pàyt/ (**-pat·ed, -pat·ing**) *vt* 1 set free from slavery or imprisonment 2 free from restrictions —**e·man·ci·pa·tion** /ɪ mànssə páysh'n/ *n* —**e·man·ci·pa·to·ry** *adj*

E·man·ci·pa·tion Proc·la·ma·tion *n* the 1863 declaration of freedom for enslaved people in all states waging war against the Union, issued by Abraham Lincoln during the US Civil War

e·mas·cu·late /ɪ máskyə làyt/ (**-lat·ed, -lat·ing**) *vt* 1 castrate (*literary*) 2 weaken the effectiveness of (*fml; sometimes offensive*) —**e·mas·cu·la·tion** /ɪ màskyə láysh'n/ *n*

em·balm /em baám/ *vt* preserve a corpse from decay after death —**em·balm·er** *n* —**em·balm·ment** *n*

em·bank·ment /em bángkmənt/ *n* a confining or supporting ridge of earth

~~embarass~~ incorrect spelling of **embarrass**

em·bar·go /em baárgō/ *n* (*pl* **-goes**) 1 an order stopping trade or another activity 2 an order halting movement of ships ■ *vt* (**-goed, -go·ing**) place an embargo on

em·bark /em baárk/ *vti* go or put on board a ship or aircraft —**em·bar·ka·tion** /èm baar káysh'n/ *n*

☐ **embark on** *vti* begin doing

~~embarass~~ incorrect spelling of **embarrass**

em·bar·rass /em bárrəss/ *vti* make or become self-conscious ○ *He's easily embarrassed.*

—em·bar·rass·ing *adj*—em·bar·rass·ing·ly *adv*—em·bar·rass·ment *n*

em·bas·sy /émbəssee/ (*pl* -sies) *n* 1 an ambassador's headquarters 2 an ambassador's staff

em·bat·tled /em bátt'ld/ *adj* 1 under assault or pressure 2 fighting or ready to fight

em·bed /em béd/ (-bed·ded, -bed·ding), im·bed *vti* 1 place or be placed solidly in a surrounding mass 2 fix or be fixed in the mind or memory

em·bel·lish /em béllish/ *vt* 1 beautify or ornament 2 add fictitious or exaggerated details to —em·bel·lish·ment *n*

em·ber /émbər/ *n* a burning fragment from a dying fire

em·bez·zle /em bézz'l/ (-zled, -zling) *vti* misuse entrusted money or property —em·bez·zle·ment *n*—em·bez·zler *n* ◊ See note at steal

em·bit·ter /em bíttər/ *vt* arouse bitter or aggrieved feelings in

em·bla·zon /em bláyz'n/ *vt* decorate with a coat of arms or vivid design

em·blem /émbləm/ *n* a symbol or image that represents something

em·blem·at·ic /èmblə máttik/, em·blem·at·i·cal /-máttik'l/ *adj* serving as an emblem of something

em·bod·y /em bóddee/ (-ied, -ies) *vt* 1 make tangible or visible 2 incorporate into an organized whole —em·bod·i·ment *n*

em·bold·en /em bóld'n/ *vt* give courage to

em·bo·lism /émbə lìzzəm/ *n* a blockage of an artery, usually caused by a blood clot

em·boss /em báwss, -bóss/ *vt* decorate with a raised pattern —em·boss·ment *n*

em·bou·chure /àam bŏŏ shŏŏr/ *n* the position of lips and tongue when playing a wind instrument

em·brace /em bráyss/ *v* (-braced, -brac·ing) 1 *vti* hug somebody or each other 2 *vt* take advantage of eagerly o *embrace an opportunity* 3 *vt* adopt as a belief or practice 4 *vt* include or encompass ■ *n* a hug

em·bra·sure /em bráyzhər/ *n* 1 a slanted opening in a fortification 2 a tapered opening in a wall, wider on the inside than outside

em·broi·der /em bróydər/ *vti* 1 sew a pattern into fabric 2 embellish a story —em·broi·der·er *n*

em·broi·der·y /em bróydəree/ (*pl* -ies) *n* 1 the making of decorative needlework 2 something with decorative needlework

em·broil /em bróyl/ *vt* involve in conflict

em·bry·o /émbree ò/ (*pl* -os) *n* an offspring of a human or other animal, or of a plant, in the initial stage of development after fertilization

em·bry·ol·o·gy /èmbree ólləjee/ *n* the study of embryos —em·bry·o·log·i·cal /èmbree ə lójjik'l/ *adj*—em·bry·ol·o·gist *n*

em·bry·on·ic /èmbree ónnik/ *adj* 1 of an embryo 2 in an early developmental stage

em·cee /em seé/ (*infml*) *n* a master or mistress of ceremonies ■ *vti* (-ceed, -cee·ing) be master or mistress of ceremonies at an event

e·mend /i ménd/ *vt* change the wording of to make more correct —e·men·da·tion /èeman dáysh'n, èmmən-, i mèn-/ *n*

em·er·ald /émmərəld, émmrəld/ *n* 1 a green precious stone, a form of beryl. Use: gems. 2 a bright green color —em·er·ald *adj*

ORIGIN Emerald comes ultimately from a Semitic word meaning "shine" that gave rise to a noun meaning "green gem" in ancient Greek. From there it passed into English via Latin and French.

e·merge /i múrj/ (e·merged, e·merg·ing) *v* 1 *vi* come out of or from behind something 2 *vti* become known or apparent o *It emerged that I had been wrong all along.* —e·mer·gence *n*—e·mer·gent *adj*

e·mer·gen·cy /i múrjənseee/ *n* (*pl* -cies) a sudden crisis requiring action ■ *adj* 1 acting or used in an emergency 2 requiring or involving immediate medical treatment o *an emergency appendectomy*

e·mer·gen·cy room *n* hospital area for urgent treatment

e·mer·i·ta /i mérritə/ *adj* retired but retaining a professional title (*of women*)

e·mer·i·tus /i mérritəss/ *adj* retired but retaining a professional title (*of men*)

Em·er·son /émmərs'n/, **Ralph Waldo** (1803–82) US essayist, lecturer, and poet —**Em·er·so·ni·an** /èmmər sónee ən/ *adj*

em·er·y /émməree/ *n* a variety of the mineral corundum. Use: abrasives.

e·met·ic /i méttik/ *adj* causing vomiting —e·met·ic *n*

emf *abbr* electromotive force

em·i·grant /émmigrənt/ *n* somebody who moves to another country —em·i·grant *adj*

em·i·grate /émmi gràyt/ (-grat·ed, -grat·ing) *vi* leave to live in another country —em·i·gra·tion /èmmi gráysh'n/ *n*

é·mi·gré /émmi gràv/ *n* a political refugee

em·i·nence /émminənss/ *n* 1 high position or status 2 a hill (*fml*) 3 **Em·i·nence** the title of a Catholic cardinal

em·i·nent /émminənt/ *adj* 1 of high standing or reputation 2 conspicuously high

em·i·nent do·main *n* governmental power to appropriate private property

em·i·nent·ly /émminəntlee/ *adv* very o *eminently qualified*

e·mir /ə meér/ *n* in some Islamic countries, an independent ruler

e·mir·ate /émmi ràyt, -ət, i meérət/ *n* a territory under an emir's rule

em·is·sar·y /émmi sèrree/ (*pl* -ies) *n* a representative sent on a diplomatic mission

e·mis·sion /i mísh'n/ n 1 the letting out of something, especially into the atmosphere 2 something given out, especially into the atmosphere ○ *harmful exhaust emissions*

e·mit /i mít/ (**e·mit·ted, e·mit·ting**) vt 1 let out, especially into the atmosphere 2 utter ○ *emitted a giggle* —**e·mit·ter** n

Em·my /émmee/ (pl **-mys**) n an award given by the American Academy of Television Arts and Sciences

e·mol·lient /i móllyənt/ adj 1 soothing to the skin 2 calming in manner (fml) —**e·mol·li·ent** n

e·mol·u·ment /i móllyəmənt/ n a payment (fml) ◊ See note at **wage**

e·mote /ə mōt/ (**e·mot·ed, e·mot·ing**) vi display exaggerated emotions

⚡ **e·mo·ti·con** /i mōtə kòn/ n a symbolic picture representing an emotion, made from computer keyboard characters and usually to be viewed sideways

e·mo·tion /i mōsh'n/ n 1 a heightened feeling such as anger or grief 2 agitation caused by strong feelings —**e·mo·tion·less** adj

e·mo·tion·al /i mōshən'l, i mōshnal/ adj 1 relating to emotions 2 easily affected by emotions —**e·mo·tion·al·ly** adv

e·mo·tive /i mōtiv/ adj causing or involving emotion —**e·mo·tive·ly** adv —**e·mo·tive·ness** n

em·pa·na·da /èmpə naádə/ n a spicy or sweet turnover in Spanish or Latin American cooking

em·pa·thize /émpə thìz/ (**-thized, -thiz·ing**) vi feel empathy ○ *empathized with them in their grief*

em·pa·thy /émpəthee/ n understanding of and identification with another's feelings —**em·pa·thet·ic** /èmpə théttik/ adj —**em·path·ic** /em páthik/ adj

~~emperer~~ incorrect spelling of **emperor**

em·per·or /émpərər, émprər/ n a man or boy ruling an empire

em·per·or pen·guin n a very large Antarctic penguin

em·pha·sis /émfəssiss/ (pl **-ses** /-sèez/) n 1 special importance ○ *puts emphasis on exercise* 2 extra spoken stress on an important word or phrase

em·pha·size /émfə sìz/ (**-sized, -siz·ing**) vt put emphasis on

em·phat·ic /em fáttik/ adj 1 expressed or done with emphasis 2 forcible and definite ○ *an emphatic refusal* —**em·phat·i·cal·ly** adv

em·phy·se·ma /èmfə séemə, -zéemə/ n a lung condition causing breathing impairment

em·pire /ém pìr/ n 1 a group of territories ruled by a single supreme authority 2 a large far-flung business

em·pire-build·ing n a tendency to enlarge a sphere of authority —**em·pire-build·er** n

em·pir·i·cal /em pírrik'l/ adj based on observation and experiment rather than theory —**em·pir·i·cal·ly** adv

em·pir·i·cism /em pírri sìzzəm/ n 1 the philosophical belief that all knowledge is derived from the experience of the senses 2 the application of observation and experiment —**em·pir·i·cist** n

em·place·ment /em pláysmənt/ n a position for large weaponry

em·ploy /em plóy/ vt 1 give paid work to 2 keep busy 3 utilize ■ n the state of employing a worker (fml) ○ *in her employ* —**em·ploy·a·ble** adj ◊ See note at **use**

em·ploy·ee /em plóy ee, èm ploy eé/ n a paid worker

em·ploy·er /em plóy ər/ n a person or organization that hires workers

em·ploy·ment /em plóymənt/ n 1 the condition of working for pay 2 work or the job done by somebody 3 the number of paid workers in a population

em·po·ri·um /em páwree əm/ (pl **-ums** or **-a** /-ə/) n a store offering a wide selection of goods

em·pow·er /em pówr/ vt 1 give authority to 2 make more confident or assertive —**em·pow·er·ment** n

em·press /émprəss/ n 1 a woman or girl ruling an empire 2 an emperor's wife

emp·ty /émptee, émtee/ adj (**-ti·er, -ti·est**) 1 containing nothing 2 unoccupied ○ *an empty chair* 3 with no passengers or load 4 insincere ○ *empty promises* 5 without meaning or purpose ○ *an empty life* ■ v (**-tied, -ties**) 1 vt remove the contents of ○ *emptied his pockets* 2 vti discharge or transfer, or be discharged or transferred ○ *The stream empties into the lake.* ■ n (pl **-ties**) a container without contents —**emp·ti·ly** adv —**emp·ti·ness** n ◊ See note at **vacant, vain**

emp·ty-hand·ed adj 1 having gained nothing ○ *came back from the negotiations empty-handed* 2 with nothing in the hands

emp·ty-head·ed adj regarded as silly and unintelligent (offensive)

e·mu /ée myòó/ (pl **e·mus** or **same**) n a large Australian flightless bird

em·u·late /émmyə làyt/ (**-lat·ed, -lat·ing**) vt 1 try to equal 2 compete successfully with —**em·u·la·tion** /èmmyə láysh'n/ n —**em·u·la·tor** n ◊ See note at **imitate**

e·mul·si·fi·er /i múlsə fī ər/ n a chemical agent that stops substances separating

e·mul·si·fy /i múlsə fī/ (**-fied, -fies**) vti convert into an emulsion —**e·mul·si·fi·ca·tion** /i mùlsəfi káysh'n/ n

e·mul·sion /i múlsh'n/ n 1 a suspension of liquid within another liquid 2 a light-sensitive photographic coating

en n a measure of printing width, half that of an em

en- *prefix* **1** put or go into, or cover with ○ *entomb* **2** cause to be ○ *enthrall* **3** thoroughly ○ *enmesh*

-en *suffix* **1** cause or come to be or have ○ *loosen* **2** made of or resembling ○ *earthen*

en·a·ble /in áyb'l, en-/ (**-bled, -bling**) *vt* **1** provide with means to do something **2** make possible ○ *enabling legislation* **—en·a·ble·ment** *n*

-enabled *suffix* made capable of using or operating with ○ *Web-enabled*

en·act /in ákt, en-/ *vt* **1** make into law **2** act out **—en·act·ment** *n*

~~enamal~~ incorrect spelling of **enamel**

e·nam·el /i námm'l/ *n* **1** a glassy decorative or protective coating **2** a paint with a hard shiny finish **3** a hard calcium-containing layer on a tooth crown ■ *vt* coat with enamel **—e·nam·el·er** *n*

en·am·ored /in ámmərd, en-/ *adj* captivated by or in love with somebody

en bloc /aaN bláwk, en blók/ *adv* all together

en·camp /in kámp, en-/ *vi* set up a camp **—en·camp·ment** *n*

en·cap·su·late /in kápsə làyt, en-/ (**-lat·ed, -lat·ing**) *v* **1** *vt* express in a concise form **2** *vti* enclose or be enclosed completely **—en·cap·su·la·tion** /in kápsə láysh'n, en-/ *n*

en·case /in káyss, en-/ (**-cased, -cas·ing**) *vt* surround closely with a case or cover **—en·case·ment** *n*

en·ceph·a·li·tis /en sèffə líⁿtiss/ *n* a brain inflammation **—en·ceph·a·lit·ic** /-líⁿttik/ *adj*

en·chant /in chánt, en-/ *vt* **1** delight **2** put under a spell **—en·chant·er** *n* **—en·chant·ing** *adj* **—en·chant·ing·ly** *adv* **—en·chant·ment** *n* **—en·chant·ress** *n*

en·chi·la·da /ènchi laàdə/ *n* a rolled tortilla with a filling

en·cir·cle /in súrk'l, en-/ (**-cled, -cling**) *vt* **1** surround **2** make a circuit of

encl. *abbr* **1** enclosed **2** enclosure

en·clave /én klàyv, óN-/ *n* **1** a region surrounded by foreign territory **2** a distinct group in a larger community

en·close /in klṓz, en-/ *vt* **1** surround **2** put a boundary around **3** insert in an envelope or package

en·clo·sure /in klṓzhər, en-/ *n* **1** something enclosed in a letter or package **2** a piece of land surrounded by a boundary **3** a boundary fence **4** the act or fact of enclosing something

⚡**en·code** /in kṓd, en-/ (**-cod·ed, -cod·ing**) *vt* **1** convert to code **2** convert into digital form for processing by computer

en·co·mi·um /en kṓmə əm/ (*pl* **-ums** *or* **-a** /-mee ə/) *n* an expression of high praise (*fml*)

en·com·pass /in kúmpəss, en-/ *vt* **1** include in its entirety **2** encircle

en·core /ón kàwr/ *n* an extra or repeated performance ■ *interj* demands

a repeat performance ■ *vt* give an encore of

en·coun·ter /in kówntər, en-/ *vt* **1** meet unexpectedly **2** meet in conflict **3** come up against ■ *n* **1** an unexpected meeting **2** a confrontation

en·cour·age /in kúr ij, en-/ (**-aged, -ag·ing**) *vt* **1** give hope, confidence, or support to **2** foster the growth or development of **—en·cour·age·ment** *n* **—en·cour·ag·ing** *adj* **—en·cour·ag·ing·ly** *adv*

en·croach /in krṓch, en-/ *vi* **1** intrude gradually or stealthily ○ *encroaching on civil liberties* **2** exceed proper limits **—en·croach·ment** *n*

en·crust·a·tion /in krust áysh'n/, **in·crust·a·tion** *n* **1** the covering of something with a hard coating or a layer of jewels **2** a hard coating or decorative layer **—en·crust** /in krúst/ *vt* **—en·crust·ed** *adj*

⚡**en·crypt** /in krípt, en-/ *vt* **1** convert into code or cipher **2** encode in a digital form using a key **—en·cryp·tion** /en krípsh'n/ *n*

en·cum·ber /in kúmbər, en-/ *vt* **1** hinder **2** load down

en·cum·brance /in kúmbrənss, en-/ *n* a burden or hindrance

en·cyc·li·cal /in síklik'l, en-/ *n* a papal statement on church doctrine sent to Roman Catholic bishops

en·cy·clo·pe·di·a /in síklə peèdee ə, en-/, **en·cy·clo·pae·di·a** *n* a comprehensive reference work

en·cy·clo·pe·dic /in síklə peèdik, en-/, **en·cy·clo·pae·dic** *adj* embracing a broadly inclusive range of knowledge

end *n* **1** the extremity of an object **2** the final part of something that has consumed time ○ *the end of the lesson* **3** a limit or boundary **4** a stopping ○ *an end to hostilities* **5** an extremity of a scale **6** a goal or purpose ○ *an end in itself* **7** a part of a communications link ○ *on the other end of the phone* **8** death or destruction ○ *met an untimely end* **9** a leftover piece **10** a share of joint responsibility ○ *your end of the bargain* **11** half of a playing field or court, defended by one side **12** in football, a player positioned at the end of a line ■ *v* **1** *vti* come or bring to a stop **2** *vi* result ○ *ended in an uproar* **3** *vi* reach a limit at a place **4** *vi* reach a tip ◇ **at loose ends** having no purpose or occupation ◇ **in the end** finally ◇ **make ends meet** be able to pay for the expenses of daily living ◇ **no end** very much indeed ◇ **on end** for an uninterrupted period ○ *rained for days on end*

☐ **end up** *vi* **1** become something eventually **2** arrive at a destination at long last

en·dan·ger /in dáynjər, en-/ *vt* put at risk **—en·dan·ger·ment** *n*

en·dan·gered spe·cies *n* a species threatened by extinction

en·dear /in deér, en-/ vt cause to be liked o *didn't endear herself to us*

en·dear·ing /in deéring, en-/ adj causing fond feelings —**en·dear·ing·ly** adv

en·dear·ment /in deérmənt, en-/ n an expression of affection

en·deav·or /in dévvər, en-/ vt try hard (fml) ■ n 1 an earnest effort to achieve something 2 an enterprise

En·de·cott /éndi kòt/, **John** (1588?–1665) English-born American colonial administrator

en·dem·ic /en démmik/ adj commonly occurring in or restricted to a particular place or group of people o *a disease endemic in the tropics* —**en·dem·i·cal·ly** adv

~~endevor~~ incorrect spelling of **endeavor**

end·game /énd gàym/ n 1 in chess, the last stage of a game 2 the last stage of a process or contest

end·ing /énding/ n the final part or tip of something o *a sad ending* o *nerve endings*

en·dive /én dìv, aaN deév/ n 1 a leafy plant used in salads and as a garnish 2 a plant cultivated for its leaves and roots

end·less /éndləss/ adj 1 seeming without end or unlimited o *endless patience* 2 forming one piece o *an endless belt* —**end·less·ly** adv

en·do·crine gland /éndəkrin-, -kreen-, -krīn-/ n a gland that secretes hormones directly into the blood or lymph

en·dog·e·nous /en dójjənəss/ adj 1 without an external cause 2 produced inside an organism

en·dor·phin /en dáwrfin/ n a natural painkiller released from the brain

en·dorse /in dáwrss, en-/ (-dorsed, -dors·ing) vt 1 give approval or public support to o *refuses to endorse either candidate* o *endorses various cosmetics* 2 sign a check on the back to obtain cash or specify a payee 3 sign to acknowledge receipt of something —**en·dorse·ment** n

en·do·scope /éndə skòp/ n a long tube with a camera on the end, inserted in the body for diagnosis or minor surgery —**en·dos·co·py** /en dóskəpee/ n

en·dow /in dów, en-/ vt 1 provide with income or property 2 provide with something desirable o *endowed with a perfect climate*

en·dow·ment /in dówmənt, en-/ n an amount of income or property provided to a person or institution

en·dur·ance /in doóranss, en-/ n 1 an ability to bear prolonged hardship 2 persistence over time

en·dure /in doór, en-/ (-dured, -dur·ing) v 1 vt bear hardship 2 vt tolerate (fml) 3 vi survive or last —**en·dur·a·ble** adj —**en·dur·ing** adj

end us·er n any of the ultimate users that a product is designed for

end·wise /énd wìz/, **end·ways** /-wàyz/ adv

1 with the end up or forward 2 with ends touching

end zone n in football, each of two scoring areas at the ends of the field

en·e·ma /énnəmə/ n an insertion of liquid into the rectum to flush out the bowels

en·e·my /énnəmee/ (pl -mies) n 1 somebody who is actively unfriendly toward another 2 a military opponent 3 something harmful or obstructive

en·er·get·ic /énnər jéttik/ adj 1 forceful 2 requiring stamina —**en·er·get·i·cal·ly** adv

en·er·gize /énnər jīz/ (-gized, -giz·ing) vt 1 give energy to 2 supply with electrical power

en·er·gy /énnərjee/ (pl -gies) n 1 vigor 2 a forceful effort o *concentrate our energies on success* 3 a power supply or source 4 (symbol *E*) the capacity of a body or system to do work

en·er·vate /énnər vàyt/ (-vat·ed, -vat·ing) vt lessen the vitality of —**en·er·va·tion** /énnər váysh'n/ n

en·fant ter·ri·ble /aaN faàN te reéblə/ n 1 somebody whose unconventional behavior is shocking 2 an avant-garde young artist

en·fee·ble /in feéb'l, en-/ (-bled, -bling) vt make weak

en·fi·lade /énfə làyd, -laàd/ n a burst of gunfire aimed along the entire length of a body of troops —**en·fi·lade** vt

~~enflict~~ incorrect spelling of **inflict**

en·fold /in fóld, en-/ vt 1 envelop 2 take in an embrace

~~enforceable~~ incorrect spelling of **enforceable**

en·force /in fáwrss, en-/ (-forced, -forc·ing) vt compel obedience to a law or rule —**en·force·a·ble** adj —**en·force·ment** n

en·forc·er /in fáwrsər, en-/ n somebody who enforces a law

en·fran·chise /in frán chīz, en-/ (-chised, -chis·ing) vt 1 give the right to vote to 2 set free —**en·fran·chise·ment** n

eng. abbr 1 engine 2 engineer 3 engineering

Eng. abbr 1 England 2 English

en·gage /in gáyj, en-/ (-gaged, -gag·ing) v 1 vt hire somebody 2 vt require the use of something o *Her writing engages most of her time.* 3 vti involve or become involved in something 4 vt attract somebody by being pleasant 5 vti activate, or become activated 6 vti fight an enemy 7 vt hold the attention of somebody 8 vti make a promise 9 vti interlock one thing with another, or become interlocked o *engaged the gears*

en·ga·gé /aaNggaa zháy/ adj politically committed

en·gaged /in gáyjd, en-/ adj 1 having agreed to marry 2 occupied or in use 3 fighting a battle 4 with parts interlocked 5 actively involved

en·gage·ment /in gáyjmənt, en-/ n 1 an agreement to marry 2 a commitment to go somewhere **3** a brief job, especially one for a performer **4** a battle ◊ See note at **fight**

en·gage·ment ring *n* a ring given by a man to his fiancée

en·gag·ing /in gáyjing, en-/ *adj* attractive or charming —**en·gag·ing·ly** *adv*

En·gels /éng g'lz/, **Friedrich** (1820–95) German political thinker and revolutionary

en·gen·der /en jéndər/ *vt* cause to exist ○ *Secrecy engenders suspicion.*

en·gine /énjin/ *n* **1** a machine that converts energy into mechanical power **2** a railroad locomotive —**en·gined** *adj*

en·gi·neer /ènjə neér/ *n* **1** an engineering professional **2** a locomotive driver **3** a soldier belonging to a unit specializing in building things ■ *vt* **1** plan or bring about, especially with ingenuity or secretiveness **2** use engineering skill to design or create

en·gi·neer·ing /ènjə neéring/ *n* the application of science to the design, construction, and maintenance of buildings and manufactured things

Eng·land /ing glənd/ country forming the southern and largest part of Great Britain and of the United Kingdom. Cap. London. Pop. 49,495,000 (1998).

Eng·lish /ing glish/ *n* **1** the Germanic language of the United Kingdom, the United States, and many other countries **2** the study of English or literature in English **3** *also* **english** in billiards, a spin applied to a ball by hitting it off-center ■ *npl* the people of England ■ *adj* **1** of the English language **2** of England or the people of England —**Eng·lish·ness** *n*

ORIGIN England and the **English** are named for the Angles, the Germanic people who invaded and settled in England in the 5C and 6C AD. They came from Angul (now Angeln) in N Germany, which got its name from its shape, somewhat resembling a fishhook. **English** has been spelled with *e* since the earliest records.

Eng·lish Chan·nel area of water between England and France linking the North Sea with the Atlantic Ocean. Length 351 mi./565 km.

Eng·lish horn *n* a double-reed woodwind instrument resembling an oboe

Eng·lish·man /ing glishmən/ (*pl* -men /-mən/) *n* a man from England

Eng·lish muf·fin *n* a flat round bread that has been cooked on a griddle, eaten toasted

Eng·lish·wom·an /ing glish wöómmən/ (*pl* -en /-wimmin/) *n* a woman from England

en·gorge /in gáwrj, en-/ (-gorged, -gorg·ing) *vti* fill with blood —**en·gorge·ment** *n*

en·grave /in gráyv, en-/ (-graved, -grav·ing) *vt* **1** carve or etch a surface **2** carve or etch a design onto a surface **3** impress something deeply on the mind —**en·grav·er** *n*

en·grav·ing /in gráyving, en-/ *n* **1** an engraved print or design **2** the act of carving or etching images

en·gross /in gróss, en-/ *vt* **1** occupy the whole attention of somebody **2** buy enough of a commodity to control the market —**en·gross·ing** *adj* —**en·gross·ing·ly** *adv*

en·gulf /in gúlf, en-/ *vt* **1** surround, cover, and swallow up **2** overwhelm —**en·gulf·ment** *n*

⚡**en·hance** /in hánss, en-/ (-hanced, -hanc·ing) *vt* **1** improve or add a desirable quality to something **2** increase the clarity of an electronic image using a computer program —**en·hance·ment** *n*

e·nig·ma /i nígmə, e-/ *n* somebody or something not easily explained or understood —**en·ig·mat·ic** /ènnig máttik/ *adj* —**en·ig·mat·i·cal·ly** *adv*

en·join /in jóyn, en-/ *vt* **1** command or impose with authority (*fml*) ○ *were enjoined to be silent* ○ *enjoined secrecy upon us* **2** forbid or prohibit —**en·join·ment** *n*

en·joy /in jóy, en-/ *vt* **1** find pleasing **2** have the use or benefit of **3** have as a good feature

en·joy·a·ble /in jóy əb'l, en-/ *adj* providing pleasure —**en·joy·a·bly** *adv*

en·joy·ment /in jóymənt, en-/ *n* **1** pleasure **2** the experiencing of something that provides pleasure **3** a source of pleasure **4** use or benefit of something, especially as a legal right

en·large /in laárj, en-/ (-larged, -larg·ing) *v* **1** *vti* make or become larger **2** *vt* make a photograph larger **3** *vti* broaden in scope **4** *vi* give more detail —**en·large·ment** *n* —**en·larg·er** *n* ◊ See note at **increase**

en·light·en /in líft'n, en-/ *vt* **1** give clarifying information to **2** free from ignorance, prejudice, or superstition —**en·light·en·ing** *adj*

en·light·ened /in líft'nd, en-/ *adj* **1** free of ignorance, prejudice, or superstition **2** well-informed

en·light·en·ment /in líft'nmənt, en-/ *n*
En·light·en·ment an 18C intellectual movement that emphasized reason and science

en·list /in líst, en-/ *vti* **1** enroll in the military **2** gain the support of, or become actively involved in an effort —**en·list·ment** *n*

en·list·ed per·son *n* a low-ranking member of the armed forces

en·liv·en /in lív'n, en-/ *vt* **1** invigorate **2** make brighter or more cheerful —**en·liv·en·ment** *n*

en masse /on máss, aaN maáss/ *adv* in a group

en·mesh /in mésh, en-/ *vt* **1** entangle **2** catch in a net

en·mi·ty /énmətee/ (*pl* -ties) *n* hostility or hatred between enemies

~~enemy~~ incorrect spelling of **enemy**

en·no·ble /i nṓb'l, e-/ (-bled, -bling) *vt* **1** make noble or more dignified (*fml*) **2** elevate to membership of the nobility —**en·no·ble·ment** *n*

en·nui /on weé/ *n* general weariness and dissatisfaction with life

e·nol·o·gy /ee nóllajee/, **oe·nol·o·gy** *n* the study of wine

e·nor·mi·ty /ə náwrmətee/ (*pl* **-ties**) *n* 1 △ enormous size or degree 2 extreme evil 3 an extremely evil act

USAGE **enormity** or **enormousness**? **Enormity** strictly means "evil" or "an evil act": *the enormity of the crime.* **Enormousness** refers to significant size or scale: *the enormousness of the task.*

e·nor·mous /ə náwrməss/ *adj* unusually large —**e·nor·mous·ly** *adv* —**e·nor·mous·ness** *n*

e·nough /i núf/ *adj* as much of as is needed or bearable ○ *enough time to shop* ○ *in enough trouble already* ■ *adv* 1 as much as is needed ○ *run fast enough* 2 adds emphasis ○ *Oddly enough, we'd met before.* 3 to a degree that can be tolerated ○ *She was arrogant enough before the promotion.* ■ *pron* the needed or tolerated amount ○ *Bring more money; we never have enough.*

en pas·sant /òN paa saàN/ *adv* in passing (*fml*)

en·quire, etc. = **inquire, etc.**

en·rage /in ráyj, en-/ (**-raged, -rag·ing**) *vt* make very angry

en·rap·ture /in rápchər, en-/ (**-tured, -tur·ing**) *vt* delight

en·rich /in rích, en-/ *vt* 1 improve the quality of 2 make wealthier —**en·rich·ment** *n*

en·roll /in róll, en-/, **en·rol** (**-rolled, -roll·ing**) *vti* enter the name of yourself or somebody else on a register or list ○ *enroll the children in school* —**en·roll·ee** /in rò lèe, en-/ *n*

en·roll·ment /in róllmənt, en-/, **en·rol·ment** *n* 1 an instance of signing up formally for something 2 the number of people registered ○ *a decline in enrollment*

en route /aan róot/ *adv* on the way

en·sconce /in skónss, en-/ (**-sconced, -sconc·ing**) *vt* settle somewhere comfortably (*fml*)

en·sem·ble /on sómb'l/ *n* 1 an outfit of clothes 2 a group of performers 3 something created by putting separate parts together 4 a section of a play or ballet in which the whole cast is involved ■ *adj* collaborative

en·shrine /in shrín, en-/ (**-shrined, -shrin·ing**) *vt* 1 protect from change, especially in law 2 keep in a shrine —**en·shrine·ment** *n*

en·shroud /in shRówd, en-/ *vt* 1 obscure 2 wrap in a shroud

en·sign (*flag*) /énsən, én sín/ (*rank*) /énsən/ *n* 1 a flag indicating a ship's nationality 2 a US Navy or Coast Guard commissioned officer of the lowest rank 3 a badge of office

en·slave /in sláyv, en-/ (**-slaved, -slav·ing**) *vt* 1 subject to a controlling influence that takes away freedom 2 make into a slave —**en·slave·ment** *n*

en·snare /in snáir, en-/ (**-snared, -snar·ing**) *vt* 1 trap in an unpleasant situation 2 catch in a trap —**en·snare·ment** *n*

en·sue /in sóo, en-/ (**-sued, -su·ing**) *vi* happen after or as a result something —**en·su·ing** *adj*

en suite /aaN sweét/ *adj, adv* (*fml*) 1 adjoining and forming part of the same unit 2 forming part of a set

en·sure /in shóor, en-/ (**-sured, -sur·ing**), **in·sure** /in-/ *vt* make certain or sure of

en·tab·la·ture /in tábblə chòor, en-/ *n* in classical architecture, the section of a structure that lies between the columns and the roof

en·tail *vt* /in táyl, en-/ 1 have something as a consequence 2 restrict the future ownership of real estate to specified descendants through a will ■ *n* /én táyl/ 1 the restriction of future ownership of real estate to specified descendants 2 an entailed piece of real estate —**en·tail·ment** *n*

en·tan·gle /in táng g'l, en-/ (**-gled, -gling**) *vt* 1 tangle up 2 put into a difficult situation —**en·tan·gle·ment** *n*

en·tente /aaN taàNt/ *n* a friendly understanding between countries

⚡**en·ter** /éntər/ *v* 1 *vti* go or come into a place 2 *vt* write or type in a book or on a computer 3 *vt* submit for formal consideration 4 *vti* register as a competitor 5 *vt* join or become involved in something ○ *enter the race for President* 6 *vti* force a way into something, e.g., the body ○ *The bullet entered here.*

□ **enter into** *vt* 1 take part in something 2 be relevant to something 3 sign up for a contract

en·ter·i·tis /èntə rítiss/ *n* inflammation of the intestines

⚡**en·ter key** *n* the return key on a computer keyboard

en·ter·prise /éntər prìz/ *n* 1 readiness to put effort into new ventures and activities 2 a daring new venture 3 a commercial business 4 organized business activities aimed at growth and profit

en·ter·pris·ing /éntər prìzing/ *adj* showing initiative —**en·ter·pris·ing·ly** *adv*

en·ter·tain /èntər táyn, éntər tàyn/ *v* 1 *vti* amuse or interest somebody or an audience 2 *vti* offer hospitality to a guest, especially in the form of food and drink 3 *vt* consider

en·ter·tain·er /èntər táynər, éntər tàynər/ *n* somebody who performs, especially professionally

en·ter·tain·ing /èntər táyning, éntər tàyning/ *adj* amusing or interesting —**en·ter·tain·ing·ly** *adv*

en·ter·tain·ment /èntər táynmənt/ *n* 1 the various ways of amusing people, especially by performing for them 2 the amount of enjoyment people get from something **3** a performance or exhibition

en·thrall /in thráwl, en-/ *vt* **1** hold the attention of in delight or fascination **2** enslave *(literary)* —**en·thrall·ment** *n*

en·throne /in thrṓn, en-/ (**-throned, -thron·ing**) *vt* **1** put on a throne as a monarch *(fml)* **2** regard as important *(literary)* —**en·throne·ment** *n*

en·thuse /in thóoz, en-/ (**-thused, -thus·ing**) *vti (disapproving)* **1** be or make enthusiastic **2** speak or say with enthusiasm

en·thu·si·asm /in thóozee àzzəm, en-/ *n* **1** excited interest **2** something somebody is passionately interested in

---

ORIGIN Enthusiasm was not always approved of. The word originally meant "possession by a god" (its root is the Greek word for "god" that gave us *theology* and related words). The frenzy associated with this led to its disapproving use as "extravagant religious emotion" in the mid-17C. More positive uses of the word did not appear until the early 18C.

---

en·thu·si·ast /in thóozee àst, en-/ *n* somebody who is passionately interested in and involved in something

en·thu·si·as·tic /in thóozee ástik, en-/ *adj* showing passionate interest —**en·thu·si·as·ti·cal·ly** *adv*

en·tice /in tíss, en-/ (**-ticed, -tic·ing**) *vt* tempt by offering something attractive —**en·tice·ment** *n* —**en·tic·ing** *adj* —**en·tic·ing·ly** *adv*

en·tire /in tír, en-/ *adj* **1** from beginning to end, or including everything ○ *rained the entire night* **2** absolute or without doubt or question ○ *The day was an entire fiasco.* —**en·tire·ly** *adv* —**en·tire·ty** /in tírətee, en-/ *n*

~~en·tirely~~ incorrect spelling of **entirely**

en·ti·tle /in tít'l, en-/ (**-tled, -tling**) *vt* **1** allow to claim something **2** give a title to —**en·ti·tle·ment** *n*

en·ti·ty /éntitee/ (*pl* **-ties**) *n* something that exists as a separate object

en·tomb /in tóom, en-/ *vt* **1** put a corpse in a tomb **2** put something in a deep or hidden place ○ *treasures entombed in secret vaults* —**en·tomb·ment** *n*

en·to·mol·o·gy /èntə mólləjee/ *n* the scientific study of insects —**en·to·mo·log·i·cal** /èntəmə lójjik'l/ *adj* —**en·to·mol·o·gist** *n*

en·tou·rage /òntə ráazh, ónta ráazh/ *n* a group of people accompanying a famous or important person

en·trails /éntrəlz, én tràylz/ *npl* **1** internal organs **2** the inner workings of something complex

en·trance[1] /éntrənss/ *n* **1** a door or gate by which to enter **2** an act of entering a room

en·trance[2] /en tránss/ (**-tranced, -tranc·ing**) *vt* **1** fascinate **2** put a spell on —**en·tranc·ing·ly** *adv*

en·trant /éntrənt/ *n* a competitor ◊ See note at **candidate**

en·trap /in tráp, en-/ (**-trapped, -trap·ping**) *vt* **1** trick into doing something wrong **2** catch in a trap —**en·trap·ment** *n*

en·treat /in treét, en-/ *vti* beg desperately —**en·treat·ing·ly** *adv*

en·treat·y /in treétee, en-/ (*pl* **-ies**) *n* a desperate plea

en·trée /ón trày, on tráy/, **en·tree** *n* **1** the main course of a meal **2** a right of entry

en·trench /in trénch, en-/ *vt* **1** dig a defensive ditch around **2** protect —**en·trench·ment** *n*

en·trenched /in tréncht, en-/ *adj* **1** firmly held ○ *deeply entrenched political views* **2** firmly established

en·tre nous /òntrə nóo/ *adv* between ourselves

en·tre·pre·neur /òntrəprə nóor, -núr/ *n* an initiator or a financial backer of new businesses —**en·tre·pre·neu·ri·al** *adj* —**en·tre·pre·neur·i·al·ism** *n* —**en·tre·pre·neur·ism** *n*

en·tro·py /éntrəpee/ *n* **1** a measure of the disorder that exists in a system **2** (*symbol* **S**) a measure of the energy in a system that is unavailable to do work —**en·tro·pic** /en tróppik/ *adj* —**en·tro·pi·cal·ly** *adv*

ORIGIN The German original of **entropy** was coined in 1865 by the German physicist Rudolph Clausius (1822–88), who developed the concept. He based it on *energy*, using the Greek word for "turning, transformation." The English form of the word appeared just a few years after the German.

---

en·trust /in trúst, en-/ *vt* give somebody responsibility for something —**en·trust·ment** *n*

en·try /éntree/ (*pl* **-tries**) *n* **1** an act of coming or going into a place **2** the right to go into a place or become a member of an organization **3** a single written item, e.g., in a diary or on a list **4** a way into a place **5** somebody or something entered in a contest

en·try-lev·el *adj* suitable for somebody who is new to a job, field, or subject

en·try·way /éntree wày/ *n* a doorway or passageway

en·twine /in twín, en-/ (**en·twined, en·twin·ing**) *vti* twist together

e·nu·mer·ate /i nóomə ràyt/ (**-at·ed, -at·ing**) *vt* **1** list a number of things individually **2** count how many there are in something —**e·nu·mer·a·ble** *adj* —**e·nu·mer·a·tion** /i nòomə ráysh'n/ *n*

e·nun·ci·ate /i núnsee àyt/ (**-at·ed, -at·ing**) *v* **1** *vti* speak or say clearly **2** *vt* state or explain clearly —**e·nun·ci·a·tion** /i nùnsee áysh'n/ *n*

en·vel·op /in vélləp, en-/ *vt* **1** wrap something up completely **2** conceal something —**en·vel·op·ment** *n* ◊ See note at **envelope**

en·ve·lope /énvə lòp, ónvə-/ *n* **1** a paper container for a letter **2** something that surrounds or encloses something else ◊ *seafood sauce in phyllo pastry envelopes* ◊ **push the envelope** try to accomplish more than is theoretically possible (*infml*)

SPELLCHECK Do not confuse the spelling of **envelope** and **envelop** ("wrap up"), which are spelled similarly but are not pronounced alike.

en·vi·a·ble /énvee əb'l/ *adj* causing feelings of envy —**en·vi·a·bly** *adv*

en·vi·ous /énvee əss/ *adj* wanting what somebody else has —**en·vi·ous·ly** *adv* —**en·vi·ous·ness** *n*

~~enviroment~~ incorrect spelling of **environment**

en·vi·ron·ment /in vírənmənt, -ví ərn-/ *n* **1** the natural world as the habitat of living things **2** a set of social and physical conditions that surround and influence the way somebody lives ◊ *a nurturing environment* —**en·vi·ron·men·tal** /in vìrən mént'l, -ví ərn-/ *adj* —**en·vi·ron·men·tal·ly** *adv*

en·vi·ron·men·tal·ist /in vìrən mént'list, -vì ərn-/ *n* **1** somebody working to protect the environment **2** somebody who believes that environment is more important than heredity to a person's development —**en·vi·ron·men·tal·ism** *n*

en·vi·ron·men·tal·ly friend·ly, en·vi·ron·ment-friend·ly *adj* minimizing harm to the natural world

en·vi·rons /in vírənz, in ví ərnz/ *npl* the surrounding area

en·vis·age /in vízzij, en-/ (**-aged, -ag·ing**) *vt* **1** *also* **en·vi·sion** /in vízh'n/ picture in the mind, especially as a future possibility **2** regard in a particular way

en·voy /én vòy/ *n* **1** an official representative of a national government **2** *also* **en·voi** the concluding part of a poem

en·vy /énvee/ *n* the feeling of wanting what somebody else has ■ *vt* (**-vied, -vies**) want what somebody else has

en·zyme /én zìm/ *n* a protein controlling biochemical reactions —**en·zy·mat·ic** /énzə máttik/ *adj*

E·o·cene /ee ə seèn/ *n* an epoch of geologic time 55–34 million years ago —**E·o·cene** *adj*

e·on /ee òn, -ən/ *n* **1** a vast unmeasurable amount of time **2** the longest unit of geologic time —**e·o·ni·an** /ee ònee ən/ *adj*

E·os /ee oss/ *n* in Greek mythology, the goddess of the dawn. Roman equivalent **Aurora**

EP *n* an extended-play phonograph record

EPA *abbr* Environmental Protection Agency

ep·au·let /éppə lèt, èppə lét/, **ep·au·lette** *n* a decoration on the shoulder of a garment, especially a uniform jacket

é·pée /e páy/ (*pl* **é·pées**) *n* a fencing sword heavier than a foil

e·phem·er·a /i fémmərə/ *n* (*pl* **-ae** /-eè/ *or* **-as**) **1** something transitory **2** a mayfly ■ *npl* collectable items originally expected to be short-lived

e·phem·er·al /i fémmərəl/ *adj* transitory —**e·phem·er·al·i·ty** /i fèmmə rállətee/ *n* —**e·phem·er·al·ly** *adv* ◊ See note at **temporary**

E·phe·sians /i feézh'nz/ *n* a book of the Bible, originally a letter from the St. Paul to the church in Ephesus. (+ *sing verb*)

Eph·e·sus /éffəsəss/ ancient Greek city on the coast of W Asia Minor, in present-day Turkey

ep·ic /éppik/ *n* **1** a long narrative poem **2** epic poetry as a genre **3** a large-scale production of a work of fiction, cinema, television, or theater ■ *adj* **1** of or like an epic **2** very large or heroic —**ep·i·cal** *adj*

ep·i·cen·ter /éppi sèntər/ *n* **1** the point on the Earth's surface above the focus of an earthquake **2** a focal point —**ep·i·cen·tral** /èppi séntrəl/ *adj*

ep·i·cure /éppi kyoòr/ *n* **1** a gourmet **2** somebody who loves luxury and sensual pleasures —**ep·i·cur·ism** *n*

ORIGIN Epicures get their name from the Greek philosopher Epicurus. He taught that the greatest good is freedom from pain and emotional disturbance, but his thought came to be associated with the pursuit of pleasure, and one of the earlier senses in English was "glutton."

ep·i·cu·re·an /èppikyə reè ən, èppi kyooree ən/ *adj* **1** devoted to sensual pleasure, especially good food **2** pleasing to an epicure —**ep·i·cu·re·an** *n* —**ep·i·cu·re·an·ism** *n*

Ep·i·cu·rus /èppi kyooərəss/ (341–270 BC) Greek philosopher

ep·i·dem·ic /èppi démmik/ *n* **1** a fast-spreading disease **2** a rapid development, especially of something bad ■ *adj* spreading unusually quickly and extensively —**ep·i·dem·i·cal·ly** *adv* ◊ See note at **widespread**

ep·i·de·mi·ol·o·gy /èppi deèmee òllajee, -dèmmee-/ *n* **1** the study of the origin and spread of diseases **2** the origin and development of a particular disease —**ep·i·de·mi·o·log·ic** /èppi deemee ə lójjik, -demmee-/ *adj* —**ep·i·de·mi·o·log·i·cal·ly** *adv* —**ep·i·de·mi·ol·o·gist** *n*

ep·i·der·mis /èppi dúrmiss/ *n* the outer layer of the skin —**ep·i·der·mal** *adj*

ep·i·du·ral /èppi dooral/ *n* an anesthetic injection into the spine

ep·i·glot·tis /èppi glóttiss/ (*pl* **-ti·ses** *or* **-tid·es** /-glótti deèz/) *n* a flap of cartilage at the base of the tongue that covers the air passages during eating or drinking —**ep·i·glot·tal** *adj*

ep·i·gram /éppi gràm/ *n* 1 a witty saying 2 a short poem

ep·i·gram·mat·ic /èppigrə máttik/, **ep·i·gram·mat·i·cal** /-máttik'l/ *adj* 1 in the form of an epigram 2 tending to use epigrams —**ep·i·gram·mat·i·cal·ly** *adv*

ep·i·graph /éppi gràf/ *n* 1 an introductory quotation in a book 2 an inscription on a monument —**ep·i·graph·ic** /èppi gráffik/ *adj* —**ep·i·graph·i·cal** *adj* —**ep·i·graph·i·cal·ly** *adv*

ep·i·lep·sy /éppi lèpsee/ *n* a medical disorder of the brain that periodically causes a sudden loss of consciousness, often with convulsions

ep·i·lep·tic /èppi léptik/ *adj* of or affected by epilepsy ■ *n* an offensive term for somebody who has epilepsy —**ep·i·lep·ti·cal·ly** *adv*

ep·i·logue /éppi lòg/, **ep·i·log** *n* 1 a short section at the end of a book, sometimes detailing the fate of the characters 2 an actor's short concluding speech, delivered directly to the audience 3 an actor who delivers an epilogue

ep·i·neph·rine /èppi néffrin/, **ep·i·neph·rin** *n* the hormone adrenaline (*technical*)

e·piph·a·ny /i píffənee/ (*pl* **-nies**) *n* 1 an appearance of a god 2 a sudden realization 3 **E·piph·a·ny** the Christian festival celebrating Jesus Christ's divinity as revealed by the Three Wise Men. Date: January 6.

ep·i·phyte /éppi fît/ *n* a plant that grows on another —**ep·i·phyt·ic** /èppi fíttik/ *adj*

e·pis·co·pa·cy /i pískəpəssee/ *n* church government by bishops

e·pis·co·pal /i pískəp'l/ *adj* 1 of bishops 2 governed by bishops

E·pis·co·pal Church *n* the independent US denomination that is in communion with the Anglican Church —**E·pis·co·pal** *adj*

e·pis·co·pa·lian /i pìskə páylee ən/ *adj* 1 believing in church government by bishops 2 **E·pis·co·pa·lian** belonging to the Episcopal Church —**e·pis·co·pa·lian** *n* —**E·pis·co·pa·lian** *n* —**e·pis·co·pa·lian·ism** *n* —**E·pis·co·pa·lian·ism** *n*

e·pis·co·pate /i pískəpət, i pískə pàyt/ *n* 1 the office or position of a bishop 2 a diocese

ep·i·sode /éppi sòd/ *n* 1 a significant incident 2 an individual part of a serialized work 3 an event in a narrative

ep·i·sod·ic /èppi sóddik/, **ep·i·sod·i·cal** /-sóddik'l/ *adj* 1 divided into episodes 2 sporadic —**ep·i·sod·i·cal·ly** *adv*

e·pis·tle /i píss'l/ *n* 1 a letter (*fml*) 2 **E·pis·tle** a letter from the apostle Paul or another early Christian writer, included as a book of the Bible

e·pis·to·lar·y /i pístə lèrree/ *adj* in the form of a letter or letters

ep·i·taph /éppi tàf/ *n* 1 an inscription on a tombstone 2 a speech or a piece of writing commemorating a dead person —**ep·i·taph·ic** /èppi táffik/ *adj*

ep·i·thet /éppi thèt/ *n* 1 an insult 2 a descriptive word added to somebody's name —**ep·i·thet·i·cal** /èppi théttik'l/ *adj*

e·pit·o·me /i píttəmee/ *n* 1 a perfect example 2 a summary of a written work (*fml*)

e·pit·o·mize /i píttə mìz/ (**-mized**, **-miz·ing**) *vt* 1 exemplify perfectly 2 summarize (*fml*) —**e·pit·o·mi·za·tion** /i pìttəmi záysh'n/ *n*

epitomy incorrect spelling of **epitome**

ep·och /éppək, éé pòk/ *n* 1 a significant period in history or in somebody's life 2 the beginning of a long and historically significant period 3 a unit of geologic time —**ep·och·al** /éppək'l, éé pòk'l/ *adj*

ep·och-mak·ing *adj* having momentous significance

e·pon·y·mous /i pónnəməss/ *adj* having the same name as the title or name of something else, e.g., the title of a book o *the eponymous hero* —**e·pon·y·mous·ly** *adv*

ep·ox·y /i póksee/, **ep·ox·y res·in** *n* a tough synthetic resin. Use: adhesives, surface coatings.

ep·si·lon /épsilòn, -lən/ *n* the 5th letter of the Greek alphabet

Ep·som salts /épsəm sáwlts/ *n* a bitter-tasting medicine. Use: to reduce swelling. (+ *sing verb*)

Ep·stein-Barr vi·rus /èp stín baàr-/ *n* a virus believed to cause infectious mononucleosis, also associated with other diseases

eq. *abbr* 1 equal 2 equation 3 equivalent

E.Q. *n* a ratio of educational attainment to chronological age. Full form **educational quotient**

eq·ua·ble /ékwəb'l, eék-/ *adj* 1 calm and not easily disturbed 2 free from marked variation and extremes —**eq·ua·bil·i·ty** /èkwə bíllətee, eèkwə-/ *n* —**eq·ua·bly** *adv*

e·qual /eékwəl/ *adj* 1 identical in size, quantity, value, or standard 2 having the same rights, opportunities, and privileges as others 3 evenly balanced between opposing sides o *hoping for an equal match in the next game* 4 equipped with the necessary qualities or means to succeed (*fml*) o *was equal to the task* 5 treating or affecting all things impartially ■ *n* somebody or something equal in quality to another ■ *vt* 1 have the same value as o *Two plus two equals four.* 2 do, produce, or achieve something to the same standard as o *equaled the world record*

e·qual·i·ty /i kwóllətee, ee-/ (*pl* **-ties**) *n* 1 the state of being equal 2 an equation with equal quantities on each side of the equal sign

e·qual·ize /eékwə lìz/ (**-ized**, **-iz·ing**) *vt* 1 make uniform or equal 2 adjust the amplitude of an electronic signal —**e·qual·i·za·tion** /eèkwəli záysh'n/ *n*

e·qual·iz·er /ˈeekwə līzər/ *n* **1** somebody or something that equalizes things **2** an electronic device that reduces distortion in a sound system

e·qual·ly /ˈeekwəlee/ *adv* **1** in the same way **2** to the same extent **3** in the same sized amounts

e·qual op·por·tu·ni·ty *n* equal treatment for all people

e·qual sign *n* a mathematical symbol (=) showing equality

e·qua·nim·i·ty /ˌeekwə nímmətee, ˌekwə-/ *n* evenness of temper even under stress —**e·quan·i·mous** /i kwónnəməss/ *adj*

e·quate /i kwáyt/ (**e·quat·ed, e·quat·ing**) *vt* **1** be, or consider something to be, equivalent to something else **2** reduce something to the same level or value as something else —**e·quat·a·ble** *adj*

e·qua·tion /i kwáyzh'n, i kwáysh'n/ *n* **1** a mathematical statement of equality **2** the act or process of equating things **3** a situation involving variable elements —**e·qua·tion·al** *adj*

e·qua·tor /i kwáytər/ *n* **1** an imaginary circle around the middle of the Earth **2** an imaginary circle around the middle of an astronomical object

> **ORIGIN** The fuller form of the medieval Latin term from which **equator** derives was *circulus aequator diei et noctis* "circle equalizing day and night."

e·qua·to·ri·al /ˌeekwə táwree əl, ˌekwə-/ *adj* **1** of or around the equator **2** situated in the plane of an equator

E·qua·to·ri·al Guin·ea country in West Africa bordering the Atlantic Ocean and comprising a mainland section, Río Muni, and several islands. Cap. Malabo. Pop. 486,060 (2001).

eq·uer·ry /ˈekwəree/ (*pl* -**ries**) *n* **1** a personal attendant of a member of the British royal family **2** formerly, an officer responsible for the royal horses

e·ques·tri·an /i kwéstree ən/ *adj* of horses or horseriding ■ *n* a skilled rider —**e·ques·tri·an·ism** *n*

e·qui·dis·tant /ˌeekwi dístənt, ˌekwi-/ *adj* equally distant —**e·qui·dis·tant·ly** *adv*

e·qui·lat·er·al /ˌeekwə láttərəl, ˌekwə-/ *adj* with sides of equal length ■ *n* **1** an equilateral figure **2** a side of an equilateral figure

e·qui·lib·ri·um /ˌeekwə líbbree əm, ˌekwə-/ (*pl* -**ums** *or* -**a**) *n* **1** emotional stability **2** a state or sense of being able to maintain bodily balance **3** a balance between forces

e·quine /ˈee kwīn, é-/ *adj* **1** of horses **2** resembling a horse ■ *n* a horse or other member of the horse family

e·qui·noc·tial /ˌeekwə nókshəl, ˌekwə-/ *adj* occurring at an equinox

e·qui·nox /ˈeekwə nòks, ékwə-/ *n* either of the times of year when the Sun crosses the

equator and day and night are of equal length everywhere on Earth

e·quip /i kwíp/ (**e·quipped, e·quip·ping**) *vt* **1** provide with the necessary tools, supplies, or clothing for a specific activity **2** provide with the necessary training or experience to succeed —**e·quip·per** *n*

equiped incorrect spelling of **equipped**

e·quip·ment /i kwípmənt/ *n* **1** the necessary tools, supplies, or clothing for a specific activity **2** the personal resources that enable a person to succeed **3** the process of providing somebody with equipment

eq·ui·ta·ble /ékwitəb'l/ *adj* **1** fair and just (*fml*) **2** of the law of equity —**eq·ui·ta·bly** *adv*

eq·ui·ty /ékwitee/ *n* **1** fairness and lack of bias **2** a system of jurisprudence that modifies common and statute law to take into account fairness **3** the value of a piece of property over and above the mortgage on it ■ **eq·ui·ties** *npl* stocks entitling the holders to a share in profits

e·quiv·a·lent /i kwívvələnt/ *adj* equal in effect, value, or meaning ■ *n* something considered to be equal or to have an equal effect, value or meaning —**e·quiv·a·lence** *n* —**e·quiv·a·lent·ly** *adv*

equivelent incorrect spelling of **equivalent**

e·quiv·o·cal /i kwívvək'l/ *adj* **1** ambiguous, often deliberately so **2** difficult to interpret or understand —**e·quiv·o·cal·i·ty** /i kwìvvə kállətee/ *n* —**e·quiv·o·cal·ly** *adv*

e·quiv·o·cate /i kwívvə kàyt/ (-**cat·ed, -cat·ing**) *vi* be deliberately unclear and evasive —**e·quiv·o·cat·ing·ly** *adv* —**e·quiv·o·ca·tion** /i kwìvvə káysh'n/ *n*

er *interj* expresses hesitation

Er *symbol* erbium

ER *abbr* **1** earned runs **2** emergency room

-er[1] *suffix* **1** somebody or something that performs or undergoes a particular action ○ *adjuster* ○ *fryer* **2** somebody connected with something, often as an occupation ○ *trucker* **3** somebody or something with a particular characteristic, quality, or form ○ *ten-pounder* **4** somebody from a particular place ○ *New Yorker*

-er[2] *suffix* more

e·ra /ˈeerə, érrə/ *n* **1** a period of time made distinctive, e.g., by a significant development ○ *the Elizabethan era* **2** a time period with a numbering system that begins at a particular significant event ○ *the Christian era* **3** a division of geologic time composed of several periods

> **ORIGIN** *Era* is based on a Latin word that came to mean a "number used as a basis for counting." In this sense it was used as a prefix before dates, and from there developed "system of numbering years from a noteworthy event," which is the sense in which *era* appeared in English in the mid-17C. As

a "period of time" it is recorded from the mid-18C.

ERA *abbr* **1** earned run average **2** Equal Rights Amendment

e·rad·i·cate /i ráddi kàyt/ (**-cat·ed, -cat·ing**) *vt* get rid of completely —**e·rad·i·ca·ble** *adj* —**e·rad·i·ca·bly** *adv* —**e·rad·i·ca·tion** /i ràddi káysh'n/ *n*

e·rase /i ráyss/ (**e·rased, e·ras·ing**) *vt* **1** remove written or typed material with an eraser or correction fluid **2** remove or destroy something —**e·ras·a·ble** *adj*

e·ras·er /i ráyssər/ *n* something used to rub out writing

E·ras·mus /i rázməss/, **Desiderius** (1466?–1536) Dutch scholar and writer

e·ra·sure /i ráyshər/ *n* **1** removal or destruction of something **2** an erased thing, e.g., a mark

er·bi·um /úrbee əm/ *n* (*symbol* **Er**) a soft silvery metallic chemical element. Use: alloys, pigment.

> **ORIGIN Erbium** is named for the town of Ytterby in Sweden, where the first mineral of the series of elements to which it belongs was discovered.

ere *prep, conj* before (*literary*) ◊ See note at **air**

Er·e·bus, Mt. /érrəbəss/ active volcano on the eastern coast of Ross Island, Antarctica. Height 12,448 ft./3,794 m.

e·rect /i rékt/ *adj* **1** in an upright position ○ *an erect plant stem* **2** firm and swollen as a result of being filled with blood, e.g., when sexually aroused ■ *vt* **1** construct something in place from basic parts and materials **2** set something upright —**e·rect·ly** *adv* —**e·rect·ness** *n*

e·rec·tile /i rékt'l, i rék tíl/ *adj* capable of swelling with blood and becoming stiff —**e·rec·til·i·ty** /i rèk tíllətee/ *n*

e·rec·tion /i réksh'n/ *n* **1** the process of constructing something or putting something up **2** a swollen stiffened state of tissue, especially of the penis **3** a building or other large structure (*fml*)

er·go /áir gò, úr gò/ *adv, conj* therefore or so

er·go·nom·ics /úrgə nómmiks/ *n* the study of workplace design (+ *sing verb*) —**er·go·nom·ic** *adj* —**er·go·nom·i·cal·ly** *adv*

Er·ic·son /érrikssən/, **Leif** (975–1020) Icelandic explorer

Er·ic the Red /èrrik-/ (950?–1000?) Norwegian explorer

E·rie /éeree/ port of entry on Lake Erie, NW Pennsylvania. Pop. 102,640 (1998).

E·rie, Lake southernmost and fourth largest of the Great Lakes

E·rie Ca·nal artificial inland waterway between Buffalo, on Lake Erie, and Albany,

New York, where it links with the Hudson River. Length 340 mi./547 km.

Er·i·tre·a /èrri treè ə/ country on the Red Sea coast in NE Africa. Cap. Asmara. Pop. 4,298,269 (2001). —**Er·i·tre·an** *n, adj*

er·mine /úrmin/ (*pl* **-mines** or same) *n* **1** a weasel, especially in its white winter coat **2** the white fur of a ermine

> **ORIGIN Ermine** probably ultimately derives from a medieval Latin name meaning "Armenian mouse." It entered English from French in the early medieval period.

Ernst /airnst, urnst/, **Max** (1891–1976) German-born French artist

e·rode /i ród/ (**e·rod·ed, e·rod·ing**) *vti* **1** wear away land, or be worn away, by wind or water **2** break down gradually ○ *Deceit will erode any friendship.* —**e·rod·i·ble** *adj*

e·rog·e·nous /i rójjənəss/ *adj* sensitive and arousing sexual feelings when touched or stroked

e·rog·e·nous zone *n* a sexually sensitive area of the body

Er·os /é ròss, ee ròss/ *n* in Greek mythology, the god of love. Roman equivalent **Cupid**

e·ro·sion /i rózh'n/ *n* **1** the process of wearing away or being worn away **2** a gradual breaking down of something —**e·ro·sion·al** *adj*

e·rot·ic /i róttik/ *adj* **1** arousing sexual feelings **2** marked by sexual desire —**e·rot·i·cal·ly** *adv*

> **ORIGIN Erotic** was adopted from French in the mid-17C. It comes from the Greek word for "sensual love," represented in mythology by the god Eros.

e·rot·i·ca /i róttikə/ *n* sexually explicit material

e·rot·i·cism /i rótti sìzzəm/, **e·ro·tism** /érrə tìzzəm/ *n* **1** an erotic quality **2** sexual desire —**e·rot·i·cist** *n*

err /ur, air/ *vi* **1** make a mistake **2** behave badly (*fml*) ◊ See note at **air**

er·rand /érrənd/ *n* **1** a short trip to do something for somebody else **2** the purpose of an errand

er·rant /érrənt/ *adj* **1** behaving badly **2** straying from an intended course —**er·rant·ly** *adv*

er·rat·ic /i ráttik/ *adj* **1** not regular or consistent and often below standard **2** often changing direction —**er·rat·i·cal·ly** *adv*

er·ra·tum /i ráatəm, i-/ (*pl* **-ta** /-tə/) *n* a printing error

er·ro·ne·ous /i rónee əss/ *adj* incorrect —**er·ro·ne·ous·ly** *adv* —**er·ro·ne·ous·ness** *n*

⨍ er·ror /érrər/ *n* **1** a mistake **2** a wrong belief **3** the state of believing or acting wrongly **4** the fact of being wrong **5** a fielding misplay in baseball **6** a problem detected by a computer program ◊ See note at **mistake**

🗲 **er·ror mes·sage** *n* a message alerting a computer user to a problem

er·satz /ér zàats/ *adj* artificial or presented as a substitute *(disapproving)*

Erse /urss/ *n* the Gaelic language —**Erse** *adj*

erst·while /úrst hwìl/ *adj* former ■ *adv* formerly *(archaic)*

er·u·dite /érryə dìt, érrə-/ *adj* knowledgeable as a result of study —**er·u·dite·ly** *adv* —**er·u·dite·ness** *n*

ORIGIN Erudite comes from a Latin word meaning "trained, instructed," which was its original English use. The Latin source is based on the word from which *rude* derives, combined with a prefix meaning "out of," so an **erudite** person has literally been trained out of rudeness.

---

er·u·di·tion /èrryə dísh'n, èrrə-/ *n* knowledge acquired by study

e·rupt /i rúpt/ *v* 1 *vti* violently release material such as gas, steam, or lava 2 *vi* burst out 3 *vi* appear as a rash on the skin —**e·rup·tion** *n* —**e·rup·tive** *adj* —**e·rup·tive·ly** *adv*

Es *symbol* einsteinium

-es *suffix* used for "-s" in words ending in -s, -ss, -x, -sh, or -ch (pronounced "ch") ◦ *buses* ◦ *birches*

🗲 **Esc** *abbr* escape (key)

es·ca·late /éskə làyt/ *(-lat·ed, -lat·ing)* *vti* become or make greater or more intense —**es·ca·la·tion** /èskə láysh'n/ *n*

es·ca·la·tor /éskə làytər/ *n* a set of moving steps that carry people between the floors of a building

es·ca·pade /éskə pàyd/ *n* a brash adventure

🗲 **es·cape** /i skáyp/ *v* *(-caped, -cap·ing)* 1 *vti* break free from captivity 2 *vt* avoid a bad situation 3 *vi* leak out 4 *vt* fail to be remembered or understood by somebody ◦ *a little village whose name escapes me* 5 *vi* exit a computer procedure ■ *n* 1 an instance of breaking free from captivity 2 an act of avoiding a bad situation 3 a means of getting away 4 a pleasant and welcome distraction 5 a computer key for exiting a program or canceling a command —**es·cap·a·ble** *adj*

es·cape art·ist *n* a performer who is skilled at escaping from restraints

es·cape clause *n* a legal way out of a contract

es·cap·ee /i skày pée, ès kay-/ *n* somebody who has escaped

es·cap·ism /i skáyp ìzzəm/ *n* 1 things that provide escape from unpleasant everyday realities 2 indulgence in fantasies to escape reality —**es·cap·ist** *adj, n*

es·cap·ol·o·gist /ès kay pólləjist/ *n* a performer who is skilled at escaping from restraints

es·ca·role /éskə ròl/ *n* a curly endive

es·carp·ment /ə skáarpmənt/ *n* 1 a steep slope at the edge of a plateau 2 a slope built in front of a fortification

Esch·er /éshər/, **M. C.** (1898–1972) Dutch graphic artist

es·chew /ass chóo/ *vt* avoid doing or using —**es·chew·al** *n*

Es·con·di·do /èss kon déedò/ city in SW California. Pop. 120,578 (1998).

es·cort *n* /éss kàwrt/ 1 a person accompanying somebody or something as a guard or as a mark of honor 2 an accompanying military vessel or aircraft 3 a man or woman hired as a social partner —**es·cort** /i skáwrt, éss kàwrt/ *vt*

es·cri·toire /èskri twáar/ *n* a writing desk

es·crow /és krò, e skró/ *n* 1 something held for somebody by an independent party until a condition is met 2 being held as an escrow ■ *vt* put in escrow

es·cu·do /e skóo dò/ *(pl -dos)* *n* the main unit of the former currency of Portugal

es·cutch·eon /ə skúchən/ *n* 1 a heraldic shield 2 a protective plate or shield, especially one fitted around a keyhole —**es·cutch·eoned** *adj*

-ese *suffix* 1 from, of, native to, or inhabiting a particular place ◦ *Taiwanese* 2 the language of a particular place ◦ *Chinese* 3 style or jargon ◦ *officialese*

~~essential~~ incorrect spelling of **essential**

Es·ki·mo /éskə mò/ *(pl -mos or same)* *n* 1 a member of a people indigenous to N Canada, Alaska, Greenland, and Siberia, comprising the Inuit and Yupik *(sometimes offensive)* 2 the language group comprising Inuit and Yupik —**Es·ki·mo** *adj* ◊ See note at **Inuit**

ESL *abbr* English as a second language

ESOL *abbr* English for speakers of other languages

e·soph·a·gus /i sóffəgəss/ *(pl -guses or -gi* /-jī, -gī/), **oe·soph·a·gus** /i sóffəgəss/ *(pl -guses or -gi)* *n* a passage from the throat to the stomach —**e·soph·a·ge·al** /i sòffə jée əl/ *adj*

es·o·ter·ic /èssə térrik/ *adj* 1 intended for or understood only by an initiated few 2 difficult to understand —**es·o·ter·i·cal·ly** *adv*

ESP *abbr* 1 English for special purposes 2 extrasensory perception

es·pa·drille /éspə drìl/ *n* a canvas shoe with a rope sole

es·pal·ier /əss pállyər, -pál yày/ *n* a tree trained to grow flat against a wall with its branches in a near horizontal position

es·par·to /ə spáar tò/ *(pl -tos)*, **es·par·to grass** *n* a coarse fibrous grass. Use: paper, ropes, mats.

es·pe·cial /i spésh'l/ *adj (fml)* 1 notable 2 particular

es·pe·cial·ly /i spésh'lee/ *adv* 1 exceptionally

2 in particular ○ *They're a helpful group, especially Mark.*

USAGE especially or **specially? Especially** means "exceptionally": *The buildings are not especially large.* **Specially** means "for a special purpose": *specially designed ramps for wheelchair access.* In rapid conversation, the first syllable of **especially** tends to be slurred or omitted, and this can affect the correct choice when the words are written.

~~especialy~~ incorrect spelling of **especially**

Es·pe·ran·to /ѐspə rántō, -raàn-/ *n* an artificial language based on root forms of words common to major European languages —**Es·pe·ran·tist** *n*

es·pi·o·nage /éspee ə naàzh/ *n* the activity of spying

es·pla·nade /ésplə naàd, -nàyd/ *n* a long wide walkway, especially by the sea

es·pous·al /əss pówz'l/ *n* **1** the adoption of something as a belief or cause **2** a marriage *(fml; often pl)*

es·pouse /i spówz/ (**-poused, -pous·ing**) *vt* **1** marry, or give in marriage *(archaic)* **2** adopt as a belief or cause —**es·pous·er** *n*

es·pres·so /e spréssō/, **ex·pres·so** /iks-/ *n* **1** very strong coffee made in a machine that forces steam through finely ground beans **2** a cup of espresso

ORIGIN Espresso is from Italian, and means literally "squeezed, pressed out." It goes back to the Latin word that also gave us *express*.

es·prit de corps /e sprèe də káwr/ *n* a pride in belonging to something

es·py /i spī/ (**-pied, -pies**) *vt* suddenly see *(literary)*

Esq. *abbr* Esquire *(in correspondence)*

-esque *suffix* in the style of, like ○ *statuesque*

es·quire /i skwīr/ *n* **1** a knight's attendant **2 Es·quire** a man's courtesy title, especially on documents

-ess *suffix* woman or girl ○ *heiress*

USAGE In recent times, the **-ess** ending has come to be regarded as sexist and old-fashioned. Words such as *authoress* and *manageress* are dropping out of use and the base term is used for both sexes.

es·say *n* /é sày, ə sáy/ **1** a piece of nonfiction writing on a particular subject, usually expressing the writer's viewpoint **2** an attempt *(fml)* **3** a test of something *(fml)* ■ *vt* /ə sáy, essay/ **1** attempt *(fml)* **2** test

es·say·ist /é sàyist/ *n* a writer of essays

es·sence /éss'nss/ *n* **1** the most basic element or feature of something **2** the perfect embodiment of something ○ *She is the essence of tact.* **3** a concentrated plant extract

ORIGIN Essence comes ultimately from the Latin verb *esse* "be."

es·sen·tial /i sénshəl/ *adj* **1** required or necessary ○ *It's essential that we arrive on time.* **2** constituting the character or feature that makes something what it is ○ *Being three-sided is essential to being a triangle.* ■ *n* something essential —**es·sen·tial·ly** *adv* ◊ See note at **necessary**

es·sen·tial oil *n* a concentrated oil extracted from a plant

EST *abbr* Eastern Standard Time

est. *abbr* **1** established **2** estimated

-est *suffix* most ○ *hardest* ○ *sloppiest*

es·tab·lish /i stábblish/ *vt* **1** start or set up something intended to continue for some time **2** place something permanently in a position or situation **3** prove the truth or validity of something

es·tab·lished /i stábblisht/ *adj* **1** accepted as true or valid **2** successful and recognized publicly as such

es·tab·lish·ment /i stábblishmənt/ *n* **1** the act of establishing something **2** something established as a business, institution, or undertaking —**es·tab·lish·men·tar·i·an** /i stàbblishmən térree ən/ *n*

es·tate /i stáyt/ *n* **1** a piece of privately owned rural land with a large house on it **2** all of somebody's property, especially that of a dead person **3** somebody's overall situation **4** a sector of society, traditionally the clergy, the nobility, or the middle class

es·tate tax *n* a tax on inherited property

es·teem /i steém/ *vt* **1** value highly **2** regard in a particular way ■ *n* **1** high regard **2** estimation of worth ◊ See note at **regard**

es·ter /éstər/ *n* a compound produced by an alcohol reacting with an acid

Es·ther /éstər/ *n* a book of the Bible that tells the story of Esther, the Jewish queen of Persia who is described as having rescued her Jewish subjects from massacre

es·thet·ic, es·thet·ics, etc. = aesthetic, etc.

es·ti·ma·ble /éstəməb'l/ *adj* admirable

es·ti·mate *vt* /éstə màyt/ (**-mat·ed, -mat·ing**) **1** calculate roughly **2** assess the cost of and submit a price ■ *n* /éstəmət/ **1** a rough calculation **2** an approximate price —**es·ti·ma·tion** /èstə máysh'n/ *n* —**es·ti·ma·tor** *n*

Es·to·ni·a /e stōnee ə/ country in NE Europe on the Gulf of Finland that gained its independence from the former Soviet Union in 1991. Cap. Tallinn. Pop. 1,423,316 (2001). —**Es·to·ni·an** *n, adj*

es·tranged /i stráynjd/ *adj* separated from a spouse —**es·trange·ment** *n*

es·tro·gen /éstrəjən/, **oes·tro·gen** *n* any hormone of the group that stimulates the development of female characteristics —**es·tro·gen·ic** /èstrə jénnik/ *adj*

es·tu·ar·y /éschoo èrree/ (*pl* **-ies**) *n* the wide lower section of a river where it meets the sea —**es·tu·ar·i·al** /èschoo érree əl/ *adj*

ET *abbr* **1** Eastern Time **2** extraterrestrial

-et *suffix* **1** small one ○ *islet* **2** something worn on ○ *anklet*

e·ta /áytə, eetə/ *n* the 7th letter of the Greek alphabet

ETA[1] *abbr* estimated time of arrival

ETA[2] /éttə/, **Eta** *n* a Basque nationalist guerrilla group

⚡**e-tail** /ée tàyl/ *n* Internet retail —**e-tail·er** *n* —**e-tail·ing** *n*

et al.[1] /et ál/ and others *(of joint authors of a book or article)*

ORIGIN This is an abbreviation of Latin *et alii.*

et al.[2] and elsewhere

ORIGIN This is an abbreviation of Latin *et alibi.*

etc. *abbr* et cetera

et cet·er·a /et séttərə, et séttrə/, **et·cet·er·a** *adv* and so on ■ *n* something or somebody unspecified

etch *v* **1** *vti* cut a design into a surface or printing plate with acid, a sharp tool, or a laser beam **2** *vt* make something clearly visible —**etch·er** *n*

etch·ing /éching/ *n* **1** a print made from an etched plate **2** the art of making etched designs

e·ter·nal /i túrn'l/ *adj* **1** existing through all time **2** unchanging ○ *eternal truths* **3** seemingly everlasting *(infml)* ○ *an eternal student* ■ *n* **E·ter·nal** God —**e·ter·nal·ly** *adv*

e·ter·nal tri·an·gle *n* a sexual or romantic relationship among three persons that involves emotional conflicts

e·ter·ni·ty /i túrnitee/ *n* **1** infinite time **2** a timeless state conceived as being experienced after death **3** a very long time *(infml)* ○ *took an eternity*

eth·a·nol /éthə nàwl/ *n* the alcohol in alcoholic beverages, also used as a solvent and in the manufacture of other chemicals

e·ther /éethər/ *n* **1** a colorless liquid with a pleasant smell. Use: solvent. **2** the sky or the air *(literary)* —**e·ther·ic** /i thérrik/ *adj*

e·the·re·al /i théeree əl/ *adj* **1** very delicate or highly refined **2** light or insubstantial **3** belonging to the heavens —**e·the·re·al·ly** *adv* —**e·the·re·al·ness** *n*

eth·ic /éthik/ *n* a set of moral principles

eth·i·cal /éthik'l/ *adj* **1** conforming to accepted standards of moral behavior **2** of ethics —**eth·i·cal·ly** *adv*

eth·ics /éthiks/ *n* the study of moral standards and their effect on conduct *(+ sing verb)* ■ *npl* a code of morality *(+ pl verb)*

E·thi·o·pi·a /eethee ópee ə/ *n* landlocked country in NE Africa. Cap. Addis Ababa. Pop. 65,891,874 (2001). —**E·thi·o·pi·an** *adj, n*

eth·nic /éthnik/ *adj* **1** of or classified according to distinctive social characteristics, e.g., of race, culture, or language **2** belonging to a particular social group, especially when living in a country where this group is a minority ○ *ethnic Albanians* ■ *n* a member of an ethnic minority —**eth·ni·cal·ly** *adv*

eth·nic cleans·ing *n* the violent elimination of an ethnic group

eth·nic·i·ty /eth níssətee/ *(pl* **-ties)** *n* ethnic affiliation or distinctiveness

eth·nic mi·nor·i·ty *n* an ethnic group that is a minority population in a country

eth·nog·ra·phy /eth nóggrəfee/ *n* the description of ethnic groups —**eth·nog·ra·pher** *n* —**eth·no·graph·ic** /èthnə gráffik/ *adj*

eth·nol·o·gy /eth nólləjee/ *n* **1** the study of ethnic groups **2** the scientific study of human cultures —**eth·nol·o·gist** *n*

e·thos /ée thòss/ *n* the distinctive character of a group or period of time

e·ti·o·lat·ed /éetee ə làytəd/ *adj* describes a plant that is pale and spindly from having been grown in poor light conditions —**e·ti·o·la·tion** /éetee ə láysh'n/ *n*

e·ti·ol·o·gy /éetee ólləjee/, **ae·ti·ol·o·gy** *n* **1** the investigation of causes and origins **2** a branch of medicine that investigates the causes and origins of disease —**e·ti·o·log·ic** /éetee ə lójjik/ *adj* —**e·ti·o·log·i·cal** —**e·ti·ol·o·gist** *n*

et·i·quette /éttikət, étti kèt/ *n* the rules of acceptable behavior

ORIGIN Etiquette is adopted from a French word that originally and literally meant "ticket." *Ticket* is, in fact, an earlier adoption of the same word. The transfer to "rules of behavior" seems to have derived from a custom of writing details of the formalities of court on small pieces of card for reference.

Et·na, Mt. /étnə/ volcano in E Sicily, Italy. Height 10,902 ft./3,323 m.

E·tru·ri·a /i trooree ə/ ancient region on the coast of NW Italy, where the Etruscan civilization flourished in the 1st millennium BC —**E·tru·ri·an** *n, adj*

E·trus·can /i trúskən/ *n* a member of an ancient people who lived in Etruria —**E·trus·can** *adj*

-ette *suffix* **1** small ○ *diskette* **2** female ○ *suffragette* **3** imitation ○ *leatherette*

é·tude /áy tòod, ay tóod/, **e·tude** *n* a short musical composition for a solo instrument intended to develop technique or display skill

et·y·mol·o·gy /èttə mólləjee/ *(pl* **-gies)** *n* **1** the study of word origins **2** the history of a word —**et·y·mo·log·i·cal** /èttəmə lójjik'l/ *adj* —**et·y·mo·log·i·cal·ly** *adv* —**et·y·mol·o·gist** *n*

ORIGIN Etymology derives ultimately from a Greek word meaning "real," and so means etymologically "the study of the real meanings of words." Its scope was later extended to include establishing the root word from which another word derives.

Eu *symbol* europium

EU *abbr* European Union

eu·ca·lyp·tus /yŏokə líptəss/ (*pl* **-tus·es** *or* **-ti** /-tī/), **eu·ca·lypt** /yŏokə lípt/ *n* an Australian evergreen tree with aromatic leaves

Eu·cha·rist /yŏokərist/ *n* **1** the Christian ceremony of communion **2** the bread and wine used during Communion —**Eu·cha·ris·tic** /yŏokə rístik/ *adj*

> **ORIGIN** Eucharist came through French and ecclesiastical Latin from a Greek word that meant "giving of thanks," and earlier "gratitude."

eu·chre /yŏokər/ *n* **1** a card game played with the highest 32 cards **2** an instance of preventing an opponent from taking tricks in euchre ■ *vt* (**-chred, -chring**) **1** prevent an opponent from taking tricks in euchre **2** *US, Can, ANZ* trick somebody

Eu·clid /yŏoklid/ (*fl* 300 BC) Greek mathematician

Eu·gene /yoo jeen/ city in W Oregon. Pop. 128,240 (1998).

eu·gen·ics /yoo jénniks/ *n* selective breeding as a proposed method of human improvement (*+ sing verb*) —**eu·gen·ic** *adj* —**eu·gen·i·cal·ly** *adv* —**eu·gen·i·cist** /yoo jénnəssist/ *n*

Eu·gé·nie /yoo jeénee, ò zhay neé/ (1826–1920) Spanish-born empress of France (1853–71)

eu·lo·gize /yŏolə jīz/ (**-gized, -giz·ing**) *vti* praise somebody or something highly —**eu·lo·giz·er** *n*

eu·lo·gy /yŏoləjee/ (*pl* **-gies**) *n* **1** a spoken or written tribute **2** high praise (*fml*) —**eu·lo·gist** *n*

Eu·men·i·des /yoo ménni deéz/ *n* in Greek mythology, three fertility goddesses later identified with the Furies

eu·nuch /yŏonək/ *n* a castrated human male

> **ORIGIN** Eunuch derives from a Greek word meaning literally "keeper of the bed." Because men attendants in the harems of Eastern courts were formerly castrated, the concept of castration became a dominant and then essential part of the word's meaning.

eu·phe·mism /yŏofə mìzzəm/ *n* **1** a less offensive synonym **2** the use of inoffensive words —**eu·phe·mis·tic** /yŏofə místik/ *adj* —**eu·phe·mis·ti·cal·ly** *adv*

eu·pho·ni·ous /yoo fṓnee əss/ *adj* pleasant-sounding —**eu·pho·ni·ous·ly** *adv* —**eu·pho·ny** /yŏofənee/ *n*

eu·pho·ni·um /yoo fṓnee əm/ *n* a brass-band instrument like a small tuba

eu·pho·ri·a /yoo fáwree ə/ *n* extreme happiness —**eu·phor·i·cal·ly** *adv*

Eu·phra·tes /yoo fráyteez/ *river* in SW Asia, rising in Turkey, flowing through Syria

and Iraq, and joining the Tigris River near the Persian Gulf. Length 1,700 mi./2,700 km.

Eur·a·sia /yoo ráyzhə, -shə/ *n* the land mass of the continents of Europe and Asia

Eur·a·sian /yoo ráyzh'n, -sh'n/ *adj* of Europe and Asia ■ *n* **1** formerly, somebody with a European and an Asian parent **2** an offensive term for somebody with a white American and a Southeast Asian parent

eu·re·ka /yoo reékə/ *interj* expresses triumph

> **ORIGIN** Eureka comes from a Greek word meaning literally "I have found." It is the exclamation traditionally said to have been uttered by the Greek mathematician Archimedes when he discovered the principle of water displacement that provided a method for establishing the purity of gold.

Eu·rip·i·des /yoo ríppi deéz/ (480?–406? BC) Greek dramatist

eu·ro /yŏorō/ (*pl* **-ros** *or* same) *n* the currency unit of the European Union, which in 2002 replaced local currency in some member states

Euro- *prefix* Europe, European ○ *Eurodollar*

euro·cent /yŏorō sènt/ the cent used in the European Union

Eu·ro·cen·tric /yŏorō séntrik/, **Eu·ro·po·cen·tric** /yoo rōpə-/ *adj* focusing on Europe, often in a way that is arrogantly dismissive of other cultures (*disapproving*) —**Eu·ro·cen·trism** *n*

Eu·ro·crat /yŏorō kràt/, **eu·ro·crat** *n* a bureaucrat in the European Union

Eu·ro·dol·lar /yŏorō dòllər/ *n* a US dollar on deposit in a European bank (*usually pl*)

Eu·ro·MP *n* a member of the European Parliament

Eu·ro·pa /yoo rṓpə/ *n* in Greek mythology, a Phoenician princess abducted by Zeus

Eu·rope /yŏorəp/ the second smallest continent after Australia, lying west of Asia, north of Africa, and east of the Atlantic Ocean. Pop. 725,962,762 (2000).

Eu·ro·pe·an /yŏorə peé ən/ *adj* **1** of Europe **2** of the European Union ■ *n* **1** somebody from Europe **2** an advocate of European union

Eu·ro·pe·an Com·mis·sion *n* an executive arm of the European Union

Eu·ro·pe·an Un·ion *n* an economic and political alliance of 15 European nations

eu·ro·pi·um /yoo rṓpee əm/ *n* (*symbol* **Eu**) a soft silvery white metallic element. Use: lasers.

Eu·ro·po·cen·tric *adj* = Eurocentric

Eu·ro·zone /yŏorō zòn/ *n* the geographic area comprising the European Union countries using the euro as a monetary unit

Eu·ryd·i·ce /yoo ríddissee/ *n* in Greek mythology, the wife of Orpheus

eu·sta·chian tube /yoo stáysh'n-/, **Eu·stachian tube** *n* a passage in the ear that equalizes air pressure on both sides of the eardrum

ORIGIN The passage is named for the Italian anatomist Bartolomeo Eustachio (1520–74), who was known for his descriptions of the human ear and heart.

eu·tha·na·sia /yòotha náyzhə/ *n* the painless killing of somebody to relieve suffering

e·vac·u·ate /i vákyoo àyt/ (-at·ed, -at·ing) v 1 *vt* make everyone leave a place 2 *vti* empty the bowels or bladder (technical) —**e·vac·u·a·tion** /i vàkyoo áysh'n/ *n*

e·vac·u·ee /i vàkyoo eé/ *n* somebody moved to a safer place to live

e·vade /i váyd/ (e·vad·ed, e·vad·ing) *vt* 1 escape or avoid somebody or something cleverly 2 avoid something difficult or unpleasant 3 be difficult for somebody to find or achieve (fml) ○ Success always evaded him. —**e·vad·er** *n*

e·val·u·ate /i vállyoo àyt/ (-at·ed, -at·ing) *vt* 1 examine and judge the value or importance of something 2 put a value on an item —**e·val·u·a·tion** /i vàllyoo áysh'n/ *n* —**e·val·u·a·tive** *adj* —**e·val·u·a·tor** *n*

ev·a·nes·cent /èvvə néss'nt/ *adj* disappearing after only a short time —**ev·a·nes·cence** *n*

e·van·gel·i·cal /èe van jéllik'l, èvvən-/ *adj* 1 *also* E·van·gel·i·cal of a Protestant denomination whose followers believe in the authority of the Bible 2 with strong beliefs and enthusiastic about encouraging people to share them 3 of the Christian Gospels ■ *n also* E·van·gel·i·cal a member of an evangelical Christian church

e·van·gel·ism /i vánjə lìzzəm/ *n* 1 the spreading of Christianity 2 enthusiastic promotion of a cause

e·van·gel·ist /i vánjəlist/ *n* 1 *also* E·van·gel·ist any of the writers of the Christian Gospels 2 a Christian who tries to convert people to Christianity —**e·van·gel·is·tic** /i vànjə lístik/ *adj*

e·van·gel·ize /i vánjə līz/ (-ized, -iz·ing) *vti* 1 try to convert people to Christianity 2 be an enthusiastic advocate for a cause —**e·van·gel·i·za·tion** /i vànjəli záysh'n/ *n*

Ev·ans·ton /évvənstən/ city in NE Illinois on Lake Michigan. Pop. 71,928 (1998).

Ev·ans·ville /évvənz vìl/ city in SW Indiana. Pop. 122,779 (1998).

e·vap·o·rate /i váppə ràyt/ (-rat·ed, -rat·ing) v 1 *vti* change liquid to vapor by heating, or be changed to vapor in this way 2 *vi* disappear gradually —**e·vap·o·ra·tion** /i vàppə ráysh'n/ *n*

e·vap·o·rat·ed milk *n* concentrated milk thickened by heating

e·va·sion /i váyzh'n/ *n* 1 the avoidance of something 2 an act of avoiding a question or an issue by giving an indirect answer

e·va·sive /i váyssiv/ *adj* 1 avoiding a question or an issue 2 intended to avoid trouble ○ took evasive action —**e·va·sive·ly** *adv* —**e·va·sive·ness** *n*

eve /eev/ *n* 1 the period immediately before an event 2 *also* **Eve** the day, evening, or night before a religious festival or public holiday 3 an evening (literary)

Eve /eev/ *n* in the Bible, the first woman

e·ven¹ /éevən/ *adj* 1 not sloping, rough, or irregular 2 at the same height 3 aligned 4 not changing or fluctuating 5 the same throughout 6 equal in amount, number, or extent 7 exactly divisible by two 8 calm and steady 9 exact in amount ■ *vti* make or become level or equal —**e·ven·ly** *adv* —**e·ven·ness** *n* ◇ **get even** take revenge

e·ven² /éevən/ *n* evening (literary)

e·ven³ /éevən/ *adv* 1 so much as 2 to a greater extent ◇ **even so** regardless of anything else

e·ven·hand·ed /èevən hándəd/ *adj* fair and impartial —**e·ven·hand·ed·ly** *adv* —**e·ven·hand·ed·ness** *n*

eve·ning /éevning/ *n* the part of the day from late afternoon to early night

eve·ning dress *n* 1 formal clothing 2 an evening gown

eve·ning gown *n* a woman's full-length formal dress

eve·ning star *n* a planet seen in the west at sunset

e·ven mon·ey *n* betting odds in which the winnings are the same as the stakes ■ *adj* as likely as not

e·vent /i vént/ *n* 1 an important incident 2 an organized occasion 3 an individual sports contest

e·ven-tem·pered *adj* not easily angered or upset —**e·ven-tem·pered·ly** *adv* —**e·ven-tem·pered·ness** *n*

e·vent·ful /i véntfəl/ *adj* 1 interesting or exciting 2 having a major effect on somebody's life —**e·vent·ful·ly** *adv*

e·ven·tide /éevən tīd/ *n* an evening (literary)

e·ven·tu·al /i vénchoo əl, i vénchəl/ *adj* happening at some, usually relatively distant, point in the future —**e·ven·tu·al·ly** *adv*

e·ven·tu·al·i·ty /i vènchoo állətee/ (pl -ties) *n* a possibility that may happen

e·ven·tu·ate /i vénchoo àyt/ (-at·ed, -at·ing) *vi* happen as a result (fml)

ev·er /évvər/ *adv* 1 at any time 2 indicates surprise ○ How ever did she do it? 3 increasingly (fml) 4 adds emphasis (infml) ○ ever so handsome 5 always ○ ever anxious to please

Mt. Everest: western shoulder of the mountain

Barnaby's

Ev·er·est, Mt. /évvərist/ mountain in the Himalaya range on the border between Nepal and China. It is the highest mountain in the world. Height 29,035 ft./8,850 m.

ev·er·glade /évvər glàyd/ n a stretch of marshy grassland

Ev·er·glades /évvər glàydz/ subtropical swamp covering much of S Florida

ev·er·green /évvər grèen/ adj with leaves throughout the year ■ n an evergreen tree ■ **ev·er·greens** npl decorative branches

ev·er·last·ing /èvvər lásting/ adj 1 lasting forever 2 lasting a long time ■ n infinity —**ev·er·last·ing·ly** adv

ev·er·more /èvvər máwr, évvər màwr/ adv forever (literary)

Ev·ers, Medgar (1925–63) US civil rights leader

ev·ery /évvree/ adj each member of a group, without exception ◇ Every life is precious. ■ det 1 the utmost ◇ every intention of succeeding 2 each, occurring intermittently or proportionately ◇ meet every two weeks ◇ **every other** each alternate thing, person, or occasion

eve·ry·day /évvree dày/ adj 1 ordinary and unremarkable 2 happening or done each day

Eve·ry·man /évvree màn/, **eve·ry·man** n an ordinary person

eve·ry·one /évvree wùn/, **eve·ry·bod·y** /-bòddee/ pron every person

eve·ry·thing /évvree thìng/ pron 1 all things 2 something all-important ◇ Family is everything.

eve·ry·where /évvree wàir, -hwàir/ adv in all places

e·vict /i víkt/ vt 1 eject a tenant from a property by legal means 2 throw somebody out of a place —**e·vict·ee** /i vìk tèe/ n —**e·vic·tion** n

ev·i·dence /évvid'nss/ n 1 something that is a sign or proof of the existence or truth of something 2 objects or information considered in relation to proof of guilt ■ vt (-denced, -denc·ing) demonstrate or prove

ev·i·dent /évvid'nt/ adj clear or obvious —**ev·i·dent·ly** adv

e·vil /éev'l/ adj 1 morally bad or wrong 2 deliberately causing harm or misfortune ■ n 1 also **E·vil** the force regarded as causing harmful or unpleasant effects 2 something unpleasant or morally wrong ◇ the social evil of alcoholism —**e·vil·ly** adv —**e·vil·ness** n

e·vil·do·er /éev'l dòo ər, èev'l dòo ər/ n somebody who does something evil —**e·vil·do·ing** n

evil eye n 1 a look of strong dislike 2 a supposed harmful magical power

e·vince /i vínss/ (**e·vinced, e·vinc·ing**) vt 1 show clearly 2 reveal by action or implication —**e·vinc·i·ble** adj

e·vis·cer·ate /i víssə ràyt/ (-at·ed, -at·ing) vt 1 disembowel a person or animal 2 remove the important part of something —**e·vis·cer·a·tion** /i vìssə ráysh'n/ n

E·vi·ta /e veétə/ ◆ Perón, Eva

e·voc·a·tive /i vókativ/ adj prompting vivid memories or images, often of the past —**e·voc·a·tive·ly** adv —**e·voc·a·tive·ness** n

e·voke /i vók/ (**e·voked, e·vok·ing**) vt 1 bring something to mind, often from the past 2 cause a particular reaction or feeling —**e·vo·ca·tion** /èvvə káysh'n, èe vō-/ n

ev·o·lu·tion /èvvə loósh'n, èèvə-/ n 1 the theoretical process by which living things develop from earlier forms 2 any developmental process —**ev·o·lu·tion·al** adj —**ev·o·lu·tion·ar·y** adj

e·volve /i vólv/ (**e·volved, e·volv·ing**) vti 1 develop or cause to develop gradually 2 develop or cause to develop via evolutionary change —**e·volve·ment** n

~~evry~~ incorrect spelling of **every**

ewe /yoo/ n a female sheep

Ew·ell /yoo əl/, **Richard Stoddert** (1817–72) US Confederate general

ew·er /yoo ər/ n a large jug with a wide spout

ex¹ n a former spouse (infml)

ex² prep 1 excluding ◇ ex dividend 2 sold from ◇ ex works

ex. abbr 1 examination 2 example 3 except

ex- prefix 1 out, outside, away ◇ exclude 2 former ◇ ex-husband

ex·ac·er·bate /ig zássər bàyt/ (-bat·ed, -bat·ing) vt make worse —**ex·ac·er·ba·tion** /ig zàssər báysh'n/ n

ex·act /ig zákt/ adj 1 correct in all details 2 precise and not allowing for variation ◇ the exact amount 3 emphasizes the significance of the thing being referred to ◇ on this the exact spot 4 rigorous and thorough ◇ an exact argument 5 characterized by precise measurements ◇ exact instruments ■ vt 1 demand and obtain 2 inflict as suffering (fml) —**ex·act·ness** n

ex·act·ing /ig zákting/ adj 1 requiring attention to detail 2 insisting on hard work —**ex·act·ing·ly** adv

ex·ac·ti·tude /ig zákti tòod/ n precision and accuracy

ex·act·ly /ig záktlee/ adv 1 no more or less ◇ exactly two miles away 2 in all details, or to the greatest degree ◇ did exactly as he was told 3 expresses agreement

exagerate incorrect spelling of **exaggerate**

ex·ag·ger·ate /ig zájjə ràyt/ (-at·ed, -at·ing) v 1 vti overstate something 2 vt make something more extreme or noticeable —**ex·ag·ger·at·ed·ly** adv —**ex·ag·ger·a·tion** /ig zàjjə ráysh'n/ n

ex·alt /ig záwlt/ vt (fml) 1 promote in rank or status 2 praise highly —**ex·al·ta·tion** /ig zàwl táysh'n/ n

ex·alt·ed /ig záwltəd/ adj (fml) 1 high in rank or status 2 noble in character —**ex·alt·ed·ly** adv —**ex·alt·ed·ness** n

ex·am /ig zám/ n 1 a test of knowledge or ability 2 a medical inspection of a patient

ex·am·i·na·tion /ig zàmmə náysh'n/ n 1 the process of looking at something and considering it carefully 2 a test of knowledge or ability 3 an interrogation in a law court

ex·am·ine /ig zámmin/ (-ined, -in·ing) vt 1 inspect something in detail 2 analyze something to understand or expose it o *examine your conscience* 3 test the knowledge or ability of somebody 4 inspect the condition of a patient 5 interrogate a witness —**ex·am·in·a·ble** adj—**ex·am·in·ee** /ig zàmmə née/ n —**ex·am·in·er** n

ex·am·ple /ig zámp'l/ n 1 something that is representative because it has typical qualities 2 somebody or something that serves as a model to be copied 3 an illustration that provides evidence o *several examples of mismanagement*

ex·as·per·ate /ig záspə ràyt/ (-at·ed, -at·ing) vt make frustrated or annoyed —**ex·as·per·at·ed·ly** adv —**ex·as·per·at·ing** adj —**ex·as·per·a·tion** /ig zàspə ráysh'n/ n ◊ See note at **annoy**

exaust incorrect spelling of **exhaust**

Ex·cal·i·bur /ek skálləbər/ n King Arthur's sword

ex·ca·vate /ékskə vàyt/ (-vat·ed, -vat·ing) v 1 vti remove earth by digging 2 vti dig a site for artifacts 3 vt form a shape or hole by digging or hollowing 4 vti uncover something with difficulty

ex·ca·va·tion /èkskə váysh'n/ n 1 the process of digging 2 a site where digging is taking place

ex·ca·va·tor /ékskə vàytər/ n 1 a mechanical digger 2 a person or animal that excavates something

excede incorrect spelling of **exceed**

ex·ceed /ik seéd/ vt 1 be greater than something 2 go beyond limits ◊ See note at **accede**

ex·ceed·ing /ik seéding/ adj very great (literary)

ex·ceed·ing·ly /ik seédinglee/ adv extremely

ex·cel /ik sél/ (-celled, -cel·ling) v 1 vti do better than before or than expected 2 vi be very good

ex·cel·lence /éksələnss/ n the quality of being outstandingly good

Ex·cel·len·cy /éksələnsee/ (pl -cies), **Ex·cel·lence** /-lənss/ n a term of address for some high officials

ex·cel·lent /éksələnt/ adj outstandingly good ■ interj agreed —**ex·cel·lent·ly** adv

ex·cept /ik sépt/ prep other than o *every house except ours* ■ conj but not or other than o *He dislikes the game except when he wins.* ■ vt exclude (fml) ◊ **except for** apart from

ex·cept·ed /ik séptəd/ adj excluded as an exception o *present company excepted*

ex·cept·ing /ik sépting/ prep, conj except for (fml)

ex·cep·tion /ik sépsh'n/ n somebody or something excluded from or not fitting into a general pattern

ex·cep·tion·a·ble /ik sépshənəb'l/ adj open to objection (fml)

ex·cep·tion·al /ik sépshən'l/ adj 1 unusual 2 outstanding —**ex·cep·tion·al·ly** adv

ex·cerpt n /ék sùrpt/ an extracted section or passage of a longer work ■ vt /ik súrpt/ take a section or passage from a longer work

ex·cess n /ik séss, ék sèss/ an amount beyond what is required ■ adj /ék sèss, ik séss/ more than what is required or wanted ◊ See note at **access**

ex·ces·sive /ik séssiv/ adj more than is considered usual, sufficient, or healthy —**ex·ces·sive·ly** adv —**ex·ces·sive·ness** n

ex·change /iks cháynj/ vt (-changed, -chang·ing) 1 give something and get something else in return o *exchange land for peace* 2 give or do something and receive the same in return o *exchange glances* 3 replace something o *exchanged the coat for a smaller size* ■ n 1 the process or an instance of giving and receiving 2 a building used for trading in commodities, securities, or other assets 3 a short conversation or argument 4 a center with equipment for interconnecting telephone lines 5 something given or received 6 the transferring of money between two currencies 7 a system of payments in which commercial documents are used instead of money —**ex·change·a·ble** adj

ex·change rate n the value of one currency if exchanged for another

ex·cheq·uer /iks chékər/, **Ex·cheq·uer** n 1 the treasury of a government or organization 2 a government's assets

ORIGIN Exchequer came via French from a Latin word meaning "chessboard," and this is in fact the earliest sense in English. The connection with revenue derives from the practice of making calculations using counters on a checkered cloth. The word then came to apply to the department of state for collecting revenues set up by the Norman kings in England. In other senses, **exchequer** was shortened to *checker*, and *checker* was shortened to *check*.

ex·cise[1] *n* /ék síz/ a tax on goods manufactured or sold within a country ■ *vt* /ik síz/ (**-cised, -cis·ing**) impose a tax on

ex·cise[2] /ik síz/ (**-cised, -cis·ing**) *vt* 1 delete (*fml*) 2 remove surgically —**ex·ci·sion** /ik sízh'n/ *n*

ex·cit·a·ble /ik sítəb'l/ *adj* easily excited —**ex·cit·a·bil·i·ty** /ik sítə bíllətee/ *n* —**ex·cit·a·ble·ness** *n* —**ex·cit·a·bly** *adv*

ex·cite /ik sít/ (**-cit·ed, -cit·ing**) *vt* 1 cause somebody to feel enjoyment or pleasurable anticipation 2 put somebody in an unpleasant state of heightened emotion 3 arouse somebody sexually 4 arouse a particular emotion 5 evoke a thought —**ex·cit·ed** *adj* —**ex·cit·ed·ly** *adv* —**ex·cit·ing** *adj* —**ex·cit·ing·ly** *adv*

ex·cite·ment /ik sítmənt/ *n* 1 the state of being excited 2 the act of stimulating something 3 an exciting event

ex·claim /ik skláym/ *vti* say something loudly and suddenly

~~exclaimation~~ incorrect spelling of **ex·clamation**

ex·cla·ma·tion /èksklə máysh'n/ *n* 1 a word, phrase, or sentence that is suddenly shouted out 2 the act of exclaiming —**ex·cla·ma·tion·al** *adj*

ex·cla·ma·tion point, ex·cla·ma·tion mark *n* a punctuation mark (!) used for exclamations

ex·clude /ik sklood/ (**-clud·ed, -clud·ing**) *vt* 1 keep somebody or something from entering or participating 2 not consider something 3 omit something

ex·clu·sion /ik slooʒh'n/ *n* 1 the act of excluding somebody or something 2 the fact of being excluded —**ex·clu·sion·ar·y** *adj*

ex·clu·sion zone *n* an area that is off-limits

ex·clu·sive /ik slooʊssiv/ *adj* 1 high-class *o an exclusive nightclub* 2 restricted in use or access *o exclusive use of the pool* 3 published or broadcast in only one place *o exclusive coverage* 4 confined to one thing ■ *n* a report printed in only one publication or broadcast in only one program —**ex·clu·sive·ly** *adv* —**ex·clu·sive·ness** *n*

ex·com·mu·ni·cate *vt* /èkskə myoóni kàyt/ (**-cat·ed, -cat·ing**) exclude somebody from the Christian community because of doctrinal differences or for morally offensive behavior ■ *adj* /-kət, -kàyt/ excommunicated ■ *n* /-kət/ an excommunicated person —**ex·com·mu·ni·ca·tion** /èkskə myoóni káysh'n/ *n*

ex·co·ri·ate /ik skáwree àyt/ (**-at·ed, -at·ing**) *vt* (*fml*) 1 criticize very strongly 2 tear the skin off *o* —**ex·co·ri·a·tion** /ik skàwree áysh'n/ *n*

ex·cre·ment /ékskrəmənt/ *n* waste material expelled from the body (*technical*) —**ex·cre·men·tal** /èkskrə mént'l/ *adj*

ex·cres·cence /ik skréss'nss/ *n* 1 an outgrowth, especially an unusual or undesirable one 2 an unsightly addition

ex·cre·ta /ik skreétə/ *npl* waste matter expelled from the body (*technical*) —**ex·cre·tal** *adj*

ex·crete /ik skreét/ (**-cret·ed, -cret·ing**) *vt* 1 expel waste from the body (*fml*) 2 eliminate waste from leaves and roots —**ex·cre·tion** *n* —**ex·cre·to·ry** /èkskrə tàwree/ *adj*

ex·cru·ci·at·ing /ik skroóshee àyting/ *adj* 1 extremely painful 2 hard to bear —**ex·cru·ci·at·ing·ly** *adv*

ex·cul·pate /ékskəl pàyt, ik skúl-/ (**-pat·ed, -pat·ing**) *vt* prove somebody innocent (*fml*) —**ex·cul·pa·tion** /èkskəl páysh'n/ *n*

ex·cur·sion /ik skúrzh'n/ *n* a short trip to a place and back

ex·cuse *vt* /ik skyoóz/ (**-cused, -cus·ing**) 1 forgive for a mistake or wrongdoing 2 make allowances for 3 release from an obligation 4 provide justification for 5 allow to leave ■ *n* /ik skyoóss/ 1 a justification 2 a false reason 3 a bad example (*infml*) —**ex·cus·a·ble** *adj* —**ex·cus·a·bly** *adv*

⨍ **exe** *abbr* a file extension indicating a program file. Full form **executable**

ex·ec /ig zék/ *n* an executive (*infml*)

ex·e·cra·ble /éksəkrəb'l/ *adj* (*fml*) 1 very bad 2 detestable —**ex·e·cra·bly** *adv*

ex·e·crate /éksə kràyt/ (**-crat·ed, -crat·ing**) *vt* (*literary or fml*) 1 feel loathing for 2 criticize severely —**ex·e·cra·tion** /èksə kráysh'n/ *n*

⨍ **ex·e·cut·a·ble** /éksə kyoótəb'l/ *adj* able to run as a computer program —**ex·e·cut·a·ble** *n*

⨍ **ex·e·cute** /éksə kyoót/ (**-cut·ed, -cut·ing**) *v* 1 *vt* kill somebody, especially as a punishment for a crime. 2 *vt* perform an action or movement 3 *vt* carry out an instruction or plan 4 *vti* run a computer file or program 5 *vt* create something *o execute a drawing* 6 *vt* carry out the terms of a legal document 7 *vt* sign a legal document before witnesses —**ex·e·cut·er** *n* —**ex·e·cu·tion** /èksə kyoósh'n/ *n* ♢ See note at **kill, perform**

ex·e·cu·tion·er /èksə kyoósh'nər/ *n* 1 the official who carries out the execution of a criminal 2 an assassin

ex·ec·u·tive /ig zékyətiv/ *n* 1 a senior manager 2 the section of a government responsible for implementing laws ■ *adj* 1 of policymaking 2 for businesspeople

ex·ec·u·tor /ig zékyətər, éksə kyoótər/ *n* 1 somebody implementing the terms of a will 2 somebody who carries something out

ex·e·ge·sis /èksə jeéssiss/ (*pl* **-ses** /-seèz/) *n* the analysis or interpretation of texts, especially biblical texts —**ex·e·get·ic** *adj*

~~exellent~~ incorrect spelling of **excellent**

ex·em·plar /ig zém plaàr, ig zémplər/ *n* (*literary*) 1 an ideal example worth copying or imitating 2 a typical example

ex·em·pla·ry /ig zémpləree/ *adj* setting a good example —**ex·em·plar·i·ly** *adv*

ex·em·pli·fy /ig zémplə fì/ (**-fied, -fies**) *vt* 1 show something by being an example of it 2 give an example of something —**ex·em·pli·fi·ca·tion** /ig zèmpləfi káysh'n/ *n*

ex·empt /ig zémpt/ *adj* not subject to something that others have to do or pay ◾ *vt* 1 free somebody from an obligation 2 release somebody from a rule that applies to others —**ex·empt·i·ble** *adj*

ex·emp·tion /ig zémpshən/ *n* 1 freedom from an obligation 2 an exempt person or thing

~~exept~~ incorrect spelling of **except**

ex·er·cise /éksər sìz/ *n* 1 physical activity designed to keep you fit 2 a series of physical movements designed to keep you fit (*often pl*) 3 the practicing of a skill or procedure (*often pl*) 4 a piece of work intended as a test 5 a set of military training operations or maneuvers 6 an activity intended to achieve a particular purpose 7 the carrying out or using of something (*fml*) ◾ *v* (**-cised, -cis·ing**) 1 *vi* take exercise in order to stay fit 2 *vt* subject a person, a part of the body, or an animal to physical exertion 3 *vt* put something to practical use 4 *vt* show a particular type of behavior ○ *exercise caution* 5 *vt* occupy or worry somebody (*fml*) ○ *The problem has exercised me greatly.* —**ex·er·cis·a·ble** *adj*

~~exercize~~ incorrect spelling of **exercise**

~~exerpt~~ incorrect spelling of **excerpt**

ex·ert /ig zúrt/ *v* 1 *vt* bring influence, pressure, or authority to bear on a situation 2 *vr* make an effort —**ex·er·tion** *n*

ex·e·unt /éksee ənt/ *vi* exit from the stage together (*as a stage direction*)

ex·fo·li·ate /eks fṓlee àyt/ (**-at·ed, -at·ing**) *v* 1 *vt* remove a thin outer layer from something, or shed such a layer 2 *vti* scrub the skin to remove the dead outer layer —**ex·fo·li·a·tion** /eks fṓlee áysh'n/ *n* —**ex·fo·li·a·tive** *adj*

ex·hale /eks háyl/ (**-haled, -hal·ing**) *v* 1 *vti* breathe out 2 *vt* give off a smell or vapor (*literary*) —**ex·ha·la·tion** /èkshə láysh'n, èksə-/ *n*

ex·haust /ig záwst/ *vt* 1 tire somebody out 2 use something up 3 try out all possibilities 4 say everything there is to say about something ◾ *n* 1 a discharge of waste gases 2 an escape system for waste gases —**ex·haust·ed** *adj* —**ex·haust·ed·ly** *adv* —**ex·haust·i·ble** *adj* —**ex·haus·tion** *n*

ex·haus·tive /ig záwstiv/ *adj* complete and detailed —**ex·haus·tive·ly** *adv* —**ex·haus·tive·ness** *n*

ex·hib·it /ig zíbbit/ *v* 1 *vti* display works of art 2 *vt* show something to others 3 *vt* show signs of something ○ *beginning to exhibit signs of metal fatigue* ◾ *n* 1 an object on display 2 a piece of evidence shown in court

ex·hi·bi·tion /èksə bísh'n/ *n* 1 a public display of works of art 2 the displaying of something 3 a demonstration of a skill

ex·hi·bi·tion·ism /èksə bísh'n ìzzəm/ *n* 1 attention-seeking behavior 2 the psychological disorder that prompts somebody to expose their genitals in public —**ex·hi·bi·tion·ist** *n*

ex·hil·a·rate /ig zíllə ràyt/ (**-rat·ed, -rat·ing**) *vt* make somebody feel happy and alive —**ex·hil·a·rat·ing·ly** *adv* —**ex·hil·a·ra·tion** /ig zìllə ráysh'n/ *n*

~~exhilerating~~ incorrect spelling of **exhilarating**

~~exhileration~~ incorrect spelling of **exhilaration**

ex·hort /ig záwrt/ *v* (*fml*) 1 *vt* urge strongly to do something 2 *vi* give somebody earnest advice —**ex·hor·ta·tion** /èg zawr táysh'n/ *n* —**ex·hor·ta·tive** /ig záwrtətiv/ *adj*

ex·hume /ig zoòm, -zyoòm, ik syoóm/ (**-humed, -hum·ing**) *vt* 1 dig up a body from a grave 2 reintroduce something neglected or forgotten —**ex·hu·ma·tion** /èksyoo máysh'n, èksoo-, ègzoo-, ègzyoo-/ *n*

~~exibition~~ incorrect spelling of **exhibition**

ex·i·gen·cy /éksəjənssee, égzə-, ig zíjj-/ (*pl* **-cies**), **ex·i·gence** /éksəjənss, égzə-/ *n* (*fml*) 1 an urgent need (*often pl*) 2 something needing immediate action —**ex·i·gent** *adj*

ex·ig·u·ous /ig zíggyoo əss, ik sígg-/ *adj* meager (*fml*) —**ex·i·gu·i·ty** /ègzi gyoó ətee, èksi-/ *n*

ex·ile /ég zîl, ék sîl/ *n* 1 unwilling absence from your own country, whether enforced by a government or made necessary by the political situation 2 somebody living unwillingly outside his or her own country ◾ *vt* (**-iled, -il·ing**) banish somebody from his or her region or country —**ex·íl·ic** /ig zíllik, ik síllik/ *adj*

ex·ist /ig zíst/ *vi* 1 be real or actual 2 be able to continue living ○ *We need food to exist.* 3 occur in a particular place or situation

~~existance~~ incorrect spelling of **existence**

ex·is·tence /ig zíst'nss/ *n* 1 the state of being real or actual 2 presence in a place or situation 3 a way of living, especially a life of hardship

ex·is·tent /ig zíst'nt/ *adj* (*fml*) 1 real or actual 2 currently existing or in operation

ex·is·ten·tial /ègzi sténshəl, èksi-/ *adj* 1 of human existence 2 of existentialism —**ex·is·ten·tial·ly** *adv*

ex·is·ten·tial·ism /ègzi sténsh'l ìzzəm, èksi-/ *n* a philosophical movement centered on individual free will and personal responsibility and denying any meaning or structure in the universe —**ex·is·ten·tial·ist** *adj, n*

ex·ist·ing /ig zísting/ *adj* currently present, in operation, or available

✱ **ex·it** /égzit, éksit/ *n* 1 a door or other means of leaving a room or building 2 a departure from a room, building, or gathering ◾ *v* 1 *vti* leave a place 2 *vi* go offstage (*refers to* *actors*) **3** *vti* terminate a computer program

ex·it poll *n* a survey of people's votes as they leave the voting place

ex·o·dus /éksədəss/ *n* **1** a departure by large numbers of people **2 Ex·o·dus** in the Bible, the flight of the Israelites from Egypt

Ex·o·dus a book of the Bible that describes the flight of the Israelites from Egypt and Moses receiving the Ten Commandments on Mount Sinai

ex of·fi·ci·o /èks ə físhee ṑ/ *adv, adj* as a consequence of the holding of a specific official position

ex·on·er·ate /ig zónnə ràyt/ (-at·ed, -at·ing) *vt* **1** free from blame or guilt **2** free from an obligation —**ex·on·er·a·tion** /ig zònnə ráysh'n/ *n*

ex·or·bi·tant /ig záwrbit'nt/ *adj* unreasonably high or large —**ex·or·bi·tance** *n* —**ex·or·bi·tant·ly** *adv*

ex·or·cise /ék sawr sìz, éksər-/ (-cised, -cis·ing), **ex·or·cize** *vt* **1** use prayers and religious rituals with the intention of freeing a person or place from evil **2** get rid of an oppressive feeling or memory

ex·or·cism /ék sawr sìzzəm, éksər-/ *n* **1** the driving out of evil spirits **2** a ceremony conducted to drive out evil spirits —**ex·or·cist** *n*

ex·o·skel·e·ton /èksō skéllət'n/ *n* the hard protective covering of many organisms, e.g., crustaceans —**ex·o·skel·e·tal** *adj*

ex·o·sphere /éksō sfèer/ *n* the outermost region of the atmosphere —**ex·o·spher·ic** /èksō sféerik, -sférrik/ *adj*

ex·ot·ic /ig zóttik/ *adj* **1** strikingly different and exciting and suggesting distant countries and cultures **2** introduced from elsewhere ○ *exotic species* ■ *n* an exotic person or thing —**ex·ot·i·cal·ly** *adv* —**ex·ot·ic·ness** *n*

ex·ot·i·ca /ig zóttikə/ *npl* highly unusual things

ex·ot·ic dancer *n* a stripper

ex·pand /ik spánd/ *v* **1** *vti* increase in scope, number, or size **2** *vti* open out after being folded **3** *v* describe something more fully —**ex·pand·a·ble** *adj* —**ex·pan·si·ble** /ik spánsəb'l/ *adj* ◊ See note at **increase**

ex·panse /ik spánss/ *n* a wide area or surface

ex·pan·sion /ik spánsh'n/ *n* **1** the process of becoming enlarged **2** an increase in scope, extent, or size **3** expanding —**ex·pan·sion·a·ry** *adj*

ex·pan·sion·ism /ik spánsh'n ìzzəm/ *n* a policy of expanding, especially territorially or economically —**ex·pan·sion·ist** *n, adj* —**ex·pan·sion·is·tic** /ik spànshə nístik/ *adj*

ex·pan·sive /ik spánsiv/ *adj* **1** talkative **2** covering a wide area, or broad in scope **3** lavish ○ *an expansive lifestyle* —**ex·pan·sive·ly** *adv* —**ex·pan·sive·ness** *n*

ex·pa·ti·ate /ek spáyshee àyt/ (-at·ed, -at·ing) *vi* speak or write at length —**ex·pa·ti·a·tion** /ek spàyshee áysh'n/ *n*

ex·pa·tri·ate *n* /eks páytree ət, -àyt/ **1** somebody who lives abroad **2** somebody without citizenship ■ *adj* /eks páytree ət, -àyt/ of people living abroad ■ *v* /eks páytree àyt/ (-at·ed, -at·ing) **1** *vi* settle abroad **2** *vt* take away somebody's citizenship —**ex·pa·tri·a·tion** /eks pàytree áysh'n/ *n*

expatriot incorrect spelling of **expatriate**

ex·pect /ik spékt/ *v* **1** *vt* confidently believe that something will happen **2** *vt* wait for an anticipated thing **3** *vt* demand something as a right or duty **4** *vti* be pregnant with or look forward to the birth of a baby (*infml; only in progressive tenses*) —**ex·pect·ed·ly** *adv* —**ex·pect·ed·ness** *n*

ex·pec·tan·cy /ik spéktənssee/ (*pl* -cies), **ex·pec·tance** /ik spéktənss/ *n* **1** excited anticipation **2** something expected

ex·pec·tant /ik spéktənt/ *adj* **1** excitedly anticipating something **2** expecting a baby —**ex·pec·tant·ly** *adv*

ex·pec·ta·tion /èk spek táysh'n/ *n* **1** a confident belief or strong hope that something will happen **2** a notion of what something will be like (*often pl*) **3** an expected standard (*often pl*) **4** excited anticipation

ex·pec·to·rant /ik spéktərənt/ *n* a medicine that stimulates the production of phlegm, as a treatment for coughs —**ex·pec·to·rant** *adj*

ex·pec·to·rate /ik spéktə ràyt/ (-rat·ed, -rat·ing) *vti* cough up and spit out phlegm —**ex·pec·to·ra·tion** /ik spèktə ráysh'n/ *n*

ORIGIN Expectorate comes from a Latin verb meaning literally "get out of the chest." *Expect* and related words also derive from Latin, but from a verb meaning "look." Both words are formed with the prefix *ex-* "out."

ex·pe·di·en·cy /ik spéedee ənssee/, **ex·pe·di·ence** /-ənss/ *n* **1** the use of fast and effective but often morally questionable methods **2** appropriateness or usefulness

ex·pe·di·ent /ik spéedee ənt/ *adj* **1** appropriate or advisable **2** advantageous for practical rather than moral reasons ■ *n* something that achieves an objective quickly —**ex·pe·di·ent·ly** *adv*

ex·pe·dite /ékspə dìt/ (-dit·ed, -dit·ing) *vt* (*fml*) **1** speed up the progress of **2** deal with quickly and efficiently

ex·pe·di·tion /èkspə dísh'n/ *n* **1** an organized trip made by a group for a specific purpose **2** an outing

ex·pe·di·tious /èkspə díshəss/ *adj* speedy or prompt

ex·pel /ik spél/ (-pelled, -pel·ling) *vt* **1** dismiss from an institution such as a school, political party, or club **2** force out

expence incorrect spelling of **expense**

ex·pend /ik spénd/ *vt* 1 use up time, energy, or another resource 2 spend money *(fml)*

ex·pend·a·ble /ik spéndəb'l/ *adj* 1 not worth preserving 2 dispensable —**ex·pend·a·ble** *n*

ex·pen·di·ture /ik spéndəchər/ *n* 1 money spent 2 the process of using something up 3 an expense

ex·pense /ik spénss/ *n* 1 an amount of money spent on something 2 the value of a resource that has been used and that can be charged against revenues ■ **ex·pens·es** *npl* money spent in the pursuit of business

~~expensiv~~ incorrect spelling of **expensive**

ex·pen·sive /ik spénsiv/ *adj* costing a lot of money —**ex·pen·sive·ly** *adv*

~~experiance~~ incorrect spelling of **experience**

ex·pe·ri·ence /ik spéeree ənss/ *n* 1 lengthy involvement in something, leading to knowledge and skill 2 knowledge and skill acquired over a period of time 3 something that happens to somebody 4 a direct personal awareness of something ■ *vt* (-enced, -enc·ing) 1 undergo or be involved in something 2 feel a sensation or emotion

ex·pe·ri·enced /ik spéeree ənst/ *adj* having knowledge and skill gained from experience

ex·pe·ri·en·tial /ik spéeree énshəl/ *adj* based on experience —**ex·pe·ri·en·tial·ly** *adv*

ex·per·i·ment *n* /ik spérrəmənt/ 1 a scientific test 2 an instance of doing something new o *switch to decaffeinated coffee as an experiment* ■ *vi* /ik spérrə mènt, ik spérrəmənt/ 1 try new things 2 carry out a scientific test —**ex·per·i·men·ta·tion** /ik spèrrəmən táysh'n/ *n*

ex·per·i·men·tal /ik spèrrə mént'l/ *adj* 1 using ideas or methods that are new and untried 2 of scientific experiments —**ex·per·i·men·tal·ly** *adv*

ex·pert *n* /ék spùrt/ a skilled or knowledgeable person ■ *adj* /ék spùrt, ik spùrt/ 1 skillful or knowledgeable 2 given or done by an expert —**ex·pert·ly** *adv* —**ex·pert·ness** *n*

ex·per·tise /èkspər téez/ *n* expert skill or knowledge

⚡ **ex·pert sys·tem** *n* a computer program that solves problems

ex·pi·ate /ékspee àyt/ (-at·ed, -at·ing) *vt* atone for wrongdoing —**ex·pi·a·tion** /èkspee áysh'n/ *n* —**ex·pi·a·to·ry** /ékspee ə tàwree/ *adj*

~~expidition~~ incorrect spelling of **expedition**

ex·pire /ik spír/ (-pired, -pir·ing) *vi* 1 come to an end or be no longer valid 2 breathe out *(technical)* —**ex·pi·ra·tion** /èkspə ráysh'n/ *n*

ex·pi·ry /ik spíree/ *n* the fact of ending or ceasing to be valid

ex·plain /ik spláyn/ *v* 1 *vti* give details about something 2 *vt* clarify the meaning of something 3 *vti* give a reason for something —**ex·plain·a·ble** *adj*

~~explaination~~ incorrect spelling of **explanation**

ex·pla·na·tion /èksplə náysh'n/ *n* 1 a statement explaining something 2 the act of giving details or reasons

ex·plan·a·to·ry /ik splánnə tàwree/, **ex·plan·a·tive** /ik splánnətiv/ *adj* explaining something

ex·ple·tive /éksplətiv/ *n* a swearword

ex·pli·ca·ble /éksplikəb'l, ik splikəb'l/ *adj* explicable —**ex·pli·ca·bly** *adv*

ex·pli·cate /ékspli kàyt/ (-cat·ed, -cat·ing) *vt* 1 explain something, especially a text, in a detailed way 2 develop a theory —**ex·pli·ca·tion** /èkspli káysh'n/ *n* —**ex·pli·ca·tive** *adj*

ex·plic·it /ik splíssit/ *adj* 1 clear and obvious 2 definite —**ex·plic·it·ly** *adv* —**ex·plic·it·ness** *n*

USAGE **explicit** or **implicit**? **Explicit** means "clear, obvious, and definite": *gave explicit directions*. **Implicit** means "implied or unstated but understood": *implicit trust*.

---

ex·plode /ik splṓd/ (-plod·ed, -plod·ing) *v* 1 *vti* burst with a sudden release of energy and a loud noise 2 *vti* burst or shatter suddenly 3 *vi* express an emotion suddenly and forcefully 4 *vi* increase dramatically o *The growth rate in home ownership exploded.*

ex·plod·ed /ik splṓdəd/ *adj* showing the parts of something separately but in their relative positions

ex·ploit *vt* /ik splóyt/ 1 take advantage of somebody 2 use something in order to gain a benefit o *fully exploit natural gas reserves* ■ *n* /ék splòyt, ik splóyt/ an exciting or daring act —**ex·ploit·a·ble** *adj* —**ex·ploi·ta·tion** /èk sploy táysh'n/ *n* —**ex·ploi·ta·tive** *adj* —**ex·ploit·er** *n*

ex·plore /ik spláwr/ (-plored, -plor·ing) *vti* 1 travel to places for the purpose of discovery 2 investigate or study something 3 search a place for natural resources —**ex·plo·ra·tion** /èksplə ráysh'n/ *n* —**ex·plor·a·to·ry** /ik spláwrə tàwree/ *adj* —**ex·plor·er** *n*

Ex·plor·er *n* a Scout aged between 14 and 21 in a program run by the Boy Scouts of America that enables young people to gain work experience

ex·plo·sion /ik splṓzh'n/ *n* 1 a sudden noisy release of energy 2 the bursting or shattering of something 3 a sudden burst of emotion 4 a dramatic increase o *an explosion in e-mail subscriptions*

ex·plo·sive /ik splṓssiv, -splṓz-/ *adj* 1 liable to explode 2 operated by exploding 3 tending toward violent anger o *an explosive temperament* ■ *n* 1 a substance that can explode *(often pl)* 2 a bomb —**ex·plo·sive·ly** *adv* —**ex·plo·sive·ness** *n*

ex·po /ék spṓ/ *n* a large exhibition or trade fair

ex·po·nent /ik spónɘnt, ék spónɘnt/ *n* **1** a supporter or promoter of a cause **2** a practitioner of an art or skill **3** a number or variable indicating the number of times the number it is attached to is to be multiplied by itself

ex·po·nen·tial /ékspɘ nénshɘl/ *adj* **1** involving numbers multiplied by themselves **2** using a base of natural logarithms **3** rapidly developing or increasing o *an exponential increase in sales* —**ex·po·nen·tial·ly** *adv*

⚡ex·port *v* /ik spáwrt/ **1** *vti* send goods abroad for sale or exchange **2** *vt* transfer computer data from one program to another ■ *n* /ék spáwrt/ **1** the selling or exchange of goods abroad **2** a product sold or exchanged abroad —**ex·por·ta·tion** / èk spàwr táysh'n/ *n* —**ex·port·er** *n*

ex·pose /ik spóz/ (-posed, -pos·ing) *v* **1** *vt* allow something to be seen **2** *vt* put somebody in an unprotected situation **3** *vt* make somebody experience something **4** *vt* reveal somebody's wrongdoings **5** *vr* reveal the genitals indecently in public **6** *vt* allow light onto a film

ex·po·sé /èks pō záy/ (*pl* -sés) *n* **1** a book or article revealing wrongdoing **2** a declaration of facts

ex·posed /ik spózd/ *adj* **1** visible or unprotected **2** with no shelter

ex·po·si·tion /ékspɘ zísh'n/ *n* **1** a large exhibition or trade fair **2** a detailed description or discussion **3** the act of describing or discussing something —**ex·pos·i·tive** /ik spózzitiv/ *adj* —**ex·pos·i·to·ry** /ik spózzi tàwree/ *adj*

ex·pos·tu·late /ik spóschɘ làyt/ (-lat·ed, -lat·ing) *vi* express disagreement or disapproval —**ex·pos·tu·la·tion** /ik spòschɘ láysh'n/ *n* —**ex·pos·tu·la·to·ry** *adj* ◊ See note at **object**

ex·po·sure /ik spózhɘr/ *n* **1** contact with or experience of something **2** the harmful effects of extreme weather conditions **3** publicity **4** the revelation of a scandal or of somebody's identity **5** the amount of time that light is allowed into a camera **6** a single section of film exposed for a photograph **7** the direction a room or building faces o *a southern exposure*

ex·pound /ik spównd/ *vti* describe and explain something —**ex·pound·er** *n*

ex·press /ik spréss/ *v* **1** *vt* state thoughts or feelings in words **2** *vt* show meaning symbolically **3** *vr* reveal your thoughts or feelings to others o *expresses herself through her music* **4** *vt* represent something as a symbol o *Express the fractions as decimal numbers.* **5** *vt* squeeze something out **6** *vt* send something by special fast delivery ■ *adj* **1** done or traveling very quickly **2** for brief transactions or a few transactions only o *use the express checkout* **3** stated clearly o *his express wish* ■ *adv* by express delivery or trans-

portation ■ *n* **1** a fast train or bus **2** a fast delivery service —**ex·press·i·ble** *adj*

ex·pres·sion /ik srésh'n/ *n* **1** a look on somebody's face **2** a word or phrase that communicates an idea **3** the conveying of thoughts or feelings **4** a way of communicating something **5** a mathematical representation of numbers or quantities —**ex·pres·sion·al** *adj*

ex·pres·sion·ism /ik srésh'n ìzzɘm/ *n* **1** an art movement concentrating on expressing feelings and moods rather than objective reality **2** a literary movement presenting stylized reality —**ex·pres·sion·ist** *n, adj* —**ex·pres·sion·is·tic** /ik srèsh'n ístik/ *adj*

ex·pres·sion·less /ik srésh'nlɘss/ *adj* showing no emotion

ex·pres·sive /ik sréssiv/ *adj* **1** full of feelings and meanings **2** conveying a particular meaning —**ex·pres·sive·ly** *adv* —**ex·pres·sive·ness** *n*

ex·press·ly /ik srésslee/ *adv* **1** specifically **2** unambiguously

ex·press·way /ik sréss wày/ *n* US, Can, Aus a wide fast highway for travel through or around a city

ex·pro·pri·ate /ik sprópree àyt/ (-at·ed, -at·ing) *vt* take away something belonging to another person —**ex·pro·pri·a·tion** /ik spròpree áysh'n/ *n*

ex·pul·sion /ik spúlshɘn/ *n* **1** dismissal from a place or from membership of a group **2** the act of forcing somebody or something out —**ex·pul·sive** *adj*

ex·punge /ik spúnj/ (-punged, -pung·ing) *vt* **1** delete something unwanted **2** put an end to something —**ex·punc·tion** /ik spúngksh'n/ *n*

ex·pur·gate /ékspɘr gàyt/ (-gat·ed, -gat·ing) *vt* edit by removing offensive parts from —**ex·pur·ga·tion** /èkspɘr gáysh'n/ *n*

ex·qui·site /ik skwízzit, ékskwizit/ *adj* **1** beautiful and delicate **2** excellent and delightful **3** sensitive and discriminating —**ex·qui·site·ly** *adv* —**ex·qui·site·ness** *n*

ext. *abbr* **1** exterior **2** external

ex·tant /ékstɘnt, ek stánt/ *adj* still in existence ◊ See note at **living**

~~extasy~~ incorrect spelling of **ecstasy**

ex·tem·po·ra·ne·ous /ik stèmpɘ ráynee ɘss/, **ex·tem·po·rar·y** /ik stémpɘ rèrree/ *adj* **1** done unrehearsed **2** prepared but said without notes **3** speaking unrehearsed —**ex·tem·po·ra·ne·i·ty** /ik stèmpɘrɘ neè ɘtee/ *n* —**ex·tem·po·ra·ne·ous·ly** *adv*

ex·tem·po·re /ik stémpɘree/ *adj, adv* without rehearsing

ex·tem·po·rize /ik stémpɘ rìz/ (-rized, -riz·ing) *vti* **1** perform something without preparation **2** handle something in a makeshift way —**ex·tem·po·ri·za·tion** /ik stèmpɘri záysh'n/ *n*

ex·tend /ik sténd/ *v* 1 *vi* occupy distance or space 2 *vi* continue for a time 3 *vi* be applicable to somebody or something ○ *The offer extends to new readers too.* 4 *vt* increase the size or limits of something 5 *vt* increase a time span 6 *vt* offer or give something —**ex·tend·a·ble** *adj* —**ex·ten·si·ble** *adj* ◊ See note at **increase**

ex·tend·ed /ik sténdəd/ *adj* 1 lasting longer than usual or expected 2 made longer or larger —**ex·tend·ed·ly** *adv*

ex·tend·ed fam·i·ly *n* a family unit consisting of parents, children, and all other relatives

⚡ **ex·ten·sion** /ik sténsh'n/ *n* 1 an addition to a building 2 an additional piece 3 an additional telephone line or telephone 4 the telephone number of an additional telephone line 5 *also* **ex·ten·sion cord** an electrical cable with a socket at one end and a plug at the other, used for plugging something into a distant power source 6 an additional period of time 7 the act of extending something or the state of being extended 8 in computing, a file extension —**ex·ten·sion·al** *adj*

ex·ten·sive /ik sténsiv/ *adj* 1 covering a large area 2 broad in scope 3 large in amount —**ex·ten·sive·ly** *adv* —**ex·ten·sive·ness** *n*

ex·tent /ik stént/ *n* the range or scope of something

ex·ten·u·ate /ik sténnyoo àyt/ *vt* (-at·ed, -at·ing) *vt* diminish the seriousness of —**ex·ten·u·at·ing** *adj* —**ex·ten·u·a·tion** /ik sténnyoo áysh'n/ *n*

ex·te·ri·or /ik stéeree ər/ *adj* 1 on or for the outside of something 2 coming from outside ○ *an exterior cause* ■ *n* 1 the outside surface, appearance, or coating of something 2 somebody's outward appearance ○ *her calm exterior*

ex·ter·mi·nate /ik stúrmə nàyt/ *vt* (-nat·ed, -nat·ing) *vt* completely kill or destroy —**ex·ter·mi·na·tion** /ik stúrmə náysh'n/ *n* —**ex·ter·mi·na·tor** *n*

ex·ter·nal /ik stúrn'l/ *adj* 1 situated on, happening on, or coming from the outside ○ *external forces* 2 for use on the outside of something 3 conveyed by outward appearance 4 outside an organization ■ **ex·ter·nals** *npl* outward appearances —**ex·ter·nal·ly** *adv*

ex·ter·nal·ize /ik stúrn'l ìz/ (-ized, -iz·ing) *vt* 1 express feelings in a visible or perceptible way 2 attribute something to external causes —**ex·ter·nal·i·za·tion** /ik stúrn'li záysh'n/ *n*

ex·tinct /ik stíngkt/ *adj* 1 having no members of a species or family still living 2 no longer in existence ○ *an extinct civilization* 3 describes a volcano that no longer erupts —**ex·tinc·tion** *n* ◊ See note at **dead**

ex·tin·guish /ik stíng gwish/ *vt* 1 put out a fire or light 2 put an end to or destroy

somebody or something —**ex·tin·guish·er** *n*

ex·tir·pate /ékstər pàyt/ (-pat·ed, -pat·ing) *vt* completely remove or destroy something undesirable *(fml)* —**ex·tir·pa·tion** /ékstər páysh'n/ *n* —**ex·tir·pa·tive** *adj*

ex·tol /ik stól/ (-tolled, -tol·ling), **ex·toll** *vt* praise enthusiastically —**ex·tol·ment** *n*

ex·tort /ik stáwrt/ *vt* obtain by force or threats

ex·tor·tion /ik stáwrsh'n/ *n* the act of obtaining something by force or threats —**ex·tor·tion·ate** *adj* —**ex·tor·tion·er** *n*

ex·tra /ékstrə/ *adj* 1 added over and above the usual or necessary amount or number 2 more and better ■ *adv* exceptionally ■ *pron* more ■ *n* 1 something additional 2 an actor with a minor nonspeaking part in a movie 3 a special edition of a newspaper

extra- *prefix* beyond or outside something ○ *extraterrestrial* ○ *extracurricular*

ex·tract *vt* /ik strákt/ 1 pull something out 2 obtain something from a source 3 get something by force 4 copy or remove a passage from a text or movie 5 derive pleasure from something 6 obtain a substance by an industrial or chemical process ■ *n* /ék stràkt/ 1 a passage taken from a text or movie 2 a purified concentrated substance ○ *vanilla extract* —**ex·tract·or** *n*

ex·trac·tion /ik stráksh'n/ *n* 1 the process of extracting something 2 the removal of a tooth 3 ethnic origin

ex·tra·cur·ric·u·lar /èkstrə kə ríkyələr/ *adj* happening or done outside the normal school curriculum

ex·tra·dite /ékstrə dìt/ (-dit·ed, -dit·ing) *vt* hand over somebody accused of a crime to a different legal authority —**ex·tra·di·tion** /èkstrə dísh'n/ *n*

ex·tra·ju·di·cial /èkstrə joo dísh'l/ *adj* 1 outside normal legal proceedings 2 outside a court's jurisdiction

ex·tra·mar·i·tal /èkstrə mérrit'l/ *adj* outside marriage

ex·tra·mu·ral /èkstrə myóorəl/ *adj* 1 outside the usual course of study 2 outside the walls or boundaries of a place or organization

ex·tra·ne·ous /ik stráynee əss/ *adj* 1 not relevant or essential 2 not essential —**ex·tra·ne·ous·ly** *adv* —**ex·tra·ne·ous·ness** *n*

ex·tra·or·di·naire /èkstrə awrd'n áir, ik stràwd'n-/ *adj* outstanding *(after nouns)* ○ *a piano player extraordinaire*

ex·traor·di·nar·y /ik stráwrd'n èrree, èkstrə áwrd'n-/ *adj* 1 unusually excellent or strange 2 additional and having a special purpose —**ex·traor·di·nar·i·ly** *adv* —**ex·traor·di·nar·i·ness** *n*

ex·trap·o·late /ik stráppə làyt/ (-lat·ed, -lat·ing) *vti* infer information from known facts —**ex·trap·o·la·tion** /ik stràppə láysh'n/ *n*

ex·tra·sen·so·ry   **per·cep·tion** /èkstrə sènsəree-/ *n* an awareness beyond the normal senses

ex·tra·ter·res·tri·al /èkstrə tə réstree əl/ *adj* existing outside the Earth ■ *n* an alien from space

ex·tra·ter·ri·to·ri·al /èkstrə teri táwree əl/ *adj* outside a territorial boundary —**ex·tra·ter·ri·to·ri·al·ly** *adv*

ex·trav·a·gance /ik strávvəgonss/, **ex·trav·a·gan·cy** /-gonssee/ (*pl* -**cies**) *n* 1 wasteful spending 2 an expensive thing

ex·trav·a·gant /ik strávvəgənt/ *adj* 1 spending too much 2 beyond what is reasonable ○ *an extravagant claim* 3 unreasonably high in price —**ex·trav·a·gant·ly** *adv* —**ex·trav·a·gant·ness** *n*

ORIGIN Extravagant derives from a medieval Latin word formed from Latin elements meaning "outside, beyond" and "wander." The second element is also the source of English *vagabond*, *vagrant*, and *vagary*. At first **extravagant** meant "divergent, irrelevant" and "strange, unsuitable." The connection with expenditure did not develop until the early 18C.

ex·trav·a·gan·za /ik strávvə gánzə/ *n* 1 a lavish entertainment 2 a spectacular display

~~extravagent~~ incorrect spelling of **extravagant**

ex·tra·vert *n*, *adj* PSYCHOL = **extrovert**

ex·treme /ik streém/ *adj* 1 highest in degree or intensity 2 beyond what is reasonable 3 farthest out 4 very strict or severe ■ *n* 1 the furthest limit or highest degree 2 somebody or something representing each of the two ends of a scale ■ **ex·tremes** *npl* drastic measures —**ex·treme·ness** *n*

ex·treme·ly /ik streémlee/ *adv* very

ex·trem·ist /ik streémist/ *n* somebody who holds extreme opinions or supports extreme measures —**ex·trem·ism** *n* —**ex·trem·ist** *adj*

ex·trem·i·ty /ik strémmətee/ (*pl* -**ties**) *n* 1 the farthest point 2 the highest degree or greatest intensity of something 3 a condition of great danger or distress 4 a hand or foot (*often pl*)

~~extremly~~ incorrect spelling of **extremely**

ex·tri·cate /èkstri káyt/ (-**cat·ed**, -**cat·ing**) *vt* release with difficulty from a place or situation —**ex·tri·ca·tion** /èkstri káysh'n/ *n*

ex·trin·sic /ik strínsik, -zik/ *adj* 1 not essential 2 coming from outside ○ *extrinsic influences* —**ex·trin·si·cal·ly** *adv*

~~extrordinary~~ incorrect spelling of **extraordinary**

ex·tro·vert /èkstrə vùrt/, **ex·tra·vert** *n* an outgoing person —**ex·tro·ver·sion** /èkstrə vùrzh'n, èkstrə vúrzh'n/ *n*

ex·trude /ik stroód/ (-**trud·ed**, -**trud·ing**) *vt* 1 force something out 2 make something

by forcing a substance through a mold or nozzle —**ex·tru·sion** *n*

ex·u·ber·ant /ig zoóbərənt/ *adj* full of enthusiasm —**ex·u·ber·ance** *n* —**ex·u·ber·ant·ly** *adv*

ex·ude /ig zoód/ (-**ud·ed**, -**ud·ing**) *v* 1 *vt* display a particular quality in manner 2 *vti* release or be released slowly

ex·ult /ig zúlt/ *vi* 1 be very happy 2 be triumphant —**ex·ul·tant** *adj* —**ex·ul·tant·ly** *adv* —**ex·ul·ta·tion** /èksəl táysh'n, ègzəl-/ *n*

-ey *suffix* = **-y** 1

ey·as /î əss/ *n* a young hawk or falcon

Eyck /îk/, **Jan van** (1390?–1441) Flemish painter

eye /î/ *n* 1 the organ of vision 2 the visible part of the eye 3 the power of sight (*often pl*) 4 somebody's gaze or attention 5 a look or facial expression 6 the ability to judge or appreciate something 7 a point of view ○ *was lovely in her eyes* 8 a new shoot on a potato 9 a hole in a needle ■ *vt* (**eyed**, **eye·ing** *or* **ey·ing**) 1 look at inquisitively 2 *UK* ogle (*infml*) —**eyed** *adj* ◊ **see eye to eye (with)** have a similar outlook or viewpoint to ◊ **turn a blind eye (to)** pretend not to be aware of ◊ **with an eye to** having as a purpose or objective ◊ **with your eyes (wide) open** fully aware of all that is involved

eye·ball /î bàwl/ *n* the round mass of the eye

eye·brow /î bròw/ *n* 1 a line of hair above the eye socket 2 a bony ridge above the eye

eye can·dy /î–/ *n* something visually attractive but intellectually undemanding (*slang*)

eye·catch·ing *adj* attracting attention —**eye·catch·er** *n* —**eye·catch·ing·ly** *adv*

eye con·tact *n* the act of looking directly into somebody's eyes

eye·ful /î fòòl/ *n* an offensive term for somebody regarded as good-looking (*slang*)

eye·glass /î glàss/ *n* 1 a single lens for correcting vision 2 an eyepiece of an optical instrument ■ **eye·glass·es** *npl* sight-correcting or protective glasses (*fml*)

eye·lash /î làsh/ *n* a hair at the edge of the eyelid

eye·let /î lət/ *n* 1 a hole for a cord to fit through 2 a metal reinforcement for an eyelet 3 an ornamented hole in embroidery

eye·lid /î lìd/ *n* a fold of skin over the eye

eye·lin·er /î līnər/ *n* a cosmetic used to darken the edges of the eyelids

eye o·pen·er *n* 1 something revealing or surprising 2 an alcoholic drink that is taken in the morning —**eye-o·pen·ing** *adj*

eye patch *n* a covering worn over one eye

eye·piece /î pèess/ *n* the lens that the user looks through in an optical instrument

eye shad·ow *n* a cosmetic used to color the eyelids

eye·sight /î sìt/ *n* the ability to see

eye sock·et *n* the part of the skull containing the eye

eye·sore /í sàwr/ *n* an ugly sight

eye·strain /í stràyn/ *n* tiredness or irritation in the eyes

eye·tooth /í tòoth/ (*pl* **-teeth** /í tèeth/) *n* a canine tooth

eye·wash /í wòsh, í wàwsh/ *n* 1 a cleansing liquid for sore eyes 2 nonsense (*infml*)

eye·wear /í wàir/ *n* glasses and contact lenses

eye·wit·ness /í wítnəss/ *n* somebody who sees something happen

ey·rie *n* = aerie

E·ze·ki·el /i zéekee əl/ *n* the book of the Bible that tells the story of the Jews' exile in Babylon in the 6C BC, traditionally attributed to Ezekiel, a Hebrew priest and prophet

⨍ e-zine /ée zéen/ *n* a website with magazine-style content and layout

Ez·ra /ézzrə/ *n* the book of the Bible that tells the story of the rebuilding of the Jewish state in Palestine 536–432 BC after the Babylonian captivity, traditionally attributed to Ezra, a Hebrew prophet

F

f¹ (*pl* **f's**), **F** (*pl* **F's** *or* **Fs**) *n* the 6th letter of the English alphabet

f² *symbol* 1 focal length 2 function

f³ *abbr* forte² *adv* (*musical direction*)

F¹ *abbr* 1 Fahrenheit 2 fail (*as a grade on a piece of work*) 3 farad 4 female

F² (*pl* **F's** *or* **Fs**) *n* the 4th note in the musical scale of C major

f. *abbr* 1 folio 2 following (*page*) 3 foul

⨍ F2F *abbr* face-to-face (*in e-mails*)

fa *n* a syllable used in singing the 4th note of a scale

FAA *n* the federal agency responsible for the aviation system in the United States. Full form **Federal Aviation Administration**

Fa·ber·gé /fàbber zháy/, **Peter Carl** (1846–1920) Russian goldsmith and jeweler

fa·ble /fáyb'l/ *n* 1 a story that teaches a lesson, especially with animals as characters 2 a legend 3 a false account 4 myths and legends collectively ■ *vt* (**-bled, -bling**) tell in fable

fa·bled /fáyb'ld/ *adj* 1 legendary 2 fictitious

fab·ric /fábbrik/ *n* 1 cloth 2 the fundamental structure or nature of something

fab·ri·cate /fábbri kàyt/ (**-cat·ed, -cat·ing**) *vt* 1 construct something from different parts 2 make up something untrue 3 forge a signature or document —**fab·ri·ca·tion** /fàbbri káysh'n/ *n*

fab·u·lous /fábbyələss/ *adj* 1 excellent (*infml*) 2 amazing 3 typical of or described in a fable —**fab·u·lous·ly** *adv* —**fab·u·lous·ness** *n*

fa·çade /fə saád/, **fa·cade** *n* 1 the front surface of a building 2 a deceptive appearance

face *n* 1 the front of the human head 2 a person being looked at (*infml*) ○ *familiar faces in the audience* 3 a facial expression or look ○ *Why the long face?* 4 an unpleasant facial expression ○ *pulling faces at people* 5 the way something looks 6 the outward appearance of somebody or something ○ *put on a brave face* ○ *the Internet changing the face of business* 7 personal reputation ○ *lose face* 8 a surface of an object presented in a particular direction ○ *the faces of a gem* 9 a visible or exposed surface of something such as a building or cliff 10 a dial on a clock or instrument ■ *v* (**faced, fac·ing**) 1 *vti* turn toward a particular person, thing, or direction 2 *vt* be in a position opposite 3 *vt* meet or confront directly ○ *forced to face the enemy* 4 *vt* accept the unpleasant facts about 5 *vt* have to contend with 6 *vt* be encountered by ○ *the problems facing them* 7 *vt* have the prospect of experiencing something unpleasant ○ *could face a jail sentence* —**face·a·ble** *adj* ◊ **fly in the face of** defy ◊ **in (the) face of** when confronted by or in spite of something (*slang*)

□ **face down** *vt* confront and prevail against

□ **face off** *vti* in some games, begin play by dropping the puck or ball between two opposing players

□ **face up to** *vt* 1 accept the unpleasant truth of 2 confront bravely

face card *n* a king, queen, or jack

face-cloth /fáyss klòth/ *n* a washcloth

face-down /fáyss dòwn/ *n* a determined confrontation between adversaries

face·less /fáyssləss/ *adj* anonymous and characterless —**face·less·ness** *n*

face-lift /fáyss lìft/ *n* 1 a surgical operation to tighten the skin of the face 2 a sprucing up

face mask *n* a covering for the face to protect or disguise it

face-off *n* 1 in some games, a beginning of play in which the referee drops the puck or ball between two opposing players 2 a confrontation

face pack *n* a cosmetic preparation for cleansing the pores of the face

face pow·der *n* cosmetic powder for the face

face-sav·ing *adj* intended to preserve somebody's reputation or dignity —**face-sav·er** *n*

fac·et /fássət/ *n* 1 an aspect of something 2 any surface of a cut gemstone —**fac·et·ed** *adj*

face time *n* 1 time spent on television 2 extra time at a place of employment

fa·ce·tious /fə seeshəss/ *adj* **1** supposed to be funny but silly or inappropriate **2** not in earnest or to be taken seriously —**fa·ce·tious·ly** *adv* —**fa·ce·tious·ness** *n*

face-to-face *adj*, *adv* **1** in each other's presence **2** directly confronting something unpleasant

face val·ue *n* **1** the value that is stated on something such as a note or coin **2** the seeming worth or meaning of something

fa·cial /fáysh'l/ *adj* on or of the face ■ *n* a beauty treatment for the face

fac·ile /fáss'l/ *adj* **1** easy to do **2** fluent but insincere **3** superficial in thought or feeling **4** working easily —**fac·ile·ly** *adv* —**fac·ile·ness** *n*

fa·cil·i·tate /fə sílli tàyt/ (-tat·ed, -tat·ing) *vt* make easy or easier to do —**fa·cil·i·ta·tion** /fə sìlli táysh'n/ *n* —**fa·cil·i·ta·tor** *n*

fa·cil·i·ty /fə sílletee/ *n* (*pl* -ties) **1** skill **2** something designed to provide a particular service or meet a particular need *(often pl)* ○ *a sports facility* ■ **fa·cil·i·ties** *npl* a toilet

fac·ing /fáyssing/ *n* a piece of fabric sewn inside a garment to neaten or decorate the edges

~~facism~~ incorrect spelling of **fascism**

fac·sim·i·le /fak símmələe/ *n* **1** an exact copy **2** a fax *(dated)*

fact *n* something known to be true ◇ **in (actual) fact** in reality

fact-find·ing *adj* for gathering information —**fact-find·er** *n*

fac·tion[1] /fáksh'n/ *n* **1** a dissenting minority within a larger group **2** conflict within a group —**fac·tion·al** *adj*

fac·tion[2] /fáksh'n/ *n* **1** writing or filmmaking that dramatizes history **2** a dramatized work based on real life

-faction *suffix* production ○ *putrefaction*

fac·tious /fákshəss/ *adj* of or causing conflict within a group —**fac·tious·ly** *adv* —**fac·tious·ness** *n*

fac·ti·tious /fak tíshəss/ *adj* **1** contrived and insincere **2** artificial or invented *(fml)*

fac·toid /fák tòyd/ *n* **1** an unreliable piece of information **2** a single fact

fac·tor /fáktər/ *n* **1** something that influences or contributes to a result **2** one of two or more quantities that when multiplied together give a particular quantity ○ *3 and 5 are factors of 15.* **3** an amount by which something is multiplied ○ *increased by a factor of three* **4** somebody who acts as an agent ■ *v* **1** *vt* calculate the factors of a given quantity **2** *vi* act as a factor ☐ **factor in** *vt* take into account

fac·tor·age /fáktərij/ *n* **1** money charged by a factor **2** the work of a factor

fac·to·ri·al /fak táwree əl/ *n* (*symbol* !) the result of multiplying a number by every whole number between itself and 1 inclusive

fac·to·ry /fáktəree/ (*pl* -ries) *n* a building where goods are manufactured

fac·to·ry floor *n* an area of a factory where manufacturing takes place

fac·to·ry ship *n* a fishing vessel equipped to process its catch

fac·to·tum /fak tótəm/ *n* somebody who does many jobs

ORIGIN **Factotum** derives from a Latin instruction "do everything!". In medieval Latin this was used in stereotypical names such as *Magister Factotum* "Mr. Do-Everything" and *Johannes Factotum* "John Do-Everything," and it is in these forms that **factotum** first appears in English in the mid-16C. The first ordinary noun use is recorded in the early 17C.

fact sheet *n* a collection of information about a product

fac·tu·al /fák choo əl, fákchəl/ *adj* **1** containing facts **2** truthful —**fac·tu·al·ly** *adv*

fac·ul·ty /fák'ltee/ (*pl* -ties) *n* **1** a mental power **2** an ability **3** the teaching staff at a school, college, or university **4** a division of a university dealing with a particular subject

fad *n* a short-lived fashion —**fad·dism** *n*

fad·dish /fáddish/ *adj* inclined to embrace fads

fade (fad·ed, fad·ing) *v* **1** *vti* lose or make lose brightness, color, or loudness gradually **2** *vi* become tired **3** *vi* disappear slowly **4** *vi* in football, drop back to pass *(refers to the quarterback)*

fade-in *n* a gradual introduction of sound or an image

fade-out *n* **1** a gradual decrease in loudness or brightness **2** a weakening of a TV or radio signal

FAE *abbr* fuel-air explosive

fa·er·ie /fáy əree, fáiree/, **fa·er·y** (*pl* -ies) *n* *(literary)* **1** fairyland **2** a fairy

Faer·oe Is·lands ▶ Faroe Islands

fag·ot /fággət/, **fag·got** *n* a bundle of sticks for firewood

Fahd /faad/ (b. 1923) king of Saudi Arabia (1982–)

Fah·ren·heit /férrən hìt/ *adj* (*symbol* **F**) of a temperature scale at which water freezes at 32°F and boils at 212°F under normal atmospheric conditions ◇ Celsius

ORIGIN The **Fahrenheit** scale is named for the German physicist Gabriel Fahrenheit (1686– 1736), who devised it.

fa·ience /fī́ aàns, fay-/, **fa·ïence** *n* pottery with a colored opaque metallic glaze

ORIGIN **Faience** derives from the French name for the town of Faenza in N Italy.

fail /fayl/ *v* **1** *vi* be unsuccessful **2** *vi* be unable or unwilling to do something ○ *failed to see what all the fuss was about* **3** *vti* not pass an exam or course **4** *vt* judge a student not good enough to pass an exam or course **5** *vi* stop functioning or growing **6** *vi* collapse financially **7** *vt* let somebody down by not doing what is expected or needed ◊ **without fail** for certain

fail·ing /fáyling/ *n* a shortcoming ■ *prep* without the occurrence of ◊ See note at **flaw**

fail-safe *adj* designed to switch to a safe condition if there is a fault or failure

⚡ **fail-soft** *adj* describes electronic equipment that can operate at a reduced level after a component or power fails

fail·ure /fáylyər/ *n* **1** lack of success, or an unsuccessful attempt **2** somebody or something that fails **3** the breakdown of something ○ *engine failure*

fain /fayn/ *(archaic) adv* happily or eagerly ■ *adj* **1** eager **2** compelled

faint /faynt/ *adj* **1** dim to the sight or hearing **2** unenthusiastic ○ *damn with faint praise* **3** dizzy and weak **4** slight or remote ○ *a faint chance* ■ *vi* lose consciousness briefly ■ *n* a sudden loss of consciousness —**faint·ly** *adv* —**faint·ness** *n*

SPELLCHECK Do not confuse the spelling of **faint** and **feint** ("a deceptive action"), which sound similar.

faint-heart·ed *adj* timid or cowardly —**faint-heart·ed·ly** *adv* —**faint-heart·ed·ness** *n* ◊ See note at **cowardly**

fair[1] /fair/ *adj* **1** reasonable or unbiased **2** according to the rules ○ *fair and free elections* **3** not stormy or cloudy **4** pleasing to look at **5** not blocked ○ *a fair view of the mountains* **6** describes light-colored hair or skin, or somebody with this **7** sizeable ○ *a fair number of responses* **8** no more than average **9** better than acceptable ○ *a fair understanding of the problems* **10** unsullied ■ *adv* **1** properly **2** directly —**fair·ness** *n* ◊ **fair and square** justly, fairly, or according to the rules

SPELLCHECK Do not confuse the spelling of **fair** and **fare** ("the cost of travel"), which sound similar.

fair[2] /fair/ *n* **1** an event with farm competitions and amusements **2** a large market for buying and selling goods **3** a commercial exhibition **4** a sale to raise money

Fair·banks /fáir bàngks/ town in E Alaska. Pop. 33,295 (1998).

fair cop·y *n* an unmarked corrected version of a document

fair game *n* a legitimate target

fair·ground /fáir gròwnd/ *n* a place where a fair is held

fair-haired *adj* with light-colored hair

fair-haired boy *n* somebody who is the favorite of a person or a group *(infml)*

fair·ly /fáirlee/ *adv* **1** honestly or justly **2** moderately **3** considerably

fair-mind·ed *adj* impartial —**fair-mind·ed·ly** *adv* —**fair-mind·ed·ness** *n*

fair·ness /fáirnəss/ *n* **1** the quality of being fair **2** beauty

fair play *n* proper conduct or play

fair sex *n* women *(literary)*

fair·way /fáir wày/ *n* a stretch of grass between a golf tee and the green

fair·y /fáiree/ *(pl* **-ies***) n* a small imaginary being with magical powers

fair·y god·moth·er *n* **1** a fairy who gives help to a specific person **2** somebody very helpful to another

fair·y·land /fáiree lànd/ *n* **1** the imaginary land of fairies **2** an enchanting place

fair·y tale *n* **1** a story about fairies or imaginary happenings **2** an unlikely explanation

fair·y-tale *adj* **1** from a fairy tale **2** very fortunate, happy, or beautiful

Fai·sal /físs'l/ (1905–75) king of Saudi Arabia (1964–75)

fait ac·com·pli /fèt ə kom plee, fàyt ə koN plee/ *(pl* **faits ac·com·plis** /*pronunc. same*/*) n* something already done or decided and unalterable

faith *n* **1** belief or trust **2** a religion or religious group **3** trust in God ◊ **on faith** without demanding proof

faith·ful /fáythfəl/ *adj* **1** with unwavering belief **2** consistently loyal **3** not adulterous or promiscuous **4** conscientious **5** in accordance with the truth ○ *a faithful account of the events* ■ *also* **Faith·ful** *npl* religious believers —**faith·ful·ly** *adv* —**faith·ful·ness** *n*

faith·less /fáythləss/ *adj* **1** disloyal **2** untrustworthy —**faith·less·ly** *adv*—**faith·less·ness** *n*

fa·ji·tas /fə heétəss/ *npl* a Mexican dish of strips of grilled meat in a soft flour tortilla

fake *n* somebody or something that is not genuine ■ *adj* not genuine ■ *v* (**faked, fak·ing**) **1** *vt* falsely present as genuine **2** *vti* pretend feeling or knowledge —**fak·er·y** *n*

fa·kir /fə keér/ *n* a religious Muslim, especially a Sufi, who lives by begging

~~falacy~~ incorrect spelling of **fallacy**

fa·la·fel /fə laáf'l/, **fe·la·fel** *n* a deep-fried ball of ground chickpeas

fal·con /fálkən, fáwl-/ *n* **1** a fast-flying bird of prey **2** a hawk trained to hunt

fal·con·ry /fálkənree, fáwl-/ *n* the training and use of falcons for hunting —**fal·con·er** *n*

Falk·land Is·lands /fáwklkland-/ group of islands and British dependency in the South Atlantic Ocean. Pop. 2,317 (1995).

fall /fawl/ *vi* (**fell** /fel/, **fall·en** /fáwlən/) **1** move downward by the force of gravity **2** drop or be lowered ○ *when the curtain falls* **3** come down suddenly from an upright position, especially by accident **4** become less or lower ○ *prices fell* **5** lose or be defeated militarily or politically **6** hang down **7** take place as if falling and enveloping something ○ *Night fell.* **8** display disappointment ○ *Her face fell.* **9** come to rest by chance ○ *His gaze fell on a book.* **10** enter a particular state or condition ○ *fell silent* **11** sin *(archaic)* ■ *n* **1** an act of falling down **2** something that has fallen ○ *a heavy fall of snow* **3** a distance down **4** the season between summer and winter **5** a waterfall *(often pl, often in place names)* ◇ **fall flat** fail to have the intended effect ◇ **fall foul** *or* **afoul of** come into conflict with ◇ **fall short** be less than is needed ◇ **fall short of** fail to meet a desired standard

□ **fall back** *vi* retreat

□ **fall back on** *or* **upon** *vt* have recourse to

□ **fall behind** *vi* fail to keep up

□ **fall for** *vt* **1** fall in love with **2** be duped by

□ **fall in** *vi* **1** form ranks **2** cave in

□ **fall in with** *vt* meet and join

□ **fall off** *vi* decline in number or quantity

□ **fall on** *or* **upon** *vt* attack *(literary)*

□ **fall out** *vi* quarrel

□ **fall through** *vi* fail to work out successfully

□ **fall to** *vt* be the duty or responsibility of

Fal·la /fáa ya, faál ya/, **Manuel de** (1876–1946) Spanish composer and pianist

fal·la·cious /fə láyshəss/ *adj* **1** containing a mistaken belief **2** deceptive —**fal·la·cious·ly** *adv* —**fal·la·cious·ness** *n*

fal·la·cy /fálləssee/ (*pl* -**cies**) *n* **1** a mistaken belief or idea **2** an invalid argument

fall·a·way /fáwlə wày/ *adj* in basketball, done while moving away from the basket

fall·back /fáwl bàk/ *n* **1** a replacement or alternative **2** a retreat or withdrawal —**fall·back** *adj*

fall·en an·gel *n* **1** an angel cast out of heaven **2** a bond with a lowered rating

fall·en wom·an *n* a woman who has had extramarital sex *(literary)*

fall guy *n (slang)* **1** somebody who is easily deceived **2** a scapegoat

fal·li·ble /fálləb'l/ *adj* tending to make mistakes —**fal·li·bil·i·ty** /fàllə bíllətee/ *n*

fall·ing-out (*pl* **fall·ings-out** *or* **fall·ings-outs**) *n* a quarrel

fall·ing star *n* a brief streak of light in the night sky created by a meteor

fall line *n* **1** an imaginary line between highland and lowland regions **2** a natural route of descent between two points on a hill

fall-off /fáwl àwf, -òf/ *n* a decrease, as in prices or demand

fal·lo·pi·an tube /fə lṓpee ən-/, **Fal·lo·pi·an tube** *n* each of two tubes through which a mammal's eggs pass from an ovary to the womb

ORIGIN The **fallopian tubes** are named for the Italian anatomist Gabriele Fallopio (1523–62), who is reputed to have discovered them.

fall·out /fáwl òwt/ *n* **1** radioactive particles that settle to Earth after a nuclear explosion or leak **2** incidental consequences, especially undesirable ones

fall·out shel·ter *n* a shelter from nuclear war

fal·low[1] /fállō/ *adj* **1** left unseeded after plowing **2** currently inactive

fal·low[2] /fállō/ *adj* of a yellowish brown color —**fal·low** *n*

fal·low deer *n* a deer of Europe and Asia, the male of which has broad flattened antlers and a spotted coat in summer

false /fawls/ (**fals·er**, **fals·est**) *adj* **1** not true or factual **2** mistaken **3** artificial **4** deliberately deceptive ○ *false promises* —**false·ly** *adv* —**false·ness** *n*

false a·larm *n* **1** a needless alarm **2** something causing needless worry

false dawn *n* **1** the light that occurs just before sunrise **2** a favorable sign whose expectations are unfulfilled

false·hood /fáwls hòod/ *n* **1** a lie **2** the telling of lies ◊ See note at **lie**

false im·pris·on·ment *n* illegal imprisonment

false move *n* an action showing an error of timing or judgment

false pre·ten·ses *npl* deception in order to gain something

false start *n* **1** an abandoned start of a race **2** an unsuccessful start

fal·set·to /fawl séttō/ (*pl* -**tos**) *n* **1** a high singing voice used by men **2** a singer who uses falsetto —**fal·set·to** *adv*

fal·si·fy /fáwlsə fī/ (-**fied**, -**fies**) *vt* **1** alter fraudulently **2** misrepresent —**fal·si·fi·ca·tion** /fàwlsəfī káysh'n/ *n*

fal·si·ty /fáwlsətee/ (*pl* -**ties**) *n* **1** the fact or state of being untrue **2** something untrue

fal·ter /fáwltər/ *v* **1** *vi* lose confidence and become hesitant **2** *vi* begin to fail **3** *vi* stumble **4** *vti* speak or say hesitantly —**fal·ter·ing** *adj* ◊ See note at **hesitate**

fame *n* the condition of being very well known

famed *adj* famous

fa·mil·ial /fə míllyəl/ *adj* of a family or families

fa·mil·iar /fə míllyər/ *adj* **1** often encountered **2** thoroughly acquainted with something **3** friendly, often to the point of impertinence ■ *n* an intimate friend *(fml)* —**fa·mil·iar·ly** *adv* —**fa·mil·iar·ness** *n*

ORIGIN Familiar came through French from a Latin word meaning "of the family."

fa·mil·iar·i·ty /fə míllee árrətee/ *n* **1** thorough knowledge **2** intimacy **3** familiar quality **4** (*pl* **fa·mil·iar·i·ties**) an unwelcome intimacy *(dated)*

fa·mil·iar·ize /fə míllyə rìz/ (-**ized**, -**iz·ing**) *vt* provide with the necessary information or experience —**fa·mil·iar·i·za·tion** /fə mìllyəri záysh'n/ *n*

~~**familier**~~ incorrect spelling of **familiar**

fam·i·ly /fámməlee/ n (pl **-lies**) 1 a group of people who live together, usually consisting of parents and children 2 a group of relatives 3 the other members of somebody's family o *spending time with her family* 4 a child or set of children born to somebody o *thinking of starting a family* 5 a group with something in common 6 a group of related languages 7 a group of related organisms ■ adj 1 used by a family 2 appropriate for children o *family viewing*

fam·i·ly court n a court dealing with families

fam·i·ly doc·tor n a doctor who treats general medical problems

fam·i·ly man n a man fond of family life

fam·i·ly name n a surname

fam·i·ly plan·ning n birth control

fam·i·ly room n a room in a home for family activities

fam·i·ly tree n a chart showing the generations of a family

fam·ine /fámmin/ n 1 a severe food shortage resulting in widespread hunger or starvation 2 a severe shortage

fam·ish /fámmish/ vti be or make extremely hungry —**fam·ished** adj

fa·mous /fáyməss/ adj 1 very well known 2 excellent (dated) —**fa·mous·ly** adv

fan[1] n 1 an electrical device with rotating blades for moving air 2 a hand-held device waved to cool the face ■ vt (**fanned, fan·ning**) 1 blow a current of air across something 2 stir up emotions 3 in baseball or hockey, miss hitting the ball or puck (slang)

ORIGIN The cooling **fan** is recorded from the mid-16C. Before that a **fan** was always a device for winnowing grain, which is the meaning of the Latin word from which it derives. **Fan** "enthusiast" is completely unrelated. It is a shortening of **fanatic**.

□ **fan out** vti spread in a fan shape

fan[2] n an enthusiast for a particular person or activity

fa·nat·ic /fə náttik/ n 1 somebody with extreme or irrational beliefs 2 somebody with an obsessive interest in something ■ adj also **fa·nat·i·cal** holding extreme or irrational beliefs or enthusiasms —**fa·nat·i·cal·ly** adv —**fa·nat·i·cism** /fə nátti sìzzəm/ n

ORIGIN Fanatic came via French from a Latin word meaning "inspired by a god, frenzied" and literally "of a temple."

fan belt n a belt that turns the cooling fan on a motor vehicle's engine

fan·ci·er /fánsee ər/ n somebody with an interest in breeding a particular plant or animal o *a pigeon fancier*

fan·ci·ful /fánsif'l/ adj 1 imaginary 2 imaginative and impractical —**fan·ci·ful·ly** adv

fan club n an organization for fans of a celebrity or performer

fan·cy /fánsee/ adj (**-ci·er, -ci·est**) 1 elaborate and ornate 2 intricately and skillfully performed o *fancy footwork* 3 describes food items of superior quality 4 expensive o *fancy prices* ■ vt (**-cied, -cies**) 1 suppose 2 imagine ■ n (pl **-cies**) 1 a sudden liking 2 an unfounded belief 3 playful imaginativeness —**fan·ci·ly** adv —**fan·ci·ness** n

fan·cy-free adj carefree

fan·cy·work /fánsee wùrk/ n decorative needlework

fan·dan·go /fan dáng gō/ (pl **-gos**) n 1 a Spanish or Latin American dance for a couple, in triple time 2 the music for a fandango

fan·fare /fán fàir/ n 1 a trumpet flourish 2 a showy display to announce or publicize something

fang n 1 a canine tooth 2 a snake's tooth —**fanged** adj

fan·light /fán lìt/ n a window above a door, traditionally semicircular

fan mail n letters from fans

fan·ny /fánnee/ (pl **-nies**) n the buttocks (slang)

fan·ny pack n a pouch for valuables strapped around the waist

fan·tab·u·lous /fan tábbyələss/ adj excellent (humorous)

fan·ta·sia /fan táyzhə, fan táyzhee ə/ n a musical composition in a free and improvisatory style

fan·ta·size /fántə sìz/ (**-sized, -si·zing**) vti imagine something pleasurable —**fan·ta·sist** n

fan·tas·tic /fan tástik/, **fan·tas·ti·cal** /-ik'l/ adj 1 excellent 2 incredible but real or true 3 imaginary 4 enormous 5 bizarre in appearance ■ interj expresses pleasure (infml) —**fan·tas·ti·cal·ly** adv

fan·ta·sy /fántəssee/ (pl **-sies**) n 1 the creative power of the imagination 2 a creation of the imagination 3 an impractical idea 4 a genre of fiction with imaginary worlds and supernatural events 5 a fantasia

ORIGIN Fantasy goes back to a Greek word meaning "appearance, imagination," formed from a verb meaning "show, make visible." It entered English through French in the 14C. By the 15C a contracted form appeared, and this developed a different range of meanings as **fancy**.

fan·zine /fán zèen/ n a fan club magazine

FAQ, FAQs abbr frequently asked questions

far adv (**far·ther** /fáarthər/ or **fur·ther** /fúrthər/, **far·thest** /fáarthəst/ or **fur·thest** /fúrthəst/) 1 a long way off 2 a long time off 3 much or many ○ *far more difficult* ■ *adj* (**far·ther** *or* **fur·ther**, **far·thest** *or* **fur·thest**) **1** remote in space or time ○ *the far distance* **2** more distant ○ *in the far corner* ◊ **far and away** without a doubt and by a large margin ◊ **far and wide** covering a great distance ◊ **far from** by no means ○ *far from over* ◊ **so far** up to this moment

far·ad /fárrəd, fá ràd/ *n* (*symbol* **F**) a unit of electrical capacitance

ORIGIN Farad is shortened from the name of Michael Faraday.

Far·a·day /fárrə dày/, **Michael** (1791–1867) British physicist and chemist

far·a·way /fáarə wày/ *adj* **1** remote **2** appearing dreamy or absent-minded

farce *n* **1** an absurd situation **2** a comic play or style of drama with absurd events

ORIGIN Farce comes from a French word meaning literally "stuffing, forcemeat," which was adopted into English with this sense in the late medieval period. The French word had already developed a metaphorical use "comic interlude," and this was separately taken into English in the early 16C. This sense arose through the practice of introducing comic interludes into religious plays in the Middle Ages.

far·ci·cal /fáarsik'l/ *adj* **1** absurd and confused **2** in the style of farce —**far·ci·cal·ly** *adv*

fare /fair/ *n* **1** an amount paid for somebody to travel **2** a paying passenger **3** food provided ■ *vi* (**fared**, **far·ing**) **1** manage in doing something ○ *How did she fare in the exam?* **2** turn out in a specified way **3** go on a trip ◊ See note at **fair**

Far East the countries of East Asia, sometimes also of Southeast Asia (*dated*) —**Far-East·ern** *adj*

~~Farenheit~~ incorrect spelling of **Fahrenheit**

fare·well /fair wél/ *interj* goodbye (*literary*) ■ *n* an expression of parting good wishes —**fare·well** *adj*

far-fetched *adj* unconvincing

far-flung *adj* **1** widespread **2** remote

Far·go /fáargō/ city in SE North Dakota. Pop. 86,718 (1998).

fa·ri·na /fə réenə/ *n* flour or meal

far·i·na·ceous /fàrrə náyshəss/ *adj* containing starch

farm *n* **1** an area of agricultural land with its buildings **2** a place where particular animals or crops are raised commercially (*usually in combination*) ○ *a trout farm* ■ *v* **1** *vti* use land for agriculture **2** *vt* rear animals, birds, or fish commercially —**farm·ing** *n*

farm·er /fáarmər/ *n* an owner or operator of a farm

farm·ers' mar·ket *n* a market for farm produce

farm hand *n* a hired worker on a farm

farm·house /fáarm hòwss/ (*pl* **-hous·es** /-hòwzəz/) *n* a house on a farm

farm·land /fáarm lànd/ *n* land suitable or used for farming

farm·stead /fáarm stèd/ *n* a farm and its buildings

farm·yard /fáarm yàard/ *n* a yard beside farm buildings

Far·oe Is·lands /fáirō-/, **Faer·oe Is·lands** group of islands and Danish territory in the North Atlantic Ocean. Cap. Tórshavn. Pop. 45,661 (2001).

far-off *adj* remote

Fa·rouk I /fə róok/ (1920–65) king of Egypt (1936–52)

far-out *adj* unusual (*slang*) —**far-out·ness** *n*

far·ra·go /fə ráa gô, -ráy-/ (*pl* **-gos** *or* **-goes**) *n* a jumble

Far·ra·gut /fárrəgət/, **David** (1801–70) US naval officer

Far·ra·khan /fárrə kàan/, **Louis Abdul** (*b.* 1933) US religious leader, leader of the Nation of Islam

far-reach·ing *adj* extensive in effect

far·row /fárrō/ *vi* give birth to piglets ■ *n* a litter of pigs

Far·si /fáarsee/ *n* the official language of Iran —**Far·si** *adj*

far·sight·ed /faar sítəd/ *adj* **1** unable to see nearby objects clearly **2** *also* **far·see·ing** able to make sound judgments regarding the future **3** *also* **far·see·ing** able to see a long way —**far·sight·ed·ly** *adv* —**far·sight·ed·ness** *n*

far·ther /fáarthər/ *adv* to a greater distance or extent ■ *adj* more distant —**far·ther·most** *adj*

far·thest /fáarthəst/ *adv* to the greatest distance or extent ■ *adj* most distant

far·thing /fáarthing/ *n* a former British coin worth one quarter of the old penny

far·thin·gale /fáarthing gàyl/ *n* a structure worn to hold out a skirt in the late 16C and early 17C

fas·ci·nate /fássə nàyt/ (**-nat·ed**, **-nat·ing**) *v* **1** *vti* captivate **2** *vt* immobilize, especially through fear —**fas·ci·nat·ing** *adj* —**fas·ci·nat·ing·ly** *adv* —**fas·ci·na·tion** /fàssə náysh'n/ *n*

fas·cism /fá shìzzəm/, **Fas·cism** *n* dictatorial government, especially combined with extreme nationalism —**fas·cist** *n*, *adj*

ORIGIN Fascism was adopted from Italian *fascismo*, the principles and organization of the *fascisti*. These were members of the *Partita Nazionale Fascista* "National Fascist Party," an Italian nationalist organization formed in 1919 by Benito Mussolini (1883–1945), initially to oppose communism. The party controlled Italy from 1922 to 1943, with Mussolini as dictator from 1925. The name was formed from *fascio* meaning "bundle" and also "group," which came from Latin *fascis* "bundle." In ancient Rome, bundles (*fasces*) of rods tied to an ax with a red string were a symbol of the total power of senior magistrates; the *fasces* were adopted as an emblem by the Italian Fascists.

fash·ion /fásh'n/ *n* **1** style in clothing or appearance **2** the current style in clothing, furnishings, or appearance ○ *no longer in fashion* **3** a manner of behaving or doing something ■ *vt* **1** give shape or form to **2** form by influence or training ○ *attitudes fashioned by his grandparents* ◇ **after a fashion** in some way but not very well

fash·ion·a·ble /fásh'nəb'l/ *adj* **1** currently popular ○ *fashionable ideas* **2** associated with rich, famous, or glamorous people ○ *a fashionable nightspot* —**fash·ion·a·bly** *adv*

fash·ion house *n* a business that designs, makes, and sells fashionable clothes

~~fashon~~ incorrect spelling of **fashion**

~~fasinating~~ incorrect spelling of **fascinating**

fast[1] *adj* **1** acting or moving rapidly **2** done quickly **3** running ahead of time ○ *My watch is ten minutes fast.* **4** conducive to great speed ○ *a fast road* **5** describes photographic film or equipment with a short exposure **6** pursuing excitement and pleasure (*infml*) ○ *in with a fast crowd* **7** not liable to fade or change color **8** strong, close, and loyal (*literary*) ○ *fast friends* **9** firmly fastened or shut ■ *adv* **1** rapidly **2** immediately or in quick succession **3** ahead of the correct time **4** soundly ○ *fast asleep* **5** firmly so as to prevent movement ○ *hold fast*

fast[2] *vi* abstain from food ■ *n* a period of fasting —**fast·er** *n*

fast-act·ing *adj* soon taking effect

fast·back /fást bàk/ *n* a car with a back that forms a continuous curve down from the roof edge

fast·ball /fást bàwl/ *n* in baseball, a fast pitch

fast-breed·er re·ac·tor *n* a nuclear reactor that produces more fissionable material than it consumes

fas·ten /fáss'n/ *vti* **1** attach or become attached securely **2** shut or be shut tightly

fas·ten·er /fáss'nər/, **fas·ten·ing** /fáss'ning/ *n* a device for fastening something

fast food *n* processed food prepared quickly

fast-for·ward *n* a function on a tape recorder or player for winding tape forward quickly ■ *vti* advance a tape rapidly

fas·tid·i·ous /fa stíddee əss/ *adj* **1** demanding about detail **2** sensitive about cleanliness

fast lane *n* **1** a passing lane of an expressway **2** the hectic lifestyle of people pursuing excitement and pleasure (*infml*) —**fast-lane** *adj*

fast·ness /fástnəss/ *n* **1** the state or quality of being fixed, firm, or secure **2** a fortress (*literary*)

fast track *n* a rapid route to progress or advancement (*infml*) —**fast-track** *adj*, *vt*

fat *n* **1** a water-insoluble chemical belonging to a group that is a main constituent of food **2** tissue containing fat **3** solidified oil or fat used in cooking **4** quantity in excess of what is needed (*infml*) ○ *a budget with no fat* ■ *adj* (**fat·ter**, **fat·test**) **1** overweight **2** containing fat **3** thick ○ *a fat book* **4** profitable ○ *fat contracts* **5** very wealthy **6** with abundant contents or supplies ○ *a fat savings account* —**fat·ness** *n*

⚡ **FAT** /fat/ *n* a table of computer information about the structure of stored files on a disk. Full form **file allocation table**

fa·tal /fáyt'l/ *adj* **1** leading to death **2** ruinous **3** decisive —**fa·tal·ly** *adv* —**fa·tal·ness** *n* ◇ See note at **deadly**

fa·tal·ism /fáyt'l lzzəm/ *n* **1** the philosophical doctrine that all events are fated to happen **2** belief in fate —**fa·tal·ist** *n* —**fa·tal·is·tic** /fàyt'l ístik/ *adj*

fa·tal·i·ty /fay tállətee, fə-/ (*pl* **-ties**) *n* a death resulting from an accident or disaster

fat cat *n* **1** somebody rich (*slang insult*) **2** a rich contributor to a political campaign (*slang*)

fate *n* **1** a force believed to predetermine events **2** an outcome or final result **3** something determined by fate ■ **Fates** *npl* in Greek mythology, the goddesses of destiny. Roman equivalent **Parcae** ■ *vt* (**fat·ed**, **fat·ing**) make inevitable —**fat·ed** *adj* ◇ **tempt fate** take a risk

fate·ful /fáytfəl/ *adj* **1** making a dire outcome inevitable **2** decided by fate

fat·head /fát hèd/ *n* a person regarded as unintelligent and thoughtless (*slang insult*) —**fat·head·ed** /fát héddəd/ *adj*

fa·ther /fáathər/ *n* **1** a male parent **2** a male ancestor, founder, or civic leader **3** **Fa·ther** God **4** **Fa·ther** used as a title for a cleric in some Christian churches ■ *vt* beget as a father —**fa·ther·hood** *n* —**fa·ther·less** *adj*

fa·ther fig·ure *n* an older man whom others look to for advice and protection

fa·ther-in-law (*pl* **fa·thers-in-law**) *n* a spouse's father

fa·ther·land /fáathər lànd/ *n* **1** somebody's homeland **2** the homeland of somebody's ancestors

fa·ther·ly /fáathərlee/ *adj* like a father —**fa·ther·li·ness** *n*

Fa·ther's Day *n* a day honoring fathers. Date: 3rd Sunday in June.

fath·om /fáthəm/ *n* a measure of water depth equal to 6 ft./1.83 m ■ *vt* **1** measure water depth using a sounding line **2** comprehend something —**fath·om·a·ble** *adj*

fath·om·less /fáthəmləss/ *adj* **1** endlessly deep **2** mystifying —**fath·om·less·ness** *n*

fa·tigue /fə teég/ *n* mental or physical exhaustion ■ **fa·tigues** *npl* informal military uniforms worn day to day and in battle ■ *vti* make or become tired —**fa·tigued** *adj*

Fat·i·ma /fáttəmə/ (606?–632 BC) youngest daughter of Muhammad

fat suit *n* a naturalistic costume designed to make an actor appear overweight

fat·ten /fátt'n/ *vti* make or become fat or plump —**fat·ten·ing** *adj*

fat·ty /fáttee/ (-ti·er, -ti·est) *adj* **1** containing fat **2** derived from fat —**fat·ti·ness** *n*

fat·ty ac·id *n* an organic acid belonging to a group occurring as fats, waxes, and oils

fat·u·ous /fáchoo əss/ *adj* showing lack of intelligence and awareness —**fat·u·i·ty** /fə toõ itee/ *n* —**fat·u·ous·ly** *adv*

fat·wa /fáttwə/, **fat·wah** *n* a decree issued by an Islamic leader

fau·cet /fáwssit/ *n* a valve that controls a flow of water

Faulk·ner /fáwknər/, **William** (1897–1962) US writer —**Faulk·ner·i·an** /fawk neéree ən/ *adj*

fault /fawlt/ *n* **1** responsibility for a mistake, failure, or wrongdoing **2** a personal shortcoming **3** a defect in something **4** a displacement in the Earth's crust, with a break in the continuity of rocks **5** in some racket games, an invalid serve ■ *vt* blame or find fault with —**fault·less** *adj* —**fault·less·ly** *adv* ◊ **find fault with** criticize ◊ **to a fault** excessively ◊ See note at **flaw**

fault·find·ing /fáwlt fìnding/ *n* criticism, especially when constant and petty —**fault·find·er** *n* —**fault·find·ing** *adj*

fault line *n* a linear feature on the Earth's surface, occurring where displaced rock layers have broken through

fault·y /fáwltee/ (-i·er, -i·est) *adj* containing defects —**fault·i·ly** *adv* —**fault·i·ness** *n*

faun /fawn/ *n* in Roman mythology, a rural god depicted as part man and part goat

SPELLCHECK Do not confuse the spelling of **faun** and **fawn** ("a young deer," "a yellowish brown color"), which sound similar.

fau·na /fáwnə/ *n* the animal life of a particular area or period —**fau·nal** *adj*

ORIGIN Fauna derives from the name of an ancient Roman rural goddess. The Swedish naturalist Carolus Linnaeus (1707–78) named his catalog of the animals of Sweden for her: *Fauna suecica* "Swedish Fauna" (1746). The use paralleled that of *flora* and quickly caught on. It is first recorded in English in 1771.

Fau·nus /fáwnəss/ *n* in Roman mythology, the god of nature. Greek equivalent **Pan**

Fau·ré /faw ráy/, **Gabriel** (1845–1924) French composer and organist

Faust /fowst/ (b. 1480?) German fortune-teller and magician reputed to have sold his soul to the devil —**Faust·i·an** *adj*

fau·vism /fó vìzzəm/, **Fau·vism** *n* a 20C artistic movement characterized by simple forms and bright colors

faux /fó/ *adj* imitation ○ *faux marble*

faux pas /fó paá/ (*pl* **faux pas** /fó paáz/) *n* a social blunder ◊ See note at **mistake**

fa·va bean /faávə-/ *n* a broad bean

fave /fayv/ *adj* favorite (*slang*)

fa·vor /fáyvər/ *n* **1** a kind act **2** an approving attitude **3** preferential treatment **4** a token of loyalty or affection **5** a small gift given to guests at a party ■ **fa·vors** *npl* sexual intimacy, especially as consented to by a woman (*dated*) ■ *vt* **1** prefer **2** express support for **3** be advantageous to ○ *tax cuts that favor the rich* **4** show preferential treatment to **5** be careful with **6** treat with particular kindness **7** resemble in appearance ○ *favors her uncle* ◊ See note at **regard**

fa·vor·a·ble /fáyvərəb'l/ *adj* **1** advantageous **2** suggesting a promising future ○ *a favorable outlook* **3** expressing or winning approval ○ *a favorable reaction* —**fa·vor·a·bly** *adv*

fa·vor·ite /fáyvərit, -vrit/ *adj* most liked ■ *n* **1** a person or thing liked most **2** a competitor considered most likely to win **3** somebody favored by a superior

fa·vor·it·ism /fáyvəri tìzzəm/ *n* the unfair favoring of a person or group

Fawkes /fawks/, **Guy** (1570–1606) English conspirator, executed for plotting to blow up the English parliament in 1605

fawn¹ /fawn/ *n* **1** a young deer **2** a yellowish brown color —**fawn** *adj* ◊ See note at **faun**

fawn² /fawn/ *vi* **1** seek favor by flattery **2** try to please by showing enthusiastic affection —**fawn·er** *n* —**fawn·ing** *adj*

fax /faks/ *n* a document or image sent electronically over telephone lines and reproduced in its original form ■ *vt* send by fax

fay *n* a fairy (*literary*)

faze /fayz/ (**fazed, faz·ing**) *vt* disconcert or fluster

SPELLCHECK Do not confuse the spelling of **faze** and **phase** ("a stage of development"), which sound similar.

FBI, F.B.I. *n* an arm of the US Justice Department that deals with national security and interstate crime. Full form **Federal Bureau of Investigation**

FCC, F.C.C. *n* the federal agency that oversees telecommunications in the US. Full form **Federal Communications Commission**

FDA, F.D.A. *n* the federal agency that oversees food and drug safety in the US. Full form **Food and Drug Administration**

FDIC, F.D.I.C. *n* the chartered organization insuring bank deposits in the United

States. Full form **Federal Deposit Insurance Corporation**

FDNY abbr Fire Department of New York

fe·al·ty /féeˈəltee/ (pl **-ties**) n allegiance to a feudal lord

fear /feer/ n **1** a feeling of anxiety that something bad will happen **2** a frightening thought **3** reverence and awe ■ v **1** vti be afraid of something **2** vt express regretfully (fml)

☐ **fear for** vt worry about the risk or danger to

fear·ful /féerfəl/ adj **1** feeling or showing fear ○ fearful for their safety **2** frightening ○ a fearful storm **3** very bad (infml) ○ a fearful headache —**fear·ful·ly** adv —**fear·ful·ness** n

fear·less /féerləss/ adj courageous —**fear·less·ly** adv —**fear·less·ness** n ♢ See note at **courage**

fear·some /féersəm/ adj **1** frightening **2** inspiring reverence and awe —**fear·some·ly** adv —**fear·some·ness** n

~~feasable~~ incorrect spelling of **feasible**

fea·si·ble /féezəbʼl/ adj **1** possible **2** plausible —**fea·si·bil·i·ty** /féezə bíllətee/ n —**fea·si·bly** adv

feast /feest/ n **1** a large meal, especially a celebratory meal for a large number of people **2** a religious celebration ■ vi **1** attend a celebratory meal **2** eat with enjoyment ○ feasting on strawberries **3** take delight ○ feasting on the view

feat /feet/ n a notable act

feath·er /féthər/ n **1** an individual part of a bird's plumage, consisting of a hollow central shaft with interlocking fine strands on both sides **2** something resembling a bird's feather ■ v **1** vt cut hair to form layers **2** vt fit or cover with feathers **3** vti turn an oar blade horizontal to decrease wind resistance **4** vt alter the position of an aircraft's propeller blades to decrease wind resistance —**feath·ered** adj

feath·er·bed·ding /féthər bèdding/ n overstaffing or limiting production to save or create jobs

feath·er dust·er n a brush made of feathers attached to a stick

feath·er·weight /féthər wàyt/ n **1** the weight category for boxers between bantamweight and lightweight **2** a boxer who competes at featherweight

feath·er·y /féthəree/ adj **1** resembling feathers **2** consisting of feathers

fea·ture /féechər/ n **1** a part of the face that makes it distinctive **2** a distinctive part ○ a geographical feature **3** a full-length motion picture **4** a regular article in a newspaper, magazine, or broadcast program **5** a prominent article in a newspaper, magazine, or broadcast program ■ v (**-tured, -tur·ing**) **1** vt contain as an important element **2** vti give or have prominence in a performance **3** vi figure in something —**fea·tured** adj

fea·ture film n a full-length movie

fea·ture-length adj as long as a full-length movie

fea·ture·less /féechərləss/ adj lacking distinctiveness

Feb. abbr February

fe·brile /fébbrəl, féebrəl/ adj of fever

Feb·ru·ar·y /fébroo èrree, fébbyoo-/ (pl **-ies**) n the 2nd month of the year in the Gregorian calendar

> **ORIGIN February** came through French from Latin, where the month was named for a Roman festival of purification that was held on the 15th.

~~Febuary~~ incorrect spelling of **February**

fe·ces /féesseez/ npl the body's solid waste —**fe·cal** /féekʼl/ adj

feck·less /fékləss/ adj **1** ineffective **2** unlikely to be successful —**feck·less·ly** adv —**feck·less·ness** n

fe·cund /féekənd, fék-/ adj **1** fertile (fml) **2** highly productive —**fe·cun·di·ty** /fi kúndətee/ n

fed past participle, past tense of **feed**

fed·er·al /féddərəl, féddrəl/ adj **1** of a form of government with some central powers and some powers retained by individual states or regions **2** of the central government in a federal system

Fed·er·al Bu·reau of In·ves·ti·ga·tion n full form of **FBI**

fed·er·al case n a federal legal matter

Fed·er·al Funds npl money lent overnight between Federal Reserve Banks

fed·er·al·ism /féddərə lìzzəm, féddrə-/ n **1** the system of federal government **2** support for the principle of federal government —**fed·er·al·ist** n, adj

Fed·er·al Re·serve Bank n in the United States, any one of the 12 reserve banks responsible for its own district

Fed·er·al Re·serve Board n the group responsible for supervising the Federal Reserve System

Fed·er·al Re·serve Sys·tem n the US banking system that regulates money supply and interest rates

fed·er·ate /fédda ràyt/ (**-ated, -at·ing**) vti unite in a federation

Fed·er·at·ed States of Mic·ro·nes·i·a ♦ **Micronesia, Federated States of**

fed·er·a·tion /fèddə ráyshʼn/ n a federal union, political system, or alliance for a common goal

fed up adj having reached the limits of tolerance or patience (infml)

fee n **1** a payment for professional services **2** a fixed charge made by an institution for membership, access, or participation **3** an inherited or heritable interest in land ◊ See note at **wage**

ORIGIN Fee and its close relatives *feudal* and *fief* take us back to the beginnings of European feudal society, when the ownership of cattle symbolized wealth. The ancient source of **fee**, denoting "livestock," is also the source of the German word *Vieh* "cattle."

fee·ble /feeb'l/ (**-bler, -blest**) *adj* **1** physically or mentally weak **2** unconvincing —**fee·ble·ness** *n* —**fee·bly** *adv* ◊ See note at **weak**

fee·ble·mind·ed *adj* an offensive term meaning below average in intelligence *(dated)* —**fee·ble·mind·ed·ly** *adv* —**fee·ble·mind·ed·ness** *n*

feed *v* (**fed**) **1** *vt* give food to a person or an animal **2** *vt* give something as food to a person or an animal ○ *fed the horse carrots* **3** *vt* be sufficient food for a person or animal ○ *This loaf won't feed us all.* **4** *vi* eat **5** *vt* sustain or support a belief or behavior ○ *Compliments feed vanity.* **6** *vt* provide something with the necessary material for operation **7** *vti* move or pass something gradually ■ *n* **1** an act or occasion of feeding **2** food, especially for animals or babies

feed·back /féed bàk/ *n* **1** noise in a loudspeaker caused by a return of part of the output **2** a response intended to provide useful information for future decisions

feed·bag /féed bàg/ *n* a bag of feed placed over a horse's muzzle

feed·er /féedər/ *n* **1** a container for food for animals or birds **2** a machine part that controls input ○ *a document feeder* **3** a tributary of a river

feed·ing fren·zy *n* a violent period of feeding by a large number of animals converging on the same food source

feed·ing ground *n* an area where wildlife regularly feeds

feed·stuff /féed stùf/ *n* livestock feed

feel *v* (**felt**) **1** *vi* seem to yourself to be in a particular emotional state ○ *Don't feel sad.* **2** *vi* cause a particular sensation ○ *The water feels cold.* **3** *vt* think that something is so ○ *I feel you're lying to me.* **4** *vti* experience an emotion or sensation ○ *felt no regret* **5** *vt* perceive something by touch **6** *vt* examine something by touching **7** *vt* make your way hesitantly **8** *vi* use touch in searching ○ *feeling around for her keys* **9** *vt* be aware of something not visible or apparent ■ *n* **1** an act of touching **2** an impression gained from touch **3** an impression sensed from something ○ *a hotel with a more traditional feel* **4** an instinct for something ◊ **feel like** have an inclination or desire for

□ **feel for** *vt* have sympathy for

feel·er /féelər/ *n* **1** an organ of touch such as an insect's antenna **2** an attempt to test the reaction of others

feel-good *adj* causing or involving a sense of well-being

feel·ing /féeling/ *n* **1** the sense of touch **2** the ability to have physical sensation **3** something experienced physically or mentally **4** affection **5** the ability to experience or express emotion ■ **feel·ings** *npl* sensibilities ■ *adj* **1** sensitive to touch **2** expressive —**feel·ing·ly** *adv*

fee split·ting *n* the practice of sharing payment for client referrals

feet plural of **foot**

feign /fayn/ *vt* **1** pretend **2** invent or make up

feind incorrect spelling of **fiend**

feint /faynt/ *n* **1** a deliberately deceptive move or action **2** a mock attack to distract attention from the main attack ■ *vti* make a feint ◊ See note at **faint**

feist·y /fístee/ (**-i·er, -i·est**) *adj* spirited *(infml)* —**feist·i·ly** *adv* —**feist·i·ness** *n*

ORIGIN Feisty means literally "like a feist," that is, a small aggressive dog. *Feist* is still used regionally. It is a variant of *fist*, a shortening of *fisting cur*, literally "dog that breaks wind," used as a term of contempt.

fe·la·fel *n* COOK = **falafel**

feld·spar /féld spaàr/, **fel·spar** /fél-/ *n* a common silicate mineral containing calcium, sodium, potassium, and other minerals —**feld·spath·ic** /feld spáthik/ *adj*

fe·lic·i·ta·tion /fə líssi táysh'n/ *n* a congratulating of somebody *(fml; often pl)*

fe·lic·i·tous /fə líssitəss/ *adj* appropriate or fortunate

fe·lic·i·ty /fə líssətee/ (*pl* **-ties**) *n* **1** happiness **2** something producing happiness **3** appropriateness

fe·line /fée lìn/ *adj* **1** of the cat family **2** resembling a cat ■ *n* a member of the cat family —**fe·lin·i·ty** /fi línnətee/ *n*

fell[1] past tense of **fall**

fell[2] *vt* **1** chop a tree down **2** knock somebody down

fell[3] *adj* fierce *(literary)*

fell[4] *n* an animal hide

Fel·li·ni /fə leénee/, **Federico** (1920–93) Italian movie director

fel·low /féllō/ *n* **1** a man or boy **2** one of a pair **3** *also* **Fel·low** a member of a learned society **4** a graduate student supported by a university department ■ *adj* being in the same group

ORIGIN Fellow comes from an ancient Scandinavian word that literally meant "somebody who lays money." Sharing costs or financial risks implies "partner, associate," and this was the original sense in English. The first element of the word is related to **fee.**

fel·low·ship /féllō shìp/ *n* **1** the sharing of common interests, goals, experiences, or views **2** a society of like-minded people

3 companionship **4** a graduate post supported by a university department

fel·low trav·el·er n **1** somebody on the same journey **2** a Communist sympathizer

fel·ly /féllee/ (pl **-lies**), **fel·loe** /féllō/ n a wheel rim

fel·on /féllən/ n somebody guilty of a felony

fel·o·ny /féllənee/ (pl **-nies**) n a serious crime such as murder —**fe·lo·ni·ous** /fə lṓnee əss/ adj

fel·spar n MINERALS = feldspar

felt[1] past tense, past participle of **feel**

felt[2] n **1** compressed wool or animal-hair fabric **2** a synthetic fabric made by the process of matting o *roofing felt* —**felt** vti

felt tip n **1** a pen point made from compressed fiber **2** a pen with a felt tip

fem. abbr **1** female **2** feminine

FEMA /féemə/ abbr Federal Emergency Management Agency

fe·male /feé màyl/ adj **1** of the sex that produces offspring **2** of women **3** describes flowers that have carpels but no stamens ■ n a female person or animal —**fe·male·ness** n

> **ORIGIN** Female is not etymologically related to *male*. Female came via French from Latin *femella*, a diminutive of *femina* "woman" (from which English gets *feminine*). *Femina* derives from a verb meaning "suck," so originates in the idea of "somebody from whom milk is sucked." *Male* developed from Latin *masculus* "man."

fem·i·nine /fémmənin/ adj **1** conventionally characteristic of or attributed to women **2** classified grammatically in the gender that includes the majority of words referring to females ■ n a feminine word or form —**fem·i·nine·ly** adv —**fem·i·nin·i·ty** /fémmə nínnətee/ n

~~**femininity**~~ incorrect spelling of **femininity**

fem·i·nism /fémmə nìzzəm/ n **1** belief in the need to secure rights and opportunities for women equal to those of men **2** the movement dedicated to securing women's rights —**fem·i·nist** n, adj

fem·i·nize /fémmə nìz/ (**-nized**, **-niz·ing**) vt make characteristic of or suitable for women —**fem·i·ni·za·tion** /fémməni záysh'n/ n

femme fa·tale /fém fə tàl, -tàal, fám-/ (pl **femmes fa·tales** /pronunc. same/) n a woman regarded as very attractive and dangerous (disapproving)

fe·mur /féemər/ (pl **fe·murs** or **fem·o·ra** /fémmərə/) n **1** the main bone in the human thigh **2** a large bone in the upper leg of vertebrates that live on land

fen n an inland marsh

fence n **1** a structure erected to enclose an area or create a barrier **2** a buyer of stolen goods (slang) ■ v (**fenced**, **fenc·ing**) **1** vt

enclose with a fence **2** vti deal in stolen goods (slang) **3** vi fight with a sword **4** vi avoid answering a question —**fenc·er** n ◊ **mend fences** restore good relations with somebody after a disagreement ◊ **sit** or **be on the fence** be unwilling or unable to choose

Fencing: As one fencer lunges forward the other prepares to parry

fenc·ing /fénsing/ n **1** fighting with slender swords **2** material for making fences **3** fences collectively

fend vt defend from harm (archaic)
□ **fend off** vt repulse

fend·er /féndər/ n **1** any of the parts of a motor vehicle or bicycle that cover each wheel **2** a metal guard for the front of a fireplace

feng shui /fang shwáy/ n a Chinese system aiming at achieving harmony between people and the places they live and work in

fen·land /fén lànd, fénlənd/ n inland marshland

fen·nel /fénn'l/ n **1** an aromatic plant with seeds and feathery leaves that have an aniseed flavor **2** a related plant with bulbous stalks that have an aniseed flavor

fen·u·greek /fénnyə grèek, fénnə-/ n **1** the aromatic seeds of a leguminous plant. Use: in medicine, food flavoring. **2** the plant that produces fenugreek

⚡ **FEP** abbr front-end processor

fe·ral /feérəl, férrəl/ adj **1** gone wild after formerly being domesticated or cultivated o *feral cats* **2** savage

Fer·di·nand I /fúrd'n ànd/ (1503–64) Holy Roman Emperor (1558–64), king of Bohemia (1526–64), and king of Germany (1531–64)

Fer·di·nand V (1452–1516) king of Castile (1474–1504); as Ferdinand II, king of Sicily (1468–1516) and of Aragon (1479–1516); as Ferdinand III, king of Naples (1503–16)

Fer·mat /fair màa/, **Pierre de** (1601–65) French mathematician

fer·ment vti /fər mént/ **1** subject to or undergo fermentation **2** cause or be in a state of commotion or agitation ■ n /fúr mènt/ a state of commotion or agitation

> **SPELLCHECK** Do not confuse the spelling of **ferment** and **foment** ("cause trouble"), which sound similar.

fer·men·ta·tion /fùrmən táysh'n, -men-/ n the breakdown of carbohydrates by micro-organisms

Fer·mi /fúrmee/, **Enrico** (1901–54) Italian-born US physicist

fer·mi·um /fúrmee əm, fér-/ n (symbol **Fm**) an artificial radioactive element. Use: tracer.

fern n a plant that has no flowers and re-produces by means of spores —**fern·y** adj

fe·ro·cious /fə róshəss/ adj 1 very fierce or savage 2 extreme —**fe·ro·cious·ly** adv —**fe·roc·i·ty** /fə róssətee/ n

fer·ret /férrət/ n a domesticated polecat bred for hunting rabbits or rats ■ vti hunt using a ferret

> **ORIGIN Ferret** comes ultimately from Latin *fur* "thief," which is also the source of *furtive*. It entered English from French.

□ **ferret out** vt locate or discover something by persistent searching

fer·ric /férrik/ adj containing iron, especially with a valence of 3

Fer·ris wheel /férriss-/, **fer·ris wheel** n an amusement ride consisting of a giant re-volving wheel with seats hanging down from it

> **ORIGIN** The **Ferris wheel** is named for the US engineer G. W. G. Ferris (1859–96), who invented it.

fer·rous /férrəss/ adj containing iron, es-pecially with a valence of 2

fer·rule /férrəl/ n a protective cap on or around a shaft or pole

fer·ry /férree/ n (pl -ries) also **ferryboat** a boat for transporting passengers, vehicles, or goods ■ vt (-ried, -ries) 1 transport pas-sengers, vehicles, or goods by ferry 2 trans-port passengers back and forth

fer·ry·man /férree màn, -mən/ (pl -men /-mèn, -mən/) n an owner or operator of a ferry

fer·tile /fúrt'l/ adj 1 able to produce offspring 2 able to produce fruits or seeds 3 describes an egg or seed that is able to develop 4 pro-ducing good crops 5 creative or productive —**fer·til·i·ty** /fur tíllətee/ n

Fer·tile Cres·cent n a fertile area in SW Asia

fer·til·i·ty drug n a drug for treating in-fertility in women

fer·ti·lize /fúrt'l ìz/ (-**lized**, -**liz·ing**) vt 1 unite a male reproductive cell with a female cell and begin the process of reproduction 2 apply fertilizer to soil or plants —**fer·til·i·za·tion** /fùrt'lə záysh'n/ n

fer·til·iz·er /fúrt'l ìzər/ n a substance added to soil to aid plant growth

fer·vent /fúrvənt/, **fer·vid** /-vid/ adj showing passionate enthusiasm —**fer·ven·cy** n —**fer·vent·ly** adv —**fer·vid·ly** adv —**fer·vid·ness** n

fer·vor /fúrvər/ n intensity of emotion

fes·cue /féskyoo/ n a grass with narrow spiky leaves. Use: lawns, pasture.

fest n a social gathering for a particular ac-tivity (infml) ○ a music fest

fes·ter /féstər/ vi 1 produce pus 2 become rotten 3 rankle

fes·ti·val /féstəv'l/ n 1 a time of celebration 2 a program of cultural events —**fes·ti·val** adj

fes·tive /féstiv/ adj 1 of celebration 2 cheerful ○ in a festive mood —**fes·tive·ly** adv —**fes·tive·ness** n

fes·tiv·i·ty /fe stívvətee/ n (pl -ties) 1 a cele-bration 2 the merrymaking typical of a celebration ■ **fes·tiv·i·ties** npl celebrations or merrymaking

fes·toon /fe stoón/ n a garland hanging in a loop or curve between two points ■ vt hang festoons on —**fes·tooned** adj

fet·a /féttə/ n a crumbly cheese used es-pecially in Greek dishes

fe·tal /féet'l/, **foe·tal** adj of a fetus

fetch vt 1 go and get 2 cause to come 3 bring as a sale price

fetch·ing /féching/ adj 1 good looking 2 having or giving an attractive quality ○ a fetching hat —**fetch·ing·ly** adv

fete /fayt, fet/, **fête** n 1 a holiday or day of celebration 2 a religious festival ■ vt (fet·ed, fet·ing; fêt·ed, fêt·ing) honor lavishly

fet·id /féttid/, **foe·tid** adj nauseating —**fet·id·ly** adv —**fet·id·ness** n

fet·ish /féttish/, **fet·ich** n 1 an object believed to have magical powers 2 an object of obses-sion ○ make a fetish of neatness 3 an object arousing sexual desire —**fet·ish·ism** n —**fet·ish·ist** n —**fet·ish·is·tic** /fètti shístik/ adj

> **ORIGIN Fetish** and *factitious* "insincere, ar-tificial" both have their origin in a Latin ad-jective meaning · "made by art." While *factitious* came directly from Latin, **fetish** came through French and Portuguese, and the Portuguese descendant of the Latin source came to be used as a noun meaning "sorcery, charm." This entered English via French in the early 17C, referring specifically to a magical object used by West African peoples.

fet·lock /fét lòk/ n a projection on the lower part of the leg of a horse or related animal

> **ORIGIN Fetlock** probably means literally "lock of hair on the foot."

fet·ter /féttər/ n (often pl) 1 a shackle for the ankles 2 a means of restraint ■ vt 1 put fetters on 2 restrain

fet·tle /fétt'l/ ◊ **in fine** or **good fettle** in good health, condition, or spirits

fet·tuc·ci·ne /fèttə cheénee/, **fet·tuc·ci·ni** n 1 narrow flat pasta (+ sing or pl verb) 2 a dish made with fettuccine

fe·tus /feetəss/, **foe·tus** n an unborn child

feud /fyood/ n a long violent dispute ■ vi participate in a feud

feu·dal /fyood'l/ adj of feudalism —**feu·dal·ly** adv

feu·dal·ism /fyood'l ĭzzəm/ n the medieval social system in which vassals held land from lords in exchange for military service —**feu·dal·is·tic** /fyood'l ĭstik/ adj

fe·ver /feevar/ n 1 an unusually high body temperature 2 a disease with fever 3 a craze 4 a state of high excitement (often in combination)

fe·ver blis·ter n a cold sore

fe·vered /feevard/ adj 1 affected by fever 2 highly excited

fe·ver·ish /feevarish/ adj 1 having a fever 2 agitated —**fe·ver·ish·ly** adv —**fe·ver·ish·ness** n

fe·ver pitch n a highly agitated state

few /fyoo/ (-**er**, -**est**) npl, pron, adj a limited number o A fortunate few escaped. o Few will ever know. o Few people came. ■ adj, pron a few some, though not many o a few books o A few escaped. —**few·ness** n

> **USAGE fewer** or **less**? **Fewer** is used with things you can count: fewer meetings, fewer people. **Less** is used with things you cannot count: less time, less prestige. The same rule applies to **fewer than** and **less than**: fewer than 20 people, less than a majority. In an exception to the rule, **less** and **less than** are often used with nouns that indicate distance, weights and measurements, sums of money, and units of time, because they are thought of as collective amounts: gifts for 50 dollars or less, arrived in less than four hours. In addition, plural nouns can precede the set phrase or less: eight items or less.

fey /fay/ adj giving an impression of other-worldliness or unworldliness

Feyn·man /finmən/, **Richard** (1918–88) US physicist

fez (pl **fez·zes**) n a flat-topped conical hat

> **ORIGIN** The **fez** is probably named for the city of Fez in Morocco. The word entered English in the early 19C from French and Turkish.

ff symbol fortissimo

fi·an·cé /fée on sáy, fee ón sày/ n the man to whom a woman is engaged to be married

fi·an·cée /fée on sáy, fee ón sày/ n the woman to whom a man is engaged to be married

Fi·an·na Fáil /fée ənə faál/ n an Irish political party, founded in 1926

fi·as·co /fee áskō/ (pl -**cos**) n a humiliating failure

> **ORIGIN Fiasco** comes from an Italian word that literally means "bottle." The origin of the English use is Italian theatrical slang, where far fiasco, literally "make a bottle," meant

"have a complete failure in a performance." The reason for this is not clear.

fi·at /fee ət, -aat/ n 1 an official authorization 2 an arbitrary order

fi·at mon·ey n money decreed to be legal tender by a government but not convertible into coin

fib (infml) n an insignificant lie ■ vi (**fibbed**, **fib·bing**) tell insignificant lies —**fib·ber** n ↕ See note at **lie**

fi·ber /fibər/, **fi·bre** n 1 a thin thread 2 thread for yarn 3 cloth made from fibers 4 the essential character of something 5 strength of character o the moral fiber of the nation 6 coarse fibrous substances in food 7 strands from the stems or leaves of some plants used for making rope and textiles 8 a long thin structure of the body tissues, e.g., muscle cells and nerve cells —**fi·bered** adj

fi·ber·board /fibər bàwrd/ n compressed wood fiber. Use: building materials.

fi·ber·glass /fibər glàss/ n 1 compressed glass fibers. Use: insulation. 2 material made from fiberglass. Use: boat hulls, car bodies.

fi·ber op·tics n the use of light transmitted through fibers to transmit information (+ sing verb) —**fi·ber-op·tic** adj

fi·bril·late /fibbrə làyt/ (-**lat·ed**, -**lat·ing**) vti beat or contract rapidly and irregularly

fib·ril·la·tion /fibbrə láysh'n/ n rapid irregular beating of the heart

fi·brin /fibrin/ n a protein that helps blood to clot

fi·brin·o·gen /fi brínnəjən/ n a protein present in the blood that is converted to fibrin

fi·broid /fi bróyd/ adj like fibers ■ n a benign growth of fibrous and muscle tissue

fi·brous /fibrəss/ adj 1 consisting of fibers 2 in elongated threads —**fi·brous·ness** n

fib·u·la /fibbyələ/ (pl -**lae** /-lèe/ or -**las**) n the outer and narrower bone in the lower leg of humans and other land-dwelling vertebrates

fiche /feesh/ n a microfiche (infml)

fick·le /fik'l/ (-**ler**, -**lest**) adj changeable in affections or intentions —**fick·le·ness** n

~~ficticious~~ incorrect spelling of **fictitious**

fic·tion /fiksh'n/ n 1 novels and stories describing imaginary people and events 2 a work of fiction 3 an untrue statement meant to deceive —**fic·tion·al** adj

fic·tion·al·ize /fikshan'l ìz/ (-**ized**, -**iz·ing**) vt make into fiction —**fic·tion·al·i·za·tion** /fikshan'li záysh'n/ n

fic·ti·tious /fik tíshəss/ adj 1 false and intended to deceive o gave a fictitious name 2 fictional —**fic·ti·tious·ly** adv —**fic·ti·tious·ness** n

fic·tive /fiktiv/ adj 1 of fiction 2 not real or true —**fic·tive·ly** adv

fid·dle /fidd'l/ *n* a violin ■ *vi* (-dled, -dling) 1 play the violin 2 toy nervously with something 3 tamper with something *(infml)* —**fid·dler** *n*

ORIGIN The ultimate source of both **fiddle** and *violin* is Latin *Vitula*, the name of a Roman goddess of joy and victory. From it was formed the verb *vitulari*, source of *vitula*, which in turn gave rise to *violin* and *viola* in the Romance languages and to English *fiddle* and German *Fiedel* in the Germanic languages.

fid·dle·sticks /fidd'l stiks/ *interj* expresses annoyance or disagreement *(infml dated)*

fid·dling /fiddling/ *adj* insignificant

fi·del·i·ty /fi déllətee/ *n* 1 loyalty 2 sexual faithfulness 3 factual accuracy or reproductive precision

fidg·et /fijjət/ *vi* move around nervously ■ *n* somebody who fidgets ■ **fidg·ets** *npl* uneasiness and restlessness

fidg·et·y /fijjətee/ *adj* 1 inclined to fidget 2 uneasy and restless —**fidg·et·i·ness** *n*

fi·do /fidó/ (*pl* -dos) *n* a coin with an error

fi·du·ci·ar·y /fi dooshee èrree, fi doosharee/ *adj* relating to trusts or the relationship between a trustee and the person acted for ■ *n* (*pl* -ies) a trustee

fief /feef/ *n* 1 a piece of land granted by a feudal lord 2 a fiefdom

fief·dom /feefdəm/ *n* 1 the lands of a feudal lord 2 something under somebody's influence or authority

⚡**field** /feeld/ *n* 1 an area of agricultural land 2 a playing area for a sport 3 an area rich in a natural resource ◇ *a gas field* 4 a broad area of something ◇ *an ice field* 5 a sphere of activity 6 a place outside an institution or workplace where practical work is undertaken 7 a battlefield 8 a group of contestants in a race or similar event 9 in physics, an area within which a force exerts an influence at every point 10 *also* **field of view** an area in the eyepiece of an optical instrument in which the image is visible 11 an area in a computer memory or screen where information can be entered and manipulated ■ *v* 1 *vt* retrieve a ball that is in play 2 *vi* be a fielder 3 *vt* deploy a group, especially for military action 4 *vt* deal with a question or complaint ◇ **play the field** date many people

Field /feeld/, **Stephen J.** (1816–99) associate justice of the US Supreme Court (1863–97)

field day *n* 1 a time of unrestrained activity or pleasure 2 a day for amateur sports or competitions

field·er /feeldər/ *n* in cricket or baseball, somebody who catches or retrieves the ball when it is struck

field e·vent *n* a throwing or jumping competition

field glass·es *npl* binoculars

field goal *n* 1 in football, a goal made with a kick 2 in basketball, a goal made in normal play

field hand *n* a farm laborer

field hock·ey *n* hockey played on ground

Field·ing /feelding/, **Henry** (1707–54) British novelist and dramatist

field mar·shal *n* the highest-ranking officer in the British army and some other armies

field mouse *n* a vole

field test *n* a test of a product under normal conditions of use —**field-test** *vt*

field trip *n* an excursion to study something firsthand

field·work /feeld wùrk/ *n* work done outside the normal place of work or study to gain firsthand experience —**field·work·er** *n*

fiend /feend/ *n* 1 a devil or evil spirit 2 somebody who is exceedingly evil 3 a mischievous person, especially a child 4 an enthusiast of a subject or activity

fiend·ish /feendish/ *adj* 1 diabolical 2 cunning and malicious 3 extremely difficult to solve or analyze —**fiend·ish·ly** *adv* —**fiend·ish·ness** *n*

~~fient~~ incorrect spelling of **feint**

fierce /feers/ (**fierc·er, fierc·est**) *adj* 1 aggressive 2 violent or intense ◇ *a fierce battle* 3 deeply and intensely felt ◇ *fierce loyalty* —**fierce·ly** *adv* —**fierce·ness** *n*

fier·y /fí əree, fíree/ (-**i·er, -i·est**) *adj* 1 glowing hot 2 bright red 3 prone to intense emotion —**fier·i·ly** *adv* —**fier·i·ness** *n*

fi·es·ta /fee éstə/ *n* 1 a religious festival, especially one in a Spanish-speaking country 2 a festival

FIFA /feefə/ *n* the international soccer governing body

ORIGIN **FIFA** is a French acronym formed from the initial letters of "Fédération Internationale de Football Association."

fife *n* a small flute without keys —**fif·er** *n*

FIFO /fí fò/ *abbr* first in, first out

fif·teen /fif téen/ *n* the number 15 —**fif·teen** *adj*, *pron* —**fif·teenth** *adj*, *adv*, *n*

fifth *n* 1 one of five parts of something 2 a 5th part of a gallon of alcoholic liquor 3 a five note interval in a diatonic musical scale 4 5th gear in a motor vehicle —**fifth** *adj*, *adv* ◇ **take the fifth** refuse to answer a self-incriminating question *(infml)*

Fifth A·mend·ment *n* a constitutional amendment protecting people against self-incrimination

fifth col·umn *n* a secret or subversive group —**fifth col·um·nist** *n*

ORIGIN The original **fifth column** was the group of supporters that General Emilio Mola claimed to have inside Madrid when he was besieging it during the Spanish Civil War

(1936–39), in addition to the four columns encircling the city.

⚡ **fifth-gen·er·a·tion** *adj* describes a highly advanced but as yet undeveloped level of computer technology

fif·ty /fíftee/ *n* the number 50 ∎ **fif·ties** *npl* **1** the numbers 50 to 59, particularly as a range of temperatures **2** the years from 50 to 59 in a century or somebody's life —**fif·ti·eth** *adj, adv, n* —**fif·ty** *adj, pron*

fif·ty-fif·ty *adj, adv* in exactly equal shares

fig *n* **1** a sweet-tasting pear-shaped fruit with many seeds **2** a fruit tree that produces figs

fig. *abbr* **1** figurative **2** figure

fight /fīt/ *v* (**fought** /fawt/) **1** *vti* use violence against somebody who resists **2** *vti* go to war with another country or group **3** *vt* carry on a contest such as an election or court case **4** *vi* struggle determinedly **5** *vti* oppose something vigorously ○ *fight injustice* **6** *vi* quarrel ∎ *n* **1** a violent encounter **2** a determined effort to achieve or resist something **3** a verbal confrontation **4** the ability or willingness to continue a battle or struggle **5** a boxing match

SYNONYMS fight, battle, war, conflict, engagement, skirmish, clash CORE MEANING: a struggle between opposing armed forces

☐ **fight back** *vt* restrain tears or emotion

☐ **fight off** *vt* **1** fend off an attacker **2** avoid succumbing to an illness or emotion

fight·er /fítər/ *n* **1** a fast military aircraft designed for attack **2** a very determined person **3** a soldier **4** a boxer

fig leaf *n* **1** a stylized representation of a leaf of the fig tree, covering the genitals in art **2** something meant to hide something else

fig·ment /fígmənt/ *n* a purely imaginary thing

fig·u·ra·tive /fíggyərətiv/ *adj* **1** not literal **2** describes art using human and animal figures —**fig·u·ra·tive·ly** *adv* —**fig·u·ra·tive·ness** *n*

fig·ure /fíggyər/ *n* **1** a symbol representing a number **2** an amount expressed numerically **3** somebody's body shape **4** a representation of a person in art **5** a human shape seen indistinctly **6** somebody within a particular context ○ *a prominent figure in her community* **7** somebody embodying a particular role ○ *a father figure* **8** an illustrative drawing or diagram in a book or article **9** a geometric form ∎ **fig·ures** *npl* mathematical calculations (*infml*) ∎ *v* (**-ured, -ur·ing**) **1** *vi* be included in something ○ *did not figure in the outcome* **2** *vt* believe or conclude (*infml*) **3** *vt* imagine or guess **4** *vti* be or happen as expected ○ *It just figures she'd show up late.* **5** *vti* calculate ○ **go figure** indicates that you think a situation you have described is odd or hard to comprehend (*slang*)

☐ **figure out** *vt* **1** find a solution or explanation for **2** decide

fig·ure eight *n* an outline of the number eight

fig·ure·head /fíggyər hèd/ *n* **1** a carved figure on the bow of a ship **2** somebody nominally in charge

fig·ure of speech *n* a nonliteral expression or use of language

fig·ure skat·ing *n* ice skating in which the skaters move in patterns —**fig·ure skat·er** *n*

fig·u·rine /fíggyə rèen/ *n* a small ornamental figure or statuette

Fi·ji /féejee/ island nation in the S Pacific Ocean north of New Zealand. Cap. Suva. Pop. 844,330 (2001).

~~filagree~~ incorrect spelling of **filigree**

fil·a·ment /fíləmənt/ *n* **1** a slender strand or fiber **2** a thin wire that produces light in a light bulb

fil·bert /fílbərt/ *n* **1** a hazelnut **2** a hazel tree

ORIGIN The **filbert** is named for the 7C abbot St. Philibert, whose feast day is toward the end of August, when hazelnuts begin to ripen.

filch *vt* steal furtively (*infml*) —**filch·er** *n* ◊ See note at **steal**

⚡ **file**[1] *n* **1** a folder, cabinet, or other container for storing papers **2** an ordered collection of documents **3** a uniquely named collection of computer instructions or data **4** a line of people or things one behind the other ∎ *v* (**filed, fil·ing**) **1** *vt* put something in order in a file **2** *vt* submit a claim or complaint to the appropriate authority **3** *vi* bring a lawsuit ○ *filed for divorce* **4** *vt* send in a news report **5** *vi* move in a line one behind the other

file[2] *n* a metal tool with sharpened ridges for smoothing an edge or surface ∎ *vti* (**filed, fil·ing**) make something smooth using a file

fi·lé /fee láy, fi láy/ *n* seasoning powder used in Cajun cooking

file cab·i·net *n* a filing cabinet

⚡ **file ex·ten·sion** *n* a sequence of characters following the period in a computer file name, identifying the file type

⚡ **file for·mat** *n* the pattern and convention by which a computer program stores information in a file

⚡ **file man·ag·er** *n* a computer program to manage files

⚡ **file·name** /fíl nàym/ *n* a title for a computer file

⚡ **file serv·er** *n* a computer in a network that other computers access

fi·let /fi láy, fèe láy/ *n* a fillet of fish or meat ∎ *vt* cut into fillets

fil·i·al /fíllee əl/ *adj* of the relationship of children to their parents —**fil·i·al·ly** *adv*

fil·i·bus·ter /fílli bùstər/ *n* **1** a tactic such as a long-winded speech used to delay or prevent the passage of legislation **2** formerly, a military adventurer —**fil·i·bus·ter** *vi*

ORIGIN A **filibuster** was a pirate who pillaged

Spanish colonies in the Caribbean in the 17C. In the mid-19C the term was used in connection with a band of Americans who fomented revolution in Latin America. It readily transferred to obstruction at home, and was used of preventing legislation in the United States in the late 19C. The word **filibuster** itself came through Spanish and French from the Dutch word that was adopted into English as **freebooter.**

fil·i·gree /fílli gree/ n lacy metal ornamentation ■ vt (-greed, -gree·ing) form into a delicate pattern —**fil·i·gree** adj

ORIGIN Filigree is an alteration of *filigrane* and was adopted from a French word that itself came from Italian *filigrano*. The elements making up the Italian original represent Latin *filum* "thread" and *granum* "seed."

fil·ing cab·i·net n a storage cabinet for files

Fil·i·pi·no /fílla peéno/ adj of the Philippines ■ n (pl -nos) 1 the official language of the Philippines 2 somebody from the Philippines

fill v 1 vti make something full, or become full 2 vt take up all the space inside something or all the surface of something ○ The room was filled with light. 3 vt cover a blank area with writing or drawing 4 vt become present or very noticeable throughout something ○ The scent of spring filled the air. 5 vt make somebody feel a strong emotion ○ were filled with joy 6 vt close up a hole 7 vt meet a need 8 vt occupy free time 9 vt carry out instructions to provide something ○ fill a prescription 10 vt choose somebody for or hold a job or office ■ n enough or plenty of something ○ I've had my fill of his complaints.

□ **fill in** vi be a substitute for somebody

□ **fill out** v 1 vt complete the blank spaces in a form or document 2 vti become or make something bigger

□ **fill up** v 1 vti become or make something full 2 vt satisfy somebody's hunger

fill·er /fíllər/ n 1 something added for bulk or to fill space 2 a substance for plugging a crack or smoothing a surface 3 an item of less important material added to take up time or space in a broadcast or publication

fil·let /fi láy/ n 1 a boneless portion of fish or meat 2 a ribbon worn around the head 3 a flat narrow architectural molding ■ vt cut into fillets

fill-in n somebody who takes another person's place temporarily

fill·ing /fílling/ n 1 a plug for the cavity in a decayed tooth 2 something used to fill the space inside something, e.g., a pillow or quilt 3 a food mixture put inside something such as a pie ■ adj satisfying hunger

fill·ing sta·tion n a gas station

fil·lip /fíllip/ n 1 something that gives you a feeling of encouragement 2 a snapping movement of the fingers —**fil·lip** vt

Fill·more /fíl màwr/, **Millard** (1800–74) 13th president of the United States (1850–53)

fil·ly /fíllee/ n (pl -lies) n a young female horse

film n 1 a movie 2 motion pictures collectively 3 the coated strip of cellulose on which still or moving pictures are captured 4 a very thin sheet of plastic. Use: wrapping. 5 a thin layer ■ v 1 vt capture somebody or something on film 2 vti make a motion picture

□ **film over** vi become covered with a thin layer of something

film·ic /fílmik/ adj characteristic of a movie

film·mak·er /film màykər/ n a movie director or producer —**film·mak·ing** n

film noir /film nwaár/ (pl **films noirs** /pronunc. same/) n a cinematic genre featuring shadowy images, cynical antiheroes, and urban settings

film·strip /film strìp/ n a strip of photographs that can be projected on a screen

film·y /fílmee/ (-i·er, -i·est) adj 1 light and transparent 2 covered with a film —**film·i·ness** n

fil·ter /fíltər/ n 1 a straining device 2 a porous material used for straining 3 a tinted screen placed over a lens to reduce light intensity 4 a device that blocks some sound frequencies and lets others through ■ v 1 vti pass through a filter 2 vi trickle ○ People filtered into the auditorium. —**fil·ter·less** adj

fil·ter tip n 1 a filtering device on a cigarette through which the smoke passes 2 a cigarette with a filter tip —**fil·ter-tipped** adj

filth·y /fílthee/ adj (-i·er, -i·est) 1 extremely dirty 2 despicable or morally objectionable ■ adv very (infml) ○ filthy rich —**filth** n —**filth·i·ly** adv —**filth·i·ness** n ◊ See note at dirty

fil·tra·tion /fil tráysh'n/ n the process of filtering something

fin n 1 an organ extending from the body of a fish or aquatic animal that helps in balance and propulsion 2 a similar part attached to the hull of a submarine 3 the upright part of an aircraft's tail —**finned** adj

fin. abbr finance

fi·na·gle /fi náyg'l/ vti get something by trickery (infml)

fi·nal /fín'l/ adj 1 last in a series ○ final reminder 2 allowing no change ○ My decision is final. ■ n the last of a series of contests ■ **fi·nals** npl 1 the last decisive rounds of a tournament 2 college exams at the end of a semester or course —**fi·nal·ly** adv

fi·na·le /fi nállee, -naálee/ n 1 a final theatrical number 2 a final musical movement

fi·nal·ist /fín'list/ n a competitor in the finals of a competition

fi·nal·i·ty /fi nálletee, fi-/ n the quality of being final

fi·nal·ize /fín'l ìz/ (-ized, -iz·ing) vt 1 put something into its final form **2** complete a transaction —**fi·nal·i·za·tion** /fīn'li záysh'n/ n

Fi·nal So·lu·tion, fi·nal so·lu·tion n the Nazis' systematic killing of Jews

~~finaly~~ incorrect spelling of **finally**

fi·nance /fī nàns, fī nàns/ n **1** the business of controlling money **2** money required to fund something ■ **fi·nanc·es** npl the money at the disposal of a person, organization, or country ■ vt (**-nanced**, **-nanc·ing**) provide the money for

ORIGIN The original idea underlying modern senses of **finance** is "finally settling a debt." The French word from which it derives is ultimately from Latin *finis* "end."

fi·nance com·pa·ny n a business that loans money

fi·nan·cial /fī nánshəl, fī-/ adj connected with money —**fi·nan·cial·ly** adv

fin·an·cier /fìnnən sèer, fínnən sèer/ n a wealthy investor who is skilled in finance

~~finantial~~ incorrect spelling of **financial**

finch n a small songbird with a short broad bill

find /fīnd/ v (**found, found** /fownd/) **1** vt discover something after searching **2** vt get something back after losing it **3** vt discover something for the first time **4** vt discover somebody or something accidentally **5** vt experience something ◇ *found them easy to get along with* **6** vt manage to get something ◇ *couldn't find the money to buy it* **7** vti reach a verdict about a defendant **8** vr become conscious of your own condition or situation ■ n a discovery

□ **find out** v **1** vti discover information about something **2** vt detect somebody's wrongdoing

find·er /fíndər/ n **1** somebody who finds things **2** a small telescope attached to a larger telescope

fin de siè·cle /fàN də syéklə/ n the last years of the 19C

✦ fine[1] adj (**fin·er, fin·est**) **1** very well or satisfactory **2** not coarse **3** sunny **4** thin, sharp, or delicate **5** much better than average ◇ *a fine wine* **6** delicately formed **7** very subtle ◇ *a fine distinction* ■ adv **1** well (infml) ◇ *It works just fine.* **2** into tiny pieces —**fine·ly** adv —**fine·ness** n

fine[2] n a sum of money paid as a punishment ■ vt (**fined, fin·ing**) punish by imposing a payment —**fin·a·ble** adj

fine art n **1** the creation of beautiful objects for their own sake **2** any art form regarded as having purely aesthetic value (often pl)

fine print n details printed in small characters

fin·er·y /fínəree/ n showy clothes

fines herbes /fèenz érb/ npl mixed fresh herbs

fi·nesse /fī néss/ n **1** elegant ability and dexterity **2** tactful treatment of a difficult situation **3** in bridge, an attempt to win a trick

with a card that is not the best in the player's hand ■ vt (**-nessed, -ness·ing**) control in a devious way

fine-tooth comb, fine-toothed comb n **1** a detailed approach to an investigation or inquiry **2** a tool with narrow tight-set teeth for combing thoroughly

fine-tune v **1** vt adjust and improve an engine's performance **2** vti get something just right —**fine-tun·ing** n

fin·ger /fíng gər/ n **1** one of the digits of the hand, sometimes excluding the thumb **2** the part of a glove that covers a finger **3** a narrow strip ■ v **1** vt touch something gently **2** vt give information about somebody to the police (slang) **3** vti play an instrument using the fingers ◇ **put your finger on** identify ◇ **twist somebody around your little finger** succeed in getting somebody to do exactly as you wish

ORIGIN Finger goes back to an ancient form that meant "five."

fin·ger bowl n a bowl for rinsing the fingers after eating

fin·ger·ing /fíng gəring/ n the use of fingers to play a musical instrument

Fin·ger Lakes group of 11 glacial lakes in W New York

fin·ger·mark /fíng gər màark/ n a dirty mark made by a finger

fin·ger·nail /fíng gər nàyl/ n the hard layer of keratin that covers the fingertip

fin·ger·print /fíng gər prìnt/ n **1** a unique pattern on the inside of every fingertip **2** a distinguishing characteristic ■ vt record the fingerprints of

fin·ger·tip /fíng gər tìp/ n a finger's end ■ adj using the fingertips ◇ **have at your fingertips** be completely familiar with

fin·ick·y /fínnikee/ (**-i·er, -i·est**), **fin·ick·ing** /-king/ adj **1** too concerned with details **2** too detailed —**fin·ick·i·ness** n ◊ See note at **careful**

fin·ish /fínnish/ v **1** vti come or bring to an end **2** vt use up **3** vt destroy (infml) **4** vt give a desired effect to a surface such as wood ■ n **1** the end part of something **2** a special top layer **3** quality of workmanship —**fin·ish·er** n

□ **finish off** vt **1** complete **2** ruin or exhaust (infml)

□ **finish with** vt not need any longer

fin·ished /fínnisht/ adj **1** done skillfully **2** having no further prospect of success

fin·ish·ing school n a private school for girls that emphasizes social skills

fi·nite /fī nìt/ adj **1** limited **2** countable or measurable **3** in a verb form that expresses person, number, and tense —**fi·nite·ly** adv —**fi·nite·ness** n

fink n **1** somebody regarded as contemptible (slang dated insult) **2** an informer (slang dated) ■ vi inform on others (slang dated)

Fin·land /fínnlənd/ country in N Europe on the Baltic Sea. Cap. Helsinki. Pop. 5,175,783 (2001). Finnish Suomi

Finn n somebody from Finland

~~finnish~~ incorrect spelling of **finish**

Finn·ish /fínnish/ n the official language of Finland —**Finn·ish** adj

fiord n GEOG = **fjord**

fir (pl **firs** or same) n an evergreen tree with needle-shaped leaves

fire n 1 the destructive burning of something ◇ fire insurance 2 a pile of burning fuel 3 the light, heat, and flames from something that is burning 4 the flame of a gas stove 5 the rapid production of light, heat, and flames from something that is burning 6 the discharge from guns 7 a gem's brilliance 8 eagerness and passion ■ v (**fired, fir·ing**) 1 vti discharge a bullet 2 vti launch something forcefully 3 vt dismiss somebody from work (infml) 4 vi begin to burn fuel and start working 5 vt stoke or fill with fuel 6 vt bake in a kiln 7 vt strike with force 8 vt excite ■ interj 1 warns people of a fire 2 commands somebody to shoot a weapon —**fired** adj ◇ **play with fire** do something dangerous or risky ◇ **under fire** 1 being shot at 2 subject to severe criticism

□ **fire off** vt direct things such as questions in sharp bursts

□ **fire up** vti make somebody very enthusiastic

fire a·larm n a bell or siren warning of a fire

fire ant n an ant with a painful sting

fire·arm /fír aàrm/ n a portable gun

fire·ball /fír bàwl/ n 1 a bright meteor 2 the center of a nuclear explosion 3 a ball of lightning

fire·bomb /fír bòm/ n a bomb designed to start a fire —**fire·bomb** vti —**fire·bomb·ing** n

fire·brand /fír brànd/ n 1 an agitator who tries to stir up others 2 a burning stick carried as a torch or weapon

fire·break /fír bràyk/ n an area cleared to halt a forest fire

fire·brick /fír brìk/ n a strong heat-resistant brick. Use: fireplaces, furnaces.

fire·bug /fír bùg/ n an arsonist (slang)

fire com·pa·ny n a group of firefighters

fire·crack·er /fír kràkər/ n an explosive paper cartridge

fire de·part·ment n a firefighting organization

fire door n 1 a fireproof door 2 an emergency exit

fire drill n a rehearsal for evacuating a building in an emergency

fire-eat·er n an entertainer who appears to swallow fire —**fire-eat·ing** n

fire en·gine n a large truck equipped to fight fires and rescue people

fire es·cape n an exterior stairway that serves as an emergency exit from a building

fire ex·tin·guish·er n a hand-held device containing chemicals for putting out small fires

fire·fight·er /fír fìtər/ n somebody whose job is putting out fires and rescuing people —**fire·fight·ing** n

fire·fly /fír flì/ (pl **-flies**) n a nocturnal beetle that produces light

fire·guard /fír gaàrd/ n a screen that protects people from sparks from an open fire

fire·house /fír hòwss/ n a fire station

fire hy·drant /fír plùg/, **fire·plug** n a water connection in the street for firefighters' emergency use

fire i·rons npl tools for tending a fire in a fireplace

fire·light /fír lìt/ n the light from an open fire

fire·man /fírmən/ (pl **-men** /-mən/) n 1 a man who is a firefighter 2 a ship's engineer

fire·place /fír plàyss/ n a low recess in a wall for an open fire

fire·pow·er /fír pòwr/ n 1 destructive military power 2 the power to achieve results

fire·proof /fír pròof/ adj unburnable or very resistant to fire —**fire·proof** vt

fire·re·tar·dant adj inhibiting the spread of fire

fire sale n a sell-off of fire-damaged goods

fire screen n a fireguard

fire·side /fír sìd/ n the part of a room by the fireplace ■ adj safe and comfortable

fire·side chat n an informal talk by a US president, broadcast to the nation

fire sta·tion n the headquarters of a team of firefighters

fire·storm /fír stàwrm/ n 1 an intense disturbance 2 a large uncontrollable blaze

fire·trap /fír tràp/ n a building that is unsafe in the event of fire

fire·truck /fír trùk/ n a fire engine

⚡**fire·wall** /fír wàwl/ n 1 a fireproof wall that confines a fire to one area 2 a piece of software that prevents unauthorized access

fire·wood /fír wòod/ n wood burned as fuel

fire·work /fír wùrk/ n an explosive object designed to make a brilliant display when lit ■ **fire·works** npl 1 a display of fireworks 2 an angry outburst (infml) 3 a spectacular display (infml)

~~firey~~ incorrect spelling of **fiery**

fir·ing line n 1 the front position in battle 2 the forefront of a movement or action

fir·ing squad n a group of soldiers who execute somebody by gunfire

firm[1] adj 1 not yielding to touch 2 securely fixed 3 determined 4 trustworthy ■ adv in a determined way ■ vti make or become firm —**firm·ly** adv —**firm·ness** n

□ **firm up** vt make more definite ◊ *firmed up the date for the meeting*

firm² n a commercial organization

fir·ma·ment /fúrməmənt/ n the sky (literary)

⚡ **firm·ware** /fúrm wàir/ n software stored on a memory chip rather than as part of a program

---

ORIGIN Firmware is "firm" in that the instructions will not be lost when power is shut off.

---

first adj 1 before the rest in numerical order or position 2 earlier than the rest 3 most important 4 fundamental 5 best ■ n 1 something that has not been done before or has never existed before 2 the person or thing that is number one in a series 3 the lowest gear in a motor vehicle 4 in baseball, first base ■ adv 1 before others 2 originally 3 initially 4 more willingly

first aid n emergency medical help

First A·mend·ment n an addition to the US Constitution that forbids Congress from interfering with a citizen's freedom of religion, speech, assembly, or petition

first base n in baseball, the initial base that a player attempts to reach after hitting the ball ◊ **get to first base** succeed in the initial phase of an activity (infml)

first-born n the oldest offspring ■ adj first in birth order

first class n 1 the highest rank or standard 2 the best accommodations offered on a plane, ship, or train 3 the postal service that offers the most speedy delivery —**first-class** adj, adv

first cous·in n a child of an uncle or aunt

first e·di·tion n 1 a copy of a book in its original printed form 2 the first copy of a newspaper subsequently changed during the day

first fam·i·ly n 1 a well-established family 2 **First Fam·i·ly** the family of the US President

first fruits npl 1 the first crop harvested 2 the first benefits of something

⚡ **first-gen·er·a·tion** adj 1 being the children of immigrant parents 2 describes the earliest form of a technology

first·hand /fúrst hánd/ adj, adv from the original source

first la·dy, First La·dy n a wife or official hostess of a US governor or president

first lan·guage n 1 somebody's native language 2 a country's main language

first lieu·ten·ant n 1 a US Army, Marine, or Air Force commissioned officer of a rank above second lieutenant 2 a naval officer responsible for maintaining a ship

first light n dawn

first·ly /fúrstlee/ adv to start with

first mate n a merchant-ship captain's second-in-command

first name n a name that comes before a family name

First Na·tion, first na·tion n in Canada, a community of indigenous people who are bound by treaty to the federal government

first night n the first public production of a play or show

first of·fend·er n a criminal convicted for the first time

first of·fi·cer n 1 a ship's first mate 2 the captain of a commercial aircraft

first per·son n 1 the form of a verb or a pronoun used to refer to the speaker or writer 2 a style of writing in the first person

first prin·ci·ple n something on which beliefs are based

first-rate adj excellent

first read·ing n the introductory stage in a legislature for a new bill

first re·fus·al n the first chance to buy something before it is offered to others

first re·spond·er /-ri spóndər/ n a volunteer paramedic

first strike n a nuclear attack that thwarts an enemy that has nuclear capabilities

First World n the main industrialized nations

First World War n World War I

fis·cal /fískəl/ adj 1 financial 2 of the public treasury —**fis·cal·ly** adv

---

ORIGIN Fiscal comes ultimately from a Latin word that literally meant "rush basket." The senses "purse" and "treasury" developed within Latin. The adjective formed from it passed into English in the mid-16C.

---

fis·cal year n a nation's or organization's 12-month period in which its budget operates

Fi·scher /físhər/, **Bobby** (b. 1943) US chess player

fish n (pl same or fish·es) 1 a vertebrate with gills that lives in water 2 fish as food 3 **Fish, Fish·es** the zodiacal sign Pisces ■ v 1 vti try to catch fish 2 vt try to catch fish in a particular place 3 vi search (infml)

fish and chips n fried fish with French fries (+ sing or pl verb)

fish·bowl /físh bòl/ n 1 a round glass bowl in which fish are kept 2 a place or lifestyle that is highly visible to the public

fish·er·man /físhərmən/ (pl -men /-mən/) n somebody who catches fish

fish·er·y /físhəree/ (pl -ies) n 1 a place for rearing fish 2 a region of water where commercial fishing is carried on 3 a business that catches or processes fish 4 the fishing industry

fish-eye lens /físh ī-/ n a very wide-angle lens on a camera

fish farm n a place for rearing fish commercially —**fish farm·er** n —**fish farm·ing** n

fish·hook /físh hòòk/ n a hook for catching fish

fish·ing /físhing/ n the activity of catching fish

fish·ing rod n a flexible pole to fish with

fish·meal /físh mèel/ n an animal feed or garden fertilizer made from fish

fish·mon·ger /físh mùng gər, -mòng-/ n somebody whose job is selling fish

fish·net /físh nèt/ n 1 a net for fishing 2 a fabric similar to netting. Use: stockings, pantyhose.

fish stick n a rectangular piece of processed fish

fish·tail /físh tàyl/ vi 1 swing from side to side 2 swing an airplane's tail from side to side to reduce speed

fish·wife /físh wìf/ n 1 a woman regarded as coarse and loud (insult) 2 a woman whose job is selling fish (archaic)

fish·y /físhee/ (-i·er, -i·est) adj 1 dubious (infml) 2 like fish in smell, taste, or feel

fis·sion /físh'n/ n 1 the splitting of an atomic nucleus, with release of energy 2 the act or process of breaking up into parts —**fis·sion·a·ble** adj

fis·sure /físhər/ n 1 a crack, especially in rock 2 the process of splitting 3 a division in a group 4 a split in a body part ■ vi (-sured, -sur·ing) split

fist n a clenched hand —**fist·ful** n

fist·fight /físt fìt/ n a fight with fists

fist·i·cuffs /físti kùfs/ npl fighting with fists (archaic or humorous)

fit¹ v (fit·ted or fit, fit·ting) 1 vti be the right size or shape for something or somebody 2 vti be appropriate for or compatible with something 3 vt try clothing on somebody and make necessary adjustments to its size and shape ■ adj (fit·ter, fit·test) 1 appropriate 2 worthy 3 physically strong and healthy 4 appearing likely to do something (infml) ◇ looked fit to drop ■ n the way that something fits ◇ **fit to be tied** very angry and exasperated (infml)

□ **fit in** v 1 vi conform well 2 vt find time for

□ **fit out** vt equip with the required items

fit² n a sudden outburst or series of convulsions ◇ **in** or **by fits and starts** starting and stopping repeatedly

fit·ful /fítfəl/ adj happening in bursts —**fit·ful·ly** adv —**fit·ful·ness** n

fit·ness /fítnəss/ n 1 the state of being physically fit 2 suitability

fit·ness cen·ter n a place with facilities for people to improve or maintain their physical fitness

fit·ted sheet n a sheet for a bed with an elastic edge or corners

fit·ter /fíttər/ n somebody who maintains or assembles machinery

fit·ting /fítting/ adj suitable ■ n 1 an instance of trying on clothes to see if they fit 2 a detachable part ■ **fit·tings** npl associated parts —**fit·ting·ly** adv —**fit·ting·ness** n

AKG London
Ella Fitzgerald

Fitz·ger·ald /fíts jérrəld/, **Ella** (1917–96) US jazz singer

Fitz·ger·ald, F. Scott (1896–1940) US writer

five /fīv/ n the number 5 —**five** adj, pron

five-and-dime, **five-and-ten**, **five-and-ten-cent store** n a type of variety store, now obsolete, that sold inexpensive merchandise

Five Civ·i·lized Na·tions, Five Civ·i·lized Tribes npl five Native North American peoples, the Choctaw, Cherokee, Chickasaw, Creek, and Seminole, who were briefly self-governing in the Indian Territory

five o'clock shad·ow n a beard growth noticeable several hours after a man shaves

five-star adj top-quality

fix v 1 vt mend or correct something 2 vt prepare something as food (infml) 3 vt agree to or arrange something 4 vt influence something dishonestly (infml) 5 vt attribute blame 6 vt direct the eyes or attention 7 vti make or become secure 8 vt sterilize an animal (infml) 9 vt hold the attention of somebody 10 vt fasten something in place 11 vt convert nitrogen to a stable biologically available form 12 vt make a photographic image permanent ■ n 1 a predicament (infml) 2 a superficial solution (infml) 3 an act of influencing something dishonestly (infml) 4 an illegal drug injection (slang) 5 a calculation of the position of something, e.g., using radar —**fix·a·ble** adj

□ **fix on** vt choose

□ **fix up** vt arrange something such as a meeting

fix·a·tion /fik sáysh'n/ n 1 an obsession 2 a childhood attachment that results in immature psychosexual behavior —**fix·at·ed** adj

fix·a·tive /fíksətiv/ n 1 a liquid sprayed onto something, e.g., a drawing, for protection 2 glue ■ adj tending to fix something

fixed adj 1 securely in position 2 not subject to change 3 unchanging in expression 4 agreed on 5 firmly or dogmatically held in the mind 6 dishonestly arranged (slang) —**fix·ed·ly** /-ədlee/ adv —**fix·ed·ness** /-ədnəss/ n

fixed as·set n a business asset that is not traded (usually pl)

fixed cost *n* a business expense that does not vary according to the amount of business, e.g., rent *(usually pl)*

fix·er /fíksər/ *n* **1** a chemical used in photography to stop the development of an image **2** somebody who solves problems

fix·i·ty /fíksiteé/ *n* the state of being fixed and unchanging

fix·ture /fíkschər/ *n* **1** an object in a fixed position **2** a person permanently established in a place or position

fizz *vi* **1** produce gas bubbles **2** hiss ■ *n* **1** effervescence **2** a hissing sound

fiz·zle /fízz'l/ *vi* (-**zled**, -**zling**) **1** peter out after a good start **2** make a hissing sound ■ *n* a hissing sound

fizz·y /fízzeé/ (-i-er, -i-est) *adj* producing or containing gas bubbles —**fizz·i·ness** *n*

fjord /fyawrd/, **fiord** *n* a narrow, steep-sided inlet of the sea in Scandinavia

fl. *abbr* **1** flourished **2** fluid

FL, Fla. *abbr* Florida

flab *n* unwanted body fat *(infml)*

flab·ber·gast /flábbər gàst/ *vt* astonish greatly *(infml)*

flab·by /flábbee/ (-**bi-er**, -**bi-est**) *adj* having unwanted body fat *(infml)* —**flab·bi·ly** *adv* —**flab·bi·ness** *n*

flac·cid /fláksid, flássid/ *adj* **1** limp **2** lacking vitality —**flac·cid·i·ty** /flak síddətee, fla-/ *n* —**flac·cid·ly** *adv*

~~flaccid~~ incorrect spelling of **flaccid**

flack *n* = flak

⚡**flag**[1] *n* **1** a colored cloth flown as an emblem, especially of national identity **2** a decoration similar to a flag **3** national identity symbolized by a flag **4** a marking device, e.g., a tag attached to something **5** an indicator generated by a computer program of a condition such as an error **6** in football, an official's flag thrown to the ground as a sign of illegal play ■ *vt* (**flagged, flag-ging**) **1** stop a vehicle by waving at the driver **2** in football, indicate illegal play with a flag **3** mark something in order to draw attention to it **4** draw attention to something **5** send information using a flag or flags

flag[2] (**flagged, flag-ging**) *vi* **1** become weak or tired **2** hang limply

flag[3] *n* a flagstone ■ *vt* (**flagged, flag-ging**) pave with flagstones —**flagged** *adj*

ORIGIN The **flag** found also in *flagstone* is probably from a Scandinavian language. Nothing is known for certain about the origin of the other **flag** words.

flag[4] *n* an iris plant

Flag Day *n* a holiday honoring the adoption of the design for the US flag. Date: June 14.

flag·el·lant /flájjələnt/ *n* a religious person who whips himself or herself as a punishment for sin —**flag·el·la·tion** /flàjjə láysh'n/ *n*

fla·gel·lum /flə jélləm/ (*pl* -**la** /-lə/ *or* -**lums**) *n* **1** a slender appendage of many microorganisms, used for movement **2** a part of an insect's antenna —**flag·el·late** /flájjələt, -làyt, flə jéllət/ *adj*

flag foot·ball *n* a form of football in which play is stopped by the removal of a flag from the waist of the ball carrier

flag·ging /flágging/ *adj* becoming weak or tired —**flag·ging·ly** *adv*

flag of con·ven·ience *n* the flag of a country under which a ship is registered because of its favorable regulations

flag·on /flággən/ *n* **1** a large wide bottle with a short neck, for alcoholic drink **2** a flagon's contents

flag·pole /flág pòl/, **flag·staff** /flág stàf/ *n* a pole on which a flag is flown

fla·grant /fláygrənt/ *adj* very obvious and objectionable —**fla·grance** *n* —**fla·gran·cy** *n* —**fla·grant·ly** *adv* ◊ See note at **blatant**

flag·ship /flág shìp/ *n* **1** the main or best ship in a fleet of ships **2** the most important or impressive thing in a group

flag·stone /flág stòn/ *n* **1** a paving stone **2** rock that splits into slabs

flag stop *n* a station where a train or bus stops only on request

flag-wav·ing *n* excessive patriotism —**flag-wav·er** *n*

flail /flayl/ *v* **1** *vti* thrash around, or move something around violently **2** *vt* hit with a whip ■ *n* **1** a manual threshing implement, consisting of a handle attached to a free swinging blade **2** a weapon shaped like a threshing flail

flair /flair/ *n* **1** talent **2** elegance ◊ See note at **flare, talent**

flak, flack *n* **1** antiaircraft fire directed from the ground **2** criticism *(infml)*

ORIGIN Flak is a German acronym formed from letters of *Fliegerabwehrkanonen*, literally "aviator defense cannons." It dates from World War II.

flake *n* **1** a small flat piece of something **2** a small individual piece of a manufactured substance ○ *soap flakes* **3** a snowflake **4** somebody regarded as odd *(infml insult)* ■ *v* (**flaked, flak-ing**) **1** *vi* fall off in flakes **2** *vt* break into flakes

flak jack·et *n* a bullet-proofed garment

flak·y /fláykee/ (-i-er, -i-est), **flak·ey** *adj* **1** regarded as unconventional or irrational *(infml)* **2** like flakes *(infml)* **3** tending to break off in flakes —**flak·i·ly** *adv* —**flak·i·ness** *n*

flam·bé /flaam báy/ (-**béed, -bés**) *vt* flavor food by pouring liquor on it, then burning it off

flam·bée /flaam báy/ *adj* served in ignited liquor

flam·boy·ant /flam bóy ənt/ *adj* **1** showy in a self-promoting way **2** brightly colored or elaborately decorated —**flam·boy·ance** *n* —**flam·boy·ant·ly** *adv*

⚡ **flame** *n* **1** a hot glowing body of burning gas **2** a strong feeling **3** a lover (*infml*) **4** an angry or abusive e-mail message ■ *v* (**flamed, flam·ing**) **1** *vi* burn producing a flame **2** *vti* criticize or abuse somebody by e-mail **3** *vi* have a fiery glow **4** *vi* feel a strong emotion —**flam·er** *n* ◇ **fan the flames** make a tense or difficult situation worse

fla·men·co /flə méngkō/ (*pl* **-cos**) *n* **1** a vigorous Spanish dance with hand clapping **2** music for a flamenco

ORIGIN Flamenco comes from a Spanish word meaning "Flemish person." In the Middle Ages the people of Flanders had a reputation for bright flamboyant dress.

flame·proof /fláym proof/ *adj* **1** describes textiles resistant to fire **2** describes cookware for use on direct heat

flame·re·tard·ant, flame·re·sist·ant *adj* resistant to catching fire

flame·throw·er *n* a weapon that projects a stream of burning liquid

⚡ **flame war** *n* an exchange of abusive e-mails

flam·ing /fláyming/ *adj* **1** producing flames **2** angry or intense **3** glowing **4** vivid in color

fla·min·go /flə míng gō/ (*pl* **-gos** *or* **-goes** *or* same) *n* a large pink tropical wading bird

ORIGIN Flamingo is first recorded in English in the mid-16C, and comes via Portuguese from obsolete Spanish *flamengo*. The Spanish may come from Dutch *Vlaming* "Flemish person," or ultimately from Latin *flamma* "flame." Whether its ultimate source is Dutch or Latin, the motivation behind the bird's name is its bright appearance. The Latin derivation would make it the "flame"-colored bird; the Dutch derivation would refer to the bright flamboyant dress of the people of Flanders (whence the Spanish dance, *flamenco*).

flam·ma·ble /flámməb'l/ *adj* able to catch fire

flan *n* **1** a custard dessert **2** an open pie with a filling

Flan·ders /flándərz/ historical region of NW Europe comprising parts of present-day W Belgium, N France, and SW Netherlands

flange /flanj/ *n* a projecting collar or rim —**flanged** *adj*

flank *n* **1** a side of the lower torso **2** a cut of meat from an animal's flank **3** a side of something, e.g., a sports field or a military formation ■ *vt* be on or at the side of

flan·nel /flánn'l/ *n* **1** soft cotton cloth. Use: clothing, sleepwear, sheets. **2** soft woolen cloth. Use: clothing. ■ **flan·nels** *npl* pants made of flannel

flan·nel·ette /flánn'l ét/ *n* light cotton flannel

flap *v*(**flapped, flap·ping**) **1** *vti* move something such as wings or arms up and down **2** *vi* fly by moving the wings **3** *vi* move or sway repeatedly ◇ *flags flapping in the breeze* **4** *vi* hit something with a broad object ■ *n* **1** a flat thin piece of something, attached at one edge, used as a cover **2** the part of a book's dust jacket that folds inside the cover **3** an act or sound of flapping **4** a movable surface on the back of an aircraft's wing used to create lift and drag **5** commotion (*infml*) —**flap·py** *adj*

flap·jack /fláp jàk/ *n* a thin flat cake cooked on a hot greased flat pan

flap·per /fláppər/ *n* a young unconventional woman of the 1920s

flare /flair/ *v* (**flared, flar·ing**) **1** *vi* burn suddenly and brightly **2** *vi* recur or intensify suddenly **3** *vi* become suddenly angry **4** *vti* widen out **5** *vt* burn off unwanted gas in the open air ■ *n* **1** a sudden or unsteady blaze of light or fire **2** a device for producing a light as a distress signal **3** a widening shape **4** in football, a short lateral pass **5** unwanted light in an optical device **6** an outburst of emotion **7** a flame for burning off waste gas **8** an area of inflammation ■ **flares** *npl* pants with wide legs below the knee —**flared** *adj*

SPELLCHECK Do not confuse the spelling of **flare** and **flair** ("talent"), which sound similar.

flare-up *n* **1** a sudden outburst of aggression (*infml*) **2** a recurrence of something

flash *v* **1** *vti* emit light suddenly, or be emitted as light suddenly **2** *vti* reflect light from another source, or be reflected in this way **3** *vti* catch or cause to catch fire suddenly **4** *vti* signal to somebody with lights **5** *vi* move quickly **6** *vti* appear or cause to appear for a moment **7** *vt* display something ostentatiously (*infml*) ■ *n* **1** a sudden burst of light **2** a sudden burst of something, e.g., inspiration **3** a brief moment **4** a device used to light a photographic subject, or the light it produces (*infml*) **5** a short news broadcast (*infml*) ◇ **a flash in the pan** a sudden brief success that is not, or not likely to be, repeated

flash·back /flásh bàk/ *n* **1** a recurring memory of a traumatic experience **2** an event or scene from the past inserted into a narrative

flash·bulb /flásh bùlb/ *n* a bulb producing a bright light for photography

flash burn *n* a burn caused by brief intense heat

flash·card /flásh kaard/ *n* a card that displays words or numbers, used as a learning aid

flash·er /fláshər/ *n* a flashing light

flash flood *n* a sudden and destructive rush of water caused by heavy rainfall

flash·gun /flásh gùn/ n a device producing a flash when a camera's shutter opens

flash·light /flásh lìt/ n a portable light source

⚡flash mem·o·ry n a read-only computer memory chip that can be erased and re-programmed in blocks

flash·point /flásh pòynt/ n 1 the temperature at which a vapor ignites 2 a trouble spot

flash·y /fláshee/ (-i·er, -i·est) adj 1 ostentatiously stylish 2 momentarily brilliant —**flash·i·ly** adv —**flash·i·ness** n

flask n 1 a small bottle used in a laboratory 2 a small flat container for alcohol

flat¹ adj (flat·ter, flat·test) 1 level and horizontal 2 even and smooth 3 lying horizontally 4 no longer bubbly 5 not inflated 6 in music, below the correct pitch 7 in music, one half-step below natural 8 lacking excitement 9 emphatically absolute ○ a flat lie ■ adv (flat·ter, flat·test) 1 below the correct musical pitch 2 very (infml) ○ flat broke 3 exactly ■ n 1 a level surface 2 a note lowered by a half-step 3 a deflated tire (infml) —**flat·ly** adv —**flat·ness** n

flat² n UK an apartment on one floor

flat·bed /flát bèd/ n a truck or trailer with an open flat area for freight

flat·car /flát kàar/ n an open railroad car without sides

flat-chest·ed /-chéstəd/ adj same with small breasts

flat·fish /flát fìsh/ (pl same or -fish·es) n any ocean fish with a flat body and both eyes on the upper side

flat-foot·ed adj having feet with low arches

Flat·head /flát hèd/ (pl same or -heads) n a member of Native North American people who lived in W Montana and N Idaho

flat·i·ron /flát ìrn/ n an iron used to press clothes

flat·land /flát lànd/ n a large stretch of level land

flat race n a horserace without jumps —**flat rac·ing** n

flat·ten /flátt'n/ v 1 vti make or become flat 2 vr stand flat against something

flat·ter /fláttər/ vt 1 compliment somebody in order to win favor 2 appeal to somebody's vanity 3 make somebody or something look good —**flat·ter·er** n —**flat·ter·ing** adj —**flat·ter·ing·ly** adv

flat·ter·y /fláttəree/ n 1 the paying of compliments to win favor 2 compliments

flat·top /flát tòp/ n a haircut that is flat on top

flat·u·lent /fláchələnt/ adj 1 full of or causing gas in the digestive system 2 pompous or self-important —**flat·u·lence** n —**flat·u·lent·ly** adv

flat·ware /flát wàir/ n 1 knives, forks, and spoons 2 flat or shallow tableware, e.g., plates

Flau·bert /flō báir/, **Gustave** (1821–80) French novelist —**Flau·ber·tian** /flō báirsh'n, -báirtee ən/ adj

flaunt /flawnt/ v 1 vt show off something 2 vr parade yourself shamelessly

---

USAGE **flaunt** or **flout**? **Flaunt** expresses the idea of shameless or ostentatious display: He flaunted his wealth. **Flout** expresses the idea of openly disobeying or defying a law or convention: drivers who flout the law.

---

flau·tist n MUSIC = **flutist**

fla·vor /fláyvər/ n 1 the characteristic taste of something 2 a representative idea of something ○ gives a flavor of the book 3 a unique characteristic ■ vt 1 give flavor to food 2 give uniqueness to something —**fla·vor·ful** adj —**fla·vor·less** adj

---

ORIGIN **Flavor** when it was first used in English meant "smell" not "taste." Smell contributes to taste, and a shift in meaning might be seen as natural, but it is not until 300 years later, in the late 17C, that the use "characteristic taste" appears.

---

fla·vor·ing /fláyvəring/ n something that adds flavor to food

flaw¹ n 1 a blemish that makes something imperfect 2 any imperfection —**flawed** adj

---

SYNONYMS **flaw, imperfection, fault, defect, failing, blemish** CORE MEANING: something that detracts from perfection

---

flaw² n 1 a gust of wind 2 a squall

flaw·less /fláwləss/ adj perfect —**flaw·less·ly** adv —**flaw·less·ness** n

flax n a fine light-colored plant fiber. Use: linen textiles.

flax·en /fláksən/ adj 1 of a pale yellow color 2 made from flax

flay vt 1 whip severely 2 strip the skin off

flea /flee/ n 1 a small leaping bloodsucking insect 2 a small beetle or crustacean that jumps like a flea

---

SPELLCHECK Do not confuse the spelling of **flea** and **flee** ("run away"), which sound similar.

---

flea·bag /flee bàg/ n a cheap shabby hotel or rooming house (infml)

flea-bit·ten adj covered with fleas or their bites

flea col·lar n a pet's collar containing flea repellent

flea mar·ket n a market selling cheap or used goods

fleck n a small mark or streak ■ vt streak or spot

fledg·ling /fléjjling/, **fledge·ling** n 1 a young bird with new flight feathers 2 somebody inexperienced ■ adj inexperienced

---

ORIGIN **Fledgling** is a relatively late (mid-19C) formation from a verb fledge, on the model of nestling. Fledge is now found mainly in full-

fledged. It means "develop feathers that are large enough for flight," and ultimately comes from an ancient root meaning "fly."

flee /flee/ (**fled**) *vi* **1** run away **2** disappear quickly (*literary*) ◊ See note at **flea**

fleece *n* **1** the woolly coat of a sheep **2** a mass of wool shorn from a sheep **3** soft fabric with a nap or pile. Use: outer garments, lining. ■ *vt* (**fleeced**, **fleec·ing**) **1** swindle somebody out of money (*infml*) **2** shear sheep —**fleec·er** *n*

fleec·y /fleéssee/ (**-i-er**, **-i-est**) *adj* made of or resembling fleece —**fleec·i·ness** *n*

fleet[1] *n* **1** a group of naval ships **2** a number of vehicles or craft under single ownership

fleet[2] (*literary*) *adj* **1** moving quickly **2** passing or fading quickly ■ *v* **1** *vi* move quickly **2** *vti* pass quickly

fleet ad·mi·ral, Fleet Ad·mi·ral *n* the highest US Navy commander

fleet·ing /fleéting/ *adj* passing or fading quickly —**fleet·ing·ly** *adv* —**fleet·ing·ness** *n* ◊ See note at **temporary**

Flem·ing /flémming/, **Sir Alexander** (1881–1955) British microbiologist. He shared a Nobel Prize in physiology or medicine (1945) with E. B. Chain and H. W. Florey for his discovery of the first antibiotic, penicillin.

Flem·ish /flémmish/ *adj* of Flanders ■ *n* one of the official languages of Belgium, closely related to Dutch ■ *npl* the people of Flanders

flesh *n* **1** the soft tissues that cover the bones of the body **2** the meat of animals **3** the pulp of fruits and vegetables **4** the physical aspect of humanity ◊ **press the flesh** greet and shake the hands of many people in public (*infml*)

□ **flesh out** *vt* amplify and add details to

flesh and blood *n* **1** relatives **2** human nature

flesh·ly /fléshlee/ (**-li-er**, **-li-est**) *adj* **1** bodily **2** of physical pleasure **3** not spiritual —**flesh·li·ness** *n*

flesh wound *n* a superficial wound

flesh·y /fléshee/ (**-i-er**, **-i-est**) *adj* **1** plump **2** with more flesh than other parts of the body —**flesh·i·ness** *n*

fleur-de-lis /flùr də leé/ (*pl* **fleurs-de-lis** /-leéz/), **fleur-de-lys** (*pl* **fleurs-de-lys**) *n* a heraldic symbol in the form of three tapering petals tied by a surrounding band

flew /floo/ past tense of **fly** ◊ See note at **flu**

flex *vti* **1** to bend something or be able to be bent easily **2** bend or contract a body part

~~flexable~~ incorrect spelling of **flexible**

flex·i·ble /fléksəb'l/ *adj* **1** able to bend without breaking **2** able to adapt to new situations —**flex·i·bil·i·ty** /fléksə billətee/ *n* —**flex·i·bly** *adv*

flex·time /fléks tìm/, **flex·i·time** /fléksee-/ *n* a system giving employees adaptable working hours

flick[1] *n* **1** a quick jerking movement **2** a quick blow ■ *v* **1** *vt* hit with a quick jerking movement **2** *vti* move jerkily **3** *vt* move or propel with a quick blow ◊ *flick a switch*

□ **flick through** *vt* read superficially while turning the pages quickly

flick[2] *n* a movie (*infml; in combination*)

flick·er[1] /flíkər/ *vi* **1** shine unsteadily **2** flutter or move jerkily ■ *n* **1** a fluctuating light **2** a short-lived feeling or expression ◊ *a flicker of joy* —**flick·er·ing·ly** *adv*

flick·er[2] /flíkər/ *n* a North American woodpecker

fli·er /flíīr/, **fly·er** *n* **1** an aircraft pilot **2** an aircraft passenger **3** a printed sheet, usually an advertisement, that is widely distributed

flight[1] /flīt/ *n* **1** the process or act of flying **2** an airplane trip **3** a series of steps between floors **4** a group of birds or planes flying together **5** an instance of imagining something strange or unreasonable ◊ *a flight of the imagination*

flight[2] /flīt/ *n* the act of running away

flight at·ten·dant *n* somebody who attends to airline passengers during a flight

flight bag *n* a small suitcase

flight deck *n* **1** the runway on an aircraft carrier **2** the part of an airplane where the pilot sits and where the controls are

flight·less /flítləss/ *adj* unable to fly

flight path *n* the course taken by an aircraft

flight plan *n* information on a proposed flight

flight re·cord·er *n* an instrument built into a plane that records details of its flight

flight sim·u·la·tor *n* a training device for pilots that mimics the conditions in a plane

flight-test *vt* test a new aircraft's performance —**flight test** *n*

flight·y /flítee/ (**-i-er**, **-i-est**) *adj* changeable and capricious —**flight·i·ly** *adv* —**flight·i·ness** *n*

flim-flam /flím flàm/ *n* a trick or swindle (*slang*) —**flim-flam** *vt* —**flim-flam·mer·y** *n*

flim·sy /flímzee/ (**-si-er**, **-si-est**) *adj* **1** fragile **2** easily torn **3** unconvincing and difficult to believe ◊ *a flimsy excuse* —**flim·si·ly** *adv* —**flim·si·ness** *n* ◊ See note at **fragile**

flinch *vi* **1** react involuntarily to pain or fear with a small backward movement **2** avoid confronting somebody or doing something —**flinch·ing·ly** *adv* ◊ See note at **recoil**

fling *v* (**flung**) **1** *vt* throw something violently **2** *vr* move forcefully **3** *vt* move your head or arms suddenly and dramatically ■ *n* (*infml*) **1** a short romantic affair **2** a period of carefree enjoyment ◊ See note at **throw**

flint *n* **1** a very hard quartz that makes sparks **2** the part of a cigarette lighter that makes the spark

flint·lock /flínt lòk/ *n* **1** a type of early firearm with a flint in the hammer **2** the firing mechanism of a flintlock

flint·y /flíntee/ (**-i·er, -i·est**) *adj* **1** stern and unemotional **2** containing flint —**flint·i·ness** *n*

flip *v* (**flipped, flip·ping**) **1** *vti* turn something over quickly, or turn quickly **2** *vt* move something with a quick light motion **3** *vti* turn the pages of a book or magazine **4** *vti* spin a coin in the air to decide something **5** *vi* suddenly become angry (*slang*) ■ *adj* (**flip·per, flip·pest**) flippant (*infml*) ■ *n* **1** the spinning of a coin in the air **2** a complete turn of the body in the air

flip chart *n* a large pad of paper mounted on an easel

flip-flop *n* **1** a backless sandal (*infml*) **2** a change of mind (*infml*) **3** a backward flip ■ *vi* (**flip-flop·ped, flip-flop·ping**) change opinion (*infml*)

flip·pant /flíppənt/ *adj* not taking something seriously enough —**flip·pan·cy** *n* —**flip·pant·ly** *adv*

flip·per /flíppər/ *n* **1** an aquatic animal's broad flat limb, used for swimming **2** a broad flat rubber extension for a swimmer's or diver's foot

flirt /flurt/ *vi* **1** express a playful sexual interest in somebody **2** consider something only casually o *flirt with the idea of moving to Chicago* ■ *n* somebody who behaves in a playfully alluring way —**flirt·ing·ly** *adv*

flir·ta·tion /flur táysh'n/ *n* **1** a playful display of sexual interest **2** a period of casual interest in something

flir·ta·tious /flur táyshəss/ *adj* tending to flirt with people —**flir·ta·tious·ly** *adv* —**flir·ta·tious·ness** *n*

flit (**flit·ted, flit·ting**) *vi* move quickly from place to place without stopping for long —**flit·ter** *n*

float /flōt/ *v* **1** *vi* rest on the surface of a liquid **2** *vt* place or move something on the surface of a liquid **3** *vi* stay up in the air **4** *vi* be heard or smelled faintly o *The scent of her perfume floated across the lawn.* **5** *vi* move gracefully (*literary*) **6** *vt* propose something as a plan (*infml*) **7** *vi* live or act without a fixed purpose or plan o *He floated from job to job.* **8** *vt* finance a company by selling stock in it to the public ■ *n* **1** a floating object that keeps another object buoyant **2** an elaborately decorated vehicle in a parade **3** a soft drink mixed with ice cream

float·er /flōtər/ *n* **1** a temporary worker (*infml*) **2** a worker who is shifted to various tasks as the need arises **3** a moving spot on the eye that interferes with vision

flock *n* **1** a group of birds or sheep **2** a crowd of people ■ *vi* go in large numbers

floe /flō/ *n* a mass of ice on the ocean

SPELLCHECK Do not confuse the spelling of **floe** and **flow** ("move freely"), which sound similar.

---

flog (**flogged, flog·ging**) *vt* beat very hard

flood /flud/ *n* **1** a large amount of water covering a previously dry area **2** a huge number of people or things o *a flood of complaints* **3** high tide **4** a floodlight **5** **Flood** in the Bible, a devastating flood that covered the Earth ■ *v* **1** *vti* cover an area with water, or be completely covered with water **2** *vi* overflow **3** *vt* supply or produce to excess —**flood·ed** *adj*

flood·gate /flúd gàyt/ *n* **1** a gate in a watercourse that controls the flow **2** something that serves to contain the potentially destructive spread of something

flood·light /flúd lìt/ *n* a powerful lamp that shines over a wide area ■ *vt* (**-light·ed** *or* **-lit** /-lìt/, **-light·ed** *or* **-lit**) light with floodlights

flood·plain /flúd plàyn/ *n* an area of low-lying flat land next to a river

flood tide *n* **1** a rising tide **2** an irresistible force

floor /flawr/ *n* **1** the part of a room on which you walk **2** one level of a building **3** the ground at the bottom of a natural feature such as a lake or forest **4** the part of a legislature where members sit **5** the part of a stock exchange where securities are traded **6** the lowest limit ■ *vt* **1** astonish somebody **2** knock somebody down

floor·board /fláwr bàwrd/ *n* **1** a wooden board joined to others to form a floor **2** a car floor

floor·ing /fláwring/ *n* materials used to make a floor

floor lamp *n* a tall lamp with a base that rests on the floor

floor plan *n* a plan of a room seen from above

floor·show /fláwr shò/ *n* an entertainment in a nightclub

floor·walk·er /fláwr wàwkər/ *n* a supervisor in a department store

flop *vi* (**flopped, flop·ping**) **1** sit or lie down heavily **2** move or hang limply **3** fail completely (*infml*) ■ *n* a total failure (*infml*)

flop·house /flóp hòwss/ (*pl* **-houses** /-hòwzəz/) *n* a cheap shabby hotel or rooming house (*infml*)

⨍ flop·py /flóppee/ *adj* (**-pi·er, -pi·est**) hanging limply ■ *n* (*pl* **-pies**) a floppy disk (*infml*) —**flop·pi·ly** *adv* —**flop·pi·ness** *n*

⨍ flop·py disk *n* a small data storage disk used in computers

---

ORIGIN A floppy disk is "floppy" only in comparison with a *hard disk*. The magnetic disk itself is flexible but the outer casing is now more rigid than it was in the earlier days of computers.

⨍ flops, FLOPS *abbr* floating-point operations per second (*indicates the speed of a computer*)

⨍ flop·ti·cal /flóptik'l/ *adj* describes a system for storing computer data on a disk that combines magnetic and optical technology

flo·ra /fláwra/ n all plants, especially all those found in a particular area *(fml)*

ORIGIN The name of the Roman goddess of flowers, Flora, was used in the Latin titles of descriptive catalogs of plants from the mid-17C. The word first appears in English use in the late 18C. *Flora* was formed from the Latin word for "flower," from which *flower* itself derives.

flo·ral /fláwrəl/ adj of, decorated with, or containing flowers —**flo·ral·ly** adv

Flor·ence /fláwrənss/ city in central Italy on the Arno River. Pop. 376,760 (1999). Italian **Firenze**

~~florescent~~ incorrect spelling of **fluorescent**

flor·id /fláwrid/ adj 1 having an unhealthy red complexion 2 ornate in wording and style —**flor·id·ly** adv —**flor·id·ness** n

Flor·i·da /fláwridə/ state in the SE United States. Cap. Tallahassee. Pop. 15,982,378 (2000). —**Flor·i·di·an** /flə ríddee ən/ adj, n

Flor·i·da Keys /-kéez/ chain of islands and reefs in S Florida, extending into the Gulf of Mexico. Length 192 mi./309 km.

flo·rist /fláwrist/ n a person or store that sells flowers and plants

floss vti clean between your teeth with special thread ■ n 1 dental floss 2 short silkworm fibers

flo·ta·tion /flō táysh'n/ n 1 the process or condition of floating 2 the selling of stock in a company to finance it

flo·ta·tion tank n a tank of salt water and minerals in which somebody floats to relax

flo·til·la /flō tíllə/ n 1 a fleet of small ships 2 an US naval unit of small warships

flot·sam /flótsəm/ n 1 wreckage floating in the sea 2 people who live on the margins of society *(sometimes offensive)*

flounce[1] /flowns/ (**flounced, flounc·ing**) vi move with an angry swagger —**flounce** n

flounce[2] /flowns/ n a decorative strip of gathered cloth on a garment or curtain

floun·der[1] /flówndər/ vi 1 move in a clumsy uncontrolled way 2 hesitate in confusion

floun·der[2] /flówndər/ (pl same or -ders) n 1 a flatfish of shallow coastal waters 2 a flounder as food

flour /flowr/ n 1 finely ground cereal grains 2 ground powder made from any dried edible plant ■ vt cover with flour —**flour·y** adj

SPELLCHECK Do not confuse the spelling of **flour** and **flower** (of a plant), which sound similar.

~~flourescent~~ incorrect spelling of **fluorescent**
~~flouride~~ incorrect spelling of **fluoride**
~~flourine~~ incorrect spelling of **fluorine**

flour·ish /flúrrish/ vi 1 be healthy or grow well 2 do well or succeed ■ n 1 a dramatic hand

or body movement 2 an embellishment to something handwritten

flout /flowt/ vt openly ignore a law or convention —**flout·ing·ly** adv ◊ See note at **flaunt**

flow /flō/ vi 1 move freely from place to place 2 circulate in the body *(refers especially to blood)* 3 be said fluently 4 be experienced as an emotion intensely and often visibly 5 derive from something *(literary)* 6 hang loosely and gracefully *(refers to clothes or hair)* ■ n 1 the movement of a fluid or an electrical charge 2 a mass or quantity that is flowing 3 a steady stream of people or things —**flow·ing·ly** adv ◊ **go with the flow** fall in with the mood or thinking of others ◊ See note at **floe**

flow chart, flow di·a·gram n a diagram showing a sequence of operations in a process

flow·er /flówr/ n 1 the colored part of a plant, containing its sexual organs 2 a single stem with a flower on it 3 a plant grown for its flowers 4 the period during which a plant is in bloom 5 the best part of something ■ vi 1 produce blooms 2 develop to maturity —**flow·ered** adj ◊ See note at **flour**

flow·er·bed /flówr bèd/ n an area of ground planted with flowers

flow·er girl n a girl who is a bridal attendant

flow·er·ing /flówring/ adj able to produce blooms ■ n a period of success

flow·er·pot /flówr pòt/ n a container for growing plants

flow·er·y /flówree/ (**-i·er, -i·est**) adj 1 full of overly elaborate expressions 2 of or decorated with flowers —**flow·er·i·ness** n

flown past participle of **fly**[1]

flow sheet n a flow chart

flu /floo/ n a viral illness producing a high fever, respiratory inflammation, and muscle pain

ORIGIN Flu is a shortening of *influenza*, first recorded in the mid-19C. *Influenza* itself originally referred specifically to a severe epidemic of 1743, which began in Italy.

SPELLCHECK Do not confuse the spelling of **flu, flue** ("a smoke or heat outlet"), and **flew** (past tense of *fly*), which sound similar.

flub (**flubbed, flub·bing**) vti blunder or mess up *(infml)* —**flub** n

fluc·tu·ate /flúkchoo àyt/ (**-at·ed, -at·ing**) vi vary in level, degree, or value —**fluc·tu·a·tion** /flúkchoo áysh'n/ n

flue /floo/ n a smoke or heat outlet ◊ See note at **flu**

flu·ent /floo ənt/ adj 1 having or showing a good command of a language 2 elegantly and effortlessly expressed —**flu·en·cy** n —**flu·ent·ly** adv

fluff /fluf/ n 1 light balls of fiber that collect on fabric 2 downy fuzz on some birds or seeds 3 a purely decorative item ■ vt 1 perform something badly (*infml*) **2** shake or pat something to get air into it

fluff·y /flúffee/ (**-i·er, -i·est**) *adj* **1** soft and light in texture **2** downy or feathery —**fluff·i·ly** *adv* —**fluff·i·ness** *n*

flu·id /flóo id/ *n* **1** anything liquid **2** in scientific usage, a liquid or gas ■ *adj* **1** flowing (*technical*) **2** smooth and graceful in movement or performance **3** likely to change ○ *The situation had remained fluid.* —**flu·id·i·ty** /floo íddətee/ *n* —**flu·id·ly** *adv*

flu·id ounce *n* **1** a US unit of liquid measurement equal to $\frac{1}{16}$ of a US pint or 29.57 ml **2** a UK unit of liquid measurement equal to $\frac{1}{20}$ of an imperial pint or 28.41 ml

fluke[1] *n* an accidental success (*infml*) —**fluk·y** *adj*

fluke[2] *n* a parasitic worm with a flattened body

fluke[3] *n* **1** either of the blades at the ends of an anchor **2** either of the lobes of a whale's tail

flume *n* a narrow gorge

flum·mox /flúmməks/ *vt* baffle and confuse (*infml*)

flung past participle, past tense of **fling**

flunk *vti* fail an exam or course (*infml*)

flunk·out /flúngk òwt/ *n* a failed student (*disapproving*)

flun·ky /flúngkee/ (*pl* **-kies**), **flun·key** (*pl* **-keys**) *n* **1** a servile assistant (*infml*) **2** a manservant in livery —**flun·ky·ism** *n*

fluo·resce /flŏo réss, flaw-/ (**-resced, -resc·ing**) *vi* experience or show fluorescence

fluo·res·cence /flŏo réss'nss, flaw-/ *n* **1** the emission of light by an object exposed to radiation **2** glowing light produced by fluorescence

fluo·res·cent /flŏo réss'nt, flaw-/ *adj* **1** capable of producing or undergoing fluorescence **2** bright and dazzling in color

fluo·res·cent lamp, fluo·res·cent light *n* an electric lamp containing a low pressure vapor in a glass tube

fluor·i·date /flŏori dàyt/ (**-dat·ed, -dat·ing**) *vt* treat water by adding small amounts of fluoride salts —**fluor·i·da·tion** /flŏori dáysh'n/ *n*

fluor·ide /flóor ìd, fláwr-/ *n* any chemical compound consisting of fluorine and another element or group

fluor·ine /flóor èen, fláwr-/ *n* (*symbol* **F**) a toxic reactive gaseous chemical element. Use: water treatment, making fluorides and fluorocarbons.

fluor·o·car·bon /flŏorō kaàrbən, flàwrō-/ *n* an inert chemical containing carbon and fluorine. Use: nonstick coatings, lubricants, refrigerants, solvents.

flur·ry /flúr ee, flúrree/ *n* (*pl* **-ries**) **1** a burst of activity **2** a short period of snowfall ■ *v* (**-ried, -ries**) **1** *vt* agitate or confuse **2** *vi* snow lightly

flush[1] *v* **1** *vi* turn red in the face **2** *vti* make water flow through a toilet to clean it after use **3** *vt* dispose of in a toilet ■ *n* **1** a sudden intense feeling **2** the beginning of an exciting or pleasurable period **3** a sudden rush of things **4** reddishness

flush[2] *adj* **1** level with something **2** beside or against something **3** temporarily rich (*infml*) ■ *adv* **1** completely level **2** directly or squarely —**flush·ness** *n*

flush[3] *vt* drive out of hiding ■ *n* birds frightened out of hiding

flush[4] *n* in poker, a hand of cards of one suit

flushed *adj* **1** red-faced **2** excited

flus·ter /flústər/ *vti* make or become nervous ■ *n* a nervous or agitated state —**flus·tered** *adj*

flute *n* **1** a wind instrument with a high-pitched sound **2** a decorative groove, especially in an architectural column ■ *vt* (**flut·ed, flut·ing**) make rounded grooves in —**flut·ed** *adj*

flut·ist /flóotist/, **flau·tist** /fláwtist, flów-/ *n* a flute player

flut·ter /flúttər/ *v* **1** *vi* move with a gentle waving motion **2** *vti* move quickly up and down or side to side **3** *vti* flap the wings rapidly **4** *vi* fly lightly or noiselessly **5** *vi* beat rapidly, either because of a disorder or from excitement (*refers to the heart*) **6** *vi* have a quivering nervous or excited feeling ■ *n* **1** a quick movement **2** agitation or excitement **3** a rapid heartbeat —**flut·ter·ing·ly** *adv* —**flut·ter·y** *adj*

flu·vi·al /flóovee əl/ *adj* of rivers

flux *n* **1** constant change **2** a substance that aids flowing, e.g., in soldering, welding, or ceramic glazes **3** flow or a rate of flow **4** the strength of a magnetic or electrical field in a particular area

fly[1] *v* (**flew** /floo/, **flown** /flōn/, **flies**) **1** *vi* move through the air **2** *vi* travel in an aircraft **3** *vt* take or send something by air **4** *vti* be the pilot of a plane **5** *vt* travel over an area by air **6** *vti* display a flag, or be displayed, as on a pole **7** *vi* move freely in the air ○ *with her hair flying* **8** *vi* go at top speed ○ *I must fly!* **9** *vi* move quickly and with explosive force ○ *sent debris flying everywhere* **10** *vi* pass quickly ○ *The time flew by.* **11** *vi* rush to do something ○ *He flew to our aid.* ■ *n* (*pl* **flies**) **1** the front opening of a pair of pants **2** the entrance flap of a tent **3** a separate outer roof of tent ◇ **fly high** enjoy a period of great success or happiness ◇ **let fly** speak angrily ◇ **on the fly 1** while in a hurry **2** while a computer program is running (*infml*)

fly[2] (*pl* **flies**) *n* **1** a two-winged insect, many of which are pests **2** any flying insect (*usually in combination*) **3** a fly-fishing lure ◇ **a fly in the ointment** a problem that spoils a good situation

fly·a·way /flí ə wày/ *adj* fine and light

fly·blown /flí blòn/ *adj* 1 maggot-ridden and contaminated 2 dirty

fly·by /flí bī/ *n* a flight close to something, especially a spaceflight close to an astronomical object

fly-by-night *adj* 1 unscrupulous in business 2 not lasting long

fly·catch·er /flí kàchər/ *n* an insect-eating songbird

fly·er *n* = flier

fly·ing /flí ing/ *adj* 1 able to fly 2 moving fast ■ *n* air travel

fly·ing but·tress *n* a proplike support built out from an outside wall

fly·ing fish *n* a fish that leaps using its large fins like wings

fly·ing fox *n* an Australasian fruit bat

⚡**fly·ing mouse** *n* a computer mouse that can be lifted and used as a pointer

fly·ing sau·cer *n* a disk-shaped UFO

fly·ing squad *n* a police or military unit that can be deployed quickly

fly·ing squir·rel *n* a nocturnal squirrel that uses a flap of skin between its front and back limbs to glide between trees

fly·leaf /flí leèf/ (*pl* **-leaves** /-leèvz/) *n* the first page in a hardcover book, attached to the inside cover page

Flynn /flin/, **Errol** (1909–59) Australian-born US actor

fly·o·ver /flí òvər/ *n* a low flight of aircraft, usually made as a spectacle for people on the ground

fly·pa·per /flí pàypər/ *n* sticky paper on which to catch flies

fly·sheet /flí sheèt/ *n* a small advertising poster

fly swat·ter *n* a tool for swatting insects

fly·weight /flí wàyt/ *n* 1 the lightest weight category for a boxer 2 a boxer who competes at this weight

fly·wheel /flí weèl, -hweèl/ *n* a heavy wheel that maintains a constant speed in a machine

Fm *symbol* fermium

FM *abbr* frequency modulation

fm. *abbr* fathom

foal /fōl/ *n* a young horse ■ *vi* give birth to a foal

foam /fōm/ *n* 1 a mass of bubbles on a liquid 2 any thick frothy substance o *shaving foam* 3 rubber, plastic, or similar material containing bubbles of air ■ *vi* produce bubbles —**foam·i·ness** *n* —**foam·y** *adj*

foam rub·ber *n* a spongy form of rubber. Use: mattresses, padding, insulation.

fob *n* 1 a chain for a pocket watch 2 an ornament or electronic device on a key ring or chain

□ **fob off** *vt* 1 mislead so as to forestall questioning 2 give something inferior or unwanted to

FOB, F.O.B., f.o.b., fob *abbr* free on board

fo·cac·cia /fə kaáchə, fō-/ *n* flat Italian bread made with yeast and olive oil and sprinkled with a topping

fo·cal /fōk'l/ *adj* 1 principal 2 of the focusing of an image —**fo·cal·ly** *adv*

fo·cal length *n* (*symbol* **f**) the distance from a lens to a focal point

fo·cal point *n* 1 the point at which rays of light meeting a lens converge or appear to diverge 2 a center of attention

fo'c's'le *n* NAUT = forecastle

fo·cus /fōkəss/ *n* (*pl* **-cus·es** *or* **-ci** /-sī/) 1 the main emphasis of something 2 an area of concern o *Our investigation has a narrow focus.* 3 a concentrated quality o *bring focus to the problem* 4 the sharpness of an image 5 the condition of seeing sharply 6 (*pl* **fo·ci**) a focal point 7 a device on a camera for adjusting the lens ■ *vti* (**-cused** *or* **-cussed**, **-cus·ing** *or* **-cus·sing**, **-cus·es** *or* **-cus·ses**) 1 direct your attention to somebody or something 2 adjust vision to see something clearly 3 adjust a lens for a clear image

fo·cused /fōkəst/, **fo·cussed** *adj* 1 concentrated 2 single-minded

fo·cus group *n* a representative group of people who are questioned about their opinions as part of political or market research

fod·der /fóddər/ *n* food for livestock

foe *n* an enemy (*fml*)

foe·tal etc. = fetal etc.

fog *n* 1 condensed water vapor in the air at or near ground level 2 something that reduces visibility 3 a state of confusion ■ *v* (**fogged, fog·ging**) 1 *vti* make or become obscured with condensation 2 *vt* make confused —**fogged** *adj*

fog bank *n* a mass of thick fog

fog·bound /fáwg bòwnd, fóg-/ *adj* 1 prevented by fog from traveling 2 shrouded in fog

fog·gy /fáwgee, fóggee/ (**-gi·er, -gi·est**) *adj* 1 filled with or obscured by fog 2 vague o *only a foggy idea* —**fog·gi·ly** *adv* —**fog·gi·ness** *n*

fog·horn /fáwg hàwrn, fóg-/ *n* a horn sounded to warn of fog

fo·gy /fōgee/ (*pl* **-gies**), **fo·gey** (*pl* **-geys**) *n* a person regarded as old-fashioned —**fo·gy·ish** *adj* —**fo·gy·ism** *n*

foi·ble /fóyb'l/ *n* a personal weakness or quirk (*usually pl*)

ORIGIN Foible is from a later form of the French word that entered English much earlier as *feeble*. It was originally used as an adjective meaning "weak," between the late 16C and early 18C. The earliest use of the noun (mid-17C) was as a technical term in fencing. The usual modern sense is recorded from the late 17C.

foie gras /fwaa graa/ *n* a fattened goose liver, or pâté made from it

foil[1] *n* 1 metal in thin sheets 2 a good contrast to something 3 a wing-shaped blade attached to the bottom of a hydrofoil

foil[2] *vt* thwart somebody's success

foil[3] *n* a long thin sword used in fencing

foist *vt* 1 force somebody to accept something undesirable 2 give somebody something inferior on the pretense that it is genuine

Fo·kine /faw keen, fō-/, **Michel** (1880–1942) Russian-born US dancer and choreographer

fold[1] /fōld/ *v* 1 *vt* bend something flat over on itself 2 *vt* make something smaller by folding it or parts of it 3 *vt* draw the arms, legs, or hands together or toward the body 4 *vt* bring the wings together or next to the body 5 *vt* put your arms around and hold somebody 6 *vi* go out of business 7 *vi* in card games, give up your hand ■ *n* 1 a folded part 2 a crease caused by folding 3 a part of something that hangs in a folded shape —**fold·a·ble** *adj* —**fold·ing** *adj*

☐ **fold in** *vt* add a food ingredient to a mixture carefully and lightly

fold[2] /fōld/ *n* 1 an enclosed area for livestock, especially sheep 2 livestock in a fold 3 a group with interests or traits in common ○ *We welcomed them back to the fold.*

-fold *suffix* 1 divided into parts ○ *manifold* 2 times ○ *tenfold*

fold·a·way /fōldə wày/ *adj* made to be folded and stored

⨍ **fold·er** /fōldər/ *n* 1 a piece of cardboard folded to make a file in which papers can be kept 2 a conceptual container for the storage of computer files in some operating systems

fold-out /fōld òwt/ *n* 1 an extra-large page in a publication, folded to fit a piece of furniture with a folding part —**fold-out** *adj*

fold-up /fōld ùp/ *adj* designed to be folded ■ *n* a failure of a business

fo·li·age /fōlee ij, fōlij/ *n* 1 leaves 2 leafy decoration

fo·li·o /fōlee ò/ *n* (*pl* -**os**) 1 a large book or manuscript 2 a large sheet of paper folded to make four pages for a book 3 a page numbered on the front ■ *adj* printed in a large format

folk /fōk/ *npl* people in general (*+ pl verb*) ■ *n* folk music (*+ sing verb*) ■ *adj* 1 traditional, especially passed down orally 2 from the ideas of ordinary people

folk dance *n* 1 a traditional dance 2 music for a traditional dance

folk he·ro *n* somebody who is admired by the public

folk·lore /fōk làwr/ *n* traditional stories, usually passed down orally —**folk·lor·ist** *n*

folk mu·sic *n* 1 traditional songs and music 2 modern music in a traditional style

folk song *n* 1 a traditional song 2 a modern song in a traditional style —**folk sing·er** *n* —**folk sing·ing** *n*

folk·sy /fōksee/ (-**si·er**, -**si·est**) *adj* 1 in the style of folk traditions 2 friendly —**folk·si·ness** *n*

folk·tale /fōk tàyl/ *n* a traditional story

fol·li·cle /fóllik'l/ *n* a small gland, cavity, or sac —**fol·lic·u·lar** /fə líkyələr/ *adj*

fol·low /fóllō/ *v* 1 *vti* come after somebody or something ○ *the main course followed by dessert* 2 *vt* add to something already done ○ *She followed her lecture with a demonstration.* 3 *vti* go after or behind somebody, moving in the same direction 4 *vt* pay close attention to 5 *vt* go along the course of ○ *follow the path* 6 *vt* go in the direction indicated by ○ *Follow that sign ahead.* 7 *vt* act or develop in accordance with 8 *vti* understand something 9 *vt* engage in as a career or profession 10 *vt* keep up to date with 11 *vi* result from something

---

SYNONYMS follow, chase, pursue, tail, shadow, stalk, trail CORE MEANING: go after or behind

---

☐ **follow through** *v* 1 *vti* take further action to complete something 2 *vi* continue the motion of a swing or throw

☐ **follow up** *vt* 1 act on information 2 do after or in addition to something ○ *will follow up the phone call with a letter*

fol·low·er /fóllō ər/ *n* 1 somebody who comes or travels after somebody or something else 2 a supporter or admirer of a person, cause, or activity

fol·low·ing /fóllō ing/ *adj* 1 next in order 2 about to be mentioned ■ *n* 1 a group of followers 2 the things about to be mentioned (*+ pl verb*) ■ *prep* after

fol·low-on *adj* continuing or resulting —**fol·low-on** *n*

fol·low-the-lead·er *n* a game in which players copy another's actions

fol·low-through *n* 1 a continuation and completion of something 2 in a sport, the concluding part of a movement

fol·low-up *n* 1 further action intended to supplement something 2 something that gives more information —**fol·low-up** *adj*

fol·ly /fóllee/ (*pl* -**lies**) *n* 1 thoughtless or reckless behavior 2 a thoughtless or reckless act or idea (*often pl*) 3 an impractical building of eccentric design

Fol·som /fólsəm/ *adj* of a prehistoric culture of North America that made leaf-shaped flint projectile points

fo·ment /fō mént/ *vt* stir up trouble or rebellion —**fo·men·ta·tion** /fōmən táysh'n, -men-/ *n* ◊ See note at **ferment**

fond *adj* 1 feeling or showing love or affection for somebody 2 liking or enjoying some-

thing **3** overly doting **4** overoptimistic ○ *fond hopes* —**fond·ly** *adv* —**fond·ness** *n* ◊
See note at **love**

Fon·da /fóndə/, **Henry** (1905–82) US movie and stage actor

fon·dant /fóndənt/ *n* **1** sugar paste. Use: filling for chocolates, coating for cakes and confectionery. **2** a soft candy made with fondant

fon·dle /fónd'l/ (**-dled**, **-dling**) *v* **1** *vt* stroke lovingly or sexually **2** touch sexually in an unwelcome way

fon·due /fon dóo, -dyóo/, **fon·du** *n* a dish eaten by dipping small pieces of food into melted cheese or hot oil

font[1] *n* **1** a receptacle for baptismal water or holy water **2** an abundant source (*literary*)

font[2] *n* a set of type or characters of the same style and size

fon·ta·nel /fòntə nél/, **fon·ta·nelle** *n* a soft, membrane-covered space between bones at the front and back of a young baby's skull

food *n* **1** substances that people, plants, and animals eat or absorb to obtain the nutrients they need **2** solid nourishment, not drinks **3** a mental stimulus

food bank *n* a place where food is collected to be given to people without the money to buy food

food chain *n* a hierarchy of feeding relationships among organisms

food court *n* a restaurant area in a shopping mall

food·ie /fóodee/, **food·y** (*pl* **-ies**) *n* somebody who enjoys good food (*infml*)

food poi·son·ing *n* inflammation of the stomach and intestines caused by eating contaminated food

food pro·ces·sor *n* an appliance that chops and blends foods

food stamp *n* a government-issued coupon exchangeable for food

food·stuff /fóod stùf/ *n* any edible substance (*usually pl*)

food web *n* the various food chains that exist within a particular ecological community

fool *n* **1** a person considered to lack good sense or judgment **2** a person considered to be or made to appear ridiculous **3** an enthusiast **4** formerly, a court entertainer **5** a creamy fruit dessert ■ *v* **1** *vt* deceive or trick **2** *vi* say something jokingly
□ **fool around** *vi* **1** behave in a silly or comical way **2** waste time
□ **fool with** *vt* play or tinker with

fool·har·dy /fóol hàardee/ *adj* bold but reckless —**fool·har·di·ness** *n*

fool·ish /fóolish/ *adj* **1** not sensible **2** feeling or appearing ridiculous ○ *a foolish grin* —**fool·ish·ly** *adv* —**fool·ish·ness** *n*

fool·proof /fóol próof/ *adj* **1** designed to function despite human error **2** infallible

fool's gold *n* any mineral with a gold luster, especially pyrites

fool's par·a·dise *n* a state of happiness based on unrealistic hopes ○ *living in a fool's paradise*

foot *n* (*pl* **feet**) **1** the part of the leg below the ankle **2** an organ of an invertebrate animal that is used to grip or move **3** (*symbol* ') a unit of length equal to 12 in./.3048 m **4** the lowest part of something **5** the part of a sock or boot that covers the foot **6** something that gives support like a foot, e.g., a shaped part at the end of the leg of a chair **7** a unit of poetic meter ■ *vt* pay the full cost of —**foot·ed** *adj* ◊ **get off on the wrong foot** begin something badly ◊ **get on** *or* **to your feet** return to a healthy or financially stable condition ◊ **have** *or* **keep both** *or* **your feet on the ground** act and think sensibly ◊ **on foot** walking ◊ **put your best foot forward** try as hard as you can to impress or please ◊ **put your feet up** stop working and relax ◊ **put your foot down** insist firmly on an opinion or decision ◊ **put your foot in it, put your foot in your mouth** make a tactless or embarrassing mistake (*infml*) ◊ **shoot yourself in the foot** do something that harms your own interests

foot·age /fóotij/ *n* **1** a filmed sequence showing an event **2** size measured in feet

foot-and-mouth dis·ease *n* a viral disease of animals with divided hoofs

foot·ball /fóot bàwl/ *n* **1** a game in which two teams of 11 players score points by carrying or kicking a ball over a goal line **2** any team game in which a ball is kicked or carried **3** a ball used in football —**foot·ball·er** *n*

foot·board /fóot bàwrd/ *n* **1** a board at the bottom of a bed **2** a support for the feet in a vehicle

foot·bridge /fóot brìj/ *n* a bridge for pedestrians

foot·er /fóottər/ *n* a piece of text below the main text of a page, especially text inserted on each page by word-processing software

foot·fall /fóot fàwl/ *n* the sound of footsteps

foot·hill /fóot hìl/ *n* a hill that forms the approach to a mountain (*often pl*)

foot·hold /fóot hòld/ *n* **1** a place where a climber's foot can get support **2** a firm base for progress

foot·ing /fóotting/ *n* **1** the secure placement of the feet when standing, walking, or running **2** a base for progress **3** a particular status, condition, or relationship ○ *put the discussion on a more scientific footing*

foo·tle /fóot'l/ *n* nonsense

foot·lights /fóot lìts/ *npl* **1** lights along the front of a stage **2** the theater as a profession

foot·lock·er /fóot lòkər/ *n* a trunk kept at the foot of a bed

foot·loose /fóot lòoss/ *adj* free to do anything or go anywhere

foot·man /fŏŏtmən/ (pl **-men** /-mən/) n a male servant in uniform

foot·mark /fŏŏt maark/ n a mark made on a surface by somebody's foot

foot·note /fŏŏt nŏt/ n 1 a piece of information at the bottom of a page 2 an additional detail

foot pas·sen·ger n a ferry passenger without a car

foot·path /fŏŏt path/ (pl **-paths** /-pathz, -paths/) n a path for walkers

⚡ **foot·print** /fŏŏt print/ n 1 a mark made on a surface by somebody's foot 2 the desk space occupied by a computer or other machine

foot·rest /fŏŏt rèst/ n something on which to rest your feet

foot·sie /fŏŏtsee/ n flirtatious play with the feet (infml) ◊ **play footsie** collaborate (infml)

foot sol·dier n an infantry soldier

foot·sore /fŏŏt sawr/ adj having aching feet

foot·step /fŏŏt stèp/ n 1 the sound of somebody's foot hitting the ground 2 a mark made by a foot ◊ **follow in somebody's footsteps** emulate another person's life or work

foot·stool /fŏŏt stŏŏl/ n a piece of furniture that supports the feet

foot·wear /fŏŏt wàir/ n shoes and boots

foot·work /fŏŏt wùrk/ n the movement of the feet in sport or dancing

fop n a man obsessed by fashion and his appearance —**fop·per·y** n —**fop·pish** adj

for prep 1 intended to be received or used by o a letter for you 2 on behalf of o acting for his client 3 toward somebody or something o heading for Paris 4 indicates how long something lasts or extends o was on vacation for a week 5 because of o did it for love 6 with the purpose of o That towel is for drying your hands. 7 in exchange for o got it for a few dollars 8 instead of o found an understudy for him 9 with reference to the normal characteristics of o It's warm for April. 10 in order to get o hoping for a promotion 11 having the same meaning as o the common term for rubella ▪ adv, prep in favor or support of somebody or something o Ten voted for, and eleven against. ▪ conj because (fml) o The trial has been adjourned, for the judge must take these motions under advisement.

for·age /fáwrij/ n 1 food for animals 2 a search, especially over a wide area or among a variety of things ▪ vi (**-aged, -ag·ing**) 1 search an area for food and supplies 2 engage in a search o foraging in the attic for the lost papers —**for·ag·er** n

For·a·ker /fáwrəkər/ mountain in the Alaska Range in S Alaska. Height 17,400 ft./5,304 m.

for·ay /fáw rày/ n 1 a sudden military raid 2 an attempt at something unfamiliar —**for·ay·er** n

for·bear[1] /fáwr báir, fər-/ (**-bore** /-báwr/, **-borne** /-báwrn/) v (fml) 1 vi hold back from doing or saying something 2 vti be tolerant of something —**for·bear·ance** n —**for·bear·ing** adj —**for·bear·ing·ly** adv

USAGE As a verb, **forbear** is the only spelling. As a noun, **forebear** ("an ancestor") is preferred.

for·bear[2] /fáwr bàir/ n = forebear

for·bid /fər bíd, fawr-/ (**-bade** /-bád, -báyd/ or **-bad** /-bád/, **-bid·den** /-bídd'n/ or **-bid, -bid·ding**) vt 1 order somebody not to do something 2 not allow something —**for·bid·dance** /fər bídd'nss, fawr-/ n

for·bid·ding /fər bídding, fawr-/ adj 1 hostile or stern 2 coldly uninviting —**for·bid·ding·ly** adv —**for·bid·ding·ness** n

~~forboding~~ incorrect spelling of foreboding

force n 1 strength o toppled by the force of the storm 2 physical power or violence used against somebody or something o the use of force as a last resort 3 the state of being in effect o The regulations come into force next week. 4 intellectual or moral power o swayed by the force of his argument 5 an influential person or thing o a force for good 6 a group of military personnel, ships, or aircraft organized to fight 7 a body of police officers 8 a group of people working together o a sales force 9 (symbol F) a physical influence that moves an object, equal to the rate of change in the object's momentum ▪ **forc·es** npl the military organizations of a country ▪ vt (**forced, forc·ing**) 1 compel somebody to do something 2 move using physical strength 3 create a way or passage using physical strength 4 obtain something by pressure o trying to force a confrontation 5 do something in a strained or unnatural way o managed to force a smile 6 make a plant mature early —**force·a·ble** adj ◊ **in force** 1 in a large group 2 valid

ORIGIN Force derives ultimately from Latin *fortis* "strong," which is also seen in *comfort, fortify,* and numerous other words. It came into English through French.

☐ **force on** or **upon** vt impose something on somebody

~~forceably~~ incorrect spelling of forcibly

forced adj 1 not natural o forced laughter 2 done out of necessity o a forced error —**forc·ed·ness** /-sədnəss/ n

forced land·ing n an emergency landing

force-feed (**force-fed**) vt 1 compel to eat 2 compel to learn

force field n in science fiction, an invisible barrier

force·ful /fáwrsfəl/ adj 1 powerful 2 impressive or persuasive —**force·ful·ly** *adv* —**force·ful·ness** *n*

force·meat /fáwrs mèet/ *n* finely chopped meat, fish, or vegetables, used for stuffing

for·ceps /fáwrsəps, fáwr sèps/ *npl* a surgical instrument resembling tongs or tweezers

forc·i·ble /fáwrsəb'l/ *adj* **1** using strength ○ *forcible entry by a burglar* **2** intensely persuasive ○ *a forcible reminder* —**forc·i·bly** *adv*

ford *n* a crossing place through shallow water —**ford** *vt* —**ford·a·ble** *adj*

Ford, Gerald R. (*b.* 1913) 38th president of the United States (1974–77)

Henry Ford

Ford, Henry (1863–1947) US industrialist

Ford, John (1895–1973) US movie director

fore *n* the front of something (*literary*) ■ *adj* positioned at the front ■ *adv* toward the front ■ *interj* in golf, warns others that you have hit a golf ball in their direction

fore- *prefix* **1** before, earlier ○ *forebear* **2** front, in front ○ *forehead*

fore·arm[1] /fáwr àarm/ *n* the lower arm

fore·arm[2] /fawr àarm/ *vt* prepare or arm in advance of an expected conflict

fore·bear /fáwr bàir/, **for·bear** *n* an ancestor (*often pl*) ◊ See note at **forbear**[1]

fore·bod·ing /fawr bṓding/ *n* **1** a premonition **2** a bad omen ■ *adj* ominous —**fore·bode** *vti* —**fore·bod·ing·ly** *adv*

fore·cast /fáwr kàst/ *vt* (**-cast** *or* **-cast·ed**) **1** predict **2** be an early sign of ■ *n* **1** a weather prediction **2** a prediction of future developments —**fore·cast·er** *n*

fore·cas·tle /fṓks'l, fáwr kàss'l/, **fo'c's'le** /fṓks'l/ *n* **1** a space in the bow of a ship for the crew's quarters **2** a raised deck at the bow of a ship

fore·close /fawr klṓz/ (**-closed**, **-clos·ing**) *v* **1** *vti* seize a property, usually for nonpayment of a mortgage **2** *vt* prevent (*fml*) —**fore·clo·sure** /fawr klṓzhər/ *n*

fore·court /fáwr kàwrt/ *n* **1** the front section of a tennis, badminton, or handball court **2** an open area at the front of a building used by the public

fore·fin·ger /fáwr fìng gər/ *n* an index finger

fore·foot /fáwr fòòt/ *n* (*pl* **-feet** /-fèet/) *n* an animal's front foot

fore·front /fáwr frùnt/ *n* **1** the leading or most important position **2** the foremost part

fore·gath·er /fawr gáth ər/ *vi* = **forgather**

fore·go /fawr gṓ/ *vt* = **forgo**

fore·go·ing /fawr gṓ ing, fáwr gṓ ing/ *adj* previously mentioned

fore·gone /fáwr gàwn, -gòn/ *adj* already completed or decided ○ *a foregone conclusion*

⚡ **fore·ground** /fáwr gròwnd/ *n* **1** the part of a picture that appears nearest the viewer **2** the leading or most important position ■ *adj* currently receiving computer commands through the keyboard, while other programs are operating ■ *vt* highlight

fore·hand /fáwr hànd/ *n* **1** in racket games, a stroke played with the palm facing forward **2** the part of a horse in front of the rider —**fore·hand** *adj, adv, vt*

fore·head /fáwrəd, fáwr hèd/ *n* the part of the face above the eyebrows

for·eign /fáwrən/ *adj* **1** of another country ○ *foreign currency* **2** dealing with another country ○ *foreign policy* **3** coming from outside ○ *a foreign body in the eye* **4** uncharacteristic ○ *foreign to her nature* —**for·eign·ness** *n*

> **ORIGIN** Foreign goes back to a Latin word meaning "out of doors," and this was an early meaning in English. The French word from which it immediately derived in the 13C was not spelled *-gn*, and neither was **foreign** until the 16C. The change seems to have come about by analogy with *sovereign*, which itself had been altered to conform to *reign*.

for·eign·er /fáwrənər/ *n* **1** somebody from another country **2** an outsider

for·eign ex·change *n* **1** dealings in foreign money **2** the currencies of foreign countries

for·eign le·gion *n* a section of an army consisting of foreign volunteers

for·eign min·is·ter *n* in some governments, the official responsible for relations with other countries

fore·knowl·edge /fawr nóllij/ *n* prior knowledge of something

fore·leg /fáwr lèg/ *n* an animal's front leg

fore·limb /fáwr lìm/ *n* a front limb

fore·lock /fáwr lòk/ *n* **1** a lock of hair growing over the human forehead **2** the front part of a horse's mane

fore·man /fáwrmən/ *n* (*pl* **-men** /-mən/) *n* **1** a man in charge of other workers **2** a male leader of a jury —**fore·man·ship** *n*

fore·mast /fáwr màst/ *n* the mast nearest the front of a ship

fore·most /fáwr mṓst/ *adj* **1** most notable **2** farthest forward ■ *adv* **1** in first position **2** to the front

fore·noon /fáwr nòòn, fawr nòòn/ *n* the morning hours

fo·ren·sic /fə rénsik, -rénzik/ *adj* **1** using science to solve crime **2** of debating —**fo·ren·si·cal·ly** *adv* —**fo·ren·sics** *n*

fore·per·son /fáwr pùrs'n/ (*pl* **-per·sons** *or*

-peo·ple /-pèep'l/ *n* **1** a person in charge of other workers **2** the head of a jury

fore·play /fáwr plày/ *n* sexual stimulation before intercourse

fore·run·ner /fáwr rùnnər/ *n* **1** a predecessor **2** somebody or something showing the future

fore·see /fawr seé/ (**-saw** /-sáw/, **-seen** /-seén/) *vti* know or expect that something will happen before it does —**fore·see·a·ble** *adj* —**fore·see·a·bly** *adv*

fore·shad·ow /fawr sháddō/ *vt* be a warning or indication of

fore·shore /fáwr shàwr/ *n* **1** the part of a shore between the high and low watermarks **2** the part of a shore between the high watermark and cultivated land

fore·short·en /fawr sháwrt'n/ *vt* make something in a drawing or painting appear shorter than it actually is to create perspective

fore·sight /fáwr sìt/ *n* the ability to think ahead —**fore·sight·ed** *adj*

fore·skin /fáwr skìn/ *n* the fold of skin covering the tip of the penis

for·est /fáwrəst/ *n* a large dense growth of trees —**for·est·ed** *adj*

fore·stall /fawr stáwl/ *vt* prevent or hinder —**fore·stall·ment** *n*

for·est·er /fáwrəstər/ *n* the manager of a forest

for·est rang·er *n* = **ranger** 1

for·est·ry /fáwrəstree/ *n* **1** the planting and growing of trees **2** the science and profession of forest management

fore·taste *n* /fáwr tàyst/ a sample of what is to come ■ *vt* /fawr tàyst, fáwr tàyst/ (**-tast·ed**, **-tast·ing**) have a foretaste of

fore·tell /fawr tél/ (**-told** /-tóld/) *vt* predict future events *(literary)* —**fore·tell·er** *n*

fore·thought /fáwr thàwt/ *n* careful thought about the future —**fore·thought·ful** *adj*

for·ev·er /faw révvər, fə-/ *adv* **1** for all time **2** for a very long time *(infml)*

for·ev·er·more /faw rèvvər máwr, fə-/ *adv* for all time *(literary)*

~~foreward~~ incorrect spelling of **forward**

fore·warn /fawr wáwrn/ *vt* warn about something that is going to happen

fore·wom·an /fáwr wòomman/ (*pl* **-wom·en** /-wìmmin/) *n* **1** a woman in charge of other workers **2** a woman leader of a jury

fore·word /fáwr wùrd, fáwrwərd/ *n* an introductory essay in a book

forex *abbr* foreign exchange

for·feit /fáwrfət/ *n* **1** the act of giving something up willingly so as to get something else **2** a penalty for wrongdoing or breaking the law **3** a penalty in a game ■ *adj* taken away as punishment ■ *vt* **1** lose something as punishment for a mistake or wrongdoing **2** give up something willingly so as to get something else **3** take some-

thing away from somebody as a penalty —**for·feit·a·ble** *adj*

for·fei·ture /fáwrfə chòor, fáwrfəchər/ *n* **1** something forfeited **2** the act of willingly giving something up so as to get something else

~~forfiet~~ incorrect spelling of **forfeit**

for·gath·er /fawr gáthər/, **fore·gath·er** *vi* assemble as a group *(fml)*

for·gave past tense of **forgive**

forge[1] *n* **1** a metal-working shop **2** a furnace for heating metal ■ *v* (**forged, forg·ing**) **1** *vti* make an illegal copy of something **2** *vt* establish something with effort ○ *forge a durable relationship* **3** *vt* shape metal by heating and hammering —**forg·er** *n*

ORIGIN Forge "make an illegal copy" came through French from the Latin verb that also gave us *fabricate*. It is recorded from the beginning of the 13C. Like its sources, **forge** at first meant simply "make, construct." The sense "shape metal" appears in the 14C. **Forge** as in *forge ahead* is unrelated and not as old, appearing in the mid-18C. Its origin is not certain, though it may be an alteration of *force*.

---

forge[2] (**forged, forg·ing**), **forge ahead** *vi* **1** move forward with a surge of speed **2** move slowly and steadily

for·ger·y /fáwrjəree/ (*pl* **-ies**) *n* **1** the illegal copying of something **2** an illegal copy

for·get /fər gét/ (**-got** /-gót/, **-got·ten** /-gótt'n/, **-get·ting**) *v* **1** *vti* not remember something **2** *vt* leave behind accidentally **3** *vti* neglect to give due attention to something **4** *vt* stop worrying about **5** *vr* lose control of your manners or emotions ○ *In his anger, he forgot himself.* —**for·get·ta·ble** *adj* ◊ See note at **neglect**

for·get·ful /fər gétfəl/ *adj* **1** absent-minded **2** neglectful of duty or responsibility *(fml)* —**for·get·ful·ly** *adv* —**for·get·ful·ness** *n*

for·get-me-not *n* a small plant with small pale-blue flowers

---

ORIGIN Forget-me-nots were worn by lovers in the 15C. The English name is recorded in the mid-16C, and is a translation from French.

---

for·give /fər gív/ (**-gave** /-gáyv/, **-giv·en** /fər gívvən/, **-giv·ing**) *v* **1** *vti* stop being angry about something **2** *vt* pardon somebody or something **3** *vt* cancel an obligation or debt —**for·giv·a·ble** *adj* —**for·giv·a·bly** *adv* —**for·give·ness** *n*

for·giv·ing /fər gívving/ *adj* **1** inclined to forgive **2** allowing for a degree of imperfection —**for·giv·ing·ly** *adv*

for·go /fawr gó/ (**-went** /-wént/, **-gone** /-gáwn, -gón/, **-goes**), **fore·go** *vt* do without

for·got past tense of **forget**

for·got·ten past participle of **forget**

~~forhead~~ incorrect spelling of **forehead**

~~foriegn~~ incorrect spelling of **foreign**

fo·rint /fáwrint/ n the main unit of Hungarian currency

fork n 1 a metal eating or serving utensil with prongs 2 a pronged garden or agricultural tool 3 a point where something divides 4 a branch of a road or river 5 a pronged machine part ■ v 1 vti move something with a fork 2 vi divide into two —**forked** adj —**fork·ful** /fáwrk fŏŏl/ n

forked light·ning n lightning that splits into two or more branches near the ground

forked tongue n untruthful or misleading speech (literary or humorous)

fork·lift /fáwrk lĭft/ n 1 an industrial device with two long steel bars for lifting loads 2 also **fork·lift truck** a vehicle equipped with a forklift —**fork·lift** vt

for·lorn /fər láwrn, fawr-/ adj 1 lonely and miserable 2 desolate —**for·lorn·ly** adv —**for·lorn·ness** n

form n 1 basic structure or shape 2 the particular way that something is or appears to be ○ bonuses in the form of extra vacation days 3 a type or kind ○ Friction is a form of energy. 4 an indistinct shape ○ a shadowy form in the distance 5 a document with blank spaces for entering information 6 the condition of a person, group, or organization ○ a violinist at the top of her form 7 the structure of an artistic work as opposed to its content 8 a mold or frame ■ v 1 vti give a shape to, or take shape 2 vti start to exist, or make exist 3 vt construct or establish 4 vt develop in the mind 5 vt influence and mold somebody or something 6 vt constitute or serve as ○ mountains forming a natural boundary

for·mal /fáwrm'l/ adj 1 in accordance with accepted conventions ○ He's terribly formal. 2 official ○ a formal invitation to the White House 3 used in serious, official, or public communications ○ a formal word 4 systematically ordered or arranged ○ a formal garden ■ n an outfit for an important, especially evening, occasion —**for·mal·ly** adv —**for·mal·ness** n

for·mal·de·hyde /fawr máldə hìd/ n a pungent gas. Use: manufacture of resins and fertilizers, preservation of organic specimens.

for·ma·lin /fáwrmalin/ n a solution of formaldehyde. Use: disinfectant, preservation of organic specimens.

for·mal·ism /fáwrm'l ìzzəm/ n emphasis on outward appearance or form rather than content or meaning —**for·mal·is·tic** /fàwrm'l ístik/ adj

for·mal·i·ty /fawr mállətee/ (pl -ties) n 1 the quality of being formal 2 an official procedure that is part of a longer procedure (often pl) 3 a necessary but insignificant procedure

for·mal·ize /fáwrm'l ìz/ (-ized, -iz·ing) vt make official or formal —**for·mal·i·za·tion** /fàwrm'li záysh'n/ n

for·mat /fáwr màt/ n 1 the way something is presented, organized, or arranged 2 the layout of a publication 3 the structure or organization of digital data ○ files in ASCII format ■ vt (-mat·ted, -mat·ting) 1 arrange the layout or organization of something 2 organize a disk for data storage

---

ORIGIN Format came through French from German in the mid-19C. It derives from the past participle of the Latin verb that gave us form, used in liber formatus "shaped book."

---

for·ma·tion /fawr máysh'n/ n 1 the development of something 2 the creation of something 3 shape or structure 4 a formal pattern —**for·ma·tion·al** adj

form·a·tive /fáwrmətiv/ adj influential in shaping or developing something

for·mer /fáwrmər/ adj 1 previous ○ met her on a former occasion 2 having previously had a particular name or status ○ the former Soviet Union 3 being the first of two things or people mentioned ■ n the first of two

for·mer·ly /fáwrmərlee/ adv in the past, but no longer

For·mi·ca /fawr míkə/ tdmk a trademark for a strong plastic laminate sheeting often used to cover surfaces

for·mic ac·id /fáwrmik-/ n an acid that occurs naturally in ants. Use: paper, textiles, insecticides, refrigerants.

for·mi·da·ble /fáwrmədəb'l, fər míddəb'l, fàwr míddəb'l/ adj 1 difficult to deal with 2 inspiring awe —**for·mi·da·bly** adv

form·less /fáwrmləss/ adj having no distinctive shape —**form·less·ly** adv —**form·less·ness** n

form let·ter n a letter with the same wording that is sent to many recipients

for·mu·la /fáwrmyələ/ (pl -las or -lae /-lèe/) n 1 a plan 2 a prescribed method of doing something 3 an established form of words 4 a set of symbols representing the chemical composition of a compound 5 a rule expressed in symbols 6 a preparation for babies used instead of human breast milk —**for·mu·la·ic** /fàwrmyə láy ik/ adj —**for·mu·la·i·cal·ly** adv

for·mu·late /fáwrmyə làyt/ (-lat·ed, -lat·ing) vt 1 devise carefully 2 say or write carefully —**for·mu·la·tion** /fàwrmyə láysh'n/ n

for·ni·cate /fáwrni kàyt/ (-cat·ed, -cat·ing) vi have sex outside marriage (fml) —**for·ni·ca·tion** /fàwrni kàysh'n/ n —**for·ni·ca·tor** n

for·prof·it adj profit-making (refers to organizations)

for·sake /fər sáyk, fawr-/ (-sook /-sŏŏk/, -sak·en /-sáykən/, -sak·ing) vt 1 abandon somebody or something 2 give up something that gives pleasure —**for·sak·en** adj

~~forsee~~ incorrect spelling of **foresee**

for·sooth /fər sóoth, fawr-/ adv indeed (archaic)

for·swear /fawr swáir/ (-swore /-swáwr/, -sworn

/-swáwrn/) v (*literary*) **1** vt reject strongly **2** vi perjure yourself

for·syth·i·a /fər síthee ə, fàwr-/ n a yellow-flowered bush

fort n a building or group of buildings with strong defenses, especially a military compound ◊ **hold the fort** take charge of something in the absence of the person usually responsible (*infml*)

For·ta·le·za /fàwrtə láyzə/ port in NE Brazil, on the Atlantic Ocean. Pop. 1,965,513 (1996).

For·tas /fáwrtəss/, **Abe** (1910–82) associate justice of the US Supreme Court (1965–69)

for·te[1] /fawrt, fáwr tày/ n somebody's strong point

for·te[2] /fáwr tày, fáwrtee/ adv in a loud manner (*musical direction*) ■ n a loud musical note or passage —**for·te** adj

~~forteen~~ incorrect spelling of **fourteen**

forth /fawrth/ adv (*fml*) **1** onward **2** out into view ◊ **and so forth** et cetera

SPELLCHECK Do not confuse the spelling of **forth** and **fourth** ("one of four parts"), which sound similar.

⚡**FORTH** /fawrth/ n a high-level computer programming language used in scientific and industrial control applications

forth·com·ing /fawrth kúmming, fàwrth kùmming/ adj **1** future ○ *a forthcoming book* **2** available when wanted ○ *Help is forthcoming.* **3** willing to give information ○ *a press secretary who is less than forthcoming*

forth·right /fáwrth rìt/ adj candid and outspoken —**forth·right·ly** adv —**forth·right·ness** n

forth·with /fawrth with/ adv immediately

for·ti·fi·ca·tion /fàwrtəfi káysh'n/ n **1** a strong structure for defending a place (*often pl*) **2** the building of defenses

for·ti·fied wine n a drink such as sherry or port made from wine to which strong alcohol has been added

for·ti·fy /fáwrtəfì/ (-fied, -fies) vt **1** make a place safer with defensive structures **2** make a structure stronger **3** add extra ingredients to something **4** strengthen or encourage somebody —**for·ti·fi·a·ble** adj

for·tis·si·mo /fawr tíssə mò/ adv very loudly (*musical direction*) ■ n (pl **-mos** or **-mi** /-mee/) a very loud musical note or passage —**for·tis·si·mo** adj

for·ti·tude /fáwrtə tòòd/ n brave determination —**for·ti·tu·di·nous** /fàwrtə tòòd'nəss/ adj

Fort Knox /-nóks/ US military reservation in central Kentucky, the repository of the nation's gold supply

Fort Lau·der·dale /-láwdər dàyl/ city in SE Florida, on the Atlantic Ocean. Pop. 153,728 (1998).

fort·night /fáwrt nìt/ n a period of two weeks

fort·night·ly /fáwrt nìtlee/ adj, adv UK every two weeks

⚡**FORTRAN** /fáwr tràn/ n an early computer programming language

ORIGIN Fortran is a blend and contraction of *formula* and *translation*.

for·tress /fáwrtrəss/ n **1** a fortified place or town with a long-term military presence **2** a place that is impossible to get into

for·tu·i·tous /fawr tòò itəss/ adj **1** accidental or unplanned **2** happening by lucky chance —**for·tu·i·tous·ly** adv

for·tu·nate /fáwrchənət/ adj **1** enjoying good luck **2** resulting from good luck —**for·tu·nate·ness** n ◊ See note at **lucky**

for·tu·nate·ly /fáwrchənətlee/ adv **1** by lucky chance **2** indicates happiness or relief ○ *Fortunately, the lion was caught.*

~~fortunatly~~ incorrect spelling of **fortunately**

for·tune /fáwrchən/ n **1** great wealth or property **2** a large sum of money (*infml*) **3** *also* **For·tune** fate **4** luck ■ **for·tunes** npl life's ups and downs

for·tune cook·ie n a Chinese cookie containing a message

for·tune hunt·er n somebody who tries to obtain wealth by marrying somebody rich (*disapproving*) —**for·tune hunt·ing** n

for·tune tell·er n somebody who claims to foretell the future —**for·tune-tell·ing** n

Fort Wayne /-wáyn/ city in NE Indiana. Pop. 185,716 (1998).

Fort Worth /-wúrth/ city in NE Texas. Pop. 491,801 (1998).

for·ty /fáwrtee/ n the number 40 ■ **for·ties** npl **1** the numbers 40 to 49, particularly as a range of temperature **2** the years from 40 to 49 in a century or in somebody's life —**for·ti·eth** adj, adv, n —**for·ty** adj, pron

for·ty-five n a .45-caliber pistol

for·ty winks n a nap (*infml*; + *sing or pl verb*)

⚡**fo·rum** /fáwrəm/ (pl **-rums** or **-ra** /-rə/) n **1** a medium for expressing an opinion or debating an issue **2** a meeting for a discussion **3** an Internet discussion group **4** a public square in an ancient Roman city

for·ward /fáwrwərd/ adv *also* **for·wards** **1** ahead **2** as progress toward a goal ○ *a step forward in employee safety* **3** to the front of a ship or an aircraft ○ *prefer a berth farther forward* ■ adj **1** directed ahead **2** directed to a future goal **3** situated at the front of a ship or an aircraft **4** unrestrained or impertinent in behavior ■ n in some team sports, an attacking player ■ vt **1** redirect mail **2** advance or promote something —**for·ward·ly** adv —**for·ward·ness** n

for·ward·ing ad·dress n a new address to which mail is to be redirected

for·ward-look·ing adj planning for or looking toward the future

Fos·se /fóssee/, **Bob** (1927–87) US dancer, choreographer, and director

Fossil: Trilobite

fos·sil /fóss'l/ n 1 the preserved remains of an animal or plant 2 somebody regarded as old-fashioned and unwilling to change (infml insult) 3 something outdated

ORIGIN Fossil was adopted from French, where it was formed from a Latin adjective meaning "dug up."

fos·sil fu·el n a fuel derived from prehistoric organisms

fos·sil·ize /fóss'l ìz/ (-ized, -iz·ing) vti 1 make or become a fossil 2 make or be unable to change —**fos·sil·i·za·tion** /fòss'li záysh'n/ n —**fos·sil·ized** adj

fos·ter /fáwstər, fóstər/ vt 1 take care of and raise a child 2 encourage and develop something 3 keep alive a feeling or thought ■ adj providing care or receiving care from adults who are not the birth parents

Fos·ter /fáwstər, fóstər/, Stephen Collins (1826–64) US songwriter

~~fotograph~~ incorrect spelling of **photograph**

Fou·cault /foo kố/, Jean-Bernard Léon (1819–68) French physicist

Fou·cault, Michel (1926–84) French philosopher

fought past tense, past participle of **fight**

foul /fowl/ adj 1 disgusting to the senses o a foul smell 2 clogged with dirt 3 contaminated 4 unpleasant (infml) 5 vulgar or obscene 6 in sports, illegal according to the rules 7 unfair or dishonest 8 stormy or wet and unpleasant 9 decaying and rotten 10 evil 11 entangled and unable to move o a foul anchor line ■ n 1 in sports, an illegal action 2 an entanglement preventing movement ■ v 1 vti in sports, act illegally against an opponent 2 vti entangle and prevent from moving, or become entangled and unable to move 3 vti obstruct, or become obstructed 4 vt make dirty —**foul·ly** adv —**foul·ness** n

SPELLCHECK Do not confuse the spelling of **foul** and **fowl** ("any edible or game bird"), which sound similar.

□ **foul out** vi be ejected from a game after committing too many fouls

□ **foul up** vti bungle, or be bungled (infml)

foul line n 1 in baseball, the lines outside which a ball cannot be legally played 2 in basketball, a line from which a free throw is taken after a foul

foul-mouthed adj using obscene language

foul play n 1 unfair behavior 2 treachery or criminal violence 3 in sports, action against the rules

foul-up n a blunder (infml)

found[1] /fownd/ vt 1 set up something such as an institution or organization 2 support something such as a conclusion with evidence or reasoning

found[2] /fownd/ vt 1 cast metal or glass 2 produce from a mold by casting

found[3] /fownd/ past tense, past participle of **find**

foun·da·tion /fown dáysh'n/ n 1 an underground support for a building (often pl) 2 the basis of a theory or idea 3 a base layer of makeup 4 the establishing of an institution 5 a charitable or educational institution —**foun·da·tion·al** adj

foun·da·tion stone n 1 a stone laid to mark the start of construction of a building 2 a basis for something

found·er[1] /fówndər/ n 1 somebody who is the first to establish something 2 **Found·er** a drafter of the US Constitution in 1787

foun·der[2] /fówndər/ v 1 vti sink, or cause to sink 2 vi collapse and fail 3 vi become stuck in soft ground or snow

found·ing fa·ther n a founder of an institution, movement, or organization

found·ling /fówndling/ n an abandoned baby

found·ry /fówndree/ (pl -ries) n a place for casting metal or glass

fount /fownt/ n (literary) 1 a source 2 a fountain or spring of water

foun·tain /fównt'n/ n 1 an ornamental water jet 2 a natural spring 3 a device producing a jet of water for drinking 4 a source of something abstract

foun·tain·head /fównt'n hèd/ n 1 a spring that is the source of a stream 2 a primary source of something abstract

four /fawr/ n the number 4 —**four** adj, pron

four-by-four, **four-by** n a four-wheel-drive vehicle

four-col·or adj using cyan, magenta, yellow, and black to print full-colored pictures

Four Cor·ners region in the SW United States, where the borders of Colorado, New Mexico, Arizona, and Utah come together

4-F n the lowest rating for military draftees

four-flush vi in poker, bet boldly though holding a bad hand

4GL abbr fourth-generation language

four-leaf clo·ver n a clover leaf with four parts that is considered lucky

four-let·ter word n a short vulgar word

401(k) /fàwr ò wun káy/ n a retirement plan

four-post·er, **four-post·er bed** n a bed with four vertical posts at each corner for a canopy or curtains

four·score /fawr skáwr/ *adj* 80 in number (*archaic*)

four·some /fáwrsəm/ *n* **1** a group of four people **2** a golf game for two pairs

four·square /fawr skwáir/ *adj* showing determination (*literary*) —**four·square** *adv*

four·teen /fawr teén/ *n* the number 14 —**four·teen** *adj, pron* —**four·teenth** *adj, adv, n*

fourth /fawrth/ *n* **1** one of four parts of something **2** a musical interval of four notes —**fourth** *adj, adv* ◊ See note at **forth**

fourth di·men·sion *n* time when used with the three other dimensions to specify the location of an event

fourth es·tate, Fourth Es·tate *n* journalists as a group

ORIGIN From medieval times, society was analyzed in terms of "estates," groups of people participating in government, either directly or through representatives. Traditionally in England there were three, originally the clergy, the barons and knights, and the commons. Different divisions were made in other European countries. A number of people and groups have been dubbed the "fourth estate," but the name has stuck to the press. The historian and essayist Thomas Carlyle attributed the first use to Edmund Burke, but it has also been claimed for the politician Lord Brougham, who is said to have used it in the House of Commons in 1823 or 1824.

fourth-gen·er·a·tion lan·guage *n* an advanced computer language resembling human speech

Fourth of Ju·ly *n* Independence Day

~~fourty~~ incorrect spelling of **forty**

4WD *abbr* four-wheel drive

four-wheel drive *n* a system in which engine power is transmitted to all four wheels of a vehicle

fowl /fowl/ (*pl same or* **fowls**) *n* **1** a chicken or related bird **2** any edible or game bird ◊ See note at **foul**

fox *n* **1** a carnivorous wild mammal resembling a dog, with reddish brown fur and a bushy tail **2** the fur of a fox **3** a trickster (*infml*) **4** a good-looking person (*slang*) ■ *vt* deceive or outwit somebody —**fox·i·ness** *n* —**fox·y** *adj*

ORIGIN Fox probably derives from an ancient root meaning "tail."

Fox (*pl same*) *n* **1** a member of a Native North American people who now live mainly in Oklahoma and Iowa **2** the Algonquian language of the Fox people —**Fox** *adj*

Fox, Charles James (1749–1806)

Fox, Vicente (*b.* 1942) president of Mexico (2000–)

fox·glove /fóks glùv/ (*pl same or* -**gloves**) *n* a plant with purple and white thimble-shaped flowers. Use: source of digitalis.

fox·hound /fóks hòwnd/ *n* a dog used for hunting foxes

fox-hunt·ing *n* the hunting of foxes on horseback with dogs

fox ter·ri·er *n* a small white dog with dark markings

fox·trot /fóks tròt/ *n* **1** a ballroom dance alternating long walking steps and short running steps **2** the music for a foxtrot **3 Fox·trot** a communications code word for the letter "F"

foy·er /fóy ər, fwaá yàỳ/ *n* **1** a lobby in a public building **2** the entrance hall in a private house

Fr *symbol* francium

fr. *abbr* from

Fr. *abbr* **1** Father **2** French

fra·cas /fráykəss, frákəss/ (*pl same*) *n* a noisy quarrel or fight

frac·tal /frákt'l/ *n* an irregular or fragmented geometric shape that can be repeatedly subdivided into smaller copies of the whole, used in computer modeling —**frac·tal** *adj*

frac·tion /frákshən/ *n* **1** a number that is not a whole number **2** a small amount o *a fraction of the cost* **3** a part **4** a component of a mixture, separated by differences in chemical or physical properties —**frac·tion·al** *adj* —**frac·tion·al·ly** *adv*

frac·tious /frákshəss/ *adj* irritable and complaining —**frac·tious·ly** *adv* —**frac·tious·ness** *n*

frac·ture /frákchər/ *n* **1** a break in a bone **2** an act of breaking something, especially a bone **3** a break or crack in an object or material ■ *vti* (-tured, -tur·ing) **1** break a bone, or be broken **2** damage something, or be damaged

frag·ile /frájjəl/ *adj* easily broken or destroyed —**fra·gil·i·ty** /frə jíllətee/ *n*

SYNONYMS fragile, delicate, frail, flimsy, frangible, friable CORE MEANING: easily broken or damaged

frag·ment *n* /frágmənt/ **1** a broken piece **2** an incomplete part of a whole ■ *vti* /frag mént/ **1** break into small pieces **2** break up —**frag·ment·ed** /frag méntəd/ *adj*

frag·men·tar·y /frágmən tèrree/ *adj* consisting only of fragments

frag·men·ta·tion /fràgmən táysh'n/ *n* **1** the breaking up of something **2** a loss of unity and cohesion **3** the shattering of an explosive device

fra·grance /fráygrənss/ *n* **1** a sweet smell **2** sweetness of smell **3** a perfume —**fra·granced** *adj* ◊ See note at **smell**

fra·grant /fráygrənt/ *adj* smelling sweet

frail (**frail·er, frail·est**) *adj* **1** physically weak **2** easy to break or damage **3** insubstantial

—**frail·ness** n —**frail·ty** n ◊ See note at fragile, weak

⚡ **frame** n 1 an underlying, supporting, or surrounding structure o *a bike with a steel frame* o *a window frame* 2 the part of a pair of eyeglasses that holds the lenses and fits around the ears 3 *UK* a piece of equipment made of bars, used, e.g., for helping somebody to walk 4 a person's body 5 a single picture on a strip of film or in a comic strip 6 in bowling, a round 7 on a computer screen, a rectangular area that contains all or a portion of a web page ■ **frames** npl a frame for eyeglasses ■ vt (**framed, fram·ing**) 1 mount a picture in a frame 2 form a surrounding framework for something 3 construct or express an idea or statement 4 cause somebody innocent to appear guilty *(slang)*

frame of mind n somebody's psychological state at a specific time

frame of ref·er·ence n 1 a set of standards used for judging or deciding something 2 a set of geometric axes for determining the location of a point in space

frame·work /fráym wùrk/ n 1 a structure consisting of interconnecting bars 2 a set of underlying ideas 3 the context in which something happens

franc n 1 the main unit of currency in several French-speaking countries 2 the main unit of the former currency in France, Belgium, and Luxembourg

ORIGIN The name **franc** probably derives from Latin *Francorum rex* "king of the Franks," which appeared on gold coins minted in the reign (1350–64) of Jean le Bon.

France largest country in W Europe. Cap. Paris. Pop. 59,551,227 (2001).

fran·chise /frán chīz/ n 1 a license to sell a company's products exclusively in a particular area 2 the area in which somebody has a commercial franchise 3 a privilege granted by an authority 4 the right to vote 5 a professional sports team in a league —**fran·chise** vt

Fran·cis (of As·si·si) /fránsiss/, St. (1182–1226) Italian mystic and preacher. He founded the Franciscan order.

Fran·cis·can /fran sískən/ n a member of a Roman Catholic order of monks and nuns largely devoted to missionary and charitable work —**Fran·cis·can** adj

fran·ci·um /fránsee əm/ n (*symbol* Fr) an unstable radioactive element

Franck /frangk, fraaNk/, **César Auguste** (1822–90) Belgian-born French composer and organist

Fran·co /frángkō/, **Francisco** (1892–1975) authoritarian head of state of Spain (1939–75)

fran·co·phone /frángkə fōn/ n a speaker of French ■ adj 1 French-speaking 2 of a French-speaking area

fran·gi·ble /fránjəb'l/ adj capable of being broken or easily damaged ◊ See note at fragile

frank[1] adj open, honest, and sometimes blunt ■ vt print an official mark over a stamp or on a piece of mail without a stamp to show that postage has been paid ■ n an official mark on a piece of mail to show that postage has been paid —**frank·ly** adv —**frank·ness** n

ORIGIN Frank derives through French from Latin *francus* "free, not enslaved or captive," and this was the first recorded sense in English. It was originally identical with the ethnic name *Frank*, because after the Franks conquered Gaul in the 6C only they and those under their protection had full political freedom. The modern senses of **frank** developed from the 16C.

frank[2] n a frankfurter *(infml)*

Frank n a member of an ancient Germanic people —**Frank·ish** adj

AKG London

Anne Frank

Frank, Anne (1929–45) German Jewish diarist

Frank·en·stein /frángkən stīn/ n 1 a creator of something destructive 2 a monster, usually represented as a large coarse-featured person 3 *also* **Frank·en·stein's mon·ster** an invention that escapes its creator's control and threatens harm or destruction

Frank·fort /fránkfərt/ capital of Kentucky. Pop. 26,418 (1998).

Frank·furt /frángkfərt, -fòort/, **Frank·furt am Main** /-aam mín/ city in west central Germany. Pop. 652,412 (1997).

frank·furt·er /frángkfərtər/, **frank·furt** n a sausage of finely ground pork or beef

ORIGIN Frankfurter is a shortening of German *Frankfurter Wurst* "sausage from Frankfurt." It is first recorded in the late 19C.

Frank·furt·er /frángkfərtər/, **Felix** (1882–1965) Austrian-born associate justice of the US Supreme Court (1939–62)

frank·in·cense /frángkən sèns/ n an aromatic resin used as incense

frank·ing ma·chine n a postage meter

Frank·lin /frángklin/, **Benjamin** (1706–90) American diplomat, printer, author, and scientist

fran·tic /frántik/ adj 1 emotionally out of control 2 excited, hurried, and confused —**fran·ti·cal·ly** adv

~~frantiely~~ incorrect spelling of **frantically**

Franz Jo·sef /frànts yṓssəf/ (1830–1916) emperor of Austria (1848–1916) and king of Hungary (1867–1916)

Franz Jo·sef Land archipelago of small islands in the Arctic Ocean, in NW Russia

frap·pé /fra páy, frap/ *adj* served chilled or poured over crushed ice ■ *n* **1** a drink served chilled poured over crushed ice **2** *also* **frap·pe** /frap/ *New England* a milk shake

Fra·ser /fráyzər, fráyzhər/ river in south central British Columbia, Canada. Length 850 mi./1,370 km.

fra·ter·nal /frə túrn'l/ *adj* **1** of brothers **2** showing friendship and mutual support **3** of fraternities **4** describes twins coming from two separate ova —**fra·ter·nal·ly** *adv*

fra·ter·ni·ty /frə túrnətee/ (*pl* **-ties**) *n* **1** a social society for men at a university or college **2** a group of people with something in common **3** brotherly love **4** a society formed for a common purpose

frat·er·nize /fráttər nìz/ (**-nized**, **-niz·ing**) *v* **1** *vi* spend time with other people socially, especially people considered unsuitable **2** *vti* socialize with somebody against military regulations —**frat·er·ni·za·tion** /fràttərni záysh'n/ *n*

frat·ri·cide /fráttri sìd/ *n* **1** the killing of a brother **2** a killer of a brother —**frat·ri·cid·al** /fràttri síd'l/ *adj*

fraud *n* **1** the crime of obtaining money or advantage by deception **2** somebody who deceives somebody else, usually for financial gain

fraud·u·lent /fráwjələnt/ *adj* designed to deceive —**fraud·u·lent·ly** *adv*

fraught /frawt/ *adj* **1** full of or accompanied by problems or dangers o *an evening fraught with hostility* **2** tense and anxious o *exhausted and fraught after the harrowing flight*

ORIGIN Fraught originally meant "laden" and applied to ships. It is related to *freight*. Fraught with "full of or accompanied by" dates from the mid-16C, but the unqualified sense "tense and anxious" is recorded only from the mid-20C.

---

fray[1] *vti* **1** wear away and hang in threads, or make something do this **2** make or become strained ■ *n* a worn part on which loose threads are showing

fray[2] *n* **1** an argument or fight **2** an exciting or lively activity or situation

fraz·zle /frázz'l/ *v* **1** *n* an exhausted state **2** a frayed state ■ *v* (**-zled**, **-zling**) **1** *vt* exhaust **2** *vi* be frayed —**fraz·zled** *adj*

freak /freek/ *n* **1** a person, animal, or plant regarded as strikingly unusual (*sometimes offensive*) **2** a highly unusual occurrence **3** a fanatic (*infml*) o *a fitness freak* ■ *adj* highly unusual or unlikely ■ *vti* become or make overexcited or overemotional (*slang*)

o *a loud explosion that freaked the cattle* —**freak·ish** *adj* —**freak·ish·ly** *adv* —**freak·y** *adj*

□ **freak out** *vti* make or become extremely upset or agitated (*slang*)

freak-out *n* an emotional outburst (*slang*)

freck·le /frék'l/ *n* a small brown mark on the human skin ■ *vti* (**-led**, **-ling**) mark or become marked with freckles —**freck·ly** *adj*

Fred·er·ick I /fréddrik/ (1123?–90) Holy Roman Emperor and king of Germany (1152–90), and king of Italy (1155–90)

Fred·er·ick II (1712–86) king of Prussia (1740–86)

Fred·er·ic·ton /fréddriktən/ capital of New Brunswick, Canada. Pop. 46,507 (1996).

free *adj* (**fre·er**, **fre·est**) **1** not controlled, restricted, or regulated o *You are free to choose.* **2** not held as a prisoner **3** not restricted in rights o *It's a free country.* **4** not ruled by a foreign country or power **5** not subject to traditional conventions or limitations o *free verse* **6** not affected by a particular thing (*often in combination*) o *a trouble-free trip* **7** not containing a particular thing (*often in combination*) o *a salt-free diet* **8** costing nothing **9** not busy **10** not being used o *Is this seat free?* **11** not attached o *grabbed the free end of the rope* **12** giving something readily o *very free with her advice* **13** not exact o *a free translation* **14** not chemically combined ■ *adv* without cost ■ *vt* (**freed**) **1** release from captivity **2** rid of something o *freed the air of smoke* **3** make available or enable —**free·ly** *adv* —**free·ness** *n*

free a·gent *n* **1** somebody able to act freely **2** a professional athlete able to sign a contract to play for any team

free as·so·ci·a·tion *n* **1** the process by which one thought is allowed to lead spontaneously to the next **2** a psychoanalytical technique for exploring somebody's unconscious by using free association —**free·as·so·ci·ate** *vi*

free·base /freé bàyss/ *n* cocaine that has been concentrated using water and a volatile liquid ■ *v* (**-based**, **-based**) **1** *vt* prepare cocaine for smoking by heating it with water and a volatile liquid **2** *vti* smoke or inhale cocaine purified by burning it with ether (*slang*)

free·bie /freébee/ *n* a promotional gift (*infml*)

free·boot·er /freé bòotər/ *n* a pirate or plunderer —**free·boot** *vi*

ORIGIN Freebooter was adopted in the late 16C from Dutch *vrijbuiter*, whose elements correspond to English *free* and *booty* and the suffix *-er*. The same Dutch word came through Spanish and French as *filibuster* "tactic to delay legislation."

---

free·born /freé bàwrn/ *adj* **1** being a free citizen

from birth **2** of people who were born as free citizens

free·dom /fréedəm/ n **1** the state of being able to act and live freely **2** release from captivity or slavery **3** a country's right to self-rule **4** the right to act or speak freely **5** the state of not being affected by something unpleasant ○ *freedom from fear* **6** ease of movement

free·dom fight·er n a fighter in an armed revolution against a regime regarded as unjust

free·dom rid·er n a member of an interracial group of civil rights activists who rode motor vehicles through the US southern states in the 1960s to challenge racial segregation

free en·ter·prise n freedom to trade without government control

free fall n **1** a descent with an unopened parachute for the first part of a parachute jump **2** an uncontrollable rapid decline —**free-fall** vi

free-float·ing adj not committed to one specific thing, especially a political party

free-for-all n a disorganized argument or fight in which all those present participate (*infml*)

free hand n complete freedom to act and decide

free-hand /frée hànd/ adj, adv drawn by hand without the aid of, e.g., a ruler or compass

free·hold /frée hòld/ n **1** legal ownership of property granting unconditional rights **2** a freehold property —**free·hold·er** n

free kick n in soccer, a kick of a stationary ball granted as a result of an infringement by an opponent

free·lance /frée làns/, **free·lanc·er** n a self-employed person who works for different clients —**free·lance** adj, adv, vi

free·load·er /frée lòdər/ n somebody who exploits somebody else's generosity (*infml*) —**free·load** vi

free love n sex without commitment

free·man /fréemən/ n (pl **-men** /-mən/) a man who is not enslaved

free mar·ket n trading without government control —**free-mar·ket** adj —**free-mar·ket·eer** n

Free·ma·son /frée màyss'n/ n a member of a worldwide society of men that has secret rites and does charitable work —**Free·ma·son·ry** n

⌁**free·net** /frée nèt/ n a free online computer information network

free port n **1** a port open to all shipping **2** a duty-free zone at a port or airport

Free·port /frée pàwrt/ city in the Bahamas. Pop. 26,574 (1990).

free rad·i·cal n a reactive atom or molecule with an unpaired electron

free-range adj **1** not caged or penned **2** produced by free-range poultry or livestock

free rein n complete freedom to act and decide

free·sia /fréezhə, -zee ə/ n a small plant with fragrant brightly colored flowers

free speech n the right to express publicly all opinions

free spir·it n somebody not afraid to flout convention —**free-spir·it·ed** adj

free-stand·ing /frée stánding/ adj not attached to a support

Free State n a US state in which slavery was not tolerated

free·style /frée stìl/ adj **1** describes a sports event that allows a free choice of style or maneuvers **2** in swimming, using the front crawl stroke ■ n a freestyle race or event —**free·styl·er** n

free·think·er /frée thíngkər/ n somebody who does not accept dogma —**free·think·ing** adj, n

free throw n in basketball, a shot at the basket awarded to a player who has been fouled

Free·town /frée tòwn/ capital, largest city, and chief port of Sierra Leone. Pop. 699,000 (1995).

free trade n international trade that is not subject to protective restrictions against imports —**free-trad·er** n

free verse n verse without a fixed metrical pattern

⌁**free·ware** /frée wàir/ n computer software that is available without cost

free·way /frée wày/ n **1** an expressway **2** a toll-free road

free·wheel /frée wéel, -hwéel/ vi **1** continue moving on a bicycle or in a vehicle without using power **2** live in a carefree way ■ n **1** a device on a bicycle that enables the rear wheel to keep rotating after pedaling has stopped **2** a device in a motor vehicle's transmission that disengages the drive shaft and allows it to rotate freely when revolving faster than the engine shaft —**free·wheel·ing** adj

free will n the power of independent action and choice

⌁**freeze** v (**froze** /frōz/, **fro·zen** /frōz'n/, **freez·ing**) **1** vti turn to solid through cold **2** vti cover or become covered with ice **3** vti block or become blocked with ice **4** vti harden through cold **5** vti stick through cold **6** vt preserve with extreme cold **7** vti feel or cause to feel very cold **8** vti harm or kill, or be harmed or killed, by cold **9** vi drop to freezing point **10** vti stop moving **11** vi come to a standstill through shock **12** vi stop responding to commands (*refers to computers*) **13** vt halt before completion **14** vt keep at the present level ○ *freeze prices* **15** vt prevent the sale or liquidation of ○ *They froze her bank account.* **16** vt stop at a specific frame and show a still image ■ n 1 a period of very cold weather 2 a restriction on something

SPELLCHECK Do not confuse the spelling of **freeze** and **frieze** ("a decorative band"), which sound similar.

freeze-frame n a single frame of film viewed as a static image

freez·er /frēzər/ n a very cold refrigerated cabinet

freez·ing /frēzing/ adj very cold ■ n also **freez·ing point** the temperature at which something freezes

freight /frayt/ n 1 goods for commercial transportation 2 the standard class of commercial transportation for goods 3 a charge for the transportation of goods 4 a train for carrying commercial goods ■ vt transport goods by commercial carrier

freight·er /fráytər/ n 1 a ship or aircraft for transporting freight 2 a freight shipper or charterer

~~freind~~ incorrect spelling of **friend**

~~freize~~ incorrect spelling of **frieze**

Fre·mont /frée mònt/ city in W California on San Francisco Bay. Pop. 204,298 (1998).

Fré·mont /frée mònt/, **John Charles** (1813–90) US army officer, explorer, and politician

French n the Romance language that is the official language of France and some other countries ■ npl the people of France —**French** adj —**French·man** n —**French·wom·an** n

French bread n crusty white bread in the form of a long slim cylindrical loaf

French Ca·na·di·an n 1 a French-speaking Canadian 2 the Canadian form of the French language —**French-Ca·na·di·an** adj

French dress·ing n 1 a salad dressing of oil, vinegar, and seasoning 2 a creamy tomato-flavored commercial salad dressing

French fries npl deep-fried potato strips

French Gui·an·a /-gee ánnə, -aànə, -gī-/ overseas region of France, on the northeastern coast of South America. Cap. Cayenne. Pop. 114,808 (1990). —**French Gui·an·an** adj, n —**French Gui·an·ese** /-geè ə neèz, -gī-/ adj, n

French horn n a brass musical instrument consisting of a coiled pipe ending in a wide bell

French kiss n a kiss in which the tongue is used

French Pol·y·ne·sia overseas territory of France, consisting of several island groups in the S Pacific Ocean. Cap. Papeete. Pop. 188,814 (1988).

French toast n sliced bread dipped in beaten egg and fried

fre·net·ic /frə néttik/ adj characterized by feverish activity, confusion, and hurry ○ frenetic activity —**fre·net·i·cal·ly** adv

fren·zy /frénzee/ n 1 uncontrolled agitated behavior 2 a burst of energetic activity —**fren·zied** adj

fre·quen·cy /frée·kwənssee/ (pl -cies) n 1 also **fre·quence** /-kwənss/ the fact of occurring frequently 2 the rate of occurrence of something 3 a broadcasting wavelength 4 (symbol v) the rate of recurrence of an oscillation, waveform, or cycle

fre·quen·cy mod·u·la·tion n radio transmission in which the frequency of the wave is varied in accordance with the particularities of the sound being broadcast

fre·quent adj /frée·kwənt/ 1 occurring often 2 habitual ■ vt /fri kwént, frée·kwənt/ go often to a particular place —**fre·quent·er** /fri kwéntər, frée·kwəntər/ n —**fre·quent·ly** adv

fres·co /fréskō/ n (pl -coes or -cos) 1 a wall or ceiling painting done on fresh plaster 2 the technique of painting on fresh plaster ■ vt (-coed, -co·ing, -coes) paint a wall or ceiling with a fresco

fresh adj 1 not stale or decaying ○ fresh milk 2 not preserved, matured, or processed ○ fresh, frozen, or canned peas 3 additional or replacing something ○ put in a fresh cartridge 4 new or clean ○ fresh towels 5 not affected by time ○ still fresh in her mind 6 excitingly different ○ fresh ideas 7 alert and full of energy ○ feeling fresh after a good night's sleep 8 describes water that is not salty 9 pleasantly clear and unpolluted ○ fresh air 10 healthy-looking ○ a fresh complexion 11 having recently arrived ○ fresh from his trip ■ adv recently (usually in combination) ○ fresh-cooked salmon —**fresh·ly** adv —**fresh·ness** n ◊ See note at **new**

fresh·en /frésh'n/ vti make or become fresh —**fresh·en·er** n

□ **freshen up** vt refill a drink

fresh·man /fréshmən/ (pl -men /-mən/) n 1 a first-year student 2 a beginner or newcomer to a post ○ Senate freshmen

fresh·wa·ter /frésh wàwtər, -wòttər/ adj 1 of water that does not contain salt 2 used on or accustomed only to inland waters

Fres·no /fréznō/ city in central California. Pop. 398,133 (1998).

fret¹ (fret·ted, fret·ting) vti 1 worry 2 wear away

fret² n a ridge on the neck of a stringed instrument —**fret·ted** adj

fret³ n an ornament or border with a geometric pattern —**fret** vt

fret·ful /frétfəl/ adj irritable and cranky —**fret·ful·ly** adv —**fret·ful·ness** n

fret·saw /frét sàw/ n a thin-bladed saw used to cut curves in wood

fret·work /frét wùrk/ n 1 ornamental woodwork with an open pattern 2 decorative designs consisting of frets

Sigmund Freud

AKG London

Freud /froyd/, **Sigmund** (1856–1939) Austrian physician and founder of psychoanalysis

Freu·di·an /fróydee ən/ adj of Freud or his theories ■ n a follower of Freud —**Freu·di·an·ism** n

Freu·di·an slip n a psychologically significant slip of the tongue

Frey·a /fráy ə/ n in Norse mythology, the goddess of love, fertility, and beauty

Fri. abbr Friday

fri·a·ble /frí əb'l/ adj brittle and crumbly —**fri·a·bil·i·ty** /frí ə bíllətee/ n ◊ See note at **fragile**

fri·ar /frír/ n a member of a Roman Catholic religious order for men —**fri·ar·ly** adj

fri·ar·y /fríree/ n (pl -ies) n 1 a community of friars 2 a building where friars live

fric·as·see /fríkə see, fríkə sèe/ n meat stewed in a white sauce —**fric·as·see** vt

fric·a·tive /fríkətiv/ adj describes a consonant made by forcing the breath through a narrow opening —**fric·a·tive** n

fric·tion /fríkshən/ n 1 the rubbing of two object against each other 2 the resistance encountered by an object moving relative to another object with which it is in contact 3 a disagreement between groups with different goals —**fric·tion·al** adj

Fri·day /frí dày, -dee/ n the 5th day of the week

ORIGIN Friday is named for Frigg, the goddess of married love and the hearth in Scandinavian mythology.

fridge n a refrigerator (infml)

fried /fríd/ adj cooked by frying

Frie·dan /free dán/, **Betty** (b. 1921) US feminist and author

~~freight~~ incorrect spelling of **freight**

friend /frénd/ n 1 a person who trusts and is fond of somebody else 2 an ally 3 an advocate of a cause 4 a patron of a charity or institution 5 **Friend** a member of the Society of Friends, also called **Quakers** —**friend·less** adj

friend·ly /fréndlee/ (-li·er, -li·est) adj 1 affectionate and trusting 2 helpful 3 allied or on the same side 4 having a pleasant and welcoming atmosphere —**friend·li·ness** n —**friend·ly** adv

friendly fire n gunfire or artillery fire accidentally directed at military personnel from their own or their allies' forces

friend·ship /frénd ship/ n 1 a relationship between friends 2 mutually friendly feelings between people

Friends of the Earth n an international environmental organization (+ sing or pl verb)

fri·er n = fryer

fries /frız/ npl deep-fried potato strips

frieze /freez/ n 1 a decorative band along the wall of a room just below the ceiling 2 a horizontal decorative band forming part of the entablature of a classical building ◊ See note at **freeze**

frig·ate /fríggət/ n 1 a medium-sized US warship larger than a destroyer and used for escort duty 2 an 18C or 19C sailing ship equipped for war

fright /frít/ n 1 a sudden feeling of fear 2 the state of being afraid 3 something very unpleasant-looking (infml) ○ My hair's a fright this morning.

fright·en /frít'n/ v 1 vti make or become afraid 2 vt scare into leaving ○ frightened him off —**fright·ened** adj —**fright·en·ing** adj

~~frightend~~ incorrect spelling of **frightened**

fright·ful /frítfəl/ adj 1 very serious or alarming ○ the frightful prospect of losing the farm 2 very bad or unpleasant ○ a frightful smell 3 very great ○ a frightful bore —**fright·ful·ly** adv

frig·id /fríjjid/ adj 1 sexually unresponsive 2 very cold 3 lacking emotional warmth —**fri·gid·i·ty** /fri jíddətee/ n —**frig·id·ly** adv

frill n a decorative band of material with many folds —**frilled** adj —**frill·y** adj

fringe n 1 a decorative edging of strands 2 a border or edging 3 an outer limit (often pl) ○ on the fringes of civilization 4 an area or activity less important than another or others (usually pl) ○ on the fringes of political life 5 a faction with views unrepresentative of the rest of a group ■ adj 1 outlying 2 outside the mainstream and regarded as unconventional ■ vt (fringed, fring·ing) 1 form a fringe around 2 decorate with a fringe —**fringed** adj

fringe ben·e·fit n 1 an additional or incidental advantage derived from an activity 2 an additional advantage provided to an employee

frip·per·y /fríppəree/ (pl -ies) n an article worn for show

Fris·bee /frízbee/ tdmk a trademark for a plastic disk thrown from person to person in a game

frisk v 1 vi leap around playfully 2 vt search somebody quickly —**frisk** n —**frisk·ing** n

frisk·y /frískee/ (-i·er, -i·est) adj feeling playful, or behaving in a playful way —**frisk·i·ly** adv —**frisk·i·ness** n

fris·son /fri sóN/ n a thrilling feeling (literary)

frit n the basic materials for glass, pottery glazes, or enamels ■ vt (frit·ted, frit·ting) fuse in order to make frit

frit·ter[1] /frítter/ *n* a small cake of fried batter

ORIGIN **Fritter** as in "fried cake" is, not unexpectedly, related to *fry*: they go back to the same Latin verb. **Fritter** as in *fritter away* comes from a noun *fritters* meaning "scraps," whose origin is not certainly known.

frit·ter[2] /frítter/ □ **fritter away** *vt* squander gradually

fritz ◇ **on the fritz** out of order or not working properly *(slang)*

friv·o·lous /frívvələss/ *adj* 1 not worth taking seriously 2 silly —**fri·vol·i·ty** /fri vóllətee/ *n* —**friv·o·lous·ly** *adv* —**friv·o·lous·ness** *n*

frizz *vti* form into tight curls ■ *n* frizzed hair

friz·zle[1] /frízz'l/ (-zled, -zling) *vti* 1 burn or shrivel 2 fry and sizzle

friz·zle[2] /frízz'l/ *vti* (-zled, -zling) form into tight curls ■ *n* a short tight curl

friz·zy /frízzee/ (-zi·er, -zi·est), **frizz·ly** /frízlee/ (friz·zli·er, friz·zli·est) *adj* in tight curls —**friz·zi·ly** *adv* —**friz·zi·ness** *n*

fro *adv* ◗ to and fro

frock *n* 1 a woman's or girl's dress *(dated)* 2 a loose outer garment traditionally worn by artists and farm workers 3 a monk's cassock

frock coat *n* a 19C man's knee-length coat for formal day wear

frog[1] *n* 1 a small tailless amphibious animal with webbed feet and long back legs used for jumping 2 a support for flowers in an arrangement 3 a nut used to secure the strings on a violin bow

frog[2] *n* an ornamental loop and button

frog·man /fráwgmən, fróg-/ (*pl* -men /-mən/) *n* an underwater swimmer with breathing equipment engaged in military, police, or rescue work

frog·march /fráwg maàrch, fróg-/ *vt* force somebody to walk somewhere with arms pinned behind the back

frol·ic /fróllik/ *vi* (-icked, -ick·ing) play lightheartedly ■ *n* 1 something lively and carefree 2 lively carefree play —**frol·ic·some** *adj*

from *prep* 1 indicates the source or beginning of something ○ *a passage from a novel* 2 indicates a range ○ *We are open from 2 to 4:30.* 3 indicates the distance between two points ○ *not far from here* 4 indicates the material or substance used to make something ○ *built from native pine* 5 indicates the cause of something ○ *low morale resulting from staff cuts*

frond *n* 1 a large leaf divided into many thin sections, found on many nonflowering plants, especially ferns or palms 2 a seaweed resembling fern leaves

front /frunt/ *n* 1 a part or surface facing forward 2 the area at the forward part of something 3 the façade of a building facing a street 4 the side of a property adjoining a river, lake, or street 5 the direction straight ahead ○ *Face the front.* 6 a leading position ○ *companies at the front of genetic research* 7 an aspect ○ *The situation looks bad on all fronts.* 8 a battle zone 9 a particular area of activity ○ *the work front* 10 a line along which one mass of air meets another differing in temperature or density 11 a group with a common purpose 12 a way of behaving adopted to deal with a situation or conceal feelings ○ *put on a brave front* 13 a cover for illegal activities 14 a figurehead leader with no real power ■ *adj* situated at the front ■ *vt* 1 face toward something 2 be a front for 3 be the leader of a group, e.g., a band

front·age /frúntij/ *n* 1 the front of a building 2 the land between a building and a street 3 the length of the front of a building or piece of land adjoining a street, lake, or river

fron·tal[1] /frúnt'l/ *adj* 1 situated at or in the front 2 showing the front of somebody or something 3 direct and very forceful ○ *made a frontal attack on her political opponent* 4 of the forehead —**fron·tal·ly** *adv*

fron·tal[2] /frúnt'l/ *n* 1 a cloth covering the front of an altar 2 the façade of a building

front bench *n* in the British parliament, one of two benches reserved for government ministers and their opposition counterparts

front burn·er *n* one of the heating elements at the rear of a stove

front door *n* 1 the main entrance to a building 2 the usual approved means of doing something

✦ front end *n* 1 the user interface of a computer system 2 a computer that performs preliminary processing on data before passing it to another computer for further processing

✦ front-end *adj* 1 of the start of a process 2 of the user interface of a computer system

front-end load *n* a high initial payment made by an investor

fron·tier /frun teér/ *n* 1 an international border 2 the edge of an area that is being settled by pioneers

fron·tis·piece /frúntiss peèss/ *n* a book illustration facing the title page

ORIGIN **Frontispiece** was assimilated to the word *piece*, but has no connection with it. Etymologically the word divides into two parts, *fronti*, a form of the Latin word for "forehead," and *spiece*, a Latin root meaning "see" (the same as in *spectator*). A **frontispiece** was at first the "façade of a building." It developed the sense "title page of a book" (now obsolete) in the early 17C, and then the modern meaning "illustration opposite the title page" in the late 17C.

front-line /frŭnt lïn/ *n also* **front line 1** the forward line of a battle, position, or formation **2** the most advanced, important, or conspicuous position ■ *adj* advanced or leading ○ *frontline research*

front-line state *n* a nation situated on the border of a war-torn or war-threatened area

front-load *vt* assign the bulk of the costs of an insurance plan or investment to an early stage

front man *n* a figurehead without real power (*infml*)

front mat-ter *n* the preliminary pages of a book before the main text

front mon-ey *n* advance payment

front of-fice *n* a management

fron-ton /frŏn tòn/ *n* a court on which jai alai is played

front-page *adj* important enough to appear on the front page of a newspaper ■ *vt* (**front-paged, front-pag-ing**) print on front page

front room *n* a living room

front-run-ner, front-run-ner /frŭnt rŭnnar/ *n* a leader in a race or contest (*infml*)

front-wheel drive *n* a system in which engine power is transmitted to the front wheels of a motor vehicle

frost *n* **1** frozen water crystals on a cold surface **2** an outdoor temperature below freezing point **3** a cold, unfriendly attitude **4** the process of freezing ■ *v* **1** *vti* cover something or be covered with frost **2** *vt* give a roughened or dull surface to glass or metal **3** *vt* put frosting on a cake **4** *vt* tint hair strands

Frost, Robert (1874–1963) US poet

frost-bite /fráwst bït/ *n* injury to body extremities caused by exposure to freezing temperatures ■ *vt* (**-bit**/-bĭt/, **-bit-ten** /-bĭtt'n/, **-bit-ing**) injure by exposure to freezing temperatures

frost-ing /fráwsting/ *n* **1** soft, rich icing **2** a rough or dull surface given to glass or metal

frost-y /fráwstee/ (**-i-er, -i-est**) *adj* **1** very cold in temperature **2** covered in frost **3** cold in manner —**frost-i-ly** *adv* —**frost-i-ness** *n*

froth /frawth, froth/ *n* **1** foam **2** foamy saliva **3** something that lacks substance or seriousness ■ *v* **1** *vt* cause to foam **2** *vi* produce foam —**froth-i-ly** *adv* —**froth-i-ness** *n* —**froth-y** *adj*

frown /frown/ *v* **1** *vi* wrinkle the brow in a displeased expression **2** *vt* express by frowning —**frown** *n* —**frown-ing-ly** *adv*
□ **frown on** *or* **upon** *vt* disapprove of

frowz-y /frówzee/ (**-i-er, -i-est**) *adj* messy and rundown

froze past tense of **freeze**

fro-zen /frŏz'n/ past participle of **freeze** ■ *adj* **1** covered by or made into ice **2** damaged or made inoperable by ice **3** extremely cold

4 preserved by freezing for eating at a later time **5** immobile **6** fixed at a particular level to avoid undesirable economic or social consequences —**fro-zen-ly** *adv* —**fro-zen-ness** *n*

fruc-tose /frúk tòz, -tòss, frook-/ *n* a sugar in fruits and honey

fru-gal /froog'l/ *adj* **1** thrifty **2** meager —**fru-gal-i-ty** /froo gállatee/ *n* —**fru-gal-ly** *adv*

fruit /froot/ *n* **1** the edible part of a plant, usually fleshy and containing seeds **2** the ovary of a plant **3** the produce of a plant, grown or harvested by humans **4** a product or consequence **5** a spore-producing part of a plant ■ *vti* produce or cause to produce fruit

fruit bat *n* a large bat of a group including many fruit-eaters

fruit-cake /froot kàyk/ *n* **1** a dense cake containing dried fruit **2** a person regarded as irrational (*slang insult*)

fruit fly *n* **1** a small plant-eating insect **2** a small insect that eats decaying fruit

fruit-ful /frootfal/ *adj* **1** bearing much fruit **2** prolific **3** successful or beneficial —**fruit-ful-ly** *adv* —**fruit-ful-ness** *n*

fru-i-tion /froo ísh'n/ *n* **1** completion **2** the enjoyment of a desired outcome

fruit-less /frootlass/ *adj* **1** unsuccessful **2** bearing no fruit —**fruit-less-ly** *adv* —**fruit-less-ness** *n*

fruit-y /frootee/ (**-i-er, -i-est**) *adj* **1** of fruit **2** rich in tone **3** considered foolish or irrational (*infml*) —**fruit-i-ness** *n*

frump *n* a woman regarded as unfashionably dressed (*infml insult*) —**frump-ish** *adj* —**frump-y** *adj*

frus-trate /frú stràyt/ (**-trat-ed, -trat-ing**) *vt* **1** thwart something or somebody **2** discourage or exasperate somebody —**frus-trat-ed** *adj* —**frus-trat-ing** *adj* —**frus-trat-ing-ly** *adv* —**frus-tra-tion** /fru stráysh'n/ *n*

fry[1] /frï/ *vti* (**fried, fries**) cook quickly in very hot fat ■ *n* (*pl* **fries**) **1** a fried dish **2** an occasion with fried food ○ *a church fish fry*

fry[2] /frï/ *npl* young fishes

fry-er /frïr/, **fri-er** *n* **1** a container for frying food (*usually in combination*) **2** a young chicken for frying

fry-ing pan, fry pan *n* a shallow metal pan with a long handle used for frying food

FSLIC *abbr* Federal Savings and Loan Insurance Corporation

ft., ft *abbr* foot *or* feet

Ft. *abbr* Fort

FTC *abbr* Federal Trade Commission

⚡ FTP *n* a standard procedure for transferring files over a network. Full form **file transfer protocol** ■ *vt* transfer files using FTP

fuch-sia /fyoosha/ *n* a plant with purplish pink or white drooping flowers

---

ORIGIN The **fuchsia** is named for the German botanist Leonhard Fuchs (1501–66).

fud·dle /fúdd'l/ vt (-dled, -dling) vt confuse, e.g., with alcohol —**fud·dle** n

fud·dy-dud·dy /fúddee dùddee/ (pl **fud·dy-dud·dies**) n a person regarded as old-fashioned and dull (infml; sometimes offensive)

fudge n a soft sugary candy ■ vti (**fudged, fudg·ing**) alter in order to deceive (infml)

fu·el /fyóō əl/ n 1 something burned to provide power or heat 2 the fissionable material burned to create nuclear energy ■ vt 1 supply something with fuel 2 stimulate or maintain an emotion o fueled her passion

fu·el-air bomb n a thermobaric bomb

fu·el cell n a device that generates electricity by converting the energy of a fuel and an antioxidant into electricity

fu·el in·jec·tion n a system for running an internal combustion engine without a carburetor by forcing fuel directly into the combustion chamber —**fu·el-in·ject·ed** adj

fu·el oil n a liquid petroleum product used to produce heat or power

Fu·en·tes /foo én tàyss, fwén-/, **Carlos** (b. 1928) Mexican writer

fug n a stuffy atmosphere

fu·gi·tive /fyóōjətiv/ n 1 somebody who runs away, especially from justice 2 something elusive ■ adj 1 running away 2 lasting only briefly o the fugitive hour of dawn 3 moving from place to place 4 hard to understand or retain (fml) o the fugitive nature of astrophysics 5 written or composed for a specific occasion (literary)

fugue /fyoog/ n 1 a musical form in which a theme is stated and varied contrapuntally 2 also **fugue state** a state in which somebody experiences temporary and selective memory loss —**fu·gal** adj

Mt. Fuji

Fu·ji, Mt. /fóōjee/, **Fu·ji-ya·ma** /fóōjee yáamə, -yaá maà/ dormant volcano and highest mountain in Japan. Height 12,387 ft./ 3,776m.

Fu·ku·o·ka /fóōkoo ōkə, -ō kaà/ port on N Kyushu Island, Japan. Pop. 1,279,671 (2000).

Ful·bright /fóol brìt/, **J. William** (1905–95) US politician and educator

ful·crum /fóolkrəm, fúlkrəm/ (pl **-crums** or **-cra** /-krə/) n 1 the pivot of a lever 2 a prop supporting something revolving about it or depending on it

ful·fill /fool fil/ vt 1 achieve something expected, desired, or promised 2 carry out a request or order 3 satisfy a standard or requirement —**ful·fill·ment** n ◊ See note at **perform**

full /fool/ adj 1 filled to capacity 2 having a large amount or number of something o full of mischief 3 greatest in degree or extent o at full speed 4 with nothing or no one missing o a full complement of staff o the full number of students 5 completely developed o in full bloom 6 having fulfilled all the requirements for something o a full colonel 7 having eaten enough 8 busy, active, and varied o live a full life 9 plump o a full figure 10 having the same parents o my full brother 11 sonorous o chanted in full voice ■ adv 1 completely o turned full around 2 exactly o took a hit full on the chest ■ n the greatest extent or fullest degree o enjoyed himself to the full —**full·ness** n —**full·y** adv ◊ **be full of yourself** be very conceited and arrogant

full·back /fool bàk/ n 1 in football, a player in the offensive backfield positioned behind the quarterback 2 in sports such as soccer, rugby, or field hockey, a defender 3 a fullback's position

full-blood·ed adj 1 thoroughbred 2 vigorous

full-blown adj 1 complete 2 fully in bloom

full dress n clothes for a ceremony or formal occasion

full-dress adj important and complete o a full-dress investigation

Ful·ler /fóollər/, **Buckminster** (1895–1983) US engineer, designer, architect, and writer

Ful·ler, Margaret (1810–50) US writer and critic

Ful·ler, Melville W. (1833–1910) chief justice of the US Supreme Court (1888–1910)

Ful·ler·ton /fóollərt'n/ city in SW California. Pop. 121,954 (1998).

⚡ **full-fea·tured** adj having the whole range of possible functions, capabilities, or options o a full-featured PC

~~**fullfill**~~ incorrect spelling of **fulfill**

full-fledged adj completely developed

full-grown adj mature or adult

full house n in poker, a hand containing three cards of the same value and a pair of another value

full-length adj describes a mirror or portrait showing the whole body

full moon n 1 the Moon appearing as a complete circle 2 the time when the Moon appears as a full circle

full-scale adj 1 life-size 2 done with total commitment of effort and resources

full-size, full-sized adj 1 of the usual size for something 2 of the standard size for a bed

full time adv during all of the time considered usual for an activity o worked full time ■ n in soccer and other sports, the end of a game

full-time *adj* **1** involving or using all the time usual or appropriate for an activity **2** occurring at or indicating the end of a game —**full-tim-er** *n*

ful-mi-nate /fŏŏlmə nàyt, fúl-/ *v* **1** speak scathingly **2** *vti* explode violently —**ful-mi-na-tion** /fŏŏlmə náysh'n, fúl-/ *n*

ful-some /fŏŏlsəm/ *adj* **1** excessively complimentary **2** lavish —**ful-some-ly** *adv*

fum-ble /fúmb'l/ (-bled, -bling) *v* **1** *vti* grope clumsily in searching for something **2** *vi* act clumsily, hesitantly, or unsuccessfully **3** *vti* in sports, drop or mishandle a ball —**fum-ble** *n* —**fum-blingl-y** *adv*

fume *v* (fumed, fum-ing) **1** *vi* be angry **2** *vi* emit gas or smoke **3** *vt* fumigate something ■ *n* (often pl) **1** smoke or gas **2** an acrid smell —**fum-ing-ly** *adv*

fu-mi-gate /fyóomi gàyt/ (-gat-ed, -gat-ing) *vti* treat something with fumes to disinfect it or kill pests —**fu-mi-ga-tion** /fyóomi gáysh'n/ *n* —**fu-mi-gant** *n* —**fu-mi-ga-tor** *n*

fun *n* **1** amusement or enjoyment **2** something amusing or enjoyable ■ *adj* amusing or enjoyable (infml) o *a fun movie*

Fu-na-fu-ti /fŏonə fóotee/ atoll and capital of Tuvalu, in the W Pacific Ocean. Pop. 3,432 (1990).

⚡**func-tion** /fúngkshən/ *n* **1** the purpose of something **2** a role assigned to somebody or something **3** a social event **4** a variable quantity determined by other values **5** a quality or characteristic that depends on and varies with another o *Success is a function of determination and ability.* **6** (symbol f) a one-to-one correspondence between members of two mathematical sets **7** a single computer operation **8** a computer program's main purpose **9** the role of a word or phrase in a construction ■ *vi* **1** serve a purpose or perform a role **2** be in working order

func-tion-al /fúngkshən'l/ *adj* **1** practical or useful **2** operational —**func-tion-al-ly** *adv*

func-tion-al-ism /fúngkshən'l lzzəm/ *n* **1** the belief that the intended function of something should determine its form **2** a philosophy emphasizing that the practical is more important than the aesthetic —**func-tion-al-ist** *n, adj* —**func-tion-al-is-tic** /fúngkshən'l ístik/ *adj*

⚡**func-tion-al-i-ty** /fùngkshə nállətee/ *n* the range of functions, capabilities, and options a computer offers

func-tion-ar-y /fúngkshə nèrree/ (pl -ies) *n* an unimportant official

⚡**func-tion key** *n* a keyboard button that instructs the computer to perform a specific action

func-tion word *n* a word whose primary purpose is to perform a syntactic function in a sentence

fund *n* **1** a supply **2** a sum of money saved or invested for a purpose ■ **funds** *npl* money ■ *vt* **1** provide money for something **2** change a short-term debt into a long-term one

fun-da-men-tal /fùndə mént'l/ *adj* **1** basic **2** central or essential ■ *n* **1** a basic principle or element (often pl) **2** the principal musical tone in a chord **3** the lowest frequency in a vibration —**fun-da-men-tal-ly** *adv*

fun-da-men-tal-ism /fùndə mént'l lzzəm/ *n* **1** a religious or political movement with a strict view of doctrine **2** the belief that religious or political doctrine should be implemented strictly —**fun-da-men-tal-ist** *n, adj*

~~**fundemental**~~ incorrect spelling of **fundamental**

fund-ing /fúnding/ *n* money to support a project

fund-rais-er /fúnd ràyzər/ *n* **1** somebody who raises money for a nonprofit organization **2** a money-raising activity or event for a nonprofit organization —**fund-rais-ing** *n*

Fun-dy, Bay of /fúndee/ inlet of the Atlantic Ocean in SE Canada, separating New Brunswick and Nova Scotia. Depth 650 ft./200 m. Length 171 mi./275 km.

fu-ner-al /fyóonərəl/ *n* **1** a ceremony for somebody who has died **2** an end to something **3** a funeral procession

fu-ner-al di-rec-tor *n* somebody who arranges funerals

fu-ner-al home, fu-ner-al par-lor *n* a business arranging or performing funerals

fu-ner-ar-y /fyóonə rèrree/ *adj* of funerals

fu-ne-re-al /fyə néeree əl/ *adj* **1** of or like a funeral **2** gloomy

fun-gi-cide /fúnjə sìd, fúng gə-/ *n* a chemical that kills fungi —**fun-gi-cid-al** /fúnjə sìd'l, fùng gə-/ *adj*

fun-goid /fúng gòyd/ *adj* of or like fungus ■ *n* a fungus

fun-gus /fúng gəss/ (pl -gi /fún jì, fúng gì/ or -gus-es) *n* a spore-producing organism of a group including molds and mushrooms —**fun-gal** *adj*

fu-nic-u-lar /fyoo níkyələr/ *adj* **1** of a rope's tension **2** operated by a rope or cable wound or pulled by a machine ■ *n* a cable-operated railroad

funk[1] *n* a musical style with a heavy rhythmic bass and backbeat —**funk-i-ly** *adv* —**funk-y** *adj*

funk[2] *n* melancholy (infml) —**funk-y** *adj*

funk-y /fúngkee/ (-i-er, -i-est) *adj* stylish and new (slang)

fun-nel /fúnn'l/ *n* **1** a cone-shaped utensil for pouring liquids into containers **2** a chimney on a steamship or steam engine ■ *v* **1** *vti* move into and through a narrow space **2** *vt* concentrate resources somewhere

fun·nel cloud *n* a funnel-shaped cloud projecting from the bottom of a thundercloud

fun·ny /fúnnee/ *adj* (**-ni·er, -ni·est**) 1 causing amusement or laughter 2 strange or puzzling 3 tricky or dishonest (*infml*) ■ **fun·nies** *npl* newspaper comic strips —**fun·ni·ly** *adv* —**fun·ni·ness** *n*

SYNONYMS **funny, comic, comical, droll, facetious, humorous, witty, hilarious, side-splitting** CORE MEANING: causing or intended to cause amusement

fun·ny bone *n* 1 the point at the outside of the elbow where a nerve is close to the longer arm bone (*infml*) 2 somebody's sense of humor

ORIGIN As well as a reference to the tingling sensation caused when the nerve at the point of the elbow is hit, the name may involve a pun on *humerus* "arm bone" and *humorous*.

fun run *n* a leisure run to promote fitness or raise money for charity

fur *n* 1 the soft dense coat of hair on a mammal 2 a dressed pelt from a mammal such as a mink. Use: garments, decoration. 3 a coat, jacket, or stole made of fur or of fake fur —**furred** *adj*

fur. *abbr* furlong

Fu·ries /fyooreez/ *npl* in Greek mythology, three avenging goddesses

fu·ri·ous /fyooree əss/ *adj* 1 very angry 2 very energetic —**fu·ri·ous·ly** *adv*

furl *vti* roll up and secure a flag or sail, or become rolled up and secure ■ *n* a furled section of a flag or sail

fur·long /fúr làwng/ *n* a measure of distance equal to 220 yards (approximately 201 meters)

ORIGIN *Furlong* means etymologically "furrow long," and so was the length of a furrow plowed across a field ten acres square.

fur·lough /fúr lō/ *n* a leave of absence, especially from military duty ■ *vt* give a leave of absence to

fur·nace /fúrnəss/ *n* an enclosure producing great heat, e.g., to heat a building or smelt metal

fur·nish /fúrnish/ *vt* 1 put furniture in a place 2 supply something (*fml*) —**fur·nished** *adj* —**fur·nish·er** *n*

fur·nish·ings /fúrnishingz/ *npl* 1 furniture, carpets, and curtains 2 clothes o *men's furnishings*

fur·ni·ture /fúrnichər/ *n* movable items such as tables and chairs in a room, garden, or patio

fu·ror /fyoor àwr/ *n* 1 an angry public reaction 2 a state of excitement 3 a craze

fur·ri·er /fúrree ər/ *n* 1 a fur dealer 2 a maker or seller of fur garments and accessories

fur·row /fúrrō/ *n* 1 a narrow trench in soil made by a plow 2 a groove 3 a wrinkle on the forehead ■ *vti* make furrows in or become marked with furrows —**fur·rowed** *adj*

fur·ry /fúree, fúrree/ (**-ri·er, -ri·est**) *adj* 1 covered in fur 2 looking or feeling like fur —**fur·ri·ness** *n*

fur·ther /fúrthər/ *adj* additional ■ *adv* 1 to a greater distance 2 to a greater degree or extent 3 in addition ■ *vt* advance —**fur·ther·most** *adj*

fur·ther·ance /fúrthərənss/ *n* advancement or progress

fur·ther·more /fúrthər màwr, fùrthər máwr/ *adv* in addition

fur·thest /fúrthəst/ *adj* most distant ■ *adv* 1 to the greatest distance 2 to the greatest degree or extent

fur·tive /fúrtiv/ *adj* 1 secretive 2 shifty —**fur·tive·ly** *adv* —**fur·tive·ness** *n* ◊ See note at **secret**

fu·ry /fyooree/ (*pl* **-ries**) *n* 1 great rage 2 a burst of violent anger 3 a wild physical force o *felt the fury of the hurricane* 4 **Fu·ry** in Greek mythology, one of the Furies ◊ See note at **anger**

furze *n* UK gorse

~~fuschia~~ incorrect spelling of **fuchsia**

fuse[1] /fyooz/ *n* an electrical circuit breaker containing a piece of metal that melts if the current is too strong ■ *vti* (**fused, fus·ing**) 1 combine 2 liquefy —**fused** *adj*

fuse[2] /fyooz/, **fuze** *n* 1 a cord or trail of a combustible substance ignited at one end to carry a flame to an explosive device 2 a mechanical or electrical detonator for a bomb or grenade ■ *vt* (**fused, fus·ing; fuzed, fuz·ing**) equip a bomb or grenade with a detonator

fu·se·lage /fyoossə làazh, fyoozə-/ *n* an airplane body, excluding the wings

Fu·shun /foo shoon/ *city* in NE China. Pop. 1,530,000 (1995).

fu·sil·ier /fyooza léer/, **fu·sil·eer** *n* a soldier with a musket

fu·sil·lade /fyoossə làad, fyoossə làyd, fyooza-/ *n* 1 a blast of gunfire from several guns at once 2 an onslaught ■ *vt* (**-lad·ed, -lad·ing**) fire at an enemy in a sustained burst from several guns at once

fu·sion /fyoozh'n/ *n* 1 the heating and liquefying of a substance 2 the blending of two or more things 3 a combination of musical styles from different traditions

fu·sion bomb *n* a hydrogen bomb using nuclear fusion

fu·sion food, fu·sion cui·sine *n* a style of cooking combining different international influences

fuss *n* 1 unnecessarily busy or excited activity 2 needless worry over trivialities 3 a protest or complaint about something trivial **4** a noisy argument **5** an excited display of affection or concern ■ *vi* **1** worry too much about trivialities **2** make nervous or aimless fiddling movements ◊ *fussed with her hair*

fuss·budg·et /fúss bùjjət/ *n* somebody who worries (*infml*)

fuss·y /fússee/ (**-i·er, -i·est**) *adj* **1** worrying too much about trivialities **2** excessively choosy **3** easily upset **4** overly elaborate, e.g., in design ◊ See note at **careful**

fus·ty /fústee/ (**-ti·er, -ti·est**) *adj* **1** smelling stale **2** outdated

fut. *abbr* future

fu·tile /fyóot'l/ *adj* vain or pointless—**fu·tile·ly** *adv*—**fu·til·i·ty** /fyoo tíllətee/ *n*

fu·ton /fóo tòn/ *n* **1** a Japanese-style mattress used as a bed **2** a sofa bed with a futon mattress

fu·ture /fyóochər/ *n* **1** a time yet to come **2** events yet to happen **3** an expected or projected state **4** the tense or verb forms used for referring to events that have not yet happened ■ **fu·tures** *npl* commodities traded for later delivery ■ *adj* **1** yet to occur **2** of or in the tense used for referring to events that have not yet happened

fu·ture per·fect *n* the form of a verb that expresses a completed action in the future, e.g., using "will have" with the past participle

fu·ture shock *n* stress caused by rapid technological change

fu·tur·ism /fyóochə rìzzəm/ *n* **1** an early 20C artistic movement valuing the beauty of technology **2** belief in the need to look to the future for personal and social fulfillment—**fu·tur·ist** *n, adj*

fu·tur·is·tic /fyòochə rístik/ *adj* **1** appearing to be ahead of the times in design or technology **2** showing life in a future time—**fu·tur·is·ti·cal·ly** *adv*

fu·tu·ri·ty /fyoo tóoratee, -chóoratee/ (*pl* **-ties**) *n* **1** the future **2** a future event (*fml*)

fu·tur·ol·o·gy /fyòochə róllajee/ *n* the study and forecasting of the future on the basis of current trends—**fu·tur·o·log·i·cal** /fyòochərə lójjik'l/ *adj*—**fu·tur·ol·o·gist** *n*

fuze *n, vt* ARMS = **fuse**²

Fu·zhou /fóo jó/ city in SE China. Pop. 1,590,000 (1995).

fuzz *n* **1** a mass of short fine hairs or fibers **2** an offensive term for the police (*slang*) ■ *vti* **1** cover or become covered with fuzz **2** blur or become blurred

fuzz·y /fúzzee/ (**-i·er, -i·est**) *adj* **1** covered with fuzz **2** consisting of fuzz **3** blurred ◊ *fuzzy vision*—**fuzz·i·ly** *adv*—**fuzz·i·ness** *n*

✦ fuzz·y log·ic *n* logic allowing for imprecision in answers to questions used in computer programming designed to mimic human intelligence

FWD *abbr* **1** four-wheel drive **2** front-wheel drive

fwd. *abbr* forward

FX *abbr* foreign exchange

FY *abbr* fiscal year

-fy *suffix* make, cause to become ◊ *modify*

✦ FYI *abbr* for your information (*in e-mails and office memos*)

G

g¹ (*pl* **g's**), **G** (*pl* **G's** *or* **Gs**) *n* the 7th letter of the English alphabet

g² *symbol* acceleration of free fall as a result of gravity

g³ *abbr* **1** gauge **2** gram

G¹ (*pl* **G's** *or* **Gs**) *n* **1** the 5th note in the musical scale of C major **2** a general-audience movie rating **3** $1,000 (*slang*)

G² *symbol* gravitational constant

G8 *n* the eight most industrialized nations. Full form **Group of Eight**

Ga *symbol* gallium

GA, Ga. *abbr* Georgia

G.A. *abbr* General Assembly (of the United Nations)

gab (**gabbed, gab·bing**) *vi* chat idly (*infml*)—**gab** *n*

gab·ar·dine /gábbər dèen/ *n* a smooth twill fabric

gab·ble /gább'l/ (**-bled, -bling**) *v* **1** *vti* speak or say unintelligibly **2** *vi* make the throaty sound of a goose—**gab·ble** *n*

ga·ble /gáyb'l/ *n* a triangular section of a building's wall where the roof slopes meet—**ga·bled** *adj*

Ga·ble /gáyb'l/, **Clark** (1901–60) US movie actor

Ga·bon /ga bón, gə bón/ country in west central Africa on the Atlantic coast. Cap. Libreville. Pop. 1,221,175 (2001).—**Ga·bon·ese** /gàbbə neéz, -neéss/ *n, adj*

Ga·bo·rone /gàbbə rónee/ capital of Botswana. Pop. 133,468 (1991).

Ga·bri·el /gáybree əl/ *n* in Christian, Islamic, and Jewish tradition, an archangel who acts as God's messenger

gad (**gad·ded, gad·ding**) *vi* be out having fun (*humorous*)

gad·a·bout /gáddə bòwt/ *n* somebody always in search of entertainment or activity (*humorous*)

Gad·da·fi /gə daáfee/, **Ga·daf·fi, Qad·da·fi** /kə-/, **Muammar al-** (*b.* 1942) Libyan soldier and national leader (1969–)

gad·fly /gád flì/ (*pl* **-flies**) *n* **1** a fly that bites livestock **2** somebody regarded as annoying

gadg·et /gájjət/ *n* **1** a small ingenious device **2** a device that is of no real use

gadg·et·ry /gájjətree/ *n* gadgets collectively

gad·o·lin·i·um /gàdd'l ínnee əm/ *n* (*symbol* Gd) a silvery-white metallic element. Use: high-temperature alloys, neutron absorber in nuclear reactors and fuels.

Gae·a = Gaia

Gael /gayl/ *n* **1** somebody who speaks Gaelic **2** a Scottish Highlander

Gael·ic /gáylik/ *n* a Celtic language spoken in Scotland and Ireland —**Gael·ic** *adj*

gaff *n* **1** a hooked pole used to hold and land fish **2** a pole used to support the upper edge of a ship's sail **3** gimmick used in a hoax ■ *vt* hold fish with a hooked pole

gaffe /gaf/ *n* a social blunder

gaf·fer /gáffər/ *n* a chief lighting electrician on a television or movie set (*infml*)

gag *n* **1** something put over a person's mouth to prevent speech **2** a restraint of free speech **3** a comic remark or action **4** a trick or practical joke (*infml*) ■ *v* (**gagged, gag·ging**) **1** *vt* put something over somebody's mouth to prevent speech **2** *vt* prevent somebody from saying or revealing something **3** *vti* choke or retch

ga·ga /gàà gàà/ *adj* foolishly enthusiastic (*infml*)

Ga·ga·rin /gə gaàrən/, **Yuri** (1934–68) Soviet cosmonaut

gage[1] (*archaic*) *n* **1** a pledge left until a debt is paid or an obligation fulfilled **2** a token thrown down or offered as a challenge to fight ■ *vt* (**gaged, gag·ing**) offer as a pledge

gage[2] *n*, *vt* = gauge

Gage, Thomas (1721–87) British-born army general and colonial administrator

gag·gle /gágg'l/ *n* **1** a group of geese **2** a group of people ○ *a gaggle of children*

gag or·der *n* a court order that forbids somebody from saying or revealing something

gag rule *n* a rule to limit debate

Gai·a /gí ə/, **Gae·a** /jée ə/, **Ge** /gay/ *n* in Greek mythology, the personification of the Earth

gai·e·ty /gáy ətee/ (*pl* -ties) *n* **1** joyfulness or lightheartedness **2** a spirited activity **3** the bright or colorful appearance of something such as clothing (*dated*)

gai·jin /gí jin/ (*pl* same) *n* a foreigner in Japan

gai·ly /gáylee/ *adv* **1** joyfully or lightheartedly **2** in bright colors (*dated*)

gain[1] *v* **1** *vt* acquire or arrive at through effort, skill, or merit ○ *gain a victory* ○ *gain access* **2** *vi* get an advantage ○ *No one stands to gain from this.* **3** *vti* get more of something gradually, or increase gradually ○ *gain in confidence* ○ *gain experience* **4** *vi* get closer to somebody being pursued or farther away from a pursuer **5** *vti* increase in or by a particular amount ○ *The dollar had gained*

two points **6** *vti* run ahead of the correct time ○ *My watch gains ten minutes every day.* **7** *vt* reach (*literary*) ○ *gained the shore* ■ *n* **1** an amount by which something has increased **2** a benefit or profit —**gain·a·ble** *adj* ◊ See note at **get**

gain[2] *n* a notch to fit something into ■ *vt* **1** cut a notch in **2** fit into a notch

gain·ful /gáynf'l/ *adj* profitable or advantageous —**gain·ful·ly** *adv*

gain·say /gayn sáy, gáyn sày/ (-**said** /-sáyd, -séd/) *vt* (*fml*) **1** deny **2** contradict —**gain·say·er** *n*

Gains·bor·ough /gáynz bùrō/, **Thomas** (1727–88) British painter

gait /gayt/ *n* **1** a manner of walking **2** a horse's pace having a specific pattern of steps

---

SPELLCHECK Do not confuse the spelling of **gait** and **gate** ("a movable barrier"), which sound similar.

---

gai·ter /gáytər/ *n* a covering for the leg from the instep to the ankle or knee (*usually pl*) —**gai·tered** *adj*

gal[1] *n* a girl or woman (*infml; sometimes offensive*)

gal[2] *n* a unit of acceleration

gal. *abbr* gallon

ga·la /gáylə, gaálə/ *n* a lavish party with food and entertainment

ga·lac·tic /gə láktik/ *adj* of galaxies or the Milky Way

ga·lac·tose /gə lák tòss, -tòz/ *n* a sugar that is a constituent of lactose

Ga·lá·pa·gos Is·lands /gə laápəgass-/, **Ga·la·pa·gos Is·lands** group of islands off W Ecuador in the Pacific Ocean. Pop. 9,785 (1990).

Ga·la·tians /gə láysh'nz/ *n* a book of the Bible believed to be a letter from St. Paul to the church in Galatia. (+ *sing verb*)

gal·ax·y /gálləksee/ (*pl* -ies) *n* **1** a large group of stars, gas, and dust forming a unit within the universe **2** a distinguished gathering **3** Gal·ax·y the Milky Way

---

ORIGIN Galaxy came via French and Latin from the Greek word for the "Milky Way," which was formed from *gala* "milk." *Milky Way* itself is a translation from Latin. The names derive from the white appearance of massed stars in the night sky.

Gal·braith /gál bràyth/, **John Kenneth** (*b.* 1908) Canadian-born US economist

gale *n* a strong wind, technically of force 8 or 9 ■ **gales** *npl* loud outbursts ○ *gales of laughter*

Ga·len /gáylən/ (129–199?) Greek physician and scholar

gal·i·lee /gállə lèe/ *n* a porch or chapel of a medieval church

Gal·i·lee /gálli lèe/ region of ancient Palestine between the Jordan River and the Sea of Galilee

Gal·i·lee, Sea of freshwater lake in NE Israel on the Jordan River

Ga·li·le·o /gàlli láy ō/ (1564–1642) Italian physicist and astronomer

gall[1] *n* **1** audacity **2** bitter feeling (*literary*)

> **ORIGIN Gall** "audacity, bitter feeling" comes from an ancient Scandinavian word meaning "yellow" (it originally referred to bile, which is of a yellowish green color). **Gall** "sore on an animal" is from an old German word, while **gall** "swelling on a plant" came via French from Latin.

gall[2] *n* a sore on an animal caused by rubbing ■ *vt* make angry or annoyed

gall[3] *n* a swelling on a tree or plant

gal·lant *adj* /gə lánt, -làant/ **1** courteous and attentive **2** brave (*literary*) ■ *n* /gə lánt, -làant, gállənt/ **1** a man courteous to women (*dated*) **2** a male lover (*archaic*) —**gal·lant·ly** *adv*

gal·lant·ry /gálləntree/ (*pl* -ries) *n* **1** courage **2** courtesy and attentiveness **3** something gallant said or done (*dated*)

Gal·lau·det /gàllə dét/, **Thomas** (1787–1851) US educator

gall·blad·der /gáwl blàddər/ *n* a sac on the right side of the liver where bile is stored

gal·le·on /gállee ən/ *n* a large three-masted sailing ship

gal·ler·y /gálləree/ (*pl* -ies) *n* **1** a place for art exhibits **2** a photographer's studio **3** a covered walkway that is open on one or both sides **4** an enclosed passageway inside a building **5** a long narrow space or room with a specific function **6** a balcony along the wall of a large building **7** *Can, Southern US* a veranda **8** *Carib* a porch at the front of a house **9** an underground passage **10** a balcony in a theater, especially the highest area, or the seats or audience in it **11** a group of spectators, especially at a tennis or golf match **12** an assorted collection —**gal·ler·ied** *adj*

gal·ley /gállee/ (*pl* -leys) *n* **1** a large ship used in ancient and medieval times, often with oars **2** a kitchen on a boat, train, or aircraft **3** *also* **galley proof** a first test copy of printed material for correction, usually not yet divided into pages

Gal·lic /gállik/ *adj* **1** French **2** Gaulish

gall·ing /gáwling/ *adj* exasperating —**gall·ing·ly** *adv*

gal·li·um /gállee əm/ *n* (*symbol* **Ga**) a rare metallic element. Use: high-temperature thermometers, semiconductors, alloys.

gal·li·vant /gállə vànt/ *vi* travel around for pleasure (*infml*)

gal·lon /gállən/ *n* a US unit of volume equal to eight US pints (approximately 3.79 liters)

gal·lop /gálləp/ *n* the fastest pace of a horse, with all four feet off the ground at the same time ■ *vti* ride a horse fast

gal·lop·ing /gálləping/ *adj* **1** fast-developing **2** like a gallop in speed or rhythm

gal·lows /gállōz/ (*pl* same) *n* a frame for hanging criminals

> **ORIGIN Gallows** comes from an ancient word meaning "pole." It was originally singular, though it occurred frequently in *pair of gallows*, from the two uprights with a cross-piece from which it was constructed. From that **gallows** came to be treated as a singular itself.

gal·lows hu·mor *n* macabre humor

gall·stone /gáwl stòn/ *n* a solid mass formed in the gallbladder

ga·lore /gə láwr/ *adj* in large quantities or numbers o *food galore*

> **ORIGIN Galore** comes from an Irish phrase meaning literally "to sufficiency." It is first recorded in the early 17C.

ga·losh·es /gə lóshəz/ *npl* waterproof over-shoes

Gals·wor·thy /gáwlz wùrthee/, **John** (1867–1933) British novelist and playwright

ga·lumph /gə lúmf/ *vi* move boisterously and clumsily (*infml*)

> **ORIGIN Galumph** is a blend of *gallop* and *triumph*, coined by Lewis Carroll in *Through the Looking-Glass* (1872).

gal·van·ic /gal vánnik/ *adj* **1** of chemically produced direct current **2** sudden or star-tling like an electric shock —**gal·van·i·cal·ly** *adv*

> **ORIGIN Galvanic**, *galvanize*, and related words are formed from the name of the Italian physiologist Luigi Galvani (1737–98), whose research led to the discovery that electricity can result from chemical action.

gal·va·nize /gálvə nīz/ (-nized, -niz·ing) *vt* **1** stimulate somebody or something to activity **2** coat metal with zinc —**gal·va·ni·za·tion** /gàlvəni záysh'n/ *n*

gal·va·nom·e·ter /gàlvə nómmətər/ *n* an instrument for measuring electric current —**gal·va·no·met·ric** /gàlvənə méttrik/ *adj* —**gal·va·nom·e·try** *n*

Gal·ves·ton /gálvist'n/ port in SE Texas. Pop. 59,567 (1998).

Gal·way /gáwl wày/ **1** seaport in the W Republic of Ireland, on **Galway Bay**, an inlet of the Atlantic Ocean. Pop. 57,000 (1996). **2** county in Connacht Province, W Republic of Ireland

Ga·ma /ga'amə/, **Vasco da** (1469?–1524) Portuguese navigator and explorer

Gam·bi·a /gámbee ə/ country on the coast of West Africa. Cap. Banjul. Pop. 1,411,205 (2001). —**Gam·bi·an** *n, adj*

gam·bit /gámbit/ *n* **1** a stratagem to secure an advantage **2** an opening move in chess

gam·ble /gámb'l/ *v* (**-bled, -bling**) **1** *vi* play games of chance **2** *vt* bet money **3** *vi* take a chance on something ◇ *gambling on nice weather* **4** *vi* endanger somebody or something ◇ *gambled with the success of the show* ■ *n* **1** a bet **2** something risky —**gam·bler** *n* —**gam·bling** *n*

ORIGIN Gamble is probably an alteration of an old word *gamel* "play games, frolic," which was a derivative of *game*. Alternatively it could have been formed directly from *game* and the suffix *-le*. It is first recorded in the early 18C. **Gamble** has no direct connection with *gambol*, which is an alteration of earlier *gambade* "horse's leap, caper." This came via French from an Italian word formed from *gamba* "leg."

gam·bol /gámb'l/ *vi* leap or skip about playfully —**gam·bol** *n*

game *n* **1** something played for fun **2** a competitive activity with rules **3** an occasion of a game **4** a style or level of playing ◇ *raise your game* **5** a stratagem or tactic **6** an occupation *(infml)* ◇ *the advertising game* **7** something not taken seriously **8** wild animals hunted for sport, or their meat ■ *adj* **1** ready and willing **2** brave ■ *vi* (**gamed, gaming**) gamble for money —**game·ly** *adv* ◇ **ahead of the game** anticipating new developments ◇ **play the game** follow the rules of a given situation, even if they are unspoken ◇ **the only game in town** the only possibility

game bird *n* a bird that is hunted for sport

game·keep·er /gáym kèepər/ *n* somebody who looks after game, as on an estate or game preserve —**game·keep·ing** *n*

game plan *n* a strategy to win a competition or achieve an objective

game point *n* **1** in racket games, a situation with the potential to win the game on the next point **2** a point that wins the game

game re·serve, game pre·serve *n* a protected area for wild animals

game show *n* a TV show with games and prizes

games·man·ship /gáymzmən shìp/ *n* **1** strategic behavior to gain an advantage **2** play of questionable fairness to gain an advantage

gam·ete /gá mèet/ *n* a cell with half the usual number of chromosomes that unites with another cell of the opposite sex in the process of sexual reproduction —**ga·met·ic** /gə méttik/ *adj*

gam·ey *adj* = **gamy**

ga·mine /gá mèen/ *n* **1** a boyish girl or young woman **2** a girl street urchin ■ *adj* appealingly boyish

gam·ing /gáyming/ *n* gambling for money

gam·ma /gámmə/ *n* the 3rd letter of the Greek alphabet

gam·ma glob·u·lin *n* a protein containing antibodies that is a component of blood serum

gam·ma ray *n* a high-energy photon emitted from a nucleus of a radioactive atom

gam·mon[1] /gámmən/ *n* **1** the lower part of a side of bacon **2** cured or smoked ham

gam·mon[2] /gámmən/ *n* a win at backgammon —**gam·mon** *vt*

Gam·ow /gámmov/, **George** (1904–68) Russian-born US theoretical physicist. He was a proponent of the theory that the universe was created in a gigantic explosion.

gam·ut /gámmət/ *n* the full range of something

ORIGIN Gamut was originally *gamma-ut*. This was the name of a note in medieval musical notation, the lowest of a particular sequence. **Gamut** came to refer to the full range of notes that a voice or instrument can produce. The modern figurative sense is first recorded in the early 17C.

gam·y /gáymee/ (**-i·er, -i·est**), **gam·ey** (**-i·er, -i·est**) *adj* **1** tasting of or like game **2** rank-smelling —**gam·i·ness** *n*

gan·der /gándər/ *n* **1** a male goose **2** a look or glance *(infml)*

Gan·dhi /gaándee/, **Indira** (1917–84) prime minister of India (1966–77, 1980–84)

Barnaby's

Mohandas Karamchand Gandhi

Gan·dhi, Mohandas Karamchand (1869–1948) Indian thinker and nationalist leader

gang *n* **1** a group of trouble-making young people **2** a group of criminals **3** a group of workers **4** a group of people who enjoy each other's company ■ *vi* form a group □ **gang up on** *vt* unite to attack or intimidate

Gan·ges /gán jèez/ river in N India and Bangladesh, emptying into the Bay of Bengal. Length 1,560 mi./2,510 km.

gang·land /gáng lànd, -lənd/ *n* the world of organized crime —**gang·land** *adj*

gan·gling /gáng gling/, **gan·gly** /-glee/ (**-gli·er, -gli·est**) *adj* awkwardly tall and thin

gan·gli·on /gáng glee ən/ (*pl* **-a** /-ə/ *or* **-ons**) *n* **1** a cluster of nerve cells **2** a swelling on a joint or tendon —**gan·gli·on·ic** /gàng glee ónnik/ *adj*

gang·plank /gáng plàngk/ *n* a movable walkway for embarking and disembarking a ship

gan·grene /gáng grèen, gang grèen/ *n* the death of an area of body tissue as a result of lack of blood ■ *vti* (**-grened, -gren·ing**) affect or become affected with gangrene —**gan·gre·nous** /gáng grənəss/ *adj*

gang·sta rap /gángstə-/ *n* rap music with lyrics about violence and gangs

gang·ster /gángstər/ *n* a member of a criminal gang —**gang·ster·ism** *n*

gang·way /gáng wày/ *n* **1** a narrow walkway **2** an entrance in a ship's side **3** a gangplank ■ *interj* make way

gan·ja /gáanjə, gán-/ *n* marijuana *(slang)*

gan·net /gánnət/ *n* a fish-eating seabird

gan·try /gántree/ (*pl* **-tries**) *n* a supporting framework for signals or machinery

gap *n* **1** an opening in a structure **2** something missing in a sequence or whole **3** an interval of time during which something stops happening ○ *after a gap of three years* **4** a disparity ○ *the gap between rich and poor* —**gap·py** *adj*

gape *vi* (**gaped, gap·ing**) **1** stare with the mouth open **2** open into a gap ■ *n* **1** an open-mouthed stare **2** an opening of the mouth —**gap·ing** *adj* ◊ See note at **gaze**

gap-toothed *adj* with gaps between the teeth

ga·rage /gə ráazh, -ráaj/ *n* **1** a building for a motor vehicle or motor vehicles **2** an establishment repairing motor vehicles ■ *vt* (**-raged, -rag·ing**) put a vehicle in a garage

ga·rage sale *n* US, Can, ANZ a sale of used or unwanted household items held in the garage of a house

Ga·ra·gum Des·ert /gàrrə gum-/ desert occupying a large portion of Turkmenistan

~~garantee~~ incorrect spelling of **guarantee**

garb *n* **1** a distinctive outfit of clothes **2** an outward appearance

⚡ **gar·bage** /gáarbij/ *n* **1** discarded food waste or unwanted material **2** nonsense **3** somebody or something worthless **4** worthless computer data

gar·bage can *n* a container for garbage or trash

gar·bage dis·pos·al *n* a device beneath a sink that grinds food so it can be washed down the pipe

gar·bage man *n* US, Can, Aus a trash collector

gar·bage truck *n* US, Can, Aus a vehicle for collecting trash

gar·ban·zo /gaar báan zṓ/ (*pl* **-zos**), **gar·ban·zo bean** *n* a chickpea

gar·ble /gáarb'l/ (**-bled, -bling**) *vt* **1** confuse a message or information so that it is misleading or unintelligible **2** scramble the transmission of a message or signal —**gar·bled** *adj*

Gar·bo /gáarbō/, **Greta** (1905–90) Swedish-born US movie actor

Gar·cí·a Lor·ca /gaar sèe ə-/ ♦ **Lorca**

Gar·cí·a Már·quez /gaar sèe ə máar kèz/, **Gabriel** (b. 1928) Colombian writer

gar·çon /gaar sṓn, -sóN/ *n* a French waiter

gar·den /gáard'n/ *n* **1** a planted area of ground **2** a park with planted areas (*often pl*) **3** a fertile farming region **4** an outdoor eating and drinking establishment ○ *a beer garden* ■ *adj* of gardens ■ *vi* look after a garden —**gar·den·er** *n*

ORIGIN Garden goes back to the same ancient root as **yard**, but it came to English through the Romance languages rather than by a direct Germanic route.

gar·den a·part·ment *n* **1** an apartment with garden access **2** an apartment building with a garden or lawn

gar·den cen·ter *n* an establishment selling plants and gardening equipment

gar·de·nia /gaar déenyə/ *n* an evergreen tree with white flowers

ORIGIN The **gardenia** is named for the Scottish-American naturalist Alexander Garden (1730?–91).

gar·den par·ty *n* a social gathering in a yard or garden

gar·den-va·ri·e·ty *adj* of the common or ordinary kind

~~gardien~~ incorrect spelling of **guardian**

Gar·field /gáar feeld/, **James A.** (1831–81) 20th president of the United States (1881)

gar·gan·tu·an /gaar gánchoo ən/ *adj* huge

ORIGIN The description **gargantuan** derives from Gargantua, a giant with an enormous appetite in the satire of that name (1534) by François Rabelais.

gar·gle /gáarg'l/ *v* (**-gled, -gling**) **1** *vti* cleanse the mouth and throat by breathing air out through liquid held in the back of the mouth **2** *vi* make a guttural sound like that made when gargling ■ *n* **1** a mouthwash **2** a guttural sound like that made when gargling

ORIGIN Gargle belongs to a set of words from an ancient root representing a sound made in the throat. It was adopted in the early 16C from a French verb formed from *gargouille* "throat." French *gargouille* is also the source of *gargoyle* "grotesque drainage spout," so called because the rainwater often ran off through a carved figure's mouth. *Gurgle* came from Latin *gurgulio* "gullet," and is closely related.

gar·goyle /gáar gòyl/ *n* a grotesque drainage spout

Gar·i·bal·di /gàrrə báwldee/, **Giuseppe** (1807–82) French-born Italian patriot

gar·ish /gérrish/ *adj* overly bright or elaborate —**gar·ish·ly** *adv* —**gar·ish·ness** *n*

gar·land /gáarlənd/ *n* **1** a flower wreath **2** a hanging flower or paper decoration ■ *vt* decorate with a garland

Gar·land /gaárlənd/, **Judy** (1922–69) US movie actor and singer

gar·lic /gaárlik/ n 1 a bulb that is divided into cloves and has a pungent odor and flavor. Use: in cooking, medicine. 2 the plant whose bulbs are garlic —**gar·lick·y** adj

gar·ment /gaármənt/ n a clothing item

gar·ner /gaárnər/ vt 1 gather in for storage 2 win or gain by an effort

Gar·ner /gaárnər/, **John N.** (1868–1967) vice president of the United States (1933–41)

gar·net /gaárnət/ n 1 a red semiprecious stone. Use: gems. 2 a dark red color —**gar·net** adj

gar·nish /gaárnish/ n 1 add an accompaniment to food or drink to enhance its flavor or appearance 2 decorate something with an ornament 3 also **gar·nish·ee** /gaárni shee/ take money or property from a debtor by legal authority o garnish wages for child support ■ n an enhancement for food or drink —**gar·nish·ing** n

gar·ret /gárrət/ n an attic

gar·ri·son /gárriss'n/ n 1 a body of stationed troops 2 a place for stationing troops ■ vt station troops at a place

Gar·ri·son /gárriss'n/, **William Lloyd** (1805–79) US abolitionist and reformer

gar·rote /gə rót, -rôt/, **gar·rotte** n 1 a method of execution by strangulation using a metal band 2 a metal band used in executions —**gar·rote** vt

gar·ru·lous /gérrələss/ adj 1 talking too much 2 wordy —**gar·ru·lous·ly** adv —**gar·ru·lous·ness** n ◊ See note at **talkative**

gar·ter /gaártər/ n a band for holding up stockings, socks, or a shirt sleeve —**gar·ter** vt

garter snake n a harmless snake with stripes running the length of its body

Gar·vey /gaárvee/, **Marcus** (1887–1940) Jamaican-born US civil rights advocate

Gar·y /gárree/ city in NW Indiana, on Lake Michigan. Pop. 108,469 (1998).

gas n 1 a substance such as air that is neither solid nor liquid and can expand indefinitely 2 a combustible gaseous substance such as natural gas or propane, used as fuel 3 gasoline 4 a gaseous substance for poisoning or asphyxiating somebody 5 a gaseous substance used as an anesthetic 6 flatulence (infml) 7 an explosive mixture of methane and air 8 somebody or something entertaining (slang) ■ v (gassed, gas·sing, gas·es or gas·ses) 1 vt attack, injure, or kill with gas 2 vi release gas

ORIGIN Gas is based on the Greek form of chaos. The first letter in Greek was pronounced like the sound of the letter g in the dialect of Flemish chemist J. B. van Helmont (1577–1644), who coined the word for a supposed highly refined form of water. The modern use arose in the early 18C.

□ **gas up** vti put gas in a car

gas·bag /gáss bàg/ n a person regarded as an idle talker (infml)

gas cham·ber n a room where people are gassed

gas·e·ous /gássee əss, gáshəss/ adj 1 resembling gas 2 containing gas

gash n a deep cut —**gash** vt

gas·hold·er /gáss hòldər/ n a storage tank for gas used as fuel

gas·i·fy /gássə fì/ (-fied, -fies) vti make into or become a gas

gas·ket /gáskət/ n 1 a rubber seal to make a joint impermeable to gas or liquid 2 a rope for securing a furled sail

gas·light /gáss lìt/ n 1 illumination from burning gas 2 a lamp fueled by gas

gas·man /gáss màn/ (pl -men /-mèn/) n a gas-meter reader

gas mask n a mask protecting the wearer against poisonous gas

gas me·ter n a device for measuring the amount of gas that has been consumed

gas·o·hol /gássə hàwl/ n automobile fuel consisting of a blend of gasoline and alcohol

gas·o·line /gássə lèen, gàssə lèen/ n automobile fuel made from petroleum

gas·om·e·ter /ga sómmətər/ n 1 a gas-measuring apparatus 2 a gasholder

gasp n 1 a sudden audible intake of breath, e.g., in surprise or pain 2 a difficult intake of breath ■ vi 1 labor to breathe 2 breathe in sharply

Gas·pé Pen·in·su·la /ga spáy-/ peninsula in SE Quebec, Canada, between the St. Lawrence River and Chaleur Bay.

gas sta·tion n a place where drivers can buy fuel

gas·sy /gássee/ (-si·er, -si·est) adj 1 full of gas 2 like gas

gas·tric /gástrik/ adj of the stomach

gastric juice n an acidic digestive secretion in the stomach

gas·tri·tis /ga strítəss/ n inflammation of the stomach lining

gas·tro·en·ter·i·tis /gàstrō entə rítəss/ n stomach and intestinal inflammation

gas·tro·en·ter·ol·o·gy /gàstrō entə rólləjee/ n the study of intestinal-tract disorders

gas·tro·in·tes·ti·nal /gàstrō in téstən'l/ adj of the stomach and intestines

gas·tron·o·my /ga strónnəmee/ (pl -mies) n 1 gourmet eating 2 a cuisine typical of a particular region —**gas·tro·nom·ic** /gàstrə nómmik/ adj

gas tur·bine n an internal-combustion engine operated by hot gases

gas·works /gáss wùrks/ (pl same) n a factory where gas for fuel is produced

ϟ **gate** /gayt/ n 1 a movable barrier across a gap in a fence or wall 2 an opening in a fence, wall, or defensive structure 3 an arrival or departure point for passengers at an airport **4** a sliding barrier or valve for regulating the passage of fluid **5** the total amount of money from ticket sales to a sporting event or entertainment **6** a logic circuit in a computer **7** an electronic switch regulating the flow of current —**gat·ed** *adj* ◊ See note at **gait**

ga·teau /ga tô, gaa-/ (*pl* -**teaux** /-tôz/ *or* -**teaus**), **gâ·teau** /*pl* -**teaux** /-tô/) *n* a rich layered cake

gate·crash·er /gáyt kràshər/ *n* an uninvited guest, or a spectator without a ticket —**gate·crash** *vti*

gat·ed com·mu·ni·ty *n* a residential community with security guards and gates

gate·fold /gáyt fòld/ *n* an oversize page that is folded to the size of other pages

gate·house /gáyt hòwss/ (*pl* -**hous·es** /-hòwzəz/) *n* a building at a gate

gate·keep·er /gáyt kèepər/ *n* **1** a guard at a gate **2** a controller of access to something or somebody

gate·leg ta·ble /gáyt leg-/ *n* a folding table with movable legs that swing out to support the leaves

gate·post /gáyt pòst/ *n* a post supporting a gate

Gates /gayts/, **Bill** (*b.* 1955) US entrepreneur and technology executive

⚡**gate·way** /gáyt wày/ *n* **1** an opening with a gate **2** an access point **3** a connection between two computer networks

gath·er /gáthər/ *v* **1** *vti* form into a group **2** *vt* harvest a crop **3** *vt* collect data from various sources **4** *vt* attract a group of people as a following or audience ○ *gathered quite a crowd* **5** *vti* accumulate **6** *vt* summon up energies or strength from within **7** *vt* surmise that something is so **8** *vt* bring somebody or something close ■ *n* each of a series of folds in fabric —**gath·er·er** *n* ◊ See note at **collect**

gath·er·ing /gáthəring/ *n* an assembly of people

ga·tor /gáytər/, **'ga·tor, ga·ter, 'ga·ter** *n* an alligator (*infml*)

GATT /gat/, **Gatt** *abbr* General Agreement on Tariffs and Trade

gauche /gōsh/ *adj* socially awkward —**gauche·ly** *adv* —**gauche·ness** *n*

gau·cho /gów chò/ (*pl* -**chos**) *n* a South American cowboy

gaud·y /gáwdee/ (-**i·er, -i·est**) *adj* brightly colored or elaborately decorated to an unpleasant or vulgar degree —**gaud·i·ly** *adv* —**gaud·i·ness** *n*

gauge /gayj/, **gage** *vt* (**gauged, gaug·ing; gaged, gag·ing**) **1** calculate the amount or extent of something **2** form a judgment of something uncertain or variable ■ *n* **1** a standard measurement or scale of measurement **2** a device for measuring an amount or quantity or for testing accuracy **3** a criterion **4** the distance between the rails of a railway

track or tramway **5** the distance between the wheels on the axle of a vehicle **6** the diameter of wire or a needle **7** the thickness of a thin material

Gau·guin /gō gáN/, **Paul** (1848–1903) French painter

Gaul /gawl/ *n* ancient region of W Europe that included large portions of modern-day France, Belgium, and neighboring countries

Gaulle ◆ **de Gaulle, Charles**

gaunt *adj* **1** thin and bony **2** stark in outline or appearance —**gaunt·ness** *n*

gaunt·let[1] /gáwntlət/ *n* a long glove with a cuff that covers part of the forearm ◊ **throw down the gauntlet** issue a challenge

gaunt·let[2] /gáwntlət/, **gant·let** /gáwntlət, gaant-/ *n* a former military punishment in which two lines of men with weapons beat somebody forced to run between them ◊ **run the gauntlet** endure attack or criticism from all sides

ORIGIN The glove the **gauntlet** has no part in *running the gauntlet*. It comes from a French word meaning "little glove." The **gauntlet** that you run was originally a *gantlope*, from Swedish *gantlopp* "passageway."

g̶a̶u̶r̶d̶ incorrect spelling of **guard**

gauze /gawz/ *n* **1** a finely woven fabric. Use: curtains, clothes. **2** a surgical dressing consisting of layers of loosely woven material —**gauz·y** *adj*

ORIGIN Gauze was probably named for Gaza on the E Mediterranean coast, which was associated with its production in the Middle Ages. The word entered English through French.

gave past tense of **give**

gav·el /gávvəl/ *n* a small hammer used for getting attention or ending something ■ *vti* use a gavel to bring an end to something

ga·votte /gə vót/ *n* **1** a French country dance like a fast minuet **2** a piece of music for a gavotte

Ga·wain /gə wáyn/ *n* in Arthurian legend, a knight who was the enemy of Sir Lancelot

gawk *vi* stare stupidly (*infml*) ◊ See note at **gaze**

gawk·y /gáwkee/ (-**i·er, -i·est**) *adj* ungainly (*infml*) —**gawk·i·ly** *adv* —**gaw·ki·ness** *n*

gay *adj* **1** homosexual **2** merry (*dated*) **3** bright in color (*dated*) ■ *n* a homosexual man or woman —**gay·ness** *n*

USAGE Gay is preferred over *homosexual.* The adjective **gay** encompasses both men and women, but when there is a need to specify both genders, as in *gay and lesbian alliances,* **gay** means men. Avoid using **gay** as a noun, as in *He's a gay* and *Four gays walked in,* because it can be taken to be offensive. Preferred substitutes are *He is gay* and *Four gay people/men/women walked in.*

Ga·za /gáazə/ seaport and principal city of the Gaza Strip, on the Mediterranean. Pop. 353,632 (1997).

Ga·za Strip region on the E Mediterranean coast bordering Egypt and Israel, under the control of the Palestinian National Authority. Pop. 1,178,119 (2001).

gaze *vi* (**gazed, gaz·ing**) look fixedly ■ *n* a steady look

SYNONYMS gaze, gape, gawk, ogle, rubberneck, stare CORE MEANING: look at somebody or something steadily or at length

ga·ze·bo /gə zeébō/ (*pl* **-bos** *or* **-boes**) *n* a small building with a view

ga·zelle /gə zél/ (*pl* **-zelles** *or* **same**) *n* a small fast antelope with long ringed horns and black face markings

ga·zette /gə zét/ *n* a newspaper

gaz·et·teer /gàzzə teér/ *n* a geographic reference book

gaz·pa·cho /gə spaáchō/ *n* a cold soup containing chopped raw tomatoes, cucumber, and other vegetables

G.B. *abbr* Great Britain

⚡**Gbyte** *abbr* gigabyte

Gd *symbol* gadolinium

G·dansk /gə dánsk/ city in N Poland, on the Gulf of Gdansk, an inlet of the Baltic Sea. Pop. 461,300 (1997). German **Danzig**

GDP *abbr* gross domestic product

GDR, G.D.R. *abbr* German Democratic Republic

Ge[1] *n* = **Gaia**

Ge[2] *symbol* germanium

gear /geer/ *n* **1** a toothed part of a machine that transmits motion by engaging with another toothed part **2** one of the fixed transmission settings in a vehicle **3** the engaged state of a vehicle's gears ○ *Put the car in gear.* **4** equipment needed for a particular activity (*infml*) **5** clothes (*infml*) ■ *vt* **1** put gears in **2** engage the gears of

☐ **gear up** *vti* get ready for something

gear·box /geér bòks/ *n* a casing around a set of gears

gear·ing /geéring/ *n* **1** a set of mechanical gears, or their power **2** the providing of something with gears

gear·shift /geér shìft/ *n* a mechanism for shifting gears

geck·o /gékō/ (*pl* **-os** *or* **-oes** /-ōz/) *n* a small tropical lizard that can climb smooth vertical surfaces

gee /jee/ *interj also* **gee wizz** expresses enthusiasm or surprise ■ *vt* (**geed**) urge an animal to move faster

geek /geek/ *n* **1** somebody regarded as socially awkward (*insult*) **2** an outrageous carnival performer —**geek·y** *adj*

geese plural of **goose**

Geh·rig /gérrig/, **Lou** (1903–41) US baseball player

Gei·ger count·er /gígər-/ *n* an instrument for detecting radiation

ORIGIN The instrument is named for the German physicist Hans Geiger (1882–1945), who invented it.

gei·sha /gáyshə, geé-/ (*pl* **same** *or* **-shas**), **gei·sha girl** *n* **1** a Japanese woman educated as a hostess for men **2** a Japanese prostitute

gel /jel/ *n* a semisolid substance with the consistency of jelly ■ *vi* (**gelled, gel·ling**) become a gel

gel·a·tin /jéllət'n/, **gel·a·tine** *n* **1** a semisolid protein. Use: foods, medicine, glue, photography. **2** a substance with the consistency of jelly

ge·lat·i·nous /jə látt'nəss/ *adj* **1** semisolid **2** of gelatin

geld /geld/ (**geld·ed** *or* **gelt** /gelt/) *vt* castrate an animal, especially a horse

geld·ing /gélding/ *n* a castrated horse

gel·ig·nite /jéllig nìt/ *n* a form of dynamite made with gelled nitroglycerine

gem /jem/ *n* **1** a precious stone that has been cut and polished **2** somebody or something excellent (*infml*)

Gem·i·ni /jémmə nì, -nèe/ *n* **1** a zodiacal constellation in the northern hemisphere. See illustration at **constellation** **2** the 3rd sign of the zodiac —**Gem·i·ni** *adj*

gem·stone /jém stòn/ *n* a stone used in jewelry

gen. *abbr* general

Gen., GEN *abbr* General

gen·darme /zhón daàrm/ *n* a French police officer

gen·der /jéndər/ *n* **1** somebody's sex **2** the categorization of nouns and pronouns in some languages according to the form taken by words that qualify them

gene /jeen/ *n* the basic unit of heredity consisting of a specific sequence of DNA or RNA in a fixed position on a chromosome

ge·ne·al·o·gy /jèenee ólləjee/ (*pl* **-gies**) *n* **1** the study of the history of families **2** a pedigree or line of family descent —**ge·ne·a·log·i·cal** /jèenee ə lójjik'l/ *adj* —**ge·ne·al·o·gist** *n*

~~geneology~~ incorrect spelling of **genealogy**

gene pool *n* all the genes of a population or species

gen·er·a plural of **genus**

gen·er·al /jénnərəl/ *adj* **1** of or including nearly all the members of a category **2** usual ○ *as a general rule* **3** widespread ○ *a general sense of urgency* **4** not specialized in knowledge ○ *for the general reader* **5** not specific ○ *in general terms* ■ *n also* **Gen·er·al** an officer of a rank above lieutenant general ◇ **in general 1** as a whole **2** in most cases

gen·er·al an·es·thet·ic n an anesthetic producing unconsciousness

gen·er·al de·liv·er·y n **1** a postal service that holds mail at the post office for the addressee **2** an address indicating mail should be held at the post office

gen·er·al e·lec·tion n an election for political representatives for the entire country

Gen·er·al Head·quar·ters n full form of GHQ

gen·er·al hos·pi·tal n a nonspecialist hospital

gen·er·al·is·si·mo /jènnərə lìssəmō/ (pl **-mos**) n a top military leader

gen·er·al·ist /jénnərəlist/ n a nonspecialist

gen·er·al·i·ty /jènnə rállətee/ (pl **-ties**) n **1** the state of being general **2** a general statement

gen·er·al·ize /jénnərə lìz/ (**-ized**, **-iz·ing**) v **1** vti express something general **2** vi make a sweeping statement **3** vti give wider use to something **4** vt make something generally known **5** vti make a general inference —**gen·er·al·i·za·tion** /jènnərəli záysh'n/ n

gen·er·al·ly /jénnərəlee/ adv **1** usually **2** as a whole ◇ not meant for the public generally **3** in general terms ◇ spoke generally

gen·er·al meet·ing n a meeting for all members of a group or organization

gen·er·al ob·li·ga·tion adj describes a municipal bond supported by the municipality's taxing and borrowing power

gen·er·al prac·tice n the work of a doctor who is not a specialist

gen·er·al prac·ti·tion·er n a family doctor (dated)

gen·er·al pur·pose adj all-purpose

gen·er·al·ship /jénnərəl shìp/ n **1** the exercising of military command **2** a general's rank or period of service

gen·er·al staff n the group of officers helping military commanders

gen·er·al store n a shop selling a wide variety of goods

gen·er·ate /jénnə ràyt/ (**-at·ed**, **-at·ing**) vt create or produce ◇ generate income ◇ generate electricity

gen·er·a·tion /jènnə ráysh'n/ n **1** a group of contemporaries **2** a single stage in the descent from a common ancestor **3** a period of time taken to produce a new generation **4** the production of power or energy —**gen·er·a·tion·al** adj

gen·er·a·tion gap n a difference between generations in their attitudes and interests that inhibits understanding

gen·er·a·tion X, Gen·er·a·tion X n the generation of young adults who were born between about 1965 and 1980, especially in the United States and Canada —**gen·er·a·tion X·er** n

ORIGIN The term comes from the title of a

novel by Douglas Coupland (b. 1961), Generation X: Tales for an Accelerated Culture.

gen·er·a·tive /jénnə ràytiv, -rətiv/ adj **1** of reproduction **2** with a productive capability

gen·er·a·tor /jénnə ràytər/ n **1** a device for producing electricity or gas **2** an originator, e.g., of an idea or plan

ge·ner·ic /jə nérrik/ adj **1** applying generally **2** of a genus **3** describes pharmaceutical products without a brand name —**ge·ner·i·cal·ly** adv

ge·ner·ic drug n a drug sold under a name that is not a trademark

gen·er·ous /jénnərəss/ adj **1** kind in giving or sharing **2** substantial in size or quantity ◇ a generous portion —**gen·er·os·i·ty** /jènnə róssətee/ n —**gen·er·ous·ly** adv —**gen·er·ous·ness** n

SYNONYMS generous, liberal, magnanimous, munificent, bountiful CORE MEANING: giving readily to others

gen·e·sis /jénnəssiss/ (pl **-ses** /-seèz/) n the time or circumstances of something's coming into being

Gen·e·sis /jénnəssiss/ n the 1st book of the Bible

Ge·net /zhə náy/, Jean (1910–86) French writer

gene ther·a·py n the treatment of disease by replacing genes

ge·net·ic /jə néttik/, **ge·net·i·cal** /-ik'l/ adj of genes or genetics —**ge·net·i·cal·ly** adv

ge·net·i·cal·ly mod·i·fied adj with an altered genetic makeup

ge·net·ic code n an order of DNA or RNA sequences that is the basis of heredity

ge·net·ic fin·ger·print·ing n = DNA fingerprinting

ge·net·ic mo·di·fi·ca·tion, ge·net·ic en·gi·neer·ing n the alteration and recombination of genetic material by technological means, resulting in transgenic organisms —**ge·net·ic en·gi·neer** n

ge·net·ics /jə néttiks/ n **1** the study of heredity and genetic variation (+ sing verb) **2** the genetic makeup of an organism (+ sing or pl verb) —**ge·net·i·cist** /jə néttəssist/ n

Ge·ne·va /jə neèvə/ city in W Switzerland. Pop. 172,809 (1998). French **Genève** —**Ge·ne·van** adj, n —**Gen·e·vese** /jènnə veèz, -veèss/ adj, n

Ge·ne·va, Lake largest lake in central Europe, between Switzerland and SE France

Gen·ghis Khan /jèng giss kaán/ (1167?–1227) Mongol conqueror

ge·ni·al /jeènyəl/ adj **1** kind and good-natured **2** mild and warm ◇ a genial climate —**ge·ni·al·i·ty** /jeènee állətee/ n —**gen·ial·ly** adv

ge·nie /jeènee/ n a magical spirit in Arabian stories that will obey the person who summons it

gen·i·tal /jénnit'l/ *adj* of the sex organs —**gen·i·tal·ly** *adv*

gen·i·tals /jénnit'lz/, **gen·i·ta·li·a** /jènni táylee ə/ *npl* the sex organs

gen·i·tive /jénnitiv/ *n* **1** a grammatical case in some languages that usually indicates possession **2** a word or form in the genitive —**gen·i·tive** *adj*

gen·ius /jeenyəss, jeènee əss/ *n* **1** somebody with outstanding talent **2** outstanding talent **3** somebody with a particular skill o *a genius with computers* **4** (*pl* **ge·ni·i** /jeènee ì/) a special quality of a place, period, or people ◊ See note at **talent**

Gen·o·a /jénnō ə/ city in NW Italy, on the Gulf of Genoa, an inlet of the Ligurian Sea. Pop. 641,437 (1999). —**Gen·o·ese** /jènnō eèz/ *n, adj*

gen·o·cide /jénnə sìd/ *n* the murder or attempted murder of an entire ethnic group —**gen·o·cid·al** /jènnə sìd'l/ *adj*

ge·nome /jee nōm/ *n* the full set of chromosomes and genes that an individual organism inherits —**ge·nom·ic** /jee nómmik/ *adj*

ge·nom·ics /jee nómmiks, -nómiks/ *n* the study and identification of gene sequences (+ *sing verb*)

gen·o·type /jénnə tìp/ *n* **1** the genetic makeup of an organism **2** a group of organisms with similar genetic makeup —**gen·o·typ·ic** /jènnə típpik/ *adj*

~~generally~~ incorrect spelling of **generally**

~~genration~~ incorrect spelling of **generation**

gen·re /zhaànrə, zhaàN-/ *n* **1** a category of artistic works **2** a type of painting depicting household scenes ◊ See note at **type**

gent /jent/ *n* a gentleman (*infml*)

gen·teel /jen teèl/ *adj* **1** well-mannered and well-bred **2** pretentiously well-mannered and respectable —**gen·teel·ly** *adv* —**gen·teel·ness** *n*

ORIGIN Genteel is a late 16C readoption of the French word that had earlier become *gentle*. It goes back to a Latin word meaning "of the same family," then later "of good family," which has also come into English as *gentile*, through a use of it in the 4C Latin version of the Bible, the Vulgate.

---

gen·tian /jénshən/ *n* **1** the dried root of a flowering plant. Use: digestive stimulant in herbal medicine. **2** a showy flowering plant whose roots are dried as gentian

gen·tile /jén tìl/ *n* **1** a non-Jewish person **2** somebody Christian as opposed to Jewish —**gen·tile** *adj*

Gen·ti·les·chi /jèntə léskee/, **Artemisia** (1593?–1651) Italian painter

gen·til·i·ty /jen tíllətee/ *n* **1** refinement and good manners **2** pretentiously refined manners and behavior

gen·tle /jént'l/ (**-tler, -tlest**) *adj* **1** mild and kind **2** moderate and not severe o *a gentle reprimand* **3** using little force o *a gentle tap on the shoulder* **4** not steep o *a gentle slope* —**gen·tle·ness** *n* —**gent·ly** *adv*

gen·tle·man /jént'lmən/ (*pl* **-men** /-mən/) *n* **1** a polite and cultured man **2** any man o *ladies and gentlemen* **3** an upper-class man —**gen·tle·man·ly** *adj*

gen·tle·man farm·er *n* **1** a farmer with independent means, who farms for pleasure **2** a farm owner who employs others to manage it

gen·tle·man's a·gree·ment, gen·tle·men's a·gree·ment *n* an agreement based on trust

gen·tle·wom·an /jént'l woòmmən/ (*pl* **-en** /-wìmmin/) *n* **1** a polite and cultured woman **2** an upper-class woman

gen·tri·fy /jéntrə fì/ (**-fied, -fies**) *vt* renovate an aging neighborhood —**gen·tri·fi·ca·tion** /jèntrəfi káysh'n/ *n*

gen·try /jéntree/ *n* **1** the upper classes **2** the English social class of people who do not belong to the nobility but who are entitled to a coat of arms

gen·u·flect /jénnyə flèkt/ *vi* **1** kneel as a gesture of respect **2** show excessive respect —**gen·u·flec·tion** /jènnyə fléksh'n/ *n*

gen·u·ine /jénnyoo in/ *adj* **1** having the qualities or value claimed **2** sincerely felt or expressed —**gen·u·ine·ly** *adv* —**gen·u·ine·ness** *n*

ge·nus /jeénəss/ (*pl* **gen·e·ra** /jénnərə/) *n* **1** a set of closely related species **2** a group with common characteristics

geo- *prefix* **1** earth, soil o *geology* **2** geography, global o *geopolitics*

ge·o·cen·tric /jee ō séntrik/ *adj* **1** describes the solar system regarded as having Earth at its center **2** measured or considered from Earth's center

ge·o·chem·is·try /jee ō kémmistree/ *n* the chemistry of the Earth and other astronomical bodies —**ge·o·chem·i·cal** *adj* —**ge·o·chem·ist** *n*

ge·o·chro·nol·o·gy /jee ō krə nólləjee/ *n* the study of the ages of geologic events and rock formations —**ge·o·chron·o·log·i·cal** /jee ō kronə lójjik'l/ *adj* —**ge·o·chro·nol·o·gist** *n*

ge·ode /jee ōd/ *n* **1** a rock with a cavity lined or filled with crystals **2** a crystal-lined cavity within a geode

ge·o·des·ic dome /jee ə déssik-/ *n* a dome made of flat sections

ge·od·e·sy /jee óddəssee/ *n* the scientific measurement of the size and shape of the Earth's surface —**ge·od·e·sist** *n*

ge·og·ra·phy /jee óggrəfee/ (*pl* **-phies**) *n* **1** the study of Earth's physical features **2** the physical features of a place or region —**ge·og·ra·pher** *n* —**ge·o·graph·ic** /jee ə gráffik/ *adj* —**ge·o·graph·i·cal** *adj* —**ge·o·graph·i·cal·ly** *adv*

ge·ol·o·gy /jee óllajee/ *n* the study of rocks and minerals —**ge·o·log·ic** /jèe ə lójjik/ *adj* —**ge·o·log·i·cal** *adj* —**ge·ol·o·gist** *n*

ge·o·met·ric /jèe ə méttrik/, **ge·o·met·ri·cal** /-ik'l/ *adj* of geometry —**ge·o·met·ri·cal·ly** *adv*

ge·o·met·ric pro·gres·sion *n* a series of numbers in which each number is separated by the same numerical step

ge·om·e·try /jee ómmətree/ *n* the mathematics of shapes —**ge·o·met·ric** *adj* —**ge·o·met·ri·cal·ly** *adv*—**ge·om·e·tri·cian** /jèe əmə trísh'n, jee òmmə-/ *n*

ge·o·phys·ics /jèe ə fízziks/ *n* the science of Earth's physical processes (+ *sing verb*) —**ge·o·phys·i·cal** *adj* —**ge·o·phys·i·cist** /-fízzəssist/ *n*

ge·o·pol·i·tics /jèe ō póllətiks/ *n* (+ *sing verb*) 1 the influences of geography on politics 2 the study of geopolitics —**ge·o·po·lit·i·cal** /jèe ō pə líttik'l/ *adj* —**ge·o·pol·i·ti·cian** /jèe ō polə tísh'n/ *n*

George /jawrj/, **St.** (*d.* 303?) patron saint of England

George I (1660–1727) king of Great Britain and Ireland (1714–27)

George II (1683–1760) king of Great Britain and Ireland (1727–60)

George III (1738–1820) king of Great Britain and Ireland (1760–1820)

George IV (1762–1830) king of Great Britain and Ireland (1820–30)

George V (1865–1936) king of Great Britain and Ireland (1910–22), then of Great Britain and Northern Ireland (1922–36)

George VI (1895–1952) king of Great Britain and Northern Ireland (1936–52)

Geor·ges Bank /jàwrjəz-/ underwater plateau in the N Atlantic Ocean, between Cape Cod, Massachusetts, and Nova Scotia. Length 175 mi./280 km.

George·town /jáwrj tòwn/ capital of Guyana. Pop. 254,000 (1995).

George Town capital of the Cayman Islands. Pop. 19,000 (1996).

Geor·gia /jáwrjə/ 1 state in the SE United States. Cap. Atlanta. Pop. 8,186,453 (2000). 2 country in S Caucasia, on the coast of the E Black Sea. Cap. Tbilisi. Pop. 4,989,285 (2001).

Geor·gian[1] /jáwrjən/ *adj* of the period 1714 to 1830 in Britain, when George I, II, III, and IV reigned in succession

Geor·gian[2] /jáwrjən/ *n* 1 the language of the Republic of Georgia 2 somebody from the US state of Georgia or the Republic of Georgia —**Georgian** *adj*

Georg·i·ev·ski /jàwrjee évskee/, **Ljubco** (*b.* 1966) prime minister of the Former Yugoslav Republic of Macedonia (1998–)

ge·o·sta·tion·ar·y /jèe ō stáysh'n èrree/ *adj* appearing to remain stationary over a point on Earth

ge·o·ther·mal /jèe ō thúrmǝl/, **ge·o·ther·mic** /-thúrmik/ *adj* of Earth's internal heat —**ge·o·ther·mal·ly** *adv*

ge·ra·ni·um /jə ráynee əm/ *n* 1 a popular garden plant with brightly colored flowers 2 a plant with saucer-shaped flowers

ger·bil /júrb'l/ *n* a small rodent resembling a mouse with long back legs

ger·i·at·ric /jèrree áttrik/ *adj* of senior citizens ■ *n* a senior citizen (*technical*)

ger·i·at·rics /jèrree áttriks/ *n* medical treatment for senior citizens (+ *sing verb*) —**ger·i·a·tri·cian** /jèrree ə trísh'n/ *n*

Gé·ri·cault /zhayri kố/, **Théodore** (1791–1824) French painter

germ /jurm/ *n* 1 a microorganism, especially one causing disease 2 the smallest element in an organism that is capable of complete development 3 the beginning of something that will develop

ORIGIN Germ goes back to a Latin word meaning "sprout, seed," which was the original sense of the word in English. It survives metaphorically in the sense "beginning," and in some fixed contexts such as *wheat germ*. The modern use "microorganism" dates from the late 19C, and springs from the idea of a germ as the source from which disease develops.

Ger·man /júrmən/ *n* 1 somebody from Germany 2 the language of Germany, Austria, and parts of Switzerland —**Ger·man** *adj*

ger·mane /jər máyn/ *adj* relevant —**ger·mane·ly** *adv* —**ger·mane·ness** *n*

Ger·man·ic /jər mánnik/ *n* 1 a NW European language group, including English, German, and the Scandinavian languages 2 the ancestor of modern Germanic languages ■ *adj* 1 of Germanic 2 of Germany

ger·ma·ni·um /jər máynee əm/ *n* (*symbol* **Ge**) a brittle gray crystalline element. Use: semiconductors, alloys.

Ger·man mea·sles *n* MED = **rubella**

Ger·man shep·herd *n* a large powerful working dog with short hair and erect ears

Ger·ma·ny /júrmənee/ country in central Europe. Cap. Berlin. Pop. 83,029,536 (2001).

ger·mi·cide /júrmə sìd/ *n* a substance that kills germs —**ger·mi·ci·dal** /júrmə síd'l/ *adj*

ger·mi·nate /júrmə nàyt/ (-nat·ed, -nat·ing) *v* 1 *vti* start growing from seed 2 *vi* be created and start to develop —**ger·mi·na·tion** /júrmə náysh'n/ *n*

germ war·fare *n* biological warfare

Geronimo

Ge·ron·i·mo /jə rónnəmō/ (1829–1909) Apache leader

ger·on·toc·ra·cy /jèrrən tókrəssee/ (*pl* **-cies**) *n* **1** government by elders **2** the elders forming a government —**ge·ron·to·crat·ic** /jə ròntə kráttik/ *adj*

ger·on·tol·o·gy /jèrrən tólləjee/ *n* the scientific study of aging —**ge·ron·to·log·i·cal** /jə ròntə lójjik'l/ *adj* —**ger·on·tol·o·gist** *n*

Ger·ry /gérree/, **Elbridge** (1744–1814) vice president of the United States (1813–14)

ger·ry·man·der /jérree màndər/ *vti* try to get extra votes unfairly, especially by changing boundaries ■ *n* an electoral area manipulated to give one political party an advantage

ORIGIN The name of Eldridge Gerry and *salamander* combined to create this word. In 1812 he changed the boundaries of electoral districts to favor his own Democratic Party. The outline of these on a map was thought to resemble a salamander.

Gersh·win /gúrshwin/, **George** (1898–1937) US composer

ger·und /jérrənd/ *n* a noun derived from a verb, e.g., in English by adding -ing —**ge·run·di·al** /jə rúndee əl/ *adj*

ge·stalt /gə shtáalt/ (*pl* **-stalts** or **-stalt·en** /-shtáalt'n/), **Ge·stalt** *n* a set of things regarded as more than the sum of its parts —**ge·stalt·ist** *n*

ge·stalt psy·chol·o·gy *n* a branch of psychology that treats behavior and perception as an integrated whole

Ge·sta·po /gə stáa pō, -shtáa-/ *n* the Nazi secret police

ORIGIN Gestapo is a German acronym formed from *Geheime Staatspolizei* "Secret State Police."

ges·ta·tion /je stáysh'n/ *n* **1** the carrying of offspring in the womb **2** the period of development of a fetus —**ges·ta·tion·al** *adj* —**ges·ta·to·ry** /jéstə tàwree/ *adj*

ges·tic·u·late /je stíkyə láyt/ (**-lat·ed, -lat·ing**) *vti* make or express by gestures —**ges·tic·u·la·tion** /je stìkyə láysh'n/ *n*

ges·ture /jéschər/ *n* **1** a body movement or an action that communicates something **2** the use of gestures ■ *vti* (**-tured, -tur·ing**) communicate by a body movement —**ges·tur·al** *adj*

ge·sund·heit /gə zóoṅt hìt/ *interj* expresses a wish for good health to somebody who has just sneezed

get /get/ (**got, got·ten** /gótt'n/) *v* **1** *vi* become or begin to have a particular quality ○ *getting hungry* **2** *vt* cause to be done ○ *got the car cleaned* **3** *vt* fetch or bring ○ *has gone to get the coats* **4** *vt* become infected by or develop ○ *got chicken pox* **5** *vi* enter or leave a particular state ○ *get ready* **6** *vi* move or arrive somewhere ○ *got home late* **7** *vt* begin (*infml*) ○ *Let's get going.* **8** forms passives ○ *got burned* **9** *vt* persuade ○ *tried to get her to go* **10** *vt* hear or understand (*infml*) **11** *vt* receive as a signal ○ *gets six channels* **12** *vt* annoy or irritate (*infml*) **13** *vt* begin to have ○ *when I get the time* **14** *vt* hit (*infml*) **15** *vt* have revenge on (*infml*) ○ *will get them in the end* —**get·a·ble** *adj* ◊ **get with it** become responsive to new styles and ideas (*infml*)

SYNONYMS **get**, acquire, obtain, gain, procure, secure CORE MEANING: come into possession of something

☐ **get across** *vti* make something understood
☐ **get ahead** *vi* be successful
☐ **get along** *vi* **1** be friendly **2** manage to make progress
☐ **get around** *v* **1** *vi* have a social life **2** *vi* become known **3** *vt* persuade somebody
☐ **get at** *vt* **1** reach **2** try to say **3** find something out
☐ **get away** *vi* **1** escape **2** leave a place
☐ **get away with** *vt* experience no bad results from something that might have been expected to produce them
☐ **get back at** *vt* take revenge on
☐ **get by** *vi* just manage to keep going
☐ **get into** *vt* get involved or interested in something
☐ **get off** *v* **1** *vi* leave **2** *vt* send a communication or package **3** *vi* have a lucky escape ○ *got off lightly*
☐ **get on** *vi* deal with and make progress in a situation
☐ **get out** *v* **1** *vti* leave, or enable somebody to leave **2** *vi* become known
☐ **get out of** *vt* avoid or enable somebody to avoid doing
☐ **get over** *vt* recover from an illness or bad experience
☐ **get through** *vt* finish
☐ **get to** *vt* **1** start dealing with **2** evoke emotions in **3** annoy
☐ **get together** *vi* meet for social or business purposes ◊ **get it together** become organized so as to perform efficiently (*slang*)
☐ **get up** *v* **1** *vti* get out of bed **2** *vt* rouse energy, strength, or similar qualities

get·a·way /géttə wày/ *n* **1** a quick departure, especially after committing a crime **2** a short vacation

Geth·sem·a·ne, Garden of /geth sémmənee/ *n* in the Bible, the olive grove just outside Jerusalem where Jesus Christ was betrayed after the Last Supper (Matthew 26:36)

get-to-geth-er /n/ a social gathering (infml)

Get-ty /géttee/, **J. Paul** (1892–1976) US oil executive

Get-tys-burg /gétteez bùrg/ borough in S Pennsylvania, site of a decisive Northern victory in 1863 during the Civil War. Pop. 7,376 (1998).

get-up /gét ùp/ n a costume or outfit (infml)

gew-gaw /gyòb gàw/ n a trinket

gey-ser /gízər/ n a spring gushing hot water and steam

Gha-na /gaánə/ country in West Africa, on the northern coast of the Gulf of Guinea. Cap. Accra. Pop. 19,894,014 (2001). —**Gha-na-ian** /gaa náy ən/ n, adj

~~Ghandi~~ incorrect spelling of **Gandhi**

ghast-ly /gástlee/ (-li-er, -li-est) adj 1 horrifying or very upsetting 2 very unpleasant o a ghastly smell —**ghast-li-ness** n

ORIGIN **Ghastly** comes from an obsolete verb gast that meant "terrify." The same element is seen in aghast. The gh spelling is modeled on ghost. It was used by the poet Edmund Spenser in the late 16C, and has since become established.

ghat /gaat/ n in South Asia, a place with steps down a river bank

ghee /gee/, **ghi** n clarified butter, especially as used in South Asian cooking

gher-kin /gúrkin/ n 1 a small cucumber. Use: pickling. 2 a prickly Caribbean fruit. Use: pickling.

ghet-to /géttō/ (pl -tos or -toes) n 1 an area of a city lived in by a minority group 2 a Jewish quarter in a city

ORIGIN The first **ghettos** were in Italy. The origin of the word is not clear, however. It may be an alteration of Italian getto "foundry," since the first ghetto established in Venice, in 1516, was on the site of a foundry; or it could be a shortening of Italian borghetto, literally "small borough."

ghet-to-ize /géttō ìz/ (-ized, -iz-ing) vt 1 segregate a minority group 2 limit the opportunities of a group of people (sometimes offensive) —**ghet-to-i-za-tion** /gèttō i záysh'n/ n

ghost /gōst/ n 1 a supposed spirit of somebody who has died, remaining after death 2 a faint trace o the ghost of a smile 3 a secondary image seen on a screen or through a telescope 4 a ghostwriter ■ vt be the ghostwriter of —**ghost-like** adj

ghost-ly /gōstlee/ (-li-er, -li-est) adj 1 pale or insubstantial like a ghost 2 reminiscent of ghosts —**ghost-li-ness** n

⚡ **ghost site** n a viewable but obsolete website

ghost sto-ry n a story about ghosts

ghost town n 1 an abandoned town 2 a deserted place (infml)

ghost-writ-er /gṓst rìtər/ n an author who writes a book to be published as the work of somebody else —**ghost-write** vti

ghoul /gool/ n 1 somebody morbidly interested in repulsive things 2 in Islamic folklore, a body-snatching demon —**ghoul-ish** adj

GHQ n the headquarters of an organization, especially a military headquarters. Full form **General Headquarters**

GHz abbr gigahertz

gi[1] abbr gill[2]

gi[2] /gee/, **gie** n a karate or judo outfit

GI n an enlisted US soldier or veteran ■ adj for GIs

ORIGIN In the 1930s and 1940s, **GI** designated items of US army equipment, indicating "government (or general) issue." This was soon extended to the soldiers themselves.

Gia-co-met-ti /jàkə méttee/, **Alberto** (1901–66) Swiss sculptor and painter

gi-ant /jī ənt/ n 1 an imaginary being who resembles a human but is much taller, larger, and stronger 2 somebody outstanding in a particular field of activity ■ adj very big

gi-ant-ess /jī əntiss/ n in fairy tales, myths, and legends, a very large being similar to a woman

gi-ant pan-da n a Chinese black-and-white panda

gib-ber /jíbbər/ vi be incoherent —**gib-ber** n

gib-ber-ish /jíbbərish/ n nonsensical or incoherent talk

gib-bet /jíbbit/ n 1 a post for exhibiting the bodies of people who have been hanged 2 a gallows

gib-bon /gíbbən/ n a small slender long-armed ape

gibe /jīb/, **jibe** n a mocking remark ■ vti (gibed, gib-ing; jibed, jib-ing) make mocking remarks about somebody —**gib-ing-ly** adv

gib-lets /jíbblits/ n the liver, heart, gizzard, and neck of an edible fowl

Gib-ral-tar /ji bráwltər/ 1 British dependency on a narrow promontory of the S Iberian Peninsula, at the western entrance to the Mediterranean Sea. Pop. 27,170 (1995). 2 city in SE Michigan. Pop. 4,550 (1998). —**Gi-bral-tar-ian** /ji brawl táiree ən/ n, adj

Gib-ral-tar, Rock of limestone and shale ridge near the tip of the S Iberian Peninsula. Height 1,398 ft./426 m.

Gib-ral-tar, Strait of channel connecting the Mediterranean Sea to the Atlantic Ocean and separating North Africa from the Rock of Gibraltar. Length 40 mi./60 km.

Gib-ran /ji braán/, **Kahlil** (1883–1931) Lebanese-born US mystic, painter, and poet

Gib-son /gíbs'n/, **Althea** (b. 1927) US tennis player and golfer

gid·dy /gíddee/ (**-di·er, -di·est**) adj **1** dizzy **2** causing dizziness —**gid·di·ly** adv —**gid·di·ness** n

Gide /zheed/, **André** (1869–1951) French writer

Giel·gud /geél gŏŏd/, **Sir John** (1904–2000) British actor

⚡ **GIF** /gif/ **1** a service mark for a format for a graphics file widely used on the World Wide Web. Full form **graphic interchange format 2** a file extension for a graphic interchange format file

gift /gift/ n **1** something given to please the recipient or to show gratitude **2** a special talent ■ vt bestow as a gift ◊ See note at **talent**

GIFT /gift/ n a method of aiding conception in which eggs and sperm are placed in a woman's fallopian tubes. Full form **gamete intrafallopian transfer**

gift cer·tif·i·cate n a slip of paper, usually purchased as a gift, that can be exchanged for goods

gift·ed /gíftəd/ adj having or showing exceptional talent or intelligence —**gift·ed·ness** n ◊ See note at **intelligent**

gift-wrap /gift ràp/, **gift-wrap·ping** /-ràpping/ n decorated wrapping paper —**gift-wrap** vt

gig¹ /gig/ n a two-wheeled one-horse carriage

gig² /gig/ n (infml) **1** a booking or performance by a musician or group at a venue where they do not play regularly **2** a temporary job

gig³ /gig/ n **1** a pronged spear **2** an arrangement of hooks used for fishing —**gig** vti

gig⁴ /gig/ (slang) n a demerit ■ vt (**gigged, gig·ging**) issue a soldier with a demerit

giga- prefix a billion ◊ gigaton

> **ORIGIN Giga-** is from the Greek word that is the source of **giant**.

⚡ **giga·bit** /gíggə bìt/ n a unit of computer network capacity equal to one megabyte of information

⚡ **gi·ga·byte** /gíggə bìt/ n a unit of computer data or storage space equal to 1,024 megabytes

⚡ **gig·a·flop** /gíggə flòp/ n a unit of computing speed equal to 1000 million floating-point operations per second

gig·a·hertz /gíggə hùrts/ (pl same) n (symbol **GHz**) a unit of frequency equal to one billion hertz, or cycles, per second

gi·gan·tic /jī gántik/ adj **1** very large, tall, or bulky **2** very great o a gigantic task —**gi·gan·ti·cal·ly** adv

gig·gle /gígg'l/ vti (**-gled, -gling**) laugh lightly or nervously ■ n a light or nervous laugh —**gig·gles** npl a fit of light or nervous laughter (infml) —**gig·gling** adj —**gig·gly** adj

⚡ **GIGO** /gí gò/ n the principle that a computer program or process is only as good as the

ideas or data put into it. Full form **garbage in, garbage out**

gig·o·lo /jíggə lò/ (pl **-los**) n **1** a man who receives payment for being a woman's sexual or social partner **2** a man who is a professional dancing partner or escort for women

Gi·la mon·ster /heélə-/ n a large brightly colored venomous lizard of US and Mexican deserts

Gi·la Riv·er /heélə-, geélə-/ river in SW New Mexico and S Arizona. Length 649 mi./1,044 km.

Gil·bert /gílbərt/, **Sir W. S.** (1836–1911) British librettist and dramatist

gild /gild/ vt **1** cover with a thin layer of gold **2** color gold (literary) ◊ See note at **guild**

gild·ed /gíldəd/ adj **1** covered with a thin layer of gold **2** wealthy and privileged o gilded youth

gill¹ /gil/ n **1** the breathing organ of fish **2** the spore-producing organ of mushrooms

gill² /jil/ n a liquid measure equal to a quarter of a pint

Gil·les·pie /gi léspee/, **Dizzy** (1917–93) US jazz trumpeter

gil·ly·flow·er /jíllee flòwr/ n **1** a clove-scented pink **2** a sweet-scented flower (archaic)

Gil·man /gílmən/, **Charlotte Perkins** (1860–1935) US social reformer and writer

gilt¹ /gilt/ n **1** a thin layer of gold **2** a government bond with a guaranteed payment (often pl) —**gilt** adj ◊ See note at **guilt**

gilt² /gilt/ n a young female pig

gilt-edged adj very safe, especially as an investment

gim·bal /gímb'l, jím-/ n a set of pivoted rings for holding an object such as a ship's compass horizontal ■ vt support on gimbals

gim·crack /jím kràk/ adj showy but shoddily made —**gim·crack** n

gim·let /gímmlət/ n **1** a tool for boring holes in wood **2** a cocktail made of vodka or gin with lime juice ■ adj piercing or penetrating o a gimlet eye

gim·mick /gímmik/ n **1** a dishonest trick **2** a hidden disadvantage to an offer or opportunity **3** something attention-grabbing **4** a gadget —**gim·mick·ry** n —**gim·mick·y** adj

gin¹ /jin/ n **1** a colorless alcoholic spirit distilled from grain and flavored with juniper berries **2** the card game gin rummy (infml)

> **ORIGIN Gin** derives its name from its chief flavoring agent, juniper. It is an abbreviation of genever, the Dutch name for the drink, which in English was often written geneva, by association with the Swiss town Geneva. Both the abbreviated and the longer form are recorded from the early 18C. **Gin** "hoist, trap"

is much older, and is a shortening of the French word that gave us *engine*.

gin[2] /jĭn/ *n* **1** a hoist operated by hand **2** a trap or snare ■ *vt* (**ginned, gin·ning**) separate cotton from its seeds

gin·ger /jínjər/ *n* **1** a hot-tasting rhizome used as a spice **2** a plant whose rhizomes are ginger —**gin·ger·y** *adj*

> **ORIGIN Ginger** has a long and complex history. It ultimately derives from an ancient language of S India and N Sri Lanka. This word passed through Sanskrit and other South Asian languages into Greek and Latin, where its initial consonant was *z*. This became *g* in the medieval period. From medieval Latin the word passed into English, and also, in a slightly different form, into French. After the Norman Conquest the French word was adopted into English, and this combined with the earlier English form to produce modern **ginger**.

gin·ger ale *n* a ginger-flavored soft drink

gin·ger beer *n* a nonalcoholic ginger-flavored drink

gin·ger·bread /jínjər brèd/ *n* **1** a ginger-flavored cake or cookie **2** elaborate decoration

> **ORIGIN Gingerbread** was adopted from French *gingembras* "preserved ginger" (the original sense in English), but was quickly assimilated to the more familiar *ginger* and *bread*. The form then influenced the application of the word, and from the 15C it was used to refer to a kind of cake.

gin·ger·ly /jínjərlee/ *adv* very cautiously or tentatively —**gin·ger·ly** *adj*

ging·ham /gíngəm/ *n* a checked cotton fabric

gin·gi·vi·tis /jìnji vítiss/ *n* gum inflammation

gink·go /gíng kò/ (*pl* **-goes**), **ging·ko** /gíng kō/ (*pl* **-koes**) *n* a Chinese tree with fan-shaped leaves

gink·go bi·lo·ba /-bī lóbə/ *n* a herbal preparation made from the pulverized leaves of the ginkgo tree

gin rum·my *n* a form of the card game rummy for two players

Gins·berg /gínzbərg/, **Allen** (1926–97) US poet

Gins·burg /gínzbərg/, **Ruth Bader** (*b*. 1933) associate justice of the US Supreme Court (1993–)

gin·seng /jín sèng/ (*pl* **-sengs** *or same*) *n* **1** a tonic medicine prepared from an aromatic root **2** a plant whose roots are prepared as ginseng

Giot·to /jáwtō, jee óttō/ (1267?–1337) Italian painter

gip·sy *n, adj* = gypsy

gi·raffe /jə ráf/ (*pl* **-raffes** *or same*) *n* a tall African mammal with a very long neck

gird /gurd/ (**gird·ed** *or* **girt** /gurt/) *v* **1** *vt* get ready for conflict or vigorous activity **2** *vt*

put a belt around, or fasten on with a belt (*literary*)

gird·er /gúrdər/ *n* a large supporting beam

gir·dle /gúrd'l/ *n* **1** a woman's elasticized undergarment extending from the waist to the thigh **2** a narrow belt worn around the waist ■ *vt* (**-dled, -dling**) surround (*literary*)

girl /gurl/ *n* **1** a female child **2** a woman (*often offensive*) **3** a girlfriend —**girl·hood** *n*

> **ORIGIN** The origin of **girl** is not really known. It appeared in the 13C, referring to a child of either sex. There are no clear examples of the modern use until the mid-16C.

Girl Fri·day *n* a young woman acting as somebody's personal assistant (*sometimes offensive*)

> **ORIGIN Girl Friday** is modeled on Man Friday, the castaway hero's all-around helper in *Robinson Crusoe* (1719) by Daniel Defoe.

girl·friend /gúrl frènd/ *n* **1** a woman or girl sweetheart or lover **2** a woman friend

girl·ie /gúrlee/ *adj* **1** showing nude women (*often offensive*) **2** noticeably or deliberately feminine (*often disapproving*) ■ *n* a little girl (*infml dated*)

girl·ish /gúrlish/ *adj* **1** of girls **2** more appropriate for a girl than a woman —**girl·ish·ly** *adv* —**girl·ish·ness** *n*

Girl Scout *n* a girl member of the Scouts

girth /gurth/ *n* **1** the distance around something thick and cylindrical **2** a band fastened round a horse's belly to keep a saddle in place ■ *vt* fasten a girth on a horse

Gish /gish/, **Lillian** (1893–1993) and her sister **Dorothy** (1898–1968) US actors

gis·mo *n* = gizmo

gist /jist/ *n* the main point or meaning of something

~~giutar~~ incorrect spelling of **guitar**

give /giv/ *v* (**gave** /gayv/, **giv·en** /gívvən/, **giv·ing**) **1** *vt* pass something into the possession of somebody ○ *gave him a present* **2** *vt* deliver something to somebody in payment or exchange for something ○ *gave me ten dollars for it* **3** *vt* administer something to somebody ○ *gave her the medicine twice a day* **4** *vt* grant something such as power, a right, or time to somebody ○ *Give me half an hour and I'll be there.* **5** *vt* communicate information or an opinion to somebody ○ *Give them my love.* **6** *vt* convey an idea or impression to somebody **7** *vt* impart a particular feeling to somebody ○ *gives us a sense of security* **8** *vt* perform an action directed at somebody ○ *gave him a quick glance* **9** *vt* provide a service for somebody ○ *gave her a massage* **10** *vt* devote something such as time or effort to something or somebody ○ *gave their lives to helping others* **11** *vt* organize or do something as an entertainment ○ *gave a party* **12** *vt* emit or utter a sound ○ *gave a sigh* **13** *vt* cause somebody to believe something

o *was given to understand that they had left*
14 *vi* yield or collapse under pressure o *The
floor gave.* **15** *vt* concede that somebody has
an advantage or a particular quality ■ *n* the
ability or tendency to yield under pressure
—**giv·er** *n*

SYNONYMS **give, present, confer, bestow,
donate, grant** CORE MEANING: hand over something to somebody

☐ **give away** *vt* **1** give something as a present
2 disclose information or a secret by
mistake **3** betray somebody by providing
information **4** present a bride to her
husband at a wedding

☐ **give back** *vt* return something

☐ **give in** *vi* **1** admit defeat **2** accept conditions

☐ **give of** *vr* contribute your time or energy

☐ **give off** *vt* emit

☐ **give out** *vt* **1** hand over or distribute **2** *vt*
emit **3** *vi* be used up **4** *vi* stop working

☐ **give over** *vt* transfer something

☐ **give up** *vt* **1** *vi* surrender **2** *vt* hand something
over **3** *vt* stop using or doing something

☐ **give up on** *vt* **1** abandon a plan **2** despair
of somebody or something

give-and-take *n* cooperation and compromise (*infml*)

give·a·way /gívvə wày/ *n* **1** something that
reveals or betrays something o *Her accent's
a dead giveaway.* **2** a gift, especially something given away as a publicity gimmick
or an incentive to buy something (*infml*)

give·back /gív bàk/ *n* a concession by employees

giv·en /gívvən/ past participle of **give** ■ *adj*
1 of a particular person or thing **2** arranged
earlier ■ *prep* **1** granted o *Given time, we'll
solve the problem.* **2** in view of o *given the
uncertainty of the situation* ■ *n* an accepted
fact

giv·en name *n* a chosen name or names as
opposed to a family name

Gi·za /géezə/ city in N Egypt on the western
bank of the Nile River, site of the Great
Pyramids and the Sphinx. Pop. 4,779,000
(1998).

giz·mo /gízmō/ (*pl* -mos), **gis·mo** *n* a complicated device or piece of equipment
(*infml*)

giz·zard /gízzərd/ *n* a part of a bird's digestive
tract where food is broken down by the
action of the muscles and small ingested
stones

gla·cé /gla sáy/ *adj* **1** glazed with a sugar
solution **2** made from powdered sugar and
water

gla·cial /gláysh'l/ *adj* **1** of a glacier or glaciers
2 icily cold

gla·ci·ate /gláyshee àyt/ (-at·ed, -at·ing) *v* **1** *vti*
cover or become covered with a glacier **2** *vt*
subject to glacial action —**gla·ci·a·tion**
/gláyshee áysh'n/ *n*

gla·cier /gláyshər/ *n* an ice mass formed in
mountain valleys or at the poles that moves
slowly

glad (**glad·der, glad·dest**) *adj* **1** delighted
2 cheerfully willing o *glad to help* **3** grateful
o *glad of the chance to relax* —**glad·ly** *adv*
—**glad·ness** *n*

glad·den /gládd'n/ *vti* be or make glad

glade *n* **1** a clearing in a forest **2** an everglade

glad hand *n* **1** an enthusiastic but insincere
handshake **2** a friendly welcome

glad·i·a·tor /gláddee àytər/ *n* a fighter in the
ancient Roman arena —**glad·i·a·to·ri·al**
/gláddee ə táwree əl/ *adj*

glad·i·o·lus /gláddee ṓləss/ (*pl same or* -**li** /-lī/
or -**lus·es**), **glad·i·o·la** /-lə/ (*pl* -**las** *or same*) *n*
a tall flowering garden plant with spikes of
funnel-shaped flowers

Glad·stone /glád stòn/, **W. E.** (1809–98) British
prime minister (1868–74, 1880–85, 1886,
and 1892–94)

glam·or·ize /glámmə rìz/ (-ized, -iz·ing),
glam·our·ize *vt* **1** make glamorous **2** ro-
manticize —**glam·or·i·za·tion** /glàmməri
záysh'n/ *n*

glam·or·ous /glámmərəss/, **glam·our·ous** *adj*
1 dressed or made up to be good-looking
2 exciting and desirable

glam·our /glámmər/, **glam·or** *n* **1** exciting
allure **2** expensive good looks —**glam·our**
adj

ORIGIN Few students would consider grammar
glamorous, but **glamour** is an alteration of
grammar. It appears in Scottish use in the
early 18C meaning "magic, enchantment."
The sense was taken from *gramarye,* an obsolete derivative of *grammar* that had moved
from "knowledge of grammar, learning" to
"knowledge of magic, occult learning." The
modern uses of **glamour** began in the mid-
19C.

glance *v* (glanced, glanc·ing) **1** *vi* look quickly
2 *vi* make a cursory examination **3** *vi* glint
4 *vt* strike at an angle ■ *n* **1** a quick look
2 a cursory examination **3** an oblique strike

glanc·ing /glánsing/ *adj* striking obliquely
—**glanc·ing·ly** *adv*

gland *n* a cell mass in the body that removes
substances from the bloodstream and ex-
cretes or modifies them —**glan·du·lar**
/glánjələr/ *adj*

glare[1] *vi* (glared, glar·ing) **1** stare intently and
angrily **2** be unpleasantly bright ■ *n* **1** an
intent and angry look **2** excessive brightness

glare[2], **glare ice** *n* black ice

glar·ing /gláiring/ *adj* **1** very obvious **2** staring
intently and angrily **3** unpleasantly bright
—**glar·ing·ly** *adv*

Glas·gow /glásskō, glássgō, gláz-/ **1** city in SW
Scotland on the Clyde River. Pop. 616,430
(1996 estimate). **2** city in S Kentucky. Pop.
14,062 (1998).

glas·nost /glaáz nòst, -nòst/ *n* a policy of government openness and accountability, especially in the last years of the Soviet Union

glass *n* **1** a transparent solid substance made from sand melted in combination with other oxides. Use: making such objects as windows, bottles, lenses. **2** something made of glass, especially a container for a drink **3** an amount contained in a glass ■ **glass·es** *npl* **1** a pair of sight-correcting lenses worn in a frame over the eyes **2** binoculars —**glass** *adj* —**glass·ful** *n*

Glass, Philip (*b.* 1937) US composer

glass ceil·ing *n* an unofficial barrier to career advancement because of gender, age, race, ethnicity, or sexual preference

glass fi·ber *n* fiberglass

glass·house /gláss hòws/ (*pl* -hous·es /-hòwzəz/) *n* a situation that attracts media attention

glass·ware /gláss wàir/ *n* glass objects

glass wool *n* a mass of glass fibers. Use: insulation, as air filters, in the manufacture of fiberglass.

glass·y /glássee/ (-i·er, -i·est) *adj* **1** smooth and slippery **2** blankly expressionless ○ *a glassy stare* —**glass·i·ly** *adv* —**glass·i·ness** *n*

glass·y-eyed *adj* blankly staring

glau·co·ma /glaw kṓmə/ *n* an eye disorder that leads to optic nerve damage —**glau·co·ma·tous** *adj*

glau·cous /gláwkəss/ *adj* **1** covered in a grayish powder **2** of a grayish green or blue color

glaze *vt* (glazed, glaz·ing) **1** cover a ceramic object with a clear or colored shiny finish **2** coat food with milk or egg to produce a shiny finish ■ *n* **1** a clear or colored shiny coating for a ceramic object **2** a coating to produce a shiny finish on food **3** a thin layer of ice —**glaz·er** *n*

gla·zier /gláyzhər/ *n* a glass fitter

glaz·ing /gláyzing/ *n* **1** a hard shiny coating **2** the covering of something with a glaze **3** the glass for a window or door

gleam /gleem/ *vi* **1** shine brightly **2** flash for a short time ■ *n* **1** a bright shining quality **2** a flash of light **3** a brief indication ○ *a gleam of interest*

gleam·ing /gléeming/ *adj* bright and clean-looking —**gleam·ing·ly** *adv*

glean /gleen/ *v* **1** *vt* obtain information gradually or in small amounts **2** *vti* gather any of the crop left behind in a harvested field

glean·ings /gléeningz/ *npl* **1** things collected over a period of time **2** the usable part of a crop left behind in a harvested field

glebe *n* land as a source of abundant produce (*literary*)

glee *n* **1** great delight **2** a gloatingly jubilant feeling —**glee·ful** *adj* —**glee·ful·ly** *adv*

glee club *n* a singing club

gleeming incorrect spelling of **gleaming**

glen *n* a long narrow valley

Glen·dale /glén dàyl/ **1** city in SW California. Pop. 185,086 (1998). **2** city in central Arizona. Pop. 193,482 (1998).

Glenn /glen/, **John** (*b.* 1921) US astronaut and senator

glib *adj* **1** fluent in an insincere way ○ *a glib talker* **2** lacking in thought or preparation ○ *a glib generalization* —**glib·ly** *adv* —**glib·ness** *n*

glide *vti* (glid·ed, glid·ing) **1** move smoothly **2** fly or land without engine power ■ *n* a smooth movement

glid·er /glídər/ *n* **1** an aircraft with no engine **2** a porch swing on an upright framework

glim·mer /glímmər/ *vi* **1** emit a dim glow **2** be present to a small extent ○ *Hope still glimmered in their hearts.* ■ *n* **1** a faint flashing light **2** a faint sign or small amount —**glim·mer·ing** *adj*

glimpse *n* **1** a brief look or sighting **2** a small indication or appearance ■ *v* (glimpsed, glimps·ing) **1** *vt* catch sight of **2** *vi* take a brief look

glint *vi* flash briefly ■ *n* **1** a brief flash **2** a slight indication

glis·san·do /gli sán dò/ (*pl* -di /-dèe/ *or* -dos) *n* a sliding movement from one note to another on a musical instrument

glis·ten /glíss'n/ *vi* **1** reflect light from a wet surface **2** have a glossy sheen (*refers to hair or an animal's pelt*) —**glis·ten** *n*

glitch *n* **1** a small problem **2** an unwanted electronic signal —**glitch·y** *adj*

glit·ter /glíttər/ *vi* sparkle or shimmer brightly ■ *n* **1** a sparkly decoration **2** sparkling light **3** glamour —**glit·ter·y** *adj*

glit·te·ra·ti /glíttə raátee/ *npl* glamorous people

ORIGIN Glitterati is a blend of *glitter* and *literati* (the literate, educated elite). It was coined by *Time* magazine in 1956.

---

glitz *n* superficial glamour —**glitz·y** *adj*

gloam·ing /glṓming/ *n* twilight (*literary*)

gloat /glṓt/ *vi* be smugly happy —**gloat** *n* —**gloat·er** *n* —**gloat·ing·ly** *adv*

glob *n* a small amount of something soft or semiliquid (*infml*)

⚡ **glob·al** /glṓb'l/ *adj* **1** worldwide **2** taking all aspects into account **3** affecting the whole of a computer system, program, or file **4** spherical —**glob·al·ly** *adv*

glob·al·ize /glṓb'l ìz/ (-ized, -iz·ing) *vti* make or become global in application or operation —**glob·al·i·za·tion** /glṓb'li záysh'n/ *n*

glob·al vil·lage *n* the whole world regarded as a single community

glob·al warm·ing *n* an increase in the world's temperatures

globe *n* **1** a map of the Earth on a sphere **2** the Earth **3** a hollow spherical object

globe ar·ti·choke *n* an artichoke

globe-trot /glób tròt/ (-trot·ted, -trot·ting) *vi* travel far and wide —**globe-trot·ter** *n*

glob·u·lar /glóbbyələr/ *adj* **1** spherical **2** having globules

glob·ule /glóbbyool/ *n* a drop of liquid or semi-liquid

glob·u·lin /glóbbyəlin/ *n* a simple globular protein

glock·en·spiel /glókən speèl, -shpeèl/ *n* a percussion instrument consisting of a set of metal bars mounted on a frame

glogg *n* mulled wine

glom (glommed, glom·ming) *vi* (slang) **1** become attached to **2** begin to understand or realize

gloom *n* **1** murky darkness **2** despondency —**gloom** *vti*

gloom·y /glóomee/ (-i·er, -i·est) *adj* **1** dark and cheerless **2** offering little hope ○ *gloomy prospects* **3** despondent —**gloom·i·ly** *adv* —**gloom·i·ness** *n*

glo·ri·fy /gláwrə fī/ (-fied, -fies) *vt* **1** make something appear better than it really is **2** extol somebody or something —**glo·ri·fied** *adj*

glo·ri·ous /gláwree əss/ *adj* **1** exceptionally lovely ○ *glorious summer weather* **2** outstanding ○ *a glorious career* **3** highly enjoyable —**glo·ri·ous·ly** *adv*

glo·ry /gláwree/ (*pl* -ries) *n* **1** fame and honor **2** an achievement that brings admiration **3** praise of a deity **4** awesome splendor **5** the idealized bliss of heaven

□ **glory in** *vt* enjoy greatly

glo·ry days *npl* a time of great success

gloss[1] *n* **1** shininess **2** deceptive and superficial attractiveness **3** *also* **gloss paint** a paint that produces a shiny finish ■ *vt* make shiny

□ **gloss over** *vt* address too lightly or omit entirely

gloss[2] *n* **1** a short definition or translation of a word or phrase **2** an interpretation or explanation ■ *vt* **1** give a gloss for a word or phrase **2** insert glosses in a text

glos·sa·ry /gláwssəree, glóss-/ (*pl* -ries) *n* an alphabetical list of terms and their meanings

gloss·y /gláwssee, glóssee/ *adj* (-i·er, -i·est) **1** shiny and smooth **2** superficially stylish (*infml*) ■ *n* (*pl* -ies) a photo with a shiny finish —**gloss·i·ly** *adv* —**gloss·i·ness** *n*

glot·tal stop /glòtt'l-/ *n* a speech sound created by opening and closing the glottis and suddenly releasing air

glot·tis /glóttiss/ (*pl* -tis·es *or* -ti·des /-ti deèz/) *n* **1** an opening between the vocal cords **2** the part of the larynx involved in producing speech

glove /gluv/ *n* **1** a covering for the hand with separate sections for the fingers and thumb **2** a protective covering for the hand worn in some sports ■ *vt* (gloved, glov·ing) put a glove on

glove com·part·ment *n* a storage space in the dashboard of a car

glow /glṓ/ *n* **1** the light from something hot **2** a soft steady light without heat or flames **3** rosiness of complexion ■ *vi* **1** emit light and heat **2** emit or reflect a soft light **3** shine with health

glow·er /glówr/ *vi* glare silently or sullenly —**glow·er** *n* —**glow·er·ing·ly** *adv*

glow·ing /glṓ ing/ *adj* **1** shining softly and steadily **2** full of praise —**glow·ing·ly** *adv*

glow-worm /glṓ wùrm/ *n* a luminous larva of some types of firefly

glox·in·i·a /glok sínnee ə/ *n* a plant with large bell-shaped flowers

---

ORIGIN The **gloxinia** is named for the 18C German botanist Benjamin P. Gloxin, who first described it.

---

glu·cosamine /gloo kóssəmin/ *n* an amino derivative of glucose. Use: food supplement, treatment for arthritis and other joint disorders

glu·cose /gloo kòss/ *n* **1** a sugar produced in plants by photosynthesis and in animals by the metabolism of carbohydrates **2** a syrupy mixture. Use: food manufacture, alcoholic fermentation.

glue *n* **1** an adhesive substance obtained from boiling animal parts **2** any adhesive substance ■ *vt* (glued, glu·ing) **1** stick things together with glue **2** cause somebody, or somebody's gaze, to remain completely still (*infml*) ○ *have been glued to the TV* —**glu·ey** *adj* —**glu·i·ness** *n*

glue-sniff·ing *n* the practice of inhaling glue fumes for their intoxicating effect —**glue-sniff·er** *n*

glug *n* **1** the sound of liquid being poured **2** a quantity of liquid poured from a bottle —**glug** *vti*

glum (glum·mer, glum·mest) *adj* quietly miserable —**glum·ly** *adv* —**glum·ness** *n*

glut *n* an excess supply ■ *vt* (glut·ted, glut·ting) **1** supply a market with too much of a product **2** give somebody enough or too much

glu·ten /glóot'n/ *n* a mixture of two proteins found in some cereal grains, especially wheat

glu·ti·nous /glóot'nəss/ *adj* sticky

glut·ton /glútt'n/ *n* an excessive eater or drinker —**glut·ton·ous** *adj*

glut·ton·y /glútt'nee/ *n* excessive eating or drinking

glyc·er·in /glíssərin/, **glyc·er·ine** /glíssərin, -reèn/, **glyc·er·ol** /glíssə ràwl/ *n* a thick sweet liquid obtained from fats and oils. Use: solvent, antifreeze, manufacture of soaps, cosmetics, lubricants, and dynamite.

gly·co·gen /glíkəjən/ n a complex carbohydrate found in the liver and muscles that is easily converted to glucose —**gly·co·gen·ic** /glíkə jénnik/ adj

glyph /glif/ n a carved vertical groove, especially in an ancient Greek frieze —**glyph·ic** adj

GM abbr 1 general manager 2 genetic modification 3 genetically modified

gm. abbr gram[1]

GMAT tdmk a trademark for a standardized test taken by applicants to business schools in the United States. Full form **Graduate Management Admission Test**

GMO abbr genetically modified organism

GMT abbr Greenwich Mean Time

gnarled /naarld/ adj 1 knotted and twisted 2 misshapen or weather-beaten

gnarl·y /naarlee/ (**-i·er, -i·est**) adj extremely risky and challenging (slang)

gnash /nash/ vt grind your teeth together

gnat /nat/ n a small biting fly

gnaw /naw/ v 1 vi chew at something 2 vt make by chewing o The mice had gnawed a hole in the box. 3 vt erode 4 vi be a source of worry o a question that had gnawed at her for years —**gnaw** n —**gnaw·ing** adj

gneiss /níss/ n a coarse rock with light and dark bands —**gneiss·ic** adj

gnome[1] /nṓm/ n in folklore and fairy tales, a tiny being resembling a dwarf, living underground and guarding treasure —**gnome·like** adj —**gnom·ish** adj

ORIGIN Gnome came through French from a Latin word coined by the 16C Swiss physician Paracelsus. He gave the name to a diminutive imaginary being living in the earth. It has no connection with **gnome** "short saying," which is from Greek.

gnome[2] /nṓm/ n a short saying

gno·mic /nṓmik/ adj 1 expressing basic truths pithily 2 cryptic

Gnos·ti·cism /nósti sìzzəm/ n a pre-Christian and early Christian religious movement teaching that salvation comes by learning esoteric spiritual truths —**Gnos·tic** n, adj

GNP abbr gross national product

gnu /noo/ (pl same or **gnus**) n a large African antelope with a head resembling that of an ox

go[1] /gṓ/ vi (**went, gone** /gawn, gon/, **goes** /gṓz/) 1 leave a place 2 move in order to do something o went to live elsewhere 3 attend o go to class 4 lead, or have as a starting point or destination 5 elapse 6 be spent or used up 7 belong o The towels go in the closet. 8 function or operate o The car won't go. 9 get weaker, fail, or break down o My eyesight is starting to go. 10 become o going nuts 11 proceed or happen in a particular way o went unchallenged o go barefoot 12 continually remain in a particular situation o go without food 13 expresses future action or intent (in progressive tenses) o What are we going to do? ■ n (pl **gos**) 1 an attempt or chance to do something 2 a turn or move in a game 3 energy and vitality (infml) ◇ **anything goes** anything is to be tolerated ◇ **make a go of** make a success of ◇ **on the go** very active and busy ◇ **to go** to be taken away from a restaurant and consumed elsewhere

□ **go about** vt deal with a problem or task

□ **go after** vt try to get

□ **go against** vt 1 oppose 2 be contrary to

□ **go ahead** vi start or continue

□ **go along** vi accompany somebody

□ **go along with** vt accept doing something, or obey somebody

□ **go around** vt/i 1 be widely known or current in a particular place 2 be enough for everyone

□ **go at** vt attempt with vigor

□ **go back on** vt change your mind about

□ **go by** v 1 vi pass in time 2 vt use as a source of information or guidance

□ **go down** vi 1 sink beneath the surface or horizon 2 be remembered in a particular way

□ **go for** vt 1 like a lot (infml) 2 apply or be relevant to o Be careful, and that goes for all of you. ◇ **go for it** aggressively pursue a goal (slang; often a command) ◇ **have something going for you** be in a situation where something is useful or helpful to you (infml)

□ **go into** vt 1 examine or look into something 2 be a factor of a number or amount

□ **go in with** vt begin a joint venture with

□ **go off** vi 1 explode or be fired 2 begin to ring or sound 3 depart

□ **go on** v 1 vi continue to happen, do something, or exist 2 vi happen or occur 3 vt be close to a particular time, age, or number (in progressive tenses) o He's going on 40.

□ **go out** vi 1 socialize or enjoy yourself away from home 2 be extinguished

□ **go over** v 1 vi change allegiance 2 vt examine or consider carefully 3 vi be received in a particular way o Her remark did not go over well.

□ **go through** vt 1 undergo unpleasantness 2 examine the parts or contents of something

□ **go under** vi fail or close down

□ **go without** vt not have something needed

go[2] /gṓ/ n a Japanese board game played with stones

GO abbr general order

goad vt 1 provoke into action 2 prod with a stick ■ n 1 a pointed animal prod 2 a stimulus to action ◊ See note at **motive**

go-a·head n permission to proceed (infml)

goal n 1 the target area in a sport 2 a score made by getting a ball or puck in the goal 3 a successful shot at a goal 4 an aim —**goal·less** adj

goal·keep·er /gṓl kèepər/, **goal·tend·er** /gṓl tèndər/, **goal·ie** /gṓlee/ *n* a player who protects the goal

goal kick *n* in soccer, a free kick by the goalkeeper near the goal

goal line *n* in games such as soccer and field hockey, the line across which the ball must be passed or carried in order to score

goal·mouth /gṓl mòwth/ (*pl* **-mouths** /-mòwthz/) *n* in games such as soccer and field hockey, the area directly in front of the goal

goal·post /gṓl pòst/ *n* each of two posts marking a goal

goal·tend·ing /gṓl tènding/ *n* **1** the protecting of the goal **2** illegal interference with a basketball player in play

goat *n* **1** (*pl* **goats** *or* **same**) a horned animal related to sheep **2** a man regarded as lecherous (*insult*) **3 Goat** the zodiacal sign Capricorn —**goat·ish** *adj*

goat·ee /gō téé/ *n* a short pointed beard

goat·herd /gṓt hùrd/ *n* a herder of goats

goat·skin /gṓt skìn/ *n* the skin of a goat

gob *n* **1** a lump of a soft wet substance (*slang*) ○ *a gob of whipped cream* **2** a massive amount (*slang humorous; often pl*)

gob·bet /góbbət/ *n* a drop of liquid or semi-liquid

gob·ble[1] /góbb'l/ (**-bled, -bling**) *vt* **1** eat quickly and greedily **2** use up (*infml humorous*) ○ *watching the pay phone gobble her money*

gob·ble[2] /góbb'l/ (**-bled, -bling**) *vi* make the sound of a male turkey —**gob·ble** *n*

gob·ble·dy·gook /góbb'ldee gòòk/, **gob·ble·de·gook** *n* nonsense or jargon (*infml*)

go·be·tween *n* somebody who mediates or carries messages between people

Go·bi De·sert /gṓbee-/ desert in N China and S Mongolia

gob·let /góbblət/ *n* **1** a piece of stemware **2** a large cup (*archaic*)

gob·lin /góbblin/ *n* in folklore and fairy tales, a tiny mischievous or evil being

go·by /gṓbee/ (*pl* **-bies** *or* **same**) *n* a small spiny-finned fish

go-cart *n* a very small open-framed car with an engine, used for racing

god *n* **1** a supernatural being that is an object of worship **2** somebody who is widely admired (*infml*) **3 God** the supreme being in some religions **4 God** in Christianity, the supreme being worshiped as the trinity ■ **gods** *npl* fate —**god·less** *adj* —**god·like** *adj*

Go·dard /gō daár/, **Jean-Luc** (*b.* 1930) French movie director

god·child /gód chìld/ (*pl* **-chil·dren** /-chìldrən/) *n* a child with a godparent or godparents

God·dard /góddərd/, **Robert** (1882–1945) US physicist

god·daugh·ter /gód dàwtər/ *n* a female godchild

god·dess /góddəss/ *n* **1** a female supernatural being that is an object of worship **2** a woman who is widely admired (*infml*)

Gö·del /gṓd'l/, **Kurt** (1906–78) Austrian-born US mathematician

~~godess~~ incorrect spelling of **goddess**

god·fa·ther /gód faàthər/ *n* **1** a man who is somebody's godparent **2** a man who heads a criminal organization (*infml*)

God-fear·ing *adj* deeply devout

god·for·sak·en /gódfər sàykən, gòdfər sáykən/ *adj* cheerless

God-giv·en *adj* inherent ○ *God-given abilities*

god·head /gód hèd/ *n* **1** the nature or essence of being divine **2 Godhead** the Christian God

god·ly /góddlee/ (**-li·er, -li·est**) *adj* **1** devout (*fml*) **2** divine —**god·li·ness** *n*

god·moth·er /gód mùthər/ *n* a woman who is somebody's godparent

go·down /gṓ dòwn/ *n* a South Asian warehouse

god·par·ent /gód pèrrənt/ *n* a sponsor of a baptized child who promises to take a special interest in him or her

god·send /gód sènd/ *n* **1** an unexpected benefit **2** something or somebody very useful

God's gift *n* an extremely valuable or gifted person (*often ironic*)

god·son /gód sùn/ *n* a male godchild

God·thåb /gód hàwb/ former name for **Nuuk**

Go·du·nov /gṓod'n àwf, gódd'n-/, **Boris Fyodorovich** (1551?–1605) tsar of Russia (1598–1605)

God·win Aus·ten, Mt. /gòddwin óstin/ ▸ **K2**

Goeb·bels /gṓbbl'z/, **Joseph** (1897–1945) German Nazi leader

go·er /gṓ ər/ *n* a regular attender (*usually in combination*)

Goe·ring /gérring, gúring/, **Gö·ring** /gṓring/, **Hermann** (1893–1946) German Nazi leader

Goe·the /gṓtə/, **Johann Wolfgang von** (1749–1832) German writer and scientist

go-get·ter *n* an enterprising person (*infml*) —**go-get·ting** *adj, n*

gog·gle /gógg'l/ *v* (**-gled, -gling**) **1** *vi* stare wide-eyed **2** *vti* roll the eyes ■ *adj* describes bulging eyes —**gog·gle** *n*

gog·gle-eyed *adj* with staring eyes

gog·gles /gógg'lz/ *npl* protective eyeglasses

Gogh ▸ **van Gogh, Vincent**

go-go *adj* energetic ■ *n* a type of music that mixes disco, funk, and Latin sounds

Go·gol /gṓ gəl, -gàwl/, **Nikolay Vasilyevich** (1809–52) Russian writer

Goh Chok Tong /gṓ chok tóng/ (*b.* 1941) prime minister of Singapore (1990–)

go·ing /gṓ ing/ *n* **1** an act of leaving a place

2 the conditions for progress or movement ○ *The going gets tough when you reach the rocky terrain.* ■ *adj* **1** currently operating successfully ○ *a going business* **2** currently accepted as standard ○ *the going rate for platinum*

go·ing-o·ver /*pl* **go·ings-o·ver**/ *n* a thorough examination (*infml*)

goi·ter /góytər/ *n* enlargement of the thyroid gland —**goi·trous** *adj*

Go·lan Heights /gō laan-/ disputed upland region on the border between Israel and Syria, northeast of the Sea of Galilee. It was annexed by Israel in 1981.

gold *n* **1** (*symbol* **Au**) a yellow metallic element. Use: jewelry, alloys. **2** a deep rich yellow color **3** things made of gold **4** wealth —**gold** *adj*

Gold·berg /góldbərg/, **Arthur J.** (1908–90) US politician and associate justice of the US Supreme Court (1962–65)

gold brick *n* **1** something that is only superficially valuable **2** a lazy person (*infml*)

gold·brick /góld brik/ *vi* avoid work (*infml*) —**gold·brick·er** *n*

gold dig·ger *n* **1** a person regarded as courting somebody for money (*insult*) **2** a gold miner —**gold-dig·ging** *n*

⚡**gold disk** *n* a master disk from which a CD is made

gold·en /góld'n/ *adj* **1** colored like gold **2** made of gold **3** excellent ○ *a golden opportunity* **4** idyllic ○ *the golden years of their lives*

gold·en age *n* **1** a period of excellence **2** in classical mythology, the earliest and best age

gold·en ea·gle *n* a large brown eagle with golden brown feathers on its head

gold·en hand·shake *n* a large payment made to an employee to compensate for the loss of a job (*infml*)

gold·en mean *n* the middle course that avoids extremes

gold·en re·triev·er *n* a medium-sized dog with golden fur

gold·en·rod /góld'n ròd/ (*pl* -**rods** *or* same) *n* a tall yellow-flowered plant that blooms in late summer

gold·en rule *n* **1** a basic rule that must be followed **2** a rule of conduct advising people to treat others as they would wish to be treated themselves

gold·en tri·an·gle *n* the part of Southeast Asia where Laos, Thailand, and Myanmar meet and where much opium is grown

gold·finch /góld finch/ *n* a small finch with yellow and black markings

gold·fish /góld fish/ (*pl* same *or* -**fish·es**) *n* a small aquarium fish

gold·fish bowl *n* a place or situation open to public scrutiny

gold leaf *n* gold in thin sheets

Gold·man /góldmən/, **Emma** (1869–1940) Russian-born US anarchist

gold med·al *n* a medal given as a first prize —**gold med·al·ist** *n*

gold mine *n* a rich source, especially of wealth

gold-plat·ed *adj* coated with gold —**gold-plate** *vt*

gold record *n* a top-selling record

gold rush *n* **1** a rush to an area where gold has been discovered **2** a rush to make money from a new source or by a new means

gold·smith /góld smith/ *n* a maker of gold articles

gold stan·dard *n* **1** a system of valuing currency in relation to the price of gold **2** the best example of its kind

Gold·wa·ter /góld wàwtər/, **Barry M.** (1909–98) US politician

Gold·wyn /góldwin/, **Samuel** (1882–1974) Russian-born US movie producer

golf *n* **1** an outdoor game in which a small ball is hit a long distance into a hole using a variety of clubs **2 Golf** a communications code word for the letter "G" ■ *vi* play golf —**golf·er** *n* —**golf·ing** *n*

golf ball *n* a ball used in golf

golf club *n* **1** a club with a long shaft and metal or wooden head used for hitting golf balls **2** a golfers' association or its premises

golf course *n* an area of land for playing golf

Gol·go·tha /gólgəthə/ ⬦ **Calvary**

go·li·ath /gə lÍ əth/, **Go·li·ath** *n* a gigantic or overpowering opponent

---

ORIGIN In the Bible, Goliath was a giant Philistine who was slain by David using a sling and a stone.

-gon *suffix* a figure having a particular number of angles ○ *hexagon*

go·nad /gó nàd/ *n* an organ that produces reproductive cells

gon·do·la /góndʻlə, gən dōlə/ *n* **1** a Venetian canal boat **2** a cable car **3** a cabin suspended below a balloon or airship **4** *also* **gon·do·la car** a long open rail car

---

ORIGIN Gondola is, as might be expected, from Venetian Italian. It is an alteration of a verb meaning "roll, rock" in a Romance dialect of the NE Alps.

---

gon·do·lier /gònd'l éer, gónd'l éer/ *n* somebody who guides a Venetian gondola

gone /gawn, gon/ past participle of **go**[1] ■ *adj* **1** absent after leaving somewhere **2** irrecoverable **3** used up **4** dead (*infml*) **5** infatuated (*infml*)

gon·er /gónnər/ *n* a person who is dead or about to die (*slang*)

gong *n* a resonant bronze plate. Use: or-

chestral percussion instrument, to summon people to meals.

gon·or·rhe·a /gònnə rée ə/, **gon·or·rhoe·a** n a sexually transmitted bacterial disease of the genitals —**gon·or·rhe·al** adj

goo n a soft sticky substance (infml)

goo·ber /goobər/, **goo·ber pea** n Can, Southern US a peanut

good /good/ adj (**bet·ter** /béttər/, **best**) 1 of high quality 2 suitable 3 skilled 4 virtuous 5 kindly 6 affording pleasure 7 not damaged or spoiled 8 ample ○ a good income 9 honorable 10 valid or allowable ○ a good explanation 11 beneficial to health 12 able to produce a desired result ○ a joke that is always good for a laugh 13 being at least ○ a good 30 minutes ■ n 1 a beneficial effect 2 a positive or useful aspect ○ take the good with the bad 3 something worth having or achieving ○ the good of the nation ◇ **for good** permanently ◇ **good and** completely (infml) ○ I'll leave when I'm good and ready. ◇ **make good** become successful

good af·ter·noon interj says hello or goodbye in the afternoon

good-bye /good bí/, **good-bye** interj expresses good wishes on parting or ending a telephone conversation ■ n an act of leaving

ORIGIN Goodbye is a contraction of "God be with you."

good eve·ning interj says hello or goodbye in the evening

good faith n honest intent

good-for-noth·ing n a person regarded as lazy (insult) —**good-for-noth·ing** adj

Good Fri·day n the Friday before Easter, when Christians remember Jesus Christ's death

good-heart·ed /good haártəd/ adj kindly and generous —**good-heart·ed·ly** adv —**good-heart·ed·ness** n

Good Hope, Cape of Cape in SW South Africa that divides the South Atlantic and Indian oceans

good-hu·mored adj cheerful —**good-hu·mored·ly** adv

good·ie n = goody

good·ish /goodish/ adj 1 rather good 2 rather large

good life n a comfortable existence

good looks npl a pleasant personal appearance, especially facial appearance —**good-look·ing** adj

good·ly /goodlee/ adj (-li·er, -li·est) 1 rather large 2 attractive (archaic) —**good·li·ness** n

Good·man /goodmən/, **Benny** (1909–86) US jazz clarinet player and band leader

good morn·ing interj says hello or goodbye in the morning

good-na·tured adj pleasant and obliging —**good-na·tured·ly** adv

good·ness /goodnəss/ n 1 the quality of being good 2 the nutrition or other benefit to be derived from something ■ interj expresses surprise

good night /good nít/ interj says goodbye at night —**good-night** adj

goods /goodz/ n items that are bought, sold, or transported (+ sing or pl verb) ■ npl portable property

Good Sa·mar·i·tan n a person who helps somebody in trouble

ORIGIN The **Good Samaritan** is the subject of a parable in the Bible (Luke 10:30–37). He stopped and helped a man who had been attacked and left for dead by thieves on the road from Jerusalem to Jericho, after others had passed him by.

good-tem·pered adj of a placid disposition —**good-tem·pered·ly** adv

good·will /good wíl, good wíl/ n 1 a friendly disposition ○ a goodwill gesture 2 willingness 3 the nontangible value of a business

good·y /goodee/ (pl -ies), **good·ie** n something sweet (often pl) ■ interj indicates delight (infml)

Good·year /good yeer/, **Charles** (1800–60) US inventor

good·y-good·y adj a person regarded as smugly virtuous (infml)

goo·ey /goo ee/ (-i·er, -i·est) adj sticky and soft —**goo·ey·ness** n

goof (infml) n 1 a careless mistake 2 a person regarded as unintelligent or incompetent (insult) ■ vi make a careless mistake □ **goof off** v waste time (infml)

goof·ball /goof báwl/ n 1 a person regarded as thoughtless or unintelligent (slang insult) 2 a barbiturate or tranquilizer in the form of a pill (slang)

goof·y /goofee/ (-i·er, -i·est) adj silly or unintelligent (infml) —**goof·i·ly** adv —**goof·i·ness** n

goon n 1 a thug 2 a person regarded as clumsy or uncouth (insult)

goose /gooss/ (pl geese /geess/) n 1 a large long-necked water bird with a honking call 2 a female goose 3 the flesh of a goose, cooked as food 4 a person regarded as silly

goose·ber·ry /gooss bèrree/ (pl -ries) n 1 an edible green or red fruit, usually eaten cooked and sweetened 2 the spiny bush that gooseberries grow on

goose bumps, goose pim·ples npl temporary pimples on the skin brought on by cold, fear, or sudden excitement

goose-flesh /gooss flèsh/ n skin affected by goose bumps

goose step n a high stiff marching step —**goose-step** vi

GOP n the Republican Party. Full form **Grand Old Party**

go·pher /gṓfər/ *n* a burrowing rodent with fur-lined cheek pouches

Mikhail Gorbachev

Gor·ba·chev /gáwrbə chàwf/, **Mikhail** (*b.* 1931) general secretary of the Soviet Communist Party (1985–91) and president of the former Soviet Union (1988–91)

Gor·di·an knot /gàwrdee ən-/ *n* a complicated problem with no apparent solution

ORIGIN The original *Gordian knot* was in the possession of Gordius, king of Gordium in ancient Phrygia, Asia Minor. Prophesy had it that it could be untied only by the future ruler of Asia, but Alexander the Great sliced through it.

Gor·di·mer /gáwrdəmər/, **Nadine** (*b.* 1923) South African novelist

gore[1] (**gored, gor·ing**) *vt* pierce the flesh with horns

ORIGIN The three English words **gore** are etymologically distinct. The origin of **gore** "pierce," which appeared in the 14C, is obscure. **Gore** "blood" is from an ancient root. It originally meant "dung, dirt, slime," and then from the mid-16C "coagulating blood." **Gore** "section of fabric" is of equally ancient origin, and in the earliest English sources meant "corner of land."

gore[2] *n* coagulating blood from a wound

gore[3] *n* a triangular section of fabric sewn together with others to form a wide skirt

Gore, Al (*b.* 1948) vice president of the United States (1993–2001)

gorge *n* 1 a deep narrow valley 2 the contents of the stomach ■ *vti* (**gorged, gorg·ing**) eat greedily

gor·geous /gáwrjəss/ *adj* 1 outstandingly beautiful or richly colored 2 very pleasant (*infml*) ○ *a gorgeous day* —**gor·geous·ly** *adv* —**gor·geous·ness** *n*

Gor·gon /gáwrgən/ *n* 1 in Greek mythology, a monstrous woman with snakes for hair, who turned those who looked at her into stone 2 *also* **gor·gon** a woman regarded as frightening or ugly (*insult*) —**Gor·go·ni·an** /gawr gṓnee ən/ *adj*

Gor·gon·zo·la /gàwrgən zṓlə/, **gor·gon·zo·la** *n* an Italian blue cheese

go·ril·la /gə rĩllə/ *n* the largest type of ape

ORIGIN The name was applied to the largest ape in 1847 by the US missionary and sci-

entist Thomas Savage. It was taken from Greek, where it was used in an account of an expedition to West Africa, explained as the name given to the women of a tribe of wild hairy people.

SPELLCHECK Do not confuse the spelling of **gorilla** and **guerrilla** ("a paramilitary soldier"), which sound similar.

Gö·ring ♦ **Goering, Hermann**

Gor·ky /gáwrkee/, **Gor·ki** former name for **Nizhniy Novgorod**

Gor·ky, Arshile (1904–48) Armenian-born US painter

~~**gorrilla**~~ incorrect spelling of **gorilla**

gorse *n* a spiny shrub with yellow flowers

go·ry /gáwree/ (**-ri·er, -ri·est**) *adj* 1 covered with blood 2 involving bloodshed 3 horrible ○ *the gory details* —**gor·i·ly** *adv* —**gor·i·ness** *n*

gosh *interj* expresses surprise (*infml*)

gos·hawk /góss hàwk/ *n* a large hawk with broad rounded wings and a long tail

gos·ling /gózzling/ *n* an immature goose

gos·pel /góspəl/ *n* 1 the absolute truth 2 *also* **gos·pel mu·sic** religious vocal music that originated among African American Christians in the S United States 3 **Gos·pel** the teachings of Jesus Christ, especially as contained in the Bible

ORIGIN **Gospel** represents what is essentially a contraction of *good spell*, with *spell* in the obsolete sense "news," and so is the "good news" preached by Jesus Christ. The first element of **gospel** came to be associated with *God* rather than *good*.

gos·sa·mer /góssəmər/ *n* 1 a fine film of cobwebs 2 a delicate fabric

gos·sip /góssip/ *n* 1 conversation about the personal details of others' lives, especially when malicious 2 casual conversation about recent events 3 somebody who habitually discusses the personal details of others' lives ■ *vi* spread rumors —**gos·sip·y** *adj*

gos·sip col·umn *n* a press feature about people's private lives —**gos·sip col·um·nist** *n*

got past participle, past tense of **get**

Goth /goth/ *n* a member of an ancient Germanic people

Goth·am /góthəm/ *n* New York City

Goth·en·burg /góth'n bùrg/ principal port in SW Sweden. Pop. 459,593 (1998). Swedish **Göteborg**

AKG London

Gothic: Interior of Cologne Cathedral, Germany (begun 1248)

Goth·ic /góthik/ *adj* **1** *also* **goth·ic** belonging to a genre of fiction characterized by gloom and darkness **2** of a medieval architectural style characterized by high ceilings and arched windows **3** of the ancient Goths

got·ten past participle of **get**

Göt·tin·gen /gúrtingən, gőtingən/ university town in central Germany. Pop. 127,519 (1997).

gouache /gwaash, goo aásh/ *n* **1** a painting technique in which opaque watercolors are mixed with gum **2** a gouache painting

Gou·da /góodə/ *n* a mild Dutch cheese

gouge /gowj/ *v* (**gouged, goug·ing**) **1** *vti* carve out a hole **2** *vti* form something roughly by cutting **3** *vt* overcharge somebody (*infml*) ■ *n* a chisel with a concave blade. Use: *cutting grooves and holes in wood.* —**goug·er** *n*

gou·lash /góo laàsh, -làsh/ *n* **1** a spicy Hungarian stew **2** an eclectic and uncoordinated mixture

Gould /goold/, **Jay** (1836–92) US financier and speculator

Gou·nod /góonō, goo nő/, **Charles François** (1818–93) French composer

gourd /gawrd/ *n* **1** any of various hard-skinned fruits whose skin is hollowed out and used for making containers **2** a gourd-producing plant

gourde /goord/ *n* the main unit of Haitian currency

gour·mand /góor maànd, góormənd/ *n* a food lover

gour·met /goor máy, góor mày/ *n* a food expert ■ *adj* describes special high-quality food

gout /gowt/ *n* **1** a disease causing swollen joints through deposits of excess uric acid **2** a large blob or clot

⚡**gov** *abbr* government organization (*in Internet addresses*)

~~governer~~ incorrect spelling of **governor**

~~goverment~~ incorrect spelling of **government**

gov·ern /gúvvərn/ *v* **1** *vti* have political authority over a country, state, or organization **2** *vt* control the actions or behavior of **3** *vt* have the controlling influence over ◇ *issues that govern the final settlement*

ORIGIN Govern came through French and

Latin from a Greek word that meant "steer a ship."

gov·er·nance /gúvvərnənss/ *n* **1** the manner of government **2** the act or state of governing

gov·ern·ess /gúvvərnəss/ *n* a woman employed to teach children at home

gov·ern·ment /gúvvərnmənt/ *n* **1** a group of people who have political authority **2** a type of political system **3** the state viewed as a ruling political power **4** the control of something **5** political science as a subject of study —**gov·ern·ment** *adj* —**gov·ern·men·tal** /gúvvərn mént'l/ *adj*

gov·er·nor /gúvvərnər/ *n* **1** a US state executive **2** a governing official **3** a member of a regulatory body **4** a device for regulating speed or amount —**gov·er·nor·ship** *n*

gov·er·nor gen·er·al (*pl* **gov·er·nors gen·er·al** *or* **gov·er·nor gen·er·als**) *n* **1** a chief governor **2** a representative of the British Crown in some Commonwealth countries —**gov·er·nor-gen·er·al·ship** *n*

govt. *abbr* government

gown *n* **1** an elegant dress **2** a long robe **3** a loose outer garment

Go·ya /góy ə/, **Francisco de** (1746–1828) Spanish painter

GP *abbr* general practitioner

GPA *abbr* US, Can, Aus grade point average

GPO *abbr* **1** general post office **2** Government Printing Office

⚡**GPRS** *n* a system that provides Internet access via cellphones and other wireless systems. Full form **general packet radio service**

GPS *n* a satellite navigation system, or a device that makes use of it. Full form **Global Positioning System**

gr. *abbr* **1** grade **2** grain **3** gram[1] **4** gross

Gr. *abbr* Greek

grab (**grabbed, grab·bing**) *v* **1** *vt* pick up or take hold of quickly, suddenly, or forcefully **2** *vti* try to grasp something ◇ *Stop grabbing or I won't give you any.* **3** *vt* seize violently or dishonestly **4** *vt* attract or impress and affect emotionally (*infml*) **5** *vt* hurriedly get (*infml*) ◇ *grab a bite to eat* —**grab** *n* —**grab·ba·ble** *adj* ◇ **up for grabs** available for the first comer to take or use (*infml*)

grab bag *n* **1** a box or bags of objects to be purchased or drawn unseen **2** a miscellaneous collection (*infml*)

Grac·chus /grákəss/, **Tiberius Sempronius** (163–133 BC) and his brother **Gaius Sempronius** (153–121 BC) Roman politicians and social reformers

grace *n* **1** elegance of form or movement **2** polite and decent behavior **3** a short prayer said at mealtimes **4** *also* **grace pe·ri·od** an extra time allowed before paying a debt **5** a pleasing or admirable quality (*usually pl*) **6** in Christianity, the love, mercy, and goodwill that is God's gift to humankind ■ *vt* (**graced, grac·ing**) 1 contribute pleasingly to an event *(often ironic)* ○ *So good of you to grace us with your presence.* 2 add elegance to something ■ *n* **Grace** a form of address used for a duke, duchess, or archbishop ■ **Gra·ces** *npl* in Greek mythology, three goddesses who had the power to grant charm, happiness, and beauty ◇ **fall from grace** lose a favored or privileged position

grace·ful /gráyssfəl/ *adj* 1 elegant and beautiful 2 poised and dignified —**grace·ful·ly** *adv* —**grace·ful·ness** *n*

grace·less /gráyssləss/ *adj* 1 without elegance 2 lacking dignity —**grace·less·ly** *adv* —**grace·less·ness** *n*

grace note *n* an extra ornamental note added to a piece of music

gra·cious /gráyshəss/ *adj* 1 kind and polite 2 elegant ○ *gracious living* ■ *interj* expresses surprise —**gra·cious·ly** *adv* —**gra·cious·ness** *n*

grack·le /grák'l/ *n* 1 a North American blackbird 2 a starling with mostly black feathers

grad *n* a graduate *(infml)*

gra·da·tion /gray dáysh'n/ *n* 1 a series of degrees, steps, or stages 2 a single degree, step, or stage 3 the arrangement of things according to size, rank, or quality —**gra·da·tion·al** *adj*

grade *n* 1 a year in school in the US and Canadian systems ○ *He's in the 9th grade.* 2 a mark indicating the quality of a student's work 3 a level in a scale of progression *(often in combination)* 4 a mark showing a stage in a process 5 a rank, e.g., in the military 6 a group of people of the same rank 7 a US classification indicating the relative quality of a food 8 a gradient or slope 9 the level at which the ground meets a building ■ *vt* (**grad·ed, grad·ing**) 1 classify things or people by rank, quality, or level 2 assign a grade to something, e.g., a student's work 3 make a road level —**grad·a·ble** *adj*

grade cross·ing *n* a railroad crossing that is level with the road

grade in·fla·tion *n* the act of grading students' work too high to compensate for lowered standards or expectations

grad·er /gráydər/ *n* a student in a particular grade at school ○ *second graders*

grade school *n* an elementary school —**grade-school·er** *n*

gra·di·ent /gráydee ənt/ *n* 1 a slope 2 the rate of slope ■ *adj* sloping

grad·u·al /grájjoo əl/ *adj* proceeding, developing, or changing slowly —**grad·u·al·ly** *adv* —**grad·u·al·ness** *n*

grad·u·ate /grájjoo ət/ 1 somebody who has completed a course of studies 2 the holder of a bachelor's degree ■ *v* /grájjoo àyt/ (**-at·ed, -at·ing**) 1 *vi* receive a diploma or degree 2 *vt* give a diploma or degree to 3 *vi*

move up in level or standard 4 *vt* mark with units of measurement ■ *adj* /grájjoo ət/ of education for students with a bachelor's degree

grad·u·at·ed /grájjoo àytəd/ *adj* 1 in stages 2 marked with units of measurement

grad·u·ate school *n* a university or university division for students who have a bachelor's degree

grad·u·a·tion /grájjoo áysh'n/ *n* 1 the completion of studies 2 a ceremony in which diplomas or degrees are given 3 a unit of measurement marked on an instrument

graf·fi·ti /grə féetee/ *n* drawings or writing on walls or other surfaces in public places

---

USAGE graffito or **graffiti**? **Graffito** comes from Italian, and its plural in Italian is **graffiti**. It is acceptable, however, to use **graffiti** as a singular noun when the meaning is "inscriptions in general" or even "an inscription."

---

graffiti incorrect spelling of **graffiti**

graft[1] *n* 1 a piece of transplanted tissue 2 a piece of a plant shoot joined to the stem of another plant ■ *vt* 1 transplant living tissue 2 join part of one plant to another

graft[2] *n* cheating for personal gain by somebody in a powerful or elected position —**graft** *vti* —**graft·er** *n*

Gra·ham /gráy əm/, **Billy** (*b.* 1918) US evangelist

Martha Graham: Performing in *Judith* (1957)

Gra·ham, Martha (1893–1991) US dancer, choreographer, and teacher

gra·ham crack·er /gráy əm-/ *n* a sweet plain whole-wheat cracker

---

ORIGIN The **graham cracker** is named for the dietary reformer Dr. Sylvester Graham (1794–1851), who advocated the type of flour from which it is made.

---

grail *n* 1 something that is eagerly sought after 2 **Grail** according to legend, the cup used by Jesus Christ at the Last Supper

grain *n* 1 cereal crops 2 a small seed 3 a tiny single piece 4 a small amount 5 the smallest unit of weight in various systems 6 any of the particles in a photographic emulsion that form an image ■ *v* 1 *vt* form grains 2 *vt* give a grain or a grainy appearance to —**grained** *adj* ◇ **go against the grain** be contrary to somebody's natural tendencies, wishes, or feelings

grain el·e·va·tor *n* a grain storehouse with a mechanism for moving the grain

Grain·ger /gráynjər/, **Percy** (1882–1961) Australian-born US pianist and composer

grain·y /gráynee/ (**-i·er, -i·est**) *adj* 1 describes a photograph in which the image is not clear 2 resembling grains in size or texture —**grain·i·ness** *n*

gram[1] *n* (*symbol* **g**) a metric unit of mass

gram[2] *n* an edible legume, e.g., green gram or black gram

-gram *suffix* 1 something written, drawn, or recorded ○ *mammogram* 2 a message delivered by a third party ○ *telegram*

gram·mar /grámmər/ *n* 1 the rules for forming words and putting them together 2 the rules that apply to words in a particular language 3 the quality of language used, in relation to standards of correctness ○ *bad grammar* 4 a book dealing with the grammar of a language

gram·mar·i·an /grə máiree ən/ *n* a grammar expert

gram·mar school *n* an elementary school

gram·mat·i·cal /grə máttik'l/ *adj* 1 in or of the rules of grammar 2 correct in terms of grammar —**gram·mat·i·cal·i·ty** /grə mätti kállətee/ *n* —**gram·mat·i·cal·ly** *adv*

~~grammer~~ incorrect spelling of **grammar**

gram·o·phone /grámmə fōn/ *n* a record player (*dated*)

Gram·pi·an Moun·tains /grámpee ən-/ mountain range in central Scotland that forms a natural division between the Highlands and Lowlands. Highest peak Ben Nevis 4,406 ft./1,343 m.

gram·pus /grámpəss/ (*pl* same or **-pus·es**) *n* a large dolphin with a blunt snout

Gra·na·da /grə naádə/ city in S Spain, site of the Alhambra. Pop. 241,471 (1998).

gran·a·ry /gránəree, gráy-/ (*pl* **-ries**) *n* a grain warehouse

Gran Cha·co /graàn chaàkō/ region in south central South America, extending from S Bolivia through Paraguay to N Argentina

grand *adj* 1 impressive in appearance or style 2 ambitious and far-reaching 3 worthy of respect 4 very enjoyable ■ *n* (*infml*) 1 1,000 dollars in money 2 a grand piano —**grand·ly** *adv* —**grand·ness** *n*

grand- *prefix* one generation further removed ○ *grandniece* ○ *grandfather*

~~grandaughter~~ incorrect spelling of **granddaughter**

Grand Banks shallow section of the Atlantic Ocean, off SE Newfoundland, Canada

Grand Can·yon gorge in NW Arizona, carved by the Colorado River. Its width varies from 5 to 18 mi./8 to 29 km, and its depth can exceed 1 mi./1.6 km. Length 277 mi./446 km.

grand·child /gránd chīld/ (*pl* **-chil·dren** /-chìldrən/) *n* a child's child

grand·dad /grán dàd/, **gran·dad** *n* a grandfather (*infml*)

grand·dad·dy /grán dàddee/, **gran·dad·dy** *n* the first or most impressive of its kind

grand·daugh·ter /grán dàwtər/ *n* a child's daughter

gran·dee /gran deé/ *n* 1 a highly respected and influential person 2 a Spanish or Portuguese nobleman

gran·deur /gránjər, -joòr/ *n* impressive appearance or style

grand·fa·ther /gránd faàthər/ *n* 1 a parent's father 2 a male ancestor ■ *vt* exempt somebody already engaged in an activity from a new law that regulates the activity —**grandfa·ther·ly** *adj*

grand·fa·ther clock *n* a tall clock that stands on the floor

grand fi·nal·e *n* a final spectacular scene or performance

Grand Forks /-fáwrks/ city in E North Dakota, on the Red River. Pop. 47,327 (1998).

gran·dil·o·quence /gran dílləkwənss/ *n* a lofty way of speaking or writing —**gran·dil·o·quent** *adj*

gran·di·ose /grándee ōss/ *adj* 1 pretentious and pompous 2 magnificent —**gran·di·ose·ly** *adv* —**gran·di·os·i·ty** /grándee óssətee/ *n*

grand ju·ry *n* in the United States and Canada, a jury called to decide if there are grounds for a criminal trial —**grand ju·ror** *n*

grand lar·ce·ny *n* the theft of high-value property

grand·ma /grán maà/ *n* a grandmother (*infml*)

grand mal /gràn'N maàl/ *n* a form of epilepsy in which there is loss of consciousness and severe convulsions

grand mas·ter /gránd màstər/, **grand·mas·ter** *n* 1 a top chess player 2 somebody who is outstanding in a particular field

grand·moth·er /grán mùthər/ *n* 1 a parent's mother 2 a female ancestor —**grand·moth·er·ly** *adj*

grand op·er·a *n* a serious opera in which all the words are sung

grand·pa /grán paà, grám paà/ *n* a grandfather (*infml*)

grand·par·ent /grán pàirənt/ *n* a parent's parent —**grand·pa·ren·tal** /gránpə rént'l/ *adj*

grand pi·an·o *n* a large harp-shaped piano with horizontal strings

Grand Prix /gròn preé, gròN-/ (*pl* same or **Grands Prix** /*pronunc. same*/) *n* 1 an important international car race 2 any important sports competition

Grand Rap·ids city in west central Michigan. Pop. 185,437 (1998).

grand slam *n* 1 the winning of all the major competitions in a series 2 any major sporting competition 3 in baseball, a home run that scores 4 runs 4 in bridge and some other card games, an instance of winning all the tricks in a game

grand·son /gránd sùn/ n a child's son

grand·stand /gránd stànd/ n 1 a structure, usually with a roof, containing rows of seats for spectators 2 the spectators in a grandstand ■ adj giving an unobstructed view ■ vi seek attention or admiration —**grand·stand·er** n

grand to·tal n a final total

grand tour n a tour of several places or all the parts of a place

~~grandure~~ incorrect spelling of **grandeur**

grange /graynj/ n 1 a granary or barn (archaic) 2 **Grange** a US farmers' organization, or one of its local branches

gran·ite /gránnit/ n a very hard coarse-grained rock. Use: building.

gran·ny /gránnee/ (pl -nies), **gran·nie** n 1 a grandmother (infml) 2 Southern US a midwife

gran·ny knot n an incorrectly tied reef knot that slips

gra·no·la /grə nólə/ n an oat breakfast cereal with other ingredients such as dried fruit and nuts

grant vt 1 comply with a request 2 allow something as a favor 3 acknowledge the truth of something 4 transfer rights or property in a legal transaction ■ n 1 a sum of money given by a government or organization for a specific purpose 2 a gift given as a favor or privilege 3 a legal transaction or document transferring money or property ◊ **take for granted** 1 fail to realize the value of 2 assume the truth of ◊ See note at **give**

Grant, Cary (1904–86) British-born US movie actor

Library of Congress

Ulysses S. Grant

Grant, Ulysses S. (1822–85) Union army general and 18th president of the United States (1869–77)

grant·ed /grántəd/ adv, conj although it is true

gran·u·lar /gránnyələr/ adj 1 made up of granules 2 with the texture or appearance of granules —**gran·u·lar·i·ty** /gránnyə lérrətee/ n

gran·u·late /gránnyə làyt/ (-lat·ed, -lat·ing) vti 1 form or make into granules 2 become or make grainy in texture or appearance —**gran·u·la·tion** /gránnyə láysh'n/ n

gran·u·lat·ed sug·ar n coarse white sugar

gran·ule /grán yòòl/ n a small grain or particle

grape n 1 a small green or purple edible berry that grows in bunches on a vine 2 also **grape·shot** small iron balls fired simultaneously from a cannon

grape·fruit /gráyp fròòt/ (pl same or -fruits) n 1 a large yellow or pink citrus fruit 2 the tree that produces grapefruit

grape·vine /gráyp vìn/ n 1 a vine that bears grapes 2 the path along which information or rumor passes informally from person to person (infml)

graph n a diagram showing relationships between two or more variable quantities ■ vt put data on a graph

graph- prefix writing (before vowels) ◊ graphology

-graph suffix 1 something written or drawn ◊ digraph 2 an instrument for writing, drawing, or recording ◊ seismograph

⚡ **graph·ic** /gráffik/ adj 1 vividly detailed 2 shown in writing 3 shown in pictures 4 also **graph·i·cal** of graphs 5 of drawing, printing, and the other graphic arts ■ n (often pl) 1 a picture produced by a computer 2 a book illustration —**graph·i·cal·ly** adv —**graph·ic·ness** n

⚡ **graph·i·cal us·er in·ter·face** n a computer operating system that relies on the use of icons, menus, and a mouse

graph·ic arts npl artistic processes based on the use of lines rather than color —**graph·ic art·ist** n

graph·ic de·sign n the art or practice of designing books, magazines, or any medium that combines images and text —**graph·ic de·sign·er** n

graph·ic nov·el n a work of fiction for adults in comic-book form

⚡ **graph·ics** /gráffiks/ n (+ sing verb) 1 the presentation of information in the form of diagrams and illustrations 2 the art of displaying, storing, and manipulating computer data as symbols, diagrams, or pictures

⚡ **graph·ics card** n a circuit board that enables a computer to display screen information

⚡ **graph·ics tab·let** n an electronic drawing device used for entering designs into a computer

graph·ite /grá fìt/ n a soft black form of carbon. Use: lubricants, carbon fibers, pencil lead.

gra·phol·o·gy /gra fóllajee/ n 1 the study of handwriting 2 the linguistic study of writing —**graph·o·log·i·cal** /gràffə lójjik'l/ adj —**gra·phol·o·gist** n

graph pa·per n paper with a series of intersecting horizontal and vertical lines

-graphy suffix 1 a particular process or technique of writing or making an image ◊ photography 2 writing about or study of a particular subject ◊ biography

grap·nel /grápnəl/ n 1 also **grap·pling i·ron**, **grap·pling hook** a device with hooks on the end of a rope that can be thrown and attached to something 2 an anchor for a small boat

grap·ple /grápp'l/ vi (-pled, -pling) 1 struggle with somebody physically 2 struggle to deal with something ■ n 1 a grapnel 2 a struggle

grasp vti 1 take or try to take hold of somebody or something 2 understand or try to understand something ■ n 1 a firm hold 2 understanding o *a poor grasp of the facts* 3 the ability to achieve something o *Success was within her grasp.*

grasp·ing /gráspɪng/ adj greedy for money

grass n 1 (pl **grass·es** or **same**) a low-growing green plant used to form lawns 2 a grass-covered area 3 (pl **grass·es** or **same**) a hollow-stemmed green plant belonging to a group that includes many cereals 4 marijuana (slang) ■ vti cover an area with grass

Grass, Günter (b. 1927) German writer and political activist

grass hock·ey n Can field hockey

grass·hop·per /gráss hòppər/ n a slender jumping insect with strong back legs

grass·land /gráss lànd/ n 1 grass-covered land 2 pasture land

grass·roots /gráss ròots/ npl 1 the ordinary people of a community or organization 2 the origin or basis of something

grass snake n a common nonpoisonous green snake

grass·y /grássee/ adj (-i·er, -i·est) adj 1 grass-covered 2 like grass —**grass·i·ness** n

grate[1] n 1 a framework of bars to keep solid fuel in a fireplace, stove, or furnace 2 a fireplace

grate[2] /grát ed, grát·ing/ v 1 vti make into small pieces using a grater 2 vti make or cause to make a harsh rubbing noise 3 vt say in a harsh voice 4 vi be a source of irritation or annoyance —**grat·ed** adj

grate·ful /gráytfəl/ adj having a desire or reason to thank somebody —**grate·ful·ly** adv —**grate·ful·ness** n

grat·er /gráytər/ n a device with sharp-edged holes on which something such as cheese can be rubbed to reduce it to small pieces

grat·i·fy /gráttɪ fī/ (-fied, -fies) vt 1 make somebody feel pleased or satisfied 2 fulfill a desire —**grat·i·fi·ca·tion** /gràttəfi káysh'n/ n —**grat·i·fy·ing** —**grat·i·fy·ing·ly** adv

grat·ing[1] /gráytɪng/ n a metal grille

grat·ing[2] /gráytɪng/ adj 1 unpleasantly rough or harsh 2 irritating or annoying —**grat·ing·ly** adv

grat·is /gráttiss, graát-, gráyt-/ adj, adv received or given without cost or payment

grat·i·tude /grátti tòod/ n a feeling of being grateful to somebody

gra·tu·i·tous /grə toò itəss/ adj 1 unnecessary and unjustifiable 2 received or given without cost or payment —**gra·tu·i·tous·ly** adv —**gra·tu·i·tous·ness** n

gra·tu·i·ty /grə toò itee/ (pl -ties) n an extra sum of money given in appreciation

grave[1] /grayv/ n a burial place in the ground

grave[2] /grayv/ (grav·er, grav·est) adj 1 solemn or serious in manner 2 involving possible harm or danger —**grave·ly** adv —**grave·ness** n

grave[3] /grayv, graav/ n the mark (`) placed above a vowel to indicate a particular pronunciation ■ adj with a grave accent

grave·dig·ger /gráyv dìggər/ n somebody who digs graves

grav·el /gráv'l/ n small stones used for paths and in concrete ■ vt cover with gravel

grav·el·ly /grávv'lee/ adj 1 sounding rough or harsh 2 like or covered with gravel

grav·en im·age n a carving of a god

Graves, Robert (1895–1985) British poet and novelist

grave·side /gráyv sìd/ n the area around an open grave

grave·stone /gráyv stòn/ n a stone that marks a grave

grave·yard /gráyv yaàrd/ n 1 an area where people are buried 2 a dumping place for old and unwanted objects and equipment

grave·yard shift n a period of work after midnight

grav·id /grávvid/ adj pregnant with young or eggs (technical) —**gra·vid·i·ty** /grə víddətee/ n —**grav·id·ly** adv

grav·i·tas /grávvi taàss/ n seriousness of tone or behavior

grav·i·tate /grávvi tàyt/ (-tat·ed, -tat·ing) v 1 vi move gradually and steadily toward somebody or something 2 vti move or cause to move under the influence of gravity

grav·i·ta·tion /gràvvi táysh'n/ n 1 gradual and steady movement in the direction of somebody or something 2 the mutual force of attraction between all things that have mass —**grav·i·ta·tion·al** adj

grav·i·ta·tion·al con·stant n a numerical factor relating force, mass, and distance

grav·i·ty /grávvitee/ n 1 the force of attraction that an astronomical object such as the Earth exerts on objects on or near its surface 2 gravitation 3 the seriousness of something considered in terms of its consequences 4 solemnity and seriousness in behavior

gra·vy /gráyvee/ (pl -vies) n 1 a sauce made with meat juices 2 money that is obtained easily (slang)

ORIGIN In the medieval period **gravy** was a kind of spiced white sauce. It came to be applied to meat juices in the late 16C. The form of the English word seems to be the result of misreading n for u (used for both u and *v* in the manuscripts of the time) in the French form *grané*.

gra·vy boat *n* a container for serving gravy

gra·vy train *n* a source of easy money (*infml*)

gray[1] *adj* (**gray·er, gray·est**) **1** of the color of ash **2** dismal or gloomy ■ *n* the color of ash ■ *vi* (**grayed, gray·ing, grays**) turn gray —**gray·ness** *n*

gray[2] *n* (*symbol* **Gy**) a unit of absorbed radiation

ORIGIN The unit is named for the English radiologist L. H. Gray (1905–65).

gray ar·e·a *n* an unclear situation or subject

gray·beard /gráy bèerd/ *n* a man of advanced years (*dated*) —**gray·beard·ed** *adj*

gray lit·er·a·ture *n* publications that have no commercial purpose

gray mat·ter *n* **1** intelligence or brains (*infml*) **2** the brownish-gray tissue in the brain

⚡**gray scale** *n* a scale for the shades of gray used in printing

gray whale *n* a baleen whale of the N Pacific

gray wolf *n* large wolf varying in color from white to black

graze[1] (**grazed, graz·ing**) *v* **1** *vti* eat grass in fields **2** *vt* allow animals to eat grass **3** *vi* eat snacks throughout the day instead of regular meals (*slang*)

graze[2] *v* (**grazed, graz·ing**) **1** *vti* touch something lightly **2** *vt* break the skin slightly ■ *n* **1** a slight break in the skin **2** a light touch

grease /greess/ **1** animal fat **2** a thick lubricant **3** oil for the hair ■ *vt* /greess, grèez/ (**greased, greas·ing**) **1** put grease on something **2** make something easier or quicker (*infml*) ◊ **grease somebody's palm** *or* **hand** bribe somebody (*infml*)

grease gun *n* a device for forcing grease into machinery

grease·paint /gréess pàynt/ *n* actors' makeup

greas·y /gréessee, gréezee/ (**-i·er, -i·est**) *adj* **1** covered with, containing, or caused by grease **2** unpleasantly friendly or flattering **3** having excessive natural oils **4** slippery —**greas·i·ly** *adv* —**greas·i·ness** *n*

great /grayt/ *adj* **1** exceptionally talented ○ *a great artist* **2** very significant or important **3** powerful **4** very good ○ *great food* **5** much ○ *It gives me great pleasure to introduce our speaker tonight.* **6** impressively large **7** large in number ○ *a great crowd of well-wishers* **8** showing much interest in something ○ *a great opera fan* **9** able to deal with something well (*infml*) ○ *great with kids* **10** bigger than others of the same kind **11** very suitable (*infml*) ○ *shoes great for walking* **12** lasting a long time ■ *n* somebody of lasting fame or influence —**great·ly** *adv* —**great·ness** *n*

great- *prefix* **1** being a parent of a grandparent ○ *great-grandmother* **2** being a grandchild's child ○ *great-grandson* **3** being a

parent's aunt or uncle ○ *great-aunt* **4** being a nephew's or niece's child ○ *great-nephew*

great ape *n* a large ape such as a gorilla, chimpanzee, or orangutan

Great Bar·ri·er Reef chain of coral reefs in the Coral Sea, off the coast of Queensland, Australia. Length 1,250 mi./2,010 km.

Great Ba·sin drainage area covering most of Nevada and parts of Utah, Oregon, Idaho, and California

Great Bear Lake freshwater lake in northwestern mainland Northwest Territories, Canada, lying astride the Arctic Circle

Great Brit·ain island of NW Europe, comprising England, Scotland, and Wales

great cir·cle *n* a circle on the surface of a sphere that has the same radius and center as the sphere

great·coat /gráyt kòt/ *n* an overcoat

Great Dane *n* a very large dog with long legs, a square head, and a deep muzzle

Great Dis·mal Swamp low-lying marshland in SE Virginia and NE North Carolina

Great·er An·til·les /gràytər an tílleez/ island group in the N Caribbean Sea, comprising Cuba, Jamaica, Hispaniola, and Puerto Rico

Great·er Sun·da Is·lands /-súndə-/ island group of Indonesia that includes Sumatra, Java, Borneo, and Sulawesi

~~greatful~~ incorrect spelling of **grateful**

great-grand·child *n* a child of a grandchild

Great Lakes group of five freshwater lakes in north central North America, comprising Lakes Superior, Michigan, Huron, Erie, and Ontario

Great Plains vast grassland region in central North America, stretching from central Canada to S Texas

Great Rift Val·ley depression of SW Asia and E Africa extending more than 3,000 mi./4,830 km from the valley of the Jordan River in Syria to Mozambique

Great Salt Lake shallow body of salt water in NW Utah

Great Slave Lake freshwater lake in the S Northwest Territories, Canada

great white shark *n* a large gray-brown and white shark that feeds on large fish and marine mammals

Great White Way *n* the historic entertainment district in Manhattan stretching along Broadway

grebe (*pl* **grebes** *or* **same**) *n* a freshwater diving bird with lobed toes

Gre·cian /gréesh'n/ *adj* in the ancient Greek style of architecture or sculpture —**Gre·cian·ize** *vt*

Gre·co /grékō/, **El** (1541–1614) Greek-born Spanish painter

Gre·co-Ro·man /grèkō rṓmən, grèekō-/ *adj* **1** of ancient Greece and Rome **2** describes a style of wrestling in which no holds are allowed below the waist

Greece /greess/ country in SE Europe, comprising the southernmost part of the Balkan Peninsula and numerous islands in the E Mediterranean. Cap. Athens. Pop. 10,623,835 (2001).

greed n a strong desire for more of something than is needed

greed·y /greedee/ (-i·er, -i·est) adj 1 eating too much 2 wanting much more of something than is needed —**greed·i·ly** adv —**greed·i·ness** n

Greek n 1 somebody from Greece 2 the language of modern or ancient Greece ∎ adj 1 of Greece or the Greeks 2 of the Greek language

Gree·ley /greelee/, **Horace** (1811–72) US politician and journalist

green adj 1 of the color of grass, between yellow and blue in the spectrum 2 having edible green leaves 3 grassy or leafy 4 not ripe 5 envious or jealous 6 naive and lacking experience ∎ n 1 the color of grass 2 a grassy area, especially one surrounding a golf hole ∎ **greens** npl 1 vegetables with green leaves and stems 2 decorative greenery ∎ vti become or make green —**green·ly** adv —**green·ness** n

green·back /green bàk/ n a piece of US paper money (slang)

Green Bay city in NE Wisconsin, on the southern shore of Lake Michigan. Pop. 102,708 (1994).

green bean n a bean with a green pod

green·belt /green bèlt/ n 1 an area of undeveloped land around a city 2 an area of irrigated land bordering a desert

green card n an identification card and work permit issued in the United States to nationals of other countries

Greene /green/, **Graham** (1904–91) British writer

green·er·y /greenaree/ n green plants

green-eyed mon·ster n jealousy

green·fly /green flī/ (pl same or -flies) n a small green aphid

green·gage /green gàyj/ n 1 a type of greenish plum 2 a tree that produces greengages

---

ORIGIN The **greengage** is named for Sir William Gage (1657–1727), who introduced it to England.

---

green·horn /green hàwrn/ n an inexperienced and unsophisticated person who is easily duped ◊ See note at **beginner**

green·house /green hòwss/ (pl -hous·es /-hówzəz/) n a glass or transparent structure in which to grow plants that need protection from the elements

green·house ef·fect n the warming of the Earth's atmosphere as a result of atmospheric pollution

green·house gas n a gas that contributes to the warming of the Earth's atmosphere

Green·land /greenlənd/ island of Denmark, in the North Atlantic and Arctic oceans, off NE Canada. Pop. 56,352 (2001). —**Green·land·er** n —**Green·land·ic** adj

green light n 1 a green-colored light that signals traffic to proceed 2 permission to begin doing something

Green Moun·tains mountain range in the Appalachian system, extending from E Canada through Vermont

green on·ion n a young onion for salads. Use: raw in salads.

Green Par·ty n an environmentalist political party

Green·peace /green peess/ n an international environmentalist pressure group

green pep·per n an unripe sweet pepper

green rev·o·lu·tion n the introduction of modern farming techniques to increase crop production

green·room /green ròom, -ròom/ n a lounge in a TV studio or concert hall where performers can relax

Greens·bor·o /greenz bùrə, -bùrō/ city in N North Carolina. Pop. 197,910 (1998).

greens·keep·er /greenz keepər/ n somebody who maintains a golf course

Green·span /green spàn/, **Alan** (b. 1926) US economist

green tea n tea made from tea leaves that have been dried but not fermented

green thumb n a high level of skill at gardening

Green·wich /grénnich, -ij/ borough of London, England, on the Thames River, site of the prime meridian, which passes through the Royal Greenwich Observatory. Pop. 211,141 (1991).

Green·wich Mean Time n = **Universal Time**

Green·wich Vil·lage /grènnich-, grìnnich-/ n an area in lower Manhattan

Greer, Germaine (b. 1939) Australian writer and feminist

greet vt 1 welcome 2 address courteously 3 respond or react to o The news was greeted with dismay. —**greet·er** n

greet·ing /greeting/ n 1 a friendly gesture 2 an act of welcoming somebody ∎ **greet·ings** npl a message of good wishes

greet·ing card n a decorated card used to send greetings

gre·gar·i·ous /grə gáiree əss/ adj 1 friendly and sociable 2 describes organisms that live in groups —**gre·gar·i·ous·ly** adv —**gre·gar·i·ous·ness** n

Gre·go·ri·an cal·en·dar /gri gàwree ən-/ n the calendar in general use worldwide

---

ORIGIN The **Gregorian calendar** is named for Pope Gregory XIII, who introduced it in 1582.

Gre·go·rian chant /grɪˈgɔːrɪən/ n a Roman Catholic liturgical chant that is sung without accompaniment

ORIGIN The **Gregorian chant** is named for Pope Gregory I (540?-604), who is credited with introducing it.

Greg·o·ry XIII /ˈgrɛgərɪ/ (1502–85) pope (1572–85)

grem·lin /ˈgrɛmlɪn/ n an imaginary creature that damages machinery (infml)

Gre·na·da /grə ˈnɑːdə/ island state in the SE Caribbean Sea, comprising the island of Grenada and some of the S **Grenadines**. Cap. St. George's. Pop. 89,227 (2001). —**Gre·na·di·an** n, adj

gre·nade /grə ˈnɑːd/ n 1 a small bomb that is thrown by hand or fired from a small weapon 2 a sealed glass projectile containing tear gas or another chemical

ORIGIN Grenade comes from a French word originally meaning "pomegranate," which was its first sense in English, in the mid-16C. The use of the word for an explosive device is recorded from the late 16C. The name was suggested by the resemblance of the shape of early grenades to a pomegranate.

gren·a·dier /ˌgrɛnə ˈdɪər/ (pl same or -diers) n 1 formerly, a grenade-carrying soldier 2 an ocean fish with no tail fin

gren·a·dine /ˌgrɛnə ˈdiːn, ˈgrɛnə diːn/ n a syrup made from pomegranates. Use: in cocktails.

Gre·no·ble /grɪ ˈnɒbl, -ˈnɔːbl/ city in SE France. Pop. 153,317 (1999).

Gretz·ky /ˈgrɛtski/, **Wayne** (b. 1961) Canadian ice hockey player

grew past tense of **grow**

grey adj, n, vti = **gray**[1]

Grey, Lady Jane (1537–54) queen of England (1553)

Grey, Zane (1875–1939) US writer

grey·hound /ˈgreɪ hoʊnd/ n a slim fast dog

ORIGIN Greyhounds do not get their name from the color gray – it has never been a significant characteristic of the breed. The first element comes from an ancient root meaning "bitch."

grid n 1 a network of reference lines on a map 2 any pattern of adjacent squares 3 a grating made of bars 4 a network for distributing electricity, gas, or water

grid·dle /ˈgrɪdl/ n a flat metal cooking surface ■ vt (-dled, -dling) cook on a griddle

grid·dle·cake /ˈgrɪdl keɪk/ n a thin pancake cooked on a griddle

grid·i·ron /ˈgrɪd aɪrn/ n 1 a grill on which food is cooked 2 a grating made of bars 3 a football field

grid·lock /ˈgrɪd lɒk/ n 1 a traffic jam 2 a deadlock —**grid·locked** adj

grief /griːf/ n 1 intense sorrow 2 a cause of intense sorrow 3 annoyance or trouble (infml) ◊ **come to grief** suffer misfortune or ruin

grief-strick·en adj deeply affected by grief

Grieg /griːg/, **Edvard** (1843–1907) Norwegian composer

griev·ance /ˈgriːvəns/ n 1 something regarded as a reason to complain 2 resentment 3 a formal objection

grieve /griːv/ (grieved, griev·ing) vti experience or cause somebody to experience intense sorrow —**griev·er** n

griev·ous /ˈgriːvəs/ adj 1 very serious or significant 2 very bad or severe —**griev·ous·ly** adv

grif·fin /ˈgrɪfɪn/, **grif·fon** /ˈgrɪfən/, **gryph·on** n a mythical monster that is part eagle and part lion

Grif·fith /ˈgrɪfɪθ/, **D. W.** (1875–1948) US movie director

grill /grɪl/ v 1 vti cook over direct heat 2 vt interrogate (infml) ■ n 1 a flat surface of metal bars used for grilling 2 food cooked on a grill 3 a restaurant serving grilled food ◊ See note at **question**

SPELLCHECK Do not confuse the spelling of **grill** and **grille** ("a lattice of bars"), which sound similar.

grille /grɪl/ n a pattern or lattice of bars, e.g., in the front of a window or the radiator of a vehicle ◊ See note at **grill**

grim (grim·mer, grim·mest) adj 1 depressingly gloomy 2 forbidding in appearance 3 sternly serious —**grim·ly** adv —**grim·ness** n

grim·ace /ˈgrɪməs, grɪ ˈmeɪs/ n a contorted facial expression indicating disgust or pain —**grim·ace** vi

grime n accumulated or ingrained dirt —**grim·y** adj

Grim·ké /ˈgrɪmkeɪ/, **Sarah Moore** (1792–1873) and her sister **Angelina Emily** (1805–79) US abolitionists and reformers

Grimm, Jacob (1785–1863) and his brother **Wilhelm Karl** (1786–1859) German philologists and folklorists

Grim Reap·er n death personified

grin (grinned, grin·ning) vi smile broadly —**grin** n

grind /graɪnd/ v (ground /graʊnd/, ground) 1 vti crush into very small pieces 2 vti rub together with a grating noise o grinding her teeth 3 vt chop food, especially meat, into tiny pieces 4 vt smooth or sharpen something by rubbing or friction ■ n 1 something boring and repetitive (infml) 2 the process of grinding something or the texture obtained from grinding o a fine grind of coffee 3 a grinding noise 4 somebody who works or studies too hard (infml) —**grind·ing·ly** adv

□ **grind on** *vi* continue in an unrelenting way

□ **grind out** *vt* produce mechanically as a result of boredom with routine ○ *grinding out articles for the local paper*

grind·stone /grínd stòn/ *n* a stone or wheel used for grinding, sharpening, or polishing

grip *n* 1 a firm hold 2 a manner of holding something 3 a handle or other holding device 4 the capability of something not to slip ○ *shoes with grip* 5 control or power ○ *in the grip of fear* ■ *v* (**gripped, grip·ping**) 1 *vt* grasp or hold firmly 2 *vti* adhere to a surface 3 *vt* capture the interest or attention of —**grip·ping** *adj*

gripe *v* (**griped, grip·ing**) 1 *vi* grumble constantly (*infml*) 2 *vt* annoy (*slang*) ■ *n* a minor complaint (*infml*) —**grip·ing** *adj* ◊ See note at **complain**

Gris /greess/, **Juan** (1887–1927) Spanish-born French artist

gris·ly /grízzlee/ (**-li·er, -li·est**) *adj* gruesomely unpleasant or horrible —**gris·li·ness** *n*

> **SPELLCHECK** Do not confuse the spelling of **grisly** and **grizzly** ("a type of bear"), which sound similar.

grist *n* grain that is ground into flour

gris·tle /gríss'l/ *n* tough cartilage in meat —**gris·tly** *adj*

grit *n* 1 sand or stone particles 2 firmness of character ■ *vt* (**grit·ted, grit·ting**) clench the teeth

grits *n* coarsely ground corn that is boiled and eaten (*+ sing or pl verb*)

grit·ty /gríttee/ (**-ti·er, -ti·est**) *adj* 1 courageous or resolute 2 starkly realistic 3 like or covered with grit —**grit·ti·ly** *adv* —**grit·ti·ness** *n*

griz·zled /grízz'ld/ *adj* 1 streaked with gray hairs ○ *his grizzled beard* 2 gray-haired

griz·zly bear /grízzlee-/, **griz·zly** (*pl* **-ies**) *n* a large brown North American bear ◊ See note at **grisly**

groan *n* 1 a long low cry of pain or misery 2 a loud creaking sound ■ *v* 1 *vt* utter or express with a groan 2 *vi* make a loud creaking sound ○ *The floorboards groaned under their weight.*

gro·cer /grṓssər/ *n* a seller of food and other household goods —**gro·cer·y** *n*

> **ORIGIN** A **grocer** was originally a "wholesaler," literally somebody selling "in gross." The word goes back through French to Latin *grossus*.

gro·cer·ies /grṓssəreez/ *npl* food and other household goods

grog *n* a mixture of rum and water

> **ORIGIN Grog** comes from the nickname (*Old Grogram*) of Admiral Edward Vernon (1684–1757), the British admiral who introduced the practice of watering down the rum that was served to sailors in the Royal Navy. His nick-

name is said to come from his habit of wearing a "**grogram**" cloak. Grogram was a coarse fabric whose name derives from French *gros grain* "coarse grain."

grog·gy /gróggee/ (**-gi·er, -gi·est**) *adj* weak or dizzy —**grog·gi·ly** *adv* —**grog·gi·ness** *n*

groin *n* the area between the thighs and the abdomen

grom·met /grómmət, grúmmət/, **grum·met** /grúmm-/ *n* a protective eyelet, or a ring that reinforces one

groom *n* 1 a bridegroom 2 somebody who cares for horses ■ *v* 1 *vti* clean the fur, skin, or feathers of an animal 2 *vt* neaten or care for the appearance of yourself or somebody else ○ *a well-groomed young man* 3 *vt* train or prepare for a particular position ○ *being groomed for the presidency*

groove *n* 1 a narrow channel in a surface 2 a settled routine (*infml*) —**groove** *vt*

groov·y /grṓovee/ (**-i·er, -i·est**) *adj* excellent or fashionable (*slang dated*) —**groov·i·ly** *adv* —**groov·i·ness** *n*

grope (**groped, grop·ing**) *v* 1 *vi* search by feeling ○ *groping for the light switch* 2 *vi* strive blindly or uncertainly ○ *groping for inspiration* 3 *vt* feel your way, e.g., in the dark 4 *vt* fondle somebody, often roughly or awkwardly (*slang*) —**grope** *n*

Gro·pi·us /grṓpee əss/, **Walter** (1883–1969) German-born US architect and educator

gross /grōss/ *adj* 1 vulgar or coarse 2 flagrantly wrong ○ *gross misconduct* 3 disgusting (*slang*) 4 measured or counted prior to deductions ○ *the gross weight of the shipment* ■ *adv* before or without deductions ○ *paid gross* ■ *adj* extremely overweight (*infml*) (*pl same*) a quantity of 144 2 (*pl* **gross·es**) a gross amount ■ *vt* earn before deductions —**gross·ly** *adv* —**gross·ness** *n*

□ **gross out** *vt* disgust (*slang*)

gross do·mes·tic prod·uct *n* the value of goods and services produced by a country excluding foreign investment income

gross na·tion·al prod·uct *n* the value of goods and services produced by a country including foreign investment income

gro·tesque /grō tésk, grə-/ *adj* 1 strangely distorted ○ *grotesque shadows* 2 bizarre or incongruous —**gro·tesque** *n* —**gro·tesque·ly** *adv* —**gro·tesque·ness** *n*

> **ORIGIN Grotesque** came through French from Italian *grottesca* "like a grotto." The Italian word was applied to wall paintings discovered in excavations of ancient buildings, many of which depicted fantastical human and animal forms interwoven with flowers and foliage.

grot·to /gróttō/ (*pl* **-toes** *or* **-tos**) *n* a natural or imitation cave with interesting features

grouch /growch/ (*infml*) *vi* complain ■ *n* 1 a complaint 2 a habitually complaining or bad-tempered person —**grouch·y** *adj*

ground[1] /grownd/ n 1 the surface of the land 2 earth or soil 3 an area of land used for a specific purpose *(often pl)* ○ *burial ground* 4 an area of knowledge or discussion ○ *Most of the ground had been covered in an earlier lecture.* 5 a reason or foundation *(often pl)* ○ *grounds for believing his story* 6 an electrical connection to the ground for safety ■ **grounds** *npl* 1 land surrounding a building 2 dregs or sediment ■ *v* 1 *vt* teach somebody the basics *(usually passive)* ○ *was well grounded in machine operation* 2 *vt* base an idea, decision, or belief on a strong foundation ○ *a decision that was grounded in personal experience* 3 *vt* connect an electric appliance safely to a ground 4 *vt* prevent a pilot or aircraft from flying 5 *vt* make a child stay at home as a punishment *(infml)* 6 *vti* go or run aground 7 *vt* put something on the ground 8 *vt* hit a ball to the ground ◇ **get off the ground** get started or operating ◇ **hit the ground running** begin to deal with a new situation without delay *(infml)*

ground[2] /grownd/ past participle, past tense of **grind**

ground ball, ground-er /grówndər/ n in baseball, a ball that bounces on the ground or rolls along after it has been hit

ground-break-ing /grównd bràyking/ adj new and innovative —**ground-break-er** n

ground cloth n 1 also **ground-sheet** /grównd sheet/ a waterproof sheet used as a tent floor 2 a waterproof cover protecting a sports field

ground cov-er n dense low-growing plants

ground floor n the floor of a building at street level ◇ **in** or **on the ground floor** involved in something at the earliest stage

ground glass n 1 glass with a roughened surface 2 glass particles. Use: abrasive.

ground-hog /grównd hòg/ n a woodchuck

Ground-hog Day n the day on which woodchuck are said to emerge from hibernation to test the weather. Date: February 2.

ground-keep-er n OCCUPATIONS = **grounds-keeper**

ground-less /grówndləss/ adj not justified or true —**ground-less-ly** adv —**ground-less-ness** n

ground-nut /grównd nùt/ n 1 the edible tuber of a climbing vine 2 *(pl* **ground-nuts** or *same)* a plant that produces groundnuts 3 a peanut

ground plan n a plan of the floor of a building

ground rule n *(often pl)* 1 a fundamental rule 2 in sports, a rule that is specific to a particular place of play

ground-sheet /grównd sheet/ n CAMPING = **ground cloth** 1

grounds-keep-er /grówndz keepər/, **ground-keep-er** /grównd-/ n somebody who maintains a playing field or the grounds of a property —**grounds-keep-ing** n

ground squir-rel n a ground-dwelling burrowing squirrel

ground-swell /grównd swèl/ n 1 a deep wide movement of the ocean 2 a rising general feeling ○ *a groundswell of public opinion*

ground wa-ter n underground water

ground-work /grównd wùrk/ n basic preparatory tasks

ground ze-ro n 1 the point above or below a nuclear explosion 2 the most basic level or starting point ○ *learning programming from ground zero* 3 **Ground Ze-ro** the huge debris field resulting from the terrorist attacks on the World Trade Center towers in New York City on September 11, 2001

group /groop/ n 1 a number of people or things considered or placed together 2 a band of musicians 3 a number of companies under common control ■ *vti* form a group ■ *adj* of or in a group or groups ○ *a group practice* ○ *group activities* —**group-ing** n

group-ie /groópee/ n a highly, often excessively, enthusiastic fan, e.g., of a film star or a popular musician or band *(infml)*

group ther-a-py n psychological treatment involving group sessions for discussing personal problems

⅋ **group-ware** /groóp wàir/ n computer software for use by groups

grouse[1] /growss/ *(pl same)* n a reddish brown ground-dwelling game bird

grouse[2] *(groused, grous-ing)* *vi* complain *(infml)* —**grouse** n ◊ See note at **complain**

grout /growt/ n mortar for filling gaps, especially between tiles ■ *vt* apply grout to

grove /grōv/ n a group or plantation of trees

Grove /grōv/, **Andy** *(b. 1936)* Hungarian-born US technology executive

grov-el /gróv'l, grúv'l/ *vi* 1 behave in a servile way 2 crawl or lie face down on the ground —**grov-el-er** n —**grov-el-ing-ly** adv

grow /grō/ *(grew* /groo/, **grown** /grōn/) *v* 1 *vi* become larger or greater 2 *vti* develop naturally ○ *Plants won't grow in this soil.* ○ *grow a moustache* ○ *grow a garden* 3 *vi* be a product of something ○ *Hatred grew out of mutual ignorance.* 4 *vi* become ○ *The night grew cold.* 5 *vt* develop and expand ○ *an attempt to grow the business* —**grow-er** n

□ **grow into** *vt* grow or develop to fit

□ **grow on** *vt* gradually become more pleasing to ○ *a song that grows on you*

□ **grow out of** *vt* become too big or mature for

□ **grow up** *vi* 1 become an adult 2 behave more maturely

grow-ing pains *npl* 1 pains in the limbs of a child or adolescent 2 early problems

growl /growl/ *vti* 1 make a low hostile sound in the throat 2 speak, say something, or communicate with a growling sound —**growl** n

grown-up adj 1 fully mature 2 for adults ■ n also **grown-up** /grōn ùp/ an adult, or somebody who is an adult and behaves like one

growth /grōth/ n 1 the process of growing 2 an increase 3 something that has grown ○ *three days' growth of beard* 4 a formation of tissue such as a tumor, with no physiological function ■ adj expanding or developing ○ *growth industries*

Groz·ny /gróznee/, **Groz·nyy** capital of Chechnya. Pop. 372,742 (1995).

grub v (grubbed, grub·bing) 1 vt dig something up, especially without proper tools 2 vt remove roots and stumps from the ground 3 vi engage in a search through or under things 4 vi work hard or toil 5 vt scrounge something (*slang*) ■ n 1 a larva 2 food (*infml*)

grub·by /grúbbee/ (-bi·er, -bi·est) adj dirty —**grub·bi·ly** adv —**grub·bi·ness** n ◊ See note at **dirty**

grub·stake /grúb stàyk/ n supplies or money given to a prospector or entrepreneur in return for a share in any future profits ■ vt (-staked, -stak·ing) give a grubstake to —**grub·stak·er** n

grudge n a feeling of resentment ■ vt (grudged, grudg·ing) 1 give something reluctantly 2 envy somebody or something —**grudg·ing** adj —**grudg·ing·ly** adv

gru·el /gróo əl, grool/ n thin weak food

gru·el·ing /gróo əling, gróol-/ adj extremely arduous —**gru·el·ing·ly** adv

grue·some /gróossəm/ adj sickening or horrifying ○ *gruesome photographs of the accident* —**grue·some·ly** adv —**grue·some·ness** n

gruff adj 1 surly 2 sounding rough or harsh —**gruff·ly** adv —**gruff·ness** n

grum·ble /grúmb'l/ (-bled, -bling) vi complain or mutter discontentedly —**grum·ble** n —**grum·bly** adj ◊ See note at **complain**

grump n a bad-tempered or sullen person (*infml*)

grump·y /grúmpee/ (-i·er, -i·est) adj bad-tempered or sullen —**grump·i·ly** adv —**grump·i·ness** n

grunge /grunj/ n rock music with punk and heavy metal elements —**grun·gy** adj

grunt v 1 vi make the noise of a pig 2 vti speak, say something, or communicate in a gruff or inarticulate way ■ n 1 a grunting sound 2 a tropical ocean fish that grunts 3 somebody doing menial tasks (*slang*) 4 a US Army infantryman (*slang*)

grunt·work /grúnt wùrk/ n boring work necessary for the completion of a task (*infml*)

Gru·yère /groo yáir/ n a hard mild Swiss cheese with holes in it

gryph·on n LEGEND = **griffin**

GSA abbr Girl Scouts of America

G-string n a piece of material covering the pubic area

GU abbr Guam

gua·ca·mo·le /gwàakə mólee/ n spiced mashed avocados and tomatoes

Gua·da·la·ja·ra /gwòdd'lə haàrə/ capital of Jalisco State, in west central Mexico. Pop. 1,633,216 (1995).

Gua·dal·ca·nal /gwaàd'lkə nál/ largest of the Solomon Islands, in the SW Pacific Ocean

Gua·de·loupe /gwàdd'l óop/ an overseas department of France consisting of a group of islands in the E Caribbean. Cap. Basse-Terre. Pop. 431,170 (2001).

guage incorrect spelling of **gauge**

Guam /gwaam/ largest of the Mariana Islands, in the NW Pacific Ocean, an unincorporated territory of the United States. Cap. Agana. Pop. 157,557 (2001). —**Gua·ma·ni·an** /gwaa máynee ən/ n, adj

Guang·zhou /gwàang jō/ capital and chief port of **Guangdong Province**, S China. Pop. 4,490,000 (1995).

gua·no /gwáanō/ n 1 the droppings of birds, bats, or seals 2 a fertilizer consisting of guano

Guan·tá·na·mo Bay /gwan taànəmō-/ inlet of the Caribbean Sea in SE Cuba. It is the site of a major US naval base.

gua·ra·ní /gwaarə neé/ (pl -ní or -nís) n the main unit of Paraguayan currency

guar·an·tee /gèrrən teé/ n 1 an assurance that something will happen ○ *no guarantee of success* 2 a promise of quality stating that faulty goods or work will be replaced, repaired, or redone 3 a promise to be responsible for somebody else's debts or obligations ■ vt (-teed) 1 assure or promise something 2 give a guarantee for goods or work 3 accept responsibility for somebody else's debts or obligations

guar·an·tor /gèrrən táwr, gérrəntər/ n somebody who gives a guarantee ◊ See note at **backer**

guar·an·ty /gérrəntee/ (pl -ties) n 1 a guarantee of responsibility for debts or obligations 2 the giving of something as security for a promise, or something so given ◊ See note at **backer**

guard /gaard/ vt 1 watch over to protect somebody or something 2 watch over to prevent the escape of a captive 3 control passage through a means of access ○ *sentries guarding the gates* 4 in basketball, prevent an opponent from scoring or playing effectively ■ n 1 the act or responsibility of guarding 2 somebody who guards 3 a defense ○ *while her guard was down* 4 a ceremonial escort 5 in basketball, a player in a defensive position 6 in football, a lineman positioned next to the center 7 a means of protection ○ *as a guard against inflation* 8 a protective device or cover to prevent injury ◊ See note at **safeguard**

□ **guard against** vt take precautions against

guard dog n a dog used for protection

guard·ed /gaardəd/ adj wary or noncommittal —**guard·ed·ly** adv —**guard·ed·ness** n ◊ See note at **cautious**

guard·house /ga·ard hòwss/ (pl **-houses** /-hòwzoz/) n a military building housing guards and prisoners

guard·i·an /ga·ardee ən/ n 1 a protector 2 somebody legally responsible for another, especially a minor —**guard·i·an·ship** n

guard·i·an an·gel n an angel supposed to look after a particular person

guard of hon·or n a body of troops acting as a ceremonial escort

guard·rail /ga·ard ràyl/ n a safety rail

guard·room /ga·ard ròom, -ròom/ n a room for military guards on duty or for military prisoners

guards·man /ga·ardzmən/ (pl **-men** /-mən/) n a member of the National Guard

Guar·ne·ri /gwaar nérree, -nyérree/ family of Italian violin makers including **Andrea** (1626–98) and his grandson **Giuseppe Antonio** (1687–1745)

~~Guatamala~~ incorrect spelling of **Guatemala**

Gua·te·ma·la /gwaàte maàla/ country in Central America, on the Gulf of Honduras. Cap. Guatemala City. Pop. 12,974,361 (2001). —**Gua·te·ma·lan** adj, n

Gua·te·ma·la Cit·y capital of Guatemala. Pop. 1,167,495 (1995).

gua·va /gwaàva/ n 1 a pear-shaped tropical fruit with red or yellow-green skin. Use: jelly. 2 a tree that produces guavas

gu·ber·na·to·ri·al /gòobərnə tàwree əl/ adj of a governor

guck, gook n an unpleasant substance (infml)

guern·sey /gúrnzee/, **Guern·sey** (pl **-seys**) n a brown-and-white dairy cow

Guern·sey /gúrnzee/ second largest of the Channel Islands, in the English Channel off France. Pop. 64,342 (2001).

guer·ril·la /gə rílla/, **gue·ril·la** n a member of an irregular paramilitary unit, usually politically motivated ◊ See note at **gorilla**

guess /gess/ v 1 vti form an opinion about something without full information o *Guess where I've been.* 2 vt arrive at the correct answer or conclusion by guessing o *I guessed it would be you.* 3 vt think or suppose o *I guess I'll have the steak.* ■ n 1 an opinion formed by guessing 2 an act or result of guessing o *Take another guess.* —**guess·a·ble** adj

guess·ti·mate /géstimət/ n an estimate based on guessing (infml) —**guess·ti·mate** /-màyt/ vti

guess·work /géss wùrk/ n the process or result of guessing

guest /gest/ n 1 a recipient of hospitality 2 a customer of a hotel or restaurant 3 somebody making a special appearance on a show ■ adj 1 appearing as a guest o *a guest star* 2 for guests

guest·house /gést hòws/ (pl **-hous·es** /-hòwzəz/) n a house for visitors

guest of hon·or n an important guest

guest·room /gést ròom, -ròom/ n a bedroom for guests

guest work·er n a nonresident foreign worker

Che Guevara

Gue·va·ra /gə vaàra/, **Che** (1928–67) Argentine-born South American revolutionary leader

guff n nonsense or empty talk (infml)

guf·faw /gə fáw/ vi laugh loudly and raucously —**guf·faw** n

⚡**GUI** abbr graphical user interface

guid·ance /gíd'nss/ n 1 advice 2 leadership 3 electronic flight-control and targeting systems

guide /gīd/ v (**guid·ed, guid·ing**) 1 vti show somebody the way 2 vt direct or steer ■ n 1 somebody or something that guides 2 somebody who leads or supervises a tour 3 also **guide-book** a tourist information book

---

SYNONYMS guide, conduct, direct, lead, steer, usher CORE MEANING: show somebody the way to a place

---

guid·ed mis·sile n a self-propelled missile steered by an electronic guidance system

guide dog n a dog trained to lead a sightless person

guide·line /gíd līn/ n 1 an official recommendation or instruction on the proper action to take 2 a line marking a correct position or route

~~guidence~~ incorrect spelling of **guidance**

guid·ing light n an example and inspiration

guild /gild/ n an association of people with a common trade or interests —**guilds·man** n —**guilds·wo·man** n

---

SPELLCHECK Do not confuse the spelling of **guild** and **gild** ("cover with gold"), which sound similar.

---

guil·der /gíldər/ n 1 the main unit of the former currency of the Netherlands 2 the main unit of currency of Suriname

guild·hall /gíld hàwl/ n a guild's meeting place

guile /gīl/ n cunning and deceitfulness —**guile·ful** adj —**guile·less** adj

guil·le·mot /gíllə mòt/ n a black-and-white diving sea bird

guil·lo·tine /gíllə tèen/ n 1 a machine for beheading people, consisting of a sliding blade in a vertical frame **2** an instrument for cutting sheet metal or paper —**guil·lo·tine** *vt*

ORIGIN The **guillotine** is named for the French physician Joseph-Ignace Guillotin (1738–1814), who suggested it as a more humane means of beheading in 1789, at the beginning of the French Revolution.

guilt /gilt/ *n* **1** the fact of having done wrong **2** awareness of wrongdoing **3** responsibility for wrongdoing **4** legal culpability —**guilt·less** *adj*

SPELLCHECK Do not confuse the spelling of **guilt** and **gilt** ("a thin layer of gold"), which sound similar.

guilt·y /gíltee/ (**-i·er, -i·est**) *adj* **1** responsible for a crime or wrongdoing **2** ashamed of wrongdoing **3** showing, suggesting, or causing guilt *o a guilty look* —**guilt·i·ly** *adv*

Guin·ea /gínnee/ country in West Africa, on the Atlantic coast. Cap. Conakry. Pop. 7,613,870 (2001). —**Guin·e·an** *adj, n*

Guin·ea-Bis·sau /gínnee bi sów/ country in West Africa, on the Atlantic coast. Cap. Bissau. Pop. 1,315,822 (2001).

guin·ea fowl *n* a plump short-tailed bird with speckled plumage. Use: food.

guin·ea pig *n* **1** a plump tailless rodent kept as a pet **2** somebody or something used as the subject of an experiment or test

Guin·e·vere /gwínni veer/ *n* legendary English queen, wife of King Arthur

Guin·ness /gínnəss/, **Sir Alec** (1914–2000) British actor

guise /gīz/ *n* **1** a deceptive outward appearance **2** a different form or appearance *o old ideas in a new guise*

gui·tar /gi taár/ *n* a stringed instrument with a long neck and flat body, played by plucking or strumming —**gui·tar·ist** *n*

Gui·yang /gwày yáng/ capital of **Guizhou Province**, S China. Pop. 1,930,000 (1995).

gu·lag /gớo laàg/ *n* a political prison or labor camp in the former Soviet Union, or a network of such prisons or camps

ORIGIN Gulag is a Russian acronym formed from letters of *Glavnoe upravlenie ispravitelno-trudovykh lagerie* "Chief administration for corrective labor camps."

gulch *n* a ravine

gulf *n* **1** a large inlet of a sea (*often in place names*) **2** a deep wide hole **3** a vast difference dividing people or groups

Gulf States *n* **1** the oil-producing countries bordering the Persian Gulf **2** the US states bordering the Gulf of Mexico

Gulf Stream *n* a warm current of the Atlantic Ocean, flowing northeast from the Gulf of Mexico along the coast of North America, then east to the British Isles

Gulf War *n* **1** a war (1991) in the Persian Gulf between US-led coalition forces and Iraq, following Iraq's invasion (1990) of Kuwait **2** = **Iran-Iraq War**

Gulf War syn·drome *n* varied symptoms including respiratory distress, rashes, and nausea experienced by some troops who served in the 1991 Gulf War

gulf·weed /gúlf weèd/ *n* floating brown seaweed

gull[1] *n* a common white-and-gray sea bird

gull[2] *vt* deceive ■ *n* a gullible person

Gul·lah /gúllə/ (*pl* **-lahs** *or same*) *n* **1** a people of African ancestry living on the coasts of North and South Carolina, Georgia, and N Florida **2** the Creole language spoken by the Gullah people —**Gul·lah** *adj*

gul·let /gúllət/ *n* the esophagus or throat

gul·li·ble /gúlləb'l/ *adj* easily deceived —**gul·li·bil·i·ty** /gùllə bíllətee/ *n*

gul·ly /gúllee/ (*pl* **-lies**) *n* a deep narrow ditch cut by water —**gul·ly** *vti*

gulp *v* **1** *vt* swallow hurriedly or in large mouthfuls **2** *vi* make a swallowing motion or sound, e.g., in fear —**gulp** *n*

gum[1] *n* **1** a sticky plant substance, especially one that hardens **2** a glue used for sticking paper **3** a tree that produces gum **4** chewing gum (*infml*) ■ *vt* (**gummed, gum·ming**) stick something to something else —**gum·my** *adj*

□ **gum up** *vt* obstruct, seal, or immobilize with or as if with a sticky substance

gum[2] *n* the flesh around the teeth (*often pl*)

gum a·ra·bic *n* a sticky substance from some acacia trees. Use: adhesives, confectionery, medicine.

gum·ball /gúm bàwl/ *n* a ball of candy-coated chewing gum

gum·bo /gúm bò/ (*pl* **-bos**) *n* **1** a stew thickened with okra **2** okra **3** sticky river soil **4** **Gum·bo** a French patois

ORIGIN Gumbo comes from a Louisiana French word of African origin, probably from a Bantu language.

gum·boil /gúm bòyl/ *n* a mouth abscess on the gum

gum boot *n* a heavy waterproof boot

gum·drop /gúm dròp/ *n* a chewy fruit-flavored candy

gump·tion /gúmpsh'n/ *n* common sense (*infml*)

gum·shoe /gúm shòo/ *n* a detective (*infml*)

gum tree *n* a tree that produces gum

gun *n* **1** a weapon that fires bullets or other projectiles **2** a device that forces something out under pressure *o a paint gun* ■ *vt* (**gunned, gun·ning**) rev up an engine (*infml*) ◊ **go great guns** do something at great speed or very effectively ◊ **jump the gun** act prematurely ◊ **stick to your guns** refuse to change your plans or opinions

ORIGIN Gun probably comes from a form of

the Scandinavian woman's name *Gunnhildr*, which is a compound of *gunnr* "battle" and *hildr* "war." It has not been uncommon throughout history for weapons to be given women's names.

□ **gun down** *vt* shoot and kill or severely injure (*infml*)

□ **gun for** *vt* (*infml*) **1** set out to attack or criticize **2** intend to get for yourself

gun·boat /gún bòt/ *n* a small ship with guns mounted on it

gun·boat di·plo·ma·cy *n* diplomacy between nations, with one nation using the threat of attack

gun dog *n* a dog of a breed trained to retrieve shot game

gun·fight /gún fìt/ *n* a fight between people with guns —**gun·fight·er** *n*

gun·fire /gún fìr/ *n* shots from a gun or guns

gung ho /gúng hò/ *adj* very enthusiastic (*infml*)

gun·man /gúnmən/ (*pl* -**men** /-mən/) *n* somebody armed with a gun, especially a criminal or assassin

gun·met·al /gún mètt'l/ *n* **1** a dark gray bronze. Use: formerly, cannon manufacture. **2** a dark gray alloy. Use: formerly, household and industrial items, toys.

gun·nel /gún'l/ *n* NAUT = **gunwale**

gun·ner /gúnnər/ *n* a soldier who fires a large gun

gun·ner·y /gúnnəree/ *n* **1** the science of guns and their design, construction, and use **2** the use of guns

gun·ny /gúnnee/ *n* coarse jute or hemp cloth. Use: sacks.

gun·play /gún plày/ *n* the shooting of guns

gun·point /gún pòynt/ ◇ **at gunpoint** under the threat of being shot and killed if orders are not obeyed

gun·pow·der /gún pòwdər/ *n* an explosive powder. Use: fireworks and other explosives, charge in some firearms.

gun·run·ning /gún rùnning/ *n* the smuggling of guns —**gun·run·ner** *n*

gun·ship /gún shìp/ *n* an aircraft with guns mounted on it

gun·shot /gún shòt/ *n* **1** the sound of a gun being fired **2** bullets or shot fired from a gun

gun·shy *adj* **1** timid or wary **2** afraid of guns or their noise

gun·sling·er /gún slìngər/ *n* an armed fighter or criminal, especially in frontier days (*infml*) —**gun·sling·ing** *n*

gun·smith /gún smìth/ *n* a maker, seller, or repairer of guns

gun·wale /gúnn'l/, **gun·nel** /gún'l/ *n* the top edge of a ship's sides above the deck (*often pl*)

ORIGIN The **gunwale** gets its name because it was used in the past to support guns. *Wales*

are the timbers forming the outside of a wooden ship.

gup·py /gúppee/ (*pl* -**pies**) *n* a small brightly colored freshwater fish

ORIGIN The **guppy** is named for the Reverend R. J. Lechmere Guppy (1836–1916), who sent the first specimen from Trinidad to the British Museum.

gur·gle /gúrg'l/ (-**gled**, -**gling**) *v* **1** *vi* make a bubbling noise (*refers to flowing liquid*) **2** *vti* make a noise or say something with a bubbling sound in the throat —**gur·gle** *n*

gur·ney /gúrnee/ (*pl* -**neys**) *n* a wheeled hospital stretcher

gu·ru /goo roo/ (*pl* -**rus**) *n* **1** a prominent or influential leader, founder, or teacher ○ *a management guru* **2** a spiritual leader or intellectual guide **3** a Hindu or Sikh religious teacher

Gu·ru Na·nak /goo roo naának/ ♦ **Nanak**

Gu·ru Na·nak Ja·nan·ti /-jə naántee/ *n* a Sikh festival marking the birthday of Guru Nanak. Date: November.

gush *vti* **1** flow or cause to flow out fast and in large quantities **2** speak, behave, or say something effusively —**gush** *n* —**gush·ing** *adj*

gush·er /gúshər/ *n* **1** a free-flowing oil well **2** an effusive person

gush·y /gúshee/ (-**i·er**, -**i·est**) *adj* overly enthusiastic or emotional —**gush·i·ly** *adv*

gus·set /gússət/ *n* a piece of fabric inserted for reinforcement or expansion

gus·sy /gússee/ (-**sied**, -**sies**) □ **gussy up** *vt* dress or decorate fancily (*infml*)

gust *n* a sudden rush of wind ■ *vi* blow in gusts —**gust·y** *adj*

gus·to /gústō/ *n* hearty enjoyment

gut *n* **1** the alimentary canal, or part of it **2** a tough fine cord made from animal intestines or a similar material **3** the place where instincts are felt ○ *a gut reaction* ■ **guts** *npl* **1** the intestines **2** inner or central parts, e.g., the workings of a machine **3** courage (*slang*) ■ *vt* (**gut·ted**, **gut·ting**) **1** remove the insides of an animal **2** destroy the interior of a building **3** make something ineffective

Gu·ten·berg /goot'n bùrg/, **Johannes** (1400?–68) German printer. He is credited with the invention of movable type.

Guth·rie /gúthree/, **Woody** (1912–67) US folk singer and composer

gut·less /gútləss/ *adj* lacking courage and determination ◇ See note at **cowardly**

guts·y /gútsee/ (-**i·er**, -**i·est**) *adj* courageous (*infml*) —**guts·i·ly** *adv* —**guts·i·ness** *n*

gut·ter /gúttər/ *n* **1** a rainwater channel on a roof **2** a drainage channel at the edge of a road **3** a poor or degraded way of life **4** a channel at the side of a bowling lane ■ *vi* **1** melt quickly (*refers to candles*) **2** flicker on the point of being extinguished *(refers to burning flames)*

~~**gutteral**~~ incorrect spelling of **guttural**

gut·ter·snipe /gúttər snīp/ *n* a dirty ragged child who lives on the streets *(dated insult)*

gut·tur·al /gúttərəl/ *adj* **1** characterized by harsh or throaty speech sounds **2** pronounced with the tongue near the soft palate

guy[1] /gī/ *(infml)* *n* a man ■ **guys** *npl* people of either sex ○ *How long have you guys been waiting?*

ORIGIN Guy is from the name of Guy Fawkes (1570–1606), one of a group of Roman Catholic conspirators who planned to blow up the British Houses of Parliament in 1605. He was hanged, and effigies of him have traditionally been burned in Britain on or around November 5. The name **guy** was originally applied to these effigies, in the early 19C. In the mid-19C the word is also recorded with the sense "grotesquely dressed person." As simply a term for a "man" or "person," **guy** began its life at the end of the 19C in the United States.

guy[2] /gī/ *n* a rope or wire tightened to support something such as a tent ■ *vt* support with guys

Guy·a·na /gee ánnə, -áanə/ country in South America, on the North Atlantic coast. Cap. Georgetown. Pop. 697,181 (2001). —**Guy·a·nese** /gī ə neéz/ *adj, n*

guz·zle /gúzz'l/ *(-zled, -zling)* *vti* drink or consume something greedily *(infml)* —**guz·zler** *n*

Gya·nen·dra /gya néndrə/ *(b. 1947)* king of Nepal (2001–)

gym /jim/ *n (infml)* **1** a gymnasium **2** physical education

gym·kha·na /jim káanə/ *n* a sporting contest

ORIGIN Gymkhana comes from an Urdu word meaning "racket court," literally "ball court." The first part of the English word has been assimilated to *gymnasium* and related forms. It began in British India in the mid-19C, referring to a public place with facilities for athletics, and later to an athletics display.

gym·na·si·um /jim náyzee əm/ *(pl* **-ums** *or* **-a** /-zee ə/) *n* **1** a large room equipped for physical exercise **2** a European academic secondary school

ORIGIN Gymnasium derives ultimately from Greek *gumnos* "naked." Exercising naked was the custom in ancient Greece. The English noun comes immediately from Latin, where it meant "school."

gym·nas·tics /jim nástiks/ *n (+ sing verb)* **1** physical training intended to develop agility and strength using exercises and equipment **2** gymnastics performed as a competitive sport or for display ■ *npl* actions demonstrating agility and skill *(+ pl verb)* ○ *verbal gymnastics* —**gym·nast** /jim nast/ *n* —**gym·nas·tic** *adj* —**gym·nas·ti·cal·ly** *adv*

gym·no·sperm /jímnə spùrm/ *n* any woody cone-bearing plant —**gym·no·sper·mous** /jímnə spúrməss/ *adj*

gy·ne·col·o·gy /gīnə kólləjee/ *n* the branch of medicine that deals with women's health, especially with the health of women's reproductive organs —**gy·ne·co·log·i·cal** /gīnəkə lójjik'l/ *adj* —**gy·ne·col·o·gist** *n*

gyp /jip/, **gip** *(infml)* *vt* (**gypped, gyp·ping**; **gipped, gip·ping**) cheat *(sometimes offensive)* ■ *n* a swindle *(sometimes offensive)*

ORIGIN The origin of **gyp** is not known for certain, but it has popularly been associated with *Gypsy*, and so regarded as a slur on Roma people.

gyp·sum /jípsəm/ *n* a white mineral of hydrated calcium sulfate. Use: cement, plaster, fertilizers.

gyp·sy /jípsee/ *(pl* **-sies**) *n* **1** somebody with a nomadic lifestyle *(infml; sometimes offensive)* **2** **Gyp·sy, Gip·sy** an offensive term for a member of the Roma people

gy·rate /jī ráyt/ *(-rat·ed, -rat·ing)* *vi* move in a circle or spiral, especially around a fixed central point —**gy·ra·tion** /jī ráysh'n/ *n*

gy·ro /jī rō, jeé-/ *(pl* **-ros**) *n* a pita sandwich with ground or sliced lamb, tomato, and onion

gy·ro·scope /jī́rə skōp/ *n* a self-stabilizing device consisting of a rotating wheel inside a circular frame. Use: compasses and other navigational aids, stabilizing mechanisms on ships and aircraft. —**gy·ro·scop·ic** /jī́rə skóppik/ *adj*

H

h *(pl* **h's**), **H** *(pl* **H's** *or* **Hs**) *n* the 8th letter of the English alphabet

H *symbol* **1** henry **2** hydrogen

h. *abbr* **1** harbor **2** height **3** *also* **H.** high

ha[1], **hah** *interj* **1** expresses various emotions such as surprise or triumph **2** indicates the sound of laughter

ha[2] *symbol* hectare

Haar·lem /haárləm/ city in W Netherlands. Pop. 148,772 (2000).

Ha·bak·kuk /hábbə kòòk, hə bákək/ *n* a book of the Bible, traditionally attributed to Habakkuk, a Hebrew priest

ha·be·as cor·pus /háybee əss káwrpəss/ *n* a

writ ordering a detained person to be brought into court

ORIGIN Habeas corpus means "you may have the body" in Latin. These are the first words of the writ.

hab·er·dash·er /hábbər dàshər/ *n* a dealer in men's clothing

ORIGIN Haberdasher seems to go back ultimately to an old French word *hapertas*, whose meaning is unclear. It could be the name of a fabric, or mean "piece of cloth," or "small goods." A **haberdasher** was originally a dealer in any small household articles, then from the 16C to the 18C usually a dealer in hats and caps.

hab·er·dash·er·y /hábbər dàshəree/ (*pl* **-ies**) *n* **1** goods sold by a haberdasher **2** a haberdasher's store or department

~~habeus corpus~~ incorrect spelling of **habeas corpus**

hab·it /hábbit/ *n* **1** a behavior pattern or regular repetitive action **2** an addiction (*slang*) **3** a long loose gown worn by monks and nuns **4** a characteristic appearance or growth pattern **5** an attitude or disposition

SYNONYMS habit, custom, tradition, practice, routine, wont CORE MEANING: established pattern of behavior

hab·it·a·ble /hábbitəb'l/ *adj* fit to live in —**hab·it·a·bil·i·ty** /hàbbitə bíllətee/ *n*

hab·i·tat /hábbi tàt/ *n* **1** the natural environment in which a plant or animal lives **2** the place where somebody or something is usually found

hab·i·ta·tion /hàbbi táysh'n/ *n* **1** the act of inhabiting **2** a place in which to live

hab·it-form·ing *adj* causing dependence and continued use ○ *habit-forming drugs*

ha·bit·u·al /hə bíchoo əl/ *adj* **1** done regularly or as a habit **2** persisting in doing something because of a tendency or desire ○ *a habitual criminal* —**ha·bit·u·al·ly** *adv* ◊ See note at **usual**

ha·bit·u·ate /hə bíchoo àyt/ (**-at·ed, -at·ing**) *vt* make somebody used to something (*fml*) ○ *People living in cities become habituated to crowds.*

ha·bit·u·é /hə bíchoo ày, hə bíchoo áy/ (*pl* **-bi·tu·és**) *n* a frequent visitor

ha·ci·en·da /hàassee éndə, hàssee-/ *n* **1** a large estate in a Spanish-speaking country **2** a house on a hacienda

⚡**hack¹** *v* **1** *vti* cut something using repeated rough or heavy blows **2** *vt* cut or divide something roughly or carelessly (*infml*) ○ *hacked a whole chunk off the article I wrote* **3** *vi* gain access to or manipulate a computer system, especially without authority **4** *vt* cope with a difficult or unpleasant situation (*infml*) **5** *vi* make a harsh dry coughing

noise ■ *n* **1** a quick chop **2** a harsh dry coughing noise

hack² *n* **1** a loyal political party worker (*disapproving*) **2** *also* **hack·ie** a taxicab driver (*infml*) **3** a mediocre worker (*disapproving*) **4** a hired writer (*disapproving*) **5** a car or carriage for hire **6** an old or worn-out horse ■ *adj* hackneyed ■ *vt* make an expression stale through overuse

ORIGIN Hack here is a shortening of *hackney*. **Hack** "cut" is of Germanic origin.

⚡**hack·er** /hákər/ *n* **1** somebody who gains unauthorized access to a computer system **2** a computer enthusiast **3** an enthusiastic amateur sportsperson

hack·ney /háknee/ *n* **1** a carriage or automobile for hire **2** a horse for riding or driving ■ *adj also* **hack·neyed** trite or unoriginal —**hack·ney·ism** *n*

ORIGIN Hackney is recorded from the medieval period, and probably derives from the name of what was then a village on the outskirts of London, England, where horses were reared and pastured. A **hackney** was originally a horse for ordinary riding, often one kept for hire, and the common condition of such horses gave rise to connotations of overuse.

hack·saw /hák sàw/ *n* a saw for cutting metal —**hack·saw** *vt*

⚡**hack·tiv·ism** /háktəv ìzzəm/ *n* political activism involving the use or sabotage of computer networks —**hack·tiv·ist** *n, adj*

had past tense, past participle of **have**

had·dock /háddək/ (*pl same or* **-docks**) *n* **1** an ocean fish related to but smaller than the cod **2** haddock as food

Ha·des /háy deèz/ *n* **1** *also* **ha·des** hell (*infml*) **2** in Greek mythology, the underworld. Roman equivalent **Dis 3** in Greek mythology, the god of the underworld. Roman equivalent **Pluto** **1** —**Had·e·an** *adj*

Ha·dith /hə deéth/, **ha·dith** *n* the collected traditions, teachings, and stories of the prophet Muhammad

hadj *n* ISLAM = **hajj**

hadj·i *n* ISLAM = **hajji**

had·n't /hád'nt/ *contr* had not

Ha·dri·an /háydree ən/ (76–138) Roman emperor (117–138)

had·ron /háddrən, hád ròn/ *n* an elementary particle that reacts strongly with other particles

had·ro·saur /háddrə sàwr/ *n* an amphibious plant-eating dinosaur with a snout resembling a duck's bill and strong hind legs

haf·ni·um /háfnee əm/ *n* (*symbol* **Hf**) a silvery metallic chemical element. Use: nuclear reactor rods, tungsten filaments.

hag *n* **1** an offensive term for a woman of advanced years considered unattractive or spiteful (*slang*) **2** a witch —**hag·gish** *adj*

Hag·ga·i /há gī, hággee ĭ/ *n* a book of the Bible that tells the story of the rebuilding of the Israelites' temple after their return to Jerusalem from exile in Babylon, traditionally attributed to Haggai, a Hebrew prophet

hag·gard /hággərd/ *adj* showing on the face signs of fatigue, anxiety, or hunger —**hag·gard·ly** *adv* —**hag·gard·ness** *n*

hag·gle /hágg'l/ (**-gled, -gling**) *vi* bargain or argue over something such as a price or a contract —**hag·gle** *n* —**hag·gler** *n*

hag·i·og·ra·phy /hàggee óggrəfee, hàyjee-/ (*pl* **-phies**) *n* **1** biography dealing with the lives of saints **2** a biography that shows undue reverence —**hag·i·og·raph·er** *n*

hah *interj* = ha¹

ha-ha /haà haá/ *interj* indicates the sound of laughter

Hahn /haan/, **Otto** (1879–1968) German physical chemist. He was awarded the Nobel Prize in chemistry in 1944 for his work on nuclear fission.

hah·ni·um /haànee əm/ *n* (*symbol* **Hn**) dubnium or hassium

Hai·da /hídə/ (*pl* same or **-das**) *n* **1** a member of a Native North American people living along and off the coast of British Columbia and the adjoining Alaskan coast **2** the language of the Haida people —**Hai·da** *adj* —**Hai·dan** *adj*

Hai·fa /hífə/ chief seaport of Israel, in the north of the country. Pop. 265,700 (1999).

hai·ku /hí kòò/ (*pl* same) *n* a 3-line Japanese poem containing 17 syllables altogether

hail¹ /hayl/ *n* **1** pellets of ice that fall like rain **2** a barrage of something unpleasant or harmful ○ *a hail of missiles* —**hail** *vi*

hail² /hayl/ *vt* **1** greet somebody **2** offer praise **3** call or signal something or somebody ○ *hail a taxi* —**hail** *n* —**hail·er** *n*
☐ **hail from** *vt* come from a particular place

hail-fel·low-well-met, **hail-fel·low** *adj* exuberantly or excessively friendly

Hail Mar·y (*pl* **Hail Mar·ys**) *n* a Christian prayer invoking the Virgin Mary's intercession

hail·stone /háyl stòn/ *n* a pellet of hail

hail·storm /háyl stàwrm/ *n* a storm with hail

Hai·phong /hí fóng/ port in N Vietnam, on the Red River delta. Pop. 783,133 (1992).

hair /hair/ *n* **1** the strands growing on the head or body **2** a single strand of hair **3** a growth on a plant resembling a hair **4** a tiny amount or degree ○ *won by a hair* ◇ **let your hair down** behave in a more relaxed way than usual (*infml*) ◇ **split hairs** argue about fine distinctions —**hair·less** *adj*

SPELLCHECK Do not confuse the spelling of **hair** and **hare** (the animal), which sound similar.

~~hair-brained~~ incorrect spelling of **harebrained**

hair·brush /háir brùsh/ *n* a brush for the hair

hair·cut /háir kùt/ *n* **1** a cutting of somebody's hair **2** the way somebody's hair is cut —**hair·cut·ter** *n* —**hair·cut·ting** *n, adj*

hair·do /háir dòò/ (*pl* **-dos**) *n* a hairstyle

hair·dress·er /háir drèssər/ *n* **1** somebody whose work is cutting and styling hair **2** a hairdresser's place of business —**hair·dress·ing** *n*

hair·line /háir lìn/ *n* **1** the line on the top of the forehead behind which hair grows **2** a very thin line

hair·net /háir nèt/ *n* a circle of netting worn to hold the hair in place

hair·piece /háir pèess/ *n* a toupee or bunch of false hair

hair·pin /háir pìn/ *n* **1** a U-shaped wire used to hold the hair in place **2** a sharp bend in a road

hair-rais·ing *adj* terrifying or thrilling —**hair-rais·er** *n*

hairs·breadth /háirz brèdth/, **hair's-breadth** *n* a very small margin

hair shirt *n* a shirt made from scratchy material, formerly worn by religious people, as a means of self-punishment

hair·split·ting /háir splìtting/ *n* excessive attention to unimportant details —**hair·split·ting** *adj*

hair spray *n* a spray used to hold a hairstyle in place

hair·style /háir stìl/ *n* the way somebody's hair is cut, styled, or arranged —**hair·styl·ing** *n* —**hair·styl·ist** *n*

hair trig·ger *n* **1** a very sensitive gun trigger **2** a very quick response —**hair-trig·ger** *adj*

hair weave *n* false hair interwoven with somebody's own hair —**hair-weave** *vt* —**hair-weav·ing** *n*

hair·y /háiree/ (**-i·er, -i·est**) *adj* **1** covered with hair **2** made of or resembling hair **3** frightening (*infml*) —**hair·i·ness** *n*

Hai·ti /háytee/ country in the N Caribbean, occupying the western third of the island of Hispaniola. Cap. Port-au-Prince. Pop. 6,964,549 (2001). —**Hai·tian** /háysh'n/ *n, adj*

hajj, hadj, haj *n* a pilgrimage to Mecca

haj·ji /hájjee/, **hadj·i** *n* a Muslim who has made a pilgrimage to Mecca

hake (*pl* same or **hakes**) *n* **1** an ocean fish resembling the cod, with two dorsal fins and an elongated body **2** hake as food

ha·kim /haà kéem/, **ha·keem** *n* **1** a Muslim doctor **2** a Muslim judge

ha·ku /haà kòò/ *n* Hawaii a crown of flowers

ha·lal /hə laàl/ *adj* describes meat from animals slaughtered according to Islamic law ■ *n* halal meat ■ *vt* (**-lalled, -lal·ling**) slaughter animals in the Islamic way

hal·cy·on days /hálsee ən-/ *npl* a tranquil happy time *(literary)*

ORIGIN The first word of **halcyon days** derives from the Greek for "kingfisher." In Greek mythology, the halcyon was a bird resembling the kingfisher with the power to calm the waves at the time of the winter solstice when it nested at sea. **Halcyon days** originally referred to two weeks of calm weather around this time.

hale[1] (**hal·er**, **hal·est**) *adj* fit and strong —**hale·ness** *n*

hale[2] (**haled**, **hal·ing**) *vt* make somebody go somewhere *(fml)*

Hale, Edward Everett (1822–1909) US cleric and writer

Hale, Nathan (1755–76) American Revolutionary hero

half /haf/ *n* (*pl* **halves** /havz/), *adj*, *pron* each of two equal parts into which a whole is or can be divided ■ *n* in sports, either of two periods into which playing time is divided ■ *adj*, *adv* **1** partial or partially ○ *a half-smile* **2** in equal parts ○ *He's half French and half Spanish.* ◇ **by half** to an excessive extent ○ *She's too friendly by half.* ◇ **not half** not at all ○ *Mmm! This cake's not half bad!*

half-and-half *n* **1** a dairy product for coffee **2** a mixture of two things in equal parts ■ *adj* containing half each of two things ■ *adv* in two equal portions

half·back /haf bàk/ *n* **1** in football, an attacking player positioned behind the front line **2** in some team sports, a player positioned in front of the last defensive line

half-baked *adj* poorly thought out *(infml)*

half-breed, half-caste *n* an offensive term for a person of mixed racial parentage *(insult)*

half broth·er *n* a brother with only one parent in common with another

half-cocked *adj* with inadequate planning or preparation

half-day *n* half a regular workday, especially when taken as vacation time

half-dol·lar *n* a US coin worth 50 cents

half-heart·ed *adj* feeling or showing little enthusiasm —**half-heart·ed·ly** *adv* —**half-heart·ed·ness** *n*

half-hour *n* **1** a period of 30 minutes **2** a point in time 30 minutes after the hour ○ *chiming on the hour and half-hour* —**half-hour·ly** *adv*, *adj*

half-life *n* **1** (*symbol* $T_\frac{1}{2}$) the time it takes a substance to lose half its radioactivity through decay **2** the time it takes for half an amount of something such as a drug to be removed from living tissue

half-mast, half-staff *n* the position to which a flag is lowered as a sign of mourning

half note *n* a note with half of the time value of a whole note

half-price *adj*, *adv* at half the usual price

half sis·ter *n* a sister with only one parent in common with another

half step, half tone *n* a semitone

half·time /háf tīm/ *n* a rest period halfway through a game

half·tone /háf tòn/ *n* **1** an intermediate shade of brightness or darkness, e.g., in a photograph **2** a process for reproducing shading in print

half-truth *n* a misleadingly incomplete statement

half·way /haf wáy, háf wày/ *adv*, *adj* **1** at or to the middle point between two things **2** only partial or partially

half·way house *n* **1** a rehabilitation center **2** a point or stopping place halfway through a long journey

half-wit /haf wit/ *n* an offensive term for a person regarded as foolish or stupid *(insult)*

hal·i·but /hálləbət/ (*pl* **-buts** or **same**) *n* **1** a large ocean flatfish **2** halibut as food

ORIGIN The **halibut** is literally a "holy flatfish." It was commonly eaten on holy days.

Hal·i·fax /hálli fàks/ capital of Nova Scotia, Canada. Pop. 113,910 (1996).

hal·i·to·sis /hálli tóssiss/ *n* bad breath

hall *n* **1** a corridor **2** an entrance room **3** a building with a large public room **4** a large room where people gather, e.g., for dining **5** a large country house **6** a campus building

hal·le·lu·jah /hàllə looyə/, **al·le·lu·ia** /àllə-/ *interj* **1** expresses praise to God **2** expresses relief —**hal·le·lu·jah** *n*

Hal·ley /hállee/, **Edmond** (1656–1742) British astronomer

hall·mark /háwl màark/ *n* **1** a mark of quality, especially on an object made of a precious metal **2** a distinguishing mark —**hall·mark** *vt*

ORIGIN The "hall" in **hallmark** is Goldsmiths' Hall in London, England, where the Goldsmiths' Company assayed and stamped gold and silver articles.

hall of fame *n* a museum dedicated to famous people in a given sphere of activity

Hal·low·een /hàllə wéen/, **Hal·low·e'en** *n* the night of October 31, the eve of All Saints' Day

hal·lu·ci·nate /hə lōoss'n àyt/ (-nat·ed, -nat·ing) *vti* imagine seeing or hearing somebody or something —**hal·lu·ci·na·tive** *adj* —**hal·lu·ci·na·to·ry** /hə lōoss'nə tàwree/ *adj*

hal·lu·ci·na·tion /hə lōoss'n áysh'n/ *n* **1** the act of hallucinating **2** a false perception sometimes caused by a psychiatric disorder or by drugs *(often pl)*

hal·lu·cin·o·gen /hə lōoss'nəjən/ *n* a drug that induces hallucinations —**hal·lu·cin·o·gen·ic** /hə lōoss'nə jénnik/ *adj*

hall·way /háwl wày/ n an entrance hall or corridor

ha·lo /háylō/ n (pl **-loes** or **-los**) **1** a circle of light around a saint's head in religious art **2** a circle of light around the Moon or Sun ■ vt (**-loed, -los**) surround with a halo

hal·o·gen /hállajan/ n any of the five electronegative chemical elements, fluorine, chlorine, iodine, bromine, or astatine ■ adj describes a light or heat source containing halogen vapor o a halogen bulb

Hals /haalss/, **Frans** (1580?–1666) Flemish-born Dutch painter

Hal·sey /háwlzee/, **William F.** (1882–1959) US naval officer

halt¹ n a temporary stop ■ interj commands somebody to stop ■ vti stop

halt² vi act hesitantly

hal·ter /háwltar/ n **1** a rope or leather device put over an animal's head and used to lead it **2** a woman's top that leaves the back and shoulders bare —**hal·ter** vt

halter neck n a garment with a halter neck —**hal·ter-neck** adj

halt·ing /háwlting/ adj hesitant o halting speech —**halt·ing·ly** adv

halve /hav/ (**halved, halv·ing**) v **1** vt divide into two equal parts **2** vti reduce or be reduced by half

halves plural of **half**

ham¹ n **1** cured meat from a hog's thigh **2** a hog's thigh **3** the back of somebody's upper leg

ham² n a performer who overacts ■ vti (**hammed, ham·ming**) overact —**ham** adj —**ham·my** adj

---

ORIGIN A **ham** actor was probably a hamfatter. This is a US slang term for an inexpert performer. Its origin is not certain, but it may represent an alteration of amateur, or it may have been inspired by a song, "The Ham-fat Man."

---

ham³ n an amateur radio operator

Ha·mas /hám àss/ n a fundamentalist Islamic Palestinian organization supporting resistance to Israel in the Israeli-occupied territories

Ham·burg /hám bùrg/ city in north central Germany. Pop. 1,705,872 (1997).

ham·burg·er /hám bùrgar/ n **1** ground beef **2** a flat patty of ground meat **3** a grilled or fried hamburger served in a bun

---

ORIGIN The **hamburger** was originally more fully a Hamburger steak (or Hamburg steak), and is named for Hamburg in Germany. It was first recorded in the 1880s in the United States.

---

ham-hand·ed, ham-fist·ed adj clumsy (infml)

Ham·il·ton /hámm'ltən/ **1** capital of Bermuda. Pop. 1,000 (1990 estimate). **2** city in SE Ontario, Canada, at the western end of Lake Ontario. Pop. 650,400 (1996).

Ham·il·ton, Alexander (1757–1804) Caribbean-born US politician and secretary of the treasury (1789–95). He was killed in a duel with his political rival Aaron Burr.

ham·let /hámmlət/ n a small village or group of houses

Ham·mar·skjöld /hámmər shòld/, **Dag** (1905–61) Swedish diplomat, secretary-general of the United Nations (1953–61)

ham·mer /hámmər/ n **1** a hand tool with a heavy head for pounding or driving in nails **2** a powered mechanical striking tool **3** a part that strikes something else, e.g., in a piano or gun ■ vti pound or drive something in with or as if with a hammer
□ **hammer away at** vt work hard at

Ham·mer, Armand (1898–1990) US industrialist, art collector, and philanthropist

Ham·mer·stein /hámmər stìn/, **Oscar II** (1895–1960) US librettist

Ham·mett, Dashiell (1894–1961) US writer

ham·mock /hámmək/ n a simple hanging bed suspended at both ends

ham·per¹ /hámpər/ vt prevent the free movement or action of ◊ See note at **hinder**

ham·per² /hámpər/ n **1** a large basket for carrying food, e.g., for a picnic **2** a large basket for laundry

Hamp·ton /hámptən/ port in SE Virginia. Pop. 136,968 (1998).

Hampton Roads deep-water channel in SE Virginia at the point where the James, Nansemond, and Elizabeth rivers empty into Chesapeake Bay

ham·ster /hámstər/ n **1** a small rodent with cheek pouches and a short tail **2** a cordless computer mouse

ham·string /hám strìng/ n **1** either of two tendons at the back of the knee **2** a muscle at the back of the thigh ■ vt (**-strung** /-strùng/) **1** cut the hamstring of **2** make powerless or ineffective o hamstrung by lack of funds

Han·cock /hán kòk/, **John** (1737–93) US patriot and the first person to sign the Declaration of Independence (1776)

hand n **1** the part at the end of the human arm below the wrist **2** an animal part corresponding to the human hand **3** a pointer on a clock or dial **4** a player's cards **5** in a card game, a round **6** a part in doing something o Who else had a hand in this? **7** help or assistance o Give me a hand. **8** a round of applause **9** possession or power o Your future is in your own hands. **10** a member of a ship's crew **11** somebody with a particular level of competence or experience o I'm an old hand at this. **12** a manual worker o a ranch hand **13** handwriting ■ vt **1** pass by hand **2** lead by the hand ◊ **at hand 1** nearby **2** about to happen ◊ **be hand in glove** cooperate, usually for a secret or illegal purpose ◊ **change hands** pass to a different owner ◊ **force somebody's hand** pressure somebody to do something against his or her will or earlier than planned ◊ **(from) hand to mouth** with barely enough to live on ◊ **in hand** under control ◊ **on hand** near and available ◊ **out of hand** immediately and without consideration ◊ **out of somebody's hands** no longer somebody's responsibility or problem ◊ **wash your hands of** refuse to continue being responsible for

☐ **hand down** vt **1** bequeath something **2** pronounce a verdict or sentence

☐ **hand in** vt submit something ∘ *handed in her resignation*

☐ **hand out** vt distribute or administer

☐ **hand over** vt surrender, give, or transfer to somebody else

Hand, Learned (1872–1961) US jurist

hand·bag /hánd bàg/ n a purse

hand·ball /hánd bàwl/ n **1** a game in which a ball is hit with the hands against a wall **2** a ball used in handball

hand·bill /hánd bìl/ n a printed sheet of paper distributed by hand

hand·book /hánd bòok/ n a small reference book, manual, or travel guide

hand·car /hánd kàar/ n a small railroad maintenance vehicle

hand·cart /hánd kàart/ n a cart pulled or pushed by hand

hand·clasp /hánd klàsp/ n a handshake

hand·craft /hánd kràft/ n skill in making things with the hands ■ vt make using manual skill

hand·cuff /hánd kùf/ n each of a pair of joined metal rings locked around somebody's wrists as a restraint *(usually pl)* ■ vt **1** put in handcuffs **2** make powerless or ineffective

Han·del /hánd'l/, **George Frideric** (1685–1759) German-born British composer

hand·ful /hánd fòol/ n **1** an amount contained by the hand **2** a small amount or number **3** a troublesome person or thing *(infml)*

hand gre·nade n a small bomb thrown by hand

hand·gun /hánd gùn/ n a gun held in one hand

⚡**hand·held** /hánd hèld/, **hand-held** adj operated while held in the hand ■ n a palmtop computer

hand·i·cap /hándee kàp/ n **1** a hindrance **2** an added advantage or disadvantage given to a competitor to balance a contest, or a contest balanced in this way **3** a physical or mental challenge *(often offensive)* ■ vt (-capped, -cap·ping) **1** hinder somebody or something **2** give a handicap to a competitor

ORIGIN Handicap is a contraction of *hand*

in cap, originally a betting game between contestants who offered to exchange items of personal property, whose difference in value was adjudicated by an umpire. The contestants placed their hands in a hat, along with some forfeit money, and the way in which they withdrew their hands – full or empty – signified whether they accepted or rejected the umpire's adjudication. If they both either accepted or rejected it, the umpire got the forfeit money; if they disagreed, the one who accepted it got the money. The application to horseracing arose in the 18C from the notion of an umpire adjudicating on the weight disadvantage to be given to a particular horse.

hand·i·capped /hándee kàpt/ adj physically or mentally challenged *(often offensive)* ■ npl an offensive term for people who are physically or mentally challenged

USAGE Although **handicapped** has a long history of use by those so affected, *physically challenged* and *people with disabilities* are preferred over the adjective and noun uses of **handicapped**.

hand·i·craft /hándee kràft/ n **1** a craft or occupation requiring manual skill **2** something made by hand

hand·i·work /hándee wùrk/ n **1** the result of somebody's action **2** work done by hand

hand·ker·chief /hángkərchif, -cheef/ (pl **-chiefs** or **-chieves** /-chivz, -cheevz/) n a square of cloth used especially for wiping the nose

han·dle /hánd'l/ n a part for holding or operating something ■ v (-dled, -dling) **1** vt touch with the hands **2** vt operate **3** vt take charge of, deal with, or control **4** vt trade in ∘ *handling stolen goods* **5** vi respond to control ∘ *a yacht that handles well in bad weather* —**han·dling** n ◊ **fly off the handle** lose your temper *(infml)* ◊ **get a handle on** understand or be able to control

han·dle·bars /hánd'l bàarz/ npl the steering handles of a bicycle or motorcycle

han·dler /hándlər/ n **1** an animal trainer **2** a manager, e.g., of a performer or a national political candidate **3** somebody who works or deals with something ∘ *a baggage handler*

hand·made /hànd máyd, hánd màyd/ adj made by hand

hand-me-down n **1** an outgrown or unwanted garment passed on to another person **2** something previously discarded by one person or group that is taken up by another

hand·out /hánd òwt/ n **1** a charitable gift **2** a document distributed to a group

hand·pick /hánd pík/ vt **1** choose carefully ∘ *handpicked the starting lineup* **2** pick or harvest by hand

hand pup·pet n a puppet fitting over the hand

hand·rail /hánd ràyl/ n a rail to hold with the hand for support

hand·saw /hánd sàw/ n a small saw for use with one hand

hands down adv 1 with great ease 2 in a way that is not open to question

hand·set /hánd sèt/ n the part of a telephone that contains the receiver and transmitter

⌁hand·shake /hánd shàyk/ n 1 a gesture of gripping and shaking somebody's hand 2 an exchange of signals establishing a link between computers or other devices —**hand·shak·ing** n

hands-off adj with no active or personal involvement

hand·some /hánsəm/ adj 1 good-looking 2 generous —**hand·some·ly** adv —**hand·some·ness** n

hands-on adj 1 involving actual use ○ a hands-on method of learning computer skills 2 involving physical touching ○ a museum with hands-on exhibits for children 3 personally or actively involved ○ a hands-on manager

hand·spring /hánd sprìng/ n an acrobatic flipping over of the body in which the hands are used

hand·stand /hánd stànd/ n an act of balancing on the hands with the legs straight up in the air

hand-to-hand adj involving bodily contact between people ○ hand-to-hand fighting —**hand to hand** adv

hand-to-mouth adj with barely enough to live on —**hand to mouth** adv

hand·work /hánd wùrk/ n work done by hand —**hand·work·er** n

hand·writ·ing /hánd rîting/ n 1 writing done by hand 2 a way of writing by hand —**hand·i·ly** adv —**hand·i·ness** n

Han·dy /hándee/, **W. C.** (1873–1958) US composer

hand·y·man /hándee màn/ n (pl -men /-mèn/) somebody who is paid to do or skilled at doing small jobs such as household repairs

hang v (hung) 1 vti fasten or hold something so that it is not supported from below, or be fastened or held in this way 2 vt put a door on its hinges 3 (past and past participle hanged) vti kill or be killed by putting a rope around the neck and removing any support for the body 4 vt decorate something by hanging things on it ○ trees hung with lights 5 vt put up wallpaper 6 vti display or be displayed by hanging (refers to pictures) 7 vt let your head droop 8 vi drape ○ The jacket hung badly on her. ■ n a way of hanging ◊ **get the hang of** learn how to do

☐ **hang around** vi loiter or waste time

☐ **hang back** vi be reluctant

☐ **hang on** vi 1 hold on tightly 2 persist in an endeavor

☐ **hang out** vi spend time casually somewhere or with somebody (slang)

☐ **hang up** v 1 vi end a telephone call 2 vti cause delay

han·gar /hángər/ n a building housing aircraft

ORIGIN Hangar is an adoption of a French word meaning "shed," whose origin is unknown. It is first recorded in English, with this more general meaning, in the late 17C. The first known use in the modern context of aircraft is from 1902, and refers to a hangar in France.

SPELLCHECK Do not confuse the spelling of hangar and hanger ("a support for hanging something"), which sound similar.

hang·dog /háng dàwg, -dòg/ adj looking guilty or sad

hang·er /hángər/ n 1 a support for hanging something, especially a frame for hanging a garment 2 somebody who hangs something ◊ See note at **hangar**

hang·er-on (pl **hang·ers-on**) n a sycophantic or parasitic follower

Hang glider

hang glid·er n an unpowered aircraft with a wing-shaped frame from which the pilot hangs —**hang-glide** vi —**hang glid·ing** n

hang·ing /hánging/ n 1 execution by putting a rope around the neck and removing any other support for the body 2 a decorative fabric hung on a wall (often pl)

hang·man /hángmən, háng màn/ (pl -men /-mən, -mèn/) n an executioner who hangs people

hang·nail /háng nàyl/ n a partly detached piece of skin beside a fingernail

ORIGIN Hangnail is an alteration of earlier agnail. The first element of this word was unfamiliar and puzzling, and was altered by popular etymology in the late 17C. In fact it represents an ancient root meaning "tight, painful."

hang·out /háng òwt/ n a place frequented by a person or group (slang)

hang·o·ver /háng òvər/ n 1 the unpleasant after effects of drinking too much alcohol 2 a remainder of the past

Hang Seng in·dex /hàng séng-/ n an index of relative prices on the Hong Kong Stock Exchange

hang-up n 1 a psychological problem or inhibition (infml) 2 a source of delay

Hang·zhou /hàng jṓ/ capital of **Zhejiang Province**, SE China, at the head of **Hangzhou Bay**, an inlet of the East China Sea. Pop. 4,210,000 (1995).

hank *n* a loose ball or coil of material such as wool or rope

han·ker /hángkər/ *vi* want something badly or persistently ○ *hankers after something she can't have* —**hank·er·ing** *n*

~~hankerchief~~ incorrect spelling of **handkerchief**

han·kie /hángkee/, **han·ky** (*pl* **-kies**) *n* a handkerchief (*infml*)

han·ky-pan·ky /hàngkee pángkee/ *n* **1** suspicious activity **2** frivolous sexual behavior

Han·ni·bal /hánnəb'l/ (247–183 BC) Carthaginian general

Ha·noi /ha nóy/ capital of Vietnam. Pop. 1,073,760 (1992).

Han·o·ver /hánnōvər/ city in NW Germany. Pop. 525,763 (1997).

Han·sard /hánsərd/ *n* the official published reports of British parliamentary proceedings

han·som /hánsəm/, **han·som cab** *n* a two-wheeled covered horse-drawn carriage

> **ORIGIN** The **hansom** is named for the British architect Joseph Aloysius Hansom (1803–82), who patented an improved design of cab in 1834.

Ha·nuk·kah /hánnəkə, haan-, khaan-/, **Ha·nu·kah, Cha·nu·kah** *n* a Jewish festival marking the rededication of the Temple in Jerusalem. Date: from 25th day of Kislev, in December, for eight days.

hao·le /hówlee/ *n* Hawaii a non-Polynesian resident of Hawaii —**hao·le** *adj*

~~hapen~~ incorrect spelling of **happen**

hap·haz·ard /hap házzərd/ *adj* unplanned, sloppy, or random —**hap·haz·ard·ly** *adv* —**hap·haz·ard·ness** *n*

> **ORIGIN Haphazard** is formed from archaic *hap* "happening, occurrence" and *hazard* in the old sense "chance."

hap·less /háppləss/ *adj* unlucky —**hap·less·ly** *adv* —**hap·less·ness** *n*

hap·pen /hápp'n/ *v* **1** *vi* occur or take place ○ *How did it happen?* **2** *vt* do something by chance ○ *if you happen to find it* **3** *vi* affect, especially in an unpleasant way ○ *I hope nothing has happened to her.* **4** *vi* be by chance ○ *It happened to be the last one in the store.*

□ **happen on** or **up·on** *vt* discover or encounter something or somebody by chance

hap·pen·ing /háppəning/ *n* something that happens

hap·pen·stance /háppən stànss/, **hap·pen-chance** /hápp'n chànss/ *n* a chance occurrence

hap·py /háppee/ (**-pi·er, -pi·est**) *adj* **1** feeling pleasure **2** causing pleasure ○ *happy news*

3 satisfied ○ *I am happy with my performance.* **4** willing ○ *happy to help* **5** fortunate ○ *a happy coincidence* —**hap·pi·ly** *adv* —**hap·pi·ness** *n*

hap·py-go-luck·y *adj* tending not to worry about the future

hap·py hour *n* a time when drinks are sold at reduced prices in bars

hap·py me·di·um *n* a satisfying compromise

~~happyness~~ incorrect spelling of **happiness**

ha·ra-ki·ri /hàrrə keéree/ *n* Japanese ritualistic suicide involving disembowelment

ha·rangue /hə ráng/ (**-rangued, -rangu·ing**) *vti* address loudly, forcefully, or angrily, usually at length —**ha·rangue** *n*

Ha·ra·re /hə raáree/ capital of Zimbabwe. Pop. 1,410,000 (1995).

ha·rass /hárrəss, hə ráss/ *vt* **1** keep bothering or attacking somebody **2** exhaust an enemy with repeated attacks —**ha·rassed** *adj* —**ha·rass·ment** *n*

Har·bin /haár bín/ capital of **Heilongjiang Province**, NE China. Pop. 4,470,000 (1995).

har·bin·ger /haárbinjər/ *n* somebody or something that announces a future event

har·bor /haárbər/ *n* **1** a sheltered place where ships can anchor or moor **2** a place of refuge ■ *vt* **1** keep in your mind for a long time ○ *harboring a secret fear of the dark* **2** provide shelter or sanctuary for

hard *adj* **1** not easily cut or bent **2** difficult ○ *a hard decision* **3** involving much effort ○ *a hard climb* **4** using much force ○ *a hard tug on the rope* **5** demanding and strict ○ *a hard taskmaster* **6** unsympathetic **7** resentful or bitter ○ *no hard feelings* **8** real or true ○ *the hard facts* **9** radical ○ *the hard left* **10** harsh or severe ○ *a hard winter* **11** describes water that contains mineral salts **12** describes beverages high in alcohol content **13** describes dangerously addictive drugs **14** describes the consonants "c" and "g" pronounced as in "come" and "go" ■ *adv* **1** with force ○ *hit the ball hard* **2** to an extreme degree ○ *pulled the truck over hard* **3** with energetic strength ○ *worked hard* **4** with concentration ○ *studied hard* —**hard·ness** *n* ◊ **be hard put to** find it difficult to

> **SYNONYMS** hard, difficult, strenuous, tough, arduous, laborious CORE MEANING: requiring effort or exertion

hard-and-fast *adj* rigidly enforced

hard-back /haárd bàk/, **hard-cov·er** /haárd kuvər/ *n* a book with a stiff cover

hard·ball /haárd bàwl/ *n* **1** baseball **2** ruthless behavior (*infml*)

hard-bit·ten *adj* tough and experienced

hard·board /haárd bàwrd/ *n* board made from compressed wood chips and sawdust

hard-boiled *adj* **1** describes an egg that is

cooked until firm **2** tough, realistic, and unsentimental (infml)

hard·bound /haárd bównd/ adj describes a book in a stiff cover

⚡**hard copy** n printed-out computer data

hard core n the committed nucleus of a group

hard-core /haárd kawr/ adj **1** uncompromising and committed **2** describes explicit pornography

hard·cov·er n PRINTING = hardback

⚡**hard disk, hard drive** n a permanent information storage unit inside a computer

hard·en /haárd'n/ vti **1** make or become hard or harder **2** make or become more determined —**hard·en·er** n

hard·hat /haárd hàt/ n **1** a protective helmet worn especially by construction workers **2** a construction worker (infml) **3** a very patriotic and conservative person (infml) —**hard·hat** adj

hard·head·ed /haárd héddad/ adj **1** logical and realistic **2** stubborn —**hard·head·ed·ly** adv —**hard·head·ed·ness** n

hard·heart·ed /haárd haártad/ adj cruel or unsympathetic —**hard·heart·ed·ly** adv —**hard·heart·ed·ness** n

hard-hit·ting adj brutally honest o a hard-hitting documentary

Har·ding /haárding/, **Warren G.** (1865–1923) 29th president of the United States (1921–23)

hard la·bor n a prison sentence including physical work

hard line n an inflexible and uncompromising position

hard·line /haárd lín/ adj inflexible —**hard·lin·er** n

hard·ly /haárdlee/ adv **1** almost not o It's hardly likely. o There are hardly any left. **2** only with difficulty o I could hardly move. **3** only just o Hardly had I rung the bell when the door was opened.

hard-nosed adj tough and shrewd (infml)

hard pal·ate n the bony front part of the roof of the mouth

hard·pan /haárd pàn/ n hard material in a layer below the soil

hard-pressed adj **1** lacking sufficient resources **2** having difficulty

hard rock n loud rock music with an insistent beat

hard sell n aggressive marketing or selling

hard·ship /haárd shìp/ n **1** difficulty or suffering caused by a lack of something **2** a cause of hardship

hard·top /haárd tòp/ n **1** a car with a fixed metal roof **2** also **hard·top con·vert·i·ble** a car with a detachable hard roof

hard up adj poor (infml)

⚡**hard·ware** /haárd wàir/ n **1** tools and implements **2** military weapons **3** computer equipment and peripherals

⚡**hard-wire** /haárd wír/ (**-wired, -wir·ing**) vt build a function into a computer with hardware

hard·wood /haárd wòod/ n **1** wood from a broad-leaved tree rather than a conifer **2** a tree that produces hardwood

har·dy /haárdee/ (**-di·er, -di·est**) adj robust and able to withstand physical hardship —**har·di·ly** adv —**har·di·ness** n

Har·dy /haárdee/, **Thomas** (1840–1928) British novelist and poet

hare /hair/ (pl same or **hares**) n a fast-running animal resembling a rabbit, with large hind legs ◊ See note at **hair**

hare-brained /háir bràynd/ adj foolish or impractical

Ha·re Krish·na /háaree–/ n **1** a Hindu religious group that worships the god Krishna **2** a member of Hare Krishna

hare·lip /háir lìp/ n an offensive term for an upper lip congenitally divided into two parts that have been only partially reunited by surgery

har·em /háirəm/ n the part of a Muslim house reserved for wives and concubines

---

ORIGIN Harem comes from an Arabic word that literally means "forbidden place." It came to be applied to the separate women's quarters in a Muslim house.

---

har·i·cot /hárri kò, -kòt/ n a white bean

hark vi listen (archaic)
□ **hark back** vi **1** think or speak again about something past **2** be similar to something past

Har·lan /haárlən/, **John Marshall** (1899–1971) associate justice of the US Supreme Court (1955–71), and his grandson **John Marshall** (1833–1911) associate justice (1877–1911)

Har·lem /haárləm/ n district of New York City, on N Manhattan Island

har·le·quin /haárləkwin, -kin/ n **1** a clown **2** **Har·le·quin** a comic character wearing diamond-patterned tights and a black mask ■ adj patterned with multicolored diamond shapes

har·lot /haárlət/ n a female prostitute (literary)

ORIGIN A **harlot** was not originally a woman. At first it meant "vagabond, rogue, beggar," as did the French word from which it was adopted.

---

harm n physical or mental damage or injury ■ vt cause harm to

SYNONYMS harm, damage, hurt, injure, wound CORE MEANING: weaken or impair something or somebody

harm·ful /haármfəl/ adj damaging —**harm·ful·ly** adv —**harm·ful·ness** n

harm·less /haármləss/ adj **1** not dangerous

2 unobjectionable or inoffensive —**harm·less·ly** adv —**harm·less·ness** n

har·mon·ic /haar mónnik/ adj produced by harmony ■ n an overtone on a stringed instrument —**har·mon·i·cal·ly** adv

har·mon·i·ca /haar mónnikə/ n a small rectangular wind instrument containing a set of metal reeds

ORIGIN The name **harmonica** was introduced by Benjamin Franklin for an instrument he devised in the early 1760s, a row of glasses turning on an axis and dipping into water, which were played by the finger. This was an improved and mechanized version of what were called "musical glasses" (and would now be called a *glass harmonica*). As a name for the wind instrument **harmonica** is recorded from the 1890s.

har·mon·ics /haar mónniks/ n the science of the physical properties of musical sound (+ sing verb)

har·mo·ni·ous /haar mốnee əss/ adj **1** of or in harmony **2** blending pleasantly —**har·mo·ni·ous·ly** adv

har·mo·ni·um /haar mốnee əm/ n an organ with a foot-operated bellows

har·mo·nize /haarmə nìz/ v **1** vti blend pleasingly **2** vi sing or play in harmony —**har·mo·ni·za·tion** /haarməni záysh'n/ n

har·mo·nized sales tax n a value-added tax in some Canadian provinces

har·mo·ny /haarmənee/ (pl -nies) n **1** a pleasing combination of musical sounds **2** a combination of notes sung or played together **3** a situation in which there is agreement **4** a pleasing effect in the arrangement of the parts of something

har·ness /haarnəss/ n **1** a set of leather straps for attaching an animal to a cart or carriage that it pulls **2** a set of straps for holding somebody in position ■ vt **1** fit an animal with a harness **2** get control of and use something —**har·ness·er** n

harp n a large triangular stringed instrument played by plucking —**harp** vi —**harp·er** n —**harp·ist** n

☐ **harp on** vti repeat something tiresomely

Har·pers Fer·ry /haarpərz-/ town in E West Virginia, at the confluence of the Potomac and Shenandoah rivers, site of John Brown's rebellion in 1859. Pop. 324 (1998).

har·poon /haar poón/ n a weapon like a spear attached to a cord and thrown or fired at a whale or other sea animal —**har·poon** vt

harp·si·chord /haárpsi kàwrd/ n a keyboard instrument played by plucking —**harp·si·chord·ist** n

har·py /haárpee/ (pl -pies) n **1** an offensive term for a woman regarded as unpleasant or greedy (insult) **2** **Har·py** In Greek mythology, a monster that was half woman and half bird of prey

harrass incorrect spelling of **harass**

har·ri·dan /hárrid'n/ n an offensive term for a woman regarded as domineering or bad-tempered (insult)

Har·ris /hárriss/, **Joel Chandler** (1848–1908) US writer

Har·ris·burg /hárrəss bùrg/ capital of Pennsylvania. Pop. 49,502 (1998).

Har·ri·son /hárriss'n/, **Benjamin** (1833–1901) 23rd president of the United States (1889–93)

Har·ri·son, William Henry (1773–1841) 9th president of the United States (1840)

har·row /hárrō/ n a farm machine for breaking up soil —**har·row** vti

har·row·ing /hárrō ing/ adj very distressing —**har·row·ing·ly** adv

har·ry /hárree/ (-ried, -ries) vt **1** distress by repeated attacks **2** raid or pillage

harsh /haarsh/ adj **1** difficult to endure o *harsh conditions* **2** severe in judgment o *harsh criticism* **3** jarring or unpleasant o *a harsh voice* o *a harsh light* —**harsh·ly** adv —**harsh·ness** n

hart (pl harts or same) n a male deer

Harte /haart/, **Bret** (1836–1902) US writer

Hart·ford /haartfərd/ capital of Connecticut. Pop. 131,523 (1998).

har·um-scar·um /hàirəm skáirəm/ adj careless and disorganized

Har·vard U·ni·ver·si·ty /haárvərd-/ n the oldest university in the United States, founded in 1636 in Massachusetts

har·vest /haárvəst/ n **1** the quantity of a crop gathered in a season o *a record harvest* **2** the gathering of a mature crop o *berries ripe for harvest* **3** the season in which crops are gathered ■ vti gather a crop

ORIGIN **Harvest** was originally the name for the third season of the year, "fall." It derives from an ancient root meaning "gather," and so always had connections with fruit and crops. Uses more directly connected with crops are recorded from the medieval period.

har·vest·er /haárvəstər/ n **1** a machine that gathers crops **2** somebody who gathers crops

har·vest moon n the full moon nearest to the autumnal equinox

has 3rd person present singular of **have**

has-been n somebody who is no longer important (infml)

hash[1] n a fried dish of potatoes and meat ■ vt chop meat or vegetables into tiny pieces

☐ **hash out, hash over** vt spend time resolving something

hash[2] n hashish (slang)

hash browns npl a fried dish of chopped potatoes

hash·ish /há sheesh, há shísh, haa sheesh/, **hash·eesh** /há sheesh, haa sheesh/ n cannabis resin used as an illegal drug

has·n't /házz'nt/ *contr* has not

hasp *n* a hinged metal fastening that fits over a staple and is secured by a pin, bolt, or padlock —**hasp** *vt*

Has·san /ha saán/, **Abdiqasim Salad** (*b.* 1942) president of Somalia (2000–)

~~hassel~~ incorrect spelling of **hassle**

has·sium /hássee əm/ *n* (*symbol* **Hs**) a rare, unstable chemical element

has·sle /háss'l/ (*infml*) *n* aggravation, or a source of aggravation ■ *vt* (**-sled, -sling**) keep bothering or annoying

has·sock /hássək/ *n* a padded stool

haste *n* great speed (*fml*)

has·ten /háyss'n/ *v* 1 *vi* do or say something immediately ○ *"And I agree," he hastened to add.* 2 *vt* speed something up ○ *would hasten his recovery* 3 *vi* go somewhere quickly (*literary*) ○ *hastened to her side*

Has·tings /háystingz/ town in S England, site of the Battle of Hastings in 1066. Pop. 81,139 (1991).

Has·tings, Warren (1732–1818) British colonial administrator

hast·y /háystee/ (**-i·er, -i·est**) *adj* done or acting too quickly —**hast·i·ly** *adv* —**hast·i·ness** *n*

hat *n* 1 a head covering 2 one of various areas of responsibility that somebody has ○ *put on her accountant's hat* —**hat·ted** *adj* ◇ **keep under your hat** keep secret ◇ **take your hat off to** acknowledge admiration for

hatch[1] *n* 1 a door in the floor or ceiling of something 2 a small hole or door between two rooms 3 *also* **hatch·back** a car with a rear door that is hinged from the roof

hatch[2] *v* 1 *vti* come or make a young organism come out of an egg 2 *vi* break open for the release of a young organism (*refers to eggs*) 3 *vt* secretly devise a plot

hatch[3] *vti* mark or be marked with parallel crossed lines to show shading —**hatch·ing** *n*

hatch·er·y /hácherree/ (*pl* **-ies**) *n* a place where fish or poultry eggs are hatched commercially

hatch·et /háchət/ *n* a small short-handled ax ◇ **bury the hatchet** make peace after a disagreement ◇ **do a hatchet job on** criticize severely (*infml*)

hatch·et man *n* (*infml*) 1 a hired killer 2 somebody hired to make cuts in staff or funding

hate *v* (**hat·ed, hat·ing**) 1 *vt* dislike somebody intensely 2 *vti* have strong distaste or aversion for something ○ *I hate cleaning the windows.* ■ *n* 1 a feeling of intense dislike 2 something hated —**hat·ed** *adj* —**hat·er** *n* ◇ See note at **dislike**

hate crime *n* a crime motivated by prejudice against a group

hate·ful /háytfəl/ *adj* 1 spitefully malevolent 2 evoking feelings of hatred —**hate·ful·ly** *adv* —**hate·ful·ness** *n*

hate mail *n* mail expressing hatred of the recipient

Hath·a·way /háthə wày/, **Anne** (1556–1623) wife of William Shakespeare

ha·tred /háytrəd/ *n* intense dislike or hostility ◇ See note at **dislike**

Hat·shep·sut /hàt shép soot/ (*fl* 15C BC) queen of Egypt (1479–57 BC)

Hat·ter·as, Cape /hátterəss/ headland in E North Carolina, renowned for treacherous weather conditions

hat trick *n* a series of three wins or successes, especially goals in a game

haugh·ty /háwtee/ (**-ti·er, -ti·est**) *adj* superior and condescending —**haugh·ti·ly** *adv* —**haugh·ti·ness** *n*

haul *vt* 1 pull or drag something with effort 2 transport something heavy and bulky ■ *n* 1 a group of stolen items 2 a distance over which something is transported or somebody travels 3 a single catch of fish —**haul·er** *n* ◇ See note at **pull**

haul·age /háwlij/ *n* 1 the transportation of goods by road or rail 2 the cost of transporting goods by road or rail

haunch *n* 1 the hip, buttock, and upper thigh 2 an animal's back leg

haunt *vt* 1 visit as a ghost 2 be a constant source of unease or worry for ■ *n* a place somebody often visits

haunt·ed /háwntəd/ *adj* 1 believed to be frequented by a ghost 2 looking frightened or worried

haunt·ing /háwnting/ *adj* evoking strong emotion —**haunt·ing·ly** *adv*

haute cou·ture /òt koo tóor/ *n* the business of designing and making exclusive clothing, or such clothing itself

haute cui·sine /òt kwi zeén/ *n* classic French cooking

hau·teur /hō túr, haw-/ *n* haughtiness

Ha·van·a[1] /hə vánnə, -vaánə/ capital, port, and largest city of Cuba. Pop. 2,184,990 (1996). —**Ha·van·an** *adj, n*

Ha·van·a[2] /hə vánnə/, **Ha·van·a ci·gar** *n* a high-quality Cuban cigar

have (*stressed*) /hav/ (*unstressed*) /həv, əv/ *v* (**had, hav·ing, has**) 1 *vt* own or possess ○ *She has a small cottage in the country.* 2 *vt* possess as a quality or characteristic ○ *He had short dark hair.* ■ *aux v* 3 forms perfect tenses ○ *Have you finished?* ○ *I have lost my keys.* ○ *would have enjoyed it* ■ *v* 4 must ○ *We have to go now.* ○ *There has to be another way.* 5 *vt* receive or obtain ○ *I had a letter from him yesterday.* 6 *vt* eat or drink ○ *He had breakfast early.* 7 *vt* think of or remember ○ *I have an idea.* 8 *vt* experience ○ *We had a great time.* 9 *vt* be affected by ○ *She has the flu.* 10 *vt* engage in ○ *They had a long talk about cars.* 11 *vt* organize ○ *We had a party last week.* 12 *vt* arrange for something to be done for you ○ *I've just had my hair cut.* 13 *vt* tolerate o *I won't have such behavior!* **14** *vt* provide accommodation or entertainment for o *We had a friend to stay for the weekend.* **15** *vt* be a prospective parent of o *We're having a baby.* **16** *vt* make something happen o *Have him phone me tomorrow.* ■ **haves** *npl* rich or privileged people ◊ **have had it** be too worn out, damaged, or exhausted to function properly *(infml)* ◊ **have had it with** have lost patience with ◊ **have it in for** want to harm ◊ **have something on somebody** have unfavorable information about somebody's activities ◊ **have it out (with)** argue over an issue with ◊ **have to do with** be relevant to ◊ **have what it takes** have the necessary skills, personality, or attitude to be successful

□ **have on** *vt* be wearing

Hav·el /háwvəl/, **Václav** (*b.* 1936) dramatist and president of Czechoslovakia (1989–92) and of the Czech Republic (1993–)

ha·ven /háyv'n/ *n* **1** a place of rest, shelter, or safety **2** an anchorage *(literary)*

have-nots *npl* people who are not rich or privileged

have·n't /háv'nt/ *contr* have not

hav·er·sack /háwvər sàk/ *n* a bag carried over one shoulder or on the back

---

ORIGIN Haversack comes via French from an obsolete German compound meaning literally "oats bag," as carried by cavalry soldiers. It is first recorded in English – for human provisions – in the mid-18C.

---

hav·oc /hávvək/ *n* **1** destruction or devastation **2** chaos

haw[1] *n* **1** a hawthorn **2** the fruit of the hawthorn

haw[2] *vi* make a sound expressing hesitation —**haw** *n*

Ha·wai·i /hə waÿ ee/ **1** state of the United States in the N Pacific Ocean, consisting of eight main islands and over 100 others. Cap. Honolulu. Pop. 1,211,537 (2000). **2** largest island in the state of Hawaii. Pop. 137,291 (1995). —**Ha·wai·ian** *n, adj*

Ha·wai·i-A·leu·tian Stan·dard Time, Ha·wai·i Stan·dard Time *n* the local standard time in Hawaii

hawk[1] *n* **1** a bird of prey with broad wings, a long tail, and a short hooked bill **2** *also* **Hawk** somebody favoring the use of force in implementing foreign policy ■ *v* **1** *vi* hunt with hawks **2** *vi* attack while flying —**hawk·ing** *n* —**hawk·ish** *adj*

hawk[2] *vti* sell goods on the streets —**hawk·er** *n*

hawk[3] *v* **1** *vi* clear the throat **2** *vt* cough up phlegm —**hawk** *n*

hawk-eyed *adj* quick to see things

haw·ser /háwzər/ *n* a cable for mooring or towing a ship

haw·thorn /háw tháwrn/ *n* a thorny tree with white or pink flowers and reddish berries

Haw·thorne /háw thawrn/, **Nathaniel** (1804–64) US writer

hay *n* cut and dried grass, often used as fodder

Haydn /híd'n/, **Joseph** (1732–1809) Austrian composer

Hayes, Rutherford B. (1822–93) 19th president of the United States (1877–81)

hay fe·ver *n* an allergic reaction to pollen

hay·loft /háy lòft/ *n* a loft for storing hay in a stable or a barn

hay·mak·er /háy màykər/ *n* **1** a machine for drying hay **2** a worker who cuts, bales, or stores hay

hay·ride /háy rìd/ *n* a pleasure ride in a wagon full of hay

hay·seed /háy sèed/ *n* **1** grass seed removed from hay **2** pieces of grass or straw that fall from hay

hay·stack /háy stàk/, **hay·rick** *n* a large pile of hay in a field

Hay·ward /háywərd/ city in NW California. Pop. 128,872 (1998).

hay·wire /háy wìr/ *adj* functioning erratically *(infml)*

haz·ard /házzərd/ *n* **1** a potential danger **2** a dangerous outcome **3** an obstacle on a golf course **4** a dice game resembling craps ■ *vt* **1** suggest tentatively **2** risk the loss of

haz·ard light *n* a flashing light on a car for warning other drivers

haz·ard·ous /házzərdəss/ *adj* potentially dangerous —**haz·ard·ous·ly** *adv* —**haz·ard·ous·ness** *n*

haz·ard·ous waste *n* a toxic byproduct of a manufacturing process or nuclear processing

haz·ard pay *n* money for dangerous work

haze[1] *n* **1** mist, cloud, or smoke in the atmosphere obscuring the view **2** a disoriented mental or physical state

haze[2] (**hazed, haz·ing**) *vti* persecute a subordinate —**haz·ing** *n*

ha·zel /háyz'l/ (*pl* **-zels** *or same*) *n* **1** *also* **ha·zel·nut** an edible brown nut **2** a small tree producing hazels **3** the wood of the hazel tree. Use: baskets, hurdles. **4** a light-brown color —**ha·zel** *adj*

Haz·litt /házlit/, **William** (1778–1830) British essayist

HAZMAT /ház màt/ *abbr* hazardous material

haz·y /háyzee/ (**-i·er, -i·est**) *adj* **1** unclear because of mist, cloud, or smoke **2** imprecise or indistinctly remembered —**haz·i·ly** *adv* —**haz·i·ness** *n*

H-bomb *n* a hydrogen bomb

⚡ **HCI** *abbr* human-computer interaction

⚡ **HD** *abbr* high density

HDR *abbr* humanitarian daily ration

he (*stressed*) /hee/ (*unstressed*) /ee/ *pron* refers to a male person or animal who has been previously mentioned or whose identity is known *(as the subject of a verb)* ■ *n* a male animal or a boy, especially a new baby

He *symbol* helium

head /hed/ *n* **1** the topmost part of a vertebrate body, containing the brain **2** the farthest forward section of an invertebrate body **3** the center of the human intellect and emotions **4** a leader **5** a crisis point **6** the wider top of a long thin object ○ *the head of a nail* **7** a flower cluster, or a compact cluster of leaves and stalks **8** the obverse of a coin that shows a leader's head **9** a title above a section of text **10** the source of a river **11** the part of a machine that records, reads, or erases sounds, images, or data **12** the pressure exerted by a liquid or gas ○ *a head of steam* ■ *adj* chief ■ *v* **1** *vt* control a group or organization **2** *vi* move in a particular direction **3** *vt* be at the front or top of something —**head·ed** *adj* —**head·less** *adj* ◊ **above** *or* **over somebody's head** too difficult for somebody to understand ◊ **go to somebody's head 1** make somebody conceited or overconfident **2** make somebody dizzy ◊ **head over heels 1** completely ○ *head over heels in love* **2** rolling or turning upside down ◊ **keep your head** remain calm ◊ **lose your head** lose self-control

☐ **head off** *vt* **1** intercept **2** forestall

head·ache /héd àyk/ *n* **1** a pain in the head **2** a source of worry *(infml)* —**head·ach·y** *adj*

head·band /héd bànd/ *n* a strip of fabric for keeping the hair in place

head·board /héd bàwrd/ *n* a board at the head of a bed

head·butt *vt* hit somebody with the head —**head-butt** *n*

head·cam /héd kàm/ *n* a video camera mounted on a person's head or on headgear

head·cheese /héd cheez/ *(pl* -**chees·es** *or* same) *n* a mixture of chopped cooked meat

head count *n* the process of counting the people in a group, or the number counted

head·dress /héd drèss/ *n* an elaborate head covering often worn as a sign of rank

⚡ **head·er** /héddər/ *n* **1** in soccer, a shot made with the head **2** a headlong fall **3** a heading on each page of a document **4** the part at the top of an e-mail for information about the message **5** a crosswise brick in a wall **6** somebody or something that makes, fits, or removes the tops of things

head·first /héd fúrst/ *adv, adj* with the head leading ■ *adv* rashly and thoughtlessly

head·gear /héd gèer/ *n* something worn on the head

head·hunt /héd hùnt/ *v* **1** *vt* attempt to recruit somebody from another company **2** *vi* cut off and collect the heads of enemies as trophies —**head·hunt·er** *n* —**head·hunt·ing** *n*

head·ing /hédding/ *n* **1** the title for a section of text **2** a ship's or aircraft's course

head·land /héddlənd, héd lànd/ *n* **1** a promontory jutting into the sea **2** an unplowed strip at the edge of a field

head·light /héd lìt/, **head·lamp** *n* a strong light on the front of a vehicle

head·line /héd lìn/ *n* the title of a newspaper article, printed in larger, heavier type ■ **head·lines** *npl* the main news items in a newspaper or news broadcast ■ *vt* (-**lined**, -**lin·ing**) **1** give a prominent heading to **2** present as the star of a show

head·lock /héd lòk/ *n* a wrestling hold in which an arm is placed around an opponent's head

head·long /héd láwng/ *adv, adj* **1** with the head foremost **2** moving fast and out of control

head·man /héd màn/ *(pl* -**men** /-mèn/) *n* **1** a community or village chief **2** a leader or overseer

head·mas·ter /héd màstər/ *n* a man in charge of a private school

head·mis·tress /héd mìstriss/ *n* a woman in charge of a private school

head of gov·ern·ment *n* the person in charge of a country's government

head of state *n* the chief representative of a country

head·on *adv, adj* with the front facing forward ■ *adv* without evasion or compromise ■ *adj* uncompromising

head·phones /héd fònz/ *npl* a device with earphones, worn on the head

head·piece /héd pèess/ *n* **1** an ornamental design printed at the beginning of a text **2** a protective covering for the head

head·quar·ter /héd kwàwrtər/ *vt* provide with headquarters

head·quar·ters /héd kwàwrtərz/ *n* (+ *sing* or *pl verb*) **1** a military commander's operational base **2** a main office or center of operations

head·rest /héd rèst/ *n* a support for the head on the back of a seat

head·room /héd ròom, -ròom/ *n* the overhead clearance in a room or vehicle, or under a bridge

head·set /héd sèt/ *n* a set of headphones with a mouthpiece

head·ship /héd shìp/ *n* the position of leader

head·stand /héd stànd/ *n* a position in which somebody balances on the head and hands

head start *n* a competitive advantage

head·stone /héd stòn/ *n* **1** a gravestone **2** *also* **head stone** a keystone

head·strong /héd stròng/ *adj* willful and stubborn —**head·strong·ness** *n*

heads-up *n* **1** a warning **2** something requiring attention ■ *adj* alert and resourceful

head-to-head *adv, adj* in or involving a direct encounter ■ *adv* with heads adjacent ■ *n* a direct encounter

head·wait·er /héd wàytər/ n the chief waiter in a restaurant

head·wa·ters /héd wàwtərz/ npl the source waters of a river

head·way /héd wày/ n 1 progress 2 forward movement 3 headroom

head·wind /héd wind/ n a wind coming from in front

head·word /héd wùrd/ n the key word at the start of a text, especially a main entry in a dictionary

head·y /héddee/ (-i·er, -i·est) adj 1 exhilarating 2 intoxicating —**head·i·ly** adv —**head·i·ness** n

heal /heel/ v 1 vt restore a person, body part, or injury to health 2 vi be repaired naturally o *The bone is healing nicely.* 3 vt correct something causing problems o *heal the rift in the party* —**heal·er** n —**heal·ing** adj, n

SPELLCHECK Do not confuse the spelling of **heal** and **heel** (of a foot), which sound similar.

health /helth/ n 1 the general condition of the body or mind in relation to the presence or absence of illness or injury 2 the general condition of something ■ adj 1 devoted to the well-being of the general public 2 promoting physical and mental well-being

health care n the provision of medical services to maintain health

health cen·ter n a place offering health care

health food n a food eaten to improve or maintain health

health·ful /hélthfəl/ adj beneficial to health

health in·sur·ance n insurance against the costs incurred through ill health

health·y /hélthee/ (-i·er, -i·est) adj 1 in good physical or mental condition 2 beneficial to health 3 suggestive of good health 4 functioning well 5 considerable (infml) o *a healthy profit* —**health·i·ly** adv —**health·i·ness** n

Hea·ney /héenee/, **Seamus** (b. 1939) Irish poet

heap /heep/ n 1 a rounded pile 2 a large amount (infml) 3 something old or battered, especially a building or car (slang) ■ vt 1 put in a pile o *heaped vegetables on his plate* 2 fill with a pile 3 give in abundance o *heaped scorn on my suggestion*

heap·ing /héeping/ adj more than filled

hear /heer/ (**heard** /hurd/) v 1 vti perceive a sound 2 vti be told or informed of something 3 vt listen to 4 vti understand by listening —**hear·a·ble** adj —**hear·er** n

SPELLCHECK Do not confuse the spelling of **hear** and **here** ("in this place"), which sound similar.

hear·ing /héering/ n 1 the ability to perceive sound 2 the distance within which something can be heard 3 a chance to be heard 4 a preliminary examination of an accused person to decide whether to go to trial

hear·ing aid n a device worn in or behind the ear to improve hearing

hear·ing-and-speech-im·paired adj unable to speak or hear

hear·ing-im·paired adj with reduced hearing ◊ See note at **deaf**

hear·ken /háarkən/ vi listen (archaic)

hear·say /héer sày/ n information heard from somebody else —**hear·say** adj

hearse /hurss/ n a vehicle that transports corpses at funerals

ORIGIN Agricultural harrows in the Middle Ages were typically toothed triangular frames, so the word for a harrow came to be applied in French to a triangular toothed frame for holding candles, particularly those placed over a coffin at funeral services. This was the meaning of **hearse** when English acquired it, and it gradually developed via "canopy placed over a coffin" and "coffin, bier" to the modern sense of "funeral vehicle."

Hearst /hurst/, **William Randolph** (1863–1951) US publisher and politician

heart /haart/ n 1 the organ in the chest that pumps blood around the body 2 the human heart considered as the basis and center of emotional life 3 somebody's essential character o *has a good heart* 4 compassion o *Have you no heart?* 5 affection o *won the hearts of the audience* 6 spirit and determination o *played with a lot of heart* 7 a mood, mental state, or frame of mind o *in good heart* 8 the distinctive and characteristic center of something o *the heart of rural America* 9 a depiction of a heart as a symbol of love 10 a playing card with one or more red heart symbols on it ◊ **eat your heart out** be consumed with envy ◊ **heart and soul** completely ◊ **learn** or **know by heart** memorize or have memorized ◊ **take to heart** take seriously ◊ **with all your heart** sincerely

heart·ache /háart àyk/ n emotional pain

heart at·tack n 1 a sudden interruption of the heart's normal function 2 a sudden severe shock (infml)

heart·beat /háart bèet/ n 1 a contraction of the heart that drives blood through the body 2 the continuous pulsation of the heart

heart·break /háart bràyk/ n intense grief —**heart·break·ing** adj

heart·break·er /háart bràykər/ n somebody with whom many people fall unhappily in love

heart·bro·ken /háart bròkən/ adj feeling intense grief —**heart·bro·ken·ly** adv

heart·burn /háart bùrn/ n an unpleasant sensation in the lower chest caused by stomach acid

heart dis·ease n a condition of the heart that impairs functioning

heart·en /haárt'n/ *vt* encourage —**heart·en·ing** *adj* —**heart·en·ing·ly** *adv*

heart·felt /haárt felt/ *adj* deeply felt

hearth /haarth/ *n* 1 the floor of a fireplace 2 the fireplace of a home, thought of as a symbol of the home and family life

hearth rug *n* a small rug placed in front of a fireplace

heart·land /haárt lànd/ *n* 1 the central part of a country 2 an area of a country with special economic, political, military, or sentimental significance *(often pl)*

heart·less /haártləss/ *adj* cruel and unfeeling —**heart·less·ly** *adv* —**heart·less·ness** *n*

heart·rend·ing /haárt rènding/ *adj* causing extreme emotional distress ◊ See note at **moving**

hearts /haarts/ *n* 1 the suit of cards marked with red heart symbols *(+ sing or pl verb)* 2 a card game in which players try to win either all or no hearts cards and the queen of spades *(+ sing verb)*

heart-search·ing *n* mental self-examination

heart·sick /haárt sìk/ *adj* very disappointed or sad —**heart·sick·ness** *n*

heart·strings /haárt stringz/ *npl* somebody's deepest feelings

heart·throb /haárt thròb/ *n* somebody considered very attractive *(infml)*

heart-to-heart *adj* very frank and intimate ■ *n* a frank intimate talk

heart·warm·ing /haárt wàwrming/ *adj* emotionally gratifying —**heart·warm·ing·ly** *adv*

heart·y /haártee/ *(-i·er, -i·est)* *adj* 1 sincere and enthusiastic 2 healthy 3 strongly felt 4 substantial and nourishing —**heart·i·ly** *adv* —**heart·i·ness** *n*

heat /heet/ *n* 1 *(symbol* **Q**) energy perceived as temperature 2 the perceptible degree of hotness 3 a source of warmth, e.g., for cooking or keeping warm 4 intense emotion 5 the time of greatest activity o *in the heat of the campaign* 6 the spiciness of some foods 7 a sexually receptive stage in a female mammal's reproductive cycle 8 a preliminary round in a race or contest to eliminate some competitors or establish a starting order 9 psychological pressure *(infml)* 10 harsh criticism *(slang)* 11 the police *(slang)* ■ *vti* make or become warm or hot

□ **heat up** *vti* make or become hotter or more intense

heat·ed /heétəd/ *adj* 1 made hot or warm 2 intense or angry o *a heated argument* —**heat·ed·ly** *adv*

heat·er /heétər/ *n* 1 a heating device 2 a heating element in a vacuum tube 3 a handgun *(slang dated)*

heat ex·haus·tion *n* physical exhaustion caused by extreme heat

heath /heeth/ *n* 1 an area of uncultivated open land covered with rough grass and small bushes 2 a low bush commonly found on heaths

hea·then /heéthən/ *n* 1 an offensive term for a person who practices a religion other than Christianity, Judaism, or Islam 2 an offensive term for somebody viewed as irreligious or uncivilized —**hea·then** *adj*

ORIGIN Etymologically a **heathen** is simply "somebody who lives on a heath." By implication such a person was savage and uncivilized. Its early association with religion may have been influenced by Latin *paganus*, which came to refer to a non-Christian but originally was also simply "somebody who lives in the country."

heath·er /héthər/ *n* a low-growing evergreen plant with spiky leaves and small flowers

heat light·ning *n* lightning without thunder

heat-proof *adj* not affected by heat in an oven or from a flame

heat rash *n* prickly heat

heat-seek·ing *adj* able to follow infrared radiation from heat

heat·stroke /heét stròk/ *n* a medical condition caused by exposure to extreme heat

heat wave *n* an unusually hot period of weather

heave /heev/ *(heaved, heav·ing)* *v* 1 *vt* move using great physical effort 2 *vi* exert physical effort in a rhythmic burst o *heave on a rope* 3 *vt* direct something heavy somewhere by tossing *(infml)* 4 *vi* rise and fall rhythmically o *His chest was heaving.* 5 *vti* vomit *(infml)* 6 *vt* laboriously utter a sigh 7 *(past* **hove** /hōv/) *vti* move or make a ship move in a particular direction —**heave** *n* ◊ See note at **throw**

heav·en /hév'n/ *n* 1 *also* **Heav·en** a place or condition of perfect happiness where good people are believed to go after death, according to some religions 2 a blissful experience ■ **heav·ens** *npl* the sky above the Earth ◊ **move heaven and earth** do everything possible to make something happen

heav·en·ly /hév'nlee/ *(-li·er, -li·est)* *adj* 1 of God and Heaven 2 in the sky or in space as seen from the Earth 3 lovely *(infml)*

heav·en·ly bod·y *n* an object that is permanently present in the sky, e.g., a star or planet

heav·en-sent *adj* happening or coming at just the right time

heav·en·ward /hév'nwərd/ *adj* directed toward heaven or the sky ■ *adv also* **heav·en·wards** toward heaven or the sky

heaves /heevz/ *n* a chronic lung disease in horses *(infml; + sing or pl verb)*

heav·y /hévvee/ *adj* *(-i·er, -i·est)* 1 weighing a lot 2 occurring or produced in large amounts o *heavy rain* 3 needing strength o *heavy physical work* 4 difficult to fulfill or cope with 5 having great force o *a heavy* *blow* **6** affected by tiredness ○ *eyes heavy with sleep* **7** dully loud ○ *a heavy thud* **8** industrial-scale ○ *heavy industry* **9** sad ○ *a heavy heart* **10** requiring concentration to be understood ○ *a heavy novel* **11** hard to digest ○ *a heavy meal* ■ *n (pl* **-ies)** **1** a villain in a play, movie, or opera *(infml)* **2** somebody powerful or influential *(slang)* —**heav·i·ly** *adv* —**heav·i·ness** *n*

heav·y cream *n* cream with a high fat content

heav·y-du·ty *adj* tough and durable

heav·y-hand·ed *adj* **1** physically or socially clumsy **2** harsh and oppressive —**heav·y-hand·ed·ly** *adv* —**heav·y-hand·ed·ness** *n*

heav·y-heart·ed *adj* feeling sad —**heav·y-heart·ed·ly** *adv* —**heav·y-heart·ed·ness** *n*

heav·y met·al *n* **1** a type of loud rock music with a very strong beat **2** a metal with a high relative density

heav·y·set /hèvwee sét/ *adj* having a large or solid build

heav·y·weight /hévwee wàyt/ *n* **1** the weight category in boxing between light heavyweight and superheavyweight **2** a boxer who competes at heavyweight **3** somebody or something powerful or influential *(infml)*

He·bra·ic /hi bráy ik/, **He·bra·i·cal** /-ik'l/ *adj* of Hebrew or the Israelites —**He·bra·i·cal·ly** *adv*

He·brew /héebroo/ *n* **1** a Semitic language, the modern form of which is one of the official languages of Israel **2** an Israelite —**He·brew** —**heck·ler** *n*

He·brews /hèe brooz/ *n* a book of the Bible, originally a letter thought to have been written toward the end of the first century AD *(+ sing verb)*

Heb·ri·des /hébbrə deez/ island group off W Scotland —**He·bri·de·an** /hèbbrə dée ən/ *adj, n*

He·bron /héeb ron, hébbron/ town in the West Bank territory. Pop. 119,401 (1997).

heck *(infml)* *interj* expresses irritation or emphasis ■ *n* emphasizes annoyance or disagreement ○ *What the heck is going on?*

heck·le /hék'l/ *(-led, -ling)* *vti* interrupt somebody giving a speech or performance by shouting —**heck·ler** *n*

hec·tare /hék tàər/ *n* a metric unit of area equal to 100 ares or 10,000 sq. m (2.471 acres)

hec·tic /héktik/ *adj* **1** constantly busy and hurried **2** hot and feverish ○ *a hectic flush* —**hec·tic·al·ly** *adv*

hecto-, hect- *prefix* one hundred ○ *hectogram*

hec·tor /héktər/ *vti* speak or address in an intimidating way

Hec·tor /héktər/ *n* a mythological Trojan hero

he'd /heed/ *contr* **1** he had **2** he would

hedge *n* **1** a close-set row of bushes forming a barrier **2** a means of protection against something, especially financial loss ■ *v*

(hedged, hedg·ing) **1** *vt* put bushes around an area **2** *vi* be evasive **3** *vi* try to offset possible financial losses

hedge fund *n* a risk-taking investment company

hedge·hog /héj hòg/ *n* a small spiny mammal that rolls into a ball when attacked

hedge·row /héj rò/ *n* a row of bushes at a roadside or around a field

he·don·ism /héed'n ìzzəm/ *n* **1** the self-indulgent pursuit of pleasure **2** the philosophy that regards pleasure as the highest good —**he·don·ist** *n* —**he·don·is·tic** /hèed'n ístik/ *adj*

hee·bie-jee·bies /hèebee jéebeez/ *npl* a feeling of nervousness *(slang)*

heed *vti* pay attention to advice or an adviser ■ *n* serious attention to advice —**heed·ful** *adj* —**heed·ful·ly** *adv* —**heed·less** *adj* —**heed·less·ly** *adv*

hee-haw /hèe hàw/ *n* a donkey's bray —**hee·haw** *vi*

heel[1] /heel/ *n* **1** the back of a foot below the ankle **2** the back part of a shoe or sock that covers the heel **3** the back of the sole of a shoe, which is thicker or taller than the rest of the shoe **4** the thicker part of the palm of the hand next to the wrist **5** a crusty end of a loaf of bread **6** a man regarded as behaving reprehensibly *(insult)* **7** the part of a golf club head to which the shaft is attached **8** the end of a violin bow that is held when playing **9** the hard rind from a wedge of cheese **10** a small piece of a plant stem left attached to a cutting to promote growth ■ *v* **1** *vt* fit or repair the heel of a shoe **2** *vi* follow by somebody's heels *(refers to dogs)* **3** *vt* dig heels into an animal that is being ridden **4** *vi* move the heels in dancing **5** *vt* mishit a golf ball with the heel of a club —**heeled** *adj* ◊ **cool your heels** wait or be kept waiting for a long time *(infml)* ◊ **dig in your heels** hold stubbornly to a position or attitude ◊ **(hard) on the heels of** soon after ◊ **to heel** under control or discipline ◊ See note at **heal**

heel[2] /heel/ *vti* lean, or make a ship lean, to one side

He·fei /hö fáy/, **Ho·fei** capital of **Anhui** Province, E China. Pop. 1,320,000 (1995).

heft *vt* **1** lift something heavy **2** estimate the weight of something by lifting it ■ *n* great weight

heft·y /héftee/ *(-i·er, -i·est)* *adj* **1** powerfully built **2** considerable ○ *a hefty sum* —**heft·i·ly** *adv* —**heft·i·ness** *n*

He·gel /háyg'l/, **G. W. F.** (1770–1831) German philosopher —**He·ge·li·an** /hə gáylee ən/ *adj, n*

he·gem·o·ny /hə jémmənee, héjjə mōnee/ *n* dominance or control, especially by one country over others —**heg·e·mon·ic** /hèjjə mónnik/ *adj*

he·gi·ra /həˈjīrə, hējˈjərə/ n 1 *also* **he·ji·ra** a flight or withdrawal from somewhere 2 **He·gi·ra, He·ji·ra** Muhammad's withdrawal from Mecca to Medina to escape persecution

Hei·deg·ger /ˈhīd ˌeggər/, **Martin** (1889–1976) German philosopher

Hei·del·berg /ˈhīdˈl bùrg/ city in SW Germany, on the Neckar River. Pop. 138,964 (1997).

heif·er /ˈhéffər/ n a young cow that has never had a calf

Hei·fetz /ˈhīfits/, **Jascha** (1901–87) Lithuanian-born US violinist

heigh-ho /ˈhī-, hay-/ *interj* expresses boredom, disappointment, or resignation

height /hīt/ n 1 the distance between the lowest and highest point of somebody or something o *a cliff about 200 feet in height* 2 the distance that somebody or something is above a point 3 the condition of being noticeably tall or high in comparison with others 4 the highest point of something 5 a high place or position *(often pl)* 6 the time of greatest intensity, activity, or success o *at the height of her powers* 7 a high level of intensity or severity *(often pl)* 8 the most extreme example of something o *the height of folly* ■ **heights** *npl* hills or mountains *(often in place names)*

height·en /ˈhīt'n/ *vti* 1 make or become greater or higher 2 appear or make brighter —**height·ened** *adj*

~~heighth~~ incorrect spelling of **height**

Heim·lich ma·neu·ver /ˈhīmlik-/ n an emergency treatment for choking that uses an upward thrust immediately below the breastbone

ORIGIN The treatment is named for Henry J. Heimlich (1920–), who devised it.

Hei·ne /ˈhīnə/, **Heinrich** (1797–1856) German poet

hei·nous /ˈháynəss/ *adj* utterly evil —**hei·nous·ly** *adv* —**hei·nous·ness** n

heir /air/ n 1 the legal inheritor of something 2 a recipient of a tradition —**heir·less** *adj* —**heir·ship** n ◊ See note at **air**

heir ap·par·ent *(pl* **heirs ap·par·ent)** n 1 somebody whose right to an inheritance cannot be altered by the birth of another heir 2 the expected successor of somebody's position

~~heirarchy~~ incorrect spelling of **hierarchy**

heir·ess /ˈáirəss/ n a woman who is the legal inheritor of something

heir·loom /ˈáir lòòm/ n 1 something valuable handed down from one generation of a family to another 2 something legally inherited by somebody

heir pre·sump·tive *(pl* **heirs pre·sump·tive)** n somebody whose right to an inheritance ceases on the birth of somebody with a stronger legal claim

Hei·sen·berg /ˈhīz'n burg/, **Werner** (1901–76) German physicist. He discovered the uncertainty principle.

heist /hīst/ n an armed robbery *(slang)* —**heist** *vt*

he·ji·ra n = **hegira**

held past tense, past participle of **hold**[1]

Hel·en /ˈhéllən/, **Hel·en of Troy** n in Greek mythology, the wife of Menelaus, a beautiful woman whose abduction by Paris was the cause of the Trojan War

Hel·e·na /ˈhél)lənə/ capital of Montana. Pop. 28,306 (1998).

hel·i·cal /ˈhéllikˈl, heé-/ *adj* in the shape of a helix or spiral —**hel·i·cal·ly** *adv*

hel·i·cop·ter /ˈhélli kòptər/ n an aircraft with rotors instead of wings ■ *vti* fly in a helicopter

ORIGIN Helicopter is formed from Greek words that mean "spiral" and "wing." The name was originally coined in French, and early examples in English sometimes have a French form. The usual modern spelling is recorded from the 1880s.

He·li·op·o·lis /ˌheélee óppəliss/ city of ancient Egypt, in the Nile delta

He·li·os /ˈheélee òss/ n in Greek mythology, the god of the sun. Roman equivalent **Sol**

he·lio·trope /ˈheélee ə tròp/ *(pl* **-tropes** *or same)* n 1 a plant with purple flowers 2 a plant with flowers that turn toward the sun

hel·i·pad /ˈhéllə pàd/ n a helicopter landing place

hel·i·port /ˈhéllə pàwrt/ n an airport for helicopters

he·li·um /ˈheélee əm/ n *(symbol* He) an inert gas. Use: inert atmospheres, cryogenic research, lasers, inflating balloons.

he·lix /ˈheéliks/ *(pl* **he·lix·es** *or* **hel·i·ces** /ˈhélli seèz, heéli-/) n something in the shape of a spiral or coil

hell n 1 *also* **Hell** a place or condition of punishment where bad people are believed to go after death, according to many religions 2 the place where everyone is believed to go after death, according to some religions 3 a situation in which there is great unpleasantness or suffering ■ *interj* expresses annoyance or surprise *(sometimes offensive)* ◊ **from hell** of the worst sort imaginable *(infml)* ◊ **give somebody hell** scold somebody severely *(infml)* ◊ **like hell** very fast or very intensely *(infml)* ◊ **raise hell** *(infml)* 1 object strongly and loudly 2 celebrate or party wildly

ORIGIN Hell goes back to an ancient form meaning "hide, conceal," and is in fact related to the second part of *conceal*.

he'll /heel/ *contr* 1 he shall 2 he will

Hel·las /ˈhélləss/ Greek name for Greece

hell-bent *adj* determined to do something, regardless of the consequences

Hel·lene /hé lèen/ *n* somebody from Greece *(fml)*

Hel·len·ic /he lénnik/ *adj* of Greece, or its people, languages, or culture

Hel·ler /héllər/, **Joseph** (1923–99) US writer

Hel·les·pont /héllis pònt/ ◆ **Dardanelles**

hell-hole /hél hòl/ *n* a dreadful place

hell·ish /héllish/ *adj* 1 very wicked or cruel 2 of hell 3 very unpleasant or difficult *(infml)* —**hell·ish·ly** *adv* —**hell·ish·ness** *n*

Hell·man /hélmən/, **Lillian** (1905–84) US playwright

hel·lo /hə lô, he-/ *interj, n (pl* **-los**) 1 expresses a greeting 2 used to attract attention ○ *Hello! Is anyone there?*

Hells Can·yon gorge in Idaho and Oregon, on the Snake River. Depth 7,900 ft./2,400 m. Length 40 mi./64 km.

helm *n* 1 a ship's steering apparatus 2 a position of control or leadership in an organization or country ■ *vt* control and direct an organization or country

hel·met /hélmət/ *n* a hard protective head covering —**hel·met·ed** *adj*

helms·man /hélmzmən/ *(pl* **-men** /-mən/) 1 somebody whose job it is to steer a ship 2 the leader of an organization or country

Hé·lo·ïse /èllô eèz/ (1098?–1164) French abbess and lover of Peter Abelard

help *v* 1 *vti* provide assistance to somebody 2 *vti* make something easier or more likely ○ *More experience would help you get a better job.* 3 *vti* bring about an improvement in an unpleasant situation ○ *I took the medication, but it didn't help.* 4 *vti* provide somebody with something needed, especially money 5 *vt* give somebody or yourself a serving of food ○ *Help yourself to some more.* 6 *vt* keep somebody or yourself from doing something *(usually in negative statements)* ○ *I couldn't help overhearing.* ■ *n* 1 assistance 2 somebody or something that assists 3 a paid employee or employees, especially domestic servants or farm laborers *(often offensive)* ■ *interj* calls for assistance —**help·er** *n* ◇ **help yourself** take something freely ◇ See note at **assistant**

ƒ help desk *n* a service providing technical support for users of a computer system or network

help·ful /hélpfəl/ *adj* providing or willing to provide help —**help·ful·ly** *adv* —**help·ful·ness** *n*

help·ing /hélping/ *n* an amount of food served to somebody

help·less /hélpləss/ *adj* 1 needing help 2 defenseless 3 unable to prevent something from happening —**help·less·ly** *adv* —**help·less·ness** *n*

help·line /hélp lìn/ *n* a telephone advice or information service

help·mate /hélp màyt/ *n* a helpful companion, especially a spouse

> **ORIGIN Helpmate** is first recorded in the early 18C, and was influenced by, if not actually based on, earlier (late 17C) *helpmeet*, with the same meaning. *Helpmeet* itself derives from a misunderstanding of a phrase in the Bible (Genesis 2:18, 20), "an help meet for him," which actually means "a helper suitable for him," with *meet* as an adjective, not a noun.

Hel·sin·ki /hel síngkee/ capital and chief port of Finland. Pop. 551,123 (2000).

hel·ter-skel·ter /hèltər skéltər/ *adv, adj* 1 hurriedly 2 haphazardly ■ *n* a hurried or confused state

~~**helth**~~ incorrect spelling of **health**

hem[1] *n* 1 a folded stitched edge on a piece of fabric 2 a hemline ■ *v* (**hemmed, hem·ming**) 1 *vti* make a hem on a fabric or garment 2 *also* **hem in** *vt* surround or confine

hem[2] (**hemmed, hem·ming**) *vi* hesitate in speech by making a noise in the throat —**hem** *interj, n* ◇ **hem and haw** hesitate while speaking or deciding about something

he-man *n* a muscular man *(infml)*

he·ma·tol·o·gy /hèemə tólləjee/ *n* the branch of medicine devoted to the study of blood and blood-producing tissues —**he·ma·to·log·ic** /hèemətə lójjik/ *adj* —**he·ma·tol·o·gist** *n*

US Office of War Information

Ernest Hemingway

Hem·ing·way /hémming wày/, **Ernest** (1899–1961) US writer

hem·i·sphere /hémmi sfeèr/ *n* 1 one half of the Earth 2 one half of a sphere 3 each of the two halves of the front part of the brain —**hem·i·spher·ic** /hèmmi sfeèrik, -sférrik/ *adj* —**hem·i·spher·i·cal** *adj*

Hem·i·spher·ic Eng·lish *n* the English spoken in the SW United States

hem·line /hém lìn/ *n* 1 the bottom edge of a skirt, dress, or coat 2 the height above or below the knee of the hem of a piece of women's clothing

hem·lock /hém lòk/ *(pl* **-locks** or same) *n* 1 a poison obtained from the fruit of an herbaceous plant 2 a poisonous plant yielding hemlock 3 an evergreen tree with short blunt needles and small cones 4 the wood of the hemlock tree. Use: construction, paper pulp.

hemo- *prefix* blood ○ *hemophilia*

he·mo·glo·bin /héemō glóbin/ *n* an oxygen-transporting substance in red blood cells

he·mo·phil·i·a /héemə fíllee ə, -feélyə/ *n* a disorder in which the blood fails to clot normally —**he·mo·phil·i·ac** *n* —**he·mo·phil·ic** *adj*

~~hemorrage~~ incorrect spelling of **hemorrhage**

hem·or·rhage /hémmərij/ *n* **1** excessive bleeding **2** an uncontrolled loss ○ *a hemorrhage of cash that threatened the firm* —**hem·or·rhage** *vti*

hem·or·rhoids /hémmə róydz/ *npl* swollen anal veins —**hem·or·rhoid·al** /hèmmə róyd'l/ *adj*

hemp *n* **1** a tough plant fiber. Use: canvas, rope, paper, cloth. **2** cannabis

hen *n* **1** an adult female chicken **2** a female bird —**hen·nish** *adj*

hence *adv* (*fml*) **1** because of this **2** later than now

hence·forth /hénss fáwrth/, **hence·for·ward** /henss fáwrwərd/ *adv* from now on

hench·man /hénchmən/ (*pl* **-men** /-mən/) *n* **1** a supporter or associate, especially of somebody involved in a criminal or dishonest cause (*disapproving*) **2** a loyal follower

ORIGIN The first part of **henchman** seems to represent *hengest*, an old form meaning "stallion." In the earliest records a **henchman** is a squire or page, but the connection with horses suggests that the word may originally have meant "groom." It fell out of use in the course of the 17C, but reappeared in the 18C for the personal attendant of a Scottish Highland chief. This was taken up by Sir Walter Scott in the early 19C, and he also appears to have been the first to extend the use to any trusty right-hand man.

hen·na /hénnə/ *n* **1** a red dye. Use: hair dye, cosmetics, fabric colorant. **2** a bush from whose leaves henna is obtained —**hen·na** *adj*, *vt*

hen·peck /hén pèk/ *vt* subject a husband to continual nagging (*offensive*)

hen·ry /hénree/ (*pl* **-ries**) *n* (*symbol* **H**) the SI unit of electrical inductance

Hen·ry I /hénree/ (1068–1135) king of the English (1100–35)

Hen·ry II (1133–89) king of the English (1154–89)

Hen·ry III (1207–72) king of England (1216–72)

Hen·ry IV (1367–1413) king of England (1399–1413)

Hen·ry IV (1553–1610) king of France (1589–1610)

Hen·ry V (1387–1422) king of England (1413–22)

Hen·ry VI (1421–71) king of England (1422–61, 1470–71)

Hen·ry VII (1457–1509) king of England (1485–1509)

Hen·ry VIII (1491–1547) king of England and Ireland (1509–47)

Hen·ry, O. (1862–1910) US short-story writer

Hen·son /hénss'n/, **Matthew** (1866–1955) US explorer

hep·a·ti·tis /hèppə títiss/ *n* inflammation of the liver

Hep·burn /hép bùrn/, **Audrey** (1929–93) Belgian-born US actor

Hep·burn, Katharine (*b.* 1907?) US actor

He·phaes·tus /hi féstəss/ *n* in Greek mythology, the god of fire. Roman equivalent **Vulcan**

hep·ta·gon /héptə gòn/ *n* a seven-sided figure —**hep·tag·o·nal** /hep tággən'l/ *adj*

her *pron* (as the object or complement of a verb or preposition) **1** refers to a woman, girl, or female animal who has been previously mentioned or whose identity is known ○ *Ask her to wait.* **2** refers to a country that has been previously mentioned or whose identity is known (*fml*) ○ *Britain and those who trade with her* **3** refers to a car, machine, or ship ○ *Fill her up, please.* ■ *adj* belonging to or associated with her ○ *That's her coat.* ○ *the Bismarck and her crew*

He·ra /héerə, hérrə/ *n* in Greek mythology, the queen of the gods. Roman equivalent **Juno** 1

Her·a·cli·tus /hérrə klítəss/ (*fl* 500? BC) Greek philosopher —**He·ra·cli·te·an** *adj*

Her·a·kles *n* in Greek mythology, a son of Zeus noted for his strength. Roman equivalent **Hercules** 1

her·ald /hérrəld/ *n* **1** a bringer of news **2** a sign of what will happen (*literary*) **3** formerly, a king's official messenger ■ *vt* **1** give or be a sign of something that is going to happen **2** welcome or announce somebody or something enthusiastically

he·ral·dic /hə ráldik/ *adj* of heraldry or heralds —**he·ral·di·cal·ly** *adv*

her·ald·ry /hérrəldree/ *n* **1** the study of coats of arms **2** coats of arms

He·rat /he rát/ city in NW Afghanistan. Pop. 177,300 (1988 estimate).

herb /urb, hurb/ *n* **1** a low-growing aromatic plant used as a seasoning or for its medicinal properties **2** a plant that does not have woody stems and forms new stems each season

her·ba·ceous /hur báyshəss, ur-/ *adj* of plants that do not have woody stems and form new stems each season

her·ba·ceous bor·der *n* a flower bed containing perennial plants

herb·al /úrb'l, húr-/ *adj* of aromatic herbs ■ *n* a book listing herbs and their properties

herb·al·ism /úrbə lìzzəm, húr-/ *n* alternative medicine based on herbs

herb·al·ist /úrbəlist, húr-/ n somebody who sells medicinal herbs or treats people with them

Her·bert /húrbərt/, **Victor** (1859–1924) Irish-born US composer

her·bi·cide /húrbə sìd, úr-/ n a chemical substance for killing weeds or unwanted plants —**her·bi·cid·al** /hùrbi síd'l, ùrbi-/ adj

her·bi·vore /húrbi vàwr, úr-/ n an animal that eats only plants

her·biv·o·rous /hur bívvərəss, ur-/ adj describes an animal that eats only plants

Her·cu·la·ne·um /hùrkyə láynee əm/ ancient Roman town near modern Naples, destroyed with its neighbor Pompeii in the eruption of Vesuvius in AD 79

Her·cu·le·an /húrkyə leé ən, hur kyóôlee ən/ adj 1 of or associated with Hercules 2 also **her·cu·le·an** needing great strength or effort

Her·cu·les /húrkyə leèz/ n 1 in Roman mythology, a son of Zeus noted for his strength. Greek equivalent **Herakles 2** (pl same or **Her·cu·les·es**) a very strong man

herd n 1 a large group of domestic animals of the same kind, especially cattle 2 a large group of wild animals of the same kind 3 a large group of people with a common interest or purpose ■ vt move or collect a group of people or animals somewhere —**herds·man** n

herd·er /húrdər/ n somebody who tends domestic animals

here /heer/ adv 1 in this place 2 at this point or stage 3 now 4 indicates an offer ○ Here's my phone number. 5 introduces a topic ○ Now, here is a question for everybody. ◇ **neither here nor there** irrelevant ◊ See note at **hear**

here·a·bouts /heerə bówts/ adv in the area

here·af·ter /heer áftər/ (fml) adv 1 after the present time 2 in any following part of a text 3 after death ■ n life after death

here·by /heer bí/ adv by this means (fml)

he·red·i·tar·y /hə réddi tèrree/ adj 1 passed on genetically 2 handed down through generations by inheritance 3 holding a right or property through inheritance

he·red·i·ty /hə réddətee/ n 1 the passing on of genetic characteristics 2 ancestry

here·in /heer ín/ adv (fml) 1 in this document 2 in this respect

here·in·af·ter /heèrin áftər/ adv later in this document (fml)

here·of /heer úv, -óv/ adv of this (fml)

her·e·sy /hérrəsee/ (pl -sies) n 1 an unorthodox religious belief 2 an unorthodox opinion in philosophy, science, or politics

her·e·tic /hérrətik/ n 1 somebody who holds an unorthodox religious belief 2 somebody who holds an unorthodox opinion in philosophy, science, or politics —**he·ret·i·cal** /hə réttik'l/ adj

here·to /heer toô/ adv to this document or matter (fml)

here·to·fore /heèrtə fáwr/ adv up until now (fml)

here·up·on /heèrə pón/ adv (fml) 1 at this 2 on this matter

here·with /heer wíth, -wíth/ adv 1 with this communication 2 by this statement (fml)

her·i·ta·ble /hérritəb'l/ adj able to be inherited —**her·i·ta·bil·i·ty** /hèrritə bíllətee/ n

her·i·tage /hérritij/ n 1 a country's history, historical buildings, and past culture considered as benefiting the present generation 2 something passing from generation to generation within a social group

her·maph·ro·dite /hər máffrə dìt/ n 1 a person, animal, or plant with both male and female sexual organs and characteristics 2 somebody or something combining contradictory elements —**her·maph·ro·dit·ic** /hər màffrə díttik/ adj —**her·maph·ro·dit·ism** n

ORIGIN Hermaphrodite derives from the name (combining the names of his parents) of Hermaphroditus, who was the son of Hermes, the messenger of the Greek gods, and Aphrodite, the Greek goddess of love. Myth has it that a nymph Salmacis desired, and achieved, complete union with him, their two bodies becoming one.

Her·mes /húr meèz/ n in Greek mythology, a god who was a messenger. Roman equivalent **Mercury 1**

her·met·ic /hər méttik/, **her·met·i·cal** /-ik'l/ adj airtight —**her·met·i·cal·ly** adv

her·mit /húrmit/ n 1 somebody who chooses to live in isolation from society 2 an early Christian living apart from society —**her·mit·ic** /hur míttik/ adj

her·mit·age /húrmitij/ n 1 a place where a hermit lives 2 **Her·mit·age** an art museum in St. Petersburg, Russia.

her·mit crab n a crab that lives in an empty mollusk shell

her·ni·a /húrnee ə/ (pl -as or -ae /-eè/) n a medical condition in which an internal organ projects through the wall of the cavity that contains it —**her·ni·al** adj

he·ro /heèrō/ (pl -roes) n 1 a very brave person 2 somebody admired 3 the main male character in a fictional plot 4 a long sandwich of meat, cheese, lettuce, and tomato

He·ro /heèrō/ n in Greek mythology, a priestess of Aphrodite whose lover Leander swam the Hellespont every night to visit her

Her·od (the Great) /hèrrəd-/ (73–4 BC) king of Judea (37–4 BC)

Her·od An·ti·pas /-ánti pàss/ (21 BC–AD 39) Galilean leader

He·rod·o·tus /hə róddətəss/ (484?–425? BC) Greek historian

he·ro·ic /hi rṓ ik/ *adj* **1** exceedingly courageous **2** of or for a hero **3** grand or extreme ■ **he·ro·ics** *npl* overdramatic behavior or talk —**he·ro·i·cal·ly** *adv*

he·ro·ic cou·plet *n* a pair of rhyming lines of iambic pentameter verse

her·o·in /hérrō in/ *n* a derivative of morphine that is an addictive illegal narcotic drug

---

SPELLCHECK Do not confuse the spelling of **heroin** and **heroine** ("a brave woman"), which sound similar.

---

her·o·ine /hérrō in/ *n* **1** a very brave woman **2** an admired woman **3** the main woman character in a fictional plot ◊ See note at **heroin**

her·o·ism /hérrō izzəm/ *n* great courage

her·on /hérrən/ *n* a long-necked freshwater wading bird

~~heros~~ incorrect spelling of **heroes**

he·ro wor·ship *n* **1** great admiration for somebody **2** the ancient Greek or Roman practice of worshiping semidivine heroes —**he·ro-wor·ship** *vt* —**he·ro-wor·ship·er** *n*

her·pes /húrpeez/ *n* a viral infection causing small painful blisters on the mouth or genitals

Her·rick /hérrik/, **Robert** (1591–1674) English poet

her·ring /hérring/ (*pl* **-rings** *or same*) *n* **1** a small ocean fish with silvery scales **2** a herring as food

her·ring·bone /hérring bṓn/ *n* a pattern of interlocking V shapes

her·ring gull *n* a large common white gull with a gray back and gray wings tipped with black

hers *pron* **1** indicates that something belongs to or is associated with a woman, girl, or female animal who has been previously mentioned or whose identity is known ○ *an uncle of hers* **2** indicates that something belongs to or is associated with a country that has been previously mentioned or whose identity is known (*fml*)

her·self /hər sélf/ *unstressed also* /ər sélf/ *pron* **1** refers to the same woman, girl, or female animal as the subject of the verb ○ *She decided to treat herself.* **2** emphasizes or clarifies which woman, girl, or female animal is being referred to ○ *a letter from the author herself* **3** shows that a woman, girl or female animal is alone or unaided ○ *sitting by herself* **4** her normal self ○ *She's not herself today.*

hertz (*pl same*) *n* (*symbol* **Hz**) the SI unit of frequency equal to one cycle per second

Hertz, Heinrich (1857–94) German physicist. His work on electromagnetic waves led to the development of the telegraph and radio. —**Hertz·i·an** *adj*

Her·ze·go·vi·na /hùrtsə gō veénə/ ◊ **Bosnia and Herzegovina**

he's *contr* **1** he has **2** he is

Hesh·van /héshvən/, **Chesh·van** /khésh vaan, -vən/ *n* the 8th month of the year in the Jewish calendar

hes·i·tant /hézzit'nt/ *adj* slow or reluctant to act because of uncertainty or doubt —**hes·i·tan·cy** *n* —**hes·i·tant·ly** *adv* ◊ See note at **unwilling**

hes·i·tate /hézzi tàyt/ (**-tat·ed, -tat·ing**) *vi* **1** be slow to act, or break off from doing something, because of uncertainty or doubt **2** be reluctant to do something —**hes·i·tat·ing·ly** *adv* —**hes·i·ta·tion** /hèzzi táysh'n/ *n*

SYNONYMS hesitate, pause, falter, stumble, waver, vacillate CORE MEANING: show uncertainty or indecision

---

~~hesitent~~ incorrect spelling of **hesitant**

Hes·se /hess, héssə/, **Hermann** (1877–1962) German novelist and poet

Hes·ti·a /héstee ə/ *n* in Greek mythology, the goddess of the hearth. Roman equivalent **Vesta**

hetero- *prefix* different, other ○ *heterosexual*

het·er·o·dox /héttərə dòks/ *adj* disagreeing with established opinions —**het·er·o·dox·y** *n*

het·er·o·ge·ne·ous /hèttərō jeénee əss/, **het·er·og·e·nous** /hèttə rójjənəss/ *adj* **1** consisting of unrelated or dissimilar parts **2** unrelated or dissimilar —**het·er·o·ge·ne·i·ty** /hèttə rō jə neé itee/ *n* —**het·er·o·ge·ne·ous·ly** *adv*

het·er·o·sex·ism /hèttərō sék sìzzəm/ *n* discrimination against homosexual men and women by heterosexuals —**het·er·o·sex·ist** *n, adj*

het·er·o·sex·u·al /hèttərō sékshoo əl/ *n* somebody sexually attracted to members of the opposite sex —**het·er·o·sex·u·al** *adj* —**het·er·o·sex·u·al·i·ty** /hèttərō sekshoo állətee/ *n*

heu·ris·tic /hyoo rístik/ *adj* of a teaching method that encourages learners to discover solutions for themselves ■ *n* a helpful procedure for getting a solution —**heu·ris·ti·cal·ly** *adv*

heu·ris·tics /hyoo rístiks/ *n* problem-solving by trial and error (+ *sing verb*)

~~heven~~ incorrect spelling of **heaven**

hew /hyoo/ (**hewn** /hyoon/ *or* **hewed**) *v* **1** *vti* cut wood or stone with an ax **2** *vt* make by cutting wood or stone

---

SPELLCHECK Do not confuse the spelling of **hew** and **hue** ("a shade of color"), which sound similar.

---

hex *n* **1** a curse or evil spell **2** a bringer of bad luck ■ *vt* **1** curse or bewitch **2** have a bad effect on

⨍ **hex·a·dec·i·mal** /hèksə déssim'l/ *adj* based on the number 16 ■ *n* **1** a number with base 16 **2** a notation for numbers with base 16

hex·a·gon /héksə gòn/ *n* a six-sided figure —**hex·ag·o·nal** /hek sággən'l/ *adj*

hex·a·gram /héksə gràm/ *n* 1 a six-pointed star-shaped figure 2 a pattern of six lines used in divination

hex·am·e·ter /hek sámmətər/ *n* a verse line of six metrical feet —**hex·a·met·ric** /hèksə méttrik/ *adj*

hey *interj* 1 demands somebody's attention (*infml*) 2 expresses amazement, delight, disappointment, or irritation 3 used as a greeting (*infml*)

hey·day /háy dày/ *n* somebody's or something's prime

ORIGIN Heyday represents a use of an old exclamation of joy or surprise, the original form of which was *heyda*. It therefore has no etymological connection with *day*, or with "making hay."

Hey·er·dahl /háy ər dàal, hí́-/, **Thor** (*b.* 1914) Norwegian anthropologist

Hf *symbol* hafnium

hi *interj* hello (*infml*)

HI *abbr* 1 Hawaii 2 hearing-impaired 3 humidity index

Hi·a·le·ah /hì ə leè ə/ *city* in SE Florida. Pop. 211,392 (1998).

hi·a·tus /hī áytəss/ (*pl* **-tus·es** *or* **same**) *n* an unexpected gap or break in continuity

Hi·a·wa·tha /hì ə wáwthə/ (*fl* 1550) Onondaga leader

hi·ber·nate /hībər nàyt/ (**-nat·ed, -nat·ing**) *vi* pass the winter in a dormant state resembling sleep —**hi·ber·na·tion** /hībər náysh'n/ *n*

Hi·ber·ni·a /hī búrnee ə/ *n* Ireland (*literary*) —**Hi·ber·ni·an** *adj, n*

hi·bis·cus /hī bískəss, hi̇́-/ *n* a bush with large brightly colored flowers

hic·cup /hí kùp, híkəp/, **hic·cough** *n* 1 a convulsive gasp produced by an abrupt involuntary contraction of the diaphragm 2 a setback in arrangements (*infml*) ■ **hic·cups** *npl* an attack of gulping intakes of breath —**hic·cup** *vti*

hick *n* a country person regarded as unsophisticated (*slang insult*)

hick·ey /híkee/ (*pl* **-eys** *or* **-ies**) *n* a threaded fitting for joining two parts

Wild Bill Hickok

Hick·ok /hík ok/, **Wild Bill** (1837–76) US law enforcer, gunfighter, and scout

hick·o·ry /híkəree/ (*pl* **-ries**) *n* 1 a hard light-colored wood. Use: tool handles, sports equipment, furniture. 2 a North American tree that produces nuts and hickory wood

hid·den a·gen·da *n* an undisclosed motive or objective

hide[1] (**hid, hid·den** /hídd'n/ *or* **hid, hid·ing**) *v* 1 *vti* move deliberately out of sight 2 *vt* keep something secret 3 *vt* block the view of something

hide[2] *n* the skin of an animal such as a deer, cow, or buffalo (*often in combination*)

hide-and-seek, hide-and-go-seek *n* a children's game in which one player lets the others hide and then tries to find them

hide·a·way /hídə wày/ *n* a secret hiding place or refuge

hide·bound /híd bòwnd/ *adj* narrow-minded and stubborn

hid·e·ous /híddee əss/ *adj* 1 horrible to see or hear 2 morally repulsive —**hid·e·ous·ly** *adv* —**hid·e·ous·ness** *n* ◊ See note at **unattractive**

hide·out /híd òwt/ *n* a place to hide in

hie /hī/ (**hied, hie·ing** *or* **hy·ing, hies**) *vi* hurry somewhere (*archaic*)

~~heifer~~ incorrect spelling of **heifer**

~~hieght~~ incorrect spelling of **height**

hi·er·ar·chy /hī́ raarkee, hī́ ə-/ (*pl* **-chies**) *n* 1 an organization or group divided into ranks 2 the controlling group in an organization or system —**hi·er·ar·chi·cal** *adj* —**hi·er·ar·chi·cal·ly** *adv*

ORIGIN Originally **hierarchy** referred to the divisions of angelic beings in early Christian theology, and for a long time after its first appearance in the 14C it is found primarily in religious and ecclesiastical contexts. This is in keeping with its Greek origins: its first element represents Greek *hieros* "sacred, holy." The general use of any group with members ranked one above the other did not develop until the 17C.

hi·er·o·glyph·ics /hīrə glíffiks, hī́ ərə-/ *n* a writing system that uses pictures or symbols (+ *sing verb*) ■ *npl* writing that is hard to decipher (*infml*; + *pl verb*)

hi·fa·lu·tin *adj* = **highfalutin**

hi-fi /hī́ fī́/ (*pl* **n**) 1 a set of high-quality audio equipment (*dated*) 2 high fidelity

hig·gle·dy-pig·gle·dy /hígg'ldee pígg'ldee/ *adj* disorganized and scattered ■ *adv* in a messy state

high /hī/ (**-er, -est**) *adj* 1 of great height ○ *a high wall* 2 reaching a particular height above a known or stated level ○ *ten feet high* 3 above average 4 raised in musical or sound pitch 5 blowing strongly (*refers to wind*) 6 important in rank 7 very favorable ○ *high esteem* 8 at a peak of activity or intensity ○ *high summer* 9 under the influence of drugs or alcohol (*slang*) ■ *adv* at, in, or into a high position ○ *flew high into the sky* ■

1 a higher than usual level or position ○ *prices reaching all-time highs* **2** a mass of high atmospheric pressure **3** a top temperature ○ *today's high of 100 degrees* **4** an elated or intoxicated state *(infml)* **5** a high gear in a motor vehicle *(infml)* ◇ **high and dry** stranded and abandoned ◇ **high and low** in every conceivable place ◇ **high and mighty** arrogant and self-important

high·ball /hī bàwl/ *n* **1** liquor mixed with water or a carbonated drink **2** a railroad signal

high·born /hī bàwrn/ *adj* born into a rich or noble family

high·boy /hī bòy/ *n* a tall chest of drawers

high·bred /hī brèd/ *adj* from good breeding stock

high·brow /hī bròw/ *adj* intellectual ■ *n* an intellectual person —**high·brow·ism** *n*

high·chair /hī chàir/ *n* a baby's chair with long legs and often a detachable tray, used at mealtimes

high-class *adj* **1** for the rich **2** sophisticated

high com·mand *n* **1** a group of senior officers who jointly control military operations **2** a military headquarters

high com·mis·sion·er *n* the head of an international commission

High Court *n* the US Supreme Court

ƒ**high-end** *adj* **1** sophisticated ○ *high-end consumers* **2** having extensive and sophisticated capabilities and features

high·er ed·u·ca·tion *n* post-secondary school education

high·er-up *n* somebody in a position of authority *(infml)*

high ex·plo·sive *n* a chemical that causes a large explosion. Use: rock blasting, military applications.

high·fa·lu·tin /hī fə lóot'n/, **hi·fa·lu·tin**, **high·fa·lu·ting** /-lóoting/ *adj* pretentious *(infml)*

high fi·del·i·ty *n* very high-quality sound reproduction

high-five *n* a gesture of greeting consisting of a slapping of raised palms *(slang)* —**high-five** *vti*

high-fli·er, **high-fly·er** *n* a high achiever

high-flown *adj* unconvincingly exalted ○ *a high-flown prose style*

high fre·quen·cy *n* a radio frequency in the range 3–30 MHz or of a wavelength of 10–100 m

high-grade *adj* of a high quality

high ground *n* **1** a raised area **2** a position of moral superiority

high-hand·ed *adj* dismissing the views of others —**high-hand·ed·ness** *n*

High Hol·i·days, **High Ho·ly Days** *npl* the period of Jewish festivals from Rosh Hashanah to Yom Kippur

high-jack *v*, *n* = hijack

high jinks, **hi-jinks** /hī jìngks/ *n* fun and games *(infml*; + *sing or pl verb)*

high jump *n* a track-and-field event in which athletes jump over a high horizontal bar —**high jump·er** *n* —**high jump·ing** *n*

high·land /hīland/ *n* an area of hilly land ■ **high·lands** *npl* a hilly or mountainous area ■ *adj* **1** of highlands **2** **High·land** of the Scottish Highlands —**high·land·er** *n*

High·land fling *n* an energetic Scottish solo dance

High·land Games *n* a meeting for Highland sports and dancing (+ *sing or pl verb)*

High·lands /hīlandz/ mountainous area of northern mainland Scotland

high-lev·el *adj* involving high-ranking people

ƒ**high-lev·el lan·guage** *n* a computer programming language approximating to natural language

high life *n* the life of fashionable people *(often ironic)* —**high lif·er** *n*

high·light /hī līt/ *n* **1** the best part of an event **2** a representative part ○ *gave us highlights of the president's speech* ■ **high·lights** *npl* light streaks in hair ■ *vt* **1** emphasize **2** put light streaks in

high·light·er /hī lītər/ *n* **1** a broad-tipped felt pen with brightly colored transparent ink **2** a cosmetic for the face, used to emphasize features

high·ly /hīlee/ *adv* **1** to an extreme degree **2** favorably **3** in a high position or rank

high-main·te·nance *adj* requiring excessive attention

High Mass *n* a fully ceremonial Roman Catholic Mass

high-mind·ed *adj* with high moral principles —**high-mind·ed·ly** *adv*

high·ness /hīnəss/ *n* **1** height **2** **High·ness** a title and form of address for a royal person

high noon *n* noon exactly

high-oc·tane *adj* with a high octane content

high-pitched *adj* **1** at the top of the sound range **2** with a steep slope

high point *n* the best part of an event

high-pow·ered *adj* **1** dynamic **2** influential

high-pres·sure *adj* **1** operating at greater than normal pressure **2** stressful **3** aggressively persistent

high priest *n* **1** the main proponent of an ideology **2** a Jewish chief priest

high pro·file *n* a position of high public prominence

ƒ**high res·o·lu·tion** *n* the use of a large number of dots to create a detailed image

high-rise *adj* **1** multistory **2** describes bicycles with high handlebars —**high-rise** *n*

high road *n* the most direct route

high school *n* an upper secondary school —**high school·er** *n*

high seas *npl* the open ocean

high sea·son *n* the peak season

high-spir·it·ed *adj* lively —**high-spir·it·ed·ly** *adv*

high-strung *adj* nervous

~~**hight**~~ incorrect spelling of **height**

high-tail /hī´ tàyl/ *vti* leave quickly (slang)

✝**high tech, hi-tech** *n* **1** advanced technology **2** plain and simple design —**high-tech** *adj*

high tech·nol·o·gy *n* modern industry, especially involving electronics and computers

high-ten·sion *adj* transmitting high voltage electricity

high tide, high wa·ter *n* the time or point when the tide is highest

high trea·son *n* treason against somebody's own country

high-wa·ter mark *n* **1** a mark showing the highest level reached by a body of water **2** the peak of something

high·way /hī´ wày/ *n* a main road

high·way·man /hī´ wàymən/ (*pl* **-men** /-mən/) *n* formerly, a roadside robber

high·way pa·trol *n* in the United States, state police officers who patrol public highways

high·way rob·ber·y *n* theft from a traveler, committed on or near a road

high wire *n* a tightrope used in a circus act

high-wire *adj* hazardous

hi·jack /hī´ jàk/, **high-jack** *vt* **1** seize an aircraft, ship, or train with force **2** take control of something for your own ends (infml) ■ *n* an act of hijacking an aircraft, ship, train, or motor vehicle —**hi·jack·er** *n* —**hi·jack·ing** *n*

hi·jinks *n* = high jinks

hike *v* (**hiked, hik·ing**) **1** *vi* take a long walk, especially for pleasure **2** *vt* raise an amount to an unreasonable level ◊ *have hiked gas prices* **3** *vt* pull something up ■ *n* **1** a pleasurable long walk **2** a sudden large increase in something —**hik·er** *n*

hi·lar·i·ous /hi láiree əss/ *adj* very funny —**hi·lar·i·ous·ly** *adv*

hi·lar·i·ty /hi lérrətee/ *n* laughter or amusement

Hil·de·gard (of Bin·gen) /híldə gaárd əv bíngən/, **St.** (1098–1179) German writer and composer

hill *n* **1** an area of high land smaller than a mountain **2** a pile or mound **3 Hill** Capitol Hill (infml) ◊ **over the hill** at an age that is supposedly past the prime of life (infml)

Hil·la·ry /hílləree/, **Sir Edmund** (b. 1919) New Zealand mountaineer and explorer who was one of the first two climbers to reach the summit of Mount Everest (1953)

hill·bil·ly /híl billee/ (*pl* **-lies**) *n* a country person regarded as unsophisticated (infml; sometimes offensive)

hill·ock /híllək/ *n* a small hill

hill·side /híl sìd/ *n* the side of a hill

hill·top /híl tòp/ *n* the summit of a hill

hill·y /híllee/ (**-i·er, -i·est**) *adj* **1** having many hills **2** having steep slopes —**hill·i·ness** *n*

hilt *n* the handle of a sword or knife

Hil·ton Head /hílton-/ one of the Sea Islands, in the Atlantic Ocean off S South Carolina

him *pron* refers to a man, boy, or male animal who has been previously mentioned or whose identity is known (as the object or complement of a verb or preposition)

Him·a·la·ya /hìmmə láy ə/, **Him·a·la·yas** mountain system in Asia, forming the northern boundary of the South Asian subcontinent. Highest peak Mt. Everest 29,028 ft./8,848 m. —**Him·a·la·yan** *adj*

Himm·ler /hímmlər/, **Heinrich** (1900–45) German Nazi official

him·self (stressed) /him sélf/ (unstressed) /im sélf/ *pron* **1** refers to the same man, boy, or male animal as the subject of the verb ◊ *He decided to treat himself.* **2** emphasizes or clarifies which man, boy, or male animal is being referred to ◊ *a letter from the author himself* **3** alone or without help ◊ *sitting by himself* **4** his normal self ◊ *He's not himself today.*

hind[1] /hīnd/ *adj* at the back

hind[2] /hīnd/ *n* a female deer

Hin·de·mith /híndə mit/, **Paul** (1895–1963) German composer and viola player

hind·er /híndər/ *vt* delay or obstruct

SYNONYMS hinder, block, hamper, hold back, impede, obstruct CORE MEANING: put difficulties in the way of progress

---

~~**hinderance**~~ incorrect spelling of **hindrance**

Hin·di /híndee/ *n* one of the official languages of India —**Hin·di** *adj*

hind·most /hīnd mòst/ *adj* farthest back (literary)

hind·quar·ter /hīnd kwàwrtər/ *n* a back part of a carcass consisting of one leg and one or two ribs ■ **hind·quar·ters** *npl* the rear of a four-legged animal

hin·drance /híndrənss/ *n* **1** something that is in the way **2** the obstructing of progress

hind·sight /hīnd sìt/ *n* understanding or knowledge after the fact

Hin·du /híndoo/ *n* a follower of Hinduism ■ *adj* **1** of Hinduism **2** of Hindus

Hin·du·ism /híndoo ìzzəm/ *n* the largest Indian religion, which believes in reincarnation and a large number of gods and goddesses

Hin·du Kush /híndoo koŏsh/ mountain system in central Asia, mainly in Afghanistan but extending into Jammu and Kashmir. Highest peak Tirich Mir 25,230 ft./7,690 m.

Hin·du·stan /híndoo staàn/ *n* formerly, the Hindi-speaking region of N India, or the wider Hindi-speaking area of South Asia

hinge *n* a movable joint that fastens two things together and allows one of them to pivot —**hinged** *adj*

☐ **hinge on** *vt* depend on ○ *Our plans hinge on the weather.*

hint *vti* suggest something indirectly ■ *n* **1** an indirect suggestion **2** a piece of advice **3** a very small amount

hin·ter·land /hintər land/ *n* **1** a remote country region **2** the land adjacent to the sea or a river

hip[1] *n* **1** the part of each side of the human body between the waist and the thigh **2** a hipbone

hip[2] (**hip·per, hip·pest**) *adj* fashionable *(slang)* —**hip·ly** *adv* —**hip·ness** *n*

hip[3] *n* a rosehip

HIP *abbr* health insurance plan

hip·bone /hip bṓn/ *n* either of the two large bones forming the sides of the pelvis

hip-hop *n* rap music *(slang)*

hip-hug·gers *npl* pants that go up only to the hips instead of the waist

~~hipocrisy~~ incorrect spelling of **hypocrisy**

hip·pie /hippee/, **hip·py** (*pl* -**pies**) *n* an unconventional young person, especially in the 1960s *(infml)* —**hip·pie·dom** *n*

hip·po /híppō/ (*pl* -**pos**) *n* a hippopotamus *(infml)*

Hip·poc·ra·tes /hi pókrə teez/ (460?–377? BC) Greek physician —**Hip·po·crat·ic** /híppə kráttik/ *adj*

Hip·po·crat·ic oath *n* a physician's promise to uphold medical ethics and standards

ORIGIN The oath is "Hippocratic" because Hippocrates reputedly formulated a similar one.

hip·po·drome /híppə drṓm/ *n* **1** a stadium used for horseracing and chariot racing in ancient Greece or Rome **2** an arena for equestrian events

hip·po·pot·a·mus /híppə póttəməss/ (*pl* -**mus·es** *or* -**mi** /-mī/) *n* a large African amphibious mammal

ORIGIN Hippopotamus comes from a Greek word meaning literally "horse of the river."

hip·py[1] /híppee/ (-**pi·er, -pi·est**) *adj* with wide hips

hip·py[2] *n* = hippie

hip·ster /hípstər/ *n* somebody who is up-to-date, especially in relation to recent developments in jazz *(slang)*

hire /hīr/ *v* (**hired, hir·ing**) **1** *vti* employ somebody **2** *vt* pay for the use of something ○ *hired the Women's Club for the reception* ■ *n* **1** the act of hiring something or somebody **2** an employee —**hir·a·ble** *adj*

hired hand *n* a paid farm worker

hire·ling /hírling/ *n* somebody who works for money, especially somebody whose only motivation is money *(disapproving)*

Hi·ro·hi·to /heerō heétō/ (1901–89) emperor of Japan (1926–89)

Hi·ro·shi·ma /hi róshimə, hìrrə sheémə/ city on SW Honshu Island, Japan. It was devastated by the first atomic bomb to be used in war, in August 1945. Pop. 1,106,922 (2000).

hir·sute /húr sòot, heér-, hər sóot/ *adj* **1** with a lot of hair **2** covered with stiff hairs —**hir·sute·ness** *n*

his *adj, pron* belonging to or associated with him

His·pan·ic /hi spánnik/ *n* a Hispanic American ■ *adj* **1** of people of Spanish descent **2** of Spain **3** of Spanish-speaking people ◊ See note at **Anglo**

USAGE Hispanic comes from a Spanish word for "Spain"; as such, it can refer to not only the Spanish-speaking people of North, Central, and South America, but to all such speakers worldwide, whose first language is Spanish and whose descent is from Spain. By contrast, *Latino* and the feminine form *Latina* are shortened from Spanish *latinamericano*, "Latin American," thus narrowing the scope of meaning to North, Central, and South America. Within the many Spanish-speaking communities of the United States, local or regional preferences are also in play, with *Latino/Latina* used more often on the West Coast and especially California, and **Hispanic** used more often in states such as Florida and Texas.

His·pan·ic A·mer·i·can *n* a US citizen of Spanish descent —**His·pan·ic-A·mer·i·can** *adj*

His·pan·io·la /hìspən yṓlə/ island in the Caribbean southeast of Cuba, divided between Haiti and the Dominican Republic

hiss *v* **1** *vi* make a sound like a continuous "s" **2** *vti* show a negative opinion of somebody or something by making this sound ■ *n* **1** a sound like a continuous "s" **2** a sound expressing disapproval

his·ta·mine /hístə mèen/ *n* a substance released by immune cells that produces allergic reactions —**his·ta·min·ic** /hístə mínnik/ *adj*

his·to·gram /hístə gràm/ *n* a statistical bar graph

his·tol·o·gy /hi stólləjee/ *n* the study of the microscopic structures of animal and plant tissue —**his·to·log·i·cal** *adj* —**his·tol·o·gist** *n*

his·to·ri·an /hi stáwree ən/ *n* **1** a student or scholar of history **2** a recorder of events

his·tor·ic /hi stáwrik/ *adj* **1** significant to history and to the future ○ *a historic decision* **2** associated with history or events in history ○ *visited the historic sites of Rome*

his·tor·i·cal /hi stáwrik'l/ *adj* **1** based on past events ○ *historical novels* **2** used in the past ○ *historical weaponry* **3** of the study of history ○ *a series of historical monographs* —**his·tor·i·cal·ness** *n*

his·tor·i·cal·ly /hi stáwrikəlee/ *adv* **1** with a view to or in terms of history **2** many times before

his·to·ri·og·ra·phy /hi stàwree óggrəfee/ *n* **1** the methods of historical research **2** the writing of history —**his·to·ri·o·graph·i·cal** *adj*

his·to·ry /hístəree/ (*pl* **-ries**) *n* **1** events that happened in the past **2** the study of the past **3** a record of events **4** an interesting past

⚡ **his·to·ry list** *n* a record of the input of previous users of a computer

his·tri·on·ic /hístree ónnik/, **his·tri·on·i·cal** /-ik'l/ *adj* **1** annoyingly overdramatic **2** of acting or actors in the theater (*fml*) —**his·tri·on·i·cal·ly** *adv*

his·tri·on·ics /hístree ónniks/ *n* overdone emotion (+ *sing or pl verb*) ■ *npl* dramatic performances (*fml; + pl verb*)

⚡ **hit** *v* (**hit, hit·ting**) **1** *vti* deliver a blow to something or somebody **2** *vti* come or bring into forceful contact ○ *His van skidded and hit a parked car.* **3** *vt* make a ball move with a bat or hand **4** *vt* strike a button or key, e.g., on a keyboard (*infml*) **5** *vt* in baseball, make a base hit **6** *vt* reach a target **7** *vt* arrive at a particular level (*slang*) ○ *The temperature hit 100 today.* **8** *vt* affect somebody badly ○ *a law that will hit investors hard* ■ *n* **1** in baseball, a base hit **2** a success **3** something that hits a target **4** a hard blow **5** a collision **6** an instance of accessing a database or Internet file **7** the effect of a drug (*slang*) **8** a professional killing (*slang*) —**hit·ter** *n* ◇ **hit it off** get along very well (*infml*)

□ **hit back** *vi* retaliate

hit-and-miss *adj* experiencing variable success

hit-and-run *adj* **1** not stopping after causing an accident ○ *a hit-and-run driver* **2** happening fast and without warning ○ *a hit-and-run attack*

hitch *v* **1** *vti* hitchhike (*infml*) **2** *vt* connect two things so that one can move the other ○ *hitched the horse to the wagon* **3** *vt* fasten something to stop it from moving ○ *hitched the horse to a fence* **4** *vi* move in jerky way ■ *n* **1** an obstacle or problem that prevents progress **2** a means of connecting two things **3** time spent in the military (*infml*) **4** a knot that unties easily **5** a sudden pull on something —**hitch·er** *n*

Hitch·cock /hích kòk/, **Sir Alfred** (1899–1980) British movie director

Sir Alfred Hitchcock

hitch·hike /hích hìk/ (**-hiked, -hik·ing**) *vi* get a free ride by signaling to drivers from the side of the road —**hitch·hik·er** *n*

⚡ **hi-tech** *n, adj* = high tech

hith·er /híthər/ *adv* to this place (*archaic*)

hith·er·to /híthər tòō, hìthər tóō/ *adv* up to now or the time in question

Hit·ler /hítlər/, **Adolf** (1889–1945) Austrian-born German Nazi dictator

hit list *n* a list of possible murder victims (*slang*)

hit man *n* a hired killer (*slang*)

hit-or-miss *adj* carelessly done

hit out (*pl* **hit outs** *or* **hits out**) *n* in field hockey, a hit that restarts the game from the 16-yard line

hit pa·rade *n* a list of pop music's bestselling recordings for a specified week (*dated*)

HIV *n* a virus that disables the immune system and can lead to AIDS. Full form **human immunodeficiency virus**

hive /hīv/ *n* **1** a home for bees **2** a colony of bees ■ *vti* (**hived, hiv·ing**) put bees into a hive

hives /hīvz/ *n* MED = urticaria (+ *sing or pl verb*)

HIV-pos·i·tive *adj* shown by a test to be infected with the HIV virus

⚡ **HLL** *abbr* high-level language

HMO *n* a healthcare organization whose members pay fees and receive medical care from participating physicians, hospitals, and other providers. Full form **health maintenance organization**

Hmong /máwng, hə máwng/ (*pl* **Hmongs** *or* **same**) *n* **1** a member of a people of S China, N Laos, Thailand, and Vietnam **2** the language of the Hmong

HMS, H.M.S. *abbr* Her Majesty's Ship

ho *interj* **1** expresses various emotions, from triumph to derision **2** attracts somebody's attention

Ho *symbol* holmium

hoa·gie /hógee/ *n* a bread roll filled with meat, cheese, and salad

hoard /hawrd/ *vti* store a supply of food or other resources —**hoard** *n* —**hoard·er** *n* ◇ See note at **collect**

SPELLCHECK Do not confuse the spelling of **hoard** and **horde** ("a large group of people"), which sound similar.

hoar frost *n* dew turned to frost

hoarse /hawrss/ (**hoars·er, hoars·est**) *adj* **1** sounding rough **2** with a harshly grating voice —**hoarse·ly** *adv* —**hoarse·ness** *n*

SPELLCHECK Do not confuse the spelling of **hoarse** and **horse** (the animal), which sound similar.

hoar·y /háwree/ (**-i·er, -i·est**) *adj* white with age —**hoar·i·ly** *adv* —**hoar·i·ness** *n*

hoax *n* a deception ∎ *vt* deceive —**hoax·er** *n*

Hobbes /hobz/, **Thomas** (1588–1679) English philosopher and political theorist —**Hobbes·i·an** *adj, n*

hob·ble /hóbb'l/ *v* (**-bled, -bling**) **1** *vt* restrict somebody's actions **2** *vi* limp along **3** *vt* limit a horse's movement by tying its legs together ∎ *n* **1** a rope or strap used for tying a horse's legs together **2** an unsteady walk

hob·by /hóbbee/ (*pl* **-bies**) *n* an enjoyable activity done for pleasure

---

ORIGIN Hobby is a variant of *Robbie*, a familiar form of the man's name *Robert*. It first occurred in *hobbyhorse*, referring to a figure of a horse's head attached to a performer in folk dance, then as a child's toy consisting of a horse's head on a stick. In the late 17C it came to mean "something pursued for pleasure," and was shortened to **hobby** in the early 19C.

---

hob·by·horse /hóbbee hàwrss/ *n* **1** a rocking horse **2** a toy consisting of an artificial horse's head on a long stick **3** a horse figure used in folk dances **4** a favorite topic

hob·by·ist /hóbbee ist/ *n* somebody with a hobby

hob·gob·lin /hób gòbblin/ *n* **1** an imaginary mischievous or evil elf or goblin **2** a fear or worry

hob·nail /hób nàyl/ *n* a nail that protects the soles of boots —**hob·nailed** *adj*

hob·nob /hób nòb/ (**-nobbed, -nob·bing**) *vi* socialize with somebody informally (*disapproving*)

ORIGIN Hobnob comes from an old toast *hob and nob*, or *hob or nob*, used with a clinking of glasses before drinking. Literally the phrase means "have and/or not have": the words are later variants of *hab*, an old form of *have*, and *nab*, its negative equivalent. The verb **hobnob** originally meant "drink together."

---

ho·bo /hó bō/ (*pl* **-boes**) *n* a poor homeless wanderer or traveler

Hob·son's choice /hóbss'nz-/ *n* a choice between the thing offered and nothing at all

---

ORIGIN Hobson's choice is named for Thomas Hobson (1554–1631), who kept a livery stable in Cambridge, England. He gave his customers the choice of the next horse or none at all.

Ho Chi Minh /hō chèe mín/ (1890–1969) resistance leader and president of North Vietnam (1954–69)

Ho Chi Minh Cit·y largest city in Vietnam. Pop. 3,015,743 (1992).

hock[1] *n* an animal's lower leg joint

hock[2] *vt* pawn (*slang*) ◊ **in hock** in debt (*slang*)

hock·ey /hókee/ *n* ice hockey

David Hockney

Hock·ney /hóknee/, **David** (*b.* 1937) British painter

ho·cus-po·cus /hókəss pókəss/ *n* a conjurer's incantation

hod *n* a trough on a pole. Use: carrying heavy building materials.

hodge·podge /hój pòj/ *n* a jumble

Hodg·kin /hójkin/, **Dorothy Mary** (1910–94) Egyptian-born British chemist. She was awarded the Nobel Prize in chemistry (1964) for work on X-rays, molecular science, and penicillin.

Hodg·kin's dis·ease *n* a malignant tumor on the lymph nodes

ORIGIN The disease is named for the British physician Thomas Hodgkin (1798–1866), who described it.

---

hoe *n* a weeding tool consisting of a blade on a long pole —**hoe** *vti*

hoe·down /hó dòwn/ *n* Can, Southern US a square dance

Hof·fa /hóffə/, **Jimmy** (1913–75?) US labor leader

hog *n* **1** a pig **2** any mammal of the pig family **3** an offensive term for a person considered to eat too much (*infml insult*) ∎ *vt* (**hogged, hog·ging**) selfishly take more of something than you need, or keep something for an unfairly long time (*infml*)

ho·gan /hógən/ *n* a traditional Navajo dwelling made of logs and mud, with a roof of earth

Ho·garth /hóg aàrth/, **William** (1697–1764) British painter and engraver —**Ho·garth·i·an** /hō gaàrthee ən/ *adj*

hogs·head /hógz hèd/ *n* a unit of measure for alcohol equal to 63 US gallons or 54 British imperial gallons

hog·tie *vt* **1** tie the legs of an animal or the feet and hands of a person together **2** impede somebody's progress (*infml*)

hog·wash /hóg wòsh/ *n* **1** nonsense (*infml*) **2** leftovers of food that are fed to hogs

hog·wild *adj* wildly excited (*slang*)

Hoh·hot /hō hót/ capital of Inner Mongolia, NE China. Pop. 1,090,000 (1995).

ho·hum *adj* indifferent (*slang*)

hoi pol·loi /hòy pə lóy/ *n* the masses of the common people (*disapproving*)

hoist vt lift, especially using a mechanical device ■ n 1 a device for lifting 2 an act of lifting something

Hok·kai·do /ho kídō/ second largest island of Japan, north of Honshu. Pop. 5,643,647 (1990).

ho·kum /hókəm/ n 1 bunk (infml) 2 unnecessary theatrics

Ho·ku·sai /hōkŏ síí/, Katsushika (1760–1849) Japanese painter and book illustrator

Hol·bein /hólbīn/, Hans, the Younger (1497–1543) and his father Hans, the Elder (1460?–1524) German painters

hold¹ v (**held**) 1 vt grasp and physically retain something 2 vt lift something and keep it in position 3 vt fix something in position 4 vt embrace somebody 5 vt contain something, usually a particular amount 6 vt retain or reserve something 7 vt stop somebody from leaving 8 vt keep possession of something by force 9 vt arrange or stage something 10 vt possess something 11 vt have a particular position and perform the duties of it ○ held the office of treasurer 12 vti keep a promise or ensure that another person keeps a promise ○ held her to her agreement 13 vt believe or feel something ○ "We hold these truths to be self-evident." 14 vt regard somebody in a particular way ○ holds her in high esteem 15 vr have a particular way of standing or walking ○ She holds herself well. 16 vt engross somebody 17 vt decide something legally 18 vi persist ○ a cold spell that has been holding all week 19 vi remain or stand firm ○ The levee held throughout the flooding. 20 vi remain valid 21 vti wait on a telephone line ■ n 1 an act of grasping and retaining the grasp 2 a wrestling technique 3 a support 4 control over somebody 5 a delaying ◇ **hold something against somebody** bear a grudge against somebody ◇ **on hold** 1 waiting to be connected or reconnected to somebody during a telephone call 2 suspended or postponed ◇ **no holds barred** with no restrictions

☐ **hold forth** vi speak at length, often tediously
☐ **hold on** vi persist
☐ **hold out** v 1 vt extend or proffer 2 vi last ○ Is the food holding out? 3 vi endure
☐ **hold over** vt defer something
☐ **hold up** v 1 vt cause to be delayed 2 vt rob at gunpoint 3 vt display or present as an example ○ The firefighter was held up as a hero. 4 vi endure

hold² n a ship's or plane's cargo space

hold·all /hóld àwl/ n a carryall

hold·back /hóld bàk/ n 1 something that hinders 2 a device on a wagon or carriage that allows a horse to push it back

hold·down n a restraint on wages or prices

hold·er /hóldər/ n 1 a container (often in combination) 2 somebody in possession of something such as a check, ticket, lease, or title (often in combination)

hold·ing /hólding/ n 1 a piece of leased land 2 a piece of property (often pl)

hold·ing com·pa·ny n a company with a controlling interest in another company or other companies

hold·ing pat·tern n the path of a plane that is awaiting permission to land

hold·out /hóld òwt/ n 1 a refusal to agree 2 somebody who holds out

hold·o·ver /hóld òvər/ n 1 a retained official ○ The Attorney General is a holdover from the last administration. 2 a student who repeats a course or grade 3 a tree left standing after others surrounding it have been felled 4 a performer or performance given an extended run

hold·up /hóld ùp/ n 1 an armed robbery 2 a delay

hole /hōl/ n 1 a cavity in an object or area 2 a gap, opening, or perforation ○ a hole in his socks 3 a burrow 4 an unpleasant, usually small and dirty, place (infml) 5 a flaw, e.g., in an argument 6 an awkward situation (infml) 7 in golf, a target in the ground ■ vt (**holed, hol·ing**) 1 make a hole or holes in 2 put in a hole —**hol·ey** adj

SPELLCHECK Do not confuse the spelling of **hole** and **whole** ("entire"), which sound similar.

hole in one n a golf shot that puts the ball in the hole from the tee

Hol·i /hólee/ n the Hindu festival of spring

hol·i·day /hóli dày/ n 1 a period of leisure 2 a legal day off ○ a public holiday 3 a holy day

Hol·i·day /hóllə dày/, Billie (1915–59) US jazz singer

ho·li·er-than-thou adj self-righteous (disapproving)

ho·li·ness /hóleenəss/ n 1 the state or quality of being holy 2 **Ho·li·ness** a title given to the pope

ho·lis·tic /hō lístik/ adj of the whole, especially taking into account all of somebody's mental, physical, and social conditions in the treatment of illness —**ho·lism** /hō lízzəm/ n —**ho·lis·ti·cal·ly** adv

Hol·land /hóllənd/ the Netherlands (infml)

hol·ler /hóllər/ vti yell loudly (infml) —**hol·ler** n

hol·low /hóllō/ adj 1 not solid 2 concave 3 echoing as if in an empty space (refers to sounds) ■ n 1 a cavity in an object or area 2 a valley ■ vti make or become hollowed —**hol·low** adv —**hol·low·ly** adv —**hol·low·ness** n ◇ See note at **vain**

hol·ly /hóllee/ (pl -**lies**) n 1 an evergreen shrub with red berries 2 holly leaves and berries used as a decoration

hol·ly·hock /hóllee hòk/ n a tall plant with showy flowers

Hol·ly·wood /hólliwŏod/ district of Los Angeles, California, a center of the US movie and television industry ■ city in SE Florida, on the Atlantic Ocean. Pop. 130,026 (1998).

Holmes /hōmz/, **Oliver Wendell** (1809–94) US physician and writer and his son **Oliver Wendell, Jr.** (1841–1935) associate justice of the US Supreme Court (1902–32).

hol·mi·um /hólmee əm/ n (symbol **Ho**) a soft silvery-white metallic element

hol·o·caust /hóllə kàwst, hóllə-/ n 1 complete destruction, especially by fire 2 **Hol·o·caust** the systematic extermination of European Jews and other ethnic groups by the Nazis during World War II

ORIGIN Holocaust came via French from a Greek word meaning "burned whole." It was originally used in English for a "burnt offering," a "sacrifice completely consumed by fire." John Milton is the first English writer recorded as using it in the wider sense "complete destruction by fire," in the late 17C, and in the succeeding centuries several precedents were set for its modern application to "nuclear destruction" and "mass murder." The specific application to the mass murder of the Jews by the Nazis during World War II was introduced by historians during the 1950s, probably as an equivalent to Hebrew *ḥurban* and *shoah* "catastrophe" (used in the same sense).

Hol·o·cene /hóllə sèen, hólə-/ n the present epoch of geologic time, which began 10,000 years ago —**Hol·o·cene** adj

hol·o·gram /hóllə gràm, hólə-/ n a three-dimensional photographic image

hol·o·graph /hóllə gràf, hólə-/ n a manuscript handwritten by its author —**hol·o·graph** adj

ho·log·raph·y /hō lóggrəfee/ n the process of making or using holograms —**hol·o·graph·ic** /hòllə gráffik, hòlə-/ adj

Hol·stein /hól stīn, -stèen/ n a black-and-white dairy cow

hol·ster /hólstər/ n a gun holder, usually worn on the hip or shoulder —**hol·ster** vt

ho·ly /hólee/ (-**li·er**, -**li·est**) adj 1 sacred ○ *holy relics* 2 saintly 3 having been consecrated ○ *holy water* —**ho·li·ly** adv

Ho·ly Com·mu·nion n Communion in the Christian church

Ho·ly Fam·i·ly n the family of Jesus Christ, especially as represented in art

Ho·ly Fa·ther n the pope

Ho·ly Ghost n in Christianity, the Holy Spirit

Ho·ly Grail n the legendary Grail

Ho·ly Land region on the eastern shore of the Mediterranean Sea, equivalent to the historic region of Palestine

ho·ly of ho·lies n 1 the inner chamber in the ancient Jewish Temple, where the Ark of the Covenant was kept 2 any sacred place

ho·ly or·ders npl 1 the rite of ordination as a Christian cleric 2 an ordained Christian cleric's rank

Ho·ly Ro·man Em·pire n a former European empire (800–1806) —**Ho·ly Ro·man Em·per·or** n

Ho·ly Spir·it n in Christianity, the third person of the Trinity

ho·ly war n a religious war

ho·ly wa·ter n blessed water in a church

Ho·ly Week n the week leading up to Easter

hom·age /hómmij, ómmij/ n 1 deference 2 a vassal's public acknowledgment of allegiance to a feudal lord

hom·bre /óm brày, ómbree/ n a man (infml)

hom·burg /hóm bùrg/ n a man's felt hat

home /hōm/ n 1 a place where somebody lives 2 a family group ○ *Theirs was a happy home, full of love.* 3 somebody's birthplace 4 an animal's native habitat 5 an establishment where full-time care is provided to people who are not wholly independent 6 in many games, the place or point that must be hit in order to score or reached in order to be safe from attack 7 in baseball, home plate ■ adj 1 domestic ○ *home furnishings* 2 of a household ○ *home life* 3 of an athletic team's own territory ○ *a home game* ■ adv 1 at or to somebody's domicile 2 effectively ○ *criticism that hit home* 3 to the center of something or as far as possible into something ○ *drove the nail home* ■ v (homed, hom·ing) 1 vi return to your domicile or operational base 2 vt be guided electronically to a target 3 vi move toward a place or point —**home·like** adj ◇ **at home** at ease or in a familiar and friendly place

□ **home in on** vt 1 proceed toward a target 2 direct attention to

⚡ **home bank·ing** n computer banking from home

home base n 1 in baseball, home plate 2 a center of operations

home·bod·y /hóm bòddee/ n (pl -**ies**) n somebody who prefers to be at home (infml)

home·boy /hóm bòy/ n a man or boy from the same place as another (slang)

home·brew /hóm brōō/ n homemade beer —**home·brewed** adj

home·com·ing /hóm kùmming/ n 1 a return home 2 an annual event in which people return to their old school for a celebration

home ec·o·nom·ics n the study in school of household management (+ sing verb)

home fries npl fried potatoes

home front n civilian activities during a war

home·girl /hóm gùrl/ n a girl from the same place as another (slang)

home·grown /hóm gròwn/ adj 1 grown in somebody's own garden 2 locally produced ○ *homegrown talent*

home·land /hóm lànd/ n 1 somebody's native country 2 formerly in South Africa under apartheid, a self-governing territory for Black people ■ *adj* of your own country ○ *homeland defense*

home·less /hómləss/ *adj* having no home ■ *npl* people with no home —**home·less·ness** *n*

home·ly /hómlee/ (**-li·er, -li·est**) *adj* regarded as not good-looking —**home·li·ness** *n* ◊ See note at **unattractive**

home·made /hóm máyd/ *adj* **1** made at home **2** makeshift

home·mak·er /hóm màykər/ *n* a manager of a household

homeo- *prefix* similar, alike ○ *homeostasis*

Home Of·fice *n* the British government department responsible for domestic affairs

ho·me·op·a·thy /hòmee óppəthee/ *n* a complementary disease-treatment system that uses small doses of natural substances —**ho·me·o·path** /hómee ə pàth/ *n* —**ho·me·o·path·ic** /hòmee ə páthik/ *adj* —**ho·me·o·path·i·cal·ly** *adv* —**ho·me·op·a·thist** *n*

ho·me·o·sta·sis /hòmee ō stáyssiss/ *n* the body's ability to maintain its temperature and other physiological processes at a constant level —**ho·me·o·stat·ic** /-státtik/ *adj*

home-own·er /hóm ònər/ *n* somebody who owns his or her home, as opposed to renting it

⚡ **home-page** /hóm pàyj/ *n* **1** a Web site's opening page **2** a personal site on the Internet

home plate *n* in baseball, the slab by which the batter stands when hitting and on which a base runner must land in order to score

hom·er /hómər/ *n* **1** in baseball, a home run (*infml*) **2** a homing device ■ *vi* in baseball, make a home run (*slang*)

Ho·mer /hómər/ (*fl* 8C BC) Greek poet

Ho·mer, Winslow (1836–1910) US artist

home rule *n* self-government

home run *n* in baseball, a hit that allows the batter to make a circuit of all four bases and score a run

home-school /hóm skòol/ *vti* teach or be taught at home —**home-school·er** *n* —**home-school·ing** *n*

home shop·ping *n* shopping done via computer or television from home

home·sick /hóm sìk/ *adj* unhappy and longing for home —**home·sick·ness** *n*

home·spun /hóm spùn/ *adj* **1** plain and simple **2** spun or woven by hand at home ■ *n* rough cloth woven from homespun thread

home·stead /hóm stèd/ *n* **1** a house, outbuildings, and land **2** an area of land occupied by a settler ■ *vi* claim and work farmland —**home·stead·er** *n*

home stretch *n* **1** the last section of a racetrack **2** the last stage of an undertaking

home·town /hóm tòwn/ *n* the town or city of somebody's birth

home·ward /hómwərd/ *adv* toward home ■ *adj* going home

home·work /hóm wùrk/ *n* **1** schoolwork done at home **2** preparatory work (*infml*)

hom·ey /hómee/ (**-i·er, -i·est**), **hom·y** *adj* having the atmosphere of a comfortable home ○ *a homey little hotel* —**hom·ey·ness** *n*

hom·i·cid·al /hòmmi síd'l/ *adj* intending or likely to commit murder

hom·i·cide /hómmi sìd/ *n* the act or result of unlawfully killing somebody

hom·i·let·ic /hòmmə léttik/ *adj* of or like a homily

hom·i·ly /hómməlee/ (*pl* **-lies**) *n* **1** a religious lecture **2** a moralizing speech (*disapproving*) —**hom·i·list** *n*

hom·ing /hóming/ *adj* **1** describes a bird that has the ability to return home **2** describes a missile or other device that is able to guide itself to a target

hom·ing pi·geon *n* a pigeon trained to return home

hom·i·nid /hómmənid/ *n* a member of a primate family including human beings —**hom·i·nid** *adj*

hom·i·ny /hómmənee/ *n* puffed and dried corn kernels cooked and eaten as food

homo- *prefix* alike, same ○ *homograph*

ho·mo·ge·ne·ous /hómmə jeenəss, hòmmə-/, **ho·mog·e·nous** /hə mójjənəss, hō-/ *adj* **1** of the same kind **2** having a uniform composition or structure throughout —**ho·mo·ge·ne·i·ty** /hòmə jə neé ətee, hòmmə-/ *n* —**ho·mo·ge·ne·ous·ly** *adv*

ho·mog·e·nize /hə mójjə nìz, hō-/ (**-nized, -niz·ing**) *v* **1** *vt* give milk or cream an even consistency **2** *vti* become or make homogeneous —**ho·mog·e·ni·za·tion** /hə mòjjəni záysh'n, hō-/ *n*

hom·o·graph /hómmə gràf, hómə-/ *n* a word with the same spelling as another but a different meaning —**hom·o·graph·ic** /hòmmə gráffik, hòmə-/ *adj*

ho·mol·o·gous /hə mólləgəss, hō-/ *adj* sharing a similar or related structure, position, function, or value

hom·o·nym /hómmənim/ *n* a word with the same spelling or pronunciation as another, but a different meaning —**hom·o·nym·ic** /hòmmə nímmik/ *adj* —**ho·mon·y·my** /hə mónnimee/ *n*

ho·mo·pho·bi·a /hòmə fóbee ə/ *n* an irrational hatred or fear of homosexuality —**ho·mo·phobe** /hómə fòb/ *n* —**ho·mo·pho·bic** /hòmə fóbik/ *adj*

hom·o·phone /hómmə fòn, hómə-/ *n* a word with the same pronunciation as another but a different meaning —**ho·moph·o·nous** /hō móffənəss/ *adj*

Ho·mo sa·pi·ens /hòmō sáypee ənz, -ènz/ *n* the species of modern human beings

ho·mo·sex·u·al /hòmə sékshoo əl, hòmō-/ *n* somebody who is sexually attracted to people of the same sex ■ *adj* **1** sexually attracted to people of the same sex **2** of homosexuality —**ho·mo·sex·u·al·i·ty** /hòmə sekshoo állətee, hòmō-/ *adj* ◊ See note at **gay**

ORIGIN Homosexual comes from Greek *homos* "same," not, as is sometimes supposed, from Latin *homo* "man."

hom·y *adj* = **homey**

hon. *abbr* **1** honorable **2** honorary

Hon. *abbr* Honorable

hon·cho /hónchō/ *n* somebody in charge (*slang*)

Hon·du·ras /hon doŏrəss/ country in Central America, with coastlines on the Caribbean Sea and the Pacific Ocean. Cap. Tegucigalpa. Pop. 6,406,052 (2001). —**Hon·du·ran** *adj*, *n*

hone /hōn/ *vt* (**honed, hon·ing**) **1** improve with refinements ◊ *honed the speech through rewrites* **2** sharpen on a whetstone ■ *n* **1** a whetstone **2** a machine tool with a rotating abrasive head

USAGE hone in or **home in? Hone** means "sharpen" (*hone a blade*) or, in an extended figurative sense, "improve, refine" (*I honed my ideas*). It is the verb **home,** meaning "move toward," that makes sense with the particle *in,* as in *He homed in on his opponent's weaknesses.*

hon·est /ónnəst/ *adj* **1** morally upright **2** truthful or true **3** impartial **4** reasonable in a particular situation ◊ *an honest mistake* —**hon·est·ly** *adv* —**hon·es·ty** *n*

hon·est bro·ker *n* an arbitrator

hon·ey /húnnee/ *n* **1** a sweet substance made by bees. Use: spread, sweetener. **2** used as an affectionate term of address (*infml*)

hon·ey·bee /húnnee beè/ *n* a bee that makes honey

hon·ey·comb /húnnee kōm/ *n* a structure of six-sided cells constructed out of wax by bees for storing honey ■ *vt* provide with a network of holes or tunnels —**hon·ey·combed** *adj*

hon·ey·dew mel·on /húnnee doo-/ *n* a melon with sweet pale green flesh

hon·eyed /húnneed/, **hon·ied** *adj* **1** ingratiating **2** pleasant-sounding

hon·ey·moon /húnnee moòn/ *n* **1** a vacation for a newly married couple **2** an initial short-lived period of good feeling —**hon·ey·moon** *vi* —**hon·ey·moon·er** *n*

hon·ey·suck·le /húnnee sùk'l/ *n* a climbing shrub with fragrant flowers

Hong Kong /hóng kòng/ special administrative region of China on the southeastern coast. Cap. Victoria. Pop. 7,210,505 (2001).

Ho·ni·a·ra /hò nee aára/ capital of the Solomon Islands. Pop. 35,288 (1990).

honk *n* **1** the sound of a car horn **2** the cry of a goose **3** a sound resembling a goose or car horn ■ *v* **1** *vti* sound a car horn **2** *vi* produce a honk

hon·ky-tonk /hóngki tòngk/ *n* **1** a cheap nightclub (*slang*) **2** ragtime piano-playing

Hon·o·lu·lu /hònnə loŏloo/ capital of Hawaii. Pop. 395,789 (1998).

hon·or /ónnər/ *n* **1** personal integrity ◊ *It's a matter of honor.* **2** respect **3** a woman's virginity or reputation for chastity (*dated*) **4** a source of pride ◊ *an honor to your parents and school* **5** a mark of distinction **6 Hon·or** a form of address used to a judge or mayor ◊ *Your Honor, may we approach the bench?* ■ **hon·ors, Hon·ors** *npl* an academic distinction ■ *vt* **1** have great respect for somebody or something **2** give somebody a special title or award **3** pay tribute to somebody **4** dignify an occasion by making an appearance **5** accept something as money ◊ *The bank won't honor a check without a signature.* **6** keep a promise —**hon·or·ee** *n*

hon·or·a·ble /ónnərəb'l/ *adj* **1** having personal integrity **2** deserving or gaining honor **3 Hon·or·a·ble** used as a title of respect because of an official position held ◊ *The Honorable Mr. Smith, the presiding judge, is on the bench.* —**hon·or·a·bly** *adv*

hon·or·a·ble dis·charge *n* official separation from the armed forces, stipulating that all duties have been honorably fulfilled

hon·o·rar·i·um /ònnə ráiree əm/ *n* (*pl* **-ums** *or* **-a** /-ə/) *n* a fee for a professional service ◊ See note at **wage**

hon·or·ar·y /ónnər èrree/ *adj* **1** awarded as an honor **2** unpaid

hon·or guard *n* a military guard assigned to a ceremony

hon·or·if·ic /ònnər íffik/ *adj* conferring honor ■ *n* **1** a title of respect **2** a form of a word used as a sign of respect

hon·or roll *n* a roster of the best students

hon·or so·ci·e·ty *n* a society for recognition of student achievement

Hon·shu /hón shoo/ largest and most populous island of Japan. Pop. 99,254,194 (1990).

hooch *n* cheap or illegally made alcohol (*slang*)

hood[1] /hoŏd/ *n* **1** a covering for the head attached to a coat **2** a cover for an appliance or machine **3** an engine cover on a vehicle **4** a part of an academic robe that hangs down at the back **5** a folding roof on a vehicle ■ *vt* cover with a hood —**hood·ed** *adj* —**hood·less** *adj*

hood[2] /hoŏd/ *n* a hoodlum (*slang*)

hood[3] /hoŏd/ *n* a neighborhood (*slang*)

-hood *suffix* **1** quality, state, condition ◊ *knighthood* **2** a group of people ◊ *brotherhood*

hood·lum /hoŏdləm, hoōd-/ *n* **1** a gangster **2** a young vandal or criminal

hoo·doo /hoŏ doŏ/ *n* **1** voodoo **2** bad luck —**hoo·doo·ism** *n*

hood·wink /hoŏd wingk/ *vt* deceive or dupe —**hood·wink·er** *n*

hoo·ey /hoŏ ee/ *n* nonsense (*infml*)

hoof /hoŏf, hoŏf/ (*pl* **hooves** /hoŏvz, hoovz/ or **hoofs**) *n* the foot of a horse, deer, or similar animal

hook /hoŏk/ *n* **1** a bent piece of metal used to attach, hang, or lift something **2** something resembling a hook **3** a fishhook **4** something that attracts somebody, especially a potential customer (*infml*) **5** a short swinging blow ■ *v* **1** *vti* fasten with a hook **2** *vt* attach one thing to another **3** *vti* bend like a hook **4** *vt* catch somebody's attention ◇ **by hook or by crook** by some means or other ◇ **hook, line, and sinker** completely (*infml*) ◇ **off the hook** free of a difficult situation (*infml*)

☐ **hook up** *vt* connect electronic devices (*infml*)

hook·ah /hoŏkə, hoŏka/ *n* a water pipe for smoking

hook and eye (*pl* **hooks and eyes**) *n* **1** a clothes fastener consisting of a hook inserted into a loop **2** a latch consisting of a hook inserted into a loop

hooked /hoŏkt/ *adj* **1** addicted (*slang*) **2** obsessed with something (*slang*) **3** shaped like a hook **4** having a hook at the end

hook·er /hoŏkər/ *n* an offensive term for a prostitute (*slang*)

Hook·er /hoŏkər/, **Joseph** (1814–79) US Union general

hook·up /hoŏk ùp/ *n* **1** a system of electronic equipment designed to operate together (*infml*) **2** a connection to a utility such as electricity or gas *o a gas hookup*

hook·worm /hoŏk wùrm/ *n* a parasitic worm with hooked mouthparts

hook·y /hoŏkee/, **hook·ey** *n* truancy (*infml*)

hoo·li·gan /hoŏligən/ *n* a young vandal or criminal (*infml*)

ORIGIN The origin of **hooligan** is not known for certain. It first appeared in print in 1898. It may derive from a stereotypical Irish surname. The *Hooligans* were a fictional rowdy Irish family in a vaudeville song of the 1890s, and a comic Irish character in a cartoon of the time was also called *Hooligan*.

---

hoop *n* **1** a ring of metal or plastic, e.g., for holding a barrel together **2** a ring through which circus animals jump **3** a stiff support for a skirt **4** a ring-shaped earring **5** the game of basketball (*slang*) ◇ **jump** or **go through hoops (for)** go to extreme lengths to please somebody (*infml*)

hoop·la /hoŏp làa, hoŏp làa/ *n* (*slang*) **1** loud celebration **2** great public uproar

hoo·ray /hoŏ ráy/, **hur·ray** /hoŏ ráy, hə-/ *interj* used as a shout of joy ■ *n* a shout of joy

hoose·gow /hoŏss gòw/ *n* a jail (*slang*)

hoot *n* **1** an owl's cry **2** the sound made by a train whistle or car horn **3** a laughing sound ■ *vi* **1** emit a hoot **2** laugh

hoot·en·an·ny /hoŏt'n ànnee/ (*pl* -**nies**) *n* an informal or impromptu performance by folk singers

Hoo·ver /hoŏvər/, **Herbert** (1874–1964) 31st president of the United States (1929–33)

Hoo·ver, J. Edgar (1895–1972) US director of the FBI (1924–72)

hooves plural of **hoof**

hop[1] *v* (**hopped, hop·ping**) **1** *vi* jump lightly on one foot **2** *vi* jump lightly with both or all feet **3** *vt* leap over something **4** *vi* get on or off a passenger vehicle (*infml*) **5** *vi* travel by airplane (*infml*) ■ *n* **1** a small quick jump **2** a short flight (*infml*) **3** a usually short journey (*infml*) **4** a dance (*infml*) **5** a bounce

hop[2] *n* a climbing vine with flowers ■ **hops** *npl* dried hop flowers. Use: flavoring beer.

hope *vti* (**hoped, hop·ing**) want or expect something ■ *n* **1** the confidence that something good will happen **2** likelihood of success *o There's not much hope that things will improve.* **3** a wish or desire

hope·ful /hópfəl/ *adj* **1** having hope **2** giving hope ■ *n* somebody who hopes or expects to be successful —**hope·ful·ness** *n*

hope·ful·ly /hópfəlee/ *adv* **1** in a hopeful way *o a hopefully worded apology* **2** △ indicates that something is hoped

---

USAGE Many people object when **hopefully** is used as a so-called sentence adverb, that is to say, as a sentence introducer that qualifies the entire sentence, as in *Hopefully, someone can resolve this.* The criticism arises from the fact that in this sentence no one is present who is meant to be doing the hoping. You can avoid the whole problem by saying *Let's hope, Let us hope,* or *It is to be hoped.*

~~hopeing~~ incorrect spelling of **hoping**

hope·less /hópləss/ *adj* **1** with no hope of success **2** feeling despair —**hope·less·ly** *adv* —**hope·less·ness** *n*

Ho·pi /hópee/ (*pl* same or -**pis**) *n* **1** a member of a Native North American people of NE Arizona **2** the language of the Hopi people —**Ho·pi** *adj*

Hop·kins /hópkinz/, **Gerard Manley** (1844–89) British poet

hop·per /hóppər/ *n* a large funnel-shaped industrial dispenser

Hop·per /hóppər/, **Edward** (1882–1967) US artist

hop·scotch /hóp skòch/ *n* a children's game in which players hop along squares marked on the ground

---

ORIGIN *Scotch* in **hopscotch** means "scratched line."

Hor·ace /háwrəss/ (65–8 BC) Roman poet —**Ho·ra·tian** /hə ráysh'n/ *adj*

horde /hawrd/ *n* a large group of people (often *pl*) ◇ See note at **hoard**

~~horizen~~ incorrect spelling of **horizon**

ho·ri·zon /hə rīz'n/ *n* the line where the land or sea meets the sky ■ **ho·ri·zons** *npl* somebody's range of experience, knowledge, or interests —**ho·ri·zon·al** *adj*

hor·i·zon·tal /hàwri zónt'l/ *adj* parallel to the horizon and at right angles to the vertical ■ *n* a horizontal line or surface —**hor·i·zon·tal·ly** *adv*

hor·mone /háwr mòn/ *n* 1 a chemical produced in one part of the body that has an effect in another part 2 a chemical in plants or insects that regulates growth —**hor·mon·al** /hawr mốn'l/ *adj*

hor·mone re·place·ment ther·a·py *n* a treatment to offset menopausal symptoms

Hor·muz, Strait of /hawr moóz, háwr mooz/ narrow waterway between Iran and the Arabian Peninsula, linking the Persian Gulf with the Arabian Sea

horn *n* 1 a device that makes a noise as a warning (often in combination) 2 a projection on an animal's head 3 any projection resembling a horn 4 a French horn 5 the hard substance of horns ■ *vt* attack something with horns (refers to horned mammals) —**horned** *adj* ◇ **pull in your horns** adopt a less active or less assertive position

Horn, Cape cape in S Chile, at the southern extremity of South America. Height 1,391 ft./424 m.

horn·bill /háwrn bỉll/ *n* a tropical bird with a large curved bill

hor·net /háwrnət/ *n* a large stinging wasp

horn·pipe /háwrn pỉp/ *n* 1 a British sailors' dance 2 the music for a hornpipe

horn·y /háwrnee/ (-i·er, -i·est) *adj* sexually excited (slang) —**horn·i·ly** *adv* —**horn·i·ness** *n*

ho·rol·o·gy /haw róllajee/ *n* 1 the measurement of time 2 the making of clocks —**hor·o·log·i·cal** *adj* —**ho·rol·o·gist** *n*

hor·o·scope /háwrə skòp/ *n* 1 a diagram of the positions of the stars and planets at a specific time 2 an astrological forecast —**hor·o·scop·ic** /hàwrə skóppik/ *adj*

Ho·ro·witz /háwrə wits/, **Vladimir** (1904–89) Russian-born US pianist

hor·ren·dous /hə réndəss, haw-/ *adj* dreadful —**hor·ren·dous·ly** *adv* —**hor·ren·dous·ness** *n*

hor·ri·ble /háwrəb'l/ *adj* 1 very unpleasant 2 causing horror 3 unkind or rude (infml) —**hor·ri·ble·ness** *n*

ORIGIN Horrible and related words go back to a Latin verb *horrere* that described hair standing on end and so came to mean "tremble, shudder."

hor·rid /háwrid/ *adj* 1 nasty (infml) 2 causing disgust or horror —**hor·rid·ly** *adv* —**hor·rid·ness** *n*

hor·rif·ic /haw ríffik/ *adj* very disturbing or frightening —**hor·rif·i·cal·ly** *adv*

hor·ri·fy /háwrə fì/ (-fied, -fies) *vt* 1 cause to feel horror 2 shock or dismay —**hor·ri·fied** *adj* —**hor·ri·fy·ing** *adj* —**hor·ri·fy·ing·ly** *adv*

hor·ror /háwrər/ *n* 1 intense fear or dislike 2 something that causes horror ■ *adj* describes grotesque and terrifying movies or literature

hor·ror sto·ry *n* 1 a frightening fictional tale 2 a report of a horrifying experience

hor·ror-struck, hor·ror-strick·en *adj* feeling horror

hors de com·bat /àwr də koN bàa/ *adj* no longer able to participate, usually because of an injury

hors d'oeuvre /awr dúrv/ (pl same or **hors d'oeuvres** /-dúrvz/) *n* an appetizer

horse /hawrss/ *n* 1 a four-legged animal used for riding and pulling vehicles 2 a piece of gymnastic equipment for vaulting 3 a frame or support ◇ **beat a dead horse** pursue a topic or course of action likely to be totally unproductive ◇ **from the horse's mouth** from a well-informed and reliable source ◇ See note at **hoarse** □ **horse around** *vi* fool around

horse·back /háwrss bàk/ *adj, adv* on a horse's back

horse chest·nut *n* 1 a shiny brown inedible seed 2 a large tree that produces horse chestnuts

horse·drawn /háwrss dràwn/ *adj* pulled by horses

horse·flesh /háwrss flèsh/ *n* a horse, or horses in general

horse·fly /háwrss flỉ/ (pl -flies) *n* a large biting fly

horse·hair /háwrss hàir/ *n* the long coarse hair from a horse. Use: upholstery, mattress filling, cloth.

horse·man /háwrssmən/ (pl -men /-mən/) *n* 1 a man who rides horses 2 a horse owner or breeder —**horse·man·ship** *n*

horse·play /háwrss plày/ *n* boisterous play

horse·pow·er /háwrss pòwr/ *n* a unit of power equal to 745.7 watts

horse·rac·ing /háwrss ràyssing/ *n* organized racing for horses and their riders

horse·rad·ish /háwrss ràddish/ *n* 1 a long pungent root. Use: in cooking as a seasoning. 2 a tall flowering plant whose roots are eaten as horseradish

horse sense *n* common sense (infml)

horse·shoe /háwrss shòo/ *n* a U-shaped piece of metal nailed to a horse's hoof for protection

horse·shoes /háwrss shòoz/ *n* a game in which players throw horseshoes at a post and score points depending on how close they land to the post (+ *sing verb*)

horse·whip /háwrss wĭp, -hwĭp/ *n* a whip for controlling a horse ■ *vt* (**-whipped, -whip·ping**) beat severely

horse·wom·an /háwrss wŏŏmmən/ (*pl* **-en** /-wĭmmĭn/) *n* 1 a woman who rides horses 2 a woman horse owner or breeder

hors·y /háwrssee/ (**-i·er, -i·est**), **hors·ey** *adj* 1 of horses 2 looking like a horse 3 interested in horses

hor·ta·to·ry /háwrtə tàwree/ *adj* urging a course of action (*fml*)

hor·ti·cul·ture /háwrti kùlchər/ *n* the science or activity of cultivating flowers, fruit, and salad vegetables in gardens or greenhouses —**hor·ti·cul·tur·al** /hàwrti kúlchərəl/ *adj* —**hor·ti·cul·tur·ist** /háwrti kúlchərist/ *n*

Ho·rus /háwrəss/ *n* the ancient Egyptian sun god

ho·san·na /hō zánnə/, **ho·san·nah** *n, interj* a shout of praise

Ho·say /hō sáy/, **Ho·sein** /hō sáyn/ *n* an Islamic religious festival marking the martyrdom of Imam Hosein. Date: 10th day of Moharram.

hose /hōz/ *n* a flexible tube through which a liquid can flow ■ *npl* stockings or tights ■ *vt* (**hosed, hos·ing**) spray or wash something or somebody with water

Ho·se·a /hō záy ə/ *n* a book of the Bible, attributed to Hosea, a Hebrew prophet

ho·sier·y /hṓzhəree/ *n* socks and stockings

hos·pice /hóspiss/ *n* a nursing home for terminally ill people

hos·pi·ta·ble /ho spíttəb'l, hóspitəb'l/ *adj* 1 cordial and generous to visitors 2 agreeable ○ *a hospitable climate* —**hos·pi·ta·bly** *adv*

hos·pi·tal /hóspit'l/ *n* an institution providing medical care

ORIGIN Hospital, hostel, and hotel all go back to the same medieval Latin word meaning "guesthouse, inn." It was formed from the Latin hospes "host, guest." Hospital came into English from an early French form in the 13C, and was originally a hostel for pilgrims and travelers. It was not used explicitly for a place for treating the sick or wounded until the mid-16C.

hos·pi·tal·i·ty /hòspi tállətee/ *n* kindness to visitors

hos·pi·tal·ize /hóspit'l ìz/ (**-ized, -iz·ing**) *vt* put somebody in a hospital —**hos·pi·tal·i·za·tion** /hóspit'li záysh'n/ *n*

⨎**host**[1] /hōst/ *n* 1 somebody who entertains guests 2 somebody who introduces guests on a show 3 the organization providing facilities for an event 4 an organism infected by a parasite 5 the landlord of an inn 6 *also* **host com·pu·ter** the main computer controlling files in a network ■ *vt* 1 accommodate an event 2 introduce guests on

a show 3 entertain guests at a social event 4 create a website for a client

host[2] /hōst/ *n* 1 a large number of people or things 2 an army (*archaic*)

Host /hōst/, **host** *n* the consecrated bread used during the Christian sacrament of Communion

hos·tage /hóstij/ *n* somebody held prisoner until specific demands are met

hos·tel /hóst'l/ *n* 1 an inexpensive lodging for young travelers 2 a cheap inn

hos·tel·ing /hóstəling/ *n* the activity of staying at hostels while traveling —**hos·tel·er** *n*

hos·tel·ry /háwstəlree/ (*pl* **-ries**) *n* an inn (*archaic*)

host·ess /hṓstəss/ *n* 1 a woman who entertains guests 2 a woman whose job is greeting customers in a restaurant —**host·ess** *vti*

hos·tile /hóst'l/ *adj* 1 very unfriendly 2 opposed to somebody or something 3 of an enemy ○ *hostile fire* —**hos·tile** *n* —**hos·tile·ly** *adv*

hos·til·i·ty /ho stíllətee/ *n* 1 intense aggression or anger 2 strong opposition ■ **hos·til·i·ties** *npl* open acts of warfare

hos·tler /hósslər, ósslər/, **os·tler** /ósslər/ *n* formerly, somebody who tended horses at an inn (*archaic*)

hot (**hot·ter, hot·test**) *adj* 1 very warm, or too warm for comfort 2 very spicy 3 controversial ○ *a hot topic* 4 quickly angered ○ *a hot temper* 5 brightly vivid in hue ○ *hot pink* 6 following closely ○ *hot on the trail* 7 topical and interesting ○ *hot news* 8 exciting (*infml*) ○ *a hot new talent* 9 very popular (*infml*) ○ *one of the hottest items for sale* 10 knowledgeable or skilled (*infml*) ○ *not very hot at math* 11 stolen (*slang*) 12 electrically charged ○ *a hot wire* 13 radioactive 14 in an elevated energy state as a result of nuclear processes —**hot·ly** *adv* —**hot·ness** *n*

hot air *n* empty statements or promises (*infml*)

hot-air bal·loon *n* a large balloon with a passenger compartment suspended from it

hot·bed /hót bèd/ *n* 1 an environment where something flourishes, especially something undesirable ○ *a hotbed of corruption* 2 a heated glass-covered planting bed

hot-blood·ed *adj* easily excited or aroused —**hot-blood·ed·ness** *n*

hot but·ton *n* something triggering a swift reaction

hot·cake /hót kàyk/ *n* a pancake ◊ **sell like hotcakes** sell very quickly (*infml*)

hot cross bun *n* a sweet bun marked with a cross, traditionally eaten on Good Friday

hot dog *n* 1 a wiener, typically served in a bun 2 a performer of stunts (*slang*)

hot-dog (**hot-dog·ged, hot-dog·ging**) *vi*

perform dangerous showy stunts *(slang)*
—**hot-dog-ging** *n*

ho-tel /hō tél/ *n* **1** a place where people pay for lodging, and where meals are often available **2 Ho-tel** a communications code word for the letter "H"

ho-te-lier /àw tel yáy, hō téllyər/ *n* a hotel proprietor

ho-tel-ing /hō télling/ *n* the act of providing temporary office desk space for somebody

hot flash *n* a sensation of body heat

hot-foot /hót fŏot/ *adv* quickly

hot-head-ed /hòt héddəd/ *adj* impetuous
—**hot-head** /hót hèd/ *n* —**hot-head-ed-ly** *adv*
—**hot-head-ed-ness** *n*

hot-house /hót hòwss/ *(pl* -**hous-es** /-hòwzəz/) *n*
1 a heated greenhouse **2** a place where something flourishes and develops ⊙ *a hothouse of technological innovation*

⚡ **hot key** *n* a computer key or combination of keys that provides a shortcut for a specific function

hot-line /hót lìn/ *n* **1** a permanent communications link between political leaders **2** a direct telephone link to a service

⚡ **hot-link** /hót lìngk/ *n* a hyperlink

⚡ **hot-list** /hót lìst/ *n* a file of a computer user's most recent hypertext link connections

hot mon-ey *n* funds transferred from one currency to another for short-term gain

hot plate *n* **1** a heated cooking surface **2** a device for keeping food warm

hot po-ta-to *n* a topic that is hard to handle

hot rod *n* a very powerful car *(slang)*

hot seat ◇ **in the hot seat** facing or liable to face criticism or difficult questioning

hot-shot /hót shòt/ *n* a self-assured expert *(infml disapproving)* —**hot-shot** *adj*

hot spot *n* **1** a place of potential unrest **2** a small area of intense heat

hot spring *n* a spring of water heated geothermally

hot stuff *n (slang)* **1** a very good person or thing **2** a person who is regarded as very sexually attractive

hot tod-dy *n* a drink of alcohol and hot water, usually sweetened

hot tub *n* a large bath for more than one person to relax or socialize in

hot-wa-ter bot-tle *n* a warming water-filled container

hot-wire *vt* start a car without a key *(infml)*

Hou-di-ni /hŏō deénee/, **Harry** (1874–1926) Hungarian-born US magician

hound /hownd/ *n* **1** a dog bred for hunting **2** any dog *(infml)* ■ *vt* **1** pursue doggedly **2** urge or nag

hour /owr/ *n* **1** a period of 60 minutes **2** the point in time at the start of an hour ⊙ *There's a bus at 20 past the hour.* **3** time of day ⊙ *at this unearthly hour* **4** a regular time for something ⊙ *her lunch hour* **5** a significant period ⊙ *your hour of glory* ■ **hours** *npl* **1** a long time ⊙ *I was waiting for hours.* **2** the times for doing particular things ⊙ *banking hours* ◇ **of the hour** currently relevant or popular ⊙ *She's the woman of the hour.*

SPELLCHECK Do not confuse the spelling of **hour** and **our** ("belonging to us"), which sound similar.

hour-glass /ówr glàss/ *n* a time-measuring device in which sand falls from one glass bulb into another

hour hand *n* the short hand on a timepiece

hou-ri /hŏoree/ *n* in Islamic belief, one of the beautiful young women who attend Muslim men in paradise

hour-ly /ówrlee/ *adj* **1** happening each hour or very regularly ⊙ *hourly news* **2** calculated or paid by the hour ⊙ *hourly wages* —**hour-ly** *adv*

house *n* /howss/ *(pl* **hous-es** /hówzəz/) **1** a building for people to live in **2** the occupants of a house **3** a building for animals **4** a restaurant or other eating establishment ⊙ *the specialty of the house* **5** a theater **6** a business operation ⊙ *a publishing house* **7** *also* **House** a lower legislative group or the building in which it meets **8** a division of the zodiac ■ *vt* /howz/ (**housed, hous-ing**) **1** give somebody a place to live **2** contain something ⊙ *a shed that houses our lawn mowers* ◇ **bring the house down** provoke a great deal of laughter or applause ◇ **on the house** given free by somebody who would normally charge ◇ **put your house in order** organize your life properly

house ar-rest *n* a form of legal confinement in which the prisoner is not allowed to leave his or her home

house-boat /hówss bòt/ *n* a large flat-bottomed boat equipped for live-aboard use

house brand *n* a product sold by only one retailer and often sold under that retailer's name

house-break-ing /hówss bràyking/ *n* illegal forcible entry into a building in order to commit a crime —**house-break-er** *n*

house-coat /hówss kòt/ *n* a woman's casual outer garment, worn at home

house-fly /hówss flì/ *(pl* -**flies**) *n* a common fly that lives in or around houses

house guest *n* a visitor to somebody's home

house-hold /hówss hòld/ *n* the people who live together in a house ■ *adj* **1** belonging to a household **2** familiar to all ⊙ *a household word*

house-hold-er /hówss hòldər/ *n* somebody who owns, rents, or is in charge of a house

house-hus-band /hówss hùzbənd/ *n* a man who manages a household full time and does not go out to work

house-keep-er /hówss kèepər/ *n* **1** somebody who manages the running of somebody else's house **2** a manager of cleaning personnel, e.g., in a hotel

house-keep-ing /hówss keeping/ n household maintenance

house-lights /hówss lĩts/ npl lights that illuminate a theater auditorium

house-man /hówssman/ (pl -men /-mən/) n a male maintenance worker

house mar-tin n a small swallow

house-mas-ter /hówss màstər/ n a man responsible for the boarders living in a house at a boarding school

house mu-sic n a style of fast and repetitive electronic dance music

house of cards n a highly unstable situation or organization, liable to collapse

House of Com-mons n the lower house of the parliaments of the United Kingdom and Canada

house of cor-rec-tion n a prison

house of ill fame, house of ill re-pute n a brothel

House of Lords n the upper house of the UK Parliament

House of Rep-re-sen-ta-tives n the lower house of the US Congress

house par-ty n **1** a large party with overnight guests at somebody's residence or at a college residence, e.g., a fraternity or sorority house **2** the guests at a house party

house-plant /hówss plànt/ n a plant grown indoors

house-sit vi take care of somebody's house while they are away

Houses of Par-lia-ment npl the buildings of the UK Parliament

house-to-house adj from one house to the next o a house-to-house search

house-wares /hówss wàirz/ npl things used in a house, especially in the kitchen

house-warm-ing /hówss wàwrming/, **house-warm-ing par-ty** n a party in a new house

house-wife /hówss wìf/ (pl -wives /-wìvz/) n a woman who manages a household full time and does not go out to work

house-work /hówss wùrk/ n household chores

hous-ing /hówzing/ n **1** living accommodations **2** the provision of living accommodations **3** a protective cover for a machine part

hous-ing de-vel-op-ment n an area of houses

hous-ing pro-ject n a low-cost housing area

Hou-ston /hyóost'n/ major port in SE Texas. Pop. 1,786,691 (1998).

Hous-ton, Sam (1793–1863) US frontiersman and politician

HOV high-occupancy vehicle

hove past tense of **heave** v 7

hov-el /húv'l/ n a small, dirty, or poorly built house

hov-er /húvvər/ vi **1** stay in the air without moving far from the same spot **2** wait nearby in a nervous or expectant way **3** stay around the same level o temperatures hovering in the low teens

hov-er-craft /húvvər kràft/ (pl same) n a vehicle that glides over water or land on a cushion of air

how /how/ adv in what way o How do I open the window? ■ conj that o Do you remember how we were ridiculed? ■ adv to what extent o How high is the roof? ■ conj in whatever way o Do it how you want. ■ adv **1** like what o How was the movie? **2** used in exclamations o How nice to see you! ■ n the way and means of accomplishing something o I'm not interested in the hows or whys this needs to be done. ◊ **how about** introduces a suggestion (infml) o How about a cup of coffee?

How-ard /hów ərd/, **Catherine** (1520?–42) queen of England (1540–42) as the fifth wife of Henry VIII

how-dah /hówdə/ n a seat on an elephant

Howe /how/, **Elias** (1819–67) US inventor

Howe, Julia Ward (1819–1910) US writer and reformer

How-ells /hów əlz/, **William Dean** (1837–1920) US writer and critic

how-ev-er /how évvər/ adv **1** to whatever degree **2** in whatever way **3** how

how-it-zer /hówitsər/ n a combat artillery cannon

howl /howl/ vi **1** make a long whining sound **2** cry out in pain or distress **3** roar with laughter (slang) ■ n **1** a long moaning cry **2** a loud cry of pain, distress, or disapproval

howl-er /hówlər/ n a ridiculous mistake (slang)

how-so-ev-er /hòwssō évvər/ adv however (fml)

hp abbr horsepower

HQ, H.Q., h.q. abbr headquarters

HR abbr **1** home run **2** also **H.R.** House of Representatives **3** human resources

hr., hr abbr hour

H.R.H. abbr **1** Her Royal Highness **2** His Royal Highness

HRT abbr hormone replacement therapy

hryv-ni-a /hrívnee ə/ (pl same or -as) n the main unit of Ukrainian currency

Hs symbol hassium

HST abbr **1** Hawaii-Aleutian Standard Time **2** hypersonic transport

⚡**html, htm** abbr a file extension for a Hyper-Text Markup Language file

⚡**HTML** n a system of tagging used to format a text document for the World Wide Web. Full form **HyperText Markup Language**

⚡**HTTP** abbr HyperText Transfer Protocol

Huang He /hwaàng hố/ second longest river in China, flowing through the north central

part of the country. Length 3,395 mi./
5,464 km.

hua·ra·che /wə raáchee/ n a sandal with the
upper part made of woven leather straps

hub n 1 the central part of a wheel or other
rotating device 2 a center of activity or
interest

Hub·ble /húbb'l/, **Edwin** (1889–1953) US
astronomer

hub·bub /hú bùb/ n 1 a confused din, especially from a number of voices speaking
at once 2 an excited fuss

hub·cap /húb kàp/ n a cover for the center of
a vehicle's wheel

hu·bris /hyoóbriss/ n 1 overweening pride and
arrogance   2   excessive   ambition
—**hu·bris·tic** /hyoo brístik/ adj

huck·le·ber·ry /húk'l bèrree/ (pl **-ries**) n 1 an
edible dark-blue berry 2 the plant that produces huckleberries

huck·ster /húkstər/ n 1 an aggressive salesperson 2 a street peddler —**huck·ster** vti

HUD abbr (Department of) Housing and
Urban Development

hud·dle /húdd'l/ n 1 a tightly packed group
2 in football, a group of players gathered
behind the line of scrimmage to hear what
the next play will be ■ vi (-dled, -dling)
1 gather tightly together 2 crouch near the
ground or in a corner 3 in football, gather
together behind the line of scrimmage to
hear what the next play will be

Hud·son /húdss'n/ river in E New York,
emptying into Upper New York Bay at
New York City. Length 306 mi./492 km.

Hud·son, Henry (1565?–1611?) English navigator

Hud·son Bay almost landlocked inland sea
of east central Canada. Depth 846 ft./258
m.

Hud·son's Bay blan·ket n Can a wool
blanket, usually cream-colored with red,
black, yellow, and indigo stripes

Hud·son Strait body of water in NE Canada
connecting Hudson Bay with the Atlantic
Ocean and separating Baffin Island from N
Quebec. Depth 2,890 ft./880 m. Length 450
mi./720 km.

hue /hyoo/ n 1 a color ◊ flowers of every hue 2 a
shade of a color ◊ a pleasing hue of green ◊
See note at **hew**

hue and cry n an uproar

huff n a fit of anger ■ vi 1 make angry
statements 2 blow or pant laboriously
—**huff·ing** n

huff·y /húffee/ (-i·er, -i·est) adj 1 easily offended or angered 2 showing irritation ◊ a
huffy silence —**huff·i·ly** adv —**huff·i·ness** n

hug v (hugged, hug·ging) 1 vti embrace somebody or something affectionately 2 vt put
your arms around something ■ n an
affectionate embrace

huge /hyooj/ (hug·er, hug·est) adj 1 enormous
2 large in scope ◊ huge talent —**huge·ly** adv
—**huge·ness** n

Hughes /hyooz/, **Charles** (1862–1947) chief
justice of the US Supreme Court (1930–41)

Hughes, Howard (1905–76) US industrialist

Langston Hughes

Hughes, Langston (1902–67) US writer

Hu·go /hyoógō/, **Victor** (1802–85) French poet,
novelist, and dramatist

Hu·gue·not /hyoógə nòt/ n a French Protestant
—**Hu·gue·not** adj

huh /hu/ interj 1 expresses surprise or disdain
2 expresses an invitation to agree ◊ Great
shot, huh?

hu·la /hoólə/ n a Polynesian dance involving
swaying hips and hand gestures

hulk n 1 a big, often clumsy person 2 a
wrecked ship's empty hull 3 an unwieldy
ship ■ vi appear as a large object

hulk·ing /húlking/, **hulk·y** /húlkee/ (-i·er, -i·est)
adj huge

hull /hul/ n 1 the body of a ship 2 the body
of a large vehicle 3 a rocket casing 4 the
outer covering of a seed or fruit ■ vt
remove the hull from a seed or fruit

Hull /hul/, **Cordell** (1871–1955) US secretary
of state (1933–44)

hul·la·ba·loo /húlləbə loó/, **hul·la·bal·loo** n a
hubbub

hum v (hummed, hum·ming) 1 vti sing with the
lips closed 2 vi make a droning sound ◊ bees
humming 3 vi give off a low steady sound
◊ a room that hummed with strange electronic
equipment 4 vi be extremely busy (infml)
◊ This place is really humming. ■ n a
humming noise

hu·man /hyoómən/ adj 1 of people 2 com-
passionately kind ■ n a human being
—**hu·man·ness** n

hu·man be·ing n a member of the human
species

hu·mane /hyoo máyn/ adj compassionate
—**hu·mane·ly** adv —**hu·mane·ness** n

hu·man e·col·o·gy n the study of people
within an environment

hu·mane so·ci·e·ty n an organization promoting kindness to animals

Hu·man Ge·nome Proj·ect n an international research initiative to sequence and
identify human genes and their positions
on chromosomes

hu·man in·ter·est *n* the power to appeal to public sympathy or curiosity —**hu·man·in·ter·est** *adj*

hu·man·ism /hyōōmə nìzzəm/ *n* **1** a belief system based on the best of human nature rather than religious faith **2** *also* **Hu·man·ism** a Renaissance cultural movement deriving from the rediscovery of the arts and philosophy of ancient Greece and Rome —**hu·man·ist** *n, adj* —**hu·man·ist·ic** /hyōōmə nístik/ *adj*

hu·man·i·tar·i·an /hyōō mànni táiree ən/ *adj* committed to improving the lives of other people —**hu·man·i·tar·i·an** *n* —**hu·man·i·tar·i·an·ism** *n*

hu·man·i·ty /hyōō mánnitee/ *n* **1** humankind **2** the qualities typical of a human being ■ **hu·man·i·ties, Hu·man·i·ties** *npl* **1** the liberal arts as subjects of study **2** classical studies

hu·man·ize /hyōōmə nìz/ (-**ized, -iz·ing**) *vti* **1** make or become human **2** make or become humane —**hu·man·i·za·tion** /hyōōmani záysh'n/ *n*

hu·man·kind /hōōmən kìnd/ *n* human beings collectively

hu·man·ly /hyōōmənlee/ *adv* **1** in a way characteristic of human beings **2** within the limits of human ability ∘ *if humanly possible* **3** according to human experience

hu·man-made /hyōōmən màyd/ *adj* made by human beings, not occurring naturally

hu·man na·ture *n* the essential character of human beings

hu·man·oid /hyōōmə nòyd/ *adj* resembling a human being —**hu·man·oid** *n*

hu·man re·sourc·es *n* employee recruitment and management (*+ sing verb*) ■ *npl* the personnel of an organization (*+ pl verb*)

hu·man rights *npl* rights such as freedom, justice, and equality that are considered to belong to everyone ■ *n* the protection or study of human rights (*+ sing verb*)

hum·ble /húmb'l/ *adj* (**-bler, -blest**) **1** modest in attitude **2** respectful **3** lowly ∘ *of humble origins* ■ *vt* (**-bled, -bling**) cause to feel less important —**hum·bled** *adj* —**hum·bling** *adj* —**hum·bly** *adv*

Hum·boldt Cur·rent /húm bòlt-/ *n* cold current of the South Pacific Ocean that flows north along the coastline of South America

hum·bug /húm bùg/ *n* **1** nonsense **2** a deception **3** somebody who deceives others as to his or her identity or history ■ *vti* (**-bugged, -bug·ging**) deceive

hum·ding·er /hùm díngər/ *n* somebody or something exceptional (*slang*)

hum·drum /húm drùm/ *adj* dull and ordinary

Hume /hyoom/, **David** (1711–76) Scottish philosopher and historian

hu·mer·us /hyōōmərəss/ (*pl* **-i** /-rì/) *n* the long bone of the human upper arm or an animal's front limb —**hu·mer·al** *adj*

hu·mid /hyōōmid/ *adj* with relatively high moisture in the air

hu·mid·i·fy /hyoo míddə fì/ (**-fied, -fies**) *vt* make more humid —**hu·mid·i·fi·ca·tion** /hyoo míddəfi káysh'n/ *n* —**hu·mid·i·fi·er** *n*

hu·mid·i·ty /hyoo míddətee/ *n* **1** atmospheric moisture **2** a high moisture level in the air

hu·mil·i·ate /hyoo míllee àyt/ (**-at·ed, -at·ing**) *vt* damage the dignity or pride of, especially publicly —**hu·mil·i·at·ing** *adj* —**hu·mil·i·a·tion** /-míllee áysh'n/ *n*

hu·mil·i·ty /hyoo míllitee/ *n* modesty or respectfulness

~~huminist~~ incorrect spelling of **humanist**

hum·int /hyōōmint/, **HUMINT** *n* intelligence information acquired from people in enemy territory. Full form **human intelligence**

hum·ming·bird /húmming bùrd/ *n* a small brightly-colored bird that hovers by rapid beating of its wings

hum·mock /húmmək/ *n* a small hill

hum·mus /hōōməss, húmməss/, **hu·mus** *n* a dip made with mashed chickpeas

hu·mor /hyōōmər/ *n* **1** amusing quality ∘ *couldn't see the humor in it* **2** the ability to see something as amusing **3** a mood or state of mind **4** a body fluid ■ *vt* do what somebody wants to keep him or her happy —**hu·mor·less** *adj* —**hu·mor·less·ly** *adv*

hu·mor·ist /hyōōmərist/ *n* **1** an amusing person **2** a comic writer or performer

hu·mor·ous /hyōōmərəss/ *adj* amusing or witty —**hu·mor·ous·ly** *adv*

~~humourous~~ incorrect spelling of **humorous**

hump *n* **1** a rounded protuberance on an animal's back **2** a pronounced outward curve of a person's upper back —**hump·y** *adj*

hump·back /húmp bàk/ *n* **1** somebody with a hump on his or her back **2** a humped back **3** *also* **hump·back whale** a large dark-colored whale with a humped back —**hump·backed** *adj*

humph *interj* expresses displeasure

Hum·phrey /húmfree/, **Hubert H.** (1911–78) vice president of the United States (1965–69)

hu·mus¹ /hyōōməss/ *n* the organic component of soil

hu·mus² *n* FOOD = **hummus**

Hun *n* **1** member of an early Asian nomadic people **2** an offensive term for a German person or the German people (*dated slang*) —**Hun·nish** *adj*

hunch *n* **1** an intuitive feeling about something **2** a stoop of the body ■ *v* **1** *vti* bend the upper body forward **2** *vi* crouch

hunch·back /húnch bàk/ *n* **1** a humped back **2** somebody with a hump on his or her back —**hunch·backed** *adj*

hun·dred /húndrəd/ *n* **1** the number 100 **2** a large number ∘ *hundreds of people* **3** the third digit to the left of a decimal point **4** a

$100 bill **5** a historical county subdivision ■ **hun·dreds** *npl* **1** the numbers 100 to 999 **2** large numbers —**hun·dred** *adj* —**hun·dredth** *n, adj*

hun·dred·weight /húndrəd wàyt/ *n* a weight of 100 lb

hung past participle, past tense of **hang**

Hun·gar·i·an /hung gáiree ən/ *n* **1** somebody from Hungary **2** the official language of Hungary —**Hun·gar·i·an** *adj*

Hun·ga·ry /húng gəree/ country in central Europe. Cap. Budapest. Pop. 10,106,017 (2001).

hun·ger /húng gər/ *n* **1** the need or desire to eat **2** a strong desire for something ○ *a hunger for knowledge* **3** starvation ■ *vi* have a strong desire for something

hun·ger strike *n* a refusal to eat as a protest —**hun·ger strik·er** *n*

hung·o·ver, hung·o·ver /hung ṓvər/ *adj* suffering from a hangover

hun·gry /húng gree/ (**-gri·er, -gri·est**) *adj* **1** needing or wanting to eat **2** wanting something greatly ○ *hungry for new experiences* —**hun·gri·ly** *adv*

hung up *adj (infml)* **1** worried **2** delayed

hunk *n* **1** a large chunk of something **2** a man with a good physique *(infml)*

hun·ker /húngkər/ *vi* crouch

□ **hunker down** *vi* settle into serious work

Hunk·pa·pa /húngk pàapə/ (*pl* same or **-pas**) *n* a member of a branch of the Teton people who now live on both sides of the border between North and South Dakota —**Hunk·pa·pa** *adj*

hun·ky-do·ry /húngkee dáwree/ *adj* fine or satisfactory *(infml)*

hunt *v* **1** *vti* pursue and kill an animal for sport or food **2** *vt* seek out and try to capture somebody **3** *vi* search for something difficult to find ■ *n* **1** a search for something **2** a search for prey —**hunt·ed** *adj* —**hunt·ing** *n*

hunt·er /húntər/ *n* **1** a person or animal that hunts for food or sport **2** a horse or dog bred or used for hunting

hunt·er-gath·er·er *n* a member of a society that forages for food instead of raising crops or livestock

hunt·ing ground *n* **1** an area for hunting **2** a source of something useful or desired ○ *a good hunting ground for antiques*

Hunt·ing·ton Beach /húntingtən-/ coastal city in S California. Pop. 195,316 (1998).

hunt·ress /húntrəss/ *n* a woman or goddess who hunts *(literary)*

hunts·man /húntsmən/ (*pl* **-men** /-mən/) *n* **1** a hunt official in charge of hounds **2** a man who goes hunting

Hunts·ville /húnts vìl/ city in N Alabama. Pop. 175,979 (1998).

hur·dle /húrd'l/ *n* **1** a light barrier for runners to jump over in some races **2** a difficulty or obstacle ■ *vt* (**-dled, -dling**) jump over a racing barrier —**hur·dler** *n*

hur·dles /húrd'lz/ *n* a footrace over light barriers (*+ sing verb*)

hur·dy-gur·dy /húrdee gúrdee, húrdee gùrdee/ (*pl* **hur·dy-gur·dies**) *n* a barrel organ or similar instrument played by turning a handle

hurl *vt* **1** throw violently **2** yell ○ *hurling abuse* —**hurl** *n* ◊ See note at **throw**

hur·ly-bur·ly /húrlee búrlee, húrlee bùrlee/ *n* noisy bustling activity

Hu·ron /hyoo̅o̅ ron/ (*pl* same or **-rons**) *n* a member of a confederacy of Native North American peoples who now live in Quebec, Ontario, and Oklahoma —**Hu·ron** *adj*

Hu·ron, Lake /hyoor on/ second largest of the Great Lakes. Depth 751 ft./229 m.

hur·rah /hoȯ ráa, hə ráa/ *interj, n* = hooray ◊ **(the) last hurrah** a final effort, experience in the limelight, or spree *(infml)* ○ *her last hurrah*

hur·ray *interj, n* = hooray

hur·ri·cane /húrri kàyn/ *n* **1** a severe tropical storm with winds above 74 mi./119km per hour **2** somebody or something that acts with speed, force, and effectiveness

ORIGIN Hurricane came via Spanish from a Native Central American word meaning "god of the storm."

hur·ri·cane lamp *n* a lantern protected with glass from the weather

hur·ry /húrree/ *v* (**-ried, -ries**) **1** *vi* move or do something with great or excessive speed **2** *vt* encourage to speed up ■ *n* **1** haste **2** urgency —**hur·ried** *adj* —**hur·ried·ly** *adv*

Hur·ston /húrst'n/, **Zora Neale** (1891–60) US writer and folklorist

hurt *v* (**hurt**) **1** *vt* injure **2** *vti* cause pain to, or experience pain **3** *vti* upset somebody's feelings, or feel upset **4** *vti* have a detrimental effect on something ○ *hurt her chances* ■ *n* **1** pain **2** an injury —**hurt** *adj* ◊ See note at **harm**

hurt·ful /húrtfəl/ *adj* emotionally painful —**hurt·ful·ly** *adv* —**hurt·ful·ness** *n*

hur·tle /húrt'l/ (**-tled, -tling**) *vi* move at very high speed

hus·band /húzbənd/ *n* the man to whom a woman is married ■ *vt* be thrifty with

hus·band·man /húzbəndmən/ (*pl* **-men** /-mən/) *n* a farmer *(archaic)*

hus·band·ry /húzbəndree/ *n* **1** farming **2** frugal management of resources

hush *vti* cause to be quiet, or become quiet ■ *n* silence

□ **hush up** *v* **1** *vt* prevent the disclosure of *(infml)* **2** *vti* keep quiet

hush-hush *adj* secret *(infml)*

hush pup·py *n* a small ball of fried cornmeal

husk *n* **1** the outer covering of some fruits, nuts, and grains **2** a useless outer shell ■ *vt* remove husks from

husk·y[1] /húskee/ (**-i·er, -i·est**) *adj* **1** burly and compact in physique **2** throaty or hoarse —**husk·i·ly** *adv* —**husk·i·ness** *n*

hus·ky[2] /húskee/ (*pl* **-kies**), **hus·kie** *n* a large working dog with a thick coat

Huss, John (1372?–1415) Bohemian nationalist and religious reformer

hus·sar /hə zaár, hoŏ-/ *n* a European light cavalry soldier

Hus·sein I /hoŏ sáyn/ (1935–99) king of Jordan (1952–99)

Hus·sein, Saddam (b. 1937) Iraqi national leader

hus·sy /hússee/ (*pl* **-sies**) *n* an offensive term for a woman or girl whose behavior is regarded as too forward (*dated*)

hust·ings /hústingz/ *n* the location or activities of a political campaign

hus·tle /húss'l/ *v* (**-tled, -tling**) **1** *vi* hurry (*infml*) **2** *vt* sell aggressively **3** *vt* convey roughly or hurriedly from a place **4** *vt* deal with quickly ■ *n* noisy activity —**hus·tler** *n*

Hus·ton /hyoŏstən/, **John** (1906–87) US movie director and actor

hut *n* a one-room building

hutch *n* **1** a shelter for housing a small animal **2** a china cabinet

Hutch·in·son /húchinss'n/, **Anne** (1591–1643) English-born American colonial religious reformer

Hux·ley /húkslee/, **Aldous** (1894–1963) British novelist and essayist

hwy *abbr* highway

hy·a·cinth /hī ə sìnth/ *n* a plant grown from a bulb, with heads of pink, white, or blue flowers

hy·ae·na /hī ee nə/ *n* ZOOL = hyena

hy·brid /hībrid/ *n* **1** a plant or animal produced by crossing genetically different forms **2** something made up of a mixture of different elements —**hy·brid** *adj*

hy·brid·ize /hībri dìz/ (**-ized, -iz·ing**) *vti* crossbreed a plant or animal —**hy·brid·i·za·tion** /hībridi záysh'n/ *n*

Hy·der·a·bad /hīdərə bàd/ **1** capital of Andhra Pradesh State, India. Pop. 2,964,638 (1991). **2** city in SE Pakistan, on the Indus River. Pop. 1,151,274 (1998).

hy·dra /hīdrə/ (*pl* **-dras** *or* **-drae** /-dree/) *n* **1** a freshwater organism that has a cylindrical body with a mouth surrounded by tentacles at one end **2 Hy·dra** a large constellation near the celestial equator

hy·dran·gea /hī dráynjə/ *n* a bush with large clusters of white, pink, or blue flowers

hy·drant /hīdrənt/ *n* a fire hydrant

hy·drate /hī dràyt/ *vt* (**-drat·ed, -drat·ing**) **1** give water to somebody or something to regulate fluid balance **2** add water to a chemical compound to form different crystals ■ *n* a chemical compound containing water molecules —**hy·dra·tion** /hīdráysh'n/ *n*

hy·drau·lic /hī dráwlik/ *adj* driven by fluid under pressure —**hy·drau·li·cal·ly** *adv*

hy·drau·lics /hī dráwliks/ *n* the study of fluids (+ *sing verb*)

hy·dro /hīdrō/ (*pl* **-dros**) *n* **1** a hydroelectric power plant **2** hydroelectric power

hydro- *prefix* **1** water, liquid, moisture ○ *hydroelectric* **2** hydrogen ○ *hydrocarbon*

hy·dro·car·bon /hīdrə kaárbən/ *n* a chemical compound containing hydrogen and carbon

hy·dro·ceph·a·lus /hīdrō séffələss/, **hy·dro·ceph·a·ly** /-séffəlee/ *n* increased fluid around the brain —**hy·dro·ce·phal·ic** /-sə fállik/ *adj*

hy·dro·chlo·ric ac·id /hīdrə kláwrik-/ *n* HCl a strong colorless acid. Use: industrial and laboratory processes.

hy·dro·dy·nam·ics /hīdrō dī námmiks/ *n* the area of fluid dynamics concerned with the study of liquids (+ *sing verb*) —**hy·dro·dy·nam·ic** *adj* —**hy·dro·dy·nam·i·cist** /-námmissist/ *n*

hy·dro·e·lec·tric /hīdrō i léktrik/ *adj* **1** generated by converting water power to electricity **2** of hydroelectric power generation —**hy·dro·e·lec·tri·cal·ly** *adv* —**hy·dro·e·lec·tric·i·ty** /hīdrō i lek tríssətee/ *n*

hy·dro·foil /hīdrə fòyl/ *n* **1** a high-speed boat with wing-shaped blades under the hull that lift the boat out of the water **2** a wing-shaped blade on a hydrofoil

hy·dro·gen /hīdrəjən/ *n* (*symbol* H) a reactive gaseous element. Use: production of ammonia, reduction of metal ores to metals.

hy·dro·gen·ate /hī drójjə nàyt/ (**-at·ed, -at·ing**) *vt* add hydrogen to —**hy·dro·gen·a·tion** /hī dròjjə náysh'n/ *n*

hy·dro·gen bomb *n* a nuclear weapon in which energy is released by the fusion of hydrogen nuclei

hy·dro·gen chlo·ride *n* HCl a colorless fuming corrosive gas. Use: manufacture of PVC.

hy·dro·gen per·ox·ide *n* H_2O_2 an unstable viscous liquid. Use: bleach, mild antiseptic, component in rocket fuel.

hy·drog·ra·phy /hī drógrəfee/ *n* the study of seas, lakes, and rivers

hydrolic incorrect spelling of **hydraulic**

hy·drol·y·sis /hī drólləssiss/ *n* the reaction of a compound with water resulting in two or more new compounds —**hy·dro·lyt·ic** /hīdrə líttik/ *adj*

hy·drom·e·ter /hī drómmətər/ *n* an instrument that determines the specific gravity of liquids —**hy·dro·met·ric** /hīdrə méttrik/ *adj* —**hy·drom·e·try** *n*

hy·drop·a·thy /hī dróppəthee/ *n* the internal

and external application of water for healing —**hy·dro·path·ic** /hídrə páthik/ adj

hy·dro·pho·bi·a /hídrə fṓbee ə/ n 1 rabies 2 fear of water —**hy·dro·pho·bic** adj

hy·dro·plane /hídrə pláyn/ n 1 a fast boat that rises up out of the water at high speed 2 a seaplane ■ vi (-planed, -plan·ing) 1 skim along the surface of water 2 skid on a wet road surface

hy·dro·pon·ics /hídrə pónniks/ n the growing of plants in a nutrient liquid (+ sing verb) —**hy·dro·pon·ic** adj

hy·dro·stat·ics /hídrə státtiks/ n the scientific study of liquids at rest (+ sing verb) —**hy·dro·stat·ic** adj

hy·dro·ther·a·py /hídrə thérrəpee/ n the external use of water for healing, e.g., exercise in a pool —**hy·dro·ther·a·pist** n

hy·drox·ide /hī dróks sìd/ n a chemical compound containing the group -OH

hy·e·na /hī éenə/, **hy·ae·na** n a scavenging wild mammal resembling a dog, with a sloping back —**hy·en·ic** adj

~~hygeine~~ incorrect spelling of **hygiene**

hy·giene /hī jèen/ n 1 the science of the preservation of health 2 cleanliness —**hy·gien·ic** /hī jénnik, -jéenik, hī jee énnik/ adj —**hy·gien·i·cal·ly** adv

hy·gien·ist /hī jéenist, -jénnist/ n somebody trained in hygiene

hy·men /hímən/ n a thin mucous membrane covering the opening of the vagina

hymn /him/ n 1 a religious song of praise 2 a song of praise ■ v 1 vt sing in praise of 2 vi sing hymns

hymn·book /hím bòok/, **hym·nal** /hímnəl/ n a book of church hymns

hype /hīp/ n excessive publicity or extravagant claims for somebody or something ■ vt (hyped, hyp·ing) publicize excessively

hy·per /hípər/ adj (infml) 1 excessively active 2 very excitable

hyper- prefix 1 over, above, beyond ○ hypertext 2 excessive, unusually high ○ hypertension

hy·per·ac·tive /hípər áktiv/ adj unusually active and unable to concentrate —**hy·per·ac·tive·ly** adv —**hy·per·ac·tiv·i·ty** /-ak tívvətee/ n

hy·per·bo·la /hī púrbələ/ (pl -las or -lae /-lee/) n a conic section formed by a point that moves in a plane so that the difference in its distance from two fixed points in the plane remains constant

hy·per·bo·le /hī púrbəlee/ n exaggeration for effect

hy·per·bol·ic /hípər bóllik/, **hy·per·bol·i·cal** /-ik'l/ adj 1 of a hyperbola 2 of hyperbole —**hy·per·bol·i·cal·ly** adv

hy·per·crit·i·cal /hípər kríttik'l/ adj excessively critical —**hy·per·crit·i·cal·ly** adv

hy·per·gly·ce·mi·a /hípər glī séemee ə/ n an excessively high level of blood sugar —**hy·per·gly·ce·mic** adj

hy·per·in·fla·tion /hípərin fláysh'n/ n very high and rapid inflation —**hy·per·in·fla·tion·ar·y** adj

⚡ **hy·per·link** /hípər lìngk/ n a link in hypertext

⚡ **hy·per·mar·ket** /hípər màarkət/ n a very large self-service store selling products usually sold in supermarkets, hardware stores, and department stores

⚡ **hy·per·me·di·a** /hípər meédee ə/ n a multimedia hypertext system

hy·per·sen·si·tive /hípər sénsitiv/ adj 1 very easily upset or offended 2 showing a strong reaction to a drug, allergen, or other agent —**hy·per·sen·si·tiv·i·ty** /-sensi tívvətee/ n

hy·per·son·ic /hípər sónnik/ adj moving at a speed at least five times the speed of sound —**hy·per·son·i·cal·ly** adv

hy·per·ten·sion /hípər ténshən/ n high blood pressure

⚡ **hy·per·text** /hípər tèkst/ n a system of storing images, text, and other computer files that allows direct links to related electronic data

⚡ **Hy·per·Text Mark·up Lan·guage** n full form of HTML

⚡ **Hy·per·Text Trans·fer Pro·to·col** n the technical rules for formatting and transmitting messages on the World Wide Web

hy·per·tro·phy /hī púrtrəfee/ n (pl -phies) a growth in size of an organ through an increase in the size, rather than the number, of its cells ■ vti (-phied, -phies) grow larger by cell enlargement —**hy·per·tro·phic** /hípər tróffik/ adj

hy·per·ven·ti·late /hípər véntə làyt/ (-lated, -lat·ing) vi breathe unusually deeply or rapidly —**hy·per·ven·ti·la·tion** /hípər venti láysh'n/ n

hy·phen /hífən/ n a dash in punctuation showing a break between syllables or parts of a compound word ■ vt hyphenate

---

USAGE A number of compound words and phrases are joined by hyphens: *thirty-seven; well-wisher; old-fashioned; mother-in-law.* For some the hyphens are optional, or inserted only when the word or phrase is used before a noun: *a coffee-table book; a well-timed attack* (but *the book on the coffee table; if the attack is well timed*). Most words with prefixes do not have a hyphen, exceptions being those where a capital letter follows the prefix (e.g., *pre-Christian*) and those where the word could be confused with another (e.g., *re-form* meaning "form again" as distinct from *reform*). A hyphen is sometimes inserted when a prefix ending in a vowel is added to a word beginning with a vowel (e.g., *co-opt, de-ice*). See **dash.**

---

hy·phen·ate /hífə nàyt/ (-at·ed, -at·ing) vt use a hyphen in —**hy·phen·a·tion** /hífə náysh'n/ n

hyp·no·sis /hip nṓssiss/ (*pl* **-ses** /-seez/) *n* 1 a state resembling sleep that can be artificially induced and that may increase suggestibility 2 the technique or practice of inducing hypnosis

hyp·no·ther·a·py /hípnō thérrəpee/ *n* the use of hypnosis to treat illness or psychological disorders —**hyp·no·ther·a·pist** *n*

hyp·not·ic /hip nóttik/ *adj* 1 of sleep or hypnosis 2 fascinating (*infml*) ■ *n* something causing sleep or drowsiness —**hyp·not·i·cal·ly** *adv*

hyp·no·tism /hípnə tìzzəm/ *n* 1 study or practice of inducing hypnosis 2 the state of hypnosis —**hyp·no·tist** *n*

hyp·no·tize /hípnə tìz/ (**-tized, -tiz·ing**) *vt* 1 put into a state of hypnosis 2 fascinate

hy·po /hípō/ (*pl* **-pos**) *n* a hypodermic injection, needle, or syringe (*infml*)

hypo- *prefix* 1 under, below ○ *hypothalamus* 2 unusually low ○ *hypoglycemia*

hy·po·al·ler·gen·ic /hípō àllər jénnik/ *adj* unlikely to cause an allergic reaction

hy·po·chon·dri·a /hípə kóndree ə/ *n* the deluded persistent conviction of being ill —**hy·po·chon·dri·ac** *adj, n*

~~hypocrasy, hypocricy~~ incorrect spelling of **hypocrisy**

hy·poc·ri·sy /hi pókrəssee/ (*pl* **-sies**) *n* 1 the pretence of having admirable principles, beliefs, or feelings 2 a hypocritical act

hyp·o·crite /híppə krìt/ *n* somebody who pretends to have admirable principles, beliefs, or feelings —**hyp·o·crit·i·cal** /hippə kríttik'l/ *adj* —**hyp·o·crit·i·cal·ly** *adv*

hy·po·der·mic /hípō dúrmik/ *adj* 1 of the area of tissue beneath the skin 2 injected or used to inject beneath the skin ■ *n* a hypodermic injection, needle, or syringe (*infml*) —**hy·po·der·mi·cal·ly** *adv*

hy·po·gly·ce·mi·a /hípō glī seemee ə/ *n* an excessively low level of blood sugar —**hy·po·gly·ce·mic** *adj*

hy·pot·e·nuse /hī pótt'n òoss/ *n* the longest side of a right triangle

hy·po·thal·a·mus /hípō thálləməss/ (*pl* **-mi** /-mī/) *n* an area of the brain that controls involuntary functions —**hy·po·tha·lam·ic** /hípōthə lámmik/ *adj*

hy·po·ther·mi·a /hípō thúrmee ə/ *n* dangerously low body temperature —**hy·po·ther·mic** *adj*

hy·poth·e·sis /hī póthəssiss/ (*pl* **-ses** /-seez/) *n* 1 a theory used as a basis for further investigation 2 an assumption made for the sake of argument

hy·poth·e·size /hī póthə sìz/ (**-sized, -siz·ing**) *vti* assume something as a hypothesis

hy·po·thet·i·cal /hípə théttik'l/, **hy·po·thet·ic** /-théttik/ *adj* assumed as a basis for further investigation or for the sake of argument —**hy·po·thet·i·cal·ly** *adv*

hy·rax /hī ràks/ (*pl* **-rax·es** *or* **-ra·ces** /-rə seez/) *n* a small Mediterranean mammal resembling a rabbit

hys·sop /híssəp/ *n* an aromatic herb similar to mint. Use: in aromatherapy and alternative medicine.

hys·ter·ec·to·my /hístə réktəmee/ (*pl* **-mies**) *n* a surgical operation to remove the womb —**hys·ter·ec·to·mize** *vt*

hys·ter·i·a /hi steéree ə/ *n* 1 emotional instability caused by a trauma 2 a state of extreme emotion, especially among a large number of people

ORIGIN Hysteria derives ultimately from the Greek word for "womb." It was given that name in the early 19C, when the condition was often believed to be peculiar to women.

hys·ter·ic /hi stérrik/ *n* somebody affected by hysteria (*dated; sometimes offensive*) ■ *adj* hysterical

hys·ter·i·cal /hi stérrik'l/ *adj* 1 of or affected by hysteria 2 extremely funny (*infml*) —**hys·ter·i·cal·ly** *adv*

hys·ter·ics /hi stérriks/ *n* (+ *sing or pl verb*) 1 uncontrollable laughter (*infml*) 2 a state of hysteria

Hz *symbol* hertz

I

i (*pl* **i's**), **I** (*pl* **I's** *or* **Is**) *n* 1 the 9th letter of the English alphabet 2 the Roman numeral for 1 ◇ **dot the i's and cross the t's** pay careful attention to the details

I[1] *pron* refers to the speaker or writer himself or herself (*as the subject of a verb*)

USAGE I or **me**? **I** is the subjective, or subject, form: *I agree; you and I* [not *you and me*] *know better than that.* **Me** is the objective, or object, form, coming after verbs and prepositions: *she agrees with me; a present for you and me.* After the verb *be* use *It is me* or *It's me. It is I,* technically correct, is used only in very formal speech or writing.

I[2] *symbol* 1 electric current 2 iodine

I[3] *abbr* interstate

-i- joins word elements ○ *fossiliferous*

IA, Ia. *abbr* Iowa

-ia *suffix* 1 place names ○ *Australia* 2 plurals ○ *memorabilia*

I·a·coc·ca /ī ə kṓkə/, **Lee** (*b.* 1924) US automobile executive

-ial *suffix* connected with or belonging to ○ *secretarial*

i·amb /ī àm/ *n* a metrical unit consisting of one short or unstressed syllable followed by one long or stressed one —**i·am·bic** /ī ámbik/ *adj*

i·am·bic pen·tam·e·ter /ī ámbik-/ *n* a poetic line consisting of five iambs

-ian *suffix* belonging to, coming from, being involved in, or being like ◊ *Italian*

⚡**IAS** *abbr* 1 immediate access store 2 indicated air speed

IATA *abbr* International Air Transport Association

IB *abbr* International Baccalaureate

ib. *abbr* ibidem

I·ba·dan /ee baád'n, -daan/ capital of Oyo State, SW Nigeria. Pop. 1,365,000 (1995).

I·be·ri·an Pen·in·su·la /ī beeree èn-/, **I·be·ri·a** /ī beeree ə/ peninsula in SW Europe, divided into Spain, Portugal, and Gibraltar —**I·be·ri·an** *adj*, *n*

i·bex /ī bèks/ (*pl same or* **i·bex·es**) *n* a wild mountain goat with long horns

ibid. *abbr* ibidem

i·bi·dem /íbbi dèm/ *adv* cites the same publication, chapter, or page previously cited

i·bis /íbiss/ (*pl* **i·bis·es** *or same*) *n* a tropical wading bird with a downward-curving bill

I·bi·za /ee beéssa/ third largest of the Balearic Islands, in the W Mediterranean Sea

-ible *suffix* 1 = **-able** ◊ *audible* 2 causing ◊ *horrible* —**ibility** *suffix*

Ibn Sa·ud /íbbən saa oód, -sówd/, **Abdul Aziz** (1880?–1953) king of Saudi Arabia (1932–53)

IBS *abbr* irritable bowel syndrome

AKG London

Henrik Ibsen

Ib·sen /íbss'n/, **Henrik** (1828–1906) Norwegian playwright

i·bu·pro·fen /íbyoo prófən/ *n* a pain-relieving and anti-inflammatory drug

-ic *suffix* 1 of or relating to, having the nature of ◊ *anarchic* 2 with a valence that is higher than that of a related compound or ion ending in *-ous* ◊ *ferric*

Ic·a·rus /íkərəss/ *n* in Greek mythology, the son of Daedalus who flew too close to the sun, which melted the wax of his artificial wings —**I·car·i·an** /ī káiree ən/ *adj*

ICBM *abbr* intercontinental ballistic missile

ice /īss/ *n* 1 frozen water 2 an expanse of frozen water 3 a substance like ice ◊ *dry ice* 4 pieces of frozen water used to cool food or drink 5 extreme unfriendliness ■ *adj* made of ice ■ *v* (**iced**, **ic·ing**) 1 *vi* develop a thin surface coating of ice 2 *vt* put icing

on a cake 3 *vt* make certain of winning a game or succeeding at something (*slang*) —**iced** *adj* ◊ **break the ice** overcome initial restraint on first meeting somebody ◊ **cut no ice** fail to impress or make a difference ◊ **on ice** in abeyance or postponed

ice age *n* 1 a period when the Earth was covered with glaciers 2 **Ice Age** the most recent ice age

ice·berg /íss bùrg/ *n* a mass of floating ice with the greater part submerged

ice·boat /íss bòt/ *n* 1 a boat with runners and a sail, used on ice 2 a ship for breaking ice —**ice·boat·ing** *n*

ice·bound /íss bównd/ *adj* immobilized by ice

ice·box /íss bòks/ *n* 1 a refrigerator 2 a cool container for food

ice·break·er /íss bràykər/ *n* 1 a ship for breaking ice 2 a talk or game that relaxes a group at a meeting or social gathering —**ice·break·ing** *n*, *adj*

ice·cap /íss kàp/, **ice cap** *n* a permanent covering of ice, e.g., on a mountain

ice-cold *adj* very cold

ice cream *n* a frozen dessert made with cream and flavorings

ice-cream so·da *n* a fizzy drink with ice cream in it

ice floe *n* a sheet of ice floating in the ocean

ice hock·ey *n* a team game played on ice by skaters using sticks and a rubber disk called a puck

ice·house /íss hòwss/ (*pl* **-hous·es** /-hòwzəz/) *n* a building for storing ice

Ice·land /íssland/ island country in the North Atlantic Ocean. Cap. Reykjavik. Pop. 277,906 (2001). —**Ice·land·er** *n*

Ice·land·ic /íss lándik/ *adj* of Iceland ■ *n* the language of Iceland

ice·man /íss màn/ (*pl* **-men** /-mèn/) *n* 1 somebody who sells or delivers ice 2 an explorer or mountaineer experienced in traveling on ice

ice milk *n* a sweet frozen food made from skim milk

ice pack *n* 1 an ice-filled cloth or bag for pressing against an injury 2 a large area of floating ice that has formed a solid mass

ice pick *n* a lightweight handheld tool for chipping or breaking ice

ice sheet *n* a long-lasting expanse of ice

ice skate *n* a boot fitted with a blade for skating on ice —**ice-skate** *vi* —**ice-skat·er** *n* —**ice skat·ing** *n*

ice storm *n* a storm in which rain turns to ice

ice wa·ter *n* 1 chilled water as a drink 2 melted ice

I Ching /ee jíng/ *n* 1 an ancient Chinese system of fortune-telling 2 the book that explains I Ching

ich·neu·mon fly /ik noõmən-/, **ich·neu·mon wasp, ich·neu·mon** n an insect resembling a wasp that is a parasite of other insects

ich·thy·ol·o·gy /ikthee óllajee/ n the scientific study of fish —**ich·thy·o·log·i·cal** /-ik'l/ adj —**ich·thy·ol·o·gist** n

ich·thy·o·saur /íkthee ə sàwr/, **ich·thy·o·sau·rus** /ikthee ə sáwrəss/ (pl -rus·es or -ri /-rī/) n a prehistoric reptile with a long snout and paddle-shaped limbs

i·ci·cle /íssik'l/ n a hanging tapered rod of ice, formed when dripping water freezes

ORIGIN Icicle is a compound of *ice* and an old word *ickle* that itself meant "icicle."

ic·ing /íssing/ n 1 glazing or frosting for cakes made from powdered sugar 2 the formation of ice on surfaces

Icon: Eastern Orthodox icon of *Christus Acheiropoietus* in the Cathedral of the Assumption, Moscow

⚡**i·con** /ī kòn/ n 1 *also* **i·kon** an image of a holy person, used in worship in Eastern Orthodox churches 2 somebody famous for and symbolizing something ○ *the all-time rock 'n' roll icon* 3 an image on a computer screen that represents something such as a program or device

i·con·ic /ī kónnik/ adj 1 of somebody or something admired as an icon 2 of a religious icon —**i·con·i·cal·ly** adv

i·con·o·clasm /ī kónnə klàst/ n 1 somebody who challenges tradition 2 a destroyer or opponent of religious images —**i·con·o·clasm** n —**i·con·o·clas·tic** /ī kònnə klástik/ adj

i·co·nog·ra·phy /īkə nóggrəfee/ n a set of images or symbols recognized as having a specific meaning —**i·co·nog·ra·pher** n —**i·con·o·graph·i·cal** adj

⚡**ICQ** n a computer program for making online contact

⚡**ICR** abbr intelligent character recognition

-ics suffix 1 a science, art, or knowledge ○ *mathematics* 2 an activity or action ○ *calisthenics*

⚡**ICT** abbr information and communications technology

ICU abbr intensive care unit

ic·y /íssee/ (-i·er, -i·est) adj 1 ice-covered 2 very cold 3 very unfriendly —**i·ci·ly** adv —**i·ci·ness** n

id n in psychoanalytic theory, a part of the human psyche that is the source of instinctive impulses

Id = Eid al-Adha, Eid al-Fitr

I'd contr 1 I had 2 I would

ID¹, Id. abbr Idaho

ID² n a proof of identity such as a card or document (infml)

id. abbr idem

I·da·ho /ídə hò/ state in the NW United States. Cap. Boise. Pop. 1,293,953 (2000). —**I·da·ho·an** adj, n

i·de·a /ī dèə ə/ n 1 an opinion 2 a suggestion ○ *was his idea to go* 3 an impression or thought ○ *get the wrong idea* 4 a plan for doing something 5 the objective or purpose of something 6 the gist of something

i·de·al /ī dèə əl/ n 1 a perfect example 2 a principle aspired to ■ adj 1 serving as the best example 2 perfect but imaginary 3 excellent or perfectly suitable —**i·de·al·ly** adv

i·de·al·ism /ī dèè ə lìzzəm/ n 1 belief in perfection 2 living by high ideals —**i·de·al·ist** n —**i·de·al·is·tic** /ī dèè ə lìstik/ adj —**i·de·al·is·ti·cal·ly** adv

i·de·al·ize /ī dèè ə līz/ (-ized, -iz·ing) vt think of or represent as perfect —**i·de·al·i·za·tion** /ī dèè əli záysh'n/ n —**i·de·al·ized** adj

~~ideally~~ incorrect spelling of **ideally**

i·dem /ī dèm, í dèm/ pron the same one, especially the one just referred to

i·den·ti·cal /ī déntik'l/ adj 1 one and the same 2 alike in every way —**i·den·ti·cal·ly** adv

i·den·ti·cal twin n either of a pair of twins developed from a single fertilized egg

~~identicle~~ incorrect spelling of **identical**

i·den·ti·fi·ca·tion /ī dèntəfi káysh'n/ n 1 recognition of the identity of somebody or something 2 a proof of identity 3 a strong feeling of affinity with another person or group

⚡**i·den·ti·fi·er** /ī déntə fīr/ n a symbol that identifies a body of data

i·den·ti·fy /ī dénti fī/ (-fied, -fies) vt 1 recognize and name 2 consider as the same —**i·den·ti·fi·a·ble** adj —**i·den·ti·fi·a·bly** adv □ **identify with** vt feel affinity with somebody

i·den·ti·ty /ī déntətee/ (pl -ties) n 1 the name or essential character that identifies somebody or something 2 sameness

i·den·ti·ty theft n theft of personal information, e.g., somebody's credit card details

id·e·o·gram /ídee ə gràm, íddee-/, **id·e·o·graph** /-gràf/ n 1 a symbol in some writing systems that represents a thing or concept rather than the word for it 2 a graphic symbol that represents a word, e.g., "@" or "&" —**id·e·o·gram·mat·ic** /ídee əgrə máttik, ìddee-/ adj —**id·e·o·graph·ic** /ídee ə gráffik, ìddee-/

i·de·o·logue /ídee ə lòg, íddee-/ *n* a zealous supporter of an ideology

i·de·ol·o·gy /ídee óllajee, íddee-/ (*pl* **-gies**) *n* a system of social, economic, or political beliefs —**i·de·o·log·i·cal** /ídee ə lójjik'l, íddee-/ *adj* —**i·de·o·log·i·cal·ly** *adv* —**i·de·ol·o·gist** *n*

id·i·o·cy /íddee əssee/ *n* an offensive term for extreme lack of intelligence or foresight

id·i·o·lect /íddee ə lèkt/ *n* the way an individual person uses language —**id·i·o·lec·tal** /íddee ə lékt'l/ *adj*

id·i·om /íddee əm/ *n* **1** a fixed expression with a nonliteral meaning **2** the natural way of using a language

id·i·o·mat·ic /íddee ə máttik, **id·i·o·mat·i·cal** /-máttik'l/ *adj* **1** characteristic of the way native speakers use a language **2** of the nature of an idiom —**id·i·o·mat·i·cal·ly** *adv*

~~idiosyncracy~~ incorrect spelling of **idiosyncrasy**

id·i·o·syn·cra·sy /íddee ə síngkrəssee/ (*pl* **-sies**) *n* a way of behaving that is peculiar to a person or group —**id·i·o·syn·crat·ic** /-ə sing kráttik/ *adj*

id·i·ot /íddee ət/ *n* a person regarded as extremely foolish (*insult*) —**id·i·ot·ic** /íddee óttik/ *adj* —**id·i·ot·i·cal·ly** *adv*

ORIGIN Idiot goes back to a Greek word that meant "private person," and deriving from that "ordinary person," and then "ignorant person." It passed into Latin in the last sense, and from there into French and English.

i·dle /íd'l/ *adj* (**i·dler, i·dlest**) **1** not working or in use **2** habitually lazy **3** frivolous and a waste of time **4** unfounded ○ *idle gossip* **5** ineffective ○ *idle threats* **6** not playing or competing ■ *n* the speed of an engine with the gear disengaged ■ *v* (**i·dled, i·dling**) **1** *vti* pass time aimlessly **2** *vi* move slowly and aimlessly **3** *vti* run with the gear disengaged —**i·dle·ness** *n* —**i·dler** *n* —**i·dly** *adv* ◊ See note at **vain**

SPELLCHECK Do not confuse the spelling of **idle** and **idol** ("an object of adoration"), which sound similar.

i·dol /íd'l/ *n* **1** an object of adoration **2** an object worshiped as a god ◊ See note at **idle**

i·dol·a·try /dóllətree/ *n* **1** extreme admiration **2** idol worship (*disapproving*) —**i·dol·a·ter** *n* —**i·dol·a·trous** *adj*

i·dol·ize /íd'l ìz/ (**-ized, -iz·ing**) *vt* **1** admire fanatically **2** worship as an idol (*disapproving*) —**i·dol·i·za·tion** /íd'li záysh'n/ *n*

⚡ **IDP** *abbr* integrated data processing

i·dyll /íd'l/, **i·dyl** *n* **1** an experience of serene happiness **2** a tranquil charming scene —**i·dyl·lic** /ī díllik/ *adj*

IE *abbr* **1** industrial engineer **2** ion exchange **3** ionization energy

i.e. *abbr* that is to say ◊ See note at **e.g.**

-ie *suffix* **1** one that is small or dear ○ *birdie* **2** one having a particular character ○ *sweetie*

~~iether~~ incorrect spelling of **either**

if *conj* **1** indicates the conditions required for something to happen ○ *If you give me the money, I'll buy one for you.* **2** indicates what may be the case ○ *If the car has broken down, we'll be late.* **3** introduces an indirect question ○ *asked if I would stay* **4** modifies a statement ○ *by Thursday, if not earlier* ■ *n* **1** a doubt **2** a condition or qualification

USAGE Substituting **would have** for **had** in an *if* clause (one stating a condition contrary to fact) is a grammatical error. Do not write: *If they would have done it right to begin with, these problems would not exist.* Write instead: *If they had done it right...* or, more formally, *Had they done it right to begin with, these problems would not exist.* Avoid the incorrect form *they'd + have,* as in *If they'd have done it right....* Here *they'd* is a contraction for *they had.* Write instead *If they'd done it right...* or *If they had done it right....*

IF *abbr* intermediate frequency

if·fy /íffee/ (**-fi·er, -fi·est**) *adj* doubtful (*infml*) —**if·fi·ness** *n*

ig·loo /ígloo/ *n* a dome-shaped Inuit house built from packed snow

Ig·na·tius Loy·o·la /ig náyshəss loy óla/, **St.** (1491–1556) Spanish priest and a founder of the Jesuits (Society of Jesus)

ig·ne·ous /ígnee əss/ *adj* **1** describes rock that was formerly molten **2** of fire (*fml*)

ig·nite /ig nít/ (**-nit·ed, -nit·ing**) *vti* set fire to, or begin to burn —**ig·nit·a·ble** *adj*

ig·ni·tion /ig nísh'n/ *n* **1** the process of igniting **2** a mechanism for starting an internal-combustion engine

ig·no·ble /ig nōb'l/ *adj* **1** dishonorable **2** not of the nobility (*fml*) —**ig·no·bly** *adv*

ig·no·min·y /ígnə mìnnee/ *n* **1** (*pl* **ig·no·min·ies**) disgrace and dishonor **2** a disgraceful act (*fml*) —**ig·no·min·i·ous** /ígnə mínnee əss/ *adj* —**ig·no·min·i·ous·ly** *adv*

ig·no·ra·mus /ígnə ráyməss/ *n* a person regarded as lacking knowledge (*insult*)

ORIGIN Ignoramus comes from a Latin verbal form meaning "we do not know," and in legal use "we take no notice." Originally it was the endorsement made by a grand jury when rejecting an indictment, occurring in phrases like *find an ignoramus* and *bring in an ignoramus.* The sense "ignorant person" dates from the early 17C, and may be taken from the title of the play *Ignoramus* (1615) by George Ruggle, a comedy satirizing lawyers.

ig·no·rant /ígnərənt/ *adj* **1** lacking knowledge or education **2** unaware ○ *ignorant of the danger* —**ig·no·rance** *n* —**ig·no·rant·ly** *adv*

ig·nore /ig náwr/ (**-nored, -nor·ing**) *vt* refuse to notice somebody or something

~~ignorent~~ incorrect spelling of **ignorant**

I·gua·çu Falls /ee gwaa soo-/ waterfall on the Iguaçu River, in S Brazil. Height 260 ft./80 m.

i·gua·na /i gwaánə/ (*pl* **-nas** *or same*) *n* a large plant-eating tropical lizard

ih·ram /ee raám/ *n* 1 a white cotton robe worn by men when they are pilgrims to Mecca 2 the state of holiness conferred or symbolized by the wearing of the ihram

Ikh·na·ton ▸ Akhenaton

IL *abbr* Illinois

-ile *suffix* of, relating to, capable of o *volatile*

~~illegal~~ incorrect spelling of **illegal**

il·e·um /íllee əm/ (*pl* **-a** /-ə/) *n* the lowest part of the small intestine —**il·e·i·tis** /íllee ítiss/ *n*

i·lex /í leks/ *n* any tree or bush related to holly

ILGWU, I.L.G.W.U. *abbr* International Ladies' Garment Workers' Union

il·i·um /íllee əm/ (*pl* **-a** /-ə/) *n* the wide flat upper portion of the pelvis

ilk /ilk/ *n* sort or type o *journalists and others of that ilk*

ill *adj* (**worse, worst** /wurst/) 1 unwell 2 resulting in harm, pain, or trouble 3 unkind and unfriendly o *ill feeling* 4 unfavorable o *an ill wind* 5 morally bad o *of ill repute* ■ *adv* (**worse, worst**) 1 badly o *ill treated* 2 unfavorably o *bodes ill* ■ *n* 1 harm or evil o *wished them ill* 2 an unfavorable opinion o *don't think ill of him*

I'll /īl/ *contr* I will

ill. *abbr* 1 illustrated 2 illustration

Ill. *abbr* Illinois

ill-ad·vised *adj* not wise to do —**ill-ad·vis·ed·ly** *adv*

ill-as·sort·ed *adj* not well matched

ill at ease *adj* uncomfortable and nervous

ill-bred *adj* rude or bad-mannered —**ill-breed·ing** *n*

ill-con·ceived *adj* not well planned or thought out

ill-con·sid·ered *adj* unwise or not well thought out

ill-de·fined *adj* not clearly or sharply defined

ill-dis·posed *adj* unfriendly or hostile

⚡ **il·le·gal** /i léeg'l/ *adj* 1 against the law or rules 2 not permitted by a computer program —**il·le·gal·i·ty** /íllee gállətee/ *n* —**il·le·gal·ly** *adv* ◊ See note at **unlawful**

il·leg·i·ble /i léjjəb'l/ *adj* impossible or hard to read —**il·leg·i·bil·i·ty** /i lèjjə bíllətee/ *n* —**il·leg·i·bly** *adv*

il·le·git·i·mate /i llə jíttəmət/ *adj* 1 against the law or rules 2 born out of wedlock —**il·le·git·i·ma·cy** *n* —**il·le·git·i·mate·ly** *adv*

ill-fat·ed *adj* ending in disaster

ill-fa·vored *adj* 1 unattractive to look at, especially facially 2 objectionable (*literary*)

ill feel·ing *n* animosity or resentment

ill-found·ed *adj* without a convincing basis

ill-got·ten *adj* acquired dishonestly or illegally

ill health *n* a poor state of general health

ill hu·mor *n* a bad mood or bad temper —**ill-hu·mored** *adj*

il·lib·er·al /i líbbərəl, -brəl/ *adj* 1 narrow-minded 2 ungenerous (*fml*)

il·lic·it /i líssit/ *adj* 1 illegal 2 unacceptable by prevailing social standards —**il·lic·it·ly** *adv* —**il·lic·it·ness** *n* ◊ See note at **elicit, unlawful**

Il·li·nois[1] /íllə nóy/ (*pl same*) *n* a member of a confederacy of Algonquian peoples who lived in an area covering N Illinois, E Iowa, and S Wisconsin, and now live in NE Oklahoma —**Il·li·nois** *adj*

Il·li·nois[2] /íllə nóy/ 1 state in the north central United States. Cap. Springfield. Pop. 12,419,293 (2000). 2 river in N Illinois. Length 420 mi./680 km. —**Il·li·nois·an** *adj*, *n*

il·liq·uid /i líkwid/ *adj* 1 hard to convert into cash 2 not having enough cash

il·lit·er·ate /i líttərət/ *adj* 1 an offensive term describing somebody unable to read and write 2 uneducated in a particular subject —**il·lit·er·a·cy** *n* —**il·lit·er·ate·ly** *adv*

ill-judged *adj* imprudent or tactless

ill-man·nered *adj* rude —**ill-man·nered·ly** *adv*

ill-na·tured *adj* bad-tempered, especially by disposition —**ill-na·tured·ly** *adv*

ill·ness /íllnəss/ *n* 1 bad health 2 a disease or sickness

il·log·i·cal /i lójjik'l/ *adj* 1 not following the rules of logic 2 unreasonable —**il·log·i·cal·i·ty** /i lòjji kállətee/ *n* —**il·log·i·cal·ly** *adv*

ill-o·mened, ill-starred *adj* apparently fated to end badly

ill-tem·pered *adj* irritable —**ill-tem·pered·ly** *adv*

ill-timed *adj* done at an unsuitable time

ill-treat *vt* 1 behave unkindly or harshly toward 2 misuse —**ill-treat·ment** *n* ◊ See note at **misuse**

il·lu·mi·nate /i loomi nàyt/ (**-nat·ed, -nat·ing**) *v* 1 *vti* light up or be lit up 2 *vt* decorate something with lights 3 *vt* make something easier to understand 4 *vt* add colored letters or designs to a manuscript or page 5 *vti* enlighten somebody (*literary*) 6 *vt* cause somebody's face to look happy and animated —**il·lu·mi·nat·ing** *adj* —**il·lu·mi·na·tor** *n*

il·lu·mi·na·tion /i lòomi náysh'n/ *n* 1 the lighting up of something 2 available light in a place or for a purpose 3 clarification and explanation

il·lu·mine /i lóomin/ (**-mined, -min·ing**) *vt* illuminate (*fml*)

ill-use *vt* treat harshly and cruelly —**ill-us-age** *n* —**ill-use** *n*

il-lu-sion /i lóozh'n/ *n* 1 something with a deceptive appearance 2 the ability of appearances to be deceptive, or of the mind to be deceived by them 3 a false idea —**il-lu-sion-ar-y** *adj*

il-lu-sion-ist /i lóozh'nist/ *n* 1 a magician 2 a painter of pictorial illusions —**il-lu-sion-is-tic** /i lòozh'n ístik/ *adj*

il-lu-so-ry /i lóossaree/, **il-lu-sive** /i lóossiv/ *adj* imaginary —**il-lu-sive-ly** *adv* —**il-lu-so-ri-ly** *adv*

il-lus-trate /íllə stràyt/ (-trat-ed, -trat-ing) *v* 1 *vt* be characteristic and revealing of 2 clarify something with examples and comparisons 3 *vt* accompany with pictures or graphics —**il-lus-tra-tor** *n*

il-lus-tra-tion /íllə stráysh'n/ *n* 1 a picture or graphic that complements a text 2 something that helps explain or exemplify something else 3 the provision of pictures or graphics to accompany a text —**il-lus-tra-tion-al** *adj*

il-lus-tra-tive /i lústrətiv/ *adj* serving as an illustration

il-lus-tri-ous /i lústree əss/ *adj* extremely distinguished —**il-lus-tri-ous-ly** *adv* —**il-lus-tri-ous-ness** *n*

ill will *n* hostility or dislike

~~illness~~ incorrect spelling of **illness**

I'm *contr* I am

IM *abbr* international master

im-age /ímmij/ *n* 1 an actual or mental picture 2 somebody who closely resembles somebody else o *She's the image of her father.* 3 a typical or extreme example o *the very image of greed* 4 a likeness seen in a mirror, seen through a lens, or produced on a screen 5 a metaphor or simile ■ *vt* (-ag-ing) 1 produce or reflect an image of 2 form a mental image of 3 describe in visual terms 4 typify —**im-ag-er** *n*

⚡**im-age com-pres-sion** *n* a technique for storing a visual image in a reduced electronic form

⚡**im-age map** *n* an electronic graphic image with areas for hypertext links

im-age-ry /ímmijree/ *n* 1 metaphors, similes, and other figurative language 2 mental or pictorial images

i-mag-i-nar-y /i májjə nèrree/ *adj* existing only in the mind

i-mag-i-nar-y u-nit *n* the positive square root of –1

i-mag-i-na-tion /i màjjə náysh'n/ *n* 1 the ability to form images in the mind, especially of things not directly experienced 2 the creative part of the mind 3 resourcefulness

i-mag-i-na-tive /i májjənətiv, -nàytiv/ *adj* 1 skilled at forming images in the mind or thinking originally 2 new and original —**i-mag-i-na-tive-ly** *adv* —**i-mag-i-na-tive-ness** *n*

i-mag-ine /i májjin/ (-ined, -in-ing) *v* 1 *vti* form an image of something in the mind 2 *vt* see or hear something unreal 3 *vt* assume or suppose something —**i-mag-i-na-ble** *adj* —**i-mag-i-na-bly** *adv* —**i-mag-in-ing** *n*

~~imaginery~~ incorrect spelling of **imaginary**

i-ma-go /i máy gò, i maà gò/ (*pl* **-goes** or **-gi-nes** /i máygə nèez, i maàgə-/) *n* a sexually mature adult insect

i-mam /i maám/ *n* 1 a leader of prayers in a mosque 2 *also* **I-mam** an Islamic religious leader regarded as a direct descendant of Muhammad or Ali —**i-mam-ate** /i maà màyt, i má-/ *n*

IMAX /í màks/ *tdmk* a trademark for a giant-screen, large-format movie and motion-simulation entertainment complex

im-bal-ance /im bállənss/ *n* a lack of balance, e.g., in emphasis or proportion —**im-bal-anced** *adj*

im-be-cile /ímbəss'l, ímbə sīl/ *n* an offensive term for somebody regarded as very foolish or unintelligent *(insult)* —**im-be-cil-ic** /ímbə síllik/ *adj* —**im-be-cil-i-ty** /-síllətee/ *n*

im-bed *vt* = **embed**

im-bibe /im bíb/ (-bibed, -bib-ing) *v* 1 *vti* drink *(fml or humorous)* 2 *vt* take in mentally *(literary)* —**im-bib-er** *n*

im-bro-glio /im brólyò/ (*pl* **-glios**) *n* a complicated situation

im-bue /im byoò/ (-bued, -bu-ing) *vt* 1 fill with a particular quality o *poetry imbued with melancholy* 2 soak with a stain or dye *(fml)*

~~imediately~~ incorrect spelling of **immediately**

IMF *abbr* International Monetary Fund

~~imformation~~ incorrect spelling of **information**

~~iminent~~ incorrect spelling of **imminent**

im-i-tate /ímmi tàyt/ (-tat-ed, -tat-ing) *vt* 1 mimic 2 follow the example or style of 3 be or look like o *a case of life imitating art* —**im-i-ta-tor** *n*

SYNONYMS **imitate, copy, emulate, mimic, take off, ape** CORE MEANING: adopt the behavior of another person

---

im-i-ta-tion /ímmi táysh'n/ *n* 1 a copy or fake 2 the imitating of somebody or something ■ *adj* not genuine —**im-i-ta-tion-al** *adj*

im-i-ta-tive /ímmi tàytiv/ *adj* 1 attempting to copy something but usually inferior 2 involving imitation —**im-i-ta-tive-ly** *adv*

im-mac-u-late /i mákyələt/ *adj* 1 completely clean 2 faultless —**im-mac-u-late-ly** *adv* —**im-mac-u-late-ness** *n*

Im-mac-u-late Con-cep-tion *n* the Roman Catholic doctrine of the Virgin Mary's freedom from original sin from the moment of her conception

im-ma-nent /ímmənənt/ *adj* 1 existing within or inherent in something *(fml)* 2 existing in

all parts of the universe —**im·ma·nence** n
—**im·ma·nent·ly** adv

SPELLCHECK Do not confuse the spelling of **immanent** and **imminent** ("about to occur"), which sound similar.

im·ma·te·ri·al /immə teéree əl/ adj 1 not relevant 2 having no physical substance —**im·ma·te·ri·al·i·ty** /immə teéree állətee/ n

im·ma·ture /immə chóor/ adj 1 not fully developed 2 childish —**im·ma·ture·ly** adv —**im·ma·tur·i·ty** n

im·meas·ur·a·ble /i mézhərəb'l/ adj vast or huge —**im·meas·ur·a·bil·i·ty** /i mèzhərə bíllətee/ n —**im·meas·ur·a·bly** adv

im·me·di·ate /i meédee ət/ adj 1 happening or done without pause or delay 2 nearest ○ his immediate family 3 needing to be dealt with first ○ the immediate problem —**im·me·di·a·cy** n

im·me·di·ate·ly /i meédee ətlee/ adv 1 without any delay 2 very closely in space or time

im·me·mo·ri·al /immə máwree əl/ adj so old that it seems always to have existed —**im·me·mo·ri·al·ly** adv

im·mense /i méns/ adj huge —**im·mense·ly** adv —**im·men·si·ty** n

im·merse /i múrs/ (-mersed, -mers·ing) v 1 vt completely submerge in liquid 2 vt baptize by submerging all or part of the body 3 vr occupy yourself totally with something —**im·mer·sion** n

im·mi·grant /ímmigrənt/ n 1 somebody settling in a new country 2 a plant or animal established in a new place —**im·mi·grant** adj

im·mi·gra·tion /immi gráysh'n/ n 1 the arrival of settlers in a new country 2 the passport control point at an airport, seaport, or border —**im·mi·grate** /ímmi gràyt/ vi

im·mi·nent /ímminənt/ adj about to occur —**im·mi·nence** n —**im·mi·nent·ly** adv ◊ See note at **immanent**

im·mo·bile /i mób'l/ adj 1 motionless 2 incapable of motion —**im·mo·bil·i·ty** /immō bíllətee, ìmmə-/ n

im·mo·bi·lize /i mób'l ìz/ (-lized, -liz·ing) vt 1 prevent from moving 2 put a machine out of action —**im·mo·bi·li·za·tion** /i mòb'li záysh'n/ n

im·mod·er·ate /i móddərət/ adj excessive —**im·mod·er·ate·ly** adv —**im·mod·er·a·tion** /i mòddə ráysh'n/ n

im·mod·est /i móddəst/ adj 1 boastful 2 indecent or offensive —**im·mod·est·ly** adv —**im·mod·es·ty** n

im·mo·late /ímmə làyt/ (-lat·ed, -lat·ing) vt kill or give up as a sacrifice (literary) —**im·mo·la·tion** /immə láysh'n/ n

im·mor·al /i máwrəl/ adj contrary to accepted moral principles —**im·mor·al·i·ty** /i maw rállətee/ n —**im·mor·al·ly** adv

im·mor·tal /i máwrt'l/ adj 1 able to have eternal life 2 famous and long remembered —**im·mor·tal** n —**im·mor·tal·i·ty** /i mawr tállətee/ n

im·mor·tal·ize /i máwrt'l ìz/ (-ized, -iz·ing) vt 1 make lastingly famous 2 give eternal life to —**im·mor·tal·i·za·tion** /i màwrt'li záysh'n/ n

im·mov·a·ble /i móovəb'l/ adj 1 unable to be moved 2 having a fixed opinion —**im·mov·a·bly** adv

im·mune /i myóon/ adj 1 protected from getting a particular disease 2 of the body's resistance to disease 3 not subject to something or susceptible to something ○ immune from prosecution

im·mune re·sponse n the response of the immune system to a disease-causing agent

im·mune sys·tem n the bodily system that recognizes and fights disease

im·mu·ni·ty /i myóonətee/ (pl -ties) n 1 resistance to disease 2 freedom from responsibility or punishment

im·mu·nize /ímmyə nìz/ (-nized, -niz·ing) vt make somebody resistant to a disease, especially by inoculation —**im·mu·ni·za·tion** /ímmyəni záysh'n/ n

immuno- prefix immune, immunity ○ immunodeficiency

im·mu·no·de·fi·cien·cy /immyənō di físh'nsee, i myóo-/ (pl -cies) n inability of the immune system to respond to and fight disease —**im·mu·no·de·fi·cient** adj

im·mu·no·glob·u·lin /ímmyənō glóbbyəlin, i myóo-/ n an antibody formed by the immune system and present in the blood

im·mu·nol·o·gy /ímmyə nólləjee/ n the scientific study of the immune system —**im·mu·no·log·i·cal** adj —**im·mu·nol·o·gist** n

im·mu·no·sup·pres·sion /ímmyənō sə présh'n, i myóo-/ n inhibition of the ability of the immune system to fight disease —**im·mu·no·sup·pres·sant** adj, n —**im·mu·no·sup·pres·sive** adj, n

im·mure /i myóor/ (-mured, -mur·ing) vt 1 imprison (literary) 2 shut away from other people (fml) —**im·mure·ment** n

im·mu·ta·ble /i myóotəb'l/ adj unchanging or unchangeable —**im·mu·ta·bil·i·ty** /i myóotə bíllətee/ n —**im·mu·ta·bly** adv

imp n 1 a mischievous child 2 a small demon

ORIGIN An imp was originally a "young plant shoot." This was metaphorically extended to "descendant of a noble family" and "child." From the 16C it could be used specifically for a "child of the devil," and this sense weakened to imply just mischief in the 17C.

imp. abbr 1 imperative 2 imperfect

im·pact n /im pákt/ 1 the hitting of one object by another 2 the force of a collision 3 a strong effect ■ vti /im pákt/ 1 strike something with force **2** △ have an effect on something —**im·pac·tion** /im páksh'n/ *n*

USAGE Many careful users of the language dislike the verb **impact** in any figurative sense, regardless of whether the verb is followed by *on*: *This impacts the company favorably* and *This impacts on the company.* The verb is undeniably common in business communication, but you can avoid it by using *affect, change,* or the like. Use of the verb is uncontroversial only in physical senses: *The car impacted the railing.*

im·pact·ed /im páktəd/ *adj* describes a tooth wedged sideways under the gum

im·pair /im páir/ *vt* weaken or damage —**im·pair·ment** *n*

im·pa·la /im páalə/ (*pl* -**las** *or* same) *n* an antelope with curving horns

im·pale /im páyl/ (-**paled,** -**pal·ing**) *vt* pierce with a pointed object —**im·pale·ment** *n*

im·pal·pa·ble /im pálpəb'l/ *adj* (*fml*) **1** unable to be touched or sensed **2** hard to understand —**im·pal·pa·bly** *adv*

im·pan·el /im pánn'l/, **em·pan·el** /em-/ *vt* **1** list people as possible jurors **2** select a jury from a list

im·part /im páart/ *vt* **1** communicate information or knowledge **2** give a particular quality

im·par·tial /im páarsh'l/ *adj* not biased in favor of one side or argument —**im·par·ti·al·i·ty** /im páarshee állətee/ *n* —**im·par·tial·ly** *adv*

im·pass·a·ble /im pássəb'l/ *adj* **1** impossible to travel on or through **2** impossible to overcome —**im·pass·a·bly** *adv*

im·passe /im pàss/ *n* a block to progress or agreement

im·pas·sioned /im pásh'nd/ *adj* showing strong feelings

im·pas·sive /im pássiv/ *adj* **1** expressionless **2** devoid of all emotion —**im·pas·sive·ly** *adv* —**im·pas·siv·i·ty** /impə sívvətee/ *n*

SYNONYMS impassive, apathetic, phlegmatic, stolid, stoic, unmoved CORE MEANING: showing no emotional response or interest

im·pa·tiens /im páysh'nz, -sh'nss/ (*pl* same) *n* a low-growing many-flowered garden plant

im·pa·tient /im páysh'nt/ *adj* **1** annoyed at being kept waiting or being delayed **2** eager —**im·pa·tience** *n* —**im·pa·tient·ly** *adv*

im·peach /im péech/ *vt* **1** accuse a serving government official with serious misconduct while in office **2** remove somebody, especially a president, from public office because of having committed crimes (*fml*) **3** bring charges against somebody **4** question the good character of somebody (*fml*) —**im·peach·a·ble** *adj* —**im·peach·ment** *n*

im·pec·ca·ble /im pékəb'l/ *adj* **1** perfect **2** free from sin —**im·pec·ca·bly** *adv*

im·pe·cu·ni·ous /impə kyóonee əss/ *adj* having little or no money

im·pe·dance /im péed'nss/ *n* **1** something that delays or prevents progress (*fml*) **2** (*symbol Z*) the opposition in an electrical circuit to the flow of alternating current

im·pede /im péed/ (-**ped·ed,** -**ped·ing**) *vt* hinder the movement or progress of ◊ See note at **hinder**

im·ped·i·ment /im péddəmənt/ *n* **1** an impairment, especially in speech **2** an obstacle

im·ped·i·men·ta /im pèddə méntə/ *npl* obstructions (*literary*)

im·pel /im pél/ (-**pelled,** -**pel·ling**) *vt* **1** force to do something **2** cause to move (*fml*)

im·pend·ing /im pénding/ *adj* imminent or threatening

im·pen·e·tra·ble /im pénnətrəb'l/ *adj* **1** impossible to get in or through **2** incomprehensible —**im·pen·e·tra·bil·i·ty** /im pènnətrə bíllətee/ *n* —**im·pen·e·tra·bly** *adv*

im·pen·i·tent /im pénnit'nt/ *adj* not repentant —**im·pen·i·tence** *n* —**im·pen·i·tent·ly** *adv*

im·per·a·tive /im pérrətiv/ *adj* **1** necessary **2** describes a mood or form of a verb expressing a command ■ *n* **1** something that must be done **2** the form of a verb used to give an order —**im·per·a·tive·ly** *adv*

im·per·cep·ti·ble /impər séptəb'l/ *adj* too small or gradual to be noticed —**im·per·cep·ti·bly** *adv*

im·per·fect /im púrfəkt/ *adj* **1** faulty or incomplete **2** describes a verb or tense that expresses incomplete action ■ *n* **1** the imperfect tense of a verb **2** a verb in the imperfect tense —**im·per·fect·ly** *adv*

im·per·fec·tion /impər fékshən/ *n* **1** a fault or defect **2** the possession of faults or defects ◊ See note at **flaw**

im·pe·ri·al /im péeree əl/ *adj* **1** belonging to an empire, emperor, or empress **2** supremely powerful **3** grand or majestic —**im·pe·ri·al·ly** *adv*

im·pe·ri·al·ism /im péeree ə lìzzəm/ *n* **1** belief in the extension of the authority of one country over colonies or other countries **2** the political, military, or economic domination of one country by another —**im·pe·ri·al·ist** *n, adj* —**im·pe·ri·al·is·tic** /im pèeree ə lístik/ *adj*

im·per·il /im pérrəl/ *vt* endanger —**im·per·il·ment** *n*

im·pe·ri·ous /im péeree əss/ *adj* haughty and domineering —**im·pe·ri·ous·ly** *adv* —**im·pe·ri·ous·ness** *n*

im·per·ish·a·ble /im pérrishəb'l/ *adj* not liable to become spoiled, weak, or damaged —**im·per·ish·a·bly** *adv*

im·per·ma·nent /im púrmənənt/ *adj* not lasting —**im·per·ma·nence** *n*

im·per·me·a·ble /im púrmee əb'l/ *adj* not permitting liquid, gas, or other fluids to pass through —**im·per·me·a·bil·i·ty** /im pùrmee ə bíllətee/ n

im·per·mis·si·ble /ímpər míssəbʹl/ adj not permitted or permissible

im·per·son·al /im púrsən'l/ adj 1 focusing on facts or events rather than people or personalities 2 not treating people as individuals o an impersonal bureaucracy —**im·per·son·al·i·ty** /im pùrs'n állətee/ n —**im·per·son·al·ly** adv

im·per·son·ate /im púrs'n àyt/ (-at·ed, -at·ing) vt 1 mimic the voice, appearance, and manners of somebody, especially in order to entertain 2 pretend to be somebody else in order to deceive —**im·per·son·a·tion** /im pùrs'n áysh'n/ n —**im·per·son·a·tor** n

im·per·ti·nent /im púrt'nənt/ adj (fml) 1 brash or disrespectful 2 irrelevant —**im·per·ti·nence** n —**im·per·ti·nent·ly** adv

im·per·turb·a·ble /ímpər túrbəbʹl/ adj consistently calm —**im·per·turb·a·bly** adv

im·per·vi·ous /im púrvee əss/ adj 1 not responsive to the suggestions or opinions of others 2 not allowing passage of something, especially liquid o impervious to damp —**im·per·vi·ous·ly** adv —**im·per·vi·ous·ness** n

im·pe·ti·go /ímpə teé gò, -tí-/ n a contagious skin disease with blisters that form scabs

im·pet·u·ous /im péchoo əss/ adj 1 acting impulsively 2 done on impulse —**im·pet·u·ous·ly** adv —**im·pet·u·ous·ness** n

im·pe·tus /ímpətəss/ n 1 the energy or motivation to do something 2 a force that maintains speed in spite of resistance

im·pi·e·ty /im pí ətee/ (pl -ties) n 1 lack of religious respect 2 an act showing lack of religious respect

im·pinge /im pínj/ (-pinged, -pinge·ing) vi 1 interfere with the usual course or extent of something (fml) o impinges on our freedom 2 strike or hit something —**im·pinge·ment** n

im·pi·ous /ímpee əs, im pí əss/ adj showing lack of religious respect —**im·pi·ous·ly** adv

imp·ish /ímpish/ adj mischievous —**imp·ish·ly** adv —**imp·ish·ness** n

im·plac·a·ble /im plákəbʹl/ adj impossible to pacify or reduce in strength —**im·plac·a·bil·i·ty** /im plàkə bíllətee/ n —**im·plac·a·bly** adv

im·plant vt /im plánt/ 1 fix in the mind or consciousness 2 insert into something that encloses 3 fix in the ground to grow 4 embed in the body surgically ■ n /im plant/ something inserted into the body during surgery —**im·plan·ta·tion** /im plànt táysh'n/ n

im·plau·si·ble /im pláwzəbʹl/ adj hard to believe —**im·plau·si·bil·i·ty** /im plàwzə bíllətee/ n —**im·plau·si·bly** adv

im·ple·ment n /ímpləmənt/ a tool or utensil ■ vt /ímplə mènt/ put into effect or action —**im·ple·men·ta·tion** /ímpləmən táysh'n/ n

im·pli·cate /ímpli kàyt/ (-cat·ed, -cat·ing) vt 1 show or suggest that somebody or something is connected with something such as a crime 2 imply something (fml)

im·pli·ca·tion /ímpli káysh'n/ n 1 something involved as a consequence o the wider implications of the decision 2 the process of implying rather than stating —**im·pli·ca·tion·al** adj

im·plic·it /im plíssit/ adj 1 implied but not stated 2 not affected by doubt or uncertainty o implicit trust 3 present as a necessary part —**im·plic·it·ly** adv ◊ See note at **explicit**

~~impliment~~ incorrect spelling of **implement**

im·plode /im plṓd/ (-plod·ed, -plod·ing) vti burst inward

im·plore /im pláwr/ (-plored, -plor·ing) vt beg or plead with somebody to do something (fml) —**im·plor·ing** adj —**im·plor·ing·ly** adv

im·plo·sion /im plṓzh'n/ n a violent inward collapse

im·ply /im plí/ (-plied, -plies) vt 1 suggest without saying 2 involve as a necessary part or condition —**im·plied** adj ◊ See note at **infer**

im·po·lite /ímpə lít/ adj rude or discourteous —**im·po·lite·ly** adv —**im·po·lite·ness** n

im·pol·i·tic /im póllətik/ adj unwise because of possible disastrous consequences —**im·pol·i·tic·ly** adv

im·pon·der·a·ble /im póndərəbʹl/ adj not measurable in terms of importance or effect ■ n something whose importance or effect is impossible to calculate (often pl) —**im·pon·der·a·bil·i·ty** /im pòndərə bíllətee/ n

⚡ **im·port** vt /im páwrt/ 1 bring in goods or materials from abroad to sell or use commercially 2 transfer computer data from one location to another 3 imply or signify something (fml) ■ n /im páwrt/ 1 something imported for sale or commercial use 2 the importing of something 3 the true significance of something —**im·por·ta·tion** /im pàwr táysh'n/ n —**im·port·er** n

im·por·tant /im páwrt'nt/ adj 1 having interest, value, or relevance 2 high-ranking or influential —**im·por·tance** n —**im·por·tant·ly** adv

~~important~~ incorrect spelling of **important**

im·por·tu·nate /im páwrchoonət/ adj (fml) 1 demanding and persistent 2 urgent or pressing —**im·por·tu·nate·ly** adv

im·por·tune /ímpər tóon, im páwrchən/ (-tuned, -tun·ing) vt ask insistently for something (fml)

im·pose /im pṓz/ (-posed, -pos·ing) v 1 vt levy or enforce something compulsory such as a tax or a punishment 2 vt make people comply with or agree to something o changes that were imposed on us 3 vti force yourself on others —**im·po·si·tion** /ímpə zísh'n/ n

im·pos·ing /im pózing/ *adj* large and impressive —**im·pos·ing·ly** *adv*

im·pos·si·ble /im póssəb'l/ *adj* 1 not able to exist or be done 2 very difficult to deal with o *an impossible child* —**im·pos·si·bil·i·ty** /im pòssə bíllətə/ *n* —**im·pos·si·bly** *adv*

im·pos·tor /im póstər/, **im·pos·ter** *n* somebody who claims to be another —**im·pos·ture** /im póschər/ *n*

im·po·tent /ímpət'nt/ *adj* 1 unable to have or maintain an erection of the penis 2 powerless —**im·po·tence** *n* —**im·po·tent·ly** *adv*

im·pound /im pównd/ *vt* 1 put a confiscated object in a confined place o *has impounded their car* 2 take goods into legal custody —**im·pound·ment** *n*

im·pov·er·ish /im póvvərish/ *vt* 1 make poor 2 spoil or reduce in quality —**im·pov·er·ish·ment** *n*

im·prac·ti·ca·ble /im práktikəb'l/ *adj* not possible to do or achieve effectively —**im·prac·ti·ca·bly** *adv*

im·prac·ti·cal /im práktik'l/ *adj* 1 not workable 2 unable to perform practical tasks or deal with practical matters —**im·prac·ti·cal·i·ty** /im pràkti kállətee/ *n* —**im·prac·ti·cal·ly** *adv*

im·pre·ca·tion /ímprə káysh'n/ *n* a curse or oath *(fml)*

im·pre·cise /ímprə síss/ *adj* not precise or accurate —**im·pre·cise·ly** *adv* —**im·pre·ci·sion** /ímprə sízh'n/ *n*

im·preg·na·ble /im prégnəb'l/ *adj* 1 impossible to capture or break into 2 unable to be shaken by outside influence o *impregnable faith* —**im·preg·na·bil·i·ty** /im prègnə bíllətee/ *n* —**im·preg·na·bly** *adv*

im·preg·nate /ím prég nàyt/ *(-nat·ed, -nat·ing)* *vt* 1 incorporate a chemical into, especially by soaking 2 make pregnant —**im·preg·na·tion** /ím preg náysh'n/ *n*

im·pre·sa·ri·o /ímprə sáaree ò, -sáiree ò/ *(pl -os)* *n* 1 a producer or promoter of commercial entertainment 2 the business head of an opera or ballet company

ORIGIN Impresario comes from an Italian word meaning literally "somebody who undertakes something." It has no connection with impressing people. The word is first recorded in English in the mid-18C.

im·press¹ /im préss/ *v* 1 *vti* affect or please somebody greatly 2 *vt* make clearly understood o *impressed the seriousness of the situation on them* 3 *vt* press a pattern or mark onto —**im·press·i·ble** /im préssəb'l/ *adj*

im·press² /ím préss/ *vt* 1 seize for public use 2 force to serve in an army or navy

im·pres·sion /im présh'n/ *n* 1 an effect that stays in somebody's mind o *made a good impression* 2 a general idea o *got the impression he was serious* 3 a pressed-in shape 4 an entertaining imitation of somebody

im·pres·sion·a·ble /im présh'nəb'l/ *adj* open to the opinions of others and easily influenced —**im·pres·sion·a·bly** *adv*

im·pres·sion·ism /im présh'n ìzzəm/, **Im·pres·sion·ism** *n* 1 a style of painting that aims to capture the immediate general effect of a scene without the details 2 a style of music expressing impressions and feelings

im·pres·sion·ist /im présh'nist/ *n* 1 *also* **Im·pres·sion·ist** a practitioner of impressionism 2 an entertainer who does impressions of people ■ *adj* *also* **Im·pres·sion·ist** of impressionism

im·pres·sion·is·tic /im prèsh'n ístik/ *adj* 1 giving a broad picture or general idea rather than detail 2 like impressionist art or music —**im·pres·sion·is·ti·cal·ly** *adv*

im·pres·sive /im préssiv/ *adj* making a deep impression on the mind or senses —**im·pres·sive·ly** *adv* —**im·pres·sive·ness** *n*

im·pri·ma·tur /ímprə máatər, -máa tòor/ *n* 1 official approval *(fml)* 2 an official license to print or publish something

im·print *n* /ím print/ 1 a pattern or mark pressed into a surface o *saw the imprint of a foot on the soil* 2 a lasting effect 3 a special mark printed or stamped on something 4 a publisher's name and other publication details printed in a book ■ *vt* /im print/ 1 produce a mark by printing or stamping 2 fix an image or thought in a vivid or lasting way —**im·print·er** *n*

im·pris·on /im prízz'n/ *vt* put in prison —**im·pris·on·ment** *n*

im·prob·a·ble /im próbbəb'l/ *adj* not likely to happen or to be true —**im·prob·a·bil·i·ty** /im pròbbə bíllətee/ *n* —**im·prob·a·bly** *adv*

im·promp·tu /im prómp tòo/ *adj* done or said without prior thought or preparation —**im·promp·tu** *adv, n*

im·prop·er /im próppər/ *adj* 1 unsuitable *(fml)* 2 not conforming to a code of conduct —**im·prop·er·ly** *adv*

im·prop·er frac·tion *n* a fraction equaling or greater than one

im·pro·pri·e·ty /ímprə prí ətee/ *(pl -ties)* *n* lack of propriety, or an inappropriate act

im·prove /im próov/ *v* 1 *vti* make or become better 2 *vt* increase the value of property —**im·prov·a·ble** *adj*

im·prove·ment /im próovmənt/ *n* 1 the process of getting better or making something better 2 a change or addition that makes something better 3 an increase in value, especially of property

im·prov·i·dent /im próvid'nt/ *adj* failing to prepare for the future —**im·prov·i·dence** *n* —**im·prov·i·dent·ly** *adv*

im·pro·vise /ímprə vìz/ *(-vised, -vis·ing)* *vti* 1 perform something not previously composed or written 2 make something out of whatever materials are available —**im·prov·i·sa·tion** /ím pròvi záysh'n,

Impravi-/ *n* —**im·prov·i·sa·to·ry** *adj* —**im·pro·vis·er** *n*

im·pru·dent /im proŏd'nt/ *adj* unwise and lacking in care or forethought —**im·pru·dence** *n* —**im·pru·dent·ly** *adv*

im·pu·dent /ímpyəd'nt/ *adj* rude and disrespectful —**im·pu·dence** *n* —**im·pu·dent·ly** *adv*

im·pugn /im pyoōn/ *vt* cast doubt on or criticize as unreliable or unworthy of respect —**im·pugn·a·ble** *adj*

im·pulse /ím pùls/ *n* **1** a sudden urge **2** an instinctive drive **3** a motive **4** a force driving something forward **5** a forward motion **6** a signal transmitted along a nerve fiber or muscle

im·pul·sive /im púlsiv/ *adj* **1** inclined to act on sudden urges **2** motivated by a sudden urge —**im·pul·sive·ly** *adv* —**im·pul·sive·ness** *n*

im·pu·ni·ty /im pyoōnatee/ *n* freedom from punishment or unpleasant consequences

im·pure /im pyoŏr/ *adj* **1** contaminated **2** mixed with something of inferior quality **3** sinful

im·pu·ri·ty /im pyoŏratee/ *n* (*pl* **-ties**) **1** lack of purity **2** a contaminant

im·pute /im pyoŏt/ (**-put·ed, -put·ing**) *vt* **1** attribute a bad action or event to **2** attribute a quality to as a source or cause —**im·pu·ta·tion** /ímpyə táysh'n/ *n*

⚡**IMS** *abbr* information management systems

in *prep* **1** indicates a place ◦ *He spent a year in Russia.* **2** indicates a state or condition being experienced ◦ *The computer industry is in flux.* **3** after a period of time **4** during **5** indicates the means by which something is expressed ◦ *The speech was in French.* **6** indicates a subject area ◦ *a degree in biology* **7** as a consequence of **8** indicates that something is covered by something ◦ *The package was in brown paper.* **9** indicates how somebody is dressed ■ *adv* **1** to or toward the inside ◦ *Come in.* **2** to or toward a place **3** at or within a place ◦ *staying in tonight* ■ *adj* **1** fashionable **2** holding power or office ◇ **in for** about to experience ◇ **in on** having knowledge about or involvement in ◇ **in that** because ◇ **in with** associated or friendly with ◇ **the ins and outs** all the details of something

In *symbol* indium

IN *abbr* Indiana

in., *in abbr* **1** inch **2** inches

in- *prefix* **1** not, lack of ◦ *inopportune* ◦ *inability* **2** in, into, toward, within ◦ *inculcate*

in·a·bil·i·ty /ínnə bíllətee/ *n* the state of not being able to do something

inable incorrect spelling of **enable**

in·ac·ces·si·ble /ínnək séssəb'l/ *adj* **1** difficult to get to **2** hard to understand —**in·ac·ces·si·bil·i·ty** /ínnək sèssə bíllətee/ *n* —**in·ac·ces·si·bly** *adv*

in·ac·cu·rate /in ákyərət/ *adj* not correct —**in·ac·cu·ra·cy** *n* —**in·ac·cu·rate·ly** *adv*

in·ac·tion /in áksh'n/ *n* **1** failure to act **2** absence of activity

in·ac·ti·vate /in ákti vàyt/ (**-vat·ed, -vat·ing**) *vt* make inactive —**in·ac·ti·va·tion** /in àkti váysh'n/ *n*

in·ac·tive /in áktiv/ *adj* **1** not taking action **2** not being used or operated **3** lazy or sedentary —**in·ac·tive·ly** *adv* —**in·ac·tiv·i·ty** /in ak tívvatee/ *n*

in·ad·e·quate /in áddəkwət/ *adj* not enough or not good enough —**in·ad·e·qua·cy** *n* —**in·ad·e·quate·ly** *adv*

in·ad·mis·si·ble /ínnəd míssəb'l/ *adj* not allowable or acceptable, especially in a court of law —**in·ad·mis·si·bil·i·ty** /ínnədmissə bíllətee/ *n*

in·ad·ver·tent·ly /ínnəd vúrt'ntlee/ *adv* without intending to or realizing —**in·ad·ver·tence** *n* —**in·ad·ver·tent** *adj*

in·ad·vis·a·ble /ínnəd vízəb'l/ *adj* not to be recommended —**in·ad·vis·a·bil·i·ty** /ínnəd vīzə bíllətee/ *n*

in·al·ien·a·ble /in áylee ənəb'l/ *adj* impossible to take away or transfer to another —**in·al·ien·a·bil·i·ty** /in àylee ənə bíllətee/ *n*

in·am·o·ra·ta /in àmmə ráatə/ (*pl* **-tas**) *n* a woman lover, or a woman whom somebody loves (*literary*)

in·ane /i náyn/ *adj* silly or time-wasting —**in·ane·ly** *adv* —**in·ane·ness** *n* —**in·an·i·ty** /i nánnətee/ *n*

in·an·i·mate /in ánnimət/ *adj* **1** not living **2** not lively —**in·an·i·mate·ness** *n*

in·ap·pli·ca·ble /in ápplikəb'l, ìnnə plíkəb'l/ *adj* not applicable, suitable, or relevant —**in·ap·pli·ca·bil·i·ty** /ínnəplikə bíllətee, in àpplikə-/ *n*

in·ap·pro·pri·ate /ínnə próppree ət/ *adj* not fitting, timely, or suitable —**in·ap·pro·pri·ate·ly** *adv* —**in·ap·pro·pri·ate·ness** *n*

in·apt /in ápt/ *adj* **1** not suitable **2** lacking skill or aptitude —**in·apt·ly** *adv* —**in·apt·ness** *n*

in·ar·tic·u·late /ín aar tíkyələt/ *adj* **1** not good at speaking effectively **2** not expressed or able to be expressed in words —**in·ar·tic·u·la·cy** *n* —**in·ar·tic·u·late·ly** *adv*

in·as·much as /ínnəz múch əz/ *conj* **1** because **2** to the extent that

in·at·ten·tion /ínnə ténsh'n/ *n* failure to pay attention —**in·at·ten·tive** *adj*

in·au·di·ble /in áwdəb'l/ *adj* impossible to hear —**in·au·di·bil·i·ty** /in áwdə bíllətee/ *n* —**in·au·di·bly** *adv*

in·au·gu·ral /i náwgyərəl/ *adj* **1** marking a beginning **2** first of several ■ *n* an inauguration or speech given at an inauguration

in·au·gu·rate /i náwgyə ràyt/ (**-rat·ed, -rat·ing**) *vt* **1** install formally into office **2** open or begin ceremonially —**in·au·gu·ra·tion** /i nàwgyə ráysh'n/ n —**in·au·gu·ra·tor** n

In·au·gu·ra·tion Day n the day in January on which a new President of the United States is inaugurated

in·aus·pi·cious /ín aw spíshəss/ adj suggesting failure or an unpromising future —**in·aus·pi·cious·ly** adv —**in·aus·pi·cious·ness** n

in·au·then·tic /ín aw théntik/ adj not authentic or genuine —**in·au·then·tic·i·ty** /ín awthən tíssətee/ n

in·be·tween adj, adv falling between others

in·board /ín bàwrd/ adj located inside a boat's hull ■ n a boat with an inboard motor

in·born /ín bàwrn/ adj innate

in·bound /ín bównd/ adj incoming

in·box n a tray for incoming paperwork

in·bred /ín brèd/ adj 1 innate 2 produced by inbreeding

in·breed·ing /ín brèeding/ n the mating of closely related individuals of a species

in·built adj innate

inc. abbr 1 included 2 also **Inc.** incorporated

In·ca /íngkə/ n (pl same or -cas) n member of a Native S American people —**In·ca** adj

in·cal·cu·la·ble /ín kálkyələb'l/ adj 1 too great to measure 2 impossible to foresee —**in·cal·cu·la·bil·i·ty** /ín kàlkyələ bíllətee/ n —**in·cal·cu·la·bly** adv

in·can·des·cent /ínkən déss'nt/ adj 1 glowing with heat 2 showing intense emotion, especially anger —**in·can·des·cence** n

in·can·ta·tion /ín kan táysh'n/ n 1 the use of supposedly magic words 2 a set of supposedly magic words —**in·can·ta·tion·al** adj

in·ca·pa·ble /ín káypəb'l/ adj 1 lacking the necessary ability 2 unable to function or perform adequately —**in·ca·pa·bil·i·ty** /ín kàypə bíllətee/ n —**in·ca·pa·bly** adv

in·ca·pac·i·tate /ínkə pássi tàyt/ (-tat·ed, -tat·ing) vt 1 deprive of power, force, or effectiveness 2 disqualify or make legally ineligible —**in·ca·pac·i·ta·tion** /ínkə passi táysh'n/ n

in·ca·pac·i·ty /ínkə pássətee/ n 1 lack of ability, force, or effectiveness 2 a physical or mental challenge

in·car·cer·ate /ín kàarsə ràyt/ (-at·ed, -at·ing) vt (fml) 1 imprison somebody 2 confine somebody —**in·car·cer·a·tion** /ín kàarsə ráysh'n/ n

in·car·nate adj /ín kàarnət/ 1 made human 2 personified ■ vt /ín kàar nàyt/ (-nat·ed, -nat·ing) 1 show in or give human form 2 personify

in·car·na·tion /ín kaar náysh'n/ n 1 the personification of a quality or idea 2 in some religious beliefs, one life in a series of lives spent in a particular body 3 **In·car·na·tion** in Christianity, God in the form of Jesus Christ

in·cau·tious /ín káwhəss/ adj careless or rash —**in·cau·tious·ly** adv —**in·cau·tious·ness** n

in·cen·di·ar·y /ín séndee èrree/ adj 1 containing chemicals that cause fire 2 likely to catch fire ■ n (pl -ies) a bomb designed to cause fire

in·cense[1] /ín sènss/ n 1 a substance burned for its fragrant smell 2 smoke or fragrance from incense

in·cense[2] /ín séns/ (-censed, -cens·ing) vt enrage —**in·censed** adj

in·cen·tive /ín séntiv/ n something that encourages somebody to do something ■ adj encouraging or motivating ◊ See note at **motive**

in·cep·tion /ín sépsh'n/ n the beginning of something (fml)

in·cer·ti·tude /ín súrtə tòod/ n 1 doubt 2 lack of self-confidence

in·ces·sant /ín séss'nt/ adj continuing uninterrupted —**in·ces·san·cy** n —**in·ces·sant·ly** adv

in·cest /ín sèst/ n sex between close relatives —**in·ces·tu·ous** adj —**in·ces·tu·ous·ly** adv —**in·ces·tu·ous·ness** n

ORIGIN Incest comes from a Latin word formed from the prefix in- "not" and the adjective castus "chaste," from which chaste also derives.

inch n 1 (symbol ") a unit of length equal to $\frac{1}{12}$ of a foot 2 a small amount ○ The committee won't budge an inch. ■ vti move slowly

in·cho·ate /ín kő ət/ adj (fml) 1 just beginning to develop 2 only partly formed

In·chon /ín chón/, **In·ch'ŏn** port in NW South Korea. Pop. 2,307,618 (1995).

in·ci·dence /ínsid'nss/ n 1 the frequency with which something occurs 2 an instance of something happening

in·ci·dent /ínsid'nt/ n 1 a single event 2 a violent public occurrence ■ adj 1 related to or occurring as a consequence of something (fml) 2 striking the surface of something

in·ci·den·tal /ínsi dént'l/ adj 1 related to or accompanying something more important 2 occasional ■ n a minor item —**in·ci·den·tal·ly** adv

in·ci·den·tal mu·sic n the background music to a movie or television program

~~incidently~~ incorrect spelling of **incidentally**

in·cin·er·ate /ín sínnə ràyt/ (-at·ed, -at·ing) vti burn something thoroughly —**in·cin·er·a·tion** /ín sìnnə ráysh'n/ n

in·cin·er·a·tor /ín sínnə ràytər/ n a furnace for burning waste

in·cip·i·ent /ín síppee ənt/ adj beginning to appear or develop —**in·cip·i·ence** n

in·cise /ín síz/ (-cised, -cis·ing) vt 1 cut into 2 engrave or carve a design into

in·ci·sion /ín sízh'n/ n a cut or the act of cutting, especially by a surgeon

in·ci·sive /in síssiv/ *adj* **1** quick to understand **2** expressed clearly —**in·ci·sive·ly** *adv* —**in·ci·sive·ness** *n*

in·ci·sor /in sízər/ *n* a flat sharp front tooth —**in·ci·sal** *adj*

in·cite /in sít/ (-cit·ed, -cit·ing) *vt* stir up feelings in or provoke action from somebody —**in·cite·ment** *n* —**in·cit·er** *n*

in·ci·vil·i·ty /ínsi víllətee/ (*pl* -ties) *n* **1** rude behavior or language **2** a rude act or remark

incl. *abbr* **1** including **2** inclusive

in·clem·ent /in klémmənt/ *adj* **1** describes weather that is not pleasant or mild **2** showing little mercy (*fml*) —**in·clem·en·cy** *n* —**in·clem·ent·ly** *adv*

in·cli·na·tion /ínkli náysh'n/ *n* **1** a feeling that influences a choice or decision **2** a tendency toward something **3** deviation from a line or plane **4** a slope —**in·cli·na·tion·al** *adj*

in·cline *vti* /in klín/ (-clined, -clin·ing) **1** be or make somebody likely to take a particular course of action **2** angle, or be angled ■ *n* /in klín/ a slope —**in·clined** *adj*

in·clude /in klood/ (-clud·ed, -clud·ing) *vt* **1** contain or have as a constituent **2** bring into a group —**in·clud·ing** *prep*

in·clu·sion /in kloozh'n/ *n* **1** the addition or presence of somebody or something in a group **2** somebody or something that is included

in·clu·sive /in kloossiv/ *adj* **1** indicates a range within which a series of items is included **2** including many things or everything —**in·clu·sive·ly** *adv* —**in·clu·sive·ness** *n*

in·cog·ni·to /ín kog neétō/ *adj, adv* in disguise

in·co·her·ent /ín kō heérənt/ *adj* **1** lacking clarity or organization **2** unable to speak or express thoughts or feelings clearly —**in·co·her·ence** *n* —**in·co·her·ent·ly** *adv*

in·com·bus·ti·ble /ín kəm bústəb'l/ *adj* not combustible —**in·com·bus·ti·bil·i·ty** /ínkəm bustə bíllətee/ *n*

in·come /ín kùm/ *n* the amount of money received over a period of time as payment for something or as profit

in·come tax *n* tax on income from employment, business, or capital

in·com·ing /ín kúmming/ *adj* **1** arriving **2** taking up a new job

in·com·men·su·rate /ínkə ménsərət, -ménshə-/ *adj* not proportionate to or up to the level of something —**in·com·men·su·rate·ly** *adv*

in·com·mode /ínkə mṓd/ (-mod·ed, -mod·ing) *vt* bother or inconvenience (*fml*)

in·com·mo·di·ous /ínkə mṓdee əss/ *adj* (*fml*) **1** uncomfortably cramped **2** causing inconvenience —**in·com·mo·di·ous·ly** *adv*

in·com·mu·ni·ca·do /ínkə myóōni kaàdō/ *adj, adv* with no means of communicating with others

in·com·pa·ra·ble /in kómpərəb'l/ *adj* **1** unequaled in quality **2** so different that a valid comparison is not possible —**in·com·pa·ra·bil·i·ty** /in kómpərə bíllətee/ *n* —**in·com·pa·ra·bly** *adv*

⨍ **in·com·pat·i·ble** /ínkəm páttəb'l/ *adj* **1** unable to cooperate or coexist **2** in computing, not able to be used with or substituted for something else —**in·com·pat·i·bil·i·ty** /ínkəm patə bíllətee/ *n* —**in·com·pat·i·bly** *adv*

in·com·pe·tent /in kómpət'nt/ *adj* **1** bad at doing something **2** lacking the necessary legal status or power for the purpose in question —**in·com·pe·tence** *n* —**in·com·pe·tent** *n* —**in·com·pe·tent·ly** *adv*

in·com·plete /ínkəm pleét/ *adj* **1** lacking something that properly belongs with it **2** unfinished in football, describes a forward pass that is not caught —**in·com·plete·ly** *adv* —**in·com·plete·ness** *n*

in·com·pre·hen·si·ble /in kómpri hénsəb'l/ *adj* impossible or very difficult to understand —**in·com·pre·hen·si·bil·i·ty** /in kómpri hensə bíllətee/ *n* —**in·com·pre·hen·si·bly** *adv*

in·com·pre·hen·sion /in kòmpri hénshən/ *n* an inability to understand

in·con·ceiv·a·ble /ínkən seévəb'l/ *adj* **1** unimaginable **2** extremely unlikely —**in·con·ceiv·a·bly** *adv*

in·con·clu·sive /ínkən klóossiv/ *adj* not providing a clear result, firm conclusion, or definite proof —**in·con·clu·sive·ly** *adv* —**in·con·clu·sive·ness** *n*

in·con·gru·ent /in kóng groo ənt, ín kon grŏŏ ənt/ *adj* not corresponding in structure or content —**in·con·gru·ence** *n* —**in·con·gru·ent·ly** *adv*

in·con·gru·ous /in kóng groo əss/ *adj* **1** unsuitable or odd **2** not in keeping or inconsistent with something —**in·con·gru·i·ty** /ínkən grŏŏ itee/ *n* —**in·con·gru·ous·ly** *adv* —**in·con·gru·ous·ness** *n*

in·con·se·quen·tial /in kònsi kwénsh'l/ *adj* unimportant —**in·con·se·quen·ti·al·i·ty** /ín kònsi kwénshee əlatee/ *n* —**in·con·se·quen·tial·ly** *adv*

in·con·sid·er·a·ble /ínkən síddərəb'l/ *adj* **1** small (*often with "not"*) **2** unworthy of consideration (*fml*) —**in·con·sid·er·a·bly** *adv*

in·con·sid·er·ate /ínkən síddərət/ *adj* failing to consider other people's feelings or wishes —**in·con·sid·er·ate·ly** *adv* —**in·con·sid·er·ate·ness** *n*

in·con·sis·tent /ínkən sístənt/ *adj* **1** containing conflicting or contradictory elements **2** varying and unpredictable —**in·con·sis·ten·cy** *n* —**in·con·sis·tent·ly** *adv*

in·con·sol·a·ble /ínkən sṓləb'l/ *adj* too distressed to be comforted —**in·con·sol·a·bly** *adv*

in·con·spic·u·ous /ínkən spíkyoo əss/ *adj* not obvious or noticeable —**in·con·spic·u·ous·ly** *adv* —**in·con·spic·u·ous·ness** *n*

in·con·stant /in kónstənt/ *adj* **1** unfaithful

in·con·stan·cy *(literary)* **2** changeable —**in·con·stan·cy** *n* —**in·con·stant·ly** *adv*

in·con·test·a·ble /ìnkən téstəb'l/ *adj* impossible to dispute —**in·con·test·a·bil·i·ty** /ìnkən testə bíllətee/ *n* —**in·con·test·a·bly** *adv*

in·con·ti·nent /in kóntənənt/ *adj* **1** unable to control the bladder or bowels **2** lacking restraint in sexual matters —**in·con·ti·nence** *n* —**in·con·ti·nent·ly** *adv*

in·con·tro·vert·i·ble /in kòntrə vúrtəb'l/ *adj* undeniable —**in·con·tro·vert·i·bly** *adv*

in·con·ven·ience /ìnkən veènyənss/ *n* **1** the fact of being annoying or bothersome **2** an annoyance ■ *vt* (**-ienced, -ienc·ing**) cause bother or difficulty to

in·con·ven·ient /ìnkən veènyənt/ *adj* causing bother or annoyance —**in·con·ven·ient·ly** *adv*

in·con·vert·i·ble /ìnkən vúrtəb'l/ *adj* not exchangeable for gold or foreign currency

in·cor·po·rate /in káwrpə ràyt/ *vti* **1** combine something or include it within something already formed **2** form or become a corporation —**in·cor·po·rat·ed** *adj* —**in·cor·po·ra·tion** /in kàwrpə ráysh'n/ *n*

in·cor·po·re·al /in kawr páwree əl/ *adj* without physical being *(fml)* —**in·cor·po·re·al·ly** *adv*

in·cor·rect /ìnkə rékt/ *adj* **1** wrong, false, or inaccurate **2** not appropriate or proper —**in·cor·rect·ly** *adv* —**in·cor·rect·ness** *n*

in·cor·ri·gi·ble /in káwrijəb'l/ *adj* **1** impossible to improve or reform **2** unruly and unmanageable —**in·cor·ri·gi·bil·i·ty** /in kàwrijə bíllətee/ *n* —**in·cor·ri·gi·bly** *adv*

in·cor·rupt·i·ble /ìnkə rúptəb'l/ *adj* **1** incapable of being corrupted **2** not subject to decomposition —**in·cor·rupt·i·bil·i·ty** /ìnkə rùptə bíllətee/ *n* —**in·cor·rupt·i·bly** *adv*

in·crease *vti* /in kreéss/ (**-creased, -creas·ing**) make or become larger or greater ■ *n* /ín kreèss/ **1** a rise to a greater number, quantity, or degree **2** the process of increasing in size —**in·creas·ing** *adj* —**in·creas·ing·ly** *adv*

SYNONYMS increase, expand, enlarge, extend, augment, intensify, amplify CORE MEANING: make larger or greater

~~incredable~~ incorrect spelling of **incredible**

in·cred·i·ble /in kréddəb'l/ *adj* beyond belief —**in·cred·i·bil·i·ty** /in krèddə bíllətee/ *n* —**in·cred·i·bly** *adv*

in·cred·u·lous /in kréjjələss/ *adj* **1** unwilling to believe **2** showing disbelief —**in·cre·du·li·ty** /ìnkrə doõlətee/ *n* —**in·cred·u·lous·ly** *adv* —**in·cred·u·lous·ness** *n*

in·cre·ment /íngkrəmənt/ *n* **1** an increase in something, especially one of a series of increases on a scale **2** the act of increasing something —**in·cre·men·tal** /ìngkrə mént'l/ *adj* —**in·cre·men·tal·ly** *adv*

in·crim·i·nate /in krímmi nàyt/ *vt* (**-nat·ed, -nat·ing**) **1** make appear guilty **2** accuse of wrongdoing —**in·crim·i·na·tion** /in krímmi náysh'n/ *n* —**in·crim·i·na·to·ry** *adj*

in·crust·a·tion *n* = encrustation

in·cu·bate /íngkyə bàyt/ (**-bat·ed, -bat·ing**) *v* **1** *vti* sit on newly laid eggs to keep them warm, or be kept warm in this way **2** *vt* keep a baby in an incubator **3** *vti* grow microorganisms in a controlled environment **4** *vi* develop to the point at which symptoms of a disease begin to appear —**in·cu·ba·tion** /ìng kyə báysh'n/ *n*

in·cu·ba·tion pe·ri·od *n* an interval between being infected with a disease and the appearance of symptoms

in·cu·ba·tor /íngkyə bàytər/ *n* a hospital apparatus in which premature or sick babies are kept in a controlled environment

in·cu·bus /íngkyəbəss/ (*pl* **-bi** /íngkyə bì/ or **-bus·es**) *n* in medieval times, a male demon who was believed to have sex with sleeping women

in·cu·des plural of **incus**

in·cul·cate /in kúl kàyt, ín kul kàyt/ (**-cat·ed, -cat·ing**) *vt* impress on somebody's mind —**in·cul·ca·tion** /ìn kul káysh'n/ *n*

in·cul·pate /in kúl pàyt/ (**-pat·ed, -pat·ing**) *vt* accuse of wrongdoing *(archaic)* —**in·cul·pa·tion** /in kul páysh'n/ *n*

in·cum·ben·cy /in kúmbənssee/ *n* the period during which somebody occupies an official post *(fml)*

in·cum·bent /in kúmbənt/ *adj* **1** necessary as a duty or obligation *(fml)* **2** currently holding a position or office ■ *n* somebody incumbent in a position or office —**in·cum·bent·ly** *adv*

in·cur /in kúr/ (**-curred, -cur·ring**) *vt* **1** experience something unpleasant o *had incurred his anger* **2** become burdened with something, especially a cost or debt —**in·cur·ra·ble** *adj* —**in·cur·rence** *n*

in·cur·a·ble /in kyóorəb'l/ *adj* **1** impossible to cure **2** impossible to change —**in·cur·a·bil·i·ty** /in kyòorə bíllətee/ *n* —**in·cur·a·bly** *adv*

in·cu·ri·ous /in kyóoree əss/ *adj* not curious or inquisitive —**in·cu·ri·os·i·ty** /in kyòoree óssətee/ *n* —**in·cu·ri·ous·ly** *adv*

in·cur·sion /in kúrzh'n/ *n* **1** a raid **2** an unwelcome intrusion *(fml)* —**in·cur·sive** /in kúrsiv/ *adj*

in·cus /íngkəss/ (*pl* **-cu·des** /ìng kyoõ deèz/) *n* a small bone shaped like an anvil in the middle ear

ind., ind *abbr* **1** independent **2** index

Ind., Ind *abbr* Indiana

in·debt·ed /in déttəd/ *adj* **1** in debt **2** obligated —**in·debt·ed·ness** *n*

in·de·cent /in deèss'nt/ *adj* **1** offending public standards, especially in sexual matters **2** improper under the circumstances o *with indecent haste* —**in·de·cen·cy** *n* —**in·de·cent·ly** *adv*

in·de·cent as·sault *n* a sexual attack that falls short of rape

in·de·cent ex·po·sure *n* the act of deliberately displaying the genitals in public

in·de·ci·pher·a·ble /ìndi sîfərəb'l/ *adj* impossible to read or understand —**in·de·ci·pher·a·bly** *adv*

in·de·ci·sion /ìndi sízh'n/ *n* the inability to decide

in·de·ci·sive /ìndi sîssiv/ *adj* **1** unable to decide **2** without a clear outcome —**in·de·ci·sive·ly** *adv* —**in·de·ci·sive·ness** *n*

in·dec·o·rous /in dékərəss/ *adj* impolite or socially unacceptable —**in·dec·o·rous·ly** *adv* —**in·de·cor·um** /ìndi káwrəm/ *n*

in·deed /in deéd/ *adv* **1** indicates agreement or confirmation **2** adds emphasis after a descriptive word or phrase o *I am willing, indeed eager, to help.*

in·de·fat·i·ga·ble /ìndi fáttigəb'l/ *adj* never tiring or losing determination —**in·de·fat·i·ga·bil·i·ty** /ìndi fáttigə bíllətee/ *n* —**in·de·fat·i·ga·bly** *adv*

in·de·fen·si·ble /ìndi fénsəb'l/ *adj* **1** too bad to be justified or excused **2** not based on fact **3** incapable of being defended —**in·de·fen·si·bil·i·ty** /ìndi fènsə bíllətee/ *n* —**in·de·fen·si·bly** *adv*

in·de·fin·a·ble /ìndi fínəb'l/ *adj* impossible to define or describe —**in·de·fin·a·bil·i·ty** /ìndi fínə bíllətee/ *n* —**in·de·fin·a·bly** *adv*

in·def·i·nite /in déffənət/ *adj* **1** unlimited **2** not clearly defined **3** vague about plans or thoughts —**in·def·i·nite·ly** *adv* —**in·def·i·nite·ness** *n*

in·def·i·nite ar·ti·cle *n* in English, either of the words "a" or "an," referring to something simply as one of its kind

in·del·i·ble /in déllab'l/ *adj* **1** permanent **2** containing indelible ink or lead o *an indelible pencil* —**in·del·i·bly** *adv*

in·del·i·cate /in déllikət/ *adj* **1** tactless or offensive **2** coarse in texture or appearance —**in·del·i·ca·cy** /-kəssee/ *n* —**in·del·i·cate·ly** *adv* —**in·del·i·cate·ness** *n*

in·dem·ni·fy /in démni fi/ (**-fied, -fies**) *vt* **1** insure against loss **2** reimburse after loss —**in·dem·ni·fi·ca·tion** /in dèmnifi káysh'n/ *n*

in·dem·ni·ty /in démnətee/ (*pl* **-ties**) *n* **1** insurance against loss or damage **2** a compensation paid for loss or damage

in·dent /in dént/ *v* /in dént/ **1** *vt* begin a line of writing or typing in from the margin **2** *vt* form a deep recess in something **3** *vt* make a jagged edge on something ■ *n* /in dént, in dént/ a space set in from the margin of a page

ORIGIN Etymologically, English has two separate words **indent**, although they have converged to a considerable extent. The one meaning "form a recess in" is simply a derivative of *dent*. **Indent** "make a jagged edge on" owes its origin to Latin *dens* "tooth." This formed the basis of a verb *indentare* that denoted the drawing up of a contract between two parties on two identical documents that were cut along a matching line of notches or "teeth" that could subsequently be rejoined to prove their authenticity.

in·dent² *vt* /in dént/ make a hole or depression in ■ *n* /in dént, in dént/ a dent or depression in a surface

in·den·ta·tion /in den táysh'n/ *n* **1** a notch or recess **2** a jagged edge **3** a space left at the beginning of a line **4** the act of indenting something

in·den·ture /in dénchər/ *n* a contract between an apprentice and a master or employer (*often pl*) ■ *vt* commit somebody to work as an apprentice or servant —**in·den·ture·ship** *n*

in·den·tured ser·vant *n* an immigrant to North America from the 17C to 19C who received passage and accommodations in exchange for several years' unpaid work

~~independant~~ incorrect spelling of **independent**

in·de·pend·ence /ìndə péndənss/ *n* **1** freedom from control by or reliance on another person, organization, or state **2** the beginning of a state's political freedom

In·de·pend·ence Day *n* US national holiday. Date: July 4.

in·de·pend·ent /ìndə péndənt/ *adj* **1** not controlled by another person, organization, or state **2** able to function by itself **3** self-supporting **4** capable of thinking and acting without the help of others ■ *n* **1** somebody or something not controlled by another **2** *also* **In·de·pend·ent** a politician or voter who does not belong to any political party —**in·de·pend·ent·ly** *adv*

in·de·pend·ent clause *n* a clause that can be a sentence

in-depth *adj* carefully considering all aspects —**in depth** *adv*

in·de·scrib·a·ble /ìndi skríbəb'l/ *adj* **1** impossible to describe **2** so great as to defy description —**in·de·scrib·a·bil·i·ty** /ìndi skríbə bíllətee/ *n* —**in·de·scrib·a·bly** *adv*

~~indespensable~~ incorrect spelling of **indispensable**

~~indestructable~~ incorrect spelling of **indestructible**

in·de·struc·ti·ble /ìndi strúktəb'l/ *adj* impossible to destroy —**in·de·struc·ti·bil·i·ty** /ìndi strùktə bíllətee/ *n* —**in·de·struc·ti·bly** *adv*

in·de·ter·min·a·ble /ìndi túrminəb'l/ *adj* **1** impossible to find out definitely **2** impossible to answer or settle —**in·de·ter·min·a·bly** *adv*

in·de·ter·mi·nate /ìndi túrminət/ *adj* **1** not known exactly **2** not precise or clear —**in·de·ter·mi·na·cy** *n* —**in·de·ter·mi·nate·ly** *adv*

✦ in·dex /ín dèks/ n (pl **-dex·es** or **-di·ces** /-di seèz/) 1 an alphabetical list in a book giving the pages on which to find specific things 2 a catalog, e.g., of books in a library 3 a publication giving a list of published works 4 an indicator or sign 5 a pointer or needle on a piece of scientific equipment 6 a character ☞ in printing that draws attention to something 7 series of labeled indentations in the pages of a book to help finding a section quickly 8 a mathematical exponent or other number given as a superscript or subscript in a mathematical expression 9 a data structure that enables quick access to data ■ v1 vti make an index for something 2 vt put in an index 3 vt indicate (fml) 4 vt subject to indexation —**in·dex·er** n

in·dex·a·tion /ín dek sáysh'n/ n the linking of something to living costs

in·dex fin·ger n the finger next to the thumb

in·dex fund n an investment fund composed of companies listed in a stock market index

In·di·a[1] /índee ə/ country in South Asia. Cap. New Delhi. Pop. 1,029,991,100 (2001).

In·di·a[2] /índee ə/ n a communications code word for the letter "I"

In·di·a ink n 1 a black pigment 2 a liquid black ink

In·di·an /índee ən/ n 1 somebody who comes from India 2 a Native North, South, or Central American (sometimes offensive) 3 in Canada, somebody of indigenous ancestry who is neither Inuit nor Metis ■ adj of India, or its peoples, languages, or cultures

---

USAGE As a name applied in error by Columbus and early European explorers, **Indian** may well be regarded as insensitive or even offensive. Some of the people in question prefer to be called American Indian(s), but others prefer the term Native American(s), this last choice being the one least likely to cause offense.

In·di·an·a /índee ánnə/ state in the north central United States. Cap. Indianapolis. Pop. 6,080,485 (2000). —**In·di·an·an** n, adj

In·di·an·ap·o·lis /índee ə náppələss/ capital of Indiana. Pop. 741,304 (1998).

In·di·an corn n 1 the corn plant 2 the grain of the corn plant

---

ORIGIN Indian corn was so called because it was cultivated by Native Americans (formerly usually called "Indians").

In·di·an O·cean ocean stretching from Asia in the north to Antarctica in the south and from Africa in the west to Australia in the east

In·di·an sum·mer n 1 a period of mild autumn weather 2 a time of calm

In·di·an Ter·ri·to·ry n land ceded to Native North Americans

in·di·cate /índi kàyt/ (-cat·ed, -cat·ing) vt 1 point to something 2 show the existence or truth of something 3 register a measurement 4 show what somebody thinks or intends —**in·di·ca·tion** /índi káysh'n/ n

in·dic·a·tive /ín díkətiv/ adj 1 indicating the existence or truth of something 2 describes the basic mood of verbs used in ordinary objective statements ■ n the basic mood of a verb, or a verb in this mood —**in·dic·a·tive·ly** adv

in·di·ca·tor /índi kàytər/ n 1 something that shows what conditions or trends exist 2 a measuring instrument 3 something such as a sign or pointer that gives information 4 a substance that shows the presence of something such as a chemical

in·dic·es plural of **index**

in·dict /ín dít/ vt 1 formally charge with a crime 2 accuse of wrongdoing —**in·dict·a·ble** adj

in·dict·ment /ín dítmənt/ n 1 a formal accusation before grand jury 2 the act of indicting somebody 3 a statement or indication that something is wrong ○ a stinging indictment of our prison system

in·die /índee/ n an independent company (slang)

in·dif·fer·ent /ín díffərənt, -díffrənt/ adj 1 showing no care or interest 2 favoring neither side —**in·dif·fer·ence** n —**in·dif·fer·ent·ly** adv

in·dig·e·nous /ín díjjənəss/ adj 1 belonging to and typical of a place 2 natural or inborn (fml) —**in·dig·e·nous·ly** adv ◊ See note at **native**

in·di·gent /índijənt/ adj lacking the bare necessities of life (fml) —**in·di·gence** n —**in·di·gent** n

in·di·gest·i·ble /índi jéstəb'l, ìn dī-/ adj difficult or impossible to digest —**in·di·gest·i·bil·i·ty** /índi jèstə bíllətee, ìn dī-/ n

in·di·ges·tion /índi jéschən, ìn dī-/ n discomfort after eating

in·dig·nant /ín dígnənt/ adj angry at unfairness —**in·dig·nant·ly** adv

in·dig·na·tion /índig náysh'n/ n anger at unfairness ◊ See note at **anger**

in·dig·ni·ty /ín dígnətee/ n (pl **-ties**) n a situation that results in humiliation

in·di·go /índi gò/ n (pl **-gos** or **-goes**) n 1 a blue dye 2 a plant that yields indigo dye

---

ORIGIN Indigo is etymologically "from India," as indeed were supplies of the dye. It is first recorded in English in the mid-16C.

In·di·o /índee ò/ n (pl **-os**) n a member of an indigenous people in a part of America or E Asia formerly ruled by Spain

in·di·rect /índi rékt, ìn dī-/ adj 1 not in a straight line 2 not occurring as the immediate or intended effect 3 not obvious or straightforward —**in·di·rect·ly** adv —**in·di·rect·ness** n

in·di·rect cost *n* a general business expense

in·di·rect ob·ject *n* a person or thing indirectly affected by the action of the verb and the direct object

in·di·rect ques·tion *n* a question in indirect speech

in·di·rect speech *n* a report of something said that does not use the speaker's actual words

in·di·rect tax *n* a tax on goods and services

in·dis·cern·i·ble /indi súrnəb'l/ *adj* impossible to see or notice —**in·dis·cern·i·bly** *adv*

in·dis·ci·pline /in díssiplin/ *n* lack of discipline

in·dis·creet /indi skréet/ *adj* carelessly tactless —**in·dis·creet·ly** *adv* —**in·dis·creet·ness** *n*

in·dis·cre·tion /indi skrésh'n/ *n* 1 tactless lack of judgment 2 something tactless or unwise

in·dis·crim·i·nate /indi skrímmənət/ *adj* 1 making no careful distinctions or choices 2 random —**in·dis·crim·i·nate·ly** *adv* —**in·dis·crim·i·nate·ness** *n*

in·dis·pen·sa·ble /indi spénsəb'l/ *adj* 1 essential 2 unavoidable ■ *n* an essential item —**in·dis·pen·sa·bil·i·ty** /indi spénsə bíllətee/ *n* —**in·dis·pen·sa·bly** *adv*◊ See note at **necessary**

~~indispensible~~ incorrect spelling of **indispensable**

in·dis·posed /indi spózd/ *adj (fml)* 1 too ill to do something 2 unwilling to say or do something

in·dis·po·si·tion /in dispə zísh'n/ *n (fml)* 1 a minor illness 2 reluctance

in·dis·put·a·ble /indi spyóotəb'l/ *adj* not to be questioned or denied —**in·dis·put·a·bly** *adv*

in·dis·sol·u·ble /indi sóllyəb'l/ *adj* incapable of being dissolved, broken, or undone —**in·dis·sol·u·bil·i·ty** /indi sòllyə bíllətee/ *n*

in·dis·tinct /indi stíngkt/ *adj* 1 not clearly seen or heard 2 not clearly expressed or remembered —**in·dis·tinct·ly** *adv* —**in·dis·tinct·ness** *n*

in·dis·tin·guish·a·ble /indi sting gwíshəb'l/ *adj* 1 very like somebody or something else 2 very hard to see, hear, or understand —**in·dis·tin·guish·a·bly** *adv*

in·di·um /índee əm/ *n (symbol* **In**) a soft silvery rare metallic element. Use: alloys, transistors, electroplating.

in·di·vid·u·al /indi víjjoo əl/ *n* 1 a particular person distinct from others in a group 2 a human being 3 a separate thing ■ *adj* 1 considered separately ○ *each individual bead is hand-sewn* 2 of or for one person 3 very distinctive —**in·di·vid·u·al·ly** *adv*

in·di·vid·u·al·ism /indi víjjoo ə lìzzəm/ *n* 1 the pursuit of personal goals 2 a personal trait

in·di·vid·u·al·ist /indi víjjoo əlist/ *n* 1 an independent thinker 2 a believer in individualism —**in·di·vid·u·al·is·tic** /indi vijoo ə lístik/ *adj*

in·di·vid·u·al·i·ty /indi víjjoo állətee/ *(pl* -**ties**) *n* 1 a specific distinguishing trait or character 2 the state of being an individual

in·di·vid·u·al·ize /indi víjjoo ə līz/ *(-ized, -iz·ing)* *vt* 1 give an individual character to 2 treat individually —**in·di·vid·u·al·i·za·tion** /indi vijoo əli záysh'n/ *n*

in·di·vid·u·ate /indi víjjoo àyt/ *(-at·ed, -at·ing)* *vt* make separate and distinct

in·di·vis·i·ble /indi vízzəb'l/ *adj* 1 not separable 2 not capable of being divided by another number without a remainder —**in·di·vis·i·bil·i·ty** /indi vizə bíllətee/ *n*

Indo- *prefix* India ○ *Indo-European*

In·do·chi·na /índō chínə/ peninsula of Southeast Asia that includes Myanmar, Thailand, Cambodia, Vietnam, Laos, and the Malay Peninsula —**In·do·chi·nese** /indō chī néez, -néess/ *adj, n*

in·doc·tri·nate /in dóktrə nàyt/ *(-nat·ed, -nat·ing)* *vt* teach a belief with the goal of discouraging independent thought —**in·doc·tri·na·tion** /in dòktrə náysh'n/ *n*

In·do-Eu·ro·pe·an *n* a family of European and Asian languages —**In·do-Eu·ro·pe·an** *adj*

in·do·lent /índələnt/ *adj* lazy —**in·do·lence** *n* —**in·do·lent·ly** *adv*

in·dom·i·ta·ble /in dómmitəb'l/ *adj* impossible to defeat or subdue —**in·dom·i·ta·bil·i·ty** /in dòmmitə bíllətee/ *n* —**in·dom·i·ta·bly** *adv*

In·do·ne·sia /índə néezhə, -néeshə/ country in Southeast Asia. Cap. Jakarta. Pop. 228,437,870 (2001). —**In·do·ne·sian** *n, adj*

in·door /ín dawr/ *adj* in a building

in·doors /in dáwrz/ *adv* in or into a building

in·du·bi·ta·ble /in doóbitəb'l/ *adj* definitely true —**in·du·bi·ta·bly** *adv*

in·duce /in doóss, -dyoóss/ *(-duced, -duc·ing)* *vt* 1 persuade or influence somebody to do something 2 produce a particular mental or physical state

in·duce·ment /in doóssmənt, -dyoóss-/ *n* 1 a reason or incentive that induces somebody to do something 2 the inducing of something ◊ See note at **motive**

in·duct /in dúkt/ *vt* 1 formally install in a position or office 2 introduce new ideas to 3 enlist for military service —**in·duct·ee** /in dùk teé/ *n*

in·duc·tance /in dúktənss/ *n* the property of an electric circuit whereby an electromotive force is created by a change of current

in·duc·tion /in dúkshən/ *n* 1 the process of inducing a state, feeling, or idea 2 the process of hastening a baby's birth by a medical intervention 3 the act of inducting somebody into a position or office 4 in logic, the process of generalizing from specific observed instances 5 the creation of electric or magnetic forces by proximity to another electric or magnetic field 6 the act

in·duc·tion coil n an electrical transformer

in·duc·tive /in dúktiv/ adj 1 of electric or magnetic induction 2 reaching a conclusion based on observation —**in·duc·tive·ly** adv —**in·duc·tive·ness** n

in·dulge /in dúlj/ (-dulged, -dulg·ing) v 1 vti allow yourself or somebody else to experience something enjoyable 2 vi drink alcohol

in·dul·gence /in dúljənss/ n 1 the act of yielding to somebody's wish 2 something allowed as a luxury

in·dul·gent /in dúljənt/ adj permissive or kind —**in·dul·gent·ly** adv

In·dus /índəss/ river in south central Asia, rising in W Tibet and flowing into the Arabian Sea. Length 1,800 mi./2,900 km.

in·dus·tri·al /in dústree əl/ adj 1 of industry 2 with many developed industries —**in·dus·tri·al·ly** adv

in·dus·tri·al ar·chae·ol·o·gy n the study of past industries

in·dus·tri·al arts n education in industrial skills (+ sing verb)

in·dus·tri·al es·pi·o·nage n the theft of trade secrets

in·dus·tri·al·ism /in dústree ə lìzzəm/ n the organization of society around industry

in·dus·tri·al·ist /in dústree əlist/ n an owner or top manager in industry

in·dus·tri·al·ize /in dústree ə lìz/ (-ized, -iz·ing) vti adapt to industrial methods of production and manufacturing —**in·dus·tri·al·i·za·tion** /in dústree əli záysh'n/ n

in·dus·tri·al park n US, Can, ANZ a special area for factories and businesses

in·dus·tri·al re·la·tions npl the relationship between management and employees

In·dus·tri·al Rev·o·lu·tion n the industrialization of Great Britain, Europe, and the United States that began in the 2nd half of the 18C

in·dus·tri·al-strength adj describes material or chemicals that are strong

in·dus·tri·ous /in dústree əss/ adj working diligently —**in·dus·tri·ous·ly** adv —**in·dus·tri·ous·ness** n

in·dus·try /índəstree/ (pl -tries) n 1 activity connected with the large-scale production of a product 2 a particular branch of industry devoted to the production of a particular thing 3 a popular activity that has become commercialized o the fitness industry 4 hard work (fml or literary)

in·e·bri·ate /i néebree àyt/ (-at·ed, -at·ing) vt 1 make intoxicated 2 excite (fml) —**in·e·bri·at·ed** adj —**in·e·bri·a·tion** /i néebree áysh'n/ n

in·ed·i·ble /in éddəb'l/ adj unfit to eat —**in·ed·i·bil·i·ty** /in èddə bíllətee/ n —**in·ed·i·bly** adv

in·ef·fa·ble /in éffəb'l/ adj unable to be expressed in words —**in·ef·fa·bil·i·ty** /in èffə bíllətee/ n —**in·ef·fa·bly** adv

in·ef·fec·tive /ínnə féktiv/ adj 1 not producing the desired result 2 lacking competence —**in·ef·fec·tive·ly** adv —**in·ef·fec·tive·ness** n

in·ef·fec·tu·al /ínnə fékchoo əl/ adj 1 incompetent or indecisive 2 incapable of producing the desired outcome —**in·ef·fec·tu·al·ly** adv

in·ef·fi·cient /ínnə físh'nt/ adj not making the best use of time and resources —**in·ef·fi·cien·cy** n

in·el·e·gant /in élləgənt/ adj 1 lacking grace, sophistication, and style 2 unnecessarily complicated or long —**in·el·e·gance** n

in·el·i·gi·ble /in élliəb'l/ adj not eligible —**in·el·i·gi·bil·i·ty** /in èllijə bíllətee/ n

in·e·luc·ta·ble /ínni lúktəb'l/ adj unavoidable (fml) —**in·e·luc·ta·bly** adv

in·ept /i népt/ adj 1 lacking in competence or skill 2 totally inappropriate —**in·ep·ti·tude** n —**in·ept·ly** adv —**in·ept·ness** n

in·e·qual·i·ty /ínnə kwóllətee/ (pl -ties) n 1 difference in social or economic status 2 lack of equal treatment

in·eq·ui·ta·ble /in ékwitəb'l/ adj unfair —**in·eq·ui·ta·bly** adv

in·eq·ui·ty /in ékwetee/ (pl -ties) n 1 unfair treatment (fml) 2 an unfair situation or action

in·e·rad·i·ca·ble /ínnə ráddikəb'l/ adj impossible to remove —**in·e·rad·i·ca·bly** adv

in·ert /i núrt/ adj 1 motionless 2 not readily changed by chemical or biological reaction —**in·ert·ly** adv —**in·ert·ness** n

ORIGIN **Inert** comes from a Latin word that literally meant "unskilled." It was formed from **in-** "not" and **art-**, the stem of **ars** "art" (from which English **art** derives). The sense "sluggish" developed in Latin.

in·er·tia /i núrshə/ n 1 apathy 2 the property of a body by which it remains at rest or continues moving in a straight line unless acted upon by a directional force —**in·er·tial** adj —**in·er·tial·ly** adv

in·es·cap·a·ble /ínnə skáypəb'l/ adj inevitable —**in·es·cap·a·bil·i·ty** /ínne skaypə bíllətee/ n —**in·es·cap·a·bly** adv

in·es·sen·tial /ínnə sénsh'l/ adj 1 not essential 2 without substance or being (literary) —**in·es·sen·tial** n —**in·es·sen·tial·ly** adv

in·es·ti·ma·ble /in éstiməb'l/ adj extremely useful or valuable —**in·es·ti·ma·bil·i·ty** /in èstimə bíllətee/ n —**in·es·ti·ma·bly** adv

in·ev·i·ta·ble /in évvitəb'l/ adj unavoidable
■ n something certain to happen —**in·ev·i·ta·bil·i·ty** /in èvvitə bíllətee/ n —**in·ev·i·ta·bly** adv

~~inevitible~~ incorrect spelling of **inevitable**

in·ex·act /ínnig zákt/ *adj* 1 not precise 2 not thorough or careful —**in·ex·act·i·tude** *n* —**in·ex·act·ly** *adv* —**in·ex·act·ness** *n*

in·ex·cus·a·ble /ínnik skyóozəb'l/ *adj* impossible to excuse or justify —**in·ex·cus·a·bil·i·ty** /ínnik skyooza bílletee/ *n* —**in·ex·cus·a·bly** *adv*

in·ex·haust·i·ble /ínnig záwstəb'l/ *adj* 1 impossible to use up 2 never tiring —**in·ex·haust·i·bil·i·ty** /ínnig zawstə bílletee/ *n* —**in·ex·haust·i·bly** *adv*

in·ex·o·ra·ble /in éksərəb'l/ *adj* 1 unstoppable (*fml*) 2 not swayed by pleas or attempts to persuade —**in·ex·o·ra·bil·i·ty** /in éksərə bílletee/ *n* —**in·ex·o·ra·bly** *adv*

in·ex·pe·di·ent /ínnik speedee ənt/ *adj* 1 inconvenient or impractical —**in·ex·pe·di·ence** —**in·ex·pe·di·ent·ly** *adv*

in·ex·pen·sive /ínnik spénsiv/ *adj* not costing much money —**in·ex·pen·sive·ly** *adv* —**in·ex·pen·sive·ness** *n*

in·ex·pe·ri·ence /ínnik speéree ənss/ *n* 1 lack of experience 2 lack of sophistication —**in·ex·pe·ri·enced** *adj*

in·ex·pert /in ékspərt/ *adj* lacking skill or experience —**in·ex·pert·ly** *adv* —**in·ex·pert·ness** *n*

in·ex·pli·ca·ble /ínnik splíkəb'l, in éksplikəb'l/ *adj* impossible to explain or justify —**in·ex·pli·ca·bil·i·ty** /ínnik splikə bílletee, in èksplikə-/ *n* —**in·ex·pli·ca·bly** *adv*

in·ex·press·i·ble /ínnik spréssəb'l/ *adj* impossible to put into words —**in·ex·press·i·bly** *adv*

in·ex·pres·sive /ínnik spréssiv/ *adj* showing no emotion —**in·ex·pres·sive·ly** *adv* —**in·ex·pres·sive·ness** *n*

in·ex·tin·guish·a·ble /ínnik stíng gwishəb'l/ *adj* impossible to put out or suppress

in ex·tre·mis /ín ik streémiss/ *adv* in desperate circumstances ■ *adj* near death

in·ex·tri·ca·ble /in ékstríkəb'l, ínnik stríkəb'l/ *adj* 1 impossible to escape from 2 impossible to separate or disentangle —**in·ex·tri·ca·bil·i·ty** /in èkstrikə bílletee, ínnik strikə-/ *n* —**in·ex·tri·ca·bly** *adv*

in·fal·li·ble /in fálləb'l/ *adj* 1 incapable of making mistakes 2 certain not to fail 3 incapable of being mistaken in matters of doctrine —**in·fal·li·bil·i·ty** /in fàllə bílletee/ *n* —**in·fal·li·bly** *adv*

in·fa·mous /ínfəməss/ *adj* 1 notorious 2 so bad as to destroy somebody's reputation —**in·fa·mous·ly** *adv*

in·fa·my /ínfəmee/ *n* 1 notoriety 2 shameful or criminal conduct

in·fan·cy /ínfənsee/ *n* 1 babyhood 2 the beginning or early stages of something

in·fant /ínfənt/ *n* a baby ■ *adj* just beginning —**in·fant·hood** *n*

ORIGIN An **infant** is etymologically "unable to speak." The word comes via French from Latin.

in·fan·ti·cide /in fántə sìd/ *n* 1 the murder of an infant 2 a killer of an infant —**in·fan·ti·cid·al** /in fàntə síd'l/ *adj*

in·fan·tile /ínfən tìl/ *adj* 1 showing a lack of maturity 2 of young children

in·fant mor·tal·i·ty rate *n* the rate of deaths during the first year of life

in·fan·try /ínfəntree/ *n* soldiers who fight on foot, or a unit of them —**in·fan·try·man** *n*

in·fat·u·a·tion /in fàchoo áysh'n/ *n* 1 a great but short-lived passion for somebody or something 2 the object of somebody's infatuation —**in·fat·u·at·ed** /in fáchoo àytəd/ *adj* ◊ See note at **love**

in·fect /in fékt/ *vt* 1 cause disease or infection in 2 affect, usually adversely —**in·fect·ed** *adj*

in·fec·tion /in fékshən/ *n* 1 the reproduction of disease-producing microorganisms in the body 2 the transmission of a disease

in·fec·tious /in fékshəss/ *adj* 1 describes a disease that can be passed on 2 caused by bacteria or other microorganisms 3 affecting the feelings of others ○ *infectious laughter* —**in·fec·tious·ly** *adv* —**in·fec·tious·ness** *n*

in·fer /in fúr/ (-**ferred**, -**fer·ring**) *v* 1 *vti* conclude something from reasoning or evidence 2 *vt* lead to as a conclusion 3 *vt* imply —**in·fer·a·ble** *adj*

USAGE infer or **imply**? **Infer** is to conclude something on the basis of reasoning or evidence: *From her comments I inferred that she supported the legislation.* **Imply** is to make something understood without expressing it directly: *Her comments implied that she supported the legislation.*

in·fer·ence /ínfərənss/ *n* 1 a conclusion drawn from reasoning or evidence 2 the process of reasoning from a premise to a conclusion —**in·fer·en·tial** /ínfə rénsh'l/ *adj* —**in·fer·en·tial·ly** *adv*

in·fe·ri·or /in feéree ər/ *adj* 1 lower in standing or rank 2 lower in quality, standard, or value 3 in a lower position than something else —**in·fe·ri·or** *n* —**in·fe·ri·or·i·ty** /in feèree áwrətee/ *n*

in·fe·ri·or·i·ty com·plex *n* a sense of being inferior

in·fer·nal /in fúrn'l/ *adj* 1 very annoying 2 of the underworld 3 diabolical in nature —**in·fer·nal·ly** *adv*

in·fer·no /in fúrnō/ (*pl* -**nos**) *n* 1 a huge destructive fire 2 a hellish place

in·fer·tile /in fúrt'l/ *adj* 1 physically incapable of having offspring 2 not producing crops —**in·fer·til·i·ty** /ín fur tílletee/ *n*

in·fest /in fést/ *vt* overrun a place to an unpleasant or harmful degree ○ *lice infesting*

their clothing —**in·fes·ta·tion** /ĭn fe stáysh'n/ *n*
—**in·fest·ed** *adj*

in·fi·del /ínfid'l/, ínfi dèl/ *n (disapproving)*
1 somebody who does not believe in a particular religion 2 somebody with no religious beliefs

in·fi·del·i·ty /ĭnfi déllətee/ *(pl* **-ties)** *n* 1 unfaithfulness, especially to a sexual partner 2 an unfaithful act

in·field /ín feeld/ *n* 1 a baseball diamond 2 the baseball players in the infield —**in·field·er** *n*

in·fight·ing /ĭn fíting/ *n* 1 internal squabbling 2 fighting at close range —**in·fight·er** *n*

in·fil·trate /ín fĭl tràyt, ĭnfíl-/ (**-trat·ed, -trat·ing)**
vti 1 cross or send somebody into an enemy territory without the enemy's knowledge 2 pass through a substance by filtration —**in·fil·tra·tion** /ĭnfil tráysh'n/ *n* —**in·fil·tra·tor** *n*

infin. *abbr* infinitive

in·fi·nite /ínfənit/ *adj* 1 without measurable limits 2 exceedingly great —**in·fi·nite** *n* —**in·fi·nite·ly** *adv* —**in·fi·nite·ness** *n*

⚡ **in·fi·nite loop** *n* a series of instructions in a computer program that repeats endlessly

in·fin·i·tes·i·mal /ĭnfini téssəm'l/ *adj* 1 tiny 2 able to assume values close to but greater than zero —**in·fin·i·tes·i·mal·ly** *adv*

in·fin·i·tive /ĭn fínnitiv/ *n* the basic form of a verb, in English usually preceded by "to"

in·fin·i·tude /ĭn fínni toòd/ *n* 1 boundlessness 2 a very large number, degree, or extent

in·fin·i·ty /ĭn fínnətee/ *(pl* **-ties)** *n* 1 limitless time, space, or distance 2 an amount or number too great to count

in·firm /ĭn fúrm/ *adj* 1 not strong or healthy 2 structurally unsound ◊ See note at **weak**

in·fir·ma·ry /ĭn fúrməree/ *(pl* **-ries)** *n* a hospital or other place where sick or injured people are cared for

in·fir·mi·ty /ĭn fúrmətee/ *n* lack of strength and vitality

in fla·gran·te de·lic·to /ĭn flə gràntee də líktō/, **in fla·gran·te** *adv* 1 in the act of committing an offense 2 in the act of having sex

in·flame /ĭn fláym/ (**-flamed, -flam·ing)** *vt* make more angry, violent, or intense —**in·flamed** *adj*

in·flam·ma·ble /ĭn flámməb'l/ *adj* 1 easily set on fire 2 easily made angry or violent —**in·flam·ma·bil·i·ty** /ĭn flàmmə bíllətee/ *n* —**in·flam·ma·ble** *n* —**in·flam·ma·bly** *adv*

in·flam·ma·tion /ĭnflə máysh'n/ *n* 1 swelling and redness produced by an infection 2 a heightening of emotion

in·flam·ma·to·ry /ĭn flámmə tàwree/ *adj* 1 likely to arouse anger or violence 2 of inflammation —**in·flam·ma·to·ri·ly** *adv*

in·flate /ĭn fláyt/ (**-flat·ed, -flat·ing)** *vti* 1 expand by filling with air or a gas 2 appear or cause to appear greater —**in·flat·a·ble** *adj*

in·flat·ed /ĭn fláytəd/ *adj* 1 exaggerated or greater than is justified ◊ *a sense of inflated*

importance 2 excessively high 3 filled with air or a gas —**in·flat·ed·ly** *adv* —**in·flat·ed·ness** *n*

in·fla·tion /ĭn fláysh'n/ *n* 1 an increase in the money supply relative to the supply of goods and services, resulting in higher prices 2 the act of inflating or condition of being inflated —**in·fla·tion·ar·y** *adj*

in·flect /ĭn flékt/ *v* 1 *vt* vary the pitch or tone of the voice 2 *vti* change the form of a word to show grammatical changes such as tense, mood, gender, or number —**in·flect·a·ble** *adj* —**in·flect·ed** *adj*

in·flec·tion /ĭn flékshən/ *n* 1 a change in the pitch or tone of the voice 2 a change in the form of a word to show grammatical changes such as tense, mood, gender, or number —**in·flec·tion·al** *adj*

in·flex·i·ble /ĭn fléksəb'l/ *adj* 1 adhering firmly to a viewpoint or principle 2 impossible to change ◊ *an inflexible rule* 3 stiff and difficult to bend —**in·flex·i·bil·i·ty** /ĭn flèksə bíllətee/ *n* —**in·flex·i·bly** *adv*

in·flict /ĭn flíkt/ *vt* 1 cause damage or harm to 2 force on somebody —**in·flic·tion** *n*

in-flight *adj* provided for passengers during a flight

in·flow /ín flo/ *n* 1 something that flows in 2 an instance or the process of flowing in —**in·flow·ing** *n*

in·flu·ence /ín floo ənss/ *n* 1 an effect on something 2 the power to affect other people's thinking or actions 3 a special advantage that comes from wealth or social status 4 somebody who can sway another person ■ *vt* (**-enced, -enc·ing)** 1 persuade or sway 2 have the power to affect ◊ **under the influence** intoxicated by the use of a chemical substance, especially alcohol *(infml)*

~~influencial~~ incorrect spelling of **influential**

in·flu·en·tial /ĭn floo énshəl/ *adj* able to influence —**in·flu·en·tial·ly** *adv*

in·flu·en·za /ĭn floo énzə/ *n* a viral illness producing high fever, respiratory inflammation, and muscle pain *(technical)* —**in·flu·en·zal** *adj*

in·flux /ín flúks/ *n* 1 arrival in large numbers 2 an inflow

in·fo[1] /ínfō/ *n* information *(infml)*

⚡ **info**[2] *abbr* general use *(in Internet addresses)*

⚡ **in·fo·me·di·ar·y** /ínfō meédee èrree/ *n* a website providing specialist information for producers of goods and customers

in·fo·mer·cial /ĭnfə múrsh'l/, ĭnfō-/, **in·for·mer·cial** /ĭn fawr múrsh'l/ *n* a television commercial made in the style of a documentary

in·form /ĭn fáwrm/ *v* 1 *vt* communicate information to 2 *vi* tell the police about somebody's wrongdoings

in·for·mal /ĭn fáwrm'l/ *adj* 1 characterized by an absence of formality and ceremony 2 unofficial 3 casual and everyday

—in·for·mal·i·ty /ˌin fawr mállətee/ n
—in·for·mal·ly adv

in·form·ant /in fáwrmənt/ n 1 somebody who supplies information 2 a police informer

⚡ in·for·ma·tion /ˌinfər máysh'n/ n 1 knowledge 2 gathered facts 3 the communication of facts and knowledge 4 computer data
—in·for·ma·tion·al adj

⚡ in·for·ma·tion re·triev·al n the systematic storage and retrieval of computer data

in·for·ma·tion sci·ence n the study of data collection, organization, and distribution, especially using computers

⚡ in·for·ma·tion tech·nol·o·gy n the use of computing, electronics, and telecommunications to process and distribute information

⚡ in·for·ma·tion the·o·ry n the mathematical analysis of data transmission, reception, storage, and retrieval

in·form·a·tive /in fáwrmətiv/ adj providing useful information —in·form·a·tive·ly adv —in·form·a·tive·ness n

in·formed /in fáwrmd/ adj 1 showing, having, or based on knowledge 2 based on full awareness —in·form·ed·ly /in fáwrmədlee/ adv

in·formed con·sent n a patient's agreement to undergo an operation or treatment after being informed of the risks

in·form·er /in fáwrmər/ n somebody who provides information about a crime to the police

in·fo·tain·ment /ˌinfō táynmənt/ n information treated or presented as entertainment —in·fo·tain·er n

in·fra /ínfrə/ adv refers a reader to a point later in a text (fml)

infra- prefix below, beneath, inferior ○ infrastructure

in·frac·tion /in frákshən/ n a failure to obey a rule

in·fra·red /ˌinfrə réd/ n electromagnetic radiation that lies outside the visible spectrum —in·fra·red adj

in·fra·struc·ture /ínfrə strùkchər/ n 1 the basic organizational structure of a company or organization 2 the public services or systems necessary to the economic activity of a country or region —in·fra·struc·tur·al /ˌinfrə strúkchərəl/ adj

in·fre·quent /in freékwənt/ adj not appearing, happening, or encountered often —in·fre·quen·cy n —in·fre·quent·ly adv

in·fringe /in frínj/ (-fringed, -fring·ing) v 1 vt disobey or disregard a law or the terms of a agreement 2 vti encroach on somebody's rights or property —in·fringe·ment n

in·fu·ri·ate /in fyooreeə àyt/ (-at·ed, -at·ing) vt make furious —in·fu·ri·at·ed adj —in·fu·ri·at·ing adj —in·fu·ri·at·ing·ly adv

in·fuse /in fyooz/ (-fused, -fus·ing) v 1 vt fill with a strong emotion 2 vt fix firmly in

somebody else's mind 3 vti steep in liquid —in·fu·sion n

-ing suffix 1 action or process ○ cooking 2 forms the present participle of verbs ○ raining 3 somebody or something that has a particular character ○ gelding

Inge /inj/, William (1913–73) US playwright

in·gen·ious /in jeényəss/ adj 1 inventive 2 clever and effective —in·gen·ious·ly adv —in·gen·ious·ness n

in·gé·nue /áNzhə nòo/ n 1 an unsophisticated girl or young woman 2 a character in a play who is a naïve young woman

in·ge·nu·i·ty /ˌinjə nòo ətee/ n inventiveness

in·gen·u·ous /in jénnyoo əss/ adj 1 innocent and unworldly 2 seeming honest and direct —in·gen·u·ous·ly adv —in·gen·u·ous·ness n

in·gest /in jést/ vt take into the body by swallowing or absorbing —in·ges·tion n

in·gle·nook /ing g'l nòok/ n 1 a recess beside a fireplace 2 a fireside seat

In·gle·wood /ing g'l wòod/ city in SW California. Pop. 111,618 (1998).

in·glo·ri·ous /in gláwree əss/ adj bringing shame or dishonor —in·glo·ri·ous·ly adv

in·got /ing gət/ n a block of metal, typically oblong

In·gra·ham /ing grəm/, Hubert (b. 1947) prime minister of the Bahamas (1992–)

in·grained /in gráynd/ adj 1 worked deep into something ○ ingrained dirt 2 long-established and confirmed ○ ingrained habits 3 impressed in somebody's mind —in·grain vt —in·grained·ness /-ədnəss/ n

in·grate /in gràyt/ n an ungrateful person

in·gra·ti·ate /in gráyshee àyt/ (-at·ed, -at·ing) vr seek to please somebody, especially to gain an advantage —in·gra·ti·at·ing adj —in·gra·ti·a·tion /in gràyshee áysh'n/ n

in·grat·i·tude /in gráttə tòod/ n lack of gratitude

~~ingredient~~ incorrect spelling of ingredient

in·gre·di·ent /in greédee ənt/ n 1 an item in a recipe 2 a required part ○ the ingredients of a good marriage

In·gres /áNgrə/, Jean-Auguste-Dominique (1780–1867) French artist

in·gress /in gréss/ n entry (fml)

in-group n a group united by common values

in·grow·ing /in gróing/ adj growing inward

in·grown /in grōn/ adj 1 grown into the flesh 2 having become a natural part of somebody's character

in·hab·it /in hábbit/ vt 1 live or reside in 2 be found or present in —in·hab·it·a·ble adj —in·hab·it·ed adj

in·hab·i·tant /in hábbit'nt/ n a person or animal that lives in a particular place

in·ha·lant /in háylənt/ adj breathed in ■ n a medicine in the form of a vapor or gas that is inhaled

in·hale /in háyl/ (**-haled, -hal·ing**) *vti* breathe something into the lungs —**in·ha·la·tion** /ínhə láysh'n/ *n*

in·hal·er /in háylər/ *n* a device for inhaling medicine

in·har·mo·ni·ous /ín haar mṓnee əss/ *adj* **1** sounding unpleasant or out of harmony **2** characterized by disagreement or conflict

in·her·ent /in héerənt, -hérrənt/ *adj* forming a basic and essential part of something —**in·her·en·cy** *n* —**in·her·ent·ly** *adv*

in·her·it /in hérrit/ *v* **1** *vti* receive something when somebody dies under the terms of a will **2** *vt* receive a genetic characteristic from a parent **3** *vt* get something from a predecessor —**in·her·it·a·ble** *adj* —**in·her·i·tor** *n*

in·her·i·tance /in hérrit'nss/ *n* **1** a sum of money, property, or a title that is inherited **2** something that is inherited from the past **3** the transmission of genetically controlled characteristics from parent to offspring

in·her·i·tance tax *n* a tax on inherited property

in·hib·it /in híbbit/ *vt* **1** prevent from continuing or developing **2** prevent from behaving freely or without self-consciousness —**in·hib·it·ed** *adj* —**in·hib·i·tive** *adj*

in·hi·bi·tion /ínnə bísh'n, ínhə-/ *n* **1** a feeling that prevents somebody from behaving freely or without self-consciousness **2** something that inhibits, or the act of inhibiting

in·hos·pi·ta·ble /in ho spíttəb'l, in hóspitəb'l/ *adj* **1** not friendly or welcoming **2** harsh and difficult to live or work in o *an inhospitable climate* —**in·hos·pi·ta·bly** *adv* —**in·hos·pi·tal·i·ty** /ín hospi tállətee/ *n*

in-house *adj, adv* within a company or organization

in·hu·man /in hyóomən/ *adj* **1** very cruel **2** unfeeling —**in·hu·man·ly** *adv* —**in·hu·man·ness** *n*

in·hu·mane /ín hyoo máyn/ *adj* not compassionate —**in·hu·mane·ly** *adv* —**in·hu·mane·ness** *n*

in·hu·man·i·ty /ín hyoo mánnətee/ (*pl* **-ties**) *n* **1** great cruelty **2** an extremely cruel act

in·im·i·cal /i nímmik'l/ *adj* (*fml*) **1** not favorable **2** hostile

in·im·i·ta·ble /i nímmitəb'l/ *adj* unique and impossible to imitate —**in·im·i·ta·bly** *adv*

in·iq·ui·ty /i níkwətee/ (*pl* **-ties**) *n* **1** injustice or immorality **2** an unjust or immoral act —**in·iq·ui·tous** *adj*

in·i·tial /i nísh'l/ *adj* **1** coming at the start **2** describes the first letter in a word ■ *n* **1** the first letter of a name, used as an abbreviation **2** a large ornate first letter ■ **in·i·tials** *npl* the first letters of somebody's names, used as an abbreviation ■ *vt* mark with initials —**in·i·tial·ly** *adv*

⚡ **in·i·tial·ize** /i nísh'l ìz/ (**-ized, -iz·ing**) *vti* prepare a computer for use, often by resetting a memory location to its original position —**in·i·tial·i·za·tion** /i nísh'li záysh'n/ *n*

in·i·ti·ate *vt* /i níshee àyt/ (**-at·ed, -at·ing**) **1** cause an event, activity, or process to begin **2** introduce somebody to a new activity or interest **3** allow somebody to take part in a ceremony, in order to become a member of a group ■ *n* /i níshee ət/ **1** somebody initiated into a group **2** somebody newly introduced to something ■ *adj* /i níshee ət/ **1** recently initiated **2** having secret or special knowledge —**in·i·ti·a·tion** /i níshee áysh'n/ *n* —**in·i·ti·a·tor** *n*

in·i·tia·tive /i níshətiv/ *n* **1** the ability to act and make decisions without help **2** a plan or strategy

in·ject /in jékt/ *v* **1** *vti* put fluid into the body with a syringe **2** *vt* force a liquid or gas into something **3** *vt* add something new to a situation o *inject a little levity* —**in·jec·tion** *n*

in-joke *n* a joke understood only by a small group

in·ju·di·cious /ín joo díshəss/ *adj* unwise —**in·ju·di·cious·ly** *adv* —**in·ju·di·cious·ness** *n*

in·junc·tion /in júngkshən/ *n* **1** a court order prohibiting something **2** a command

in·jure /ínjər/ (**-jured, -jur·ing**) *vt* **1** cause physical harm to **2** cause distress to by being unkind ◊ See note at **harm**

in·ju·ry /ínjəree/ (*pl* **-ries**) *n* **1** physical damage to the body **2** a wound **3** harm done to somebody's reputation —**in·ju·ri·ous** /in jóoree əss/ *adj*

in·ju·ry time *n* in soccer, time added for injury stoppages

~~injust~~ incorrect spelling of **unjust**

in·jus·tice /in jústiss/ *n* unfair treatment, or an instance of this

ink *n* **1** liquid for writing, drawing, or printing **2** a dark liquid ejected by an octopus, squid, or related organism to deter predators ■ *vt* write something with ink —**ink·er** *n* —**ink·y** *adj*

ink·blot /íngk blòt/ *n* **1** a stain or spot of spilled ink **2** a pattern of blots or dots for analysis in a psychological test

⚡ **ink-jet print·er** *n* a printer that prints using droplets of ink from tiny ink jets

in·kling /íngkling/ *n* **1** a faint idea **2** a hint

ink·stand /íngk stànd/ *n* a stand on a desk for ink, pens, and other writing materials

ink·well /íngk wèl/ *n* a jar of ink, especially one that fits into a hole in a desk

in·laid /ín làyd/ *adj* **1** set into a surface **2** decorated with an inlaid pattern

in·land /in lànd, ínlənd/ *adj* not near a coast or border ■ *adv* in or into the interior of a country

In·land Sea arm of the Pacific Ocean in Japan, between the islands of Honshu, Shikoku, and Kyushu. Length 270 mi./430 km.

in-law *n* a relative by marriage (*infml*)

in·lay /ín lày/ *vt* (**-laid**) **1** set into a surface **2** decorate with an inlaid design ■ *n* **1** pieces of material set into a surface **2** a decorative pattern formed by inlaying —**in·lay·er** /ín láy ər/ *n*

in·let /ín lèt, ínlət/ *n* **1** a narrow stretch of water extending inland from a coast **2** a stretch of water between two islands

in-line skates *npl* roller skates with wheels in a single line —**in-line skat·ing** *n*

~~inlist~~ incorrect spelling of **enlist**

in lo·co pa·ren·tis /ín-lòkò pə réntiss/ *adv* responsible as a parent for somebody else's child

in·mate /ín màyt/ *n* somebody confined to an institution

in me·mo·ri·am /ín mə máwree əm/ *prep, adv* in memory of somebody (*in epitaphs and obituaries*)

in·most *adj* = innermost

inn *n* **1** a place providing lodging for travelers (*often in the names of establishments*) **2** a bar or restaurant

ORIGIN **Inn** is related to *in*, being etymologically a place you stay "in." In its earliest uses it could be a permanent lodging or home. The sense "place providing lodging" began to develop in the 14C.

~~innaccurate~~ incorrect spelling of **inaccurate**

in·nards /ínnərdz/ *npl* (*infml*) **1** the internal organs of the body **2** the internal parts of a machine

in·nate /í náyt/ *adj* **1** present from birth **2** integral —**in·nate·ly** *adv* —**in·nate·ness** *n*

in·ner /ínnər/ *adj* **1** near or closer to the center **2** being or occurring inside **3** of the mind

in·ner cit·y *n* the central area of a city —**in·ner-cit·y** *adj*

in·ner·most /ínnər mòst/, **-most** /ín mòst/ *adj* **1** most private or personal **2** farthest from the outside

in·ner tube *n* a rubber tube inside a tire

in·ning /ínning/ *n* a division of a baseball game in which each team bats until it makes three outs

in·nings /ínningz/ (*pl same*) *n* in cricket, a team's turn at batting

inn·keep·er /ín kèepər/ *n* somebody in charge of an inn

in·no·cent /ínnəss'nt/ *adj* **1** not guilty of a crime **2** harmless in intention **3** pure and uncorrupted by evil **4** naive ■ *n* a blameless or naive person —**in·no·cence** *n* —**in·no·cent·ly** *adv*

In·no·cent III /ínnəss'nt/ (1160?–1216) pope (1198–1216)

~~inoculation~~ incorrect spelling of **inoculation**

in·noc·u·ous /í nókyoo əss/ *adj* **1** unlikely to offend **2** harmless —**in·noc·u·ous·ly** *adv* —**in·noc·u·ous·ness** *n*

in·no·vate /ínnə vàyt/ (**-vat·ed, -vat·ing**) *vi* try out new ideas —**in·no·va·tive** /-vàytiv/ *adj* —**in·no·va·tive·ly** *adv* —**in·no·va·tive·ness** *n* —**in·no·va·tor** *n*

in·no·va·tion /ínnə váysh'n/ *n* **1** the process of inventing or introducing new things **2** a new invention, idea, or method —**in·no·va·tion·al** *adj*

Inns·bruck /ínz brŏŏk/ capital of Tirol Province, W Austria. Pop. 110,997 (1999).

in·nu·en·do /ínnyoo éndō/ (*pl* **-does** *or* **-dos**) *n* a remark that hints at something improper

in·nu·mer·a·ble /í nŏŏmərəb'l/ *adj* countless —**in·nu·mer·a·bil·i·ty** /í nŏŏmərə bíllətee/ *n* —**in·nu·mer·a·bly** *adv*

in·nu·mer·ate /í nŏŏmərət/ *adj* unable to do arithmetic

~~inocence~~ incorrect spelling of **innocence**

in·oc·u·late /í nókyə làyt/ (**-lat·ed, -lat·ing**) *vt* inject or introduce a substance that protects against a disease —**in·oc·u·la·tion** /í nòkyə láysh'n/ *n*

in·of·fen·sive /ínnə fénsiv/ *adj* not harmful, annoying, or offensive —**in·of·fen·sive·ly** *adv* —**in·of·fen·sive·ness** *n*

in·op·er·a·ble /ín óppərəb'l, -ópprə-/ *adj* **1** too far advanced for effective surgery **2** not workable

in·op·er·a·tive /ín óppərətiv, in ópprətiv/ *adj* **1** not functioning properly **2** ineffective or unenforceable —**in·op·er·a·tive·ly** *adv*

in·op·por·tune /ín òppər tóŏn/ *adj* happening at an inconvenient time —**in·op·por·tune·ly** *adv* —**in·op·por·tu·ni·ty** *n*

in·or·di·nate /ín áwrd'nət/ *adj* excessive in amount or degree —**in·or·di·nate·ly** *adv*

in·or·gan·ic /ín awr gánnik/ *adj* **1** composed of minerals rather than living material **2** describes a chemical compound that contains no carbon —**in·or·gan·i·cal·ly** *adv*

in·or·gan·ic chem·is·try *n* the study of inorganic compounds

in·pa·tient /ín pàysh'nt/ *n* somebody receiving medical treatment that requires a hospital stay ■ *adj* for inpatients

⚡ **in·put** /ín pŏŏt/ *n* **1** comments or suggestions made **2** the energy that operates a machine **3** data entered into computer ■ *v* (**-put·ted** *or* **-put, -put·ting**) **1** *vt* contribute information (*infml*) **2** enter data into a computer

in·quest /ín kwèst/ *n* **1** a formal inquiry, usually before a jury **2** an investigation into what went wrong (*literary*)

in·qui·e·tude /ín kwí ə tŏŏd/ *n* restlessness of mind (*literary*)

in·quire /ín kwír/ (**-quired, -quir·ing**), **en·quire** /en-/ *v* **1** *vti* ask something **2** *vi* try to find out the facts —**in·quir·er** n —**in·quir·ing** adj —**in·quir·ing·ly** adv

in·qui·ry /in kwíree, ínkwəree/ (pl **-ies**), **en·qui·ry** /en kwíree, énkwəree/ n 1 a formal investigation 2 a request for information

in·qui·si·tion /ínkwə zísh'n/ n 1 a period of intense questioning 2 **In·qui·si·tion** a former Roman Catholic tribunal for judging heretics —**in·qui·si·tion·al** adj

in·quis·i·tive /in kwízzətiv/ adj 1 eager for knowledge 2 too curious —**in·quis·i·tive·ly** adv —**in·quis·i·tive·ness** n

in·quis·i·tor /in kwízzitər/ n 1 a relentless interrogator 2 also **In·quis·i·tor** a member of the Roman Catholic Inquisition —**in·quis·i·to·ri·al** /in kwìzzə táwree əl/ adj

in re /in rée, in ráy/ prep with regard to

in·roads /ín ròdz/ npl an encroachment

in·rush /ín rùsh/ n an influx

INS abbr Immigration and Naturalization Service

ins. abbr 1 inches 2 insurance

in·sa·lu·bri·ous /ínsə lóobree əss/ adj unwholesome or unpleasant —**in·sa·lu·bri·ty** /ínsə lóobritee/ n

in·sane /in sáyn/ adj 1 legally incompetent or irresponsible because of a psychiatric disorder 2 wildly unreasonable or unwise (infml) —**in·sane·ly** adv —**in·san·i·ty** /in sánnətee/ n

in·san·i·tar·y /in sánnə tèrree/ adj dirty or unhygienic

in·sa·tia·ble /in sáyshəb'l/ adj always wanting more —**in·sa·tia·bil·i·ty** /in sàyshə bíllətee/ n —**in·sa·tia·bly** adv

in·scribe /in skríb/ (**-scribed, -scrib·ing**) vt 1 put writing or engraving on a surface 2 write a dedication on a book or photograph

in·scrip·tion /in skrípsh'n/ n 1 words or letters written or engraved on something 2 a dedication written in a book or on a photograph —**in·scrip·tion·al** adj

in·scru·ta·ble /in skróotəb'l/ adj not expressing anything clearly and hard to interpret o an inscrutable expression —**in·scru·ta·bil·i·ty** /in skròotə bíllətee/ n —**in·scru·ta·bly** adv

in·seam /ín seem/ n an inside pant leg seam, or its measurement

in·sect /ín sèkt/ n 1 a small six-legged animal with a segmented body 2 any small organism that resembles an insect (not in technical use)

ORIGIN Insect derives from Latin insectum, which means literally "something cut up or into." The name refers to the segmented structure of an insect body. The Latin was itself a direct translation from Greek entomon, which is seen in English entomology. **Insect** is first recorded in 1601.

in·sec·ti·cide /in sékti sìd/ n a chemical substance used to kill insects —**in·sec·ti·cid·al** /in sèkti síd'l/ adj

in·sec·ti·vore /in sékti vàwr/ n an insect-eating organism —**in·sec·tiv·o·rous** /ín sek tívvərəss/ adj

in·se·cure /ínsə kyóor/ adj 1 not confident 2 not safe —**in·se·cure·ly** adv —**in·se·cu·ri·ty** /ínsə kyóorətee/ n

in·sem·i·nate /in sémmi nàyt/ (**-nat·ed, -nat·ing**) vt 1 put semen into the reproductive tract of a woman or female animal 2 introduce something such as a new idea or principle —**in·sem·i·na·tion** /in sèmmi náysh'n/ n

in·sen·sate /in sèn sàyt/ adj 1 inanimate and thus unable to feel 2 irrational (fml)

in·sen·si·ble /in sénsəb'l/ adj 1 without feeling or consciousness 2 not aware or responsive —**in·sen·si·bil·i·ty** /in sènsə bíllətee/ n

in·sen·si·tive /in sénsətiv/ adj 1 thoughtless of others 2 not responsive to physical stimulus —**in·sen·si·tive·ly** adv —**in·sen·si·tiv·i·ty** /in sènsə tívvətee/ n

in·sen·tient /in sénshənt/ adj without life, consciousness, or perception —**in·sen·tience** n

in·sep·a·ra·ble /in séppərəb'l, -sépprə-/ adj 1 always together 2 unable to be separated —**in·sep·a·ra·bil·i·ty** /in sèppərə bíllətee, -sèpprə-/ n —**in·sep·a·ra·bly** adv

in·sert vt /in súrt/ 1 put inside or into something 2 add to something written ■ n /ín sùrt/ 1 an advertising supplement in a magazine 2 an added part —**in·ser·tion** n

in-serv·ice adj 1 happening during full-time employment o in-service training 2 working as a full-time employee

in·set /in sét/ (**-set, -set·ting**) vt insert into a larger thing —**in·set** /ín sét/ n

in·shal·lah /in shálla/, **in·sh'al·lah** interj an expression meaning "if God wills," used to suggest that something in the future is uncertain

in·shore /ín sháwr/ adj near a coast ■ adv toward a coast

in·side /in síd, ín síd/ adj, prep happening or coming from within an organization o inside knowledge of the buyout ■ adv, prep 1 within a place o I looked inside. o Everyone's inside the office. 2 within or into somebody's inner feelings ■ prep within a particular time (infml) ■ adj 1 inner or interior o an inside pocket 2 farthest from the center of a road o an inside lane ■ n 1 an interior or inner part 2 the part of a road farthest from the center 3 a position that gives access to information ■ **in·sides** npl internal organs of the body (infml) ◊ **inside out** with the part that is normally inside facing out ◊ **know something inside out** know something extremely well

in·side in·for·ma·tion n something that only insiders know

in·sid·er /in sídər/ n a member of a group who has access to information about the group

in·sid·er trad·ing, in·sid·er deal·ing n stock transactions made with inside information

in·side track n 1 the inner lane of a racetrack 2 a position of advantage

in·sid·i·ous /in síddee əss/ adj gradual and harmful —**in·sid·i·ous·ly** adv —**in·sid·i·ous·ness** n

in·sight /ín sìt/ n 1 perceptiveness 2 a clear perception —**in·sight·ful** /in sítf'l, in sítf'l/ adj —**in·sight·ful·ly** adv

in·sig·ni·a /in sígnee ə/ (pl same or -as) n 1 a badge of authority or membership 2 an identifying mark

in·sig·nif·i·cant /ín sig níffikənt/ adj 1 without importance 2 without meaning —**in·sig·nif·i·cance** n —**in·sig·nif·i·cant·ly** adv

in·sin·cere /ín sin séer/ adj not having or expressing genuine feelings —**in·sin·cere·ly** adv —**in·sin·cer·i·ty** /ín sin sérrətee/ n

in·sin·u·ate /in sínnyoo àyt/ (-at·ed, -at·ing) v 1 vti hint or suggest something indirectly 2 vr worm your way in —**in·sin·u·at·ing·ly** adv —**in·sin·u·a·tion** /in sínnyoo áysh'n/ n

in·sip·id /in síppid/ adj 1 dull and unexciting 2 flavorless —**in·si·pid·i·ty** /ínsi píddətee/ n —**in·sip·id·ly** adv

in·sist /in síst/ vti 1 state or demand firmly despite opposition 2 be persistent in a demand o insist on punctuality

~~insistant~~ incorrect spelling of **insistent**

in·sis·tent /in sístənt/ adj 1 persistent in demanding something 2 demanding attention o insistent pleas —**in·sis·tence** n —**in·sis·tent·ly** adv

in si·tu /in sí too, in seé too/ adv, adj in its natural or original place

in·so·far as /in sō faàr-/ conj to the extent that

in·sole /ín sòl/ n 1 a shoe lining 2 a removable pad inside a shoe

in·so·lent /ínsələnt/ adj openly disrespectful —**in·so·lence** n —**in·so·lent·ly** adv

in·sol·u·ble /in sóllyəb'l/ adj 1 not dissolvable 2 impossible to solve —**in·sol·u·bil·i·ty** /in sòllyə bíllətee/ n

in·solv·a·ble /in sólvəb'l/ adj impossible to solve —**in·solv·a·bil·i·ty** /in sòlvə bíllətee/ n

in·sol·vent /in sólvənt/ adj unable to pay debts —**in·sol·ven·cy** n

in·som·ni·a /in sómnee ə/ n difficulty in sleeping —**in·som·ni·ac** adj, n

in·so·much as /ínsō mùch àz/ conj because

in·sou·ci·ance /in sóossee ənss/ n a carefree attitude —**in·sou·ci·ant** adj

in·spect /in spékt/ vt 1 look at critically 2 survey

in·spec·tion /in spéksh'n/ n 1 a critical examination 2 an official examination

in·spec·tor /in spéktər/ n 1 an official exam-

iner 2 a police officer of middle rank —**in·spec·tor·ship** n

in·spec·tor·ate /in spéktərət/ n a group of inspectors

in·spi·ra·tion /ínspə ráysh'n/ n 1 the stimulus to do creative work 2 a person or thing that inspires somebody 3 creativeness 4 a good idea 5 supposed divine influence —**in·spi·ra·tion·al** adj

in·spire /in spír/ (-spired, -spir·ing) vt 1 stimulate somebody to greater effort, enthusiasm, or creativity 2 arouse a particular feeling —**in·spired** adj

inst., Inst. abbr institute

in·sta·bil·i·ty /ínstə bíllətee/ n 1 the quality of being unstable or unpredictable 2 lack of steadiness or firmness

~~instalation~~ incorrect spelling of **installation**

⚡ **in·stall** /in stáwl/, **in·stal** (-stalled, -stall·ing) vt 1 fit or connect equipment and make it ready for use 2 load software onto a computer 3 place somebody in an official post —**in·stall·er** n

in·stal·la·tion /ínstə láysh'n/ n 1 the process of installing equipment 2 something that has been installed 3 a military base 4 the appointment of somebody to a position

in·stall·ment /in stáwlmənt/, **in·stal·ment** n 1 a partial repayment 2 a part in a series

in·stall·ment plan n a credit system

in·stance /ínstənss/ n 1 an example 2 an occurrence ■ vt (-stanced, -stanc·ing) offer or serve as an example

in·stant /ínstənt/ adj 1 happening immediately, without delay o an instant dislike 2 in a form that is quickly and easily prepared o instant cocoa 3 achieved suddenly and effortlessly o an instant success ■ n 1 a very short time 2 a moment in time

> **ORIGIN Instant** goes back to a Latin verb meaning "be present." Its original sense in English was "urgent," and it later also meant "current" and "imminent." The modern sense "happening immediately" did not develop until the late 16C.

in·stan·ta·ne·ous /ínstən táynee əss/ adj 1 happening immediately 2 indicating the value of a varying quantity at a given instant —**in·stan·ta·ne·i·ty** /in stàntə neè ətee, ìnstəntə-/ n —**in·stan·ta·ne·ous·ly** adv

in·stant·ly /in stəntlee/ adv immediately ■ conj as soon as

in·stant mes·sag·ing n a system for electronic communication by means of live e-mail or chat rooms

in·stant re·play n an immediate playback of a videotape, especially of a sports play

in·stead /in stéd/ adv in somebody's or something's place ◊ **instead of** as an alternative to or substitute for

in·step /in stèp/ n the upper part of the foot between the ankle and toes

in·sti·gate /ínsti gàyt/ (-gat·ed, -gat·ing) vt
1 get a process started 2 start trouble
—in·sti·ga·tion /ínsti gáysh'n/ n
—in·sti·ga·tor n

in·still /in stíl/, **in·stil** (-stilled, -still·ing) vt
1 introduce something such as an idea or
principle to somebody's mind by repetition 2 pour a liquid into something drop
by drop —in·still·ment n

in·stinct /ín stíngkt/ n 1 an inborn pattern of
behavior 2 a strong natural impulse
—in·stinc·tive /in stíngtiv/ adj
—in·stinc·tive·ly adv —in·stinc·tive·ness n
—in·stinc·tu·al /in stíngkchoo əl/ adj

in·sti·tute /ínsti toòt/ vt (-tut·ed, -tut·ing) 1 start
or initiate formally 2 set up or establish
■ n 1 an organization for promoting something such as an art or science 2 an educational institution, especially for technical
subjects 3 a seminar

in·sti·tu·tion /ínsti toósh'n/ n 1 a large and
influential organization 2 an established
practice o the institution of marriage 3 the
initiation or establishment of something
4 a long-established person or thing (infml)
5 a place where people who are mentally
or physically challenged are cared for
—in·sti·tu·tion·al adj

in·sti·tu·tion·al·ize /ínsti toòshən'l īz/ (-ized,
-iz·ing) vt 1 put into an institution such as
a hospital or prison 2 make an accepted
part of a large organization or society
—in·sti·tu·tion·al·i·za·tion /ínsti toòshən'li
záysh'n/ n

in·sti·tu·tion·al·ized /ínstə toòshən'l īzd,
-toòshnə īzd/ adj unable to think and act
independently outside an institution such
as a prison

in·store adj within a store o an in-store deli

in·struct /in strúkt/ v 1 vti train or teach 2 vt
give an order to 3 vt give information to ◊
See note at **teach**

in·struc·tion /in strúkshən/ n 1 teaching, or
the facts and skills taught 2 an order or
command ■ **in·struc·tions** npl information
on how to use or make something
—in·struc·tion·al adj

in·struc·tive /in strúktiv/ adj providing useful
information or insight —in·struc·tive·ly
adv —in·struc·tive·ness n

in·struc·tor /in strúktər/ n 1 a teacher or trainer
2 a low-ranking college teacher
—in·struc·tor·ship n

in·stru·ment /ínstrəmənt/ n 1 a tool or mechanical device, especially one for precise
work 2 an object used to produce music
3 a measuring device 4 a means of doing
something 5 a legal document (fml)

in·stru·men·tal /ínstrə mént'l/ adj 1 for or
played by musical instruments, not voices
2 important in having achieved a result
■ n a piece of music played by instruments
—in·stru·men·tal·ly adv

in·stru·men·tal·ist /ínstrə mént'list/ n somebody who plays a musical instrument

in·stru·men·ta·tion /ínstrəmən táysh'n, -men-
/ n 1 the arrangement of music for instruments 2 equipment for the control or
operation of something

in·stru·ment pan·el n a mounted set of
control devices

in·sub·or·di·nate /ínsə báwrd'nət/ adj disobedient or rebellious —in·sub·or·di·na·
tion /ínsə bawrd'n áysh'n/ n

in·sub·stan·tial /ín səb stánsh'l/ adj 1 not very
large, solid, or strong 2 not tangible or real

in·suf·fer·a·ble /in súffərəb'l/ adj unbearable
—in·suf·fer·a·bly adv

in·suf·fi·cient /ínsə físh'nt/ adj not adequate
to satisfy a purpose or standard
—in·suf·fi·cien·cy /in súf·fi·cient·ly adv

in·su·lar /ínsələr, ínsyələr/ adj 1 limited in
outlook 2 of islands —in·su·lar·ism n
—in·su·lar·i·ty /ínsə lérrətee, ínsyə-/ n

in·su·late /ínsə làyt, ínsyə-/ (-lat·ed, -lat·ing) vt
1 protect or isolate somebody from something 2 prevent or reduce the flow of heat,
electricity, or sound from or through something —in·su·la·tor n

in·su·la·tion /ínsə láysh'n, ínsyə-/ n 1 material
used to insulate something 2 the process
of insulating something

in·su·lin /ínsəlin/ n a hormone that regulates
the glucose level in blood

in·sult v /in súlt/ 1 vti do or say something
rude or insensitive to somebody 2 vt show
a lack of respect for ■ n /in súlt/ 1 a rude or
insensitive remark or action that offends
somebody 2 something that shows a lack
or respect —in·sult·ing adj —in·sult·ing·ly
adv

in·su·per·a·ble /in soòpərəb'l/ adj impossible
to overcome —in·su·per·a·bly adv

in·sup·port·a·ble /ínsə páwrtəb'l/ adj 1 impossible to endure 2 unjustifiable
—in·sup·port·a·bly adv

in·sur·ance /in shoóronss/ n 1 financial protection against loss or harm 2 a payment
made to obtain insurance 3 the insurance
business 4 a means of protection

in·sur·ance pol·i·cy n a contract providing
insurance

in·sure /in shoór/ (-sured, -sur·ing) v 1 vti cover
something with insurance 2 vt = **ensure**
—in·sur·a·ble adj —in·sured adj, n
—in·sur·er n

~~insurence~~ incorrect spelling of **insurance**

in·sur·gent /in súrjənt/ n 1 a rebel against
authority, especially one involved in an uprising 2 a political party member who
rebels against party leadership
—in·sur·gence n —in·sur·gent adj

in·sur·mount·a·ble /ínsər mówntəb'l/ adj too
great to overcome —in·sur·mount·a·bil·i·ty
/ínsər mowntə bíllətee/ n —in·sur·mount·a·ble

in·sur·rec·tion /ínsə rékshən/ n rebellion against a country's government or rulers —**in·sur·rec·tion·al** adj —**in·sur·rec·tion·ism** n —**in·sur·rec·tion·ist** n, adj

⚡ **int** abbr international organization (in Internet addresses)

int. abbr 1 interest 2 also **Int.** international 3 intransitive

in·tact /in tákt/ adj 1 whole and undamaged 2 with all the necessary parts —**in·tact·ness** n

in·ta·glio /in tállyō, in taályō/ (pl -**glios** or -**gli** /-tállyee/) n a design carved into stone or hard metal

in·take /ín tàyk/ n 1 an amount taken in 2 the act of taking something in 3 an opening through which fluid passes

in·tan·gi·ble /in tánjəb'l/ adj 1 not able to be touched or seen 2 hard to define or describe —**in·tan·gi·bil·i·ty** /in tànjə bíllətee/ n —**in·tan·gi·ble** n —**in·tan·gi·bly** adv

in·tan·gi·ble as·set n a valuable but unquantifiable business asset such as goodwill

in·te·ger /íntəjər/ n a positive or negative whole number

in·te·gral /íntəgrəl, in téggrəl/ adj 1 necessary or constituent 2 composed of parts that together form a whole 3 with no parts missing —**in·te·gral·ly** adv

in·te·grate /íntə gràyt/ (-**grat·ed**, -**grat·ing**) v 1 vti fit in with a group and its activities 2 vt combine parts or objects into a functioning whole 3 vt make a group, community, or place and its opportunities available to all, regardless of race, ethnic group, religion, gender, or social class —**in·te·gra·ble** adj —**in·te·grat·ed** adj —**in·te·gra·tion** /íntə gráysh'n/ n

⚡ **in·te·grat·ed cir·cuit** n a tiny complex of electronic components on a wafer of semiconducting material —**in·te·grat·ed cir·cuit·ry** n

⚡ **in·te·gra·tor** /íntə gràytər/ n 1 a computer component that solves equations 2 somebody or something that integrates

in·teg·ri·ty /in téggrətee/ n 1 the possession of high moral principles or professional standards 2 the state of being complete and undivided (fml) 3 the state of being sound and undamaged (fml)

in·teg·u·ment /in téggyəmənt/ n an outer protective layer of an organism

~~intellectual~~ incorrect spelling of **intellectual**
~~intelligence~~ incorrect spelling of **intelligence**

in·tel·lect /ínt'l èkt/ n 1 mental ability 2 an intelligent person

in·tel·lec·tu·al /ínt'l ékchoo əl/ adj 1 of thought and reasoning 2 intelligent and knowledgeable 3 for intelligent people ■ n an intellectual person —**in·tel·lec·tu·al·ly** adv

in·tel·lec·tu·al·ize /ínt'l ékchoo ə lìz/ (-**ized**, -**iz·ing**) vti consider or explain something using reasoning alone —**in·tel·lec·tu·al·i·za·tion** /ínt'l ékchoo əli záysh'n/ n

in·tel·lec·tu·al prop·er·ty n original creative work that can be protected by law

in·tel·li·gence /in téllijənss/ n 1 the ability to think and learn 2 secret information, or its collection

in·tel·li·gence quo·tient n full form of **IQ**

⚡ **in·tel·li·gent** /in téllijənt/ adj 1 having a high level of intelligence 2 sensible or rational 3 able to store and process data electronically —**in·tel·li·gent·ly** adv

---

SYNONYMS intelligent, bright, quick, smart, clever, able, gifted CORE MEANING: having the ability to learn and understand easily

---

in·tel·li·gent·si·a /in tèlli jéntsee ə/ n the most intellectual or highly educated members of a society

in·tel·li·gi·ble /in téllijəb'l/ adj understandable —**in·tel·li·gi·bil·i·ty** /in tèllijə bíllətee/ n —**in·tel·li·gi·bly** adv

in·tem·per·ate /in témpərət, -prət/ adj 1 drinking alcohol to excess 2 lacking self-control —**in·tem·per·ance** n —**in·tem·per·ate·ly** adv

in·tend /in ténd/ vt 1 mean to do 2 do, say, or produce for a particular purpose

in·ten·dant /in téndənt/ n an administrative official in some countries

in·tend·ed /in téndəd/ adj 1 aimed at or designed for 2 planned for the future 3 said or done deliberately ■ n a future husband or wife (dated or humorous)

in·tense /in téns/ adj 1 extreme in a way that can be felt ○ intense heat 2 involving great effort or activity 3 narrowly focused ○ an intense stare —**in·tense·ly** adv —**in·tense·ness** n —**in·ten·si·ty** /in ténsitee/ n

in·ten·si·fy /in ténsə fì/ (-**fied**, -**fies**) vti make or become greater or more intense —**in·ten·si·fi·ca·tion** /in tènsəfi káysh'n/ n ◊ See note at **increase**

in·ten·sive /in ténsiv/ adj 1 involving concentrated effort 2 making heavy use of something (often in combination) ○ capital-intensive 3 describes a modifier, e.g., "extremely" that emphasizes the word it modifies ■ n also **in·ten·si·fi·er** an intensive modifier —**in·ten·sive·ly** adv —**in·ten·sive·ness** n

in·ten·sive care n a hospital department for patients who need constant monitoring

in·tent /in tént/ n 1 a plan or purpose (fml) 2 somebody's state of mind when committing or planning a crime ■ adj 1 with fixed attention 2 determined —**in·tent·ly** adv —**in·tent·ness** n ◊ **to all intents and purposes** in effect

in·ten·tion /in ténsh'n/ n 1 an aim or objective 2 the quality of having a purpose in mind ○ act without intention

in·ten·tion·al /in ténshən'l/ adj done on purpose —**in·ten·tion·al·i·ty** /in tènshə nállətee/ n —**in·ten·tion·al·ly** adv

in·ter /in túr/ (-terred, -ter·ring) vt bury in a grave or tomb

inter- prefix 1 between, among o intercut 2 mutual, reciprocal o interchange

in·ter·act /ìntər ákt/ vi 1 act on each other 2 communicate or work with somebody else or together

in·ter·ac·tion /ìntər ákshən/ n 1 the process of interacting 2 any of the forces that exist between elementary particles, namely gravitational, electromagnetic, strong, and weak —**in·ter·ac·tion·al** adj

⚡ **in·ter·ac·tive** /ìntər áktiv/ adj 1 communicating or collaborating 2 allowing or involving user-machine communication —**in·ter·ac·tive·ly** adv —**in·ter·ac·tiv·i·ty** /ìntər ak tívvətee/ n

in·ter a·li·a /ìntər áylee ə, -áalee ə/ adv among other things

in·ter·breed /ìntər bréed/ (-bred /-bréd/) vti 1 mate with a member of a different breed or species 2 breed or make something breed within a closed group or a narrow range of types

in·ter·cede /ìntər seéd/ (-ced·ed, -ced·ing) vi 1 plead or speak on somebody's behalf 2 mediate in a dispute

in·ter·cept /ìntər sépt/ v 1 vti prevent people or objects from reaching their destination or target 2 vt in sports, get possession of the ball when it was intended for an opponent —**in·ter·cept** n —**in·ter·cep·tion** n

in·ter·cep·tor /ìntər séptər/, **in·ter·cept·er** n a fast fighter plane or guided missile designed to intercept enemy aircraft or missiles

in·ter·ces·sion /ìntər sésh'n/ n 1 the act of interceding on somebody's behalf 2 a prayer on another's behalf —**in·ter·ces·sion·al** adj —**in·ter·ces·sor** n

in·ter·change vti /ìntər cháynj/ (-changed, -chang·ing) 1 switch places or the places of two things 2 alternate with each other in a series ■ n /ìntər cháynj/ 1 an exchange of ideas or information 2 the act of alternating or changing places 3 a highway intersection at which vehicles do not cross other traffic to change direction

in·ter·change·a·ble /ìntər cháynjəb'l/ adj usable instead of another or each other —**in·ter·change·a·bly** /ìntər cháynjəblee/ adv

in·ter·change fee n a fee paid by one bank to another to cover cardholder costs until payment is made

in·ter·cit·y /ìntər síttee/ adj happening or traveling between cities

in·ter·col·le·giate /ìntər kə leéjee ət/ adj happening between colleges

in·ter·com /ìntər kòm/ n a communication system between parts of a building

in·ter·com·mu·ni·cate /ìntər kə myoóni kàyt/ (-cat·ed, -cat·ing) vi 1 talk to each other 2 connect and have access to each other o intercommunicating hotel rooms —**in·ter·com·mu·ni·ca·tion** /ìntərkə myoóni káysh'n/ n —**in·ter·com·mu·ni·ca·tive** adj

in·ter·con·nect /ìntər kə nékt/ vti 1 join onto one another 2 relate two or more things —**in·ter·con·nec·tion** n

in·ter·con·ti·nen·tal /ìntər kontə nént'l/ adj happening or traveling between continents

in·ter·course /ìntər káwrs/ n 1 penetration of a woman's vagina by a man's penis 2 mutual dealings

in·ter·cut /ìntər kút/ (-cut, -cut·ting) vt alternate scenes during editing of a movie to show events occurring simultaneously

in·ter·de·nom·i·na·tion·al /ìntər di nòmmi náyshən'l, -shnəl/ adj involving different religious denominations

in·ter·de·part·men·tal /ìntər deè paart mént'l/ adj involving different departments

in·ter·de·pend·ent /ìntər di péndənt/ adj 1 depending on each other to exist 2 relying on mutual support or cooperation —**in·ter·de·pend** vi —**in·ter·de·pend·ence** n —**in·ter·de·pend·ent·ly** adv

in·ter·dict n /ìntər díkt/ an official order prohibiting something ■ vt /ìntər díkt/ 1 ban by law 2 prevent somebody from entering illegally —**in·ter·dic·tion** n

in·ter·dis·ci·pli·nar·y /ìntər díssəplə nèrree/ adj involving different subjects or fields of study

in·ter·est /íntrəst/ n 1 curiosity or concern 2 a power, quality, or aspect that attracts attention 3 an enjoyable activity (often pl) 4 the good or advantage of something o in the interests of peace 5 a borrowing charge or payment for a loan 6 a share in something ■ **in·ter·ests** npl a group of people, especially influential people, who share a goal ■ vt 1 get the attention of 2 cause to want to have something

in·ter·est·ed /íntrəstəd/ adj 1 curious or concerned 2 wanting something 3 affected by or involved in something —**in·ter·est·ed·ly** adv

in·ter·est·ing /íntrəsting/ adj 1 arousing curiosity or attention 2 not boring —**in·ter·est·ing·ly** adv

⚡ **in·ter·face** n /ìntər fàyss/ 1 a surface or point forming a common boundary 2 a point of interaction 3 a common boundary between devices, or a person and a device, across which data flows 4 a piece of software that allows communication between devices or between a computer and operator ■ vti /ìntər fàyss, ìntər fáyss/ (-faced, -fac·ing) 1 meet or join at a common boundary 2 interact —**in·ter·fa·cial** /ìntər fáysh'l/ adj

~~interference~~ incorrect spelling of **interference**

in·ter·fere /ìntər feér/ (-fered, -fer·ing) vi 1 delay or obstruct the course of something

2 meddle in the affairs of others **3** cause electronic interference **4** obstruct, block, or hinder illegally an opponent in a sport —**in·ter·fer·ing** adj—**in·ter·fer·ing·ly** adv

in·ter·fer·ence /ɪntər féerənss/ n **1** meddling in other people's affairs **2** the delay or obstruction of the course of something **3** the illegal interfering with an opponent in a sport **4** in football, the legal blocking of defensive players **5** a signal that disrupts radio, telephone, or television reception —**in·ter·fer·en·tial** /ɪntərfə rénshəl/ adj

in·ter·fer·on /ɪntər feér òn/ n a protein produced by cells in response to virus infection that inhibits viral replication

in·ter·ga·lac·tic /ɪntərgə láktik/ adj occurring, moving, or situated between galaxies

in·ter·gov·ern·men·tal /ɪntər gùvvərn mént'l/ adj between two or more governments

in·ter·im /ɪntərim/ adj **1** having a temporary effect **2** holding office until a permanent replacement can be elected or appointed ■ n the intervening time between events

in·te·ri·or /in teéeree ər/ n **1** the inside of something **2** the inside of a building or room **3** the part of a country that is farthest from the coast **4** **In·te·ri·or** the internal affairs of a country ■ adj **1** located inside **2** central or inland **3** occurring in the mind **4** **In·te·ri·or** of the internal affairs of a country

in·te·ri·or dec·o·ra·tion, in·te·ri·or de·sign n **1** the planning of the decoration and furnishings of a room or building **2** the decorations and furnishings of a room or building —**in·te·ri·or dec·o·ra·tor** n

in·ter·ject /ɪntər jékt/ vti interrupt with a comment —**in·ter·jec·to·ry** adj

in·ter·jec·tion /ɪntər jékshən/ n **1** an exclamation expressing an emotion **2** a comment made abruptly —**in·ter·jec·tion·al** adj

in·ter·lace /ɪntər láyss/ (-laced, -lac·ing) v **1** vti weave together **2** vt break up the flow or monotony of something with something else —**in·ter·lace·ment** n

in·ter·lard /ɪntər laárd/ vt vary or interrupt speech or writing by inserting contrasting material

in·ter·leave /ɪntər leév/ (-leaved, -leav·ing) vt add extra pages between the pages of a book

in·ter·link /ɪntər língk/ vti connect in several ways

in·ter·lock /ɪntər lók/ vti **1** fit together closely **2** operate or cause to operate as a unit

in·ter·loc·u·tor /ɪntər lókyətər/ n a participant in a discussion or conversation (fml)

in·ter·lop·er /ɪntər lṓpər/ n **1** an intruder **2** somebody who interferes in other people's affairs —**in·ter·lope** vi

in·ter·lude /ɪntər lṓod/ n **1** a period of time during which something different happens

2 a short piece of entertainment performed during a break

in·ter·mar·ry /ɪntər márree/ (-ried, -ries) vi **1** marry a member of another group **2** marry within a group —**in·ter·mar·riage** n

in·ter·me·di·ar·y /ɪntər meédee èrree/ n (pl -ies) **1** a go-between or mediator **2** a means or medium for bringing something about ■ adj **1** mediating **2** lying in between

in·ter·me·di·ate[1] /ɪntər meédee ət/ adj being between two different states or extremes —**in·ter·me·di·ate** n —**in·ter·me·di·ate·ly** adv

in·ter·me·di·ate[2] /ɪntər meédee àyt/ (-at·ed, -at·ing) vi act as a go-between or mediator

in·ter·ment /in túrmənt/ n the burial of a corpse

in·ter·mez·zo /ɪntər mét sṑ/ (pl -zos or -zi /-métsee/) n **1** a short movement in a longer musical work **2** a short piece of music

in·ter·mi·na·ble /in túrminəb'l/ adj seemingly endless —**in·ter·mi·na·bly** adv

in·ter·min·gle /ɪntər míng g'l/ (-gled, -gling), **in·ter·mix** vti mix together

in·ter·mis·sion /ɪntər mísh'n/ n **1** a break in a performance **2** a pause in an activity

in·ter·mit·tent /ɪntər mítt'nt/ adj happening from time to time —**in·ter·mit·tent·ly** adv ◊ See note at **periodic**

in·tern /ɪntərn/ n also **in·terne 1** a junior doctor in a hospital **2** a trainee ■ v **1** vi work as an intern **2** vt detain in confinement on grounds of national security —**in·tern·ment** n —**in·tern·ship** n

in·ter·nal /in túrn'l/ adj **1** located inside o internal organs **2** intended for use inside **3** inherent or natural **4** occurring within a country **5** occurring within the mind —**in·ter·nal·ly** adv

in·ter·nal-com·bus·tion en·gine n an engine that burns fuel in chambers within it

in·ter·nal·ize /in túrn'l ìz/ (-ized, -iz·ing) vt **1** adopt others' beliefs or attitudes **2** keep a problem to yourself and not express it —**in·ter·nal·i·za·tion** /in tùrn'li záysh'n/ n

in·ter·nal med·i·cine n the branch of medicine dealing with the internal organs

In·ter·nal Rev·e·nue Ser·vice n the US tax collection agency

in·ter·na·tion·al /ɪntər náshən'l, -náshnəl/ adj **1** involving several countries or people from several countries **2** crossing national boundaries ■ n **1** an international organization **2** **In·ter·na·tion·al** any of various international socialist organizations —**in·ter·na·tion·al·i·ty** /ɪntər nashə nállətee/ n —**in·ter·na·tion·al·ly** adv

In·ter·na·tion·al A·tom·ic Time n a precise system of measuring time in which a second is defined in terms of atomic events

In·ter·na·tion·al Date Line *n* an internationally agreed imaginary line where the date changes by one day

in·ter·na·tion·al·ism /ĭntər náshən'l ĭzzəm, -náshnə ĭizzəm/ *n* cooperation between countries

in·ter·na·tion·al·ize /ĭntər náshən'l ĭz, -náshnə ĭiz/ (-ized, -iz·ing) *vt* 1 make international 2 put under international control or protection —**in·ter·na·tion·al·i·za·tion** /ĭntər nash'nəli záysh'n, -nàshnəli záysh'n/ *n*

in·ter·na·tion·al re·la·tions *npl* relations between countries ■ *n* the study of relations between countries (+ *sing verb*)

in·terne *n* = intern

in·ter·nec·ine /ĭntər né sèen, -nèe sèen/ *adj* 1 occurring within a group or organization 2 mutually destructive

ORIGIN The original meaning of **internecine** is "attended by great slaughter." Its modern connotations of "conflict within a group" arose from the standard interpretation of *inter-* as "among, between," but in fact in the case of Latin *internecinus* it was being used simply to add emphasis.

in·tern·ee /ĭntər nèe/ *n* a prisoner who has been interned

⚡**In·ter·net** /ĭntər nèt/ *n* a global computer network giving access to services such as e-mail and the World Wide Web

⚡**In·ter·net ho·tel** *n* a place with many computers handling Internet traffic for businesses

⚡**In·ter·net pro·to·col** *n* a data transmission standard for the Internet

⚡**In·ter·net ser·vice pro·vid·er** *n* a business offering Internet access to subscribers

in·ter·nist /ĭn túrnist/ *n* a specialist in diseases affecting the internal organs

in·ter·pen·e·trate /ĭntər pénnə tràyt/ (-trat·ed, -trat·ing) *vti* mix or weave together thoroughly —**in·ter·pen·e·tra·tion** /ĭntər pènnə tráysh'n/ *n*

in·ter·per·son·al /ĭntər púrsən'l/ *adj* of relationships between people —**in·ter·per·son·al·ly** *adv*

in·ter·plan·e·tar·y /ĭntər plánnə tèrree/ *adj* between planets

in·ter·play /ĭntər plày/ *n* mutual effect and interaction

In·ter·pol /ĭntər pàwl/ *n* an association of national police forces that promotes international cooperation in apprehending criminals. Full form **International Criminal Police Organization**

in·ter·po·late /ĭn túrpə làyt/ (-lat·ed, -lat·ing) *vt* 1 insert something into something else 2 add words to a text —**in·ter·po·la·tion** /ĭn túrpə láysh'n/ *n*

in·ter·pose /ĭntər pōz/ (-posed, -pos·ing) *v* 1 *vti* interrupt by saying something when somebody else is speaking 2 *vt* place something

or yourself between people or things —**in·ter·po·si·tion** /ĭntərpə zĭsh'n/ *n*

~~interpretation~~ incorrect spelling of **interpretation**

in·ter·pret /ĭn túrprət/ *v* 1 *vt* establish or explain the meaning of something 2 *vt* ascribe a meaning to something o *interpreted her response as a rejection* 3 *vt* perform something in a way that reflects your understanding of it or feelings about it 4 *vti* translate what somebody is saying in another language —**in·ter·pret·a·ble** *adj* —**in·ter·pre·ta·tive** *adj* —**in·ter·pret·er** *n* —**in·ter·pre·tive** *n*

in·ter·pre·ta·tion /ĭn túrprə táysh'n/ *n* 1 the establishment of the meaning of something 2 an ascription of a particular meaning to something —**in·ter·pre·ta·tion·al** *adj*

in·ter·ra·cial /ĭntər ráysh'l/ *adj* occurring between or involving different races —**in·ter·ra·cial·ly** *adv*

in·ter·reg·num /ĭntər régnəm/ (*pl* -nums *or* -na /-régnə/) *n* a time between one reign and the next —**in·ter·reg·nal** *adj*

in·ter·re·late /ĭntər láyt/ (-lat·ed, -lat·ing) *vti* have or bring into a relationship —**in·ter·re·la·tion** *n*

⚡**in·ter·ro·gate** /ĭn térrə gàyt/ (-gat·ed, -gat·ing) *vt* 1 question somebody thoroughly 2 request a response from a computer device or program —**in·ter·ro·ga·tion** /ĭn tèrrə gáysh'n/ *n* —**in·ter·ro·ga·tor** *n* ◊ See note at **question**

in·ter·rog·a·tive /ĭntə róggətiv/ *adj* 1 questioning 2 consisting of or used in asking a question o *an interrogative pronoun* ■ *n* 1 a word used to form a question 2 the form of a sentence that is used to ask a question —**in·ter·rog·a·tive·ly** *adv*

in·ter·rupt /ĭntə rúpt/ *v* 1 *vti* stop a speaker or a speaker's utterance 2 *vti* disturb somebody or somebody's work 3 *vt* cause something to stop 4 *vt* take a break from doing something —**in·ter·rup·tion** *n*

in·ter·scho·las·tic /ĭntər skə lástik/ *adj* occurring between schools

in·ter·sect /ĭntər sékt/ *vti* 1 cross 2 overlap

in·ter·sec·tion /ĭntər sékshən/ *n* 1 the act of intersecting 2 a place where two roads or paths cross 3 a point or set of points common to intersecting geometric figures —**in·ter·sec·tion·al** *adj*

in·ter·sperse /ĭntər spúrs/ (-spersed, -spers·ing) *vt* 1 break the continuity of something with something else 2 put something here and there in or among something else —**in·ter·sper·sion** *n*

in·ter·state /ĭntər stàyt/ *adj* occurring between or connecting states ■ *n* a major highway between cities

in·ter·stel·lar /ĭntər stéllər/ *adj* occurring between stars

in·ter·stice /ĭn túrstiss/ *n* a small space between two things or parts

⚡ **in·ter·sti·tial** /ĭntər stĭsh'l/ *adj* of interstices ■ *n* an unsolicited advertisement on the World Wide Web that briefly precedes a selected page

in·ter·twine /ĭntər twīn/ (**-twined, -twin·ing**) *vti* **1** twist together **2** link together —**in·ter·twine·ment** *n*

~~interrupt~~ incorrect spelling of **interrupt**

in·ter·val /ĭntərvəl/ *n* **1** an intervening period of time **2** an intervening distance **3** a difference in musical pitch between two notes

in·ter·vene /ĭntər veĕn/ *vi* **1** act to change what is happening **2** prevent or delay something by happening **3** elapse before an event or time ○ *the intervening years* —**in·ter·ven·tion** /ĭntər vĕnshən/ *n*

in·ter·ven·tion·ism /ĭntər vĕnshə nĭzzəm/ *n* **1** involvement in another country's affairs **2** government interference in economic matters —**in·ter·ven·tion·ist** *n, adj*

in·ter·view /ĭntər vyoo/ *n* a meeting for asking somebody questions ■ *n* **1** *vt* ask somebody questions in an interview **2** *vi* perform in an interview ○ *interviews well* —**in·ter·view·ee** /ĭntər vyoo eĕ/ *n* —**in·ter·view·er** *n*

in·ter·war /ĭntər wáwr/ *adj* occurring between wars

in·ter·weave /ĭntər weĕv/ (**-wove /-wóv/, -woven /-wóv'n/, -weav·ing**) *vti* **1** weave together **2** combine

in·tes·tate /ĭn té stàyt, ĭn tĕstət/ *adj* leaving no legally valid will —**in·tes·ta·cy** /ĭn tĕstəssee/ *n*

in·tes·tine /ĭn téstin/ *n* a part of the digestive tract between the stomach and the anus or an equivalent structure (*often pl*) —**in·tes·ti·nal** *adj*

in·ti·fa·da /ĭnti faáda/ *n* the Palestinian uprising in the West Bank and Gaza Strip that started in 1987

in·ti·mate[1] /ĭntəmət/ *adj* **1** of a close personal relationship **2** private and personal **3** involving or having a sexual relationship (*euphemistic*) **4** thorough and based on personal experience ■ *n* a close friend —**in·ti·ma·cy** *n* —**in·ti·mate·ly** *adv*

in·ti·mate[2] /ĭntə màyt/ (**-mat·ed, -mat·ing**) *vt* hint quietly or subtly —**in·ti·ma·tion** /ĭntə máysh'n/ *n*

in·tim·i·date /ĭn tímmə dàyt/ (**-dat·ed, -dat·ing**) *vt* **1** persuade or dissuade by frightening **2** cause to feel overawed or inadequate —**in·tim·i·dat·ing·ly** *adv* —**in·tim·i·da·tion** /ĭn tímmə dáysh'n/ *n*

in·to /(*stressed*) /ĭntoo/ (*unstressed*) /ĭntə/ *prep* **1** indicates movement to the interior or inner part ○ *came into the house* **2** indicates movement to the midst of ○ *leapt into the water* **3** indicates beginning to do or be involved in ○ *burst into action* ○ *went into marketing* **4** indicates contact with ○ *bumped into them* **5** indicates the result of change ○ *turned into a frog* **6** indicates the result

of influence or persuasion ○ *talked me into going* **7** indicates division ○ *9 into 63 equals 7.* ○ *divided the cake into six* **8** enthusiastic about (*infml*) ○ *really into tennis*

in·tol·er·a·ble /ĭn tóllərəb'l/ *adj* **1** impossible to bear **2** very unpleasant —**in·tol·er·a·bly** *adv*

in·tol·er·ant /ĭn tóllərənt/ *adj* **1** easily annoyed **2** not willing to accept cultural or ethnic differences —**in·tol·er·ance** *n* —**in·tol·er·ant·ly** *adv*

~~intolerent~~ incorrect spelling of **intolerant**

in·to·na·tion /ĭntə náysh'n/ *n* **1** the rising and falling pitch of the voice **2** an intoning —**in·to·na·tion·al** *adj*

in·tone /ĭn tón/ (**-toned, -ton·ing**) *vt* say something in a solemn or chanting way (*fml*) —**in·tone·ment** *n*

in to·to /ĭn tótō/ *adv* as a whole

in·tox·i·cant /ĭn tóksikənt/ *n* an intoxicating substance —**in·tox·i·cant** *adj*

in·tox·i·cate /ĭn tóksi kàyt/ (**-cat·ed, -cat·ing**) *vt* **1** make drunk or stupefied **2** make highly excited —**in·tox·i·cat·ed** *adj* —**in·tox·i·cat·ed·ly** *adv* —**in·tox·i·cat·ing** *adj* —**in·tox·i·ca·tion** /ĭn tóksi káysh'n/ *n*

intra- *prefix* within or inside ○ *intracompany*

In·tra·coas·tal Wa·ter·way /ĭntrə kóst'l-/ system of protected waterways in the E and SE United States. Length 2,485 mi./4,000 km.

in·tra·com·pa·ny /ĭntrə kúmpənee/ *adj* occurring within a company

in·trac·ta·ble /ĭn tráktəb'l/ *adj* **1** strong-willed and rebellious (*fml*) **2** difficult to deal with or solve —**in·trac·ta·bly** *adv* ◊ See note at **unruly**

in·tra·mu·ral /ĭntrə myoorəl/ *adj* occurring within a school or other institution

⚡ **in·tra·net** /ĭntrə nèt/ *n* a computer network within an organization

in·tran·si·gent /ĭn tránsəjənt, -zəjənt/, **in·tran·si·geant** /ĭn-/ *adj* refusing to compromise —**in·tran·si·gence** *n*

in·tran·si·tive /ĭn tránzətiv/ *adj* describes a verb that does not require a direct object to complete its meaning —**in·tran·si·tive** *n* —**in·tran·si·tive·ly** *adv*

in·tra·pre·neur /ĭntrə prə núr, -noŏr/ *n* an entrepreneur within a company —**in·tra·pre·neur·i·al** *adj*

in·tra·state /ĭntrə stáyt/ *adj* within one state

in·tra·u·ter·ine /ĭntrə yootərin, -rĭn/ *adj* occurring or designed for use inside the womb

in·tra·u·ter·ine de·vice *n* a contraceptive device inserted into the womb

in·tra·ve·nous /ĭntrə veĕnəss/ *adj* **1** occurring within or administered into a vein **2** used in administering fluids or drugs into the veins —**in·tra·ve·nous·ly** *adv*

in-tray *n* an in-box

in·trep·id /in tréppid/ *adj* fearless and persistent —**in·tre·pid·i·ty** /ìntrə píddətee/ *n* —**in·trep·id·ly** *adv*

intrest incorrect spelling of **interest**

in·tri·cate /íntrikət/ *adj* 1 with many small or detailed parts 2 complex and difficult to understand or resolve —**in·tri·ca·cy** *n* —**in·tri·cate·ly** *adv*

in·trigue *n* /ín treeg, in treeg/ 1 secret plotting 2 a secret plot ∎ *v* /in treeg/ (**-trigued, -trigu·ing**) 1 *vt* interest or arouse the curiosity of 2 *vi* scheme —**in·trigu·er** *n* —**in·trigu·ing·ly** *adv*

in·trin·sic /in trínzik, -sik/, **in·trin·si·cal** /-zik'l, -sik'l/ *adj* 1 basic and essential to what something is 2 by or in itself —**in·trin·si·cal·ly** *adv*

in·tro /íntrō/ *n* an introduction (*infml*)

intro- *prefix* 1 in, into ○ *introduce* 2 inward ○ *introvert*

in·tro·duce /íntrə dóoss, -dyóoss/ (**-duced, -duc·ing**) *vt* 1 present yourself or another person to a stranger 2 bring in something new 3 cause somebody to experience something new 4 preface something with something else 5 talk about something for the first time

in·tro·duc·tion /íntrə dúkshən/ *n* 1 an explanatory section at the beginning of a book or other text 2 something giving the basic facts about something 3 the act of introducing somebody or something 4 a first experience

in·tro·duc·to·ry /íntrə dúktəree/ *adj* 1 introducing what is to come 2 providing the basic facts or skills

in·tro·spec·tion /íntrə spéksh'n/ *n* the examination of your own feelings —**in·tro·spec·tive** *adj* —**in·tro·spec·tive·ly** *adv*

in·tro·vert *n* /íntrə vùrt/ 1 a reserved person 2 somebody focusing on his or her own self ∎ *vt* /íntrə vùrt, íntrə vúrt/ turn something inward —**in·tro·ver·sion** /íntrə vúrzh'n, -sh'n/ *n* —**in·tro·vert·ed** *adj*

in·trude /in tróod/ (**-trud·ed, -trud·ing**) *vi* 1 invade somebody's privacy 2 have an unpleasant effect

in·trud·er /in tróodər/ *n* 1 somebody who enters illegally 2 an unwelcome person

in·tru·sion /in tróozh'n/ *n* 1 a disturbance of somebody's peace or privacy 2 something unwelcome —**in·tru·sive** /in tróossiv/ *adj* —**in·tru·sive·ly** *adv*

in·tu·it /in tóo it/ *vt* know instinctively

in·tu·i·tion /íntoo ísh'n, ìntyoo-/ *n* 1 instinctive knowledge, or the ability to know things instinctively 2 something known instinctively —**in·tu·i·tion·al** *adj* —**in·tu·i·tive** /in tóo itiv/ *adj* —**in·tu·i·tive·ly** *adv* —**in·tu·i·tive·ness** *n*

inuendo incorrect spelling of **innuendo**

In·u·it /ínnoo it, -yoo-/ (*pl same or* **-its**), **In·nu·it** *n* 1 a member of an Arctic or Greenlandic people 2 the language of the Inuit people —**In·u·it** *adj*

USAGE The Inuit Circumpolar Conference, held in 1977 in Barrow, Alaska, chose officially to replace the term *Eskimo* with **Inuit** (which means "the real people"). Although *Eskimo* remains in common use, care should be exercised in using this word.

in·un·date /ínnən dàyt/ (**-dat·ed, -dat·ing**) *vt* 1 overwhelm with a huge quantity of things 2 flood with water —**in·un·da·tion** /ínnən dáysh'n/ *n*

in·vade /in vàyd/ (**-vad·ed, -vad·ing**) *v* 1 *vti* enter a country by military force 2 *vt* enter and spread through something, especially causing damage 3 *vt* go somewhere in large numbers ○ *has been invaded by tourists* 4 *vt* spoil something by interrupting or intruding on it ○ *invading our privacy* —**in·vad·er** *n*

in·va·lid¹ /in vállid/ *adj* 1 not legal 2 based on a mistake —**in·va·lid·i·ty** /ìnvə líddətee/ *n* —**in·va·lid·ly** *adv*

in·va·lid² /ínvəlid/ *n* somebody with an incapacitating disease or medical condition —**in·va·lid** *adj*

in·val·i·date /in vállə dàyt/ (**-dat·ed, -dat·ing**) *vt* 1 make not legal 2 show to be wrong or worthless —**in·val·i·da·tion** /in vàllə dáysh'n/ *n* ◊ See note at **nullify**

in·val·u·a·ble /in vállyoo əb'l/ *adj* extremely useful or valuable —**in·val·u·a·bly** *adv*

in·var·i·a·ble /in váiree əb'l/ *adj* never changing ∎ *n* a constant quantity —**in·var·i·a·bil·i·ty** /in vàiree ə bíllətee/ *n* —**in·var·i·a·bly** *adv*

in·va·sion /in váyzh'n/ *n* 1 an entry into a country by military force 2 an arrival in large numbers 3 a spoiling of something by interrupting or intruding on it

in·va·sive /in váyssiv/ *adj* 1 involving military invasion 2 intruding on somebody's privacy or rights —**in·va·sive·ly** *adv*

in·vec·tive /in véktiv/ *n* abusive language (*fml*)

in·veigh /in váy/ *vi* speak out angrily

ORIGIN When first adopted in the late 15C, **inveigh** meant "carry in, introduce." This accords with the etymological meaning of Latin *invehere*, from which it derives. *Vehere* is also the source of *vehicle*. Latin *invehere* had also developed a form meaning "attack, assault with words," and this was taken into English in the early 16C.

in·vei·gle /in váyg'l/ (**-gled, -gling**) *vt* 1 persuade or entice 2 obtain by persuasion —**in·vei·gle·ment** *n*

in·vent /in vént/ *vt* 1 create something new 2 make up something false ○ *invented a reason for being late* —**in·ven·tor** *n*

in·ven·tion /in vénshən/ n 1 a newly created thing 2 the creating of something new

in·ven·tive /in véntiv/ adj 1 skilled at inventing 2 displaying creativity —**in·ven·tive·ly** adv —**in·ven·tive·ness** n

in·ven·to·ry /ínvən tàwree/ n (pl -ries) 1 a list of items 2 a record of a business's assets, or the assets themselves 3 a stock of goods ■ vt (-ried, -ries) make an inventory of

in·verse /in vúrs, ín vùrs/ adj opposite to or reversing something —**in·verse** n —**in·verse·ly** adv

in·ver·sion /in vúrzh'n, -sh'n/ n a reversal of the order or position of the parts of something

in·vert /in vúrt/ vt 1 reverse the order or position of the parts of something 2 make something the opposite of what it was before —**in·vert·ed** adj —**in·vert·i·ble** adj

in·ver·te·brate /in vúrtəbrət, -bràyt/ n an animal without a backbone —**in·ver·te·brate** adj

in·vest /in vést/ v 1 vti use money to buy stocks or bonds 2 vt contribute time or effort to something 3 vt give something a particular quality 4 vt confer something such as authority on a person or group —**in·ves·tor** n

in·ves·ti·gate /in vésti gàyt/ v 1 vt carry out an official examination or inquiry into something 2 vi go and take a look —**in·ves·ti·ga·tion** /in vésti gáysh'n/ n —**in·ves·ti·ga·tive** adj —**in·ves·ti·ga·tor** n

in·ves·ti·ture /in vésta chòor, -chər/ n the formal installation of somebody in an official position

in·vest·ment /in véstmənt/ n 1 the use of money for future profit 2 an amount of money invested 3 something invested in 4 the contribution of time or effort to an activity

in·vest·ment an·a·lyst n a stock exchange researcher

in·vest·ment com·pa·ny n a company holding securities for investment only

in·vest·ment deal·er n Can a broker for an investment company

in·vest·ment trust n a legally constituted group of investors

in·vet·er·ate /in véttərət/ adj 1 doing something habitually 2 firmly established —**in·vet·er·a·cy** n —**in·vet·er·ate·ly** adv

in·vid·i·ous /in víddee əss/ adj 1 involving an unfair distinction 2 unpleasant and likely to cause resentment —**in·vid·i·ous·ly** adv —**in·vid·i·ous·ness** n

in·vig·or·ate /in víggə ràyt/ vt (-at·ed, -at·ing) fill with energy —**in·vig·or·at·ing** adj —**in·vig·or·at·ing·ly** adv —**in·vig·or·a·tion** /in víggə ràysh'n/ n

in·vin·ci·ble /in vínsəb'l/ adj 1 unbeatable 2 too great or difficult to overcome —**in·vin·ci·bil·i·ty** /in vìnsə bíllətee/ n —**in·vin·ci·bly** adv

in·vi·o·la·ble /in vī ələb'l/ adj 1 secure from infringement 2 secure from attack —**in·vi·o·la·bil·i·ty** /in vì ələ bíllətee/ n —**in·vi·o·la·bly** adv

in·vi·o·late /in vī ələt/ adj not subject to detrimental change —**in·vi·o·late·ly** adv

in·vis·i·ble /in vízzəb'l/ adj 1 impossible to see 2 hidden —**in·vis·i·bil·i·ty** /in vízzə bíllətee/ n —**in·vis·i·bly** adv

in·vis·i·ble ink n a liquid used to write things that remain invisible until the paper is treated in some way

in·vi·ta·tion /ínvi táysh'n/ n 1 a spoken or written message inviting somebody 2 the act of inviting —**in·vi·ta·tion·al** adj, n

in·vite vt /in vít/ (-vit·ed, -vit·ing) 1 ask to come somewhere or participate in something 2 welcome 3 provoke ■ n /ín vìt/ an invitation (infml)

in·vit·ing /in víting/ adj suggesting or offering pleasure o an inviting smell —**in·vit·ing·ly** adv

in vi·tro /in veétrō/ adj, adv in an artificial environment such as a test tube

in vi·tro fer·til·i·za·tion n fertilization achieved in laboratory conditions outside a living organism

in·vo·ca·tion /ínvə káysh'n/ n 1 a calling upon a higher power 2 a prayer forming part of a service —**in·vo·ca·tion·al** adj

in·voice /ín vòyss/ n a written record of goods or services provided and a request for payment ■ vt (-voiced, -voic·ing) send an invoice to

in·voke /in vók/ (-voked, -vok·ing) vt 1 call upon a higher power 2 use something in support of an argument or case

in·vol·un·tar·y /in vóllən tèrree/ adj 1 required or done against somebody's will 2 spontaneous and automatic —**in·vol·un·tar·i·ly** adv

in·volve /in vólv/ (-volved, -volv·ing) vt 1 contain as a necessary element 2 concern or have to do with 3 cause to participate 4 embroil or implicate —**in·volved** adj —**in·volve·ment** n —**in·volv·ing** adj

in·vul·ner·a·ble /in vúlnərəb'l/ adj 1 unable to be hurt 2 safe from attack —**in·vul·ner·a·bil·i·ty** /in vùlnərə bíllətee/ n —**in·vul·ner·a·bly** adv

in·ward /ínnwərd/ adj 1 situated inside 2 of the mind or spirit ■ adv also **in·wards** /ínnwərdz/ 1 toward the inside or center 2 toward the mind or spirit —**in·ward·ness** n

in·ward-look·ing adj preoccupied with your own concerns

in·ward·ly /ínnwərdlee/ adv 1 to or in yourself 2 on or to the inside

I/O abbr input/output

i·o·dine /ī ə dìn, -din, -dèen/ n 1 (symbol I) a nonmetallic crystalline halogen element. Use: pharmaceuticals, dyes, isotopes in medicine and industry. **2** an antiseptic containing dissolved iodine

ORIGIN Iodine was coined by Sir Humphry Davy in 1814 as an extension of French *iode*, the name given to the element by the French physicist Joseph-Louis Gay-Lussac (1778–1850). He based it on Greek *iōdēs* "violet-colored," because heated iodine crystals produce a purple vapor.

i·o·dize /ī ə dīz/ (**-dized, -diz·ing**) *vt* treat with iodine **—i·o·di·za·tion** /ī ədi zāysh'n/ *n*

i·on /ī ən, ī òn/ *n* an electrically charged atom or atom group **—i·on·ic** /ī ónnik/ *adj*

-ion *suffix* **1** action or process o *eruption* o *erosion* **2** result of an action or process o *abrasion*

Io·nes·co /ēē ə néskō/, **Eugène** (1912–94) Romanian-born French dramatist

I·o·ni·a /ī ōnee ə/ ancient region of W Asia Minor, on the Aegean coast **—I·o·ni·an** *adj, n*

I·o·ni·an Sea /ī ōnee èn seé/ arm of the Mediterranean Sea between SE Italy and W Greece

I·on·ic /ī ónnik/ *adj* of a classical architectural order characterized by columns with a scroll-like ornamentation at the top

i·on·ize /ī ə nīz/ (**-ized, -iz·ing**) *vti* change into ions **—i·on·i·za·tion** /ī əni záysh'n/ *n*

i·on·o·sphere /ī ónnə sfèer/ *n* the ionized layers in the upper atmosphere **—i·on·o·spher·ic** /ī ònnə sfeérik, -sférrik/ *adj*

i·o·ta /ī ṓtə/ *n* **1** the 9th letter of the Greek alphabet **2** a very small amount o *anyone with an iota of sense*

IOU *n* a written record of a debt

I·o·wa /ī əwə/ state in the north central United States. Cap. Des Moines. Pop. 2,926,324 (2000). **—I·o·wan** *n, adj*

⚡IP *abbr* **1** image processing **2** innings pitched **3** Internet protocol

⚡IPL *abbr* initial program load

IPO *abbr* initial public offering

ip·so fac·to /ípsō fáktō/ *adv* because of a particular fact

IQ, I.Q. *n* a measure of intelligence obtained through a series of aptitude tests. Full form **intelligence quotient**

Ir *symbol* iridium

⚡IR *abbr* **1** information retrieval **2** infrared (radiation)

IRA¹ *n* an Irish nationalist organization. Full form **Irish Republican Army**

IRA² *n* a savings plan for retirement. Full form **Individual Retirement Account**

I·ran /i ràn, i rán/ country in SW Asia. Cap. Tehran. Pop. 66,128,965 (2001).

I·ra·ni·an /i ráynee ən/ *n* **1** a large group of languages spoken in the region northeast of the Persian Gulf **2** somebody from Iran **—I·ra·ni·an** *adj*

Iran-Iraq War, Gulf War *n* the war (1980–88) between Iran and Iraq, following Iraq's invasion of border territory in Iran

I·raq /i rák, i ráak/ country in SW Asia. Cap. Baghdad. Pop. 23,331,985 (2001).

I·ra·qi /i rákee, i ráakee/ *n* **1** somebody from Iraq **2** the Arabic dialect of Iraq **—I·ra·qi** *adj*

i·ras·ci·ble /i rássəb'l/ *adj* quick-tempered **—i·ras·ci·bil·i·ty** /i ràssə bíllətee/ *n* **—i·ras·ci·bly** *adv*

i·rate /ī ráyt/ *adj* very angry **—i·rate·ly** *adv* **—i·rate·ness** *n*

~~irational~~ incorrect spelling of **irrational**

⚡IRC *abbr* Internet relay chat (*in e-mails*)

ire *n* great anger ◊ See note at **anger**

Ire·land /īrlənd/ **1** island of NW Europe, in the North Atlantic Ocean, comprising the Republic of Ireland and the British province of Northern Ireland **2** country occupying most of the island of Ireland. Cap. Dublin. Pop. 3,840,838 (2001).

Ire·land, North·ern ♦ Northern Ireland

ir·i·des·cent /írri déss'nt/ *adj* having lustrous rainbow colors **—ir·i·des·cence** *n*

i·rid·i·um /i ríddee əm/ *n* (*symbol* **Ir**) a silver-white metallic element. Use: corrosion-resistant alloys.

i·ris /īriss/ *n* **1** the colored part of an eye **2** a flowering plant with large sword-shaped leaves

I·rish /īrish/ *adj* **1** of Ireland **2** of the Gaelic language of Ireland **3** of the English dialect of Ireland ■ *n* **1** *npl* the people from Ireland ■ *n* the Gaelic language of Ireland **—I·rish·man** *n* **—I·rish·ness** *n* **—I·rish·wom·an** *n*

I·rish cof·fee *n* coffee with Irish whiskey, topped with whipped cream

I·rish Gael·ic *n* an official language of the Republic of Ireland **—I·rish Gael·ic** *adj*

I·rish moss *n* an edible seaweed

I·rish Sea arm of the N Atlantic Ocean between Great Britain and Ireland

I·rish set·ter *n* a large dog with a reddish coat

I·rish stew *n* a lamb and potato stew

I·rish whis·key *n* whiskey made in Ireland

irk *vt* annoy slightly ◊ See note at **annoy, bother**

irk·some /úrksəm/ *adj* slightly annoying **—irk·some·ly** *adv* **—irk·some·ness** *n*

Ir·kutsk /ur kŏŏtsk, eer-/ city in S Siberian Russia. Pop. 668,449 (1995).

i·ron /īrn/ *n* **1** (*symbol* **Fe**) a metallic element. Use: engineering and structural products. **2** a hard, strong, or unyielding quality o *a will of iron* **3** a heated tool made of iron or steel o *a soldering iron* **4** an appliance with a flat metal base, used for pressing clothes **5** a metal-headed golf club ■ *n npl* manacles or fetters for the arms or legs ■ *adj* **1** made of iron **2** very strong or tough

3 determined or cruel ■ *vti* press clothes with an iron ◊ **pump iron** do weightlifting exercises (*slang*)

□ **iron out** *vt* settle a problem or resolve a dispute by removing difficulties

I·ron Age *n* the archaeological period immediately after the Bronze Age, when iron was increasingly used

i·ron·clad /ˈīrnˌklad/ *adj* **1** covered or protected with iron plates **2** not liable to be contradicted or changed ◊ *an ironclad agreement*

I·ron Cur·tain *n* the militarized border and policy of isolation that prevented W and E Europeans from communicating freely during the Cold War

i·ron·ic /ī rónnik/, **i·ron·i·cal** /ī rónnik'l/ *adj* **1** involving irony **2** △ involving a surprising or apparently contradictory fact —**i·ron·i·cal·ly** *adv* ◊ See note at **sarcastic**

USAGE Do not use **irony**, **ironic**, and **ironically** to refer to coincidental or improbable situations, as opposed to truly incongruous ones: *Coincidentally* [not *Ironically*], *both the defense counsel and the prosecutor graduated from Yale Law School.*

---

i·ron·ing /ˈīrning/ *n* **1** the act of pressing clothes **2** clothes for pressing

i·ron·ing board *n* a board for ironing clothes on

i·ron·man *n* **1** a strong man **2** *also* **I·ron Man** a men's sports competition held on a beach and including a variety of disciplines

i·ron·stone /ˈīrnˌstōn/ *n* **1** an iron-bearing sedimentary rock **2** a hard white pottery

I·ron Wom·an *n* a women's sports competition held on a beach and including a variety of disciplines

i·ron·work /ˈīrnˌwûrk/ *n* something made of iron, e.g., a decorative gate

i·ron·works /ˈīrnˌwûrks/ (*pl same*) *n* a factory where iron is smelted or heavy iron goods are made (+ *sing* or *pl verb*)

i·ro·ny /ˈīrənee/ *n* **1** humor based on words suggesting the opposite of their literal meaning **2** incongruity between what actually happens and what might be expected ◊ See note at **ironic**

ORIGIN Irony has nothing to do with **iron**. It came through Latin from a Greek word that meant "pretended ignorance." It referred particularly to a device taught by the philosopher Socrates as a way of getting the better of an opponent in argument, and this was one of its earliest meanings in English.

Ir·o·quois /ˈirrəˌkwoy/ (*pl same*) *n* a member of a former confederacy of six Native North American peoples, the Mohawk, Oneida, Seneca, Onondaga, Cayuga, and Tuscarora —**Ir·o·quoi·an**, **Ir·o·quois** *adj*

ir·ra·di·ate /i ˈraydee ayt/ (**-at·ed**, **-at·ing**) *vt* **1** expose to radiation **2** light up —**ir·ra·di·a·tion** /i ˌraydee áysh'n/ *n*

ir·ra·tion·al /i ráshən'l, i ráshnəl/ *adj* **1** contrary to or lacking in reason or logic **2** unable to think clearly —**ir·ra·tion·al·i·ty** /i ˌràsh'n álətee/ *n* —**ir·ra·tion·al·ly** *adv*

ir·ra·tion·al num·ber *n* a real number that is not rational

Ir·ra·wad·dy /ˈirrə wóddee/ principal river of Myanmar. Length 1,300 mi./2,100 km.

ir·rec·on·cil·a·ble /i ˈrèkən sīləb'l, i ˌrékən sīləb'l/ *adj* **1** incompatible **2** unresolvable —**ir·rec·on·cil·a·bly** *adv*

ir·re·cov·er·a·ble /ˈirri kúvvərəb'l/ *adj* incapable of being regained or repaired —**ir·re·cov·er·a·bly** *adv*

ir·re·deem·a·ble /ˈirri deeməb'l/ *adj* **1** unable to be bought back or paid off **2** not convertible into coins **3** incapable of reforming or being saved **4** irrecoverable —**ir·re·deem·a·bly** *adv*

ir·re·duc·i·ble /ˈirri doossəb'l/ *adj* **1** incapable of being decreased **2** incapable of simplification —**ir·re·duc·i·bly** *adv*

ir·ref·u·ta·ble /ˈirrə fyoótəb'l, i ˈréffyə-/ *adj* incapable of being refuted or disproved —**ir·ref·u·ta·bly** *adv*

ir·re·gard·less /ˈirri gaárdləss/ *adv* △ regardless (*nonstandard*)

USAGE Since the prefix **ir-** means "not" (as it does in *irrespective*), and the suffix *-less* means "without," **irregardless** is a double negative and is regarded as nonstandard. Use instead *irrespective* or *regardless*.

---

ir·reg·u·lar /i réggyələr/ *adj* **1** not of uniform appearance **2** occurring at odd intervals **3** not conforming to accepted rules, standards, or practices **4** not following the usual rules of word formation ◊ *an irregular verb* —**ir·reg·u·lar·i·ty** /i ˌrèggyə lérrətee/ *n* —**ir·reg·u·lar·ly** *adv*

ir·rel·e·vant /i rélləvənt/ *adj* not relevant —**ir·rel·e·vance** *n* —**ir·rel·e·vant·ly** *adv*

~~irrelevent~~ incorrect spelling of **irrelevant**

ir·re·li·gious /ˈirri llíjəss/ *adj* **1** lacking any religious faith **2** against religion —**ir·re·li·gious·ly** *adv* —**ir·re·li·gious·ness** *n*

ir·re·me·di·a·ble /ˈirri méedee əb'l/ *adj* incapable of being remedied —**ir·re·me·di·a·bly** *adv*

ir·rep·a·ra·ble /i réppərəb'l/ *adj* not repairable or able to be put right —**ir·rep·a·ra·bly** *adv*

ir·re·place·a·ble /ˈirri pláyssəb'l/ *adj* incapable of being replaced —**ir·re·place·a·bly** *adv*

ir·re·press·i·ble /ˈirri préssəb'l/ *adj* not able to be controlled —**ir·re·press·i·bil·i·ty** /ˈirri ˌprèssə billətee/ *n* —**ir·re·press·i·bly** *adv*

ir·re·proach·a·ble /ˈirri prṓchəb'l/ *adj* beyond criticism —**ir·re·proach·a·bly** *adv*

~~irresistable~~ incorrect spelling of **irresistible**

ir·re·sis·ti·ble /ˈirri zístəb'l/ *adj* **1** unable to be resisted or successfully opposed **2** very desirable —**ir·re·sis·ti·bil·i·ty** /ɪrri zɪstə bíllətee/ n —**ir·re·sis·ti·bly** adv

ir·res·o·lute /i rézzə lóot/ adj incapable of deciding —**ir·res·o·lute·ly** adv —**ir·res·o·lu·tion** /i rèzzə lóosh'n/ n

ir·re·spec·tive /írri spéktiv/ adj regardless —**ir·re·spec·tive·ly** adv ◊ **irrespective of** without taking into account ◊ See note at **irregardless**

ir·re·spon·si·ble /írri spónsəb'l/ adj not caring about the consequences of personal actions ■ n an irresponsible person —**ir·re·spon·si·bil·i·ty** /írri spònsə bíllətee/ n —**ir·re·spon·si·bly** adv

ir·re·triev·a·ble /írri treévəb'l/ adj 1 not recoverable after being lost 2 irreparable —**ir·re·triev·a·bil·i·ty** /írri treévə bíllətee/ n —**ir·re·triev·a·bly** adv

~~irrevelant~~ incorrect spelling of **irrelevant**

~~irreverant~~ incorrect spelling of **irreverent**

ir·rev·er·ent /i révvərənt/ adj lacking in respect —**ir·rev·er·ence** n —**ir·rev·er·ent·ly** adv

ir·re·vers·i·ble /írri vúrsəb'l/ adj incapable of reversal —**ir·re·vers·i·bil·i·ty** /írri vùrsə bíllətee/ n —**ir·re·vers·i·bly** adv

ir·rev·o·ca·ble /i révvəkəb'l/ adj impossible to revoke, undo, or change —**ir·rev·o·ca·bil·i·ty** /i rèvvəkə bíllətee/ n —**ir·rev·o·ca·bly** adv

ir·ri·gate /írri gàyt/ (-gat·ed, -gat·ing) vt 1 supply a dry area with water for growing crops 2 make water or liquid medication flow through or over a body part or wound —**ir·ri·ga·ble** adj —**ir·ri·ga·tion** /írri gáysh'n/ n

ir·ri·ta·ble /írritəb'l/ adj 1 easily annoyed 2 sensitive, especially to inflammation —**ir·ri·ta·bil·i·ty** /írritə bíllətee/ n —**ir·ri·ta·bly** adv

ir·ri·ta·ble bow·el syn·drome n a bowel condition in which there is recurrent pain with constipation or diarrhea

ir·ri·tant /írritənt/ adj causing irritation —**ir·ri·tant** n

ir·ri·tate /írri tàyt/ (-tat·ed, -tat·ing) v 1 vti annoy somebody 2 vt produce a painful reaction in —**ir·ri·tat·ing** adj —**ir·ri·tat·ing·ly** adv —**ir·ri·ta·tion** /írri táysh'n/ n ◊ See note at **anger, annoy**

ir·rupt /i rúpt/ vi 1 enter abruptly 2 increase quickly —**ir·rup·tion** n

IRS abbr Internal Revenue Service

Ir·vine /úr vîn/ city in SW California. Pop. 136,446 (1998).

Ir·ving /úrving/, **Washington** (1783–1859) US writer

is /iz/ 3rd person present singular of **be**

⚡**IS** abbr information services

is. abbr island

Is. abbr Island (in place names)

I·saac n in the Bible, the son of Abraham

Is·a·bel·la I /ízzə béllə/ queen of Castile and León (1474–1504)

I·sa·iah /ɪ záy ə/ n a book of the Bible that contains prophecies and apocalyptic material, traditionally attributed to Isaiah, a Hebrew prophet

ISBN abbr International Standard Book Number

⚡**ISDN** n a digital telephone network that can transmit sound and data. Full form **Integrated Services Digital Network**

-ish suffix 1 characteristic of, like, tending to o babyish 2 of or relating to, from o Polish 3 somewhat, approximately o brownish

Ish·er·wood /íshər wŏod/, **Christopher** (1904–86) British-born US writer

i·sin·glass /íz'n glàss, ízing-/ n 1 a gelatin used as a clarifying agent and in adhesives and jellies 2 mica

I·sis /íssiss/ n Egyptian mother goddess

isl. abbr 1 island 2 isle

Is·lam /íss laám, iz-, íz laám, íss-/ n 1 the religion of Muslims, based upon the teachings of Muhammad 2 the Muslim world —**Is·lam·ic** /íss laámik, iz-/ adj

Is·lam·a·bad /íss laámmə bad/ capital of Pakistan. Pop. 791,085 (1998).

Is·lam·ism /íssla mìzzəm, ízz-/ n 1 a conservative Islamic political movement 2 the religion or principles of Islam —**Is·lam·ist** adj, n

Is·lam·ize /íssla mìz, ízzlə-/ (-ized, -iz·ing) vt 1 convert to Islam 2 make subject to Islamic law —**Is·lam·i·za·tion** /íssləmi záysh'n, izzləmi-/ n

is·land /ílənd/ n 1 a land mass surrounded by water (often in place names) 2 something like an island in being isolated or surrounded by something different —**is·land·er** n

---

ORIGIN Despite their similarity, **island** and **isle** have completely different origins. **Island** goes back to a compound formed from an ancient root meaning "water" combined with the word land. **Isle** comes from Latin insula, meaning "island." The resemblance is due to a 16C change in the spelling of **island** under the influence of the semantically close isle.

---

isle /îl/ n an island (literary) ◊ See note at **aisle**

Isle of Man island in the Irish Sea, a self-governing Crown dependency of the United Kingdom. Cap. Douglas. Pop. 69,788 (1991).

Isle of Wight /-wît/ island off S England. Pop. 125,100 (1995).

is·let /ílət/ n a small island

-ism suffix 1 action, process o mesmerism 2 characteristic behavior or manner o despotism 3 state, condition o conservatism 4 doctrine, system of beliefs o defeatism 5 prejudice o sexism

is·n't /ízz'nt/ contr is not

ISO abbr 1 in search of 2 International Organization for Standardization

i·so·bar /ˈisə bàär/ n a line on a weather map connecting places with equal atmospheric pressure —**i·so·bar·ic** /isə bérrik/ adj

~~isoceles~~ incorrect spelling of **isosceles**

i·so·late /ˈisə làyt/ (-lat·ed, -lat·ing) vt 1 separate from others 2 put in quarantine —**i·so·la·tion** /isə làysh'n/ n

i·so·lat·ed /ˈisə làytəd/ adj 1 far away from other inhabited areas 2 alone or lonely 3 rare and unlikely to recur ◇ an isolated incident

i·so·la·tion·ism /isə làysh'n izzəm/ n a national policy of avoidance of international relations —**i·so·la·tion·ist** n, adj

i·so·mer /ˈisəmər/ n 1 one of two or more molecules with the same number of atoms but different chemical structures 2 one of two or more nuclides with the same mass number but different energy states —**i·so·mer·ic** /isə mérrik/ adj

i·so·met·ric /isə méttrik/, **i·so·met·ri·cal** /isə méttrik'l/ adj 1 equal in dimension or measurement 2 involving pushing the muscles against something —**i·so·met·ri·cal·ly** adv

i·so·met·rics /isə méttriks/ n isometric exercise (+ sing or pl verb)

i·sos·ce·les /ī sóssə leèz/ adj describes a triangle with two sides of equal length ◇ an isosceles triangle

i·so·therm /ˈisə thùrm/ n a line on a weather map connecting places with equal or constant temperature —**i·so·ther·mal** adj

i·so·ton·ic /isə tónnik/ adj 1 of muscle contraction under relatively constant tension 2 containing the same concentration of salts and minerals as the body ◇ isotonic drinks —**i·so·ton·i·cal·ly** adv

i·so·tope /ˈisə tòp/ n each of two or more forms of an element with the same atomic number —**i·so·top·ic** /isə tóppik/ adj

⚡ **ISP** abbr Internet service provider

Is·ra·el /ˈizree əl/ country in SW Asia, on the eastern shore of the Mediterranean Sea. Cap. Jerusalem. Pop. 5,938,093 (2001). —**Is·rae·li** /iz ráylee/ n, adj

Is·ra·el·ite /ˈizzree ə lìt/ n a member of an ancient Hebrew people descended from Jacob —**Is·ra·el·it·ic** /izzree ə lìttik/ adj

~~Isreal~~ incorrect spelling of **Israel**

is·sue /ˈishoo/ n 1 a subject of concern 2 a copy of a publication for a particular date 3 a set of things made available for sale at the same time 4 the official distribution of something ◇ the issue of parking permits 5 offspring ◇ died without issue 6 ⚠ a source of conflict, misgiving, or emotional distress (infml) ◇ had issues with some of her suggestions ■ v (-sued, -su·ing) 1 vt supply or distribute officially 2 vt release as a public statement or warning 3 vt publish 4 vi come out from somewhere ◇ Smoke issued from

the burning building. —**is·su·er** n ◇ **at issue** under discussion or to be decided ◇ **take issue** disagree

---

USAGE Avoid using **issue** as a vague substitute for problem, difficulty, or point of disagreement or to denote intentionally unstated problems, typically emotional or mental, as in He's one of those people who always has issues.

-ist suffix 1 somebody practicing a particular skill or profession ◇ psychologist 2 somebody following a particular belief or school of thought ◇ idealist 3 somebody playing a particular instrument ◇ guitarist —**-istic** suffix

Is·tan·bul /ˈis tan bool, -taan-/ largest city in Turkey, on the Bosporus. Pop. 8,274,921 (1997).

isth·mus /ˈissməss/ (pl -mus·es or -mi /ˈiss mī/) n 1 a narrow strip of land connecting two larger masses 2 a narrow connection or passage between body parts —**isth·mi·an** /ˈssmee ən/ adj, n

it pron 1 refers to an object, animal, or abstraction 2 indicates a particular situation or point of view ◇ won't talk about it ◇ It's strange. 3 indicates something reported ◇ It was said that 4 indicates weather or temperature ◇ It's raining and cold. 5 indicates time ◇ It's six o'clock. 6 emphasizes a following clause ◇ It's you who's always complaining. ■ n the player in children's games who must catch or find the others

⚡ **IT** abbr information technology

I·tal·ian /i tállyən/ n 1 somebody from Italy 2 the language of Italy —**I·tal·ian** adj —**I·tal·ian·ate** adj

i·tal·ic /i tállik/ adj printed, written, or using letters sloping to the right ■ n 1 an italic letter (often pl) 2 **I·tal·ic** the language family that includes Latin

i·tal·i·cize /i tálli sìz/ (-cized, -ciz·ing) vt print in italic type —**i·tal·i·ci·za·tion** /i tàllissi záysh'n/ n

It·a·ly /ˈitt'lee/ country in S Europe. Cap. Rome. Pop. 57,679,825 (2001).

itch v 1 vti make somebody want to scratch the skin 2 vi be eager ■ n 1 a feeling of wanting to scratch 2 an eager longing for something —**itch·i·ness** n —**itch·ing** n —**itch·y** adj

it'd contr 1 it had 2 it would

-ite suffix 1 mineral, rock, ore, soil, fossil ◇ graphite 2 descendant or follower of ◇ Trotskyite 3 native or resident of ◇ urbanite 4 salt or ester of an acid with a name ending in -ous ◇ sulfite

i·tem /ˈitəm/ n 1 one thing in a collection 2 one thing in a list 3 a broadcast or published report 4 a couple in a relationship (infml)

i·tem·ize /ˈitə mìz/ (-ized, -iz·ing) v 1 vt list the individual things in a set of related things ◇ an itemized bill 2 vi list deductions on a tax return —i·tem·i·za·tion /ítəmi záysh'n/ *n*

it·er·a·tion /ittə ráysh'n/ *n* a repetition —**it·er·ate** /íttə ràyt/ *vt* —**it·er·a·tive** /íttə ràytiv/ *adj*

i·tin·er·ant /t́ tínnərənt/ *adj* traveling to find or perform work —**i·tin·er·ant** *n*

i·tin·er·ar·y /t́ tínnə rèrree/ (*pl* -**ies**) *n* 1 a list of places to be visited 2 a record of a journey

-itis *suffix* inflammation, disease o *dermatitis*

it'll *contr* it will

its *adj* of or belonging to it

USAGE its or **it's**? The possessive form of the pronoun *it* is **its**, even though it does not have an apostrophe before the *s*: *The cat is licking its* [not *it's*] *paws.* **It's** is a contraction for *it is* or *it has*: *It's* [not *Its*] *going to rain tonight.*

it's *contr* 1 it has 2 it is

it·self /it sélf/ *pron* 1 refers back to something that is the subject of the verb o *His ignorance finally revealed itself.* 2 emphasizes something just mentioned o *The house itself was cheap.*

ITV *abbr* instructional television

IUD *abbr* intrauterine device

IV *abbr* 1 intravenous 2 intravenously

I·van IV /ívən/ (1530–84) tsar of Russia (1547–84)

I've *contr* I have

-ive *suffix* tending to or performing o *illustrative*

Ives /ívz/, **Charles** (1874–1954) US composer

IVF *abbr* in vitro fertilization

i·vo·ry /ívəree/ *n* 1 the material of the tusks of elephants and some other animals 2 a creamy-white color ■ **i·vo·ries** *npl* 1 piano keys (*infml*) 2 teeth (*slang*) —**i·vo·ry** *adj*

I·vo·ry Coast /ívəree-/ former name for **Côte d'Ivoire**

i·vo·ry tow·er *n* a state or situation separated from real-life problems

ORIGIN Ivory tower is a translation of French *tour d'ivoire*, which was first used in 1837 by the writer Charles-Augustin Sainte-Beuve (1804–69) to refer to the aloofness from everyday realities of the poet Alfred de Vigny (1797–1863).

i·vy /ívee/ (*pl* -**vies** or same) *n* an evergreen climbing plant —**i·vied** *adj*

I·vy League *n* a group of prestigious US universities —**I·vy League** *adj* —**I·vy Leagu·er** *n*

I·wo Ji·ma /éèwə jéèmə, èéwō-/ largest of the Volcano Islands of Japan, in the W Pacific Ocean, east of Taiwan

I·yar /éè yaàr/ *n* the 2nd month of the year in the Jewish calendar

-ize *suffix* 1 cause to be, make o *formalize* 2 treat with or as o *lionize* 3 become, become like o *crystallize* —**-ization** *suffix*

Iz·mir /íz meèr/ seaport in W Turkey. Pop. 2,130,359 (1997).

J

j¹ (*pl* **j's**), **J** (*pl* **J's** or **Js**) *n* the 10th letter of the English alphabet

j² *abbr* joule

J *symbol* joule

J. *abbr* 1 Journal 2 Judge

jab *vti* (**jabbed, jab·bing**) 1 punch sharply 2 make a short fast punch at an opponent ■ *n* 1 a sharp pushing or poking movement 2 a short sharp punch

jab·ber /jábbər/ *vti* talk or say something very fast —**jab·ber** *n*

jack *n* 1 a portable device for lifting heavy objects 2 a playing card with a picture of a young man on it, ranking between a ten and a queen 3 an electrical socket into which a plug is inserted 4 an object used in the game of jacks 5 the male of various animals 6 a flag on a ship indicating its nationality ■ *vt* raise with a jack

ORIGIN The various uses of **jack** all come from the name *Jack*, a nickname for *John*. The term often implies "ordinary" or "small."

□ **jack up** *vt* increase the amount of

jack·al /ják'l/ (*pl* -**als** or same) *n* a wild animal resembling a dog

jack·ass /ják ass/ *n* 1 a male ass 2 a person regarded as unintelligent (*slang insult*)

jack·boot /ják boòt/ *n* a military boot that comes up to or over the knee

jack·daw /ják dàw/ *n* a large black bird

jack·et /jákət/ *n* 1 a short coat 2 an outer covering or casing ■ *vt* put a jacket on

Jack Frost *n* frost personified

jack·ham·mer /ják hàmmər/ *n* a hand-held pounding power tool

jack-in-the-box (*pl* **jacks-in-the-box** or **jack-in-the-box·es**) *n* a child's toy consisting of a puppet on a spring inside a box

jack·knife /ják nìf/ *n* (*pl* -**knives** /-nìvz/) 1 a large pocketknife 2 a dive in which the diver bends the body to touch the toes and then straightens out ■ *vi* (-**knifed, -knif·ing**) 1 lose control so that the trailer swings around to be at an angle to the cab (*refers to tractor-trailers*) 2 do a jackknife dive

jack-of-all-trades (*pl* **jacks-of-all-trades**) *n* somebody who can do many types of work

jack-o'-lan·tern *n* a lantern made from a hollowed-out pumpkin

jack·pot /ják pòt/ *n* the most valuable cash prize, e.g., in a lottery

jack rab·bit *n* a large hare

Jack Rob·in·son ◊ **before you can** *or* **could say Jack Robinson** without the slightest delay or hesitation *(infml)*

jacks *n* a game that involves picking up small metal or plastic pieces between bouncing or throwing and catching a small ball (+ *sing verb*)

Jack·son /jáks'n/ capital of Mississippi. Pop. 188,419 (1998).

Andrew Jackson

Jack·son, Andrew (1767–1845) 7th president of the United States (1829–37)

Jack·son, Jesse (*b.* 1941) US civil rights leader, minister, and politician

Jack·son, Stonewall (1824–63) US Confederate general

Jack·son·ville /jáks'n vil/ city in NE Florida. Pop. 693,630 (1998).

Jac·o·be·an /jàkə beé ən, jàykə-/ *adj* of the reign of James I of England and Ireland —**Jac·o·be·an** *n*

ORIGIN **Jacobean** and **Jacobite** are from the Latin form of "James," *Jacobus*.

Jac·o·bite /jákə bìt/ *n* a supporter of James II and his descendants in their claim to the British throne —**Jac·o·bite** *adj* —**Jac·o·bit·ism** *n*

Ja·cuz·zi /jə koõzee/ *tdmk* a trademark for a whirlpool bath

jade *n* a semiprecious stone. Use: ornaments, jewelry.

ORIGIN Despite the close association of **jade** with China and Japan, its name has no Asian connections. A derivative of Latin *ilia* "flanks," the part of the body where the kidneys are situated, passed into Spanish as *ijada*. It was thought that jade could cure pain in the renal area, so the Spanish called it *piedra de ijada*, literally "stone of the flanks," eventually reduced to *ijada*. In French it became *ejade*. Subsequently *l'ejade* "the jade" became *le jade*, from which English **jade** is derived.

jad·ed /jáydəd/ *adj* 1 bored through having or doing too much of something 2 exhausted —**jad·ed·ness** *n*

Jaf·fa /jáffə/, **Jaf·fa or·ange** *n* a variety of thick-skinned juicy orange

jag *n* a period of overindulgence or loss of control *(infml)*

Jag·de·o /jágdee ò/, **Bharrat** (*b.* 1964) president of Guyana (1999–)

jag·ged /jággəd/ *adj* 1 pointy 2 uneven —**jag·ged·ly** *adv* —**jag·ged·ness** *n*

jag·uar /jág waar/ *n* a big wild cat related to the leopard

jai a·lai /hí π, hí ə lí/ *n* a game derived from pelota

jail /jayl/ *n* a secure place where criminals and suspects awaiting trial are kept ■ *vt* put in jail

ORIGIN **Jail** goes back to Latin *cavea* "cave," and would literally have meant "little cave." The form **jail** came through French.

jail·bird /jáyl bùrd/ *n* a current or former prisoner in a jail *(slang)*

jail·break /jáyl bràyk/ *n* an escape from jail

jail·er /jáylər/, **jail·or** *n* a prison guard

Jain /jīn/, **Jai·na** /jínə/ *n* a believer in Jainism —**Jain** *adj*

Jain·ism /jínìzzəm/ *n* an ancient branch of Hinduism that advocates deep respect for all living things —**Jain·ist** *adj*

Jai·pur /jī poõr/ capital of Rajasthan State, N India. Pop. 1,458,483 (1991).

Ja·kar·ta /jə kaártə/ capital and largest city of Indonesia. Pop. 7,764,764 (1997).

ja·la·pe·ño /hàalə páyn yō/ (*pl* **-ños**), **ja·la·pe·ño pep·per** *n* a small hot pepper

ja·lop·y /jə lóppee/ (*pl* **-ies**) *n* an old or dilapidated car *(dated infml)*

jal·ou·sie /jálləssee/ *n* a slatted window covering

jam *v* (**jammed**, **jam·ming**) 1 *vt* push something forcibly into a tight space 2 *vt* fill something with people or things crushed together 3 *vti* stop or cause to stop working through sticking or locking ○ *The photocopier jammed.* 4 *vt* block something up and prevent passage 5 *vt* interfere with broadcasting signals 6 *vt* overwhelm a switchboard with telephone calls 7 *vt* apply brakes hard ○ *jammed on the brakes* 8 *vi* improvise music together ■ *n* 1 a spread made of fruit boiled with sugar 2 a difficult situation *(infml)* 3 a stoppage —**jam·mer** *n*

Ja·mai·ca /jə máykə/ island country in the N Caribbean Sea. Cap. Kingston. Pop. 2,665,636 (2001). —**Ja·mai·can** *n*, *adj*

jamb /jam/ *n* an upright support of a door or window frame

jam·bo·ree /jàmbə reé/ *n* 1 a big celebration 2 an international meeting of Boy Scouts

ORIGIN The origin of **jamboree** is not known. It first appears in the United States in the 1860s. It was adopted as the title for the 1920 International Rally of Boy Scouts, and has been used by the Boy Scouts ever since.

James¹ /jaymz/ *n* a book of the Bible, originally a letter believed to have been written by James, a brother of Jesus Christ

James² /jaymz/ river in W Virginia. Length 340 mi./547 km.

James¹, St. "James the Great" (*fl* 1C AD) in the Bible, one of the 12 apostles of Jesus Christ

James², St. "James the Less" (*d.* AD 62?) traditionally regarded as the brother of Jesus

James I (1566–1625) king of England and Ireland (1603–25), also James VI of Scotland (1567–1625)

James II (1633–1701) king of England, Scotland, and Ireland (1685–88)

James, Henry (1843–1916) US-born British novelist

James, Jesse (1847–82) US outlaw

James, William (1842–1910) US philosopher and psychologist

James Bay southern extension of Hudson Bay, between W Quebec and NE Ontario, Canada

James·town /jáymz tòwn/ **1** city in SW New York. Pop. 32,166 (1998). **2** former village in SE Virginia, the first permanent English settlement in America

Jam·mu and Kash·mir /júmmoo–/ state in N India, a section of the disputed territory of Kashmir. Cap. Srinagar. Pop. 7,720,000 (1991).

jam ses·sion *n* a session of musical improvisation

Jan. *abbr* January

Ja·ná·ček /yaànə chèk/, **Leoš** (1854–1928) Czech composer

Jane Doe /jàyn dó/ *n* **1** an average woman **2** an anonymous woman

jan·gle /jáng g'l/ (**-gled, -gling**) *vti* **1** make or cause to make a harsh metallic sound **2** irritate somebody's nerves —**jan·gle** *n* —**jan·gly** *adj*

jan·i·tor /jánnətər/ *n* somebody employed to clean and maintain a building —**jan·i·to·ri·al** /jànnə táwree əl/ *adj*

Jan·u·ar·y /jánnyoo èrree/ (*pl* **-ys**) *n* the 1st month of the Gregorian calendar

ORIGIN January is named for *Janus*, a Roman god of beginnings and of gates and doors, who was represented with two faces looking in opposite directions (in the case of the month, behind to the old year and ahead to the new).

Ja·pan /jə pán/ country in East Asia, comprising four large islands and more than 1,000 others. Cap. Tokyo. Pop. 126,771,660 (2001).

Ja·pan, Sea of arm of the W Pacific Ocean between Korea and Japan

Jap·a·nese /jàppə néez, jáppə neez/ (*pl* same) *n* **1** somebody from Japan **2** the official language of Japan —**Jap·a·nese** *adj*

Jap·lish /jápplish/ *n* Japanese with a mixture of English words and phrases

ja·pon·i·ca /jə pónnikə/ *n* a camellia

jar¹ *n* a cylindrical storage container with a wide opening

jar² *v* (**jarred, jar·ring**) **1** *vti* shake abruptly **2** *vti* irritate or disturb o *That constant drilling really jars my nerves.* **3** *vti* make or cause to make a grating sound **4** *vi* clash or conflict ■ *n* **1** a physical jolt **2** a grating sound —**jar·ring** *adj*

jar·di·nière /jàard'n éer, jaàrd'n eer, jàard'n yáir, jaàrd'n yair/ *n* a pot for house plants

jar·gon /jaárgən/ *n* **1** specialist or technical language **2** unintelligible language (*disapproving*) —**jar·gon·is·tic** /jàargə nístik/ *adj*

jas·mine /jázmin/ (*pl* same or **-mines**), **jes·sa·mine** /jéssəmin/ *n* a climbing plant with fragrant flowers

jas·per /jáspər/ *n* a red iron-bearing form of quartz. Use: jewelry, ornaments.

jaun·dice /jáwndiss/ *n* an illness causing yellowing of the skin, tissues, and whites of the eyes ■ *vt* (**-diced, -dic·ing**) **1** make cynical, jealous, or prejudiced **2** affect with jaundice —**jaun·diced** *adj*

jaunt *n* a short excursion —**jaunt** *vi*

jaun·ty /jáwntee/ (**-ti·er, -ti·est**) *adj* **1** carefree **2** perky and casually fashionable —**jaun·ti·ly** *adv* —**jaun·ti·ness** *n*

ja·va /jaávə/ *n* brewed coffee (*infml*)

Ja·va /jaávə/ island in Southeast Asia, the most populous island in Indonesia. Pop. 114,733,500 (1995).

jave·lin /jávvlən, -vələn/ *n* **1** a light spear thrown as a weapon or in competitions **2** a throwing contest using a javelin

jaw *n* **1** either of two bones anchoring the teeth and forming the structural basis of the mouth in vertebrates **2** an invertebrate body part with a function or structure similar to a vertebrate jaw **3** a gripping part of a tool or machine

jaw·bone /jáw bòn/ *n* a bone in the jaw, especially the lower jaw

jaw·break·er /jáw bràykər/ *n* **1** a hard candy (*infml*) **2** a crushing machine **3** an unpronounceable word (*infml*)

jay *n* a noisy brightly colored bird of the crow family

Jay, John (1745–1829) first chief justice of the US Supreme Court (1789–95)

jay·vee /jày vée/ *n* a junior varsity player

jay·walk /jáy wàwk/ *vi* cross a street anywhere other than at a designated crossing place —**jay·walk·er** *n* —**jay·walk·ing** *n*

jazz *n* **1** a type of syncopated popular music of African American origin **2** unnamed things (*slang*) o *a new motorcycle and all the jazz that comes with it* ■ *vi* **1** play or dance to jazz **2** exaggerate (*slang*)

ORIGIN The term *jazz* originated in the S United States (it is first recorded in 1909, applied to a type of ragtime dance), and it is tempting to speculate that its ancestor crossed the Atlantic on the slave ships from Africa. In the absence of any certain origin, various colorful theories have been put forward – for example, that **jazz** came from the nickname of a certain Jasbo Brown, an itinerant musician along the banks of the Mississippi ("Jasbo" perhaps being an alteration of "Jasper").

□ **jazz up** *vt* make more lively or interesting (*infml*)

jazz·y /jázzee/ (**-i·er, -i·est**) *adj* showy (*slang*) —**jazz·i·ness** *n*

⚡**JCL** *n* a powerful computer language used for batch processing. Full form **Job Control Language**

jeal·ous /jélləss/ *adj* 1 bitterly envious 2 suspicious of rivals —**jeal·ous·ly** *adv* —**jeal·ous·ness** *n* —**jeal·ous·y** *n*

jeans /jeenz/ *npl* hard-wearing casual pants with raised seams, usually made of denim

ORIGIN **Jeans** were originally made of *jean*, a strong twill cotton. The name goes back to a French form of Genoa, the Italian city where the cloth was first made.

Jed·da ♦ Jiddah

Jeep /jeep/ *tdmk* a trademark for a four-wheel-drive vehicle suitable for rough terrain

jeer *vti* express derision of somebody or something vocally —**jeer** *n* —**jeer·ing·ly** *adv*

Library of Congress

Thomas Jefferson

Jef·fer·son /jéffərs'n/, **Thomas** (1743–1826) 3rd president of the United States (1801–09)

Jef·fer·son Cit·y capital of Missouri. Pop. 34,911 (1998).

Jeff·reys /jéffreez/, **Sir Alec J.** (b. 1950) British geneticist. He developed the technique for establishing an individual's genetic identification, known as genetic fingerprinting.

Je·ho·vah /jə hóvə/ *n* in the Bible, a form of the Hebrew name of God

Je·ho·vah's Wit·ness *n* a member of a religious group believing in the imminence of Jesus Christ's reign on Earth

je·june /jə jóon/ *adj* 1 boring and intellectually undemanding 2 childish

je·ju·num /jə jóonəm/ *n* the middle part of the small intestine —**je·ju·nal** *adj*

Je·kyll and Hyde /jék'l ən híd/ *n* a person who has two distinct personalities, one good and the other evil

ORIGIN The term comes from *The Strange Case of Dr. Jekyll and Mr. Hyde* (1886), by Robert Louis Stevenson.

jell *vti* 1 solidify 2 take shape, or cause to take shape

Jell-O /jéllō/ *tdmk* a trademark for a gelatin-based dessert

jel·ly /jéllee/ *n* 1 a semisolid fruit preserve 2 a substance with the consistency of jelly ■ *vti* (**-lied, -lies**) set into a jelly —**jel·lied** *adj*

jel·ly·bean /jéllee been/ *n* a bean-shaped candy with a hard coating and a soft jelly center

jel·ly·fish /jéllee fish/ (*pl* **-fish·es** *or* same) *n* a stinging invertebrate marine animal

jel·ly roll *n* a rolled up cake made with sponge and jelly

~~jelous~~ incorrect spelling of **jealous**

je ne sais quoi /zhō nə say kwaa/ *n* an undefinable quality

ORIGIN **Je ne sais quoi** means literally "I do not know what" in French.

Jen·ner /jénnər/, **Edward** (1749–1823) British physician. He discovered a vaccine against smallpox.

jen·ny /jénnee/ (*pl* **-nies**) *n* a female of various animals o *a jenny wren*

jeop·ard·ize /jéppər dīz/ (**-ized, -iz·ing**) *vt* endanger

jeop·ard·y /jéppərdee/ *n* the risk of loss, harm, or death

ORIGIN **Jeopardy** derives from French *jeu parti* literally "divided game," and so originally referred to chances being even or uncertain. Early on, however, the emphasis began to fall on the riskiness and danger of the uncertainty rather than the equal chance of a successful outcome.

~~jepardy~~ incorrect spelling of **jeopardy**

jer·bo·a /jər bṓ ə/ (*pl* **-as**) *n* a small rodent of Asia and Africa

jer·e·mi·ad /jérrə mí əd/ *n* a lengthy complaint (*fml*)

Jer·e·mi·ah /jérrə mí ə/ *n* a book of the Bible that contains prophecies about the fall of Judah and Jerusalem and the Israelites' captivity in Babylon, traditionally attributed to Jeremiah, a Hebrew prophet

Jer·i·cho /jérrikō/ *n* town in the Jordan Valley. According to the Bible, the ancient town was destroyed by Joshua after he led the Israelites back from captivity in Egypt. Pop. 14,744 (1997).

jerk[1] *v* 1 *vt* pull suddenly 2 *vti* move joltingly 3 *vt* make ice cream refreshments ■ *n* 1 a sudden pull 2 a jolting motion 3 a person

regarded as behaving foolishly *(slang insult)*
4 an overhead lift in weightlifting

jerk² *vt* preserve meat in strips by sun-drying or smoking

jer·kin /júrkin/ *n* a close-fitting sleeveless jacket

jerk·wa·ter /júrk wàwtər, -waàtər/ *adj* **1** remote from population centers and considered small and unimportant **2** lacking significance

ORIGIN The name was originally applied to remote locations on railroad lines, where steam engines had to be supplied with water from streams using a bucket on a rope.

jerk·y¹ /júrkee/ (**-i·er, -i·est**) *adj* moving with sudden stops and starts —**jerk·i·ly** *adv* —**jerk·i·ness** *n*

jerk·y² /júrkee/ *n* strips of meat preserved by sun-drying or smoking

jer·o·bo·am /jèrrə bố əm/ *n* a large wine bottle holding the equivalent of four standard bottles

ORIGIN In the Bible, Jeroboam was "a mighty man of valor" (I Kings 11:28).

Je·rome /jə róm/, **St.** (347?–419?) Croatian-born monk and scholar. He was the first translator of the Bible into Latin.

jer·ry-built /jérree bìlt/ *adj* shoddily built

jer·ry can *n* a can for gas or water

jer·sey /júrzee/ (*pl* **-seys**) *n* **1** a plain knitted fabric used for clothing **2** a sweater **3 Jer·sey** a breed of pale brown dairy cattle

ORIGIN The fabric **jersey** was originally a woolen worsted made on the island of Jersey.

Jer·sey largest and southernmost of the Channel Islands, in the English Channel. Pop. 89,361 (2001).

Jer·sey Cit·y port and industrial center in NE New Jersey. Pop. 232,429 (1998).

Je·ru·sa·lem /jə roòssələm, -roòzə-/ historic city lying at the intersection of Israel and the West Bank. The whole of the city is claimed by Israel as its capital, but this is disputed internationally. Pop. 633,700 (1999).

Je·ru·sa·lem ar·ti·choke *n* **1** an edible tuber with a knobby skin and white flesh **2** a perennial plant that produces edible tubers

ORIGIN Jerusalem artichokes do not come from Jerusalem. The name is an alteration of Italian *girasole* "sunflower," because the plant does belong to the sunflower family.

jes·sa·mine /jéssamin/ *n* = jasmine

jest *(literary) n* a joke or playful act ■ *vi* be witty about something —**jest·ing·ly** *adv*

jest·er /jéstər/ *n* **1** an entertainer employed at a medieval court **2** somebody who jokes

Jes·u·it /jézhoo it, jézzoo-/ *n* a member of the Society of Jesus, a Roman Catholic religious order —**Jes·u·it·ic** /jèzhoo íttik, jèzzoo-/ *adj* —**Jes·u·it·i·cal** *adj*

Je·sus Christ /jéezəss-/, **Je·sus** *n* a religious teacher whose life and teachings form the basis of Christianity

jet¹ *n* **1** a pressurized stream of fluid **2** a hole through which fluid is forced **3** *also* **jet en·gine** an engine that produces forward thrust using discharged gases o *using jet technology* **4** an aircraft powered by a jet engine ■ *v* (**jet·ted, jet·ting**) **1** *vi* travel by jet aircraft **2** *vti* flow or send out forcefully in a thin stream

ORIGIN The verb **jet** was adopted from French *jeter* "throw" in the late 16C. It originally meant "protrude, stick out." This sense is best preserved in related *jetty* "projecting pier," while the underlying meaning "throw" is still present in *jettison* "throw something overboard." **Jet** began to be used for "spurt out in a forceful stream" in the 17C. The notion of using such a stream to create forward motion was first encapsulated in the term *jet propulsion* in the mid-19C, but it did not take concrete form until the term *jet engine* was recorded in 1943.

jet² *n* **1** a black mineral. Use: jewelry, ornaments. **2** *also* **jet black** a dark black color —**jet** *adj*

jet lag *n* fatigue and disorientation following a long flight across different time zones —**jet-lagged** *adj*

jet plane *n* a jet-propelled airplane

jet·sam /jétsəm/ *n* **1** cargo or equipment discarded by a ship in distress **2** discarded things

jet set *n* the social set of rich international travelers *(infml)* —**jet-set·ter** *n*

Jet Ski *tdmk* a trademark for a jet-propelled personal watercraft

jet stream *n* a permanent high-level wind current moving east

jet·ti·son /jéttiss'n/ *vt* **1** throw overboard **2** reject o *plans that had to be jettisoned*

jet·ty /jéttee/ (*pl* **-ties**) *n* **1** a breakwater **2** a landing pier

Jew *n* **1** a believer in Judaism **2** a member of a Semitic people descended from the ancient Hebrews and following Judaism

jew·el /jóo əl/ *n* **1** a personal ornament made from a gemstone **2** a gemstone **3** a small crystal or gemstone used as a watch bearing **4** a prized example ■ *vt* adorn with jewels

jew·el box, jew·el case *n* **1** a box for jewelry **2** a hinged plastic case for a CD

jew·el·er /jóo ələr/, **jew·el·ler** *n* a maker, seller, or repairer of jewelry

~~jewelery~~ incorrect spelling of **jewelry**

jew·el·ry /jóo əlree/ *n* ornaments for the body, e.g., necklaces, bracelets, earrings, and rings o *a jewelry box*

jew·el·weed /jōō əl weed/ (*pl* **-weeds** or *same*) *n* a plant with seed pods that burst when ripe

Jew·ess /jōō əss/ *n* a taboo term for a Jewish woman or girl (*dated*)

Jew·ish /jōō ish/ *adj* **1** of Judaism **2** of Jews —**Jew·ish·ly** *adv* —**Jew·ish·ness** *n*

Jew·ry /jōōree/ *n* Judaism or its followers

jew's harp *n* a musical instrument held between the teeth and played by plucking a protruding metal tongue

Jez·e·bel /jézzə bèl/, **jez·e·bel** *n* an offensive term for a woman regarded as sexually immoral (*insult*)

ORIGIN The original **Jezebel** was a Phoenician princess of the 9C BC who became the wife of Ahab, king of Israel, as related in the Bible (1 Kings 21:5–15, 2 Kings 9:30–37).

Jiang Qing /jyàang chíng/ (1914–91) Chinese political activist

Jiang Ze·min /jyàang zay m-n/ (b. 1926) president of the People's Republic of China (1993–)

jib *n* **1** a small triangular sail in front of the main mast of a sailing vessel **2** a crane's projecting arm

jibe¹ /jīb/ *vti* (**jibed, jib·ing**) **1** swing, or make a sail swing, across a boat or ship **2** change direction, or cause a boat or ship to change direction, as a result of a sail's jibing ■ *n* an act of jibing

jibe² /jīb/ (**jibed, jib·ing**) *vi* be in accord (*infml*)

jibe³ /jīb/ *n*, *vti* = **gibe**

ji·ca·ma /heékəmə/ *n* the sweet edible root of a tropical plant

Jid·dah /jíddə/, **Jed·da** /jéddə/ port in W Saudi Arabia, on the Red Sea. Pop. 1,490,000 (1995).

jif·fy /jíffee/, **jiff** /jif/ *n* a brief moment (*infml*) ○ *I'll be ready in a jiffy.*

jig *n* **1** a lively dance in triple time **2** a device for holding a piece of work in place and guiding a tool to cut or drill it ■ *vi* (**jigged, jig·ging**) dance a jig

jig·ger /jíggər/ *n* **1** a measure for alcoholic spirits, around 1.5 fl. oz **2** a jig operator **3** a small sail at the stern of a small sailboat

jig·gle /jígg'l/ (**-gled, -gling**) *vti* shake with small repeated movements —**jig·gle** *n* —**jig·gly** *adj*

jig·saw /jíg sàw/ *n* **1** *also* **jig·saw puz·zle** a game consisting of a set of irregularly shaped interlocking pieces fitted together to make a picture **2** a power saw for cutting curves ■ *vt* cut with a jigsaw

ji·had /ji hàad/ *n* a holy war by Muslims against people or countries regarded as hostile to Islam

Ji·lin /jeéllin/ province in NE China. Cap. Changchun. Pop. 1,420,000 (1995).

jilt *vt* reject a lover

Jim Crow /jìm krṓ/, **Jim Crow·ism** /jìm krṓ ìzzəm/ *n* a taboo term for discrimination against Black people, especially of a systematic kind (*taboo offensive*)

Ji·nan /jeè naàn/, **Chi·nan** capital of Shandong Province, E China. Pop. 3,470,000 (1995).

jin·gle /jíng g'l/ *n* **1** a metallic tinkle **2** a catchy tune used for advertising a product ■ *vti* (**-gled, -gling**) make or cause to make a metallic tinkling sound —**jin·gly** *adj*

jin·go·ism /jíng gō ìzzəm/ *n* aggressive nationalism —**jin·go·ist** *adj, n* —**jin·go·is·tic** /jíng gō ístik/ *adj*

ORIGIN The context of the coining of **jingoism** was British foreign policy of the late 1870s. The Prime Minister, Benjamin Disraeli, favored sending gunboats to halt the advance of the Russian fleet out of their own waters into the Mediterranean. This gave rise to a music-hall song, written in 1878 by G.W. Hunt, the refrain of which went: "We don't want to fight, yet by Jingo! if we do, We've got the ships, we've got the men, and got the money too." Opponents of the policy picked up on the word **jingo** and used it as an icon of blind patriotism.

jin·ni /jínnee/ (*pl* **jinn** /jin/), **djin·ni** (*pl* **djinn**) *n* an Islamic magic spirit

jinx *n* a supposed cause of misfortune ■ *vt* bring misfortune on —**jinxed** *adj*

jit·ney /jítnee/ (*pl* **-neys**) *n* a small bus that takes passengers on a regular route for a small fare

jit·ter·bug /jíttər bùg/ *n* a fast 1940s dance for couples

jit·ter·y /jíttəree/ *adj* **1** nervous **2** jerky

jiu·jit·su *n* MARTIAL ARTS = **jujitsu**

jive *n* **1** jazz or swing music of the 1930s and 1940s **2** insincere talk (*slang*) ■ *vi* (**jived, jiv·ing**) dance the jive —**jiv·er** *n*

jnr., Jnr. *abbr* junior

Joan of Arc /jṑn əv aàrk/, **St.** (1412–31) French patriot and saint

job /job/ *n* **1** a paid occupation **2** a task or piece of work **3** a crime (*infml*) ○ *a bank job* ■ *v* (**jobbed, job·bing**) **1** *vi* take occasional or casual work **2** *vti* deal in wholesale merchandise —**job·less** *adj* —**job·less·ness** *n*

Job /jōb/ a book of the Bible that describes the afflictions and eventual reward of Job, a righteous man whose faith withstood severe testing by God

job ac·tion *n* a workers' protest

job·ber /jóbbər/ *n* **1** somebody taking occasional or casual work **2** a wholesaler —**job·bing** *adj*

job de·scrip·tion *n* a written description of the responsibilities of a specific job

job lot *n* an assortment of articles

Jobs /jobz/, **Steve** (b. 1955) US entrepreneur and technology executive

Job's com·fort·er /jòbz-/ *n* somebody who causes more misery in an attempt to offer comfort

job seek·er *n* somebody looking for a job

job-shar·ing *n* the dividing up of a full-time job between part-time workers —**job-share** *n*, *vi* —**job-shar·er** *n*

jock[1] *n* a disc jockey (*infml*)

jock[2] *n* (*infml*) **1** an athlete **2** a jockstrap

jock·ey /jókee/ *n* (*pl* **-eys**) a racehorse rider ■ *v* (**-eyed, -ey·ing**) **1** *vti* ride a racehorse **2** *vi* maneuver to try to gain an advantage

jock·strap /jók stràp/ *n* a support for a sportsman's genitals

jo·cose /jō kóss/ *adj* playful and humorous (*literary*) —**jo·cose·ly** *adv* —**jo·cos·i·ty** /jō kóssətee/ *n*

joc·u·lar /jókyələr/ *adj* **1** playful and joking **2** intended to be humorous —**joc·u·lar·i·ty** /jòkyə lérrətee/ *n* —**joc·u·lar·ly** *adv*

joc·und /jókənd/ *adj* cheerful and good-humored (*literary*) —**jo·cun·di·ty** /jə kúndətee/ *n*

jodh·purs /jódpərz/ *npl* riding breeches that are wide at the hip and narrow at the calves

Joe Blow *n* US, Can, Aus an average man

Jo·el /jō əl, jōl/ *n* a book of the Bible that contains the prophecies of Joel, a Hebrew prophet

jo·ey /jō ee/ *n* Aus a young kangaroo

jog[1] (**jogged, jog·ging**) *v* **1** *vi* run at a slow steady pace **2** *vt* nudge **3** *vi* go slowly but steadily —**jog** *n* —**jog·ging** /jógging/ *n*

jog[2] *n* a sharp turn ■ *vi* (**jogged, jog·ging**) make sharp turn

jog·ger /jóggər/ *n* somebody who jogs for exercise ■ **jog·gers** *npl* loose pants for jogging

jog·gle /jógg'l/ (**-gled, -gling**) *vti* shake gently —**jog·gle** *n*

jog trot *n* **1** a slow running pace **2** a boring pace of life

Jo·han·nes·burg /jō haánnəss bùrg/ capital of **Gauteng Province**, NE South Africa. Pop. 2,172,000 (1995).

john /jon/ *n* a toilet (*infml*)

John *n* **1** the 4th of the gospels of the Bible in which the life and teachings of Jesus Christ are described **2** a book of the Bible, originally written as a letter and traditionally attributed to St. John.

John /jon/, **St.** (*d*. 101?) in the Bible, one of the 12 apostles of Jesus Christ. By tradition he is considered to be the author of the fourth Gospel, three Epistles, and the Book of Revelations.

John (1167–1216) king of England (1199–1216)

John (of Gaunt) /-gáwnt/, **Duke of Lancaster** (1340–99) English soldier and politician

John (the Bap·tist), St. (8? BC–AD 27?) Judaean prophet

John Birch So·ci·e·ty /-búrch-/ *n* a conservative political organization

John Bull *n* **1** the personification of England **2** an archetypal Englishman —**John Bull·ish** *adj* —**John Bull·ish·ness** *n* —**John Bull·ism** *n*

ORIGIN The original **John Bull** was a character representing the English nation in the satire *Law is a Bottomless Pit*, the first in a collection of pamphlets called *The History of John Bull* issued in 1712 by John Arbuthnot (1667–1735). These advocated ending the war with France in which Britain was engaged at the time.

John Doe /-dō/ *n* **1** an average man (*infml*) **2** an anonymous man

john·ny /jónnee/ *n* (*pl* **-nies**) a short hospital gown, tied at the back

John·ny Ap·ple·seed /áppˈl seèd/ **◆ Chapman, John**

john·ny·cake /jónnee kàyk/ *n* Can, Northeast US a flat bread made with cornmeal

John Paul II (*b*. 1920) pope (1978–)

Johns, Jasper (*b*. 1930) US artist

John·son /jónssˈn/, **Andrew** (1808–75) 17th president of the United States (1865–69)

John·son, Claudia Alta Taylor, "Lady Bird" (*b*. 1912) US first lady (1963–69)

The White House

Lyndon Baines Johnson and Lady Bird Johnson

John·son, Lyndon Baines (1908–73) 36th president of the United States (1963–69)

John·son, Magic (*b*. 1959) US basketball player

John·son, Philip (*b*. 1906) US architect

John·son, Samuel (1709–84) British critic, poet, and lexicographer —**John·so·ni·an** /jon sóneeən/ *adj*

joie de vi·vre /zhwàa də veévrə/ *n* exuberance and love of living

join *v* **1** *vti* bring or come together **2** *vt* connect two or more things ○ *join the dots* **3** *vti* become part of a group **4** *vt* meet or share the company of somebody ○ *I'll join you for dinner*. —**join·a·ble** *adj*

□ **join in** *vti* participate in an activity

join·er /jóynər/ *n* a construction carpenter, especially one who makes finished woodwork

join·er·y /jóynəree/ *n* **1** the finished woodwork in a building **2** the work of a joiner, or the techniques that a joiner uses

joint *n* **1** a junction between bones **2** a place on a plant stem from which leaves or branches grow **3** a place where parts or things are joined **4** a large piece of roasted meat **5** a bar or nightclub *(slang)* **6** a marijuana cigarette *(slang)* ■ *adj* **1** done together **2** sharing the same role **3** owned in common **4** combined ○ *the joint ravages of the weather and pollution* ■ *vt* **1** fit parts or things together with a joint **2** divide a carcass into pieces for cooking —**joint·ly** *adv* ◊ **out of joint 1** dislocated or painfully displaced **2** disturbed or disrupted

Joint Chiefs of Staff *npl* the highest US military advisory group to the President

joint stock *n* stock held jointly in a company

joint ven·ture *n* a business enterprise jointly undertaken by two or more companies

joist *n* a beam supporting a floor, roof, or ceiling

joke *n* **1** a funny story **2** something said or done to amuse people **3** something laughably inadequate *(slang)* ■ *vti* (joked, jok·ing) make jokes or say something to amuse people —**jok·ing·ly** *adv*

jok·er /jṓkər/ *n* **1** a teller or player of jokes **2** a playing card bearing the picture of a jester, which can sometimes be substituted for any other card

jok·ey /jṓkee/ (-i·er, -i·est), **jok·y** *adj* good-humored and amusing —**jok·ily** *adv*

Jol·li·et /jṓlee ét/, **Jo·li·et**, Louis (1645–1700) French-Canadian explorer

jol·li·fi·ca·tion /jòllifi káysh'n/ *n* an enthusiastic celebration

jol·li·ty /jóllətee/ *n* fun or cheerful celebration

jol·ly /jóllee/ (-li·er, -li·est) *adj* **1** friendly and cheerful **2** happily festive *(dated)*

Jol·ly Rog·er *n* a pirates' black flag showing a white skull and crossbones

jolt /jōlt/ *v* **1** *vti* shake or jerk violently **2** *vt* bring abruptly back to reality **3** *vi* bump up and down or from side to side while moving ■ *n* **1** a shock or sudden reminder **2** a sudden violent movement —**jolt·ing·ly** *adv* —**jolt·y** *adj*

Jo·nah /jṓnə/ *n* **1** somebody thought to be a bringer of bad luck **2** a book in the Bible that tells the story of Jonah —**Jo·nah·esque** /jṓnə ésk/ *adj*

ORIGIN In the Bible, Jonah was a Hebrew prophet of the 8C BC who disobeyed God and attempted to escape by sea. He was thrown overboard in a storm as a bringer of bad luck, but was swallowed by a great fish and vomited out three days later, unharmed.

Jones, John Paul (1747–92) Scottish-born US naval officer

jon·quil /jóngkwəl/ *n* a narcissus with small fragrant flowers

Jon·son /jónssən/, **Ben** (1572–1637) English playwright and poet

Corbis-Bettmann
Scott Joplin

Jop·lin /jóplin/, **Scott** (1868–1917) US composer

Jor·dan /jáwrd'n/ **1** country in SW Asia. Cap. Amman. Pop. 5,153,378 (2001). **2** river in SW Asia, rising in Syria and flowing south through the Sea of Galilee to the Dead Sea. Length 200 mi./320 km. —**Jor·da·nian** /jàwr dáynee ən/ *adj, n*

Jor·dan, Michael (b. 1963) US basketball player

Jo·seph (1840?–1904) Nez Percé leader

Jo·seph, St. (fl 1C BC) in the Bible, the husband of Mary, the mother of Jesus

Jo·sé·phine /jṓzə feen/ (1763–1814) empress of the French (1804–09)

josh *vti* tease good-humoredly *(infml)* —**josh·ing·ly** *adv*

Josh·u·a /jóshoo ə/ *n* a book of the Bible that contains a narrative of the Hebrew invasion and partition of Canaan under the command of Joshua, Moses' successor

Jos·pin /zhóss paN/, **Lionel** (b. 1937) prime minister of France (1997–)

joss stick /jóss-/ *n* a stick of incense

jos·tle /jóss'l/ (-tled, -tling) *vti* knock against somebody deliberately

jot *vt* (jot·ted, jot·ting) write quickly ■ *n* a tiny bit

joule /jool/ *n* (symbol J) the SI unit of energy or work

ORIGIN The **joule** is named for the British physicist James Prescott Joule (1818–89).

jour·nal /júrn'l/ *n* **1** a magazine or periodical **2** a diary

jour·nal·ese /jùrn'l eéz/ *n* the writing style regarded as typical of journalists *(disapproving)*

jour·nal·ism /júrn'l ìzzəm/ *n* **1** the job of gathering, editing, and publishing news in the media **2** writing or reporting for the media as a literary genre —**jour·nal·ist** *n* —**jour·nal·is·tic** /jùrn'l ístik/ *adj* —**jour·nal·is·ti·cal·ly** *adv*

~~**journel**~~ incorrect spelling of **journal**

jour·ney /júrnee/ *n* (pl -neys) **1** a trip or expedition from one place to another **2** a gradual passing from one state to a more advanced state ○ *a spiritual journey* ■ *vi* (-neyed, -ney·ing) travel from one place to another —**jour·ney·er** *n*

jour·ney·man /júrnimən/ (*pl* **-men** /-mən/) *n* **1** a qualified artisan working for an employer **2** somebody with ordinary competence at something

ORIGIN One of the strands in the history of *journey* is the meaning "a day's work," which existed alongside "a day's travel" in the French word from which it was adopted. A **journeyman** was originally one qualified to work for a daily wage rather than as an apprentice.

joust /jowst/ *n* a medieval tournament in which mounted knights charged each other with lances ■ *vi* **1** engage in a joust **2** engage in a contest

Jove /jōv/ *n* the Roman god Jupiter —**Jo·vi·an** /jōvee ən/ *adj*

jo·vi·al /jōvee əl/ *adj* cheerful in mood or disposition —**jo·vi·al·i·ty** /jōvee állətee/ *n* —**jo·vi·al·ly** *adv*

jowl[1] /jowl/ *n* **1** the lower jaw **2** a cheek

jowl[2] /jowl/ *n* **1** the hanging part of a double chin **2** a piece of hanging flesh under the chin of an animal or bird

joy *n* **1** great happiness **2** something that brings great happiness —**joy·less** *adj* —**joy·less·ly** *adv* —**joy·less·ness** *n*

Joyce /joyss/, **James** (1882–1941) Irish novelist

joy·ful /jóyf'l/ *adj* **1** feeling or showing joy **2** causing joy —**joy·ful·ly** *adv* —**joy·ful·ness** *n*

joy·ous /jóy əss/ *adj* expressing, causing, or full of joy —**joy·ous·ly** *adv* —**joy·ous·ness** *n*

joy·rid·ing /jóy rīding/ *n* the crime of high-speed driving in a stolen car —**joy·ride** *n*, *vi* —**joy·rid·er** *n*

⚡**joy·stick** /jóy stik/ *n* **1** a control lever of an aircraft or small vehicle **2** a hand-held lever for controlling cursor movement or a video game symbol

J.P., JP *abbr* Justice of the Peace

⚡**jpeg** /jáy pèg/, **jpg** *abbr* a file extension for a Joint Photographic Experts Group file

⚡**JPEG** /jáy pèg/ *n* a format for a compressed graphics file widely used on the World Wide Web. Full form **Joint Photographic Experts Group**

jr., Jr. *abbr* junior

Juan Car·los /waàn kaàrlōss, hwaàn-/ (*b.* 1938) king of Spain (1975–)

Juan de Fu·ca, Strait of /waàn də fóokə/ body of water between S Vancouver Island, Canada, and NW Washington. Length 99 mi./160 km.

Juá·rez /waàr ez, hwaàr-/, **Benito Pablo** (1806–72) Mexican president (1861–63 and 1867–72) and national hero

ju·bi·lant /jóobilənt/ *adj* triumphantly joyful —**ju·bi·lant·ly** *adv*

ju·bi·la·tion /jóobə láysh'n/ *n* uninhibited rejoicing and celebration

ju·bi·lee /jóobə lèe, jòobə lée/ *n* **1** a special anniversary of an event **2** a time of celebration

ORIGIN **Jubilee** goes back to a Hebrew word meaning literally "ram." This derives from the ram's horn with which the Jewish year of jubilee was proclaimed every 50 years. There was originally no connection with words like *jubilant* and *jubilation*, to which **jubilee** might now appear to be related (they come from Latin *jubilare* "call out, shout for joy"). Association with them did, however, reinforce the celebratory aspects of **jubilee**, so that the idea of a 50-year period has in many contexts been lost. We now refer to a 50th anniversary as a *golden jubilee*, but before the 19C **jubilee** alone would have meant just that.

Ju·da·ism /jóodee ìzzəm/ *n* **1** the religion of the Jewish people **2** the Jewish way of life —**Ju·da·is·tic** /jóodee ístik/ *adj*

Ju·das /jóodəss/ *n* *also* **Ju·das Is·car·i·ot** /-iz kárree ət/ one of the 12 apostles of Jesus Christ, who betrayed him **2** a person regarded as a traitor (*literary*)

jud·der /júddər/ *vi* shake violently —**jud·der** *n*

Jude /jood/ *n* a book of the Bible, traditionally attributed to Jude

Jude /jood/, **St.** (*fl* AD 1C) one of the 12 apostles of Jesus Christ

Ju·de·a /joo dee ə/, **Ju·dae·a, Ju·dah** /jóodə/ historic region in SW Asia, incorporating parts of present-day Israel and the West Bank —**Ju·de·an** *adj*, *n*

judge *n* **1** a senior court official who supervises trials, decides cases, instructs juries, and pronounces sentence **2** an adjudicator in a contest or competition ■ *v* (**judged, judg·ing**) **1** *vt* act as a judge in a court case, contest, or competition **2** *vti* assess the quality or likelihood of something **3** *vt* form an opinion of

Judges *n* a book of the Bible that tells the story of the Israelites from the 13C BC to 11C BC (+ *sing verb*)

judg·ment /júj'mənt/, **judge·ment** *n* **1** the decision in a court case **2** discernment or good sense **3** an opinion formed after considering something **4** the judging of a case, contest, or competition **5** **Judg·ment, Judg·ment Day** in various religions, God's judgment on humanity at the end of the world

judg·men·tal /juj mént'l/ *adj* tending to judge or criticize people —**judg·men·tal·ly** *adv*

ju·di·ca·ture /jóodikə chŏor/ *n* the position or authority of a judge

ju·di·cial /joo dísh'l/ *adj* **1** of judges, court judgments, or the justice system **2** enforced by a law court —**ju·di·cial·ly** *adv*

ju·di·ci·ar·y /joo díshee èrree/ *n* (*pl* **-ies**) **1** the branch of government that dispenses justice **2** the court system ■ *adj* of judges

ju·di·cious /joo díshəss/ *adj* sensible and wise —**ju·di·cious·ly** *adv* —**ju·di·cious·ness** *n*

Ju·dith /jóodəth/ *n* a book in the Roman Catholic version of the Bible and the Protestant Apocrypha that tells the story of heroism of Judith, a Jewish woman, in saving her people

ju·do /joodó/ *n* a Japanese martial art that makes use of balance and body weight —**ju·do·ist** *n*

jug *n* 1 a large container for liquids with a handle and a cork stopper 2 *also* **jug·ful** the liquid contained in a jug 3 prison *(humorous)*

jug·ger·naut /júggər nàwt/ *n* 1 an irresistible crushing force 2 **Jug·ger·naut** a form of the Hindu god Krishna

ORIGIN **Juggernaut** is one of the forms taken by the Hindu god Krishna. Every year in Puri in NE India a statue of Juggernaut is pulled through the town on a huge chariot. It used to be said, fictitiously, that worshipers of Krishna threw themselves under the wheels of the Juggernaut wagon in an access of religious ecstasy, so **juggernaut** came to be used in English for an irresistible crushing force.

jug·gle /júgg'l/ (-**gled**, -**gling**) *v* 1 *vti* keep several objects in the air at once by throwing and catching them in quick succession 2 *vt* arrange things to fit into a schedule —**jug·gler** *n*

jug·u·lar /júggyələr/, **jug·u·lar vein** *n* the vein returning blood from the head ■ *adj* of the neck

juice /jooss/ *n* 1 the liquid from fruit or vegetables 2 the liquid from cooking meat 3 a natural fluid or secretion of the body ○ *gastric juices* 4 electricity *(infml)* ■ *vt* (**juiced**, **juic·ing**) extract juice from

juice box *n* an individual box of fruit juice

juic·er /jóossər/ *n* a kitchen appliance for extracting fruit or vegetable juice

juic·y /jóossee/ (-**i·er**, -**i·est**) *adj* 1 containing a lot of juice 2 interesting or titillating —**juic·i·ness** *n*

ju·jit·su /joo jítsoo/, **jiu·jit·su** *n* a Japanese system of unarmed fighting devised by the samurai

ju·ju /joojoo/ *n* 1 an object thought to possess magical powers 2 the supposed magical power of a juju —**ju·ju·ism** *n*

juke·box /jook bòks/ *n* a coin-operated machine that plays selected records or compact discs

ORIGIN The first element of **jukebox** is probably ultimately of West African origin. It seems to have come into English from a word meaning "disorderly" or "wicked" in a creole language spoken by people in the SE United States and on neighboring islands. The first known written record of the word dates from 1935, and that for **jukebox** from 1939.

Jul. *abbr* July

✦ Jul·ian date /joolyən-/ *n* in computer programming, a date expressed as the number of days since January 1 of the current year

ju·li·enne /jooʹlee èn, zhóolee-/ *adj* describes food cut into long thin strips

Ju·li·et /joolee ət/ *n* a communications code word for the letter "J"

Ju·ly /joo líʹ/ (*pl* -**lies**) *n* the 7th month of the year in the Gregorian calendar

ORIGIN **July** is named for Julius Caesar, who was born in that month.

Ju·ma·da /joo maádaa/ *n* either the 5th or the 6th month of the year in the Islamic calendar

jum·ble /júmb'l/ *vti* (-**bled**, -**bling**) 1 put things out of order 2 mix things up mentally ■ *n* a muddled mass

jum·bo /júmbò/ *n* 1 somebody or something larger than usual 2 *also* **jum·bo jet** a large wide-bodied passenger jet aircraft

ORIGIN The word **jumbo** was popularized through Jumbo, a very large elephant at the zoo in London, England, who was sold to Barnum and Bailey's circus in 1882.

jump *v* 1 *vi* leave a surface with both feet 2 *vt* pass over an obstacle by jumping 3 *vt* move quickly in a particular direction ○ *Jump in and I'll drive you home.* 4 *vi* rise suddenly by a large amount 5 *vt* ambush somebody *(infml)* 6 *vi* start in surprise or fright 7 *vti* leave the track accidentally *(refers to trains)* 8 *vi* move abruptly or discontinuously ○ *jumping from one thing to another* 9 *vt* leave a place, or abandon a commitment ○ *jumped bail* ○ *jump ship* ■ *n* 1 a jumping movement, or the distance jumped 2 an obstacle or apparatus used in jumping competitions or races

☐ **jump at** *vt* accept eagerly

jump ball *n* in basketball, a restarting of play in which a referee throws the ball up between two opponents who each try to tip it toward a team member

jump·er[1] /júmpər/ *n* a sleeveless dress worn over a blouse or sweater

jump·er[2] /júmpər/ *n* 1 a person or animal that jumps 2 a short wire for making an electrical connection

jump·er ca·bles *npl* electric cables for starting the engine of a vehicle with a dead battery

jump·ing jack *n* an exercise in which the legs are flung apart while the hands are clapped above the head

jump·ing-off point *n* 1 a place from which to start a trip 2 a basis for beginning something

jump jet *n* a jet aircraft that takes off and lands vertically

jump-off *n* 1 the start of a race or military

attack 2 the deciding round of a jumping contest

jump rope n a rope jumped over as a game

jump shot n a basketball shot from midair —**jump shoot-er** n

jump-start vt start a vehicle using jumper cables —**jump-start** n

jump-suit n 1 a woman's one-piece suit combining top and pants 2 a parachutist's one-piece garment

jump-y /júmpee/ (-i-er, -i-est) adj very nervous or anxious —**jump-i-ly** adv —**jump-i-ness** n

jun. abbr junior

Jun. abbr June

junc-tion /júngkshən/ n a place where things join —**junc-tion-al** adj

junc-tion box n an enclosed box containing electrical connections

junc-ture /júngkchər/ n 1 a point in time 2 a place where things join (fml)

June n the 6th month of the year in the Gregorian calendar

ORIGIN June is named for Juno, the queen of the gods in Roman mythology.

Ju-neau /joo nō/ port and capital of Alaska. Pop. 30,191 (1998).

Jung /yoŏng/, Carl Gustav (1875–1961) Swiss psychiatrist —**Jung-i-an** adj

jun-gle /júng'l/ n 1 a tropical forest 2 an area thickly covered with vegetation

jun-gle gym n a framework on which children can climb

jun-ior /jóonyər/ adj 1 of or for youth or childhood 2 also **Ju-nior** identifies the younger of two family members with the same name, e.g., father and son 3 of low rank or little experience 4 smaller than the standard size 5 of third-year high-school or college students ■ n 1 somebody younger than another being referred to o three years his junior 2 a person of low rank or little experience 3 a child younger than a teenager 4 a third-year high-school or college student

jun-ior col-lege n a college offering a two-year course of study

jun-ior var-si-ty n a high-school or college sports team that competes at a level below varsity

ju-ni-per /jóonipər/ n 1 the oil from small purple cones resembling berries. Use: to flavor gin. 2 an evergreen bush or tree whose cones produce juniper oil

junk[1] n 1 unwanted or worthless objects (infml) 2 cheap low-quality goods (infml) 3 nonsense (infml) 4 heroin (slang) ■ vt discard (infml) —**junk-y** adj

junk[2] n a flat-bottomed Chinese sailing boat

junk bond n a high-risk investment bond with a possible high return

jun-ket /júngkət/ n 1 an expense-paid trip, especially one taken by a politician at public expense 2 an outing, excursion, or party 3 a milk dessert set with rennet ■ v 1 vti throw a party for somebody 2 vi go on an expense-paid trip

junk food n highly processed food lacking nutritional balance

junk-ie /júngkee/, **junk-y** (pl -ies) n a drug addict (slang)

junk mail n unsolicited mail, especially advertisements

junk shop n a store selling secondhand goods or low quality antiques

junk-yard /júngk yaàrd/ n a place where junk is collected

Ju-no /jóonō/ n in Roman mythology, the queen of the gods. Greek equivalent **Hera** —**Ju-no-esque** /jóonō ésk/ adj

jun-ta /hóontə/ n a group of military rulers in charge of a country after a coup (+ sing or pl verb)

Ju-pi-ter /jóopitər/ n 1 in Roman mythology, the ruler of the gods. Greek equivalent **Zeus** 2 the largest planet in the solar system

Ju-ras-sic /joo rássik/ n a period of geologic time 205–142 million years ago —**Ju-ras-sic** adj

ju-rid-i-cal /joo ríddik'l/, **ju-rid-ic** /-ríddik/ adj of the law or judges

ju-ris-dic-tion /jóoriss díksh'n/ n 1 the authority to enforce laws or make legal judgments 2 the area over which legal authority extends —**ju-ris-dic-tion-al** adj

ju-ris-pru-dence /jóoriss prood'nss/ n 1 the philosophy of law 2 the law as it applies in a particular place or situation —**ju-ris-pru-dent** adj, n —**ju-ris-pru-den-tial** /jóoriss proo dénsh'l/ adj

ju-rist /jóorist/ n a legal expert —**ju-ris-tic** /joor ístik/ adj —**ju-ris-ti-cal** adj

ju-ror /jóorər/ n a jury member

ju-ry /jóoree/ (pl -ries) n 1 a group of people chosen to decide a legal case 2 a group of people judging a competition

ju-ry box n the part of a court where the jury sits

ju-ry du-ty n service as juror

ju-ry-rig (ju-ry-rigged, ju-ry-rig-ging) vt build or fit out in a makeshift manner

just adv 1 a very short time ago o He just left. 2 at this moment (also with "about to" and "going to") o I was just about to tell you. 3 only or merely o got off with just a warning 4 barely o arrived just in time 5 emphasizes a statement o It's just plain wrong. 6 exactly o just what I need ■ adj 1 fair and impartial 2 morally correct —**just-ly** adv —**just-ness** n ◊ **just about** almost ◊ **just now** 1 a very short time ago 2 at this very moment ◊ **just so** done or arranged precisely

jus-tice /jústiss/ n 1 fairness or reasonableness in treating people or making decisions 2 the legal system, or the application of law **3** a judge ◊ **do justice to** convey the true merits of

jus·tice of the peace *n* a local magistrate

jus·ti·fi·a·ble /jústi fī əb'l, jùsti fī əb'l/ *adj* able to be justified —**jus·ti·fi·a·bil·i·ty** /jùsti fī ə bíllətee/ *n* —**jus·ti·fi·a·bly** *adv*

jus·ti·fi·a·ble hom·i·cide *n* lawful killing

jus·ti·fi·ca·tion /jùstifi káysh'n/ *n* **1** something that justifies an action or attitude **2** the act of justifying something

jus·ti·fy /jústi fī/ (-**fied**, -**fies**) *vt* **1** give or serve as an acceptable reason or excuse for something **2** adjust the spacing of a line to align the margins of a text

Jus·tin·i·an I /ju stínnee ən/ (483–565) Roman emperor (527–65)

just-in-time *n* a manufacturing system in which goods are produced and delivered as they are required

jut (**jut·ted**, **jut·ting**) *vti* stick out —**jut** *n* —**jut·ting** *adj*

jute *n* **1** a coarse plant fiber. Use: sacking, rope. **2** either of two plants that provide jute

Jute *n* a member of a Germanic people who invaded SE England in the 5C

Ju·ve·nal /joovən'l/ (AD 65?–128?) Roman satirist

ju·ve·nile /joovən'l/ *adj* **1** youthful **2** of or for young people **3** childish ■ *n* a young person —**ju·ve·nile·ly** *adv* —**ju·ve·nile·ness** *n*

ju·ve·nile de·lin·quent *n* a young criminal —**ju·ve·nile de·lin·quen·cy** *n*

jux·ta·pose /júkstə pṓz/ (-**posed**, -**pos·ing**) *vt* put side by side —**jux·ta·po·si·tion** /júkstəpə zísh'n/ *n*

JV *abbr* **1** joint venture **2** junior varsity

Jy·ais·tha /jī ástə/ *n* the 3rd month of the year in the Hindu calendar

K

k[1] (*pl* **k's**), **K** (*pl* **K's** *or* **Ks**) *n* the 11th letter of the English alphabet

k[2] *abbr* **1** karat **2** kilo- **3** knit

K[1] *symbol* **1** kelvin **2** kinetic energy **3** one thousand **4** one thousand dollars **5** potassium

⚡**K**[2] *abbr* **1** kilobyte **2** kilometer **3** kindergarten **4** king **5** knight

K-12 /káy twélv/ *n* the school system from kindergarten through 12th grade

K2 /káy tóo/ second highest mountain in the world, in the Karakorum Range in the W Himalaya range. Height 28,251 ft./8,611 m.

ka·bob *n* FOOD = kebab

Ka·bul /kaʻá bôōl, kə bôōl/ capital of Afghanistan. Pop. 700,000 (1993).

Kaf·ka /kaʻáfkə/, **Franz** (1883–1924) Austrian (Czech) novelist

Kaf·ka·esque /kaʻáfkə ésk/ *adj* **1** of Kafka's work **2** impersonal and overcomplex

kaf·tan *n* = caftan

~~kahki~~ incorrect spelling of **khaki**

Frida Kahlo: Photographed in 1930 by Edward Weston

Kah·lo /kaʻál ô/, **Frida** (1907–54) Mexican painter

Kahn /kaan/, **Louis** (1901–74) Estonian-born US architect and teacher

ka·hu·na /kə hoʻonə/ *n* **1** a Hawaiian priest or traditional healer **2** an important person (*infml*)

kai·ser roll /kízər-/ *n* a crusty round roll, often sprinkled with seeds

Ka·la·ha·ri De·sert /kaʻálə haʻáree-/ dry region in Botswana, Namibia, and South Africa

Ka·lash·ni·kov /kə laʻáshni kàwf/ *n* a Russian-made semi-automatic rifle used among terrorists and paramilitary groups

---

ORIGIN The **Kalashnikov** is named for its Russian developer M. T. Kalashnikov (1919–).

---

kale *n* a variety of cabbage with dark-green curly leaves

ka·lei·do·scope /kə lídə skôp/ *n* **1** a cylindrical optical toy with mirrors and shifting colors inside that create colored patterns **2** a complex shifting scene or pattern —**ka·lei·do·scop·ic** /kə lídə skóppik/ *adj*

ORIGIN The **kaleidoscope** was given its name in 1817 by its inventor, the British physicist Sir David Brewster. He formed it from the Greek word for "beautiful" that is also seen in *calligraphy*, a Greek word meaning "shape," and the ending *-scope* used for optical instruments.

~~kaleidoscope~~ incorrect spelling of **kaleidoscope**

Ka·ma·ku·ra /kaʻámə koʻorə/ city on SE Honshu Island, Japan. Pop. 169,945 (2000).

Kam·chat·ka Pen·in·su·la /kam chàt kə-/ peninsula of E Russia that separates the Sea of Okhotsk from the Bering Sea and the Pacific Ocean

Ka·me·ha·me·ha I /kə màyəmáy ə/ (1758–1819) king of Hawaii (1782–1819)

ka·mi·ka·ze /kaˈami kaˈazee/ *n* **1** a Japanese suicide pilot in World War II **2** an aircraft used by a kamikaze **3** somebody reckless and self-destructive (*infml*) —**ka·mi·ka·ze** *adj*

Kam·pa·la /kaam paˈala/ capital of Uganda. Pop. 773,463 (1991 estimate).

Kam·pu·che·a /kàmpoˈo cheˈe ə/ former name for Cambodia —**Kam·pu·che·an** *n, adj*

Kan·chen·jun·ga /kùnchən júng gə, -joˈong-/ third highest mountain in the world, in the Himalaya range, on the border between Nepal and India. Height 28,209 ft./8,598 m.

Kan·da·har /kàəndə haˈar, kùndə-/ capital of **Kandahar Province**, S Afghanistan. Pop. 225,500 (1988 estimate).

Kan·din·sky /kan dínskee/, **Wassily** (1866–1944) Russian painter

kan·ga·roo /kàng gə roˈo/ (*pl* -**roos**) *n* a large long-tailed marsupial with powerful hindquarters

kan·ga·roo court *n* an unofficial or mock court delivering summary judgment

Kan·pur /kaˈan poor, kaan poˈor/ city in N India, on the Ganges River. Pop. 1,874,409 (1991).

Kans. *abbr* Kansas

Kan·sa /kánzə, kánssə/ (*pl* -**sas** *or* same) *n* **1** a member of a Native North American people who now live mainly in E Oklahoma **2** the language of the Kansa people —**Kan·sa** *adj*

Kan·sas /kánzəss/ state in the central United States. Cap. Topeka. Pop. 2,688,418 (2000). —**Kan·san** *n, adj*

Kan·sas Cit·y 1 largest city in Missouri. Pop. 441,574 (1998). **2** city in NE Kansas, directly across the state line from Kansas City, Missouri. Pop. 141,297 (1998).

Kant, Immanuel (1724–1804) German philosopher —**Kant·i·an** *adj* —**Kant·i·an·ism** *n*

Kao·hsiung /kòw shyoˈong/ city in SW Taiwan, on the Taiwan Strait. Pop. 1,462,302 (1999).

ka·o·lin /káy əlin/, **ka·o·line** *n* a white clay. Use: porcelain, ceramics, medicines.

ORIGIN Kaolin comes ultimately from the name of a hill in Jiangxi province, N China, where fine white china clay is found. The name means literally "high hill" in Chinese.

ka·pok /káy pòk/ *n* a silky fiber obtained from the seed covering of a tropical tree. Use: stuffing, padding.

kap·pa /káppə/ *n* the 10th letter of the Greek alphabet

ka·put /kaa poˈot, -poˈot, kə-/ *adj* broken or out of order (*infml*)

ORIGIN Kaput came immediately from German in the late 19C, but the German itself was taken from a French term used in some card games, meaning "without tricks."

Ka·ra·chi /kə raˈachee/ seaport and largest city of Pakistan. Pop. 9,269,265 (1998).

Ka·ra·ko·rum Range /kàrrə káwrəm-/ mountain range in south central Asia, in the W Himalaya range. Highest peak K2 28,250 ft./8,611 m.

kar·a·o·ke /kèrree óˈkee/ *n* a form of entertainment in which amateurs sing to prerecorded music

kar·at /kérrət/ *n* a measure of gold content

Karate

ka·ra·te /kə raˈatee/ *n* a Japanese martial art using fast kicks and blows —**ka·ra·te·ist** *n*

kar·ma /kaˈarmə/ *n* in the Hindu and Buddhist belief that the quality of people's current and future lives is determined by their behavior in this and past lives —**kar·mic** *adj*

Kart·ti·ka /kaˈartəkə/, **Kar·ti·ka** *n* the 8th month of the year in the Hindu calendar

Kar·zai /kaar zíˈ/, **Hamid** (*b.* 1955?) chairman of the Interim Administration of Afghanistan (2001–02)

Kash·mir /kásh mèer/ disputed territory in the northern part of South Asia

Kas·pa·rov /káspə ràwf/, **Garry** (*b.* 1963) Armenian chess player

Kat·man·du /kàt man doˈo/, **Kath·man·du** capital of Nepal. Pop. 533,000 (1995).

Kat·zav /kát zàv/, **Qat·zav, Moshe** (*b.* 1945) president of Israel (2000–)

Kau·ai /kòw wíˈ/ fourth largest island in Hawaii. Pop. 55,983 (1995).

Kauff·man /kówfmən/, **Angelica** (1741–1807) Swiss painter

Ka·un·da /kaa óˈondə/, **Kenneth** (*b.* 1924) president of Zambia (1964–91)

Ka·wa·sa·ki /kàawə saˈakee/ city on east central Honshu Island, Japan, beside Tokyo Bay. Pop. 1,218,233 (2000).

kay·ak /kíˈ àk/ *n* **1** a sports canoe propelled by double-bladed paddles **2** a traditional Inuit animal-skin boat propelled by one or two people using double-bladed paddles —**kay·ak** *vti* —**kay·ak·er** *n*

Ka·zakh·stan /kàzzək staˈan, kə zaˈak-/ country in central Asia, on the Caspian Sea. Cap. Astana. Pop. 16,731,303 (2001).

ka·zoo /kə zoˈo/ (*pl* -**zoos**) *n* a simple toy instrument that makes a buzzing sound when blown

⚡**KB** *abbr* kilobyte

⚡**kbyte** *abbr* kilobyte

K.C. abbr Kansas City

Kea·ton /keét'n/, **Buster** (1895–1966) US silent movie comedian

Keats /keets/, **John** (1795–1821) British poet —**Keats·i·an** adj

ke·bab /kə baáb/, **ka·bob** /-bób/ n a selection of small pieces of food threaded onto a stick and grilled

ked·ger·ee /kéjjə reè, kèjjə reé/ n 1 a dish of South Asian origin consisting of lentils, rice, and sometimes fish 2 a dish of rice, smoked fish, and hard-boiled eggs

keel n the main structural member of a ship, stretching along the bottom from bow to stern ◇ **on an even keel** in a stable condition

□ **keel over** vi collapse or fall over (infml)

keel·haul /keél hàwl/ vt drag somebody from one side to the other under the keel of a ship as a punishment

keen[1] adj 1 intense ○ keen competition 2 sensitive or finely tuned ○ a keen sense of smell 3 enthusiastic 4 with a sharp edge (literary) ○ a keen razor 5 cold and biting ○ a keen wind 6 fine or very good (slang dated) ○ a keen new bike 7 quick to understand things —**keen·ly** adv —**keen·ness** n

keen[2] vi lament loudly for the dead

~~keeness~~ incorrect spelling of **keenness**

keep v 1 vti hold or maintain in your possession ○ The sample is yours to keep. 2 vt maintain in a particular place or condition ○ Keep your arm up. 3 vt store somewhere when not in use ○ kept the keys in a drawer 4 vti continue, or cause to continue, in a particular way ○ kept working 5 vt not tell anybody about ○ keep a secret 6 vt adhere faithfully to ○ kept his word 7 vt fulfill as a religious duty ○ keep the Sabbath 8 vt create or maintain as a record ○ keep a diary 9 vi not spoil or decay 10 vt detain or delay ○ I won't keep you a moment. 11 vt take care of as an owner ○ keep pets ■ n 1 food and lodging ○ work for your keep 2 the innermost fortified part of a castle ◇ **for keeps** permanently or forever (infml) ◇ **keep something to yourself** refrain from revealing something

□ **keep down** vt 1 maintain in a state of inferiority or oppression 2 maintain at a low level

□ **keep on** vt continue to employ

□ **keep up** v 1 vt maintain at the present level 2 vi go or progress at the same pace as somebody or something 3 vt maintain in good condition

keep·er /keépər/ n 1 somebody in charge of a building (usually in combination) ○ a lighthouse keeper 2 somebody whose job is to take care of or protect animals 3 a prison guard 4 a gamekeeper 5 somebody who maintains something ○ a good record keeper 6 in football, a play in which the quarterback runs toward the goal with the ball

keep·ing /keéping/ n 1 taking care of somebody or something 2 somebody's charge or possession ○ in his keeping ◇ **in keeping with** consistent with or appropriate for

keep·sake /keép sàyk/ n a small item kept as a memento

keg n a small barrel ■ vt (**kegged**, **keg·ging**) store beer in a barrel

kei·ret·su /kay rétsoo/ (pl same) n a Japanese business conglomerate

Kel·ler /kéllər/, **Helen** (1880–1968) US author and lecturer

Kel·ly /kéllee/, **Gene** (1912–96) US movie actor, dancer, and director

Kel·ly, Grace (1929–82) US movie actor

kelp n 1 a brown seaweed with thick broad fronds 2 seaweed ash. Use: source of potash and iodine.

kel·vin /kélvin/ n (symbol **K**) the SI unit of absolute temperature

Kel·vin /kélvin/, **William Thomson, 1st Baron** (1824–1907) British physicist

ken n knowledge

Ken. abbr Kentucky

Ken·ne·dy, Cape /kénnədee/ former name for **Canaveral, Cape**

Ken·ne·dy /kénnədee/, **Anthony M.** (b. 1936) associate justice of the US Supreme Court (1988–)

Ken·ne·dy, Jackie (1929–94) US first lady (1961–63)

John F. Kennedy

Ken·ne·dy, John F. (1917–63) 35th president of the United States (1961–63)

Ken·ne·dy, Robert F. (1925–68) US attorney general (1961–64)

ken·nel /kénn'l/ n 1 a place where dogs are boarded, trained, or bred 2 a doghouse ■ vti put or stay in a kennel

ORIGIN Kennel derives ultimately from Latin *canis* "dog," which also gave us *canine* and other words.

Ken·tuck·y /ken túkee/ state in the east central United States. Cap. Frankfort. Pop. 4,041,769 (2000). —**Ken·tuck·ian** n, adj

Ken·ya /kényə/ country in E Africa. Cap. Nairobi. Pop. 30,765,916 (2001). —**Ken·yan** n, adj

Ken·yat·ta /ken yaáta/, **Jomo** (1891–1978) prime minister (1963–64) and president of Kenya (1964–78)

Kep·ler /képplər/, **Johannes** (1571–1630) German astronomer

kept past tense, past participle of **keep** ■ *adj* supported financially by a lover

ke·ra·tin /kérrətin/ *n* a fibrous protein that is the main constituent of nails, hair, and hooves

kerb *n*, *vt* UK = **curb**

ker·chief /kúrchif, -cheéf/ *n* a woman's square scarf

Ke·ren·sky /kərénskee/, **Aleksandr Fyodorovich** (1881–1970) Russian revolutionary leader

ker·nel /kúrn'l/ *n* 1 the edible content of a nut or fruit stone 2 the grain of a cereal that contains a seed and husk 3 the central part ◊ See note at **colonel**

ker·o·sene /kérrə seén, kèrrə seén/ *n US, Can, ANZ* a colorless flammable oil distilled from petroleum. Use: fuel.

Ker·ou·ac /kérrə wàk/, **Jack** (1922–69) US novelist

kes·trel /késtrəl/ *n* a small falcon

ketch *n* a small two-masted sailing ship

ketch·up /kéchəp/, **catch·up** /káchəp, kéchəp/, **cat·sup** /kátsəp, káchəp, kéchəp/ *n* a thick cold tomato sauce

ket·tle /kétt'l/ *n* 1 a teakettle 2 a metal cooking pot with a lid ◊ *a fish kettle*

ket·tle·drum /kétt'l drùm/ *n* a percussion instrument consisting of a large metal drum with a parchment skin top —**ket·tle·drum·mer** *n*

ʄ key[1] /kee/ *n* 1 a metal bar with notches or grooves that is turned to operate a lock's mechanism 2 a device such as a plastic card for opening a door or lock 3 a lever or button on a musical instrument that is pressed to produce a sound 4 a system of related musical notes in a scale beginning on a particular note ◊ *in the key of E* 5 a tool that is turned to wind, set, or calibrate a mechanism 6 a means of achieving, understanding, accessing, or controlling something ◊ *the key to success* ◊ *the key to the riddle* 7 a list of the answers to a test or exercise 8 a computer or typewriter keyboard button 9 the pitch or quality of a voice or expressive sound 10 in cryptography, a sequence of symbols or characters for encoding or decoding 11 an explanatory text or list 12 a field in a database record that uniquely identifies that record ■ *adj* crucial ■ *v* (keyed, key·ing) 1 *vt* provide with an explanatory key 2 *vt* regulate the pitch of 3 *vti* type characters using a computer keyboard 4 *vt* lock or adjust with a key

key[2] /kee/ *n* a small low island of sand or coral in the Gulf of Mexico or the Caribbean

Key /kee/, **Francis Scott** (1779–1843) US poet and lawyer. He wrote the lyrics to "The Star Spangled Banner" (1814).

ʄ key·board /kee bàwrd/ *n* 1 a set of keys in a row or rows for a computer or musical instrument 2 a musical instrument with a keyboard ■ *vti* input data using a computer keyboard —**key·board·er** *n*

key·board·ist /kee bàwrdist/ *n* a keyboard instrument player

key card *n* a plastic card with an encoded metal strip giving access to a door or mechanism

ʄ key da·ta·base *n* in e-commerce, a database that holds all keys used by a certificate authority

keyed up *adj* excited or tense (*infml*)

ʄ key es·crow *n* a computer data encryption system in which the decoding key is held by a third party

key·hole /kee hòl/ *n* the hole in a lock for a key

key·hole sur·ger·y *n* surgery performed using instruments inserted through a small incision in the body and manipulated externally

Key Lar·go /-laàrgō/ one of the largest of the Florida Keys, off the tip of SE Florida. Length 30 mi./48 km.

Keynes /kaynz/, **John Maynard, 1st Baron Keynes of Tilton** (1883–1946) British economist —**Keynes·i·an** *n, adj*

key·note /kee nòt/ *n* 1 the main theme of something 2 the tonic in a musical scale ■ *adj* containing the main theme ■ *v* (-not·ed, -not·ing) 1 *vti* deliver an important speech to a conference or meeting 2 *vt* outline an important policy in a speech or report

ʄ key·pad /kee pàd/ *n* 1 a small keyboard with numbers on the pad 2 the part of a computer keyboard containing the number and command keys

key ring *n* a metal ring for holding keys

key sig·na·ture *n* a group of sharps or flats at the beginning of a piece of music showing what key it is in

key·stone /kee stòn/ *n* 1 the central stone in an arch 2 something upon which other related things depend

ʄ key·stroke /kee stròk/ *n* a single stroke of a keyboard key

Key West city in S Florida, on Key West Island. Pop. 25,701 (1998).

key·word /kee wùrd/ *n* 1 a word used as a reference point for further information or as an indication of the contents of a document 2 a word used as a key to a code

kg *symbol* kilogram

KGB *n* the former Soviet secret police

khak·i /kákee, kaàkee/ *n* 1 a brownish yellow color 2 a tough brownish yellow cloth. Use: pants, military uniforms. ■ **khak·is** *npl* pants or a uniform made of khaki —**khak·i** *adj*

Kha·me·nei /kaà me neé/, **Ali, Ayatollah** (*b.*

1939) supreme spiritual leader of Iran (1989–)

Khar·toum /kaar toʻom/ capital of Sudan and of Khartoum Province. Pop. 924,505 (1993).

Kha·ta·mi /kaʻa taa meʻe, khaʻa-/, **Mohammad** (b. 1943) president of Iran (1997–) and cleric

Khmer /kmair/ (pl same or **Khmers**) n 1 a member of a people of Cambodia 2 the official language of Cambodia

Kho·mei·ni /kō máynee/, **Ruhollah, Ayatollah** (1900?–89) Iranian religious and political leader

Khru·shchev /króosh chef, -chawf/, **Nikita** (1894–1971) premier of the former Soviet Union (1958–64)

Khy·ber Pass /kíbər-/ mountain pass in W Asia, the most important pass connecting Afghanistan and Pakistan

kHz abbr kilohertz

kib·ble /kíbb'l/ n ground meal that has been formed into pellets, especially for pet food ■ vt (-bled, -bling) grind into small pieces

kib·butz /ki bŏots, -bŏots/ (pl **-but·zim** /-bŏot'seèm, -bŏot-/) n a collective farm or factory in Israel

kib·itz /kíbbits/ vi (infml) 1 interfere or give unwanted advice 2 chat

kib·lah /kíbblə/ n the direction of Mecca that Muslims must face when praying

ki·bosh /kí bósh, ki bósh/ vt put a stop to

kick v 1 vti strike somebody or something with the foot 2 vti move something by striking it with the foot 3 vti make a thrashing movement with the legs 4 vti raise the leg high quickly 5 vi recoil (refers to firearms) ■ n 1 a blow with the foot 2 a thrashing leg movement 3 a swift raising of the leg 4 the act or an instance of kicking a ball 5 a pleasurable feeling (infml) 6 a sudden stimulant effect produced by something such as alcohol 7 a temporary strong interest (infml) ◊ on a health kick 8 the recoil of a gun

☐ **kick around** v 1 vt mistreat (infml) 2 vi travel aimlessly around

☐ **kick in** vti US, Can, ANZ contribute toward the cost of something (infml)

☐ **kick off** vi in football, start play by kicking the ball to the receiving team

☐ **kick out** vt expel or send away (infml)

Kick·a·poo /kíkə pŏo/ (pl same or **-poos**) n a member of a Native North American people who now live in Kansas, Oklahoma, and Texas —**Kick·a·poo** adj

kick·back /kík bàk/ n a bribe paid to gain an advantage (infml)

kick·ball /kík bàwl/ n a children's game similar to baseball but using a large ball that is kicked instead of batted

kick·box·ing /kík bòksing/ n a form of boxing with kicking as well as punching —**kick·box·er** n

kick·er /kíkər/ n 1 somebody that kicks 2 an unexpected or surprising problem or fact (infml)

kick·off /kík àwf/ n 1 in football, the place kick at the beginning of a game or half or after a goal 2 the start of something, or the time at which something starts (infml) 3 in soccer, the place kick that begins the game 4 the starting time of a soccer or football game

kick·stand /kík stànd/ n a pivoting metal bar on a bicycle or motorcycle used to keep it upright when stationary

kick-start vt 1 start a motorcycle by stepping down on the starter 2 start a process or activity quickly and forcefully ■ n also **kick-start·er** the pedal on a motorcycle that starts it when stepped on forcefully

kid[1] n 1 a child or young person (infml) 2 a young goat 3 soft leather from a young goat ■ adj younger (infml) ◊ my kid sister ■ vti (**kid·ded, kid·ding**) give birth to a young goat ◊ See note at **youth**

kid[2] (**kid·ded, kid·ding**) v 1 vti say or speak in fun or teasing 2 vt deceive (infml) ◊ Don't kid yourself.

Kidd, William (1645?–1701) Scottish-born American pirate

kid·die /kíddee/, **kid·dy** (pl **-dies**) n a small child (infml)

kid glove ◊ **handle with kid gloves** deal with using great care or delicacy

kid·nap /kíd nàp/ (**-napped** or **-naped, -nap·ping** or **-nap·ing**) vti abduct and hold somebody, usually for ransom —**kid·nap·per** n

kid·ney /kídnee/ (pl **-neys**) n either of two organs in the vertebrate abdomen for filtering waste liquid

kid·ney bean n 1 a small dark-red kidney-shaped edible bean 2 a plant producing kidney beans

Kier·ke·gaard /keèrkə gàard/, **Søren** (1813–55) Danish philosopher

Ki·ev /keè ev/ capital and largest city of Ukraine. Pop. 2,600,000 (1998).

Ki·ga·li /ki gaàlee/ capital of Rwanda. Pop. 286,000 (1995).

Kil·i·man·ja·ro, Mt. /kílləmən jaàrō/ highest mountain in Africa, in NE Tanzania. Height 19,341 ft./5,895 m.

kill[1] v 1 vti cause a person or animal to die 2 vt ruin or end something 3 vt cause severe pain to somebody (infml) ◊ My feet are killing me! 4 vr overexert yourself (infml; often ironic) ◊ killed herself to finish on time 5 vt use up spare time (infml) ◊ an hour to kill 6 vt stop a plan or the passage of a bill ■ n 1 the moment or an act of killing a person or animal 2 the prey killed by a person or animal 3 the destruction of an enemy airplane, ship, or tank (slang) —**kill·ing** n, adj

---

SYNONYMS **kill, murder, assassinate,**

execute, put to death, slaughter, slay, put down, put to sleep CORE MEANING: deprive of life

kill[2] *n regional* a waterway *(archaic)*

kill·er /kíllər/ *n* **1** somebody or something that kills **2** something very difficult *(infml)* **3** something excellent or exceptional *(slang)*

kill·er in·stinct *n* **1** the urge to kill **2** a strong will to win at any cost

kill·er whale *n* a black-and-white toothed whale inhabiting colder seas

kill·ing fields *npl* a place of carnage

kill·joy /kíl jòy/ *n* somebody who spoils the fun of others

kiln *n* an industrial oven ■ *vt* process in a kiln

ki·lo /keélō/ *n* **1** *(symbol* k*)* a kilogram *(infml)* **2** a communications code word for the letter "K"

kilo- *prefix* **1** *(symbol* k*)* a thousand (10³) ○ *kilogram* **2** a binary thousand ○ *kilobyte*

⨍ **kil·o·bit** /kíllə bìt/ *n* 1,024 bits

⨍ **kil·o·byte** /kíllə bìt/ *n* 1,024 bytes

kil·o·gram /kíllə gràm/ *n* *(symbol* kg*)* 1,000 grams

kil·o·hertz /kíllə hùrts/ *n* 1,000 hertz

kil·om·e·ter /ki lómmətər/ *n* 1,000 meters

kil·o·watt /kíllə wòt/ *n* 1,000 watts

kilt *n* a Scottish tartan garment like a skirt, traditionally worn by men —**kilt·ed** *adj*

kil·ter /kíltər/ *n* good working order

Kim Dae Jung /kím dī jóng/ (b. 1925) president of South Korea (1998–)

Kim Jong Il /kím jong íl/ (b. 1941) premier of North Korea (1994–)

ki·mo·no /kə mṓnə, -mṓnō/ *(pl* **-nos***)* *n* **1** a full-length loose traditional Japanese garment **2** a Western garment resembling a kimono, especially a dressing gown —**ki·mo·noed** *adj*

kin *n* **1** somebody's family group *(+ pl verb)* **2** a member of a group that shares characteristics with another group **3** a blood relation ■ *adj* related

ki·na /keénə/ *n* the main unit of Papua New Guinean currency

kind[1] /kīnd/ *adj* **1** generous, warm, or compassionate ○ *You're very kind.* ○ *a kind act* **2** not harsh, unpleasant, or dangerous ○ *a detergent that is kind to the environment* ◊ See note at **generous**

kind[2] /kīnd/ *n* **1** a group of people or things that share features ○ *What kind of fruit is this?* **2** an example of something regarded as inferior or unsatisfactory ○ *a kind of apology* ◊ **kind of** rather *(infml)* ◊ **in kind** **1** with goods or services and not money **2** with something of the same sort ◊ **of a kind** alike in only some respects ◊ See note at **type**

kin·der·gar·ten /kíndər gaàrt'n, -gaàrd'n/ *n US, ANZ* a school or class for young children

before they start formal education —**kin·der·gart·ner** *n*

kind·heart·ed /kīnd haártəd/ *adj* friendly, sympathetic, and generous by nature —**kind·heart·ed·ly** *adv* —**kind·heart·ed·ness** *n*

kin·dle /kínd'l/ *(-dled, -dling)* *vti* **1** start burning **2** excite or interest, or become excited or interested

kin·dling /kíndling/ *n* material that burns easily, used for starting a fire

kind·ly /kíndlee/ *adj* *(-li·er, -li·est)* **1** friendly, sympathetic, and generous **2** pleasant, mild, or comfortable ■ *adv* **1** please **2** in a kind way —**kind·li·ness** *n*

kind·ness /kíndnəss/ *n* **1** generosity, warmth, and compassion **2** a generous, warm, or compassionate act

kin·dred /kíndrəd/ *adj* close to somebody or something because of similar qualities or interests ■ *n* **1** a blood relationship **2** somebody's family group *(+ pl verb)* —**kín·dred·ship** *n*

ki·net·ic /ki néttik, kī-/ *adj* of motion

ki·net·ic en·er·gy *n* *(symbol* T *or* Eₖ*)* the energy that a body has because of its motion

ki·net·ics /ki néttiks, kī-/ *n (+ sing verb)* **1** the study of motion **2** the branch of chemistry that studies rates of reactions

kin·folk /kín fòk/ *npl* somebody's relatives

king *n* **1** a man or boy who rules as monarch **2** an animal considered the best, strongest, or biggest of its kind **3** the foremost man in a particular field **4** a high-value playing card with a picture of a king on it **5** the principal chess piece **6** a crowned piece in checkers **7** **King** in Christianity, God or Jesus Christ —**king·li·ness** *n* —**king·ly** *adj* —**king·ship** *n*

King, Billie Jean (b. 1943) US tennis player

Martin Luther King, Jr.

King, Martin Luther, Jr. (1929–68) US civil rights leader and minister

King, William Lyon Mackenzie (1874–1950) prime minister of Canada (1921–26, 1926–30, 1935–48)

king·dom /kíngdəm/ *n* **1** the territory or people ruled by a monarch **2** a sphere of activity in which somebody or something dominates **3** any of the three groups, animal, vegetable, and mineral, into which natural things are traditionally divided

king·fish·er /kíng físhər/ *n* a brightly colored bird that feeds on fish

King James Bi·ble, King James Ver·sion *n* an English version of the Bible of 1611

king·mak·er /kíng màykər/ *n* somebody with the power to appoint people to important positions

king·pin /kíng pìn/ *n* 1 the most important person in a group or place *(infml)* 2 in bowling, the front pin in a pin layout

Kings *n* each of two books of the Bible that relate the histories of Israel and the kings of Judah *(+ sing verb)*

king-size, king-sized *adj* 1 larger than standard 2 describes an extra-large bed 3 very great *(infml)*

King·ston /kíngstən/ 1 chief seaport and capital of Jamaica. Pop. 538,100 (1995). 2 city in SE Ontario Province, Canada, on Lake Ontario at the mouth of the St. Lawrence River. Pop. 112,610 (1996).

Kings·town /kíngz tòwn/ capital and principal port of St. Vincent and the Grenadines, on St. Vincent Island. Pop. 16,130 (1995).

kink *n* 1 a tight twist or coil in an otherwise straight section of something 2 a minor difficulty *(infml)* 3 a muscular spasm *(infml)* 4 an eccentricity in somebody's personality or behavior ■ *vti* contain a kink, or give a kink to

kink·y /kíngkee/ (-i·er, -i·est) *adj* 1 tightly twisted or coiled 2 of or engaging in unusual sexual practices *(slang)* 3 sexually provocative *(slang)* —**kink·i·ly** *adv* —**kink·i·ness** *n*

Kin·sey /kínzee/, **Alfred** (1894–1956) US biologist, best known for his studies of male (1948) and female (1953) sexuality (the *Kinsey Reports*)

kins·folk /kínz fòk/ *npl* somebody's relatives

Kin·sha·sa /kin shaássa/ capital of the Democratic Republic of the Congo. Pop. 4,655,313 (1994).

kin·ship /kín shìp/ *n* 1 relationship by blood or marriage 2 relationship through common characteristics or a common origin

kins·man /kínzmən/ (*pl* -men /-mən/) *n* a male relative

kins·wom·an /kínz wòomman/ (*pl* -en /-wìmmin/) *n* a female relative

ki·osk /kée òsk, kee ósk/ *n* a small roofed street booth

Ki·o·wa /kí ə wàw, -ə wàà/ (*pl same or* -was) *n* 1 a member of a Native North American people who now live in Oklahoma 2 the language of the Kiowa people —**Ki·o·wa** *adj*

kip (*pl same*) *n* the main unit of currency of Laos

Kip·ling /kípling/, **Rudyard** (1865–1936) British writer and poet

kip·per /kíppər/ *n* 1 a male salmon in the spawning season 2 a smoked herring ■ *vt* smoke herring

Ki·ri·ba·ti /kéerrə baátee/ independent island state in the west central Pacific Ocean, part of Micronesia. Cap. Tarawa. Pop. 94,149 (2001).

Kirk /kurk/ *n* the Church of Scotland

kirsch /keershl/, **kirsch·was·ser** /kéersh vaàssər/ *n* cherry brandy from Germany or France

Ki·san·ga·ni /kèessan gaánee/ capital of Orientale Region, in N Democratic Republic of the Congo. Pop. 417,517 (1994).

Kis·lev /kíssləf/ *n* the 9th month of the year in the Jewish calendar

kis·met /kíz mèt, -mət/ *n* 1 fate 2 Allah's will

kiss *vti* touch with the lips —**kiss·a·ble** *adj*

kiss·er /kíssər/ *n* 1 somebody who kisses 2 a mouth *(slang)*

Kis·sin·ger /kíssinjər/, **Henry** (*b.* 1923) German-born US secretary of state (1973–77)

kiss of death *n* somebody or something that will cause failure or disaster

kit *n* 1 a set of articles, tools, or equipment used for a particular purpose or activity 2 a set of parts to be assembled

Ki·ta·kyu·shu /kèetə kyóoshoo/ city in the north of Kyushu Island, Japan. Pop. 1,005,353 (2000).

kit bag *n* a soft cylindrical shoulder bag

kitch·en /kíchən/ *n* a room or area where food is prepared and cooked

kitch·en cab·i·net *n* a political leader's unofficial advisers

Kitch·e·ner /kíchənər/ city in S Ontario, Canada. Pop. 178,420 (1996).

kitch·en·ette /kìchə nét/ *n* a small kitchen area

kitch·en gar·den *n* a garden for growing vegetables, herbs, and sometimes fruit, for a household

kitch·en·ware /kíchən wàir/ *n* utensils for preparing and cooking food

kite *n* 1 a fabric- or paper-covered framework flown in the wind at the end of a string 2 a small slim hawk

kith /kith/ ◇ **kith and kin** somebody's friends and relatives

kitsch /kich/ *n* 1 artistic tastelessness 2 tasteless decorative objects —**kitsch·y** *adj*

kit·ten /kítt'n/ *n* a young cat ■ *vi* give birth to young cats

kit·ten·ish /kítt'nish/ *adj* 1 frisky 2 flirtatious —**kit·ten·ish·ness** *n*

kit·ty¹ /kíttee/ (*pl* -ties) *n* a cat *(infml)*

kit·ty² /kíttee/ (*pl* -ties) *n* 1 a fund of money to which people have contributed in order to buy something in common 2 a pool of bets

Kit·ty Hawk /kíttee hàwk/ town in NE North Carolina, on the Atlantic Ocean, site of the

Wright brothers' successful glider and airplane experiments. Pop. 2,336 (1998).

ki·wi /kéewee/ (*pl* same or **-wis**) *n* **1** a flightless New Zealand bird **2** *also* **ki·wi fruit** a sweet green fruit with a brownish skin

Klans·man /klánzmən/ (*pl* **-men** /-mən/) *n* a member of Ku Klux Klan

Klee /klay/, **Paul** (1879–1940) Swiss painter

Kleen·ex /klée nèks/ *tdmk* a trademark for a soft facial tissue

klep·to·ma·ni·a /klèptə máynee ə/ *n* an obsessive desire to steal **—klep·to·ma·ni·ac** *n*

Klerk ◊ de Klerk, F. W.

Klimt, Gustav (1862–1918) Austrian painter

Klon·dike /klón dik/ region of NW Yukon Territory, Canada, named for the Klondike River, which traverses it

klutz *n* an offensive term for somebody regarded as physically or socially clumsy (*slang insult*) **—klutz·i·ness** *n* **—klutz·y** *adj*

⚡ km *abbr* **1** kilometer **2** Comoros (*in Internet addresses*)

knack /nak/ *n* **1** an easy clever way of doing something **2** a natural ability or talent ◊ See note at **talent**

knap·sack /náp sàk/ *n* a bag designed for carrying personal items on a hiker's back

knave /nayv/ *n* a jack in card games

knead /need/ *v* **1** *vti* work dough or clay until it is smooth **2** *vt* massage a body part to relax the muscles ◊ See note at **need**

knee /nee/ *n* **1** the joint of the human leg between the thigh and the lower leg **2** the area around the knee joint **3** the upper part of the thigh of somebody sitting down o *Come and sit on my knee.* **4** the middle joint of a four-legged animal's hind leg or of a bird's leg **5** a growth from a tree root protruding above the surface of water ■ *vt* (**kneed**) hit with the knee

knee·cap /née kàp/ *n* the flat bone at the front of the knee joint

knee-deep *adj* **1** standing in something as high as the knees o *knee-deep in water* **2** reaching as high as the knees

knee-high *adj* up to the knees

knee jerk *n* an involuntary contraction of the thigh muscle, producing a sudden extension of the leg below the knee

knee-jerk *adj* tending to react predictably and without thinking, or happening as a result of such a reaction (*infml*) o *a knee-jerk politician* o *a knee-jerk opinion*

kneel /neel/ (**knelt** /nelt/ *or* **kneeled**) *vi* rest on or get down on both knees

knell /nel/ *n* **1** the sound of a bell rung slowly, especially in mourning **2** an ominous signal for somebody or something (*literary*)

knew past tense of **know**

knick·ers /níkərz/, **knick·er·bock·ers** /níkər

bòkərz/ *npl* loose short breeches gathered at the knee

ORIGIN Knickers is a shortening of *knickerbockers*. *Knickerbockers* is taken from the name Diedrich Knickerbocker, given by Washington Irving to the pretended author of his *History of New York* (1809). He presumably invented *Knickerbocker* as a typical Dutch-sounding name. The transfer to *knickerbockers* is said to derive from the breeches' resemblance to Dutchmen's knee breeches as depicted in William Cruikshank's original illustrations for the *History of New York*. By the 1880s it was shortened to *knickers*.

knick·knack /ník nàk/ *n* a small ornament

knife /nīf/ *n* (*pl* **knives** /nīvz/) **1** a tool consisting of a sharp blade with a handle for cutting **2** a knife designed as a stabbing weapon ■ *vt* (**knifed, knif·ing**) stab **—knif·er** *n* ◊ **under the knife** undergoing surgery (*infml*)

knife-edge *n* a point in a situation at which it is balanced precariously between two possible outcomes

knife·point /nīf pòynt/ ◊ **at knifepoint** while being threatened with a knife

knight /nīt/ *n* **1** an early-medieval mounted soldier of low social rank **2** a late-medieval mounted soldier of high social rank **3** a man with a nonhereditary title "Sir" **4** a member of a religious or secret brotherhood **5** a champion of a cause **6** a protector of a woman **7** a chess piece shaped like a horse's head ■ *vt* make a man a knight **—knight·ly** *adv*

SPELLCHECK Do not confuse the spelling of **knight** and **night** ("period of darkness"), which sound similar.

knight-er·rant (*pl* **knights-er·rant**) *n* a wandering medieval knight **—knight·er·rant·ry** *n*

knight·hood /nīt hòod/ *n* **1** the rank or title of a knight **2** chivalry and honor

Knights of the Round Ta·ble *npl* the order of knights of Arthurian legend

knit /nit/ *v* (**knit·ted** *or* **knit, knit·ting**) **1** *vti* interlock yarn loops to make a garment or fabric **2** *vt* unite **3** *vi* grow together again after fracture (*refers to bone*) **4** *vt* draw the brows together in a frown ■ *n* something made by knitting **—knit·ter** *n* **—knit·ting** *n*

SPELLCHECK Do not confuse the spelling of **knit** and **nit** ("an egg of a louse"), which sound similar.

knit·ting nee·dle *n* a long thin rod used in knitting

knives plural of **knife**

knob /nob/ *n* **1** a rounded handle or switch **2** a rounded projection **—knob·by** *adj*

knock /nok/ *v* **1** *vi* make a noise by hitting something, often repeatedly o *knock at the door* o *branches knocking against the window*

2 *vt* strike with a blow o *knocked the vase off the table* **3** *vti* collide, or cause to collide o *knocked my head on a low beam* **4** *vt* criticize *(slang)* ■ *n* **1** a blow or collision **2** a sound of knocking

□ **knock around** *or* **a·bout** *vi* travel around an area *(infml)*

□ **knock down** *vt* **1** cause fall **2** cut the price of *(infml)*

□ **knock off** *v* **1** *vi* stop work for a break or at the end of a day *(infml)* **2** *vt* produce with ease or speed *(infml)* **3** *vt* kill *(slang)*

□ **knock out** *vt* **1** in boxing, defeat with a knockout **2** make unconscious

knock·down /nók dòwn/ *adj* **1** very powerful o *a knockdown blow* **2** easily disassembled

knock·down-drag-out /-drág òwt/ *adj* intensely violent or bitter —**knock·down-drag-out** *n*

knock·er /nókər/ *n* a fixture used for knocking on a door

knock·off /nók àwf/ *n* a cheap copy of a piece of well-known merchandise *(infml)*

knock·out /nók òwt/ *n* **1** a punch that wins a boxing match **2** a boxing victory won by a knockout **3** somebody or something stunning or excellent *(infml)*

~~knoledge~~ incorrect spelling of **knowledge**

knoll /nōl/ *n* a small rounded hill

Knos·sos /nóssəss, knóssəss/ ruined city in N Crete, the center of the Minoan civilization from about 3,000 BC to 1,100 BC

knot /not/ *n* **1** a lump-shaped object formed when a strand is interlaced with itself or another strand and pulled tight **2** a tangled mass of strands **3** a deep bond, especially marriage **4** a dark whorl in lumber **5** a lump, e.g., on a tree trunk or in the body **6** *(symbol* **kn***)* a unit of speed equal to one nautical mile per hour **7** a tight group o *a knot of people* **8** a tense feeling o *a knot in my stomach* ■ *v* (**knot·ted, knot·ting**) **1** *vt* tie in a knot **2** *vti* tangle —**knot·ty** *adj* ◇ **tie (up) in knots** confuse utterly ◇ **tie the knot** get married *(infml)*

SPELLCHECK Do not confuse the spelling of **knot** and **not** (indicating a negative), which sound similar.

know /nō/ (**knew** /noo/, **known** /nōn/) *v* **1** *vti* have information in the mind **2** *vti* be certain about something **3** *vt* have learned o *know how to operate a computer* **4** *vt* be acquainted or familiar with **5** *vt* be able to distinguish o *know right from wrong* —**know·a·ble** *adj* ◇ **in the know** possessing information that is secret or restricted

SPELLCHECK Do not confuse the spelling of **know** and **no** (indicating a negative response), which sound similar.

know-how *n* practical ability and knowledge *(infml)*

know·ing /nó ing/ *adj* **1** indicating secret knowledge o *a knowing smile* **2** shrewd or clever **3** intentional —**know·ing·ly** *adv*

knowl·edge /nóllij/ *n* **1** information in the mind **2** awareness **3** all that can be known

knowl·edge·a·ble /nóllijəb'l/, **knowl·edg·a·ble** *adj* knowing a great deal —**knowl·edge·a·bly** *adv*

⚡ **knowl·edge base** *n* data used for solving problems

knowl·edge man·age·ment *n* the organization of intellectual resources and information systems within a company

~~knowlegable~~ incorrect spelling of **knowledgeable**

known past participle of **know**

Knox /noks/, **Henry** (1750–1806) American Revolutionary soldier

Knox, John (1513?–72) Scottish religious reformer

Knox·ville /nóks vìl, nóksvəl/ city in E Tennessee. Pop. 165,540 (1998).

knuck·le /núk'l/ *n* **1** a finger joint **2** the rounded projection of a knuckle when a fist is made *(often pl)* ■ *vt* (**-led, -ling**) rub, hit, or press with the knuckles

□ **knuckle down** *vi* work hard *(infml)*

□ **knuckle under** *vi* submit

KO *(infml)* *n* (*pl* **KO's**) a knockout ■ *vt* (**KO'd, KO'ing, KO's**) knock out, especially in boxing

ko·a·la /kō áalə/, **ko·a·la bear** *n* a gray furry marsupial resembling a bear

Ko·be /kṓbèè, kṓ bày/ seaport on S Honshu Island, Japan, on Osaka Bay. Pop. 1,461,678 (2000).

Ko·dá·ly /kṓ dī/, **Zoltán** (1882–1967) Hungarian composer

Ko·di·ak Is·land /kṓdee ak-/ island of SW Alaska, in the Gulf of Alaska

kohl /kōl/ *n* a preparation used as dark eye makeup

kohl·ra·bi /kōl ráabee, -rábbee/ *n* **1** (*pl* **kohl·ra·bies**) a turnip-shaped cabbage stem eaten as a vegetable **2** a plant that produces kohlrabies

koi (*pl* **same**), **koi carp** *n* a brightly-colored carp kept as a pond fish

Koi·zu·mi /koy zṓmee/, **Junichiro** (b. 1942) Japanese prime minister (2001–))

Ko·la Penin·sula /kōlə-/ peninsula in NW European Russia, between the Barents Sea and the White Sea

Kol·ka·ta /kol káttə/ capital of West Bengal state and port in NE India. Pop. 4,580,544 (2001).

kook *n* a person regarded as eccentric *(slang insult)* —**kook·y** *adj*

kook·a·bur·ra /kóokə bùrrə/ (*pl* **-ras** *or* **same**) *n* a large Australian kingfisher with a laughing call

Koo·te·nay /kóot'n ày/, **Koo·te·nai** river of the NW United States and SW Canada. Length 407 mi./655 km.

Ko·ran /kə raΛn, kaw-/, **Qur·'an** n the sacred text of Islam —**Ko·ran·ic** /kə raΛnik, -rΛnnik, kaw-/ adj

Ko·re·an /kə rée ən/ n 1 somebody from North or South Korea 2 the language of North and South Korea —**Ko·re·an** adj

ko·ru·na /káwrə naΛə/ (pl -run or -ru·nas) n the main unit of Czech and Slovak currency

Kos ♦ **Cos**

Kos·ci·i·usz·ko, Mt. /kòssee úskō/ highest mountain in Australia, in the Snowy Mountains in SE New South Wales. Height 7,310 ft./2,228 m.

Koś·ci·usz·ko /kòssee úsk ō/, **Tadeusz** (1746–1817) Polish soldier and revolutionary

ko·sher /kóshər/ adj 1 describes food prepared according to Jewish law 2 lawful or proper (infml) —**ko·sher** vt

Ko·so·vo /káwssə vò/ former autonomous province in SW Serbia. Pop. 1,956,196 (1991). Albanian **Kosova** —**Ko·so·van** n, adj —**Ko·so·var** /-vaΛar/ n, adj

Kos·tu·ni·ca /kosh tóonitsə/, **Vojislav** (b. 1944) president of the Federal Republic of Yugoslavia (2000–)

Ko·sy·gin /kə séegin/, **Aleksey** (1904–80) premier of the former Soviet Union (1964–80)

Kow·loon /kòw lóon/ peninsula in SE China, forming part of Hong Kong. Pop. 2,030,683 (1991).

kow·tow /kòw tów, ków tòw/ vi 1 kneel and touch the forehead to the ground to show respect 2 be servile —**kow·tow** n

ORIGIN Kowtow comes from a Chinese compound word meaning literally "strike head." The Chinese custom was first described in English in the early 1800s, but it took only until the 1820s for it to become extended to any servile act and to be used as a verb.

kph, k.p.h. abbr kilometers per hour

Kr symbol krypton

Krafft-E·bing /kràft ébbing/, **Richard, Freiherr von** (1840–1902) German neuropsychologist

kraft, kraft pa·per n thick brown paper. Use: bags, wrapping paper.

Kra·ka·tau /kràkə tów/, **Kra·ka·to·a** /-tṓ ə/ 1 small volcanic island in SW Indonesia, in the Sunda Strait between Java and Sumatra 2 volcano on the island of Krakatau, Indonesia. Height 2,667 ft./813 m.

Kra·ków /kraΛ kòw, krá kòw/, **Cra·cow** city in S Poland. Pop. 740,500 (1997)

Krei·sler /krísslər/, **Fritz** (1875–1962) Austrian-born US violinist and composer

Krem·lin /krémmlin/ n 1 a walled compound in Moscow housing the Russian government 2 the former Soviet government

krill (pl same) n a tiny crustacean resembling a shrimp

Krish·na /kríshnə/ n the Hindu god often depicted as a young man tending cattle who is an incarnation of Vishnu —**Krish·na·ism** n

Kriss Kring·le /kríss kríng g'l/ n Santa Claus (humorous or literary)

Kri·zan·o·vic /kri zhánnə vìch/, **Jozo** (b. 1944) Croat representative of the presidency of Bosnia and Herzegovina (2001–), which rotates between a Serb, a Bosnian Muslim, and a Croat

Kroc /krok/, **Ray** (1902–84) US restaurateur

kro·na /krónə/ (pl -nor /-nər/) n the main unit of Swedish currency

kró·na /krónə/ n the main unit of Icelandic currency

kro·ne /krónə/ (pl -ner /-nər/) n the main unit of currency in Denmark and Norway

kroon /kroon/ (pl **kroons** or **kroon·i** /króonee/) n the main unit of Estonian currency

Kro·to /krótō/, **Sir Harold Walter** (b. 1939) British chemist. He codiscovered the molecular family of carbon called fullerenes.

kryp·ton /kríp tòn/ n (symbol Kr) a gaseous chemical element. Use: fluorescent lamps, lasers.

KS abbr Kansas

Kt, Kt. abbr 1 karat 2 knight

kt. abbr 1 knight 2 knot

Kua·la Lum·pur /kwaΛalə lòōm p'óor/ capital of Malaysia. Pop. 1,145,342 (1996).

Ku·blai Khan /kòoblī kaΛan/ (1215–94) Mongol leader and emperor of China (1279–94)

Ku·brick /kyóobrik/, **Stanley** (1928–99) US movie director

ku·dos /kóo dòz/ n praise or honor (+ sing verb)

USAGE Careful writers and speakers avoid the form kudo, created in the erroneous belief that kudos is a plural.

Ku Klux Klan /kòo klùks klán/ n a white supremacist group

kum·quat /kúm kwòt/ n 1 a small orange edible fruit 2 a tree that produces kumquats

ku·na /kónə/ (pl -ne /kónə/) n the main unit of Croatian currency

kung fu /kùng fóo, kòong-/ n a Chinese martial art using circular movements of the arms and legs

Kun·lun Moun·tains /kòon lóon-/ mountain range in W China. Height 25,338 ft./7,723 m. Length 2,000 mi./3,000 km.

Kun·ming /kòon míng/ capital of **Yunnan Province**, SW China. Pop. 1,740,000 (1995).

Kurd n a member of a people of SW Asia —**Kurd·ish** adj

Kurd·i·stan /kúrdə stàn/ region in SW Asia, encompassing parts of Turkey, Iraq, Iran, Armenia, and Syria, considered the homeland of the Kurdish people. Pop. 26,000,000 (early 1990s).

Ku·ril Is·lands /kóoril-/, **Ku·rile Is·lands** island chain in the Pacific Ocean extending from NE Hokkaido in Japan to S Kamchatka Peninsula in Russia. Pop. 25,000 (1990).

Ku·ro·sa·wa /koʹoro saʹawa/, **Akira** (1910–98) Japanese movie director

Ku·wait /koo wáyt/ country in SW Asia, at the northwestern tip of the Persian Gulf. Cap. Kuwait City. Pop. 2,041,961 (2001). —**Ku·wait·i** n, adj

Ku·wait Cit·y capital of Kuwait. Pop. 28,259 (1995).

kW, kw abbr kilowatt

kwa·cha /kwaʹacha/ n the main unit of currency in Malawi and Zambia

Kwa·ki·utl /kwaʹakee oótʹl/ (pl same or **-utls**) n 1 a member of a Native North American people who live on Vancouver Island and on the adjacent coast of British Columbia 2 the language of the Kwakiutl people —**Kwa·ki·utl** adj

kwan·za /kwaʹanza/ (pl **-zas** or same) n the main unit of Angolan currency

Kwan·zaa /kwaʹanza/, **Kwan·za** n African American holiday. Date: December 26 to January 1.

KY, Ky. abbr Kentucky

kyat /chaat/ n the main unit of currency in Myanmar

Kyo·to /kyótō/ city on S Honshu Island, Japan. Pop. 1,388,267 (2000).

Kyrg·yz·stan /keʹergi stàn/ country in Central Asia. Cap. Bishkek. Pop. 4,753,003 (2001).

Kyu·shu /kee oóshoo, kyoóshoo/ southernmost of the four major islands of Japan. Pop. 13,269,000 (1990).

L

l[1] (pl **l's**), **L** (pl **L's** or **Ls**) n 1 the 12th letter of the English alphabet 2 the Roman numeral for 50

l[2] abbr liter

L[1] symbol luminosity

L[2] abbr 1 large 2 learner

l. abbr 1 left 2 length 3 line

⚡**L8R** abbr later (in e-mails)

la[1] interj used to show surprise or emphasis

la[2], **lah** n a syllable used in singing the 6th note of a scale

La symbol lanthanum

LA abbr 1 also **L.A.** Los Angeles 2 also **La.** Louisiana

lab n a laboratory (infml)

Lab. abbr Labrador

la·bel /láybʹl/ n 1 an informative piece of paper or fabric attached to something 2 a descriptive word or phrase ∎ vt (**-beled** or

-belled, -bel·ing or **-bel·ling**) 1 attach a label to 2 use a particular word to describe ○ resents being labeled as a troublemaker

la·bi·al /láybee əl/ adj of the lips

la·bor /láybər/ n 1 physical work 2 labor unions collectively 3 a task, especially a difficult one (often pl) 4 the process of childbirth ∎ vi 1 work hard 2 do something with difficulty —**la·bor·er** n ◊ See note at **work**
□ **labor under** vt be at a disadvantage because of believing something to be true that is not ○ laboring under the misconception that the problem had been solved

lab·o·ra·to·ry /lábbrə tàwree/ (pl **-ries**) n 1 a place for scientific research and experimentation 2 a place for the manufacture of drugs or chemicals

La·bor Day n a US and Canadian public holiday honoring working people. Date: 1st Monday in September.

la·bored /láybərd/ adj showing obvious effort or difficulty

la·bo·ri·ous /lə báwree əss/ adj requiring or involving much effort. —**la·bo·ri·ous·ly** adv ◊ See note at **hard**

la·bor of love n something demanding or difficult done for pleasure rather than money

la·bor-sav·ing /láybər sàyving/ adj describes a device intended to save human effort

la·bor un·ion n a workers' organization to promote the interests and rights of its members

Lab·ra·dor[1] /lábbrə dàwr/ n a large dog with a short thick coat

Lab·ra·dor[2] /lábbrə dàwr/ mainland portion of Newfoundland, Canada, on the Labrador Sea

Lab·ra·dor Cur·rent cold ocean current that flows south past Newfoundland, Canada, and W Greenland to join the Gulf Stream

Lab·ra·dor Pen·in·su·la large peninsula in E Canada, including much of Quebec and the mainland portion of Newfoundland

Lab·ra·dor Sea arm of the Atlantic Ocean that separates Canada from Greenland

~~laboratory~~ incorrect spelling of **laboratory**

la·bur·num /lə búrnəm/ n a tree with yellow drooping clusters of flowers

lab·y·rinth /lábbə rìnth/ n a confusing network of paths or passages —**lab·y·rin·thine** /lábbə rínthin, -theen, -thin/ adj

La·can /ləkaʹan/, **Jacques** (1901–81) French psychoanalyst

lace /layss/ n 1 a delicate fabric with a pattern of holes 2 a cord used to tie edges together, especially on footwear ∎ vt (**iaced, lac·ing**) 1 fasten something with a lace or laces 2 add alcohol or drugs to a drink

lac·er·ate /lássə ràyt/ (**-at·ed, -at·ing**) vt 1 cut the flesh jaggedly 2 distress somebody deeply —**lac·er·a·tion** /lássə ráysh'n/ n

lach·ry·mose /lákrə mòss/ *adj* (*literary*) **1** crying or tending to cry easily and often **2** so sad as to make people cry

lack *n* a shortage or absence ■ *v* **1** *vt* be without or in need of **2** *vi* have too little of something

SYNONYMS lack, shortage, deficiency, deficit, want, dearth CORE MEANING: an insufficiency or absence of something

lack·a·dai·si·cal /làkə dáyzik'l/ *adj* without enthusiasm or effort —**lack·a·dai·si·cal·ly** *adv*

lack·ey /lákee/ (*pl* -**eys**) *n* **1** a servile follower **2** a male servant (*archaic*) —**lack·ey** *vi*

ORIGIN Lackey goes back to an Arabic word meaning "the judge." It came to English through Catalan and French, where it had come to mean "foot soldier" and then "footman."

lack·ing /láking/ *adj* **1** without something necessary o *lacking in good taste* **2** not present or available

lack·lus·ter /lák lùstər/ *adj* lacking energy or passion

la·con·ic /lə kónnik/ *adj* using few words —**la·con·i·cal·ly** *adv*

lac·quer /lákər/ *n* **1** a solution that dries to form a hard glossy decorative or protective coating **2** hair spray (*dated*) —**lac·quer** *vt* —**lac·quer·er** *n*

Popperfoto

Lacrosse

la·crosse /lə kráwss/ *n* a team sport played with a netted stick and a small hard ball

ORIGIN Lacrosse was originated by Native North Americans. French-speakers in Canada gave it the name *jeu de la crosse* "game of the hooked stick." As an English word it is first recorded in the mid-19C.

lac·tate /lák tàyt/ (-**tat·ed**, -**tat·ing**) *vi* produce milk in the body (*refers to female mammals*) —**lac·ta·tion** /lak táysh'n/ *n*

lac·tic ac·id *n* $C_3H_6O_3$ a colorless organic acid produced by muscles and found in sour milk

lac·tose /lák tòss, -tòz/ *n* **1** a sugar found in milk **2** a form of lactose derived from whey. Use: in food products and pharmaceuticals.

la·cu·na /lə kyoonə, -koonə/ (*pl* -**nae** /-nèe/ or -**nas**) *n* **1** a gap (*literary*) **2** a small cavity, e.g., in bone or cartilage —**la·cu·nal** *adj*

lac·y /láyssee/ (-**i·er**, -**i·est**) *adj* **1** made of lace **2** like lace in appearance o *lacy clouds* —**lac·i·ness** *n*

lad *n* **1** a boy or young man **2** a man (*infml*)

La·dakh /lə dáak/ mountainous region of NW India, Pakistan, and China

lad·der /láddər/ *n* a portable device with parallel sides and rungs to climb up or down

~~ladel~~ incorrect spelling of **ladle**

lad·en /láyd'n/ *adj* **1** heavily loaded (*often in combination*) o *fruit-laden boughs* **2** oppressed or weighed down o *laden with guilt*

La·den ♦ bin Laden, Osama

la·dies' man, la·dy's man *n* a man who likes flirting with women

la·dle /láyd'l/ *n* a long spoon with a deep bowl ■ *vt* (-**dled**, -**dling**) serve using a ladle

la·dy /láydee/ (*pl* -**dies**) *n* **1** a woman **2** an aristocratic woman **3 La·dy** a title for some female members of the aristocracy

ORIGIN Lady means literally "bread-kneader." In origin it is a compound of *hlaf*, an early form of *loaf*, and -*dige*, which represents an ancient root meaning "knead" that also gave us *dough*.

la·dy·bug /láydee bùg/ *n* a small red beetle with black spots

la·dy·fin·ger /láydee fing gər/ *n* a small finger-shaped sponge cake

la·dy-in-wait·ing (*pl* **la·dies-in-wait·ing**) *n* a female attendant for a queen or princess

la·dy-kill·er *n* a man who is very attractive to women

la·dy·like /láydee lìk/ *adj* polite and dignified

La·dy·ship /láydee ship/ *n* a form of address for a woman with the title of "Lady"

la·dy's man *n* = ladies' man

La·fay·ette /làffee ét/, **Marie Joseph Paul Yves Roch Gilbert du Motier, Marquis de** (1757–1834) French soldier and politician

lag[1] *vi* (**lagged, lag·ging**) **1** fall behind compared with others **2** decrease in intensity o *Interest in the scandal has never lagged.* ■ *n* a period of time between events

lag[2] (**lagged, lag·ging**) *vt* insulate a water pipe or tank

la·ger /láagər/ *n* light-colored beer

ORIGIN Lager was originally more fully *lager beer*. This was a partial translation of German *Lager-Bier*, literally "storehouse beer," beer made for keeping. It is recorded in English from the 1850s.

lag·gard /lággərd/ *n* somebody or something who falls behind —**lag·gard·ly** *adv*, *adj*

lag·ging /lágging/ *n* insulating material for water pipes and tanks

la·goon /lə goon/ *n* a partly enclosed area of seawater

La·gos /láy gòss/ largest city, chief port, and

former capital of Nigeria. Pop. 1,484,000 (1995).

La·gos Es·co·bar /laàgoss éskō baàr/, **Ricardo** (b. 1938) president of Chile (2000–)

La Guar·di·a /lə gwaárdee ə/, **Fiorello Henry** (1882–1947) US politician and mayor of New York City (1934–45)

La·hore /lə háwr/ capital of Punjab Province, NE Pakistan. Pop. 5,063,499 (1998).

laid past tense, past participle of **lay**[1]

laid-back adj relaxed and easygoing (infml)

Lai·lat al-Mi·raj /lày lat al mi raáj/ n an Islamic festival marking the ascent of Muhammad to heaven. Date: 27th of Rajab.

Lai·lat ul-Qa·dr /láy lat ōol kaàdər/ n an Islamic festival marking the sending down of the Koran to Muhammad. Date: 27th of Ramadan.

lair n 1 a wild animal's den 2 a retreat or hideaway (infml)

lais·sez-faire /lè say fáir/, **lais·ser-faire** n 1 a principle of noninterference, especially lack of government regulation of private industry 2 letting people do as they please

la·i·ty /láy ətee/ npl lay people, especially people who do not belong to the clergy

lake n 1 an inland body of water 2 a pool of liquid

lakh /laak/ (pl **lakhs** or **same**) n S Asia a hundred thousand, especially 100,000 rupees

Lak·shmi /lúkshmee/, **Lak·smi** n the Hindu goddess of prosperity, the wife of Vishnu

lam n a hasty escape

la·ma /laáma/ n a Tibetan or Mongolian Buddhist monk

La·ma·ism /laáma ìzzəm/ n a form of Buddhism practiced in Tibet and Mongolia, with elements from other religions —**La·ma·ist** n, adj

La·mar /lə maár/, **Lucius Quintus Cincinnatus** (1825–93) associate justice of the US Supreme Court (1888–93)

La·marck /lə maárk/, **Jean-Baptiste Pierre Antoine de Monet, Chevalier de** (1744–1829) French naturalist and evolutionist. His theory that evolution proceeded by the inheritance of acquired characteristics was superseded by Darwin's theory of natural selection. —**La·marck·i·an** adj, n

lamb /lam/ n 1 a young sheep 2 the meat of a lamb ■ vti bear a lamb —**lamb·ing** n

Lamb /lam/, **Charles** (1775–1834) British essayist. Pseudonym **Elia**

lam·ba·da /lam baáda/ n 1 a fast rhythmic Latin-American dance 2 the music for a lambada

lam·baste /lam báyst/ (-**bast·ed, -bast·ing**), **lam·bast** /-bást/ vt criticize severely

lamb·da /lámda/ n the 11th letter of the Greek alphabet

lam·bent /lámbənt/ adj 1 glowing or flickering

(literary) 2 with a light but brilliant touch o lambent wit —**lam·ben·cy** n

lamb·skin /lám skin/ n 1 a woolly lamb's pelt 2 leather from a lamb's hide

lame (**lam·er, lam·est**) adj 1 walking unevenly because of a leg injury or impairment (offensive of a person) 2 unconvincing (sometimes offensive) —**lame** vt —**lame·ly** adv —**lame·ness** n

la·mé /la máy/ n a fabric interwoven with metallic threads

lame duck n 1 an outgoing office holder with weakened power 2 somebody or something regarded as weak or unfortunate (offensive of a person)

la·ment /lə mént/ vti express sadness or disappointed regret about something ■ n 1 an expression of sadness or regret 2 a song or poem of mourning —**lam·en·ta·tion** /làmmən táysh'n/ n

la·men·ta·ble /lə méntəb'l, lámməntəb'l/ adj pitiful or deplorable —**lam·en·ta·bly** adv

Lam·en·ta·tions /làmmən táysh'nz/ n a book of the Bible written in the form of elegies, traditionally, by Jeremiah, a Hebrew prophet (+ sing verb)

lam·i·nate vt /lámmə nàyt/ (-**nat·ed, -nat·ing**) 1 cover something with a thin protective sheet 2 bond layers together ■ n /lámmə nàyt, -nit/ material made up of bonded layers ■ adj /lámmə nit, -nàyt/ in layers —**lam·i·na·tion** /làmmə náysh'n/ n

lamp n 1 a device producing light, especially electric light 2 a device producing ultraviolet light or infrared heat radiation

lamp·black /lámp blàk/ n powdered carbon. Use: pigment, printing ink, in electrodes.

lam·poon /lam póon/ n a satirical attack in writing or verse —**lam·poon** vt —**lam·poon·er** n —**lam·poon·ist** n

ORIGIN **Lampoon** was adopted from French lampon in the mid-17C, but its origins in French are not altogether clear. It may come from lampons "let us drink," used as a refrain in songs.

lamp·post /lámp pòst/ n a post supporting a streetlight

lamp·shade /lámp shàyd/ n a decorative cover for a lamp

⚡**LAN** /lan/ abbr local area network

lance /lanss/ n a long weapon with a metal point ■ vt (**lanced, lanc·ing**) pierce with a sharp instrument o lance a blister

lance cor·po·ral n a marine of the US Marine Corps of a rank above private first class and below corporal

Lan·ce·lot /lánsələt/ n in Arthurian legend, one of the knights of the Round Table

lan·cet /lánsət/ n 1 a scalpel 2 a narrow pointed arch, or a window with this shape

land n 1 the dry solid part of the Earth's surface 2 a particular kind of ground o low-

lying land 3 ground used for agriculture ○ *working on the* land 4 an area of owned ground ○ *Get off my* land! 5 a country ○ *her native* land ○ *foreign* lands 6 an imagined place ○ *the* land *of make-believe* ■ v 1 vi arrive by aircraft ○ come or bring down from the air onto water or solid ground 3 vt obtain something desired ○ *landed a job in Hollywood* 4 vti go or put ashore from a ship 5 vt strike a blow 6 vti end up or cause to end up somewhere unpleasant ○ *landed him in jail* 7 vi appear or arrive unexpectedly or unwelcomely 8 vt čatch and bring in a fish —**land·er** n —**land·less** adj

Land, Edwin Herbert (1909–91) US inventor and entrepreneur

land·ed /lándəd/ adj 1 owning land 2 consisting of land

land·fall /lánd fàwl/ n 1 arrival on or sighting of land after a sea journey 2 the first land reached after a journey

land·fill /lánd fìl/ n 1 an area where refuse is buried 2 the burial of waste material

land·ing /lánding/ n 1 the act of coming down to the ground 2 a level area between flights of stairs

land·ing gear n an aircraft's undercarriage

land·ing stage n a platform for loading and unloading passengers and goods from a boat

land·ing strip n an airstrip

land·la·dy /lánd làydee/ (pl -dies) n a woman who rents out property or lodgings

land·line /lánd lìn/ n a telecommunications cable on land

land·locked /lánd lòkt/ adj surrounded by land

land·lord /lánd làwrd/ n somebody who rents out property or lodgings

land·lub·ber /lánd lùbbər/ n somebody who is clumsy aboard a ship due to lack of experience at sea —**land·lub·ber·ly** adj

land·mark /lánd màʌrk/ n 1 a prominent structure or feature that identifies a location 2 a significant or historic event or development 3 a structure or site preserved because of historical significance

land·mass /lánd màss/ n a huge area of land

land·mine /lánd mìn/ n a buried explosive device

land of·fice n a government office that administers and records sales and transfers of public land

land-of·fice bus·i·ness n a very brisk trade *(infml)*

land·own·er /lánd ònər/ n an owner of land —**land·own·ing** n, adj

land·scape /lánd skàyp/ n 1 an expanse of scenery 2 a picture of scenery ■ vt (-scaped, -scap·ing) improve the appearance of an area of land by reshaping and planting

land·slide /lánd sìd/ n 1 a sudden collapse

of land on a mountainside or cliff 2 an overwhelming victory

land·ward /lándwərd/ adj facing land ■ adv also **land·wards** toward land

lane n 1 a division of a road for a single line of vehicles or a particular type of vehicle 2 a track assigned to a single runner or swimmer in a race 3 a narrow road or path 4 a shipping route

Lang, Fritz (1890–1976) Austrian-born US movie director

Lange /lang/ /láng/, **Dorothea** (1895–1965) US photographer

Lang·ley /lánglee/, **Samuel Pierpont** (1834–1906) US aviation pioneer

lan·gous·tine /láang goo steèn, làang goo steèn/ n a large prawn or small lobster

⚡ **lan·guage** /láng gwij/ n 1 the system of words, sounds, and grammar used by a particular group of people for communication 2 communication with words 3 a specialist vocabulary 4 a style of verbal expression 5 a set of symbols and rules for writing computer programs ◇ **speak the same language** have values or interests in common

ORIGIN Language goes back to Latin *lingua* "tongue." The suffix *-age* was added in French, from which the word was adopted in the 13C.

SYNONYMS language, vocabulary, idiolect, tongue, dialect, slang, jargon, parlance, lingo CORE MEANING: communication by words

lan·guid /láng gwid/ adj 1 without energy 2 slow-moving —**lan·guid·ly** adv

lan·guish /láng gwish/ vi 1 be neglected or deprived 2 become weaker or less successful

lan·guor /lángər, láng gər/ n 1 a pleasant feeling of weariness 2 listlessness and indifference —**lan·guor·ous** adj

lan·iard n = lanyard

lank adj 1 long and slender 2 limp and straight ○ *lank hair* —**lank·ly** adv —**lank·ness** n

lank·y /lángkee/ (-i·er, -i·est) adj tall and thin in an ungraceful way —**lank·i·ly** adv —**lank·i·ness** n

lan·o·lin /lánn'lin/, **lan·o·line** /-l eèn/ n fat from sheep's wool. Use: in skin creams and ointments.

Lan·sing /lánsing/ capital of Michigan. Pop. 127,825 (1998).

lan·tern /lántərn/ n a portable lamp with transparent sides

lan·tha·nide /lánthə nìd/ n any of a group of rare-earth elements

lan·tha·num /lánthənəm/ n (symbol **La**) a rare-earth metallic element. Use: glass manufacture.

lan·yard /lánnyərd/, **lan·iard** n 1 a cord worn around the neck for carrying something 2 a short rope used aboard a ship

Lan·zhou /làn jṓ/, **Lan-chou, Lan-chow** capital of **Gansu Province**, N China. Pop. 1,194,640 (1990).

Laos /lowss/ independent state of Southeast Asia. Cap. Vientiane. Pop. 5,635,967 (2001). —**La·o·tian** /lay ṓsh'n, lówsh'n/ n, adj

Lao-tzu /lṓw dzóö/ (570?–490? BC) Chinese philosopher

lap[1] n the top of a seated person's thighs

lap[2] n 1 a circuit of a racetrack 2 a stage, e.g., of a journey ■ v (**lapped, lap·ping**) 1 vt overtake a competitor by a complete lap 2 vt enfold or wrap (literary) 3 vti overlap (literary)

lap[3] (**lapped, lap·ping**) vti 1 drink liquid with the tongue (refers to animals) 2 wash gently against a surface

□ **lap up** v 1 vti = **lap**[3] 1 2 vt enjoy something eagerly and uncritically

lap·a·ros·co·py /làppə róskəpee/ (pl -**pies**) n an internal abdominal examination through a tube-shaped instrument —**lap·a·ro·scope** /láppərə skōp/ n —**lap·a·ro·scop·ic** /làppərə skóppik/ adj

La Paz /lə páz, laa páss/ capital of Bolivia. Pop. 758,141 (1997).

lap·dog /láp dàwg, -dòg/ n a small pet dog

la·pel /lə pél/ n the folded-back front edge of a jacket

la·pis laz·u·li /làppiss lázzyə lī̇́, -lázhə-, -lázzyəlee/ n a deep blue semiprecious stone. Use: jewelry.

Lap·land /láppland/ Arctic region extending across the northern parts of Norway, Sweden, Finland, and the Kola Peninsula of Russia —**Lap·lan·der** n

Lapp n an offensive term for a member of the Saami people —**Lapp** adj

lapse n 1 a momentary fault or failure in behavior or morality 2 a gap in continuity 3 a passage of time 4 a failure to exercise a legal right in time ■ vi (**lapsed, laps·ing**) 1 gradually end or stop doing something 2 become null and void through disuse, negligence, or death 3 decline in value, quality, or conduct —**lapsed** adj

⚡ **lap·top** /láp tòp/ n a small portable computer

⚡ **lap·ware** /láp wàir/ n computer software for children

lap·wing /láp wìng/ (pl -**wings** or same) n a bird of the plover family with a long crest

ORIGIN Early forms of **lapwing** show it to be composed of **leap** and an ancient root related to **wink** that meant "move from side to side." Its name derives from the manner of its flight.

~~laquer~~ incorrect spelling of **lacquer**

La Ra·za /laa raás-/ n Mexicans, Mexican Americans, or Spanish-speaking people of the Americas, considered as a group

~~larceny~~ incorrect spelling of **larceny**

lar·ce·ny /laársənee/ n theft of personal property —**lar·ce·nist** n —**lar·ce·nous** adj

larch (pl **larch·es** or same) n 1 a deciduous tree of the pine family 2 the durable wood of a larch tree

lard n white pork fat used in cooking ■ v 1 vti add strips of fat to meat before cooking 2 vt add to speech or writing o larded with quotations

lar·der /laárdər/ n 1 a room or cupboard for storing food 2 a food supply

La·re·do /lè ráydō/ city in S Texas, on the border with Mexico. Pop. 175,783 (1998).

large (**larg·er, larg·est**) adj 1 big in size 2 general in scope o a large view of the subject —**large·ness** n ◊ **at large** 1 as a widely based and general group of people 2 escaped or free and possibly dangerous ◊ **by and large** speaking generally

large in·tes·tine n the last section of the alimentary canal

large·ly /laárjlee/ adv 1 mainly 2 on a grand scale

larg·er-than-life adj impressive and flamboyant

large-scale adj 1 big and detailed 2 extensive

lar·gesse /laar jéss/, **lar·gess** n 1 generosity 2 gifts

lar·go /laárgō/ adv fairly slowly (musical direction) —**lar·go** adj, n

la·ri /laáree/ (pl same or -**ris**) n the main unit of Georgian currency

lar·i·at /lárree ət/ n 1 a lasso 2 a rope for tethering an animal

lark[1] n a small brownish songbird

lark[2] n 1 a piece of harmless mischief or adventurous fun o did it for a lark 2 an amusing prank ■ vi act mischievously

lark·spur /laárk spùr/ n a delphinium plant

lar·va /laárvə/ (pl -**vae** /-vee/ or -**vas**) n the immature worm-shaped form of an insect —**lar·val** adj

lar·yn·gi·tis /làrrən jītiss/ n inflammation of the larynx —**lar·yn·git·ic** /-jíttik/ adj

lar·ynx /lárringks/ (pl **la·ryn·ges** /lə rín jèez/ or **lar·ynx·es**) n the part of the respiratory tract containing the vocal cords

la·sa·gna /lə zaányə/ (pl -**gnas** or -**gne** /-nyə/), **la·sa·gne** (pl -**gnes** or same) n 1 pasta in the form of thin sheets 2 a dish made up of alternate layers of thin sheets of pasta, tomato sauce, and cheese

La Salle /lə sál, laa-/, **René-Robert Cavelier, Sieur de** (1643–87) French explorer

Las Ca·sas /laass kaássəss/, **Bartolomé de** (1474–1566) Spanish missionary

las·civ·i·ous /lə sívvee əss/ adj 1 lewd 2 erotic —**las·civ·i·ous·ly** adv

la·ser /láyzər/ *n* a device emitting a highly focused beam of light

> **ORIGIN** Laser is an acronym formed from initial letters of "light amplification by stimulated emission of radiation."

⚡**la·ser print·er** *n* a computer printer that uses a laser beam to transfer the image

la·ser visa *n* a visa for Mexican nationals entering the United States, similar to a credit card

lash[1] *n* **1** a stroke with a whip **2** an eyelash ■ *v* **1** *vti* strike a surface with violence ○ *Heavy rain lashed the windows.* **2** *vti* criticize somebody severely ○ *lashing into her former colleagues* **3** *vt* strike with a whip **4** *vti* flick something to and fro, or move in this way

lash[2] *vt* tie something tightly or securely to something else

lass /lass/ *n* a girl or young woman (*sometimes offensive*)

las·si·tude /lássi tòod/ *n* tiredness and apathy

las·so /lássō, la soó/ *n* (*pl* -**sos**) a rope with a sliding noose ■ *vt* (-**soed, -soing, -sos**) catch an animal with a lasso

last[1] *adj* **1** most recent **2** being or occurring after all the others **3** final or only remaining **4** least suitable, desirable, or likely ○ *the last thing I wanted to hear* ■ *adv* **1** most recently **2** after all the others ■ *n* **1** somebody or something that is last **2** the final moment ○ *cheerful to the last* —**last·ly** *adv* ◊ **at last** finally ◊ **at long last** eventually ◊ **every last** every one

last[2] *vti* be sufficient for or remain available to somebody for a period of time

last[3] *n* a foot-shaped block used by a shoemaker or cobbler

last-ditch *adj* final and desperate

last hur·rah *n* a final effort

last·ing /lásting/ *adj* permanent, or continuing for a long time —**last·ing·ly** *adv*

Last Judg·ment *n* in some beliefs, God's final judgment on humankind at the end of the world

last min·ute *n* the latest possible time —**last-min·ute** *adj*

last name *n* somebody's surname

last rites *npl* **1** a Roman Catholic ceremony for a dying person **2** religious burial rites

Last Sup·per *n* Jesus Christ's last meal with his disciples

last word *n* **1** the final remark in a discussion or argument **2** the ultimate decision **3** the best ○ *the last word in luxury*

Las Ve·gas /laas váygass/ city in S Nevada. Pop. 404,288 (1998).

lat /laat/ (*pl* **lat·i** /láttee/ *or* **lats**) *n* the main unit of Latvian currency

lat. *abbr* latitude

latch *n* **1** a device for keeping a door shut consisting of a movable bar that fits into a notch **2** a door lock that needs a key to be opened from the outside but not the inside ■ *vt* secure with a latch

☐ **latch onto** *vt* (*infml*) **1** cling or stick to, especially in an unwelcome way **2** adopt something enthusiastically

latch·key /lách kèe/ (*pl* -**keys**) *n* a door key

latch·key child, latch·key kid *n* a child who returns to an empty home after school

late /layt/ *adj, adv* (**lat·er, lat·est**) **1** after the expected or usual time **2** near the end of a period of time ○ *late morning* **3** recent or recently ■ *adj* dead ○ *her late uncle* —**late·ness** *n* ◊ **of late** recently ◊ See note at **dead**

late·com·er /láyt kùmmər/ *n* **1** somebody who arrives late **2** somebody who has recently become involved with or interested in something

late·ly /láytlee/ *adv* recently

la·tent /láyt'nt/ *adj* **1** present or existing, but in an undeveloped or unexpressed form **2** having the potential to develop —**la·ten·cy** /láyt'nssee/ *n*

lat·er /láytər/ comparative of **late** ■ *adv* after the present time or a specific period of time

lat·er·al /láttərəl/ *adj* **1** of or at the side **2** sideways —**lat·er·al·ly** *adv*

lat·er·al think·ing *n* an unconventional approach to solving problems

lat·est /láytəst/ superlative of **late** ■ *adj* newest, most recent, or most up-to-date —**lat·est** *n*

la·tex /láy tèks/ (*pl* -**ti·ces** /-seèz/ *or* -**tex·es**) *n* **1** a milky liquid produced by some plants **2** a mixture of rubber or plastic particles in water. Use: manufacture of emulsion paints, adhesives, and synthetic rubber products.

lath /lath/ *n* a thin wooden strip used to support plaster or tiles —**lath** *vt*

lathe /layth/ *n* a machine that turns and cuts wood or metal

lath·er /láthər/ *n* **1** foam produced by soap or detergent used with water **2** white foam produced during periods of heavy exercise, especially by horses **3** an agitated state (*infml*) ■ *v* **1** *vti* produce or cause to produce lather **2** *vt* cover with soapy lather —**lath·er·y** *adj*

Lat·in /látt'n/ *n* **1** the language of ancient Rome, adopted in medieval Europe as the language of education, culture, religion, and government **2** somebody who speaks a Romance language, especially somebody from S Europe or Latin America —**Lat·in** *adj* —**Lat·in·ize** *vt*

Lat·i·na /lə teénə/ *n* a Latin-American woman or girl

Lat·in A·mer·i·ca the entire western hemisphere south of the United States —**La·tin-A·mer·i·can** *adj, n*

La·ti·no /lə teenō/ (pl -nos) n 1 somebody from Latin America 2 a Latin-American living in the United States ◊ See note at **Anglo, Hispanic**

lat·i·tude /láttə tōōd/ n 1 an imaginary line around the Earth parallel to the equator, or its angular distance from the equator 2 an area of the Earth's surface near a particular latitude *(often pl)* ○ *the northern latitudes* 3 scope for freedom of action ○ *It's a very creative job, allowing me a great deal of latitude.* —**lat·i·tu·din·al** /látta tōōd'nal/ *adj*

lat·ke /látka/ n a fried grated potato cake

la·trine /lə treen/ n a toilet, especially a communal one on a military base

lat·te /láatay/ n an espresso coffee with steamed milk

lat·ter /láttər/ n, adj the second of two ■ adj coming relatively near the end ○ *in the latter part of his life*

lat·ter-day adj resembling somebody or something from the past ○ *thought of himself as a latter-day Roosevelt*

lat·ter·ly /láttərlee/ adv recently

lat·tice /láttiss/ n 1 *also* **lat·tice·work** /láttiss wùrk/ a crisscross framework of interwoven strips 2 a regular geometrical arrangement of points, e.g., the atoms in a crystal —**lat·ticed** adj

Lat·vi·a /láatvee ə/ country in NE Europe, bordering the Baltic Sea. Cap. Riga. Pop. 2,385,231 (2001). —**Lat·vi·an** n, adj

laud /lawd/ vt praise highly —**laud·a·to·ry** /láwdə tàwree/ adj

laud·a·ble /láwdəb'l/ adj praiseworthy —**laud·a·bly** adv

lau·da·num /láwd'nəm/ n a solution of opium in alcohol. Use: formerly, for pain relief.

Laud·er /láwdər/, **Estée** (b. 1908) US entrepreneur

laugh /laf/ vi 1 make sounds in the throat expressing amusement 2 mock or show contempt for somebody or something ■ n 1 a sound made when laughing 2 somebody or something funny or entertaining *(infml)* —**laugh·er** n —**laugh·ing·ly** adv ◊ **have the last laugh** be proved right or triumph in the end

laugh·a·ble /láffəb'l/ adj ridiculously inadequate —**laugh·a·bly** adv

laugh·ing·stock /láffing stòk/ n an object of ridicule

laugh·ter /láftər/ n the sound or act of laughing

launch¹ /lawnch/ vt 1 fire a spacecraft or missile into the air 2 put a boat or ship into the water 3 begin or initiate a planned activity ○ *launched an investigation* 4 put a new product on sale 5 hurl yourself at something or somebody —**launch** n —**launch·er** n

launch² /lawnch/ n a large motorboat

launch pad, launch·ing pad n 1 a platform for launching rockets 2 a starting point for success

laun·der /láwndər/ vt 1 wash clothes or linen 2 pass money through a legitimate account to disguise its illegal origins

laun·der·ette /láwndə rét/ n an establishment with coin-operated washing machines

Laun·dro·mat /láwndrə màt/ *US, Can, Aus* a service mark for a self-service coin-operated commercial laundry

laun·dry /láwndree/ (pl -dries) n 1 dirty clothes to be laundered 2 freshly laundered clothes 3 a place where clothes and linen are laundered

ORIGIN Laundry is a contraction of an obsolete word *lavendry*, which goes back to the Latin verb *lavare* "wash." **Laundry** is first recorded early in the 16C. It was based on, and reinforced by, the related *launder*, which is now a verb but was originally a noun, "a person who washes linen."

lau·re·ate /láwree ət/ n 1 an award winner in the arts or sciences 2 a poet laureate —**lau·re·ate** adj —**lau·re·ate·ship** n

lau·rel /láwrəl/ n 1 the bay tree 2 an evergreen tree or bush with dark or spotted leaves and berries 3 a wreath of bay leaves awarded as an honor in classical times ■ **lau·rels** npl honors won for achievement ◊ **rest on your laurels** be satisfied with your success and do nothing to improve on it

Lau·ren·tian Moun·tains /law rènshən-/ mountain range in S Quebec, Canada, that runs north of the St. Lawrence River. Height 3,905 ft./1,190 m.

Lau·ri·er /láwree ày/, **Sir Wilfrid** (1841–1919) Canadian lawyer, journalist, and prime minister (1896–1911)

la·va /láavə, lávvə/ n 1 molten rock flowing from a volcano 2 rock formed from solidified lava

La·val /lə vál/ city in S Quebec Province, Canada. Pop. 330,393 (1996).

lav·a·to·ry /lávvə tàwree/ (pl -ries) n a toilet —**lav·a·to·ri·al** /làvvə táwree əl/ adj

lav·en·der /lávvəndər/ n 1 a plant with fragrant leaves and flowers 2 dried lavender flowers and leaves. Use: essential oil, perfume for clothes, linen, or toiletries. 3 a pale purple color —**lav·en·der** adj

la·ver¹ /láyvər/ n a basin for ritual washing in synagogues

la·ver² /láyvər/ n a dried edible seaweed

La Vé·ren·drye /lə vèrraaN dree/, **Sieur Pierre Gaultier de Varennes de** (1685–1749) Canadian explorer and fur trader

lav·ish /lávish/ adj 1 abundant 2 generous or extravagant ■ vt give or spend lavishly ○ *lavished attention on the child* —**lav·ish·ly** adv —**lav·ish·ness** n

La·voi·sier /lə vwàà zyày, laav waa zyáy/, **Antoine Laurent** (1743–94) French chemist. He published the first proper table of the chemical elements.

law *n* **1** a binding or enforceable rule **2** a piece of legislation **3** the body of laws of a community or of a particular area of activity **4** control or authority ◇ *the rule of law* **5** the legal profession **6** the police **7** a statement of scientific truth ◇ **lay down the law** express an opinion in an overbearing or dogmatic way

law·a·bid·ing *adj* obeying the law

law and or·der *n* **1** enforcement of the law **2** social stability resulting from observance of the law

law·break·er /láw bràykər/ *n* somebody who breaks the law —**law·break·ing** *n, adj*

law·ful /láwf'l/ *adj* permitted or authorized by law —**law·ful·ly** *adv* —**law·ful·ness** *n* ◇ See note at **legal**

law·less /láwləss/ *adj* **1** unregulated **2** having no laws —**law·less·ly** *adv* —**law·less·ness** *n*

law·mak·er /láw màykər/ *n* somebody who drafts and enacts laws —**law·mak·ing** *n, adj*

lawn[1] *n* an area of short cultivated grass

lawn[2] *n* a fine light fabric. Use: clothing, household linen.

USAGE The material **lawn** is probably named for Laon, a town in France that was noted for linen manufacture.

lawn bowl·ing *n* a game in which heavy wooden balls are rolled towards a smaller target

lawn mow·er *n* a machine for cutting grass

law of the jun·gle *n* aggressive or competitive behavior motivated by self-interest or survival

AKG London

D. H. Lawrence

Law·rence /láwrənss/, **D. H.** (1885–1930) British writer

Law·rence, T. E. (1888–1935) British soldier and author

law·ren·ci·um /law rénsee əm/ *n* (*symbol* **Lr**) a radioactive metallic chemical element

ORIGIN **Lawrencium** is named for the US physicist Ernest O. Lawrence (1901–58).

law·suit /láw sòot/ *n* a court case between individuals

law·yer /láwyər/ *n* somebody qualified to practice law —**law·yer·ly** *adj*

lax *adj* **1** not strict or careful enough **2** not tight or tense —**lax·i·ty** *n* —**lax·ly** *adv* —**lax·ness** *n*

lax·a·tive /láksətiv/ *n* a drug used to promote bowel movements —**lax·a·tive** *adj*

lay[1] *v* (laid) **1** *vt* put something or somebody down in a horizontal position **2** *vt* put or place something ◇ *laid emphasis on this fact* **3** *vt* place something over a surface **4** *vt* cause something to lie flat **5** *vti* produce eggs **6** *vt* devise or prepare something ◇ *lay a trap* ■ *n* the way something lies ◇ **be laid low** become ill or incapacitated ◇ **lay it on (thick)** flatter with exaggerated praise

☐ **lay by** *vt* set something aside for the future

☐ **lay down** *vt* **1** surrender or sacrifice something **2** formulate a rule

☐ **lay in** *vt* acquire and store for the future

☐ **lay into** *vt* hit forcefully

☐ **lay off** *v* **1** *vt* stop employing somebody when there is insufficient work **2** *vti* stop doing or using something (*infml*)

☐ **lay out** *vt* **1** plan or design something **2** spend money

☐ **lay over** *vi* make a stop during a trip

☐ **lay up** *vt* **1** store something for future use **2** confine somebody with an injury or illness

lay[2] *adj* **1** not belonging to the clergy **2** without specialist knowledge or professional training

lay[3] *n* **1** a poem for singing **2** a song

lay[4] past tense of **lie**[1]

lay·a·bout /láy ə bòwt/ *n* a person regarded as lazy or idle

lay·er /láyr/ *n* **1** a flat covering or single thickness **2** somebody who lays something (*usually in combination*) ◇ *a bricklayer* ■ *v* **1** *vti* arrange in or form into layers **2** *vt* cut hair in different lengths

lay·ette /lay ét/ *n* a set of clothing and accessories for a baby

lay·man /láymən/ (*pl* **-men** /-mən/) *n* a layperson, especially a man

lay·off /láy àwf/ *n* **1** the laying off of employees **2** a period of unemployment

lay·out /láy òwt/ *n* **1** the way things are arranged, or a design showing this **2** the design or arrangement of printed matter on a page

lay·o·ver /láy òvər/ *n* a stop during a journey

lay·per·son /láy pùrs'n/ (*pl* **-peo·ple** /-peep'l/) *n* **1** somebody without specialist knowledge or professional training **2** somebody who is not a member of the clergy

lay read·er *n* a layperson who acts as a reader in church services

lay·wom·an /láy wòomman/ (*pl* **-en** /-wìmmin/) *n* a female layperson

Laz·a·rus /lázzərəss/, **Emma** (1849–87) US writer

laze (**lazed, laz·ing**) *vi* relax or be idle

la·zy /láyzee/ (**-zi·er, -zi·est**) *adj* **1** not wanting to work or make an effort **2** conducive to idleness —**la·zi·ly** *adv* —**la·zi·ness** *n*

la·zy·bones /láyzee bònz/ (*pl same*) *n* a person regarded as lazy (*infml*)

la·zy Su·san /-soóz'n/ *n* a revolving circular tray used on a dining table

lb, lb. *abbr* pound or pounds

LB *abbr* linebacker

lc, l.c. *abbr* lowercase

LCD *abbr* liquid-crystal display

lea /lee, lay/ *n* a grassy field (*literary*)

leach /leech/ *vti* drain away from soil when dissolved in rainwater (*refers to minerals and chemicals*)

lead[1] /leed/ *v* (**led** /led/) **1** *vti* show the way to others, usually by going ahead **2** *vi* be the way somewhere ○ *a path leading to the canal* **3** *vt* bring a person or animal by pulling **4** *vti* direct or command others **5** *vt* cause somebody to do something **6** *vi* result in something ○ *leading to confusion* **7** *vt* live a particular kind of life **8** *vti* be at the beginning or front of something **9** *vti* be ahead of others ■ *n* **1** the front position, first place, or principal role **2** a distance between competitors **3** a starring role or actor **4** an example or precedent **5** a tip or clue —**lead·er** *n* —**lead·er·ship** *n* ◊ See note at **guide**

☐ **lead off** *vi* begin first

☐ **lead on** *vt* entice with a false promise

☐ **lead up to** *vt* approach a subject indirectly

lead[2] /led/ *n* **1** (*symbol* Pb) a heavy bluish gray metallic chemical element. Use: car batteries, pipes, solder, radiation shields. **2** a weight on a line for measuring depth **3** a stick of graphite in a pencil ■ *vt* cover with lead —**lead·less** *adj*

SPELLCHECK Do not confuse the spelling of **lead** (a noun meaning "heavy metallic chemical element") and **led** (past tense and past participle of the verb **lead**), which sound similar.

---

lead bal·loon /lèd-/ *n* a complete failure

Lead·bel·ly /léd bèllee/ (1888–1949) US singer and guitarist

lead·ed /léddəd/ *adj* **1** containing lead **2** with small glass panes secured by lead strips

lead·en /léd'n/ *adj* **1** of lead **2** dull and gray **3** tired and heavy —**lead·en·ly** *adv*

lead-in /leéd-/ *n* **1** an introductory remark **2** an antenna wire

lead·ing[1] /leéding/ *adj* **1** very important or well known **2** ahead

lead·ing[2] /lédding/ *n* **1** lead strips around glass panes **2** the spacing around lines of type

lead·ing edge /leéding-/ *n* **1** the forefront of development ○ *at the leading edge of tech-*

nology **2** the forward edge of an aircraft wing, propeller, or airfoil

lead·ing la·dy /leéding-/ *n* somebody who plays the main female role in a play or movie

lead·ing light /leéding-/ *n* an outstanding or influential person

lead·ing man /leéding-/ *n* somebody who plays the main male role in a play or movie

lead·ing ques·tion /leéding-/ *n* a question that prompts the desired answer

lead-off /leéd àwf/ *n* the first in a series

lead time /leéd-/ *n* the time needed to do something, e.g., between ordering and delivery of goods

leaf /leef/ (*pl* **leaves** /leevz/) *n* **1** a flat green part that grows from the stem or branch of a plant and whose main function is photosynthesis **2** leaves, or the state or time of having leaves ○ *when the trees are in leaf* **3** a sheet of paper in a book **4** very thin metal foil **5** a hinged, sliding, or removable part of a table top, door, or shutter —**leaf·less** *adj* ◊ **turn over a new leaf** start to behave in a more acceptable way

☐ **leaf through** *vt* turn the pages of

leaf·let /leéflət/ *n* **1** a piece of printed material distributed free **2** a small leaf ■ *vti* (**-let·ed** *or* **-let·ted, -let·ing** *or* **-let·ting**) distribute leaflets in a place or to a group

leaf·y /leéfee/ (**-i·er, -i·est**) *adj* **1** with many leaves or trees **2** describes vegetables with edible leaves —**leaf·i·ness** *n*

~~leag, leage~~ incorrect spelling of **league**

league /leeg/ *n* **1** a group of states or organizations with common interests or goals **2** a group of sports clubs or teams that compete with each other —**league** *vti*

leak /leek/ *n* **1** a hole or crack through which something escapes or enters **2** an accidental escape or entry of gas, liquid, or electricity **3** a disclosure of confidential information ■ *vti* **1** let something in or out accidentally through a hole or crack, or escape or enter in this way **2** disclose confidential information unofficially or covertly, or be disclosed in this way —**leak·age** *n* —**leak·i·ness** *n* —**leak·proof** *adj* —**leak·y** *adj*

SPELLCHECK Do not confuse the spelling of **leak** and **leek** (the vegetable), which sound similar.

Lea·key /leékee/ family of British archaeologists and paleontologists including **Louis** (1903–72), his wife **Mary** (1913–96), and their son **Richard** (*b.* 1944)

lean[1] /leen/ *v* **1** *vi* bend or incline **2** *vti* rest against something for support **3** *vi* show a tendency or preference ○ *leaning toward a more tolerant approach* —**lean** *n* —**lean·ing** *n*

☐ **lean on** *vt* be dependent on or supported by

lean² /leen/ *adj* 1 without excess body fat 2 not fatty o *lean meat* 3 not productive or profitable 4 economical and efficient ■ *n* meat without fat —**lean·ly** *adv* —**lean·ness** *n* ◊ See note at **thin**

Le·an·der /lee ándər/ *n* in Greek mythology, the lover of Hero who drowned in the Hellespont while swimming to visit her

lean-to (*pl* **lean-tos**) *n* a structure with a sloping roof built against a wall

leap /leep/ (**leaped** *or* **leapt** /lept/) *vi* 1 jump high or a long distance 2 move, change, or increase abruptly or substantially —**leap** *n* ◊ **in** *or* **by leaps and bounds** extremely rapidly

leap-frog /leep fràwg, -fròg/ *n* a game in which players vault over each other ■ *v* (**-frogged, -frog·ging**) 1 *vt* vault over somebody in leapfrog, or over something as if in leapfrog 2 *vi* advance quickly by passing others

leap year a year with 366 days, occurring usually once every four years

Lear /leer/, **Edward** (1812–88) British writer and artist

learn /lurn/ (**learned** *or* **learnt** /lurnt/) *vti* 1 acquire knowledge of a subject or skill 2 find out something —**learn·er** *n*

learn·ed /lúrnəd/ *adj* having or showing much education and knowledge —**learn·ed·ness** *n*

learn·er's per·mit *n* a learner's driver's license

learn·ing /lúrning/ *n* 1 the acquisition of knowledge 2 acquired knowledge

learn·ing curve *n* 1 the rate of learning something new 2 a graph plotting the rate of learning against the time spent

learn·ing dis·a·bil·i·ty *n* a condition that prevents or hinders somebody from learning basic skills such as reading and mathematics —**learn·ing-dis·a·bled** *adj*

lease /leess/ *n* 1 a rental contract 2 the period of time covered by a lease ■ *vt* (**leased, leas·ing**) rent —**leas·a·ble** *adj* —**leas·er** *n*

lease·back /leéss bàk/ *n* an arrangement that involves selling property then renting it from the new owner

lease·hold /leéss hòld/ *n* the holding of a property through a lease —**lease·hold·er** *n*

leash /leesh/ *n* 1 a strap, chain, or rope attached to the collar or harness of an animal 2 a restraint ■ *vt* 1 fit with a leash 2 restrain

least /leest/ *pron* the smallest or lowest ■ *adj* smallest or lowest ■ *adv* to or in the smallest or lowest degree ◊ **at least** 1 not less than 2 in any case o *At least you still have a job.* ◊ **not (in) the least** not at all ◊ **not least** especially

least com·mon de·nom·i·na·tor *n* the lowest multiple shared by all the denominators in a set of fractions

least com·mon mul·ti·ple *n* the lowest whole number divisible without a remainder by all members of a set of numbers

leath·er /léthər/ *n* the tanned and dressed hide of animals —**leath·er** *adj* —**leath·er·y** *adj*

leave¹ /leev/ (**left**, **leav·ing**) *v* 1 *vti* go away from a person or place 2 *vt* cause something to remain 3 *vt* let something remain behind accidentally 4 *vt* give something in a will 5 *vt* not change the condition of something 6 *vt* have something remaining o *6 minus 4 leaves 2.* 7 *vt* set something aside 8 *vt* abandon a person or place 9 *vt* have somebody as a survivor 10 *vti* give up your position in something 11 *vt* give a task to another person o *Leave it to me.* ◊ **leave much to be desired** be highly unsatisfactory

□ **leave behind** *vt* 1 progress faster than 2 forget about o *leaving your cares behind you*

□ **leave off** *v* 1 *vi* stop doing something 2 *vt* stop using or wearing

leave² *n* 1 a period of permitted absence 2 permission (*fml*)

leav·en /lév'n/ *n also* **leav·en·ing** /lév'ning/ 1 a rising agent in dough 2 something that enlivens (*literary*) ■ *vt* 1 make bread or cake rise 2 enliven something (*literary*)

leave of ab·sence *n* 1 permission to be absent 2 time away from work

leaves plural of **leaf**

leave-tak·ing *n* a farewell (*literary*)

leav·ings /leévingz/ *npl* scraps

Leb·a·non /lébbənən, -nòn/ country in SW Asia, on the Mediterranean Sea. Cap. Beirut. Pop. 3,627,774 (2001). —**Leb·a·nese** /lèbbə neéz, -neéss/ *n, adj*

lech·er /léchər/ *n* a man regarded as lustful (*disapproving*) —**lech·er·ous** *adj* —**lech·er·ous·ly** *adv* —**lech·er·y** *n*

ORIGIN Lecher comes from a French word meaning literally "licker." The verb from which it derives had come to mean "live a life of debauchery or gluttony" as well as "lick."

Le Cor·bu·sier /lə kawr boo zyáy/ (1887–1965) Swiss-born French architect and designer

lec·tern /léktərn/ *n* a reading stand

lec·ture /lékchər/ *n* 1 an instructional speech 2 a teaching session at which a lecture is given —**lec·ture** *vti*

lec·ture hall *n* a room or building for holding lectures

lec·tur·er /lékchərər/ *n* 1 a college teacher, usually a part-time faculty member without tenure 2 a professional or experienced speaker about a specific topic

led /led/ past tense, past participle of **lead¹** ◊ see note at **lead²**

LED *n* a semiconductor used for indicator lights on electronic equipment. Full form **light-emitting diode**

ledge /lej/ n 1 a flat surface projecting from a rock face 2 a narrow shelf fixed to a wall 3 a raised surface underwater, especially near a shore —**ledged** adj

ledg·er /léjjər/ n a financial record book with columns for debits and credits

lee n 1 the side of a ship that is away from the wind 2 shelter from the elements

Lee, Ann (1736–84) British-born American religious leader

Lee, Henry (1756–1818) American Revolutionary leader

Lee, Richard Henry (1732–94) American politician

Robert E. Lee

Lee, Robert E. (1807–70) US Confederate general

Lee, Spike (b. 1957) US movie writer and director

leech n 1 a blood-sucking worm 2 an exploiter of other people

Leeds /leedz/ city in N England. Pop. 726,939 (1996).

leek /leek/ n a slender edible plant with green leaves and a white stem and bulb ◊ See note at **leak**

Lee Kuan Yew /lee kwáan yóo/ (b. 1923) prime minister of Singapore (1959–90)

leer vi look lasciviously or maliciously —**leer** n —**leer·ing** adj

leer·y /leeree/ (-i-er, -i-est) adj suspicious or wary —**leer·i·ness** n

lees /leez/ npl wine sediment

lee·ward /leeword/ (nautical) /loo ərd/ adj, adv away from the wind

Lee·ward Is·lands /leeword-/ group of islands in the NE Caribbean. The principal islands include Antigua and Barbuda, Guadeloupe, Montserrat, and St. Kitts.

lee·way /lee wày/ n a margin for variation

left[1] adj 1 on or toward the west when somebody is facing north 2 also **Left** advocating liberal, socialist, or communist political and social changes or reform ■ adv on or toward the left side ■ n 1 the left side of somebody or something 2 also **Left** people who support liberal, socialist, or communist political and social changes or reform 3 a position to the left of somebody or something, or a turn toward the left —**left·ism** n —**left·ist** n, adj

ORIGIN The earliest meaning of **left** is "weak." It came to refer to the left, or "weaker," side of the body around the beginning of the 13C.

left[2] past tense, past participle of **leave**[1]

⚡ **left-click** vti click with the left mouse button

left field n 1 the part of the outfield to the batter's left 2 the position of the baseball player responsible for fielding balls hit to left field 3 a position differing from mainstream beliefs and not taken seriously (infml) —**left field·er** n

left-hand adj 1 on or toward the left 2 intended for or done by the left hand

left-hand·ed adj 1 using the left hand, rather than the right, for tasks such as writing 2 done with the left hand 3 not sincere o a left-handed compliment —**left-hand·ed** adv

left-hand·er n somebody who uses his or her left hand for most things

left·o·ver /léft òvər/ adj remaining unused ■ n something remaining ■ **left·o·vers** npl food saved from a previous meal

left·ward /léftword/ adj moving toward or located on the left ■ adv also **left·wards** /léftwərdz/ to or at the left

left wing n the members of an organization who most favor change —**left-wing** adj —**left-wing·er** n

left·y /léftee/ (pl -ies) n a left-handed person (infml)

leg n 1 a lower limb that a person or animal uses for support or motion 2 a supporting pole 3 meat from the leg of an animal or bird 4 a part of a piece of clothing that covers the leg 5 a section of a trip or course 6 the part of a relay race completed by one athlete 7 a portion of a sports competition that has its own winner ◊ **a leg up** an advantage ◊ **have legs** be likely to enjoy a sustained period of success (infml) ◊ **on your last legs** on the verge of collapse —**leg·less** adj

leg·a·cy /léggəssee/ n (pl -cies) 1 a bequest made in a will 2 something from the past that still exists or has an effect ■ adj still in use although technically superseded o legacy software

le·gal /leeg'l/ adj 1 of the law 2 of or for lawyers 3 established or permitted by law —**le·gal·ly** adv

SYNONYMS legal, lawful, decriminalized, legalized, legitimate, licit CORE MEANING: describes something that is permitted, recognized, or required by law

le·gal aid n free or low-cost lawyers' services for people who cannot afford to pay

le·gal·ese /leeg'l eéz, -eéss/ n law jargon

le·gal·ism /leeg'l ìzzəm/ n strict adherence to the letter of the law, rule, or religious or moral code —**le·gal·is·tic** /leeg'l ístik/ adj

le·gal·i·ty /lee gállətee/ n conformity to the law

le·gal·ize /leeg'l ìz/ (-ized, -iz·ing) vt make lawful —**le·gal·i·za·tion** /leeg'li záysh'n/ n

le·gal ten·der n valid currency

leg·ate /léggət/ n 1 a pope's representative 2 a government representative or diplomat —**leg·ate·ship** n

leg·a·tee /lègga teé/ n a recipient of a legacy

le·ga·tion /lə gáysh'n/ n a group of diplomats on a mission

le·ga·to /lə gaá tō/ adv smoothly (musical direction) —**le·ga·to** adj, n

leg·end /léjjənd/ n 1 an old story presented as history but unlikely to be true 2 old stories in general 3 a celebrity 4 an inscription on an object 5 an explanation of symbols on a map —**leg·en·dar·y** adj

leg·er·de·main /lèjjərdə máyn/ n a show of skill or cleverness, especially with deceitful intent

-legged /léggəd/ suffix 1 with a particular number of legs o four-legged 2 with a particular type or position of legs o bandy-legged o cross-legged

leg·ging /légging/ n a protective covering for the lower leg ■ **leg·gings** npl close-fitting pants

leg·gy /léggee/ (**-gi·er**, **-gi·est**) adj with long or shapely legs

leg·i·ble /léjjəb'l/ adj clear enough to be read —**leg·i·bil·i·ty** /lèjjə bíllətee/ n —**leg·i·bly** adv

le·gion /léejən/ n 1 a large body of soldiers 2 a multitude ■ adj many —**le·gion·ar·y** adj —**le·gion·naire** /lèejə náir/ n

le·gion·naires' dis·ease /lèejə náirz-/ n virulent bacterial pneumonia

ORIGIN **Legionnaires' disease** is so called because the first recognized outbreak was at an American Legion convention in Philadelphia in 1976.

leg·is·late /léjji slàyt/ (**-lat·ed**, **-lat·ing**) v 1 vi make laws 2 vt bring about by making laws —**leg·is·la·tor** n

leg·is·la·tion /lèjji sláysh'n/ n 1 the process of making laws 2 a law or body of laws

leg·is·la·tive /léjji slàytiv/ adj of lawmaking or a lawmaking body

leg·is·la·ture /léjji slàychər/ n a body of people authorized to make laws

legitamate incorrect spelling of **legitimate**

le·git·i·mate adj /lə jíttimət/ 1 legal 2 conforming to acknowledged standards 3 well-founded o legitimate concerns about water quality 4 born of legally married parents ■ vt /lə jítti mayt/ (**-mat·ed**, **-mat·ing**) legalize something —**le·git·i·ma·cy** n —**le·git·i·mate·ly** adv

le·git·i·mize /lə jítti mīz/ (**-mized**, **-miz·ing**) vt = legitimate, 2 —**le·git·i·mi·za·tion** /lə jìttimi záysh'n/ n

leg·room /lég ròom, -ròòm/ n space for your legs to move

Le Guin /lə gwín/, **Ursula** (b. 1929) US science-fiction writer

leg·ume /lé gyòom, lə gyòom/ n 1 an edible seed or pod such as a bean or pea 2 a plant that produces legumes —**le·gu·mi·nous** /lə gyóomeenəss/ adj

leg·work /lég wùrk/ n basic research (infml)

lei[1] /lay, láy ee/ (pl **leis**) n in Polynesia and Hawaii, a flower garland worn around the neck

lei[2] /lay/ plural of **leu**

Leib·niz /líb nits/, **Leib·nitz**, **Gottfried Wilhelm von**, **Baron** (1646–1716) German philosopher and mathematician —**Leib·niz·i·an** /líb nítsee ən/ adj, n

Leices·ter /léstər/ city in central England. Pop. 299,080 (1997).

Leip·zig /lípsig/ city in east central Germany. Pop. 481,526 (1997).

lei·sure /leézhər, lézhər/ n free time —**lei·sured** adj

lei·sure·ly /leézharlee, lézh-/ adj slow and relaxed ■ adv in an unhurried way —**lei·sure·li·ness** n

leit·mo·tif /lít mō teèf, lít mō teèf/, **leit·mo·tiv** n 1 a thematic passage in a piece of music 2 a main recurring theme

leitu incorrect spelling of **lieu**

lek n the main unit of Albanian currency

Le·maî·tre /lə méttrə/, **Georges-Henri** (1894–1966) Belgian astrophysicist and priest. He was a proponent of the "big bang" theory of the universe.

lem·ming /lémming/ n 1 a rodent with a small thick furry body 2 a conformist mindlessly following a destructive course of action

lem·on /lémmən/ n 1 an oval yellow citrus fruit with sour juicy flesh 2 a tree that produces lemons 3 something that is defective or disappointing (infml) —**lem·on·y** adj

lem·on·ade /lémmə nàyd/ n a drink made from lemons

lem·on·grass /lémmən gràss/ n a type of grass that produces perfumed oil and is used in cooking

lem·on sole n 1 an edible flatfish 2 lemon sole as food

lemon-squeez·er n a device for extracting juice from citrus fruit

lem·pi·ra /lem peèrə/ n the main unit of Honduran currency

le·mur /leémər/ n a primate that lives in Madagascar

Le·na /leénə/ river in Siberian Russia, emptying into the Laptev Sea. Length 2,700 mi./4,300 km.

lend (**lent**) v 1 vt let somebody borrow something 2 vti give somebody money for a limited time 3 vt add a quality to something o lend an air of intimacy —**lend·er** n ◇ **lend itself to** be appropriate for a particular purpose

L'En·fant /laàN faàN/, **Pierre Charles** (1754–1825) French architect and soldier who planned the layout of Washington, D.C.

length /length/ n 1 the distance from end to end 2 the time something takes from beginning to end 3 a long piece of something narrow o *a length of copper piping* 4 in a race, a unit of distance between two competitors, measured as the length of one competitor o *two lengths ahead* 5 the degree to which somebody pursues an action or a thought o *going to great lengths to win* ◊ **at length 1** in great detail and for a long time *(fml)* **2** after a long while or a delay

length·en /léngthən/ vti become or make longer

length·wise /léngth wìz/, **length·ways** /-wàyz/ adv, adj along or parallel to the longest side

length·y /léngthee/ (-i·er, -i·est) adj long, or too long —**length·i·ly** adv —**length·i·ness** n

le·ni·ent /léenee ənt/ adj not harsh —**le·ni·ence, le·ni·en·cy** n —**le·ni·ent·ly** adv

AKG London

Vladimir Ilyich Lenin

Le·nin /lénnin/, **Vladimir Ilyich** (1870–1924) Russian revolutionary leader

Len·in·grad /lénnin gràd/ former name for **St. Petersburg**

Len·in·ism /lénnə nìzzəm/ n Lenin's theories developed from Marxism —**Len·in·ist** n, adj

lens /lenz/ n 1 a piece of curved and polished glass or other transparent material that forms an image by focusing light 2 a system of lenses used in a camera or other optical instrument 3 a contact lens 4 the part of the eye that focuses light on the retina

lent past participle, past tense of **lend**

Lent n in the Christian calendar, the period of 40 weekdays before Easter

ORIGIN **Lent**, like earlier *Lenten*, of which it is a shortened form, was originally the season of spring. It comes from the same ancient root as *long*, with reference to the lengthening of the days at that time of year. Because the ecclesiastical period of **Lent** fell within spring, however, it came increasingly to have that more restrictive sense.

~~**lenth**~~ incorrect spelling of **length**

len·til /lént'l/ n 1 an edible seed that is sold dried and split 2 a plant that produces lentils

len·to /lén tò/ adv slowly (*musical direction*) —**len·to** adj, n

Le·o /lée ò/ n 1 a zodiacal constellation in the northern hemisphere 2 the 5th sign of the zodiac —**Le·on·i·an** /lee ṓnee ən/ n

Le·o X /lée ò/ (1475–1521) pope (1513–21)

Le·o·nar·do da Vin·ci /lée ə naàr dō də vínchee/ (1452–1519) Italian painter, sculptor, architect, engineer, and scientist

le·one /lee ṓn/ n the main unit of Sierra Leonean currency

le·o·nine /lée ə nìn/ adj of or like a lion

leop·ard /léppərd/ n a large slender wild cat with a brown to red coat with black spots

le·o·tard /lée ə taàrd/ n a tight stretchy garment that covers the torso, worn especially by dancers, gymnasts, and athletes ■ **le·o·tards** npl a dancer's one-piece garment, covering the body from the neck or waist to the feet

ORIGIN The **leotard** is named for the French trapeze artist Jules Léotard (1830–70), who designed it.

lep·er /léppər/ n 1 somebody with leprosy 2 somebody whom other people avoid

lep·re·chaun /léprə kàwn/ n in Irish folklore, a mischievous elf

ORIGIN **Leprechaun** comes from an Irish word meaning literally "little body." It was first used in English in the early 17C.

lep·ro·sy /léprəssee/ n a tropical disease of the skin and nerves —**lep·rous** adj

lep·ton /lép tòn/ n a subatomic particle that interacts only weakly with other particles —**lep·ton·ic** /lep tónnik/ adj

Ler·mon·tov /lúrmən tàwf/, **Mikhail Yuryevich** (1814–41) Russian poet and novelist

les·bi·an /lézbee ən/ n a woman who is sexually attracted to other women —**les·bi·an** adj —**les·bi·an·ism** n

Les·bos /léz boss/ island in E Greece, in the Aegean Sea. Pop. 103,700 (1991). —**Les·bi·an** adj

le·sion /léezh'n/ n a damaged area in part of the body, especially a skin wound

Le·so·tho /lə sótò, -sóotoo/ country in southern Africa, bordered on all sides by South Africa. Cap. Maseru. Pop. 2,177,062 (2001).

less adj, pron a smaller amount ■ adv to a smaller degree ■ prep with the subtraction of ◊ **less than** not o *has been less than pleasant*

-less suffix 1 without, lacking o *headless* o *restless* 2 unable to be o *fathomless*

les·see /le séé/ n somebody who holds a lease

less·en /léss'n/ vti make or become less

Les·seps /léssops/, **Ferdinand Marie, Vicomte de** (1805–94) French diplomat and engineer

less·er /léssər/ adj, adv not as big or important

Less·er An·til·les /-an tílleez/ island group in the Caribbean, stretching from Puerto Rico southeastward to the coast of Venezuela and comprising the Virgin Islands, Leeward Islands, and Windward Islands

Les·ser Sun·da Is·lands ♦ Sunda Islands

Express Newspapers

Doris Lessing

Les·sing /léssing/, **Doris** (b. 1919) British novelist, raised in southern Africa

les·son /léss'n/ n 1 a period of time spent teaching or studying 2 the material taught in a lesson 3 new or better knowledge 4 a useful experience that teaches you something 5 a rebuke ○ *gave her a lesson in manners* 6 *also* **Les·son** a Bible passage read during a church service

---

ORIGIN Lesson came via French from a Latin word meaning "reading." This etymological sense survives in the **lesson** read in church. From "something to be read" it came to mean "something to be studied," and then a "period of time spent teaching or studying."

---

les·sor /lé sàwr/ n somebody who grants a lease

lest conj in case

let¹ (**let**, **let·ting**) vt 1 not prevent 2 give permission to do something ○ *Dad won't let me.* 3 expresses a suggestion ○ *Let us pray.* 4 expresses resignation or indifference ○ *Let them try!* 5 rent out ◇ **let alone** even less ○ *a region barely explored, let alone mapped* ◇ **let somebody go** dismiss somebody from his or her employment ◇ **let somebody have it** attack somebody physically or verbally ◇ **let yourself go** 1 start acting in a much more relaxed way than usual 2 stop caring about your appearance

□ **let down** vt 1 lower something 2 disappoint somebody

□ **let on** vi share a secret (infml)

□ **let out** v 1 vt make a loud yell 2 vi end a session or term and release students

□ **let up** vi 1 become slower 2 relax

let² n in tennis or squash, a replayed serve

-let suffix 1 small one ○ *droplet* 2 something worn on ○ *bracelet*

let·down /lét dòwn/ n a disappointment

le·thal /léethəl/ adj 1 deadly 2 harmful —**le·thal·i·ty** /lee tháll ətee/ n —**le·thal·ly** adv ◇ See note at **deadly**

leth·ar·gy /léthərjee/ n 1 sluggishness 2 lack of enthusiasm —**le·thar·gic** /lə tháarjik/ adj —**le·thar·gi·cal·ly** adv

let's contr let us

let·ter /léttər/ n 1 a message sent by mail 2 a symbol representing a sound or sounds and used to spell words 3 a badge of excellence, especially in a varsity sport ■ v 1 vt write letters or words on 2 vi earn a badge of excellence, especially in a varsity sport

⚡ **let·ter bomb** n 1 a package containing explosives that is sent by mail 2 a destructive e-mail

let·tered /léttərd/ adj 1 with letters written on it 2 educated

let·ter·head /léttər hèd/ n 1 headed stationery for writing letters on 2 a printed name and address on stationery

let·ter·ing /léttəring/ n the act or a style of writing

let·ter of cred·it n an official bank document authorizing somebody to draw money from another bank

let·ter-per·fect adj 1 knowing or performing something perfectly 2 known or performed perfectly

⚡ **let·ter-qual·i·ty** adj describes printing of high quality

let·tuce /léttəss/ n a plant grown for its edible leaves, which are eaten raw in salads

---

ORIGIN Lettuce goes back to Latin *lac* "milk," which is also the first element of *lactate*. The name refers to the milky sap of its stalk.

---

let-up /lét ùp/ n a pause (infml)

le·u /lé òò/ (pl **lei** /lay/) n the main unit of currency in Romania and Moldova

leu·ke·mi·a /loo keémee ə/ n a cancer in which white blood cells displace normal blood —**leu·ke·mic** adj, n

~~**leutenant**~~ incorrect spelling of **lieutenant**

lev /lev/ (pl **lev·a** /lévvə/) n the main unit of Bulgarian currency

Le·vant /lə vánt/ former name for the region in the E Mediterranean comprising modern-day Lebanon, Israel, and parts of Syria and Turkey —**Le·van·tine** /lévv'n tìn, -tèen, lə ván- / n, adj

lev·ee /lévvee/ n a natural or artificial embankment beside a river

lev·el /lévv'l/ adj 1 flat and horizontal, with an even surface 2 equal to or even with another person or group ○ *level at three games all* 3 steady ○ *maintaining a level pressure* 4 smooth or even 5 next to or alongside ■ n 1 a position from which height is measured ○ *10,000 feet above sea level* 2 height from a reference point ○ *the low level of the river* 3 a particular position relative to a rank or scale 4 an amount or concentration 5 the position of a particular floor in a structure ○ *ground level* 6 a tool for determining levelness 7 a horizontal surface ■ v (-eled or -elled, -el·ing or -el·ling) 1 vt make something level 2 vt demolish and flatten a building 3 vt aim a gun 4 vt direct attention 5 vi be honest with somebody (infml) —**lev·el·ly** adv —**lev·el·ness** n ◇ **on the level** honest and trustworthy (infml)

□ **level off** *vti* **1** *also* **level out** start to fly level with the ground, or make an aircraft do this **2** make or become steady

lev·el·er /lévvlər/, **lev·el·ler** *n* **1** something that makes situations more equal **2** a believer in equality

lev·el-head·ed *adj* calm and sensible —**lev·el-head·ed·ly** *adv* —**lev·el-head·ed·ness** *n*

lev·er /lévvər, leévər/ *n* **1** a rigid bar that pivots on a fulcrum and is used for moving a load at one end by means of force applied at the other end **2** a projecting part of a device or machine used for controlling it ■ *vt* move with a lever

lev·er·age /lévvərij/ *n* **1** the mechanical advantage gained by using a lever **2** the power to get things done **3** the use of borrowed money to purchase an asset in the hope of increasing the return on the investment ■ *v* (-**aged**, -**ag·ing**) **1** *vti* borrow money in order to buy a company **2** *vt* optimize

lev·er·aged buy·out *n* a way of buying a company using borrowed money secured by the assets of the target company

lev·er·et /lévvərət/ *n* a young hare

Le·vesque /lə vék/, **Rene** (b. 1922) Canadian journalist and political leader

Le·vi /lévvee, láyvee/, **Primo** (1919–87) Italian novelist, poet, and scientist

le·vi·a·than /lə ví əthən/ *n* **1** something huge **2** a whale (*literary*)

ORIGIN Leviathan was a sea monster in the Bible.

Le·vi-Strauss /lay vee strówss/, **Claude Gustave** (b. 1908) French social anthropologist

lev·i·tate /lévvi tàyt/ (-**tat·ed**, -**tat·ing**) *vti* rise in the air, or cause to rise —**lev·i·ta·tion** /lévvi táysh'n/ *n*

Le·vit·i·cus /lə víttikəss/ *n* a book of the Bible containing the priestly tradition of the Levites

Lev·itt /lévvit/, **William J.** (1907–94) US housing developer

lev·i·ty /lévvətee/ *n* flippancy

lev·y /lévvee/ *vt* (-**ied**, -**ies**) **1** impose a tax **2** raise an army ■ *n* (*pl* -**ies**) **1** a tax **2** the raising of tax **3** an army —**lev·i·a·ble** *adj*

lewd /lood/ *adj* sexual in an offensive way —**lewd·ly** *adv* —**lewd·ness** *n*

Lew·is /loo iss/, **Carl** (b. 1961) US athlete

Lew·is, C. S. (1898–1963) Irish-born British critic, scholar, and novelist

Lew·is, Meriwether (1774–1809) US explorer

Lew·is, Sinclair (1885–1951) US novelist

lex·i·cal /léksik'l/ *adj* **1** of words **2** of a lexicon —**lex·i·cal·ly** *adv*

lex·i·cog·ra·phy /léksi kóggrəfee/ *n* the process or activity of writing dictionaries

—**lex·i·cog·ra·pher** *n* —**lex·i·co·graph·ic** /lèksikə gráffik/ *adj*

lex·i·col·o·gy /léksi kólləjee/ *n* the study of word meanings and origins —**lex·i·co·log·i·cal** /lèksikə lójjik'l/ *adj* —**lex·i·col·o·gist** *n*

lex·i·con /léksəkən, -kòn/ (*pl* -**cons** *or* -**ca** /-kə/) *n* **1** a dictionary **2** the vocabulary of a particular field of activity

Lex·ing·ton /léksingtən/ **1** city in north central Kentucky. Pop. 241,749 (1998). **2** town in NE Massachusetts, site of the first battle of the American Revolution in 1775. Pop. 28,974 (1996).

lex·is /léksiss/ *n* the entire vocabulary of a language

Lha·sa /laássə, lássə/ city and capital of the autonomous region of Tibet, SW China. Pop. 161,788 (1991).

Li *symbol* lithium

li·a·bil·i·ty /lí ə bíllətee/ (*pl* -**ties**) *n* **1** obligation under the law **2** a debt **3** a disadvantage **4** somebody who is a burden

li·a·ble /líəb'l/ *adj* **1** legally responsible **2** susceptible or likely to experience something

li·aise /lee áyz/ (-**aised**, -**ais·ing**) *vi* cooperate closely

li·ai·son /leèə ay zòn, lee áy-/ *n* **1** exchange of information or planning of joint efforts **2** a love affair between people who are not married to each other

li·ar /lír/ *n* somebody who tells lies

~~Liase~~ incorrect spelling of **liaise**

~~Liason~~ incorrect spelling of **liaison**

Lib. *abbr* Liberal

~~libary~~ incorrect spelling of **library**

li·ba·tion /lī báysh'n/ *n* **1** the pouring of a liquid as a religious offering, or the liquid poured **2** an alcoholic drink (*humorous*) —**li·ba·tion·al** *adj*

li·bel /líb'l/ *n* **1** a false public statement that damages somebody's reputation **2** the making of a libel ■ *vt* defame —**li·bel·er** *n* —**li·bel·ist** *n* —**li·bel·ous** *adj* ◊ See note at **malign**

ORIGIN Libel came via French from a Latin word meaning literally "little book." A **libel** in English was originally a "formal document" or "written statement." In the early 16C it also developed the sense "pamphlet, leaflet," and was applied especially to one defaming somebody's character. It is out of this that the modern sense "false damaging statement" arose in the early 17C.

lib·er·al /líbbərəl, líbbrəl/ *adj* **1** broad-minded and tolerant **2** favoring gradual political or social reforms, especially those that extend democracy, distribute wealth more evenly, and protect individual freedom **3** generous with money, time, or another asset ◊ *liberal in her bequests* **4** culturally oriented ◊ *a liberal education* **5** **Lib·er·al** of the Liberal

Party ■ *n* 1 a liberal person 2 **Lib·er·al** a member of the Liberal Party —**li·ber·al·ly** *adv* ◊ See note at **generous**

lib·er·al arts *npl* education in culturally rather than vocationally oriented subjects

lib·er·al·ism /líbbərə lìzzəm, líbbrə-/ *n* belief in tolerance and gradual reform in moral, religious, or political matters —**lib·er·al·is·tic** /líbbərə lístik, líbbrə-/ *adj*

lib·er·al·i·ty /líbbə rállətee/, **lib·er·al·ness** /líbbərəlnəss, líbbrál-/ *n* 1 generosity with money, time, or another asset 2 largeness in size or amount

lib·er·al·ize /líbbərə līz, líbbrə-/ (-ized, -iz·ing) *vti* make or become less strict —**lib·er·al·i·za·tion** /líbbərəlí záysh'n, líbbrəli-/ *n*

Lib·er·al Par·ty *n* a major Canadian political party

lib·er·ate /líbbə ràyt/ (-at·ed, -at·ing) *vt* 1 set somebody free physically 2 release somebody from social constraints —**lib·er·at·ing·ly** *adv* —**lib·er·a·tion** /líbbə ráysh'n/ *n* —**lib·er·a·tion·ist** *n* —**lib·er·a·tor** *n*

Li·be·ri·a /lī béeree ə/ country in West Africa, on the North Atlantic Ocean. Cap. Monrovia. Pop. 3,225,837 (2001). —**Li·be·ri·an** *adj, n*

lib·er·tar·i·an /líbbər táiree ən/ *n* an advocate of individual responsibility or freedom —**lib·er·tar·i·an·ism** *n*

lib·er·tine /líbbər teèn/ *n* somebody who leads an immoral life —**lib·er·tine** *adj* —**lib·er·tin·ism** *n*

lib·er·ty /líbbərtee/ (*pl* -ties) *n* 1 freedom from constraint or force 2 freedom from captivity 3 a basic political, social, and economic right to choose how to think or act (*often pl*) 4 a short authorized leave from naval duties

li·bid·i·nous /li bídd'nəss/ *adj* having or expressing strong sexual desire

li·bi·do /li bée dṓ/ (*pl* -dos) *n* 1 sex drive 2 in some theories, the psychic and emotional energy linked to sexuality —**li·bid·i·nal** /lə bídd'nəl/ *adj*

Li·bra /léebrə, lī́-/ *n* 1 a zodiacal constellation in the southern hemisphere 2 the 7th sign of the zodiac —**Li·bra** *adj* —**Li·bran** *n, adj*

li·brar·i·an /lī bráiree ən/ *n* a library worker

li·brar·y /líb rèrree, líbrəree/ (*pl* -ies) *n* 1 a place where books or other research materials are kept 2 a collection of books, newspapers, records, tapes, or other research materials

Li·brar·y of Con·gress *n* the US national library

~~library~~ incorrect spelling of **library**

li·bret·to /li bréttṓ/ (*pl* -tos *or* -ti /-tèe/) *n* the words of an opera —**li·bret·tist** *n*

Li·bre·ville /léebrə vìl/ chief port and capital of Gabon. Pop. 365,650 (1993 estimate).

Lib·y·a /líbbee ə/ country in North Africa, on the Mediterranean Sea. Cap. Tripoli. Pop. 5,240,599 (2001). —**Lib·y·an** *n, adj*

Lib·y·an Des·ert arid region in NE Africa, in Libya, Egypt, and Sudan, the northeastern part of the Sahara Desert

lice plural of **louse**

li·cence *n* UK = **license**

li·cense /líss'nss/ *n* 1 an official permit to own or do something 2 legal authorization to do something 3 freedom to bend the truth, especially for artistic purposes ■ *vt* (-censed, -cens·ing) formally allow —**li·cens·a·ble** *adj*

li·censed prac·ti·cal nurse *n* a nurse who gives basic care

li·cens·ee /líss'n seé/ *n* somebody with an official license to do something

li·cense plate *n* a flat piece of metal showing the registration number of a vehicle

li·cen·ti·ate /lī sénshee ət/ *n* somebody authorized to practice a profession

li·cen·tious /lī sénshəss/ *adj* sexually immoral

li·chen /lī́kən/ *n* a complex organism consisting of fungi and algae growing together that often appears as gray, green, or yellow patches on rocks and trees —**li·chen·ous** *adj*

Lich·ten·stein /líktən stìn/, **Roy** (1923–97) US painter, graphic artist, and sculptor

lic·it /líssit/ *adj* allowed by law ◊ See note at **legal**

lick *v* 1 *vt* pass the tongue over something 2 *vti* brush against something 3 *vt* defeat a competitor convincingly (*infml*) ■ *n* 1 a movement of the tongue over something 2 a bit of something (*infml*)

lick·e·ty-split /líkətee splít/ *adv* quickly (*infml*)

lick·ing /líking/ *n* (*infml*) 1 a beating 2 a convincing defeat

lic·o·rice /líkərish/ *n* 1 a dried black plant root. Use: laxative, confectionery, brewing. 2 a kind of soft black or red candy

ORIGIN *Licorice* comes ultimately from Greek *glukurrhiza*, literally "sweet root." Its first element is related to *glucose* and its second to *rhizome*.

lid *n* 1 a top for a container 2 an eyelid 3 a restraint or control that keeps something within acceptable bounds (*infml*) —**lid·ded** *adj*

lie¹ /lī/ (**lay**, **lain**, **ly·ing** /lī́ ing/) *vi* 1 stretch out on a surface 2 be placed flat on a surface ○ *A book lay open on the table.* 3 be located in a particular place ○ *lying due south of here* 4 be buried 5 be in a particular condition or state ○ *lay hidden for years* 6 be still to come ○ *Years of work lie ahead of us.* 7 stay undisturbed

☐ **lie back** *vi* recline and relax

☐ **lie down** *vi* 1 lie on a surface 2 rest in bed

lie² /lī/ *vi* (**lied**, **ly·ing** /lī́ ing/) 1 deliberately say something untrue in order to deceive 2 give a false impression ■ *n* **1** something said or written that is untrue **2** a false impression

SYNONYMS lie, untruth, falsehood, fabrication, fib, white lie CORE MEANING: something that is not true

Liech·ten·stein /líkt'n stīn/ independent principality in central Europe. Cap. Vaduz. Pop. 32,528 (2001).

lie de·tec·tor *n* a machine for sensing untruthfulness during questioning

lief /leef, leev/ *adv* willingly (archaic)

liege /leej, leezh/ *n* **1** a feudal lord **2** a vassal —**liege·dom** *n*

lien /leen, lèè ən/ *n* a legal claim on somebody's property

~~liesure~~ incorrect spelling of **leisure**

lieu /loo/ ◊ **in lieu (of)** instead or in place of something else

Lieut. *abbr* Lieutenant

lieu·ten·ant /loo ténnənt/ *n* **1** a deputy **2** an officer in the US Army, Air Force, or Marine Corps of a rank of first lieutenant or second lieutenant, the lowest officer ranks **3** an officer in the US Navy or Coast Guard of a rank above lieutenant junior grade **4** a US police officer or firefighter of the rank above sergeant —**lieu·ten·an·cy** *n*

ORIGIN A **lieutenant** is literally somebody "holding the place," somebody deputizing for another. The French word from which it was adopted in the 14C was formed from *lieu* (as in *in lieu* of "in place of") and *tenant* "holding," from which English *tenant* derives. **Lieutenant** did not come to refer to a specific rank until the 16C.

lieu·ten·ant colo·nel *n* in some armed forces, an officer of a rank above major

lieu·ten·ant com·man·der *n* an officer in the US, British, or Canadian navies, or in the US Coast Guard, of a rank above lieutenant

lieu·ten·ant gen·er·al *n* in some armed forces, an officer of a rank above major general

lieu·ten·ant gov·er·nor *n* **1** an elected official in a state government of a rank below governor **2** a Canadian provincial official representing the British monarch —**lieu·ten·ant gov·er·nor·ship** *n*

lieu·ten·ant jun·ior grade (*pl* **lieu·ten·ants jun·ior grade**) *n* an officer in the US Navy or Coast Guard of a rank above an ensign

life (*pl* **lives** /līvz/) *n* **1** the quality that distinguishes living organisms from dead ones or inanimate matter **2** a living being, especially a person (*usually pl*) ◊ *dozens of lives lost* **3** living things considered together ◊ *an expert on Amazonian plant life* **4** the whole time that somebody is alive **5** a time when something functions **6** some part of somebody's life ◊ *social life* **7** human activity **8** the character or conditions of somebody's existence ◊ *had a hard life* **9** a

characteristic way of living ◊ *country life* **10** vitality ◊ **get a life** do something to make your existence less boring (slang)

life belt *n* a belt or ring that keeps the wearer afloat

life·blood /līf blùd/ *n* **1** blood regarded as necessary for life (literary) **2** something vital to a whole

life·boat /līf bōt/ *n* **1** a boat kept on a larger ship for use in emergencies **2** a rescue boat

life buoy *n* a buoyant float for keeping somebody's head and shoulders above water in an emergency

life cy·cle *n* **1** the stages of development of a living organism **2** all the stages in the development of something

life ex·pec·tan·cy *n* somebody's expected length of life

life form *n* any living organism

life·guard /līf gaàrd/ *n* a trained person who watches over swimmers and saves those in danger

life his·to·ry *n* **1** all the stages of an organism's life **2** somebody's life story

life im·pris·on·ment *n* punishment requiring a convicted criminal to remain in prison until he or she dies

life in·sur·ance *n* insurance that pays named beneficiaries a specific sum when the policyholder dies

life jack·et *n* a jacket that keeps the wearer afloat

life·less /līfləss/ *adj* **1** dead **2** lacking animation —**life·less·ly** *adv* —**life·less·ness** *n* ◊ See note at **dead**

life·like /līf līk/ *adj* true to life

life·line /līf līn/ *n* **1** a safety cable attached to somebody performing a dangerous maneuver **2** a vital means of communication or support

life·long /līf làwng/ *adj* lasting for life

life part·ner *n* a long-term romantic or sexual partner

life pre·serv·er *n* a ring, belt, or jacket that keeps the wearer afloat

life raft *n* an inflatable lifeboat

life·sav·er /līf sàyvər/ *n* a provider of greatly needed help

life·sav·ing /līf sàyving/ *adj* rescuing or reviving ■ *n* techniques or efforts to rescue people, especially from drowning

life sen·tence *n* a judgment of life imprisonment

life-size *adj* as big as the real thing

life span *n* **1** an expected length of life **2** the length of time something is expected to last or function

life·style /līf stīl/ *n* a manner of living

life-sup·port sys·tem, **life sup·port** *n* **1** a piece of technical equipment that provides living conditions for people in environments in which these are unavailable

2 a piece of technical equipment that temporarily performs a vital body function, e.g., respiration —**life sup·port** adj

life-threat·en·ing adj very dangerous

life·time /líf tìm/ n **1** the length of time that somebody or something remains alive **2** the length of time that something remains useful or functional

life vest n a life jacket

LIFO abbr last in, first out

lift v **1** vti go or raise to a higher position **2** vt take and move something **3** vt revoke an order o lift a ban **4** vti make or become cheerful o visibly lifted his spirits **5** vi disappear or become less severe o until the fog lifts **6** vt steal something (infml) **7** vt make a sound louder o lift their voices ■ n **1** a rise in spirits **2** a ride to a destination in somebody else's vehicle (infml) **3** the combination of upward forces acting on an aircraft **4** the process of raising something **5** the degree to which something rises **6** the force needed to raise something **7** a mechanical raising device —**lift·a·ble** adj —**lift·er** n

□ **lift off** vi leave a launch pad (refers to spacecraft)

lift-off /líft àwf/ n **1** the moment when a rocket leaves a launch pad **2** the initial thrust that launches a rocket

lig·a·ment /líggəmənt/ n **1** a band of tough tissue connecting body parts **2** a connector —**lig·a·men·tal** /líggə mént'l/ adj

lig·a·ture /líggəchər, líggə chòor/ n **1** something used for tying **2** a character consisting of joined letters **3** a curved line in a musical score used for combining the duration of notes

Li·ge·ti /li géttee/, **György** (b. 1923) Hungarian composer

light[1] /lit/ n **1** electromagnetic radiation, particularly in the range visible to the human eye **2** an artificial source of light **3** a particular kind of light o fading light **4** somebody's share or access to light o standing in my light **5** daylight **6** dawn **7** a traffic signal **8** general notice o came to light **9** the way that something is viewed o regarded in exceptionally bad light **10** a source of fire, especially a match ■ adj **1** full of brightness **2** pale o decorated in light green **3** served with milk o light coffee ■ v (lit or light·ed) **1** vti make or start to burn **2** vt illuminate something **3** vt give something an animated look o A smile lit his face. **4** vt lead somebody with a light —**light·ness** n ◇ **bring to light** reveal ◇ **in (the) light of** taking into consideration ◇ **see the light** suddenly understand or appreciate something

light[2] /lit/ adj **1** not heavy in weight **2** not dense **3** not forceful **4** easy to do **5** consuming small quantities of something **6** not severe o a light sentence **7** not intellectually demanding **8** lacking the usual or expected quantity of something, especially alcohol **9** not burdened by worry o a light heart **10** slightly dizzy o a light head **11** nimble **12** easily digested or not filling o a light snack **13** delicately flavored **14** easily awakened or disturbed o a light sleeper **15** carrying small weights **16** manufacturing small products without heavy machinery ■ adv **1** leniently **2** with little luggage ■ vi (light·ed or lit) come to rest (refers to birds) —**light·ly** adv —**light·ness** n ◇ **make light of** treat as unimportant

light bulb n a glass sphere with a filament that produces light

light·en[1] /lít'n/ vti make or become less heavy or burdensome

light·en[2] /lít'n/ v **1** vti make or become pale **2** vi glow

light·er[1] /lítər/ n **1** a small device for lighting cigarettes **2** somebody or something that lights something (usually in combination)

light·er[2] /lítər/ n a flat-bottomed cargo boat

light-fin·gered adj **1** likely to steal things **2** nimble with the fingers

light-foot·ed /lít fóotəd/, **light-foot** adj able to walk or run with agility —**light-foot·ed·ly** adv

light-head·ed /lít héddəd/ adj **1** dizzy or euphoric **2** tending to behave in a silly way —**light-head·ed·ly** adv —**light-head·ed·ness** n

light-heart·ed /lít haártəd/ adj **1** happy and relaxed **2** entertaining in a carefree way —**light-heart·ed·ly** adv —**light-heart·ed·ness** n

light heav·y·weight n **1** the weight category in boxing between middleweight and heavyweight **2** a boxer who competes at light heavyweight

light·house /lít hòwss/ (pl **-houses** /-hòwzəz/) n a tall coastal building with a flashing light to guide sailors

light·ing /líting/ n **1** a type or quality of light, or the equipment that produces it **2** equipment for providing light effects on a stage or movie set **3** the effect produced by lights on a stage or movie set

light·ning /lítning/ n a discharge of atmospheric electricity appearing as flashes of light in the sky ■ adj very fast or sudden

light·ning bug n a firefly

light·ning rod n **1** a metal rod protecting a building from lightning **2** a focus of public feelings

light·ning strike n an unexpected attack

⚡ **light pen, light sty·lus** n a pen-shaped computer device for manipulating information on a screen

lights npl the lungs of a domestic animal used as food

light show n **1** a display of moving lights, often at a rock or pop concert **2** an entertainment consisting of colored lights synchronized with recorded music

lights out n 1 a time when people must sleep 2 a signal sounded at lights out

light·weight /ˈlīt ˌwāt/ adj 1 not heavy in weight or texture 2 lacking intellectual depth ■ n 1 somebody or something regarded as insignificant (infml) ○ a political lightweight 2 the weight category in boxing between featherweight and welterweight 3 a boxer who competes at lightweight

light-year, light year n the distance that light travels in a vacuum in one solar year, approximately 5.88 trillion mi./9.46 trillion km ■ **light-years** npl a long way (infml)

lig·ne·ous /ˈlignee əss/ adj of or like wood

lig·nite /ˈlig ˌnīt/ n soft brown-black coal —**lig·nit·ic** /lig ˈnittik/ adj

Li·gu·ri·an Sea /li ˈgooree ən-/ arm of the Mediterranean Sea between NW Italy and Corsica and Elba

lik·a·ble /ˈlīkəb'l/, **like·a·ble** adj pleasant and friendly —**lik·a·bly** adv

like¹ prep 1 resembling 2 such as 3 indicates characteristics (often in questions) ○ What's it like there at this time of year? 4 typical of (often negative) ○ It's not like him to be this late. 5 inclined toward ○ felt like screaming 6 with a suggestion of ○ It looks like rain. ■ conj 1 as 2 △ as if or as though (nonstandard) ■ adv 1 in a particular way (infml) ○ looked like new 2 △ used as a filler or for emphasis (nonstandard) 3 △ introduces direct speech (nonstandard) ■ n 1 something similar 2 an exact counterpart ■ adj alike ◊ **the likes of** people or things of the particular sort

USAGE Avoid using the conjunction **like** to mean "as" or "as if" or "as though" with a following verb: It sounds like she may resign. Say instead: It sounds as if she may resign. Avoid also using **like** as a meaningless filler: "Once, when I was, like, 13 or 14…", or to introduce speech: She was like, "Don't worry."

like² v (liked, lik·ing) 1 vt regard as enjoyable 2 vt consider to be pleasant ○ I really like her. 3 vt want to have or do ○ Would you like a drink? 4 vt regard in a positive way 5 vi have a preference ○ if you like ■ n a preference

-like suffix resembling or characteristic of ○ workmanlike

like·li·hood /ˈlīklee hŏŏd/ n 1 a degree of probability 2 a probable event

like·ly /ˈlīklee/ adj (-li·er, -li·est) 1 probable 2 plausible (often ironic) 3 suitable ■ adv probably

~~likelyhood~~ incorrect spelling of **likelihood**

like-mind·ed adj sharing the same opinions —**like-mind·ed·ness** n

lik·en /ˈlīkən/ vt compare with another, especially to point out similarities

like·ness /ˈlīknəss/ n 1 a representation of somebody 2 similarity in appearance

like·wise /ˈlīk ˌwīz/ adv 1 in the same way 2 also

lik·ing /ˈlīking/ n 1 fondness or enjoyment 2 preference ◊ See note at **love**

~~likly~~ incorrect spelling of **likely**

li·lac /ˈlīlək/ (pl **-lacs** or same) n 1 a small tree with fragrant white or purple flowers 2 a pale purple color tinged with blue —**li·lac** adj

li·lan·ge·ni /li ˈlaang gènnee/ (pl **em·a·lan·ge·ni** /èmmə laang génnee/) n the main unit of currency of Swaziland

Li·li·u·o·ka·la·ni /lə ˈlēe ō kə laánee/ (1838–1917) queen of Hawaii (1891–93)

Lil·li·pu·tian /lillə pyōōsh'n/, **lil·li·pu·tian** n a very small person or thing ■ adj 1 tiny 2 trivial or petty

ORIGIN *Lilliputian* originally referred to Lilliput, an imaginary country in Jonathan Swift's *Gulliver's Travels* (1726), whose inhabitants were only 6 in. (15 cm) tall.

⚡ **LILO** /ˈlīlō/ n last in, last out data storage

Li·long·we /li ˈlóng way/ capital and second largest city of Malawi. Pop. 1,000,000 (1998).

lilt n 1 a pleasant rising and falling variation in voice pitch 2 a cheerful piece of music —**lilt·ing** adj

lil·y /ˈlillee/ (pl **-ies**) n 1 a perennial plant with large, sometimes trumpet-shaped, flowers 2 a plant resembling a lily ◊ **gild the lily** try to improve something that is already good or beautiful enough

lil·y-liv·ered /-ˈlivərd/ adj cowardly (dated)

lil·y of the val·ley (pl **lil·ies of the val·ley** or same) n a small perennial plant with sweet-smelling, bell-shaped white or pink flowers on a single stem

lil·y pad n a leaf of a water lily

lil·y-white adj 1 pale and unblemished 2 blameless

Li·ma¹ /ˈleema/ n a communications code word for the letter "L"

Li·ma² /ˈleemə/ capital of Peru. Pop. 6,464,693 (1998).

li·ma bean /ˈlīmə-, ˈleemə-/ n a pale green flattish edible bean

limb /lim/ n 1 an arm, leg, wing, flipper, or similar appendage 2 a large tree branch ◊ **be out on a limb** in an isolated position, without support

lim·ber /ˈlimbər/ adj 1 supple and agile 2 flexible —**lim·ber·ness** n
□ **limber up** vi do gentle physical exercises to loosen the muscles

lim·bo¹ /ˈlimbō/, **Lim·bo** n in Roman Catholic theology, a place for the souls of unbaptized children

lim·bo² /ˈlimbō/ (pl **-bos**) n a Caribbean dance

that involves bending backward and passing under a bar

lime[1] /līm/ n 1 calcium oxide 2 a form of calcium used for improving soil ■ vt (limed, lim·ing) spread or treat with lime

lime[2] n 1 a round green citrus fruit with sour juicy flesh 2 *also* **lime tree** an evergreen tree that produces limes

lime[3] n 1 *also* **lime tree** a linden tree 2 the wood of a lime tree

lime·ade /lī máyd/ n a carbonated drink made from or tasting of lime juice

lime·light /līm līt/ n 1 the focus of attention 2 an early form of stage lighting in which quicklime was heated to produce a brilliant light, or the light so produced

lim·er·ick /límmərik/ n a five-line humorous poem with regular meter and rhyme patterns

ORIGIN The **limerick** is said to derive its name from a Victorian custom of singing nonsense songs with this rhyme scheme, with the refrain "Will you come up to Limerick?" The first known use of the word dates from 1896.

lime·scale /līm skàyl/ n a deposit of lime on the inside of a teakettle or boiler

lime·stone /līm stòn/ n a sedimentary rock that consists mainly of the skeletons of ocean organisms

lim·it /límmit/ n 1 the farthest point, degree, or amount 2 a maximum or minimum amount or number allowed 3 a boundary of an area (often pl) o the city limits ■ vt 1 restrict 2 be a boundary to —**lim·it·less** adj —**lim·it·less·ly** adv —**lim·it·less·ness** n

lim·i·ta·tion /límmi táysh'n/ n 1 an imposed restriction 2 a disadvantage or weakness (often pl)

lim·it·ed /límmitəd/ adj 1 existing within imposed limits or restrictions 2 lacking full scope, extent, or authority o limited powers 3 with less talent or skill than expected or required —**lim·i·ted·ly** adv —**lim·i·ted·ness** n

lim·it·ed e·di·tion n an edition of a book or art print produced in limited numbers

lim·it·ed li·a·bil·i·ty n an investor's liability for a company's debts that is limited to the value of his or her stake

lim·o /límmō/ (pl -os) n a limousine (infml)

Li·món /li món/, **José** (1908–72) Mexican-born US dancer and choreographer

lim·ou·sine /límmə zèen, límmə zèen/ n 1 a large, luxurious, chauffeur-driven automobile 2 a vehicle transporting people to and from an airport

ORIGIN Limousine in French means literally "woman from Limousin (a former province of central France)." However it was also used as the name of a type of cloak with a cape worn by cart drivers in Limousin, and it is this that seems to have suggested the name **limousine**.

The driver's separate compartment in early limousines, at the beginning of the 20C, was outside, though covered with a roof.

limp[1] vi 1 walk unevenly because of an injury or disability 2 proceed with difficulty ■ n an impaired gait (sometimes offensive)

limp[2] adj 1 not stiff or rigid 2 lacking strength, energy, or enthusiasm —**limp·ly** adv —**limp·ness** n

lim·pet /límpət/ (pl -pets or same) n a marine organism with a rough conical shell that clings to rocks

lim·pid /límpid/ adj 1 transparent 2 lucid —**lim·pid·ly** adv

Lim·po·po /lim pốpō/ river in SE Africa, rising in N South Africa and flowing through S Mozambique to the Indian Ocean. Length 1,100 mi./1,800 km.

linch·pin /línch pìn/, **lynch·pin** n 1 a pin through an axle that stops a wheel from coming off 2 an essential element in the success of something

Lin·coln /língkən/ capital of Nebraska. Pop. 213,088 (1998).

Library of Congress

Abraham Lincoln

Lin·coln, Abraham (1809–65) 16th president of the United States (1861–65) —**Lin·coln·esque** /língkə nésk/ adj

Lin·coln, Mary Todd (1818–82) US first lady (1861–65)

linc·tus /língktəss/ n a cough syrup

Lind·bergh /línd bùrg/, **Charles Augustus** (1902–74) US aviator and engineer

lin·den /líndən/ (pl -dens or same) n a deciduous tree with heart-shaped leaves

Lind·say /línzee/, **Vachel** (1879–1931) US poet

line[1] n 1 a long narrow mark 2 a row of people or things 3 in geometry, a one-dimensional path traced by a moving point or drawn between two fixed points 4 a facial wrinkle (often pl) 5 a border 6 a row of words on a page 7 a characteristic contour (often pl) o the car's sleek lines 8 a transport company 9 a rope, wire, or cable 10 in football, a line of scrimmage, or the players on the forward line 11 a type of merchandise 12 a version of something o uttered the official line 13 a brief written message 14 a specialized area of work ■ **lines** npl an actor's spoken words ■ vt (lined, lin·ing) 1 mark a line on 2 arrange or be arranged in a line or along an edge o shrubs lining the driveway ◊ **draw the line**

set limits ◊ **in line for** likely to receive ◊ **lay it on the line** speak frankly *(infml)* ◊ **lay** or **put something on the line** risk the loss of something valuable *(infml)* ◊ **out of line** not conforming with what is expected or acceptable behavior *(infml)* ◊ **read between the lines** deduce something that is not explicit *(infml)* ◊ **toe the line** comply with expectations

□ **line out** *vi* in baseball, be put out after a line drive

□ **line up** *v* 1 *vti* arrange in or form a row 2 *vi* form a line 3 *vt* organize or provide o *lined up a keynote speaker*

line² (**lined, lin·ing**) *vt* 1 cover or reinforce the inside surface of 2 cover the surface of o *walls were lined with books*

lin·e·age /línnee ij/ *n* 1 a line of descent 2 a related group of people

lin·e·al /línnee əl/ *adj* in a direct line from an ancestor —**lin·e·al·ly** *adv*

lin·e·a·ment /línnee əmənt/ *n* a feature or contour *(literary)*

lin·e·ar /línnee ər/ *adj* 1 of lines 2 of a straight line —**lin·e·ar·i·ty** /línnee árrətee/ *n* —**lin·e·ar·ly** *adv*

line·back·er /lín bàkər/ *n* a football player positioned behind the defensive line —**line·back·ing** *n*

line danc·ing *n* a dance performed in rows to country and western music —**line dance** *n*, *vi* —**line danc·er** *n*

line draw·ing *n* a drawing made using only lines

line·man /línmən/ (*pl* -**men** /-mən/) *n* 1 somebody maintaining phone or power lines 2 a football player on the forward line

lin·en /línnən/ (*pl* same or -**ens**) *n* 1 thread or fabric made from flax 2 clothes or household items made from linen *(often pl)*

line of cred·it *n* the limit of available credit

line of scrim·mage *n* in football, an imaginary line across the field where the ball is resting, where the teams line up to start a play

lin·er¹ /línər/ *n* 1 a passenger ship or plane 2 eyeliner

lin·er² /línər/ *n* 1 a lining, or material used for making lining 2 a protective cover for a record or CD

lin·er notes *npl* information about a recording that is printed on the packaging

lines·man /línzmən/ (*pl* -**men** /-mən/) *n* in some sports, an official who signals when the ball is out of bounds

line·up /lín ùp/ *n* 1 in sports, a list of players and their positions 2 a television schedule 3 a group of people assembled by the police that a witness or victim of a crime inspects to help police identify a crime suspect

ling (*pl* same or **lings**) *n* 1 an edible ocean fish related to the cod 2 ling as food

-ling *suffix* 1 one connected with or resembling o *sapling* 2 a small one o *gosling*

lin·ger /líng gər/ *vi* 1 put off leaving because of reluctance to go 2 wait around or move about idly 3 remain alive while gradually dying —**lin·ger·ing** *adj*

lin·ge·rie /làanzhə ráy, làanzhəree, làaNzh-/ *n* women's underwear

lin·go /líng gò/ (*pl* -**goes**) *n* *(infml)* 1 a language that is not the speaker's native language 2 a set of specialized terms

lin·gua fran·ca /líng gwə frángkə/ (*pl* **lin·gua fran·cas** or **lin·guae fran·cae** /-gwee frángkee/) *n* 1 a language used in common by speakers of different languages 2 formerly, a traders' language that was a mixture of several Mediterranean languages

lin·gual /líng gwəl/ *adj* of the tongue —**lin·gual·ly** *adv*

lin·gui·ne /líng gweénee/, **lin·gui·ni** *n* pasta in long narrow flat strips

lin·guist /líng gwist/ *n* 1 a speaker of several languages 2 a student of linguistics

lin·guis·tic /líng gwístik/ *adj* 1 of language 2 of linguistics —**lin·guis·ti·cal·ly** *adv*

lin·guis·tics /líng gwístiks/ *n* the study of language (+ *sing verb*)

lin·i·ment /línnəmənt/ *n* a liquid rubbed into the skin to relieve pain

lin·ing /líning/ *n* an interior covering, or the material from which it is made

⚡ **link** *n* 1 a ring or loop forming part of a chain 2 a connection 3 a hypertext connection allowing direct access to related electronic text, images, and other data 4 a part of a transportation system 5 a broadcasting unit for relaying signals ■ *vti* connect, or be connected

link·age /língkij/ *n* 1 a connection, or the fact of being connected 2 a system of interconnected parts

links *n* a golf course (+ *sing* or *pl verb*)

link·up /língk up/ *n* a connection

Lin·nae·us /li née əss/, **Carolus** (1707–78) Swedish naturalist. He devised the standard system of binomial nomenclature for plants and animals. —**Lin·nae·an** *adj*

lin·net /línnət/ (*pl* -**nets** or same) *n* a small brown songbird of the finch family

li·no·cut /líno kùt/ *n* a print from a design cut in linoleum

li·no·le·um /li nólee əm/ *n* a tough washable floor covering

lin·seed /lín seéd/ *n* 1 the seed of the flax plant, which yields oil 2 flax grown as an oilseed crop

lint *n* 1 small pieces of fiber or fluff 2 soft absorbent material used for medical dressings —**lint·y** *adj*

lin·tel /lint'l/ *n* a supporting beam above a window or door

li·on /lí ən/ n 1 a large wild cat with a tawny coat, the male of which has a shaggy mane 2 somebody who is brave and strong 3 **Li·on** the constellation Leo ◊ **the lion's share** the largest or best part

li·on·ess /lí ənəss/ n a female lion

li·on·heart·ed /lí ən haártəd/ adj courageous —**li·on·heart·ed·ness** n

li·on·ize /lí ə nìz/ (**-ized, -iz·ing**) vt treat somebody as a celebrity —**li·on·i·za·tion** /lí əni záysh'n/ n

lip n 1 either of two fleshy folds around the mouth 2 something shaped like a lip 3 impertinence (slang) 4 any of two sets of folds of skin at the opening of the vulva

lip balm n moisturizing ointment for lips

lip gloss n a shiny lip cosmetic

lip·id /líppid, lípíd/, **lip·ide** /lí pìd, lí-/ n a biological compound that is not soluble in water, e.g., a fat —**lip·id·ic** /li píddik, lī-/ adj

lip·o·suc·tion /líppə sùksh'n, lípə-/ n cosmetic surgery to remove body fat

Lip·pi /líppee/, **Fra Filippo** (1406?–69) Italian painter

lip-read /líp reèd/ (**lip-read** /-red/) vti understand what is said by watching a speaker's lips move —**lip-read·er** /líp reèdər/ n

lip ser·vice n insincere respect or agreement

lip·stick /líp stìk/ n a cosmetic for coloring the lips

lip-synch, lip-sync vti match lip movements to recorded sound

liq·ue·fy /líkwə fì/ (**-fied, -fies**), **liq·ui·fy** vti become or make liquid —**liq·ue·fac·tion** /líkwə fáksh'n/ n

~~liquer~~ incorrect spelling of **liqueur**

li·queur /li kúr, -kyoor/ n a sweet alcoholic drink

liq·uid /líkwid/ n any flowing substance similar to water in consistency ■ adj 1 in the form of a liquid 2 describes assets easily converted into cash 3 clear and shining —**liq·uid·ly** adv

liq·ui·date /líkwi dàyt/ (**-dat·ed, -dat·ing**) v 1 vti pay a debt 2 vti shut down a business 3 vt turn assets into cash —**liq·ui·da·tion** /líkwi dáysh'n/ n —**liq·ui·da·tor** n

liq·uid-crys·tal dis·play n a display of characters created by applying electricity to cells made of liquid crystal to make some of them change color

li·quid·i·ty /li kwíddətee/ n 1 the quality of being liquid 2 the quality of being easily converted into cash

liq·uid·ize /líkwi dìz/ (**-ized, -iz·ing**) vti make or become liquid

liq·uor /líkər/ n an alcoholic beverage produced by distillation rather than fermentation

liq·uor store n a store that sells alcoholic beverages

li·ra /leérə/ (pl **-re** /leér ay, -rə/) n 1 the main unit of currency of Turkey and Malta 2 the former unit of Italian currency

Lis·bon /lízbən/ capital of Portugal. Pop. 601,180 (1995).

lisle /lìl/ n fine smooth cotton thread. Use: stockings.

lisp n 1 a speech defect in which "s" sounds are pronounced as a soft "th" 2 a speech sound made by somebody with a lisp —**lisp** vti —**lisp·ing** adj, n —**lisp·ing·ly** adv

⚡ **LISP** /lisp/ n a programming language used in artificial intelligence

---

ORIGIN LISP is a contraction of "list processor." It was coined in the 1950s.

---

lis·some /líssəm/, **lis·som** adj 1 gracefully slender and flexible 2 quick and graceful in moving —**lis·some·ly** adv —**lis·some·ness** n

list[1] n a series of words, names, numbers, or other pieces of information written one after the other ■ v 1 vt arrange items as an ordered series 2 vt include somebody or something in an ordered series 3 vt admit a security for trading on an exchange ○ is listed on the New York Stock Exchange 4 vti set or have an official retail price ○ lists at $40

list[2] vi lean to one side ■ n a sideways tilt

lis·ten /líss'n/ vi 1 make a conscious effort to hear 2 pay attention and take into account —**lis·ten·a·ble** adj —**lis·ten·er** n

lis·ten·ing post n 1 in the military, a forward position for detecting enemy movements 2 a place for gathering intelligence

Lis·ter /lístər/, **Joseph, 1st Baron** (1827–1912) British surgeon. His development of antiseptic techniques greatly reduced surgical mortality.

lis·te·ri·a /lə steéree ə/ n a rod-shaped disease-causing bacterium found in food

list·ing /lísting/ n 1 an entry in a list, catalog, or directory 2 a list, catalog, or directory ■ **list·ings** npl published lists of cultural events

list·less /lístləss/ adj weary or unwilling to make an effort —**list·less·ly** adv —**list·less·ness** n

Lis·ton /lístən/, **Sonny** (1932–70) US boxer

list price n a published retail price that a seller may discount

⚡ **list·serv** /líst sùrv/ n an Internet service allowing users to have online discussions

Franz Liszt

Liszt /list/, **Franz** (1811–86) Hungarian pianist, composer, and conductor

lit past participle, past tense of **light¹**

lit. *abbr* 1 liter 2 literary 3 literature

lit·a·ny /lítt'nee/ (*pl* **-nies**) *n* 1 a series of prayers including invocations from a priest or minister and responses from the congregation 2 a long repetitious list

li·tas /lée tàass/ (*pl same*) *n* the main unit of Lithuanian currency

lite *adj* low in calories, sugar, fat, or alcohol (*in labeling or advertising foods and beverages*)

li·ter /léetar/ *n* a measure of volume equal to 1 cubic decimeter or 1.056 liquid quarts

lit·er·a·cy /líttərəssee, líttrəssee/ *n* 1 ability to read and write 2 competence in a particular subject ○ *computer literacy*

lit·er·al /líttəral/ *adj* 1 word for word ○ *a literal transcript* 2 strictly adhering to the basic meaning of an original text ○ *a literal interpretation* 3 including or dealing only with the facts 4 using alphabetical letters —**lit·er·al·ness** *n*

lit·er·al·ly /líttərəlee/ *adv* 1 strictly adhering to basic meaning 2 △ adds emphasis (*infml*) ○ *I was literally freezing.*

USAGE In formal contexts, avoid using **literally** for emphasis, especially when combined with a colorful figure of speech: *The principal is literally breathing fire.* Say instead *The principal is absolutely furious* or *The principal is really livid.*

lit·er·ary /líttə rèrree/ *adj* 1 of literature 2 formally expressed —**lit·er·ar·i·ness** *n*

lit·er·ate /líttərət/ *adj* 1 able to read and write 2 competent in a particular subject ○ *computer-literate* 3 well-educated or cultured —**lit·er·ate** *n* —**lit·er·ate·ly** *adv* —**lit·er·ate·ness** *n*

lit·er·a·ti /líttə ràatee/ *npl* (*fml*) 1 highly educated people 2 authors and others deeply involved in literature

lit·er·a·ture /líttərəchər, líttrəchər, -chóor/ *n* 1 creative written works such as fiction, poetry, drama, and criticism 2 a body of written works of a language, culture, or period ○ *Russian literature* 3 writings on a specific subject ○ *scientific literature* 4 printed information ○ *the company's promotional literature*

lithe /līth/ (**lith·er**, **lith·est**) *adj* flexible and supple —**lithe·ly** *adv* —**lithe·ness** *n* —**lithe·some** *adj*

lith·i·um /líthee əm/ *n* (*symbol* Li) a soft silverwhite chemical element that is the lightest metal known. Use: alloys, ceramics, batteries, medical treatment for bipolar disorder.

li·thog·ra·phy /li thóggrəfee/ *n* a printing process using a plate on which only the image to be printed takes up ink —**lith·o·graph** /líthə gràf/ *n*, *vti* —**li·thog·raph·er** *n* —**lith·o·graph·ic** /líthə gráffik/ *adj*

Lith·u·a·ni·a /líthōō áynee ə/ country in NE Europe, bordering the Baltic Sea. Cap. Vilnius. Pop. 3,610,535 (2001). —**Lith·u·a·ni·an** *n*, *adj*

lit·i·gate /lítti gàyt/ (**-gat·ed**, **-gat·ing**) *vi* pursue or be involved in a lawsuit —**lit·i·gant** *n*, *adj* —**lit·i·ga·tor** *n*

lit·i·ga·tion /lítti gáysh'n/ *n* the process or state of bringing a lawsuit

li·ti·gious /li tíjjəss/ *adj* 1 of legal action 2 inclined to take legal action

lit·mus /lítməss/ *n* a powdery substance obtained from lichens. Use: indicator for acids or bases, turning red in acids and blue in bases.

lit·mus pa·per *n* paper treated with litmus,

lit·mus test *n* 1 a test using litmus paper to identify whether something is an acid or base 2 a test in which a single factor determines the outcome ○ *making the nominee's stand on trade a litmus test for their support*

li·to·tes /líta teèz, lítta-, π tō-/ (*pl same*) *n* understatement for effect, often involving a negative, or an example of this

~~litrature~~ incorrect spelling of **literature**

li·tre *n* UK = **liter**

lit·ter /líttər/ *n* 1 scattered trash 2 a group of young animals born in a single birth 3 bedding for animals 4 material for a pet's toilet box 5 a stretcher (*dated*) 6 formerly, a couch with poles for carrying somebody ■ *v* 1 *vti* drop trash 2 *vt* cover a place with scattered objects —**lit·ter·er** *n*

~~litterature~~ incorrect spelling of **literature**

lit·ter·bug /líttər bùg/ *n* somebody who leaves litter in public places (*infml disapproving*)

lit·tle /lítt'l/ *adj* (**-tler**, **-tlest**) 1 small or of less than average size 2 young 3 describes a younger sister or brother ○ *my little sister* 4 small in a pleasant way ○ *his cute little habits* 5 short or quick ○ *gave a little smile* ■ *pron* a small amount (*after "a"*) ○ *I only ate a little.* ■ *adj* (**-tler**, **-tlest**), *pron* not much ○ *had little or no effect* ■ *adv* 1 hardly ○ *little did they know* 2 not often ○ *visiting them little* —**lit·tle·ness** *n* ◇ **little by little** gradually

Lit·tle Big·horn /-bíg hawrn/ river in S Montana. General George Armstrong Custer and his army were defeated and killed by Native Americans on its banks in June 1876. Length 90 mi./145 km.

lit·tle fin·ger *n* the smallest finger of the human hand

Lit·tle League *n* baseball league for children from 8 to 12 years old —**Lit·tle Leag·uer** *n*

lit·tle peo·ple *npl* 1 people who have small or average incomes and minimal influence 2 small imaginary beings such as fairies and elves

Lit·tle Rock capital of Arkansas. Pop. 175,303 (1998).

lit·tle toe *n* the smallest toe of the human foot

lit·to·ral /líttərəl/ *adj* 1 on or near a shore 2 living on or near a shore ◼ *n* a shore

lit·ur·gy /líttərjee/ (*pl* **-gies**) *n* 1 a form of worship set down by a church 2 *also* **Lit·ur·gy** the form of service used for celebrating Communion in a Christian church —**li·tur·gi·cal** /li túrjik'l/ *adj*

liv·a·ble /lívvəb'l/, **live·a·ble** *adj* 1 comfortable to live in o *a livable town* 2 endurable and worthwhile

live[1] /liv/ (**lived** /livd/, **liv·ing** /lívving/) *v* 1 *vi* be alive 2 *vi* stay alive o *lived through a serious illness* 3 *vi* reside in a particular place or way o *lives alone* 4 *vti* have a particular kind of life o *life comfortably* 5 *vi* make a living in a particular way o *lives by waiting tables* 6 *vti* fully enjoy life o *really knew how to live* 7 *vi* persist o *Her fame lives on.* 8 *vt* experience or go through o *living a nightmare* o **live it up** live or celebrate in an extravagant way (*slang*)

☐ **live down** *vt* cause something shameful to be forgotten by living in a commendable way

☐ **live off** *vt* rely on financially

☐ **live on** *vt* 1 live off somebody or something 2 eat a particular food to survive

☐ **live out** *vt* 1 do something previously imagined 2 live until the end of a particular period

☐ **live up to** *vt* meet expectations

☐ **live with** *vt* tolerate something

live[2] /liv/ *adj* 1 living 2 broadcast as it happens 3 appearing performing, or performed in person o *I'd rather dance to live music.* 4 recorded during a performance 5 relevant to current concerns o *a live issue* 6 connected to a power source 7 charged with an explosive o *live ammunition* 8 burning or glowing o *live coals* 9 describes a volcano that is still active 10 containing living bacteria ◼ *adv* 1 in front of an audience 2 broadcast while the event happens

lived-in /lívd-/ *adj* 1 slightly untidy but homey 2 careworn

live-in /lív-/ *adj* 1 living at your place of work 2 sharing a home with a sexual partner

live·li·hood /lívlee hood/ *n* a job or other source of income

live·long /lív làwng/ *adj* emphasizes how long a period of time seems to last (*literary*)

live·ly /lívlee/ (**-li·er, -li·est**) *adj* 1 full of energy 2 animated, exciting, or stimulating 3 enthusiastic o *takes a lively interest in everything* 4 full of movement o *a lively dance* —**live·li·ly** *adv* —**live·li·ness** *n*

~~livelyhood~~ incorrect spelling of **livelihood**

li·ven /lív'n/ *vti* make or become lively

live oak /lív-/ *n* an evergreen oak with a short broad trunk and leathery leaves

liv·er /lívvər/ *n* 1 a large glandular organ in vertebrates that secretes bile and stores and filters blood 2 the liver of a mammal, fowl, or fish as food

Liv·er·pool /lívvər pool/ port in NW England, on the Mersey River. Pop. 467,995 (1996).

. **liver spot** *n* a brown spot on the skin

liv·er·wurst /lívvər wùrst/ *n* sausage made with liver

liv·er·y /lívvəree/ (*pl* **-ies**) *n* 1 a uniform, especially one worn by servants 2 the professional care or renting of horses —**liv·er·ied** *adj*

liv·er·y·man /lívvəreemən, lívvreemən/ (*pl* **-men** /-mən/) *n* an owner or employee of a livery stable

live·stock /lív stòk/ *n* animals raised for food or other products or kept for use, especially on a farm

live wire /lív-/ *n* 1 a wire connected to a power source 2 an energetic person (*infml*)

liv·id /lívvid/ *adj* 1 furious 2 with a bluish bruised color 3 ashen —**li·vid·i·ty** /li víddətee/ *n* —**liv·id·ly** *adv*

liv·ing /lívving/ *adj* 1 alive 2 realistic or true to life o *the living image of her mother* 3 still in use o *a living language* ◼ *n* 1 a means of earning money to live on, or the money somebody so earns o *What do you do for a living?* 2 the maintaining of life o *the cost of living* 3 quality or manner of life o *healthy living* ◼ *npl* people who are alive

---

SYNONYMS living, alive, animate, extant
CORE MEANING: having life or existence

---

liv·ing death *n* a period of unrelieved misery

liv·ing room *n* a room in a house for relaxing or entertaining

Liv·ing·stone /lívving stən/, **David** (1813–73) British physician, missionary, and explorer

liv·ing wage *n* a wage that can support a family in reasonable comfort

liv·ing will *n* a document in which the signer declines to be kept alive artificially by life-support systems if he or she becomes terminally ill

Liv·y /lívvee/ (59 BC–AD 17) Roman historian

liz·ard /lízzərd/ *n* 1 a four-legged reptile with a long scaly body, movable eyelids, and a long tapering tail 2 a large reptile such as an alligator or crocodile that resembles a lizard

Lju·blja·na /lyoŏ blaánaa/ capital of Slovenia. Pop. 330,000 (1997).

ll, ll. *abbr* lines

'll *contr* 1 shall 2 will

lla·ma /laáma/ *n* a domesticated long-haired mammal related to camels

LL.D. *abbr* Doctor of Laws

Lloyd /loyd/, **Harold** (1893–1971) US movie actor

Lloyd George /lòyd jáwrj/, **David, 1st Earl of**

Dwyfor (1863–1945) British prime minister (1916–22)

⚡**load** /lōd/ n 1 something carried or transported 2 the amount that is carried or dealt with at one time (often in combination) ○ a boat load of passengers ○ a small load of dirty shirts 3 the amount of work that a person or machine is required to do ○ my teaching load 4 a mental burden 5 a single charge of ammunition for a gun 6 the total force and weight that a structure is designed to withstand 7 a charge added to the price of some mutual fund shares ■ **loads** npl a large amount or a lot of (infml) ○ loads of visitors ■ v 1 vti put ammunition in a firearm 2 vti put cargo or passengers on a vehicle, ship, or aircraft 3 vt put a load on an animal, or give a load to a person to carry 4 vt in baseball, put runners on all three bases ○ loading the bases with a line drive 5 vt put something in a device for it to function or operate on ○ load a camera with film 6 vt add surcharge to an insurance premium 7 vt weight one side of a die or a roulette wheel to prevent it from operating randomly ○ He must have loaded the dice. —**load·er** n

load·ed /lōdəd/ adj 1 carrying a full load 2 describes a weapon containing ammunition 3 with a hidden implication ○ a loaded question 4 rich (slang) 5 very drunk (slang) 6 describes dice or a roulette wheel weighted unfairly 7 supplied with many extras ○ the car comes loaded

load·ing /lōding/ n 1 a load or weight carried 2 material added to increase weight 3 an additional insurance premium

loaf[1] /lōf/ (pl **loaves**) n 1 a quantity of bread shaped and baked as a whole 2 a quantity of food shaped in a rectangular block (in combination) ○ meatloaf

loaf[2] /lōf/ vi spend time lazily

ORIGIN Loafing has no connection with bread. The verb loaf was extracted from loafer, which was itself probably taken from German Landläufer "tramp" (literally "land-runner"). Loaf is first recorded in the 1830s.

loaf·er /lōfər/ n a lazy person

loam /lōm/ n 1 fertile workable soil 2 clay and sand mixed for building —**loam·y** adj

loan /lōn/ n 1 an amount of money lent 2 the act of lending something ■ vt lend —**loan·er** n

loan shark n an unethical moneylender (disapproving)

loan·word /lōn wùrd/, **loan word**, **loan** n a word borrowed from another language

loath /lōth, lōth/, **loth** adj reluctant ◊ See note at **unwilling**

loathe /lōth/ (**loathed**, **loath·ing**) vt dislike intensely —**loath·ing·ly** adv

~~loathesome~~ incorrect spelling of **loathsome**

loath·ing /lōthing/ n intense dislike ◊ See note at **dislike**

loath·some /lōthsəm/ adj repulsive —**loath·some·ness** n

loaves plural of **loaf**[1]

lob v(**lobbed, lob·bing**) 1 vti hit a ball in a high arc 2 vt throw casually ■ n a high arching shot

lob·by /lóbbee/ n (pl **-bies**) 1 an entrance area in a public building 2 a public area in a legislative building 3 a group trying to influence political policy ■ vti (**-bied, -bies**) petition politicians or influential people —**lob·by·er** n —**lob·by·ism** n —**lob·by·ist** n

lobe n 1 an earlobe 2 any rounded body part

lo·be·li·a /lō beelee ə, lō beelyə/ n a plant with white or purple flowers

lo·bot·o·my /lə bóttəmee/ n (pl **-mies**) n a surgical operation to sever the nerves connecting the front part of the brain to the thalamus —**lo·bot·o·mize** vt

lob·ster /lóbstər/ n 1 a hard-shelled sea animal with a pair of large pincers 2 a crustacean related to the lobster

lob·ster pot n a lobster trap

lo·cal /lōk'l/ adj 1 in or for a nearby area 2 characteristic of a particular area 3 not widespread 4 of a comparatively small governmental region 5 affecting only a particular part of the body 6 stopping at all stops ○ a local train ■ n 1 somebody who comes from a particular area 2 a train or bus that stops at all stops 3 a branch of an organization, especially a union 4 a regional news item —**lo·cal·ly** adv —**lo·cal·ness** n

lo·cal an·es·thet·ic n a drug that eliminates pain in a particular part of the body

⚡**lo·cal ar·e·a net·work** n a network of personal computers within a small area

lo·cal col·or n interesting characteristic features of a particular place

lo·cale /lō kál/ n the location of an event or story

lo·cal gov·ern·ment n 1 the government of a city, county, or region 2 elected officials at the local level

lo·cal·i·ty /lō kállətee/ n (pl **-ties**) 1 a particular place 2 situation at a particular point in space or time

lo·cal·ize /lōk'l īz/ (**-ized, -iz·ing**) vt 1 confine to a place 2 find the location of —**lo·cal·i·za·tion** /lōk'li záysh'n/ n

lo·cate /lō kàyt, lō káyt/ (**-cat·ed, -cat·ing**) v 1 vt find a new place 2 vi establish a residence or business in a place 3 vt position or situate

lo·ca·tion /lō káysh'n/ n 1 the site or position of something 2 a movie setting 3 the discovery of something —**lo·ca·tion·al** adj

loch /lok, lawkh/ n Scotland 1 a lake 2 a long narrow inlet

lock[1] n 1 a fastening mechanism usually operated by a key 2 a gated section of a waterway 3 a wrestling hold 4 the part of a gun that causes the explosion ■ v 1 vti fasten using a lock **2** *vt* put something or somebody in a locked place **3** *vti* fix or be fixed in place **4** *vt* hold somebody tightly —**lock-able** *adj* ◊ **lock, stock, and barrel** completely

□ **lock away** *vt* **1** imprison **2** store in a locked place

□ **lock out** *vt* prevent somebody from entering by locking a door

lock² *n* a piece of hair ■ **locks** *npl* human hair *(literary)*

lock·box /lók bòks/ *n* a lockable box

Locke, John (1632–1704) English philosopher

lock·er /lókər/ *n* **1** a lockable compartment for personal belongings **2** a freezer **3** a trunk used for storage

lock·er room *n* a changing room with lockers

lock·et /lókət/ *n* a small decorative case for a picture or memento worn on a neck chain

lock·jaw /lók jàw/ *n* a sustained spasm of the jaw muscles that is an early symptom of tetanus

lock·keep·er /lók kèepər/, **lock·mas·ter** /lók màstər/ *n* a person in charge of a waterway lock

lock·out /lók òwt/ *n* a refusal by management to allow workers into the workplace

lock·smith /lók smìth/ *n* somebody who installs and repairs locks

lock·step /lók stèp/ *n* **1** military marching with soldiers close together **2** a mindless routine

lock·up /lók ùp/ *n* **1** a place with prison cells **2** the securing of a building, or the time when this is done

Lock·wood /lók wòod/, **Belva Ann Bennet** (1830–1917) US lawyer, reformer, and women's rights activist

lo·co /ló kò/ *adj* wildly irrational *(infml)*

lo·co·mo·tion /lòkə mṓsh'n/ *n* movement from one place to another

lo·co·mo·tive /lòkə mṓtiv/ *n* a railroad engine ■ *adj* of locomotion

lo·co·weed /lókò wèed/ *n* a plant of the pea family that is toxic to animals

lo·cus /lókəss/ (*pl* **-ci** /ló sì, lóssee, lókee/) *n* **1** a place where something happens **2** a set of points, the positions of which satisfy a set of algebraic conditions

lo·cust /lókəst/ *n* **1** a swarming grasshopper **2** a deciduous N American tree with clusters of fragrant flowers **3** a pod-bearing tree such as the carob

lo·cu·tion /lə kyóosh'n, lə kyóosh'n/ *n* **1** a typical phrase **2** somebody's style of speech

lode *n* **1** a deposit of ore **2** an abundant supply

lode·star /lṓd stàar/ *n* **1** the North Star **2** a guiding principle *(literary)*

lode·stone /lṓd stṓn/ *n* **1** magnetite **2** an attraction

lodge *n* **1** a small building providing temporary accommodation in the country **2** a building in a vacation resort **3** an inn or hotel **4** a branch of a union or organization **5** a meeting hall **6** a Native North American dwelling **7** a small gatekeeper's house **8** a beaver's den ■ *v* (**lodged, lodg·ing**) **1** *vt* make a complaint or appeal **2** *vt* deposit something in a safe place **3** *vti* stick or get stuck **4** *vi* live in somebody else's house *(dated)* **5** *vt* place somebody in temporary accommodation **6** *vt* give somebody the power to act

lodg·er /lójjər/ *n* a paying guest

lodg·ing /lójjing/ *n* somewhere to stay, especially temporarily ■ **lodg·ings** *npl* a rented room or rooms in a boarding house or private home *(dated)*

Lodz /lòoj, lodz/, **Łódź** /wooj/ city in central Poland. Pop. 812,300 (1997).

loft *n* **1** the upper floor of a barn **2** a gallery in a church **3** the upper floor of a warehouse or factory, converted to living space **4** a raised sleeping platform in a room **5** the slanting angle on a golf club ■ *vt* hit a ball high

loft·y /lóftee/ (**-i·er, -i·est**) *adj* **1** haughty **2** exalted **3** very high

log¹ *n* **1** a piece cut from a tree **2** a record of a journey **3** a record of events **4** a device for measuring speed ■ *v* (**logged, log·ging**) **1** *vt* record an event in a log **2** *vti* cut up a tree for logs **3** *vt* travel a particular distance or speed —**log·ger** *n* —**log·ging** *n* ◊ **sleep like a log** sleep very soundly

□ **log off** *or* **out** *vi* end a computer session

□ **log on** *or* **in** *vti* enter a computer system

log² *n* a logarithm *(infml)*

Lo·gan, Mt. /lṓgən/ highest peak in Canada, in the St. Elias Range in SW Yukon Territory. Height 19,551 ft./5,959 m.

lo·gan·ber·ry /lṓgən bèrree/ (*pl* **-ries**) *n* **1** a purplish-red fruit like a large raspberry **2** the plant that produces loganberries

ORIGIN The **loganberry** is named for the US horticulturist James H. Logan (1841–1928), who first cultivated it.

log·a·rithm /lóggə rìthəm/ *n* the power to which a base must be raised to equal a given number —**log·a·rith·mic** /lóggə rìthmik/ *adj* —**log·a·rith·mi·cal·ly** *adv*

ORIGIN The word **logarithm** was coined in the early 17C by the British mathematician John Napier. He formed it from Greek *logos* "ratio" and *arithmos* "number."

log·book /lóg bòok/ *n* a book containing a record of a journey

log cab·in *n* a simple house made of logs

loge /lṓzh/ *n* **1** the front of the balcony in a theater **2** a box in a theater

log·ger·head /lóggər hèd/ ◊ **at loggerheads** involved in a quarrel or feud

✦log·ic /lójjik/ *n* **1** the branch of philosophy that deals with the theory of reasoning **2** a system of reasoning **3** sensible argument and thought **4** the design of a computer's circuit

log·i·cal /lójjik'l/ *adj* **1** sensible and based on facts **2** able to think rationally —**log·i·cal·i·ty** /lòjji kállətee/ *n* —**log·i·cal·ly** *adv*

⚡**log·ic bomb** *n* a piece of software that acts as a virus

⚡**log·ic cir·cuit** *n* a computer switching circuit that performs operations on input signals

lo·gis·tics /lə jístiks, lō jístiks/ *n (+ sing or pl verb)* **1** the organization of a complex task **2** the organization of troop movements

log·jam /lóg jàm/ *n* **1** a deadlock **2** a river blockage caused by floating logs

lo·go /lố gố/ *(pl* **-gos)** *n* a design used as a symbol of an organization

⚡**log·on** /lóggon/, **log·in** /lóggin/ *n* **1** the act of logging on to a computer **2** a password used to log on

log·roll·ing /lóg ròling/ *n* **1** the exchange of political support **2** mutual support **3** a balancing game

loin /loyn/ *n* **1** the part of the back between the ribs and the hips **2** meat cut from the loin of an animal ◼ **loins** *npl* the area below the waist at the front of the body and above the thighs *(literary)*

loin·cloth /lóyn klòth/ *n* a cloth worn around the hips to cover the genitals

Loire /lwaar/ longest river in France, rising in the southeast and flowing to the Bay of Biscay in the northwest. Length 634 mi./1,020 km.

loi·ter /lóytər/ *vi* **1** stand around idly **2** proceed slowly —**loi·ter·er** *n*

loll *vi* **1** lounge in a relaxed way **2** droop

lol·li·pop /lóllee pòp/, **lol·ly·pop** *n* piece of hard candy on a stick

lol·lop /lólləp/ *vi* move in a bouncy uncontrolled way

Lom·bar·dy /lómbərdee, lúm-/ autonomous region in north central Italy. Cap. Milan. Pop. 9,028,913 (1998). —**Lom·bar·dic** /lom báərdik, lum-/ *adj*

Lo·mé /lố mày/ capital of Togo. Pop. 700,000 (1997).

Lon·don /lúndən/ **1** capital of the United Kingdom, in SE England. Pop. 7,074,265 (1996). **2** city in SW Ontario, Canada. Pop. 325,646 (1996). —**Lon·don·er** *n*

Lon·don, Jack (1876–1916) US writer

lone *adj* only one *o a lone survivor*

lone·ly /lốnlee/ *(-li·er, -li·est) adj* **1** feeling alone and sad **2** isolated —**lone·li·ness** *n*

lone·ly-hearts *adj* of or for people who are looking for a romantic relationship

~~lonelyness~~ incorrect spelling of **loneliness**

lon·er /lốnər/ *n* somebody who likes being alone

lone·some /lốnsəm/ *adj* **1** sad from being alone **2** desolate —**lone·some·ly** *adv* —**lone·some·ness** *n*

lone wolf *n* a loner

long¹ /lawng, long/ *adj* **1** extending a considerable distance **2** going on or back for a lengthy period **3** having many items **4** of a particular length **5** with a greater length than width **6** extending in time or space beyond what is usual or desirable **7** having plenty of a particular thing *(infml)* ◦ *long on rhetoric* ◼ *adv* **1** for a long time **2** for a particular length of time ◦ *all day long* **3** at a much earlier or later time ◦ *long after he left* ◼ *n* a long time ◦ *Are you here for long?* ◇ **as** *or* **so long as 1** because of the fact that **2** on the condition that ◇ **before long** before much time passes ◇ **long since** a long time ago ◇ **no longer** not now

long² *vi* have a strong desire or yearning for somebody or something ◦ *She longed for summer.* ◇ See note at **want**

long. *abbr* longitude

long-a·wait·ed *adj* hoped for and expected for a long time

Long Beach city in SW California. Pop. 430,905 (1998).

long·bow /lávng bồ, lóng-/ *n* a large handdrawn bow —**long·bow·man** *n*

long-dis·tance *adj* **1** between distant telephones **2** relating to foot races of over one mile/1,500 m long ◼ *n* the provision of long-distance telephone service ◼ *adv* using a long-distance telephone line

long di·vi·sion *n* a method of division of large numbers that shows each step

long-drawn-out *adj* prolonged

lon·gev·i·ty /lon jévvətee/ *(pl* **-ties)** *n* **1** long life **2** the duration of life

long face *n* a sad expression —**long-faced** *adj*

Long·fel·low /láwng fèlồ, lóng-/, **Henry Wadsworth** (1807–82) US poet

long·hand /láwng hànd, lóng-/ *n* handwriting as opposed to typing

long·horn /láwng hàwrn, lóng-/ *(pl* **-horns** *or* 'same) *n* a reddish brown cow with long horns formerly common in the United States

long·ing /láwnging, lónging/ *n* a steady strong desire ◼ *adj* showing yearning —**long·ing·ly** *adv*

Long Is·land island in SE New York. Queens and Brooklyn, two boroughs of New York City, are situated at its western end. Pop. 6,882,362 (1997).

Long Is·land Sound inlet of the Atlantic Ocean between N Long Island, New York, and S Connecticut

lon·gi·tude /lónji tòod/ *n* the angular distance of a place from the prime meridian in Greenwich, England

lon·gi·tu·di·nal /lònji toõd'nəl/ *adj* **1** going from top to bottom **2** of longitude —**lon·gi·tu·di·nal·ly** *adv*

long johns *npl* underwear with full-length legs

long jump *n* a competition in which athletes jump for distance rather than height

long-last·ing *adj* lasting a long time

long-lived *adj* living or existing for a long time

long-lost *adj* not seen for a long time (*humorous*)

Lon·go /láwng ỏ/, **Robert** (b. 1953) US painter, sculptor, filmmaker, and performance artist

long-play·ing rec·ord *n* full form of **LP**

long-range *adj* **1** extending well into the future **2** traveling long distances

long·shore·man /láwng shàwrmən, lóng-/ (*pl* **-men** /-mən/) *n* a dock worker

long shot *n* **1** somebody or something unlikely to win or succeed **2** a camera shot of a distant object ◇ **not) by a long shot** (not) in any way at all (*infml*)

long-sight·ed *adj* able to see distant objects better than nearby ones —**long-sight·ed·ly** *adv* —**long-sight·ed·ness** *n*

long-stand·ing *adj* having existed for a long time

long-suf·fer·ing *adj* patiently enduring unpleasantness

long term *n* a time lasting from now far into the future

long-term *adj* **1** of or affecting the long term **2** long-lasting

long-time /láwng tìm, lóng-/ *adj* having existed for years

lon·gueur /lawng gúr, lòng-/ *n* a period of boredom

long wave *n* a radio wave over 1,000m

long-wind·ed *adj* **1** using too many words **2** not easily becoming short of breath —**long-wind·ed·ness** *n* See note at **wordy**

look *v* **1** *vi* turn the eyes toward or on something **2** *vi* use the eyes to search **3** *vi* appear in a particular way **4** *vi* consider ◇ *look at the problem* **5** *vt* fit something by appearance ◇ *looks his age* **6** *vi* face a particular way ◇ *The house looks over the lake.* ■ *n* **1** an act or instance of looking **2** the way somebody or something appears **3** a facial expression ■ **looks** *npl* outward appearance

□ **look after** *vt* take care of

□ **look ahead** *vi* think about the future

□ **look back** *vi* think about the past

□ **look down on** or **upon** *vt* treat as inferior

□ **look into** *vt* investigate carefully

□ **look on** *v* **1** *vi* be a spectator **2** *also* **look upon** *vt* regard

□ **look out** *vi* be careful

□ **look out for** *vt* **1** watch for (*infml*) **2** take care of

□ **look to** *vt* rely on

□ **look up** *v* **1** *vt* search for in a reference book **2** *vi* improve **3** *vt* visit

□ **look up to** *vt* respect and admire

look-a·like *n* somebody or something that looks very much like another (*infml*)

look·er /loôkər/ *n* somebody who watches

look·er-on (*pl* **look·ers-on**) *n* an onlooker

look·ing glass *n* a mirror (*archaic*)

look·out /loôk òwt/ *n* **1** a careful watch **2** somebody watching for danger **3** a place that gives a good view

⚡ **look-up** *n* a computer procedure that matches a term against stored information

loom[1] *vi* **1** appear as a large shape **2** be about to happen

loom[2] *n* a weaving apparatus

loon *n* a diving bird of northern waters

loon·y /loônee/ (**-i·er**, **-i·est**), **loon·ey** *adj* **1** an offensive term meaning affected by a psychiatric disorder **2** considered silly or strange (*infml*) —**loon·i·ness** *n* —**loon·y** *n*

⚡ **loop** *n* **1** a circle or oval made by a line curving over itself **2** a loop of string or other material **3** a closed circuit **4** a set of commands in a computer program ■ *v* **1** *vti* be in or form into a loop **2** *vt* fasten, join, or arrange something using a loop ◇ **in** or **out of the loop** be or not be among the people who are decision-makers or are fully informed (*infml*)

loop·hole /loôp hòl/ *n* **1** a gap in a law **2** a slit in a wall

loop·y /loôpee/ (**-i·er**, **-i·est**) *adj* **1** having loops **2** an offensive term meaning irrational

loose /looss/ *adj* (**loos·er**, **loos·est**) **1** not firmly fixed **2** not fastened or pulled tight **3** not tight-fitting **4** free ◇ *broke loose* **5** not packaged **6** not dense or compact **7** imprecise ◇ *a loose translation* **8** considered sexually promiscuous (*dated; disapproving*) ■ *adv* (**loos·er**, **loos·est**) freely ■ *v* (**loosed**, **loos·ing**) **1** *vt* set a person or animal free **2** *vt* untie a knot **3** *vti* make or become less tight **4** *vt* fire a missile —**loose·ly** *adv* —**loose·ness** *n*

USAGE loose or **lose**? **Lose** is a verb only, as in *Don't lose* [not *loose*] *possession of the ball, or you'll lose the game.* **Loose** is an adjective, adverb, and verb, as in *loose* [not *lose*] *floorboards; dogs running loose* [not *lose*]; *loosed her grip.*

---

loose end ◇ **at loose ends** not knowing what to do with yourself (*infml*)

loose-leaf *adj* having removable pages

loos·en /loôss'n/ *v* **1** *vti* make or become less tight **2** *vt* untie hair or a knot **3** *vt* relax control or strictness

loot *n* **1** things taken during a war or riot **2** stolen goods **3** money (*infml*) ■ *vti* take things from a place during a war or riot —**loot·er** *n*

lop (lopped, lop·ping) *vt* **1** cut a branch off a tree **2** cut something off

lope /lōp/ *v* (loped, lop·ing) **1** *vi* run with long easy strides **2** *vti* canter or make a horse canter ■ *n* a gait with long strides

lop-eared *adj* with long hanging ears

Lo·pe de Ve·ga /lòpay de váyga/ (1562–1635) Spanish playwright and poet

lop·sid·ed /lóp sīdəd, lop sīdəd/ *adj* **1** leaning to one side **2** unevenly balanced

lo·qua·cious /lō kwáyshəss/ *adj* talkative —**lo·qua·cious·ly** *adv* —**lo·qua·ci·ty** /lō kwássətee/ *n* ◊ See note at **talkative**

AKG London

Federico García Lorca

Lor·ca /láwrkə/, **Federico García** (1898–1936) Spanish poet and playwright

lord *n* **1** any powerful man **2** an aristocrat **3** a feudal superior **4** **Lord** the Christian or Jewish God **5** **Lord** a title given to some noblemen **6** **Lord** a title given to some high-ranking British officials ■ *interj* **Lord** expresses surprise ■ **Lords** *npl* the British House of Lords —**Lord·ship** *n*

> **ORIGIN Lord** means literally "bread guardian." In origin it is a compound of *hlaf*, an early form of *loaf*, and *ward*.

lord·ly /láwrdlee/ (-li·er, -li·est) *adj* **1** arrogant **2** impressive —**lord·li·ness** *n*

Lord's Prayer *n* the most important Christian prayer

lore /lawr/ *n* **1** knowledge handed down verbally **2** knowledge acquired from teaching or experience

Lor·rain /law ráyn/, **Claude** (1600–82) French painter

lor·ry /láwree/ (*pl* -ries) *n UK* a large motor truck

Los Al·a·mos /los álla mòss/ city in central New Mexico, site of a major nuclear weapons research facility. Pop. 11,420 (1996).

Los An·ge·les /los ánjələss, -lèez/ city in SW California, the second most populous city in the United States. Pop. 3,597,556 (1998).

lose /lōoz/ *v* (lost, los·ing) *v* **1** *vt* be unable to find something **2** *vti* fail to win **3** *vt* fail to keep something **4** *vt* make somebody fail to win something ◊ *a mistake that lost us the game* **5** *vt* not use something such as time to your advantage **6** *vt* be unable to control something, e.g., *your temper* **7** *vt* experience a reduction in something **8** *vt* cease to have something **9** *vt* no longer see

or hear something **10** *vt* have a loved one die **11** *vt* leave somebody behind **12** *vt* confuse somebody **13** *vti* be or become slow by an amount of time *(refers to timepieces)* —**los·a·ble** *adj* ◊ **lose it** (*infml*) **1** become removed from reality **2** be unable to maintain emotional control or composure ◊ See note at **loose**

☐ **lose out** *vi* fail to win or obtain something (*infml*)

~~loseing~~ incorrect spelling of **losing**

los·er /lóozər/ *n* **1** somebody who has not won **2** somebody who is habitually unsuccessful or unlucky (*insult*)

loss *n* **1** the fact of no longer having something **2** somebody or something lost **3** death **4** money spent in excess of income (*often pl*) **5** a sad feeling deriving from an absence **6** a reduction in level or amount **7** an instance of losing a contest **8** death, damage, or injury claimed under an insurance policy ◊ **at a loss** uncertain what to say or do ◊ **cut your losses** withdraw from a situation in which there is no possibility of winning

loss lead·er *n* an article deliberately sold at a loss to attract customers

lost *v* past tense, past participle of **lose** ■ *adj* **1** mislaid **2** unable to find the way **3** wasted **4** no longer in existence **5** preoccupied **6** confused by something complicated

lost and found *n* a place where mislaid items may be held

lost cause *n* something that cannot succeed

lot *pron* a large number of people or things ■ *n* **1** a set of people or things **2** an item in an auction **3** somebody's destiny ◊ *our lot in life* **4** a piece of land ■ **lots** *npl* large numbers or a large amount (*infml*)

> **USAGE a lot** or **alot**? The one-word spelling **alot** is nonstandard usage and should be avoided. In formal writing avoid **a lot** in favor of *much, many, a great deal of,* and the like.

Lot *n* in the biblical Book of Genesis, the son of Haran, brother of Abraham

loth *adj* = **loath**

lo·ti /lótee/ (*pl* **ma·lo·ti** /maa lótee/) *n* the main unit of currency in Lesotho

lo·tion /lósh'n/ *n* a liquid skin cream

lot·ter·y /lóttəree/ (*pl* -ies) *n* **1** a large-scale gambling game **2** a situation in which the outcome depends on chance

lot·to /lóttō/ *n* **1** a game resembling bingo **2** *also* **Lot·to** a state-run lottery in some US states and in Australia

lo·tus /lótəss/ (*pl* **-tus·es** *or* same) *n* **1** in Greek mythology, a fruit causing drowsiness **2** a water plant with large rounded leaves and pink flowers

lo·tus-eat·er *n* **1** a lazy and indulgent person **2** in Greek mythology, somebody who lived in a state of idle stupor after eating the lotus fruit

louche /loosh/ *adj* disreputable

loud *adj* 1 high in volume of sound 2 expressing something noisily o *loud protests* 3 shockingly bright in color or bold in design ■ *adv* loudly —**loud·ly** *adv* —**loud·ness** *n*

loud-mouth /lówd mòwth/ (*pl* -**mouths** /-mòwthz/) *n* a loud boaster (*infml*) —**loud-mouthed** /lówd mòwthd, -mòwthd/ *adj*

loud-speak·er /lówd speékər/ *n* a device for converting electrical signals into sound

Lou·is XIV /lóò ee/ (1638–1715) king of France (1643–1715)

Lou·is XV (1710–74) king of France (1715–74)

Lou·is XVI (1754–93) king of France (1774–93)

Lou·is /lóò iss/, **Joe** (1914–81) US boxer

Lou·is·bourg /lóò iss bùrg/ former town on Cape Breton Island, E Nova Scotia, Canada. It is Canada's national historic site.

Lou·i·si·an·a /loo eèzee ánnə/ state in the S United States, on the Gulf of Mexico. Cap. Baton Rouge. Pop. 4,468,976 (2000). —**Lou·i·si·an·an** *n, adj*

Lou·i·si·an·a Pur·chase territory of the W United States purchased from France in 1803. It extended from the Gulf of Mexico northward to the Canadian border and from the Mississippi River westward to the Rocky Mountains.

Lou·is Phi·lippe /lóò ee fə leép/ (1773–1850) king of France (1830–50)

Lou·is·ville /lóò i vìl, -ee vìl/ largest city in Kentucky. Pop. 255,045 (1998).

lounge *vi* (**lounged, loung·ing**) 1 lie or sit lazily 2 pass time lazily ■ *n* a public room for relaxing

loung·er /lównjər/ *n* 1 somebody who lounges around 2 a reclining chair or couch

lour *vi, n* = **lower**[2]

Lourdes /lóòrd, lòòrdz/ town in SW France, a major site of Roman Catholic pilgrimage. Pop. 15,203 (1999).

louse /lowss/ *n* (*pl* **lice** /līss/) 1 a parasitic insect 2 a small invertebrate animal (*often in combination*) 3 a person regarded as contemptible (*insult*) ■ *vt* (**loused, lous·ing**) rid a person or animal of lice

□ **louse up** *vti* bungle something (*infml*)

lous·y /lówzee/ (-**i·er, -i·est**) *adj* (*infml*) 1 inferior 2 unpleasant —**lous·i·ly** *adv* —**lous·i·ness** *n*

lout /lowt/ *n* a person regarded as ill-mannered (*insult*)

lou·ver /lóòvər/, **lou·vre** *n* 1 a frame with angled horizontal slats 2 a slat in a louver

Louv·re /lóòvrə, lóòvər/ *n* the French national art museum

lov·a·ble /lúvvəb'l/, **love·a·ble** *adj* worthy of love —**lov·a·bly** *adv*

love /luv/ *n* 1 very strong affection 2 passionate attraction and sexual desire 3 somebody who is loved 4 a romantic affair 5 a strong liking 6 something that you feel enthusiastic about 7 a score of zero ■ *v* (**loved, lov·ing**) 1 *vti* feel tender affection for a person or animal 2 *vti* feel romantic and sexual desire for somebody 3 *vt* like something very much 4 *vt* show kindness to somebody o *love your enemies* —**love·less** *adj*

SYNONYMS love, liking, affection, fondness, passion, infatuation, crush CORE MEANING: a strong positive feeling toward somebody or something

love af·fair *n* 1 a sexual or romantic relationship 2 an intense liking

love-bird /lúv bùrd/ *n* 1 a small parrot 2 a lover (usually *pl*)

love child *n* a child of unmarried parents

loved one *n* somebody who is dear to you

~~loveing~~ incorrect spelling of **loving**

love-lorn /lúv làwrn/ *adj* very unhappy because of romantic problems

love·ly /lúvlee/ (-**li·er, -li·est**) *adj* 1 beautiful and pleasing 2 delightful —**love·li·ness** *n*

love-mak·ing /lúv màyking/ *n* 1 sexual activity 2 courtship (*dated*)

lov·er /lúvvər/ *n* 1 a sexual partner 2 somebody who likes or is devoted to a particular thing (*often in combination*) —**lov·er·ly** *adj, adv*

love seat *n* a small sofa

love-sick /lúv sìk/ *adj* unhappy because of love —**love-sick·ness** *n*

lov·ing /lúvving/ *adj* 1 showing affection 2 done with careful attention —**lov·ing·ly** *adv* —**lov·ing·ness** *n*

lov·ing cup *n* a two-handled drinking or ornamental vessel

lov·ing kind·ness *n* compassion

~~lovly~~ incorrect spelling of **lovely**

low[1] /lō/ *adj* 1 close to the ground 2 with relatively little height 3 below average or standard 4 small in value or importance 5 near depletion 6 turned down or dimmed 7 quiet 8 deep in pitch 9 near the bottom of a scale 10 dispirited 11 providing slow vehicular speed 12 lacking status ■ *adv* 1 in a low position 2 with a deep tone 3 quietly ■ *n* 1 a low position or degree 2 a region of low atmospheric pressure 3 an unhappy or unsuccessful period —**low·ness** *n*

low[2] /lō/ *n* the mooing sound of a cow ■ *vi* moo

low-born /lō bàwrn/ *adj* born to low-class parents

low-brow /lō bròw/ *adj* unsophisticated (*disapproving*) ■ *n* an unsophisticated person

low-cal *adj* with relatively few calories

Low Coun·tries region in NW Europe, made up of Belgium, the Netherlands, and Luxembourg. Pop. 26,016,000 (1995).

low·down /lŏ dòwn/ *n* the inside information about somebody or something *(infml)*

low-down *adj* mean *(infml)* ○ *a low-down trick*

Low·ell, Amy Lawrence (1874–1925) US poet and critic

Low·ell, James Russell (1819–91) US magazine editor and diplomat

Low·ell, Robert (1917–77) US poet

low·er[1] /lŏ ər/ *v* 1 *vt* bring something to a lower level 2 *vti* reduce or be reduced 3 *vt* move your head or eyes downward 4 *vr* humiliate yourself 5 *vt* reduce the volume or pitch of a sound ○ *lower your voice* ■ *adj* 1 below another 2 reduced or less ○ *lower wages* 3 closer to the bottom ○ *the lower slopes* 4 of less importance 5 earlier in a geologic period 6 describes organisms that are less advanced in terms of development or complexity ○ *a lower life form*

low·er[2] /lŏr, lowr/, **lour** *vi* 1 be overcast 2 look angry ■ *n* a scowl —**low·er·ing** *adj*

Low·er Cal·i·for·ni·a /lŏ ər kàlli fáwrnee ə/ ▸ **Baja California**

low·er·case /lŏ ər káyss/ *n* small letters, not capitals —**low·er·case** *adj, vt*

low·er class *n* the lowest social group *(often pl)* —**low·er-class** *adj*

low·er house, low·er cham·ber *n* one of the two branches of a legislature

low·est com·mon de·nom·i·na·tor *n* 1 MATH = least common denominator 2 the mass of ordinary people regarded as undiscerning

low·est com·mon mul·ti·ple *n* MATH = least common multiple

low-fat *adj* describes food with relatively little fat

low fre·quen·cy *n* a radio frequency ranging from 30 to 300 kilohertz

low-grade *adj* 1 inferior in quality 2 describes a medical condition that is mild and not serious

low-hang·ing fruit *n* a target that is easy to accomplish, or a problem that is easy to solve

low-key, low-keyed *adj* 1 restrained or understated 2 subdued in color

low·land /lŏlond/ *n* an area of relatively low or flat land —**low·land** *adj*

Low·lands /lŏlondz/ region of Scotland lying south of the Highlands —**Low·land·er** *n*

low-lev·el *adj* 1 situated or done at lower than the usual level 2 low in status or intensity

⚡**low-lev·el lan·guage** *n* a computer programming language that is closer to machine language than to ordinary speech

low-life /lŏ lìf/ *n* 1 a criminal or somebody who associates with criminals *(infml)* 2 criminal or immoral people *(infml insult)* —**low-life** *adj*

low·lights /lŏ lìts/ *npl* strands of hair dyed to a darker shade

low·ly /lŏlee/ *adj* (-li·er, -li·est) 1 low in status 2 meek ■ *adv* (-li·er, -li·est) in a meek way —**low·li·ness** *n*

low·ly·ing *adj* relatively close to sea level

low-main·te·nance *adj* needing little effort or expense to keep in good condition

low-pitched *adj* 1 low in tone 2 shallow in slope

low point *n* the least enjoyable or successful period

low-pres·sure *adj* 1 having or exerting little pressure 2 relaxed

low pro·file *n* behavior that avoids public attention

⚡**low-res·o·lu·tion, low-res** *adj* describes a computer screen or printer with ill-defined text or graphics

low rise *n* a building of few stories —**low-rise** *adj*

low-slung *adj* close to the ground

low tech·nol·o·gy, low tech *n* simple technology, especially that used to make basic items or perform basic tasks —**low-tech** *adj*

low tide, low wa·ter *n* 1 the lowest tide level, or the time when the tide is at this level 2 the worst point in something

low-wa·ter mark *n* 1 a line marking low tide 2 the worst point in something

lox[1] *n* smoked salmon

lox[2] *n* liquid oxygen

loy·al /lóy əl/ *adj* 1 faithful 2 showing a feeling of devotion or duty to somebody or something —**loy·al·ly** *adv* —**loy·al·ness** *n*

loy·al·ist /lóy əlist/ *n* 1 somebody who is loyal to his or her country or government 2 **Loy·al·ist** an American who supported the British during the American Revolution —**loy·al·ism** *n*

loy·al·ty /lóy əltee/ (*pl* -ties) *n* 1 the state of being loyal 2 a feeling of devotion or duty to somebody or something *(often pl)*

loz·enge /lózzənj/ *n* 1 a medicated candy or tablet 2 a diamond shape

LP *n* a long-playing record

LPG *abbr* liquefied petroleum gas

LPGA *abbr* Ladies Professional Golf Association

LPN, L.P.N. *abbr* licensed practical nurse

Lr *symbol* lawrencium

LSAT *abbr* Law School Admissions Test

LSD *n* a hallucinogenic drug

ORIGIN LSD is an acronym formed from letters of German *Lysergsäure Diathylamid* "lysergic acid diethylamide."

---

lt. *abbr* light

Lt., LT *abbr* Lieutenant

Ltd., ltd. *abbr* limited (liability) *(after the name of a British company)*

Lu *symbol* lutetium

Lu·an·da /loo ándə/ capital of Angola. Pop. 2,080,000 (1995).

Lub·bock /lúbbək/ city in north central Texas. Pop. 190,974 (1998).

lube *US, Can, Aus (infml)* n lubricant ■ vt (lubed, lub·ing) lubricate

lu·bri·cant /loöbrikənt/ n 1 a friction-reducing substance 2 an element that eases a difficult situation —**lu·bri·cant** adj

lu·bri·cate /loöbri kàyt/ (-cat·ed, -cat·ing) vt 1 apply lubricant to 2 make slippery —**lu·bri·ca·tion** /loöbri káysh'n/ n

lu·bri·cious /loo bríshəss/, **lu·bri·cous** /loöbrikəss/ adj (literary) 1 lewd or obscene 2 slippery —**lu·bric·i·ty** n

Lu·bum·ba·shi /loöboöm baáshee/ capital of Shaba Administrative Region, SE Democratic Republic of the Congo. Pop. 851,381 (1994).

Lu·cas /loökass/, **George** (b. 1944) US movie director and producer

Luce /looss/, **Clare Boothe** (1903–87) US playwright, politician, and diplomat

Luce, Henry Robinson (1898–1967) US editor and publisher

Lu·cerne /loo súrn/ city in central Switzerland. Pop. 57,193 (1998).

Lu·cerne, Lake of /loo súrn/ lake in central Switzerland

lu·cid /loössid/ adj 1 easily understood 2 shining 3 rational —**lu·cid·i·ty** /loo síddətee/ n —**lu·cid·ly** adv —**lu·cid·ness** n

Lu·ci·fer /loössəfər/ n 1 Satan 2 the morning star

~~lucious~~ incorrect spelling of **luscious**

luck n 1 good fortune 2 a fortunate or unfortunate event, or a series of such events o *Our luck had changed.* ◊ **push** or **press your luck** depend unreasonably on your good luck to continue

☐ **luck into** vt get something good by luck

☐ **luck out** vi succeed by chance

luck·i·ly /lúkilee/ adv as the result of good luck

luck·less /lúkləss/ adj unfortunate

Luck·now /lúk now/ capital of Uttar Pradesh State, N India. Pop. 1,619,115 (1991).

luck·y /lúkee/ (-i·er, -i·est) adj 1 having good luck 2 bringing good luck 3 resulting from good luck —**luck·i·ness** n

SYNONYMS lucky, fortunate, happy, providential, serendipitous CORE MEANING: relating to advantage or good fortune

lu·cra·tive /loökrətiv/ adj producing profit or wealth —**lu·cra·tive·ly** adv —**lu·cra·tive·ness** n

lu·cre /loökər/ n money (dated or humorous)

Lud·dite /lúd dìt/ n 1 an opponent of new technology 2 a 19C protester against technology —**Lud·dism** /lúd dìzzəm/ n —**Lud·dite** adj

ORIGIN According to tradition, the **Luddites** were named for Ned Ludd, an 18C farm

worker from Leicestershire, England, who destroyed two machines in a fit of rage.

lu·di·crous /loödikrəss/ adj absurdly ridiculous —**lu·di·crous·ly** adv —**lu·di·crous·ness** n

lug¹ (lugged, lug·ging) vt pull something heavy or bulky with effort

lug² n 1 a projecting part used for grabbing or turning 2 a small projection on a boot or tire improving traction 3 a person regarded as clumsy or unintelligent (infml insult)

luge /loozh/ n a racing toboggan —**luge** vi —**lug·er** n

lug·gage /lúggij/ n suitcases and bags

lug·gage rack n 1 a frame on top of a car, used for carrying things 2 an overhead frame in a train or bus for luggage

Lu·go·si /loo góssee/, **Bela** (1882–1956) Hungarian-born US actor

lu·gu·bri·ous /loo goöbree əss, lə-/ adj mournful or gloomy

Luke n the third of the gospels of the Bible in which the life and teachings of Jesus Christ are described, traditionally attributed to St. Luke.

Luke, St. (fl AD 1C) evangelist. By tradition he is considered to be the author of the biblical Acts of the Apostles and the third Gospel of the New Testament.

luke·warm /loök wàwrm/ adj 1 warm but not hot 2 showing little enthusiasm —**luke·warm·ly** adv —**luke·warm·ness** n

lull vt 1 soothe or calm somebody or something 2 give somebody a false sense of security ■ n a period of calm

lull·a·by /lúllə bì/ (pl -bies) n 1 a gentle song for soothing a child to sleep 2 the music for a lullaby

lum·ba·go /lum báy gō/ n pain in the lower back

lum·bar /lúmbər, -baàr/ adj of the lower back

SPELLCHECK Do not confuse the spelling of **lumbar** and **lumber** ("logs sawed for use"), which sound similar.

lum·bar punc·ture n the insertion of a needle into the spinal cord to draw out a sample of spinal fluid

lum·ber¹ /lúmbər/ n logs sawed for use ■ vti turn trees into lumber ◊ See note at **lumbar**

lum·ber² /lúmbər/ vi move clumsily

lum·ber·jack /lúmbər jàk/ n somebody who fells trees for lumber

lum·ber·yard /lúmbər yaàrd/ n a business that sells lumber

lu·mi·nar·y /loömə nèrree/ (pl -ies) n 1 an eminent person 2 a sun, moon, or star (literary)

lu·mi·nes·cence /loömə néss'nss/ n the emission of light without heat —**lu·mi·nes·cent** adj

lu·mi·nos·i·ty /lòòmə nóssətee/ n 1 the state of being luminous 2 (symbol L) the energy radiated by an astronomical object

lu·mi·nous /lòomənəss/ adj 1 emitting light 2 bright 3 illuminated —**lu·mi·nous·ly** adv

lum·mox /lúmməks/ n a person regarded as clumsy (infml insult)

lump[1] n 1 a solid chunk 2 a tumor ■ v 1 vt group people or things together, often without good reason 2 vi move heavily ■ adj in lumps

lump[2] vt put up with (infml)

lump·ec·to·my /lum péktəmee/ (pl -mies) n the removal of a breast tumor

lum·pen /lúmpən, lòóm-/ adj (disapproving) 1 living on the margins of society 2 not educated or enlightened

lump·ish /lúmpish/ adj 1 moving awkwardly 2 considered unintelligent and lethargic (insult)

lump sum n a single payment of a total amount

lump·y /lúmpee/ (-i·er, -i·est) adj with unwanted lumps —**lump·i·ly** adv —**lump·i·ness** n

lu·na·cy /lòónəssee/ n behavior regarded as irrational or misguided

lu·nar /lòónər/ adj 1 of the Moon 2 used for travel to the Moon

lu·nar mod·ule n a spacecraft that lands on the Moon's surface

lu·nar month n 1 a period between new moons 2 a 28-day period

lu·na·tic /lòónətik/ adj considered thoughtless or reckless —**lu·na·tic** n

lu·na·tic fringe n members of a group or society whose views are regarded as extreme (insult)

lunch n 1 a midday meal 2 the food eaten at midday ■ vi eat lunch ◊ **out to lunch** regarded as being out of touch with reality (insult)

ORIGIN **Lunch** is an abbreviation of *luncheon*. The origin of the latter is not known for certain. It may be an alteration of *nuncheon* "light refreshment, snack," the constituents of which are early forms of *noon* and obsolete *shench* "drink, cupful." *Luncheon* is recorded from the mid-17C, and **lunch** from the early 19C.

lunch·box /lúnch bòks/ n a container used to carry food such as sandwiches to work or school

lunch·eon /lúnchən/ n 1 lunch (fml) 2 a midday gathering with food

lunch·eon meat n cold processed meat

lunch·room /lúnch ròom, -ròòm/ n a room in an office or school where people can eat lunch

lunch·time /lúnch tìm/ n the time when lunch is usually eaten

lung n a respiratory organ, especially in vertebrates —**lung·ful** n

lunge /lunj/ n 1 a sudden attacking forward movement 2 a quick thrust ■ vi (**lunged**, **lung·ing**) 1 move suddenly forward in a threatening way 2 make a quick thrust

lunk·head /lúngk hèd/ n somebody regarded as unintelligent (infml insult)

Luo·yang /lwŏ yaàng/ city in east central China. Pop. 1,370,000 (1995).

lu·pine[1] /lòópən/, **lu·pin** n a plant with tall flower spikes

lu·pine[2] /lòó pìn/ adj 1 of a wolf 2 ravenous

lurch[1] vi 1 pitch suddenly to one side 2 move unsteadily —**lurch** n —**lurch·ing·ly** adv

lurch[2] n a losing position in cribbage

lure vt (**lured**, **lur·ing**) entice somebody ■ n 1 something that entices 2 attraction 3 a device that attracts a fish

lu·rid /lóòrid/ adj 1 horrifying or shocking 2 unattractively bright —**lu·rid·ly** adv —**lu·rid·ness** n

⚡ **lurk** vi 1 move or wait furtively 2 exist unsuspected 3 read messages in an online forum but make no contributions (slang) —**lurk·er** n —**lurk·ing** adj

Lu·sa·ka /loo saàka/ capital of Zambia. Pop. 1,317,000 (1995).

lus·cious /lúshəss/ adj 1 sweet and juicy 2 appealing to the senses 3 sexually desirable (infml) —**lus·cious·ly** adv —**lus·cious·ness** n

lush[1] adj 1 growing vigorously 2 sweet and juicy 3 luxurious —**lush·ly** adv —**lush·ness** n

lush[2] n a heavy drinker (slang)

lust n 1 strong sexual desire 2 eagerness ■ vi 1 feel strong sexual desire 2 feel a great eagerness —**lust·ful** adj —**lust·ful·ly** adv

lus·ter /lústər/ n 1 a soft sheen of reflected light 2 shininess 3 splendor

lus·trous /lústrəss/ adj shining —**lus·trous·ly** adv —**lus·trous·ness** n

lust·y /lústee/ (-i·er, -i·est) adj 1 strong and healthy 2 energetic or enthusiastic —**lust·i·ly** adv —**lust·i·ness** n

lute[1] n a musical instrument resembling a guitar with a pear-shaped body —**lu·te·nist** n

lute[2] n paste or other substance used as a sealant ■ vt seal with lute

lu·te·ti·um /loo teeshee əm/ n (symbol Lu) a metallic element. Use: catalyst in the nuclear industries.

Lu·ther, Martin (1483–1546) German theologian and religious reformer

Lu·ther·an /lòóthərən/ n a member of the Protestant church founded by Martin Luther

Lux·em·bourg /lúksəm bùrg/ country in W Europe. Cap. Luxembourg (City). Pop. 442,972 (2001). —**Lux·em·bourg·er** n

Lux·em·burg /lúksəm bùrg/, **Rosa** (1871–1919) Polish-born German political activist

~~luxery~~ incorrect spelling of **luxury**

lux·u·ri·ant /lug zhóoree ənt, luk shóoree-/ adj with a great deal of thick healthy growth —**lux·u·ri·ance** n —**lux·u·ri·ant·ly** adv

lux·u·ri·ate /lug zhóoree àyt, luk shóoree-/ (-at·ed, -at·ing) vi 1 derive great enjoyment 2 grow vigorously

lux·u·ri·ous /lug zhóoree əss, luk shóoree-/ adj 1 comfortable and expensive 2 enjoying luxury —**lux·u·ri·ous·ly** adv

lux·u·ry /lúgzhəree, lúkshəree/ (pl -ries) n 1 pleasurable self-indulgent activity 2 a nonessential item

Lu·zon /loo zón/ largest island in the Philippines. Pop. 30,759,000 (1990).

ly·ce·um /lī sée əm/ n 1 a concert hall or theater (usually in names of buildings) 2 a sponsor of public events

ly·chee /leéchee/, **li·tchi, li·chee** n the small round fruit of a Chinese tree

lych·gate /lích-/, **lich·gate** n a covered gateway into a churchyard

Lyd·i·a /líddee ə/ ancient country in present-day NW Turkey, on the Aegean Sea —**Lyd·i·an** adj, n

Lyme dis·ease /lím-/ n a serious infectious disease transmitted by ticks

> **ORIGIN** The disease is named for a town in Connecticut, where an outbreak occurred.

lymph /limf/ n a body fluid containing white cells

lym·phat·ic /lim fáttik/ adj of lymph or the system that transports lymph ■ n a vessel that transports lymph

lymph node n an organ that filters microorganisms and other particles from lymph

lynch /linch/ vt put to death illegally without trial, usually by hanging —**lynch·ing** n

> **ORIGIN** Lynching derives its name from Captain William Lynch (1724–1820), a planter and justice of the peace who organized an illegal tribunal in Virginia in 1780.

lynch mob n a group of people who lynch somebody

lynch·pin n ENG = linchpin

lynx /lingks/ n 1 (pl same or lynx·es) a short-tailed medium-sized wildcat 2 **Lynx** a faint constellation of the northern hemisphere

Ly·ons /lee óN/, **Ly·on** city in east central France. Pop. 445,452 (1999).

lyre /lír/ n a U-shaped stringed instrument of ancient Greece

lyr·ic /lírrik/ adj 1 of poetry expressing personal feelings 2 singing with a lightness of voice ■ n 1 the words of a song (often pl) 2 a short personal poem —**lyr·i·cist** /-sist/ n

lyr·i·cal /lírrik'l/ adj 1 lyric 2 gushingly complimentary —**lyr·i·cal·ly** adv

lyr·i·cism /lírrə sìzzəm/ n 1 a lyric style in poetry or music 2 enthusiastically emotional expression

Ly·sen·ko /li séngk ō/, **Trofim Denisovich** (1898–1976) Russian geneticist and agronomist. His erroneous belief that acquired characteristics can be inherited dominated Soviet agricultural policy (1940–65).

M

m[1] (pl **m's**), **M** (pl **M's** or **Ms**) n 1 the 13th letter of the English alphabet 2 the Roman numeral for 1,000

m[2] symbol 1 mass 2 meter 3 million 4 minute(s)

M abbr 1 male 2 mass 3 medium (of clothes size) 4 million

m. abbr 1 male 2 married 3 masculine 4 mile 5 minute(s) 6 month

M. abbr 1 male 2 Monsieur

⚡**M8** abbr mate (in e-mails)

mA symbol milliampere(s)

MA, M.A. abbr Massachusetts

ma'am /mam/ n a formal or respectful form of address for a woman

MAC /mak/ n a type of satellite television transmission system. Full form **multiplexed analog component**

Mac- /mək/ prefix also **Mc-, M'-** /mə/ son of (in proper names)

ma·ca·bre /mə kaåbrə, -kaåbr/ adj horribly gruesome —**ma·ca·bre·ly** adv

> **ORIGIN** Macabre in its usual modern sense is recorded from the late 19C. Before then it appeared only in dance macabre (and earlier than that, dance of macabre), translating French danse macabre, the "Dance of Death," in which a figure representing Death entices people to dance with him until they collapse and die. It is thought that macabre here is an alteration of Macabé and that the whole phrase translates medieval Latin chorea Machabaeorum "dance of the Maccabees." The Maccabees were a Jewish family involved in a religious revolt in biblical times, and their slaughter may have been represented in a medieval miracle play, giving rise to the idea of a deadly dance.

mac·ad·am /mə káddəm/ n a smooth hard road surface containing broken stones

> **ORIGIN** Macadam is named for the Scottish civil engineer John Loudon McAdam (1756–1836), who developed the system of making such road surfaces.

mac·a·ro·ni /màkə rṓnee/ n small pasta tubes

mac·a·roon /màkə roòn/ n a light cookie containing ground almonds or coconut

Mac·Ar·thur /mik áarthər/, **Douglas** (1880–1964) US general

Ma·cau /mə ków/, **Ma·cao** Special Administrative Region in SE China. Pop. 453,733 (2001).

ma·caw /mə káw/ (pl **-caws** or same) n a large tropical parrot

Mac·beth /mək béth/ (c. 1005–57) king of Scotland (1040–57)

Mac·ca·bees /mákəbeez/ npl four books of Jewish history, the first two of which are included in the Apocrypha

mac·chi·a·to /màakee áàtō/ n an espresso coffee with a touch of milk

Mac·don·ald /mək dónn'ld/, **Sir John Alexander** (1815–91) Scottish-born lawyer, business executive, and prime minister of Canada (1867–73 and 1878–91)

Mac·Don·ald, Ramsay (1866–1937) British prime minister (1924, 1929–35)

mace[1] n 1 a ceremonial staff of office 2 a spiked metal club

mace[2] n a spice made from the case of a nutmeg seed

Mace tdmk a trademark for an aerosol used to immobilize an attacker for a brief time

Mac·e·do·ni·a /màssə dónee ə/ 1 also **Mac·e·don** /mássədən, -dòn/ ancient kingdom in N Greece 2 country in SE Europe. Cap. Skopje. Pop. 2,046,209 (2001). Official name **Former Yugoslav Republic of Macedonia** 3 mountainous region of NE Greece. Cap. Thessaloniki. Pop. 1,710,513 (1991). 4 district in SW Bulgaria —**Mac·e·do·ni·an** n, adj

mac·er·ate /mássə ràyt/ (**-at·ed, -at·ing**) vti 1 soften or be softened by soaking 2 separate or become separated by soaking —**mac·er·a·tion** /màssə ráysh'n/ n

Mach /makh/, **Ernst** (1838–1916) Austrian physicist and philosopher

ma·chet·e /mə shéttee, -chéttee/ n a large heavy knife

Mach·i·a·vel·li /màkee ə véllee, mà kya-/, **Niccolò** (1469–1527) Italian historian, politician, and philosopher

Mach·i·a·vel·li·an /màkee ə véllee ən, mà kya-/ adj 1 cunning and unscrupulous 2 of Machiavelli —**Mach·i·a·vel·li·an** n —**Mach·i·a·vel·li·an·ism** n

ma·chine /mə sheen/ n 1 a mechanical device with moving parts, often powered by electricity 2 a simple unpowered device such as a lever or pulley 3 a powered form of transportation 4 a group of people in political control ■ vti (**-chined, -chin·ing**) cut or shape using a machine —**ma·chine·like** adj

ma·chine gun n an automatic weapon, often mounted, that fires a rapid series of shots —**ma·chine-gun** vt

⚡ **ma·chine lan·guage, ma·chine code** n computer instructions written in binary code

⚡ **ma·chine-read·a·ble** adj able to be used directly by a computer

ma·chin·er·y /mə sheenəree/ n 1 mechanical parts 2 machines 3 a set of processes or procedures

ma·chine tool n a machine that shapes and finishes metals —**ma·chine-tooled** adj

⚡ **ma·chine trans·la·tion** n computer translation

ma·chin·ist /mə sheenist/ n 1 somebody who cuts or shapes something using a machine 2 a US naval officer assigned to the engine room

ma·chis·mo /mə kízmō, mə chízmō/ n stereotypical masculinity

Mach num·ber /maak-/ n the speed of an object relative to the speed of sound

ma·cho /máachō/ adj stereotypically masculine —**ma·cho·ism** n

Machu Picchu

Ma·chu Pic·chu /máachoo peekchoo, -peechoo/ ruined Inca city

Mac·ken·zie /mə kénzee/ river in the Northwest Territories, Canada. Length 1,120 mi./1,800 km.

Mac·Ken·zie /mə kénzee/, **William Lyon** (1795–1861) Canadian insurgent and politician

Mac·ken·zie Moun·tains mountain range in W Canada, spanning the border between the Northwest Territories and the Yukon Territory. Highest peak Keele Peak 9,750 ft./2,972 m.

mackeral incorrect spelling of **mackerel**

mack·er·el /mákrəl/ (pl **-els** or same) n 1 an oily fish of the N Atlantic 2 any fish similar to the mackerel

Mack·i·nac, Straits of /máki nàw/ channel in N Michigan connecting Lake Huron and Lake Michigan. Length 30 mi./48 km.

Mack·i·nac Is·land island in the Straits of Mackinac, N Michigan

Mack·in·tosh /mákin tàwsh/, **Charles Rennie** (1868–1928) British architect and interior designer

Mac·Leish /mə kleésh/, **Archibald** (1892–1982) US poet, playwright, and public official

Ma·con /máykən/ city in central Georgia. Pop. 114,336 (1998).

mac·ra·mé /mákrə mày/ n decorative work in knotted string

↯ **mac·ro** /mákrō/ (*pl* **-ros**), **mac·ro·in·struc·tion** /mákrō in strúksh'n/ *n* a computer instruction that initiates several additional instructions

macro- *prefix* 1 large, inclusive ○ *macrocosm* 2 long ○ *macrobiotics*

mac·ro·bi·ot·ics /màkrō bī óttiks/ *n* a vegan diet said to prolong life (*+ sing verb*) —**mac·ro·bi·ot·ic** *adj*

mac·ro·cosm /mákrə kòzzəm/ *n* a complex system seen as a single unit —**mac·ro·cos·mic** /màkrə kózmik/ *adj*

mac·ro·ec·o·nom·ics /màkrō eekə nómmiks, -ekə-/ *n* the study of large-scale economic systems (*+ sing verb*) —**mac·ro·ec·o·nom·ic** *adj* —**mac·ro·e·con·o·mist** /-i kónnəmist/ *n*

mad (**mad·der**, **mad·dest**) *adj* 1 very angry 2 an offensive term meaning affected by a psychiatric disorder 3 very unwise or rash (*sometimes offensive*) 4 frantic (*sometimes offensive*) 5 passionate about something (*often in combination, sometimes offensive*) 6 describes an animal with rabies —**mad·ly** *adv* —**mad·ness** *n*

Mad·a·gas·car /màddə gáskər/ island country in the Indian Ocean, off the coast of SE Africa. Cap. Antananarivo. Pop. 15,982,563 (2001). —**Mad·a·gas·can** *adj, n*

Mad·am /máddəm/ (*pl* **Mes·dames** /may dám, -dáam/ *or* **Mad·ams**) *n* 1 addresses a woman in a letter (*fml*) 2 addresses a female official, used before the name of her position 3 a woman who runs a brothel 4 **mad·am** (*pl* **mes·dames** /may dám, -dàam/) a polite term of address for a woman (*fml*)

Ma·dame /máddəm, mə dáam/ (*pl* **Mes·dames** /may dám, -dàam/) *n* the title of a Frenchwoman, used before her name or as a polite term of address

mad·cap /mád kàp/ *adj* reckless —**mad·cap** *n*

mad cow dis·ease *n* VET = BSE

MADD /mad/ *abbr* Mothers Against Drunk Driving

mad·den /mádd'n/ *vt* 1 make very angry 2 make irrational —**mad·den·ing** *adj* —**mad·den·ing·ly** *adv*

made past tense, past participle of **make**

Ma·dei·ra /mə deérə/ *n* a fortified wine made on the Madeira Islands

Ma·dei·ra Is·lands /mə deérə-/ group of islands in the E North Atlantic Ocean, an autonomous region of Portugal. Pop. 256,000 (1992).

mad·e·moi·selle /màdmwə zél, màdmə-/ (*pl* **mes·de·moi·selles** /màydə-/ *or* **mad·e·moi·selles**) *n* 1 a young Frenchwoman 2 **Mad·e·moi·selle** the title of a young Frenchwoman, used before her name or as a polite form of address (*sometimes offensive*)

made-to-or·der *adj* 1 custom-made 2 perfectly suitable

made-up *adj* 1 untrue 2 wearing cosmetics

mad·house /mád hòwss/ (*pl* **-hous·es** /-howzəz/) *n* 1 an offensive term for a hospital for people with psychiatric disorders 2 a scene of chaos or confusion (*infml; sometimes offensive*)

mad·i·son /máddiss'n/ *n* a cycling relay race

Mad·i·son /máddiss'n/ capital of Wisconsin. Pop. 209,306 (1998).

Mad·i·son, Dolley (1768–1849) US first lady (1809–17)

James Madison

Mad·i·son, James (1751–1836) 4th president of the United States (1809–17)

Mad·i·son Av·e·nue *n* the US advertising industry

ORIGIN **Madison Avenue** is the street in New York that is the center of the advertising industry.

mad·man /mád màn, -mən/ (*pl* **-men** /-mèn, -mən/) *n* an offensive term for a man with a psychiatric disorder

Ma·don·na /mə dónnə/ *n* 1 the Virgin Mary 2 *also* **ma·don·na** an image of the Virgin Mary

mad·ras /máddrəss, mə dráss/ *n* a type of strong fine cloth, often with a striped or checked design

Mad·ras /mə dráass/ former name for **Chennai**

ma·dra·sa /mə dráassə/ *n* 1 a school for the study of Islamic religion and thought 2 an Islamic religious school for boys

Ma·drid /mə dríd/ capital of Spain. Pop. 2,881,506 (1998).

mad·ri·gal /máddrig'l/ *n* 1 an English part song for unaccompanied voices 2 a medieval Italian song —**mad·ri·gal·ist** *n*

ORIGIN **Madrigal** goes back ultimately to the Latin word for "womb." This formed a derivative meaning "of a mother" and from that "uncomplicated." This passed into Italian, and then into English in the late 16C. A **madrigal** was originally a simple song, presumably of the kind a mother would sing to a child.

ma·dro·ña /mə drōnə/, **ma·dro·ño** /mə drō nò/ (*pl* **-ños**) *n* a N American tree with smooth crimson peeling bark

mad·wom·an /mád wòommən/ (*pl* **-en** /-wimmin/) *n* an offensive term for a woman with a psychiatric disorder

mael·strom /máylstrəm/ *n* 1 a whirlpool 2 a turbulent or violent situation

maes·tro /místrō/ (*pl* **-tros** *or* **-tri** /-tree/) *n* an expert, especially a musician, conductor, or composer

Ma·fi·a /maáfee ə/ *n* 1 an international secret criminal organization 2 *also* **ma·fi·a** a mutually supportive clique

Ma·fi·o·so /maáfee ōssō, -ōzō/ (*pl* **-si** /-see, -zee/ *or* **-sos**), **ma·fi·o·so** *n* a Mafia member

mag·a·zine /mággə zèen/ *n* 1 a periodical publication 2 a bullet or cartridge holder 3 a storehouse for military supplies 4 a photographic slide holder

---

ORIGIN Magazine came through French and Italian from an Arabic word meaning "storehouse," which was also the original sense in English in the late 16C. The "publication" sense derived from the idea of a storehouse of information. **Magazine** came to be used as a title for books providing information in the mid-17C, and developed its familiar modern use of "periodical publication" in the mid-18C.

Ma·gel·lan, Strait of /mə géllən/ channel separating mainland South America and Tierra del Fuego, between the Atlantic and Pacific oceans. Length 350 mi. / 560 km.

Ma·gel·lan, Ferdinand (1480?–1521) Portuguese explorer

ma·gen·ta /mə jéntə/ *n* a purplish pink color —**ma·gen·ta** *adj*

mag·got /mággət/ *n* the larva of a fly

Mag·ha /múggə/ *n* the 11th month in the Hindu calendar

Ma·gi /máy jī, májjī/ *npl* in the Bible, the three wise men who came to celebrate the birth of Jesus Christ —**Ma·gi·an** /-jee ən, -jən/ *adj*, *n* —**Ma·gi·an·ism** *n*

mag·ic /májjik/ *n* 1 conjuring tricks or illusions 2 a mysterious quality, talent, or skill 3 a supposed supernatural power that makes impossible things happen 4 the practice of magic ■ *adj* 1 of or for magic 2 particularly important ■ *vt* (-**icked**, -**ick·ing**) cause to appear, disappear, change, or move by magic

mag·i·cal /májjik'l/ *adj* 1 apparently produced by magic 2 wonderful —**mag·i·cal·ly** *adv*

mag·ic bul·let *n* 1 a drug that cures a serious disease with no undesirable side effects on the patient 2 an easy solution

mag·ic car·pet *n* an imaginary flying carpet

ma·gi·cian /mə jísh'n/ *n* 1 an entertainer who performs conjuring tricks and illusions 2 somebody who supposedly has the supernatural power to use magic

Mag·ic Mark·er *tdmk* a trademark for a highlighting pen that comes in various colors of ink

mag·ic wand *n* 1 a stick used by a magician 2 something that is able to work wonders

mag·is·te·ri·al /màjjə steeree əl/ *adj* 1 dignified 2 domineering 3 authoritative

mag·is·trate /májji stràyt, -strət/ *n* 1 a judge in a lower court 2 a local law officer —**mag·is·trate·ship** *n*

mag·ma /mágmə/ *n* molten rock —**mag·mat·ic** /mag máttik/ *adj*

Mag·na Car·ta /màgnə kaártə/, **Mag·na Char·ta** *n* 1 an important medieval social charter that established civil rights in England 2 any document that establishes rights

mag·na cum lau·de /màgnə kum lówdə, -lówdee/ *adv, adj* with a high academic distinction *(refers to college or university degrees)*

ORIGIN The phrase is Latin, and literally means "with great praise."

---

mag·nan·i·mous /mag nánnəmass/ *adj* very generous or forgiving —**mag·na·nim·i·ty** /màgnə nímmətee/ *n* —**mag·nan·i·mous·ly** *adv* ◊ See note at **generous**

mag·nate /mág nàyt, -nət/ *n* somebody who is rich and powerful —**mag·nate·ship** *n*

mag·ne·sia /mag néezhə, -néeshə/ *n* a white powder. Use: antacid, laxative.

mag·ne·si·um /mag néezee əm/ *n* (*symbol* Mg) a light silver-white metallic element. Use: alloys, photography, fireworks.

mag·net /mágnət/ *n* a piece of metal that attracts or clings to iron or steel objects

mag·net·ic /mag néttik/ *adj* 1 having the power of a magnet 2 able to be magnetized 3 of or using magnetism 4 powerfully charming 5 of the Earth's magnetism —**mag·net·i·cal·ly** *adv*

⚡**mag·net·ic bub·ble** *n* a small magnetic region in a film of magnetic material. Use: to store data in computer memory.

⚡**mag·net·ic disk** *n* a computer disk

mag·net·ic field *n* a region surrounding a magnetized body

mag·net·ic north *n* the direction of the north magnetic pole

mag·net·ic pole *n* 1 either of the two points at the end of a magnet 2 either of two regions near the Earth's geographic poles at which the Earth's magnetic field is strongest

⚡**mag·net·ic re·cord·ing** *n* 1 the storing of data on a magnetized medium 2 a surface containing magnetically recorded information

mag·net·ic res·o·nance im·ag·ing *n* a medical imaging technique that uses electromagnetic radiation

⚡**mag·net·ic stripe, mag·net·ic strip** *n* a strip of a magnetic medium encoded with information on a plastic card

⚡**mag·net·ic tape** *n* thin tape coated with iron oxide, used to record sounds, images, or data

mag·net·ism /mágnə tìzzəm/ n 1 the phenomenon of physical attraction for iron 2 the force exerted by a magnetic field 3 strong attractiveness, e.g., the power of somebody's personality to influence others

mag·net·ite /mágnə tìt/ n a common black magnetic mineral

mag·net·ize /mágnə tìz/ (-ized, -iz·ing) v 1 vti make or become magnetic 2 vt attract somebody strongly —**mag·net·i·za·tion** /mágnəti záysh'n/ n

mag·net school n a specialized public school

~~magnificent~~ incorrect spelling of **magnificent**

mag·ni·fi·ca·tion /mágnəfi káysh'n/ n 1 the process of making something appear physically larger 2 an increase of actual size

mag·nif·i·cent /mag níffiss'nt/ adj 1 beautiful and impressive 2 very good (infml) —**mag·nif·i·cence** n —**mag·nif·i·cent·ly** adv

mag·ni·fy /mágnə fì/ (-fied, -fies) vt 1 increase the apparent size of something, especially by using a microscope or lens 2 increase the actual size of something 3 overstate the importance of something —**mag·ni·fi·er** n

mag·ni·fy·ing glass n a hand-held lens used to make objects appear larger

mag·ni·tude /mágnə tòod/ n 1 greatness of size, volume, or extent 2 importance 3 a measure of the energy of an earthquake 4 a number assigned to a mathematical quantity 5 the brightness of an astronomical object

mag·no·lia /mag nólyə/ (pl -no·lia or -no·lias) n 1 a small tree or bush with flowers of various colors 2 a creamy-white color —**mag·no·lia** adj

mag·num[1] /mágnəm/ n 1 a wine bottle that holds the equivalent of two normal bottles 2 the contents of a magnum

mag·num[2] /mágnəm/ adj describes a firearm cartridge with a more powerful charge than others of the same caliber ■ n a powerful gun

mag·num o·pus n a great work of art or literature

mag·pie /mág pì/ n 1 a black-and-white bird of the crow family 2 a talkative person (infml)

ORIGIN A magpie was originally just a pie. The name came via French from Latin pica, which probably goes back to an ancient root meaning "pointed" (with reference to a bird's beak). Mag- was added in the late 16C. In origin it represents Mag, a shortened form of the name Margaret, but the reason for the addition is not known.

Ma·gritte /maa greèt/, **René** (1898–1967) Belgian painter

ma·ha·ra·jah /maahə ráəjə, -ráazhə/, **ma·ha·ra·ja** n an Indian prince of a rank above a rajah

ma·ha·ra·ni /maahə ráanee/ n 1 a maharajah's wife 2 an Indian princess of a rank above a rani

ma·ha·ri·shi /maahə reèshee/ n in Hinduism, a religious instructor

ma·hat·ma /mə haátmə, -hát-/ n S Asia a title bestowed on somebody deeply revered

Mah·di /maadee/ n in Islamic belief, a prophet who is expected to appear before the world ends

Mah·fouz /maa foòz/, **Naguib** (b. 1911) Egyptian novelist and screenwriter

Ma·hi·can /mə heèkən/ n 1 a member of a Native North American confederacy of peoples whose descendants now live in Wisconsin and Oklahoma 2 the Algonquian language of the Mahican people —**Ma·hi·can** adj

mah·jongg /maa zhóng, -jóng/, **mah·jong** n a Chinese game using tiles marked with designs

Mah·ler /maalər/, **Gustav** (1860–1911) Czechborn Austrian composer and conductor

ma·hog·a·ny /mə hóggənee/ (pl -nies) n 1 a reddish brown hardwood. Use: construction, furniture-making. 2 a tropical tree that produces mahogany

ma·hout /mə hówt/ n an elephant driver

maid /mayd/ n 1 a woman servant 2 a young unmarried woman (literary; sometimes offensive)

maid·en /mayd'n/ n a young unmarried woman (sometimes offensive) ■ adj first (sometimes offensive) o the ship's maiden voyage —**maid·en·ly** adj

maid·en·head /mayd'n hèd/ n (literary) 1 a hymen 2 a woman's virginity

maid·en name n a married woman's surname at birth

maid of hon·or n 1 a chief bridesmaid 2 an unmarried attendant of a queen or princess

✏**mail**[1] n 1 items sent through the postal service 2 the postal system 3 a particular collection or delivery of mail 4 a vehicle transporting mail 5 e-mail (infml) ■ vt send by mail or e-mail —**mail·er** n

mail[2] n flexible armor

mail·bag /máyl bàg/ n 1 a sack for transporting mail 2 a mail carrier's bag 3 mail received

mail·box /máyl bòks/ n 1 a public collection box in which letters are mailed 2 US, ANZ a box into which mail is delivered

mail car·ri·er n a post office employee

mail·drop /máyl dròp/ n 1 a container for mail 2 a delivery place

Mail·er /máylər/, **Norman** (b. 1923) US writer

mail·ing list n a list of names and addresses to which advertising material or information is sent

mail·man /máyl màn, -mən/ (pl -men /-mèn, -mən/) n a man who delivers mail

✏**mail merge** n a word-processing technique for creating a series of individualized documents

mail or·der n buying and selling by mail

maim vt wound or disable severely

main /mayn/ adj 1 greatest in size or importance 2 utmost ◊ *main force* ■ n 1 a large pipe or cable for distributing water, gas, or electricity 2 the open sea *(literary)* ◊ **in the main** largely or in general

Main /mīn, mayn/ river in south central Germany. Length 325 mi./523 km.

main course n the principal dish of a meal

Maine /mayn/ state in the NE United States. Cap. Augusta. Pop. 1,274,923 (2000).

⚡ main·frame /máyn fràym/ n a powerful computer accommodating several users simultaneously

main·land /máynlənd, -lànd/ n the principal landmass of a country or continent —**main·land·er** n

main line n a major rail route

main·line /máyn līn/ vti (**-lined, -lin·ing**) inject drugs intravenously *(slang)* ■ adj 1 established 2 of a major rail route —**main·lin·er** n

main·ly /máynlee/ adv usually or mostly

main·mast /máyn màst, máynməst/ n the principal mast on a sailing vessel

⚡ main mem·o·ry n a computer's random access memory

main·sail /máynsəl, máyn sàyl/ n a vessel's principal sail

main·spring /máyn spring/ n 1 the principal spring in a watch or clock 2 the chief reason for an action

main·stay /máyn stày/ n 1 the chief support ◊ *the mainstay of the country's economy* 2 a line securing a mainmast

main·stream /máyn stréem/ n the most widely accepted current of thought or behavior ■ vti enroll students with physical or learning disabilities in general classes —**main·stream** adj

Main Street /máyn-/ n the inhabitants of a small town as a group

main·street·ing /máyn stréeting/ n Can political campaigning on the streets

⚡ main·tain /màyn táyn/ vt 1 cause something to continue 2 keep something in working order by regular checks and repairs 3 provide somebody with financial support 4 insist on the truth of something ◊ *maintained that she knew nothing about it* 5 update a website or software package —**main·tain·a·ble** adj

main·te·nance /máyntənənss/ n 1 regular repair work 2 continuation or preservation 3 the provision of financial support 4 money paid to an ex-spouse

~~maintenence~~ incorrect spelling of **maintenance**

maî·tre d'hô·tel /màytrə dō tél/ (pl **maî·tres d'hô·tel** /pronunc. same/) n 1 a headwaiter 2 a senior male servant

maize n UK the cereal corn, or its grains

Maj., MAJ abbr Major

maj·es·ty /májəstee/ n 1 great dignity 2 supreme power 3 **Maj·es·ty** a title for a king or queen —**ma·jes·tic** /mə jéstik/ adj —**ma·jes·ti·cal·ly** adv

Maj. Gen. abbr Major General

ma·jor /máyjər/ n 1 an army officer, or an officer of the US and Canadian air forces and the US Marine Corps, of a rank above captain 2 US, Can, ANZ a particular subject in which a college or university student chooses to specialize 3 US, Can, ANZ a student specializing in a particular subject ◊ *a philosophy major* ■ **ma·jors** npl the major leagues ■ adj 1 of high standing ◊ *a major recording artist* 2 large or significant 3 serious ■ vi US, Can, ANZ study a particular course ◊ *majoring in philosophy*

ORIGIN Major derives from the comparative (meaning "larger, greater") of Latin *magnus*. As a military term it was adopted from French in the mid-17C. It represents a shortening of *sergent-major* "sergeant major," a rank that was formerly more senior than it is now.

Ma·jor·ca /mə yáwrkə/, **Mal·lor·ca** largest of the Balearic Islands, in the W Mediterranean Sea. Pop. 736,885 (1994). —**Major·can** n, adj

ma·jor·do·mo /máyjər dṓmṓ/ (pl **ma·jor·do·mos**) n the chief male servant of a large household

ma·jor·ette /màyjə rét/ n Can a young woman marching with a band and twirling a baton

ma·jor gen·er·al n an army officer, or an officer of the US Marine Corps, of a rank above brigadier general

ma·jor·i·ty /mə jáwrətee/ (pl **-ties**) n 1 more than one-half of a group of people or things (+ sing or pl verb) 2 the number of votes by which a person or group wins 3 the age of legal responsibility

ma·jor·i·ty lead·er n the head of a majority party in a legislature

ma·jor league n 1 a main baseball league 2 a top sports league —**ma·jor-league** adj —**ma·jor-leagu·er** n

ma·jor med·i·cal n health insurance that covers most or all costs incurred during a serious illness

ma·jor scale n a musical scale with a semitone between the third and fourth notes and the seventh and eighth notes

Mak·a·lu /múkə lòò/ mountain in the Himalaya range, on the Nepal-China border. Height 27,825 ft./8,481 m.

make vt (made, mak·ing) 1 do or perform an action 2 produce, construct, or manufacture something 3 prepare or arrange something 4 create or form something 5 formulate something ◊ *make a promise* 6 reckon or estimate something ◊ *What time do you make it?* 7 cause somebody or something to be something particular o *made him unhappy* o *made it illegal to sell fireworks* **8** change something into something else o *making wood into charcoal* **9** appoint somebody to a particular position **10** cause somebody or something to do a particular thing o *made me lose my place* **11** force somebody to do something o *You can't make her stay.* **12** earn a sum of money **13** score **14** amount to a total ■ *n* **1** a brand of a product **2** the process of making something —**mak·a·ble** *adj* —**mak·er** *n* ◇ **have it made**, **got it made** be in a position to succeed without serious problems *(infml)* ◇ **make do (with something)** use something as a substitute ◇ **make it** be successful *(infml)* ◇ **on the make 1** trying hard to succeed *(infml)* **2** trying to find a sexual partner *(slang)*

☐ **make out** *v* **1** *vt* see or hear indistinctly **2** *vt* understand **3** *vt* complete in writing o *make out a check* **4** *vi* engage in sexual activities *(slang)*

☐ **make over** *vt* change the appearance of

☐ **make up** *v* **1** *vt* prepare something by putting things together **2** *vt* constitute something **3** *vt* invent a story or excuse **4** *vti* apply cosmetics to the face **5** *vti* resolve a quarrel **6** *vi* compensate for something

make-be·lieve *n* imaginary situations or events that somebody pretends are true

make-o·ver /máyk òvər/ *n* a change of physical appearance

make·shift /máyk shíft/ *adj* providing a temporary substitute —**make·shift** *n*

make·up /máyk ùp/ *n* **1** facial cosmetics **2** the way parts or qualities are combined or arranged **3** an exam for students who failed or missed the previous one

make-work *n* a task given to prevent idleness

mak·ing /máyking/ *n* **1** production or manufacture **2** the cause of somebody's success ■ **mak·ings** *npl* **1** required ingredients **2** potential o *He has the makings of a great musician.*

mal- *prefix* bad, badly o *malpractice*

Mal·a·bar Coast /mállə baar-/ coastal region of SW India, extending from Goa southward

Mal·a·bo /mállə bò/ capital, port, and largest city of Equatorial Guinea, on N Bioko Island. Pop. 30,000 (1995).

Ma·lac·ca, Strait of /mə lákə/ strait in Southeast Asia between the Malay Peninsula and Sumatra. Length 500 mi./800 km.

Mal·a·chi /mállə kì/ *n* a book of the Bible containing writings by Malachi, a Hebrew prophet

mal·a·chite /mállə kìt/ *n* a green mineral. Use: decorative stones, source of copper.

mal·ad·just·ed /mállə jústəd/ *adj* unable to cope with everyday social situations —**mal·ad·just·ment** *n*

mal·ad·min·is·tra·tion /málləd mínni stráysh'n/ *n* incompetent or dishonest management

mal·a·droit /mállə dróyt/ *adj* clumsy or insensitive —**mal·a·droit·ly** *adv* —**mal·a·droit·ness** *n*

mal·a·dy /mállədee/ (*pl* **-dies**) *n* **1** an illness **2** a problem

Má·la·ga /málləgə/ port in S Spain. Pop. 528,079 (1998).

mal·aise /mə láyz, ma-, -léz/ *n* **1** a general feeling of illness **2** a general feeling of discontent

Mal·a·mud /málləməd/, **Bernard** (1914–86) US novelist and short-story writer

mal·a·mute /mállə myòòt/, **mal·e·mute** *n* an Alaskan working dog

mal·a·prop·ism /mállə pro pìzzəm/ *n* the unintentional use of a wrong word that sounds similar

---

ORIGIN The original perpetrator of **malapropisms** was Mrs. Malaprop, a character in Richard Sheridan's play *The Rivals* (1775). Her name is based on *malapropos* "inappropriate(ly)," from French *mal à propos*, literally "badly to the purpose."

---

ma·lar·i·a /mə láiree ə/ *n* a recurring illness transmitted by mosquitoes —**ma·lar·i·al** *adj*

ORIGIN **Malaria** was adopted in the mid-18C from Italian *mal' aria*, literally "bad air." Originally it was associated particularly with Rome, and referred to a condition of the air around marshes and swamps that was thought to cause fevers.

---

ma·lar·key /mə laárkee/, **ma·lar·ky** *n* nonsense or insincere talk *(infml)*

Ma·la·wi /mə láawee/ country in SE Africa. Cap. Lilongwe. Pop. 10,548,250 (2001). —**Ma·la·wi·an** *n, adj*

Ma·la·wi, Lake lake in southeast central Africa, lying between Malawi, Mozambique, and Tanzania. Also called **Nyasa, Lake**

Ma·lay /mə láy, máy làyʹ/ *n* **1** a member of a Southeast Asian ethnic group **2** the language of Malaysia —**Ma·lay** *adj*

Ma·lay Ar·chi·pel·a·go largest system of island groups in the world, in the South Pacific Ocean southeast of Asia and north of Australia, and including Indonesia and the Philippines

Ma·lay Pen·in·su·la peninsula in Southeast Asia between the South China Sea and the Strait of Malacca, including parts of Myanmar, Thailand, and Malaysia. Length 750 mi./1,210 km.

Ma·lay·sia /mə láyzhə, -láyshə/ country in Southeast Asia. Cap. Kuala Lumpur. Pop. 22,229,040 (2001). —**Ma·lay·sian** *n, adj*

Mal·colm X /málkəm éks/ (1925–65) US political activist

mal·con·tent /málkən tènt/ n a person who is discontented with something, e.g., a political system —**mal·con·tent** adj

Mal·dives /máwl dèevz, mál dīvz/ island country in the N Indian Ocean. Cap. Male. Pop. 310,764 (2001). —**Mal·div·i·an** /mawl dívvən, mal-/ n, adj

male adj 1 of the sex that produces sperm 2 of men or boys 3 capable of fertilizing a female sex cell 4 describes a flower or plant that bears only stamens and does not produce fruit —**male** n —**male·ness** n

male chau·vin·ist n a man who believes that men are superior to women (disapproving) —**male chau·vin·ism** n

mal·e·dic·tion /màllə díkshən/ n (fml) 1 a curse 2 slander

mal·e·fac·tor /málla fàktər/ n a wrongdoer —**mal·e·fac·tion** /màllə fáksh'n/ n

ma·lef·i·cent /mə léffiss'nt/ adj harmful or evil —**ma·lef·i·cence** n

male men·o·pause n midlife anxiety in men

mal·e·mute n ZOOL = malamute

ma·lev·o·lent /mə lévvələnt/ adj 1 wanting to harm others 2 harmful or evil —**ma·lev·o·lence** n —**ma·lev·o·lent·ly** adv

mal·fea·sance /mal feéz'nss/ n (fml) 1 misconduct 2 an unlawful act

mal·for·ma·tion /màl fawr máysh'n/ n an unusual shape or structure —**mal·formed** /màl fáwrmd/ adj

mal·func·tion /mal fúngkshən/ vi fail to work correctly —**mal·func·tion** n

Ma·li /máalee/ country in West Africa. Cap. Bamako. Pop. 11,008,518 (2001).

mal·ice /málliss/ n the desire or intention to do harm —**ma·li·cious** /mə líshəss/ adj —**ma·li·cious·ly** adv —**ma·li·cious·ness** n

ma·lign /mə lín/ vt say or write something bad about ■ adj 1 harmful or evil 2 wishing to harm others —**ma·lig·ni·ty** /mə lígnətee/ n —**ma·lign·ly** adv

SYNONYMS **malign**, **defame**, **slander**, **libel**, **vilify** CORE MEANING: say or write something damaging about somebody

ma·lig·nant /mə lígnənt/ adj 1 showing a desire to harm others 2 likely to cause harm 3 likely to spread through the body o a malignant tumor —**ma·lig·nan·cy** n —**ma·lig·nant·ly** adv

ma·lin·ger /mə líng gər/ vi feign illness

mall /mawl/ n 1 a large indoor shopping complex 2 a shady avenue 3 a pedestrian shopping area along a street

ORIGIN The shopping mall derives from **mall** as a name for the alley used in pall-mall, a game rather like croquet that was once highly fashionable in Britain. An alley in St. James's Park, London, England, came to be used as a walk, and the name of the Mall was then transferred to any sheltered promenade. These 17C and 18C uses were invoked in the 20C with the introduction of the pedestrian or enclosed shopping area.

mal·lard /mállərd/ (pl -lards or same) n a wild duck in which the male has a dark green head

Mal·lar·mé /màl aar máy/, **Stéphane** (1842–98) French poet

mal·le·a·ble /mállee əb'l/ adj 1 able to be shaped and bent 2 easily persuaded or influenced —**mal·le·a·bil·i·ty** /màllee ə bíllətee, màllə-/ n ◊ See note at pliable

mal·let /mállət/ n 1 a tool with a large cylindrical wooden or metal head 2 a stick with a cylindrical head used in croquet or polo

mal·le·us /mállee əss/ (pl -i /-ī/) n the outermost of the three small bones in the middle ear. ◊ incus, stapes

Mal·lor·ca ◆ Majorca

mal·low /málló/ (pl -lows or same) n a flowering plant with hairs on the stem and leaves

Mal·mö /málmö/ port in SW Sweden. Pop. 254,904 (1998).

mal·nour·ished /mal núr risht/ adj having a diet that is inadequate or inappropriate —**mal·nour·ish·ment** n

mal·nu·tri·tion /màl noo trísh'n/ n unhealthy or inadequate nutrition

mal·o·dor·ous /mal ódərəss/ adj smelling bad

ma·lo·ti plural of loti

mal·prac·tice /mal práktiss/ n wrong or negligent conduct of a professional or official —**mal·prac·ti·tion·er** /màl prak tísh'nər/ n

Mal·raux /mal rố/, **André** (1901–76) French novelist, art theorist, archaeologist, and public servant

malt n partly germinated grain. Use: brewing beer, distilling whiskey. ■ v 1 vti change grain into malt 2 vt make or mix something with malt —**malt** adj

Mal·ta /máwltə/ island country in the central Mediterranean Sea. Cap. Valletta. Pop. 394,583 (2001).

malt·ed milk, **malt·ed** n 1 a soluble powder of dried milk and malted grain 2 a drink made from malted milk

Mal·tese /mawl teéz, -teéss/ (pl same) n 1 somebody from Malta 2 the language of Malta —**Mal·tese** adj

Mal·tese cross n a cross with arms like inward-pointing arrowheads

Mal·thus /málthəss/, **Thomas Robert** (1766–1834) British economist —**Mal·thu·sian** /mal thoózh'n, -thoózee ən/ adj, n —**Mal·thu·sian·ism** n

mal·tose /máwl tòss, -tòz/ n a white crystalline sugar

mal·treat /mal treét/ vt treat badly —**mal·treat·ment** n ◊ See note at misuse

malt whis·key n whiskey distilled from malted barley

ma·ma /maámə, mámmə/, **mam·ma** n mother (infml; usually used by or to children)

mam·ba /maámbə/ n a large venomous snake of tropical Africa

mam·bo /maámbō/ (pl -bos) n 1 a dance resembling the rumba 2 the music for a mambo —**mam·bo** vi

Mam·et /mámmit/, **David** (b. 1947) US playwright and movie director

mam·mal /mámm'l/ n a class of warm-blooded vertebrate animals in which the female has milk-producing organs —**mam·ma·li·an** /mə máylee ən/ adj

ORIGIN The taxonomic name *Mammalia* was coined in Latin by the Swedish naturalist Carolus Linnaeus. He based it on Latin *mamma* "breast," as it refers to the class of animals that suckle their young. The word was Anglicized as the plural **mammals** in the early 19C.

mam·ma·ry /mámməree/ adj of a milk-producing organ such as a breast or udder

mam·mo·gram /mámmə gràm/ n an X-ray of the breast

mam·mog·ra·phy /ma móggrəfee/ n X-ray examination of a breast

mam·mon /mámmən/, **Mam·mon** n wealth regarded as an evil influence

mam·moth /mámməth/ n (pl -moths or same) 1 an extinct hairy elephant 2 something enormous ■ adj huge

ORIGIN Mammoth was adopted in the early 18C from Russian. It came ultimately from a Siberian word meaning literally "earth, soil." The first remains of **mammoths** to be found were dug out of the frozen soil of Siberia, and it came to be believed that the animals burrowed in the earth. The adjectival use of **mammoth** for "huge" dates from the early 19C.

mam·my /mámmee/ (pl -mies), **mam·mie** n mother (infml; usually used by children)

Ma·mo·ré /maa mō ráy/ river in N Bolivia, flowing northward into the Madeira River. Length 1,200 mi./1,900 km.

man n (pl **men**) 1 an adult male human being 2 a person (often offensive if used of women) 3 a man with a particular occupation or nationality (usually in combination) 4 the human race (often offensive as excluding women) 5 an employee or worker (often offensive as excluding women) 6 a husband or male companion (slang) 7 a term of address (slang; sometimes offensive) 8 a piece used in board games ■ vt (**manned**, **man·ning**) (often offensive) 1 supply with workers or a crew 2 be ready to operate or defend —**man·like** adj

Man, Isle of ◊ Isle of Man

MAN /man/ abbr metropolitan area network

Man. abbr Manitoba

man a·bout town (pl **men a·bout town**) n a sophisticated man in fashionable society (dated)

man·a·cle /mánnək'l/ n each of a pair of joined rings around a prisoner's wrist (usually pl) —**man·a·cle** vt

man·age /mánnij/ (-**aged**, -**ag·ing**) v 1 vti administer or run a business, department, or project 2 vti achieve something with difficulty ○ eventually managed to open the door 3 vi cope in a difficult situation 4 vt deal with a situation or process that requires skillful control ○ managing patient care 5 vt discipline or control a person or animal —**man·age·a·ble** adj —**man·age·a·bly** adv

man·aged care n a system for providing medical care in which costs are monitored and limited

man·age·ment /mánnijmənt/ n 1 administration 2 managers as a group 3 successful or skillful handling ○ crisis management —**man·age·men·tal** /mànnij mént'l/ adj

⚡ man·age·ment in·for·ma·tion sys·tem n a system that helps managers run a company, especially a computerized system

man·ag·er /mánnijər/ n 1 somebody who manages a business, department, or project 2 an organizer of somebody's business affairs 3 an organizer of training and other affairs for an athlete or team —**man·a·ge·ri·al** /mànni jeéree əl/ adj —**man·ag·er·ship** n

man·ag·ing di·rec·tor n Can, UK, ANZ a person in charge of a company

~~managment~~ incorrect spelling of **management**

Ma·na·gua /mə naágwə/ capital of Nicaragua. Pop. 1,200,000 (1995).

Ma·na·ma /mə naámə/ capital of Bahrain. Pop. 148,000 (1995).

ma·ña·na /maa nyaánə/ adv 1 tomorrow 2 later

Ma·nas·sas /mə nássəss/ city in NE Virginia, the site of the two Civil War battles of Bull Run in 1861 and 1862. Pop. 35,300 (1998).

man·at /mánnət/ n the main unit of currency in Azerbaijan and Turkmenistan

man·a·tee /mánnə teè/ n a large aquatic plant-eating mammal with front flippers and a broad flattened tail

Ma·naus /mə nówss/ capital of Amazonas State, NW Brazil. Pop. 1,157,357 (1996).

Man·ches·ter /mán chestər/ 1 city in NW England, connected by the **Manchester Ship Canal** with the Irish Sea. Pop. 430,818 (1996). 2 largest city in New Hampshire. Pop. 102,524 (1998).

Man·chu·ri·a /man choóree ə/ historical name for a region of NE China comprising Heilongjiang, Jilin, and Liaoning provinces —**Man·chu·ri·an** n, adj

man·da·la /mándələ/ *n* in Buddhism or Hinduism, a circular design representing the universe

Man·da·lay /màndə láy/ city in central Myanmar. Pop. 532,949 (1983).

man·da·mus /man dáyməss/ (*pl* -mus·es) *n* an order from a high court

Man·dan /mán dàn/ (*pl same or* -dans) *n* 1 a member of a Native American people of North Dakota who now mainly live near Lake Sakakawea 2 the language of the Mandan people

man·da·rin /mándərin/ *n* 1 a high-ranking official in the Chinese Empire 2 a high-ranking civil servant 3 **Man·da·rin, Man·da·rin Chi·nese** Modern Standard Chinese, the official language of the People's Republic of China 4 *also* **man·da·rin or·ange** a small orange citrus fruit with a loose skin 5 a tree that produces mandarins —**Man·da·rin** *adj* —**man·da·ri·nate** *n*

ORIGIN **Mandarin** is not ultimately from Chinese, as might have been expected. It goes back to a Sanskrit root meaning "think," and entered English through Malay and Portuguese. The fruit is probably called a **mandarin** because of its color. Chinese mandarins traditionally wore yellow robes.

man·date /mán dàyt/ *n* 1 an authoritative order 2 authority bestowed by an electoral victory 3 a territory placed by the League of Nations under the administration of a member state ■ *vt* (-dat·ed, -dat·ing) make something mandatory

man·da·to·ry /mándə tàwree/ *adj* 1 compulsory 2 with the power of a mandate —**man·da·to·ri·ly** *adv*

South African Embassy

Nelson Mandela

Man·de·la /man déllə, -dáylə/, **Nelson** (b. 1918) president of South Africa (1994–99)

Man·del·stam /mánd'l stàm/, **Osip Ye·mjlyevich** (1891?–1938?) Russian poet

man·di·ble /mándib'l/ *n* 1 the lower jaw of a person or animal (*technical*) 2 each of the upper and lower parts of a bird's beak —**man·dib·u·lar** /man díbbyələr/ *adj*

man·do·lin /mándə lín, mánd'lin/ *n* a stringed instrument of the lute family with a pear-shaped body

man·drake /mán dràyk/ *n* a plant with a forked root formerly believed to have magical powers

man·drill /mándril/ *n* a large baboon with a colorful muzzle in the male

mane *n* 1 long hair on an animal's neck 2 thick long hair on somebody's head (*literary or infml*) —**maned** *adj*

Ma·net /man áy/, **Édouard** (1832–83) French painter

ma·neu·ver /mə noóvər/ *n* 1 a skilled movement or action 2 a military movement or exercise (*often pl*) ■ *v* 1 *vti* move skillfully o *maneuvered the boat into the berth* 2 *vti* do military exercises 3 *vt* manipulate for personal advantage —**ma·neu·ver·a·bil·i·ty** /mə noóvərə bíllətee/ *n* —**ma·neu·ver·a·ble** *adj*

ORIGIN **Maneuver** was adopted in the late 18C from a French verb that had previously entered English in the 14C as *manure* "manage, occupy, or till land."

man·ful /mánfəl/ *adj* brave and determined as a man is traditionally supposed to be —**man·ful·ly** *adv* —**man·ful·ness** *n*

man·ga·nese /máng gə nèez, -nèess/ *n* (*symbol* **Mn**) a brittle grayish-white metallic element. Use: alloys, strengthening steel.

mange /maynj/ *n* a skin disease of animals that causes itching and hair loss —**mang·y** *adj*

man·ger /máynjər/ *n* an eating trough for animals

man·gle¹ /máng g'l/ *vt* 1 mutilate by tearing or crushing 2 ruin by carelessness or incompetence

ORIGIN The two English words **mangle** are not related, though shared ideas of crushing could easily suggest that they are. The verb meaning "mutilate by crushing or tearing" was adopted in the 14C from the French verb that also gave us *maim*. The "machine for pressing fabric" is considerably later, late 17C, and comes from Dutch *mangel*, a shortening of *mangelstok* "crushing roller." The second element is related to English *stock*. The first goes back to Greek *magganon* "engine of war, axis of a pulley."

man·gle² /máng g'l/ *n* a machine for pressing fabric —**man·gle** *vt*

man·go /máng gō/ (*pl* -goes *or* -gos) *n* 1 a juicy sweet red or green fruit 2 a tropical evergreen tree that produces mangoes

man·grove /mán gròv, máng-/ *n* a tropical evergreen tree of tidal coasts with exposed intertwined roots

man·han·dle /mán hànd'l/ *vt* (-dled, -dling) 1 handle somebody or something roughly 2 move something unwieldy by hand

Man·hat·tan¹ /man hátt'n/, **man·hat·tan** *n* a whiskey and vermouth cocktail

Man·hat·tan² 1 borough of New York City, mainly on **Manhattan Island** at the northern end of New York Bay. Pop. 1,487,536

(1990). **2** city in NE Kansas. Pop. 41,318 (1998).

man·hole /mán hòl/ *n* a covered opening giving access to a sewer

man·hood /mán hòod/ *n* **1** the state of being a man **2** manliness

man·hour *n* the work of one person per hour (*sometimes offensive*)

man·hunt /mán hùnt/ *n* a search for a criminal

ma·ni·a /máynee ə/ *n* **1** an obsessive interest or enthusiasm **2** a psychiatric disorder involving excessive activity and impulsive behavior

-mania *suffix* an excessive enthusiasm for o *pyromania*

ma·ni·ac /máynee àk/ *n* **1** an offensive term for somebody regarded as irrational because of a psychiatric disorder **2** an obsessive enthusiast —**ma·ni·a·cal** /mə nî ək'l/ *adj* —**ma·ni·a·cal·ly** *adv*

man·ic /mánnik/ *adj* **1** of mania **2** hectic (*infml; sometimes offensive*) —**man·i·cal·ly** *adv*

man·ic-de·pres·sive *n* a person with bipolar disorder —**man·ic-de·pres·sive** *adj*

man·i·cure /mánni kyòor/ *n* a cosmetic treatment of the hands and fingernails ■ *vt* (**-cured, -cur·ing**) **1** treat with a manicure **2** cut and shape carefully o *a neatly manicured lawn* —**man·i·cur·ist** *n*

man·i·fest /mánnə fèst/ *adj* obvious ■ *v* **1** *vt* show clearly **2** *vi* appear ■ *n* a list of cargo or passengers —**man·i·fest·ly** *adv*

man·i·fes·ta·tion /mànnə fes táysh'n/ *n* **1** a manifesting or being manifested **2** a sign of the presence or existence of something **3** a public demonstration

Man·i·fest Des·ti·ny *n* a 19C doctrine that the United States has a right to expansion

man·i·fes·to /mànnə féstō/ *n* (*pl* **-tos** *or* **-toes**) *n* a declaration of principles, policies, and objectives

man·i·fold /mánnə fòld/ *adj* **1** many and various **2** having many parts or forms ■ *n* a chamber or pipe with several openings

man·i·kin /mánnikin/, **man·ni·kin** *n* **1** a dummy for displaying clothes **2** an anatomical model of the human body

ma·nil·a /mə níllə/, **Ma·nil·a** *n* a cigar made in Manila **2** *also* **Ma·nil·a pa·per** strong pale-brown paper

Ma·nil·a /mə níllə/ capital of the Philippines. Pop. 1,580,924 (1999).

man in the street *n* the average person (*sometimes offensive*)

ϟ **ma·nip·u·late** /mə níppyə làyt/ (**-lat·ed, -lat·ing**) *vt* **1** operate or handle something skillfully **2** work with data on a computer **3** control somebody or something deviously **4** falsify something for personal advantage **5** examine or treat a body part by moving it with the hands —**ma·nip·u·la·tion** /mə níppyə láysh'n/ *n* —**ma·nip·u·la·tive** /-lətiv,

-làytiv/ *adj* —**ma·nip·u·la·tor** *n* —**ma·nip·u·la·to·ry** *adj*

Man·i·to·ba /mànni tóbə/ province in south central Canada. Cap. Winnipeg. Pop. 1,147,880 (2000). —**Man·i·to·ban** *adj, n*

man·kind /mán kìnd/ *n* **1** all human beings (*often offensive*) **2** men as distinct from women (*dated*)

man·ly /mánlee/ (**-li·er, -li·est**) *adj* **1** conventionally typical of or appropriate to a man **2** having manly qualities —**man·li·ness** *n*

man-made, man·made /mán màyd/ *adj* artificial or synthetic and not natural (*often offensive*)

Mann /man, maan/, **Thomas** (1875–1955) German-born US novelist and critic

man·na /mánnə/ *n* **1** in the Bible, divinely provided sustenance **2** an unexpected benefit

man·ne·quin /mánnikin/ *n* **1** a dummy for displaying clothes **2** a fashion model (*dated*)

man·ner /mánnər/ *n* **1** the way something is done **2** a way of behaving ■ **man·ners** *npl* **1** social behavior **2** customs and practices ◊ **to the manner born** thoroughly adapted to something

man·nered /mánnərd/ *adj* **1** affected **2** behaving in a particular way (*usually in combination*) o *an ill-mannered child*

man·ner·ism /mánnər ìzzəm/ *n* **1** an idiosyncrasy **2** affected behavior **3** *also* **Man·ner·ism** a late-16C style of art and architecture characterized by stylized and elongated forms

man·ner·ly /mánnərlee/ *adj* polite

man·ni·kin *n* = **manikin**

Man·ning /mánning/, **Patrick Augustus Mervyn** (*b.* 1946) prime minister of Trinidad and Tobago (1991–95, 2001–)

man·nish /mánnish/ *adj* **1** suitable for a man rather than a woman (*often offensive*) o *a mannish haircut* **2** like or typical of a man

man of let·ters *n* a writer (*fml*)

man of the cloth *n* a clergyman

man-of-war (*pl* **men-of-war**) *n* **1** a warship **2** a Portuguese man-of-war

ma·nom·e·ter /mə nómmətər/ *n* an instrument for measuring gas pressure —**man·o·met·ric** /mànnə méttrik/ *adj* —**ma·nom·e·try** *n*

man·or /mánnər/ *n* **1** a large house and the land surrounding it, especially a feudal estate controlled by a lord **2** in North America before 1776, an inheritable piece of land granted by royal charter **3** *also* **man·or house** the residence of the lord or lady of a manor —**ma·no·ri·al** /mə náwree əl/ *adj*

~~manouver~~ incorrect spelling of **maneuver**

man·pow·er /mán pòwr/ *n* power in terms of

the number of people available or needed (*sometimes offensive*)

man·qué /maaN káy/ *adj* frustrated in your ambitions ◇ *a poet manqué*

man·sard roof /mán saàrd-/ *n* a roof with a double slope on all sides

manse /manss/ *n* 1 a Christian minister's house 2 a large house

man·ser·vant /mán sùrvənt/ (*pl* **men·ser·vants** /mén sùrvənts/) *n* a male servant, especially a valet

Mans·field /mánss feeld/, **Katherine** (1888–1923) New Zealand-born British writer

man·sion /mánshən/ *n* 1 a large and grand house 2 a division of the zodiac

man·sized, man·size *adj* 1 larger than the ordinary size 2 of the size of a man ◇ *a man-sized hole*

man·slaugh·ter /mán slàwtər/ *n* the unpremeditated killing of a human being

Man·te·gna /man ténnyə/, **Andrea** (1431–1506) Italian painter

man·tel /mánt'l/ *n* an ornamental fireplace frame

man·tel·piece /mánt'l peèss/ *n* a mantel or its projecting top

man·tel·shelf /mánt'l shèlf/ (*pl* **-shelves** /-shèlvz/) *n* the projecting top of a mantel

man·til·la /man teéyə, -tíllə/ *n* a lace scarf covering the head and shoulders

man·tis /mántiss/ (*pl* **-tis·es** *or* **-tes** /-teèz/) *n* a large predatory insect with grasping front legs

man·tis·sa /man tíssə/ *n* a fractional part of a logarithm

man·tle /mánt'l/ *n* 1 a covering (*literary*) 2 a sleeveless cloak 3 an incandescent circle of wire mesh around a lamp flame 4 the part of the Earth between the crust and the core 5 ARCHIT = **mantel** —**man·tle** *vt*

man-to-man *adj* honest and intimate ◇ *a man-to-man talk* —**man-to-man** *adv*

man·tra /mántrə/ *n* 1 a sacred word repeated in meditation 2 an often repeated expression or idea

man·u·al /mánnyoo əl/ *adj* 1 of or using the hands 2 involving physical rather than mental effort 3 operated by a person rather than a machine ■ *n* a small book that contains information and instructions —**man·u·al·ly** *adv*

man·u·al al·pha·bet *n* a finger alphabet for hearing-impaired people

Ma·nuel·i·to /mànnwe leétō/ (1818–93) Navajo leader

man·u·fac·ture /mànnyə fákchər/ (**-tured, -tur·ing**) *v* 1 *vti* make something, or produce something industrially 2 *vt* invent an excuse —**man·u·fac·ture** *n* —**man·u·fac·tur·er** *n* —**man·u·fac·tur·ing** *n, adj*

man·u·fac·tured home *n* 1 a prefabricated dwelling 2 a mobile home

ma·nure /mə noór/ *n* fertilizer made from dung —**ma·nure** *vt*

ORIGIN Manure came into English in the 14C as a verb, from a French word meaning "manage, occupy, or till land" (the same verb was readopted in a later form as *maneuver*). It had developed from Latin words meaning literally "work with the hands." The English noun that means "dung as a fertilizer" was formed from the verb in the mid-16C.

man·u·script /mánnyə skrìpt/ *n* 1 a handwritten book 2 an author's original text

Manx /mangks/ *adj* of the Isle of Man ■ *n* a Celtic language of the Isle of Man ■ *npl* the Manx people —**Manx·man** *n* —**Manx·wom·an** *n*

man·y /ménnee/ *adj, pron* a considerable number

man·y-sid·ed *adj* having many sides or aspects

Mao·ism /mów ìzzəm/ *n* the doctrines and teachings of Mao Zedong —**Mao·ist** *n, adj*

Mao·ri /mówree/ (*pl* same) *n* 1 a member of a New Zealand people 2 the language of the Maori people —**Mao·ri** *adj*

Mao Zedong

Mao Ze·dong /mòw tsay toóng/, **Mao Tse-tung** (1893–1976) chairman of the People's Republic of China (1949–76)

map *n* 1 a geographic diagram showing locations 2 a diagram showing relative positions, e.g., of the stars ■ *vt* (**mapped, map·ping**) create a map of —**map·pa·ble** *adj* ◊ **on the map** in a prominent position (*slang*)

☐ **map out** *vt* plan

ma·ple /máyp'l/ *n* 1 a deciduous tree with winged seeds 2 the wood of the maple tree. Use: furniture, flooring.

ma·ple syr·up *n* a sweet syrup made from the sap of a particular maple

Ma·pu·to /mə poótō/ capital of Mozambique. Pop. 1,098,000 (1991 estimate).

ma·qui·la·do·ra /mə kèelə dáw ràa, maa keèlaa-/, **ma·qui·la** /mə keèlə, maa keè làà/ *n* a factory in Mexico in which imported materials are assembled into products for export

mar (**marred, mar·ring**) *vt* spoil

mar. *abbr* 1 maritime 2 married

Mar. *abbr* March

mar·a·bou /márrə bòò/ n 1 a large African stork 2 down from a marabou's tail. Use: trimming for clothes.

mar·a·bout /márrə bòò/ n 1 a Muslim hermit or monk 2 the tomb of a marabout

ma·ra·ca /mə raákə/ n a rattle usually used in pairs as a percussion instrument

Ma·ra·cai·bo, Lake /màrrə kíbō/ largest lake in South America, in NW Venezuela

Ma·ra·ñón /màrrə nyón/ river in N South America, flowing northward from the Andes into the Amazon River. Length 990 mi./1,600 km.

mar·a·schi·no /màrrə skeénō, -sheénō/ n a cherry liqueur

mar·a·schi·no cher·ry n a cocktail cherry preserved in maraschino-flavored syrup

mar·a·thon /márrə thòn/ n 1 a long-distance running or walking race 2 a lengthy and difficult task —**mar·a·thon·er** n

ORIGIN According to tradition, when the Greek army defeated the Persians at Marathon, on the northeastern coast of Attica, in 490 BC, the runner Pheidippides was dispatched to bring the good news to Athens (in fact there is no contemporary evidence for the story, which is not recorded until 700 years after the event). When the modern Olympic Games were first held, in Athens in 1896, a long-distance race was introduced to commemorate the ancient feat, run over a course supposedly equal in distance to the journey from Marathon to Athens (about 22 mi./35 km). The present distance was established at the 1948 Olympics in London, England.

ma·raud·ing /mə ráwding/ adj roving around attacking and looting —**ma·raud·er** n

mar·ble /maárb'l/ n 1 a dense crystallized rock. Use: building, sculpture, and monuments. 2 a small glass ball used in games ■ **mar·bles** npl mental abilities (infml) ○ *lost his marbles* ■ vt (-bled, -bling) color paper with mottled streaks

mar·bling /maárbling/ n 1 coloring like marble 2 streaks of fat in meat

Mar·burg dis·ease /maár bùrg-/ n a severe, often lethal, viral infection

ORIGIN The disease is named for the city of Marburg in Germany, where the first major outbreak occurred.

mar·ca·site /maárkə sìt, -zìt/ n 1 a yellow mineral. Use: jewelry. 2 a decorative piece of polished metal

march[1] /maárch/ v 1 vi walk in military fashion, with regular movements of the arms and legs at a steady rhythmic pace 2 vti move in military-style formation ○ *marched the troops off to battle* 3 vi walk with determination ○ *marched into the store and demanded to see the manager* 4 vt force somebody to go somewhere ○ *grabbed the boys and marched them into the house* 5 vi

walk with others in a protest or demonstration 6 vi pass steadily ○ *Time marches on.* ■ n 1 an act of marching ○ *a four-hour march back to the camp* ○ *a protest march* 2 a marching speed 3 a steady forward movement ○ *the march of time* 4 a piece of music in marching rhythm ◇ **steal a march on somebody** do something before somebody else to your own advantage

march[2] n a border area between two countries

March n the 3rd month of the year in the Gregorian calendar

ORIGIN March is named for Mars, the Roman god of war.

march·ing or·ders npl orders to set off on a military expedition

mar·chio·ness /maárshənəss, màarshə néss/ n a noblewoman ranking between a duchess and a countess

Mar·co·ni /maar kónee/, **Guglielmo, Marchese** (1874–1937) Italian electrical engineer. He pioneered the practical development of radio signaling.

Mar·cos /maárk oss/, **Ferdinand** (1917–89) Philippine national leader and president-dictator of the Philippines (1965–86)

Mar·cus Au·re·li·us ◊ **Aurelius, Marcus**

Mar·di Gras /maárdee graá/ (pl **Mar·dis Gras** /pronunc. same/) n 1 the Tuesday before Lent 2 a carnival before Lent

mare[1] /mair/ n an adult female horse

ma·re[2] /maá rày, maáree/ (pl **-ri·a** /-ree ə/ or **-res**) n a dark plain on the Moon or Mars

Mare ◊ **de la Mare, Walter**

mar·ga·rine /maárjərin/ n a yellow fatty substance used as a spread and in cooking

ORIGIN Margarine comes from French. The substance was originally made from clarified beef fat. The name is based on Greek *margaron* "pearl," through the name (*margaric acid* in English) of a fatty acid that was believed to be a constituent of animal fats (including beef fat) and whose crystals had a pearly luster.

mar·ga·ri·ta /maárgə reétə/ n a tequila cocktail

Mar·gas·ir·sa /maárgə seérsə/ n the 9th month of the year in the Hindu calendar. Also called **Agrahayana**

mar·gin /maárjin/ n 1 a blank space at the side of a page 2 an outer edge 3 a part farthest from the center (often pl) ○ *on the margins of society* 4 the difference between amounts or numbers ○ *won by a small margin* 5 an additional amount allowed as a precaution ○ *no margin for error*

mar·gin·al /maárjin'l/ adj 1 in or on a margin 2 small in scale or importance 3 on the fringes of a group —**mar·gin·al·ly** adv

mar·gin·al·ize /maárjin'l ìz/ (-ized, -iz·ing) vt prevent from having power or commanding attention —**mar·gin·al·i·za·tion** /màarjin'li záysh'n/ *n*

mar·gue·rite /màargə reet, -gyə reet/ *n* a garden plant resembling a daisy

ma·ri·a·chi /màaree aàchee, màrree-/ (*pl* **-chis**) *n* 1 a Mexican street band 2 traditional Mexican folk music played by a mariachi

~~mariage~~ incorrect spelling of **marriage**

Ma·ri·an·a Is·lands /màrree aánə-/ island group in the W North Pacific Ocean, east of the Philippines, comprising Guam and the Commonwealth of the Northern Mariana Islands. Pop. 226,500 (2000).

Ma·ri·a The·re·sa /mə rèe ə tə ráyzə/ (1717–80) archduchess of Austria and queen of Hungary and Bohemia (1740–80)

Ma·ri·co·pa /màrri kópə/ (*pl same or* **-pas**) *n* 1 a member of a Native North American people who live in Arizona 2 the language of the Maricopa people —**Ma·ri·co·pa** *adj*

Ma·rie An·toi·nette /mə rèe àntwə nét/ (1755–93) queen of France as the wife of Louis XVI

Ma·rie de Mé·di·cis /mə rèe də méddi chee/ (1573–1642) queen and regent of France (1600–17)

mar·i·gold /màrrə gòld/ *n* a garden plant with yellow or orange flowers

mar·i·jua·na /màrrə waànə, -hwaànə/, **mar·i·hua·na** *n* 1 a drug derived from the hemp plant 2 the hemp plant

ma·rim·ba /mə rímbə/ *n* a musical instrument like a xylophone with resonators beneath the bars

Ma·rin /márrin/, **John** (1870–1953) US painter

ma·ri·na /mə rèenə/ *n* a harbor for pleasure boats

mar·i·nade *n* /màrrə náyd/ a flavored liquid in which food may be soaked before cooking ■ *vti* /márrə nàyd/ (**-nad·ed, -nad·ing**) marinate

ORIGIN The word **marinade** is related to *marine*. It came via French from a verb meaning "pickle in brine" in Spanish and Italian and deriving from Latin *aqua marina* "seawater, brine." **Marinade** is first recorded in English in the early 18C; related *marinate* is a little older (mid-17C).

mar·i·nate /márrə nàyt/ (**-nat·ed, -nat·ing**) *vti* soak in a marinade before cooking —**mar·i·na·tion** /màrrə náysh'n/ *n*

ma·rine /mə rèen/ *adj* 1 of the sea 2 of ships or sailing ■ *n* 1 *also* **Ma·rine** a seagoing soldier 2 a fleet of ships (*fml*)

Ma·rine Corps *n* a branch of the US armed forces operating on land and at sea

mar·i·ner /márrənər/ *n* a sailor

mar·i·o·nette /màrree ə nét/ *n* a puppet worked by strings

mar·i·tal /márrət'l/ *adj* of marriage —**mar·i·tal·ly** *adv*

mar·i·time /márrə tìm/ *adj* of or close to the sea

Mar·i·time Prov·inc·es, Mar·i·times collective name for the E Canadian provinces of New Brunswick, Nova Scotia, and Prince Edward Island —**Mar·i·tim·er** *n*

mar·jo·ram /máarjərəm/ *n* an aromatic herb used in cooking

mark[1] /maark/ *n* 1 a spot, line, patch, or impression on a surface 2 a symbol (*often in combination*) ○ *a question mark* 3 an indication ○ *as a mark of respect* 4 a sign of influence or involvement ○ *left his mark on the company* 5 an identifying feature or characteristic 6 a number or letter indicating somebody's assessment of correctness, quality, or performance 7 a target, aim, or goal 8 a guide to position or direction 9 a starting line in a race ■ *v* 1 *vti* make a mark or marks on something ○ *The vase has marked the table.* 2 *vt* make visible or identifiable with a mark 3 *vt* be an indicator of ○ *marks the end of an era* 4 *vt* celebrate or give prominence to ○ *mark the occasion* 5 *vt* assess and indicate the quality or correctness of 6 *vt* take notice of (*often a command*) ○ *Mark my words, this will make a difference.* —**mark·er** *n*

SPELLCHECK Do not confuse the spelling of **mark** and **marque** ("a commercial brand"), which sound similar.

☐ **mark down** *vt* lower the price of

☐ **mark up** *vt* increase the price of

mark[2] /maark/ *n* MONEY = **deutsche mark**

Mark /maark/ *n* the second of the gospels in the Bible in which the life and teachings of Jesus Christ are described, traditionally attributed to St. Mark

Mark /maark/, **St.** (*fl* 1C) evangelist. By tradition he is considered to be the author of the second Gospel in the Bible.

mar·ka /múrkə/ *n* the main unit of currency in Bosnia and Herzegovina

Mark An·to·ny ♦ Antony, Mark

mark·down /máark dòwn/ *n* a price reduction

marked /maarkt/ *adj* 1 noticeable 2 singled out for something unpleasant —**mark·ed·ly** /máarkədlee/ *adv*

mar·ket /máarkət/ *n* 1 a gathering for buying and selling 2 a place where a market is held 3 a collection of small shops or stalls 4 the area of economic activity involving buying and selling 5 a shop or store, especially a specialized one 6 the buying and selling of a particular commodity 7 a group of potential customers 8 demand for a particular product or service 9 the stock market ■ *vt* offer something for sale in a way that makes people want to buy it —**mar·ket·er** *n* —**mar·ket·ing** *n* ◇ **on the market** available for customers to buy

mar·ket·a·ble /máarkətəb'l/ *adj* 1 fit to be sold

○ *a highly marketable property* **2** in demand
○ *skills that are readily marketable*

mar·ket e·con·o·my *n* an economy regulated by the laws of supply and demand

mar·ket·eer /maàrkə teèr/ *n* **1** somebody who trades at or in a market **2** a supporter of a particular type of market *(usually in combination)* ○ *a free marketeer*

mar·ket gar·den *n* a plot for growing produce for sale —**mar·ket gar·den·er** *n* —**mar·ket gar·den·ing** *n*

mar·ket lead·er *n* a company with the largest market share

mar·ket mak·er *n* somebody who buys and sells securities

mar·ket·place /maàrkət plàyss/ *n* **1** an open space for a market **2** the sphere of trading

mar·ket price *n* the current price of something

mar·ket re·search *n* the study of consumers' wants and purchases —**mar·ket re·search·er** *n*

mar·ket share *n* a share of the total sales of a product

mar·ket val·ue *n* the amount for which something can be sold on the open market

mark·ing /maàrking/ *n* **1** a mark or pattern of marks *(often pl)* **2** the assessment and grading of written work

mark·ka /maàr kàa, -ka/ *(pl* **-kaa** *or* **-kas***) n* the main unit of the former Finnish currency

marks·man /maàrksmən/ *(pl* **-men** /-mən/*) n* **1** somebody skilled in shooting **2** a man considered a good or bad shot —**marks·man·ship** *n*

marks·wo·man /maàrks woòmmən/ *(pl* **-men** /-wimmin/*) n* **1** a woman skilled in shooting **2** a woman considered a good or bad shot

⚡ **mark·up** /maàrk up/ *n* **1** an amount added to a price **2** the addition to a text of coding or instructions for layout and style

⚡ **mark·up lan·guage** *n* a computer coding system specifying the layout and style of a document

marl *n* a mixture of clay and lime. Use: fertilizer, water softener. —**marl·y** *adj*

mar·lin /maàrlin/ *(pl* **-lins** *or* **same***) n* a game fish with an elongated upper jaw

Mar·lowe /maàrlō/, **Christopher** (1564–93) English playwright

mar·ma·lade /maàrmə làyd/ *n* a preserve of citrus fruit containing shredded rind

ORIGIN **Marmalade** was originally "quince jam." The word is first recorded in English in the late 15C. It came via French from Portuguese, where it was formed from *marmelo* "quince." This goes back to a Greek word that referred to a kind of apple grafted onto a quince.

Mar·ma·ra, Sea of /maàrmərə/, **Mar·mo·ra, Sea of** inland sea in NW Turkey, connected

with the Black Sea by the Bosporus and with the Aegean Sea by the Dardanelles

mar·mo·re·al /maar máwree əl/ *adj* of marble *(literary)*

mar·mo·set /maàrmə sèt, -zèt/ *(pl* **-sets** *or* **same***) n* a small furry monkey with tufted ears and a long tail

mar·mot /maàrmət/ *(pl* **-mots** *or* **same***) n* a stout-bodied burrowing rodent

ma·roon[1] /mə roòn/ *n* a deep purplish-red color —**ma·roon** *adj*

ORIGIN The two English words **maroon** are as unrelated as their meanings suggest. The color came via French and Italian from a Greek word meaning "chestnut." The verb **maroon** was formed from a noun, a name given to descendants of runaway slaves in Suriname and the Caribbean islands. This came from a French shortening of American Spanish *cimarrón*, literally "wild, untamed."

ma·roon[2] /mə roòn/ *vt* leave isolated without any means of escape

marque /maark/ *n* a commercial brand, especially of a luxury or high-performance product ◊ See note at **mark**

mar·quee /maar keé/ *n* a permanent canopy projecting over an entrance to a hotel or theater ■ *adj* having public appeal ○ *a movie star with marquee value*

Mar·que·sas Is·lands /maar káyssəss-/ group of volcanic islands in French Polynesia, in the South Pacific Ocean. Pop. 7,538 (1988).

mar·quess /maàrkwəss/ *n* a nobleman ranking between a duke and an earl —**mar·ques·sate** /maàrkwə sàyt, -zàyt/ *n*

mar·que·try /maàrkətree/ *n* **1** decorative designs made of inlaid wood or other materials **2** the craft of making marquetry

Mar·quette /maar két/, **Jacques** (1637–75) French missionary and explorer

Már·quez /maàr kez/ ◊ **García Márquez, Gabriel**

mar·quis /maàrkwiss, maar keé/ *(pl* **-quis·es** /-kwissəz/ *or* **-quis** /-keéz/*) n* in various European countries, a nobleman ranking above a count —**mar·quis·ate** /maàrkwəzət, -wəssət/ *n*

mar·quise /maar keèz/ *n* **1** in some European countries, a noblewoman ranking above a countess **2** a marquee

~~marrage~~ incorrect spelling of **marriage**

Mar·ra·kesh /màrrə késh/, **Mar·ra·kech** city in W Morocco. Pop. 745,541 (1994).

mar·riage /márrij/ *n* **1** a legal relationship between two people living together as sexual partners **2** a married relationship between two particular people ○ *They have a happy marriage.* **3** the joining of two people in marriage **4** a union of two things —**mar·riage·a·bil·i·ty** /màrrijə bĺllətee/ *n* —**mar·riage·a·ble** *adj*

mar·riage of con·ven·ience *n* a marriage

for practical or political purposes rather than love

mar·ried /márreed/ adj 1 having a spouse 2 of marriage ■ **mar·rieds** npl married people

mar·row /márrō/ n a soft tissue in the central cavity of bones

mar·row·bone /márrō bòn/ n a bone that contains edible marrow

mar·ry /márree/ (-ried, -ries) v 1 vti take somebody in marriage 2 vt join in marriage 3 vt give in marriage 4 vt acquire by marriage ○ hoping to marry money 5 vti match or combine successfully

Mars /maarz/ n 1 in Roman mythology, the god of war. Greek equivalent **Ares** 2 the 4th planet from the Sun

Mar·sa·la /maar saála/ n a Sicilian fortified wine

Mar·seil·laise /màarssə yéz, -ə láyz/ n the French national anthem

Mar·seilles /maar sáy/, **Mar·seille** port in SE France. Pop. 798,430 (1999).

marsh n an area of soft wet ground —**marsh·y** adj

mar·shal /máarsh'l/ n 1 a high-ranking officer in some armed forces 2 somebody in charge of an event such as a parade or a race 3 a parade honoree 4 a federal law enforcement officer 5 the head of a fire or police department in some US cities ■ v (-shaled or -shalled, -shal·ing or -shal·ling) 1 vt arrange in appropriate order ○ marshal your thoughts 2 vt gather and organize 3 vt guide or lead ceremonially 4 vti act as a marshal at an event

SPELLCHECK Do not confuse the spelling of **marshal** and **martial** ("military," "warlike"), which sound similar.

mar·shal·ing yard n a place where trains are made up

Mar·shall /máarsh'l/, **George Catlett** (1880–1959) US military commander and secretary of state (1947–49)

Mar·shall, John (1755–1835) chief justice of the US Supreme Court (1801–35)

Mar·shall, Thurgood (1908–93) US civil rights lawyer and associate justice of the US Supreme Court (1967–91)

Mar·shall Is·lands island country in the central N Pacific Ocean. Cap. Majuro. Pop. 70,822 (2001).

marsh gas n methane formed by decomposing plant matter in the absence of air

marsh·land /máarsh lànd, -lənd/ n marshy ground

marsh mal·low n a medicinal herb with pink flowers

marsh·mal·low /máarsh mèllō/ n a soft spongy candy —**marsh·mal·low·y** adj

ORIGIN Marshmallow was originally made from the root of the marsh mallow plant.

marsh mar·i·gold n a plant with yellow flowers that grows in marshy ground

mar·su·pi·al /maar soópee əl/ n an animal with a pouch in which the young develop

mart n a market

mar·ten /máart'n/ (pl same or -tens) n a short-legged bushy-tailed mammal with a long slender body that lives in trees

Mar·tha's Vine·yard /máarthəz-/ island in SE Massachusetts, in the Atlantic Ocean. Pop. 8,900 (1990).

Mar·tí /maartee´é/, **José Julian** (1853–95) Cuban revolutionary leader and poet

mar·tial /máarsh'l/ adj 1 military 2 fierce or hostile —**mar·tial·ly** adv ◊ See note at **marshal**

mar·tial art n a system of combat and self-defense such as judo or karate

mar·tial law n control of civilians by armed forces

Mar·tian /máarsh'n/ adj of the planet Mars ■ n a supposed inhabitant of Mars

mar·tin /máart'n/ n a bird related to the swallow

mar·ti·net /màart'n ét/ n a rigid disciplinarian

ORIGIN The original **martinet** was the 17C French soldier Jean Martinet, who invented a system of military drill.

mar·ti·ni /maar teénee/ n a cocktail of gin or vodka with vermouth

Mar·ti·nique /màartə neék, màart'n eék/ island department of France in the E Caribbean Sea. Pop. 418,454 (2001).

Mar·tin Lu·ther King Day n a legal holiday. Date: 3rd Monday in January.

Mar·ti·nů /máarti noo/, **Bohuslav Jan** (1890–1959) Czech composer

mar·tyr /máartər/ n 1 somebody who chooses to die rather than deny a belief 2 somebody who makes sacrifices for a cause ■ vt kill somebody for a belief —**mar·tyr·dom** n

~~marvelous~~ incorrect spelling of **marvelous**

mar·vel /máarv'l/ n 1 a wonderful thing 2 a very skillful person ■ vi be amazed

mar·vel·ous /máarvələss/, **mar·vel·lous** adj 1 amazingly impressive 2 extremely good —**mar·vel·ous·ly** adv

Karl Marx

Marx /maarks/, **Karl** (1818–83) German political philosopher —**Marx·i·an** adj

Marx Broth·ers (fl early 20C) US comedians. **Chico** (born Leonard, 1891–1961), **Groucho**

(born Julius Henry, 1895–1977), and **Harpo** (born Adolph, 1888–1964), the three most prominent of the brothers, appeared in movies such as *A Night at the Opera* (1935).

Marx·ism /maárk sìzzəm/ *n* Karl Marx's political and economic theories about class struggle leading to social change —**Marx·ist** *n, adj*

Marx·ism-Len·in·ism *n* a further development of Marxism including the theories of Lenin —**Marx·ist-Len·in·ist** *n, adj*

Mar·y /máiree/ *n* in the Bible, the mother of Jesus Christ

Mar·y I /máiree/ (1516–58) queen of England and Ireland (1553–58)

Mar·y II (1662–94) queen of England, Scotland, and Ireland (1689–94)

Mar·y (Queen of Scots) (1542–87) queen of Scotland (1542–67)

Mar·y·land /máirilənd/ state in the E United States. Cap. Annapolis. Pop. 5,296,486 (2000). —**Mar·y·land·er** *n*

Mar·y Mag·da·lene /-mágdə lèen/ *n* follower of Jesus Christ

mar·zi·pan /maárzə pàn, maártsə-/ *n* a paste made from ground almonds and sugar

---

ORIGIN Marzipan goes back ultimately to Arabic *mawtabān*, literally "enthroned king." The Saracens used it as the name of a medieval Venetian coin that had a figure of the seated Jesus Christ on it. In the Italian dialect of Venice the word became *matapan*, and, eventually, in general Italian, *marzapane*. Its meaning supposedly progressed from the "coin" via "measure of weight or capacity," "box of such capacity," and "such a box containing confectionery" to "the contents of such a box." English acquired the word and it became *marchpane*. Around the 19C *marzipan* was borrowed from German. This was an alteration of Italian *marzapane*, based on the misconception that it came from Latin *marci panis* "St. Mark's bread."

Ma·sac·cio /mə saáchee ō/ (1401?–27) Italian painter

masc. *abbr* masculine

mas·car·a /ma skárrə, mə-/ *n* a cosmetic for eyelashes ■ *vt* —**mas·car·a** *vt*

mas·car·po·ne /màaskaar pónee/ *n* a rich Italian cream cheese

mas·cot /más kòt, máskət/ *n* something or somebody believed to bring good luck

mas·cu·line /máskyəlin/ *adj* **1** of men and boys **2** traditionally associated with men rather than women **3** of a grammatical gender including the majority of words referring to males ■ *n* the masculine grammatical gender, or a word or form in this gender —**mas·cu·line·ly** *adv* —**mas·cu·lin·i·ty** /màskyə línnətee/ *n*

Mase·field /máyss fèeld/, **John** (1878–1967) British poet

Mas·er·u /mázzə rōō/ capital of Lesotho. Pop. 297,000 (1995).

mash *n* **1** a mixture of grain and water used to make alcohol **2** ground animal food **3** a pulpy mass ■ *vt* **1** soak grain **2** crush something to a pulp

MASH /mash/, **M.A.S.H.** *abbr* mobile army surgical hospital

mas·int /mássint/, **MASINT** *n* intelligence data acquired, typically electronically, about possible attacks using weapons of mass destruction. Full form **materials intelligence**

mask *n* **1** a covering for the eyes or face **2** something that conceals or disguises something ○ *a mask for his true feelings* **3** a mold of a face **4** an animal's face markings ■ *vt* **1** conceal or disguise something **2** shield part of something, e.g., from paint or light —**masked** *adj*

masked ball *n* a dance at which the guests wear disguises

mask·ing tape *n* adhesive tape used to shield parts of a surface when painting

mas·och·ism /mássə kìzzəm/ *n* **1** sexual pleasure derived from being hurt or humiliated **2** the tendency to seek and enjoy suffering —**mas·o·chist** *n* —**mas·o·chis·tic** /màssə kístik/ *adj*

ORIGIN Masochism was explored by the Austrian novelist Leopold von Sacher-Masoch (1835–95), whose name became permanently associated with it.

---

ma·son /máyss'n/ *n* **1** somebody who works with stone **2** **Ma·son** a Freemason —**Ma·son·ic** /mə sónnik/ *adj*

Ma·son-Dix·on Line /màyss'n díks'n-/ *n* the boundary between free and slave states before the American Civil War

---

ORIGIN The Mason-Dixon Line was surveyed in 1763–67 by Charles Mason and Jeremiah Dixon.

Ma·son·ite /máyssə nìt/ *tdmk* a trademark for fiberboard products

Ma·son jar /máyss'n-/ *n* a glass container used in canning food

ma·son·ry /máyss'nree/ *n* **1** a mason's trade **2** a mason's work **3** stonework **4** **Ma·son·ry** Freemasonry

Mas·qat ▸ Muscat

masque /mask/ *n* a dramatic entertainment with masked performers

mas·quer·ade /màskə ráyd/ *n* **1** a party where people wear masks and costumes **2** a disguise or pretense ■ *vi* (-ad·ed, -ad·ing) pretend to be somebody or something else

mass *n* **1** a lump of matter **2** a collection of things **3** a large unspecified quantity *(often pl)* ○ *masses of work to do* **4** the majority **5** the physical property of an object that is based on the amount of matter it contains ■ —**mass·es** *npl* the ordinary people ■ *vti* gather in a mass ■ *adj* **1** involving a large number o *a mass demonstration* **2** general

Mass, mass *n* **1** in some Christian churches, the ceremony of Communion **2** a musical setting of a Roman Catholic Mass

Mass. *abbr* Massachusetts

Mas·sa·chu·sett /màssə chōossət/ (*pl same or* -setts), **Mas·sa·chu·set** (*pl same or* -sets) *n* **1** a member of a Native North American people who lived in the Massachusetts Bay area **2** an extinct Algonquian language of the Massachusett people —**Mas·sa·chu·sett** *adj*

Mas·sa·chu·setts /màssə chōossəts/ state in the NE United States. Cap. Boston. Pop. 6,349,097 (2000).

Mas·sa·chu·setts Bay inlet of the Atlantic Ocean, in E Massachusetts

mas·sa·cre /mássəkər/ *n* **1** the killing of many people **2** a bad defeat (*infml*) —**mas·sa·cre** *vt*

mas·sage /mə saa<u>zh</u>, -saaj/ *n* a treatment that involves rubbing or kneading the muscles ■ *vt* (-saged, -sag·ing) **1** rub or knead the muscles of **2** manipulate statistics or other information deceptively —**mas·sag·er** *n*

Mas·se·net /mássə nay/, **Jules Émile Frédéric** (1842–1912) French composer

mas·seur /ma súr, mə súr, ma sóor/ *n* a man whose job is massaging

mas·seuse /ma sóoss, -sōoz, -sōz/ *n* a woman whose job is massaging

mas·sif /ma seéf/ *n* a mountain range or large mountain mass

mas·sive /mássiv/ *adj* **1** bulky and heavy **2** extremely large in amount or degree —**mas·sive·ly** *adv* —**mas·sive·ness** *n*

mass-mar·ket *adj* appealing to a wide range of people ■ *vt* sell to many people

mass me·di·a *n* the communications media in general (*+ sing or pl verb*)

mass noun *n* a noun representing something that cannot be counted, e.g., "water"

mass-pro·duce *vt* make products in large quantities —**mass-pro·duc·er** *n* —**mass pro·duc·tion** *n*

mast[1] *n* **1** a vertical pole, especially one supporting a sail or flag **2** a tall broadcasting antenna

mast[2] *n* nuts used as hog feed

mas·tec·to·my /ma stéktəmee/ (*pl* -mies) *n* the surgical removal of a breast

mas·ter /mástər/ *n* **1** somebody in authority or control (*sometimes offensive as excluding women*) **2** the owner of an animal **3** somebody highly skilled at something **4** a skilled worker qualified to teach apprentices (*usually in combination*) o *a master craftsman* **5** an original from which copies are made **6** the captain of a merchant ship **7** a machine or device that controls others (*sometimes offensive*) **8** a prefix to a boy's surname ■ *adj* (*sometimes offensive*) **1** con-

trolling o *the master switch* **2** principal o *the master bedroom* ■ *vt* **1** learn thoroughly or well **2** control or overcome (*sometimes offensive*) —**mas·ter·less** *adj*

mas·ter chief pet·ty of·fi·cer *n* a noncommissioned officer of the highest rank in the US Navy or Coast Guard

mas·ter class *n* a class given by an expert (*sometimes offensive*)

mas·ter·ful /mástərfəl/ *adj* **1** expert (*sometimes offensive*) **2** able or tending to lead —**mas·ter·ful·ly** *adv* —**mas·ter·ful·ness** *n*

mas·ter gun·ner·y ser·geant *n* a noncommissioned officer in the US Marine Corps, of a rank above master sergeant and below sergeant major

mas·ter key *n* a key that will open all the locks in a place

mas·ter·ly /mástərlee/ *adj* brilliantly skilled —**mas·ter·li·ness** *n*

mas·ter·mind /mástər mìnd/ *n* somebody who plans and oversees a complex process —**mas·ter·mind** *vt*

Mas·ter of Arts *n* a usually postgraduate degree in a nonscience subject

mas·ter of cer·e·mo·nies *n* the host of a formal event (*sometimes offensive*)

Mas·ter of Sci·ence *n* a usually postgraduate degree in a science subject

mas·ter·piece /mástər pèess/, **mas·ter·work** /-wùrk/ *n* **1** a great artistic work **2** somebody's best piece of work

Mas·ters /mảastərz/, **Edgar Lee** (1869–1950) US poet

Mas·ter's de·gree *n* a Master of Arts or Master of Science degree

mas·ter ser·geant *n* in the US Army and Marine Corps, a noncommissioned officer of a rank above sergeant major, and in the US Air Force above technical sergeant

Mas·ter·son /mảastərssən/, **Bat** (1853–1921) Canadian-born US sheriff

mas·ter·stroke /mástər stròk/ *n* a brilliant idea or tactic

mas·ter·work /mástər wùrk/ *n* a masterpiece

mas·ter·y /mástəree/ *n* **1** expert skill **2** complete control (*sometimes offensive*)

mast·head /mást hèd/ *n* **1** a newspaper's title as displayed on the front page **2** the top of a mast

mas·tic /mástik/ *n* **1** an aromatic resin. Use: lacquer, varnish, adhesives, condiments. **2** a flexible cement. Use: filler, adhesive, sealant.

mas·ti·cate /másti kàyt/ (-cat·ed, -cat·ing) *vti* chew food —**mas·ti·ca·tion** /màsti káysh'n/ *n*

mas·tiff /mástif/ *n* a big smooth-haired dog

ORIGIN Mastiff goes back to a Latin word meaning "tame," literally "used to the hand." It entered English through a French word that ended in -*in*. Where the -*iff* came from is not known.

mas·ti·tis /ma stítiss/ *n* inflammation of a woman's breast or a cow's udder

mas·to·don /mástə dòn/ *n* a large shaggy extinct mammal

mas·toid proc·ess /mást oyd-/ *n* a bony protuberance on the skull behind the ear

mas·tur·bate /mástər bàyt/ (-bat·ed, -bat·ing) *vi* stroke the genitals for sexual pleasure —**mas·tur·ba·tion** /màstər báysh'n/ *n* —**mas·tur·ba·to·ry** /-bə tàwree/ *adj*

mat[1] *n* **1** a piece of material placed on the floor or other surface for decoration or protection **2** a thick mass ■ *vti* (**mat·ted, mat·ting**) form or form into a tangled mass —**mat·ted** *adj*

mat[2] *n* **1** a border placed around a picture for framing **2** *also* **matte** a flat finish ■ *vt* (**mat·ted, mat·ting**) frame with a mat

mat., mat *abbr* matinée

M.A.T. *abbr* Master of Arts in Teaching

mat·a·dor /máttə dàwr/ *n* a bullfighter who kills the bull

Ma·ta Ha·ri /màatə hàaree/ (1876–1917) Dutch dancer and spy

match[1] *n* **1** a contest **2** a close likeness of somebody or something **3** an equal or counterpart **4** one half of a pair **5** a marital partnership or partner ■ *v* **1** *vt* be similar or identical to **2** *vt* compete equally with ○ *I can match him for speed.* **3** *vti* make a pleasing combination with something **4** *vt* be or find a match for —**match·a·ble** *adj*

ORIGIN The two words **match** are unrelated. The first is an ancient Germanic word, the earliest English sense of which was "husband or wife, sexual partner." The second was adopted in the 14C from French. It originally meant "wick of a candle or lamp." The modern **match** dates from the mid-19C.

match[2] *n* **1** a thin stick with a tip that ignites **2** an explosives fuse

match·book /mách bòok/ *n* a cardboard folder containing matches

match·box /mách bòks/ *n* a box for matches

match·less /máchləss/ *adj* unrivaled

match·mak·er /mách màykər/ *n* somebody who arranges relationships or marriages

match point *n* the final point of a game or match

match·stick /mách stìk/ *n* the stem of a match —**match·stick** *adj*

match·up /mách ùp/ *n* a matching of competitors

mate[1] *n* **1** a deck officer **2** a partner in sex or marriage **3** a skilled worker's helper **4** something that matches **5** a breeding partner ■ *v* (**mat·ed, mat·ing**) **1** *vti* breed **2** *vi* have sex **3** *vt* connect two objects

mate[2] (**mat·ed, mat·ing**) *n, vt, interj* checkmate

ma·té /máa tày, maa táy/ *n* a tea-like drink made from the dried leaves of a South American tree

ma·te·ri·al /mə téeree əl/ *n* **1** a substance used to make things **2** information used in the making of a book, movie, or similar work **3** cloth or fabric ■ **ma·te·ri·als** *npl* equipment ■ *adj* **1** physical **2** worldly **3** relevant or important —**ma·te·ri·al·ly** *adv*

ma·te·ri·al·ism /mə téeree ə lìzzəm/ *n* **1** the theory that physical matter is the only reality **2** devotion to wealth and possessions —**ma·te·ri·al·ist** *n* —**ma·te·ri·al·is·tic** /mə tèeree ə lístik/ *adj*

ma·te·ri·al·ize /mə téeree ə līz/ (-ized, -iz·ing) *vi* **1** become real **2** assume a physical form —**ma·te·ri·al·i·za·tion** /mə tèeree əli záysh'n/ *n*

ma·té·ri·el /mə tèeree él/, **ma·te·ri·el** *n* military supplies and equipment

ma·ter·nal /mə túrn'l/ *adj* **1** of or like a mother **2** on or from the mother's side of a family ○ *my maternal grandfather* —**ma·ter·nal·ly** *adv*

ma·ter·ni·ty /mə túrnətee/ *n* **1** motherhood **2** the period during pregnancy or around the time of childbirth (*usually in combination*) ○ *maternity clothes*

ma·ter·ni·ty leave *n* leave from work around the time of childbirth

math /math/ *n* mathematics (*infml*)

math·e·mat·i·cal /màthə máttik'l/ *adj* **1** of mathematics **2** very accurate —**math·e·mat·i·cal·ly** *adv*

math·e·mat·ics /màthə máttiks/ *n* the study of relationships among numbers, shapes, and quantities (+ *sing verb*) ■ *npl* calculations (+ *pl verb*) —**math·e·ma·ti·cian** /màthəmə tísh'n/ *n*

ORIGIN The central importance of mathematics is reflected in its origins. It goes back to a Greek root that meant simply "learn." In the Middle Ages **mathematics** referred to the four subjects that formed the basis of medieval scientific knowledge: geometry, arithmetic, astronomy, and music.

Ma·ther /máthər/, **Cotton** (1663–1728) American minister and theologian

Ma·ther, Increase (1639–1723) American minister

~~mathematics~~ incorrect spelling of **mathematics**

mat·i·née /màtt'n áy/, **mat·i·nee** *n* an afternoon performance

mat·ins /mátt'nz/ *n* in some Christian churches, a morning ceremony or liturgy

Henri Matisse: Photographed in 1948 working on his paper cut-outs

Ma·tisse /mə teéss/, **Henri** (1869–1954) French artist

~~matress~~ incorrect spelling of **mattress**

ma·tri·arch /máytree àark/ n 1 a female head of a family or community 2 a woman in a position of great power or respect —**ma·tri·ar·chal** /máytree áark'l/ adj

ma·tri·ar·chy /máytree àarkee/ n a social order, community, or organization in which women are in charge

mat·ri·cide /máttrə sìd/ n 1 the killing of a mother by her child 2 somebody who commits matricide —**mat·ri·ci·dal** /màttrə síd'l/ adj

ma·tric·u·late /mə tríkyə làyt/ (-lat·ed, -lat·ing) vti admit or be admitted as a college or university student —**ma·tric·u·la·tion** /mə tríkyə láysh'n/ n

mat·ri·mo·ny /máttrə mōnee, máttrəmənee/ n 1 the married state 2 the marriage ceremony —**mat·ri·mo·ni·al** /màttrə mōnee əl/ adj

ma·trix /máytriks/ (pl -tri·ces /-tri seèz/ or -trix·es) n 1 a substance in which something is embedded 2 a situation in which something develops 3 a rectangular arrangement of mathematical elements

ma·tron /máytrən/ n a mature woman

ma·tron·ly /máytrənlee/ adj 1 of or like a matron 2 mature and full-figured

ma·tron of hon·or n a bride's married attendant

matte n = matt²1

mat·ter /máttər/ n 1 something to be considered or dealt with 2 a substance or material o reading matter 3 the material substance of the universe 4 the cause of a problem o What's the matter? 5 printed text 6 the subject of speech or writing ■ **matters** npl circumstances o We were under a lot of stress, which didn't improve matters. ■ vi 1 have importance 2 make a difference ◊ **for that matter** as far as that is concerned ◊ **no matter what** regardless of what happens ◊ See note at **subject**

Mat·ter·horn /máttər hàwrn/ mountain in the Pennine Alps, on the Italian-Swiss border. Height 14,692 ft./4,478 m.

mat·ter of fact n 1 something that is true and cannot be denied 2 a question settled by a court that involves deciding on the truth of a statement ◊ **as a matter of fact** really or actually

mat·ter-of-fact adj 1 straightforward and not emotional 2 factual —**mat·ter-of-fact·ly** adv

Mat·thew /máthyoo/ n the first of the gospels of the Bible in which the life and teachings of Jesus Christ are described, traditionally attributed to St. Matthew

Mat·thew /máthyoo/, **St.** (fl AD 1C) one of the 12 apostles of Jesus Christ

mat·ting /mátting/ n 1 material woven from natural fibers. Use: mats, coverings. 2 mats

mat·tock /máttək/ n a tool like a pickax with a flattened blade at right angles to the handle

mat·tress /máttrəss/ n a pad containing springs or a soft material on which to sleep

ma·ture /mə choor/ adj 1 showing characteristics typical of an adult 2 experienced 3 fully grown or fully developed 4 old and of good flavor 5 involving a period of serious thought o on mature reflection 6 due for payment or repayment o mature bonds ■ vti (-tured, -tur·ing) make or become mature —**mat·u·ra·tion** /màchə ráysh'n/ n —**ma·ture·ly** adv —**ma·ture·ness** n —**ma·tur·i·ty** n

ma·ture stu·dent n a student who has gone into higher education later than usual

mat·zo /maátsə/, **mat·zoh** n (pl -zos or -zoth /maàts òt/; pl -zohs or -zoth) unleavened bread traditionally eaten during Passover ■ adj of or for matzo o matzo meal

Mauch·ly /máwklee/, **John W.** (1907–80) US physicist. He worked with John Eckert on the ENIAC project (1943–46) that developed the first general-purpose electronic digital computer.

maud·lin /máwdlin/ adj tearfully or excessively sentimental

ORIGIN **Maudlin** represents a development of Magdalen, the name given to the woman Mary to whom Jesus Christ was said to have appeared after his resurrection (John 20:1–18). Mary Magdalen became identified with the sinner described in another of the gospels (Luke 8:37), and in art she was shown weeping in repentance. Initially the adjective **maudlin** referred specifically to the weepy stage of drunkenness, first recorded in maudlin-drunk in the early 16C. The more general use of tearfully or excessively sentimental developed in the mid-17C.

Maugham /mawm/, **W. Somerset** (1874–1965) British author

Mau·i /mów ee/ second largest island of Hawaii. Pop. 105,336 (1995).

maul /mawl/ vt 1 batter or tear at o was mauled by a tiger 2 handle roughly 3 criticize fiercely ■ n a pile-driving hammer, usually with a wooden head

maul·vi /mówl weè/ (pl -vis) n an Islamic scholar or instructor in a religious school

Mau·na Ke·a /mòwnə káy ə, màwnə-/ dormant volcano on north central Hawaii Island, Hawaii, the highest peak in the state 13,796 ft./4,205 m

Mau·na Lo·a /-lō ə/ active volcano on south central Hawaii Island, Hawaii. Height 13,680 ft./4,170 m.

maun·der /máwndər/ v 1 vti speak or say in a vague or incoherent way 2 vi move or act aimlessly

Maun·dy Thurs·day /máwndee-/ n a Christian holy day marking the Last Supper. Date: Thursday before Easter Day.

Mau·pas·sant /mố pass oN, mò pass aàN/, **Guy**

de (1850–93) French novelist and short-story writer

Mau·ri·er ♦ du Maurier, Dame Daphne

Mau·ri·ta·ni·a /màwrə táynee ə/ country in NW Africa, on the Atlantic Ocean. Cap. Nouakchott. Pop. 2,747,312 (2001). —**Mauri·ta·ni·an** n, adj

Mau·ri·tius /mə ríshəss/ island country in the SW Indian Ocean, east of Madagascar. Cap. Port Louis. Pop. 1,189,825 (2001). —**Mauri·tian** n, adj

mau·so·le·um /màwzə leě əm, màwssə-/ (pl -ums or -a /-ə/) n 1 a large grand tomb 2 an ornate building that contains tombs

ORIGIN The original **mausoleum** was built in the 4C BC for Mausolus, the king of Caria in Asia Minor, by his widow Artemisia. The word came from Greek through Latin.

mauve /mōv/ n a pale purplish color —**mauve** adj

ma·ven /máyvən/, **ma·vin** n an expert or enthusiast

mav·er·ick /mávərik, mávvrik/ n 1 an independent person who refuses to conform 2 an unbranded animal

ORIGIN Mavericks are probably named for the Texas cattle owner Samuel Augustus Maverick (1803–70), who did not brand some of his calves.

maw n an animal's mouth, throat, or stomach

mawk·ish /máwkish/ adj sentimental in a contrived way —**mawk·ish·ly** adv —**mawk·ish·ness** n

Maw·lid al-Na·bi /màwlid al naàbee/ n in Islam, the celebrations marking the prophet Muhammad's birthday. Date: 12th day of Rabi I.

max n the maximum (infml)
☐ **max out** vti reach the limit of a resource (slang)

max·i /máksee/ n an ankle-length garment ■ adj ankle-length

max·il·la /mak síllə/ (pl -lae /-leě/ or -las) n 1 either of a fused pair of bones forming the upper jaw of vertebrates 2 a mouthpart of an insect or other arthropod —**maxil·lar·y** adj

max·im /máksim/ n 1 a pithy saying with some truth to it 2 a general rule

max·i·mal /máksim'l/ adj 1 of a maximum 2 best possible —**max·i·mal·ly** adv

Max·i·mil·ian /màksi míllyən/ (1832–67) archduke of Austria and emperor of Mexico (1863–67)

max·i·mize /máksi mīz/ (-mized, -miz·ing) vt increase something to the maximum —**max·i·mi·za·tion** /màksimi záysh'n/ n

max·i·mum /máksiməm/ n 1 the greatest possible amount 2 the highest amount or level reached ■ adj of the greatest possible amount or value

may modal v 1 an auxiliary verb indicating that something is possibly true ○ That may be the best way. 2 an auxiliary verb indicating that something ought to happen ○ The crash may have been caused by faulty brakes. 3 an auxiliary verb indicating permission (fml) ○ You may go now. 4 an auxiliary verb indicating a right to do something ○ You may withdraw money from this account at any time. 5 an auxiliary verb indicating polite requests or suggestions ○ May I be of service? 6 an auxiliary verb indicating a wish (fml) ○ May you have a safe journey. ◊ **be that as it may** nevertheless ◊ See note at **can**

May n the 5th month of the year in the Gregorian calendar

ORIGIN May is named for the Roman fertility goddess Maia.

May, Cape cape at the southern tip of New Jersey

Ma·ya[1] /maà yə/ (pl same or -yas), **Ma·yan** /-yən/ n 1 a member of a Native American people of Central America and S Mexico whose classical culture flourished from the 4C to the 8C AD 2 the language of the Maya people —**Ma·ya** adj —**Ma·yan** adj

Ma·ya[2] /maà yə/ n the mother of the Buddha

may·be /máybee/ adv perhaps ○ Maybe he'll come later. ○ "Can I have a new bike?" "Maybe."

may·day /máy dày/ n a distress call from a ship or aircraft

May Day n 1 a day for celebrating the coming of spring. Date: May 1. 2 a holiday in honor of workers. Date: May 1:

May·er /máy ər/, **Louis B.** (1885–1957) Russian-born US movie producer

may·flow·er /máy flòwr/ (pl -ers or same) n 1 a plant that flowers in May 2 a trailing arbutus

may·fly /máy flī/ (pl -flies) n a short-lived flying insect

may·hem /máy hèm/ n 1 chaos or severe disruption 2 malicious injury that disfigures or disables a person

ORIGIN Mayhem is recorded from the late 15C. Another form of the French word from which it derives had been adopted earlier as a noun maim "permanent injury or disfigurement," which is no longer used. The French noun was formed from the verb that gave us maim, which is therefore closely related to mayhem.

may·n't /máynt/ contr may not

may·o /máy ō/ n mayonnaise (infml)

~~mayonaise~~ incorrect spelling of **mayonnaise**

may·on·naise /máy ə nàyz, mày ə náyz/ n a creamy sauce made from egg yolks and oil

ORIGIN There are several conflicting theories about the origin of **mayonnaise**, among them that it is an alteration of *bayonnaise*, as if the sauce originated in Bayonne, in SW France, and that it goes back to French *mayou* "egg yolk." But the early variant spelling *mahonnaise* suggests that it originally meant literally "of Mahon," and that the sauce was so named to commemorate the taking of Port Mahon, the capital of the Balearic island of Menorca, Spain, by the duc de Richelieu in 1756.

may·or /máy ər/ *n* the head of a city or town government —**may·or·al** *adj* —**may·or·ship** *n*

may·or·al·ty /máy ərəl tee/ (*pl* -ties) *n* a mayor's official position or period of office

may·pole /máy pòl/ *n* a decorated pole for May Day celebrations

Mays /mayz/, **Willie** (*b.* 1931) US baseball player

Maz·a·rin /mázər ìn, ma za ráN/, **Jules, Cardinal** (1602–61) Italian-born French cardinal

maze *n* **1** an area of connecting paths designed to be difficult to find a way through **2** a confusing network of paths

Mb *abbr* millibar

⚡ **MB** *abbr* **1** Manitoba **2** megabyte **3** message board (*in e-mails*)

M.B.A., MBA *abbr* Master of Business Administration

Mba·bane /əmba baánee/ capital of Swaziland. Pop. 61,000 (1995).

Mbe·ki /əm békee/, **Thabo** (*b.* 1942) South African president (1999–)

MBO *abbr* management buyout

⚡ **Mbyte** *abbr* megabyte

MC *abbr* **1** Marine Corps **2** master of ceremonies

MCAT /ém kàt/ *tdmk* a trademark for a standardized test taken by applicants to medical schools in the United States. Full form **Medical College Admissions Test**

Mc·Car·thy /mə kaárthee/, **Joseph R.** (1908–57) US politician

Mc·Car·thy·ism /mə kaárthee ìzzəm/ *n* **1** the practice of publicly accusing somebody of having Communist sympathies **2** the practice of unfairly accusing or investigating people —**Mc·Car·thy·ist** *n, adj* —**Mc·Car·thy·ite** *n, adj*

Mc·Clel·lan /mə kléllən/, **George Brinton** (1826–85) US Union army commander

Mc·Cor·mick /mə káwrmik/, **Cyrus Hall** (1809–84) US inventor

Mc·Coy /mə kóy/ ◊ **the real McCoy** a genuine person or thing (*infml*)

Mc·Cul·lers /mə kúllərz/, **Carson** (1917–67) US writer

Mc·En·roe /mákən rò/, **John** (*b.* 1959) US tennis player

Mc·Kin·ley, Mt. /mə kínnlee/ highest mountain in North America, in the Alaska Range,

in south central Alaska. Height 20,320 ft./6,194 m. Also called **Denali**

Mc·Kin·ley, William (1843–1901) 25th president of the United States (1897–1901)

Md *symbol* mendelevium

MD, M.D. *abbr* **1** Doctor of Medicine **2** *also* **Md.** Maryland **3** muscular dystrophy

m/d, M/d *abbr* months after date

MDT *abbr* Mountain Daylight Time

me¹ *pron* refers to the speaker or writer (*as the object or complement of a verb or preposition*) ○ Listen to me. ◊ See note at I¹

me² *n* MUSIC = mi

ME *abbr* **1** *also* **Me.** Maine **2** mechanical engineer **3** mining engineer

me·a cul·pa /máy ə koõl paá/ *interj* expresses an admission of guilt or fault (*fml or humorous*) —**me·a cul·pa** *n*

mead /meed/ *n* an alcoholic drink made from honey

Mead, Lake /meed/ artificial lake on the Arizona-Nevada border, formed by the Hoover Dam on the Colorado River

Mead, Margaret (1901–78) US anthropologist

Meade /meed/, **George Gordon** (1815–72) US Union general

mead·ow /méddō/ *n* a grassy field, sometimes used for producing hay or grazing livestock

mead·ow·lark /méddō laàrk/ (*pl* -larks *or same*) *n* a brown songbird with a yellow breast

mea·ger /meégər/, **mea·gre** *adj* **1** unsatisfactorily small **2** of bad quality —**mea·ger·ly** *adv* —**mea·ger·ness** *n*

meal¹ /meel/ *n* **1** a substantial amount of food eaten at one time **2** a time for eating a meal

meal² /meel/ *n* **1** a cereal ground to a powder **2** a ground-up substance

meals on wheels *n* a service bringing hot meals to people who are unable to leave their homes (*+ sing verb*)

meal tick·et *n* **1** a dependable source of money or support (*infml*) **2** a ticket for a meal

meal·time /meél tìm/ *n* the usual time of a meal

meal·y-mouthed /meèlee-/ *adj* lacking frankness or directness (*disapproving*)

mean¹ /meen/ (**meant** /ment/) *vt* **1** have a particular sense ○ What does this word mean? **2** intend to express a particular idea ○ That's not what I meant. **3** intend to do something ○ didn't mean to upset you **4** be serious in expressing an opinion or intention ○ I'm leaving you. And I mean it this time. **5** be a cause or sign of something ○ This means we'll have to go back.

mean² /meen/ *adj* **1** unkind or malicious **2** cruel **3** shabby **4** excellent (*infml*) ○ He *plays a mean sax.* **5** base or unworthy **6** not generous —**mean·ly** *adv* —**mean·ness** *n*

SYNONYMS mean, nasty, vile, low, base, ignoble CORE MEANING: below normal standards of decency

---

mean³ /meen/ *n* **1** a value intermediate between other values **2** an alternative in the middle of a range of possibilities ■ *adj* **1** medium **2** in an intermediate position

me·an·der /mee ándər/ *vi* **1** follow a twisting route **2** wander slowly and aimlessly ■ *n* **1** a relaxed walk **2** a twist or bend in a route —**me·an·der·ing·ly** *adv*

ORIGIN The original **meandering** river was the Maeander in ancient Phrygia (now the Büyük Menderes in Turkey).

---

mean·ing /meening/ *n* **1** what a word or symbol means **2** what somebody wants to express **3** what something signifies or indicates —**mean·ing·less** *adj* —**mean·ing·less·ly** *adv* —**mean·ing·less·ness** *n*

mean·ing·ful /meeningfəl/ *adj* **1** with a discernible meaning **2** conveying a meaning that is not directly expressed *o a meaningful look* —**mean·ing·ful·ly** *adv* —**mean·ing·ful·ness** *n*

means /meenz/ *n* something enabling somebody to do something (+ *sing or pl verb*) ■ *npl* available money and resources (+ *pl verb*) ◊ **by all means** certainly ◊ **by no means** not at all

means test *n* an examination of somebody's income to establish eligibility for financial aid —**means test·ing** *n*

meant past participle, past tense of **mean¹**

mean·time /meen tìm/ *n* the time between events

mean·while /meen wìl/ *adv* **1** during the time between events **2** while something is happening

Mean·y /meenee/, **George** (1894–1980) US labor leader

mea·sles /meez'lz/ *n* a contagious viral disease producing a rash of red spots (+ *sing or pl verb*) ■ *npl* measles spots (+ *pl verb*)

mea·sly /meezlee/ (-**sli·er**, -**sli·est**) *adj* **1** unsatisfactorily small *(infml)* **2** infected with measles

meas·ure /mézhər/ *n* **1** the size of something **2** a system or standard for determining the size of something **3** a way of evaluating something **4** a unit in a system for determining the size of something **5** an action taken for a particular purpose *(often pl)* **6** something such as a ruler or spoon used to determine size or quantity **7** a standard amount of something such as alcohol **8** a limited, appropriate, or particular extent or amount *o contributed in no small measure to our success* **9** a reasonable or appropriate limit *o His rage had no measure.* **10** a unit

of time into which all music is divided, according to beats **11** a bill or law **12** the rhythm or meter of a piece of poetry ■ *vt* (-**ured**, -**ur·ing**) **1** find the size, length, quantity, or rate of something using a suitable instrument or device **2** assess the effect or quality of something **3** be a particular size, length, quantity, or rate **4** determine the size of somebody for clothes **5** compare the size or quality of something with something else —**meas·ur·a·ble** *adj* —**meas·ur·a·bly** *adv* —**meas·ure·less** *adj* ◊ **for good measure** beyond the amount required

□ **measure up** *vi* be good enough

meas·ured /mézhərd/ *adj* **1** unhurried or reasonable **2** determined by measuring

meas·ure·ment /mézhərmənt/ *n* **1** the size of something measured **2** the measuring of something

meat /meet/ *n* **1** edible animal flesh **2** the edible part of something **3** the important part of something

---

ORIGIN Originally **meat** just meant "food" (as it still does in the phrase *meat and drink*). The restriction to animal flesh developed from the 13C. The word goes back to an ancient root meaning "measure," through reference to a measured portion of food. Another early use, "kind of food," survives in *sweetmeat*.

SPELLCHECK Do not confuse the spelling of **meat** and **meet** ("encounter"), which sound similar.

---

meat and po·ta·toes *n* the most basic or important part (+ *sing or pl verb*) —**meat-and-po·ta·toes** *adj*

meat·ball /meet bàwl/ *n* **1** a small ball of a ground meat **2** somebody regarded as unintelligent *(slang insult)*

meat loaf *n* a loaf-shaped ground meat mixture

meat·pack·ing /meet pàking/ *n* the industry that deals with butchering animals for meat —**meat·pack·er** *n*

meat·y /meetee/ (-**i·er**, -**i·est**) *adj* **1** containing or tasting of meat **2** interesting and thought-provoking —**meat·i·ness** *n*

mec·ca /mékə/ *n* an important or popular center for something

Mec·ca /mékə/ city in W Saudi Arabia. The birthplace of the Prophet Muhammad, it is the holiest city of Islam. Pop. 770,000 (1995).

me·chan·ic /mə kánnik/ *n* somebody who repairs or operates machinery or engines

me·chan·i·cal /mə kánnik'l/ *adj* **1** machine-operated **2** involving or located in a machine or engine **3** done automatically without thinking or feeling —**me·chan·i·cal·ly** *adv*

me·chan·i·cal en·gi·neer·ing *n* the branch of engineering involving machines —**me·chan·i·cal en·gi·neer** *n*

me·chan·i·cal pen·cil *n* a pencil with replaceable lead

me·chan·ics /mə kánniks/ *n* 1 the study of the effect of energy and forces on systems (+ *sing verb*) 2 the design, making, and running of machines (+ *sing or pl verb*) ■ *npl* the details of how something works or is done (+ *pl verb*)

mech·a·nism /mékə nìzzəm/ *n* 1 a machine or machine part that performs a particular task 2 something like a machine o *the fragile mechanism of the planet's ecology* 3 a method or means of doing something 4 the way that something works

mech·a·nis·tic /mèkə nístik/ *adj* 1 explaining natural phenomena by physical causes and processes 2 typical of a machine rather than a thinking feeling human being —**mech·a·nis·ti·cal·ly** *adv*

mech·a·nize /mékə nìz/ (-nized, -niz·ing) *vt* 1 use machinery to do something 2 equip somebody or something with machinery —**mech·a·ni·za·tion** /mèkəni záysh'n/ *n* —**mech·a·nized** *adj*

Mech·e·len /mékələn, mékh-/ city in N Belgium. Pop. 75,689 (1991).

med. *abbr* 1 medical 2 medicine 3 medieval 4 medium

M.Ed. *abbr* Master of Education

med·al /médd'l/ *n* 1 a small flat piece of metal, usually inscribed, given as an award 2 a piece of metal with a religious image, worn as an accessory ■ *vi* (-aled *or* -alled, -al·ing *or* -al·ling) win a medal in a competition

ORIGIN A **medal** is etymologically "something made of metal," and goes back to the Latin and Greek words from which *metal* is derived. **Medal** came into English in the late 16C through French and Italian.

med·al·ist /médd'list/ *n* 1 somebody awarded a medal 2 somebody who designs, makes, or collects medals

me·dal·lion /mə dállyən, -dàllee yáwN/ *n* 1 a large medal 2 a large decorative metal disk worn on a neck chain

Me·dan /may daàn/ city on N Sumatra, Indonesia. Pop. 1,974,300 (1997).

med·dle /médd'l/ (-dled, -dling) *vi* interfere in somebody else's concerns —**med·dler** *n* —**med·dle·some** *adj*

~~medecine~~ incorrect spelling of **medicine**

~~medeval~~ incorrect spelling of **medieval**

Me·del·lín /màydə yeèn/ city in northwest central Colombia. Pop. 1,958,000 (1999).

med·e·vac /méddə vàk/ *n* 1 the evacuation of injured people to a medical facility 2 a helicopter used to evacuate injured people —**med·e·vac** *vt*

me·di·a /meèdee ə/ *n* television, newspapers, and radio collectively (+ *sing or pl verb*) ■ plural of **medium**

USAGE When **media** means the broadcast and print press in general, it takes a singular verb: *The media has covered the story already.* If **media** indicates separate journalistic outlets and their activities, it takes a plural verb: *The media have taken different approaches to coverage of war.* Use **medium**, not **media**, to refer to a single system or method of communication: *Cable television is a relatively inexpensive advertising medium.* Never use the false plural "medias."

me·di·ae·val *adj* = medieval

me·di·al /meèdee əl/ *adj* at the middle —**me·di·al·ly** *adv*

me·di·an /meèdee ən/ *n* 1 a middle point 2 = median strip 3 the middle value of a set of ordered values 4 a midpoint in a frequency distribution 5 a line connecting the vertex of a triangle and the midpoint of the opposite side ■ *adj* 1 in, to, or through the middle 2 of or involving a statistical median

me·di·an strip *n US, Can, Aus* a central strip separating traffic lanes

me·di·a stud·ies *n* the study of the mass media as an academic subject (+ *sing or pl verb*)

me·di·ate /meèdee àyt/ (-at·ed, -at·ing) *v* 1 *vi* intervene to resolve a conflict 2 *vt* achieve a solution to a dispute by bringing both sides to an agreement —**me·di·a·tion** /meèdee áysh'n/ *n* —**me·di·a·tor** *n*

med·ic /méddik/ *n* a member of an army medical corps

Med·i·caid /méddi kàyd/ *n* a program funded by the US and state governments for people who are unable to pay some or all of their medical expenses

med·i·cal /méddik'l/ *adj* of medicine ■ *n* a physical examination by a doctor to determine somebody's state of health —**med·i·cal·ly** *adv*

med·i·cal ex·am·in·er *n* a physician establishing the cause of somebody's death

⌁**med·i·cal te·le·mat·ics** *n* the use of computer networks for the international exchange and retrieval of medical data (+ *sing verb*)

me·dic·a·ment /mə díkəmənt, méddikə-/ *n* a substance used to treat an illness

Med·i·care /méddi kàir/ *n* 1 a US health insurance program under which medical expenses for senior citizens are partially paid by the government 2 **med·i·care** a Canadian health insurance scheme

med·i·cate /méddi kàyt/ (-cat·ed, -cat·ing) *vt* 1 treat a patient with a drug 2 add a drug to —**med·i·cat·ed** *adj*

med·i·ca·tion /mèddi káysh'n/ *n* 1 a drug used to treat an illness 2 treatment of an illness using drugs

Med·i·ci /méddə cheè/ family of Italian bankers and politicians including **Cosimo**

de' (1389–1464), **Lorenzo de'** (1449–92), and **Cosimo I de'** (1519–74)

me·dic·i·nal /mə díssin'l, -díssnəl/ *adj* **1** having properties that can be used to treat illness **2** intended to improve somebody's well-being —**me·dic·i·nal·ly** *adv*

med·i·cine /méddəssin/ *n* **1** a drug or remedy used for treating illness **2** the diagnosis and treatment of illnesses and injuries

med·i·cine man *n* a healer believed to use supernatural powers, especially among Native North American peoples

med·i·co /méddi kò/ (*pl* **-cos**) *n* a doctor or medical student (*infml*)

me·di·e·val /méedee éev'l, mèddee-/, **me·di·ae·val** *adj* **1** of the Middle Ages **2** old-fashioned

Me·di·na /mə déenə/ city in west central Saudi Arabia, site of the Prophet Muhammad's tomb and a holy city of Islam. Pop. 608,300 (1992).

me·di·o·cre /mèe dee ókər, mèe dee òkər/ *adj* adequate but not very good —**me·di·oc·ri·ty** /méedee ókrətee/ *n*

med·i·tate /méddi tàyt/ (**-tat·ed, -tat·ing**) *vi* **1** empty or concentrate the mind for spiritual purposes or relaxation **2** think carefully —**med·i·ta·tion** /mèddi táysh'n/ *n* —**med·i·ta·tive** *adj* —**med·i·ta·tor** *n*

Med·i·ter·ra·ne·an /mèdditə ráynee ən/ *n* **1** the Mediterranean Sea or the surrounding area **2** somebody from around the Mediterranean Sea

Med·i·ter·ra·ne·an Sea inland sea of Europe, Asia, and Africa, linked to the Atlantic Ocean at its western end by the Strait of Gibraltar

~~Mediterranean~~ incorrect spelling of **Mediterranean**

me·di·um /méedee əm/ *adj* **1** neither large nor small **2** cooked between rare and well-done ■ *n* (*pl* **-a** /-ə/ *or* **-ums**) **1** an intermediate state between extremes **2** a means of mass communication **3** a means of conveying ideas or information **4** a substance that carries or transmits something **5** somebody believed to transmit messages between the living and the dead **6** the means by which something is achieved **7** a material for storing or preserving something **8** an artistic method or type of art

me·di·um of ex·change *n* something used like money

me·di·um wave *n* a radio wave of intermediate length

med·ley /méddlee/ (*pl* **-leys**) *n* **1** a musical sequence of different tunes or songs **2** a mixture of things **3** a swimming race with sections using different strokes

me·dul·la /mə dúllə/ (*pl* **-las** *or* **-lae** /-lee/) *n* the innermost part of an organ of a plant or animal —**me·dul·lar** *adj*

meek *adj* **1** mild or quiet by nature **2** submissive and lacking initiative or determination —**meek·ly** *adv* —**meek·ness** *n*

meer·kat /méer kàt/ *n* a South African mongoose

meet[1] /meet/ *v* (**met**) **1** *vti* encounter or get together by chance or arrangement **2** *vti* encounter or be introduced for the first time **3** *vt* go and greet or fetch somebody **4** *vi* gather for a discussion **5** *vti* join or cross ○ *where the two roads meet* **6** *vti* experience something such as a challenge or success ○ *met with failure* **7** *vt* satisfy what is required **8** *vt* agree with somebody about something ○ *meet you on a price* ■ *n* a sports occasion for numbers of competitors and spectators ◊ See note at **meat**

meet[2] /meet/ *adj* appropriate (*archaic*) —**meet·ly** *adv*

meet·ing /méeting/ *n* **1** a gathering of people for a discussion or an event **2** the people at a meeting **3** an occasion when somebody meets somebody else

meet·ing·house /méeting hòwss/ *n* a place where some religious groups, especially Quakers, meet for worship

⚡ **mega-** *prefix* **1** one million (10^6) ○ *megavolt* **2** a binary million (2^{20}) ○ *megabyte* **3** very large or great ○ *megastar* **4** very (*slang*) ○ *megarich*

⚡ **meg·a·bit** /méggə bìt/ *n* **1** 1,048,576 bits **2** one million bits

⚡ **meg·a·byte** /méggə bìt/ *n* **1** 1,048,576 bytes **2** one million bytes

meg·a·death /méggə dèth/ *n* one million deaths

meg·a·dose /méggə dòss/ *n* a very large dose of a medical drug or food supplement

meg·a·hertz /méggə hùrts/ (*pl same*) *n* (*symbol* **MHz**) one million hertz

meg·a·lith /méggə lìth/ *n* a large prehistoric standing stone —**meg·a·lith·ic** /mèggə líthik/ *adj*

meg·a·lo·ma·ni·a /mèggəlō máynee ə, mèggələ-/ *n* **1** the enjoyment of or craving for power **2** a psychiatric disorder in which somebody has delusions of great power and importance —**meg·a·lo·ma·ni·ac** *n, adj* —**meg·a·lo·ma·ni·a·cal** /mə nī ək'l/ *adj*

meg·a·lop·o·lis /mèggə lóppəliss/ *n* **1** an area consisting of several large cities **2** a very large city

meg·a·phone /méggə fòn/ *n* a funnel-shaped device for amplifying the voice ■ *vti* (**-phoned, -phon·ing**) speak through a megaphone

meg·a·star /méggə stàar/ *n* a very well-known celebrity

meg·a·ton /méggə tùn/ *n* **1** a unit of explosive power equivalent to one million tons of TNT **2** one million tons —**meg·a·ton·nage** *n*

meg·a·watt /méggə wòt/ *n* one million watts —**meg·a·watt·age** /méggə wòttij/ *n*

Mei·ji Ten·no /may jèe ténnō/ (1852–1912) emperor of Japan (1867–1912)

mei·o·sis /mī ṓssiss/ *n* the process of cell division in which the nucleus divides into four nuclei, each containing half the usual number of chromosomes —**mei·o·tic** /mī óttik/ *adj*

AKG London

Golda Meir

Me·ir /mī ər, may eêr/, **Golda** (1898–1978) Russian-born Israeli prime minister (1969–74)

meit·ner·i·um /mīt néeree əm/ *n* (*symbol* **Mt**) an unstable radioactive chemical element

Me·ji·a /me hèe a/, **Hipólito** (*b.* 1941) president of the Dominican Republic (2000–)

Me·kong /mee kóng/ major river in Southeast Asia, flowing from SE China through the Indochinese peninsula and into the South China Sea in Vietnam. Length 2,610 mi./ 4,200 km.

mel·a·mine /méllə mèen/ *n* **1** a white crystalline solid. Use: manufacture of synthetic resins, in leather tanning. **2** a type of resin or plastic made from melamine

mel·an·cho·li·a /mèllən kṓlee ə/ *n* depression as a form of psychiatric disorder (*dated*)

mel·an·chol·ic /mèllən kóllik/ *adj* pensively sad

mel·an·chol·y /méllən kòllee/ *adj* feeling or causing pensive sadness ■ *n* pensive sadness

ORIGIN Medieval medical thought attributed physical and mental states to the balance of four bodily substances, of which one was "black bile." Excess of "black bile" was considered to cause depression or **melancholy**, and "black bile" is the literal meaning of the Greek word from which **melancholy** derives.

Mel·a·ne·sia /mèllə néezee ə, -néezhə/ ethnographic grouping of islands of the W Pacific Ocean south of the equator, including New Guinea, the Solomon Islands, New Caledonia, Vanuatu, and Fiji —**Mel·a·ne·sian** *adj, n*

mé·lange /may láaNzh, -láaNzh/, **me·lange** *n* a mixture of things (*literary or fml*)

mel·a·nin /méllənin/ *n* a brown skin pigment

mel·a·no·ma /mèllə nṓmə/ (*pl* **-mas** *or* **-ma·ta** /-mətə/) *n* a malignant skin tumor

mel·a·to·nin /mèllə tṓnin/ *n* a hormone that causes changes in the color of the skin

Mel·ba toast /mélbə-/ *n* thin crisp curling toast

ORIGIN **Melba toast** is named for the Australian opera singer Dame Nellie Melba (1859–1931). It formed part of her diet during an illness in 1897.

Mel·bourne /mélbərn/ capital of Victoria, Australia. Pop. 3,371,300 (1998).

meld[1] *vti* combine or blend —**meld** *n*

meld[2] *vti* show a hand of cards to score points —**meld** *n*

me·lee /máy lày, may láy/, **mê·lée** /me láy/ *n* **1** a confused fight **2** a confused mingling of people or things

mel·lif·lu·ous /mə líffloo əss/, **mel·lif·lu·ent** /-ənt/ *adj* pleasant to hear

mel·low /méllō/ *adj* **1** soft and rich in color or tone **2** smooth and rich in taste **3** fully ripe **4** easygoing —**mel·low** *vti* —**mel·low·ly** *adv* —**mel·low·ness** *n*

me·lod·ic /mə lóddik/ *adj* of, consisting of, or characteristic of melody —**me·lod·i·cal·ly** *adv*

me·lo·di·ous /mə lṓdee əss/ *adj* **1** having a pleasant melody **2** characterized by melody —**me·lo·di·ous·ly** *adv* —**me·lo·di·ous·ness** *n*

mel·o·dra·ma /méllə draàmə, -dràmmə/ *n* **1** a dramatic or literary work with stereotyped characters, exaggerated emotions and language, and sensationalized events **2** an exaggerated or excessively dramatic situation or type of behavior

mel·o·dra·mat·ic /mèllə drə máttik/ *adj* **1** exaggeratedly theatrical **2** of melodrama —**mel·o·dra·mat·i·cal·ly** *adv*

mel·o·dy /mélladee/ (*pl* **-dies**) *n* **1** a series of musical notes forming a tune **2** the main tune in a piece of music

mel·on /méllən/ *n* **1** a round edible fruit with a tough rind and sweet juicy flesh **2** a plant that produces melons

ORIGIN **Melon** goes back to a Greek word that actually meant "apple." It formed a compound with another word meaning "gourd," which passed into Latin. In late Latin this compound was shortened, but etymologically speaking the wrong element was dropped, and the part meaning literally "apple" was left referring to a gourd.

melt *v* **1** *vti* change from a solid to a liquid state because of heat **2** *vti* dissolve **3** *vi* disappear or merge gradually **4** *vti* move or be moved emotionally ■ *n* **1** a period during which snow and ice thaw **2** a grilled sandwich with melted cheese on top

melt·down /mélt dòwn/ *n* **1** the melting of nuclear reactor fuel rods that results in a radiation leak **2** complete collapse (*infml*)

melt·ing /mélting/ *adj* full of or causing sweet and tender emotions —**melt·ing·ly** *adv*

melt·ing point *n* the temperature at which something changes from a solid to a liquid form

melt·ing pot *n* a society composed of many different cultures

Mel·ville /mélvil/, **Herman** (1819–91) US writer

Mel·ville Is·land uninhabited island in NW Canada

mem·ber /mémbər/ *n* **1** somebody who belongs to a particular group or organization **2** *also* **Mem·ber** a representative elected to a legislative body **3** a limb **4** an individual part of a whole

Mem·ber of Par·lia·ment *n* somebody elected to a parliament

mem·ber·ship /mémbər ship/ *n* **1** the state of belonging to a particular group or organization **2** the members of an organization

mem·brane /mém bràyn/ *n* **1** a thin layer of animal or plant tissue covering, lining, or separating organs **2** a thin pliable porous sheet of material —**mem·bra·nous** /-brənəss/ *adj*

me·men·to /mə méntô/ (*pl* **-tos** *or* **-toes**) *n* a souvenir

mem·o /mémmô/ (*pl* **-os**) *n* **1** a written communication circulated in an office **2** a note serving as a reminder

mem·oir /mém wàar/ *n* a biography or historical account written from personal knowledge ■ **mem·oirs** *npl* **1** an autobiography **2** the proceedings of a learned society —**mem·oir·ist** *n*

mem·o·ra·bil·i·a /mèmmərə bíllee ə/ *npl* **1** objects connected with a famous person **2** personal souvenirs

mem·o·ra·ble /mémmərəb'l/ *adj* **1** worth remembering **2** easily remembered —**mem·o·ra·bil·i·ty** /mèmmərə bíllətee/ *n* —**mem·o·ra·bly** *adv*

mem·o·ran·dum /mèmmə rándəm/ (*pl* **-dums** *or* **-da** /-də/) *n* **1** an office memo **2** a note serving as a reminder

me·mo·ri·al /mə máwree əl/ *n* **1** a commemorative object or event **2** a statement of facts accompanying a petition ■ *adj* commemorative —**me·mo·ri·al·ly** *adv*

Me·mo·ri·al Day *n* a US holiday to commemorate soldiers who died in war. Date: last Monday in May.

mem·o·rize /mémmə rìz/ (**-rized, -riz·ing**) *vt* learn and remember —**mem·o·ri·za·tion** /mèmməri záysh'n/ *n*

⚡ **mem·o·ry** /mémməree/ (*pl* **-ries**) *n* **1** the ability to retain and retrieve knowledge of past events and experiences **2** somebody's stock of retained knowledge and experience **3** the retained impression of a particular person, event, or subject **4** the act of remembering **5** *also* **mem·o·ry bank** the part of a computer where data is stored for quick retrieval **6** the data storage capacity of a computer

Mem·phis /mémfiss/ **1** ruined city and capital

of ancient Egypt **2** city in SW Tennessee. Pop. 603,507 (1998). —**Mem·phi·an** *n, adj*

mem·sa·hib /mem saáb/ *n S Asia* a former way of addressing a married European woman

men·ace /ménnəss/ *n* **1** a possible source of danger **2** a nuisance (*infml*) ■ *v* (**-aced, -ac·ing**) **1** *vt* be dangerous to **2** *vti* threaten —**men·ac·ing** *adj* —**men·ac·ing·ly** *adv*

mén·age /may naázh/ *n* (*fml*) **1** a household **2** the management of a house

mén·age à trois /màv naazh aa trwaá/ (*pl* **mén·ages à trois** /*pronunc. same*/) *n* a sexual arrangement involving three people

me·nag·er·ie /mə nájjəree/ *n* **1** a collection of captive wild animals exhibited to the public **2** an enclosure for exhibited wild animals

Menck·en /méngkən/, **H. L.** (1880–1956) US journalist and critic

mend *v* **1** *vti* restore something to a satisfactory condition **2** *vt* remove damage such as a hole **3** *vti* improve **4** *vi* recover or heal ■ *n* a repair —**mend·a·ble** *adj* —**mend·er** *n*

men·da·cious /men dáyshəss/ *adj* **1** having a tendency to tell lies **2** deliberately untrue —**men·dac·i·ty** /men dássətee/ *n*

Men·del /ménd'l/, **Gregor Johann** (1822–84) Austrian monk and scientist. He developed the principles of heredity and laid the basis of modern genetics. —**Men·de·li·an** /mèn déelyən/ *adj*

men·de·le·vi·um /mèndə léevee əm/ *n* (*symbol* **Md**) a synthetic short-lived radioactive element

Men·de·le·yev /mèndə líyəv/, **Dmitry Ivanovich** (1834–1907) Russian chemist. He formulated the periodic law of elements and devised the periodic table (1869).

Men·dels·sohn /ménd'lssən/, **Felix** (1809–47) German composer

men·di·cant /méndikənt/ *adj* begging and living on charity ■ *n* **1** a beggar (*fml*) **2** a member of a religious order that lives by begging

Men·e·la·us /mènnə láyəss/ *n* in Greek mythology, the king of Sparta and husband of Helen of Troy

men·folk /mén fôk/, **men·folks** /-fôks/ *npl* **1** the men associated with a family or group **2** men in general

men·hir /mén hèer/ *n* a single standing stone erected by prehistoric people

me·ni·al /méenee əl/ *adj* **1** of or involving unskilled work that confers low social status on those doing it **2** of servants ■ *n* a domestic servant —**me·ni·al·ly** *adv*

men·in·gi·tis /mènnin jítiss/ *n* a severe illness involving inflammation of the membranes around the brain and spinal cord —**men·in·git·ic** /-jíttik/ *adj*

Men·non·ite /ménnə nìt/ *n* a member of a Protestant group emphasizing adult baptism and pacifism —**Men·non·it·ism** n

ORIGIN Mennonite was adopted from German in the mid-16C. It comes from the name of Menno Simons (1496–1561), an early leader of the group.

men·o·pause /ménnə pàwz/ n the time in a woman's life when she stops menstruating —**men·o·paus·al** /mènnə páwz'l/ adj

me·no·rah /mə náwrə/ n 1 a six-branched ceremonial candlestick used in the Jewish Temple 2 an eight-branched candlestick lit during Hanukkah

Me·not·ti /mə nóttee/, **Gian-Carlo** (b. 1911) Italian-born US composer

Men·sa /ménssə/ n a constellation in the southern hemisphere that forms part of the larger Magellanic Cloud

men·ses /mén seèz/ n (technical; + sing or pl verb) 1 menstruation 2 menstrual discharge

men's room n a public toilet for men

men·stru·al /ménstroo əl/ adj of menstruation

men·stru·al cy·cle n the month-long cycle during which a woman menstruates once (fml)

men·stru·ate /ménstroo àyt/ (-at·ed, -at·ing) vi discharge blood and other matter from the womb as part of the menstrual cycle —**men·stru·a·tion** /mènstroo áysh'n/ n

men·tal /mént'l/ adj 1 of the mind 2 carried out in the mind ○ mental arithmetic —**men·tal·ly** adv

men·tal age n a measure of intellectual development according to the norms of children of the same age

men·tal·i·ty /men tállətee/ (pl -ties) n 1 somebody's habitual way of thinking 2 somebody's intellectual ability

men·thol /mén thàwl/ n a mint-tasting compound made from peppermint oil. Use: flavorings, perfumes, mild anesthetic. —**men·tho·lat·ed** adj

men·tion /ménshən/ v 1 vti use a particular word or name when speaking or writing 2 vt acknowledge somebody for exceptional conduct ■ n an honorable mention —**men·tion·a·ble** adj ◇ **not to mention** besides

men·tor /mén tàwr, méntər/ n 1 an experienced adviser and guide for somebody younger 2 somebody who trains and helps a junior colleague

ORIGIN In Greek mythology, Mentor was the teacher and protector of Odysseus' son Telemachus.

⚡**men·u** /ménnyoò/ n 1 a list of available dishes at a restaurant or formal meal 2 a list of options, e.g., program options on a computer

⚡**men·u-driv·en** adj operated using computer menus

me·ow /mee ów/ n a characteristic cry of a cat ■ vi utter meows

Meph·i·stoph·e·les /mèffi stóffə leèz/, **Me·phis·to** /mə fístó/ n in medieval mythology, a subordinate of Satan —**Me·phis·to·phe·le·an** /mə fìstə feélyən, -feèlee ən/ adj

mer·can·tile /múrkən tìl/ adj of merchants or trading

Mer·ca·tor /mur káytər/, **Gerardus** (1512–94) Flemish geographer, cartographer, and mathematician

mer·ce·nar·y /múrs'n èrree/ (pl -ies) n 1 a professional soldier paid to fight in the army of another country 2 somebody motivated only by money —**mer·ce·nar·y** adj

mer·chan·dise n /múrchən dìz, -dìss/ goods for sale ■ v /múrchən dìz/ (-dised, -dis·ing) also **mer·chan·dize** (-dized, -diz·ing) 1 vti trade in goods commercially 2 vt promote a product for sale —**mer·chan·dis·er** n

mer·chan·dis·ing /múrchən dìzing/ n 1 the promotion of products for sale 2 spin-off products from a movie, TV program, sports team, or event

mer·chant /múrchənt/ n 1 a dealer in wholesale goods 2 a retailer ■ adj 1 of trade or merchants 2 of a merchant marine

⚡**mer·chant ac·count** n a bank account for depositing payments made by credit card, used especially in Internet trading

mer·chant cer·tif·i·cate au·thor·i·ty n a certificate authority supplying certificates to merchants

mer·chant·man /múrchəntmən/ (pl -men /-mən/), **mer·chant ship** n an oceangoing cargo ship

mer·chant ma·rine n a country's merchant ships, or the sailors who serve in them

Mer·ci·a /múrshee ə, múrshə/ ancient Anglo-Saxon kingdom of central England —**Mer·ci·an** adj, n

mer·ci·ful /múrssif'l/ adj 1 showing mercy 2 welcome because of ending something unpleasant —**mer·ci·ful·ly** adv

mer·ci·less /múrsiləss/ adj 1 showing no mercy 2 strict and intolerant —**mer·ci·less·ly** adv —**mer·ci·less·ness** n

mer·cu·ri·al /mər kyóoree əl/ adj 1 lively and unpredictable 2 containing mercury

mer·cu·ry /múrkyəree/ n 1 (symbol Hg) a poisonous liquid metallic element. Use: in thermometers and barometers, dental fillings, lamps. 2 the mercury in a weather thermometer or barometer, or the temperature or pressure it indicates

Mer·cu·ry /múrkyəree/ n 1 in Roman mythology, the god of commerce who was the messenger of the gods. Greek equivalent **Hermes** 2 the planet in the solar system nearest the Sun

mer·cy /múrsee/ (pl -cies) n 1 compassion or forgiveness 2 a compassionate forgiving disposition **3** something to be thankful for

Mer·cy Corps *n* a group of trained American Red Cross volunteers, ready to assist during sudden disasters

mer·cy kill·ing *n* euthanasia, or an act of euthanasia

mere /meer/ (*superlative* **mer·est**) *adj* **1** just what is specified and nothing more ○ *She was no mere journalist.* **2** by itself and without anything more ○ *the mere mention of his name* —**mere·ly** *adv*

mer·e·tri·cious /mèrrə tríshəss/ *adj* **1** superficially attractive but without real value *(fml)* **2** misleadingly plausible or significant ○ *swayed by a meretricious argument*

merge /murj/ (**merged, merg·ing**) *vti* **1** combine into a single entity **2** blend together gradually —**merg·ing** *n*

merg·er /múrjər/ *n* **1** a combining of two or more companies **2** a blend or combination

Mé·ri·da /mérree dàà/ capital of Yucatán State, SE Mexico. Pop. 649,770 (1995).

me·rid·i·an /mə ríddee ən/ *n* **1** a line of longitude between the North and South poles **2** either half of the circle of the meridian, from pole to pole **3** a great circle of the celestial sphere passing through the celestial poles **4** *Midwest* a median separating traffic lanes

me·ringue /mə ráng/ *n* **1** a cooked mixture of whipped egg whites and sugar **2** a meringue cookie or shell

mer·it /mérrit/ *n* **1** value that deserves respect and acknowledgment **2** a good quality *(often pl)* ■ **mer·its** *npl* the facts of a matter considered objectively ■ *vt* be worthy of or deserve

mer·i·toc·ra·cy /mèrri tókrəssee/ (*pl* -**cies**) *n* **1** a social system based on ability **2** an elite group of people who achieved their position on the basis of their ability —**mer·it·o·crat·ic** /mèrritə kráttik/ *adj*

mer·i·to·ri·ous /mèrri táwree əss/ *adj* deserving honor and recognition —**mer·i·to·ri·ous·ly** *adv*

Mer·lin /múrlin/ *n* in Arthurian legend, a magician and adviser to King Arthur

mer·maid /múr màyd/ *n* a mythical sea creature with the upper body of a woman and the tail of a fish instead of legs

ORIGIN The *mer-* of **mermaid** represents an old word *mere* "sea." *Mere* goes back to the same root as Latin *mare* "sea," from which words like *marine* and *mariner* derive.

mer·ry /mérree/ (-**ri·er**, -**ri·est**) *adj* lively and cheerful ○ *a merry laugh* —**mer·ri·ly** *adv* —**mer·ri·ment** *n* —**mer·ri·ness** *n*

mer·ry-go-round *n* **1** an amusement park ride consisting of a rotating platform with moving seats shaped like animals **2** a revolving piece of playground equipment for children to sit on and push or be pushed

mer·ry·mak·ing /mérree màyking/ *n* lively celebration —**mer·ry·mak·er** *n*

Mer·sey /múrzee/ river in NW England. Length 70 mi./110 km.

me·sa /máyssə/ *n* a flat steep-sided elevated area in the SW United States

Me·sa /máyssə/ city in south central Arizona. Pop. 360,076 (1998).

Me·sa·bi Range /mə sáabee-/ range of hills in NE Minnesota, known for their rich deposits of iron ore. Length 130 mi./210 km.

mes·cal /mess kál/ (*pl* -**cals** *or same*) *n* **1** a Mexican liquor distilled from some species of agave **2** the peyote cactus

mes·ca·line /méskə lèen, mésskəlin/ *n* a hallucinogenic drug extracted from the nodules of the peyote cactus

Mes·dames 1 plural of **Madame 2** plural of **Madam**

mes·de·moi·selles plural of **mademoiselle**

mesh *n* **1** material like net ○ *wire mesh* **2** one of the openings in the threads or wires of a net **3** the threads or wires of a net **4** something that traps or entangles *(often pl)* ■ *vti* **1** fit together **2** catch or entangle, or become caught or entangled **3** make gear teeth engage, or become engaged

Me·sic /máysich/, **Stjepan** (*b.* 1934) president of Croatia (2000–)

mes·mer·ic /mez mérrik/ *adj* fascinating or hypnotic —**mes·mer·i·cal·ly** *adv*

mes·mer·ize /mézmə rìz/ (-**ized**, -**iz·ing**) *vt* **1** absorb the attention of **2** hypnotize —**mes·mer·i·za·tion** /mèzməri záysh'n/ *n* —**mes·mer·iz·ing·ly** *adv*

ORIGIN The first people to be **mesmerized** were patients of the Austrian doctor Franz Anton Mesmer (1734–1815), who conducted experiments in which he induced trance-like states in his subjects.

mes·on /mé zòn, mée-/ *n* an elementary particle that has a mass between that of an electron and proton and participates in the strong interaction —**me·son·ic** /me zónnik, mée-/ *adj*

Mes·o·po·ta·mi·a /mèssəpə táymee ə/ ancient region of W Asia, between the Tigris and Euphrates rivers in present-day Iraq. It was the site of several early civilizations, including Babylonia. —**Mes·o·po·ta·mi·an** *n, adj*

mes·o·sphere /mézzə sfèer, méssə-/ *n* the atmospheric layer between the stratosphere and thermosphere —**mes·o·spher·ic** /mèzzə sférrik, mèssə-, -sféerik/ *adj*

Mes·o·zo·ic /mèzzə zố ik, mèssə-/ *n* an era of geologic time 248–65 million years ago —**Mes·o·zo·ic** *adj*

mes·quite /me skéet/ (*pl same or* -**quites**) *n* **1** a hard wood often burned in a barbecue to flavor food **2** a small spiny tree that produces mesquite wood

mess n 1 an untidy condition or dirty state 2 a chaotic state 3 a place for communal meals 4 a group of people who eat communally 5 a serving or quantity of food ■ v 1 vi meddle 2 vi use something carelessly so as to cause a problem or damage ○ *messing with his computer* 3 vt make untidy or dirty
□ **mess up** vti bungle something (*infml*)

mes·sage /méssij/ n 1 a communication in speech, writing, or signals 2 a lesson or moral that somebody wants to communicate, e.g., in a work of art ■ vt (-saged, -sag·ing) send a message to —**mes·sag·ing** n

✦ **mes·sage board** n an online bulletin board
~~messanger~~ incorrect spelling of **messenger**

mes·sen·ger /méss'njər/ n 1 somebody carrying a message 2 a paid courier ■ vt send by messenger

mess hall n a place for communal meals, especially in the armed forces

Mes·siaen /mèss yaáN, -yaàN, Olivier** (1908–92) French composer and organist

mes·si·ah /mə sí ə/ n 1 a savior or liberator 2 **Mes·si·ah** in the Hebrew Bible, an anointed king who will lead the Jews back to the land of Israel and establish justice in the world 3 **Mes·si·ah** in Christianity, Jesus Christ regarded as the Messiah prophesied in the Hebrew Bible

mes·si·an·ic /mèssee ánnik/ adj 1 also **Mes·si·an·ic** of the Messiah 2 involving great enthusiasm —**mes·si·an·i·cal·ly** adv

Mes·sieurs plural of **Monsieur**

Mes·si·na /me seénə/ city in NE Sicily, Italy. Pop. 261,134 (1999).

Messrs. plural of **Mr.**

mess·y /méssee/ (-i·er, -i·est) adj 1 dirty or untidy 2 difficult to resolve or deal with —**mess·i·ly** adv —**mess·i·ness** n

mes·ti·zo /mes teézō/ (pl -zos or -zoes) n a person of mixed ancestry, especially Native American and European

met past tense, past participle of **meet**[1]

meta- prefix 1 later, behind ○ *metacarpus* ○ *metatarsus* 2 beyond, transcending, encompassing ○ *metalanguage*

me·tab·o·lism /mə tábbə lìzzəm/ n 1 the processes by which food is converted into the energy and products needed to sustain life 2 the biochemical activity of a particular substance in a living organism —**met·a·bol·ic** /mèttə bóllik/ adj —**met·a·bol·i·cal·ly** adv

me·tab·o·lite /mə tábbə lìt/ n a byproduct of metabolism

me·tab·o·lize /mə tábbə lìz/ (-lized, -liz·ing) vti subject or be subjected to metabolism

met·a·car·pus /mèttə kaàrpəss/ (pl -pi /-pì/) n 1 a set of five long bones in the human hand between the wrist and fingers 2 the forefoot or hand of a vertebrate between the wrist and digits —**met·a·car·pal** adj, n

Met·a·com·et /méttə kòmət/, **Met·a·com** /méttə kòm/ ♦ **Philip**

Met·ai·rie /méttə rèe/ city in SE Louisiana. Pop. 149,428 (1996).

met·al /métt'l/ n 1 a solid shiny chemical element that is malleable, ductile, and able to conduct heat and electricity well 2 a mixture of one or more metals 3 heavy metal music (*slang*) ■ vt (-aled or -alled, -al·ing or -al·ling) cover or provide with metal —**met·al·loid** n, adj

met·a·lan·guage /méttə làng gwij/ n language used to describe language

met·al de·tec·tor n 1 a device for detecting buried metal objects 2 a screening device for detecting weapons

me·tal·lic /mə tállik/ adj 1 of, containing, or typical of metal 2 shiny 3 tasting of metal —**me·tal·li·cal·ly** adv

met·al·lur·gy /métt'l ùrjee/ n the study of metals and the procedures for extracting, refining, and making things from them —**met·al·lur·gic** /métt'l úrjik/ adj —**met·al·lur·gi·cal** adj —**met·al·lur·gist** n

met·al·work /métt'l wùrk/ n 1 the making of metal objects 2 metal objects —**met·al·work·er** n —**met·al·work·ing** n

met·a·mor·phic /mèttə máwrfik/, **met·a·mor·phous** /-fəss/ adj 1 by or from metamorphism 2 of metamorphosis

met·a·mor·phose /mèttə máwr fòz, -fòss/ (-phosed, -phos·ing) vti change or cause to change by metamorphosis

met·a·morph·ism /mèttə máwr fìzzəm/ n the process by which the physical structure of rocks changes as a result of heat and pressure

met·a·mor·pho·sis /mèttə máwrfəssiss/ (pl -ses /-seèz/) n 1 a change of physical form, appearance, or character 2 a supposed supernatural transformation

met·a·phor /méttə fàwr/ n 1 the application of a word or phrase to somebody or something, meant not literally, but to make a comparison, e.g., saying that somebody is a snake 2 figurative language —**met·a·phor·i·cal** /méttə fáwrik'l/ adj —**met·a·phor·i·cal·ly** adv

met·a·phys·i·cal /mèttə fízzik'l/ adj 1 of metaphysics 2 based on speculative reasoning 3 abstract or theoretical —**met·a·phys·i·cal·ly** adv

met·a·phys·ics /mèttə fízziks/, **met·a·phys·ic** /-fízzik/ n the branch of philosophy dealing with the nature of being and beings (+ sing verb)

me·tas·ta·sis /mə tástəssiss/ (pl -ses /-seèz/) n 1 the spread of cancer through the body 2 a malignant tumor that has developed as a result of the spread of cancer cells —**met·a·stat·ic** /mèttə státtik/ adj

met·a·tar·sus /mèttə táarsəss/ (pl -si /-sì, -see/) n 1 a set of five long bones in the human foot between the ankle and the toes

2 the hind foot of a vertebrate between the ankle and toes —**met·a·tar·sal** *adj, n*

mete /meet/ (**met·ed, met·ing**) ☐ **mete out** *vt* give out something such as punishment or justice, especially in a harsh or unfair way

me·te·or /meetee ər, -àwr/ *n* **1** a mass of rock from space that burns up on entering the atmosphere **2** the light from a burning meteor

me·te·or·ic /meetee áwrik/ *adj* **1** of meteors **2** very fast or brilliant —**me·te·or·i·cal·ly** *adv*

me·te·or·ite /meetee ə rìt/ *n* a rock from outer space that has reached the Earth

me·te·or·ol·o·gy /meetee ə róllajee/ *n* the scientific study of the weather —**me·te·or·o·log·i·cal** /-ərə lójjik'l/ *adj* —**me·te·or·ol·o·gist** *n*

me·ter¹ /meetər/ *n* a rhythmic pattern in verse or music

me·ter² /meetər/ *n* (*symbol* **m**) the basic SI unit of length, equivalent to 39.37 in

me·ter³ /meetər/ *n* **1** a device for measuring the amount or flow of something **2** a parking meter —**me·ter** *vt*

-meter *suffix* measuring device ○ *thermometer*

meth·a·done /métha dòn/, **meth·a·don** /-dòn/ *n* a synthetic painkilling drug. Use: substitute for heroin in the treatment of addiction.

meth·am·phet·a·mine /mèth am fétta mèen, -min/ *n* a form of the stimulant amphetamine

meth·ane /mé thàyn/ *n* a colorless odorless flammable gas that is the main constituent of natural gas. Use: fuel.

meth·a·nol /métha nàwl/ *n* a colorless volatile poisonous liquid. Use: solvent, fuel, in antifreeze for motor vehicles.

me·thinks /mi thíngks/ (**-thought** /-tháwt/) *vi* it seems to me (*humorous or archaic*)

meth·od /méthad/ *n* **1** a planned way of doing something **2** orderliness

me·thod·i·cal /ma thóddik'l/, **me·thod·ic** /-ik/ *adj* systematic or painstaking —**me·thod·i·cal·ly** *adv* —**me·thod·i·cal·ness** *n*

Meth·od·ist /méthadist/ *n* an evangelical Protestant church founded in the 18C by John Wesley and his followers —**Meth·od·ism** *n* —**Meth·od·ist** *adj* —**Meth·od·is·tic** /mètha dístik/ *adj*

meth·od·ol·o·gy /mètha dóllajee/ (*pl* **-gies**) *n* **1** the methods or organizing principles underlying an area of study **2** in philosophy, the study of organizing principles and underlying rules —**meth·od·o·log·i·cal** /méthada lójjik'l/ *adj* —**meth·od·o·log·i·cal·ly** *adv* —**meth·od·ol·o·gist** *n*

me·thu·se·lah /ma thóozala/, **Me·thu·se·lah** *n* a wine bottle holding the equivalent of 8 normal bottles

ORIGIN According to the Bible, Methuselah

was an ancestor of Noah and lived 969 years (Gen 5: 21–27).

meth·yl al·co·hol /méthal-/ *n* methanol

meth·yl·at·ed spir·it /métha laytad-/, **meth·yl·at·ed spir·its** *n* ethanol with methanol and a violet dye added. Use: fuel, solvents.

met·i·cal /métti kàl, mètti kaál/ (*pl* **-cais** or **-cals**) *n* the main unit of Mozambican currency

me·tic·u·lous /ma tíkyaless/ *adj* precise and painstaking —**me·tic·u·lous·ly** *adv* —**me·tic·u·lous·ness** *n* ◊ See note at **careful**

mé·tier /me tyáy, may-/, **me·tier** *n* **1** somebody's occupation or trade **2** an activity that somebody is particularly good at

Me·tis /may tée, -teéss/ (*pl* **-tis** /-teéz/) *n* a Canadian of mixed Aboriginal and European descent

me·ton·y·my /ma tónnamee/ *n* a figure of speech in which an attribute of a thing stands for the thing itself

me·tre *n* UK = **meter²**

met·ric /méttrik/ *adj* **1** of the metric system **2** *also* **met·ri·cal** of poetic meter —**met·ri·cal·ly** *adv*

met·ric sys·tem *n* a decimal system of weights and measures based on units such as the kilogram and the meter

met·ric ton *n* (*symbol* **t**) a unit of weight equal to 1000 kg

met·ro·nome /méttra nòm/ *n* a device that indicates a given musical tempo, either aurally or visually —**met·ro·nom·ic** /mèttra nómmik/ *adj*

me·trop·o·lis /ma tróppaliss/ *n* a large city ◊ See note at **city**

ORIGIN Metropolis goes back to a Greek word meaning literally "mother city." It entered English via Latin in the mid-16C.

met·ro·pol·i·tan /mèttra póllit'n/ *adj* **1** forming a large city **2** of or characteristic of a metropolis **3** of the home territory of a country rather than its territories elsewhere ■ *n* **1** an inhabitant of a metropolis **2** in Christianity, a high-ranking church official **3** the head of the Russian Orthodox Church

Met·ter·nich /méttar nĭkh/, **Klemens Wenzel Nepomuk Lothar von, Prince of Metternich-Winneburg-Beilstein** (1773–1859) German-born Austrian chancellor of the Hapsburg Empire (1821–48)

met·tle /métt'l/ *n* **1** spirit or strength of character **2** somebody's temperament —**met·tle·some** *adj* ◊ See note at **courage**

ORIGIN Mettle is actually a form of *metal*. Both spellings were formerly used for both words, even into the 19C, though 18C dictionaries had recognized the distinction. Although mettle is in origin a figurative or metaphorical use of *metal*, any conscious mental association between the two was lost long ago.

mew[1] /myoo/ *vi* make a high-pitched cry (*refers to cats and kittens*) —**mew** *n*

mew[2] /myoo/ *n* a seagull

mewl /myool/ *vi* cry weakly

Mex·i·cal·i /mèksə kálleé/ city in NW Mexico. Pop. 696,034 (1995).

Mex·i·can A·mer·i·can *n* an American of Mexican descent

Mex·i·co /méksi kò/ country in S North America. Cap. Mexico City. Pop. 101,879,170 (2001). —**Mex·i·can** /méksikən/ *adj, n*

Mex·i·co, Gulf of arm of the Atlantic Ocean, east of Mexico and south of the United States

Mex·i·co City capital of Mexico. Pop. 9,800,000 (1995).

mez·za·nine /mézz'n eën, mèzz'n eën/ *n* **1** *also* **mez·za·nine floor** a low story, especially one between the 1st and 2nd floors of a building **2** the lowest balcony in a theater ■ *adj* describes an intermediate range of investment

mez·zo /métsō, médzō/ *adv* moderately (*musical direction*) ■ *n* (*pl* **-zos**) *also* **mez·zo·so·pran·o** a woman singer with a range between a soprano and a contralto

mez·zo·tint /métsō tìnt, médzō-/ *n* **1** an engraving process that involves scraping and burnishing a copper plate **2** a mezzotint print —**mez·zo·tint** *vt*

M.F.A. *abbr* Master of Fine Arts

mg *symbol* milligram

Mg *symbol* magnesium

MG *abbr* Major General

mgr. *abbr* manager

Mgr. *abbr* Monsignor

MHz *symbol* megahertz

mi /mee/, **me** *n* a syllable used in singing the 3rd note of a scale

MI *abbr* **1** Michigan **2** Military Intelligence

mi. *abbr* mile

MIA *n* a soldier reported missing in action. Full form **missing in action**

Mi·am·i /mī ámmee/ city in SE Florida. Pop. 368,624 (1998).

Mi·am·i Beach city in SE Florida, on an island opposite Miami. Pop. 97,053 (1998).

mi·as·ma /mī ázmə, mee-/ (*pl* **-mas** *or* **-ma·ta** /-mətə/) *n* **1** a harmful or poisonous vapor **2** an unwholesome atmosphere

mi·ca /míkə/ *n* a shiny mineral compound of aluminum and silicon. Use: electrical insulators, heating elements.

Mi·cah /míkə/ *n* a book of the Bible, traditionally attributed to Micah, a Hebrew prophet

mice plural of **mouse**

Mich. *abbr* Michigan

Mich·ael·mas /mík'lməss/ (*pl* **-mas·es**) *n* a traditional Christian feast day. Date: September 29.

Mi·chel·an·ge·lo /mìk'l ánjəlō/ (1475–1564) Italian sculptor, painter, architect, and poet

Mich·i·gan /míshigən/ state in the N United States. Cap. Lansing. Pop. 9,938,444 (2000). —**Mich·i·gan·der** /mìshi gándər/ *n* —**Mich·i·gan·ite** *n, adj*

Mich·i·gan, Lake third largest of the Great Lakes, in the N United States

Mic·mac *n, adj* PEOPLES, LANG = **Mi'kmaq**

mi·cro /míkrō/ *adj* very small

micro- *prefix* **1** small, minute ○ *microcosm* **2** using a microscope or requiring magnification ○ *microbiology* **3** one millionth (10^{-6}) ○ *microgram* ○ *microsecond* **4** of a small area or on a small scale ○ *micromanage*

mi·crobe /mī krōb/ *n* a microscopic organism that transmits disease —**mi·cro·bi·al** /mī krōbee əl/ *adj*

ORIGIN Microbe is formed from Greek elements that mean literally "small life." It was coined in French in 1878, and adopted into English a few years later.

---

mi·cro·bi·ol·o·gy /mìkrō bī óllə jee/ *n* the scientific study of microscopic organisms —**mi·cro·bi·o·log·i·cal** /mìkrō bī ə lójjik'l/ *adj*

mi·cro·brew·e·ry /mìkrō bròo əree/ (*pl* **-ries**) *n* a small brewery —**mi·cro·brew·er** *n* —**mi·cro·brew·ing** *n*

⚡**mi·cro·chip** /míkrə chìp/ *n* a small wafer of semiconductor material on which an integrated circuit is laid out

mi·cro·cli·mate /míkrō klìmət/ *n* the climate of a confined space or small geographic area —**mi·cro·cli·mat·ic** /mìkrō klī máttik/ *adj* —**mi·cro·cli·ma·tol·o·gist** /mìkrō klīmə tólləjist/ *n* —**mi·cro·cli·ma·tol·o·gy** *n*

⚡**mi·cro·com·put·er** /míkrō kəm pyòotər/ *n* a small computer

mi·cro·cosm /míkrə kòzzəm/ *n* a small version of something larger —**mi·cro·cos·mic** /mìkrə kózmik/ *adj*

mi·cro·dot /míkrə dòt/ *n* a tiny photograph about the size of a dot

⚡**mi·cro·e·lec·tron·ics** /mìkrō i lek trónniks/ *n* the design, development, and construction of very small electronic circuits (+ *sing verb*) —**mi·cro·e·lec·tron·ic** *adj* —**mi·cro·e·lec·tron·i·cal·ly** *adv*

mi·cro·fi·ber /míkrō fībər/ *n* a very fine synthetic thread

mi·cro·fiche /míkrō feèsh/ (*pl same or* **-fich·es**) *n* a sheet of microfilm containing pages of information

mi·cro·film /míkrə fìlm/ *n* a strip of film containing tiny photographs ■ *vti* photograph on microfilm

mi·cro·form /míkrə fàwrm/ *n* the miniaturized

reproduction on film or paper of pages of information

⚡ **mi·cro·in·struc·tion** /mĭkrō in strúkshən/ n a single low-level programming instruction

mi·cro·man·age /mĭkrō mánnij/ (**-aged, -ag·ing**) vt manage a business or organization by attending to small details —**mi·cro·man·age·ment** n —**mi·cro·man·ag·er** n

mi·cro·me·ter /mī krómmətər/ n a device for measuring small distances accurately —**mi·cro·met·ric** /mĭkrō méttrik/ adj —**mi·crom·e·try** n

mi·cron /mí kròn/ n one millionth of meter

Mic·ro·ne·sia /mĭkrō neézhee ə, -neésha/ ethnographic grouping of islands of the W Pacific Ocean east of the Philippines and mainly north of the equator —**Mi·cro·ne·sian** adj, n

Mic·ro·ne·sia, Fed·er·at·ed States of island nation in the W Pacific Ocean. Cap. Palikir. Pop. 134,597 (2001).

mi·cro·or·gan·ism /mĭkrō áwrgə nìzzəm/ n a microscopic organism

mi·cro·phone /mĭkrə fòn/ n a device for converting sounds into electrical signals for amplification, transmission, or recording

⚡ **mi·cro·proc·es·sor** /mĭkrō pró sèssər/ n a microcomputer's central processing unit consisting of a single chip

⚡ **mi·cro·pro·gram** /mĭkrō prògrəm/ n a computer program built into a microprocessor

⚡ **mi·cro·pro·gram·ming** /mĭkrō prògrəming/ n a means of programming a computer's central processing unit by breaking down instructions into small steps

mi·cro·scope /mĭkrə skòp/ n an instrument that uses a lens or system of lenses to produce a greatly magnified image of an object

mi·cro·scop·ic /mĭkrə skóppik/ adj 1 very small 2 thorough and detailed 3 also **mi·cro·scop·i·cal** invisible without the use of a microscope —**mi·cro·scop·i·cal·ly** adv

mi·cro·sur·ger·y /mĭkrō súrjəree/ n surgery using miniaturized instruments and a specially designed microscope —**mi·cro·sur·gi·cal** adj

mi·cro·wave /mĭkrə wàyv/ n 1 a short electromagnetic wave. Use: radar, radio transmissions, cooking or heating devices. 2 an oven using microwaves to heat or cook food quickly —**mi·cro·wav·a·ble** adj —**mi·cro·wave** vt

mid /mid/ adj occupying a middle or central position

'mid /mid/, **mid** prep amid

mid- prefix middle o midfield

mid·air /mid áir/ n a point in the air above a surface —**mid·air** adj

Mi·das /mídəss/ n in Greek mythology, a king who turned objects to gold by touching them

mid·At·lan·tic adj North American and British in style

mid·day /míd dày/ n the middle of the day

mid·den /mídd'n/ n a pile of dung or refuse

mid·dle /mídd'l/ adj 1 equidistant from the sides, edges, or ends of something 2 halfway between the beginning and end of a period 3 occupying an intermediate position, e.g., in age or status ■ n 1 the part or position farthest from the sides, edges, or ends of something 2 the period halfway between the beginning and end of something 3 a position between highest and lowest 4 the inside or central part of something 5 the waist, stomach, or central part of the body (infml) 6 the center of a team's formation

mid·dle age n the period between youth and later life —**mid·dle-aged** adj

Mid·dle Ag·es n the period in European history between antiquity and the Renaissance

Mid·dle A·mer·i·ca n 1 the socially traditional US middle class 2 the Midwest —**Mid·dle A·mer·i·can** adj, n

mid·dle·brow /mídd'l bròw/ n somebody with moderate and conventional cultural and intellectual interests (infml) —**mid·dle·brow** adj

mid·dle class n the social class between the poor and the wealthy —**mid·dle-class** adj

mid·dle dis·tance n the area between the foreground and the background

mid·dle ear n the central part of the ear containing the bones that transmit sound

Mid·dle East n 1 the region from Egypt to Iran 2 the historical area from Iran to Myanmar —**Mid·dle East·ern** adj —**Mid·dle East·ern·er** n

Mid·dle Eng·lish n the English language from 1100 to 1500

mid·dle fin·ger n the finger between the forefinger and the third finger

mid·dle ground n 1 the area between the foreground and the background 2 a position between extremes

mid·dle·man /mídd'l màn/ (pl **-men** /-mèn/) n 1 somebody who buys goods from a producer and sells them to retailers or consumers 2 a go-between

mid·dle man·age·ment n the tier of managers below top executives —**mid·dle man·ag·er** n

mid·dle name n a name between somebody's first name and surname

mid·dle-of-the-road adj 1 moderate and not extreme 2 intended to have broad music appeal —**mid·dle-of-the-road·er** n

mid·dle school n a school for children between the ages of about 11 and 14

mid·dle-sized adj of average size

⚡ **mid·dle·ware** /mídd'l wàir/ n software that

manages the connection between a client and a database

mid·dle·weight /middʹl wàyt/ n **1** a weight category for boxers between welterweight and light heavyweight **2** a boxer who competes at middleweight

Mid·dle West n = Midwest

mid·dling /middling/ adj **1** medium, moderate, or average **2** ordinary and unexceptional —**mid·dling·ly** adv

mid·dlings /middlingz/ npl Southern US a cut of pork taken from between the ham and shoulder

mid·dy /middee/ (pl -dies) n also **mid·dy blouse** a blouse with a sailor collar

Mid·east /mid eest/ n the Middle East

mid·field /mid feeld/ n **1** the central area of a sports field **2** the players in the midfield (+ sing or pl verb) —**mid·field·er** n

midge /mij/ n a biting insect that flies in swarms

midg·et /mijjit/ n **1** an offensive term for an unusually short person **2** a very small version of something —**midg·et** adj

mid·i /middee/ (pl -is) n a skirt or coat ending just below the knee

⚡ **MIDI** /middee/ n the interface between an electronic musical instrument and a computer. Full form **musical instrument digital interface**

Mid·lands /midlandz/ region of central England —**Mid·land·er** n

mid·night /mid nìt/ n twelve o'clock at night —**mid·night·ly** adj, adv

mid·night sun n the sun when visible at midnight in the Arctic or Antarctic circles in summer

mid·point /mid pòynt/ n **1** the point on a line, journey, or distance halfway between the beginning and end **2** the point of time halfway through a period

mid·range /mid ràynj/ n the middle of a series or range ■ adj covering a medium distance

mid·riff /midrif/ n the front area of the human body between the chest and the waist

mid·ship·man /mid shipmən/ (pl -men /-mən/) n a student training to be a naval officer

midst n the center of something ■ prep amid (literary)

mid·stream /mid streem/ n **1** the middle part of a river or stream **2** a point halfway through something —**mid·stream** adv

mid·sum·mer /mid sùmmər/ n the middle period of the summer

Mid·sum·mer Day n the day of the summer solstice in Europe. Date: June 24.

mid·term /mid tùrm/ n **1** the midpoint of an academic term or term of office **2** an exam taken halfway through a college or university term (often pl) **3** the period midway through a pregnancy —**mid·term** adj

mid·town /mid tòwn/ n the central area of city

mid·way /mid wàyʹ/ adv, adj **1** halfway between two points **2** halfway through a period ■ n an area for sideshows at a fair

Mid·way Is·lands /mid way-/ island group in the NW Hawaiian Islands, administered by the United States. In 1942 it was the site of an important Allied victory in World War II.

mid·week /mid week/ n the middle part of a week —**mid·week** adj, adv —**mid·week·ly** /mid weeklee/ adj, adv

Mid·west /mid wéstʹ/, **Mid·dle West** n the northern part of the central United States —**Mid·west·ern** adj —**Mid·west·ern·er** n

mid·wife /mid wìfʹ/ n (pl -wives /-wìvz/) **1** somebody trained to help deliver babies **2** somebody who helps to create something ■ vt (-wifed or -wived /-wìvd/, -wif·ing or -wiv·ing /-wìving/) assist in the birth of a baby —**mid·wife·ry** /mid wìffəree, mid wìfəree/ n

ORIGIN Mid is an obsolete preposition meaning "with," and wife formerly meant simply "woman." A midwife is therefore literally a woman who is with another woman giving birth.

mid·win·ter /mid wìntər/ n the middle period of the winter

mien /meen/ n somebody's manner or appearance taken as an indication of character (fml)

Mies van der Ro·he /meèz van dər rố ə/, **Ludwig** (1886–1969) German-born US architect and designer

might[1] /mīt/ modal v **1** indicates the possibility that something is true or will happen o might still be alive **2** prefaces advice or a suggestion o You might want to phone first. **3** indicates that somebody ought to do or have done something o You might have told me!

SPELLCHECK Do not confuse the spelling of **might** and **mite** ("a tiny eight-legged animal"), which sound similar.

might[2] /mīt/ n great power or strength

might-have-been n something that might have happened

might·n't /mītʹnt/ contr might not

might·y /mítee/ adj (-i·er, -i·est) **1** strong and powerful **2** big and impressive ■ adv US, regional extremely —**might·i·ly** adv —**might·i·ness** n

migrain incorrect spelling of **migraine**

mi·graine /mí gràyn/ n a recurrent extremely bad headache, often affecting one side of the head

ORIGIN Migraine goes back to Greek hemikranion, literally "half skull," the idea being of a pain in one side of the head.

mi·grant /mígrənt/ n **1** somebody who moves from place to place **2** a migratory animal —**mi·grant** adj

mi·grate /mī́ grāyt/ (**-grat·ed, -grat·ing**) *vi* 1 move from one region or country to another 2 move between habitats in response to seasonal changes 3 move within an organism or substance —**mi·gra·tion** /mī gráysh'n/ *n* —**mi·gra·tion·al** *adj* —**mi·gra·to·ry** /mī́grə tàwree/ *adj*

mih·rab /mee̍rab/ *n* a niche in a mosque pointing toward Mecca

mike (*infml*) *n* a microphone ■ *vt* (**miked, mik·ing**) fit somebody or transmit something with a microphone

Mike *n* a communications code word for the letter "M"

Mi'k·maq /mĭk màk/ (*pl same or* **-maqs**), **Mic·mac** (*pl same or* **-macs**) *n* 1 a member of a group of Native North American people living in E Canada 2 the Algonquian language of the Mi'kmaq people —**Mi'k·maq** *adj*

mil[1] *n* one thousandth of an inch

⚡ mil[2] *abbr* 1 military 2 military organization (*in Internet addresses*) 3 militia

mi·la·dy /mi láydee/ (*pl* **-dies**) *n* a British gentlewoman or female aristocrat (*archaic or humorous*)

Mi·lan /mi laán/ city in N Italy. Pop. 1,307,785 (1999). —**Mil·a·nese** /mílla neéz, -neéss/ *n, adj*

mild /mīld/ *adj* 1 gentle and amiable 2 lightly flavored 3 pleasant and temperate o *a mild evening* 4 not severe or harsh o *a mild disagreement* 5 not dangerous o *a mild earthquake* 6 not containing chemicals that might harm the skin or clothes —**mild·ly** *adv* —**mild·ness** *n*

mil·dew /míl do͞o/ *n* 1 a fungal disease of plants 2 a gray or white fungus on damp walls or materials ■ *vti* affect or be affected by mildew —**mil·dew·y** *adj*

mild-man·nered *adj* gentle and polite

mile *n* 1 a unit of distance equivalent to 5,280 ft. or 1,760 yd. or 1.6 km 2 a nautical mile ■ **miles** *npl* a long way (*infml*)

ORIGIN The **mile** was originally a Roman unit of distance equal to 1,000 paces. The word comes ultimately from Latin *mille* "thousand." The mile came to be associated with measurements that derived from agricultural rather than military practices, and its length varied greatly over history before it came to be standardized at 1,760 yards.

mile·age /mílij/, **mil·age** *n* 1 a distance in miles 2 the number of miles a vehicle has traveled 3 the miles a vehicle can travel on a particular amount of fuel 4 a travel allowance paid at a fixed rate per mile 5 the advantage or usefulness of something (*infml*)

~~millennium~~ incorrect spelling of **millennium**

mile·post /míl pòst/ *n* a roadside post showing the distance to a place

mil·er /mílər/ *n* a competitor in a one-mile race

mile·stone /míl stòn/ *n* 1 a roadside stone showing the distance to a place 2 an important event in the course of something

Mi·let·us /mə leétəss/ ruined ancient Ionian city in SW Asia Minor, in present-day Turkey

mi·lieu /mil yo͞o, mi lyö́/ (*pl* **-lieus** *or* **-lieux** /-lyö́/) *n* the surroundings that somebody lives in or is influenced by

mil·i·tant /míllit'nt/ *adj* 1 very actively or aggressively defending or supporting a cause 2 engaged in fighting or warfare —**mil·i·tan·cy** *n* —**mil·i·tant** *n* —**mil·i·tant·ly** *adv*

mil·i·ta·rism /míllitə rìzzəm/ *n* 1 the pursuit of military aims 2 the strong influence of military personnel on a government —**mil·i·ta·rist** *n* —**mil·i·ta·ris·tic** /míllitə ristík/ *adj*

mil·i·ta·rize /míllitə rīz/ (**-rized, -riz·ing**) *vt* 1 equip or train for war 2 convert for military use —**mil·i·ta·ri·za·tion** /míllitəri záysh'n/ *n*

mil·i·tar·y /mílli tèrree/ *adj* 1 of war or the armed forces 2 of the army or soldiers ■ *n* the armed forces, or its high-ranking officers —**mil·i·tar·i·ly** *adv*

mil·i·tar·y a·cad·e·my *n* 1 a training school for military officers 2 a school with military discipline

mil·i·tar·y po·lice *n* a police force within the armed forces

mil·i·tate /mílli tàyt/ (**-tat·ed, -tat·ing**) *vi* have an influence, especially a negative one, on something

USAGE militate or **mitigate**? **Mitigate** means "lessen the impact or degree of seriousness of something undesirable": *how to mitigate the worst effects of the recession* There were *mitigating circumstances.* **Militate**, usually followed by *against*, means "have an influence, especially a negative one, on something": *Poor refereeing militated against a satisfactory outcome to the contest.*

mi·li·tia /mə líshə/ *n* 1 an emergency army of soldiers who are civilians 2 an unauthorized quasi-military group —**mi·li·tia·man** *n*

milk *n* 1 a nutritious white fluid produced by mammals to feed their young 2 a white liquid from a plant 3 a white liquid cosmetic or pharmaceutical product ■ *v* 1 *vti* take milk from a cow 2 *vt* exploit something (*infml*)

milk choc·o·late *n* chocolate made with milk

milk cow *n* a cow that produces milk

milk·maid /mílk màyd/ *n* a woman who milks cows

milk·man /mílk màn, -mən/ (*pl* **-men** /-mèn, -mən/) *n* a man who delivers milk door-to-door

milk shake *n* a cold whisked drink made from flavored milk and usually ice cream

milk toast *n* toast in hot milk

milk·weed /mílk weèd/ *n* a plant with a milky sap and seed pods that release silky tufted seeds

milk·y /mílkee/ (**-i·er, -i·est**) *adj* 1 like milk in color or consistency 2 containing milk 3 cloudy or opaque —**milk·i·ness** *n*

Milk·y Way *n* the galaxy to which the Earth belongs

mill[1] *n* 1 a flour-making factory 2 a plant or machine for processing raw materials 3 a small device for grinding raw coffee, pepper, or salt 4 a machine for performing a simple manufacturing procedure such as stamping or cutting metal ■ *v* 1 *vt* grind grain by machine 2 *vt* manufacture a product from raw materials by machine 3 *vt* put ridges on a coin edge 4 *vi* move around in a confused or restless group —**milled** *adj*

mill[2] *n* a thousandth of a dollar

Mill, James (1773–1836) British philosopher and economist

Mill, John Stuart (1806–73) British philosopher and economist

Mil·lay /mi láy/, **Edna St. Vincent** (1892–1950) US poet and playwright

Mille ◊ de Mille, Agnes

~~millenium~~ incorrect spelling of **millennium**

mil·len·ni·um /mi lénnee əm/ (*pl* **-ums** *or* **-a** /-ə/) *n* 1 a period of 1,000 years 2 the thousand-year period of peace on earth prophesied in the Bible on the Second Coming of Jesus Christ 3 a hoped-for utopian age 4 a thousandth anniversary —**mil·len·ni·al** *adj*

mil·le·pede *n* INSECTS = millipede

mill·er /míllər/ *n* 1 a mill operator 2 a milling machine

Arthur Miller

Mil·ler /míllər/, **Arthur** (*b.* 1915) US playwright

mil·let /míllit/ *n* 1 a pale shiny cereal grain. Use: flour, alcoholic drinks, birdseed, fodder. 2 a cereal plant that produces millet grain

Mil·let /miláy/, **Jean-François** (1814–75) French painter

milli- *prefix* one thousandth (10⁻³) o *milligram* o *millisecond*

mil·li·bar /mílli baàr/ *n* a unit of atmospheric pressure equal to one thousandth of a bar

mil·li·gram /mílli gràm/ *n* a unit of mass and weight equal to one thousandth of a gram

mil·li·li·ter /mílli leètər/ *n* a unit of volume equal to one thousandth of a liter

mil·li·me·ter /mílli meètər/ *n* a unit of length equal to one thousandth of a meter

mil·li·ner /míllənər/ *n* a maker of women's hats —**mil·li·ner·y** *n*

ORIGIN **Milliner** originally meant somebody from the Italian city of Milan (a "Milaner"). In the 16C it began to be used to refer to sellers of fancy goods and accessories of a type made in Milan, including *Milan bonnets*. Eventually **milliner** came to be restricted to makers of women's hats.

mil·lion /míllyən/ *n* 1 a thousand thousand 2 a large number (*infml; often pl*) 3 a million units of a currency ■ **mil·lions** *npl* several million people or things —**mil·lion** *adj* —**mil·lionth** *adj, n*

mil·lion·aire /míllyə náir, míllyə nàir/ *n* somebody worth more than one million units of currency

mil·lion·air·ess /míllyə náirəss/ *n* a woman worth more than one million units of currency

~~millionnaire~~ incorrect spelling of **millionaire**

mil·li·pede /mílli peèd/, **mil·le·pede** *n* an arthropod with a segmented tubular body on many pairs of legs

mil·li·watt /mílli wòt/ *n* (*symbol* **mW**) an electrical unit

mill·pond /míl pònd/ *n* a pond made by damming a stream in order to create a flow to drive a mill wheel

mill·stone /míl stòn/ *n* 1 a grain-grinding stone 2 a burdensome responsibility

mill wheel *n* a wheel that powers a mill

Milne /miln/, **A. A.** (1882–1956) British writer

Mi·lo·se·vic /mi lóssə vìch/, **Mi·lo·še·vic, Slobodan** (*b.* 1941) Yugoslavian president of Serbia (1989–97) and the Federal Republic of Yugoslavia (1997–2000)

Mi·łosz /mee losh, mee wosh/, **Czeslaw** (*b.* 1911) Lithuanian-born US writer

milque·toast /mílk tòst/, **Milque·toast** *n* somebody regarded as timid, especially a man (*dated insult*)

ORIGIN The original **milquetoast** was Caspar Milquetoast, a cartoon character created by H. T. Webster in 1924.

milt *n* fish semen

Mil·ton /míltən/, **John** (1608–74) English poet —**Mil·to·ni·an** /mil tónee ən/ *adj* —**Mil·ton·ic** /mil tónnik/ *adj*

Mil·wau·kee /mil wáwkee/ city in SE Wisconsin. Pop. 578,364 (1998). —**Mil·wau·kee·an** *adj, n*

mime *n* 1 acting using only gesture and action 2 *also* **mime art·ist** a performer who uses mime ■ *vti* (**mimed, mim·ing**) express something in mime

mi·met·ic /mi méttik, mī-/, **mi·met·i·cal** /mi méttik'l/ adj 1 of imitation 2 of mimicry in plants and animals —**mi·met·i·cal·ly** adv

mim·ic /mímmik/ v (**-icked, -ick·ing**) 1 copy somebody or the mannerisms or appearance of somebody 2 mock somebody through imitation 3 resemble something, e.g., in style 4 take on the appearance of another plant or animal, e.g., to discourage predators ■ n somebody who imitates others, especially for comic effect ◊ See note at **imitate**

mim·ic·ry /mímmikree/ n 1 the imitation of others, often for comic effect 2 a plant's or animal's resemblance to another species or to its surroundings

mi·mo·sa /mi mōssə, -mōzə/ n 1 a flowering tree whose leaves are sensitive to touch 2 a cocktail of champagne and orange juice

min. abbr 1 minimum 2 minute[1]

min·a·ret /mínnə rét/ n a tall slender tower attached to a mosque, from which the muezzin calls the faithful to prayer

min·a·to·ry /mínnə tàwree/ adj menacing (fml)

mince (**minced, minc·ing**) v 1 vt chop food into tiny pieces 2 vi walk in an affectedly dainty way 3 vt use tact in choosing words —**minc·er** n

mince·meat /mínss meèt/ n 1 a chopped fruit and spice mixture 2 finely ground meat

mind /mīnd/ n 1 the center of consciousness that generates thoughts, feelings, and perceptions and stores knowledge and memories 2 the capacity to think and understand 3 a way of thinking ○ changed my mind 4 a state of thought or feeling regarded as usual ○ out of my mind 5 the desire to act in a particular way ○ had a mind to go ■ v 1 vt pay attention to ○ Mind the traffic. 2 vt control ○ Mind your temper. 3 vti object or object to 4 vt temporarily watch over 5 vt remember ○ Mind what I told you. —**mind·er** n

Min·da·na·o /mínda naa ō, -nów/ island in S Philippines. Pop. 14,536,000 (1990).

mind-blow·ing adj extremely exciting, surprising, or shocking (infml) —**mind-blow·ing·ly** adv

mind-bog·gling adj mentally overwhelming (infml) —**mind-bog·gling·ly** adv

mind·ed /míndəd/ adj inclined to do something

mind·ful /míndfəl/ adj aware and attentive —**mind·ful·ly** adv —**mind·ful·ness** n ◊ See note at **aware**

mind·less /míndləss/ adj 1 requiring little or no mental effort 2 purposeless or irrational —**mind·less·ly** adv —**mind·less·ness** n

mind-numb·ing adj exceedingly boring —**mind-numb·ing·ly** adv

Min·do·ro /min dáwrō/ island in W Philippines. Pop. 282,593.

mind read·er n somebody who is able to sense other people's thoughts —**mind reading** n

mind·set /mínd sèt/ n a set of beliefs or thought processes that affect somebody's attitude or behavior

mine[1] n 1 an excavated area in the earth from which minerals are extracted 2 the buildings, machinery, and people needed to work a mine 3 an area where there is a mineral deposit 4 a rich source of something ○ a mine of information 5 an underground or underwater explosive device ■ v (**mined, min·ing**) 1 vti remove minerals from the earth 2 vt lay explosive mines in an area 3 vt dig a tunnel beneath something

mine[2] pron indicates possession by the speaker or writer ■ adj my (archaic; before vowels)

mine·field /mín feèld/ n 1 an area containing explosive mines 2 a hazardous situation

min·er /mínər/ n 1 a worker in a mine 2 somebody who lays explosive mines

SPELLCHECK Do not confuse the spelling of **miner** and **minor** ("small or insignificant," "somebody not legally an adult"), which sound similar.

min·er·al /mínnərəl/ n 1 an inorganic substance that occurs naturally in the ground 2 a mined substance 3 an inorganic nutritive substance in food —**min·er·al** adj

min·er·al·o·gy /mínnə róllajee/ (pl **-gies**) n 1 the scientific study of minerals 2 a profile of an area's mineral deposits —**min·er·a·log·i·cal** /mínnərə lójjik'l/ adj —**min·er·al·o·gist** n

min·er·al wa·ter n drinkable water with a high mineral salt or gas content

Mi·ner·va /mi núrvə/ n in Roman mythology, the goddess of wisdom. Greek equivalent **Athena**

min·e·stro·ne /mínnə strōnee/ n an Italian vegetable soup

mine·sweep·er /mín sweèpər/ n a ship that detects explosive mines

min·gle /míng g'l/ (**-gled, -gling**) v 1 vti mix or be mixed gently or gradually 2 vi circulate among people at a party

min·i /mínnee/ n a smaller version of something (infml)

mini- prefix small, short, miniature ○ minibus

min·i·a·ture /mínnee ə chər, -ə chŏor, mínnichər/ n 1 a smaller-than-usual example or copy of something 2 a tiny detailed painting, especially a portrait ■ adj smaller than usual

ORIGIN It could easily be assumed that **miniature** is related to forms from the Latin words **minor** "smaller, less" and minimus "smallest, least." In fact, **miniature** goes back to Latin minium "red lead." Red lead was used in ancient and medieval times to make a red ink used in decorating manuscripts. Italian *miniatura*, formed from a verb from Latin *minium*, meant "painting, illumination," and was particularly used for the small paintings in manuscripts. English adopted this word in the late 16C, and it was immediately broadened to include any small image. The superficial resemblance to words such as *minor* and *minute* contributed to the development of the adjectival use "smaller than usual," which is recorded from the early 18C.

min·i·a·tur·ist /mínnee ə chŏorist, -əchərist/ *n* a painter of miniatures

min·i·a·tur·ize /mínnee əchə rìz, mínnichə rìz/ (-ized, -iz·ing) *vt* make a version of in a smaller size —**min·i·a·tur·i·za·tion** /mínnee əchəri záysh'n, mínnichəri záysh'n/ *n*

min·i·bar /mínnee baar/ *n* a refrigerator in a hotel room stocked with alcoholic drinks

min·i·bus /mínnee bùss/ *n* a small bus for short trips

⚡**min·i·com·put·er** /mínnee kəm pyŏotər/ *n* a computer intermediate in power between a personal computer and a mainframe

min·im /mínnəm/ *n* 1 a unit of fluid measure equal to approximately one drop 2 a half note

min·i·mal /mínnəm'l/ *adj* 1 very small 2 smallest possible in amount or extent —**min·i·mal·ly** *adv*

min·i·mal·ism /mínnəm'l ìzzəm/ *n* 1 simplicity of style in art, design, or literature 2 a trend in music toward simplicity of rhythm and tone —**min·i·mal·ist** *adj*, *n*

min·i·mize /mínnə mìz/ (-mized, -miz·ing) *vt* 1 reduce to a minimum 2 play down the extent or seriousness of —**min·i·mi·za·tion** /mínnəmi záysh'n/ *n*

min·i·mum /mínnəməm/ (*pl* -mums *or* -ma /-mə/) *n* 1 the lowest possible, recorded, or permissible amount or degree 2 a minimum amount of money that a restaurant or nightclub requires a patron to spend —**min·i·mum** *adj*

min·i·mum wage *n* 1 the lowest rate of pay allowed by law 2 a living wage

min·ing /míning/ *n* 1 the process of removing minerals from the earth 2 the process of laying explosives

min·ion /mínnyən/ *n* 1 a servile or slavish follower of somebody 2 a servant (*literary*)

~~miniscule~~ incorrect spelling of **minuscule**

min·i·se·ries /mínnee seeriz/ (*pl* same) *n* a short series of TV programs

min·i·skirt /mínnee skùrt/ *n* a skirt with the hemline well above the knee

min·is·ter /mínnistər/ *n* 1 a member of the Christian, especially Protestant, clergy 2 a senior officer of state in a government department 3 a diplomat, especially of a rank below an ambassador ■ *vi* 1 give help to somebody in need (*fml*) 2 perform the duties of a member of the clergy

—**min·is·te·ri·al** /mínni steéree əl/ *adj*
—**min·is·ter·ship** *n*

ORIGIN A **minister** was originally just a servant or agent of another, a relatively minor person as its origin in Latin *minus* "less" would suggest. Early in its history, however, it came to refer especially to a functionary of the Christian Church, and in the 16C specifically to an ordained member of the clergy. **Minister** was not applied to a political appointee until the 17C.

min·is·try /mínnistree/ (*pl* -tries) *n* 1 the work or period of service of a Christian minister 2 ministers collectively (+ *sing* or *pl verb*) 3 *also* **Min·is·try** a government department 4 a government building

~~miniture~~ incorrect spelling of **miniature**

min·i·van /mínnee vàn/ *n* a small van for passengers and cargo

mink /mingk/ *n* 1 (*pl* **minks** *or* same) a webtoed member of the weasel family 2 the fur of a mink

Minn. *abbr* Minnesota

Min·ne·ap·o·lis /mínnee áppəliss/ city in SE Minnesota. Pop. 351,731 (1998).

Min·ne·so·ta /mínnə sótə/ state in the north central United States. Cap. St. Paul. Pop. 4,919,479 (2000). —**Min·ne·so·tan** *adj*, *n*

min·now /mínnō/ *n* 1 a small fish used as bait 2 any small fish

Mi·no·an /mi nó ən/ *adj* of a Bronze Age civilization on Crete lasting from around 3000 to 1100 BC

mi·nor /mínər/ *adj* 1 relatively small in quantity, size, or degree 2 low in rank 3 low in severity or danger 4 describes a musical scale that has a semitone interval between the 2nd and 3rd, 5th and 6th, and sometimes 7th and 8th notes 5 describes a musical key based on a minor scale 6 not legally an adult ■ *n* 1 somebody who is not legally an adult 2 a musical key or harmony based on a minor scale 3 a subject chosen as a secondary specialization 4 a student who takes a secondary course of study ■ *vi* study a secondary subject ◊ See note at **miner**

mi·nor·i·ty /mi náwrətee, mī-/ (*pl* -ties) *n* 1 a small group within a larger group 2 a group that has insufficient votes to win 3 a group of people within a society whose ethnic, racial, national, religious, sexual, political, or linguistic characteristics differ from the rest of society 4 an offensive term for a member of a minority group 5 the period when somebody is a legal minor —**mi·nor·i·ty** *adj*

mi·nor league *n* a professional sports league that is not part of any major league

Mi·nos /mín oss/ *n* in Greek mythology, a king of Crete who kept the Minotaur in a labyrinth

Min·o·taur /mínnə tàwr, mínə-/ *n* in Greek mythology, a monster with the body of a man and the head of a bull

Minsk capital of Belarus. Pop. 1,680,000 (1999).

min·ster /mínstər/ *n* a large or important cathedral or church, usually one originally connected with a monastery

min·strel /mínstrəl/ *n* 1 a medieval traveling musician 2 a member of a troupe of entertainers who wore makeup to make themselves appear black and performed in variety shows *(a form of entertainment now usually considered racist and highly offensive)*

mint[1] *n* 1 a plant with aromatic leaves. Use: food flavoring. 2 a piece of mint-flavored candy —**mint·y** *adj*

mint[2] *n* 1 a place where coins used as currency are made 2 a large amount of money *(infml)* ■ *vt* 1 make coins 2 invent something, especially a word or phrase ■ *adj* in perfect condition

mint ju·lep *n* an alcoholic drink with a mint garnish

min·u·et /mínnyoo ét/ *n* 1 a stately 17C French court dance in triple time 2 the music for a minuet

ORIGIN The **minuet** takes its name from the "small or dainty" (French *menuet*) steps taken in the dance.

Min·u·it /mínn yoo ít/, **Peter** (1580–1638) Dutch-born American colonial administrator

mi·nus /mínəss/ *prep* 1 reduced by subtracting a number 2 lacking ■ *adj* 1 showing subtraction 2 less than zero 3 having a detrimental effect ■ *n* 1 *also* **mi·nus sign** a symbol (-) of subtraction or a negative quantity 2 a negative quantity 3 a disadvantage

min·us·cule /mínnə skyóol/ *adj* extremely small

min·ute[1] /mínnit/ *n* 1 a unit of time equal to 60 seconds or 1/60th of an hour 2 a very short time 3 a particular moment 4 *(symbol ')* a unit of measurement of angles equivalent to 1/60th of a degree ■ **min·utes** *npl* the official record of what was said at a meeting

mi·nute[2] /mī nóot/ *(-nut·er, -nut·est)* *adj* 1 very small 2 insignificant —**mi·nute·ly** *adv* —**mi·nute·ness** *n*

min·ute hand /mínnit-/ *n* the longer hand on a clock, which indicates minutes

min·ute·man /mínnit màn/ *(pl* -men /-mèn/) *n* a militiaman in the Revolutionary War

mi·nu·ti·ae /mī nóoshee èe/ *npl* small details

Mi·o·cene /mī ə sèen/ *n* an epoch of geologic time 23.3–5.2 million years ago —**Mi·o·cene** *adj*

✦ **MIPS** /mips/, **mips** *abbr* million instructions per second

mir·a·cle /mírrək'l/ *n* 1 an event regarded as an act of God 2 an amazing event

mi·rac·u·lous /mi rákyələss/ *adj* 1 regarded as caused by supernatural intervention 2 extraordinary —**mi·rac·u·lous·ly** *adv* —**mi·rac·u·lous·ness** *n*

mi·rage /mi raázh/ *n* 1 an optical illusion of water in the distance 2 something unreal or imagined

Mi·ran·da rights /mi rándə-/ *npl* the rights of a person being arrested to remain silent or to have an attorney present during questioning

ORIGIN The rights are named for Miranda vs Arizona, the case that led to the US Supreme Court ruling on a suspect's right to legal advice and silence.

mire /mīr/ *n* 1 thick mud 2 a bog 3 a difficult situation ■ *v (mired, mir·ing)* 1 *vti* sink or make sink into mud and become stuck 2 *vt* make muddy 3 *vt* involve or entangle in difficulties —**mir·y** *adj*

Mi·ró /mee ró/, **Joan** (1893–1983) Spanish painter, sculptor, and printmaker

✦ **mir·ror** /mírrər/ *n* 1 a highly reflective surface or piece of material that reflects an image 2 something that accurately reproduces or depicts something else 3 *also* **mir·ror site** a copy of a website maintained on a different file server so as to spread the distribution load or to protect data from loss ■ *vt* 1 reflect something in a surface 2 be similar to or reproduce something else 3 maintain an exact copy of a program, data, or a website, usually on another file server

mir·ror im·age *n* a reversed image

mirth /murth/ *n* enjoyment, especially accompanied by laughter —**mirth·ful** *adj* —**mirth·ful·ly** *adv* —**mirth·less** *adj* —**mirth·less·ly** *adv*

✦ **MIS** *abbr* management information system

mis- *prefix* 1 badly, wrongly ○ *mishandle* 2 bad, wrong ○ *misdeed*

mis·ad·ven·ture /mìssəd vénchər/ *n* an unfortunate event

mis·a·lign /mìssə lín/ *vt* position or arrange incorrectly —**mis·a·lign·ment** *n*

mis·al·li·ance /mìssə lī ənss/ *n* an alliance of mismatched partners

mis·an·thrope /míss'n thròp/, **mis·an·thro·pist** /mi sánthrəpist/ *n* somebody who hates people —**mis·an·throp·ic** /mìss'n thróppik/ *adj* —**mis·an·thro·py** /mi sánthrəpee/ *n*

mis·ap·ply /mìssə plí/ *(-plied, -plies)* *vt* use incorrectly —**mis·ap·pli·ca·tion** /miss àpplə káysh'n/ *n*

mis·ap·pre·hen·sion /miss àppri hénsh'n/ *n* a false impression or incorrect understanding —**mis·ap·pre·hend** *vt*

mis·ap·pro·pri·ate /mìssə própree àyt/ *(-at·ed, -at·ing)* *vt* take or use dishonestly —**mis·ap·pro·pri·a·tion** /miss əpròpree áysh'n/ *n* ◊ See note at **steal**

mis·be·got·ten /mìssbi gótt'n/ *adj* **1** ill-conceived and generally bad **2** dishonestly obtained **3** born illegitimately

mis·be·have /mìssbi háyv/ (-haved, -hav·ing) *vi* be naughty and troublesome

mis·be·hav·ior /mìssbi háyvyər/ *n* unacceptable behavior

misc. *abbr* miscellaneous

mis·cal·cu·late /miss kálkyə làyt/ (-lat·ed, -lat·ing) *vti* **1** calculate something wrongly **2** make a wrong assessment about something or somebody —**mis·cal·cu·la·tion** /miss kàlkyə láysh'n/ *n*

mis·car·riage /miss kérrij/ *n* **1** the premature expulsion of a fetus that is too immature to survive **2** the mishandling or failure of an undertaking *(fml)*

mis·car·riage of jus·tice *n* a failure of the legal system to come to a just decision

mis·car·ry /miss kérree/ (-ried, -ries) *vi* **1** lose a fetus through a miscarriage **2** be expelled from the womb at too early a stage to be able to survive **3** fail *(fml)*

mis·cast /miss kást/ (-cast) *vt* **1** give an actor an unsuitable part **2** choose the wrong actor for a part

mis·ceg·e·na·tion /mìssijə náysh'n/ *n* sexual relations, marriage, or cohabitation between people of different races *(offensive when used disapprovingly, as often formerly)*

~~miscelaneous~~ incorrect spelling of **miscellaneous**

mis·cel·la·ne·ous /mìssə láynee əss/ *adj* **1** composed of varied things **2** each being different —**mis·cel·la·ne·ous·ly** *adv*

mis·cel·la·ny /míssə làynee/ (*pl* -nies) *n* **1** a miscellaneous collection **2** a collection of miscellaneous writings

mis·chance /miss chánss/ *n* **1** misfortune **2** a piece of bad luck

~~mischeif~~ incorrect spelling of **mischief**

mis·chief /mísschif/ *n* **1** naughty behavior **2** the tendency to behave naughtily

mis·chief-mak·er *n* a troublemaker or spreader of gossip

~~mischievous~~ incorrect spelling of **mischievous**

mis·chie·vous /mísschivəss/ *adj* **1** playfully naughty or troublesome **2** damaging *(fml)* —**mis·chie·vous·ly** *adv* —**mis·chie·vous·ness** *n* ◊ See note at **bad**

mis·con·ceive /mìskən seév/ (-ceived, -ceiv·ing) *vt* fail to understand

mis·con·ceived /mìskən seévd/ *adj* resulting from a wrong understanding

mis·con·cep·tion /mìskən sépsh'n/ *n* a mistaken idea

mis·con·duct /miss kón dùkt/ *n* **1** immoral, unethical, or unprofessional behavior **2** incompetence

mis·con·strue /mìskən stroō/ (-strued, -stru·ing) *vt* misunderstand or misinterpret

mis·count *vti* /miss kównt/ count things incorrectly ■ *n* /miss kòwnt/ an incorrect count

mis·cre·ant /mískree ənt/ *n* a wrongdoer *(literary)*

mis·cue /miss kyoō/ *n* a faulty shot in billiards or snooker —**mis·cue** *vti*

mis·deed /miss deéd/ *n* a wicked act

mis·de·mean·or /mìssdi meénər/ *n* a minor crime or misdeed

mis·di·al /miss dī əl/ *vti* dial a telephone number incorrectly —**mis·di·al** /miss dī əl/ *n*

mis·di·rect /mìssdi rékt/ *vt* **1** give somebody wrong directions to a place **2** wrongly address mail

mi·ser /mízər/ *n* **1** somebody who hoards money **2** an ungenerous or selfish person —**mi·ser·li·ness** *n* —**mi·ser·ly** *adj*

mis·er·a·ble /mízzərəb'l/ *adj* **1** very unhappy **2** very unpleasant **3** contemptible **4** inadequate —**mis·er·a·bly** *adv*

mis·er·y /mízzəree/ (*pl* -ies) *n* **1** great unhappiness **2** a source of great unhappiness **3** poverty

mis·fire *vi* /miss fīr/ (-fired, -fir·ing) **1** fail to fire a bullet or shell properly **2** fail to ignite the fuel mixture in the cylinder properly *(refers to an internal-combustion engine)* **3** go wrong ■ *n* /miss fīr, miss fír/ a malfunction in firing

mis·fit /miss fít/ *n* **1** somebody who does not fit comfortably into a situation or environment **2** something that fits badly

mis·for·tune /miss fáwrchən/ *n* **1** bad luck **2** an unhappy event

mis·giv·ing /miss gívving/ *n* a feeling of doubt or apprehension *(often pl)*

mis·guid·ed /miss gídəd/ *adj* mistaken or inappropriate —**mis·guid·ed·ly** *adv* —**mis·guid·ed·ness** *n*

mis·han·dle /miss hánd'l/ (-dled, -dling) *vt* **1** deal with incompetently **2** treat roughly

mis·hap /miss hàp/ *n* **1** an accident **2** bad luck *(fml)*

mis·hear /miss heér/ (-heard /-húrd/) *vti* not hear correctly

Mi·shi·ma /mi sheémə/, **Yukio** (1925–70) Japanese novelist

mis·hit /miss hít/ (-hit, -hit·ting) *vt* hit in the wrong direction or with too little force

mish·mash /mísh màsh/ *n* a disorderly or confusing mixture

mis·in·form /mìssin fáwrm/ *vt* give wrong information to —**mis·in·for·ma·tion** /miss infər máysh'n/ *n*

mis·in·ter·pret /mìssin túrprət/ *vt* understand or explain incorrectly —**mis·in·ter·pre·ta·tion** /miss in turprə táysh'n/ *n* —**mis·in·ter·pret·er** *n*

mis·judge /miss júj/ (-judged, -judg·ing) *vti* make a bad judgment about somebody or something —**mis·judg·ment** *n*

mis·lay /miss láy/ (-laid /-láyd/) *vt* lose temporarily

mis·lead /miss leéd/ (-led /-léd/) vt 1 inform falsely 2 lead into bad actions 3 lead in the wrong direction —**mis·lead·ing** adj —**mis·lead·ing·ly** adv

mis·man·age /miss mánnij/ (-aged, -ag·ing) vt manage incompetently —**mis·man·age·ment** n

mis·match n /miss màch/ an unlikely or ill-suited pair ■ vt /miss mách/ match or pair unsuitably

mis·no·mer /miss nṓmər/ n an unsuitable name

mi·sog·y·ny /mi sójjənee/ n hatred of women —**mi·sog·y·nist** n —**mi·sog·y·nis·tic** /mi sòjjə nístik/ adj

misspelling incorrect spelling of **misspelling**

mis·place /miss pláyss/ (-placed, -plac·ing) vt 1 mislay something 2 place trust or confidence in somebody or something unworthy or inappropriate —**mis·place·ment** n

mis·print n /miss prìnt, miss prínt/ a mistake in printing ■ vt /miss prínt/ print incorrectly

mis·pro·nounce /mìsprə nównss/ (-nounced, -nounc·ing) vt pronounce incorrectly —**mis·pro·nun·ci·a·tion** /mìsprə nùnsee áysh'n/ n

mis·quote /miss kwót/ (-quot·ed, -quot·ing) vti quote somebody or something inaccurately —**mis·quo·ta·tion** /miss kwō táysh'n/ n

mis·read /miss reéd/ (-read /-réd/) vt 1 read inaccurately 2 misinterpret

mis·re·port /mìssri páwrt/ vt report in an inaccurate or distorted way —**mis·re·port** n

mis·rep·re·sent /miss rèppri zént/ vt 1 give a false account of 2 not represent truly —**mis·rep·re·sen·ta·tion** /miss rèppri zen táysh'n/ n

mis·rule /miss roól/ vt (-ruled, -rul·ing) rule a nation badly or unjustly ■ n 1 bad or unjust government 2 public disorder

miss[1] v 1 vti not hit a target 2 vt fail to be present at or on time for 3 vt not hear, see, or understand 4 vt not take advantage of 5 vt fail to achieve 6 vt manage to escape or avoid 7 vt feel sorry because of the absence of ■ n 1 a failure to hit a target 2 any failure —**miss·a·ble** adj

miss[2] n 1 a way of addressing a young woman 2 a young woman 3 **Miss** a title given to a young or unmarried woman

Miss. abbr Mississippi

mis·sal /míss'l/ n a Roman Catholic prayer book

mis·shap·en /miss sháypən/, **mis·shaped** /miss sháypt/ adj having an undesirable shape —**mis·shap·en·ness** n

mis·sile /míss'l/ n 1 a rocket-propelled warhead 2 an object thrown or launched as a weapon

miss·ing /míssing/ adj 1 absent 2 disappeared

miss·ing link n 1 a theoretical animal that makes the evolutionary link between apes and humans 2 something required to complete something

mis·sion /mísh'n/ n 1 an assigned task 2 a calling or vocation 3 a space vehicle's trip 4 a group of representatives or missionaries 5 a permanent diplomatic delegation 6 a building used by missionaries

mis·sion·ar·y /mísh'n èrree/ (pl -ies) n 1 somebody sent to a foreign country by a church to spread its faith or do medical or social work 2 somebody who tries to persuade others to accept or join something —**mis·sion·ar·y** adj

mis·sion·ar·y po·si·tion n a sexual position with the man on top facing the woman

mis·sion creep n a tendency of military operations to increase gradually in scope and demand further commitment of personnel and resources

mis·sion state·ment n a formal statement of the aims of an organization

Mis·sis·sip·pi /míssi síppee/ 1 major river in the United States. It flows southward from N Minnesota to Louisiana, emptying into the Gulf of Mexico. Length 2,340 mi./3,770 km. 2 state in the SE United States. Cap. Jackson. Pop. 2,844,658 (2000). —**Mis·sis·sip·pi·an** n, adj

mis·sive /míssiv/ n a letter or written message

missile incorrect spelling of **missile**

Mis·sou·la /mi zoólə/ city in W Montana. Pop. 52,239 (1998).

Mis·sou·ri /mi zooree/ 1 longest river in the United States. It flows from SW Montana southeastward to join the Mississippi River in Missouri. Length 2,315 mi./3,726 km. 2 state in the central United States. Cap. Jefferson City. Pop. 5,595,211 (2000). —**Mis·sou·ri·an** n, adj

mis·spell /miss spél/ vt spell incorrectly —**mis·spell·ing** n

mis·spend /miss spénd/ (-spent /-spént/) vt squander time or money

mis·step /miss stép/ n 1 a wrong step 2 an error in judgment or conduct

mist n 1 thin fog 2 condensed water vapor on a surface 3 a fine spray ■ vi 1 become obscured by mist 2 become blurred by tears

mis·take /mi stáyk/ n 1 an incorrect act or decision 2 an error ■ vt (-took /-toók/, -tak·en /-táykən/, -tak·ing) 1 misunderstand 2 identify incorrectly —**mis·tak·a·ble** adj

SYNONYMS mistake, error, inaccuracy, slip, blunder, faux pas CORE MEANING: something incorrect or improper

mis·tak·en /mi stáykən/ adj 1 wrong in your opinion 2 based on incorrect information —**mis·tak·en·ly** adv —**mis·tak·en·ness** n

mis·ter /místər/ n 1 a way to address a man 2 **Mis·ter** the full form of "Mr."

Mis·ti /meéstee/ dormant volcano in the Andes, in S Peru. Height 19,101 ft./5,822 m.

mis·time /miss tím/ (**-timed, -tim·ing**) vt fail to do at the correct time

mis·tle·toe /míss'l tò/ n 1 an evergreen bush with white berries in winter 2 a Christmas decoration consisting of a sprig of mistletoe

ORIGIN **Mistle** in **mistletoe** is itself the ancient word for "mistletoe." The second element means "twig." The short and longer forms were used alongside each other in English until the late 17C, when **mistletoe** finally prevailed.

mis·tral /místrəl, mi straál/ n a powerful wind in S France

mis·treat /miss treét/ vt treat badly or roughly —**mis·treat·ment** n ◊ See note at **misuse**

mis·tress /místrəss/ n 1 a woman with whom a man has a long extramarital affair 2 the woman who owns or controls something 3 a highly skilled woman 4 a woman who keeps a pet 5 **Mrs. Mistress** Mrs. (archaic)

mis·tri·al /miss trī əl, -trí/ n 1 a trial made invalid by a mistake such as an error in procedure 2 an inconclusive trial

mis·trust /miss trúst/ n suspicion or lack of trust ■ vt be suspicious or distrustful of —**mis·trust·ful** adj

mist·y /místee/ (**-i·er, -i·est**) adj 1 covered in mist 2 like mist 3 dim and indistinct —**mist·i·ly** adv —**mist·i·ness** n

mist·y-eyed adj 1 with tears in the eyes 2 sentimental

mis·un·der·stand /míss undər stánd/ (**-stood** /-stood/) vt fail to understand the true meaning, nature, or intentions of

mis·un·der·stand·ing /míss undər stánding/ n 1 a failure to understand or interpret something correctly 2 a minor dispute

mis·use n /miss yoóss/ 1 the incorrect or improper use of something 2 cruel treatment ■ vt /miss yoóz/ (**-used, -us·ing**) 1 use incorrectly or improperly 2 treat somebody cruelly —**mis·used** adj

SYNONYMS **misuse, abuse, ill-treat, maltreat, mistreat** CORE MEANING: treat wrongly or badly

MIT abbr Massachusetts Institute of Technology

Mitch·ell /míchəl/, **Keith C.** (b. 1947) prime minister of Grenada (1995–)

Mitch·ell, Margaret (1900–49) US writer

mite[1] /mīt/ n a tiny eight-legged organism related to ticks ◊ See note at **might**

mite[2] /mīt/ n a small amount

mi·ter /mítər/ n 1 a Christian bishop's or abbot's ceremonial headdress 2 also **mi·ter joint** in woodwork, a corner joint made by joining two pieces of wood that have been cut at 45° angles ■ vt join pieces of wood using a miter joint

Mith·ras /míthrass/ n in Persian mythology, the god of light, truth, and goodness

mit·i·gate /mítti gàyt/ (**-gat·ed, -gat·ing**) vt 1 partly excuse a crime 2 make something less severe —**mit·i·gat·ing** adj —**mit·i·ga·tion** /mítti gáysh'n/ n ◊ See note at **militate**

mi·to·chon·dri·on /mítə kóndree ən/ (pl **-a** /-ə/) n a component of a cell that contains DNA and produces enzymes for the metabolic conversion of food to energy —**mi·to·chon·dri·al** adj

mi·to·sis /mī tóssiss/ n the process by which a cell divides into two daughter cells, each having the same number of chromosomes as the original cell —**mi·tot·ic** /mī tóttik/ adj

mitt n 1 a mitten (infml) 2 a hand covering similar to a mitten 3 a hand (slang) 4 a baseball player's padded glove

mit·ten /mítt'n/ n a glove with two sections, one for the thumb and one for the four fingers

mitz·vah /mítsvə, mítts vaá/ (pl **-voth** /-vòt, -vòth/ or **-vahs**) n 1 a Jewish religious duty 2 an act of kindness done by or for a Jewish person

mix v 1 vt combine ingredients 2 vi become combined, or be capable of combining ◦ Oil and water don't mix. 3 vt make something by combining ingredients 4 vt add something ◦ Mix the flour into the water. 5 vt closely associate one thing with another ◦ mix business with pleasure 6 vi go well together 7 vi meet people socially 8 vt crossbreed plants or animals ■ n 1 an act of mixing 2 a combination ◦ an intriguing mix of styles 3 a substance consisting of a number of ingredients from which something is prepared ◦ a cake mix —**mix·a·ble** adj

□ **mix up** v 1 vt mistake the identity of people, or one person for another 2 vt change the order of things 3 vti involve or become involved in something

mixed adj 1 consisting of a mixture or combination 2 with good and bad elements

mixed bag n a diverse group or collection

mixed bless·ing n something that is both good and bad

mixed dou·bles n a tennis, table tennis, or badminton match played by two pairs, each consisting of a man and a woman (+ sing verb)

mixed e·con·o·my n an economy with both government-owned and privately owned businesses and industries

mixed farm·ing n the growing of crops and rearing of animals on the same farm

mixed mar·riage n a marriage between people of different ethnic origins or religions

mixed-race adj having or involving different racial backgrounds

mix·er /míksər/ n 1 a mixing device or machine 2 a nonalcoholic drink such as fruit juice that is often mixed with alcohol 3 a sociable person 4 a get-together

Mix·tec /méess tek/ (pl same or -tecs), **Mix·tec·an** /méess tékən/ (pl -ans or same) n 1 a member of a Native American people who are now spread throughout Mexico 2 the language of the Mixtec people —**Mix·tec** adj

mix·ture /míkschər/ n 1 a blend of ingredients 2 a number of different things existing or brought together 3 a substance formed by combining substances without a chemical reaction 4 the process of mixing things (fml)

SYNONYMS mixture, blend, combination, compound, alloy, amalgam CORE MEANING: something formed by mixing materials

mix-up n a state of confusion, or a mistake

miz·zen /mízz'n/ n a mizzenmast or its sail ■ adj of or used on a mizzenmast

miz·zen·mast /mízz'n màst, mízz'nməst/ n the 3rd mast from the front on a ship with three or more masts

mks, MKS abbr meter-kilogram-second

ml abbr milliliter

Mlle. abbr Mademoiselle

Mlles. abbr Mesdemoiselles

mm abbr millimeter

MM. abbr Messieurs

Mme. abbr Madame

Mmes. abbr Mesdames

Mn symbol manganese

MN abbr 1 Minnesota 2 magnetic north

mne·mon·ic /ni mónnik/ n a short rhyme, phrase, or other mental technique that aids memory —**mne·mon·ic** adj —**mne·mon·i·cal·ly** adv

Mo symbol molybdenum

MO, Mo. abbr Missouri

mo. abbr month

M.O., m.o. abbr 1 mail order 2 modus operandi

Mo·ab /mó àb/ ancient kingdom situated to the east of the Dead Sea, in modern-day Jordan —**Mo·ab·ite** /mó ə bìt/ n, adj

moan /mōn/ v 1 vi make a low sound expressing pain or misery, or a similar sound 2 vti complain (infml) ■ n 1 a sound of somebody moaning 2 a sound similar to a moan made by something such as the wind 3 a complaint (infml) —**moan·er** n

moat /mōt/ n a ditch around a castle or fort dug for protection from attack

mob /mob/ n 1 a large and unruly crowd 2 UK a group of people (infml) 3 ordinary people, especially regarded collectively as unintelligent or irrational (infml) 4 **Mob** the Mafia or the world of organized crime (infml) ■ vt (mobbed, mob·bing) 1 crowd

around somebody or into a place 2 attack a person or animal in large numbers

ORIGIN Mob is a shortening of an archaic noun *mobile*, which was itself shortened from Latin *mobile vulgus* "the fickle or excitable crowd."

mo·bile /mób'l, mó bèel, -bìl/ adj 1 easy to move 2 operating from a vehicle 3 changing from one social or professional class to another ■ n a hanging sculpture or decoration that moves with air currents —**mo·bil·i·ty** /mō bíllətee/ n

Mo·bile /mō bèel/ city in SW Alabama. Pop. 202,181 (1998).

-mobile suffix automobile, vehicle ○ snowmobile

mo·bile home n a large transportable trailer that is usually connected to utilities and left on one site

mo·bile phone n a portable wireless telephone

mo·bi·lize /móbə lìz/ (-lized, -liz·ing) vti prepare forces for action —**mo·bi·li·za·tion** /móbəli záysh'n/ n

mob·ster /móbstər/ n a gangster (infml)

Mo·bu·tu Se·se Se·ko /mə boòtoo sayssay sáykó/ (1930–97) Congolese soldier and president of Zaïre (Democratic Republic of the Congo) (1965–97)

~~moccasin~~ incorrect spelling of **moccasin**

moc·ca·sin /mókəssin/ n 1 a soft leather Native North American shoe 2 a low-heeled leather shoe with prominent stitching

mo·cha /mókə/ n 1 a dark brown strong Arabian coffee 2 a coffee and cocoa flavoring used in baking

mock v 1 vti treat something or somebody with scorn 2 vt mimic as a way of making fun of somebody ■ adj 1 imitation ○ mock leather 2 done as an act, especially to be amusing —**mock·ing** adj —**mock·ing·ly** adv ◊ See note at ridicule

mock·er·y /mókəree/ n scorn

mock-he·ro·ic adj describes poetry that satirizes the heroic style ■ n a verse written in mock-heroic style

mock·ing·bird /móking bùrd/ n a long-tailed grayish bird that imitates other birds' calls

mock-up n 1 a full-scale model 2 a preliminary layout of a newspaper or magazine

mod·al /mód'l/ adj 1 describes a verb expressing a grammatical mood such as possibility or necessity 2 of musical modes —**mod·al·ly** adv

mode n 1 a manner or form 2 a style or fashion 3 a machine setting 4 a musical scale that can be played over an octave using only the white keys of a piano 5 the most frequent value in a statistical range

mod·el /módd'l/ n 1 a copy of an object, especially on a smaller scale 2 a particular version of a manufactured article **3** something used as a basis for a related idea, process, or system **4** somebody who is paid to display clothing or merchandise in shows or photographs **5** a simplified version of something used for analysis **6** a perfect example **7** somebody who poses for an artist ■ *v* **1** *vti* display clothes as a fashion model **2** *vi* be an artist's model **3** *vt* base one thing on another **4** *vt* make something by shaping a material such as clay —**mod·el·er** *n*

⚡ **mo·dem** /mó dèm/ *n* a device that connects computers via a phone line

ORIGIN Modem is a blend of *modulator* and *demodulator*.

mod·er·ate *adj* /móddərət/ **1** not large, great, or severe ○ *a moderate portion* **2** not excessive or unreasonable ○ *a moderate eater* **3** not extreme or radical ○ *moderate views* **4** neither particularly good nor particularly bad ■ *n* /móddərət/ somebody with moderate views ■ *vti* /móddə ràyt/ (-at·ed, -at·ing) **1** make or become less extreme **2** preside over a meeting or discussion —**mod·er·ate·ly** *adv* —**mod·er·ate·ness** *n*

mod·er·a·tion /móddə ráysh'n/ *n* **1** the state of being moderate **2** the limiting or controlling of something so that it becomes or remains moderate **3** the position or function of a moderator

mod·er·a·tor /móddə ràytər/ *n* somebody who presides over an assembly or discussion

mod·ern /móddərn/ *adj* **1** belonging to the present day **2** of or using the latest ideas, equipment, or techniques ■ *n* a modern person —**mod·ern·ly** *adv* —**mod·ern·ness** *n* ◊ See note at **new**

mod·ern-day /móddərn dáy/ *adj* **1** resembling somebody or something from the past **2** existing in the present day

mod·ern·ism /móddər nìzzəm/ *n* **1** the latest styles, tastes, attitudes, or practices **2** modern styles in art, architecture, and literature —**mod·ern·ist** *n, adj* —**mod·ern·is·tic** /móddər nístik/ *adj*

mod·ern·ize /móddər nìz/ (-ized, -iz·ing) *vti* make something more modern —**mod·ern·i·za·tion** /móddərni záysh'n/ *n*

mod·est /móddəst/ *adj* **1** not unduly proud of your own achievements or abilities **2** not extreme or excessive ○ *a modest income* **3** not showy or elaborate ○ *a modest dwelling* **4** not overtly sexual —**mod·est·ly** *adv* —**mod·es·ty** *n*

Mo·des·to /mə déstō/ city in central California. Pop. 182,016 (1998).

mod·i·cum /móddikəm/ *n* a small amount

mod·i·fy /móddə fì/ (-fied, -fies) *vt* **1** make changes to something **2** make something less extensive, severe, or extreme **3** affect the meaning of a word, usually by describing or limiting it with an adjective,

noun, or phrase —**mod·i·fi·a·ble** *adj* —**mod·i·fi·ca·tion** /móddəfi káysh'n/ *n* —**mod·i·fi·er** *n* ◊ See note at **change**

Mo·di·glia·ni /móddil yaánee/, **Amedeo** (1884–1920) Italian painter and sculptor

mod·ish /módish/ *adj* fashionable —**mod·ish·ly** *adv* —**mod·ish·ness** *n*

Mo·dred /máwdrəd/, **Mor·dred** /máwrdrəd/ *n* in Arthurian legend, the knight who killed King Arthur

mod·u·lar /mójjələr/ *adj* consisting of separate modules —**mod·u·lar·i·ty** /mòjjə lérrətee/ *n* —**mod·u·lar·ly** *adv*

mod·u·late /mójjə làyt/ (-lat·ed, -lat·ing) *vt* **1** change the tone, pitch, or volume of a sound **2** alter something to make it less strong, forceful, or severe **3** vary the characteristics of a radio wave —**mod·u·la·tion** /mòjjə láysh'n/ *n* —**mod·u·la·tor** *n*

mod·ule /mójjool/ *n* **1** an independent interchangeable unit of a structure or system **2** a self-contained part of a space vehicle

mo·dus op·er·an·di /mōdəss oppə rándee, -dì/ (*pl* **mo·di op·er·an·di** /mōdee oppə rándee, mō dì oppə rán dì/) *n* a particular method of doing things

mo·dus vi·ven·di /mōdəss vi véndee, -dì/ (*pl* **mo·di vi·ven·di** /mōdee vi véndee, mō dì vi vén dì/) *n* **1** a compromise that allows conflicting groups, parties, or ideas to coexist **2** a way of life for a particular group or person

Mog·a·dish·u /mòggə díshoō/ capital of Somalia. Pop. 982,000 (1995).

mo·gul¹ /mōg'l, mō gùl/ *n* a powerful person, especially in the media

mo·gul² /mōg'l, mō gùl/ *n* a skiing obstacle consisting of a mound of packed snow

mo·hair /mō hàir/ *n* the wool of an Angora goat

ORIGIN Mohair comes from an Arabic word that means literally "preferred, select, choice." It was adopted into English in the late 16C, and began to be assimilated to *hair* during the 17C.

Mo·ha·ve /mō haávee/ (*pl* same or -ves), **Mo·ja·ve** *n* **1** a member of a Native North American people who lived along the Colorado River **2** the language of the Mohave people —**Mo·ha·ve** *adj*

Mo·hawk /mō hàwk/ (*pl* same or -hawks) *n* **1** a member of a Native North American people who now live mainly in Ontario and New York **2** the language of the Mohawk people **3** **mo·hawk** a hairstyle in which the sides of the head are shaved and the hair on top is left sticking up —**Mo·hawk** *adj*

Mo·he·gan /mō héegən/ (*pl* same or -gans) *n* **1** a member of a Native North American people who live mainly in SE Connecticut and Wisconsin **2** the Algonquian language of the Mohegan people —**Mo·he·gan** *adj*

Mo·hen·jo-da·ro /mō hènjō daárō/ ruined ancient city of a Bronze Age civilization in modern-day S Pakistan

Mo·hi·can /mō heékən, mə-/ (*pl same or* **-cans**) *n* a Mahican, or the Mahican language (*dated*) —**Mo·hi·can** *adj*

moi·e·ty /móy əteeí/ (*pl* **-ties**) *n* **1** one of two parts (*fml*) **2** among Native South Americans and Aboriginal Australians, one of two divisions of society for ritual and marriage purposes

moi·ré /mwaa ráy/ *n* **1** a wavy pattern on fabric created using engraved rollers **2** fabric with a wavy pattern and reflective finish —**moi·ré** *adj*

moist *adj* **1** slightly wet **2** pleasantly fresh, not dry or stale —**mois·ten** *vt* —**moist·ly** *adv* —**moist·ness** *n* ◊ See note at **wet**

mois·ture /móyschər/ *n* slight wetness

mois·tur·ize /móyschə rìz/ (**-ized, -iz·ing**) *v* **1** *vti* apply cream or lotion to the skin of the face to keep it from drying out **2** *vt* make something moist —**mois·tur·iz·er** *n*

Mo·ja·ve *n, adj* PEOPLES, LANG = **Mohave**

Mo·ja·ve Des·ert /mō haávee-/ dry region in S California

mo·jo /mó jò/ (*pl* **-joes** *or* **-jos**) *n* (*slang*) **1** magic **2** a supposed magic charm

mol /mōl/ *symbol* **mole**[4]

mo·lar[1] /mólər/ *n* a back tooth

mo·lar[2] /mólər/ *adj* **1** of a mole of a substance **2** containing one mole per liter of solution —**mo·lar·i·ty** /mō lárrətee/ *n*

mo·las·ses /mə lássəz/ *n* syrup produced during sugar refining

ORIGIN **Molasses** goes back to Latin *mel* "honey." It entered English in the 16C from Portuguese.

mold[1] /mōld/ *n* **1** a container into which a molten or liquid substance is poured to make a shape **2** a frame on which something is formed **3** an object made in a mold **4** the general shape of something **5** distinctive character or nature ○ *a leader in the heroic mold* ■ *vt* **1** make in a mold **2** give a particular shape to **3** influence the character and development of

mold[2] /mōld/ *n* **1** a fungus that causes organic matter to decay **2** a growth of mold on something, or the discoloration it causes ■ *vi* become covered with mold

mold[3] /mōld/ *n* soil that is rich in humus

Mol·da·vi·a /mol dáyvee ə/ region and former principality of E Europe, in modern-day Romania and Moldova —**Mol·da·vi·an** *n, adj*

mold·board /mōld báwrd/ *n* the curved blade of a plow, bulldozer, or snowplow

mold·er /mṓldər/ *vi* crumble and decay through natural processes

mold·ing /mṓlding/ *n* **1** a decorative strip on

a wall or a piece of furniture **2** something made in a mold

Mol·do·va /mol dóvə/ country in SE Europe. Cap. Chisinau. Pop. 4,431,570 (2001). —**Mol·do·van** *n, adj*

mold·y /mṓldee/ (**-i·er, -i·est**) *adj* **1** with mold growing on it **2** stale or unpleasant from age or rot —**mold·i·ness** *n*

mole[1] /mōl/ *n* **1** a small burrowing mammal with large forelimbs, no external ears, minute eyes, and dense velvety fur **2** a spy within an organization who discloses secret information about the organization

mole[2] /mōl/ *n* a dark raised growth on the skin

mole[3] /mōl/ *n* **1** a massive sea wall **2** a harbor protected by a mole

mole[4] /mōl/ *n* (*symbol* **mol**) an International System unit of amount of substance equal to the same number of elementary units as the number of atoms in 12 grams of carbon-12

ORIGIN The name of the unit was adopted from German, and is a shortening of *Molekul* "molecule."

mo·le[5] /mólee/ *n* a spicy Mexican chocolate sauce

mo·lec·u·lar bi·ol·o·gy *n* the branch of biology concerned with the nature and function of biological phenomena at the molecular level

mo·lec·u·lar weight *n* the total of all the atomic weights of the atoms in a molecule

mol·e·cule /mólla kyoòl/ *n* **1** the smallest physical unit of a substance that can exist independently **2** a tiny amount —**mo·lec·u·lar** /mə lékyələr/ *adj*

mole·hill /mṓl hìl/ *n* a small mound of earth dug up by a burrowing mole

mole·skin /mṓl skìn/ *n* **1** the fur of a mole **2** a strong cotton fabric with a brushed surface

mo·lest /mə lést/ *vt* **1** abuse somebody sexually, especially a child **2** bother, pester, or disturb a person or animal —**mo·les·ta·tion** /mō le stáysh'n/ *n* —**mo·lest·er** *n*

Mo·lière /mōl yáir/ (1622–73) French dramatist

moll /mol/ *n* a gangster's woman companion (*slang*)

mol·li·fy /mólla fì/ (**-fied, -fies**) *vt* **1** pacify somebody who is angry or upset **2** make something less intense or severe —**mol·li·fi·ca·tion** /mòlləfi káysh'n/ *n*

mol·lusk /mólləsk/, **mol·lusc** *n* an invertebrate with a soft unsegmented body, usually protected by a shell —**mol·lus·kan** /mə lúskən/ *adj, n*

mol·ly·cod·dle /móllee kòdd'l/ (**-dled, -dling**) *vt* treat in an overprotective and over-indulgent way

Mo·lo·kai /mṓlō kí, mṓlə kì/ volcanic island in

central Hawaii, between Maui and Oahu. Pop. 6,838 (1995).

Mo·lo·tov cock·tail /móla tàwf-, máwla-, mólə-/ *n* a simple bomb made of a bottle filled with flammable liquid

ORIGIN **Molotov cocktails** are so called because Vyacheslav Mikhailovich Molotov (1890–1986), Soviet premier (1930–41) and foreign minister (1939–49), ordered their large-scale production after the Nazi invasion of Russia.

molt /mōlt/ *vi* shed feathers, fur, or skin periodically to allow for replacement with new growth ■ *n* 1 the shedding of feathers, fur, or skin 2 the feathers, fur, hair, or skin that are shed —**molt·er** *n*

mol·ten /mōlt'n/ *adj* melted and glowing with heat

mol·to /mōltō/ *adv* very (*in musical directions*)

Mo·luc·cas /mə lúkəz/ group of islands in E Indonesia. Pop. 1,741,800 (1998). —**Mol·uc·can** *n, adj*

mo·lyb·de·num /mə líbdənəm/ *n* (*symbol* Mo) a very hard silvery metallic element. Use: strengthening steel alloys.

mom *n* mother (*infml*) ◇ **Mom, Pop, and apple pie** the virtues that US citizens regard as desirable in their culture

mom-and-pop, ma-and-pa *adj* 1 family-run 2 friendly and informal

Mom·ba·sa /mom bássə/ port in SE Kenya, on the Indian Ocean. Pop. 465,000 (1989).

mo·ment /mōmənt/ *n* 1 a short interval of time 2 a specific instant or time 3 the present time 4 a short period of excellence (*often pl*) ◇ *It's not great opera, but it has its moments.* 5 importance (*fml*) ◇ *a decision of great moment*

mo·men·tar·i·ly /mōmən térrəlee/ *adv* 1 briefly 2 very soon

mo·men·tar·y /mōmən tèrree/ *adj* 1 very brief 2 present or happening at every moment —**mo·men·tar·i·ness** *n*

~~momento~~ incorrect spelling of **memento**

mo·men·tous /mō méntəss/ *adj* highly significant —**mo·men·tous·ly** *adv* —**mo·men·tous·ness** *n*

mo·men·tum /mō méntəm/ *n* 1 the power to increase or develop at an ever-growing pace ◇ *in danger of losing momentum* 2 the speed or force of a forward moving object

mom·my /mómmee/ (*pl* -mies), **mom·ma** /-mə/ *n* mother (*infml*)

mom·my track *n* a career route taken by a working mother (*infml*)

Mon. *abbr* Monday

mon- *prefix* = **mono-** (*before vowels*)

Mon·a·co /mónnəkō/ independent principality forming a coastal enclave in SE France. Cap. Monaco. Pop. 31,842 (2001). —**Mon·a·can** *n, adj*

mon·arch /mónnərk/ *n* 1 a king, queen, or other supreme ruler of a state 2 *also* **mon·arch but·ter·fly** a large migrating orange and black butterfly —**mo·nar·chal** /mə naárk'l/ *adj*

mo·nar·chic /mə naárkik/, **mo·nar·chi·cal** /-ik'l/ *adj* of a monarch or monarchy —**mo·nar·chi·cal·ly** *adv*

mon·ar·chy /mónnərkee/ (*pl* -chies) *n* 1 a political system in which a monarch rules 2 a royal family

mon·as·ter·y /mónnə stèrree/ (*pl* -ies) *n* 1 the residence of a community of monks 2 a community of monks —**mon·as·te·ri·al** /mònnə steéree əl/ *adj*

mo·nas·tic /mə nástik/ *adj* 1 of monks, nuns, or monasteries 2 *also* **mo·nas·ti·cal** reclusive or austere ■ *n* a monk

~~monastry~~ incorrect spelling of **monastery**

Mon·dale /món dàyl/, **Walter** (*b.* 1928) US vice president (1977–81) and diplomat

Mon·day /mún dày, múndee/ *n* the first day of the traditional working week

ORIGIN **Monday** is literally the "day of the moon." The same name appears in other Germanic languages, and was translated from Latin *lunae dies*, from which Romance forms such as French *lundi* derive directly.

Mon·dri·an /mòndree aán, móndree aan/, **Piet** (1872–1944) Dutch painter

Mo·net /mō náy/, **Claude** (1840–1926) French painter

mon·e·tar·ism /mónnətə rìzzəm/ *n* 1 the theory that economic changes are caused by changes in the money supply 2 the policy of controlling an economy by making gradual changes in the money supply —**mon·e·tar·ist** *n, adj*

mon·e·tar·y /mónnə tèrree/ *adj* of money or a currency

mon·e·tar·y u·nit *n* a country's basic unit of currency

mon·e·tize /mónnə tìz/ (-tized, -tiz·ing) *vt* make something the legal tender of a country —**mon·e·ti·za·tion** /mònnəti záysh'n/ *n*

mon·ey /múnnee/ *n* 1 the amount of coins and bills in somebody's possession or available to somebody 2 a national currency 3 an official or unofficial medium of exchange ■ **mon·eys, mon·ies** *npl* a sum of money ◇ *state education monies* ◇ **for somebody's money** in somebody's opinion ◇ **in the money** having a lot of money

mon·ey-back *adj* promising a refund

mon·ey-chang·er /múnnee chàynjər/ *n* 1 a foreign currency exchanger 2 a machine dispensing coins in exchange for paper money

mon·eyed /múnneed/, **mon·ied** *adj* 1 rich 2 consisting of or resulting from money

mon·ey-grub·ber /múnnee grùbbər/ *n* somebody intent on making money (disapproving) —**mon·ey-grub·bing** adj, n

mon·ey-lend·er /múnnee lèndər/ n somebody who lends money at interest —**mon·ey-lend·ing** n

mon·ey-mak·er /múnnee màykər/ n **1** somebody who is good at making money **2** a project or business that makes a lot of money —**mon·ey-mak·ing** n, adj

mon·ey mar·ket n **1** short-term trade in low-risk securities **2** a mutual fund that sells its shares to buy short-term securities

mon·ey or·der n an order for a specific amount of money that can be used to make payments

mon·ey sup·ply n the amount of money circulating in an economy

-monger suffix seller, dealer, promoter ◇ fishmonger

Mon·gol /móng g'l, móng gòl/ n **1** somebody from Mongolia **2** mon·gol a former term, now offensive, for somebody affected by Down syndrome (dated) —**Mon·gol** adj

Mon·go·li·a /mong gólee ə, mon-/ country in Central Asia. Cap. Ulaanbaatar. Pop. 2,654,999 (2001). —**Mon·go·li·an** n, adj

mon·gol·oid /móng gə lòyd/ adj an offensive term meaning affected by Down syndrome (dated)

Mon·gol·oid adj **1** of an E Asian racial group in an obsolete classificatory system **2** mon·gol·oid an offensive term meaning affected by Down syndrome (dated) —**Mon·gol·oid** n

mon·goose /món gòoss/ (pl -goos·es) n an animal that resembles a ferret and kills snakes

---

ORIGIN Mongoose was adopted from a South Asian language in the late 17C. It has no connection at all with geese.

---

mon·grel /móng grəl/ n **1** a dog of mixed breed **2** any animal or plant of mixed breed ■ adj mixed in origin or character (sometimes offensive) —**mon·grel·ism** n

mon·ied adj = moneyed

mon·ies plural of money

mon·i·ker /mónnikər/, **mon·ick·er** n a name or nickname (slang)

⚡**mon·i·tor** /mónnitər/ n **1** a closed-circuit television set or viewing device **2** a computer video display **3** a computer program that observes and controls other programs in a system **4** somebody who ensures proper conduct **5** a school student who helps a teacher by being given a special duty ■ vt **1** watch over somebody to ensure his or her proper conduct **2** check something regularly for developments **3** listen to broadcasts or telephone conversations **4** check the quality of transmitted signals —**mon·i·to·ri·al** /mònni táwree əl/ adj

monk /mungk/ n a man who lives in a religious community —**monk·ish** adj

AKG London
Thelonious Monk

Monk /mungk/, **Thelonious** (1920–82) US jazz pianist and composer

mon·key /múngkee/ n (pl -keys) **1** a medium-sized primate belonging to the group that includes baboons, marmosets, capuchins, and macaques **2** a mischievous child (infml) ■ vt (-keyed, -key·ing) mimic (archaic) □ **monkey around** vi behave in a silly careless way

mon·key bars npl a structure of poles and bars for children to climb on

mon·key busi·ness n illegal, dishonest, or dubious activity (infml)

mon·key-shines /múngkí shìnz/ npl silly or mischievous behavior (infml)

mon·key wrench n a wrench with an adjustable jaw

mon·o¹ /mónnō/ n monophonic reproduction

mon·o² /mónnō/ n infectious mononucleosis (infml)

mono- prefix **1** one, single, alone ◇ monoculture **2** containing a single atom, radical, or group ◇ monoxide

mon·o·chro·mat·ic /mònnə krō máttik/ adj having only one color —**mon·o·chro·mat·i·cal·ly** adv

mon·o·chrome /mónnə króm/ adj **1** created or displayed in shades of one color or black and white **2** lacking interest or distinctiveness ■ n **1** a black-and-white photograph or transparency **2** a piece of artwork in shades of one color **3** the artistic technique of using one color —**mon·o·chro·mic** /mònnə krómik/ adj

mon·o·cle /mónnək'l/ n an eyeglass for one eye

mon·o·clo·nal /mònnə klón'l/ adj describes cells or products of cells belonging to a single clone

mon·o·cot·y·le·don /mònnə kòtt'l éed'n/ n a plant belonging to the group that has a single seed leaf in the seed —**mon·o·cot·y·le·don·ous** adj

mon·o·cul·ture /mónnə kùlchər/ n the practice of growing only one crop in a field or larger area —**mon·o·cul·tur·al** /mònnə kúlchərəl/ adj

mo·nog·a·my /mə nóggəmee/ n **1** the practice of only having one sexual partner or mate during a period of time **2** marriage to one person at a time —**mo·nog·a·mist** n —**mo·nog·a·mous** adj

mon·o·gram /mónnə gràm/ *n* a set of decorative initials ■ *vt* (**-grammed** or **-gramed**, **-gram·ming** or **-gram·ing**) put a monogram on —**mon·o·gram·mat·ic** /mònnəgrə máttik/ *adj* —**mon·o·grammed** *adj*

mon·o·graph /mónnə gràf/ *n* a scholarly piece of writing on a particular topic —**mo·nog·ra·pher** /mə nóggrəfər/ *n* —**mon·o·graph·ic** /mònnə gráffik/ *adj*

mon·o·lin·gual /mònnə líng gwəl/ *adj* 1 able to speak only one language 2 produced in only one language —**mon·o·lin·gual·ism** *n*

mon·o·lith /mónnə lìth/ *n* 1 a pillar of rock standing by itself 2 a large block of building material 3 something large and immovable, especially a long-established organization —**mon·o·lith·ic** /mònnə líthik/ *adj*

mon·o·lith·ic tech·nol·o·gy *n* a technology used in electronics manufacture in which all circuit components are mounted on a single piece of material

mon·o·logue /mónnə lòg/, **mon·o·log** /n/ 1 an actor's long speech 2 a long uninterrupted speech by anyone 3 a series of jokes or amusing stories told by a comedian —**mo·nol·o·gist** /mə nólləjist, mónnə lòggist/ *n*

mon·o·ma·ni·a /mònnə máynee ə/ *n* an obsessive preoccupation with a single thing —**mon·o·ma·ni·ac** *n*

mon·o·mer /mónnəmər/ *n* a simple molecule that can join in long chains with other molecules —**mon·o·mer·ic** /mònnə mérrik/ *adj*

Mo·non·ga·he·la /mə nòng gə héelə/ river in West Virginia and Pennsylvania. Length 130 mi./210 km.

mon·o·nu·cle·o·sis /mònnō nooklee ṓssiss/ *n* a condition marked by a significant rise in the number of atypical white blood cells in the blood

mon·o·phon·ic /mònnə fónnik/ *adj* using one channel to reproduce sound

mon·o·plane /mónnə plàyn/ *n* an airplane with a single set of wings

mo·nop·o·list /mə nóppəlist/ *n* 1 a controller of a monopoly 2 a supporter of policies favoring monopolies —**mo·nop·o·lis·tic** /mə nòppə lístik/ *adj*

mo·nop·o·lize /mə nóppə lìz/ (**-lized, -liz·ing**) *vt* 1 have exclusive commercial control of 2 dominate selfishly —**mo·nop·o·li·za·tion** /mə nòppəli záysh'n/ *n*

mo·nop·o·ly /mə nóppəlee/ (*pl* **-lies**) *n* 1 a situation in which one company has exclusive control of the supply of a product or service 2 a company with a monopoly —**mo·nop·o·lism** *n*

mon·o·rail /mónnə ràyl/ *n* a railroad in which the trains straddle or are suspended from a single beam

mon·o·so·di·um glu·ta·mate /mònnə sṓdee əm glóotə màyt/ *n* a flavor enhancer used in the food industry

mon·o·syl·lab·ic /mònnə si lábbik/ *adj* 1 describes a statement or answer that is brief and unhelpful 2 containing only one syllable ○ *a monosyllabic word* —**mon·o·syl·lab·i·cal·ly** *adv* —**mon·o·syl·lab·ic·i·ty** /mònnə silə bíssətee/ *n*

mon·o·syl·la·ble /mónnə sìlləb'l/ *n* a word consisting of one syllable

mon·o·the·ism /mónnə thee ìzzəm/ *n* belief in a single God —**mon·o·the·ist** *n, adj* —**mon·o·the·is·tic** /mònnə thee ístik/ *adj*

mon·o·tone /mónnə tòn/ *n* 1 a sound that does not rise or fall in pitch 2 a series of sounds that stay at the same pitch ■ *adj* lacking variety in pitch, color, or another quality —**mon·o·ton·ic·i·ty** /mònnə tō níssətee/ *n*

mo·not·o·nous /mə nótt'nəss/ *adj* 1 repetitious and uninteresting 2 uttered in an unvaried tone —**mo·not·o·nous·ly** *adv* —**mo·not·o·ny** *n*

mon·o·un·sat·u·rat·ed /mònnō un sácʜə ràytəd/ *adj* describes a fatty acid with only one carbon double bond

mon·o·va·lent /mònnə váylənt/ *adj* 1 describes a chemical element or isotope with a valence of one 2 containing only one type of antibody —**mon·o·va·lence** *n* —**mon·o·va·len·cy** *n*

mon·ox·ide /mə nók sìd/ *n* an oxide containing one oxygen atom

mon·o·zy·got·ic /mònnō zī góttik/ *adj* describes twins derived from a single fertilized egg

Mon·roe /mən rṓ/, **James** (1758–1831) 5th president of the United States (1817–25)

Mon·roe, Marilyn (1926–62) US actor

Mon·ro·vi·a /mən rṓvee ə/ capital of Liberia. Pop. 421,058 (1984).

Mon·sieur /mə syúr/ (*pl* **Mes·sieurs** /may syúr, -syúrz/) *n* 1 a French title equivalent to "Mr." 2 a French word used to address a man

Mon·si·gnor /mon séenyər/ (*pl.*-**gnors** or -**gnor·i** /-seen yáwree/) *n* a title for a high-ranking Roman Catholic cleric —**Mon·si·gnor·i·al** /mòn seen yáwree əl/ *adj*

mon·soon /mon sṓn/ *n* 1 a wind system that reverses direction seasonally 2 a period of heavy rainfall, especially during the summer in South Asia —**mon·soon·al** *adj*

mon·ster /mónstər/ *n* 1 an imaginary or mythical being that is ugly and terrifying 2 somebody who is inhumane and vicious 3 something extraordinarily large (*infml*)

mon·stros·i·ty /mon stróssətee/ (*pl* -**ties**) *n* 1 a very ugly thing 2 a monstrous quality

mon·strous /mónstrəss/ *adj* 1 shocking and morally unacceptable 2 extremely large 3 resembling a mythical monster —**mon·strous·ly** *adv* —**mon·strous·ness** *n*

Mont. *abbr* Montana

mon·tage /mon táazʜ/ *n* 1 an artwork created from a collection of materials and pieces of things **2** the technique of creating a montage **3** a sequence of overlapping film clips

Mon·taigne /mon táyn, -tényə/, **Michel Eyquem de** (1533–92) French essayist

Mon·tan·a /mon tánə/ state in the NW United States. Cap. Helena. Pop. 902,195 (2000). —**Mon·tan·an** n, adj

Mon·tauk /món tàwk/ (pl same or **-tauks**) n a member of a Native North American people who lived in the eastern part of Long Island, New York —**Mon·tauk** adj

Mont Blanc /mònt blángk, mòN blaáN/ highest mountain in the Alps and W Europe, in E France, on the Italian border. Height 15,771 ft./4,807 m.

Mont·calm /mont kaám, moN kálm/, **Louis-Joseph de, Marquis de Montcalm** (1712–59) French soldier

Mon·te Car·lo /mòntee kaárlō/ resort town in Monaco. Pop. 13,154 (1982).

Mon·te·ne·gro /mòntə neègrō, -néggrō/ constituent republic of the Federal Republic of Yugoslavia, in the southwest of the country. Cap. Podgorica. Pop. 673,981 (2001). —**Mon·te·ne·grin** n, adj

Mon·ter·rey /mòntə ráy/ capital of Nuevo Leon State, NE Mexico. Pop. 1,088,143 (1995).

Mon·tes·quieu /mòntə skyoó/, **Charles Louis de Secondat, Baron de la Brède et de** (1689–1755) French jurist and writer

Mon·tes·so·ri /mòntə sáwree/, **Maria** (1870–1952) Italian physician and educator

Mon·te·ver·di /mònti váirdee/, **Claudio** (1567–1643) Italian composer

Mon·te·vi·de·o /mòntəvi dáy ō/ capital of Uruguay. Pop. 1,378,707 (1996).

Mon·te·zu·ma II /mònti zoómə/ (1466–1520) Aztec emperor (1502–20)

Mont·gol·fier /mont gólfee ər, moN gòl fyáy/, **Joseph Michel** (1740–1810) and his brother **Jacques Etienne** (1745–99) French inventors who developed the hot-air balloon

Mont·gom·er·y /mont gúmməree, -gúmree/ capital of Alabama. Pop. 197,014 (1998).

Mont·gom·er·y, Bernard Law, 1st Viscount Montgomery of Alamein (1887–1976) British military commander

month /munth/ n **1** a major named division of the year in various calendar systems **2** a period of four weeks or 30 days **3** an interval between dates in consecutive months **4** one twelfth of a solar year **5** the time between one new moon and the next ■ **months** npl a long period of time

month·ly /múnthlee/ adj **1** happening or produced once a month **2** lasting a month ■ adv once a month ■ n (pl **-lies**) a magazine issued every month

Mont·pel·ier /mont peélyər/ capital of Vermont. Pop. 7,734 (1998).

Mon·tre·al /mòntree áwl/ city in S Quebec, Canada. Pop. 1,016,376 (1996).

Mont-Saint-Mi·chel /mòN saN mi shél/ granite islet off the coast of NW France, known for its Benedictine abbey

Mont·ser·rat /mòntsə rát/ island in the E Caribbean Sea, a dependency of the United Kingdom. Pop. 12,771 (1996).

mon·u·ment /mónnyəmənt/ n **1** a large stone statue or carving serving as a tribute **2** a famous place or building **3** a carved headstone

mon·u·men·tal /mònnyə mént'l/ adj **1** huge in size, importance, or intensity **2** of or in the form of a monument —**mon·u·men·tal·ly** adv

moo (**mooed, moo·ing, moos**) vi make the deep drawn-out noise of a cow —**moo** n

⚡ **MOO** /moo/ n a virtual space in which participants can discuss a topic online. Full form **multi-user domain, object-oriented**

mooch vti get something for nothing from another person (infml) —**mooch·er** n

mood¹ n **1** a state of mind **2** the general feeling of a group

mood² n a set of verb forms expressing a particular attitude

mood·y /moódee/ (**-i·er, -i·est**) adj **1** tending to change mood unpredictably **2** displaying unhappiness or anger —**mood·i·ly** adv —**mood·i·ness** n

moon n **1** also **Moon** the Earth's only natural satellite **2** any planet's natural satellite ■ vi wander around in a dreamy or listless state

moon·beam /moón beèm/ n a shaft of moonlight

moon·light /moón lìt/ n light from the Moon ■ vi work at a second job in addition to a main job, often secretly (infml) —**moon·light·er** n —**moon·light·ing** n

moon·lit /moón lìt/ adj brightened by moonlight

moon·scape /moón skàyp/ n **1** a view of the Moon's surface **2** a bare deserted landscape

moon·shine /moón shìn/ n (infml) **1** illegally made alcohol **2** nonsense —**moon·shin·er** n

moon·shot /moón shòt/ n a launch of a spacecraft to the moon

moon·stone /moón stòn/ n a semiprecious translucent variety of feldspar. Use: gems.

moon·struck /moón strùk/ adj **1** in a daze, often because of love (infml humorous) **2** behaving in a wildly confused way (dated literary)

moor¹ n a large wild area of treeless land, covered with bracken, heather, coarse grasses, or moss (often pl)

moor² vti secure or be secured with ropes, cables, or an anchor

Moor n a member of a nomadic people of Arab and Berber descent whose civilization flourished in North Africa from the 8C to the 15C —**Moor·ish** adj

Moore /moŏr, mawr/, **Marianne** (1887–1972) US poet

moor·hen /moŏr hèn/ n a black water bird with a red bill

moor·land /moŏr lànd, -lənd/ n an area of moor

moose (pl same) n a large mammal of the deer family with long legs and, in the male, flat antlers

moot /moōt/ adj 1 arguable 2 irrelevant 3 legally insignificant because of having already been decided or settled —**moot·ness** n

SPELLCHECK Do not confuse the spelling of **moot** and **mute** ("unable to speak or make a sound"), which sound similar.

moot court n a court in which law students try hypothetical cases as part of their training

mop n 1 a long-handled tool for washing floors 2 a short-handled tool for washing dishes ■ vt (mopped, mop·ping) 1 wash with a mop 2 wipe to remove perspiration □ **mop up** vt 1 deal with remaining enemy forces to secure an area after a victory 2 clear up the final details of a task (infml)

MOP n somebody who has assets that are nominally worth a million dollars or pounds but that may never be realizable in cash. Full form **millionaire on paper**

mope /mōp/ (moped, mop·ing) vi be miserable, listless, and full of self-pity —**mop·er** n —**mop·ey** adj

mo·ped /mō pèd/ n a motorized bicycle

mo·raine /mə ráyn/ n a mass of earth and rock debris left by a retreating glacier

mor·al /máwrəl/ adj 1 involving issues of right and wrong 2 based on personal conscience 3 regarded in terms of what is known to be right or just o a moral victory 4 good or right by accepted standards ■ n a rule governing behavior given as a conclusion of a story ■ **mor·als** npl standards of behavior —**mor·al·ly** adv

mo·rale /mə rál, maw-/ n the general level of confidence or optimism in a group

mor·al·ist /máwrəlist/ n 1 a student, teacher, or critic of morals 2 somebody with high moral standards —**mor·al·is·tic** /màwrə lístik/ adj

mo·ral·i·ty /mə rállətee, maw-/ n 1 accepted moral standards 2 the rightness or wrongness of something

mor·al·ize /máwrə līz/ (-ized, -iz·ing) v 1 vi criticize the morals of other people 2 vt analyze in terms of morality —**mor·al·i·za·tion** /màwrəli záysh'n/ n —**mor·al·iz·er** n —**mor·al·iz·ing** n

mo·rass /mə ráss, maw-/ n 1 an area of soggy ground 2 an overwhelming or frustrating situation that slows progress

mor·a·to·ri·um /màwrə táwree əm/ (pl -ums or -a /-ə/) n 1 an agreed halt or period of postponement 2 an authorized delay in meeting an obligation

mor·bid /máwrbid/ adj 1 interested in gruesome or gloomy subjects 2 gruesome or gloomy 3 of or resulting in illness —**mor·bid·ly** adv —**mor·bid·ness** n

mor·bid·i·ty /mawr bíddətee/ n 1 the presence of illness or disease 2 the relative frequency of occurrence of a disease

more /mawr/ adv 1 to a greater extent, or in a larger number or amount (forming the comparative of some adjectives and adverbs) o is more beautiful o behaved more sensibly 2 the comparative of "much" o wanted it more 3 for a longer time o chatted a bit more ■ adv, pron with greater frequency or intensity o The more you listen, the more you hear. o are now going to the theater more ■ adj, pron additional or further (pronoun + sing or pl verb) o There aren't any more of these. o No more is expected. o needs more light ◊ **more or less** 1 approximately 2 essentially or basically

More /mawr/, **Sir Thomas, St.** (1478–1535) English politician and scholar

more·o·ver /mawr ṓvər/ adv furthermore or besides

mo·res /máw ràyz, -rèez/ npl established customs and rules in a society or group

~~morgage~~ incorrect spelling of **mortgage**

Mor·gan /máwrgən/, **John Pierpont** (1837–1913) US financier

Mor·gan le Fay /màwrgən lə fáy/ n in Arthurian legend, an evil sorceress who was the half-sister and enemy of King Arthur

morgue /mawrg/ n 1 a room or building run by a state or local government where dead bodies are kept for autopsy or identification 2 a file of information in a newspaper office, used for reference

ORIGIN The Morgue was a mortuary in Paris, France, where unidentified bodies were laid out. It was first used as an English word in the mid-19C.

mor·i·bund /máwrə bùnd/ adj 1 nearly dead 2 becoming obsolete —**mor·i·bun·di·ty** /màwrə búndətee/ n

Mo·ri·sot /màwree zṓ/, **Berthe** (1841–95) French painter

Mor·mon /máwrmən/ n a member of the Church of Jesus Christ of Latter-day Saints —**Mor·mon** adj —**Mor·mon·ism** n

morn n a morning (literary)

morn·ing /máwrning/ n 1 the early part of the day, before noon 2 the period from midnight to noon 3 dawn

morn·ing-af·ter pill n a contraceptive pill taken after sexual intercourse

morn·ing dress n a man's formal daytime suit

morn·ing glo·ry *n* a climbing plant with showy flowers

morn·ing sick·ness *n* nausea in pregnant women

morn·ing star *n* a planet seen clearly at dawn

mo·roc·co /mə rókō/, **mo·roc·co leath·er** *n* very soft goatskin leather

Mo·roc·co /mə rókō/ country in NW Africa. Cap. Rabat. Pop. 30,645,305 (2001). —**Mo·roc·can** *n, adj*

mo·ron /máw ròn/ *n* **1** an offensive term for somebody regarded as unintelligent *(insult)* **2** an offensive term for somebody with learning difficulties —**mo·ron·ic** /mə rónnik, maw-/ *adj* —**mo·ron·i·ty** /mə rónnətee, maw-/ *n*

mo·rose /mə róss, maw-/ *adj* having a withdrawn gloomy personality —**mo·rose·ly** *adv* —**mo·rose·ness** *n*

morph[1] *n* one of two or more variant forms of an animal or plant

⚡ **morph**[2] *vti* **1** transform from one image to another by means of computer graphics, or be transformed in this way **2** transform in appearance completely and instantaneously

-morph *suffix* something that has a particular form, shape, or structure o *polymorph* —**morphic** *suffix* —**morphism** *suffix* —**morphous** *suffix* —**morphy** *suffix*

mor·pheme /máwr feèm/ *n* the smallest meaningful unit of speech or writing —**mor·phem·ic** /mawr feèmik/ *adj*

mor·phine /máwr feèn/ *n* an opium-based pain-relieving drug

mor·phol·o·gy /mawr fóllajee/ (*pl* **-gies**) *n* **1** the form and structure of organisms, or the study of this **2** the structure of words in a language, or the study of this —**mor·pho·log·i·cal** /màwrfə lójjik'l/ *adj* —**mor·phol·o·gist** *n*

Mor·ris /mórriss/, **Gouverneur** (1752–1816) American federalist leader

Mor·ris, **Robert** (1734–1806) American patriot and financier

Mor·ris, **William** (1834–96) British artist, poet, and social activist

Popperfoto

Toni Morrison

Mor·ris·on /mórriss'n/, **Toni** (*b.* 1931) US writer

mor·row /mórrō/ *n* the next day *(literary)*

Morse /mawrss/, **Morse code** *n* a system for representing letters and numbers with short and long signals of sound or light that are printed out as dots and dashes

Morse /mawrss/, **Samuel F. B.** (1791–1872) US inventor and artist. He invented the electric telegraph (1837) and the Morse code.

mor·sel /máwrs'l/ *n* **1** a small piece of food **2** a small amount of anything ■ *vt* (**-seled** *or* **-selled**, **-sel·ing** *or* **-sel·ling**) divide into portions

~~mortgage~~ incorrect spelling of **mortgage**

mor·tal /máwrt'l/ *adj* **1** certain to die eventually **2** human **3** fatal **4** continuing until somebody dies o *mortal combat* **5** of death **6** hated o *a mortal enemy* **7** intense ■ *adj, adv* adds emphasis *(dated)* ■ *n* a human being —**mor·tal·ly** *adv* ◊ See note at **deadly**

mor·tal·i·ty /mawr tállətee/ *n* **1** the condition of being certain to die eventually **2** the number of deaths that occur at a given time, in a given group, or from a given cause

mor·tal sin *n* in the Roman Catholic Church, a sin that brings damnation

mor·tar /máwrtər/ *n* **1** a mixture of cement, sand, and water. Use: in building to hold bricks and stones together. **2** a cannon with a short wide barrel **3** a bowl in which a substance is ground with a pestle

mor·tar·board /máwrtər bàwrd/ *n* **1** a board for carrying mortar **2** a hat with a square flat top and a tassel, worn on formal academic occasions

mort·gage /máwrgij/ *n* **1** a loan to buy property that is security for the loan **2** the contract for a mortgage that exists between a borrower and a lender **3** the money borrowed in a mortgage ■ *vt* (**-gaged**, **-gag·ing**) give as security for a loan —**mort·gage·a·ble** *adj*

> **ORIGIN Mortgage** was adopted from French, and means literally "dead pledge." The idea is presumably that the property is "dead" or lost to the mortgagor if the loan is not repaid.

mort·ga·gee /màwrgi jeè/ *n* the lender in a mortgage agreement

mort·gage rate *n* an interest rate on a mortgage loan

mort·ga·gor /màwrgi jáwr, máwrgi jər/, **mort·gag·er** *n* the borrower in a mortgage agreement

mor·ti·cian /mawr tísh'n/ *n* a funeral director

mor·ti·fy /máwrtə fì/ (**-fied**) *vt* **1** shame and humiliate **2** use self-inflicted hardship or pain to control desires and passions —**mor·ti·fi·ca·tion** /màwrtəfi káysh'n/ *n* —**mor·ti·fy·ing** *adj* —**mor·ti·fy·ing·ly** *adv*

mor·tise /máwrtiss/, **mor·tice** *n* a hole cut to receive a projecting part to form a joint ■ *vt* (**-tised**, **-tis·ing**; **-ticed**, **-tic·ing**) **1** cut a mortise in **2** join by means of a mortise and tenon

Mor·ton /máwrt'n/, **Jelly Roll** (1885–1941) US jazz pianist

mor·tu·ar·y /máwrchoo èrree/ *n* (*pl* **-ies**) a room or building where dead bodies are kept until burial or cremation ■ *adj* of death

mo·sa·ic /mō záy ik/ *n* **1** a picture or design made with small pieces of colored material stuck onto a surface **2** the art of making mosaics

Mo·sa·ic /mō záy ik/, **Mo·sa·i·cal** /-ik'l/ *adj* of Moses, the Hebrew prophet who, according to the Bible, led the Israelites out of slavery in Egypt

Mos·cow /móskow, -kō/ capital of Russia. Pop. 10,666,935 (1995).

Mo·selle /mō zél/ river in NE France and NW Germany. Length 342 mi./550 km.

Mos·es /mṓziz/ (*fl* 14–13C BC) in the Bible, a Hebrew who led the Israelites out of slavery in Egypt

mo·sey /mṓzee/ (**-seyed, -sey·ing, -seys**) *vi* walk unhurriedly (*infml*)

mosh *vt* dance in a frenzied way to rock music (*infml*)

Mos·lem /mózzləm, móssləm/ (*pl* **-lems** or same) *n* ISLAM = **Muslim**

USAGE *Muslim* is to be preferred over **Moslem**.

mosque /mosk/ *n* a Muslim place of worship

ORIGIN **Mosque** goes back to an Arabic word meaning literally "place of bowing down." It entered English through Italian and French.

mos·qui·to /mə skéetō/ (*pl* **-toes** or **-tos**) *n* a small slender fly that feeds on the blood of mammals and transmits diseases such as yellow fever and malaria

mos·qui·to net *n* a fine net curtain used as protection against mosquitoes

moss /mawss/ *n* a simple nonflowering plant that inhabits moist shady sites —**moss·y** *adj*

most /mōst/ *adj, pron* greatest in number, amount, extent, or degree o *the candidate winning the most votes* o *The most I can lend you is $50.* ■ *adv* **1** to the greatest extent (forming the superlative of some adjectives and adverbs) o *the most expensive* **2** the superlative of "much" o *He likes her most.* **3** very o *a most enjoyable day* **4** almost (*infml*) o *Most everyone was invited.*

-most *suffix* **1** nearest to or toward o *topmost* **2** most o *southernmost*

most·ly /mṓstlee/ *adv* **1** mainly **2** usually

mote *n* a speck or particle

mo·tel /mō tél/ *n* a hotel for motorists

~~moter~~ incorrect spelling of **motor**

mo·tet /mō tét/ *n* a vocal composition based on a sacred text

moth /mawth/ *n* a night-flying insect resembling a butterfly

moth·ball /máwth bàwl/ *n* a moth-repellent ball of a solid chemical substance ■ *vt* **1** put something off indefinitely **2** take a factory out of operation

moth-eat·en *adj* **1** eaten by moth larvae **2** worn-out

moth·er /múthər/ *n* **1** a female parent **2** a woman acting as a parent **3** a woman who is the originator of something **4** the origin or stimulus of something o *Necessity is the mother of invention.* **5** **Moth·er** a title for a nun ■ *vt* **1** look after somebody with care, sometimes with excessive care **2** give birth to and bring up a baby —**moth·er·hood** *n* —**moth·er·less** *adj* —**moth·er·li·ness** *n* —**moth·er·ly** *adj*

⚡ **moth·er·board** /múthər bàwrd/ *n* the main circuit board of a computer

moth·er coun·try *n* **1** the country that colonists have left **2** somebody's country of birth

moth·er hen *n* a woman who is regarded as overprotective and fussing

moth·er-in-law (*pl* **moth·ers-in-law**) *n* a spouse's mother

moth·er-in-law a·part·ment *n* a small apartment attached to a house that is suitable for a parent to live in independently

moth·er·land /múthər lànd/ *n* somebody's country of birth

Moth·er Na·ture *n* the forces of nature regarded as a willful being

Moth·er of God *n* a title given to the mother of Jesus Christ, especially by Roman Catholics

moth·er-of-pearl *n* the pearly inside layer of some shells. Use: decorative inlays.

Moth·er's Day *n* the 2nd Sunday in May, when people give their mothers cards and presents

moth·er ship *n* a ship or spaceship that provides services and supplies for smaller ships

moth·er su·pe·ri·or (*pl* **moth·er su·pe·ri·ors** or **moth·ers su·pe·ri·or**) *n* the head of a convent or community of Christian nuns

moth·er-to-be (*pl* **moth·ers-to-be**) *n* a pregnant woman

moth·er tongue *n* the first language somebody learns as a child at home

Moth·er·well /múthər wèl/, **Robert** (1915–91) US artist

mo·tif /mō téef/ *n* **1** a repeated design **2** a sewn or printed decoration

mo·tion /mṓsh'n/ *n* **1** the process or a way of moving **2** a movement or gesture **3** the power of movement **4** a formal proposal put forward for discussion or a vote ■ *vti* signal to somebody —**mo·tion·less** *adj* —**mo·tion·less·ly** *adv* —**mo·tion·less·ness** *n*

mo·tion pic·ture *n* a movie (*technical*)

mo·tion sick·ness *n* sick feeling caused by movement —**mo·tion sick** *adj*

mo·ti·vate /mṓtə vàyt/ (**-vat·ed, -vat·ing**) *vt* provide with an incentive —**mo·ti·vat·ed**

adj —**mo·ti·va·tion** /mòtə váysh'n/ *n* —**mo·ti·va·tion·al** *adj* —**mo·ti·va·tor** *n*

mo·tive /mótiv/ *n* **1** a reason or incentive **2** a motif in literature, art, or music ■ *adj* **1** causing motion **2** driving somebody to do something —**mo·tive·less** *adj*

SYNONYMS motive, incentive, inducement, spur, goad CORE MEANING: something that prompts action

mot juste /mò zhoóst/ (*pl* **mots justes** /*pronunc. same*/) *n* the right word or words to express something

mot·ley /móttlee/ (**-li·er, -li·est**) *adj* **1** made up of different types that do not combine well **2** of varied colors

mo·to·cross /mótō kràwss/ *n* motorcycle racing over rough ground

mo·tor /mótər/ *n* **1** a machine that creates motion **2** an engine ■ *adj* **1** of vehicles **2** motor-driven **3** causing motion **4** of muscle activity

mo·tor·bike /mótər bìk/ *n* **1** a light motorcycle **2** a bicycle with a motor

mo·tor·boat /mótər bòt/ *n* a small boat with an engine —**mo·tor·boat·er** *n* —**mo·tor·boat·ing** *n*

mo·tor·cade /mótər kàyd/ *n* a procession of cars escorting somebody important

mo·tor·car /mótər kàar/ *n* a car (*dated or fml*)

mo·tor·cy·cle /mótər sìk'l/ *n* a two-wheeled motor-powered vehicle ■ *vi* (**-cled, -cling**) ride on a motorcycle —**mo·tor·cy·clist** *n*

mo·tor home *n* a motor vehicle with living facilities

mo·tor·ist /mótərist/ *n* a driver of a motor vehicle

mo·tor·ize /mótə rìz/ (**-ized, -iz·ing**) *vt* **1** fit something with a motor **2** equip troops with vehicles —**mo·tor·i·za·tion** /mótərr záysh'n/ *n*

mo·tor neu·ron dis·ease *n* a disease that causes muscle weakness and wasting

mo·tor pool *n* vehicles kept by an organization for its employees

mo·tor scoot·er *n* a light motorcycle

mo·tor ve·hi·cle *n* any road vehicle powered by an engine

Mo·town /mó tòwn/ *tdmk* a trademark for a music company based in Detroit whose music, consisting of elements of pop, soul, and gospel, was especially popular during the 1960s and 1970s

Mott /mot/, **Lucretia** (1793–1880) US feminist and abolitionist

mot·tle /mótt'l/ (**-tled, -tling**) *vt* mark something with different colors

mot·to /móttō/ (*pl* **-toes** *or* **-tos**) *n* **1** a rule to live by **2** a saying on a coat of arms

moue /moo/ *n* a pout

mound /mownd/ *n* **1** a small hill **2** a constructed pile of something **3** a pile of objects **4** a large amount **5** the raised part of a baseball field where the pitcher plays —**mound** *vt*

Mound Build·er *n* a member of an early Native North American people who built burial mounds and earthwork fortifications in what is now the Midwest and Southeast of the United States

mount[1] /mownt/ *v* **1** *vt* climb something such as stairs or a hill **2** *vti* get onto a horse to ride **3** *vt* begin a course of action **4** *vt* organize an event or spectacle **5** *vi* increase **6** *vt* put somebody onto or sit on a form of transportation **7** *vt* get onto something higher **8** *vi* go up into the air **9** *vt* secure something to something else **10** *vt* put something onto a support or into a position for use ■ *n* **1** a support or holder for fixing something in place **2** an animal used for riding

mount[2] /mownt/ *n* a mountain (*literary; often in place names*)

moun·tain /mównt'n/ *n* **1** a very high point of land **2** a large pile **3** a large amount (*infml; often pl*)

moun·tain ash *n* a shrub with red or orange berries

moun·tain bike *n* a bicycle for rough terrain

moun·tain board·ing *n* the sport of traveling down hillsides on a board similar to a skateboard but with bigger wheels

moun·tain·eer /mòwnt'n eér/ *n* **1** a mountain climber **2** an inhabitant of mountains ■ *vi* climb mountains —**moun·tain·eer·ing** *n*

moun·tain goat *n* a wild North American goat

moun·tain lau·rel *n* an evergreen North American shrub with pink or white flowers

moun·tain li·on *n* a large wild cat

moun·tain·ous /mównt'nəss/ *adj* **1** having mountains **2** very large

moun·tain range *n* a connected series of mountains

moun·tain·side /mównt'n sìd/ *n* the sloping side of a mountain

Moun·tain Stan·dard Time, Moun·tain Time *n* standard time in W North America

moun·tain·top /mównt'n tòp/ *n* the peak of a mountain

moun·te·bank /mówntə bàngk/ *n* (*literary*) **1** somebody who deceives other people **2** a seller of fake medicines

mount·ed /mówntəd/ *adj* **1** on horseback **2** fixed in place

Mount·ie /mówntee/, **Mount·y** (*pl* **-ies**) *n* a member of the Royal Canadian Mounted Police (*infml*)

mount·ing /mównting/ *n* a supporting device ■ *adj* becoming greater

mourn /mawrn/ *v* **1** *vti* express or feel sadness at somebody's death **2** *vi* express sadness at the loss of something —**mourn·er** *n*

mourn·ful /máwrnfəl/ *adj* **1** feeling sad, or expressing sadness **2** causing sadness —**mourn·ful·ly** *adv* —**mourn·ful·ness** *n*

mourn·ing /máwrning/ *n* a show of deep sadness following somebody's death

⚡ **mouse** /mowss/ *n* (*pl* **mice**) **1** a small rodent with a long mostly hairless tail **2** (*pl* **mous·es** *or* **mice**) a handheld input device for controlling a computer ■ *vi* (**moused, mous·ing**) hunt mice

⚡ **mouse but·ton** *n* a push button on a computer mouse

⚡ **mouse pad, mouse mat** *n* a surface on which to move a computer mouse

mous·er /mówssər/ *n* an animal that catches mice

mouse·trap /mówss tràp/ *n* a device used to catch mice ■ *vt* (**-trapped, -trap·ping**) trap by clever deception

mous·sa·ka /moo saákə, mòossə kaà/ *n* a Greek dish of eggplant and ground meat

mousse /mooss/ *n* **1** a light sweet food with a base of whipped cream and egg **2** a foam for setting or styling hair ■ *vt* (**moussed, mouss·ing**) style hair with mousse

mous·y /mówssee/ (**-i·er, -i·est**), **mous·ey** *adj* **1** dull brown in color **2** timid

mouth *n* /mowth/ (*pl* **mouths** /mowthz/) **1** the organ through which food is taken in and from which sound is emitted **2** the feature of the face that is the visible part of the mouth **3** the place where a river enters the sea **4** an opening in the earth **5** the opening of a container **6** an opening between parts of a tool ■ *vt* /mowth/ (**mouthed, mouth·ing, mouths**) **1** say loudly or insincerely **2** mumble
□ **mouth off** *vi* (*infml*) **1** talk back rudely **2** express forcefully

mouth·ful /mówthfool/ *n* **1** a quantity of food or drink taken at one time **2** a small amount of food **3** a word or phrase that is hard to pronounce

mouth or·gan *n* a harmonica

mouth·part /mówth paàrt/ *n* a body part near the mouth of an insect or other arthropod that it uses to gather or chew food

mouth·piece /mówth peèss/ *n* **1** a part of a musical instrument, telephone, or other device held to the mouth **2** *also* **mouth guard** a device to protect an athlete's teeth **3** a person or publication expressing the views of an organization (*sometimes disapproving*)

mouth-to-mouth, mouth-to-mouth re·sus·ci·ta·tion *n* a revival method in which the rescuer blows air into the victim's mouth and lungs

mouth·wash /mówth wàwsh/ *n* a solution used for gargling

mouth·wa·ter·ing /mówth wàwtəring/ *adj* whetting the appetite —**mouth·wa·ter·ing·ly** *adv*

mouth·y /mówthee, mówthee/ (**-i·er, -i·est**) *adj* tending to talk loudly or too much (*infml*) —**mouth·i·ness** *n*

mov·a·ble /móovəb'l/, **move·a·ble** *adj* **1** easily moved **2** changing date from year to year ○ *Easter is a movable holiday.* ■ *n* a piece of easily moved property (*often pl*) —**mov·a·bil·i·ty** /móovə billətee/ *n* —**mov·a·ble·ness** *n*

mov·a·ble feast *n* a festival that falls on a different day each year

move /moov/ *v* (**moved, mov·ing**) **1** *vti* change or cause to change position **2** *vti* change your residence, job, or school, or make somebody change residence, job, or school **3** *vi* take action **4** *vi* change your view **5** *vti* improve or progress, or cause something to improve or progress **6** *vi* formally propose action **7** *vt* stir somebody's emotions **8** *vti* sell or be sold **9** *vti* empty the bowels, or be emptied ■ *n* **1** an instance of moving **2** a step in a series **3** somebody's turn to play in a board game **4** a maneuver ◇ **on the move** going forward, or making progress
□ **move in** *vi* start living or working somewhere
□ **move in on** attempt to take control of

move·ment /móovmənt/ *n* **1** an act of moving **2** a way of moving **3** a collective effort to achieve a social or political goal **4** the moving parts of a clock or watch **5** a self-contained section of a long musical work **6** an act of emptying the bowels ■ **move·ments** *npl* somebody's activities and whereabouts

mov·er /móovər/ *n* **1** somebody or something that causes motion **2** somebody with a particular social circle **3** a company or person that moves people's property from one location to another

mov·ie /móovee/ *n* a series of moving pictures ■ **mov·ies** *npl* **1** the motion picture industry **2** the showing of a movie ○ *go to the movies*

mov·ie·go·er /móovee gòr/ *n* a viewer of movies

mov·ie star *n* a popular actor in motion pictures

mov·ie the·a·ter, mo·vie house *n* a theater where motion pictures are shown

mov·ing /móoving/ *adj* **1** making people feel emotion **2** able to move **3** in motion (*usually in combination*) ○ *slow-moving* —**mov·ing·ly** *adv*

SYNONYMS moving, pathetic, pitiful, poignant, touching, heartwarming, heartrending
CORE MEANING: arousing emotion

---

mov·ing pic·ture *n* a motion picture (*dated*)

mov·ing van *n* a large truck used to transport furniture

mow¹ /mō/ (**mowed, mown** /mōn/ *or* **mowed**) *vt* cut grass with a lawn mower or scythe
□ **mow down** *vt* kill many people quickly

mow² /mō/ *n* **1** a storage place for hay **2** a pile of stored hay

mox·ie /móksee/ *n* courage (*slang*)

Mo·zam·bique /mò zəm beék/ country in SE Africa. Cap. Maputo. Pop. 19,371,057 (2001). —**Mo·zam·bi·can** n, adj

Mo·zart /mòts aart/, **Wolfgang Amadeus** (1756–91) Austrian composer —**Mo·zar·ti·an** adj

moz·za·rel·la /mòtsə réllə/ n a white cheese used in cooking, especially on pizza

MP, M.P. abbr 1 Member of Parliament 2 military police 3 mounted police

✦ **mp3** /èm pee threé/ abbr a file extension indicating a sound file that can be downloaded from the Internet

✦ **mpeg** /èm pèg/ abbr a file extension for an MPEG file

✦ **MPEG** /èm pèg/ n a computer file standard for storing and transmitting digital video and audio. Full form **Moving Pictures Experts Group**

✦ **mpg** abbr 1 also **m.p.g.** miles per gallon 2 a file extension for a Moving Pictures Experts Group file

mph, m.p.h. abbr miles per hour

M.Phil. /èm fíl/ abbr Master of Philosophy

MPV n a car similar to a van, typically with three rows of seats. Full form **multipurpose vehicle**

Mr. /místər/ n the customary courtesy title for a man, used before his name or job title o Mr. Lee o Mr. President

MRI abbr magnetic resonance imaging

Mrs. /míssiz/ n the customary courtesy title for a married woman, used before her name

MS abbr 1 Mississippi 2 multiple sclerosis

ms., MS. abbr manuscript

Ms. /miz/ n the customary courtesy title for a woman that makes no distinction between married and unmarried status

M.S., M.Sc. abbr Master of Science

✦ **MS-DOS** /èm ess dáwss, èm ess dóss/ tdmk a trademark for a widely used computer operating system

MSG abbr monosodium glutamate

Msgr. abbr Monsignor

mss., MSS. abbr manuscripts

MST, M.S.T. abbr Mountain Standard Time

MT abbr 1 machine translation 2 megaton 3 metric ton 4 Montana 5 Mountain Time

mt. abbr megaton

Mt. abbr 1 Mount 2 Mountain

MTBE n an antiknock additive in unleaded gasoline. Full form **methyl tertiary-butyl ethyl**

mtg. abbr meeting

M-the·o·ry n a theory describing the forces and matter that make up the universe that incorporates existing theories and suggests the existence of 11 dimensions

mts., Mts. abbr mountains

mu /myoo, moo/ n the 12th letter of the Greek alphabet

Mu·bar·ak /moo baárək, moo-/, **Hosni** (b. 1928) Egyptian president (1981–)

much adv 1 to a great extent (often in combination) o much-loved 2 often o don't go there much ■ adj, pron great in quantity or extent o Much of the day was spent packing. o caused much joy ◊ **as much** precisely that ◊ **(as) much as** although, or even though

mu·ci·lage /myoóossəlij/ n 1 a thick water-based glue 2 a sticky plant product

mu·ci·lag·i·nous /myoóossə lájjənəss/ adj 1 producing mucilage 2 moist and sticky

muck (infml) n sticky dirt ■ vt make something dirty
□ **muck up** vt spoil (infml)

muck-rake /múk ràyk/ (-raked, -rak·ing) vi seek out and expose scandal —**muck-rak·er** n —**muck-rak·ing** n

muck·y /múkee/ (-ier, -i·est) adj filthy (infml) —**muck·i·ly** adv—**muck·i·ness** n

mu·cous /myoókəss/ adj of mucus

mu·cous mem·brane n a moist membrane that lines body cavities open to the exterior

mu·cus /myoókəss/ n a slimy secretion that lines mucous membranes —**mu·coid** /myoó kòyd/ adj

mud n 1 wet dirt 2 defamatory material

✦ **MUD** /mud/ n a virtual space for multiple users. Full form **multiuser domain**

mud-bath /múd bàth/ (pl **-baths** /-bàths, -bàthz/) n a beauty treatment involving immersion in mud

mud·dle /múdd'l/ v (-dled, -dling) 1 vt mix things together in disorder 2 confuse things 3 make somebody confused ■ n 1 a confused state 2 a mix-up —**mud·dled** adj
□ **muddle through** vi succeed despite a lack of organization

mud·dle-head·ed /mùdd'l héddəd/ adj 1 unable to think clearly 2 badly thought-out —**mud·dle-head·ed·ly** adv —**mud·dle-head·ed·ness** n

mud·dy /múddee/ adj (-di·er, -di·est) 1 made dirty with mud 2 resembling mud 3 lacking brightness or transparency 4 confused ■ vt (-died, -dies) make dirty or unclear —**mud·di·ly** adv—**mud·di·ness** n

mud flap, mud·guard /múd gaàrd/ n a flap behind a wheel of a vehicle to keep mud out

mud-pack /múd pàk/ n a cleansing facial treatment in which a preparation is smeared on the skin and allowed to dry

mud pie n a mass of mud shaped by a child

mud·room /múd ròom, -ròòm/ n a room where dirty shoes or other clothing may be removed before entering the main rooms of a house

mud·slide /múd slìd/ n a destructive flow of mud

mud·sling·ing /múd slìnging/ n defamation of an opponent —**mud·sling·er** n

⚡**MUD vir·tu·al** /n a virtual space for a collaborative project

mues·li /myoózlee/ n a breakfast food consisting of cereals, nuts, and dried fruits

mu·ez·zin /myoo ézzin, myoó əzin, moo-/ n a man who calls Muslims to prayer

muff[1] /n a furry cylinder used to put both hands in to keep them warm

muff[2] vt 1 fail to catch a ball 2 do something badly

muf·fin /múffin/ n a small round cake for one person

muf·fle /múff'l/ vt (-fled, -fling) 1 wrap something to stifle sound 2 make something less loud 3 prevent something from being expressed ■ n a device that muffles sound —**muf·fled** adj

muf·fler /múfflər/ n 1 a scarf worn round the neck 2 US, Can, ANZ a silencer on a car exhaust

muf·ti /múftee, moóftee/ n 1 civilian clothes when worn by somebody who usually wears a uniform 2 also **Muf·ti** an expert on Islamic law

mug[1] n 1 a large round straight-sided drinking cup 2 the contents of a mug —**mug·ful** n

mug[2] n 1 somebody's face (slang) 2 a violent man ■ v (mugged, mug·ging) 1 vt rob somebody in the street 2 vi make faces —**mug·ger** n —**mug·ging** n

Mu·ga·be /moò gaábee/, **Robert** (b. 1924) national leader and president (1987–) of Zimbabwe

mug·gy /múggee/ (-gi·er, -gi·est) adj very hot and humid —**mug·gi·ness** n

mug shot n a photograph of a face, especially one taken by the police

Mu·ham·mad /moò hámmid, mə-/, **Mo·ham·med** (570?–632) Arabian founder of Islam

Mu·ham·mad, Elijah (1897–1975) US political activist

Mu·har·ram /moo hárrəm/, **Mo·har·ram** n the 1st month of the Islamic calendar

Muir /myoor/, **John** (1838–1914) Scottish-born US naturalist and explorer

mu·ja·hed·din /moò jaahə deén, moòjahə-/, **mu·ja·he·deen, mu·ja·hi·din** npl Islamic guerrillas

muk·luk /múk lùk/ n 1 a large waterproof boot 2 an Inuit sealskin boot

mu·lat·to /moò láttō, -laátō/ (pl -tos or -toes) n (dated) 1 an offensive term for somebody who has one Black and one Caucasian parent 2 an offensive term for somebody who has both Black and Caucasian parents or ancestors

mul·ber·ry /múl bèrree/ (pl -ries) n 1 a small purple fruit 2 the tree that produces mulberries

mulch n a covering of organic material laid over the soil around plants to suppress weeds or retain moisture —**mulch** vti

mule[1] /myool/ n a cross between a horse and a donkey

mule[2] /myool/ n a backless slipper or shoe

mu·le·teer /myoólə teér/ n a mule driver

mul·ish /myoólish/ adj stubborn —**mul·ish·ly** adv —**mul·ish·ness** n

mull[1] /mul/
□ **mull over** vt think about something carefully

mull[2] /mul/ vt heat and flavor wine, beer, or cider

mul·lah /múllə, moólla/ n 1 a Muslim scholar 2 a title of respect given to a learned Muslim man

mul·let /múllət/ n 1 (pl mul·lets or same) a thick-bodied fish typically found in inshore waters 2 mullet as food

mul·li·ga·taw·ny /mùlligə táwnee/ n a spicy meat and vegetable soup

mul·lion /múllyən/ n a vertical bar that divides the panes of a window —**mul·lioned** adj

Mul·ro·ney /mul roónee/, **Brian** (b. 1939) prime minister of Canada (1984–93)

multi- prefix many, multiple, more than one or two ○ multimedia

⚡**mul·ti·ac·cess** /múltee ák sess, mùltī-/ adj allowing several users access at the same time

⚡**mul·ti·cast·ing** /múltee kàsting/ n the process of sending data to many network users simultaneously —**mul·ti·cast** vt

mul·ti·col·or /múlti kùllər/, **mul·ti·col·ored** /-kùllərd/ adj 1 of different colors 2 producing several colors at once

mul·ti·cul·tur·al /mùltee kúlchərəl, mùltī-/ adj 1 of more than one culture 2 supporting ethnic integration —**mul·ti·cul·tur·al·ism** n

mul·ti·dis·ci·pli·nar·y /mùltee díssipli nèrree, mùltī-/, **mul·ti·dis·ci·pline** /mùltee díssiplin, mùltī-/ adj involving a range of subjects

mul·ti·fac·et·ed /mùltee fássətəd, mùltī-/ adj 1 with diverse qualities 2 describes a gemstone with many facets

mul·ti·far·i·ous /mùltə fáiree əss/ adj with much variety

mul·ti·lat·er·al /mùlti láttərəl/ adj 1 involving several parties or nations 2 many-sided —**mul·ti·lat·er·al·ly** adv

mul·ti·lin·gual /mùltee líng gwəl, mùltī-/ adj of or speaking several languages —**mul·ti·lin·gual·ly** adv

⚡**mul·ti·me·di·a** /mùltee meédee ə, mùltī-/ n 1 sound and video on computers 2 in teaching, the use of video, film, and music in addition to other methods 3 the use of various materials and media in art 4 in advertising, the use of all the communications media —**mul·ti·me·di·a** adj

mul·ti·mil·lion /mùltee míllyən, mùltī-/ adj involving millions of a monetary unit

mul·ti·mil·lion·aire /múltee millyə náir, mùltī-/ *n* a very rich person

mul·ti·na·tion·al /múltee náshən'l, -náshnəl, mùltī-/ *adj* **1** operating in several countries **2** involving people from several countries ■ *n* a large company that operates in several countries —**mul·ti·na·tion·al·ism** *n*

mul·ti·ple /múltip'l/ *adj* involving several things ■ *n* a number that is divisible by another —**mul·ti·ply** /-plee/ *adv*

mul·ti·ple-choice *adj* offering several possible answers

mul·ti·ple scle·ro·sis *n* a serious progressive disease of the nervous system

⚡ **mul·ti·plex** /múltə pléks/ *n* **1** a movie theater complex with several units **2** multiple transmission of signals along one communications line ■ *adj* complex ■ *vt* send signals by multiplex

⚡ **mul·ti·plex·er** /múltə pléksər/, **mul·ti·plex·or** *n* **1** a device for sending several data streams down a single communications line **2** a film-to-video system

mul·ti·pli·ca·tion /múltipli káysh'n/ *n* **1** an arithmetic operation in which a number is added to itself a stated number of times **2** a marked increase —**mul·ti·pli·ca·tion·al** *adj* —**mul·ti·pli·ca·tive** /múltə plíkətiv, múltəpli káytiv/ *adj*

mul·ti·pli·ca·tion sign *n* a symbol that indicates multiplication, e.g., x

mul·ti·pli·ca·tion ta·ble *n* a table giving the numbers 1 through 12 or 10 and all their multiples

mul·ti·plic·i·ty /múltə plíssətee/ *n* **1** a great variety **2** complexity

mul·ti·ply /múltə plí/ (-**plied, -plies**) *v* **1** *vti* combine numbers by multiplication **2** *vti* increase in amount **3** *vi* breed —**mul·ti·plic·a·ble** /-plíkəb'l/ *adj*

mul·ti·ply /múltəplí/ *adj* with more than one layer

⚡ **mul·ti·port** /múlti pàwrt/ *adj* describes a computer network with several connection points

⚡ **mul·ti·pro·cess·ing** /múltee pró sèssing, mùltī-/ *n* the use of several processing units in a single computer

⚡ **mul·ti·pro·ces·sor** /múltee pró sèssər, mùltī-/ *n* a computer system for parallel processing

mul·ti·pur·pose /múltee púrpəss, mùltī-/ *adj* with several uses

mul·ti·ra·cial /múltee ráysh'l, mùltī-/ *adj* of more than one race or ethnic group —**mul·ti·ra·cial·ly** *adv*

mul·ti·sto·ry /múlti stàwree/, **mul·ti·sto·ried** /múlti stàwreed/ *adj* with several stories

mul·ti·task·ing /múlti tàsking/ *n* the simultaneous management of two or more tasks by a computer or a person

mul·ti·tude /múlti tòod/ *n* **1** a crowd **2** a large number (*often pl*)

mul·ti·tu·di·nous /mùlti tóod'nəss/ *adj* very numerous

⚡ **mul·ti·us·er** /múlti yóozər/ *adj* used by several people

mul·ti·vi·ta·min /múltə vîtəmin/ *n* a pill containing several vitamins —**mul·ti·vi·ta·min** *adj*

mum[1] *adj* silent (*infml*) ■ *interj* keep quiet

mum[2] *n* a chrysanthemum (*infml*)

Mum·bai /móom bî/ port and capital of Maharashtra, west central India. Pop. 9,925,891 (1991).

mum·ble /múmb'l/ *vti* (-**bled, -bling**) say something quietly and unclearly ■ *n* an indistinct way of speaking —**mum·bling** *adj* —**mum·bly** *adj*

mum·bo jum·bo /múmbō júmbō/ *n* confusing language, especially technical jargon (*infml*)

mum·mer /múmmər/ *n* **1** a masked partygoer **2** an actor taking part in a pantomime, folk play, or mime show **3** a mime artist

mum·mi·fy /múmmə fí/ (-**fied, -fies**) *vt* preserve a corpse for burial by embalming and wrapping it in cloth —**mum·mi·fi·ca·tion** /mùmməfi káysh'n/ *n*

mum·my /múmmee/ (*pl* -**mies**) *n* **1** a body that has been embalmed and wrapped in cloth **2** a naturally preserved body

ORIGIN The name for an Egyptian **mummy** derived from an Arabic word that referred both to an embalmed body and to a substance like bitumen whose exact composition is not known, but which was reputed to have medicinal properties. These ideas seem to have blended to some extent as the word traveled through Latin and French, and **mummy** reached English as a medicinal substance that was supposed to be derived from mummified remains.

mumps *n* a contagious disease that causes swelling of the salivary glands (+ *sing or pl verb*)

ORIGIN **Mumps** is in origin the plural of an obsolete noun meaning "grimace." The name presumably derives from the contortion of the face caused by swollen glands.

munch /munch/ *vti* chew noisily

Munch /móongk/, **Edvard** (1863–1944) Norwegian painter

munch·kin /múnchkin/ *n* **1** a small person **2** an insignificant person (*infml*)

ORIGIN The original **munchkin** was a creature invented by L. Frank Baum in *The Wizard of Oz* (1900).

mun·dane /mun dáyn/ *adj* **1** commonplace **2** of this world —**mun·dane·ly** *adv* —**mun·dan·i·ty** /-dánnətee/ *n*

mung bean *n* **1** a small green or yellow bean **2** the plant that produces mung beans

Mu·nich /myoonik/ capital of Bavaria, SE Germany. Pop. 1,244,676 (1997).

mu·nic·i·pal /myoo níssəp'l/ *adj* of a municipality ■ *n* a municipal bond —**mu·nic·i·pal·ly** *adv*

mu·nic·i·pal bond *n* a security issued by a local government, usually to pay for public improvements

mu·nic·i·pal·i·ty /myoo nissə pállətee/ (*pl* -ties) *n* 1 a town or city with its own government 2 the members of a local government ◊ See note at **city**

mu·nif·i·cent /myoo niffiss'nt/ *adj* very generous —**mu·nif·i·cence** *n* —**mu·nif·i·cent·ly** *adv* ◊ See note at **generous**

mu·ni·tion /myoo nísh'n/ *vt* supply with weapons ■ **mu·ni·tions** *npl* military supplies —**mu·ni·tion·er** *n*

mu·ni·tion·ize /myoo nísh'n ìz/ (-ized, -iz·ing) *vt* process chemical, nuclear, or biological material so that it can be deployed as a weapon

Mu·ñoz Ma·rin /moo nyòz ma rín/, **Luis** (1898–1980) Puerto Rican politician

Mun·ro /mən rố/, **Alice** (b. 1931) Canadian writer

Mün·ster /moónstər, mûnstər/ inland port in NW Germany. Pop. 264,887 (1997).

mu·on /myoo òn/ *n* an elementary particle with a mass about 200 times that of an electron —**mu·on·ic** /myoo ónnik/ *adj*

mu·ral /myoorəl/ *n* a painting on a wall ■ *adj* of walls —**mu·ral·ist** *n*

Mu·ra·sa·ki /moòr aa saàkee/, **Shikibu** (978?–1026?) Japanese court lady and writer

mur·der /múrdər/ *n* the crime of killing somebody deliberately ■ *v* 1 *vti* kill somebody illegally and deliberately 2 *vt* kill somebody brutally 3 *vt* destroy or completely spoil (*slang*) —**mur·der·er** *n* —**mur·der·ess** *n* ◊ See note at **kill**

mur·der·ous /múrdərəss/ *adj* 1 likely to commit murder 2 difficult (*infml*) —**mur·der·ous·ly** *adv*

Express Newspapers

Dame Iris Murdoch

Mur·doch /múr dok/, **Dame Iris** (1919–99) Irish-born British novelist and philosopher

Mur·doch, Rupert (b. 1931) Australian-born US media proprietor

murk *n* gloomy darkness

murk·y /múrkee/ (-i·er, -i·est) *adj* 1 dark and gloomy 2 hard to see through 3 difficult to understand —**murk·i·ly** *adv* —**murk·i·ness** *n*

~~murmer~~ incorrect spelling of **murmur**

mur·mur /múrmər/ *n* 1 a continuous hum 2 something said quietly 3 a complaint 4 a sound usually heard via a stethoscope that indicates heart trouble ■ *v* 1 *vti* say something softly 2 *vi* complain discreetly —**mur·mur·ing·ly** *adv* —**mur·mur·ous** *adj*

Mur·phy's Law /múrfeez-/ *n* the principle that if anything can go wrong, it will (*infml*)

Mur·ray /múrree/ river in SE Australia. Length 1,609 mi./2,589 km.

Mur·rum·bidg·ee /mùrrəm bíjjee/ river in New South Wales, Australia. Length 980 mi./1,600 km.

mus·cat /mú skàt, múskət/ *n* a white grape. Use: wine making, raisins.

Mus·cat /mús kàt/, **Mas·qat** /máss gàt/ capital of Oman. Pop. 635,000 (1995).

mus·ca·tel /mùskə tél/, **mus·ca·del** /-dél/ *n* a sweet white wine

mus·cle /múss'l/ *n* 1 body tissue that is specialized to undergo repeated contraction and relaxation, thereby producing movement of body parts 2 an organ composed of muscle tissue 3 power and influence 4 power and physical strength (*infml*) —**mus·cly** *adj*

ORIGIN **Muscle** goes back to Latin *musculus*, literally "little mouse." It seems that the shape and movement of some muscles under the skin reminded observers of a mouse. The same Latin word gave rise to *mussel*.

SPELLCHECK Do not confuse the spelling of **muscle** and **mussel** ("an edible marine organism"), which sound similar.

☐ **muscle in** *vi* get involved by force or against the wishes of others (*infml*)

mus·cle-bound /múss'l bòwnd/, **mus·cle-bound** *adj* 1 with overdeveloped muscles 2 rigid and inflexible

mus·cle·man /múss'l màn/ (*pl* -men /-mèn/) *n* a strong man with developed muscles

Mus·co·vite /múskə vìt/ *n* somebody from Moscow, Russia ■ *adj* Russian (*archaic*)

mus·cu·lar /múskyələr/ *adj* 1 of the muscles 2 strong and with developed muscles —**mus·cu·lar·i·ty** /mùskyə lérrətee/ *n*

mus·cu·lar dys·tro·phy *n* a muscle-wasting disease

mus·cu·la·ture /múskyələchər, -chòor/ *n* the arrangement of muscles in the body

muse¹ /myooz/ *vti* 1 think about something 2 say something thoughtfully —**mus·ing·ly** *adv*

ORIGIN **Muse** "think" is unrelated to **muse** "inspiration" and the *Muses*. It came through French from a medieval Latin word meaning "animal's muzzle or mouth," probably from the idea of staring open-mouthed.

muse² /myooz/ n 1 the source of an artist's inspiration 2 an artist's particular talent 3 **Muse** in Greek mythology, one of the nine daughters of Zeus who presided over the creative arts

mu·se·um /myoo zée əm/ n a place where objects of artistic, historical, or scientific importance are preserved, studied, and displayed

---

ORIGIN A **museum** is literally devoted to the Muses, who preside over the creative arts. The word first occurs in English in the early 17C as the name of a university building erected in Alexandria in Egypt in the 3C BC. The modern sense appears in the mid-17C.

---

mu·se·um piece n 1 a valuable and interesting object 2 somebody or something dismissed as old-fashioned (infml)

mush¹ /mush/ n 1 pulp 2 sentimental words or ideas 3 cooked cereal ■ vt mash —mush·i·ness n —mush·y adj

mush² /mush/ interj a command to sled dogs to move forward —mush·er n

Mu·shar·raf /moo shárraf/, **Pervez** (b. 1943) president of Pakistan (1999–)

mush·room /músh room/ n 1 any of various types of umbrella-shaped fungi, many of which are edible 2 a fast-growing thing ■ vi 1 grow quickly 2 become mushroom-shaped

mush·room cloud n a mushroom-shaped cloud caused by a nuclear explosion

mu·sic /myóozik/ n 1 sounds that are made in order to create an effect 2 the art of producing and arranging sounds to create an effect 3 written notation for music ◊ **face the music** deal with a difficult or unpleasant consequence

mu·si·cal /myóozik'l/ adj 1 of or for music 2 pleasant-sounding 3 good at music ■ n a play or movie with songs —mu·si·cal·ly adv —mu·si·cal·ness n

mu·sic box n a box that plays a tune

mu·sic hall n an auditorium

mu·si·cian /myoo zísh'n/ n somebody who plays a musical instrument —mu·si·cian·ship n

mu·si·col·o·gy /myóozi kóllajee/ n the study of music —mu·si·co·log·i·cal /myóozika lójjik'l/ adj —mu·si·col·o·gist n

mu·sic stand n a stand for holding a player's sheets of music

musk n a glandular secretion of a deer. Use: perfume manufacture. —musk·i·ness n —musk·y adj

mus·kel·lunge /múska lùnj/ (pl -lun·ges or same) n 1 a large freshwater fish of the pike family 2 muskellunge as food

mus·ket /múskət/ n a long-barreled gun of former times

ORIGIN Musket came via French from Italian moschetta "crossbow bolt." Early muskets

could fire crossbow bolts as well as bullets. The Italian word was formed from mosca "fly (the insect)," which also gave rise to moschetto "sparrow hawk," because the bird's markings were thought to suggest a fly. This word may have reinforced the name for the weapon, as early guns were often named for birds of prey.

---

mus·ket·eer /múska tèer, mùska téer/ n 1 an infantryman who carried a musket 2 a royal bodyguard in 17C and 18C France

Mus·ko·gee /mus kógee/ (pl same or -gees) n a member of a Native North American people who lived in SE North America

musk·rat /músk kràt/ (pl same or -rats) n 1 a large amphibious rodent 2 the fur of a muskrat

~~musle~~ incorrect spelling of **muscle**

Mus·lim /múzzlam, móoz-/ n a follower of Islam ■ adj of Islam

mus·lin /múzzlin/ n a thin cotton fabric. Use: curtains, sheets, dresses.

ORIGIN Muslin is named for Mosul, a town in Iraq where such fabric was made. The word came into English in the early 17C through French from Italian.

---

muss (infml) vt mess up ■ n mess

mus·sel /múss'l/ n 1 an edible marine organism with a blue-black shell 2 a freshwater mollusk whose shell is a source of mother-of-pearl ◊ See note at **muscle**

Mus·so·li·ni /móossa leénee/, **Benito** (1883–1945) Italian fascist leader

Mus·sorg·sky /ma záwrgskee, -sáwrgskee/, **Modest Petrovich** (1839–81) Russian composer

must¹ modal v (must) 1 be compelled to do something ○ must vacate the building 2 be important or necessary to do or be something ○ must be simple to use 3 be certain that something is the case 4 indicates belief based on the available evidence ○ They must have left earlier. 5 intend ○ I must be going. 6 suggests or invites somebody to do something ○ You must see a doctor. ■ n something regarded as essential ■ prefix absolutely necessary (infml; added to a verb to form a noun or adjective) ○ a must-see

must² n grape juice before it is fermented into wine

must³ n a musty condition

mus·tache /mú stàsh, ma stásh/ n 1 a line of hair above the upper lip 2 hair around an animal's mouth —mus·tached adj

mus·ta·chi·o /ma stáshee ô/ (pl -os) n a thick or fancy mustache (archaic or humorous; often pl) —mus·ta·chi·oed adj

mus·tang /mú stàng/ n a North American wild horse

mus·tard /mústərd/ n 1 a spicy condiment consisting of or made from powdered seeds 2 a plant with pungent seeds from which mustard is made **3** a dark yellow color —**mus·tard** *adj* —**mus·tard·y** *adj* ◊ **cut the mustard** be up to the desired standard *(infml)*

mus·tard gas *n* a poison gas that is an evaporated oily liquid

mus·ter /mústər/ *v* **1** *vti* come together as a group, or order military personnel or a ship's crew to come together **2** *vt* summon up something such as strength or courage ■ *n* a gathering of military personnel or a ship's crew for a particular reason ◊ **pass muster** measure up to set standards

must-have *n* something regarded as essential —**must-have** *adj*

must·n't /múss'nt/ *contr* must not

must·y /mústee/ (-i·er, -i·est) *adj* **1** with an old damp smell **2** stale —**must·i·ness** *n*

mu·ta·ble /myóotəb'l/ *adj* **1** tending to change **2** capable of change —**mu·ta·bil·i·ty** /myóotə bíllətee/ *n* —**mu·ta·bly** *adv*

mu·ta·gen /myóotəjən/ *n* something that increases the rate of mutation of cells —**mu·ta·gen·ic** /myóotə jénnik/ *adj*

mu·tant /myóot'nt/ *n* something that has mutated ■ *adj* resulting from mutation

mu·tate /myóo táyt, myoo táyt/ (-tat·ed, -tat·ing) *vti* undergo or cause to undergo mutation —**mu·ta·tive** /myóo táytiv, -tətiv/ *adj*

mu·ta·tion /myoo táysh'n/ *n* **1** a random change in a gene or chromosome resulting in a new trait or characteristic that can be inherited **2** something that has mutated **3** the act or process of changing —**mu·ta·tion·al** *adj*

mu·ta·waa /moo taã waa/ *n* in some Muslim countries, a police force whose duty is to ensure that the population complies with the laws of Islam

mute /myoot/ *adj* **1** unwilling or unable to speak **2** making no sound **3** not expressed in words **4** not pronounced ■ *n* **1** an offensive term for somebody who is unable to speak *(dated)* **2** a device that reduces or softens an instrument's tone **3** a silent letter ■ *vt* (**mut·ed, mut·ing**) **1** moderate the volume of a sound **2** make something less bright **3** reduce or soften an instrument's tone —**mute·ly** *adv* —**mute·ness** *n* ◊ See note at **moot**

mut·ed /myóotəd/ *adj* **1** not bright or intense **2** not loud **3** understated —**mut·ed·ly** *adv*

mu·ti·late /myóot'l àyt/ (-lat·ed, -lat·ing) *vt* **1** injure severely by damaging or removing body parts **2** ruin by removing parts —**mu·ti·la·tion** /myóot'l áysh'n/ *n* —**mu·ti·la·tor** *n*

mu·ti·nous /myóot'nəss/ *adj* **1** involving mutiny **2** refusing to obey

mu·ti·ny /myóot'nee/ *n* (pl **-nies**) rebellion against a legal authority, especially by soldiers or sailors against their officers ■ *vi* (**-nied, -nies**) participate in a mutiny —**mu·ti·neer** /myóot'n eer/ *n*

mutt *n* a mongrel dog *(slang)*

mut·ter /múttər/ *v* **1** *vti* say something quietly **2** *vi* grumble —**mut·ter** *n* —**mut·ter·er** *n*

mut·ton /mútt'n/ *n* meat from a mature sheep —**mut·ton·y** *adj*

mut·ton·chops /mútt'n chòps/ *npl* elaborately shaped whiskers that leave the chin bare

mu·tu·al /myóochoo əl/ *adj* **1** felt and expressed by each person ◊ *mutual admiration* **2** with the same feelings or relationship ◊ *mutual friendship* **3** shared by two people or groups **4** describes a financial company in which the members constitute the stockholders —**mu·tu·al·i·ty** /myóochoo állətee/ *n* —**mu·tu·al·ly** *adv*

mu·tu·al fund *n* a type of investment that uses members' capital to buy stocks from other companies

mu·tu·al·ize /myóochoo ə ìtz/ (-ized, -iz·ing) *vt* alter the organization of a company to assign the majority of shares to employees and customers —**mu·tu·al·i·za·tion** /myóochoo əli záysh'n/ *n*

muu-muu /móo mòo/ (pl **-muus**), **mu·mu** (pl **-mus**) *n* a loose Hawaiian dress

Mu·zak /myóo zàk/ *tdmk* a trademark for recorded background music played in stores, restaurants, elevators, and other public places

muz·zle /múzz'l/ *n* **1** an animal's nose and jaws **2** a restraining device fitted on an animal's muzzle **3** the end of a gun barrel ■ *vt* (**-zled, -zling**) **1** put a muzzle on an animal **2** prevent somebody's free expression

muz·zy /múzzee/ (-zi·er, -zi·est) *adj* **1** not thinking clearly **2** vague

MVP *abbr* most valuable player (award)

mW *abbr* milliwatt

MW *abbr* **1** medium wave **2** megawatt

my /mī/ *adj* belonging to or associated with me ■ *interj* expresses sudden emotion

my·al·gi·a /mī áljee ə, -áljə/ *n* muscle pain —**my·al·gic** *adj*

Myan·mar /myaàn maàr/ country in Southeast Asia. Cap. Yangon. Pop. 41,994,678 (2001).

my·ce·li·um /mī séelee əm/ (pl -a /-ə/) *n* the body of a fungus —**my·ce·li·al** *adj*

My·ce·nae /mī séenee/ ancient Greek city —**My·ce·nae·an** /mîssə née ən/ *n, adj*

my·col·o·gy /mī kólləjee/ *n* **1** the study of fungi **2** the fungi of a particular area —**my·co·log·i·cal** /mîkə lójjik'l/ *adj* —**my·col·o·gist** *n*

my·co·tox·in /mîkə tóksin/ *n* a fungal poison

my·e·lin /mí əlin/ *n* the material that surrounds nerve cells

my·e·lo·ma /mī ə lṓmə/ (pl -**mas** or -**ma·ta** /-mətə/) *n* a malignant tumor of the bone marrow

my·nah /mína/, **my·nah bird**, **my·na**, **my·na bird** *n* a bird of the starling family, some of which are capable of imitating human speech

my·o·pi·a /mī ṓpee ə/ n 1 nearsightedness 2 lack of foresight —**my·op·ic** /mī óppik/ adj

myr·i·ad /meeree əd/ adj 1 too numerous to count 2 consisting of many different elements ■ n a large number o a myriad of stars

myrrh /mur/ n an aromatic resinous gum. Use: in perfume, incense, medicinal preparations.

myr·tle /múrt'l/ n 1 an evergreen tree with blue-black berries 2 PLANTS = periwinkle

my·self /mī sélf/ pron 1 refers to me as the subject of the verb o I hurt myself. 2 emphasizes or clarifies that I am being referred to o I saw it myself. 3 shows that I am alone or unaided o sitting by myself 4 my normal self o I'm not myself today.

mys·te·ri·ous /mi steeree əss/ adj involving or full of mystery —**mys·te·ri·ous·ly** adv —**mys·te·ri·ous·ness** n

~~mysterous~~ incorrect spelling of **mysterious**

mys·ter·y /místəree/ (pl -ies) n 1 a puzzling event or situation 2 an unknown person or thing 3 a story about a puzzling event, especially an unsolved crime 4 something knowable only by divine revelation 5 also **mys·ter·y play** a medieval drama based on the life of Jesus Christ

mys·tic /místik/ n a follower of mysticism ■ adj mystical

mys·ti·cal /místik'l/ adj 1 with a divine meaning 2 of mysticism 3 with a supernatural significance —**mys·ti·cal·ly** adv —**mys·ti·cal·ness** n

mys·ti·cism /místə sìzzəm/ n 1 belief in intuitive spiritual revelation 2 a system of religious belief followed in order to achieve personal union with the divine

mys·ti·fy /místə fī/ (-fied, -fies) vt 1 puzzle greatly 2 make mysterious —**mys·ti·fi·ca·tion** /mìstəfi káysh'n/ n —**mys·ti·fy·ing** adj —**mys·ti·fy·ing·ly** adv

mys·tique /mi steek/ n a mysterious quality

myth /mith/ n 1 an ancient story about heroes or supernatural beings 2 myths collectively 3 a symbolic character or story 4 a fictitious person or thing

myth·i·cal /míthik'l/, **myth·ic** /míthik/ adj 1 of myths 2 imaginary —**myth·i·cal·ly** adv

myth·mak·er /míth màykər/ n a creator of myths —**myth·mak·ing** n

my·thol·o·gize /mi thóllə jīz/ (-gized, -giz·ing) v 1 vt make into a myth 2 vi create myths —**my·thol·o·giz·a·tion** /mi thòllajī záysh'n/ n

my·thol·o·gy /mi thóllajee/ (pl -gies) n 1 the body of myths belonging to a particular culture 2 myths collectively —**myth·o·log·i·cal** /mìthə lójjik'l/ adj—**my·thol·o·gist** n

myx·o·ma·to·sis /mik sòmə tṓssiss/ n a highly infectious viral disease of rabbits

N

n¹ (pl n's), **N** (pl N's or Ns) n the 14th letter of the English alphabet

n² n an indefinite whole number

n³ symbol neutron

N¹ symbol nitrogen

N² abbr 1 knight (in chess) 2 neutral (on gearshifts) 3 north 4 northern

Na symbol sodium

n/a abbr 1 not applicable 2 not available

NAACP, N.A.A.C.P. abbr National Association for the Advancement of Colored People

nab /nab/ (**nabbed, nab·bing**) vt (infml) 1 grab something 2 catch and arrest a criminal or fugitive

na·bob /náy bòb/ n a European person who made a fortune in India

Na·bo·kov /nə bŏk of, -bók-, nábbə kof/, **Vladimir** (1899–1977) Russian-born US writer

Nab·u·lus /nábbə lòoss/, **Nab·lus** /nábbləss/ city in the West Bank Territory. Pop. 100,231 (1997).

na·chos /naa chŏz/ npl a hot dish of tortilla chips covered in cheese or salsa

na·cre /náykər/ n mother-of-pearl

Na·der /náydər/, **Ralph** (b. 1934) US attorney and consumer-protection advocate

na·dir /náydər, -deer/ n 1 the lowest point in something, e.g., somebody's life 2 a point on the celestial sphere that is directly opposite the zenith

> **ORIGIN Nadir** derives from an Arabic word meaning "opposite." The full form from which it was shortened was an astronomical term, "opposite the zenith."

NAFTA /náftə/ n a free-trade agreement between the United States, Canada, and Mexico. Full form **North American Free Trade Agreement**

nag¹ v (**nagged, nag·ging**) 1 vti repeatedly ask somebody to do something 2 vti keep criticizing somebody 3 vi be persistently painful or bothersome ■ n a person regarded as somebody who nags (insult) —**nag·ging** n —**nag·ging·ly** adv ◊ See note at **complain**

nag² n an old horse

Na·ga·sa·ki /nàggə saakee/ city on W Kyushu, Japan. Pop. 423,021 (2000).

Na·go·ya /na góy ə/ city on S Honshu, Japan. Pop. 2,101,877 (2000).

Na·hua·tl /naa waat'l/ (pl same or **-hua·tls** or **-hua** or **-huas**) n 1 a member of a Native Central American people 2 also **Na·hua, Na·huat·lan** the language of the Nahuatl people —**Na·hua·tl** adj

Na·hum /náyhəm, náy əm/ n a book of the Bible that records the prophecies of Nahum, a Hebrew prophet

nai·ad /náy əd, -àd, nī àd/ (pl **-ads** or **-a·des** /-ə dèez, nī ə-/) n 1 in Greek mythology, a water nymph 2 an aquatic larva

nail /nayl/ n 1 a short pointed metal pin hammered into a surface to fix something 2 the horny covering on the end of a finger or toe ■ vt 1 fasten, attach, or secure something with nails 2 catch or convict a guilty person (infml) o nailed him for insider trading 3 establish or achieve something precisely or conclusively (infml) o nailed the jump 4 in baseball, tag a runner out —**nail·er** n —**hit the nail on the head** absolutely correct

□ **nail down** v establish or agree something clearly and conclusively

nail·brush /náyl brùsh/ n a brush for cleaning fingernails

nail clip·pers npl a tool for trimming fingernails and toenails

nail file n a small file for fingernails and toenails

nail pol·ish, nail var·nish n lacquer to decorate fingernails and toenails

nail scis·sors n small scissors for trimming fingernails (+ sing or pl verb)

Nai·paul /nī pawl/, **V. S.** (b. 1932) Trinidadian-born British novelist

nai·ra /nírə/ n the main unit of Nigerian currency

Nai·ro·bi /nī róbee/ capital of Kenya. Pop. 1,810,000 (1995).

na·ive /naa éev/ (**-iv·er, -iv·est**), **na·ïve** /-īv·er, -īv·est), **na·ïf** /-éef/ (**-ïf·er, -ïf·est**) adj 1 with an extremely simple and trusting view of the world 2 not shrewd or sophisticated 3 in art, rejecting sophisticated techniques —**na·ive·ly** adv

na·ked /náykəd/ adj 1 without clothing 2 lacking the usual covering 3 not concealed o naked aggression 4 unadorned o the naked truth —**na·ked·ly** adv —**na·ked·ness** n

SYNONYMS **naked, bare, nude, undressed, unclothed** CORE MEANING: devoid of clothes or covering

na·ked eye n unaided vision

nak·fa /nák fə/ n the main unit of Eritrean currency

N. Am. abbr 1 North America 2 North American

nam·by-pam·by /nàmbee pámbee/ adj feeble and lacking strength of character (infml; sometimes offensive) —**nam·by-pam·by** n

ORIGIN **Namby-pamby** was an insulting nickname given to the English poet Ambrose Philips (1674–1749), playing on his first name. Philips was noted for feebly sentimental pastorals, which were ridiculed by the author Henry Carey in Namby Pamby

(1726). The name was again publicly used by Alexander Pope in his poem The Dunciad. The generalized use first appears in the phrase "namb-pamby style," attributed to Jonathan Swift, who died in 1745.

name n 1 what somebody or something is called 2 an uncomplimentary description o called him names 3 a reputation o made a name for herself as a designer ■ vt (**named, nam·ing**) 1 give a name to 2 identify by name 3 decide on and specify o name the day 4 appoint to an office ◊ **in the name of** 1 by the authority of 2 for the sake of ◊ **the name of the game** what something is all about (infml)

name day n the feast day of the saint for whom somebody is named

name-drop·ping n the practice of mentioning the names of famous acquaintances —**name-drop** vi —**name-drop·per** n

name·less /náymləss/ adj 1 lacking a name 2 anonymous 3 indescribable o nameless fears —**name·less·ness** n

name·ly /náymlee/ adv specifically

name·plate /náym plàyt/ n a plaque marked with somebody's name

name·sake /náym sàyk/ n somebody with the same name as another person

name·tag /náym tàg/ n a badge marked with somebody's name

Na·mib·i·a /nə míbbee ə/ country in SW Africa. Cap. Windhoek. Pop. 1,797,677 (2001). —**Na·mib·i·an** n, adj

nan /naan, nan/ n a flat South Asian bread

Na·nak /náanək/, **Gu·ru Na·nak** (1469–1539) Indian religious leader who founded Sikhism

Nan·chang /náan cháang/ capital of Jiangxi Province, SE China. Pop. 1,410,000 (1995).

⚡ **NAND** /nand/ (pl **NANDs**), **NAND gate** n a type of logical operator used in computers. Full form **not and**

Nan·ga Par·bat /nùng gə paàr baat/ mountain in the W Himalaya range, in NW Kashmir. Height 26,657 ft./8,125 m.

Nan·jing /náan jíng/ capital of Jiangsu Province, E China, on the Yangtze River. Pop. 2,960,000 (1995).

Nan·ning /nan níng/ capital of Guangxi Zhuangzu Autonomous Region, SE China. Pop. 1,370,000 (1995).

nan·ny /nánnee/ (pl **-nies**), **nan·nie** n somebody employed to take care of a family's children

nan·ny goat n a female goat

nano- prefix 1 extremely small o nanotechnology 2 one billionth (10^{-9}) o nanosecond

nan·o·sec·ond /nánnə sèkənd/ n one billionth of a second

nan·o·tech·nol·o·gy /nànnō tek nólləjee/ (pl **-gies**) n the technology used to build microscopic devices

Nan·sen /nánss'n/, **Fridtjof** (1861–1930) Norwegian explorer

Nan·tuck·et /nan túkət/ island in SE Massachusetts, on **Nantucket Sound**. Pop. 3,124 (1996).

nap[1] *n* a short sleep ■ *vi* (**napped**, **nap·ping**) **1** sleep lightly **2** be off guard

nap[2] *n* the pile on a fabric ■ *vt* (**napped**, **nap·ping**) raise the pile of a fabric by brushing it

na·palm /náy pàam, -pàalm/ *n* **1** a highly flammable jelly. Use: in flamethrowers and fire bombs. **2** an aluminum-based thickening agent. Use: manufacture of jellied gasoline. ■ *vt* attack with napalm

Nap·a Val·ley /náppə-/ region of west central California, famous for its vineyards

nape /nayp/ *n* the back of the neck

Na·pi·er /náypee ər/, **John** (1550–1617) Scottish mathematician who invented logarithms

nap·kin /nápkin/ *n* a piece of cloth for protecting clothes and wiping the mouth during eating

Na·ples /náyp'lz/ **1** capital of Campania Region, S Italy, on the **Bay of Naples**. Pop. 1,020,120 (1999). **2** city in SW Florida. Pop. 19,404 (1998).

AKG London

Napoleon I, emperor of the French: Portrait (1807) by Andrea Appiani

Na·po·le·on I /nə pólee ən, -pólyən/ (1769–1821) emperor of the French (1804–14, 1815) —**Na·po·le·on·ic** /nə pòlee ónnik/ *adj*

Na·po·le·on III (1808–73) emperor of the French (1852–70)

~~narative~~ incorrect spelling of **narrative**

narc /naark/ *n* a narcotics agent *(slang)*

nar·cis·sism /náarsə sìzzəm/ *n* **1** excessive self-admiration **2** a personality disorder marked by an excessive need for admiration —**nar·cis·sist** *n* —**nar·cis·sis·tic** /nàarsə sístik/ *adj*

nar·cis·sus /naar síssəss/ (*pl* **-si** /-sì/ *or* **-sus·es** *or* **same**) *n* a spring plant with yellow or white flowers

nar·co·lep·sy /náarkə lèpsee/ *n* a condition characterized by uncontrollable bouts of deep sleep —**nar·co·lep·tic** /nàarkə léptik/ *adj, n*

nar·co·sis /naar kṓssiss/ *n* drug-induced stupor

nar·cot·ic /naar kóttik/ *n* **1** a drug that reduces pain and induces sleep or stupor **2** an illegal drug ■ *adj* causing sleep, stupor, or altered mental states through chemical properties

Nar·ra·gan·set /nàrrə gánsət/ (*pl* **-sets** *or* **same**), **Nar·ra·gan·sett** (*pl* **-setts** *or* **same**) *n* **1** a member of a Native North American people who lived in Rhode Island **2** the extinct Iroquoian language of the Narraganset people —**Nar·ra·gan·set** *adj*

Nar·ra·gan·sett Bay /nàrrə gànssət-/ inlet of the Atlantic Ocean in SE Rhode Island. Length 26 mi. /42 km.

nar·rate /ná ràyt/ (**-rat·ed**, **-rat·ing**) *vt* **1** tell a story **2** give the commentary on a movie or television program —**nar·ra·tion** /na ráysh'n/ *n* —**nar·ra·tion·al** *adj* —**nar·ra·tor** *n*

nar·ra·tive /nárrətiv/ *n* **1** a story **2** the process of narrating ■ *adj* **1** telling a story **2** of narration

nar·row /nárrō/ *adj* **1** small in width **2** limited in size or scope *o a narrow range of options* **3** limited in outlook *o a narrow view of events* **4** just enough for success *o a narrow escape* ■ *vti* *also* **nar·row down** make or become narrow in width, limit, or scope —**nar·row·ly** *adv* —**nar·row·ness** *n*

nar·row·band /nárrō bànd/ *adj* using a narrow band of broadcasting frequencies

nar·row gauge *n* **1** a distance between the two rails of a railroad track under 4 ft. 8.5 in. /143.5 cm **2** a track or train with a narrow gauge —**narrow-gauge** *adj*

nar·row-mind·ed *adj* with a limited and often prejudiced outlook —**nar·row-mind·ed·ly** *adv* —**nar·row-mind·ed·ness** *n*

nar·rows /nárrōz/ *n* a narrow stretch of river or sea (+ *sing or pl verb*)

nar·y /náiree/ *adj* none *(literary)*

NASA /nássə/ *n* the US space agency. Full form **National Aeronautics and Space Administration**

na·sal /náyz'l/ *adj* **1** of the nose **2** pronounced through the nose —**na·sal·i·ty** /nay zállətee/ *n* —**na·sal·ly** *adv*

na·sal·ize /náyz'l ìz/ (**-ized**, **-iz·ing**) *vti* make a speech sound nasal —**na·sal·i·za·tion** /nàyz'li záysh'n/ *n*

NASCAR /náss kàar/ *abbr* National Association of Stock Car Auto Racing

nas·cent /náyss'nt, náss'nt/ *adj* just beginning to develop —**nas·cence** *n* —**nas·cen·cy** *n*

NASDAQ /náz dàk/ *n* a US financial market for over-the-counter securities. Full form **National Association of Securities Dealers Automated Quotation System**

~~nash~~ incorrect spelling of **gnash**

Nash /nash/, **Ogden** (1902–71) US writer and lyricist

Nash·u·a /náshōō ə/ city in S New Hampshire. Pop. 82,169 (1998).

Nash·ville /násh vìl/ capital of Tennessee. Pop. 510,274 (1998).

Nas·sau /ná sàw/ capital of the Bahamas. Pop. 172,000 (1997).

Gamal Abdel Nasser

Nas·ser /nássər, naássər/, **Gamal Abdel** (1918–70) president of Egypt (1956–70)

Nast /nast/, **Thomas** (1840–1902) German-born US satirical cartoonist

nas·tur·tium /nə stúrshəm, na-/ n a plant with pungent round leaves and yellow to red flowers

nas·ty /nástee/ (-ti·er, -ti·est) adj 1 spiteful 2 repugnant to the senses ○ a nasty smell 3 unpleasant or uncomfortable ○ nasty weather 4 likely to harm or be painful ○ a nasty bruise 5 morally offensive (infml) 6 difficult to solve or deal with (infml) —**nas·ti·ly** adv —**nas·ti·ness** n ◊ See note at **mean**

na·tal /náyt'l/ adj of birth

Na·than /náyth'n/, **S. R.** (b. 1924) president of Singapore (1999–)

na·tion /náysh'n/ n 1 a community of people in a land under a single government 2 a community of people of the same ethnic origin, whether living together in one territory or not 3 a Native American people or federation —**na·tion·hood** n

Na·tion /náysh'n/, **Carry** (1846–1911) US temperance leader

na·tion·al /náshən'l, náshnəl/ adj 1 of a nation 2 for a whole nation 3 characteristic of the people of a particular nation ■ n a citizen of a particular nation —**na·tion·al·ly** adv

na·tion·al an·them n the official song of a country

na·tion·al as·sem·bly n a national legislative body

na·tion·al debt n the total debts of a government

na·tion·al dress, na·tion·al cos·tume n the traditional clothes of a country

Na·tion·al Guard n a US military reserve

na·tion·al·ism /náshən'l Izzəm, náshnə-/ n 1 a desire for political independence 2 patriotism —**na·tion·al·ist** n, adj —**na·tion·al·is·tic** /náshən'l Istik, náshnə-/ adj

na·tion·al·i·ty /náshə nállətee/ (pl -ties) n 1 citizenship of a particular nation 2 the people forming a nation-state 3 an ethnic group within a larger entity

na·tion·al·ize /náshən'l Iz, náshnə-/ (-ized, -iz·ing) vt 1 transfer a private business to government ownership 2 give something a national character —**na·tion·al·i·za·tion** /nàshən'li záysh'n, nàshnə-/ n —**na·tion·al·ized** adj

na·tion·al mon·u·ment n an important place protected by the government

na·tion·al park n an area of public land protected by the government

na·tion·al se·cu·ri·ty n the protection of a nation from danger

Na·tion·al Se·cu·ri·ty Coun·cil n a council consisting of the president, the secretary of state, and top advisers that maintains national security

na·tion·al ser·vice n compulsory service in a country's armed forces

Na·tion of Is·lam n a Black Islamic movement

na·tion-state n an independent country

na·tion·wide /náysh'n wíd/ adj, adv everywhere in a nation

na·tive /náytiv/ adj 1 inborn ○ native intelligence 2 born or originating in a particular place ○ native to the Southwest 3 of the indigenous inhabitants of a place (dated; often considered offensive) 4 occurring naturally ■ n 1 someone born in a particular place ○ a native of Boston 2 an original inhabitant (dated; often considered offensive) —**na·tive·ly** adv —**na·tive·ness** n

SYNONYMS native, aboriginal, indigenous, autochthonous CORE MEANING: originating in a particular place

USAGE Avoid use of the lowercase noun and adjective **native** to mean "an indigenous inhabitant of a place" and "relating to the indigenous people of a place," as in the natives of Guam and the native people of Haiti. Prefer the indigenous or original or aboriginal people of Guam or the Haitians. Capitalized Native, totally acceptable, now refers not only to Native North and South Americans but also to indigenous peoples of places such as Hawaii and Alaska, i.e., Native Alaskans, Alaska Natives, and Native Hawaiians.

Na·tive A·las·kan n an Alaska Native

Na·tive A·mer·i·can n a member of any of the indigenous peoples of North, Central, or South America —**Na·tive A·mer·i·can** adj ◊ See note at **Indian**

Na·tive Ha·wai·ian n a member of the indigenous people of Hawaii

na·tive speak·er n a speaker of a language learned in infancy

na·tiv·i·ty /nə tívvətee/ (pl -ties) n 1 birth or origin 2 **Na·tiv·i·ty** the birth of Jesus Christ

NATO /náytō/, **Na·to** n an international military alliance. Full form **North Atlantic Treaty Organization**

nat·ty /náttee/ (-ti·er, -ti·est) adj neat and smart in appearance —**nat·ti·ly** adv —**nat·ti·ness** n

nat·u·ral /náchərəl, náchrəl/ adj 1 of nature 2 conforming with nature ○ natural signs *of aging* **3** produced by nature ○ *a natural sapphire* **4** of the physical world ○ *striking natural features* **5** like human nature ○ *a natural desire for independence* **6** innate ○ *his natural charm* **7** behaving in a sincere unaffected way **8** not artificial ○ *all natural ingredients* **9** related by blood ○ *her natural mother* **10** describes a musical note that is not sharp or flat ■ *n* **1** somebody with innate skills or abilities **2** a musical sign canceling a sharp or flat —**nat·u·ral·ness** *n*

nat·u·ral child·birth *n* childbirth with little medical help

nat·u·ral gas *n* a combustible mixture of hydrocarbon gases

nat·u·ral his·to·ry *n* the study and description of the natural world

nat·u·ral·ism /nácherə lìzzəm, náchrə-/ *n* in art or literature, a movement or school advocating realistic description

nat·u·ral·ist /nácherəlist, náchrə-/ *n* **1** somebody studying natural history **2** an advocate of naturalism —**nat·u·ral·ist** *adj*

nat·u·ral·is·tic /nàcherə lístik, nàchrə-/ *adj* reproducing nature or reality in a faithful way —**nat·u·ral·is·ti·cal·ly** *adv*

nat·u·ral·ize /nácherə līz, náchrə-/ (**-ized, -iz·ing**) *v* **1** *vti* grant citizenship to somebody **2** *vt* introduce something foreign into general use **3** *vti* acclimatize a plant or animal —**nat·u·ral·i·za·tion** /nàcherəli záysh'n, nàchrə-/ *n* —**nat·u·ral·ized** *adj*

nat·u·ral lan·guage *n* a naturally evolved human language, especially as opposed to a computer language

ϟ **nat·u·ral lan·guage proc·ess·ing** *n* the use of computers to process natural language

nat·u·ral·ly /nácherəlee, náchrəlee/ *adv* **1** as expected **2** of course **3** by nature **4** in a normal way **5** without artificial aid or treatment

nat·u·ral re·source *n* a naturally occurring exploitable material

nat·u·ral sci·ence *n* any of the sciences that deal with phenomena observable in nature —**nat·u·ral sci·en·tist** *n*

nat·u·ral se·lec·tion *n* the Darwinian theory that the organisms that survive and pass on their genetic characteristics are those that adapt best to their natural environment

na·ture /náychər/ *n* **1** the physical world **2** *also* **Na·ture** the forces controlling the physical world **3** a type or sort of thing **4** the intrinsic character of a person or thing **5** a temperament **6** universal human behavior

na·ture re·serve, na·ture pre·serve *n* a protected area for animals or plants, especially rare ones

na·ture trail *n* a walking route designed to draw attention to interesting natural features

na·tur·ism /náychə rìzzəm/ *n* **1** the practice of wearing no clothes, derived from the belief

that nudity is a natural healthy state **2** nature worship

na·tur·op·a·thy /nàychə róppəthee/ *n* drug-free medical treatment —**na·tur·o·path** /náychərə pàth/ *n* —**na·tur·o·path·ic** /nàychərə páthik/ *adj*

naught /nawt/ *n* **1** a zero **2** nothing *(literary)* ■ *adv* not at all *(archaic)* ■ *adj* worth nothing *(archaic)*

naugh·ty /náwtee/ (**-ti·er, -ti·est**) *adj* **1** badly behaved **2** mildly indecent *(humorous)* —**naugh·ti·ly** *adv* —**naugh·ti·ness** *n* ◊ See note at **bad**

Na·u·ru /naˈa ōˈ ōˈ ōˈroo/ island country in the central Pacific Ocean, just south of the Equator. Cap. Yaren. Pop. 12,088 (2001). —**Na·u·ru·an** *n, adj*

nau·se·a /náwzee ə, náwshə/ *n* **1** an unsettled feeling in the stomach **2** disgust *(literary)*

nau·se·ate /náwzee àyt, náwshee-/ (**-at·ed, -at·ing**) *vti* **1** make somebody sick or nauseous **2** disgust somebody —**nau·se·at·ing** *adj* —**nau·se·at·ing·ly** *adv*

nau·seous /náwzee əss, náwshəss/ *adj* **1** causing sickness in the stomach **2** having an unsettled feeling in the stomach

nau·ti·cal /náwtik'l/ *adj* of sailors, ships, or seafaring —**nau·ti·cal·ly** *adv*

nau·ti·cal mile *n* (symbol **M**) an international measure of distance at sea

nau·ti·lus /náwt'ləss/ (*pl* **-lus·es** *or* **-li** /-lī/) *n* a shellfish with a spiral shell

NAV *abbr* net asset value

Nav·a·jo /náwvə hô, naˈavə-/ (*pl same or* **-jos**), **Nav·a·ho** (*pl same or* **-hos**) *n* **1** a member of a Native North American people who live mainly in N New Mexico and Arizona **2** the language of the Navajo people —**Nav·a·jo** *adj*

na·val /náyv'l/ *adj* of navies or warships —**na·val·ly** *adv*

SPELLCHECK Do not confuse the spelling of **naval** and **navel** ("hollow on the stomach"), which sound similar.

Na·varre /nə vaˈar/ autonomous region in NE Spain. Cap. Pamplona. Pop. 530,819 (1998).

nave /nayv/ *n* **1** the long central part of a cross-shaped church **2** a hub

na·vel /náyv'l/ *n* a hollow on the surface of the stomach where the umbilical cord was tied ◊ See note at **naval**

na·vel-gaz·ing *n* pointless self-analysis

na·vel or·ange *n* a seedless orange with a smaller secondary fruit

ϟ **nav·i·ga·ble** /náviɡəb'l/ *adj* **1** passable by ship **2** followable by links with related sections that users can move through

nav·i·gate /návi gàyt/ (**-gat·ed, -gat·ing**) *v* **1** *vti* find or follow a route through a place **2** *vi* give instructions how to drive a car on the right route —**nav·i·ga·tion** /nàvvi gáysh'n/ *n* —**nav·i·ga·tion·al** *adj* —**nav·i·ga·tor** *n*

Nav·ra·ti·lo·va /nàvrə ti lóvə/, **Martina** (*b.* 1956) Czech-born US tennis player

na·vy /náyvee/ (*pl* **-vies**) *n* **1** a country's sea-going military force **2** a fleet of ships **3** *also* **na·vy blue** dark blue —**na·vy** *adj*

na·vy bean *n* a white variety of kidney bean

ORIGIN **Navy beans** are so called because they were formerly a staple food in the US Navy.

nay /nay/ *n* a no vote ■ *adv* introduces a correction (*literary*) ■ *interj* no (*archaic*)

nay·say·er /náy sày ər/ *n* a dissenter

Naz·a·reth /názzərəth/ town in N Israel. Pop. 57,200 (1999).

Na·zi /naátsee, nát-/ (*pl* **-zis**) *n* a member or supporter of the fascist German National Socialist Party under Adolf Hitler —**Na·zi** *adj* —**Na·zi·fy** *vt* —**Na·zism** *n*

Nb *symbol* niobium

NB, N.B. *abbr* New Brunswick

N.B., NB, n.b., nb *interj* calls attention to something in writing. Full form **nota bene**

NBA, N.B.A. *abbr* **1** National Basketball Association **2** National Boxing Association

NC *abbr* **1** no charge **2** *also* **N.C.** North Carolina

NC-17 /én see sèw'n téen/ *n* a rating for movies with adult content

NCAA, N.C.A.A. *abbr* National Collegiate Athletic Association

NCO, N.C.O. *abbr* noncommissioned officer

Nd *symbol* neodymium

ND, N.D. *abbr* North Dakota

N'Dja·me·na /ən jaàmənə/ capital of Chad. Pop. 530,965 (1993).

né /nay/ *adj* (*for a man*) **1** born with a particular name **2** formerly known as

Ne *symbol* neon

NE *abbr* **1** Nebraska **2** *also* **N.E.** New England **3** northeast **4** northeastern

NEA *abbr* **1** National Education Association **2** National Endowment for the Arts

Ne·an·der·tal man /nee àndər taal-/, **Ne·an·der·thal man** /-thawl-/ *n* an extinct species of early Stone Age humans

ORIGIN **Neandertal man** is named for the valley (German *Tal*) of the Neander River in W Germany, where a skull providing the first evidence for the species was found in 1857.

Ne·a·pol·i·tan /nee ə póllət'n/ *adj* of Naples, S Italy —**Ne·a·pol·i·tan** *n*

neap tide /néep-/ *n* a tide that shows the least range between high and low tides

near /neer/ *adv, prep, adj* **1** a short distance away **2** a short time away ○ *near the end of the week* ○ *the near future* ■ *adv, adj* **1** at a point not far away in state, resemblance, or number ○ *a sensation near to being a champion* **2** almost ○ *near total failure* ■ *adj* **1** on the left side **2** closely

related ■ *vti* approach a place, time, or state —**near·ness** *n*

ORIGIN Etymologically, **near** means "nearer" and not "near." The ancient Germanic positive of which it is a comparative is represented by English **nigh**, and the superlative by **next**. The immediate source of **near** is an old Scandinavian word, which already simply meant "close."

⚡ **NEAR** /neer/ *n* a binary operator used in text searches that returns true if its operands occur within a specified proximity to each other, and false otherwise

near beer *n* a low-alcohol drink

near·by /neer bī/ *adj, adv* not far off

Near East *n* = Middle East **1** —**Near East·ern** *adj*

near·ly /néerlee/ *adv* **1** almost but not quite the case **2** closely in time, proximity, or relationship

near miss *n* **1** a shot that comes close to a target but does not quite hit it **2** a near collision

near·sight·ed /néer sìtəd/ *adj* with bad distance vision —**near·sight·ed·ly** *adv* —**near·sight·ed·ness** *n*

neat /neet/ *adj* **1** orderly in appearance **2** orderly by nature **3** simple and elegant ○ *a neat solution to a problem* **4** excellent (*infml*) **5** skillfully performed **6** undiluted **7** compact —**neat·en** *vt* —**neat·ly** *adv* —**neat·ness** *n*

neath /neeth/, **'neath** *prep* beneath (*literary*)

Neb., Nebr. *abbr* Nebraska

neb·bish /nébbish/ *n* an offensive term for somebody regarded as weak-willed (*insult*)

Ne·bras·ka /nə bráskə/ state in the central United States. Cap. Lincoln. Pop. 1,711,263 (2000). —**Ne·bras·kan** *n, adj*

Neb·u·chad·nez·zar II /nèbbyŏokəd nézzər/ (*fl* 6C BC) Babylonian king (605–562 BC)

neb·u·la /nébbyələ/ (*pl* **-lae** /-lèe/ *or* **-las**) *n* a region or cloud of interstellar dust and gas —**neb·u·lar** *adj*

neb·u·lize /nébbyə līz/ (**-lized, -liz·ing**) *vt* convert liquid to spray

neb·u·liz·er /nébbyə līzər/ *n* a device that releases a medicinal spray

neb·u·lous /nébbyələss/ *adj* **1** unclear **2** of nebulae —**neb·u·lous·ly** *adv* —**neb·u·lous·ness** *n*

~~neccessary, necessary~~ incorrect spelling of necessary

nec·es·sar·i·ly /nèssə sérrəlee/ *adv* **1** inevitably **2** unavoidably

nec·es·sar·y /néssə sèrree/ *adj* **1** essential or required **2** following inevitably ■ *n* (*pl* **nec·es·sar·ies**) something that is essential (*infml*)

SYNONYMS necessary, essential, vital, indispensable, requisite, needed CORE

MEANING: describes something that is required

ne·ces·si·tate /nə séssi tàyt/ (-tat·ed, -tat·ing) vti 1 make something necessary 2 oblige somebody to do something (fml) —ne·ces·si·ta·tion /nə sèssi táysh'n/ n

ne·ces·si·tous /nə séssitəss/ adj 1 in a state of poverty (literary) 2 necessary (fml)

ne·ces·si·ty /nə séssətee/ (pl -ties) n 1 something that is essential, especially a basic need o food, shelter, and the other necessities 2 requirement dictated by circumstances o issuing replacements as necessity dictates

neck /nek/ n 1 the part of the body between the head and the torso 2 the part of a garment that fits around the neck 3 a cut of meat from an animal's neck 4 a long narrow opening o the neck of a bottle 5 a strip of land or water 6 a long narrow fingerboard on a stringed instrument 7 in horseracing, a narrow winning margin o won the race by a neck —necked adj ◊ be breathing down somebody's neck 1 be close behind somebody 2 be putting pressure on somebody to do something more quickly ◊ break your neck try very hard to achieve something (infml) ◊ neck and neck even in a competition (infml) ◊ neck of the woods a particular area (infml) ◊ stick your neck out take a risk (infml)

neck·er·chief /nékər chìf, -cheef/ (pl -chiefs or -chieves /-chìvz, -cheevz/) n a square of cloth worn tied around the neck

neck·lace /nékləss/ n a decorative chain or string of jewels worn around the neck

neck·line /nék lìn/ n the line formed by the edge of a garment under the neck

neck·tie /nék tì/ n a strip of cloth worn under the collar of a man's shirt

nec·ro·man·cy /nékrə mànssee/ n 1 the practice of supposedly predicting the future by communicating with the spirits of the dead 2 witchcraft (literary) —nec·ro·man·cer n —nec·ro·man·tic /nèkrə mántik/ adj

nec·ro·phil·i·a /nèkrə fíllee ə/ n sexual desire for dead bodies —nec·ro·phil·i·ac n —nec·ro·phil·ic adj

ne·crop·o·lis /ne króppəliss/ (pl -lis·es or -leis /-làyss/) n a cemetery

ne·cro·sis /ne króssiss/ n the death of cells in tissue or organs —ne·crot·ic /-króttik/ adj

nec·tar /néktər/ n 1 the liquid that plants produce to attract insects 2 in Greek and Roman mythology, the drink of the gods 3 any enjoyable drink (infml) —nec·tar·y adj

nec·tar·ine /néktə reen/ n 1 a smooth-skinned peach 2 the tree that produces nectarines

née /nay/, nee adj 1 born with a particular name (of a woman) 2 formerly known as (refers to women)

need /need/ vti require something ■ modal v indicates that something is desirable or

necessary ■ n a requirement ◊ See note at knead, necessary

need·ful /needfəl/ adj (fml) 1 required 2 requiring —need·ful·ly adv —need·ful·ness n

nee·dle /need'l/ n 1 a sharp metal tool used to carry the thread in sewing 2 a pointed rod used in knitting 3 a stylus on a record player 4 a pointer on a dial 5 a hypodermic syringe 6 a pointed leaf of a conifer ■ vt (-dled, -dling) provoke or annoy (infml) —nee·dler n

nee·dle ex·change n the provision of needles for drug users

nee·dle·point /need'l pòynt/ n 1 embroidery stitched on canvas to resemble tapestry 2 lace made with a needle and a paper pattern

need·less /needləss/ adj without reason or justification —need·less·ly adv —need·less·ness n

nee·dle·wom·an /need'l wòommən/ (pl -en /-wìmmin/) n a seamstress

nee·dle·work /need'l wùrk/ n 1 crafts involving sewing or knitting 2 a piece of sewing or embroidery —nee·dle·work·er n

need·n't /neednt/ contr need not

need·y /needee/ (-i·er, -i·est) adj 1 in a state of poverty 2 having a strong need for affection or emotional support —need·i·ly adv —need·i·ness n

ne'er /nair/ adv never (literary)

ne'er-do-well n a person regarded as lazy and irresponsible —ne'er-do-well adj

ne·far·i·ous /nə férree əss/ adj utterly immoral or wicked —ne·far·i·ous·ly adv

Nef·er·ti·ti /néffər teètee/ ancient Egyptian queen

ne·gate /nə gáyt/ (-gat·ed, -gat·ing) vt (fml) 1 deny or prove false 2 invalidate —ne·ga·tion n —ne·ga·tor n ◊ See note at nullify

neg·a·tive /néggətiv/ adj 1 indicating refusal, denial, or disagreement o a negative response 2 contributing to an unhappy situation o negative feelings 3 pessimistic 4 indicating the absence of something tested for 5 less than zero 6 of the same magnitude as, but opposite to, something positive 7 having the same electric charge as an electron ■ n 1 a photographic image with tones and colors reversed 2 an answer of "no" 3 a word that implies "no" 4 something or somebody undesirable or discouraging (infml) ■ interj no (fml) ■ vt (-tived, -tiv·ing) say "no" to something (fml) —neg·a·tive·ly adv —neg·a·tiv·i·ty /nèggə tívvətee/ n

neg·a·tive eq·ui·ty n a situation in which real estate is worth less than the outstanding mortgage on it

Ne·gev /né gev/, Ne·geb /né geb/ desert region in Israel, comprising the southern half of the country

ne·glect /nə glékt/ *vt* **1** fail to care properly for **2** fail to do ○ *neglected to tell him* ■ *n* neglecting or being neglected —**ne·glect·ful** *adj* —**ne·glect·ful·ly** *adv*

SYNONYMS neglect, forget, omit, overlook
CORE MEANING: fail to do something

neg·li·gee /nèggli zháy, néggli zháy/, **neg·li·gée, neg·li·gé** *n* a woman's long dressing gown made of light fabric

neg·li·gence /négglijənss/ *n* **1** the condition of being negligent **2** a civil wrong causing injury or harm

neg·li·gent /négglijənt/ *adj* **1** habitually careless or irresponsible **2** in law, guilty of negligence —**neg·li·gent·ly** *adv*

neg·li·gi·ble /négglijəb'l/ *adj* insignificant

ne·go·tia·ble /nə góshəb'l, -góshee ə-/ *adj* **1** open to negotiation **2** exchangeable for money —**ne·go·tia·ble** *n*

ne·go·ti·ate /nə góshee àyt/ (-at·ed, -at·ing) *v* **1** *vti* come to an agreement on something through discussion and compromise **2** *vt* exchange a check or security for money **3** *vt* get past or deal with something successfully —**ne·go·ti·a·tion** /nə góshee áysh'n/ *n* —**ne·go·ti·a·tor** *n*

Ne·gress /neégrəss/ *n* an offensive term for a Black woman (*dated*)

Ne·gro[1] /neégrō/ (*pl* -groes) *n* a now usually offensive term for a Black person

USAGE Though *Negro* is still used in certain restricted formulaic expressions, it is not the preferred term for people of color such as African Americans. Use instead *African American, woman of color, man of color,* or *people of color.*

Ne·gro[2] /náy grō, néggrō/ **1** river in NW South America that rises in E Colombia and flows southeastward to empty into the Amazon in N Brazil. Length 1,400 mi./ 2,300 km. **2** river in central Argentina flowing eastward into the Atlantic Ocean. Length 400 mi./640 km.

Ne·groid /neé gròyd/ *adj* an offensive term, no longer in scientific use, describing a racial group that originated in Africa (*dated*)

Ne·he·mi·ah /neè hə mí ə/ *n* a book of the Bible, recounting the rebuilding of Jerusalem in the 5C BC, traditionally attributed to Nehemiah, a Jewish leader

Neh·ru /náy ròò/, **Jawaharlal** (1889–1964) first prime minister of independent India (1947–64)

~~neice~~ incorrect spelling of *niece*

neigh /nay/ *n* the long high-pitched sound a horse makes —**neigh** *vi*

neigh·bor /náybər/ *n* **1** somebody living nearby **2** something or somebody located next to or very near another ■ *vti* be next to or very near something or somebody ○ *neighboring countries*

neigh·bor·hood /náybər hòòd/ *n* **1** a local community **2** an approximation (*infml*) ○ *in the neighborhood of $175,000*

neigh·bor·ly /náybərlee/ *adj* friendly or kind like a good neighbor

nei·ther /neéthər, nī-/ *det, pron, conj* not either ■ *adv* also not ○ *I don't tell tales, and neither should you.*

ORIGIN *Neither* was not formed directly from *either*, though the spelling has been changed under its influence. It was originally a compound formed from obsolete *na* "not" and the ancestor of *whether* used in the sense "which of two."

Nel·son /néls'n/, **Horatio, Viscount** (1758–1805) British naval commander

nem·a·tode /némmə tòd/ *n* a tiny worm with an unsegmented body

nem·e·sis /némməssiss/ (*pl* -ses /-seez/) *n* **1** unbeatable opponent (*literary*) **2** a source of harm or ruin (*literary*) **3** deserved punishment resulting in downfall (*literary*) **4** an avenging person or force (*literary*) **5** **Nem·e·sis** the Greek goddess of retribution

neo- *prefix* new, recent ○ *neoclassical* ○ *neoNazi*

Neoclassical: Front porch of Monticello, Charlottesville, Virginia (begun 1770)

ne·o·clas·si·cal /neè ō klássik'l/, **ne·o·clas·sic** /-sik/ *adj* of the revival of classical style or forms in the arts —**ne·o·clas·si·cism** *n* —**ne·o·clas·si·cist** *n*

ne·o·co·lo·ni·al·ism /neè ō kə lónee ə lìzzəm/ *n* economic domination of a weaker nation —**ne·o·co·lo·ni·al·ist** *n*

ne·o·dym·i·um /neè ō dímmee əm/ *n* (*symbol* Nd) a silvery-white or yellowish rare-earth metallic element. Use: lasers, glass manufacture.

Ne·o·lith·ic /neè ə líthik/ *n* the latest period of the Stone Age —**Ne·o·lith·ic** *adj*

ne·ol·o·gism /nee óllə jìzzəm/, **ne·ol·o·gy** /nee ólləjee/ (*pl* -gies) *n* **1** a new word or meaning **2** the coinage of new words —**ne·ol·o·gis·tic** /nee òllə jístik/ *adj* —**ne·ol·o·gize** *vi*

ne·on /neè òn/ *n* (*symbol* Ne) a gaseous chemical element that glows orange when electricity passes through it

ne·o·nate /neè ə nàyt/ *n* a newborn child —**ne·o·na·tal** /neè ə náyt'l/ *adj*

ne·o·Na·zi /n 1 a modern-day advocate of Nazism 2 a white racist —**ne·o·Na·zism** n

ne·on light, ne·on lamp n a light filled with neon

ne·o·phyte /neè ə fīt/ n 1 a beginner 2 a recent convert

ne·o·plasm /neè ə plàzzəm/ n a tumor or tissue containing a growth

ne·o·prene /neè ə preèn/ n a synthetic material resembling rubber. Use: in the manufacture of equipment for which waterproofing is important.

Ne·pal /nə paál/ country in South Asia, on the NE border of India, in the Himalaya range. Cap. Katmandu. Pop. 25,284,463 (2001). —**Nep·al·ese** /nèpp leèz, -leéss/ n, adj —**Ne·pal·i** n, adj

neph·ew /néffyoo/ n the son of a brother, sister, brother-in-law, or sister-in-law

ne·phri·tis /ni frītiss/ n kidney inflammation

nep·o·tism /néppə tìzzəm/ n favoritism shown to relatives —**nep·o·tis·tic** /nèppə tístik/ adj

Nep·tune /nép toòn/ n 1 the 8th planet from the Sun 2 in Roman mythology, the god of the sea. Greek equivalent **Poseidon**

nep·tu·ni·um /nep toònee əm/ n (symbol **Np**) a silvery radioactive chemical element. Use: neutron detection.

nerd n a single-minded enthusiast of highly technical things (often in combination; sometimes offensive) —**nerd·ish** adj —**nerd·y** adj

Ne·ro /neèrō/ (AD 37–68) Roman emperor (AD 54–68)

Ne·ru·da /ne roòda, -roòtha/, **Pablo** (1904–73) Chilean poet and diplomat

nerve n 1 a fiber bundle transmitting impulses within the body 2 the sensitive tissue in a tooth 3 courage 4 impudence ■ **nerves** npl 1 somebody's ability to tolerate stress 2 nervousness (infml) ◊ See note at **courage**

nerve cen·ter n 1 a control center 2 a group of nerve cells that performs a specific function

nerve gas n a gas that attacks the nervous system

nerve·less /núrvləss/ adj 1 numb or weak 2 calm and fearless —**nerve·less·ly** adv —**nerve·less·ness** n

nerve-rack·ing, nerve-wrack·ing adj causing great anxiety or distress

nerv·ous /núrvəss/ adj 1 apprehensive or uneasy 2 easily worried or frightened 3 of the nerves —**nerv·ous·ly** adv —**nerv·ous·ness** n

nerv·ous break·down n a psychiatric disorder caused by stress or anxiety

nerv·ous sys·tem n the network of nerves in the body

nerv·y /núrvee/ (-i·er, -i·est) adj (infml) 1 fearless 2 aggressive

ness n a projecting section of coastline (often in place names)

Ness, Loch lake in N Scotland. Length 23 mi./37 km.

-ness suffix state, condition, quality ○ sadness

nest n 1 a structure built by birds or other animals to live in 2 something shaped like a bird's nest 3 a place where something bad flourishes ■ v 1 vi build a nest 2 vti group together or one inside another

nest egg n a sum of money saved

nes·tle /néss'l/ v 1 vti settle or put into a comfortable position 2 vi be in a sheltered place ○ a village nestling in the foothills

nest·ling /néstling, néssling/ n a young bird

net¹ n 1 a mesh of loosely interwoven threads 2 a bag-shaped piece of net used to hold or catch something ○ a fishing net 3 a light open-weave fabric 4 a system for selecting or restricting ○ slip through the net 5 a broadcasting, telecommunications, or computer network 6 a strip of net across a sports court 7 a piece of net forming part of the goal in some sports 8 **Net** the Internet (infml) ■ vt (net·ted, net·ting) 1 catch in a net 2 protect by covering with a net

net² adj 1 remaining after deductions ○ net pay 2 of the contents only, excluding packaging ○ net weight 3 overall ○ the net result ■ vt (net·ted, net·ting) earn or gain as profit after deductions ■ n a net amount

net³ abbr networking organization (in Internet addresses)

Net·an·ya·hu /nètt'n yaàhoo/, **Binyamin** (b. 1949) Israeli prime minister (1996–99)

net as·set val·ue n the value of mutual-fund securities

neth·er /néthər/ adj lower —**neth·er·most** adj

Neth·er·lands /néthərlandz/ country in NW Europe, on the North Sea. Cap. Amsterdam. Pop. 15,981,472 (2001). —**Neth·er·land·er** n —**Neth·er·land·ish** adj

Neth·er·lands An·til·les two island groups in the Caribbean Sea, an overseas territory of the Netherlands. Cap. Willemstad. Pop. 212,226 (2001).

net·i·quette /nétti kèt/ n rules for communication on the Internet (infml)

net·phone /nét fōn/ n a phone that uses the Internet to make connections and carry voice messages

net·ting /nétting/ n mesh ○ wire netting

net·tle /nétt'l/ n a plant with stinging leaves ■ vt (-tled, -tling) 1 irritate or annoy (infml) 2 sting with a nettle leaf

net·war /nét wàwr/ n nontraditional warfare carried out by dispersed groups of activists without a central command, often communicating electronically

net·work /nét wùrk/ n 1 a system of interconnected lines 2 a coordinated system of people or things 3 a group of broadcasting affiliates 4 a system of linked computers 5 netting ■ v 1 vt broadcast a program simultaneously within a network 2 vt link computers 3 *vi* maintain relationships with useful contacts —**net·work·er** *n* —**net·work·ing** *n*

Neu·mann /nyōomən/ ♦ von Neumann, John

neu·ral /nōorəl/ *adj* of nerves —**neu·ral·ly** *adv*

neu·ral·gia /noo rálje/ *n* pain along the path of a nerve —**neu·ral·gic** *adj*

⚡**neu·ral net·work** *n* 1 an interconnecting system of nerve cells 2 *also* **neu·ral net** a computer system that mimics the human brain

neuro- *prefix* nerve, neural ○ *neurosurgery*

⚡**neu·ro·com·put·er** /nóorō kəm pyōotər/, **neu·ral com·put·er** *n* a computer that mimics the human brain —**neu·ro·com·put·ing** *n*

neu·rol·o·gy /noo róllajee/ *n* the branch of medicine that deals with the nervous system —**neu·ro·log·ic** /nóorə lójjik/ *adj* —**neu·ro·log·i·cal** *adj* —**neu·rol·o·gist** *n*

neu·ron /nóor òn/, **neu·rone** /-ôn/ *n* a nerve cell —**neu·ron·al** /nóo rôn'l, nóoranal/ *adj*

neu·ro·sis /noo róssiss/ (*pl* **-ses** /-séez/) *n* a mild psychiatric disorder characterized by anxiety, depression, and hypochondria

neu·ro·sur·ger·y /nóorō súrjaree/ *n* surgery on the nervous system, including the brain —**neu·ro·sur·geon** *n* —**neu·ro·sur·gi·cal** *adj*

neu·rot·ic /noo róttik/ *adj* 1 affected by a neurosis 2 overanxious or obsessive (*often offensive*) —**neu·rot·ic** *n*

neu·ro·trans·mit·ter /noo rō transs míttər/ *n* a chemical that carries communication between nerves

neu·ter /nóotər/ *vt* remove the testicles or ovaries of ■ *adj* 1 without sex organs 2 grammatically neither masculine nor feminine in gender ■ *n* 1 a neutered animal 2 a grammatically neuter word

neu·tral /nóotral/ *adj* 1 belonging to, supporting, or assisting no side 2 without distinctive qualities 3 neither acidic nor alkaline ■ *n* 1 a disengaged gear position 2 a nonaligned person or country —**neu·tral·i·ty** /noo trállətee/ *n* —**neu·tral·ly** *adv*

neu·tral·ize /nóotrə līz/ (**-ized**, **-iz·ing**) *vt* 1 make ineffective 2 make neutral —**neu·tral·i·za·tion** /nóotrali záysh'n/ *n*

neu·tri·no /noo trée nō/ (*pl* **-nos**) *n* a neutral elementary particle with a zero rest mass and no charge

neu·tron /nóo tròn/ *n* an elementary particle with a zero electric charge —**neu·tron·ic** /noo trónnik/ *adj*

neu·tron bomb *n* a nuclear bomb with low radioactive contamination

neu·tron star *n* the remnant of a collapsed star, composed entirely of neutrons

Nev. *abbr* Nevada

Ne·vad·a /nə vaådə/ state in the W United

States. Cap. Carson City. Pop. 1,998,257 (2000). —**Ne·vad·an** *n*, *adj*

Nev·el·son /névl'ssən/, **Louise** (1900–88) Russian-born US sculptor

nev·er /névvər/ *adv* 1 at no time 2 not in any circumstances ■ *interj* expresses great surprise

nev·er-end·ing *adj* continuous and apparently unlikely ever to stop —**nev·er-end·ing·ly** *adv*

nev·er-mar·ried *adj* describes someone who has never been married

nev·er·more /névvər máwr/ *adv* never again (*literary*)

nev·er-nev·er land *n* an imaginary place where wonderful things happen

> **ORIGIN** *Never Never Land* was the fantasy land to which Peter Pan took the Darling children in J. M. Barrie's play *Peter Pan* (1904). The name was popularized through Barrie, but it has in fact been recorded earlier, in the subtitle of a one-act play by Israel Zangwill that was performed in 1900.

nev·er·the·less /névvər thə léss/ *adv* in spite of that

Nev·is, Ben ♦ Ben Nevis

nev·us /néevəss/ (*pl* **-i** /-ī/) *n* a birthmark

new /noo/ *adj* 1 recently created or invented 2 not used or second-hand 3 introduced or acquired as a replacement ○ *new rules* ○ *our new home* 4 recently discovered 5 at the start of a period ○ *in the new year* 6 having recently acquired a particular status ○ *the new president* 7 unfamiliar —**new·ness** *n*

> **SYNONYMS** new, fresh, modern, new-fangled, novel, original CORE MEANING: never experienced before or having recently come into being

New Age *adj* of a modern cultural movement emphasizing spirituality ■ *n* a style of music intended to induce serenity —**New Ag·er** *n*

New·ark /nóo ark/ city in NE New Jersey. Pop. 267,823 (1998).

⚡**new·bie** /nóobee/ *n* a new user of the Internet

new·born /nóo báwrn/ *adj* 1 born very recently 2 newly discovered or recovered ○ *newborn faith* —**new·born** *n*

New Bruns·wick /-brúnzwik/ province in SE Canada. Cap. Fredericton. Pop. 756,598 (2000).

New Cal·e·do·ni·a island in the SW Pacific Ocean, east of Australia, with nearby islands, an overseas territory of France. Cap. Nouméa. Pop. 204,863 (2001).

New·cas·tle up·on Tyne /nóo kass'l ə pon tín/ port in NE England. Pop. 282,338 (1996).

new·com·er /nóo kúmmər/ *n* a recent arrival

New Deal *n* 1 the reform policies introduced in the 1930s by the US president Franklin

D. Roosevelt. **2** the period of Roosevelt reforms —**New Deal·er** n

New Del·hi capital of India. Pop. 301,000 (1991).

new e·con·o·my n the economy of the information age

new·el /nōō əl/ n **1** also **new·el post** a post supporting a handrail of a staircase on a landing **2** a vertical pillar supporting a spiral staircase

New Eng·land region of the NE United States, comprising the states of Maine, New Hampshire, Vermont, Massachusetts, Rhode Island, and Connecticut —**New Eng·land·er** n

Newf. abbr Newfoundland

new·fan·gled /nōō fáng g'ld/ adj puzzlingly or suspiciously new ◊ See note at **new**

ORIGIN The -fangled part of **newfangled** represents an ancient verb meaning "capture, seize." The original meaning of **newfangled** was "easily carried away by new things."

---

new·found /nōō fównd/ adj recently discovered

New·found·land, Is·land of /nōōfəndlənd, -lànd/ island in the Atlantic Ocean, part of the Canadian province of Newfoundland and Labrador. Pop. 538,099 (1991). —**New·found·land·er** n

New·found·land and Lab·ra·dor easternmost province in Canada, comprising the island of Newfoundland and part of Labrador. Cap. St. John's. Pop. 538,823 (2000).

New·found·land Stan·dard Time, New·found·land Time n the local standard time in Newfoundland, Canada

New Guin·ea island in the W Pacific Ocean, north of Australia, divided between Irian Jaya in the west and Papua New Guinea in the east. Pop. about 5,300,000 (1995). —**New Guin·e·an** n, adj

New Hamp·shire state in the NE United States. Cap. Concord. Pop. 1,235,786 (2000). —**New Hamp·shir·ite** n

New Ha·ven city in S Connecticut. Pop. 123,189 (1998).

New Jer·sey state on the eastern coast of the United States. Pop. 8,414,350 (2000). —**New Jer·sey·an** n, adj —**New Jer·sey·ite** n

new·ly /nōōlee/ adv **1** recently or lately **2** again

new·ly·wed /nōōlee wèd/ n somebody recently married —**new·ly·wed** adj

New·man /nōōmən, nyōōmən/, **John Henry, Cardinal** (1801–90) British theologian

New Man n a modern sensitive man who shares domestic chores and parenting

New Mex·i·co state in the SW United States. Cap. Santa Fe. Pop. 1,819,046 (2000). —**New Mex·i·can** n, adj

new mon·ey n recently acquired wealth

new moon n the Moon, or the phase of the Moon, when it is invisible or seen as a narrow crescent

New Neth·er·land /-néthərlənd/ former Dutch colony in E North America, in present-day New York and New Jersey

New Or·leans /-áwrlee ənz, -áwrlinz/ port in SE Louisiana. Pop. 465,538 (1998). —**New Or·lea·ni·an** /-awr lée nee ən/ n

New·port News /nōō pawrt nōōz/ city in SE Virginia. Pop. 178,615 (1998).

news /nōōz/ n **1** information about recent events ○ Any news from the hospital? **2** information about current events provided by the media **3** a radio or television broadcast about the day's events **4** something previously unknown ○ It's news to me.

news a·gen·cy n a newsgathering organization

news·cast /nōōz kàst/ n a broadcast of news —**news·cast·er** n

news con·fer·ence n a press conference

news·deal·er /nōōz dèelər/ n a newspaper seller

news desk n an area where news is prepared for publication or broadcasting

news flash n a brief news item interrupting a program

⨍ news·group /nōōz grōōp/ n an Internet discussion group

news·hound /nōōz hownd, nyōōz hownd/ n a journalist who covers news (infml)

news·let·ter /nōōz lèttər/ n a printed report containing news of interest to a group

news·pa·per /nōōz pàypər, nōōss-/ n **1** a daily or weekly publication containing news and advertisements **2** the pages of a newspaper used for some other purpose ○ wrapped in newspaper —**news·pa·per·man** n —**news·pa·per·wom·an** n

news·print /nōōz prìnt/ n inexpensive low-quality paper for newspapers

news·reel /nōōz rèel/ n a news film

news·room /nōōz ròòm, -ròòm/ n a room where news is prepared for publication or broadcasting

news·stand /nōōz stànd/ n a stall selling newspapers

⨍ news·wire /nōōz wìr/ n an Internet news service

news·wor·thy /nōōz wúrthee/ (-thi·er, -thi·est) adj interesting enough to be reported as news —**news·wor·thi·ness** n

news·y /nōōzee/ (-i·er, -i·est) adj filled with news ○ a newsy letter

newt /nōōt/ n a small amphibian with short legs and a tail

ORIGIN "A newt" was originally "an ewt." The initial n was gained when this common combination of words was misinterpreted. The origin of ewt itself is unknown.

New Ter·ri·to·ries area of Hong Kong situated mostly on the Chinese mainland north of Kowloon

New Tes·ta·ment *n* the second section of the Christian Bible, dealing with the life and teachings of Jesus Christ

new·ton /noŏt'n/ *n* (*symbol* **N**) an SI unit of force equivalent to the force that produces an acceleration of one meter per second on a mass of one kilogram

New·ton /noŏt'n, nyoo-/, **Sir Isaac** (1642–1727) English scientist. He discovered gravitation and formulated the laws of motion. —**New·to·ni·an** /noo tōnee ən/ *adj*

new town *n* a self-sufficient planned town

new wave *n* **1** an innovative arts movement **2** post-punk rock music

New World *n* the western hemisphere (*dated*)

New Year's Day *n* the first day of the year. Date: January 1.

New Year's Eve *n* the last day of the year. Date: December 31.

New York 1 *also* **New York City** city in SE New York State, at the mouth of the Hudson River. It comprises the boroughs of Manhattan, Queens, Brooklyn, the Bronx, and Staten Island. Pop. 7,420,166 (1998). **2** state in the NE United States. Cap. Albany. Pop. 18,976,457 (2000). —**New York·er** *n*

New Zea·land /-zeeland/ country in the SW Pacific Ocean, southeast of Australia, comprising mainly the North Island and the South Island. Cap. Wellington. Pop. 3,864,129 (2001). —**New Zea·land·er** *n*

next /nekst/ *adj, adv* immediately following ■ *adj* **1** following this one ○ *getting married next week* **2** adjoining ○ *in the next room* **3** closest ○ *several miles from the next village* ◇ **next to 1** adjacent to or beside **2** closest to, in comparison with something else **3** almost ○ *There was next to nothing left.*

next door *adv* **1** in or into the next house or room **2** very close ■ *adj* immediately adjacent

next of kin *n* somebody's nearest relative or relatives (+ *sing or pl verb*)

nex·us /néksəss/ (*pl same or* **-us·es**) *n* **1** a connection or link **2** a group of connected people or things **3** the center or focus of something

Nez Per·cé /nez púrss, ness-, -pur sáy/ (*pl same or* **Nez Per·cés**), **Nez Per·ce** /nez púrss, ness-/ (*pl same or* **Nez Per·ces**) *n* **1** a member of a Native North American people who live mainly in W Idaho and NE Washington **2** the language of the Nez Percé people —**Nez Per·cé** *adj*

NFL *abbr* National Football League

⚡**NFS** *abbr* **1** network file service **2** network file system **3** not for sale

ng *abbr* nanogram

NGO *n* Nongovernment Organization

Ngo Dinh Di·em /'ng gŏ din dee ém, 'ng gŏ din dyém/ (1901–63) president of South Vietnam (1955–63)

ngul·trum /əng gŏoltrəm, -gŏol-/ *n* the main unit of Bhutanese currency

NH, N.H. *abbr* New Hampshire

NHL *abbr* National Hockey League

Ni *symbol* nickel

ni·a·cin /nī´əssin/ *n* a B complex vitamin found in meat and dairy products

Ni·ag·a·ra /nī ággrə, nī ággərə/ river in NE North America, flowing from Lake Erie into Lake Ontario and forming part of the US-Canadian border. Length 35 mi./56 km.

Ni·ag·a·ra Falls waterfall in the Niagara River, divided by Goat Island into American Falls and Horseshoe, or Canadian, Falls. Height 182–187 ft./55–57 m.

Nia·mey /nyaa máy/ capital of Niger. Pop. 587,000 (1995).

~~niave~~ incorrect spelling of **naive**

nib *n* a detachable metal writing tip for a pen

nib·ble /níbb'l/ *vti* (**-bled, -bling**) **1** take small quick or cautious bites of something **2** bite gently and playfully ■ *n* **1** an act of nibbling **2** a tiny amount of food (*infml*)

Ni·cae·a /nī seeə/ ancient Byzantine city of Asia Minor, on the site of present-day Iznik, NW Turkey

Nic·a·ra·gua /níkə raágwə/ largest country in Central America, situated between the North Pacific Ocean and the Caribbean Sea. Cap. Managua. Pop. 4,918,393 (2001). —**Nic·a·ra·guan** *n, adj*

nice /nīss/ (**nic·er, nic·est**) *adj* **1** pleasant **2** kind **3** respectable **4** attractive **5** subtle —**nice·ly** *adv* —**nice·ness** *n*

ORIGIN Nice has changed its meaning dramatically over the centuries. The original sense was "foolish, stupid": it came through French from a Latin verb meaning "not know." In English it transformed through "neat, dainty," "shy," "fastidious" and numerous other shades of meaning to reach its modern use as a general term of approval in the early 18C.

Nice /neess/ city in SE France. Pop. 342,738 (1999).

ni·ce·ty /níssətee/ (*pl* **-ties**) *n* (*often pl*) **1** a fine distinction or detail **2** a refined feature

niche /nich, neesh/ *n* **1** a suitable place or activity for somebody ○ *She carved out her own niche in the industry.* **2** a specialized market **3** a recess in a wall —**niche** *vt*

Nich·o·las, **St.** (*fl* 4C) prelate and saint from Asia Minor

Nich·o·las I (1796–1855) tsar of Russia (1825–55)

Nich·o·las II (1868–1918) tsar of Russia (1894–1917)

nick *n* a small cut or notch ■ *vt* make a nick in ◊ **in the nick of time** at the last possible moment

nick·el /nĭk'l/ *n* **1** (*symbol* Ni) a silvery white metallic element. Use: alloys, batteries, electroplating, catalyst. **2** a five-cent coin

ORIGIN **Nickel** is a shortening of German *Kupfernickel* "copper nickel" (an important ore of nickel). A *Nickel* was a dwarf or mischievous demon, and the ore was given that name because it yielded no copper. A similar reference to malicious supernatural thwarting of mining is seen in *cobalt* from German *Kobold*, literally a harmful goblin.

nick·el·o·de·on /nĭkə lōdee ən/ *n* **1** an early coin-operated jukebox **2** an early 5-cent movie theater

Nick·laus /nĭk lowss/, **Jack** (*b.* 1940) US golfer

~~nickle~~ incorrect spelling of **nickel**

nick·nack *n* HOUSEHOLD = **knickknack**

nick·name /nĭk nàym/ *n* **1** a name used instead of somebody's or something's real name **2** a shortened form of a name —**nick·name** *vt*

ORIGIN "A **nickname**" was originally "an ekename." The initial *n* was gained when this common combination of words was misinterpreted. *Eke* itself is an obsolete word meaning "addition" that is closely related to the verb *eke out*. A **nickname** is thus etymologically a name in addition to your proper name.

Nic·o·bar Is·lands /nĭkə baàr-/ island group in the Indian Ocean, east of Sri Lanka, part of the Indian union territory of the Andaman and Nicobar Islands. Pop. 39,022 (1991).

Nic·o·si·a /nĭkə seè ə/ capital of Cyprus. Pop. 194,000 (1997).

nic·o·tine /nĭkə teèn/ *n* a toxic alkaloid derived from tobacco. Use: insecticide. —**nic·o·tin·ic** /nĭkə tínnik/ *adj*

ORIGIN **Nicotine** is named for the French courtier Jacques Nicot (1530–1604), who was ambassador to Lisbon in Portugal and introduced tobacco to France.

nic·o·tine patch *n* a nicotine-impregnated patch worn on the skin by somebody trying to give up smoking

niece /neess/ *n* the daughter of a brother, sister, brother-in-law, or sister-in-law

~~nieghbor~~ incorrect spelling of **neighbor**

niels·bohr·i·um /neèlz báwree əm/ *n* an artificially produced radioactive chemical element

ORIGIN **Nielsbohrium** is named for the Danish physicist Niels Bohr.

~~neither~~ incorrect spelling of **neither**

Nie·tzsche /neéchə, neéchee/, **Friedrich Wilhelm** (1844–1900) German philosopher —**Nie·tzsche·an** *n, adj*

nif·ty /nĭftee/ (**-ti·er, -ti·est**) *adj* very good or effective (*infml*) —**nif·ti·ly** *adv* —**nif·ti·ness** *n*

Ni·ger /nĭjər/ **1** country in West Africa, north of Nigeria. Cap. Niamey. Pop. 10,355,156 (2001). **2** river in W Africa, rising in S Guinea and flowing through Mali, Niger, and Nigeria into the Gulf of Guinea. Length 2,600 mi./4,180 km.

Ni·ge·ri·a /nī jeèree ə/ country in West Africa. Cap. Abuja. Pop. 126,635,630 (2001). —**Ni·ge·ri·an** *n, adj*

nig·gard·ly /nĭggərdlee/ *adj* (**-li·er, -li·est**) **1** reluctant to give or spend anything **2** small or inadequate ■ *adv* in a miserly or stingy way —**nig·gard** *n*

nig·gle /nĭg'l/ (**-gled, -gling**) *vi* **1** criticize in a petty way **2** be preoccupied with details —**nig·gle** *n* —**nig·gling** *adj* —**nig·gling·ly** *adv*

nigh /nī/ *adv, adj* near ■ *adv* almost

night /nīt/ *n* **1** the daily period of darkness between sunset and sunrise **2** the time spent in bed **3** an evening spent in a particular way ◊ *a night at the theater* **4** nightfall —**night** *adj* ◊ See note at **knight**

night·cap /nīt kàp/ *n* **1** a drink before going to bed **2** a last event **3** a cap worn in bed

night·clothes /nīt klò͞thz, -klòz/ *npl* clothes for wearing in bed

night·club /nīt klùb/ *n* a place of entertainment open late —**night·club·bing** *n*

night crawl·er *n* an earthworm used as bait

night de·pos·i·to·ry *n* a safe in a bank wall with access from outside for depositing money

night·dress /nīt drèss/ *n* a nightgown

night·fall /nīt fàwl/ *n* the beginning of night

night·gown /nīt gòwn/ *n* a loose lightweight dress worn in bed

night·hawk /nīt hàwk/ *n* a nightjar with black, white, and buff plumage

night·ie /nītee/, **night·y** (*pl* **-ies**) *n* a nightgown (*infml*)

night·in·gale /nīt'n gàyl, nĭting-/ *n* a brownish songbird of the thrush family that sings at night

ORIGIN **Nightingale** means literally "night singer" (*gale* is ultimately related to *yell*). There was originally no *n* in the middle of the word, but it began to be inserted in the 13C.

AKG London

Florence Nightingale

Night·in·gale /nīting gàyl/, **Florence** (1820–1910) British nursing pioneer

night·jar /nít jàar/ *n* a nocturnal bird that feeds on insects caught in flight

night·life /nít lìf/ *n* evening entertainment

night·light /nít lìt/ *n* a small light left on at night

night·long /nít làwng/ *adj, adv* throughout the entire night

night·ly /nítlee/ *adj* 1 happening every night 2 occurring at night ■ *adv* every night

night·mare /nít màir/ *n* 1 a very bad dream 2 a very upsetting or difficult experience —**night·mare** *adj* —**night·mar·ish** *adj*

> **ORIGIN** The *mare* of **nightmare** is a spirit or monster that was supposed to settle on sleepers' chests and give them feelings of suffocation and bad dreams.

night owl *n* somebody who stays up late (*infml*)

night school *n* a school with evening classes

night shift *n* 1 a nighttime work period 2 a group of people working at night

night·shirt /nít shùrt/ *n* a long loose shirt-like garment worn in bed

night·spot /nít spòt/ *n* a nightclub

night·stick /nít stik/ *n* a police officer's club

night·time /nít tìm/ *n* the period of night

night watch *n* a guard or watch kept at night

night watch·man *n* somebody who guards a place at night

NIH *abbr* National Institutes of Health

ni·hil·ism /nī ə lìzzəm, neé ə-, nīhi-/ *n* 1 the total rejection of morality and religion or political authority 2 the belief that nothing is worthwhile —**ni·hil·ist** *n* —**ni·hil·is·tic** /nī ə lístik, neè ə-/ *adj*

Ni·jin·sky /ni zhínskee, jín-/, **Vaslav** (1890–1950) Russian ballet dancer

Ni·ke /nī kee/ *n* in Greek mythology, the goddess of victory

Nik·kei In·dex /ni káy-/ *n* a Tokyo stock exchange index of stocks

nil *n* zero

Nile /nīl/ river in NE Africa, rising in Lake Victoria, Uganda, and flowing northward to empty into the Mediterranean Sea in Egypt. Length 4,160 mi./6,695 km.

nim·ble /nímb'l/ (**-bler, -blest**) *adj* 1 fast and agile 2 able to think quickly and cleverly —**nim·ble·ness** *n* —**nim·bly** *adv*

nim·bus /nímbəss/ (*pl* **-bus·es** *or* **-bi** /-bī/) *n* 1 a dark rain-bearing cloud 2 a cloud of light or a halo around a representation of a deity or saint

NIMBY[1] /nímbee/ (*pl* **-BYs**), **Nim·by** (*pl* **-bys**) *n* somebody who objects to the location of something undesirable near his or her home (*infml*) —**Nim·by·ism** *n*

NIMBY[2] *abbr* not in my backyard

Nim·itz /nímmits/, **Chester William** (1885–1966) US naval officer

nine /nīn/ *n* 1 the number 9 2 a baseball team —**nine** *adj, pron* —**ninth** *n, adj, adv* ◇ **dressed (up) to the nines** very elaborately or formally dressed

9–11 /nīn i lévv'n/ *n* the coordinated terrorist attacks in the United States on September 11, 2001

nine·pin /nín pìn/ *n* a pin used in ninepins

nine·pins /nín pìnz/ *n* a bowling game using ninepins (+ *sing verb*)

nine·teen /nìn teén/ *n* the number 19 —**nine·teen** *adj, pron* —**nine·teenth** *n, adj, adv*

~~nineth~~ incorrect spelling of **ninth**

nine·ty /nîntee/ *n* the number 90 ■ **nine·ties** *npl* 1 the numbers between 90 and 99, particularly as a range of temperatures 2 the years from 90 to 99 in a century or somebody's life —**nine·ti·eth** *n, adj, adv* —**nine·ty** *adj, pron*

Nin·e·veh /nínnəvə/ ancient capital of Assyria, in present-day N Iraq

nin·ja /nínjə/ (*pl* **-jas** *or* same) *n* a feudal Japanese mercenary trained in the martial arts

~~ninty~~ incorrect spelling of **ninety**

ni·o·bi·um /nī ōbee əm/ *n* (*symbol* Nb) a lustrous light gray ductile metallic element that is a superconductor. Use: steel alloys.

nip[1] *vt* (**nipped, nip·ping**) 1 pinch between two surfaces 2 sever by pinching, biting, or clipping 3 sting with cold 4 halt the growth of 5 steal (*infml*) ■ *n* 1 an act of nipping 2 a chill ◇ *a nip in the air* ◇ **nip and tuck** very closely and evenly contested (*infml*)

nip[2] *n* a small drink of something ■ *vti* (**nipped, nip·ping**) sip

> **ORIGIN** Nip "small drink" is probably a shortening of obsolete *nipperkin* "small vessel for alcoholic drink," which was recorded in the early 17C. A *nip* was originally (late 18C) a half pint of ale, and only later a small drink.

nip·per /níppər/ *n* a large claw of a crustacean, especially a lobster or crab ■ **nip·pers** *npl* pliers or clippers

nip·ple /nípp'l/ *n* 1 the tip of a mammary gland 2 a rubber bottle top 3 a baby's pacifier

nip·py /níppee/ (**-pi·er, -pi·est**) *adj* **1** chilly **2** sharp-tasting —**nip·pi·ness** *n*

nir·va·na /neer vaánə, nur-/ *n* **1** *also* **Nir·va·na** in Hir duism, Buddhism, and Jainism, spiritual enlightenment **2** an ultimate experience of something pleasurable

Ni·san /níss'n, nee saán/ *n* the 1st month of the Jewish calendar

nit /nit/ *n* the egg or larva of a louse —**nit·ty** *adj* ◊ See note at **knit**

ni·ter /nítər/ *n* potassium nitrate or sodium nitrate

nit·pick /nít pìk/ *vti* criticize insignificant details of something —**nit·pick·er** *n* —**nit·pick·ing** *n* ◊ See note at **criticize**

ni·trate /ní tràyt/ *n* **1** a salt or ester of nitric acid **2** a fertilizer consisting of a nitrate —**ni·trate** *vt* —**ni·tra·tion** /ní tráysh'n/ *n*

ni·tric ac·id /nítrik-/ *n* a corrosive liquid. Use: manufacture of explosives, fertilizers, and rocket fuels.

ni·tri·fy /nítrə fì/ (**-fied, -fies**) *vt* **1** treat or combine something with nitrogen **2** fertilize soil with nitrogen —**ni·tri·fi·ca·tion** /nítrəfi káysh'n/ *n*

ni·tro·gen /nítrəjən/ *n* (*symbol* **N**) a colorless odorless gaseous chemical element. Use: manufacture of ammonia, explosives, and fertilizers.

ni·tro·glyc·er·in /nítrō glíssərin, nìtrə-/, **ni·tro·glyc·er·ine** *n* a thick oily explosive liquid. Use: manufacture of explosives, treatment of angina pectoris.

ni·trous ox·ide /nítəss-/ *n* a sweet-smelling gas. Use: anesthetic.

nit·ty-grit·ty /níttee gríttee/ *n* the basic, important, or practical details of something (*infml*) —**nit·ty-grit·ty** *adj*

nit·wit /nít wìt/ *n* a person regarded as unintelligent (*insult*)

nix /niks/ *vt* say no to (*slang*) ■ *n* nothing (*slang dated*) ■ *interj* stop! (dated *slang*) —**nixed** *adj*

Richard Nixon

Nix·on /níks'n/, **Richard Milhous** (1913–94) 37th president of the United States (1969–74)

Nizh·niy Nov·gor·od /nízhnee nóvgə ròd, -náwvgə ràwd/ port in W Russia. Pop. 1,840,212 (1995).

NJ, N.J. *abbr* New Jersey

Nko·mo /əng kốmô/, **Joshua** (1917–99) Zimbabwean nationalist leader

Nkru·mah /'n kròomə, 'ng-/, **Kwame** (1909–72) first prime minister (1957–60) and president (1960–66) of Ghana

⚡ **NLP** *abbr* natural language processing

NLRB, N.L.R.B. *abbr* National Labor Relations Board

NM *abbr* **1** nautical mile **2** *also* **N.M.** New Mexico

NMD *abbr* National Missile Defense

N. Mex. *abbr* New Mexico

no[1] /nô/ *adv, interj* **1** indicates refusal, denial, or disagreement **2** indicates agreement with a negative statement ○ *"Nobody ever takes any notice." "No, they don't."* **3** indicates shock or disbelief ■ *n* (*pl* **noes** or **nos**) **1** an answer or vote of "no" **2** somebody who votes "no" ◊ See note at **know**

no[2] /nô/ *adj* **1** not any at all ○ *no money* **2** not at all ○ *She's no fool.*

No[1] /nô/, **Noh** *n* a highly stylized form of Japanese drama

No[2] *symbol* nobelium

no., No. *abbr* **1** north **2** northern **3** number

No·ah /nô ə / *n* in the Bible, a Hebrew patriarch who built an ark and saved human and animal life from the Flood

No·bel /nō bél/, **Alfred** (1833–96) Swedish chemist and inventor of dynamite. He established the original Nobel Prizes.

no·bel·i·um /nō bèelee əm/ *n* (*symbol* **No**) an artificially produced radioactive chemical element

No·bel Prize *n* an international award for achievement —**No·bel prize·win·ner** *n*

no·bil·i·ty /nō bíllətee/ (*pl* **-ties**) *n* **1** the class of nobles **2** aristocratic rank **3** excellent moral character

no·ble /nốb'l/ *adj* (**-bler, -blest**) **1** of the nobility **2** having or showing high moral principles **3** chemically inactive ■ *n* a titled aristocrat —**no·ble·man** —**no·ble·wom·an** *n* —**no·bly** *adv*

no·blesse o·blige /nō blèss ə blèezh/ *n* the idea that aristocrats must behave honorably and generously toward the lower classes

no·bod·y /nốbədee, -bòddee, -bùddee/ *pron* not one single person ■ *n* (*pl* **-ies**) an unimportant person

no·brain·er /-bráynər/ *n* something self-evident or easy (*slang*)

noc·tur·nal /nok túrn'l/ *adj* **1** occurring at night **2** describes animals that are active at night —**noc·tur·nal·ly** *adv*

noc·turne /nók tùrn/ *n* **1** a piece of tranquil dreamy music **2** a painting of a night scene

nod (**nod·ded, nod·ding**) *v* **1** *vti* move the head up and down in agreement **2** *vi* doze **3** *vi* droop or sway in the wind —**nod** *n*

⚡ **node** /nōd/ *n* **1** a lump or swelling **2** a point of leaf attachment on a plant stem **3** a point where lines meet or intersect in a diagram or graph **4** a point in a computer network where a message can be created or received —**nod·al** *adj*

nod·ule /nó jòòl/ *n* a small lump or protuberance —**nod·u·lar** /nójjələr/ *adj*

No·el /nō él/, **No·ël** *n* Christmas

no-fly-zone *n* an area of the sky forbidden to aircraft

no-frills *adj* describes a service or establishment that is basic *(infml)*

no-go ar·e·a *n* an area forbidden to unauthorized people

noise /noyz/ *n* 1 a sound, especially a loud or unpleasant sound 2 a combination of sounds ○ *too much noise in the room* 3 electric disturbance that makes a signal unclear ■ *vt* (**noised, nois·ing**) spread a rumor or gossip ○ *a story being noised around in newsrooms* —**noise·less** *adj* —**noise·less·ly** *adv* —**noise·less·ness** *n* —**nois·i·ly** *adv* —**nois·i·ness** *n* —**nois·y** *adj*

ORIGIN Noise derives from the same Latin word as *nausea*. *Nausea* came directly from Latin, and specifically meant "seasickness." The fuss and commotion surrounding attacks of seasickness presumably led to its association with sound as the word reached English via French to become **noise**.

noise pol·lu·tion *n* irritating noise from the environment

noi·some /nóyssəm/ *adj* 1 foul or disgusting 2 dangerous —**noi·some·ness** *n*

no-load *adj* free from commission or fees

no·lo con·ten·de·re /nōlō kən téndəree/ *n* a plea accepting charges without admitting guilt

no·mad /nó màd/ *n* 1 a member of a people who move from place to place 2 a wanderer —**no·mad·ic** /nō máddik/ *adj*

no man's land *n* 1 territory between opposing armed forces 2 unclaimed land 3 a situation in which rules or boundaries are uncertain

nom de guerre /nòm də gáir/ (*pl* **noms de guerre** /nòm-/) *n* a pseudonym

nom de plume /nòm də plóom/ (*pl* **noms de plume** /nòm-/) *n* a writer's pseudonym

Nome /nōm/ city in W Alaska, on the Seward Peninsula. Pop. 3,899 (1998).

no·men·cla·ture /nṓmən klàychər/ *n* 1 the assigning of names to organisms in a scientific classification system 2 a system of names

nom·i·nal /nómmən'l/ *adj* 1 in name only 2 very low in amount ○ *a nominal fee* 3 of a noun —**nom·i·nal·ly** *adv*

nom·i·nal val·ue *n* par value

nom·i·nate /nómmə nàyt/ (**-nat·ed, -nat·ing**) *vt* 1 propose for election or for an award 2 appoint —**nom·i·na·tion** /nòmmə náysh'n/ *n*

nom·i·na·tive /nómmə nàytiv/ (*grammatical case*) /nómmənətiv/ *n* 1 the grammatical case

of the subject of a verb or sentence 2 a word in the nominative —**nom·i·na·tive** *adj*

nom·i·nee /nòmmə neé/ *n* somebody nominated

non- *prefix* not, without, the opposite of ○ *nonrenewable* ○ *nonstick* ○ *nonviolence*

non·ac·cep·tance /nòn ək séptənss/ *n* refusal or rejection

non·a·ge·nar·i·an /nònnəjə nérree ən, nònə-/ *n* somebody in his or her nineties —**non·a·ge·nar·i·an** *adj*

non·a·gon /nónnə gòn, nónə-/ *n* a nine-sided geometric figure —**non·ag·o·nal** /nō nággən'l/ *adj*

non·al·co·hol·ic /nòn alkə háwllik/ *adj* containing no alcohol

non·a·ligned /nònnə línd/ *adj* not allied with another nation —**non·a·lign·ment** *n*

non·ap·pear·ance /nònnə peéronss/ *n* a failure to turn up

non·at·ten·dance /nònnə téndənss/ *n* a failure to be present —**non·at·ten·der** *n*

non·bank /non bángk/ *n* a financial enterprise that is not a bank but performs some bank functions —**non·bank·ing** *adj*

non·busi·ness /non bíznəss/ *adj* not relating to business

nonce /nonss/ *n* the present time *(archaic)* ○ *for the nonce*

nonce word *n* a word coined for a single occasion

non·cha·lant /nònshə laánt, nónshə laànt/ *adj* calm and unconcerned —**non·cha·lance** *n* —**non·cha·lant·ly** *adv*

ORIGIN Etymologically **nonchalant** means "not hot." The idea of being hot and bothered readily led the French verb "be hot" to mean also "be concerned." **Nonchalant** was adopted into English from French in the mid-18C.

non·com·bat·ant /nònkəm bátt'nt/ *n* 1 a civilian in wartime 2 a nonfighting member of the armed forces

non·com·mis·sioned of·fi·cer /nònkə mish'nd-/ *n* an officer who has been appointed from the lower ranks

non·com·mit·tal /nònkə mítt'l/ *adj* not expressing an opinion —**non·com·mit·tal·ly** *adv*

non·com·pet·i·tive bid /nònkəm petitiv-/ *n* a method of purchasing US Treasury bills at an average weekly price

non·com·pli·ance /nònkəm plî ənss/ *n* failure to comply —**non·com·pli·ant** *adj*

non com·pos men·tis /non kòmpəss méntiss/ *adj* in law, not mentally competent to understand what is happening to and to make important decisions

non·con·form·ist /nònkən fáwrmist/ *n* 1 an unconventional person 2 *also* **Non·con·form·ist** a member of a Protestant church that is not the established church —**non·con·form·ist** *adj*

non·con·form·i·ty /nònkən fáwrmətee/ *n* 1 unconventionality 2 lack of agreement with something

non·con·trib·u·to·ry /nònkən tríbbyə tàwree/ *adj* not requiring contributions from an employee or member ○ *a noncontributory pension plan*

non·co·op·er·a·tion /nònkō opə ráysh'n/ *n* 1 refusal to cooperate 2 civil disobedience —**non·co·op·er·a·tive** /nònkō óppərətiv, -ràytiv/ *adj*

non·cus·to·di·al /nònkə stódee əl/ *adj* 1 not involving imprisonment ○ *a noncustodial sentence* 2 not having custody of child

non·de·duct·i·ble /nòndi dúktəb'l/ *adj* not deductible from taxable income

non·de·liv·er·y /nòn di lívvəree/ *n* failure to deliver something

non·de·script /nòndi skrípt/ *adj* unremarkable

⚡**non·dig·i·tal** /non díjit'l/ *adj* 1 not involving computers or the Internet 2 not processing or representing data by numbers

none /nun/ *pron* 1 nobody 2 not any ◇ **have none of** refuse to tolerate ◇ **none the** in no degree *(with comparative adjectives)* ○ *none the wiser* ◇ **none too** not very ○ *none too pleased*

non·en·ti·ty /non éntətee/ (*pl* -ties) *n* 1 an insignificant person 2 something nonexistent

non·es·sen·tial /nòn i sénshəl/ *adj* 1 not absolutely necessary 2 not essential in the diet —**non·es·sen·tial** *n*

none·the·less /nùnthə léss/ *adv* nevertheless

non·e·vent /nòn i vént/ *n* a disappointingly unexciting occasion

non·ex·ist·ent /nòn ig zístənt/ *adj* not existing —**non·ex·ist·ence** *n*

non·fat /non fát/ *adj* without fat, or with the fat content removed

non·fic·tion /non fíksh'n/ *n* prose that consists of factual information —**non·fic·tion·al** *adj*

non·flam·ma·ble /non flámməb'l/ *adj* difficult to burn

non·gov·ern·men·tal /nòn gùvvərn mént'l/ *adj* not run by a government

non·in·ter·ven·tion /nòn intər vénsh'n/ *n* lack of interference in other countries' affairs —**non·in·ter·ven·tion·ist** *n, adj*

non·in·va·sive /nòn in váyssiv/ *adj* 1 not involving entering or cutting into the body 2 describes a medical condition that is not likely to spread to other parts of the body

non·mar·ket·a·ble /nòn máarkətəb'l/ *adj* 1 not able to be marketed 2 not convertible into cash

non·mem·ber /nòn mémbər/ *n* a person or group that is not a member

non·met·al /non métt'l/ *n* a chemical element without the properties of a metal —**non·me·tal·lic** /nòn mə tállik/ *adj*

non·ne·go·tia·ble /nòn nə góshee əb'l, nòn nə-/ *adj* 1 not open to negotiation 2 not legally transferable

non·nu·cle·ar /nòn nóoklee ər/ *adj* not using nuclear power or weapons

no-no (*pl* **no-nos**) *n* something not allowed *(infml)*

non·ob·ser·vance /nònnəb zúrvənss/ *n* failure to obey a rule or practice

no-non·sense *adj* 1 direct and practical 2 basic and unadorned

non·pa·reil /nònpə rél, nónpə rèl/ *n* 1 somebody or something without an equal 2 a sugar-covered chocolate disk ■ *adj* peerless

non·par·ti·san /nòn paártizən/ *adj* not supporting any political party —**non·par·ti·san** *n*

non·pay·ment /non páymənt/ *n* failure to pay

non·per·son /non púrs'n/ *n* 1 somebody ignored by a political regime 2 an insignificant person

non·plus /non plúss/ (-**plussed** *or* -**plused**, -**plus·sing** *or* -**plus·ing**, -**plus·ses**) *vt* confuse or fluster —**non·plussed** *adj*

⚡**non·print·ing** /nòn prínting/ *adj* describes a character used for formatting that does not appear on a printout

non·prof·it /nòn próffit/ *n* an organization that is not run with the aim of making a profit ○ *a nonprofit organization*

non·pro·lif·er·a·tion /nòn prə liffə ráysh'n/ *n* limitation of the spread of something, especially nuclear weapons ○ *a nonproliferation agreement*

non·re·fund·a·ble /nòn ri fúndəb'l/ *adj* for which payment cannot be claimed back ○ *a nonrefundable deposit*

non·re·new·a·ble /nòn ri nóo əb'l/ *adj* 1 not replaceable once used 2 not renewable once expired

non·res·i·dent /non rézzidənt/ *adj* 1 not living or staying in a place 2 not involving living at the workplace —**non·res·i·dent** *n*

non·re·stric·tive /nòn ri stríktiv/ *adj* describes a relative clause giving nonessential additional information

non·sense /nón sènss, nónsənss/ *n* 1 meaningless language or behavior 2 a pointless act or statement 3 irritating behavior ○ *won't stand for any nonsense* ■ *interj* expresses emphatic contradiction —**non·sen·si·cal** /non sénsik'l/ *adj* —**non·sen·si·cal·i·ty** /-sènssi kállətee/ *n* —**non·sen·si·cal·ly** *adv* —**non·sen·si·cal·ness** *n*

non se·qui·tur /non sékwitər/ *n* a statement apparently unrelated to what preceded it

non·slip /non slíp/ *adj* preventing slipping

non·smok·er /non smókər/ *n* 1 somebody who does not smoke 2 a railroad car or compartment where smoking is forbidden

non·smok·ing /non smóking/ *adj* 1 restricted to nonsmokers 2 not smoking

non·spe·cif·ic /nòn spə síffik/ *adj* 1 general 2 without a particular medical cause

non·stan·dard /non stándərd/ adj 1 not of an accepted standard 2 not used in standard language

non·start·er /non staártər/ n something or somebody unlikely to succeed (infml)

non·state ac·tor /nòn stayt-/ n an individual or body acting independently of a state or government, e.g., a terrorist group

non·stick /non stík/ adj preventing food from sticking during cooking

non·stop /non stóp/ adj, adv 1 without a stop 2 without interruption

non·trans·fer·a·ble /nòn trans fúr əb'l/, **non-trans·ferra·ble** adj for use only by the specified person

non·un·ion /non yoonyən/ adj 1 not belonging to a labor union 2 not using labor union members —**non·un·ion·ized** adj

non·ver·bal /non vúrb'l/ adj not involving words —**non·ver·bal·ly** adv

non·vi·o·lence /non ví əlanss, -víIanss/ n the principle of refraining from using violence —**non·vi·o·lent** adj

⚡ non·vol·a·tile /non vóllat'l/ adj 1 not likely to evaporate 2 retaining data when the power is off

non·vot·ing /non vóting/ adj describes stock that does not give the holder the right to vote

non·white /non wít, -hwít/, **non-White** n somebody from a dark-skinned ethnic group (sometimes offensive) —**non·white** adj

noo·dle /nood'l/ n a long thin strip of pasta (often pl)

nook /nook/ n 1 a quiet private place 2 a small corner or recess

noon /noon/ n 12 o'clock midday

ORIGIN **Noon** derives from Latin *nona* "ninth," as a shortening of a compound meaning "ninth hour." In ancient Rome the hours of the day were counted from sunrise, so the ninth hour fell at about three o'clock in the afternoon. This is what **noon** originally meant in English. Three o'clock was also an hour of prayer in the Roman Catholic Church, and the word **noon** was used for this office. It may be that the taking of a meal in preparation for this hour of prayer led **noon** to refer to an earlier part of the day. Obsolete *noonmeat* "noon meal" is recorded in the 10C, followed by **noon** itself in the 12C for the midday meal, with the sense "midday" following hard on its heels.

noon·day /noon dày/ adj of or happening at midday (literary) —**noon·day** n

no one pron nobody

noon·time /noon tìm/ n noon or the middle of the day

noose /nooss/ n a loop in a rope tied with a sliding knot

Noot·ka /nootkə/ (pl -kas or same) n 1 a member of a Native North American people of the coast of W Vancouver Island, British Columbia, and Cape Flattery, on the Olympic Peninsula in Washington State 2 the language of the Nootka people —**Noot·ka** adj

nope /nōp/ adv, interj no (slang)

nor /nawr/ conj and not either ○ Neither he nor his brother was involved. ■ adv also not ○ She doesn't want to go, and nor do I.

⚡ NOR n logical operator

ORIGIN **NOR** is a blend of *not* and *or*, and not a use of the conjunction *nor*.

Nor. abbr North

NORAD /náwr àd/ abbr North American Aerospace Defense Command

Nor·dic /náwrdik/ adj 1 Scandinavian 2 tall, fair, and blue-eyed —**Nor·dic** n

Nor·folk /náwrfək/ city and port in SE Virginia. Pop. 215,215 (1998).

Nor·kay ♦ Tenzing Norkay

norm /nawrm/ n 1 a standard pattern of behavior 2 the usual situation or circumstances

nor·mal /náwrm'l/ adj 1 usual 2 healthy ■ n the usual standard or level —**nor·mal·i·ty** /nawr máll∂tee/ n —**nor·mal·ly** adv

nor·mal·ize /náwrm'l īz/ (-ized, -iz·ing) v 1 vti make or become what is usual or regular 2 vt cause to conform —**nor·mal·i·za·tion** /nàwrm'li záysh'n/ n

Nor·man /náwrmən/ n 1 a member of a Viking people who settled in Normandy and later invaded England 2 somebody from Normandy —**Nor·man** adj

Nor·man /náwrmən/, **Jessye** (b. 1945) US operatic soprano

Nor·man·dy /náwrməndee/ region of NW France, bordering on the English Channel. Cap. Rouen.

nor·ma·tive /náwrmətiv/ adj (fml) 1 of standards 2 creating or prescribing standards

Norse /nawrs/ npl 1 the Vikings 2 the people of Scandinavia ■ n early Norwegian, Danish, Icelandic, or a related language

nor·te·ño /nawr táynyō/ n 1 a type of Mexican dance music, characterized by rolling accordion riffs 2 somebody from N Mexico

north /nawrth/ n 1 the direction to the left of somebody facing the rising sun 2 the compass point that is opposite south 3 also **North** the part of an area or country that is in the north ■ adj 1 in the north 2 blowing from the north ■ adv toward the north —**north·bound** adj

North /nawrth/, **Frederick, 8th Baron North** (1732–92) British prime minister (1770–82)

North Af·ri·ca northern part of the African continent, comprising Morocco, Mauritania, Algeria, Tunisia, Libya, and Egypt —**North Af·ri·can** adj, n

North A·mer·i·ca continent in the western hemisphere, extending northward from

NW South America to the Arctic Ocean. It comprises Central America, Mexico, the United States, Canada, and Greenland. Pop. 405,000,000 (2000). —**North A·mer·i·can** *adj, n ◊* See note at **America**

North Car·o·li·na /-kèrrə lînə/ state on the coast of the E United States. Cap. Raleigh. Pop. 8,049,313 (2000). —**North Car·o·lin·i·an** *adj, n*

North Da·ko·ta state of the north central United States. Cap. Bismarck. Pop. 642,200 (2000). —**North Da·ko·tan** *adj, n*

north·east /nawrth ēest/ *nautical usage* /nawr ēest/ *n* 1 a direction or compass point between north and east 2 *also* **North·east** the part of an area or country that is in the northeast ■ *adj* 1 *also* **North·east** in the northeast 2 blowing from the northeast ■ *adv* toward the northeast

north·east·er /nawrth ēestər/ *nautical usage* /nawr ēestər/ *n* a storm or wind from the northeast

north·east·er·ly /nawrth ēestərlee/ *nautical usage* /nawr ēestərlee/ *adj* 1 in the northeast 2 blowing from the northeast —**north·east·er·ly** *adv*

north·east·ern /nawrth ēestərn/ *nautical usage* /nawr ēestərn/ *adj* 1 in the northeast 2 facing northeast 3 blowing from the northeast 4 *also* **North·east·ern** of the northeast —**north·east·ern·er** *n*

north·east·ward /nawrth ēestward/ *nautical usage* /nawr ēestward/ *adj* in the northeast ■ *n* a direction toward or point in the northeast ■ *adv* also **north·east·wards** toward the northeast

north·er·ly /náwrthərlee/ *adj* 1 in the north 2 blowing from the north ■ *n (pl* **-lies**) a wind from the north —**north·er·ly** *adv*

north·ern /náwrthərn/ *adj* 1 in the north 2 north of the equator 3 facing north 4 blowing from the north 5 *also* **North·ern** of the north —**north·ern·most** *adj*

North·ern Al·li·ance *n* a loose coalition of Afghan military forces that ended Taliban rule in Afghanistan in 2001

north·ern·er, North·ern·er *n* somebody from the north of a country or region

north·ern hem·i·sphere *n* the half of the Earth north of the equator

North·ern Ire·land province of the United Kingdom, in NE Ireland. Cap. Belfast. Pop. 1,689,000 (1998).

north·ern lights *npl* the aurora borealis

North·ern Mar·i·an·a Is·lands /-màrree ánnə-/ island group in the W Pacific Ocean, a self-governing commonwealth of the United States. Pop. 71,912 (2000).

North Is·land northernmost principal island of New Zealand. Pop. 2,749,980 (1996).

North Ko·re·a /-kə rēə ə, -kō rēē ə/ country in East Asia, in the north of the Korean Peninsula. Cap. Pyongyang. Pop. 21,968,228 (2001). —**North Ko·re·an** *n, adj*

north pole *n* 1 *also* **North Pole** the northern end of the Earth's axis 2 *also* **north mag·net·ic pole** the point on the Earth's surface to which a compass needle is attracted

North Sea arm of the Atlantic Ocean lying between the NE United Kingdom and continental Europe

North Star *n* Polaris

North·um·bri·a /nawr thúmbree ə/ ancient Anglo-Saxon kingdom in N Great Britain —**North·um·bri·an** *adj, n*

North Viet·nam former republic in Southeast Asia, occupying the northern part of modern-day Vietnam —**North Viet·nam·ese** *n, adj*

north·ward /náwrthward/ *adj* moving in a direction toward the north ■ *n* a point in the north ■ *adv* also **north·wards** toward the north —**north·ward·ly** *adj, adv*

north·west /nawrth wést/ *nautical usage* /nawr wést/ *n* 1 a direction or compass point between north and west 2 **North·west** the NW states of Washington, Oregon, and Idaho 3 *also* **North·west** the part of an area or country that is in the northwest 4 **North·west** the area of Canada north and west of the Great Lakes ■ *adj* 1 in the northwest 2 blowing from the northwest ■ *adv* toward the northwest

north·west·er /nawrth wéstar/ *nautical usage* /nawr wéstar/ *n* a storm or wind from the northwest

north·west·er·ly /nawrth wéstarlee/ *nautical usage* /nawr wéstarlee/ *adj* 1 in the northwest 2 blowing from the northwest ■ *n (pl* **-lies**) a wind from the northwest —**north·west·er·ly** *adv*

north·west·ern /nawrth wéstarn/ *nautical usage* /nawr wéstarn/ *adj* 1 in the northwest 2 facing northwest 3 blowing from the northwest 4 *also* **North·west·ern** of the northwest —**north·west·ern·er** *n*

North·west Pas·sage sea passage along the coast of N North America, connecting the Atlantic and Pacific oceans

North·west Ter·ri·to·ries territory of NW Canada, extending north of the provinces between Yukon Territory and Hudson Bay. Cap. Yellowknife. Pop. 42,083 (2000).

North·west Ter·ri·to·ry historic territory of the north central United States, extending from the Ohio and Mississippi rivers northward to the Great Lakes, and comprising present-day Ohio, Indiana, Illinois, Michigan, Wisconsin, and E Minnesota

north·west·ward /nawrth wéstword/ *nautical usage* /nawr wéstward/ *adj* in the northwest ■ *n* a direction toward or point in the northwest ■ *adv* also **north·west·wards** toward the northwest

Nor·way /náwr way/ country in N Europe, in W Scandinavia. Cap. Oslo. Pop. 4,503,440 (2001).

Nor·we·gian /nawr weèjən/ *n* **1** somebody from Norway **2** the official language of Norway —**Nor·we·gian** *adj*

nos., Nos. *abbr* numbers

nose /nōz/ *n* **1** the part of the face or head through which a person or animal breathes and smells **2** the sense of smell **3** an intuitive ability to detect or recognize something **4** a part resembling a nose, e.g., the projecting front part of an aircraft or vehicle ■ *v* (**nosed, nos·ing**) **1** *vi* pry or snoop (*infml*) **2** *vi* search for or discover something by or as if by scent ○ *nosed out my secret hoard of chocolate* **3** *vti* advance or cause to advance with caution ○ *nosed into the stream of traffic* ◇ **keep your nose clean** avoid getting into trouble (*infml*) ◇ **keep** *or* **put your nose to the grindstone** keep working hard without taking a break ◇ **look down your nose at** regard as inferior ◇ **on the nose** absolutely correctly (*infml*) ◇ **put somebody's nose out of joint** make somebody feel thwarted or offended ◇ **thumb your nose at** express defiance or contempt of ◇ **turn up your nose at** refuse as unworthy of you (*infml*) ◇ **under somebody's nose** in full view of or very close to somebody

nose·bleed /nōz blèed/ *n* a flow of blood from the nose

nose·dive /nōz dìv/ *n* **1** a steep plunge through the air by an aircraft **2** a sharp decrease —**nose·dive** *vi*

nose·gay /nōz gày/ *n* a small bouquet of flowers

nos·ey *adj* = nosy

nosh /nosh/ (*infml*) *n* a snack ■ *v* **1** *vt* eat **2** *vi* eat a snack

no-show *n* somebody expected who does not arrive

nos·tal·gi·a /no stáljə, nə-/ *n* **1** sentimental recollection **2** things that arouse nostalgia —**nos·tal·gic** *adj* —**nos·tal·gi·cal·ly** *adv*

Nos·tra·da·mus /nòstrə daàməss, -dáyməss/ (1503–66) French astrologer and physician

nos·tril /nóstrəl/ *n* a breathing hole in the nose

nos·trum /nóstrəm/ *n* **1** an ineffective remedy for a social, political, or economic problem **2** a quack medicine

nos·y /nózee/ (**-i·er, -i·est**), **nos·ey** *adj* intrusively inquisitive (*infml*) —**nos·i·ly** *adv* —**nos·i·ness** *n*

not *adv* **1** forms negatives (often contracted in *infml* English to "n't") **2** avoids repetition when indicating denial, refusal, or negation ○ *I don't think I'll be late, at least I hope not.* **3** indicates the opposite (*humorous*) ○ *You're really going to enjoy this – not!* ◇ See note at **knot**

⚡ **NOT** *n* a computer logic circuit

no·ta·ble /nótəb'l/ *adj* **1** worthy of note **2** interesting or significant **3** distinguished or famous —**no·ta·ble** *n* —**no·ta·bly** *adv*

no·ta·rize /nóta rìz/ (**-rized, -riz·ing**) *vt* certify legally —**no·ta·ri·za·tion** /nòtəri záysh'n/ *n*

no·ta·ry /nótəree/ (*pl* **-ries**) *n* somebody legally authorized to certify authenticity

no·ta·tion /nō táysh'n/ *n* **1** a set of written symbols used to represent something **2** a set of symbols to represent something **3** a note **4** noting or writing down

notch /noch/ *n* **1** a small V-shaped cut **2** a degree on a scale, especially when measuring achievement ■ *vt* **1** make a notch in **2** achieve or score (*slang*) ○ *notched up another win* —**notch·y** *adj*

note /nōt/ *n* **1** a jotted record or reminder **2** an informal letter **3** a musical or vocal sound **4** a symbol in music **5** a key on a keyboard instrument **6** a comment or an item of supplementary information in a text **7** distinction **8** an indication of mood **9** a piece of paper money **10** a tune (*archaic*) ■ **notes** *npl* a summary for future reference ■ *vt* (**not·ed, not·ing**) **1** notice or remember **2** mention **3** write down

~~noteable~~ incorrect spelling of **notable**

⚡ **note·book** /nót bòk/ *n* **1** a small book of blank or lined paper **2** a small personal computer

note card *n* a decorative card for a short letter

not·ed /nótəd/ *adj* **1** well-known **2** marked or significant —**not·ed·ly** *adv*

note·pad /nót pàd/ *n* a small pad of blank or lined paper

note·pa·per /nót pàypər/ *n* paper for writing letters

note·wor·thy /nót wùrthee/ (**-thi·er, -thi·est**) *adj* deserving attention —**note·wor·thi·ly** *adv* —**note·wor·thi·ness** *n*

noth·ing /núthing/ *pron* **1** not anything **2** something of no importance **3** a quantity or number that when added to another does not change it ■ *n* a totally unimportant person or thing

noth·ing·ness /núthingnəss/ *n* **1** absence of everything **2** complete worthlessness or meaninglessness **3** nonexistence

~~noticable~~ incorrect spelling of **noticeable**

no·tice /nótiss/ *n* **1** a public sign **2** a written announcement **3** warning **4** a period of warning **5** official notification of the end of employment **6** attention **7** a critical review ■ *v* (**-ticed, -tic·ing**) **1** *vti* observe or catch sight of something ○ *Did you notice what he had in his hand?* **2** *vti* perceive or become aware of something ○ *I noticed that he avoided mentioning her name.* **3** *vt* mention **4** *vt* write a critical review of

no·tice·a·ble /nótissəb'l/ *adj* **1** easily perceived **2** noteworthy —**no·tice·a·bly** *adv*

no·ti·fi·a·ble /nótə fì əb'l/ *adj* describes an infectious disease that must be reported

no·ti·fy /nótə fì/ (**-fied, -fies**) *vt* **1** tell officially **2** make known —**no·ti·fi·ca·tion** /nòtəfi káysh'n/ *n*

no·tion /nṓsh'n/ n 1 an idea or concept 2 a vague impression ■ **no·tions** npl small items used in sewing

no·tion·al /nṓshan'l, nṓshnal/ adj abstract, imaginary, or hypothetical —**no·tion·al·ly** adv

no·to·ri·ous /na táwree ass, nō-/ adj famous for something bad —**no·to·ri·e·ty** /nṓta rī ́atee/ n —**no·to·ri·ous·ly** adv

Not·ting·ham /nṓttingam/ city in central England. Pop. 283,969 (1996).

not·with·stand·ing /nòt with stánding, -with-/ (fml) prep despite (often after nouns) o The lack of a catalog notwithstanding, it was a very interesting exhibition. ■ adv nevertheless ■ conj although

Nouak·chott /nwaak shót/ capital of Mauritania. Pop. 707,000 (1990).

nou·gat /nṓogat/ n a chewy candy made with egg whites and honey and usually containing nuts

nought n UK = naught ₁

noun /nown/ n a word used to name things, people, or places

nour·ish /núr ish/ vt 1 give food to 2 encourage or strengthen —**nour·ish·ing** adj —**nour·ish·ment** n

nous /nooss, nowss/ n 1 the capacity to reason and acquire knowledge 2 the part of the human spirit capable of rational thought

nou·veau riche /nóovō réesh/ (pl **nou·veaux rich·es** /pronunc. same/) n somebody with newly acquired wealth —**nouveau riche** adj

nou·velle cui·sine /noo véi kwi zeèn, -kwee-/ n a lighter style of French cooking

Nov. abbr November

no·va /nṓva/ (pl **-vas** or **-vae** /-vee/) n a star that has a temporary dramatic increase in brightness

No·va Sco·tia /nṓva skṓsha/ province in E Canada. Cap. Halifax. Pop. 940,996 (2000). —**No·va Sco·tian** n, adj

nov·el[1] /nóvv'l/ n a relatively long fictional prose work

nov·el[2] /nóvv'l/ adj refreshingly new ◊ See note at **new**

nov·el·ette /nòvv'l ét/ n a sentimental or short novel

nov·el·ist /nóvv'list/ n a writer of novels

nov·el·la /nō vélla/ n a short novel

nov·el·ty /nóvv'ltee/ (pl **-ties**) n 1 a small toy or trinket 2 newness and originality 3 a new thing or experience

No·vem·ber /nō vémbar/ n 1 the 11th month of the year in the Gregorian calendar 2 a communications code word for the letter "N"

ORIGIN November comes from a Latin word literally meaning "ninth month." In ancient Rome the calendar started the year in March.

Nov·go·rod /nóvga ròd/ city in NW Russia. Pop. 288,910 (1995).

nov·ice /nóvviss/ n 1 a beginner 2 a member of a religious order who has not yet taken vows ◊ See note at **beginner**

no·vi·ti·ate /nō víshat, nō víshee at/, **no·vi·ci·ate** n 1 the period of being a novice 2 religious novices' living quarters

No·vo·cain /nṓva kàyn/ tdmk a trademark for a synthetic drug. Use: local anesthetic.

No·vo·si·birsk /nòvvassa beérsk/ city in south central Russia. Pop. 1,428,141 (1995).

now /now/ adv 1 at the present time 2 immediately 3 given the current situation o It doesn't matter now. 4 up to the present time o for six months now 5 prefaces a remark or calls for attention o Now, what would you like to drink? ■ conj since or in view of the fact that ■ n the present time ■ adj fashionable (infml)

now·a·days /nów a dàyz/ adv in the present ~~nowadays~~ incorrect spelling of **nowadays**

no·where /nṓ wàir, -hwàir/ adv in or to no place ■ n a remote place

no·wise /nṓ wīz/ adv in no manner at all

nox·ious /nókshass/ adj 1 physically or morally harmful 2 disgusting —**nox·ious·ly** adv

noz·zle /nózz'l/ n 1 a projecting spout 2 a short tapered tube used for directing or accelerating a flow

nr abbr near

NRA abbr National Rifle Association

NRC abbr Nuclear Regulatory Commission

⌇NRN abbr no reply necessary (in e-mails)

NS, N.S. abbr 1 not sufficient (funds) 2 Nova Scotia 3 nuclear ship

NSE abbr National Stock Exchange

NST abbr Can Newfoundland Standard Time

NT, N.T. abbr 1 Newfoundland Time 2 Can Northwest Territories

nth /enth/ adj indefinitely large numerically

nu /noo, nyoo/ (pl **nus**) n the 13th letter of the Greek alphabet

nu·ance /noò àans/ n a subtle difference —**nu·anced** adj

nub n 1 the central issue 2 a small lump or projection —**nub·by** adj

Nu·bi·a /noòbee a, nyoò-/ region of NE Africa, in S Egypt and N Sudan —**Nu·bi·an** n, adj

nu·bile /noòb'l, noò bīl/ adj ready for marriage (dated) —**nu·bil·i·ty** /noo billatee/ n

nu·cle·ar /noòklee ar/ adj 1 of or forming a nucleus 2 of nuclear weapons or nuclear energy

nu·cle·ar en·er·gy n energy produced by combining or splitting atoms or atomic nuclei

nu·cle·ar fam·i·ly n a social unit of parents with their children

nu·cle·ar fis·sion n the production of

nuclear energy by splitting atoms or atomic nuclei

nu·cle·ar fu·sion *n* the process in which light atoms combine and form heavier atoms, releasing a great amount of energy

nu·cle·ar phys·ics *n* the branch of physics in which nuclear structures and forces are studied (*+ sing verb*) —**nu·cle·ar phys·i·cist** *n*

nu·cle·ar pow·er *n* power produced by combining or splitting atoms or atomic nuclei —**nu·cle·ar-pow·ered** *adj*

nu·cle·ar re·ac·tor *n* a device producing nuclear energy

nu·cle·ar waste *n* unwanted material produced by nuclear reactors

nu·cle·ar weap·on *n* an explosive nuclear device

nu·cle·ar win·ter *n* a cold dark period after a nuclear war

nu·cle·ic ac·id /noo klee ik-, -klay-/ *n* an acid, e.g., DNA or RNA, found in all living cells and conveying genetic information

nu·cle·us /nookleə əss/ (*pl* -i /-i/ -klee i/ *or* -us·es) *n* 1 an important central element or part 2 the positively charged central region of an atom 3 the central part of a living cell

nu·clide /nook lid/ *n* one or more atomic nuclei identifiable as being of the same element by having the same number of protons and neutrons and the same energy content

~~nucular~~ incorrect spelling of **nuclear**

nude /nood/ *adj* 1 unclothed 2 for unclothed people ■ *n* an unclothed figure —**nu·di·ty** *n*
◊ See note at **naked**

nudge (nudged, nudg·ing) *vt* 1 push somebody or something gently 2 have nearly reached a level *o profits nudging the 100 million mark* —**nudge** *n*

nud·ist /noodist/ *n* somebody preferring to be nude, especially in designated public places —**nud·ism** *n* —**nud·ist** *adj*

nue·vo sol /nwáyvó sól/ (*pl* **nue·vos sol·es** /nwàyvòs sólays/) *n* MONEY = **sol²**

nu·ga·to·ry /nóogə tàwree/ *adj* 1 trivial 2 not legally valid

nug·get /núggət/ *n* 1 a lump of precious metal 2 a small precious thing

nui·sance /nóoss'nss/ *n* 1 somebody or something irritating 2 something that causes harm or offense and is illegal

nuke /nook/ (*slang*) *vt* (nuked, nuk·ing) attack with nuclear weapons ■ *n* 1 a nuclear weapon 2 a nuclear power plant

~~nukular~~ incorrect spelling of **nuclear**

null *adj* 1 invalid 2 valueless 3 amounting to nothing ■ *n* zero (*literary*) —**nul·li·ty** *n*

nul·li·fy /núllə fì/ (-fied, -fies) *vt* 1 make legally invalid 2 cancel out

SYNONYMS **nullify**, **abrogate**, **annul**, **repeal**,

invalidate, **negate** CORE MEANING: put an end to the effective existence of something

numb /num/ *adj* 1 without sensation 2 unable to feel emotion —**numb** *vt* —**numb·ing** *adj* —**numb·ly** *adv* —**numb·ness** *n*

num·ber /númbər/ *n* 1 an identifying figure or group of figures *o a fax number o a number 6 shirt* 2 a figure used in counting 3 a countable quantity 4 a piece of popular music 5 an unspecified quantity *o taught me a number of things* 6 a thing (*infml*) 7 in grammar, quantity expressed by the form of a word 8 a single thing in a series 9 counting ■ *v* 1 *vt* identify by a number 2 *vt* include in a group *o was numbered among the best* 3 *vti* reach a particular total ◊ **have somebody's number** understand somebody's true motives or character

USAGE **Number** is a collective noun that can take a singular or plural verb depending on how you use it. If you put the definite article *the* in front of **number** you must use a singular verb: *The number of styles available is limited.* If you put the indefinite article *a* before **number**, you must use a plural verb: *A number of styles are available.*

⚡**num·ber crunch·er** *n* (*slang*) 1 a computer that performs calculations 2 somebody whose job is to perform calculations —**num·ber crunch·ing** *n*

num·ber·less /númbərləss/ *adj* 1 countless 2 not numbered

num·ber one *n* 1 the first in a series or hierarchy 2 somebody's own self and interests (*infml*) ■ *adj* 1 most important 2 excellent (*infml*)

Num·bers /númbərz/ *n* the fourth book of the Bible (*+ sing verb*)

num·bers game *n* an illegal gambling game in which people bet on undetermined numbers

numb·skull *n* = **numskull** (*insult*)

nu·mer·a·cy /nóomərəssee/ *n* mathematical competence

nu·mer·al /nóomərəl/ *n* a symbol representing a number —**nu·mer·al** *adj*

nu·mer·ate *adj* /nóomərət/ mathematically competent ■ *vt* /nóomə ràyt/ (-at·ed, -at·ing) enumerate things (*archaic*)

nu·mer·a·tor /nóomə ràytər/ *n* in mathematics, a part of a common fraction appearing above the line and representing the number of parts of a whole

nu·mer·i·cal /noo mérrik'l/, **nu·mer·ic** /-mérrik/ *adj* 1 consisting of numbers 2 in terms of the numbers of things —**nu·mer·i·cal·ly** *adv*

⚡**nu·mer·ic key·pad** *n* a part of a computer keyboard containing keys that are numbered like a calculator

nu·mer·ol·o·gy /nóomə róllajee/ *n* the study of the supposed influence of numbers

—**nu·mer·o·log·i·cal** /noŏmərə lójjik'l/ adj
—**nu·mer·ol·o·gist** n

nu·mer·ous /noŏmərəss/ adj many in number
—**nu·mer·ous·ly** adv —**nu·mer·ous·ness** n

nu·mi·nous /noŏmənəss/ adj mysteriously associated with a deity (fml)

nu·mis·mat·ics /noŏmiz máttiks, -miss-/ n the collecting of coins and medals (+ sing verb)
—**nu·mis·ma·tist** /noo mízmətist/ n

⚡ **Num Lock** n a keyboard feature that cancels the usual functions of the numeric keypad and allows it to be used to input numbers

num·skull /núm skúl/, **numb·skull** n a person regarded as unintelligent (insult)

nun n a woman who belongs to a religious order

ORIGIN Nun goes back to a Latin word that was used of anyone of advanced or advancing age. It came to be applied specifically to monks and nuns, although in English nun has always applied to a member of a women's community.

Nun·a·vut /noŏnə voŏt/ territory of N Canada. Cap. Iqaluit. Pop. 27,692 (2000).

nun·ci·o /núnsee ŏ, noŏn-/ (pl -os) n a representative of the pope in a country

nun·ner·y /núnnəree/ (pl -ies) n a convent of nuns

nup·tial /núpshəl, núpchəl/ adj of marriage or a wedding ■ **nup·tials** npl a wedding (fml)
—**nup·tial·ly** adv

Nu·rem·berg /noŏrəm bùrg/ city in SE Germany. Pop. 495,845 (1997).

CORBIS/Bettmann

Rudolf Nureyev

Nu·re·yev /noŏree ef, noo ráy-/, Rudolf (1938–93) Russian-born ballet dancer and choreographer

nurse /nurss/ n 1 somebody trained to look after sick and injured people 2 a nanny (dated) 3 somebody who breast-feeds another woman's baby ■ v (nursed, nurs·ing) 1 vti breast-feed a baby 2 vt look after a sick or injured person 3 vt consume something slowly ○ nursing a drink 4 vt keep a negative feeling in the mind, often letting it develop ○ nurses a grudge 5 vt hold or manage somebody or something carefully and with devotion 6 vt take care with a part of the body affected by sickness or injury ○ nurse a sprained ankle 7 vi work as a nurse

nurse·maid /núrss máyd/ n a woman who looks after young children (dated)

nurse prac·ti·tion·er n a nurse trained in primary health care to assume some of the responsibilities of a doctor

nurs·er·y /núrssəree, núrssree/ (pl -ies) n 1 a business that grows plants commercially 2 a hospital room for newborn children 3 an infant's room in a house 4 also **nurs·er·y school** a school for children under five 5 a place that provides childcare

nurs·er·y·man /núrssəreemən, núrssreemən/ (pl -men /-mən/) n a commercial grower of plants

nurs·er·y rhyme n a song or poem for a child

nurs·ing /núrssing/ n 1 caring for sick and injured people 2 breast-feeding

nurs·ing home n a long-term residential health care facility

nurs·ling /núrssling/ n (literary) 1 a baby who is being breast-fed 2 a child who is cared for by somebody other than the parents

nur·ture /núrchər/ vt (-tured, -tur·ing) 1 care for a young child, animal, or plant during development 2 encourage somebody or something to flourish ■ n 1 care or encouragement given to a young child, animal, or plant 2 environmental influence, especially as opposed to genetic factors —**nur·tur·er** n

nut n 1 a fruit with a hard outer shell that contains a seed 2 an edible kernel of a nut 3 a fastening screwed onto a bolt 4 an enthusiast (infml) 5 an offensive term for somebody with a psychiatric disorder

nut·crack·er /nút kràkər/ n 1 a tool for cracking nuts' shells 2 a bird that eats pine nuts

nut·meg /nút mèg/ n 1 a spice produced by grating a hard nut, or the nut itself 2 a tropical evergreen tree that produces nutmegs

nu·tra·ceu·ti·cal /noŏtrə soŏtik'l/, **nu·tri·ceu·ti·cal**, **neu·tra·ceu·ti·cal** n a foodstuff that is promoted as having medical and health benefits

nu·tri·ent /noŏtree ənt/ n a substance providing nourishment —**nu·tri·ent** adj

nu·tri·ment /noŏtrəmənt/ n nourishing food

nu·tri·tion /noo trísh'n/ n 1 the processing of food by the body 2 the science of food —**nu·tri·tion·al** adj —**nu·tri·tion·ist** n

nu·tri·tious /noo tríshəss/ adj providing nutrition

nu·tri·tive /noŏtrətiv/ adj 1 containing nutrients 2 of nourishment —**nu·tri·tive·ly** adv

nuts adj (slang) 1 an offensive term meaning affected by a psychiatric disorder 2 enthusiastic about something (sometimes offensive)

nut·shell /nút shèl/ n the hard outer shell of a nut ◇ **in a nutshell** in very few words

nut·ty /núttee/ (-ti·er, -ti·est) adj 1 containing or tasting of nuts 2 an offensive term meaning affected by a psychiatric disorder (slang) —**nut·ti·ness** n

nuz·zle /núzz'l/ (**-zled, -zling**) vti rub something with the nose or face —**nuz·zle** n

NV abbr 1 Nevada 2 nonvoting

nvCJD abbr new variant CJD

NW abbr 1 northwest 2 northwestern

N.W.T. abbr Can Northwest Territories

NY, N.Y. abbr New York

⚡ **nyb·ble** /níbb'l/ n half of a byte

> **ORIGIN Nybble** is a humorous alteration of *nibble* with *y* from *byte* and a play on *bite*.

ny·lon /ní lòn/ n a synthetic material. Use: clothing, food containers, brush bristles. ■ **ny·lons** npl women's stockings (dated)

> **ORIGIN** The word **nylon** was coined in 1938 by Du Pont, the inventors of the material. The ending *-on* was taken from other fabric names such as *cotton* and *rayon*, but *nyl-* has no particular significance.

nymph /nimf/ n 1 in mythology, a spirit of nature depicted as a beautiful young woman 2 an insect larva that develops directly into an adult without a pupa stage

nym·phet /ním fèt, -fət/, **nym·phette** /nim fét/ n a young woman regarded as sexually desirable

nym·pho·ma·ni·a /nìmfə máynee ə/ n a supposed compulsive sexual desire in some women (often offensive) —**nym·pho·ma·ni·ac** adj, n

NYSE abbr New York Stock Exchange

NZ abbr New Zealand

O

o (pl **o's**), **O** (pl **O's** or **Os**) n the 15th letter of the English alphabet

o' contr of

O¹ n 1 a zero 2 a human blood type containing a specific antigen

O² interj 1 begins a strong plea or wish 2 expresses wonder (literary)

O³ symbol oxygen

O. abbr ocean

-o suffix forms abbreviated or informal forms of words o *beano* o *demo*

-o- connects words and suffixes

oaf /ōf/ n a person regarded as clumsy or ignorant (insult) —**oaf·ish** adj

O·a·hu /ə waŏ hoo, ō aǎ-/ island in central Hawaii. Pop. 870,761 (1995).

oak /ōk/ n 1 a tree that produces acorns and has leaves with several rounded or pointed lobes 2 the hard wood of an oak tree. Use: furniture-making, flooring. —**oak·en** adj

oak ap·ple n a rounded hollow growth on an oak tree caused by wasp infestation

Oak·land /ōkland/ city in W California. Pop. 365,874 (1998).

Oak·ley /óklee/, **Annie** (1860–1926) US sharpshooter

oa·kum /ókəm/ n tar-soaked rope formerly used to seal gaps between planks in a boat's hull

oar /awr/ n 1 a pole with one broad flat end, used to propel a boat 2 also **oars·man, oars·wom·an** somebody rowing with an oar

> **SPELLCHECK** Do not confuse the spelling of **oar**, **or** (indicating an alternative), or **ore** ("a mineral from which metal is extracted"), which sound similar.

oar·lock /áwr lòk/ n a rest for an oar

o·a·sis /ō áyssiss/ (pl **-ses** /-sèez/) n an area of fertile land in a desert

oat /ōt/ n a cereal plant with edible seeds ■ **oats** npl the edible seeds of an oat plant

oath /ōth/ (pl **oaths** /ōthz/) n 1 a solemn promise 2 a swearword

oat·meal /ót mèel/ n 1 crushed oats 2 a breakfast cereal made from rolled oats

OAU abbr Organization of African Unity

Oa·xa·ca /wə haǎkə, waa khaǎ kaa/ capital of Oaxaca State, S Mexico. Pop. 212,818 (1990).

Ob' /awb, ob/ river in W Siberian Russia that flows northward into the **Gulf of Ob'**. Length 2,290 mi./3,680 km.

o·ba /ōbə/ n a traditional ruler of the Yoruba people of West Africa

O·ba·di·ah /òbə dí ə/ n a book of the Bible containing the prophecies of Obadiah, a Hebrew prophet

O·ba·san·jo /ōbə saǎnjō/, **Olusegun** (b. 1937) president of Nigeria (1999–)

ob·bli·ga·to /òbbli gaàtō/, **ob·li·ga·to** adj not to be left out (musical direction) ■ n (pl **-tos** or **-ti** /-tee/) an obbligato part

ob·du·rate /ób doorət/ adj 1 stubborn 2 hardhearted —**ob·du·ra·cy** n —**ob·du·rate·ly** adv

o·be·ah /ōbee ə/, **o·bi** /ōbee/ n a Caribbean religion involving witchcraft

~~obedience~~ incorrect spelling of **obedience**

o·be·di·ent /ō beèdee ənt, ə-/ adj following demands or orders —**o·be·di·ence** n —**o·be·di·ent·ly** adv

o·bei·sance /ō báyss'nss, ə-/ n a respectful gesture or attitude (fml)

ob·e·lisk /óbbəlìsk/ n 1 a tall stone pillar with a square base and sides that taper to a pointed top 2 a dagger sign used in printing

o·bese /ō beèss/ adj unhealthily overweight —**o·be·si·ty** n

o·bey /ō báy/ (**o·beyed, o·bey·ing, o·beys**) vti 1 follow instructions or comply with a rule or law **2** be controlled by somebody or something

ob·fus·cate /óbfə skàyt/ (-cat·ed, -cat·ing) v **1** vti make something obscure or unclear **2** vt confuse somebody —**ob·fus·ca·tion** /òbfə skáysh'n/ n —**ob·fus·ca·to·ry** /ob fúskə tàwree/ adj

ob·gyn /ó bee jèe wī én, ò bee gín/, **ob/gyn** n obstetrics and gynecology (infml)

Ob'·Ir·tysh /àwb eer tísh, òb-/ river system in W Siberian Russia, incorporating the Irtysh and Ob' rivers. Length 3,362 mi./5,410 km.

o·bit·u·ar·y /ə bíchoo èrree, ō-/ (pl -ies) n an announcement of somebody's death, often with a short biography

⚡ **ob·ject** n /óbjəkt, ób jèkt/ **1** something visible or tangible **2** a focus of attention or emotion **3** a goal or purpose **4** a noun or pronoun affected by the action of a verb or governed by a preposition **5** a block of information that can be selected and manipulated on a computer ■ v /əb jékt/ **1** vi be opposed to or express opposition to something **2** vt state as an objection —**ob·ject·or** n

---

SYNONYMS object, protest, demur, remonstrate, expostulate CORE MEANING: indicate opposition to something

---

⚡ **ob·ject code** n the binary version of a computer program that is used by the computer to run the program

ob·jec·ti·fy /ob jéktə fī/ (-fied, -fies) vt **1** think of or represent as actual **2** reduce to the status of an object

ob·jec·tion /ob jékshən/ n **1** a feeling or expression of opposition **2** a reason for a feeling or expression of opposition

ob·jec·tion·a·ble /ob jékshənəb'l/ adj causing disapproval or offense —**ob·jec·tion·a·bly** adv

ob·jec·tive /ob jéktiv/ adj **1** free of bias or prejudice **2** based on facts or observable evidence **3** of or being the case of a noun or pronoun that is the object of a verb or preposition ■ n **1** a goal or purpose **2** the objective case, or a word in the objective case —**ob·jec·tive·ly** adv —**ob·jec·tive·ness** n —**ob·jec·tiv·i·ty** /òb jek tívvətee/ n

⚡ **ob·ject lan·guage** n the language that a computer interprets when it runs programs

ob·ject les·son n a concrete illustration of how to do something

⚡ **ob·ject-o·ri·ent·ed graph·ics** npl graphic images present in a computer as instructions to draw objects

⚡ **ob·ject-o·ri·ent·ed pro·gram·ming** n computer programming based on objects arranged in a branching hierarchy

ob·jet d'art /òb zhay daár/ (pl **ob·jets d'art** /pronunc. same/) n an object with artistic value

ob·late /ó blàyt, o blàyt/ adj shaped like a flattened sphere —**ob·late·ly** adv

ob·la·tion /ə bláysh'n, ō-/ n an offering of a gift to a deity —**ob·la·tion·al** adj

ob·li·gate /óbbli gàyt/ (-gat·ed, -gat·ing) vt **1** compel legally or morally **2** commit funds to fulfill an obligation

ob·li·ga·tion /òbbli gáysh'n/ n **1** something that must be done because of legal or moral duty **2** the state of being morally or legally compelled to do something **3** a feeling of gratitude that makes somebody believe a favor must be returned —**ob·li·ga·tion·al** adj

o·blig·a·to·ry /ə blíggə tàwree/ adj legally, morally, or religiously required —**o·blig·a·to·ri·ly** adv

o·blige /ə blíj/ (o·bliged, o·blig·ing) vt **1** require somebody to do something for legal, moral, or religious reasons **2** force somebody to do something **3** cause somebody to feel indebted **4** do a favor for somebody

o·blig·ing /ə blíjing/ adj willing to be helpful —**o·blig·ing·ly** adv —**o·blig·ing·ness** n

o·blique /ō bléek, ə-/ adj **1** sloping or slanting **2** indirect o an oblique reference **3** not parallel or perpendicular **4** not right-angled **5** of or being a grammatical case of a noun or pronoun other than the nominative or vocative ■ adv changing direction to or at an angle of 45° ■ n something oblique —**o·blique·ly** adv —**o·blique·ness** n

o·blit·er·ate /ə blíttə ràyt, ō-/ (-at·ed, -at·ing) vt **1** destroy utterly **2** erase or obscure —**o·blit·er·a·tion** /ə blíttə ráysh'n, ō-/ n

o·bliv·i·on /ə blívvee ən/ n **1** the state of being completely forgotten **2** the state of forgetting everything completely

o·bliv·i·ous /ə blívvee əss/ adj **1** unaware **2** forgetting —**o·bliv·i·ous·ly** adv

ob·long /ób làwng/ adj describes a shape that is longer than it is wide —**ob·long** n

ob·lo·quy /óbbləkwee/ n (fml or literary) **1** severe criticism or defamation of somebody **2** disgrace resulting from defamation

ob·nox·ious /ob nókshəss, əb-/ adj thoroughly objectionable —**ob·nox·ious·ly** adv —**ob·nox·ious·ness** n

o·boe /ó bō/ n a woodwind instrument with a double reed and keys —**o·bo·ist** n

---

ORIGIN The **oboe** was earlier called the hautboy, which came from the French name hautbois, literally "high wood," referring to the instrument's high pitch. It is recorded from the mid-16C. The French word also came into English via Italian as **oboe** and is recorded from the early 18C.

---

ob·scene /ob seén, əb-/ adj **1** indecent, especially by being sexually explicit **2** morally disgusting or outrageous —**ob·scene·ly** adv —**ob·scen·i·ty** /ob sénnətee, əb-/ n

ob·scure /əb skyóor, ob-/ adj **1** hard to understand **2** indistinct **3** unimportant or un-

known **4** known to few people —**ob·scure**
vt —**ob·scure·ly** *adv* —**ob·scu·ri·ty** *n*

SYNONYMS obscure, abstruse, recondite,
arcane, cryptic, enigmatic CORE MEANING: difficult to understand

~~obsene~~ incorrect spelling of **obscene**

ob·se·quies /óbsəkweez/ *npl* funeral rites

ob·se·qui·ous /əb seékwee əss, ob-/ *adj* too
eager to please or obey —**ob·se·qui·ous·ly**
adv —**ob·se·qui·ous·ness** *n*

ob·ser·vance /əb zúrvənss/ *n* **1** compliance
with laws, instructions, or customs **2** a
ritual or ceremony

ob·ser·vant /əb zúrvənt/ *adj* **1** attentive and
alert **2** complying with laws, instructions,
or customs —**ob·ser·vant·ly** *adv*

ob·ser·va·tion /óbzər váysh'n/ *n* **1** attentive
watching **2** a remark or comment **3** a record
of something seen or noted **4** the observing
of laws, instructions, or customs —**ob·
ser·va·tion·al** *adj*

ob·ser·va·tion post *n* a military position
from which soldiers can watch enemy
movements

ob·ser·va·to·ry /əb zúrvə tàwree/ (*pl* -**ries**) *n* **1** a
place for scientific observations, especially
of astronomical phenomena **2** a place for
looking at a view

ob·serve /əb zúrv/ (-**served**, -**serv·ing**) *v* **1** *vt* see
or notice **2** *vti* watch somebody or some-
thing attentively **3** *vti* be a formal witness
to something **4** *vt* say as a comment on what
has been seen or noted **5** *vt* comply with a
law, instruction, or custom —**ob·serv·a·ble**
adj —**ob·serv·er** *n*

ob·sess /əb séss, ob-/ *v* **1** *vt* preoccupy to an
unhealthy degree **2** *vi* think or worry about
something constantly

ob·ses·sion /əb sésh'n, ob-/ *n* **1** an unhealthy
preoccupation **2** the state of being obsessed
—**ob·ses·sion·al** *adj*—**ob·ses·sive** /əb séssiv,
ob-/ *adj* —**ob·ses·sive·ly** *adv* —**ob·ses·
sive·ness** *n*

ob·ses·sive-com·pul·sive dis·or·der *n* a
psychiatric condition involving obsessive
thoughts and compulsive behavior

ob·sid·i·an /əb síddee ən, ob-/ *n* jet-black volcanic glass

ob·so·les·cent /óbsə léss'nt/ *adj* becoming obsolete —**ob·so·les·cence** *n*

ob·so·lete /óbsə leét/ *adj* **1** no longer in use
2 out-of-date —**ob·so·lete·ly** *adv*

ob·sta·cle /óbstək'l/ *n* **1** a hindrance to progress **2** something blocking the way

ob·sta·cle course *n* **1** a training area where
soldiers have to get past various obstacles
2 a course for an obstacle race

ob·sta·cle race *n* a race with obstacles that
competitors must get past

ob·stet·rics /ob stéttriks/ *n* the branch of medicine that deals with pregnancy and child-

birth (+ *sing verb*) —**ob·stet·ric** *adj* —**ob·
ste·tri·cian** /óbstə trísh'n/ *n*

~~obsticle~~ incorrect spelling of **obstacle**

ob·sti·nate /óbstinət/ *adj* **1** stubborn **2** difficult
to control or remove o *an obstinate stain*
—**ob·sti·na·cy** *n* —**ob·sti·nate·ly** *adv*

ob·strep·er·ous /əb stréppərəss/ *adj* noisily argumentative or unruly ◊ See note at **unruly**

ob·struct /əb strúkt, ob-/ *vt* **1** prevent or hinder
passage through **2** hinder the progress of
3 hide from sight by being in the way
—**ob·struc·tor** *n* ◊ See note at **hinder**

ob·struc·tion /əb strúkshən, ob-/ *n* **1** a block or
hindrance **2** the obstructing of somebody
or something **3** the state of being obstructed

ob·struc·tion·ist /əb strúkshənist, ob-/ *adj*
using delaying tactics —**ob·struc·tion·ist** *n*

ob·struc·tive /əb strúktiv, ob-/ *adj* **1** uncooperative **2** of or caused by obstruction
—**ob·struc·tive·ly** *adv*

ob·tain /əb táyn/ *v* **1** *vt* get possession of **2** *vi*
be established or current o *the conditions
that obtained at that time* —**ob·tain·a·ble** *adj*
◊ See note at **get**

ob·trude /əb troöd/ (-**trud·ed**, -**trud·ing**) *v* **1** *vti*
impose yourself or your opinions on other
people **2** *vt* push out —**ob·tru·sion**
/-troözh'n/ *n* —**ob·tru·sive** /-troössiv/ *adj* —**ob·
tru·sive·ly** *adv*

ob·tuse /əb toöss, ob-/ *adj* **1** slow to understand something **2** describes an angle
between 90° and 180° —**ob·tuse·ly** *adv*
—**ob·tuse·ness** *n*

ob·verse *n* /ób vùrss, ob vúrs, əb-/ **1** the main
side of a coin or medal **2** a counterpart,
complement, or opposite ■ *adj* /ob vúrs,
əb-, ób vùrs/ **1** facing an observer **2** being a
counterpart, complement, or opposite

ob·vi·ate /óbvee àyt/ (-**at·ed**, -**at·ing**) *vt* **1** make
something unnecessary (*fml*) **2** avoid or
prevent an anticipated difficulty —**ob·vi·
a·tion** /óbvee áysh'n/ *n*

ob·vi·ous /óbvee əss/ *adj* **1** easy to see
2 unsubtle —**ob·vi·ous·ly** *adv* —**ob·vi·
ous·ness** *n*

~~occasionally~~ incorrect spelling of **occasionally**

oc·ca·sion /ə káyzh'n/ *n* **1** a particular time,
especially when something happens **2** a
chance or opportunity **3** a cause or reason
4 a need o *never had occasion to use it* **5** an
important event ■ *vt* cause

oc·ca·sion·al /ə káyzhən'l, -káyzhnəl/ *adj* occurring from time to time **2** of or for a
special event ◊ See note at **periodic**

oc·ca·sion·al·ly /ə káyzhən'lee, ə káyzhnəlee/
adv sometimes, but not regularly or frequently

oc·ci·dent /óksidənt, óksi dènt/ *n* **1** the west
(*fml*) **2 Oc·ci·dent** the western hemisphere,
especially the countries of Europe and
the Americas (*dated*) —**oc·ci·den·tal** /óksi
dént'l/ *adj*

oc·clud·ed /ə klóoded/ *adj* blocked or stopped up *(technical)* ○ *occluded arteries*

oc·cult /ə kúlt/ *adj* **1** supposedly supernatural or magic **2** not understandable by ordinary human beings **3** describes symptoms not visible to the naked eye *(technical)* ■ *n* the realm of the supposed supernatural

oc·cult·ism /ə kúl tìzzəm/ *n* belief in the supposed supernatural —**oc·cult·ist** *n*

oc·cu·pant /ókyəpənt/ *n* a holder of a position, or the resident of a place —**oc·cu·pan·cy** *n*

oc·cu·pa·tion /ókyə páysh'n/ *n* **1** a job done for a living **2** an activity **3** an act of occupying or the state of being occupied **4** the invasion and control of a country or area by military forces —**oc·cu·pa·tion·al** *adj*

oc·cu·pa·tion·al ther·a·py *n* treatment of an illness or condition by periods of productive activity —**oc·cu·pa·tion·al ther·a·pist** *n*

oc·cu·py /ókyə pī/ (-**pied**, -**pies**) *vt* **1** live in or be the regular occupant of a place **2** engage the attention of somebody **3** fill a space or an amount of time **4** invade and take control of a country or area —**oc·cu·pi·er** *n*

oc·cur /ə kúr/ (-**curred**, -**cur·ring**) *vi* **1** take place **2** exist or be present **3** enter somebody's mind ○ *didn't occur to me to stop*

~~occurance~~, ~~occurence~~ incorrect spelling of **occurrence**

~~occured~~ incorrect spelling of **occurred**

oc·cur·rence /ə kúr rənss/ *n* **1** something that happens **2** the fact of occurring

o·cean /ṓsh'n/ *n* **1** a large sea **2** the whole body of the Earth's seas **3** a large amount or expanse —**o·ce·an·ic** /ṓshee ánnik/ *adj*

ORIGIN The ancient Greeks conceived of the world as surrounded by a great river or sea, to which they gave the name from which **ocean** ultimately derives. In early use in English, too, **ocean** presupposed a single body of water. The use of the word did not recognize individual **oceans** until the 14C.

O·ce·an·i·a /ṓshee ánnee ə/ the smaller islands of the central and S Pacific Ocean, including Micronesia, Melanesia, and Polynesia, and sometimes Australasia —**O·ce·an·i·an** *n, adj*

o·cean·og·ra·phy /ṓshə nóggrəfee/ *n* the scientific study of oceans —**o·cean·og·ra·pher** *n* —**o·cean·o·graph·ic** /ṓsh'nə gráffik/ *adj*

O·cean·side /ṓsh'n sìd/ city in SW California. Pop. 152,367 (1998).

oc·e·lot /óssə lòt, ṓss-/ (*pl* -**lots** or same) *n* a small wildcat resembling a leopard

o·cher /ṓkər/, **o·chre** *n* a brownish-yellow color —**o·cher** *adj*

o'clock /ə klók/ *adv* as a particular hour in telling the time ○ *arrive at 7 o'clock*

O'Con·nell /ṓ kónn'l/, **Daniel** (1775–1847) Irish politician, supporter of Irish independence

O'Con·nor /ṓ kónnər/, **Flannery** (1925–64) US writer

O'Con·nor, Sandra Day (b. 1930) associate justice of the US Supreme Court (1981–)

⨎ OCR *abbr* **1** optical character reader **2** optical character recognition

Oct. *abbr* October

oc·ta·gon /óktə gòn/ *n* an eight-sided geometric figure —**oc·tag·o·nal** /ok tággən'l/ *adj*

⨎ oc·tal no·ta·tion /ókt'l-/ *n* a computer-programming number system using the numerals 0 to 7, each unit being three bits

oc·tane /ók tàyn/ *n* C_8H_{18} a liquid hydrocarbon found in petroleum

oc·tane num·ber, oc·tane rat·ing *n* a measure of the ability of motor fuel to prevent misfiring or knocking

oc·tave /óktiv, ók tàyv/ *n* **1** an interval of eight notes on the diatonic musical scale **2** a group of eight lines of poetry

oc·tet /ok tét/ *n* **1** a group of eight, especially musicians **2** a musical composition for a group of eight

Oc·to·ber /ok tṓbər/ *n* the tenth month of the year in the Gregorian calendar

ORIGIN October comes from a Latin word literally meaning "eighth month." In ancient Rome the calendar started the year in March.

oc·to·ge·nar·i·an /óktə jə náiree ən/ *n* somebody in his or her eighties

oc·to·pus /óktəpəss/ *n* a sea animal with a soft oval body and eight arms with suckers

oc·u·lar /ókyələr/ *adj* of the eyes or eyesight ■ *n* an eyepiece of an optical instrument

oc·u·list /ókyəlist/ *n* an optometrist or ophthalmologist *(dated)*

~~occupation~~ incorrect spelling of **occupation**

~~occur~~ incorrect spelling of **occur**

~~occurred~~ incorrect spelling of **occurred**

~~occurrence~~ incorrect spelling of **occurrence**

OD[1] *abbr* **1** Doctor of Optometry **2** *also* **O/D, o/d** overdraft **3** *also* **O/D, o/d** overdrawn

OD[2] /ṓ deé/ *(slang)* *vi* (**OD'ed, OD'ing**) take an overdose of a drug ■ *n* (*pl* **ODs**) an overdose

o.d. *abbr* on demand

odd *adj* **1** unusual or strange **2** describes a number not divisible exactly by 2 **3** leftover ○ *a few odd coins* **4** separated or different from the rest of a pair or set ○ *wearing odd socks* **5** irregular or occasional ○ *gets the odd day off* **6** slightly greater than a particular number ○ *50-odd dollars* —**odd·ly** *adv* —**odd·ness** *n*

odd·ball /ód bàwl/ *n* a person regarded as unconventional *(infml insult)*

odd·i·ty /óddətee/ (*pl* -**ties**) *n* somebody or something different from the rest

odd job *n* an occasional small job *(often pl)*

odd·ment /ódmənt/ *n* something left over *(usually pl)*

odds *npl* **1** the chances of something happening **2** the predicted chances in betting **3** a handicap or advantage used in competition ◊ **at odds (with)** in disagreement or conflict with

odds-and-ends *npl* miscellaneous items

odds-on *adj* likeliest to win, succeed, or happen *(infml)*

ode /ōd/ *n* a lyric poem with a complex style and structure

O·der /ōdər/ river in north central Europe, flowing northward from the Czech Republic into the Baltic Sea. Length 563 mi./906 km.

O·des·sa /ō déssə/, **O·des·a** port in south central Ukraine, on the Black Sea. Pop. 1,027,000 (1998).

O·dets /ō déts/, **Clifford** (1906–63) US playwright

O·din /ōdin/ *n* in Norse mythology, the king of the gods

o·di·ous /ōdee əss/ *adj* hateful —**o·di·ous·ly** *adv* —**o·di·ous·ness** *n*

~~odissey~~ incorrect spelling of **odyssey**

o·di·um /ōdee əm/ *n* general hatred or disapproval directed at somebody

o·dom·e·ter /ō dómmətər/ *n* a device that records distance

o·don·tol·o·gy /ō don tólləjee/ *n* the study of teeth —**o·don·to·log·i·cal** /ō dòntə lójjik'l/ *adj* —**o·don·tol·o·gist** *n*

o·dor /ōdər/ *n* **1** a smell **2** a pervasive quality ○ *the odor of sanctity* —**odor·less** *adj* ◊ See note at **smell**

o·dor·if·er·ous /ōdə ríffərəss/ *adj* having a strong odor *(technical)*

o·dor·ous /ōdərəss/ *adj* having a strong odor *(literary)*

O·dys·seus /ō díss yōoss, ō díssee əss/ *n* in Greek mythology, a hero of the Trojan War who spent ten years returning home. Roman equivalent **Ulysses**

od·ys·sey /ōddəssee/ (*pl* -**seys**) *n* a long series of travels and adventures

OECD *abbr* Organization for Economic Cooperation and Development

oe·de·ma *n* MED = **edema**

Oed·i·pus /éddəpəss, eéd-/ *n* in Greek mythology, a man who unwittingly killed his father and married his mother

Oed·i·pus com·plex *n* in psychoanalysis, a theorized unconscious sexual desire in a male child for his mother

Ō·e Ken·za·bu·rō /ō ay kènzə bōorō/ (b. 1935) Japanese writer

o'er /awr/ *prep, adv* over *(literary)*

oe·soph·a·gus *n* ANAT = **esophagus**

oes·tro·gen *n* BIOCHEM = **estrogen**

oeu·vre /ōvrə, ōōvrə/ *n* an artistic work, or an artist's works collectively

of /uv, ov/ unstressed form /əv/ *prep* **1** indicates the person or thing affected by or performing an action ○ *the birth of their daughter* **2** used after quantities to indicate what is being measured ○ *millions of dollars* **3** connected with ○ *the president of France* **4** containing ○ *a mug of coffee* **5** being part of ○ *a slice of cake* **6** made from ○ *a rod of iron* **7** indicates relationship or association ○ *thinking of you* **8** relating to as a feeling or quality ○ *sure of himself* ○ *kind of you* **9** indicates a particular type ○ *something of an expert* **10** having a particular quality ○ *a musician of great talent* ○ *the gentleness of his manner* **11** indicates amount ○ *a limit of eight characters* **12** before the hour of ○ *a quarter of ten*

off /awf, of/ *prep, adv* **1** so as to get out of or leave ○ *getting off the bus* **2** so as to keep away from ○ *Keep off the grass.* **3** away from work ○ *a day off* **4** as a reduction on ○ *10 percent off everything* **5** so as to be removed from ○ *washes off easily* ■ *adv* **1** further away in space or time ○ *two miles off* ○ *a week off* **2** as a measurement or division ○ *the distance marked off on the map* **3** to completion ○ *paid off* **4** into a particular state ○ *dozed off* ■ *prep* **1** abstaining from ○ *stay off caffeine* **2** on a diet of ○ *living off vegetables* **3** not far away from, or leading away from ○ *just off the main street* ■ *adv, adj* **1** not in operation ○ *switch off* **2** canceled ○ *The deal's off.* ■ *adj* **1** no longer fresh ○ *The milk's off.* **2** in a particular condition with regard to something ○ *How are you off for cash?* **3** in error or out of alignment ◊ **off and on** occasionally

---

USAGE In formal writing, avoid **off** plus *of*: *The actors stepped off* [not *off of*] *the stage.* Avoid also using **off** after verbs like *buy* or *borrow*: *I bought the computer from* [not *off*] *my roommate.*

---

off. *abbr* **1** office **2** officer **3** official

off-air *adj* happening during a recording but not broadcast —**off air** *adv*

of·fal /áwf'l, óff'l/ *n* **1** the edible internal organs of an animal **2** something thrown away

off·beat *n* an unaccented musical beat

off·beat /áwf beét, óf-/ *adj* unconventional

off-Broad·way *n* professional New York shows away from the Broadway area

off-cen·ter *adj* **1** not at the center, especially when this causes a problem **2** slightly eccentric —**off cen·ter** *adv*

off chance *n* a slight possibility ◊ **on the off chance** just in case something happens

off-cut /áwf kùt, óf-/ *n* a remaining scrap of something that has been cut

Of·fen·bach /áwf'n bàakh, -bàak/, **Jacques** (1819–80) German-born French composer

of·fence *n* UK = **offense**

of·fend /ə fénd/ *v* **1** *vti* cause somebody anger,

resentment, or hurt **2** *vi* break a law —**of·fend·er** *n* —**of·fend·ing** *adj*

ORIGIN Offend goes back to a Latin verb meaning "strike against." Some early uses retain the aspect of physical attack or contact, as do the related words *offense* and *offensive*, but during the 18C senses relating to feelings, morals, conduct, and society took over **offend** completely.

of·fense /ö fénss/ *n* **1** a legal or moral crime **2** an offensive **3** the attacking players on a team **4** anger or resentment felt at something

of·fen·sive /ö fénssiv/ *adj* **1** causing anger, resentment, or moral outrage **2** unpleasant to the senses **3** demonstrating aggression **4** designed for use in an attack **5** in possession of the ball or puck ■ *n* an attack or assault —**of·fen·sive·ly** *adv* —**of·fen·sive·ness** *n*

of·fer /áwfər, óf-/ *vt* **1** present something for acceptance or rejection **2** provide something for those who want it o *The town offers many attractions.* **3** volunteer to do something **4** have something for sale or rent **5** *also* **of·fer up** give something to God as part of worship **6** exhibit a quality o *offered little resistance* **7** make a bid or financial proposal o *offered $40 for it* ■ *n* a proposal

of·fer·ing /áwfəring, óf-/ *n* **1** the making of an offer, or an offer made **2** a gift for a deity

of·fer price, of·fer·ing price *n* the price of something being sold

~~offered~~ incorrect spelling of **offered**

of·fer·to·ry /áwfər tàwree, óffər-/ (*pl* -**ries**) *n* **1** in Christianity, an offering of Communion bread and wine **2** a church collection

off-guard *adj* not anticipating a possible attack or approach

off·hand /awf hánd, of-, áwf hánd, óf-/ *adv* **1** casually **2** without preparation or research ■ *adj* *also* **off·hand·ed 1** unconcerned and uncaring **2** done casually or without planning —**off·hand·ed·ly** *adv*

of·fice /áwfiss, óf-/ *n* **1** a room used for business activity **2** a place of business **3** a commercial or professional organization **4** the workers in an office **5** a government agency or department **6** a position of responsibility **7** a set form of a Christian service ■ **of·fic·es** *npl* something done on behalf of another (*fml*)

of·fice build·ing *n* a large building with offices

of·fice-free *adj* not needing an office from which to work

of·fice hold·er *n* **1** an official in government **2** somebody who holds office in a society, club, or voluntary organization

of·fice hours *npl* the times during which a business is open

of·fi·cer /áwfissər, óf-/ *n* **1** somebody with a commission in the armed forces **2** an

elected or appointed official **3** a member of a police force **4** somebody licensed to be in authority on a ship

of·fi·cial /ö físh'l/ *n* somebody holding office ■ *adj* **1** of a governmental body **2** approved by some authority **3** formal or ceremonial o *the building's official opening* —**of·fi·cial·ly** *adv*

of·fi·cial·dom /ö físh'ldəm/ *n* bureaucrats and bureaucracy (*infml*)

of·fi·cial·ese /ö fish'l éez, -éess/ *n* pompous, wordy language considered characteristic of official documents

of·fi·ci·ate /ö físhee àyt/ *vi* act in an official capacity —**of·fi·ci·ant** *n*

of·fi·cious /ö físhəss/ *adj* meddlesome and interfering —**of·fi·cious·ly** *adv* —**of·fi·cious·ness** *n*

off·ing /áwfing, óf-/ ◊ **in the offing** expected or likely in the future

off-key *adj* **1** out of tune **2** inappropriate —**off-key** *adv*

off-lim·its *adj* out of bounds

✦ **off-line** *adj* **1** describes a computer or peripheral device disconnected or functioning separately from an associated computer or network **2** involved in preparing but not transmitting broadcast material —**off line** *adv*

off-load /awf lód, of-, áwf lód, óf-/ *v* **1** *vti* unload goods **2** *vt* get rid of something unwanted by passing it on to somebody else

off-peak *adj* of the least busy time —**off peak** *adv*

off-piste *adj* not on regular ski-runs —**off piste** *adv*

off·print /áwf prìnt, óf-/ *n* a printed version of a single article from a periodical

off-put·ting *adj* irritating or disconcerting —**off-put·ting·ly** *adv*

off-ramp *n* a road leading away from a highway

off-road *adj* taking place or for use away from public roads

off-road ve·hi·cle *n* a vehicle used on rough terrain

off-screen *adj* **1** not visible on a screen **2** occurring in ordinary life rather than on television or in a movie o *their off-screen romance* —**off screen** *adv*

off-sea·son *n* a time of year when an activity is stopped or at a low level ■ *adv* in the off-season

off·set *n* /áwf sèt, óf-/ **1** something counterbalancing or compensating for something else **2** an abrupt bend in a straight line **3** a printing process in which ink is transferred to paper from another surface **4** something set apart ■ *v* /áwf sèt, óf-, awf sèt, óf-/ (**-set, -set·ting**) **1** *vt* counteract or compensate for **2** *vti* print by offset printing **3** *vti* form or be an offset in something

off·shoot /áwf shòot, óf-/ *n* **1** a shoot growing from the main stem of a plant **2** something that comes from something else

off·shore /awf sháwr, of-/ *adv* **1** from water to land o *blowing offshore* **2** in water some way from a shore o *anchored offshore* ■ *adj* **1** blowing or positioned offshore **2** at sea some way from a shore **3** based in a foreign country

off·side /áwf síd, óf-/ *adj* in sports, illegally beyond the advance of the ball or puck during play —**off·side** *adv*

off·site /áwf sìt, óf-/ *adj* not on the main site —**off·site** *adv*

off·spring /áwf spring, óf-/ (*pl* same or -springs) *n* **1** the child, children, young, or descendants of a person or animal **2** a result or product of something

off·stage /áwf stáyj, óf-/ *adv* **1** outside the area of a stage used for acting **2** in private life, as opposed to when performing in the theater —**off·stage** *adj*

off-street *adj* not in the street but in a parking lot, garage, or driveway

off-the-cuff *adj* said without preparation —**off the cuff** *adv*

off-the-rack *adj* not tailor-made —**off the rack** *adv*

off-the-rec·ord *adj* said unofficially and not to be repeated or attributed to the speaker —**off the rec·ord** *adv*

off-the-shelf *adj* available from existing stock —**off the shelf** *adv*

off-the-wall *adj* bizarrely unusual (*infml*) —**off the wall** *adv*

off-white *adj* near-white in color —**off-white** *n*

off year *n* a year without a presidential election —**off-year** *adj*

oft /awft, oft/ *adv* often (*literary; now often in combination*) o *her oft-quoted remark*

of·ten /áwf'n, óff'n/ *adv* at short intervals or repeatedly ◇ **every so often** regularly but at fairly long intervals

ORIGIN The older word for "often" is *oft*. **Often** is an extended form of this, perhaps formed on the analogy of *selden*, an earlier form of *seldom*.

of·ten·times /áwf'n tìmz, óff'n-/, **oft·times** /áwft tìmz, óft-/ *adv* often (*literary*)

Og·la·la /og laálə/ (*pl* same or -las) *n* a member of a branch of the Teton people who live mainly in South Dakota —**Og·la·la** *adj*

o·gle /óg'l/ (**o·gled, o·gling**) *vti* stare at somebody with sexual interest —**o·gle** *n* ◊ See note at **gaze**

O·gle·thorpe /óg'l thàwrp/, **James Edward** (1696–1785) British North American colonist

o·gre /ógər/ *n* **1** in fairy tales, an evil giant or monster **2** a person regarded as frightening —**o·gre·ish** *adj*

o·gress /ógrəss/ *n* **1** in fairy tales, a mean female monster **2** a woman regarded as frightening

oh /ō/ *interj* **1** expresses strong emotion **2** introduces a strong reaction o *Oh what a fool I've been.* **3** introduces a response **4** shows thought or hesitation

OH *abbr* Ohio

O·hi·o /ō hī ō/ **1** river in the E United States, flowing southwestward from Pittsburgh into the Mississippi River. Length 981 mi./1,580 km. **2** state in the north central United States. Cap. Columbus. Pop. 11,353,140 (2000). —**O·hi·o·an** *adj, n*

ohm /ōm/ *n* (*symbol* Ω) the SI unit of electrical resistance

ORIGIN The **ohm** is named for the German physicist Georg Simon Ohm (1787–1854).

o·ho /ō hó/ *interj* expresses surprise or jubilation

oil *n* **1** a liquid fat that does not dissolve in water and will burn **2** petroleum, or a petroleum derivative used as a fuel or lubricant **3** a thick oily liquid **4** an oil paint (*usually pl*) ■ *vt* apply oil to —**oiled** *adj*

oil cake *n* livestock feed made from the solid residue remaining after extraction of the oil from some seeds

oil·can /óyl kàn/ *n* a metal container for oil

oil·cloth /óyl klàwth/ *n* oil-treated cloth. Use: table coverings.

oil field *n* an oil-producing area

oil·man /óyl màn, -mən/ (*pl* **-men** /-mèn, -mən/) *n* an executive or worker in the oil industry

oil paint *n* a paint containing oil that dries

oil paint·ing *n* **1** a picture made using oil paints **2** the use of oil paints

oil pan *n* a reservoir of motor oil in a vehicle

oil rig *n* a platform and other equipment used in drilling for oil

oil·skin /óyl skìn/ *n* **1** fabric treated with oil to make it waterproof **2** a garment made of oilskin

oil slick *n* a film of oil, especially on water

oil well *n* a borehole for extracting oil

oil·y /óylee/ (**-i·er, -i·est**) *adj* **1** dirty with oil o *don't want to get my hands oily* **2** containing or like oil **3** ingratiating —**oil·i·ness** *n*

oink /oyngk/ *interj, n* the characteristic sound made by a hog —**oink** *vi*

oint·ment /óyntmənt/ *n* a greasy soothing or softening substance used on the skin

OJ, oj *abbr* orange juice

O·jib·wa /ō jíbbwə, ō jíb wày/ (*pl* **-was** or same), **O·jib·way** /ō jíb wày/ (*pl* **-ways** or same) *n* **1** a member of a Native North American people living in territories ranging from Saskatchewan across to Michigan **2** the Algonquian language of the Ojibwa people —**O·jib·wa** *adj*

OK[1] /ō káy/, **o·kay** (*infml*) *interj* indicates agreement ■ adj 1 allowable 2 rather good or pleasant ■ vt (OK'ed, OK'ing; o·kayed, o·kay·ing) give or obtain approval for ■ n (pl OK's; pl o·kays) somebody's approval or consent

ORIGIN Of the many competing theories about the origins of OK, the one now most widely accepted is that the letters stand for *oll* or *orl korrect*, a facetious early 19C American phonetic spelling of *all correct*. This was reinforced by the fact that they were also co-incidentally the initial letters of *Old Kinderhook*, the nickname of US president Martin Van Buren (who was born in Kinderhook, New York State), which were used as a slogan in the presidential election of 1840 (a year after the first record of OK in print).

OK[2] *abbr* Oklahoma

O·ka·na·gan, Lake /ŏkə naʼagən/ lake in S British Columbia, Canada

o·ka·pi /ŏ kaʼapee/ (*pl* **-pis** *or same*) *n* a plant-eating mammal resembling a small giraffe

O·kee·cho·bee, Lake /ŏki chŏbee/ lake in S Florida, in the N Everglades

Popperfoto

Georgia O'Keeffe

O'Keeffe /ŏ keéf/, **Georgia** (1887–1986) US artist

O·ke·fe·no·kee Swamp /ŏkifə nŏkee-/ swamp in SE Georgia and NE Florida

Ok·hotsk, Sea of /ŏ kótsk, ə khótsk/ arm of the NW Pacific Ocean, lying off the coast of E Siberia

O·ki·na·wa /ŏki naʼawə/ **1** city on south central Okinawa Island, Japan. Pop. 122,356 (2000). **2** largest of the Ryukyu Islands, SW Japan. Pop. 1,229,000 (1991).

Okla. *abbr* Oklahoma

O·kla·ho·ma /ŏklə hŏmə/ state in the south central United States. Cap. Oklahoma City. Pop. 3,450,654 (2000). —**O·kla·ho·man** *adj, n*

O·kla·ho·ma City capital of Oklahoma. Pop. 472,221 (1998).

o·kra /ŏkrə/ *n* **1** a green finger-shaped pod used as a vegetable **2** the plant that produces okra **3** a thick stew made with okra

old /ŏld/ *adj* (**old·er, old·est**) **1** having lived for a long time compared with others **2** originating years ago **3** showing characteristics sometimes associated with having lived long **4** wise or mature **5** having existed for a particular time

(*usually in combination*) **6** of the remote past **7** former **8** familiar **9** existing or used over time **10** used for emphasis (*infml*) ◇ *any old time* **11** expresses familiarity or affection (*infml*) ◇ *Good old Charlie!* ■ *n* a person of a particular age (*in combination*) ◇ *three-year-olds* ■ *npl* an offensive term for people who have lived a long time —**old·ness** *n*

old age *n* the later years of a life lived out to its full term

old coun·try *n* an immigrant's country of origin

old·en /ŏld'n/ *adj* of the distant past (*literary*)

Old·en·burg /ŏld'n bûrg/, **Claes** (*b.* 1929) Swedish-born US sculptor

Old Eng·lish *n* the earliest form of the English language, used up to about AD 1150 —**Old Eng·lish** *adj*

Old Eng·lish sheep·dog *n* a large shaggy dog with a white and gray coat

old-fash·ioned *adj* **1** out of date **2** maintaining the ways of an earlier time ■ *n* a cocktail made with whiskey, bitters, and fruit

SYNONYMS old-fashioned, outdated, antiquated, archaic, obsolete, passé, antediluvian CORE MEANING: no longer in current use or no longer considered fashionable

Old Glo·ry *n* the US flag

old guard *n* the long-established and conservative members of a group

old hand *n* a very experienced person

old hat *adj* boringly familiar (*infml*)

old·ie /ŏldee/ *n* an old thing, especially a popular song (*infml*)

old mas·ter *n* **1** a great European painter between the Middle Ages and the 18C **2** a painting by an old master

old school *n* a group adhering to traditional values and practices —**old-school** *adj*

Old Tes·ta·ment *n* the first section of the Christian Bible, corresponding to the Hebrew Bible

old-time *adj* **1** old-fashioned **2** long-established

old-tim·er *n* **1** a senior citizen, especially a man (*sometimes offensive*) **2** a resident or worker who has been at a particular place for a long time

Ol·du·vai Gorge /ŏldə vī, -vày, -wày-/ ravine in N Tanzania, where fossil remains of early humans and hominids have been found. Length 30 mi./50 km. Depth 300 ft./91 m.

old wives' tale *n* a superstitious or erroneous belief

Old World *n* the eastern hemisphere

old-world *adj* typical of a former age

o·lé /ŏ láy/ *interj* expresses triumph, approval, or encouragement, especially at a bullfight ■ *n* a cry of "olé"

o·le·ag·i·nous /ŏlee ájjənəss/ *adj* **1** containing or like oil **2** ingratiating

o·le·an·der /ōlee ándər/ (*pl* **-ders** *or same*) *n* a poisonous evergreen shrub with leathery leaves and sweet-smelling flowers

ol·fac·to·ry /ol fáktəree/ *adj* of the sense of smell

ol·i·gar·chy /ólli gaárkee/ (*pl* **-chies**) *n* 1 a small governing group 2 a country or organization ruled by an oligarchy 3 government by an oligarchy —**ol·i·gar·chic** /ólli gaárkik/ *adj*

Ol·i·go·cene /ólli gō seen, ə líggə-/ *n* an epoch of geologic time 34–24 million years ago —**Ol·i·go·cene** *adj*

ol·ive /ólliv/ *n* 1 a small green or black fruit with a stone 2 the tree that produces olives

ol·ive branch *n* 1 a conciliatory gesture 2 a branch of an olive tree used as a symbol of peace

ol·ive drab *n* 1 a grayish green color 2 an olive drab military uniform

ol·ive oil *n* oil from olives. Use: salad dressings, cooking, in soap and cosmetics.

Ol·ives, Mount of /óllivz, -əvz/ ridge of hills in the West Bank, east of Jerusalem. Height 2,737 ft./834 m.

O·liv·i·er /ə livvee əy/, **Laurence, 1st Baron Olivier of Brighton** (1907–89) British actor and director

Olm·sted /ólm stèd/, **Frederick Law** (1822–1903) US landscape architect

O·lym·pi·a /ə límpee ə, ō lím-/ 1 plain in SW Greece, site of the ancient Olympic Games 2 capital of Washington. Pop. 39,188 (1998).

O·lym·pi·ad /ō límpee àd/ *n* 1 a single Olympic Games 2 a four-year period for calculating dates

O·lym·pi·an /ō límpee ən/ *adj* 1 enormous 2 of Mount Olympus or the Greek gods 3 aloof or superior 4 of Olympia ■ *n* 1 an Olympic athlete 2 a superior person 3 in Greek mythology, a god 4 somebody from Olympia

O·lym·pic /ō límpik, ō-/ *adj* of the Olympic Games

O·lym·pic Games, O·lym·pics *npl* 1 a large-scale international sports contest, held every four years 2 an ancient Greek festival of athletic, literary, and musical contests, held every four years

O·lym·pus, Mt. /ə límpəss, ō lím-/ highest mountain in Greece, the mythological home of the Greek gods. Height 9,570 ft./2,917 m.

Om /óm/ *n* a sacred syllable chanted in Hindu and Buddhist mantras

O·ma·ha¹ /ōmə haà/ (*pl* **-has** *or same*) *n* 1 a member of a Native North American people who live in NE Nebraska 2 the language of the Omaha people —**O·ma·ha** *adj*

O·ma·ha² /ōmə haà/ city in E Nebraska, on the Missouri River. Pop. 371,291 (1998).

O·man /ō maán/ country on the SE Arabian Peninsula. Cap. Muscat. Pop. 2,622,198 (2001). —**O·man·i** *adj, n*

O·man, Gulf of arm of the Arabian Sea, situated between Oman and SE Iran

O·mar Khay·yam /ō maar kī aám/ (1050?–1122) Persian poet, mathematician, and astronomer

om·buds·man /ómbŭdzmən, -bŏŏdz-, -bùdz-/ (*pl* **-men** /-mən/) *n* an independent investigator of complaints against government, companies, or other organizations —**om·buds·man·ship** *n*

ORIGIN The word **ombudsman** was adopted from 19C Swedish. The first **ombudsman** in an English-speaking country was appointed in New Zealand in 1962; the United Kingdom followed in 1966.

Om·dur·man /ómdoor maàn, -mán/ city in east central Sudan. Pop. 1,267,077 (1993).

o·me·ga /ō máygə/ *n* the 24th and final letter of the Greek alphabet

om·e·let /ómmlət/, **om·e·lette** *n* a dish of beaten eggs cooked in a thin layer

ORIGIN The **omelet** seems to take its name from its thin flat shape. It derives ultimately from Latin *lamina* "thin plate," and entered English via French in the early 17C.

o·men /ómən/ *n* a prophetic sign ■ *vti* indicate the future of somebody or something

om·i·cron /ómi kròn, ómmi-/ *n* the 15th letter of the Greek alphabet

om·i·nous /ómminəss/ *adj* threatening something bad —**om·i·nous·ly** *adv* —**om·i·nous·ness** *n*

o·mis·sion /ō míshˈn/ *n* 1 something omitted 2 the omitting of something

o·mit /ō mít/ (**o·mit·ted, o·mit·ting**) *vt* 1 leave somebody or something out 2 fail to do something —**o·mis·si·ble** /ō míssəbˈl/ *adj* See note at **neglect**

~~omission~~ incorrect spelling of **omission**

~~ommited, ommitted~~ incorrect spelling of **omitted**

omni- *prefix* all o omnipresent

om·ni·bus /ómni bùss, -bəss/ *n* 1 a book collecting several related works 2 a bus (*archaic or fml*) ■ *adj* bringing many different things together as a single unit

om·ni·di·rec·tion·al /ómnee di rékshən'l/ *adj* able to transmit or receive signals in or from any direction

om·nip·o·tent /om níppətənt/ *adj* all-powerful ■ *n* Om·nip·o·tent God —**om·nip·o·tence** *n*

om·ni·pres·ent /ómnee prézz'nt/ *adj* 1 always present everywhere 2 found everywhere —**om·ni·pres·ence** *n*

om·nis·cient /om níshənt/ *adj* all-knowing —**om·nis·cience** *n*

om·ni·vore /ómnə vàwr/ *n* 1 an animal that eats any type of food 2 somebody with

wide interests **—om·niv·o·rous** /om
nĩvvərəss/ adj

Omsk /awmsk/ city in SW Russia. Pop.
1,437,781 (1995).

on prep **1** above and in contact with o *sitting
on the bed* **2** attached to or supported by
o *mounted on the wall* **3** being carried by
o *no cash on me* **4** located in or near o *on
the coast* **5** at a time during o *on Tuesday*
6 relating to o *a talk on international relations*
7 by means of or using o *on horseback* **8** in
a circumstance or position o *on vacation* o *on
equal terms* **9** directed toward o *shone a light
on them* ■ adv **1** in contact with something
o *an envelope with a stamp on* **2** into a
condition of attachment or suspension
o *sewing a button on* **3** over part of the body
o *put gloves on* **4** so as to continue o *stayed
on at the college* **5** in or into performance or
operation o *put a concert on* ■ adj **1** taking
place at the present time **2** arranged or
planned o *Is the game still on?* ◇ **be on to**
be aware of the real nature of *(infml)* ◇ **on
and off** occasionally ◇ **on and on** in a
continuous, persistent way

ON abbr Ontario

-on suffix **1** a subatomic particle o *electron* **2** a
unit, quantum o *photon*

once /wunss/ adv **1** at a time in the past **2** on
one occasion only **3** multiplied by one
o *Once three is three.* **4** by one step or degree
of relationship o *a cousin once removed* ■
conj as soon as ◇ **at once 1** immediately
2 all at the same time ◇ **for once** only on
this particular occasion ◇ **once and for all**
permanently or definitively

once-o·ver n a quick appraising look *(infml)*

on·col·o·gy /ong kóllajee/ n the branch of
medicine that deals with cancer **—on·co·
log·i·cal** /ôngka lójjik'l/ adj **—on·col·o·gist** n

on·com·ing /ón kùmming/ adj heading directly toward somebody or something

one /wun/ adj, pron **1** a unique or separate
person or thing o *the one exception* o *from one
place to another* **2** a single person or thing
o *one hour later* o *gave me only one* ■ adj
1 definite but not identified o *one August
afternoon* **2** a particular but unknown o *a
letter from one Lee Smith* ■ pron **1** any person
(fml) o *One can eat well here.* **2** refers to somebody or something previously mentioned
o *an old vase, and a cracked one at that* ■ n the
number 1 **—one·ness** n ◇ **one and all** everyone in a group ◇ **one by one** individually in
sequence

one another pron each to the other or others

one-horse adj **1** small, dull, and insignificant
2 with only one candidate or competitor
who is likely to win

O·nei·da /ō nída/ (pl same or **-das**) n **1** a
member of a Native North American
people who now live mainly in Ontario,
New York, and Wisconsin **2** the Iroquoian
language of the Oneida people **—O·nei·da**
adj

O'Neill /ō néel/, **Eugene** (1888–1953) US playwright

one-lin·er n a brief joke or witticism, usually
in one sentence

one-man band n **1** a street musician who
plays several instruments at once **2** an organization in which one person does
everything

one-night stand n **1** a sexual or romantic
encounter that occurs only once *(infml)* **2** a
performance on one night only

one-on-one adj **1** personal **2** directly against
each other ■ n in sports, a game or practice
involving only two players **—one-on-one**
adv

on·er·ous /ónnərəss, ônərəss/ adj difficult
—on·er·ous·ly adv **—on·er·ous·ness** n

one·self /wun sélf/ pron *(fml)* **1** any person's
own self **2** any person's normal self

one-shot adj *(infml)* **1** happening only once
2 effective at the first attempt

one-sid·ed adj **1** unfairly favoring one competitor **2** biased **—one-sid·ed·ness** n

one-stop adj providing a variety of goods or
services in one place

one-time /wún tīm/ adj **1** former **2** also **one-
time** happening only once

one-to-one adj with pairings between
members of two mathematical sets that
leave no remainder **—one-to-one** adv

one-track adj focused on or obsessed with
one subject

one-two punch, one-two n **1** two successive
punches **2** two quick sequential actions or
events

one-up·man·ship /wun úpmən shĩp/ n the
attempt to do better than or show up rivals

one-way adj **1** in one direction only **2** not
allowing a return journey **3** involving only
one of two people

on·go·ing /ón gō ing/ adj continuing

on·ion /únnyən/ n **1** a pungent edible bulb
used as a vegetable **2** a plant that produces
onions **—on·ion·y** adj

⚡ **on·line** /ón lĩn/, **on-line** adj **1** attached to or
available through a central computer or
computer network **2** connected to a computer network via the Internet, or available
via the Internet **—on·line** adv

⚡ **on-line ban·king** n a banking service accessed from a commercial online network

⚡ **on·lin·er** /ón lĩnər/ n a user of online services

on·look·er /ón lòokər/ n an observer of an
event **—on·look·ing** adj

on·ly /ónlee/ adv **1** solely or exclusively o *for
members only* o *applying only to residents* **2** indicates the condition for something to
happen or be true o *only if you come too*
3 merely o *could only stand and watch* **4** no
more and no less o *only two people here* **5** as
recently as o *only yesterday* **6** indicates an
event that happens immediately after the
one mentioned o *arrived only to find that*

they'd left ■ *adj* indicates the single person or thing involved ◊ *the only candidate* ◊ *an only child* ■ *conj* except that ◊ **only too** very

on·o·mat·o·poe·ia /ŏnnə matə pēē ə/ *n* the formation of words that imitate a sound —**on·o·mat·o·poe·ic** *adj*

On·on·da·ga /ŏnnən dáwgə, -dáàgə, -dáygə/ (*pl same or* -**gas**) *n* **1** a member of a Native North American people who live in central New York and Ontario **2** the language of the Onondaga people —**On·on·da·ga** *adj*

on·rush /ŏn rùsh/ *n* a forward rush —**on·rush·ing** *adj*

on-screen /ŏn skreen/ *adj, adv* appearing on a TV or movie screen

on·set /ŏn sèt/ *n* **1** the beginning of something, especially something unpleasant **2** an initial military attack

on·shore /ŏn shàwr/ *adj* **1** on land as opposed to the sea **2** in the direction of land —**on·shore** *adv*

on·side /on sīd/ *adj, adv* in sports, keeping a position that is allowed within the rules of the game

on·side kick *n* in football, a type of kickoff

on·slaught /ŏn slàwt/ *n* an overwhelming assault or force

on·stage /on stáyj/ *adj, adv* performed or happening on the stage of a theater

on-stream *adj, adv* in or into operation or production

On·tar·i·o /on táiree ō/ province of east central Canada. Cap. Toronto. Pop. 11,669,344 (2000). —**On·tar·i·an** *n, adj*

On·tar·i·o, Lake smallest and easternmost of the Great Lakes, on the border between NW New York and SE Ontario, Canada

on·to /ŏn tòo, óntə/ *prep* **1** so as to be on top of ◊ *putting it onto the top shelf* **2** toward and into contact with ◊ *splashed water onto her face* **3** making or about to make a discovery ◊ *The police are onto them.*

on·tog·e·ny /on tójjənee/, **on·to·gen·e·sis** /òntə jénnəssiss/ *n* development of an individual to maturity —**on·to·gen·ic** /òntə jénnik/ *adj*

on·tol·o·gy /on tólləjee/ (*pl* -**gies**) *n* **1** the study of the nature of existence **2** a theory of existence —**on·to·log·i·cal** /òntə lójjik'l/ *adj* —**on·tol·o·gist** *n*

o·nus /ōnəss/ *n* **1** a duty or responsibility **2** the blame for something

on·ward /ónnwərd/ *adj* moving forward ■ *adv* also **on·wards** at or to a point ahead

on·yx /ónniks/ *n* a fine-grained mineral with colored bands. Use: gems, cameo work.

oo·dles /ōod'lz/ *npl* a large amount (*infml*)

↯ **OOG** *abbr* object-oriented graphics

ooh /oo/ *vi* express surprise or pleasure

oomph /ŏomf/ *n* **1** energy **2** sexual attractiveness (*slang*)

oops /ŏops, oops/ *interj* acknowledges clumsiness (*infml*)

ooze[1] *vti* (**oozed, ooz·ing**) **1** flow or leak slowly **2** overflow with some quality or emotion ■ *n* a very slow flow —**ooz·y** *adj*

ooze[2] *n* thick mud or slime at the bottom of a river or lake

OP *abbr* out of print

o·pac·i·ty /ō pássətee/ *n* the state of being opaque

o·pal /ōpəl/ *n* noncrystalline silica. Use: gems.

o·pal·es·cent /ōpə léss'nt/ *adj* shimmering with milky colors —**o·pal·es·cence** *n*

o·paque /ō páyk/ *adj* **1** not transparent or translucent **2** hard to understand —**o·paque·ly** *adv*

op art, Op Art *n* an abstract art movement using geometric shapes and color —**op art·ist** *n*

OPEC /ō pèk/ *abbr* full form **Organization of Petroleum Exporting Countries**

op-ed /op éd/ *n* the page of a newspaper opposite the editorial page, containing contributed articles and personal views

o·pen /ōpən/ *adj* **1** not closed, enclosed, sealed, blocked, or locked **2** apart, wide, or unfolded **3** frank and honest **4** public or freely accessible ◊ *open hearings* **5** receptive ◊ *open to suggestions* **6** vulnerable ◊ *open to criticism* **7** available to do business **8** vacant for applicants ◊ *The position is still open.* **9** not predetermined or decided ◊ *keeping my options open* ■ *v* **1** *vti* unfasten or unfold from a locked, closed, or sealed position or state **2** *vti* move apart, or part the lips or eyelids **3** *vti* start trading, or allow customers access to in order to trade **4** *vti* start or get something under way **5** *vi* start being shown to or performed for the general public for the first time **6** *vt* remove obstructions from something ◊ *opened its borders* **7** *vi* give access to a place (*refers to part of a building*) ◊ *opens onto a courtyard* ■ *n* **1** a competition anyone can enter **2** a large and unobstructed outdoor space **3** a public state ◊ *get the facts into the open* —**o·pen·ly** *adv* —**o·pen·ness** *n*

☐ **open up** *vi* speak freely

o·pen-air *adj* outdoor

o·pen-and-shut *adj* decisively clear

o·pen bar *n* a bar where free drinks are served at a social function

o·pen-end *adj* **1** not having limits **2** allowing increased borrowing

o·pen-end·ed *adj* **1** without a prearranged end or limit **2** easily modified —**o·pen-end·ed·ly** *adv* —**o·pen-end·ed·ness** *n*

o·pen-end in·vest·ment com·pa·ny *n* FIN = **mutual fund**

o·pen·er /ōpənər/ *n* a device for opening something ◊ **for openers** firstly (*infml*)

o·pen-eyed *adj* **1** watchful **2** with eyes wide in wonder

o·pen-faced sand·wich *n* a sandwich on only one piece of bread

o·pen·hand·ed /ṓpən hándəd/ adj generous with money and material things —**o·pen·hand·ed·ly** adv —**o·pen·hand·ed·ness** n

o·pen·heart·ed /ṓpən haártəd/ adj kindly and generous in spirit —**o·pen·heart·ed·ness** n

o·pen-heart sur·ger·y n heart surgery during which the heart is exposed and blood is circulated outside the body by mechanical means

o·pen house n 1 a situation or occasion when visitors are welcome at any time 2 a school visiting day 3 a viewing period before a sale

o·pen·ing /ṓpəning/ n 1 a gap or hole in something 2 the first part or start of something 3 the occasion when something is formally opened 4 an opportunity 5 a job vacancy

o·pen·ing night n the night of the first public performance of a play or other show

o·pen let·ter n a letter to somebody that is published

o·pen mar·ket n trading without commercial restrictions

o·pen-mind·ed adj unprejudiced and receptive to new ideas —**o·pen-mind·ed·ly** adv —**o·pen-mind·ed·ness** n

o·pen mort·gage n Can a mortgage without fixed repayment terms

o·pen-mouthed adj with the mouth open in surprise or wonder

o·pen-plan adj having a large space left open rather than divided up into smaller units

o·pen sea·son n a period when restrictions on hunting are lifted

o·pen se·cret n something that is supposed to be secret but is widely known

o·pen ses·a·me /-séssəmee/ n a key to success

⚡ **o·pen sys·tem** n a computer design system with uniform industry standards

⚡ **o·pen trad·ing pro·to·col** n a standardized computer protocol for payments

o·pen wa·ter n an expanse of unenclosed and unobstructed water

o·pen·work /ṓpən wùrk/ n 1 decorative work using patterns of holes 2 embroidery with decorated holes

op·er·a¹ /ṓppərə, ópprə/ n 1 a drama set to music 2 operas as a genre

op·er·a² /ṓpərə, óppərə/ plural of **opus**

op·er·a·ble /ṓppərəb'l, ópprəb'l/ adj 1 surgically treatable 2 able to be done

op·er·a glass·es npl small binoculars for the theater

⚡ **op·er·and** /ṓppə rànd/ n 1 an entity that is to have a mathematical operation performed on it 2 a part of a computer instruction that specifies the location of the data to be manipulated

op·er·ate /ṓppə ràyt/ (-at·ed, -at·ing) v 1 vti work or function, or make something work or function 2 vi perform surgery

operater incorrect spelling of operator

op·er·at·ic /ṓppə ráttik/ adj of opera —**op·er·at·i·cal·ly** adv

op·er·at·ing room n a room in a hospital where surgical operations are performed

⚡ **op·er·at·ing sys·tem** n a master control program in a computer

op·er·at·ing ta·ble n a table used for surgical operations

op·er·a·tion /ṓppə ráysh'n/ n 1 the controlling or operating of something 2 a functioning state 3 something carried out, especially something complex 4 a surgical procedure 5 an organized action or campaign 6 a mathematical process ■ **op·er·a·tions** npl the controlling of organized actions

op·er·a·tion·al /ṓppə ráyshən'l, -shnəl/ adj 1 able to operate or be used 2 of the operating of something or the way something operates

op·er·a·tive /ṓppərətiv, ópprətiv/ adj 1 in place and having an effect 2 significant ■ n 1 a skilled worker 2 a detective 3 a spy —**op·er·a·tive·ly** adv

op·er·a·tor /ṓppə ràytər/ n 1 somebody operating machinery or equipment 2 an owner or manager of a business 3 a manipulative person (infml) 4 a symbol or other entity performing or describing a mathematical operation

op·e·ret·ta /ṓppə réttə/ n a comic opera with dancing —**op·e·ret·tist** n

oph·thal·mic /op thálmik, of-/ adj of the eye

oph·thal·mol·o·gy /ṓpthal mólləjee, ṓfthal-/ n the medical study and treatment of eyes —**oph·thal·mo·log·i·cal** /ṓpthalmə lójjik'l, ṓfthalmə-/ adj —**oph·thal·mol·o·gist** n

o·pi·ate /ṓpee ət/ n 1 an opium-containing drug 2 a sleep-inducing substance ■ adj containing opium

o·pine /ō pín/ (**o·pined, o·pin·ing**) vti state an opinion (fml)

o·pin·ion /ə pínnyən/ n 1 a personal view about an issue 2 an estimation of worth 3 an expert view

o·pin·ion·at·ed /ə pínnyə nàytəd/ adj unwilling to change strongly held opinions

o·pin·ion poll n a survey of the public's views

o·pi·um /ṓpee əm/ n an addictive drug prepared from the seeds of a poppy

opponent incorrect spelling of opponent

O·por·to ◆ Porto

opportunity incorrect spelling of opportunity

opposite incorrect spelling of opposite

o·pos·sum /ə póssəm/ (pl -**sums** or same) n a small nocturnal marsupial

opp. abbr opposite

Op·pen·hei·mer /ṓppən hímər/, J. Robert (1904–67) US nuclear physicist, leader of the team that developed the atomic bomb

~~opperation~~ incorrect spelling of **operation**

~~oppinion~~ incorrect spelling of **opinion**

op·po·nent /ə pṓnənt/ n 1 a rival in a contest 2 somebody opposing a course of action or a belief —**op·po·nent** adj

op·por·tune /òppər tòon, òppər tóon/ adj fitting or fortunate and well-timed —**op·por·tune·ly** adv —**op·por·tune·ness** n

op·por·tun·ist /òppər tóonist/ n an unprincipled resourceful person —**op·por·tun·ism** n

op·por·tun·is·tic /òppər too nístik/ adj 1 taking advantage of opportunities, especially in an unprincipled way 2 usually minor but potentially life-threatening when immunity is low ○ *opportunistic infections*

op·por·tu·ni·ty /òppər tóonətee, òppər tóonətee/ (pl -ties) n 1 an advantageous chance 2 favorable conditions

op·por·tu·ni·ty cost n the cost of a business decision regarded as the value of the alternative that is forgone

op·pose /ə pṓz/ (-posed, -pos·ing) v 1 vti be actively against something 2 vt set in contrast to 3 vt put opposite 4 vt compete with as opponents —**op·pos·a·ble** adj —**op·pos·ing** adj

op·posed /ə pṓzd/ adj actively against something

op·po·site /óppəzit/ adj 1 on the side that faces something or is at the farthest distance away 2 facing or moving away from each other 3 totally different ■ n 1 somebody or something different from another 2 an antonym ■ adv in the opposite position ■ prep 1 across from 2 in a complementing acting role to

op·po·site num·ber n somebody's counterpart in another department or organization

op·po·site sex n men as a group as opposed to women, or women as a group as opposed to men

op·po·si·tion /òppə zísh'n/ n 1 an actively hostile attitude 2 a sports opponent 3 also **Op·po·si·tion** an out-of-power political party —**op·po·si·tion·al** adj

op·press /ə préss/ vt 1 dominate harshly 2 be a source of stress or worry —**op·pres·sion** n —**op·pres·sor** n

op·pres·sive /ə préssiv/ adj 1 dominating harshly 2 causing stress or discomfort —**op·pres·sive·ly** adv —**op·pres·sive·ness** n

op·pro·bri·um /ə próbree əm/ n 1 scorn 2 disgrace

~~opression~~ incorrect spelling of **oppression**

opt vi choose from alternatives

□ **opt out** v choose not to do something (infml)

opt. abbr 1 optical 2 optimum 3 optional

~~opthalmology~~ incorrect spelling of **ophthalmology**

op·tic /óptik/ adj of the eyes or vision ■ n an instrument's lens

op·ti·cal /óptik'l/ adj 1 of visible light or optics 2 of vision —**op·ti·cal·ly** adv

⚡ **op·ti·cal char·ac·ter read·er** n a device for reading printed text into a computer by optical character recognition

⚡ **op·ti·cal char·ac·ter rec·og·ni·tion** n the use of light-sensing methods to convert an image or text into digital form

⚡ **op·ti·cal disk, op·ti·cal disc** n a rigid computer disk read by a laser

op·ti·cal fi·ber n a fiber used to transmit information in the form of pulses of laser light

op·ti·cal il·lu·sion n 1 visual perception of something that is not actually there 2 a source of optical illusion

⚡ **op·ti·cal mouse** n a computer mouse operated by light-emitting diodes

⚡ **op·ti·cal scan·ner** n a device that converts an image or text into digital form

op·ti·cian /op tísh'n/ n a maker and seller of lenses and eyeglasses

op·tics /óptiks/ n the study of light (+ sing verb)

op·ti·mal /óptəm'l/ adj most desirable or favorable —**op·ti·mal·ly** adv

op·ti·mism /óptə mìzzəm/ n 1 the tendency to expect or hope for the best 2 the philosophical doctrine that this is the best of all possible worlds —**op·ti·mist** n —**op·ti·mis·tic** /óptə místik/ adj —**op·ti·mis·ti·cal·ly** adv

---

ORIGIN Optimism was coined in French (as *optimisme*) in 1737 as a term for the doctrine of the German philosopher Leibniz that the actual world is the best of all possible worlds. The word is based on Latin *optimus* "best."

---

op·ti·mize /óptə mìz/ (-mized, -miz·ing) vt 1 make something function at its best, or use something to its best advantage 2 solve a technical problem in the best way possible —**op·ti·mi·za·tion** /óptəmi záysh'n/ n

op·ti·mum /óptəməm/ (pl -ma /-mə/ or -mums) n the best of several possible options or outcomes —**op·ti·mum** adj

op·tion /ópshən/ n 1 a choice 2 freedom of choice 3 the right to buy or sell something at a fixed price within a given period

op·tion·al /ópshən'l/ adj not compulsory —**op·tion·al·ly** adv

op·tom·e·trist /op tómmətrist/ n a licensed eye examiner and lens prescriber —**op·to·met·ry** n

~~optomist~~ incorrect spelling of **optimist**

~~optomistic~~ incorrect spelling of **optimistic**

op·u·lent /óppyələnt/ adj 1 characterized by a lavish display 2 in ample supply —**op·u·lence** n —**op·u·lent·ly** adv

o·pus /ṓpəss/ (pl o·per·a /ṓpərə, óppərə/ or o·pus·es) n 1 one of a series of numbered musical works by the same composer **2 a** creative work

or /awr/ *unstressed* /ər/ *conj* **1** joins alternatives ○ *Either you typed the wrong name, or something is wrong with the equipment.* ○ *Do you prefer tea or coffee?* **2** indicates approximation ○ *one or two* **3** rephrases a statement ○ *German measles, or rubella* **4** otherwise ○ *You'd better leave or you'll be late.* ◇ **or other** not exactly identified or definite ○ *some play or other* ◇ **or so** approximately ○ See note at **oar**

⚡ **OR**[1] /awr/ *n* a Boolean operator whose result is true if one or both of its operands are true and false otherwise

OR[2] /awr/ *abbr* **1** *also* **O.R.** operating room **2** Oregon

-or *suffix* **1** somebody or something that does or performs ○ *sailor* **2** condition, state, activity ○ *horror*

or·a·cle /áwrək'l/ *n* **1** a source of wisdom or prophesy **2** a shrine of an ancient Greek or Roman prophetic deity **3** an ancient Greek or Roman prophetic deity —**or·rac·u·lar** /aw rákyələr, ə-/ *adj*

o·ral /áwrəl/ *adj* **1** of the mouth **2** designed for use in the mouth **3** spoken **4** describes medicines that are taken by mouth ■ *n* a test requiring spoken answers *(often pl)* —**o·ral·ly** *adv* ◇ See note at **verbal, aural**

oral con·tra·cep·tive *n* a pill taken to prevent pregnancy

oral his·to·ry *n* **1** history recorded on tape by participants in events **2** a written work of history based on interviews with or recordings of participants —**o·ral his·to·ri·an** *n*

or·ange /áwrənj/ *n* **1** a round juicy citrus fruit with a skin between red and yellow in color **2** a tree that produces oranges **3** a color between red and yellow, like that of a ripe orange —**or·ange** *adj* —**or·ang·ey** *adj*

Or·ange /áwrənj/ **1** river in South Africa, flowing westward from Lesotho into the Atlantic Ocean. Length 1,300 mi./2,100 km. **2** city in SW California. Pop. 123,820 (1998). **3** city in NE New Jersey. Pop. 29,925 (1996).

or·ange·ade /àwrən jáyd/ *n* an orange-flavored drink

or·ange·ry /áwrənjree/ *(pl* **-ries)** *n* a large greenhouse where orange trees are grown

o·rang·u·tan /ə ràngə tàn, aw-/, **o·rang·u·tang** /ə ràngə táng/ *n* a large reddish-brown ape

ORIGIN Orangutan comes from the Malay name, meaning literally "forest person" or "wild man." It is first recorded in English in the late 17C.

o·rate /aw ráyt, áw ràyt/ *(-rat·ed, -rat·ing)* *vi* **1** make a formal public speech *(fml)* **2** speak pompously

o·ra·tion /aw ráysh'n/ *n* **1** a formal public speech **2** a pompous speech

or·a·tor /áwrətər/ *n* somebody skilled in making speeches

or·a·to·ri·o /àwrə táwree ò/ *(pl* **-os)** *n* a piece of classical music for instruments and voices on a religious theme

or·a·to·ry[1] /áwrə tàwree/ *n* **1** the art of public speaking **2** skill at public speaking —**or·a·tor·i·cal** /àwrə táwrik'l/ *adj*

or·a·to·ry[2] /áwrə tàwree/ *(pl* **-ries)** *n* a small private room for prayer or worship

orb *n* **1** a sphere **2** a spherical astronomical object **3** a jeweled sphere with a small cross on top that forms part of a king's or queen's regalia **4** an eye or eyeball *(literary)* —**or·bic·u·lar** /awr bíkyələr/ *adj*

or·bit /áwrbit/ *n* **1** the path of a planet, satellite, or moon around another larger astronomical object **2** a revolution of one astronomical object around another larger one **3** an area of interest **4** an eye socket ■ *v* **1** *vti* move around an astronomical object **2** *vt* put into astronomical orbit —**or·bit·al** *adj*

or·bit·er /áwrbitər/ *n* a spacecraft or satellite designed to orbit an astronomical object but not to land on it

or·ca /áwrkə/ *n* a killer whale

or·chard /áwrchərd/ *n* an area of fruit or nut trees, or the trees planted in such an area

or·ches·tra /áwrkəstrə/ *n* **1** a large group of musicians directed by a conductor **2** the part of a theater in front of the stage where the musicians sit **3** the main floor of a theater, especially the sections of seats nearest the stage —**or·ches·tral** /awr késtrəl/ *adj*

ORIGIN In a theater in ancient Greece, the **orchestra** was a semicircular area in front of the stage where the chorus (who commented in unison on the action of the play) danced and sang; in ancient Rome, it was an area in front of the stage with seats for senators and other important people. These are the contexts in which **orchestra** appeared in English during the 17C. In the early 18C, however, it began to refer to the place in a theater or opera house where musicians sat (usually just in front of the stage), and then to the musicians themselves.

or·ches·trate /áwrkə stràyt/ *(-trat·ed, -trat·ing)* *vt* **1** arrange music for an orchestra **2** organize unobtrusively ○ *carefully orchestrated the visit* —**or·ches·tra·tion** /àwrkə stráysh'n/ *n* —**or·ches·tra·tor** *n*

or·chid /áwrkid/ *n* a plant prized for its beautiful fragrant flowers —**or·chi·da·ceous** /àwrki dáyshəss/ *adj*

ORIGIN The word **orchid** was introduced in 1845. It was taken from the modern Latin name of the family of plants to which the orchid belongs, where *orchid-* had wrongly been used as a form of *orchis*, the classical Latin name. Latin *orchis* came from a Greek word literally meaning "testicle" and applied to the plant from the shape of the tubers.

or·dain /awr dáyn/ *vt* **1** make somebody officially a priest, minister, or rabbi **2** order something formally *(fml)* —**or·dain·ment** *n*

or·deal /awr deel/ *n* a difficult or harrowing experience

or·der /áwrdər/ *n* **1** a command or instruction to somebody to do something **2** an instruction to bring or supply something **3** something brought or supplied in response to an instruction **4** neatness **5** an arrangement or sequence of items **6** the absence of crime o *maintaining order on our streets* **7** a properly functioning condition **8** the arrangement of society into groups or classes and the relationship among them **9** a type of something o *a different order of intelligence* **10** *also* **Or·der** a religious community whose members live by a particular set of rules **11** *also* **Or·der** a group of people honored for services to their country, or the decoration indicating such an honor o *the Order of the Garter* ■ **or·ders** *npl* holy orders ■ *v* **1** *vt* command somebody to do something **2** *vt* give an instruction for something to be done **3** *vti* give an instruction for something to be brought or supplied **4** *vt* arrange things in a neat or sensible order ◊ **a tall order** a request that is very difficult to fulfill *(infml)* ◊ **in order to** *or* **that** with the object or purpose of ◊ **on order** requested but not yet supplied or delivered

or·der·ly /áwrdərlee/ *adj* **1** well-behaved or peaceful **2** neatly arranged ■ *n* (*pl* **-lies**) **1** a hospital worker who does not provide medical care **2** a soldier who is a senior officer's personal assistant —**or·der·li·ness** *n*

or·di·nal /áwrd'nəl/ *adj* showing position in a sequence of numbers ■ *n also* **or·di·nal num·ber** a number such as 1st or 10th that shows position in a sequence

or·di·nance /áwrd'nənss/ *n* a law or rule made by an authority, especially a municipal government

SPELLCHECK Do not confuse the spelling of **ordinance** and **ordnance** ("military weapons systems"), which sound similar.

~~ordinarly~~ incorrect spelling of **ordinarily**

or·di·nar·y /áwrd'n èrree/ *adj* **1** usual **2** unremarkable **3** of a common everyday kind —**or·di·nar·i·ly** *adv* —**or·di·nar·i·ness** *n*

or·di·na·tion /àwrd'n áysh'n/ *n* the act or ceremony of making somebody officially a priest, minister, or rabbi

ord·nance /áwrdnənss/ *n* **1** military weapons and equipment **2** the military department responsible for weapons and supplies ◊ See note at **ordnance**

Or·do·vi·cian /àwrdə vísh'n/ *n* a period of ge-

ologic time 495–443 million years ago —**Or·do·vi·cian** *adj*

or·dure /áwrjər/ *n* excrement *(fml)*

ore /awr/ *n* a mineral from which metal is extracted ◊ See note at **oar**

Ore., Oreg. *abbr* Oregon

o·reg·a·no /ə réggə nò/ *n* **1** the leaves of an aromatic herb used as a flavoring **2** an aromatic plant whose leaves are used as oregano

Or·e·gon /áwrəgən, órrə-/ *often by outsiders* /-gon/ state in the NW United States. Cap. Salem. Pop. 3,421,399 (2000). —**Or·e·go·ni·an** /àwrə gónee ən, òrrə-/ *n, adj*

Ø·re·send /úrrə sùn, -sòond/, **Ö·re·sund** strait between SW Sweden and E Denmark. Length 65 mi./100 km.

Orff /awrf/, **Carl** (1895–1982) German composer

ϟ **org** /awrg/ *abbr* noncommercial organization *(in Internet addresses)*

or·gan /áwrgən/ *n* **1** a large musical keyboard instrument producing sound when air passes through its pipes **2** an instrument without pipes that makes a sound similar to an organ **3** an independent part of an animal or plant with a specific function **4** a newspaper or magazine regarded as a means of communication *(fml)*

or·gan·dy /áwrgəndee/, **or·gan·die** *n* a lightweight transparent cotton fabric. Use: dressmaking.

or·gan·elle /àwrgə nél/ *n* a specialized component of a cell that has its own particular function, e.g., a nucleus or mitochondrion

or·gan grind·er *n* a street musician playing a barrel organ, traditionally accompanied by a small monkey for collecting money

or·gan·ic /awr gánnik/ *adj* **1** of living things **2** occurring or developing naturally **3** consisting of efficiently combined elements in a seemingly natural relationship **4** produced without the use of synthetic agricultural chemicals **5** of the body's organs **6** describes chemical compounds based on carbon —**or·gan·i·cal·ly** *adv*

or·gan·ic chem·is·try *n* the scientific study of carbon-based compounds

or·gan·ism /áwrgə nìzzəm/ *n* **1** a living thing **2** a functioning system of interdependent parts

or·gan·ist /áwrgənist/ *n* an organ player

or·gan·i·za·tion /àwrgəni záysh'n/ *n* **1** a group of people with a shared interest or purpose **2** coordination of separate elements into a unit or structure **3** the relationships between separate elements arranged into a whole —**or·gan·i·za·tion·al** *adj*

or·gan·ize /áwrgə nìz/ (**-ized, -iz·ing**) *v* **1** *vti* form or cause people to form a structured group **2** *vt* coordinate the various elements of something **3** *vt* arrange the elements of something so as to create a structure **4** *vt* make somebody or something become more effective —**or·gan·ized** adj

or·gan·ized crime n a large-scale network of professional criminals

ƒ **or·gan·iz·er** /áwrgə nìzər/ n **1** somebody who organizes projects **2** a small portable date-book in book or computer form

or·gan·o·phos·phate /àwrgənō fóss fàyt, awr gànnə-/ n an organic compound containing phosphate groups, which may be toxic. Use: pesticides, fertilizers.

or·gan·za /awr gánzə/ n a stiff transparent silk or synthetic fabric. Use: dressmaking.

or·gasm /áwr gàzzəm/ n the climax of sexual excitement —**or·gasm** vi —**or·gas·mic** /awr gázmik/ adj

or·gy /áwrjee/. n **1** a party where group sex occurs **2** a debauched party —**or·gi·as·tic** /àwrjee ástik/ adj

o·ri·ent v /áwree ent/ **1** vt put in position facing a particular direction **2** vr find your position and the direction you need to travel in **3** vt direct something in a particular way ○ advertising oriented toward teenage girls **4** vt make somebody or yourself familiar with a new situation ■ adj /áwree ənt/ eastern (archaic) ■ n /áwree ənt/ also **O·ri·ent** the countries of East Asia, especially China, Japan, and their neighbors (dated) —**o·ri·en·tate** vti —**o·ri·en·ta·tion** /àwree ən táysh'n/ n

O·ri·ent /áwree ənt/, **o·ri·ent** n the countries of East Asia, especially China, Japan, and their neighbors (dated)

O·ri·en·tal /àwree ént'l/, **o·ri·en·tal** adj of East Asia (dated) ■ n a taboo term for somebody from East Asia

or·i·en·teer·ing /àwree ən teering/ n a sport that combines cross-country running and map-reading —**or·i·en·teer** n, vi

or·i·fice /áwrəfiss/ n an opening in the body

o·ri·ga·mi /àwri gáamee/ n the Japanese art of paper-folding

or·i·gin /áwrəjin/ n (often pl) **1** the starting point or first cause of something **2** the source from which something comes or develops **3** somebody's ancestry, social class, or country

SYNONYMS **origin, source, derivation, provenance, root** CORE MEANING: the beginning of something

o·rig·i·nal /ə ríjjən'l/ adj **1** first **2** completely new and not derivative **3** creative ■ n **1** the first version from which copies or alternative versions are made **2** an authentic piece of art —**o·rig·i·nal·i·ty** /ə ríjjə nállətee/ n —**o·rig·i·nal·ly** adv◊ See note at **new**

o·rig·i·nal sin n the sinful state that Christians believe all people are born into

o·rig·i·nate /ə ríjjə nàyt/ (-nat·ed, -nat·ing) v **1** vi have an origin somewhere **2** vt invent or introduce —**o·rig·i·na·tor** n

O·ri·no·co /àwri nṓkō/ river in Venezuela, flowing northward into the Atlantic Ocean. Length 1,590 mi. /2,560 km.

o·ri·ole /áwree ōl/ n a black-and-yellow songbird

Ork·ney Is·lands /áwrknee-/ island group in NE Scotland. Pop. 19,450 (1991).

Or·lan·do /awr lándō/ city in N Florida. Pop. 181,175 (1998).

Or·lé·ans /awr lay áaN, -lèe ənz/ capital of Loire Department, north central France. Pop. 113,126 (1999).

or·mo·lu /áwrmə lòō/ n a gold-colored alloy of copper and zinc. Use: decorating furniture, jewelry, moldings.

or·na·ment n /áwrnəmənt/ **1** a decorative object put on display **2** decoration or decorative quality **3** something that decorates something else ■ vt /áwrnə mènt/ add decorative elements or items to —**or·na·men·ta·tion** /àwrnə men táysh'n, -mən-/ n

or·na·men·tal /àwrnə mént'l/ adj **1** decorative and with no practical purpose **2** describes a plant grown for its beauty ■ n an ornamental plant —**or·na·men·tal·ly** adv

or·nate /awr náyt/ adj **1** elaborately or excessively decorative **2** using elaborate language —**or·nate·ly** adv

or·ner·y /áwrnəree/ adj uncooperative and irritable (infml) —**or·ner·i·ness** n

or·ni·thol·o·gy /àwrnə thóllajee/ n the study of birds —**or·ni·tho·log·i·cal** /àwrnəthə lójjik'l/ adj —**or·ni·thol·o·gist** n

ƒ **OROM** abbr optical read-only memory

o·ro·tund /áwrə tùnd/ adj (fml) **1** loud, clear, and strong **2** pompous or bombastic

ORIGIN **Orotund** was formed from Latin ore rotundo, literally "with a round mouth." The Latin phrase was used in English writing from the early 18C, and **orotund** itself appeared in the late 18C.

or·phan /áwrfən/ n **1** a child whose parents are dead **2** a young animal without a mother ■ vt make somebody an orphan —**or·phan·hood** n

or·phan·age /áwrfənij/ n a home for orphans

Or·phe·us /áwrfee əss, áwrfyooss/ n in Greek mythology, a poet and musician, who descended to the underworld to seek his wife, Eurydice, after her death but failed to bring her back

or·tho·don·tics /àwrthə dóntiks/, **or·tho·don·tia** /-dónshə/ n the correction of teeth irregularities —**or·tho·don·tic** adj —**or·tho·don·tist** n

or·tho·dox /áwrthə dòks/ adj **1** following traditional doctrine **2** **Or·tho·dox** of the Eastern Orthodox Church **3** **Or·tho·dox** of the branch of Judaism that accepts the Torah as the literal work of God **4** customary —**or·tho·dox·y** n

Or·tho·dox Church n the Eastern Orthodox Church

or·thog·o·nal /awr thóggən'l/ adj of right angles —**or·thog·o·nal·ly** adv

or·thog·ra·phy /awr thóggrəfee/ (pl -phies) n 1 correct spelling 2 the study of how letters are arranged in words 3 the relationship between sounds and letters

or·tho·pe·dic /àwrthə peédik/, **or·tho·pae·dic** adj 1 of orthopedics 2 of bone, joint, ligament, or muscle disorders —**or·tho·pe·dist** n

or·tho·pe·dics /àwrthō peédiks/, **or·tho·pae·dics** n the branch of medicine dealing with bone, joint, ligament, or muscle disorders (+ sing verb)

or·thot·ics /awr thóttiks/ n the science of the design and fitting of medical devices such as braces (+ sing verb) —**or·thot·ic** adj —**or·thot·ist** /àwrthətist/ n

AKG London

George Orwell

Or·well /áwr wèl/, **George** (1903–50) British writer —**Or·well·i·an** /àwr wéllee ən/ adj

-ory suffix 1 of or relating to ○ compulsory ○ illusory 2 place or thing connected with or used for ○ refectory ○ oratory

o·ryx /áwriks/ (pl same or **o·ryx·es**) n an antelope with a black-and-white face and a hump

Os symbol osmium

⚡**OS** abbr 1 operating system 2 ordinary seaman 3 also **o.s.** out of stock

O·sage /ó sàyj, ō sáyj/ (pl same or **O·sag·es**) n 1 a member of a Native North American people who live mainly in Oklahoma 2 the language of the Osage people —**O·sage** adj

O·sa·ka /ō saákə, òsaa kaá/ port on SE Honshu, Japan. Pop. 2,471,100 (2000).

Os·car /óskər/ n a communications code word for the letter "O"

Os·ce·o·la /òssee ólə/ (1800?–38) Seminole leader

os·cil·late /óssə làyt/ (-lat·ed, -lat·ing) vi 1 swing rhythmically between two points 2 be indecisive —**os·cil·la·tion** /òssə láysh'n/ n —**os·cil·la·tor** n

os·cil·lo·scope /ə síllə skòp/ n a device for showing electrical current on a screen

os·cu·late /óskyə làyt/ (-lat·ed, -lat·ing) v 1 vt kiss (fml or humorous) 2 vi make contact (technical) —**os·cu·la·tion** /òskyə láysh'n/ n

-ose suffix full of, having the qualities of, resembling ○ verbose

OSHA /óshə/ abbr Occupational Safety and Health Administration

⚡**OSI** abbr open systems interconnection

o·sier /ózhər, ózee ər/ n 1 a willow tree with long flexible stems used for making baskets 2 a willow branch

O·si·ris /ō síriss/ n the ancient Egyptian god of the underworld

Os·lo /ózzlō, óss-/ capital of Norway. Pop. 499,693 (1998).

os·mi·um /ózmee əm/ n (symbol **Os**) a hard white metallic element, the densest known. Use: catalyst, alloy for pen nibs.

os·mo·sis /oz móssiss, oss-/ n 1 the diffusion of solvent through a semipermeable membrane from a dilute to a more concentrated solution 2 the gradual absorption of knowledge through continued exposure rather than study —**os·mot·ic** /oz móttik, oss-/ adj

os·prey /óspree, óss prà
y/ (pl -preys or same) n a fish-eating hawk with long wings and a white head

os·si·fy /óssə fì/ (-fied, -fies) vti 1 harden into bone 2 make or become rigidly conventional in attitude or behavior —**os·si·fi·ca·tion** /òssəfi káysh'n/ n

os·ten·si·ble /o sténsəb'l/, **os·ten·sive** /o sténssiv/ adj seeming to be true, but open to doubt —**os·ten·si·bly** adv

os·ten·ta·tion /òs ten táysh'n, òstən-/ n showiness

os·ten·ta·tious adj showy —**os·ten·ta·tious·ly** adv

osteo- prefix bone ○ osteoporosis

os·te·o·ar·thri·tis /òstee ō aar thrítəss/ n a form of arthritis involving loss of cartilage in the joints

os·te·op·a·thy /òstee óppəthee/ n the treatment of bodily misalignments through manipulation —**os·te·o·path** /óstee ə pàth/ n —**os·te·o·path·ic** /òstee ə páthik/ adj

os·te·o·po·ro·sis /òstee ō pə róssiss/ n a disease in which the bones become very brittle

os·tra·cize /óstrə sìz/ (-cized, -ciz·ing) vt exclude from society or a group —**os·tra·cism** n

ORIGIN **Ostracize** comes from a Greek verb based on ostrakon "pottery fragment." In ancient Athens, when it was proposed that a particular person should be sent into exile because he was becoming a danger to the state, a vote was taken on the matter. The method of voting was to inscribe the name of the prospective exile on a piece of broken pottery (ostrakon). If enough votes were cast against him, he was sent away for ten years.

os·trich /óstrich, óstrij/ (pl -trich·es or same) n a large long-necked flightless bird

OT abbr 1 occupational therapy 2 also **O.T.** Old Testament 3 also **O.T.**, **o.t.** overtime

OTB abbr off-track betting

OTC, O.T.C. *abbr* over-the-counter

oth·er /úthər/ *adj, pron* **1** additional or further to somebody or something mentioned ○ *Let me make one other suggestion.* **2** different from somebody or something mentioned ○ *This issue, more than any other, has divided opinion.* **3** of the remaining people in a group ○ *She left earlier with the other kids.* **4** being the second of two things when the first is known ○ *Where's my other glove?* ■ *pron* **oth·ers** other people or things (+ *pl verb*) —**oth·er·ness** *n* ◊ **other than** apart from

oth·er·world·ly /úthər wúrldlee / *adj* not being or seeming to be of this world

oth·er·wise /úthər wìz/ *adv* **1** or else ○ *I overslept; otherwise I would have called.* **2** differently ○ *Come at three unless you hear otherwise.* **3** in other ways ○ *It was noisy, but otherwise fun.* ■ *adj* different ○ *lots of information, digital and otherwise*

o·ti·ose /óshee òss, ótee-/ *adj* **1** not effective **2** worthless

O·tis /ótiss/, **James** (1725–83) American colonial leader

⚡**OTP** *abbr* open trading protocol

OTS, O.T.S. *abbr* Officers' Training School

Ot·ta·wa[1] /óttəwə, -waà/ (*pl same or* -**was**) *n* **1** a member of a Native North American people who live mainly in Ontario, Michigan, Kansas, and Oklahoma **2** the Algonquian language of the Ottawa people —**Ot·ta·wa** *adj*

Ot·ta·wa[2] /óttəwə, -waà/ **1** river in Ontario and Quebec, Canada, flowing into the St. Lawrence River. Length 696 mi./1,120 km. **2** capital of Canada, in SE Ontario. Pop. 323,340 (1996).

ot·ter /óttər/ (*pl same or* -**ters**) *n* **1** a fish-eating mammal with smooth brown fur and webbed feet **2** otter fur

Ot·to I /óttó/ (912–973) Holy Roman emperor (962–973) and king of Germany (936–973)

ot·to·man /óttəmən/ *n* **1** a low upholstered stool **2** a long upholstered box used as a seat **3 Ot·to·man** a member of a Turkish people who conquered Asia Minor in the 13C —**Ot·to·man** *adj*

Ouach·i·ta /wóshi tàw/ river flowing southeastward from Arkansas into Louisiana. Length 605 mi./974 km.

Ouach·i·ta Moun·tains mountain range in central Arkansas and E Oklahoma

Oua·ga·dou·gou /waàgə dóogoo/ capital of Burkina Faso. Pop. 634,479 (1991).

ou·bli·ette / óoblee ét/ *n* a dungeon with a trapdoor in the ceiling

ouch /owch/ *interj* expresses pain

ought[1] /awt/ *modal v* **1** indicates a duty or obligation or that it is morally right to do something ○ *You ought to be ashamed.* **2** indicates that something is important or a good idea ○ *You ought to see a doctor.* **3** in-

dicates probability or expectation ○ *We ought to be there by now.* **4** indicates a desire or wish ○ *You ought to come for dinner sometime.*

ought[2] /awt/ *n* a zero

ou·gui·ya /oo gée yə/ *n* the main unit of Mauritanian currency

ounce[1] /ownss/ *n* **1** a unit of weight equal to one-sixteenth of a pound **2** a fluid ounce

> **ORIGIN** The **ounce** in weight goes back through French to Latin *uncia* "twelfth part," the same word that gave us *inch*.

ounce[2] /ownss/ (*pl same or* **ounc·es**) *n* a snow leopard

our /owr/ *adj* **1** belonging to us **2** belonging to everyone ◊ See note at **hour**

Our Fa·ther *n* in Christianity, the Lord's Prayer

Our La·dy *n* in Christianity, a title for Mary, the mother of Jesus Christ

ours /owrz/ *pron* that or those belonging to us ○ *Her house is OK, but I like ours better.* ○ *Ours are over there.*

our·selves /owr sélvz/ *pron* **1** refers to the speaker or writer and at least one other person (as the object of a verb or preposition when the subject refers to the same people) ○ *We didn't injure ourselves.* **2** refers to people in general ○ *secrets that we find difficult to admit even to ourselves* **3** refers emphatically to the speaker or writer and at least one other person ○ *We ourselves must bear the responsibility.* **4** our usual selves ○ *somewhere where we can really be ourselves*

-ous *suffix* **1** full of, having the qualities of ○ *virtuous* **2** having a lower valence than a corresponding compound or ion the name of which ends in *-ic* ○ *ferrous*

oust /owst/ *vt* **1** force somebody out of a place **2** remove somebody from office

oust·er /ówstər/ *n* the removal of somebody from a place or position

out /owt/ *adv* **1** away from a place, especially the inside of something **2** so as to be removed from inside something ○ *took out her laptop* **3** outside ○ *It's cold out.* **4** in another place far away ○ *She's out in Australia.* **5** indicates a goal achieved in the action specified by the verb ○ *stuck it out to the end* **6** in or into existence ○ *one of the best albums out* ■ *adj, adv* **1** away from the home or workplace ○ *He's out at the moment.* **2** no longer alight or burning ○ *The fire's gone out.* **3** available to buy ○ *now out in paperback* **4** in baseball, in such a way as to retire a batter or team ■ *adj* **1** no longer allowed to take part in a game **2** unacceptable or impossible ○ *Tomorrow's definitely out for me.* **3** unfashionable **4** intent on something ○ *out for what he can get* **5** unconscious **6** used up or finished **7** not working ○ *All the phones are out.* **8** in baseball, retired from offensive play **9** open about being a homosexual man or woman ■ *vt* expose somebody as being a homosexual man or woman ■ *n* 1 a way of avoiding undesirable consequences *(infml)* 2 in baseball, a play that retires a batter or base runner —**out·most** *adj* ◊ **out of 1** so as to leave a place ○ *came out of the building* 2 so as to remove something from a place ○ *took a pen out of her bag* 3 toward the outside of ○ *looking out of the window* 4 no longer having ○ *We're out of butter.* 5 using as a source or material ○ *made out of scrap metal* 6 motivated by ○ *did it out of spite* 7 so as not or no longer to be in a situation ○ *stayed out of trouble* ◊ **out of it** very drunk, or under the influence of drugs *(infml)*

out·age /ówtij/ *n* 1 a temporary loss of electrical power 2 an amount missing after delivery or storage

out-and-out *adj* thorough or utter

out·back *n* /ówt bàk/ a remote area, especially in Australia —**out·back** *adj*

out·bid /ówt bíd/ (-**bid·ded**, -**bid·ding**) *vt* bid higher than somebody else

out·board /ówt bàwrd/ *adj* located on the outside of a boat —**out·board** *adv*

out·bound /ówt bównd/ *adj* traveling away from a place

out·box *n* a tray for finished paperwork

out·break /ówt bràyk/ *n* a sudden occurrence of something unpleasant

out·build·ing /ówt bílding/ *n* a barn or shed situated away from the main building on a property

out·burst /ówt bùrst/ *n* 1 a sudden display of emotion 2 a sudden intense period of activity

out·cast /ówt kàst/ *n* somebody rejected by others —**out·cast** *adj*

out·class /ówt kláss/ *vt* be significantly better than

out·come /ówt kùm/ *n* a result

out·crop /ówt kròp/, **out·crop·ping** /-kròpping/ *n* a part of a rock formation projecting from the ground —**out·crop** *vi*

out·cry /ówt krí/ (*pl* -**cries**) *n* 1 a strong widespread reaction against something 2 a clamor from a group of people

out·dat·ed /ówt dáytəd/ *adj* no longer in fashion or in use ◊ See note at **old-fashioned**

out·dis·tance /ówt dístənss/ (-**tanced**, -**tanc·ing**) *vt* 1 go faster than other competitors in a race 2 be much better than others

out·do /ówt dóo/ (-**did** /-díd/, -**done** /-dún/, -**do·ing**) *vt* do more or better than

out·door /ówt dáwr/ *adj* located in, belonging to, or suited to the open air

out·doors /ówt dáwrz/ *adv* outside a building ■ *n* the open air, especially when away from populated areas

out·draw /ówt dráw/ (-**drew** /-dróo/, -**drawn** /-dráwn/) *vt* 1 draw a gun faster than 2 attract a larger audience than

out·er /ówtər/ *adj* 1 on the outside of something 2 away from the center of something —**out·er·most** *adj*

out·er space *n* interplanetary and interstellar space

out·er·wear /ówtər wàir/ *n* clothing for outdoors worn over other clothing

out·face /ówt fáyss/ (-**faced**, -**fac·ing**) *vt* 1 stare somebody down 2 defy somebody

out·fall /ówt fàwl/ *n* the outlet of a sewer, drain, or stream that empties into a larger body of water

out·field /ówt feèld/ *n* the part of a baseball or softball field beyond the diamond —**out·field·er** *n*

out·fit /ówt fìt/ *n* 1 a set of clothes worn together 2 a set of tools or equipment for a particular activity 3 a small team or organization *(infml)* ■ *vt* (-**fit·ted**, -**fit·ting**) 1 equip 2 provide with a set of clothes

out·fit·ter /ówt fìttər/ *n* a store selling outdoor leisure equipment

out·flank /ówt flángk/ *vt* 1 go around the main body of an enemy force and attack it from the side or behind 2 outwit or bypass somebody

out·flow /ówt flò/ *n* 1 the process of flowing out or away 2 an amount of a liquid, gas, or money that moves away from a place

out·fox /ówt fóks/ *vt* outwit

out·go /ówt gó/ (*pl* -**goes**) *n* an amount of money paid out

out·go·ing /ówt góing/ *adj* 1 departing or going out 2 leaving a job ○ *the outgoing president* 3 sociable —**out·go·ing·ness** *n*

out·grow /ówt gró/ (-**grew** /-gróo/, -**grown** /-grón/) *vt* 1 get too large for something 2 move beyond previous interests

out·growth /ówt gròth/ *n* 1 a natural development or result of something 2 an offshoot

out·guess /ówt géss/ *vt* gain an advantage over somebody by guessing that person's thoughts or intentions

out·gun /ówt gún/ (-**gunned**, -**gun·ning**) *vt* have more or better weapons than

out·house /ówt hòwss/ (*pl* -**hous·es** /-hòwzəz/) *n* 1 an outdoor toilet 2 an outbuilding

out·ing /ówting/ *n* 1 an excursion 2 a walk outdoors 3 the practice or an instance of revealing somebody to be homosexual or bisexual

out·land·ish /ówt lándish/ *adj* strikingly peculiar —**out·land·ish·ly** *adv*

out·last /ówt lást/ *vt* exist or survive longer than

out·law /ówt làw/ *n* 1 a known criminal who is at liberty or a fugitive 2 somebody officially without legal rights ■ *vt* 1 make illegal 2 take away legal rights from —**out·law** *adj* —**out·law·ry** *n*

out·lay *n* /ówt làly/ 1 the spending of money or expending of resources 2 an amount of

money spent ■ *vt* /owt láy/ (**-laid** /-láyd/)
spend money

out·let /ówt lèt, -lət/ *n* **1** a vent **2** a release for
the emotions **3** a place where something is
sold **4** a market providing goods or services **5** a receptacle for an electric plug to
make a connection with a power supply

out·li·er /ówt lìr/ *n* **1** a separate part of a
system, organization, or body that is at
some distance from the main part
2 somebody living at a distance from work

out·line /ówt lìn/ *n* **1** the edge or outer shape
of something **2** a line drawn around the
outside of something **3** a rough plan or
explanation of something **4** a summary ■
vt (**-lined, -lin·ing**) **1** draw as an outline
2 describe the essential elements of

out·live /owt lív/ (**-lived, -liv·ing**) *vt* **1** live
longer than **2** outlast

out·look /ówt lòok/ *n* **1** an attitude **2** the likely
future of something

out·ly·ing /ówt lì ing/ *adj* situated away from
the central part of something

out·ma·neu·ver /ówt mə nóovər/ *vt* **1** outwit
2 surpass other vehicles in maneuver-
ability

out·mod·ed /owt módəd/ *adj* **1** old-fashioned
2 obsolete

out·num·ber /owt númbər/ *vt* be more numerous than

out-of-court *adj* arranged without going to
a court of law

out-of-date *adj* old-fashioned or not current

out-of-pock·et *adj* **1** requiring somebody to
spend cash o *out-of-pocket travel expenses*
2 having lost money

out-of-state *adj* from or of another state

out-of-the-way *adj* **1** far from a populated
area **2** unusual

out-of-town *adj* from or in another town

out·pace /owt páyss/ (**-paced, -pac·ing**) *vt* be
better or faster than

out·pa·tient /ówt pàysh'nt/ *n* a patient receiving treatment in a hospital without
staying overnight

out·per·form /ówt pər fáwrm/ *vt* perform better
than

out·place·ment /ówt plàyssmənt/ *n* a service
provided by a company to help dismissed
employees find new jobs

out·play /owt pláy/ *vt* play better than

out·post /owt pòst/ *n* **1** a group of troops stationed away from the main force **2** a small
remote military base **3** a remote or frontier
settlement

out·pour·ing /ówt pàwring/ *n* something that
floods out o *an outpouring of generosity* o *an
outpouring of lava*

⚡**out·put** /ówt pòot/ *n* **1** an amount of something
produced in a fixed period of time **2** energy or power produced by a system **3** information produced by a computer
—**out·put** *vt*

out·rage /ówt ràyj/ *n* **1** a violent, cruel, or
offensive act **2** anger or indignation pro-
voked by an outrage ■ *vt* (**-raged, -rag·ing**)
1 attack violently or cruelly **2** make angry
or indignant

ORIGIN Outrage is not connected etymologically to either *out* or *rage*. It is an adoption
of a French noun (with the noun suffix *-age*)
formed from a verb *outrer* "exceed, exaggerate," which goes back ultimately to
Latin *ultra* "beyond."

out·ra·geous /owt ráyjəss/ *adj* **1** extraordinary
and unconventional **2** morally shocking
3 excessive —**out·ra·geous·ly** *adv* —**out·ra·
geous·ness** *n*

~~outragious, outrageus~~ incorrect spelling of
outrageous

~~outrageous~~ incorrect spelling of **outrageous**

out·rank /owt rángk/ *vt* have a higher rank or
status than

ou·tré /oo tráy/ *adj* unconventional or bizarre

out·reach *vt* /owt réech/ **1** reach farther than
somebody or something **2** exceed a limit
■ *n* /ówt rèech/ **1** the provision of community services to particular social groups
2 the extent of the reach of somebody or
something

out·ride /owt ríd/ (**-rode** /-ród/, **-rid·den** /-rídd'n/,
-rid·ing) *vt* ride better or faster than somebody

out·rid·er /ówt rìdər/ *n* a rider acting as an
escort for a carriage, vehicle, or racehorse

out·rig·ger /ówt rìggər/ *n* **1** a stabilizing float
on the side of a canoe **2** a boat or canoe
fitted with an outrigger

out·right *adv* /ówt rìt, òwt rít/ **1** wholly and
completely o *owns the business outright* **2** instantly o *refused our offer outright* ■ *adj* /ówt
rìt/ **1** absolute o *an outright lie* **2** without
restrictions or limitations o *an outright gift*
—**out·right·ly** *adv*

out·ri·val /owt rív'l/ *vt* surpass

out·run /owt rún/ (**-ran** /-rán/, **-run, -run·ning**) *vt*
1 run faster or farther than **2** escape by
running away from

out·sell /owt sél/ (**-sold** /-sóld/) *vt* **1** be sold
more quickly or in greater quantities than
2 be a better salesperson than

out·set /ówt sèt/ *n* the start of something

out·shine /owt shín/ (**-shone** /-shón/ *or* **-shined,
-shin·ing**) *vt* **1** shine brighter than **2** surpass
in excellence or quality

out·side /owt síd, ówt sìd/ *adv, prep, adj*
1 located on or beyond the outer surface
or edge of something o *standing outside the
circle* **2** out of doors o *went outside to sun-
bathe* **3** beyond the immediate environment
o *in the world outside* ■ *adj* **1** slight or
remote o *an outside chance* **2** the maximum
possible or probable o *an outside estimate of
three months* ■ *prep* beyond the scope of
o *outside my comprehension* ■ *n* **1** the outer
surface or appearance of something o *The*

outside of the house needs painting. **2** the part farthest from the side of a road or the center of a race track ○ *coming up fast on the outside* ◇ **at the outside** at the most ◇ **outside of** other than

out·sid·er /owt sídər/ n **1** somebody who does not belong to a group **2** a competitor or candidate considered unlikely to win

out·size /owt síz/ n an extra large size ■ *adj also* **out·sized** extra large

out·skirts /ówt skùrts/ npl the outlying areas of a town or city

out·smart /owt smaärt/ vt outwit

out·sold past participle, past tense of **outsell**

out·source /ówt sàwrss/ (-sourced, -sourc·ing) vt buy goods or services normally produced or provided within a company from an outside source

out·spo·ken /owt spókən/ adj fearlessly candid —**out·spo·ken·ness** n

out·spread /owt spréd/ adj extended or spread out flat —**out·spread** vt

out·stand·ing /owt stánding/ adj **1** unusually excellent **2** not yet resolved —**out·stand·ing·ly** adv

out·stare /owt stáir/ (-stared, -star·ing) vt stare somebody down

out·stay /owt stáy/ vt **1** stay longer than **2** show greater endurance than

out·stretch /owt stréch/ vt extend or hold out

out·strip /owt stríp/ (-stripped, -strip·ping) vt **1** do better or go faster than **2** exceed

out·take /ówt tàyk/ n a section cut from the final version of a movie, television program, or musical recording

out·tray n an out-box

out·vote /owt vót/ (-vot·ed, -vot·ing) vt defeat by voting

out·ward /ówtwərd/ adj **1** located outside or on or toward the exterior of something **2** visible ○ *gave no outward indication that she was upset* **3** of the physical body ○ *His outward appearance belied his inner turmoil.* **4** apparent or superficial ○ *shouldn't judge by outward appearances* ■ adv also **out·wards** toward the outside and away from the inside or middle —**out·ward·ly** adv

out·ward-bound adj making an outgoing trip

out·weigh /owt wáy/ vt **1** be more important or valuable than **2** weigh more than

out·wit /owt wít/ (-wit·ted, -wit·ting) vt gain an advantage over somebody through cunning

out·worn /owt wáwrn/ adj no longer current or useful

ou·zo /óozō/ n a colorless Greek aniseed-flavored alcoholic drink

o·va plural of **ovum**

o·val /óvəl/ adj egg-shaped or elliptical ■ n an egg shaped or elliptical form

O·val Of·fice n **1** the US president's office in the White House **2** the US presidency

o·va·ry /óvəree/ (pl -ries) n **1** either of the two female reproductive organs that produce eggs **2** the part of a pistil that bears ovules and ripens into a fruit —**o·var·i·an** /ō váiree ən/ adj

o·va·tion /ō váysh'n/ n a loud and long round of applause

ov·en /úv'n/ n a heated compartment used for baking, roasting, or drying

ov·en-proof /úv'n proof/ adj capable of being used in an oven without being damaged by the heat

ov·en·ware /úv'n wàir/ n dishes for baking and serving

o·ver /óvər/ resting on the top of something or above the top of something with a space in between ○ *A cloud of smoke hung over the town.* ○ *wearing a shirt over his T-shirt* ■ prep, adv **1** on or to the other side of ○ *jumped over the fence* **2** throughout ○ *all over town* **3** more than ○ *people over thirty* ■ adv **1** across an intervening space ○ *reached over and turned off the TV* **2** so as to change position ○ *knocked over the vase* **3** remaining ○ *food left over from the party* **4** again or from the beginning again ○ *have to start over* ■ prep **1** by means of a communications device ○ *talking over the phone* **2** about or concerning ○ *grieving over the death of her husband* **3** as an effect or influence on somebody or something ○ *exercising more control over file access* **4** during ○ *discussed it over lunch* **5** recovered from an illness or something unpleasant ○ *was still getting over a cold* **6** in preference to somebody or something ○ *chose him over me* ■ adj **1** finished ○ *It's all over now.* **2** no longer fashionable (infml) ■ interj indicates that somebody speaking in a radio communication has finished talking ◇ **over again** once more ◇ **over against** in contrast with, or in opposition to ◇ **over and above** in addition to or in excess of ◇ **over and over** repeatedly

over- prefix **1** excessively ○ *overconfident* ○ *overact* **2** extremely ○ *overjoyed* **3** above something, extra ○ *overshoe* ○ *overtime* **4** above, over, on top ○ *overcast* ○ *overlap* **5** so as to turn over, completely ○ *overthrow*

o·ver·act /ōvər ákt/ vti act with exaggerated emphasis —**o·ver·ac·tion** n

o·ver·ac·tive /ōvər áktiv/ adj too active —**o·ver·ac·tiv·i·ty** /ōvər ak tívvətee/ n

o·ver·age[1] /ōvər áyj/ adj **1** too old for something **2** no longer useful (offensive of people)

o·ver·age[2] /óvərij/ n a surplus

o·ver·all adj /óvər àwl/, adv /òvər áwl/ **1** from one end to the other **2** in total ■ adj considered as a whole ■ adv on the whole

o·ver·alls npl **1** a one-piece garment worn to protect a worker's clothes **2** loose-fitting work trousers with a bib and shoulder straps

o·ver·arch·ing /ōvər aárching/ adj including or overshadowing everything

o·ver·arm /ōvər aárm/ adj, adv with the arm or hand raised above the shoulder and rotating forward

o·ver·ate past tense of **overeat**

o·ver·awe /ōvər áw/ (-awed, -aw·ing) vt cause feelings of awe in

o·ver·bal·ance /ōvər báIlənss/ (-anced, -anc·ing) v 1 vti lose or make lose balance 2 vt be more important than

o·ver·bear·ing /ōvər báiring/ adj arrogant and bossy —**o·ver·bear·ing·ly** adv

o·ver·bite /ōvər bīt/ n a dental condition in which the upper front teeth project too far over the lower teeth

o·ver·blown /ōvər blṓn/ adj 1 exaggerated 2 pretentious

o·ver·board /ōvər báwrd/ adv over the side of a ship ◊ **go overboard** behave with extreme enthusiasm

o·ver·book /ōvər bŏŏk/ vti take too many reservations for

o·ver·bur·den vt /ōvər búrd'n/ overload

o·ver·came past tense of **overcome**

o·ver·ca·pac·i·ty /ōvər kə pássətee/ n an ability to produce more than demand requires

o·ver·cap·i·tal·ize /ōvər káppit'l īz/ (-ized, -iz·ing) vt 1 provide a business with too much capital 2 overvalue a business

o·ver·cast adj /ōvər kást/ 1 cloudy 2 sewn along the edge with loose stitches to prevent unraveling ■ v /ōvər kást/ 1 vi become cloudy 2 vt sew an edge with loose stitches to prevent unraveling

o·ver·charge v /ōvər chaárj/ (-charged, -charg·ing) 1 vti charge somebody too much 2 vt put excessive power into a battery or circuit ■ n /ōvər chaárj/ 1 an excessive charge for something 2 the act of charging too much for something

o·ver·cloud /ōvər klṓwd/ vti 1 cloud over 2 make or become dim and gloomy (fml)

o·ver·coat /ōvər kṓt/ n 1 a thick outer coat worn over other clothes 2 a top layer of paint or varnish, or the process of applying such a layer

o·ver·come /ōvər kúm/ (-came /-káym/, -come, -com·ing) v 1 vt make somebody incapacitated or helpless ○ was completely overcome with emotion 2 vt conquer a problem 3 vti defeat somebody or something (fml) ◊ See note at **defeat**

o·ver·com·pen·sate /ōvər kómpən sàyt/ (-sat·ed, -sat·ing) v 1 vi try too hard to make up for something 2 vti reward somebody too much —**o·ver·com·pen·sa·tion** /ōvər kòmpən sáysh'n/ n

o·ver·cook /ōvər kŏŏk/ vt cook too long

o·ver·crowd /ōvər krṓwd/ vt make too crowded —**o·ver·crowd·ed** adj —**o·ver·crowd·ing** n

o·ver·do /ōvər dṓo/ (-did /-díd/, -done /-dún/)

vt 1 do to excess 2 spoil the effect of by exaggeration 3 overcook

o·ver·dose n /ōvər dṓss/ a dangerously large amount of a drug ■ vti /ōvər dṓss/ (-dosed, -dos·ing) take or give an overdose

o·ver·draft /ōvər dráft/ n 1 a negative balance in a bank account 2 a borrowing limit for a negative balance in a bank account

o·ver·drawn /ōvər dráwn/ adj having withdrawn more money than a bank account contains

o·ver·drive n /ōvər drīv/ 1 an engine gear in an automobile that saves gas at high speeds 2 an especially intense level of activity (infml) ○ Production has gone into overdrive. ■ vt /ōvər drīv/ (-drove /-drṓv/, -driv·en /-drív'n/, -driv·ing) drive too hard

o·ver·due /ōvər dṓo/ adj late or delayed

o·ver·eat /ōvər eét/ (-ate /-áyt/, -eat·en /-eét'n/) vi eat too much food

o·ver·em·pha·sis /ōvər émfəsiss/ n excessive emphasis —**o·ver·em·phat·ic** /ōvər em fáttik/ adj

o·ver·em·pha·size /ōvər émfə sìz/ (-sized, -siz·ing) vt give too much emphasis to

o·ver·es·ti·mate vt /ōvər ésta máyt/ (-mat·ed, -mat·ing) 1 calculate at too high a limit 2 give excessive merit or importance to ■ n /ōvər éstəmət/ an excessively high estimate —**o·ver·es·ti·ma·tion** /-èstə máysh'n/ n

o·ver·ex·pose /ōvər ik spṓz/ (-posed, -pos·ing) vt 1 expose film to too much light 2 allow somebody, or expose somebody to, too much of something —**o·ver·ex·po·sure** /-ik spṓzhər/ n

o·ver·ex·tend /ōvər ik sténd/ 1 vr risk financial ruin by borrowing or spending too much 2 vt force beyond a reasonable limit 3 vt prolong beyond the expected duration

o·ver·fill /ōvər fíll/ vti make or become too full

o·ver·flow v /ōvər flṓ/ 1 vti pour out over the edge of a container 2 vi flood 3 vt spread beyond the limits of ■ n /ōvər flṓ/ 1 the excess liquid contents of something 2 the excess quantity of people or things in a place 3 an outlet that allows liquid to escape before it runs over the top of its container 4 an amount in excess of a limit

o·ver·fly /ōvər flī/ (-flew /-flṓo/, -flown /-flṓn/, -flies) vti 1 fly above an area 2 overshoot

o·ver·ground /ōvər grṓwnd/ adj, adv on or above the ground

o·ver·grown /ōvər grṓn/ adj covered with unchecked vegetation

o·ver·hand /ōvər hànd/ adj, adv with the hand raised above the shoulder and rotating forward

o·ver·hang v /ōvər háng/ (-hung /-húng/) 1 vti project over 2 vt loom over ■ n /ōvər hàng/ something that projects over the space beneath

o·ver·haul vt /ōvər háwl, ōvər háwl/ 1 look for mechanical defects in a machine 2 repair a machine extensively **3** revise something thoroughly ■ n /óvər hàwl/ an extensive repair of something

o·ver·head adv /òvər héd/ directly above ■ adj /óvər hèd/ **1** positioned directly above **2** in racket games, describes a shot hit hard downward with the racket above the head ■ n /óvər hèd/ ongoing business costs

o·ver·head pro·jec·tor n a piece of equipment for projecting an image on a transparency onto a wall or screen

o·ver·hear /òvər heè ər/ (-heard /-húrd/) vti hear what is said to others

o·ver·heat /òvər heèt/ vti **1** become or make too hot **2** grow or make an economy grow too quickly —**o·ver·heat·ed** adj

o·ver·hung past tense, past participle of **overhang**

~~override~~ incorrect spelling of **override**

o·ver·in·dulge /òvər in dúlj/ (-dulged, -dulg·ing) v **1** vti give in to a desire too much, especially in eating or drinking too much **2** vt be too indulgent with somebody —**o·ver·in·dul·gence** n —**o·ver·in·dul·gent** adj

o·ver·in·vest·ment /òvər in véstmənt/ n the act of investing too much money in a company

o·ver·joyed /òvər jóyd/ adj extremely delighted

o·ver·kill /óvər kìl/ n **1** a response that far exceeds what is needed **2** a greater destructive capacity than is needed

o·ver·land /óvər lànd/ adv by or across land

o·ver·lap /òvər láp/ (-lapped, -lap·ping) v **1** vti place or be over the edge of something **2** vt extend beyond —**o·ver·lap** /óvər làp/ n

o·ver·lay /òvər láy/ (-laid /-láyd/) vt **1** place a covering or covering layer on top of something **2** be a covering on the surface of something —**o·ver·lay** /óvər làv/ n

o·ver·leaf /òvər leèf/ adv on the other side of the page

o·ver·load vt /òvər lód/ **1** put an excessive load on somebody or something or in something **2** use more current than an electrical system can handle ■ n /óvər lòd/ **1** an excessive electrical load on a system **2** an excessive physical weight **3** an excessive mental or emotional burden

o·ver·long /òvər láwng/ adj too long ■ adv for too long a time

o·ver·look vt /òvər loòk/ **1** fail to notice something **2** ignore a shortcoming or fault **3** provide a view of something from above **4** be located above something ■ n /óvər loòk/ a place that gives a view down over something ◊ See note at **neglect**

o·ver·lord /óvər làwrd/ n **1** a ruler with power over other rulers **2** somebody powerful

o·ver·ly /óvərlee/ adv too much

o·ver·much /òvər múch/ adv to excess ■ adj excessive

o·ver·night /òvər nít, óvər nìt/ adv **1** throughout or during the night **2** in the course of one night or very suddenly ■ adj **1** lasting one night **2** occurring at night **3** extremely quick

o·ver·night·er /òvər nítər/ n somebody on an overnight stay

o·ver·op·ti·mis·tic /òvər opti místik/ adj excessively optimistic —**o·ver·op·ti·mism** /-ópti mìzzəm/ n —**o·ver·op·ti·mis·ti·cal·ly** adv

o·ver·pass /óvər pàss/ n US, Can, ANZ a road or bridge that crosses over another route

o·ver·pay /òvər páy/ (-paid /-páyd/) vti **1** pay more than a job warrants **2** pay too much by mistake —**o·ver·paid** adj

o·ver·play /òvər pláy/ v **1** vt overstate something **2** vti overact a part **3** vt hit or kick a ball too hard or far

o·ver·pow·er /òvər pówr/ vt **1** subdue physically **2** overwhelm mentally —**o·ver·pow·er·ing** adj

o·ver·print vti /òvər print, óvər prìnt/ print something additional on a printed surface ■ n /óvər prìnt/ **1** an additional printing on a printed surface **2** an overprinted postage stamp

o·ver·pro·duce /òvər prə dóoss/ (-duced, -duc·ing) vti produce too much of something —**o·ver·pro·duc·tion** /-prə dúksh'n/ n

o·ver·qual·i·fied /òvər kwóllə fìd/ adj with more academic qualifications or experience than is necessary for a particular job

o·ver·rate /òvər ráyt/ (-rat·ed, -rat·ing) vt overvalue —**o·ver·rat·ed** adj

o·ver·reach /òvər reèch/ v **1** vr fail through excessive ambitiousness **2** vti extend too far or beyond something

o·ver·re·act /òvər ree ákt/ vi react too strongly —**o·ver·re·ac·tion** n

o·ver·ride vt /òvər ríd/ (-rode /-ród/, -rid·den /-rídd'n/, -rid·ing) **1** cancel somebody's action or decision **2** outweigh something **3** take manual control of an automatic control system ■ n /óvər rìd/ **1** the act of overriding an automatic control system **2** a switch for overriding an automatic control system

o·ver·rid·ing /òvər ríding/ adj most important —**o·ver·rid·ing·ly** adv

o·ver·ripe /òvər rìp/ adj too ripe

o·ver·rule /òvər roòl/ (-ruled, -rul·ing) vt **1** reject somebody's argument as unsound **2** decide against somebody or something

o·ver·run v /òvər rún/ (-ran /-rán/, -run, -run·ning) **1** vt spread rapidly over and crowd **2** vt conquer and take over the territory of **3** vti exceed a fixed limit **4** vt go farther than intended beyond **5** vti overflow or spill over something ■ n /óvər rùn/ **1** the amount by which something overruns **2** the act of overrunning something

⚡o·ver·scan /ōvər skán/ *adj* extending beyond the viewing boundary of a computer screen

o·ver·seas /ōvər seèz/ *adv* across an ocean, especially in another country ■ *adj* /ōvər seéz/ 1 of or from a place across an ocean ○ *overseas visitors* 2 involving travel across an ocean ■ *n* /ōvər seèz/ a place or places across an ocean (+ *sing verb*) ○ *come from overseas*

o·ver·see /ōvər seé/ (-**saw** /-sáw/, -**seen** /-seén/) *vt* supervise

o·ver·se·er /ōvər seé ər/ *n* a supervisor

o·ver·sell /ōvər sél/ (-**sold** /-sóld/) *v* 1 *vt* praise somebody or something to an implausible extent 2 *vti* sell something too aggressively 3 *vti* sell too much or too many of something

o·ver·sen·si·tive /ōvər sénssətiv/ *adj* excessively sensitive —**o·ver·sen·si·tiv·i·ty** /-sensə tívvətee/ *n*

o·ver·sexed /ōvər sékst/ *adj* with excessive sex drive

o·ver·shad·ow /ōvər sháddō/ *vt* 1 take attention away from by appearing more important 2 cast a shadow over

o·ver·shoe /ōvər shoò/ *n* a protective shoe worn over an ordinary shoe

o·ver·shoot *vti* /ōvər shoòt/ (-**shot** /-shót/) 1 send or go farther than intended 2 fail to take off or land before the end of a runway 3 exceed a fixed limit ■ *n* /ōvər shoòt/ 1 the overshooting of a runway 2 the amount by which something exceeds a fixed limit

o·ver·sight /ōvər sìt/ *n* 1 a mistake resulting from a failure to do or notice something 2 supervision of something (*fml*)

o·ver·sim·pli·fy /ōvər símplə fì/ (-**fied**, -**fies**) *vt* distort something by excessive simplification —**o·ver·sim·pli·fi·ca·tion** /-símpləfi káysh'n/ *n*

o·ver·size /ōvər sìz/ *adj also* **o·ver·sized** larger than usual or necessary

o·ver·sleep /ōvər sleép/ (-**slept** /-slépt/) *v* 1 *vi* sleep longer than intended 2 *vt* sleep too late for

o·ver·sold past participle, past tense of **oversell**

o·ver·spend /ōvər spénd/ (-**spent** /-spént/) *vti* spend too much

o·ver·spill *n* /ōvər spíl/ something that has spilled over ■ *vti* /ōvər spíl/ (-**spilled** *or* -**spilt** /-spílt/) spill over

o·ver·state /ōvər stáyt/ (-**stat·ed**, -**stat·ing**) *vt* exaggerate —**o·ver·state·ment** *n*

o·ver·stay /ōvər stáy/ *vti* stay longer than the time intended for something

o·ver·step /ōvər stép/ (-**stepped**, -**step·ping**) *vt* exceed a limit or boundary

o·ver·stock *v* /ōvər stók/ 1 *vti* stock too much of something 2 *vt* keep too many animals on a piece of land ■ *n* /ōvər stòk/ an excessive supply of something

o·ver·stored /ōvər stáwrd/ *adj* having too many stores

o·ver·stretch /ōvər stréch/ *v* 1 *vti* stretch too far so as to cause injury or damage 2 *vt* try to do too much with available resources

o·vert /ō vúrt, ṓ vùrt/ *adj* open and unconcealed —**o·vert·ly** /ō vúrtlee, ṓ vùrtlee/ *adv* —**o·vert·ness** *n*

o·ver·take /ōvər táyk/ (-**took** /-toòk/, -**tak·en** /-táykən/, -**tak·ing**) *v* 1 *vti* go past somebody or something traveling in the same direction 2 *vt* do better than somebody or something

o·ver·tax /ōvər táks/ *vt* 1 impose too great a strain on 2 levy excessive tax on

o·ver·the·count·er *adj* 1 describes securities bought and sold electronically 2 buyable without a prescription

o·ver·the·top *adj* excessive and exaggerated (*infml*)

o·ver·throw *vt* /ōvər thrṓ/ (-**threw** /-throó/, -**thrown** /-thrṓn/) 1 remove somebody from power by force 2 pitch a baseball too hard 3 throw a ball too far ■ *n* /ōvər thrṓ/ 1 the removal of somebody from power by force 2 a throw of a ball that goes too far

o·ver·time /ōvər tìm/ *n* 1 time worked in addition to the normal hours of employment 2 pay for additional time worked 3 extra time added to a game, often to break a tie ■ *adv* beyond the normal length of time

o·ver·tone /ōvər tòn/ *n* 1 a subtle supplementary meaning or nuance ○ *an overtone of malice in his manner* 2 a musical tone whose frequency is a multiple of a fundamental tone

o·ver·took past tense of **overtake**

o·ver·ture /ōvər choòr/ *n* 1 a single orchestral movement introducing a longer musical work such as an opera 2 an introductory proposal or initiative 3 a self-standing orchestral piece in one movement

o·ver·turn /ōvər túrn/ *v* 1 *vti* tip upside down 2 *vt* overthrow somebody or something 3 *vt* reverse a previous decision by using legal procedures

~~overrun~~ incorrect spelling of **overrun**

o·ver·use *n* /ōvər yoòss/ excessive use ■ *vt* /ōvər yoòz/ (-**used**, -**us·ing**) use too much

o·ver·val·ue /ōvər vállyoo/ (-**ued**, -**u·ing**) *vt* put too high a value on

o·ver·view /ōvər vyoò/ *n* 1 a broad survey 2 a summary

o·ver·ween·ing /ōvər weéning/ *adj* 1 intolerably arrogant 2 excessive

o·ver·weight /ōvər wáyt/ *adj* 1 too heavy for good health 2 above an allowed weight limit ■ *vt* 1 overemphasize 2 overload

o·ver·whelm /ōvər wélm, -hwélm/ *vt* 1 surge over and cover somebody or something 2 overcome somebody physically 3 overpower somebody emotionally 4 provide somebody with a huge amount of something —**o·ver·whelm·ing** *adj* —**o·ver·whelm·ing·ly** *adv*

o·ver·win·ter /ōvər wíntər/ *v* 1 *vti* keep livestock or plants alive throughout the winter by sheltering them, or be kept alive in this manner 2 *vi* live somewhere during the winter

o·ver·with·hold /ōvər with hṓld, -with-/ (-**held** /-héld/) *vti* deduct too much tax from a salary or investment

o·ver·work /ōvər wúrk/ *v* 1 *vti* do or force to do too much work 2 *vt* overuse something, especially a word or expression ■ *n* excessive work

⌀ o·ver·write /ōvər rít/ (-**wrote** /-rṓt/, -**writ·ten** /-rítt'n/, -**writ·ing**) *vti* 1 replace a computer file with another with the same name 2 write in too elaborate or polished a style

o·ver·wrought /ōvər ráwt/ *adj* 1 very upset 2 too elaborate

Ov·id /óvvid/ (43 BC–AD 17) Roman poet —**vid·i·an** /ṓ víddee ən/ *adj*

o·void /ṓ vòyd/ *adj* with the form of an egg —**o·void** *n*

o·vu·late /óvyə làyt, óvvyə-/ (-**lat·ed**, -**lat·ing**) *vi* release an egg from the ovary —**o·vu·la·tion** /óvyə láysh'n, òvvyə-/ *n*

o·vule /ṓ vyòol, ó-/ *n* 1 the structure in a plant that develops into a seed after fertilization 2 an immature egg —**o·vu·lar** /óvyələr, óvvyələr/ *adj*

o·vum /óvəm/ (*pl* **o·va** /óvə/) *n* a female reproductive cell

ow /ŏ/ *interj* expresses pain

OW *abbr* one-way

owe /ŏ/ (**owed**, **ow·ing**) *v* 1 *vt* be obligated to pay somebody money o *owes the bank a lot of money* 2 *vti* be financially in debt to somebody o *doesn't owe anyone* 3 *vt* be indebted for something to somebody o *owed his success to her* 4 *vt* feel that a response is due somebody o *I owe you an explanation.*

Ow·en /ṓ in/, **Robert** (1771–1858) British social reformer

Ow·en, Wilfred (1893–1918) British poet

Jesse Owens: Photographed in the long jump competition at the Berlin Olympics (1936)

Ow·ens /ṓ inz/, **Jesse** (1913–80) US athlete

ow·ing /ṓ ing/ *adj* due to be paid ◊ **owing to** as a result of

owl /owl/ *n* 1 a nocturnal bird of prey with a large head, a flat face, and a hooting call

2 somebody with a quality or habit attributed to owls, e.g., wisdom or staying up late —**owl·et** *n* —**owl·ish** *adj*

own /ōn/ *adj, pron* 1 emphasizes that somebody or something belongs to a particular person or thing o *has her own business* 2 indicates that somebody does something without help or interference o *makes his own clothes* ■ *v* 1 *vt* have as your property o *doesn't own a car* 2 *vti* acknowledge *(fml)* o *owned that the struggle was hard* —**own·er** *n* —**own·er·ship** *n* ◊ **come into your own** start to be really effective, useful, or successful ◊ **hold your own** 1 put up effective resistance in an argument or contest 2 remain in a stable condition after an illness or injury ◊ **on your own** alone

ox /oks/ (*pl* **ox·en** /óksən/) *n* 1 an adult castrated bull, used as a draft animal 2 a cow or bull

ox·bow /óks bò/ *n* a bend in a river

ox·eye /óks ì/ *n* 1 a daisy 2 a plant with flower heads like a daisy's

ox·ford /óksfərd/ *n* 1 *also* **Ox·ford** a sturdy leather lace-up shoe 2 a strong cotton used for making shirts, or a shirt made of this material

Ox·ford /óks fərd/ city in south central England. Pop. 137,343 (1996).

ox·i·dant /óksidənt/ *n* a substance that oxidizes other substances

ox·i·da·tion /òksi dáysh'n/ *n* 1 addition of oxygen to a chemical or compound 2 loss of electrons from a chemical or compound

ox·ide /ók stíd/ *n* a compound containing oxygen, especially in combination with a metal

ox·i·dize /óksi dìz/ (-**dized**, -**diz·ing**) *vti* 1 react, or make a chemical react, with oxygen 2 lose, or make a chemical element or compound lose, electrons —**ox·i·di·za·tion** /òksidi záysh'n/ *n* —**ox·i·diz·er** *n*

ox·tail /óks tàyl/ *n* an ox's tail as food

ox·y·a·cet·y·lene /òksee ə séttʹl èen, -séttʹlin/ *n* an oxygen and acetylene mixture that produces a hot flame. Use: cutting, welding metal.

ox·y·gen /óksijən/ *n* (*symbol* **O**) a colorless odorless gaseous chemical element essential for breathing

---

ORIGIN Oxygen was coined in French in the late 18C by the chemist Lavoisier, originally as an adjective (in *principe oxygène* "acidifying principle"), then as a noun. He gave the gas the name, from Greek words meaning "acid forming," because it was at that time believed to be an essential component in the formation of acids.

---

ox·y·gen·ate /óksijə nàyt/ (-**at·ed**, -**at·ing**) *vti* combine with oxygen

ox·y·gen mask *n* a device fitting over the nose and mouth for providing oxygen for breathing

ox·y·gen tent *n* a transparent plastic structure into which oxygen is pumped for helping a patient in bed to breathe

ox·y·mo·ron /ōksee máw ròn/ (*pl* **-ra** /-rə/) *n* a combination of two words with contradictory meanings that are used together for a special effect

o·yez /ō yéz, -yéss, -yáy/, **o·yes** *interj* calls for silence before an announcement or at the opening of a session in a court of law, usually spoken three times in succession ■ *n* a cry of "oyez"

oys·ter /óystər/ *n* a shellfish with a rough irregularly shaped two-part shell

oys·ter·catch·er /óystər kàchər/ *n* a shore bird with a long red bill and black-and-white plumage that lives on shellfish and worms

⚡**oz, oz.** *abbr* 1 Australia *(in Internet addresses)* 2 ounce

O·zark Plat·eau /ō zaark-/, **O·zarks**, **O·zark Moun·tains** mountainous region of the south central United States, extending from SW Missouri across NW Arkansas and E Oklahoma

o·zone /ō zōn/ *n* 1 a form of oxygen produced by electrical discharge 2 fresh air, especially ocean air *(infml)*

o·zone-friend·ly *adj* not harming the ozone layer

o·zone lay·er, **o·zo·no·sphere** /ō zōnə sfeer, ō zónnə-/ *n* the layer of the upper atmosphere that absorbs harmful ultraviolet solar radiation

P

p[1] (*pl* **p's**), **P** (*pl* **P's** *or* **Ps**) *n* the 16th letter of the English alphabet ◊ **mind** *or* **watch your p's and q's** be careful to be polite and well-behaved

p[2] *symbol* piano *(musical direction)*

P *symbol* phosphorus

P *abbr* 1 parity 2 park *(on gearshifts)* 3 pawn *(in chess)* 4 pressure

p. *abbr* 1 page 2 part 3 participle 4 past 5 peso 6 pint

⚡**P2P** /pèe tə pée/ *adj* 1 describes payments or linkups made between two people via the Internet. Full form **person-to-person** 2 describes software enabling Internet users to communicate without the use of intermediaries such as servers. Full form **peer-to-peer**

Pa *symbol* 1 pascal 2 protactinium

PA[1] *abbr also* **Pa.** Pennsylvania

PA[2] *n* an electronic sound-amplification system in a public place. Full form **public-address system**

P.A. *abbr* 1 physician's assistant 2 prosecuting attorney

pa'an·ga /paàng gə, paa aàng gə/ *n* the main unit of Tongan currency

PABA /pábbə, paàbə/ *n* a component of the B vitamin complex. Use: sunscreen. Full form **para-aminobenzoic acid**

PAC *abbr* political action committee

pace[1] /payss/ *n* 1 speed of movement or progress 2 a step in walking or running 3 the distance covered in a step 4 a way of walking ○ *an uneven pace* 5 the gait of a horse at different speeds ■ *v* (**paced**, **pac·ing**) 1 *vti* walk back and forth in an area 2 *vti* walk along with regular strides 3 *vti* measure by counting steps 4 *vt* set the speed at which somebody runs or does something 5 *vr* run or work at a controlled rate

pa·ce[2] /paà chày, páyssee/ *prep* with all respect to

pace·mak·er /páyss màykər/ *n* 1 *also* **pace·set·ter** /-sèttər/ a competitor who sets the pace 2 *also* **pace·set·ter** a leader in a field of activity 3 an electrical device inserted into the body to regulate the heartbeat

pa·chi·si /pə chéezee/ *n* an ancient South Asian board game similar to backgammon

Pa·chu·ca /pə choòkə, paa choò kaa/ capital of Hidalgo State, central Mexico. Pop. 179,440 (1990).

pach·y·derm /páki dùrm/ *n* a large thick-skinned mammal such as an elephant, rhinoceros, or hippopotamus —**pach·y·der·mal** /pàki dúrm'l/ *adj*

pa·cif·ic /pə síffik/ *adj* 1 bringing peace 2 having a peaceful temperament

Pa·cif·ic /pə síffik/, **Pa·cif·ic O·cean** largest ocean in the world, stretching from the Arctic Ocean in the north to Antarctica in the south, and from North and South America in the east to East Asia, the Malay Archipelago, and Australia in the west —**Pa·cif·ic** *adj*

Pa·cif·ic Is·lands, Trust Ter·ri·to·ry of the former U.N. trust territory in the W Pacific Ocean administered by the United States, comprising 2,000 islands including the Caroline, Marshall, and Mariana islands

Pa·cif·ic North·west region of the NW United States that includes Washington and Oregon and sometimes SW British Columbia, Canada

Pa·cif·ic Rim *n* the countries bordering the Pacific Ocean considered as an economic unit

Pa·cif·ic Stan·dard Time, Pa·cif·ic Time *n* the local standard time in W North America

pac·i·fi·er /pássə fīr/ *n* 1 somebody or something that pacifies 2 a rubber or plastic object that babies suck

pac·i·fism /pássə fizzəm/ *n* **1** opposition to war or violence **2** refusal to participate in a war for moral or religious reasons —**pac·i·fist** *n* —**pac·i·fis·tic** /pàssə fístik/ *adj*

pac·i·fy /pássə fī/ (**-fied, -fies**) *vt* **1** calm **2** bring peace to —**pac·i·fi·ca·tion** /pàssəfi káysh'n/ *n*

⚡ **pack**[1] *n* **1** a collection of things in a package **2** a commercial container **3** the contents of a pack, or the amount contained in it **4** a large amount (*infml*) o *a pack of lies* **5** a group of animals living and hunting together **6** a large group of people acting together **7** a group of Cub Scouts **8** the main body of competitors in a race **9** a set of 52 playing cards **10** a bag carried on the back ■ *v* **1** *vti* put belongings into a container for transporting **2** *vti* put products into containers for sale, transport, or storage **3** *vt* create a package or bundle **4** *vt* fill something tightly o *book packed with useful information* **5** *vti* crowd into or fill a place **6** *vt* compress a computer file **7** *vti* make or become compacted **8** *vt* press something around an object to hold or protect it **9** *vti* carry a gun (*infml*) —**packed** *adj*

ORIGIN Pack "container, put in container" was adopted in the 12C from Dutch or German. Pack "fill with supporters" is probably an alteration of *pact*, and dates from the early 16C.

☐ **pack off** *vt* send away unceremoniously (*infml*) o *packed the kids off to camp*

pack[2] *vt* fill a jury or committee with supporters

pack·age /pákij/ *n* **1** a parcel **2** a container in which goods are packed **3** a number of different things constituting a single item or proposal o *a good severance package* **4** *also* **pack·age tour** a fully organized vacation tour ■ *vt* (**-aged, -ag·ing**) **1** put into a package **2** present attractively —**pack·ag·er** *n*

pack·age deal *n* a set of proposals offered as a single item

pack·ag·ing /pákijing/ *n* **1** the wrapping or container for something **2** the design or style of the wrapping or container for something **3** the presentation of somebody or something in a way intended to be appealing

pack an·i·mal *n* **1** an animal that carries loads **2** an animal that lives and hunts in a pack

pack·er /pákər/ *n* **1** somebody or something that packs goods **2** a person or company that processes and packages food

⚡ **pack·et** /páckit/ *n* **1** a small container for goods **2** a small parcel **3** a data unit in a computer network **4** *also* **pack·et boat** a passenger or cargo boat on a regular short run

⚡ **pack·et switch·ing** *n* the transmission of data as packets over a channel occupied only during transmission

pack·horse /pák hàwrs/ *n* a horse for carrying loads

pack ice *n* floating ice in a solid mass

pack·ing /páking/ *n* **1** the act of putting things into containers for storage or transport **2** material for protecting a packed object

pack rat *n* **1** a woodland rat that collects and stores objects **2** somebody who hoards objects (*infml*)

pack·sad·dle /pák sàdd'l/ *n* a saddle for carrying loads

pact *n* an agreement between two or more people or groups

pad[1] *n* **1** a piece of soft material for protecting, shaping, cleaning, or absorbing something **2** a protective covering for part of the body, especially when playing a sport **3** a block of sheets of paper **4** a piece of ink-filled material on which a rubber stamp is pressed **5** an area where a helicopter takes off and lands or a rocket is launched **6** a sanitary napkin **7** a piece of backing material for something laid on a surface **8** a fleshy cushion on an animal's paw **9** the fleshy tip of a finger or toe **10** somebody's living quarters (*slang dated*) **11** a broad floating leaf of a water plant ■ *vt* (**pad·ded, pad·ding**) **1** use soft material to fill, protect, or shape something or make it more comfortable **2** add unnecessary material to a piece of writing

pad[2] *vti* (**pad·ded, pad·ding**) walk or walk along something quietly ■ *n* the sound of quiet footsteps

pad·ded cell *n* a lockable room with padded walls and floor in a psychiatric hospital

pad·ding /pádding/ *n* **1** thick soft material for filling, protecting, or shaping something **2** unnecessary additions to a piece of writing

pad·dle[1] /pádd'l/ *n* **1** a short flat-bladed oar for propelling a canoe or small boat **2** a table tennis racket ■ *v* (**-dled, -dling**) **1** *vti* propel or carry in a canoe with a paddle **2** *vt* stir with a paddle

pad·dle[2] /pádd'l/ (**-dled, -dling**) *vti* dabble the hands or feet in water —**pad·dle** *n*

pad·dle·boat /pádd'l bòt/ *n* a boat propelled by one or more paddle wheels

pad·dle wheel *n* a bladed wheel attached to an engine and propelling a ship

pad·dock /páddək/ *n* **1** an enclosed field for horses **2** an area at a racetrack for mounting racehorses

pad·dy /páddee/ (*pl* **-dies**) *n* *also* **pad·dy field** a rice field kept under shallow water

pad·dy wag·on *n* US, Can, ANZ a police vehicle for transporting suspects or criminals

Pa·de·rew·ski /pàddə réfskee/, **Ignace Jan** (1860–1941) Polish pianist, composer, and prime minister (1919)

pad·lock /pád lòk/ *n* a small detachable lock with a semicircular bar at the top —**pad·lock** *vt*

pa·dre /paá drày, paádree/ *n* used to address a Roman Catholic priest in a Spanish, Portuguese, or Italian-speaking country

pae·an /pée ən/ *n* a written, spoken, or musical expression of joy or praise

pa·el·la /paa áy yàa, paa élla/ *n* a Spanish dish of rice, chicken, and shellfish

pa·gan /páygən/ *n* **1** a follower of a religion that is not one of the main world religions (*sometimes offensive*) **2** a follower of an ancient polytheistic or pantheistic religion —**pa·gan** *adj* —**pa·gan·ism** *n*

Pa·ga·ni·ni /pàggə néenee/, **Niccolò** (1782–1840) Italian composer and violinist

⚡**page**[1] *n* **1** one side of a sheet of paper **2** a single sheet in book **3** the amount of writing on a page **4** the amount of computer data printing out as a page **5** the amount of data that can be seen on a computer screen at one time ■ *v* (**paged, pag·ing**) **1** *vi* look through pages **2** *vt* number each page of

page[2] *n* **1** a boy attendant on a ceremonial occasion **2** a youth who runs errands or carries messages in a hotel or club ■ *vt* (**paged, pag·ing**) **1** summon by calling out a name **2** contact on a pager

pag·eant /pájjənt/ *n* **1** a large-scale spectacle representing a historical event **2** an elaborate and colorful procession

pag·eant·ry /pájjəntree/ *n* magnificent ceremonial display

page·boy /páyj bòy/ *n* a medium-length smooth hairstyle with the ends curled under

⚡**page break** *n* an indication where a computer printer will start a new page

~~pagent~~ incorrect spelling of **pageant**

pag·er /páyjər/ *n* an electronic device for contacting somebody

pag·i·nate /pájjə nàyt/ (**-nat·ed, -nat·ing**) *vt* number each page of

pag·i·na·tion /pàjjə náysh'n/ *n* **1** the page numbers of a book or document **2** the process of numbering the pages of a book

⚡**pag·ing**[1] /páyjing/ *n* the transfer of computer data from main memory to auxiliary memory to speed up performance

pag·ing[2] /páyjing/ *n* **1** the use of a pager **2** a facility that enables somebody to be contacted via a pager

pa·go·da /pə gódə/ *n* **1** a Buddhist temple with projecting roofs **2** a building designed like a Buddhist pagoda

Pah·la·vi /paálə vèe/, **Muhammad Reza Shah** (1919–80) shah of Iran (1941–79)

paid past participle, past tense of **pay** ■ *adj* done to earn money ○ *paid employment*

paid-up *adj* **1** not owing anything **2** fully paid for

pail *n* a bucket

pain /payn/ *n* **1** an acutely unpleasant physical sensation resulting from being hit, injured, or sick **2** a feeling of pain in a particular part of the body (*often pl*) **3** severe emotional distress **4** somebody or something annoying (*infml*) ■ **pains** *npl* trouble taken to do something ■ *v* **1** *vt* sadden or distress **2** *vti* feel or cause to feel physical pain —**pain·less** *adj* —**pain·less·ly** *adv* ◊ **on** or **under pain of** at the risk of the penalty of ○ *on pain of instant dismissal*

SPELLCHECK Do not confuse the spelling of **pain** and **pane** (of a window), which sound similar.

Paine /payn/, **Thomas** (1737–1809) British-born American writer, political philosopher, and revolutionary

pained *adj* expressing pain or wounded or disappointed feelings

pain·ful /páynfəl/ *adj* **1** causing physical or mental pain **2** hurting as a result of an injury or disease —**pain·ful·ly** *adv*

pain·kill·er /páyn killər/ *n* a pain-reducing drug —**pain·kill·ing** *adj*

pains·tak·ing /páynz tàyking/ *adj* taking or showing great care and attention to detail —**pains·tak·ing·ly** *adv* ◊ See note at **careful**

paint /paynt/ *n* **1** a colored liquid applied to a surface to decorate or protect it, or to create a painting **2** dried paint on a surface **3** *also* **paint horse** a horse with irregular patches of white and another color on its coat ■ *v* **1** *vti* cover something with paint **2** *vti* create a picture using paint **3** *vt* mark designs or words on a surface using paint **4** *vt* apply liquid to a surface with a brush **5** *vt* apply cosmetics to the face or nails **6** *vt* describe something vividly in words

paint·ball /páynt bàwl/ *n* a combat game between teams with guns that fire a marking dye —**paint·ball·er** *n* —**paint·ball·ing** *n*

paint·brush /páynt brùsh/ *n* a brush for applying paint

Paint·ed Des·ert plateau region of north central Arizona, noted for its vividly colored rocks

paint·er[1] /páyntər/ *n* **1** an artist who paints pictures **2** a worker who paints houses

pain·ter[2] /páyntər/ *n* a rope attached to the front of a boat for tying it up

paint·ing /páynting/ *n* **1** a painted picture **2** the activity of applying paint

paint·work /páynt wùrk/ *n* painted surfaces

pair /pair/ *n* **1** a set of two similar matching things used together ○ *a pair of socks* **2** something with two matching or identical joined parts ○ *a pair of binoculars* **3** two people or animals doing something together or connected in some way **4** one of two matching articles ○ *lost the pair to his* *cuff link* ■ *v* **1** *vti* form or cause to form a pair **2** *vt* match two things together

SPELLCHECK Do not confuse the spelling of **pair, pare** ("cut off"), or **pear** (the fruit), which sound similar.

pais·ley /páyzlee/ *n* a bold pattern with curving shapes —**pais·ley** *adj*

Pai·ute /pí yóot/ (*pl* **-utes** *or same*), **Pi·ute** *n* **1** a member of each of two Native North American peoples, the Northern Paiutes, living in Oregon, Nevada, and NE California, and the Southern Paiutes living in Utah **2** the language of the Paiute people —**Pai·ute** *adj*

pa·ja·mas /pə jaàməz, pə jámməz/ *npl* light loose-fitting pants and a matching shirt for wearing in bed

Pak·i·stan /páki stàn, paàki staàn/ country in South Asia, bordering the Arabian Sea. Cap. Islamabad. Pop. 144,616,640 (2001). —**Pak·i·stan·i** /pàki staànee, paàki-/ *n, adj*

pal *n* a friend (*infml*) ■ *vi* (**palled, pal·ing**) become friends, or spend time together as friends

pal·ace /páiləss/ *n* **1** the official residence of a sovereign **2** a large imposing building

ORIGIN The original **palace** was the *Palatium* built on (and named for) the Palatine Hill in Rome by the emperor Augustus. The name came to be used for all grand and imposing residences. Latin *palatium* passed into English via French.

pal·a·din /pálləd'n, -din/ *n* a medieval champion or chivalric hero

pal·an·quin /pàlən keén/ *n* a covered seat carried on poles on the shoulders of two or four people

pal·at·a·ble /pál lətəb'l/ *adj* **1** having a good enough taste to be eaten or drunk **2** acceptable to somebody's sensibilities

pal·ate /pállət/ *n* **1** the roof of the mouth **2** somebody's sense of taste —**pal·a·tal** *adj*

SPELLCHECK Do not confuse the spelling of **palate, palette** ("a board for artist's paints"), or **pallet** ("a tray for stacking loads on"), which sound similar.

pa·la·tial /pə láysh'l/ *adj* **1** luxurious **2** of or fit for a palace

pa·lat·i·nate /pə látt'n àyt, pə látt'nət/ *n* the territory or status of a palatine

pal·a·tine /pállə tīn/ *n* **1** a powerful feudal lord in central Europe **2** a court official in the late Roman and Byzantine empires ■ *adj* **1** of or suitable for a palace **2** being or of a palatine

Pa·lau /paa lów/ country in the W Pacific Ocean comprising a group of islands that are part of the Caroline Islands. Cap. Koror. Pop. 19,092 (2001).

pa·lav·er /pə lávvər, -laàvər/ *n* empty talk —**pa·lav·er** *vti*

pale¹ *adj* (**pal·er, pal·est**) **1** lacking color or intensity o *pale yellow* **2** with a whitish complexion, usually from illness or worry ■ *vi* (**paled, pal·ing**) **1** become whiter or paler **2** become less important —**pale·ness** *n*

pale² *n* **1** a fence stake **2** a boundary fence ◊ **beyond the pale** outside the limits of what is considered to be acceptable

Pa·le·o·cene /páylee ə seèn/ *n* the epoch of geologic time when placental mammals first appeared, 65 to 55 million years ago —**Pa·le·o·cene** *adj*

pa·le·og·ra·phy /páylee óggrəfee/ *n* the study of ancient handwriting and manuscripts —**pa·le·og·ra·pher** *n* —**pa·le·o·graph·i·cal** /páylee ə gráffik'l/ *adj*

Pa·le·o·lith·ic /páylee ə líthik/ *n* the early Stone Age —**Pa·le·o·lith·ic** *adj*

pa·le·on·tol·o·gy /páylee on tólləjee/ *n* the study of life in prehistoric times —**pa·le·on·to·log·i·cal** /páylee ontə lójjik'l/ *adj* —**pa·le·on·tol·o·gist** *n*

Pa·le·o·zo·ic /páylee ə zṓ ik/ *n* the era of geologic time when fish, insects, amphibians, reptiles, and land plants first appeared, about 600 million to 230 million years ago —**Pa·le·o·zo·ic** *adj*

Pa·ler·mo /pə lúrmō, -láir-/ port on NW Sicily, Italy. Pop. 685,551 (1999).

Pal·es·tine /pálə stìn/ **1** historical region in SW Asia on the coast of the E Mediterranean Sea, the biblical land of Canaan **2** former country in SW Asia, between the Dead Sea and the Mediterranean Sea, divided in 1947 between Israel and Jordan. In 1993 Palestinians gained limited self-rule in Israeli-held territories in the Gaza Strip and on the West Bank of the Jordan River. —**Pal·es·tin·i·an** /pàlə stínnee ən/ *n, adj*

pal·ette /pállət/ *n* **1** a board on which an artist arranges and mixes paints **2** the range of colors used by an artist ◊ See note at **palate**

pal·frey /páwlfree/ (*pl* **-freys**) *n* a woman's riding horse (*archaic*)

pal·i·mo·ny /pálli mṓnee/ (*pl* **-nies**) *n* alimony for an unmarried ex-lover

pal·imp·sest /pálimp sèst/·*n* a manuscript written over a partly erased older manuscript

pal·in·drome /pállin drṓm/ *n* a text reading the same backward and forward —**pal·in·dro·mic** /pàllin drómmik, -drṓmik/ *adj*

pal·ing /páyling/ *n* **1** a fence of stakes **2** a stake in a fence

pal·i·sade /pàlli sáyd, pálli sàyd/ *n* a fence made of wooden stakes

pall¹ *n* **1** a covering that makes a place dark and gloomy **2** a gloomy atmosphere **3** a cloth covering for a casket

pall² *vi* become boring or insipid

Pal·la·di·o /pə laàdee ô/, **Andrea** (1508–80) Italian architect

pal·la·di·um /pə láydee əm/ n (symbol **Pd**) a soft, silvery-white metal. Use: catalyst, alloys.

ORIGIN **Palladium** was named for *Pallas*, an asteroid discovered in 1803, shortly before the element. *Pallas* itself is another name for Athena, the Greek goddess of wisdom and warfare.

pall·bear·er /páwl bàirər/ n somebody who carries a casket

pal·let¹ /pállət/ n a platform on which cargo is stored or transported ◊ See note at **palate**

pal·let² /pállət/ n 1 a makeshift bed 2 a straw mattress

pal·li·ate /pállee àyt/ (-at·ed, -at·ing) vt 1 reduce the intensity or severity of something 2 make an offense seem less serious 3 alleviate a symptom of a medical condition —**pal·li·a·tion** /pàllee áysh'n/ n

pal·lid /pállid/ adj 1 unhealthily pale 2 lackluster —**pal·lid·i·ty** /pa líddətee, pə-/ n

pal·lor /pállər/ n an unhealthy-looking paleness

palm¹ /paam/ n the inner surface of the hand ■ vt 1 hide something in the hand 2 take something stealthily

ORIGIN The two English words **palm** go back to the same Latin word, which meant both "palm of the hand" and "palm tree." The tree was so called because a cluster of palm leaves was thought to look like a hand and fingers. The two branches of Latin *palma* reached English by different routes: "palm of the hand" through ancient Germanic forms, and "palm tree" through early Romance words and French.

☐ **palm off** vt 1 give something in a deceitful way 2 pass on something unwanted

palm² /paam/ n 1 a tropical tree or plant with fronds 2 a palm leaf used as a victory sign

palm·cord·er /paàm kàwrdər/ n a small camcorder

Palm·er /paàmər, paàlmər/, **Arnold** (b. 1929) US golfer

palm·is·try /paàmistree/ n examining the palms of the hands to predict a person's destiny —**palm·ist** n

palm oil n oil from the fruit of some palm trees. Use: lubricants, soap, cosmetics, foods.

Palm Springs city in S California. Pop. 43,942 (1998).

Palm Sun·day n a Christian festival marking Jesus Christ's entry into Jerusalem. Date: Sunday before Easter.

⚡ **palm·top** /paàm tòp/ n a computer that is small enough to hold in one hand

palm·y /paàmee/ (-i·er, -i·est) adj 1 of palm trees 2 prosperous or flourishing, especially formerly (literary)

Pal·o·mar, Mt. /pállə maàr/ mountain in S California, site of an astronomical observatory. Height 6,138 ft./1,871 m.

pal·o·mi·no /pàllə meénô/ (pl -nos) n a golden-colored horse with a pale mane and tail

pal·pa·ble /pálpəb'l/ adj 1 so intense as almost to produce a physical sensation 2 obvious or easily observed 3 able to be felt by the hands, especially in a medical examination —**pal·pa·bly** adv

pal·pate /pál pàyt/ (-pat·ed, -pat·ing) vt examine medically by touching

pal·pi·tate /pálpi tàyt/ (-tat·ed, -tat·ing) vi beat irregularly (refers to the heart) —**pal·pi·tant** adj

pal·sy /páwlzee/ n a muscular inability to move (archaic)

pal·try /páwltree/ (-tri·er, -tri·est) adj 1 insignificant o a paltry sum of money 2 despicable —**pal·tri·ness** n

~~pamflet~~ incorrect spelling of **pamphlet**

Pa·mirs /pə meérz/ mountainous region of central Asia, located mainly in Tajikistan and extending to NE Afghanistan and NW China. Highest peak Ismail Samani Peak, 24,590 ft./7,495 m.

pam·pas /pámpəz, -pəss/ n treeless grassland in South America (+ sing or pl verb) —**pam·pe·an** /pámpee ən, pam peé ən/ adj

pam·pas grass n a very tall ornamental grass

pam·per /pámpər/ vt 1 treat lavishly and indulgently 2 indulge or gratify

pam·phlet /pámflət/ n an informational or political leaflet

ORIGIN *Pamphilet* and *Pamflet* were popular names of a short anonymous 12C Latin love poem, *Pamphilus, seu de Amore*. The word came to be applied to any short text. **Pamphlet** began to establish itself as the standard form in the 16C.

pam·phlet·eer /pàmflə teér/ n a writer of political pamphlets —**pam·phlet·eer** vi

Pam·plo·na /pam plóna/ city in NE Spain. Pop. 171,150 (1998).

pan¹ /pan/ n 1 a cooking pot, usually of metal 2 a shallow dish or container ■ v (panned, pan·ning) 1 vt criticize severely, especially in a review (infml) 2 vi wash or shake soil or gravel to separate precious metals

☐ **pan out** vi turn out well or successfully (infml)

pan² /pan/ (panned, pan·ning) vti move a camera horizontally from a fixed point —**pan** n

pan³ /paan/ n 1 a betel leaf 2 a rolled betel leaf containing spices

Pan /pan/ n 1 in Greek mythology, the god of nature. Roman equivalent **Faunus** 2 the innermost moon of Saturn

PAN abbr Mexico National Action Party. Full form **Partido Acción Nacional**

pan- *prefix* all, any, everyone ◇ *pantheism*

pan·a·ce·a /pànnə seè ə/ *n* a supposed cure for all diseases or problems —**pan·a·ce·an** *adj*

pa·nache /pə násh, -naàsh/ *n* **1** dashing style **2** a plume of feathers on a helmet

pan·a·ma /pánnə maà/, **Pan·a·ma** *n* a man's lightweight hat made of braided leaves or straw

Pan·a·ma /pánnə maà/ country in Central America. Cap. Panama City. Pop. 2,845,647 (2001). —**Pan·a·ma·ni·an** /pànnə máynee ən/ *n, adj*

Pan·a·ma, Isth·mus of isthmus connecting North and South America

Pan·a·ma Ca·nal canal across the Isthmus of Panama, connecting the Pacific Ocean and the Caribbean Sea. Length 40 mi./64 km.

Pan·a·ma Cit·y capital of Panama. Pop. 668,927 (1996).

pan·a·tel·la /pànnə téllə/, **pan·a·tel·a** *n* a thin straight cigar

pan·cake /pán kàyk/ *n* a very thin fried cake

Pan·chen La·ma /pàanchən-/ *n* in Tibetan Buddhism, a lama of the second highest rank

pan·cre·as /pángkree əss, pánkree-/ *n* a gland that produces insulin and digestive enzymes —**pan·cre·at·ic** /pàngkree áttik, pànkree-/ *adj*

pan·da /pándə/ *n* **1** *also* **pan·da bear** a large black-and-white Chinese mammal **2** a red panda

pan·dem·ic /pan démmik/ *adj* having a widespread effect ■ *n* a very widespread disease or medical condition

pan·de·mo·ni·um /pàndə mônee əm/ *n* chaos and uproar

ORIGIN The English poet John Milton coined *Pandemonium* as the name of the capital of hell in his epic poem *Paradise Lost* (1667). It is formed from Greek words meaning "of all the demons." From the late 18C a *pandemonium* was applied to a place of vice, confusion, or uproar, and the sense "chaos and uproar" developed in the mid-19C.

---

pan·der /pándər/ *vi* **1** indulge another person's weaknesses or questionable tastes ◇ *tired of pandering to their children's demands* **2** procure sexual favors for somebody (*disapproving*) ■ *n* *also* **Pan·der·er** (*disapproving*) **1** somebody who indulges another person's weaknesses or questionable tastes **2** a go-between in a romantic or sexual relationship

pan·dit /pándit/ *n* a wise and learned Brahman

P & L *abbr* profit and loss

Pan·do·ra /pan dáwrə/ *n* in Greek mythology, the first woman, sent with a container of evils to avenge Prometheus's theft of fire

Pan·do·ra's box *n* **1** in Greek mythology, the container from which the evils of the world were released **2** a source of troubles

pane /payn/ *n* **1** a glazed section of a window or door **2** a piece of glass in a window or door ◊ See note at **pain**

pan·e·gyr·ic /pànnə jírrik, -jírrik/ *n* praise expressed in formal speech or writing —**pan·e·gyr·ist** *n* —**pan·e·gyr·ize** *vt*

pan·el /pánn'l/ *n* **1** a flat rectangular part of something such as a door or wall, often raised above or sunk in the surface **2** a strip of fabric in a garment **3** a wooden surface for painting **4** a surface on which measuring instruments are mounted **5** a group of people who discuss an issue or debate before an audience **6** a list of people for jury duty ■ *vt* supply something with panels

pan·el·ing /pánn'ling/ *n* **1** a decorative wooden wall covering **2** a panel-covered wall

pan·el·ist /pánn'list/ *n* a member of a panel

pan·el truck *n* a small enclosed delivery truck or van

pang *n* **1** a sharp pain **2** an intense emotion

Pan·ge·a /pan jeè ə/ *n* a hypothetical ancient supercontinent thought to have incorporated all the Earth's major landmasses before the beginning of continental drift

pan·go·lin /páng gəlin, pang gólin/ *n* a scaly mammal with a long snout and a sticky tongue for catching ants and termites

pan·han·dle /pán hànd'l/ *n* **1** a handle of a cooking pan **2** *also* **Pan·han·dle** a strip of land that extends away from the state it belongs to ■ *v* (-**dled**, -**dling**) **1** *vi* beg money from strangers **2** *vt* get by begging **3** *vt* beg money from —**pan·han·dler** *n*

pan·ic /pánnik/ *n* overpowering fear or anxiety ■ *adj* of or caused by panic ◇ *panic selling on the stock market* ■ *vti* (-**icked**, -**ick·ing**) be or make extremely afraid —**pan·ick·y** *adj*

ORIGIN *Panic* is based on a Greek word meaning "of Pan." Pan, the god of nature in Greek mythology, was believed to frequent lonely spots and to frighten people by suddenly appearing or making noises. The earliest use of *panic* is as an adjective, in phrases such as *panic terror*, which came via French from modern Latin *panicus terror*. The adjective and noun are both recorded from the early 17C.

---

pan·ic at·tack *n* a sudden overpowering feeling of fear or anxiety

pan·ic but·ton *n* an alarm for summoning help

pan·ic-strick·en, pan·ic-struck *adj* affected by panic

~~panicy~~ incorrect spelling of **panicky**

Pan·ja·bi *n, adj* LANGUAGE = **Punjabi**

Emmeline Pankhurst

Pank·hurst /pángk hùrst/, **Emmeline** (1858–1928) British campaigner for woman's suffrage

pan·nier /pánnyər, pánnee ər/ *n* 1 a basket or bag on an animal, bicycle, or motorcycle, used for carrying things 2 a basket carried on somebody's back

pan·o·ply /pánnəplee/ (*pl* **-plies**) *n* 1 an impressive display or array 2 full armor 3 a protective covering

pan·o·ram·a /pànnə rámmə, -ráàmə/ *n* 1 a 360° view 2 a comprehensive survey 3 a picture with a wide view —**pan·o·ram·ic** /-rámmik/ *adj*

ORIGIN Panorama is formed from Greek words meaning "all" and "view." It was coined in the late 1780s by an Irish artist called Robert Barker for a method he had invented for painting a scene on the inside of a cylinder in such a way that its perspective would seem correct to somebody viewing it from inside the cylinder. In 1793 he opened his "Panorama," a large building in Leicester Square, London, where the public could come and gaze at such all-encompassing scenes. The modern abstract meaning was in use by the early 19C.

pan·pipes /pán pìps/ *npl* a wind instrument consisting of a set of reeds of different lengths, bound together

pan·sy /pánzee/ (*pl* **-sies**) *n* a flower with bright velvety petals

ORIGIN Pansy comes from a French word meaning literally "thought." The flower was so called because of its lowered head, thought to suggest a state of engrossed thoughtfulness.

pant *v* 1 *vi* take short fast shallow breaths 2 *vt* say breathlessly ■ *n* a shallow breath

pan·ta·loons /pàntə lóonz/ *npl* wide pants gathered at the ankle

ORIGIN Pantaloons get their name from a stock character in a form of Italian popular comedy that developed during the 16C and 17C. Pantaloon (*Pantalone* in Italian) wore tight-fitting pants in the style of the day, and these were the original **pantaloons**. The name was used again of a late 18C and early 19C fashion, and eventually became generic in application. In this general sense it was shortened to *pants*.

pan·the·ism /pánthee ìzzəm/ *n* 1 the belief that God is present in everything 2 a belief in all or many deities —**pan·the·ist** *n* —**pan·the·is·tic** /pànthee ístik/ *adj*

pan·the·on /pánthee ən, -òn/ *n* 1 a temple dedicated to all deities 2 of a specific religion 3 a memorial to dead heroes 4 the most important people in a particular field

pan·ther /pánthər/ (*pl* **-thers** *or same*) *n* 1 a black leopard 2 a mountain lion

pant·ies /pánteez/ *npl* women's or girls' underpants (*infml*)

pan·to·mime /pántə mìm/ *n* 1 a mime artist 2 a theatrical performance in ancient Rome in which one masked actor played all the characters in mime —**pan·to·mim·ist** *n*

~~pantomime~~ incorrect spelling of **pantomime**

pan·try /pántree/ (*pl* **-tries**) *n* a large cupboard or small room for storing food

pants *npl* 1 *US, Can, Aus* men's or women's trousers 2 an item of underwear that covers the buttocks and the genitals

ORIGIN Pants is a shortening of *pantaloons* that originated in North America in the mid-19C.

pant·suit /pánt sòot/, **pants suit** *n* a matching jacket and pants

pant·y·hose /pántee hòz/, **pant·y hose**, **pan·ti·hose** /pántee hòz/ *npl* a tight sheer leg covering stretching from a woman's waist to her toes

pant·y·waist /pántee wàyst/ *n* an offensive term for an effeminate man (*slang*)

pap *n* 1 semiliquid food 2 material lacking depth or substance —**pap·py** *adj*

pa·pa /paàpə, pə paá/ *n* 1 a father (*dated*) 2 **Pa·pa** /paàpə/ a communications code word for the letter "P"

pa·pa·cy /páypəssee/ (*pl* **-cies**) *n* 1 papal power or status 2 a pope's period in power

Pa·pa Doc /paàpə dók/ ♦ **Duvalier, François**

Pa·pa·go /páppə gò, paàpə-/ (*pl same or* **-gos**) *n* 1 a member of a Native North American people who live mainly in N Mexico and S Arizona 2 the language of the Papago people —**Pa·pa·go** *adj*

pa·pal /páypʹl/ *adj* of the pope

pa·pa·raz·zo /pàapə raàt sò/ (*pl* **-zi** /-seè/), **pa·pa·raz·zi** *n* a scandal-seeking photographer

pa·pa·ya /pə pí ə/ *n* 1 a tropical fruit with orange pulp and numerous seeds 2 the tree that produces papayas

pa·per /páypər/ *n* 1 a thin flat material made from wood pulp. Use: for writing and printing on, for wrapping things in, for covering walls. 2 one or more sheets of paper 3 a newspaper 4 a student's essay 5 an academic article or talk 6 wallpaper (*infml*) 7 a commercial negotiable document ■ **pa·pers** *npl* 1 personal identity documents 2 an assortment of documents ■ *adj* 1 made of or resembling paper

2 existing in documentary form ■ *vt* cover a wall with wallpaper —**pa·per·er** *n* —**pa·per·y** *adj* ◊ **on paper** in theory, but not in fact

pa·per·back /páypər bàk/ *n* a book with a thin flexible cover —**pa·per·back** *adj*

pa·per·boy /páypər bòy/ *n* a boy who delivers newspapers

pa·per chase *n* a thorough search or collation of documents

pa·per·clip /páypər klìp/, **pa·per clip** *n* a clip for holding papers together

pa·per·girl /páypər gùrl/ *n* a girl who delivers newspapers

pa·per·hang·er /páypər hàngər/ *n* somebody who hangs wallpaper

pa·per·knife /páypər-/ (*pl* **-knives** /-nìvz/) *n* a knife for opening envelopes

pa·per·less /páypərləss/ *adj* using electronic records or communications, rather than paper

pa·per mon·ey *n* bills

pa·per prof·it *n* an unrealized gain (*often pl*)

pa·per route *n* a newspaper delivery job or route

pa·per-thin *adj* extremely thin —**pa·per-thin** *adv*

pa·per ti·ger *n* a person or thing that appears to be powerful but is not

pa·per trail *n* a sequence of documents from which a series of actions can be traced (*infml*)

pa·per·weight /páypər wàyt/ *n* an object used for keeping papers in place

pa·per·work /páypər wùrk/ *n* routine clerical work

pa·pier-mâ·ché /pàypər mə sháy, pà pyay maa sháy/ *n* sheets of paper pulp and glue stuck together in layers to form objects —**pa·pier-mâ·ché** *adj*

ORIGIN Papier-mâché is a French word meaning literally "chewed paper," adopted into English in the mid-18C.

Pap·i·neau /páppinò/, **Louis Joseph** (1786–1871) Canadian politician

pa·pist /páypist/ *n* an offensive term for a member of the Roman Catholic Church —**pa·pist·ry** *n*

pa·poose /pa poóss, pə-/ *n* an offensive term for a Native North American baby or young child

pa·pri·ka /pa preékə, pə-, pápprikə/ *n* **1** a mild red spice made from sweet red peppers **2** a sweet red pepper

Pap smear *n* a test for cancer of the neck of the womb

ORIGIN Pap is shortened from the name of the Greek-born US anatomist George Papanicolaou (1883–1962).

Pap·u·a New Guin·ea /pàppyoo ə noo gínnee/ nation in the SW Pacific Ocean, comprising E New Guinea and several hundred smaller islands. Cap. Port Moresby. Pop. 5,049,055 (2001). —**Pap·u·a New Guin·e·an** *n, adj*

pa·py·rus /pə píross/ (*pl* **-ri** /-rī/ *or* **-rus·es**) *n* **1** an ancient writing material resembling paper **2** a papyrus document **3** a tall marsh plant from which papyrus was made

par *n* **1** an average level or standard **2** the accepted value of a currency **3** the value of a security at issue **4** a standard score assigned to each hole on a golf course ■ *adj* average ■ *vt* (**parred, par·ring**) in golf, score a par on a hole

para- *prefix* **1** beside, near, along with o *parameter* **2** beyond o *paranormal* **3** resembling **4** assistant, auxiliary o *paralegal* **5** parachute o *parasailing*

par·a·ble /párrəb'l/ *n* **1** a moral or religious story **2** a story ascribed to Jesus Christ

pa·rab·o·la /pə rábbələ/ *n* a curve formed by the intersection of a cone with a plane parallel to its side

par·a·chute /párrə shoot/ *n* a canopy for slowing somebody's fall from an aircraft ■ *vti* (**-chut·ed, -chut·ing**) drop by parachute —**par·a·chut·ist** *n*

pa·rade /pə ráyd/ *n* **1** a celebratory procession **2** a succession of people or things **3** a gathering of troops in formation **4** a flamboyant or flaunting exhibition of something ■ *vi* **1** march in a parade **2** assemble for a military parade

pa·rade ground *n* an area where troops gather for inspection or training

~~paradice~~ incorrect spelling of **paradise**

par·a·digm /párrə dīm/ *n* **1** an example that is typical or serves as a basis **2** a set of all possible inflections of a word, used as an example —**par·a·dig·mat·ic** /párrə dig máttik/ *adj* —**par·a·dig·mat·i·cal·ly** *adv*

par·a·digm shift *n* a radical change in somebody's basic assumptions or approach

par·a·dise /párrə dìss, -dìz/ *n* **1** a place or state of perfect happiness **2** a place that is ideally suited to somebody (*infml*) **3** also **Par·a·dise** heaven —**par·a·di·sa·ic** /párrədi sáy ik, -záy-/ *adj* —**par·a·dis·al** /párrə díss'l, -dìz'l/ *adj*

par·a·dox /párrə dòks/ *n* **1** something that is absurd or contradictory **2** a self-contradictory statement —**par·a·dox·i·cal** /párrə dóksik'l/ *adj* —**par·a·dox·i·cal·ly** *adv*

par·af·fin /párrəfin/ *n* **1** also **par·af·fin wax** a white waxy solid mixture of hydrocarbons. Use: in candles, pharmaceuticals, cosmetics, as a sealant. **2** a mixture of liquid hydrocarbons obtained from petroleum. Use: fuel. —**par·af·fin·ic** /párrə fínnik/ *adj*

~~parafin~~ incorrect spelling of **paraffin**

par·a·glid·ing /párrə glìding/ *n* the sport of gliding with a parachute —**par·a·glid·er** *n*

par·a·gon /párrə gòn, -gən/ *n* an example of excellence

par·a·graph /párrə gràf/ *n* **1** a section of written matter that begins on a new or indented line and contains a distinct idea **2** a short news story

Par·a·guay /párrə gwî, -gwày/ river in SW Brazil and Paraguay. Length 1,580 mi./2,550 km. ■ country in south central South America. Cap. Asunción. Pop. 5,734,139 (2001). —**Par·a·guay·an** /pàrrə gwî ən, -gwáy-/ *n, adj*

par·a·keet /párrə kèet/ *n* a small tropical parrot

par·a·le·gal /pàrrə leėg'l/ *n* a lawyer's assistant who has specialist legal training —**par·a·le·gal** *adj*

~~paralel~~ incorrect spelling of **parallel**

~~paralized~~ incorrect spelling of **paralyzed**

par·al·lax /párrə làks/ *n* **1** the apparent change in the position of an object caused by a change in the observer's position **2** the angle used to measure an astronomical object's distance from the Earth —**par·al·lac·tic** /pàrrə láktik/ *adj*

⚡ **par·al·lel** /párrə lèl/ *adj* **1** describes lines, planes, and curved surfaces that are always the same distance apart **2** having many characteristics in common **3** of a computer that processes several items of information simultaneously ■ *n* **1** each of a set of parallel lines or planes **2** somebody or something that shares many characteristics with another **3** a comparison **4** an imaginary line around the Earth that is parallel to the equator and represents a degree of latitude **5** a configuration of electrical components that distributes current evenly ■ *vt* **1** run parallel to **2** follow a similar course to ■ *adv* in a parallel manner or position —**par·al·lel·ism** *n*

par·al·lel bars *npl* two bars on upright supports used for gymnastic exercises (+ *pl verb*) ■ *n* the sports event in which gymnasts use the parallel bars (+ *sing verb*)

par·al·lel·o·gram /pàrrə léllə gràm/ *n* a four-sided geometrical figure in which opposite sides are parallel and of equal length

⚡ **par·al·lel port** *n* a computer connection point through which data can be sent and received simultaneously

⚡ **par·al·lel pro·cess·ing** *n* the use of multiple processors to run different parts of the same computer program concurrently

pa·ral·y·sis /pə rálləssiss/ *n* **1** the loss of voluntary movement as a result of damage to nerve or muscle function **2** failure to take action or make progress

par·a·lyt·ic /pàrrə líttik/ *adj* relating to loss of voluntary movement

par·a·lyze /párrə lìz/ (-**lyzed**, -**lyz·ing**) *vt* **1** cause somebody to lose the ability to move a part of the body **2** make temporarily unable to move, e.g., with fear **3** bring to a standstill

Par·a·mar·i·bo /pàrrə márrə bõ/ capital of Suriname. Pop. 289,000 (1997).

par·a·med·ic /pàrrə méddik/ *n* somebody trained to give treatment in a medical emergency —**par·a·med·i·cal** *adj*

pa·ram·e·ter /pə rámmətər/ *n* **1** a limiting factor or restriction o *working within the parameters of our budget* **2** a measurable variable quantity in a set that determines a system **3** a variable mathematical value —**par·a·met·ric** /pàrrə méttrik/ *adj*

par·a·mil·i·tar·y /pàrrə míllə tèrree/ *adj* **1** military in style **2** assisting official military forces **3** using military tactics and weapons against the official ruling power ■ *n* (*pl* -**ies**) a member of a paramilitary organization

par·a·mount /párrə mòwnt/ *adj* greatest in importance or significance —**par·a·mount·ly** *adv*

par·a·mour /párrə mòor/ *n* a lover (*literary*)

Pa·ra·ná /pàrrə naá/ **1** river flowing southward from SW Brazil through east central South America into the Río de la Plata in Argentina. Length 1,740 mi./2,800 km. **2** city in NE Argentina. Pop. 207,041 (1991).

par·a·noi·a /pàrrə nóy ə/ *n* **1** extreme suspicion or distrust **2** a psychiatric disorder involving delusion —**par·a·noid** /párrə nòyd/ *adj, n*

par·a·nor·mal /pàrrə náwrm'l/ *adj* not able to be explained scientifically ■ *n* paranormal events or phenomena —**par·a·nor·mal·ly** *adv*

par·a·pet /párrəpət, párrə pèt/ *n* **1** a low wall at the edge of a bridge or balcony **2** a protective wall of earth along the edge of a military trench

~~paraphanalia~~ incorrect spelling of **paraphernalia**

par·a·pher·na·lia /pàrrəfər náylee ə/ *n* assorted objects or items of equipment

ORIGIN Paraphernalia was originally a legal term for property that remained a woman's own when she married, in contrast to her dowry, which belonged to her husband. It derives from a Greek word meaning literally "beside the dowry." Paraphernalia came to be used for any personal belongings and bits and pieces in the mid-18C.

par·a·phrase /párrə fràyz/ *vt* (-**phrased**, -**phras·ing**) rephrase and simplify ■ *n* a paraphrased version —**par·a·phras·tic** /pàrrə frástik/ *adj*

par·a·ple·gi·a /pàrrə pleèjə, -pleèjee ə/ *n* inability to move the lower body —**par·a·ple·gic** *adj, n*

par·a·psy·chol·o·gy /pàrrə sī kólləjee/ *n* the study of unexplained mental phenomena —**par·a·psy·cho·log·i·cal** /pàrrə sīkə lójjik'l/ *adj* —**par·a·psy·chol·o·gist** *n*

para·sail·ing /párrə sàyling/ *n* the activity of

hanging from a parachute behind a speedboat

par·a·scend·ing /párrə sènding/ *n* the activity of parachuting to earth after rising into the air while being towed

par·a·site /párrə sìt/ *n* **1** an organism living on or in another without benefit to the host **2** a scrounger —**par·a·sit·ic** /párrə síttik/ *adj*

par·a·sol /párrə sàwl/ *n* an umbrella that provides shade from the sun

par·a·stat·al /párrə stáyt'l/ *adj* indirectly controlled by a state ■ *n* a parastatal organization

par·a·troop·er /párrə tròopər/ *n* a soldier trained to use a parachute —**par·a·troops** *npl*

par·boil /paár bòyl/ *vt* partly cook by boiling

Par·cae /paársee/ *npl* in Roman mythology, the Fates. Greek equivalent **Moirai**

par·cel /paárs'l/ *n* **1** something wrapped up in paper or other packaging **2** a piece of land split off a larger piece ■ *vt* wrap into a parcel

□ **parcel out** *vt* divide and distribute

par·cel post *n* the postal service for parcels

parch *vt* make extremely dry by depriving of water

parched *adj* **1** very thirsty (*infml*) **2** dry from lack of rainfall ◊ See note at **dry**

parch·ment /paárchmənt/ *n* **1** a former writing material made from animal hide **2** a document written on parchment **3** thick high-quality paper

ORIGIN Ultimately **parchment** is named for two places: the city of Pergamum in Asia Minor, and the ancient kingdom of Parthia, in the northeast of present-day Iran. Pergamum was noted for its writing materials, and Parthia for a scarlet leather. Two Latin words became blended and resulted in the French word that English adopted as **parchment**.

par·don /paárd'n/ *vt* **1** forgive somebody for wrongdoing **2** excuse somebody for something impolite ■ *n* **1** the act of releasing somebody from punishment **2** a document authorizing freedom from punishment —**par·don·a·ble** *adj* —**par·don·a·bly** *adv*

pare /pair/ (**pared, par·ing**) *vt* **1** remove the skin of a vegetable or fruit **2** trim fingernails or toenails ◊ See note at **pair**

par·ent /páirənt/ *n* **1** a mother, father, or legal guardian **2** the origin or source of something ■ *vt* act as a parent to a child —**pa·ren·tal** /pə rént'l/ *adj* —**par·ent·hood** *n* —**par·ent·ing** *n*

par·ent·age /páirəntij/ *n* **1** somebody's parents **2** the origin of something

pa·ren·the·sis /pə rénthəssiss/ (*pl* -**ses** /-seez/) *n* **1** one of a pair of curved signs, (), used to distinguish qualifying words and phrases from surrounding text **2** a word or phrase within parentheses —**par·en·thet·i·cal** /párrən théttik'l/ *adj*

Par·ent-Teach·er As·so·ci·a·tion *n* a school organization of parents and teachers

pa·reve /paárəvə/, **par·veh** /paárvə/, **par·ve** *adj* describes food that, under Jewish law, is neither meat nor a dairy product

par ex·cel·lence /paar èksə laáNss/ *adj* of the highest quality

par·fait /paar fáy/ *n* **1** a dessert of ice cream, fruit, syrup, and whipped cream **2** a creamy frozen dessert

par·he·li·on /paar héelee ən, -héelyən/ (*pl* -**a** /-lee ə/) *n* a bright spot on either side of the Sun, caused by ice crystals in the atmosphere diffracting light

pa·ri·ah /pə rí ə/ *n* **1** an outcast **2** somebody of low caste in South Asia

par·ing knife *n* a small kitchen knife for paring vegetables and fruit

Par·is[1] /párriss/ *n* in Greek mythology, the Trojan prince whose abduction of Helen started the Trojan War

Par·is[2] /párriss/ *French* /pa rée/ capital of France. Pop. 2,125,246 (1999). —**Pa·ri·si·an** /pə réezh'n/ *adj, n*

par·ish /párrish/ *n* **1** a district with its own church **2** the people of a parish

pa·rish·ion·er /pə ríshənər/ *n* a member of a parish

par·i·ty /párrətee/ *n* **1** equality of status, pay, or value **2** equivalence in the exchange rate between currencies

park *n* **1** an area of land for public recreation **2** a protected area of countryside **3** an area of land developed for commercial enterprises ○ *an industrial park* **4** a stadium or sports field ■ *v* **1** *vti* stop and leave a vehicle **2** *vti* maneuver a motor vehicle into a space **3** *vt* leave something somewhere (*slang*) —**park·ing** *n*

par·ka /paárkə/ *n* **1** a long, hooded jacket **2** an Arctic coat made of animal skin

par·kade /paár kàyd/ *n* *Can* a multilevel parking lot

Par·ker /paárkər/, **Bonnie** (1910–34) US outlaw. With Clyde Barrow she robbed banks and killed 12 people.

Par·ker, Charlie (1920–55) US jazz saxophonist and composer

Par·ker /paárkər/, **Dorothy** (1893–1967) US writer, critic, and humorist

park·ing light *n* a small light on a vehicle

park·ing lot *n* a place where people park their motor vehicles

park·ing me·ter *n* a coin-operated roadside meter for buying parking time

Par·kin·son's dis·ease /paárkins'nz-/ *n* a progressive nervous disorder marked by trembling and a slow shuffling walk

ORIGIN Parkinson's disease is named for the British physician James Parkinson (1755–1824), who described it.

Par·kin·son's law *n* the theory that work expands to fill the available time

ORIGIN Parkinson's law is named for the British historian C. Northcote Parkinson (1909–93), who formulated it.

park·land /páark lànd/ *n* the land in a park

Rosa Parks

Parks, Rosa (*b.* 1913) US civil rights leader

park·way /páark wày/ *n* US, Can, Aus a wide road bordered by grass and trees

~~parlement~~ incorrect spelling of **parliament**

par·lance /páarlənss/ *n* 1 a style of speech or writing 2 speech

par·lay /páar làv, -leē/ *vt* (-layed, -lay·ing) 1 stake an original bet and its winnings on 2 make good use of an advantage ■ *n* a parlaying of a bet

SPELLCHECK Do not confuse the spelling of **parlay** and **parley** ("negotiate"), which sound similar.

par·ley /páarleē/ *vi* (-leyed, -ley·ing) talk or negotiate ■ *n* (*pl* -leys) a round of talks or negotiations ◊ See note at **parlay**

par·lia·ment /páarləmənt/ *n* 1 a nation's legislative body 2 **Par·lia·ment** the legislative body of the United Kingdom and other countries —**par·lia·men·ta·ry** /pàarlə méntəree, -méntree/ *adj*

ORIGIN Parliament is adopted from French *parlement*, which was formed from *parler* "speak." The French word meant originally "conversation, conference," and then "consultative body." Both these meanings passed into English, though only the second survives. The *-ia-* spelling derives from the form of the word in texts written in England using Latin.

par·lia·men·tar·i·an /pàarlə men táiree ən, -mən-/ *n* 1 a member of a parliament 2 an expert in parliamentary procedures and history

par·lor /páarlər/ *n* 1 a living room for entertaining guests 2 a room equipped to provide particular goods or services (*often in combination*) ○ *a beauty parlor*

par·lor car *n* a comfortable North American railroad passenger car

par·lous /páarləss/ *adj* unsafe or uncertain (*archaic or humorous*)

Par·ma /páarmə/ city in north central Italy. Pop. 167,523 (1999).

Par·men·i·des /paar ménni deèz/ (*fl* 500 BC) Greek philosopher

Par·me·san /páarmə zàn, -zàan/ *n* a pale hard strong-tasting cheese

ORIGIN Parmesan means literally "of Parma," the Italian city where the cheese is traditionally made. The actual form of the word comes from French. *Parmesan cheese* is first recorded in English in the early 16C.

Par·nas·sus /paar nássəss/ mountain in central Greece. Height 8,061 ft./2,457 m.

Par·nell /paar nél, páarn'l/, **Charles Stewart** (1846–91) Irish politician

pa·ro·chi·al /pə rṓkee əl/ *adj* 1 limited in interests and perspective 2 of a parish —**pa·ro·chi·al·ism** *n*—**pa·ro·chi·al·ly** *adv*

pa·ro·chi·al school *n* a school affiliated with a church

par·o·dy /párrədee/ *n* (*pl* -dies) 1 a comic or satirical imitation of a literary or artistic work 2 parodies in general ■ *vt* (-died, -dies) write or perform a parody of —**pa·rod·i·cal** /pə róddik'l/ *adj*—**par·o·dist** *n*

pa·role /pə rṓl/ *n* 1 the early release of a prisoner conditional on good behavior 2 a promise given by a prisoner of war as a condition of release ■ *vt* (-roled, -rol·ing) release a prisoner on parole

~~parrot~~ incorrect spelling of **parrot**

par·ox·ysm /párrək sìzzəm/ *n* 1 a sudden outburst of emotion 2 a sudden onset or intensification of a symptom

par·quet /paar káy/ *n* 1 flooring consisting of wood blocks laid in a decorative pattern 2 the main floor of a theater ■ *vt* cover a floor with parquet

Parr /paar/, **Catherine** (1512–48) queen of England (1543–47) as the sixth wife of Henry VIII

~~parrallel~~ incorrect spelling of **parallel**

par·ri·cide /párrə sìd/ *n* 1 the murder of a parent or close relative 2 somebody who commits parricide —**par·ri·cid·al** /pàrrə síd'l/ *adj*

par·rot /párrət/ *n* 1 a brightly colored tropical bird, some species of which can mimic speech 2 somebody who repeats the words of another by rote ■ *vt* repeat by rote —**par·rot·er** *n*

par·rot·fish /párrət fìsh/ (*pl same or* -fish·es) *n* a tropical fish with a beak-like jaw

par·ry /párree/ (-ried, -ries) *v* 1 *vti* turn a blow aside 2 *vt* avoid answering a question —**par·ry** *n*

⨍ parse /paarss/ (parsed, pars·ing) *v* 1 *vti* describe the grammatical role of a word or structure of a sentence 2 *vt* analyze computer input in a specified language against the formal grammar of that language

Par·see /paar seè, páar seè/, **Par·si** /n a member of a Zoroastrian group living in South Asia —**Par·see** *adj*—**Par·see·ism** *n*

⚡ **pars·er** /paársər/ n a computer program for analyzing input

par·si·mo·ni·ous /paàrsə mṓnee əss/ adj frugal —**par·si·mo·ni·ous·ly** adv —**par·si·mo·ny** /paársə mṓnee/ n

pars·ley /paárslee/ n an herb of the carrot family with compound leaves. Use: in cooking, as a garnish.

pars·nip /paársnip/ n 1 a whitish root vegetable shaped like a carrot 2 the plant that produces parsnips

par·son /paárs'n/ n 1 an Episcopal minister 2 a Protestant minister

ORIGIN Parson is in origin the same word as *person*, and in early texts both forms are used in both senses. How the meaning "minister" developed is not clear: suggestions include that the minister was an "important person," or that he was the "person" legally responsible for the parish.

par·son·age /paárs'nij/ n a parson's house

part n 1 a portion or section 2 a separable piece or component 3 an integral or essential feature or component ○ *be a part of the community* 4 an actor's role 5 somebody's involvement or influence ○ *his part in the crime* 6 somebody's side or viewpoint ○ *You always take her part.* 7 a separate musical role 8 a dividing line in hair ■ **parts** npl a region (infml) ○ *unheard of in these parts* ■ v 1 vti move or be moved apart ○ *Part them to keep them from fighting.* 2 vti divide or be divided into parts 3 vt divide hair along a line 4 vi end a relationship ■ adj partial ■ adv partially ◇ **for the most part** in general, or mostly ◇ **in part** to an extent ◇ **part and parcel** an indivisible element ◇ **take part** be actively involved

□ **part with** vt give something up or away

par·take /paar táyk/ (-took /-tŏŏk/, -tak·en /-táykən/, -tak·ing) vi 1 eat or drink something 2 participate —**par·tak·er** n

par·the·no·gen·e·sis /paárthənō jénnəssiss/ n reproduction without fertilization —**par·the·no·ge·net·ic** /-jə néttik/ adj

par·tial /paársh'l/ adj 1 not complete or total 2 affecting parts but not the whole 3 having a strong liking 4 biased —**par·tial·ly** adv —**par·tial·ness** n

par·ti·al·i·ty /paárshee állətee/ n 1 fondness for something 2 a biased attitude or biased behavior

par·tic·i·pant /paar tíssəpənt/ n somebody who takes part in something ■ adj participating

par·tic·i·pate /paar tíssə pàyt/ (-pat·ed, -pat·ing) vi take part in something —**par·tic·i·pa·tion** /paar tíssə páysh'n/ n —**par·tic·i·pa·to·ry** /-tíssəpə tàwree/ adj

par·ti·ci·ple /paárti sípp'l/ n a verb form that is used to form complex tenses —**par·ti·cip·i·al** /paárti síppee əl/ adj

~~particlar~~ incorrect spelling of **particular**

par·ti·cle /paártik'l/ n 1 a tiny piece or speck ○ *airborne particles* 2 a tiny amount ○ *not a particle of truth in it* 3 a unit of matter smaller than the atom or its main components 4 an adverb or preposition that forms part of a phrasal verb

par·ti·cle·board /paártik'l bàwrd/ n US, NZ board from bonded sawdust or wood particles

par·ti·cle phys·ics n the branch of physics that deals with the study of subatomic particles (+ sing verb)

par·ti·col·ored, par·ty·col·ored adj multicolored

par·tic·u·lar /pər tíkyələr/ adj 1 that is one out of several 2 personal and different from others ○ *a particular dislike* 3 great or more than usual ○ *take particular care* 4 special and worth mentioning ○ *I have no particular objection.* 5 fussy or choosy ■ n an individual fact, detail, or item (often pl) —**par·tic·u·lar·ly** adv ◇ **in particular** specifically or especially

par·tic·u·lar·i·ty /pər tíkyə lérrətee/ n (pl -ties) (fml) 1 concern for accuracy 2 an individual fact, detail, or item

par·tic·u·lar·ize /pər tíkyələ rìz/ (-ized, -iz·ing) vt 1 make particular to one person or thing 2 provide with specific examples

part·ing /paárting/ n a leaving or departing ■ adj done, made, or given while leaving

part·ing shot n a final hostile remark made on leaving

par·ti·san /paártiz'n, -zàn/, **par·ti·zan** n 1 a strong supporter 2 a resistance fighter ■ adj showing strong and sometimes biased support —**par·ti·san·ship** n

par·ti·tion /paar tísh'n/ n 1 a structure that divides a space 2 the division of a country into separate countries 3 a division into parts (fml) ■ vt 1 divide a room with a partition 2 split a country into separate countries —**par·ti·tion·ist** n

par·ti·tive /paártətiv/ adj 1 separating (fml) 2 describes a grammatical construction that expresses a part of something ■ n a partitive construction

part·ly /paártlee/ adv not wholly

part·ner /paártnər/ n 1 somebody who shares in an activity 2 each member of a couple in a relationship 3 somebody joined in a dance or game with somebody else 4 a business associate ■ vt be the partner of

part·ner·ship /paártnər ship/ n 1 a relationship between partners 2 cooperation 3 a group of people working together 4 a company owned by partners

part of speech n a grammatical category of words with the same function in sentences

par·took past tense of **partake**

par·tridge /paártrij/ n 1 a medium-sized game bird 2 the meat of a partridge

part-time *adj, adv* for less than the usual amount of time —**part-tim·er** *n*

par·tu·ri·tion /pàart⋅a rísh'n, pàarcha-/ *n* the act of giving birth (*fml or technical*)

part·way /paàrt wày/ *adv* some of the way

par·ty /paàrtee/ *n* (*pl* **-ties**) **1** a social gathering for enjoyment **2** a group of people doing something together **3** a political organization that seeks office or power **4** one side in an agreement or dispute ■ *vi* (**-tied, -ties**) socialize or enjoy yourself at a party (*infml*) —**par·ty·er** *n*

par·ty·go·er /paàrtee gò ar/ *n* an attender of a party

par·ty line *n* **1** the official policy of a political party **2** a telephone line shared by more than one user

par·ty pol·i·tics *n* party-oriented political activity (+ *sing or pl verb*) —**par·ty-po·lit·i·cal** *adj*

par val·ue *n* the value of a security at issue

par·ve·nu /paàrva noò, paàrva noó/ *n* (*pl* **-nus**) somebody who is newly rich or influential

Pas·a·de·na /pàssa deéna/ **1** city in SW California. Pop. 134,587 (1998). **2** city in SE Texas. Pop. 133,964 (1998).

pas·cal /pa skál, paa skaàl/ *n* (*symbol* **Pa**) a unit of pressure or stress equal to one newton per square meter

ORIGIN The **pascal** is named for the 17C French philosopher and mathematician Blaise Pascal.

⚡ Pas·cal /pa skál, paa skaàl/ *n* a high-level computer programming language

ORIGIN The name **Pascal** alludes to the 17C French philosopher and mathematician Blaise Pascal, but was also seen as an acronym from French *programme appliqué à la sélection et la compilation automatique de la littérature.*

Pas·cal /pa skál, paa skaàl/, **Blaise** (1623–62) French philosopher and mathematician

pas de deux /paà da dǿ/ (*pl* **pas de deux** /*pronunc. same*/) *n* a ballet dance for two people

~~passenger~~ incorrect spelling of **passenger**

pash·mi·na /pàsh meéna/ *n* (*pl* **-nas**) **1** a fine fabric made from goat's wool **2** a shawl made from pashmina

Pash·to /púshtô/ (*pl* **same** or **-tos**) *n* **1** an official language of Afghanistan **2** somebody whose native language is Pashto —**Pash·to** *adj*

Pash·tun /push toón/ (*pl* **-tuns** or **same**) *n* a member of a people who live in E and S Afghanistan and NW Pakistan

pass *v* **1** *vti* move past a place or person **2** *vti* throw a ball, or hit a puck, to another player **3** *vt* hand something over **4** *vti* move or be moved in a particular way ○ *passed his hand along the banister* **5** *vi* extend past, through,

or along something **6** *vi* undergo change **7** *vt* spend time **8** *vi* elapse **9** *vi* come to an end **10** *vti* be successful in an exam or subject **11** *vti* approve or get approval for something such as legislation **12** *vi* die (*fml*) **13** *vi* in card games, not raise a bid **14** *vt* excrete something from the body **15** *vt* give a judgment, opinion, or comment ■ *n* **1** a document granting something such as a privilege **2** an act of passing a ball or puck to another player **3** a successful grade in an exam or subject **4** a way through mountains (*often in place names*) **5** an uninvited attempt to kiss or touch somebody sexually **6** in card games, a failure to bid ◊ **let something pass** make no comment or intervention ◊ See note at **past**

☐ **pass away** or **on** *vi* die

☐ **pass out** *vi* faint

☐ **pass up** *vt* forgo

pass·a·ble /pássab'l/ *adj* **1** acceptable **2** able to be crossed or traveled on —**pass·a·bly** *adv*

SPELLCHECK Do not confuse the spelling of **passable** and **possible** ("likely"), which sound similar.

pas·sage /pássij/ *n* **1** a corridor or pathway **2** a way through an obstruction **3** a section of a piece of writing or music **4** the process of time passing **5** a trip **6** the right to travel as a passenger **7** the approval of a new law **8** a tube in the body

pas·sage·way /pássij way/ *n* a corridor or pathway

pass·book /páss boök/ *n* a customer's book containing a record of bank transactions

pas·sé /pa sáy/ *adj* **1** out of date **2** no longer in prime condition

pas·sen·ger /pássanjar/ *n* somebody traveling in a vehicle

pas·sen·ger seat *n* the seat in the front of a vehicle next to the driver's seat

pas·ser·by /pl **pas·sers-by**/ *n* somebody who happens to be going past a place

pas·sim /pássim/ *adv* indicates various occurrences in a book

pass·ing /pássing/ *adj* **1** going past **2** transitory **3** brief and without paying much attention ■ *n* **1** the fact of ceasing to exist **2** the elapsing of time **3** death (*euphemistic*) ◊ See note at **temporary**

pas·sion /pásh'n/ *n* **1** intense emotion **2** strong sexual desire **3** intense enthusiasm **4** an object of an enthusiasm **5 Pas·sion** in Christianity, the sufferings of Jesus Christ after the Last Supper ■ **pas·sions** *npl* emotions —**pas·sion·less** *adj* ◊ See note at **love**

pas·sion·ate /pásh'nat/ *adj* **1** showing sexual desire **2** showing intense emotion —**pas·sion·ate·ly** *adv*

pas·sion·flow·er /pásh'n flòwr/ *n* a climbing vine with large flowers

pas·sion fruit *n* the edible fruit of the passionflower

Pas·sion play *n* a play about Jesus Christ's sufferings

pas·sive /pássiv/ *adj* 1 not actively taking part 2 obeying readily 3 affected or produced by something external ○ *passive solar heat gain* 4 describes a verb form or voice that expresses an action done to the subject of the verb ■ *n* the passive voice, or a verb in the passive voice —**pas·sive·ly** *adv* —**pas·sive·ness** *n* —**pas·siv·ism** *n* —**pas·siv·i·ty** /pa sívvətee/ *n*

pas·sive re·sis·tance *n* nonviolent resistance —**pas·sive re·sist·er** *n*

pas·sive smok·ing *n* the breathing in of other people's tobacco smoke

pass·key /páss kèe/ (*pl* -keys) *n* 1 a master key 2 a skeleton key

Pass·over /páss òvər/ *n* a Jewish festival marking the exodus of the Israelites from Egypt. Date: seven or eight days from the 14th day of Nisan.

pass·port /páss pàwrt/ *n* 1 an official identification document giving the bearer the right to travel 2 a means of access

pass-through *n* an opening in a kitchen wall

passtime incorrect spelling of **pastime**

⚡ **pass·word** /páss wùrd/ *n* 1 a word that must be used to gain access 2 a sequence of keyed characters giving access to a computer system or program

past[1] *prep, adv* 1 moving beyond a person or thing ○ *walked past without saying a word* 2 later than a time ○ *past his bedtime* ■ *prep* 1 on the farther side of ○ *the bakery past the school* 2 beyond a number, amount, or point ○ *Do what you like; I'm past caring.* ◇ **not put it past somebody** believe that somebody is capable of doing something (*infml*)

past[2] *adj* 1 elapsed or gone by ○ *the past few days* 2 having existed or occurred at an earlier time 3 one-time or former 4 describes a verb tense that expresses an action that took place previously ■ *n* 1 the time before the present 2 somebody's previous history 3 a shameful personal history 4 the past tense, or verb on the past tense

USAGE past or **passed**? Do not confuse these two words. Consider these examples: *He passed me at 80 mph; She is the past president of our sorority.* In the first example, the past tense of the verb *pass*, which is **passed**, is required: *He passed me....* In the second sentence the adjective **past** ("one-time, former") is required: *She is the past president....*

pas·ta /paástə, pástə/ *n* 1 a food made from flour, eggs, and water and formed into many shapes 2 a dish made with cooked pasta

⚡ **paste** /payst/ *n* 1 a soft adhesive mixture 2 a semisolid mixture 3 a soft food substance such as a spread or pastry dough 4 glass used to make imitation gems 5 porcelain clay ■ *vt* (past·ed, past·ing) 1 stick things together or on a surface using paste 2 place text, data, or an image in a document electronically

paste·board /páyst bàwrd/ *n* thick stiff paper ■ *adj* flimsy ○ *pasteboard houses*

pas·tel /pa stél/ *adj* having a pale soft color ■ *n* 1 a pale soft color 2 a paste used for making artists' crayons 3 an artist's crayon 4 a drawing done with pastels —**pas·tel·ist** *n*

pas·tern /pástərn/ *n* the part of a horse's foot between the fetlock and the top of the hoof

Pas·ter·nak /pástər nàk/, **Boris Leonidovich** (1890–1960) Soviet poet and author

paste-up *n* a number of sheets with printed pages pasted on them for checking

Pas·teur /pas túr, pas tyúr, paass-/, **Louis** (1822–95) French scientist. He developed the process of pasteurization and vaccinations to induce immunity against certain viral diseases.

pas·teur·ize /páscha rìz, pástə-/ (-ized, -iz·ing) *vt* treat a liquid by heating it in order to destroy harmful bacteria —**pas·teur·i·za·tion** /pàschəri záysh'n, pàstəri-/ *n*

pas·tiche /pa steésh, paa-/ *n* a literary or artistic work that borrows from or imitates other works

pas·tille /pa steél/ *n* 1 a lozenge 2 a substance burned as an incense or fumigant

pas·time /páss tìm/ *n* an agreeable activity

past mas·ter *n* an expert

pas·tor /pástər/ *n* a religious minister —**pas·tor·ship** *n*

pas·tor·al /pástərəl/ *adj* 1 rural 2 idealizing rural life 3 of religious ministers or their duties —**pas·tor·al·ly** *adv*

past par·ti·ci·ple *n* a participle expressing completed action in the past

past per·fect *n* the verb tense that uses "had" plus a past participle —**past per·fect** *adj*

pas·tra·mi /pə straámee/ *n* spicy smoked beef eaten cold in thin slices

Pas·tra·na /pa straánə/, **Andrés** (*b.* 1954) president of Colombia (1998–)

pas·try /páystree/ *n* 1 dough for pies 2 food, or an item of food, made from pastry

pas·tur·age /páschərij/ *n* 1 land for grazing 2 the grazing of livestock

pas·ture /páschər/ *n* 1 land for grazing 2 plants that animals graze on ■ *vti* (-tured, -tur·ing) graze, or put to graze

pas·ture·land /páschər lànd/ *n* land used for pasture

pasturized incorrect spelling of **pasteurized**

past·y /páystee/ (-i·er, -i·est) *adj* 1 unhealthily pale 2 resembling paste —**past·i·ness** *n*

PA sys·tem *n* a sound-amplification system. Full form **public-address system**

pat[1] *vt* (**pat·ted, pat·ting**) 1 hit lightly with the palm of the hand 2 touch repeatedly with the palm of the hand to show affection 3 shape with the hands ■ *n* 1 a light blow or touch 2 a piece of a soft substance, especially butter 3 a soft sound

pat[2] *adv* 1 exactly or fluently o *He has his part down pat.* 2 at the most appropriate time or place ■ *adj* glib o *a pat answer*

pa·ta·ca /pə táakə/ *n* the main unit of currency of Macau

Pat·a·go·ni·a /pàttə gṓnee ə/ region of S Argentina, between the Andes Mountains and the South Atlantic Ocean —**Pat·a·go·ni·an** *n, adj*

⚡**patch** *n* 1 a piece of material that covers or mends a hole 2 a small area within a larger one 3 a small area of land where something is grown o *a cabbage patch* 4 a pad or shield worn over a damaged eye 5 a cover for a wound 6 a sewn-on badge 7 a fix or update for a bug in software ■ *vt* 1 mend or repair with a patch 2 sew from cloth pieces o *patched up their friendship* 3 fix or update with a software patch

patch·ou·li /pə chōolee, páchəlee/, **pach·ou·li** *n* 1 an aromatic oil. Use: perfumes, aromatherapy. 2 a bush of the mint family whose leaves produce patchouli

patch·work /pách wùrk/ *n* 1 needlework in which patches of cloth are sewn together 2 a collection of dissimilar parts

patch·y /páchee/ (**-i·er, -i·est**) *adj* 1 occurring in patches 2 of varying quality —**patch·i·ly** *adv* —**patch·i·ness** *n*

pate *n* a head (*archaic or humorous*)

pâ·té /paa táy/ *n* a spreadable food made from meat, fish, or vegetables

pâ·té de foie gras /paa tày də fwaa graá/ *n* pâté made from the livers of fattened geese

pa·tel·la /pə téllə/ (*pl* **-lae** /-lee/ *or* **-las**) *n* the kneecap (*technical*) —**pa·tel·lar** *adj*

pat·ent *n* /páttˈnt/ 1 an exclusive right to make and sell an invention 2 an invention protected by a patent 3 a land ■ *adj* /páytˈnt, páttˈnt/ 1 clear or obvious 2 protected by patent ■ *vt* /páttˈnt/ 1 protect by patent 2 grant a patent to —**pat·ent·ly** *adv*

pat·ent leath·er *n* leather with a glossy surface

pat·ent med·i·cine *n* a nonprescription medicine

pa·ter·fa·mil·i·as /pàytər fə mílee əss, pàatər-/ (*pl* **-tres·fa·mil·i·as** /pàytreez-, pàatreez-/) *n* a man in the role of father or head of household

pa·ter·nal /pə túrnˈl/ *adj* 1 of fathers or fatherhood 2 related through or inherited from a father —**pa·ter·nal·ly** *adv*

pa·ter·nal·ism /pə túrnˈl ìzzəm/ *n* an approach to relationships or management in which the desire to help and advise neglects personal choice and responsibility —**pa·ter·nal·is·tic** /pə tùrnˈl ístik/ *adj*

pa·ter·ni·ty /pə túrnətee/ *n* 1 fatherhood 2 descent from a father

pa·ter·ni·ty leave *n* time off work granted to a new father

pa·ter·ni·ty suit *n* a lawsuit for financial support brought by a woman against a man who she claims is her child's father

pa·ter·ni·ty test *n* a genetic test to determine fatherhood

pa·ter·nos·ter /pàatər nóstər, pàytər-/, **Pa·ter·nos·ter** *n* in Roman Catholicism, the Lord's Prayer

path /paath/ *n* 1 a track made by people repeatedly walking on it 2 a surfaced track for walking or cycling 3 a route along which something moves o *the Earth's path around the Sun* 4 a course of action

-path *suffix* 1 somebody with a particular disorder o *sociopath* 2 somebody who practices a particular type of remedial treatment o *osteopath*

pa·thet·ic /pə théttik/ *adj* 1 arousing or expressing pity 2 contemptibly or laughably inadequate (*infml*) —**pa·thet·i·cal·ly** *adv* ◊ See note at **moving**

path·find·er /páth fìndər/ *n* a discoverer of a way through uncharted territory or knowledge —**path·find·ing** *n*

path·o·gen /páthəjən/ *n* an agent of disease such as a virus or bacterium —**path·o·gen·ic** /pàthə jénnik/ *adj*

path·o·log·i·cal /pàthə lójjik'l/ *adj* 1 uncontrolled or unreasonable o *a pathological liar* 2 of disease 3 of pathology —**path·o·log·i·cal·ly** *adv*

pa·thol·o·gy /pə thólləjee/ (*pl* **-gies**) *n* 1 the processes of a particular disease 2 a condition that is not expected or usual 3 the scientific study of disease —**pa·thol·o·gist** *n*

pa·thos /páy thàwss/ *n* 1 a quality that arouses pity 2 the expression of pity

path·way /páth wày/ *n* 1 a path or route 2 a sequence of biochemical reactions in a metabolic process

pa·tience /páysh'nss/ *n* the capacity for waiting without becoming annoyed

pa·tient /páysh'nt/ *adj* capable of waiting without becoming annoyed ■ *n* somebody who is receiving medical treatment —**pa·tient·ly** *adv*

pat·i·na /páttˈnə, pə téenə/ (*pl* **-nas** *or* **-nae** /-nee/) *n* 1 a thin green layer of corrosion on copper 2 a surface sheen

pat·i·o /páttee ò/ (*pl* **-os**) *n* 1 a paved area outside a house, used for dining or recreation 2 a roofless courtyard

pat·i·o doors *npl* doors opening onto a patio

pa·tis·se·rie /pə tíssəree/ *n* 1 a bake shop 2 pastries or cakes

Pat·na /pútnə/ capital of Bihar State, NE India. Pop. 917,243 (1991).

pat·ois /pát wàa, pa twáa/ (*pl same*) *n* 1 a regional dialect 2 a jargon of a particular group 3 **Pat·ois** a Creole language spoken on some islands of the Caribbean —**Pat·ois** *adj*

Pa·ton /páytn/, **Alan** (1903–88) South African writer and politician

patriachal incorrect spelling of **patriarchal**

pa·tri·arch /páytree aàrk/ *n* 1 the male head of a family or group 2 a respected senior man 3 a senior bishop of the Eastern Orthodox Church or one of the Eastern Christian churches that recognize papal supremacy

pa·tri·ar·chal /páytree aàrk'l/, **pa·tri·ar·chic** /-aàrkik/ *adj* 1 of a patriarch 2 of or characteristic of a culture in which men dominate

pa·tri·ar·chy /páytree aàrkee/ (*pl* **-chies**) *n* a social system or society in which men dominate

pa·tri·cian /pə trísh'n/ *n* 1 a member of an aristocracy 2 somebody with qualities associated with the aristocracy —**pa·tri·cian** *adj*

pat·ri·cide /páttri sìd/ *n* 1 the murder of a father by his child 2 somebody who commits patricide —**pat·ri·cid·al** /páttri sìd'l/ *adj*

Pat·rick /páttrik/, **St.** (389?–461?) British-born Irish cleric and the patron saint of Ireland

pat·ri·lin·e·al /páttrə línnee əl/, **pat·ri·lin·e·ar** /-ər/ *adj* tracing descent through the male line

pat·ri·mo·ny /páttrə mònee/ (*pl* **-nies**) *n* an inheritance from a male ancestor —**pat·ri·mo·ni·al** /páttrə mónee əl/ *adj*

pa·tri·ot /páytree ət, -òt/ *n* somebody who proudly supports his or her own country —**pat·ri·ot·ic** /páytree óttik/ *adj* —**pa·tri·ot·i·cal·ly** *adv* —**pa·tri·ot·ism** *n*

Pa·tri·ot Day *n* in the United States, a day commemorating those who died in the terrorist attacks of 2001. Date: September 11.

pa·trol /pə tról/ *n* 1 a regular tour of a place made by a guard 2 somebody carrying out a patrol 3 a military unit on a mission ■ *vti* (**-trolled, -trol·ing**) go on a patrol of an area

pa·trol·man /pə trólmən/ (*pl* **-men** /-mən/) *n* a patrolling police officer

pa·tron /páytrən/ *n* 1 somebody who gives money or other support 2 a regular customer —**pa·tron·al** *adj* —**pa·tron·ly** *adj* ◊ See note at **backer**

pa·tron·age /páytrənij, páttrə-/ *n* 1 appointments given by a politician to loyal supporters 2 the power to make appointments 3 regular purchasing from a store 4 the support given by a patron 5 condescending kindness

pa·tron·ize /páytrə nìz, páttrə-/ (**-ized, -iz·ing**) *vt* 1 be condescending to 2 be a regular customer of (*fml*) —**pa·tron·iz·ing** *adj* —**pa·tron·iz·ing·ly** *adv*

pa·tron saint *n* a saint believed to be a special guardian

pat·ro·nym·ic /páttrə nímmik/ *adj* derived from a male ancestor's name —**pat·ro·nym·ic** *n*

pat·sy /pátsee/ (*pl* **-sies**) *n* a person regarded as open to victimization or manipulation (*infml insult*)

pat·ter /páttər/ *vi* 1 make a quick tapping sound 2 step lightly ■ *n* a light tapping noise

ORIGIN Although both English words **patter** contain an element of speed in their meaning, there is no etymological connection between them. **Patter** "make a quick tapping sound" is a derivative of *pat* in the sense "hit." **Patter** "fast talk" is a shortening of *paternoster* "the Lord's Prayer." The modern meaning evolved from "mumble prayers quickly," the way the paternoster was said in church.

pat·ter /páttər/ *n* 1 glib and rapid talk 2 jargon

pat·tern /páttərn/ *n* 1 a repeated decorative design 2 a prototype 3 a plan or model used as a guide for making something 4 a regular or repetitive arrangement, occurrence, or way of behaving 5 a good example ■ *vt* decorate or make using a pattern

pat·terned /páttərnd/ *adj* decorated with pattern

Pat·ter·son /páttərs'n/, **Percival James** (*b.* 1935) prime minister of Jamaica (1992–)

USMA Archives, West Point

George S. Patton

Pat·ton /pátt'n/, **George S.** (1885–1945) US general

pat·ty /páttee/ (*pl* **-ties**) *n* 1 a flat individual portion of food 2 a small pie

pau·ci·ty /páwssətee/ *n* 1 an inadequacy or lack of something 2 a small number of things

Paul /pawl/, **St.** (AD 3?–62?) early Christian missionary —**Paul·ine** /páw lìn, -leèn/ *adj*

Paul III (1468–1549) pope (1534–49)

Paul, Alice (1885–1977) US feminist and social reformer

Pau·ling /páwling/, **Linus** (1901–94) US chemist and peace activist

paunch /pawnch/ *n* a big stomach —**paunch·y** *adj*

pau·per /páwpər/ *n* 1 a very poor person 2 a recipient of public aid —**pau·per·ism** *n*

Paus·a /páwzə/ n the 10th month of the Hindu calendar

pause /pawz/ vi (**paused**, **paus·ing**) 1 briefly stop doing something 2 stay briefly 3 hesitate ■ n 1 a brief stop 2 a short silence 3 a hesitation 4 a musical symbol indicating that a note is to be held longer —**paus·al** adj ◊ **give somebody pause** make somebody hesitate or reconsider ◊ See note at **hesitate**

pave /payv/ (**paved**, **pav·ing**) vt cover with a hard surface for walking or traveling on ◊ **pave the way** prepare for and facilitate

pave·ment /páyvmənt/ n a paved surface of a road

pa·vil·ion /pə vílyən/ n 1 an open, often ornamental, building in a garden or park 2 an exhibition tent 3 a large ornate tent 4 a detached building forming part of a building complex

~~pavillion~~ incorrect spelling of **pavilion**

pav·ing /páyving/ n 1 the construction of a paved surface 2 pavement 3 material for making a paved surface

Pav·lov /páv lov, -làwf/, **Ivan Petrovich** (1849–1936) Russian physiologist famous for his studies on conditioned reflexes with dogs

Pav·lo·va /pav lóvə, pávləvə/, **Anna** (1882–1931) Russian ballet dancer

paw n 1 a mammal's foot with claws or nails 2 a human hand (infml) ■ vti 1 strike something repeatedly with a paw or hoof 2 touch clumsily

pawn[1] vt 1 deposit something with a pawnbroker 2 pledge your honor, word, or life ■ n 1 an object deposited with a pawnbroker 2 a hostage

pawn[2] n 1 the chess piece of lowest value 2 a person manipulated by another

---

ORIGIN The chess **pawn** came via French from a medieval Latin word meaning "foot soldier." **Pawn** "deposit, pledge" was also adopted immediately from French, but it goes back to an ancient Germanic source.

---

pawn·bro·ker /páwn bròkər/ n a moneylender who accepts personal items as security

Paw·nee /páwnee/ (pl same or **-nees**) n 1 a member of a confederation of Native North American peoples who lived in Nebraska and Kansas and who are now mainly dispersed 2 the language of the Pawnee people —**Paw·nee** adj

pawn·shop /páwn shòp/ n a place to pawn things

paw·paw /páwpaw/ n a papaya

pax n 1 a kiss of peace given during a Roman Catholic Mass 2 a tablet kissed during a Roman Catholic Mass

pay v (**paid**) 1 vti give somebody money in return for work, goods, or services 2 vti settle a debt 3 vti bring in money ◊ How much does the job pay? 4 vti punish, or be

punished 5 vt yield interest on an investment 6 vi be profitable or beneficial ◊ Crime doesn't pay. 7 vt bestow a compliment or give attention 8 vt make a visit ■ n money given in return for work, goods, or services ■ adj requiring payment to function ◊ pay TV —**pay·ee** /pay eé/ n ◊ **put paid to** put an end to or ruin (infml) ◊ See note at **wage**

□ **pay off** v 1 vt repay in full 2 vt bribe (infml) 3 vi prove successful

pay·a·ble /páy əb'l/ adj 1 requiring payment 2 granting payment to a particular person ■ **pay·a·bles** npl liabilities

pay-as-you-go n the practice of paying debts or costs as they arise

pay·back /páy bàk/ n a return on an investment

pay·check /páy chèk/ n 1 a salary or wage check 2 wages or a salary

pay·day /páy dày/ n the day on which employees are paid

pay dirt n 1 a potentially profitable discovery 2 a mineral deposit worth mining

pay·down /páy dòwn/ n a reduction of a debt

~~payed~~ incorrect spelling of **paid**

pay·load /páy lòd/ n 1 a quantity of cargo 2 the passengers and equipment carried by an aircraft or spacecraft 3 an explosive charge of a missile

pay·mas·ter /páy màstər/ n a person in charge of paying employees

pay·ment /páymənt/ n 1 an amount paid 2 a reward or punishment 3 the act of paying

⚡ **pay·ment gate·way** n an Internet payments interface

pay·off /páy àwf, -òf/ n 1 full payment of a debt 2 a final settlement or outcome 3 ultimate benefit or advantage 4 a bribe (infml)

pay·o·la /pay óla/ n a bribe for promoting a product

pay·out /páy òwt/ n the act of paying money, or the sum paid

pay-per-view n a cable or satellite TV system in which individual programs can be watched for a fee

pay·phone /páy fòn/ n a public telephone requiring coin or card payment

pay·roll /páy ròl/ n 1 a list of paid employees 2 the total wages paid to employees

pay·stub /páy stùb/ n a pay statement

pay tel·e·vi·sion, pay TV n a system in which only viewers who have paid for unscrambling equipment can watch broadcasts

⚡ **pay·ware** /páy wàir/ n commercial software

Octavio Paz

Paz /pass, paz/, **Octavio** (1914–98) Mexican writer

Pb *symbol* lead

PBS *abbr* Public Broadcasting Service

PC[1] *abbr* **1** Peace Corps **2** politically correct

⚡**PC**[2] *n* **1** a personal computer **2** a computer compatible with IBM PCs and MS-DOS

p.c. *abbr* percent

⚡**PCI** *n* a specification for extending a computer's internal circuitry by adding circuit boards. Full form **peripheral component interconnect**

Pd *symbol* palladium

pd. *abbr* paid

p.d. *abbr* per diem

P.D. *abbr* **1** police department **2** per diem

⚡**PDA** *abbr* personal digital assistant

⚡**pdf** *n* a format or file extension for a computer document file that enables a document to be processed and printed on any computer using any printer or word-processing program. Full form **portable document format**

⚡**PDN** *abbr* public data network *(in e-mails)*

PDT *abbr* Pacific Daylight Time

PE[1] *adv* used as a non-Christian equivalent to AD in dates. Full form **Present Era**

PE[2] *abbr* Prince Edward Island

P.E. *abbr* physical education

P/E *abbr* price-earnings

pea /pee/ *n* **1** a round green seed that grows in a pod, eaten as a vegetable **2** a leguminous plant with peas in pods ■ **peas** *npl* pea pods

~~peacable~~ incorrect spelling of **peaceable**

peace /peess/ *n* **1** freedom from war **2** mental calm **3** a peace treaty **4** law and order **5** a state of harmony ■ *interj* be calm or silent ◇ **at peace** in a state of calm and serenity ◇ **hold your peace** refrain from speaking *(dated)* ◇ **keep the peace** refrain from or prevent conflict

> **SPELLCHECK** Do not confuse the spelling of **peace** and **piece** ("a part"), which sound similar.

Peace /peess/ river in central British Columbia and N Alberta, Canada. Length 1,195 mi./1,923 km.

peace·a·ble /péessəb'l/ *adj* **1** disposed toward peace **2** tranquil —**peace·a·bly** *adv*

Peace Corps *n* a US government organization of volunteers who work in developing countries

peace·ful /péessfəl/ *adj* **1** quiet and calm **2** mentally calm —**peace·ful·ly** *adv* —**peace·ful·ness** *n*

peace·keep·ing /péess kéeping/ *n* the preservation of peace, especially between formerly warring groups —**peace·keep·er** *n*

peace·mak·er /péess màykər/ *n* somebody who establishes peace

peace of·fer·ing *n* something given to an enemy to encourage reconciliation

peace pipe *n* a ceremonial Native North American pipe

peace·time /péess tìm/ *n* a period without war

peach /peech/ *n* **1** a large orange-yellow fruit with a pit **2** a tree that produces peaches **3** an excellent person or thing *(infml)*

> **ORIGIN** Etymologically the **peach** is "from Persia." The word goes back to Latin *malum persicum*, literally "Persian apple." The **peach** is actually from China, but only became familiar to western Europeans after its cultivation had spread to Persia.

peach mel·ba *n* a dessert of peaches and vanilla ice cream with a raspberry sauce

> **ORIGIN** The dish was created in honor of the Australian opera singer Dame Nellie Melba (1859–1931).

peach·y /péechee/ (**-i·er, -i·est**) *adj* resembling a peach in color, taste, or texture —**peach·i·ly** *adv*

pea·cock /pée kòk/ *n* **1** a male peafowl, whose long iridescent tail can be held up like an open fan **2** a peafowl of either sex

pea·fowl /pée fòwl/ (*pl* same *or* **-fowls**) *n* a large Asian pheasant

pea·hen /pée hèn/ *n* a female peafowl

peak /peek/ *n* **1** a pointed mountain top **2** a mountain with a pointed top **3** the point of greatest success, strength, or development **4** a pointed part ■ *vi* **1** reach the peak of success, strength, or development **2** form a peak ■ *adj* **1** maximum or highest o *peak efficiency* **2** during maximum use or demand o *peak viewing time*

> **SPELLCHECK** Do not confuse the spelling of **peak, peek** ("look quickly"), or **pique** ("bad mood"), which sound similar.

peaked[1] /peekt, péekəd/ *adj* having a peak —**peak·ed·ness** /péekədnəss/ *n*

peaked[2] /péekəd/ *adj* sickly

peak sea·son *n* the most popular time of the year for vacations

peal /peel/ *n* **1** a ringing of bells **2** a set of tuned bells **3** a noisy outburst or loud repetitive sound ○ *peals of laughter* ○ *a peal of thunder* ■ *vti* ring bells, or ring, loudly

SPELLCHECK Do not confuse the spelling of **peal** and **peel** ("remove an outer layer"), which sound similar.

Peale /peel/, **Charles Willson** (1741–1827) US artist

pea·nut /pée nùt/ *n* 1 an oily edible seed that grows underground 2 the plant that produces peanuts ■ **pea·nuts** *npl* a small amount of money (*infml*)

pea·nut but·ter *n* a spreadable food made from peanuts

pear /pair/ *n* 1 a fruit with a teardrop shape and white flesh 2 the tree that produces pears ◊ See note at **pair**

pearl /purl/ *n* 1 a small lustrous sphere formed in an oyster or other mollusk. Use: gems. 2 mother-of-pearl 3 a highly valued person or thing —**pearl·y** *adj*

pearl bar·ley *n* polished barley grains

Pearl Har·bor inlet of the Pacific Ocean on S Oahu, Hawaii. Japanese planes attacked the US naval base there on December 7, 1941, prompting the United States' entry into World War II.

Pearse /peerss/, **Patrick Henry** (1879–1916) Irish nationalist leader

pear-shaped *adj* 1 shaped like a pear 2 clear and resonant

Pear·son /péerss'n/, **Lester** (1897–1972) prime minister of Canada (1963–68)

Pea·ry /péeree/, **Robert** (1856–1920) US explorer

peas·ant /pézz'nt/ *n* 1 an agricultural laborer or small farmer 2 a country-dweller

peas·ant·ry /pézz'ntree/ *n* peasants as a class

pea·shoot·er /pée shōotər/ *n* a toy pipe through which dried peas can be blown

pea soup *n* a soup made with peas

peat /peet/ *n* 1 a deposit of compacted organic debris 2 a piece of peat used for fuel —**peat·y** *adj*

peb·ble /pébb'l/ *n* a small rounded smooth stone ■ *vt* (**-bled, -bling**) give an irregular grainy surface to leather —**peb·bly** *adj*

pe·can /pi kaàn, -kán, pée kàn/ *n* 1 an edible nut resembling a long walnut 2 the tree that produces pecans

pec·ca·dil·lo /pèkə dílló/ (*pl* **-loes** *or* **-los**) *n* a trifling offense

peck¹ /pek/ *v* 1 *vt* pick up with the beak 2 *vti* strike with the beak 3 *vi* nibble at food, eating little ■ *n* 1 a swift blow with the beak 2 a light kiss (*infml*)

peck² *n* a unit of dry measure equal to 8 quarts/9.09 liters

peck·ing or·der *n* a social hierarchy

Pe·cos /páykəss/ river flowing from E New Mexico into the Rio Grande in W Texas. Length 926 mi./1,490 km.

pecs *npl* the pectoral muscles (*infml*)

pec·tin /péktin/ *n* a substance found in plant cell walls. Use: gelling agent. —**pec·tic** *adj* —**pec·tin·ous** *adj*

pec·to·ral /péktərəl/ *adj* of the chest ■ *n* a chest muscle

pec·to·ral fin *n* a fin near a fish's gills

pe·cu·liar /pi kyóolyər/ *adj* 1 unusual or strange ○ *The situation was very peculiar.* 2 unique —**pe·cu·li·ar·i·ty** /pi kyòol yérrətee, -lee érrətee/ *n* —**pe·cu·liar·ly** *adv*

~~peculier~~ incorrect spelling of **peculiar**

pe·cu·ni·ar·y /pi kyóonee èrree/ *adj* of money

ped·a·gogue /péddə gòg/ *n* a teacher, often a dogmatic one

ped·a·go·gy /péddə gòjjee/, **ped·a·gog·ics** /pèddə gójjiks/ *n* teaching —**ped·a·gog·i·cal** *adj*

ped·al /pédd'l/ *n* a foot-operated lever for a machine or musical instrument ■ *vti* 1 ride a bicycle 2 operate or play using a pedal ■ *adj* of the foot

SPELLCHECK Do not confuse the spelling of **pedal**, **petal** ("of a flower"), or **peddle** ("sell goods"), which sound similar.

ped·al push·ers *npl* calf-length women's pants

ped·ant /pédd'nt/ *n* 1 somebody who is too concerned with rules and details 2 somebody who shows off his or her knowledge —**pe·dan·tic** /pə dántik/ *adj* —**ped·ant·ry** *n*

~~pedastool~~ incorrect spelling of **pedestal**

ped·dle /pédd'l/ *vt* (**-dled, -dling**) 1 sell goods, especially while traveling from place to place 2 sell drugs —**ped·dler** *n* ◊ See note at **pedal**

ped·er·ast /péddə ràst/ *n* a man who has sexual relations with a boy (*fml*) —**ped·er·as·ty** *n*

ped·es·tal /péddəst'l/ *n* 1 the base of a column 2 the supporting base of a piece of furniture 3 a position of being exalted or admired

pe·des·tri·an /pə déestree ən/ *n* somebody who is on foot ■ *adj* ordinary or unexceptional —**pe·des·tri·an·ism** *n*

pe·des·tri·an·ize /pə déestree ə nìz/ (**-ized, -iz·ing**) *vt* make a street into a pedestrian area —**pe·des·tri·an·i·za·tion** /pə dèstree əni záysh'n/ *n*

pe·di·at·rics /pèedee áttriks/ *n* the branch of medicine concerned with children's development and diseases (*+ sing verb*) —**pe·di·at·ric** *adj* —**pe·di·a·tri·cian** /pèedee ə trísh'n/ *n*

ped·i·cure /péddi kyoòr/ *n* 1 medical care of the feet 2 a cosmetic treatment for the feet —**ped·i·cur·ist** *n*

ped·i·gree /péddi grèe/ *n* 1 the line of ancestors of a pure-bred animal 2 a document listing an animal's ancestors 3 a family tree —**ped·i·greed** *adj*

ped·i·ment /péddimənt/ n 1 a gable on a row of columns 2 a broad flat rock surface

pe·dom·e·ter /pə dómmətər/ n an instrument for measuring the distance walked

peek /peek/ vi look quickly —**peek** n ◊ See note at **peak**

peek·a·boo /peekə bòo/ n a children's game of hiding and uncovering the face and saying "peekaboo"

peel /peel/ v 1 vt remove the skin or outer layer of 2 vt pull something away from a surface 3 vi lose an outer layer ○ *Her nose was peeling.* 4 vi come off in thin strips or pieces ■ n the skin of a fruit or vegetable —**peel·er** n ◊ See note at **peal**

peep¹ /peep/ v 1 vi look quickly or secretly 2 vti make or make become visible only briefly —**peep** n

peep² /peep/ vi 1 make a short high-pitched noise 2 make a quiet noise, or speak in a quiet voice —**peep** n

peep·hole /peep hòl/ n a small opening to look through

peep·show /peep shò/, **peep show** n 1 an erotic show viewed from a private booth 2 in former times, a sequence of pictures viewed through a lens or hole

peer¹ /peer/ vi 1 look closely 2 be partially or briefly visible

---

SPELLCHECK Do not confuse the spelling of **peer** and **pier** ("a walkway jutting into the sea"), which sound similar.

---

peer² /peer/ n 1 a person of equal standing with another 2 a member of the nobility in Great Britain and Northern Ireland

peer·age /peerij/ n 1 nobles considered as a group 2 the rank or title of a member of the nobility

peer·ess /peerəss/ n 1 a woman peer 2 the wife of a peer

peer group n a social group of equals

peer·less /peerləss/ adj without equal —**peer·less·ly** adv

peer pres·sure n the social pressure on people to behave like their peers

peer re·view n evaluation of a piece of work by experts

peeve /peev/ (infml) vt (**peeved, peev·ing**) annoy ■ n an annoying thing

pee·vish /peevish/ adj irritable —**pee·vish·ly** adv —**pee·vish·ness** n

~~peform~~ incorrect spelling of **perform**

peg /peg/ n 1 a pin or bolt for fastening or marking something 2 a hook for hanging things on 3 a part for tuning a string on a musical instrument 4 a degree or step 5 a fast throw ■ vt (**pegged, peg·ging**) 1 secure or mark something with pegs 2 put a peg in something 3 fix a cost or value at a certain level 4 categorize somebody or something ◊ **bring** or **take down a peg (or two)** make more humble

peg·board /pég bàwrd/ n a board with holes for playing games or keeping score

Popperfoto

I. M. Pei

Pei /pay/, **I. M.** (b. 1917) Chinese-born US architect

P.E.I., PEI abbr Prince Edward Island

~~peice~~ incorrect spelling of **piece**

~~peir~~ incorrect spelling of **pier**

Peirce /peerss/, **Charles Sanders** (1839–1914) US philosopher and physicist

pe·jo·ra·tive /pə jáwrətiv, péjjə ràytiv, peejə-/ adj expressing disapproval (fml) —**pe·jo·ra·tive** n —**pe·jo·ra·tive·ly** adv

Pe·king /pèe kíng/ former name for **Beijing**

Pe·king·ese /peeking eez, -eess/, **Pe·kin·ese** /peekənèez, -neess/ n a small dog with a flat nose and long silky hair

pe·koe /peekō/ n a high-quality black tea

pe·lag·ic /pə lájjik/ adj found in the open sea rather than near the shore

Express Newspapers

Pelé

Pe·lé /pél ay/ (b. 1940) Brazilian soccer player

pel·i·can /péllikən/ n a large water bird that has a bill with a pouch

pel·lag·ra /pə lággrə, pə láygrə/ n a disease caused by a dietary deficiency of niacin

pel·let /péllət/ n 1 a small ball of compressed material 2 a small bullet or piece of shot —**pel·let** vt

pell-mell /pèl mél/ adv 1 in a disorderly rush 2 in a confused or untidy manner —**pell-mell** adj, n

pel·lu·cid /pə loóssid/ adj 1 transparent or translucent (literary) 2 clear in meaning (fml)

Pel·o·pon·ne·sus /pèlləpə neéssəss/ peninsula forming the southern part of mainland Greece —**Pel·o·pon·ne·sian** /pèlləpə neézh'n, -neésh'n/ n, adj

pe·lo·ta /pə lótə/ n a game in which baskets are used to hit a ball against a wall and catch it

pelt[1] *n* an animal skin ■ *vt* remove the skin of an animal

pelt[2] *v* 1 *vt* bombard with blows or missiles 2 *vt* beat against 3 *vi* rain heavily 4 *vi* move quickly ■ *n* a strong blow —**pelt·er** *n*

pel·vis /pélviss/ (*pl* **-vis·es** *or* **-ves** /-veez/) *n* the basin-shaped structure formed by the hip bones and sacrum —**pel·vic** *adj*

pen[1] *n* 1 an instrument for writing in ink 2 a particular style of writing ■ *vt* (**penned, pen·ning**) write —**pen·ner** *n*

ORIGIN The **pen** for writing goes back to Latin *penna* "feather," and was adopted from French. The origins of **pen** "enclosure" and **pen** "female swan" are unknown. **Pen** "prison" is a shortening of *penitentiary*.

pen[2] *n* 1 a small enclosure for animals 2 an area where somebody or something is confined —**pen** *vt*

pen[3] *n* a penitentiary (*slang*)

pen[4] *n* a female swan

PEN /pen/ *abbr* International Association of Poets, Playwrights, Editors, Essayists, and Novelists

pe·nal /peen'l/ *adj* of punishment

pe·nal code *n* a body of laws relating to the punishment of crime

pe·nal·ize /peen'l iz/ (**-ized, -iz·ing**) *vt* 1 impose a penalty on 2 put at a disadvantage —**pe·nal·i·za·tion** /peen'li záysh'n/ *n*

pe·nal ser·vi·tude *n* confinement in a remote place of imprisonment and punishment

pen·al·ty /pénn'ltee/ (*pl* **-ties**) *n* 1 a legal or official punishment for a crime or offense 2 a fine for breaking a contract 3 an unpleasant consequence o *paying the penalty of being too lenient* 4 in sports, a disadvantage imposed for breaking a rule

pen·al·ty ar·e·a *n* an area in front of a soccer goal where the goalkeeper may handle the ball

pen·al·ty kick *n* in soccer, a free kick at an opposing team's goal

pen·al·ty shoot·out *n* in soccer, a tiebreaker involving a series of penalty kicks

pen·ance /pénnənss/ *n* 1 self-imposed punishment for wrongdoing 2 a Christian sacrament of confession and forgiveness of sins —**pen·ance** *vt*

~~penatrate~~ incorrect spelling of **penetrate**

pen·chant /pénchənt/ *n* a liking or tendency

pen·cil /péns'l/ *n* 1 an instrument containing a stick of graphite used for drawing and writing 2 something resembling a pencil in shape or function o *an eyebrow pencil* o *a pencil of light* —**pen·cil** *vt*

pen·cil push·er *n* somebody whose job involves mainly paperwork (*infml*)

⚡ **pen com·put·er** *n* a computer that recognizes handwriting

pen·dant /péndənt/ *n* 1 a hanging ornament

or piece of jewelry 2 a necklace with a hanging ornament

pen·dent /péndənt/ *adj* (*fml or literary*) 1 hanging or suspended 2 overhanging

pend·ing /pénding/ *adj* 1 not yet dealt with or settled 2 about to happen ■ *prep* 1 until 2 during

pen·du·lous /pénjələss, péndyələss/ *adj* hanging loosely —**pen·du·lous·ly** *adv*

pen·du·lum /pénjələm, péndyələm/ *n* 1 a weight swinging freely from a fixed point 2 a swinging weighted rod controlling a clock mechanism —**pen·du·lar** *adj*

~~penecillin~~ incorrect spelling of **penicillin**

pen·e·trate /pénnə tràyt/ (**-trat·ed, -trat·ing**) *v* 1 *vti* enter or pass through something 2 *vt* permeate or spread through something 3 *vt* see into or through something dark or obscure —**pen·e·tra·ble** *adj* —**pen·e·tra·tion** /pènnə tráysh'n/ *n* —**pen·e·tra·tive** *adj*

pen·e·trat·ing /pénnə tràyting/ *adj* 1 able or tending to penetrate o *a penetrating odor* 2 piercing or probing o *a penetrating stare* 3 loud and shrill

pen·guin /péng gwin/ *n* an upright black-and-white seabird that cannot fly

ORIGIN The origin of **penguin** is somewhat mysterious. The word first appears in the late 16C, referring to both the penguin we know and a large flightless sea bird of N Atlantic coasts that is now extinct. A narrative of 1582 suggested that the word was Welsh, and *pen gwyn* "white head" has been suggested. The familiar **penguin**, however, has a black head.

pen·i·cil·lin /pènni síllin/ *n* an antibiotic originally derived from mold

pen·in·su·la /pə nínsyələ, pə nínsələ/ *n* a strip of land projecting into a body of water —**pen·in·su·lar** *adj*

pe·nis /péenəss/ (*pl* **-nis·es** *or* **-nes** /-neez/) *n* the male organ of copulation, in many mammals also used for urination —**pe·nile** /pée níl/ *adj*

pen·i·tent /pénnitənt/ *adj* feeling regret for wrongdoing ■ *n* a penitent person —**pen·i·tence** *n* —**pen·i·ten·tial** /pènni ténshəl/ *adj* —**pen·i·tent·ly** *adv*

pen·i·ten·tia·ry /pènni ténshəree/ *n* (*pl* **-ries**) a prison ■ *adj* 1 of penance 2 of punishment or reform of offenders

pen·knife /pén nìf/ (*pl* **-knives** /-nìvz/) *n* a pocketknife

pen·man·ship /pénmən shìp/ *n* the art or technique of writing by hand

Penn, William (1644–1718) English-born American Quaker reformer and colonialist

Penn., Penna. *abbr* Pennsylvania

pen name *n* a false name used by a writer

pen·nant /pénnənt/ *n* 1 a triangular flag, especially displayed on a ship 2 *US, Can, Aus* a flag symbolizing a sports championship

pen·ne /pé này/ *n* short tube-shaped pasta cut diagonally at the ends

pen·ni·less /pénnìləss/ *adj* without any money

Pen·nine Hills /pén ĭn-/ range of hills in N England, forming the "spine" of the country. Highest peak Cross Fell 2,930 ft./893 m.

pen·non /pénnən/ *n* a long narrow flag carried on a lance

Penn·syl·va·nia /pènsəl váynyə/ state in the NE United States. Cap. Harrisburg. Pop. 12,281,054 (2000). —**Penn·syl·va·nian** *n, adj*

pen·ny /pénnee/ (*pl* -**nies**) *n* 1 (*symbol* p) a subunit of currency in the United Kingdom 2 a US and Canadian coin worth one cent

pen·ny an·te *n* a game of poker in which the bets are small

pen·ny pinch·er *n* a stingy person (*infml*) —**pen·ny-pinch·ing** *adj*

pen·ny stock *n* a security that often sells for less than a dollar a share

pen·ny whis·tle *n* a high-pitched flutelike musical instrument

pen pal *n* a friend made through letter-writing

pen·sion[1] /pénsh'n/ *n* money paid regularly to a retired person or as compensation o *a widow's pension* ■ *vt* pay a pension to —**pen·sion·a·ble** *adj*

pen·sion[2] /paàn syáwn/ *n* a small hotel or boarding house in continental Europe

pen·sion·er /pénshənər/ *n* somebody who receives a pension

pen·sive /pénsiv/ *adj* deeply thoughtful. —**pen·sive·ly** *adv* —**pen·sive·ness** *n*

penta- *prefix* five o *pentagon*

pen·ta·gon /péntə gòn/ *n* 1 a five-sided geometric figure 2 **Pen·ta·gon** the US Department of Defense, or the building that houses it —**pen·tag·o·nal** /pen tággən'l/ *adj*

pen·ta·gram /péntə gràm/ *n* a five-pointed star

pen·tam·e·ter /pen támmətər/ *n* a line of poetry made up of five units of rhythm

pen·tath·lon /pen táthlon, -táth lòn/ *n* a sporting competition consisting of five events

Pen·te·cost /péntə kòst/ *n* a Christian festival marking the descent of the Holy Spirit upon the apostles. Date: 7th Sunday after Easter.

ORIGIN Pentecost goes back to the Greek word for "fifty." The Jewish festival to which the word originally referred is observed on the 50th day after the 2nd day of Passover.

Pen·te·cos·tal /pèntə kóst'l/ *adj* 1 of a Christian denomination that emphasizes the workings of the Holy Spirit 2 of Pentecost —**Pen·te·cos·tal** *n* —**Pen·te·cos·tal·ism** *n* —**Pen·te·cos·tal·ist** *n, adj*

pent·house /pént hòwss/ (*pl* -**houses** /-hòwzəz/) *n* 1 an expensive top-floor or rooftop apartment 2 a sloping roof or shed attached to a building

ORIGIN A **penthouse** is not etymologically a type of house. It derives from a shortening of an old French word *apentis* meaning "lean-to," which goes back to the Latin verb that is also the source of *append*. English adopted the word in the 14C, and it began to be linked to *house* in the 16C.

pent-up *adj* repressed or stifled o *pent-up emotions*

pe·nul·ti·mate /pə núltimət/ *adj* second to last —**pe·nul·ti·mate·ly** *adv*

pe·num·bra /pə númbrə/ (*pl* -**brae** /-bree/ *or* -**bras**) *n* a partial shadow, e.g., in an eclipse

pe·nu·ri·ous /pə noōree əss/ *adj* (*literary*) 1 having little money 2 not generous with money

pen·u·ry /pénnyəree/ *n* extreme poverty

pe·on /pee òn, -ən/ *n* 1 a farm laborer, especially one working off a debt 2 a drudge 3 a low-paid worker

pe·o·ny /pee ənee/ (*pl* -**nies**) *n* an ornamental plant with showy flowers

peo·ple /peep'l/ *n* a nation, community, or ethnic group ■ *npl* 1 human beings collectively 2 subordinates, e.g., subjects or employees 3 close relatives (*infml*) 4 ordinary men and women ■ *vt* (-**pled**, -**pling**) populate

peo·ple per·son *n* somebody who likes being with others

Pe·or·i·a /pee áwree ə/ city in central Illinois. Pop. 111,148 (1998).

pep *n* liveliness (*infml*) —**pep·pi·ly** *adv* —**pep·py** *adj*

□ **pep up** *vt* make lively (*infml*)

pep·per /péppər/ *n* 1 a hot seasoning made from ground dried berries 2 a plant that produces berries used to make pepper 3 a hollow fruit eaten as a vegetable 4 a plant that produces peppers ■ *v* 1 *vt* sprinkle or season with pepper 2 *vt* bombard with small missiles 3 sprinkle or scatter liberally o *manuscripts peppered with typing errors*

pep·per-and-salt *adj* salt-and-pepper

pep·per·corn /péppər kàwrn/ *n* a small dried berry that is ground to make pepper

pep·per mill *n* a pepper grinder

pep·per·mint /péppər mìnt/ *n* 1 a flavoring made from the aromatic oil of a mint plant. Use: food industry, pharmaceuticals. 2 a candy flavored with peppermint 3 a plant with leaves that produce peppermint

pep·per·o·ni /pèppə rónee/ *n* a spicy sausage, often used on pizzas

pep·per spray *n* a pepper-based aerosol spray, used to disable an aggressive or violent person

pep·per·y /péppəree/ *adj* 1 strongly flavored with pepper 2 angry and critical

pep ral·ly *n* a meeting for generating enthusiasm

pep·sin /pépsin/ *n* a stomach enzyme that digests protein

pep talk *n* an encouraging talk (*infml*)

pep·tic ul·cer /péptik-/ *n* an ulcer in the upper digestive tract

pep·tide /pép tīd/ *n* a linear molecule made up of two or more linked amino acids —**pep·tid·ic** /pep tíddik/ *adj*

Pepys /peeps, péppiss/, **Samuel** (1633–1703) English diarist

Pe·quot /péė kwòt/ (*pl* same *or* -**quots**) *n* 1 a member of a Native North American people of E Connecticut 2 the Algonquian language of the Pequot people —**Pe·quot** *adj*

per *prep* 1 for each ○ *50 miles per hour* 2 according to ○ *per instructions*

per·am·bu·late /pə rámbyə làyt/ (-**lat·ed**, -**lat·ing**) *vti* walk around a place (*fml*) —**per·am·bu·la·tion** /pə ràmbyə láysh'n/ *n*

per an·num /pər ánnəm/ *adv* in every year, or by the year

per·cale /pər káyl/ *n* a smooth cotton or polyester fabric. Use: sheets, clothing.

per cap·i·ta /pər káppitə/ *adv*, *adj* for each person

per·ceive /pər séėv/ (-**ceived**, -**ceiv·ing**) *vt* 1 become aware of using the senses 2 understand in a particular way ○ *the action was perceived as a conciliatory gesture* —**per·ceiv·a·ble** *adj*

per·cent /pər sént/ *adv* (*symbol %*) expresses a proportion in hundredths ■ *n* (*pl* same) 1 one hundredth 2 a percentage

per·cent·age /pər séntij/ *n* 1 a proportion expressed in hundredths 2 a part or proportion 3 a commission or share (*infml*) 4 advantage (*infml*) ○ *There's no percentage in accepting the proposal.*

> **USAGE** If you put the definite article *the* before **percentage**, you must use a singular verb after it: *The percentage of errors in the report is large.* If you put the indefinite article *a* before **percentage**, use a singular or plural verb, depending on whether what follows is regarded as a single unit or a plural: *A large percentage of the electorate remains undecided. A large percentage of the errors are found in this report.*

per·cen·tile /pər sén tìl/ *n* a statistical measure on a scale of 100

per·cep·ti·ble /pər séptəb'l/ *adj* detectable —**per·cep·ti·bly** *adv*

per·cep·tion /pər sépshən/ *n* 1 the process or result of perceiving 2 an attitude, impression, or understanding ○ *altered the public's perception of the issue* 3 the ability to be perceptive —**per·cep·tion·al** *adj*

per·cep·tive /pər séptiv/ *adj* 1 quick to understand or discern things 2 of perception —**per·cep·tive·ly** *adv* —**per·cep·tive·ness** *n*

per·cep·tu·al /pər sépchoo əl/ *adj* of perception

perch[1] *n* 1 a place for a bird to sit 2 a temporary resting place 3 an advantageous or prominent position 4 a unit of length equal to 5½ yd./5.03 m. ■ *v* 1 *vti* sit precariously ○ *He was perched on a high stool.* 2 *vt* situate in a high place 3 *vi* land or sit on a perch (*refers to birds*)

perch[2] (*pl* **perch·es** *or* same) *n* 1 a freshwater fish with rough scales 2 perch as food

per·chance /pər cháns/ *adv* perhaps (*literary*)

~~perceive~~ incorrect spelling of **perceive**

per·cip·i·ent /pər síppee ənt/ *adj* perceptive, observant, or discerning —**per·cip·i·ence** *n*

per·co·late /púrkə làyt/ (-**lat·ed**, -**lat·ing**) *v* 1 *vti* pass through a filter 2 *vi* pass or spread slowly ○ *news percolating through to the hostages* 3 *vti* make coffee in a percolator, or be made in a percolator —**per·co·la·tion** /pùrkə láysh'n/ *n*

per·co·la·tor /púrkə làytər/ *n* a coffeepot in which boiling water circulates through a basket of coffee grounds

per·cus·sion /pər kúsh'n/ *n* 1 the group of musical instruments that produce sound by being struck 2 impact, or the noise or shock of an impact (*fml*)

per·cus·sion cap *n* a detonator that explodes when struck, formerly used to fire some pistols

per·cus·sion·ist /pər kúsh'nist/ *n* a musician who plays a percussion instrument

per·cus·sive /pər kússiv/ *adj* having the effect of an impact

per di·em /pər deė əm/ *adv*, *adj* by the day ■ *n* a daily payment or allowance

per·di·tion /pər dísh'n/ *n* 1 everlasting punishment in Hell 2 Hell

per·e·gri·nate /pérrəgri nàyt/ (-**nat·ed**, -**nat·ing**) *vti* travel (*literary*)

per·e·gri·na·tion /pèrrəgri náysh'n/ *n* a journey (*literary*)

per·e·grine fal·con /pérrəgrin-, -greėn-/, **per·e·grine** *n* a large falcon with a blue-gray back and white underparts

> **ORIGIN** The **peregrine falcon** is literally a "traveling falcon." Falconers formerly captured them full-grown while migrating, and did not take them from their nests while young as with other birds.

per·emp·to·ry /pə rémptəree/ *adj* 1 dictatorial 2 ending or closed to further discussion or action —**per·emp·to·ri·ly** *adv*

~~perennial~~ incorrect spelling of **perennial**

per·en·ni·al /pə rénnee əl/ *adj* 1 describes a plant that lasts for more than two growing seasons 2 recurring or enduring —**per·en·ni·al** *n* —**per·en·ni·al·ly** *adv*

Pé·rez de Cuél·lar /pè ress də kwáy yaar/, **Javier** (*b.* 1920) Peruvian diplomat and secretary-general of the United Nations (1982–91)

per·fect *adj* /púrfikt/ **1** without faults, flaws, or errors **2** complete and whole **3** excellent or ideal **4** especially suitable **5** utter or absolute ○ *perfect happiness* **6** describes a verb aspect or form expressing completed action ■ *vt* /pər fékt/ make perfect ■ *n* /púrfikt/ the perfect aspect, or a form of a verb in the perfect aspect —**per·fect·i·ble** *adj* —**per·fect·ly** *adv*

per·fec·tion /pər féksh'n/ *n* **1** the state or quality of being perfect **2** the process of perfecting

per·fec·tion·ist /pər fékshənist/ *n* somebody who strives for or demands perfection —**per·fec·tion·ism** *n*

per·fi·dy /púrfidee/ *n* deliberate treachery *(fml)* —**per·fid·i·ous** /pər fíddee əss/ *adj*

per·fo·rate /púrfə ràyt/ (**-ra·ted, -rat·ing**) *vt* **1** puncture **2** make a line of holes in for tearing —**per·fo·rat·ed** *adj*

per·fo·ra·tion /pùrfə ráysh'n/ *n* **1** a hole **2** a line of holes for tearing **3** perforating or being perforated

per·force /pər fáwrs/ *adv* unavoidably *(literary)*

per·form /pər fáwrm/ *v* **1** *vt* begin and bring an action to completion **2** *vt* fulfill what is required **3** *vti* present an artistic work such as a play or piece of music to an audience **4** *vi* function or behave in a particular way ○ *performs well under pressure* —**per·form·er** *n*

SYNONYMS perform, do, carry out, fulfill, discharge, execute CORE MEANING: complete a task

per·form·ance /pər fáwrmənss/ *n* **1** a presentation of an artistic work to an audience **2** a manner of functioning ○ *a high-performance car* **3** the process of performing

per·form·ance art *n* art that combines static and dramatic artistic media —**per·form·ance art·ist** *n*

per·form·ing arts *npl* drama, dance, and music

per·fume /púr fyòom, pər fyóom/ *n* **1** a fragrant liquid **2** a pleasant smell —**per·fume** *vt* ◊ See note at **smell**

per·fum·er·y /pər fyóoməree/ (*pl* **-ies**) *n* **1** perfumes in general **2** a place where perfumes are made or sold

per·func·to·ry /pər fúngktəree/ *adj* **1** done routinely ○ *a perfunctory kiss* **2** hasty and superficial ○ *a perfunctory search* —**per·func·to·ri·ly** *adv*

Per·ga·mum /púrgəməm/ ancient Greek and Roman city in NW Asia Minor, in present-day W Turkey

per·go·la /púrgələ/ *n* a structure of posts and latticework that supports climbing plants

per·haps /pər háps, -áps/ *adv* possibly

peri- *prefix* **1** around, surrounding ○ *perianth* **2** near ○ *perinatal*

per·i·anth /pérree ànth/ *n* the outer structure of a flower including the petals

Per·i·cles /pérrə kleèz/ (495?–429? BC) Athenian political leader —**Per·i·cle·an** /pèrrə kleè ən/ *adj*

per·i·gee /pérrəjee/ *n* the point at which a satellite, moon, or planet comes nearest to the object it is orbiting

per·il /pérrəl/ *n* **1** exposure to risk **2** a source of danger —**per·il·ous** *adj* —**per·il·ous·ly** *adv*

pe·rim·e·ter /pə rímmitər/ *n* **1** a boundary enclosing an area **2** a curve enclosing an area, or the length of such a curve

per·i·na·tal /pèrrə náyt'l/ *adj* around the time of childbirth —**per·i·na·tal·ly** *adv*

per·i·ne·um /pèrrə neè əm/ (*pl* **-a** /-ə/) *n* the area of the body surrounding the genitals and anus —**per·i·ne·al** *adj*

pe·ri·od /peèree əd/ *n* **1** an interval of time **2** a particular interval of time, e.g., in history ○ *the early Victorian period* **3** an occurrence of menstruation **4** a unit of geologic time shorter than an era and longer than an epoch **5** the punctuation mark (.) ■ *adj* of a particular historical time ○ *in period costume*

USAGE A **period** is used at the end of a sentence that is not a question or exclamation: *It rained last Saturday.* It is also used after some abbreviations: *at 11 a.m. on Aug. 7, 2000.* The period is increasingly omitted in abbreviations, especially in contractions (e.g., *Dr, St, Ltd*) and after capital letters (e.g., *VCR*). Shortened forms used as words in their own right (e.g., *gym, disco, pub*) and acronyms pronounced as words (e.g., *AIDS, laser, NATO*) should not be written with periods. The same mark is used in decimal notation (*2.5 children*), where it is read as "point." It is also used in Internet addresses, where it is read as "dot" (*.com*).

pe·ri·od·ic /peèree óddik/ *adj* **1** recurring from time to time **2** occurring at regular intervals —**pe·ri·od·i·cal·ly** *adv* —**pe·ri·o·dic·i·ty** /peèree ə díssətee/ *n*

SYNONYMS periodic, intermittent, occasional, sporadic CORE MEANING: recurring over a period of time

pe·ri·od·i·cal /peèree óddik'l/ *n* a magazine or journal ■ *adj* **1** published at regular intervals **2** periodic

pe·ri·od·ic ta·ble *n* a table of chemical elements arranged according to their atomic numbers

pe·ri·od piece *n* something such as a piece of furniture or work of art that dates from or evokes a particular historical period

per·i·pa·tet·ic /pèrrəpə téttik/ *adj* traveling from place to place ■ *n* a peripatetic worker

⚡**pe·riph·er·al** /pə ríffərəl/ *adj* 1 at the edge 2 minor or incidental ■ *n* a computer device external to but controlled by the central processing unit —**pe·riph·er·al·ly** *adv*

pe·riph·er·y /pə ríffəree/ (*pl* -ies) *n* the area around the edge

pe·riph·ra·sis /pə rífrrəssiss/ (*pl* -ses /-sèèz/) *n* 1 the use of more words than necessary to avoid saying something directly 2 an expression that states something indirectly

per·i·scope /pérrə skòp/ *n* a tubular optical instrument used to see something not in a direct line of sight

per·ish /pérrish/ *vi* die (*literary*)

per·ish·a·ble /pérrishəb'l/ *adj* liable to rot or spoil ■ *n* something perishable, especially a food item

per·i·stal·sis /pèrrə stáwlsiss/ (*pl* -ses /-sèèz/) *n* the involuntary contractions of the muscles of the intestine —**per·i·stal·tic** *adj*

per·i·style /pérrə stìl/ *n* a line of columns encircling a building or courtyard

per·i·to·ni·tis /pèrrət'n ítiss/ *n* inflammation of the membrane lining the abdomen

per·i·wig /pérrə wìg/ *n* a 17C and 18C man's wig

per·i·win·kle /pérrə wìngk'l/ *n* a trailing plant with blue or white flowers

~~perjorative~~ incorrect spelling of **pejorative**

per·jure /púrjər/ /-jured, -jur·ing/ *vt* tell lies under oath —**per·jur·er** *n* —**per·ju·ry** *n*

perk *n* an additional benefit ○ *one of the perks of the job*

☐ **perk up** *vti* 1 make or become more cheerful, lively, or refreshed 2 stick up straight ○ *The dog's ears perked up.*

Per·kins /púrkinz/, **Frances** (1880–1965) US secretary of labor (1933–45)

perk·y /púrkee/ (-i·er, -i·est) *adj* 1 lively and cheerful 2 overly self-confident —**perk·i·ly** *adv* —**perk·i·ness** *n*

Perl·man /púrlmən/, **Itzhak** (*b.* 1945) Israeli-born US violinist

perm *n* a hair treatment that gives long-lasting curls or waves —**perm** *vt*

Perm /purm, pairm/, **Perm'** city in E European Russia. Pop. 1,275,482 (1995).

per·ma·frost /púrmə fràwst/ *n* permanently frozen subsoil

~~permament~~ incorrect spelling of **permanent**

per·ma·nent /púrmənənt/ *adj* 1 lasting forever 2 unchanging ■ *n* a perm (*fml*) —**per·ma·nence** *n* —**per·ma·nent·ly** *adv*

per·ma·nent press *n* a fabric treatment that gives shape and wrinkle resistance

per·ma·nent wave *n* a perm

per·me·a·ble /púrmee əb'l/ *adj* allowing liquids or gases to pass through

per·me·ate /púrmee àyt/ (-at·ed, -at·ing) *vti* 1 enter and spread through something 2 pass, or make pass, through tiny openings in a porous substance or membrane —**per·me·a·tion** /pùrmee áysh'n/ *n*

~~permenent~~ incorrect spelling of **permanent**

Per·mi·an /púrmee ən/ *n* a period of geologic time 290–248 million years ago —**Per·mi·an** *adj*

~~permissable~~ incorrect spelling of **permissible**

per·mis·si·ble /pər míssəb'l/ *adj* allowable or permitted —**per·mis·si·bil·i·ty** /pər missə bíllətee/ *n* —**per·mis·si·bly** *adv*

per·mis·sion /pər mísh'n/ *n* agreement to allow something

per·mis·sive /pər míssiv/ *adj* 1 allowing freedom to behave in ways others might consider unacceptable 2 giving permission —**per·mis·sive·ly** *adv* —**per·mis·sive·ness** *n*

per·mit *vti* /pər mít/ (-mit·ted, -mit·ting) 1 agree to allow something 2 make something possible ■ *n* /púrmit, pər mít/ a document giving permission

~~permited~~ incorrect spelling of **permitted**

per·mu·ta·tion /pùrmyə táysh'n, pùrmyoo-/ *n* 1 an arrangement created by moving or reordering items 2 a transformation 3 an ordered arrangement of elements from a set

per·ni·cious /pər níshəss/ *adj* 1 causing serious harm 2 malicious —**per·ni·cious·ly** *adv*

per·ni·cious a·ne·mi·a *n* a severe form of anemia

~~perogative~~ incorrect spelling of **prerogative**

AKG London

Eva Perón

Pe·rón /pə rón/, **Eva** (1919–52) Argentine political figure. Married to President Juan Perón, she was extremely popular but never held public office.

Pe·rón, Isabel de (*b.* 1931) president of Argentina (1974–76)

Pe·rón, Juan (1895–1974) president of Argentina (1946–55 and 1973–74) —**Per·o·nist** /pə rónist/ *n, adj*

per·o·rate /pérrə ràyt/ (-rat·ed, -rat·ing) *vi* (*fml*) 1 end a speech by summarizing its main points 2 give a long-winded speech —**per·o·ra·tion** /pèrrə ráysh'n/ *n*

per·ox·ide /pə rók sìd/ *n* 1 a chemical compound containing oxygen atoms 2 a substance used to lighten hair ○ *a peroxide blonde* —**per·ox·ide** *vt*

per·pen·dic·u·lar /pùrpən díkyələr/ *adj* 1 at right angles 2 vertical 3 *also* **Per·pen-**

dic·u·lar of a late Gothic style of architecture 4 very steep —**per·pen·dic·u·lar** n

per·pe·trate /púrpə tràyt/ (-trat·ed, -trat·ing) vt do something illegal or morally wrong —**per·pe·tra·tion** /pùrpə tráysh'n/ n —**per·pe·tra·tor** n

per·pet·u·al /pər péchoo əl/ adj 1 lasting forever or indefinitely 2 occurring repeatedly —**per·pet·u·al·ly** adv

per·pet·u·ate /pər péchoo àyt/ (-at·ed, -at·ing) vt 1 cause to last for a long time 2 cause to be remembered —**per·pet·u·a·tion** /-pèchoo áysh'n/ n

per·pe·tu·i·ty /pùrpə toó ətee/ n 1 the condition of being perpetual 2 eternity

per·plex /pər pléks/ vt puzzle or confuse —**per·plexed** adj —**per·plex·i·ty** n

per·qui·site /púrkwəzit/ n a perk (fml)

Per·rault /pe ró, pə ró/, **Charles** (1628–1703) French writer and collector of fairy stories

~~perrenial~~ incorrect spelling of **perennial**

per·ry /pérree/ n a drink made from fermented pear juice

Per·ry /pérree/, **Matthew Calbraith** (1794–1858) US naval officer

Per·ry, **Oliver Hazard** (1785–1819) US naval officer

per se /pər sáy/ adv in itself

per·se·cute /púrsə kyoòt/ (-cut·ed, -cut·ing) vt 1 oppress or treat cruelly, e.g., because of ethnic origin or religious beliefs 2 pester or harass —**per·se·cu·tion** /pùrsə kyoósh'n/ n —**per·se·cu·tor** n

Per·sep·o·lis /pər séppəlìss/ ruined ancient Persian city in present-day SW Iran

per·se·vere /pùrsə veér/ (-vered, -ver·ing) vi persist determinedly despite difficulties —**per·se·ver·ance** n

~~perseverence~~ incorrect spelling of **perseverance**

Per·shing /púrshing/, **John J.** (1860–1948) US general

Per·sia /púrzhə/ 1 former name for **Iran** 2 ancient empire in SW Asia that stretched eastward from the E Mediterranean Sea to the Indus River in present-day Pakistan

Per·sian /púrzh'n/ n 1 somebody from Iran 2 a member of a people of ancient Persia 3 the language of the ancient Persians 4 a domestic cat with long silky hair —**Per·sian** adj

Per·sian Gulf arm of the Arabian Sea, between the NE Arabian Peninsula and SW Iran

per·sim·mon /pər símmən/ n 1 a smooth-skinned orange-red fruit 2 a tree that produces persimmons

per·sist /pər síst/ vi 1 continue steadily or obstinately 2 continue happening or existing —**per·sist·ence** n —**per·sist·ent** adj —**per·sist·ent·ly** adv

~~persistant~~ incorrect spelling of **persistent**

per·snick·e·ty /pər sníkətee/ adj 1 excessively concerned with details (infml) 2 requiring attention to detail

per·son /púrs'n/ (pl **peo·ple** /peép'l/ or **per·sons** formal) n 1 a human being 2 somebody's body, including clothing o objects found on her person 3 a form of verbs and pronouns denoting the speaker, person addressed, or person referred to o the third person singular —**person** suffix

per·so·na /pər sónə/ (pl **-nas** or **-nae** /-nee/) n 1 a character in literature (often pl) 2 an assumed identity or role 3 somebody's public image

per·son·a·ble /púrsənəb'l/ adj having a pleasant personality and appearance

per·son·age /púrsənij/ n (fml) 1 an important person 2 a historical figure or fictional character

per·son·al /púrs'n'l, púrsnəl/ adj 1 of somebody's private life 2 of a particular person o personal opinion 3 done by a person himself or herself o that personal touch 4 intended for a specific person 5 referring offensively to somebody in particular o making personal remarks about his appearance 6 of the body o personal hygiene ■ n a personal message or notice in the classified section of a newspaper or magazine (often pl)

per·son·al as·sis·tant n an employee who performs secretarial and administrative tasks for somebody

per·son·al col·umn n a section of a magazine or newspaper in which personals are printed

✦ **per·son·al com·put·er** n a computer intended for use by one person

✦ **per·son·al dig·i·tal as·sis·tant** n a portable electronic notebook

✦ **per·so·nal i·den·ti·fi·ca·tion num·ber** full form of **PIN**

✦ **per·son·al in·for·ma·tion man·ag·er** n a piece of software that organizes notes, contacts, and appointments

per·son·al·i·ty /pùrs'n állətee/ (pl **-ties**) n 1 the totality of somebody's character and traits 2 distinctive or appealing personal characteristics o lacking in personality 3 a famous person

per·son·al·i·ty dis·or·der n a psychiatric disorder that affects social interaction

per·son·al·ize /púrsən'l īz/ (-ized, -iz·ing) vt 1 put somebody's initials or name on something 2 change something to reflect its owner's or occupier's personality —**per·son·al·i·za·tion** /pùrsən'li záysh'n/ n

per·son·al·ly /púrsən'lee/ adv 1 in your own opinion or experience o Personally, I think they should be banned. 2 as a person

✦ **per·son·al or·gan·iz·er** n 1 an appointment calendar with replaceable pages 2 a handheld computer that can function as a calendar, address book, and calculator

per·son·al pro·noun *n* a pronoun that refers to a person, e.g., "I" or "her"

per·son·al ster·e·o *n* a small audio cassette or CD player with earphones

per·son·al wa·ter·craft *n* a water motorcycle

per·so·na non gra·ta /pər sôna nön graáta/ (*pl* **per·so·nae non gra·tae** /pər sônee nön graátee/) *n* an unwelcome or unacceptable person —**per·so·na non gra·ta** *adj*

~~personel, personell~~ incorrect spelling of **personnel**

per·son·i·fy /pər sónna fī/ (**-fied**, **-fies**) *vt* 1 be an embodiment or perfect example of something 2 represent something abstract as human —**per·son·i·fi·ca·tion** /pər sònnəfi káysh'n/ *n*

per·son·nel /pùrsə nél/ *n* the department of an organization that deals with employment and staffing issues ■ *npl* the people employed in an organization

per·son-to-per·son *adj* 1 face-to-face and direct 2 describes a telephone call chargeable only when the recipient is reached ■ *adv* to be paid if the recipient answers

per·spec·tive /pər spéktiv/ *n* 1 a personal or subjective viewpoint ○ *a different perspective on the matter* 2 a measured or objective assessment ○ *keep things in perspective* 3 the way distant objects appear to an observer

per·spi·ca·cious /pùrspi káyshəss/ *adj* perceptive —**per·spi·ca·ci·ty** /-kassətee/ *n*

per·spic·u·ous /pər spíkyoo əss/ *adj* clear and comprehensible —**per·spi·cu·i·ty** /pùrspi kyoó ətee/ *n* —**per·spic·u·ous·ly** *adv*

per·spi·ra·tion /pùrspə ráysh'n/ *n* 1 sweat 2 the process or act of sweating

per·spire /pər spír/ (**-spired**, **-spir·ing**) *vti* secrete sweat —**per·spir·ing·ly** *adv*

per·suade /pər swáyd/ (**-suad·ed**, **-suad·ing**) *vt* 1 make somebody do something by reasoning, pleading, or coaxing 2 convince somebody of something —**per·suad·a·ble** *adj*

per·sua·sion /pər swáyzh'n/ *n* 1 the process of persuading 2 the ability to persuade 3 a set of beliefs

per·sua·sive /pər swáyssiv/ *adj* persuading, or able to persuade —**per·sua·sive·ly** *adv* —**per·sua·sive·ness** *n*

~~persue~~ incorrect spelling of **pursue**

~~persuit~~ incorrect spelling of **pursuit**

~~persumably~~ incorrect spelling of **presumably**

pert *adj* 1 amusingly bold 2 jaunty and stylish —**pert·ly** *adv* —**pert·ness** *n*

PERT /purt/ *n* a method of prioritizing complex activities. Full form **program evaluation and review technique**

per·tain /pər táyn/ *vi* 1 have relevance 2 be appropriate

Perth /purth/ capital of Western Australia. Pop. 1,341,900 (1998).

per·ti·na·cious /pùrti náyshəss/ *adj* 1 resolute 2 persistent —**per·ti·nac·i·ty** /-nássətee/ *n*

per·ti·nent /púrt'nənt/ *adj* relevant —**per·ti·nence** *n* —**per·ti·nent·ly** *adv*

per·turb /pər túrb/ *vt* disturb and trouble or worry —**per·turb·a·ble** *adj* —**per·tur·ba·tion** /pùrtər báysh'n/ *n*

per·tus·sis /pər tússiss/ *n* whooping cough (*technical*) —**per·tus·sal** *adj*

Pe·ru /pə roó/ country in W South America. Cap. Lima. Pop. 27,483,864 (2001). —**Pe·ru·vi·an** /-an/ *adj*, *n*

pe·ruse /pə roóz/ (**-rused**, **-rus·ing**) *vt* read carefully —**pe·rus·al** *n*

per·vade /pər váyd/ (**-vad·ed**, **-vad·ing**) *vt* spread throughout —**per·va·sion** /pər váyzh'n/ *n* —**per·va·sive** /pər váyssiv/ *adj* —**per·va·sive·ly** *adv*

per·verse /pər vúrs/ *adj* 1 purposely unreasonable, awkward, or stubborn 2 perverted —**per·verse·ly** *adv* —**per·ver·si·ty** *n*

per·ver·sion /pər vúrzh'n/ *n* 1 a sexual practice considered unusual or unacceptable 2 perverting or being perverted

per·vert *vt* /pər vúrt/ 1 lead away from what is good, moral, or proper 2 misinterpret or distort 3 use improperly ■ *n* /púr vùrt/ an offensive term for somebody whose sexual behavior is considered unusual or unacceptable (*insult*) —**per·vert·er** *n* —**per·vert·i·ble** *adj*

per·vi·ous /púrvee əss/ *adj* susceptible to permeation —**per·vi·ous·ly** *adv*

pe·se·ta /pə sáytə/ *n* the main unit of the former Spanish currency

Pe·sha·war /pe shaáwər/ city in N Pakistan, near the Khyber Pass. Pop. 988,055 (1998).

pes·ky /péskee/ (**-ki·er**, **-ki·est**) *adj* troublesome or irritating (*infml*) —**pes·ki·ly** *adv*

pe·so /páyssō/ (*pl* **-sos**) *n* the main unit of currency in several South and Central American countries

pes·sa·ry /péssəree/ (*pl* **-ries**) *n* a vaginal suppository

pes·si·mist /péssəmist/ *n* somebody who always expects the worst to happen —**pes·si·mism** *n* —**pes·si·mis·tic** /péssə místik/ *adj* —**pes·si·mis·ti·cal·ly** *adv*

pest *n* 1 a damaging organism 2 an annoying person or thing (*infml*)

ORIGIN Pest originally referred to a fatal epidemic disease, especially bubonic plague. It was adopted in the late 15C from French.

---

pes·ter /péstər/ *vt* annoy constantly, especially by harassing with demands

pes·ti·cide /pésti sīd/ *n* a chemical substance used to kill pests —**pes·ti·cid·al** /pèsti síd'l/ *adj*

pes·ti·lence /péstilənss/ *n* an epidemic of disease (*archaic*)

pes·ti·lent /péstilənt/ *adj* deadly —**pes·ti·len·tial** /pèsti lénsh'l/ *adj*

pes·tle /péss'l/ *n* an object with a rounded

end for crushing or grinding substances in a mortar —**pes·tle** *vt*

pes·to /péstõ/ *n* a sauce made of basil, pine nuts, oil, Parmesan cheese, and garlic

pet[1] *n* 1 an animal kept for companionship or amusement 2 a favorite person ■ *adj* 1 kept as a pet 2 special or favorite o *a pet topic* ■ *v* (**pet·ted, pet·ting**) 1 *vt* stroke 2 *vt* treat indulgently 3 *vi* touch each other for sexual pleasure —**pet·ting** *n*

ORIGIN The origin of neither English word **pet** is known. The use of an animal or person is of Scottish and N English origin. It is first recorded in the early 16C meaning "indulged or spoiled child," and then applying to an animal in the mid-16C. The word referring to a "sulky mood" also first appears in the mid-16C.

pet[2] *n* a sulky mood

peta- *prefix* one million billion o *petabyte*

⨍ **pet·a·byte** /pétta bìt/ *n* a quadrillion bytes

pet·al /pétt'l/ *n* one of the colored outer parts of a flower —**pet·aled** *adj* ◊ See note at pedal

pe·tard /pə taárd/ *n* an explosive charge for breaching a door, wall, or fortification ◊ **be hoist with your own petard** be the victim of your own attempt to harm somebody else

pe·ter /peétər/ *vi* become less
□ **peter out** *vi* dwindle and finally stop or disappear

Pe·ter /peétər/ *n* either of two books in the Bible, originally written as letters and traditionally attributed to St. Peter.

Pe·ter, **St.** (*d.* AD 64?) one of the 12 apostles of Jesus Christ

Pe·ter (the Great) (1672–1725) tsar of Russia (1682–1725)

Pe·ter Prin·ci·ple *n* the theory that people are promoted until they reach their level of incompetence

ORIGIN The principle is named for the US author Laurence Johnston Peter (1919–90), who formulated it.

Pe·ter·son /peétərs'n/, **Oscar** (*b.* 1925) Canadian jazz pianist

pet·i·ole /péttee òl/ *n* a leaf stalk (*technical*) —**pet·i·o·late** /-ə làyt/ *adj*

pet·it bour·geois /péttee boor zhwaá, pə tèe-/ (*pl* **pe·tits bour·geois** /péttee-/) *n* a member of the lower middle-class —**pe·tite bour·geoi·sie** /pə tèet boor zhwaa zeé/ *n*

pe·tite /pə teét/ *adj* small and delicately built

pet·it four /péttee fáwr, pə teè fáwr/ (*pl* **pe·tits fours** /péttee fáwrz, pəteè-/) *n* a bite-size sweet cake served after a meal

pe·ti·tion /pə tísh'n/ *n* 1 a demand for official action signed by many people 2 an appeal or request to a higher authority ■ *v* 1 *vt* give or address a petition to 2 *vi* make a demand or request using a petition o *petitioning for his release* —**pe·ti·tion·er** *n*

pet·it mal /pèttee mál/ *n* a mild form of epilepsy

pet·it point /pèttee póynt/ (*pl* **pe·tits points** /*pronunc. same*/) *n* 1 a small stitch used in needlepoint for details 2 embroidery with small stitches

pet name *n* a name showing endearment

Pe·tra /peétra, péttra/ ancient ruined city in present-day SW Jordan

Pe·trarch /peé traark, pét raàrk/ (1304–74) Italian poet and scholar —**Pe·trarch·an** /pi traárkən/ *adj*

pet·rel /péttrəl/ *n* a seabird with a hooked beak and tubular nostrils

ORIGIN The **petrel** is perhaps named for St. Peter, who is described as walking on water (Matthew 14:29). The bird flies close to the sea, touching the water with its feet.

Pe·tri dish /peétree-/ *n* a flat-bottomed dish for growing bacterial cultures

ORIGIN The **Petri dish** is named for the German bacteriologist Julius Petri (1852–92), who invented it.

pet·ri·fy /péttrə fì/ (**-fied, -fies**) *v* 1 *vt* immobilize with fear 2 *vti* change into stone —**pet·ri·fi·ca·tion** /pèttrəfi káyshən/ *n*

pet·ro·chem·i·cal /pèttrō kémmik'l/ *n* a derivative of petroleum or natural gas —**pet·ro·chem·i·cal** *adj*

pet·ro·dol·lar /péttrō dòllər/ *n* a unit of currency earned by an oil-exporting nation

pet·rol /péttrəl/ *n UK* gasoline

pe·tro·le·um /pə trólee əm/ *n* crude oil found in sedimentary rocks

pe·tro·le·um jel·ly *n* a greasy gelatinous substance derived from petroleum. Use: ointment base, lubricant, protective covering.

pe·trol·o·gy /pə tróllajee/ *n* the study of rocks —**pet·ro·log·i·cal** /pèttrə lójjik'l/ *adj* —**pe·trol·o·gist** *n*

pet·ti·coat /péttee kòt/ *n* a woman's underskirt or slip

pet·ti·fog·ging /péttee fògging/ *adj* 1 petty or trivial 2 quibbling (*insult*) —**pet·ti·fog** *vi* —**pet·ti·fog·ger** *n*

pet·ting zoo *n* a collection of animals for petting

pet·tish /péttish/ *adj* peevish

pet·ty /péttee/ (**-ti·er, -ti·est**) *adj* 1 insignificant 2 narrow-minded 3 mean or spiteful —**pet·ti·ly** *adv* —**pet·ti·ness** *n*

pet·ty cash *n* money kept in an office for small business expenses

pet·ty of·fi·cer *n* a noncommissioned naval officer in the US Navy or Coast Guard, and in the Canadian Navy

pet·u·lant /péchələnt/ *adj* ill-tempered and sulky —**pet·u·lance** *n* —**pet·u·lant·ly** *adv*

pe·tu·nia /pə toŏnee ə/ *n* a plant with bright funnel-shaped flowers

pew /pyoo/ *n* a church or synagogue bench with a straight back

pe·wee /pée weé/, **pee·wee** *n* a drab medium-sized flycatcher

pew·ter /pyoŏtər/ *n* 1 a silver-gray alloy of tin and lead 2 objects made of pewter collectively

pe·yo·te /pay ṓtee/ *n* 1 a spineless globe-shaped cactus 2 *also* **pe·yo·te but·ton** a nodule containing mescaline on the stem of a peyote

PG *tdmk* a rating indicating that a movie may be seen by anyone, but parental guidance is suggested for children

PG-13 /-thùr teén/ *tdmk* a rating indicating that a movie may be seen by anyone, but parental guidance is suggested for children under the age of 13

PGA *abbr* Professional Golfers' Association

⚡**PGP** *n* a computer encryption program. Full form **Pretty Good Privacy**

pH *n* a measure of acidity (low pH) or alkalinity (high pH). Full form **potential of hydrogen**

pha·e·ton /fáy ət'n, fáyt'n/ *n* 1 a light four-wheeled horse-drawn carriage 2 an old-fashioned touring car

ORIGIN The **phaeton** was named in French in the mid-18C for a figure in Greek mythology. The god of the sun drove his golden chariot across the sky from east to west each day. His son Phaethon begged his father to let him drive it, but lost control of the horses, and threatened catastrophe to the earth. To prevent this, Zeus, the king of the gods, killed him with a thunderbolt.

phag·o·cyte /fággə sìt/ *n* a cell that removes unwanted substances from the body —**phag·o·cyt·ic** /fággə síttik/ *adj*

pha·lanx /fáy lànks, fá-/ (*pl* **-lanx·es** *or* **-lan·ges** /fə lánjeez, fay-/) *n* 1 a tight group 2 a body of troops in close formation —**pha·lan·ge·al** /fə lánjee əl, fay-/ *adj*

Phal·gu·na /pál goŏnə, fál-/ *n* the 12th month of the Hindu calendar

phal·lus /fálləss/ (*pl* **-lus·es** *or* **-li** /-lì/) *n* 1 a stylized representation of a penis 2 an erect penis —**phal·lic** *adj*

Phan·er·o·zo·ic /fànnərə zṓ ik/ *n* the present eon of geologic time, which began 570 million years ago —**Phan·er·o·zo·ic** *adj*

phan·tasm /fán tàzzəm/ *n* 1 a ghost or spirit 2 a delusion or illusion —**phan·tas·mal** /fan tázm'l/ *adj*

phan·tas·ma·go·ri·a /fàntazmə gáwree ə/ *n* 1 a series of bizarre images 2 an ever-changing scene —**phan·tas·ma·gor·i·cal** /-gáwrik'l/ *adj*

phan·tom /fántəm/ *n* 1 an unreal presence 2 an illusion —**phan·tom** *adj*

Phar·aoh /fáirṓ/, **phar·aoh** *n* a ruler of ancient Egypt —**Phar·a·on·ic** /fàir ay ónnik/ *adj*

Phar·i·see /férri seé/ *n* 1 a member of an ancient Jewish religious group 2 *also* **phar·i·see** a person regarded as self-righteous or hypocritical (*disapproving*) —**Phar·i·sa·ic** /fèrri sáy ik/ *adj* —**Phar·i·see·ism** *n*

phar·ma·ceu·ti·cal /fàarmə soŏtik'l/ *adj* of the preparation and sale of medicinal drugs ■ *n* a medicinal drug (*usually pl*)

phar·ma·cist /fáarməssist/ *n* somebody who dispenses medicinal drugs

phar·ma·col·o·gy /fàarmə kólləjee/ (*pl* **-gies**) *n* 1 the study of drugs 2 the effects of a drug —**phar·ma·co·log·i·cal** /fàarməkə lójjik'l/ *adj* —**phar·ma·col·o·gist** *n*

phar·ma·co·poe·ia /fàarməkə peé ə/, **phar·ma·co·pe·ia** *n* 1 a book describing drugs and their uses 2 a collection of drugs

~~pharmacuetical~~ incorrect spelling of **pharmaceutical**

phar·ma·cy /fáarməsee/ (*pl* **-cies**) *n* 1 the dispensing of medicinal drugs 2 a shop selling or dispensing medicinal drugs

phar·yn·gi·tis /fàrrən jítiss/ *n* a sore throat

phar·ynx /fárringks/ (*pl* **pha·ryn·ges** /fə rínjeez/ *or* **phar·ynx·es**) *n* the throat

phase /fayz/ *n* 1 a stage of development 2 a temporary pattern of behavior 3 a part or aspect 4 a recurring visible form of the Moon or a planet ■ *vt* (**phased, phas·ing**) 1 do something in stages ○ *a takeover that is being phased to minimize disruption* 2 synchronize two or more things —**pha·sic** *adj* ◊ See note at **faze**

□ **phase in** *vt* introduce gradually

□ **phase out** *vt* discontinue gradually

phase-out /fáyz òwt/ *n* a gradual discontinuation

Ph.D. *abbr* Doctor of Philosophy

pheas·ant /fézz'nt/ (*pl* **-ants** *or* **same**) *n* 1 a large long-tailed game bird 2 a pheasant as food

ORIGIN The **pheasant** is ultimately named for the Phasis, a river in the Caucasus (now the Rioni River in W Georgia) that was thought to be its original home. The name entered English via French and Latin from Greek.

phe·nix *n* MYTHOL = **phoenix**

phe·no·bar·bi·tal /féenō baàrbi tàwl/ *n* a crystalline barbiturate used as a sedative

phe·nol /fée nàwl/ *n* a poisonous caustic compound. Use: manufacture of resins, dyes, and pharmaceuticals, antiseptic, disinfectant.

phe·nom·e·nal /fə nómmən'l/ *adj* remarkably impressive —**phe·nom·en·al·ly** *adv*

~~phenomenom~~ incorrect spelling of **phenomenon**

phe·nom·e·non /fə nómmə nòn, -nən/ (*pl* **-na**

/-nə/ or -**nons**/ n 1 an observable occurrence 2 something extraordinary

USAGE The plural of **phenomenon**, which comes from Greek, is *phenomena*, not *phenomenas*. Never use the false singular *phenomena*.

phe·no·type /féenə tīp/ n the visible characteristics of an organism resulting from genetic and environmental interaction —**phe·no·typ·i·cal** /-k'l/ adj

pher·o·mone /férrə mōn/ n a chemical secreted by animals that has a developmental and behavioral influence on other members of the species —**pher·o·mon·al** /fèrrə mōn'l/ adj

phew /fyoo/ interj expresses tiredness, relief, or disgust

phi /fī/ (pl **phis**) n the 21st letter of the Greek alphabet

phi·al /fī əl/ n a small medicine bottle

Phi Be·ta Kap·pa n 1 an academic honor society 2 a honor society member

Phid·i·as /fíddee əss/ (fl 490–430 BC) Greek sculptor

Phil·a·del·phi·a /fíllə délfee ə/ port in SE Pennsylvania. Pop. 1,436,287 (1998).

phi·lan·der /fi lándər/ vi have casual affairs with women (disapproving) —**phi·lan·der·er** n

phi·lan·thro·py /fi lánthrəpee/ (pl -**pies**) n 1 a desire to improve the welfare of humanity 2 a philanthropic act or group —**phil·an·throp·ic** /fíllən thróppik/ adj —**phil·an·throp·i·cal** adj —**phil·an·throp·i·cal·ly** adv —**phi·lan·thro·pist** n

phi·lat·e·ly /fi látt'lee/ n stamp collecting —**phil·a·tel·ic** /fíllə téllik/ adj —**phi·lat·e·list** n

ORIGIN Monsieur Herpin, a French stamp collector, was looking for an impressive and learned-sounding term for his hobby. Because the Greeks and Romans did not have postage stamps, there was no classical term for them. So he went back a stage beyond stamps, to the days of franking with a postmark. In France, such letters were marked with the words *franc de port* "carriage-free." The nearest he could get to this in Greek was *ateleia*, and from it he created *philatélie*, the English form of which made its first recorded appearance in 1865.

-**phile** suffix somebody or something that loves or has an affinity for o *bibliophile* —**philic** suffix —**philous** suffix —**phily** suffix

Phi·le·mon /fi léemən/ n a book in the Bible, written by St. Paul, appealing to Philemon to take pity on his slave who had escaped and converted to Christianity.

phil·har·mon·ic /fíl haar mónnik/ adj performing or promoting music ■ n a philharmonic orchestra, choir, or society

-**philia** suffix 1 intense or unusual attraction to 2 tendency toward o *hemophilia* —**philiac** suffix

Phil·ip /fílləp/, **St.** (fl AD 1stC) one of the 12 apostles of Jesus Christ

Phil·ip /fílləp/ (d. 1676) Wampanoag leader. Born **Metacomet**

Phil·ip II /fíllip/ (1527–98) king of Spain (1556–98)

Phil·ip II (382–336 BC) king of Macedonia (359–336 BC)

~~Philipines~~ incorrect spelling of **Philippines**

Phi·lip·pi /fílli pī, fi lí ppī/ ancient town of Macedonia, in present-day NE Greece

Phi·lip·pi·ans /fi líppee ənz/ n a book of the Bible, originally a letter from St. Paul to the church in Philippi. (+ sing verb)

Phil·ip·pines /fíllə péenz/ country in Southeast Asia, comprising over 7,000 islands in the W Pacific Ocean. Cap. Manila. Pop. 82,841,518 (2001). —**Phil·ip·pine** adj

Phil·ip·pine Sea section of the W Pacific Ocean, between S Japan and NE Philippines

phil·is·tine /fílli stèen, -stìn/ n 1 **Phil·is·tine** a member of a people of ancient Palestine 2 somebody who does not appreciate artistic and intellectual achievements (disapproving) ■ adj 1 **Phil·is·tine** of the Philistines 2 uncultured —**phi·lis·tin·ism** n

~~Philipines~~ incorrect spelling of **Philippines**

phi·lol·o·gy /fi lólləjee/ n 1 the study of the history and relationship of languages 2 the study of ancient texts —**phil·o·log·i·cal** /fíllə lójjik'l/ adj —**phi·lol·o·gist** n

phi·los·o·pher /fi lóssəfər/ n 1 somebody who studies the principles of existence and reality 2 somebody who thinks deeply about life in general

phi·los·o·pher's stone, phi·los·o·phers' stone n a substance that medieval alchemists believed could turn other metal into gold

phil·o·soph·i·cal /fíllə sóffik'l/, **phil·o·soph·ic** /-sóffik/ adj 1 of philosophy 2 showing calmness and resignation —**phil·o·soph·i·cal·ly** adv

phi·los·o·phize /fi lóssə fīz/ (-phized, -phiz·ing) vi 1 discuss the nature of reality 2 express opinions or moralize in a superficial or tedious way —**phi·los·o·phiz·er** n

phi·los·o·phy /fi lóssəfee/ (pl -**phies**) n 1 the study of basic concepts such as truth, existence, and reality 2 a school of thought 3 a set of guiding or underlying principles

phil·ter /fíltər/, **phil·tre** n a potion (literary)

~~phisical~~ incorrect spelling of **physical**

phle·bi·tis /flə bítiss/ n inflammation of the wall of a vein

phlegm /flem/ n 1 thick mucus in the respiratory passages 2 unflappability —**phlegm·y** adj

phleg·mat·ic /fleg máttik/, **phleg·mat·i·cal** /-máttik'l/ adj not easily excited or worried ◊ See note at **impassive**

~~phlem~~ incorrect spelling of **phlegm**

phlo·em /flṓ èm/ n the nutrient-carrying tissue of vascular plants

phlox (pl same or **phlox·es**) n a garden plant with clusters of scented flowers

Phnom Penh /pə nòm pén, nòm-/ capital of Cambodia. Pop. 429,000 (1995).

-phobe suffix somebody fearing or disl.. ing ○ technophobe

pho·bi·a /fṓbee ə/ n strong fear or dislike ○ a phobia about traveling in elevators —**pho·bic** adj, n

-phobia suffix an exaggerated or irrational fear of ○ claustrophobia —**-phobic** suffix

Phoe·ni·cia /fə nísha/ ancient region of coastal city-states in SW Asia —**Phoe·ni·cian** n, adj

phoe·nix /féeniks/, **phe·nix** n a mythological bird that burned itself, and from whose ashes another phoenix arose

Phoe·nix /féeniks/ capital of Arizona. Pop. 1,198,064 (1998).

phone /fōn/ n a telephone ■ vti (phoned, phon·ing) telephone

-phone suffix 1 a device that emits or receives sounds ○ saxophone ○ microphone 2 a telephone ○ cellphone 3 a speech sound ○ homophone —**-phonic** suffix —**-phony** suffix

phone book n a telephone book

phone booth n a telephone booth

phone·card /fōn kaärd/ n a plastic card used instead of money in a public telephone

pho·neme /fṓ nèem/ n a speech sound that is the smallest unit that can distinguish one word from another —**pho·ne·mic** /fə néemik, fō-/ adj

pho·net·ic /fə néttik, fō-/ adj 1 of speech sounds or phonetics 2 showing pronunciation —**pho·net·i·cal·ly** a v

pho·net·ics /fə néttiks, fō-/ n (+ sing verb) 1 the study of speech sounds and how they are produced 2 the sound system of a language —**pho·ne·ti·cian** /fōnə tísh'n/ n

pho·ney adj, n = **phony**

phon·ic /fónnik/ adj 1 of or using phonics 2 of sound 3 of speech sounds

phon·ics /fónniks/ n a reading method that involves associating letters with sounds (+ sing verb)

pho·no·graph /fōnə gràf/ n a record player

pho·nol·o·gy /fə nólləjee, fō-/ (pl -gies) n 1 the study of the pattern of speech sounds in language 2 the sound system of a language —**pho·no·log·i·cal** /fōnə lójjik'l/ adj

pho·ny /fōnee/, **pho·ney** (-ni·er, -ni·est) adj 1 not genuine 2 giving a false impression —**pho·ny** n —**pho·ni·ly** adv —**pho·ni·ness** n

phos·phate /fóss fàyt/ n 1 a salt or ester of phosphoric acid 2 a carbonated drink

phos·pho·res·cence /fòsfə réss'nss/ n the continued emission of light after exposure to and removal of a source of electromagnetic radiation —**phos·pho·resce** vi —**phos·pho·res·cent** adj

phos·phor·ic ac·id n a transparent liquid or solid acid. Use: fertilizer, rust-proofing, in soft drinks, pharmaceuticals, and animal feeds.

phos·pho·rus /fósfərəss/ n 1 (symbol P) a poisonous nonmetallic chemical element that ignites in air and glows in the dark. Use: matches, fireworks, incendiary devices, fertilizers. 2 a phosphorescent substance —**phos·phor·ic** /foss fáwrik/ adj —**phos·pho·rous** adj

ORIGIN Phosphorus goes back to a Greek word meaning literally "light-bringer," which was also used as a name for the planet Venus as it appears in the morning (as the "morning star"). It was applied from the early 17C to any substance or organism that glowed, and when the chemical element was isolated in the mid-17C it was adopted as its name, since **phosphorus** ignites when exposed to the air.

pho·to /fṓtō/ (pl -tos) n a photograph —**pho·to** vt

photo- prefix 1 light, radiant energy ○ photosensitive 2 photographic ○ photocopy

⚡**pho·to CD** n a compact disk storing images from photographs

pho·to·cop·y /fōtə kòppee/ (pl -ies) n a copy of a text or picture produced by a photographic process —**pho·to·cop·i·er** n —**pho·to·cop·y** vti

pho·to·e·lec·tric cell /fōtō i léktrik-/ a photosensitive device controlling an electric current, e.g., in a burglar alarm or exposure meter

~~photoes~~ incorrect spelling of **photos**

pho·to fin·ish n the end of a race so close that the result must be determined from a photograph

pho·to·gen·ic /fōtə jénnik/ adj looking attractive in photographs

pho·to·graph /fōtə gràf/ n a picture produced from an image recorded on light-sensitive film or a digitized array in a camera ■ v 1 vti take a photograph of somebody or something 2 vi be photographed with a particular result ○ Scenes like this photograph best in bright sunlight. —**pho·tog·ra·pher** /fə tóggrəfər/ n

pho·to·graph·ic /fōtə gráffik/ adj 1 of photography 2 like a photograph in accuracy or detail ○ a photographic memory —**pho·to·graph·i·cal·ly** adv

pho·tog·ra·phy /fə tóggrəfee/ n the art, hobby, or profession of producing pictures with a camera

pho·to·jour·nal·ism /fōtō júrn'l ìzzəm/ n journalism using mainly photographs —**pho·to·jour·nal·ist** n

pho·tom·e·try /fō tómmətree/ n the measurement of the intensity of light —**pho·tom·e·ter** n —**pho·to·met·ric** /fōtə méttrik/ adj

pho·ton /fó tòn/ n a quantum of visible light or other form of electromagnetic radiation demonstrating both particle and wave properties —**pho·ton·ic** /fō tónnik/ adj

pho·to op·por·tu·ni·ty n an opportunity for taking newsworthy photographs

pho·to·sen·si·tive /fōtō sénsətiv/ adj reacting to light —**pho·to·sen·si·tiv·i·ty** /fōtō sènsə tívvətee/ n

pho·to·syn·the·sis /fōtō sínthəssiss/ n the production by plants and some other organisms of carbohydrates and oxygen from carbon dioxide and water using light and chlorophyll —**pho·to·syn·the·size** vti —**pho·to·syn·thet·ic** /fōtō sin théttik/ adj

pho·to·vol·ta·ic cell /fōtō vol táy ik-, -vòl-/ n a photoelectric cell that uses the potential difference between dissimilar materials exposed to electromagnetic radiation

phras·al verb n a verb combined with an adverb or preposition in an idiomatic way

phrase /frayz/ n 1 a string of words forming a grammatical unit that is not a complete sentence 2 a fixed expression ■ vt (phrased, phras·ing) express in a particular way —**phras·al** adj

phrase book n a book of translated phrases for travelers abroad

phra·se·ol·o·gy /fràyzee óllajee/ n 1 the phrases used in a particular sphere of activity 2 the way words and phrases are chosen and put together —**phra·se·o·log·i·cal** /fràyzee ə lójjik'l/ adj

phras·ing /fráyzing/ n 1 the way words are chosen and put together 2 the way musical notes are grouped into phrases

phre·nol·o·gy /frə nóllajee/ n the study of the bumps on the skull, formerly believed to indicate character —**phre·nol·o·gist** n

Phryg·i·a /fríjjee ə/ ancient country in Asia Minor, in present-day west central Turkey

phy·lac·ter·y /fi láktəree/ (pl -ies) n a Jewish aid to prayer consisting of each of two small leather boxes containing scriptures (often pl)

phyl·lo /féelō/, **phyl·lo pas·try** n fine-layered Greek pastry

phy·lum /fîləm/ (pl -la /-lə/) n 1 a major taxonomic group in zoological classification 2 a large group of languages or language stocks thought to be historically related, e.g., Indo-European

phys·ic /fízzik/ (archaic) n a medicine, especially a purgative ■ vt (-icked, -ick·ing) treat with a medical remedy

phys·i·cal /fízzik'l/ adj 1 of the body 2 real and touchable 3 needing bodily strength

4 involving bodily contact 5 describes sciences that deal with nonliving things ■ n a physical examination (infml) —**phys·i·cal·i·ty** /fízzi kállətee/ n —**phys·i·cal·ly** adv

phys·i·cal ed·u·ca·tion n physical exercise as a school subject

phys·i·cal ex·am·i·na·tion n a general medical examination to check that somebody is fit and healthy

phys·i·cal ge·og·ra·phy n the study of the natural features of the Earth's surface

phys·i·cal·ly chal·lenged adj unable to perform some of the activities of daily life

phys·i·cal sci·ence n a science that deals with nonliving things, e.g., physics or chemistry

phys·i·cal ther·a·py n physiotherapy —**phys·i·cal ther·a·pist** n

phy·si·cian /fi zísh'n/ n 1 a medical doctor 2 a doctor who diagnoses and treats diseases and injuries using methods other than surgery

phys·ics /fízziks/ n the study of matter, energy, force, and motion (+ sing verb) ■ npl the physical properties or behavior of something (+ pl verb) —**phys·i·cist** /fízzisist/ n

physio- prefix physical ○ physiotherapy

phys·i·og·no·my /fízzee ógnəmee/ (pl -mies) n 1 somebody's facial features, especially viewed as a guide to character 2 the character or appearance of something —**phys·i·og·no·mist** n

phys·i·ol·o·gy /fízzee óllajee/ n 1 the study of the functioning of living things 2 the body's internal processes —**phys·i·o·log·i·cal** /fízzee ə lójjik'l/ adj —**phys·i·o·log·i·cal·ly** adv —**phys·i·ol·o·gist** n

phys·i·o·ther·a·py /fízzee ō thérrəpee/ n the treatment of injuries by means such as exercise and massage —**phys·i·o·ther·a·peu·tic** /fízzee ō therrə pyóotik/ adj —**phys·i·o·ther·a·pist** n

phy·sique /fi zeék/ n the shape and size of somebody's body

pi /pī/ n 1 the 16th letter of the Greek alphabet 2 a mathematical constant equal to the circumference of a circle divided by its diameter, approximately 3.142

⚡**PIA** abbr peripheral interface adaptor

Pi·af /pée af/, **Édith** (1915–63) French singer

Pia·get /pèeə zháy/, **Jean** (1896–1980) Swiss psychologist

pi·a·nis·si·mo /pèe ə níssi mō/ adv very softly (musical direction) —**pi·a·nis·si·mo** adj

pi·an·ist /pée ənist, pee ánnist/ n a piano player

pi·an·o¹ /pee ánnō/ (pl -os) n a large musical instrument with a keyboard through which stretched wire strings are struck with hammers

ORIGIN Piano is a shortening of pianoforte, which in Italian (the language from which both terms derive) means literally "soft loud." The name referred to the ability of the instrument to vary volume using felt-covered blocks, a characteristic not shared by the harpsichord and other earlier keyboard instruments. **Piano** is recorded in English in the early 19C, and **pianoforte** in the mid-18C.

pi·a·no² /pee aáno/ *adv* softly *(musical direction)* —**pi·a·no** *adj*

pi·an·o·for·te /pee ànnò fáwr tày/ *(pl* **-tes)** *n* a piano *(fml)*

pi·az·za /pee aátsə/ *(pl* **-ze** /-áatsay/) *n (pl* **pi·az·ze)** an Italian public square

pic·a·dor /píkə dàwr/ *n* a bullfighter on horseback

pic·a·resque /pìkə résk/ *adj* **1** of rogues **2** describes prose fiction about the adventures of a roguish hero

Pablo Picasso: Photographed in 1933 by Man Ray

AKG London

Pi·cas·so /pi kaássò, -kássò/, **Pablo** (1881–1973) Spanish painter and sculptor

pic·ca·lil·li /pìkə líllee/ *n* pickle relish

pic·co·lo /píkə lò/ *(pl* **-los)** *n* the smallest member of the flute family of musical instruments

pick¹ *vt* **1** remove fruit or flowers from a plant **2** choose somebody or something from a group **3** remove something in small pieces **4** open a lock without a proper key **5** start a fight or argument **6** play a stringed instrument by plucking the strings ■ *n* **1** a choice ○ *take your pick* **2** the best —**pick·er** *n*

☐ **pick at** *vt* scrape with the fingernails

☐ **pick on** *vt* persistently criticize or bully

☐ **pick out** *vt* choose

☐ **pick up** *v* **1** *vt* lift or collect something or somebody **2** *vt* gather dropped things **3** *vti* take on a passenger or passengers **4** *vt* learn something in a casual or unsystematic way **5** *vi* become better *(infml)* **6** *vt* arrest *(infml)*

pick² *n* **1** a tool for breaking up hard surfaces, consisting of a long handle and a curved metal head **2** a device for plucking guitar strings —**pick** *vti*

pick·ax /pík àks/ *n* a pick with a metal head that has one pointed and one flattened end

ORIGIN The **pickax** is etymologically not strictly an ax at all. The word came via French from Latin *picus* "woodpecker." It was altered by association with *ax* in the 15C.

pick·et /píkit/ *n* **1** a pointed post stuck in the ground **2** a soldier or group of soldiers on

guard **3** a protester or group of protesters outside a place, e.g., during a strike ■ *v* **1** *vt* enclose or mark with pickets **2** *vt* guard with or as a picket **3** *vti* hold or take part in a protest outside a place —**pick·et·er** *n*

pick·et fence *n* a simple fence of pointed stakes

pick·et line *n* a line of protesters picketing a place

Pick·ett /píkit/, **George Edward** (1825–75) US Confederate general

Pick·ford /píkfərd/, **Mary** (1893–1979) Canadian-born US actor and producer

pick·ings /píkingz/ *npl* things available

pick·le /pík'l/ *n* **1** a vegetable preserved in vinegar or brine **2** liquid for pickling food **3** an awkward situation *(infml)* ■ *vt* **(-led, -ling)** preserve in vinegar or brine —**pick·ler** *n*

pick·led /pík'ld/ *adj* preserved in vinegar or brine

pick-me-up *n* an energizing drink *(infml)*

~~picknick~~ incorrect spelling of **picnic**

pick·pock·et /pík pòkət/ *n* a thief who steals from people's pockets and bags —**pick·pock·et·ing** *n*

pick·up /pík ùp/ *n* **1** the collection of something to be taken somewhere else **2** somebody or something picked up **3** *also* **pick·up truck** a light open-backed truck with a hinged tailgate **4** an improvement or increase *(infml)* **5** a power to accelerate *(infml)*

pick·y /píkee/ **(-i·er, -i·est)** *adj* hard to please or satisfy —**pick·i·ly** *adv* —**pick·i·ness** *n*

pic·nic /pík nik/ *n* **1** a meal taken on an outing and eaten outdoors **2** an easy or pleasant thing *(infml)* ○ *Moving house is no picnic.* **3** a shoulder cut of pork ■ *vi* **(-nicked, -nick·ing)** eat a picnic —**pic·nick·er** *n*

~~picnicing~~ incorrect spelling of **picnicking**

pic·to·ri·al /pik táwree əl/ *adj* **1** of pictures **2** illustrated by pictures ■ *n* a highly illustrated periodical —**pic·to·ri·al·ly** *adv*

pic·ture /píkchər/ *n* **1** a visual representation of something or somebody on a flat surface **2** a photograph **3** the image on a television screen **4** a movie **5** a mental image **6** a description in writing or music **7** a situation in its context ■ *vt* **(-tured, -tur·ing) 1** imagine **2** describe

pic·ture book *n* a book with many illustrations, especially one for children

pic·ture-per·fect *adj* without disorder or dirt

pic·tur·esque /pìkchə résk/ *adj* very attractive or scenic —**pic·tur·esque·ly** *adv* —**pic·tur·esque·ness** *n*

pic·ture win·dow *n* a large window, usually with a single pane of glass

PID *abbr* pelvic inflammatory disease

pid·dle /pídd'l/ **(-dled, -dling)** *vi* spend time on unimportant things —**pid·dle** *n*

pid·dling /píddling/ *adj* very small or trivial (*infml*) —**pid·dling·ly** *adv*

pidg·in /píjjin/ *n* a simplified language made up of elements of different languages and used as a common second language

---

ORIGIN Pidgin represents a Chinese alteration of *business*, and is itself an example of *pidgin* English, the altered and simplified English used in trade and other communications in China and East Asia in the 19C.

---

pie /pī/ *n* **1** a baked dish consisting of a filling encased in pastry **2** a divisible whole ◊ **pie in the sky** a pipe dream

---

ORIGIN The origin of *pie* is not certain, but it may be named for the magpie (or *pie*, as it was earlier called). The fillings of early *pies* characteristically consisted of a mixture of ingredients, and may have been likened to the miscellaneous items collected by magpies.

---

pie·bald /pī báwld/ *adj* pinto —**pie·bald** *n*

piece /peess/ *n* **1** a part detached from a whole **2** an individual item or article ○ *a piece of equipment* **3** an interconnecting part ○ *a 500-piece jigsaw* **4** an example of something ○ *a piece of luck* **5** a statement of opinion ○ *I've said my piece.* **6** an artistic work **7** a published article **8** a coin **9** an object moved in a board game ■ *vt* (**pieced, piec·ing**) **1** put together bit by bit ○ *piece together the events of that night* **2** mend by adding a patch or piece ◊ **fall** *or* **go to pieces** become unable to cope ◊ See note at **peace**

pi·èce de ré·sis·tance /pee èss də rə zeéss taàns, -ray zeéss-/ (*pl* **pi·èces de ré·sis·tance** /pee èss də rə zeéss taàns, pee èss də ray zeéss taàns/) *n* **1** the most impressive thing **2** the most important dish of a meal (*fml*)

piece·meal /peéss meèl/ *adv* **1** gradually **2** in separate parts ■ *adj* done part by part

piece·work /peéss wùrk/ *n* work paid by the amount done

pie-chart /pī chaàrt/ *n* a graphical representation in the form of a circle divided into sections

pied-à-terre /pee àydə táir/ (*pl* **pieds-à-terre** /-táir/) *n* a small secondary residence used for business purposes or vacations

Pied·mont Pla·teau /peèd mont-/ upland region of the E United States, extending from New York to Alabama between the Appalachian Mountains and the Atlantic Coastal Plain

pied pip·er /pīd-/ *n* somebody who attracts supporters and followers

---

ORIGIN In German folklore, the Pied Piper was a visiting piper whose entrancing music rid the town of Hamelin of its rats. The story is the basis of a poem (1842) by Robert Browning.

---

pier /peer/ *n* **1** a walkway on stilts jutting into the sea **2** a vertical structural support, e.g., for a bridge or wall ◊ See note at **peer**

pierce /peers/ (**pierced, pierc·ing**) *v* **1** *vi* bore into something with a pointed object **2** *vt* make a hole through something **3** *vti* penetrate a barrier **4** *vti* sound or shine suddenly and intensely through silence or darkness

Pierce, Franklin (1804–69) 14th president of the United States (1853–57)

pierc·ing /peérsing/ *adj* **1** unpleasantly loud and shrill **2** acutely perceptive **3** intensely cold ■ *n* the practice of making holes in parts of the body so that ornamental rings can be inserted —**pierc·ing·ly** *adv*

Pie·ro del·la Fran·ce·sca /pyàirò dellə fran chéskə/ (1420?–92) Italian painter

Pierre /peer/ capital of South Dakota. Pop. 13,267 (1998).

Pier·rot /peé ə rò, pye rő/ *n* a traditional French pantomime clown with a white face and costume

pi·e·ty /pī ətee/ (*pl* **-ties**) *n* **1** religious devotion **2** a devout act **3** a conventional or hypocritical statement or observance of a belief

pif·fle /pífl'l/ *n* nonsense (*infml dated*)

pig *n* **1** a short fat farm animal with a broad snout and a curly tail **2** pork **3** a person regarded as greedy or coarse (*infml insult*) **4** a rough block of cast metal **5** an offensive term for a police officer (*slang*) ■ *vi* (**pigged, pig·ging**) give birth to pigs ◊ **a pig in a poke** something that is bought or obtained without being inspected
□ **pig out** *vi* eat greedily (*infml*)

pi·geon /píjjən/ *n* a stocky medium-sized gray-and-white bird that is common in cities

pi·geon·hole /píjjən hòl/ *n* **1** one of a set of small compartments for putting messages in for different people **2** a category into which somebody or something is put without much thought ■ *vt* **1** put into a category without much thought **2** postpone

pi·geon-toed *adj* walking with the toes turning in

pig·ger·y /píggəree/ (*pl* **-ies**) *n* **1** a place for raising pigs **2** greedy or coarse behavior

pig·gish /píggish/, **pig·gy** /píggee/ (**-gier, -gi·est**) *adj* **1** greedy **2** obstinate —**pig·gish·ly** *adv*

pig·gy /píggee/ (*pl* **-gies**) *n* a pig or piglet (*baby talk*)

pig·gy·back /píggee bàk/ *n* **1** a ride on somebody's back **2** transportation of one vehicle on another —**pig·gy·back** *adj, adv, vt*

pig·gy bank *n* a child's savings bank, often in the shape of a pig

pig·head·ed /pig héddəd/ *adj* obstinate —**pig·head·ed·ly** *adv* —**pig·head·ed·ness** *n*

pig i·ron *n* iron in rough blocks

pig·let /pígglət/ n a young pig

pig·ment n /pígmənt/ 1 a substance added to give something such as paint or ink its color 2 a natural coloring substance in plant or animal tissue ■ vt /pígmənt, pig mént/ give color to —**pig·men·tar·y** adj

pig·men·ta·tion /pígmən táysh'n/ n the natural color of plants and animals

pig·pen /píg pèn/, **pig·sty** /píg stì/ (pl -sties) n 1 a building or pen for pigs 2 a dirty place

pig·skin /píg skìn/ n 1 leather from a pig 2 a football —**pig·skin** adj

pig·tail /píg tàyl/ n a braid or bunch of hair gathered together —**pig·tailed** adj

pi·ka /peéka, píka/ (pl -kas or same) n a small short-eared burrowing mammal related to the rabbit

pike[1] (pl pikes or same) n a large sharp-toothed freshwater fish

ORIGIN Pike as a name for a fish comes from an earlier word meaning "pointed object," from the shape of its jaws. The same word is also the second element of turnpike, of which pike "road" is a shortening (a turnpike was originally a "spiked barrier," and then a "toll gate"). The weapon name was adopted from French in the early 16C, and is formed from a verb meaning "prick, irritate," which is also the source of pique. The diving and gymnastic pike is the most recent, dating from the early 20C, but its etymology has never been established.

pike[2] n formerly, a weapon consisting of a pole with a spike on top

pike[3] n a turnpike

pike[4] n a diving or gymnastic position in which the body is bent double

Pike, Zebulon Montgomery (1779–1813) US explorer and soldier

Pikes Peak mountain in the Rocky Mountains, in east central Colorado. Height 14,110 ft./4,301 m.

pike·staff /pík stàf/ n 1 the shaft of a pike 2 a walking stick with a metal point

pi·laf /pí laaf, peé laáf/, **pi·lau** /pí lów, peé lòw/ n a rice dish, often with chopped vegetables, fish, or meat added

pi·las·ter /pi lástər/ n an ornamental column on a wall

Pi·late /pílət/, **Pontius** (fl 1C) Roman administrator

pil·chard /pílchərd/ (pl -chards or same) n 1 a small ocean fish 2 a pilchard as food

pile[1] n 1 a mound of things 2 a large quantity or amount (infml; often pl) 3 a large impressive building ■ v (piled, pil·ing) 1 vt heap 2 vt place large amounts on 3 vi go as a crowd

pile[2] n a support for a building that is driven into the ground

pile[3] n the surface of a carpet or a fabric such as velvet, formed of fiber loops

pile driv·er n a machine that hammers piles into the ground

piles npl hemorrhoids (infml)

pile-up /pí l ùp/ n 1 a collision involving several vehicles (infml) 2 an accumulation of things

pil·fer /pílfər/ vti steal small things of little value —**pil·fer·er** n —**pil·fer·ing** n ◊ See note at **steal**

pil·grim /pílgrim/ n 1 a traveler to a holy place for religious reasons 2 a traveler on a special journey (literary) 3 Pil·grim a Plymouth Colony founder —**pil·grim·age** n

~~pilgrimmage~~ incorrect spelling of **pilgrimage**

pill n 1 a round tablet of medicine taken orally 2 also **Pill** an oral contraceptive

pil·lage /pílij/ vti (-laged, -lag·ing) 1 plunder a place 2 steal possessions as plunder ■ n 1 the plundering of somebody's possessions 2 possessions stolen as plunder —**pil·lag·er** n

pil·lar /pílər/ n 1 a column used for support or decoration 2 something tall and narrow

pill·box /píl bòks/ n 1 a small container for pills 2 also **pill·box hat** a woman's brimless flat-topped hat

pil·lion /pílyən/ n a passenger seat behind the driver of a motorcycle or the rider of a horse —**pil·lion** adv

pil·lo·ry /pílləree/ n (pl -ries) a wooden frame with holes into which somebody's head and hands could be locked, formerly a method of public punishment ■ vt (-ried, -ries) 1 ridicule 2 punish in a pillory

pil·low /pílō/ n 1 a cushion for the head in bed 2 a soft base for supporting the tools used in lace-making ■ vt 1 rest the head on a pillow 2 provide a soft and comfortable surface for something

pil·low·case /pílō kàyss/, **pil·low·slip** /-slìp/ n a removable cover for a pillow

pil·low talk n intimate talk in bed

pi·lot /pílət/ n 1 somebody who flies an aircraft or spacecraft 2 somebody who steers ships in ports or through difficult areas 3 a leader or guide 4 a television or radio program intended to form the basis for a series ■ vt 1 fly an aircraft or spacecraft 2 navigate a ship 3 be in charge of running something

pi·lot·age /pílətij/ n the piloting of an aircraft, spacecraft, or ship

pil·sner /pílznər, pílsnər/ n 1 a Czech lager beer with a strong hops flavor 2 also **pil·sner glass** a glass for drinking beer

⚡**PIM** abbr personal information manager

Pi·ma /peéma/ n 1 a member of a Native North American people who live mainly in central Arizona 2 the language of the Pima people —**Pi·ma** adj

pi·men·to /pi méntō/ n 1 also **pi·mien·to** a large sweet red pepper. Use: paprika, olive stuffing, garnish. **2** a plant that produces pimentos

pim·per·nel /pímpər nèl, -nəl/ (pl **-nels** or same) n a small flowering plant with long trailing stems

pim·ple /pímp'l/ n an inflamed skin blemish —**pim·ply** adj

pin n **1** a small thin metal stick with a sharp point and a round head, used for holding pieces of fabric together **2** something resembling a pin in shape or function, e.g., a safety pin, bobby pin, or rolling pin **3** a decorative object attached to clothing by means of a sharp metal point **4** a bowling pin **5** in golf, a pole with a flag on it, used to mark a hole ■ vt (**pinned, pin·ning**) **1** fasten with a pin **2** keep from moving

□ **pin down** vt **1** determine with certainty **2** force to keep a commitment or come to a decision

⚡ **PIN** /pin/, **PIN num·ber** n a multidigit number used by a person to gain access to cash, a computer, or a telephone system. Full form **personal identification number**

~~pinacle~~ incorrect spelling of **pinnacle**

pi·ña co·la·da /pèenyə kə laádə/ n a cocktail made from pineapple juice, rum, and coconut

pin·a·fore /pínnə fàwr/ n a sleeveless garment like an apron

pi·ña·ta /pin yaátə, peen yaátə/ n a decorated container that is broken by a blindfolded person with a stick to get the gifts inside it

Pi·na·tu·bo, Mt. /pínnə toóbō/ active volcano on central Luzon, Philippines. Height 5,840 ft./1,780 m.

pin·ball /pín bàwl/ n an indoor game played on a sloping electronic table in which a player flicks a ball past obstacles to score points

pince-nez /pìns náy/ (pl **pince-nez** /-náyz/) n glasses that are clipped to the bridge of the nose

pin·cer move·ment /pínsər-/, **pin·cers move·ment** /pínsərs-/ n a military maneuver in which two columns of troops converge on an enemy in a curving movement from opposite sides

pin·cers /pínsərz/ npl **1** the large front claws of some crustaceans and arachnids, e.g., the lobster **2** a tool for gripping things

pinch v **1** vti grip something between two objects, especially a finger and thumb **2** vti be too tight and painful for a part of the body **3** vt make somebody or something wither or shrink ■ n **1** a painful squeeze, especially with the thumb and finger **2** a very small amount of something ◊ **3** a critical time ◊ **feel the pinch** have financial problems ◊ See note at **steal**

pinch hit n in baseball, a hit by a substitute batter —**pinch-hit** vi —**pinch hit·ter** n

pin·cush·ion /pín koòsh'n/ n a pad for storing pins on

pine[1] n **1** wood from an evergreen tree. Use: furniture-making, construction, finishing material. **2** an evergreen coniferous tree grown for its wood

pine[2] (**pined, pin·ing**) vi **1** yearn **2** waste away as a result of grief or longing

pine·ap·ple /pī nàpp'l/ n **1** a large fruit with juicy yellow flesh, a thick lumpy brown skin, and a tuft of leaves at the top **2** (pl **pine·ap·ples** or same) a plant that produces pineapples

ORIGIN The **pineapple** was given its name because it was thought to resemble a pine cone (the earlier and original sense of the word).

pine cone n the seed case of a pine tree

pine nee·dle n the needle-shaped leaf of a pine tree

pine nut n an edible pine seed

ping n **1** a single light ringing sound **2** a knock in an engine ■ vi knock (refers to engines)

pin·head /pín hèd/ n the rounded end of a pin

pin·hole /pín hòl/ n a tiny hole or puncture

pin·ion[1] /pínnyən/ n a bird's wing, especially the tip ■ vt **1** restrain somebody by holding or tying his or her arms **2** keep a bird from flying by removing or binding its wing feathers

pin·ion[2] /pínnyən/ n a small gear wheel that engages with a larger gear or a rack

pink[1] n **1** a pale reddish color **2** a plant with fragrant pink, red, or white flowers **3** the highest degree or best example of something ■ adj of a pale reddish color —**pink·ness** n

ORIGIN The Dutch phrase pinck oogen meant literally "small eyes." It was adopted into English in the partially translated form pink eyes, which may have been used as the name of plants related to the **pink**. The abbreviated form **pink** emerged as a plant name in the 16C. Many of these plants have pale red flowers, and by the 18C **pink** was being used as a color term.

pink[2] vt **1** cut with pinking shears **2** punch little holes in something such as leather as a decoration

pink-col·lar adj of jobs once done by women

pink·ie /píngkee/, **pink·y** (pl **-ies**) n US, Can, Scotland the little finger (infml)

pink·ing shears, pink·ing scis·sors npl scissors with a serrated blade for cutting cloth

pink slip n a termination of employment notice (infml)

pin mon·ey n **1** money for buying personal nonessential things **2** money that a man gives his wife for personal use (dated)

pin·na·cle /pínnək'l/ n **1** the highest point or level of something **2** a mountain peak

⚡**PIN num·ber** *n* BANKING, COMPUT = **PIN**

pi·noch·le /peé nùk'l, -nôk'l/, **pi·noc·le** *n* a card game played with incomplete decks

pi·ñon /pín yòn, pínnyən/ (*pl* **-ñons** *or* **-ño·nes** /pín yōneez/), **pin·yon** *n* 1 *also* **pi·ñon nut** a small sweet nut 2 a pine tree that produces piñons

pin·point /pín pòynt/ *vt* identify or locate something correctly ■ *n* something small or trivial ■ *adj* exact

pin·prick /pín prik/ *n* 1 a small hole made by a pin or something similar 2 a slight wound 3 a minor irritant

pins and need·les *n* a tingling sensation in a body part (+ *sing or pl verb*)

pin·stripe /pín strìp/ *n* 1 a narrow line in a fabric 2 fabric with very narrow lines. Use: business suits. —**pin-striped** *adj*

pint /pīnt/ *n* a unit of liquid or dry measure equal to one eighth of a gallon

Pin·ter /píntər/, **Harold** (*b.* 1930) British playwright and director —**Pin·ter·esque** /pìntə résk/ *adj*

pin·to /píntō/ *adj* describes a horse that is marked with patches of white ■ *n* (*pl* **-tos** *or* **-toes**) a pinto horse

pin·to bean *n* 1 an edible mottled brown and pink kidney-shaped bean 2 a plant that produces pinto beans

pint-size, pint-sized *adj* very small (*infml*)

pin-up /pín ùp/ *n* a posed picture of a sexually attractive person ■ *adj* designed to hang on wall

pin·wheel /pín weèl, -hweèl/ *n* 1 a rotating toy 2 a firework that spins

pin·yon *n* FOOD, TREES = **piñon**

pi·o·neer /pì ə neér/ *n* the first person to do or develop something or to explore a territory ■ *vt* develop or explore something new

pi·ous /pí əss/ *adj* 1 devoutly religious 2 acting in a falsely moralizing way 3 holy or sacred —**pi·ous·ly** *adv*

pip[1] *n* a small hard seed of a fruit such as an apple that usually has several seeds

pip[2] *n* 1 a spot on a die or domino 2 a symbol on a playing card

pipe /pīp/ *n* 1 a tube for transporting liquid or gas 2 a tubular object, part, or organ 3 a small bowl with a hollow stem for smoking 4 the amount in a smoker's pipe 5 a tubular musical instrument played by blowing 6 a tubular part of a musical organ 7 a high-pitched noise ■ **pipes** *npl* bagpipes ■ *v* (**piped, pip·ing**) 1 *vt* carry liquid or gas by pipe 2 *vti* install and connect pipes in something 3 *vt* play a tune on a pipe or bagpipes 4 *vt* send piped music through a place 5 *vt* decorate something with piping 6 *vti* sing, speak, or say something in a high-pitched voice —**pipe·ful** *n*

□ **pipe down** *vi* stop talking or become quieter (*infml; often a command*)

□ **pipe up** *vi* begin to speak in order to interrupt or explain

pipe clean·er *n* a flexible wire covered with fluffy material for cleaning a tobacco pipe

piped mu·sic *n* background music in a public place

pipe dream *n* an unrealistic notion

pipe·line /pīp līn/ *n* 1 a long pipe system for transporting oil or gas 2 a channel of communications —**pipe·line** *vt* ◊ **in the pipeline** in preparation but not yet ready

pip·er /pīpər/ *n* 1 a pipe player 2 a bagpiper ◊ **pay the piper** to take the consequences for something

pi·pette /pī pét/ *n* a small glass tube for sucking up liquid to measure it before transferring it to another container

pip·ing /pīping/ *n* 1 a system of pipes 2 a fabric-covered cord. Use: decorating clothes, upholstery. 3 a decorative effect on food using something such as lines of frosting 4 the art or skill of playing a pipe or bagpipes 5 a shrill noise 6 the sound of a pipe or bagpipes ■ *adj* shrill

pip·it /píppit/ *n* a small long-tailed songbird

pip·pin /píppin/ *n* a cultivated variety of apple

pip·squeak /píp skweèk/ *n* a person or thing regarded as small or insignificant (*infml*)

pi·quant /peékənt, -kàant, pee kàant/ *adj* 1 spicy, pungent, or salty 2 stimulating or provocative —**pi·quan·cy** *n* —**pi·quant·ly** *adv*

pique /peek/ *n* a feeling of resentment caused by an insult ■ *vt* (**piqued, piqu·ing**) 1 make resentful 2 arouse or provoke ◊ *piqued my curiosity* ◊ See note at **peak**

pi·qué /pi kày, pee-, peé kày/ *n* a closely woven ribbed fabric. Use: clothes.

pi·ra·cy /pírəssee/ *n* the activity of a pirate

Pi·rae·us /pī reé əss, pi rày-/ city in east central Greece, the port of Athens. Pop. 182,671 (1991).

Pi·ran·del·lo /pìrrən déllō/, **Luigi** (1867–1936) Italian playwright

pi·ra·nha /pi ràanyə, -rànnyə, -ràanə, -ránnə/ (*pl* **-nhas** *or same*), **pi·ra·ña** (*pl* **-ñas** *or same*) *n* a small tropical fish with sharp teeth that attacks in large numbers

pi·rate /pírət/ *n* 1 a robber operating on the high seas 2 a ship used by sea robbers 3 somebody using copyrighted material without permission —**pi·rate** *vt* —**pi·rat·ic** /pī ráttik/ *adj*

pi·rogue /pi rōg/ *n* a dugout canoe

pir·ou·ette /peéroo ét/ *n* a spin on one foot in ballet

Pi·sa /peézə/ city in west central Italy. Pop. 93,303 (1997).

pis·ca·to·ri·al /pìskə táwree əl/, **pis·ca·to·ry** /pískə tàwree/ *adj* of fish or fishing (*fml*)

Pi·sces /pí seèz/ *n* 1 a zodiacal constellation in the northern hemisphere 2 the 12th sign of the zodiac —**Pi·sce·an** /písee ən/ n —**Pi·sces** adj

Pis·sar·ro /pi saárō/, **Camille** (1830–1905) French painter

pis·soir /pee swaár/ n a public urinal in a street

pis·ta·chi·o /pi stáshee ò, -staáshee-/ (pl **-os**) n 1 also **pis·ta·chi·o nut** a nut with an edible green kernel 2 (pl **pis·ta·chi·os** or same) a tree that produces pistachios

piste /peest/ n a snow-covered slope for skiing

pis·til /píst'l/ n the female reproductive part of a plant

pis·tol /píst'l/ n a small gun designed to be held in one hand ■ vt shoot with a pistol

pis·tol-whip vt hit with the butt or barrel of a pistol

pis·ton /pístən/ n 1 a metal cylinder that slides within a tube 2 a valve in a brass instrument used for altering the pitch

pit[1] n 1 a big hole in the ground 2 a hole or shaft in the ground for mining 3 a small circular scar left by a disease or skin disorder 4 the very bottom of something ○ in the pit of my stomach 5 a pitfall 6 the part of a theater where the orchestra sits 7 a servicing area for racing cars (often pl) 8 an arena for cocks or dogs to fight in 9 the trading area on the floor of an exchange 10 in track and field, a sandy area where jumpers land 11 Hell (literary) ■ **pits** npl the worst possible thing, person, or place (infml) ■ vt (**pit·ted, pit·ting**) 1 set up in opposition 2 mark with small holes or indentations

pit[2] n the hard seed of a fruit such a peach that has only one seed ■ vt (**pit·ted, pit·ting**) remove the kernel from a fruit

pi·ta /peétə/, **pi·ta bread** n a flat round unleavened bread that can be opened to insert a filling

pit-a-pat /pittə pát/ adv with a series of quick tapping sounds —**pit-a-pat** n, vi

pit bull, pit bull ter·ri·er n a large and muscular bull terrier

Pit·cairn Is·land /pít kairn-/ island in the central South Pacific Ocean, the main island of a group forming a dependency of the United Kingdom. Pop. 61 (1991).

pitch[1] v 1 vti throw or hurl something 2 vt throw something away 3 vti in baseball, throw a ball to the batter 4 vt set up a tent, camp, or other temporary structure 5 vt secure something in the ground 6 vti fall, or make somebody or something fall down 7 vi slant in a particular way 8 vt set something at a particular intellectual level 9 vi move up and down (refers especially to ships and aircraft) 10 vti in golf, hit a ball high in the air with some backspin 11 vt set a musical instrument to a particular key ■ n 1 in baseball, a throw of the ball to the batter 2 a particular degree of something ○ such a pitch of anxiety 3 the degree of slope

of something 4 the level of a sound in a scale, according to its frequency 5 in golf, a high shot with some backspin 6 an aggressive speech trying to sell or promote something (infml)

□ **pitch in** vi 1 help willingly 2 begin to do something enthusiastically

pitch[2] n 1 a dark sticky substance obtained from tar. Use: waterproofing roofs. 2 a natural tarry substance such as asphalt ■ vt spread pitch on

pitch-black, pitch-dark adj extremely dark

pitched bat·tle n 1 a fierce battle at a prearranged location 2 a fierce conflict or argument

pitch·er[1] /píchər/ n a large single-handled water jug

pitch·er[2] /píchər/ n in baseball, the player who throws the ball to the batter

pitch·fork /pích fàwrk/ n a pronged long-handled farming tool for moving hay ■ vt use a pitchfork to move hay

pitch·out /pích òwt/ n 1 in baseball, a high pitch that is intentionally thrown outside of the strike zone 2 in football, a lateral pass behind the line of scrimmage

pitch pine n a pine tree that yields pitch or turpentine

pit·e·ous /píttee əss/ adj deserving or arousing pity —**pit·e·ous·ly** adv

pit·fall /pít fàwl/ n 1 a potential difficulty or disaster 2 a trap consisting of a disguised hole in the ground

pith /pith/ n 1 the white tissue under the rind of citrus fruits 2 the tissue inside the stem of a vascular plant 3 the central or most important part of something 4 vigor or stamina

pith hel·met n a sun hat made from dried pith

pith·y /píthee/ (-i·er, -i·est) adj 1 brief and to the point 2 of or resembling pith —**pith·i·ly** adv

pit·i·ful /píttif'l/, **pit·i·a·ble** /píttee əb'l/ adj 1 arousing pity 2 arousing contempt or derision —**pit·i·a·bly** adv —**pit·i·ful·ly** adv

pit·i·less /píttiləss/ adj 1 lacking in pity 2 very severe —**pit·i·less·ly** adv

pi·ton /peé tòn/ n a spike for securing a rope when climbing

pit stop n 1 a refueling stop for a car during a race 2 a brief stop during a road journey to rest, refuel, or eat (infml)

pit·tance /píttnss/ n a very small sum of money

pit·ter-pat·ter /píttər pàttər/ n a rapid continuous tapping sound —**pit·ter-pat·ter** adv, vi

pittiful incorrect spelling of pitiful

Pitts·burgh /píts bùrg/ city in SW Pennsylvania. Pop. 340,520 (1998).

pi·tu·i·tar·y gland /pi toó i tèrree-/ n a gland at

the base of the brain that produces growth hormones

pit·y /píttee/ n **1** a feeling of sympathy **2** something regrettable ■ vt (-ied, -ies) feel pity for —**pit·y·ing·ly** adv

pitiful incorrect spelling of **pitiful**

Pi·us XII /pí əss/ (1876–1958) pope (1939–58)

piv·ot /pívvət/ n **1** an object on which a larger object turns or swings **2** a turning movement on a pivot ■ vi turn on or as if on a pivot

piv·ot·al /pívvət'l/ adj **1** vitally important **2** acting as a pivot —**piv·ot·al·ly** adv

pix n CHR = **pyx**

pix·el /píks'l, -sèl/ n a tiny dot of light that is the basic unit of a video screen image

> **ORIGIN** Pixel is a compound of pix "pictures" and a shortening of element.

pix·ie /píksee/, **pix·y** (pl -ies) n a mischievous fairy or elf

pix·i·lat·ed /píksə làytəd/ adj made up of pixels

> **ORIGIN** Pixilated is formed from pixel in imitation of an earlier word that meant "bewildered" or "drunk" and was humorously created from pixie and the ending of words like elated and titillated.

Pi·zar·ro /pi zaárō/, **Francisco** (1476?–1541) Spanish explorer

piz·za /péetsə/ n a flat round piece of baked dough with a topping, usually of cheese, tomato sauce, and other ingredients

piz·zazz /pi záz/, **piz·zaz** n energy and style (infml)

piz·ze·ri·a /péetsə rée ə/ (pl -as), **piz·za par·lor** n a pizza restaurant

piz·zi·ca·to /pítsee kaátō/ by plucking the strings of a bowed instrument (musical direction) ■ n (pl -ti /-tee/) a piece of music played pizzicato —**piz·zi·ca·to** adj

pl. abbr plural

Pl. abbr Place (in addresses)

PL/1 abbr a high-level computer programming language. Full form **programming language 1**

plac·ard /plá kaàrd, -kərd/ n **1** a large piece of stiff paper or board with writing on it displayed or carried in public **2** a small card or metal plaque with a name on it ■ vt **1** put placards on **2** advertise or announce with placards

pla·cate /pláy kàyt, plá-/ (-cat·ed, -cat·ing) vt make less angry —**plac·a·ble** /plákəb'l, pláy-/ adj —**pla·ca·tion** /play káysh'n/ n

place /playss/ n **1** an area or portion of space **2** a geographical locality such as a town, country, or region **3** a relatively open area in a town **4** a home **5** an area where something in particular happens o his place of business **6** a particular point or position in something o lost my place **7** somebody's

natural responsibility or right o not your place to tell me what to do **8** somewhere to sit o three places at the table **9** somebody's position in a ranking o finished in last place **10** the second position in a horse race ■ v (**placed, plac·ing**) **1** vt put in a particular position or state **2** vt recognize or remember o can't place him **3** vt assign to a position or location **4** vt have accepted and dealt with o placed an order for a new car **5** vt assign a finishing position o placed fourth overall **6** vi finish second, especially in a horse race ◇ **go places** become successful (infml) ◇ **put somebody in his** or **her place** humble somebody who is behaving in an arrogant or insolent way (infml) ◇ **take place** happen

> **ORIGIN** Place came into English via French from Latin platea "broad way." The "broad" element is seen more clearly in piazza and plaza, words for an "open square" that developed (through Italian and Spanish respectively) from the same Latin word.

pla·ce·bo /plə séebō/ (pl -bos or -boes) n **1** something prescribed for a patient that has no physical effect but can produce a psychological improvement **2** an inactive substance given as a control to a participant in a clinical trial of a new drug

> **ORIGIN** Placebo means "I shall please" in Latin. Its meaning of a medicine given more to please and have a psychological effect on the patient than for any physical benefit began in the late 18C.

pla·ce·bo ef·fect n a positive psychological effect felt simply from knowing that treatment has been given

place card n a card on a dining table showing where somebody is to sit

place kick n in football or rugby, a kick in which the ball is propped or held up on the ground —**place-kick** vt

place mat n a table mat for somebody's plate

place·ment /pláyssmənt/ n **1** the act of placing something, or the state of being placed **2** the process of matching somebody to a particular job or situation

pla·cen·ta /plə séntə/ (pl -tas or -tae /-tee/) n **1** an organ that develops in the uterus of a pregnant mammal to feed the fetus **2** the part of the ovary of a flowering plant that bears ovules —**pla·cen·tal** adj, n

place set·ting n a set of silverware, plates, and glasses for one person, arranged on a table

plac·id /plássid/ adj **1** calm by nature **2** complacent —**pla·cid·i·ty** /plə síddətee/ n —**plac·id·ly** adv

pla·gia·rize /pláyjə rìz/ (-rized, -riz·ing) vti copy somebody else's work and claim it is your own —**pla·gia·rism** n —**pla·gia·rist** n —**pla·gia·ris·tic** /plàyjə rístik/ adj

plague /playg/ n 1 an epidemic disease that kills many people 2 bubonic plague 3 the appearance of something harmful or unpleasant in large numbers ■ vt (**plagued, plagu·ing**) 1 afflict 2 annoy or pester constantly

plaice /playss/ (pl same) n a large flatfish

plaid /plad/ n 1 a long piece of tartan cloth worn over the shoulder as part of traditional Scottish Highland dress 2 a tartan pattern —**plaid** adj

plain /playn/ adj 1 simple and ordinary 2 clearly visible 3 clear in meaning 4 frank 5 not combined with another substance 6 uncolored or unpatterned 7 not pretty 8 absolute ■ adv 1 absolutely 2 frankly ■ n 1 a flat expanse of land 2 the simplest knitting style or stitch —**plain·ly** adv —**plain·ness** n◊ See note at **unattractive**

SPELLCHECK Do not confuse the spelling of **plain** and **plane** ("an aircraft," "a flat surface"), which sound similar.

plain clothes, plain-clothes /pláyn klóthz, -klóz/ npl civilian clothes worn by a police officer on duty —**plain-clothes** adj

Plain Peo·ple npl the Amish or the Mennonites

plain sail·ing n something that is easy to do

Plains In·di·an n a member of any of the Native American peoples who formerly lived on the Great Plains of North America

plain·song /pláyn sàwng/ n church music consisting of unaccompanied singing in unison

plain-spo·ken adj candid —**plain-spo·ken·ness** n

plaint /playnt/ n 1 an expression of grief (literary) 2 a complaint

plain text /plán tèkst/, **plain-text** n the form of a message that is in ordinary readable language, not in code

plain·tiff /pláyntif/ n somebody who brings a civil action

plain·tive /pláyntiv/ adj sad-sounding —**plain·tive·ly** adv —**plain·tive·ness** n

plait /playt, plat/ n a length of something such as hair or dough consisting of strands woven over and under each other ■ vt form into a plait

plan n 1 a method worked out in order to achieve an objective 2 something that somebody intends or has arranged to do (often pl) 3 a diagram or chart of the layout or structure of something ■ vti (**planned, plan·ning**) 1 work out a plan for something 2 intend to do something

Planck /plangk/, **Max** (1858–1947) German physicist

plane[1] /playn/ n 1 an airplane 2 a flat or two-dimensional surface 3 a level of existence, mental activity, or achievement ■ adj flat or two-dimensional ◊ See note at **plain**

plane[2] /playn/ n 1 a tool with an adjustable metal blade at an angle, for smoothing wood 2 a tool with a flat metal blade, for smoothing clay or plaster —**plane** vt

plane[3] /playn/, **plane tree** n a tall deciduous tree that has leaves with pointed lobes and peeling bark

plan·et /plánnət/ n 1 an astronomical object that orbits a star 2 in astrology, the Sun, Moon, or any of the planets of the solar system, except the Earth, considered to influence people's lives —**plan·e·tar·y** adj

ORIGIN A **planet** goes back through French and Latin to a Greek word meaning literally "wanderer." The **planets** (in ancient and medieval astronomy including the Sun and Moon) were astronomical objects that moved in relation to the fixed stars. The modern use dates from the mid-17C.

plan·e·tar·i·um /plànnə táiree əm/ (pl **-ums** or **-a** /-ə/) n 1 a building with a domed ceiling on which images of the night sky are projected 2 a projector used in a planetarium

plan·gent /plánjənt/ adj 1 expressing or suggesting sadness (literary) 2 resonant

plank n 1 a long flat piece of wood for use in building 2 a policy that is part of a political party's platform ■ vt cover with planks —**plank·ing** n

plank·ton /plángktən/ n a mass of tiny floating organisms eaten by aquatic animals —**plank·ton·ic** /plangk tónnik/ adj

planned ob·so·les·cence n the policy of ensuring that something soon becomes obsolete, so that consumers will have to buy a replacement

plan·ner /plánnər/ n 1 somebody who plans 2 a chart or book for planning future events

plant n 1 a vegetable organism that grows in earth or water and usually has green leaves 2 a smaller vegetable organism such as a flower or herb that does not have a permanent woody stem 3 a factory or other industrial complex ■ v 1 vt put something into the ground to grow 2 vti place young plants or sow seeds in an area of ground ○ planted the bed with pansies 3 vt put something down firmly 4 vt put an idea in somebody's mind 5 vt place something in a concealed position 6 vt introduce somebody into a group to spy on or influence it (infml) —**plant·a·ble** adj —**plant-like** adj

ORIGIN There did exist a Latin noun planta that meant "shoot, cutting," of uncertain origin, but the meaning of the English noun **plant** is not found. It is likely that this sense developed after the classical Latin period and is linked with the action of pressing on a shovel, or some other tool, with the planta "sole of the foot" in order to work the soil for planting.

plan·tain[1] /plántən/ n a small wild plant with

leaves growing from its base and a greenish flower spike

plan·tain[2] /plántɪn/ n 1 a green fruit like a banana, eaten cooked 2 a plant that produces plantains

plan·tar wart /plántər-, -taàr-/ n a wart on the sole of the foot

plan·ta·tion /plan táysh'n/ n 1 a large estate or farm for growing crops such as cotton, coffee, tea, or rubber 2 a group of cultivated crop plants

plant·er /plántər/ n 1 an owner or manager of a plantation 2 a large decorative container for houseplants 3 a machine for planting seeds, tubers, or bulbs

plaque /plak/ n 1 an inscribed or decorated flat piece of metal or stone fixed to a surface, especially to commemorate somebody or something 2 a deposit that builds up on the surface of teeth and can lead to gum disease 3 a distinct raised patch or deposit, e.g., on the skin or an artery wall, as part of a medical condition

plas·ma /plázmə/ n 1 the clear yellowish fluid component of blood 2 a blood substitute prepared by removing the cells and corpuscles of sterile blood 3 a hot ionized gas found in the Sun, stars, and fusion reactors —**plas·mat·ic** /plaz máttik/ adj

plas·ter /plástər/ n 1 a mixture of lime, sand, and water for covering interior walls and ceilings 2 also **plas·ter of Paris** a white powder mixed with water to form a quick-hardening paste. Use: sculpting, casts for broken limbs. ■ vt 1 cover interior walls and ceilings with plaster 2 apply something thickly over a surface (infml) 3 stick a mass of things over a surface 4 make a name, story, or image appear in many locations —**plas·ter·er** n —**plas·ter·y** adj

plas·ter·board /plástər bàwrd/ n plaster sandwiched between two layers of strong paper. Use: interior walls.

plas·ter cast n 1 a rigid plaster covering for a broken limb 2 a plaster copy of something

plas·ter·work /plástər wùrk/ n the plaster finish on surfaces or decorative plaster moldings on interior walls and ceilings

plas·tic /plástik/ n 1 a moldable synthetic material made from the polymerization of organic compounds 2 credit cards (infml) ■ adj 1 made of plastic 2 artificial and unnatural 3 able to be molded 4 of molding, modeling, or sculpting —**plas·tic·i·ty** /pla stíssətee/ n

plas·tic bul·let n a large PVC bullet used for riot control

plas·tic ex·plo·sive /pla steék-/, **plas·tique** n a soft moldable explosive

plas·tic sur·ger·y n surgery to repair damaged tissue or improve somebody's appearance —**plas·tic sur·geon** n

plas·tid /plástid/ n a component of a photosynthetic plant cell that contains DNA and is involved in food synthesis and storage

Pla·ta, Rí·o de la /plaátə/ marine inlet in SE South America between Uruguay and Argentina. Length 190 mi./300 km.

plat du jour /plaà də zhoòr/ (pl **plats du jour** /pronunc. same/) n the dish of the day on a restaurant menu

plate n 1 a flat or shallow dish, especially one from which food is eaten or served 2 the contents of a plate 3 a particular platter of served food ○ a low-calorie plate 4 in baseball, home plate 5 a coating of gold or silver on a base metal 6 metal in thin sheets 7 an artificial palate fitted with false teeth 8 a sensitized sheet of glass for receiving a photographic image 9 a flat piece of material with an inscription or engraving on it (often in combination) 10 a thin sheet of a substance 11 a section of the Earth's crust that moves in relation to other segments 12 a prize of a gold or silver cup, especially for a horse race, or a competition for one 13 an engraved metal sheet or a typeset page from which to print 14 a full-page illustration in a book, especially on glossy paper 15 a print taken from an engraved surface ■ vt (**plat·ed**, **plat·ing**) 1 cover a base metal with a gold or silver coating 2 cover something with sheets of armor plating —**plat·ed** adj —**plate·ful** n ◊ **have something on your plate** have something that requires your attention (infml)

pla·teau /pla tó/ n (pl **-teaus** or **-teaux** /-tóz/) 1 a raised area of land with a level top 2 a stable phase ■ vi level out

plate glass n strong thick glass in large sheets

plate·let /pláytlət/ n a particle in the blood that is important in the clotting process

plate tec·ton·ics n the theory that continental drift and volcanic and seismic activity are due to movement of segments of the Earth's crust (+ sing verb)

platéau incorrect spelling of **plateau**

⚡ **plat·form** /plát fàwrm/ n 1 a raised floor or flat structure, higher than an adjacent area 2 a raised area providing access to trains 3 a particular policy of a party seeking election 4 also **plat·form shoe** a shoe with a thickened sole 5 a standard configuration of computer hardware or a particular operating system

Plath /plath/, **Sylvia** (1932–63) US poet

CORBIS/Bettmann

Sylvia Plath

plat·ing /pláyting/ n 1 a thin covering of gold or silver applied to a base metal 2 a protective covering of metal plates on a ship or tank

plat·i·num /plátt'nəm/ n (symbol **Pt**) a precious silvery-white metallic element. Use: jewelry, catalyst, electroplating.

plat·i·tude /plátta tòod/ n 1 a pointless or unoriginal statement 2 the use of platitudes

Pla·to /pláytō/ (428?–347 BC) Greek philosopher

pla·ton·ic /plə tónnik/ adj 1 involving friendship or affection without sexual relations 2 **Pla·ton·ic** of Plato —**pla·ton·i·cal·ly** adv

pla·toon /plə tōōn/ n 1 a subdivision of a company of soldiers 2 a group of people with a common aim

---

ORIGIN Platoon was adopted (in the mid-17C) from a French word meaning literally "little ball." Its meaning had been extended to a "small group of people" and a tight unit such as a **platoon**.

Platte /plat/ river in central Nebraska. Length 310 mi./500 km.

plat·ter /pláttər/ n 1 a large flat dish for serving food 2 a particular type of served food (often in combination) o a seafood platter

plat·y·pus /pláttəpəss, -pòoss/ (pl -pus·es or -pi /-pì/) n an Australian egg-laying waterdwelling mammal with webbed feet and a snout like a duck's bill

plau·dit /pláwdit/ n an expression of praise

~~plausable~~ incorrect spelling of **plausible**

plau·si·ble /pláwzəb'l/ adj 1 believable and appearing likely to be true 2 persuasive —**plau·si·bil·i·ty** /plàwzə bíllətee/ n —**plau·si·bly** adv

play v 1 vi engage in an enjoyable activity for amusement 2 vti take part in a game or sport 3 vt compete against somebody in a game or sport 4 vti assign or be assigned to a position on a sports field 5 vt use a ball, piece, or card in a game 6 vt perform music on an instrument 7 vti reproduce recorded music for listening, or be reproduced for listening 8 vti deal with a situation in a particular way to achieve an aim o play it safe 9 vti act a part in a theatrical work, television show, or movie 10 vti direct light or water somewhere, or be so directed ■ n 1 enjoyable recreational activities 2 an action or move in a game 3 the action during a game 4 the amount of looseness in, e.g., a rope 5 a dramatic composition for, e.g., the stage —**play·a·ble** adj ◊ **play fast and loose** act irresponsibly or recklessly ◊ **play hard to get** pretend not to be interested or available ◊ **play it by ear** improvise your response to a situation as it develops

□ **play around** vi behave irresponsibly

□ **play at** vt pretend to do or be something

□ **play back** vti replay a recording

□ **play down** vt minimize the importance of

□ **play on** vt take advantage of somebody's emotional weakness to achieve an aim

□ **play up** vt emphasize

□ **play with** vt 1 think about or deal with halfheartedly 2 treat carelessly

play·back /pláy bàk/ n 1 the replaying of a recording 2 a device or facility for re-playing recordings

play·bill /pláy bìl/ n 1 a theater program 2 a poster advertising a play (dated)

play·boy /pláy bòy/ n a wealthy pleasure-seeking man

play-by-play adj giving a live and detailed description, especially of a sports event ■ n a spoken description of an event as it happens

play-down n Can, Scotland a match or matches played to decide a championship

played out adj 1 exhausted 2 no longer popular or fashionable

play·er /pláy ər/ n 1 somebody who takes part in a sport or game (often in combination) 2 somebody who plays a musical instrument (usually in combination) o a trumpet player 3 a participant in an activity o a major player in the direct banking sector 4 a stage actor 5 a device for playing recorded sound o a CD player

play·ful /pláyf'l/ adj 1 enjoying fun and games 2 said or done in fun —**play·ful·ly** adv —**play·ful·ness** n

play·go·er /pláy gò ər/ n somebody who attends the theater

play·ground /pláy grównd/ n an outdoor play area for children

play·group /pláy gròop/ n a supervised meeting for preschool children to play together

play·house /pláy hòwss/ (pl -houses /-hòwzəz/) n 1 a theater 2 a small model house for children

play·ing card n a card belonging to a set used for playing card games

play·ing field n an area for organized team games

play·list /pláy lìst/ n a list of recordings for playing on a radio program or station

play·mate /pláy màyt/ n somebody, especially a child, who plays with another

play·off /pláy àwf, -òf/ n 1 a deciding game to find the winner of a tied contest 2 one of a series of games that decides a championship

play·pen /pláy pèn/ n a structure for a baby to play in safely

~~playright~~ incorrect spelling of **playwright**

play·room /pláy ròòm, -ròòm/ n a room for children to play in

play·thing /pláy thìng/ n 1 a toy 2 somebody or something treated as a toy

play·time /pláy tìm/ *n* a period for playing, especially as a break for children at school

play·wright /pláy rìt/ *n* a writer of plays

~~playwrite~~ incorrect spelling of **playwright**

pla·za /plàazə, plázzə/ *n* **1** an open square in a town or city, especially in a Spanish-speaking country **2** a shopping center

plea /plee/ *n* **1** an urgent emotional request **2** a defendant's answer to a charge **3** a statement of a defendant's or claimant's case **4** an excuse

plea-bar·gain·ing *n* the practice of pleading guilty to a lesser charge to avoid being tried for a more serious charge —**plea bar·gain** *n* —**plea-bar·gain** *vi*

plead /pleed/ (**plead·ed** *or* **pled**) *v* **1** *vi* beg earnestly **2** *vt* offer something as an excuse **3** *vt* answer "guilty" or "not guilty" to a charge in a court —**plead·ing·ly** *adv*

pleas·ant /plézz'nt/ *adj* **1** enjoyable **2** good-natured —**pleas·ant·ly** *adv* —**pleas·ant·ness** *n*

pleas·ant·ry /plézz'ntree/ (*pl* -**ries**) *n* a polite or witty remark

please /pleez/ *adv, interj* used in polite or urgent requests ○ *Please be quiet.* ■ *interj* expresses indignation ○ *Please! Do you expect me to believe that?* ■ *v* (**pleased, pleas·ing**) **1** *vti* give pleasure to somebody **2** *vt* be the wish or will of somebody (*fml or literary*) **3** *vi* like or wish to do something ○ *Do as you please.* —**pleased** *adj* —**pleas·ing** *adj* —**pleas·ing·ly** *adv*

~~pleasent~~ incorrect spelling of **pleasant**

pleas·ur·a·ble /plézhərəb'l/ *adj* giving pleasure —**pleas·ur·a·bly** *adv*

pleas·ure /plézhər/ *n* **1** happiness or satisfaction **2** sensual or sexual gratification **3** recreation, relaxation, or amusement **4** a source of satisfaction ■ *vt* (-**ured, -ur·ing**) give sexual pleasure to —**pleas·ure·less** *adj*

pleat /pleet/ *n* a vertical fold sewn or pressed in a fabric ■ *vt* put pleats in

plebe /pleeb/ *n* a first-year US military or naval student

ple·be·ian /plə bée ən/ *n* **1** an ordinary ancient Roman citizen **2** somebody from a lower social class (*insult*) —**ple·be·ian** *adj*

~~plebian~~ incorrect spelling of **plebeian**

pleb·i·scite /plébbi sìt/ *n* a vote of all the electorate on a question of importance

plec·trum /pléktrəm/ (*pl* -**tra** /-trə/ *or* -**trums**) *n* a pick for plucking the strings of a musical instrument such as a guitar

pled past participle, past tense of **plead**

pledge *n* **1** a solemn vow **2** something given as security or as a token **3** a promise to donate money, e.g., to a charity or to a political cause **4** a fraternity or sorority recruit **5** a deposit of property **6** the state of being held as security ■ *v* (**pledged, pledg·ing**) **1** *vt* promise to do something **2** *vti* promise to

join a fraternity or sorority **3** *vt* enroll a student in a society **4** *vt* bind by a pledge **5** *vt* give something as security (*dated*) —**pledg·a·ble** *adj* —**pledg·er** *n*

Pledge of Al·le·giance *n* an oath promising loyalty to the United States

Pleis·to·cene /plístə sèen/ *n* an epoch of geologic time 1.8 million–10,000 years ago —**Pleis·to·cene** *adj*

ple·na·ry /pléenəree, plénnə-/ *adj* **1** attended by every member or delegate **2** full or unlimited (*fml*) ■ *n* (*pl* -**ries**) a plenary meeting

plen·i·po·ten·ti·a·ry /plènnəpə ténshəree/ *adj* having or conferring full power to act independently ■ *n* (*pl* -**ies**) an official with full powers

plen·i·tude /plénnə tòod/ *n* (*literary*) **1** abundance **2** completeness or fullness

plen·te·ous /pléntee əss/ *adj* (*literary*) **1** abundant **2** productive —**plen·te·ous·ly** *adv*

plen·ti·ful /pléntif'l/ *adj* **1** abundant or in good supply **2** productive —**plen·ti·ful·ly** *adv*

plen·ty /pléntee/ *pron* an adequate or abundant amount or quantity ■ *n* prosperity ■ *adv* sufficiently (*infml*)

ple·o·nasm /plèe ə nàzzəm/ *n* **1** the use of superfluous words **2** an example of using superfluous words —**ple·o·nas·tic** /plèe ə nástik/ *adj*

~~pleasant~~ incorrect spelling of **pleasant**

ple·si·o·saur /pléessee ə sàwr, pleezee-/ *n* an extinct marine reptile of the Mesozoic era

pleth·o·ra /pléthərə/ *n* a large or excessive amount or number of something

pleu·ri·sy /plóorissee/ *n* an inflammation of the lung membrane —**pleu·rit·ic** /ploō rittik/ *adj*

Plex·i·glas /pléksi glàss/ *tdmk* a trademark for a tough transparent acrylic plastic that can be used in place of glass

plex·us /pléksəss/ (*pl* -**us·es** *or same*) *n* **1** a network of nerves or blood vessels in the body **2** a complex network

pli·a·ble /plí əb'l/ *adj* **1** flexible **2** easily influenced —**pli·a·bil·i·ty** /plí ə bíllətee/ *n*

SYNONYMS pliable, ductile, malleable, elastic, pliant CORE MEANING: able to be bent or molded

---

pli·ant /plí ənt/ *adj* **1** supple **2** adaptable —**pli·an·cy** *n* —**pli·ant·ly** *adv* ◊ See note at **pliable**

pli·ers /plí ərz/ *npl* a tool with two hinged arms ending in jaws for gripping something

plight[1] /plìt/ *n* an unfortunate condition

plight[2] /plìt/ (**plight·ed** *or* **plight**) *vt* make a vow

plinth /plinth/ *n* a square supporting block for a column or statue

Plin·y (the El·der) /plínnee-/ (AD 23–79) Roman scholar

Plin·y (the Young·er) (AD 62–113) Roman politician and writer

Pli·o·cene /plí ə seèn/, **Plei·o·cene** n an epoch of geologic time 5.3–1.8 million years ago —**Pli·o·cene** adj

PLO abbr Palestine Liberation Organization

plod vi (**plod·ded**, **plod·ding**) 1 walk heavily 2 work slowly but steadily ■ n 1 a walk with slow heavy steps 2 the sound of somebody walking with slow heavy steps —**plod·ding** adj—**plod·ding·ly** adv

plop n the sound of something dropping into water without a large splash ■ v (**plopped**, **plop·ping**) 1 vti fall or let fall with a plop 2 vi drop down quickly and heavily —**plop** adv

plo·sive /plóziv, plóssiv/ adj describes a consonant that is pronounced with a suddenly released breath —**plo·sive** n

plot n 1 a secret plan to do something illegal or subversive 2 a story line 3 a small piece of ground ■ v (**plot·ted**, **plot·ting**) 1 vti make secret plans to do something illegal or subversive 2 vt mark the course of a ship or aircraft on a chart 3 vti mark points or a line on a graph, or be marked on a graph —**plot·less** adj

⚡**plot·ter** /plóttər/ n 1 somebody who secretly plans to do something illegal or subversive 2 a computer device for drawing graphs

plough n, vti UK = **plow**

plov·er /plúvvər/ n a wading shore bird with a short bill and tail and long pointed wings

plow /plow/ n 1 a farm implement for breaking up soil and making furrows 2 a heavy tool or machine for cutting or clearing a channel or route ■ v 1 vti make furrows in land 2 vti cut or force a way through something ◇ plough my way through the crowd 3 vt make a channel or cleared route in something 4 vt put something under the soil with a plow 5 vti work methodically at something

□ **plow into** vt crash into

□ **plow on** vi keep going

□ **plow under** vt overwhelm

plow·man /plówmən/ (pl -men /-mən/) n 1 somebody who operates a plow 2 a farm laborer

plow·share /plów shàir/ n the part of a plow that cuts the soil

ploy n a deceptive tactic

pluck v 1 vt take away quickly 2 vt pull off the feathers or hair of 3 vt pull off or out of something else ◇ plucking flowers 4 vti tug at 5 vt play by pulling and releasing the strings of ■ n 1 bravery 2 an act of plucking something ◇ See note at **courage**

pluck·y /plúkee/ (**-i·er**, **-i·est**) adj brave —**pluck·i·ly** adv—**pluck·i·ness** n

plug n 1 something used to fill and close a hole tightly 2 a stopper for a sink or bathtub 3 an electrical connection with prongs or pins that fit into a wall socket 4 an electrical wall socket (infml) 5 an unofficial favorable mention of something in order to publicize

it (infml) 6 a cake of chewing tobacco ■ v (**plugged**, **plug·ging**) 1 vt fill and close up a hole 2 vt give something an unofficial favorable mention in order to publicize it (infml) 3 vt shoot somebody (slang) 4 vi work steadily (infml) ◇ **pull the plug on** bring abruptly to an end

□ **plug in** vti connect to a power source

⚡**plug and play** n a technical standard that allows a peripheral device to connect to a computer and function immediately without the need for further configuration of the system —**plug-and-play** adj

⚡**plug-in** adj connectible by a plug to a power source ■ n 1 a device that can be connected by a plug to a power source 2 a data file that alters an application

plum /plum/ n 1 a dark reddish purple smooth-skinned fruit containing a flattened stone 2 a fruit tree that produces plums 3 a dark reddish purple color 4 something highly desirable (infml) —**plum** adj

> **ORIGIN** Plum goes back to a Latin word that is also the source of prune (the dried fruit). It was adopted into ancient Germanic languages, where the form with l rather than r developed. Prune came through French.

> **SPELLCHECK** Do not confuse the spelling of **plum** and **plumb** ("a weight attached to a line"), which sound similar.

plum·age /plóomij/ n the feathers of a bird

plumb /plum/ n 1 a weight attached to a line, used for finding the depth of water or establishing a true vertical position 2 a true vertical position ■ adv 1 in true vertical position 2 exactly (infml) 3 completely (infml) ■ adj vertical ■ vt 1 fully comprehend something mysterious 2 experience something unpleasant to an extreme degree 3 find the depth or true vertical position of something ◇ See note at **plum**

plumb·er /plúmmər/ n somebody who installs and fixes pipes and water fixtures in buildings

plumb·ing /plúmming/ n 1 the work of a plumber 2 the pipes and water fixtures in a building

plumb line n a line with a weight attached, used for finding the depth of water or establishing a true vertical position

plume /ploom/ n 1 a large or ornamental feather 2 a feather or bunch of feathers used as a decorative crest 3 a rising column of something such as smoke or dust ■ v (**plumed**, **plum·ing**) 1 vt preen the feathers 2 vr pride yourself on something —**plumed** adj

plum·met /plúmmət/ vi fall or drop steeply downward —**plum·met** n

plump[1] adj 1 slightly overweight (sometimes offensive) 2 having a satisfactory amount of flesh o *a plump chicken* ■ *vti* make or become fatter or rounder —**plump·ness** *n*

plump[2] *vti* drop abruptly or heavily ■ *n* an abrupt or heavy fall, or the sound of one ■ *adv* **1** heavily **2** directly

plum pud·ding *n* a rich steamed suet pudding containing dried fruit

plum to·ma·to *n* an elongated firm-textured tomato

plun·der /plúndər/ *vti* rob a place or person or steal goods using violence and causing damage, especially in a war ■ *n* **1** goods stolen by force, especially in a war **2** the theft of goods by force or fraud —**plun·der·er** *n*

plunge *v* (plunged, plung·ing) **1** *vti* move suddenly downward or forward **2** *vt* put somebody or something suddenly in an unpleasant condition **3** *vt* thrust something quickly or firmly into a liquid or container **4** *vi* become involved enthusiastically in an activity **5** *vi* embark recklessly on a course of action **6** *vi* drop suddenly in value ■ *n* **1** a leap into something, especially water **2** a sudden sharp fall in value **3** a place to swim —**plung·ing** *adj* ◇ **take the plunge** commit to doing something

plunge pool *n* a small deep swimming pool used for cooling the body

plung·er /plúnjər/ *n* **1** a tool for clearing clogged drains, consisting of a rubber suction cup on a handle **2** a part of a device with a plunging movement

plunk, plonk *vti* **1** pluck the strings of a musical instrument **2** drop down suddenly and heavily —**plunk** *n, adv*

plu·per·fect /ploo púrfikt/ *n* the past perfect tense of a verb ■ *adj* **1** utterly perfect **2** in the pluperfect

plu·ral /plóorəl/ *adj* **1** referring grammatically to more than one person or thing **2** of more than one person or thing ■ *n* **1** the plural number category **2** the plural form of a word

plu·ral·ism /plóorə lìzzəm/ *n* the existence of different ethnic, religious, or political groups within a society —**plu·ral·ist** *n* —**plu·ral·is·tic** /plóorə lístik/ *adj*

plu·ral·i·ty /plóo rállətee/ (*pl* -ties) *n* **1** the condition of being plural **2** a great number or part of something **3** the votes gained by a winning candidate when no one else has more than 50 percent of the total vote

plus /pluss/ *prep* used for adding one number or amount to another (*often written as "+"*) o *Two plus two equals four.* ■ *adj* **1** showing or involving addition **2** with a figure or value on the positive side of a scale (*often written as "+"*) **3** advantageous o *on the plus side* **4** somewhat more than a particular number ■ *n* (*pl* plus·es *or* plus·ses) **1** *also* **plus sign** the symbol "+," used to show addition or a positive quantity **2** a positive quantity **3** an advantageous factor (*infml*)

■ *conj* (*infml*) **1** △ and also **2** △ and furthermore

USAGE Avoid using **plus** to introduce an independent clause: *He is the chair of the department, plus has his own consulting firm.* Use instead: *As well as being the chair of the department, he has his own consulting firm.* In formal writing avoid using **plus** in place of *and* as a conjunction joining two subjects in a sentence: *Lack of practice and* [not *plus*] *a knee injury have caused her to drop out.*

---

plush *n* a rich smooth fabric with a long soft nap ■ *adj also* **plush·y** luxurious (*infml*) —**plush·ness** *n*

Plu·tarch /plóo taàrk/ (46–120) Greek historian, biographer, and philosopher

Plu·to /plóotō/ *n* **1** in Roman mythology, the god of the underworld. Greek equivalent **Hades 2** the smallest, and on average, the most distant planet in the solar system

plu·toc·ra·cy /ploo tókrəssee/ (*pl* -cies) *n* **1** rule by the wealthy **2** a society ruled by the wealthy —**plu·to·crat** /plóotə kràt/ *n* —**plu·to·cra·tic** /plóotə kráttik/ *adj*

plu·to·ni·um /ploo tónee əm/ *n* (*symbol* **Pu**) a silvery radioactive metallic element. Use: production of atomic energy and weapons.

ply[1] (plied, plies) *v* **1** *vti* work hard at an occupation **2** *vt* use a tool or weapon diligently or skillfully **3** *vt* offer goods or services for sale **4** *vt* supply somebody with or subject somebody to something in an insistent way **5** *vti* travel a route regularly

ply[2] *n* (*pl* plies) (*often in combination*) **1** a twisted strand of yarn or rope **2** a thin layer of something such as wood or a tire ■ *vti* (plied, plies) twist or fold things together

Plym·outh /plímməth/ **1** port in SW England. Pop. 260,000 (1996). **2** town in SE Massachusetts, settled by the Pilgrims. Pop. 7,258 (1996).

ply·wood /plí wòod/ *n* board made by gluing thin layers of wood together

Pm *symbol* promethium

P.M., p.m. *adv* between twelve noon and midnight. Full form **post meridiem**

P-mail /peé màyl/ *n* regular mail sent through the postal service

PMS *abbr* premenstrual syndrome

pneu·mat·ic /noo máttik/ *adj* using or filled with compressed air —**pneu·mat·i·cal·ly** *adv*

pneu·mo·co·ni·o·sis /nòomō kónee óssis/ *n* a lung disease caused by inhaling dust

pneu·mo·nia /noo mónee ə, nyoo-/ *n* an inflammation of one or both lungs

~~pnuematic~~ incorrect spelling of **pneumatic**

~~pnuemonia~~ incorrect spelling of **pneumonia**

Po[1] *symbol* polonium

Po[2] /pố/ river in N Italy, flowing eastward

into the Adriatic Sea. Length 405 mi./652 km.

PO, P.O. *abbr* **1** Petty Officer **2** *also* **p.o.** postal order **3** post office **4** purchase order

poach[1] *vti* **1** catch fish or game illegally **2** appropriate or remove somebody or something unfairly or secretly

poach[2] *vt* cook by simmering in liquid

poach·er[1] /póchər/ *n* somebody who poaches fish or game

poach·er[2] /póchər/ *n* a pan for poaching eggs

AKG London

Pocahontas: Posthumous portrait (1666)

Po·ca·hon·tas /pòkə hóntəss/ (1595?–1617?) Powhatan princess

pock·et /pókət/ *n* **1** a small pouch in a piece of clothing for holding small items **2** somebody's personal money ○ *paid for it out of his own pocket* **3** a small area differentiated from neighboring areas in a particular way **4** a cavity or opening, or the contents of one ■ *vt* **1** put something in a pocket **2** take something dishonestly ■ *adj* **1** small enough to carry in a pocket **2** small of its type —**pock·et·ful** *n* ◊ **have deep pockets** have large financial resources ◊ **in somebody's pocket** fully under somebody's control ◊ **line your pocket(s)** profit at the expense of others

pock·et·book /pókət bòok/ *n* **1** a small case for money and documents carried in a pocket **2** a purse **3** somebody's financial resources **4** a small book

pock·et·knife /pókət nìf/ (*pl* **-knives** /-nìvz/) *n* a small knife with one or more blades that fold into the handle

pock·et-sized, pock·et-size *adj* **1** small enough to be carried in a pocket **2** small

pock·et ve·to *n* **1** an indirect presidential veto **2** an indirect veto by a state governor

pock·mark /pók maàrk/ *n* (*often pl*) **1** a small circular scar on the skin left by smallpox, chickenpox, or acne **2** a small hollow disfiguring mark

pod[1] *n* **1** a long narrow seed case holding the seeds of plants such as peas and beans **2** a detachable compartment of a spacecraft **3** a streamlined housing for equipment on an aircraft or submarine

pod[2] *n* a small group of ocean mammals

-pod, -pode *suffix* foot, part like a foot ○ *arthropod* — **-podous** *suffix*

Pod·go·ri·ca /pòdgo reétsə/ capital of Montenegro, S Yugoslavia. Pop. 163,493 (1998).

po·di·a·try /pə dí ətree/ *n* medical care and treatment for the feet —**po·di·at·ric** /pòdee áttrik/ *adj* —**po·di·a·trist** *n*

po·di·um /pódee əm/ (*pl* **-ums** *or* **-a** /-ə/) *n* a small raised platform for an orchestra conductor, lecturer, or speaker

Poe /pō/, **Edgar Allan** (1809–49) US writer and critic

po·em /pó əm/ *n* a piece of writing in verse, using rhythm, imagery, and often rhyme

~~peeple~~ incorrect spelling of **people**

po·e·sy /pó əzee, -əssee/ *n* poetry (*literary*)

po·et /pó ət/ *n* somebody who writes poems

po·et·as·ter /pó ə tàstər/ *n* a bad poet (*literary*)

po·et·ic /pō éttik/, **po·et·i·cal** /-ik'l/ *adj* of or resembling poetry —**po·et·i·cal·ly** *adv*

po·et·ic jus·tice *n* just retribution for something

po·et·ic li·cense *n* the freedom to disobey writing conventions to achieve a special effect

po·et lau·re·ate (*pl* **po·ets lau·re·ate** *or* **po·et lau·re·ates**) *n* **1** a British court poet who writes poems celebrating great events **2** a poetry consultant to the Library of Congress

po·et·ry /pó ətree/ *n* **1** the work of a poet **2** poems collectively or as a genre **3** the writing of poems **4** a poetic quality

po·go stick /pógō-/ *n* a pole with a spring and footrests at the bottom used for hopping around

po·grom /pə gróm, pógrəm/ *n* an organized campaign to kill a minority group

poign·ant /póynyənt/ *adj* causing sadness or pity —**poign·ance** *n* —**poign·an·cy** *n* —**poign·ant·ly** *adv* ◊ See note at **moving**

poin·set·ti·a /poyn séttee ə, -sétta/ (*pl* **-as** *or* **same**) *n* a bush with red leaves like petals

point *n* **1** an opinion, idea, or fact put forward **2** the essential idea **3** a purpose **4** an item in a list or plan **5** a distinguishing quality **6** a specific location **7** a moment in time **8** a particular stage, level, or degree **9** the sharp or tapering end of something **10** a prominent headland (*often in place names*) **11** the act of pointing **12** a dot or punctuation mark, especially a period **13** a unit used in scoring, evaluating, or measuring something **14** a mark on a compass indicating bearing or direction ■ *v* **1** *vi* extend a finger to draw attention to somebody or something **2** *vt* aim the end of an object at a target **3** *vi* be turned toward or aimed in a particular direction **4** *vt* direct somebody toward a destination **5** *vi* suggest that something is the case ○ *It all points to one conclusion.* **6** *vi* call attention to a fact or situation as being important ◊ **beside the point** irrelevant or unimportant ◊ **in point of fact** in reality ◊ **stretch a point** exaggerate ◊ **to the point** relevant ◊ **(up) to a point** to a certain extent, but not completely

□ **point out** *vt* **1** indicate where somebody or something is **2** draw attention to something

□ **point up** *vt* emphasize

⚡**point-and-click** *adj* describes a computer interface that allows a user to interact via a mouse click —**point-and-click** *vi*

point-blank *adv* **1** at close range **2** directly and bluntly —**point-blank** *adj*

point-ed /póyntəd/ *adj* **1** ending in a point **2** made with emphasis and implying criticism —**point-ed-ly** *adv* —**point-ed-ness** *n*

⚡**point-er** /póyntər/ *n* **1** a stick or cane used for pointing **2** an indicator on a measuring device **3** a helpful piece of advice or information **4** a hunting dog that indicates the position of game **5** an arrow on a computer screen showing the position of the mouse

poin-til-lism /pwaántee lìzzəm, póynt'l lìzzəm/ *n* a style of 19C painting using dots of color to create a picture —**poin-til-list** *n*, *adj*

point-less /póyntləss/ *adj* **1** without purpose or benefit **2** scoreless —**point-less-ly** *adv* —**point-less-ness** *n*

point man *n* **1** a lead soldier in a military formation **2** somebody in the forefront of an activity

point of or-der *n* a question about procedure in a debate or meeting

⚡**point of pres-ence** *n* a place where a user can connect to a computer network

point-of-sale *adj* located at the place where a product is sold —**point of sale** *n*

point of view *n* **1** a way of thinking about a subject **2** somebody's personal opinion on a subject

point-to-point *n* a cross-country steeplechase ■ *adj* from one place to another

⚡**Point-to-Point Pro-to-col** *n* a protocol for dial-up access to the Internet

point-y /póyntee/ (**-i-er, -i-est**) *adj* with a pointed end —**poin-ti-ness** *n*

poise /poyz/ *n* **1** composure **2** controlled grace in movement ■ *vti* (**poised, pois-ing**) balance or suspend, or be balanced or suspended

poised /poyzd/ *adj* **1** ready to act ○ *We are now poised to take over the company.* **2** ready to move **3** calm and composed

~~poison~~ incorrect spelling of **poison**

poi-son /póyz'n/ *n* a toxic substance that causes illness or death if taken into the body ■ *vt* **1** harm or kill a person or animal with a toxic substance **2** add poison to something **3** pollute the environment **4** corrupt or undermine somebody or something —**poi-son-er** *n* —**poi-son-ous** *adj*

ORIGIN A **poison** is etymologically simply a "drink." It goes back to the Latin word that also gave us **potion**, which was a derivative of

the verb *potare* "drink." The application to toxic substances developed in Latin.

poi-son gas *n* a toxic gas used as a weapon

poi-son i-vy *n* **1** a vine that causes an itching rash **2** the rash produced by poison ivy

poi-son oak *n* **1** a plant related to poison ivy that causes an itching rash **2** the rash produced by poison oak

poi-son-pen let-ter *n* an anonymous abusive letter

poi-son pill *n* a company strategy intended to deter a hostile takeover

Poi-ti-er /pwaátee ay/, **Sidney** (*b.* 1924) US actor and director

poke¹ *v* (**poked, pok-ing**) **1** *vti* prod somebody or something with a finger, elbow, or stick **2** *vt* make a hole in something by pushing at it with a finger or sharp object **3** *vt* push something into a hole **4** *vti* protrude or make protrude from something **5** *vi* search haphazardly ○ *poking around in a second-hand bookstore* **6** *vt* stir a fire with a poker ■ *n* a prod with a finger, elbow, or stick

poke² *n* regional a bag

pok-er¹ /pókər/ *n* a card game involving betting on combinations of cards

pok-er² /pókər/ *n* a metal rod for stirring a fire

po-key /pókee/ (*pl* **-keys** *or* **-kies**), **po-ky** (*pl* **-kies**) *n* a jail (*slang*)

pok-y /pókee/ (**-i-er, -i-est**), **pok-ey** slow (*infml*) —**pok-i-ness** *n*

pol *n* a politician (*infml*)

pol. *abbr* **1** political **2** politics

Po-land /póland/ country in E Europe, bordering on the Baltic Sea. Cap. Warsaw. Pop. 38,633,912 (2001).

po-lar /pólər/ *adj* **1** of or near either of the Earth's poles **2** of the pole of a rotating body, magnet, or electrically charged object

po-lar bear *n* a white Arctic bear

Po-lar-is /pə lérriss/ *n* the brightest star of the Big Dipper, near the celestial north pole

po-lar-i-ty /pō lérrətee/ (*pl* **-ties**) *n* **1** an extreme difference between individuals or groups **2** the condition of having opposite characteristics at different points in a system, especially with regard to electric charge or magnetic properties

po-lar-ize /pólə rìz/ (**-ized, -iz-ing**) *vti* **1** make differences between groups or ideas even more extreme, or become even more extreme **2** acquire or cause something to acquire polarity —**po-lar-i-za-tion** /póləri záysh'n/ *n*

Po-lar-oid /pólə ròyd/ *tdmk* **1** a trademark for a camera that produces instant pictures, or the film used in such a camera **2** a trademark for a transparent plastic that allows polarized light through and is used to reduce glare in sunglasses

pole¹ /pōl/ *n* **1** the North or South Pole **2** each of the two endpoints of the axis of a sphere

3 each of two opposites **4** each of the two ends of a magnet or an electric terminal **5** each of the two ends of an electric terminal

---

SPELLCHECK Do not confuse the spelling of **pole** and **poll** ("an election or survey"), which sound similar.

---

pole² /pōl/ *n* a long straight piece of wood or metal with a round cross-section that can be held in the hand

Pole /pōl/ *n* somebody from Poland

pole·ax /pṓ làks/ *n* **1** an ax with a hammer face opposite the blade, formerly used for slaughtering animals **2** a battle-ax with a hammer or spike opposite the blade

pole·cat /pṓl kàt/ *n* **1** a small animal related to the weasel that emits a foul smell when disturbed **2** a skunk

---

ORIGIN The first part of **polecat** may come from a French word meaning "hen, fowl" (the source of *poultry* and *pullet*), because the animal related to the weasel was known to take hens from farmyards.

---

po·lem·ic /pə lémmik/ *n* a passionate argument against somebody or something —**po·lem·ic** *adj* —**po·lem·i·cal** *adj* —**po·lem·i·cist** *n*

po·lem·ics /pə lémmiks/ *n* the art of making polemical arguments (+ *sing verb*)

po·len·ta /pō léntə/ *n* Italian-style cornmeal

pole po·si·tion *n* the best starting position in a horserace or auto race

pole·star /pṓl stàar/, **Pole Star** *n* Polaris

pole vault *n* **1** a field event in which competitors attempt to clear a high crossbar using a pole to propel them into the air **2** a jump in the pole vault —**pole-vault** *vti* —**pole-vault·er** *n*

po·lice /pə lṓess/ *n* **1** a civil organization responsible for maintaining law and order **2** police officers collectively (+ *pl verb*) **3** a specialized force responsible for enforcing rules and procedures in a particular sphere of activity ■ *vt* (**-liced, -lic·ing**) **1** maintain law and order in a place using the police **2** enforce rules and procedures in a particular sphere of activity **3** clear an area of litter

po·lice dog *n* **1** a dog trained to work with the police **2** a German shepherd

po·lice force *n* an organized body of police officers within a particular area

po·lice·man /pə lṓessmən/ (*pl* **-men** /-mən/) *n* a man who is a police officer

po·lice of·fi·cer *n* a member of a police force

po·lice state *n* a country in which the government uses the police to exercise repressive control over the population

po·lice sta·tion *n* the local headquarters of a police force

po·lice·wom·an /pə ˈleess wŏommən/ (*pl* **-wom·en** /-wimmin/) *n* a woman police officer

pol·i·cy /pṓlləssee/ (*pl* **-cies**) *n* **1** a course of action adopted by an individual or group **2** prudence in the pursuit of a course of action **3** an insurance contract

pol·i·cy·hol·der /pṓlləssee hòldər/ *n* an insured person or organization

po·li·o /pṓlee ò/, **po·li·o·my·e·li·tis** /pṓlee ō mī ə lítiss/ *n* a disease that inflames the brain stem and spinal cord, sometimes leading to paralysis —**po·li·o·my·e·lit·ic** /pṓlee ō mī ə líttik/ *adj*

pol·ish /pṓllish/ *v* **1** *vti* make or become smooth or glossy **2** *vt* remove the outer layers of brown rice **3** *vti* make or become more refined or elegant ■ *n* **1** a substance used for polishing **2** the smoothness or glossiness of something that has been polished **3** a rub given to something to make it smooth or glossy **4** refinement

□ **polish off** *vt* finish quickly and completely

Po·lish /pṓlish/ *npl* the people of Poland ■ *n* the official language of Poland —**Po·lish** *adj*

Pol·it·bu·ro /pṓllit byoòrō/ *n* the executive committee of a governing Communist Party

po·lite /pə līt/ (**-lit·er, -lit·est**) *adj* **1** well-mannered **2** elegant and refined —**po·lite·ly** *adv* —**po·lite·ness** *n*

po·li·tic /pṓllətik/ *adj* prudent, shrewd, or cunning —**pol·i·tic·ly** *adv*

po·lit·i·cal /pə líttik'l/ *adj* **1** of party politics **2** of government —**po·lit·i·cal·ly** *adv*

po·lit·i·cal·ly cor·rect *adj* describes language or behavior that deliberately avoids giving offense, e.g., in regard to ethnic origin or sexual orientation —**po·lit·i·cal cor·rect·ness** *n*

po·lit·i·cal·ly in·cor·rect *adj* describes language or behavior that could give offense, e.g., in regard to ethnic origin or sexual orientation

po·lit·i·cal pris·on·er *n* somebody imprisoned for his or her political beliefs

po·lit·i·cal sci·ence *n* the study of government —**po·lit·i·cal sci·en·tist** *n*

pol·i·ti·cian /pòllə tísh'n/ *n* **1** somebody actively or professionally involved in politics **2** a member of a branch of government

po·lit·i·cize /pə lítti sìz/ (**-cized, -ciz·ing**) *v* **1** *vti* introduce an issue into the political arena, or be introduced there **2** *vt* give political awareness to somebody or a political flavor to something

pol·i·tick·ing /pṓllə tìking/ *n* political campaigning

po·lit·i·co /pə lítti kò/ (*pl* **-cos**) *n* a politician (*infml*)

pol·i·tics /pṓllətiks/ *n* **1** the theory and practice of government (+ *sing verb*) **2** the activity within a political party that is concerned with debate and the creation and carrying out of policies (+ *sing or pl verb*) **3** the relationships in a particular field involving power, authority, or influence (+ *sing or pl verb*) ◦ *the politics of education* **4** the use of tactics and strategy to gain advancement in a group (+ *sing or pl verb*) ■ *npl* (+ *pl verb*) **1** political activity **2** political beliefs

pol·i·ty /póllatee/ (*pl* -ties) *n* a particular form of government

Polk /pōk/, **James Knox** (1795–1849) 11th president of the United States (1845–49)

pol·ka /pólka, pókə/ *n* **1** a lively dance for couples involving three quick steps and a hop **2** the music for a polka —**pol·ka** *vi*

pol·ka dot *n* a dot repeated to form a regular pattern on fabric

poll /pōl/ *n* **1** an election **2** a survey of public opinion on an issue **3** the number of votes cast in an election ■ **polls** *npl* a place in which to vote in an election ■ *vt* **1** sample opinion methodically **2** receive a particular number of votes **3** record jury votes **4** remove an animal's coat or horns ◊ See note at **pole**

ORIGIN The original meaning of **poll**, underlying all its senses, is "head." The voting **poll** reflects the idea of counting heads.

pol·lack /póllək/ (*pl* same), **pol·lock** *n* **1** a N Atlantic fish of the cod family **2** a pollack as food

pol·lard /póllərd/ *n* **1** a tree that has had its branches cut back to encourage growth **2** an animal whose horns have been removed or shed ■ *vt* cut branches or horns

pol·len /póllən/ *n* a powdery substance containing male reproductive cells produced by flowering plants

pol·len count *n* the amount of pollen in the air

pol·li·nate /pólla nàyt/ (-nat·ed, -nat·ing) *vt* transfer pollen from a male to a female part of a flower and so fertilize the plant —**pol·li·na·tion** /pólla náysh'n/ *n*

pol·li·wog /póllee wòg/, **pol·ly·wog** *n* a tadpole

pol·lock *n* ZOOL = **pollack**

Pol·lock /póllək/, **Jackson** (1912–56) US artist

poll·ster /pólstər/ *n* somebody who conducts opinion polls

poll tax *n* a tax levied equally on all members of the population

pol·lut·ant /pə lóōt'nt/ *n* something that causes pollution

pol·lute /pə lóōt/ (-lut·ed, -lut·ing) *vt* **1** contaminate the natural environment **2** corrupt or defile —**pol·lu·tion** *n*

Pol·ly·an·na /pòllee ánnə/ *n* an eternal optimist

ORIGIN The original *Pollyanna* was the central character in children's stories written by the

author Eleanor Hodgman Porter (1868–1920).

pol·ly·wog *n* ZOOL = **polliwog**

po·lo /pólō/ *n* a team game played on horseback and using mallets and a wooden ball to score goals

Po·lo /pólō/, **Marco** (1254–1324) Venetian merchant and traveler

pol·o·naise /pòllə náyz, pòlə-/ *n* a slow formal dance for couples in triple time

po·lo·ni·um /pə lóneeəm/ *n* (*symbol* Po) a rare radioactive metallic element. Use: removal of static electricity.

po·lo shirt *n* a casual cotton shirt with a buttoned opening at the neck

Pol Pot /pòl pót/ (1928–98) Cambodian prime minister (1975–79) and leader of the Khmer Rouge

pol·ter·geist /póltər gÌst/ *n* a supposed noisy and troublesome supernatural spirit

pol·troon /pol tróōn/ *n* a person regarded as a contemptible coward (*archaic insult*)

~~polution~~ incorrect spelling of **pollution**

poly- *prefix* more than one ◦ *polygamy*

pol·y·an·dry /póllee àndree/ *n* **1** the custom of having multiple husbands **2** in female animals, the practice of having multiple mates in a breeding season —**pol·y·an·drous** /pòllee ándrəss/ *adj*

pol·y·an·thus /pòllee ánthəss/ (*pl* -thus·es or -thi /-thÌ/) *n* a hybrid primrose

pol·y·es·ter /pòllee èstər, pòllee éstər/ *n* **1** a synthetic polymer. Use: resins, plastics, textile fibers. **2** a strong synthetic fabric

pol·y·eth·yl·ene /pòllee éthə lèen/ *n* synthetic polymer. Use: manufacture of containers, packaging, and electrical insulation.

po·lyg·a·my /pə líggəmee/ *n* **1** the custom of having multiple spouses **2** in animals, the practice of having multiple mates in a breeding season —**po·lyg·a·mist** *n* —**po·lyg·a·mous** *adj*

pol·y·glot /póllee glòt/ *adj* **1** able to speak many languages **2** written in many languages —**pol·y·glot** *n*

pol·y·gon /póllee gòn/ *n* a flat many-sided geometric figure —**po·lyg·o·nal** /pə líggən'l/ *adj*

pol·y·graph /póllee gràf/ *n* **1** a device that records pulse, perspiration, and other involuntary responses, often used as a lie detector **2** a test using a polygraph —**pol·y·graph·ic** /pòllee gráffik/ *adj*

pol·y·he·dron /pòllee heédrən/ (*pl* -drons or -dra /-drə/) *n* a many-sided solid geometric figure —**pol·y·he·dral** *adj*

pol·y·math /póllee màth/ *n* somebody with wide-ranging knowledge —**pol·y·math·ic** /pòllee máthik/ *adj*

pol·y·mer /pólləmər/ *n* a compound consisting of large molecules made up of smaller identical molecules —**pol·y·mer·ic** /pòllə mérrik/ *adj* —**po·lym·er·i·za·tion** /pə límməri zàysh'n/ *n* —**pol·y·mer·ize** *vt*

pol·y·mer·ase /póllimə ràyz, pə límmə ràyz, -ràyss/ *n* an enzyme that catalyzes a polymer

pol·y·morph /póllee màwrf/ *n* an organism, part of an organism, protein, or chemical compound that is found in different forms —**pol·y·mor·phic** /póllee máwrfik/ *adj*

pol·y·mor·phism /-máwr fizzəm/ *n* **1** the characteristic of existing in different forms **2** a difference in DNA sequence between individuals

Pol·y·ne·sia /pòllə neézhə/ ethnographic grouping of islands in the central and S Pacific Ocean —**Pol·y·ne·sian** *n*, *adj*

pol·yp /póllip/ *n* **1** a marine invertebrate that remains attached to a rock **2** a usually benign growth on the skin or a mucous membrane —**pol·yp·oid** *adj*

po·lyph·o·ny /pə líffənee/ *n* music with several melodies sounded together —**po·lyph·o·nous** *adj*

pol·y·pro·pyl·ene /pòllee própə leèn/, **pol·y·pro·pene** /-prṓ peèn/ *n* a versatile type of plastic. Use: pipes, industrial fibers, molded objects.

pol·y·sty·rene /pòllee stí reèn/ *n* a synthetic packing and insulating material

pol·y·syl·la·ble /póllee síllab'l/ *n* a word with many syllables —**pol·y·syl·lab·ic** /-si lábbik/ *adj*

pol·y·tech·nic /póllee téknik/ *n* a college offering mostly vocational courses

pol·y·the·ism /póllee thee ìzzəm, pòllee theé-/ *n* belief in several or many deities —**pol·y·the·ist** —**pol·y·the·is·tic** /pòllee thee ístik/ *adj*

pol·y·un·sat·u·rat·ed /pòllee un sáchə ràytəd/ *adj* describes a fat containing several double or triple bonds between carbon atoms, and less likely than some other fats to be converted into cholesterol in the body

pol·y·ure·thane /pòllee yoörə thàyn/ *n* a thermoplastic polymer. Use: resins, coatings, insulation, adhesives, foams, fibers.

po·made /pō máyd, pə-, -maàd/ *n* a perfumed oil or ointment for hair —**po·made** *vt*

po·man·der /pṓ màndər, pō mán-/ *n* **1** a mixture of aromatic substances kept in a container **2** a container for a pomander

pome·gran·ate /pómmə grànnət, púmmə-, póm gràn-, púm-/ *n* **1** a round red fruit with numerous seeds within juicy red flesh **2** the tropical Asian tree that produces pomegranates

~~pomegranite~~ incorrect spelling of **pomegranate**

Pom·er·a·ni·an /pòmmə ráynee ən/ *n* a small dog with a long silky coat

pom·mel /púmm'l, póm-/ *n* **1** the front part of a saddle that curves upward **2** the knob on the hilt of a sword

pom·mel horse *n* **1** a gymnastics apparatus consisting of a raised oblong pad with handles on top **2** a gymnastics event using a pommel horse

Po·mo·na /pə mṓnə/ *n* in Roman mythology, the goddess of fruit

pomp *n* **1** ceremonial splendor **2** excessive self-importance

pom·pa·dour /pómpə dàwr, -doòr/ *n* **1** a woman's hairstyle in which the hair is swept back high off the face **2** a similar man's hairstyle

Pom·pa·dour /pómpə dàwr, -doòr/, **Marquise de** (1721–64) French mistress of Louis XV and patron of the arts

Pompeii: View of the Forum, with Vesuvius in the background

Pom·pe·ii /pom páy, pom páy ee/ ancient Roman city in present-day S Italy, buried by volcanic ash during the eruption of Mount Vesuvius in AD 79

pom-pom /póm pòm/ *n* **1** a cheerleader's tasseled paper ball on a handle **2** a small tufted wool ball used as a decoration on clothes

pom·pous /pómpəss/ *adj* **1** self-important **2** revealing self-importance —**pom·pos·i·ty** /pom póssətee/ *n* —**pom·pous·ly** *adv*

Pon·ce /páwn say/ port in S Puerto Rico. Pop. 187,749 (1990).

Ponce (de Le·ón) /pónss də lee ón, pón sə də leé ən, -pònth ay də lee ón-/, **Juan** (1460–1521) Spanish explorer

pon·cho /pónchō/ (*pl* -**chos**) *n* **1** a simple cloak that fits over the head **2** a similar raincoat

pond *n* a small body of still water

pon·der /póndər/ *vti* consider something carefully —**pon·der·a·ble** *adj*, *n*

pon·der·ous /póndərəss/ *adj* **1** moving heavily **2** lacking liveliness or wit —**pon·der·ous·ly** *adv* —**pon·der·ous·ness** *n*

pone /pṓn/ *n Southern US* cornpone

pon·iard /pónnyərd/ *n* a small dagger (*literary*)

Pon·ti·ac /póntee ak/ (1720?–69) Ottawa leader

pon·tiff /póntif/ *n* a pope

pon·tif·i·cal /pon tíffik'l/ *adj* **1** of a pontiff **2** pompous ■ **pon·tif·i·cals** *npl* a pontiff's vestments

pon·tif·i·cate *vi* /pon tíffi kàyt/ (-**cat·ed**, -**cat·ing**) **1** speak pompously **2** officiate as a bishop ■ *n* /pon tíffikət, -kàyt/ a pope's or bishop's term of office —**pon·tif·i·ca·tion** /pon tìffi káysh'n/ *n*

pon·toon /pon tóon/ n 1 a floating support for a bridge 2 a float on a seaplane

po·ny /pónee/ (pl -nies) n 1 any breed of small horse 2 a horse used in polo

po·ny·tail /pónee tàyl/ n a hairstyle with long hair tied together at the back —**po·ny·tailed** adj

Pon·zi scheme /pónzee-/ n a pyramid investment swindle in which supposed profits are paid to early investors from money actually invested by later participants

ORIGIN The name comes from Charles Ponzi (?-1949), who perpetrated such a swindle in the United States in 1919.

pooch n a dog (infml)

poo·dle /poód'l/ n a curly-haired dog

pooh interj expresses disdain

Pooh-Bah /poo baa/, **pooh-bah** n 1 a pompous but useless official 2 an important person

ORIGIN The original **Pooh-Bah** was a character in The Mikado (1885), an operetta by W. S. Gilbert and Sir Arthur Sullivan.

pooh-pooh vt show scorn for

pool[1] n 1 a swimming pool 2 a puddle 3 a small body of still water 4 a deep or still part of a river or stream 5 an arrangement of light that resembles a pool ○ The floodlights bathed her in a pool of pink light. —**pool** vi

pool[2] n 1 a game played on a table with a cue and a number of balls 2 a form of gambling in which stakes are placed in a common fund that is then shared by the winners 3 the total amount staked in a gambling game 4 any collective resource, e.g., of vehicles or typists 5 an agreement between businesses to control production and sales to guarantee profits ■ vt share resources

pool·room /poól ròom, -room/ n a place where pool is played

pool·side /poól sìd/ n the area bordering a swimming pool

poop[1] vt tire out (infml) —**pooped** adj
□ **poop out** vi quit doing something because of exhaustion (slang)

poop[2] n information (slang)

poop[3] n 1 a raised area at the rear of a ship 2 a poop deck

poop deck n a raised deck at the stern of a ship, with cabins below

poor /poor, pawr/ adj 1 lacking money or possessions 2 inferior 3 lacking skill or ability 4 low or inadequate 5 weak 6 deficient (often in combination) 7 deserving pity ■ npl people who are poor —**poor·ness** n

poor boy n regional a long sandwich

poor·house /poór hòwss, páwr-/ (pl -hous·es /-hòwzəz/) n formerly, a publicly funded accommodation for poor people

poor law n a law for the support of poor people

poor·ly /poórlee, páwr-/ adv 1 inadequately 2 unfavorably

poor re·la·tion n an inferior version of something or somebody

pop[1] n 1 a sudden bursting sound 2 Midwest a bubbly soft drink (infml) 3 a gunshot ■ v (popped, pop·ping) 1 vti make or cause to make a bursting sound 2 vti burst open, or cause to burst open 3 vi bulge (refers to somebody's eyes) 4 vt move quickly into a particular position or place (infml) ◇ **a pop** for each one (slang)

pop[2] n 1 also **Pop** a father (infml) 2 an offensive way of addressing an older man (slang dated)

pop[3] n 1 pop music 2 pop art ■ adj 1 musically commercial 2 popular (infml)

POP abbr 1 point of purchase 2 persistent organic pollutant

pop. abbr population

pop art n a 1960s artistic movement that sought to incorporate popular culture into art

pop·corn /póp kàwrn/ n 1 corn kernels heated until puffy and light 2 packing material consisting of small pieces of polystyrene or a similar material

pope, Pope n the head of the Roman Catholic Church —**pope·dom** n

Pope, Alexander (1688-1744) English poet

pope's nose n the tail end of a cooked bird (sometimes offensive)

pop-eyed /póp ìd/ adj 1 with bulging eyes 2 wide-eyed

pop fly n in baseball, a short high fly ball

pop·gun /póp gùn/ n a toy gun that makes a popping noise

pop·lar /pópplər/ n 1 a slender quick-growing tree of the willow family 2 the wood of a poplar

pop·lin /pópplin/ n a plain cotton fabric with fine ribbing. Use: clothes, upholstery.

pop mu·sic n modern commercial music aimed at the general public, especially young people

Po·po·ca·té·petl /pòpə káttə pètt'l, pò paw kaa té pètt'l/ volcano in south central Mexico. Height 17,887 ft./5,452 m.

pop·o·ver /póp òvər/ n a hollow muffin-shaped quick bread

pop·pa·dom /póppədəm/, **pop·pa·dum** n a South Asian crispy bread

pop·per /póppər/ n a corn-popping device

pop·py /póppee/ (pl -pies) n a plant with cup-shaped seed pods and red, orange, or white flowers

pop·py·cock /póppee kòk/ n nonsense (infml dated)

pop·py seed n the seed of a poppy. Use: in baking.

pop quiz *n* an unannounced test

pops *n* an orchestra that plays popular classical music or pop music

Pop·si·cle /pópsik'l/ *tdmk* a trademark for a colored flavored ice on one or two sticks

pop·u·lace /póppyəlass/ *n* **1** the inhabitants of a place **2** the general public

---

SPELLCHECK Do not confuse the spelling of **populace** and **populous** ("highly populated"), which sound similar.

---

pop·u·lar /póppyələr/ *adj* **1** appealing to the general public **2** well-liked **3** of the general public **4** believed by people in general —**pop·u·lar·i·ty** /pòppyə lérrətee/ *n* —**pop·u·lar·ly** *adv*

pop·u·lar front *n* a left-wing coalition

pop·u·lar·ize /póppyələ rìz/ (**-ized**, **-iz·ing**) *vt* **1** make popular **2** make understandable to a general audience —**pop·u·lar·i·za·tion** /pòppyələri záysh'n/ *n*

pop·u·late /póppyə làyt/ (**-lat·ed**, **-lat·ing**) *vt* **1** put people in a place **2** inhabit a place in numbers —**pop·u·lat·ed** *adj*

pop·u·la·tion /póppyə láysh'n/ *n* **1** all the people in a place **2** the total number of people in a place **3** all the plants or animals of a particular species in a place

pop·u·lism /póppyə lìzzəm/ *n* **1** politics based on principles considered unfavorable to a perceived elite **2** a focus on ordinary people, e.g., in the arts —**pop·u·list** *n*, *adj*

pop·u·lous /póppyələss/ *adj* highly populated —**pop·u·lous·ness** *n* ◊ See note at **populace**

⚡**pop-up** *adj* **1** with a mechanism that makes something lift upward quickly **2** presented on a computer screen temporarily **3** containing cut-out figures that rise up as a page is opened ○ *a pop-up book* ■ *n* in baseball, a pop fly

por·ce·lain /páwrsələn, páwrslən/ *n* **1** a hard translucent ceramic material **2** items or an object made of porcelain —**por·ce·la·ne·ous** /páwrssə láynee əss/ *adj*

porch *n* **1** a covered shelter at the entrance to a building **2** a roofed room on the outside of a building

por·cine /páwr sìn, páwrs'n/ *adj* of pigs

por·cu·pine /páwrkyə pìn/ *n* a rodent with long protective quills

pore¹ /pawr/ *n* **1** a tiny opening in the skin **2** a tiny opening in a plant leaf or stem

pore² (**pored**, **por·ing**) *vi* **1** look at something concentratedly **2** think about something carefully ◊ See note at **pour**

pork *n* meat from a hog

pork bar·rel *n* government projects affording political opportunism (*infml*)

pork·er /páwrkər/ *n* a fat young hog

pork rinds *npl* small pieces of fried pork rind eaten as a snack

porn, por·no /páwrnō/ *n* pornography (*infml*)

por·nog·ra·phy /pawr nóggrəfee/ *n* **1** the sex industry **2** sexually explicit material —**por·nog·ra·pher** *n* —**por·no·graph·ic** /pàwrnə gráffik/ *adj* —**por·no·graph·i·cal·ly** *adv*

po·rous /páwrəss/ *adj* **1** permeable **2** with pores or cavities —**po·ros·i·ty** /paw róssətee/ *n* —**po·rous·ly** *adv*

por·phy·ry /páwrfəree/ *n* **1** a reddish-purple rock **2** a rock with isolated large crystals

por·poise /páwrpəss/ (*pl* **-pois·es** or same) *n* a sea mammal like a dolphin with a blunt nose

por·ridge /páwrij/ *n* UK oatmeal, as a breakfast food

port¹ *n* **1** a large harbor **2** a town with a large harbor **3** a waterfront

---

ORIGIN The six English words **port** are all ultimately related. **Port** "harbor" is adopted from Latin *portus* in the same sense. The **port** side of a ship, recorded from the mid-16C, was probably originally the side turned toward the "harbor," and so derived from that **port**. **Port** "opening in a ship" came via French from Latin *porta* "gate," which is closely related to *portus*. The drink **port** is named for the town of Porto or Oporto (literally "the port") at the mouth of the river Douro in Portugal, from which the wine was shipped. Latin *portus* gave rise to a verb *portare*, which probably originally meant "bring into port" but came to mean just "carry," and it is from this verb that English **port** "carry a weapon across the body" derives: it came via French in the mid-16C. The most recent **port**, a verb used in computing, is either a specialized development of the "carrying" word or from the computing sense of the noun **port²**.

⚡**port²** *n* **1** an opening in the side of a boat for loading and unloading **2** an external computer connection **3** a valve-operated opening

port³ *n* the left side of a ship or plane —**port** *adj*, *adv*

port⁴ *n* a strong sweet fortified wine

port⁵ *vt* carry a weapon across the body

⚡**port⁶** *vt* convert software for a different computer system

⚡**port·a·ble** /páwrtəb'l/ *adj* **1** easily moved around **2** easy to convert to another computer operating system —**port·a·ble** *n* —**port·a·bly** *adv*

⚡**port·a·ble doc·u·ment for·mat** *n* full form of **pdf**

port·age /páwrtij, pawr taázh/ *n* the process of carrying boats overland ■ *vt* (**-aged**, **-ag·ing**) carry a boat overland to a waterway

⚡**por·tal** /páwrt'l/ *n* **1** a large gate or entrance (*literary*) **2** *also* **por·tal site** a home site for a web browser

Port-au-Prince /-ō prínss/ capital of Haiti. Pop. 1,461,000 (1995).

port·cul·lis /pàwrt kúlliss/ *n* a heavy castle gate that can slide up and down

Port E·liz·a·beth city in SE South Africa. Pop. 1,035,000 (1995).

por·tend /pawr ténd/ *vt* **1** be an omen of something unpleasant **2** indicate something

por·tent /páwr tènt/ *n* **1** an omen **2** ominous significance

por·ten·tous /pawr téntəss/ *adj* **1** very significant for the future **2** pompous

por·ter[1] /páwrtər/ *n* **1** somebody who carries people's luggage **2** an attendant on a railroad car

por·ter[2] /páwrtər/ *n* a type of dark beer

Por·ter /páwrtər/, **Cole** (1891–1964) US composer and lyricist

Por·ter, Katherine Anne (1890–1980) US writer

Porter, William Sydney ♦ Henry, O.

port·fo·li·o /pawrt fôlee ô/ (*pl* **-os**) *n* **1** a large flat case for carrying documents or works of art **2** the contents of a portfolio, especially samples of somebody's creative work **3** a group of investments **4** a government minister's responsibilities

port·fo·li·o work·er *n* an employee who acquires skills and experience in a number of different areas

port·hole /páwrt hòl/ *n* a round window in a ship

por·ti·co /páwrti kò/ (*pl* **-coes** *or* **-cos**) *n* **1** a porch **2** a covered walkway

por·tion /páwrsh'n/ *n* **1** a helping of food **2** a part or section **3** somebody's fate (*literary*) ■ *vt* divide something into parts

Port·land /páwrtlənd/ **1** city in SW Maine. Pop. 62,786 (1998). **2** city in NW Oregon. Pop. 503,891 (1998).

Port Lou·is /-lòō is, -lòō ee/ capital of Mauritius. Pop. 147,131 (1998).

port·ly /páwrtlee/ (**-li·er, -li·est**) *adj* regarded as slightly overweight —**port·li·ness** *n*

port·man·teau /pawrt mántò, pàwrt man tó/ (*pl* **-teaus** *or* **-teaux** /-tòz/) *n* a large suitcase

> **ORIGIN Portmanteau** was adopted in the mid-16C from a French word meaning literally "carry a mantle or cloak." In French the *portmanteau* was originally an official who carried the king's cloak, then the bag in which he carried it, and hence any large bag carrying items for a journey.

port·man·teau word *n* a word that combines the sounds and meanings of two other words

Port Mores·by /-máwrzbee/ capital of Papua New Guinea. Pop. 193,242 (1990).

Por·to /páwrtò/, **O·por·to** /ò páwrtò/ port in NW Portugal. Pop. 285,320 (1995).

Por·to A·le·gre /páwrtò ə léggrə/ capital of Rio Grande do Sul State, SE Brazil. Pop. 1,288,879 (1996).

port of call *n* a foreign port visited by a ship

port of en·try *n* an international border crossing

Port-of-Spain, Port of Spain capital of Trinidad and Tobago. Pop. 45,284 (1995).

Por·to-No·vo /pàwrto nóvò/ capital of Benin. Pop. 200,000 (1994).

por·trait /páwrtrət/ *n* **1** a picture of a person **2** a description of somebody or something —**por·trait·ist** *n*

por·trai·ture /páwrtrə chòòr, -trəchər/ *n* **1** the making of portraits **2** portraits in general

por·tray /pawr tráy/ *vt* **1** depict somebody or something visually **2** describe somebody or something in words **3** play a role in a play or movie —**por·tray·a·ble** *adj* —**por·tray·al** *n*

Port Sa·id /-saa éed/ city in NE Egypt. Pop. 469,000 (1998).

Ports·mouth /páwrtsməth/ **1** city in SE Virginia. Pop. 98,936 (1998). **2** city in S England. Pop. 192,000 (1996).

Port Stan·ley ♦ Stanley

Port Su·dan city in NE Sudan. Pop. 305,385 (1993).

Por·tu·gal /páwrchəgəl/ country in SW Europe, in the W Iberian Peninsula. Cap. Lisbon. Pop. 10,066,253 (2001).

~~Portugese~~ incorrect spelling of **Portuguese**

Por·tu·guese /pàwrchə géez, -géess/ *n* **1** the language of Portugal and Brazil **2** somebody from Portugal —**Por·tu·guese** *adj*

Por·tu·guese man-of-war *n* a sea organism resembling a jellyfish

POS *abbr* point of sale

pose[1] /pòz/ *v* (**posed, pos·ing**) **1** *vti* adopt a physical posture for a photograph or painting, or position somebody or something for this purpose **2** *vi* impersonate somebody **3** *vi* behave in a pretentious way (*disapproving*) **4** *vt* ask a question **5** *vt* cause something to exist ○ *pose* a threat to peace ■ *n* **1** a posture **2** a pretense (*disapproving*)

pose[2] /pòz/ (**posed, pos·ing**) *vt* baffle (*archaic*)

Po·sei·don /pə síd'n, pō-/ *n* in Greek mythology, the god of the sea. Roman equivalent **Neptune**

pos·er[1] /pózər/ *n* somebody who poses for a photograph or painting

pos·er[2] /pózər/ *n* a challenging problem

~~posess~~ incorrect spelling of **possess**

~~posession~~ incorrect spelling of **possession**

po·seur /pò zúr/ *n* a person regarded as pretentious (*disapproving*)

posh *adj* elegant, fashionable, and expensive (*infml*) —**posh·ly** *adv* —**posh·ness** *n*

> **ORIGIN** The legend has become widely circulated that **posh** is an acronym formed from the initial letters of "port out, starboard home," an allusion to the fact that wealthy British passengers could afford the more ex-

pensive cabins on the port side of the ships going out to India, and on the starboard side returning home, which kept them out of the heat of the sun. Pleasant as this story is, it has never been substantiated. Another possibility is that **posh** may be the same word as the now obsolete *posh* "dandy, swell," a slang term current around the end of the 19C.

pos·it /pózzit/ *vt* put forward for consideration or as an assumption *(fml)*

po·si·tion /pə zísh'n/ *n* 1 the place where somebody or something is 2 a bodily posture 3 the way in which something is placed or arranged 4 a particular set of circumstances 5 a rank or role 6 a viewpoint or policy 7 the correct or usual place 8 a job or post ■ *vt* 1 put in a particular position 2 determine the site or location of —**po·si·tion·al** *adj*

po·si·tion pa·per *n* an in-depth report giving an official view

pos·i·tive /pózzətiv/ *adj* 1 not in doubt 2 impossible to disprove 3 confident and optimistic 4 producing good results ○ *a very positive experience* 5 indicating agreement or approval ○ *positive feedback* 6 in test results, indicating the presence of a particular organism or component 7 adds emphasis *(infml)* ○ *a positive disaster* 8 (symbol +) more than zero 9 with an electrical charge like that of a proton 10 describes a photographic image with shading that matches the subject 11 not comparative or superlative in degree ■ *n* 1 a positive photographic image 2 a positive number or value 3 an adjective or adverb in the positive degree —**pos·i·tive·ly** *adv* —**pos·i·tive·ness** *n* —**pos·i·tiv·i·ty** /pòzzə tívvətee/ *n*

pos·i·tiv·ism /pózzəti vìzzəm/ *n* the theory that knowledge can only be acquired through direct observation or experience —**pos·i·tiv·ist** *n*, *adj* —**pos·i·tiv·is·tic** /pòzzəti vístik/ *adj*

pos·se /póssee/ *n* 1 a group of citizens called upon to help a sheriff 2 any assembled group *(infml)* 3 a search party

ORIGIN **Posse** is a mid-17C shortening of *posse comitatus* (early 17C), in Latin literally "force of the county," the body of men above the age of 15 in a county whom a sheriff could summon to quell a riot or for some other purpose. The briefer **posse** was always more common in the United States.

pos·sess /pə zéss/ *vt* 1 have or own 2 have as an ability or quality 3 influence the behavior or thinking of 4 have sex with *(dated; sometimes offensive)* —**pos·ses·sor** *n*

pos·sessed /pə zést/ *adj* 1 controlled by a supposed supernatural force or a strong feeling 2 being the possessor of something ○ *possessed of wealth and beauty* 3 calm and self-controlled

pos·ses·sion /pə zésh'n/ *n* 1 the fact of possessing something 2 something that somebody owns 3 a colony *(often pl)* 4 the state of being controlled by a supposed supernatural force or strong feeling 5 control of the ball or puck in a team game 6 the fact of having something illegal 7 occupancy of property ■ **pos·ses·sions** *npl* personal property

pos·ses·sive /pə zéssiv/ *adj* 1 demanding all of somebody's attention or love 2 selfish 3 of ownership 4 showing possession in grammatical terms ■ *n* the possessive form of words, or a possessive form —**pos·ses·sive·ly** *adv* —**pos·ses·sive·ness** *n*

pos·si·bil·i·ty /pòssə bíllətee/ *n* (*pl* -ties) 1 something that is possible 2 the state of being possible ■ **pos·si·bil·i·ties** *npl* potential

pos·si·ble /póssəb'l/ *adj* 1 able or likely to happen, be done, exist, or be true 2 potential —**pos·si·bly** *adv* ◊ See note at **passable**

POSSLQ *abbr* person of the opposite sex sharing living quarters *(infml)*

pos·sum /póssəm/ *n* an opossum *(infml)* ◊ **play possum** feign sleep

⚡ **post** /pōst/ *n* 1 an upright pole or stake 2 a military base 3 an upright part of a frame 4 a position of employment ■ *v* 1 *vt* update a computer database 2 *vt* send somebody to a particular place to work ■ *n* a message on an Internet newsgroup ■ *v* 1 *vti* send a message to an Internet newsgroup 2 *vt* pay bail to set somebody free ■ *n* 1 *UK* a system for sending and delivering items 2 *UK* letters and packages mailed to people ■ *v* 1 *vt* transfer a soldier to a new unit 2 *vt* score a point or points in a game 3 *vt* appoint somebody to a military command 4 *vt* publish text electronically ■ *n* 1 a workplace or assigned station 2 a veterans' organization ■ *v* *vt* display information in a public place

⚡ **POST** *abbr* Power On Self-Test

post- *prefix* after, later ○ *postwar* ○ *postdate*

post·age /pṓstij/ *n* 1 the price paid for delivery of an item of mail 2 stamps or other marks showing payment

post·age me·ter *n* a postage machine

post·age stamp *n* a paper stamp stuck on an item to show that postage has been paid ■ *adj* tiny ○ *a postage-stamp bikini*

post·al /pṓst'l/ *adj* of a post office or mail service ◊ **go postal** become extremely angry, often in a violent way *(slang)*

post·al code *n* *Can, UK* a series of letters and numbers ending an address

post·bel·lum /-béllm/, **post·bel·lum** *adj* after a war

post·card /pṓst kaàrd/ *n* a card on which to write a short message to be mailed

post·date /pōst dáyt/ (-dat·ed, -dat·ing) *vt* 1 put a later date on a check in order to delay payment 2 happen later than something

post·doc·tor·al /pōst dóktərəl/ *adj* of academic work undertaken after a doctorate

post·er /pṓstər/ *n* a printed picture used as a decoration or advertisement

post·er child *n* 1 a person who appears in advertising, especially for a charity 2 a person or thing appearing as a representative or illustrative example (*sometimes offensive*)

pos·te·ri·or /po steerēe ər, pō-/ *adj* 1 situated at the rear of something 2 near the back of the body ■ *n* the buttocks (*humorous*)

pos·ter·i·ty /po stérrətee/ *n* (*fml*) 1 all future generations 2 all of somebody's descendants

post·grad·u·ate /pōst grájjoo ət/, **post·grad** *informal* /pōst gràd/ *adj* of education for students who already have a bachelor's degree ■ *n* a student with a bachelor's degree who is studying for a higher degree

post·haste /pōst háyst/ *adv* quickly

post hoc /pōst hók/ *n* the error of arguing that a previous event necessarily caused a subsequent event

post·hu·mous /póschəməss/ *adj* 1 after somebody's death 2 published after the writer's death —**post·hu·mous·ly** *adv*

post·in·dus·tri·al /pōst in dústree əl/ *adj* after the decline of heavy industry

ⵏ**post·ing** /pṓsting/ *n* a message on an Internet newsgroup

Post-it *tdmk* a trademark for a self-sticking slip of paper sold in pad form

post·man /pṓstmən/ *n* (*pl* -men /-mən/) *n* a person who delivers mail

post·mark /pōst maárk/ *n* an official stamp that shows when an item was mailed —**post·mark** *vt*

post·mas·ter /pōst màstər/ *n* an official in charge of a postal district

post·mis·tress /pōst místrəss/ *n* a woman official in charge of a postal district (*dated*)

post·mod·ern·ism /pōst móddər nìzzəm/ *n* a style or trend in architecture, art, and literature that developed from modernism

post·mor·tem /pōst máwrtəm/ *adj* occurring after death ■ *n* 1 a medical examination of a corpse 2 a retrospective analysis

post·na·tal /pōst náyt'l/ *adj* after birth —**post·na·tal·ly** *adv*

post of·fice *n* 1 a place where people can mail items and buy stamps 2 a national mail system

post of·fice box *n* a numbered box at a post office where mail is kept until the addressee collects it

post·op·er·a·tive /pōst óppərətiv/ *adj* occurring after surgery

post·paid /pōst páyd/ *adj* with the postage paid in advance

post·par·tum de·pres·sion /pōst paártəm-/ *n* a woman's severe depression after giving birth

post·pone /pōst pṓn, pṓss-/ *vt* put off until a later time —**post·pone·ment** *n*

post·pran·di·al /pōst prándee əl/ *adj* after a meal (*fml or humorous*)

post·script /pōst skrìpt/ *n* a short message added to a letter below the signature

post·struc·tur·al·ism *n* an intellectual movement that developed from structuralism

post·trau·mat·ic stress dis·or·der *n* a psychological condition that affects some people who have suffered a severe trauma

pos·tu·lant /póschələnt/ *n* somebody who applies to join a religious order (*fml*) —**pos·tu·lan·cy** *n*

pos·tu·late *vt* /póschə làyt/ (-lat·ed, -lat·ing) 1 assume to be true 2 make a claim for ■ *n* /póschəlat, -làyt/ 1 something postulated 2 a statement underpinning a theory —**pos·tu·la·tion** /pòschə láysh'n/ *n*

pos·ture /póschər/ *n* 1 the way somebody carries his or her body when standing or walking 2 a position that the body can assume 3 an attitude or pose ■ *vi* (-tured, -tur·ing) 1 assume a false attitude in order to impress people 2 put your body into a particular posture —**pos·tur·al** *adj*

post·vi·ral syn·drome /pōst vírəl-/ *n* MED = chronic fatigue syndrome

post·war /pōst wàwr, pòst wáwr/ *adj* after a war

po·sy /pṓzee/ (*pl* -sies) *n* a blooming flower or bunch of flowers

pot[1] *n* 1 a watertight container for cooking or storage 2 a similar container, e.g., a flowerpot or teapot 3 a dish or container made from clay 4 the total money bet in one hand of a card game 5 a common fund (*infml*) ■ *vt* (pot·ted, pot·ting) 1 put a plant in a pot 2 preserve food in a pot —**pot·ful** *n* ◇ **go to pot** deteriorate (*infml*)

pot[2] *n* marijuana (*slang*)

po·ta·ble /pṓtəb'l/ *adj* suitable for drinking

pot·ash /pót àsh/ *n* a potassium compound used in fertilizers

po·tas·si·um /pə tássee əm/ *n* (*symbol* K) a highly reactive metallic element. Use: coolant in nuclear reactors, in fertilizers.

ORIGIN The name **potassium** was coined in 1807 by Sir Humphry Davy. The basis of the word is *potash*, in which potassium is found. French *potasse*, the equivalent of *potash*, was adopted into English as *potass*, a form now obsolete. Davy formed **potassium** from this obsolete English word or the original *potash*.

po·tas·si·um bro·mide *n* a white crystalline compound. Use: in lithography, medicine, photography.

po·tas·si·um ni·trate *n* a white crystalline salt. Use: in fireworks, explosives, matches, as fertilizer, meat preservative.

po·ta·to /pə táytō/ (*pl* **-toes**) *n* **1** a rounded white tuber cooked in various ways as a vegetable **2** the plant that produces potatoes

po·ta·to chip *n US, Can, ANZ* a thin deep-fried slice of potato

~~potatoe~~ incorrect spelling of **potato**

pot·bel·ly /pót bèllee/ (*pl* **-lies**) *n* a bulging stomach —**pot·bel·lied** *adj*

pot·bel·ly stove, pot·bel·lied stove *n* a household stove heated with coal or wood

pot·boil·er /pót bòylər/ *n* a book or movie of low quality

> **ORIGIN** The purpose of a **potboiler** is to "keep the pot boiling," to provide an author with enough money to be able to continue to buy food and eat.

pot·bound /pót bównd/ *adj* describes a plant that is too big for its current container

po·tent /pṓt'nt/ *adj* **1** strong and effective **2** capable of having an erection and sexual intercourse —**po·ten·cy** *n* —**po·tent·ly** *adv*

po·ten·tate /pṓt'n tàyt/ *n* a powerful person, especially a ruler

po·ten·tial /pə ténshəl/ *adj* possible but not yet realized ■ *n* **1** the capacity to develop and be successful **2** the work required to bring a unit of positive electric charge from infinity to a specified point in an electric field —**po·ten·tial·ly** *adv*

po·ten·tial en·er·gy *n* (*symbol V or* E_p) the energy stored in a body or system

pot·hold·er /pót hòldər/ *n* a fabric pad used to handle hot cooking pots and utensils

pot·hole /pót hòl/ *n* **1** a hole in a road surface **2** a vertical hole in a limestone area

po·tion /pṓsh'n/ *n* a medicinal, magical, or poisonous drink

pot·luck /pót lùk/ *n* the food that is available to an unexpected guest ■ *adj* describes a meal to which everyone brings a dish

Po·to·mac /pə tṓmək/ river of the E United States, flowing eastward from West Virginia into Chesapeake Bay. Length 383 mi./616 km.

pot·pour·ri /pōpə reé/ (*pl* **-ris**) *n* **1** a collection of fragrant dried flowers **2** a miscellaneous mixture

~~potray~~ incorrect spelling of **portray**

pot roast *n* a piece of beef cooked in its own juices in a covered pot —**pot-roast** *vti*

Pots·dam /póts dàm/ city in NE Germany. Pop. 138,268 (1997).

pot·sherd /pót shùrd/, **pot·shard** /-shaárd/ *n* a piece of broken pottery

pot·shot /pót shòt/ *n* **1** an easy shot in sports **2** a criticism leveled at an easy target

pot·ted /póttəd/ *adj* **1** growing in a pot **2** preserved in a pot

pot·ted plant *n* a plant grown in a flowerpot

pot·ter /póttər/ *n* a maker of pottery

Beatrix Potter

Pot·ter /póttər/, **Beatrix** (1866–1943) British children's writer and illustrator

pot·ter's wheel *n* a rotating device for making pottery by hand

pot·ter·y /póttəree/ *n* **1** objects made of baked clay **2** the activity of making pottery

pot·ting soil *n* nutrient-enriched soil for potted plants

pot·ty /póttee/ (*pl* **-ties**) *n* a bowl used as a toilet for a small child

POTUS /pótəss/ *n* the US president. Full form **President of the United States**

pouch /powch/ *n* **1** a small soft bag **2** a pocket of skin in an animal

poul·tice /pṓltiss/ *n* a warm moist substance applied to an injury

poul·try /pṓltree/ *n* **1** domestic fowl (+ *sing or pl verb*) **2** the meat from poultry

pounce /powns/ *vi* **1** jump or swoop suddenly on somebody or something **2** move quickly in attacking or taking something —**pounce** *n*

pound[1] /pownd/ *v* **1** *vti* strike something hard and repeatedly **2** *vt* beat something to a pulp or powder **3** *vi* throb **4** *vt* attack somebody continuously **5** *vi* run with heavy steps

pound[2] /pownd/ *n* **1** an avoirdupois unit of weight divided into 16 ounces **2** the main unit of the former currency of the Republic of Ireland **3** a troy unit of weight divided into 12 ounces **4** the main unit of currency in the United Kingdom and several other countries **5** a British unit of force

pound[3] /pownd/ *n* **1** an enclosure for stray animals **2** an enclosure for vehicles or other goods being held by an authority

Pound /pownd/, **Ezra** (1885–1972) US writer

pound·age /pówndij/ *n* **1** payment per pound of weight **2** weight in pounds

pound cake *n* rich yellow cake

pound sign *n* **1** the symbol (£) that indicates pound sterling **2** the symbol (#)

pound ster·ling (*pl* **pounds ster·ling**) *n* the official name for the unit of currency used in the United Kingdom

pour /pawr/ *v* **1** *vt* make a substance flow **2** *vti* serve a drink from a container **3** *vi* flow in large quantities **4** *vi* rain heavily **5** *vi* come or go in large numbers **6** *vt* express feelings in an unrestrained way

USAGE pour or pore? You **pour** from the pot into a coffee cup, **pore** over a text (=study it carefully), and have **pores** in your skin.

pout /powt/ *v* **1** *vti* push the lips outward in sulkiness or sexiness **2** *vi* sulk —**pout** *n* —**pout·y** *adj*

pou·tine /poo teen/ *n Can* a Quebec dish of fried potatoes and cheese

pov·er·ty /póvvərtee/ *n* **1** the state of lacking money or possessions **2** a lack of something

pov·er·ty line, pov·er·ty lev·el *n* an income below which somebody is thought to live in poverty

pov·er·ty-strick·en *adj* lacking money or possessions to a problematic degree

POW *abbr* prisoner of war

pow·der /pówdər/ *n* **1** a substance in the form of tiny loose particles **2** gunpowder ■ *v* **1** *vt* put powder on the face **2** *vti* turn into powder —**pow·der·y** *adj*

pow·der keg *n* **1** a keg for gunpowder **2** a tense situation

pow·der puff *n* a pad used to powder the skin of the face

pow·der room *n* **1** a bathroom for women **2** a bathroom for guests

Department of Defense, Washington, D.C.

Colin Powell

Pow·ell /pów əl/, **Colin** (b. 1937) US general and US Secretary of State (2001–)

Pow·ell, Lewis Franklin, Jr. (1907–98) associate justice of the US Supreme Court (1971–87)

⚡ **pow·er** /pówr/ *n* **1** the ability or capacity to do something **2** physical strength **3** control and influence **4** political control of a country **5** the authority to act **6** a person or organization with power **7** an important country **8** persuasiveness **9** a skill **10** (*symbol P*) a measure of the rate of doing work or transferring energy **11** the energy that drives machinery **12** electricity **13** the number of times a quantity is to be multiplied by itself **14** the magnifying ability of a lens ■ *adj* **1** run by electricity or fuel **2** intended for business success o *a power tie* ■ *v* **1** *vt* provide the operating energy for **2** *vi* move energetically —**pow·er·less** *adj* —**pow·er·less·ly** *adv* —**pow·er·less·ness** *n* ◇ **the powers that be** the people in authority

□ **power down** *vti* turn a computer off
□ **power up** *vti* turn a computer on

pow·er base *n* the foundation of somebody's political power

pow·er·boat /pówr bòt/ *n* a powerful motorboat —**pow·er·boat·ing** *n*

pow·er brok·er *n* somebody with political or commercial influence

pow·er·ful /pówrfl/ *adj* **1** influential **2** physically strong **3** effective —**pow·er·ful·ly** *adv* —**pow·er·ful·ness** *n*

pow·er·house /pówr hòwss/ (*pl* -**hous·es** /-hòwzəz/) *n* somebody or something very productive (*infml*)

pow·er line *n* a cable carrying electricity

pow·er lunch *n* an important lunchtime business meeting

pow·er of at·tor·ney *n* the legal authority to act for another person

pow·er plant, pow·er sta·tion *n* **1** a plant for generating electricity **2** a unit that powers a self-propelled object

pow·er pol·i·tics *n* political relations based on power (+ *sing or pl verb*)

pow·er steer·ing *n* a vehicle steering system in which supplementary engine power makes steering easier

pow·er walk·ing *n* quick walking for exercise —**pow·er walk·er** *n*

Pow·ha·tan /pow hátt'n, pòw ə tán/ (1550?–1618) Algonquian leader

pow·wow /pów wòw/ *n* **1** a Native American ceremony during which a shaman performs rituals **2** a meeting for discussion (*infml*) —**pow·wow** *vi*

pox *n* any disease that causes scarring spots on the skin

Poz·nań /pôz nàn, -nàan/ city in west central Poland. Pop. 580,000 (1997).

pp *abbr* pianissimo

pp. *abbr* pages

p.p. *abbr* **1** by proxy (*used when signing documents on behalf of sb else*) **2** parcel post **3** past participle

PPO *abbr* preferred-provider organization

PR *abbr* **1** *also* **P.R.** Puerto Rico **2** public relations

pr. *abbr* pronoun

prac·ti·ca·ble /práktikəb'l/ *adj* **1** capable of being done **2** usable

prac·ti·cal /práktik'l/ *adj* **1** concerned with facts and experience, not with theory **2** useful **3** good at solving problems **4** practicing **5** suitable for everyday use **6** virtual (*infml*) o *a practical disaster* —**prac·ti·cal·i·ty** /práktì kállətee/ *n*

prac·ti·cal joke *n* a trick played on somebody for amusement —**prac·ti·cal jok·er** *n*

prac·ti·cal·ly /práktikəlee/ *adv* **1** almost **2** in a practical way

prac·ti·cal nurse *n* a nurse holding basic qualifications

prac·tice /práktiss/ v (-ticed, -tic·ing) 1 vti repeat something to get better 2 vt do something as a habit or custom 3 vti work in law or medicine 4 vt follow a religion ■ 1 repetition done in order to improve performance 2 the performance of a religion, profession, or custom 3 the process of carrying out an idea 4 the work of a professional person 5 a habit or custom ◊ See note at **habit**

prac·ticed /práktist/ adj expert

prac·tic·ing /práktissing/ adj pursuing a particular activity

~~practicle~~ incorrect spelling of **practical**

~~practicly~~ incorrect spelling of **practically**

prac·ti·tion·er /prak tísh'nər/ n somebody who practices a profession

prag·mat·ic /prag máttik/ adj 1 concerned with practical results 2 of philosophical pragmatism —**prag·mat·i·cal·ly** adv

prag·mat·ics /prag máttiks/ n the study of language in use (+ sing verb)

prag·ma·tism /prágma tìzzəm/ n 1 the attitude of somebody who thinks about practical results rather than principles 2 the theory that something should be evaluated according to its practical success —**prag·ma·tist** n

Prague /praag/ capital of the Czech Republic. Pop. 1,193,270 (1999).

Prai·a /prí ə/ capital of the Republic of Cape Verde, in SE São Tiago island. Pop. 95,000 (1998).

prai·rie /práiree/ n an area of North American grassland ■ **prai·ries** npl Can the provinces of Manitoba, Alberta, and Saskatchewan

prai·rie dog n a North American burrowing rodent

prai·rie schoo·ner n a 19C covered wagon

praise /prayz/ n 1 an expression of admiration 2 worship and thanks to God or a deity ■ vt (praised, prais·ing) 1 express admiration for 2 worship and thank

praise·wor·thy /práyz wùrthee/ adj admirable —**praise·wor·thi·ness** n

pra·line /práy leèn/ n 1 a paste made from crushed caramelized nuts 2 a chocolate candy with a praline filling

ORIGIN Praline represents part of the name of the French military officer Marshal de Plessis-Praslin (1598–1675), whose cook invented it.

pram n UK BABYWARE = **baby carriage**

prance (pranced, pranc·ing) v 1 vi move in a lively exaggerated way 2 vti jump, or make a horse jump, forward on the back legs —**prance** n —**pranc·ing** adj

prank[1] n a practical joke —**prank·ster** n

prank[2] vti decorate or display something, somebody, or yourself ostentatiously

~~prarie~~ incorrect spelling of **prairie**

pra·se·o·dym·i·um /práyzee ō dímmee əm/ n

(symbol **Pr**) a rare metallic element. Use: alloys, coloring for glass.

prate /prayt/ (prat·ed, prat·ing) vi talk annoyingly or about trivial things —**prate** n —**prat·ing·ly** adv

prat·fall /prát fàwl/ n a comic fall (slang)

prat·tle /prátt'l/ (-tled, -tling) vi talk idly or childishly —**prat·tle** n —**prat·tling·ly** adv

prawn n an edible crustacean like a large shrimp ■ vi fish for prawns —**prawn·er** n

prax·is /práksiss/ n (fml) 1 the performance or practical application of a skill 2 an established practice

Prax·it·e·les /prak síttə leèz/ (390?–330? BC) Greek sculptor

pray /pray/ vti 1 speak to God, a deity, or a saint 2 hope for something strongly 3 make an earnest request ■ interj emphasizes a question or command (dated or humorous)

> **SPELLCHECK** Do not confuse the spelling of **pray** and **prey** ("a hunted animal or person"), which sound similar.

prayer /prair/ n 1 a spoken or unspoken communication with God, a deity, or a saint 2 the act of communicating with God, a deity, or a saint 3 a religious service with prayers (often pl) 4 an earnest request or desire 5 a slight chance

prayer beads npl a string of beads for counting prayers

prayer book n a book of set prayers for religious services

pray·ing man·tis n an insect with raised forelegs

pre- prefix 1 before, earlier, in advance ○ preschool ○ predate ○ prerequisite 2 in front of ○ premolar

preach /preech/ v 1 vti give a religious sermon 2 vi give advice in an irritating way 3 vt urge people to accept something —**preach·er** n —**preach·y** adj

pre·am·ble /prée àmb'l, pree ámb'l/ n 1 an introductory explanation 2 something that precedes something else

Pre·cam·bri·an /pree kámbree ən/ n the earliest geologic period —**Pre·cam·bri·an** adj

pre·car·i·ous /prə káiree əss/ adj 1 dangerously uncertain or insecure 2 not well founded (fml) —**pre·car·i·ous·ly** adv

pre·cast /pree kást/ adj allowed to harden in a mold before positioning ○ precast concrete —**pre·cast** vt

pre·cau·tion /prə káwsh'n/ n something done to give protection against a possible undesirable event —**pre·cau·tion·ar·y** adj

pre·cede /prə seèd/ (-ced·ed, -ced·ing) vt 1 come or go before something 2 say or do something before something else

> **SPELLCHECK** Do not confuse the spelling of **precede** and **proceed** ("begin or continue with an action"), which sound similar.

prec·e·dence /préssəd'nss/, **prec·e·den·cy** /-d'nssee/ n 1 relative importance in status 2 priority

prec·e·dent /préssəd'nt/ n 1 something used as an example for later action or as justification for a later decision 2 an established practice ■ adj preceding (fml)

pre·ced·ing /prə seeding/ adj coming before

~~preceed~~ incorrect spelling of **precede**

~~preceence~~ incorrect spelling of **presence**

pre·cept /preé sèpt/ n a principle or instruction guiding conduct (fml)

pre·cinct /preé sinkt/ n 1 an electoral district 2 a city area patrolled by a police unit ■ **pre·cincts** npl the area around a place

pre·ci·os·i·ty /prèshee óssətee/ (pl -ties) n ridiculous overrefinement

pre·cious /préshəss/ adj 1 worth a lot of money 2 greatly valued 3 not to be wasted 4 fastidious or affected ■ adv very o have precious little time —**pre·cious·ness** n

pre·cious met·al n gold, silver, or platinum

pre·cious stone n a gemstone

prec·i·pice /préssəpiss/ n 1 a high cliff or crag 2 a very dangerous situation —**prec·i·piced** adj

pre·cip·i·tate v /prə síppi tàyt/ (-tat·ed, -tat·ing) 1 vt make something happen quickly 2 vt send somebody or something rapidly 3 vi fall from the sky as rain, snow, or hail 4 vti separate a solid out of a solution, or be separated from a solution ■ adj /prə síppi tət/ 1 done or acting rashly 2 hurried 3 sudden ■ n /prə síppi tàyt, -tət/ a suspension of small particles formed in a solution —**pre·cip·i·tate·ly** adv —**pre·cip·i·ta·tive** adj

pre·cip·i·ta·tion /prə síppi táysh'n/ n 1 rain, snow, or hail 2 the formation of rain, snow, or hail 3 the formation of a suspension in a solution 4 great haste (fml)

pre·cip·i·tous /prə síppitəss/ adj 1 done rashly 2 high and steep —**pre·cip·i·tous·ly** adv —**pre·cip·i·tous·ness** n

pré·cis /práy see, pray seé/ (pl same) n a summary —**pré·cis** vt

pre·cise /prə síss/ adj 1 exact or detailed 2 careful about details 3 indicates something specific o at that precise moment 4 able to deal with small details 5 distinct and correct —**pre·cise·ly** adv —**pre·cise·ness** n

pre·ci·sion /prə sízh'n/ n 1 exactness 2 mathematical accuracy ■ adj made with exactness or accuracy o precision instruments

pre·clude /prə klood/ (-clud·ed, -clud·ing) vt 1 prevent or make impossible (fml) 2 exclude in advance —**pre·clu·sion** /-kloossivl/ —**pre·clu·sive** /-kloossivl/ adj

pre·co·cious /prə kóshəss/ adj mentally advanced compared to other children of the same age, often irritatingly so —**pre·co·cious·ly** adv —**pre·co·cious·ness** n —**pre·coc·i·ty** /prə kóssətee/ n

pre·cog·ni·tion /preè kog nísh'n/ n the supposed ability to foresee the future —**pre·cog·ni·tive** /preè kógnətiv/ adj

pre·con·ceived /preè kən seévd/ adj formed in the mind in advance —**pre·con·ceive** vt —**pre·con·cep·tion** /preè kən sépshən/ n

pre·con·di·tion /preè kən dísh'n/ n something that must be done first ■ vt prepare for a particular event or state

pre·cur·sor /preè kùrsər/ n somebody or something that comes earlier

pre·date /pree dáyt/ (-dat·ed, -dat·ing) vt exist earlier than

pred·a·tor /préddətər/ n 1 a carnivorous animal or destructive organism 2 somebody who plunders or destroys —**pred·a·to·ry** adj

pre·de·cease /preè di seéss/ (-ceased, -ceas·ing) vt die before —**pre·de·cease** n

pred·e·ces·sor /préddə sèssər, preédə-/ n 1 the previous holder of a job 2 something that was replaced by something else

pre·de·fined /preè di fínd/ adj established in advance

pre·des·ti·na·tion /preè destə náysh'n/ n the doctrine that God or fate has decided everything in advance

pre·de·ter·mine /preè də túrmən/ (-min·ed, -min·ing) vt decide or arrange in advance

pre·dic·a·ment /prə díkəmənt/ n a difficult situation

pred·i·cate n /préddikət/ 1 the part of a sentence that contains all elements except the subject 2 something affirmed or denied ■ vt /préddi kàyt/ (-cat·ed, -cat·ing) 1 base an opinion, action, or result on something 2 state something about the subject of a statement —**pred·i·ca·tion** /prèddi káysh'n/ n

pre·dict /prə díkt/ vt say what will happen —**pre·dict·a·ble** adj —**pre·dict·a·bly** adv —**pre·dic·tion** n —**pre·dic·tor** n

✦ **pre·dic·tive** /prə díktiv/ adj 1 relating to the forecasting of a likely result or outcome o a predictive medical test 2 using technology that anticipates the word a computer user is in the process of keying o predictive indexing

pred·i·lec·tion /prèdd'l ékshən/ n a particular liking

pre·dis·pose /preèdi spóz/ (-posed, -pos·ing) vt (fml) 1 cause to be favorable to something 2 cause to be liable or inclined to do something —**pre·dis·pos·al** n —**pre·dis·po·si·tion** /preè dispə zísh'n/ n

pre·dom·i·nant /prə dómmənənt/ adj 1 most common 2 most important —**pre·dom·i·nance** n —**pre·dom·i·nant·ly** adv

pre·dom·i·nate (-nat·ed, -nat·ing) vi /prə dómmə nàyt/ 1 be in the majority 2 be more important

~~predominately~~ incorrect spelling of **predominantly**

pree·mie /preeemee/, **pre·mie** n ■ a prematurely born infant

pre·em·i·nent /pree émminənt/ adj highly distinguished or outstanding —**pre·em·i·nence** n —**pre·em·i·nent·ly** adv

pre·empt /pree émpt/ vt **1** act to prevent **2** occupy to acquire the right to buy later **3** take the place of —**pre·emp·tion** n —**pre·emp·to·ry** adj

pre·emp·tive /pree émptiv/ adj **1** done before others can act **2** intended to prevent an attack —**pre·emp·tive·ly** adv

preemptory incorrect spelling of **peremptory**

preen v **1** vi groom the feathers with the beak **2** vti spend a long time grooming and dressing in a fussy way

pre·fab /preè fàb/ n a prefabricated building (infml)

pre·fab·ri·cate /pree fábbrə kàyt/ (-cat·ed, -cat·ing) vt produce in standard sections for assembly elsewhere —**pre·fab·ri·ca·tion** /pree fabbrə káysh'n/ n

pref·ace /préffəss/ n **1** an introductory part of a text **2** a preliminary action ■ vt (-aced, -ac·ing) **1** introduce with a preface **2** serve as an introduction to

ORIGIN In spite of appearances, **preface** has no etymological connection with **face**. It derives through French from Latin *praefatio*, which is literally "something said beforehand" and so an exact parallel with the more basically English formation *foreword*.

pref·a·to·ry /préffə tàwree/ adj acting as a preface —**pref·a·to·ri·ly** /prèffə táwrəlee/ adv

pre·fect /preè fèkt/ n **1** a high-ranking regional administrative official in France or Italy **2** in ancient Rome, a senior administrative or military official **3** a student who assists a teacher with discipline —**pre·fec·to·ri·al** /prèè fek tàwree əl/ adj

pre·fec·ture /preè fèkchər/ n the district over which a prefect has jurisdiction —**pre·fec·tur·al** /pree fékchərəl/ adj

pre·fer /pri fúr/ (-ferred, -fer·ring) vt like better or want more than something else

pref·er·a·ble /préffərəb'l/ adj more desirable —**pref·er·a·bly** adv

preferance incorrect spelling of **preference**

prefered incorrect spelling of **preferred**

pref·er·ence /préffərənss/ n **1** the view that one person or thing is better than another **2** a right to express a choice o *We exercised our preference.* **3** somebody or something regarded as better than others

pref·er·en·tial /prèffə rénsh'l/ adj showing favoritism o *preferential treatment* —**pref·er·en·tial·ism** n —**pref·er·en·tial·ly** adv

pre·fer·ment /pri fúrmənt/ n (fml) **1** promotion to a higher position **2** a high-ranking position

pre·ferred pro·vid·er or·gan·i·za·tion n an organization that contracts with hospitals and physicians to provide health care to subscribers

pre·ferred stock n equity stock whose holders are the first to receive dividends

pre·fig·ure /pree fíggyər/ (-ured, -ur·ing) vt **1** represent or suggest something important that develops later **2** think about something beforehand —**pre·fig·ur·a·tive** adj —**pre·fig·ure·ment** n

pre·fix /preè fíks/ n a word element that is attached to the beginning of words to change their meaning ■ vt **1** put in front of something else **2** add a prefix to —**pre·fix·al** /pree fíks'l/ adj —**pre·fix·a·tion** /prèè fik sáysh'n/ n

pre·fron·tal lo·bot·o·my /pree frùnt'l-/ n a surgical operation to cut nerves connecting parts of the brain

preg·nant /prégnənt/ adj **1** carrying unborn offspring within the body **2** significant or full of meaning —**preg·nan·cy** n —**preg·nant·ly** adv

pre·heat /pree heèt/ vt heat in advance

pre·hen·sile /pree héns'l/ adj able to take hold of things, especially by wrapping round them o *a prehensile tail* —**pre·hen·sil·i·ty** /prèè hen síllətee/ n

pre·his·tor·ic /preè hi stáwrik/ adj of the period before recorded history —**pre·his·to·ri·an** n —**pre·his·tor·i·cal·ly** adv —**pre·his·to·ry** /pree hístəree/ n

pre·judge /pree júj/ (-judged, -judg·ing) vt judge prematurely —**pre·judg·ment** n

prej·u·dice /préjjədiss/ n **1** an opinion formed beforehand and based on irrational feelings, insufficient knowledge, or stereotyping **2** the holding of ill-informed opinions **3** disadvantage or harm ■ vt (-diced, -dic·ing) **1** cause to form an irrational opinion in advance **2** affect adversely —**prej·u·diced** adj —**prej·u·di·cial** /prèjjə dísh'l/ adj —**prej·u·di·cial·ly** adv ◇ **without prejudice** in law, without doing any harm to somebody's legal rights or any claim that somebody has (fml)

prel·ate /préllət/ n a high-ranking member of the clergy —**pre·lat·ic** /prə láttik/ adj

pre·lim·i·na·ry /pri límmə nèrree/ adj coming before something and leading up to it ■ n (pl -ies) an introductory or preparatory activity (often pl) —**pre·lim·i·nar·i·ly** adv

pre·lit·er·ate /pree líttərət/ adj without written language

prel·ude /prél yood, práy lòod/ n **1** a piece of classical music that introduces or precedes another one **2** an introductory event or occurrence ■ vt (-ud·ed, -ud·ing) act as prelude to

pre·mar·i·tal /pree mérrət'l/ adj before marriage

pre·ma·ture /preèmə choòr/ adj **1** happening earlier than is usual or desirable **2** born before completing the usual gestation period —**pre·ma·ture·ly** adv

pre·med·i·tate /pree méddi tàyt/ (-tat·ed, -tat·ing) v 1 *vt* plan beforehand 2 *vti* ponder something in advance —**pre·med·i·tat·ed** *adj* —**pre·med·i·tat·ed·ly** *adv*

pre·med·i·ta·tion /pree mèddi táysh'n/ *n* 1 in law, the act of planning and intending a crime beforehand 2 reflection before action

pre·men·stru·al /pree ménstroo əl/ *adj* immediately before a menstrual period

pre·men·stru·al syn·drome *n* symptoms such as irritability and headache experienced by some women immediately before a menstrual period

pre·mier /pri meér/ *adj* best or most important ■ *n* a prime minister —**pre·mier·ship** *n*

pre·miere /pri meér/ *n* the first public performance or showing of something ■ *vti* (-miered, -mier·ing) present or be presented publicly for the first time

prem·ise /prémmiss/ *n* 1 a statement given as the evidence for a conclusion 2 the basis of an argument ■ *vti* (-ised, -is·ing) propose something as a premise in an argument

prem·is·es /prémmissəz/ *npl* a piece of land and the buildings on it

pre·mi·um /preemee əm/ *n* 1 the regular sum of money paid for an insurance policy 2 an additional sum of money 3 a prize 4 the amount above its nominal value for which something sells ■ *adj* high-quality

pre·mo·lar /pree mólər/ *n* a grinding tooth between a canine and molar —**pre·mo·lar** *adj*

pre·mo·ni·tion /prèmmə nísh'n, preemə-/ *n* 1 a strong but irrational feeling that something is going to happen 2 a warning about the future —**pre·mon·i·to·ry** *adj*

pre·na·tal /pree náyt'l/ *adj* before childbirth —**pre·na·tal·ly** *adv*

pre·nup·tial a·gree·ment /pree núpshəl-/, **pre·nup** /pree nùp/ *n* a financial agreement between marriage partners made before the marriage

pre·oc·cu·pa·tion /prèe òkyə páysh'n/, **pre·oc·cu·pan·cy** /pree ókyəpənsee/ (*pl* -cies) *n* 1 the fact of constantly thinking about something 2 the focus of somebody's constant attention

pre·oc·cu·pied /pree ókyə pìd/ *adj* 1 completely absorbed in thinking about something 2 already occupied —**pre·oc·cu·py** *vt*

pre·owned /pree ónd/ *adj* US, ANZ secondhand

prep. *abbr* 1 preparation 2 preposition

prep·a·ra·tion /prèppə ráysh'n/ *n* 1 the work involved in preparing something 2 the state of being prepared 3 a mixture made for a particular purpose

pre·par·a·to·ry /pri párrə tàwree/ *adj* 1 serving to make something ready 2 introductory

pre·par·a·to·ry school *n* 1 a private secondary school 2 a British private elementary school

pre·pare /pri páir/ (-pared, -par·ing) v 1 *vti* make something ready for use or action 2 *vt* get ready, or make somebody ready, for something 3 *vt* make by putting things together 4 *vt* plan in advance —**pre·pared** *adj*

pre·pay /pree páy/ (-paid /-páyd/) *vt* pay for beforehand —**pre·pay·a·ble** *adj* —**pre·pay·ment** *n*

~~preperation~~ incorrect spelling of **preparation**

pre·pon·der·ate /pri póndə ràyt/ (-at·ed, -at·ing) *vi* be greater or dominant —**pre·pon·der·ance** *n* —**pre·pon·der·ant** *adj* —**pre·pon·der·ant·ly** *adv*

prep·o·si·tion /prèppə zísh'n/ *n* a word used before a noun or pronoun to express connections and relationships —**prep·o·si·tion·al** *adj*

> **LANGUAGE NOTE** In certain circumstances a **preposition** can go at the end of a sentence; for instance, in the case of the phrasal verbs *attend to* and *put up with*: *Are you being attended to? This noise is hard to put up with.* Some questions and clauses opening with *what*, *which*, or *who*, for example, typically have the preposition at the end, as in *What on earth were they thinking about?* Some infinitive clauses also have prepositions at their ends, as in *I've been invited to the dance, but I need someone to go with*

pre·pos·sess·ing /prèe pə zéssing/ *adj* giving a pleasing impression —**pre·pos·sess·ing·ly** *adv*

pre·pos·ter·ous /pri póstərəss/ *adj* outrageous or absurd —**pre·pos·ter·ous·ly** *adv* —**pre·pos·ter·ous·ness** *n*

> **ORIGIN Preposterous** comes from a Latin word meaning "inverted," and this sense was once used in English. The development to "absurd, perverse" had already taken place in Latin, however, and this was also adopted. Both senses appeared in the mid-16C, but after the 18C "inverted" was usually accompanied by a self-conscious reference to the literalness of the use.

prep·py /préppee/, **prep·pie** (*infml*) *adj* of young well-educated affluent people ■ *n* (*pl* -pies; *pl* -pies) a preparatory school student —**prep·pi·ly** *adv*

⚡ **pre·proc·ess** /pree pró sèss/ *vt* analyze and process something, e.g., computer data, beforehand

pre·pro·fes·sion·al /prèe prə féshən'l, -féshnəl/ *adj* preparing for a profession

⚡ **pre·pro·gram** /pree pró gràm/ (-grammed *or* -gramed, -gram·ming *or* -gram·ing) *vt* 1 program a computer in advance 2 prepare somebody in such a way that a desired response is later assured

prep school *n* a preparatory school (*infml*)

pre·pu·bes·cent /prèepyoo béss'nt/ *adj* of the

period just before puberty ■ *n* a pre-pubescent child

pre·quel /preékwəl/ *n* an earlier part of a story told in a previous book or movie

Pre-Raph·a·el·ite /pree ráffee ə lìt/ *n* a member of a 19C group of painters who aimed to revive an early naturalistic style of Italian painting —**Pre-Raph·a·el·ite** *adj* —**Pre-Raph·a·el·it·ism** *n*

ORIGIN The **Pre-Raphaelites** are so called because they aimed to revive the style of Italian painting before Raphael (1483–1520).

pre·re·cord /prèe ri káwrd/ *vt* record in advance

pre·req·ui·site /pree rékwizit/ *n* something needed as a prior condition —**pre·req·ui·site** *adj*

pre·rog·a·tive /pri róggətiv/ *n* **1** a privilege restricted to people occupying a particular rank or position **2** an individual right or privilege

Pres. *abbr* President

pres·age /préssij, pri sáyj/ *n* **1** a portent or omen **2** a feeling that a particular thing is going to happen ■ *vt* (**pre·saged**, **pre·sag·ing**) be a warning that something will happen

pres·by·ter /prézbitər/ *n* **1** an ordained member of the clergy in many Christian churches **2** a lay official in a Presbyterian church

pres·by·te·ri·an /prèzbi teéree ən/ *adj* **1** of church administration by elected lay members **2 Pres·by·te·ri·an** of the Reformed churches ■ *n* **1** a supporter of church administration by elected lay officials **2 Pres·by·te·ri·an** a member of a Presbyterian church —**Pres·by·te·ri·an·ism** *n*

pres·by·ter·y /prézbi tèrree/ (*pl* **-ies**) *n* **1** a group of presbyters **2** the governing body of a Presbyterian church **3** a part of a church for the use of the clergy only

pre·school /prèe skòol/ *adj* **1** under school age **2** for preschool children ■ *n* a school for very young children —**pre·school·er** *n* —**pre·school·ing** *n*

pre·sci·ent /preéshee ənt, pré-, -sh'nt/ *adj* knowing in advance —**pre·science** *n*

pre·scribe /pri skríb/ (**-scribed**, **-scrib·ing**) *v* **1** *vti* order the use of a particular medication **2** *vt* recommend a remedy **3** *vt* lay down a rule —**pre·scrib·a·ble** *adj*

pre·scrip·tion /pri skrípshən/ *n* **1** a written order for medicine or corrective lenses **2** a prescribed medication **3** a proven formula for something **4** the establishing of regulations

pre·scrip·tion drug *n* a drug available only by prescription

pre·scrip·tive /pri skríptiv/ *adj* making or adhering to rules or regulations —**pre·scrip·tive·ly** *adv* —**pre·scrip·tive·ness** *n*

pres·ence /prézzənss/ *n* **1** the fact of being present **2** the area within sight or earshot of somebody **3** an impressive appearance or bearing **4** a person who is present **5** military or diplomatic personnel stationed in a place

pres·ence of mind *n* the ability to stay calm in a crisis

pre·sent[1] *v* /pri zént/ **1** *vt* give something to **2** *vt* make somebody a gift or an award of **3** *vt* show or display something ○ *presented his best side to the camera* **4** *vt* pose or be the cause of ○ *presented a threat to national security* **5** *vt* bring a legal charge against **6** *vt* introduce formally **7** *vt* bring before the public **8** *vr* appear or arise ○ *when opportunity presents itself* ■ *n* /prézzənt/ a gift —**pre·sent·er** *n* ◊ See note at **give**

pre·sent[2] /prézzənt/ *adj* **1** currently happening or in existence **2** in a particular place ■ *n* **1** the current time **2** the verb tense used for indicating the present time, or a form in this tense

pre·sent·a·ble /pri zéntəb'l/ *adj* **1** fit to appear in public **2** fit to be displayed or given —**pre·sent·a·bly** *adv*

pres·en·ta·tion /prèzz'n táysh'n/ *n* **1** the act of presenting something **2** a prepared talk or performance for an audience **3** the way something appears when presented

pres·ent-day *adj* existing in modern times

pre·sen·ti·ment /pri zéntəmənt/ *n* a feeling that something will happen

pres·ent·ly /prézz'ntlee/ *adv* **1** soon (*fml* or *literary*) **2** at the present time (*sometimes objected to*)

pres·ent par·ti·ci·ple *n* the form of a verb that ends in "-ing" in English and suggests a progressive or active sense

pres·ent per·fect *n* the form of a verb formed with "has" or "have" and a past participle

pres·er·va·tion /prèzzər váysh'n/ *n* **1** protection from harm **2** the fact or process of keeping something unchanged —**pres·er·va·tion·ism** *n* —**pres·er·va·tion·ist** *n*

pre·ser·va·tive /pri zúrvətiv/ *n* something that prevents spoilage or decay, especially a food additive —**pre·ser·va·tive** *adj*

pre·serve /pri zúrv/ *vt* (**-served**, **-serv·ing**) **1** make sure that something does not change or deteriorate **2** keep up or maintain something **3** make jam **4** protect somebody or something from danger or harm (*fml* or *literary*) ■ *n* **1** somebody's private place or particular area of activity **2** fruit jelly or jam (*often pl*) **3** an area where wildlife is protected —**pre·serv·a·ble** *adj*

pre·set *vt* /pree sét/ (**-set**, **-set·ting**) set a machine to switch on later ■ *n* /pree sèt/ a control that turns a machine on later

pre·side /pri zíd/ (**-sid·ed**, **-sid·ing**) *vi* be officially in charge or responsible

pres·i·dent /prézzid'nt/, **Pres·i·dent** n 1 the head of state of a republic 2 the highest-ranking member of an association 3 the head of a company 4 the head of some educational or governmental establishments —**pres·i·den·cy** n —**pres·i·den·tial** /prèzzə dénshəl/ adj

pres·i·dent-e·lect /pl pres·i·dents-e·lect/ n a president who has been elected but has not yet taken office

Pres·i·dents' Day n an official holiday commemorating the birthdays of George Washington and Abraham Lincoln. Date: 3rd Monday in February.

pre·sid·i·um /prə síddee əm/ (pl **-a** /-ə/ or **-ums**) n an executive committee in the former Soviet Union and other Communist countries

Elvis Presley

Pres·ley /prézzlee/, **Elvis** (1935–77) US singer and actor

press[1] v 1 vti push against something steadily 2 vt squeeze the juice out of 3 vt smooth using a hot iron 4 vt change the shape of by squeezing or applying a steady weight 5 vt hold tightly 6 vt force to do something 7 vt try to obtain something from o pressed him for an apology ■ n 1 the act of pressing something 2 a tightly packed crowd, or the force they exert 3 a device for pressing something 4 a device for flattening clothes o a trouser press 5 newspapers or reporters in general 6 comments by reporters o got a good press 7 a machine for printing 8 a publishing company (in names) 9 the process of printing o about to go to press —**pressed** adj —**press·er** n
□ **press for** vti emphatically demand something of somebody

press[2] vt force somebody into military service ■ n the forcing of people into military service

press a·gen·cy n a news agency

press a·gent n somebody employed to get publicity for a client

press box n an area where reporters sit to report on an event

press con·fer·ence n an arranged meeting with reporters

press gal·ler·y n a balcony for reporters to watch proceedings

press gang n formerly, a group with the job of forcing people into military service

press-gang vt force somebody to do something

press·ing /préssing/ adj 1 urgent 2 very persistent —**press·ing·ly** adv —**press·ing·ness** n

press of·fi·cer n somebody providing news to reporters about an organization's activities

press re·lease n a statement or account of a news event supplied to reporters

press sec·re·tar·y n an employee who handles news coverage

pres·sure /préshər/ n 1 the process of applying a steady weight or force 2 a constant state of stress and urgency 3 an outside influence or requirement that affects behavior or feelings 4 (symbol p) the force acting on a surface divided by the area over which it acts ■ vt (-sured, -sur·ing) try to persuade somebody to do something o They were pressured into selling by the rest of the family.

pres·sure cook·er n a heavy cooking pot that steams food at high pressure and temperatures —**pres·sure-cook** vt

pres·sure group n a group working for social or political change

pres·sure point n a point on the body where an artery can be compressed

pres·sur·ize /préshə rìz/ (-ized, -iz·ing) vt increase the air pressure in an enclosed space or container —**pres·sur·i·za·tion** /prèshəri záysh'n/ n

pres·tige /pre steèzh, -steéj/ n 1 respect associated with high quality, success, or high rank 2 glamour —**pres·ti·gious** /pre steèjəss, -stíjjəss/ adj —**pres·ti·gious·ly** adv

pres·to /préstō/ adv 1 very fast (musical direction) 2 suddenly (infml) ■ interj at once —**pres·to** adj

pre·sum·a·bly /pri zóoməblee/ adv it is reasonable to suppose

pre·sume /pri zoóm/ (-sumed, -sum·ing) v 1 vti accept that something is true 2 vi behave arrogantly or overconfidently (usually in negative statements) —**pre·sum·a·ble** adj —**pre·sum·ing** adj

pre·sump·tion /pri zúmpshən/ n 1 something believed without actual evidence 2 rudeness or arrogance 3 a legal inference

~~presumptious~~ incorrect spelling of **presumptuous**

pre·sump·tive /pri zúmptiv/ adj probable (fml) —**pre·sump·tive·ly** adv —**pre·sump·tive·ness** n

pre·sump·tu·ous /pri zúmpchoo əss/ adj rude or arrogant —**pre·sump·tu·ous·ly** adv

pre·sup·pose /prèe sə pōz/ (-posed, -pos·ing) vt 1 assume in advance 2 require as a prior condition —**pre·sup·po·si·tion** /prèe supə zísh'n/ n

pre·tax /pree táks/ adj before the deduction of tax

pre·teen /pree teén/, **pre·teen·ag·er** /-teén
àyjər/ *adj* **1** for children between ages 9 and
12 **2** between 9 and 12 years old ■ *n* a child
between 9 and 12 years old

pre·tence *n* UK = pretense

pre·tend /pri ténd/ *v* **1** *vti* act as if something
were true **2** *vt* make an insincere claim
about ○ *I don't pretend to be an expert.* **3** *vt*
mislead somebody about ○ *pretending to be
sick* **4** *vi* claim ownership of or a right to
something (*fml*) ○ *pretends to the throne*
—**pre·tend·ed** *adj* —**pre·tend·er** *n*

pre·tense /preé téns, pri téns/ *n* **1** an insincere
or feigned action or a false appearance **2** an
unwarranted claim (*often in the negative*)
○ *makes no pretense of expertise* **3** make-
believe

pre·ten·sion /pri ténshən/ *n* **1** a questionable
claim to something (*often pl and with
negatives*) **2** affected and usually ostentatious behavior

pre·ten·tious /pri ténshəss/ *adj* **1** self-
important and affected **2** made to look or
sound important —**pre·ten·tious·ly** *adv*
—**pre·ten·tious·ness** *n*

pret·er·it /préttərit/, **pret·er·ite** *n* the past tense
of a verb —**pret·er·it** *adj*

pre·ter·nat·u·ral /preétər náchərəl/ *adj* **1** exceeding what is usual in nature (*fml or
literary*) **2** supernatural or uncanny (*literary*)
—**pre·ter·nat·u·ral·ly** *adv*

pre·text /preé tèkst/ *n* a made-up excuse

Pre·to·ri·a /pri táwree ə/ administrative
capital of South Africa. Pop. 1,314,000
(1995).

pret·ti·fy /prítta fī/ (**-fied, -fies**) *vt* make pretty,
especially superficially —**pret·ti·fi·ca·tion**
/prìttəfi káysh'n/ *n*

pret·ty /príttee/ *adj* (**-ti·er, -ti·est**) **1** having a
pleasant face **2** nice to look at or listen to
3 large in amount (*infml*) ○ *cost a pretty
penny* **4** very bad (*infml*) ○ *got into a pretty
mess* ■ *adv* to a fairly large extent (*infml*)

pret·zel /préts'l/ *n* a salted knot-shaped or
stick-shaped snack biscuit

pre·vail /pri váyl/ *vi* **1** be unbeaten and in
control **2** be the most common or frequent
3 exist currently (*fml*) —**pre·vail·ing** *adj*
—**pre·vail·ing·ly** *adv*

□ **prevail on** or **up·on** *vt* persuade

prev·a·lent /prévvələnt/ *adj* found commonly
or widely. —**prev·a·lence** *n* —**prev·a·
lent·ly** *adv* ◊ See note at **widespread**

pre·var·i·cate /pri vérrə kàyt/ (**-cat·ed, -cat·ing**)
vi avoid giving a direct or honest answer
or opinion —**pre·var·i·ca·tion** /pri vèrrə
káysh'n/ *n* —**pre·var·i·ca·tor** *n*

~~prevalant~~ incorrect spelling of **prevalent**

pre·vent /pri vént/ *vt* **1** stop from taking place
2 stop from doing something
—**pre·vent·a·ble** *adj* —**pre·ven·tion** *n*

pre·ven·tive /pri véntiv/, **pre·ven·ta·tive** /pri
véntətiv/ *adj* done with or having the

purpose of preventing something
—**pre·ven·ta·tive** *n* —**pre·ven·tive** *n*

pre·view /preé vyoo/ *n* **1** a showing of something, e.g., a movie or exhibition, in
advance **2** a description of a forthcoming
broadcast ■ *vt* show or describe in advance

pre·vi·ous /preévee əss/ *adj* **1** coming before
somebody or something of the same kind
2 already arranged ○ *a previous engagement*
—**pre·vi·ous·ly** *adv*

pre·war /preé wáwr/ *adj* before the war

prey /pray/ (*pl same or* **preys**) *n* animals
hunted by other animals as food ◊ See note
at **pray**

□ **prey on** or **upon** *vt* **1** hunt and kill other
animals for food **2** victimize somebody

PRI *n* the Mexican Institutional Revolutionary Party. Full form **Partido Re-
volucionario Institucional**

price *n* **1** the cost of something bought or
sold **2** something sacrificed to get something else ■ *vt* (**priced, pric·ing**) decide,
mark, or find out the price of ◊ **at a price**
for a lot of money ◊ **at any price** no matter
how much it costs ◊ **beyond price** priceless

Price, Leontyne (*b.* 1927) US operatic soprano

price-earn·ings ra·tio *n* the ratio of a stock's
price to its earnings

price fix·ing *n* the artificial setting of prices
by producers or a government

price·less /príssləss/ *adj* very valuable

price tag *n* a label saying what something
costs

price war *n* intense market competition

pric·ey /príssee/ (**-i·er, -i·est**), **pric·y** *adj* expensive (*infml*) —**pric·ey·ness** *n*

prick /prik/ *vt* **1** make a small hole through
or in **2** cause to feel sudden unease ○ *His
conscience pricked him.* **3** mark out on a
surface with tiny holes ■ *n* **1** a quick sharp
pain **2** a small puncture ◊ **prick up your
ears** listen intently

prick·le /prík'l/ *n* **1** a sharp pointed projection
on a plant part **2** a tingling feeling ■ *vti*
(**-led, -ling**) hurt in a stinging way

prick·ly /príklee/ (**-i·er, -i·est**) *adj* **1** with small
sharp spikes **2** irritating to the skin **3** easily
offended or annoyed (*infml*) **4** especially
difficult and likely to upset people (*infml*)
—**prick·li·ness** *n*

prick·ly heat *n* a rash caused by heat

prick·ly pear *n* a cactus with pear-shaped
fruits

pric·y *adj* = pricey (*infml*)

pride *n* **1** a feeling of personal superiority **2** a
proper sense of your own value **3** satisfaction with something you have done or
possess **4** a source of personal satisfaction
5 a group of lions —**pride·ful** *adj* —**pride·
ful·ly** *adv* ◊ **pride of place** the most important position

priest /preest/ *n* **1** an ordained minister in
some Christian denominations **2** a spiritual

leader or teacher in a non-Christian religion —**priest·hood** n —**priest·ly** adj

priest·ess /préestəss/ n a woman who is a spiritual leader of a pagan religion

Priest·ley /préestlee/, **Joseph** (1733–1804) British chemist and religious radical

prig n a smug morally upright person (disapproving) —**prig·ger·y** n —**prig·gish** adj

prim (**prim·mer**, **prim·mest**) adj **1** prudish **2** formal and proper in manner or appearance —**prim·ly** adv —**prim·ness** n

pri·ma bal·le·ri·na /préemə-/ n a principal woman dancer in a ballet company

pri·ma·cy /prímǝssee/ (pl -**cies**) n **1** the state of being first in importance ○ Speech is regarded as having primacy over writing. **2** the position or period of office of a church primate

pri·ma don·na /prèemə dónnə/ (pl **pri·ma don·nas**) n **1** a leading woman opera singer **2** a person regarded as demanding and difficult to please (insult)

pri·ma fa·cie /príma fáyshee, -fáyshee èe, prèemə-/ adv at first glance ■ adj **1** clear from a first impression **2** legally sufficient to establish a fact

pri·mal /prím'l/ adj **1** first or original **2** primary or most significant

pri·mar·i·ly /prí mérrilee/ adv **1** mainly or mostly **2** originally or at first

pri·mar·y /prí mèrree, prímərree/ adj **1** first in a sequence or development **2** most important ■ n (pl -**ies**) a preliminary election of candidates for a government post

pri·mar·y care n the level of professional health care given by a family doctor or nurse

pri·mar·y col·or n any of the basic colors from which all other colors can be produced

pri·mar·y school n a school for the first years of a child's compulsory education, including grades one through four or five

pri·mate n /prí màyt/ **1** a member of an order of mammals including human beings, apes, and monkeys **2** also **Pri·mate** an archbishop or high-ranking bishop —**pri·ma·tial** /prí máysh'l/ adj

~~**primative**~~ incorrect spelling of **primitive**

prime[1] adj **1** of the best quality **2** first in importance or rank ■ n **1** the best stage of something ○ in the prime of life **2** the earliest period of something **3** also **prime num·ber** a whole number that is not divisible without a remainder except by itself and one —**prime·ness** n

prime[2] v **1** vti make or become ready for use **2** vt prepare a surface for painting **3** vt put a charge in a gun **4** vt put liquid in a pump to get it started **5** vt brief somebody on how to behave or answer questions

prime cost n the cost of the material and labor necessary to make a product

prime in·ter·est rate n = prime rate

prime min·is·ter n **1** the head of a cabinet and chief executive in a parliamentary democracy **2** a ruler's chief minister —**prime min·is·te·ri·al** adj —**prime min·is·ter·ship** n

prime mov·er n the most important person or thing in initiating and continuing a process

prim·er[1] /prímmər/ n **1** a book used to teach young children to read **2** an introductory text

prim·er[2] /prímər/ n an undercoat of paint or sealant

prime rate, prime in·ter·est rate n the lowest lending rate available from a bank at a given time

prime time n the hours of highest television viewing —**prime-time** adj

pri·me·val /prí meev'l/ adj ancient and original

prim·i·tive /prímmitiv/ adj **1** at or of the first stages of something **2** of or appearing in an early stage of biological development **3** very simple in design or construction **4** not relying on modern technology for comfort ○ primitive camping facilities ■ n **1** somebody or something from an original stage **2** somebody from a culture with simple technologies (often offensive) **3** an untrained artist, or a work by one —**prim·i·tive·ly** adv —**prim·i·tive·ness** n

pri·mo·gen·i·tor /prímō jénnitər/ n (fml) **1** the first ancestor of a people or group **2** any ancestor

pri·mo·gen·i·ture /prímō jénni chòòr/ n (fml) **1** status as a first-born child **2** a first-born child's right of inheritance

pri·mor·di·al /prí máwrdee əl/ adj **1** existing at the beginning of time or the development of something **2** basic or essential

primp vti groom in a fussy way

prim·rose /prím rōz/ n a small perennial plant with colorful flowers

prince n **1** a son of a monarch or of a monarch's son **2** a man who rules a principality **3** a high-ranking nobleman in some European countries —**prince·dom** n

prince charm·ing, Prince Charm·ing n a charming man

> **ORIGIN** The original **prince charming** is the prince whom the fairy-tale character Cinderella was able to meet at a ball with the help of her fairy godmother, after being left at home by her sisters. The story was popularized by a 1697 collection of traditional tales set down by the French writer Charles Perrault (1628–1703).

Prince Ed·ward Is·land island province in SE Canada. Cap. Charlottetown. Pop. 138,928 (2000). —**Prince Ed·ward Is·land·er** n

prince·ly /prínslee/ (-**li·er**, -**li·est**) adj **1** of a prince **2** very expensive or generous —**prince·li·ness** n

prin·cess /prínsəss, -sèss, prin séss/ (*pl* -cess·es) n 1 a daughter of a monarch or of a monarch's daughter 2 a prince's wife 3 a woman who rules a principality 4 a high-ranking noblewoman in some European countries

prin·ci·pal /prínsəp'l/ adj of primary importance ■ n 1 the leading or most highly ranked person 2 a significant participant 3 a head administrator of a school 4 a lead performer 5 the original amount invested or borrowed, or what remains of that 6 a person represented by another in a legal matter —**prin·ci·pal·ly** adv —**prin·ci·pal·ship** n

> **USAGE** principal or principle? Principle is a noun only, as in the principles of a democratic system and a woman of principle. Principal, as a noun, means "a school administrator," "an important participant," and "a monetary amount invested." As an adjective it means "main": our principal [not principle] reason for an appeal.

prin·ci·pal·i·ty /prínsə pállətee/ n (*pl* -ties) a territory ruled by a prince or princess ■ **prin·ci·pal·i·ties** npl one of the orders of angels in the traditional Christian hierarchy

prin·ci·pal parts npl 1 the basic verb forms from which other forms are derived in an inflected language 2 the infinitive, past tense, and participial forms of an English verb

prin·ci·ple /prínsəp'l/ n 1 a basic law or assumption in a system of thought 2 an ethical standard 3 the basic way in which something works —**prin·ci·pled** adj ◊ **in principle** in theory, or in the essentials ◊ **on principle** because of belief in a particular ethical standard ◊ See note at **principal**

⨍ **print** n 1 a mark made by pressing something onto a surface 2 characters printed or written on a surface ○ in small print 3 status as a published text or author ○ wants to get into print 4 an artwork made by inking a raised design and pressing it onto paper or another surface 5 fabric with an inked or painted design ○ a print dress 6 a photograph made from a negative 7 a copy of a motion picture ■ vti 1 make a document or publication using a printing press or computer printer 2 publish something on paper 3 mark something with lettering or a design using pressure ○ prints the logo on T-shirts 4 write something using separated letters rather than cursive script 5 make a copy of a photograph from a negative ■ adj of the published media

□ **print out** vt produce a printed copy of data from a computer

print·a·ble /príntəb'l/ adj 1 suitable for printing or publication 2 able to be printed

print·ed cir·cuit n an electronic circuit in which components and connections are formed by etching a metallic coating on an insulating board

print·ed mat·ter n published material such as books, magazines, and catalogs

print·er /príntər/ n 1 a person or company in the printing trade 2 a machine for printing text or images

print·ing /prínting/ n 1 the production of copies of documents, publications, or images 2 printed characters 3 letters written separately rather than in cursive script, or the writing of such letters

print·ing press n a machine for pressing inked set type or etched plates onto paper or textiles

⨍ **print·out** /prínt òwt/ n a paper copy of data printed from a computer

print run n the production or output of one session of printing

pri·on /prée òn, prí ən/ n an infectious protein particle

pri·or[1] /prír/ adj 1 earlier 2 more important or basic

pri·or[2] /prír/ n 1 an officer in a monastery of a rank below abbot 2 a man who heads a religious community

pri·or·ess /prírəss/ n 1 an officer in a convent of a rank below abbess 2 a woman who heads a religious community

pri·or·i·tize /prī áwrə tìz, prírə tìz/ (-tized, -tiz·ing) v 1 vti rank things according to importance or urgency 2 vt rank as the most important or urgent —**pri·or·i·ti·za·tion** /prī àwrə ti záysh'n/ n

pri·or·i·ty /prī áwrətee/ n (*pl* -ties) n 1 the state of having greater or the greatest importance or urgency 2 somebody or something ranked as having great importance or urgency 3 the state of having preceded something else

pri·or·y /príree/ n (*pl* -ies) n a religious community headed by a prior or prioress, or the home of such a community

prise vt = **prize**[3]

pris·m /prízzəm/ n 1 a polygonal solid for separating white light into a spectrum of colors 2 a cut-glass object

pris·mat·ic /priz máttik/, **pris·mat·i·cal** /priz máttik'l/ adj 1 of a prism 2 describes light separated into the colors of the spectrum by a prism

pris·on /prízz'n/ n a place where criminals and people awaiting trial are confined

pris·on camp n 1 a camp for prisoners of war 2 a minimum security prison

pris·on·er /prízz'nər/ n 1 somebody held in prison 2 somebody held against his or her will

pris·on·er of con·science n somebody imprisoned by a state because of his or her beliefs

pris·on·er of war n a soldier captured and imprisoned by the enemy

~~prissoner~~ incorrect spelling of **prisoner**

pris·sy /príssee/ (-si·er, -si·est) *adj* very prudish and proper —**pris·si·ly** *adv* —**pris·si·ness** *n*

Priš·tin·a /préeshtinə/ city in central Kosovo, Federal Republic of Yugoslavia. Pop. 155,496 (1991).

pris·tine /prí steen, pri steen/ *adj* **1** immaculately clean and neat **2** in or of an original state

pri·va·cy /prívəssee/ *n* **1** the state of being apart from others **2** freedom from the observation, intrusion, and attention of others

pri·vate /prívət/ *adj* **1** not for others to see or know about **2** secluded **3** not open to the public **4** acting in a personal rather than official capacity **5** not supported by government funding o *private enterprise* **6** requiring special knowledge to understand o *a private joke* ■ *n* a soldier or marine of the lowest rank —**pri·vate·ly** *adv* —**pri·vate·ness** *n*

pri·vate bank·ing *n* management by a bank of a customer's wealth in its entirety

pri·vate en·ter·prise *n* **1** business not owned or regulated by the government **2** a privately owned company

pri·va·teer /prívə téer/ *n* **1** a private ship authorized to engage in war **2** somebody sailing on a privateer

pri·vate eye *n* a private investigator (*infml*)

pri·vate first class (*pl* **pri·vates first class**) *n* a soldier in the US Army or Marine Corps of a rank above private

pri·vate in·come *n* income not derived from working

pri·vate in·ves·ti·ga·tor *n* a detective who is not a member of the police and is available for private hire

pri·va·tion /prī váysh'n/ *n* **1** the lack of life's necessities **2** depriving somebody of something

pri·va·tize /prívə tīz/ (-tized, -tiz·ing) *vt* take out of state ownership or control —**pri·va·ti·za·tion** /prívəti záysh'n/ *n*

~~privilage, privilege, priviledge~~ incorrect spelling of **privilege**

priv·et /prívət/ *n* a common evergreen shrub used for hedges

priv·i·lege /prívəlij, prívlij/ *n* **1** a right or benefit that is not available to everyone **2** the advantages enjoyed by an elite group **3** a special honor o *a privilege to work with you* ■ *vt* (-leged, -leg·ing) grant a privilege or privileges to —**priv·i·leged** *adj*

priv·y /prívee/ *adj* **1** sharing secret knowledge o *privy to the planned surprise* **2** of somebody, especially the British monarch, as a private individual rather than in an official capacity ■ *n* (*pl* -ies) an outside toilet (*infml*)

prize[1] *n* **1** an award for a winner of a contest or competition **2** something highly valued, especially because it is hard to get ■ *vt* (prized, priz·ing) value very highly ■ *adj* worthy of or given a prize

---

ORIGIN The two nouns **prize** are etymologically distinct. **Prize** "award" is in fact a variant form of **price** and derives ultimately from Latin *pretium* "price," which also gave us the verb *praise*. **Prize** "captured ship" was adopted from French, where it meant literally "something seized or taken." The verb **prize** "lever" may be related to it.

---

prize[2] *n* a captured ship or ship's cargo

prize[3] (prized, priz·ing), **prise** (prised, pris·ing) *vt* **1** force something open with a lever **2** extract information

prize·fight /príz fīt/ *n* a boxing match for money —**prize·fight·er** *n* —**prize·fight·ing** *n*

prize·win·ner /príz winnər/ *n* somebody or something that wins a prize —**prize·win·ning** *adj*

pro[1] /prō/ *n* (*pl* **pros**) **1** an argument in favor of something **2** a person or side arguing in favor of something ■ *prep* in favor of ■ *adv* in favor

pro[2] /prō/ (*pl* **pros**) *n* **1** a professional, especially a sportsperson (*infml*) **2** a skilled person or expert —**pro** *adj*, *adv*

⨍ pro[3] /prō/ *abbr* professional practice (*in Internet addresses*)

pro- *prefix* **1** substituting for, acting in place of o *pronoun* **2** in favor of o *pro-life* **3** before, earlier than o *prognosis* **4** in front of o *prognathous*

pro·ac·tive /prō áktiv/ *adj* taking the initiative rather than reacting to events —**pro·ac·tive·ly** *adv*

pro-am /prō ám/ *adj* combining professionals and amateurs ■ *n* a pro-am competition

prob·a·bil·i·ty /próbbə billətee/ (*pl* -ties) *n* **1** the state of being probable **2** something likely to happen **3** the mathematical likelihood of an event

prob·a·ble /próbbəb'l/ *adj* likely to exist, occur, or be true ■ *n* somebody or something likely to be chosen or to do something —**prob·a·bly** *adv*

pro·bate /prō bàyt/ *n* legal certification of the validity of a will ■ *vt* (-bat·ed, -bat·ing) certify that a will is valid

pro·bate court *n* a court that probates wills

pro·ba·tion /prō báysh'n/ *n* **1** the supervision of an offender in the community by a probation officer **2** a period of testing somebody's suitability for a job or other role —**pro·ba·tion·ar·y** *adj* —**pro·ba·tion·er** *n*

pro·ba·tion of·fi·cer *n* a supervisor of offenders released into the community under condition of good behavior

probe *n* **1** a thorough investigation **2** an exploratory expedition or device o *a space probe* **3** a long thin surgical instrument for exploring or examining ■ *vti* (probed, prob·ing) **1** investigate thoroughly

2 explore or examine using a probe —**prob·ing·ly** adv

pro·bi·ty /prōbitee/ n moral integrity and honesty

prob·lem /próbbləm/ n **1** a situation or person presenting a difficulty **2** a puzzle to be solved ■ adj hard to deal with

SYNONYMS problem, mystery, puzzle, riddle, conundrum, enigma CORE MEANING: something difficult to solve or understand

prob·lem·at·ic /próbblə máttik/, **prob·lem·at·i·cal** /-máttik'l/ adj presenting a problem or difficulty —**prob·lem·at·i·cal·ly** adv

~~probly~~ incorrect spelling of probably

pro bo·no /prō bố nố/ adj, adv done for the public good without compensation

pro·bos·cis /prō bóssiss, -bóss kiss/ (pl -cis·es or -ces /-ees/ or -ci·des /-si dèez/) n **1** a long flexible snout, especially an elephant's trunk **2** a large nose (humorous)

~~precede~~ incorrect spelling of proceed

pro·ce·dure /prō seéjər/ n **1** an established or correct method of doing something **2** any means of doing something —**pro·ce·dur·al** adj

pro·ceed /prō seéd, prə-/ vi **1** go on to do something **2** continue with a course of action **3** progress **4** go in a particular direction, especially forward **5** bring a legal action against somebody **6** arise or develop from something ◊ See note at precede

pro·ceed·ings /prō seédingz/ npl **1** a series of events **2** legal action **3** an official record of a meeting

pro·ceeds /prő seédz/ npl the money obtained from a transaction

⚡ **proc·ess**¹ /pró sèss, prő-/ n **1** a series of actions directed toward a particular aim **2** a series of natural occurrences producing a change or development **3** a summons to appear in court **4** the entire proceedings in a lawsuit **5** a natural outgrowth on an organism ■ vt **1** prepare or treat something using a set procedure or a particular process **2** deal with somebody or something according to a set procedure **3** use a computer program to work on data

proc·ess² /prə sèss/ vi move in a procession

pro·ces·sion /prə sésh'n/ n **1** a group of people or vehicles moving forward in a line as part of a celebration, commemoration, or demonstration **2** forward movement in a procession

pro·ces·sion·al /prə séshən'l, -séshnəl/ adj of or for a procession ■ n a piece of music for a procession, especially a church procession

⚡ **pro·ces·sor** /pró sèssər, prố sèssər/ n **1** somebody or something that processes things **2** a central processing unit of a computer

pro·choice adj advocating access to legalized abortion

pro·claim /prō kláym, prə-/ vt announce or declare publicly or formally —**proc·la·ma·tion** /pròklə máysh'n/ n

pro·cliv·i·ty /prō klívvətee/ (pl -ties) n a natural tendency

~~proclomation~~ incorrect spelling of **proc·lamation**

pro·cras·ti·nate /prō krásti nàyt, prə-/ (-nat·ed, -nat·ing) vti postpone doing something, especially habitually —**pro·cras·ti·na·tion** /prō kràsti náysh'n, prə-/ n —**pro·cras·ti·na·tor** n

pro·cre·ate /prőkree àyt/ (-at·ed, -at·ing) vti produce offspring —**pro·cre·a·tion** /prőkree áysh'n/ n —**pro·cre·a·tive** /prőkree àytiv/ adj

proc·tor /próktər/ n a supervisor at a school examination ■ vt supervise an exam —**proc·to·ri·al** /prok táwree əl/ adj —**proc·tor·ship** n

pro·cure /prō kyoór, prə-/ (-cured, -cur·ing) v **1** vt acquire, especially by effort **2** vti provide somebody for prostitution —**pro·cur·a·ble** adj —**pro·cure·ment** n ◊ See note at get

prod vti (prod·ded, prod·ding) **1** jab or poke with a finger, elbow, or pointed object **2** incite somebody to action ■ n **1** a jab or poke **2** an incitement to action **3** an instrument used for prodding a person or animal

prod·i·gal /próddig'l/ adj **1** extravagantly wasteful **2** giving or producing generous amounts —**prod·i·gal·ly** adv

pro·di·gious /prə díjjəss/ adj **1** great in amount, size, or extent **2** marvelous or exceedingly impressive —**pro·di·gious·ly** adv —**pro·di·gious·ness** n

prod·i·gy /próddəjee/ (pl -gies) n **1** somebody with exceptional talent at an early age **2** something marvelous or exceedingly impressive

pro·drug /pró drùg/ n a substance converted to active drug in the body

pro·duce v /prō doóss/ (-duced, -duc·ing) **1** vti make or create something **2** vt cause something to happen or arise **3** vti yield or bring forth something **4** vt present or show something **5** vt organize and supervise the making of something ○ produce a new album ■ n /prő doóss/ farm or garden products —**pro·duc·er** n —**pro·duc·i·ble** adj

prod·uct /pró dùkt/ n **1** something made or created **2** a consequence **3** a result of multiplying quantities

pro·duc·tion /prə dúkshən/ n **1** the producing of something **2** something produced **3** the presentation of a play, opera, or musical ○ appearing in a new production

pro·duc·tive /prə dúktiv/ adj **1** producing something in large quantities **2** producing worthwhile results —**pro·duc·tive·ly** adv —**pro·duc·tiv·i·ty** /prő duk tívvətee/ n

prof n a professor (infml)

Prof. abbr Professor

pro·fane /prō fáyn, prə-/ adj 1 showing disrespect for God or religion (fml) 2 not relating to religion ■ vt (-faned, -fan·ing) treat irreverently —**pro·fan·a·to·ry** /prō fánnə tàwree, prə-/ adj —**pro·fane·ly** adv

ORIGIN **Profane** goes back to a Latin word meaning literally "outside the temple." Its root is also found in *fanatic*.

pro·fan·i·ty /prō fánnətee, prə-/ (pl -ties) n 1 profane language or behavior 2 a profane word or phrase

pro·fess /prō féss, prə-/ (-fess·es) v 1 vti acknowledge something publicly 2 vt claim something falsely 3 vt follow a particular religion —**pro·fessed** adj —**pro·fess·ed·ly** /prō féssədlee, prə-/ adv

pro·fes·sion /prō fésh'n, prə-/ n 1 an occupation requiring extensive education 2 the people in a particular profession o *the legal profession* 3 a declaration or public acknowledgment of something

pro·fes·sion·al /prō féshən'l, -féshnəl, prə-/ adj 1 of a profession 2 engaged in an occupation or activity as a paid job rather than a hobby 3 highly competent —**pro·fes·sion·al** n —**pro·fes·sion·al·ly** adv

pro·fes·sion·al·ism /prō féshən'l ìzzəm, -féshnə lìzzəm, prə-/ n the skills and standards of a profession

pro·fes·sion·al·ize /prō féshən'l ìz, -féshnə lìz, prə-/ (-ized, -iz·ing) vt cause to meet professional standards

pro·fes·sor /prə féssər/ n 1 a college or university teacher of the highest academic rank 2 a teacher —**pro·fes·so·ri·al** /pròffə sáwree əl/ adj —**pro·fes·sor·ship** n

prof·fer /próffər/ vt 1 hold out for somebody to take 2 propose for consideration

proffesor incorrect spelling of **professor**

pro·fi·cient /prō físh'nt/ adj very skilled —**pro·fi·cien·cy** n —**pro·fi·cient·ly** adv

pro·file /prō fíl/ n 1 the side view of something, especially somebody's face 2 a short biographical article 3 a set of data that indicates the extent to which something conforms to a standard 4 a degree of attracting public attention o *kept a low profile* ■ vt (-filed, -fil·ing) 1 write a short biographical article on 2 show the facial profile of —**pro·fil·er** n

prof·it /próffit/ n 1 the excess of income over expenditure, especially in business 2 money made from an investment or transaction (often pl) 3 an advantage or benefit derived from an activity ■ v 1 vi make a profit 2 vti benefit or cause to benefit from something —**prof·it·less** adj

SPELLCHECK Do not confuse the spelling of **profit** and **prophet** ("a foreteller of the future"), which sound similar.

prof·it·a·ble /próffitəb'l/ adj 1 making a profit

2 useful to somebody —**prof·it·a·bil·i·ty** /pròffitə bíllətee/ n —**prof·it·a·bly** adv

prof·it·eer /pròffi teér/ vi make excessive profits from scarce or essential goods —**prof·it·eer·ing** n

pro·fit·e·role /prə fíttə ròl/ n a cream puff with chocolate sauce

prof·li·gate /próffligət, -gàyt/ adj 1 wasteful or extravagant 2 with low moral standards —**prof·li·ga·cy** n —**prof·li·gate** n

pro for·ma /prō fáwrmə/ adj done or existing only as a formality

pro·found /prə fównd/ adj 1 very great or intense 2 showing or requiring great understanding or knowledge —**pro·found·ly** adv —**pro·fun·di·ty** /prə fúndətee/ n

pro·fuse /prə fyóoss/ adj 1 given or giving freely and extravagantly 2 existing in large amounts —**pro·fuse·ly** adv —**pro·fu·sion** /prə fyóozh'n/ n

pro·gen·i·tor /prō jénnitər/ n 1 an ancestor 2 an originator or a prototype

prog·e·ny /prójjənee/ (pl same or -nies) n 1 the offspring of a person, animal, or plant 2 something developing or resulting from something else

pro·ges·ter·one /prō jéstə ròn/ n a sex hormone produced in women that prepares the womb for a fertilized ovum and maintains pregnancy

prog·na·thous /prógnəthəss/, **prog·nath·ic** /prog náthik/ adj having a projecting jaw

prog·no·sis /prog nóssiss/ (pl -ses /-seez/) n 1 an opinion on the likely course of a disease 2 a prediction of how something will develop

prog·nos·tic /prog nóstik/ adj of or acting as a prognosis or prediction ■ n a prediction

prog·nos·ti·cate /prog nósti kàyt/ (-cat·ed, -cat·ing) vti predict or foretell future events —**prog·nos·ti·ca·tion** /-nòsti káysh'n/ n —**prog·nos·ti·ca·tor** n

☡ **pro·gram** /prō gràm/ n 1 a list of instructions for a computer in a programming language 2 a set of coded operating instructions for a machine 3 a plan of action 4 a radio or television show 5 a booklet giving details of a public performance 6 a public performance 7 a set of activities with a specific goal ■ v (-grammed or -gramed, -gram·ming or -gram·ing) 1 vti write a program for a computer 2 vt give coded operating instructions to a machine 3 vt schedule something 4 vt train somebody to do something automatically —**pro·gram·ma·ble** /prō gràmməb'l/ adj —**pro·gram·mat·ic** /prògrə máttik/ adj

pro·gramme n, vt UK = **program**

☡ **pro·gram·mer** /prō gràmmər/, **pro·gram·er** n somebody who programs computers

☡ **pro·gram·ming** /prō gràmming/, **pro·gram·ing** n 1 creating of computer programs 2 selection and scheduling of broadcasts

⚡ **pro·gram·ming lan·guage** *n* a special vocabulary and set of rules for instructing a computer

pro·gress /pró grèss, prô-/ 1 improvement or development ○ *making progress in the talks* 2 movement forward or onward ■ *vi* /prə grèss, prô-/ 1 improve or develop 2 move forward or onward

pro·gres·sion /prə grésh'n/ *n* 1 a gradual advance from one stage to another 2 movement forward or onward 3 a series of related things 4 a sequence of numbers related by a constant formula —**pro·gres·sion·al** *adj*

pro·gres·sive /prə gréssiv/ *adj* 1 developing gradually over a period of time 2 favoring social, economic, or political reform 3 describes taxation with higher rates for higher incomes 4 of an aspect of a verb expressing continuous action ■ *n* 1 a supporter of social, economic, or political reform 2 the progressive aspect of a verb, or a verb in the progressive aspect —**pro·gres·sive·ly** *adv* —**pro·gres·sive·ness** *n*

pro·hib·it /prō híbbit/ *vt* 1 forbid by a law or rule 2 prevent

pro·hi·bi·tion /prō ə bísh'n/ *n* 1 the forbidding of something by a law or rule, or an order that forbids something 2 the outlawing of the production of and trade in alcoholic beverages

pro·hib·i·tive /prō híbbitiv/ *adj* 1 too expensive for most people 2 forbidding something —**pro·hib·i·tive·ly** *adv*

pro·hib·i·to·ry /prō híbbi tàwree/ *adj* 1 likely to prevent or forbid something *(fml)* 2 preventing or forbidding something

proj·ect *n* /pró jèkt/ 1 a task requiring time and planning 2 an extensive organized unit of work ○ *a class project* 3 a housing project *(often pl)* ■ *v* /prə jèkt/ 1 *vt* estimate something future using present data ○ *project a 3% growth rate* 2 *vti* stick out beyond something 3 *vt* communicate an impression of something or yourself ○ *projects himself as a confident speaker* 4 *vt* unconsciously attribute your own feelings to others 5 *vt* direct light or an image onto a surface 6 *vti* make the voice clearly heard at a distance —**pro·jec·tion** /prə jékshən/ *n*

pro·jec·tile /prə jékt'l/ *n* a missile or shell ■ *adj* impelled forward

pro·jec·tion·ist /prə jékshənist/ *n* an operator of a film projector

pro·jec·tor /prə jéktər/ *n* a piece of equipment for projecting film or slides onto a screen

Pro·ko·fi·ev /prə káwfee ef/, **Sergey Sergeyevich** (1891–1953) Russian composer

pro·lapse /prō láps/ *n* a slippage of an internal organ from its usual position —**pro·lapsed** *adj*

pro·le·tar·i·an /prôlə táiree ən/ *adj* of the working class —**pro·le·tar·i·an** *n* —**pro·le·tar·i·an·ism** *n*

pro·le·tar·i·at /prôlə táiree ət/ *n* the working class

ORIGIN The original **proletariat** was a social class in ancient Rome whose members owned no property and who were regarded as serving the state only in the production of offspring. The word was originally formed in French from Latin *proles* "offspring," and first used in English in the mid-19C.

pro-life *adj* in favor of protection of the human embryo or fetus, especially by opposing open access to abortion —**pro-lif·er** *n*

pro·lif·er·ate /prə líffə ràyt/ *(-at·ed, -at·ing)* *v* 1 *vi* increase greatly 2 *vti* reproduce rapidly —**pro·lif·er·a·tion** /prə líffə ráysh'n/ *n*

pro·lif·ic /prə líffik/ *adj* 1 highly productive 2 producing a lot of fruit or many offspring —**pro·lif·i·cal·ly** *adv*

pro·lix /prō líks, prô líks/ *adj* wordy —**pro·lix·i·ty** /prō líksətee/ *n* ◊ See note at wordy

pro·logue /prô lòg/, **pro·log** *n* an introductory passage or speech in a novel, play, or poem ■ *vt* *(-logued, -logu·ing; -loged, -log·ing)* preface with a prologue

pro·long /prə láwng/ *vt* cause to go on longer —**pro·lon·ga·tion** /prō lawng gáysh'n/ *n*

prom *n* a formal student dance

⚡ **PROM** /prom/ *abbr* programmable read-only memory

prom·e·nade /pròmmə náyd, -naàd/ *(fml)* *n* a walk taken for pleasure or to be seen ■ *vti* *(-nad·ed, -nad·ing)* take a stroll in a public place

prom·e·nade deck *n* a covered upper deck of a ship where passengers can walk

Pro·me·the·us /prə meéthee əss/ *n* in Greek mythology, a Titan who gave fire to humankind

pro·me·thi·um /prə meéthee əm/ *n* *(symbol* **Pm***)* a radioactive metallic element. Use: phosphorescent paints, X-ray source.

ORIGIN Promethium is named for Prometheus. The element is the result of the ability to use the energy of nuclear fission, and this suggested a parallel with the Titan's original giving of fire.

prom·i·nence /prómminənss/ *n* 1 conspicuous importance 2 something that sticks out

prom·i·nent /prómminənt/ *adj* 1 sticking out 2 noticeable 3 eminent or well-known —**prom·i·nent·ly** *adv*

~~promiscous~~ incorrect spelling of **promiscuous**

pro·mis·cu·ous /prə mískyoo əss/ *adj* *(disapproving)* 1 sexually indiscriminate 2 choosing without discriminating —**prom·is·cu·i·ty** /prómmi skyoó ətee/ *n* —**pro·mis·cu·ous·ly** *adv*

prom·ise /prómmiss/ v (-ised, -is·ing) 1 vti assure somebody that something will happen or be done ○ *promised to come* ○ *promised that the patient would recover* 2 vt pledge to give something to somebody ○ *promised them a kitten* 3 vti make somebody expect something ○ *The sky promised rain.* ■ n 1 a solemn assurance or undertaking 2 a good indication for the future ○ *showed great promise*

prom·is·ing /prómmissing/ adj likely to be successful or turn out well —**prom·is·ing·ly** adv

prom·is·so·ry /prómmi sáwree/ adj containing a promise

prom·is·so·ry note n a signed agreement to pay money

prom·on·to·ry /prómmən tàwree/ (pl -ries) n a projecting point of land

pro·mote /prə mót/ (-mot·ed, -mot·ing) vt 1 advance to a more senior job or rank 2 support, encourage, or advocate 3 advertise —**pro·mot·a·ble** adj —**pro·mo·tion** n —**pro·mo·tion·al** adj

pro·mot·er /prə mótər/ n 1 an arranger of a public event such as an entertainment or sporting contest 2 a supporter or advocate of something

⚡ **prompt** adj 1 done immediately 2 quick to act ■ v 1 vt urge into action 2 vt bring about 3 vti provide an actor with lines that he or she has forgotten ■ n 1 a reminder of words to a performer who has forgotten them 2 a symbol or message informing a computer user that input is required —**prompt·er** n —**prompt·ly** adv —**prompt·ness** n

prom·ul·gate /prómml gàyt, prə múl gàyt/ (-gat·ed, -gat·ing) vt (fml) 1 announce or declare officially 2 make widely known —**prom·ul·ga·tion** /prómm'l gáysh'n/ n

pron. abbr 1 pronoun 2 pronunciation

prone /prōn/ adj 1 inclined to do or be affected by something 2 lying face down —**prone·ness** n

prong n a sharp point at the end of something ■ vt pierce with something sharp —**pronged** adj

pro·nom·i·nal /prō nómmən'l/ adj acting as a pronoun —**pro·nom·i·nal** n

pro·noun /prō nòwn/ n a member of a class of words replacing a noun or noun phrase

pro·nounce /prə nówns/ (-nounced, -nounc·ing) vti 1 articulate speech sounds or words 2 formally declare something —**pro·nounce·a·ble** adj —**pro·nounce·ment** n

pro·nounced /prə nównst/ adj 1 noticeable 2 voiced or spoken —**pro·nounc·ed·ly** /prə nównsədlee/ adv

~~pronounciation~~ incorrect spelling of **pronunciation**

pron·to /próntō/ adv immediately or fast (infml)

pro·nun·ci·a·tion /prə nùnsee áysh'n/ n the way in which speech sounds or words are articulated

proof n 1 conclusive evidence 2 the relative strength of a drink's alcoholic content measured against a standard 3 a printed copy used for checking errors in something printed or reproduced 4 a sequence of steps to validate a solution 5 a photographic print from a negative ■ adj 1 impervious or resistant to something 2 having a particular relative alcoholic strength (often in combination) ■ vt make impervious or resistant

proof·read /próof reèd/ (-read /-rèd/) vti check a proof for errors in printing or reproduction —**proof·read·er** n

prop[1] n 1 a rigid support 2 a comforting person or thing ■ vt (propped, prop·ping) support with a prop

prop[2] n an object used in a theatrical performance or movie

prop·a·gan·da /próppə gándə/ n 1 publicity to promote an idea or cause 2 misleading information that is systematically spread —**prop·a·gan·dist** n, adj —**prop·a·gan·dize** vti

---

ORIGIN The first **propaganda**, etymologically, was sent out by the Congregation for the Propagation of the Faith (in Latin *Propaganda Fide*), a committee of Roman Catholic cardinals who supervised foreign missions and trained priests to serve in them. The modern sense of "publicity" dates from the early 20C.

---

prop·a·gate /próppə gàyt/ (-gat·ed, -gat·ing) v 1 vti reproduce, or cause an organism to reproduce 2 vt spread something widely —**prop·a·ga·tion** /próppə gáysh'n/ n —**prop·a·ga·tor** n

pro·pane /prő pàyn/ n C_3H_8 a flammable hydrocarbon gas. Use: fuel, propellant, refrigerant.

pro·pel /prə pél/ (-pelled, -pel·ling) vt 1 push forward 2 cause to happen

pro·pel·lant /prə péllənt/, **pro·pel·lent** n 1 a substance burned to give upward thrust to a rocket 2 an explosive charge for projecting a bullet from a gun —**pro·pel·lant** adj

pro·pel·ler /prə péllər/ n a revolving shaft with spiral blades that causes a ship or aircraft to move

~~propeller~~ incorrect spelling of **propeller**

pro·pen·si·ty /prə pénsətee/ (pl -ties) n a tendency to behave in a particular way

prop·er /próppər/ adj 1 appropriate or correct ○ *in its proper perspective* 2 fulfilling all requirements ○ *proper medical care* 3 with correct manners 4 as narrowly identified ○ *in the city proper* —**prop·er·ly** adv —**prop·er·ness** n

prop·er frac·tion n a fraction in which the numerator is less than the denominator

prop·er noun, prop·er name *n* a capitalized name of a specific person or thing

prop·er·ty /próppərtee/ (*pl* **-ties**) *n* **1** something owned by a specific person **2** owned land or real estate **3** a trait, attribute, or quality (often *pl*) **4** a theatrical prop (*fml*) —**prop·er·tied** *adj*

proph·e·cy /próffəssee/ (*pl* **-cies**) *n* **1** a prediction considered to reveal the will of a deity **2** a prediction

USAGE **prophecy** or **prophesy**? **Prophecy**, a noun, means "a prediction," as in *a dire economic prophecy.* The verb **prophesy** means "predict," as in *had already prophesied a recession.*

proph·e·sy /próffə sì/ (**-sied, -sies**) *v* **1** *vti* predict something **2** *vi* reveal the will of a deity with respect to the future ◊ See note at **prophecy**

proph·et /próffət/ *n* **1** somebody who interprets and transmits the will of a deity **2** somebody who predicts the future **3** an inspired leader **4 Proph·et** Muhammad, the founder of Islam ◊ See note at **profit**

proph·et·ess /próffətəss/ *n* a woman who is a prophet

pro·phet·ic /prə féttik/ *adj* **1** correctly predicting the future **2** of a prophet —**pro·phet·i·cal** *adj* —**pro·phet·i·cal·ly** *adv*

pro·phy·lac·tic /prōfə láktik, próffə-/ *adj* protecting against disease ■ *n* **1** a condom **2** a drug that guards against disease

pro·phy·lax·is /prōfə láksiss, próffə-/ (*pl* **-es** /-eez/) *n* treatment, such as vaccination, that prevents disease

pro·pin·qui·ty /prə píngkwətee/ *n* nearness (*fml*)

pro·pi·ti·ate /prō píshee àyt/ (**-at·ed, -at·ing**) *vt* conciliate or win the favor of —**pro·pi·ti·a·tion** /prō píshee áysh'n/ *n* —**pro·pi·ti·a·to·ry** *adj*

pro·pi·tious /prō píshəss/ *adj* **1** favorable to success **2** kindly (*fml*) —**pro·pi·tious·ly** *adv*

~~propaganda~~ incorrect spelling of **propaganda**

pro·po·nent /prə pṓnənt/ *n* an advocate of something

pro·por·tion /prə páwrsh'n/ *n* **1** a quantity that is part of a whole **2** the relationship between quantities **3** the correct or desirable relative size or importance ◊ *in proportion* **4** a relationship between two variables that remains constant ■ **pro·por·tions** *npl* **1** the size or shape of something **2** the importance of something ■ *vt* **1** maintain a proportional relationship **2** give pleasing proportions to

pro·por·tion·al /prə páwrshən'l, -shnəl/ *adj* **1** in the correct relationship of size, quantity, or degree **2** related by a constant ratio —**pro·por·tion·al·ly** *adv*

pro·por·tion·ate /prə páwrsh'nət/ *adj* proportional in size, quantity, or degree —**pro·por·tion·ate·ly** *adv*

pro·pos·al /prə pṓz'l/ *n* **1** an idea or plan put forward for consideration **2** the proposing of something

pro·pose /prə pṓz/ (**-posed, -pos·ing**) *v* **1** *vt* put forward as a suggestion **2** *vt* state as an intention (*fml*) **3** *vt* nominate for an elected position or for promotion **4** *vti* make an offer of marriage to **5** *vt* ask others to join in a toast —**pro·pos·er** *n*

prop·o·si·tion /próppə zísh'n/ *n* **1** a proposal for consideration **2** a statement of opinion or judgment **3** an invitation to have sexual intercourse **4** a private deal or agreement **5** somebody or something to be dealt with (*infml*) ■ *vt* **1** invite to have sexual intercourse **2** offer a deal to —**prop·o·si·tion·al** *adj*

pro·pound /prə pównd/ *vt* suggest an idea or explanation —**pro·pound·er** *n*

pro·pri·e·tar·y /prə prī ə tèrree/ *adj* **1** of owners or ownership **2** privately owned **3** manufactured or sold by somebody with an exclusive legal right to do so

pro·pri·e·tor /prə prī ətər/ *n* the owner of something, especially a business —**pro·pri·e·to·ri·al** /prə prī ə táwree əl/ *adj* —**pro·pri·e·tor·ship** *n*

pro·pri·e·ty /prə prī ətee/ *n* **1** socially correct or appropriate behavior **2** the quality of being socially appropriate ■ **pro·pri·e·ties** *npl* the rules of etiquette

ORIGIN **Propriety** derives from the same French word as *property*, and "property" was one of its early senses. The better-developed strand of meaning, however, is based on "appropriateness." This emerged in the early 17C, though the modern sense of "socially correct behavior" is not recorded until the late 18C.

pro·pul·sion /prə púlsh'n/ *n* the process or force by which something is moved —**pro·pul·sive** *adj*

pro ra·ta /prō ráytə, -raatə/ *adv, adj* in a fixed proportion

pro·rate /prō ráyt/ (**-rat·ed, -rat·ing**) *vti* calculate or divide something on a pro rata basis —**pro·ra·tion** *n*

pro·sa·ic /prō záy ik/ *adj* **1** lacking imagination **2** straightforward —**pro·sa·i·cal·ly** *adv*

pros and cons *npl* advantages and disadvantages

pro·sce·ni·um /prō seénee əm/ *n* the part of a stage in front of the curtain

pro·sciut·to /prō shóotō/ *n* dried and smoked Italian ham

pro·scribe /prō skríb/ (**-scribed, -scrib·ing**) *vt* **1** condemn or ban **2** banish —**pro·scrib·er** *n*

prose /prōz/ *n* ordinary writing or speech without the structure of poetry

pros·e·cute /próssə kyòot/ (**-cut·ed, -cut·ing**) *vti* **1** take legal action against somebody **2** try to prove that somebody is guilty in a court of law —**pros·e·cut·a·ble** *adj* —**pros-**

e·cu·tion /pròssə kyōōsh'n/ n —**pros·e·cu·tor** n

~~prosecuter~~ incorrect spelling of **prosecutor**

pros·e·lyte /pròssə līt/ n somebody converted to a new belief ■ vti (**-lyt·ed, -lyt·ing**) = **proselytize** —**pros·e·ly·tism** /próssələ tizzəm/ n

pros·e·ly·tize /próssələ tīz/ (**-tized, -tiz·ing**) vti try to convert somebody to a new belief —**pros·e·ly·ti·za·tion** /pròssələti záysh'n/ n —**pros·e·ly·tiz·er** n

pros·o·dy /próssədee/ n the study of the structure of poetry —**pros·sod·ic** /prə sóddik/ adj

pros·pect /pró spèkt/ n 1 a possibility of something happening soon 2 something that is expected to happen soon 3 a wide view or scene 4 the direction in which something faces 5 a prospective customer 6 somebody or something with the potential to succeed ■ **pros·pects** npl expectations of success ■ vti search an area for mineral deposits

pro·spec·tive /prə spéktiv/ adj likely to become or happen —**pro·spec·tive·ly** adv

pros·pec·tor /pró spèktər/ n somebody who looks for mineral deposits

pro·spec·tus /prə spéktəss/ n an official document giving advance information about something

pros·per /próspər/ vi succeed and flourish, especially financially

pros·per·i·ty /pro spérrətee/ n wealth or success

pros·per·ous /próspərəss/ adj 1 successful and flourishing, especially financially 2 wealthy —**pros·per·ous·ly** adv —**pros·per·ous·ness** n

pros·tate /pró stàyt/, **pros·tate gland** n a gland surrounding the urethra below the bladder in male mammals that secretes a fluid into the semen —**pros·tat·ic** /pro státtik/ adj

pros·the·sis /pros théessiss/ n (pl **-ses** /-seez/) 1 an artificial body part 2 the replacement of body parts with artificial devices —**pros·thet·ic** /pros théttik/ adj —**pros·thet·ics** n

pros·ti·tute /próstə tōōt/ n 1 somebody paid for sexual intercourse 2 somebody who degrades his or her talent for money ■ vt (**-tut·ed, -tut·ing**) 1 misuse for gain 2 offer as a prostitute —**pros·ti·tu·tion** /pròstə tōōsh'n/ n

pros·trate /pró stràyt/ v (**-trat·ed, -trat·ing**) 1 vr lie face downward 2 vt lay or throw flat on the ground 3 vt make weak or helpless ■ adj 1 lying flat, facing downward 2 lying down 3 drained of energy —**pros·tra·tion** /pro stráysh'n/ n

pros·y /prózee/ adj (**-i·er, -i·est**) dull and unimaginative —**pros·i·ness** n

pro·tac·tin·i·um /prò tak tínnee əm/ n (symbol **Pa**) a radioactive metallic chemical element

pro·tag·o·nist /prò tággənist/ n 1 the main character in a story 2 a leading figure in a contest or dispute

pro·te·an /prótee ən, prō teé ən/ adj 1 variable in nature, appearance, or behavior 2 versatile

> **ORIGIN** Being **protean** was originally an attribute of Proteus, a prophetic sea god in Greek mythology who could change his shape at will.

pro·tect /prə tékt/ vt keep safe from harm or damage —**pro·tec·tive** adj —**pro·tec·tive·ly** adv —**pro·tec·tive·ness** n ◊ See note at **safeguard**

⚡ **pro·tect·ed** /prə téktəd/ adj 1 classified as an endangered species 2 sheltered 3 locked against changes by unauthorized computer users

pro·tec·tion /prə tékshən/ n 1 the protecting of somebody or something 2 something that protects 3 insurance coverage 4 payment extorted by threatening harm or damage to property (infml) 5 also **pro·tec·tion·i·sm** the imposition of duties on imports, designed to protect domestic industries against foreign competition

pro·tec·tor /prə téktər/ n 1 somebody or something that protects 2 also **Pro·tec·tor** somebody ruling in place of a monarch —**pro·tec·tor·al** adj —**pro·tec·tor·ship** n

pro·tec·tor·ate /prə téktərət/ n 1 a state dependent on another, or the relationship between such states 2 the position or term of office of a protector

pro·té·gé /prótə zhày, pròtə zháy/ n somebody under the patronage of another

pro·té·gée /prótə zhày, pròtə zháy/ n a woman or girl under somebody's patronage

pro·tein /pró teen/ n 1 a complex natural compound composed of linked amino acids 2 food rich in protein

> **ORIGIN** The word **protein** was coined around 1838 (in a French form) by the Dutch chemist Gerardus Johannes Mulder (1802–80). He based it on Greek prōteios "primary," a derivative of protos "first." It was originally applied to a substance regarded as the primary constituent of all animal and vegetable bodies, but when chemical advances proved the single substance not to exist, the word continued to appear appropriate for the group of substances that are now called **proteins.**

pro tem adv, adj for the time being

Prot·er·o·zo·ic /pròtərə zó ik/ n an eon of geologic time 2,500–570 million years ago —**Prot·er·o·zo·ic** adj

pro·test vti /prə tést, prō-, pró tèst/ 1 complain or object strongly about something 2 say firmly that something is true ■ n /pró tèst/ 1 a strong complaint or objection 2 a demonstration of public opposition or disapproval —**prot·es·tant** /prə tést'nt, pró

tést'nt/ *n, adj* —**pro·test·er** *n* ◊ See note at **complain, object**

Prot·es·tant /próttəstənt/ *n* a member of a Western Christian church that rejects papal authority —**Prot·es·tant** *adj* —**Prot·es·tant·ism** *n*

⚡ **pro·to·col** /prótə kàwl/ *n* **1** the etiquette of state occasions **2** a code of conduct **3** an international agreement **4** a written record or draft of an agreement **5** a set of rules for exchanging information between computers

pro·ton /pró tòn/ *n* (*symbol* **p**) a stable positively charged nuclear particle —**pro·ton·ic** /prō tónnik/ *adj*

pro·to·plasm /prótə plàzzəm/ *n* the contents of a living cell including the nucleus and cytoplasm —**pro·to·plas·mic** /prótə plázmik/ *adj*

pro·to·type /prótə tìp/ *n* **1** an original used as a model for later forms or stages **2** a standard example —**pro·to·typ·al** /prótə típ'l/ *adj* —**pro·to·typ·i·cal** /prótə típpik'l/ *adj* —**pro·to·typ·i·cal·ly** *adv*

pro·to·zo·an /prótə zṓ ən/ (*pl* **-ans** *or* **-a** /-ə/) *n* a single-celled organism such as an amoeba —**pro·to·zo·an** *adj* —**pro·to·zo·ic** *adj*

pro·tract /prō trákt, prə-/ *vt* make something last longer —**pro·trac·tion** *n*

pro·tract·ed /prō tráktəd, prə-/ *adj* lasting a long time

pro·trac·tor /prō tráktər, prə-/ *n* a flat semicircular instrument for measuring angles

pro·trude /prō trōōd/ (**-trud·ed**, **-trud·ing**) *vti* stick or push out —**pro·tru·sion** *n* —**pro·tru·sive** *adj*

pro·tu·ber·ance /prō tōōbərənss/, **pro·tu·ber·an·cy** /-rənsee/ (*pl* **-cies**) *n* **1** something that sticks out **2** the fact of sticking out —**pro·tu·ber·ant** *adj*

proud *adj* **1** pleased and satisfied **2** fostering feelings of pride ◦ *the proudest moment* **3** having self-respect **4** arrogant **5** looking impressive **6** *Midwest, Southern US* feeling pleased or delighted —**proud·ly** *adv* —**proud·ness** *n*

SYNONYMS proud, arrogant, conceited, egotistic, vain CORE MEANING: describing somebody who is pleased with himself or herself

Marcel Proust

Proust /proost/, **Marcel** (1871–1922) French novelist —**Prous·ti·an** *adj*

prove /proov/ (**proved, proved** *or* **prov·en** /proóvən/, **prov·ing**) *v* **1** *vt* establish or demonstrate the truth of **2** *vt* subject something to scientific analysis to determine its worth or characteristics **3** *vti* turn out to be a particular thing or of a particular character ◦ *It proved impossible to dislodge the rock.* —**prov·a·ble** *adj*

prov·e·nance /próvvənənss, -naàns/ *n* **1** the place of origin of something **2** the source and ownership history of something such as an artwork ◊ See note at **origin**

Pro·vence /prə vaànss/ region of SE France

prov·en·der /próvvəndər/ *n* **1** food for livestock (*archaic*) **2** food (*literary or humorous*)

prov·erb /pró vùrb/ *n* a short well-known saying

pro·ver·bi·al /prə vúrbee əl/ *adj* **1** expressed as a proverb **2** used in a proverb

Prov·erbs /pró vùrbz/ *n* a book of the Bible made up of the sayings of wise men, including Solomon

pro·vide /prə víd/ (**-vid·ed**, **-vid·ing**) *v* **1** *vt* supply somebody with, or be a source of, something needed or wanted **2** *vt* require something as a condition (*fml*) **3** *vi* take precautions ◦ *provide against disaster* **4** *vi* supply a means of support ◦ *providing for her family* —**pro·vid·er** *n*

pro·vid·ed /prə vídəd/, **pro·vid·ed that** *conj* on condition that

prov·i·dence /próvvid'nss, -dènss/, **Prov·i·dence** *n* **1** guidance and care believed to be provided by God **2** God perceived as a guiding and caring force

Prov·i·dence /próvvidənss/ capital of Rhode Island. Pop. 150,890 (1998).

prov·i·dent /próvvid'nt, -dènt/ *adj* **1** preparing for future needs **2** economical or frugal

prov·i·den·tial /próvvi dénshəl/ *adj* **1** of providence **2** very lucky ◊ See note at **lucky**

pro·vid·ing /prə víding/, **pro·vid·ing that** *conj* on condition that

prov·ince /próvvins/ *n* **1** an administrative division of a country **2** an area of knowledge ■ **prov·inc·es** *npl* the parts of a country outside the capital and main cities

pro·vin·cial /prə vínshəl/ *adj* **1** of a province or the provinces **2** unsophisticated and narrow-minded (*disapproving*) ■ *n* **1** somebody from the provinces **2** an unsophisticated person (*disapproving*) —**pro·vin·cial·ism** *n* —**pro·vin·cial·ly** *adv*

prov·ing ground *n* a place where something or somebody is tested

pro·vi·sion /prə vízh'n/ *n* **1** the supplying of something **2** an action taken to meet a possible or expected need **3** a legal clause stating a condition ■ **pro·vi·sions** *npl* food and other supplies ■ *vt* provide with food and other supplies —**pro·vi·sion·er** *n*

pro·vi·sion·al /prə vízhən'l, -vízhnəl/ *adj* temporary or conditional —**pro·vi·sion·al·ly** *adv*

pro·vi·so /prə vízō/ (*pl* **-sos** *or* **-soes**) *n* 1 a clause added to a contract 2 a condition within an agreement

Pro·vo /prōvō/ city in N Utah. Pop. 110,419 (1998).

prov·o·ca·tion /pròvvə káysh'n/ *n* 1 the provoking of somebody or something 2 a cause of anger

pro·voc·a·tive /prə vókətiv/ *adj* 1 making people angry or excited 2 deliberately sexually arousing —**pro·voc·a·tive·ly** *adv* —**pro·voc·a·tive·ness** *n*

pro·voke /prə vōk/ (**-voked, -vok·ing**) *vt* 1 make somebody feel angry 2 cause or stir somebody to an emotion or response —**pro·vok·ing·ly** *adv*

pro·vost /prṓ vṓst, prṓvəst, prṓvost/ *n* 1 an important university administrator 2 a senior dignitary of a cathedral

prow /prowl/ *n* 1 the front part of a ship 2 a projecting front part

prow·ess /prṓw əss/ *n* 1 superior skill 2 valor and ability in combat

prowl /prowl/ *vti* roam an area stealthily in search of prey, food, or opportunity ■ *n* an act of prowling —**prowl·er** *n*

prox·i·mate /próksəmət/ *adj* 1 nearest 2 very close in space or time —**prox·i·ma·tion** /pròksə máysh'n/ *n*

prox·im·i·ty /prok símmətee/ *n* closeness

prox·y /próksee/ (*pl* **-ies**) *n* 1 the function or power of somebody authorized to act for another 2 somebody authorized to act for another

---

ORIGIN Proxy is a contraction of *procuracy*, a word that is now rare, meaning "the managing of somebody else's affairs, acting on behalf of another." It goes back to the same Latin verb as *procure*.

---

prude *n* somebody easily shocked by matters relating to sex or nudity —**prud·er·y** *n* —**prud·ish** *adj* —**prud·ish·ly** *adv* —**prud·ish·ness** *n*

pru·dent /prōōd'nt/ *adj* 1 having good sense in dealing with practical matters 2 carefully considering consequences —**pru·dence** *n* —**pru·dent·ly** *adv* ◊ See note at **cautious**

pru·den·tial /prōō dénshəl/ *adj* resulting from, depending on, or using prudence

prune[1] *n* a dried plum

prune[2] (**pruned, prun·ing**) *v vti* cut branches from a plant to encourage fuller growth 2 vt reduce something by removing unwanted material

pru·ri·ent /prōōree ənt/ *adj* marked by unwholesome sexual interest —**pru·ri·ence** *n*

Prus·sia /prúshə/ historical region of Germany and former kingdom in north central Europe —**Prus·sian** *adj, n*

prus·sic ac·id /prússik-/ *n* a colorless weak acid that smells of almonds

pry[1] (**pried, pries**) *vi* inquire nosily —**pry·ing·ly** *adv*

pry[2] *vt* (**pried, pries**) 1 force open with a lever 2 get information with difficulty ■ *n* (*pl* **pries**) a tool for applying leverage

P.S. *abbr* 1 *also* **p.s.** postscript 2 public school

psalm /saam, saalm/, **Psalm** *n* a sacred song or poem of praise —**psalm·ist** *n*

ORIGIN Psalm goes back to a Greek verb that originally meant "pluck" but was extended to "pluck harp strings." The noun derived from it was used in the Greek translation of the Hebrew Bible, the Septuagint, and from there passed into Latin and the Germanic and Romance languages.

Psalms /saamz, saalmz/ *n* a book of the Bible made up of 150 poems and hymns to God, traditionally attributed to King David

Psal·ter /sáwltər/, **psal·ter** *n* a book containing psalms

psal·ter·y /sáwltəree/ (*pl* **-ies**) *n* an ancient musical instrument with numerous strings

pseu·do /sōōdō/ *adj* not genuine

pseudo- *prefix* false, spurious ○ *pseudoscience*

pseu·do·nym /sōōdə nim/ *n* a false name —**pseu·don·y·mous** /soo dónnəməss/ *adj*

pseu·do·sci·ence /sōōdō sī́ ənss/ *n* a theory or method mistakenly held to be scientific

psi /sī́, psī́/ *n* the 23rd letter of the Greek alphabet

psit·ta·co·sis /sìttə kṓssiss/ *n* a bacterial disease of parrots and related birds that can be transmitted to humans

pso·ri·a·sis /sə rī́ əssiss/ *n* a skin disease marked by red scaly patches

PST *abbr* Pacific Standard Time

~~psuedonym~~ incorrect spelling of **pseudonym**

psych /sīk/ *v* 1 *vt* intimidate 2 *vr* = **psych up** □ **psych out** *vt* (*infml*) 1 intimidate 2 guess the thought processes of □ **psych up** *vt* prepare yourself or somebody else mentally (*infml*)

psy·che /sī́kee/ *n* 1 the human spirit or soul 2 the human mind

psy·che·de·li·a /sī́kə deélee ə/ *n* the subculture of psychedelic drugs

psy·che·del·ic /sī́kə déllik/ *adj* 1 of hallucinogenic drugs 2 resembling images and sounds experienced under the influence of hallucinogenic drugs —**psy·che·del·i·cal·ly** *adv*

psy·chi·a·try /sī kī́ ətree, sī-/ *n* the branch of medicine concerned with mental or behavioral disorders —**psy·chi·at·ric** /sī́kee áttrik/ *adj* —**psy·chi·a·trist** *n*

psy·chic /sī́kik/ *adj* 1 of the mind 2 supposedly sensitive to supernatural forces ■ *n* somebody supposedly sensitive to the supernatural —**psy·chi·cal·ly** *adv*

psycho- prefix **1** mind, mental o psychoactive **2** psychology, psychological o psychobabble

psy·cho·ac·tive /sīkō áktiv/ adj describes drugs that affect mood or behavior

psy·cho·a·nal·y·sis /sīkō ə nálləssiss/ n **1** a method of psychiatric therapy based on the theory that mental life functions on both conscious and unconscious levels **2** treatment by psychoanalysis, involving the interpretation of dreams and the patient's free association of ideas —**psy·cho·an·a·lyst** /sīkō ánn'list/ n —**psy·cho·an·a·lyt·i·cal** /-lĭttik'l/ adj —**psy·cho·an·a·lyze** /sīkō ánnə līz/ vt

psy·cho·bab·ble /sīkō bàbb'l/ n psychological jargon

~~psychedelic~~ incorrect spelling of **psychedelic**

psy·cho·dra·ma /sīkə draằmə, -drámmə/ n a form of psychotherapy in which patients perform roles in dramas that illustrate their problems

psy·cho·gen·ic /sīkō jénnik/ adj arising from mental or emotional processes —**psy·cho·gen·i·cal·ly** adv

psy·cho·ki·ne·sis /sīkō ki néessiss, -kī-/ n the supposed moving of objects with the mind —**psy·cho·ki·net·ic** /-ki néttik, -kī-/ adj

psy·cho·log·i·cal /sīkə lójjik'l/ adj **1** of psychology **2** of the mind —**psy·cho·log·i·cal·ly** adv

psy·cho·log·i·cal war·fare n **1** warfare by propaganda **2** the use of psychological tactics to disadvantage somebody

psy·chol·o·gy /sī kólləjee/ (pl **-gies**) n **1** the study of the mind **2** the characteristic mental makeup of a person or group —**psy·chol·o·gist** n

psy·cho·path /sīkə pàth/ n an offensive term for somebody with a personality disorder that leads to violent antisocial behavior —**psy·cho·path·ic** /sīkə páthik/ adj

psy·cho·pa·thol·o·gy /sīkō pə thólləjee/ n the study of psychiatric disorders —**psy·cho·path·o·log·i·cal** /-pàthə lójjik'l/ adj —**psy·cho·pa·thol·o·gist** n

psy·cho·sex·u·al /sīkō sékshoo əl/ adj of the mental and emotional aspects of sexuality

psy·cho·sis /sī kóssiss/ (pl **-ses** /-séez/) n a psychiatric disorder marked by loss of contact with reality —**psy·chot·ic** /sī kóttik/ adj —**psy·chot·i·cal·ly** adv

psy·cho·so·mat·ic /sīkə sə máttik/ adj **1** describes a physical illness that is mentally induced **2** of both the mind and body —**psy·cho·so·mat·i·cal·ly** adv

psy·cho·ther·a·py /sīkō thérrəpee/ n the treatment of mental disorders by psychological methods —**psy·cho·ther·a·peu·tic** /-thèrrə pyootik/ adj —**psy·cho·ther·a·pist** n

~~psycology~~ incorrect spelling of **psychology**

Pt symbol platinum

PT abbr **1** part-time **2** physical therapy

pt. abbr **1** part **2** pint **3** point **4** port

Pt. abbr (in place names) **1** Point **2** Port

PTA, P.T.A. abbr Parent Teacher Association

ptar·mi·gan /taàrmigən/ (pl same or **-gans**) n a grouse of cold regions that turns white in winter

pter·o·dac·tyl /tèrrə dákt'l/ n an extinct flying reptile with a rudimentary beak

pter·o·saur /tèrrə sàwr/ n an extinct flying reptile with membranous wings

p.t.o. abbr please turn over

Ptol·e·my /tólləmee/ (AD 100?–170?) Greek astronomer, mathematician, and geographer

Ptol·e·my I (367?–283? BC) Macedonian king of Egypt (305–283? BC)

Pu symbol plutonium

pub n UK a bar selling alcohol and sometimes food

pu·ber·ty /pyóobərtee/ n the stage of becoming physiologically mature —**pu·ber·tal** adj

pu·bes·cent /pyoo béss'nt/ adj **1** reaching or having reached puberty **2** covered with down or fine hair —**pu·bes·cence** n

pu·bic /pyóobik/ adj of the pubis

pu·bis /pyóobiss/ (pl **-bes** /-bèez/) n the lower front of the hipbone

pub·lic /públik/ adj **1** of, for, or belonging to all members of the community o public health **2** open to all **3** of the state or state agencies **4** done openly **5** describes companies whose stock is available for anyone to buy ■ n **1** the community as a whole **2** a particular part of the community o the reading public —**pub·lic·ly** adv

pub·lic-ad·dress sys·tem n full form of **PA**

~~publically~~ incorrect spelling of **publicly**

pub·li·can /públikən/ n a tax collector in the Roman Empire

pub·li·ca·tion /públi káysh'n/ n **1** the publishing of something **2** a published item, especially one in printed form, e.g., a book or magazine

pub·lic de·fend·er n a publicly funded attorney representing the less well-off

pub·lic do·main n **1** government land **2** the state of not being protected by a patent or copyright

pub·lic fig·ure n a well-known person

pub·lic hous·ing n government-provided housing at low rent

pub·li·cist /públissist/ n somebody who arranges for publicity for a client

pub·lic·i·ty /pu blíssətee/ n **1** the stimulation of public interest in or awareness of something or somebody **2** interest or awareness created among the general public or media **3** the business of publicizing things

pub·li·cize /públi sìz/ (**-cized, -ciz·ing**) vt make generally known

pub·lic o·pin·ion n the general attitude of the public toward something

pub·lic pros·e·cu·tor n a government prosecutor of criminal actions on behalf of the community

pub·lic re·la·tions n (+ sing or pl verb) 1 the promotion of a favorable image and good relationship with the public 2 the particular image and relationship a person or organization has with the public

pub·lic school n 1 a state-funded school in the United States 2 an independent fee-charging secondary school in the United Kingdom

pub·lic ser·vant n a holder of a government position

pub·lic ser·vice n 1 government employment 2 the provision of essential services 3 a service run for the benefit of the general public, e.g., a utility

pub·lic-spir·it·ed adj concerned for the community's welfare

pub·lic tel·e·vi·sion n noncommercial television

pub·lic works npl civil-engineering projects undertaken or financed by the government

pub·lish /públish/ v 1 vti prepare and produce material in printed or electronic form for distribution 2 vt make something public knowledge —**pub·lish·a·ble** adj —**pub·lish·er** n —**pub·lish·ing** n

Puc·ci·ni /poo cheenee/, **Giacomo** (1858–1924) Italian composer

puce /pyooss/ adj purplish-red —**puce** n

puck n a disc that the players hit in hockey

Puck n also **puck** a mischievous spirit in English folklore

puck·er /púkər/ vti gather into wrinkles ■ n a small wrinkle

puck·ish /púkish/ adj mischievous or naughty

pud·ding /pŏodding/ n a sweet creamy cooked dessert thickened with flour (often in combination)

ORIGIN A **pudding** was originally a sausage: an animal's stomach or intestine stuffed with chopped meat and other ingredients and boiled. Other foods cooked in a bag came to be called **puddings**, then dishes made with flour and enclosed in a casing made with flour, until eventually neither the ingredients, nor the shape, nor the manner of cooking could determine what was and what was not a **pudding**.

pud·dle /púdd'l/ n a shallow pool of liquid, especially water

pu·den·dum /pyoo déndəm/ (pl -da /-déndə/) n the external genitals —**pu·den·dal** adj

pudg·y /pújjee/ (-i·er, -i·est) adj short and overweight (infml; sometimes offensive) —**pudg·i·ness** n

Pueb·la /pwébblaa/ capital of Puebla State, central Mexico. Pop. 1,222,569 (1995).

pueb·lo /pwébblō/ (pl -los) n 1 a Native North or Central American village with multi-story stone or adobe houses 2 a village in a Spanish-speaking country

Pueb·lo /pwébblō/ (pl same or -los) n a member of a Native North or Central American people who live in or lived in pueblos —**Pueb·lo** adj

pu·er·ile /pyoorəl, pyoor il, pyoo ərəl/ adj silly and childish —**pu·er·il·i·ty** /pyoor ríllətee/ n

pu·er·per·al /pyoo úrpərəl/ adj of childbirth

Puer·to Ri·co /pwèrtə reekō/ island in the N Caribbean Sea, east of Hispaniola, a self-governing commonwealth of the United States. Cap. San Juan. Pop. 3,937,316 (2001). —**Puer·to Ri·can** n, adj

puff n 1 a short sudden rush of air, steam, or smoke 2 the sound made by a puff 3 a short exhalation of breath 4 an inhaling followed by exhaling when smoking 5 also **puff pas·try** a light flaky multilayered pastry 6 a piece of exaggerated praise or publicity ■ v 1 vi breathe quickly and heavily 2 vti emit steam, smoke, or gas in short blasts 3 vti inhale and exhale smoke from a cigarette, cigar, or pipe 4 vi move while emitting puffs of smoke or steam 5 vi move while panting 6 vti swell, e.g., with air or pride

puff·ball /púf bàwl/ n a round fungus that produces a cloud of dark spores if disturbed

puffed-up adj self-important

puf·fin /púffin/ (pl -fins or same) n a black-and-white diving bird with a short neck and a triangular colorful bill

puff·y /púffee/ (-i·er, -i·est) adj 1 swollen 2 short of breath —**puff·i·ness** n

pug[1] n a small dog with a wrinkled face, short coat, and curled tail

pug[2] vt (pugged, pug·ging) 1 knead clay with water 2 fill a gap with clay or mortar ■ n clay suitable for molding —**pug·gy** adj

Pu·get Sound /pyóojət-/ arm of the Pacific Ocean, in NW Washington

pu·gi·lism /pyóojə lìzzəm/ n the sport of boxing —**pu·gi·list** n —**pu·gi·lis·tic** /pyóojə lístik/ adj

pug·na·cious /pug náyshəss/ adj quarrelsome and aggressive —**pug·na·cious·ly** adv —**pug·na·cious·ness** n —**pug·nac·i·ty** /pug nássətee/ n

puke /pyook/ (puked, puk·ing, pukes) vti vomit (slang) —**puke** n

pu·la /pŏolə/ (pl same) n the main unit of Botswanan currency

Pu·las·ki /pə láskee/, **Casimir** (1747–79) Polish-born American army officer

pul·chri·tude /púlkrə tòod/ n beauty (literary or humorous) —**pul·chri·tu·di·nous** /pùlkrə tōod'nəss/ adj

Pu·lit·zer /pŏollitsər, pyŏolitsər/, **Joseph** (1847–1911) Hungarian-born US journalist and patron of the arts

pull /pŏol/ v 1 vti draw something or somebody nearer 2 vt remove something forcibly 3 *vt* draw a load along 4 *vti* tug at or jerk something or somebody 5 *vt* strain and damage a muscle 6 *vt* attract a crowd (*infml*) 7 *vt* take out a weapon in readiness to fight (*infml*) 8 *vt* apply force to a trigger 9 *vt* open or close curtains 10 *vti* tear or rip something 11 *vt* stretch something elastic, e.g., taffy ■ *n* 1 a pulling or being pulled 2 a pulling force 3 the power to attract an audience or supporters (*infml*) 4 something such as a tab or handle used for pulling (*often in combination*) —**pull·er** *n*

SYNONYMS pull, drag, draw, haul, tow, tug, yank CORE MEANING: move something toward you or in the same direction as you

☐ **pull off** *vt* achieve despite difficulties (*infml*)

☐ **pull out** *vti* depart from a stopping place and join the traffic

☐ **pull through** *vti* recover from illness or difficulties

☐ **pull up** *vi* arrive and stop

pull·back /poól bàk/ *n* a withdrawal of troops

⚡ **pull-down** *adj* made to appear on a computer screen by clicking on a heading —**pull-down** *n*

pul·let /poóllət/ *n* a young domestic hen

pul·ley /poóllee/ (*pl* **-leys**) *n* a wheel with a grooved rim over which a belt or chain can run to change the direction of a pulling force

Pull·man /poólmən/ *n* a comfortable train car

pull·out /poól òwt/ *n* 1 a removable section of a publication 2 a withdrawal from an obligation or difficult circumstance 3 a retreat from a place or military involvement

pull·o·ver /poól òvər/ *n* a garment that is pulled on over the head, especially a sweater

pull-tab *n* a ring pulled to open a drink can

pul·mo·nar·y /poólmə nèrree, púlmə-/ *adj* of the lungs

pulp /pulp/ *n* 1 the soft fleshy tissue inside a fruit or vegetable 2 the pith inside a plant stem 3 a soft or soggy mass of material 4 crushed wood for paper 5 cheap books and magazines 6 the sensitive tissue inside a tooth ■ *vti* crush or be crushed into pulp —**pulp·y** *adj*

pul·pit /poól pit, púl pit/ *n* a raised platform in a church where the priest or minister stands

pulp·wood /púlp woòd/ *n* soft wood used to make paper

pul·sar /púl saàr/ *n* a small dense star that emits brief intense bursts of visible radiation, radio waves, and X-rays

pul·sate /púl sàyt/ (**-sat·ed, -sat·ing**) *vi* 1 expand and contract with a regular beat (*refers to blood vessels*) 2 vibrate or throb —**pul·sat·ing** *adj* —**pul·sa·tion** /púl sáysh'n/ *n*

pulse[1] /puls/ *n* 1 the regular expansion and contraction of an artery, caused by the pumping of blood through the body 2 a rhythmical beat or throb 3 a sudden change in a constant quantity, or a repeating change in magnitude ■ *vi* (**pulsed, puls·ing**) 1 beat rhythmically 2 undergo brief sudden changes in quantity, e.g., in voltage

pulse[2] /puls/ *n* 1 an edible seed from a pod ○ *eats peas, beans, and other pulses* 2 a plant that has pods as fruit

pul·ver·ize /púlvə rìz/ (**-ized, -iz·ing**) *vt* crush to a powder —**pul·ver·i·za·tion** /pùlvəri záysh'n/ *n*

pu·ma /poomə, pyoomə/ (*pl* **-mas** *or same*) *n* a mountain lion

pum·ice /púmmiss/ *n* a type of light rock full of air spaces

pum·mel /púmm'l/ *vt* hit repeatedly

pump[1] /pump/ *vt* 1 force a liquid or gas to flow in a particular direction 2 move something up and down energetically ○ *frantically pumping the brakes* 3 question somebody persistently ■ *n* a device for making a liquid or gas flow in a particular direction

☐ **pump out** *vt* 1 produce a great deal of 2 remove fluid from

☐ **pump up** *vt* 1 inflate something 2 make somebody excited (*infml*) ○ *pumped them up for the game*

pump[2] /pump/ *n* a plain low-cut woman's shoe

pum·per·nick·el /púmpər nik'l/ *n* dark rye bread

pump·kin /púmpkin, púmkin/ *n* 1 a large orange fruit with a thick rind and many seeds 2 a plant that produces pumpkins

pun *n* a play on words —**pun** *vi* —**pun·ny** *adj*

punch[1] /punch/ *vt* 1 hit somebody with the fist 2 poke 3 press a button or key 4 herd cattle ■ *n* 1 a blow with the fist 2 vigor ◇ **pack a punch** be very powerful (*infml*) ◇ **not pull any** *or* **your punches, pull no punches** speak bluntly ◇ **roll with the punches** adapt easily to a difficult situation (*infml*)

ORIGIN Of the three English words **punch**, two are ultimately related. **Punch** "hit" derives from a French verb meaning "prick," which developed from Latin. The tool **punch** is probably an abbreviation of an earlier word *puncheon* "wooden support," which is ultimately from the same Latin root. The odd one out, **punch** the drink, appears to go back to a Sanskrit word meaning "five," because there were originally five essential ingredients. It was encountered in South Asia in the 17C.

punch[2] *n* 1 a tool for making holes 2 a stamping tool —**punch** *vt*

punch[3] *n* a drink of mixed fruit juices

punch-bowl /púnch bòl/ *n* a bowl for serving punch

punch-drunk *adj* disoriented by punches to the head

punch·ing bag *n* a boxers' training device

punch·line /púnch lïn/ *n* the funny ending of a joke

punch·y /púnchee/ (**-i·er, -i·est**) *adj (infml)* 1 forceful o *a good punchy slogan* 2 punch-drunk

punc·til·i·ous /pungk tíllee əss/ *adj* 1 careful about correct behavior 2 taking great care over details —**punc·til·i·ous·ly** *adv* ◊ See note at **careful**

punc·tu·al /púngkchoo əl/ *adj* keeping to the arranged time —**punc·tu·al·i·ty** /pùngkchoo állətee/ *n* —**punc·tu·al·ly** *adv*

punc·tu·ate /púngkchoo àyt/ (**-at·ed, -at·ing**) *v* 1 *vti* add punctuation to a text 2 *vt* interrupt frequently

punc·tu·a·tion /pùngkchoo áysh'n/ *n* 1 the marks used to organize writing into clauses, phrases, and sentences 2 the use of punctuation

punc·tu·a·tion mark *n* a sign used to punctuate text

punc·ture /púngkchər/ *n* a small hole ■ *v* (**-tured, -tur·ing**) 1 *vti* make a hole in or get a hole 2 *vt* ruin somebody's confidence —**punc·tur·a·ble** *adj*

pun·dit /púndit/ *n* somebody who expresses an opinion, especially in the media

Pu·ne /póonə/ city in west central India. Pop. 1,566,651 (1991).

pun·gent /púnjənt/ *adj* 1 strong-smelling or strong-tasting 2 expressed in a witty and biting manner —**pun·gen·cy** *n* —**pun·gent·ly** *adv*

pun·ish /púnnish/ *vt* 1 make somebody undergo a penalty for an offense o *crimes formerly punished by death* 3 treat somebody or something harshly —**pun·ish·a·ble** *adj* —**pun·ish·er** *n* —**pun·ish·ing** *adj* —**pun·ish·ing·ly** *adv*

pun·ish·ment /púnnishmənt/ *n* 1 the act of punishing 2 the penalty for doing something wrong 3 rough treatment or heavy use

pu·ni·tive /pyóonətiv/ *adj* 1 of or as punishment o *punitive air strikes* 2 causing hardship o *punitive taxation* —**pu·ni·tive·ly** *adv*

Pun·jab /pún jàab, pun jáab/ 1 state in NW India, bordering the province of Punjab in Pakistan. Cap. Chandigarh. Pop. 21,695,000 (1994). 2 province of NE Pakistan, bordering the Indian state of Punjab. Cap. Lahore. Pop. 72,585,000 (1998).

Pun·ja·bi /pun jáabee, -jábbee/, **Pan·ja·bi** *n* the official language of Punjab —**Pun·ja·bi** *adj*

punk *n* 1 a 1970s youth movement marked by confrontational antiestablishment attitudes 2 a member of the punk movement 3 *also* **punk rock** the fast loud music of the punk movement 4 an offensive term for a young man regarded as worthless or aggressive *(insult)* 5 dried wood ■ *adj* of the punk movement or punk rock

punt[1] *vti* drop a football and kick it before it hits the ground —**punt** *n* —**punt·er** *n*

punt[2] *n* a narrow flat-bottomed boat propelled using a long pole ■ *vti* propel or go in a punt —**punt·er** *n*

pu·ny /pyóonee/ *adj* 1 small and weak 2 inadequate —**pu·ni·ness** *n*

ORIGIN Puny is an alteration of a form *puisne* that more clearly reflects its origins. It is an adoption of a French word meaning literally "born afterward." The original meaning of **puny** and *puisne* was "junior."

---

pup *n* 1 a young dog 2 a young seal or other animal ■ *vi* (**pupped, pup·ping**) give birth to pups

pu·pa /pyóopə/ (*pl* **-pae** /-pèè/ *or* **-pas**) *n* a developing insect inside a cocoon —**pu·pal** *adj*

pu·pate /pyoó pàyt/ (**-pat·ed, -pat·ing**) *vi* develop from a larva into a pupa

pu·pil[1] /pyoóp'l/ *n* a student

ORIGIN The two words **pupil** are closely related. **Pupil** "student" goes back to Latin forms meaning "orphan, ward," diminutives of *pupus* "boy" and *pupa* "girl." "Orphan" was in fact the original English meaning of **pupil**, with the need for orphan children to be cared for and taught leading to the "student" sense in the mid-16C. The connection with the **pupil** of the eye derives from the extension of Latin *pupa* to mean "doll." The small reflected images that people see in each other's eyes when they stand close prompted the part of the eye where the "doll" was seen also to be called a *pupa*.

---

pu·pil[2] /pyoóp'l/ *n* the dark circular opening at the center of the eye

---

ORIGIN Pupil goes back to Latin *pupa* "girl," which was extended to mean "doll." The small reflected images that people see in each other's eyes when they stand close prompted the part of the eye where the "doll" was seen also to be called a *pupa*.

---

pup·pet /púppət/ *n* 1 a doll with movable parts used in entertainment 2 somebody who can be manipulated

pup·pet·eer /pùppə teér/ *n* somebody who operates puppets —**pup·pet·ry** /púppətree/ *n*

pup·py /púppee/ (*pl* **-pies**) *n* a young dog —**pup·py·ish** *adj*

ORIGIN Puppy was adopted in the late 15C from a French word meaning "doll, toy," and originally referred to a small dog kept as a pet or plaything. The movement from "toy dog" to "young dog" took place in the late 16C. The French form goes back to a Latin word for "girl" that is also the source of *puppet* and *pupil*.

---

pup·py love *n* adolescent love or infatuation

pu·pus /poŏpōōss/ *npl Hawaii* hors d'oeuvres

pur·blind /púr blīnd/ *adj* lacking understanding (*fml*)

pur·chase /púrchəss/ *vt* (-chased, -chas·ing) get by paying money ■ *n* **1** the act of buying something **2** an item bought **3** a firm grip or hold —**pur·chas·a·ble** *adj* —**pur·chas·er** *n*

pur·chas·ing pow·er *n* **1** wealth regarded as the ability to spend **2** the value of currency

pur·dah /púrdə/ *n* the Hindu and Islamic practice of keeping women from public view

pure /pyoor/ (**pur·er, pur·est**) *adj* **1** not mixed with another substance **2** free from contamination **3** complete or utter ○ *pure terror* **4** chaste (*literary*) **5** describes sound or color that is clear and vivid **6** involving theory, not practice ○ *pure science* **7** of unmixed ancestry —**pure·ly** *adv* —**pure·ness** *n* —**pu·ri·ty** *n*

pure·bred /pyoor brèd/ *adj* with ancestors of the same breed —**pure·bred** *n*

pu·rée /pyoŏ ráy, pyə-/, **pu·ree** *n* food made into a thick paste ■ *vti* (-réed; -reed) make food into a purée

pur·ga·tive /púrgətiv/ *n* a substance that causes evacuation of the bowels (*fml*) —**pur·ga·tive** *adj*

pur·ga·to·ry /púrgə tàwree/ *n* **1** *also* **Pur·ga·to·ry** in Roman Catholic doctrine, a place where the souls of dead people go until they have made amends for their sins **2** a miserable situation —**pur·ga·to·ri·al** /pùrgə táwree ol/ *adj*

⚡ **purge** (**purged, purg·ing**) *vt* **1** remove opponents from a place or organization **2** remove something undesirable or no longer wanted **3** free somebody from guilt or sin (*fml*) **4** delete computer data from a storage device —**purge** *n*

pu·ri·fy /pyoŏrə fī/ (-fied, -fies) *vt* **1** remove impurities from **2** make spiritually pure —**pu·ri·fi·ca·tion** /pyoŏrəfi káysh'n/ *n*

Pu·rim /poŏrim, poo rím/ *n* a Jewish festival. Date: 14th day of Adar.

pur·ist /pyoŏrist/ *n* an upholder of traditional standards —**pur·ism** *n* —**pu·ris·tic** /pyoŏ rístik/ *adj*

pu·ri·tan /pyoŏrət'n/ *n* **1** somebody with a strict moral code who is suspicious of pleasure **2** **Pu·ri·tan** a member of a Protestant group of the 16C and 17C that advocated simple rites and a strict moral code —**pu·ri·tan** *adj* —**pu·ri·tan·i·cal** /pyoŏrə tán·nik'l/ *adj* —**pu·ri·tan·ism** *n*

purl *n* a reverse plain knitting stitch —**purl** *vti*

pur·lieu /púrlyoo, púrloo/ *n* an outlying district ■ **pur·lieus** *npl* environs or outskirts (*fml*)

pur·loin /pur lóyn/ *vt* steal (*fml or humorous*) —**pur·loin·er** *n* ◊ See note at **steal**

pur·ple /púrp'l/ *n* **1** a color that combines red and blue **2** a purple robe, worn as a sign

of high rank ■ *adj* **1** of a red-blue color **2** elaborate or exaggerated in style ○ *purple prose* —**pur·ple·ness** *n*

pur·port *vt* /pər páwrt/ claim to be something or somebody ■ *n* /púr páwrt/ (*fml*) **1** meaning **2** intent —**pur·port·ed** *adj* —**pur·port·ed·ly** *adv*

pur·pose /púrpəss/ *n* **1** the reason for which something exists, is done, or has been made **2** the desired effect of something **3** determination —**pur·pose·less** *adj* —**pur·pose·less·ly** *adv* ◊ **on purpose** deliberately

pur·pose·ful /púrpəssfəl/ *adj* **1** determined **2** having a goal —**pur·pose·ful·ly** *adv*

pur·pose·ly /púrpəsslee/ *adv* intentionally

purr *n* **1** a cat's low regular murmuring noise **2** any similar sound ■ *v* **1** *vi* emit a purr **2** *vti* say something in a soft throaty voice —**purr·ing·ly** *adv*

purse *n* **1** a woman's bag for carrying everyday belongings **2** an amount of prize money **3** an amount of available money ■ *vt* (**pursed, purs·ing**) draw your lips together at the sides

purs·er /púrsər/ *n* an officer on a ship or aircraft who manages money and, on a passenger ship, looks after passengers

purse strings *npl* control over finances

pur·su·ance /pər soŏ ənss/ *n* the process of doing something as required (*fml*)

pur·su·ant /pər soŏ ənt/ ◊ **pursuant to** in accordance with (*fml*)

pur·sue /pər soŏ/ (-sued, -su·ing) *v* **1** *vti* follow or chase somebody or something **2** *vt* try to accomplish **3** *vt* continue or follow up on **4** *vt* be an ever-present problem for —**pur·su·a·ble** *adj* —**pur·su·er** *n* ◊ See note at **follow**

pur·suit /pər soŏt/ *n* **1** the act of pursuing somebody or something ○ *in pursuit of the stolen car* ○ *the pursuit of excellence* **2** a hobby

pur·vey /pər váy/ *vt* **1** supply goods (*fml*) **2** circulate gossip —**pur·vey·or** *n*

pur·view /púr vyoŏ/ *n* **1** scope or range **2** the main enacting part of written legislation

pus /puss/ *n* a yellowish liquid formed at sites of infection

Pu·san /poo saán/ city and port in SE South Korea. Pop. 3,813,814 (1995).

push /poŏsh/ *v* **1** *vti* press against somebody or something in order to move them **2** *vti* advance or cause to advance using pressure or force **3** *vt* encourage somebody strongly **4** *vt* exploit something to the limit ○ *Don't push your luck.* **5** *vt* force something to change ○ *push prices down* **6** *vt* try to sell something **7** *vt* sell drugs (*slang*) ■ *n* **1** an application of pressure **2** the process of advancing **3** an energetic effort **4** a military advance **5** a stimulus —**push·ing** *adj* —**push·ing·ly** *adv* ◊ **be pushing ...** be approaching a particular age (*infml*) ◊ **when** *or* **if push comes to shove** at the point when something must be done or a decision must be made

push-but-ton *adj* 1 operated by pushing a button 2 equipped with automatic devices

push-cart /póŏsh kaàrt/ *n* a lightweight cart pushed by hand

⚡**push-down** /póŏsh dòwn/ *n* a computer storage technique in which the last item stored is the first retrieved

push-er /póŏshər/ *n* a seller of illegal drugs (*slang*)

Push-kin /póŏshkin/, **Aleksandr Sergeyevich** (1799–1837) Russian writer

push-o-ver /póŏsh òvər/ *n* (*infml*) 1 an easy victim 2 something that is easy to do

⚡**push tech-nol-o-gy** *n* Internet technology providing customized information

⚡**push-up** /póŏsh ùp/ *n* 1 *US, Can, Aus* an exercise performed by pushing your body upward from the floor using your arms 2 a computer storage technique in which the first item stored is the first retrieved

push-y /póŏshee/ (**-i-er, -i-est**) *adj* unpleasantly competitive or forceful (*infml*) —**push-i-ly** *adv* —**push-i-ness** *n*

pu-sil-lan-i-mous /pyóosil lánniməss/ *adj* cowardly —**pu-sil-la-nim-i-ty** /pyóosilə nímmətee/ *n* ◊ See note at **cowardly**

puss[1] /póŏss/ *n* a cat (*dated infml*)

puss[2] /póŏss/ *n* a face (*slang*)

puss-y[1] /póŏssee/ (*pl* **-ies**) *n* a cat (*infml; often by or to children*)

pus-sy[2] /pússee/ (**-si-er, -si-est**) *adj* containing pus

puss-y-cat /póŏssee kàt/ *n* 1 a cat (*often used by or to children*) 2 somebody who is gentle and amiable (*infml*)

puss-y-foot /póŏssee fòŏt/ *vi* behave hesitantly or speak vaguely (*infml*)

puss-y wil-low *n* a willow tree with grayish catkins

pus-tule /pús chŏŏl/ *n* a pimple or similar pus-filled inflammation —**pus-tu-lar** /púschələr/ *adj*

put /póŏt/ *vt* (**put, put-ting**) 1 move something or somebody into a particular place or position 2 cause somebody or something to be in a particular place or situation 3 make somebody or something do something ○ *put her to work in the garden* 4 make somebody be affected by something ○ *put pressure on them* 5 use or apply something ○ *Put your mind to it.* 6 invest money in something 7 express something in a particular way 8 bring something up as a question or proposal 9 estimate something to be a particular amount ○ *put him in his late 30s* 10 throw the heavy metal ball in the shot put ■ *n* a throw of the heavy metal ball in the shot put

□ **put across** *vt* communicate clearly

□ **put down** *vt* 1 write something 2 suppress a

rebellion 3 disparage or belittle somebody (*infml*)

□ **put off** *vt* 1 postpone or delay 2 make disgusted 3 discourage ◊ **put somebody off his** *or* **her stride** distract somebody and cause him or her to perform less well

□ **put on** *vt* 1 cover part of your body with something such as clothing 2 tease somebody (*infml*) ○ *You're putting me on.*

□ **put out** *vt* 1 extinguish a light or fire 2 annoy or upset somebody 3 cause somebody inconvenience 4 in baseball, retire a batter or base runner

□ **put over** ◊ **put one over (on somebody)** trick somebody (*infml*)

□ **put up with** *vt* tolerate

pu-ta-tive /pyóotətiv/ *adj* 1 generally accepted as being a particular thing ○ *the putative father of the child* 2 thought to exist —**pu-ta-tive-ly** *adv*

put-back *n* a rebound in basketball

put-down /póŏt dòwn/ *n* a crushing remark (*infml*)

Pu-tin /póŏtin/, **Vladimir** (*b.* 1952) Russian president (2000–)

put-on *adj* false ■ *n* (*infml*) 1 an act of teasing somebody 2 a false outer appearance

put out *adj* annoyed, upset, offended, or inconvenienced

put-out /póŏt òwt/ *n* in baseball, a play in which somebody is retired

pu-tre-fy /pyóotri fī/ (**-fied, -fies**) *vti* make or become putrid —**pu-tre-fac-tion** /pyóotrə fáksh'n/ *n*

pu-tres-cent /pyoo tréss'nt/ *adj* 1 decaying 2 of decay —**pu-tres-cence** *n*

pu-trid /pyóotrid/ *adj* decaying with a foul smell —**pu-trid-i-ty** /pyoo tríddətee/ *n* —**pu-trid-ly** *adv*

putsch /póŏch/ *n* a sudden attempt by a group to overthrow a government

putt /pút/ *vti* hit a golf ball with a gentle tapping stroke —**putt** *n*

put-ter[1] /púttər/ *vi* pass time with trivial things

put-ter[2] /púttər/ *n* 1 a golf club for use on the green 2 a golfer who is putting

put-to /póŏ tŏ/ (*pl* **-ti** /-tèe/) *n* in art, a cherub

put-ty /púttee/ *n* 1 a paste used to fill holes in wood or to fix glass in window frames 2 a paste used as a finishing coat on plaster

Pu-tu-ma-yo /póotoo mĩyó/ tributary of the Amazon in NW South America. Length 1,000 mi./1,610 km.

put-up-on *adj* badly treated

puz-zle /púzz'l/ *vt* (**-zled, -zling**) confuse somebody by being hard to understand ■ *n* 1 a game or toy involving skill or intelligence 2 somebody or something difficult to understand —**puz-zle-ment** *n* ◊ See note at **problem**

□ **puzzle out** *vt* solve or understand something by reasoning or logic

□ **puzzle over** *vt* think hard about something confusing or complicated

puz·zler /púzzlər/ *n* something that is confusing or mystifying

PVC *n* a tough synthetic material. Use: flooring, piping, clothing. Full form **polyvinyl chloride**

Pvt., PVT *abbr* Private

p.w. *abbr* per week

pyg·my /pígmee/, **pig·my** *n̄* (*pl* **-mies**) 1 an offensive term for somebody of shorter than average height 2 **Pyg·my, Pig·my** a member of an African or Asian people of small stature ■ *adj* of a small breed *(sometimes offensive)*

py·ja·mas UK = pajamas

py·lon /pí lòn, pílən/ *n* 1 a metal tower supporting high-voltage cables 2 a tower at an airfield that marks the course for pilots to follow 3 a monumental gateway or pillar

Pyong·yang /pyáwng yàng/ capital of North Korea. Pop. 2,500,000 (1995).

py·or·rhe·a /pī ə reè ə/ *n* inflammation of the gums with a discharge of pus

pyr·a·mid /pírrəmid/ *n* 1 a huge ancient Egyptian stone tomb in the shape of a pyramid 2 a solid shape with a square base and sloping triangular sides 3 a system with a gradually expanding structure —**pyr·am·i·dal** /pi rámmidd'l/ *adj* —**pyr·a·mid·ic** /pírrə míddik/ *adj*

pyr·a·mid sell·ing *n* the sale of goods to a number of distributors, each of whom sells the goods to a number of other distributors, and so on

pyre /pīr/ *n* a pile of burning material, especially one on which a body is cremated

Pyr·e·nees /peérə neèz/ mountain range forming a natural boundary between France and Spain. Highest peak Pic d'Aneto 11,168 ft./3,404 m.

Py·rex /pí rèks/ *tdmk* a trademark for a type of glass that is resistant to heat and chemicals

py·rites /pī ríteez, pī rītis/, **py·rite** /pí rīt/ *n* a mineral with a metallic luster. Use: a source of iron and sulfur.

py·ro·ma·ni·a /pírō máynee ə, -máynyə/ *n* an uncontrollable desire to burn things —**py·ro·ma·ni·ac** *n*

py·ro·tech·nics /pírə tékniks/ *n* (+ *sing* or *pl verb*) 1 a fireworks display 2 any showy display —**py·ro·tech·nic** *adj* —**py·ro·tech·ni·cal** *adj*

Pyr·rhic vic·to·ry /pírrik-/ *n* a victory won at such great cost that it amounts to a defeat

ORIGIN The original **Pyrrhic victory** was won by Pyrrhus, king of the ancient Greek province of Epirus, who invaded Italy and defeated the Roman army at Heraclea (280 BC) and Asculum (279 BC), but sustained huge losses to his troops.

Py·tha·gor·as /pi thággərəss/ (582?–500? BC) Greek philosopher and mathematician —**Py·thag·o·re·an** /pi thàggə reè ən, pī-/ *adj*, *n*

py·thon /pí thòn/ *n* a large constricting snake

ORIGIN In Greek mythology, Python was a huge serpent or monster killed by the god Apollo near Delphi. The name **python** was adopted for a real snake in the mid-19C.

pyx /piks/, **pix** *n* 1 a box for Communion wafers 2 a container for coins at a mint

Q

q (*pl* **q's**), **Q** (*pl* **Q's** or **Qs**) *n* the 17th letter of the English alphabet

Q *abbr* queen

q. *abbr* 1 quart 2 quarter 3 quarto 4 question

Qad·da·fi /gə daáfee, kə-/ ♦ Gaddafi, Muammar al-

Q & A /kyoò ənd áy/ *abbr* question and answer

Qa·tar /kaà taàr, kə taàr/ country in E Arabia. Cap. Doha. Pop. 769,152 (2001). —**Qa·tar·i** /kə taàree/ *adj*, *n*

qb *abbr* quarterback

QC *abbr* Quebec

QED *adv* indicates that a particular fact is proof of the theory that has just been advanced

Q fe·ver *n* an infectious bacterial disease

Qing·dao /ching dów/ city in E China, on the Yellow Sea. Pop. 3,140,000 (1995).

Qi·qi·har /cheè chee haàr, -haà ər/ port in NE China. Pop. 1,520,000 (1995).

⚡**QL** *abbr* query language

Qom /kōm/, **Qum** /koòm/ city in west central Iran. Pop. 777,677 (1996).

qt. *abbr* quart

q.t. ◇ **on the q.t.** quietly and secretly *(infml)*

qua /kway, kwaa/ *prep* as *(fml)*

quack[1] /kwak/ *n* the harsh sound made by a duck

quack[2] /kwak/ *n* 1 a fake doctor 2 a fraud —**quack·er·y** *n*

ORIGIN Quack is a shortening of the now obsolete *quacksalver*, a word that was adopted from Dutch in the late 16C. Its elements mean "chatter, prattle" and "remedy" (the second Dutch element is related to English *salve*), so that *quacksalvers* were people who constantly proclaimed the virtues of their remedies and medicines. The shortened form **quack** is recorded from the mid-17C.

quad[1] /kwod/ *n* a quadruplet *(infml)*

quad² /kwod/ n a quadrangle (infml)

quad·ran·gle /kwód ràng g'l/ n 1 a four-sided shape 2 an open area surrounded by buildings —**quad·ran·gu·lar** /kwod ráng gyələr/ adj

quad·rant /kwóddrənt/ n 1 a quarter of the circumference of a circle 2 a quarter of the area of circle 3 a quarter of a surface 4 a device for measuring the angle of a star

quad·ra·phon·ic /kwòddrə fónnik/, **quad·ri·phon·ic** adj using a four-channel sound system —**quad·ra·phon·ics** n

quad·rat·ic e·qua·tion /kwo dràttik-/ n an equation containing squared terms

quadri- prefix four, fourth o quadrilateral

quad·ri·ceps /kwóddri sèps/ (pl same or **-cep·ses** /-sèpseez/) n a large muscle at the front of the thigh

quad·ri·lat·er·al /kwòddri láttərəl, -láttrəl/ n a four-sided figure ■ adj four-sided

qua·drille /kwo dríl, kwə-, kə-/ n 1 a square dance of French origin 2 the music for a quadrille

quad·ril·lion /kwo dríllyən/ (pl **-lions** or same).n the number written as one followed by 15 zeros —**quad·ril·lion** adj, pron —**quad·ril·lionth** adj, n

quad·ri·ple·gi·a /kwòddrə plèejee ə, -plèejə/ n inability to move all four limbs or the entire body below the neck —**quad·ri·pleg·ic** n, adj

quad·ru·ped /kwóddrə pèd/ n a four-footed animal ■ adj four-footed —**quad·ru·pe·dal** /kwo dróopəd'l/ adj

quad·ru·ple /kwo dróop'l/ vti (-**pled, -pling**) increase fourfold ■ adj 1 multiplied by four 2 with four parts ■ n a quantity that is four times as great as another

quad·ru·plet /kwo dróoplət/ n one of four babies born to the same mother at the same time

quaff /kwof/ vti drink alcohol quickly or heartily (literary or humorous) —**quaff** n

quag·mire /kwág mìr/ n 1 swamp 2 a difficult situation

qua·hog /kwáw hàwg, kwô hòg/, **qua·haug** n a thick-shelled edible clam

quail¹ /kwayl/ (pl same or **quails**) n 1 a small bird with mottled brown plumage 2 any small North American game bird

quail² /kwayl/ vi tremble or shrink with fear or apprehension ◊ See note at recoil

quaint /kwaynt/ adj attractively old-fashioned —**quaint·ly** adv —**quaint·ness** n

quake /kwayk/ vi (**quaked, quak·ing**) 1 tremble with fear 2 shake ■ n an earthquake (infml) —**quak·y** adj

Quak·er /kwáykər/ n a member of a Christian group who believe in God's direct approach to each person, without formal sacraments, ministry, or creeds —**Quak·er·ism** n —**Quak·er·ly** adj

qual·i·fi·ca·tion /kwòllifi káysh'n/ n 1 an attribute or skill that makes somebody suitable for a specific job or activity 2 an official requirement for eligibility, e.g., passing an examination (often pl) 3 the meeting of requirements for eligibility 4 something that modifies or restricts something

qual·i·fy /kwóllə fì/ (-**fied, -fies**) v 1 vti be or make suitable 2 vti have or give eligibility 3 vt limit or change 4 vt moderate 5 vt modify or restrict the meaning of —**qual·i·fied** adj —**qual·i·fi·er** n

qual·i·ta·tive /kwóllə tàytiv/ adj of quality —**qual·i·ta·tive·ly** adv

qual·i·ty /kwóllətee/ (pl **-ties**) n 1 a distinguishing characteristic 2 an essential property 3 the general standard of something 4 excellence

qual·i·ty con·trol n the process or job of controlling the quality of manufactured products

qual·i·ty of life n the degree of somebody's contentment with everyday life

qual·i·ty time n time devoted exclusively to somebody that strengthens mutual bonds

qualm /kwaam/ n a feeling of unease —**qualm·ish** adj

quan·da·ry /kwóndəree, -dree/ (pl **-ries**) n a dilemma

~~quandry~~ incorrect spelling of **quandary**

quan·ta plural of **quantum**

quan·ti·fi·er /kwónta fìr/ n a word such as "all" or "some" that indicates the range of things referred to

quan·ti·fy /kwónta fì/ (-**fied, -fies**) vt determine the number, amount, degree, or extent of something —**quan·ti·fi·a·ble** /kwòntə fì əb'l/ adj —**quan·ti·fi·ca·tion** /-fi káysh'n/ n

quan·ti·ta·tive /kwónta tàytiv/ adj 1 relating to quantity 2 measurable —**quan·ti·ta·tive·ly** adv

quan·ti·ty /kwóntatee/ (pl **-ties**) n 1 an amount or number of something 2 a large amount or number o imported in quantity 3 a mathematical entity with a numerical value

quan·tum /kwóntəm/ n (pl **-ta** /-tə/) 1 the smallest quantity of energy 2 the smallest unit used to measure a physical property ■ adj major —**quan·tal** adj

quan·tum leap n a sudden change or advance

quan·tum me·chan·ics n the study and analysis of the interactions of atoms and elementary particles based on quantum theory (+ sing or pl verb) —**quan·tum me·chan·i·cal** adj

quan·tum phys·ics n the branch of physics that uses quantum theory (+ sing verb)

quan·tum the·o·ry n a theory of elementary particles or energy states that assumes that energy is subdivided into discrete amounts and that matter possesses wave properties

quar·an·tine /kwáwrən tèen/ n 1 isolation to prevent spread of disease 2 a place of isolation ■ vt (-**tined, -tin·ing**) 1 isolate in order to avoid the spread of disease **2** detain for social or political reasons

ORIGIN A period of **quarantine** originally lasted for 40 days: the word goes back to the Latin word for "forty." The medical use entered English from Italian in the mid-17C, when ships with passengers or crew suspected of illness were prevented from entering Italian ports for 40 days.

quarentine incorrect spelling of **quarantine**

quark /kwawrk/ n an elementary particle with an electric charge that is believed to be a constituent of baryons and mesons

ORIGIN The **quark** was named by its discoverer, the US physicist Murray Gell-Mann. He associated its coinage with a nonsense word used in James Joyce's *Finnegan's Wake* (1939): "Three quarks for Muster Mark." The particle name **quark** first appeared in print in 1964.

quar·rel /kwáwrəl/ n **1** an angry dispute **2** a reason to argue ■ vi **1** argue vehemently **2** disagree

quar·rel·some /kwáwrəlsəm/ adj argumentative —**quar·rel·some·ness** n

quar·ry¹ /kwáwree/ (pl -ries) n **1** a hunted animal or bird **2** an object of pursuit

quar·ry² /kwáwree/ n (pl -ries) an excavation from which stone or other material is extracted ■ vti (-ried, -ries) obtain stone or other material from a quarry

quart /kwawrt/ n a unit of measurement equal to two pints

quar·ter /kwáwrtər/ n **1** one of four equal parts of something **2** a number equal to one divided by four **3** a period of three months **4** 25 cents, or a coin worth this amount **5** 15 minutes before or after the hour **6** also **Quar·ter** a district of a town **7** an unspecified person or group (often pl) ○ help from any quarter **8** mercy **9** an academic term ■ **quar·ters** npl accommodations, e.g., for military personnel or household employees ■ adj divided by four ■ vt **1** divide something into four **2** cut a human body into four following execution

quar·ter·back /kwáwrtər bàk/ n in football, the player who calls the signals for offensive plays

quar·ter·deck /kwáwrtər dèk/ n the rear part of the upper deck on a ship

quar·ter·fi·nal /kwáwrtər fìn'l, kwáwrtər fìn'l/ n a match before a semifinal —**quar·ter·fi·nal·ist** n

quar·ter horse n a strong horse bred for racing over short distances

quar·ter·ly /kwáwrtərlee/ adj happening every three months ■ adv every three months ■ n (pl -lies) a journal published every three months

quar·ter·mas·ter /kwáwrtər màstər/ n **1** an army officer with responsibility for food and equipment **2** a naval officer with duties including navigation and signals

quar·ter note n a musical note with one-quarter the time value of a whole note

quar·tet /kwawr tét/, **quar·tette** n **1** a group of four singers or musicians **2** a piece of music for a quartet

quar·tile /kwáwr tìl, kwáwrt'l/ n any one of the four equal groups into which a statistical sample can be divided

quar·to /kwáwrtō/ (pl -tos) n **1** a page size created by folding a standard sheet of printing paper in half twice, creating four leaves or eight pages **2** a book with quarto pages

quartz /kwawrts/ n a crystalline mineral. Use: electronics, gems.

qua·sar /kwáy zàar/ n a remote astronomical object that emits large amounts of energy

quash¹ /kwosh/ vt suppress

quash² /kwosh/ vt declare null and void

qua·si /kwáy zì, kwaázee/ adj almost but not quite

quasi- prefix as if, resembling ○ quasi-stellar object

qua·si-stel·lar ob·ject n ASTRON = quasar

qua·ter·cen·ten·a·ry /kwòttər sen ténnəree/ (pl -ries) n a 400th anniversary

Qua·ter·nar·y /kwóttər nèrree/ n the present period of geologic time, which began 1.8 million years ago —**Qua·ter·nar·y** adj

quat·rain /kwó tràyn/ n a four-line verse

quat·re·foil /káttrə fòyl/ n **1** a design or symbol in the shape of a flower with four petals or a leaf with four parts **2** an architectural ornament with four lobes

qua·ver /kwáyvər/ v **1** vi tremble slightly **2** vti say something in a trembling voice —**qua·ver** n —**qua·ver·ing·ly** adv

quay /kee/ n a waterside platform in a port or harbor

Quayle /kwayl/, **Dan** (b. 1947) vice president of the United States (1989–93)

quay·side /kée sìd/ n the edge of a quay

Que. abbr Quebec

quea·sy /kwéezee/ (-si·er, -si·est) adj **1** nauseated **2** easily nauseated **3** causing uneasiness **4** causing nausea —**quea·si·ly** adv —**quea·si·ness** n

Que·bec¹ /kwi bék, ki-/, **Qué·bec** /kay-/ **1** also **Qué·bec, Que·bec Ci·ty, Qué·bec Ci·ty** capital of Quebec Province, Canada,. Pop. 167,264 (1996). **2** province in E Canada. Cap. Quebec. Pop. 7,372,448 (2000). —**Que·bec·er** n

Que·bec² /kwə bék, kə-, kay-/ n a communications code word for the letter "Q"

Qué·bé·cois /kày be kwaá/, **Qué·be·cois, Que·be·cois** adj of Quebec ■ n (pl same) somebody from Quebec

Quech·ua /kéchwə/ (pl same or -uas) n **1** a member of a Native South American people living in the Andes **2** the language of the Quechua people —**Quech·ua** adj

queen /kween/ n **1** a female ruler **2** the wife or widow of a king **3** a playing card with a picture of a queen on it **4** a woman, place, or thing admired above all others **5** an egg-laying bee, ant, or termite **6** the most powerful chess piece —**queen·li·ness** n —**queen·ly** adj

queen bee n a fertile female bee

queen moth·er n a monarch's widowed mother

Queens /kweenz/ borough of New York City, on W Long Island. Pop. 1,951,598 (1990).

Queen's Eng·lish n standard British English

queen-size adj larger than standard

queer /kweer/ adj (dated) **1** strange or unusual **2** considered eccentric **3** an offensive term meaning gay ■ n an offensive term for a gay man (insult) ■ vt thwart or compromise —**queer·ly** adv —**queer·ness** n

quell /kwel/ vt **1** bring to an end, usually by force **2** allay a feeling

quench /kwench/ vt **1** satisfy a thirst or a desire **2** extinguish a fire **3** subdue a feeling —**quench·less** adj

quer·u·lous /kwérrələss/ adj **1** tending to complain **2** whining —**quer·u·lous·ly** adv

que·ry /kweeree/ n (pl **-ries**) **1** a question **2** a doubt ■ vt (**-ried, -ries**) **1** express doubts about something **2** ask a question

quest /kwest/ n **1** a search **2** an adventurous expedition ■ vti go in search of something (literary) —**quest·ing·ly** adv

ques·tion /kwéschən/ n **1** a written or spoken inquiry **2** a doubt **3** a matter that is the subject of discussion **4** an examination problem ■ vt **1** interrogate somebody **2** raise doubts about something —**ques·tion·er** n —**ques·tion·ing** adj —**ques·tion·ing·ly** adv ◊ **beg the question** take for granted the very point that needs to be proved ◊ **be out of the question** be impossible or unacceptable ◊ **call into question** raise doubts about ◊ **in question** under discussion or being dealt with

---
SYNONYMS question, quiz, interrogate, grill
CORE MEANING: ask for information

---

ques·tion·a·ble /kwéschənəb'l/ adj **1** open to doubt or disagreement **2** not respectable or morally acceptable o questionable motives —**ques·tion·a·bly** adv

~~questionaire~~ incorrect spelling of **questionnaire**

ques·tion mark n the punctuation mark (?) used at the end of a direct question

ques·tion·naire /kwéschə náir/ n a list of questions used to gather information

quet·zal /ket sáal/ n (pl **-zals** or **-za·les** /-sáa làyz/) n **1** a bird with bright green and red plumage **2** the main unit of Guatemalan currency

ʃ queue /kyoo/ n a set of computer tasks waiting to be performed ■ vt (**queued, queu·ing** or **queue·ing**) add a job to a computer's list of tasks

quib·ble /kwíbb'l/ vi (**-bled, -bling**) make trivial objections —**quib·ble** n —**quib·bling·ly** adv

quiche /keesh/ n a pie filled with a mixture of eggs and various meat or vegetable ingredients

quick /kwik/ adj **1** acting fast **2** showing alertness or sharp perception **3** nimble **4** done without delay **5** brief ■ n **1** the flesh under a nail **2** somebody's deepest feelings or most private emotions ■ adv fast (infml) —**quick·ly** adv —**quick·ness** n ◊ **quick and dirty** hastily produced to meet an immediate or pressing need (infml) ◊ See note at **intelligent**

quick·en /kwíkən/ v **1** vti make or become faster **2** vti stimulate or be stimulated **3** vi begin to come to life

quick·ie /kwíkee/ n an activity done hurriedly, especially an act of sex (infml)

quick·lime /kwík lìm/ n calcium oxide

quick·sand /kwík sànd/ n **1** a deep mass of wet sand that sucks down any heavy object on its surface **2** a dangerous situation

quick·sil·ver /kwík sìlvər/ n mercury (literary) ■ adj changing unpredictably

quick·step /kwík stèp/ n **1** a fast marching step **2** a fast ballroom dance **3** the music for a quickstep

quick-tem·pered adj easily angered —**quick-tem·pered·ness** n

quick-wit·ted adj able to think quickly —**quick-wit·ted·ly** adv —**quick-wit·ted·ness** n

quid /kwid/ n a piece of chewing tobacco

quid pro quo /kwìd prō kwó/ (pl **quid pro quos**) n **1** something done in exchange **2** the act of returning a favor

qui·es·cent /kwee éss'nt/ adj inactive —**qui·es·cence** n

qui·et /kwí ət/ adj **1** making little noise **2** peaceful or relaxing **3** done in private **4** free from trouble **5** not showy ■ n the absence of noise ■ vti make or become quiet —**qui·et·ly** adv —**qui·et·ness** n ◊ See note at **silent**

SPELLCHECK Do not confuse the spelling of **quiet** and **quite** ("somewhat"), which sound similar.

---

qui·et·ism /kwí ə tìzzəm/ n a form of Christian mysticism —**qui·et·ist** adj, n

qui·e·tude /kwí ə tòod/ n calmness or tranquillity (literary)

qui·e·tus /kwī eetəss/ n (literary) **1** a release from a debt or duty **2** death

quill /kwil/ n **1** a large feather **2** a pen made from the shaft of a feather **3** a spine on the body of a porcupine or similar animal

quilt /kwilt/ *n* a thick bed cover made of two layers of fabric stitched together ∎ *vt* make something by sewing two layers of fabric together with a filling in between —**quilt·ing** *n*

quince /kwins/ *n* 1 a pear-shaped fruit that is edible only when cooked. Use: preserves. 2 a tree that produces quinces

ORIGIN The **quince** takes its name from Cydonia (now Khania), a port in NW Crete from which the fruit was exported.

qui·nine /kwī nī́n/ *n* a drug made from cinchona bark. Use: treatment of malaria.

quint /kwint/ *n* a quintuplet (*infml*)

quin·tal /kwíntəl/ *n* 1 a metric unit of weight equal to 100 kg 2 a hundredweight

quin·tes·sence /kwin téss'nss/ *n* 1 the embodiment of something 2 the purest extract of a substance that contains all its properties —**quin·tes·sen·tial** /kwíntə sénsh'l/ *adj*

quin·tet /kwin tét/, **quin·tette** /-/ *n* 1 a group of five singers or musicians 2 a piece of music for a quintet

quin·tu·plet /kwin túpplət, -toõplət/ *n* one of five babies born to the same mother at the same time

quip /kwip/ *n* a witticism ∎ *vti* (**quipped, quip·ping**) say something wittily

quire /kwīr/ *n* a set of 24 or 25 sheets of paper, equal to one twentieth of a ream

quirk /kwurk/ *n* 1 an odd turn of events 2 an odd mannerism —**quirk·i·ly** *adv* —**quirk·i·ness** *n* —**quirk·y** *adj*

quis·ling /kwízling/ *n* a traitor

ORIGIN The original **quisling** was Vidkun Quisling, a Norwegian politician who from 1933 led the National Union Party, the Norwegian fascist party. (Quisling was not his real name—he was originally Abraham Lauritz Jonsson.) When the Germans invaded Norway in 1940 he gave them active support, urging his fellow Norwegians not to resist them, and in 1942 he was installed by Hitler as a puppet premier. In 1945 he was shot for treason.

quit /kwit/ (**quit** *or* **quit·ted, quit·ting**) *v* 1 *vti* resign or give up a job 2 *vti* stop doing something 3 *vt* leave a place (*archaic*)

quite /kwīt/ *adv* 1 to some degree, but not greatly ○ *The film was quite good, but I wouldn't bother seeing it again.* 2 entirely or altogether ○ *not quite as bad as all that* 3 very or really 4 adds emphasis ○ *That was quite a party!* ◊ See note at **quiet**

Qui·to /keétō/ capital of Ecuador. Pop. 1,444,363 (1996).

quits /kwits/ *adj* on even terms, especially after repayment or retaliation (*infml*)

quit·tance /kwítt'nss/ *n* exemption

quit·ter /kwíttər/ *n* somebody who gives up easily (*infml*)

quiv·er¹ /kwívvər/ *vi* tremble —**quiv·er** *n* —**quiv·er·y** *adj*

quiv·er² /kwívvər/ *n* 1 a case for arrows 2 the arrows in a quiver

quix·ot·ic /kwik sóttik/ *adj* romantic and impractical —**quix·ot·i·cal·ly** *adv*

ORIGIN The original **quixotic** person was Don Quixote, the hero of a romance (1605–15) by the Spanish writer Miguel de Cervantes.

quiz /kwiz/ *n* a short test ∎ *vt* (**quizzed, quiz·zing**) 1 test a student or class 2 interrogate ◊ See note at **question**

quizes incorrect spelling of **quizzes**

quiz·mas·ter /kwíz màstər/ *n* the emcee on a quiz show

quiz·zi·cal /kwízzik'l/ *adj* questioning —**quiz·zi·cal·ly** *adv*

Qum ▸ **Qom**

quoits /kwoyts, koyts/ *n* a game in which rings are thrown over short posts (+ *sing verb*)

quon·dam /kwóndəm, -dàm/ *adj* former (*literary*)

quo·rum /kwáwrəm/ *n* the minimum number of people required to be present at a meeting for its business to be valid

quo·ta /kwốtə/ *n* 1 a proportional share 2 a maximum permitted number or amount

quot·a·ble /kwốtəb'l/ *adj* 1 worth quoting 2 officially able to be quoted in a publication

quo·ta·tion /kwō táysh'n/ *n* 1 a piece of quoted speech or writing 2 the act of quoting what somebody has said or written 3 an estimate of the cost of proposed work 4 the current price of a stock —**quo·ta·tion·al** *adj*

quo·ta·tion mark *n* one of a pair of punctuation marks (" ") used at the beginning and end of a direct quotation

quote /kwốt/ *vti* (**quot·ed, quot·ing**) 1 repeat somebody's exact words 2 refer to something in support of an argument 3 give an estimate of the cost of proposed work ∎ *n* 1 a quotation (*infml*) 2 a quotation mark (*often pl*) 3 an estimate for work

quoth /kwōth/ *vt* said (*literary*)

quo·tid·i·an /kwō tíddee ən/ *adj* (*fml*) 1 commonplace 2 daily

quo·tient /kwốsh'nt/ *n* the number that results from the division of one number by another

Qur'an, Qur-an *n* = **Koran**

✦ **QWERTY key·board** /kwúrtee-/ *n* a standard computer keyboard

R

r¹ (*pl* **r's**), **R** (*pl* **R's** *or* **Rs**) *n* the 18th letter of the English alphabet ◊ **the three R's** the basic skills of reading, writing, and arithmetic

r² *symbol* **1** radius **2** resistance

R¹ (*pl* **R's** *or* **Rs**) *n* movie rating indicating that a movie can be seen by children under 17 only if accompanied by an adult. Full form **restricted**

R² *symbol* **1** radical **2** Réaumur scale **3** resistance

R³ *abbr* **1** radius **2** Republican **3** registered trademark **4** rook **5** run

r. *abbr* right

R. *abbr* **1** rabbi **2** rector **3** river

Ra *symbol* radium

Ra·bat /rə baàt, raa-/ capital of Morocco. Pop. 1,385,872 (1994).

rab·bet /rábbət/ *n* a groove cut for a wood joint ■ *vt* **1** cut a rabbet in something **2** join pieces with a rabbet

rab·bi /rá bī/ *n* **1** the leader of a Jewish congregation or synagogue **2** a Jewish scholar —**rab·bi·ni·cal** /rə bínnik'l/ *adj*

rab·bin·ate /rábbə nàyt, -nət/ *n* **1** the post or term of office of a rabbi **2** rabbis collectively

rab·bit /rábbit/ (*pl* **-bits** *or* **same**) *n* **1** a small burrowing mammal with long ears and a short tail **2** a hare (*infml*) **3** the fur of a rabbit

rab·bit ears *npl* an antenna on top of a television

rab·bit punch *n* a blow to the back of the neck —**rab·bit-punch** *vt*

rab·ble /rább'l/ *n* **1** an unruly crowd **2** an offensive term for ordinary people (*insult*; + *sing or pl verb*)

rab·ble-rous·er *n* an agitator (*disapproving*) —**rab·ble-rous·ing** *n*, *adj*

Ra·be·lais /rábbə lày, ràbbə láy/, **François** (1493?–1553) French humanist and writer —**Ra·be·lai·si·an** /ràbbə láyzee ən, -láyzh'n/ *adj*, *n*

Ra·bi /ráabee/, **Ra·bi·a** /rə bee ə/ *n* either the 3rd or the 4th month of the Islamic calendar

rab·id /rábbid/ *adj* **1** having rabies **2** fanatical (*disapproving*) —**ra·bid·i·ty** /rə bíddətee/ *n* —**rab·id·ly** *adv*

ra·bies /ráy beèz/ *n* a severe viral disease that affects the nervous system and is transmitted in the saliva of an infected animal

Ra·bin /raa beén/, **Yitzhak** (1922–95) Israeli prime minister (1974–77 and 1992–95)

rac·coon /ra koón/ (*pl* **-coons** *or* **same**), **ra·coon** *n* **1** a small ring-tailed mammal **2** the fur of a raccoon

race¹ *n* **1** a contest of speed **2** any competitive effort between rivals ■ **rac·es** *npl* horse-races or horseracing ■ *v* (**raced, rac·ing**) **1** *vti* compete against somebody in a race **2** *vi* move very fast **3** *vi* beat fast (*refers to the heart*) **4** *vti* run or make an engine run at high speed —**rac·er** *n* —**rac·ing** *n*

race² *n* **1** any of the groups into which human beings are divided on the basis of physical characteristics **2** the fact of belonging to a particular race

race·car /ráyss kaàr/ *n* a car used for racing

race card ◊ **play the race card** use the issue of race, e.g., in legal argumentation or in a debate, to win an advantage or make a point (*infml*)

race·course /ráyss kàwrss/ *n* a track for cars or runners

race·horse /ráyss hàwrss/ *n* a horse bred for participating in races

ra·ceme /ray seém, rə-/ *n* a type of flower cluster that has flowers along a long main stem

race·track /ráyss tràk/ *n* a track for holding races

AKG London

Sergey Rachmaninoff

Rach·ma·ni·noff /raak maànnə nàwf/, **Sergey** (1873–1943) Russian-born composer and pianist

ra·cial /ráysh'l/ *adj* **1** existing between races ◊ *racial harmony* **2** of a particular race of people —**ra·cial·ly** *adv*

ra·cial pro·fil·ing *n* the alleged tendency of some police officers to attribute criminal intentions to members of particular ethnic groups and to stop and question them in disproportionate numbers without probable cause

Ra·cine /rə seén/, **Jean Baptiste** (1639–99) French playwright

ra·cism /ráy sìzzəm/ *n* **1** prejudice against or animosity toward people of other races **2** the belief that some races of people are inherently superior —**rac·ist** *adj*, *n*

rack¹ *n* **1** a framework for holding things **2** a toothed bar that engages the teeth of a pinion or gear to turn rotary motion into linear motion **3** a former instrument of torture that stretched a person's body **4** a frame for positioning the balls in a cue game, or the balls so positioned ■ *vt* **1** cause somebody great pain **2** stretch or strain something violently ◊ *racked my brain* **3** torture somebody on a rack ◊ **off the rack** ready to wear

ORIGIN Rack "framework" was adopted from Dutch in the 14C (the cut of meat **rack** may represent a development of this). **Rack** "ruin" is a late-16C variant of *wrack* in the same sense. *Wrack* originally meant "vengeance," and is related to *wreak*.

□ **rack up** *vt* accumulate something such as points *(infml)*

rack[2] *n* a cut of meat consisting of one or both sides of the front ribs

rack[3] ◊ **go to rack and ruin** deteriorate into a state of neglect or ruin

rack·et[1] /rákət/, **rack·quet** *n* **1** a bat with a network of strings, used in sports such as tennis and badminton **2** a snowshoe in the shape of a racket

rack·et[2] *n* **1** a loud disturbing noise **2** an illegal scheme

rack·et·eer /rákə teér/ *n* somebody who profits from illegal activities —**rack·et·eer** *vi* —**rack·et·eer·ing** *n*

rack·ets /rákəts/, **rac·quets** *n* an indoor sport similar to squash in which long-handled rackets are used *(+ sing verb)*

rac·on·teur /rà kon túr/ *n* somebody who tells entertaining stories

ra·coon *n* zool = **raccoon**

rac·quet *n* RACKET GAMES, LEISURE = **racket**[1]

rac·quet·ball /rákət báwl/ *n* an indoor sport similar to squash in which short-handled rackets are used

rac·y /ráyssee/ (-i-er, -i-est) *adj* **1** mildly indecent **2** pungent —**rac·i·ly** *adv* —**rac·i·ness** *n*

ra·dar /ráy daàr/ *n* **1** an object-locating system that uses reflected radio waves **2** a piece of object-locating equipment ◊ **be on somebody's radar screen** be a focal point of interest *(infml)*

ra·dar gun *n* handheld radar device for monitoring motorists' speed

ra·dar trap *n* a police speed trap

rad·dled /rádd'ld/ *adj* haggard

ra·di·al /ráydee əl/ *adj* **1** running from the center outward **2** of a radius ■ *n* a tire in which the foundation fabric cords run at right angles to the circumference —**ra·di·al·ly** *adv*

ra·di·an /ráydee ən/ *n* (*symbol* **rad**) a unit of angular measurement equivalent to the angle between two radii that enclose a section of the circumference of a circle equal in length to the length of the radius

ra·di·ant /ráydee ənt/ *adj* **1** showing happiness, energy, or good health **2** shining with bright or glowing light **3** describes heat, light, or energy emitted in the form of waves or rays **4** emitting radiant energy —**ra·di·ance** *n* —**ra·di·ant·ly** *adv*

ra·di·ate *vti* /ráydee àyt/ (-at-ed, -at-ing) **1** send out energy, or be sent out, as rays or waves **2** show a feeling or quality clearly, or be shown clearly **3** spread or cause to spread from the center ■ *adj* /ráydee ət/ with parts radiating from the center —**ra·di·a·tive** *adj*

ra·di·a·tion /ráydee áysh'n/ *n* **1** energy particles emitted by substances whose atoms are not stable and are spontaneously decaying **2** energy emitted in the form of rays

or waves **3** the emission of energy in the form of waves **4** radiotherapy

ra·di·a·tion sick·ness *n* a medical condition caused by overexposure to radiation

ra·di·a·tor /ráydee àytər/ *n* **1** a room heater, especially one connected to a central boiler **2** an engine-cooling device

rad·i·cal /ráddik'l/ *adj* **1** basic **2** far-reaching **3** favoring major changes ■ *n* **1** somebody with radical views **2** a mathematical root of another number or quantity —**rad·i·cal·ly** *adv* —**rad·i·cal·ness** *n*

rad·i·cal·ism /ráddik'l 'izzəm/ *n* political policies or attitudes that advocate major changes

rad·i·cal·ize /ráddik'l 'iz/ (-ized, -iz·ing) *vti* **1** change fundamentally **2** make or become politically radical —**rad·i·cal·i·za·tion** /ràddik'li záysh'n/ *n*

rad·i·cal sign *n* the mathematical symbol √ indicating a square root or higher root

ra·dic·chi·o /rə deékee ò, raa-/ (*pl* -os) *n* a reddish purple variety of chicory

ra·di·o /ráydee ò/ *n* **1** the use of electromagnetic waves for communication **2** a device that receives sound broadcasts **3** sound broadcasts transmitted by means of radio waves ■ *vti* (-oed, -o·ing, -os) communicate with somebody by radio

radio- *prefix* **1** radiation o *radioactive* **2** radio o *radiotelephone*

ra·di·o·ac·tive /ráydee ò áktiv/ *adj* **1** emitting radiation **2** of or using radioactive substances —**ra·di·o·ac·tive·ly** *adv*

ra·di·o·ac·tiv·i·ty /ráydee ò ak tívvətee/ *n* **1** the radioactive nature of a substance **2** radiation

ra·di·o as·tron·o·my *n* the branch of astronomy dealing with radio waves from space —**ra·di·o as·tron·o·mer** *n*

⚡ **ra·di·o but·ton** *n* a symbol on a computer screen that represents one of a set of options from which a choice must be made

ra·di·o·car·bon dat·ing *n* GEOL = **carbon dating**

ra·di·o·con·trolled *adj* remotely controlled using radio signals

ra·di·o·gram /ráydee ò gràm/ *n* a telegram

ra·di·o·graph /ráydee ò gràf/ *n* a photograph taken using radiation other than visible light, especially X-rays ■ *vt* take a radiograph of —**ra·di·og·ra·pher** /ráydee óggrəfər/ *n* —**ra·di·o·graph·ic** /-ò gráffik/ *adj* —**ra·di·og·ra·phy** /-óggrəfee/ *n*

ra·di·ol·o·gy /ráydee ólləjee/ *n* **1** the branch of medicine that uses X-rays **2** the science of radiation and radioactive substances —**ra·di·o·log·i·cal** /ráydee ə lójək'l/ *adj* —**ra·di·ol·o·gist** *n*

ra·di·o·tel·e·phone /ráydee ò téllə fòn/ *n* a telephone that uses radio waves —**ra·di·o·te·leph·o·ny** /-tə léffənee/ *n*

ra·di·o tel·e·scope n an instrument for studying radio waves emitted by astronomical objects

ra·di·o·ther·a·py /ráydee ō thérrəpee/ n medical treatment using radiation —**ra·di·o·ther·a·peu·tic** /-thèrrə pyóotik/ adj —**ra·di·o·ther·a·pist** n

ra·di·o wave n an electromagnetic wave of a frequency between 10 kHz and 300,000 MHz

rad·ish /ráddish/ n 1 an edible red or white root, eaten raw 2 a plant that produces radishes

Rad·i·sic /ráddisich/, Zivko (b. 1936) Serb representative of the presidency of Bosnia and Herzegovina (1998–) which rotates between a Serb, a Bosnian Muslim and a Croat

ra·di·um /ráydee əm/ n (symbol Ra) a white radioactive chemical element. Use: luminous coatings, treatment of cancer.

ra·di·us /ráydee əss/ (pl -i /-dee ī/ or -us·es) n 1 (symbol r) a line from the center of a circle to its edge 2 (symbol r) the length of a radius 3 the area of a circle with a particular radius ◊ all the houses within a radius of two miles 4 the range of somebody's effectiveness or influence 5 the shorter and thicker of the two bones in the human forearm

ra·don /ráy dón/ n (symbol Rn) a gaseous radioactive element. Use: radiotherapy.

RAF, R.A.F. abbr Royal Air Force

raf·fi·a /ráffee ə/ n 1 a fiber taken from the leaves of a palm tree. Use: mats, baskets. 2 also **raf·fi·a palm** a tree that produces raffia

raff·ish /ráffish/ adj 1 charmingly unconventional or disreputable 2 showy

raf·fle /ráff'l/ n a lottery with objects rather than money as prizes

raft[1] n 1 a flat floating structure used for transportation or as a platform 2 an inflatable boat or mat ■ vi travel on a raft —**raft·ing** n

raft[2] n a large number or amount (infml)

raf·ter /ráftər/ n a sloping timber that supports a roof —**raf·tered** adj

rag[1] n 1 a small piece of scrap cloth 2 an inferior newspaper (infml) ■ **rags** npl worn-out clothes

rag[2] (ragged, rag·ging) v 1 vti tease or taunt somebody (dated) 2 vt scold persistently —**rag·ging** n

ra·ga /raàgə/ n a type of classical South Asian music

rag·a·muf·fin /rággə mùffən/ n a neglected child dressed in tattered clothes (dated)

ORIGIN Ragamuffin is probably formed from rag and a second element that may just be fanciful or may be based on the Dutch word meaning "mitten" that gave us muff.

rag·bag /rág bàg/ n a miscellany (infml)

rag doll n a stuffed cloth doll

rage n 1 extreme anger 2 the object of a short-lived fashion or enthusiasm 3 force or intensity ■ vi (raged, rag·ing) 1 act with or feel rage 2 occur with violence ◊ See note at anger

~~rageing~~ incorrect spelling of **raging**

rag·ged /rággəd/ adj 1 frayed or torn 2 with an uneven edge or surface 3 of varying quality 4 wearing rags 5 unkempt —**rag·ged·ly** adv —**rag·ged·ness** n

rag·ged·y /rággədee/ adj (infml) 1 tattered 2 rough or uneven

rag·ing /ráyjing/ adj 1 very angry 2 very severe or painful

rag·lan /rágglən/ adj 1 describes a sleeve that extends to the collar 2 having raglan sleeves ■ n a garment with raglan sleeves

rag·man /rág màn, rágmən/ (pl -men /-mèn, -mən/) n a dealer in rags

ra·gout /ra góo/ n stew

rag·pick·er /rág pìkər/ n a rag and junk dealer

rag·tag /rág tàg/ adj 1 mixed and often of dubious quality 2 messy

rag·time /rág tìm/ n a form of syncopated popular music of the early 20C

rag·weed /rág wèed/ n a wild plant with small green flowers that produce large amounts of pollen

rag·wort /rág wùrt, -wàwrt/ n a wild plant with yellow flowers like daisies

raid n 1 a sudden attack made in an attempt to seize or destroy something 2 an attempt to lure employees, members, or clients away from a competing organization ■ v 1 vti make a raid on a place 2 vt steal 3 vt lure somebody away —**raid·er** n

ORIGIN Raid is actually a Scottish variant of road. The forms are related to ride, and "riding with hostile intent" and "raid" were early senses of road. The use had effectively died out when Sir Walter Scott revived raid in the early 19C, and its existence has never since looked in danger.

rail[1] n 1 a long piece of wood or metal 2 a fence or railing (often pl) 3 a steel bar that forms a railroad track ◊ **go off the rails** begin to go wrong and lose direction

rail[2] vi complain bitterly

rail[3] (pl **rails** or same) n a wading bird with short wings and long toes

rail·ing /ráyling/ n a structure with rails and posts

rail·ler·y /ráyləree/ (pl -ies) n 1 good-humored teasing 2 a joking remark

rail·road /ráyl ròd/ n 1 a track made of rails for trains to run on 2 a transportation system that consists of trains ■ vt 1 force a decision through quickly without discussion 2 force somebody to act hastily (infml) —**rail·road·er** n

rail·road flat *n* an apartment with rooms in a straight line

rail·way /ráyl wày/ *n* a light rail system —**rail·way·man** *n*

rai·ment /ráymənt/ *n* clothes *(literary)*

rain /rayn/ *n* condensed water falling from clouds ■ **rains** *npl* a period of rainy weather ■ *v* 1 *vi* drop rain 2 *vti* come or deliver in great numbers

> **SPELLCHECK** Do not confuse the spelling of **rain**, **reign** ("of a monarch"), or **rein** ("strap for guiding a horse"), which sound similar.

rain·bow /ráyn bò/ *n* an arc of light in the sky that has been separated into its constituent colors by moisture ■ *adj* 1 with varied colors 2 containing many different elements

rain check *n* 1 a ticket for a rescheduled event 2 a guarantee of a future offer

rain·coat /ráyn kòt/ *n* a waterproof coat

rain date *n* a date that an event will be rescheduled to if rain forces cancellation

rain·fall /ráyn fàwl/ *n* 1 the amount of rain that falls in a particular period 2 the occurrence of rain

rain for·est *n* a thick tropical forest

rain gauge *n* a rain-measurement device

Rai·nier III /ray neér, rə nyáy/ prince of Monaco (1949–)

Rai·nier, Mt. /rə neér, ray-/ dormant volcano in west central Washington, the highest peak in the Cascade Range. Height 14,410 ft./4,392 m.

rain·mak·er /ráyn màykər/ *n* 1 somebody who achieves outstanding results in business or politics *(infml)* 2 somebody who causes or is believed to cause rain —**rain·mak·ing** *n*

rain·storm /ráyn stàwrm/ *n* a storm with rain

rain·wa·ter /ráyn wàwtər/ *n* water that has fallen as rain

rain·y /ráynee/ (-i-er, -i-est) *adj* with a lot of rain —**rain·i·ness** *n*

raise /rayz/ *v* (raised, rais·ing) 1 *vt* move something higher 2 *vt* act as a parent or guardian to a child ○ *raised by relatives* 3 *vt* make something larger or greater 4 *vt* grow crops or breed animals 5 *vt* erect something 6 *vt* offer something for consideration ○ *raised another point* 7 *vt* collect something together ○ *raising money for charity* 8 *vti* increase a bet or bid 9 *vt* contact somebody by radio or telephone 10 *vt* end a siege 11 *vt* improve something ○ *raised his spirits* 12 *vt* cause something to appear, occur, or arise ■ *n* 1 *US, Can, Aus* a pay increase 2 the act of increasing something —**rais·er** *n*

raised /rayzd/ *adj* with projecting surface

rai·sin /ráyz'n/ *n* a dried grape

rai·son d'ê·tre /rày zawn déttrə/ (*pl* **rai·sons d'ê·tre** /rày zawn-/) *n* a reason for living or a justification for existing

Raj /raaj/ *n* the period of British rule in South Asia

Raj·ab /rújjəb/ *n* the 7th month of the year in the Islamic calendar

ra·jah /rààjə/, **ra·ja** *n* a Hindu ruler

rake¹ *n* a long-handled gardening tool with a toothed head ■ *v* (raked, rak·ing) 1 *vt* move, clear, or smooth with a rake 2 *vti* search through

> **ORIGIN Rake** the tool is an old word of Germanic origin. **Rake** is recorded from the early 17C, but its origins are unknown. The immoral **rake** was originally a *rakehell*. The longer form is recorded from the mid-16C, and **rake** itself from the mid-17C.

□ **rake in** *vt* gather in large quantities *(infml)*
□ **rake up** or **o·ver** *vt* mention something from the past *(infml)*

rake² *n* an immoral seeker of pleasure

rake³ *n* 1 a slant or slope 2 the angle of a wing or propeller ■ *vti* (raked, rak·ing) angle or be angled

rake-off *n* a share *(infml)*

rak·ish /ráykish/ *adj* 1 dashingly stylish 2 streamlined in a way that suggests speed —**rak·ish·ness** *n*

Ra·leigh /ráwlee, ràà-/ capital of North Carolina. Pop. 259,423 (1998).

Ra·leigh, Sir Walter (1554–1618) English navigator and writer

ral·ly /rállee/ *n* (*pl* -lies) 1 a recovery or improvement 2 a large gathering of people 3 a renewed buying of stocks 4 an automobile race on public or rough roads 5 an exchange of shots in a racket sport ■ *v* (-lied, -lies) 1 *vti* gather together for a purpose 2 *vti* revive after a setback or illness 3 *vti* increase in value 4 *vi* exchange shots in a racket sport 5 *vti* reorganize after a setback —**ral·li·er** *n*

ram *n* 1 a male sheep 2 a battering or crushing device 3 **Ram** the zodiacal sign Aries ■ *v* (rammed, ram·ming) 1 *vti* strike horizontally with great force 2 *vt* collide with deliberately 3 *vt* force into place

⚡ RAM /ram/ *n* random-access memory

Ra·ma /ràámə/ *n* an incarnation of the Hindu god Vishnu

Ram·a·dan /ràámə dààn/ *n* the 9th month of the year in the Islamic calendar, during which Muslims fast between dawn and dusk

ram·ble /rámb'l/ *vi* (-bled, -bling) 1 talk or write aimlessly and at length 2 walk for pleasure, usually in the countryside 3 follow a changing course 4 grow in a random way ■ *n* a walk for pleasure, usually in the countryside —**ram·bler** *n* —**ram·bling** *adj, n* —**ram·bling·ly** *adv*

ram·bunc·tious /ram búngkshəss/ *adj* unruly —**ram·bunc·tious·ly** *adv*

ram·e·kin /rámməkin/, **ram·e·quin** *n* 1 a small

baking dish for a single serving of food **2** a food served in a ramekin

ra·men /ráymən/ *n* a Japanese dish of long thin noodles in soup or stock

Ram·e·ses II /rámmə sèez/, **Ram·ses II** /rám sèez/ (*fl* 13C BC) Egyptian pharaoh

ram·ie /rámmee, ráymee/ *n* fiber from the bark of an Asian bush. Use: textiles, rope.

ram·i·fi·ca·tion /rámməfə káysh'n/ *n* **1** a complicating result **2** the process of dividing into branches or sections

ram·i·fy /rámmə fì/ (-fied, -fies) *vi* **1** divide into branches or sections **2** have complicating results

ramp *n* a sloping path or surface ■ *vt* build with a slope —**ramped** *adj*

□ **ramp up** *vt* increase sharply

ram·page *n* /rám pàyj/ an outburst of violent or riotous behavior ■ *vi* /rám pàyj, ram páyj/ (-paged, -pag·ing) act violently or riotously —**ram·pag·ing** *adj*

ram·pant /rámpənt/ *adj* **1** occurring or growing unchecked **2** describes a heraldic animal on its hind legs —**ram·pan·cy** *n* —**ram·pant·ly** *adv*

ram·part /rám pàart/ *n* a fortified embankment, often with a low wall on top

ram·rod /rám ròd/ *n* **1** a rod for loading a charge into a gun or cannon **2** a cleaning rod for a gun ■ *adv* emphasizes rigidity or uprightness ○ *ramrod straight*

Ram·say /rámzee/, **Sir William** (1852–1916) British chemist. He discovered the noble gases.

ram·shack·le /rám shàk'l/ *adj* badly built or run-down

ORIGIN **Ramshackle** ultimately derives from *ransack*. A derivative *ransackle* was formed from this, and in the late 17C its past participle *ransackled* was altered to *ramsackled* and used to mean "disorderly." **Ramshackle** appears in dialect use with the same sense in the early 19C. The modern meaning developed in the mid-19C.

ran past tense of **run**

ranch *n* **1** a livestock farm on rangeland **2** *also* **ranch house** a house on a ranch **3** *also* **ranch house** a single-story house ■ *v* **1** *vi* work on a ranch **2** *vt* raise animals on a ranch —**ranch·ing** *n*

ranch dress·ing *n* creamy salad dressing

ranch·er /ránchər/ *n* **1** a ranch owner **2** a single-story house

ran·che·ra /ran chérrə/ *n* a traditional Mexican ballad featuring guitars and vocals

Ran·cho Cu·ca·mon·ga /ránchō kòokə múng gə/ city in SW California. Pop. 120,047 (1998).

ran·cid /ránsəd/ *adj* with the disagreeable taste or smell of decomposing fats or oils —**ran·cid·i·ty** /ran síddətee/ *n*

ran·cor /rángkər/ *n* deep-seated ill-will or resentment —**ran·cor·ous** *adj* —**ran·cor·ous·ly** *adv*

rand (*pl* same) *n* the main unit of South African currency

r & b, R & B *abbr* rhythm and blues

R & D *abbr* research and development

Ran·dolph /rán dòlf/, **A. Philip** (1889–1979) US labor leader

ran·dom /rándəm/ *adj* **1** done or occurring without a pattern **2** not uniform or regular **3** of a set in which all the members have the same probability of occurrence ○ *a random sampling* —**ran·dom·ly** *adv* —**ran·dom·ness** *n* ◇ **at random** with no set plan, system, or connection

↯ **ran·dom-ac·cess** *adj* retrieving data stored in an arbitrary sequence

↯ **ran·dom-ac·cess mem·o·ry** *n* the primary working memory of a computer

ran·dom·ize /rándə mìz/ (-ized, -iz·ing) *vti* make or become random —**ran·dom·i·za·tion** /rándəmi záysh'n/ *n*

R and R, R & R *abbr* **1** rest and recreation **2** rest and relaxation

ra·nee *n* POL = **rani**

rang past tense of **ring**[2]

range /raynj/ *n* **1** a number or variety of different things ○ *dealing with a wide range of people* **2** a number of similar or related things, e.g., products for sale **3** a category defined by its limits ○ *the age range from 25 to 45* **4** an area of effective operation, or the limit of this area **5** a practice area ○ *a shooting range* **6** an area of open land for grazing farm animals **7** all the notes that a singer or a musical instrument can produce **8** a row of mountains **9** movement over an area **10** a stove for cooking ■ *v* **1** *vi* vary between limits **2** *vti* move freely and extensively over an area **3** *vt* align according to something, e.g., attributes ○ *The cadets were ranged into platoons by height.* **4** *vt* arrange in line ○ *ranged the chess pieces on the board* **5** *vi* include or deal with a number of things ○ *Her interests range from parapsychology to parachuting.*

rang·er /ráynjər/ *n* **1** an official overseeing a state or national forest **2** *also* **Rang·er** a member of an armed state law enforcement unit, especially in Texas

Ran·goon /rang gōon/ former name for **Yangon**

rang·y /ráynjee/ (-i·er, -i·est) *adj* slim and long-limbed

ra·ni /ráanee, ràanée/, **ra·nee** *n* an Indian queen or princess, or the wife of a rajah

rank[1] *n* **1** an official position within an organization, especially a military or police force **2** a degree of importance or excellence relative to others ○ *a political journalist of the first rank* **3** high status **4** a line of people or things side by side ■ **ranks** *npl* **1** enlisted soldiers **2** people in a specific group or category ○ *joined the ranks of the* *unemployed* ■ *v* 1 *vti* have or give a rating ○ *ranks high on my list of desirable improvements* 2 *vt* outrank ○ *A colonel ranks a major.* 3 *vti* position or stand people or things in rows 4 *vi* seem most important

rank[2] *adj* 1 utter or unmitigated 2 strong- or foul-smelling ○ *the rank odor of rotten eggs* 3 describes vegetation that is growing too vigorously —**rank·ly** *adv* —**rank·ness** *n*

rank and file *n* 1 ordinary members ○ *the union's rank and file* 2 enlisted troops —**rank-and-file** *adj* —**rank and fil·er** *n*

Ran·kin /ráŋkin/, **Jeannette** (1880–1973) US politician and legislator

rank·ing /ráŋking/ *adj* 1 holding the highest rank 2 foremost ■ *n* a position relative to others

ran·kle /ráŋk'l/ *vi* cause continuing bitter feelings

ORIGIN Nowadays feelings **rankle**, but originally the verb was used of parts of the body, wounds, and sores that festered or suppurated. In the course of its history the word lost an initial *d-*. It goes back through a French verb to the Latin noun *draco* "serpent" (from which *dragon* also derives). The original idea was therefore of an ulcer caused by the bite of a snake.

ran·sack /ránsak/ *vt* 1 search something very thoroughly 2 rob and despoil, e.g., a captured city

ORIGIN Ransack was adopted from an old Scandinavian compound formed from words meaning "house" and "search." The second element *-sack* is related to *seek*.

ran·som /ráns'm/ *n* 1 a sum of money demanded for releasing a captive 2 release of a captive in return for payment ■ *vt* pay money for the release of a captive

rant *vti* speak or say in a loud or aggressive manner —**rant** *n*

rap[1] *n* (**rapped, rap·ping**) 1 *vti* hit something sharply 2 *vt* criticize or rebuke 3 *vt* say sharply ■ *n* 1 a sound of knocking 2 unfair blame *(slang)* ○ *a bum rap* 3 a sharp blow 4 a criminal charge *(slang)* 5 a jail sentence *(slang)* ◇ **beat the rap** avoid conviction on a charge *(slang)* ◇ **take the rap (for)** take the blame or punishment for something *(slang)*

rap[2] *n* 1 popular music with spoken rhyming vocals 2 an informal talk *(slang)* —**rap** *vi* —**rap·per** *n*

ra·pa·cious /rə páyshəss/ *adj* greedy and destructive —**ra·pa·cious·ly** *adv* —**ra·pa·ci·ty** /rə pássətee/ *n*

rape[1] *n* 1 the crime of forcing somebody to have sexual intercourse 2 an instance of rape 3 violent destructive treatment ○ *the rape of the countryside* —**rape** *vt* —**rap·ist** *n*

rape[2] *n* a plant with bright yellow flowers grown commercially. Use: oil, fodder.

rape shield law *n* a law prohibiting the defense at a rape trial from questioning the plaintiff about her or his prior sexual experiences

Raph·a·el /ráffee èl, ràaffee él/ (1483–1520) Italian artist

rap·id /ráppid/ *adj* quick or fast ■ **rap·ids** *npl* a fast-moving turbulent part of a river —**ra·pid·i·ty** /rə píddətee/ *n* —**rap·id·ly** *adv* —**rap·id·ness** *n*

Rap·id Cit·y city in W South Dakota. Pop. 57,513 (1998).

rap·id-fire *adj* 1 coming in very quick succession 2 designed to fire very quickly

ra·pi·er /ráypee ər/ *n* a sword with a long slender blade

rap·ine /ráppən, rá pīn, ráy pīn/ *n* use of force to seize property *(literary)*

rap·pel /rə pél/ *vi* descend a steep mountainside by a rope

rap·port /ra páwr, rə-/ *n* a friendly relationship or emotional bond

rap·proche·ment /ràa prawsh maàN/ *n* establishment or renewal of friendly relations

rapt *adj* 1 completely engrossed 2 blissfully happy —**rapt·ly** *adv* —**rapt·ness** *n*

rap·ture /rápchər/ *n* 1 bliss or ecstasy 2 mystical transportation ■ **rap·tures** *npl* a state of great happiness or enthusiasm ○ *went into raptures about the meal* —**rap·tur·ous** *adj*

rare[1] /rair/ (**rar·er, rar·est**) *adj* 1 not often happening or found 2 unusually great or excellent 3 describes air containing little oxygen —**rare·ly** *adv* —**rare·ness** *n* —**rar·i·ty** /ráirətee/ *n*

rare[2] (**rar·er, rar·est**) *adj* describes lightly cooked meat that remains raw inside

rare-earth el·e·ment *n* a metallic element of the lanthanide group

rar·e·fied /ráirə fīd/, **rar·i·fied** *adj* 1 describes an atmosphere with a low oxygen content 2 esoteric or elitist

~~rasberry~~ incorrect spelling of **raspberry**

ras·cal /rásk'l/ *n* 1 a mischievous person *(humorous)* 2 a dishonest person

rase *vt* = **raze** *(literary)*

rash[1] *adj* thoughtless and impetuous —**rash·ly** *adv* —**rash·ness** *n*

rash[2] *n* 1 a reddish itchy patch on the skin 2 a series of instances in a brief period ○ *a rash of robberies*

rash·er /ráshər/ *n* a slice of bacon

rasp *n* 1 a file with large teeth 2 a harsh grating sound ■ *vt* 1 say in a harsh voice 2 smooth or scrape with a rasp —**rasp·y** *adj*

rasp·ber·ry /ráz bèrree/ (*pl* **-ries**) *n* 1 a small red fruit made up of many tiny fleshy parts 2 a plant that produces raspberries

AKG London

Grigory Yefimovich Rasputin

Ras·pu·tin /rass pyŏotin/, **Grigory Yefimovich** (1869?–1916) Russian peasant and self-proclaimed holy man

Ras·ta·far·i·an /ràstə férree ən/ n a member of an Afro-Caribbean religious group that venerates the former emperor of Ethiopia, Haile Selassie —**Ras·ta·far·i·an** adj —**Ras·ta·far·i·an·ism** n

⚡ **rast·er** /rástər/ n the pattern of horizontal scanning lines that create the image on a television or computer screen

⚡ **ras·ter font** n a bit-mapped font

⚡ **ras·ter·ize** /rástə rīz/ (**-ized, -iz·ing**) vt convert a digitized image for display or printing

rat n 1 a long-tailed rodent resembling a large mouse 2 a person regarded as untrustworthy or disloyal (slang insult) ■ vi (**rat·ted, rat·ting**) hunt or catch rats —**rat·ter** n ◊ **smell a rat** be suspicious (slang)

□ **rat on** vt betray or inform on (infml)

rat-a-tat-tat /ràttə tat tát/, **rat-tat-tat, rat-tat** n the sound of sharp knocking

rat·a·tou·ille /ràttə tŏo ee/ n a dish of stewed tomatoes, onions, peppers, eggplant, and zucchini

ratch·et /ráchət/ n 1 a turning mechanism allowing movement in one direction 2 also **ratch·et wheel** a toothed wheel forming part of a ratchet ■ v 1 vt force something to rise or fall in stages 2 vti move with a ratchet

rate n 1 a speed 2 an amount expressed in relation to something else ○ the mortality rate 3 an amount of money charged ■ v (**rat·ed, rat·ing**) 1 vti have or regard as having a particular value or position relative to others 2 vt deserve 3 vt classify —**rat·a·ble** adj —**rate·a·ble** adj ◊ **at any rate** whatever else may be true

rate of ex·change n FIN = exchange rate

rate of re·turn n an amount of income generated by an investment

rate·pay·er /ráyt pày ər/ n somebody who pays for utility consumption

rath·er /ráthər/ adv 1 more willingly ○ I'd rather go to the mountains. 2 with more justification or precision ○ praise them rather than blame 3 to some extent or degree ○ rather tall ○ rather attractive 4 on the contrary

ORIGIN Rather is in origin the comparative of an obsolete adjective rathe meaning "quick." "More quickly" became "more willingly" early in its history. The sense "to some extent" did not develop until the late 16C.

rat·i·fy /ráttə fī/ (**-fied, -fies**) vt formally approve —**rat·i·fi·ca·tion** /ràttəfə káysh'n/ n

rat·ing /ráyting/ n 1 an assessment or classification 2 a classification of somebody by occupation ■ **rat·ings** npl a list showing the size of a television or radio audience

ra·tio /ráyshō, ráyshi ō/ (pl **-tios**) n 1 a proportional relationship 2 the relationship between two quantities arrived at by dividing one by another

ra·tion /rásh'n, ráysh'n/ n a fixed amount allocated to a person ■ **ra·tions** npl an amount of food officially allocated ■ vt restrict the amount of something a person can have ○ Gasoline was rationed during the crisis.

□ **ration out** vt distribute in limited quantities

ra·tion·al /rásh'n'l/ adj 1 able to think clearly and sensibly 2 in accordance with logic or scientific knowledge ○ a rational explanation 3 able to reason 4 expressible as a ratio of two integers —**ra·tion·al·i·ty** /ràshə nállətee/ n —**ra·tion·al·ly** adv

ra·tion·ale /ràshə nál/ n a set or statement of underlying reasons or principles

ra·tion·al·ism /ráshən'l lzzəm, ráshno llzzəm/ n 1 reasoning as the basis of action 2 reason as the source of truth —**ra·tion·al·ist** n —**ra·tion·al·is·tic** /ràshən'l ístik, ràshnə lístik/ adj

ra·tion·al·ize /rásh'n'līz/ (**-ized, -iz·ing**) v 1 vti offer a reasonable explanation for behavior 2 vt make rational 3 vt interpret logically 4 vti make a business or operation more efficient and profitable, e.g., by reducing the workforce —**ra·tion·al·i·za·tion** /ràsh'n'li záysh'n/ n

rat race n a struggle to survive in the competitive environment of modern life (infml)

rat·tan /ra tán, rə-/ n the stems of a tropical Asian climbing plant. Use: wickerwork, furniture, canes.

rat-tat, rat-tat-tat n = rat-a-tat-tat

rat·tle /rátt'l/ v (**-tled, -tling**) 1 vti make or cause to make short sharp knocking sounds 2 vt disconcert ■ n 1 a succession of short sharp knocking sounds 2 a baby's toy or other device that makes a rattling sound 3 the tip of rattlesnake's tail

□ **rattle off** vt say very quickly

□ **rattle on** vi talk quickly, inconsequentially, and at length

rat·tle·snake /rátt'l snàyk/ n a large venomous snake with vibrating horny segments in the tail

rat·ty /ráttee/ (**-ti·er, -ti·est**) adj 1 dilapidated (infml) 2 infested with rats 3 of or like a rat —**rat·ti·ly** adv —**rat·ti·ness** n

rau·cous /ráwkəss/ adj unpleasantly loud or harsh —**rau·cous·ly** adv —**rau·cous·ness** n

raun·chy /ráwnchee/ (-chi·er, -chi·est) adj sexually explicit or obscene (infml) —**raun·chi·ly** adv —**raun·chi·ness** n

rav·age /rávvij/ vt (-aged, -ag·ing) 1 wreck or destroy 2 plunder o a village ravaged of all its valuables by army deserters ■ **rav·ag·es** npl damaging effects o the ravages of time —**rav·ag·er** n

rave /rayv/ vi (raved, rav·ing) 1 speak loudly and angrily 2 speak wildly and incoherently ■ n 1 enthusiastic praise (infml) o rave reviews 2 an act of raving ■ adj very enthusiastic (infml) o rave reviews —**rav·er** n —**rav·ing** n, adj

rav·el /rávv'l/ (-eled or -elled, -el·ing or -el·ling) vti 1 fray 2 tangle

Ra·vel /rə vél/, **Maurice** (1875–1937) French composer

ra·ven /ráyv'n/ n a large black bird of the crow family ■ adj black and shiny (literary)

rav·en·ous /rávv'nəss/ adj extremely hungry —**rav·en·ous·ly** adv —**rav·en·ous·ness** n

ra·vine /rə veen/ n a deep narrow valley

ra·vi·o·li /rávvee ólee/ (pl -lis) n filled square parcels of pasta

rav·ish /rávvish/ vt 1 sexually assault (literary) 2 carry off forcibly (literary) —**rav·ish·er** n

raw adj 1 not cooked 2 unprocessed or unrefined 3 inflamed and sore 4 unpleasantly cold o a raw wind 5 inexperienced 6 brutally realistic o the raw facts 7 coarse, vulgar, and crude o a raw joke —**raw·ly** adv —**raw·ness** n

Ra·wal·pin·di /ráàwəl píndee/ city in NE Pakistan. Pop. 1,406,214 (1998).

raw·hide /ráw hīd/ n 1 untanned hide 2 a whip or rope made of rawhide

ray¹ n 1 a beam of light or other radiant energy 2 a trace of something positive such as hope or comfort 3 a straight line that extends from a point infinitely in one direction —**rayed** adj

ray² n a fish with a flat body and broad fins

Ray, Man (1890–1976) US artist

ray gun n in science fiction, a gun that fires energy rays that stun or destroy

ray·on /ráy òn/ n a synthetic textile fiber

raze (razed, raz·ing), **rase** (rased, rasing) vt completely destroy a place

ra·zor /ráyzər/ n an instrument for shaving —**ra·zor** vt

ra·zor blade n a disposable blade for a razor

razz vt tease (slang)

razz·ma·tazz /rázmə táz/ n exciting showiness

Rb symbol rubidium

RBI, rbi abbr runs batted in

RC abbr Red Cross

RCMP, R.C.M.P. abbr Royal Canadian Mounted Police

Rd. abbr Road (in addresses)

re¹ /ray/ n a syllable used in singing the 2nd note of a scale

re² /ray, ree/ prep with reference to

're contr are

Re symbol 1 rhenium 2 rupee

re- prefix 1 again, anew o reinvest 2 back, backward o recall

reach /reech/ v 1 vti stretch out or extend as far as a particular place 2 vi move the hand toward something to touch or grasp it 3 vt arrive at 4 vti influence or have an impact on people 5 vt communicate with ■ n 1 an act or extent of reaching 2 a range of power o beyond the reach of the law ■ **reach·es** npl an area or level of something o the upper reaches of the Amazon

re·act /ree ákt/ vi 1 say or do one thing as a result of another thing said or done to you 2 undergo physical or chemical change, e.g., as a result of contact with something —**re·ac·tive** adj

re·ac·tion /ree áksh'n/ n 1 one thing said or done as a result of another thing said or done to you 2 the process of reacting physically or chemically 3 an adverse response by the body to a substance 4 an equal but opposite force exerted by a body when a force acts upon it 5 strong conservatism (disapproving) 6 a nuclear process resulting in a structural change of atomic nuclei

re·ac·tion·ar·y /ree áksh'n èrree/ adj opposed to liberal or progressive change (disapproving) —**re·ac·tion·ar·y** n

re·ac·ti·vate /ree ákti vàyt/ (-vat·ed, -vat·ing) vti make or become active again —**re·ac·ti·va·tion** /ree àkti váysh'n/ n

re·ac·tor /ree áktər/ n 1 somebody or something that reacts or takes part in a reaction 2 a device in which nuclear fission or fusion occurs, producing energy 3 a component in an electrical circuit

ⅇ **read** /reed/ v (read /red/) 1 vti interpret written words 2 vti utter written words 3 vti learn something by reading o He read law instead of going to law school. 4 vt interpret nonverbal material, e.g., signs, symbols, or signals o read a map o read music 5 vt understand something intuitively o must have read my mind 6 vti interpret something in a specific way o However you read it, her idea is impractical. 7 vt have a particular wording o a sign reading KEEP OUT 8 vti receive and understand a radio message 9 vt indicate or display data o The thermometer reads zero. 10 vti transfer data into computer memory ■ n 1 literary material of a particular quality for reading (slang) o a novel that is an excellent read 2 a spell of reading

SPELLCHECK Do not confuse the spelling of **read** and **reed** (the plant), which sound similar.

read·a·ble /reedab'l/ adj 1 legible 2 enjoyable to read —**read·a·bly** adv

re·ad·dress /reè ə dréss/ *vt* **1** put a new address on **2** attend to again

⚡**read·er** /reédər/ *n* **1** somebody who reads **2** a reading device connected to a computer **3** an educational book

read·er·ship /reédər shìp/ *n* the people who read a specific publication

read·i·ly /rédd'lee/ *adv* **1** without hesitation **2** with ease

read·ing /reéding/ *n* **1** an interpretation of written material **2** material that is read **3** an occasion when something is read ○ *a poetry reading* **4** a text read to an audience or congregation **5** a measurement or other information taken from a piece of equipment

re·ad·just /reè ə júst/ *vi* rearrange or make small changes to something —**re·ad·just·ment** *n*

⚡**README file** /reédmee-/ *n* a computer text file containing information about the installation or operation of software

re·ad·mit /reè əd mít/ (**-mit·ted, -mit·ting**) *vt* allow to enter, have access, or belong again —**re·ad·mis·sion** *n*

⚡**read-on·ly** *adj* describes a computer file that cannot be changed or deleted

⚡**read-on·ly mem·o·ry** *n* a small permanent computer memory for storing data that cannot be changed

⚡**read·out** /reéd òwt/ *n* **1** data retrieved by a computer **2** a display of information on a piece of equipment

read-through *n* the reading of a play before full rehearsals begin

⚡**read-write head** *n* a device in a computer that reads and writes data

read·y /réddee/ *adj* (**-i·er, -i·est**) **1** prepared for something **2** finished and available for use **3** on the point of doing something ○ *worked until I was ready to drop* **4** willing or eager to do something ○ *ready to help* **5** quickly produced ○ *a ready answer* **6** prepared in advance (*often in combination*) ○ *ready-sliced cheese* **7** intelligent or alert ○ *a ready wit* ■ *vt* (**-ied, -ies**) prepare —**read·i·ness** *n*

read·y-made *adj* **1** already prepared or made **2** thought out in advance ○ *ready-made excuses* ■ *n* a ready-to-wear garment

re·af·firm /reè ə fúrm/ *vt* confirm that something is still true or right —**re·af·fir·ma·tion** /reè afər máysh'n/ *n*

The White House

Ronald Reagan

Rea·gan /ráygən/, **Ronald** (*b.* 1911) 40th president of the United States (1981–89)

re·a·gent /ree áyjənt/ *n* a substance that takes part in a chemical reaction

re·al[1] /reè əl/ *adj* **1** physically existing **2** verifiable as actual fact ○ *her real name* **3** not artificial or synthetic **4** traditional and authentic **5** sincere **6** adds emphasis ○ *a real professional* ○ *be in real trouble* **7** of land and fixed property ■ *adv* very (*infml*) ■ *n* real things or reality —**real·ness** *n* ◇ **for real** seriously, not as a joke or as a practice (*infml*)

> **SPELLCHECK** Do not confuse the spelling of **real** and **reel** (of thread), which sound similar.

re·al[2] /ray áal, ree-/ (*pl* **-als** *or* **-al·es** /ray áales/) *n* the main unit of Brazilian currency

re·al es·tate *n US, Can, ANZ* land and any immovable property on it

re·a·lign /reè ə lín/ *v* **1** *vt* put back into a straight line **2** *vti* change to fit a different situation —**re·a·lign·ment** *n*

re·al·ism /reè ə lìzzəm/ *n* **1** the ability to view situations in a practical and objective way **2** the lifelike representation of people and objects in art and literature —**re·al·ist** *n*

re·al·is·tic /reè ə lístik/ *adj* **1** practical and objective **2** reasonable ○ *a realistic price* **3** representing real life as it is —**re·al·is·ti·cal·ly** *adv*

~~realisticly~~ incorrect spelling of **realistically**

re·al·i·ty /ree állətee/ (*pl* **-ties**) *n* **1** real existence **2** all that actually exists or happens **3** something that exists or happens

re·al·ize /reè ə líz/ (**-ized, -iz·ing**) *v* **1** *vti* know and understand something **2** *vti* be or become aware of something **3** *vt* achieve something hoped or worked for **4** *vt* convert something into money, usually by selling it ○ *realize our assets* —**re·al·iz·a·ble** *adj* —**re·al·i·za·tion** /reè əli záysh'n/ *n* ◇ See note at **accomplish**

re·al-life *adj* real rather than fictional

re·al·lo·cate /ree állə kàyt/ (**-cat·ed, -cat·ing**) *vt* allocate differently —**re·al·lo·ca·tion** /ree ələ káysh'n/ *n*

re·al·ly /reè əlee, reélee/ *adv* **1** in actual fact **2** in a genuine way ○ *felt really sorry* **3** adds emphasis ○ *really exciting* **4** properly ○ *You should really apply for the job in writing.* ■ *interj* expresses surprise, doubt, or exasperation

realm /relm/ *n* **1** an area or domain, e.g., of thought or knowledge ○ *within the realm of reason* **2** a kingdom

re·al·po·li·tik /ray áal poli teék/ *n* politics based on practical considerations

⚡**real time** *n* **1** the time it takes for a computer system to process input data and no more **2** the actual time of occurrence —**real-time** *adj*

Re·al·tor /reè əltər/ *tdmk* a trademark for a member of the US National Association of Realtors or the Canadian Association of Real Estate Boards

re·al·ty /rée əltee/ *n* real estate

re·al-world *adj* relevant to everyday life

realy incorrect spelling of **really**

ream[1] /reem/ *n* a quantity of paper, usually 500 sheets ■ **reams** *npl* a large quantity, especially of written material

ream[2] /reem/ *vt* form, enlarge, or shape a hole with a special tool —**ream·er** *n*

reap /reep/ *vt* 1 cut and gather a crop 2 obtain something as a result —**reap·er** *n*

re·ap·pear /rée ə peér/ *vi* appear again —**re·ap·pear·ance** *n*

re·ap·praise /rée ə práyz/ (-praised, -prais·ing) *vt* consider something again, often with a view to change —**re·ap·prais·al** *n*

rear[1] *v* 1 *vt* raise animals or children 2 *vi* rise on the hind legs (*refers to animals*)

rear[2] /reer/ *n* 1 the back of something 2 the part of an army that is farthest from the front 3 somebody's buttocks, or the similar part of an animal (*infml*) ■ *adj* back —**rear·most** *adj* ◊ **bring up the rear** be at the back

rear ad·mi·ral *n* an officer of a rank above captain in the US Navy or Coast Guard, or above commodore in the British or Canadian navies

rear-end *vt* crash into the back of a vehicle —**rear-end·er** *n*

rear·guard /reér gaárd/ *n* 1 troops protecting the rear of a retreating army 2 members of an organization who oppose change or progress (*disapproving*) —**rear·guard** *adj*

re·arm /rée aárm/ *vti* equip a person, group, or nation with weapons again —**re·ar·ma·ment** /rée aármamant/ *n*

re·ar·range /rée ə ráynj/ (-ranged, -rang·ing) *vt* 1 change the order or position of 2 change the appointed time of —**re·ar·range·ment** *n*

rear·view mir·ror /reér vyoo-/ *n* a mirror providing a view of the road behind a vehicle

rear·ward /reérward/ *adv* also **rear·wards** toward the rear ■ *adj* in or near the rear

rea·son /reéz'n/ *n* 1 a justification 2 a motive 3 a cause that explains something 4 the power of ordered or logical thought ■ *vi* 1 think logically 2 use rational argument to persuade somebody —**rea·soned** *adj* —**rea·son·ing** *n* ◊ **it stands to reason** it seems obvious or logical ◊ See note at **deduce**

USAGE The word **reason** is correctly followed by *that* rather than by *because* in sentences of the type *The reason I left is that* [not *because*] *I was bored.* Alternatively, simply use: *I left because I was bored.*

rea·son·a·ble /reéz'nab'l/ *adj* 1 capable of making rational judgments 2 being in accordance with common sense 3 not expecting or demanding more than is possible 4 fairly good 5 fairly large 6 not exorbitant —**rea·son·a·bly** *adv* ◊ See note at **valid**

re·as·sure /rée ə shoór/ (-sured, -sur·ing) *vt* make somebody feel less worried —**re·as·sur·ance** *n* —**re·as·sur·ing** *adj* —**re·as·sur·ing·ly** *adv*

re·a·wak·en /rée ə wáykən/ *v* 1 *vti* wake again 2 *vt* stimulate again

re·badge /ree báj/ (-badged, -badg·ing) *vt* change the identifying marks of a product or business

re·bate /rée bàyt/ *n* a sum of money returned or deducted —**re·bate** /rée bàyt/ *vt*

reb·el /rébb'l/ *n* 1 somebody who defies or protests authority 2 a soldier who opposes a ruling government 3 an unconventional person ■ *vi* /ri bél/ (re·belled, re·bel·ling) 1 fight to overthrow a government 2 protest by defying authority 3 refuse to conform 4 have or show intense dislike for something —**re·bel·lious** /ri béllyəss/ *adj*

rebelion incorrect spelling of **rebellion**

re·bel·lion /ri béllyən/ *n* 1 an attempt to overthrow a government 2 defiance of authority

re·birth /ree búrth/ *n* 1 regeneration of something dead or destroyed 2 revival of ideas or forces

⚡**re·boot** /ree boot/ *vti* restart a computer —**re·boot** *n*

re·born /ree báwrn/ *adj* having been regenerated or renewed

re·bound /ree bównd/ *v* 1 *vi* spring back 2 *vi* recover from a setback 3 *vti* in basketball, take possession of the ball off the backboard —**re·bound** /ree bównd/ *n* ◊ **on the rebound** starting something new after a disappointment or setback

re·buff /ri búf/ *vt* 1 reject or snub 2 repel or drive back —**re·buff** *n*

re·build /ree bíld/ (-built /-bílt/) *vt* 1 build again 2 restore *o rebuilt her confidence*

re·buke /ri byoók/ (-buked, -buk·ing) *vt* criticize or reprimand —**re·buke** *n*

re·bus /reébass/ (*pl* -bus·es) *n* a word puzzle made up of pictures, letters, or numbers

re·but /ri bút/ (-but·ted, -but·ting) *vti* refute —**re·but·tal** *n*

re·cal·ci·trant /rə kálsitrənt/ *adj* resisting control —**re·cal·ci·trance** *n* —**re·cal·ci·trant** *n* ◊ See note at **unruly**

ORIGIN Recalcitrant derives ultimately from the Latin word for "heel." A **recalcitrant** person therefore literally "kicks back" at the cause of restraint or offense. The word was adopted from French in the mid-19C.

re·call *v* /ri káwl/ 1 *vti* remember 2 *vt* order to return *o recalled the ambassador to Washington* 3 *vt* request the return of, e.g., because of defects *o The manufacturer has recalled all models built in 2001.* 4 *vt* bring to mind *o a style that recalls the Kennedy years* ■ *n* /ree káwl/ 1 a manufacturer's request to return a defective product 2 dismissal of an elected official from office by popular vote **3** the act of recalling **4** memory

re·cant /ri kánt/ *vti* deny a belief —**re·can·ta·tion** /rèe kan táysh'n/ *n*

re·cap[1] /rèe kàp/ (-capped, -cap·ping) *vti* restate the main points of something —**re·cap** *n*

re·cap[2] *US, ANZ n* /rèe kàp/ a retread ■ *vt* /ree káp/ (-capped, -cap·ping) retread a tire

re·ca·pit·u·late /rèeka pícha làyt/ (-lat·ed, -lat·ing) *vti* restate the essence of something (*fml*) —**re·ca·pit·u·la·tion** /rèeka pícha láysh'n/ *n*

re·cap·ture /ree kápchər/ (-tured, -tur·ing) *vt* **1** capture again **2** experience again ○ *an attempt to recapture their youth* —**re·cap·ture** *n*

re·cast /ree kást/ (-cast) *vt* change the form of

~~reccommend~~ incorrect spelling of **recommend**

re·cede /ri séed/ (-ced·ed, -ced·ing) *vi* **1** go back or down ○ *waiting for the flood waters to recede* **2** become more distant **3** slope backward

re·ceipt /ri séet/ *n* **1** a written acknowledgment that something has been received **2** an act of receiving ■ **re·ceipts** *npl* the amount received, especially in business ■ *v* **1** *vt* acknowledge payment of a bill with a signature **2** *vti* give a receipt for money or goods

re·ceiv·a·ble /ri séevəb'l/ *adj* **1** suitable to be received **2** due to be paid ■ **re·ceiv·a·bles** *npl* money owed

re·ceive /ri séev/ (-ceived, -ceiv·ing) *v* **1** *vti* get or take something given or sent **2** *vti* pick up and convert electronic signals **3** *vt* meet with, experience, or be subjected to **4** *vt* react to ○ *The proposals were not well received.* **5** *vti* greet or entertain visitors **6** *vt* catch or hold ○ *a barrel that receives rainwater* **7** *vt* allow to enter ○ *was received into the scholarly community*

re·ceived /ri séevd/ *adj* generally accepted ○ *received opinion*

re·ceiv·er /ri séevər/ *n* **1** the part of a telephone that contains the mouthpiece and earpiece **2** a device for picking up signals **3** somebody appointed by a court to manage a bankrupt business **4** somebody who receives

re·ceiv·er·ship /ri séevər ship/ *n* being in the hands of a receiver

re·cent /rées'nt/ *adj* **1** having happened not long ago **2** modern —**re·cen·cy** *n* —**re·cent·ly** *adv* —**re·cent·ness** *n*

re·cep·ta·cle /ri séptək'l/ *n* a container

re·cep·tion /ri sépshən/ *n* **1** a formal party **2** the way somebody or something is received **3** the quality of a radio or television signal received **4** the act of receiving **5** the place where visitors to a hotel, business, or public building are first received

re·cep·tion·ist /ri sépshənist/ *n* an employee who greets visitors, customers, or patients

re·cep·tion room *n* a room where clients or patients can wait

re·cep·tive /ri séptiv/ *adj* **1** willing to accept something ○ *receptive to new ideas* **2** quick to learn **3** able to receive something —**re·cep·tive·ly** *adv* —**re·cep·tive·ness** *n* —**re·cep·tiv·i·ty** /rèe sep tívvətee/ *n*

re·cep·tor /ri séptər/ *n* a nerve ending that converts stimuli into nerve impulses

re·cess /rée sèss, ri séss/ *n* **1** a break between academic classes **2** a break from work, business, or other activity **3** a remote place (*often pl*) ○ *the recesses of her mind* **4** an indentation or hollowed-out space, e.g., a niche or alcove ■ *v* **1** *vti* suspend proceedings **2** *vt* put in a niche **3** *vt* make a niche in

re·ces·sion /ri sésh'n/ *n* **1** a decline in economic activity **2** the process of receding —**re·ces·sion·a·ry** *adj*

re·ces·sion·al /ri séshən'l, -séshnəl/ *n* a ceremonial withdrawal from a building at the conclusion of a formal ceremony, e.g., a wedding

re·ces·sive /ri séssiv/ *adj* **1** describes a gene that produces an effect in some conditions only **2** describes a characteristic determined by a recessive gene **3** engaged in receding ○ *recessive tides*

re·charge /ree chaárj/ (-charged, -charg·ing) *vt* replenish the electricity in a battery —**re·charge·a·ble** *adj* —**re·charg·er** *n*

re·cher·ché /rə shàir sháy/ *adj* rare or obscure

re·cid·i·vism /ri síddə vízzəm/ *n* relapsing into crime —**re·cid·i·vist** *n, adj*

~~receipt~~ incorrect spelling of **receipt**

~~recieve~~ incorrect spelling of **receive**

Re·ci·fe /rə séefə/ capital of Pernambuco State, NE Brazil. Pop. 1,346,045 (1996).

rec·i·pe /réssə pèe/ *n* **1** a set of instructions for preparing food **2** something likely to have a particular result ○ *the recipe for success* ○ *a recipe for disaster*

ORIGIN Recipe was originally an instruction at the beginning of medical prescriptions (rather like *take* in "Take three pills daily"). It is the imperative form of Latin *recipere* "receive, take." **Recipe** came first to be used as a noun in the sense "prescription, remedy" in the late 16C. The modern cooking sense did not appear until the early 18C. The earlier word in both these noun senses was *receipt*.

---

re·cip·i·ent /ri síppee ənt/ *n* somebody who receives something ■ *adj* in the process of receiving

re·cip·ro·cal /ri síprrək'l/ *adj* **1** given or shown by each side **2** given or done in return **3** describes a number or quality that is related to another by the fact that when multiplied together the product is one

—re·cip·ro·cal n **—re·cip·ro·cal·i·ty** /ri sìpprə kállətee/ n **—re·cip·ro·cal·ly** adv

re·cip·ro·cate /ri sípprə kàyt/ (-cat·ed, -cat·ing) vti **1** give something mutually or in return for something similar **2** move backward and forward **—re·cip·ro·ca·tion** /ri sìpprə káysh'n/ n

rec·i·proc·i·ty /rèssə próssətee/ (pl -ties) n a reciprocal relationship or act

re·cit·al /ri sít'l/ n **1** a solo performance of music or dance **2** the reciting of something in public **—re·ci·tal·ist** n

rec·i·ta·tion /rèssə táysh'n/ n **1** the reciting of something, e.g., a poem **2** a student's oral response to a teacher's questions

re·cite /ri sít/ (-cit·ed, -cit·ing) vt **1** repeat from memory or read aloud **2** give a detailed account or list of

reck·less /réklòss/ adj showing a lack of thought about danger **—reck·less·ly** adv **—reck·less·ness** n

reck·on /rékən/ v **1** vti count or calculate **2** vt regard or consider o reckoned to be the best in her field **3** vt include o reckon him among my friends **4** vt think or believe

□ **reckon with** vt face or deal with o If he lets you down he'll have me to reckon with.

reck·on·ing /rékəning/ n **1** a calculation **2** the settlement of an account **3** a time to account for wrongs

re·claim /ree kláym/ vt **1** claim something back **2** convert wasteland for cultivation **3** extract a useful substance for reuse **—re·claim·a·ble** adj **—rec·la·ma·tion** /rèklə máysh'n/ n

re·cline /ri klín/ (-clined, -clin·ing) v **1** vi lie back or down **2** vti tilt back o Do these seats recline? **—re·clin·er** n

re·cluse /ré klòoss, ri klóoss/ n **1** somebody who lives alone and avoids social contact **2** somebody who lives a solitary life of prayer **—re·clu·sive** adj **—re·clu·sive·ness** n

rec·og·ni·tion /rèkəg nísh'n/ n **1** an act of recognizing, or the fact of being recognized **2** appreciation for an achievement **3** acknowledgment of validity or truth

re·cog·ni·zance /ri kógniz'nss/ n a formal agreement to do something, e.g., appear in court, or the sum of money pledged for this o was released on her own recognizance **—re·cog·ni·zant** adj

rec·og·nize /rékəg nìz/ (-nized, -niz·ing) vt **1** identify somebody or something seen before **2** acknowledge or show appreciation of somebody else's achievement **3** accept the validity or truth of something **—rec·og·niz·a·ble** adj **—rec·og·niz·a·bly** adv **—rec·og·nized** adj

re·coil /ri kóyl/ vi **1** move back suddenly and violently **2** draw back in horror or disgust **—re·coil** /ree kòyl, ri kóyl/ n

SYNONYMS recoil, flinch, quail, shrink,

wince CORE MEANING: draw back in fear or distaste

rec·ol·lect /rèkə lékt/ vti remember **—rec·ol·lec·tion** n

re·com·bi·na·tion /rèè kombə náysh'n/ n any process that produces offspring with genes different from those of either parent

~~recommend~~ incorrect spelling of recommend

rec·om·mend /rèkə ménd/ vt **1** suggest as being most suitable **2** endorse as worthy or pleasing **3** make appealing or attractive o The film has little to recommend it. **—rec·om·mend·a·ble** adj **—rec·om·men·da·tion** /rèkə men dáysh'n/ n

SYNONYMS recommend, advise, advocate, counsel, suggest CORE MEANING: put forward ideas to somebody deciding on a course of action

rec·om·pense /rékəm pènss/ vt (-pensed, -pens·ing) **1** pay or reward o was recompensed for her heroism **2** give compensation to or for ■ n **1** remuneration **2** compensation

rec·on·cile /rékən sìl/ vt (-ciled, -cil·ing) vt **1** make disputing people friendly again **2** make somebody accept something unpleasant o reconciled herself to the fact that her career was over **3** make conflicting things consistent or compatible **—rec·on·cil·a·ble** adj **—rec·on·cile·ment** n **—rec·on·cil·i·a·tion** /rèkən silee áysh'n/ n **—rec·on·cil·i·a·to·ry** /rèkən síllee ə tàwree/ adj

rec·on·dite /rékən dìt, ri kón-/ adj understood only by experts **—rec·on·dite·ness** n ◊ See note at obscure

re·con·di·tion /rèè kən dísh'n/ vt repair and replace the worn-out parts of ◊ See note at renew

~~reconize~~ incorrect spelling of recognize

~~reconnaisance~~ incorrect spelling of reconnaissance

re·con·nais·sance /ri kónnəss'nss/ n exploration of an area to gather information

re·con·noi·ter /rèekə nóytər, rèkə-/ vti explore an area to gather information

re·con·sid·er /rèekən síddər/ vti think about something again, usually with a view to changing a decision **—re·con·sid·er·a·tion** /rèekən sidə ráysh'n/ n

re·con·sti·tute /ree kónstə tòot/ vt (-tut·ed, -tut·ing) **1** bring something back to its original state, e.g., by adding water to a concentrated form **2** alter the form of something **—re·con·sti·tu·tion** /rèè konstə tóosh'n/ n

re·con·struct /rèekən strúkt/ vt **1** put something back together **2** replicate something from the past on the basis of evidence **3** restore government and the rule of law to a destroyed nation **—re·con·struc·tive** adj

re·con·struc·tion /rèekən strúksh'n/ n 1 the act or process of reconstructing something, or something that has been reconstructed 2 **Re·con·struc·tion** the period (1865–77) during which the states that had seceded during the Civil War were reorganized under federal control

⨍ **re·cord** n /rékərd/ 1 a lasting account, usually in writing 2 the greatest accomplishment so far ○ *broke the record for the high jump* ○ *in record time* 3 a disk of recorded music for a phonograph (dated) 4 a body of information or statistics (often pl) ○ *the hottest summer on the meteorological record* 5 a list of past accomplishments or crimes 6 a document containing history 7 a written account of proceedings 8 a collection of related data items in a computer database ■ v /rɪ káwrd/ 1 vti make a copy of sounds or images on a tape or disk 2 vti indicate a measurement 3 vt make a note of 4 vt make a lasting account of —**re·cord·a·ble** adj ◊ **off the record** not intended to be made public ◊ **set the record straight** put right a mistake or misunderstanding

---

ORIGIN Record goes back to Latin *cor* "heart," and so to record something is etymologically to put it to your heart.

---

re·cord·er /rɪ káwrdər/ n 1 a machine for recording 2 a person who makes a written record 3 a wind instrument with a whistle-shaped mouthpiece and finger holes

re·cord·ing /rɪ káwrding/ n 1 a copy of sounds or images 2 the making of a tape or CD, especially of music

re·count vt /rɪ kównt/ tell a story

re·count /rèe kównt/ vti count again —**re·count** /rèe kównt/ n

re·coup /rɪ kóop/ vt 1 regain something lost or obtain an equivalent 2 reimburse somebody —**re·coup·a·ble** adj

~~recouperate~~ incorrect spelling of **recuperate**

re·course /rèe káwrss, rɪ káwrss/ n 1 the seeking of assistance ○ *without recourse to further borrowing* 2 a source of help or a solution ○ *our only recourse*

re·cov·er /rɪ kúvvər/ v 1 vt regain 2 vi return to a previous or usual state, e.g., of health 3 vt reclaim from waste 4 vi return to the right position ○ *The goaltender recovered and blocked the incoming puck.* 5 vt compensate for ○ *working hard to recover their losses* —**re·cov·er·a·ble** adj —**re·cov·er·y** n

re·cov·er /rèe kúvvər/ vt 1 put a new cover on 2 cover again

rec·re·ant /rékree ənt/ adj (fml) 1 disloyal 2 cowardly —**rec·re·ant** n

re·cre·ate /rèe kree áyt/ (-**cre·at·ed**, -**cre·at·ing**) vt create again —**re·cre·a·tion** n ◊ See note at **copy**

rec·re·a·tion /rèkree áysh'n/ n 1 an activity engaged in for pleasure or relaxation 2 engagement in enjoyable activities, especially after work —**re·cre·ate** /-áyt/ vi —**rec·re·a·tion·al** adj

rec·re·a·tion·al ve·hi·cle n a large motor vehicle used for recreational activities such as camping

rec·re·a·tion room n 1 a room in a house, used for relaxation and recreation 2 a room in a public building for games and social events

re·crim·i·na·tion /rɪ krìmmə náysh'n/ n an accusation made against somebody who has made another accusation —**re·crim·i·nate** /rɪ krímmə náyt/ vi —**re·crim·i·na·to·ry** adj

re·cruit /rɪ króot/ v 1 vti engage a person or people for military service or work 2 vt raise an armed force ■ n a new member, especially of a military force —**re·cruit·er** n —**re·cruit·ment** n

rec·ta plural of **rectum**

rec·tan·gle /rék tàng g'l/ n a four-sided figure with four right angles —**rec·tan·gu·lar** /rek táng gyələr/ adj

rec·ti·fi·er /réktə fìə/ n an electronic device that converts alternating current to direct current

rec·ti·fy /réktə fì/ (-**fied**, -**fies**) vt 1 correct errors in 2 purify, especially by distillation —**rec·ti·fi·a·ble** adj —**rec·ti·fi·ca·tion** /rèktəfi káysh'n/ n

rec·ti·lin·e·ar /rèktə línnee ər/, **rec·ti·lin·e·al** /-əl/ adj 1 having straight lines 2 moving in a straight line

rec·ti·tude /réktə tòod/ n 1 moral integrity 2 correctness of judgment (fml)

rec·to /réktō/ (pl -**tos**) n 1 the front of a printed sheet 2 a right-hand page

rec·tor /réktər/ n 1 a cleric in charge of a Roman Catholic congregation or community 2 a cleric in charge of an Episcopal parish 3 the head of some educational institutions —**rec·tor·ship** /réktər shìp/ n

rec·to·ry /réktəree/ (pl -**ries**) n a religious rector's house

rec·tum /réktəm/ (pl -**tums** or -**ta** /-tə/) n the lower part of the large intestine —**rec·tal** adj —**rec·tal·ly** adv

---

ORIGIN Rectum is a form of Latin *rectus* "straight." It is short for *intestinum rectum* "straight intestine" ("straight" in contrast with the twisting shape of the rest of the intestine).

---

re·cum·bent /rɪ kúmbənt/ adj lying down flat (literary) ○ *a recumbent statue of the general*

re·cu·per·ate /rɪ kóopə ràyt/ (-**at·ed**, -**at·ing**) v 1 vi recover from an illness or injury 2 vt get back something lost ○ *recuperate investment losses* —**re·cu·per·a·tion** /rɪ kóopə ráysh'n/ n —**re·cu·per·a·tive** adj

re·cur /rɪ kúr/ (-**curred**, -**cur·ring**) vi 1 occur again 2 occur as an infinitely repeated digit or series of digits at the end of a decimal fraction —**re·cur·rence** n —**re·cur·rent** /rɪ kúrənt/ adj

re·cy·cle /ree sı̄k'l/ (-cled, -cling) v 1 vti process used material for later reuse 2 vti save something for later reprocessing or reuse 3 vt use again unimaginatively ◊ *recycling the same old ideas* —**re·cy·cla·ble** adj —**re·cy·cling** n

red adj (red·der, red·dest) 1 of the color of blood 2 describes hair that is reddish brown 3 blushing or flushed 4 also **Red** Socialist or Communist (infml disapproving) ■ n 1 the color of blood 2 also **Red** a Socialist or Communist (infml disapproving) —**red·dish** adj —**red·ness** n ◊ **in the red** in debt ◊ **see red** become very angry (infml)

red a·lert n a warning of or state of heightened readiness for an emergency

Red Ar·my n the former Soviet Army

red blood cell n a blood cell carrying oxygen

red-blood·ed adj strong, vigorous, determined, and high-spirited

red·breast /réd brèst/ (pl -breasts or same) n a robin or other bird with a red chest

red card n in soccer, a referee's card displayed when ejecting a player

red car·pet n 1 a strip of carpet laid down for important visitors 2 VIP treatment

AKG London

Red Cloud

Red Cloud (1822–1909) Oglala Sioux leader

red·coat /réd kòt/, **Red·coat** n a British soldier, especially during the American Revolution

Red Cres·cent n the Red Cross in Islamic countries

Red Cross n an international organization that provides medical care

red cur·rant n 1 a sharp-tasting red berry. Use: jellies. 2 a bush that produces red currants

red·den /rédd'n/ vti make or become red

re·dec·o·rate /ree dékə ràyt/ (-rat·ed, -rat·ing) vti renew the interior decoration of a house or room —**re·dec·o·ra·tion** /reè dèkə ráysh'n/ n

re·deem /ri deem/ vt 1 make something acceptable in spite of negative qualities 2 restore a good opinion of somebody 3 buy something back 4 exchange a voucher or coupon for money or goods 5 pay off a debt 6 atone for human sin (refers to Jesus Christ) —**re·deem·a·ble** adj —**re·deem·er** n —**re·deem·ing** adj —**re·demp·tion** /ri démpsh'n/ n —**re·demp·tive** /ri démptiv/ adj

re·de·ploy /reèdi plóy/ vti move people or equipment to a different area or activity —**re·de·ploy·ment** n

re·de·vel·op /reèdi vélləp/ vt improve a rundown area —**re·de·vel·op·ment** n

red flag n 1 a flag symbolizing Communism or Socialism 2 an incitement to anger 3 a warning signal

red-hand·ed adj in the act of committing an offense ◊ *caught red-handed*

red·head /réd hèd/ n somebody with reddish brown hair —**red·head·ed** adj

red her·ring n something introduced to divert attention or mislead

red-hot adj 1 glowing red with heat 2 very hot 3 very exciting (infml) ◊ *red-hot news*

re·di·al /ree dī əl/ vti dial a telephone number again

~~rediculous~~ incorrect spelling of **ridiculous**

re·did past tense of **redo**

re·di·rect /reèdi rékt, -dī-/ vt 1 send something received to another place ◊ *redirecting the previous tenant's mail* 2 reroute traffic —**re·di·rec·tion** n

re·dis·trib·ute /reèdi strí byoòt/ (-ut·ed, -ut·ing) vt 1 distribute again 2 apportion differently —**re·dis·tri·bu·tion** /reèdistrə byoòsh'n/ n

red-let·ter day n a very special day

red light n a warning signal

red·line /réd lìn/ (-lined, -lin·ing) v 1 vti refuse financial services to people or businesses in a supposedly high-risk area 2 vt earmark for dismissal

red meat n meat that is red when raw

re·do /ree doó/ (-did /-díd/, -done /-dún/, -do·ing, -does /-dúz/) vt do again or differently

red·o·lent /rédd'lənt/ adj 1 aromatic (literary) 2 having a particular smell ◊ *redolent of beeswax* 3 suggestive or reminiscent of something ◊ *redolent of corruption* —**red·o·lence** n

Re·don /rə dón, rə doN/, **Odilon** (1840–1916) French painter and lithographer

re·dou·ble /ree dúbb'l/ (-bled, -bling) vti increase considerably ◊ *redoubled our efforts*

re·doubt /ri dówt/ n 1 a stronghold (literary) 2 a temporary fortification

re·doubt·a·ble /ri dówtəb'l/ adj with formidable personal qualities —**re·doubt·a·bly** adv

re·dound /ri dównd/ vi 1 have a particular result ◊ *a decision that redounded to his credit* 2 return as a consequence to a person or group (fml) ◊ *His attempts at revenge redounded upon his own head.*

red pan·da n a reddish animal resembling a raccoon

red pep·per n a hollow red fruit eaten as a vegetable

re·draw /ree dráw/ (-drew /-droò/, -drawn

/-dráwn/ *vt* **1** reposition a boundary **2** draw something again or differently

re-dress *n* /ree drèss, ri dréss/ compensation or reparation ■ *vt* /ri dréss/ **1** make up for a loss or wrong **2** impose fairness or equality on a situation

Red Riv-er river of the south central United States, flowing eastward along the Oklahoma-Texas border and into the Mississippi River in Louisiana. Length 1,220 mi./1,970 km.

Red Sea inland sea between Arabia and NE Africa

red-shirt /réd shùrt/ *n* a college athlete barred from varsity competition for one year so as to extend eligibility or improve skills

red tape *n* bureaucracy (*infml*)

re-duce /ri dōōss/ (-duced, -duc-ing) *v* **1** *vti* decrease **2** *vt* bring to an undesirable state ○ *reduce to tears* **3** *vt* make cheaper **4** *vt* simplify **5** *vt* analyze systematically **6** *vt* demote **7** *vti* thicken by the evaporation of water **8** *vti* undergo or cause to undergo a chemical reaction in which there is a loss of oxygen or a gain of hydrogen —**re-duc-i-ble** *adj*

re-duc-tion /ri dúkshən/ *n* **1** a reducing or a being reduced **2** the amount by which something is reduced —**re-duc-tive** *adj*

re-dun-dan-cy /ri dúndənssee/ *n* **1** the state of being superfluous **2** duplication as a safety measure **3** use of superfluous words —**re-dun-dant** *adj* —**re-dun-dant-ly** *adv*

red-wood /réd wòod/ *n* **1** a tall tree with reddish bark **2** red-colored wood

re-ech-o /ree ékō/ (-oed, -o-ing, -oes) *v* **1** *vi* echo back **2** *vt* repeat something

reed /reed/ *n* **1** a tall water plant **2** the stalk of a reed. Use: thatching, basketry. **3** a vibrating part in a musical instrument that produces sound when air passes it ◊ See note at **read**

Reed /reed/, **John** (1887–1920) US writer and revolutionary

Reed, Walter (1851–1902) US army surgeon and bacteriologist. He discovered that yellow fever is transmitted by mosquitoes.

re-ed-u-cate /ree éjjə kàyt/ (-cat-ed, -cat-ing), **re-ed-u-cate** *vt* teach or train again to change or update knowledge, skills, or behavior

reed-y /réedee/ (-i-er, -i-est) *adj* **1** full of reeds **2** high-pitched —**reed-i-ness** *n*

reef[1] *n* a ridge of rock or coral in a body of water

reef[2] *vt* gather in part of a sail ■ *n* the part of a reefed sail that is gathered in

reef-er /réefər/ *n* a marijuana cigarette (*slang*)

reek /reek/ *vi* **1** have a very strong unpleasant smell **2** give clear evidence of something unpleasant ○ *The document reeks of the double standard.* ■ *n* a strong unpleasant smell ○ *the reek of disinfectant* ◊ See note at **smell**

SPELLCHECK Do not confuse the spelling of **reek** and **wreak** ("cause havoc or destruction"), which sound similar.

reel[1] /reel/ *n* **1** a cylindrical or wheel-shaped device on which something such as thread or tape is wound **2** a section of a movie **3** a winder on a fishing rod ■ *vt* wind onto or off a reel ◊ See note at **real**

□ **reel off** *vt* list quickly and easily

reel[2] /reel/ *vi* **1** stagger backward **2** move unsteadily **3** feel giddy or confused ○ *still reeling from the shock* —**reel** *n*

reel[3] /reel/ *n* a lively dance for sets of couples

re-e-lect /rèe i lékt/, **re-e-lect** *vt* elect somebody again —**re-e-lec-tion** *n*

⚡ **re-en-ter** /ree éntər/, **re-en-ter** *v* **1** *vti* go into a place again **2** *vt* enter data again

re-en-try /ree éntree/ (*pl* -tries), **re-en-try** *n* **1** the act of reentering **2** a return to Earth's atmosphere from space

re-es-tab-lish /rèe ə stábblish/, **re-es-tab-lish** *vt* establish again —**re-es-tab-lish-ment** *n*

re-ex-am-ine /rèe ig zámmin/ (-ined, -in-ing), **re-ex-am-ine** *vt* **1** examine again **2** question again after cross-examination —**re-ex-am-i-na-tion** /rèe ig zami náysh'n/ *n*

ref. *abbr* reference

re-fec-to-ry /ri féktəree/ (*pl* -ries) *n* a dining hall

re-fer /ri fúr/ (-ferred, -fer-ring) *v* **1** *vi* make or have reference to somebody or something ○ *referred to him by name* ○ *This clause refers to you as the tenant.* **2** *vi* consult somebody or something for information ○ *refer to the manual* **3** *vt* direct to a source of help —**re-fer-ral** *n*

ref-e-ree /rèffə reé/ *n* an official overseeing a sports contest or a team game —**ref-e-ree** *vti*

ref-er-ence /réffərənss/ *n* **1** a spoken or written mention **2** the process of referring **3** relevance or connection **4** a source of information ○ *a reference book* **5** a note directing a reader to a source of information **6** a statement of somebody's character and qualifications

ref-er-en-dum /rèffə réndəm/ (*pl* -dums *or* -da /-də/) *n* a vote by an whole population on an issue

~~referrence~~ incorrect spelling of **reference**

re-fill *vti* /ree fíl/ fill again ■ *n* /rée fíl/ a replacement for the contents of a container —**re-fill-a-ble** *adj*

re-fine /ri fín/ (-fined, -fin-ing) *vti* **1** make or become purer **2** make or become more cultured or elegant **3** make or become more effective or sophisticated ○ *refining my technique* —**re-fined** *adj* —**re-fin-er** *n*

re-fine-ment /ri fínmənt/ *n* **1** elegance, politeness, and good taste **2** an improvement

3 the process of refining **4** superior quality and sophistication ○ *a dish of great refinement*

re·fin·er·y /ri fínəree/ (*pl* **-ies**) *n* a place for processing and purifying substances such as oil or sugar

re·fit /ree fít/ (**-fit·ted, -fit·ting**) *vti* repair and equip again —**re·fit** /rée fit/ *n*

re·fla·tion /ree fláysh'n/ *n* the process of bringing an economy out of recession

re·flect /ri flékt/ *v* **1** *vt* send light, sound, or heat back from a surface **2** *vti* show a mirror image of something **3** *vt* show or indicate something ○ *The election results reflect discontent among voters.* **4** *vi* think seriously **5** *vt* have or express a particular thought ○ *reflected that withdrawal might be the safest option* **6** *vti* bring credit or discredit to somebody or something ○ *an action that reflects badly on the school*

re·flec·tion /ri flékshən/ *n* **1** the act of reflecting or being reflected **2** a reflected image **3** careful thought **4** a considered idea **5** an indication or result ○ *a reflection of your hard work*

re·flec·tive /ri fléktiv/ *adj* **1** thoughtful **2** able to reflect —**re·flec·tive·ness** *n*

re·flec·tor /ri fléktər/ *n* something that reflects light

re·flex /rée flèks/ *adj* **1** automatic and involuntary **2** without thought or preparation **3** describes an angle of between 180° and 360° **4** *also* **re·flexed** bent or folded back ○ *reflex leaves* ■ *n* an involuntary physiological reaction, such as a sneeze

re·flex·ive /ri fléksiv/ *adj* **1** describes a pronoun ending in "-self," used to refer back to the subject of a sentence or clause **2** describes a verb denoting self-directed action —**re·flex·ive** *n* —**re·flex·ive·ly** *adv*

re·flex·ol·o·gy /rée flek sóllajee/ *n* massage of the feet or hands to relax or heal other parts of the body —**re·flex·ol·o·gist** *n*

re·form /ri fáwrm/ *v* **1** *vt* improve by removing faults **2** *vti* adopt or cause to adopt a more acceptable way of behaving ■ *n* **1** political or social reorganization and improvement **2** an improving change —**re·form·er** *n* —**re·form·ism** *n* —**re·form·ist** *adj, n*

re-form /ree fáwrm/ *vti* form again

↯ re·for·mat /ree fáwr màt/ (**-mat·ted, -mat·ting**) *vt* format computer data again or differently

ref·or·ma·tion /rèffər máysh'n/ *n* **1** a process of reforming **2 Ref·or·ma·tion** the 16C religious movement that established Protestantism —**ref·or·ma·tion·al** *adj*

re·for·ma·to·ry /ri fáwrmə tàwree/ *n* (*pl* **-ries**) *also* **re·form school** a house of corrections for young offenders ■ *adj* intended to reform (*fml*)

Re·form Ju·da·ism *n* a branch of Judaism that seeks to adapt religious practice to modern times

re·fract /ri frákt/ *vt* alter the course of a wave of energy, as water does to light —**re·frac·tion** *n* —**re·frac·tive** *adj* —**re·frac·tiv·i·ty** /rèe frak tívvətee/ *n*

re·frac·to·ry /ri fráktəree/ *adj* **1** stubborn, rebellious, and uncontrollable **2** highly heat-resistant ■ *n* a material that is able to withstand high temperatures without melting —**re·frac·to·ri·ly** *adv*

re·frain[1] /ri fráyn/ *vi* hold yourself back from doing something —**re·frain·ment** *n*

> **ORIGIN** The two English words **refrain** are unrelated, though both were adopted from French in the 14C. **Refrain** "hold back" goes back to Latin *frenum* "bridle." **Refrain** "chorus" derives ultimately from Latin *frangere* "break," the idea being of a chorus breaking off and then resuming.

re·frain[2] *n* **1** a recurring piece of verse in a poem **2** the chorus in a song

~~reference~~ incorrect spelling of **reference**

↯ re·fresh /ri frésh/ *vt* **1** renew the energy of somebody with rest, food, or drink **2** prompt the memory **3** replenish something **4** update a visual display or electronic device with data —**re·fresh·er** *adj* —**re·fresh·ing** *adj* —**re·fresh·ing·ly** *adv*

re·fresh·er course *n* a course of study updating previous training

re·fresh·ment /ri fréshmənt/ *n* **1** something that refreshes **2** an act of refreshing or being refreshed ■ **re·fresh·ments** *npl* food and drink

~~refrigerator~~ incorrect spelling of **refrigerator**

re·frig·er·ant /ri fríjjərənt/ *n* a substance used to cool or freeze something

re·frig·er·ate /ri fríjjə ràyt/ (**-at·ed, -at·ing**) *vt* make or keep something cool —**re·frig·er·a·tion** /-fríjjə ráysh'n/ *n*

re·frig·er·a·tor /ri fríjjə ràytər/ *n* an artificially cooled appliance for storage

re·fu·el /ree fyóo əl/ *v* **1** *vti* refill with fuel **2** *vt* provide new material or impetus for something such as a debate

ref·uge /ré fyóoj/ *n* **1** shelter or protection **2** a place providing refuge

ref·u·gee /rèffyə jée/ *n* somebody who seeks refuge in a foreign country

re·fund *vt* /ri fúnd, rée fùnd/ return money to somebody ■ *n* /rée fùnd/ an amount of money refunded —**re·fund·a·ble** *adj*

re·fur·bish /ree fúrbish/ *vt* restore something to good condition —**re·fur·bish·er** *n* —**re·fur·bish·ment** *n*

re·fus·al /ri fyóoz'l/ *n* **1** an act of refusing **2** the chance to accept or reject something before others ○ *gave us right of first refusal*

re·fuse[1] /ri fyóoz/ (**-fused, -fus·ing**) *v* **1** *vti* indicate that you will not do something **2** *vt* not accept something —**re·fus·a·ble** *adj*

ref·use[2] /ré fyóoss/ *n* things thrown away as garbage

re·fute /ri fyóot/ (**-fut·ed, -fut·ing**) vt 1 prove false or wrong by providing evidence to the contrary 2 deny —**re·fut·a·ble** /ri fyóotəb'l, réffyətəb'l/ adj —**re·fut·a·bly** /-fyóotəblee/ adv —**ref·u·ta·tion** /réffyə táysh'n/ n

reg. abbr 1 region 2 registrar 3 registry 4 regular

re·gain /rə gáyn, ree-/ vt 1 get something back 2 reach a place again

re·gal /réeg'l/ adj characteristic of or suitable for a monarch —**re·gal·ly** adv

re·gale /ri gáyl/ (**-galed, -gal·ing**) vt 1 entertain somebody, e.g., by storytelling 2 give somebody plenty to eat and drink

re·ga·lia /ri gáylyə/ n (+ sing or pl verb) 1 the ceremonial objects and clothing of royalty or other holders of high office 2 the distinctive clothing or symbols of a particular group of people

re·gard /ri gaárd/ vt 1 consider ○ regards her as a friend 2 have a particular feeling about ○ regarded the prospect with horror 3 judge the quality or worth of ○ is highly regarded in the community 4 look at attentively ■ n 1 attention or concern ○ little regard for their safety 2 favorable opinion ■ **re·gards** npl friendly greetings —**re·gard·ful** adj ◇ **in this** or **that regard** as far as this or that is concerned (fml)

SYNONYMS **regard, admiration, esteem, favor, respect, reverence, veneration** CORE MEANING: appreciation of the worth of somebody or something

re·gard·ing /ri gaárding/ prep about or on the subject of

re·gard·less /ri gaárdləss/ adv in spite of everything ■ adj heedless —**re·gard·less·ly** adv ◇ See note at **irregardless**

re·gat·ta /ri gaátə, -gáttə/ n a series of boat races

ORIGIN The original **regattas** were gondola races on the Grand Canal in Venice. The word means a "fight, struggle" in the Venetian dialect of Italian. The first recorded use for a boat race in England was in 1775, when a **regatta** was held on the Thames River in London.

re·gen·cy /réejənsee/ (pl **-cies**) n 1 a group of people ruling on behalf of a monarch 2 the authority or rule of a regent

re·gen·er·ate v /ri jénnə ràyt/ (**-at·ed, -at·ing**) 1 vti form again 2 vti recover or cause to recover from decline 3 vt restore somebody spiritually ■ adj /-jénnərət/ 1 spiritually reborn or renewed 2 newly formed or grown —**re·gen·er·a·tion** /ri jénnə ráysh'n/ n —**re·gen·er·a·tive** /-rətiv/ adj

re·gen·er·a·tive med·i·cine n the branch of medicine that deals with repairing or replacing tissues and organs by using advanced materials and methodologies, e.g., cloning

re·gent /réejənt/ n 1 somebody ruling on behalf of a monarch 2 a university or other educational official —**re·gent** adj

reg·gae /ré gày/ n popular music of Jamaican origin combining rock, calypso, and soul

reg·i·cide /réjji sìd/ n 1 the killing of a king 2 somebody who kills a king —**reg·i·ci·dal** adj

re·gime /ray zhéem, ri-/, **ré·gime** n 1 a form of government 2 a specific government, especially an oppressive one 3 an established way of doing things

reg·i·men /réjjəmən, -mèn/ n a program of diet, exercise, and other measures to improve health

reg·i·ment n /réjjəmənt/ 1 a military unit made up of two or more battalions 2 a large number of people or things ■ vt /réjjə mènt/ 1 control strictly 2 group systematically —**reg·i·men·tal** /réjjə mént'l/ adj —**reg·i·men·ta·tion** /réjjəmən táysh'n/ n

Re·gi·na /ri jínə/ capital of Saskatchewan, Canada. Pop. 180,400 (1996).

re·gion /réejən/ n 1 a geographic, political, cultural, or ecological area 2 an administrative unit 3 a large indefinite area 4 the range within which a particular figure falls ○ in the region of $1,000

re·gion·al /réejən'l/ adj 1 of a region 2 characteristic of or limited to a specific area of a country ○ a regional accent —**re·gion·al·i·za·tion** /réejən'li záysh'n/ n —**re·gion·al·ize** vt —**re·gion·al·ly** adv

re·gion·al·ism /réejən'l ìzzəm/ n 1 division into administrative areas 2 a regional linguistic feature

ƒ reg·is·ter /réjjistər/ n 1 an official list 2 a book for official records, e.g., of attendance 3 a device that automatically records numbers or quantities 4 a grate in a heating system 5 a computer memory location 6 a musical range ■ v 1 vti record something, or cause something to be recorded, in a register 2 vti enroll 3 vt show something as a measurement 4 vt display or express a feeling ○ registered her disapproval 5 vti note or be noted mentally —**reg·is·trant** n

reg·is·tered mail n a secure mail service

reg·is·tered nurse n US, Can, ANZ a qualified licensed nurse

reg·is·tered trade·mark n an official trademark

reg·is·trar /réjji straár/ n 1 an official who keeps student records in a college or university 2 somebody who keeps official records 3 an official responsible for stock records 4 a hospital admissions officer —**reg·is·trar·ship** n

reg·is·tra·tion /réjji stráysh'n/ n 1 the act of registering, or the state of being registered 2 legal proof of ownership of a vehicle 3 an entry in a register, or a document certifying its making 4 the number of people registering together

reg·is·tra·tion num·ber *n* an identifying sequence of letters and numbers displayed on a vehicle

reg·is·try /réjjistree/ (*pl* **-tries**) *n* 1 a records office 2 registration

re·gress /ri gréss/ *v* 1 *vi* return to an earlier worse condition 2 *vi* go back or move backward 3 *vti* cause to go back to an earlier psychological period or state —**re·gress** /reé gréss/ *n* —**re·gres·sion** *n*

re·gres·sive /ri gréssiv/ *adj* 1 regressing 2 describes a tax system in which less well-off people pay proportionally more in taxes —**re·gres·sive·ly** *adv*

re·gret /ri grét/ *vt* (**-gret·ted, -gret·ting**) 1 wish you had not done or said something 2 be sorry to say o *We regret to tell you that the hotel is full.* ■ *n* a feeling of regretting something —**re·gret·ful** *adj* —**re·gret·ful·ly** *adv* —**re·gret·ful·ness** *n* —**re·gret·ta·ble** *adj* —**re·gret·ta·bly** *adv*

re·group /ree groop/ *v* 1 *vti* form into an organized body again 2 *vi* recover and prepare for further effort

reg·u·lar /réggyələr/ *adj* 1 separated by equal times or spaces 2 happening frequently 3 usual 4 following a routine or pattern 5 of a standard or medium size o *a regular coffee* 6 symmetrical 7 proper or qualified o *not a regular doctor* 8 belonging to a professional force o *a regular army officer* 9 thorough and absolute (*infml*) o *a regular tyrant in the office* 10 pleasant and reliable (*infml*) o *a regular guy* ■ *n* 1 a frequent visitor or customer (*infml*) 2 a professional soldier (*often pl*) —**reg·u·lar·i·ty** /règgyə lárrətee/ *n* —**reg·u·lar·i·za·tion** /règgyələri záysh'n/ *n* —**reg·u·lar·ize** *vt* —**reg·u·lar·ly** *adv*

reg·u·late /réggyə làyt/ (**-lat·ed, -lat·ing**) *vt* 1 control something 2 adjust machinery so that it works correctly 3 make something regular —**reg·u·la·tive** *adj* —**reg·u·la·to·ry** *adj*

reg·u·la·tion /règgyə láysh'n/ *n* 1 an official rule or law (*often pl*) 2 an act of regulating, or the state of being regulated ■ *adj* 1 officially approved for use 2 standard

reg·u·la·tor /réggyə làytər/ *n* a control mechanism (*often in combination*)

re·gur·gi·tate /ri gúrji tàyt/ (**-tat·ed, -tat·ing**) *vt* 1 bring food back up from the stomach 2 repeat information mechanically —**re·gur·gi·ta·tion** /ri gúrji táysh'n/ *n*

re·hab /rée hàb/ *n* rehabilitation (*infml*)

re·ha·bil·i·tate /reè ə bíllə tàyt, reè hə-/ (**-tat·ed, -tat·ing**) *vt* 1 help somebody return to good health or to life away from a hospital or prison 2 restore somebody to a rank or rights —**re·ha·bil·i·ta·tive** *adj*

re·ha·bil·i·ta·tion /reè ə bilə táysh'n, reè hə-/ *n* the process of rehabilitating somebody, especially after confinement in a hospital or prison

re·hash /ree hásh/ *vt* repeat or reuse old material or ideas —**re·hash** /reé hàsh/ *n*

re·hearse /ri húrs/ (**-hearsed, -hears·ing**) *v* 1 *vti* practice something before performing it 2 *vt* train somebody for a performance —**re·hears·al** *n*

ORIGIN Rehearse goes back to a French word meaning "large agricultural rake" (from which *hearse* also derives). Its etymological meaning is therefore "rake over," and saying something over again was what rehearsing originally implied. The sense of practicing for a performance developed in the late 16C.

re·heat /ree heét/ *vti* heat something again

Rehn·quist /rén kwìst/, **William H.** (b. 1924) chief justice of the US Supreme Court (1986–)

re·ho·bo·am /reè ə bố əm/ *n* a large wine bottle, six times the size of a normal bottle

ORIGIN In the Bible, Rehoboam was the son of Solomon and king of ancient Judah (922?–915? BC), who "fortified the strongholds, and put captains in them . . . and stores of oil and wine" (2 Chronicles 11:11).

re·house /ree hówz/ (**-housed, -hous·ing**) *vt* move somebody to better housing

Reich /rík, ríkh/ *n* the German state or empire in any of its various historical manifestations

reign /rayn/ *n* 1 a period of royal rule 2 control or influence ■ *vi* 1 rule a nation, especially as a monarch 2 be the overarching influence o *After he spoke, silence reigned.* ◊ See note at **rain**

reign of ter·ror *n* a time of systematic violence or intimidation

re·im·burse /reè im búrs/ (**-bursed, -burs·ing**) *vt* pay back money spent by somebody —**re·im·burs·a·ble** *adj* —**re·im·burse·ment** *n*

Reims /reemz/, **Rheims** city in NE France. Pop. 187,206 (1999).

rein /rayn/ *n* a strap for controlling a horse ■ **reins** *npl* means of exercising power o *held the reins of government for eight years* ■ *vt* tightly restrain or control o *had to rein back inflation* ◊ **give (free) rein to** impose no restraints or limitations on ◊ **have** or **keep a (tight) rein on** maintain strict control over ◊ See note at **rain**

□ **rein in** *v* 1 *vti* stop or slow a horse 2 *vt* restrain or control o *Let's rein in the rhetoric.*

re·in·car·na·tion /reè in kaar náysh'n/ *n* 1 in some religions, rebirth of the soul in a new body 2 in some religions, a body in which somebody is reborn —**re·in·car·nate** /reè in kaár nàyt/ *vt* —**re·in·car·nate** /-kaárnət/ *adj*

rein·deer /ráyn deèr/ (*pl same or* **-deers**) *n* a large deer with branched antlers

re·in·force /reè in fáwrs/ (**-forced, -forc·ing**) *vt* 1 strengthen or support something with something additional 2 provide a military force with more troops or weapons 3 influence behavior by reward or punishment —**re·in·forc·er** n

re·in·forced con·crete n concrete strengthened with metal

re·in·force·ment /rèe in fáwrsmənt/ n 1 the addition of strength or support 2 material added to reinforce something ■ **re·in·force·ments** npl additional troops, weapons, or resources

re·in·state /rèe in stáyt/ (-stat·ed, -stat·ing) vt 1 restore to a former job or position 2 bring back into use or force —**re·in·state·ment** n

re·in·tro·duce /rèe intrə doóss/ (-duced, -duc·ing) vt bring or take back to a place o a plan to reintroduce wild boar to the forests —**re·in·tro·duc·tion** /rèe intrə dúksh'n/ n

re·in·vent /rèe in vént/ vt 1 invent again 2 create a new version of —**re·in·ven·tion** n

re·in·vest /rèe in vést/ vti 1 invest income made on a previous investment 2 invest profits in improving the business that produced them —**re·in·vest·ment** n

REIT abbr real estate investment trust

re·it·er·ate /ree íttə ráyt/ (-at·ed, -at·ing) vt repeat —**re·it·er·a·tion** /ree íttə ráysh'n/ n —**re·it·er·a·tive** adj

re·ject vt /ri jékt/ 1 not accept, believe, or make use of 2 deny love, kindness, or friendship to ■ n /rèe jèkt/ something or somebody rejected as unsuitable —**re·jec·tion** n

re·jig·ger /ree jíggər/ vt alter, rearrange, or readjust (infml)

re·joice /ri jóyss/ (-joiced, -joic·ing) vi feel or express great happiness (literary) —**re·joic·ing** n

re·join[1] /ree jóyn/ v 1 vt return to somebody after being apart 2 vti become a member of something again

re·join[2] /ri jóyn/ vti reply immediately and orally (fml)

re·join·der /ri jóyndər/ n a reply or retort (fml) ◊ See note at **answer**

re·ju·ve·nate /ri jóovə nàyt/ (-nat·ed, -nat·ing) vt 1 make somebody feel or look young again 2 restore something to its original condition —**re·ju·ve·na·tion** /-jòovə náysh'n/ n

re·kin·dle /ree kínd'l/ (-dled, -dling) vt 1 revive a feeling 2 make a fire burn again

re·lapse /ri láps/ (-lapsed, -laps·ing) vi 1 go back to a former undesirable state 2 become ill again after an apparent recovery —**re·lapse** /rèe láps/ n

re·late /ri láyt/ (-lat·ed, -lat·ing) v 1 vi have a connection with something else 2 vt find or show a connection between 3 vi involve or apply to somebody or something else 4 vi respond favorably, or form a friendly relationship based on understanding (infml) o I just can't relate to him. 5 vt tell or describe o related a tale of sorrow —**re·lat·a·ble** adj

re·lat·ed /ri láytəd/ adj 1 connected by similarity or a common origin 2 belonging to the same family —**re·lat·ed·ness** n

re·la·tion /ri láysh'n/ n 1 connection based on similarity or relevance 2 a member of the same family ■ **re·la·tions** npl 1 contacts between groups or people 2 sexual intercourse (euphemistic)

⚡ re·la·tion·al /ri láyshən'l, -láyshnəl/ adj 1 involving a relationship 2 describes a computer database organized or presented as a set of tables

re·la·tion·ship /ri láysh'n ship/ n 1 a connection or similarity 2 feelings for or behavior toward somebody else 3 a close friendship, especially one involving sex

rel·a·tive /réllətiv/ adj 1 in comparison with each other or another o discussed the relative merits of commuting by car pool or by public transportation 2 changing with circumstances or context 3 dependent on or in proportion to something else ■ n a member of the same family —**rel·a·tive·ly** adv

rel·a·tive clause n a clause that provides additional information about a preceding noun or pronoun

rel·a·tive den·si·ty n (symbol d) the ratio of the density of a substance to the density of a standard substance at the same temperature and pressure

rel·a·tive hu·mid·i·ty n the ratio of the amount of water vapor in the air at a given temperature to the maximum amount air can hold at the same temperature, expressed as a percentage

rel·a·tive pro·noun n a pronoun, e.g., "that" or "which," that introduces a relative clause

rel·a·tiv·ism /réllǝti vìzzǝm/ n the belief that concepts such as right and wrong are not absolute —**rel·a·tiv·is·tic** /rèllǝti vístik/ adj

rel·a·tiv·i·ty /rèllǝ tívvǝtee/ n 1 a theory showing that mass, length, and time change with velocity, or a similar theory relating to gravitation and acceleration 2 dependence on a variable factor

re·lax /ri láks/ v 1 vi spend time at ease 2 vti make or become less anxious or hostile 3 vti make or become less formal or strict 4 vti make or become less tense or tight —**re·lax·ant** n, adj —**re·lax·a·tion** /rèe lak sáysh'n/ n —**re·laxed** adj —**re·lax·ing** adj

re·lay /ree lày/ 1 the passing of something to somebody else 2 also **re·lay race** a race for teams in which each member covers part of the total distance (infml) 3 a replacement team of people or animals 4 a switching device that regulates another device or a system 5 an apparatus that receives and retransmits signals ■ vt /ri láy, rèe láy/ 1 pass something on to somebody or something else o relay a message 2 receive and retransmit a signal

re-lay /ree láy/ (**re-laid** /-láyd/, **re-laid** /-láyd/) vt lay again

re-lease /ri leéss/ vt (**-leased**, **-leas-ing**) 1 set somebody or something free 2 stop holding something 3 let something out ○ *released a plume of smoke* 4 free somebody from an obligation 5 fire or lay off an employee (fml) 6 make something available, e.g., for sale or publication 7 operate a mechanism to let something work ○ *released the clutch* ■ n 1 an act of releasing or being released 2 something made available to the public 3 the deliberate or accidental introduction of an industrial product into the environment 4 a control mechanism 5 a document confirming the surrender or relinquishment of something —**re-leas-a-ble** adj —**re-leas-er** n

rel-e-gate /réllə gàyt/ (**-gat-ed**, **-gat-ing**) vt move somebody or something to a lower or less important position or category than before —**rel-e-ga-tion** /réllə gáysh'n/ n

~~**releive**~~ incorrect spelling of **relieve**

re-lent /ri lént/ vi 1 become less strict and stop refusing to permit or do something 2 become less intense

re-lent-less /ri léntləss/ adj 1 ceaseless and intense 2 persistently hostile and merciless —**re-lent-less-ly** adv —**re-lent-less-ness** n

rel-e-vant /rélləvənt/ adj 1 having a logical connection 2 having current significance —**rel-e-vance** n —**rel-e-vant-ly** adv

~~**relevent**~~ incorrect spelling of **relevant**

re-li-a-ble /ri lī əb'l/ adj 1 able to be trusted or relied on 2 likely to be accurate —**re-li-a-bil-i-ty** /-lī ə bíllətee/ n —**re-li-a-bly** adv

re-li-ance /ri lī ənss/ n 1 dependence ○ *a reliance on painkillers* 2 trust or confidence —**re-li-ant** adj

rel-ic /réllik/ n 1 something old surviving from the past 2 a keepsake 3 something from a dead holy person

re-lief /ri leéf/ n 1 a freeing from suffering, anxiety, or boredom 2 a source of relief 3 somebody who replaces another 4 prominence caused by contrast 5 the projection of figures or shapes from a surface, e.g., in sculpture 6 aid provided to those in need 7 the freeing of a besieged town 8 the variations in the height of land

re-lief map n a map showing variations in the height of land

re-lieve /ri leév/ (**-lieved**, **-liev-ing**) v 1 vt stop something unpleasant 2 vt replace another person in a job or position 3 vt remove a burden from somebody 4 vr urinate 5 vt make less anxious (usually passive) 6 vt free a besieged place

re-li-gion /ri líjjən/ n 1 people's beliefs about and worship of deities 2 a particular system of such beliefs 3 a set of strongly held personal beliefs or values —**re-lig-ion-less** adj

re-li-gious /ri líjjəss/ adj 1 of religion 2 believing in a higher being 3 thorough or conscientious —**re-lig-ious-ly** adv —**re-lig-ious-ness** n

~~**religous**~~ incorrect spelling of **religious**

re-lin-quish /ri língkwish/ vt 1 renounce or surrender 2 abandon or let go of —**re-lin-quish-ment** n

rel-i-quar-y /rélli kwèrree/ (pl **-ies**) n a container or shrine for relics

rel-ish /réllish/ vt 1 take great pleasure in 2 enjoy the taste of ■ n 1 enjoyment 2 a spicy side dish or accompaniment to food 3 interest or excitement ○ *added relish to an otherwise dull weekend*

ORIGIN Relish is an adoption of a French noun formed from the verb that is the source of *release*. The idea is of a taste or smell being released to or left on the senses.

re-live /ree lív/ (**-lived**, **-liv-ing**) vt experience again

~~**rellevant**~~ incorrect spelling of **relevant**

re-lo-cate /ree lố kàyt, rèe lō káyt/ (**-cat-ed**, **-cat-ing**) vti move to a new place —**re-lo-ca-tion** /rèe lō káysh'n/ n

re-luc-tant /ri lúktənt/ adj 1 not willing or enthusiastic 2 uncooperative —**re-luc-tance** n —**re-luc-tant-ly** adv ◊ See note at **unwilling**

re-ly /ri lí/ (**-lied**, **-lies**) vi 1 depend on somebody or something 2 trust somebody or something

re-main /ri máyn/ vi 1 stay or wait somewhere 2 continue in a particular state 3 be left 4 be left to be dealt with ○ *The question still remains.* —**re-main-ing** adj

re-main-der /ri máyndər/ n 1 the part of something that is left over 2 the amount left over when a number or quantity cannot be divided exactly by another 3 an unsold copy of a book ■ vt sell unsold copies of a book at a reduced price

re-mains /ri máynz/ npl 1 all that is left of something 2 a corpse 3 ancient ruins

re-make n /rèe màyk/ a new version of something, especially a movie ■ vt /ree màyk/ (**-made** /-máyd/, **-mak-ing**) produce again

re-mand /ri mánd/ vt 1 return a prisoner or accused person to custody 2 send a case back to lower court ■ n the return of a prisoner or accused person to custody pending trial —**re-mand-ment** n

re-mark /ri maárk/ n 1 a casual comment 2 the making of a remark ■ v 1 vti comment on something 2 vt observe or notice (fml)

re-mark-a-ble /ri maárkəb'l/ adj 1 worth commenting on 2 unusual or exceptional —**re-mark-a-bly** adv

Re-marque /rə maárk/, **Erich Maria** (1898–1970) German-born US writer

re-mar-ry /ree márree/ (**-ried**, **-ries**) vi marry a second or subsequent time —**re·mar·riage** n

re·mas·ter /rée mástər/ vt make an improved master recording or movie of

re·match /rée màch/ n a second match between opponents —**re·match** /ree mách/ vt

Rem·brandt van Rijn /rém brànt vaan rín, -braànt-/ (1606–69) Dutch artist

re·me·di·al /ri meédee əl/ adj 1 acting as a remedy 2 helping to improve skills

re·me·di·a·tion /ri meédee áysh'n/ n the use of remedial methods, especially to improve skills or reverse environmental damage

rem·e·dy /rémmədee/ n (pl -dies) 1 a treatment for disease 2 a way of putting something right ■ vt (-died, -dies) 1 cure a disease 2 put something right —**re·me·di·a·ble** /ri meédee əb'l/ adj

re·mem·ber /ri mémbər/ v 1 vti recall something forgotten 2 vti keep something in your memory 3 vt keep somebody in mind 4 vt give greetings to somebody from somebody else ○ Remember me to your parents.

re·mem·brance /ri mémbrənss/ n 1 remembering or being remembered 2 the process of honoring the memory of a person or event 3 something remembered 4 a memento

Re·mem·brance Day n a day for the commemoration of war dead. Date: November 11.

re·mind /ri mínd/ vt cause to remember or think of ○ Remind me to collect the drycleaning. ○ He reminds me of his father. —**re·mind·er** n

Rem·ing·ton /rémmingtən/, Frederic (1861–1909) US artist

~~reminice~~ incorrect spelling of **reminisce**

rem·i·nisce /rèmmə níss/ (-nisced, -nisc·ing) vi talk or think about the past

rem·i·nis·cence /rèmmə níss'nss/ n 1 recollection of the past 2 something remembered from the past

rem·i·nis·cent /rèmmə níss'nt/ adj 1 suggestive of somebody or something else 2 suggestive of the past —**rem·i·nis·cent·ly** adv

re·miss /ri míss/ adj careless or negligent

re·mis·sion /ri mísh'n/ n 1 the easing or disappearance of the symptoms of a disease 2 release from a debt or obligation

re·mit /ri mít/ (-mit·ted, -mit·ting) v 1 vt send a payment 2 vt cancel or not enforce something 3 vti reduce in intensity 4 vt pardon or forgive something —**re·mit·tal** n

re·mit·tance /ri mítt'nss/ n 1 the sending of payment 2 money sent as payment

re·mix vt /ree míks/ produce a new version of a piece of recorded music by adding or altering tracks ■ n /reè míks/ a remixed recording

rem·nant /rémnənt/ n 1 a small part left over 2 a trace of something

re·mod·el /ree móddʹl/ vt renovate or alter the structure or style of —**re·mod·el·er** n

re·mon·strance /ri mónstrənss/ n 1 a forceful argument 2 a formal protest

re·mon·strate /ri món stràyt/ (-strat·ed, -strat·ing) vi argue strongly —**re·mon·stra·tion** /ri mòn stráysh'n, rèmmən-/ n —**re·mon·stra·tive** /-ətiv/ adj ◊ See note at object

re·morse /ri máwrs/ n a strong feeling of guilt and regret —**re·morse·ful** adj —**re·morse·ful·ly** adv

re·morse·less /ri máwrsləss/ adj 1 showing no compassion 2 continuing unabated —**re·morse·less·ly** adv —**re·morse·less·ness** n

re·mort·gage /ree máwrgij/ (-gaged, -gag·ing) vt change the terms of a mortgage on a property —**re·mort·gage** n

⚡**re·mote** /ri mót/ adj (-mot·er, -mot·est) 1 far away 2 away from populated areas 3 distantly related 4 distant in time 5 slight ○ a remote possibility 6 aloof 7 operated from a distance ■ n 1 a remote control (infml) 2 a computer situated far from a central computer —**re·mote·ly** adv —**re·mote·ness** n

⚡**re·mote ac·cess** n access to a computer from a separate terminal

re·mote con·trol n 1 a handheld control that operates something from a distance 2 operation from a distance —**re·mote-con·trolled** adj

re·mount /ree mównt/ v 1 vt mount again or differently 2 vti get back onto a horse

re·move /ri móov/ v (-moved, -mov·ing) 1 vt take away from somebody or something 2 vti go or take to a new place 3 vt take off ○ removed his hat 4 vt get rid of ○ removed the stain 5 vt dismiss from office ■ n the degree of distance between people or things —**re·mov·a·ble** adj —**re·mov·al** n

re·moved /ri móovd/ adj 1 distant 2 distantly related —**re·mov·ed·ness** /-ədnəss/ n

REM sleep /rém-/ n a stage of sleep marked by dreaming and rapid eye movements

re·mu·ner·ate /ri myóonə ràyt/ (-at·ed, -at·ing) vt give payment to —**re·mu·ner·a·ble** adj —**re·mu·ner·a·tion** /ri myóonə ráysh'n/ n —**re·mu·ner·a·tive** adj

Re·mus /reéməss/ n in Roman mythology, the son of Mars and twin brother of Romulus, the founder of the city of Rome

ren·ais·sance /rénnə saànss, rènnə saànss, ri náyss'nss/, **re·nas·cence** /ri náss'nss, -náyss'nss/ n 1 a rebirth or revival 2 **Ren·ais·sance** the period of European history that followed the Middle Ages and was characterized by cultural revival and scientific development —**Ren·ais·sance** adj

Ren·ais·sance man n a man with wide-ranging interests and talents

re·nal /réen'l/ *adj* of the kidneys

re·name /ree náym/ (**-named, -nam·ing**) *vt* give a new name to

re·nas·cent /ri náss'nt, -náyss'nt/ *adj* newly active

rend (**rent** or **rend·ed**) *v* **1** *vti* tear apart violently **2** *vt* disturb or pierce with a loud sound ○ *A scream rent the air.* **3** *vt* cause pain or distress to ◊ See note at **tear**

ren·der /réndar/ *vt (fml)* **1** give help or provide a service **2** translate something **3** portray something artistically **4** submit something for action **5** give what is due **6** put somebody into a particular state ○ *were rendered powerless* —**ren·der·a·ble** *adj* —**ren·der·ing** *n*

ren·dez·vous /ráan day voò, raàndɔ-/ *n (pl* **-vous** /-voòz/) **1** a meeting **2** the location of an arranged meeting ■ *vti* (**-voused** /-voòd/, **-vous·ing** /-voò ing/, **-vouses** /-voòz/) meet

ren·di·tion /ren dísh'n/ *n* **1** a version of a musical or theatrical piece **2** a translation

ren·e·gade /rénnə gàyd/ *n* **1** a traitor **2** a rebel

ren·ege /ri níg, -nég, -neèg/ (**-neged, -neg·ing**) *vi* **1** break a promise **2** in cards, not follow suit when able to

re·new /ri noó/ *vt* **1** begin again **2** make effective or available for a longer period of time ○ *renewed the contract* **3** repair or replace **4** revitalize —**re·new·al** *n* —**re·newed** *adj*

SYNONYMS renew, recondition, renovate, restore, revamp CORE MEANING: improve the condition of something

---

re·new·a·ble /ri noó əb'l/ *adj* able to be sustained or renewed ○ *renewable resources* —**re·new·a·bly** *adv*

ren·net /rénnət/ *n* **1** a preparation made from the stomach lining of calves. Use: cheese making. **2** a substance containing rennet, used in cheese making

Re·no /reénō/ city in W Nevada. Pop. 163,334 (1998).

AKG London

Pierre Auguste Renoir

Re·noir /rén waàr, rən waàr/, **Pierre Auguste** (1841–1919) French painter and sculptor

re·nounce /ri nównss/ (**-nounced, -nounc·ing**) *vt* **1** give up a claim to something **2** reject or disavow a belief —**re·nounce·ment** *n*

ren·o·vate /rénnə vàyt/ (**-vat·ed, -vat·ing**) *vt* restore to good condition —**ren·o·va·tion** /rènnə váysh'n/ *n* —**ren·o·va·tor** *n* ◊ See note at **renew**

re·nown /ri nówn/ *n* widespread acclaim —**re·nowned** *adj*

rent[1] *n* **1** regular payment by a tenant for the use of property **2** payment for the use of equipment ■ *vti* **1** pay to use somebody's property **2** allow the use of property for payment —**rent·a·ble** *adj* —**rent·er** *n*

rent[2] past tense, past participle of **rend** ■ *n* **1** a hole made by tearing **2** a rift in a relationship

rent·al /rént'l/ *n* **1** the amount of money paid or received in rent **2** the renting of something **3** something rented ■ *adj* for rent

rent-free *adj* free of charge ■ *adv* at no cost

re·nun·ci·a·tion /ri nùnsee áysh'n/ *n* **1** the denial or rejection of something **2** a formal declaration giving something up —**re·nun·ci·a·to·ry** /-núnsee ə tàwree/ *adj*

re·o·pen /ree ṓpən/ *vti* **1** open again **2** start again ○ *reopen the discussion*

re·or·gan·ize /ree áwrgə nìz/ (**-ized, -iz·ing**) *vti* **1** organize again after being disturbed **2** organize differently —**re·or·gan·i·za·tion** /ree àwrgəni záysh'n/ *n*

rep[1], **repp** *n* a ribbed fabric

rep[2] *n* a sales representative *(infml)*

rep[3] *n* a reputation *(infml)*

rep[4] *n* a repetition of a fitness exercise *(infml)*

rep. *abbr* reprint

Rep. *abbr* **1** Representative **2** Republic **3** Republican

re·paid past tense, past participle of **repay**

re·pair[1] /ri páir/ *vt* **1** restore something damaged or broken to good condition ○ *in need of repair* **2** put something right ■ *n* **1** the act of repairing something **2** the condition of something ○ *no longer in good repair* —**re·pair·a·ble** *adj* —**re·pair·er** *n*

re·pair[2] /ri páir/ *vi* go somewhere

rep·a·ra·ble /réppərəb'l/ *adj* able to be repaired —**rep·a·ra·bly** *adv*

rep·a·ra·tion /rèppə ráysh'n/ *n* **1** amends **2** the repairing of something *(fml)* ■ **rep·a·ra·tions** *npl* compensation for damage requested by the victorious side in a war —**re·par·a·to·ry** /ri párrə tàwree/ *adj*

rep·ar·tee /rèppər teè, -táy, -paar-/ *n* **1** witty talk **2** a witty remark

re·past /ri pást/ *n* a meal *(literary)*

re·pa·tri·ate *vt* /ree páytree àyt/ (**-at·ed, -at·ing**) send somebody back to his or her own country of birth, citizenship, or origin ■ *n* /ree páytree ət, -àyt/ somebody who has been repatriated —**re·pa·tri·a·tion** /ree pàytree áysh'n/ *n*

re·pay /ri páy/ (**-paid** /-páyd/) *vt* **1** pay back money to somebody **2** return a favor —**re·pay·a·ble** *adj* —**re·pay·ment** *n*

re·peal /ri peél/ *vt* revoke a law ■ *n* the repealing of a law —**re·peal·a·ble** *adj*

re·peat /ri peét/ *v* **1** *vti* say, do, or experience something again **2** *vti* echo somebody's words 3 *vt* tell what you have heard 4 *vt* say something memorized ■ *n* /reè peèt/ something such as a broadcast, pattern, or customer order that is repeated or recurs —**re·peat·a·ble** *adj* —**re·peat·ed** *adj* —**re·peat·ed·ly** *adv*

re·pel /ri pél/ (-pelled, -pel·ling) *vt* 1 resist an attack 2 keep something away 3 exert a force that tends to push something away 4 spurn somebody 5 disgust somebody

~~repellant~~ incorrect spelling of **repellent**

re·pel·lent /ri péllənt/ *adj* 1 resistant or impervious to something (often in combination) 2 causing disgust 3 pushing or driving away ■ *n* 1 a substance that drives away insects 2 a substance that makes a surface resistant to something —**re·pel·lence** *n* —**re·pel·lent·ly** *adv*

re·pent /ri pént/ *v* 1 *vti* be sorry for something 2 *vi* abandon bad habits or ways —**re·pen·tance** *n* —**re·pen·tant** *adj* —**re·pen·tant·ly** *adv*

~~repentence~~ incorrect spelling of **repentance**

re·per·cus·sion /reèpər kúsh'n/ *n* 1 an indirect or undesirable result of an action (often pl) 2 the rebounding of a force after impact —**re·per·cus·sive** *adj*

rep·er·toire /réppər twaàr/ *n* 1 a stock of artistic material that somebody can perform 2 a range of resources that somebody has

rep·er·to·ry /réppər tàwree/ (*pl* -ries) *n* 1 a system in which a theater company presents a set of plays during a single season 2 a performer's repertoire —**rep·er·to·ri·al** /réppər tàwree əl/ *adj*

rep·e·ti·tion /réppə tísh'n/ *n* 1 the process of repeating something 2 something that is the same as something that happened before

rep·e·ti·tious /réppə tíshəss/ *adj* full of repeated material

re·pet·i·tive /ri péttitiv/ *adj* involving repetition, especially to a boring degree —**re·pet·i·tive·ly** *adv* —**re·pet·i·tive·ness** *n*

re·phrase /ree fráyz/ *vt* say or write in different words

~~repitition~~ incorrect spelling of **repetition**

re·place /ri pláyss/ (-placed, -plac·ing) *vt* 1 take or fill the place of 2 put back in its place —**re·place·a·ble** *adj*

USAGE replace or **substitute**? These words take different constructions, although the resulting meaning is the same. You **replace** item B with (or less often by) item A, but **substitute** item A for item B.

re·place·ment /ri pláyssmənt/ *n* 1 the process of replacing something or somebody 2 a person or thing that takes another's place

re·play *vt* /ree pláy/ 1 play a game, match, or contest again 2 play a recording again ■ *n* /reè plày/ 1 a contest, match, or game played

again 2 a second playing of recorded material

re·plen·ish /ri plénnish/ *vt* replace used items in a stock —**re·plen·ish·ment** *n*

re·plete /ri pleét/ *adj* 1 amply or fully equipped 2 having eaten enough —**re·plete·ness** *n*

rep·li·ca /répplikə/ *n* an accurate reproduction

rep·li·cate /réppli kàyt/ (-cat·ed, -cat·ing) *vt* 1 repeat, copy, or reproduce something 2 reproduce by copying cellular or genetic material —**rep·li·ca·tion** /réppli káysh'n/ *n* ◊ See note at **copy**

re·ply /ri plí/ *v* (-plied, -plies) 1 *vti* respond to what somebody says or writes 2 *vi* respond to an action or gesture with an action or gesture ■ *n* (*pl* -plies) 1 a spoken or written answer 2 an action performed as a response —**re·pli·er** *n* ◊ See note at **answer**

re·port /ri páwrt/ *v* 1 *vti* tell somebody about something that happened 2 *vti* tell people news using the media 3 *vt* inform the authorities about something 4 *vt* give details about research results or an investigation 5 *vi* inform somebody of your arrival 6 *vi* be under somebody's authority ■ *n* 1 an account of something 2 a news item or broadcast 3 a document giving information about something 4 an unconfirmed account of something 5 a sharp loud noise —**re·port·a·ble** *adj*

re·port·age /ri páwrtij/ *n* 1 the reporting of news by the media 2 a body of reported news

re·port card *n* a written account of child's schoolwork

re·port·ed·ly /ri páwrtədlee/ *adv* according to unconfirmed reports

re·port·er /ri páwrtər/ *n* somebody who gathers and reports the news —**rep·or·to·ri·al** /réppər tàwree əl, reèpər-/ *adj*

re·pose¹ /ri póz/ *n* 1 rest 2 tranquility, calmness, or peace of mind ■ *v* (-posed, -pos·ing) (fml) 1 *vti* lie somewhere resting 2 *vi* be dead (euphemistic) —**re·pos·al** *n*

re·pose² /ri póz/ (-posed, -pos·ing) *vt* put faith or confidence in somebody or something (fml)

re·pos·i·to·ry /ri pózzə tàwree/ (*pl* -ries) *n* 1 a place or receptacle for storage 2 somebody with extensive knowledge

re·pos·sess /reèpə zéss/ *vt* reclaim goods or property that a buyer has not paid for —**re·pos·ses·sion** *n*

rep·re·hen·si·ble /réppri hénssəb'l/ *adj* deserving to be censured —**rep·re·hen·si·bly** *adv*

rep·re·sent /réppri zént/ *vt* 1 act or speak on behalf of 2 symbolize 3 go somewhere on behalf of 4 be the equivalent of 5 depict as being something in particular —**rep·re·sent·a·ble** *adj*

rep·re·sen·ta·tion /rèpprəzən táysh'n/ n 1 the fact of being represented by somebody else 2 an electoral system of representatives, or the representatives elected 3 a depiction of something 4 action or speech on behalf of somebody else

rep·re·sen·ta·tion·al /rèpprəzən táyshən'l, -táyshnəl/ adj 1 of or characterized by representation 2 describes art that portrays recognizable objects

rep·re·sen·ta·tive /rèpprə zéntətiv/ n 1 somebody who speaks or acts for another 2 a member of a legislature 3 also **Rep·re·sen·ta·tive** a member of the US House of Representatives or of a state legislature 4 a commercial agent or salesperson ■ adj 1 characteristic of something 2 involving or made up of elected representatives 3 made up of all types —**rep·re·sen·ta·tive·ly** adv —**rep·re·sen·ta·tive·ness** n

~~represententive~~ incorrect spelling of **representative**

re·press /ri préss/ vt 1 curb an action that would show feelings 2 use authority to control people's freedom 3 block something from the conscious mind —**re·pressed** adj —**re·press·i·ble** adj —**re·pres·sion** n —**re·pres·sive** adj —**re·pres·sive·ly** adv

re·prieve /ri préev/ vt (-prieved, -priev·ing) 1 halt or delay somebody's punishment 2 offer respite to somebody ■ n a halt to or delay of punishment —**re·priev·a·ble** adj

rep·ri·mand /rèpprə mànd/ vt rebuke for wrongdoing ■ n a rebuke

re·print vt /ree prínt/ print again ■ n /rée prìnt/ 1 PUBL = **offprint** 2 a reissue of a printed work

re·pri·sal /ri prízˈl/ n 1 a retaliation in war 2 any strong or violent retaliation

re·prise /ri príz/ n 1 a repeat of a musical passage 2 the chorus of a song ■ vt (-prised, -pris·ing) repeat a passage of music or a showing of a movie

re·proach /ri próch/ v 1 vt criticize somebody for wrongdoing 2 vr feel blameworthy ■ n 1 adverse criticism 2 discredit —**re·proach·a·ble** adj

re·proach·ful /ri próchfəl/ adj disapproving —**re·proach·ful·ly** adv —**re·proach·ful·ness** n

rep·ro·bate /rèpprə bàyt/ n somebody who lives an immoral life

re·pro·cess /ree pró sèss, -pró-/ vt process something again in order to reuse it

re·pro·duce /rèeprə dóoss/ (-duced, -duc·ing) v 1 vti duplicate or be duplicated by a process such as photography or scanning 2 vt repeat 3 vi produce offspring 4 vt remember or imagine again —**re·pro·duc·i·ble** adj ◊ See note at **copy**

re·pro·duc·tion /rèeprə dúkshən/ n 1 a copy of an object in an earlier style 2 the process

of reproducing 3 a printed, electronic, or photographic duplicate 4 the recording of sound 5 the production of offspring by sexual or asexual means

re·pro·duc·tive /rèeprə dúktiv/ adj involving the production of offspring —**re·pro·duc·tive·ness** n

⚡**re·pro·gram** /ree pró gràm/ (-grammed or -gramed, -gram·ming or -gram·ing) vt program a computer system differently —**re·pro·gram·ma·ble** adj

re·proof /ri próof/ n severe criticism

re·prove /ri próov/ (-proved, -prov·ing) vt criticize severely —**re·prov·ing·ly** adv

rep·tile /rép tìl, répt'l/ n a cold-blooded scaly vertebrate —**rep·tile** adj —**rep·til·i·an** /rep tíllee ən/ adj, n

re·pub·lic /ri púbblik/ n 1 a political system with elect representatives to exercise power and an elected representative, not a monarch, at its head 2 also **Re·pub·lic** a country whose political system is a republic

---

ORIGIN Republic came through French from Latin *res publica*, literally "public matter." It was adopted into English in the late 16C, and in early use could mean "the state, the general good" as well as "a state in which the people hold supreme power."

---

re·pub·li·can /ri púbblikən/ n 1 a supporter of republics as a form of government 2 **Re·pub·li·can** a member of the US Republican Party 3 **Re·pub·li·can** somebody who wants or works for a united Ireland —**re·pub·li·can·ism** n

Re·pub·li·can Par·ty n one of the two main US political parties

re·pu·di·ate /ri pyóodee àyt/ (-at·ed, -at·ing) vt 1 disapprove of and refuse to be associated with 2 deny the truth or validity of 3 refuse to acknowledge or pay ◊ *repudiate a debt*

re·pug·nant /ri púgnənt/ adj 1 offensive and unacceptable 2 revolting —**re·pug·nance** n —**re·pug·nant·ly** adv

re·pulse /ri púlss/ vt (-pulsed, -puls·ing) 1 repel an attacking force 2 disgust (infml) ■ n 1 a rejection 2 the process of repelling an attacking force

re·pul·sion /ri púlshən/ n 1 disgust 2 a repelling force between two bodies of like electric charge or magnetic polarity

re·pul·sive /ri púlsiv/ adj 1 disgusting 2 tending to repel —**re·pul·sive·ly** adv —**re·pul·sive·ness** n

re·pur·chase a·gree·ment /ree púrchəss-/ n 1 an agreement between a dealer and investor for the dealer to buy back securities 2 an agreement to buy something back

rep·u·ta·ble /rèppyətəbˈl/ adj known to be honest, reliable, or respectable

rep·u·ta·tion /rèppyə táyshˈn/ n the views that

are generally held about somebody or something

re·pute /ri pyóot/ *n* (*fml*) **1** estimation of character **2** good reputation

re·put·ed /ri pyóotəd/ *adj* generally believed —**re·put·ed·ly** *adv*

re·quest /ri kwést/ *vt* **1** ask politely for something **2** ask somebody to do something ■ *n* **1** the polite expression of a wish **2** something asked for

req·ui·em /rékwee əm/, **Req·ui·em** *n* **1** a Roman Catholic service for somebody who has died **2** the music for a requiem

re·quire /ri kwír/ (**-quired, -quir·ing**) *vt* **1** need for a particular purpose or as a precondition **2** demand by law **3** insist on —**re·quired** *adj* —**re·quire·ment** *n*

req·ui·site /rékwizit/ *adj* essential (*fml*) ■ *n* something that is essential ◊ See note at **necessary**

req·ui·si·tion /rèkwi zísh'n/ *n* **1** a formal demand or request for something **2** the process of making a formal demand or request ■ *vt* demand and take officially

re·quite /ri kwít/ (**-quit·ed, -quit·ing**) *vt* return a kindness or hurt in kind —**re·quit·al** *n*

re·re·lease /rèe ri leéss/ *vt* (**-leased, -leas·ing**) distribute a music recording or movie again ■ *n* a rereleased recording or movie

re·route /ree rówt, -róot/ (**-rout·ed, -rout·ing**) *vt* direct vehicles or people another way

re·run /ree rún/ (**-ran** /-rán/, **-run, -run·ning**) *vt* show a broadcast again —**re·run** /rèe rùn/ *n*

re·sale /rèe sàyl/ *n* **1** the selling of something again **2** the selling of something secondhand —**re·sal·a·ble** /rèe sáyləb'l/ *adj*

re·sched·ule /rée skéjjool/ (**-uled, -ul·ing**) *vt* **1** change the time fixed for something **2** extend the repayment period of a loan

re·scind /ri sínd/ *vt* cancel or abolish something —**re·scind·a·ble** *adj*

res·cue /réskyoo/ *v* (**-cued, -cu·ing**) **1** *vt* save from danger or harm **2** save from being discarded ■ *n* **1** removal from danger or harm **2** an instance of providing help to somebody in a difficult situation —**res·cu·a·ble** *adj* —**res·cu·er** *n*

res·cue work·er *n* a member of a medical or emergency service

re·search *n* /rée sùrch, ri súrch/ methodical study or investigation to discover facts or establish a theory ■ *vti* /ri súrch, rèe sùrch/ study something methodically —**re·search·er** *n*

re·search and de·vel·op·ment *n* investigation and development of new or improved products

re·sell /rèe sél/ (**-sold** /-sóld/) *vt* sell something previously purchased to a new buyer

re·sem·blance /ri zémblənss/ *n* similarity, especially in appearance, to somebody or something else

re·sem·ble /ri zémb'l/ (**-bled, -bling**) *vt* be similar to

~~resemblence~~ incorrect spelling of **resemblance**

re·sent /ri zént/ *vt* be annoyed about or toward a perceived unfairness —**re·sent·ment** *n*

re·sent·ful /ri zéntfəl/ *adj* annoyed about something regarded as unfair —**re·sent·ful·ly** *adv* —**re·sent·ful·ness** *n*

res·er·va·tion /rèzzər váysh'n/ *n* **1** an arrangement by which something such as a room or seat is booked in advance **2** the process of arranging something in advance **3** an area of land set aside for a particular purpose, especially for the use of a Native North American people **4** a limiting condition ■ **res·er·va·tions** *npl* doubts or misgivings

re·serve /ri zúrv/ *vt* (**-served, -serv·ing**) **1** set something aside for future use or a specific purpose **2** book a place beforehand **3** retain something such as a right for your own benefit **4** postpone a decision ○ *reserve judgment* ■ *n* **1** coolness of manner **2** a substitute player **3** a part or member of the armed services not on active duty at a given time **4** a country's supply of gold and foreign currency kept as a contingency **5** a supply of a natural resource not yet utilized **6** *Can* a Native North American reservation ■ **re·serves** *npl* inner strengths drawn on in an emergency —**re·serv·a·ble** *adj*

re·serve bank *n* one of 12 banks in the US Federal Reserve system

re·serve cur·ren·cy *n* a foreign currency held by a central bank for settling international transactions

re·served /ri zúrvd/ *adj* **1** booked in advance **2** set aside for a specific use **3** reticent or emotionally restrained —**re·serv·ed·ly** /-ədlee/ *adv* —**re·serv·ed·ness** *n*

re·serv·ist /ri zúrvist/ *n* a member of a military reserve force

res·er·voir /rézzər vwàar/ *n* **1** a lake or tank for storing water **2** a part of a machine or device where liquid is stored

re·set /rèe sét/ (**-set, -set·ting**) *vt* **1** set something again **2** put a dial or counter back to its original setting

re·set·tle /rèe sétt'l/ (**-tled, -tling**) *vt* relocate a population —**re·set·tle·ment** *n*

~~resevoir~~ incorrect spelling of **reservoir**

re·shape /rèe sháyp/ (**-shaped, -shap·ing**) *vt* **1** change or restore the shape of **2** change the organization of

re·shuf·fle /rèe shúff'l/ *n* **1** a shuffling of cards again **2** a redistribution of jobs —**re·shuf·fle** *vti*

re·side /ri zíd/ (**-sid·ed, -sid·ing**) *vi* **1** live somewhere **2** be present

res·i·dence /rézzid'nss/ *n* **1** a place where somebody lives **2** the fact or time of living somewhere **3** medical training in a specialty following internship

res·i·den·cy /rézzid'nsee/ (*pl* **-cies**) *n* **1** medical training in a specialty following internship **2** the fact or time of living somewhere

⨍ **res·i·dent** /rézzid'nt/ *n* **1** somebody who is living in a place **2** a doctor who is completing a residency **3** a member of a government intelligence agency who lives in and oversees operations in a foreign country ■ *adj* **1** living in a particular place **2** living somewhere as part of a job **3** permanently retained in a computer's random-access memory for quick access —**res·i·dent·ship** *n*

res·i·den·tial /rèzzi dénshəl/ *adj* **1** consisting of private housing rather than offices or factories **2** providing living accommodations ○ *a residential post*

re·sid·u·al /ri zíjjoo əl/ *adj* left over ■ *n* **1** something left over **2** a fee paid to writers, performers, and directors when their work is broadcast again —**res·id·u·al·ly** *adv*

res·i·due /rézzi doò/ *n* something left over after another part has been removed

re·sign /ri zín/ *v* **1** *vti* give up a job or position **2** *vr* accept something reluctantly —**re·signed** *adj* —**re·sign·ed·ly** /-əèdlee/ *adv*

re·sign /ree sín/ *vti* sign or have a player sign another contract

res·ig·na·tion /rèzzig náysh'n/ *n* **1** the act of resigning, or a formal notification of this **2** reluctant acceptance of something

re·sil·ient /ri zíllyənt/ *adj* **1** recovering quickly from setbacks **2** elastic —**re·sil·ience** *n* —**re·sil·ien·cy** *n* —**re·sil·ient·ly** *adv*

res·in /rézzin/ *n* **1** a semisolid substance secreted in the sap of some plants **2** a synthetic compound resembling natural resin. Use: manufacture of petrochemicals and plastics. —**res·in·ous** *adj*

re·sist /ri zíst/ *v* **1** *vti* oppose or stand firm against **2** *vt* refuse to accept or comply with **3** *vt* be unaffected by ○ *ability to resist infection* **4** *vti* say no to something tempting —**re·sis·ter** *n* —**re·sist·i·ble** *adj*

re·sis·tance /ri zístənss/ *n* **1** opposition **2** refusal to accept or comply with something **3** the ability to remain undamaged by something **4** (*symbol* R *or* r) a force that opposes or slows another force **5** (*symbol* R) the opposition that a device or substance presents to the flow of electricity **6** **Re·sis·tance** a secret organization that fights for freedom against an occupying power —**re·sist·ant** *adj*

~~resistence~~ incorrect spelling of **resistance**

re·sis·tor /ri zístər/ *n* a component that controls the flow of electricity

re·sold past tense, past participle of **resell**

res·o·lute /rézzə loòt/ *adj* determined and purposeful —**res·o·lute·ly** *adv* —**res·o·lute·ness** *n*

res·o·lu·tion /rèzzə loòsh'n/ *n* **1** the process of resolving something such as a dispute **2** a formal expression of the consensus of a group, usually as the result of a vote **3** a firm decision **4** determination **5** the quality of the detail on a screen or in a photographic image **6** a solution to a problem

re·solve /ri zólv/ *v* (**-solved, -solv·ing**) **1** *vt* come to a firm decision about **2** *vti* split into constituent parts **3** *vt* express formally as the consensus of a group **4** *vt* find a solution to **5** *vt* dispel ○ *resolved all doubts* **6** *vt* bring to a satisfactory conclusion ■ *n* **1** determination **2** a firm decision —**re·solv·a·ble** *adj* —**re·solved** *adj*

res·o·nance /rézzənənss/ *n* **1** the resonant quality of something **2** an underlying meaning of an event or work of art **3** an intense and prolonged sound produced by sympathetic vibration

res·o·nant /rézzənənt/ *adj* **1** deep and rich in sound **2** continuing to sound for some time —**res·o·nant·ly** *adv*

res·o·nate /rézzə nàyt/ (**-nat·ed, -nat·ing**) *v* **1** *vti* resound or echo, or cause to resound or echo **2** *vi* have an impact beyond that which is apparent

res·o·na·tor /rézzə nàytər/ *n* a resonating device or part that produces sound or microwaves

re·sort /ri záwrt/ *n* **1** a place popular with people on vacation **2** a source of help **3** the act of turning to somebody or something for help ◊ **resort to** have recourse to something, often an extreme measure, in order to achieve something ○ *had to resort to blackmail*

re·sort /ree sáwrt/ *vt* sort again

re·sound /ri zównd/ *vi* **1** be filled with a reverberating sound **2** sound loudly and clearly **3** make a reverberating sound

re·sound·ing /ri zównding/ *adj* **1** clear and emphatic **2** echoing loudly —**re·sound·ing·ly** *adv*

re·source /reè sàwrs, ri sáwrs/ *n* **1** a source of help **2** a supply of something needed **3** the ability to find solutions to problems ■ **re·sour·ces** *npl* **1** inner abilities drawn on when necessary **2** natural, economic, or military assets ■ *vt* provide with resources

re·source al·low·ance *n Can* a tax benefit for some producers

re·source·ful /ri sáwrsfəl/ *adj* ingenious and enterprising —**re·source·ful·ly** *adv* —**re·source·ful·ness** *n*

re·spect /ri spékt/ *n* **1** an individual characteristic ○ *satisfactory in all respects* **2** an attitude of admiration and deference **3** the state of being respected **4** consideration or thoughtfulness ■ **re·spects** *npl* polite greetings ■ *vt* **1** feel or show admiration and deference toward **2** pay attention to or not violate o *respect the law* **3** be considerate of or toward —**re·spect·ed** *adj* —**re·spect·er** *n* ◊ See note at **regard**

re·spect·a·ble /ri spéktəb'l/ *adj* **1** reflecting accepted standards of correctness or decency **2** satisfactory **3** of a presentable appearance *(infml)* —**re·spect·a·bil·i·ty** /-spèktə bíllətee/ *n* —**re·spect·a·bly** *adv*

re·spect·ful /ri spéktfəl/ *adj* showing respect —**re·spect·ful·ly** *adv* —**re·spect·ful·ness** *n*

re·spec·tive /ri spéktiv/ *adj* relating to each one considered separately o *returning to their respective homes* —**re·spec·tive·ly** *adv*

res·pi·ra·tion /rèspə ráysh'n/ *n* **1** breathing **2** the process in living organisms that produces energy by the exchange of gases with the environment —**res·pi·ra·to·ry** /réspərə tàwree, ri spírə-/ *adj*

res·pi·ra·tor /réspə ràytər/ *n* **1** a machine that artificially maintains breathing **2** a protective mask through which somebody breathes

re·spire /ri spīr/ (-**spired**, -**spir·ing**) *v* **1** *vti* breathe **2** *vi* undergo the process of respiration

res·pite /réspit/ *n* **1** a brief period of rest or relief **2** a temporary delay or reprieve

~~resplendant~~ incorrect spelling of **resplendent**

re·splen·dent /ri spléndənt/ *adj* dazzlingly impressive —**re·splen·dence** *n* —**re·splen·dent·ly** *adv*

re·spond /ri spónd/ *v* **1** *vti* provide an answer **2** *vi* react

~~respondant~~ incorrect spelling of **respondent**

re·spon·dent /ri spóndənt/ *n* **1** somebody who replies to something **2** the defendant in a divorce case or an appeal —**re·spon·dent** *adj*

~~responsability~~ incorrect spelling of **responsibility**

re·sponse /ri spónss/ *n* **1** a reply to a question **2** a reaction **3** a reply made by the church choir or congregation during some services ◊ See note at **answer**

⌁ **re·sponse time** *n* **1** a reaction time **2** a time from issuing an instruction to action

re·spon·si·bil·i·ty /ri spònssə bíllətee/ (*pl* -**ties**) *n* **1** the state of being responsible **2** blame for something o *take full responsibility* **3** something for which somebody is responsible **4** the authority to act

re·spon·si·ble /ri spónssəb'l/ *adj* **1** accountable to somebody for something **2** requiring trustworthiness and conscientiousness o *a responsible position* **3** being to blame for something **4** in charge of somebody or something **5** reliable **6** rational and accountable for your actions **7** authorized to act —**re·spon·si·bly** *adv*

re·spon·sive /ri spónssiv/ *adj* **1** showing a positive response **2** done in response to

something —**re·spon·sive·ly** *adv* —**re·spon·sive·ness** *n*

rest¹ *n* **1** a state or period of refreshing freedom from exertion **2** the repose of sleep **3** a stopping of movement **4** the repose of death **5** freedom from anxiety o *put her mind at rest* **6** a pause in music **7** a place to stop and relax **8** a support, especially on a piece of furniture ■ *v* **1** *vti* regain or cause to regain energy by means of relaxation or sleep **2** *vi* be tranquil **3** *vi* be dead **4** *vti* stop moving or working temporarily **5** *vi* be subject to no further attention o *Let the matter rest.* **6** *vti* support or be supported **7** *vi* depend on somebody or something —**rest·ed** *adj*

rest² *n* the remainder (+ *sing or pl verb*) ■ *vi* continue to be *(usually a command)*

~~restaraunt~~ incorrect spelling of **restaurant**

rest ar·e·a *n* US, Can, ANZ a stopping place for drivers

re·start /ree staárt/ *vti* start again —**re·start** /reé staàrt/ *n*

res·tau·rant /réstərənt, -ront/ *n* a place where meals are sold and served to customers

---

ORIGIN A **restaurant** is literally a place where people are "restored" or refreshed. The word was adopted from French in the early 19C.

---

res·tau·ra·teur /rèstərə túr/, **res·tau·ran·teur** /réstərəntər, -ròntər/ *n* a restaurant owner or manager

rest·ful /réstfəl/ *adj* **1** providing rest **2** calm or tranquil —**rest·ful·ly** *adv* —**rest·ful·ness** *n*

rest home *n* a supervised home for infirm senior citizens and chronically ill people

res·ti·tu·tion /rèsti tóosh'n/ *n* **1** the return of something to its owner **2** compensation for loss, damage, or injury

res·tive /réstiv/ *adj* impatient and on the verge of resisting control —**res·tive·ly** *adv* —**res·tive·ness** *n*

rest·less /réstləss/ *adj* **1** constantly moving, or unable to be still **2** seeking change because of discontent **3** unable to rest or sleep —**rest·less·ly** *adv* —**rest·less·ness** *n*

re·stock /ree stók/ *vti* replenish a stock of something

res·to·ra·tion /rèstə ráysh'n/ *n* **1** the returning of something to its former condition or state **2** **Res·to·ra·tion** the return to monarchy in England in 1660

re·stor·a·tive /ri stáwrətiv/ *adj* restoring strength or vigor —**re·stor·a·tive** *n*

re·store /ri stáwr/ (-**stored**, -**stor·ing**) *vt* **1** give or put back **2** return to an earlier or better condition or position —**re·stor·er** *n* ◊ See note at **renew**

re·strain /ri stráyn/ *vt* **1** prevent from doing something **2** control or keep within limits —**re·strain·a·ble** *adj* —**re·strained** *adj*

re·straint /ri stráynt/ *n* **1** moderate or controlled behavior o *showing admirable re-*

straint **2** something that restrains, controls, or limits ○ *impose trade restraints* **3** a device for limiting somebody's freedom of movement

~~restraunt~~ incorrect spelling of **restaurant**

re·strict /ri stríkt/ *vt* keep within limits —**re·strict·ed** *adj* —**re·strict·ed·ness** *n* —**re·stric·tion** *n*

re·stric·tive /ri stríktiv/ *adj* **1** tending to restrict **2** limiting the range of reference or application of a word, phrase, or clause —**re·stric·tive·ly** *adv* —**re·stric·tive·ness** *n*

rest·room /rést ròom, -ròom/ *n* a room that includes a toilet, especially in a public building

re·struc·ture /ree strúkchər/ (-tured, -tur·ing) *v* **1** *vti* change the basic structure of something **2** *vt* alter the terms of a loan

re·sult /ri zúlt/ *vi* **1** follow as a consequence **2** cause a particular outcome ■ *n* **1** something that is caused by another action, condition, or event **2** a score, e.g., in a sporting competition or on a test ■ **re·sults** *npl* the desired outcome

re·sul·tant /ri zúltn't/ *adj* resulting from something ■ *n* something that results from something else

re·sume /ri zóom/ (-sumed, -sum·ing) *v* **1** *vti* continue after a pause **2** *vt* take, assume, or occupy again —**re·sump·tion** /ri zúmpshən/ *n*

ré·su·mé /rézzə màyÎ, re·su·mé, re·su·me /n* **1** *US, Can, ANZ* a summary of somebody's work and educational experience **2** a summary

re·sur·face /ree súrfəss/ (-faced, -fac·ing) *v* **1** *vi* come to the surface again **2** *vi* appear again **3** *vt* put a new surface on

re·sur·gence /ri súrjənss/ *n* a rising or strengthening again ○ *a resurgence of a patriotism* —**re·surg·ent** *adj*

res·ur·rect /rèzzə rékt/ *vt* **1** raise from the dead **2** bring back into use

res·ur·rec·tion /rèzzə rékshən/ *n* **1** in some belief systems, a rising from or raising of somebody from the dead **2 Res·ur·rec·tion** in Christian belief, Jesus Christ's rising from the dead **3** the revival of something

re·sus·ci·tate /ri sússi tàyt/ (-tat·ed, -tat·ing) *vti* revive, or be revived, from unconsciousness —**re·sus·ci·ta·tion** /ri sùssi táysh'n/ *n* —**re·sus·ci·ta·tive** *adj*

re·tail /reé tàyÎ/ *n* the sale of goods to consumers ■ *adv* from a store in small quantities at the consumer price ■ *vti* sell goods to consumers —**re·tail·er** *n* —**re·tail·ing** *n*

re·tain /ri táyn/ *vt* **1** keep possession of **2** remember **3** keep in a particular place or position **4** pay a fee in order to reserve the professional services of —**re·tain·a·ble** *adj* —**re·tain·ment** *n*

re·tain·er /ri táynər/ *n* **1** a device for holding something in place **2** a paid servant in a household **3** a fee paid to reserve professional services ◊ **on (a) retainer** paid

regularly in order to be consulted whenever necessary

re·tain·ing wall *n* a wall built to keep earth or water in place

re·take /ree táyk/ (-took /-tóok/, -tak·en /-táykən/, -tak·ing) *vt* **1** recapture from an enemy **2** record, photograph, or film again —**re·take** /reé tàyk/ *n*

re·tal·i·ate /ri tállee àyt/ (-at·ed, -at·ing) *vi* deliberately harm somebody in revenge —**re·tal·i·a·tion** /ri tàllee àysh'n/ *n* —**re·tal·i·a·to·ry** /ri tállee ə tàwree/ *adj*

re·tard /ri taárd/ *vt* slow or delay the progress of —**re·tar·da·tion** /reè taar dáysh'n/ *n*

re·tard·ed /ri taárdid/ *adj* **1** underdeveloped **2** an offensive term meaning intellectually or emotionally challenged

retch /rech/ *vi* **1** experience a vomiting spasm **2** vomit ■ *n* a vomiting spasm

SPELLCHECK Do not confuse the spelling of **retch** and **wretch** ("somebody who is pitied"), which sound similar.

retd. *abbr* **1** retired **2** returned

re·ten·tion /ri ténsh'n/ *n* the process of retaining something or the condition of being retained

re·ten·tive /ri téntiv/ *adj* able to retain something **2** with a good memory —**re·ten·tive·ness** *n*

re·think /ree thíngk/ (-thought /-tháwt/) *vti* think about something again with a view to changing opinions or plans

ret·i·cent /réttiss'nt/ *adj* **1** tending not to talk openly or much **2** reluctant —**ret·i·cence** *n* —**ret·i·cent·ly** *adv* ◊ See note at **silent**

ret·i·na /rétt'nə/ (*pl* **-nas** *or* **-nae** /-nee/) *n* the light-sensitive membrane at the back of the eye —**ret·i·nal** *adj*

ret·i·nue /rétt'n ò͡o/ *n* a group of followers or attendants

re·tire /ri tír/ (-tired, -tir·ing) *v* **1** *vi* stop working permanently and voluntarily **2** *vi* go to bed **3** *vi* leave a place or position ○ *has retired from public life* **4** *vt* take out of service **5** *vt* in baseball, end a term at bat by putting out **6** *vti* withdraw from a sports contest —**re·tire·ment** *n*

re·tired /ri tírd/ *adj* **1** no longer working **2** having withdrawn

re·tir·ee /ri tì reé/ *n* somebody who has retired from work

re·tir·ing /ri tíring/ *adj* **1** shy and reserved **2** involving or undergoing retirement —**re·tir·ing·ly** *adv*

re·tool /ree tóol/ *v* **1** *vti* replace the equipment in a place **2** *vt* reorganize something in order to maximize efficiency

re·tort[1] /ri táwrt/ *vt* **1** respond sharply or wittily **2** put forward as an argument in reply to ■ *n* a sharp or witty answer ◊ See note at **answer**

re·tort² /ri táwrt/ *n* **1** a glass container with a long spout used in distillation **2** a closed container for heating substances ■ *vt* heat in a retort

re·touch /ree túch/ *vt* remove imperfections from, or make small finishing changes to —**re·touch** /ree tùch, ree túch/ *n*

re·trace /ri tráyss/ (**-traced, -trac·ing**) *vt* go back over a path or route again

re·tract /ri trákt/ *v* **1** *vti* move or draw in from an extended position **2** *vt* withdraw a statement or promise —**re·tract·a·ble** *adj* —**re·trac·tion** *n*

re·train /ree tráyn/ *vti* teach or learn a new skill —**re·train·a·ble** *adj*

re·tread /ree tréd/ **1** a tire with new tread **2** a remake ■ *vt* /ree tréd/ bond new tread to a tire

re·tread /ree tréd/ (**re·trod** /-tród/, **re·trod·den** /-tródd'n/) *vt* walk a route again

re·treat /ri tréet/ *n* **1** a movement away from danger or confrontation **2** a withdrawal of military forces, or a signal for this **3** a withdrawal from a previously held point of view **4** a place or period of time for rest, meditation, or privacy ■ *vi* **1** move away, especially from danger or confrontation **2** make a military withdrawal

re·trench /ri trénch/ *vi* economize —**re·trench·ment** *n*

re·tri·al /ree trī əl/ *n* a second trial following a flawed or inconclusive trial

ret·ri·bu·tion /rèttrə byóosh'n/ *n* punishment or vengeance —**re·trib·u·tive** /ri tríbbyətiv/ *adj* —**re·trib·u·to·ry** /ri tríbbyə tàwree/ *adj*

⚡**re·trieve** /ri tréev/ (**-trieved, -triev·ing**) *vt* **1** get something back **2** save something from being lost or damaged **3** remedy a situation **4** get data from a computer storage device —**re·triev·a·ble** *adj* —**re·triev·al** *n*

re·triev·er /ri tréevər/ *n* **1** a large dog belonging to a breed originally used to fetch game shot by a hunter **2** somebody or something that retrieves

ret·ro /réttrō/ *adj* modeled on something from the past ■ *n* (*pl* **-ros**) **1** the use of past styles **2** a retrorocket

retro- *prefix* back, backward, after ○ *retrorocket* ○ *retrofit*

ret·ro·ac·tive /rèttrō áktiv/ *adj* applying to the past and continuing into the present ○ *retroactive pay increases*

ret·ro·fit /réttrō fít/ *vt* modify something old with a newly available part —**ret·ro·fit** *n*

ret·ro·flex /réttrō fléks/, **ret·ro·flexed** /-flèksd/ *adj* bent backward

ret·ro·grade /réttrō gràyd/ *adj* **1** moving backward **2** returning to an earlier worse state

ret·ro·gress /rèttrō gréss/ *vi* **1** return to an earlier worse condition **2** go backward —**ret·ro·gres·sion** *n* —**ret·ro·gres·sive** *adj* —**ret·ro·gres·sive·ly** *adv*

ret·ro·rock·et /réttrō ròkət/ *n* a small rocket engine that produces thrust to act against the main engines

ret·ro·spect /réttrə spèkt/ ◇ **in retrospect** when reviewing the past, especially from a new perspective or with new information

ret·ro·spec·tion /rèttrə spéksh'n/ *n* the act of looking back over the past

ret·ro·spec·tive /rèttrə spéktiv/ *adj* **1** reviewing the past **2** containing an artist's past works ■ *n* an exhibition of an artist's past work

re·try /ree trī/ *v* (**-tried, -tries**) **1** *vt* try again in a court of law **2** *vti* attempt again ■ *n* (*pl* **-tries**) a second attempt

ret·si·na /rétsinə, ret seénə/ *n* a resin-flavored wine from Greece

⚡**re·turn** /ri túrn/ *v* **1** *vi* come or go back to a place or former condition **2** *vi* mention or consider something again **3** *vi* appear or happen again **4** *vt* put, give, send, or bring something back **5** *vt* yield a profit **6** *vt* reelect somebody to office **7** *vt* give a verdict in court **8** *vt* in racket sports, hit a ball back ■ *n* **1** a going or coming back to a place or previous condition **2** the act of returning something **3** something returned **4** the reappearance of something **5** a response to something done or given ○ *give love in return* **6** a profit (*often pl*) **7** also **re·turns** *npl* election results ■ *adj* **1** of going or coming back to a place **2** happening again —**re·turn·a·ble** *adj*, *n* —**re·turn·ee** /ri tùr neé/ *n*

re·turn·ing of·fi·cer *n Can, UK, Aus* an election official responsible for overseeing the count

re·u·ni·fy /ree yoōnə fī/ (**-fied, -fies**) *vti* reunite after being divided —**re·u·ni·fi·ca·tion** /-yoōnəfi káysh'n/ *n*

re·un·ion /ree yoōnyən/ *n* **1** the act of reuniting or being reunited **2** a gathering of relatives, old friends, or former colleagues

re·u·nite /rèe yoo nít/ (**-nit·ed, -nit·ing**) *vti* come or bring back together after separation

re·use *vt* /ree yooz/ (**-used, -us·ing**) use again ■ *n* /ree yooss/ the reusing of something —**re·us·a·ble** *adj*

Reu·ters /róytərz/ *n* a British news agency providing international news reports

Reu·ther /roōthər/, **Walter Philip** (1907–70) US labor leader

re·ut·il·ize /ree yoōt'l ìz/ (**-ized, -iz·ing**) *vt* utilize something again —**re·ut·il·i·za·tion** /rèeyoot'li záysh'n/ *n*

rev *vti* (**revved, rev·ving**) increase the speed of an engine ■ *n* a single engine revolution (*infml; usually pl*)

rev. *abbr* **1** revenue **2** reverse **3** review **4** revised **5** revolution

Rev., Revd. *abbr* Reverend

re·val·ue /ree vállyoo/ (**-ued**, **-u·ing**), **re·val·u·ate** /-àyt/ (**-at·ed**, **-at·ing**) vt **1** raise the value of a currency **2** reassess the value of something

re·vamp /reè vámp/ vt alter for the better —**re·vamp** n ◊ See note at **renew**

re·veal /ri veél/ vt **1** make known **2** expose to view

re·veal·ing /ri veéling/ adj **1** showing parts of the body that are normally covered **2** disclosing new or surprising information —**re·veal·ing·ly** adv

re·veil·le /révvəlee/ n a bugle call to awaken military personnel

rev·el /révv'l/ vi **1** take pleasure in something **2** enjoy a party ■ n a noisy celebration (often pl) —**rev·el·er** n

revelant incorrect spelling of **relevant**

rev·e·la·tion /rèvvə láysh'n/ n **1** a piece of new or surprising information that is disclosed **2** an unexpectedly good or valuable new experience **3** a demonstration of divine will **4 Rev·e·la·tion, Rev·e·la·tions** a book of the Bible that includes a description of the end of the world —**rev·e·la·to·ry** /révvələ tàwree, ri véllə-/ adj

rev·el·ry /révv'lree/ (pl **-ries**) n noisy celebrating (often pl)

re·venge /ri vénj/ vt (**-venged**, **-veng·ing**) administer punishment in retaliation for something ■ n **1** the desire to punish somebody in retaliation **2** punishment administered in retaliation for harm done —**re·venge·ful** adj —**re·veng·er** n

rev·e·nue /révvə noo/ n the income of a business or government

rev·e·nue bond n a bond issued by a government

rev·e·nue shar·ing n distribution of a portion of federal income to state and local governments

re·verb /ri vúrb/ n **1** an electronically produced echo in music **2** an echo-producing device —**re·verb** vi

re·ver·ber·ate /ri vúrbə ràyt/ (**-at·ed**, **-at·ing**) v **1** vti echo or cause to echo **2** vi have a continuing or far-reaching effect —**re·ver·ber·ant** adj —**re·ver·ber·a·tion** /ri vùrbə ráysh'n/ n

ORIGIN Reverberate derives from a Latin verb meaning "beat back," which was formed from verbera "whips, rods." "Beat or drive back" was the original English sense, lasting from the late 15C to the late 18C. Figurative senses such as "echo" developed from the late 16C.

re·vere /ri veér/ (**-vered**, **-ver·ing**) vt treat or regard with admiring respect

Re·vere /ri veér/, **Paul** (1735–1818) American silversmith and patriot

rev·er·ence /révvərənss/ n **1** feelings of deep respect **2** also **Rev·er·ence** a form of address for a member of the Christian clergy ■ vt (**-enced**, **-enc·ing**) show deep respect for (fml) ◊ See note at **regard**

rev·er·end /révvərənd/ adj **1** of the Christian clergy **2** respected (fml) ■ n **1** a member of the Christian clergy (infml) **2 Rev·er·end** a form of address for a member of the Christian clergy

Rev·er·end Moth·er n a form of address for a Mother Superior

rev·er·en·tial /rèvvə rénshəl/ adj **1** also **rev·er·ent** /révvərənt/ deeply respectful **2** deserving respect —**rev·er·en·tial·ly** adv

rev·er·ie /révvəree/ (pl **-ies**) n a daydream

re·ver·sal /ri vúrs'l/ n **1** a change to the opposite direction **2** a setback **3** the reversing of something

re·verse /ri vúrs/ adj **1** opposite to the usual or previous arrangement **2** on the back side **3** for backward movement ■ n **1** the opposite of something **2** the back side of something **3** a change to the opposite direction or position **4** a setback **5** the gear in a vehicle for backward movement ■ v (**-versed**, **-vers·ing**) **1** vt change something to the opposite direction or position **2** vti go or cause to go backward **3** vt turn something inside out **4** vt revoke an earlier ruling

re·verse dis·crim·i·na·tion n discrimination against dominant social groups

re·verse en·gi·neer·ing n piracy of a competitor's technology by dismantling and reproducing its product —**re·verse-en·gi·neer** vt

re·verse mort·gage n a mortgage in which a bank pays an annuity to a homeowner and charges it against the home's equity

re·verse take·o·ver n a sale of a company to avoid a hostile takeover

↯ re·verse vid·e·o n the reversal of the usual color combination on a computer screen

re·vers·i·ble /ri vúrsəb'l/ adj able to be changed or undone —**re·vers·i·bil·i·ty** /-vùrsə billətee/ n

re·ver·sion /ri vúrzh'n/ n **1** a return to a former condition or point of view **2** restoration of an organism's original genetic characteristics, by a second mutation **3** the return of property to the former owner, or property so returned

re·vert /ri vúrt/ vi **1** return to a previous state **2** return to an earlier topic in a discussion **3** return to old habits **4** become the property of the former owner

re·view /ri vyoó/ n **1** a survey of past actions, performance, or events **2** a journalistic article giving an assessment of something **3** a publication featuring reviews **4** a reexamination **5** a discussion of subject matter in preparation for a test **6** a military inspection ■ v **1** vt look at something critically **2** vt give an opinion on the quality of something **3** vt consider something again **4** vi study for test **5** vt look back on something **6** *vt* reconsider an earlier judicial decision **7** *vt* subject troops to military inspection —**re·view·er** *n*

SPELLCHECK Do not confuse the spelling of **review** and **revue** ("musical variety show"), which sound similar.

re·vile /ri víl/ (**-viled**, **-vil·ing**) *v* **1** *vt* attack verbally **2** *vi* use abusive language —**re·vile·ment** *n*

re·vise /ri víz/ (**-vised**, **-vis·ing**) *vt* **1** rethink something **2** make a previous estimate more accurate or realistic **3** prepare a new version of text —**re·vi·sion** /ri vízh'n/ *n*

re·vi·sion·ism /ri vízh'n ìzzəm/ *n* **1** the reconsidering of accepted truths **2** an anti-Marxist socialist movement that advocates gradual reform —**re·vi·sion·ist** *adj, n*

re·vis·it /ree vízzit/ *vt* **1** go to a place again **2** reconsider something ■ *n* a subsequent visit

re·vi·tal·ize /ree vít'l ìz/ (**-ized**, **-iz·ing**) *vt* give new life or energy to —**re·vi·tal·i·za·tion** /-vìt'li záysh'n/ *n*

re·viv·al /ri vív'l/ *n* **1** a renewal of interest in something **2** a new production of a play **3** the reviving of something or somebody **4** an evangelical Christian meeting

re·viv·al·ism /ri vív'l ìzzəm/ *n* **1** the desire to foster new interest in something **2** an evangelical religious movement —**re·viv·al·ist** *adj*

re·vive /ri vív/ (**-vived**, **-viv·ing**) *v* **1** *vti* recover or cause to recover consciousness **2** *vti* make or become active, accepted, or popular again **3** *vt* cause an experience or feeling to return **4** *vt* stage a play again —**re·viv·a·ble** *adj*

re·viv·i·fy /ree vívvə fì/ (**-fied**, **-fies**) *vt* give new life or energy to —**re·viv·i·fi·ca·tion** /ree vìvvəfi káysh'n/ *n*

re·voke /ri vók/ (**-voked**, **-vok·ing**) *vt* formally cancel or withdraw —**rev·o·ca·tion** /rèvvə káysh'n, rèe võ-/ *n*

re·volt /ri vólt/ *v* **1** *vi* rebel against the state or authority **2** *vt* cause to feel disgust ■ *n* **1** an uprising against a government **2** a defiance of authority —**re·volt·ing** *adj* —**re·volt·ing·ly** *adv*

rev·o·lu·tion /rèvvə lóosh'n/ *n* **1** an overthrow of a political system, or an attempt to do so **2** a major change **3** a complete circular turn

rev·o·lu·tion·ar·y /rèvvə lóosh'n èrree/ *adj* **1** of or advocating political revolution **2** new and different ■ *n* (*pl* **-ies**) somebody committed to political revolution

rev·o·lu·tion·ize /rèvvə lóosh'n ìz/ (**-ized**, **-iz·ing**) *vt* cause radical change in

re·volve /ri vólv/ (**-volved**, **-volv·ing**) *v* **1** *vti* move in a circle on an axis or around a point **2** *vi* be focused on something or somebody —**re·volv·a·ble** *adj*

re·volv·er /ri vólvər/ *n* a pistol with a revolving cylinder of chambers

re·volv·ing cred·it *n* a credit plan that imposes regular repayments

re·volv·ing door *n* **1** a door with sections that turn around a central pivot **2** a system in which people are constantly entering and leaving, e.g., by being hired and fired

re·volv·ing fund *n* a fund that can be drawn upon and repaid as desired

re·vue /ri vyóo/ (*pl* **-vues**) *n* a musical variety show ◊ See note at **review**

re·vul·sion /ri vúlsh'n/ *n* **1** a feeling of disgust **2** a pulling or turning back (*fml*)

re·ward /ri wáwrd/ *n* **1** something good given or received in return for something done **2** an amount of money offered for information about a criminal or the return of lost property ■ *vt* **1** give somebody something as a reward **2** repay somebody's efforts —**re·ward·a·ble** *adj* —**re·ward·ing** *adj* —**re·ward·ing·ly** *adv*

re·wind *vt* /ree wínd/ (**-wound** /-wównd/) wind back to an earlier point or onto the original spool ■ *n* /rée wìnd/ the rewinding process or function

re·wire /ree wír/ (**-wired**, **-wir·ing**) *vt* provide with new electrical wiring

re·word /ree wúrd/ *vt* revise the wording of

re·work /ree wúrk/ *vt* **1** make changes or improvements to **2** amend for reuse in a different context

⚡ re·writ·a·ble /ree rítəb'l/ *adj* describes magnetic media that can be written on repeatedly

re·write *vt* /ree rít/ (**-wrote** /-rṓt/, **-writ·ten** /-rìtt'n/, **-writ·ing**) **1** change the wording or structure of text **2** change the way that history is perceived ■ *n* /rée rìt/ a rewritten text —**re·writ·er** *n*

Rex *n* the title of a reigning king

Rey·kja·vik /ràykyə vík/ capital of Iceland. Pop. 108,351 (1998).

Rey·nolds /rénn'ldz/, **Sir Joshua** (1723–92) British painter

Rf *symbol* rutherfordium

RFD *abbr* rural free delivery

Rh *symbol* rhodium

rhap·so·dize /rápsə dìz/ (**-dized**, **-diz·ing**) *vi* express great enthusiasm

rhap·so·dy /rápsadee/ (*pl* **-dies**) *n* **1** a free-form musical composition **2** an expression of intense enthusiasm (*often pl*) —**rhap·sod·ic** /rap sóddik/ *adj*

Rhee /ree/, **Syngman** (1875–1965) president of South Korea (1948–60)

Rheims ♦ Reims

rhe·ni·um /réenee əm/ *n* (*symbol* **Re**) a rare heavy metallic element. Use: catalyst, alloyed with tungsten in thermocouples.

rhe·sus mon·key /réessəss-/ *n* a brown monkey of the macaque family

rhet·o·ric /réttərik/ *n* **1** persuasive speech or writing **2** pretentious or empty language **3** the art or study of using language ef-

fectively —**rhe·tor·i·cal** /ri tórrik'l/ *adj*
—**rhe·tor·i·cal·ly** *adv* —**rhet·o·ri·cian** /rèttə
ríshʹnʹ/ *n*

rhe·tor·i·cal ques·tion *n* a question asked
for effect and requiring no answer

rheu·mat·ic /roo máttik/ *adj* of or affected by
rheumatism

rheu·mat·ic fe·ver *n* a childhood disease
that causes fever and joint swelling and
often damage to the heart valves

rheu·ma·tism /roomə tìzzəm/ *n* **1** pain and
stiffness in the joints or muscles **2** rheu-
matoid arthritis

ORIGIN Rheumatism was once thought to be
caused by the flow of watery discharges within
the body, and the name is based on Latin and
Greek *rheuma* "bodily fluid." It was adopted
into English from French in the 17C.

---

rheu·ma·toid ar·thri·tis /roomə tòyd-/ *n* a
chronic disease of the joints that causes
painful stiffness and swelling

rheu·ma·tol·o·gy /roomə tóllojee/ *n* the branch
of medicine that deals with rheumatic diseases —**rheu·ma·tol·o·gist** *n*

Rh fac·tor *n* an antibody-producing substance in red blood cells

---

ORIGIN Rh factor is short for *Rhesus factor*.
The antigen was given this name because it
was first discovered in the blood of rhesus
monkeys.

Rhine /rīn/ river in W Europe, flowing northwestward from SE Switzerland through
Germany and the Netherlands, emptying
into the North Sea. Length 820 mi./1,320
km.

rhine·stone /rín stòn/ *n* a small fake gem

rhi·ni·tis /rī nítiss/ *n* inflammation of the
mucous membrane of the nose

rhi·no /rí nò/ (*pl same or* -**nos**) *n* a rhinoceros
(*infml*)

rhi·noc·er·os /rī nóssərəss/ (*pl* -**os·es** *or same
or* -i-ỉ/) *n* a massive thick-skinned mammal
with a horn or horns on its nose

ORIGIN Rhinoceros is formed from Greek
words meaning literally "nose horn."

~~rhinocerous~~ incorrect spelling of **rhinoceros**

rhi·zome /rí zòm/ *n* a horizontal underground
stem

rho /rò/ (*pl* **rhos**) *n* the 17th letter of the Greek
alphabet

Rhode Is·land /ròd-/ state in the NE United
States. Cap. Providence. Pop. 1,048,319
(2000). —**Rhode Is·land·er** *n*

Rhodes /ròdz/ largest island of the Dodecanese, Greece. Pop. 87,831 (1981).

Rho·de·sia /rò déezhə/ former name for Zimbabwe —**Rho·de·sian** *adj, n*

rho·di·um /ròdee əm/ *n* (*symbol* Rh) a hard
corrosion-resistant metallic element. Use:
alloys, in plating other metals.

rho·do·den·dron /ròdə déndrən/ *n* an ornamental evergreen flowering tree

rhom·boid /róm bòyd/ *n* a parallelogram with
unequal adjacent sides ■ *adj* **1** rhom-
boid-shaped **2** of a rhombus

rhom·bus /rómbəss/ (*pl* -**bus·es** *or* -**bi** /-bī/) *n* an
oblique-angled parallelogram —**rhom·bic**
adj

Rhône /ròn/ river in Switzerland and France,
flowing southwestward from the Alps into
the Mediterranean Sea. Length 505 mi./813
km.

rhu·barb /roo baarb/ *n* **1** the pink stalks of a
perennial plant, cooked as a fruit **2** the
plant whose stalks are rhubarb

ORIGIN The Greeks had two words for **rhubarb**:
rhēon (which evolved into Latin *rheum*, now
the plant's scientific name) and *rha*, which is
said to have come from *Rha*, an ancient name
of the Volga River, in allusion to the fact that
rhubarb was grown on its banks. **Rhubarb** is
native to China, and was once imported to
Europe via Russia, and in medieval Latin
became known as *rha barbarum* "barbarian
rhubarb, foreign rhubarb." In due course association with Latin *rheum* altered this to
rheubarbarum.

---

rhyme /rīm/ *n* **1** similarity in the sound of
word endings **2** a word whose ending
sounds similar to another **3** a short poem
■ *v* (**rhymed, rhym·ing**) **1** *vi* have a word
ending that sounds similar **2** *vt* match a
word with another as a rhyme ◊ **without
rhyme or reason** without any rational explanation

rhym·ing slang *n* slang that uses rhyming
expressions as substitutes for words

rhythm /ríthəm/ *n* **1** the pattern of beats in
music, or a particular pattern of beats **2** the
pattern of stress in poetry, or a particular
stress pattern **3** any regular or characteristic pattern —**rhyth·mic** /ríthmik/ *adj*
—**rhyth·mi·cal·ly** *adv*

rhythm and blues *n* a style of music that
combines elements of blues and jazz

rhythm meth·od *n* a method of contraception
that relies on knowing a woman's fertile
period

rhythm sec·tion *n* the instruments in a band
that provide the basic rhythm

RI, R.I. *abbr* Rhode Island

ri·al /ree aál/ *n* the main unit of currency in
Iran and Oman

rib *n* **1** any of the curved bones of the chest
2 a cut of meat that contains a rib or ribs
3 a ridged pattern in knitting **4** a raised
vein on a leaf ■ *v* (**ribbed, rib·bing**) **1** *vti*
tease somebody (*infml*) **2** *vt* shape, support,
or fit with ribs —**rib·bing** *n*

rib·ald /ríbb'ld, rī bàwld/ *adj* coarse and funny
—**rib·ald·ry** *n*

Rib·ben·trop /ríbbən tròp/, **Joachim von** (1893–
1946) German Nazi official

rib·bon /ríbbən/ n **1** a decorative strip of fabric **2** a strip of inked material in a typewriter or printer **3** a long narrow strip of anything ■ **rib·bons** npl tatters

rib cage n the ribs as a unit

ri·bo·fla·vin /ríbə flàyvin, ríbə fláyvin/ n a vitamin that is the yellow component of the B complex group

ri·bo·nu·cle·ic ac·id /ríbō noo klèe ik-/ n full form of **RNA**

Ri·car·do /ri kaárdō/, **David** (1772–1823) British economist

rice /ríss/ n **1** the edible seeds of a cereal plant **2** a cereal plant that grows in warm countries and produces rice grains

rice pa·per n **1** thin edible paper made from plants, used to prevent some foods sticking during baking **2** artists' paper made from the pith of a Chinese tree

rice pud·ding n rice baked in milk and sugar

rich adj **1** having a lot of money or property **2** expensive and fine **3** with a good supply of a resource o *a city rich in culture o cotton-rich fabric* **4** plentiful **5** productive or fertile **6** with a high proportion of fatty ingredients **7** deeply and fully saturated with color **8** having a deep full sound ■ npl rich people o *the rich and famous* —**rich·ly** adv —**rich·ness** n

Rich·ard I /ríchərd/ (1157–99) king of England (1189–99)

Rich·ard II (1367–1400) king of England (1377–99)

Rich·ard III (1452–85) king of England (1483–85)

Rich·ard·son /ríchərdss'n/, **H. H.** (1838–86) US architect

Rich·ard·son, Samuel (1689–1761) British novelist

Rich·e·lieu /ríshə lòò, reeshə lyő/, **Armand Jean du Plessis, Duc de** (1585–1642) French religious and political leader

✦ **rich e-mail** n an e-mail with a voice message attached

rich·es /ríchəz/ npl **1** great wealth **2** plentiful natural resources

Rich·mond /ríchmənd/ capital of Virginia. Pop. 194,173 (1998).

Rich·ter scale /ríktər-/ n a scale for measuring the magnitude of earthquakes

ORIGIN The scale is named for the US seismologist Charles Francis Richter (1900–85), who devised it.

✦ **rich text** n computer text that includes formatting codes

rick n a stack of hay or straw

rick·ets /ríkits/ n a bone-softening disease

rick·et·y /ríkətee/ (-i·er, -i·est) adj **1** unstable **2** infirm **3** affected by rickets

Rick·o·ver /rík òvər/, **Hyman** (1900–86) Russian-born US naval officer

rick·shaw /rík shàw/, **rick·sha** n **1** a two-wheeled passenger vehicle pulled by a person **2** a three-wheeled passenger vehicle pedaled by a driver

ric·o·chet /ríkə shày, ríkə sháy/ vi (-cheted /ríkə shàyd, ríkə sháyd/, -chet·ing /ríkə shày ing, ríkə shày ing/) rebound ■ n a rebounding action

ri·cot·ta /ri kóttə/ n soft cheese used mostly in cooking

rid (**rid**, **rid·ding**) vt free a place, thing, or person of something undesirable

rid·dance /rídd'nss/ n the removal or destruction of something undesirable

rid·dle¹ /rídd'l/ n **1** a word puzzle **2** a puzzling thing ■ vi (-dled, -dling) talk in riddles —**rid·dler** n

rid·dle² /rídd'l/ (-dled, -dling) vt **1** make holes in something **2** affect every part of something —**rid·dler** n ◊ See note at **problem**

ride /ríd/ v (**rode** /rōd/ or **rid·den** /rídd'n/, **rid·ing**) **1** vti sit on and control a horse or other animal **2** vti travel on a bike or motorbike **3** vti travel as a passenger in a vehicle **4** vti use a surfboard, skateboard, or similar piece of sports equipment **5** vti travel in an elevator **6** vt travel over an area o *ride the range* **7** vi be easy or difficult to handle (refers to vehicles) **8** vti move on or as if on water o *riding the air currents* **9** vi do something effortlessly **10** vi depend on something o *Her future rides on this interview.* **11** vi be allowed to continue o *Let it ride for now.* ■ n **1** a trip by vehicle or animal, especially one taken for pleasure **2** a means of transportation **3** the quality of travel in a vehicle **4** an entertainment at a fairground or amusement park **5** a path on which to ride horses ◊ **be riding high** be enjoying a period or feeling of success ◊ **ride roughshod over 1** treat somebody very inconsiderately **2** disregard a rule, law, or agreement ◊ **take somebody for a ride** cheat or deceive somebody

☐ **ride out** vt deal with a problem and survive

Ride /ríd/, **Sally Kirsten** (b. 1951) US astronaut

rid·er /rídər/ n **1** somebody riding a horse, bike, skateboard, or snowboard **2** an additional clause to a bill or contract

rid·er·ship /rídər shìp/ n the number of passengers using public transportation

ridge n **1** a long narrow raised area **2** a raised land formation **3** the line formed where the sloping sides of a roof meet ■ vti (**ridged, ridg·ing**) form ridges or make ridges in

rid·i·cule /ríddi kyōbl/ vt (-culed, -cul·ing) mock ■ n mocking laughter, behavior, or comments

SYNONYMS ridicule, deride, laugh at, mock, send up CORE MEANING: belittle by making fun of

ri·dic·u·lous /ri díkyələss/ adj **1** unreasonable **2** completely silly —**ri·dic·u·lous·ly** adv —**ri·dic·u·lous·ness** n

rid·ing[1] /rídīng/ n the activity of sitting on and controlling a moving horse ■ adj used while on horseback

rid·ing[2] /rídīng/ n Can a Canadian constituency

ORIGIN Riding comes from an old Scandinavian word meaning "third part."

Rief·en·stahl /reef'n stäal, -shtäal/, **Leni** (b. 1902) German movie director and photographer

ri·el /ree él/ n the main unit of Cambodian currency

~~**rien**~~ incorrect spelling of **rein**

RIF n the laying off of members of a workforce. Full form **reduction in force**

rife /rīf/ adj 1 widespread and plentiful 2 full of something undesirable ◊ See note at **widespread**

riff n a short distinctive series of notes in rock music or jazz

rif·fle /ríff'l/ (-fled, -fling) v 1 vti flick through the pages of something 2 vt shuffle cards by making two piles, raising the corners, and letting them fall and overlap —**rif·fle** n

riff·raff /rif ràf/ n an offensive term for people regarded as socially inferior (insult)

ri·fle[1] /ríff'l/ n a gun with a long barrel that is fired from the shoulder ■ vt (-fled, -fling) cut a gun barrel with spiral grooves

ri·fle[2] /ríff'l/ (-fled, -fling) v 1 vti search vigorously 2 vt rob —**ri·fler** n

ri·fle·man /ríf'lmən/ (pl -men /-mən/) n a soldier with a rifle

ri·fle range n an area for shooting practice

rift n 1 a gap or break 2 a disagreement 3 a displacement of rock layers caused by stress ■ vti split

rift val·ley n a valley formed by a geologic rift

rig[1] vt (rigged, rig·ging) 1 equip a ship with rigging 2 provide somebody or something with equipment 3 construct something hastily and without proper materials ■ n 1 a drilling structure for oil 2 an arrangement of sails and masts 3 specialist equipment 4 a large truck (infml)

rig[2] vt (rigged, rig·ging) arrange the outcome of dishonestly ■ n a trick

Ri·ga /reega/ capital of Latvia. Pop. 796,732 (1999).

rig·a·ma·role n = **rigmarole**

rig·a·to·ni /rígga tōnee/ n pasta in the form of thick tubes

rig·ging /rígging/ n a system of ropes, wires, and pulleys

right /rīt/ adj 1 consistent with facts or belief o the right answer 2 socially approved 3 conforming to what is usual or expected 4 proper with regard to use 5 most suitable or desirable o waiting for the right offer 6 on or toward the east when somebody is facing north 7 main or most prominent o right side up 8 perpendicular ■ adv 1 properly o did it right 2 just or exactly o right at that moment 3 straight 4 correctly 5 morally and appropriately 6 on or toward the right side 7 used as part of a title ■ n 1 the morally appropriate thing 2 something correct or true 3 an entitlement or freedom (often pl) 4 a legal entitlement 5 a claim to property (often pl) 6 also **Right** political conservatives as a group 7 the right side of somebody or something 8 a right-hand turn ■ v 1 vti put something into an upright position 2 vt correct a mistake 3 vt make amends for a wrong —**right·a·ble** adj —**right·ly** adv —**right·ness** n ◊ **in your own right** because of your birth, ability, or other entitlement ◊ **set** or **put something to rights** put something into the correct or ordered state

right an·gle n a 90° angle —**right·an·gled** adj

⚡**right-click** vi press the right-hand mouse button

right·eous /ríchəss/ adj 1 always observing a religious or moral code 2 justifiable —**right·eous·ly** adv —**right·eous·ness** n

right field n 1 in baseball, the part of the outfield to the batter's right 2 in baseball, the position of the player responsible for fielding balls hit to right field —**right field·er** n

right·ful /rítfəl/ adj having or owned by somebody with a legal or moral claim —**right·ful·ly** adv —**right·ful·ness** n

right-hand adj 1 on or to the right 2 for the right hand 3 most important and trusted

right-hand·ed adj 1 preferring to use the right hand 2 done with or designed for the right hand ■ adv with the right hand —**right-hand·ed·ly** adv —**right-hand·ed·ness** n

right-hand·er n somebody who is right-handed

Right Hon·our·a·ble n Can a Canadian title given for life to certain eminent people, e.g., a governor general

right·ist /rítist/ adj of or favoring political conservatism ■ n a political conservative —**right·ism** n

right-mind·ed /rìt míndəd/ adj sensible and fair —**right-mind·ed·ness** n

right of way n 1 a vehicle's right to proceed ahead of another 2 a lawful route across somebody's property, or the right to use it

rights is·sue n an offering of stock to existing stockholders on favorable terms

right-size (right-sized, right-siz·ing) vi make a company the size considered appropriate by dismissing employees

right-think·ing adj sensible and fair

right tri·an·gle n a triangle with one right angle

right·ward /rítwərd/ adj directed to the right ■ adv also **right·wards** toward the right

right wing *n* the conservative membership of a group —**right-wing** *adj* —**right-wing·er** *n*

rig·id /ríjjid/ *adj* **1** firm and stiff **2** applied strictly **3** refusing to change —**ri·gid·i·ty** /ri jíddətee/ *n* —**rig·id·ly** *adv* —**rig·id·ness** *n*

rig·ma·role /rígmə ròl/, **rig·a·ma·role** /ríggəmə-/ *n* **1** a ridiculously complicated process **2** an overelaborate explanation or account

ORIGIN Rigmarole is first recorded in the mid-18C, and appears to be a contraction of *ragman roll*. A ragman roll was a parchment scroll used in a medieval gambling game. The roll had things such as names written on it, with pieces of string attached to them, and participants had to select a string at random. The word *ragman* may have been a contraction of *ragged man*, perhaps in allusion to the appearance of the scroll, with all its bits of string hanging from it. *Ragman roll* eventually came to be used for any list or catalog, and *ragman* itself denoted a "long rambling discourse" in 16C Scottish English – a meaning that seems to have transferred itself eventually to **rigmarole**.

rig·or /ríggər/ *n* **1** the application of demanding standards **2** severity in dealings with people **3** harshness or hardship

rig·or mor·tis /-máwrtiss/ *n* the progressive stiffening of the body after death

rig·or·ous /ríggərəss/ *adj* **1** strict or difficult ○ *rigorous training* **2** precise and exacting ○ *rigorous standards* —**rig·or·ous·ly** *adv*

Riis /reess/, **Jacob** (1849–1914) Danish-born US journalist and social reformer

rile /rīl/ (**riled**, **ril·ing**) *vt* make somebody angry (*infml*)

Ri·ley /rílee/ ◇ **the life of Riley** a comfortable life with no worries

Ril·ke /rílkə/, **Rainer Maria** (1875–1926) Bohemian-born German poet

rim *n* the outer edge of something circular or rounded ■ *vt* (**rimmed**, **rim·ming**) form a rim around —**rimmed** *adj*

rime[1] /rīm/ *n* a coating of frost —**rim·y** *adj*

rime[2] /rīm/ (*archaic*) *n* a rhyme ■ *vti* (**rimed**, **rim·ing**) rhyme

Rim·sky-Kor·sa·kov /rímskee káwrssə kàwf/, **Nikolay** (1844–1908) Russian composer

rind /rīnd/ *n* the tough outer layer of a fruit or other food

ring[1] /ring/ *n* **1** a hard circular band of something **2** a circular piece of jewelry worn on a finger **3** a circular mark, arrangement, or device **4** a circular motion **5** a group of people operating dishonestly **6** a circular area for a performance, exhibition, or contest **7** a platform for boxing or wrestling ■ *vt* **1** form a circle around something **2** encircle with ring

SPELLCHECK Do not confuse the spelling of

ring and wring ("twist forcefully"), which sound similar.

ring[2] /ring/ *v* (**rang**, **rung**) **1** *vti* make or cause to make the sound of a bell **2** *vti* echo loudly **3** *vi* call somebody by sounding a bell or buzzer **4** *vi* make a particular impression on somebody ○ *His excuse didn't ring true.* **5** *vi* hear continuous high-pitched sounds ○ *My ears are ringing.* ■ *n* **1** the sound of a bell **2** a sound like a bell **3** a general impression **4** a loud repeated sound

□ **ring up** *vt* accomplish

ring bind·er *n* a stiff cover with metal rings inside for holding papers

ring·er /ríngər/ *n* somebody entered fraudulently in a competition (*infml*)

ring·ette /ring ét/ *n* Can a game similar to hockey

ring fin·ger *n* the finger next to the little finger, especially on the left hand

ring·git /ríng git/ *n* the main unit of currency of Malaysia

ring·ing /rínging/ *n* a continuing sound like a bell ■ *adj* stated loudly and unmistakably

ring·lead·er /ríng lèedər/ *n* the chief troublemaker in a group

ring·let /rínglət/ *n* a curly lock of hair

ring·mas·ter /ríng màstər/ *n* a member of a circus who announces events

ring·side /ríng sìd/ *n* the area next to a boxing or wrestling ring

ring·worm /ríng wùrm/ *n* a fungal skin disease

rink *n* **1** an area of ice used for sports **2** a surface used for roller-skating

rinse /rinss/ *vt* (**rinsed**, **rins·ing**) **1** lightly wash or clean in liquid **2** flush with water after washing or cleaning ■ *n* **1** an act of rinsing something **2** a cosmetic treatment for coloring hair

Ri·o de Ja·nei·ro /rèe ō day zhə náir ō, -neèrō/ city in SE Brazil, the capital of **Rio de Janeiro State**. Pop. 5,551,538 (1996).

Ri·o Gran·de /rèe ō gránd, -grándee/ river of SW North America, flowing from SW Colorado into the Gulf of Mexico and forming part of the Texas-Mexico border. Length 1,900 mi./3,100 km.

ri·ot /rí ət/ *n* **1** a violent public disturbance **2** an extremely entertaining event or person (*infml*) ■ *vi* take part in a violent public disturbance —**ri·ot·er** *n* ◇ **read (somebody) the riot act** reprimand somebody severely ◇ **run riot** behave in a wild and uncontrolled way

ri·ot·ous /rí ətəss/ *adj* **1** unrestrained **2** rioting or likely to riot (*fml*) —**ri·ot·ous·ly** *adv*

ri·ot po·lice *n* police officers equipped for controlling a riot

rip *v* (**ripped**, **rip·ping**) **1** *vti* tear or be torn roughly **2** *vt* use force to remove something that is firmly attached **3** *vi* move with extreme speed ■ *n* a place where something has been torn ◇ **let it** *or* **her rip**

proceed without restraint (infml) ◊ **let rip**
speak without restraint (infml) ◊ See note
at **tear**

□ **rip off** vt (infml) **1** treat unfairly over money
2 steal

R.I.P. abbr rest in peace

rip·cord /ríp kàwrd/ n **1** a cord pulled to open
a parachute **2** a cord that releases some of
the gas in a hot-air balloon

ripe /rip/ (**rip·er, rip·est**) adj **1** mature and
ready to harvest or eat **2** mature and full
of flavor ○ ripe cheese **3** at the most suitable
stage for something to happen ○ The time is
ripe for asking for a raise. —**ripe·ness** n

rip·en /rípən/ vti **1** make or become ripe
2 reach or cause to reach the right stage of
development —**rip·en·ing** adj, n

rip·off n something not worth the price asked
or paid for it (infml)

ri·poste /ri póst/ n **1** a quick and clever response **2** a quick fencing thrust made after
parrying an attack ◊ See note at **answer**

⚡ **rip·per** n a program for copying digital music
from a CD to a computer —**rip·ping** n

rip·ple /rípp'l/ v (**-pled, -pling**) **1** vti have or
cause to have tiny gentle waves **2** vti have
or cause to have a gentle wavy pattern **3** vi
make a lapping sound ■ n **1** a tiny wave
or a series of tiny waves **2** a gentle wavy
shape or mark **3** a sound that passes
through a group or place, increasing and
decreasing in loudness ■ **rip·ples** npl re-
percussions or consequences

rip·ple ef·fect n a spreading series of re-
percussions or consequences

rip·tide /ríp tìd/ n a strong turbulent current
that opposes other currents

⚡ **RISC** /risk/ abbr reduced-instruction-set computer

rise /riz/ vi (**rose** /rōz/, **ris·en** /rízz'n/, **ris·ing**)
1 stand up **2** ascend **3** increase in height
or level **4** increase in amount, degree, or
intensity **5** achieve greater status **6** extend
upward ○ The tower rose above the village.
7 swell in size ○ allow the bread to rise
8 engage in a revolt **9** have a beginning or
source ○ a stream rising in the hills **10** spring
up or grow **11** get up after sleeping
12 appear over the horizon **13** become res-
urrected ■ n **1** an increase **2** a process of
coming to public notice and acclaim **3** an
upward slope **4** higher ground **5** an ascent
◊ **get a rise out of** provoke an angry reaction from by teasing (infml) ◊ **give rise
to** cause or produce

ris·er /rízər/ n **1** somebody who gets out of
bed at a particular time ○ an early riser **2** the
vertical part of a step

ris·i·ble /rízzab'l/ adj **1** causing laughter
2 inclined to laugh (fml) —**ris·i·bly** adv

risk n **1** the chance or possibility of danger
or harm **2** a factor, state, or course that
poses a possible danger ■ vt **1** endanger
2 do something despite a possible danger

—**risk·i·ly** adv —**risk·i·ness** n —**risk·y** adj
◊ **at risk** in danger of injury, damage, or
loss

ri·sot·to /ri zóttō/ n a dish of rice and other
ingredients cooked in stock

ris·qué /ri skáy/ adj sexually suggestive

ris·sole /ri sól, rìssôl/ n a small fried cake of
meat coated in breadcrumbs

rite /rit/ n **1** a ceremonial or formal procedure
(often pl) **2** a system of ceremonial procedures

rite of pas·sage n **1** a significant transitional
event in human life **2** a ceremony marking
somebody's passage from one stage of life
to another

rit·u·al /ríchoo əl/ n **1** an established and prescribed pattern of observance, e.g., in a religion **2** the performance of actions in a set,
ordered, and ceremonial way ■ adj of a
rite —**rit·u·al·is·tic** /ríchoo ə lístik/ adj
—**rit·u·al·ly** adv

ritz·y /rítsee/ (**-i·er, -i·est**) adj expensively
stylish (infml)

ri·val /rív'l/ n **1** a person or group competing
with another for something or somebody
2 a person or thing that can equal or
surpass another in a specific respect ■ v
1 vt equal or surpass **2** vi compete with ■
adj competing —**ri·val·ry** n

ORIGIN A **rival** is etymologically "somebody
using the same stream as another," and therefore a competitor for the same resources. The
word was adopted from Latin in the late 16C,
and goes back to Latin rivus "stream."

---

riv·en /rívv'n/ adj torn apart (literary)

riv·er /rívvər/ n **1** a large natural channel of
flowing fresh water **2** a large flow of something (often pl) ◊ **sell down the river** betray
or desert (infml)

Ri·ve·ra /ri vérrə/, **Diego** (1886–1957) Mexican
artist

riv·er·bank /rívvər bàngk/ n the ground rising
up beside a river's edge

riv·er·bed /rívvər bèd/ n the ground over
which a river flows

riv·er·front /rívvər frùnt/ n the area of a town
or property facing a river

riv·er·side /rívvər sìd/ n the area of land by a
river —**riv·er·side** adj

Riv·er·side /rívvər sìd/ city in SW California.
Pop. 262,140 (1998).

riv·et /rívvit/ n a short metal fastener for two
metal sheets ■ vt **1** firmly fix the attention
(infml) **2** fasten something with a rivet

riv·et·ing /rívviting/ adj fascinating (infml)
—**riv·et·ing·ly** adv

~~rivetting~~ incorrect spelling of **riveting**

Riv·i·er·a /rìvvee érrə/ coastal region of SE
France and NW Italy

riv·u·let /rívvyələt/ n **1** a little stream (literary)
2 a small flow of something

Ri·yadh /rèe yaàd/ capital of Saudi Arabia. Pop. 2,620,000 (1995).

ri·yal /ri yaàl/ *n* the main unit of currency in Qatar, Saudi Arabia, and Yemen

Rn *symbol* radon

RN, R.N. *abbr* registered nurse

RNA *n* a nucleic acid containing ribose and found in all living cells. Full form **ribonucleic acid**

roach[1] /rōch/ (*pl* **same** *or* **roach·es**) *n* 1 a European freshwater fish 2 a small North American sunfish

roach[2] /rōch/ *n* a cockroach (*infml*)

road *n* 1 a long surfaced route for vehicles 2 a course of action leading to a particular outcome ◊ **down the road** in the future

road·block /rōd blòk/ *n* 1 a barrier across a road to stop traffic 2 an obstacle

road hog *n* a motorist regarded as selfish and inconsiderate (*infml*)

road·house /rōd hòwss/ (*pl* **-hous·es** /-hòwzəz/) *n* a hotel or tavern located beside a road

road·ie /rōdee/ *n* somebody whose job is to take care of and set up equipment for a band of musicians when traveling

road·kill /rōd kìl/ *n* an animal killed by a vehicle

road map, road·map /rōd màp/ *n* a map for motorists showing roads and distances

road rage *n* uncontrollable anger experienced by a driver in difficult road conditions

road·run·ner /rōd rùnnər/ *n* a fast-running desert bird

road·show /rōd shò/ *n* 1 a performance by a touring company of entertainers or broadcasters 2 a group traveling from place to place to publicize or promote something

road·side /rōd sìd/ *n* an area at a road's edge

road sign *n* a sign by the side of a road providing directions for road users

road·ster /rōdstər/ *n* an open-top sports car (*dated*)

road test *n* 1 a test of a vehicle or tire under actual operating conditions 2 an official practical driving test —**road-test** *vt*

road·way /rōd wày/ *n* the driving area of a road

road·work /rōd wùrk/ *n* 1 repairs to a road 2 a form of exercise consisting of running on roads

road·wor·thy /rōd wùrthee/ *adj* fit to be driven safely —**road·wor·thi·ness** *n*

roam /rōm/ *vti* wander aimlessly —**roam·er** *n*

roan /rōn/ *adj* describes an animal with a reddish-brown, brown, or black coat speckled with white ■ *n* a roan horse

Ro·a·noke /rō ə nòk/ city in SW Virginia. Pop. 93,749 (1998).

roar /rawr/ *v* 1 *vi* growl loudly 2 *vti* shout loudly 3 *vi* laugh loudly 4 *vi* make a continuous deep sound ◊ *A fire roared in the grate.* ■ *n* 1 a loud shout 2 a loud laugh 3 a loud growl 4 a continuous deep sound ◊ *the roar of the tempest*

Roar·ing Twen·ties *npl* the 1920s, when thought of as a time of exuberance and prosperity

roast /rōst/ *v* 1 *vti* cook in an oven using fat 2 *vti* prepare coffee beans or nuts by drying or browning, or be prepared in this way 3 *vti* overheat 4 *vt* criticize harshly (*infml*) ■ *n* 1 an oven-cooked piece of meat 2 an open-air meal with food cooked on open fires ■ *adj* oven-cooked

roast·ing /rōsting/ *adj* very hot (*infml*)

rob (**robbed, rob·bing**) *vt* 1 steal from a person or place 2 deprive somebody unfairly —**rob·ber** *n*

rob·ber bar·on *n* 1 an unscrupulous 19C US industrialist 2 a medieval nobleman who stole from travelers passing through his lands

rob·ber·y /róbbəree/ (*pl* **-ies**) *n* a theft of property

Rob·bins /róbbinz/, **Jerome** (1918–98) US dancer and choreographer

robe *n* 1 a long loose ceremonial garment (*often pl*) 2 a dressing gown or bathrobe ■ *vti* (**robed, rob·ing**) dress in a robe

Rob·ert I /róbbərt-/, "**Rob·ert the Bruce**" /-brooss/ (1274–1329) king of Scotland (1306–29)

Paul Robeson

Robe·son /róbsən/, **Paul** (1898–1976) US singer and actor

Robes·pierre /róbz pee àir, -pyair/, **Maximilien** (1758–94) French lawyer and revolutionary

rob·in /róbbin/ *n* 1 a large North American thrush with a rust-colored breast 2 a small brown European thrush, the male of which has a red chest

Rob·in·son /róbbins'n/, **Arthur** (*b.* 1926) prime minister (1986–91) and president (1997–) of Trinidad and Tobago

Rob·in·son, Edwin Arlington (1869–1935) US poet

Rob·in·son, Jackie (1919–72) US baseball player and civil rights activist

ro·bot /rō bòt, róbət/ *n* 1 a machine programmed to perform tasks normally done by people 2 an imaginary machine functioning like a human 3 somebody who

behaves like a machine —**ro·bot·ic** /rō·
bóttik/ *adj*

ORIGIN The first **robots** appeared in the play
R. U. R. (*Rossum's Universal Robots*) (1920)
by the Czech dramatist Karel Čapek. Čapek
coined the name from Czech *robota* "forced
labor," and it entered English via German.
The first English use is recorded in 1923.

ro·bot·ics /rō·bóttiks/ *n* the design and use of
robots (+ *sing verb*)

Rob Roy (1671–1734) Scottish brigand

ro·bust /rō·búst, rố·bùst/ *adj* **1** strong and
healthy **2** full-flavored —**ro·bust·ly** *adv*
—**ro·bust·ness** *n*

Roch·es·ter /róchistər/ **1** city in SE Minnesota.
Pop. 78,173 (1998). **2** city in W New York.
Pop. 216,887 (1998).

rock[1] *n* **1** a hard aggregate of more than one
mineral **2** a boulder **3** somebody dependable **4** a diamond (*infml*) ◇ **between
a rock and a hard place** faced with two
equally undesirable choices ◇ **on the rocks**
served with ice cubes

rock[2] *v* **1** *vti* sway to and fro **2** *vti* shake
violently **3** *vt* shock (*infml*) **4** *vi* play or
dance to rock music (*infml*) ■ *n* **1** an act of
rocking **2** a type of pop music derived from
rock and roll

rock·a·bil·ly /róka bîllee/ *n* a type of pop
music combining rock and roll with
country music

rock and roll, rock'n'roll /rókən rốl/ *n* **1** pop
music with a heavy beat, played on electric
instruments **2** dancing done to rock and
roll —**rock and roll** *vi* —**rock and roll·er** *n*

rock bot·tom *n* the lowest possible level or
price —**rock-bot·tom** *adj*

rock can·dy *n* hard sugar candy

Rock·e·fel·ler /róka fèllar/ family of US in-
dustrialists and philanthropists including
John D. (1839–1937) and his son **John D., Jr.**
(1874–1960) and grandson **Nelson A.** (1908–
79), vice president of the United States
(1974–77).

rock·er /rókər/ *n* **1** a rocking device **2** a curved
piece of wood or metal that allows a
rocking chair or cradle to rock **3** a rocking
chair **4** a rock musician or fan (*infml*)

rock·et[1] /rókət/ *n* **1** a space vehicle **2** a device
that burns fuel and oxidizer, producing
thrust by expelling the hot gases **3** a rocket-
propelled weapon **4** a firework or flare containing combustible propellants ■ *vi*
1 move fast **2** increase quickly (*infml*)

ORIGIN The earliest sense of **rocket**, "self-
propelled flare," is recorded from the early
17C. The word was adopted from Italian *roc-
chetta*, literally "small distaff" (a rod for
thread used in spinning by hand), and **rockets**
were so called because of their shape. The
name for the salad leaf is unrelated. It came
from French in the late 15C.

rock·et[2] /rókət/ *n* a plant with peppery leaves
used in salads

rock·et sci·ence *n* any complex and intellectually demanding activity (*infml*)

Rock·ford /rókfərd/ city in N Illinois. Pop.
143,656 (1998).

rock gar·den /rókaree/, **rock·er·y** (*pl* **-ies**) *n* a
decorative garden with rocks

Rock·ies /rókeez/ ❱ **Rocky Mountains**

rock·ing chair *n* a chair on rockers for
rocking backward and forward

rock·ing horse *n* a child's model horse on
rockers for rocking backward and forward
on

rock'n'roll *n, vi* MUSIC, DANCE = **rock and roll**

rock salt *n* common salt found in mineral
deposits, usually sold as small chunks

rock-sol·id *adj* **1** firm and unshakable **2** hard
and unlikely to break

rock stead·y *n* a type of Jamaican reggae

Rock·well /rók wèl/, **Norman** (1894–1978) US
illustrator

rock·y[1] /rókee/ (**-i·er, -i·est**) *adj* **1** consisting
of or covered with rocks **2** hard like rock
—**rock·i·ness** *n*

rock·y[2] /rókee/ (**-i·er, -i·est**) *adj* **1** full of difficulties **2** unsteady —**rock·i·ness** *n*

Rock·y Moun·tains major mountain system
of W North America, extending more than
3,000 mi./4,800 km from N Alaska to New
Mexico. Highest peak Mt. Elbert 14,433
ft./4,399 m.

~~**rococco**~~ incorrect spelling of **rococo**

Rococo: Detail of stucco at Wies church,
Bavaria, Germany (1745–54)

ro·co·co /rə kốkō, rō-, rốka kồ/, **Ro·co·co** *n* an
ornate 18C style of art or music —**ro·co·co**
adj

rod *n* **1** a narrow cylindrical length of a material such as wood, metal, or plastic **2** a
pole for fishing **3** a stick or bundle of sticks
for beating somebody **4** a surveying pole
5 a staff of office **6** oppressive power **7** a
receptor cell in the eye that is sensitive to
dim light but not color **8** an obsolete unit of
length equal to 5.5 yd./5.03 m **9** an obsolete
unit of area equal to 30.25 sq. yd./25.3 sq. m

rode past tense of **ride**

ro·dent /rốd'nt/ *n* a small mammal such as a
rat or a mouse with large gnawing incisor
teeth

ro·de·o /rốdee ò, rō dáy ò/ (*pl* **-os**) *n* **1** a competition involving cowboy skills **2** a cattle round-up

Rodg·ers /rójjərz/, **Richard** (1902–79) US composer

Ro·din /rō dáN/, **Auguste** (1840–1917) French sculptor

Rod·ney /ródnee/, **Caesar** (1728–84) American patriot

roe[1] /rō/ *n* fish eggs or sperm

roe[2] /rō/ (*pl same or* **roes**) *n* a reddish brown woodland deer

Roent·gen /réntgən, réntjən/, **Wilhelm Conrad** (1845–1923) German physicist. He discovered X-rays, originally known also as "Roentgen rays."

Roeth·ke /rétkee, rétkə/, **Theodore** (1908–63) US poet

rog·er /rójjər/ *interj* indicates that a message has been received and understood (*in telecommunications*)

Rog·ers /rójjərz/, **Ginger** (1911–95) US dancer and actor

Rog·ers, Will (1879–1935) US humorist

Ro·get /rō zháy, rō zhày/, **Peter Mark** (1779–1869) British physician and compiler of *Roget's Thesaurus of English Words and Phrases* (1852)

rogue /rōg/ *n* **1** somebody dishonest, especially somebody who is also likable **2** somebody mischievous **3** a plant inferior to others of the same type ■ *adj* **1** describes an animal that is solitary and dangerous **2** unorthodox and unpredictable —**rogu·er·y** /rṓgəree/ *n* —**rogu·ish** *adj* —**rogu·ish·ly** *adv*

⚡ **rogue site** *n* a website that acquires visitors by having a domain name similar to that of a popular site

rogue state *n* a nation believed by Western countries to sabotage international political stability, sponsor terrorists, and develop weapons of mass destruction

Ro·he ♦ Mies van der Rohe, Ludwig

ROI *abbr* return on investment

roil *v* **1** *vti* make or become opaque and cloudy **2** *vt* irritate or annoy

role, rôle /rōl/ *n* **1** a part played by somebody in a play, movie, opera, or other performance **2** the function that somebody or something performs in an action or event **3** a part played by somebody in a social context that demands a particular pattern of behavior

role mod·el *n* somebody who is a good example for others to copy

role-play, role-play·ing *n* the acting out of a part, especially that of somebody with a particular social role, in order to understand it better —**role-play** *vti*

Rolf·ing /rólfing/ a service mark for a therapy using vigorous massage to alleviate physical or psychological tension

roll /rōl/ *v* **1** *vti* turn over and over **2** *vti* move on wheels or rollers **3** *vti* move while rocking from side to side **4** *vi* extend in a series of gentle slopes **5** *vti* move in a steady flowing motion **6** *vi* get a project under way (*infml*) ○ *We're ready to roll.* **7** *vt* trill a sound, especially an "r" **8** *vi* reverberate loudly **9** *vti* throw dice, or score a number by throwing dice **10** *vt* flatten something with a roller or rolling pin **11** *vti* form into a round or cylindrical shape **12** *vti* start to operate, e.g., a movie camera ■ *n* **1** an official list of people in a group **2** a tube, cylinder, or coil **3** a small individual bread product, or a sandwich made with one **4** an act of rolling **5** a toss of a die or dice **6** a rolling movement **7** a trilling sound **8** a rumbling noise **9** a series of drum beats ◇ **be rolling in it** be very rich (*infml*) ◇ **on a roll** enjoying a period of success (*infml*)

☐ **roll back** *vt* decrease prices or wages

☐ **roll out** *vt* introduce a product into a market

roll·back /rōl bàk/ *n* a cut in prices or wages

roll call *n* **1** an attendance check **2** a time for a roll call

roll·er /rṓlər/ *n* **1** a rolling tube for applying paint or ink **2** a small solid wheel with no spokes **3** a large heavy revolving cylinder with a handle for flattening lawns **4** a hair curler **5** a long heavy wave that only breaks on reaching the shore

⚡ **roll·er·ball** /rṓlər bàwl/ *n* a device containing a ball that is used instead of a computer mouse

Roll·er·blade /rṓlər blàyd/ *tdmk* a trademark for a type of roller skate on which the wheels are arranged in one straight line

roll·er coast·er *n* **1** an amusement park ride consisting of open cars on a narrow rail track with extreme peaks and troughs and sharp bends **2** a situation with sudden extreme changes

roll·er skate *n* **1** a frame with wheels that attaches to a shoe **2** a special shoe fitted with wheels —**roll·er-skate** *vi* —**roll·er-skate** skat·er *n* —**roll·er skat·ing** *n*

rol·lick·ing /rólliking/ *adj* boisterous

roll·ing /rṓling/ *adj* **1** having gentle slopes **2** developing gradually in stages ○ *a rolling program of reform*

roll·ing pin *n* a cylindrical kitchen utensil for flattening dough or pastry

roll-on *adj* applied to the skin with a rotating ball in the top of the container ■ *n* a deodorant with a rotating ball applicator

roll·out *n* the launch of a product into a market

roll·o·ver /rōl ṓvər/ *n* **1** a transfer of funds from one investment to another **2** an accident in which a vehicle overturns

roll-top desk, roll-top *n* a writing desk with a rounded slatted cover that can be pulled down over the writing area

Ro·lo·dex /rōlə dèks/ *tdmk* a trademark for a desktop filing system in which cards containing names, addresses, and telephone numbers are attached to a central cylinder

ro·ly-po·ly /rōlee pōlee/ *adj* overweight (*sometimes offensive*)

Rom /rōm/ (*pl same or* **Ro·ma** /rōmə/) *n* a group of nomadic people who migrated from India in the 15C (+ *pl verb*)

⚡ **ROM** /rom/ *abbr* read-only memory

rom., rom *abbr* roman

ro·maine /rō máyn/, **ro·maine let·tuce** *n* a variety of lettuce with long leaves

Ro·man /rōmən/ *adj* 1 of modern or ancient Rome 2 of the Roman Catholic church 3 **ro·man** in or of the upright type used as the standard type in printing ■ *n* 1 somebody from modern or ancient Rome 2 **ro·man** roman type

Ro·man al·pha·bet *n* the Western writing system of 26 letters

Ro·man can·dle *n* a short cylindrical freestanding firework

Ro·man Cath·o·lic *adj* of the Catholic Church headed by the Pope in Rome ■ *n* a member of the Roman Catholic Church —**Ro·man Ca·thol·i·cism** *n*

ro·mance *n* /rō mánss, rō mànss/ 1 a love affair 2 exciting or intense love 3 a feeling of adventure and excitement 4 a love story 5 a medieval story of chivalry 6 a fictitious narrative of exciting or mysterious adventures 7 **Ro·mance** the group of Indo-European languages that are descended from Latin ■ *vt* /rō máns/ (**-manced, -manc·ing**) treat somebody romantically —**Ro·mance** *adj* —**ro·manc·er** /rō mánsər/ *n*

ORIGIN The original **romances** were written in *Romance*, then a name for the vernacular language of France as opposed to Latin. They were medieval tales of chivalry or extraordinary adventures. The French word from which **romance** derives means literally "of Rome."

Ro·man Em·pire *n* 1 the territories ruled by Roman emperors 2 the rule of Roman emperors

CORBIS/Andrea Jemolo

Romanesque: Carved stone capital (1127–45) from Pamplona Cathedral, Spain

Ro·man·esque /rōmə nésk/ *adj* of an early European architectural or artistic style of the 11C and 12C —**Ro·man·esque** *n*

Ro·ma·ni·a /rō máynee ə/ country in SE Europe, bordering the Black Sea. Cap. Bucharest. Pop. 22,364,022 (2001). —**Ro·ma·ni·an** *n, adj*

Ro·man nose *n* a high-bridged nose

Ro·man nu·mer·al *n* a letter or letters representing a number used by the ancient Romans

Ro·mans /rōmənz/ *n* a book of the Bible, originally a letter from St. Paul to the church in Rome.

Ro·mansch /rō maánsh, -mánsh/, **Ro·mansh** *n* a Romance language that is one of the official languages of Switzerland —**Ro·mansch** *adj*

ro·man·tic /rō mántik/ *adj* 1 involving exciting or intense sexual love 2 suitable for lovemaking or tender emotions 3 idealistic and impractical 4 **Ro·man·tic** of a musical, literary, and artistic movement of the late 18C and early 19C that emphasized feelings, nature, and interest in other cultures ■ *n* 1 a romantic person 2 **Ro·man·tic** a composer, writer, or artist involved in the Romantic movement—**ro·man·ti·cal·ly** *adv*—**ro·man·ti·cism** /-sìzzəm/ *n*—**ro·man·ti·cist** *n*

ro·man·ti·cize /rō mánti sìz/ (**-cized, -ciz·ing**) *v* 1 *vt* make something appear glamorous 2 *vi* think romantically

Rom·a·ny /rómmənee, rōmənee/ (*pl* **-nies**), **Rom·a·ni** *n* 1 the language of the Roma people 2 a member of the Roma people (*dated*) —**Rom·a·ny** *adj*

Rome /rōm/ capital of Italy. Pop. 2,646,408 (1999).

Ro·me·o /rōmee ō/ (*pl* **-os**) *n* 1 an amorous man 2 a communications code word for the letter "R"

ORIGIN The original **Romeo** was the young lover of Juliet in Shakespeare's play *Romeo and Juliet* (1594).

Rom·mel /rómməl/, **Erwin** (1891–1944) German general

romp *vi* 1 play boisterously 2 win easily (*infml*) ■ *n* 1 boisterous activity 2 an easy victory (*infml*)

Rom·u·lus /rómyələss/ *n* in Roman mythology, the founder of the city of Rome

⚡ **ROM·ve·lope** /rómvə lòp/, **rom·ve·lope** *n* a protective cardboard cover for a CD-ROM

rood *n* 1 a crucifix 2 a unit of area equal to a quarter of an acre

roof /roof, rŏŏf/ *n* 1 the outer covering of the top of a building 2 the top covering of something 3 the top of the inside of a cavity ■ *vt* build a roof on ◊ **hit the roof** become extremely angry ◊ **go through the roof** rise to an extremely high level

roof·er /roofər, rŏŏffər/ *n* somebody who builds or repairs roofs

roof gar·den *n* 1 a garden on top of a building 2 a restaurant at the top of a building

roof·ing /roófing, roóffing/ n material for making a roof

roof·top /roof tòp, roof-/ n the outer surface of the roof of a building

rook[1] /roŏk/ n a large black bird that nests in colonies in treetops ■ vt swindle (slang)

rook[2] /roŏk/ n a chess piece that can be moved any distance in a straight line

rook·er·y /roókaree/ (pl -ies) n 1 a colony of rooks 2 a breeding place for rooks

rook·ie /roókee/ n (infml) 1 somebody inexperienced in an activity or job 2 a first-year player in professional sports

room /room, roŏm/ n 1 available space that may or may not be filled with something or where something can happen o need more room 2 a part of a building consisting of four walls and a ceiling 3 the people in a room 4 scope or opportunity for something to exist or happen o there's room for improvement ■ rooms npl accommodations for rent ■ vi share living quarters —**room·ful** n

~~roomate~~ incorrect spelling of **roommate**

room·er /roómar, roŏmar/ n somebody who rents a room

room·mate /room màyt, roŏm-/ n somebody sharing a room

room ser·vice n a hotel service providing guests with food and drink in their rooms

room·y /roómee, roŏmmee/ (-i·er, -i·est) adj spacious —**room·i·ness** n

Roo·se·velt /rózə vèlt, róz-, roóz-/, **Eleanor** (1884–1962) US first lady (1933–45), social activist, and writer

Franklin D. Roosevelt

Roo·se·velt, Franklin D. (1882–1945) 32nd president of the United States (1933–45)

Theodore Roosevelt

Roo·se·velt, Theodore (1858–1919) 26th president of the United States (1901–09)

roost n a place where birds sleep ■ vi go to sleep in a roost ◊ **rule the roost** be in charge

roost·er /roóstar/ n 1 an adult male domestic fowl 2 an arrogant man

root[1] /root, roŏt/ n 1 the underground base of a plant that gets water from the soil 2 the underground edible part of a plant 3 the portion of a body part such as a tooth or hair embedded in tissue 4 the base of something o the root of the tongue 5 the fundamental cause of something 6 a number multiplied by itself a particular number of times 7 the core part of a word left when any affixes are removed ■ roots npl somebody's cultural or family origins ■ vti 1 grow or cause to grow roots 2 become or cause to become fixed or embedded ◊ **take root** become established ◊ See note at **origin**

☐ **root up** vt dig up a plant

root[2] /root, roŏt/ v 1 vti dig in the ground with the snout 2 vi rummage

☐ **root out** vt remove completely

root[3] /root, roŏt/ vi 1 cheer or shout in support 2 provide with support

Root /root/, **Elihu** (1845–1937) US lawyer and politician

root beer n a soft drink made from root extracts

⚡ **root di·rec·to·ry** n the top-level directory in a computer's filing system

root·ed /roótad/ adj 1 fixed in the ground by roots 2 well established 3 seemingly unable to move —**root·ed·ness** n

root·stock /roót stòk, roŏt-/ n 1 a rhizome 2 a root used in grafting

root veg·e·ta·ble n a vegetable grown for its edible root

rope n 1 a strong cord made by twisting fibers together 2 a row of things strung or twisted together ■ ropes npl the usual procedures (infml) ■ vt (roped, rop·ing) 1 secure somebody or something with rope 2 enclose an area with ropes ◊ **on the ropes** in a hopeless position and likely to fail (infml)

Ro·sa·ri·o /rō zaáree ō, -saáree-/ city in east central Argentina. Pop. 1,157,372 (1991).

ro·sa·ry /rózaree/ (pl -ries) n 1 a series of Roman Catholic prayers 2 a string of beads used in counting the prayers said in a rosary

ORIGIN Rosary comes from a Latin word meaning "rose garden," and this is one of its early senses in English. In the early 16C it came also to refer to a series of Roman Catholic prayers. It was a common stylistic device at the time to name collections of verse or similar short pieces after bunches of flowers (anthology comes from the Greek word for "flower").

rose[1] n 1 a prickly bush with ornamental flowers 2 a flower of the rose ■ adj of, having, or resembling roses

rose² past tense of **rise**

ro·sé /rō záy/ *n* a pink wine

ro·se·ate /rōzee àyt, -ee ət/ *adj* **1** rose-colored **2** optimistic

Ro·seau /rō zố/ capital of Dominica. Pop. 15,853 (1991).

rose·bud /róz bùd/ *n* the unopened flower of a rose

rose·bush /róz bòosh/ *n* a rose that grows as a bush

rose·hip /róz hìp/ *n* the fruit of the rose plant. Use: jelly, herbal tea, medicinal syrups.

rose·mar·y /róz`mèrree/ *n* **1** aromatic gray green needle-shaped leaves. Use: food flavoring, perfume. **2** a bush that produces rosemary

ORIGIN The earlier form of **rosemary** was *rosmarine*, which gives a clearer clue to its etymology. It originally had no connection with roses or the name Mary, but derived from a Latin word meaning literally "dew of the sea" (because it grew near sea coasts and its blossoms were thought to resemble dew). The earlier form was altered during the 14C by association with *rose* and *Mary*, probably referring to the mother of Jesus Christ.

ro·sette /rō zét/ *n* a decoration resembling a rose

rose wa·ter *n* water scented with rose petals

rose win·dow *n* a round window with tracery in a pattern resembling a rose

rose·wood /róz wòod/ *n* **1** the dark rose-scented wood of various tropical trees. Use: furniture. **2** a tree from which rosewood is obtained

Rosh Ha·sha·nah /ráwsh hə sháwnə, -shaắanə/, **Rosh Ha·sha·na** *n* Jewish New Year Festival. Date: 1st and 2nd of Tishri in the autumn.

Ross /ross/, **Betsy** (1752–1836) US seamstress and reputed maker of the first US flag

Ross, Sir James Clark (1800–62) British explorer

Ross, John (1790–1866) Cherokee leader

AKG London

Christina Rossetti

Ros·set·ti /rō zéttee/, **Christina** (1830–94) British poet

Ros·set·ti, Dante Gabriel (1828–82) British painter and poet

Ros·si·ni /rō seẻnee/, **Gioacchino Antonio** (1792–1868) Italian composer

Ross Sea arm of the S Pacific Ocean, extending into E Antarctica between Victoria Land and Marie Byrd Land, and incorporating the **Ross Ice Shelf**

ros·ter /róstər/ *n* **1** a list of names of employees, athletes, or members of the armed forces, usually detailing their periods of duty **2** the people on a roster ■ *vt* put on a roster

Ros·tock /róst òk, ráwst àwk/ city and port in NE Germany. Pop. 232,634 (1997).

Ros·tov /rə stáwf/ city in SW European Russia, on the Don River. Pop. 1,127,339 (1995).

ros·trum /róstrəm/ (*pl* **-trums** *or* **-tra** /-trə/) *n* a platform for public speaking

ros·y /rōzee/ (**-i·er, -i·est**) *adj* **1** pinkish red **2** having a pinkish complexion **3** promising **4** optimistic o *takes a rosy view of things* —**ros·i·ly** *adv* —**ros·i·ness** *n*

rot *v* (**rot·ted, rot·ting**) **1** *vti* break down organically or decompose **2** *vi* deteriorate badly ■ *n* the process of decaying

ro·ta·ry /rótəree/ (*pl* **-ries**) *n* **1** a rotating part or machine **2** a traffic circle

Ro·ta·ry Club *n* a local branch of an organization of business and professional people that encourages service to the community —**Ro·tar·i·an** /rō térree ən/ *n* —**Ro·tar·i·an·ism** *n*

ro·tate /rō tàyt/ (**-tat·ed, -tat·ing**) *vti* **1** turn around an axis **2** alternate or vary —**ro·ta·tion** *n*

ROTC *abbr* Reserve Officers' Training Corps

rote *n* mechanical repetition in order to remember something

Roth, Philip (b. 1933) US writer

Roth·ko /róth kồ/, **Mark** (1903–70) Russian-born US artist

Roth·schild /róth chìld, rôths-/ family of German and British financiers including **Mayer Amschel** (1743–1812), his sons **Salomon** (1774–1855) and **Nathan Mayer** (1777–1836), and grandson **Lionel Nathan** (1808–79)

ro·tis·se·rie /rō tíssəree/ *n* **1** a roasting spit **2** a shop or restaurant where meat is roasted and sold

rot·ten /róttʼn/ *adj* **1** decayed **2** of a low standard or quality (*infml*) **3** very bad or unwell (*infml*) —**rot·ten·ly** *adv* —**rot·ten·ness** *n*

Rot·ter·dam /-dàam, róttər dàm/ port in SW Netherlands. Pop. 593,321 (2000).

rott·wei·ler /rótt wîtər, -vîtər/ *n* a large powerful black dog with tan markings

ro·tund /rō túnd/ *adj* **1** overweight **2** rich in sound —**ro·tun·di·ty** *n*

ro·tun·da /rō túndə/ *n* a round domed building or room

Rou·ault /roo ố/, **Georges Henri** (1871–1958) French painter and engraver

rou·ble *n* MONEY = ruble

rouge /roozh/ *n* **1** reddish makeup for the

cheeks *(dated)* **2** a reddish polish in powder form —**rouge** *vt*

rough /ruf/ *adj* **1** not having a smooth or flat surface **2** coarse in texture **3** windy or turbulent **4** not gentle **5** not refined or polite **6** harsh in sound or taste **7** general and approximate **8** makeshift o *a rough shelter made from branches* **9** crude o *a rough wooden carving* **10** severe or unpleasant **11** rowdy ■ *n* **1** the part of a golf course where the grass is left long **2** a preliminary version ■ *vt* **1** roughen **2** use violence on an opposing player —**rough·ly** *adv* —**rough·ness** *n* ◇ **rough it** live in a less comfortable way than usual *(infml)*

SPELLCHECK Do not confuse the spelling of **rough** and **ruff** ("a stiff pleated collar"), which sound similar.

□ **rough out** *vt* outline in broad terms
□ **rough up** *vt* beat somebody violently *(infml)*
rough·age /rúffij/ *n* fiber in food
rough-and-read·y *adj* **1** crude but serviceable **2** not refined or polite but friendly and kind
rough-and-tum·ble *n* a situation that lacks rules or order —**rough-and-tum·ble** *adj*
rough·en /rúff'n/ *vti* make or become rough
rough-hewn *adj* **1** cut without precision and not smoothed **2** crudely made
rough·house /rúf hòwss/ *(infml)* *n* a violent or rowdy situation ■ *vti* (**-housed, -hous·ing**) behave or treat in a violent or rowdy way
rough·neck /rúf nèk/ *n* somebody rough and bad-mannered *(infml)*
rou·lette /roo lét/ *n* a gambling game in which a ball is rolled onto a spinning horizontal wheel divided into compartments
round¹ /rownd/ *adj* **1** circular or spherical **2** curved **3** not less or more than o *a round dozen* **4** expressed by an integer o *a round number* **5** considerable o *a round sum* —**round·ish** *adj* —**round·ness** *n*
round² /rownd/ *n* **1** a round shape or object **2** a session of a particular event o *the first round of talks* **3** a stage of a competition **4** a game of golf in which all the holes are played **5** a turn of play, as in a card game **6** a charge of ammunition **7** a gun discharge **8** a series of regular visits *(often pl)* **9** a set of drinks bought, one for each person in a group **10** an outburst of applause **11** a song for several voices, each starting at a different time **12** a circular dance **13** a cut of beef from between the rump and the shank ◇ **in the round** with the stage in the center and the audience seated around it
round³ /rownd/ *v* **1** *vt* move in a curve past something **2** *vti* express a number as the nearest significant number above or below it
□ **round down** *vt* express a number as the nearest significant number below it

□ **round off** *vt* **1** make more rounded **2** finish in a pleasing way
□ **round out** *vti* make or become more complete
□ **round up** *vt* **1** gather people or animals together **2** express a number as the nearest significant number above it
round⁴ /rownd/ *prep, adv* **1** around **2** in a partial circuit of something o *coming round the corner* **3** turning on an axis o *cylinders going round at 1,000 revolutions per second*
round·a·bout /równdə bòwt/ *adj* indirect and not straightforward
round·ly /równdlee/ *adv* severely o *was roundly criticized*
round rob·in *n* a tournament in which everyone plays everyone else
round-ta·ble /równd tàyb'l/ *n* a discussion in which all the participants are on equal terms
Round Ta·ble *n* the legendary circular table at which King Arthur and his knights sat
round-the-clock *adj* 24 hours a day
round trip *n* a trip to a place and back
round-up /równd ùp/ *n* **1** a gathering of people or animals **2** a summary
round·worm /równd wùrm/ *n* a parasitic worm found in the human intestine
rouse /rowz/ (**roused, rous·ing**) *v* **1** *vti* wake **2** *vt* shake somebody out of apathy **3** *vt* provoke a feeling in somebody
rous·ing /rówzing/ *adj* **1** inciting emotion **2** lively —**rous·ing·ly** *adv*
Rous·seau /roo só/, **Henri** (1844–1910) French painter
Rous·seau, Jean Jacques (1712–78) French philosopher and writer
roust *vt* force to get up
roust·a·bout /rówstə bòwt/ *n* an unskilled laborer
rout /rowt/ *n* **1** a disorderly retreat by a defeated army **2** a crushing defeat ■ *vt* **1** force to retreat **2** defeat thoroughly
route /root, rowt/ *n* **1** a way to travel from one place to another **2** the course that something follows or the way it progresses **3** a regular journey usually consisting of a series of stops ■ *vt* (**rout·ed, rout·ing**) send along a particular route
⚡ **rout·er** /róotər, rówtər/ *n* a computer switching program for transferring messages
⚡ **rou·tine** /roo téen/ *n* **1** the usual sequence for a set of activities **2** something boringly repetitive **3** a rehearsed set of actions or speeches making up a performance **4** a part of a computer program that performs a particular task ■ *adj* **1** usual or standard **2** boringly repetitive —**rou·tine·ly** *adv* —**rou·tine·ness** *n* ◇ See note at **habit, usual**
roux /roo/ *n* a base of flour and fat for a sauce
rove /rōv/ (**roved, rov·ing**) *v* **1** *vti* wander or travel over an area aimlessly **2** *vi* move

in changing directions ◇ *as his gaze roved around the room*

rov·er /rṓvər/ *n* 1 a wanderer 2 a small vehicle for exploring the surface of a planet

rov·ing /rṓving/ *adj* 1 moving about 2 erratic or fickle

row[1] /rṓ/ *n* 1 a line of people or things placed next to each other 2 a narrow street lined by houses ◇ **in a row** one after the other ◇ **a tough** *or* **hard row to hoe** something difficult to do

row[2] /rṓ/ *vti* propel a boat with oars —**row·er** *n* —**row·ing** *n*

row[3] /rów/ *n* 1 a noisy argument 2 an unpleasant loud noise ■ *vi* argue noisily

row·boat /rṓ bòt/ *n* a small boat propelled by oars

row·dy /rówdee/ *adj* (**-di·er, -di·est**) unruly ■ *n* (*pl* **-dies**) a noisy person —**row·di·ly** *adv* —**row·di·ness** *n* —**row·dy·ism** *n*

row house /rṓ-/, **row home** /rṓ-/ *n* a house adjoining others to which it is similar

Row·ling /rṓling/, **J. K.** (*b.* 1965) British author

roy·al /róy əl/ *adj* 1 of kings and queens 2 enjoying royal patronage 3 excellent ◇ *given a royal welcome* 4 extremely bad (*infml*) ◇ *a royal pain in the neck*

roy·al blue *adj* of a deep bright blue color —**roy·al blue** *n*

roy·al flush *n* in poker, a hand consisting of the top five cards of a suit

Roy·al High·ness *n* a title used for a member of a royal family other than a king or queen

roy·al·ist /róy əlist/ *n* 1 somebody in favor of a monarchy 2 **Roy·al·ist** a Cavalier in the English Civil War —**roy·al·ism** *n* —**roy·al·ist** *adj*

roy·al·ly /róy əlee/ *adv* generously or splendidly

roy·al·ty /róy əltee/ *n* (*pl* **-ties**) 1 a royal person or royal people collectively 2 a royal person's status 3 a percentage of the income from a book, piece of music, or invention paid to its creator (*often pl*)

rpm, r.p.m. *abbr* revolutions per minute

RR, R.R. *abbr* 1 railroad 2 rural route

R.S.V.P., r.s.v.p. used on an invitation to request a response to it

ORIGIN RSVP is an abbreviation of French *répondez s'il vous plaît* "please reply."

⚡**RT** *abbr* real time (*in e-mails*)

⚡**RTDS** *abbr* real-time data system

⚡**rtf**[1] *n* a computer document file that contains formatting codes. Full form **rich text format**

rtf[2] *abbr* a file extension for a rich text format file

Rt. Hon. *abbr* Right Honourable

Ru *symbol* ruthenium

⚡**RU** *abbr* are you (*in e-mails*)

rub *v* (**rubbed, rub·bing**) 1 *vt* move the hand or an object over the surface of something,

pressing down with repeated circular or backward and forward movements 2 *vi* make dragging contact with a surface 3 *vti* cause soreness on the skin as a result of repeated friction ■ *n* 1 a rubbing action 2 a massage 3 a difficulty ◇ **rub the wrong way** irritate or annoy

☐ **rub down** *vt* massage

☐ **rub off** *vi* be passed on

☐ **rub out** *v* 1 *vti* obliterate 2 *vt* kill (*slang*)

rub·ber[1] /rúbbər/ *n* 1 a natural elastic substance made from the dried sap of various tropical trees 2 an elastic synthetic substance using or resembling natural rubber 3 a waterproof overshoe (*usually pl*) 4 a condom (*slang; sometimes offensive*) —**rub·ber·y** *adj*

rub·ber[2] /rúbbər/ *n* 1 in card games, a deciding game 2 in card games, a match or session of play (*infml*)

rub·ber band *n* a rubber loop for holding things together

rub·ber·ize /rúbbə rìz/ (**-ized, -iz·ing**) *vt* treat with rubber

rub·ber·neck /rúbbər nèk/ *vi* gawk (*infml*) —**rub·ber·neck·er** *n* ◇ See note at **gaze**

rub·ber plant *n* a plant with thick glossy leaves and a rubbery sap, often grown as houseplant

rub·ber stamp *n* 1 a stamping device consisting of an embossed rubber pad that is inked 2 an automatic authorization or approval —**rub·ber-stamp** *vt*

rub·bing /rúbbing/ *n* an impression of a surface made by covering it with paper and rubbing it with a drawing implement

rub·bish /rúbbish/ *n* 1 trash 2 worthless things 3 nonsense —**rub·bish·y** *adj*

rub·ble /rúbb'l/ *n* 1 fragments of broken buildings 2 rough stones used as filler or bulk between walls

rub·down /rúb dòwn/ *n* a massage or vigorous drying after exercise

ru·bel·la /roo béllə/ *n* a contagious childhood disease that causes swelling of the lymph glands and a reddish rash (*technical*)

Ru·bens /rṓbənz/, **Peter Paul** (1577–1640) Flemish painter

Ru·bi·con /rṓbi kòn/, **ru·bi·con** *n* a point of no return

ORIGIN The **Rubicon** was a stream in N Italy (now called the Rubicone) that formerly constituted part of the boundary between Gaul and Italy. By crossing it with his army en route to Rome in 49 BC, Julius Caesar broke a law forbidding a general to lead an army out of his own province, and so committed himself to civil war against the Roman Senate and his rival Pompey.

ru·bi·cund /rṓbikənd/ *adj* having a healthy reddish skin color (*literary*)

ru·bid·i·um /roo bíddee əm/ *n* (*symbol* **Rb**) a

silvery white radioactive chemical element. Use: photocells.

Ru·bin·stein /róobin stǐn/, Artur (1887–1982) Polish-born US pianist

ru·ble /róob'l/, **rou·ble** n the main unit of currency in Russia, Belarus, and Tajikistan

ru·bric /róobrik/ n 1 a printed title or heading 2 a category

ru·by /róobee/ (pl -bies) n a red precious stone. Use: jewelry, manufacture of watches, precision instruments.

ruck·sack /rúk sàk, róok-/ n a bag carried on the back

ruck·us /rúkəss/ n a noisy disturbance

rud·der /rúddər/ n 1 a pivoting blade under the water at the stern of a ship for steering it 2 an airfoil on the tail of an aircraft for steering it

rud·dy /rúddee/ (-di·er, -di·est) adj 1 having a healthy reddish skin color 2 reddish —**rud·di·ness** n

rude (rud·er, rud·est) adj 1 ill-mannered or discourteous 2 sudden and unpleasant o *a rude awakening* 3 roughly made —**rude·ly** adv —**rude·ness** n

ru·di·ment /róodəmənt/ n 1 something basic to a subject (often pl) 2 an undeveloped body part

ru·di·men·ta·ry /róodə méntəree/ adj 1 basic 2 still developing

Ru·dolph /róodolf/, Wilma Glodean (1940–94) US athlete

rue¹ /roo/ (rued, ru·ing) vti feel regret for something

rue² /roo/ (pl rues or same) n a flowering plant once used medicinally

rue·ful /róof'l/ adj regretful —**rue·ful·ly** adv —**rue·ful·ness** n

ruff¹ /ruf/ n 1 a fancy pleated collar worn in the 16C and 17C 2 a growth of long bushy neck hair or feathers on an animal or bird —**ruffed** adj ◊ See note at **rough**

ruff² /ruf/ n in bridge or whist, the act of playing a trump card

ruf·fi·an /rúffee ən/ n somebody rough or violent (dated) —**ruf·fi·an** adj —**ruf·fi·an·ly** adj

ruf·fle /rúff'l/ v (-fled, -fling) 1 vt disorder somebody's hair 2 vti disturb or ripple a surface, or become disturbed or rippled 3 vt make the feathers erect 4 vt annoy somebody 5 vt gather or pleat material to use as trim ■ n 1 something uneven or disordered in a surface 2 something irritating 3 a trim of gathered or pleated fabric 4 a ruff on an animal or bird —**ruf·fled** adj

ru·fi·yaa /roo fee yaa, ròo fee yàa/ (pl same) n the main unit of currency in the Maldives

rug n 1 a fabric covering for an area of floor 2 a mat of animal skin

rug·by /rúgbee/, **rug·by foot·ball** n a team

sport played with an oval ball that is passed by hand or kicked

ORIGIN The game was named for Rugby School, a private school in Warwickshire, central England, where it was reputedly invented. Legend has it that a boy called William Webb Ellis picked up the ball and ran with it during an ordinary game of soccer in 1823. The name itself is first recorded in the 1860s.

rug·ged /rúggəd/ adj 1 with a rough, irregular surface 2 strong-featured 3 physically resilient 4 strongly built —**rug·ged·ly** adv —**rug·ged·ness** n

rug rat n a young child (infml humorous)

ru·in /róo in/ n 1 the physical remains of a destroyed building or city (often pl) 2 a state of complete loss or destruction 3 a cause of destruction ■ vt 1 destroy something completely 2 destroy somebody financially 3 damage something beyond repair —**ru·in·a·tion** /róo ə náysh'n/ n —**ru·ined** adj

ru·in·ous /róo inəss/ adj 1 causing destruction 2 decayed or deteriorated beyond repair

rule n 1 a principle governing conduct 2 a prevailing condition or quality 3 a governing or reigning power 4 a reign or period of government ■ v (ruled, rul·ing) 1 vti govern 2 vt control or restrain 3 vt make a straight line 4 vti dominate 5 vti issue a legal decision or order

□ **rule out** vt 1 exclude 2 prevent

rule·book /róol bòok/ n 1 a publication containing the rules of an activity 2 the approved way of doing something

rul·er /róolər/ n 1 somebody who rules 2 a straight calibrated plastic, wood, or metal strip for measuring and for drawing straight lines

rul·ing /róoling/ adj 1 governing 2 most powerful ■ n an official or binding decision by an authority

rum n an alcoholic liquor made from sugar cane

rum·ba /rúmbə, róom-, ròom-/, **rhum·ba** n 1 a rhythmically complex Cuban dance 2 a ballroom dance based on the Cuban rumba 3 the music for a rumba ■ vi (-baed, -baed /-bad/, -ba·ing, -bas) dance a rumba

rum·ble /rúmb'l/ v (-bled, -bling) 1 vi make a deep rolling sound 2 vt say something with a deep rolling voice 3 vi US, Can, NZ take part in a street fight (slang) ■ n 1 a deep rolling sound 2 US, Can, NZ a street fight (slang)

rum·bling /rúmbling/ n 1 a deep rolling sound 2 a first indication of discontent or an unpleasant event (often pl)

rum·bus·tious /rum búschəss/ adj noisy and exuberant

ru·men /róo men, róomən/ (pl -mi·na /-mənə/ or

-mens *n* the first stomach of a ruminant animal

ru·mi·nant /roomənənt/ *n* any cud-chewing hoofed mammal with an even number of toes and a stomach with multiple chambers ■ *adj* **1** of ruminants **2** thoughtful and reflective

ru·mi·nate /roomə nàyt/ (-nat·ed, -nat·ing) *v* **1** *vi* chew partially digested food *(refers to ruminants)* **2** *vti* think carefully about something —**ru·mi·na·tion** /roomə náysh'n/ *n* —**ru·mi·na·tive** *adj*

rum·mage /rúmmij/ *v* (-maged, -mag·ing) **1** *vti* search through things in a messy way **2** *vt* find by rummaging ■ *n* **1** a messy search through things **2** secondhand articles

rum·mage sale *n* a sale of secondhand items for charity

rum·my /rúmmee/ *n* a card game in which players try to get cards of the same value or a run of cards of one suit

ru·mor /roomər/ *n* **1** an unverified report **2** idle speculation ■ *vt* pass on as a rumor

ru·mor·mon·ger /roomər mùng gər, -mòng-/ *n* somebody who habitually spreads rumors ■ *vi* spread rumors habitually

rump *n* **1** an animal's hindquarters **2** beef from an animal's hindquarters **3** somebody's buttocks *(infml)*

rum·ple /rúmp'l/ *vti* (-pled, -pling) make or become creased or unkempt ■ *n* a crease

rum·pus /rúmpəss/ *n* a noisy disturbance

rum·pus room *n US, Can, ANZ* a room in a house for parties and play

run *v* (ran, run, run·ning) **1** *vi* go on foot fast **2** *vt* travel a particular distance by running **3** *vti* participate in a race **4** *vt* perform something ○ *run a test* **5** *vti* leave or cause to leave quickly ○ *take the money and run* **6** *vt* speed across, over, or through something ○ *running the rapids* **7** *vt* transport ○ *ran me into town* **8** *vi* turn to somebody for help ○ *ran to his brother for money* **9** *vi* visit a place briefly ○ *ran out to the mountains for the weekend* **10** *vti* move smoothly over or through something ○ *ropes running easily through the pulleys* **11** *vti* be or make somebody be a candidate in an election **12** *vi* enter a state or condition ○ *Supplies were running low.* **13** *vti* operate ○ *Let the engine run.* **14** *vt* direct the activities, affairs, or operation of something ○ *runs the whole department* **15** *vti* flow or cause to flow ○ *run a faucet* **16** *vti* spread or leak undesirably ○ *The colors have run.* **17** *vi* range between particular limits ○ *The work ran from difficult to impossible.* **18** *vti* extend along a route or for a particular distance ○ *ran the cable under the road* **19** *vt* continue for a particular length or time ○ *a report running ten pages* **20** *vt* experience something ○ *running a high temperature* **21** *vti* total a particular amount ○ *The bill runs to four figures.* **22** *vi* recur ○ *Stubbornness runs in the family.* **23** *vti*

unravel ■ *n* **1** a fast pace on foot **2** a gallop **3** an act of running **4** a foot race **5** a regular trip **6** a distance or period covered **7** a brief trip **8** free use of a place ○ *the run of the house* **9** a period when a condition or circumstance prevails ○ *a run of bad luck* **10** an operating period of, e.g., a machine **11** a series of continuous performances **12** an urgent demand for something ○ *a run on coffee* **13** the general tendency of things ○ *the usual run of events* **14** an average or typical kind ○ *the general run of merchandise* **15** a place in a knitted garment with unraveled stitches **16** an animal enclosure **17** a baseball score made by traveling around all the bases ◊ **be on the run** be fleeing from somebody or something ◊ **give somebody a run for his or her money** provide somebody with serious competition

☐ **run along** *vi* leave *(usually a command)*

☐ **run away** *vi* flee or escape

☐ **run down** *v* **1** *vti* stop or cause to stop functioning through loss of power **2** *vt* hit with a vehicle **3** *vt* belittle **4** *vt* catch eventually

☐ **run out** *vi* exhaust supplies

☐ **run over** *v* **1** *vt* knock down with a vehicle **2** *vti* go beyond a set limit

☐ **run through** *vt* **1** use up quickly **2** rehearse quickly

run·a·bout /rúnnə bòwt/ *n* **1** a small vehicle for short trips **2** a wanderer

run·a·round /rúnnə ròwnd/ *n* delaying or misleading tactics

run·a·way /rúnnə wày/ *n* somebody who escapes ■ *adj* **1** escaped from captivity or harm **2** out of control **3** easily won *(infml)*

run·down /rún dòwn/ *n* a summary of the main points of something

run-down *adj* **1** tired and not in normal good health **2** shabby and neglected

rune *n* **1** a character in an ancient Germanic alphabet **2** a magical symbol or spell —**run·ic** *adj*

rung¹ *n* **1** a step of a ladder **2** a crosspiece of a chair

rung² past participle of **ring**²

run-in *n* an argument *(infml)*

~~runing~~ incorrect spelling of **running**

run·nel /rúnn'l/ *n* **1** a small stream **2** a narrow water channel

run·ner /rúnnər/ *n* **1** an athlete or horse in a race **2** a messenger **3** in football, a player who carries the ball **4** a smuggler *(often in combination)* ○ *gun runner* **5** a manager or operator of a business or machine **6** a door or drawer slide **7** a blade on a sled or ice skate **8** a long narrow strip of carpet **9** a thin horizontal plant stem that grows roots

run·ner-up (*pl* **run·ners-up**) *n* somebody in second place

run·ning /rúnning/ *n* the sport or exercise of running ■ *adj* **1** used or worn by runners ○ *running shoes* **2** long-standing ○ *a running* joke ■ *adv* consecutively ○ *for five days running* ◇ **be in** or **out of the running** have or not have a chance of success

run·ning board *n* a narrow step beneath the doors of some early vehicles

run·ning mate *n* a nominee for a lesser office

run·ny /rúnnee/ (**-ni·er, -ni·est**) *adj* 1 of a liquid consistency 2 releasing mucus —**run·ni·ness** *n*

run·off /rún àwf, -òf/ *n* 1 rainfall not absorbed by the soil 2 waste products carried by rainfall into surface waters 3 a tie-breaking contest

run-of-the-mill *adj* unexceptional

run-on *adj* added to a line of text without a line break ■ *n* 1 a section of text added without a line break 2 an undefined word appearing at the end of a dictionary entry

runs /runz/ *n* diarrhea (*infml*; *+ sing or pl verb*)

runt *n* 1 the smallest and weakest animal in a litter 2 somebody regarded as small and weak (*insult*) —**runt·y** *adj*

run-through *n* 1 a rehearsal 2 a brief review

run·way /rún wày/ *n* 1 a strip for aircraft landings and takeoffs 2 an extension of a stage into the audience

ru·pee /roo peé, roópee/ *n* the main unit of currency in India, Mauritius, Nepal, Pakistan, the Seychelles, and Sri Lanka

ru·pi·ah /roo peé ə/ (*pl* **-ahs** *or same*) *n* the main unit of Indonesian currency

rup·ture /rúpchər/ *n* 1 a break in or breaking apart of something 2 a tear in or tearing of bodily tissue ■ *vti* (**-tured, -tur·ing**) 1 break, burst, or tear 2 cause or undergo a rift in a relationship 3 cause or undergo a tearing of bodily tissue

ru·ral /róorəl/ *adj* 1 outside the city 2 characteristic of the countryside —**ru·ral·ly** *adv*

ruse /rooz, rooss/ *n* something done to deceive others

rush¹ /rush/ *v* 1 *vi* move fast 2 *vt* hurry somebody or something along 3 *vt* take or send somebody or something to a place urgently 4 *vt* do something hastily 5 *vt* attack suddenly ■ *n* 1 a hurry, or a need for hurry 2 a sudden fast movement by somebody toward a place 3 a busy time 4 a sudden attack 5 a sudden quick flow ■ **rushes** *npl* the first unedited prints of movie scenes ■ *adj* done or needing to be done quickly —**rushed** *adj*

rush² /rush/ *n* 1 the stem of a plant that grows in wet areas. Use: weaving baskets and mats. 2 the plant from which rushes are obtained

rush hour *n* the peak period of travel to or from work

Rush·more, Mt. /rúsh mȧwr/ mountain in the Black Hills, SW South Dakota, carved with the heads of presidents Washington, Jefferson, Lincoln, and Theodore Roosevelt, a national memorial. Height 5,725 ft./1,745 m.

rusk *n* a crisp bread for children

Rus·kin /rússkin/, **John** (1819–1900) British art and social critic

Rus·sell /rúss'l/, **Bertrand, 3rd Earl Russell** (1872–1970) British philosopher and mathematician

rus·set /rússat/ *n* a reddish brown color —**rus·set** *adj*

Rus·sia /rúshə/ country in E Europe and N Asia, extending from the Baltic Sea to the Pacific Ocean, and from the Arctic Ocean to the Caucasus. Cap. Moscow. Pop. 145,470,200 (2001).

Rus·sian /rúsh'n/ *n* 1 somebody from Russia 2 the official language of Russia ■ *adj* 1 of Russia 2 of the former Soviet Union (*dated*)

Rus·sian rou·lette *n* 1 a game in which people take turns aiming a revolver containing one bullet at their own heads 2 a dangerous action or activity

ORIGIN The game is "Russian" because it was reportedly played by Russian officers in Romania in 1917, though their version of the game was even more deadly in that only one bullet was removed from the revolver.

rust *n* 1 a reddish brown coating of iron oxide on iron or steel 2 a plant disease caused by a fungus ■ *vti* corrode with rust

rust belt, Rust Belt *n* a declining area of heavy industry

rus·tic /rústik/ *adj* 1 of a country lifestyle 2 plain and simple ■ *n* somebody who lives in the country (*sometimes offensive*) —**rus·ti·cal·ly** *adv* —**rus·tic·i·ty** /ru stíssətee/ *n*

rus·tle¹ /rúss'l/ (**-tled, -tling**) *v* 1 *vti* make or cause to make a soft crackling sound 2 *vi* move with a rustling sound —**rus·tle** *n* —**rus·tling·ly** *adv*

□ **rustle up** *vt* prepare food quickly (*infml*)

rus·tle² /rúss'l/ (**-tled, -tling**) *vti* steal livestock —**rus·tler** *n*

rust·proof /rúst proof/ *adj* not susceptible to rust ■ *vt* make metal rustproof —**rust·proof·ing** *n*

rust·y /rústee/ (**-i·er, -i·est**) *adj* 1 corroded 2 out of practice —**rust·i·ly** *adv* —**rust·i·ness** *n*

rut¹ *n* 1 a narrow groove made by a vehicle wheel 2 a boring situation ■ *vt* (**rut·ted, rut·ting**) make ruts in

rut² *n* an annual period of sexual excitement in male ruminants —**rut** *vi* —**rut·tish** *adj*

ru·ta·ba·ga /róotə bàygə/ *n* 1 a root vegetable similar to a turnip 2 a European turnip plant that produces rutabagas

Ruth /rooth/ *n* the book of the Bible that tells the story of Ruth, an ancestor of King David

Babe Ruth

Ruth /rooth/, **Babe** (1895–1948) US baseball player

ru·the·ni·um /roo thëènee əm/ *n* (*symbol* **Ru**) a white metallic element. Use: hardening of platinum and palladium alloys.

Ruth·er·ford /rúthər fùrd/, **Ernest, 1st Baron Rutherford of Nelson and Cambridge** (1871–1937) New Zealand-born British physicist. He discovered the nuclear structure of the atom (1909).

ruth·er·ford·i·um /rùthər fáwrdee əm/ *n* (*symbol* **Rf**) a radioactive chemical element produced artificially in atomic collisions

ruth·less /róothləss/ *adj* having or showing no pity —**ruth·less·ly** *adv* —**ruth·less·ness** *n*

Rut·ledge /rút lij/, **John** (1739–1800) chief justice of the US Supreme Court (1795)

RV *abbr* **1** recreational vehicle **2** reentry vehicle

Rwan·da /roo áandə/ country in east central Africa. Cap. Kigali. Pop. 7,312,756 (2001). —**Rwand·an** /n, adj —**Rwand·ese** /roo àan deèz, -deèss/ *n, adj*

rye *n* **1** the edible seeds of a cereal plant, also used to produce whiskey **2** a cereal plant that produces rye grains **3** *also* **rye whis·key** a whiskey distilled from fermented rye

~~ryme~~ incorrect spelling of **rhyme**

~~rythm~~ incorrect spelling of **rhythm**

Ry·u·kyu Is·lands /ree oʻo koo-/ archipelago in SW Japan. Pop. 1,222,458 (1990).

S

s¹ (*pl* **s's**), **S** (*pl* **S's** *or* **Ss**) *n* the 19th letter of the English alphabet

s² *symbol* second

S¹ *symbol* **1** entropy **2** sulfur

S² *abbr* **1** satisfactory **2** small (*in clothes sizes*) **3** south **4** strike (*in baseball*)

-'s *suffix* forms the possessive of nouns ○ *school's* ○ *men's*

-s, -es *suffix* **1** forms the plural of many regular nouns ○ *dogs* ○ *bananas* **2** forms the 3rd person present singular of regular verbs and most irregular verbs ○ *speaks*

Saa·mi /sáamee/ (*pl same or* -**mis**) *n* a member of an indigenous people of Lapland

Sab·bath /sábbəth/ *n* **1** Sunday as a day of Christian religious worship and rest **2** in Judaism and some Christian groups, Saturday as a day of worship and rest

sab·bat·i·cal /sə báttik'l/ *n* a period of leave from work for research, study, or travel —**sab·bat·i·cal** *adj*

sa·ber /sáybər/ *n* **1** a heavy sword with a curved blade **2** a fencing sword with a tapering blade

sa·ber-rat·tling *n* an aggressive show of force

sa·ber-toothed ti·ger *n* an extinct member of the cat family with long curving upper canine teeth

Sa·bin /sáybin/, **Albert** (1906–93) Polish-born US microbiologist and immunologist. He developed an oral, live-virus polio vaccine.

sa·ble /sáyb'l/ (*pl* -**bles** *or same*) *n* **1** a marten with soft dark fur **2** sable fur

sab·o·tage /sábbə tàazh/ *n* **1** deliberate damaging or destroying of property or equipment, e.g., by enemy agents or disgruntled workers **2** an action taken to hinder somebody's efforts —**sab·o·tage** *vt*

ORIGIN Sabotage derives ultimately from a French word meaning "clog." The underlying idea was of clattering along in clogs. Through the implication of clumsiness, this came to mean "do work badly," and then "destroy deliberately."

sab·o·teur /sàbbə túr/ *n* somebody who sabotages property or equipment

sac /sak/ *n* a small bag or pouch formed by a membrane in an animal or plant

SPELLCHECK Do not confuse the spelling of **sac** and **sack** ("a large bag"), which sound similar.

Sac /sak, sawk/ *n, adj* PEOPLES, LANG = **Sauk**

SAC *abbr* Strategic Air Command

Sac·a·ga·we·a /sàkəjə weè ə/ (1784–1812 or 1884) Shoshone interpreter and guide

sac·cha·rin /sákərin/ *n* $C_7H_5NO_3S$ a white crystalline compound. Use: sugar substitute.

sac·cha·rine /sákərin, -rèen/ *adj* **1** of or like sugar **2** too sweet and insincere

Sac·co /sákō/, **Nicola** (1891–1927) Italian-born US anarchist

sac·er·do·tal /sàssər dôt'l, sàkər-/ *adj* of a priest or the priesthood

sa·chem /sáychəm/ *n* a chief of a Native North American people

sa·chet /sa sháy/ *n* a bag containing perfumed powder or potpourri for scenting clothes

sack¹ /sak/ *n* **1** a large bag made of coarse cloth or heavy paper **2** dismissal from a job (*infml*) **3** a bed (*infml*) ■ *vt* **1** dismiss from employment (*infml*) **2** put in a sack

—sack·er n ◊ **hit the sack** go to bed (infml) ◊ See note at **sac**

ORIGIN The two words **sack** entered English by different routes, but are ultimately related. Sack "bag" is derived from Latin *saccus*, which is of Semitic origin. Sack "destroy and plunder" goes back to the same Latin word, probably through the idea of carrying off plunder in bags, but came through Italian and French.

sack² /sak/ vt destroy and plunder **—sack** n

sack·cloth /sák klàwth/ n **1** coarse cloth for sacks **2** clothes made from sackcloth worn in mourning or penitence

sack·ing /sáking/ n coarse cloth made from hemp or jute. Use: sacks.

sack race n a race in which competitors jump along in a sack

sa·cra plural of **sacrum**

~~sacrafice~~ incorrect spelling of **sacrifice**

sac·ra·ment /sákrəmənt/ n **1** a Christian religious rite or ceremony considered to bring divine grace **2** also **Sac·ra·ment** the consecrated elements of the Christian Communion

Sac·ra·men·to /sàkrə méntō/ capital of California, on the **Sacramento River**. Pop. 404,168 (1998).

sa·cred /sáykrid/ adj **1** dedicated to a deity or a religious purpose **2** of religion **3** worthy of worship or respect **—sa·cred·ness** n

sa·cred cow n somebody or something exempt from criticism

~~sacreligious~~ incorrect spelling of **sacrilegious**

sac·ri·fice /sákrə fìss/ n **1** the giving up of somebody or something valuable in exchange for somebody or something considered more worthwhile **2** something valued and given up **3** something or somebody offered to a god ■ v (-ficed, -fic·ing) **1** vt give up as a sacrifice **2** vti make an offering of an animal or person to a god **—sac·ri·fice·a·ble** adj **—sac·ri·fi·cial** /sàkrə físh'l/ adj

sac·ri·lege /sákrəlij/ n **1** theft or desecration of something considered holy **2** disrespect toward something others consider worthy of respect **—sac·ri·le·gious** /sàkrə líjjəss/ adj

sac·ris·tan /sákristən/ n **1** somebody responsible for objects kept in a Christian church **2** a sexton (dated)

sac·ris·ty /sákristee/ n (pl -ties) a room for sacred objects in a Christian church

sac·ro·il·i·ac /sàkrō íllee àk/ adj of the bones joining the back and the hip

sac·ro·sanct /sákrō sàngkt/ adj **1** sacred **2** not to be criticized or tampered with

sa·crum /sáykrəm, sák-/ n (pl -crums or -cra /-krə/) a triangular bone in the lower back

sad (sad·der, sad·dest) adj **1** feeling or showing unhappiness **2** causing or containing unhappiness ○ sad news **—sad·ly** adv **—sad·ness** n

ORIGIN Sad originally meant "satisfied" or "sated" and is related to Latin *satis* "enough." The modern senses developed through "weary" and "dignified, grave, solemn."

SAD abbr seasonal affective disorder

AKG London

Anwar al-Sadat

Sa·dat /sə dáat/, **Anwar al-** (1918–81) president of Egypt (1970–81)

sad·den /sádd'n/ vti make or become sad

sad·dle /sádd'l/ n **1** a seat for riding an animal **2** a seat on a bicycle or motorcycle **3** a cut of meat including part of the backbone and both loins ■ vt (-dled, -dling) strap a saddle onto ◊ **in the saddle** in control

□ **saddle with** vt burden somebody with something

sad·dle·bag /sádd'l bàg/ n a bag attached to a saddle on a horse, bicycle, or motorcycle

sad·dler /sáddlər/ n a maker, repairer, or seller of saddlery

sad·dler·y /sáddləree/ n **1** saddles and other equipment for horses **2** the job of a saddler

sad·dle sore n a sore on a rider's buttocks or leg caused by the rubbing of a saddle **—sad·dle-sore** adj

Sad·du·cee /sájjəssee, sáddyəssee/ n a member of an ancient Jewish group of priests and aristocrats **—Sad·du·ce·an** /sàjjə sée ən, sàddyə-/ adj **—Sad·du·cee·ism** n

Sade /saad/, **Marquis de** (1740–1814) French philosopher and novelist

sa·dism /sáy dìzzəm/ n the deriving of pleasure, especially sexual pleasure, from inflicting pain on others **—sa·dist** n **—sa·dis·tic** /sə dístik/ adj **—sa·dis·ti·cal·ly** adv

sa·do·mas·o·chism /sàydō mássə kìzzəm, sàddō-/ n sexual practices involving sadism and masochism **—sa·do·mas·o·chist** n **—sa·do·mas·o·chis·tic** /sàydō massə kìstik, sàddō-/ adj

Sa·far /sə fàar/ n the 2nd month of the year in the Islamic calendar

sa·fa·ri /sə fàaree/ n a cross-country expedition, especially in Africa, to hunt or observe wild animals

safe adj (saf·er, saf·est) **1** not dangerous **2** not in danger **3** unharmed or undamaged **4** sure to be successful ○ a safe bet **5** probably correct ○ safe to assume that **6** cautious and conservative **7** in baseball, having reached a base or home without being put out ■ *n* a strong metal container for valuables —**safe·ly** *adv* —**safe·ness** *n*

safe-con·duct *n* **1** the official guaranteeing of a traveler's safety **2** a document or escort guaranteeing a traveler's safety

safe-de·pos·it box *n* a strong metal box for storing valuables at a bank

safe·guard /sáyf gàard/ *n* a protective measure ■ *vt* keep safe

---

SYNONYMS safeguard, protect, defend, guard, shield CORE MEANING: keep safe from actual or potential damage or attack

---

safe house *n* a house used as a hiding place from enemies or pursuers

safe·keep·ing /sàyf kéeping, sáyf kéeping/ *n* **1** protection from harm, damage, loss, or theft **2** a system whereby banks keep customers' canceled checks

safe sex *n* sexual activity in which precautions are taken to prevent the spread of sexually transmitted disease

safe·ty /sáyftee/ (*pl* **-ties**) *n* **1** freedom from danger **2** lack of danger **3** the fact of being unharmed or undamaged ○ *She led them to safety.* **4** a device preventing the unintentional operation of a mechanism **5** in football, a play awarding points to the defensive team

safe·ty belt *n* **1** a seat belt in a car **2** a strap to prevent somebody from falling

safe·ty cur·tain *n* a fireproof curtain in a theater at the front of the stage

safe·ty glass *n* shatterproof glass

safe·ty match *n* a match that has to be struck against a special surface in order to be lighted

safe·ty net *n* **1** a net below a high place to catch somebody falling **2** something intended to help people in the event of difficulty or hardship

safe·ty pin *n* a loop-shaped pin that fastens into itself with its point under a cover

safe·ty ra·zor *n* a razor with a partially covered blade to minimize the risk of accidental injury

safe·ty valve *n* **1** a valve that releases fluid when pressure reaches a dangerous level **2** a means of releasing emotion or energy

saf·fron /sáffron/ *n* **1** a spice made from the stigmas of a crocus. Use: food colorant or flavoring. **2** a bright orange yellow color —**saf·fron** *adj*

~~saftey, safty~~ incorrect spelling of **safety**

sag (**sagged, sag·ging**) *v* **1** *vti* bend under weight **2** *vi* become weaker or lose enthusiasm —**sag·gy** *adj*

sa·ga /saága/ *n* **1** an epic tale in Norse literature **2** a long novel or series of novels **3** a long and complicated series of events (*infml*)

---

sa·ga·cious /sə gáyshəss/ *adj* wise or shrewd —**sa·gac·i·ty** /sə gássətee/ *n*

sage[1] (*literary*) *n* a wise person ■ *adj* wise —**sage·ly** *adv* —**sage·ness** *n*

sage[2] (*pl* **sag·es** or *same*) *n* **1** a plant with aromatic grayish green leaves. Use: flavoring food. **2** a sagebrush

sage·brush /sáyj brùsh/ (*pl* **-brush·es** or *same*) *n* a bush with silvery wedge-shaped leaves and large flower clusters

Sag·it·tar·i·us /sàjjə táiree əss/ *n* **1** a zodiacal constellation in the southern hemisphere **2** the 9th sign of the zodiac —**Sag·it·tar·i·an** *adj*, *n*

sa·go /sáygō/ *n* a starchy substance obtained from the pith of a palm. Use: cooking, stiffening fabric.

sa·gua·ro /sə gwaárō, -waárō/ (*pl* **-ros** or *same*), **sa·hua·ro** /sə waárō/ *n* a large cactus of the SW United States and Mexico

Sa·har·a /sə hárrə, -háirə/ largest desert in the world, covering much of North Africa —**Sa·har·an** *adj*, *n*

Sa·hel /sə háyl, sá hil/ dry zone in North Africa, extending from Sudan westward to Senegal

sa·hib /saá lb, -éeb, -híb/, **sa·heb** /saab, saá heb/ *n* S Asia a polite form of address for European men used in South Asia in colonial times

said /sed/ *v* past tense, past participle of **say** ■ *adj* previously mentioned ○ *discovered the said car*

Sai·gon /sī gón/ former name for **Ho Chi Minh City**

sail /sayl/ *n* **1** a large piece of fabric for catching the wind to propel a boat **2** a trip or voyage in a boat or ship, especially one with a sail or sails **3** the sails of a vessel collectively ○ *under full sail* **4** something resembling a sail in form or function ■ *v* **1** *vti* travel by boat or ship across a stretch of water **2** *vti* move across water driven by wind or engine power ○ *ships that sailed the seas* **3** *vt* control the movements of a boat or ship, especially using sails **4** *vi* begin a sea journey ○ *We sail at noon.* **5** *vi* move smoothly or swiftly —**sail·ing** *n* ◇ **set sail** depart in a boat or ship ◇ **under sail** with sails hoisted, and not propelled by an engine

---

SPELLCHECK Do not confuse the spelling of **sail** and **sale** (of goods), which sound similar.

---

sail·board /sáyl bàwrd/ *n* a surfboard with a sail —**sail·board** *vi* —**sail·board·er** *n*

sail·boat /sáyl bòt/ *n* a boat with a sail or sails

sail·fish /sáyl físh/ (*pl* same or **-fish·es**) *n* a fish with a large sail-shaped fin

sail·or /sáylər/ *n* somebody who serves in the navy or works on a ship

sail·plane /sáyl plàyn/ *n* a light glider —**sail·plane** *vi* —**sail·plan·er** *n*

saint /saynt/ *n* **1** in Christianity, somebody formally recognized after death as having led a holy life **2** a virtuous person ■ *vt* in Christianity, declare officially to be a saint —**saint·ed** *adj* —**saint·hood** *n* —**saint·li·ness** *n* —**saint·ly** *adj*

St. Au·gus·tine /saynt áwgə steèn/ city in NE Florida. Pop. 12,573 (1998).

St. Ber·nard /-bər naárd/ *n* a large dog bred to rescue lost mountain travelers

St. Croix /-króy/ largest of the US Virgin Islands. Pop. 50,139 (1990).

St. E·li·as, Mt. /-ə líʉ əss/ second highest mountain in Canada, on the Alaska-Yukon Territory border. Height 18,008 ft./5,489 m.

St. El·mo's fire /-élmōz-/ *n* a luminous region of electrical discharge

Saint-Ex·u·pé·ry /sàN teg zoópə reè/, **Antoine Marie Roger de** (1900–44) French aviator and writer

Saint-Gau·dens /saynt gáwd'nz/, **Augustus** (1848–1907) Irish-born US sculptor

St. He·le·na /-hə leénə/ British island in the S Atlantic Ocean, off the coast of West Africa, the site of Napoleon's death in exile in 1821. Pop. 7,266 (1998).

St. Hel·ens, Mt. /-héllənz/ active volcano in SW Washington State. Height 8,365 ft./2,550 m.

St. John's /-jónz/ **1** capital of Newfoundland, Canada. Pop. 101,936 (1996). **2** capital of Antigua and Barbuda. Pop. 23,000 (1990).

St. Kitts and Ne·vis /-kíts ənd neéviss/ independent state in the Caribbean, comprising two islands of the Leeward Islands group. Cap. Basseterre. Pop. 38,756 (2001).

St. Law·rence /-láwrənss/ river in SE Canada, flowing northeastward from Lake Ontario into the Gulf of St. Lawrence. Length 800 mi./1,300 km.

St. Law·rence, Gulf of deep inlet of the Atlantic Ocean between Newfoundland and the Canadian mainland

St. Law·rence Sea·way waterway in SE Canada and the NE United States that permits oceangoing vessels to navigate between the Atlantic Ocean and the Great Lakes

St. Lou·is /-loò iss/ city in E Missouri, on the Mississippi River. Pop. 339,316 (1998).

St. Lu·cia /-loòshə/ independent island state in the Caribbean, one of the Windward Islands. Cap. Castries. Pop. 158,178 (2001).

St. Mar·tin /-maárt'n/ one of the Leeward Islands, divided between a dependency of Guadeloupe in the north and part of the Netherlands Antilles in the south. Pop. 65,774 (1994).

St. Paul /-páwl/ capital of Minnesota. Pop. 257,284 (1998).

St. Pe·ters·burg /-peétərz bùrg/ **1** second-largest city in Russia. Pop. 5,149,689 (1995).

2 city in west central Florida. Pop. 236,029 (1998).

St.-Pi·erre and Mi·que·lon /san peèr ən meèkə lòn, saN pyàir ən meè klòN/ two small islands in the N Atlantic Ocean, off the coast of Newfoundland, Canada, an overseas territory of France. Cap. St. Pierre. Pop. 6,928 (2001).

Saint-Saëns /saN saáNss/, **Camille** (1835–1921) French composer

saint's day *n* a day commemorating a specific saint

St. Thom·as /-tómməss/ island of the US Virgin Islands, in the Caribbean, east of Puerto Rico. Pop. 48,166 (1990).

St. Val·en·tine's Day /-vállən tīnz-/ the day on which valentines are traditionally sent. Date: February 14

St. Vin·cent and the Gren·a·dines /-vínsənt ənd thə grènnə deénz/ independent state in the Caribbean comprising the island of St. Vincent and 32 of the islands of the Grenadine group. Cap. Kingstown. Pop. 115,942 (2001).

sake¹ /sayk/ *n* **1** somebody's or something's good, benefit, or welfare *o for my sake* **2** the motive for or objective of something *o for the sake of arriving early*

sa·ke² /saákee/, **sa·ki** *n* a Japanese alcoholic drink made from fermented rice

Sa·kha·lin /sákə leèn, sàkhə lyeén/ island of E Russia, in the Sea of Okhotsk. Pop. 660,000 (1983).

Sa·kha·rov /saákə ràwf/, **Andrei Dmitriyevich** (1921–89) Soviet physicist and political dissident

sa·laam /sə laám/ *n* a deep bow with the palm of the right hand on the forehead —**sa·laam** *vti*

sal·a·ble /sáyləb'l/, **sale·a·ble** *adj* suitable for selling —**sal·a·bil·i·ty** /sàylə billətee/ *n*

sa·la·cious /sə láyshəss/ *adj* explicitly sexual or lewd —**sa·la·cious·ly** *adv*

sal·ad /sálləd/ *n* **1** a dish made of a mixture of raw vegetables **2** a cold dish of a particular food or type of food *o fruit salad o potato salad*

sal·ad bar *n* a counter in a grocery store or restaurant serving or selling salads

sal·ad dress·ing *n* a sauce for putting on salad

Sal·a·din /sállədin/ (1138–93) sultan of Egypt and Syria (1174–93)

Sal·a·man·ca /sàllə mángkə/ city in west central Spain. Pop. 158,457 (1998).

sal·a·man·der /sállə màndər/ *n* a small amphibious animal resembling a lizard

sa·la·mi /sə laámee/ *n* a spicy sausage, usually served cold in thin slices

sal·a·ry /sálləree, sállree/ (*pl* -ries) *n* a fixed sum of money paid at regular intervals to an employee —**sal·a·ried** adj ◊ See note at **wage**

ORIGIN The first **salary** was money paid to soldiers in the army of ancient Rome for the purchase of salt (Latin *sal*). Salt was then a valued and valuable commodity.

sa·la·ry·man /sálləree màn/ (pl **-men** /-mèn/) n in Japan, a loyal and unambitious employee of a large corporation

sale /sayl/ n 1 the selling of goods or services 2 a period of time when a shop sells goods at a discount 3 an auction 4 an amount sold (often pl) ◊ **for sale** available for purchase ◊ See note at **sail**

sale·a·ble adj = **salable**

Sa·lem /sáyləm/ 1 city in NE Massachusetts, site of witchcraft trials in 1692. Pop. 38,351 (1998). 2 capital of Oregon. Pop. 126,702 (1998).

Sa·ler·no /sə lúrnō/ capital of **Salerno Province**, Italy. Pop. 142,458 (1999).

~~salery~~ incorrect spelling of **salary**

sales·clerk /sáylz klùrk/ n somebody serving customers in a store

sales force n a body of salespeople employed by a company

sales·man /sáylzmən/ (pl **-men** /-mən/) n a man employed to sell goods or services —**sales·man·ship** n

sales·per·son /sáylz pùrss'n/ (pl **-peo·ple** /-pèep'l/ or **-per·sons**) n somebody employed to sell goods or services

sales pitch n the statements, arguments, or assurances made by somebody trying to sell something

sales rep·re·sen·ta·tive n somebody who visits prospective customers to sell a company's products

sales re·sis·tance n buyers' opposition to a seller's tactics

sales slip n a proof of purchase or sale

sales tax n a government tax on retail merchandise collected at the point of sale by the retailer

sales·wom·an /sáylz wòommən/ (pl **-wom·en** /-wimmin/) n a woman employed to sell goods or services

sal·i·cyl·ic ac·id /sàlli sillik-/ n a white crystalline acid. Use: preservative, manufacture of aspirin and dyes.

sa·li·ent /sáy lee ənt, sáylyənt/ adj 1 particularly noticeable, striking, or relevant 2 projecting from a surface —**sa·li·ence** n —**sa·li·en·cy** n

sa·line /sáy lèen, -līn/ adj containing salt —**sa·lin·i·ty** /sə linnətee/ n

Sal·in·ger /sállinjər/, **J. D.** (b. 1919) US writer

Salis·bur·y Plain /sàwlz beree-/ area of rolling, chalky downs in SW England, site of Stonehenge

Sa·lish /sáylish/ n 1 a small family of Native North American languages spoken in the NW United States and British Columbia 2 a member of a Salish-speaking Native North American people who live in British Columbia —**Sa·lish·an** adj, n

sa·li·va /sə līvə/ n the liquid secreted by glands into the mouth in mammals

sal·i·var·y gland /sállə veree-/ n a saliva-producing gland

sal·i·vate /sállə vàyt/ (**-vat·ed, -vat·ing**) vi produce saliva, especially in expectation of food —**sal·i·va·tion** /sàllə váysh'n/ n

Salk /sawlk/, **Jonas** (1914–95) US physician and epidemiologist. He developed the first vaccine against polio.

sal·low /sállō/ adj unnaturally pale and yellowish —**sal·low·ness** n

sal·ly /sállee/ n (pl **-lies**) 1 an attack from a defensive position 2 a witty remark ■ vi (**-lied, -lies**) 1 make a sally from a defensive position 2 set out from indoors or on an excursion

salm·on /sámmən/ (pl same or **-ons**) n 1 a large fish that migrates up freshwater rivers to spawn 2 the pinkish flesh of the salmon as food

sal·mo·nel·la /sàlmə néllə/ (pl **-lae** /-lee/) n a bacterium that can cause food poisoning

sa·lon /sə lón, sa láwN/ n 1 an elegant sitting room in a large house 2 a social gathering of intellectuals 3 a place for hairdressing or beauty treatments

Sa·lo·ni·ka /sə lónnikə, sàllə néekə/ ♦ **Thes·saloníki**

sa·loon /sə loòn/ n 1 a place where alcohol can be bought and drunk 2 a large room on a ship for passengers to sit in

sal·sa /saálssə/ n 1 a spicy sauce of chopped vegetables eaten with Mexican foods 2 Latin American dance music combining jazz and rock elements with Cuban melodies

salt /sawlt/ n 1 small white crystals consisting largely of sodium chloride. Use: food seasoning and preservative. 2 a crystalline chemical compound formed from the neutralization of an acid by a base containing a metal or group acting like a metal 3 something that adds zest 4 dry wit 5 a sailor with long experience ■ **salts** npl a chemical or crystalline solution used for a particular purpose ○ smelling salts ■ adj 1 preserved with salt ○ salt cod 2 containing salt ○ salt tears 3 containing or associated with salt water ○ a salt marsh ■ vt season, preserve, or treat with salt ◊ **take with a grain** or **pinch of salt** listen to without fully believing ◊ **the salt of the earth** a very good, worthy person or group ◊ **worth your salt** productive

☐ **salt away** vt put money aside for future use

SALT /sawlt/ abbr Strategic Arms Limitation Talks (or Treaty)

salt-and-pep·per adj describes hair flecked with dark and light colors

salt·box /sáwlt bòks/ *n* a wood-frame house with a sloping roof that has two stories at the front and one in the back

salt·cel·lar /sáwlt sèllər/ *n* a small container for salt, especially one for use at the table

---

ORIGIN Saltcellars are not etymologically cellars. The second part represents *saler*, an old word that itself meant "saltcellar." The strictly redundant *salt* had been added, and the spelling changed to *cellar*, before *saler* finally fell into disuse in the early 16C. It had come into English from French, and goes back to Latin *sal* "salt."

---

sal·tine /sawl téen/ *n* a thin salty cracker

Salt Lake Ci·ty capital of Utah. Pop. 174,348 (1998).

salt lick *n* a deposit or block of salt that animals lick

salt marsh *n* a marsh that regularly floods with salt water

salt·pe·ter /sàwlt péetər/ *n* 1 sodium nitrate 2 potassium nitrate

salt·shak·er /sáwlt shàykər/ *n* a perforated salt dispenser

salt wa·ter *n* 1 water containing a lot of salt 2 seawater

salt·wa·ter /sáwlt wàwtər/ *adj* 1 consisting of or containing salt water 2 living in salt water

salt·y /sáwltee/ (-i·er, -i·est) *adj* 1 tasting of salt 2 lively and amusing and sometimes mildly indecent —**salt·i·ness** *n*

sa·lu·bri·ous /sə loóbree əss/ *adj* good for the health —**sa·lu·bri·ty** *n*

sal·u·tar·y /sállyə tèrree/ *adj* 1 useful or valuable 2 healthful (*fml*)

sal·u·ta·tion /sállyə táysh'n/ *n* 1 an expression or act of greeting 2 the opening phrase of a letter or speech

sa·lu·ta·to·ri·an /sə loòtə táwree ən/ *n* a student in a graduating class who is second highest in academic ranking

sa·lute /sə loót/ *v* (-lut·ed, -lut·ing) 1 *vti* give a formal gesture of respect to another member of the armed forces or to a flag 2 *vt* greet 3 *vt* formally praise or honor ◼ *n* 1 an act of saluting somebody or something 2 a firing of guns as a military honor

Sal·va·dor /sálvə dàwr/ capital of Bahia State, E Brazil. Pop. 2,211,539 (1996).

Sal·va·dor, El ▶ El Salvador

Sal·va·do·ran /sàlvə dáwrən/, **Sal·va·do·ri·an** /-dáwree ən/, **Sal·va·do·re·an** *n* somebody from El Salvador ◼ *adj* of El Salvador

sal·vage /sálvij/ *vt* (-vaged, -vag·ing) save something from destruction or loss ◼ *n* 1 the rescue of property from destruction or loss 2 the rescue of a ship or its cargo or crew from the sea 3 rescued goods —**sal·vage·a·ble** *adj*

sal·va·tion /sal váysh'n/ *n* 1 the saving of somebody or something from harm or loss 2 a means of salvation 3 in Christian doctrine, deliverance from sin through Jesus Christ —**sal·va·tion·al** *adj*

Sal·va·tion Ar·my *n* a worldwide evangelical Christian organization that provides help to those in need

salve /sav, salv/ *n* 1 a soothing ointment 2 something that eases worry or distress ◼ *vt* (salved, salv·ing) ease pain, worry, or distress

sal·ver /sálvər/ *n* a serving tray

ORIGIN A **salver** is etymologically for making something safe, and in actuality was used for presenting food that had been tested for poison to the Spanish king. It came through French *salve* from Spanish *salva* in the mid-17C, but on entering English was altered on the model of *platter* or some similar word.

---

sal·vo /sálvō/ (*pl* **-vos** *or* **-voes**) *n* 1 a simultaneous discharge of weapons 2 an outburst of applause or cheering

Sal·ween /sál wèen/ river in Southeast Asia, flowing through SW China and Myanmar into the Gulf of Martaban. Length 1,740 mi./2,800 km.

Salz·burg /sálts bùrg, zaálts-/ capital of **Salzburg Province**, W Austria. Pop. 143,991 (1999).

SAM /sam/ *abbr* surface-to-air missile

Sa·mar·i·a /sə máiree ə/ city and state in ancient Palestine, in present-day NW Jordan —**Sam·ar·i·an** *n*, *adj*

Sa·mar·i·tan /sə márrətən/ *n* 1 somebody from Samaria 2 a helper of somebody in trouble —**Sa·mar·i·tan·ism** *n*

sa·mar·i·um /sə máiree əm/ *n* (*symbol* **Sm**) silvery gray metallic element. Use: strong magnets, carbon-arc lighting, laser materials, neutron absorber.

Sa·mar·kand /sámmər kànd/ city in S Uzbekistan. Pop. 368,000 (1994).

sam·ba /sámbə, saámbə/ *n* 1 a Brazilian dance with strong African influences 2 the music for a samba —**sam·ba** *vi*

same *adj, pron, adv* 1 alike in every significant respect *o the same age o thinks much the same o look the same* 2 not changed or changing *o wore the same hat as yesterday* ◼ *adj, pron* previously mentioned or described *o went because he was bored and I left for the same reason* —**same·ness** *n*

same-sex *adj* of homosexual men or women

Sa·mo·a /sə mố ə/ island country in the S Pacific Ocean. Cap. Apia. Pop. 179,058 (2001). —**Sa·mo·an** *n*, *adj*

Sam·o·set /sámmə sèt/ (1590?–1655?) Abenaki Algonquin leader

sam·o·var /sámmə vaàr/ *n* a large Russian tea urn

sam·pan /sám pàn/ *n* a small Southeast Asian boat with a flat bottom

sam·ple /sámp'l/ n 1 a small amount used as an example of something 2 a piece of recorded sound taken from an existing recording ■ vti (-pled, -pling) take a sample of something

sam·pler /sámplər/ n 1 somebody who tests samples for quality 2 an embroidered cloth containing rows of different stitches 3 a representative selection 4 an electronic equipment for sampling musical phrases

Sam·son /sámss'n/ n a very strong man —**Sam·so·ni·an** /sam sónee ən/ adj

ORIGIN In the Bible, Samson was an Israelite judge and warrior who used his enormous strength to fight the Philistines.

Sam·u·el /sámmyoo əl/ n either of two books of the Bible that tell the history of the Israelites from the birth of Samuel, the first prophet after Moses, to the end of the reign of King David

sam·u·rai /sámmə rì/ (pl same or -rais) n a member of the former aristocratic Japanese warrior class

San[1] /san/ n used as a title, usually in place names, before the name of a man saint

San[2] (pl same or **Sans**) n a member of a southern African people

San An·dre·as Fault /sàn an drày əss-/ n a geologic fault zone in California

San An·to·ni·o /-an tónee ò/ city in south central Texas. Pop. 1,114,130 (1998).

san·a·to·ri·um /sànnə táwree əm/ (pl -ums or -a /-ə/), **san·i·tar·i·um** /sànnə táiree əm/ n 1 a medical facility for long-term illness 2 a health resort (dated)

San Ber·nar·di·no /-bərnər deènò/ city in S California. Pop. 186,402 (1998).

sanc·ti·fy /sángktə fì/ (-fied, -fies) vt 1 make holy 2 give a religious blessing to ○ sancti-fied the marriage —**sanc·ti·fi·ca·tion** /sàngktəfì káysh'n/ n

sanc·ti·mo·ni·ous /sàngktə mónee əss/ adj making an exaggerated show of holiness or moral superiority (disapproving) —**sanc·ti·mo·ni·ous·ly** adv —**sanc·ti·mo·ny** /sángktə mònee/ n

sanc·tion /sángksh'n/ n 1 official authorization 2 a penalty imposed for breaking a rule 3 a punitive measure to pressure a country to conform to international law or opinion (often pl) ○ imposed trade sanc-tions ■ vt 1 authorize 2 approve of —**sanc·tion·a·ble** adj

sanc·ti·ty /sángktətee/ n sacredness or holiness

sanc·tu·ar·y /sángkchoo èrree/ (pl -ies) n 1 a place of refuge 2 a place where wildlife is protected 3 a holy place such as a church, temple, or mosque

sanc·tum /sángktəm/ (pl -tums or -ta /-tə/) n 1 a sacred inner place 2 a quiet private place

sand n 1 material made of tiny grains of rock and minerals, found especially on beaches and in deserts 2 an area of sand ■ vt 1 smooth using sandpaper 2 sprinkle or fill with sand

Sand /sand, saaN/, **George** (1804–76) French writer

san·dal /sánd'l/ n a light open shoe with straps —**san·daled** adj

ORIGIN Sandals have no etymological connection with sandalwood, though they were in fact originally made of wood. Sandal derives through Latin from Greek, and though its exact origins are unknown they are probably in an Asian language. Sandal in sandalwood goes back through Greek, Persian, and Arabic to a known Sanskrit word.

sand·bag /sánd bàg/ n a sealed sack of sand. Use: building defenses, as ballast. ■ vt (-bagged, -bag·ging) protect with sandbags —**sand·bag·ger** n

sand·bank /sánd bàngk/ n a mound of sand that is usually submerged

sand·bar /sánd baàr/ n a long ridge of sand caused by currents or the tide

sand·blast /sánd blàst/ vti clean or polish something using a jet of pressurized air or steam mixed with sand —**sand·blast** n

sand·box /sánd bòks/ n a container of sand for children's play

Sand·burg /sánd bùrg/, **Carl** (1878–1967) US poet, folklorist, and historian

sand·cas·tle /sánd kàss'l/ n a small model of a castle made of damp sand

sand dol·lar n a flat circular sea animal related to the starfish and sea urchin

sand·er /sándər/ n a power tool for smoothing surfaces

sand fly n a tropical biting fly resembling a moth

San Di·e·go /-dee áygò/ city in SW California, on **San Diego Bay**. Pop. 1,220,666 (1998).

S & L n a savings and loan association

sand·man /sánd màn/ n in folklore, a character who makes children sleep by sprinkling sand in their eyes

sand·pa·per /sánd pàypər/ n strong paper coated on one side with sand or another abrasive material ■ vt smooth using sand-paper

sand·pi·per /sánd pìpər/ (pl -pers or same) n a long-billed shore bird

sand·stone /sánd stòn/ n a type of rock made of sand bound together with a mineral cement

sand·storm /sánd stàwrm/ n a strong wind carrying sand

sand trap n a bunker on a golf course

sand·wich /sándwich, sám-/ n 1 a snack consisting of slices of bread with a filling in between 2 something arranged in layers or made up of things squashed together

■ *vt* fit tightly between two other things or people in space or time

ORIGIN The **sandwich** was named for John Montague, 4th earl of Sandwich (1718–92). He is said to have been so addicted to the gambling table that in order to sustain him through an entire 24-hour session uninterrupted, he had a portable meal of cold beef between slices of toast brought to him. The idea was not new, but the earl's patronage ensured that it became a vogue.

sand·wich board *n* a pair of boards carrying notices hanging from the shoulders

~~sandwitch~~ incorrect spelling of **sandwich**

sand·y /sándee/ (**-i·er, -i·est**) *adj* **1** made up of, covered with, or full of sand **2** resembling sand in texture or color —**sand·i·ness** *n*

sane (**san·er, san·est**) *adj* **1** mentally healthy **2** based on rational thinking —**sane·ly** *adv* —**sane·ness** *n*

San Fer·nan·do Val·ley /-fər nándō-/ residential and industrial region in S California. Pop. 1,300,000 (1998).

San Fran·cis·co /-frən sískō/ city in W California. Pop. 745,774 (1998). —**San Fran·cis·can** *n, adj*

San Fran·cis·co Bay inlet of the Pacific Ocean in W California. Length 60 mi./100 km.

sang past tense of **sing**

Sang·er /sángər/, **Frederick** (*b.* 1918) British biochemist, noted for his work on insulin, the structure of proteins, and the nucleotide sequence of nucleic acids

Library of Congress

Margaret Sanger

Sang·er, Margaret (1883–1966) US social reformer

sang-froid /sàng frwaá, saàng-/ *n* calmness under pressure

san·gri·a /sang graé ə/ *n* a drink made with red wine, brandy, lemonade or soda, and fruit juice, served chilled

san·gui·nar·y /sáng gwə nèrree/ *adj* (*fml*) **1** involving bloodshed **2** bloodthirsty

san·guine /sáng gwin/ *adj* **1** cheerfully optimistic **2** having a healthy rosy color ○ *a sanguine complexion* —**san·guin·i·ty** /sang gwínnətee/ *n*

san·i·tar·i·um /n HEALTH SERV = **sanatorium**

san·i·tar·y /sánnə tèrree/ *adj* **1** of public health, especially general hygiene **2** clean and hygienic

san·i·tar·y pad, san·i·tar·y nap·kin *n* a pad for absorbing blood during menstruation

san·i·tar·y pro·tec·tion *n* sanitary pads and tampons

san·i·ta·tion /sànnə táysh'n/ *n* **1** the study and maintenance of public health, especially through water and sewage systems **2** sewage and garbage collection and disposal

san·i·ta·tion work·er *n* somebody employed to haul away trash

san·i·tize /sánnə tīz/ (**-tized, -tiz·ing**) *vt* **1** clean by disinfecting or sterilizing **2** make less likely to offend ○ *a sanitized version of the article* —**san·i·ti·za·tion** /sànnati záysh'n/ *n*

~~sanitorium~~ incorrect spelling of **sanatorium**

san·i·ty /sánnətee/ *n* **1** the condition of being mentally healthy **2** good sense

San Jo·se /-hō sáy/ city in W California. Pop. 861,284 (1998).

San Jo·sé /-hō sáy/ capital of Costa Rica. Pop. 329,154 (1997).

San Juan /-waàn, -hwaàn/ capital of Puerto Rico. Pop. 426,832 (1990).

sank past tense of **sink**

San Lu·is Po·to·sí /-loo éess pòttō seé/ capital of **San Luis Potosí State**, central Mexico. Pop. 625,466 (1995).

San Ma·ri·no /-mə reénō/ small independent enclave in NE Italy. Cap. San Marino. Pop. 27,336 (2001).

San Mar·tín /-maar teén/, **José Francisco de** (1778–1850) Argentine revolutionary leader

San Mig·uel de Tu·cu·mán /-mi gèl də too koo maán/ capital of **Tucumán Province**, NW Argentina. Pop. 470,809 (1991).

San Sal·va·dor /-sálvə dàwr/ capital of El Salvador. Pop. 415,346 (1992).

San·skrit /sánskrit/ *n* an ancient South Asian language that is the language of classical Hindu texts —**San·skrit** *adj* —**San·skrit·ist** *n*

sans ser·if /san sérrif/, **san·ser·if** *n* a style of typeface with no small horizontal lines at the ends of the main strokes

San·ta A·na /sàntə ánnə/ city in SW California. Pop. 305,955 (1998).

San·ta An·na /-ánnə/, **Antonio Lopez de** (1794–1876) general and president of Mexico (1833–36, 1844, 1847, and 1853–55)

San·ta Bar·ba·ra Is·lands /-baàrbərə/ island group of S California, in the Pacific Ocean

San·ta Claus /-sántə klàwz/ *n* an imaginary old man with a white beard and a red suit who brings presents to children at Christmas

San·ta Cruz /-kroóz/ city in central Bolivia. Pop. 914,795 (1997).

San·ta Fe /-fáy/ capital of New Mexico. Pop. 67,879 (1998). —**San·ta Fe·an** *n, adj*

San·ta Ro·sa /-rōzə/ city in NW California. Pop. 126,891 (1998).

San·ta·ya·na /sàntee yánnə/, **George** (1863–1952) Spanish-born US philosopher

San·ti·a·go /sàntee aàgò/ capital of Chile. Pop. 4,703,954 (1998).

San·ti·a·go de Com·po·ste·la /-də kompo stéllə/ capital of Galicia, NW Spain, formerly a major place of Christian pilgrimage. Pop. 93,584 (1998).

San·ti·a·go de Cu·ba /-koòbə/ second largest city in Cuba. Pop. 432,396 (1996).

San·to Do·min·go /sàntò də míng gò/ capital of the Dominican Republic. Pop. 3,166 (1995).

São Pau·lo /sow pówlò/ capital of São Paulo State, SE Brazil. Pop. 9,839,436 (1996).

São To·mé and Prín·ci·pe /-tò mày ənd prínsəpə/ island country off the coast of Gabon, in the Gulf of Guinea. Cap. São Tomé. Pop. 165,034 (2001).

sap[1] *n* **1** a watery fluid containing nutrients that circulates through the tissues of plants **2** energy or vitality **3** an offensive term for somebody regarded as thoughtless or unintelligent *(slang insult)* —**sap·py** *adj*

sap[2] *n* a covered trench leading to enemy territory ■ *v* (**sapped, sap·ping**) **1** *vti* dig a sap or a tunnel that undermines enemy fortifications **2** *vt* gradually take away somebody's energy ○ *sapping his strength*

~~saphire~~ incorrect spelling of **sapphire**

sa·pi·ent /sáypee ənt/ *adj* wise —**sa·pi·ence** *n*

sap·ling /sáppling/ *n* a young tree

sap·per /sáppər/ *n* **1** a military engineer specializing in trenches and tunnels **2** a military engineer who lays, detects, and disarms mines

sap·phire /sá fìr/ *n* **1** a deep blue variety of corundum. Use: gems. **2** a brilliant blue color —**sap·phire** *adj*

Sap·pho /sáffò/ (*fl* 7C BC) Greek poet

Sap·po·ro /sa páwrò/ city on W Hokkaido Island, Japan. Pop. 1,801,327 (2000).

sap·ro·phyte /sápprə fìt/ *n* an organism that lives on decaying organic matter —**sap·ro·phyt·ic** /sàpprə fíttik/ *adj*

sap·suck·er /sáp sùkər/ *n* a small woodpecker that drills holes in trees in order to drink the sap

Sar·a·cen /sárrəss'n/ *n* **1** a Muslim who fought the Christian Crusaders in the Middle Ages **2** a member of an ancient desert people of Syria and Arabia —**Sar·a·cen** *adj*

Sar·a·gos·sa /sàrrə góssə/ ♦ **Zaragoza**

Sa·ra·je·vo /sàrrə yáyvò/ capital of Bosnia-Herzegovina. Pop. 360,000 (1997).

sa·ran /sə rán/ *n* a thermoplastic resin produced from a vinyl compound. Use: fabrics, plastic wrap.

Sa·ra·wak /sə ráa wàak/ state in NW Borneo, Malaysia. Cap. Kuching. Pop. 1,954,300 (1997).

sar·casm /saàr kàzzəm/ *n* language meaning the opposite of what it says and intended to mock or deride

sar·cas·tic /saar kástik/ *adj* using or characterized by sarcasm —**sar·cast·ic·al·ly** *adv*

SYNONYMS sarcastic, ironic, sardonic, satirical, caustic CORE MEANING: describes remarks that are designed to hurt or mock

sar·co·ma /saar kṓmə/ (*pl* **-mas** *or* **-ma·ta** /-mətə/) *n* a malignant tumor that begins growing in connective tissue

sar·coph·a·gus /saar kóffəgəss/ (*pl* **-gi** /-gī/ *or* **-gus·es**) *n* a stone coffin

ORIGIN Sarcophagus came through Latin from a Greek word meaning literally "flesh eater." The Greek word originally referred to a stone that was fabled to consume the flesh of dead bodies and that was used for coffins.

sar·dine /saar deèn/ *n* **1** a tiny ocean fish related to the herring **2** a sardine as food

Sar·din·i·a /saar dínnee ə/ Italian island in the W Mediterranean Sea. Cap. Cagliari. Pop. 1,659,466 (1995). —**Sar·din·i·an** *adj*, *n*

Sar·dis /saàrdiss/ ancient city of W Asia Minor, near present-day Izmir, Turkey, the capital of the ancient kingdom of Lydia

sar·don·ic /saar dónnik/ *adj* disdainfully or ironically mocking —**sar·don·i·cal·ly** *adv*◊ See note at **sarcastic**

Sar·gas·so Sea /saar gàssò-/ section of the North Atlantic Ocean between the Greater Antilles and the Azores, noted for its predominantly still waters

Sar·gent /saárjənt/, **John Singer** (1856–1925) Italian-born US artist

sa·ri /saàree/, **sa·ree** *n* a South Asian woman's garment consisting of a long rectangle of fabric wrapped around the body and over the shoulder

sar·in /saárin/ *n* a toxic gas that attacks the central nervous system, causing convulsions and death

Sar·noff /saàr nàwf/, **David** (1891–1971) Russian-born US broadcasting executive

sa·rong /sə ráwng/ *n* a traditional garment of Malaysia and Java consisting of a length of fabric wrapped around the body

Sa·roy·an /sə róy ən/, **William** (1908–81) US playwright and novelist

sar·sa·pa·ril·la /sàaspə ríllə/ (*pl* **-las** *or same*) *n* **1** the dried root of a tropical creeper or temperate plant. Use: traditional or herbal medicine, flavoring in soft drinks. **2** a tropical vine or similar plant whose roots are dried as sarsaparilla **3** a soft drink flavored with sarsaparilla

Sar·to ♦ **Andrea del Sarto**

sar·to·ri·al /saar táwree əl/ *adj* of tailoring or tailored clothing

AKG London

Jean-Paul Sartre

Sar·tre /saártrə, saart/, **Jean-Paul** (1905–80) French philosopher, playwright, and novelist

SAS *n* a UK military force trained for dangerous clandestine operations. Full form **Special Air Service**

SASE *abbr* self-addressed stamped envelope

sash *n* **1** a fabric belt **2** a wide ribbon worn across the chest

sa·shay /sa sháy/ *vi* **1** walk with an exaggerated sway to attract attention (*humorous*) **2** perform a sequence of steps in square dancing

sa·shi·mi /saa sheémee/ *n* a Japanese dish of sliced raw fish, usually served with a dip

sash win·dow *n* a window consisting of two frames, one above the other, that are able to overlap in vertical grooves

Sask. *abbr* Saskatchewan

Sas·katch·e·wan /sa skáchəwən/ province in central Canada. Cap. Regina. Pop. 1,023,636 (2000). —**Sas·katch·e·wa·ni·an** /sa skàchə waánee ən/ *n, adj*

Sas·ka·toon /sàskə toón/ second largest city in Saskatchewan, Canada. Pop. 193,647 (1996).

sas·quatch /sás kwòch, sás kwàwch/ *n* a large hairy humanoid said to live in NW Canada

sass *n* back talk (*infml*) —**sass** *vt*

sas·sa·fras /sássə fràss/ (*pl same*) *n* **1** the aromatic dried root bark of a tree. Use: flavoring, perfumes, medicines. **2** a deciduous tree whose root bark is dried as sassafras

~~sassafrass~~ incorrect spelling of **sassafras**

sas·sy /sássee/ (**-si·er, -si·est**) *adj* **1** impudent or disrespectful **2** high-spirited —**sas·si·ly** *adv* —**sas·si·ness** *n*

sat past tense, past participle of **sit**

SAT /sat/ *tdmk* a trademark for a standardized test taken by applicants to colleges in the United States. Full form **Scholastic Aptitude Test**

Sat. *abbr* Saturday

~~satalite~~ incorrect spelling of **satellite**

Sa·tan /sáyt'n/ *n* in Christianity, the devil

sa·tan·ic /sə tánnik/ *adj* **1** of Satan or the worship of Satan **2** extremely evil —**sa·tan·i·cal·ly** *adv*

Sa·tan·ism /sáyt'n ìzzəm/ *n* Satan worship

sa·tay /saà tay/ *n* a Southeast Asian kebab served with peanut sauce

satch·el /sáchəl/ *n* a small bag for carrying things such as books, often with a shoulder strap

sate (**sat·ed, sat·ing**) *vt* **1** fully gratify the hunger or desire of **2** provide with too much

~~satellite~~ incorrect spelling of **satellite**

sat·el·lite /sátt'l īt/ *n* **1** an object sent into space that orbits a planet and relays information to Earth **2** a moon orbiting another astronomical object **3** a country dependent on another more powerful country

sat·el·lite dish *n* a dish-shaped antenna for receiving television signals broadcast via satellite

sat·el·lite tel·e·vi·sion *n* television broadcast via satellite

~~Saterday~~ incorrect spelling of **Saturday**

sa·ti·ate /sáyshee àyt/ (**-at·ed, -at·ing**) *vt* **1** fully gratify hunger or desire **2** provide somebody with too much of something desirable

Sa·tie /saa teé/, **Erik** (1866–1925) French composer

sa·ti·e·ty /sə tí ətee/ *n* the state of having been satiated

sat·in /sátt'n/ *n* a glossy silk or rayon fabric ■ *adj* **1** made of satin **2** glossy like satin —**sat·in·y** *adj*

ORIGIN Satin is ultimately named for the port of Tseutung (now Tsinkiang) in S China, from where it was exported. It came to English via French from an Arabic form of the name.

sat·in·wood /sátt'n wòod/ *n* **1** a smooth hard yellow brown wood. Use: furniture making. **2** a tree that produces satinwood

sat·ire /sá tīr/ *n* **1** use of wit to attack vice and folly **2** a literary work using satire —**sa·tir·i·cal** /sə tírrik'l/ *adj* —**sa·tir·i·cal·ly** *adv* —**sat·i·rist** /sáttərist/ *n*

sat·i·rize /sáttə rìz/ (**-rized, -riz·ing**) *vt* use satire against —**sat·i·ri·za·tion** /sàttəri záysh'n/ *n*

sat·is·fac·tion /sàttəs fáksh'n/ *n* **1** the feeling of pleasure that comes when a need or desire is fulfilled **2** fulfillment of a need or desire **3** contentment with something such as an arrangement or performance

sat·is·fac·to·ry /sàttəs fáktəree/ *adj* good enough to meet a requirement or expectation —**sat·is·fac·to·ri·ly** *adv*

sat·is·fy /sáttəs fī/ (**-fied, -fies**) *v* **1** *vt* make somebody feel pleased or content **2** *vti* fulfill a need or desire **3** *vt* resolve the doubts of somebody **4** *vt* meet a requirement or condition **5** *vt* pay a debt in full —**sat·is·fied** *adj* —**sat·is·fy·ing·ly** *adv*

sa·to·ri /saa táwree/ *n* in Zen Buddhism, a state of spiritual enlightenment

sat·su·ma /sat sōoma/ n 1 a cultivated variety of mandarin orange 2 a citrus tree that produces satsumas

~~satellite~~ incorrect spelling of **satellite**

sat·u·rate /sácha ràyt/ (-rat·ed, -rat·ing) vt 1 soak something with liquid 2 fill something completely 3 supply a market fully —**sat·u·rat·ed** adj —**sat·u·ra·tion** /sácha ráysh'n/ adj

sat·u·rat·ed fat n fat from animal products in which the carbon atoms are fully combined with hydrogen

sat·u·ra·tion point n a limit to the scope for expansion or absorption

Sat·ur·day /sáttər dày, -dee/ n the 7th day of the week

ORIGIN **Saturday** is named for the Roman god Saturn.

Sat·ur·day night spe·cial n a cheap handgun (infml)

Sat·urn /sáttərn/ n 1 in Roman mythology, the god of agriculture and ruler of the universe until deposed by his son Zeus. Greek equivalent **Cronus** 2 the 6th planet from the Sun —**Sa·tur·ni·an** /sa túrnee ən/ adj

sat·ur·na·li·a /sáttər náylee ə/ n (pl -as or same) a wild celebration ■ **Sat·ur·na·li·a** npl the ancient Roman festival in celebration of Saturn. Date: mid-December.

sat·ur·nine /sáttər nìn/ adj gloomy and morose

sa·tyr /sáytər, sáttər/ n 1 in Greek mythology, a woodland creature that is half-man, half-goat 2 a man displaying inappropriate or excessive sexual behavior

sauce /sawss/ n 1 a thick liquid added to food 2 stewed fruit served with a meal o cranberry sauce 3 something that adds zest or excitement ■ vt (sauced, sauc·ing) add a sauce to food

sauce·boat /sáwss bòt/ n a low pitcher for sauce or gravy

sauce·pan /sáwss pàn/ n a deep cooking pan with a handle

sau·cer /sáwssər/ n 1 a small circular dish for holding a cup 2 a round flat object

sauc·y /sáwssee/ (-i·er, -i·est) adj 1 impudent 2 pert —**sau·ci·ly** adv —**sau·ci·ness** n

Sa·ud ♦ Ibn Saud, Abdul Aziz

Sa·ud (1902–69) king of Saudi Arabia (1953–64)

Sau·di A·ra·bi·a /sòwdee ə ráybee ə/ country in SW Asia, on the Arabian Peninsula. Cap. Riyadh. Pop. 22,757,092 (2001). —**Sau·di A·ra·bi·an** n, adj

sau·er·bra·ten /sów ər braàt'n/ n a dish of beef roast marinated and cooked in vinegar

sau·er·kraut /sów ər kròwt/ n shredded cabbage fermented in its own juice with salt

Sauk /sawk/ (pl same or **Sauks**), **Sac** /sak, sawk/ (pl same or **Sacs**) n 1 a member of a Native North American people who now live mainly in Oklahoma 2 the Algonquian language of the Sauk people —**Sauk** adj

Saul /sawl/ (fl 11C BC) first king of ancient Israel (about 1020–00 BC)

Sault Sainte Ma·rie Ca·nals /sòo saynt mə rèe-/ series of ship canals in the United States and Canada, on the St. Marys River, between lakes Superior and Huron.

sau·na /sáwnə, sównə/ n 1 a steam bath followed by a plunge in cold water or a light brushing with birch or cedar boughs 2 a room for a sauna

saun·ter /sáwntər/ vi walk at an easy pace ■ n 1 an easy walking pace 2 a walk at an easy pace

~~saurkraut~~ incorrect spelling of **sauerkraut**

sau·sage /sáwssij/ n spicy chopped meat and other ingredients in a casing

Saus·sure /sō sóor, -syóor/, **Ferdinand de** (1857–1913) Swiss linguist

sau·té /sō táy/ vt fry lightly in a little fat ■ n a sautéed dish

sav·age /sávvij/ adj 1 vicious or violent 2 severe in effect o savage job cuts 3 an offensive term meaning belonging or relating to a culture perceived as uncivilized ■ n 1 a vicious or violent person 2 an offensive term for a member of a people considered to be uncivilized ■ vt (-aged, -ag·ing) 1 attack violently 2 criticize cruelly —**sav·age·ly** adv —**sav·age·ness** n —**sav·age·ry** n

sa·van·na /sə vánnə/, **sa·van·nah** n a grassy plain

Sa·van·nah /sə vánnə/ 1 river rising in NW South Carolina and flowing along the South Carolina-Georgia border into the Atlantic Ocean. Length 314 mi./505 km. 2 city in SE Georgia, at the mouth of the Savannah River. Pop. 131,674 (1998).

sa·vant /sa vaánt/ n a learned person

⚡ save¹ /sayv/ v (saved, sav·ing) 1 vt rescue somebody or something from harm or danger 2 vti set aside and accumulate money for later use 3 vt avoid wasting or using something o save time o switched it off to save the batteries 4 vti reduce expense o saving on fuel 5 vti store a copy of computer data on a storage medium 6 vt redeem somebody from the consequences of sin ■ n an action that prevents an opponent from scoring a goal —**sav·er** n

save² /sayv/ prep, conj except o everybody save me

sav·er /sáyvər/ n something that conserves resources (in combination) o a great time-saver

sav·ing /sáyving/ n 1 an amount kept from being spent, wasted, or used 2 the rescuing of somebody or something from harm or danger ■ **sav·ings** npl money set aside ■ prep, conj except (literary)

sav·ing grace *n* a redeeming quality or feature

sav·ings ac·count *n* a bank account for saving money

sav·ings and loan as·so·ci·a·tion *n* a co-operative bank that invests savings mainly in home mortgage loans

sav·ings bank *n* a bank that invests savings and pays interest

sav·ings bond *n* 1 a US government bond 2 *Can* a Canadian government-issued bond

sav·ior /sáyvyər/ *n* 1 somebody who saves another from harm or danger 2 **Sav·ior** in Christianity, Jesus Christ

sa·voir-faire /sàv waar fáir/ *n* social adeptness

Sa·vo·na·ro·la /sàvvənə róla/, **Girolamo** (1452–98) Italian religious leader and martyr

sa·vor /sáyvor/ *vt* 1 enjoy unhurriedly 2 enjoy the taste or smell of ■ *n* 1 the taste or smell that something has 2 a distinctive quality

sa·vor·y¹ /sáyvoree/ *adj* 1 appetizing 2 salty or sharp-tasting rather than sweet

sa·vor·y² *n* an herb with aromatic leaves. Use: flavoring food.

sav·vy /sávvee/ *(infml) adj* shrewd and well informed ■ *n* shrewdness and practical knowledge

saw¹ *n* a tool with a toothed metal blade for cutting ■ *vti* (**sawed** *or* **sawn** /sawn/) cut something using a saw

saw² *n* a trite old saying

saw³ past tense of **see¹**

saw-buck /sáw bùk/ *n* 1 a sawhorse 2 a ten-dollar bill *(slang)*

> **ORIGIN** *Sawbuck* was borrowed from Dutch in the mid-19C. The sense "ten-dollar bill" derives from the resemblance between the X-shaped end of a sawhorse and the roman numeral for 10.

saw·dust /sáw dùst/ *n* fine particles of wood produced during sawing

sawed-off *adj* 1 with one end cut short o *a sawed-off shotgun* 2 an offensive term meaning of small stature *(slang)*

saw·fish /sáw fìsh/ *(pl same or* -**fish·es**) *n* a fish with a long toothed snout

saw·horse /sáw hàwrss/ *n* a support for wood during sawing

saw·mill /sáw mìl/ *n* a factory where wood is sawed

sawn past participle of **saw¹**

saw·yer /sáwyər/ *n* somebody who saws wood for a living

sax *n* a saxophone *(infml)*

sax·i·frage /sáksi frij, -fràyj/ *(pl* -**frages** *or same) n* a plant with small flowers that grows on rocky ground

Sax·on /sáks'n/ *n* 1 a member of an ancient Germanic people who established kingdoms in S Britain 2 the language of the ancient Saxons —**Sax·on** *adj*

sax·o·phone /sáksə fòn/ *n* a metal wind instrument with keys and a reed —**sax·o·phon·ist** *n*

> **ORIGIN** The **saxophone** is named for the Belgian instrument-maker Antoine Joseph ("Adolphe") Sax (1814–94), who devised it. The name first appears in English in 1851 in the catalog of the Great Exhibition of that year held in London, England.

say *v* (**said** /sed/) 1 *vt* utter in a normal voice 2 *vti* express something verbally 3 *vt* indicate in numbers or symbols o *The clock said midnight.* 4 *vt* suppose o *Let's say we can't afford it.* 5 *vt* recite o *says his prayers* ■ *n* 1 a chance to speak o *have your say* 2 the right to give an opinion and have it considered o *had no say in the decision* ■ *adv* approximately o *if we get, say, three gallons* ■ *interj (infml)* 1 expresses surprise, admiration, or protest 2 attracts attention —**say·er** *n* ◇ **it goes without saying** it is obvious or self-evident

Say·ers /sáy arz/, **Dorothy L.** (1893–1957) British writer

say·ing /sáy ing/ *n* a proverbial expression

sa·yo·na·ra /sì ə náara/ *interj* good-bye *(infml)*

say-so *n* permission or authorization from somebody *(infml)*

Sb *symbol* antimony

SBA¹ *n* a radio navigation system that signals aircraft during the approach to landing. Full form **standard beam approach**

SBA² *abbr* Small Business Administration

sc, s.c. *abbr* small capital

Sc *symbol* scandium

SC *abbr* 1 Security Council 2 *also* **S.C.** South Carolina

scab *n* 1 a crust over a healing wound 2 a strikebreaker *(disapproving)* ■ *vi* (**scabbed, scab·bing**) 1 become covered with a scab 2 work during a strike *(disapproving)*

scab·bard /skábbərd/ *n* a sheath for a sword or dagger

scab·by /skábbee/ (-**bi·er**, -**bi·est**) *adj* having or covered with scabs —**scab·bi·ness** *n*

sca·bies /skáybeez/ *n* a contagious skin disease caused by a mite, with itching, inflammation, and small red lumps

sca·bi·ous /skáybee əss, skábbee əss/ *(pl* -**ous·es** *or same) n* a plant with dome-shaped flowers

scab·rous /skábbrəss, skáybrəss/ *adj* with a rough scaly or hairy surface

scads *npl* large quantities *(infml)*

scaf·fold /skáff'ld, -fòld/ *n* 1 a framework of poles and planks erected against or around a building to support workers 2 a platform for executions by hanging or beheading —**scaf·fold·er** *n*

scaf·fold·ing /skáff'lding, ská fòlding/ *n* 1 a system of scaffolds 2 the materials for building a scaffold

scal·a·ble /skáyləb'l/ *adj* **1** climbable **2** describes computer graphics fonts whose size can be altered

sca·lar /skáylər/ *n* a quantity with magnitude but not direction

scal·a·wag /skálla wàg/, **scal·ly·wag** /skállee- */n* **1** a mischievous or rascally person (*dated infml*) **2** a white Southerner who collaborated with the federal government during Reconstruction

ORIGIN *Scalawag* is thought variously to derive from the name *Scallaway* of Scotland's Shetland Islands, or from an obsolete Scots word *scallag*, "a farm servant." Its first recorded appearance in the United States is understood to be 1848, with the spelling *scalaway*. In western New York State a *scala-way* meant "a mean rascal." During Reconstruction a *scalawag* referred to a white southern operative who assisted the federal government in implementing its policies throughout the South, often profiteering in the process. But its earlier political meaning, first recorded in 1862, was "an intriguer, especially in politics."

scald *vt* **1** burn with hot liquid or steam **2** heat to near boiling point ■ *n* a burn caused by hot liquid or steam

scald·ing /skáwlding/ *adj* **1** extremely hot **2** scathing

scale¹ *n* **1** any of the small flat bony or horny overlapping plates on fish and some reptiles and mammals **2** a thin flat piece or flake **3** a deposit formed inside a kettle or boiler ■ *v* (**scaled, scal·ing**) **1** *vt* clean scales or scale from ○ *scaling the fish* **2** *vi* flake off

scale² *n* **1** a measuring instrument with graduated markings **2** a measuring system based on a series of marks at regular intervals representing numerical values **3** the extent or relative size of something ○ *the scale of the devastation* **4** a series of musical notes arranged according to pitch ■ **Scales** *npl* the zodiacal sign Libra ■ *vt* (**scaled, scal·ing**) **1** climb up or over **2** make or draw to scale ◇ **to scale** with the same proportion of reduction or enlargement throughout
□ **scale down** *or* **back** *vt* reduce
□ **scale up** *vt* increase

scale³ *n* a weighing machine (*sometimes pl*)

scale in·sect, scale *n* a destructive plant-sucking insect that covers itself with a waxy secretion resembling scales

sca·lene /skáy lèen, skay léen/ *adj* describes a triangle in which each side is a different length

Sca·li·a /skə lée ə/, **Antonin** (*b.* 1936) associate justice of the US Supreme Court (1986–)

scal·lion /skállyən/ *n* a small onion with long leaves

ORIGIN The **scallion** is ultimately named for Ascalon, a port in ancient Palestine. Its Latin

name meant "onion of Ascalon," but in French the "onion" part was dropped, and in some forms of French the initial vowel sound was also lost. An alteration of the same French word became the ancestor of *shallot*, a name for a similar vegetable.

scal·lop /skóllap/ *n* **1** a sea mollusk with a wavy fan-shaped shell **2** the flesh of a scallop as food **3** a wavy ornamental fabric edging **4** a thin slice of meat ■ *vt* make a series of curves along the edge of fabric —**scal·loped** *adj* —**scal·lop·ing** *n*

scal·ly·wag *n* = scalawag

scalp *n* the skin and underlying tissue on top of the head ■ *vt* **1** cut off the scalp of **2** resell for a quick profit ○ *scalping tickets* —**scalp·er** *n*

scal·pel /skálpəl/ *n* a surgical knife with a short blade

scal·y /skáylee/ (**-i·er, -i·est**) *adj* covered in scales —**scal·i·ness** *n*

scam (*slang*) *n* a dishonest scheme for making money ■ *vt* (**scammed, scam·ming**) trick with a scam

scam·per /skámpər/ *vi* run quickly or playfully —**scam·per** *n*

scam·pi /skámpee/ *n* shrimp with garlic and lemon

scan *vt* (**scanned, scan·ning**) **1** examine something thoroughly or intently ○ *scanning the horizon* **2** look through or read something quickly **3** analyze verse in terms of its meter **4** direct a light-sensitive device over a surface in order to convert an image into digital or electronic form ■ *n* **1** an image produced by scanning something **2** the scanning of something —**scan·na·ble** *adj*

scan·dal /skánd'l/ *n* **1** something causing public outrage or censure **2** an outburst of public outrage or censure **3** malicious talk or gossip

scan·dal·ize /skánd'l ìz/ (**-ized, -iz·ing**) *vt* offend by shocking behavior —**scan·dal·i·za·tion** /skánd'li záysh'n/ *n*

scan·dal·mon·ger /skánd'l mùng gər, -mòng-/ *n* a spreader of malicious gossip —**scan·dal·mon·ger·ing** *n*

scan·dal·ous /skánd'ləss/ *adj* **1** causing or deserving public outrage or censure **2** defamatory —**scan·dal·ous·ly** *adv*

Scan·di·na·vi·a /skàndə náyvee ə/ region in N Europe comprising Norway, Sweden, Denmark, Finland, Iceland, and the Faroe Islands —**Scan·di·na·vi·an** *n, adj*

scan·di·um /skándee əm/ *n* (*symbol* Sc) a rare silvery white metallic element. Use: tracer.

~~scandle~~ incorrect spelling of **scandal**

scan·ner /skánnər/ *n* **1** a device for scanning written or recorded data **2** a device for converting an image or text into digital form **3** a device for scanning the internal organs or structure of the body

scan·sion /skánshən/ n 1 the analysis of verse in terms of the rules of poetic meter 2 the meter of a line, poem, or verse

scant adj 1 not enough 2 only or not quite a particular amount o *a scant twenty votes* —**scant·ly** adv

scant·y /skántee/ (-i·er, -i·est) adj 1 hardly covering the body 2 not much and less than is needed 3 only just enough —**scant·i·ly** adv —**scant·i·ness** n

-scape suffix a scene or view o *landscape*

scape·goat /skáyp gòt/ n 1 somebody made to take the blame for others 2 somebody wrongly blamed ■ vt make a scapegoat of

scap·u·la /skáppyələ/ (pl **-lae** /-lee/ or **-las**) n either of two flat triangular bones forming the back of the shoulder

scar n 1 a mark left on the skin after a wound heals 2 a lasting mental effect of a distressing experience ■ vt (**scarred, scar·ring**) mark with scars

scar·ab /skérrab/ n 1 a large black beetle sacred to the ancient Egyptians 2 a representation of a scarab

scarce /skairss/ (**scar·cer, scar·cest**) adj 1 in insufficient supply 2 rarely found —**scarce·ness** n ◊ **make yourself scarce** go or stay away (infml)

scarce·ly /skáirsslee/ adv 1 only just o *scarcely arrived when she was put to work* 2 hardly at all o *scarcely slept all night* 3 almost certainly not o *scarcely a good reason*

scar·ci·ty /skáirssətee/ (pl **-ties**) n 1 an insufficient supply 2 a rarity

scare /skair/ v (**scared, scar·ing**) 1 vt frighten 2 vi be or become frightened ■ n 1 a sudden fright 2 a situation causing general alarm o *another food scare*

scare·crow /skáir krò/ n an object in the shape of a person set up for scaring birds away

scared /skaird/ adj frightened

scarf¹ (pl **scarfs** or **scarves**) n a cloth worn around the neck, head, or shoulders

scarf² n 1 also **scarf joint** a joint made between corresponding notched ends of boards 2 either of the notched ends of a scarf joint —**scarf** vt

scar·i·fy /skárrə fì/ (**-fied, -fies**) vt make scratches on the skin —**scar·i·fi·ca·tion** /skàrrəfi káysh'n/ n

scar·la·ti·na /skaarlə teénə/ n scarlet fever (technical)

Scar·lat·ti /skaar laátee/, **Alessandro** (1659–1725) and his son **Domenico** (1685–1757) Italian composers

scar·let /skáarlət/ n a bright red color —**scar·let** adj

scar·let fe·ver n a contagious disease with fever, sore throat, and a red rash, mainly affecting children

scarp n a steep slope or cliff

scarves plural of **scarf¹**

scar·y /skáiree/ (-i·er, -i·est) adj frightening (infml) —**scar·i·ly** adv —**scar·i·ness** n

scat¹ (**scat·ted, scat·ting**) vi leave quickly (infml; usually a command)

scat² n a jazz vocal style using nonsense syllables —**scat** vi

scath·ing /skáything/ adj highly critical and scornful —**scath·ing·ly** adv

sca·tol·o·gy /ska tólləjee, skə-/ n a preoccupation with excrement or obscene language —**scat·o·log·i·cal** /skàtt'l ójjik'l/ adj —**sca·tol·o·gist** n

scat·ter /skáttər/ v 1 vt throw things around over a wide area 2 vti disperse in different directions

SYNONYMS scatter, broadcast, distribute, disseminate CORE MEANING: spread around

scat·ter-brain /skáttər bràyn/ n a person regarded as incapable of organized thought —**scat·ter-brained** adj

scat·ter cush·ion n a throw pillow

scat·tered /skáttərd/ adj 1 dispersed 2 infrequent or isolated

scat·ter·ing /skáttəring/ n a small amount or number spread irregularly

scat·ter rug n a small rug

scat·ter-shot /skáttər shòt/ adj unsystematic

scav·enge /skávvənj/ (**-enged, -eng·ing**) vti 1 look for something usable among discarded material 2 feed on carrion or scraps —**scav·en·ger** n

~~seedule~~ incorrect spelling of **schedule**

~~sceince~~ incorrect spelling of **science**

~~sceeme~~ incorrect spelling of **scheme**

sce·nar·i·o /sə nárree ò, -nérree-, -náaree-/ (pl **-os**) n 1 a possible situation or sequence of events 2 an outline of the plot of a play or opera

scene /seen/ n 1 a division of an act of a play or opera, presenting continuous action in one place 2 a view or picture 3 a short section of a play, opera, movie, or work of literature, presenting a single event o *the love scene* 4 a place where something happens o *the scene of the crime* 5 the scenery for a dramatic work o *a quick scene change* 6 an embarrassing public display of emotion 7 the setting or environment of a particular activity o *the fashion scene* ◊ **behind the scenes** in private and away from public view

scen·er·y /seénəree/ n 1 the set or backdrop for a piece of theater or movie 2 landscape or natural surroundings, especially when picturesque

sce·nic /seénik, sénnik/ adj 1 picturesque 2 of natural scenery

scent /sent/ n 1 a characteristic pleasant smell 2 a smell left behind by a person or animal and used as a trail 3 cosmetic fragrances or perfume ■ v 1 vti perceive by smelling 2 vt detect as imminent **3** *vt* fill with a pleasant smell ◊ See note at **smell**

scep·ter /séptər/ *n* **1** a staff used as a royal emblem **2** royal authority

scep·tic *n* UK = skeptic

scha·den·freu·de /sháad'n fróydə/, **Scha·den·freu·de** *n* malicious or smug pleasure at somebody else's misfortune

sched·ule /skéjjool, skéjjəl/ *n* **1** a list of meetings, commitments, or appointments **2** a plan of work to be done **3** a list of arrivals and departures ■ *vt* (**-uled, -ul·ing**) **1** plan for a particular time **2** make a list of, or include in a list —**sched·u·ler** *n*

Schel·ling /shélling/, **Friedrich Wilhelm Joseph von** (1775–1854) German philosopher

sche·ma /skeémə/ (*pl* **-ma·ta** /skee máatə, ski máttə/) *n* a diagram or plan showing the basic outline of something

sche·mat·ic /skee máttik, ski-/ *adj* showing the basic form or layout of something —**sche·mat·i·cal·ly** *adv*

sche·ma·tize /skeémə tíz/ (**-tized, -tiz·ing**) *vt* arrange systematically or in schematic form —**sche·ma·ti·za·tion** /skèemətì záysh'n/ *n*

scheme /skeem/ *n* **1** a secret plot or plan **2** a systematic plan of action or arrangement of parts ■ *v* (**schemed, schem·ing**) **1** *vi* make a secret plan **2** *vt* plan systematically —**schem·er** *n*

scher·zo /skáirtsō/ (*pl* **-zos** *or* **-zi** /-tsee/) *n* a fast and lighthearted musical movement or piece

Schie·le /sheélə/, **Egon** (1890–1918) Austrian painter

Schil·ler /shíllər/, **Friedrich von** (1759–1805) German poet, dramatist, historian, and philosopher

schil·ling /shílling/ *n* the main unit of the former Austrian currency

schism /skízzəm, sízzəm/ *n* a division into factions, especially within a religion or religious denomination

schis·mat·ic /skiz máttik, siz-/ *adj* of a schism ■ *n* a participant in or promoter of a schism

schist /shist/ *n* a rock that splits into layers

schiz·oid /skíts òyd/ *adj* **1** tending toward schizophrenia **2** an offensive term describing a personality that suggests violent inner conflicts

schiz·o·phre·ni·a /skìtsə freénee ə/ *n* a severe psychiatric disorder with symptoms of withdrawal into the self —**schiz·o·phren·ic** /-frénnik/ *adj, n*

schle·miel /shlə meél/ *n* an offensive term for somebody regarded as bungling, inept, or unlucky (*slang insult*)

schlep /shlep/ (**schlepped, schlep·ping**) *vt* carry clumsily or with difficulty (*infml*)

Schlie·mann /shleé màan/, **Heinrich** (1822–90) German archaeologist

schlock /shlok/ *n* something of inferior quality (*slang*) —**schlock** *adj*

schmaltz /shmaalts, shmawlts/, **schmalz** *n* **1** cloying or exaggerated sentimentality (*infml*) **2** cooking fat —**schmaltz·y** *adj*

schmooze /shmooz/ (**schmoozed, schmooz·ing**) *vt* be ingratiating toward

schmuck /shmuk/, **shmuck** *n* an offensive term for somebody regarded as worthless (*slang insult*)

schnapps /shnaps/ *n* flavored liquor

~~schnaps~~ incorrect spelling of **schnapps**

schnit·zel /shníts'l/ *n* a fried thin slice of meat

Schoen·berg /shúrn bùrg, shön bairk/, **Arnold** (1874–1951) Austrian composer

schol·ar /skóllər/ *n* **1** a learned person **2** a student with a scholarship —**schol·ar·li·ness** *n* —**schol·ar·ly** *adj*

schol·ar·ship /skóllər shìp/ *n* **1** a sum of money granted to a student for expenses **2** academic learning

scho·las·tic /skə lástik, sko-/ *adj* **1** of schools, scholarship, or studying **2** of scholasticism

scho·las·ti·cism /skə lásti sìzzəm, sko-/ *n* medieval theology and philosophy based on the writings of Aristotle

school[1] /skool/ *n* **1** a building or institution where children are taught **2** a college or university **3** a university department specializing in a particular subject ○ *business school* **4** an institution teaching a nonacademic skill ○ *a riding school* **5** the staff and students of a school **6** a group of artists or writers sharing the same approach ■ *vt* **1** instruct in a particular skill **2** educate in school **3** discipline

---

ORIGIN The **school** for children and the **school** for fish are unrelated. The first was adopted into the ancient Germanic languages from Latin; the second came around 1400 from a Dutch word meaning "troop, multitude," and is related to *shoal*.

---

school[2] /skool/ *n* a large group of fish or ocean mammals swimming together ■ *vi* form or swim in a school

school age *n* the age at which children are legally required to attend school —**school-age** *adj*

school board *n* a local body overseeing schools

school·boy /skoól bòy/ *n* a boy attending school ■ *adj* appropriate to schoolboys

school·child /skoól chìld/ (*pl* **-chil·dren** /-chìldrən/) *n* a child attending school

school day *n* **1** a day on which school is conducted **2** the part of the day spent at school

school dis·trict *n* an administrative area of public schools

school·girl /skoól gùrl/ *n* a girl attending school

school·house /skool howss/ (pl **-houses** /-howzəz/) n **1** a building used as a school **2** a teacher's house attached to a school

school·ing /skooling/ n **1** education at school **2** systematic instruction or training

school·marm /skool maarm/ n an offensive term for a woman schoolteacher, especially one regarded as prim or old-fashioned (dated insult)

school·mas·ter /skool màstər/ n a man schoolteacher (dated)

school·mate /skool màyt/ n a friend or another pupil attending the same school

school of thought n a shared way of thinking about something

school·room /skool room, -room/ n a school classroom

school·teach·er /skool teechər/ n a teacher in a school below college level —**school·teach·ing** n

school·work /skool wùrk/ n work done by a student in or after school

school·yard /skool yaàrd/ n a play area for schoolchildren

school year n **1** the months when schools are open **2** a 12-month period during which pupils are assigned to the same class

schoo·ner /skoonər/ n **1** a sailing vessel with two or more masts **2** US, Can, Aus a beer glass

Scho·pen·hau·er /shópən hòwər/, **Arthur** (1788–1860) German philosopher

Schrö·der /shrúrdər/, **Gerhard** (b. 1944) chancellor of Germany (1998–)

Schrö·ding·er /shródingər, shró-/, **Erwin** (1887–1961) Austrian physicist. He made a major contribution to quantum theory.

Schu·bert /shoobərt/, **Franz** (1797–1828) Austrian composer

Schulz /shoolts/, **Charles** (1922–2000) US cartoonist

Schu·mann /shoo maàn, shoomən/, **Robert** (1810–56) German composer

schwa /shwaa, shvaa/ n an unstressed vowel sound, e.g., the "a" in "above," or the symbol "ə" used to represent it

Barnaby's

Albert Schweitzer

Schweit·zer /shwítsər/, **Albert** (1875–1965) German-born theologian, musicologist, and missionary

sci·at·i·ca /sī áttikə/ n pain in the hip and leg caused by pressure on a nerve

sci·ence /sī ənss/ n **1** the study of the physical world by systematic observation and experiment **2** a branch of science ○ the life sciences **3** knowledge gained from science **4** a systematic body of knowledge

sci·ence fic·tion n fiction based on futuristic science and technology

sci·ence park n a place for commercial scientific research

sci·en·tif·ic /sī ən tíffik/ adj **1** of science **2** systematic or methodical —**sci·en·tif·i·cal·ly** adv

sci·en·tist /sī əntist/ n an expert in or student of science

sci-fi /sī fī/ n science fiction (infml)

scim·i·tar /símmətər, -taàr/ n a sword with a curved blade that broadens toward the point

scin·til·la /sin tíllə/ n a small amount

scin·til·late /sínt'l àyt/ (-lat·ed, -lat·ing) vi **1** sparkle **2** be dazzlingly lively or clever —**scin·til·lat·ing** adj —**scin·til·la·tion** /sínt'l áysh'n/ n

sci·on /sī ən/ n **1** a living shoot or twig of a plant used for grafting **2** a descendant

Scip·i·o /síppee ō, skíppee ō/, **Publius Cornelius** (d. 211 BC) Roman general

Scip·i·o Af·ri·ca·nus (the El·der) /síppee ō afri kaànəss/ (234?–183 BC) Roman general

scis·sors /sízzərz/ (pl same) n **1** a cutting instrument consisting of two crossed blades with ring-shaped handles (+ sing or pl verb) **2** a movement of the legs resembling the opening and closing of scissors ○ a scissors kick —**scis·sor** vti

scle·ro·sis /sklə róssəss/ (pl -ses /-seez/) n the hardening and thickening of body tissue —**scle·rot·ic** /sklə róttik/ adj

scoff vi express derision or scorn —**scoff** n —**scoff·er** n

scoff·law /skóf làw, skáwf-/ n a person who violates the law (infml)

scold /skōld/ vti criticize somebody sharply ■ n somebody who scolds —**scold·ing** adj, n

sconce /skonss/ n a wall bracket for candles or light bulbs

scone /skōn/ n a small sweetened or unsweetened bread

ORIGIN **Scone** is probably a shortening of early Dutch schoonbroot "fine bread." For the first three hundred years of its life, from the early 16C, the word was largely confined to Scotland.

scoop n **1** a utensil shaped like a small deep shovel **2** a utensil with a bowl-shaped head used to serve soft food in round portions **3** the digging part of a machine **4** an exclusive news story (infml) ■ vt **1** make a hollow with a scoop or similar object ○ scooped a hole in the ground **2** remove something with a scoop or cupped hand ○ scooped up a handful of sand **3** lift some-

body or something swiftly **4** publish or broadcast a news item before rivals

scoot *vi (infml)* **1** go away quickly *(often a command)* **2** move quickly —**scoot** *n*

scoot·er /skóotər/ *n* **1** a wheeled toy with a footboard and handlebars **2** a light motorcycle

scope *n* **1** freedom or space to act **2** the range covered by an activity or topic

-scope *suffix* an instrument for viewing or observing ○ *telescope* —**-scopic** *suffix* —**-scopy** *suffix*

Scopes, John T. (1900–70) US teacher and subject of a controversial court case (1925) about the teaching of evolution

scorch *vti* **1** burn on the surface **2** dry out with intense heat ■ *n* a surface burn

scorched-earth pol·i·cy *n* **1** the policy of destroying everything of use to an advancing enemy **2** a company strategy of avoiding a hostile takeover by appearing financially unattractive

score *n* **1** in a game or match, the number of points made by a team or a player **2** a record of points made ○ *Who's keeping score?* **3** an exam result **4** *(pl same or scores)* a group of 20 *(often in combination)* **5** a written or printed copy of a musical composition **6** a superficial cut **7** a grudge ○ *settling old scores* ■ **scores** *npl* a great many ■ *v* (**scored, scor·ing**) **1** *vti* make a point or points **2** *vti* record or award the points in a game or competition **3** *vt* grade an exam **4** *vti* get a number of points in an exam **5** *vt* cut notches or lines in the surface of something **6** *vt* orchestrate or arrange a piece of music —**score·less** *adj* —**scor·er** *n* ◊ **on this** or **that score** as far as this or that is concerned

---

ORIGIN Score can be traced to an ancient root meaning "cut," from which *shear* and *short* also derive. It was adopted from an old Scandinavian word meaning both "notch" and "20." Senses connected with counting derive from making notches on a surface to keep a tally or count. The **score** of a game is an 18C development of meaning. The musical **score** may refer to the bar line linking together related staffs.

---

score·board /skáwr bàwrd/ *n* a board at a sports place where the score is displayed

score·card /skáwr kàard/ *n* **1** a card for recording a player's score **2** a card listing players in a game

scorn *n* contempt and lack of respect ■ *vt* **1** disdain or hold in contempt **2** reject contemptuously ○ *scorned our offer of help* —**scorn·ful** *adj* —**scorn·ful·ly** *adv*

Scor·pi·o /skáwrpee ò/ *n* **1** *also* **Scor·pi·us** a zodiacal constellation in the southern hemisphere **2** the 8th sign of the zodiac —**Scor·pi·o** *adj*

scor·pi·on /skáwrpee ən/ *n* an arachnid with a poisonous stinger at the tip of its upturned tail

Scor·se·se /skawr sáysee, -sézzee/, **Martin** (*b.* 1942) US movie director

Scot *n* **1** somebody from Scotland **2** a member of an ancient people of Ireland and N Britain

scotch *vt* put a stop to ○ *scotch a rumor*

Scotch *n* **1** whiskey produced in Scotland **2 Scots** ■ *adj* of or from Scotland

scot-free *adv* without punishment or penalty

ORIGIN The Scots do not lend their name to **scot-free**. It comes from a completely unrelated word meaning "payment, tax."

Scot·land /skóttlənd/ country forming the northernmost part of Great Britain and of the United Kingdom. Cap. Edinburgh. Pop. 5,120,000 (1998).

Scots *adj* of Scotland ■ *n* a form of English spoken in parts of Scotland —**Scots·man** *n* —**Scots·wom·an** *n*

Scott, Dred (1795–1858) US enslaved laborer who sued for his freedom in 1846. The case was among the causes of the American Civil War.

Scott, Robert Falcon (1868–1912) British naval officer and explorer

Scott, Sir Walter (1771–1832) Scottish novelist and poet

Scott, Winfield (1786–1866) US general

Scot·tish /skóttish/ *adj* of Scotland ■ *npl* the people of Scotland ■ *n* Scots —**Scot·tish·ness** *n*

Scotts·dale /skóts dàyl/ city in south central Arizona. Pop. 195,394 (1998).

scoun·drel /skówndrəl/ *n* a dishonorable or unprincipled person

scour[1] /skowr/ *vt* clean or remove by rubbing with something abrasive —**scour** *n* —**scour·er** *n*

scour[2] /skowr/ *vti* **1** search something carefully **2** move quickly over or through an area

scourge /skurj/ *n* **1** somebody or something that torments or punishes **2** a whip —**scourge** *vt*

scout /skowt/ *n* **1** a soldier sent to gather information **2** somebody sent to find talented new people **3 Scout** a member of the Boy Scouts or the Girl Scouts ■ *v* **1** *vi* search an area **2** *vi* gather information **3** *vti* seek out talented new people

---

ORIGIN A **scout** may be thought of as looking out for things, but etymologically a **scout** listens. The word is shortened from early French *escouter* "listen" (*écouter* in modern French).

Scout·ing /skówting/ *n* Boy or Girl Scout activities

scout·mas·ter /skówt màstər/ *n* the adult leader of a troop of Scouts

scowl /skowl/ *n* a frown of anger or displeasure —**scowl** *vi*

scrab·ble /skrább'l/ (-bled, -bling) *vi* 1 scratch or grope with hurried movements of the fingers or claws 2 climb hastily or clumsily 3 struggle to get something —**scrab·ble** *n*

scrag·gly /skrágglee/ (-gli·er, -gli·est) *adj* messy and uneven in appearance

scrag·gy /skrággee/ (-gi·er, -gi·est) *adj* 1 scrawny 2 jagged ◊ See note at **thin**

scram (scrammed, scram·ming) *vi* leave quickly (*infml; often a command*)

scram·ble /skrámb'l/ (-bled, -bling) *v* 1 *vi* climb hastily using the hands and feet 2 *vi* hurry urgently 3 *vi* compete frantically 4 *vt* mix things together 5 *vt* beat and cook eggs 6 *vt* make a transmitted signal unintelligible 7 *vti* take off quickly or cause aircraft to take off quickly in an military emergency —**scram·ble** *n*

scram·bled eggs *n* cooked beaten eggs (+ *sing or pl verb*)

scrap¹ *n* 1 a small piece 2 waste material to be reprocessed or reused ■ **scraps** *npl* leftovers ■ *vt* (scrapped, scrap·ping) 1 get rid of 2 convert to scrap

scrap² *n* a minor fight (*infml*) ■ *vi* (scrapped, scrap·ping) fight or disagree

scrap·book /skráp bòok/ *n* an album used to collect pictures, clippings, and other material

scrape *v*(scraped, scrap·ing) 1 *vti* move something hard, sharp, or rough across the surface of something 2 *vt* remove by scraping 3 *vt* damage or injure by scraping 4 *vti* make or cause to make a grating noise ■ *n* 1 an act of scraping 2 a light scratch 3 a grating sound 4 a dangerous or awkward situation (*infml*) —**scrap·er** *n*
□ **scrape together** *or* **up** *vt* gather with difficulty

scrap·heap /skráp hèep/ *n* a place for discarded things or people (*infml*)

scra·pie /skráypee/ *n* a disease of the nervous system in sheep and goats

scrap·py¹ /skráppee/ (-pi·er, -pi·est) *adj* 1 consisting of fragments 2 disjointed or disconnected —**scrap·pi·ness** *n*

scrap·py² /skráppee/ (-pi·er, -pi·est) *adj* (*infml*) 1 plucky, determined, and willing to fight or argue 2 belligerent or quarrelsome

scratch *vti* 1 mark the surface of something with something sharp or rough 2 tear the skin of a person or animal 3 make or cause to make a scraping movement or noise 4 rub the nails or claws over an itchy part of the body 5 withdraw from a competition ■ *n* 1 a mark or wound caused by scratching 2 an act or sound of scratching ■ *adj* 1 done randomly 2 assembled hastily —**scratch·er** *n* ◊ **from scratch** right from

the beginning, or with nothing having been done previously (*infml*)

scratch card *n* a card with one or more sections that can be scratched to reveal a possible prize

⚡ **scratch file** *n* a temporary computer file

⚡ **scratch·pad** /skrách pàd/ *n* 1 a pad of paper for making rough notes 2 a temporary storage area in a computer memory

scratch·y /skráchee/ (-i·er, -i·est) *adj* 1 causing itchiness 2 making a scratching sound —**scratch·i·ly** *adv* —**scratch·i·ness** *n*

scrawl *vti* write or draw something untidily or hastily —**scrawl** *n* —**scrawl·y** *adj*

scraw·ny /skráwnee/ (-ni·er, -ni·est) *adj* very thin and bony —**scraw·ni·ness** *n* ◊ See note at **thin**

scream /skreem/ *n* 1 a piercing cry 2 a high-pitched noise 3 somebody or something highly amusing (*infml*) ■ *v* 1 *vi* utter a scream 2 *vt* shout in a piercing voice 3 *vi* make a high-pitched noise —**scream·ing·ly** *adv*

scree *n* 1 rock debris at the base of a hill 2 a scree-covered slope

screech *n* 1 a shrill scream 2 a loud high-pitched grating sound ◊ *the screech of brakes* —**screech** *vi* —**screech·y** *adj*

screed *n* a lengthy piece of writing

⚡ **screen** *n* 1 a flat vertical structure used for concealment, partitioning, protection, or decoration 2 something that conceals or shelters ◊ *protected by a screen of leaves* 3 a surface on which images such as movies or data are displayed or projected 4 the movie industry 5 a sieve ■ *v* 1 *vt* conceal, protect, or partition with a screen 2 *vt* protect from something unpleasant or dangerous 3 *vt* show in a movie theater or on television ◊ *The program will be screened next month.* 4 *vti* test or examine people for a disease or for suitability 5 *vt* sift —**screen·ful** *n* —**screen·ing** *n*

⚡ **screen dump** *n* the printing or saving of data on a computer screen

⚡ **screen font** *n* a font used on a computer screen

screen·play /skréen plày/ *n* a movie script

⚡ **screen sav·er** *n* a utility that provides a moving display for a computer screen during periods of inactivity

screen test *n* a filmed audition for a part in a movie —**screen-test** *vti*

screen·writ·er /skréen rìtər/ *n* a writer of screenplays —**screen·writ·ing** *n*

screw *n* 1 a tapering threaded piece of metal used to fasten parts together 2 a propeller ■ *v* 1 *vti* fasten with screws 2 *vti* rotate along a thread to attach or tighten ◊ *screw the bulb into the socket* 3 *vt* crumple into a tight ball ◊ *screwed up the letter and threw it away* 4 *vti* contort or be contorted ◊ *screwed* *up her eyes against the glare* —**screw·a·ble** *adj*

☐ **screw up** *vti* an offensive term meaning make a mess of something *(slang)*

screw·ball /skroʻo bàwl/ *n* 1 a pitch that curves in a direction opposite to that of a curve ball 2 an offensive term for somebody regarded as unconventional or eccentric *(slang insult)*

screw·driv·er /skroʻo drìvər/ *n* 1 a tool for turning screws 2 a vodka and orange juice cocktail

screw·y /skroʻo ee/ (**-i·er, -i·est**) *adj* an offensive term meaning regarded as odd or irrational *(slang)*

scrib·ble /skríbb'l/ (**-bled, -bling**) *vti* 1 write hastily or untidily 2 make meaningless markings —**scrib·ble** *n* —**scrib·bly** *adj*

scribe *n* 1 somebody who copies documents or manuscripts 2 a clerk —**scrib·al** *adj*

scrim·mage /skrímmij/ *n* 1 a practice game 2 in football, the action from the time the ball is snapped to the end of the play 3 a confused struggle —**scrim·mage** *vti*

scrimp *vi* economize drastically or excessively

scrip[1] *n* temporary paper currency

scrip[2] *n* a small satchel or wallet

⚡ **script** *n* 1 the text of a play, movie, or broadcast 2 handwriting 3 a system of writing 4 a sequence of automated computer commands that tells a program to execute a specific procedure ■ *vt* write the script for

scrip·ture /skrípchər/, **Scrip·ture** *n* 1 biblical or other sacred writings 2 a biblical or other sacred text —**scrip·tur·al** *adj*

script·writ·er /skrípt rìtər/ *n* a writer of movie, radio, or television scripts —**script·writ·ing** *n*

scrof·u·la /skróffyələ/ *n* tuberculosis of the lymph glands of the neck

⚡ **scroll** /skrōl/ *n* 1 a roll of parchment or paper for writing a document 2 an ornamental design resembling a scroll ■ *vti* move text or graphics up, down, or across a computer screen

⚡ **scroll bar** *n* a bar on a computer screen for moving through a display

scrooge /skrooj/, **Scrooge** *n* a miser *(infml)*

ORIGIN The original **scrooge** was Ebenezer Scrooge, a character in *A Christmas Carol* (1843) by Charles Dickens.

scro·tum /skrōtəm/ (*pl* **-tums** *or* **-ta** /-tə/) *n* the pouch containing the testicles —**scro·tal** *adj*

scrounge /skrownj/ *vti* beg or borrow *(infml)* —**scroung·er** *n*

scrub[1] (**scrubbed, scrub·bing**) *v* 1 *vti* clean something by rubbing hard, e.g., with a brush 2 *vt* remove dirt by scrubbing 3 *vt* cancel *(infml)* —**scrub** *n*

scrub[2] *n* 1 a stunted tree or bush 2 low straggly vegetation, or an area covered with this —**scrub·by** *adj*

scruff *n* the back of the neck

scruff·y /skrúffee/ (**-i·er, -i·est**) *adj* messy or shabby —**scruff·i·ly** *adv* —**scruff·i·ness** *n*

scrum *n* *also* **scrum·mage** /skrúmmij/ in rugby, a play to get the ball by forwards with linked arms and heads down ■ *vi* (**scrummed, scrum·ming**) form a rugby scrum

scrump·tious /skrúmpshəss/ *adj* delightful or delicious *(infml)* —**scrump·tious·ness** *n*

scrunch *v* 1 *vt* crumple, crush, or squeeze 2 *vi* hunch or crouch down

scrunch·ie /skrúnchee/ *n* a fabric-covered elasticized band for fastening hair

scru·ple /skroʻop'l/ *n* 1 a moral or ethical consideration 2 a unit of weight equal to about 1.3 g ■ *vi* (**-pled, -pling**) hesitate because of scruples ○ *wouldn't scruple to cheat*

scru·pu·lous /skroʻopyələss/ *adj* 1 having or showing moral integrity 2 very precise —**scru·pu·los·i·ty** /skroʻopyə lóssətee/ *n* —**scru·pu·lous·ly** *adv* —**scru·pu·lous·ness** *n* ⟡ See note at **careful**

scru·ti·nize /skroʻot'n īz/ (**-nized, -niz·ing**) *vt* examine closely and carefully

scru·ti·ny /skroʻot'nee/ *n* 1 careful inspection 2 observation

⚡ **SCSI** /skúzee/ *n* a high-speed computer interface specification. Full form **small computer systems interface**

scu·ba /skoʻobə/ *n* an underwater breathing apparatus consisting of a portable canister of compressed air and a mouthpiece

scud *vi* (**scud·ded, scud·ding**) move swiftly and smoothly ○ *clouds scudding across the sky* ■ *n* 1 a swift smooth movement 2 clouds driven by the wind

Scud mis·sile *n* a surface-to-surface missile

scuff *vti* 1 lightly scrape the surface of something, or become scraped superficially 2 scrape the feet while walking ■ *n* 1 a mark made by scuffing 2 a flat backless shoe

scuf·fle /skúff'l/ *n* a disorderly fight at close quarters ■ *vi* (**-fled, -fling**) 1 engage in a scuffle 2 shuffle quickly

scull *n* 1 a single oar at the back of a boat 2 a light racing boat —**scull** *vti* —**scull·er** *n*

scul·ler·y /skúlləree/ (*pl* **-ies**) *n* a room for kitchen chores

scul·lion /skúllyən/ *n* a kitchen servant *(archaic)*

sculpt *vti* 1 make a sculpture 2 carve or model material

~~sculpter~~ incorrect spelling of **sculptor**

sculp·tor /skúlptər/ *n* an artist who makes sculptures

~~sculpture~~ incorrect spelling of **sculpture**

sculp·ture /skúlpchər/ *n* 1 the creation of three-dimensional art 2 a three-dimensional work of art ■ *vti* (**-tured, -tur·ing**) **1** make a sculpture **2** carve or model material —**sculp·tur·al** *adj*

scum *n* **1** a filmy layer on the surface of liquid **2** an offensive term for a person or group of people regarded as disreputable or worthless *(slang insult)* —**scum·my** *adj*

scup·per[1] /skúppər/ *n* an opening for draining water, e.g., from a ship's deck

scup·per[2] *vt* wreck or ruin a plan or chance

scur·ri·lous /skúrrələss/ *adj* abusive or defamatory —**scur·ril·i·ty** /skə rílləteé/ *n* —**scur·ri·lous·ly** *adv*

scur·ry /skúr ee, skúrree/ (**-ried, -ries**) *vi* **1** move briskly with small steps **2** move around agitatedly or with a swirling motion —**scur·ry** *n*

scur·vy /skúrvee/ *n* a disease caused by a deficiency of vitamin C ■ *adj* (**-vi·er, -vi·est**) despicable —**scur·vi·ness** *n*

scut·tle[1] /skútt'l/ *n* a small covered hatch in a ship's deck or hull ■ *vt* (**-tled, -tling**) **1** sink a ship by letting water into the hull **2** destroy or end something

scut·tle[2] /skútt'l/ *n* a coal container used indoors

scut·tle[3] /skútt'l/ (**-tled, -tling**) *vi* move with short fast steps —**scut·tle** *n*

scut·tle·butt /skútt'l bùt/ *n* gossip or rumors *(slang)*

Scyl·la /sílla/ *n* a mythological sea monster

scythe /sīth/ *n* a tool with a curved blade for mowing or reaping —**scythe** *vti*

SD *abbr* **1** *also* **S.D., S. Dak.** South Dakota **2** standard deviation

SDI, S.D.I. *abbr* Strategic Defense Initiative

Se *symbol* selenium

SE *abbr* **1** southeast **2** southeastern

sea /see/ *n* **1** the salt waters of the Earth **2** a body of salt water **3** a large lake **4** the state of the sea's surface ◇ *big seas* **5** a large number or quantity ◇ *a sea of faces* ◇ **at sea** bewildered and confused

---

SPELLCHECK Do not confuse the spelling of **sea** and **see** ("look at"), which sound similar.

---

sea a·nem·o·ne *n* a small sea animal with tentacles that is usually attached to a rock

sea·bed /seé bèd/ *n* the floor of the ocean

sea·bird /seé bùrd/ *n* a bird that lives near the ocean

sea·board /seé bàwrd/ *n* land near the sea

sea·bor·gi·um /see báwrgee əm/ *n* (*symbol* **Sg**) an unstable radioactive chemical element

sea breeze *n* a breeze blowing from the sea

sea change *n* a great change

sea·far·ing /seé fàiring/ *adj* **1** regularly going to sea **2** of sea travel or transportation ■ *n* a sailor's way of life —**sea·far·er** *n*

sea·food /seé foòd/ *n* edible fish and shellfish

sea·front /seé frùnt/ *n* a seaside waterfront

sea·go·ing /seé gò ing/ *adj* **1** for sailing on the open ocean **2** regularly going to sea

sea·gull /seé gùl/ *n* a common white-and-gray sea bird

sea horse *n* a bony fish that has a head like a horse's and swims upright

seal[1] /seel/ *n* **1** a tight or perfect closure **2** a closure that must be broken to open something **3** an authenticating stamp, or a piece of wax marked with one **4** an ornamental adhesive stamp ■ *vt* **1** close tightly or securely **2** make watertight or airtight **3** authenticate with a seal **4** confirm or settle ◇ *seal a contract* —**seal·a·ble** *adj* —**seal·er** *n*

seal[2] /seel/ *n* **1** a fish-eating sea mammal with flippers **2** sealskin ■ *vi* hunt seals —**seal·er** *n*

SEAL /seel/ *abbr* sea, air, land (team)

sea·lane *n* an established route for large ships at sea

seal·ant /seélənt/ *n* a substance used to make something watertight or airtight

sea lev·el *n* the level of the surface of the sea relative to the land

sea li·on *n* a large seal with external ears

seal·skin /seél skìn/ *n* **1** a seal's pelt **2** leather made from a seal's skin

seam /seem/ *n* **1** a line or ridge where pieces are joined, especially by sewing **2** a linear indentation, such as a wrinkle ■ *vt* **1** join pieces along their edges **2** mark with lines

---

SPELLCHECK Do not confuse the spelling of **seam** and **seem** ("appear to be"), which sound similar.

---

sea·man /seémən/ (*pl* **-men** /-mən/) *n* a sailor —**sea·man·ship** *n*

seam·less /seémləss/ *adj* **1** without seams **2** smoothly continuous —**seam·less·ly** *adv*

seam·stress /seémstrəss/ *n* a woman who sews

seam·y /seémee/ (**-i·er, -i·est**) *adj* having unpleasant qualities associated with a degraded way of living —**seam·i·ness** *n*

se·ance /sáy àanss, -àaNss/ *n* a meeting at which a spiritualist attempts to communicate with the dead

sea·plane /seé plàyn/ *n* an aircraft that can land on water

sea·port /seé pàwrt/ *n* a town or city's harbor where seagoing ships can berth

sea pow·er *n* **1** a nation with naval strength **2** naval strength

sear /seer/ *v* **1** *vt* burn or scorch **2** *vti* wither or dry up —**sear** *n*

search /surch/ *v* **1** *vti* examine something thoroughly in order to find somebody or something **2** *vt* examine the clothing or body of somebody for concealed items **3** *vt* discover something by investigation ◇ *searched out the relevant file* —**search** *n* —**search·a·ble** *adj*

⚡ **search en·gine** *n* a computer program that

searches for specific words, especially on the Internet

search·ing /súrching/ *adj* penetrating or probing —**search·ing·ly** *adv*

search·light /súrch lìt/ *n* **1** an apparatus for projecting a powerful beam of light **2** the light from a searchlight

search par·ty *n* a group that is looking for a missing person

search war·rant *n* a court order authorizing a search of somebody's property

sea salt *n* coarse salt produced from seawater

sea·scape /seé skàyp/ *n* an ocean view, or a picture of the ocean

sea ser·pent *n* **1** a legendary giant snake reportedly seen in the ocean **2** *also* **sea snake** a venomous snake that swims

sea·shell /seé shèl/ *n* the empty shell of a sea mollusk

sea·shore /seé shàwr/ *n* land lying next to the ocean, especially a beach

sea·sick /seé sìk/ *adj* nauseated from the rocking of a ship or boat —**sea·sick·ness** *n*

sea·side /seé sìd/ *n* land bordering the ocean —**sea·side** *adj*

sea·son /seéz'n/ *n* **1** a traditional division of the year based on weather conditions **2** a period of the year marked by something such as a particular activity or the availability of a particular food ○ *mating season* ○ *the asparagus season* **3** a period of time of unspecified length ■ *v* **1** *vti* add salt, pepper, herbs, or spices to food **2** *vt* enliven by adding something ○ *a speech seasoned with wit* **3** *vti* dry out before use *(refers to timber)* **4** *vt* cause to gain experience or toughness ○ *seasoned troops* —**sea·son·ing** *n* ◇ **in season 1** plentifully available and at a peak of quality **2** allowed to be hunted, caught, or killed

ORIGIN Season goes back to a Latin verb meaning "sow, plant," and so is etymologically the "time for sowing seeds." In French, the immediate source of **season**, it developed the sense "suitable time for doing something," and from there it began to refer to divisions of the year characterized by distinctive conditions that made the **season** suitable for particular activities.

sea·son·a·ble /seéz'nəb'l/ *adj* **1** typical of the season **2** opportune —**sea·son·a·bly** *adv*

sea·son·al /seézən'l, seéznəl/ *adj* **1** dependent on season **2** limited to particular times —**sea·son·al·ly** *adv*

sea·son·al af·fec·tive dis·or·der *n* depression related to winter

sea·son tick·et *n* a ticket valid for multiple use during a specific period of time

seat /seet/ *n* **1** a place to sit **2** something to sit on **3** the part of a garment covering the buttocks **4** a position as member of an official group ○ *a seat on the council* **5** a place

where something is located *(fml)* ○ *the seat of emotions* **6** a center of power ■ *vt* **1** place in a seat **2** provide seats for ◇ **by the seat of your pants** using intuition and guesswork

seat belt *n* a strap designed to keep somebody in a vehicle or aircraft seat

seat·ing /seéting/ *n* **1** seats provided **2** the arrangement of seats or sitters

seat·mate /seét màyt/ *n* somebody in an adjacent seat

Se·at·tle /see átt'l/ city in west central Washington. Pop. 536,978 (1998).

sea ur·chin *n* a sea animal with a spiny spherical shell

sea wall *n* a wall built to hold back the ocean waves

sea·ward /seéwərd/, **sea·wards** /-wərdz/ *adv* toward the sea ■ *adj* situated or directed toward the sea

sea·wa·ter /seé wàwtər/ *n* salt water from the sea

sea·way /seé wày/ *n* **1** an inland waterway for seagoing ships **2** a route across the sea

sea·weed /seé weèd/ *n* plants that grow in the sea

sea·wor·thy /seé wùrthee/ *adj* fit to sail safely on the sea —**sea·wor·thi·ness** *n*

se·ba·ceous /sə báyshəss/ *adj* of or producing a waxy substance that lubricates the hair and skin

Se·bas·to·pol /sə bástə pòl/, **Se·vas·to·pol** /-vástə-/ city in S Ukraine. Pop. 356,000 (1998).

sec[1] *adj* describes wine that is dry in taste

sec[2] *abbr* secant

se·cant /seékənt/ *n* **1** a straight line that intersects with a curve in two or more places **2** the ratio of the hypotenuse to the side adjacent to a given angle in a right triangle

se·cede /si seéd/ (**-ced·ed, -ced·ing**) *vi* withdraw formally from an alliance

~~seceed~~ incorrect spelling of **secede**

se·ces·sion /si sésh'n/ *n* **1** formal withdrawal from an alliance **2** **Se·ces·sion** the withdrawal of 11 States from the Union in 1860–61 —**se·ces·sion·ist** *n, adj*

se·clude /sə kloód/ (**-clud·ed, -clud·ing**) *vt* **1** isolate somebody **2** make a place private —**se·clud·ed** *adj* —**se·clud·ed·ness** *n* —**se·clu·sion** *n*

sec·ond[1] /sékənd/ *adj* **1** coming immediately after the first **2** another **3** additional and less important ■ *n* **1** the one after the first in a series **2** another person or thing **3** a boxer's or duelist's assistant **4** an imperfect article sold cheap **5** in a car, the forward gear between first and third ■ *vt* state support for a motion or nomination proposed by another ■ *adv* **1** except for one ○ *the second-highest mountain in the world* **2** secondly

sec·ond[2] /sékənd/ *n* **1** *(symbol* **s***)* a unit of time equal to $\frac{1}{60}$th of a minute **2** *(symbol* **"***)* a unit of measurement of angles equal to $\frac{1}{360}$th of a degree **3** a very short time

sec·ond·ar·y /sékən dèrree/ *adj* **1** less important than something else **2** happening as result of something else ○ *secondary tumors* **3** for students aged between 11 and 18 ○ *a secondary school* —**sec·ond·ar·i·ly** /sèkən dérrəlee/ *adv* —**sec·ond·ar·y** *n*

sec·ond base *n* in baseball, the base directly opposite home plate, or the player positioned close to it

sec·ond best *adj* **1** surpassed only by the best ○ *my second-best suit* **2** inferior to the best —**sec·ond best** *n*

sec·ond class *n* **1** the category immediately below the best **2** a mail delivery service for newspapers and periodicals ■ *adj* **1** of the second class ○ *second-class mail* **2** inferior ○ *treated as second-class citizens* —**sec·ond-class** *adv*

Sec·ond Com·ing *n* the prophesied return of Jesus Christ at the end of the world

sec·ond cous·in *n* a child of a parent's first cousin

sec·ond gen·er·a·tion *n* **1** the children of immigrants **2** a later stage in the development of something —**sec·ond-gen·er·a·tion** *adj*

sec·ond-guess *vti* **1** criticize after the event **2** predict what will happen or what somebody will do

sec·ond hand *n* a hand on a clock or watch that shows the time in seconds

sec·ond·hand /sèkənd hánd/ *adj* **1** previously owned by somebody else **2** selling secondhand goods **3** not original ■ *adv* **1** in secondhand condition ○ *bought it secondhand* **2** through an intermediary ○ *acquires the information secondhand*

sec·ond-in-com·mand *n* a deputy

sec·ond lieu·ten·ant *n* an officer of the lowest commissioned rank

sec·ond·ly /sékəndlee/ *adv* as the second point in an argument or discussion

sec·ond mort·gage *n* an additional mortgage on a mortgaged property

sec·ond na·ture *n* an ingrained habit

sec·ond o·pin·ion *n* an opinion or assessment by another expert

sec·ond per·son *n* the form of a verb or pronoun used when addressing somebody

sec·ond sight *n* clairvoyance —**sec·ond-sight·ed** *adj*

sec·ond thought *n* a reconsideration (*often pl*) ○ *having second thoughts about going*

sec·ond wind *n* renewed energy

Sec·ond World War *n* = **World War II**

~~secretary~~ incorrect spelling of **secretary**

se·cre·cy /séekrəssee/ *n* **1** the state of being secret ○ *talks held in secrecy* **2** the keeping of a secret or secrets ○ *sworn to secrecy*

se·cret /séekrət/ *adj* **1** withheld from general knowledge **2** undercover **3** not confessed

or admitted ○ *a secret admirer* **4** private and secluded ■ *n* **1** a piece of secret information **2** a mystery —**se·cret·ly** *adv*

SYNONYMS secret, clandestine, covert, furtive, stealthy, surreptitious CORE MEANING: conveying a desire or need for concealment

---

se·cret a·gent *n* a spy

sec·re·tar·i·at /sèkrə térree ət/ *n* **1** an administrative department **2** the secretarial staff of a secretary-general

sec·re·tar·y /sékrə tèrree/ (*pl* **-ies**) *n* **1** somebody who does clerical or administrative work for a person or organization **2** *also* **Sec·re·tar·y** a cabinet member or head of a major government department **3** a cabinet incorporating a writing desk —**sec·re·tar·i·al** /sèkrə táiree əl/ *adj*

sec·re·tar·y-gen·er·al (*pl* **sec·re·tar·ies-gen·er·al**) *n* the chief executive officer of an organization such as the United Nations

Sec·re·tar·y of State *n* the US cabinet-level official in charge of foreign affairs

se·crete¹ /sə kréet/ (**-cret·ed, -cret·ing**) *vti* produce and discharge a substance from a gland or organ —**se·cre·tion** *n* —**se·cre·to·ry** *adj*

se·crete² /sə kréet/ (**-cret·ed, -cret·ing**) *vt* put in a hidden place

se·cre·tive /séekrətiv/ *adj* unwilling to reveal information —**se·cre·tive·ly** *adv* —**se·cre·tive·ness** *n*

se·cret ser·vice *n* **1** an undercover government organization **2 Se·cret Ser·vice** a US president's security officers

sect *n* **1** a religious group with beliefs at variance with an established group **2** a denomination of a larger religious group

---

ORIGIN Sect goes back to the past participle of Latin *sequi* "follow." In spite of appearances it is not related to *section* or *sector*, but to *sequence* and *second*. The immediate source of *sect* was French.

---

sec·tar·i·an /sek térree ən/ *adj* **1** of relations between religious groups **2** of a single religious group —**sec·tar·i·an** *n* —**sec·tar·i·an·ism** *n*

sec·tion /séksh'n/ *n* **1** a distinct part or subdivision **2** a functional area **3** a view of something cut through ■ *vt* divide

sec·tion·al /sékshən'l/ *adj* **1** of a particular section **2** divided into or consisting of sections —**sec·tion·al·ly** *adv*

sec·tion·al·ism /sékshn'l ìzzəm/ *n* excessive concern for the interests of a particular group —**sec·tion·al·ist** *n, adj*

Sec·tion Eight *n* **1** a military discharge for physical or psychological reasons **2** a soldier discharged under Section Eight regulations

sec·tor /séktər/ *n* **1** a component of an integrated system, e.g., an economy or society **2** a part of an area of military operations **3** a part of a circle bounded by two radii —**sec·tor** *vt* —**sec·tor·i·al** /sek táwree əl/ *adj*

sec·u·lar /sékyələr/ *adj* **1** not concerned with religion **2** not religious or spiritual **3** not belonging to a monastic order ○ *secular clergy* —**sec·u·lar·i·ty** /sèkyə lárrətee/ *n* —**sec·u·lar·ly** *adv*

sec·u·lar·ism /sékyələ rìzzəm/ *n* **1** the exclusion of religion from public affairs **2** rejection of religion —**sec·u·lar·is·tic** /sèkyələ rístik/ *adj*

sec·u·lar·ize /sékyələ rìz/ (-ized, -iz·ing) *vt* **1** transfer from religious to state control **2** make secular —**sec·u·lar·i·za·tion** /sèkyələri záysh'n/ *n*

se·cure /sə kyoor/ *adj* **1** not troubled by fear or doubt **2** firmly fixed or attached **3** unlikely to fail or be lost ○ *a secure investment* **4** safe from attack or theft ■ *vt* (-cured, -cur·ing) **1** fix or attach firmly **2** make safe **3** acquire —**se·cure·ly** *adv* —**se·cure·ment** *n* ◊ See note at **get**

⚡ **se·cure serv·er** *n* an Internet server suitable for confidential communications, e.g., e-commerce payments

se·cu·ri·ty /sə kyoorətee/ (*pl* -ties) *n* **1** the state or feeling of safety **2** something giving assurance **3** protection against attack, crime, espionage, or other danger **4** people entrusted to guard a building or organization **5** an asset deposited to guarantee repayment **6** a guarantor **7** a financial instrument such as a stock certificate or bond

se·cu·ri·ty blan·ket *n* a familiar object, e.g., a blanket, that a child carries around

se·cu·ri·ty guard *n* a guard employed to protect a building or site

se·cu·ri·ty risk *n* somebody or something considered likely to compromise security

se·dan /sə dán/ *n* **1** *US, Can, ANZ* a car with a permanent roof, front and rear seats, and a separate trunk **2** *also* **se·dan chair** an enclosed chair carried on poles

se·date /sə dáyt/ *adj* dignified and unhurried ■ *vt* give a sedative to —**se·date·ly** *adv* —**se·date·ness** *n* —**se·da·tion** *n*

sed·a·tive /séddətiv/ *n* a drug that induces a state of calm or drowsiness —**sed·a·tive** *adj*

sed·en·tar·y /sédd'n tèrree/ *adj* **1** involving a great deal of sitting **2** taking little exercise

Se·der /sáydər/ *n* a Jewish feast on either of the first two nights of Passover, commemorating the exodus of the Jews from Egypt

sedge *n* a plant resembling grass

sed·i·ment /séddimənt/ *n* **1** settled matter at the bottom of a liquid **2** eroded material transported and deposited elsewhere

sed·i·men·ta·ry /sèddə méntəree/ *adj* **1** of or forming sediment **2** describes rock formed from eroded material

sed·i·men·ta·tion /sèddəmən táysh'n/ *n* the formation of sedimentary rocks or sediment

se·di·tion /sə dísh'n/ *n* rebellion against government authority, or incitement to rebel —**se·di·tious** *adj* —**se·di·tious·ly** *adv*

se·duce /sə dooss/ (-duced, -duc·ing) *vt* **1** induce to have sexual relations **2** tempt or win over —**se·duc·er** *n* —**se·duc·tion** /sə dúksh'n/ *n* —**se·duc·tive** /sə dúktiv/ *adj* —**se·duc·tive·ly** *adv*

sed·u·lous /séjjələss/ *adj* painstaking (*literary*) —**se·du·li·ty** /sə dóolətee/ *n*

see¹ /see/ (saw, seen) *v* **1** *vti* perceive with the eyes **2** *vi* have vision **3** *vti* view or watch something **4** *vti* understand something **5** *vt* meet, visit, consult, or have an interview with somebody **6** *vt* have a romantic relationship with somebody **7** *vt* imagine something **8** *vt* consider somebody or something in a particular way ○ *see her as a potential rival* **9** *vt* undergo or experience something ○ *saw active service* **10** *vt* escort somebody **11** *vt* make sure that something happens ○ *See that they wash their hands.* **12** *vt* find out ○ *see what he wants* ◊ See note at **sea**

☐ **see through** *vt* perceive the truth beneath the exterior ○ *I saw through his bravado.*

see² /see/ *n* **1** a bishop's diocese **2** a bishop's authority

seed /seed/ *n* **1** a plant part produced by sexual reproduction containing the embryo of a new plant **2** plant parts used for propagation, as a whole **3** a source or beginning ○ *the seeds of doubt* **4** descendants (*literary*) **5** a graded competitor ■ *vt* **1** plant seeds in **2** remove seeds from **3** rank a player —**seed·less** *adj*

seed·bed /seed bèd/ *n* **1** a plot of ground for growing seedlings **2** a place where something develops

seed·ling /seedling/ *n* a young plant grown from a seed

seed mon·ey *n* initial funding

seed·y /seedee/ (-i·er, -i·est) *adj* **1** shabby or disreputable **2** having many seeds

see·ing /see ing/ *conj* in view of the fact ○ *Seeing that you're an old friend, I'll give you a special price.*

seek /seek/ (sought /sawt/, sought) *v* **1** *vti* try to find **2** *vt* try to obtain or reach **3** *vt* attempt ○ *seeking to exploit the rift between them* —**seek·er** *n*

seem /seem/ *vti* give an impression of being or doing something ○ *It's not as easy as it seems.* ○ *We seem to have a misunderstanding.* ◊ See note at **seam**

seem·ing /seeming/ *adj* apparent but not necessarily true or real —**seem·ing·ly** *adv*

seem·ly /seemlee/ (-li·er, -li·est) *adj* suitable and correct —**seem·li·ness** *n*

seen past participle of **see¹**

seep *vi* 1 pass slowly through a small opening *(refers to liquids or gases)* 2 enter or depart gradually —**seep** *n* —**seep·age** *n*

seer /seer, see ər/ *n* 1 somebody believed to be able to predict the future 2 somebody with supposed supernatural powers

seer·suck·er /seer sùkər/ *n* a lightweight fabric with alternate puckered and smooth stripes

ORIGIN Seersucker derives via Hindi from a Persian phrase meaning literally "milk and honey," which came to refer to a striped linen garment. The word is first recorded in English in the early 18C.

see·saw /see sàw/ *n* 1 a playground toy on which people go up and down at opposite ends of a bar 2 an up-and-down or other alternating movement ■ *vi* 1 ride on a seesaw 2 move like a seesaw

seethe /seeth/ (**seethed**, **seeth·ing**) *vi* 1 be angry 2 be full of bustling activity 3 boil or appear to boil —**seeth·ing** *adj*

see-through *adj* made of transparent material

seg·ment *n* /ségmənt/ a component or section ■ *vt* /ség mént/ split into segments —**seg·men·tal** /seg mént'l/ *adj* —**seg·men·ta·tion** /ségmən táysh'n/ *n*

Se·go·vi·a /si góvee ə, say gáwvyaa/, **Andrés** (1893–1987) Spanish guitarist

seg·re·gate /séggrə gàyt/ (**-gat·ed**, **-gat·ing**) *v* 1 *vt* separate people or groups 2 *vti* keep different groups within a population separate —**seg·re·ga·tion** /sèggrə gáysh'n/ *n* —**seg·re·ga·tion·al** *adj*

ORIGIN Segregate comes from a Latin word meaning literally "separate from the flock." It was adopted into English in the mid-16C.

se·gue /sé gwày, sáy-/ (**-gued**, **-gue·ing**, **-gues**) *vi* 1 in music, continue by playing another piece or passage without a pause 2 make a smooth transition —**se·gue** *n*

~~seige~~ incorrect spelling of **siege**

Seine /sayn, sen/ river rising in E France and flowing northwestward through Paris into the English Channel. Length 482 mi./776 km.

seis·mic /sízmik/ *adj* 1 of earthquakes 2 extremely large or great *(infml)* ○ *had a seismic impact* —**seis·mi·cal·ly** *adv*

seis·mo·graph /sízmə gràf/ *n* a device for detecting and measuring earthquakes —**seis·mog·ra·pher** /sīz móggrəfər/ *n* —**seis·mo·graph·ic** /sìzmə gráffik/ *adj* —**seis·mog·ra·phy** /sīz móggrəfee/ *n*

seis·mol·o·gy /sīz mólləjee/ *n* the study of earthquakes —**seis·mo·log·i·cal** /sìzmə lójjik'l/ *adj* —**seis·mol·o·gist** *n*

~~seive~~ incorrect spelling of **sieve**

seize /seez/ (**seized**, **seiz·ing**) *vt* 1 take hold of quickly and firmly 2 take advantage of eagerly and immediately 3 affect suddenly

4 appropriate or confiscate 5 take into custody

sei·zure /seezhər/ *n* 1 the act of seizing, or the state of being seized 2 an attack of an illness or condition, e.g., of epilepsy

sel·dom /séldəm/ *adv* rarely —**sel·dom·ness** *n*

se·lect /sə lékt/ *vti* choose from among others ■ *adj* 1 of particularly good quality 2 having limited membership 3 especially chosen —**se·lect·ee** /sə lèk teé/ *n* —**se·lect·ness** *n*

se·lect com·mit·tee *n* a Congressional investigative group

se·lec·tion /sə léksh'n/ *n* 1 somebody or something chosen 2 the act of choosing, or the state of being chosen 3 the available choice

se·lec·tive /sə léktiv/ *adj* 1 not universal 2 discerning —**se·lec·tive·ly** *adv* —**se·lec·tive·ness** *n* —**se·lec·tiv·i·ty** /sə lèk tívvətee/ *n*

se·lec·tive ser·vice *n* a conscription system for US military service

se·le·ni·um /sə leénee əm/ *n* (*symbol* **Se**) a nonmetallic chemical element. Use: photocells, photocopiers.

self *n* (*pl* **selves**) 1 somebody's perceived personality ○ *not his usual self* 2 self-interest 3 somebody's individual personality ○ *develop a sense of self* ■ *pron* myself, yourself, himself, or herself *(infml)* ○ *not enough to sustain self and family* ■ *adj* 1 self-colored 2 of the same fabric

self- *prefix* of, by, for, or in itself ○ *self-assured* ○ *self-control*

self-ab·sorbed *adj* preoccupied with yourself —**self-ab·sorp·tion** *n*

self-ad·dressed *adj* addressed to the sender ○ *enclose a self-addressed envelope*

self-ad·he·sive *adj* having a sticky surface

self-a·nal·y·sis *n* analysis of your own personality

self-ap·point·ed *adj* assuming a particular role personally ○ *a self-appointed arbiter of good taste*

self-as·sem·bly *n* construction from a kit of parts

self-as·sured *adj* relaxed and self-confident —**self-as·sur·ance** *n*

self-cen·tered *adj* thinking only of yourself —**self-cen·tered·ness** *n*

self-col·ored *adj* all of one color

self-con·fessed *adj* according to your own admission

self-con·fi·dence *n* confidence in yourself and your abilities —**self-con·fi·dent** *adj* —**self-con·fi·dent·ly** *adv*

self-con·grat·u·la·tion *n* smugness —**self-con·grat·u·la·to·ry** *adj*

self-con·scious *adj* 1 ill at ease in the company of others 2 highly conscious of the impression you make on others —**self-con·scious·ly** *adv* —**self-con·scious·ness** *n*

self-con·tained adj 1 having everything required 2 keeping feelings and opinions private —**self-con·tain·ment** n

self-con·trol n the ability to control your own reactions or impulses —**self-con·trolled** adj

self-de·feat·ing adj thwarting its own objectives

self-de·fense n 1 the use of force to defend yourself, or the legal right to do this 2 martial arts or other unarmed combat techniques

self-de·ni·al n denial of your own desires —**self-de·ny·ing** adj

self-dep·re·cat·ing, self-dep·re·ca·to·ry adj belittling yourself or your achievements

self-de·struct /-də strúkt/ vi 1 destroy itself automatically 2 ruin your own life —**self-de·struct** adj

self-de·struc·tion n 1 an act of self-destructing 2 suicide —**self-de·struc·tive** adj

self-de·ter·mi·na·tion n 1 the right to decide for yourself 2 the right of a people to choose their own government

self-dis·ci·pline n the ability to motivate or control yourself —**self-dis·ci·plined** adj

self-dis·cov·er·y n learning about yourself

self-doubt n lack of self-confidence

self-ef·fac·ing adj modest and reserved —**self-ef·fac·ing·ly** adv

self-em·ployed adj working independently or running your own business —**self-em·ploy·ment** n

self-es·teem n self-respect

self-ev·i·dent adj obvious without explanation or proof —**self-ev·i·dent·ly** adv

self-ex·am·i·na·tion n 1 reflection on your own thoughts and behavior 2 the regular examination of parts of your own body for signs of disease

self-ex·plan·a·to·ry adj easy to understand by itself

self-ex·pres·sion n expression of your personality and feelings, e.g., through art

self-fi·nanc·ing adj financed without outside support

self-ful·fill·ing adj 1 happening because expected 2 satisfying —**self-ful·fill·ment** n

self-gov·ern·ing, self-gov·ern·ed adj 1 using self-control 2 governed or run by its own inhabitants or employees

self-gov·ern·ment n democracy or political independence

self-help n the solving of problems without outside professional or government help

self-hood /sélf hǒod/ n 1 individuality 2 a sense of self 3 somebody's character or personality

self-im·age n your opinion of your own worth or attractiveness

self-im·por·tance n excessively high evaluation of your own importance —**self-im·por·tant** adj —**self-im·por·tant·ly** adv

self-im·posed adj taken on by choice o a self-imposed deadline

self-im·prove·ment n improvement of yourself by your own effort

self-in·crim·i·na·tion n implication of your own guilt, especially during court testimony —**self-in·crim·i·nat·ing** adj —**self-in·crim·i·na·to·ry** adj

self-in·duced adj resulting from your own actions

self-in·dul·gence n excessive pursuit of your own pleasure or satisfaction —**self-in·dul·gent** adj —**self-in·dul·gent·ly** adv

self-in·flict·ed adj done to yourself o a self-inflicted wound

self-in·ter·est n 1 selfishness 2 your own advantage —**self-in·ter·est·ed** adj

self·ish /sélfish/ adj looking after your own interests, needs, and desires —**self·ish·ly** adv —**self·ish·ness** n

self-knowl·edge n understanding of yourself

self·less /sélfləss/ adj putting others' needs ahead of your own —**self·less·ly** adv —**self·less·ness** n

self-made adj 1 successful as a result of your own efforts 2 made without others' help

self-o·pin·ion·at·ed adj 1 certain of being right 2 very conceited

self-per·pet·u·at·ing adj having the power to preserve or renew itself indefinitely

self-pit·y n feeling sorry for yourself —**self-pit·y·ing** adj —**self-pit·y·ing·ly** adv

self-por·trait n a portrait or written description of the artist or writer who made it

self-pos·sessed adj in control of emotions —**self-pos·ses·sion** n

self-pres·er·va·tion n the instinct to keep yourself safe

self-pro·claimed adj claiming to be a particular thing

self-pro·mo·tion n action to attract attention to yourself or your abilities

self-re·gard n 1 concern or admiration only for yourself 2 self-respect

self-re·proach n criticizing or blaming yourself —**self-re·proach·ful** adj

self-re·spect n belief in your own worth and dignity —**self-re·spect·ing** adj

self-re·straint n control over what you say and do

self-right·eous adj sure of your moral superiority (disapproving) —**self-right·eous·ly** adv —**self-right·eous·ness** n

self-rule n the right of a people to choose their own government

self-sac·ri·fice n the giving up of personal needs for the sake of others —**self-sac·ri·fic·ing** adj

self·same /sélf sàym/ adj identical

self-seek·ing adj selfish —**self-seek·ing** n

self-ser·vice adj describes a store or machine where people help themselves —**self-ser·vice** n

self-serv·ing adj putting personal considerations first

self-styled adj claiming to be as stated ◊ See note at **so-called**

self-suf·fi·cient adj 1 able to provide everything you need without buying from others 2 able to manage alone —**self-suf·fi·cien·cy** n

self-sup·port·ing adj 1 getting along financially without outside help 2 standing without being held —**self-sup·port** n

self-taught adj having learned something without formal instruction

self-ten·der n an offer made by a company to buy back its own shares

self-worth n a belief in your own value

Sel·juk /sél jòòk, sel jóòk/ n a member of a Turkish ruling family before the Ottoman Empire —**Sel·juk** adj

sell (sold) v 1 vti exchange something for money 2 vt offer something for sale 3 vi be bought in quantity 4 vt make people want to buy a product 5 vt persuade somebody to accept an idea ○ need to sell the proposal to stockholders —**sell·er** n ◊ **sell short** undervalue the quality and worth of somebody or something ○ Don't sell yourself short. ◊ **sell yourself** emphasize your positive qualities as a candidate for a particular job ◊ **sold on** enthusiastic about something (infml)

□ **sell out** vti 1 sell all of something 2 betray your own principles (infml)

sell-by date n the date something perishable should be sold by

sell·er's mar·ket n a time when demand is greater than supply, resulting in higher prices

sell·ing point n a feature of a product or idea that makes people want to buy or accept it

sell·out /sél òwt/ n 1 an event for which no more tickets are available 2 a betrayal (infml) 3 a betrayer of a principle (infml)

selves plural of **self**

se·man·tic /sə mántik/ adj 1 of the meanings of words 2 of semantics —**se·man·ti·cal·ly** adv

se·man·tics /sə mántiks/ n (+ sing verb) 1 the study of meaning in language 2 the study of symbols —**se·man·ti·cist** /-tissist/ n

sem·a·phore /sémma fàwr/ n 1 a system of signaling using hand-held flags 2 a mechanical signaling device —**sem·a·phore** vti

sem·blance /sémblənss/ n 1 a trace of a quality 2 an outward appearance

se·men /séemən/ n fluid containing sperm ejaculated by a male

se·mes·ter /sə méstər/ n a division of the academic year lasting 15 to 18 weeks or 6 months

sem·i /sémmee, sémmī/ n a semifinal (infml)

semi- prefix 1 partial, partially, somewhat ○ semiconductor 2 half ○ semibreve 3 resembling, having some characteristics of ○ semitropical 4 occurring twice during a particular period ○ semiweekly

sem·i·au·to·mat·ic /sèmmee àwtə máttik, sèmmī-/ adj 1 describes a weapon that reloads automatically 2 partially automated —**sem·i·au·to·mat·ic** n

sem·i·cir·cle /sémmi sùrk'l/ n a half circle —**sem·i·cir·cu·lar** /sèmmi súrkyəlàr/ adj

sem·i·co·lon /sémmi kòlən/ n a punctuation mark separating parts of a sentence or list

USAGE A **semicolon** is used to separate two related parts of a sentence when each part could stand alone as a sentence: The building is chiefly a tourist attraction; it is rarely used as a church these days. Semicolons may also be used instead of commas to separate parts of a list: We invited Jack and Kate, who live next door; Maria, my sister-in-law; and some of our colleagues from work. See also **colon**.

sem·i·con·duc·tor /sèmmee kən dúktər, sèmmī-/ n a solid material that has partial electrical conductivity —**sem·i·con·duc·tive** adj

sem·i·con·scious /sèmmee kónshəss, sèmmī-/ adj partially conscious —**sem·i·con·scious·ness** n

sem·i·fi·nal /sèmmee fín'l, sèmmī-/ n a round of a competition immediately before the final —**sem·i·fi·nal** adj —**sem·i·fi·nal·ist** n

sem·i·nal /sémmin'l/ adj 1 influential, especially in stimulating further thought or research 2 capable of development

sem·i·nar /sémmə nàar/ n 1 a meeting for the presentation or discussion of a specialized subject 2 a meeting of students for study or discussion with an academic supervisor

sem·i·nar·y /sémmə nèrree/ (pl -ies) n a school for training the clergy —**sem·i·nar·i·an** /sèmmə nérree ən/ n

Sem·i·nole /sémmə nòl/ (pl same or -noles) n 1 a member of a Native North American people who now live mainly in Oklahoma and Florida 2 the language of the Seminole people —**Sem·i·nole** adj

se·mi·ot·ics /sèmmee óttiks, sèemee-/ n (+ sing verb) 1 the study of signs and symbols 2 the study of symptoms of diseases —**se·mi·ot·ic** adj —**se·mi·o·ti·cian** /sèmmee ə tísh'n, sèemee-/ n

sem·i·per·ma·nent /sèmmee púrmənənt, sèmmī-/ adj lasting for a long time

sem·i·per·me·a·ble /sèmmee púrmee əb'l, sèmmī-/ adj filtering selectively

sem·i·pre·cious /sèmmee préshəss, sèmmī-/ adj describes moderately valuable stones and minerals

sem·i·pro·fes·sion·al /sèmmee prə féshən'l, sèmmī-/ *adj* **1** participating in a sport or artistic activity for pay but not as a fulltime professional **2** for semiprofessional athletes or players —**sem·i·pro·fes·sion·al** *n* —**sem·i·pro·fes·sion·al·ly** *adv*

sem·i·qua·ver /sémmee kwàyvər, sémmī-/ *n* MUSIC = **sixteenth note**

sem·i·skilled /sèmmee skĭld, sèmmī-/ *adj* with or requiring some skill or training

sem·i·sol·id /sèmmee sóllid, sèmmī-/ *adj* half solid, half liquid

Sem·ite /sé mĭt/ *n* a member of a Semiticspeaking people

Se·mit·ic /sə mĭttik/ *n* a group of languages spoken in North Africa and SW Asia, including Hebrew and Arabic ■ *adj* **1** of Semitic **2** speaking a Semitic language

sem·i·tone /sémmee tòn, sémmī-/ *n* the smallest interval in a musical scale —**sem·i·ton·ic** /-tónnik/ *adj*

sem·i·trail·er /sémmee tràylər, sémmī-/ *n* a trailer without front wheels

sem·i·trop·i·cal /sèmmee tróppik'l, sèmmī-/ *adj* subtropical

sem·i·week·ly /sèmmee weèklee, sèmmī-/ *adj* happening or published twice a week —**sem·i·week·ly** *adv*

sem·o·li·na /sèmmə leénə/ *n* grains of ground wheat. Use: pasta, couscous, other foods.

sen·ate /sénnət/ *n* **1** *also* **Sen·ate** the upper legislative body of government, e.g., in the United States **2** the highest council of ancient Rome

ORIGIN The original Roman **senate** was literally an "assembly of elders." The word is formed from Latin *senex* "man of advanced years, elder."

sen·a·tor /sénnətər/ *n* a member of a senate —**sen·a·to·ri·al** /sènnə táwree əl/ *adj*

send (**sent**) *vt* **1** cause somebody or something to go **2** communicate a message **3** tell or command somebody to go somewhere **4** cause something to happen or be received **5** propel something ○ *A gust of wind sent the papers swirling around the room.* **6** drive somebody into a particular state ○ *The delay is sending her into fits of frustration.* —**send·er** *n*
□ **send up** *vt* mock by imitation (*infml*)

send-off /sénd àwf/ *n* a farewell

send-up /sénd ùp/ *n* a parody (*infml*)

Sen·e·ca[1] /sénnəkə/ (*pl* same *or* -**cas**) *n* **1** a member of a Native North American people who live in W New York and S Ontario **2** the language of the Seneca people —**Sen·e·ca** *adj* —**Sen·e·can** *adj*

Sen·e·ca[2] /sénnəkə/ (4? BC–AD 65) Spanishborn Roman philosopher and writer

Sen·e·gal /sénni gáwl, -gàal/ country in West Africa, on the Atlantic Ocean. Cap. Dakar.

Pop. 10,284,929 (2001). —**Sen·e·gal·ese** /sénni gaw leèz, -gə-/ *n, adj*

~~senery~~ incorrect spelling of **scenery**

se·nes·cent /sə néss'nt/ *adj* aging —**se·nes·cence** *n*

se·nile /seé nīl, sé-/ *adj* **1** mentally less acute in later life **2** of later life ○ *senile dementia* —**se·nile·ly** *adv* —**se·nil·i·ty** /sə nĭllətee/ *n*

sen·ior /seényər/ *adj* **1** more advanced in age **2** higher in rank —**sen·ior** *n*

sen·ior cit·i·zen *n* somebody of retirement age or older

sen·ior·i·ty /seen yáwrətee/ (*pl* -**ties**) *n* **1** status accorded to greater age or higher rank **2** the state of being senior to somebody else

sen·na /sénnə/ *n* **1** dried plant leaves or pods. Use: purgative, laxative. **2** the plant from which senna is obtained

se·ñor /sen yáwr, sin-/ (*pl* **-ñors** *or* **-ñor·es** /-yáwress/) *n* the Spanish equivalent of Mr.

se·ño·ra /sen yáwrə, sin-/ *n* the Spanish equivalent of Mrs.

se·ño·ri·ta /sàynyə reétə, sènnyə-/ *n* the Spanish equivalent of Miss

sen·sa·tion /sen sáysh'n/ *n* **1** a physical feeling **2** the power to perceive through the sense organs **3** a mental impression **4** a state or cause of avid public interest

sen·sa·tion·al /sen sáyshən'l/ *adj* **1** exceptionally good **2** extraordinary ○ *a sensational defeat* **3** involving sensationalism —**sen·sa·tion·al·ly** *adv*

sen·sa·tion·al·ism /sen sáyshən'l ìzzəm/ *n* emphasis on the most shocking, lurid, or emotive aspects of something —**sen·sa·tion·al·ist** *n, adj* —**sen·sa·tion·al·ize** *vt*

sense *n* **1** a physical faculty for acquiring information about the world, e.g., sight or smell **2** a feeling derived from the senses or intuition ○ *a sense of security* **3** the ability to perceive or appreciate a particular quality ○ *a sense of humor* **4** intelligence or sound judgment **5** a useful purpose or good reason **6** a meaning ■ **sens·es** *npl* a rational state of mind ■ *vt* (**sensed, sens·ing**) **1** perceive **2** understand intuitively —**sen·sate** /sén sàyt/ *adj* ◇ **in a sense** considered from one point of view ◇ **make sense** be understandable and consistent with reason ◇ **make sense of** understand

sense·less /sénssləss/ *adj* **1** having lost consciousness **2** with no apparent purpose ○ *a senseless crime* —**sense·less·ly** *adv* —**sense·less·ness** *n*

sense or·gan *n* an organ such as the eye or ear that receives stimuli from the physical world and transmits them to the brain

sen·si·bil·i·ty /sènssə bĭllətee/ *n* the capacity to respond emotionally ■ **sen·si·bil·i·ties** *npl* sensitivity about moral or ethical issues

sen·si·ble /sénssəb'l/ *adj* **1** showing intelligence and sound judgment **2** able to be perceived **3** aware of something *(fml)* —**sen·si·ble·ness** *n* —**sen·si·bly** *adv* ◊ See note at **aware**

sen·si·tive /sénssətiv/ *adj* **1** easily damaged or irritated ○ *sensitive teeth* **2** acutely perceptive **3** affected by an external stimulus *(often in combination)* ○ *sensitive to light* ○ *a touch-sensitive screen* **4** thoughtful and sympathetic **5** easily offended, annoyed, or upset —**sen·si·tive·ly** *adv* —**sen·si·tiv·i·ty** /sénssə tívvətee/ *n*

sen·si·tize /sénssə tīz/ (**-tized, -tiz·ing**) *vt* **1** make sensitive to a particular substance —**sen·si·ti·za·tion** /sénssəti záysh'n/ *n*

sen·sor /sénssər/ *n* a detecting device

sen·so·ry /sénssəree/ *adj* of sensation and the senses

sen·su·al /sénshoo əl/ *adj* **1** of physical or sexual pleasure **2** of the senses rather than the intellect —**sen·su·al·ly** *adv* —**sen·su·al·ness** *n*

sen·su·ous /sénshoo əss/ *adj* **1** of sense stimulation **2** causing or appreciating pleasurable sense stimulation —**sen·su·ous·ly** *adv* —**sen·su·ous·ness** *n*

sent past tense, past participle of **send**

~~sentance~~ incorrect spelling of **sentence**

sen·tence /sént'nss/ *n* **1** a complete meaningful linguistic unit **2** a judgment specifying punishment for a crime ■ *vt* (**-tenced, -tenc·ing**) allocate a punishment to a criminal

sen·tence ad·verb *n* an adverb modifying a whole sentence

sen·ten·tious /sen ténshəss/ *adj* **1** full of aphorisms **2** overly moralizing —**sen·ten·tious·ly** *adv*

sen·tient /sénshənt, sénshee ənt/ *adj* **1** capable of feeling and perception **2** capable of responding with feeling —**sen·tience** *n*

sen·ti·ment /séntəmənt/ *n* **1** an idea based on a feeling or emotion **2** a general feeling or opinion ■ **sen·ti·ments** *npl* a view or opinion

sen·ti·men·tal /séntə mént'l/ *adj* **1** affected acutely by emotional matters **2** displaying too much emotion **3** appealing to tender feelings —**sen·ti·men·tal·ist** *n* —**sen·ti·men·tal·i·ty** /séntəmən tállətee/ *n* —**sen·ti·men·tal·ize** *vti* —**sen·ti·men·tal·ly** *adv*

sen·ti·nel /séntən'l, sént'nəl/ *n* a lookout or guard —**sen·ti·nel** *vt*

sen·try /séntree/ (*pl* **-tries**) *n* a member of the armed services posted as a lookout or guard

sen·try box *n* a shelter for a sentry

Seoul /sōl/ capital and largest city of South Korea. Pop. 10,229,262 (1995).

Sep. *abbr* September

Se·pal /seép'l, sépp'l/ *n* a modified leaf that encloses the petals of a flower

sep·a·rate *adj* /séppərət/ **1** not touching or connected **2** distinct or unrelated ■ *v*/séppə ràyt/ (**-rat·ed, -rat·ing**) **1** *vt* move or keep apart **2** *vt* be positioned between **3** *vt* be the factor that distinguishes **4** *vi* come apart or become detached **5** *vi* cease living as a couple **6** *vt* categorize or sort **7** *vti* divide —**sep·a·ra·ble** *adj* —**sep·a·rate·ly** *adv* —**sep·a·rate·ness** *n* —**sep·a·ra·tion** /séppə ráysh'n/ *n* —**sep·a·ra·tor** *n*

□ **separate out** *vti* come or cause to come out of a mixture

sep·a·rat·ed /séppə ràytəd/ *adj* no longer living together but still married

sep·a·ra·tist /séppərətist/ *n* an advocate of breaking away from a group or country —**sep·a·ra·tism** *n* —**sep·a·ra·tist** *adj*

~~seperate~~ incorrect spelling of **separate**

se·pi·a /seépee ə/ *n* **1** a reddish brown pigment or color **2** a sepia-tinted drawing or photograph —**se·pi·a** *adj*

sep·sis /sépsiss/ *n* the condition caused by the presence of microorganisms or their toxins in body tissue or blood

Sept. *abbr* September

Sep·tem·ber /sep témbər/ *n* the 9th month of the year in the Gregorian calendar

> **ORIGIN September** comes from a Latin word literally meaning "seventh month." In ancient Rome the calendar started the year in March.

sep·tet /sep tét/, **sep·tette** /sep tét/ *n* **1** a group of seven musical performers **2** a piece of music for seven performers

sep·tic /sép tik/ *adj* **1** affected by sepsis and full of pus **2** of sepsis —**sep·tic·i·ty** /sep tíssətee/ *n*

sep·ti·ce·mi·a /séptə seémee ə/ *n* the presence of microorganisms in the bloodstream —**sep·ti·ce·mic** *adj*

sep·tic tank *n* a container in which human waste is decomposed by bacteria

sep·tu·a·ge·nar·i·an /sép too əjə nérree ən, sèp choo-/ *n* somebody who is between 70 and 79 years old —**sep·tu·a·ge·nar·i·an** *adj*

Sep·tu·a·gint /sép too ə jint, sép choo-/ *n* a Greek version of the Hebrew Bible made in the 3C and 2C BC

sep·ul·cher /sépp'lkər/ *n* **1** a burial vault **2** a container for relics —**sep·ul·cher** *vt*

se·pul·chral /sə púlkrəl, -poolkrəl/ *adj* **1** dismal or gloomy **2** of sepulchers *(fml)*

se·quel /seékwəl/ *n* **1** a movie, book, or television program that continues the story of an earlier one **2** something that follows on

se·quence /seékwənss/ *n* **1** a series of things arranged or connected in a particular way, or happening one after another **2** the order in which things happen or are arranged ■ *vt* (**-quenced, -quenc·ing**) put or do things in order —**se·quen·tial** /si kwénsh'l/ adj —**se·quen·tial·ly** adv

✦**se·quen·tial ac·cess** n a method of accessing and reading a computer file by starting at the beginning

se·ques·ter /si kwéstər/ vt 1 put somebody into isolation *(fml)* 2 take somebody's property temporarily until an obligation is discharged

se·quin /séekwin/ n 1 a small shiny decoration on clothing or accessories 2 a former gold coin used in Venice and Turkey —**se·quined** adj

se·quoi·a /si kwóy ə/ *(pl same or -as)* n a very tall Californian redwood tree

ORIGIN The **sequoia** was named in 1847 for the Cherokee leader Sequoya.

Se·quoy·a /si kwóy ə/, **Se·quoi·a** (1766?–1843) Cherokee leader

se·ra plural of **serum**

se·ra·glio /sə rállyō, sə raalyō/ *(pl -glios)* n 1 a Muslim harem 2 a Turkish palace

ser·aph /sérrəf/ *(pl -aphs or -a·phim* /-əffim/*)* n an angel of the highest rank —**se·raph·ic** /sə ráffik/ adj

Ser·bi·a /súrbee ə/ republic in SE Europe that, together with Montenegro, makes up the Federal Republic of Yugoslavia. Cap. Belgrade. Pop. 10,003,309 (2001). —**Ser·bi·an** n, adj

Ser·bo-Cro·a·tian /súrbō krō áysh'n/, **Ser·bo-Cro·at** /-krō at/ n 1 the Slavic languages spoken by the Serbians and Croatians 2 a speaker of Serbo-Croatian ■ adj of Serbo-Croatian

sere /seer/, **sear** adj dry and withered *(literary)*

ser·e·nade /sèrrə náyd, sérrə nàyd/ n 1 a love song performed for the loved one, traditionally in the evening outside a window 2 an instrumental composition for a small ensemble —**ser·e·nade** vt —**ser·e·nad·er** n

ORIGIN Serenades are traditionally sung in the evening, but this was not originally part of the meaning. The word came through French from Italian *serenata*, which was formed from *sereno* "serene" but came to be associated with *sera* "evening."

ser·en·dip·i·ty /sèrrən díppətee/ n a talent for making useful discoveries by chance —**ser·en·dip·i·tous** adj —**ser·en·dip·i·tous·ly** adv ◊ See note at **lucky**

ORIGIN Serendipity was coined by the British writer Horace Walpole (1717–97), who introduced it in a letter to a friend dated January 28, 1754. He formed it from the title of a fairy tale, *The Three Princes of Serendip*, whose heroes possessed the talent. *Serendip* is said to be an old name for Sri Lanka.

se·rene /sə réen/ adj 1 calm and untroubled 2 cloudless —**se·rene·ly** adv —**se·ren·i·ty** /sə rénnətee/ n

serf n 1 a medieval farmworker treated as the landowner's property 2 any enslaved laborer —**serf·dom** n

~~**sergant**~~ incorrect spelling of **sergeant**

serge n a type of strong cloth

ORIGIN Serge is etymologically related to *silk*. It came via French from Latin *sericus* in its feminine form *lana serica*, literally "wool of the Seres." *Seres* was the name given to the people of China and other countries from where silk was obtained, and *sericus* gave rise to the word *silk*.

ser·geant /saárjənt/ n 1 in various armed forces, a noncommissioned officer of a rank above corporal 2 a police officer of a rank below lieutenant —**ser·gean·cy** n

ser·geant ma·jor *(pl ser·geants ma·jor or ser·geant ma·jors)* n in various armed forces, a noncommissioned officer of the highest rank

se·ri·al /séeree əl/ n 1 a story that is published or broadcast in parts 2 a regular newspaper or magazine ■ adj 1 happening or doing something repeatedly 2 produced in parts —**se·ri·al·ly** adv ◊ See note at **cereal**

se·ri·al·ize /séeree ə līz/ *(-ized, -iz·ing)* vt produce a story in parts —**se·ri·al·i·za·tion** /sèeree əli záysh'n/ n

se·ri·al kill·er n somebody who murders many people over a period of time —**se·ri·al kill·ing** n

se·ri·al num·ber n an identification number

✦**se·ri·al port** n a computer socket for peripherals

se·ries /séer eez/ *(pl same)* n 1 a number of things that come one after another 2 a set of broadcast programs 3 a set of games between the same teams 4 an arrangement of electric elements

USAGE If you use **series** to mean "a single set of things," use a singular verb even if **series** is followed by the preposition *of* and a plural noun: *A series of meetings is planned for next year.* If you use **series** to mean "two or more sets of things," use a plural verb: *Three series of meetings are planned for next year.*

ser·if /sérrif/ n a decorative line finishing a stroke of a printed letter

se·ri·ous /séeree əss/ adj 1 very bad or great 2 important and grave 3 thoughtful or thought-provoking 4 not lighthearted —**se·ri·ous·ly** adv —**se·ri·ous·ness** n

ser·mon /súrmən/ n 1 a religious talk that forms part of a church service 2 a long lecture on behavior

ser·mon·ize /súrmə nìz/ *(-ized, -iz·ing)* vti lecture somebody about his or her behavior

se·ro·to·nin /sèrrə tṓnin/ n a chemical in the body that acts as a transmitter of nerve impulses

ser·pent /súrpənt/ n 1 a snake *(literary)* 2 a treacherous person

ser·pen·tine /súrpən tèen, -tīn/ *adj* **1** winding or curving **2** resembling a snake *(literary)* ■ *n* a green or brown mineral. Use: ornamental stone.

ser·ra·tion /sə ráysh'n/ *n* a series of notches like the teeth of a saw

ser·rat·ed /səráytid/ *adj* with notches or projections

ser·ried /sérreed/ *adj* close together *(literary)*

se·rum /séerəm/ (*pl* **-rums** *or* **-ra** /-rə/) *n* **1** the liquid part of blood without clotting agents **2** MED = **antiserum**

ser·vant /súrvənt/ *n* **1** somebody employed to do household jobs **2** somebody who works for the public

serve *v* (**served, serv·ing**) **1** *vti* work for somebody as a servant **2** *vi* be of use **3** *vti* prepare and supply food or drink **4** *vti* give food or drink to somebody **5** *vt* provide goods or services for a customer **6** *vt* spend a particular length of time in prison **7** *vi* be in the military **8** *vti* have a particular effect **9** *vt* deliver a legal document to somebody *(fml)* **10** *vi* in racket games, put the ball or shuttlecock into play ■ *n* in racket games, a hit that starts a point ◇ **serve somebody right** be a deserved punishment

⚡**serv·er** /súrvər/ *n* **1** somebody who serves customers **2** in racket sports, somebody who starts a point **3** a tray or utensil for serving food or drinks **4** the central computer in a network

~~serviceable~~ incorrect spelling of **serviceable**

ser·vice /súrvəss/ *n* **1** work done for somebody else **2** a system that meets a public need, e.g., for transport **3** a government agency **4** a branch of the armed forces **5** a maintenance operation for machinery **6** current use or operation ◇ *not in service* **7** a religious ceremony **8** a set of dishes **9** the act or job of serving somebody **10** in racket sports, the act of serving a ball or shuttlecock ■ **ser·vic·es** *npl* armed forces ■ *vt* (**-viced, -vic·ing**) **1** provide a service to the community **2** clean and adjust machinery ■ *adj* **1** providing a service, not goods **2** used by employees or for deliveries —**ser·vic·er** *n*

ser·vice·a·ble /súrvəssəb'l/ *adj* **1** likely to withstand hard wear **2** in working condition —**ser·vice·a·bly** *adv*

ser·vice ar·e·a *n* **1** a complex of facilities for highway travelers **2** an area over which a broadcasting company can achieve a satisfactory signal

ser·vice charge *n* an amount of money added to a bill for service

ser·vice con·tract *n* a repair contract

ser·vice in·dus·try *n* an industry that provides services

ser·vice·man /súrvəssman/ (*pl* **-men** /-mən/) *n* **1** a soldier **2** *also* **ser·vice man** a repairman

ser·vice mark *n* the logo used by the providers of a particular service

ser·vice·per·son /súrvəss pùrss'n/ (*pl* **-peo·ple** /-pèep'l/ *or* **-per·sons**) *n* **1** a soldier **2** *also* **ser·vice per·son** a person who undertakes repairs

⚡**ser·vice pro·vid·er** *n* **1** a business that connects people to the Internet **2** a company that provides services

ser·vice road *n* a minor road beside a main road

ser·vice sta·tion *n* a place that sells gasoline to motorists

ser·vice·wom·an /súrvəss wòommən/ (*pl* **-en** /-wimmin/) *n* **1** a woman soldier **2** *also* **ser·vice wom·an** a woman who undertakes repairs

ser·vile /súrv'l, -vīl/ *adj* **1** too obedient **2** menial —**ser·vile·ly** *adv* —**ser·vil·i·ty** /sur víllətee/ *n*

serv·ing /súrving/ *n* a quantity of food served to one person

ser·vi·tor /súrvitər, -tawr/ *n* a servant *(archaic)*

ser·vi·tude /súrvi tòod/ *n* **1** the state of being a slave **2** work imposed as a punishment

ses·a·me /séssəmee/ (*pl* **-mes** *or* **same**) *n* **1** the seeds of a tropical plant. Use: cooking, oil extraction. **2** the tropical plant that produces sesame seeds

ses·sion /sésh'n/ *n* **1** a meeting of an official body **2** a series of official meetings **3** a time when classes are held in a school or university **4** a period during which a specific thing is done ■ **ses·sions** *npl* the sittings of a justice of the peace —**ses·sion·al** *adj*

set[1] *v* (**set, set·ting**) **1** *vt* put something somewhere **2** *vt* put somebody into a particular condition **3** *vt* make something happen **4** *vt* focus on something **5** *vt* prepare something to be used **6** *vti* become or make solid **7** *vt* adjust a measuring device **8** *vt* decide on or impose something, e.g., a price **9** *vt* be an example **10** *vt* establish a record **11** *vt* arrange hair using styling products or clips **12** *vt* put a gem into a setting **13** *vt* put a broken bone back into position **14** *vi* heal after being broken *(refers to bones)* **15** *vt* provide the music for something **16** *vt* portray something in a particular setting **17** *vt* position the sails on a boat **18** *vi* go below the horizon *(refers to the Sun)* **19** *vi* get ready to start a race **20** *vi* become permanent *(refers to a dyes or colors)* ■ *n* **1** the condition of being solid **2** an arrangement of theatrical scenery **3** a hairstyle created using styling products or clips **4** INDUST, ZOOL = **sett** ■ *adj* **1** established **2** inflexible **3** ready **4** determined

☐ **set about** *vt* begin

☐ **set apart** *vt* make conspicuous or different

☐ **set aside** *vt* **1** reserve **2** reject a previous decision

☐ **set back** *vt* delay something

☐ **set down** *vt* write down

☐ **set forth** *v* **1** *vt* state **2** *vi* leave *(literary)*

□ **set off** v **1** vi start out on a trip **2** vt make something operate **3** vt make somebody start doing something **4** vt make something start to happen **5** vt make something look attractive

□ **set out** v **1** vi begin a journey **2** vt display or lay out **3** vt present

□ **set up** v **1** vt erect something **2** vti prepare the equipment for an event **3** vt organize something **4** vti start a business

set[2] n **1** a collection considered as or forming a unit **2** a social group **3** a device that receives radio or television signals **4** a main division of a tennis match ■ vi (**set, set·ting**) dance facing a partner

set·back /sét bàk/ n **1** something that delays progress **2** a shelf or recess in a wall

set-in adj built-in

Se·ton /séet'n/, **St. Elizabeth Ann** (1774–1821) US educator and religious leader

set piece n **1** a carefully planned action **2** a formal work of art **3** a piece of scenery

sett n **1** a rectangular paving stone **2** a badger's burrow

set·tee /se tée/ n **1** a comfortable seat for two people **2** a bench with a back

set·ter /séttər/ n a long-haired dog belonging to various breeds trained as bird dogs

set·ting /sétting/ n **1** a set of surroundings **2** a chosen point or level in the operation of a machine **3** the metal fixture of a jewel **4** the utensils for one person at a table **5** the period or place in which a story takes place

set·tle /sett'l/ v (**-tled, -tling**) **1** vti decide on something **2** vt solve a problem or end a dispute **3** vti make or become resident in a particular place **4** vti cause a cloudy liquid to become clear, or become clear by forming a sediment **5** vt pay a debt **6** vi move downward and come to rest **7** vti end a legal dispute **8** vti make or become calm **9** vt put something in order **10** vti make somebody or yourself comfortable in a particular position ■ n a long wooden seat with a high back

set·tle·ment /sétt'lmənt/ n **1** a colony **2** an agreement reached after discussion **3** a small community **4** an arrangement transferring property to somebody

set·tler /séttlər/ n an early resident in a new place

set-to (pl **set-tos**) n an argument or fight (infml)

set-up /sét ùp/ n **1** the organization of something **2** a set of prepared objects for a particular task **3** a dishonest plan or trick (infml)

Seu·rat /sə ráa/, **Georges** (1859–91) French painter

Seuss /sooss/, **Dr.** (1904–91) US writer and illustrator

sev·en /sév'n/ n the number 7 —**sev·en** adj, pron

sev·en·teen /sèv'n téen/ n the number 17 —**sev·en·teen** adj, pron —**sev·en·teenth** adj, adv, n

sev·enth /sév'nth/ n **1** one of seven parts of something **2** in music, an interval of seven notes —**sev·enth** adj, adv

Sev·enth-Day Ad·vent·ist /-ádvəntist, -ad véntist/ n a member of a Protestant Christian denomination that observes the Sabbath on Saturday

sev·enth heav·en n **1** a state of perfect happiness **2** in Islamic and Talmudic belief, the highest heaven

sev·en·ty /sév'ntee/ n the number 70 ■ **sev·en·ties** npl **1** the numbers 70 to 79, particularly as a range of Fahrenheit temperatures **2** the years from 70 to 79 in a century or somebody's life —**sev·en·ti·eth** adj, adv, n —**sev·en·ty** adj, pron

sev·en·ty-eight, 78 n a phonograph record played at 78 revolutions per minute

sev·er /sévvər/ vti **1** cut through something, or cut something off **2** break off a tie **3** separate something

sev·er·al /sévvərəl/ adj, pron a small number, though more than two or three o several days ago o several of them ■ adj **1** various or different o went their several ways **2** separate or individual o joint and several liability

sev·er·al·ly /sévvərəlee/ adv (fml or literary) **1** separately or individually **2** in turn or respectively

sev·er·ance /sévvərənss/ n **1** the act of severing something **2** loss of employment because of lack of available work **3** also **sev·er·ance pay** compensation for the loss of a job

sev·er·ance tax n a state tax on a natural resource to be used in another state

se·vere /sə veér/ adj **1** strict or harsh **2** extremely bad or dangerous o severe injuries **3** extremely unpleasant or difficult **4** exacting **5** looking stern or serious **6** plain or austere in style —**se·vere·ly** adv —**se·vere·ness** n —**se·ver·i·ty** /sə vérrətee/ n

Sev·ern /sévvərn/ river in NW Ontario, Canada, flowing northeastward into Hudson Bay. Length 610 mi./982 km.

Se·ville /sə víl/ capital of **Sevilla Province** and the autonomous region of Andalusia, SW Spain. Pop. 701,927 (1998).

~~seviral~~ incorrect spelling of **several**

sew /sō/ (**sewn** /sōn/ or **sewed**) vti make or repair things with a needle and thread —**sew·er** n

SPELLCHECK Do not confuse the spelling of **sew, so** ("in order that"), and **sow** ("plant seed"), which sound similar.

□ **sew up** vt finish successfully

sew·age /soo ij/ n waste matter from homes carried off in drains

sew·age plant n a place where sewage is treated

Sew·ard /soŏ ərd/, **William H.** (1801–72) US secretary of state (1861–69)

sew·er /soŏ ər/ n an underground drain for waste

sew·er·age /soŏ ərij/ n 1 a system of sewers 2 the removal of toilet waste from homes

sew·ing /só ing/ n 1 the activity of using a needle and thread 2 material being sewn

sew·ing ma·chine n a machine for sewing

sewn past participle of **sew**

sex n 1 the male or female gender 2 sexual activity or sexual intercourse ■ adj of sex ■ vt determine the sex of an animal

sex- prefix six ◊ **sextet**

sex·a·ge·nar·i·an /séksəjə náiree ən/ n somebody aged between 60 and 69 —**sex·a·ge·nar·i·an** adj

sex·ism /sék sɪzzəm/ n 1 discrimination on the grounds of sex 2 sexual stereotyping —**sex·ist** adj, n

sex·less /séksləss/ adj 1 without sexual activity 2 without sexual characteristics —**sex·less·ness** n

sex·ol·o·gy /sek sólləjee/ n the study of human sexuality —**sex·o·log·i·cal** /sèksə lójjik'l/ adj —**sex·ol·o·gist** n

sex·tant /sékstənt/ n a navigational instrument incorporating a telescope and an angular scale

sex·tet /sek stét/, **sex·tette** n 1 a group of six musicians or singers 2 any group of six people or things

sex·ton /sékstən/ n a church caretaker

Sex·ton /sékstən/, **Anne** (1928–74) US poet

sex·tup·let /sek stúpplət, -stoŏplət/ n 1 one of six offspring born together 2 a group of six musical notes

sex·u·al /sékshoo əl, séksh'l/ adj 1 of sexual activity 2 of both sexes or either sex —**sex·u·al·ly** adv

sex·u·al ha·rass·ment n unwanted sexual advances

sex·u·al in·ter·course n sex involving penetration

sex·u·al·i·ty /sèkshoo állətee/ n 1 the state or fact of being sexual 2 involvement in sexual activity 3 sexual appeal

sex·u·al·ly trans·mit·ted dis·ease, sex·u·al·ly trans·mit·ted in·fec·tion n a disease caught through sexual activity

sex·u·al o·ri·en·ta·tion n the direction of somebody's sexual desire toward people of the opposite sex, the same sex, or both sexes

sex·y /séksee/ (**-i·er, -i·est**) adj 1 arousing sexual desire 2 appealing (infml) ◊ a sexy new slogan —**sex·i·ly** adv —**sex·i·ness** n

Sey·chelles /say shélz/ island country in the W Indian Ocean. Cap. Victoria. Pop. 79,715 (2001). —**Sey·chell·ois** /sày shel waá/ adj, n

Sey·mour /sée màwr/, **Jane** (1509?–37) queen

of England (1536–37) as the 3rd wife of Henry VIII

Sg suffix seaborgium

⚡SGML n a method of representing text electronically by defining the relationship between form and structure. Full form **Standard Generalized Markup Language**

Sgt., SGT abbr Sergeant

Sha'·ban /shə baàn, shaa-/, **Sha·ban, Shaa·ban** n the 8th month of the year in the Islamic calendar

Shab·bat /shə baàt/ n the Jewish Sabbath, celebrated on Saturday

shab·by /shábbee/ (**-bi·er, -bi·est**) adj 1 worn and threadbare 2 wearing worn clothes 3 inferior or inconsiderate 4 inferior in quality —**shab·bi·ly** adv —**shab·bi·ness** n

shack n a small flimsy building

shack·le /shák'l/ n a metal locking band fastened around the wrists or ankles of prisoners (often pl) ■ vt (**-led, -ling**) 1 restrict the freedom of ◊ felt shackled by the rules 2 restrain or secure with shackles

Shack·le·ton /shák'ltən/, **Sir Ernest Henry** (1874–1922) Irish explorer

shade n 1 an area out of direct sunlight 2 a variation on a basic color 3 something that blocks out light 4 a window blind 5 a small amount 6 a variation or nuance ■ **shades** npl sunglasses (infml) ■ v (**shad·ed, shad·ing**) 1 vt protect something from sunlight 2 vt darken a part of a picture 3 vi change slightly or gradually

shad·ing /sháyding/ n 1 a dark area in a picture 2 a slight difference

shad·ow /sháddō/ n 1 a darkened shape of somebody or something blocking the light 2 darkness in a place or painting 3 a hint of something 4 ominous gloom 5 a dark area under the eyes 6 a ghost ■ vt 1 protect something from light 2 follow somebody secretly ◊ See note at **follow**

shad·ow·y /sháddō ee/ (**-i·er, -i·est**) adj 1 full of shadows 2 not clearly seen

shad·y /sháydee/ (**-i·er, -i·est**) adj 1 having little natural light 2 dishonest —**shad·i·ly** adv —**shad·i·ness** n

shaft n 1 a long handle 2 a vertical passage 3 a passage for ventilation in a building 4 a rotating rod that provides motion or power for a machine 5 a beam of light 6 a pole on a cart to which a horse is harnessed 7 an arrow or spear (literary) 8 the long thin body of a spear or similar weapon 9 the main part of an architectural column ■ vt treat unfairly (slang)

shag[1] n 1 a carpet with a long pile 2 long pile on a textile

shag[2] n a small cormorant

shag·gy /shággee/ (**-gi·er, -gi·est**) adj 1 long and tangled 2 having coarse long hair or wool —**shag·gi·ness** n

shag·gy-dog sto·ry n a long story with a weak ending

shah /shaa/ n a former hereditary monarch of Iran

Shah Ja·han /shàa jə haán/ (1592–1666) emperor of India (1628–58)

shai·tan /shī taàn, shày-/ n 1 in Islamic countries, an evil spirit or person 2 **Shai·tan** in Islamic belief, the devil

shake v (**shook** /shŏŏk/, **shak·en** /sháykən/, **shak·ing**) 1 vti move or cause to move back and forth in short quick movements 2 vi tremble or quaver 3 vti get or put into a particular state by shaking 4 vt shock and upset somebody 5 vti clasp hands as a greeting, farewell, or sign of agreement 6 vt move your head to express "No" ■ n 1 an act of shaking 2 a vibration 3 a milk shake 4 a handshake 5 a reasonable chance ○ *a fair shake for everybody* ■ **shakes** npl uncontrollable trembling ◊ **no great shakes** not very good or important (*infml*)

□ **shake down** vt 1 extort money from (*slang*) 2 search thoroughly (*infml*)

□ **shake up** vt 1 make major changes to or in 2 shock or upset

shake·down /sháyk dòwn/ n 1 an act of extortion (*slang*) 2 a thorough search (*infml*)

shake·out /sháyk òwt/ n a change resulting in losses

shak·er /sháykər/ n 1 a container for dispersing the contents in fine particles 2 a container for mixing drinks 3 **Shak·er** a member of an ascetic Christian denomination

~~Shakespear, Shakespeare~~ incorrect spelling of **Shakespeare**

William Shakespeare

Shake·speare /sháyks peer/, **William** (1564–1616) English poet and playwright —**Shake·spear·e·an** /shayk speéree ən/ adj, n —**Shake·spear·i·an** adj, n

shake-up n a major change

shak·y /sháykee/ (**-i·er**, **-i·est**) adj 1 trembling 2 likely to collapse 3 weak and not likely to last —**shak·i·ly** adv —**shak·i·ness** n

shale n a dark rock composed of layers of dark sediment and clay —**shal·y** adj

shall stressed /shal/ unstressed /shəl/ modal v 1 indicates that something will or ought to happen in the future 2 indicates determination 3 indicates that something must happen because of a rule 4 makes offers and suggestions (*in questions*) ○ *Shall we go now?*

LANGUAGE NOTE shall or **will**? The traditional rule, often stated in grammars and usage books, is that to express a simple future tense **shall** is used after *I* and *we* (*I shall leave promptly at noon*) and **will** in other cases (*They/you will leave at noon*). To express intention, command, or wish their roles are reversed: *I will do this right or die trying*; *Passengers shall present two photo IDs prior to ticketing*. It is unlikely that this rule has ever been regularly observed, however, and many examples in the printed works of the best writers contradict it.

shal·lot /shə lót/ n 1 a vegetable like a small onion 2 the plant that produces shallots

shal·low /shállō/ adj 1 not physically deep 2 not thinking or feeling deeply ■ **shallows** npl an area of shallow water —**shallow·ly** adv —**shal·low·ness** n

sha·lom /shaa lốm/ interj used as a Jewish greeting or farewell

sham n 1 a fake 2 an impostor 3 a pillow cover ■ adj not genuine ■ vti (**shammed**, **sham·ming**) feign

sha·man /shaámən, sháymən/ n a spiritual leader with healing powers —**sha·man·ic** /shə mánnik, shay-/ adj —**sha·man·ism** n

sham·ble /shámb'l/ vi (**-bled**, **-bling**) shuffle along clumsily ■ n a shuffling walk

ORIGIN The verb **shamble** is probably from a dialect adjective meaning "ungainly." This may be related to *shambles*, through the phrase *shamble legs*, referring to the legs of trestle tables set up for a meat market or "shambles."

sham·bles /shámb'lz/ n 1 a disorganized failure 2 a state of disorder or chaos

ORIGIN A *shamble* was originally a stool or table. The word gradually acquired the specialized meaning "meat table," being applied to meat sellers' stalls at markets. The plural form **shambles** came to denote a slaughterhouse, and hence metaphorically any place of carnage. The milder modern sense "state of disorder" did not emerge until the early 20C.

shame n 1 a feeling that combines dishonor, unworthiness, and embarrassment 2 the capacity to feel unworthy 3 a state of disgrace 4 a cause for regret ■ vt (**shamed**, **sham·ing**) 1 cause to feel ashamed 2 force to do something through shame ◊ **put to shame** cause to seem inferior by comparison

shame·faced /sháym fàyst/ adj 1 showing shame 2 timid —**shame·fac·ed·ly** /sháym fàysədlee, -fàystlee/ adv

ORIGIN **Shamefaced** originally had no connection with the face. The word was *shame-*

fast, and the literal meaning "held fast by shame." It was altered under the influence of *face* in the mid-16C.

shame·ful /sháymf'l/ *adj* disgraceful or scandalous —**shame·ful·ly** *adv* —**shame·ful·ness** *n*

shame·less /sháymləss/ *adj* feeling or showing no shame —**shame·less·ly** *adv* —**shame·less·ness** *n*

Sha·mir /shə meér/, **Yitzhak** (b. 1914) Polish-born Israeli prime minister (1983–84, 1986–92)

sham·my /shámmee/ (*pl* -mies) *n* a chamois cloth used for household cleaning

sham·poo /sham poó/ *n* 1 a liquid soap for cleaning the hair 2 a sudsy detergent for cleaning upholstery and carpets ■ *vt* (-pooed, -poo·ing, -poos) clean with shampoo

sham·rock /shám ròk/ *n* a three-leafed clover

Shan·dong /sháàn dóng/ province in east central China, bordering on the Yellow Sea. Cap. Jinan. Pop. 87,380,000 (1997).

shan·dy /shándee/ *n* a mixture of beer and lemon-lime soda

Shang·hai /shàng hí/ port in E China. Pop. 13,580,000 (1995). —**Shang·hai·nese** /shàng hī neéz/ *npl*

Shan·gri-la /shàng gree laá/ *n* an imaginary utopia

> **ORIGIN** The original **Shangri-la** was an imaginary land in *The Lost Horizon* (1933) by the British novelist James Hilton.

shank *n* 1 a long, narrow part of something 2 a cut of meat from an animal's leg 3 the lower part of an animal's leg 4 the lower part of the human leg

Ravi Shankar

Shan·kar /shángk aar/, **Ravi** (b. 1920) Indian sitarist, composer, and teacher

Shan·non /shánnən/ longest river in the British Isles, rising in north central Republic of Ireland and flowing southwestward to the Atlantic Ocean. Length 230 mi./370 km.

shan't /shant/ *contr* shall not

shan·ty /shántee/ (*pl* -ties) *n* a crude shack

shan·ty·town /shántee tòwn/ *n* a settlement consisting of crudely made shacks

shape *n* 1 the outline of something or somebody 2 something that is not clearly seen 3 a geometric form such as a square or cone 4 general health or condition 5 a mold or form ■ *vt* (shaped, shap·ing) 1 influence greatly 2 decide on the character of 3 give a particular shape to
□ **shape up** *vi* 1 improve (*infml*) 2 reach an acceptable standard

shape·less /sháypləss/ *adj* lacking precise shape or structure —**shape·less·ly** *adv* —**shape·less·ness** *n*

shape·ly /sháyplee/ (-li·er, -li·est) *adj* having a pleasing shape —**shape·li·ness** *n*

shard, sherd *n* a fragment of glass, metal, or pottery

share /shair/ *v* (shared, shar·ing) 1 *vti* use something along with other people 2 *vti* take responsibility for something together 3 *vt* let somebody use or have part of something 4 *vt* divide something equally between people 5 *vt* have a similar feeling or experience ■ *n* 1 the part of something that somebody has been allotted 2 a part of a company's stock —**shar·er** *n*

share·crop·per /sháir kròppər/ *n* a tenant farmer working for a share in the value of the crop

share·hold·er /sháir hòldər/ *n* FIN = **stockholder**

⨍ share·ware /sháir wàir/ *n* software that is available free for a trial period and is paid for voluntarily afterward

sha·ri·a /shaa reé ə/, **sha·ri'·a, sha·ri'·ah** *n* Islamic religious law, based on the Koran

shark *n* 1 a large carnivorous fish 2 a ruthless or dishonest person (*infml*)

Sha·ron /sha rón/, **Ariel** (b. 1928) Israeli soldier, politician, and prime minister (2001–)

sharp *adj* 1 able to cut and puncture things 2 pointed 3 quick-witted 4 critical and unsympathetic 5 sudden and significant 6 distinct ○ *in sharp contrast* 7 clearly detailed 8 piercing in sound 9 strong and bitter or acidic in taste 10 describes a musical note that is higher by a half step 11 describes a musical note that has too high a pitch 12 stylish ■ *adv* 1 precisely 2 at slightly too high a pitch ■ *n* 1 (symbol ♯) a note that is higher by a half step, or a printed symbol for this 2 a sharp medical instrument (*usually pl*) 3 also **sharp·er** /sháarpər/ a skillful cheat (*infml*) —**sharp·en** *vti* —**sharp·en·er** *n* —**sharp·ly** *adv* —**sharp·ness** *n*

sharp-eyed *adj* 1 alert to detail 2 having good eyesight

Sharps·burg /sháarps bùrg/ village in NW Maryland, site of one of the bloodiest battles in the Civil War on September 17, 1862

sharp·shoot·er /sháarp shòotər/ *n* 1 somebody who shoots firearms precisely 2 an accurate finder of a target

sharp-tongued *adj* critical or sarcastic

sharp-wit·ted *adj* mentally keen —**sharp-wit·ted·ly** *adv*

Shas·ta /shásta/ (pl same or **-tas**) n 1 a member of a group of Native North American people who live in the highlands of N California 2 the language of the Shasta people, almost extinct —**Shas·ta** adj

Sha·sta, Mt. /shásta/ extinct volcano in N California. Height 14,162 ft./4,317 m.

Shat·ten /shátt'n/, **Gerald·P.** (b. 1949) US developmental biologist. He led the research team that produced the first genetically modified monkey.

shat·ter /sháttar/ v 1 vti smash into pieces 2 vt destroy hope or belief

shat·ter·proof /sháttar proof/ adj resistant to shattering

shave /shayv/ v (**shaved, shaved** or **shav·en** /sháyv'n/, **shav·ing**) 1 vti remove hair with a razor 2 vt reduce an amount slightly 3 vt barely touch something in passing 4 vt remove a thin layer ■ n an act of shaving hair off, especially off the face

shav·en /sháyv'n/ v past participle of **shave** ■ adj (often in combination) 1 without any beard or other facial hair 2 trimmed

shav·er /sháyvar/ n a device for shaving facial hair

Sha·vu·oth /sha voo ŏt, -ŏth/, **Sha·vu·ot** /-òt/ n a Jewish festival marking the giving of the Law to Moses. Date: 6th of Sivan, in May or June.

Shaw, George Bernard (1856–1950) Irish playwright

shawl n a fabric square for the head and shoulders or to wrap a baby in

Shaw·nee /shaw nee/ (pl same or **-nees**) n 1 a member of a Native North American people who now live mainly in Oklahoma 2 the Algonquian language of the Shawnee people, almost extinct —**Shawnee** adj

Shaw·wal /sha wól/ n the 10th month of the year in the Islamic calendar

she stressed /shee/ unstressed /shi/ pron refers to a female person or animal, or an object perceived as female, that has been previously mentioned or whose identity is known (as the subject of a verb) ■ n a female person or animal, especially a new baby

s/he /shèe awr hée/ pron she or he (intended to avoid sexism in writing)

sheaf /sheef/ (pl **sheaves** /sheevz/) n 1 a bundle of harvested grain stalks 2 any bundle

shear /sheer/ v (**sheared** or **shorn** /shawrn, shōrn/) 1 cut something off 2 cut hair, wool, or foliage from something ■ n 1 the removal of an animal's fleece 2 the wool cut off an animal 3 a cutting tool with blades like scissors —**shear·er** n

SPELLCHECK Do not confuse the spelling of **shear** and **sheer** ("complete and utter"), which sound similar.

shears /sheerz/ (pl same) n a cutting tool like a large pair of scissors (+ sing or pl verb)

sheath /sheeth/ n (pl **sheaths** /sheethz, sheeths/) 1 a case for a blade 2 a close-fitting covering 3 a closely fitting dress ■ vt sheathe

sheathe /sheeth/ (**sheathed, sheath·ing**) vt 1 put into a sheath 2 enclose something with a covering or case

sheath·ing /sheething/ n a protective covering

sheath knife n a knife carried in a sheath

sheaves plural of **sheaf**

She·ba /sheeba/ ancient kingdom of SW Arabia, in present-day Yemen

she·bang /sha báng/ ◊ **the whole shebang** everything (infml)

she·been /sha been/ n an illegal drinking establishment

shed[1] (**shed, shed·ding**) v 1 vt cause tears or blood to flow 2 vt radiate light 3 vti lose something such as hair or fur naturally 4 vt get rid of something

shed[2] n 1 a small building used for storage or shelter 2 a large open building used for storage or shelter or as a work area

she'd /sheed/ contr 1 she had 2 she would

sheen n a glossy appearance

sheep (pl same) n 1 a domesticated hooved mammal kept for its wool and meat 2 a submissive person

sheep-dip n 1 a disinfectant for sheep 2 a bath containing sheep-dip

sheep·dog /sheep dàwg/ n a breed of dog used to herd sheep

sheep·fold /sheep fōld/ n a pen for sheep

sheep·ish /sheepish/ adj 1 embarrassed 2 timid —**sheep·ish·ly** adv —**sheep·ish·ness** n

sheep·skin /sheep skìn/ n 1 sheep leather with or without wool 2 a diploma (infml)

sheer[1] /sheer/ adj 1 complete and utter 2 pure or unadulterated 3 nearly vertical or perpendicular ■ n a nearly transparent fabric —**sheer** adv —**sheer·ness** n ◊ See note at **shear**

sheer[2] /sheer/ vi swerve from a course —**sheer** n

sheet[1] /sheet/ n 1 a cloth used on a bed 2 a flat thin rectangular piece 3 a broad thin expanse 4 a flat baking pan

sheet[2] /sheet/ n a rope for changing a sail's position ■ **sheets** npl spaces at the bow and stern of a ship

sheet·ing /sheeting/ n thin material for covering

sheet light·ning n lightning that appears in a broad sheet

sheet met·al n metal in sheet form

sheet mu·sic n printed music on unbound sheets

Shef·field /shé feeld/ city in N England. Pop. 530,375 (1996).

sheik /sheek, shayk/, **sheikh** n 1 the leader of an Arab family or village 2 an Islamic religious leader —**sheik·dom** n

shei·ka /sháy kaa/, **shei·kha** n a sheik's wife

shield incorrect spelling of **shield**

shek·el /shék'l/ n 1 the main unit of Israeli currency 2 an ancient Jewish unit of weight

shelf (pl **shelves**) n 1 a flat surface on which to put objects 2 the contents of a shelf 3 a ledge of rock or ice —**shelf·ful** n

shelf life n a period of time during which a product remains fresh

shell n 1 the hard protective covering of a turtle, crab, other mollusk or crustacean, or of an insect 2 the covering of an egg or nut 3 a protective casing 4 the framework of a building 5 a pastry case 6 a hollow or empty thing 7 a large explosive projectile 8 a gun cartridge 9 a narrow racing boat 10 a group of electrons with similar energy in similar orbits around the nucleus of an atom ■ v 1 vt take something out of a shell 2 vti bombard a target 3 vi collect seashells □ **shell out** vti pay out money (infml)

she'll /sheel/ contr 1 she shall 2 she will

shel·lac /shə lák/, **shel·lack** n 1 purified resin from a tropical insect 2 a varnish made from shellac dissolved in alcohol ■ vt (**-lacked, -lack·ing; -lacked, -lack·ing**) 1 apply shellac to 2 defeat easily (slang)

shell com·pa·ny n a company that exists largely in name only and has no independent assets

Mary Shelley

Shel·ley /shéllee/, **Mary** (1797–1851) British writer

Shel·ley, Percy Bysshe (1792–1822) British poet

shell-fire /shél fìr/ n 1 fired artillery shells 2 the act or noise of firing artillery shells

shell-fish /shél fìsh/ (pl **same** or **-fish·es**) n an edible water animal with a shell

shell game n 1 a gambling game in which an object is hidden under one of three cups 2 a fraudulent scheme

shell shock n a psychiatric disorder caused by the stress of warfare (dated) —**shell-shocked** adj

shel·ter /shéltər/ n 1 a structure providing protection or covering 2 an establishment for people who need to leave a violent or otherwise dangerous situation 3 protection or cover 4 a place in which to live ■ vti provide with or find shelter

shel·tered /shéltərd/ adj 1 protected from the elements 2 not exposed to the rigors or unpleasantness of life

shelve[1] (**shelved, shelv·ing**) vt 1 put on a shelf 2 set aside

shelve[2] (**shelved, shelv·ing**) vi slope gradually

shelves plural of **shelf**

shelv·ing /shélving/ n 1 shelves 2 material used for making shelves

Shen·an·do·ah Val·ley /shènnən dóə-/ valley of the **Shenandoah River** in N Virginia. Length 140 mi./225 km.

Shen·yang /shèn yúng/ city in NE China. Pop. 5,120,000 (1995).

shepard, sheppard incorrect spelling of **shepherd**

Shep·ard /shéppərd/, **Alan, Jr.** (1923–98) US astronaut

Shep·ard /shéppərd/, **Sam** (b. 1943) US playwright and actor

shep·herd /shéppərd/ n somebody who tends sheep ■ v 1 vti tend sheep 2 vt guide a group of people somewhere

shep·herd's pie n a dish of ground meat topped with mashed potato

sher·bet /shúrbət/, **sher·bert** /-bərt/ n a frozen dessert made with fruit juice, milk, and egg white

ORIGIN **Sherbet** goes back to an Arabic verb meaning "drink," from which **syrup** also derives. The noun formed from this verb made its way through Persian and Turkish to enter English as **sherbet**, a cooling drink, in the early 17C. By a diversion through Italian and French the Arabic noun also made an appearance as **sorbet**.

sherd n = **shard**

Sher·i·dan /shérrid'n/, **Philip Henry** (1831–88) US Union general

Sher·i·dan, Richard Brinsley (1751–1816) Irish-born British playwright

sher·iff /shérrif/ n 1 the chief law enforcement officer in a US county 2 a Canadian court officer

ORIGIN A **sheriff** is etymologically a **shire reeve**, the representative of royal authority in an English shire (county).

Sher·lock Holmes /shùrlok hómz/ n somebody with exceptional powers of deduction and perception (humorous)

ORIGIN The original **Sherlock Holmes** was a detective in stories by Sir Arthur Conan Doyle (1859–1930).

Sher·man /shúrmən/, **Roger** (1721–93) American patriot

Sher·man, William T. (1820–91) US Union general

Sher·pa /shúrpə/ (pl **-pas** or **same**) n a member of a Himalayan people

Popperfoto

~~sherrif~~ incorrect spelling of **sheriff**

sher·ry /shérree/ n a fortified Spanish wine

Sher·wood For·est /shùr wood-/ ancient forest in central England

she's /sheez/ contr 1 she has 2 she is

Shet·land Is·lands /shétlənd-/ island group of N Scotland, comprising about 150 islands in the Atlantic Ocean. Cap. Lerwick. Pop. 23,232 (1996). —**Shet·land·er** n

Shet·land po·ny n a small sturdy pony with a long shaggy mane and tail

She·vat /shə vót/, **She·bat** /-bót, -vót/ n the 11th month of the year in the Jewish calendar

shh interj = sh

Shi·a /shée ə/, **Shi·'a**, **Shi·'ah** n one of the major branches of Islam

shi·at·su /shee áat soo/, **shi·at·zu** n a form of massage applying pressure to acupuncture points

shib·bo·leth /shíbbə lèth/ n 1 a catchword or slogan 2 an identifying pronunciation, word, or custom

> **ORIGIN Shibboleth** derives from a Hebrew word meaning "stream." According to the Bible, the people of Gilead, east of the Jordan River, used the word *Sibbōleṯ* as a password, for they knew their enemies the Ephraimites, from west of the Jordan, could not pronounce the initial /sh/ properly (Judges 12:5–6).

~~shiek~~ incorrect spelling of **sheik**

shield /sheeld/ n 1 a flat or convex piece of armor carried on the arm 2 something that provides protection or a defense 3 something resembling a shield in shape ■ vti protect with or act as a shield ◊ See note at **safeguard**

⚡ **shift** v 1 vti move to a different position 2 vti change or exchange something for something else 3 vti change gears 4 vi provide for your own needs 5 vi press the shift key on a computer keyboard ■ n 1 a change made at any of the periods into which a 24-hour working day is divided, or the people working during one 3 also **shift key** a keyboard key that makes letters capitals 4 a loose-fitting dress 5 a woman's undergarment resembling a shirt ◊ See note at **change**

shift·less /shíftləss/ adj lacking ambition —**shift·less·ness** n

shift·y /shíftee/ (-i·er, -i·est) adj untrustworthy or evasive —**shift·i·ly** adv —**shift·i·ness** n

Shi·ite /shée ìt/, **Shi·'ite** n a follower of the Shia branch of Islam —**Shi·ite** adj —**Shi·it·ic** /shee íttik/ adj

shi·ka·ri /shi káaree/ n S Asia a big-game hunter or guide

shill n 1 a pretended customer or gambler 2 a self-interested promoter ■ v 1 vi be a shill 2 vt promote as a shill

shil·ling /shílling/ n the main unit of currency in several East-African countries

shil·ly-shal·ly /shíllee shàllee/ (**shil·ly-shal·lied**, **shil·ly-shal·lies**) vi 1 hesitate or vacillate 2 waste time

Shi·loh /shílō/ site in SW Tennessee where a major battle of the Civil War was fought on April 6–7, 1862

shim·mer /shímmər/ vti 1 shine with a wavering light 2 be or make visible as a wavering image ■ n 1 a wavering light or glow 2 a wavering image or appearance —**shim·mer·y** adj

shim·my /shímmee/ n 1 a popular dance of the 1920s involving shaking of the body from the shoulders down 2 a quick movement of the body to the side ■ vi (-**mied**, -**mies**) 1 dance the shimmy 2 move quickly to the side

shin n 1 the front of the lower leg 2 also **shin·bone** the bone at the front of the lower leg 3 a cut of beef used for stew ■ vti (**shinned**, **shin·ning**) climb using the arms and legs

shin·dig /shín dìg/ n a noisy party (infml)

shine /shīn/ v (**shone** /shōn/, **shined**) 1 vi emit light 2 vi be bright 3 vt direct light somewhere 4 vi excel 5 vt polish ■ n 1 brightness from a light source 2 a bright surface 3 an act of polishing something

shin·er /shínər/ n a black eye (infml)

shin·gle¹ /shíng g'l/ n 1 a small flat roof or wall tile 2 a sign or nameplate ■ vt (-**gled**, -**gling**) 1 cover a roof or wall with shingles 2 cut hair to taper at the back —**shin·gler** n

shin·gle² /shíng g'l/ n 1 pebbles on a beach 2 a beach covered in shingle

shin·gles /shíng g'lz/ n a viral disease related to chickenpox causing inflammation and pain along a nerve path

shin·ny¹ /shínnee/ (-**nied**, -**nies**) vi climb quickly

shin·ny² /shínnee/, **shin·ney** n (pl -**nies**; pl -**neys**) 1 a North American game resembling field hockey 2 a stick used in shinny ■ vi (-**nied**, -**ny·ing**, -**nies**; -**neyed**, -**ney·ing**, -**neys**) play shinny

Shin·to /shín tò/ n a Japanese religion with numerous gods and spirits of the natural world —**Shin·to·ism** n —**Shin·to·ist** n, adj

shin·y /shínee/ (-i·er, -i·est) adj 1 bright and polished 2 worn smooth and glossy —**shin·i·ness** n

ship n a large boat designed to carry passengers or cargo ■ vt (**shipped**, **ship·ping**) 1 transport something in a ship or by a common carrier 2 send something or somebody somewhere 3 take in water over the sides of a ship or boat

-ship suffix 1 condition, state, or quality ○ companionship 2 skill, art, craft ○ musicianship 3 office, title, position, profession ○ governorship 4 a group of people collectively ○ *membership* **5** something showing a particular quality or condition ○ *township* **6** a person holding a particular title ○ *ladyship*

ship·board /shíp bàwrd/ *adj* occurring on board a ship

ship·build·er /shíp bìldər/ *n* a person or business that makes ships —**ship·build·ing** *n*

ship·load /shíp lòd/ *n* the amount carried in a ship

ship·mate /shíp màyt/ *n* a sailor or passenger on the same ship as another

ship·ment /shípmənt/ *n* **1** a quantity of goods shipped together **2** the act of shipping goods

ship·per /shíppər/ *n* a transporter of goods

ship·ping /shípping/ *n* **1** the act of transporting goods **2** ships generally

ship·shape /shíp shàyp/ *adj* in good order —**ship·shape** *adv*

ship·wreck /shíp rèk/ *n* **1** the sinking or destruction of a ship **2** a sunken ship ■ *vt* **1** involve somebody in a shipwreck **2** destroy a ship

ship·yard /shíp yàard/ *n* a place where ships are built

shire /shīr/ *n UK* a county in England or Wales

shirk *v* **1** *vt* avoid an obligation, task, or responsibility **2** *vi* avoid work or duty

shirt *n* **1** a garment for the upper body, usually with sleeves, a collar, and a front opening **2** a man's undergarment with sleeves ◊ **keep your shirt on** control your temper *(infml; usually a command)* ◊ **lose your shirt** lose everything you have

ORIGIN Shirt derives from the ancient Germanic root that gave us *short*, and also, through a Scandinavian language, *skirt*.

shirt·sleeve /shúrt slèev/ *adj* needing no jacket

shirt·tail /shúrt tàyl/ *n* a piece at the end of a newspaper article ■ *adj* **1** too small **2** young

shirt·waist /shúrt wàyst/ *n* a blouse that resembles a man's shirt

shish ke·bab /shísh-/ *n* a dish of grilled meat and vegetables on a skewer

Shi·va /sheéva/, **Si·va** /seéva/ *n* an important Hindu god, called the Destroyer

shiv·er[1] /shívvar/ *vi* tremble because of cold, fear, or illness ■ *n* a body tremor —**shiv·er·y** *adj*

shiv·er[2] /shívvar/ *n* a fragment ■ *vti* shatter into fragments

Sho·ah /shó ə, -àa/ *n* the Holocaust

shoal[1] /shōl/ *n* **1** a large school of fish **2** a large group of people

shoal[2] /shōl/ *n* **1** an area of shallow water **2** an underwater sandbank ■ *adj also* **shoal·y** /shólee/ shallow

shock[1] *n* **1** something surprising and up-

setting **2** the feelings of distress or numbness experienced after a shock **3** a state of physiological collapse **4** a forceful physical impact **5** an electric shock **6** a shock absorber ■ *v* **1** *vt* surprise and upset **2** *vti* offend or disgust, or be offended or disgusted —**shock·a·ble** *adj* —**shock·proof** *adj*

shock[2] *n* a group of sheaves of drying grain or corn

shock[3] *n* a mass of shaggy hair

shock ab·sorb·er *n* a device on a vehicle for absorbing shocks

shock·er /shókər/ *n (infml)* **1** something unpleasant **2** a shocking story, play, or movie

shock·ing /shóking/ *adj* **1** outrageous **2** distressing **3** very bad *(infml)* ■ *adj, adv* very bright in color —**shock·ing·ly** *adv* —**shock·ing·ness** *n*

shock jock *n* a provocative host of a radio program *(slang)*

Shock·ley /shóklee/, **William B.** (1910–89) US physicist

shock tac·tics *npl* methods that are likely to shock people, used to achieve a goal

shock ther·a·py, shock treat·ment *n* electric shock treatment for psychiatric disorders

shock troops *npl* soldiers trained to lead an assault

shock wave *n* **1** a wave of heat and air pressure produced by an explosion, earthquake, or movement of a supersonic body **2** a surprised reaction *(often pl)*

shod past participle, past tense of **shoe**

shod·dy /shóddee/ *adj* (-di·er, -di·est) **1** poorly made **2** of inferior material ■ *n (pl* -**dies**) something inferior —**shod·di·ly** *adv* —**shod·di·ness** *n*

shoe /shoo/ *n* **1** a stiff outer covering for the human foot **2** a horseshoe **3** a part of a machine that protects against wear **4** a device on an electric train that connects to the electrified rail ■ *vt* (**shod** or **shoed**) **1** fit a horse with horseshoes **2** supply a person with shoes ◊ **be in somebody's shoes** be in somebody else's position *(infml)*

shoe·box /shoo bòks/ *n* a box for a pair of shoes

shoe·horn /shoo hàwrn/ *n* a device to help a person's heel into a shoe ■ *vt* squeeze somebody or something into a space

shoe·lace /shoo làyss/ *n* a cord for fastening a shoe

shoe·mak·er /shoo màykər/ *n* somebody who makes or repairs shoes

shoe·shine /shoo shìn/ *n* an instance of polishing shoes

shoe·string /shoo string/ *adj* **1** consisting of little money **2** long and narrow ◊ **on a shoestring** using very little money

shoe·tree /shoo trèe/ *n* a device inserted into a boot or shoe to keep it in shape

sho·far /shō fàar/ (*pl* **-fars** *or* **-froth** /shō frõt/) *n* a ram's horn blown in a synagogue on Rosh Hashanah and Yom Kippur

sho·gun /shōgən, shō gùn/ *n* a military commander in feudal Japan —**sho·gun·al** *adj*

~~sholder~~ incorrect spelling of **shoulder**

shone past tense, past participle of **shine**

shoo *interj* used to get an animal to leave ■ *vt* (**shooed, shoo·ing, shoos**) wave an animal away

shoo-in *n* a certainty to win or succeed

shook past tense of **shake**

shoot /shoot/ *v* (**shot**) 1 *vti* fire a weapon or projectile 2 *vt* hit somebody or something with a bullet 3 *vti* move or cause to move fast 4 *vt* travel over a stretch of water fast 5 *vti* record something on film 6 *vti* kick or throw a ball in an attempt to get a point 7 *vt* move a bolt into place 8 *vi* begin to grow or germinate 9 *vt* play a cue game ■ *n* a newly grown aerial part of a plant, e.g., a leaf bud or branch ◊ See note at **chute**

□ **shoot up** *v* 1 *vi* increase suddenly 2 *vi* get taller 3 *vti* inject an illegal drug *(slang)*

shoot·er /shootər/ *n* somebody or something that shoots

shoot·ing gal·ler·y *n* a place to practice shooting

shoot·ing star *n* a meteor

shoot·ing stick *n* a walking stick with a handle that folds out to make a seat

shoot-out /shoot owt/ *n* a decisive fight with guns

shop *n* 1 a retail business 2 a workshop 3 a schoolroom for woodwork ■ *v* (**shopped, shop·ping**) 1 *vi* visit stores 2 *vt* visit a particular store —**shop·per** *n* ◊ **talk shop** talk about your work

shop·keep·er /shóp keepər/ *n* a retail storekeeper

shop·lift /shóp lìft/ *vti* steal goods from a store —**shop·lift·er** *n* —**shop·lift·ing** *n*

shop·ping /shópping/ *n* the activity of going to stores

⚡ **shop·ping a·gent** *n* a computer program used to browse websites for products and services

shop·ping bag *n* a strong bag with handles in which to carry purchases

shop·ping cart *n* a wheeled cart in which to put purchases

shop·ping list *n* 1 a list of items to shop for 2 a list of things wanted

shop·ping mall *n* a large shopping center

shop stew·ard *n* a union official who represents workers in talks with management

shop-worn /shóp wàwrn/ *adj* 1 faded or otherwise spoiled from being on display in a store 2 describes trite or stale ideas

shore[1] /shawr, shōr/ *n* the strip of land at the edge of water

shore[2] /shawr, shōr/ *vt* (**shored, shor·ing**) 1 prop up a structure 2 help to stop something from failing ■ *n* a prop to support something

shore leave *n* 1 permission for a sailor to go ashore 2 the time a sailor spends ashore

shore·line /sháwr lìn, shōr-/ *n* the line where water meets land

shorn /shawrn, shōrn/ past participle of **shear** ■ *adj* 1 having short hair 2 deprived of something

short *adj* 1 not long or tall 2 lasting briefly 3 concise 4 having less than needed 5 recalling only recent events ○ *a short memory* 6 curtly discourteous 7 full of fat and so flaky ○ *short pastry* ■ *adv* 1 in an abrupt way 2 before reaching a target ■ *n* 1 a movie of less than full length 2 a short circuit ■ **shorts** *npl* 1 short pants above the knee 2 men's underpants ■ *vti* shortcircuit —**short·ness** *n* ◊ **short of** 1 not having something, or not having enough of something 2 less than 3 without actually doing something

short·age /sháwrtij/ *n* a lack of something needed or wanted ◊ See note at **lack**

short·bread /sháwrt brèd/ *n* a rich buttery cookie

short·cake /sháwrt kàyk/ *n* 1 a dessert consisting of a sponge-cake base with fruit and cream 2 a sponge cake used as a base for shortcake

short-change /shàwrt cháynj/ (**-changed, -chang·ing**) *vt* 1 give a customer too little change 2 treat somebody unfairly

short-cir·cuit *vti* have or cause a failure in an electrical circuit —**short cir·cuit** *n*

short·com·ing /sháwrt kùmming/ *n* a defect or deficiency *(often pl)*

short·cut /sháwrt kùt/ *n* 1 a shorter route 2 a more direct method that saves time or trouble —**short·cut** *vti*

short·en /sháwrt'n/ *v* 1 *vti* become or make something shorter 2 *vti* reduce the odds on a bet, or be reduced 3 *vt* reduce the area of a sail

short·en·ing /sháwrt'ning/ *n* fat added to pastry dough

short·fall /sháwrt fàwl/ *n* 1 an amount that is lacking 2 a failure to meet a goal

short·hand /sháwrt hànd/ *n* 1 a quick way of writing by using symbols 2 a shorter way of saying something

short·hand·ed *adj* short of workers

short-haul *adj* for short distances

short list *n* a final list from which to make a selection

short-lived /sháwrt lívd, -lìvd/ *adj* lasting only a short time ◊ See note at **temporary**

short·ly /sháwrtlee/ *adv* 1 in a short time 2 curtly

short-range *adj* 1 operating over a short distance 2 concerning the near future

short shrift n unsympathetic treatment

short-sight-ed adj failing to consider potential difficulties in the long term —**short-sight-ed-ly** adv —**short-sight-ed-ness** n

short-staffed adj with fewer workers than are needed

short-stop /sháwrt stòp/ n 1 in baseball, an infielder position 2 a player at shortstop

short sto-ry n a short work of prose fiction

short-tem-pered adj quick to become angry

short-term adj 1 not lasting long 2 payable or maturing relatively soon

short ton n MEASURE = **ton** 1

short wave n a radio wave that is shorter than 100 meters

Sho-sho-ne /shō shónee/ (pl **-nes** or same), **Sho-sho-ni** (pl **-nis** or same) n 1 a member of a Native North American people who live mainly in Nevada, Idaho, Wyoming, and Utah 2 the language of the Shoshone people —**Sho-sho-ne** adj —**Sho-sho-ne-an** n, adj

Shos-ta-ko-vich /shòstə kóvich/, **Dmitri** (1906–75) Russian composer

shot[1] n 1 a single occasion of shooting a gun 2 somebody who shoots a gun with a particular level of skill 3 a bullet or cannonball 4 small metal pellets 5 in sports, an attempt to score 6 in sports, an act of hitting a ball 7 the shot put 8 a particular view from a movie camera 9 a continuous uninterrupted film sequence 10 an attempt 11 a guess (infml) 12 a hypodermic injection (infml) 13 a small amount of alcohol (infml) ◊ **deliver** or **fire a shot across somebody's bows** warn somebody of what might happen ◊ **like a shot** very eagerly and quickly

shot[2] past tense, past participle of **shoot** ■ adj 1 two-tone in color 2 streaked with a different color 3 filled with a particular quality

shot-gun /shót gùn/ n a gun that shoots a load of small pellets

shot-gun wed-ding, shot-gun mar-riage n a marriage arranged hastily owing to pregnancy

shot put n 1 an athletics competition in which a heavy ball is thrown from the shoulder 2 the ball used in the shot put —**shot-put-ter** n

should /shŏŏd, shəd/ modal v 1 expresses desirability or rightness o You should work less. 2 expresses likelihood or probability o I should hear next week. 3 expresses conditions or consequences o If anything should happen, let me know. 4 would o I should love to meet her. 5 reports a past viewpoint about the future o He was keen that I should meet his publisher friend. ◊ See note at **would**

shoul-der /shóldər/ n 1 either part of a human body where an arm attaches to the trunk 2 in vertebrate animals, a joint that attaches a forelimb to the trunk 3 meat from an animal's shoulder 4 something that is sloped like a shoulder 5 a strip of land beside a road ■ **shoul-ders** npl 1 the upper area of the back 2 the capacity to handle responsibility ■ vt 1 carry or place something on your shoulders 2 accept responsibility ◊ **rub shoulders with** associate with ◊ **shoulder to shoulder** side by side

shoul-der bag n a bag carried by means of a shoulder strap

shoul-der blade n a flat triangular bone in the back of the shoulder

shoul-der strap n a strap that goes over a shoulder to carry a bag or support clothing

should-n't /shŏŏd'nt/ contr should not

shout vti call out something loudly ■ n a loud cry —**shout-er** n ◊ **nothing to shout about** not very good (infml)

shove /shuv/ (**shoved, shov-ing**) v 1 vt move something with force 2 vti push somebody or something roughly —**shove** n
□ **shove off** vi leave (infml)

shov-el /shúv'l/ n 1 a scooping tool with a long or short handle 2 a machine for digging earth ■ v 1 vti dig with a shovel for something 2 vt put or throw large amounts of something carelessly —**shov-el-ful** n

show /shō/ v (**shown** /shōn/) 1 vt make or be visible 2 vti exhibit or display publicly, or be exhibited or displayed 3 vt guide somewhere 4 vt point out 5 vt demonstrate as a quality or attitude 6 vt establish, demonstrate, or present as an argument or information 7 vi arrive or put in an appearance (infml) 8 vi come in third or better in a horserace ■ n 1 an expression or demonstration of something 2 a public entertainment, performance, or exhibition 3 an appearance or outward display 4 an impressive display 5 a third place finish —**show-ing** n ◊ **get the** or **this show on the road** begin an activity or start an event (infml) ◊ **steal the show** attract the most attention
□ **show off** v 1 vi try to impress others 2 vt present for approval

show-and-tell n a classroom activity in which each child tells about an object

show biz n show business (infml)

show-boat /shō bòt/ n a riverboat theater ■ vi show off for attention (infml)

show busi-ness n the entertainment industry

show-case /shō kàyss/ n 1 a glass case for displaying objects 2 the most favorable setting for something ■ vt (**-cased, -cas-ing**) present to advantage

show-down /shó dòwn/ n a confrontation

show-er /shów ər/ n 1 a wash under a spray of water 2 a place or the equipment for a shower 3 a brief period of rain, snow, sleet, or hail 4 a sudden fall of something from the sky o a meteor shower 5 a large amount

6 *US, Can, ANZ* a party at which gifts are given to somebody ■ *v* **1** *vi* wash under a shower **2** *vti* fall or make things fall like a spray —**show·er·y** *adj*

show·er gel *n* gel soap for washing in a shower

show·girl /shṓ gùrl/ *n* a young woman performing in a stage chorus

show jump·ing *n* a competition in which people on horseback jump over obstacles —**show·jump** *vi* —**show·jump·er** *n*

show·man /shṓmən/ (*pl* **-men** /-mən/) *n* a gifted entertainer —**show·man·ship** *n*

shown past participle of **show**

show-off *n* somebody who tries to impress others (*infml*)

show of hands *n* a vote in which opinions are expressed by raised hands

show·piece /shṓ pèess/ *n* an excellent example

show·place /shṓ plàyss/ *n* **1** a place visited for its beauty or historical importance **2** something that is exceptionally beautiful

show·room /shṓ ròòm, -ròòm/ *n* a room where retail products are displayed

show·stop·per /shṓ stòppər/ *n* **1** a performance that receives prolonged applause from an audience **2** something so striking that it stops action

show tri·al *n* a trial held for political reasons

show·y /shṓ ee/ (**-i·er**, **-i·est**) *adj* **1** making an impressive display **2** ostentatious —**show·i·ly** *adv* —**show·i·ness** *n*

shrank past participle of **shrink**

shrap·nel /shrápnəl/ *n* **1** fragments from an explosive device **2** a shell that scatters metal fragments

> **ORIGIN Shrapnel** is named for General Henry Shrapnel (1761–1842), a British artillery officer who invented an exploding shell.

shred *n* **1** a long torn strip **2** a small part ■ *vt* (**shred·ded**, **shred·ding**) **1** tear something into shreds **2** put something through a shredder

shred·der /shréddər/ *n* a machine for destroying documents or cutting wood into chips

Shreve·port /shreév pàwrt/ city in NW Louisiana. Pop. 188,319 (1998).

shrew *n* **1** a small insect-eating nocturnal mammal with a pointed nose **2** an offensive term for a woman regarded as quarrelsome or ill-tempered

shrewd *adj* good at judging people or situations —**shrewd·ly** *adv* —**shrewd·ness** *n*

> **ORIGIN Shrewd** is formed from *shrew*, in the obsolete uses "wicked person" and as a verb meaning *curse*. The animal was formerly believed to have a poisonous bite and was considered by the superstitious to be evil. The original meaning of **shrewd** was "evil, vile."

The modern sense "clever, good at judging people" did not develop until the early 16C.

shrew·ish /shróo ish/ *adj* quarrelsome or ill-tempered —**shrew·ish·ly** *adv* —**shrew·ish·ness** *n*

shriek /shreek/ *v* **1** *vi* make a loud shrill sound **2** *vt* say something in a loud shrill voice —**shriek** *n*

shrift *n* (*archaic*) **1** confession to a priest **2** absolution

shrill *adj* **1** penetratingly high-pitched **2** tending to talk in a shrill voice ■ *v* **1** *vi* make a shrill sound (*literary*) **2** *vt* say something in a piercing voice —**shrill·ness** *n* —**shril·ly** *adv*

shrimp *n* (*pl* same *or* **shrimps**) **1** a small ocean crustacean with ten legs **2** something undersize (*infml*) ■ *vi* fish for shrimp —**shrimp·er** *n*

shrine /shrīn/ *n* **1** a holy place of worship **2** a container for holy relics **3** the tomb of a holy person **4** an alcove in a church for a religious icon

shrink /shringk/ *v* (**shrank** /shrangk/ *or* **shrunk** /shrungk/, **shrunk** *or* **shrunk·en** /shrúngkən/) **1** *vti* make or become smaller or less **2** *vi* move away in disgust or fear ■ *n* a psychiatrist (*slang; sometimes offensive*) —**shrink·a·ble** *adj* ◊ See note at **recoil**

shrink·age /shríngkij/ *n* **1** the amount lost when something shrinks **2** the act of shrinking

shrink·ing vi·o·let *n* a meek person (*infml*)

shrive /shrīv/ (**shrove** /shrōv/ *or* **shrived**, **shriv·en** /shrív'n/ *or* **shrived**, **shriv·ing**) *vt* **1** absolve somebody of sins **2** impose penance

shriv·el /shrív'l/ *vti* **1** make or become shrunken and wrinkled **2** weaken

shroud /shrowd/ *n* **1** a burial cloth **2** a covering, especially one designed for protection **3** a piece of wire that supports a mast ■ *vt* **1** wrap a corpse in a shroud **2** cover or conceal something

Shrove Tues·day /shrōv-/ *n* the day of the Christian calendar that comes before Ash Wednesday

> **ORIGIN Shrove** is an irregular use of the past tense of *shrive*, a verb used in the Christian Church and meaning "hear the confession of and give absolution to." *Shrive* itself derives from Latin *scribere* "write."

shrub¹ *n* a woody plant with several stems growing from the base

shrub² *n* an alcoholic fruit juice drink

shrub·ber·y /shrúbbəree/ (*pl* **-ies**) *n* **1** a part of a garden with shrubs **2** shrubs collectively

shrub·by /shrúbbee/ (**-bi·er**, **-bi·est**) *adj* **1** with shrubs **2** like a shrub

shrug /shrug/ (**shrugged**, **shrug·ging**) *vti* raise and drop your shoulders briefly to indicate lack of interest or knowledge —**shrug** *n*

□ **shrug off** *vt* dismiss as unimportant

shrunk past tense, past participle of **shrink**

shrunk·en past participle of **shrink**

shuck /shŭk/ *n* 1 the husk or shell of something 2 an oyster or clam shell ■ *vt* 1 take something from a husk 2 get rid of *(infml)* —**shuck·er** *n*

shucks *interj* expresses disappointment *(infml)*

shud·der /shŭddər/ *vi* 1 shiver violently 2 vibrate rapidly —**shud·der** *n*

shuf·fle /shŭff'l/ (**-fled, -fling**) *v* 1 *vi* walk or dance without lifting your feet 2 *vt* change where things are located 3 *vt* mix things up 4 *vti* rearrange the order of playing cards in a random way —**shuf·fle** *n* —**shuf·fler** *n*

shuf·fle·board /shŭff'l bàwrd/ *n* 1 a game of guiding disks into numbered scoring areas 2 a surface for shuffleboard

shun (**shunned, shun·ning**) *vt* deliberately avoid —**shun·ner** *n*

shunt *v* 1 *vt* move somebody or something elsewhere 2 *vti* change or cause a train to change tracks 3 *vt* get rid of a responsibility 4 *vt* divert an electric current ■ *n* a device for diverting electric current

shush /shŏŏsh, shush/ *interj* be quiet ■ *vt* silence *(infml)*

shut *v* (**shut, shut·ting**) 1 *vti* close an opening, or be closed 2 *vt* stop access to or exit from a place 3 *vt* close something by bringing its covering parts together 4 *vti* stop operations in a place ■ *adj* secured

□ **shut in** *vt* confine or enclose

□ **shut off** *v* 1 *vti* stop operating, or cause to stop operating 2 *vt* cut off the flow of something 3 *vt* block off

□ **shut out** *vt* 1 stop from scoring 2 keep from scoring

□ **shut up** *v* 1 *vi* stop talking *(infml)* 2 *vt* confine somebody somewhere

shut·down /shŭt dòwn/ *n* the permanent closing of a business

shut·eye /shŭt ì/ *n* sleep *(infml)*

shut·in *n* somebody who is rarely or never able to leave home, especially because of illness or lack of physical mobility *(infml)*

shut·off /shŭt àwf/ *n* 1 a valve or other device that shuts something off 2 an interruption or temporary stoppage

shut·out /shŭt òwt/ *n* 1 an occasion when management prevents workers from entering the workplace 2 a game in which one side scores no points

shut·ter /shŭttər/ *n* 1 a hinged door or window cover 2 the part of a camera that opens the lens aperture to let light in ■ *vt* 1 close a door or window using shutters 2 fit something with shutters

shut·tle /shŭtt'l/ *n* 1 the part of a loom that holds the weft and passes it between the warp threads 2 a spindle or bobbin for holding thread 3 a passenger vehicle that makes frequent trips between places 4 a space shuttle 5 the act of going back and forth ■ *vti* (**-tled, -tling**) travel or take something frequently between two places

shut·tle·cock /shŭtt'l kòk/ *n* in badminton, a cone-shaped object of feathers or plastic in a rounded base that is hit over the net

shut·tle di·plo·ma·cy *n* diplomatic negotiations in which the mediator travels back and forth between countries

shy¹ *adj* (**shi·er, shi·est**) 1 reserved and uncomfortable in the company of others 2 cautious 3 reluctant 4 short of a desired amount ■ *vi* (**shied, shies**) 1 move suddenly in fright 2 behave evasively ■ *n* (*pl* **shies**) a sudden move —**shy·ly** *adv* —**shy·ness** *n*

shy² (**shied, shies**) *vti* throw something quickly —**shy** *n*

shy·ster /shístər/ *n* a person regarded as unscrupulous *(slang insult)*

ORIGIN Shyster first appeared in the United States in the 1840s, but its precise origin is not certain. It may be from German *Scheisser*, an offensive term of abuse.

Si *symbol* silicon

SI *abbr* International System of Units. Full form **Système international (d'unités)**

Si·am /sī ám/ former name for **Thailand** —**Si·a·mese** /sì ə meèz/ *n, adj*

Si·a·mese cat /sì ə meez-/ *n* a short-haired domestic cat with a cream-colored body and dark ears, paws, face, and tail

Si·a·mese twins *npl* twins born physically joined together

ORIGIN The two most famous such twins, Chang and Eng (1811–74), were born in Siam (modern Thailand).

Si·be·li·us /sə báylee əss, -báylyəss/, **Jean** (1865–1957) Finnish composer

Si·be·ri·a /sī beèree ə/ vast region of E Russia, extending from the Ural Mountains to the Pacific Ocean —**Si·be·ri·an** *n, adj*

sib·i·lant /síbbilənt/ *adj* pronounced with a hissing sound ■ *n* a sibilant consonant —**sib·i·lance** *n*

sib·ling /síbbling/ *n* a brother or sister

sib·yl /síbb'l/ *n* 1 in ancient Greece or Rome, a woman prophet 2 a woman fortune teller —**si·byl·lic** /sī bíllik/ *adj*

sic¹ /sik/ *adv* thus or so

sic² /sik/ (**sicced** *or* **sicked, sic·cing** *or* **sick·ing**), **sick** *vt* 1 attack or chase somebody 2 incite a person or animal to attack or chase somebody

Si·chuan /si chwaán/, **Sze·chwan** /se-/ province of S China. Cap. Chengdu. Pop. 114,300,000 (1997).

Si·ci·ly /síssəlee/ island of S Italy, the largest in the Mediterranean Sea. Pop. 5,082,697 (1995). —**Si·cil·ian** /si síllee ən/ *n, adj*

sick *adj* **1** affected by an illness **2** of or for illness **3** likely to vomit **4** an offensive term meaning thought to have a psychiatric disorder **5** in bad taste (*infml*) **6** distraught **7** very bored ○ *I'm sick of listening to you.* **8** yearning **9** disgusted or repelled **10** impaired ○ *a sick economy* ■ *npl* sick people

sick-bay /sík bày/ *n* **1** a ship's hospital **2** a treatment facility in a large building

sick-bed /sík bèd/ *n* a sick person's bed

sick build-ing syn-drome *n* a set of symptoms associated with working in buildings that have poor ventilation or contain toxic building materials

sick-en /síkən/ *vti* **1** make or become nauseated **2** make or feel disgusted —**sick-en-ing** *adj* —**sick-en-ing-ly** *adv*

sick-le /sík'l/ *n* a tool with a curved blade and a handle, used for cutting tall grass or grain crops

sick leave *n* absence from work due to illness

sick-le-cell a-ne-mi-a *n* a hereditary form of anemia

sick-ly /síklee/ (-li-er, -li-est) *adj* **1** often ill ○ *a sickly child* **2** produced by illness **3** causing illness or nausea **4** feeble —**sick-li-ness** *n*

sick-ness /síknəss/ *n* **1** an illness **2** nausea

sick pay *n* the salary given to an employee who is absent from work because of illness

sick-room /sík ròòm, -ròòm/ *n* a room to which a sick person is confined

side *n* **1** a line forming part of the edge of something **2** a surface of something, especially a vertical surface **3** either of the surfaces of something flat **4** the left or right part of something **5** a place or direction relative to a central point or to the observer ○ *the east side of the city* **6** either of the areas separated by a barrier ○ *the south side of the river* **7** an area at the edge of something ○ *the side of the road* **8** either half of the body, especially the area from shoulder to hip **9** the place next to somebody or something ○ *standing at my side* **10** a person or group opposing another person or group **11** an opinion in a dispute **12** an aspect or view of an issue or event ○ *saw the funny side* **13** a line of descent ○ *on his father's side* ■ *adj* **1** at or on a side **2** from the side **3** incidental or of subsidiary importance ○ *a side issue* ■ *vi* (**sid-ed, sid-ing**) align with or against one of the people or groups in a dispute ◇ **on the side 1** illegally or secretly **2** in addition to a main job or activity ◇ **side by side** close beside each other ◇ **take sides** support one person or group against another ◇ **the other side of the coin** the contrasting or contrary aspect of something

side-bar /síd bàar/ *n* **1** a boxed supplementary news story printed alongside a featured story **2** a judge-lawyer discussion

side-board /síd bàwrd/ *n* a piece of dining room furniture for storing tableware and linen

side-burns /síd bùrnz/ *npl* hair in front of the ears

ORIGIN Sideburns were originally *burnsides*, and named for General Ambrose Burnside, who wore them.

---

side-car /síd kàar/ *n* a passenger vehicle attached to a motorcycle

side dish *n* food served with a main dish

side ef-fect *n* an undesirable secondary effect, especially of a drug or medical treatment

side-kick /síd kìk/ *n* a companion (*infml*)

side-light /síd lìt/ *n* a piece of incidental information

side-line /síd lìn/ *n* **1** either of two lines marking the side boundaries of a sports field **2** a supplementary source of income ■ **side-lines 1** the area of a sports field outside its boundaries **2** the position of being uninvolved in something ■ *vt* (**-lined, -lin-ing**) **1** keep a player out of a game **2** exclude somebody from participation

side-long /síd làwng/ *adj* directed to the side —**side-long** *adv*

side or-der *n* a portion of food ordered to accompany a main dish

si-de-re-al /sī déeree əl/ *adj* of the stars

side-sad-dle /síd sàdd'l/ *n* a saddle designed for women in long skirts ■ *adv* with both legs on the same side of the horse

side-show /síd shò/ *n* a minor attraction at a circus or fair

side split *n* *Can* a split-level house

side-split-ting /síd splìtting/ *adj* hilarious

side-step /síd stèp/ *vti* (**-stepped, -step-ping**) **1** step aside to avoid somebody or something **2** avoid saying or discussing something ■ *n* a sideways movement

side street *n* a small street off a main street

side-swipe /síd swìp/ *n* a glancing blow ■ *vt* (**-swiped, -swip-ing**) strike with a glancing blow

side-track /síd tràk/ *v* **1** *vt* divert from the original subject or activity **2** *vti* shunt a train ■ *n* a railroad siding

side-walk /síd wàwk/ *n* a paved path for pedestrians

side-ward /sídwərd/ *adj* toward or at one side ■ *adv* *also* **side-wards** toward one side

side-ways /síd wàyz/, **side-wise** /-wìz/ *adj, adv* **1** to or toward one side **2** from the side **3** with the side facing the front

sid-ing /síding/ *n* a short railroad track leading off the main track

si-dle /síd'l/ (**-dled, -dling**) *v* **1** *vi* edge along furtively **2** *vti* move sideways —**si-dle** *n*

Si·don /síd'n/ city in SW Lebanon. Pop. 38,000 (1998).

SIDS *abbr* sudden infant death syndrome

siege /seej/ *n* 1 a military or police operation in which a place is surrounded until the people inside surrender 2 a prolonged effort or period ■ *vt* (**sieged, sieg·ing**) subject a place to a siege

Si·en·a /see énna/ capital of Siena Province, Tuscany Region, in north central Italy. Pop. 54,769 (1997). —**Si·e·nese** /seè ə néez/ *n, adj*

~~sience~~ incorrect spelling of **science**

~~siene~~ incorrect spelling of **scene**

si·en·na /see énna/ *n* artists' paint made with iron-rich soil —**si·en·na** *adj*

ORIGIN Sienna is named for the city of Siena in Italy, where the pigment was originally produced.

---

si·er·ra /see érrə/ *n* 1 a range of mountains with jagged peaks 2 **Si·er·ra** a communications code word for the letter "S" —**si·er·ran** *adj*

Si·er·ra Le·one /see èrrə lee ón/ country in West Africa. Cap. Freetown. Pop. 5,426,618 (2001). —**Si·er·ra Le·on·e·an** /-lee ónee ən/ *n, adj*

Si·er·ra Ma·dre /-maádray/ mountain system in Mexico, extending from the US border in the north to the border with Guatemala in the south. Length 680 mi./1,100 km. Highest peak Orizaba, 18,406 ft./5,610 m.

Si·er·ra Ne·va·da /-nə vaádə/ mountain range in E California. Highest peak Mt. Whitney, 14,491 ft./4,417 m.

si·es·ta /see éstə/ *n* an early afternoon rest or nap

ORIGIN Siesta came through Spanish from Latin *sexta* "6th" in *sexta hora* "6th hour (of the day)."

---

sieve /siv/ *n* a meshed utensil used for straining or sifting ■ *vt* (**sieved, siev·ing**) put something through a sieve

~~sieze~~ incorrect spelling of **seize**

sift *v* 1 *vti* pass a substance through a sieve to separate out the larger particles 2 *vt* separate out with a sieve or by selection 3 *vti* sort or examine minutely —**sift·er** *n*

sigh /sī/ *vi* 1 breathe deeply and audibly in relief or tiredness 2 make a sound like somebody sighing o *The wind sighed in the trees.* 3 yearn ■ *n* the act or sound of sighing

sight /sīt/ *n* 1 the ability to see 2 the perception of something or somebody with the eyes 3 the range or field of vision 4 something seen 5 something worth seeing *(often pl)* 6 somebody or something unpleasant to look at *(infml)* 7 an alignment device on a gun or surveying instrument ■ *v* 1 *vt* see or notice 2 *vti* observe or measure something using an optical device 3 *vti* aim at something with a gun

—**sight·ed** *adj* —**sight·ed·ness** *n* ◊ **at or on sight** as soon as something or somebody is seen ◊ **out of sight** no longer able to be seen ◊ **set or have your sights on something** decide to try to get something ◊ **sight unseen** without seeing or inspecting first ◊ See note at **cite**

sight draft *n* a bill payable on demand

sight·ing /sī́ting/ *n* an occasion of seeing something

sight·less /sī́tləss/ *adj* unable to see —**sight·less·ness** *n*

sight-read /sī́t rèed/ *vti* read or perform something such as music without practicing or seeing it beforehand —**sight-read·er** *n*

sight·see·ing /sī́t sèe ing/ *n* the visiting of places of interest

sig·int /sí́ggint/, **SIGINT** *n* intelligence data acquired electronically. Full form **signals intelligence**

sig·ma /sígmə/ *n* the 18th letter of the Greek alphabet

sign /sīn/ *n* 1 an indication of the existence or presence of something o *a sign of wealth* o *a sign of illness* 2 an act or gesture that conveys an idea or information 3 a public notice bearing advertising, directions, instructions, or a warning 4 an omen 5 one of the 12 divisions of the zodiac, each represented by a symbol 6 a symbol used in math, logic, or music ■ *vti* 1 write your name in a characteristic way on something 2 approve a document by signing it 3 employ or become employed by a signed agreement 4 communicate in sign language —**sign·er** *n*

SPELLCHECK Do not confuse the spelling of **sign** and **sine** ("a trigonometric function"), which sound similar.

☐ **sign away** *vt* give up rights or property with a signed document

☐ **sign off** *v* 1 *vi* end a form of communication 2 *vt* approve something *(infml)*

☐ **sign over** *vt* transfer ownership of something with a signed document

☐ **sign up** *vti* enlist for military service

sig·nal /sígn'l/ *n* 1 an action, gesture, or sign used as a means of communication 2 a piece of information communicated by a signal 3 a piece of information transmitted by electrical current or electromagnetic wave ■ *adj* notable o *a signal accomplishment* ■ *v* 1 *vti* communicate by sending a signal 2 *vt* indicate o *The event signaled the end of the conflict.* —**sig·nal·er** *n* —**sig·nal·ly** *adv*

sig·nal·man /sígnəlmən/ (*pl* **-men** /-mən/) *n* 1 somebody in the military who sends and receives signals 2 a railroad employee in charge of operating signals

sig·na·to·ry /sígnə tàwree/ *n* (*pl* **-ries**) a party to a treaty or contract ■ *adj* bound by a treaty or contract

sig·na·ture /sígnəchər, sígnə chöor/ *n* **1** somebody's signed name **2** a distinctive identifying characteristic **3** a key signature

⚡ **sig·na·ture file** *n* a text file containing the user's name and address serving as a signature at the end of an e-mail

sign·board /sín bàwrd/ *n* a board bearing a notice or advertisement

sig·net /sígnət/ *n* **1** a small seal, especially one engraved on a ring **2** a seal for stamping official documents

sig·net ring *n* a finger ring with an engraved seal

sig·nif·i·cance /sig níffikənss/ *n* **1** importance or value **2** implied or intended meaning

sig·nif·i·cant /sig níffikənt/ *adj* **1** having or expressing a meaning **2** having a hidden or implied meaning **3** momentous and influential **4** substantial —**sig·nif·i·cant·ly** *adv*

sig·nif·i·cant oth·er *n* somebody's spouse or long-term sexual partner

sig·ni·fi·ca·tion /sígnəfi káysh'n/ *n* **1** the meaning of something **2** the act of signifying

~~significant~~ incorrect spelling of **significant**

sig·ni·fy /sígni fì/ (**-fied, -fies**) *v* **1** *vt* mean **2** *vt* be a sign of **3** *vi* be important

sign·ing /síning/, **sign lan·guage** *n* communication by gestures, especially a system used by or to people who are hearing-impaired

sign·ing bo·nus *n* an extra amount of money paid for signing a contract

sign·off *n* the end of a transmission period

sign·post /sín pòst/ *n* **1** a pole with a sign on it giving directions or information **2** something that gives a clue or indication

Si·ha·nouk /sée ənòök/, **Norodom** (*b.* 1922) king of Cambodia (1993–)

Sikh /seek/ *n* a member of a monotheistic religion founded in N India in the 16C —**Sikh** *adj* —**Sikh·ism** *n*

Sik·kim /síkim/ state in NE India. Cap. Gangtok. Pop. 444,000 (1994). —**Sik·kim·ese** /síki méez, -méess/ *n, adj*

Si·kor·sky /si káwrskee/, **Igor** (1889–1972) Russian-born US aeronautical engineer and corporate executive

si·lage /sílij/ *n* animal fodder consisting of partly fermented green plant material

si·lence /sílənss/ *n* **1** the absence or lack of noise **2** a refusal, failure, or inability to speak ■ *vt* (**-lenced, -lenc·ing**) **1** stop from speaking or making a noise **2** suppress the expression of ◇ *silence criticism*

si·lenc·er /sílənssər/ *n* a device for muffling the noise of a gun

si·lent /sílənt/ *adj* **1** without noise or sound **2** not speaking **3** inclined to say little **4** unspoken **5** unable or forbidden to speak

6 describes a letter that is not pronounced —**si·lent·ly** *adv* —**si·lent·ness** *n*

SYNONYMS silent, quiet, reticent, taciturn, uncommunicative CORE MEANING: not speaking or not saying much

si·lent ma·jor·i·ty *n* the greater part of a population who do not express their opinions

si·lent part·ner *n* a capital investor in a business who takes no part in its management

Si·le·sia /sī léeshə/ historic region in east central Europe, lying mostly within present-day SW Poland —**Si·le·sian** *n, adj*

sil·hou·ette /sílloo ét/ *n* **1** a picture of somebody or something as a black shape against a lighter background **2** something dark against a light background ■ *vt* (**-et·ted, -et·ting**) cause to appear as a silhouette

ORIGIN The **silhouette** was named in French for the author and politician Etienne de Silhouette (1709–67). As French finance minister in the late 1750s, he gained a reputation for stinginess, and **silhouette** came to be used for anything skimped. One account of the application of the word to a simple picture showing a dark shape against a light background is that it carries on this notion of "simplicity" or "lack of finish," but an alternative theory is that Silhouette himself was in the habit of making such pictures.

sil·i·ca /sílikə/ *n* a naturally occurring colorless transparent solid with a high melting point. Use: manufacture of glass, abrasives, concrete.

sil·i·cate /sílli kàyt, -kət/ *n* a common rock-forming mineral containing silicon and oxygen

sil·i·con /sílikən, -kon/ *n* (*symbol* Si) a brittle nonmetallic chemical element. Use: alloys, semiconductors, building materials.

sil·i·con chip *n* a wafer of silicon on which an integrated circuit is laid out

sil·i·cone /sílli kòn/ *n* a silicon-based synthetic substance in the form of a grease, oil, or plastic. Use: lubricants, insulators, water-repellents, adhesives, coatings, prosthetics.

Sil·i·con Val·ley /síllikən-, -kon-/ region in W California, an important center for the electronics and computer industries

sil·i·co·sis /sílli kóssiss/ *n* a chronic lung disease caused by inhalation of silica dust

silk *n* **1** the fine fiber secreted by silkworms to make their cocoons. Use: threads, fabrics. **2** silk thread or fabric **3** the fine fiber secreted by spiders to make their webs

silk·en /sílkən/ *adj* **1** made of silk **2** like silk in texture or appearance

silk·screen *vti* print a design on paper or fabric by forcing ink through areas of a silk screen that are not blocked out with an impermeable substance ■ *n* **1** a print produced by silk-screening **2** *also* **silk-screen print·ing** a method of printing designs by silk-screening

silk·worm /sílk wùrm/ *n* a moth larva that produces silk

silk·y /sílkee/ (**-i·er, -i·est**) *adj* **1** looking or feeling like silk **2** made of silk **3** smooth or unctuous in manner —**silk·i·ly** *adv* —**silk·i·ness** *n*

sill *n* **1** a window ledge **2** the bottom of a window or door frame

sil·ly /síllee/ (**-li·er, -li·est**) *adj* **1** lacking common sense **2** trivial —**sil·li·ly** *adv* —**sil·li·ness** *n*

> **ORIGIN** The meaning of **silly** has undergone one of the most astonishing changes in the history of English word development. In a thousand years it has gone from "blessed, happy" to "foolish." The transformation began with "blessed" becoming "pious." This led on via "innocent, harmless," "pitiable," and "feeble" to "feeble in mind, foolish."

si·lo /sílo/ *n* (*pl* **-los**) **1** a cylindrical tower for storing grain or animal feed or for making silage **2** a chamber for storing and launching missiles ■ *vt* store in a silo

~~silouette~~ incorrect spelling of **silhouette**

silt *n* sediment in a river or lake ■ *vti* clog up with silt —**sil·ta·tion** /sil táysh'n/ *n* —**silt·y** *adj*

Si·lu·ri·an /si lóoree ən, sī-/ *n* a period of geologic time 443–417 million years ago —**Si·lu·ri·an** *adj*

sil·van *adj* = **sylvan**

sil·ver /sílvər/ *n* **1** (*symbol* **Ag**) a shiny grayish white metallic element. Use: ornaments, solders, photographic chemicals, conductors. **2** tableware or other household goods made of or covered with silver **3** coins made of silver or a silver-colored metal **4** a lustrous grayish white color ■ *adj* **1** made of silver **2** of the color or luster of silver **3** 25th **4** resonant and clear ■ *v* **1** *vt* coat with silver **2** *vti* make or become silver in color

sil·ver birch *n* a tree with silvery-white bark

sil·ver·fish /sílvər físh/ *n* (*pl same or* **-fish·es**) a small silvery wingless insect that feeds on starch in household materials

sil·ver med·al *n* a silver disk awarded for coming second in a race or competition —**sil·ver med·al·ist** *n*

sil·ver plate *n* **1** a thin coating of silver on a base metal **2** items coated with silver

sil·ver screen *n* movies and the movie industry

sil·ver ser·vice *n* a silver coffee or tea set

sil·ver·smith /sílvər smìth/ *n* somebody who makes or repairs silver objects

sil·ver-tongued *adj* eloquent or persuasive

sil·ver·ware /sílvər wàir/ *n* **1** metal tableware **2** silver items, especially tableware

sil·ver·y /sílvəree/ *adj* **1** like silver in color or luster **2** containing or coated with silver

~~simbol~~ incorrect spelling of **symbol**

Si·me·non /seema náwN/, **Georges** (1903–89) Belgian-born French writer

sim·i·an /símmee ən/ *adj* of or like monkeys and apes ■ *n* a monkey or ape

sim·i·lar /símmələr/ *adj* **1** sharing some qualities **2** describes geometric figures that differ in size or proportion but not in shape or angular measurements —**sim·i·lar·ly** *adv*

> **USAGE** In its meaning "sharing some qualities," **similar** is followed by *to*, not *as*: *I had a similar experience to* [not *as*] *yours*.

sim·i·lar·i·ty /símmə lárrətee/ (*pl* **-ties**) *n* **1** the quality of being similar **2** a shared characteristic

sim·i·le /símmələe/ *n* a figure of speech drawing a comparison between two things

~~similer, simlar~~ incorrect spelling of **similar**

~~similie~~ incorrect spelling of **simile**

⨍ **SIMM** /sim/ *n* a module plugged into a computer's motherboard to add memory. Full form **single inline memory module**

sim·mer /símmər/ *v* **1** *vti* cook or remain just below the boiling point **2** *vi* be filled with unexpressed emotion, especially anger —**sim·mer** *n*

□ **simmer down** *vi* become calm

Si·mon /símən/ *n* (*fl* AD 1C) one of the 12 apostles of Jesus Christ

sim·pa·ti·co /sim paáti kō, -pátti-/ *adj* compatible in temperament or interests

sim·per /símpər/ *v* **1** *vt* say something with a simpering smile **2** *vi* smile in an affectedly coy manner —**sim·per** *n* —**sim·per·ing** *adj*, *n* —**sim·per·ing·ly** *adv*

sim·ple /símp'l/ (**-pler, -plest**) *adj* **1** easy **2** lacking decoration or embellishment **3** consisting of only one part **4** uncomplicated **5** ordinary or straightforward **6** an offensive term meaning having limited intellectual ability **7** naive or guileless **8** humble and unsophisticated —**sim·ple·ness** *n* —**sim·ply** *adv* ◊ See note at simplistic

sim·ple frac·tion *n* a fraction that consists of two whole numbers separated by a horizontal or slanting line, as opposed to a decimal fraction

sim·ple in·ter·est *n* interest on an investment that is not compounded

sim·ple-mind·ed *adj* **1** showing a lack of due thought or consideration **2** an offensive term meaning having limited intellectual ability —**sim·ple-mind·ed·ly** *adv* —**sim·ple-mind·ed·ness** *n*

sim·ple·ton /símp'ltən/ *n* an offensive term for somebody regarded as lacking intelligence or judgment

~~simpley~~ incorrect spelling of **simply**

sim·plic·i·ty /sim plíssətee/ (*pl* **-ties**) *n* **1** lack of complexity, embellishment, or difficulty **2** a simple quality or thing

sim·pli·fy /símplə fī/ (**-fied, -fies**) *vt* make less complicated or easier to understand —**sim·pli·fi·ca·tion** /símpləfi káysh'n/ *n* —**sim·pli·fi·er** *n*

sim·plis·tic /sim plístik/ *adj* **1** naively simple **2** tending to oversimplify something —**sim·plis·ti·cal·ly** *adv*

USAGE **simple** or **simplistic**? **Simplistic** implies that something is oversimplified and shows disapproval: *far too simplistic an approach to the problem*. It should not be used as an alternative or stronger word for **simple**: *I recommended a simple* [not *simplistic*] *solution to the problem*.

sim·u·la·crum /símmyə láykrəm, -lákrəm/ (*pl* **-cra** /-krə/) *n* **1** a representation or image **2** something vaguely similar to something else

sim·u·late /símmyə làyt/ (**-lat·ed, -lat·ing**) *vt* **1** reproduce a feature or features of something, especially by computer **2** fake, feign, or imitate something —**sim·u·la·tion** /símmyə láysh'n/ *n* —**sim·u·la·tor** *n*

si·mul·cast /sím'l kàst, símm'l-/ *n* **1** a simultaneous television and radio broadcast **2** a live broadcast of an event on closed-circuit television —**si·mul·cast** *vt*

si·mul·ta·ne·ous /sīm'l táynee əss/ *adj* happening at the same time —**si·mul·ta·ne·i·ty** /sīm'ltə neè ətee/ *n* —**si·mul·ta·ne·ous·ly** *adv*

~~simultanious~~ incorrect spelling of **simultaneous**

sin[1] *n* **1** a transgression of a religious law **2** an offense against a moral or ethical principle **3** in Christianity, being denied God's grace because of having committed a sin —**sin** *vi* —**sin·ner** *n*

sin[2] *abbr* sine

SIN *abbr Can* Social Insurance Number

Si·nai /sí nī/ peninsula of NE Egypt, bounded on the east by the Gulf of Aqaba and on the west by the Gulf of Suez

Si·nai, Mt. mountain in NE Egypt on the south central Sinai Peninsula. Height 7,500 ft./2,888 m.

Si·na·tra /si naátrə/, **Frank** (1915–98) US singer and actor

since *prep, conj* happening after the time mentioned ■ *adv* subsequently ■ *conj* because

sin·cere /sin seér/ (**-cer·er, -cer·est**) *adj* **1** honest and open **2** not feigned —**sin·cer·i·ty** /sin sérrətee/ *n*

sin·cere·ly /sin seérlee/ *adv* in an honest and open way

~~sincerly~~ incorrect spelling of **sincerely**

Sin·clair /sing kláir/, **Upton** (1878–1968) US writer and reformer

sine /sīn/ *n* for an angle in a right triangle, a trigonometric function equal to the length of the side opposite the angle divided by the hypotenuse ◊ See note at **sign**

si·ne·cure /sínə kyòor/ *n* **1** a paid job requiring little work **2** a paid church office without duties

si·ne di·e /sìni dī ée, sìn ay deé àv/ *adv* without a day being fixed for a further meeting

si·ne qua non /sìnni kwaa nón, -nón, sìnee-/ an essential condition

sin·ew /sínnyoo/ *n* **1** a tendon **2** strength or power (*literary*)

sin·ew·y /sínnyoo ee/ *adj* **1** thin and strong **2** consisting of or containing tendons or stringy parts resembling tendons

sin·ful /sínf'l/ *adj* **1** committing or characterized by sin **2** morally or ethically wrong —**sin·ful·ly** *adv* —**sin·ful·ness** *n*

sing (**sang, sung**) *v* **1** *vti* use the voice to produce musical sounds **2** *vti* perform songs professionally **3** *vti* make a characteristic tuneful sound (*refers to animals*) **4** *vi* make a whistling, humming, or ringing sound ○ *The wind made the wires sing.* **5** *vt* put in a particular state by singing ○ *sang the baby to sleep* **6** *vi* confess to or implicate others in a crime (*slang*) —**sing·er** *n*

sing·a·long *n* an occasion when people sing together

Sin·ga·pore /síng gə pàwr, -pòr, síngə-/ city-state in Southeast Asia, comprising one major island and several islets south of the Malay Peninsula. Cap. Singapore. Pop. 4,300,419 (2001). —**Sin·ga·por·e·an** /síng gə páwree ən, sìngə-/ *n, adj*

singe /sinj/ *v* **1** *vti* burn slightly on the surface or edge **2** *vt* remove feathers or hair from a carcass with flame —**singe** *n*

Sing·er /síngər/, **Isaac Bashevis** (1904–91) Polish-born US writer

Sin·gha·lese /n, adj* PEOPLES, LANG = Sinhalese

sin·gle /síng g'l/ *adj* **1** unmarried **2** for one person **3** considered individually ○ *every single time* **4** one ○ *didn't get a single reply* **5** consisting of one thing or part ■ *n* **1** a room or bed for one person **2** a recording consisting of one song with a secondary song on the other side **3** one dollar **4** in baseball, a hit that allows the batter to reach first base ■ *vti* in baseball, hit a single —**sin·gle·ness** *n* —**sin·gly** *adv*

□ **single out** *vt* choose from a group for a particular purpose

sin·gle-breast·ed *adj* with a slight overlap at the front and a single row of buttons

sin·gle file *n* a single line of people, animals, or vehicles ■ *adv* moving in a single line

sin·gle-hand·ed *adj* **1** unaided **2** using or requiring only one hand ■ *adv* without help —**sin·gle-hand·ed·ly** *adv*

sin·gle-mind·ed *adj* **1** with a single aim **2** preoccupied with one task —**sin·gle-mind·ed·ness** *n*

sin·gle par·ent *n* somebody who raises a child alone —**sin·gle-par·ent·ing** *n*

sin·gles /síng g'lz/ *n* (*pl same*) a racket game between two players ■ *npl* unmarried people

sing·song /síng sàwng/ *adj* with rising and falling intonation ■ *n* a rising and falling intonation in speech

sin·gu·lar /síng gyələr/ *adj* 1 referring to one person or thing 2 exceptional or unusual ■ *n* a singular word or form —**sin·gu·lar·i·ty** /síng gyə lárrətee/ *n* —**sin·gu·lar·ly** *adv*

Sin·ha·lese /sìnhə léez/ (*pl same*), **Sin·gha·lese** /sìng gə-, sìngə-/ *n* 1 a member of a Sri Lankan people 2 the language of the Sinhalese —**Sin·ha·lese** *adj*

sin·is·ter /sínnəstər/ *adj* suggesting evil or trouble —**sin·is·ter·ly** *adv*

sink /singk/ *v* (**sank** /sangk/ or **sunk** /sungk/, **sunk**) 1 *vti* go beneath the surface of a liquid 2 *vi* appear to descend to or below the horizon 3 *vi* become lower 4 *vi* fall or collapse gently ○ *sank to his knees* 5 *vi* drill a well, tunnel, or shaft in the ground 6 *vti* penetrate or cause to penetrate a surface or an object ○ *sank its fangs into her leg* 7 *vi* become quieter 8 *vi* diminish or decline 9 *vt* invest money in a business or project 10 *vt* bring somebody or something to ruin 11 *vt* make a successful shot or hit (*infml*) ■ *n* 1 a basin fixed to a wall with a piped water supply and drainage 2 *also* **sink·hole** a natural depression in the ground —**sink·a·ble** *adj* ◇ **sink or swim** succeed or fail based on unaided effort

---

SPELLCHECK Do not confuse the spelling of **sink** and **sync** ("synchronization"), which sound similar.

□ **sink in** *vi* 1 become absorbed 2 finally become understood

sink·er /síngkər/ *n* a weight on a fishing line

sink·ing fund *n* a fund reserved to pay debt

sin·u·ous /sínnyoo əss/ *adj* 1 moving in graceful curves 2 full of bends and curves —**sin·u·ous·ly** *adv* —**sin·u·ous·ness** *n*

si·nus /sínəss/ *n* 1 a cavity filled with air in the bones of the skull, especially in the nasal passages 2 a widened channel in the body containing blood, especially venous blood

si·nus·i·tis /sìnə sítiss/ *n* inflammation of the sinus lining

Siou·an /sóo ən/ *n* 1 a family of Native North American languages that includes Dakota, Omaha, and Choctaw 2 somebody speaking a Siouan language —**Siou·an** *adj*

Sioux /soo/ (*pl same*) *n* a member of a group of Native North American peoples who lived throughout the Great Plains, and now live mainly in North and South Dakota —**Sioux** *adj*

Sioux Falls city in SE South Dakota. Pop. 116,762 (1998).

sip *vti* (**sipped, sip·ping**) drink slowly in very small amounts ■ *n* a small amount of drink taken into the mouth

si·phon /sífən/, **sy·phon** *v* 1 *vt* draw liquid through a tube from one container to another using atmospheric pressure 2 *vti* illegally tap funds or resources ■ *n* a bent tube for siphoning liquids

sir (*stressed*) /sur/ (*unstressed*) /sər/ *n* 1 a polite form of address for a man 2 **Sir** a title used before the name of a knight or baronet

sire /sīr/ *vt* (**sired, sir·ing**) father offspring ■ *n* 1 the male parent of a four-legged animal 2 *also* **Sire** a respectful form of address for a king or lord (*archaic*)

si·ren /sírən/ *n* 1 a warning device that produces a loud wailing sound 2 in Greek mythology, a woman believed to lure sailors onto rocks with her singing

sir·loin /súr lòyn/ *n* a prime cut of beef from the lower ribs or upper loin

---

ORIGIN One of the most persistent of etymological fictions is that the **sirloin** got its name because a particular English king found the cut of beef so excellent that he knighted it. The monarch has been variously identified as Henry VIII, James I, and Charles II, but none of these is chronologically possible, and the story has no truth to it at all. **Sirloin** actually comes from an Old French word meaning "above the loin." The spelling *sir-*, which began to replace the original *sur-* "above" in the 18C, no doubt owes something to the "knighting" story.

---

si·roc·co /sə rókō/ (*pl* -**cos**), **sci·roc·co** *n* an oppressive hot Mediterranean wind

sir·ree /sə reé/ *n* sir

sis /siss/ *n* a way of addressing a sister (*infml*)

si·sal /síss'l, sīz'l/, **si·sal hemp** *n* 1 a strong fiber obtained from the leaves of the agave plant. Use: rope, rugs. 2 a plant from which sisal is obtained

~~scissors~~ incorrect spelling of **scissors**

sis·sy /síssee/ (*pl* -**sies**) *n* an offensive term for a boy or man regarded as lacking in strength or courage (*infml*) —**sis·sy·ish** *adj*

sis·ter /sístər/ *n* 1 a female sibling 2 a stepsister or half-sister 3 *also* **Sis·ter** a nun 4 a woman who supports feminism 5 a fellow African American woman ■ *adj* closely associated —**sis·ter·li·ness** *n* —**sis·ter·ly** *adj, adv*

sis·ter·hood /sístər hòòd/ *n* 1 solidarity among women 2 a group of women with a shared aim or interest 3 the status of a sister

sis·ter-in-law (*pl* **sis·ters-in-law**) *n* 1 a spouse's sister 2 a brother's wife

sit (**sat, sit·ting**) *v* 1 *vi* rest on a surface with the weight on the buttocks 2 *vt* place somebody or yourself in a seat 3 *vi* rest the body on the lowered hindquarters (*refers to four-legged animals*) 4 *vi* perch, roost, or cover eggs (*refers to birds*) 5 *vi* pose for a portrait

6 *vi* be or remain idle ○ *sat around all day* **7** *vi* be placed or situated somewhere ○ *The dishes were still sitting on the table.* **8** *vti* babysit *(infml)* **9** *vt* have seating space for a particular number of people **10** *vi* be accepted or considered in a particular way ○ *The news didn't sit well with her.* **11** *vi* rest, weigh, hang, or lie in a particular way ○ *The responsibility sat heavily on his shoulders.* ◊ **sit tight** refrain from moving or acting *(infml)* ◊ **sitting pretty** in a favorable position *(infml)*

☐ **sit down** *vti* seat or become seated

☐ **sit in** *vi* attend something without taking an active part

☐ **sit on** *vt* **1** be a member of a decision-making group **2** suppress or delay dealing with something *(infml)*

☐ **sit up** *vi* **1** sit upright or rise to a sitting position **2** stay up late

Si·ta /seeˈtə, seeˈtaa/ *n* an incarnation of the Hindu goddess Lakshmi

si·tar /si ˈtaar/ *n* a South Asian stringed instrument —**si·tar·ist** *n*

sit·com /sitˈkòm/ *n* a situation comedy *(infml)*

sit-down *adj* served to people sitting at a table ■ *n* **1** *also* **sit-down strike** a strike in which workers sit down in their place of work and refuse to work or leave **2** *also* **sit-in** the occupation of a building by a group of people as a protest

site /sīt/ *n* **1** a place where something stands **2** a place where a significant event happened ■ *vt* (**sit·ed, sit·ing**) position or locate somewhere ◊ See note at **cite**

sit·ter /sítter/ *n* **1** somebody hired to take care of something or somebody *(often in combination)* **2** an artist's or photographer's model

sit·ting /sítting/ *n* **1** one of the periods when a meal is served in a place not large enough to seat everyone simultaneously **2** a period spent seated, e.g., while posing for a portrait **3** a session of a public body ■ *adj* **1** seated or for being seated **2** currently in office

Sitting Bull

Sit·ting Bull (1831?–90) Sioux leader

sit·ting duck *n* an easy target *(infml)*

sit·ting room *n* a room in a home used for sitting with guests

sit·u·ate /síchoo àyt/ *vt* place in a location or context —**sit·u·at·ed** *adj*

sit·u·a·tion /síchoo áysh'n/ *n* **1** a set of conditions or circumstances, e.g., in a place or in somebody's life **2** the location of a property **3** a job or position of employment *(fml)* —**sit·u·a·tion·al** *adj*

sit·u·a·tion com·e·dy *n* a TV or radio comedy series based on everyday situations

sit-up *n* an abdominal exercise done by lying on the back with the legs bent and raising the upper body

sitz bath /sits-, zits-/ *n* **1** a bathtub shaped like a chair **2** an act of bathing in a sitz bath

SI u·nit *n* an internationally accepted unit of measurement

Si·van /sivˈn/ *n* the 3rd month of the Jewish calendar

six *n* the number 6 —**six** *adj, pron* —**sixth** *n, adj, adv*

six·fold /síks fòld/ *adj* **1** six times greater **2** with six parts ■ *adv* by six times as much or as many

Six Na·tions *n* a confederacy of six Iroquois peoples, the Cayuga, Mohawk, Oneida, Onondaga, Seneca, and Tuscarora, that was formed in 1722

six-pack *n* six cans or bottles sold together as a unit

six·teen /síks teèn, síks teèn/ *n* the number 16 —**six·teen** *adj, pron* —**six·teenth** *n, adj, adv*

six·teenth note /síks teenth-, síks teenth-/ *n* a note with one 16th the time value of a whole note

sixth sense *n* a supposed extra sense allowing somebody to perceive things not detectable by the other senses

six·ty /síkstee/ *n* (*pl* -ties) the number 60 ■ **six·ties** *npl* **1** the numbers 60 to 69, particularly as a range of temperatures **2** the years from 60 to 69 in a century or somebody's life —**six·ti·eth** *n, adj, adv* —**six·ty** *adj, pron*

siz·a·ble /sízəb'l/, **size·a·ble** *adj* fairly large —**siz·a·bly** *adv*

size[1] /sīz/ *n* **1** the amount, extent, or degree of something of how large or small it is **2** the largeness of something **3** a standard measurement of a manufactured item ■ *vt* (**sized, siz·ing**) sort according to size —**sized** *adj* ◊ **cut down to size** cause to be less self-important and arrogant

☐ **size up** *vt* assess

size[2] /sīz/ *n* a gelatinous mixture made from glue, starch, or varnish. Use: filling pores in the surface of paper, textiles, or plaster. —**size** *vt*

siz·zle /sízz'l/ (**-zled, -zling**) *vi* **1** make the noise of food frying **2** be hot *(infml)* —**siz·zle** *n* —**siz·zling** *n*

S.J. *abbr* Society of Jesus

Sjæl·land /syélland/ main island of Denmark, on which Copenhagen, the country's capital, is situated. Pop. 2,159,260 (1994).

SK *abbr* Saskatchewan

ska /skaa/ *n* a type of popular Jamaican dance music

skate[1] *n* **1** an ice skate **2** a roller skate ■ *vi* (**skat·ed, skat·ing**) move on skates —**skat·er** *n* —**skat·ing** *n*

skate[2] (*pl* **skates** *or* **same**) *n* **1** a bottom-dwelling ocean fish **2** skate as food

skate·board /skáyt bàwrd/ *n* a wheeled board on which to ride standing up or to perform stunts —**skate·board** *vi* —**skate·board·er** *n* —**skate·board·ing** *n*

skeet shooting, skeet *n* a form of clay-pigeon shooting

> **ORIGIN** *Skeet* was the winning entry in a competition to name the sport in 1926. An invented word, it was said by its proposer, Mrs. Gertrude Hurlbutt of Dayton, Montana, to be a very old form of *shoot*.

skein /skayn/ *n* **1** a length of yarn wound loosely and coiled together **2** a flock of geese in flight

skel·e·tal /skéllət'l/ *adj* **1** of a skeleton **2** very thin

skel·e·ton /skéllət'n/ *n* **1** the framework of bones of a person or animal **2** the supportive protective structure of an invertebrate **3** the basic frame something is built around **4** something with only the essential parts left **5** an outline description of something

skel·e·ton key *n* a key that can unlock many doors

skep·tic /sképtik/ *n* **1** a doubter of accepted beliefs **2** a doubter of religious teachings —**skep·ti·cal** *adj* —**skep·ti·cal·ly** *adv* ◇ See note at **doubtful**

skep·ti·cism /sképti sìzzəm/ *n* a doubting attitude toward accepted beliefs or religious teachings

sketch *n* **1** a picture drawn quickly and roughly **2** a short comic performance **3** a rough description or explanation **4** a short piece of writing ■ *vti* make a sketch of something —**sketch·er** *n*

sketch·book /skéch bòok/, **sketch·pad** /-pàd/ *n* a book of plain paper in which to make sketches

sketch·y /skéchee/ (**-i·er, -i·est**) *adj* **1** superficial **2** giving only the main points —**sketch·i·ly** *adv* —**sketch·i·ness** *n*

skew /skyoo/ *v* **1** *vti* make or become slanted or unsymmetrical **2** *vt* misrepresent or distort ■ *adj* slanted or unsymmetrical ■ *n* a slanted position

skew·er /skyoo ər/ *n* **1** a thin pointed rod pushed through pieces of food to hold them during cooking **2** a thin pointed object used to pierce something and hold it in place ■ *vt* **1** pierce with or as if with a skewer **2** criticize pointedly

ski /skee/ *n* (*pl* **skis**) either of a pair of long thin boards used to slide across snow or in waterskiing ■ *vti* (**skied, ski·ing, skis**) move across snow or water on skis —**ski·er** *n* —**ski·ing** *n*

skid *n* **1** an uncontrolled slide in a wheeled vehicle **2** a runner on an aircraft **3** a pallet on which goods are loaded **4** one of two or more poles or logs forming a track on which to slide something heavy **5** a block used to prevent a wheel from turning ■ *v* (**skid·ded, skid·ding**) **1** *vti* slide or cause to slide dangerously across a surface **2** *vi* slide over a surface without turning and gripping it (*refers to wheels*) ◇ **on the skids** heading for failure (*slang*)

skid row *n* a rundown part of town (*infml*)

skiff *n* a small flat-bottom boat

skif·fle /skiff'l/ *n* a type of 1950s pop music played by a small group with guitars and improvised instruments

ski jump *n* **1** a steep artificial slope from which skiers jump **2** a jump made from a ski jump —**ski jump·er** *n* —**ski jump·ing** *n*

ski lift *n* an apparatus for transporting skiers up a mountainside

skill *n* **1** the ability to do something well **2** something requiring experience or training to do well —**skilled** *adj* ◇ See note at **ability**

skil·let /skíllit/ *n* a frying pan

skill·ful /skílf'l/ *adj* **1** particularly adept at something **2** requiring or done with a special skill —**skill·ful·ly** *adv* —**skill·ful·ness** *n*

~~skillfull~~ incorrect spelling of **skillful**

skim (**skimmed, skim·ming**) *v* **1** *vt* scoop a substance such as fat from the top of a liquid **2** *vt* rid a liquid of material accumulating on its surface **3** *vti* pass closely over a surface **4** *vti* glance quickly through a book or paper **5** *vt* send something bouncing lightly along the surface of water —**skim** *n*

skim milk *n* milk with the fat removed

skimp *v* **1** *vti* use or provide too little of something **2** *vt* do something inadequately

skimp·y /skímpee/ (**-i·er, -i·est**) *adj* **1** done using barely enough of the necessary materials **2** stingy —**skimp·i·ness** *n*

skin *n* **1** the external protective membrane or covering of an animal's body **2** a thin outer layer, especially of a fruit or vegetable **3** a hide or pelt of an animal **4** a thin pliant layer that forms on a liquid **5** the outer covering of a structure such as an aircraft ■ *vt* (**skinned, skin·ning**) **1** remove the skin or outer layer of something **2** scrape the skin accidentally from a part of the body ◇ **be no skin off somebody's back** not matter to somebody (*infml*) ◇ **by the skin of your teeth** by a very narrow margin (*infml*) ◇ **get under somebody's skin** annoy or irritate somebody (*infml*) ◇ **save somebody's skin** prevent somebody from suffering hurt, loss, or punishment (*infml*)

skin-deep *adj* superficial and without depth
■ *adv* superficially

skin div·ing *n* the sport of underwater diving with a snorkel, mask, and flippers —**skin-dive** *vi* —**skin div·er** *n*

skin-flint /skín flìnt/ *n* a miser

~~sking~~ incorrect spelling of **skiing**

skin graft *n* a piece of skin taken from part of the body to replace damaged skin

Skin·ner /skínnər/, **B. F.** (1904–90) US psychologist —**Skin·ner·i·an** /ski neèree ən/ *adj, n*

skin·ny /skínnee/ (-ni·er, -ni·est) *adj* very thin ◊ See note at **thin**

skin-tight /skín tít/ *adj* fitting close to the body

skip *v* (**skipped**, **skip·ping**) 1 *vi* move with small hopping steps 2 *vti* jump repeatedly over a rope swung over the head and under the feet 3 *vti* omit or pass over something 4 *vt* not attend an event or activity (*infml*) 5 *vt* promote a student one grade beyond the next in succession, or be promoted in this way 6 *vti* leave quickly and secretly (*infml*) ○ *He skipped town.* 7 *vti* move or cause to move in a series of small bounces ■ *n* 1 a small hopping step 2 an omission

skip·per /skíppər/ *n* 1 somebody in charge of a boat or ship 2 the leader of a team (*infml*) ■ *vt* be the skipper of (*infml*)

skir·mish /skúrmish/ *n* 1 a small brief battle in a war 2 a short fight or argument —**skir·mish** *vi* —**skir·mish·er** *n* ◊ See note at **fight**

skirt *n* 1 a garment that hangs from the waist and does not divide into separate legs 2 the section from the waist to the hem on a dress, coat, or robe 3 something that hangs down like a skirt ■ *v* 1 *vti* form a border around the outside of an area or object 2 *vti* move around the outside of an area or object 3 *vt* avoid giving proper attention to

skit *n* a short comic dramatic performance or piece of writing, especially a satirical one

skit·ter /skíttər/ *vi* 1 scamper 2 skid lightly across a surface

skit·tish /skíttish/ *adj* 1 nervous 2 silly and irresponsible —**skit·tish·ly** *adv* —**skit·tish·ness** *n*

skit·tle /skíttʼl/ *n* ninepin

Skop·je /skóp yee/ capital of the Former Yugoslav Republic of Macedonia, in the north central part of the country. Pop. 440,577 (1994).

SKU /èss kay yoò, skyoó/, **Sku** *n* a unique code assigned to a inventory item for identification and inventory control. Full form **stockkeeping unit**

skul·dug·ger·y /skul dúggəree/, **skull-dug·ger·y** *n* unfair or dishonest tricks carried out secretively against somebody (*humorous*)

skulk *vi* move furtively

skull /skul/ *n* the bony part of the head encasing the brain

skull and cross·bones *n* 1 a representation of a skull above two crossed bones, used as a symbol of danger or death 2 a black flag bearing a white skull and crossbones, used by pirates

skull·cap /skúl kàp/ *n* 1 a small round brimless hat fitting over the crown of the head 2 a yarmulke

skunk *n* (*pl* **skunks** *or same*) 1 a black-and-white mammal that defends itself by ejecting a foul-smelling liquid from an anal gland 2 an offensive term for a person regarded as despicable (*slang insult*) ■ *vt* defeat soundly (*slang*)

sky (*pl* **skies**) *n* 1 the region above the Earth 2 the way the sky appears in a particular place or at a particular time (*often pl*) ◊ **the sky's the limit** there is no upper limit (*infml*)

sky·cap /skí kàp/ *n* an airport porter

sky·dive /skí dìv/ (-**dived** *or* -**dove** /-dṓv/, -**div·ing**) *vi* jump from an airplane and free-fall before opening a parachute —**sky div·er** *n* —**sky·div·ing** *n*

Skye /skí/ largest island in the Inner Hebrides, W Scotland. Pop. 8,843 (1991).

sky-high *adj* extremely high ■ *adv* high into the air or in all directions, and often in pieces

sky·jack /skí jàk/ *vt* hijack an aircraft —**sky·jack·er** *n* —**sky·jack·ing** *n*

sky·lark /skí làark/ *n* a lark that sings melodiously while high in the air

sky·light /skí lìt/ *n* a window in a roof

sky·line /skí lìn/ *n* 1 the outline of buildings or landscape features against the sky 2 the horizon

sky mar·shal *n* a federal law enforcement officer who provides in-flight security on commercial passenger aircraft

sky·rock·et /skí ròkət/ *vti* increase dramatically and quickly (*infml*) ■ *n* a brilliant firework that explodes high in the air

sky·scrap·er /skí skràypər/ *n* a very tall building

sky·surf·ing /skí sùrfing/ *n* the sport of jumping from an aircraft and performing various maneuvers before parachuting to the ground —**sky-surf** *vi* —**sky·surf·er** *n*

sky·ward /skíwərd/ *adv, adj* toward the sky

sky·writ·ing /skí rìting/ *n* writing with colored smoke released from an aircraft, or the resulting message —**sky·write** *vti*

slab *n* a thick flat broad piece of something

slack *adj* 1 not taut 2 not showing enough care 3 not busy ■ *adv* loosely ■ *n* 1 looseness or give in something 2 unused productive potential in an organization or system 3 time that is not busy ■ **slacks** *npl* casual pants ■ *v* 1 *vi* avoid work or not work hard 2 *vti* make or become slower or less intense **—slack·er** n **—slack·ly** adv **—slack·ness** n

slack·en /slákən/ vti **1** make or become slower or less intense **2** loosen or relax

slag n waste material from smelting

slag heap n a mound of waste from a coal mine or factory

slain past participle of **slay**

slake (**slaked, slak·ing**) v **1** vt satisfy a need, especially a thirst **2** vti treat lime with water to make calcium hydroxide, or undergo this process

Popperfoto

Slalom

sla·lom /slaaləm/ n **1** a downhill zigzag ski race **2** a zigzag race ■ vi follow a zigzag course

slam[1] v (**slammed, slam·ming**) **1** vti close forcefully and noisily **2** vti put down violently or land heavily **3** vti hit suddenly or violently **4** vt criticize forcefully (infml) ■ n **1** a loud forceful blow or impact **2** a forceful criticism

slam[2] n the winning of all the tricks in a hand of bridge or whist

slam dunk n in basketball, a forceful dunk shot **—slam-dunk** vt

slam·mer /slámmər/ n a jail (slang)

slan·der /slándər/ n a false statement that is damaging to somebody's reputation, or the making of such a statement ■ vt utter a slander against **—slan·der·er** n **—slan·der·ous** adj **—slan·der·ous·ly** adv ◊ See note at **malign**

slang n **1** very casual speech or writing **2** a form of language used by a particular group **—slang** adj **—slang·y** adj

slang·ing match n Can, UK an exchange of insults

slant v **1** vti be or set at an angle **2** vt make appealing to a particular group of people ○ a magazine slanted toward the youth market **3** vt present in a biased way ■ n **1** a slope **2** a particular point of view or perspective ○ a new slant on the events **—slant·ed** adj **—slant·ing** adj

slap n **1** a blow with the open hand or a flat object **2** the noise of a slap ■ v (**slapped, slap·ping**) **1** vt hit with the open hand or a flat object **2** vi strike sharply and noisily ○ water slapping against the hull **3** vt put down sharply **4** vt apply quickly and carelessly ○ slapped on a coat of paint

slap·dash /sláp dàsh/ adj careless **—slap·dash** adv

slap·stick /sláp stìk/ n comedy that depends on physical action

⚡ **slash** vt **1** make long cuts in **2** attack with sweeping strokes of a sharp object **3** criticize **4** reduce or shorten greatly ○ slash prices ■ n **1** a sweeping stroke made with a sharp object **2** a long cut **3** a keyboard character in the form of a leaning diagonal line **—slash·er** n

slash-and-burn adj of a form of agriculture in which trees and vegetation are cut down and burned in order to plant crops

slat n a thin narrow wooden or metal strip **—slat·ted** adj

slate n **1** a fine-grained rock that splits easily into layers **2** something such as a roofing tile or writing tablet made of slate **3** a dark gray color **4** a list of electoral candidates ■ vt (**slat·ed, slat·ing**) **1** cover with slate **2** include in a list of electoral candidates **3** designate for a task or position **—slate** adj **—slat·y** adj

slath·er /sláthər/ vt spread thickly on something ○ slather jelly on toast

slat·tern /sláttərn/ n an offensive term for a woman regarded as having poor standards of hygiene or grooming (dated) **—slat·tern·ly** adj

slaugh·ter /sláwtər/ n **1** the killing of animals for their meat **2** the brutal killing of a person or large numbers of people ■ vt **1** kill an animal for its meat **2** kill a person or large numbers of people brutally **—slaugh·ter·er** n **—slaugh·ter·ous** adj ◊ See note at **kill**

slaugh·ter·house /sláwtər hòwss/ (pl **-hous·es** /-hòwzəz/) n a place where animals are killed for their meat

slave /slayv/ n **1** formerly, a person forced to work for another for no payment and regarded as that person's property **2** a person dominated by somebody or something **3** somebody who works very hard, in bad conditions, and for low pay ■ vi (**slaved, slav·ing**) work very hard

slav·er[1] /sláyvər/ n **1** a slave owner or dealer **2** also **slave ship** a ship used to carry captured and enslaved people

slav·er[2] /slávvər, sláyvər/ vi dribble saliva from the mouth ■ n saliva dribbling from somebody's mouth

slav·er·y /sláyvəree/ n **1** a system based on the use of enslaved labor **2** being an enslaved laborer **3** very hard work in bad conditions and for low pay

Slav·ic /slaávik/, **Sla·von·ic** /slə vónnik/ n an Eastern European language group that includes Bulgarian, Russian, and Polish **—Slav·ic** adj

slav·ish /sláyvish/ adj (sometimes offensive) **1** servile **2** unoriginal **—slav·ish·ly** adv

slaw n coleslaw

slay /slay/ (**slew** /sloo/, **slain** /slayn/) vt kill (fml or literary) —**slay·er** n

SPELLCHECK Do not confuse the spelling of **slay** and **sleigh** ("a horse-drawn carriage used on snow"), which sound similar.

slea·zy /sléezee/ (**-zi·er**, **-zi·est**) adj 1 sordid 2 dishonest or immoral —**sleaze** n —**slea·zi·ly** adv —**slea·zi·ness** n

sled n a small vehicle with runners for traveling or transporting goods over snow

sledge n a large sled used for transporting goods

sledge·ham·mer /sléj hàmmər/ n a large heavy hammer ■ adj very forceful

sleek adj 1 smooth and shiny 2 well-groomed and healthy-looking ■ vt make sleek —**sleek·ly** adv —**sleek·ness** n

sleep n 1 the state of resting while not being awake 2 an inactive or dormant state resembling sleep ■ v (**slept**) 1 vi go into or be in a state of sleep 2 vi be inactive or dormant 3 vt provide beds for a particular number of people ◊ **not lose (any) sleep over** not worry unnecessarily about ◊ **put to sleep** kill an animal in a humane way ◊ **sleep on it** postpone a decision

□ **sleep with** vt have sex with (infml; euphemistic)

sleep·er /sléepər/ n 1 somebody who sleeps in a particular way 2 a train car with beds 3 somebody or something that is belatedly successful (infml)

sleep-in adj living at your place of work

sleep·ing bag n a padded or lined fabric bag for sleeping in, especially while camping

sleep·ing car n a railroad car where passengers sleep

sleep·ing pill n a pill containing a sleep-inducing drug

sleep·ing sick·ness n 1 a tropical disease spread by tsetse flies 2 a form of encephalitis causing lethargy

sleep·less /sléepləss/ adj 1 without sleep, or unable to sleep 2 always awake or active —**sleep·less·ly** adv —**sleep·less·ness** n

sleep·o·ver /sléep òvər/ n an overnight stay for children at somebody else's house (infml)

sleep·walk /sléep wàwk/ vi walk while asleep —**sleep·walk·er** n —**sleep·walk·ing** n

sleep·y /sléepee/ (**-i·er**, **-i·est**) adj 1 drowsy 2 quiet and without much activity —**sleep·i·ly** adv —**sleep·i·ness** n

sleep·y·head /sléepee hèd/ n a drowsy person (infml) —**sleep·y·head·ed** adj

sleet n 1 partly frozen rain 2 a thin coating of ice formed when rain freezes ■ vi fall as sleet

sleeve n 1 either of the parts of a garment that cover the arms 2 a tubular piece fitting in or over a cylinder 3 a protective cover, e.g., for a record —**sleeved** adj

—**sleeve·less** adj ◊ **up your sleeve** kept hidden or secret but available for use

sleigh /slay/ n an open horse-drawn vehicle with runners for use on snow ■ vi travel in a sleigh ◊ See note at **slay**

sleight of hand /slīt-/ n 1 skill with the hands in conjuring or card tricks 2 skill in doing something without revealing how

slen·der /sléndər/ adj 1 small in circumference or width in proportion to height or length 2 slim 3 limited in degree, extent, or size ◊ **win by a slender margin** —**slen·der·ness** n ◊ See note at **thin**

slept past tense, past participle of **sleep**

sleuth /slooth/ n a detective (infml) ■ vi investigate as or like a detective

slew¹ /sloo/ past tense of **slay**

slew² /sloo/, **slue** n a large number of something (infml)

slew³ /sloo/ n GEOG = **slough¹**

slice /slīss/ n 1 a thin broad piece cut from something 2 a share of something 3 in golf, a shot in which the ball curves away to the side 4 in tennis, a shot that makes the ball spin and stay low ■ v (**sliced**, **slic·ing**) 1 vt cut into slices 2 vti cut cleanly 3 vi move swiftly and cleanly, especially through air or water 4 vt cut something off something else 5 vt in golf or tennis, hit the ball with a slice —**slic·er** n

slick adj 1 smooth or slippery 2 crafty (infml) 3 superficially impressive or persuasive ■ n a slippery patch of something ■ vt make smooth —**slick·ly** adv —**slick·ness** n

slick·er /slíkər/ n 1 a shiny raincoat 2 somebody sophisticated but untrustworthy (infml)

slide /slīd/ v (**slid** /slid/, **slid·ing**) 1 vti move smoothly across a surface 2 vti move or pass unobtrusively 3 vi change to a worse condition 4 vi lose your grip or secure footing on a surface ■ n 1 a sliding movement 2 a structure with a smooth slope for children to slide down 3 a small positive photograph viewed by projection on a screen 4 a downhill displacement of rock, mud, or earth 5 a glass holder for viewing a specimen under a microscope 6 a sliding part ◊ **let things or something slide** let a situation gradually deteriorate

slide rule n a calculating device consisting of two rulers marked with graduated logarithmic scales

slid·ing scale n a scale that varies according to changes in another factor

~~slieght of hand~~ incorrect spelling of **sleight of hand**

slight /slīt/ adj 1 very small in size or degree 2 thin ■ vt 1 ignore or treat disrespectfully 2 treat as unimportant ■ n a disrespectful act —**slight·ly** adv —**slight·ness** n ◊ **not in the slightest** not at all (infml)

slim adj (**slim·mer**, **slim·mest**) 1 smaller in width, thickness, or girth than height or length 2 pleasingly thin ■ v (**slimmed**, **slim·ming**) 1 vi lose weight, especially by dieting 2 vt reduce in size or scope —**slim·mer** n —**slim·ming** n, adj —**slim·ness** n ◊ See note at **thin**

slime /slīm/ n 1 an unpleasantly thick slippery liquid 2 a mucous secretion of some organisms such as snails —**slim·i·ness** n —**slim·y** adj

sling[1] n 1 a wide bandage tied around the neck for supporting an injured arm or hand 2 a carrying strap for something such as a rifle 3 a loop or net for moving something heavy 4 a weapon consisting of a leather loop used for launching stones ■ v (**slung**) 1 vt throw with force 2 carry or move in a sling —**sling·er** n

sling[2] n a drink containing alcohol, sugar, lemon or lime juice, and water

sling·back /slīng bàk/ n a woman's shoe with an open back and a strap for the heel

sling·shot /slīng shòt/ n a small Y-shaped weapon used to propel stones

slink /slingk/ (**slunk** /slungk/ or **slinked**) vi 1 move furtively 2 move sexily

slink·y /slíngkee/ (**-i·er**, **-i·est**) adj 1 seductive in appearance or movement 2 attractively close-fitting —**slink·i·ly** adv· —**slink·i·ness** n

slip[1] v (**slipped**, **slip·ping**) 1 vti move smoothly 2 vti put on or take off something quickly and easily 3 vi lose your footing or grip on a surface 4 vti move accidentally out of place 5 vi go quietly or unobtrusively 6 vt put or give secretly 7 vi do something wrong 8 vi get worse ■ n 1 a loss of footing or grip on a surface 2 an error 3 a light sleeveless woman's undergarment 4 a place between two piers for a ship to dock 5 a cloth covering, e.g., for a pillow ◊ **give somebody the slip** escape from somebody ◊ **let slip** 1 reveal without meaning to 2 allow somebody or something to escape ◊ See note at **mistake**

slip[2] n 1 a stem or branch of a plant cut off and used to start a new plant 2 a slightly built young person 3 a small piece of paper such as a receipt

⚡**SLIP** /slip/ n a protocol for dial-up access to the Internet. Full form **serial line Internet protocol**

slip·cov·er /slíp kùvvər/ n a cover for furniture ■ vt cover furniture

slip·knot /slíp nòt/ n 1 a knot that slips easily along the rope around which it is tied 2 a knot that can be unfastened by pulling

slip·on n a shoe or garment that is easy to put on —**slip-on** adj

slip·page /slíppij/ n 1 an act or the process of slipping 2 the amount that something slips

slip·per /slíppər/ n an indoor shoe

slip·per·y /slíppəree/ (**-i·er**, **-i·est**) adj 1 causing sliding 2 hard to hold firmly

3 untrustworthy —**slip·per·i·ly** adv —**slip·per·i·ness** n

slip·pery slope n a dangerous situation that can lead to disaster

slip·shod /slíp shòd/ adj 1 carelessly done 2 untidy

slip·stream /slíp streem/ n 1 the air behind a propeller 2 the area of reduced air pressure behind a fast-moving vehicle

slip-up n an error (infml)

slip·way /slíp wày/ n a ramp used to launch, land, build, or repair boats

slit (**slit**, **slit·ting**) vt make a long straight cut in —**slit** n ◊ See note at **tear**

slith·er /slíthər/ v 1 vti slide without control 2 vi move with a sliding snake-like motion —**slith·er** n

sliv·er /slívvər/ n 1 a thin piece of something that has been split, cut, or broken off 2 a small portion or slice of something —**sliv·er** vti

sliv·o·vitz /slívvə vìts/ n an E European plum brandy

slob n an offensive term for a person regarded as lazy, messy, or bad-mannered —**slob·bish** adj

slob·ber /slóbbər/ v 1 vti dribble saliva 2 vi be excessively sentimental or emotional ■ n 1 dribbled saliva 2 excessively sentimental or emotional writing or talk

sloe /slō/ (pl **sloes** or same) n 1 a sour blue-black fruit of the blackthorn 2 a blackthorn

sloe gin n a liqueur made of gin flavored with sloes

slog (**slogged**, **slog·ging**) vi 1 walk slowly and with effort 2 work long and hard —**slog** n

slo·gan /slógən/ n 1 a motto 2 a catchy advertising phrase

sloop n a single-masted sailing boat

slop n 1 something spilled 2 mud or slush 3 unappealing watery food (often pl) ■ **slops** npl kitchen waste used as hog feed ■ v (**slopped**, **slop·ping**) 1 vti spill a liquid or be spilled 2 vt serve food messily

slope /slōp/ n 1 a piece of ground that inclines 2 the side of a hill or mountain 3 a slant or something slanted ■ vti (**sloped**, **slop·ing**) go or cause to go up or down at an angle —**slop·ing** adj

slop·py /slóppee/ (**-pi·er**, **-pi·est**) adj 1 messy or in disorder 2 slushy, muddy, or wet 3 not done well (infml)

slop·py joe n ground beef cooked in a spiced tomato sauce, served in a bun

slosh v 1 vt spill or splash a liquid over something 2 vti move or splash in a liquid (infml) —**slosh·y** adj

sloshed adj drunk (slang)

⚡**slot** n 1 a narrow opening into which something can be inserted 2 a place and time scheduled for somebody or something 3 a job in an organization 4 a receptacle for an expansion card in a computer ■ v (**slot·ted**,

slot·ting 1 *vti* put or be put in a slot 2 *vt* cut a slot in

sloth /slawth, slōth, sloth/ *n* 1 laziness 2 a slow-moving tree-dwelling mammal

sloth·ful /sláwthf'l, slóthf'l, slóthf'l/ *adj* lazy —**sloth·ful·ly** *adv*

slot ma·chine *n* a coin-operated gambling or vending machine

slouch *vti* walk, stand, or sit in a lazy drooping way, or make a part of the body sag lazily ■ *n* a lazy or inept person (*infml; usually in negative statements*)

slough[1] /sloo, slowl, **slew** /sloo/ *n* 1 a muddy hole 2 a swampy area 3 a spiritual low point —**slough·y** *adj*

slough[2] /sluf/ *n* 1 the dead outer skin shed by a reptile or amphibian 2 a layer of dead skin shed after an infection ■ *v* 1 *vti* shed or be shed 2 *vt* ignore

Slo·va·ki·a /slō vaakee ə/ country in east central Europe. Cap. Bratislava. Pop. 5,414,937 (2001). —**Slo·vak** /slō vàk/ *n, adj* —**Slo·va·ki·an** *n, adj*

Slo·ve·ni·a /slō veenee ə/ country in E Europe, on the Balkan Peninsula. Cap. Ljubljana. Pop. 1,930,132 (2001). —**Slo·vene** /slō veen/ *n, adj* —**Slo·ve·ni·an** *n, adj*

slov·en·ly /slúvv'nlee/ (**-li·er, -li·est**) *adj* an offensive term meaning dirty and messy —**slov·en·li·ness** *n*

slow /slō/ *adj* 1 not moving quickly 2 taking a long time 3 taking too much time 4 describes a clock or watch showing a time that is earlier than the correct time 5 hesitant 6 lacking the usual volume of sales or customers 7 regarded as unintelligent (*infml insult*) 8 dull and boring ■ *adv* 1 behind the correct time or pace 2 slowly ■ *vti* 1 make or become slow 2 delay or be delayed —**slow·ly** *adv* —**slow·ness** *n*

slow·down /slō dòwn/ *n* a reduction in work

slow mo·tion *n* a method or effect in movies or videos that shows action happening more slowly than in reality —**slow·mo·tion** *adj*

slow·poke /slōw pòk/ *n* somebody who is slow (*infml*)

slow·worm /slō wùrm/ *n* a lizard without legs

sludge /sluj/ *n* 1 watery mud or slush 2 the solids in sewage that separate out during treatment —**sludg·y** *adj*

slug[1] *n* 1 a bullet 2 a single shot of strong alcoholic drink (*infml*) 3 a disk used as an illegal coin

slug[2] *n* a slow-moving land mollusk without a shell

slug[3] (**slugged, slug·ging**) *vt* hit hard —**slug** *n*

slug·gard /slúggərd/ *n* a lazy person (*archaic*) —**slug·gard·ly** *adj*

slug·gish /slúggish/ *adj* 1 moving slowly or very little 2 not very responsive 3 lacking alertness and energy —**slug·gish·ly** *adv* —**slug·gish·ness** *n*

sluice /slooss/ *n* 1 an artificial water channel controlled by a valve or floodgate 2 a valve or floodgate controlling the water in a sluice 3 a drainage channel 4 a trough for separating gold from sand or gravel ■ *v* (**sluiced, sluic·ing**) 1 *vt* flush something with water 2 *vt* wash gold in a sluice 3 *vti* release or be released from a sluice

slum *n* a poor area of a city (*often pl*) ■ *v* (**slummed, slum·ming**) 1 *vti* accept lower living standards than usual (*often humorous*) 2 *vi* visit a slum out of curiosity

slum·ber /slúmbər/ *vi* 1 sleep 2 be inactive or resting ■ *n* 1 an act or period of sleeping 2 inactivity —**slum·ber·less** *adj*

slum·ber par·ty *n* a party at which a group of children spend the night at one of the children's homes

slum·lord /slúm làwrd/ *n* an owner of slum housing

slump *vi* 1 collapse 2 slouch ■ *n* 1 a slouched posture 2 an economic decline 3 a period of poor performance

slung past tense, past participle of **sling**[1]

slunk past tense, past participle of **slink**

slur *v* (**slurred, slur·ring**) 1 *vti* speak or say indistinctly 2 *vt* insult or disparage somebody 3 *vt* gloss over something 4 *vt* play musical notes in a smooth uninterrupted way ■ *n* 1 an insulting or disparaging remark 2 an indistinct pronunciation or sound 3 a curved line connecting musical notes to show that they are to be played in a smooth uninterrupted way

slurp *vti* drink noisily ■ *n* the sound of something being slurped —**slurp·ing·ly** *adv*

slur·ry /slúr ee/ *n* a mixture of water and an indissoluble solid

slush *n* 1 melting snow or ice 2 a semiliquid substance 3 excessively sentimental speech or writing —**slush·i·ness** *n* —**slush·y** *adj*

slush fund *n* an amount of money set aside for illegal activities

slut *n* an offensive term for a woman regarded as sexually promiscuous or having poor standards of hygiene —**slut·tish** *adj* —**slut·ty** *adj*

sly (**sli·er, sli·est**) *adj* 1 crafty 2 evasive —**sly·ly** *adv* —**sly·ness** *n* ◊ **on the sly** without the knowledge or permission of others

Sm *symbol* samarium

smack[1] *v* 1 *vti* slap somebody 2 *vi* hit an object or surface noisily 3 *vt* press the lips together and then open them with a short loud noise ■ *n* 1 a slap 2 a noisy smacking sound 3 a loud kiss ■ *adv* 1 with a loud noise 2 exactly or directly

smack[2] *n* 1 a distinctive taste of something 2 a hint of something ■ *vi* 1 be distinctively flavored 2 suggest or hint at something ◊ *an appointment that smacks of nepotism*

smack³ *n* a fishing vessel

smack⁴ *n* heroin *(slang)*

smack·er /smákər/ *n (infml)* **1** a loud kiss **2** a dollar

small *adj* **1** little in size **2** little in quantity or value **3** insignificant **4** limited in scale **5** young **6** petty and mean-spirited **7** humiliated ■ *adv* **1** in or into little pieces **2** in a moderate or limited way ■ *n* a narrow or small part of something o *the small of the back* —**small·ish** *adj* —**small·ness** *n*

small change *n* **1** low-denomination coins **2** something trivial

small-claims court *n* a local court for claims involving small amounts of money

Smal·ley /smáwlee/, **Richard E.** (*b.* 1943) US chemical physicist. He jointly discovered the molecular family of carbon called fullerenes.

small fry *npl* **1** young children *(infml)* **2** young fish

small hours *n* the early morning hours after midnight

small in·tes·tine *n* the part of the digestive tract where digestion of food and most absorption of nutrients takes place

small-mind·ed *adj* petty —**small-mind·ed·ly** *adv* —**small-mind·ed·ness** *n*

small po·ta·toes *npl* somebody or something insignificant *(infml)*

small·pox /smáwl pòks/ *n* a highly contagious viral disease that leaves distinctive scars

small print *n* fine print

small-scale *adj* **1** limited in scope or size **2** made in a smaller version

small talk *n* casual conversation

small-time *adj* unimportant *(infml)*

smarm·y /smaármee/ (**-i·er, -i·est**) *adj* excessively ingratiating —**smarm·i·ly** *adv* —**smarm·i·ness** *n*

⚡smart *adj* **1** intelligent **2** shrewd **3** witty and amusing **4** insolent **5** neat and orderly in appearance **6** fashionable **7** lively and vigorous **8** fitted with a microprocessor ■ *vi* **1** cause or have a stinging pain **2** feel embarrassed ■ *adv* in a smart manner ■ *n* a stinging pain ■ **smarts** *npl* intelligence *(infml)* —**smart·ly** *adv* —**smart·ness** *n* ¢ See note at **intelligent**

smart al·eck /-àllik/, **smart al·ec** *n* somebody who likes to show how clever he or she is *(infml)* —**smart-al·eck** *adj*

smart bomb *n* a missile guided by laser or radio beams

⚡smart card *n* an electronic card storing personal data and used for identification and financial transactions

smart·en /smaárt'n/ *vt* **1** improve the appearance of **2** speed up

□ **smarten up** *vti* **1** make or become livelier **2** make or become wiser

smart mon·ey *n* **1** an investment or bet that is likely to succeed **2** people who know

what to invest in or bet on to make a profit

⚡smart ter·mi·nal *n* a network terminal that carries out processing but uses another computer for data storage

smash *v* **1** *vti* break into pieces **2** *vti* break with force **3** *vti* hit against an object or surface **4** *vt* defeat or destroy **5** *vt* in racket games, hit downward with force with an overhead stroke ■ *n* **1** a loud noise of something hitting something else and breaking into pieces **2** a great success **3** a heavy blow **4** a collision **5** in racket games, an overhead stroke hit downward with force ■ *adv* with the sound of a smash —**smash·er** *n*

smashed *adj* intoxicated *(infml)*

smash-up /smásh ùp/ *n* **1** a wreck **2** a complete collapse or defeat

smat·ter·ing /smáttəring/ *n* **1** a slight knowledge of something **2** a small amount of something

smear /smeer/ *v* **1** *vti* spread a greasy, sticky, or liquid substance over something, or be spread in this way **2** *vt* spread damaging rumors about ■ *n* **1** an act of smearing or a smeared patch of something **2** a harmful rumor —**smear·y** *adj*

smear cam·paign *n* a deliberate sustained attempt to harm somebody's reputation

smell *v* (**smelled** *or* **smelt**) **1** *vti* detect, recognize, or assess something by means of the nose **2** *vi* have a particular smell o *Something smells good.* **3** *vi* have an unpleasant smell o *That really smells!* **4** *vt* detect the presence of something undesirable ■ *n* **1** the sense based on the nerves in the nose that distinguish odors **2** the quality of something detected by the nose **3** an act of smelling something in order to judge or identify it —**smell·er** *n*

SYNONYMS **smell, odor, aroma, bouquet, scent, perfume, fragrance, stink, stench, reek** CORE MEANING: the way something smells

---

smell·ing salts *npl* a mixture of ammonium carbonate and perfume. Use: formerly, to revive somebody who felt faint or had become unconscious.

smell·y /sméllee/ (**-i·er, -i·est**) *adj* with a strong or unpleasant smell —**smell·i·ness** *n*

smelt¹ *vti* melt ore in order to get metal, or undergo this process

smelt² (*pl* **smelts** *or* **same**) *n* **1** a small silvery fish of northern waters **2** smelt as food

smelt³ past tense, past participle of **smell**

smelt·er /sméltər/ *n* **1** somebody who smelts ore **2** a smelting apparatus or factory

Smet·a·na /sméttənə/, **Bedřich** (1824–84) Czech composer

smid·gen /smíjjən/, **smid·gin, smid·geon, smidge** *n* a small amount *(infml)*

smile /smíl/ *v* (**smiled, smil·ing**) **1** *vti* raise the corners of the mouth in an expression of amusement or pleasure **2** *vi* look happy or pleased **3** *vi* show favor to somebody ■ *n*

1 an expression of amusement or pleasure made by smiling **2** an appearance of pleasure or approval *(often pl)* —**smil·ing·ly** *adv*

⚡ **smil·ey** /smíflee/ *adj* (**-i·er, -i·est**) smiling ■ *n* (*pl* **-eys**) a symbol :-) used in e-mails to express pleasure, approval, or humor

smirk *n* an insolent smile ■ *vi* smile insolently

smite /smīt/ (**smote** /smōt/, **smit·ten** /smítt'n/ *or* **smote**, **smit·ing**) *v* **1** *vti* hit hard *(literary)* **2** *vt* affect somebody strongly or disastrously *(literary)* **3** *vt* fill somebody with love *(literary; often passive)*

smith /smith/ *n* **1** somebody who makes or repairs metal objects **2** a blacksmith

Smith /smith/, **Adam** (1723–90) British philosopher and economist

Smith, Bessie (1894–1937) US blues singer

Smith, David (1906–65) US sculptor

Smith, Joseph (1805–44) US founder of the Church of Jesus Christ of Latter-Day Saints

Smith, Margaret Chase (1897–1995) US politician and senator (1948–72)

smith·er·eens /smíthə reenz/ *npl* very small broken pieces *(infml)*

Smith·son /smíths'n/, **James** (1765–1829) British mineralogist and chemist whose legacy helped to establish the Smithsonian Institution (1846)

smith·y /smíthee, smíthee/ (*pl* **-ies**) *n* **1** a blacksmith's workplace **2** a blacksmith

smit·ten past participle of **smite**

smock *n* a loose garment worn to protect the clothes ■ *vt* sew with decorative gathering stitches

smock·ing /smóking/ *n* decorative stitching used to gather fabric

smog *n* a mixture of fog and smoke or exhaust fumes —**smog·gy** *adj*

smoke /smōk/ *n* **1** a cloud of tiny particles rising from something burning **2** minute particles suspended in a gas **3** an act of smoking a cigarette, cigar, or pipe **4** a cigarette *(infml)* ■ *v* (**smoked, smok·ing**) **1** *vti* inhale smoke from burning tobacco or another substance in a cigarette, cigar, or pipe **2** *vi* give off smoke **3** *vt* cure food with smoke **4** *vt* fumigate something with smoke ◊ **go up in smoke** fail to happen as planned or hoped

☐ **smoke out** *vt* drive from hiding with smoke

smoke a·larm, smoke de·tec·tor *n* a device that sounds an alarm when it detects smoke

smoke and mir·rors *n* something intended to divert attention from something else

smoke bomb *n* a weapon producing irritating chemical smoke, used for forcing people or animals out of a place

smoke hood *n* a plastic head covering with a breathing apparatus

smoke·less /smókləss/ *adj* producing no smoke

smok·er /smókər/ *n* **1** somebody who smokes tobacco **2** a railroad car designated for smoking **3** an apparatus for smoking food

smoke screen *n* **1** an action intended to mislead somebody or obscure something **2** a mass of smoke used for hiding ship or troop movements

smoke sig·nal *n* a signal made with a column of smoke

smoke·stack /smók stàk/ *n* a large, often cylindrical, outlet for combustible gases and smoke

smok·ing gun *n* a piece of conclusive evidence or proof of wrongdoing

smok·ing room *n* a room for smokers

smok·y /smókee/ (**-i·er, -i·est**) *adj* **1** filled with smoke **2** colored like smoke **3** tasting of smoke **4** giving off excessive smoke —**smok·i·ly** *adv* —**smok·i·ness** *n*

smol·der /smóldər/, **smoul·der** *vi* **1** burn slowly without a flame **2** have or exist as a suppressed emotion ■ *n* **1** thick smoke from a slow-burning fire **2** a slow-burning fire

Smo·lensk /smə lénsk, smə-/ city in W Russia. Pop. 398,405 (1995).

Smol·lett /smóllət/, **Tobias George** (1721–71) British novelist

smooch *(infml)* *vti* kiss and caress ■ *n* an act or period of smooching

smooth /smooth/ *adj* **1** not having a rough or bumpy surface **2** without lumps **3** proceeding without upheaval or difficulties **4** without jerks or jolts **5** not harsh, sharp, or sour **6** insincerely pleasant or flattering ■ *vt* **1** remove roughness or bumps from something **2** remove lines and creases from something **3** remove obstacles or difficulties from something ■ *n* **1** an act or the process of smoothing **2** a smooth part of something —**smooth·ly** *adv* —**smooth·ness** *n*

☐ **smooth over** *vt* lessen difficulties or tensions

smooth·ie /smóothee/ *n* **1** *also* **smooth·y** (*pl* **-ies**) an insincerely charming man *(infml)* **2** a puréed fruit drink, often with milk, yogurt, or ice cream

smor·gas·bord /smáwrgəss bàwrd/ *n* a buffet meal with a large variety of dishes

smote past tense of **smite**

smoth·er /smúthər/ *v* **1** *vti* deprive or be deprived of air **2** *vti* kill or die by suffocation **3** *vt* overwhelm somebody with affection **4** *vt* put out a fire **5** *vt* suppress or hide a feeling —**smoth·er·ing·ly** *adv*

smoul·der *vi, n* = smolder

⚡ **SMS** *n* a service for sending short textual messages, e.g., between cellular phones and pagers. Full form **short message service**

smudge /smuj/ *n* **1** a patch of smeared ink or paint **2** a dirty mark **3** a blurred or indistinct area **4** smoke for protecting trees from frost or insects, or a fire producing such smoke ■ vti (**smudged, smudg·ing**) 1 smear or be smeared 2 make or become dirty —**smudg·y** adj

smug /smug-ger, smug-gest/ adj self-satisfied —**smug·ly** adv —**smug·ness** n

smug·gle /smúgg'l/ (-**gled, -gling**) v 1 vti bring goods into a country illegally 2 vt bring or take away secretly —**smug·gler** n

smut n 1 obscene jokes, stories, or pictures 2 a fungal plant disease characterized by sooty spores on leaves 3 a small piece of soot or dirt —**smut·ti·ness** n —**smut·ty** adj

Sn symbol tin

⚡**SNA** abbr systems network architecture

snack n 1 a small quick meal 2 food eaten between meals —**snack** vi

snack bar n a small restaurant selling snacks

snaf·fle /snáff'l/, **snaf·fle bit** n a jointed bit with rings at either side for attaching a horse's reins

sna·fu /sna foó/ n a bad situation caused by incompetence (infml)

⚡**SNAFU** abbr situation normal all fouled up (in e-mails)

snag n 1 a small problem that impedes progress 2 a sharp point on which something may catch and tear 3 a small hole or loose thread in a fabric ■ v (**snagged, snag·ging**) 1 vti catch on a snag 2 vt obstruct the progress of 3 vt obtain by luck —**snag·gy** adj

snail n a small animal with a coiled shell and a retractable muscular foot on which it crawls

⚡**snail mail** n postal mail (infml)

snake /snayk/ n 1 a legless reptile with a scaly tubular body 2 an offensive term for somebody regarded as untrustworthy ■ v (**snaked, snak·ing**) 1 vi move or extend in curves like a snake 2 vt drag by a rope or chain

Snake river in the NW United States, rising in NW Wyoming and flowing into the Columbia River in SE Washington. Length 1,040 mi./1,670 km.

snake·bite /snáyk bìt/ n the bite of a poisonous snake

snake charm·er n an entertainer who elicits a swaying movement from snakes with music

snake oil n worthless medicine

snake·skin /snáyk skìn/ n 1 a snake's skin 2 leather made of snakes' skins

snak·y /snáykee/ (-i·er, -i·est) adj 1 bending or twisting 2 treacherous —**snak·i·ly** adv

snap v (**snapped, snap·ping**) 1 vti break with a sharp noise 2 vti move or operate with a sharp noise 3 vti say something angrily 4 vt take a photograph of somebody or something (infml) 5 vti bite or grasp somebody or something suddenly 6 vti move sharply 7 vt in football, pass the ball back to the quarterback from the line of scrimmage ■ n

1 a sharp sound 2 a fastener that clicks together 3 something that is easy to do 4 a short period of cold weather 5 liveliness o *His campaign needs more snap.* 6 in football, a pass from the line of scrimmage back to the quarterback ■ adj decided without reflection o *a snap decision*

snap·drag·on /snáp dràggən/ n a garden plant with spikes of flowers

snap·per /snáppər/ n 1 (pl **snap·pers** or same) a carnivorous tropical fish 2 also **snap·ping tur·tle** a freshwater turtle with powerful jaws 3 snapper as food

snap·pish /snáppish/ adj showing irritation or impatience —**snap·pish·ly** adv

snap·py /snáppee/ (-pi·er, -pi·est) adj 1 stylish (infml) 2 interesting and to the point (infml) 3 showing irritation or impatience 4 hasty —**snap·pi·ly** adv

snap·shot /snáp shòt/ n a photograph taken quickly and casually

snare[1] /snair/ n 1 an animal trap 2 something designed to trap an unwary person ■ vt (**snared, snar·ing**) 1 catch in a trap 2 entrap by alluring deception

snare[2] /snair/ n a set of metal cords on the underside of a drum (often pl)

snare drum n a drum with a snare on its underside that makes a harsh metallic sound when the drum is hit

snarl[1] v 1 vi growl 2 vti say something angrily —**snarl** n —**snarl·ing·ly** adv

snarl[2] n 1 a tangled mass of something 2 a state of confusion 3 a knot in wood ■ vti 1 tangle or become tangled 2 become or cause to become confused or congested

snatch vt 1 grab or take quickly 2 move or remove quickly 3 take or get when the opportunity arises 4 kidnap somebody (infml) ■ n 1 an act of snatching something 2 a small amount —**snatch·er** n

snaz·zy /snázzee/ (-zi·er, -zi·est) adj attractively new, bright, or fashionable (infml) —**snaz·zi·ly** adv

sneak /sneek/ v (**sneaked** or **snuck**) 1 vi go or move stealthily 2 vt do without being noticed 3 vt bring or take stealthily ■ n 1 a person regarded as untrustworthy (insult) 2 a stealthy departure ■ adj stealthily done

sneak·er /snéekər/ n US, Can, ANZ a sports shoe with a rubber sole (often pl)

sneak·ing /snéeking/ adj slight but persistent o *a sneaking suspicion*

sneak·y /snéekee/ (-i·er, -i·est) adj underhanded —**sneak·i·ly** adv —**sneak·i·ness** n

sneer n an expression of scorn in which the upper lip is raised ■ v 1 vi feel or show scorn 2 vt say with scorn —**sneer·ing** adj —**sneer·ing·ly** adv

sneeze n an involuntary explosive expulsion of air through the nose and mouth —**sneeze** vi

snick *n* a small cut —**snick** *vi*

snick·er /sníkər/, **snig·ger** /snígɡər/ *vi* laugh disrespectfully in a stifled way —**snick·er** *n*

snide /snīd/ (**snid·er, snid·est**) *adj* derisively sarcastic —**snide·ly** *adv*

sniff *v* 1 *vti* breathe in through the nose, e.g., in smelling something 2 *vt* have a suspicion of ○ *began to sniff trouble* ■ *n* 1 an act or sound of sniffing 2 a suspicion
□ **sniff out** *vt* find out (*infml*)

⚡ **sniff·er** /sníffər/ *n* 1 a device that monitors data transmission 2 a program on a computer system designed legitimately or illegitimately to capture data being transmitted on a network

snif·fle /snífflʼl/ *vi* (**-fled, -fling**) 1 inhale mucus 2 weep quietly ■ *n* an act or sound of sniffling

snif·ter /snífftər/ *n* a glass for serving brandy

snig·ger *vti, n* = snicker

snip *vti* (**snipped, snip·ping**) cut using small strokes ■ *n* 1 a small cut 2 a small piece that has been snipped off 3 an act or sound of snipping

snipe /snīp/ *n* (*pl* **snipes** *or* **same**) a wading bird with a long straight bill ■ *vi* (**sniped, snip·ing**) a shot fired from a concealed position —**snip·er** *n*

snip·pet /sníppət/ *n* a small piece of something such as information or music

snip·py /sníppee/ (**-pi·er, -pi·est**) *adj* sharp-tongued (*infml*) —**snip·pi·ly** *adv* —**snip·pi·ness** *n*

snit *n* a fit of temper

snitch (*slang*) *v* 1 *vt* pilfer 2 *vi* inform on somebody ■ *n* an informer

sniv·el /snívvʼl/ (**-eled** *or* **-elled, -el·ing** *or* **-el·ing**) *vi* 1 sniff audibly 2 behave in a tearful or self-pitying way —**sniv·el** *n* —**sniv·el·er** *n* —**sniv·el·ing** *n, adj*

snob *n* 1 somebody who looks down on people who are not cultivated or not from a high social class 2 somebody who disdains things that he or she considers inferior —**snob·ber·y** *n* —**snob·bish** *adj* —**snob·bish·ly** *adv* —**snob·bism** *n* —**snob·by** *adj*

ORIGIN Snob originally meant "shoemaker" (a sense that survives in places). In England Cambridge University students of the late 18C adopted it as a slang term for a "townsman, somebody not a member of the university," and it seems to have been this usage that formed the basis in the 1830s for a new general sense "member of the lower classes." The modern senses began as "somebody who admires and cultivates social superiors," and this use received a considerable boost when Thackeray used it in his *Book of Snobs* (1848). The suggestion that the word itself comes from *s.nob.*, short for Latin *sine nobilitate* "without nobility," is ingenious but ignores the word's early history.

snook[1] /snook, snŏŏk/ (*pl* **same** *or* **snooks**) *n* a large fish of warm seas and rivers

snook[2] /snook, snŏŏk/ *n* a rude gesture made with the thumb on the nose and the fingers outstretched

snoop /snoop/ *vi* pry in a furtive way (*infml*) —**snoop·er** *n* —**snoop·y** *adj*

snoot /snoot/ *n* a nose (*infml*)

snoot·y /snootee/ (**-i·er, -i·est**) *adj* showing haughty condescension (*infml*) —**snoot·i·ly** *adv*

snooze (**snoozed, snooz·ing**) *vi* sleep lightly (*infml*) —**snooze** *n*

snore /snawr, snōr/ (**snored, snor·ing**) *vi* breathe noisily while asleep —**snore** *n* —**snor·er** *n*

snor·kel /snáwrkʼl/ *n* 1 an underwater breathing apparatus consisting of a U-shaped tube 2 a ventilator on a submarine ■ *vi* swim with a snorkel —**snor·kel·er** *n* —**snor·kel·ing** *n*

snort *v* 1 *vi* force air through the nose explosively 2 *vi* show contempt by snorting 3 *vti* inhale an illegal drug, especially cocaine (*slang*) ■ *n* 1 a harsh sound made by snorting 2 a gulp of alcohol (*infml*) —**snort·ing** *n, adj*

snot *n* 1 an offensive term for the mucus produced in the nose (*slang*) 2 an offensive term for somebody regarded as arrogant (*slang insult*) —**snot·ti·ly** *adv* —**snot·ty** *adj*

snout /snowt/ *n* an animal's nose —**snout·ed** *adj*

snow /snō/ *n* 1 water vapor in the form of falling flakes of ice crystals 2 snow on the ground 3 cocaine or heroin in the form of a white powder (*slang*) 4 a fall of snow ○ *had a heavy snow last night* ■ *v* 1 *vi* fall as snow (*refers to rain and snow*) ○ *It's snowing!* 2 *vt* persuade somebody with glib talk (*slang*) ○ *was snowed into buying some worthless land*

Snow /snō/, **C. P., Baron Snow of Leicester** (1905–80) British novelist and critic

snow·ball /snō báwl/ *n* 1 a ball of compacted snow that is thrown, especially by children 2 a frozen snack made from crushed ice and colored, flavored syrup ■ *vti* 1 increase or cause to increase rapidly 2 throw snowballs at somebody

Snow·belt /snō bèlt/ *n* the N United States

snow·blow·er /snō blŏ ər/ *n* a machine for clearing snow from roads

snow·board /snō báwrd/ *n* a board for sliding downhill on snow ■ *vi* use a snowboard —**snow·board·er** *n* —**snow·board·ing** *n*

snow·bound /snō bównd/ *adj* prevented by snow from leaving or traveling

snow cone *n US, Can, Carib* a flavored crushed ice snack

snow·drift /snō drìft/ *n* a bank of snow blown together by the wind

snow·drop /snō dròp/ *n* a plant that bears white flowers in early spring

snow·fall /snṓ fàwl/ n 1 a fall of snow 2 the amount of fallen snow in a particular place or a given period

snow·field /snṓ feèld/ n a large permanently snow-covered area

snow·flake /snṓ flàyk/ n an individual mass of ice crystals falling as snow

snow leop·ard n a large mountain cat with a thick pale gray or brown coat marked with dark splotches

snow line n the boundary of a snowfield or the line of altitude above which there is permanent snow

snow·man /snṓ màn/ n (pl **-men** /-mèn/) n a roughly human figure made out of compacted snow

snow·mo·bile /snṓmə beèl, -mō-/ n a small vehicle for traveling over snow **—snow·mo·bil·er** n **—snow·mo·bil·ing** n

snow pea n US, Can, ANZ a variety of pea with a thin flat edible pod

snow·plow /snṓ plòw/ n 1 a vehicle for clearing snow 2 a turning or braking technique in skiing in which the skis are pointed toward each other ■ vi ski in the snowplow position

snow·shoe /snṓ shòo/ n a framework attached to a boot for walking over snow **—snow·sho·er** n

snow·storm /snṓ stàwrm/ n a storm with heavy snow

snow tire n a tire used in snow

snow·y /snṓ ee/ adj 1 covered in snow 2 like snow **—snow·i·ness** n

snub vt (**snubbed, snub·bing**) treat somebody rudely, especially by excluding or ignoring them ■ n an action intended to humiliate somebody

snub-nosed adj 1 with a short barrel or blunt end 2 with a short turned-up nose

snuck past tense, past participle of **sneak**

snuff vt 1 extinguish a flame 2 trim off the burned end of a candlewick 3 put an end to somebody or something (infml)

snuff² n powdered tobacco for inhaling through the nostrils ■ vi take snuff

snuff³ v 1 vt inhale through the nose 2 vti sniff ■ n a sniffing sound

snuff·box /snúf bòks/ n a box for storing snuff

snuff·er /snúffər/ n a long-handled candle extinguisher

snuf·fle /snúff'l/ v (**-fled, -fling**) 1 vi breathe noisily 2 vti say something nasally ■ n a sound of snuffling **—snuf·fly** adj

snug (**snug·ger, snug·gest**) adj 1 cozy 2 small but comfortable 3 sheltered 4 close-fitting **—snug·ly** adv **—snug·ness** n

snug·gle /snúgg'l/ (**-gled, -gling**) vi 1 cuddle up to somebody 2 settle into a warm and comfortable position

so¹ /sō/ conj 1 in order that ○ held her tight so she wouldn't fall 2 introduces a result ○ Everything is done on a shoestring, so their prices are very low. 3 indicates similarity ○ Just as my circumstances have changed, so too have my aims in life. ■ adv 1 indicates that what is true of one person or thing is also true of another (followed by an auxiliary or modal verb, or by the main verb "do," "have," or "be") ○ If you can keep a secret, so can I. 2 as described ○ The company has the potential to be very successful, and will soon be so. 3 refers back to something mentioned earlier ○ for those who would like to do so 4 to such an extent 5 emphasizes a quality ○ I was so scared. 6 therefore or in consequence ○ She said that she would like to see me again so I gave her my phone number. 7 introduces a comment or question ○ So I see you've changed your mind. 8 indicates something using actions or gestures ○ Hold onto the boat like so. 9 indeed (nonstandard) ○ "You never explained what to do." "I did so!" ◊ **and so on** or **forth** and other similar things ◊ **so much, so many** a limited or unspecified degree or amount ◊ **so much for** indicates a particular person or thing has not been useful or helpful (infml) ◊ See note at **sew**

so² /sō/ n MUSIC = **sol**¹

soak /sōk/ v 1 vti immerse or be immersed in liquid for a time 2 vt make very wet 3 vti absorb or be absorbed 4 vi permeate ■ n 1 an act of soaking 2 a habitual drinker (slang)

soak·ing /sṓking/ n an act or the process of immersing something in liquid ■ adj very wet (infml)

so-and-so (pl **so-and-sos**) n 1 an unnamed person or thing (infml) 2 a person regarded as unpleasant or annoying (infml insult)

soap /sōp/ n 1 a solid, liquid, or powdered preparation used for washing or cleaning 2 a soap opera (infml) 3 a metallic salt combined with a fatty acid. Use: bases for waterproofing agents, ointments, greases. ■ vt put soap on

soap·box /sṓp bòks/ n a platform for impromptu public speaking

soap op·e·ra n a serial melodrama on television or radio

ORIGIN In the early days of radio and television in the United States, serials were often sponsored by soap manufacturers, hence the name **soap opera**.

soap pow·der n a powdered detergent for use in washing machines

soap·stone /sṓp stòn/ n a soft variety of the mineral talc. Use: decorative carving.

soap·suds /sṓp sùdz/ npl water with a soapy lather **—soap·suds·y** adj

soap·y /sṓpee/ (**-i·er, -i·est**) adj 1 full of or covered with soap 2 like soap **—soap·i·ness** adv

soar /sawr/ vi 1 fly, glide, or rise high in the air 2 increase rapidly **—soar** n

SPELLCHECK Do not confuse the spelling of

soar and **sore** ("painful"), which sound similar.

sob (sobbed, sob·bing) v 1 vi cry with gasping sounds 2 vt say while sobbing —**sob** n —**sob·bing·ly** adv

so·ber /sóbər/ adj 1 not drunk 2 tending not to drink alcohol 3 serious in demeanor 4 lacking vitality or brightness in appearance 5 based on rational thinking ■ vti lessen intoxication —**so·ber·ing** adj —**so·ber·ing·ly** adv —**so·ber·ly** adv —**so·ber·ness** n

□ **sober up** vti make or become sober after being drunk

so·bri·e·ty /sə brí ətee, sō-/ n 1 the state of not being drunk 2 seriousness

so·bri·quet /sóbri kày, -kèt, sòbri káy, -két/, **sou·bri·quet** n a nickname

sob sto·ry n a story that is intended to provoke pity (infml)

so-called adj 1 popularly known as 2 incorrectly known as

USAGE Do not put quotation marks around expressions following **so-called** and self-styled, which already convey the ideas "popularly called or known" and "incorrectly or falsely called or known," respectively: a so-called generalissimo of capitalism, not a so-called "generalissimo of capitalism."

soc·cer /sókər/ n a game in which two teams of 11 players try to score by kicking or butting a ball into goals on either end of a field

soc·cer mom n a mother who is preoccupied with her children's leisure activities

~~soccity~~ incorrect spelling of **society**

so·cia·ble /sóshəb'l/ adj 1 enjoying the company of other people 2 friendly —**so·cia·bil·i·ty** /sóshə bíllətee/ n —**so·cia·bly** adv

so·cial /sóshəl/ adj 1 of society 2 of the way people interact 3 describes animals that live in communities o social insects such as ants 4 offering opportunities for interaction o a social club 5 of human welfare o social programs ■ n an informal get-together —**so·cial·ly** adv

so·cial climb·er n somebody who seeks social advancement (disapproving)—**so·cial climb·ing** n

so·cial de·moc·ra·cy n the principle of a gradual shift from capitalism to socialism —**so·cial dem·o·crat** n —**so·cial dem·o·crat·ic** adj

so·cial en·gi·neer·ing n the practical application of a social science in solving social problems

so·cial·ism /sóshə lìzəm/ n 1 a political system of communal ownership 2 also **So·cial·ism** a political movement based on socialism —**so·cial·ist** n —**so·cial·is·tic** /sóshə lístik/ adj

so·cial·ite /sóshə lìt/ n somebody who is well known in fashionable society

so·cial·ize /sóshə līz/ (-ized, -iz·ing) v 1 vi take part in social activities 2 vt train to be a fit member of society o socialize a child 3 vt place under public ownership or control —**so·cial·i·za·tion** /sòshəli záysh'n/ n —**so·cial·iz·er** n

so·cial·ized med·i·cine n health care subsidized by the government

so·cial mo·bil·i·ty n the ability of people to change their social status

so·cial sci·ence n 1 the study of societies 2 a discipline in which a specific area of society is studied, e.g., sociology, economics, or anthropology —**so·cial sci·en·tist** n

so·cial se·cu·ri·ty n 1 also **So·cial Se·cu·ri·ty** a government program that provides economic security to people who are retired, unemployed, or unable to work 2 money paid to somebody under the Social Security program

So·cial Se·cu·ri·ty num·ber n a person's reference number within the Social Security system

so·cial ser·vice n any of the public services provided for the welfare of a person or community (often pl)

so·cial ser·vic·es n an agency providing social services (+ sing verb)

so·cial stud·ies n a school subject involving the study of society (+ sing verb)

so·cial wel·fare n the social services provided by a state or private organization

so·ci·e·ty /sə sí ətee/ (pl -ties) n 1 the sum of the social relationships among groups of people or animals 2 a structured community of people 3 the customs of a community and the way it is organized 4 a subset of a society 5 the prominent or fashionable people in a community 6 companionship 7 a group of people who share a common interest —**so·ci·e·tal** adj

So·ci·e·ty of Friends n the Christian group also known as the Quakers

So·ci·e·ty of Je·sus n a Roman Catholic order engaged in missionary and educational work worldwide

socio- prefix society, social o sociopath o socioeconomic

so·ci·o·ec·o·nom·ic /sòssee ō èkə nómmik, sòshee-, -èekə nómmik/ adj involving economic and social factors —**so·ci·o·ec·o·nom·i·cal·ly** adv

so·ci·ol·o·gy /sòssee óllajee, -shee-/ n 1 the study of human societies 2 the study of an individual social institution —**so·ci·o·log·i·cal** /sòssee ə lójjik'l, -shee-/ adj —**so·ci·ol·o·gist** n

so·ci·o·path /sóssee ō pàth, -shee-/ n an offensive term for somebody whose personality disorder leads to violent antisocial behavior —**so·ci·o·path·ic** /sòssee ō páthik,

-shee-/ adj —**so·ci·op·a·thy** /sòssee óppəthee, -shee-/ n

so·ci·o·po·lit·i·cal /sòssee ō pə líttik'l, -shee-/ adj involving social and political factors

sock[1] n (pl **socks** or **sox**) a soft covering for the foot and lower leg

sock[2] vt hit hard, especially with the fist (infml)

sock·et /sókət/ n 1 a shaped hole that receives a part to make a connection 2 a hollow in the body into which a joint or other part fits ■ vt put in a socket

Soc·ra·tes /sókrə teez/ (469–399 BC) Greek philosopher

sod n a layer or piece of earth with growing grass

so·da /sódə/ n 1 a effervescent soft drink 2 soda water 3 a refreshment made of ice cream in flavored effervescent water 4 sodium that is chemically combined with other elements

so·da foun·tain n 1 a soda water dispenser 2 a counter where beverages, ice cream, and snacks are sold (dated)

so·da pop n an effervescent soft drink (infml)

so·da wa·ter n water made effervescent by the addition of carbon dioxide

sod·den /sódd'n/ adj 1 thoroughly wet 2 drunk —**sod·den·ly** adv —**sod·den·ness** n

so·di·um /sódee əm/ n (symbol Na) an abundantly occurring chemical element. Use: catalyst, tracer, in chemical processes.

so·di·um bi·car·bon·ate n a white crystalline powder. Use: leavening agent, antacid, in effervescent drinks and fire extinguishers.

so·di·um chlo·ride n a colorless crystalline compound, commonly known as salt. Use: food seasoning, preservative.

so·di·um ni·trate n a white crystalline salt. Use: curing of meats, rocket propellant, fertilizer, manufacture of explosives and glass.

sod·om·y /sóddəmee/ n an offensive term for anal intercourse or sexual intercourse with an animal

so·fa /sófə/ n an upholstered seat for more than one person

so·fa bed n a sofa that converts to a bed

So·fi·a /sófee ə/ capital of Bulgaria. Pop. 1,141,712 (1996).

soft /sáwft, soft/ adj 1 easily shaped or cut 2 yielding to physical pressure ○ a soft cushion 3 with a smooth texture ○ soft fur 4 quiet 5 without glare or intensity of light or color 6 gentle 7 lenient 8 undemanding (infml) ○ a soft job 9 incapable of enduring hardship 10 describes water in which soap lathers easily 11 lacking significance ○ soft news 12 based on negotiation, flexibility, and good will ○ a soft sell 13 of a currency or system not backed by gold 14 describes the consonant sounds "c" and "g" as in

"dance" and "age" ■ adv softly —**soft·ly** adv —**soft·ness** n

soft·back /sáwft bàk/ n a paperback —**soft·back** adj

soft·ball /sáwft bàwl, sóft-/ n 1 baseball played with a larger softer ball 2 the ball used for softball

soft·boiled adj describes a boiled egg with a liquid yolk

soft·bound /sáwft bòwnd, sóft-/ adj paperback

⚡**soft cop·y** n data stored on a computer, not printed on paper

soft·core adj sexually suggestive without being explicit

soft drink n a cold and usually effervescent nonalcoholic drink

soft drug n an illegal drug regarded as less dangerous or addictive than heroin and cocaine

soft·en /sáwf'n, sóffən/ vti 1 make or become less hard 2 make or become kinder 3 make or become less resilient or determined —**soft·en·er** n

soft fo·cus n the deliberate blurring of a photographic image

soft·heart·ed adj kind —**soft·heart·ed·ly** adv —**soft·heart·ed·ness** n

soft·ie n = softy

soft land·ing n the safe landing of a spacecraft

soft pal·ate n the soft upper back part of the mouth

soft ped·al n a piano pedal that reduces volume

soft-ped·al vti 1 play a piano's soft pedal 2 play something down (infml)

soft sell n a subtle selling approach (infml)

soft-shell crab n an edible crab that has recently shed its shell

soft soap n persuasive flattery (infml)

soft-soap vt persuade by flattery (infml)

soft-spo·ken adj with a quiet gentle voice

soft spot n a weak spot ◇ **have a soft spot for** have especially tender feelings or affection for

soft top n a car with a fabric roof that can be folded back

⚡**soft·ware** /sáwft wàir, sóft-/ n programs and applications for computers

⚡**soft·ware en·gi·neer·ing** n the design and implementation of computer programs

soft·wood /sáwft wòod, sóft-/ n 1 the wood of any coniferous tree 2 a coniferous tree

soft·y /sáwftee, sóftee/ n (pl -ies), **soft·ie** n a weak, timid, or sentimental person (infml)

sog·gy /sóggee, sáwgee/ (-gi·er, -gi·est) adj 1 thoroughly wet 2 with too much liquid —**sog·gi·ness** n

soh n MUSIC = sol[1]

soil[1] n 1 the top layer of the ground 2 a particular type of earth ○ sandy soil 3 a country (literary) ○ their native soil

soil² /soyl/ vt 1 make dirty 2 bring dishonor on ■ n 1 dirt 2 feces

soi·ree /swaa ráy/, **soi·rée** n an evening party

so·journ /sṓ jùrn/ (literary) n a brief visit ■ vi stay for a time —**so·journ·er** n

sol¹ /sol/, **so** /sṓ/, **soh** /sṓ/ n a syllable used in singing the 5th note of a scale

sol² /sol/ (pl **sol·es** /sṓlays/) n the main unit of currency in Peru

Sol /sol/ n in Roman mythology, the sun god. Greek equivalent **Helios**

sol·ace /sṓlləss/ n 1 comfort or relief from emotional distress 2 a source of solace ■ vt (-aced, -ac·ing) provide with solace

so·lar /sṓlər/ adj 1 of or from the Sun 2 operating using energy from the Sun

so·lar cell n an electric cell that converts solar radiation directly into electricity

so·lar en·er·gy n energy from the Sun

so·lar·i·um /sə láirree əm, sṓ-/ (pl **-a** /-ə/ or **-ums**) n a room built for enjoying sunlight

so·lar pan·el n a panel that collects solar energy

so·lar plex·us n 1 a mass of nerve cells in the upper abdomen 2 a point on the upper abdomen just below where the ribs separate

ORIGIN The nerves form a radial network and so were likened to the sun's rays and called "solar."

so·lar sys·tem n the Sun and the bodies orbiting it

sold past participle, past tense of **sell**

sol·der /sóddər/ n 1 an alloy for joining metal 2 something that unites people or things ■ vti 1 join or be joined with solder 2 unite to form a whole —**sol·der·er** n

sol·der·ing iron n a tool for melting and applying solder

~~soldier~~ incorrect spelling of **soldier**

sol·dier /sṓljər/ n 1 somebody who serves in an army 2 an army member below officer rank 3 a dedicated worker for a cause ■ vi serve in an army —**sol·dier·ly** adj

ORIGIN Soldier goes back to Latin solidus, an ancient Roman gold coin (literally a "solid" coin), and so a soldier is etymologically one who fights for pay. It was adopted into English from French.

sol·dier of for·tune n a soldier who enlists or serves for money or adventure

sol·dier·y /sṓljəree/ n 1 soldiers collectively 2 a soldier's work or skill

sold-out adj with no tickets left

sole¹ /sol/ n 1 the underside of a foot 2 the bottom of a shoe ■ vt (**soled, sol·ing**) put a sole on a shoe

SPELLCHECK Do not confuse the spelling of **sole** and **soul** ("a person's spirit"), which sound similar.

sole² /sol/ adj 1 of which there is only one ○ the sole reason 2 belonging to one person or group ○ has sole responsibility for the department —**sole·ness** n

sole³ /sol/ (pl **soles** or **same**) n 1 a fish with a flat body 2 sole as food

sol·e·cism /sólla sìzzəm, sṓlə-/ n 1 a grammatical mistake 2 something incorrect or inappropriate, e.g., a breach of etiquette —**sol·e·cis·ti·cal** /sólla sístik'l, sṓlə-/ adj

sole·ly /sṓl lee/ adv 1 only ○ sold the company solely for commercial reasons 2 exclusively ○ He is solely to blame.

~~solemly~~ incorrect spelling of **solemnly**

sol·emn /sólləm/ adj 1 serious or earnest 2 humorless 3 formal —**sol·emn·ly** adv —**sol·emn·ness** n

so·lem·ni·ty /sə lémnətee/ (pl **-ties**) n 1 the solemn quality of something 2 a solemn ceremony (often pl)

sol·em·nize /sólləm nìz/ (-nized, -niz·ing) vt 1 celebrate or observe with a ceremony or formality 2 make dignified —**sol·em·ni·za·tion** /sòlləmnì záysh'n/ n

sol·fa /sṓl faa/ n a system of using syllables to denote degrees of a musical scale

so·lic·it /sə líssit/ vt 1 try to get something by making repeated pleas 2 vt ask somebody for something 3 vti offer people sex for money —**so·lic·i·ta·tion** /sə lìssə táysh'n/ n

so·lic·i·tor /sə líssətər/ n 1 the top legal officer in a city, town, county, or government department 2 somebody who solicits orders or financial contributions 3 UK an attorney who draws up legal documents and does preparatory work for barristers

so·lic·i·tor gen·er·al (pl **so·lic·i·tors gen·er·al**) n 1 a US law officer who is in charge of appeals 2 **So·lic·i·tor Gen·er·al** Can a member of a federal or provincial cabinet responsible for law enforcement, prisons, and some forms of licensing 3 a state law officer equivalent to a state attorney general

so·lic·i·tous /sə líssətəss/ adj 1 expressing an attitude of concern 2 ready and willing —**so·lic·i·tous·ly** adv —**so·lic·i·tous·ness** n

so·lic·i·tude /sə líssə tòod/ n concern and consideration, especially when expressed

sol·id /sólləd/ adj 1 not soft or yielding 2 not hollow 3 unadulterated or unmixed 4 of strong and secure construction 5 uninterrupted ○ worked for a solid two hours 6 unanimous ○ Support for the proposal was solid. 7 reliable 8 financially secure 9 three-dimensional 10 without spaces between words or lines of type ■ n 1 a solid thing 2 a three-dimensional figure 3 a substance that retains its shape, unlike a liquid or gas —**so·lid·i·ty** /sə líddətee/ n —**sol·id·ly** adv —**sol·id·ness** n

sol·i·dar·i·ty /sòllə dárrətee/ n mutual agreement and support

so·lid·i·fy /sə líddə fì/ (**-fied, -fies**) *vti* **1** make or become solid **2** make or become strong and united —**so·lid·i·fi·ca·tion** /sə líddəfi káysh'n/ *n*

so·lil·o·quy /sə lílləkwee/ (*pl* **-quies**) *n* **1** the act of talking when alone **2** a speech made by an actor alone on stage

sol·ip·sism /sóllǝp sìzzǝm, sól-/ *n* a belief in the self as the only reality —**sol·ip·sist** *n* —**sol·ip·sis·tic** /sòllǝp sístik, sòlǝp-/ *adj*

sol·i·taire /sóllǝ tàir/ *n* **1** a card game for one **2** a single gemstone that is set in a ring

sol·i·tar·y /sóllǝ tèrree/ *adj* **1** done alone **2** preferring to be or live alone **3** remote or apart from others **4** single o *a solitary boat on the river* **5** describes animals that live alone or in pairs rather than in colonies or social groups ■ *n* (*pl* **-ies**) **1** a recluse **2** *also* **sol·i·tar·y con·fine·ment** imprisonment in an isolated cell —**sol·i·tar·i·ly** *adv* —**sol·i·tar·i·ness** *n*

sol·i·tude /sóllǝ tòod/ *n* **1** the state of being alone **2** remoteness

so·lo /sólō/ *n* (*pl* **-li** /-lee/) **1** a musical piece or passage performed by one person **2** any performance by one person ■ *adj* **1** for a single performer **2** done by one person ■ *adv* alone ■ *vi* (**-loed, -lo·ing**) do something without help or accompaniment

so·lo·ist /sólō ist/ *n* somebody who performs a musical solo

Sol·o·mon Is·lands /sóllǝmǝn-/ country comprising over 35 islands and atolls in the South Pacific Ocean. Cap. Honiara. Pop. 480,442 (2001). —**Sol·o·mon Is·land·er** *n*

sol·stice /sólstiss, sól-/ *n* **1** the longest or shortest day of the year **2** either of the points on the ecliptic when the Sun reaches its northernmost or southernmost point —**sol·sti·tial** /sol stísh'l, sòl-/ *adj*

sol·u·ble /sóllyǝb'l/ *adj* **1** able to be dissolved in liquid **2** able to be solved —**sol·u·bil·i·ty** /sòlyǝ bíllǝtee/ *n* —**sol·u·bly** *adv*

so·lu·tion /sǝ lóosh'n/ *n* **1** a way of resolving a problem or difficulty **2** the answer to a puzzle or question **3** the act of finding a solution **4** a fluid with a substance dissolved in it **5** the process of forming a solution

solve /solv, sawlv/ (**solved, solv·ing**) *vt* **1** deal with a problem successfully **2** find the answer to a puzzle **3** work out the solution to an equation or other mathematical problem —**solv·a·bil·i·ty** /sòlvǝ bíllǝtee/ *n* —**solv·a·ble** *adj*

sol·vent /sólvǝnt/ *adj* **1** having enough money to cover expenses and debts **2** able to dissolve substances ■ *n* a substance that dissolves other substances —**sol·ven·cy** *n*

Sol·zhe·ni·tsyn /sòlzhǝ nee̱tsin, sǝlzhǝ nyee̱tsin/, **Aleksandr Isayevich** (*b.* 1918) Russian writer

som /som/ (*pl* **same**) *n* the main unit of currency of Kyrgyzstan

So·ma·li·a /sō maálee ǝ, sǝ-/ country in E Africa. Cap. Mogadishu. Pop. 7,488,773 (2001). —**So·ma·li·an** *n, adj*

So·ma·li·land /sō maálee lànd, sǝ-/ region of NE Africa, comprising Somalia, Djibouti, and part of Ethiopia

so·mat·ic /sō máttik/ *adj* affecting the body

so·mat·ic cell *n* any body cell except a reproductive cell

som·ber /sómbǝr/ *adj* **1** dark and gloomy **2** dark in color **3** serious and melancholy —**som·ber·ly** *adv* —**som·ber·ness** *n*

som·bre·ro /som brérrō/ (*pl* **-ros**) *n* a wide-brimmed hat

some *stressed* /sum/ *unstressed* /sǝm/ *adj, pron* indicates an unspecified number, quantity, or proportion o *I agree with you to some extent.* o *Some of you will not agree with me.* ■ *adj* **1** quite a few o *We have been debating this problem for some months now.* **2** particular but unspecified o *some medical book* **3** adds emphasis o *That was some performance!* ■ *adv* **1** approximately o *for some 30 years* **2** to a small extent (*infml*) o *I do write some.* **3** a great deal (*infml*) o *I'll have to study some.*

-some *suffix* **1** characterized by a particular quality, condition, or thing o *troublesome* **2** a group containing a particular number of members o *threesome*

some·bod·y /súm bòddee, súmbǝdee/, **some·one** /súm wùn/ *pron* some unspecified person ■ *pron, n* (*pl* **-ies**; *pl* **someones**) an important or well-known person

some·day /súm dày/ *adv* at an unspecified time in the future

some·how /súm hòw/ *adv* **1** in some way, often with great effort or difficulty o *He somehow managed to climb back up.* **2** for an unknown reason o *She somehow forgot to tell anyone where she was going.*

some·place /súm plàyss/ *adv* somewhere (*infml*)

som·er·sault /súmmǝr sàwlt/ *n* an acrobatic rolling of the body in a complete circle ■ *vi* perform a somersault

ORIGIN **Somersault** came from a French word deriving ultimately from Latin *super* "above" and *saltus* "leap". It is recorded in English from the mid-16C.

some·thing /súm thing/ *pron* **1** an unspecified thing o *I knew there was something wrong.* **2** an unspecified amount o *something over 50%* **3** suggesting a resemblance o *something of the athlete about him* **4** rather o *something of a disappointment* ■ *adv* **1** to some extent o *Your voice sounds something like hers.* **2** to an extreme degree (*infml*) o *It hurts something awful.* ◊ **something else** somebody or something really special or remarkable (*infml*) ◊ **have something to do with** be connected with or involve

some·time /súm tìm/ *adv* at an unspecified time in the future ○ *They intend to marry sometime soon.* ■ *adj* 1 former ○ *a sometime student of this university* 2 occasional ○ *an author and sometime lecturer*

some·times /súm tìmz/ *adv* on some occasions or from time to time ○ *We go to the theater sometimes.*

some·way /súm wày/, **some·ways** /-wàyz/ *adv* using some means that is not yet known or stated ○ *We'll figure it out someway.*

some·what /súm wòt, súm hwòt/ *adv* to some extent

some·where /súm wàir, súm hwàir/ *adv* 1 in some unspecified place ○ *He lives somewhere in Vermont.* 2 expresses approximation ○ *somewhere between three and four hundred* ◇ **get somewhere** make progress toward achieving something

Somme /som, sawm/ river in N France, flowing into the English Channel. Length 150 mi./241 km.

som·nam·bu·late /som námbyə làyt/ (-**lat·ed**, -**lat·ing**) *vi* sleepwalk (technical) —**som·nam·bu·la·tion** /som nàmbyə láysh'n/ *n* —**som·nam·bu·la·tor** *n*

som·nam·bu·lism /som námbyə lìzzəm/ *n* sleepwalking (technical) —**som·nam·bu·list** *n*

som·no·lent /sómnələnt/ *adj* 1 sleepy 2 lacking activity —**som·no·lence** *n* —**som·no·lent·ly** *adv*

~~something~~ incorrect spelling of **something**

son /sun/ *n* 1 somebody's male child 2 a male descendant 3 a man or boy connected with a particular place or period ○ *the achievements of the sons of the Industrial Revolution* 4 **Son** in Christianity, Jesus Christ —**son·less** *adj*

SPELLCHECK Do not confuse the spelling of **son** and **sun** ("a star"), which sound similar.

so·nar /só naàr/ *n* 1 a system for detecting underwater objects by means of sound waves 2 a device that uses sonar

so·na·ta /sə naátə/ *n* a classical composition for one or more solo instruments

Sond·heim /sónd hìm/, **Stephen** (b. 1930) US composer and lyricist

son et lu·mière /sàwn ay loo myáir/ *n* an outdoor spectacle with music and lights

song /sawng, song/ *n* 1 a set of words that are sung 2 singing as an activity or form of expression 3 an instrumental work in the style of a song 4 the characteristic sound of a bird or insect ◇ **for a song** very cheaply (infml)

song·bird /sáwng bùrd, sóng-/ *n* a bird with a musical call

song·book /sáwng bò‍ok, sóng-/ *n* a book of songs

Song of Sol·o·mon, Song of Songs *n* a book

of the Bible consisting of a set of love poems traditionally attributed to King Solomon

song·ster /sáwngstər, sóngstər/ *n* 1 a singer 2 a songbird

song·writ·er /sáwng rìtər/ *n* a writer of songs

son·ic /sónnik/ *adj* 1 of sound or sound waves 2 of the speed of sound in air

sonic boom *n* a loud boom produced when an aircraft flies faster than the speed of sound

son-in-law (*pl* **sons-in-law**) *n* a daughter's husband

son·net /sónnət/ *n* a fourteen-line rhyming poem with a set structure

So·no·ran De·sert /sə nàwrən-/ desert in SW Arizona, S California, and NW Mexico

so·no·rous /sónnərəss, sə náwrəss/ *adj* 1 producing sound 2 sounding with loud deep tones —**so·no·rous·ly** *adv*

soon *adv* 1 after a short time ○ *She soon realized that she had made a mistake.* 2 quickly ○ *How soon will you be ready?* 3 early ○ *It's a little bit soon to be thinking of leaving, isn't it?* ◇ **as soon as** immediately after ◇ **no sooner...than** immediately after one thing had happened, another took place ◇ **sooner or later** at some as yet unspecifiable time in the future

soot /sò‍ot, soot/ *n* the black dust given off by a fire —**soot·y** *adj*

soothe /sooth/ (**soothed, sooth·ing**) *vt* 1 ease pain 2 calm somebody down —**sooth·ing** *adj* —**sooth·ing·ly** *adv*

sooth·say·er /sò‍oth sày ər/ *n* somebody who predicts the future —**sooth·say** *vi*

sop *n* 1 something given to satisfy a discontented person 2 a piece of food dipped in liquid ■ *vti* (**sopped, sop·ping**) soak in liquid

□ **sop up** *vt* soak up liquid

soph·ism /sóffizzəm/ *n* an apparently clever but flawed argument —**soph·ist** *n* —**so·phis·tic** /sə fístik/ *adj* —**so·phis·ti·cal·ly** *adv*

so·phis·ti·cate *vt* /sə fístə kàyt/ (-**cat·ed**, -**cat·ing**) 1 make somebody more cultured or worldly 2 make something more complex ■ *n* /sə fístəkət/ a cultured or worldly person

so·phis·ti·cat·ed /sə fístə kàytəd/ *adj* 1 knowledgeable and cultured 2 suitable for sophisticated people 3 advanced, complex, and up-to-date ○ *a sophisticated computer network* —**so·phis·ti·cat·ed·ly** *adv* —**so·phis·ti·ca·tion** /sə fístə káysh'n/ *n*

ORIGIN Sophisticated originally meant "adulterated, impure," and later "falsified, dishonest." It did not acquire positive associations until the late 19C. Like *sophistry*, **sophisticated** ultimately refers to the Sophists, a group of Greek philosophers in the 5C BC who became discredited because of their specious reasoning and moral skepticism.

soph·is·try /sóffistree/ n apparently clever but flawed reasoning

~~sophmore~~ incorrect spelling of **sophomore**

Soph·o·cles /sóffə kleèz/ (496?–406? BC) Greek dramatist

soph·o·more /sóffə màwr, sóf màwr/ n 1 a second-year student in a high school, college, or university 2 somebody in the second year of a project or activity

soph·o·mor·ic /sòffə máwrik/ adj 1 immature 2 of sophomores

sop·o·rif·ic /sòppə ríffik, sòpə-/ adj 1 causing sleep or drowsiness 2 feeling sleepy ■ n a sleep-inducing drug

sop·ping /sópping/, **sop·ping wet** adj thoroughly wet

sop·py /sóppee/ (-pi·er, -pi·est) adj very wet —**sop·pi·ly** adv —**sop·pi·ness** n

so·pran·o /sə pránnō, sə praànō/ (pl -os) n 1 a woman or boy with the highest singing voice 2 the highest singing voice, or a part written for this voice

sor·bet /sáwrbət, -bay/ n a frozen dessert made with fruit syrup

sor·cer·y /sáwrssəree/ n the supposed supernatural use of magic —**sor·cer·er** n —**sor·cer·ess** n —**sor·cer·ous** adj

sor·did /sáwrdəd/ adj 1 demonstrating the worst aspects of humanity 2 dirty and depressing —**sor·did·ly** adv —**sor·did·ness** n

sore /sawr, sōr/ adj (sor·er, sor·est) 1 painful 2 causing anger, embarrassment, or distress ○ His dismissal has always been a sore point. 3 angry or upset (infml) 4 urgent ○ in sore need of help ■ n a painful open skin infection —**sore·ness** n ◊ See note at **soar**

sore·ly /sáwrlee, sórlee/ adv very ○ I was sorely tempted to give her the money.

sor·ghum /sáwrgəm/ (pl -ghums or same) n a cereal crop grown in warm areas of the world

So·rop·ti·mist /sə róptimist/ n a member of a professional women's club that promotes public service

so·ror·i·ty /sə ráwrətee, -rórrətee/ (pl -ties) n a social society for women students

sor·rel[1] /sáwrəl, sórrəl/ (pl -rels or same) n a plant with sharp-tasting leaves. Use: salad greens, medicines.

sor·rel[2] /sáwrəl, sórrəl/ adj reddish brown ■ n 1 a reddish brown color 2 a reddish brown horse

sor·row /sórrō, sáwrō/ n 1 a feeling of deep sadness 2 a cause of sorrow ■ vi grieve (literary)

ORIGIN Sorrow and sorry look as though they should be closely related, but in fact they are not. Sorrow comes from an ancient Germanic root meaning "care." Sorry also represents a Germanic word, but is related to sore.

sor·row·ful /sórrōf'l, sáwrōf'l/ adj sad —**sor·row·ful·ly** adv

sor·ry /sórree, sáwree/ adj (-ri·er, -ri·est) 1 apologetic 2 sympathetic 3 pitiful ■ interj 1 expresses apology 2 asks somebody to repeat something (infml) —**sor·ri·ness** n

⚡ sort n 1 a category 2 something similar to a particular thing ○ It's a sort of play with dancing. 3 the process of arranging electronic data in a set order ■ vt 1 put in categories 2 put in a set order —**sort·er** n ◊ **of a sort, of sorts** of a mediocre kind ◊ **out of sorts** 1 not in a very good mood 2 slightly unwell ◊ **sort of** somewhat (infml) ◊ See note at **type**

⚡ sor·ta·tion /sawr táysh'n/ n the process of sorting things, especially when done by a machine or computer

sor·tie /sáwrtee/ n 1 an attack on an enemy 2 a combat aircraft mission ■ vi (-tied) make a sortie

SOS /èss ō éss/ n a distress signal

so-so /sō sō/ adj neither good nor bad (infml)

sot n an offensive term for somebody who habitually drinks a lot of alcohol (literary)

So·to ◆ de Soto, Hernando

sot·to vo·ce /sòttō vóchee, -chày/ adv in a quiet voice —**sot·to vo·ce** adj

sou·bri·quet n = sobriquet

~~souce~~ incorrect spelling of **source**

souf·flé /soo fláy/ n a light dish containing whisked egg whites —**souf·flé** adj

sought past tense, past participle of **seek**

sought-af·ter adj in demand

souk /sook/, **suq** n an outdoor Arab market

soul /sōl/ n 1 the nonphysical aspect of a person 2 a person's spirit regarded as surviving after death 3 somebody's feelings ○ Her soul was in turmoil. 4 spiritual depth ○ The work lacked soul. 5 the essence of a people or nation ○ discover the soul of the Russian people 6 a type of person 7 an individual person (usually pl) ○ a country of some 10 million souls 8 a perfect example or personification of something ○ the soul of discretion 9 the quality that characterizes African American culture 10 a kind of African American music that developed out of blues and gospel music ◊ See note at **sole**

soul food n African American food

soul·ful /sōlf'l/ adj deeply or sincerely emotional —**soul·ful·ly** adv —**soul·ful·ness** n

soul·less /sōl ləss/ adj 1 lacking warmth or feeling 2 lacking interesting or engaging qualities

soul mate n a friend with whom somebody shares deep feelings and attitudes

soul-search·ing n thorough examination of personal thoughts and feelings

sound[1] /sownd/ n 1 something that can be heard 2 vibrations sensed by the ear 3 the sensation produced in the ear by vibrations

4 reproduced music or speech **5** the activity of recording music or speech **6** an impression formed from available information ○ *From the sound of it she's finally found a job she likes.* **7** earshot ○ *within sound of the church bells* **8** a basic element of speech formed by the vocal tract and interpreted through the ear ■ *v* **1** *vi* seem from what is reported ○ *The meal sounded awful.* **2** *vi* indicate a particular condition by means of speech ○ *He sounded exhausted.* **3** *vi* have a particular quality when heard **4** *vti* make or cause to make a noise ○ *An alarm sounded.* **5** *vt* articulate an element of speech **6** *vt* make a bodily organ emit a sound as a test of its physical condition —**sound·less** *adj* —**sound·less·ly** *adv*

sound² /sownd/ *adj* **1** not damaged **2** healthy **3** sensible **4** completely acceptable **5** deep and peaceful **6** complete or thorough **7** with little financial risk **8** logically or legally valid ■ *adv* deeply ○ *sound asleep* —**sound·ly** *adv* —**sound·ness** *n* ◊ See note at **valid**

sound³ /sownd/ *v* **1** *vti* measure the depth of water **2** *vi* dive suddenly and swiftly *(refers to whales)* **3** *vt* examine with a probe ■ *n* a surgical probe

sound⁴ /sownd/ *n* **1** a wide channel **2** an ocean inlet

sound bar·ri·er *n* a sudden increase in the force of air opposing a moving body as it approaches the speed of sound, producing a sonic boom

sound bite *n* a brief broadcast remark, especially one by a politician

⚡ sound card *n* a circuit board for computer sound

sound ef·fect *n* a recording or imitation of a sound used in a broadcast or performance ■ **sound ef·fects** *npl* movie sounds other than dialogue and music

sound·ing /sównding/ *n* **1** a measurement of the depth of water **2** a measurement of atmospheric conditions at a particular altitude ■ **sound·ings** *npl* a preliminary inquiry into people's opinions

sound·ing board *n* **1** somebody asked for a preliminary opinion **2** a structure that reflects sound

sound·proof /sównd proof/ *adj* impenetrable to noise ■ *vt* make soundproof

sound sys·tem *n* a set of equipment for amplifying sound

sound·track /sównd tràk/ *n* **1** the sound recorded for a movie **2** a strip on film that carries the sound

sound wave *n* an audible pressure wave caused by a disturbance in air or water

soup /soop/ *n* a liquid food made by cooking ingredients such as meat, fish, or vegetables in water, milk, or stock

ORIGIN **Soup** was adopted from French *soupe*,

which meant "soup" but also "broth poured on slices of bread." This gives a better clue to the origin of the word, which goes back to a Latin verb meaning "soak."

□ **soup up** *vt* modify a car to make it more powerful *(infml)*

soup·çon /soop sáwN, soop sòn/ *n* a tiny amount

soup kitch·en *n* a place that serves free meals to needy people

soup·y /soópee/ (**-i·er, -i·est**) *adj* like soup

sour /sowr/ *adj* **1** with a naturally sharp acidic taste **2** with a bad taste because of unwanted fermentation **3** characterized by bitter feelings **4** unfriendly or unpleasant ■ *vti* **1** make or become sour **2** make or become dissatisfied ■ *n* a cocktail with lemon or lime —**sour·ly** *adv* —**sour·ness** *n*

source /sawrss, sòrss/ *n* **1** the place where something begins or the thing that something derives from **2** a provider of information ○ *a reliable source* **3** the beginning of a river ■ *vt* (**sourced, sourc·ing**) locate something for use ◊ See note at **origin**

⚡ source code *n* a computer code that can be converted into machine code

sour cream *n* cream that has been artificially soured

sour·dough /sówr dò/ *n* **1** fermenting dough reserved for use as a leavening **2** bread made with sourdough

sour grapes *n* an affected scorn for something secretly desired

ORIGIN **Sour grapes** alludes to the fable *The Fox and the Grapes* by Aesop, in which the fox disparages some grapes as sour when he cannot reach them.

sour·puss /sówr pòoss/ *n* a bad-tempered person *(infml)*

Sou·sa /soóza, -sa/, **John Philip** (1854–1932) US military bandmaster and composer

souse /sowss/ *v* (**soused, sous·ing**) **1** *vt* steep food in vinegar or brine to preserve it **2** *vti* drench or soak something, or become drenched or soaked **3** *vt* make somebody intoxicated *(slang)* ■ *n* **1** a liquid used in pickling **2** pickled food

Sout·er /soótər/, **David** (*b.* 1939) associate justice of the US Supreme Court (1990–)

south /sowth/ *n* **1** the direction to the right of somebody facing the rising sun **2** the compass point that is opposite north **3** *also* **South** the part of an area or country that is in the south ■ *adj* **1** *also* **South** in the south **2** blowing from the south ■ *adv* toward the south —**south·bound** *adj*

South Af·ri·ca country in southern Africa. Cap. Pretoria. Pop. 43,586,097 (2001). —**South Af·ri·can** *n, adj*

South A·mer·i·ca fourth largest continent in the world, lying between the Atlantic and Pacific oceans southeast of North America and stretching from the isthmus of Panama southward to Cape Horn. Pop. 317,846,000 (1996).

South·amp·ton /sow thámptən, sowth hámptən/ port in S England. Pop. 214,859 (1996).

South A·sia region comprising Bangladesh, Bhutan, India, the Maldives, Nepal, Pakistan, and Sri Lanka —**South A·sian** n, adj

South Bend city in N Indiana. Pop. 99,417 (1998).

South Car·o·li·na state of the SE United States. Cap. Columbia. Pop. 4,012,012 (2000). —**South Car·o·lin·i·an** n, adj

South Chi·na Sea part of the China Sea, bounded by SE China, Vietnam, Malaysia, and the Philippines

South Da·ko·ta state of the north central United States. Cap. Pierre. Pop. 754,844 (2000). —**South Da·ko·tan** n, adj

south·east /sowth éest/ n 1 the compass point between south and east 2 also **South·east** the part of an area or country that is in the southeast ■ adj 1 also **South·east** in the southeast 2 blowing from the southeast ■ adv toward the southeast —**south·east·ward** adj, adv

South·east A·sia region comprising Brunei, Cambodia, Indonesia, Laos, Malaysia, Myanmar, the Philippines, Singapore, Thailand, and Vietnam —**South·east A·sian** n, adj

south·east·er·ly /sowth éestərlee/ adj 1 in the southeast 2 blowing from the southeast ■ n (pl **-lies**) also **south·east·er** /sowth éestər/ a wind from the southeast

south·east·ern /sowth éestərn/ adj 1 in the southeast 2 facing southeast 3 also **South·east·ern** of the southeast

south·er·ly /súthərlee/ adj 1 in or toward the south 2 blowing from the south ■ n (pl **-lies**) a wind from the south

south·ern /súthərn/ adj 1 in the south 2 south of the equator 3 facing south 4 also **South·ern** of the southern part of a country —**south·ern·most** adj

South·ern Alps mountain range on the South Island, New Zealand. Highest peak Mt. Cook, 12,316 ft./3,754 m.

South·ern Cross n a constellation in the southern hemisphere

south·ern·er /súthərnər/, **South·ern·er** n somebody from the south of a country

south·ern hem·i·sphere n the half of the Earth south of the equator

South Is·land largest island of New Zealand. Pop. 931,566 (1996).

South Ko·re·a /-kə rée ə, -kó rée ə/ country in East Asia, occupying the S Korean Peninsula. Cap. Seoul. Pop. 47,904,370 (2001). —**South Ko·re·an** n, adj

south·paw /sówth pàw/ n somebody who is left-handed, especially a pitcher or boxer (infml)

South Pole n the southern end of the Earth's axis

South Seas npl 1 the South Pacific 2 the seas of the southern hemisphere

South Vi·et·nam former country in Southeast Asia, occupying the southern part of modern-day Vietnam —**South Vi·et·nam·ese** n, adj

south·ward /sówthwərd/ adj in or toward the south ■ n a point in the south ■ adv also **south·wards** toward the south —**south·ward·ly** adv, adj

south·west /sowth wést/ n 1 the compass point between south and west 2 also **South·west** the part of an area or country that is in the southwest ■ adj 1 also **South·west** in the southwest 2 blowing from the southwest ■ adv toward the southwest

south·west·er /sowth wéstər, sow-/ n 1 a storm from the southwest 2 also **sou'west·er** /sow wéstər/ a broad-brimmed waterproof hat

south·west·er·ly /sowth wéstərlee, sow-/ adj 1 in or toward the southwest 2 blowing from the southwest ■ n (pl **-lies**) a wind from the southwest

south·west·ern /sowth wéstərn/ adj 1 in the southwest 2 facing southwest 3 also **South·west·ern** of the southwest

~~souvenier~~ incorrect spelling of **souvenir**

sou·ve·nir /sòovə néer/ n an object that reminds you of the place where you got it

sou'west·er n = southwester

sov·er·eign /sóvvrən/ n 1 a monarch 2 an old British gold coin worth one pound ■ adj 1 politically independent 2 with complete power 3 outstanding or excellent

sov·er·eign·ty /sóvvrəntee/ n 1 supreme authority over a state 2 political independence

~~soveriegn~~ incorrect spelling of **sovereign**

~~soverign~~ incorrect spelling of **sovereign**

so·vi·et /sóvee ət, -èt/ n 1 a Communist council in the former Soviet Union 2 an early Russian revolutionary council 3 **So·vi·et** somebody from the former Soviet Union ■ adj **So·vi·et** of the former Soviet Union —**so·vi·et·ism** n

So·vi·et Un·ion /sòvee ət yóonyən/ former federation of Communist states in E Europe and northern and central Asia from 1922 until 1991

sow /sō/ (**sown** /sōn/ or **sowed**) v 1 vti plant seeds 2 vt cause a feeling or idea to arise or become widespread —**sow·er** n ◊ See note at **sew**

So·we·to /sə wáytō, sə wéttō/ township in NE South Africa. Pop. 596,632 (1991).

sox plural of **sock**[1] n (infml)

soy /soy/, **soy·a** /sóy ə/ n 1 a soybean plant 2 also **soy sauce** a dark salty liquid made from soybeans. Use: flavoring foods. ■ adj made or derived from soybeans

soy·bean /sóy bèen/ *n* **1** the edible seed of a South Asian plant. Use: soy sauce, soy milk, tofu, textured vegetable protein. **2** the plant that produces soybeans

So·yin·ka /shaw yíngka/, **Wole** (*b.* 1934) Nigerian writer and political activist

spa /spaa/ *n* **1** an establishment with relaxation facilities **2** a resort with mineral springs **3** a whirlpool bath

space *n* **1** the region beyond the Earth's atmosphere **2** the region that exists between all astronomical objects **3** the three-dimensional expanse where matter exists **4** an interval of time ○ *In the space of two hours the situation was resolved.* **5** an area set apart for a particular purpose **6** a blank area between printed words or lines **7** an empty or available area ■ *v* (**spaced, spac·ing**) **1** *vt* set things apart from each other **2** *vti* become or cause to become inattentive or dazed (*slang*)

space age *n* the era of space exploration —**space-age** *adj*

space bar *n* a keyboard bar pressed to introduce a space

space cap·sule *n* the part of a spacecraft where the crew and passengers travel

space·craft /spáyss kràft/ (*pl same or* -**crafts**), **space·ship** /spáyss shìp/ *n* a vehicle for space travel

spaced-out *adj* inattentive or dazed (*slang*)

space heat·er *n* a portable appliance used to heat a small area

space·man /spáyss màn, -mən/ (*pl* -**men** /-mèn, -mən/) *n* **1** an astronaut **2** an extraterrestrial

space probe *n* a spacecraft with no crew that is used to explore distant regions of space and send data back to Earth

space shut·tle *n* a reusable spacecraft

space sta·tion, space plat·form *n* a satellite used as a base in space

Spacesuit: Astronaut Buzz Aldrin on the Moon

space·suit /spáyss sòot/ *n* an astronaut's suit

space·walk /spáyss wàwk/ *n* an astronaut's excursion out of a spacecraft ■ *vi* go out of a spacecraft in space —**space·walk·er** *n*

space·wom·an /spáyss woòmman/ (*pl* -**wom·en** /-wìmmin/) *n* **1** a woman astronaut **2** a female extraterrestrial

spa·cial *adj* = spatial

spac·ing /spáyssing/ *n* **1** the space between things, e.g., between printed words or lines **2** the arranging of things in spaces

spa·cious /spáyshəss/ *adj* containing ample space —**spa·cious·ly** *adv* —**spa·cious·ness** *n*

spade[1] /spayd/ *n* a digging tool with a long handle and a wide flat blade ■ *vt* (**spad·ed, spad·ing**) dig or remove with a spade

spade[2] /spayd/ *n* a playing card of the suit with black spear-shaped symbols

spade·work /spáyd wùrk/ *n* **1** digging **2** preliminary work

~~spagetti~~ incorrect spelling of **spaghetti**

spa·ghet·ti /spə géttee/ *n* **1** string-shaped pasta **2** a dish of cooked spaghetti

spa·ghet·ti West·ern *n* a Western made in Europe by an Italian movie company

Spain /spayn/ country in SW Europe on the Iberian Peninsula. Cap. Madrid. Pop. 40,037,995 (2001).

spake past tense of **speak** (*archaic*)

⚡ **spam** *n* electronic junk mail ■ *vti* (**spammed, spam·ming**) send unwanted electronic messages

span[1] *n* **1** the distance between two limits or extremities, e.g., the wing tips of an airplane **2** the distance between two supports of a bridge or other structure **3** a period of time ■ *vt* (**spanned, span·ning**) **1** extend over or across **2** measure with the hand

span[2] *n* a pair of horses or other animals driven together

span·dex /spán dèks/ *n* a synthetic stretch fabric

span·gle /spáng g'l/ *n* **1** a small shiny decoration **2** a small sparkling spot or object ■ *v* (-**gled, -gling**) **1** sprinkle or decorate with spangles **2** *vi* glitter with spangles —**span·gly** *adj*

Spang·lish /spáng glish/ *n* a variety of Spanish with many English borrowings

Span·iard /spánnyərd/ *n* somebody from Spain

span·iel /spánnyəl/ *n* a medium-sized dog with a wavy coat and large drooping ears

Span·ish /spánnish/ *n* a Romance language spoken in most of Spain and much of Central and South America ■ *npl* the people of Spain ■ *adj* **1** of Spain **2** of the Spanish language

Span·ish A·mer·i·ca the part of America that was colonized by the Spanish from the 16C and where Spanish is still widely spoken, including much of Central and South America and some Caribbean islands —**Span·ish A·mer·i·can** *n, adj*

Span·ish Main the part of the Caribbean Sea crossed by Spanish ships in colonial times

Span·ish om·e·let *n* an omelet served with a spicy tomato sauce

Span·ish Sa·ha·ra former name for **Western Sahara**

spank /spangk/ *vt* slap the buttocks of —**spank** *n*

spank·ing /spángking/ *n* a beating on the buttocks with the open hand ■ *adj* 1 exceptional (*infml*) 2 brisk ■ *adv* very ○ *a spanking new car*

spar[1] *n* a thick strong pole that supports the rigging on a ship

spar[2] *vi* (**sparred, spar·ring**) 1 box, especially for practice 2 argue ■ *n* a practice bout of boxing

spar[3] *n* any light-colored mineral that splits easily

spare /spair/ *vt* (**spared, spar·ing**) 1 refrain from harming 2 treat leniently 3 save from doing something 4 withhold or avoid 5 use frugally 6 afford ○ *I can't spare any time to exercise.* ■ *adj* 1 kept in reserve 2 superfluous 3 lean 4 scanty ■ *n* 1 something extra 2 in bowling, an instance of knocking down all the pins with two balls —**spare·ly** *adv* —**spare·ness** *n* ◇ **to spare** more than what is needed

spare time *n* leisure time

spare tire *n* 1 an extra tire carried in case of a puncture 2 a band of extra flesh around the waist (*humorous*)

spar·ing /spáiring/ *adj* 1 frugal 2 scanty —**spar·ing·ly** *adv*

spark *n* 1 a fiery particle thrown from something that is burning or rubbing 2 an electric discharge 3 something that activates or initiates something ○ *a spark of interest* ■ *v* 1 *vi* throw off sparks 2 *vt* stimulate or incite

spar·kle /spáark'l/ *vi* (**-kled, -kling**) 1 throw off sparks 2 shine with a flickering reflected light 3 perform in an impressive or lively way ■ *n* 1 a shining particle 2 animation —**spark·ly** *adj*

spar·kler /spáarklor/ *n* a hand-held firework that throws off sparks

spar·kling /spáarkling/ *adj* 1 reflecting glittering light 2 describes drinks that are effervescent 3 vivacious

spark plug *n* a device that ignites the fuel in an engine

sparks *n* a radio operator (*infml; + sing verb*)

spark·y /spáarkee/ (**-i·er, -i·est**) *adj* lively

spar·ring part·ner *n* 1 somebody who spars with a boxer 2 a debating partner

spar·row /spárrō/ *n* 1 a small brownish songbird 2 a finch resembling a sparrow

spar·row hawk *n* 1 a small North American falcon 2 a small European and Asian hawk

sparse /spaarss/ (**spars·er, spars·est**) *adj* thinly distributed —**sparse·ly** *adv* —**sparse·ness** *n*

Spar·ta /spáarta/ town in the S Peloponnesus, Greece, the site of an ancient city-state that was an important military power between the 6C and 4C BC. Pop. 14,084 (1991).

Spar·ta·cus /spáartakass/ (*d.* 71 BC) Roman enslaved laborer and rebel leader

Spar·tan /spáart'n/ *n* 1 a native of ancient Sparta 2 a person with a strong character ■ *adj* 1 of ancient Sparta 2 **spar·tan** marked by discipline and austerity —**Spar·tan·ism** *n* —**spar·tan·ly** *adv*

spasm /spázzəm/ *n* 1 an involuntary muscle contraction 2 a sudden burst of activity

spas·mod·ic /spaz móddik/ *adj* 1 affected by spasms 2 intermittent —**spas·mod·i·cal·ly** *adv*

spas·tic /spástik/ *adj* 1 affected by spasms 2 an offensive term describing somebody who lacks physical coordination (*dated*) ■ *n* an offensive term for somebody with a disability that affects physical coordination (*dated*) —**spas·ti·cal·ly** *adv*

spat[1] *n* a petty quarrel ■ *vi* (**spat·ted, spat·ting**) quarrel pettily

spat[2] past tense, past participle of **spit**[1]

spat[3] *n* a fabric covering for the upper part of a shoe

spate /spayt/ *n* 1 a flood or a state of flooding 2 an outburst

spa·tial /spaysh'l/, **spa·cial** *adj* of space —**spa·tial·ly** *adv*

spat·ter /spáttər/ *v* 1 *vti* come or force out in scattered drops 2 *vt* splash with a liquid ■ *n* a droplet of something spattered

spat·u·la /spácholə/ *n* a flat utensil used to lift or mix food and other substances

spawn *n* 1 a mass of eggs produced by a water animal 2 offspring ■ *v* 1 *vi* deposit eggs 2 *vi* produce young 3 *vt* give rise to

spay *vt* remove a female animal's ovaries

SPCA *abbr* Society for the Prevention of Cruelty to Animals

~~speech~~ incorrect spelling of **speech**

speak /speek/ (**spoke** /spōk/ *or* **spake** /spayk/ *archaic*, **spo·ken** /spōkən/) *v* 1 *vti* utter words with the voice 2 *vi* converse or communicate 3 *vt* be able to use a particular language 4 *vi* be on good terms ○ *They're not speaking anymore.* 5 *vi* deliver a speech ◇ **so to speak** in one way of expressing it ◇ **something speaks for itself** something has an obvious meaning ◇ **to speak of** worth mentioning

☐ **speak out** *vi* speak frankly

☐ **speak up** *vi* 1 talk loudly 2 talk frankly

-speak /speek/ *suffix* the way of speaking or vocabulary characteristic of a particular group or field ○ *adspeak*

speak·eas·y /speek eezee/ (*pl* **-ies**) *n* a place where alcohol is sold illegally

speak·er /speekər/ *n* 1 somebody who speaks 2 somebody who makes a speech 3 a spokesperson 4 a loudspeaker 5 **Speak·er** the presiding officer of a legislative body

speak·er·phone /speekər fōn/ *n* a phone with a loudspeaker and microphone

spear[1] /speer/ *n* 1 a long-handled weapon with a blade that is thrown from the shoulder 2 a weapon with a sharp point and barbs for catching fish ■ *vt* 1 pierce or stab with a spear or a pointed utensil 2 catch a ball with a thrust of the arm —**spear·man** n

spear² /speer/ n a young shoot of some plants

spear·head /spéer hèd/ n 1 the pointed head of a spear 2 the leading forces in a military attack ■ vt act as the leader of an undertaking

spear·mint /spéer mìnt/ (pl same or -mints) n a common mint plant. Use: flavoring.

spec n a detailed description, especially one providing information needed to make or build something (infml) ◊ **on spec** UK with a chance of making a profit but no certainty of it (infml)

spe·cial /spésh'l/ adj 1 unusual or superior in comparison to others 2 held in esteem 3 reserved ○ It's my special chair. 4 made or arranged for a particular purpose ■ n 1 something designed or reserved for a particular purpose 2 a television program that is not part of a schedule 3 a temporary reduction in price —**spe·cial·ness** n

spe·cial de·liv·er·y n the delivery of mail with priority treatment or outside normal times

spe·cial ed·u·ca·tion n teaching for students with special needs

Spe·cial Forc·es npl a branch of the US Army trained in guerrilla warfare and counterinsurgency tactics

spe·cial-in·ter·est group, spe·cial in·ter·est n a group trying to influence government policy on a particular issue

spe·cial·ist /spéshəlist/ n 1 somebody specializing in a particular interest, activity, or field 2 a doctor who practices in a particular field only 3 an enlisted person in the US Army with special technical skills

spe·cial·ize /spéshə lìz/ (-ized, -iz·ing) v 1 vt adapt to suit a specific purpose 2 vi devote time to a particular activity, skill, or field of study —**spe·cial·i·za·tion** /spèshəlì záysh'n/ n

~~speciall~~ incorrect spelling of **special**

spe·cial·ly /spésh'lee/ adv for a particular purpose or occasion ◊ See note at **especially**

spe·cial needs npl the particular educational requirements that some people have because of physical challenges or learning difficulties

Spe·cial O·lym·pics n a competition for athletes who are physically or mentally challenged (+ sing or pl verb)

spe·cial op·er·a·tions, spe·cial ops n a branch of a military force engaged in covert operations (+ sing or pl verb)

spe·cial plead·ing n 1 a request for a court to consider new evidence 2 an argument presenting only one aspect of an issue

spe·cial school n a school for students with special needs

spe·cial·ty /spésh'ltee/ (pl -ties) n 1 an interest or field that somebody specializes in 2 a product or service that somebody is spe-

cialized in producing 3 a distinctive mark or quality

spe·cie /spéeshee, -ssee/ n money in the form of coins

~~special~~ incorrect spelling of **special**

spe·cies /spée sheez, spèe seez/ (pl same) n 1 a biological classification that is a subdivision of a genus 2 the organisms in a species 3 a type, sort, or variety of something ◊ See note at **type**

spe·cif·ic /spə síffik/ adj 1 precise 2 of a particular thing 3 of a biological species 4 describes a treatment that is effective for a particular medical condition ■ n 1 a detail 2 a medication that is effective against a particular disease —**spe·cif·i·cal·ly** adv —**spec·i·fic·i·ty** /spèsə físsətee/ n

spec·i·fi·ca·tion /spèssəfi káysh'n/ n 1 a detailed description, especially one providing information needed to make or build something 2 something specified 3 the act of specifying something

spe·cif·ic grav·i·ty n PHYS = relative density

~~specifically~~ incorrect spelling of **specifically**

spec·i·fy /spéssə fì/ (-fied, -fies) vt 1 state explicitly 2 state as a condition ○ The rules specify that pets cannot be kept here. 3 include something in a specification —**spec·i·fi·a·ble** /spéssə fì əb'l, spèssə fì əb'l/ adj

~~speciman~~ incorrect spelling of **specimen**

spec·i·men /spéssəmən/ n 1 something that is representative because it is typical of its kind or of a whole ○ a specimen of his handwriting 2 a sample, e.g., of urine or blood, for testing and diagnosis

spe·cious /spéeshəss/ adj 1 apparently true but actually false 2 deceptively attractive —**spe·cious·ly** adv —**spe·cious·ness** n

speck n 1 a small spot 2 a particle ■ vt mark with specks

speck·le /spék'l/ n a small colored spot, e.g., on plumage or an eggshell ■ vt (-led, -ling) mark with speckles —**speck·led** adj

spec·ta·cle /spéktək'l/ n 1 something remarkable that is seen 2 a lavish performance or display

spec·ta·cles /spéktək'lz/ npl eyeglasses worn to correct vision

spec·tac·u·lar /spek tákyələr/ adj 1 visually impressive 2 remarkable ■ n a lavish artistic production —**spec·tac·u·lar·ly** adv

spec·ta·tor /spék tàytər/ n somebody who watches an event —**spec·tate** vi

spec·ta·tor sport n a sport that is interesting to watch

spec·ter /spéktər/, **spec·tre** n 1 a ghost 2 an unpleasant prospect ○ the specter of nuclear war

spec·tral /spéktrəl/ adj 1 ghostly 2 of or produced by a spectrum

spec·trum /spéktrəm/ (pl -tra /-trə/ or -trums) n 1 the distribution of colored light produced when white light is dispersed 2 a radiation frequency range with a particular property **3** any range, especially between two extremes

spec·u·late /spékyə làyt/ (**-lat·ed**, **-lat·ing**) v **1** vti form an opinion based on incomplete or available facts **2** vi consider possibilities **3** vi make risky deals for profit —**spec·u·la·tion** /spèkyə láysh'n/ n —**spec·u·la·tive** /spékyə làytiv, -lətiv/ adj —**spec·u·la·tive·ly** adv —**spec·u·la·tive·ness** n —**spec·u·la·tor** n

sped past tense, past participle of **speed**

speech n **1** the ability to speak **2** communication by speaking **3** spoken language ○ recordings of human speech **4** a talk given to an audience **5** a particular way of speaking

speech com·mu·ni·ty n a group that includes all the speakers of a particular language

speech·less /spéechləss/ adj **1** temporarily unable to speak **2** permanently unable to speak **3** remaining silent —**speech·less·ly** adv —**speech·less·ness** n

✚ **speech rec·og·ni·tion** n a computer's ability to understand human speech

✚ **speech syn·the·sis** n a computer's ability to imitate human speech

speech ther·a·py n the treatment of speech disorders —**speech ther·a·pist** n

speech·writ·er /spéech rìtər/ n somebody who writes speeches that other people deliver

speed n **1** the rate at which something moves or happens **2** rapidity **3** an amphetamine drug (slang) ■ v (**sped** or **speed·ed**) **1** vti go or move quickly, or cause to go or move quickly **2** vi drive faster than the speed limit **3** vi pass or happen quickly —**speed·er** n —**speed·ing** adj ◇ **be** or **get up to speed** be or become fully informed about the latest developments

☐ **speed up** vti increase or cause to increase in rate or speed

speed·boat /spéed bòt/ n a fast motorboat

speed bump n a bump in the road made to slow down motorists

speed lim·it n the maximum permitted speed on a stretch of road

speed·om·e·ter /spə dómmətər/ n an instrument in a vehicle that shows its speed

speed skat·ing n the sport of racing on ice with skates

speed trap n an area monitored by traffic police, usually with radar equipment

speed·up /spéed up/ n **1** an increase in speed **2** a demand for an increase in productivity without an increase in pay

speed·way /spéed wày/ n **1** a racetrack for motor vehicles **2** a fast road

speed·y /spéedee/ (**-i·er**, **-i·est**) adj **1** fast **2** capable of moving fast —**speed·i·ly** adv —**speed·i·ness** n

speak incorrect spelling of **speak**

spe·le·ol·o·gy /spèelee óllajee/ n the study of caves —**spe·le·o·log·i·cal** /spèelee ə lójjik'l/ adj —**spe·le·ol·o·gist** n

spell[1] v **1** vti name or write the letters of a word **2** vt form a particular word **3** vt signify something ○ conditions that could spell disaster

☐ **spell out** vt state explicitly

spell[2] n **1** a word or set of words believed to have magical power **2** the influence of a spell **3** a fascination or attraction

spell[3] n **1** a short period (infml) **2** a period of particular weather **3** a bout of illness **4** a period of work or duty ■ vt US, ANZ, Scotland relieve somebody who is working

spell·bind·ing /spél bìnding/ adj captivating —**spell·bind** vt —**spell·bind·ing·ly** adv —**spell·bound** /spél bównd/ adj

✚ **spell·check·er** /spél chèkər/ n a computer program that corrects spelling errors —**spell·check** n, v

spell·er /spéllər/ n **1** somebody with a particular level of skill at spelling ○ an excellent speller **2** a book for teaching or improving spelling

spell·ing /spélling/ n **1** the ability to spell **2** the act of forming words by ordering letters **3** the way a word is actually spelled

spell·ing bee n a spelling contest

spe·lunk·ing /spə lúngking, spì-/ n the sport of exploring caves —**spe·lunk·er** n

spend (**spent**) v **1** vti pay money in exchange for goods or services **2** vt devote time or effort to something ○ spent a lot of time thinking about it **3** vt pass a particular amount of time in a particular place or way ○ spent two weeks in Japan **4** vt use something up —**spend·er** n

spend·ing mon·ey n cash for personal expenses

spend·thrift /spénd thrìft/ n an extravagant spender ■ adj wasteful with money

ORIGIN Thrift is used in **spendthrift** in the old sense "savings, earnings."

Spen·ser /spénssər/, **Edmund** (1552?–99) English poet —**Spen·se·ri·an** /spen seèree ən/ adj

spent past tense, past participle of **spend** ■ adj **1** used ○ tossed the spent match into the fire **2** exhausted ○ felt totally spent by the end of the day

sperm (pl same or **sperms**) n **1** semen **2** also **sper·mat·o·zo·on** /spur màttə zŏ on, spùrmətə zŏ on/ (pl **-a** /-zŏ ə/) a male reproductive cell —**sper·mat·ic** /spur máttik/ adj

sper·ma·ce·ti /spùrmə séttee/ n a white waxy solid from sperm whales. Use: formerly, in cosmetics, candles, and ointments.

sperm bank n a place where semen is stored

sperm count n the concentration of sperm in

somebody's semen, or a test to determine this

sper·mi·cide /spúrmə sìd/ *n* a sperm-killing agent used as a contraceptive —**sper·mi·cid·al** /spúrmə síd'l/ *adj*

sperm oil *n* a pale yellow oil from the head of a sperm whale. Use: formerly, industrial lubricant.

sperm whale *n* a whale whose massive square head has a cavity filled with a mixture of sperm oil and spermaceti

ORIGIN Sperm here is short for *spermaceti*.

spew *vti* 1 vomit 2 pour or flow out forcefully ■ *n* vomit

Spe·yer /spí ər, shpí ər/ city in SW Germany, scene in 1529 of a protest by supporters of Martin Luther. Pop. 45,100 (1989).

SPF *n* a lotion's sun protection rating. Full form **sun protection factor**

sphag·num /sfágnəm/ *n* a type of moss that forms peat

sphere /sfeer/ *n* 1 a ball-shaped object 2 a perfectly round solid figure 3 a field of knowledge or activity 4 an area of control or influence 5 a group within a society —**spher·al** *adj* —**spher·i·cal** /sféerək'l, sfér-/ *adj* —**spher·i·cal·ly** *adv* —**spher·i·cal·ness** *n* —**sphe·ric·i·ty** /sfe ríssətee/ *n*

sphe·roid /sfeer oyd, sfé royd/ *n* something that is like a sphere but is not perfectly round —**sphe·roi·dal** /sfi róyd'l, sfe-/ *adj*

sphinc·ter /sfíngktər/ *n* a circular band of muscle around the opening of a body passage —**sphinc·ter·al** *adj*

Sphinx, Giza, Egypt

sphinx /sfingks/ (*pl* **sphinx·es** *or* **sphin·ges** /sfín jèez/) *n* 1 in Greek mythology, a winged creature with a lion's head and woman's body 2 in Egyptian mythology, a creature with a lion's body and the head of a man, ram, or bird 3 a statue of a sphinx

spic-and-span *adj* = spick-and-span

spice /spīss/ *n* 1 an aromatic substance derived from the nonleafy parts of plants and used as a flavoring 2 a source of excitement or interest 3 a strong smell ■ *vt* (**spiced, spic·ing**) 1 season with spice 2 make more exciting

~~spicey~~ incorrect spelling of **spicy**

spick-and-span /spɪk-/, **spic-and-span** *adj* 1 neat 2 in perfect condition

spic·y /spíssee/ (**-i·er, -i·est**) *adj* 1 seasoned with spice 2 arousing interest because of its sexual impropriety (*infml*) —**spic·i·ness** *n*

⚡**spi·der** /spídər/ *n* 1 an eight-legged invertebrate animal that spins webs 2 a computer program that searches for information to be added to a search engine's index

spi·der·web /spídər wèb/ *n* a web spun by a spider

spi·der·y /spídəree/ *adj* 1 thin and irregular 2 spider-infested

spiel /speel, shpeel/ *n* a speech designed to convince somebody, especially a salesperson's patter (*infml*) —**spiel** *vi*

Steven Spielberg

Spiel·berg /spéel bùrg/, **Steven** (*b.* 1947) US movie director and producer

spiff·y /spíffee/ (**-i·er, -i·est**) *adj* stylish (*infml*) —**spiff·i·ly** *adv*

spig·ot /spíggət/ *n* 1 a faucet 2 a tap attached to a cask

spike[1] *n* 1 a pointed metal or wooden piece, especially one along the top of a railing or wall 2 a large nail 3 a metal point on the sole of a running shoe (*often pl*) 4 a sharp point 5 a sudden surge in voltage 6 a graphic image of a sudden peak and fall 7 a sudden brief increase ■ **spikes** *npl* a pair of running shoes with spikes on the soles ■ *v* (**spiked, spik·ing**) 1 *vt* sneakily add something, e.g., a drug or alcohol, to a drink 2 *vt* injure or disable somebody or something with a spike or spikes 3 *vi* rise abruptly 4 *vt* render something useless or ineffective (*infml*) —**spiked** *adj*

spike[2] *n* 1 an ear of grain 2 a long cluster of flowers attached directly to a stem with the newest flowers at the tip

spik·y /spíkee/ (**-i·er, -i·est**) *adj* with one or several spikes —**spik·i·ness** *n*

spill *v* (**spilled** *or* **spilt**) 1 *vti* flow or cause to flow accidentally from a container 2 *vi* come out of a confined space in large numbers or quantities o *The fans spilled onto the field.* 3 *vti* fall or cause to fall off a horse or bike (*infml*) ■ *n* 1 a fall from a horse or bike (*infml*) 2 something that flows accidentally from a container o *working to contain the spill* —**spill·er** *n*

spill·age /spíllij/ *n* 1 the spilling of something 2 a quantity spilled

spill·o·ver /spíl òvər/ *n* 1 a quantity spilled

due to excess **2** a spread due to excess **3** an indirect effect

spin *v* (**spun**, **spin·ning**) **1** *vti* rotate or turn around quickly **2** *vti* create thread or yarn from raw materials **3** *vti* make a web or cocoon **4** *vti* present information in the best possible light **5** *vti* go or cause to go into a deep spiral dive *(refers to aircraft)* **6** *vt* tell an improbable story as though it were true **7** *vti* remove water, especially from washed clothes, by spinning in a machine **8** *vi* become dizzy ○ *My head was spinning.* ■ *n* **1** a quick rotating movement **2** favorable bias or distortion in presenting information **3** a spiraling dive by an aircraft **4** a short trip taken for pleasure in a vehicle *(infml)* **5** a dizzy state —**spin·ner** *n*

□ **spin out** *v* **1** *vi* lose control of a vehicle **2** *vt* make supplies last by careful management **3** *vt* prolong something

spi·na bif·i·da /spìnə bíffidə/ *n* a condition in which part of the spinal cord or surrounding membrane protrudes through a cleft in the spinal column

spin·ach /spínich/ *n* a plant with edible leaves. Use: cooked vegetable, raw in salads.

spi·nal /spín'l/ *adj* of the spinal column

spi·nal col·umn *n* the interconnected bones of a vertebrate animal's back

spi·nal cord *n* a thick cord of nerve tissue extending from the bottom of the brain and down the spinal column

spin·dle /spínd'l/ *n* **1** a handheld rod for spinning thread **2** a mechanical thread-spinning device **3** a rotating rod for operating a device

spin·dly /spíndlee/ *adj* (**-dli·er**, **-dli·est**), **spin·dling** /spíndling/ *adj* long or tall and thin

spin doc·tor /spín mìstər/ *n* somebody who imparts a favorable bias to information given to the public or media *(slang)*

spin·drift /spín drìft/ *n* spray from waves

spine *n* **1** the spinal column **2** the vertical back of a book's cover **3** a hard sharp projection on an animal or a plant

spine·less /spínləss/ *adj* **1** weak and cowardly **2** without a spine —**spine·less·ly** *adv* —**spine·less·ness** *n* ◊ See note at **cowardly**

spin·et /spínnit/ *n* **1** a small upright piano **2** a small harpsichord with strings set at a slant to the keyboard

spine-tin·gling *adj* frightening or exciting —**spine-tin·gling·ly** *adv*

spin·na·ker /spínnəkər/ *n* a large triangular sail at the front of a yacht

spin·ner·et /spínnə rét, spínnə rèt/ *n* a spider's silk-producing organ

spin·ning wheel *n* a domestic device for spinning yarn by means of a large wheel driven by hand or a treadle

spin-off /spín àwf/ *n* **1** a product, material, or service derived incidentally from something else **2** a subsidiary that is divested by distributing stock to stockholders of the parent company

spin-out /spín òwt/ *n* an uncontrollable skid

Spi·no·za /spi nózə/, **Baruch** (1632–77) Dutch philosopher

spin·ster /spínstər/ *n* an offensive term for a woman who has remained unmarried beyond the usual age *(dated)* —**spin·ster·hood** *n*

ORIGIN A **spinster** was originally a woman who made her livelihood by spinning yarn.

spin·y /spínee/ *adj* (**-i·er**, **-i·est**) *adj* with spines or thorns —**spin·i·ness** *n*

spir·a·cle /spírək'l, spírrək'l/ *n* **1** a blowhole of a whale, dolphin, or similar ocean mammal *(technical)* **2** a small aperture for breathing, e.g., in an insect's side

spi·ral /spírəl/ *n* **1** a flat curve or series of curves that constantly increase or decrease in size in circling around a central point **2** a helix **3** something with the shape of a spiral or helix ■ *adj* of or with the shape of a spiral or helix ■ *v* (**-raled** *or* **-ralled**, **-ral·ing** *or* **-ral·ling**) **1** *vti* move in a spiral **2** *vi* change with ever increasing speed **3** *vti* shape or be shaped like a spiral —**spi·roid** *adj*

spi·ral stair·case *n* a staircase that winds around a central axis

spire[1] *n* **1** a narrow tapering structure topping a roof, tower, or steeple, or a tower or steeple with one **2** a slender, upward-pointing part of a plant

spire[2] *n* **1** a spiral or coil **2** a convolution of a spiral or coil

spir·it /spírrət/ *n* **1** a vital force that characterizes a human being **2** a person's will or sense of self **3** enthusiasm and energy for living **4** a person's disposition **5** the attitude or state of mind of a person or group ○ *in the spirit of compromise* **6** the intention behind something rather than its literal meaning **7** a supernatural being without a physical body **8** **Spir·it** in Christianity, the Holy Spirit **9** a strong alcoholic drink made by distillation *(often pl)* ■ **spir·its** *npl* mood ■ *vt* remove secretly or mysteriously

spir·it·ed /spírrətəd/ *adj* **1** lively **2** behaving in a particular way *(usually in combination)* ○ *mean-spirited* —**spir·it·ed·ly** *adv* —**spir·it·ed·ness** *n*

spir·it lamp *n* a lamp that burns alcohol

spir·it·less /spírrətləss/ *adj* lacking in courage or energy

spir·it lev·el *n* a calibrated tube with an air bubble in it for measuring whether surfaces are horizontal

spir·i·tu·al /spírrichoo əl/ *adj* **1** of the soul or spirit **2** of religion or sacred things ■ *n* a religious song arising from African

American culture —**spir·i·tu·al·i·ty** /spɪrrichoo álletee/ n —**spir·i·tu·al·ly** adv —**spir·i·tu·al·ness** n

spir·i·tu·al·ism /spírrichoo ə lìzzəm/ n belief in the possibility of communication with dead people, especially through a medium —**spir·i·tu·al·ist** n

spit v (spit or spat, spit·ting) 1 vi eject saliva from the mouth 2 vt expel from the mouth 3 vi make a sputtering or hissing sound 4 vi rain or snow lightly ■ n 1 saliva ejected from the mouth 2 an expulsion of something from the mouth

□ **spit up** vt regurgitate or vomit (refers to babies)

spit² n 1 a thin rod on which meat is impaled for roasting 2 an elongated point of land projecting from a shore ■ vt (spit·ted, spit·ting) impale on a spit

spit·ball /spít bàwl/ n 1 a chewed paper wad thrown as a prank 2 an illegal baseball pitch using a moistened ball

spite n petty ill will ■ vt (spit·ed, spit·ing) act maliciously toward ◊ **in spite of** notwithstanding, or without taking account of

spite·ful /spítf'l/ adj vindictive in a petty way —**spite·ful·ly** adv —**spite·ful·ness** n

spit·fire /spít fìr/ n somebody excitable and quick-tempered

spit·ting im·age n an exact likeness of somebody (infml)

spit·tle /spítt'l/ n 1 saliva ejected from the mouth 2 something resembling frothy saliva

spit·toon /spi toón/ n a receptacle for spittle

splash v 1 vti scatter liquid on something 2 vi be scattered or fly up in drops or larger amounts (refers to liquid) 3 vti move through water, scattering it about 4 vt display prominently ◊ splashed it across the front page ■ n 1 a noise of liquid splashing 2 a small patch of color 3 a tiny amount of liquid (infml) 4 a drop or larger amount of liquid splashed 5 a prominent display

splash·y /spláshee/ (-i·er, -i·est) adj 1 attracting a lot of notice (infml) 2 colorful 3 making splashes —**splash·i·ness** n

splat n a wet smacking sound —**splat** adv

splat·ter /spláttər/ vti spatter or splash —**splat·ter** n

splay vti 1 spread wide and outward, especially awkwardly 2 have or give slanting sides ■ adj also **splayed** spread flat and outward

spleen n 1 an organ in the abdomen that helps to destroy old red blood cells, form cells for the immune system, and store blood 2 bad temper —**spleen·ful** adj

splen·did /spléndəd/ adj 1 magnificent 2 reflecting light brilliantly 3 excellent —**splen·did·ly** adv —**splen·did·ness** n

splen·dif·er·ous /splen dífferəss/ adj magnificent (humorous) —**splen·dif·er·ous·ly** adv

splen·dor /spléndər/ n 1 magnificence 2 something splendid ◊ the splendors of Egypt —**splen·dor·ous** adj

sple·net·ic /splə néttik/ adj bad-tempered (literary)

splice /splīss/ vt (spliced, splic·ing) join different strands or pieces of a material ■ n a connection made by splicing

splint n 1 a rigid device to immobilize a broken bone 2 a strip of wood used in basketry —**splint** vt

splin·ter /splíntər/ n a thin sharp fragment ■ vti 1 break into sharp fragments 2 divide into factions —**splin·ter·y** adj

splinter group n a group split from another because of a disagreement

split v (split, split·ting) 1 vti divide lengthwise 2 vti burst or rip apart 3 vti separate into parts or factions 4 vti share among a group ◊ split the proceeds 5 vti depart (slang) ■ n 1 a splitting of something 2 a crack or lengthwise break in something 3 a division or separation caused by disagreement 4 a share, especially a share of money (infml) ■ adj 1 broken, cracked, or separated into parts 2 divided because of a disagreement —**split·ter** n ◊ See note at **tear**

□ **split up** vi end a relationship

Split /splít/ port in S Croatia, on the Adriatic Sea. Pop. 189,388 (1991).

split in·fin·i·tive n a phrase in which "to" and its verb are separated by another word or words

split-lev·el adj with the floor of a story on different levels ◊ a split-level house —**split-lev·el** n

split pea n a dried pea used in soup

split per·son·al·i·ty n 1 a psychological disorder in which somebody appears to have two or more different personalities 2 a tendency to mood swings

split screen n a television or movie screen divided into more than one image

split sec·ond n a very short time

split shift n a single work period divided into two or more sessions with a long break between them

split·ting /splítting/ adj very painful ◊ a splitting headache

split-up n a separation and ending of a relationship

splotch n a large irregular spot

splurge (splurged, splurg·ing) vi indulge in something extravagant or expensive (infml)

splut·ter /splúttər/ v 1 vi make a spitting or choking sound 2 vti say something incoherently —**splut·ter** n —**splut·ter·ing** n, adj

Dr. Spock

Spock, Dr. (1903–98) US pediatrician and political activist

spoil *v* (**spoiled** *or* **spoilt**) **1** *vt* impair, damage, or ruin **2** *vt* harm the character of by overindulgence **3** *vi* become rotten ∎ **spoils** *npl* **1** property seized by a victor **2** the rewards and benefits of winning ◊ **be spoiling for** be eager for

spoil·age /spóylij/ *n* **1** the process of decaying or becoming damaged, or the resulting condition **2** waste arising from decay or damage

spoiled *adj* **1** ruined by decay or damage **2** willful or selfish because of having been overindulged

spoil·er /spóylər/ *n* **1** a device on the back of an automobile to deflect air and keep its wheels on the ground **2** somebody or something that can ruin another's success

spoil·sport /spóyl spàwrt/ *n* somebody who spoils others' fun

spoilt past tense, past participle of **spoil**

Spo·kane /spō kán/ city in E Washington, on the falls of the Spokane River. Pop. 184,058 (1998).

spoke[1] *n* **1** a supporting rod extending from the hub of a wheel to its rim **2** a rung of a ladder

spoke[2] past tense of **speak**

spo·ken /spókən/ past participle of **speak** ∎ *adj* **1** expressed with the voice **2** speaking in a particular way (*in combination*) ◊ **spoken for** already owned or reserved by somebody ◊ See note at **verbal**

spokes·man /spóksmən/ (*pl* **-men** /-mən/) *n* somebody speaking on behalf of another or others

spokes·per·son /spóks pùrss'n/ *n* somebody speaking on behalf of another or others

spokes·wom·an /spóks wòomman/ (*pl* **-en** /-wimmən/) *n* a woman speaking on behalf of another or others

spo·li·a·tion /spòlee áysh'n/ *n* the seizing or plundering of things by force

sponge /spunj/ *n* **1** an invertebrate ocean animal with a porous fibrous skeleton **2** a lightweight absorbent piece of a sponge's skeleton, or a piece of synthetic material resembling this. Use: bathing, cleaning. **3** an absorbent contraceptive device ∎ *v* (**sponged, spong·ing**) **1** *vt* clean or remove with a sponge **2** *vi* live off the generosity of others (*infml*) —**spong·er** *n*

sponge bath *n* a body wash without immersion

sponge cake *n* a light open-textured cake made with flour, eggs, and sugar, and usually without shortening

spong·y /spúnjee/ (**-i·er, -i·est**) *adj* **1** open-textured **2** absorbent and elastic —**spong·i·ness** *n*

~~sponser~~ incorrect spelling of **sponsor**

spon·sor /spónssər/ *n* **1** a radio or television advertiser who pays for programming **2** a contributor to an event's funding **3** a legislator who proposes and supports a bill **4** a supporter of a person or activity **5** a godparent (*fml*) ∎ *vt* act as a sponsor to ◊ See note at **backer**

> **ORIGIN** A **sponsor** is etymologically, in Latin, "somebody who makes a solemn promise." The word was adopted into English in the mid-17C in the sense "godparent," which had developed during the Christian era.

spon·ta·ne·ous /spon táynee əss/ *adj* **1** arising from an internal or natural cause **2** arising from impulse or inclination —**spon·ta·ne·i·ty** /spòntə neé ətee, -náy ətee/ *n* —**spon·ta·ne·ous·ly** *adv*

spon·ta·ne·ous com·bus·tion *n* ignition caused by internal heat generation

~~spontanious~~ incorrect spelling of **spontaneous**

spoof *n* **1** a good-humored hoax **2** an amusing satire —**spoof** *vt*

> **ORIGIN Spoof** was invented by the British comedian Arthur Roberts (1852–1933) as the name of a game of his creation that involved hoaxing. It was first mentioned in print in 1884.

spook *n* (*infml*) **1** a ghost **2** a spy or secret agent ∎ *vt* **1** haunt as a ghost **2** startle

spook·y /spóokee/ (**-i·er, -i·est**) *adj* **1** scarily suggestive of the supernatural (*infml*) **2** strange or amazing (*infml*) **3** easily frightened —**spook·i·ly** *adv* —**spook·i·ness** *n*

spool *n* **1** a cylinder on which something is wound **2** an amount on a spool ∎ *v* **1** *vti* wind something on a spool **2** *vi* transfer computer data to a memory store for printing later

spoon *n* **1** an eating utensil consisting of a shallow oval bowl attached to a handle **2** a shiny fishing lure ∎ *vt* eat or transfer using a spoon —**spoon·ful** *n*

spoon·bill /spòon bíl/ *n* a tropical wading bird with a long flat bill

spoon·er·ism /spóonə rìzzəm/ *n* an accidental verbal error in which the initial sounds of words are transposed

> **ORIGIN** The **spoonerism** is named for the

British educator Reverend William Spooner (1844–1930), who was known for such slips.

spoon-feed (spoon-fed) *vt* 1 feed with a spoon 2 provide with everything, so that no independent thought or effort is required

spoor /spoor, spawr/ *n* an animal's track or trail

Spor·a·des /spórrə dèez/ group of Greek islands in the Aegean Sea

spo·rad·ic /spə ráddik/ *adj* occurring at irregular intervals ◊ See note at **periodic**

spore *n* an asexual reproductive structure in seedless plants, algae, fungi, and some protozoans ■ *vi* (**spored, spor·ing**) produce spores

spor·ran /spáwrən, spórrən/ *n* a pouch worn at the front of a kilt

sport *n* 1 a competitive physical activity governed by rules, or such activities as a group (*often pl*) 2 an active pastime 3 somebody who remains cheerful in losing circumstances (*infml*) ■ *v* 1 *vt* wear proudly or flamboyantly (*infml*) 2 *vi* play happily (*fml*) —**sport·ful** *adj*

sport·ing /spáwrting/ *adj* 1 used in sports 2 in keeping with the principles of fair competition —**sport·ing·ly** *adv*

sporting chance *n* a fair chance of success

spor·tive /spáwrtiv/ *adj* 1 playful 2 done as a joke —**spor·tive·ly** *adv* —**spor·tive·ness** *n*

sports car *n* a small fast car

sports·cast /spáwrts kàst/ *n* a sports broadcast —**sports·cast·er** *n*

sports drink *n* a thirst-quenching drink for use during or after physical exercise

sports jacket *n* a man's casual jacket worn with nonmatching trousers

sports·man /spáwrtsmən/ (*pl* -men /-mən/) *n* 1 a man engaging in sports 2 somebody fair and honorable —**sports·man·like** *adj*

sports·man·ship /spáwrtsmən shìp/ *n* 1 fair and honorable conduct 2 participation in sports

sports·per·son /spáwrts pùrss'n/ *n* a person engaging in sport

sports sup·ple·ment *n* a dietary supplement to enhance physical performance

sports·wear /spáwrts wàir/ *n* casual clothes

sports·wom·an /spáwrts woomman/ (*pl* -wom·en /-wìmmən/) *n* 1 a woman engaging in sports 2 a fair and honorable woman

sport-u·til·i·ty ve·hi·cle, sport-u·til·i·ty *n* a four-wheel-drive vehicle larger than a car, suitable for rough terrain

sport·y /spáwrtee/ (-i·er, -i·est) *adj* 1 for sports 2 enthusiastic about sports 3 similar to a sports car 4 fair or sporting

spot *n* 1 a distinct small round area on a surface 2 a mark on the skin 3 a particular place, point, position, or location 4 an awkward situation (*infml*) 5 a small amount ■ *adj* made or available immediately ■ *v* (spot·ted, spot·ting) 1 *vt* see or detect suddenly 2 *vti* make or become stained 3 *vt* mark with dots 4 *vt* remove stains from —**spot·ted** *adj* ◊ **hit the spot** be just what is required for total satisfaction (*infml*) ◊ **in a spot** in a difficult or embarrassing position (*infml*) ◊ **on the spot** 1 immediately 2 in a difficult situation or under pressure

spot check *n* a random inspection —**spot-check** *vt*

spot·less /spótless/ *adj* 1 immaculately clean 2 beyond reproach —**spot·less·ly** *adv* —**spot·less·ness** *n*

spot·light /spót lìt/ *n* 1 a strong beam of light illuminating a small area, or a lamp producing such a light 2 the focus of attention ■ *vt* (-lit /-lìt/ or -light·ed) 1 illuminate with a spotlight 2 focus attention on

spot price *n* a current market price

spot·ter /spóttər/ *n* somebody watching out for something (*often in combination*)

spot·ty /spóttee/ (-ti·er, -ti·est) *adj* 1 inconsistent 2 marked with spots —**spot·ti·ly** *adv* —**spot·ti·ness** *n*

spouse /spowss, spowz/ *n* a husband or wife —**spou·sal** /spówz'l/ *adj* —**spou·sal·ly** *adv*

spout *vti* 1 discharge or be discharged in a jet or stream 2 talk about something at great length ■ *n* 1 a tube or opening for pouring liquid 2 a stream of liquid

sprain *n* an injury to ligaments ■ *vt* injure the ligaments of

sprang past tense of **spring**

sprat *n* 1 (*pl* **sprats** or **same**) a small edible fish of the herring family 2 a sprat as food

sprawl *vi* 1 sit or lie with arms and legs spread awkwardly 2 extend in a disordered way ■ *n* 1 a sprawling position 2 the unchecked growth of an urban area —**sprawl·ing** *adj*

spray[1] *n* 1 a moving cloud or mist of water or other liquid particles 2 a jet of liquid from an atomizer or pressurized container 3 a container for releasing liquid in a spray ■ *vt* 1 disperse or discharge as a spray 2 apply a spray to —**spray·er** *n*

spray[2] *n* 1 a shoot or branch of a plant, with flowers, leaves, or berries on it 2 a flower arrangement

spray can *n* a container of liquid under pressure

spray gun *n* a device with a trigger for applying liquid under pressure

spread /spred/ *v* (spread) 1 *vt* open or extend something fully 2 *vti* extend or disperse over a large area 3 *vti* extend over a period of time 4 *vti* extend over a wider range than before 5 *vt* separate things by stretching or pulling 6 *vti* make or become widely known 7 *vt* coat something with a layer of a substance 8 *vti* send or go out in all directions ■ *n* 1 the extension or distribution of something over an area 2 a wide variety of things **3** the limit of extension of something **4** the distance or range between two points or things **5** an expanse of land **6** a bed or table cover **7** a food for spreading on bread or crackers **8** a pair of facing pages of a newspaper, magazine, or book **9** a large meal laid out on a table *(infml)* —**spread·able** *adj*

spread bet·ting *n* betting on the movement of a stock price in relation to a given range of high and low values

spread ea·gle *n* **1** the image of an eagle with its wings and legs outstretched **2** a way of standing or lying that resembles this —**spread-ea·gle** *adj*

⚡**spread·sheet** /spréd sheèt/ *n* **1** a computer program for numerical or other data in cells forming rows and columns **2** a display or printout of a spreadsheet

spree *n* a period of extravagant or self-indulgent activity

sprig *n* a small shoot or twig from a plant

spright·ly /sprītlee/ (-li-er, -li-est) *adj* light and vigorous —**spright·li·ness** *n*

spring *v* (**sprang, sprung**) **1** *vi* move suddenly, especially upward or forward, in a single movement **2** *vi* leap over **3** *vi* rapidly resume an original position o *branches springing back* **4** *vi* appear or emerge rapidly or suddenly **5** *vi* originate from a particular source **6** *vi US, Can, Aus* pay for *(slang)* o *I'll spring for lunch.* **7** *vt* operate by releasing a mechanism ■ *n* **1** a coil of metal that can regain its shape after pressure **2** the ability to regain an original position or shape **3** the season of the year between winter and summer **4** an onward or upward leap **5** a stream of water emerging from underground

spring·board /spríng bàwrd/ *n* **1** a flexible diving board **2** a flexible board on which gymnasts jump before vaulting

spring·bok /spríng bòk/ *n* (*pl* **same** or **spring·boks**) a small gazelle that can leap high in the air

spring-clean *vti* clean a house or room thoroughly at the end of winter

spring·er /spríngər/, **spring·er span·iel** *n* a small spaniel with a long wavy coat and floppy ears

spring fe·ver *n* feelings of restlessness or longing aroused by springtime

Spring·field /spríng feèld/ **1** capital of Illinois. Pop. 117,098 (1998). **2** city in south central Massachusetts. Pop. 148,144 (1998).

spring-load·ed *adj* fixed in place or controlled by a spring

spring roll *n* a snack or starter consisting of minced vegetables and meat wrapped in a pancake and fried

spring tide *n* a tide with a greater than average range that occurs near the times of the new moon and full moon

spring·time /spríng tìm/ *n* the season of spring

spring·y /spríngee/ (-i-er, -i-est) *adj* returning readily to shape after pressure —**spring·i·ly** *adv* —**spring·i·ness** *n*

sprin·kle /spríngk'l/ *v* (-kled, -kling) **1** *vt* scatter small drops or particles over a surface **2** *vi* rain very slightly **3** *vt* scatter or be scattered randomly among other things o *fields sprinkled with poppies* ■ *n* a light rain

sprin·kler /spríngklər/ *n* **1** a device for sending out a spray of water **2** a perforated nozzle for fitting onto a watering can or hose

sprin·kling /spríngkling/ *n* a small amount scattered or distributed thinly

sprint *n* **1** a short race at high speed **2** a fast finishing run at the end of a longer race ■ *vi* go at top speed —**sprint·er** *n*

sprite *n* **1** a supernatural being like an elf or fairy **2** a ghost or spirit

spritz *vt* spray through a nozzle —**spritz** *n*

spritz·er /spríItsər/ *n* a drink of wine and effervescent water

sprock·et /sprókət/ *n* **1** a tooth on a wheel **2** *also* **sprock·et wheel** a wheel with sprockets that engage with perforations on film or the links of a chain

sprout *v* **1** *vti* develop buds or shoots **2** *vi* begin to grow from a seed ■ *n* **1** a new growth on a plant **2** a Brussels sprout ■ **sprouts** *npl* newly sprouted seeds or beans

spruce¹ (*pl* **spruc·es** or **same**) *n* **1** an evergreen tree of the pine family **2** the soft light wood of a spruce tree

---

ORIGIN No connection is now perceived between **spruce** the tree and **spruce** "neat and trim," but they may have the same ultimate origin. *Spruce* was an old name for Prussia, and the tree is literally a "Prussian fir." **Spruce** "neat and trim" may be shortened from obsolete *spruce leather*, a leather from Prussia formerly used especially for jerkins.

---

spruce² *vti* (**spruced, spruc·ing**) make neater or smarter in appearance ■ *adj* looking neat and trim —**spruce·ly** *adv*

sprung past participle of **spring**

spry /sprī/ (**spry·er** or **spri·er, spry·est** or **spri·est**) *adj* agile and energetic —**spry·ly** *adv* —**spry·ness** *n*

spud *n* **1** a potato *(slang)* **2** a spade with a sharp narrow blade

spume *n* foam on the surface of a liquid, especially the ocean *(literary)* —**spu·mous** *adj* —**spum·y** *adj*

spun past tense, past participle of **spin**

spunk *n* pluckiness *(infml)* —**spunk·i·ly** *adv* —**spunk·y** *adj*

spur *n* **1** a device attached to a rider's heel, used to encourage a horse to go faster **2** an inducement to take action **3** a short section of railroad track off a main line **4** a mountain ridge that projects outward **5** a short road off a major road ■ *vt* (**spurred,**

spur·ring) 1 encourage somebody to take action or try harder 2 use spurs on a horse —**spurred** *adj* ◊ **on the spur of the moment** without thinking or making preparations ◊ **win** *or* **gain your spurs** gain recognition and respect for the first time ◊ See note at **motive**

spu·ri·ous /spyo͝oree əs/ *adj* not genuine or valid —**spu·ri·ous·ly** *adv* —**spu·ri·ous·ness** *n*

spurn *vt* reject with disdain —**spurn·er** *n*

spur-of-the-mo·ment *adj* done or occurring on impulse

spurt *n* 1 a jet of liquid or gas 2 a sudden increase, e.g., of energy ■ *vti* expel or gush out in a jet

sput·nik /spo͝otnik, spút-/ *n* an Earth-orbiting satellite launched by the former Soviet Union

sput·ter /spútter/ *vi* 1 make a popping and spitting sound 2 spit out food and saliva 3 speak in explosive bursts —**sput·ter** *n*

spu·tum /spyo͞otəm/ (*pl* **-ta** /-tə/) *n* a substance that is coughed up, such as phlegm

spy /spī/ *n* (*pl* **spies**) 1 somebody employed by a government to obtain secret information about other countries 2 an employee who obtains information about rival organizations ■ *v* (**spied, spies**) 1 *vi* act as a spy 2 *vt* catch sight of
☐ **spy out** *vt* discover or examine covertly

spy·glass /spī glàss/ *n* a small telescope

⚡ **spy·ware** /spī wàir/ *n* software surreptitiously installed on a hard disk to relay encoded information via an Internet connection

sq. *abbr* square *adj* 3

Sq. *abbr* square *n* 3 (*in addresses*)

⚡ **SQL** *n* a computer language for obtaining information from databases. Full form **structured query language**

squab·ble /skwóbb'l/ *n* a petty argument —**squab·ble** *vi*

squad /skwod/ *n* 1 a group of soldiers 2 a group of police officers 3 a team of people

squad car *n* a police car

squad·ron /skwóddrən/ *n* 1 a naval unit containing two or more divisions of a fleet 2 an air force unit containing two or more flights

squal·id /skwólləd/ *adj* 1 neglected and dirty 2 lacking in dignity, honesty, or morals —**squal·id·ly** *adv* —**squal·id·ness** *n* ◊ See note at **dirty**

squall[1] /skwawl/ *n* 1 a sudden windstorm, often with heavy rain or snow 2 a brief but noisy disturbance ■ *vi* blow strongly and suddenly (*refers to winds*) —**squall·y** *adj*

squall[2] /skwawl/ *vi* yell or cry noisily —**squall** *n*

squal·or /skwóllər/ *n* 1 shabbiness and dirtiness 2 moral degradation

squan·der /skwóndər/ *vt* use wastefully or extravagantly

Squan·to /skwóntō/ (1585?–1622) Wampanoag interpreter

square /skwair/ *n* 1 a geometric figure with four right angles and four equal sides 2 an object shaped like a square 3 an open space in an urban area where two streets meet 4 the result of multiplying a number or term by itself ■ *adj* 1 shaped like a square or cube 2 forming a right angle 3 describes a measurement of surface area according to the length of each side of a square ○ *100 square feet* 4 describes a square with sides of a particular length ○ *10 feet square* 5 completely fair 6 boring and old-fashioned (*slang dated*) ■ *v* (**squared, squar·ing**) 1 *vt* make something square 2 *vt* multiply a number by itself 3 *vt* divide something into squares 4 *vt* move something so that it is straight or level 5 *vti* concur or make something agree ○ *does not square with what we know* ■ *adv* at right angles —**square·ness** *n*
☐ **square up** *vi* settle debts

square brack·et *n* a bracket used for enclosing and separating text

square dance *n* a country dance in which sets of four couples form squares —**square danc·ing** *n*

square·ly /skwáirlee/ *adv* 1 directly and forcefully 2 honestly

square meal *n* a filling and nourishing meal

square-rigged *adj* describes a ship with its principal sails at right angles to its length

square root *n* a number that when multiplied by itself produces the given number

squash[1] (*pl* **same** *or* **squash·es**) *n* 1 a vegetable of the gourd family 2 a plant that produces squashes

squash[2] /skwosh/ *v* 1 *vt* flatten or crush something with pressure 2 *vti* force your way into or put something into a small space 3 *vt* put down a rebellion ■ *n* 1 a racket game played in a walled court with a hard rubber ball 2 the action or noise of squashing

squash·y /skwóshee/ (**-i·er, -i·est**) *adj* easily squashed

squat /skwot/ *vi* (**squat·ted, squat·ting**) 1 crouch down with the knees bent and the thighs resting on the calves 2 occupy property without a legal claim ■ *adj* (**squat·ter, squat·test**) 1 short and solid 2 in a crouched posture ■ *n* 1 the action of squatting 2 a squatting position —**squat·ness** *n*

squat·ter /skwóttər/ *n* 1 an illegal occupant of land or property 2 an early North American homesteader

squaw *n* an offensive term for a Native North American woman or wife (*dated*)

squawk *v* 1 *vi* utter a loud harsh cry 2 *vti* complain or say loudly and annoyingly (*infml*) —**squawk** *n*

squeak /skweek/ *v* 1 *vi* make a high-pitched

sound or cry **2** *vt* say shrilly **3** *vi* barely manage something *(infml)* —**squeak** *n*

squeak·y /skweékee/ (**-i·er**, **-i·est**) *adj* **1** tending to squeak **2** designed to make a squeaking noise when pressed —**squeak·i·ly** *adv* —**squeak·i·ness** *n*

squeak·y-clean *adj* extremely clean

squeal /skweel/ *n* **1** a short shrill cry **2** a loud high sound made by tires when a vehicle brakes suddenly ■ *v* **1** *vti* give a short high cry, or say in a shrill voice **2** *vi* become an informer *(slang disapproving)* —**squeal·er** *n*

squea·mish /skweémish/ *adj* **1** easily made to feel sick **2** easily offended or disgusted —**squea·mish·ly** *adv* —**squea·mish·ness** *n*

squee·gee /skweé jeé/ *n* a T-shaped implement edged with plastic or rubber, used in cleaning windows to remove water from the surface

squeeze *v* (**squeezed**, **squeez·ing**) **1** *vt* press something from two sides **2** *vt* press somebody's hand or other part of the body affectionately or reassuringly **3** *vti* exert pressure on something **4** *vt* push a person or object into a gap **5** *vi* push into or through a small space **6** *vt* find time for somebody or something in a busy schedule **7** *vt* press fruit to obtain juice **8** *vi* barely manage to do something ○ *squeezed through the exam* ■ *n* **1** a squeezing action **2** something squeezed out —**squeeza·ble** *adj*

squelch /skwelch/ *v* **1** *vi* make a sucking or gurgling sound like that of trampling on muddy ground **2** *vt* crush something by trampling **3** *vt* silence something such as a rumor or an unwanted remark *(slang)* —**squelch** *n* —**squel·chy** *adj*

squib *n* **1** a short satirical piece **2** a small firecracker **3** a faulty firecracker that burns without exploding

squid (*pl same or* **squids**) *n* **1** an invertebrate ocean animal with ten arms and a long tapered body **2** squid as food

squig·gle /skwíg'l/ *n* **1** a wavy line or mark **2** an illegible word —**squig·gly** *adj*

squint *vi* **1** partly close the eyes to see better **2** have eyes that do not look in parallel **3** glance at something sideways ■ *n* **1** a condition in which the eyes do not look in parallel **2** a quick glimpse *(infml)* **3** a narrowing of the eyes to see better —**squint·y** *adj*

squire *n* **1** a rural landowner, especially the main local landowner **2** an attendant to a knight in the Middle Ages

squirm /skwurm/ *vi* **1** wriggle from discomfort **2** feel or show signs of emotional distress and embarrassment —**squirm** *n* —**squirm·er** *n* —**squirm·y** *adj*

squir·rel /skwúr əl/ *n* a small bushy-tailed rodent that lives in trees ■ *vt* hoard ○ *squirreled away some money*

squirt /skwurt/ *v* **1** *vti* force or spurt out from a narrow opening **2** *vt* squirt liquid at or

over ■ *n* **1** a small stream of squirted liquid **2** an offensive term for a young or small person *(infml insult)*

squirt gun *n* a toy gun that shoots water

squish *v* **1** *vt* squeeze or crush **2** *vi* make a soft splashing noise ■ *n* a soft splashing noise —**squish·y** *adj*

Sr *symbol* strontium

sr. *abbr* senior

Sr. *abbr* **1** senior **2** señor **3** sister

⚡ **SRAM** *abbr* static random access memory

Sra·va·na /sraávənə/ *n* the 5th month of the year in the Hindu calendar

Sreb·re·ni·ca /srèbbrə neétsə/ town in E Bosnia-Herzegovina. Pop. 37,211 (1991).

Sri Lan·ka /shree lángkə/ island country in South Asia, off the tip of SE India. Cap. Colombo. Pop. 19,408,635 (2001). —**Sri Lan·kan** *n, adj*

SS[1] *abbr* steamship

SS[2] *n* a Nazi paramilitary force acting as Hitler's bodyguard

SS. *abbr* Saints

SSI *abbr* Supplemental Security Income

SSN *abbr* Social Security Number

ST *abbr* standard time

St. for saints, see under first name ■ *abbr* **1** Saint. See also under **Saint 2** Strait **3** Street *(in addresses)*

stab *v* (**stabbed**, **stab·bing**) **1** *vt* thrust a knife or other sharp pointed instrument into **2** *vti* jab a finger or object at something or somebody **3** *vi* hurt suddenly and sharply ■ *n* **1** an act of stabbing ○ *a stab wound* **2** a sudden brief painful feeling **3** an attempt *(infml)* —**stab·bing** *adj*

~~stabalize~~ incorrect spelling of **stabilize**

sta·bil·i·ty /stə bíllətee/ *n* the state or quality of being stable

sta·bi·lize /stáyb'l ìz/ (**-lized**, **-liz·ing**) *v* **1** *vti* make or become stable **2** *vt* maintain the level of something —**sta·bi·li·za·tion** /stàyb'li záysh'n/ *n*

sta·bi·liz·er /stáyb'l ìzər/ *n* **1** an airfoil that keeps an aircraft aligned with the direction of flight **2** a pair or set of fins to control a ship's rolling **3** a chemical compound added to another substance to make it resistant to change

sta·ble[1] /stáyb'l/ *adj* **1** steady and not liable to change or move **2** not excitable or liable to mental illness **3** not subject to changes in chemical or physical properties —**sta·ble·ness** *n* —**sta·bly** *adv*

sta·ble[2] *n* **1** a building in which horses are kept **2** a group of horses owned by one person or kept or trained together ■ *vti* (**sta·bled**, **sta·bling**) put, keep, or live in a stable

sta·ble door *n* a door with separate upper and lower sections

~~stablize~~ incorrect spelling of **stabilize**

stac·ca·to /stə káatō/ *adv* in quick separate notes *(musical direction)* —**stac·ca·to** *adj, n*

stack *n* 1 a pile of things arranged one on top of another 2 a large pile of hay, straw, or grain stored outdoors 3 a tall chimney or group of chimneys 4 a large number or amount *(infml)* ■ **stacks** *npl* an area of book storage in a library that is not usually open to the public ■ *v* 1 *vti* put or be arranged in a stack 2 *vt* load or heap with objects —**stack·a·ble** *adj*

stacked *adj* dishonestly arranged

stack·up /sták ùp/ *n* a number of aircraft waiting a turn to land

sta·di·um /stáydee əm/ (*pl* **-ums** *or* **-a** /-dee ə/) *n* an arena, usually open, with tiered seats for spectators of sports or other activities

Staël /staal/, **Madame de** (1766–1817) French writer

staff *n* 1 the people who work for an employer or in a particular section of an organization 2 a group of officers assisting a military commander 3 (*pl* **staffs** *or* **staves**) a large heavy stick 4 (*pl* **staffs** *or* **staves**) a pole on which a flag is flown 5 a set of five horizontal lines for writing music ■ *vt* provide with employees

staff·er /stáffər/ *n* a member of the staff of an organization *(infml)*

staff of·fi·cer *n* a military officer aiding a commander or working as a planner or adviser at headquarters

staff ser·geant *n* a noncommissioned officer of a rank above a sergeant

stag *n* a mature male deer ■ *adj* restricted to men *(infml)* ■ *adv* without a woman companion on a social occasion *(infml)*

stage *n* 1 the area in a theater where the action takes place 2 the profession of actors 3 a platform where speeches are made or ceremonies performed 4 a period or step during a process ■ *vt* (**staged, stag·ing**) 1 organize or carry out something, e.g., a show or a protest 2 set a play in a particular place or time —**stage·a·ble** *adj*

stage·coach /stáyj kōch/ *n* a large horse-drawn coach

stage·craft /stáyj kràft/ *n* the technique or art of putting on plays

stage di·rec·tion *n* an instruction directing an actor in the script of a play

stage door *n* an outside door into the backstage part of a theater

stage fright *n* fear of performing for an audience

stage·hand /stáyj hànd/ *n* a helper on a stage set

stage left *n* the side of a stage on the actor's left

stage-man·age *v* 1 *vt* tightly control every aspect of an event 2 *vti* serve as stage manager for a play —**stage-man·age·ment** *n*

stage man·ag·er *n* somebody who manages backstage activities in a theater

stage right *n* the side of a stage on the actor's right

stage-struck *adj* loving the theater and desperately wanting to be involved in it, especially as a performer

stage whis·per *n* a loud whisper

stag·ey *adj* = **stagy**

stag·fla·tion /stag fláysh'n/ *n* a period of inflation and little growth in an economy —**stag·fla·tion·ar·y** *adj*

stag·ger /stággər/ *v* 1 *vi* move unsteadily, nearly falling 2 *vt* make a person or animal stumble 3 *vt* astonish or shock somebody 4 *vt* arrange activities for separate or partly overlapping times 5 *vt* arrange things so that they do not form a straight line *(often passive)* —**stag·ger** *n* —**stag·gered** *adj* —**stag·ger·er** *n*

stag·ger·ing /stággəring/ *adj* amazing —**stag·ger·ing·ly** *adv*

stag·ing /stáyjing/ *n* 1 the process or technique of presenting a stage play 2 a structure of scaffolding for a building

stag·ing ar·e·a *n* a place for assembling a military force

stag·nant /stágnənt/ *adj* 1 still and not flowing 2 foul or stale from lack of motion 3 not developing or making progress —**stag·nan·cy** *n* —**stag·nant·ly** *adv*

stag·nate /stág nàyt/ (**-nat·ed, -nat·ing**) *vi* 1 stop flowing or moving 2 become foul or stale from lack of motion 3 fail to develop or make progress —**stag·na·tion** /stag náysh'n/ *n*

stag·y /stáyjee/ (**-i·er, -i·est**), **stag·ey** *adj* exaggerated or artificial in manner, as if in a play *(disapproving)* —**stag·i·ness** *n*

staid /stayd/ *adj* sedate and settled in habits or temperament —**staid·ly** *adv* —**staid·ness** *n*

stain *n* 1 a discolored patch 2 a color finish for wood 3 a dye used to color microscopic specimens 4 something that detracts from a person's good reputation ■ *v* 1 *vti* leave a discolored mark on something 2 *vt* finish or dye with a stain 3 *vt* disgrace or detract from —**stain·less** *adj*

stained glass *n* colored glass often used in windows

stain·less steel *n* corrosion-resistant steel containing chromium

stair /stair/ *n* 1 a single step in a series leading from one floor or level to another 2 a series of stairs ■ **stairs** *npl* a set or several sets of stairs

SPELLCHECK Do not confuse the spelling of **stair** and **stare** ("look fixedly"), which sound similar.

stair·case /stáir kàyss/ *n* a flight of stairs inside a building

stair·way /stáir wày/ *n* a passageway between floors or levels that contains stairs

stair·well /stáir wèl/ *n* a vertical shaft for a staircase

stake[1] /stayk/ *n* 1 a thin pointed post driven into the ground 2 a former method of execution in which somebody was tied to a post and burned ■ *vt* (**staked, stak·ing**) 1 support or strengthen with a stake 2 tie or tether to a stake 3 mark or fence with stakes 4 assert rights over

---

SPELLCHECK Do not confuse the spelling of **stake** and **steak** ("a thick cut of meat or fish"), which sound similar.

□ **stake out** *vt* 1 watch continuously from a hiding place *(infml)* 2 establish the boundaries of

stake[2] *n* 1 an amount of money risked in gambling 2 a share or interest in something ■ **stakes** *npl* 1 the degree of risk in a situation ■ the prize or winnings available ■ *vt* (**staked, stak·ing**) 1 wager 2 put down as an investment in something ◊ **at stake** at risk of being lost

---

ORIGIN The origin of **stake** "money risked" is not certain, but it may be a use of **stake** "post," deriving from a supposed former custom of putting whatever was wagered (for example, your shirt) on a post before the start of the contest being bet on. It is first recorded in the mid-16C. **Stake** meaning "post" is from an ancient Germanic root.

---

stake·hold·er /stáyk hòldər/ *n* a person or group with a direct interest or investment in something —**stake·hold·ing** *n*

stake·out /stáyk òwt/ *n* hidden surveillance, especially by the police *(infml)*

sta·lac·tite /stə lák tìt/ *n* a conical limestone pillar hanging in a cave —**stal·ac·tit·ic** /stàllək títtik/ *adj*

ORIGIN Stalactite is formed from a Greek word meaning "dripping." Its companion *stalagmite* is based on a related Greek word meaning "dropping." Both were taken from modern Latin in the late 17C.

---

sta·lag·mite /stə lág mìt/ *n* a conical limestone pillar rising from a cave floor —**stal·ag·mit·ic** /stàlləg míttik/ *adj*

stale (**stal·er, stal·est**) *adj* 1 no longer fresh 2 frequently heard and boring —**stale** *vti*

stale·mate /stáyl màyt/ *n* 1 a situation in which no side can take any further effective action 2 a chess situation with no winner because neither player can move without being in check —**stale·mate** *vt*

Joseph Stalin

Sta·lin /staalin/, **Joseph** (1879–1953) Georgian-born general secretary of the Communist Party of the USSR (1922–53)

Sta·lin·grad /staalin gràd/ former name for **Volgograd**

Sta·lin·ism /staalə nìzzəm/ *n* the political and economic theories of Stalin, developed from Marxism-Leninism —**Sta·lin·ist** *n, adj*

stalk[1] /stawk/ *n* 1 a fleshy main stem of a plant, or a part that supports a leaf or flower 2 a slender supporting part of an object

stalk[2] /stawk/ *v* 1 *vt* follow stealthily 2 *vi* walk stiffly and angrily 3 *vi* proceed steadily and malevolently 4 *vt* harass with persistent and inappropriate attention —**stalk** *n* —**stalk·er** *n*

stalk·ing horse *n* 1 a means to disguise an objective 2 a candidate whose motive is to conceal somebody else's candidacy or to divide or assess the opposition

stall[1] *n* 1 a booth, counter, or other small structure set up to sell goods or dispense information 2 a compartment in a building for a large animal 3 a situation in which an engine stops abruptly in an undesired way 4 a small room or partitioned space for a shower or toilet 5 a sudden dive by an aircraft 6 a pew or enclosed seat in a church 7 a space for parking ■ *vti* 1 stop suddenly, or make an engine stop suddenly, in an undesired way 2 go into a dive, or cause an aircraft to go into a dive

stall[2] *v* 1 *vti* delay somebody with hesitation, evasion, or obstruction, or use delaying tactics 2 *vi* in football or basketball, prolong holding the ball to prevent an opponent from scoring —**stall** *n*

stal·lion /stállyən/ *n* an uncastrated male horse

stal·wart /stáwlwərt/ *adj* 1 dependable and loyal 2 sturdy and strong ■ *n* a hard-working loyal supporter —**stal·wart·ly** *adv* —**stal·wart·ness** *n*

sta·men /stáymən/ (*pl* **-mens** *or* **-mi·na** /stáymənə, stámmənə/) *n* the male reproductive organ of a flower —**sta·mi·nal** /stáymən'l, stámm ə-/ *adj*

Stam·ford /stámfərd/ city in SW Connecticut. Pop. 110,689 (1998).

stam·i·na /stámmənə/ *n* resilient energy and strength —**stam·i·nal** *adj*

ORIGIN Stamina was originally a plural word

meaning "original or essential elements" and "strong elements of a person's constitution, innate strength." It was adopted in the late 17C from the plural of Latin *stamen* "warp of a fabric," applied also in the plural to the threads of life spun by the Fates in Greek and Roman mythology. The modern sense of "resilient strength" developed in the early 18C.

stam·mer /stámmər/ *vti* speak or say with hesitations and repetitions ■ *n* a speech condition that makes somebody stammer —**stam·mer·er** *n*

stamp *n* 1 a small piece of gummed paper showing payment for postage or official acknowledgment 2 a small block for printing a design 3 a design printed onto paper with a stamp 4 a characteristic or distinguishing sign 5 the banging down of a foot ■ *v* 1 *vt* stick or press a stamp on something 2 *vti* bang a foot down 3 *vi* walk forcefully —**stamped** *adj*

□ **stamp out** 1 eradicate 2 extinguish 3 cut out using a sharp tool

Stamp Act *n* a British law of 1765 taxing legal documents and some printed material in the North American colonies

stamp col·lect·ing *n* the collecting of postage stamps as a hobby —**stamp col·lec·tor** *n*

stam·pede /stam peéd/ *n* 1 a headlong rush, especially of animals 2 a sudden rush of people to do something ■ *v* (-ped·ed, -ped·ing) 1 *vti* rush forward in a frightened headlong surge, or make animals or people do this 2 *vt* force somebody into doing something prematurely or ill-advisedly

stamp·ing ground *n* a habitual haunt or gathering place (*infml*)

stance /stanss/ *n* 1 an attitude toward something 2 a way of standing

stanch[1] /stawnch, staanch, stanch/, **staunch** /stáwnch/ *v* 1 *vti* stop the flow of a liquid, or stop flowing 2 *vt* stop a wound from bleeding —**stanch·er** *n*

stanch[2] *adj* = **staunch**[1]

stan·chion /stánchən/ *n* an upright supporting pole

stand *v* (**stood** /stood/) 1 *vti* be or set upright 2 *vi* get up onto the feet from a sitting or lying posture 3 *vi* be situated in a particular place 4 *vi* be in a particular state o *stands in need of renovation* 5 *vi* remain motionless or unused 6 *vi* remain valid or in existence 7 *vt* tolerate 8 *vt* undergo without harm or damage 9 *vt* submit to or be subjected to o *stand trial* 10 *vi* be a candidate 11 *vt* pay for something for somebody else o *stood them all a drink* ■ *n* 1 the action or a period of standing 2 an attitude toward something 3 a supporting structure 4 a piece of furniture on which things are hung or in which things are held upright (*often in combination*) o *an umbrella stand* 5 a booth

or stall where something is sold, distributed, or exhibited (*often in combination*) o *a refreshment stand* 6 a place for witnesses in court ■ **stands** *npl* a large seating area for spectators —**stand·ee** /stan deé/ *n*

□ **stand for** *vt* 1 mean or represent 2 believe in and fight for 3 put up with

□ **stand out** *vi* 1 be conspicuous 2 project or protrude

□ **stand up** *v* 1 *vti* rise to or put in an upright position 2 *vi* resist scrutiny o *evidence that won't stand up in court*

□ **stand up for** *vt* defend the interests of

□ **stand up to** *vt* resist or refuse to be cowed by

⌁ **stand-a·lone** *adj* operating independently of a computer network or system

stan·dard /stándərd/ *n* 1 a level of quality, excellence, or achievement 2 an authorized model or specification by which things are measured or judged 3 a flag with an emblematic design 4 a supporting base ■ *adj* 1 constituting or not differing from the norm 2 widely used and respected 3 regarded as linguistically correct ■ **stan·dards** *npl* principles governing behavior —**stan·dard·ly** *adv*

stan·dard-bear·er *n* 1 a leader or inspiring representative or advocate of something 2 somebody who carries a standard or flag

stan·dard de·vi·a·tion *n* a statistical measure of the amount by which a set of values differs from the arithmetical mean

stan·dard·ize /stándər dìz/ (-ized, -iz·ing) *v* 1 *vti* conform or cause to conform to a standard 2 *vt* assess by comparison with a standard —**stan·dard·i·za·tion** /stàndərdi záysh'n/ *n*

stan·dard·ized test *n* a test for assessing a student's aptitude

stan·dard of liv·ing *n* a level of material comfort experienced by a person or group

stan·dard time *n* the time of day in any of the established time zones

stand·by /stánd bì/ *n* 1 a person or thing that can be relied on or is available as a substitute or in an emergency 2 an unreserved travel ticket, or a passenger having no prior reservation ■ *adj* 1 able to be used as a substitute or in an emergency 2 describes a ticket that is unreserved and subject to availability, or a person using such a ticket ■ *adv* on a standby basis

stand-down *n* a return to normal after an alert or a military presence

stand-in *n* 1 a temporary replacement 2 a movie actor's double —**stand-in** *vi*

stand·ing /stánding/ *n* 1 somebody's status and reputation 2 the duration of something ■ *adj* 1 performed while upright 2 permanently in existence or effect 3 not flowing

stand·ing ar·my *n* a professional military

force maintained in times of peace as well as war

stand·ing com·mit·tee *n* a permanent committee for dealing with a particular issue

stand·ing or·der *n* an order or rule that remains in force on all relevant occasions until it is specifically revoked

stand·ing room *n* space for people to stand but not sit

Stan·dish /stándish/, **Miles** (1584?–1656) English-born American colonist

stand-off /stánd àwf, -òf/ *n* a deadlock

stand·off·ish /stànd áwfish, -óffish/ *adj* aloof or uncommunicative —**stand·off·ish·ly** *adv* —**stand·off·ish·ness** *n*

stand·out /stánd òwt/ *n* somebody or something outstanding (*infml*)

stand·pipe /stánd pìp/ *n* a vertical open-ended pipe attached to a pipeline to regulate pressure

stand·point /stánd pòynt/ *n* a point of view

stand·still /stánd stìl/ *n* a complete halt

stand-up /stánd ùp/ *adj* **1** performing or performed by standing alone on stage and telling jokes **2** a *standup comedy* **2** at which people stand, especially to eat or drink **3** erect and not folded down ■ *n* standup comedy or a standup comedian

stank past tense of **stink**

Stan·ley /stánlee/ capital of the Falkland Islands. Pop. 1,232 (1986).

Stan·ley, Sir H. M. (1841–1904) British journalist and explorer

Stan·ton /stánt'n/, **Elizabeth Cady** (1815–1902) US social reformer

stan·za /stánzə/ *n* a group of lines forming a division of a poem —**stan·za·ic** /stan záy ik/ *adj*

sta·pes /stáy peèz/ *n* (*pl* same *or* -**pe·des** /stə peè deèz/) *n* a stirrup-shaped bone in the middle ear —**sta·pe·di·al** /stə peèdee əl/ *adj*

sta·ple[1] /stáyp'l/ *n* **1** a small thin piece of bent wire used to fasten papers and sheets of other thin materials together **2** a U-shaped piece of strong metal wire with two sharp points, driven into wood or masonry to fasten something ■ *vt* fasten with a staple or staples

sta·ple[2] /stáyp'l/ *n* **1** a basic ingredient of a diet **2** a principal or recurring element or feature **3** the most important article of trade **4** a raw material **5** wool, cotton, or flax fiber graded according to length and fineness —**sta·ple** *adj*

sta·ple gun *n* a powerful device used to drive staples into wood or masonry

sta·pler /stáyplər/ *n* a device for stapling papers together

star *n* **1** an astronomical object visible as a point of light in the night sky **2** a shape with four or more triangular points radiating from a center **3** an asterisk **4** a very famous or successful performer **5** an especially important or proficient person ■ *v* (**starred, star·ring**) **1** *vt* have as a leading actor **2** *vi* be a leading performer in something such as a movie or show **3** *vt* mark with an asterisk ■ *adj* very important or successful

star·board /staárbərd/ *n* the right-hand side of somebody facing the front of a ship or aircraft —**star·board** *adj, adv*

ORIGIN Starboard has no connection with the stars. *Star*- represents a form related to *steer* and meaning "paddle." The name derives from the ancient custom of steering boats by means of a paddle on the right-hand side.

---

star·burst /staár bùrst/ *n* a radiating pattern of lines or light

starch *n* **1** a natural carbohydrate substance made by plants. Use: food, production of alcohol. **2** a white powder extracted from potatoes and grain. Use: stiffening fabric. ■ *vt* stiffen fabric with starch

star cham·ber *n* a harsh and arbitrary tribunal

starch·y /staárchee/ (-**i·er**, -**i·est**) *adj* **1** of or containing starch **2** formal and appearing to lack warmth and humor —**starch·i·ness** *n*

star-crossed *adj* believed to be destined to be unhappy

star·dom /staárdəm/ *n* star status in sports or entertainment

star·dust /staár dùst/ *n* a magical or dreamy quality or feeling, or the imaginary substance supposed to induce this

stare /stair/ *vi* (**stared, star·ing**) **1** look directly and fixedly **2** be wide open with shock or amazement (*refers to eyes*) ■ *n* **1** a long concentrated look **2** a facial expression with the eyes wide open ◊ See note at **stair, gaze**

star·fish /staár fìsh/ (*pl* same *or* -**fish·es**) *n* a star-shaped invertebrate ocean animal

star fruit *n* a yellow tropical fruit with a star-shaped cross section

star·gaz·er /staár gàyzər/ *n* a daydreamer

stark *adj* **1** forbiddingly bare and plain **2** presented in unambiguous and harsh terms **3** complete or utter ■ *adv* utterly —**stark·ly** *adv* —**stark·ness** *n*

star·let /staárlət/ *n* a young woman actor seen as a possible future star

star·light /staár lìt/ *n* light from the stars

star·ling /staárling/ *n* a common bird with glossy greenish black plumage

star·lit /staár lìt/ *adj* lit by starlight

Star of Da·vid /staár/ *n* a six-pointed star formed by two equilateral triangles superimposed on each other, used as a symbol of Judaism and the state of Israel

star·ry /staáree/ (-**ri·er**, -**ri·est**) *adj* **1** with many stars shining **2** covered or decorated with stars

star·ry-eyed adj naively idealistic

Stars and Stripes n the national flag of the United States (+ sing or pl verb)

star sign n a sign of the zodiac

Star-Span·gled Ban·ner n 1 the national anthem of the United States 2 the Stars and Stripes

star·struck /staär strŭk/ adj fascinated by stars of the entertainment world and by stardom

star·stud·ded adj with many movie or stage stars

start v 1 vti do something that was not being done before ○ started work ○ started to laugh 2 vti come or bring into being, or get under way ○ starts at one o'clock ○ starting a new business 3 vti begin working, or make an engine begin to work 4 vi begin at a particular level ○ Prices start at $15. 5 vi make a sudden or involuntary movement ■ n 1 the first part of something that proceeds through time 2 the place or time at which something starts 3 a quick sudden or involuntary movement 4 a position ahead of others 5 a set of conditions at the beginning of something ○ a good start in life

START /staart/ abbr Strategic Arms Reduction Talks

start·er /staärtər/ n 1 a starting device for an engine 2 somebody signaling the start of a race 3 a competitor who starts in a race 4 a first course of a meal

start·er home n a small property suitable for a first-time buyer

start·ing block n a support for a runner's feet at the start of a race

start·ing gate n a line of gated stalls from which horses leave to start a race

start·ing grid n a pattern of lines marking starting positions on an auto racing track

start·ing gun n a gun fired to start a race

start·ing line n a line on a racetrack behind which runners start

star·tle /staärt'l/ (-tled, -tling) vt disconcert or frighten into making an involuntary movement —**star·tling** adj —**star·tling·ly** adv

start-up /staärt ŭp/ n 1 something such as a company that is just beginning operations 2 the beginning of an activity or project —**start-up** adj

star·va·tion /staar váysh'n/ n severe lack of food or the physical condition caused by this

starve (**starved, starv·ing**) v 1 vti weaken or die because of hunger, or cause somebody to do this 2 vi be very hungry (infml) 3 vt deprive of something vitally needed

starve·ling /staärvling/ n a very thin person (archaic)

stash n a hidden store or supply (infml) —**stash** vt

sta·sis /stáyssiss, stássiss/ n 1 a motionless or unchanging state 2 a stoppage of the flow of body fluids

state n 1 a condition that somebody or something is in 2 a developmental stage of an animal or plant 3 a mostly autonomous region of a federal country 4 a country with its own independent government 5 a country's government and government-controlled institutions 6 a nervous, upset, or excited condition 7 a ceremonious way of doing something 8 any form that a physical substance can be in ■ **States** npl the United States (infml) ■ adj 1 of a country's government 2 done with full ceremony ■ vt (**stat·ed, stat·ing**) express or announce in words

state at·tor·ney n a state's attorney

state·craft /stáyt kráft/ n the art of governing well

State De·part·ment n the US department of foreign affairs

state·hood /stáyt hŏŏd/ n the status of a state in a federal union

state·house /stáyt hòwss/ (pl -hous·es /-hòwzəz/) n in the United States, a building in which a state legislature convenes

state·less /stáytləss/ adj having no official nationality

state line n a boundary between two states

state·ly /stáytlee/ (-li·er, -li·est) adj 1 impressively weighty and dignified 2 grand and imposing

state·ment /stáytmənt/ n 1 an expression in words of something definite 2 an account of facts relating to a crime or legal case 3 an expression of an idea through a medium other than words 4 a printed record of the transactions relating to an account

Sta·ten Is·land /stàtt'n-/ one of the five boroughs of New York. Pop. 378,977 (1990).

state of af·fairs n a particular set of circumstances

state of con·cern n a rogue state (fml)

state of the art n the most advanced level of technology —**state-of-the-art** adj

state room n a large room used on state occasions

state·room /stáyt ròom, -ròòm/ n a luxurious private cabin or compartment on a ship

state's at·tor·ney, state at·tor·ney n a prosecutor who acts on behalf of the state

state se·cret n a secret important to national security and revealed only to authorized people

state·side /stáyt sīd/ adv in or toward the United States ■ adj of the United States

states·man /stáytsmən/ (pl -men /-mən/) n a leading or senior man politician —**states·man·like** adj —**states·man·ship** n

states·wo·man /stáyts wŏŏmən/ (pl -men /-wĭmmin/) n a leading or senior woman politician

state troop·er n a police officer who patrols the state highways

state·wide /stáyt wíd, stàyt wíd/ *adj* affecting an entire state —**state·wide** *adv*

stat·ic /státtik/ *adj* **1** motionless or unchanging **2** of forces or pressures that act without causing movement **3** of stationary electric charges **4** of or caused by electrical interference in a radio or television broadcast ■ *n* **1** electrical interference in a radio or television broadcast **2** *also* **stat·ic e·lec·tric·i·ty** a stationary electric charge that builds up on an insulated object —**stat·i·cal·ly** *adv*

stat·in /státtin/ *n* a drug belonging to a group that reduces cholesterol in the blood

sta·tion /stáysh'n/ *n* **1** a stop on a railroad or bus route **2** a local branch or headquarters of an organization such as the police force, fire department, or ambulance service **3** a building specially equipped to perform a function ◊ *a pumping station* **4** a building equipped to make and transmit radio or television broadcasts **5** a broadcasting channel **6** a place where somebody is assigned to be ■ *vt* assign to a place

sta·tion·ar·y /stáysha nèrree/ *adj* **1** not moving or at a standstill **2** fixed and not able to be moved **3** unchanging

> **SPELLCHECK** Do not confuse the spelling of **stationary** and **stationery** ("paper and envelopes"), which sound similar.

sta·tion break *n* an interval on television or radio used for an announcement or commercial

sta·tion·er /stáysh'nər/ *n* a seller of stationery

> **ORIGIN** In medieval Latin a *stationarius* was originally a "trader who kept a permanent stall." The word's Latin source meant literally "standing, keeping still." Of the comparatively rare stores that existed in the Middle Ages, the commonest were bookstores, licensed by the universities, and so English adopted the Latin term. It has since come down in the world somewhat to "seller of paper, pens, etc." (a sense first recorded in the mid-17C).

sta·tion·er·y /stáysha nèrree/ *n* paper, envelopes, pens, and other things used for writing ◊ See note at **stationary**

sta·tion house *n* a building housing a police or fire department

sta·tion·mas·ter /stáysh'n màstər/ *n* a railroad official in charge of a station

sta·tion wag·on *n* US, Can, ANZ a large car with an extended area behind the rear seats and a tailgate

sta·tis·tic /stə tístik/ *n* **1** an element of data from a collection **2** a numerical value or function used to describe a sample —**sta·tis·ti·cal** *adj* —**sta·tis·ti·cal·ly** *adv*

sta·tis·tics /stə tístiks/ *n* the branch of mathematics that deals with numerical data in terms of samples and populations (+ sing *verb*) ■ *npl* a collection of numerical data (+ pl *verb*) ◊ *this month's sales statistics* —**stat·is·ti·cian** /stàttə stísh'n/ *n*

sta·tive /státiv/ *adj* describes a verb expressing a state, not an action —**sta·tive** *n*

statment incorrect spelling of **statement**

stat·u·ar·y /stáchoo èrree/ *n* **1** statues considered collectively **2** the art of making statues

stat·ue /stáchoo/ *n* a carved or cast three-dimensional image of a human or animal

stat·u·esque /stàchoo ésk/ *adj* attractive in a stately way

stat·u·ette /stàchoo ét/ *n* a small statue

stat·ure /stáchər/ *n* **1** the height of a person or animal in a standing position **2** a person's social or professional standing

sta·tus /státtəss, státtəss/ *n* **1** rank in society or a group **2** prestige or high standing **3** a situation that is subject to change **4** somebody's legal standing

sta·tus bar *n* a bar on a computer screen that displays information about an application being used

sta·tus quo /-kwố/ *n* the way things are now

sta·tus sym·bol *n* a sign of wealth or prestige

stat·ute /stáchoot/ *n* **1** a law enacted by a legislature **2** an established rule or law

stat·ute book *n* a record of acts passed by a legislature and remaining in force

stat·ute law *n* law enacted by a legislature

stat·u·to·ry /stácho tàwree/ *adj* of a statute

stat·u·to·ry rape *n* sexual relations with a minor

staunch[1] /stawnch, staanch/, **stanch** *adj* **1** loyal **2** sturdy —**staunch·ly** *adv* —**staunch·ness** *n*

staunch[2] *vt* = **stanch**[1]

stave /stayv/ *n* **1** a band of wood used in making the hull of a boat or the body of a barrel **2** a rung or bar of wood or other material **3** a wooden staff or stick **4** a musical staff ■ *v* (**staved** *or* **stove, staved, stav·ing**) **1** *vt* break the staves of a boat or barrel **2** *vti* cause something to break inward

☐ **stave off** *vt* avoid or prevent something unpleasant, often only temporarily

stay[1] *v* **1** *vi* continue to be in the same position or state **2** *vi* live temporarily or permanently in a place **3** *vti* pass a particular length of time in a place or in doing something **4** *vt* persevere in doing or supporting something ◊ *stay the course* **5** *vi* linger or pause ◊ *Stay a moment.* **6** *vt* put a stop to something **7** *vt* postpone or hinder something ■ *n* **1** a short period spent away from home **2** a curb or check **3** a temporary halt in legal proceedings ◊ **stay put** remain in a place or position

stay[2] *n* **1** a support such as a brace, prop, or buttress **2** a small piece of hard material used to stiffen a corset or girdle ■ **stays** *npl* a stiffened corset ■ *vt* support or prop up (*archaic*)

stay³ *n* 1 a rope or cable supporting a mast 2 a rope used to steady or guide something

stay-at-home *adj* not leaving home much by choice —**stay-at-home** *n*

stay·ing pow·er *n* the ability to keep doing something or to keep trying

STD *abbr* sexually transmitted disease

stead /sted/ *n* the position or role of another ◊ **stand somebody in good stead** be useful to somebody

stead·fast /stéd fàst/ *adj* 1 firm in purpose, loyalty, or resolve 2 firmly fixed or constant —**stead·fast·ly** *adv* —**stead·fast·ness** *n*

stead·y /stéddee/ *adj* (**-i·er, -i·est**) 1 stable or not easily moved 2 staying the same 3 constant or continuous 4 reliable but dull or routine 5 not easily upset or excited 6 staid or serious ■ *vti* (**-ied, -ies**) make or become steady —**stead·i·ly** *adv* —**stead·i·ness** *n*

steak /stayk/ *n* 1 a thick cut of lean beef 2 a thick piece of other meat or of fish ◊ See note at **stake**

steak·house /stáyk hòwss/ (*pl* **-hous·es** /-hòwzəz/) *n* a restaurant serving steaks

steak tar·tare /-taar taár/ *n* a dish of uncooked ground beef with raw egg and chopped onions

steal /steel/ *v* (**stole, sto·len** /stôlən/) 1 *vti* take another's property unlawfully 2 *vt* take something furtively or through trickery 3 *vi* go quietly or unobtrusively 4 *vt* take and use another's ideas ■ *n* 1 an act of stealing 2 a bargain (*infml*)

SPELLCHECK Do not confuse the spelling of **steal** and **steel** (the metal), which sound similar.

SYNONYMS steal, pinch, nick, filch, purloin, pilfer, embezzle, misappropriate
CORE MEANING: the taking of property unlawfully

---

stealth /stelth/ *n* 1 the doing of something slowly, quietly, and covertly to avoid detection 2 furtiveness ■ *adj* virtually undetectable by radar —**stealth·ful** *adj*

stealth·y /stélthee/ (**-i·er, -i·est**) *adj* 1 done in a deliberately slow, careful, and quiet way 2 furtive or cunning —**stealth·i·ly** *adv* —**stealth·i·ness** *n* ◊ See note at **secret**

steam /steem/ *n* 1 the vapor that is formed when water is boiled 2 the visible mist of condensed water vapor ■ *adj* driven by or using steam ■ *v* 1 *vi* produce steam 2 *vi* move by steam 3 *vti* cook in the steam of boiling water

□ **steam up** *vti* become or make clouded with condensed water vapor

steam·boat /steém bòt/ *n* a boat powered by steam

steam en·gine *n* an engine powered by steam

steam·er /steémər/ *n* 1 a steamboat or steamship 2 a covered pan for steaming food

steam·ing /steéming/ *adj* very angry (*infml*)

steam i·ron *n* an iron with a chamber for water that produces steam to dampen the laundry

steam·rol·ler /steém ròlər/ *n* 1 a vehicle with large heavy rollers as wheels for flattening roads 2 a crushing force that eliminates resistance ■ *vt also* **steam-roll** 1 flatten with a steamroller 2 ruthlessly crush

steam·ship /steém shìp/ *n* a ship powered by steam

steam·y /steémee/ (**-i·er, -i·est**) *adj* 1 full of steam 2 hot and clammy 3 overtly sexual (*infml*) —**steam·i·ly** *adv*

ste·a·tite /steé ə tìt/ *n* soapstone

steed /steed/ *n* a spirited horse (*literary*)

steel /steel/ *n* 1 a strong alloy of iron and carbon 2 something made of steel ■ *vt* 1 coat or edge with steel 2 prepare or brace for a setback or trial —**steel** *adj* ◊ See note at **steal**

steel band *n* a musical group playing steel drums

steel drum, steel pan *n* a Caribbean percussion instrument made from an oil drum

Steele /steel/, **Sir Richard** (1672–1729) English playwright and essayist

steel gui·tar *n* a guitar played on a horizontal stand with a plectrum and metal slide

steel wool *n* a clump of abrasive steel strands. Use: cleaning, polishing.

steel·works /steél wùrks/ *n* a steel-making factory

steel·y /steélee/ *adj* 1 like steel 2 determined and tough —**steel·i·ness** *n*

steep¹ *adj* 1 sloping sharply 2 excessively high, especially in cost (*infml*) 3 very large ◊ *a steep decline in demand* —**steep·en** *vti* —**steep·ly** *adv* —**steep·ness** *n*

steep² *v* 1 *vti* immerse or soak in liquid 2 *vt* permeate —**steep** *n*

stee·ple /steep'l/ *n* 1 a church tower 2 a spire

stee·ple·chase /steép'l chàyss/ *n* 1 a horse race with jumps on the track 2 a track event with hurdles and a water jump ■ *vi* (**-chased, -chas·ing**) run a steeplechase —**stee·ple·chas·er** *n*

stee·ple·jack /steép'l jàk/ *n* a builder or repairer of steeples and other tall structures

steer¹ *v* 1 *vti* guide a vehicle or ship by a device such as a wheel or rudder 2 *vt* influence somebody to go in a particular direction or take a particular course —**steer·a·ble** *adj* ◊ See note at **guide**

steer² *n* a young castrated ox

steer·age /steérij/ *n* 1 the cheapest accommodations on a passenger ship, usually near the rudder and steering gear 2 the process of steering a boat

steer·ing col·umn *n* a part of a motor vehicle connecting the steering wheel with the main steering mechanism

steer·ing com·mit·tee *n* a group of people selected to set agendas, decide topics for discussion, and prioritize business

steer·ing wheel *n* a wheel in a vehicle or ship that is turned to change its direction

steers·man /stéerzmən/ (*pl* **-men** /-mən/) *n* somebody who steers a boat or ship

Steich·en /stík'n/, **Edward** (1879–1973) Luxembourg-born US photographer

stein /stīn/ *n* **1** an earthenware or pewter beer mug, often with a lid **2** the quantity of beer held by a stein

Stein /stīn/, **Gertrude** (1874–1946) US writer

Viking Press

John Steinbeck

Stein·beck /stín bèk/, **John Ernst** (1902–68) US writer

Stein·em /stínəm/, **Gloria** (*b.* 1934) US feminist

Stein·er /stínər, shtínər/, **Rudolf** (1861–1925) Austrian philosopher

Stel·la /stéllə/, **Frank** (*b.* 1936) US artist

stel·lar /stéllər/ *adj* **1** of or like a star or stars **2** exceptionally good

stem[1] *n* **1** the main stalk of a plant **2** a secondary stalk of a plant, bearing a leaf, bud, or flower **3** a narrow part of an object, e.g., a wine glass or tobacco pipe **4** the main part of a word, to which inflections and affixes are added ■ *v* (**stemmed, stem·ming**) **1** *vi* originate **2** *vt* remove the stem of **3** *vt* provide with a stem —**stemmed** *adj*

stem[2] (**stemmed, stem·ming**) *vt* prevent from flowing

stem·ware /stém waìr/ *n* glassware with stems

stench *n* a horrible smell ◊ See note at **smell**

sten·cil /sténss'l/ *n* **1** a plate with a cut-out design that is marked on a surface when paint or ink is applied **2** a pattern or lettering marked using a stencil ■ *vt* (**-ciled** *or* **-cilled, -cil·ing** *or* **-cil·ling**) **1** apply a design or lettering using a stencil **2** decorate a surface using a stencil —**sten·cil·er** *n*

Stend·hal /sten daál/ (1783–1842) French novelist

ste·nog·ra·phy /stə nóggrəfee/ (*pl* **-phies**) *n* **1** shorthand writing or typing **2** something written or typed in shorthand —**ste·nog·ra·pher** *n* —**sten·o·graph·ic** /stènnə gráffik/ *adj* —**sten·o·graph·i·cal·ly** *adv*

sten·to·ri·an /sten táwree ən/ *adj* loud or declamatory

ORIGIN The original **stentorian** voice belonged to Stentor, a Greek herald in the stories of the Trojan War in Greek mythology.

step /step/ *n* **1** a short movement made by raising one foot and putting it down ahead of the other **2** the distance of a step **3** the sound of a footfall **4** a way of walking **5** a very short distance **6** a raised surface for the foot, especially one of a series going up or down **7** a stage in progress **8** a degree, grade, or interval ■ **steps** *npl* **1** outdoor stairs **2** a path or course made by somebody else ■ *v* (**stepped, step·ping**) **1** *vi* move a foot onto something or in a particular direction **2** *vi* walk a short distance **3** *vi* move forward by taking steps **4** *vt* arrange in or provide with steps —**stepped** *adj* ◊ **be in** *or* **out of step** agree or disagree with somebody or something ◊ **step by step** gradually ◊ **step on it** hurry (*slang; usually a command*) ◊ **take steps** take action ◊ **watch your step** be careful and cautious

SPELLCHECK Do not confuse the spelling of **step** and **steppe** ("a wide grassy plain"), which sound similar.

□ **step up** *vt* raise in stages

step- *prefix* related because of remarriage, not by blood ○ *stepson* ○ *stepmother*

step·broth·er /stép brùthər/ *n* a son of a stepparent

step change *n* a significant change

step·child /stép chìld/ (*pl* **-chil·dren** /-chìldrən/) *n* a stepson or stepdaughter

step·daugh·ter /stép dàwtər/ *n* a daughter of somebody's spouse from a previous marriage

step-down *adj* **1** decreasing in stages **2** lowering voltage —**step-down** *n*

step·fam·i·ly /stép fàmməlee/ (*pl* **-lies**) *n* a family with a stepparent

step·fa·ther /stép faàthər/ *n* a mother's subsequent husband

step·lad·der /stép làddər/ *n* a folding ladder with steps and a supporting frame

step·moth·er /stép mùthər/ *n* a father's subsequent wife

step·par·ent /stép pàirənt/ *n* a stepfather or stepmother

steppe /step/ *n* a vast dry and grass-covered plain ■ **Steppes** *npl* the plains of Russia and Ukraine ◊ See note at **step**

step·ping stone *n* **1** a stone to put a foot on to cross a stream or wet area **2** a step toward a goal

step·sis·ter /stép sìstər/ *n* a daughter of a stepparent

step·son /stép sùn/ *n* a son of somebody's spouse from a previous marriage

step-up *adj* **1** increasing in stages **2** raising voltage —**step-up** *n*

stere /steer/ *n* a cubic meter

ster·e·o /stérree ō, steér-/ (*pl* **-os**) *n* **1** a device producing stereophonic sound **2** stereophonic reproduction —**ster·e·o** *adj*

ster·e·o·phon·ic /stèrree ə fónnik, stèeree ə-/ *adj* using two soundtracks and transmission channels for recorded sound —**ster·e·o·phon·i·cal·ly** *adv*

ster·e·o·scop·ic /stèrree ə skóppik, stèeree-/ *adj* producing a three-dimensional effect when seen —**ster·e·o·scop·i·cal·ly** *adv*

ster·e·o·type /stérree ə tīp, stèeree-/ *n* **1** a conventional oversimplified or standardized conception of a person or group **2** a metal printing plate cast from a mold ■ *vt* (**-typed**, **-typ·ing**) **1** reduce to a stereotype **2** print using a stereotype —**ster·e·o·typ·i·cal** /stérree ə típpik'l, stèeree-/ *adj* —**ster·e·o·typ·i·cal·ly** *adv*

ster·ile /stérrəl, -īl/ *adj* **1** incapable of producing offspring **2** incapable of supporting vegetation **3** free of bacteria and other organisms —**ste·ril·i·ty** /stə ríllətee/ *n*

ster·il·ize /stérrə līz/ (**-ized**, **-iz·ing**) *vt* make sterile —**ster·il·i·za·tion** /stèrrəli záysh'n/ *n*

~~sterie~~ incorrect spelling of **stereo**

ster·ling /stúrling/ *n* **1** *also* **ster·ling sil·ver** an alloy containing at least 92.5% silver **2** British currency ■ *adj* **1** of sterling silver **2** admirable

stern¹ *adj* **1** strict and uncompromising **2** showing disapproval or anger —**stern·ly** *adv* —**stern·ness** *n*

stern² *n* the rear of a ship or boat —**stern** *adj*

Stern·berg ◆ **von Sternberg, Josef**

Sterne /sturn/, **Laurence** (1713–68) Irish novelist

ster·num /stúrnəm/ (*pl* **-nums** *or* **-na** /-nə/) *n* the breastbone (*technical*) —**ster·nal** *adj*

ster·oid /steér òyd, sté ròyd/ *n* any of a group of organic compounds including the sex hormones —**ste·roid·al** /steer óyd'l, sté róyd'l/ *adj*

steth·o·scope /stéthə skōp/ *n* a medical instrument for listening to breathing and heartbeats —**steth·o·scop·ic** /stèthə skóppik/ *adj*

Steu·ben /stoóbən, styoóbən/, **Friedrich Wilhelm Ludolf Gerhard Augustin von, Baron von** (1730–94) Prussian-born American Revolutionary soldier

ste·ve·dore /steévə dàwr/ *n* a longshoreman who loads and unloads ships —**ste·ve·dore** *vti*

Ste·vens /steévənz/, **John Paul** (b. 1920) associate justice of the US Supreme Court (1975–)

AKG London

Wallace Stevens

Ste·vens, Wallace (1879–1955) US poet

Ste·ven·son /steévənssən/, **Adlai** (1900–65) US politician, presidential candidate (1952, 1956), and diplomat

Ste·ven·son, Robert Louis (1850–94) Scottish writer

stew /stoo, styoo/ *n* a simmered dish, usually of meat and vegetables ■ *v* **1** *vti* cook by simmering **2** *vi* be troubled or agitated ◇ **in a stew** agitated, anxious, or in a difficult situation (*infml*)

stew·ard /stoó ərd, styoó-/ *n* **1** a passenger attendant on an aircraft or ship **2** somebody in charge of meals on a ship or at a hotel or club **3** a property or household manager **4** an official at a public event —**stew·ard** *vti* —**stew·ard·ship** *n*

Stew·art /stoó ərt, styoó-/, **Jimmy** (1908–97) US movie actor

Stew·art, Potter (1915–85) associate justice of the US Supreme Court (1958–81)

STI *abbr* sexually transmitted infection

stick¹ *n* **1** a thin branch **2** a long often cylindrical piece of wood or other material used for a particular purpose ○ *a hockey stick* ○ *a walking stick* **3** a stick-like part or piece ○ *a stick of celery* ■ **sticks** *npl* a remote place (*infml*)

stick² *v* (**stuck**) **1** *vti* fasten or be fixed on contact, usually by means of a viscous substance **2** *vt* fasten with a pointed object **3** *vt* pierce or stab **4** *vti* protrude **5** *vt* put somewhere (*infml*) **6** *vi* be or become unable to move **7** *vt* puzzle ○ *was stuck for an answer* **8** *vi* stay in the mind **9** *vt* impose something unpleasant on ○ *I always get stuck with the boring jobs.* ■ *n* ability to adhere ◇ **stick it to** treat somebody unfairly or harshly ◇ **stick it out** persist with something to the end

☐ **stick around** *vi* remain or wait (*infml*)
☐ **stick by** *or* **with** *vt* stay loyal to
☐ **stick out** *vti* extend or protrude
☐ **stick up** *v* **1** *vti* point upward **2** *vt* rob at gunpoint (*infml*)

stick·ball /stík bàwl/ *n* a game with baseball rules played with a stick

stick·er /stíkər/ *n* **1** a small piece of adhesive paper or plastic, e.g., a label **2** something that sticks

stick·er price *n* a car's list price

stick·ing point *n* a point likely to cause deadlock

stick in·sect *n* an insect resembling a twig

stick-in. the-mud *n* somebody determinedly old-fashioned (*infml*)

stick·le·back /stík'l bàk/ (*pl* **-backs** or same) *n* a small spiny fish

stick·ler /stíklər/ *n* somebody insistent about details and correctness

stick pin *n* a long ornamental pin

stick shift *n* a manual transmission, its gear shift, or a vehicle with a manual transmission

stick-to-it-ive-ness /stik toò itivnəss/ *n* perseverance

stick·up /stík ùp/ *n* an armed robbery (*infml*)

⚡ **stick·y** /stíkee/ (**-i·er, -i·est**) *adj* 1 covered in something gluey 2 able to stick to a surface 3 humid and hot 4 difficult (*infml*) 5 describes a website that attracts and retains visitors (*infml*) —**stick·i·ly** *adv* —**stick·i·ness** *n*

Stieg·litz /steéglits/, **Alfred** (1864–1946) US photographer

stiff *adj* 1 rigid or hard to move 2 painful and not supple 3 severe 4 difficult 5 forceful *o a stiff breeze* 6 potent *o a stiff drink* 7 very formal in manner ■ *adv* 1 totally *o bored stiff* 2 in a stiff way ■ *n* a corpse (*slang*) ■ *vt* cheat out of money owed (*slang*) —**stiff·en** *vti* —**stiff·ly** *adv* —**stiff·ness** *n*

stiff-necked *adj* obstinately proud

sti·fle /stíf'l/ (**-fled, -fling**) *v* 1 *vti* suffocate 2 *vt* check or repress *o stifle opposition o stifle a yawn*

sti·fling /stífling/ *adj* 1 uncomfortably hot and stuffy 2 repressive —**sti·fling·ly** *adv*

stig·ma /stígmə/ *n* 1 a sign of social unacceptability 2 the part of a flower's female reproductive organ that receives the male pollen grains —**stig·ma·tic** /stig máttik/ *adj*

stig·ma·ta /stig máatə, stígmətə/ *n*, ¹ marks resembling crucifixion wounds on the hands and feet

stig·ma·tize /stígmə tìz/ (**-tized, -tiz·ing**) *v* 1 *vt* label as socially undesirable 2 *vti* mark with a stigma or stigmata —**stig·ma·ti·za·tion** /stígməti záysh'n/ *n*

stile /stíl/ *n* a step or steps for climbing over a fence

SPELLCHECK Do not confuse the spelling of **stile** and **style** ("a way of doing something"), which sound similar.

sti·let·to /sti léttō/ (*pl* **sti·let·tos** or **sti·let·toes**) *n* 1 a small dagger 2 a woman's shoe with a high pointed heel

still¹ *adj* 1 not moving 2 describes a drink that is not carbonated 3 calm or quiet ■ *adv* silently or without motion ■ *n* 1 silence or peace (*literary*) *o the still of the night* 2 a photograph of a scene from a motion picture ■ *v* 1 *vti* make or become

still 2 *vt* relieve *o stilled our fears* —**still·ness** *n*

still² *adv* 1 now as before *o It's still my favorite.* 2 even at this time *o He may still be around.* 3 even more (*often with a comparative*) *o better still*

still³ *n* an apparatus for distilling

still·born /stíl bàwrn/ *adj* 1 dead at birth 2 useless from the start —**still·birth** *n*

~~stilleto, stilletto~~ incorrect spelling of **stiletto**

still life (*pl* **still lifes**) *n* a picture of something inanimate

stilt *n* 1 each of a pair of poles with footrests on which somebody balances and walks 2 a supporting post

stilt·ed /stíltəd/ *adj* 1 describes speech or writing that does not flow naturally 2 unduly formal —**stilt·ed·ly** *adv*

Stil·ton /stíltən/ *n* a strong British cheese usually with blue veins

stim·u·lant /stímmyələnt/ *n* 1 a source of a stimulus 2 a drug producing an increase in functional activity —**stim·u·lant** *adj*

stim·u·late /stímmyə làyt/ (**-lat·ed, -lat·ing**) *vt* 1 cause to begin or develop *o stimulate discussion* 2 make interested or excited 3 cause physical activity in something such as a nerve or an organ —**stim·u·lat·ing** *adj* —**stim·u·la·tion** /stímmyə láysh'n/ *n* —**stim·u·la·tive** *adj*

stim·u·lus /stímmyələss/ (*pl* **-li** /-lī/) *n* 1 something that encourages something to begin, increase, or develop 2 something that causes a physical response in an organism

sting *v* (**stung**) 1 *vti* prick the skin of a person or animal and inject a poisonous or irritant substance (*usually refers to insects and plants*) 2 *vti* feel or cause to feel a sharp pain 3 *vt* upset ■ *n* 1 a wound caused by stinging 2 an organ used for stinging 3 a sharp pain 4 an undercover operation to catch criminals (*slang*) —**sting·er** *n*

sting·ray /stíng rày/ (*pl* **-rays** or same) *n* a ray with a flexible tail that has poisonous spines

stin·gy /stínjee/ (**-gi·er, -gi·est**) *adj* not giving or spending much —**stin·gi·ly** *adv* —**stin·gi·ness** *n*

stink *vi* (**stank** or **stunk, stunk**) 1 smell horrible 2 be very bad or worthless (*infml*) ■ *n* 1 a foul smell 2 a scandal (*infml*) —**stink·y** *adj* ◊ See note at **smell**

stink bomb *n* a practical joker's device emitting a foul smell

stink·er /stíngkər/ *n* something of very poor quality (*slang*)

stink·ing /stíngking/ *adj* very smelly ■ *adv* adds emphasis (*infml*) *o stinking rich* —**stink·ing·ly** *adv*

stint *v* 1 *vi* be miserly or too sparing *o Don't stint on the cream.* 2 *vt* deny somebody something ■ *n* 1 a fixed period of work or duty 2 a limitation —**stint·er** *n*

sti·pend /stí pènd, -pənd/ n a fixed allowance or salary, especially one paid to a cleric ◊ See note at **wage**

stip·ple /stípp'l/ (-pled, -pling) vt paint, mark, or apply with dabbing strokes —**stip·ple** n —**stip·pling** n

stip·u·late /stíppyə làyt/ (-lat·ed, -lat·ing) vt state or demand as a condition —**stip·u·la·tion** /stíppyə láysh'n/ n

stir[1] v (stirred, stir·ring) 1 vt mix ingredients with a spoon or similar implement 2 vti move slightly 3 vi get up after resting 4 vt goad somebody into action 5 vt arouse a feeling or memory (fml) 6 vti arouse strong emotions in somebody ■ n 1 an act of stirring 2 a commotion
□ **stir up** vt cause trouble

stir[2] n prison (slang)

stir-cra·zy adj made unsettled by confinement (infml or humorous)

stir-fry vt fry food rapidly over a high heat, stirring continuously ■ n a stir-fried dish

stir·ring /stúr ing/ adj 1 causing an emotional reaction 2 lively —**stir·ring·ly** adv

stir·rup /stúr əp/ n a foot support hanging from a horse's saddle

stitch n 1 a length of thread passed through material in sewing or skin in surgery 2 a loop of yarn made in knitting or crochet 3 a style of sewing or knitting 4 a sudden pain in the side of the abdomen ■ vt 1 sew something 2 close a wound with stitches —**stitch·er** n —**stitch·er·y** n ◊ **in stitches** laughing a great deal

stoat (pl **stoats** or **same**) n an ermine

stock n 1 a supply of goods for sale 2 a supply held in reserve 3 the shares issued by a company, or the money raised by selling them 4 an individual investor's share (often pl) 5 farm animals 6 ancestry or descent 7 the original variety from which others are descended 8 a related group of animals or plants 9 broth used as a base for soups, stews, and sauces 10 a supporting part or frame 11 the system of presenting a set of plays during a single season ■ vt 1 have or keep a product in stock 2 fill something with a supply of goods o a well-stocked pantry ■ adj unoriginal ◊ **take stock** think carefully about a situation

stock·ade /sto káyd/ n 1 a defensive barrier 2 the area inside a stockade 3 a military prison —**stock·ade** vt

stock·breed·er /stók brèedər/ n a breeder of farm animals —**stock·breed·ing** n

stock·bro·ker /stók bròkər/ n somebody who deals in the stock market for clients —**stock·bro·ker·age** n

stock car n 1 a car modified for racing 2 a railroad car for livestock

stock cer·tif·i·cate n a certificate of stock ownership

stock ex·change n a stock market, or the building in which it is located

Stock·haus·en /shtók hòwz'n, stók-/, **Karlheinz** (b. 1928) German composer

stock·hold·er /stók hòldər/ n an owner of company stock —**stock·hold·ing** n

Stock·holm /stók hòm/ capital of Sweden. Pop. 736,113 (1998).

stock·ing /stóking/ n a thin close-fitting knit covering for a woman's foot and leg (often pl) —**stock·inged** adj

ORIGIN The use of **stocking** to mean leg coverings may have arisen from the humorous comparison of the stocks in which people's legs were restrained as punishment with "leggings, hose."

stock-in-trade n 1 a basic resource 2 goods and equipment

stock·man /stókmən, -màn/ (pl **-men** /-mən, -mèn/) n 1 somebody who owns, breeds, or looks after farm animals 2 a man working in warehouse

stock mar·ket n 1 a financial market for trading in stocks and shares 2 trading in stocks and shares

stock op·tion n a benefit by which an employee of a company can buy its stock at a special price

stock·pile /stók pìl/ (-piled, -pil·ing) vti amass large quantities of something —**stock·pile** n ◊ See note at **collect**

stock·room /stók ròòm, -ròòm/ n a storeroom in a shop, office, or factory

stocks n a wooden frame with holes for the hands and feet or head and hands, formerly used for public punishment (+ sing or pl verb)

stock-still adv completely still

stock·tak·ing /stók tàyking/ n 1 evaluation of a situation 2 counting and listing store or business inventory

Stock·ton /stóktən/ city in central California. Pop. 240,143 (1998).

stock·y /stókee/ (-i·er, -i·est) adj short, broad, and strong-looking —**stock·i·ly** adv —**stock·i·ness** n

stock·yard /stók yaàrd/ n a temporary animal enclosure

sto·ic /stó ik/ n 1 somebody who endures adversity patiently and impassively 2 **Sto·ic** a member of an ancient Greek school of philosophy that accepted life's ups and downs with equanimity —**sto·ic** adj —**Sto·ic** adj —**sto·i·cal** adj —**sto·i·cal·ly** adv —**sto·i·cism** n —**Sto·i·cism** n ◊ See note at **impassive**

stoke (stoked, stok·ing) vti 1 add fuel to a fire and stir it up 2 tend a boiler or furnace —**stok·er** n

stole[1] past tense of **steal**

stole[2] n 1 a woman's scarf or shawl 2 a long narrow ecclesiastical scarf

sto·len past participle of **steal**

stol·id /stóllǝd/ adj solemn and impassive
—**sto·lid·i·ty** /stǝ líddǝtee/ n —**stol·id·ly** adv
◊ See note at **impassive**

sto·ma /stṓmǝ/ (pl **-ma·ta** /-mǝtǝ/) n a plant
pore —**sto·ma·tal** adj

stom·ach /stúmmǝk/ n 1 a sac-like digestive
organ in vertebrates 2 the abdomen (infml)
3 an appetite or desire ○ no stomach for a
fight ■ vt tolerate

stom·ach·ache /stúmmǝk àyk/ n a pain in the
abdomen

stomp v 1 vi walk with heavy steps 2 vt tread
heavily on (infml) ■ n 1 a jazz dance with
stamping foot movements 2 the music for
a stomp —**stomp·ing·ly** adv

stone /stōn/ n 1 the hard substance that rocks
are made of 2 a rock fragment 3 a shaped
piece of stone, e.g., a gravestone (often in
combination) 4 a small hard mass (usually in
combination) 5 a gem 6 a hard central part
containing the seed of a fruit 7 a small hard
mineral mass that forms in an organ ■ adv
adds emphasis ○ stone sober ■ vt (stoned,
ston·ing) 1 throw stones at somebody or
something 2 remove the stone from a fruit
◊ be carved or set or cast in (tablets of)
stone be firmly established and impossible
to alter ◊ leave no stone unturned make
every possible effort

Stone, Harlan Fiske (1872–1946) chief
justice of the US Supreme Court (1941–46)

Stone, Lucy (1818–93) US feminist and abolitionist

Stone Age n the earliest period of human
history

stone-cold adj completely cold

stoned /stōnd/ adj 1 under the influence of
drugs (slang) 2 intoxicated (infml)

stone-ground /stōn grównd/ adj ground with
millstones

Stone·henge /stōn hénj/ prehistoric monument on Salisbury Plain, S England, consisting of two concentric circles of large
standing stones

stone·ma·son /stōn máyss'n/ n somebody
who works with stone as a building
material —**stone·ma·son·ry** n

stone·wall /stōn wáwl/ v 1 vti refuse to cooperate with somebody (infml) 2 vi deliberately create a delay —**stone·wall·er** n

stone·ware /stōn wàir/ n dense opaque
pottery

stone·washed /stōn wòsht/ adj given a worn
faded look by washing with small pumice
pebbles

stone·work /stōn wùrk/ n 1 the stone parts of
a building 2 the process of building with
stone —**stone·work·er** n

ston·y /stṓnee/ (-i·er, -i·est), **ston·ey** adj
1 covered with stones 2 of or like stone
3 emotionless —**ston·i·ly** adv —**ston·i·**
ness n

stood past tense, past participle of **stand**

stooge /stooj/ n 1 a comedian's partner who
is the butt of the jokes 2 a person regarded
as being easily exploited by others (slang
insult) 3 a police informer (slang)

stool n 1 a simple backless seat 2 a piece of
excrement

stool pi·geon n 1 a police informer (slang)
2 a pigeon used as a hunter's decoy

ORIGIN Pigeons used as decoys were originally
tied to stools or wooden platforms. The term
stool pigeon is first recorded in 1830.

---

stoop[1] v 1 vti bend the head and upper body
forward and downward while walking or
standing 2 vi behave in a degrading way
3 vi condescend ■ n a stooping posture
—**stoop·ing** adj

stoop[2] n a small porch

stop v (stopped, stop·ping) 1 vti cease or cause
to cease doing something or moving 2 vti
end 3 vt prevent something 4 vi pause or
interrupt a trip before continuing 5 vt fill,
block, or plug something ■ n 1 an end of
movement or action 2 a break in a trip, or
a place visited on the way 3 a place where
a bus or train pauses for passengers 4 a
plug that blocks something 5 a device preventing movement (often in combination) ○ a
doorstop 6 a subset of organ pipes, or a knob
controlling them ◊ pull out all the stops
make every possible effort

stop·cock /stóp kòk/ n a valve for controlling
flow

~~stoped~~ incorrect spelling of **stopped**

stop·gap /stóp gàp/ n a temporary substitute
—**stop·gap** adj

stop·light /stóp līt/ n 1 a traffic light 2 a light
on the rear of a vehicle that is activated by
the brakes

stop·o·ver /stóp ṑvǝr/ n 1 a halt made during
a trip 2 a place where a stopover is made

stop·page /stóppij/ n stopping or being
stopped

stop·per /stóppǝr/ n a cork or plug —**stop·per**
vt

stop·watch /stóp wòch/ n a watch that can
be started and stopped instantly to time
somebody or something

⚡ **stor·age** /stáwrij/ n 1 storing or being stored
2 space for storing things 3 a device or
medium for storing computer data 4 the
price charged for storing something

⚡ **stor·age dump** n a printout of all stored computer data

store vt (stored, stor·ing) 1 put away for future
use 2 put into safekeeping, e.g., in a warehouse 3 fill or provide ■ n 1 a place that
sells goods at retail 2 a quantity saved for
future use 3 a place where goods are kept
in quantity ■ stores npl supplies ◊ in
store about to happen ◊ set great store
by consider to be important or valuable
—**stor·a·ble** adj

store-bought *adj* bought from a store

store·front /stáwr frùnt/ *n* **1** the side of a store that faces the street **2** a room or building with a storefront

store·house /stáwr hòwss/ *(pl* **-hous·es** /-hòwzəz/*) n* **1** a building where things are stored **2** an abundant source or collection

store·keep·er /stáwr kèepər/ *n* **1** a retail store owner **2** somebody in charge of supplies

store·room /stáwr ròom, stáwr ròòm/ *n* a room used for storage

sto·rey *n* UK = **story²**

sto·ried /stáwreed/ *adj* interesting, famous, or celebrated in stories *(literary)*

stork *(pl* **storks** *or same) n* a large black-and-white wading bird with long legs and a long neck

storm *n* **1** a spell of violent weather **2** a heavy bombardment of objects **3** a sudden outburst of strong feeling **4** a sudden strong attack on a defended position ■ *v* **1** *vt* attack a place violently **2** *vi* be violently and noisily angry **3** *vi* rush with violence or anger ○ *stormed out of the room* **4** *vi* blow strongly with or without precipitation —**storm·i·ly** *adv* —**storm·i·ness** *n* —**storm·y** *adj* ◊ **take by storm 1** capture or overwhelm suddenly and with great force **2** make a great and immediate impression on

storm cel·lar *n* a shelter underground used as a refuge during a windstorm

storm cloud *n* **1** a cloud indicating bad weather **2** a sign of impending trouble, especially war

storm troop·er *n* **1** a member of the Nazi militia **2** a member of a military attack force

sto·ry¹ /stáwree/ *(pl* **-ries** *) n* **1** a factual or fictional narrative **2** a short piece of prose fiction **3** *also* **sto·ry line** the plot of a novel, play, or motion picture **4** an account of facts ○ *changed her story several times* **5** a falsehood *(infml)*

ORIGIN *Story* "narrative" goes back to the same Latin and Greek words as *history. Story* came from Latin *historia* through French, whereas *history* was taken directly from Latin. *Story* "floor or level in a building" derives from a particular use of Latin *historia* found in texts written in England, perhaps because historical scenes were often painted on the façades of medieval buildings.

sto·ry² /stáwree/ *(pl* **-ries** *) n* a floor or level in a building —**sto·ried** *adj*

Sto·ry /stáwree/, **Joseph** (1779–1845) associate justice of the US Supreme Court (1811–45)

sto·ry·book /stáwree bòòk/ *n* a book of children's stories ■ *adj* typical of children's stories

sto·ry·tell·er /stáwree tèllər/ *n* a teller or writer of stories —**sto·ry·tell·ing** *n*

stoup /stoop/ *n* a basin for holy water

stout /stowt/ *adj* **1** thickset or heavy **2** courageous and determined **3** strong and substantial ○ *stout footwear* ■ *n* a dark strong beer —**stout·ly** *adv* —**stout·ness** *n*

stout·heart·ed /stòwt hártəd/ *adj* courageous or unyielding —**stout·heart·ed·ly** *adv* —**stout·heart·ed·ness** *n*

stove¹ /stōv/ *n* an appliance for cooking or heating

stove² /stōv/ past tense, past participle of **stave**

stove·pipe hat *n* a man's tall silk hat

stow /stō/ *vt* **1** put away neatly **2** fill with tightly packed things **3** store for later use □ **stow away** *vi* hide on a ship or aircraft to travel free

stow·age /stō ij/ *n* **1** stowing or being stowed **2** a place or space for stowing something

stow·a·way /stō ə wày/ *n* somebody who stows away on a ship or aircraft

Harriet Beecher Stowe

Stowe /stō/, **Harriet Beecher** (1811–96) US writer and abolitionist

strad·dle /strádd'l/ (-dled, -dling) *v* **1** *vt* sit or stand with legs astride something **2** *vt* be on both sides of something ○ *The city straddles the river.* **3** *vt* belong or apply to more than one category or situation **4** *vti* appear to favor both sides of an issue —**strad·dle** *n* —**strad·dler** *n*

Stra·di·va·ri /stràddə váiree, -vaàree/, **Antonio** (1644–1737) Italian violin maker

Strad·i·var·i·us /stràddə váiree əss/ *n* a violin made by Stradivari

strafe /strayf/ *vt* attack with gunfire from a low-flying aircraft —**strafe** *n*

strag·gle /strágg'l/ (-gled, -gling) *vi* **1** stray from a path, or fall behind a group **2** be or become spread out —**strag·gle** *n* —**strag·gler** *n* —**strag·gly** *adj*

straight /strayt/ *adj* **1** not curved or bent **2** level **3** correct or accurate **4** candid or direct ○ *a straight answer* **5** honest and fair ○ *straight dealings* **6** consecutive **7** not diluted **8** neat and tidy **9** not comic ○ *a straight actor* **10** heterosexual *(slang)* **11** conventional *(slang)* ■ *adv* in a straight manner or course ■ *n* **1** something straight, e.g., part of a racing track **2** a poker hand containing five cards in sequence **3** a heterosexual person *(slang)* **4** a conventional person *(slang)* —**straight·ish** *adj* —**straight·ly** *adv* —**straight·ness** *n*

SPELLCHECK Do not confuse the spelling of

straight and strait ("a sea channel"), which sound similar.

straight ar·row *n* a steadfast person *(infml)* —**straight-ar·row** *adj*

straight·a·way /stráyt ə wày/ *adv* immediately ■ *n* a straight track ■ *adj* without curves

straight·en /stráyt'n/ *vti* make or become straight

□ **straighten out** *vti* make or become clear or satisfactory

straight·for·ward /stràyt fáwrwərd/ *adj* 1 frank or honest 2 not difficult or complicated —**straight·for·ward·ly** *adv* —**straight·for·ward·ness** *n*

straight man *n* a comedian's partner who sets up or responds to a joke

straight-to-vid·e·o *adj* describes a movie released only in video format

straight·way /stráyt wày/ *adv* 1 immediately 2 by a direct route

strain[1] *v* 1 *vti* pull or stretch tight, or be pulled or stretched tight 2 *vi* make the utmost effort 3 *vt* use to the utmost 4 *vt* injure by twisting, stretching, or overexertion 5 *vti* be or make tense or stressed 6 *vti* pass through a strainer 7 *vt* remove using a strainer ■ *n* 1 straining or being strained 2 a pulling or stretching force 3 mental or physical stress 4 a cause of stress 5 a great exertion 6 an injury caused by twisting, stretching, or overexertion

strain[2] *n* 1 a line of ancestry 2 a subgroup of a species of organism distinguished by specific characteristics 3 an inherited quality or trait 4 a trace 5 the character, mood, or theme of something

strain·er /stráynər/ *n* a device for removing solids from liquids

strait /strayt/ *n (often pl)* 1 a channel joining two seas 2 a difficult situation ■ *adj (archaic)* 1 narrow or confined 2 strict or rigid ◊ See note at **straight**

strait·ened /stráyt'nd/ *adj* made difficult or restricted ○ *living in straitened circumstances*

strait·jack·et /stráyt jàkət/, **straight·jack·et** *n* 1 a jacket-shaped garment with sleeves that can be tied to restrain somebody 2 something that limits or restricts —**strait·jack·et** *vt*

strait-laced *adj* excessively strict in morals

strand[1] *n* a strip of land at the water's edge ■ *v* 1 *vti* go or leave ashore or aground 2 *vt* leave somebody in difficulty, especially in a strange or remote place —**strand·ed** *adj*

strand[2] *n* 1 a single fiber or filament, often twisted with others 2 a length of something such as wire or string 3 a string of beads

strange /straynj/ (**strang·er**, **strang·est**) *adj* 1 unexpected or unusual 2 unfamiliar 3 hard to explain 4 from a different place, or of a different kind —**strange·ly** *adv* —**strange·ness** *n*

strang·er /stráynjər/ *n* 1 an unfamiliar person 2 a newcomer 3 an outsider

stran·gle /stráng g'l/ *vti* 1 kill by squeezing the throat 2 suppress the utterance of ○ *strangled a sob* —**stran·gler** *n*

stran·gle·hold /stráng g'l hòld/ *n* 1 a state of complete power 2 a choking wrestling hold

stran·gu·late /stráng gyə làyt/ (**-lat·ed**, **-lat·ing**) *v* 1 *vt* strangle 2 *vti* constrict a part of the body, or become constricted, until the natural flow of blood or air is prevented —**stran·gu·la·tion** /stràng gyə láysh'n/ *n*

strap *n* 1 a flexible strip, e.g., of leather, used to bind or secure something 2 a loop of flexible material used as a handle, e.g., for a bag 3 a thin strip of material that forms part of a garment and passes over the shoulder ■ *vt* (**strapped, strap·ping**) 1 secure with a strap 2 beat with a strap —**strap·less** *adj*

strapped *adj* short of something *(infml)* ○ *strapped for cash*

strap·ping /strápping/ *adj* robust *(infml)* ■ *n* 1 straps 2 material for straps

Stras·bourg /stráz bùrg/ city in NE France. Pop. 264,115 (1999).

stra·ta plural of **stratum**

strat·a·gem /stráttəjəm/ *n* 1 a military tactic or maneuver for deceiving an enemy 2 a clever ruse

~~strategy~~ incorrect spelling of **strategy**

stra·te·gic /strə teejik/, **stra·te·gi·cal** /-ik'l/ *adj* 1 of or involving strategy 2 done for reasons of strategy —**stra·te·gi·cal·ly** *adv*

strat·e·gist /stráttəjist/ *n* somebody skilled in strategy

strat·e·gize /stráttə jìz/ (**-gized, -giz·ing**) *vi* plan a strategy

strat·e·gy /stráttəjee/ (*pl* **-gies**) *n* 1 the planning and conducting of a military campaign 2 a plan of action in any field, or the development and execution of such a plan ○ *business strategy*

Strat·ford-up·on-A·von /stràtfərd ə pon áyvən/ town in west central England, birthplace of William Shakespeare. Pop. 111,211 (1996).

strat·i·fy /stráttə fì/ (**-fied, -fies**) *vti* 1 form into layers 2 separate into groups based on social status —**strat·i·fi·ca·tion** /stràttəfi káysh'n/ *n*

strat·o·sphere /stráttə sfèer/ *n* 1 the region of the Earth's atmosphere between the troposphere and mesosphere 2 a very high level or position —**strat·o·spher·ic** /stràttə sféerik, -sférrik/ *adj*

stra·tum /stráytəm, strát-/ (*pl* **-ta** /-tə/ or **-tums**) *n* 1 a layer, especially of sedimentary rock *(fml)* 2 a level of society —**stra·tal** *adj*

USAGE The plural of **stratum** is **strata**, reflecting the word's Latin history. Do not use the false plural *stratas* or the incorrect false Latin plural *stratae*: *in all strata* [not *stratas* or *stratae] of society.* A variant plural *stratums* exists but is relatively infrequent.

stra·tus /stráytəss, strát-/ (*pl* **-ti** /-tee/) *n* a flat gray cloud formation

Strauss /strowss, shtrowss/ family of Austrian composers including **Johann, the Elder** (1804–49) and his son **Johann, the Younger** (1825–99)

Strauss, Richard (1864–1935) German conductor and composer

Igor Stravinsky

Stra·vin·sky /strə vín skee/, **Igor** (1882–1971) Russian-born US composer

straw *n* **1** the stalks of threshed cereal crops **2** a thin tube for sucking up a drink **3** a dried grass stalk **4** something worthless ■ *adj* worthless ◊ **clutch** *or* **grasp at straws** be willing to try anything that may help in a desperate situation ◊ **draw the short straw** be chosen to do a difficult or unpleasant task

straw·ber·ry /stráw bèrree/ (*pl* **-ries**) *n* **1** a small soft red fruit **2** a plant that produces strawberries

ORIGIN The connection between *straw* and the *strawberry* is obscure. One suggestion is that the long trailing shoots of the plants reminded people of straw laid on the floor. Another is that *straw* was used in an obsolete sense "small piece of chaff or straw," referring to the appearance of the external seeds on the fruit.

straw·ber·ry blond *adj* describes hair that is blond with a reddish tinge —**straw·ber·ry blond** *n*

straw·ber·ry mark *n* a red birthmark

straw man *n* a front for somebody else's questionable or illegal activities

straw poll, straw vote *n* an unofficial vote

stray *vi* **1** wander away from a place or group **2** wander about aimlessly **3** digress from a subject ■ *adj* **1** lost or homeless ◊ *a stray dog* **2** scattered or separated ■ *n* somebody or something lost or homeless, especially a domestic animal

streak /streek/ *n* **1** a thin stripe of contrasting color **2** a short period or unbroken run ◊ *a winning streak* **3** a contrasting characteristic **4** a layer or strip of something **5** a lightning flash ■ *v* **1** *vti* mark with or form streaks **2** *vi* dash or rush **3** *vi* run naked through a public place (*infml*) —**streaked** *adj* —**streak·er** *n* —**streak·y** *adj*

stream /streem/ *n* **1** a small river **2** a constant flow **3** an air or water current **4** a continuous series ■ *v* **1** *vi* flow in large quantities **2** *vi* move in the same direction **3** *vti* produce a flow of liquid ◊ *His nose streamed blood.* **4** *vi* float freely ◊ *with her hair streaming behind* **5** *vi* pour out in a trail or beam **6** *vt* broadcast on the Internet —**stream·ing** *n*

stream·er /streemər/ *n* **1** a narrow flag **2** a decorative paper strip

stream·line /streem lìn/ (**-lined, -lin·ing**) *vt* **1** design or build with an aerodynamic shape **2** make more efficient —**stream·lined** *adj* —**stream·lin·ing** *n*

stream of con·scious·ness *n* **1** a literary style that presents a flow of thoughts **2** a flow of thoughts

~~strech~~ incorrect spelling of **stretch**

street *n* **1** a public road in a town or city **2** the buildings or inhabitants of a street ■ *adj* of modern urban society ◊ **the man** *or* **person** *or* **woman in the street** the average person

street·car /streèt kàar/ *n* a passenger vehicle running on rails

street cred·i·bil·i·ty *n* popularity and acceptance, especially among the young

street·light /streèt lìt/, **street·lamp** /-làmp/ *n* a light on a post that illuminates a street

street smarts *npl* the ability to survive in difficult and dangerous situations in a modern city

street val·ue *n* the price obtainable for something illegal, especially drugs

street·walk·er /streèt wàwkər/ *n* a prostitute (*infml*) —**street·walk·ing** *n*

street·wise /streèt wìz/, **street-smart** *adj* able to survive in difficult and dangerous situations in a modern city (*infml*)

strength *n* **1** physical power **2** emotional toughness ◊ *strength of mind* **3** the ability to withstand force or pressure **4** defensive ability **5** degree of intensity, e.g., of light or sound **6** persuasive power ◊ *the strength of her argument* **7** potency, e.g., of alcohol or drugs **8** the number of people needed for something ◊ **in strength** in large numbers ◊ **on the strength of** on the basis of

strength·en /stréngth'n/ *vti* make or become stronger

~~strenous~~ incorrect spelling of **strenuous**

~~strenth~~ incorrect spelling of **strength**

stren·u·ous /strénnyoo əss/ *adj* **1** requiring great effort or strength **2** energetic or determined —**stren·u·ous·ly** *adv* —**stren·u·ous·ness** *n* ◊ See note at **hard**

strep·to·coc·cus /strèptə kókəss/ (*pl* **-ci** /-sì, -kì/) *n* a round bacterium that can cause disease —**strep·to·coc·cal** *adj*

strep·to·my·cin /strèptə míssən/ *n* an antibiotic. Use: treatment of bacterial infections.

stress *n* 1 a feeling of anxiety and tiredness, often caused by personal problems or overwork 2 a cause of stress 3 special importance or emphasis 4 a more forceful pronunciation of a syllable or playing of a note ■ *vt* 1 emphasize 2 pronounce or play forcefully 3 subject to stress —**stressed** *adj* —**stress·ful** *adj* —**stres·sor** *n* ◊ See note at **worry**

stress frac·ture *n* a small bone fracture caused by repeated physical strain

stress mark *n* a mark showing a syllable to be stressed

stretch *v* 1 *vti* make or become longer or wider 2 *vi* be capable of expanding and regaining its original shape 3 *vti* extend the body or part of it to full length 4 *vti* make or become taut 5 *vt* suspend something between two points 6 *vti* extend in space or time 7 *vt* make a small amount go further 8 *vt* exceed a limit or break a rule ■ *n* 1 an act of stretching 2 a length or expanse 3 a period of time 4 a prison term *(slang)* 5 elasticity ■ *adj* 1 elastic 2 extended to provide extra space ○ *a stretch limousine* —**stretch·a·ble** *adj* —**stretch·y** *adj*

stretch·er /strécher/ *n* a device for carrying somebody in a lying position —**stretch·er** *vt*

stretch mark *n* a mark on skin that has been stretched, especially during pregnancy *(often pl)*

stretch-out *n* 1 an extension of a period of time in which to do something 2 a requirement of additional work without additional pay

strew /stroo/ (**strewn** *or* **strewed**) *vt* 1 scatter untidily or over a large area 2 cover with strewn things

stri·at·ed /strí áytəd/ *adj* marked with parallel grooves, ridges, or narrow bands —**stri·a·tion** /strī áysh'n/ *n*

strick·en /stríkən/ *adj* 1 deeply or badly affected *(often in combination)* ○ *grief-stricken* 2 affected by illness

~~strickly, stricly~~ incorrect spelling of **strictly**

strict *adj* 1 severe in maintaining discipline 2 enforced rigorously 3 precise 4 closely observing rules or practices —**strict·ly** *adv* —**strict·ness** *n*

stric·ture /stríkchər/ *n (fml)* 1 a severe criticism 2 a limit or restriction

stride *vi* (**strode, strid·den** /strídd'n/, **strid·ing**) walk with long regular steps ■ *n* 1 a long step or the distance covered by it 2 an advance toward improving or developing something ◊ **take something in stride** accept something without being unduly upset

stri·dent /stríd'nt/ *adj* 1 loud or harsh 2 strongly expressed —**stri·den·cy** *n* —**stri·dent·ly** *adv*

strife *n* bitter conflict or rivalry

strike *v* (**struck, struck** *or* **strick·en** /strík'n/, **strik·ing**) 1 *vti* hit a person or thing 2 *vti* deliver a blow 3 *vti* collide with a person or thing 4 *vti* attack an opponent 5 *vi* stop working as a protest 6 *vti* produce fire by friction, or light a match 7 *vti* discover something suddenly, e.g., oil 8 *vt* press a key on a keyboard or musical instrument 9 *vti* indicate the time by making a sound *(refers to clocks)* 10 *vt* make something, e.g., a coin, by stamping 11 *vt* make an impression on somebody 12 *vti* affect somebody suddenly ○ *was stricken with a heart attack* 13 *vt* cross something out 14 *vt* lower a flag or sail ■ *n* 1 a hit or blow 2 a sound of striking 3 a work stoppage as a protest 4 a refusal to do something as a protest ○ *a hunger strike* 5 a military attack 6 a sudden discovery of something 7 in bowling, the knocking down of all the pins with a single ball 8 in baseball, a pitch swung at but missed ◊ **strike it rich** become extremely wealthy or successful

> **ORIGIN Strike** goes back to the same ancient root as **stroke**, and like **stroke** originally implied a light touch. More forcible senses developed from the 13C. The use "stop working" is first recorded in the mid-18C, and probably belongs to the strand of meaning "lower" (as in the **striking** of a sail or flag), referring to the laying down of tools.

☐ **strike out** *vti* in baseball, put a batter out or be put out by three strikes

☐ **strike up** *v* 1 *vti* begin to play a piece of music, or cause to begin playing 2 *vt* begin ○ *struck up a friendship*

strike·break·er /strík bràykər/ *n* 1 somebody who works while colleagues strike 2 somebody hired to replace a striker

strike-out *n* in baseball, an out made by a batter charged with three strikes

strik·er /stríkər/ *n* 1 somebody who is on strike 2 an attacking player in a soccer team

strik·ing /stríking/ *adj* 1 conspicuous 2 attractive or impressive —**strik·ing·ly** *adv*

Strind·berg /strínd bùrg, strín-/, **August** (1849–1912) Swedish dramatist —**Strind·berg·i·an** /strind búrgee ən/ *adj*

string *n* 1 a thin cord used for fastening, hanging, or tying 2 something resembling string 3 a succession of items 4 a line of things 5 a sequence of similar elements, e.g., letter or numbers 6 a set of objects threaded together 7 a cord stretched across a musical instrument, a sports racket, or an archer's bow ■ **strings** *npl* the stringed instruments of an orchestra, or the musicians playing them ■ *vt* (**strung**) 1 thread onto a string 2 hang between two points 3 arrange or extend in a line 4 provide with a string or strings —**string** *adj* —**stringed** *adj* —**string·i·ness** *n* —**string·y** *adj* ◊ **pull strings** use influence to try to gain an advantage ◊ **with no strings (attached)** unconditionally

string bean *n* **1** a slim green bean pod cooked as a vegetable **2** the plant that produces string beans

stringed in·stru·ment, string in·stru·ment *n* a musical instrument with strings that are bowed or plucked

strin·gent /strínjənt/ *adj* rigorous or severe —**strin·gen·cy** *n* —**strin·gent·ly** *adv*

string·er /stríngər/ *n* **1** a freelance or part-time journalist **2** a horizontal structural timber **3** a player on a team ranked according to ability *(usually in combination)*

string quar·tet *n* **1** a group of four musicians playing stringed instruments **2** a piece of music for a string quartet

strip[1] *v* **(stripped, strip·ping)** **1** *vi* undress **2** *vi* do a striptease **3** *vt* remove something covering a surface ○ *strip the walls of paper* ○ *strip the paper from the walls* **4** *vt* remove the entire contents of a place **5** *vt* deprive somebody of his or her status **6** *vt* take something apart in order to clean or repair it ■ *n* a striptease —**strip·per** *n*

strip[2] *n* **1** a long narrow flat piece **2** an airstrip **3** a series of cartoons that tell a story or joke

stripe[1] *n* **1** a long narrow band of a different color or texture **2** a pattern of stripes **3** a symbol of rank sewn onto a uniform —**stripe** *vt* —**striped** *adj* —**strip·y** *adj*

stripe[2] *n* a blow from a whip or cane

strip·light *n* a row of lamps used to light a stage

strip·ling /stríppling/ *n* an adolescent boy

strip mall *n* a long building divided into individual stores

strip mine *n* a surface mine —**strip min·ing** *n*

strip pok·er *n* a card game in which losing players gradually remove their clothes

strip-search *vti* search the clothing and body of a suspect —**strip search** *n*

strip·tease /stríp téez, strìp téez/ *n* an erotic entertainment in which somebody slowly undresses

strive /strīv/ **(strove** /strōv/ *or* **strived, striv·en** /strívv'n/ *or* **strived, striv·ing)** *vi* **1** try hard **2** fight or compete

strobe light, strobe *n* a high-intensity flashing light

strob·o·scope /strōbə skōp/ *n* a flashing device that makes moving objects appear stationary —**stro·bo·scop·ic** /strōbə skóppik/ *adj*

strode past tense of **stride**

Stro·heim ⸓ **von Stroheim, Erich**

stroke *n* **1** a blockage or rupture of a blood vessel in the brain **2** a sudden occurrence ○ *a stroke of luck* **3** an act or way of hitting a ball **4** a swimming style or movement **5** a single mark or movement of a pen or brush **6** a sound made by a striking clock **7** a hit or blow **8** a caressing movement **9** a single movement in a series, e.g., of an oar, wing,

or piston ■ *vt* **(stroked, strok·ing)** **1** move the hand gently over **2** push gently

stroll /strōl/ *v* **1** *vti* walk unhurriedly **2** *vi* do something effortlessly ■ *n* a leisurely walk

stroll·er /strōlər/ *n* **1** *US, Can, Aus* a light chair with wheels in which a young child can be pushed **2** somebody who is strolling

strong *adj* **1** physically powerful **2** forceful **3** not easily damaged or broken **4** healthy and well **5** thriving ○ *a strong economy* **6** convincing ○ *a strong argument* **7** skillful or knowledgeable **8** exerting influence or authority **9** felt or expressed powerfully or forcefully **10** bold, clearly defined, and prominent ○ *strong features* **11** extreme ○ *strong measures* **12** having an intense effect on the senses **13** containing a lot of the main ingredient ○ *strong black coffee* **14** containing a lot of alcohol **15** well defended —**strong·ly** *adv* ◇ **come on strong** behave or express something aggressively *(slang)* ◇ **going strong** thriving and doing well

strong-arm *adj* using force or coercion *(infml)*

strong·box /stróng bòks/ *n* a secure container for valuables

strong·hold /stróng hòld/ *n* **1** a fortified place **2** a place where a particular group or activity is concentrated

strong·man /stróng màn/ *(pl -men /-mèn/)* *n* **1** a powerful leader **2** a performer of feats of strength

strong·room /stróng ròom, -ròom/ *n* a reinforced room for safe storage

stron·ti·um /strónshee əm, -tee-/ *n* *(symbol* Sr*)* a silvery white metallic chemical element. Use: fireworks, flares, alloys.

ORIGIN **Strontium** is ultimately named for Strontian in Scotland, where one of its compounds was found in lead mines. The current form of the name was introduced in 1808 by the British chemist Sir Humphry Davy.

strop *n* a leather strap for sharpening a razor —**strop** *vt*

strove past tense of **strive**

struck past tense, past participle of **strike**

struc·tur·al·ism /strúkchərə lìzzəm/ *n* the study of literature, language, and society as a network of interrelated elements —**struc·tur·al·ist** *n, adj*

struc·ture /strúkchər/ *n* **1** something built or assembled from parts **2** an orderly system of interrelated parts **3** the way that parts link or work together ■ *vt* **(-tured, -tur·ing)** organize or arrange into a system —**struc·tur·al** *adj* —**struc·tur·al·ly** *adv*

⸓ **struc·tured que·ry lan·guage** *n* full form of SQL

stru·del /stroōd'l/ *n* a filled rolled pastry

strug·gle /strúgg'l/ *vi* **(-gled, -gling)** **1** make a great physical or mental effort to do something difficult **2** fight by grappling **3** wriggle forcefully to escape **4** move with difficulty ■ n 1 a great effort 2 a fight 3 a hard task —**strug·gler** n

strum (strummed, strum·ming) vti play a musical instrument by brushing the strings —**strum** n

strum·pet /strúmpət/ n an offensive term for a woman prostitute or a woman regarded as sexually promiscuous (archaic)

strung past tense, past participle of **string** ■ adj overwrought

strung out adj 1 weakened by long-term drug use (slang) 2 overwrought (slang)

strut v (strut·ted, strut·ting) 1 vi walk in an arrogant or pompous way 2 vt show off ■ n 1 a long rigid supporting structural member 2 a strutting walk

strych·nine /strík nìn, -nèen/ n a poisonous plant product. Use: rodent control, nervous system stimulant.

Stu·art /stóo ərt, styóo-/, **Charles Edward** (1720–88) grandson of James II of England, Scotland, and Ireland and claimant to the British throne

Stu·art, Gilbert (1755–1828) US artist

Stu·art, James Ewell Brown (1833–64) US Confederate general

stub n 1 a remaining part 2 a detachable part, e.g., of a ticket or check, retained as a record ■ vt (stubbed, stub·bing) bang the toe against something

☐ **stub out** vt extinguish a cigarette or cigar

stub·ble /stúbb'l/ n 1 a short growth of beard 2 short stalks left in the ground after harvesting —**stub·bly** adj

stub·born /stúbbərn/ adj 1 unreasonably and obstructively determined 2 dogged 3 hard to remove or deal with —**stub·born·ly** adv —**stub·born·ness** n

~~stubborness~~ incorrect spelling of **stubbornness**

stub·by /stúbbee/ adj short and thick or thickset

stuc·co /stúkō/ n 1 wall plaster 2 decorative plaster work —**stuc·co** vt

stuck past tense, past participle of **stick**[2] ■ adj 1 jammed, caught, or unable to move o The drawer's stuck o We were stuck in traffic. 2 unable to find a solution

stuck-up adj snobbish and conceited (infml)

stud[1] n 1 a stallion or other male animal used for breeding 2 a sexually attractive or skillful man (infml)

stud[2] n 1 a fastener for a shirt 2 a simple earring 3 a vertical support for a wall 4 a decorative metal knob ■ vt (stud·ded, stud·ding) 1 be present or visible throughout o a star studded sky 2 fit or decorate with studs

stud·book /stúd bòok/ n a record book of horse or dog pedigrees

stu·dent /stóod'nt/ n 1 somebody who studies at a school, college, or university 2 somebody knowledgeable about or interested in a particular thing o a student of human foibles ■ adj in training for a profession o a student teacher

stu·dent bod·y n a school's students

stu·dent coun·cil n an elected high school student group

stu·dent gov·ern·ment n a representative assembly of college students

stud·ied /stúddeed/ adj not spontaneous

~~studing~~ incorrect spelling of **studying**

stu·di·o /stóodee ò/ n 1 a room or building for the production of films, broadcasts, or musical recordings 2 a small apartment 3 a movie production company 4 an artist's workplace 5 a dance school

stu·di·ous /stóodee əss/ adj 1 inclined to study 2 careful and painstaking —**stu·di·ous·ly** adv —**stu·di·ous·ness** n

stud·y /stúddee/ v (-ied, -ies) 1 vti learn about a subject 2 vti take an educational course 3 vt investigate by research 4 vt look at or read carefully ■ n (pl -ies) 1 the process of studying 2 an investigation 3 a report on research 4 a room for studying, reading, or writing 5 a preparatory work of art

stud·y hall n 1 study time in school 2 a schoolroom for independent study

stuff vt 1 fill something with stuffing 2 push things into a container 3 put something somewhere hurriedly 4 eat or feed somebody a lot of food ■ n 1 miscellaneous or unspecified things or material 2 personal possessions 3 personal qualities o the stuff that heroes are made of 4 special skill or knowledge o She knows her stuff. 5 foolish words or action 6 woolen fabric —**stuffed** adj —**stuff·er** n ◊ **do your stuff** do what is required or expected

stuffed shirt n a pompous person (infml)

stuff·ing /stúffing/ n 1 a well-flavored filling for meat or vegetables 2 a soft filling for cushions, pillows, or toys

stuff·y /stúffee/ (-i·er, -i·est) adj 1 airless 2 strait-laced —**stuff·i·ness** n

stul·ti·fy /stúltə fì/ (-fied, -fies) vt 1 diminish interest by being tedious or boring 2 make somebody seem stupid —**stul·ti·fi·ca·tion** /stùltəfə káysh'n/ n

stum·ble /stúmb'l/ (-bled, -bling) vi 1 trip when walking or running 2 walk unsteadily 3 speak or act hesitatingly 4 make a minor mistake 5 find something by chance o stumbled across a vital piece of evidence —**stum·ble** n —**stum·bling·ly** adv◊ See note at **hesitate**

stum·bling block n an obstacle

stump n 1 the remaining base of a felled tree 2 a small part remaining after the rest has been removed ■ v 1 vt baffle 2 vt campaign (infml) 3 vi walk heavily —**stump·er** n ◊ **on the stump** engaged in making campaign speeches (infml)

stump·y /stúmpee/ (**-i·er, -i·est**) *adj* short and thick

stun (**stunned, stun·ning**) *vt* **1** make unconscious **2** shock

stung past tense, past participle of **sting**

stunk past tense, past participle of **stink**

stun·ning /stúnning/ *adj* outstandingly impressive or attractive —**stun·ning·ly** *adv*

stunt[1] *n* **1** a dangerous feat done for entertainment **2** something underhanded done for attention o *a publicity stunt*

stunt[2] *vt* restrict the growth of something

stunt·man /stúnt màn/ (*pl* **-men** /-mèn/) *n* somebody who replaces an actor in a dangerous scene

stunt·wom·an /stúnt wŏomman/ (*pl* **-en** /-wĭmmin/) *n* a woman who replaces an actor in a dangerous scene

stu·pe·fy /stóopə fĭ/ (**-fied, -fies**) *vt* **1** amaze **2** make unable to think clearly —**stu·pe·fac·tion** /stòopə fáksh'n/ *n* —**stu·pe·fy·ing·ly** *adv*

stu·pen·dous /stoo péndəss/ *adj* impressively great —**stu·pen·dous·ly** *adv*

stu·pid /stóopəd/ *adj* **1** regarded as unintelligent **2** silly —**stu·pid·i·ty** /stoo píddətee/ *n* —**stu·pid·ly** *adv*

~~stupify~~ incorrect spelling of **stupefy**

stu·por /stóopər/ *n* **1** a dazed state **2** a state of near-unconsciousness —**stu·por·ous** *adj*

stur·dy /stúrdee/ (**-di·er, -di·est**) *adj* **1** solidly made **2** with a strong build —**stur·di·ly** *adv* —**stur·di·ness** *n*

> **ORIGIN** Sturdy goes back to the Latin intensive prefix *ex-* and *turdus* "thrush" (the songbird). These formed a French word meaning "dazed, stupefied" and also "reckless, violent," which was adopted into English in the latter sense. The meaning "strongly built" developed in the 14C. How thrushes came to represent drunkenness is not altogether clear, but perhaps they ate fermenting wine grapes and were seen staggering as a consequence.

stur·geon /stúrj'n/ (*pl* **-geons** or same) *n* **1** a large fish that is a source of caviar **2** sturgeon as food

stut·ter /stúttər/ *vti* say or speak with a stammer —**stut·ter** *n* —**stut·ter·er** *n* —**stut·ter·ing** *adj*

Stutt·gart /stóot gàart/ capital of Baden-Württemberg State, SW Germany. Pop. 588,482 (1997).

Stuy·ve·sant /stívisənt/, **Peter** (1610?–72) Dutch colonial administrator in North America

sty[1] (*pl* **sties**) *n* an enclosure for hogs —**sty** *vt*

sty[2] (*pl* **sties**), **stye** *n* a swelling on an eyelid

style /stíl/ *n* **1** a distinctive form **2** a way of doing something (*often in combination*) o *a hands-on management style* **3** the way something is written or performed o *Style is more important than content.* **4** flair or good taste **5** fashionable status **6** a way in which clothes or hair are cut or shaped **7** luxuriousness o *dining in style* ■ *vt* (**styled, styl·ing**) **1** give a style to **2** cause to conform to a style —**styl·er** *n* —**sty·lis·tic** *adj* ◊ **cramp somebody's style** restrict what somebody is able to do (*infml*) ◊ See note at **stile**

styl·ish /stílish/ *adj* sophisticated, elegant, and fashionable —**styl·ish·ly** *adv* —**styl·ish·ness** *n*

styl·ist /stílist/ *n* **1** a hairdresser **2** somebody whose creative work shows an accomplished style

styl·ize /stíl ìz/ (**-ized, -iz·ing**) *vt* give a distinctive or artificial style to —**styl·i·za·tion** /stìli záysh'n/ *n*

⚡ **sty·lus** /stíləss/ (*pl* **-li** /-lĭ/) *n* **1** a phonograph needle **2** an engraving or writing tool **3** a pointed device for use on a computer screen that responds to pressure

sty·mie /stímee/, **sty·my** (**-mied, -mies**) *vt* hinder the progress of —**sty·mie** *n*

styp·tic /stíptik/ *adj* able to stop bleeding

Sty·ron /stírən/, **William** (*b.* 1925) US writer

suave /swaav/ (**suav·er, suav·est**) *adj* charming, especially in an insincere way —**suave·ly** *adv* —**suave·ness** *n* —**suav·i·ty** *n*

sub *n* **1** a substitute (*infml*) **2** a submarine **3** a sandwich made with a long roll ■ *vi* (**subbed, sub·bing**) act as a substitute (*infml*)

sub- *prefix* **1** under, below, beneath o *subconscious* **2** subordinate, secondary o *sublet* **3** less than completely o *subhuman* **4** subdivision o *subcontinent*

sub·al·tern /su báwltərn, súbb'l tùrn/ *n* **1** a British army officer of a rank below captain **2** a subordinate person ■ *adj* subordinate

sub·arc·tic /sùb aárktik/ *adj* of or like the area south of the Arctic Circle

sub·a·tom·ic /sùbbə tómmik/ *adj* **1** smaller than or part of an atom o *a subatomic particle* **2** on a scale smaller than the atom, or involving phenomena at this level

sub·com·mit·tee /súbkə mìttee/ *n* a special-purpose group within a committee

sub·com·pact /sub kóm pàkt/ *n* a very small car

sub·con·scious /sub kónshəss/ *adj* existing unknown in the mind ■ *n* the part of the mind not consciously perceived —**sub·con·scious·ly** *adv* —**sub·con·scious·ness** *n*

sub·con·ti·nent /sub kónt'nənt/ *n* a separate part of a continent, e.g., the area of Asia containing India, Pakistan, and Bangladesh —**sub·con·ti·nen·tal** /sùb kont'n ént'l/ *adj, n*

sub·con·tract /sub kón tràkt, súb kòn trakt/ *n* a secondary contract in which a person or company hired to do something passes on some or all of the work to another —**sub·con·tract** *vti* —**sub·con·trac·tor** *n*

sub·cul·ture /súb kùlchər/ *n* a separate social group within a larger culture

sub·cu·ta·ne·ous /sùbkyə táynee əss/ *adj* under the skin —**sub·cu·ta·ne·ous·ly** *adv*

⚡ **sub·di·rec·to·ry** /súbdi réktəree, sùb dī-/ (*pl* -ries) *n* a directory within another directory on a storage device such as a hard drive

sub·di·vide /sùbdi víd/ (-vid·ed, -vid·ing) *vti* divide further —**sub·di·vid·er** *n* —**sub·di·vi·sion** /sùb di vízh'n, súbdi vízh'n/ *n*

⚡ **sub·do·main name** /sùbdə máyn-, -dô-/, **sub·do·main** *n* a subdivision or second level of an Internet domain name

sub·due /səb doó/ (-dued, -du·ing) *vt* 1 bring under control, often using force 2 make less intense —**sub·dued** *adj*

sub·group /súb gròop/ *n* a distinct group within a larger group

sub·hu·man /sub hyóomən, -yóomən/ *adj* of or displaying behavior inferior to that expected of human beings

sub·ject *n* /súb jèkt/ 1 a matter being discussed, examined, or otherwise dealt with 2 a course of study 3 somebody who is the focus of an activity ○ *not an appropriate subject for hypnosis* 4 a person ruled by a monarch or other authority 5 somebody or something represented in a picture or written about in a book ○ *the subject of her latest biography* 6 in grammar, the performer of a verb's action, e.g., "she" in "Where does she live?" ■ *adj* /súb jèkt/ 1 prone or susceptible ○ *areas subject to flooding* 2 ruled or controlled ○ *not subject to the laws of this country* ■ *adv* /súb jèkt/ depending ○ *subject to your approval* ■ *vt* /səb jèkt/ 1 cause to undergo something, especially an unpleasant experience ○ *were subjected to rigorous training* 2 bring under the power of another person or group —**sub·jec·tion** /səb jéksh'n/ *n*

SYNONYMS subject, topic, subject matter, matter, theme, burden CORE MEANING: what is under discussion

sub·jec·tive /səb jéktiv/ *adj* 1 based on personal feelings or opinions 2 existing only in the mind 3 of the subject of a verb —**sub·jec·tive·ly** *adv* —**sub·jec·tiv·i·ty** /sùb jek tívvətee/ *n*

⚡ **sub·ject line** *n* an e-mail line indicating the subject of the message

sub·ject mat·ter *n* the material dealt with, e.g., in a book, documentary, or discussion ◊ See note at **subject**

sub ju·di·ce /sub joodəssee, -yoodə kày/ *adj* being examined in court and therefore not for public comment

sub·ju·gate /súbjə gàyt/ (-gat·ed, -gat·ing) *vt* conquer or force into submission —**sub·ju·ga·tion** /sùbjə gáysh'n/ *n* —**sub·ju·ga·tor** *n*

sub·junc·tive /səb júngktiv/ *n* a grammatical mood expressing doubts, wishes, and possibilities, or a verb in this mood —**sub·junc·tive** *adj*

sub·lease *n* /súb lèess/ an arrangement to rent a property from a tenant —**sub·lease** *vt*

sub·let /sùb lét/ *vti* (-let, -let·ting) rent property under a sublease ■ *n* a property rented under a sublease

sub·li·mate /súbblə màyt/ *v* (-mat·ed, -mat·ing) 1 *vt* redirect impulses or energies towards a more acceptable activity 2 *vti* change directly from a solid to a gas or vice versa ■ *n* a sublimated solid or gas —**sub·li·ma·tion** /sùbblə máysh'n/ *n*

sub·lime /sə blím/ *adj* (-lim·er, -lim·est) 1 awe-inspiringly beautiful 2 of the highest moral or spiritual value ■ *vti* (-limed, -lim·ing) change directly from a solid to a gas or vice versa —**sub·lime·ly** *adv* —**sub·lim·i·ty** /sə blímmətee/ *n*

sub·lim·i·nal /sub límmin'l/ *adj* below the threshold of conscious awareness —**sub·lim·i·nal·ly** *adv*

sub·ma·chine gun /sùbmə sheén-/ *n* a hand-held machine gun

sub·ma·rine /súbmə reèn/ *n* 1 an underwater boat that can travel long distances 2 a sandwich made with a long roll ■ *adj* underwater —**sub·ma·rin·er** /sùb mə reénər, -márrinər/ *n*

sub·merge /səb múrj/ (-merged, -mer·ging) *v* 1 *vti* put or go under the surface of water or other liquid 2 *vt* suppress —**sub·merged** *adj* —**sub·mer·gence** *n*

sub·mers·i·ble /səb múrssəb'l/ *adj* for underwater use ■ *n* an underwater boat

sub·mis·sion /səb mísh'n/ *n* 1 yielding, or readiness to yield 2 something submitted for consideration

sub·mis·sive /səb míssiv/ *adj* ready to submit to others —**sub·mis·sive·ly** *adv*

sub·mit /səb mít/ (-mit·ted, -mit·ting) *v* 1 *vt* propose or hand in 2 *vi* yield 3 *vi* agree to undergo something 4 *vi* defer to somebody —**sub·mit·tal** *n* ◊ See note at **yield**

sub·nor·mal /sub náwrm'l/ *adj* lower than usual or average —**sub·nor·mal·i·ty** /sùb nawr mállətee/ *n*

⚡ **sub·note·book** /sub nót bòok/ *n* a portable computer smaller than a notebook

sub·or·bi·tal /sub áwrbət'l/ *adj* 1 below the eye socket 2 not making a full orbit of a planet

sub·or·di·nate *adj* /sə báwrd'nət/ 1 lower in rank 2 of secondary importance ■ *n* /sə báwrd'nət/ somebody of lower rank than another ■ *vt* /sə báwrd'n àyt/ (-at·ed, -at·ing) 1 treat as less important than something else 2 place in a lower rank —**sub·or·di·nate·ly** *adv* —**sub·or·di·na·tion** /sə bàwrd'n áysh'n/ *n*

sub·orn /sə báwrn/ *vt* persuade to do wrong —**sub·or·na·tion** /sùb awr náysh'n/ *n*

sub·plot /súb plòt/ *n* **1** a story secondary to the main story **2** a smaller section of a plot of land

sub·poe·na /sə peénə/, **sub·pena** *n* a legal order summoning a witness or demanding evidence —**sub·poe·na** *vt*

⚡ **sub·rou·tine** /súbroo teèn/ *n* an independent sequence of computer programming instructions

sub·scribe /səb skríb/ (-**scribed**, -**scrib·ing**) *v* **1** *vi* make advance payment for something **2** *vti* promise to give money regularly or invest in something **3** *vi* support a theory or view —**sub·scrib·er** *n*

sub·script /súb skrìpt/ *n* a character printed slightly below another character

sub·scrip·tion /səb skrípsh'n/ *n* advance payment for something, or an agreement to pay for something to be received over a period of time

sub·sec·tion /súb sèkshən/ *n* a division of a section, e.g., in a document

sub·se·quent /súbsəkwənt/ *adj* later in time or order —**sub·se·quent·ly** *adv*

sub·ser·vi·ent /səb súrvee ənt/ *adj* **1** too eager to obey **2** secondary in importance —**sub·ser·vi·ence** *n* —**sub·ser·vi·ent·ly** *adv*

sub·set /súb sèt/ *n* a mathematical set whose elements are contained in another set

sub·side /səb síd/ (-**sid·ed**, -**sid·ing**) *vi* **1** diminish in intensity **2** drop to a lower level

sub·si·dence /səb síd'nss, súbsədənss/ *n* **1** the sinking of land **2** the decreasing of something

sub·sid·i·ar·i·ty /səb síddee árrətee/ *n* **1** the assignment of power to the smallest possible political units **2** being subsidiary

sub·sid·i·ar·y /səb síddee àrree/ *adj* **1** secondary in importance **2** helping or supporting ■ *n* (*pl* -**ar·ies**) **1** a subsidiary person or thing **2** a company controlled by a larger one —**sub·sid·i·ar·i·ly** *adv*

sub·si·dize /súbssə dìz/ (-**dized**, -**diz·ing**) *vt* give a subsidy to —**sub·si·di·za·tion** /súbssədi záysh'n/ *n*

sub·si·dy /súbssədee/ (*pl* -**dies**) *n* **1** a grant of money given by a government to a private organization **2** a contribution to help with expenses

sub·sist /səb síst/ *vi* manage to live on only just enough food or money —**sub·sis·tent** *adj*

sub·sis·tence /səb sístənss/ *n* **1** subsisting **2** existence

sub·sis·tence farm·ing *n* farming that feeds the farmer's family alone —**sub·sis·tence farm·er** *n*

sub·sis·tence lev·el *n* a barely adequate standard of living

sub·soil /súb sòyl/ *n* the soil beneath the topsoil

sub·son·ic /sub sónnik/ *adj* **1** slower than the speed of sound **2** flying at subsonic speed —**sub·son·i·cal·ly** *adv*

sub·spe·cies /súb speèsheez, -seez/ (*pl* same) *n* a distinct plant or animal category within a species

sub·stance /súbstənss/ *n* **1** a kind of matter or material **2** tangible physical matter **3** real or practical value **4** material wealth **5** the gist or actual meaning of something

sub·stance a·buse *n* excessive consumption or misuse of any substance, especially drugs or alcohol

~~substancial~~ incorrect spelling of **substantial**

sub·stan·dard /sub stándərd/ *adj* below the expected or required standard

sub·stan·tial /səb stánsh'l/ *adj* **1** considerable **2** solid or sturdy **3** filling and satisfying **4** wealthy **5** real and tangible —**sub·stan·tial·ly** *adv*

sub·stan·ti·ate /səb stánshee àyt/ (-**at·ed**, -**at·ing**) *vt* **1** prove or support **2** make real or actual —**sub·stan·ti·a·tion** /səb stànshee áysh'n/ *n*

sub·stan·tive *adj* /súbstəntiv/ **1** with practical importance **2** basic or essential **3** of or used like a noun ■ *n* /súbstəntiv, səb stántiv/ a noun —**sub·stan·tive·ly** *adv*

sub·sta·tion /súb stàysh'n/ *n* **1** a branch of power station where electrical power is modified or redistributed **2** a subsidiary post office or station

sub·sti·tute /súbstə tòot/ *vti* (-**tut·ed**, -**tut·ing**) put in or take the place of another ■ *n* **1** something used in place of something else **2** somebody who replaces another, especially as a teacher or during a sports game —**sub·sti·tu·tion** /súbstə tóosh'n/ *n* ◊ See note at **replace**

sub·sti·tute teach·er *n* a temporary replacement teacher

sub·stra·tum /súb stràytəm, -stràttəm/ (*pl* -**ta** /-tə/) *n* an underlying base or layer, e.g., subsoil or bedrock —**sub·stra·tal** *adj*

sub·struc·ture /súb strúkchər/ *n* **1** the foundation of a building **2** an underlying structure —**sub·struc·tur·al** /sub strúkchərəl/ *adj*

sub·sume /səb sóom/ (-**sumed**, -**sum·ing**) *vt* **1** include in a larger category **2** make subject to a rule

sub·ten·ant /súb ténnənt/ *n* somebody renting property from a tenant —**sub·ten·an·cy** *n*

sub·tend /səb ténd/ *vt* **1** extend from one side to the other, opposite an angle or side of a geometric figure **2** lie underneath and enclose

sub·ter·fuge /súbtər fyòoj/ *n* something designed to hide a real objective

sub·ter·ra·ne·an /súbtə ráynee ən/, **sub·ter·ra·ne·ous** /-nee əss/ *adj* **1** underground **2** secret

sub·text /súb tèkst/ *n* an underlying meaning —**sub·tex·tu·al** /sub tékschoo əl/ *adj*

sub·ti·tle /súb tìt'l/ n 1 a printed text or translation of what is being said on television or in a movie 2 a subsidiary and often explanatory title —**sub·ti·tle** vt

sub·tle /súttl/ adj 1 slight and not obvious 2 pleasantly understated 3 able to make refined judgments —**sub·tle·ness** n —**sub·tle·ty** n —**sub·tly** adv

subtley incorrect spelling of **subtly**

sub·to·tal /súb tòt'l/ n the total of part of a set of figures —**sub·to·tal** vt

sub·tract /səb trákt/ v 1 vti perform the arithmetical calculation of deducting one number or quantity from another 2 vt remove something from something larger —**sub·trac·tion** n

sub·trop·i·cal /sub tróppik'l/ adj located between tropical and temperate areas —**sub·trop·ics** npl

sub·u·nit /súb yòonit/ n a unit that forms part of a larger unit

sub·urb /sú bùrb/ n a residential area on the edge of a city —**sub·ur·ban** /sə búrbən/ adj

sub·ur·ban·ite /sə búrbə nìt/ n an inhabitant of a suburb

sub·ur·bi·a /sə búrbee ə/ n suburbs or suburbanites in general

sub·ven·tion /səb vénsh'n/ n a grant or subsidy

sub·ver·sive /səb vúrssiv/ adj intended or likely to subvert ◼ n somebody involved in subversive activities —**sub·ver·sive·ly** adv —**sub·ver·sive·ness** n

sub·vert /səb vúrt/ vt undermine or overthrow a government or other institution —**sub·ver·sion** n

sub·way /súb wày/ n US, Can, Scotland an underground railroad

sub·ze·ro /súb zeèrō/ adj below zero degrees

succede incorrect spelling of **succeed**

suc·ceed /sək seéd/ v 1 vi achieve what is planned or attempted 2 vi gain fame, wealth, or power 3 vti follow after in a position or role ◊ succeed to a title 4 vt come after in time

succesful incorrect spelling of **successful**

succesive incorrect spelling of **successive**

suc·cess /sək séss/ n 1 the achievement of an objective 2 the attainment of fame, wealth, or power 3 something or somebody that turns out well

suc·cess·ful /sək séssf'l/ adj 1 achieving what is planned or attempted 2 popular and making a lot of money ◊ a successful play 3 prosperous or well known —**suc·cess·ful·ly** adv

suc·ces·sion /sək sésh'n/ n 1 a series of people or things coming one after another ◊ a succession of blows 2 the taking over of a title or position —**suc·ces·sion·al** adj

suc·ces·sive /sək séssiv/ adj following in sequence —**suc·ces·sive·ly** adv

suc·ces·sor /sək séssər/ n somebody who succeeds another to a position

suc·cess sto·ry n a successful person or thing

suc·cinct /sək síngkt/ adj brief and to the point —**suc·cinct·ly** adv —**suc·cinct·ness** n

suc·cor /súkər/ n help or relief (literary)

suc·co·tash /súkə tàsh/ n a cooked bean and corn dish

suc·cu·lent /súkyələnt/ adj 1 juicy and tasty 2 describes a plant with fleshy water-storing parts ◼ n a succulent plant —**suc·cu·lence** n —**suc·cu·lent·ly** adv

suc·cumb /sə kúm/ vi 1 yield 2 die from an illness or injury ◊ See note at **yield**

suceed incorrect spelling of **succeed**

sucessful incorrect spelling of **successful**

sucessive incorrect spelling of **successive**

such adj 1 of the kind mentioned ◊ beware of such offers 2 so great ◊ Don't be such a fool. ◼ adv very ◊ such lovely flowers ◼ n this or something of this kind ◊ Such was his fate. ◊ **such as** introduces an example ◊ **such as it is** being what it is and no more

such and such adj unspecified ◼ pron something unspecified

such·like /súch lìk/ pron others of the same kind (infml) ◼ adj similar to those just mentioned

suck v 1 vti draw liquid out of something with the mouth 2 vti make something dissolve in the mouth 3 vt draw something in or out ◊ Fuel is sucked into the cylinder. 4 vt pull with a powerful force 5 vi be very bad (slang) —**suck** n

suck·er /súkər/ n 1 somebody regarded as easily fooled, influenced, or exploited (infml) 2 a lollipop (infml) 3 an organ, e.g., of a sea animal, that clings by suction 4 an organ for sucking in food 5 a shoot growing from an underground stem or root 6 a freshwater fish with a sucking mouth ◼ vt trick (infml)

suck·le /súk'l/ (-led, -ling) v 1 vti feed from a breast, teat, or udder 2 vt nourish (literary)

suck·ling /súkling/ n a baby or young animal

su·crose /sóo kròss, -krōz/ n a sugar found naturally in many plants

suc·tion /súksh'n/ n 1 the process of sucking 2 a force created by a difference in pressure

suc·tion cup n an attachment that adheres to a surface by suction

Su·dan /soo dán/ 1 country in NE Africa. Cap. Khartoum. Pop. 36,080,373 (2001). 2 region of savanna and dry grassland in north central Africa, south of the Sahara —**Su·da·nese** /sòodʹneéz, sòodʹn eéss/ n, adj

sud·den /súdd'n/ adj happening quickly and unexpectedly —**sud·den·ly** adv —**sud·den·ness** n

sud·den death n in sports, the continuation of play until a decisive goal or point is scored

sud·den in·fant death syn·drome *n* crib death *(technical)*

suds *npl* bubbles on soapy water ■ *n* beer *(slang)* —**suds·y** *adj*

sue /soo/ (**sued, su·ing**) *v* **1** *vti* undertake legal proceedings against somebody **2** *vi* make a formal request *(fml)* ○ *sued for peace after the long siege* —**su·er** *n*

suede /swayd/ *n* **1** leather with a velvety surface **2** fabric resembling suede

su·et /sóo ət/ *n* hard fat from sheep and cattle kidneys. Use: cooking, tallow.

Sue·to·ni·us /swee tónee əss/, **Gaius Tran·quillus** (69?–140) Roman biographer and historian

Su·ez /sóo əz/ port in NE Egypt, at the head of the Gulf of Suez. Pop. 417,000 (1998).

Su·ez Ca·nal canal in NE Egypt, connecting the Mediterranean and the Red Sea. Length 121 mi./195 km.

suf·fer /súffər/ *v* **1** *vti* feel pain or great discomfort in body or mind **2** *vti* undergo something unpleasant **3** *vti* tolerate something **4** *vi* have an illness ○ *suffers from asthma* **5** *vi* appear to be less good ○ *suffers in comparison* **6** *vi* be adversely affected —**suf·fer·a·ble** *adj* —**suf·fer·er** *n*

~~sufferage~~ incorrect spelling of **suffrage**

suf·fer·ance /súffərənss/ *n* **1** tolerance of something prohibited **2** endurance of difficulty or pain

suf·fer·ing /súffəring/ *n* mental or physical pain

suf·fice /sə físs/ (**-ficed, -fic·ing**) *vi* be enough

~~sufficient~~ incorrect spelling of **sufficient**

suf·fi·cient /sə físh'nt/ *adj* enough —**suf·fi·cien·cy** *n* —**suf·fi·cient·ly** *adv*

suf·fix /súffiks/ an element added at the end of a word ■ *vt* /súffiks, sə fíks/ add as suffix —**suf·fix·a·tion** /súffik sáysh'n/ *n*

suf·fo·cate /súffə kàyt/ (**-cat·ed, -cat·ing**) *vti* **1** stop or cause to stop breathing **2** die from a lack of air, or kill by cutting off air **3** not allow or be allowed to develop —**suf·fo·cat·ing** *adj* —**suf·fo·ca·tion** /súffə káysh'n/ *n*

suf·fra·gan /súffrəgən/ *n* **1** an assistant bishop **2** a bishop working as an assistant to an archbishop —**suf·fra·gan** *adj*

suf·frage /súffrij/ *n* **1** the right to vote **2** the act of voting *(archaic)*

suf·fra·gette /súffrə jét/ *n* a woman who campaigned for women's voting rights

suf·fra·gist /súffrəjist/ *n* an advocate of extending voting rights —**suf·fra·gism** *n*

suf·fuse /sə fyóoz/ (**-fused, -fus·ing**) *vt* spread throughout and over —**suf·fu·sion** *n* —**suf·fu·sive** /sə fyóossiv, -ziv/ *adj*

Su·fi /sóofee/ (*pl* **-fis**) *n* a Muslim mystic —**Su·fi** *adj* —**Su·fic** *adj* —**Su·fism** *n* —**Su·fis·tic** /soo fístik/ *adj*

~~sufficient~~ incorrect spelling of **sufficient**

sug·ar /shóoggər/ *n* **1** a sweet-tasting substance in the form of tiny white or brown grains. Use: food sweetener, drinks. **2** a portion of sugar **3** any simple carbohydrate that is sweet-tasting, crystalline, and soluble in water **4** used as a term of endearment *(infml)* ■ *vt* **1** add sugar to something **2** try to make something more agreeable —**sug·ared** *adj*

sug·ar beet *n* a variety of beets grown for the sugar in its root

sug·ar cane *n* a tall plant whose sap is a source of sugar

sug·ar dad·dy *n* a rich older man who spends money lavishly on a much younger partner *(infml)*

sug·ar·y /shóoggəree/ *adj* **1** containing sugar **2** like sugar in taste or appearance **3** exaggeratedly and often insincerely pleasant

sug·gest /səg jést, sə jést/ *vt* **1** propose for consideration as a possible choice or course of action **2** remind somebody of **3** express indirectly ◊ See note at **recommend**

sug·gest·i·ble /səg jéstəb'l, sə jést-/ *adj* easily influenced —**sug·gest·i·bil·i·ty** *n*

sug·ges·tion /səg jéschən, sə jés-/ *n* **1** an idea or proposal put forward for consideration **2** a slight trace **3** the act of suggesting something

sug·ges·tive /səg jéstiv, sə jést-/ *adj* **1** conjuring up ideas or images **2** implying something improper —**sug·ges·tive·ly** *adv* —**sug·ges·tive·ness** *n*

Su·har·to /sə haártō, soo-/ (b. 1921) president of Indonesia (1967–98)

su·i·cid·al /sóo i síd'l/ *adj* **1** wanting to commit suicide **2** of suicide **3** extremely dangerous —**su·i·cid·al·ly** *adv*

su·i·cide /sóo i sìd/ *n* **1** the act of killing yourself **2** somebody who commits suicide

su·i·cide bomb·ing *n* a bomb attack in which the bomber dies —**su·i·cide bomb·er** *n*

su·i·cide pact *n* an agreement between people to kill themselves together

su·i·cide watch *n* a regular check by prison guards on inmates suspected of having suicidal impulses

suit /soot/ *n* **1** a set of clothes for wearing together, usually made of the same material **2** a set of clothes for a particular purpose *(often in combination)* **3** a set of playing cards bearing the same symbols **4** a case brought to a law court **5** the wooing of a woman *(archaic)* ■ *v* **1** *vti* be right or appropriate for somebody or something **2** *vt* be pleasing or satisfying to somebody **3** *vt* look good on somebody **4** *vt* make something suitable **5** *vr* please yourself ◊ **be somebody's strong suit** something at which somebody is particularly good ◊ **follow suit 1** do the same as somebody else has done **2** play a card of the same suit as the previous player

suit·a·ble /sóotəb'l/ *adj* right for a particular purpose —**suit·a·bil·i·ty** /sóotə bíllətee/ *n* —**suit·a·bly** *adv*

suit·case /sóot kàyss/ *n* a rectangular container for carrying belongings while traveling

⚡**suite** /sweet/ *n* 1 a set of rooms 2 a set of cmatching furniture 3 a set of instrumental works performed together 4 the people accompanying an important person 5 an integrated software package

SPELLCHECK Do not confuse the spelling of **suite** and **sweet** ("sugary"), which sound similar.

suit·or /sóotər/ *n* 1 a man who is wooing a woman *(fml)* 2 somebody seeking to take over a business 3 somebody who brings a lawsuit

Su·kar·no /soo kaàrnó/ (1901–70) president of Indonesia (1945–68)

Su·kar·no·pu·tri /soo kaàrnə póotree/, **Mega·wati** (b. 1947) Indonesian president (2001–)

Suk·koth /soo kót, -kôth, -kôss, -kəss/, **Suc·coth, Suk·kot** *n* a Jewish harvest festival. Date: from the eve of the 15th of Tishri.

Su·la·we·si /sóolə wáyssee/ island in Indonesia, in the Malay Archipelago east of Borneo. Pop. 13,732,500 (1995).

Su·lei·man I (the Mag·ni·fi·cent) /sóolli maàn, sòoli-, sôol ay-/, **Su·lay·man I** (1494–1566) Ottoman sultan

sul·fa drug /súlfə-/ *n* an antibacterial drug now rarely used

sul·fate /súl fàyt/ *n* a salt or ester of sulfuric acid

sul·fide /súl fíd/ *n* a compound in which sulfur is typically combined with one or more elements or groups with a positive electric charge

sul·fite /súl fít/ *n* a salt or ester of sulfurous acid

sul·fur /súlfər/, **sul·phur** *n* (symbol **S**) a yellow nonmetallic chemical element. Use: manufacture of sulfuric acid, matches, fungicides, and gunpowder.

sul·fur di·ox·ide /-dī óksīd/ *n* a strong-smelling toxic gas. Use: food preservative, fumigant, bleaching agent, manufacture of sulfuric acid.

sul·fu·ric /sul fyóorik/ *adj* containing sulfur, especially with a valence of six

sul·fu·ric ac·id *n* a strong corrosive acid. Use: batteries, manufacture of fertilizers, explosives, detergents and dyes.

sul·fur·ize /súlfyə rīz/ (-ized, -iz·ing) *vt* treat or combine something with sulfur or a sulfur compound

sul·fur·ous /súlfərəss, súlfyə-/, **sul·fur·e·ous** /sul fyóoree əss/ *adj* 1 containing sulfur, especially with a valence of four 2 similar to burning sulfur, especially in color or smell

sul·fur·ous ac·id *n* a weak colorless acid. Use: food preservative, disinfectant, bleaching agent.

sulk *vi* be angrily silent or aloof ■ *n* 1 a period or state of sulking 2 somebody who sulks —**sulk·er** *n*

sulk·y /súlkee/ *adj* (-i·er, -i·est) angrily silent or aloof ■ *n* (*pl* -ies) a horse-drawn vehicle for one person —**sulk·i·ly** *adv* —**sulk·i·ness** *n*

sul·len /súllən/ *adj* maintaining a hostile silence —**sul·len·ly** *adv* —**sul·len·ness** *n*

Sul·li·van /súlləvən/, **Sir Arthur** (1842–1900) British composer

Sul·li·van, Louis (1856–1924) US architect

sul·ly /súllee/ (-lied, -lies) *vt* 1 spoil or tarnish ○ *a reputation sullied by scandal* 2 make dirty —**sul·lied** *adj*

sul·phur *n* CHEM ELEM = sulfur

sul·tan /súltən/ *n* especially formerly, a Muslim ruler —**sul·tan·ship** *n*

sul·tan·a /sul tánnə/ *n* 1 a dried grape 2 a sultan's woman relative

sul·tan·ate /súltənət, súltə nàyt/ *n* 1 a country ruled by a sultan 2 the rank of sultan

sul·try /súltree/ *adj* 1 hot and damp 2 sensual —**sul·tri·ness** *n*

Su·lu Sea /sóoloo-/ arm of the Pacific Ocean west of the Philippines and northeast of Borneo

sum[1] /sum/ *n* 1 a total 2 an amount of money 3 an arithmetical calculation 4 the gist of something (*literary*) ■ *vt* (**summed, sum·ming**) add up (*fml*)

ORIGIN Sum came through French from a Latin word literally meaning "highest thing." The development in meaning from "highest" to "sum total" resulted from the Roman practice of counting columns of figures from the bottom upward, the total being written at the top.

□ **sum up** *vti* summarize something

sum[2] /soom/, **som** *n* the main unit of currency in Uzbekistan

su·mac /sóo màk, shóo-/ *n* 1 a tree of the cashew family 2 ground and dried leaves from one kind of sumac tree. Use: tanning, dyeing.

~~summary~~ incorrect spelling of **summary**

Su·ma·tra /soo maàtrə/ island in W Indonesia, separated from the Malay Peninsula by the Strait of Malacca. Pop. 40,830,400 (1995). —**Su·ma·tran** *n, adj*

Su·mer /sóomər/ ancient country of S Mesopotamia, in present-day Iraq

Su·me·ri·an /soo méeree ən, -méree-/ *n* 1 a member of a people of ancient Babylonia 2 the language of ancient Sumer —**Su·me·ri·an** *adj*

sum·ma cum lau·de /sóommə kóom lów dày, sóomə koom-, -lówdee/ *adv* with the highest academic distinction —**sum·ma cum lau·de** *adj*

sum·ma·rize /súmmə rìz/ (**-rized, -riz·ing**) vt make a summary of —**sum·mar·ist** n —**sum·ma·ri·za·tion** /sùmmərì záysh'n/ n

sum·ma·ry /súmməree/ n (pl **sum·ma·ries**) a short version of something, containing the main points ■ adj 1 done immediately and with little discussion or attention to formalities ○ a summary execution 2 giving only the main points —**sum·mar·i·ly** /sə mérrəlee, súmmərəlee/ adv —**sum·ma·ri·ness** n

sum·ma·ry court-mar·tial n a court-martial tried by a single officer

sum·ma·tion /su máysh'n/ n 1 a final argument in court 2 a summary of something said 3 a total 4 arithmetic addition —**sum·ma·tive** /súmmətiv/ adj

sum·mer /súmmər/ n 1 the warmest season of the year 2 the warm weather associated with summer ■ vi spend the summer somewhere —**sum·mer·y** adj

sum·mer camp n a place of summer recreation for children, usually in the country

sum·mer·house /súmmər hòwss/ (pl **-hous·es** /-hòwzəz/) n a light shelter in a garden or park

sum·mer school n a course of study attended in the summer

sum·mer·time /súmmər tìm/ n the season of summer

sum·mit /súmmit/ n 1 the highest point of a mountain 2 a conference between heads of government on a matter of great importance 3 the highest point of anything

sum·mon /súmmən/ v 1 vt order somebody to appear in court 2 vt send for somebody 3 vt convene a group 4 vi gather resources such as courage or strength

sum·mons /súmmənz/ n an official order to appear in a specific place, especially in court, at a specific time ■ vt serve somebody with a summons

Sum·ner /súmnər/, **Charles** (1811–74) US senator (1851–74) and abolitionist

su·mo /soomo/ n a Japanese style of wrestling

sump n 1 a low-lying spot or place that receives liquid runoff 2 a cesspool for waste

sump pump n a pump for removing especially water from a basement

~~sumptious~~ incorrect spelling of **sumptuous**

sump·tu·ous /súmpchoo əss/ adj 1 splendid in appearance 2 lavish or extravagant —**sump·tu·ous·ly** adv —**sump·tu·ous·ness** n

sum to·tal n 1 everything put together 2 a final total

sun /sun/ n 1 also **Sun** the star around which the Earth revolves 2 any star 3 light or heat from the Sun ■ v (**sunned, sun·ning**) 1 vr bask in the sun 2 vt warm or dry in the sun —**sun·less** adj ◊ **under the sun** in the whole world ◊ See note at **son**

Sun. abbr Sunday

sun-baked /sún bàykt/ adj hardened, dried, or baked by the sun

sun-bathe /sún bàyth/ vi expose the body to the rays of the sun —**sun-bath·er** n —**sun-bath·ing** n

sun·beam /sún bèem/ n a ray of sunlight

Sun-belt /sún bèlt/, **Sun Belt** n the US states in the South and Southwest

sun·block /sún blòk/ n a cream or lotion applied to the skin to block out ultraviolet rays

sun·burn /sún bùrn/ n a painful inflammation or blistering of the skin as the result of overexposure to the sun ■ vti (**-burned** or **-burnt** /-bùrnt/) suffer or cause to suffer sunburn —**sun-burned** adj

sun·burst /sún bùrst/ n 1 a sudden burst of sunshine 2 a design consisting of rays extending from a central circle

sun·dae /sún dày/ n an ice-cream dessert with toppings

Sun·da Is·lands /súndə-, soondə-/ island group of the Malay Archipelago comprising the Greater Sunda Islands, which include Sumatra, Java, and Borneo, and the Lesser Sunda Islands, which include Bali and Timor

sun dance n a Native North American prairie ceremonial dance in honor of the Sun

Sun·day /sún dày, -dee/ n 1 the 7th day of the week 2 the Christian Sabbath day ■ adj 1 of Sunday 2 for special occasions

ORIGIN The origin of **Sunday** is exactly what it appears to be, the "day of the Sun."

Sun·day school n a class offering religious education on Sundays

sun deck n US, ANZ a balcony or terrace used for sunbathing

sun·der /súndər/ vti break or be broken apart (literary)

sun·di·al /sún dì əl/ n an instrument that shows the time by a sun-generated shadow

sun·down /sún dòwn/ n sunset

sun-drenched /sún drèncht/ adj describes a place that enjoys much hot sunshine

sun·dress /sún drèss/ n a sleeveless dress worn in hot weather

sun-dried adj dried in the sun

sun·dry /súndree/ adj various ■ **sun·dries** npl various miscellaneous items or goods

sun·fish /sún fìsh/ (pl same or **-fish·es**) n a North American spiny-finned freshwater fish, often with iridescent colors

sun·flow·er /sún flòwr/ n a tall plant with large yellow-rayed flowers

sung past participle of **sing**

sun·glass·es /sún glàssəz/ npl tinted eyeglasses that protect the eyes against strong sunlight

sunk past participle, past tense of **sink**

sunk·en /súngkən/ *adj* 1 submerged 2 appearing hollow ○ *sunken cheeks* 3 situated at a lower level than the surrounding area ○ *a sunken garden*

sun·lamp /sún làmp/ *n* an ultraviolet lamp used for tanning or therapeutic purposes

sun·light /sún lìt/ *n* light from the sun —**sun·lit** /sún lìt/ *adj*

Sun·ni /sónnee/ (*pl same or* -**nis**) *n* 1 one of the main branches of Islam 2 a member of the Sunni branch of Islam

sun·ny /súnnee/ (-**ni·er**, -**ni·est**) *adj* 1 full of sunshine 2 full of sunlight 3 cheerful —**sun·ni·ness** *n*

sun·ny-side up *adj* describes an egg that is fried on one side only

Sun·ny·vale /súnnee vàyl/ city in N California. Pop. 127,444 (1998).

sun·rise /sún rìz/ *n* the coming up of the sun, or the time when this occurs

sun·roof /sún ròof/ *n* a window in the roof of a car

sun·screen /sún skrèen/ *n* a substance applied to the skin to prevent sunburn when tanning

sun·set /sún sèt/ *n* the going down of the sun, or the time when this occurs

sun·shade /sún shàyd/ *n* an awning, parasol, or similar object that gives shade from the sun

sun·shine /sún shìn/ *n* 1 direct sunlight 2 a place where the sun's rays can be felt 3 a source of good feelings —**sun·shin·y** *adj*

sunshine law *n* a law that prohibits closed meetings of public bodies

sun·spot /sún spòt/ *n* a dark patch on the Sun

sun·stroke /sún stròk/ *n* an illness caused by overexposure to the sun

sun·tan /sún tàn/ *n* a darkening of the skin from exposure to the sun —**sun-tanned** *adj*

sun-up /sún ùp/ *n* sunrise

Sun Yat-sen /sóon yát sén/ (1866–1925) Chinese revolutionary leader

sup[1] *vt* (**supped**, **sup·ping**) 1 sip liquid 2 eat something by the spoonful ■ *n* a sip of liquid

sup[2] (**supped**, **sup·ping**) *vi* have supper (*fml or literary*)

su·per /sóopər/ (*infml*) *adj* 1 excellent 2 very great ■ *adv* especially ■ *n* 1 a building superintendent 2 *ANZ* superannuation ■ *interj* expresses great enthusiasm or approval

super- *prefix* 1 something larger, stronger, or faster than others of its kind ○ *superstore* 2 over, above, on ○ *superstructure* 3 exceeding the usual limits ○ *superheat* 4 in addition to, over and above ○ *supernumerary*

su·per·a·gen·cy /sóopər àyjənssee/ (*pl* -**cies**) *n* a huge government agency made up of or controlling other agencies

su·per·an·nu·at·ed /sóopər ánnyoo àytəd/ *adj* 1 retired 2 worn out 3 out-of-date

su·perb /soo púrb, sə-/ *adj* 1 excellent 2 grand —**su·perb·ly** *adv*

Su·per Bowl a service mark for the championship game of the National Football League, played each year between the champions of the National Football Conference and the American Football Conference

su·per·bug /sóopər bùg/, **su·per·germ** /-jùrm/ *n* an antibiotic-resistant bacterium

~~supercede~~ incorrect spelling of **supersede**

su·per·charg·er /sóopər chàarjər/ *n* a device used to increase an engine's power

su·per·cil·i·ous /sóopər síllee əss/ *adj* contemptuously indifferent —**su·per·cil·i·ous·ly** *adv*

ORIGIN Supercilious comes from a Latin adjective formed from *supercilium* "eyebrow" (from *super* "above" and *cilium* "eyelid"). It refers to raised eyebrows as a sign of haughty disdain.

su·per·class /sóopər klàss/ *n* a taxonomic category of organisms above a class

⚡**su·per·com·put·er** /sóopər kəm pyóotər/ *n* a high-speed computer

su·per·con·duc·tiv·i·ty /sóopər kòndək tívvitee/ *n* the ability to conduct electricity without resistance —**su·per·con·duc·tive** /-dúktiv/ *adj* —**su·per·con·duc·tor** /-dúktər/ *n*

su·per·fi·cial /sóopər físh'l/ *adj* 1 concerned only with the obvious or main parts of something 2 of or on the surface 3 without depth of character 4 only apparent 5 insignificant —**su·per·fi·ci·al·i·ty** /-fishee állətee/ *n* —**su·per·fi·cial·ly** *adv*

su·per·fine /sóopər fín, sòopər fín/ *adj* 1 extremely fine grain or texture 2 of the highest quality

su·per·flu·i·ty /sóopər flóo ətee/ (*pl* -**ties**) *n* 1 something inessential 2 an excessive quantity

su·per·flu·ous /sə púrfloo əss/ *adj* 1 more than necessary 2 not essential —**su·per·flu·ous·ly** *adv*

su·per·germ *n* = **superbug**

su·per·glue /sóopər glòo/ *n* a fast-acting strong glue

su·per·group /sóopər gròop/ *n* a world-famous rock music band

su·per·heat /sóopər hèet/ *vt* heat something to an extremely high degree or beyond its boiling point

su·per·heav·y·weight /sóopər hévvee wàyt/ *n* 1 the heaviest weight category for boxers 2 a boxer who competes at superheavyweight

su·per·he·ro /sóopər hèerō/ (*pl* -**roes**) *n* a superhuman cartoon character who fights crime

su·per·high·way /sòopər hí wày/ *n* a wide multilane highway

su·per·hu·man /sòopər hyóomən, -yóomən/ *adj* 1 beyond human capability, or having more-than-human capabilities 2 supernatural —**su·per·hu·man·ly** *adv*

su·per·im·pose /sòopərim póz/ (**-posed, -pos·ing**) *vt* lay something over something else —**su·per·im·po·si·tion** /sòopərimpə zísh'n/ *n*

su·per·in·tend /sòopərin ténd/ *vt* be in charge of

~~superintendant~~ incorrect spelling of **superintendent**

su·per·in·ten·dent /sòopərin téndənt/ *n* 1 somebody in charge 2 somebody in charge of the maintenance of a building 3 a high-ranking police officer ■ *adj* in charge —**su·per·in·ten·dence** *n* —**su·per·in·ten·den·cy** *n*

su·pe·ri·or /sə péeree ər/ *adj* 1 higher in quality, degree, rank, or position 2 above average 3 condescending 4 above being affected by something ○ *regarded herself as superior to spurious gossip* 5 written or printed higher than the main characters ■ *n* 1 somebody or something higher or better than others 2 somebody in charge of a religious order —**su·pe·ri·or·i·ty** /sə péeree áwratee/ *n* —**su·pe·ri·or·ly** *adv*

Su·pe·ri·or, Lake /sə péeree ər/ westernmost of the Great Lakes, between the north central United States and S Ontario, Canada. Depth 1,333 ft./406 m. Length 350 mi./560 km.

su·pe·ri·or court *n* in some US states, a court lower than an appellate court

su·per·la·tive /soo púrlətiv/ *adj* 1 excellent 2 highest in degree of grammatical comparison ■ *n* 1 the form of an adjective or adverb that expresses the highest degree of grammatical comparison 2 a superlative adjective or adverb 3 somebody or something of the highest degree of excellence —**su·per·la·tive·ly** *adv*

su·per·man /sòopər màn/ (*pl* **-men** /-mèn/) *n* 1 a man who is a high achiever 2 Nietzsche's ideal man

ORIGIN **Superman** was introduced by the British playwright George Bernard Shaw as a translation of German *Übermensch*, a coinage by Friedrich Nietzsche. Shaw used it in the title of his play *Man and Superman* (1903).

su·per·mar·ket /sòopər màarkət/ *n* a large grocery store

su·per·mod·el /sòopər mòdd'l/ *n* a famous and highly paid fashion model

su·per·nat·u·ral /sòopər náchərəl/ *adj* 1 not of the natural world 2 of a deity ■ *n* 1 supernatural things 2 the realm of supernatural things —**su·per·nat·u·ral·ly** *adv*

su·per·no·va /sòopər nòvə, sòopər nòvə/ (*pl* **-vae** /-vèe/ *or* **-vas**) *n* an exploding star

su·per·nu·mer·ar·y /sòopər nóomə rèrree/ *adj* 1 exceeding the usual number 2 employed as a substitute or extra worker ■ *n* (*pl* **-ies**) 1 somebody or something extra 2 an actor without a speaking part

su·per·or·di·nate /sòopər áwrd'nət/ *n* 1 a word whose meaning includes another more specific word 2 somebody or something superior —**su·per·or·di·nate** *adj*

su·per·pow·er /sòopər pòwr/ *n* 1 a powerful nation 2 extremely high electric or mechanical power —**su·per·pow·ered** *adj*

su·per·script /sòopər skript/ *n* a letter, number, or symbol written or printed higher than the main characters —**su·per·script** *adj*

su·per·sede /sòopər séed/ (**-sed·ed, -sed·ing**) *vt* 1 replace something less efficient, modern, or appropriate 2 succeed somebody or something else, e.g., in a position (*fml*) —**su·per·sed·ence** *n*

⚡ **su·per·serv·er** /sòopər súrvər/ *n* a powerful computer that controls a network

su·per·son·ic /sòopər sónnik/ *adj* capable of exceeding the speed of sound —**su·per·son·i·cal·ly** *adv*

su·per·star /sòopər stàar/ *n* a very famous person in sports or entertainment

su·per·sti·tion /sòopər stísh'n/ *n* 1 an irrational belief that something bad or good will happen if a specific thing is done 2 irrational beliefs in general

su·per·sti·tious /sòopər stíshəss/ *adj* 1 believing in superstitions 2 based on an irrational belief

su·per·store /sòopər stàwr/ *n* a very large store selling, e.g., books or groceries

su·per·struc·ture /sòopər strúkchər/ *n* 1 a ship's upper structure 2 the visible part of a building 3 the part of something that has developed from a base —**su·per·struc·tural** /sòopər strúkchərəl/ *adj*

su·per·tank·er /sòopər tàngkər/ *n* a big tanker ship

Su·per Tues·day *n* a Tuesday in a presidential election year on which many primaries are held

su·per·vise /sòopər vìz/ (**-vised, -vis·ing**) *vt* oversee an activity or a group of people —**su·per·vis·ion** /sòopər vízh'n/ *n*

~~superviser~~ incorrect spelling of **supervisor**

su·per·vi·sor /sòopər vìzər/ *n* 1 a boss 2 the teacher who oversees the teaching of a subject —**su·per·vi·so·ry** /sòopər vìzəree, sòopər vízəree/ *adj*

su·per·wom·an /sòopər wòomman/ (*pl* **-en** /-wimmən/) *n* a woman regarded as superhuman

su·pine /soo pín/ *adj* 1 lying on the back 2 passive or lethargic

~~supose~~ incorrect spelling of **suppose**

sup·per /súppər/ *n* 1 a small evening meal eaten before bedtime 2 the main evening meal

sup·per·time /súppər tìm/ n the time when supper is eaten

sup·plant /sə plánt/ vt 1 take somebody's place by force 2 take the place of something outmoded or irrelevant —**sup·plan·ta·tion** /sù plan táysh'n/ n

sup·ple /súpp'l/ (-**pler**, -**plest**) adj 1 flexible 2 moving with ease and grace —**sup·ple·ly** adv —**sup·ple·ness** n

sup·ple·ment n /súppləmənt/ 1 an addition 2 a publication that enlarges on or corrects something previously published 3 an additional section in a newspaper or magazine 4 a food substance taken to improve the diet 5 an extra charge ■ vt /súpplə mènt/ 1 make an addition to 2 be an additional part of —**sup·ple·men·tal** /sùpplə mént'l/ adj —**sup·ple·men·ta·tion** /sùpplə men táysh'n/ n —**sup·ple·ment·er** n

sup·ple·men·ta·ry /sùpplə méntəree/ adj 1 additional 2 making up for something lacking

sup·pli·ant /súpplee ənt/ adj making a humble appeal (fml) —**sup·pli·ance** n

sup·pli·cant /súppləkənt/ n somebody who makes a supplication (fml)

sup·pli·ca·tion /sùpplə káysh'n/ n (fml) 1 a humble appeal made to somebody in authority 2 the addressing of wishes to somebody able to grant them —**sup·pli·cate** /súpplə kàyt/ vti —**sup·pli·ca·to·ry** /súppləkə tàwree/ adj

~~suppliment~~ incorrect spelling of **supplement**

sup·ply /sə plí/ vt (-**plied**, -**plies**) 1 provide something wanted or needed by somebody 2 satisfy a need (fml) ■ n (pl -**plies**) 1 the available amount of something 2 the act of providing something ■ **sup·plies** npl basic things needed to survive or operate —**sup·pli·er** n

sup·ply-side ec·o·nom·ics n the economics of production (+ sing or pl verb)

sup·port /sə páwrt/ vt 1 keep from falling 2 bear the weight of 3 sustain financially 4 give help or encouragement to 5 be in favor of 6 give comfort to 7 corroborate ■ n 1 something that supports 2 assistance, encouragement, or approval 3 a supportive person —**sup·port·a·ble** adj —**sup·port·er** n —**sup·port·ive** adj

sup·port group n a group of people who meet to discuss their problems and help one another

sup·port hose npl stockings that support the veins in the lower legs

sup·pose /sə pṓz/ (-**posed**, -**pos·ing**) vt 1 believe or imagine to be true 2 consider or imagine as possible 3 take or require as a precondition 4 require or expect to do something (usually passive) ○ You're supposed to be in school.

sup·posed /sə pṓzd, -pṓzəd/ adj accepted as true but doubtful —**sup·pos·ed·ly** /-ədlee/ adv

sup·pos·ing /sə pṓzing/ conj if it is assumed that (infml)

sup·po·si·tion /sùppə zísh'n/ n 1 a hypothesis 2 the mental act of supposing —**sup·po·si·tion·al** adj

sup·pos·i·to·ry /sə pózzə tàwree/ (pl -**ries**) n a small medicated solid designed to dissolve in the rectum or vagina

sup·press /sə préss/ vt 1 put an end to something by force ○ swiftly suppressed the student protest 2 prevent or restrain something 3 stop the spread or publication of information 4 resist feelings or memories consciously —**sup·pres·sant** n —**sup·press·i·ble** adj —**sup·pres·sion** n

su·pra /sóopra/ adv above

supra- prefix transcending ○ supranational

su·pra·na·tion·al /sòopra násh'n'l/ adj multinational —**su·pra·na·tion·al·ism** n

su·prem·a·cist /sə prémməssəst, soo-/ n a believer in the superiority of a particular racial group (usually in combination)

su·prem·a·cy /sə prémməssee, soo-/ n a position of superiority or authority

su·preme /sə préem, soo-/ adj 1 above all others in power or status 2 highest in degree —**su·preme·ly** adv

su·prême /sə prém, soo-/ adj describes food served with a rich cream sauce

Su·preme Be·ing n God

Su·preme Court n 1 the highest US federal court 2 a highest state court 3 the highest court in a country

~~supress~~ incorrect spelling of **suppress**

~~suprise~~ incorrect spelling of **surprise**

Su·ra·ba·ya /sòora bí ə/ city on NE Java Island, Indonesia. Pop. 2,351,303 (1997).

Su·rat /sŏŏ rát, sŏŏrət/ port in W India. Pop. 1,498,817 (1991).

sur·charge /súr chàarj/ vti (-**charged**, -**charg·ing**) 1 charge a customer an additional amount 2 overcharge a customer ■ n an extra charge

sure /shoor/ adj (**sur·er**, **sur·est**) 1 definitely true 2 firmly believing something 3 certain to happen 4 certain to be obtained 5 very confident 6 always effective 7 firm and secure ■ adv (infml) 1 undoubtedly 2 yes —**sure·ness** n ◊ **for sure** without a doubt (infml) ◊ **sure enough** as was expected ○ Sure enough, the cat came back.

sure-fire adj certain to succeed (infml)

sure-foot·ed adj unlikely to stumble or fall —**sure-foot·ed·ly** adv —**sure-foot·ed·ness** n

sure·ly /shŏŏrlee/ adv 1 invites a response, e.g., of confirmation or denial ○ Surely you don't mean that! 2 without fail 3 without doubt

sure·ty /shŏŏrətee/ (pl -**ties**) n a guarantor —**sure·ty·ship** n

⚡ surf n foamy waves ■ v 1 vi ride waves on a surfboard 2 vt visit various sites on the

Internet in search of something, often casually —**surf·er** n —**surf·ing** n

sur·face /súrfəss/ n (pl -fac·es) 1 the outermost or uppermost part of something 2 a solid flat area 3 a thin layer applied to the outside of something 4 a superficial part ■ adj 1 used on or applied to a surface 2 superficial ■ vi (-faced, -fac·ing) 1 come up to the surface of water 2 appear 3 become known ◊ **on the surface** as an outward appearance or when examined superficially ◊ **scratch the surface** deal with only a very small or relatively unimportant part of something

sur·face mail n the ordinary mail service, as opposed to air mail

sur·face ten·sion n (symbol γ or σ) the naturally elastic quality of the surface of a liquid

sur·face-to-air adj describes a missile launched from the ground or a ship against an air target

surf·board /súrf bàwrd/ n a board on which to ride ocean waves —**surf·board·er** n —**surf·board·ing** n

sur·feit /súrfət/ n 1 an excessive number or amount 2 overindulgence in food or drink ■ vt give somebody an overage of something

surge vi (**surged, surg·ing**) 1 move like a wave 2 make a concerted rush 3 increase suddenly ■ n 1 a surging movement 2 a sudden increase in an emotion or feeling 3 a sudden power increase

sur·geon /súrjən/ n a doctor who specializes in performing operations

ORIGIN **Surgeon** goes back ultimately to the Greek words for "hand" and "work," so a **surgeon** is one who performs manual operations.

⚡ **surge pro·tec·tor** n a device that protects electrical equipment against power surges

sur·ger·y /súrjəree/ n (pl -ies) 1 medical treatment involving operations 2 the branch of medicine that deals with operations

sur·gi·cal /súrjik'l/ adj 1 of surgery 2 resulting from surgery —**sur·gi·cal·ly** adv

Su·ri·ba·chi, Mt. /sòorə baáchee/ n hill on Iwo Jima, site of the raising of the US flag by US Marines during World War II on February 23, 1945

Su·ri·name /sóori naáma/ country in NE South America. Cap. Paramaribo. Pop. 433,998 (2001). —**Su·ri·na·mese** /sòorə na méez, -méess/ n, adj

sur·ly /súrlee/ (-li·er, -li·est) adj bad-tempered and rude —**sur·li·ness** n

ORIGIN **Surly** means etymologically "like a lord or sir." It is a mid-16C alteration of obsolete *sirly* "lordly, haughty, imperious." **Surly** shared these early meanings, but they did not survive far into the 18C, and from the late 16C the modern sense of "bad-tempered" dominated.

sur·mise /sur míz/ vti make a guess about something ■ n guesswork or conjecture —**sur·mis·a·ble** adj

sur·mount /sur mównt/ vt 1 overcome a difficulty 2 get to the top of something (fml) 3 be placed on top of something (fml) —**sur·mount·a·ble** adj

sur·name /súr nàym/ n somebody's family name —**sur·name** vt

~~suround~~ incorrect spelling of **surround**

sur·pass /sur páss/ vt 1 go beyond or be greater or better than 2 do better than

sur·pass·ing /sur pássing/ adj outstanding (literary) —**sur·pass·ing·ly** adv

sur·plice /súrpləss/ n a white ecclesiastical outer garment

sur·plus /súrpləss/ n an excess amount ■ adj additional to requirements

sur·prise /sər príz/ vt (-prised, -pris·ing) 1 make somebody amazed 2 catch somebody or something unawares 3 give somebody something unexpectedly ■ n 1 something surprising or unexpected 2 amazement —**sur·pris·ing** adj —**sur·pris·ing·ly** adv

~~surprize~~ incorrect spelling of **surprise**

sur·re·al /sə rée əl/ adj 1 bizarrely unreal or dreamlike 2 of surrealism —**sur·re·al** n —**sur·re·al·ly** adv

sur·re·al·ism /sə rée ə lìzzəm/ n 1 an early 20C artistic and literary movement that represented the subconscious with fantastic imagery and the juxtaposition of contradictory elements 2 surreal art or literature —**sur·re·al·ist** n, adj —**sur·re·al·is·tic** /sə rèe ə lístik/ adj —**sur·re·al·is·ti·cal·ly** adv

sur·ren·der /sə réndər/ v 1 vi stop fighting because you are unable to win 2 vt give up possession or control of 3 vt give up or abandon 4 vi give yourself up to something such as an emotion ■ n the act of surrendering ◊ See note at **yield**

sur·rep·ti·tious /sùr əp tíshəss/ adj secret and stealthy —**sur·rep·ti·tious·ly** adv ◊ See note at **secret**

sur·rey /súr ree/ n (pl -reys) n a 19C horse-drawn carriage with two or four seats

sur·ro·gate adj /súr əgət/ taking the place of somebody or something else ■ n /súr əgət/ 1 a substitute 2 a woman who bears a child for another 3 in some states, a judge who probates wills and settles estates ■ vt /súr ə gàyt/ (-gat·ed, -gat·ing) appoint as a stand-in —**sur·ro·ga·cy** n —**sur·ro·gate·ship** n —**sur·ro·ga·tion** /sùr ə gáysh'n/ n

sur·round /sə równd/ vt 1 occupy the space all around 2 encircle in order to close off all means of escape ■ n an area around something

sur·round·ings /sə równdingz/ npl the landscape, events, circumstances, or objects around somebody or something

sur·tax /súr tàks/ n 1 an additional tax 2 a higher tax that applies above a specific level

~~surveilance~~ incorrect spelling of **surveillance**

sur·veil·lance /sər váylənss/ n continual close observation

sur·vey .vt /sər váy/ (-veyed, -vey·ing, -veys) 1 look at or consider something generally 2 look at or consider something carefully 3 plot a map of an area 4 question people in a poll ■ n /súr vày/ (pl -veys) 1 a general view 2 an opinion poll, or an analysis of the results —**sur·vey·a·ble** adj

~~surveyer~~ incorrect spelling of **surveyor**

sur·vey·or /sər váy ər/ n somebody who surveys land

sur·viv·al /sər vív'l/ n 1 the fact of surviving 2 the act or process of surviving in adverse conditions

sur·vive /sər vív/ (-vived, -viv·ing) v 1 vi remain alive or in existence 2 vt stay alive longer than somebody 3 vt live through something difficult or unpleasant —**sur·viv·a·ble** adj

~~surviver~~ incorrect spelling of **survivor**

sur·vi·vor /sər vívər/ n 1 somebody who survives a difficult or dangerous experience 2 a close relative who outlives another

~~susceptable, suseptible~~ incorrect spelling of **susceptible**

sus·cep·ti·ble /sə séptəb'l/ adj 1 easily affected 2 likely to be affected —**sus·cep·ti·bil·i·ty** /sə sèptə bíllətee/ n —**sus·cep·ti·bly** adv

su·shi /sóoshee, soo-/ n small cakes of rice mixed with fish or vegetables and wrapped in seaweed

~~suspecious~~ incorrect spelling of **suspicious**

sus·pect vt /sə spékt/ 1 think that somebody may be guilty 2 doubt the truth or validity of something 3 believe something to be so ■ n /súss pèkt/ a person suspected of wrongdoing ■ adj /súss pèkt/ 1 likely to be false or untrustworthy 2 likely to contain something illegal or dangerous o inspected the suspect luggage

~~suspence~~ incorrect spelling of **suspense**

sus·pend /sə spénd/ vt 1 hang something from above 2 stop something for a period of time 3 bar somebody for a period of time 4 postpone something 5 disperse particles in a liquid or gas

sus·pend·ed an·i·ma·tion n 1 the temporary slowing of biological functions 2 an unconscious state resembling death

sus·pend·ed sen·tence n a penal sentence that will be served only if the offender commits a similar offense within the stated period

sus·pend·er /sə spéndər/ n a strap for holding up pants (usually pl)

sus·pense /sə spénss/ n 1 uncertainty 2 enjoyable tension —**sus·pense·ful** adj

sus·pen·sion /sə spénsh'n/ n 1 a temporary stopping or postponement of something 2 the temporary removal of somebody, e.g., from a job, school, or team, usually as a punishment 3 a system that reduces the effects of vibration in a vehicle 4 a dispersion of particles in a liquid or gas

sus·pen·sion bridge n a bridge suspended from cables

sus·pi·cion /sə spísh'n/ n 1 the feeling that somebody has done something wrong 2 mistrust 3 the condition of being suspected

sus·pi·cious /sə spíshəss/ adj 1 arousing suspicion 2 tending to suspect 3 indicating suspicion —**sus·pi·cious·ly** adv —**sus·pi·cious·ness** n

Sus·que·han·na /sùskwə hánnə/ river in New York and Pennsylvania, emptying into Chesapeake Bay in Maryland. Length 447 mi./719 km.

Sus·que·han·nock /sùskwə hánnək/ (pl same or -nocks), **Sus·que·han·na** /-hánnə/ (pl same or -nas) n a member of an extinct Native North American people who lived along the Susquehanna River

sus·tain /sə stáyn/ vt 1 continue something in spite of difficulties 2 experience something such as injury or loss 3 make something continue to exist 4 nourish somebody 5 support something from below 6 provide somebody with moral support 7 decide that something, e.g., an objection, is valid 8 confirm something o sustained the lower court's ruling

sus·tain·a·ble /sə stáynəb'l/ adj 1 able to be maintained 2 exploiting natural resources without destroying ecological balance o sustainable agriculture —**sus·tain·a·bly** adv

sus·te·nance /sústənənss/ n 1 nourishment 2 livelihood 3 the condition of being sustained

Suth·er·land /súthərlənd/, **Dame Joan** (b. 1926) Australian operatic soprano

~~sutle~~ incorrect spelling of **subtle**

Sut·lej /súttlij/ river in South Asia, flowing through SW Tibet, N India, and E Pakistan. Length 901 mi./1,450 km.

su·tra /sóotrə/ n 1 a summary of Hindu teachings 2 also **sut·ta** /sóott ə/ a Buddhist religious text

su·ture /sóochər/ n 1 material used for surgical stitching 2 the line of a seam or join, e.g., between the edges of a wound 3 an immovable joint between bones ■ vt (-tured, -tur·ing) close a wound with sutures —**su·tur·al** adj

SUV abbr sport-utility vehicle

Su·va /sóovə/ capital of Fiji. Pop. 77,366 (2000).

~~suviver~~ incorrect spelling of **survivor**

svelte /svelt, sfelt/ *adj* graceful and slender

Sven·ga·li /sven gaˈalee, sfen-/ *n* an evil manipulator

> **ORIGIN** The original **Svengali** was a villainous hypnotist in the novel *Trilby* (1894) by the French-born novelist and illustrator George du Maurier (1834–96).

⚡**SVGA** *n* a video screen specification. Full form **super video graphics array**

SW *abbr* **1** short wave **2** southwest **3** southwestern

swab /swob/ *n* **1** a piece of soft material for soaking up blood **2** a small ball of cotton attached to a short stick **3** a specimen of mucus or other secretion taken using a swab **4** a mop ■ *vt* (**swabbed, swab·bing**) **1** clean or treat with a swab **2** mop

swad·dle /swódd'l/ (**-dled, -dling**) *vt* **1** wrap somebody in something **2** wrap a baby up tightly

swag *n* **1** a curtain that hangs in a curve **2** a festoon **3** loot *(slang)* ■ *vi* (**swagged, swag·ging**) move with a lurch

swag·ger /swággər/ *vi* **1** walk in an arrogant way **2** speak boastfully —**swag·ger** *n* —**swag·ger·er** *n* —**swag·ger·ing·ly** *adv*

Swa·hi·li /swaa heélee, swə-/ (*pl same or* -**lis**) *n* **1** a member of an E African people **2** the Bantu language of the Swahili people —**Swa·hi·li** *adj*

swain *n* a woman's male admirer or lover *(literary)*

swal·low[1] /swóllō/ *v* **1** *vti* take in something through the mouth and down the throat **2** *vi* make the movement of swallowing food or drink with the throat **3** *vt* engulf or destroy something **4** *vt* suppress feelings **5** *vt* believe something *(infml)* **6** *vt* endure something ■ *n* **1** the act of swallowing food or drink **2** an amount of food or drink swallowed

swal·low[2] /swóllō/ *n* a small songbird with pointed wings and a forked tail

swam past tense of **swim**

swa·mi /swaámee/ *n* a respected Hindu religious teacher

swamp /swomp/ *n* an area of wetland ■ *v* **1** *vt* overburden somebody or something **2** *vt* inundate an area **3** *vti* become, or cause a boat to become, full of water and sink —**swamp·y** *adj*

swamp·land /swómp lànd/ *n* an area of wetland

swan /swon/ *n* a large long-necked water bird

swank *adj* very showy ■ *n* elegance —**swank·i·ness** *n* —**swank·y** *adj*

swans·down /swónz dòwn/, **swan's-down** *n* swan feathers

Swan·sea /swónzee/ port in S Wales. Pop. 230,180 (1996). Welsh **Abertawe**

swan song *n* a final public performance or act

swap /swop/, **swop** *(infml)* *vti* (**swapped, swap·ping; swopped, swop·ping**) trade things ■ *n* an exchange —**swap·pa·ble** *adj*

> **ORIGIN Swap** originally meant "hit." The sense "trade" emerged in the 16C from the idea of striking hands to seal a bargain.

swap con·tract *n* a contract that involves a reciprocal exchange of some kind, e.g., one in which the contracting parties agree to exchange cash flows

swap·tion /swópsh'n/ *n* an option on a contract

sward /swawrd/ *n* an area of grass

swarf /swawrf/ *n* **1** space debris that orbits the Earth *(infml)* **2** metal shavings

swarm[1] /swawrm/ *n* **1** a group of insects **2** a large mass of people ■ *vi* **1** form a flying group **2** move in a mass **3** be overrun

> **ORIGIN** The two English words **swarm** are etymologically distinct. The **swarm** of bees goes back to an ancient root that was an imitation of the sound of buzzing. The origin of **swarm** "climb," which appeared in the mid-16C, is unknown.

swarm[2] *vi* climb using the arms and legs

swarth·y /swáwrtheé/ (**-i·er, -i·est**) *adj* having a dark complexion —**swar·thi·ness** *n*

swash·buck·ler /swósh bùklər/ *n* **1** an adventurer **2** a novel or movie about an adventurer —**swash·buck·ling** *adj*

swas·ti·ka /swóstikə/ *n* **1** a Nazi symbol consisting of a cross with four arms of the same length bent clockwise **2** an ancient religious symbol consisting of a cross with four arms of the same length bent clockwise or counterclockwise

swat /swot/, **swot** *vti* (**swat·ted, swat·ting; swot·ted, swot·ting**) strike or slap somebody or something ■ *n* **1** a sharp blow **2** attempt —**swat·ter** *n*

SWAT /swot/ *n* a special police unit with military training. Full form **Special Weapons and Tactics**

swatch /swoch/ *n* a fabric sample

swath /swoth/, **swathe** /swayth/ *n* **1** the width cut by a mowing machine **2** a path cut through a growing crop

swathe /swayth/ *vt* (**swathed, swath·ing**) **1** wrap completely **2** enfold ■ *n* a wrapping

sway *v* **1** *vti* swing or move back and forth **2** *vi* lean to one side or from side to side in turn **3** *vti* waver, or cause somebody to waver, between opinions **4** *vt* persuade or influence ■ *n* **1** a swaying motion **2** control over a person or area —**sway·a·ble** *adj* ◊ **hold sway** have control or influence

Swa·zi·land /swaázee lànd/ landlocked country in southern Africa. Cap. Mbabane. Pop. 1,104,343 (2001).

swear /swair/ (**swore, sworn**) *v* **1** *vti* affirm the truth of something **2** *vti* solemnly promise something **3** *vi* use blasphemous or obscene language **4** *vti* take an oath **5** *vti* declare something under oath

□ **swear in** *vt* make somebody take an oath when taking up an office

□ **swear off** *vt* renounce a bad habit

swear·word /swáir wùrd/ *n* an offensive or taboo word

sweat /swet/ *n* **1** moisture exuded on the skin, e.g., as a result of heat or anxiety **2** the state of having sweat on the skin **3** moisture condensed or exuded on a surface **4** hard or boring work ■ **sweats** *npl* matching casual pants and shirt worn for exercising *(infml)* ■ *v* **1** *vti* produce or cause to produce sweat **2** *vt* wet or mark with sweat **3** *vti* cook in its own juices **4** *vi* work hard *(slang)* ◇ **no sweat** it can be done with ease *(slang)*

□ **sweat out** *vt* endure something to the end *(slang)*

sweat·band /swét bànd/ *n* a strip of cloth worn around the head or wrist to absorb sweat

sweat eq·ui·ty *n* **1** equity from contributed labor **2** labor for equity **3** work in lieu of payment

sweat·er /swéttər/ *n* a knitted garment for the upper body, usually with long sleeves

sweat gland *n* a small tubular organ in the skin from which sweat is released

sweat·shop /swét shòp/ *n* a workplace staffed with overworked, underpaid employees

sweat·y /swéttee/ (**-i·er, -i·est**) *adj* **1** damp with sweat **2** causing sweating —**sweat·i·ness** *n*

Swede /sweed/ *n* somebody from Sweden

Swe·den /swéed'n/ country in NW Europe. Cap. Stockholm. Pop. 8,875,053 (2001).

Swe·den·borg /swéed'n bàwrg/, **Emanuel** (1688–1772) Swedish scientist and theologian —**Swe·den·bor·gi·an** /swéed'n báwrjee ən, -gee ən/ *n, adj*

Swed·ish /swéedish/ *n* the official language of Sweden ■ *adj* of Sweden or Swedish

sweep *v* (**swept**) **1** *vti* clean a place with a broom or brush **2** *vt* move something with a horizontal stroke **3** *vti* brush against the ground when moving **4** *vti* move with speed, force, or dignity **5** *vti* spread through a place **6** *vt* carry somebody or something along **7** *vti* win something overwhelmingly **8** *vt* stretch out in an arc, or extend broadly ■ *n* **1** an instance of cleaning with a broom or brush **2** a brushing stroke **3** a long smooth movement **4** a long smooth curve **5** a wide expanse **6** a curved or broad range **7** an overwhelming victory ■ **sweeps** *npl* television ratings in a specific period ◇ **make a clean sweep (of)** get rid of everything or everyone unwanted or unnecessary

sweep·back /swéep bàk/ *n* an aircraft wing that is angled backward

sweep·er /swéepər/ *n* **1** a person or a machine that sweeps floors or carpets **2** in soccer, a roving defensive player

sweep·ing /swéeping/ *adj* **1** on a large scale **2** too general ○ *sweeping statements* **3** overwhelming ○ *a sweeping victory* —**sweep·ing·ly** *adv*

sweep·ings /swéepingz/ *npl* things swept up

sweep·stakes /swéep stàyks/ (*pl* same) *n* a lottery in which the payout depends on the amount paid in

sweet /sweet/ *adj* **1** tasting or smelling of sugar **2** containing sugar **3** not bitter or sour **4** fresh **5** not salty **6** pleasing to the senses **7** satisfying ○ *a sweet victory* **8** kindly **9** charming or endearing ■ *adv* in a pleasant way ■ *n* **1** something that is pleasing to the emotions or feelings ○ *had to take the bitter with the sweet* **2** a term of endearment **3** FOOD = **candy** ■ **sweets** *npl* sweet-tasting food of any kind, especially sweet creations —**sweet·ly** *adv* —**sweet·ness** *n* ◇ See note at **suite**

sweet-and-sour *adj* containing sugar and vinegar flavorings

sweet·bread /swéet brèd/ *n* an animal's pancreas or thymus gland eaten as food

sweet corn *n* **1** a type of corn with sweet kernels **2** corn kernels eaten as food

sweet·en /swéet'n/ *v* **1** *vti* increase in sweetness **2** *vt* improve the taste or smell of **3** *vt* make more desirable ○ *sweeten a deal* **4** *vt* soften or persuade **5** *vt* make less acid

sweet·en·er /swéet'nər/ *n* a substance added to make something sweet or sweeter

sweet·en·ing /swéet'ning/ *n* **1** a substance making something sweet or sweeter **2** the act of making something sweet or sweeter

sweet·heart /swéet hàart/ *n* **1** a boyfriend or girlfriend *(dated)* **2** used as an affectionate term of address **3** a kindly person

sweet·ie /swéetee/ *n* an endearing person or pet *(infml)*

sweet·meat /swéet mèet/ *n* candy or confectionery served after a meal *(archaic)*

sweet noth·ings *npl* romantic words

sweet pea *n* a climbing plant with pastel-colored flowers

sweet pep·per *n* **1** a bell-shaped pepper eaten as a vegetable **2** the plant that produces sweet peppers

sweet po·ta·to *n* the fleshy orange root of a tropical plant, eaten as a vegetable

sweet spot *n* the most effective place on a racket or a bat on which you can hit a ball

sweet-talk *vti* use unctuously persuasive language to somebody *(infml)*

sweet tooth *n* a fondness for sweet food

sweet wil·liam /-wíllyəm/ (*pl* **sweet wil·liams** or same) *n* a plant with variously colored flowers

swell *v* (**swelled** or **swol·len** /swólən/) **1** *vti* increase in size, quantity, or degree **2** *vi* become temporarily larger than usual **3** *vti* increase and decrease in loudness **4** *vti* fill with emotion ■ *n* **1** the undulation of the sea surface **2** a rounded part that sticks out **3** an increase in size or number **4** in music, a crescendo followed by a diminuendo **5** a fashionable person (*dated infml*) **6** somebody of high status (*dated infml*) ■ *adj* **1** good (*slang*) ○ *did a swell job* **2** grandly stylish or fashionable (*dated*)

swell·ing /swélling/ *n* **1** an enlargement of something such as tissue **2** a lump or protuberance

swel·ter /swéltər/ *vi* be oppressed by heat ■ *n* unpleasant heat or an unpleasant sensation of hotness —**swel·ter·ing** *adj*

swept past tense, past participle of **sweep**

swept-back /swépt bàk, swèpt bák/ *adj* describes an aircraft wing that is angled backward

swerve *vti* (**swerved, swerv·ing**) turn suddenly away from a direct course ■ *n* an abrupt change in direction

swift *adj* **1** happening or done fast **2** moving or acting fast ■ *adv* quickly ■ *n* (*pl same or swifts*) a small bird that resembles a swallow —**swift·ly** *adv* —**swift·ness** *n*

Swift, Jonathan (1667–1745) Anglo-Irish author and cleric —**Swift·ian** *adj*

swig (*infml*) *vti* (**swigged, swig·ging**) drink something in large gulps ■ *n* a large gulp of a drink

swill *v* **1** *vt* wash or rinse with water **2** *vti* move, or cause liquid to move, around in a container **3** *vt* drink greedily or in large amounts (*disapproving*) ■ *n* **1** watery feed for hogs **2** kitchen waste **3** any sloppy liquid mixture

swim *v* (**swam, swum, swim·ming**) **1** *vi* move unsupported through water by moving parts of the body **2** *vt* travel a particular distance or cross a particular stretch of water by swimming **3** *vt* swim with a particular stroke **4** *vi* be dizzy **5** *vi* seem to move or spin **6** *vi* be covered in liquid ○ *meat swimming in gravy* —**swim·mer** *n* —**swim·ming** *n*

~~swiming~~ incorrect spelling of **swimming**

swim·ming·ly /swímminglee/ *adv* smoothly and successfully

swim·ming pool *n* an artificial body of water in which to swim

swim·ming trunks *npl* men's or boys' shorts worn for swimming

swim·suit /swím sòot/ *n* an outfit worn for swimming

swim·wear /swím wàir/ *n* clothing worn for swimming

swin·dle /swínd'l/ *vt* (**-dled, -dling**) obtain something from somebody by fraud ■ *n* a fraudulent transaction —**swin·dler** *n*

swine (*pl same*) *n* **1** a hog raised domestically **2** a man regarded as extremely unpleasant (*insult*) —**swin·ish** *adj*

swing *v* (**swung**) **1** *vti* move to and fro **2** *vti* pivot or rotate **3** *vti* move in a curve **4** *vi* walk with a swaying motion **5** *vti* strike or attempt to strike somebody or something with a sweeping blow **6** *vi* ride on a swinging seat **7** *vi* fluctuate or vacillate **8** *vt* arrange or manipulate (*infml*) ○ *swing a deal* **9** *vi* be hanged as a punishment (*infml*) **10** *vi* swap sexual partners (*dated slang*) ■ *n* **1** a hanging seat that moves backward and forward **2** a swinging movement **3** the range of movement of something that swings **4** a sweeping stroke or blow **5** a shift or fluctuation **6** a circular tour ○ *a swing around the block* **7** *also* **swing music** a style of jazz music suitable for dancing —**swing·er** *n* —**swing·ing** *adj* ◇ **in full swing** in vigorous progress ◇ **get into the swing of things** get into the established routine

swing bridge *n* a movable bridge that pivots horizontally

swing-by *n* a deliberate change in a space vehicle's course to accommodate the gravitational pull of a nearby object

swing shift *n* **1** a shift between day and night shifts **2** workers on a swing shift

swing vot·er *n* a voter without a fixed political allegiance who is capable of affecting the outcome of a close election

swipe *v* (**swiped, swip·ing**) **1** *vti* hit somebody or something hard with a sweeping blow **2** *vt* steal something (*infml*) ■ *n* **1** a sweeping blow **2** a critical attack (*infml*)

swipe card *n* a card containing coded information that can be passed through and read by an electronic device

swirl *v* **1** *vti* turn or cause to turn with a circular motion **2** *vi* be dizzy ■ *n* **1** a circular motion **2** a spiral —**swirl·y** *adj*

swish *vti* make or move with a smooth whistling or rustling sound ■ *n* a swishing sound or movement —**swish·y** *adj*

Swiss *n* (*pl same*) **1** somebody from Switzerland **2** the dialect of German, French, or Italian that is spoken in Switzerland ■ *adj* of Switzerland

Swiss chard *n* a leafy vegetable similar to spinach

Swiss steak, swiss steak *n* braised beef

switch *n* **1** a button or lever that controls an electrical circuit **2** a sudden change **3** a substitution **4** a thin rod or cane **5** the tip of an animal's tail **6** a device for shifting trains between tracks **7** a railroad siding **8** a routing device used within telephone exchanges ■ *v* **1** *vti* change from one thing to another **2** *vti* exchange or be exchanged **3** *vti* move a train between tracks **4** *vti* flick or swing to and fro **5** *vt* beat somebody with a switch —**switch·a·ble** *adj* —**switch·er** *n*

☐ **switch off** *vti* turn off a piece of electrical equipment (*infml*)

☐ **switch on** *vt* turn on a piece of electrical equipment

switch·back /swĭch bǎk/ *n* a twisty road with many hills

switch·blade /swĭch blǎyd/ *n* a knife with a spring-operated blade

switch·board /swĭch bàwrd/ *n* **1** a manual device for connecting telephone lines **2** a control panel containing electrical devices

Swit·zer·land /swĭtsər lànd/ country in west central Europe. Cap. Bern. Pop. 7,283,274 (2001).

swiv·el /swĭv'l/ *vti* pivot or rotate ■ *n* a device that allows a mechanical part to turn

swiv·el chair *n* a chair that can rotate

swiz·zle stick /swĭzz'l-/ *n* a small rod used to stir an alcoholic drink

swol·len past participle of **swell**

swoon *vi* **1** feel faint with joy **2** fall in a faint ■ *n* a loss of consciousness

swoop *vi* **1** make a sweeping descent **2** execute a pounce ■ *n* **1** a sudden descent **2** a sudden attack ◊ **at** *or* **in one fell swoop** in a single fast action

swoosh /swoosh, swōōsh/ *vti* make or move with a rushing sound —**swoosh** *n*

swop *vti, n* = **swap**

sword /sawrd/ *n* a hand-held weapon with a long blade

sword dance *n* a dance performed over crossed swords laid on the floor

sword·fish /sáwrd fĭsh/ (*pl* same *or* **-fish·es**) *n* **1** a large ocean fish with a sword-shaped jaw **2** swordfish as food

sword·play /sáwrd plày/ *n* sword fighting

swords·man /sáwrdzmən/ (*pl* **-men** /-mən/) *n* somebody who fights with a sword —**swords·man·ship** *n*

swore past tense of **swear**

sworn past participle of **swear** ■ *adj* **1** legally binding **2** unwavering in resolve

swot *vti, n* = **swat**

swum past participle of **swim**

swung past tense, past participle of **swing**

syc·a·more /síkə màwr/ (*pl* **-mores** *or* same) *n* **1** a maple tree with winged seeds **2** a large spreading plane tree

syc·o·phant /síkəfənt, -fànt, síkəfənt, -fànt/ *n* a fawning flatterer —**syc·o·phan·cy** /síkə fántik, sìkə-/ *adj* —**syc·o·phan·ti·cal·ly** *adv*

Syd·ney /sídnee/ capital of New South Wales, SE Australia. Pop. 3,986,700 (1998).

Syd·ney O·pera House *n* an arts center in Sydney Harbor, Australia

~~sylable~~ incorrect spelling of **syllable**

~~sylabus~~ incorrect spelling of **syllabus**

syl·lab·ic /si lábbik/ *adj* **1** of syllables **2** describes a consonant that forms a syllable without a vowel, such as the "l" in "bottle" **3** marked by clear enunciation

syl·la·ble /síllab'l/ *n* **1** a unit of spoken language containing a single vowel sound or syllabic consonant **2** a letter or group of letters that corresponds to a spoken syllable

syl·la·bub /síllə bùb/, **sil·la·bub** *n* a dessert of cream whipped with brandy or wine

syl·la·bus /síllabass/ (*pl* **-bi** /-bī/ *or* **-bus·es**) *n* an outline of a course of study

> **ORIGIN Syllabus** has its origins in a misprint. In an early edition of some of Cicero's letters, the Latin word *sittybas* "labels, tables of contents" was printed as *syllabos*. This was then wrongly referred to a nonexistent Greek noun (supposed to be from the verb *sullambanein* "gather together," from which *syllable* derives), and a Latin equivalent *syllabus* was formed.

syl·lo·gism /síllə jĭzzəm/ *n* **1** a logical argument involving three propositions **2** deductive reasoning

sylph /sĭlf/ *n* **1** a slim and graceful girl or woman **2** an imaginary female being inhabiting the air —**sylph·like** *adj*

syl·van /sílvən/, **sil·van** *adj* (*literary*) **1** of a forest **2** wooded

sym·bi·o·sis /sìm bī óssiss, -bee-/ (*pl* **-ses** /-séez/) *n* **1** a close association of animals or plants that is usually mutually beneficial **2** any mutually beneficial relationship —**sym·bi·ot·ic** /sìm bī óttik, sìmbee-/ *adj* —**sym·bi·ot·i·cal** *adj* —**sym·bi·ot·i·cal·ly** *adv*

~~symble~~ incorrect spelling of **symbol**

sym·bol /símb'l/ *n* **1** something that represents something else **2** a sign with a specific meaning ◊ See note at **cymbal**

sym·bol·ic /sim bóllik/, **sym·bol·i·cal** /-ik'l/ *adj* **1** of or using symbols **2** representing something else —**sym·bol·i·cal·ly** *adv*

⚡ **sym·bol·ic lan·guage** *n* **1** an artificial language that uses symbols extensively **2** a computer programming language that uses symbols

sym·bol·ism /símbə lĭzzəm/ *n* **1** the use of symbols **2** a system of symbols **3** symbolic meaning —**sym·bol·ist** *n, adj*

sym·bol·ize /símbə līz/ (**-ized, -iz·ing**) *vt* **1** be a symbol of **2** represent by means of a symbol —**sym·bol·i·za·tion** /sìmbəli záysh'n/ *n*

~~symetrical~~ incorrect spelling of **symmetrical**

~~symetry~~ incorrect spelling of **symmetry**

sym·met·ri·cal /si méttrik'l/, **sym·met·ric** /-méttrik/ *adj* **1** exhibiting symmetry **2** equally or evenly balanced **3** describes body parts that have the same function but are situated on opposite sides of an organ or the body —**sym·met·ri·cal·ly** *adv*

sym·me·try /símmətree/ (*pl* **-tries**) *n* **1** the property of sameness on both sides of a dividing line **2** the beauty that derives from balanced proportions

sym·pa·thet·ic /sìmpə théttik/ *adj* **1** feeling or showing sympathy **2** showing agreement or approval **3** provoking sympathy

4 suited to something —**sym·pa·thet·i·cal·ly** adv

sym·pa·thize /símpə thìz/ (-**thized**, -**thiz·ing**) vi 1 feel or show sympathy 2 be of the same opinion —**sym·pa·thiz·er** n

sym·pa·thy /símpəthee/ (pl -**thies**) n 1 the capacity to understand and share somebody else's feelings 2 sorrow for another person's pain or trouble 3 the inclination to think or feel the same as somebody else 4 agreement or harmony o *a plan in sympathy with our wishes* 5 allegiance or loyalty (often pl) o *party sympathies*

sym·pa·thy strike n a labor strike to support other strikers

sym·pho·ny /símfənee/ (pl -**nies**) n 1 a complex musical composition 2 a symphony orchestra 3 a harmonious composition or arrangement —**sym·phon·ic** /sim fónnik/ adj —**sym·phon·i·cal·ly** adv

sym·pho·ny or·ches·tra n a large orchestra that includes wind, string, and percussion instruments

sym·po·si·um /sim pózee əm/ (pl -**ums** or -a /-zee ə/) n 1 a formal meeting for the discussion of a subject 2 a published collection of opinions —**sym·po·si·ac** adj

---

ORIGIN A **symposium** was originally a convivial affair with drinking. The word is ultimately formed from Greek *sym-* "together" and *potēs* "drinker." When first adopted into English from Latin in the late 16C, it especially applied to meetings held in ancient Greece for drinking and conversation. The modern, drier sense of "formal meeting for discussion" emerged in the late 18C.

---

symp·tom /símptəm/ n 1 an indication of illness felt by a patient 2 a sign of something to come o *early symptoms of a recession*

symp·to·mat·ic /símptə máttik/ adj 1 indicating illness 2 typical or indicative of something —**symp·to·mat·i·cal·ly** adv

syn·a·gogue /sínnə gòg/ n 1 a place of worship for a Jewish congregation 2 a Jewish congregation —**syn·a·gog·al** /sìnnə gógg'l/ adj

sync /singk/, **synch** n synchronization (infml) ◊ See note at **sink**

syn·chro·mesh /síngkrō mèsh/ n a gear system with synchronized parts —**syn·chro·mesh** adj

syn·chron·ic /sin krónnik/ adj studying something at a point in time rather than over its history —**syn·chron·i·cal·ly** adv

syn·chro·nic·i·ty /sìngkrə níssətee/ n the coincidence of events that seem related

syn·chro·nize /síngkrə nìz/ (-**nized**, -**niz·ing**) v 1 vi happen together 2 vi go or work together or in unison 3 vt make things happen or work at the same time or rate 4 vt align the sound with the image of a movie —**syn·chro·ni·za·tion** /sìngkrəni záysh'n/ n

syn·chro·nized swim·ming n stylized group swimming in which swimmers perform choreographed movements

syn·chro·nous /síngkrənəss/ adj 1 occurring simultaneously 2 working at the same rate —**syn·chro·nous·ly** adv —**syn·chro·ny** n

syn·co·pa·tion /síngkə páysh'n/ n the modifying of a musical rhythm by placing the accent on a weak beat —**syn·co·pa·te** /síngkə pàyt/ vti —**syn·co·pa·ted** adj

~~**syncronous**~~ incorrect spelling of **synchronous**

syn·di·cal·ism /síndikə lìzzəm/ n 1 a revolutionary political doctrine that advocates workers' seizure of the means of production 2 a system of government in which unionized workers control the means of production —**syn·di·cal·ist** adj, n

syn·di·cate n /síndəkət/ 1 a group of businesses 2 a business that sells news to the media 3 a group of newspapers under a single owner 4 a group of people who combine for a common purpose ■ vt /síndə kàyt/ (-**cat·ed**, -**cat·ing**) 1 sell something for multiple publication 2 sell TV programs to independent stations 3 control something as a syndicate

syn·drome /sín dròm/ n 1 a group of identifying signs and symptoms 2 a set of things that form a pattern

syn·er·gy /sínnərjee/ (pl -**gies**) n the combined effort or action of two or more things, people, or organizations that is greater than the sum of its parts —**syn·er·get·ic** /sìnnər jéttik/ adj —**syn·er·gic** /si núrjik/ adj

J. M. Synge: Portrait by John B. Yeats

Synge /sing/, **J. M.** (1871–1909) Irish dramatist

syn·od /sínnəd/ n a church council —**syn·od·al** /sínnəd'l, si nódd'l/ adj

~~**synonim**~~ incorrect spelling of **synonym**

~~**synonomous**~~ incorrect spelling of **synonymous**

syn·o·nym /sínnə nìm/ n a word that means the same as another —**syn·o·nym·i·ty** /sìnnə nímmətee/ n —**syn·on·y·mous** /si nónnəməss/ adj

syn·on·y·my /si nónnəmee/ (pl -**mies**) n 1 equivalence of meaning 2 the study of synonyms 3 an annotated list of synonyms

syn·op·sis /si nópsiss/ (pl -**ses** /-sèez/) n 1 a summary of a text 2 a summary of a subject

syn·tac·tic /sin táktik/, **syn·tac·ti·cal** /-ik'l/ adj 1 of syntax 2 conforming to the rules of syntax —**syn·tac·ti·cal·ly** adv

syn·tax /sín tàks/ *n* **1** the organization of words in sentences **2** the branch of grammar that deals with syntax **3** the rules of syntax **4** the rules governing the structure of computer programs

syn·the·sis /sínthǝssiss/ (*pl* **-ses** /-seèz/) *n* **1** a unified whole resulting from the combining of different elements **2** the combining of different elements into a new whole *(fml)* **3** the formation of compounds through one or more chemical reactions involving simpler substances **4** the producing of sound with a synthesizer —**syn·the·sist** *n*

syn·the·size /sínthǝ sìz/ (**-sized, -siz·ing**) *v* **1** *vti* combine different elements into a new whole, or be combined in this way **2** *vt* produce a substance or material by chemical or biological synthesis —**syn·the·si·za·tion** /sìnthǝssí záysh'n/ *n*

syn·the·siz·er /sínthǝ sìzǝr/ *n* an electronic musical instrument with a keyboard

syn·thes·pi·an /sin théspee ǝn/ *n* **1** a computer simulation of a well-known actor **2** an actor used in animation

syn·thet·ic /sin théttik/ *adj* **1** made artificially by chemical synthesis, especially so as to resemble a natural product **2** insincere ■ *n* a chemically produced substance or material —**syn·thet·i·cal** *adj* —**syn·thet·i·cal·ly** *adv*

syph·i·lis /síffǝliss/ *n* a sexually transmitted disease that affects many parts of the body —**syph·i·lit·ic** /sìffǝ líttik/ *adj*

sy·phon *n, vt* = **siphon**

Syr·a·cuse /sírrǝ kyòoss/ city in central New York. Pop. 152,215 (1998).

Sy·ria /sírree ǝ/ country in SW Asia. Cap. Damascus. Pop. 16,728,808 (2001). —**Syr·i·an** *n, adj*

sy·ringe /si rínj/ *n* **1** an instrument for injecting or withdrawing fluids **2** a device for pumping and spraying fluids ■ *vt* (**-ringed, -ring·ing**) use a syringe on

syr·up /sírrǝp/, **sir·up** *n* **1** a sweet liquid consisting of sugar dissolved in water **2** a thick flavored sweet liquid **3** medicine in the form of a thick liquid **4** maple syrup —**syr·up·y** *adj*

ORIGIN Syrup goes back to an Arabic verb meaning "drink," from which *sherbet* also derives. Since many Arabic drinks are sweetened, the words tended to be adopted into Western languages with the association "sweet drink."

---

sys·tem /sístǝm/ *n* **1** a number of parts organized into a complex whole **2** a set of principles **3** a way of proceeding **4** a transport network **5** a set of organs or structures in the body that have a common function **6** the whole human body **7** an assembly of components **8** a set of computer hardware, software, and peripherals functioning together **9** the state of being orderly **10** a group of astronomical objects **11** the established order in society ◇ **game the system** manipulate and take unfair advantage of loopholes in rules and regulations to engage in risky, typically illegal, schemes *(slang)*

sys·tem·at·ic /sìstǝ máttik/, **sys·tem·at·i·cal** /-ik'l/ *adj* **1** done methodically **2** well organized **3** of, constituting, or based on a system —**sys·tem·at·i·cal·ly** *adv*

sys·tem·a·tize /sístǝmǝ tìz/ (**-tized, -tiz·ing**), **sys·tem·ize** /sístǝ mìz/ *vti* make or become systematic —**sys·tem·a·ti·za·tion** /sìstǝmǝti záysh'n/ *n* —**sys·tem·a·tiz·er** *n*

sys·tem·ic /si stémmik/ *adj* **1** of a system or affecting all elements in a system **2** affecting the whole body **3** affecting all the tissues of a plant o *a systemic herbicide* —**sys·tem·i·cal·ly** *adv*

sys·tem op·er·a·tor *n* the operator of an electronic bulletin board

sys·tems a·nal·y·sis *n* analysis of an organization's data-processing requirements —**sys·tems an·a·lyst** *n*

Szcze·cin /shché chin/ capital of Szczecin Province, NW Poland. Pop. 419,000 (1997).

Sze·chwan = **Sichuan**

T

t¹ (*pl* **t's**), **T** (*pl* **T's** *or* **Ts**) *n* the 20th letter of the English alphabet ◇ **to a T** exactly

t² *symbol* **1** time **2** troy

T *symbol* **1** absolute temperature **2** kinetic energy **3** period **4** surface tension **5** temperature **6** tritium

t. *abbr* **1** tare **2** teaspoon **3** tense **4** transitive

T. *abbr* tablespoon

T1 line, T-1 line *n* a dedicated Internet phone line

Ta *symbol* tantalum

tab¹ *n* **1** an attachment for holding, lifting, or opening something **2** a check in a bar or restaurant *(infml)* **3** a tag or label ◇ **keep tabs on** keep a close watch on *(infml)*

tab² *n* a key on a computer keyboard that moves the cursor several spaces or from one field to the next

tab·ard /tábbǝrd/ *n* a sleeveless tunic

tab·by /tábbee/ *n* (*pl* **-bies**) **1** a striped cat **2** a pet female cat **3** silk with a striped or wavy pattern ■ *adj* striped or brindled

---

ORIGIN The fabric **tabby** is ultimately named for a quarter in Baghdad, where it was made. It was originally striped, and this feature led to its application to **tabby** cats. The name for the fabric entered English through Arabic and

---

French in the late 16C. The first recorded use of "**tabby cat**" occurs a century later.

tab·er·na·cle /tábbər nàk'l/ *n* **1** *also* **Tab·er·na·cle** a portable tent used by the Israelites as a sanctuary for the Ark of the Covenant **2** an evangelical place of worship **3** a container for holy bread and wine —**tab·er·nac·u·lar** /tábbər nákyələr/ *adj*

tab·la /taáblə/ *n* a South Asian percussion instrument

ta·ble /táyb'l/ *n* **1** an item of furniture with legs and a flat top on which to put things **2** a flat surface used for working on **3** the quality or quantity of food served **4** the people eating at a table **5** an arrangement of information in columns or a condensed list **6** a slab on which an inscription is engraved ■ *vt* (**-bled, -bling**) postpone discussion of something ◊ **on the table** presented for discussion at a meeting ◊ **turn the tables (on)** gain the advantage from somebody who previously held it

tab·leau /tá blò, ta blô/ (*pl* **-leaux** /-lòz/ *or* **-leaus**) *n* **1** a picturesque display **2** any striking visual scene **3** *also* **tab·leau vi·vant** /-vee vaàN/ a group of costumed people posing silent and motionless to recreate a famous scene

ta·ble·cloth /táyb'l klàwth/ *n* a cloth cover for a dining table

ta·ble d'hôte /taàb'l dòt, taàblə-/ *n* a fixed-price meal from a limited menu

ta·ble·land /táyb'l lànd/ *n* an elevated flat region

ta·ble·spoon /táyb'l spoòn/ *n* **1** a serving spoon **2** *also* **ta·ble·spoon·ful** a measure based on the capacity of a tablespoon

tab·let /tábblət/ *n* **1** a compressed powdered drug to be swallowed **2** a small flat cake of a substance such as soap **3** an inscribed stone or wooden slab **4** a number of sheets of paper fastened together

ta·ble ten·nis *n* a game similar to tennis played with small paddles and light hollow balls on a table

ta·ble·ware /táyb'l wàir/ *n* plates, glasses, and other items used at meals

ta·ble wine *n* inexpensive wine served with everyday meals

tab·loid /táb lòyd/, **tab·loid news·pa·per** *n* a small-format popular newspaper with short, often sensationalist articles ■ *adj* sensationalist

ORIGIN Tabloid was registered as a proprietary name for a brand of tablet in 1884 by Burroughs, Wellcome, and Company. It was the underlying notion of "compression" or "condensation" that led to its application to newspapers of small page size and "condensed" versions of news stories, which emerged at the beginning of the 20C.

ta·boo /tə boò/ *adj* **1** socially or culturally forbidden **2** sacred and prohibited ■ *n* (*pl*

-boos *or* **-bus**) **1** a social or cultural prohibition **2** a subject or type of behavior that is forbidden or deeply disapproved of **3** prohibition on the grounds of being sacred —**ta·boo** *vt*

tab·u·lar /tábbyələr/ *adj* **1** arranged in a table **2** having a flat surface **3** broad and flat —**tab·u·lar·ly** *adv*

tab·u·la ra·sa /tábbyələ raássə, -raázə/ (*pl* **tab·u·lae ra·sae** /-raássee, -raázee/) *n* **1** the supposed state of the mind prior to experiences **2** a chance to start afresh

tab·u·late /tábbyoo làyt/ (**-lat·ed, -lat·ing**) *vt* **1** arrange information in a table **2** make something flat —**tab·u·la·tion** /tàbbyə láysh'n/ *n*

tab·u·la·tor /tábbyə láytər/ *n* **1** somebody or something that tabulates data **2** a tab key on a computer keyboard, or a similar device on a typewriter

tach·o·graph /táko gràf/ *n* a device in a commercial vehicle that records speeds and distances traveled

ta·chom·e·ter /ta kómmətər/ *n* a device in a motor vehicle for measuring rotation speed —**tach·o·met·ric** *adj* —**ta·chom·e·try** /ta kómmətree/ *n*

tac·it /tássit/ *adj* implied but not expressed —**tac·it·ly** *adv* —**tac·it·ness** *n*

tac·i·turn /tássi tùrn/ *adj* uncommunicative —**tac·i·tur·ni·ty** /tàssi túrnətee/ *n* —**tac·i·turn·ly** *adv* ◊ See note at **silent**

Tac·i·tus /tássitəss/ (AD 55?–117?) Roman historian

tack[1] *n* **1** a small sharp broad-headed nail **2** a thumbtack **3** a course of action or method of approach **4** a loose temporary stitch ■ *v* **1** *vt* fasten something with or as if with a tack or tacks **2** *vt* sew something loosely and temporarily **3** *vti* change the direction of a sailing vessel so that the wind is blowing on the opposite side —**tack·er** *n* □ **tack on** *vt* add as an extra

tack[2] *n* saddles, bridles, and harnesses

tack·le /ták'l/ *n* **1** in some ball games, an attempt to stop an opposing player's progress **2** equipment for a particular activity **3** ropes and pulleys used for lifting ■ *vt* (**-led, -ling**) **1** deal with something difficult **2** confront somebody **3** make a tackle on an opposing player

tack·y[1] /tákee/ (**-i·er, -i·est**) *adj* slightly sticky —**tack·i·ly** *adv* —**tack·i·ness** *n*

tack·y[2] /tákee/ (**-i·er, -i·est**) *adj* in bad taste —**tack·i·ly** *adv* —**tack·i·ness** *n*

ta·co /taákō/ (*pl* **-cos**) *n* a filled crisp tortilla shell

Ta·co·ma /tə kōmə/ city in W Washington State. Pop. 179,814 (1998).

tact *n* **1** the ability to avoid giving offense **2** discretion —**tact·ful** *adj* —**tact·ful·ly** *adv* —**tact·ful·ness** *n* —**tact·less** *adj* —**tact·less·ly** *adv* —**tact·less·ness** *n*

tac·tic /táktik/ *n* a means to achieve a goal

tac·ti·cal /táktik'l/ *adj* 1 of tactics 2 done or used to support a military objective 3 serving as a means to an end 4 showing skilled planning —**tac·ti·cal·ly** *adv*

tac·tics /táktiks/ *n* (+ *sing verb*) 1 the science of directing forces in battle to achieve an objective 2 the art of finding and implementing means to achieve immediate aims —**tac·ti·cian** /tak tíshʹn/ *n*

tac·tile /tákt'l, ták tíl/ *adj* 1 of the sense of touch 2 tangible —**tac·tile·ly** *adv* —**tac·til·i·ty** /tak tíllǝtee/ *n*

tad *n* a small amount (*infml*) ◇ **a tad** somewhat (*infml*)

tad·pole /tád pōl/ *n* a frog or toad larva

Ta·dzhik·i·stan ▸ Tajikistan

tae kwon do /tī kwon dố/ *n* a Korean martial art including kicking moves

taf·fe·ta /táffǝtǝ/ *n* a stiff shiny silk or similar fabric. Use: women's clothes.

taf·fy /táffee/ *n* a chewy candy made from boiled sugar

Taft, William Howard (1857–1930) 27th president of the United States (1909–13) and chief justice of the US Supreme Court (1921–30)

⚡**tag**[1] *n* 1 a label 2 a classifying label for a piece of data to facilitate retrieval 3 a plastic or metal tip at the end of a shoelace 4 an electronic monitoring device 5 a descriptive word or phrase used about somebody or something 6 *also* **tag ques·tion** a short added clause turning a statement into a question 7 a graffiti artist's signature ■ *v* (**tagged, tag·ging**) 1 *vt* label something with a tag 2 *vt* add something on at the end 3 *vt* give somebody a nickname 4 *vt* attach an electronic monitoring tag to an offender 5 *vti* follow somebody closely

tag[2] *n* 1 a children's chasing game 2 in baseball, an instance of tagging a runner ■ *vt* (**tagged, tag·ging**) 1 catch and touch a player in a game of tag 2 in baseball, put a runner out by touching the runner with the ball

tag·a·long /tággǝ làwng/ *n* a follower

tag·li·a·tel·le /tàllyǝ téllǝ/ *n* pasta in long narrow ribbons

tag line *n* 1 a punch line 2 a slogan

Popperfoto

Rabindranath Tagore

Ta·gore /tǝ gáwr/, **Rabindranath** (1861–1941) Indian writer

Ta·gus /táygǝss/ river flowing through central Spain and central Portugal to the Atlantic Ocean. Length 626 mi./1,007 km. Portuguese **Tejo**. Spanish **Tajo**

ta·hi·ni /tǝ heénee/, **ta·hi·na** /-nǝ/ *n* a paste made from crushed sesame seeds. Use: seasoning.

Ta·hi·ti /tǝ heétee/ island of French Polynesia, in the S Pacific Ocean. Pop. 115,820 (1998). —**Ta·hi·tian** /tǝ heésh'n/ *n, adj*

Ta·hoe, Lake /táǝhō/ lake in the W United States, on the border of Nevada and California

tai chi /tī cheé/, **tai chi chuan** /-chwaʹan/ *n* a Chinese system of exercise characterized by very slow and deliberate balletic body movements

tail /tayl/ *n* 1 the rearmost part of an animal's body, or the movable extension to it 2 the rear, last, or lowest part of something 3 the rearmost part of an aircraft, missile, or bomb 4 the luminous stream of gas behind a comet ■ **tails** *npl* 1 a tail coat 2 a man's formal evening clothes 3 the reverse of a coin ■ *vt* follow secretly (*infml*) —**tail·less** *adj* ◇ **turn tail** run away

SPELLCHECK Do not confuse the spelling of **tail** and **tale** ("a factual or fictional narrative"), which sound similar.

tail-coat /táyl kōt/ *n* a man's formal short-fronted coat with two long tapering parts at the back

tail end *n* the last or rear part of something

tail·gate /táyl gàyt/ *n* a gate at the back of a truck that drops down for loading or unloading ■ *vti* (-**gat·ed, -gat·ing**) drive close behind another vehicle —**tail·gat·er** *n*

tail·light /táyl lìt/ *n* a red light at the rear of a motor vehicle

tai·lor /táylǝr/ *n* a maker of clothes ■ *v* 1 *vti* make clothes 2 *vt* adapt something to a particular purpose

tai·lored /táylǝrd/ *adj* 1 made to fit neatly 2 made for a particular purpose

tai·lor-made *adj* 1 ideal for somebody or something 2 made by a tailor

tail·piece /táyl pèess/ *n* 1 something forming an end or added at the end 2 a decoration at the bottom of a page

tail·pipe /táyl pìp/ *n* a pipe letting out the exhaust gases from an engine

tail·plane /táyl plàyn/ *n* the horizontal part of an aircraft tail

tail·spin /táyl spìn/ *n* a rapid spiral descent by an aircraft

tail·wind /táyl wìnd/ *n* a wind blowing in the direction in which something is traveling

taint /taynt/ *vt* 1 pollute 2 corrupt morally ■ *n* 1 an imperfection detracting from the quality of something 2 something that pollutes

Tai·pei /tì páy, -báy/, **T'ai·pei** capital and largest city of Taiwan. Pop. 2,639,939 (1999).

Tai·wan /tì waàn/ island country of Southeast Asia, administered independently since 1949 by the Chinese Nationalist government. It is claimed as a province by the People's Republic of China. Cap. Taipei. Pop. 22,370,461 (2001). —**Tai·wan·ese** /tì waa neèz/ n, adj

Tai·yu·an /tì ywán, tì yoo án/ capital of **Shanxi Province**, east central China. Pop. 2,100,000 (1995).

Ta·jik·i·stan /taa jíki stàn, -staàn/, **Ta·dzhik·i·stan** country in SE Central Asia. Cap. Dushanbe. Pop. 6,578,681 (2001).

ta·ka /taáka/ n the main unit of Bangladeshi currency

Ta·kak·kaw Falls /táka kaw-/ highest falls in Canada, in SE British Columbia. Height 1,650 ft./503 m.

take /tayk/ v (**took** /töok/, **tak·en** /táykan/, **tak·ing**) 1 vt remove or steal something belonging to somebody else 2 vt get hold of somebody or something 3 vt convey somebody or something somewhere 4 vt capture or win something o took the city 5 vt perform or do something 6 vt get into or onto something o Please take a seat. 7 vt claim or assume something such as credit, glory, or blame 8 vt enable somebody to go somewhere, or go along a course leading somewhere o Will this road take us to the beach? o Take the first road on the left. 9 vt agree to perform or assume the duties associated with something o has decided to take the job 10 vt be willing to accept something o wouldn't take my credit card 11 vt be able to bear something o can't take criticism 12 vt react to something o took the news badly 13 vt travel by a particular means 14 vt be able to contain a particular amount 15 vt write something o took notes 16 vt make a photograph 17 vt study something o taking Spanish 18 vt start to perform or occupy something o took office last month 19 vt carry something out o take action 20 vt consider or discuss something o Let's take your last point first. 21 vt require a particular thing o took courage to speak out 22 vt experience an emotion or have a particular view o taking pity on us 23 vt interpret or understand somebody or something in a particular way o took that to mean he agreed 24 vt consume or ingest something o take medicine 25 vi work or be successful o The perm didn't take. 26 vt measure something with a device or procedure o took his temperature 27 vi become ill o took sick 28 vt subtract a number from something 29 vt assume charge of something ■ n 1 money obtained in business transactions (infml) 2 an uninterrupted recording by a camera or sound equipment 3 a personal impression (infml) o her take on his presentation

—**tak·er** n ◊ **on the take** taking or willing to take bribes (infml) ◊ **take it** 1 be able to tolerate a difficult situation 2 assume that something is true ◊ **take it or leave it** either accept a thing the way it is or refuse it (usually spoken)

☐ **take after** vt resemble

☐ **take back** vt withdraw something said or written

☐ **take for** vt believe somebody to be, often mistakenly o took you for your sister

☐ **take in** vt 1 include something 2 go and see a performance or sports event 3 understand and remember something

☐ **take off** v 1 vi begin flying 2 vt remove a garment 3 vi jump o took off from the diving board

☐ **take out** vt 1 take somebody as a companion to a social event 2 remove something

☐ **take over** vti take control of something from somebody else

☐ **take to** vt 1 form a liking for somebody or something 2 start doing something habitually

☐ **take up** vt begin doing something regularly as an occupation or hobby

take·a·way /táyk ə wày/, **take·a·way** n in football, an interception or recovered fumble that gives the defensive team possession of the ball

take-home pay n pay left after deductions

take-off /táyk àwf, -òf/ n 1 the process of leaving the ground at the beginning of a flight 2 a point of rapid growth 3 the beginning of a jump

take-out /táyk òwt/ adj 1 prepared for eating elsewhere 2 selling takeout food ■ n 1 prepared food bought for eating elsewhere 2 a store selling food for eating elsewhere

take-o·ver /táyk òvər/ n the act of assuming control of something, especially a business

take-up n 1 the part of a mechanism onto which something passing through it is wound 2 the level of acceptance of an offer

ta·la /taála/ (pl same or -las) n the main unit of Samoan currency

talc /talk/ n 1 a soft mineral consisting of hydrated magnesium silicate 2 also **tal·cum pow·der** a powder for the skin made from talc

tale /tayl/ n 1 a narrative or account of events 2 a short piece of fiction 3 an untrue story or report ◊ See note at **tail**

tal·ent /tállənt/ n 1 a natural ability to do something well 2 a person or people with an exceptional ability 3 an ancient unit of weight and money —**tal·ent·ed** adj

---

SYNONYMS talent, gift, aptitude, flair, bent, knack, genius CORE MEANING: the natural ability to do something well

tal·ent scout *n* a discoverer and recruiter of talented people

tal·ent show *n* a performance by amateur entertainers competing for a prize

Tal·i·ban /táali bàan/ *npl* a strict Islamic group that controlled Afghanistan from 1996 to 2001

tal·is·man /tállissmən, tálliz-/ *n* **1** an object believed to give protection, magical powers, or good fortune to somebody carrying or wearing it **2** something believed to have magical power —**tal·is·man·ic** /tàlliss mánnik, tàlliz-/ *adj*

> **ORIGIN** Talisman is not a compound of *man* (and so forms its plural as *-mans* not *-men*). It was adopted in the mid-17C from French or Spanish, and appears to be ultimately from Greek.

talk /tawk/ *v* **1** *vti* speak or express something by speaking **2** *vi* have a conversation ○ *talked for an hour* **3** *vti* discuss a subject ○ *talk business* **4** *vi* communicate or negotiate **5** *vti* speak a language ○ *talks Italian* **6** *vi* reveal information when interrogated **7** *vi* gossip **8** *vt* persuade somebody ○ *talked her out of going* ■ *n* **1** a conversation **2** the things said in a conversation **3** a speech or lecture **4** gossip **5** empty speech ○ *He's all talk.* **6** a subject of discussion or gossip ○ *the talk of the town* ■ **talks** *npl* negotiations ■ *adj* made up of informal interviews or telephone calls ○ *the talk broadcast culture* —**talk·er** *n*

□ **talk back** *vi* reply impudently

□ **talk over** *vt* discuss

talk·a·tive /táwkətiv/ *adj* inclined to talk readily and at length —**talk·a·tive·ness** *n*

> **SYNONYMS** talkative, chatty, gossipy, garrulous, loquacious CORE MEANING: talking a lot

talk·fest /táwk fèst/ *n* a long period of talking

talk·ing book *n* a book recorded on an audio cassette

talk·ing point *n* an item for discussion

talk·ing-to *n* a scolding *(infml)*

talk ra·di·o *n* a broadcast format involving interviews, discussions, and telephone call-ins

talk show *n* a television or radio show with a discussion or interview format

tall /tawl/ *adj* **1** reaching or having grown to a considerable or above-average height **2** having grown to a particular height ○ *five feet tall* **3** substantial, demanding, or difficult ○ *a tall order* **4** improbable or exaggerated ○ *a tall story* ■ *adv* proudly ○ *walking tall* —**tall·ish** *adj* —**tall·ness** *n*

Tal·la·has·see /tàllə hássee/ capital of Florida. Pop. 136,628 (1998).

Tal·ley·rand /tállee rànd/, **Charles Maurice de** (1754–1838) French politician and diplomat

Tal·linn /tállin, taálin/ capital of Estonia. Pop. 420,470 (1997).

tal·lith /táalith, taa leét/ *(pl -lith·im* /táalə theém/ *or -liths)* *n* a Jewish prayer shawl

tal·low /tálló/ *n* a fatty substance extracted from the fat of sheep or cattle. Use: candles, soap. —**tal·low·y** *adj*

tall ship *n* a square-rigged sailing ship

tal·ly /tállee/ *v (-lied, -lies)* **1** *vti* agree, correspond, or come to the same amount, or cause to do so **2** *vti* make a score in a contest **3** *vt* count up ○ *tally a score* ■ *n (pl -lies)* **1** a record of items ○ *kept a tally of what I had bought* **2** the score achieved by somebody

Tal·mud /táal mŏod, tálməd/ *n* the collection of ancient Jewish writings used as the basis for Jewish law —**Tal·mu·dic** /taal mŏodik, tal-/ *adj* —**Tal·mu·di·cal** *adj* —**Tal·mud·ist** *n*

tal·on /tállən/ *n* **1** a hooked claw of a bird of prey **2** something resembling a claw —**tal·oned** *adj*

ta·ma·le /tə maálee/ *n* a Mexican dish of meat and peppers rolled in cornmeal dough and wrapped in corn husks

tam·a·rack /támmə ràk/ *n* **1** the wood of a North American larch **2** a larch that produces tamarack

ta·ma·ri /tə maáree/ *n* a rich Japanese soy sauce

tam·a·rind /támmərind/ *n* **1** a pod containing many seeds in an acidic pulp. Use: preserves, drinks, medicines. **2** a tree that produces tamarinds

tam·a·risk /támmərisk/ *n* a tree with leaves resembling scales

tam·bou·ra /tam bŏorə/ *n* an Asian stringed instrument resembling a lute

tam·bou·rine /tàmbə reén/ *n* a circular lid-shaped percussion instrument with jingling metallic discs —**tam·bou·rin·ist** *n*

tame *adj* **(tam·er, tam·est)** **1** no longer wild **2** describes an animal that is unafraid of human contact **3** bland ○ *a tame rendition of the anthem* ■ *vt* **(tamed, tam·ing)** **1** domesticate a wild animal or make land cultivable **2** bring somebody or something under control **3** moderate something —**tam·a·ble** *adj* —**tame·ly** *adv* —**tame·ness** *n* —**tam·er** *n*

Tam·er·lane /támmər làyn/, **Tam·bur·laine** /támbər-/ (1336–1405) Turkic ruler and conqueror

Tam·il /támm'l, taám'l/ *(pl -ils or same)* *n* **1** a member of a people who live in S India and N Sri Lanka **2** the language of the Tamil people —**Tam·il** *adj*

Tam·ma·ny Hall /támmənee-/ *n* a corrupt political organization —**Tam·ma·ny·ism** *n* —**Tam·ma·ny·ite** *n*

Tam·muz /taá mŏoz, taa mŏoz/ *n* the 4th month of the year in the Jewish calendar

tam-o'-shan·ter /tàmmə shántər/ *n* a brimless

Scottish woolen hat with a pom-pom in the center

tamp *vt* **1** pack something down by tapping **2** pack sand or earth into a drill hole above an explosive

Tam·pa /támpə/ seaport in west central Florida, on **Tampa Bay**, an arm of the Gulf of Mexico. Pop. 289,156 (1998).

tam·per /támpər/ *vi* **1** interfere with something in a way that causes harm or damage **2** influence a person or process corruptly ◇ *tampering with the jury*

Tam·pi·co /tam peekó/ seaport in E Mexico. Pop. 278,933 (1995).

tam·pon /tám pòn/ *n* **1** a plug of soft material used during menstruation **2** an absorbent pad used to control bleeding, especially during surgery

tan[1] *n* **1** a suntan **2** a light brown color ■ *v* **(tanned, tan·ning) 1** *vti* get or give a suntan **2** *vt* convert hide to leather **3** *vt* give a beating to (*infml*) ■ *adj* (**tan·ner, tan·nest**) **1** of a light brown color **2** sun-bronzed

tan[2] *abbr* tangent

tan·a·ger /tánnəjər/ *n* a small brightly colored songbird with a conical bill

Ta·nan·a·rive /tə nànnə reév, taa nàanə reév/ former name for **Antananarivo**

tan·dem /tándəm/ *n* **1** a bicycle for two riders, one behind the other **2** a team of two horses harnessed one behind the other, or a carriage drawn by such a team ■ *adv* with one behind the other ◇ **in tandem 1** in partnership or cooperation **2** with one behind the other

tan·door·i /tan doóree/ *adj* cooked in a clay oven after marination in yogurt and spices

Ta·ney /táwnee/, **Roger** (1777–1864) chief justice of the US Supreme Court (1836–64)

tang *n* **1** a strong sharp taste or smell **2** a slight suggestion of something ◇ *a tang of lemon* —**tang·y** *adj*

~~tangable~~ incorrect spelling of **tangible**

Tan·gan·yi·ka /tàng gən yeéka/ former country in East Africa, constituting the mainland part of what is now Tanzania —**Tan·gan·yi·kan** *n, adj*

Tan·gan·yi·ka, Lake lake in east central Africa, with shorelines in Burundi, Tanzania, Zambia, and the Democratic Republic of the Congo. Length 420 mi./680 km.

tan·ge·lo /tánjə lò/ (*pl* **-los**) *n* **1** a citrus fruit with smooth skin and orange flesh **2** a hybrid between a tangerine tree and a grapefruit tree that produces tangelos

tan·gent /tánjənt/ *n* **1** a line, curve, or surface that touches another but does not cross or intersect it **2** for a given angle in a right triangle, a trigonometric function equal to the length of the side opposite the angle divided by the length of the adjacent side ■ *adj* **1** *also* **tan·gen·tial** /tan jénshəl/ straying

away from the current subject **2** *also* **tan·gen·tial** of a tangent **3** touching but not crossing or intersecting —**tan·gen·cy** *n* —**tan·gen·tial·ly** *adv* ◇ **go off at** *or* **on a tangent** change to a different subject or line of thought

tan·ger·ine /tànjə reén, tánjə rèen/ *n* **1** a small orange citrus fruit **2** a tree that produces tangerines **3** a bright orange color —**tan·ger·ine** *adj*

ORIGIN The fruit is named for Tangier in Morocco, from where it was exported to Britain in the 1840s. The color name dates from the late 19C.

tan·gi·ble /tánjəb'l/ *adj* **1** able to be touched **2** actual or real ■ *n* something with a physical form, especially a financial asset (*often pl*) —**tan·gi·bil·i·ty** /tànjə bíllətee/ *n*

Tan·gier /tan jeér/ city in N Morocco. Pop. 526,215 (1994).

tan·gle /táng g'l/ (**-gled, -gling**) *v* **1** *vti* make or become twisted into a jumbled mass **2** *vt* catch and entwine **3** *vi* become involved in a conflict or disagreement with somebody ◇ *Don't tangle with those people.* —**tan·gle** *n* —**tan·gle·ment** *n*

tan·go /táng gò/ (*pl* **tan·gos**) *n* **1** a Latin American ballroom dance with gliding steps and sudden pauses **2** the music for a tango **3 Tan·go** a communications code word for the letter "T" —**tan·go** *vi* —**tan·go·ist** *n*

Tang·shan /táang shàan/ city in NE China. Pop. 1,540,000 (1995).

tank *n* **1** a large container for liquids or gases **2** the amount held by a tank **3** a large armored combat vehicle with tracks, a rotating turret, and a heavy gun **4** *also* **tank top** a close-fitting sleeveless shirt ■ *vi* decline sharply or fail (*slang*) —**tank·ful** *n*

ORIGIN Tank "container for liquids" originated in a South Asian word for "pond, cistern" and was first used in English in the early 17C. It was a code name for an armored vehicle used for secrecy during its development in 1915, supposedly because the new machine resembled a tank for benzene.

tank·ard /tángkərd/ *n* a big beer mug

tanked, tanked-up *adj* very drunk (*slang*)

tank·er /tángkər/ *n* a ship, truck, or aircraft transporting large quantities of liquid or gas

tank farm *n* a group of fuel storage tanks located together

tank suit *n* a swimsuit

tan·ner /tánnər/ *n* somebody who tans hides

tan·ner·y /tánnəree/ (*pl* **-ies**) *n* a place for tanning hides

tan·nin /tánnin/ *n* a brownish or yellowish plant compound. Use: tanning, dyes, astringents.

tan·ning /tánning/ *n* **1** the conversion of animal skin into leather **2** the browning of skin in sunlight or ultraviolet light **3** a sound thrashing

tan·ning bed /tánzee/ *n* an apparatus for lying on to get a tan

tan·sy /tánzee/ (*pl* -sies) *n* a plant with yellow flowers and divided leaves

tan·ta·lize /tánt'līz/ (-lized, -liz·ing) *vt* tease or torment by showing but not giving something desired —**tan·ta·li·za·tion** /tànt'li záysh'n/ *n* —**tan·ta·liz·ing** *adj* —**tan·ta·liz·ing·ly** *adv*

ORIGIN To **tantalize** a person is to subject him or her to the same torments as Tantalus in Greek mythology.

tan·ta·lum /tánt'ləm/ *n* (*symbol* Ta) a blue-gray metallic element. Use: electronic components, alloys, plates and pins for orthopedic surgery.

Tan·ta·lus /tánt'ləss/ *n* in Greek mythology, a king who was tormented by having fruit and water kept just outside his reach

tan·ta·mount /tántə mòwnt/ *adj* equivalent

tan·trum /tántrəm/ *n* a childish fit of temper

Tan·za·ni·a /tànzə née ə/ country in E Africa. Cap. Dodoma. Pop. 36,232,074 (2001).

Tao /tow, dow/ *n* in Taoist philosophy, the ultimate reality or energy, and a person's relationship to it

Tao·ism /tów īzzəm, dów-/ *n* **1** a Chinese philosophy advocating a simple life and non-interference with the natural course of things **2** a Chinese religion based on Taoism —**Tao·ist** *n*, *adj* —**Tao·is·tic** /tow ístik, dow-/ *adj*

Taos /towz, dowz/ (*pl* same) *n* a member of a Native North American people of the Pueblo group

tap[1] *v* (tapped, tap·ping) **1** *vti* hit somebody or something lightly **2** *vt* hit an object lightly against something else **3** *vt* make a sound by tapping **4** *vt* move making a series of light sounds **5** *vt* select and appoint somebody for a role or job ○ *tapped her as the publicity chair* ■ *n* **1** a light blow **2** the sound of a light blow **3** a metal part on a tap-dancing shoe —**tap·per** *n*

tap[2] *n* **1** a faucet **2** a stopper in a cask or barrel **3** beer from a cask **4** a listening device secretly installed in telecommunications equipment ■ *vt* (tapped, tap·ping) **1** install a secret listening device in telecommunications equipment **2** attach a tap to something **3** draw liquid from something **4** get into a power supply and divert energy from it **5** make an internal screw thread in something ◊ **on tap** available for immediate use (*infml*)

ta·pas /táa pàass/ *npl* Spanish snacks served as appetizers with alcoholic drinks

tap dance *n* a dance performed wearing shoes with metal tips to make a rhythmic sound —**tap-dance** *vi* —**tap danc·er** *n* —**tap-danc·ing** *n*

tape *n* **1** a strip of adhesive material on a roll **2** a video or audio cassette **3** a long narrow strip of material used to secure or tie something **4** *also* **tape re·cord·ing** a recording on magnetic tape **5** magnetic tape **6** a long strip of material marking the finish line in a race ■ *v* (taped, tap·ing) **1** *vti* record on magnetic tape **2** *vt* secure or tie with tape

tape deck *n* an electric device for playing and recording audio tapes

tape meas·ure *n* a calibrated strip for measuring lengths

ta·per /táypər/ *vti* **1** become or make gradually narrower at one end **2** reduce gradually ■ *n* a slim candle narrowing at the top —**ta·per·ing** *adj* —**ta·per·ing·ly** *adv*

tape re·cord·er *n* a machine for recording or playing cassette or reel-to-reel tapes —**tape-re·cord** *vt*

tap·es·try /táppəstree/ (*pl* -tries) *n* **1** a heavy fabric or wall hanging with a woven or embroidered design **2** embroidery resembling tapestry **3** something varied and intricate

tape·worm /táyp wùrm/ *n* a parasitic worm found in the guts of vertebrates

tap·i·o·ca /táppee óka/ *n* a starch obtained from the root of a cassava plant. Use: puddings, thickener for sauces.

ta·pir /táypər/ (*pl* -pirs *or* same) *n* a nocturnal hoofed mammal with a fleshy snout

tap·root /táp ròot/ *n* the large main root of some plants

taps *n* a bugle call given to signal lights out or at a military funeral or memorial service (+ *sing or pl verb*)

tap wa·ter *n* water from a domestic or commercial water supply, as opposed to mineral water or rainwater

ta·que·ri·a /táakə rée ə/ *n* an establishment that prepares and sells Mexican food such as tacos and burritos

tar *n* **1** a thick black liquid distilled from wood or coal **2** the residue from tobacco smoke ■ *vt* (tarred, tar·ring) cover with tar —**tar·ry** *adj*

ta·ra·ma·sa·la·ta /táà raa maa sə láàtə/ *n* a fish roe paste

tar·an·tel·la /tàrrən téllə/ *n* **1** an Italian whirling dance **2** the music for a tarantella

ORIGIN The **tarantella** is ultimately named for Taranto, a town in Italy, which also gave its name to the *tarantula* (since the spider was found near there). Between the 15C and 17C, S Italy saw many cases of a nervous disorder characterized by uncontrollable body movements and popularly attributed to the tarantula's bite. The most effective cure for the condition was thought to be a whirling dance that mimicked its symptoms, which was consequently called the **tarantella**.

ta·ran·tu·la /tə ránchələ/ (*pl* -las *or* -lae /-lee/) *n* **1** a large hairy tropical or subtropical

American spider **2** a European wolf spider

Ta·ra·wa /tə raáwə, tárrə waá/ capital of Kiribata, a W Pacific Ocean island group, retaken in World War II by US Marines from the Japanese in November 1943

Tar·bell /taárbəl/, **Ida** (1857–1944) US journalist

tar·dy /taárdee/ adj (-di-er, -di-est) late ■ n (pl -dies) an instance of being late —**tar·di·ly** adv —**tar·di·ness** n

tare[1] /tair/ n a vetch plant or seed

tare[2] /tair/ n **1** the weight of the packaging on goods, or an allowance made for this **2** a vehicle's unladen weight

tar·get /taárgət/ n **1** a round object marked with concentric circles, aimed at in shooting sports **2** somebody or something aimed at **3** an objective **4** the focus or object of an action ◊ *the target of her anger* ■ vt **1** make the focus or object of something ◊ *a campaign that targets under-35s* **2** aim at or direct toward a person, thing, or place ◊ *missiles targeted on the capital*

⚡**tar·get·cast** /taárgət kàst/ (-cast or -cast·ed) vi broadcast a website to a selected audience

tar·iff /tárrif/ n **1** a duty levied on imported or exported goods **2** a list of tariffs **3** a list of fees, fares, or prices

Tar·king·ton /taárkingtən/, **Booth** (1869–1946) US writer

tar·mac /taár màk/ n surfacing material for roads and runways ■ vt (-macked, -mack·ing) **1** cover with tarmac **2** park an airplane

tarn n a small mountain lake formed by glacier action

tar·nish /taárnish/ v **1** vti become or make dull and discolored from oxidation or rust **2** vt damage somebody's reputation ■ n dullness and discoloration caused by oxidation or rust —**tar·nish·a·ble** adj

ta·ro /taárō, tárrō/ n (pl -ros) a plant with edible starchy tubers

tar·ot /tárrō, tə rṍ/ n **1** a system of fortune-telling with cards **2** also **tar·ot card** a card used for fortune-telling

tarp n a tarpaulin (infml)

tar·pa·per /taár pàypər/ n paper coated with tar. Use: waterproofing.

tar·pau·lin /taar páwlin, taárpəlin/ n **1** a heavy waterproof canvas material. Use: covering. **2** a sheet of tarpaulin

tar·pon /taárpən/ n (pl same or -pons) n an ocean fish with a streamlined body and thick silvery scales

Tar·quin·i·us Su·per·bus /taar kwinnee əss soo púrbəss/, **Lucius** (fl 6C BC) king of Rome (534–510 BC)

tar·ra·gon /tárrə gòn, -gən/ n an herb with aromatic leaves. Use: flavoring food.

~~tarrif~~ incorrect spelling of **tariff**

tar·ry /tárree/ (-ried, -ries) vi **1** remain temporarily **2** linger **3** wait

tar·sus /taársəss/ (pl -si /-sī, -seè/) n the ankle bones of a vertebrate —**tar·sal** adj

tart[1] adj **1** sour or sharp-tasting **2** sharply critical —**tart·ly** adv —**tart·ness** n

tart[2] n a pie without a top crust

tart[3] n an offensive term for a woman prostitute or a woman regarded as sexually provocative (slang insult)

tar·tan /taárt'n/ n a multicolored checked pattern associated with a Scottish clan or regiment, or fabric in this pattern

tar·tar /taártər/ n **1** a hard deposit on teeth **2** a deposit that forms in wine casks —**tar·tar·ous** adj

Tar·tar /taártər/ n a member of the Tatar people —**Tar·tar** adj

tar·tar sauce /taártər-/, **tar·tare sauce** n a cold sauce for fish made from mayonnaise with chopped capers and pickles

Tash·kent /tash ként, tàash-/ capital of Uzbekistan. Pop. 2,282,000 (1995).

task n **1** an assigned job **2** an important or difficult piece of work ■ vt **1** assign a task to ◊ *tasked me with writing the letter* **2** burden with work ◊ **take to task** scold or criticize

⚡**task·bar** /tásk baàr/ n a bar on a computer screen with buttons showing which programs are running

task force n **1** a temporary military group for a mission **2** a temporary group for performing a task

task·mas·ter /tásk màstər/ n **1** somebody who supervises work demandingly **2** a demanding discipline or responsibility

Tas·ma·ni·a /taz máynee ə/ Australian island state off SE Australia. Cap. Hobart. Pop. 471,100 (1998). —**Tas·ma·ni·an** n, adj

Tas·man Sea /tàzmən-/ region of the South Pacific Ocean between Australia and New Zealand

tas·sel /táss'l/ n **1** a bunch of loose threads tied together at one end and used as a decoration **2** a tuft at the top of a corn stem ■ v (-seled or -selled, -sel·ing or -sel·ling) **1** vt decorate with tassels **2** vi produce a tassel (refers to corn)

taste n **1** the sense that perceives flavors through the sensory organs of the tongue **2** the sensation stimulated in the taste buds on contact with food or drink **3** an act of perceiving the flavor of something **4** a small quantity of something eaten or drunk to perceive its taste **5** a brief or first experience of something **6** a liking for something ◊ *a taste for expensive clothes* **7** the ability to make good aesthetic judgments **8** a sense of what is socially acceptable ◊ *a remark in poor taste* ■ v (tast·ed, tast·ing) **1** vt discern the flavor of something with the taste buds **2** vt test something for its flavor **3** vti experience something briefly or for the first time **4** vi have a particular flavor ◊ *tastes fishy* —**tast·a·ble** adj

taste bud *n* one of the sensory receptors on the tongue that is involved in the sense of taste

taste·ful /táystfəl/ *adj* showing good aesthetic taste —**taste·ful·ly** *adv* —**taste·ful·ness** *n*

taste·less /táystləss/ *adj* 1 without flavor 2 showing a lack of good aesthetic taste —**taste·less·ly** *adv* —**taste·less·ness** *n*

tast·er /táystər/ *n* 1 a judge of the quality of food or drink 2 somebody testing an important person's food or drink for poison by tasting it first

tast·y /táystee/ (-i-er, -i-est) *adj* having a pleasant flavor —**tast·i·ly** *adv* —**tast·i·ness** *n*

tat (tat·ted, tat·ting) *vti* work at or produce tatting

ta·ta·mi /tə ta´amee, taa-/ (*pl same or* -mis) *n* a Japanese straw mat

Ta·tar /táatər/ *n* a member of a people of Central Asia —**Ta·tar** *adj*

tatoo incorrect spelling of **tattoo**

tat·tered /táttərd/ *adj* 1 ragged or in shreds 2 dressed in rags

tat·ting /tátting/ *n* 1 lace made with a shuttle 2 the process of making tatting —**tat·ter** *n*

tat·tle /tátt'l/ *vi* (-tled, -tling) engage in gossiping ■ *n* 1 somebody who gossips 2 gossip and tale-telling —**tat·tler** *n*

tat·tle·tale /tátt'l tàyl/ *n* somebody who reveals somebody else's secrets or bad behavior

tat·too[1] /ta toó, tə-/ *n* (*pl* -toos) a permanent picture or design made on the skin ■ *vt* (-tooed, -toos) make a tattoo on —**tat·too·er** *n* —**tat·too·ist** *n*

ORIGIN Tattoo "design on the skin" was adopted from a Polynesian language in the mid-18C. Tattoo "military signal or display" is a century older. It came from Dutch *taptoe*, literally "tap to," an instruction to shut off the tap of beer barrels at closing time in taverns. The earliest use in English was "a call summoning soldiers back to their quarters."

tat·too[2] /ta toó, tə-/ *n* (*pl* -toos) 1 an evening military display performed as entertainment 2 a regular beating on a surface o *the tattoo of rain on a flat roof* 3 a bugle or drum call telling soldiers to return to their · quarters in the evening ■ *vti* beat with a steady rhythm

tat·ty /táttee/ (-ti-er, -ti-est) *adj* in poor condition —**tat·ti·ness** *n*

tau /tow, taw/ *n* the 19th letter of the Greek alphabet

tau cross *n* a cross shaped like T

taught past tense, past participle of **teach**

taunt *vt* 1 provoke or mock hurtfully 2 tantalize ■ *n* a hurtfully mocking or provocative remark —**taunt·ing·ly** *adv*

taupe /tōp/ *n* a brownish gray color —**taupe** *adj*

Tau·rus /táwrəss/ (*pl* -rus·es *or* -ri /-rī/) *n* 1 a zodiacal constellation in the northern hemisphere 2 the 2nd sign of the zodiac 3 somebody born under Taurus —**Tau·re·an** *n* —**Tau·rus** *adj*

Tau·rus Moun·tains /táwross-/ mountain range in S Turkey. Highest peak Aladag 12,251 ft./3,734 m.

taut /tawt/ *adj* 1 stretched tightly 2 firm and flexed 3 stressed or anxious 4 concise o *taut prose* —**taut·ly** *adv* —**taut·ness** *n*

tau·tol·o·gy /taw tóllajee/ (*pl* -gies) *n* 1 the redundant repetition of meaning in different words 2 an instance of tautology —**tau·to·log·i·cal** /tàwtə lójjik'l/ *adj*

tav·ern /távvərn/ *n* a bar, café, or inn

taw·dry /táwdree/ (-dri-er, -dri-est) *adj* gaudy and of poor quality —**taw·dri·ly** *adv* —**taw·dri·ness** *n*

ORIGIN Tawdry is a 17C shortening of *tawdry lace*, itself an alteration of *St. Audrey's lace*. The name *Audrey* is a contracted form of *Etheldreda*, and the Etheldreda in question was a 7C Anglo-Saxon queen of Northumbria, England. She was very fond in her youth of fine lace neckerchiefs, and when she later developed a fatal tumor of the neck, she regarded it as divine retribution for her former extravagance. After her death in 679 she was canonized and made patron saint of Ely in E England. In the Middle Ages fairs were held in her memory, known as "St. Audrey's fairs," at which lace neckties were sold. These were often made from cheap gaudy material, and by the 17C the eroded form *tawdry* was being used generally for "cheap and gaudy."

taw·ny /táwnee/ (-ni-er, -ni-est) *adj* 1 of an orangey brown color 2 describes port wine that has matured for more than ten years in the barrel —**taw·ni·ness** *n*

tax *n* 1 an amount of money paid to a government by its citizens, used to run the country 2 a strain or heavy demand ■ *vt* 1 make somebody pay a tax on something 2 strain or make heavy demands on somebody or something 3 accuse or charge somebody o *She was taxed for failure to appear in court.* —**tax·a·ble** *adj* —**tax·a·bly** *adv*

tax·a·tion /tak sáysh'n/ *n* 1 the levying of taxes, or a system of doing this 2 money collected in taxes —**tax·a·tion·al** *adj*

tax a·void·ance *n* the paying of the minimum amount of tax possible by claiming all allowable deductions

tax-de·duct·i·ble *adj* able to be deducted as an expense from taxable income

tax-deferred *adj* not taxable until a later time

tax e·va·sion *n* illegal failure to pay taxes

tax-ex·empt *adj* legally exempt from taxation

tax-free *adj* not subject to taxation

tax ha·ven *n* a country with favorable tax rates

tax·i /táksee/ *n* (*pl* **-is** *or* **-ies**) *also* **tax·i·cab** /-kàb/ a car that carries paying passengers ■ *vti* (**-ied, -i·ing** *or* **-y·ing, -is** *or* **-ies**) **1** make an aircraft move along the ground before takeoff or after landing, or move in this way **2** transport or travel in a taxi

tax·i·der·my /táksi dùrmee/ *n* the art of stuffing dead animals for display —**tax·i·der·mist** *n*

tax·ing /táksing/ *adj* demanding —**tax·ing·ly** *adv*

tax·i stand *n* an area for parked taxicabs

tax·i·way /táksee wày/ *n* a path used by taxiing aircraft

tax loss *n* a transaction resulting in a reduced tax liability

tax·on·o·my /tak sónnəmee/ (*pl* **-mies**) *n* **1** the classification of organisms **2** the principles of classification —**tax·o·nom·ic** /tàksə nómmik/ *adj* —**tax·on·o·mist** *n*

tax·pay·er /táks pày ər/ *n* somebody who pays a tax or taxes, especially income tax —**tax·pay·ing** *adj*

tax re·turn *n* a government form for recording income and expenses in order to calculate tax liability

tax shel·ter *n* an investment intended to reduce income tax liability —**tax-shel·tered** *adj*

Tay·lor /táylər/, **Elizabeth** (*b.* 1932) British-born US movie actor

Tay·lor, Zachary (1784–1850) 12th president of the United States (1849–50)

Tay-Sachs dis·ease /tày sáks-/ *n* a genetic disease causing ultimate loss of sight and brain function

> **ORIGIN** The disease is named for Warren Tay (1843–1927), a British ophthalmologist, and Bernard Sachs (1858–1944), a US neurologist.

Tb *symbol* terbium

TB, T.B. *abbr* tuberculosis

TBA, tba *abbr* to be announced

Tbi·li·si /təbə leéssee/ capital of the Republic of Georgia. Pop. 1,268,000 (1990 estimate).

T-bill *n* a Treasury bill

T-bone steak *n* a large steak containing a T-shaped bone

tbs., tbsp., TBSP *abbr* tablespoon

Tc *symbol* technetium

T cell *n* a white blood cell from the thymus, important to the immune system

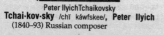

Peter IlyichTchaikovsky

Tchai·kov·sky /chī káwfskee/, **Peter Ilyich** (1840–93) Russian composer

✚ TCP/IP *abbr* transmission control protocol/Internet protocol

TD *abbr* touchdown

Te *symbol* tellurium

tea /tee/ *n* **1** the dried shredded leaves of an Asian plant, used for making a drink by adding boiling water **2** a tea drink **3** a drink made by the infusion of plant leaves or flowers **4** an Asian evergreen bush whose leaves are used to make tea **5** a snack or light meal of cakes, sandwiches, and tea

> **SPELLCHECK** Do not confuse the spelling of **tea** and **tee** ("a T-shirt," "a golf peg"), which sound similar.

tea bag *n* a small bag containing tea leaves that is placed in boiling water to make a tea drink

teach /teech/ (**taught** /tawt/) *v* **1** *vt* impart knowledge or skill to somebody by instruction **2** *vt* give lessons to a person or animal **3** *vt* make somebody understand through experience **4** *vti* be a teacher in an institution ○ *teaches college* —**teach·a·ble** *adj*

> **SYNONYMS** teach, educate, train, instruct, coach, tutor, school, drill CORE MEANING: impart knowledge or skill in something

teach·er /teechər/ *n* **1** somebody who teaches, especially professionally **2** something that teaches ○ *Experience is a great teacher.* —**teach·er·ly** *adj*

teach-in *n* an extended period of speeches and lectures as part of a protest

teach·ing /teeching/ *n* **1** the practice or profession of being a teacher **2** something taught (*often pl*) ■ *adj* **1** used for teaching **2** involved in teaching

teach·ing hos·pi·tal *n* a hospital that trains medical students

teak /teek/ *n* **1** a durable red-brown wood. Use: furniture, shipbuilding. **2** a tree from which teak is obtained

tea·ket·tle /tee kètt'l/ *n* a container with a handle, spout, and lid for boiling water

teal /teel/ (*pl* same *or* **teals**) *n* **1** a small duck with iridescent blue or green wing patches **2** a greenish blue color —**teal** *adj*

team /teem/ *n* **1** a group of people forming one side in a sports competition **2** a number of people functioning cooperatively as a group **3** a group of animals made to work together ■ *v* **1** *vti* form into a team **2** *vt* transport using a team of animals **3** *vi* drive a team of animals

> **SPELLCHECK** Do not confuse the spelling of **team** and **teem** ("be full of"), which sound similar.

team·mate /teém màyt/ *n* a member of the same team

team play·er *n* somebody who works cooperatively

team spir·it n enthusiasm about working as a team

team·ster /téemstər/ n a truck driver

team·work /téem wùrk/ n 1 cooperative work by a group 2 the results produced by group work

tea·pot /tée pòt/ n a container with a spout and handle for infusing and serving tea

tear¹ /tair/ v (tore /tawr, tōr/, torn /tawrn, tōrn/) 1 vti pull something such as paper or fabric apart, or come apart in this way 2 vt separate something using force 3 vi move or act very quickly (infml) o tearing down the road 4 vt cause something to become divided or fragmented 5 vt make a hole in something by tearing 6 vt cut something such as flesh leaving jagged edges 7 vt injure a muscle or ligament so that some of the tissue is pulled apart and separated ■ n 1 an act of tearing 2 a split caused by tearing

SYNONYMS tear, rend, rip, split CORE MEANING: pull apart forcibly

□ **tear apart** vt 1 divide or separate by tearing 2 distress somebody

□ **tear down** vt demolish or dismantle

tear² /teer/ n a drop of salty fluid from the eye ■ **tears** npl 1 weeping, e.g., from grief or pain 2 the salty liquid that moistens and protects the eyes —**tear·i·ly** adv —**tear·i·ness** n —**tear·y** adj

SPELLCHECK Do not confuse the spelling of **tear** and **tier** ("a row of seats"), which sound similar.

tear·drop /téer dròp/ n 1 a drop of salty fluid from the eye 2 a shape resembling a teardrop, or something having this shape

tear·ful /téerfəl/ adj 1 crying or about to cry 2 sad enough to cause tears —**tear·ful·ly** adv

tear gas /téer-/ n a chemical agent that incapacitates people by irritating their eyes —**tear-gas** vt

tear·jerk·er /téer jùrkər/ n an excessively sentimental story, play, or movie (infml) —**tear·jerk·ing** adj

tear-off /táir-/ adj produced so that individual sheets can be removed easily

tea·room /tée ròom, -ròom/ n a restaurant serving tea and light refreshments

tease /teez/ v (teased, teas·ing) 1 vti annoy a person or animal on purpose 2 vti make fun of somebody 3 vt urge somebody by coaxing 4 vt arouse physical desire in somebody without intending to give satisfaction 5 vt comb hair toward the scalp to make it look thicker 6 vt pull fibers apart by combing or carding 7 vt raise a nap on cloth by combing ■ n 1 a provocative opening remark 2 an act of teasing —**teas·ing** adj —**teas·ing·ly** adv

tea·sel /téez'l/ n 1 a plant that produces flowers covered with hooked leaves 2 an implement used to raise fabric nap

teas·er /téezər/ n 1 somebody who teases somebody else 2 a tricky problem 3 an advertisement offering a gift

tea ser·vice, tea set n a set of matching articles for serving tea

tea·spoon /tée spòon/ n 1 a small spoon for stirring tea 2 also **tea·spoon·ful** the amount held by a teaspoon 3 also **tea·spoon·ful** a measure equal to one-third of a tablespoon

teat /teet, tit/ n a protuberance on the breast or udder of a female mammal through which milk is excreted

tea tow·el n a dishtowel

Te·bet n JUDAISM, CALENDAR = Tevet

tech /tek/ n (infml) 1 technology 2 a technical college or university (often capitalized in names) o Cal Tech ■ adj 1 technical 2 technological

⚡**tech·ie** /tékee/, **tek·kie** n somebody competent in technology (infml)

tech·ne·ti·um /tek néeshee əm/ n (symbol Tc) a silvery gray radioactive metallic element. Use: tracer, corrosion-resistant materials.

tech·ni·cal /téknik'l/ adj 1 of industrial techniques or applied science 2 specializing or skilled in practical or scientific subjects 3 belonging to a specific subject or profession o a technical glossary 4 exhibiting or deriving from technique 5 strictly interpreted —**tech·ni·cal·ly** adv

tech·ni·cal·i·ty /tèkni kállətee/ (pl -ties) n 1 a detail or term understood only by a specialist 2 a trivial point arising from the strict application of rules o a legal technicality 3 the quality of being technical

⚡**tech·ni·cal sup·port** n a repair or advice service offered by computer or software manufacturers

tech·ni·cian /tek nísh'n/ n 1 a specialist in industrial techniques 2 a laboratory employee

Tech·ni·col·or /tékni kùllər/ tdmk a trademark for an early color process for making motion pictures

~~techniqe~~ incorrect spelling of **technique**

tech·nique /tek néek/ n 1 the procedure or skill required for a specific task 2 treatment of the basics of something such as an artistic work or a sport 3 skill or expertise in doing a specific thing

tech·no /téknō/ n fast electronic dance music using digitally synthesized instruments

techno- prefix technology, technological o technocrat

tech·noc·ra·cy /tek nókrəssee/ (pl -cies) n 1 a government or social system in which scientists, engineers, and technicians are politically powerful 2 a philosophy promoting technocracy

tech·no·crat /téknə kràt/ *n* **1** a bureaucrat who is a technical expert **2** a proponent of technocracy —**tech·no·crat·ic** /tèknə kráttik/ *adj*

tech·nol·o·gy /tek nólləjee/ (*pl* -gies) *n* **1** the development and application of tools, machines, and methods for manufacturing and other processes **2** a method of applying technical knowledge or tools —**tech·no·log·i·cal** /tèknə lójjik'l/ *adj* —**tech·no·log·i·cal·ly** *adv* —**tech·nol·o·gist** *n*

⚡**tech·no·phile** /téknə fìl/ *n* somebody who likes or is interested in new technology or computerization

⚡**tech·no·phobe** /téknə fòb/ *n* somebody who dislikes or is intimidated by new technology or computerization —**tech·no·pho·bi·a** /tèknə fóbee ə/ *n*

~~tecnical~~ incorrect spelling of **technical**

~~tecnique~~ incorrect spelling of **technique**

tec·ton·ic /tek tónnik/ *adj* **1** of the forces that produce movement or deformation of the Earth's crust **2** of construction and architecture —**tec·ton·ics** *n*

Te·cum·seh /tə kúmssə/ (1768?–1813) Shawnee leader

ted·dy¹ /téddee/ (*pl* -dies), **ted·dy bear** *n* a soft furry toy bear

> **ORIGIN Teddies** are named for president Theodore Roosevelt, who was fond of bear hunting. His nickname, "Teddy," was used in a humorous poem in the *New York Times* about the adventures of two bears. Their names (Teddy B and Teddy G) were then appropriated to two bears in the Bronx Zoo whose popularity caused toy manufacturers to market toy bears as *teddy bears.*

ted·dy² /téddee/ (*pl* -dies) *n* a woman's one-piece short undergarment

te·di·ous /téedee əss/ *adj* boringly long or repetitive —**te·di·ous·ly** *adv* —**te·di·ous·ness** *n*

te·di·um /téedee əm/ *n* the quality of being tedious

tee¹ /tee/ *n* a T-shirt (*infml*)

tee² /tee/ *n* **1** a peg with a cupped end placed in the ground to hold a golf ball **2** an area on a golf course where play for a new hole starts ▪ *vti* (**teed**) put a golf ball on a tee ◊ See note at **tea**
□ **tee off** *vi* in golf, hit a ball from a tee at the start of a hole

teed off *adj* annoyed (*infml*)

tee-hee, te-hee *interj* expresses laughter —**tee-hee** *vi*

teem /teem/ *vi* be full of people or animals —**teem·ing·ly** *adv* ◊ See note at **team**

teen (*infml*) *adj* teenage ▪ *n* a teenager

teen·age /teen àyj/, **teen·aged** /-àyjd/ *adj* **1** aged between 13 and 19 **2** of teenagers

teen·ag·er /teen àyjər/ *n* a young person aged between 13 and 19 ◊ See note at **youth**

teens *npl* **1** the numbers ending in "-teen" **2** the years between 13 and 19 in somebody's life or a century

teen·sy-ween·sy /téensi weensee/, **teen·y-ween·y** /téeni weenee/ *adj* quite tiny (*infml*)

tee·ny /téenee/ (-ni·er, -ni·est) *adj* quite tiny (*infml*)

tee·pee *n* CULTL ANTHROP = **tepee**

tee shirt *n* CLOTHING = **T-shirt**

tee·ter /téetər/ *vi* move totteringly

tee·ter-tot·ter *n* a seesaw

teeth plural of **tooth**

teethe /teeth/ (**teethed, teeth·ing**) *vi* grow your first teeth

tee·to·tal /tee tòt'l/ *adj* abstaining from alcohol —**tee·to·tal·er** *n* —**tee·to·tal·ism** *n*

> **ORIGIN** The *tee* of **teetotal** represents an emphatic repetition of the initial consonant of *total.* The adjective "abstaining from alcohol" is attributed to a Richard Turner of Preston, Lancashire, England, who is said to have used it in a speech to a temperance society in September 1833.

TEFL *abbr* teaching (of) English as a foreign language

Tef·lon /téf lòn/ *tdmk* a trademark for polytetrafluoroethylene, a plastic with nonstick properties that is used as a coating, e.g., for cookware

Te·gu·ci·gal·pa /te gòossee gálpə/ capital of Honduras. Pop. 813,900 (1995).

te-hee *interj, vi* = **tee-hee**

Teh·ran /te raàn, -rán/ capital of Iran. Pop. 6,758,845 (1996).

tek·kie *n* = **techie** (*infml*)

tel. *abbr* **1** telegram **2** telegraph **3** telephone

Tel A·viv /tèl ə veev/, **Tel A·viv-Jaf·fa** /-jáffə/ city in west central Israel. Pop. 348,100 (1999).

⚡**tel·co ho·tel** /télkō-/ *n* an Internet hotel

tele- *prefix* **1** distant, operating at a distance ○ *telecommute* **2** television ○ *telegenic* **3** telegraph, telephone ○ *telebanking*

tel·e·bank·ing /téllə bàngking/ *n* a system of banking carried out by telephone

tel·e·cast /téllə kàst/ *n* a television broadcast ▪ *vti* (**-cast** *or* **-cast·ed**) broadcast a television program —**tel·e·cast·er** *n*

tel·e·com·mu·ni·ca·tion /tèlli kə myōoni káysh'n/ *n* electronic communication using wires or radio signals

tel·e·com·mu·ni·ca·tions /tèlli kə myōoni káysh'nz/ *n* the science of transmitting information electronically by wires or radio signals (*+ sing or pl verb*)

⚡**tel·e·com·mute** /tèllə kə myōot/ (-mut·ed, -mut·ing) *vi* work from home on a computer linked to the workplace via a modem —**tel·e·com·mut·er** *n* —**tel·e·com·mut·ing** *n*

tel·e·con·fer·enc·ing /téllə kònfərənsing, -kònfrənsing/ *n* videoconferencing using telephone lines —**tel·e·con·fer·ence** *n, vi*

tel·e·gen·ic /tèllə jénnik/ *adj* looking good on television

tel·e·gram /tèllə gràm/ *n* a telegraph message —**tel·e·gram·mat·ic** /tèlləgrə máttik/ *adj*

tel·e·graph /tèllə gràf/ *n* **1** a method of long-distance communication by coded electrical impulses transmitted through wires **2** a telegram ■ *v* **1** *vti* send a message to somebody by telegraph **2** *vt* communicate something indirectly or without words ○ *had telegraphed her annoyance with a frown* —**te·leg·ra·pher** /tə léggrəfər/ *n* —**te·leg·ra·phist** /tə léggrəfist/ *n* —**te·leg·ra·phy** /tə léggrəfee/ *n*

tel·e·graph·ic /tèllə gráffik/ *adj* **1** of telegraphy or telegrams **2** concise or elliptical —**tel·e·graph·i·cal·ly** *adv*

tel·e·ki·ne·sis /tèllə ki neessiss, -kī-/ *n* the supposed power to move an object without using any physical means —**tel·e·ki·net·ic** /-néttik/ *adj*

Te·le·mann /táylə màan/, **Georg Philipp** (1681–1767) German composer

tel·e·mar·ket·ing /tèllə màarkəting/ *n* selling or promoting goods and services by telephone —**tel·e·mar·ket·er** *n*

⨍ tel·e·mat·ics /tèllə máttiks/ *n* the science of data transmission (+ *sing verb*) —**tel·e·mat·ic** *adj*

tel·e·med·i·cine /tèllə mèddissin/ *n* the use of telecommunications systems to transmit medical information

te·lep·a·thy /tə léppəthee/ *n* supposed communication directly from one person's mind to another —**tel·e·path** /tèllə pàth/ *n* —**tel·e·path·ic** /tèllə páthik/ *adj* —**tel·e·path·i·cal·ly** *adv*

tel·e·phone /tèllə fòn/ *n* **1** an electronic device containing a receiver and transmitter and linked to a telecommunications system **2** a system of communication using telephones ■ *vti* (-phoned, -phon·ing) **1** speak to somebody using the telephone **2** send a message by telephone —**tel·e·phon·ic** /tèllə fónnik/ *adj*

tel·e·phone book, tel·e·phone di·rec·to·ry *n* an alphabetical listing of names, addresses, and telephone numbers of people or businesses

tel·e·phone booth *n* a structure with a payphone in it

tel·e·phone ex·change *n* a center housing equipment for interconnecting telephone lines

tel·e·phone pole *n* a pole for telephone wires

te·leph·o·ny /tə léffənee/ *n* the science or a system of communication using telephones

tel·e·pho·to lens /tèllə fó tō-/ *n* a camera lens that makes distant objects seem nearer or larger

tel·e·play /tèllə plày/ *n* a play written for television

tel·e·port /tèllə pàwrt/ *v* **1** *vt* move something supposedly using mental power **2** *vi* in science fiction, move somewhere instantly without traveling —**tel·e·por·ta·tion** /tèllə pawr táysh'n/ *n*

tel·e·print·er /tèllə príntər/ *n* a teletypewriter

⨍ tel·e·proc·ess·ing /tèllə pró sèssing/ *n* use of remote computer terminals to process data

Tel·e·PrompT·er /tèllə prómptər/ *tdmk* a trademark for a device showing text for somebody speaking on television to read

tel·e·scope /tèllə skòp/ *n* **1** a device using compound lenses or concave mirrors for looking at distant objects **2** a radio telescope ■ *v* (-scoped, -scop·ing) **1** *vi* slide concentric parts neatly inside each other **2** *vt* condense

tel·e·scop·ic /tèllə skóppik/ *adj* **1** of telescopes **2** able to make distant objects seem nearer or larger **3** with concentric parts that slide inside each other —**tel·e·scop·i·cal·ly** *adv*

tel·e·shop·ping /tèllə shòpping/ *n* the purchase of goods advertised on television by telephone or computer —**tel·e·shop** *vi* —**tel·e·shop·per** *n*

tel·e·text /tèllə tèkst/ *n* a system of broadcasting written information on television over or instead of the picture

tel·e·thon /tèllə thòn/ *n* a lengthy television broadcast combining entertainment with appeals for donations to a charity

tel·e·type·writ·er /tèllə tī̄p rī̄tər/ *n* a piece of equipment for telegraphic communication that uses a device like a typewriter for data input and output

tel·e·van·ge·list /tèllə vánjəlist/ *n* a Christian evangelist whose services are broadcast on TV —**tel·e·van·gel·ism** *n*

tel·e·vise /tèllə vīz/ (-vised, -vis·ing) *vt* broadcast on television

tel·e·vi·sion /tèllə vìzh'n/ *n* **1** a system of capturing images and sounds, broadcasting them electronically, and reproducing them for viewing and listening **2** also **tel·e·vi·sion set** an electronic device for receiving and reproducing the images and sounds of a television signal **3** the television broadcasting industry —**tel·e·vi·sual** /tèllə vízhoo əl/ *adj*

ORIGIN The word **television** is first recorded in English in 1907. Its literal meaning is "far vision." During its early history it was criticized for being a hybrid of elements of Greek (*tēle* "far off") and Latin origin, but nothing now could sound more familiar.

---

tel·ex /té lèks/ *n* **1** a communications system using teletypewriters **2** a message sent or received by telex ■ *vti* send a message to somebody by telex

tell (told /tōld/) *v* **1** *vt* relate events or facts **2** *vt* express a particular thing in speech ○ *tell a lie* **3** *vt* inform somebody of something **4** *vti* express thoughts or feelings to somebody in words **5** *vt* order somebody to do something **6** *vt* distinguish two or more things ○ *couldn't tell one pup from the other* **7** *vt* ascertain or perceive something ○ *couldn't tell whether she was pleased or not* **8** *vt* purport to reveal the future ○ *tell fortunes* **9** *vi* reveal a secret ○ *Don't worry, I won't tell.* ◇ **all told** altogether ◇ **tell it like it is** give an accurate account of something *(infml)*

□ **tell off** *vt* scold *(infml)*

Tell, William *n* legendary Swiss patriot

tel·ler /téllər/ *n* **1** somebody who tells something ○ *a teller of tall tales* **2** a bank employee who receives and pays out money

Tel·ler /téllər/, **Edward** (*b.* 1908) Hungarian-born US physicist. He helped construct the first atomic bomb and was the principal architect of the hydrogen bomb.

tell·ing /télling/ *adj* **1** inadvertently revealing something ○ *a telling look* **2** highly effective ○ *written in telling detail* —**tell·ing·ly** *adv*

tell·tale /tél tàyl/ *adj* clearly showing or indicating something secret ■ *n* **1** a sign of a hazard **2** somebody who reveals somebody else's secrets or wrongdoing

tel·lu·ri·um /tə loóree əm, te-/ *n* (*symbol* Te) a semimetallic chemical element. Use: alloys, various manufacturing processes.

tem·blor /témblər, -blàwr/ *n* an earthquake

te·mer·i·ty /tə mérrətee/ *n* reckless boldness

temp *n* a temporary worker, especially one hired from an agency ■ *vi* work as a temp ○ *She's temping with a bank.*

Tem·pe /témpee/ city in central Arizona. Pop. 167,622 (1998).

tem·per /témpər/ *n* **1** an emotional condition of a particular kind ○ *an even temper* **2** a tendency to get angry easily **3** an angry state **4** a calm state ○ *lost his temper* **5** the hardness of a metal ■ *vt* **1** make something less harsh or more acceptable by adding something else ○ *temper criticism with kindness* **2** make somebody stronger through exposure to hardship **3** harden metal by heating and cooling it

tem·per·a /témpərə/ *n* **1** a painting technique using colors made from pigment mixed with water and egg yolk **2** a painting done in tempera

tem·per·a·ment /témprəmənt, témpərə-/ *n* **1** a quality of mind that characterizes somebody **2** the state of being excessively excitable and irritable

tem·per·a·men·tal /tèmprə mént'l, tèmpərə-/ *adj* **1** easily upset and irritated **2** unpredictable ○ *a temperamental car* **3** of temperament —**tem·per·a·men·tal·ly** *adv*

tem·per·ance /témprənss, -pərənss/ *n* **1** self-restraint **2** abstinence from alcohol

~~temperary~~ incorrect spelling of **temporary**

tem·per·ate /témprət, -pərət/ *adj* **1** mild or restrained in behavior or attitude **2** describes a climate without temperature extremes —**tem·per·ate·ly** *adv* —**tem·per·ate·ness** *n*

Tem·per·ate Zone *n* the parts of the Earth that have hot summers, cold winters, and intermediate falls and springs

tem·per·a·ture /témpərə chòor, -chər, témprə-/ *n* **1** the degree of heat of an object or place **2** the degree of heat of a person's body **3** an unusually high body temperature in excess of 98.6° F/37.0° C ○ *running a temperature*

~~temperment~~ incorrect spelling of **temperament**

~~temperture~~ incorrect spelling of **temperature**

tem·pest /témpəst/ *n* a severe storm *(literary)*

tem·pes·tu·ous /tem péschoo əss/ *adj* **1** with severe storms **2** emotionally turbulent —**tem·pes·tu·ous·ly** *adv* —**tem·pes·tu·ous·ness** *n*

tem·plate /témplət/ *n* a pattern from which other similar things can be made

tem·ple[1] /témp'l/ *n* **1** a building for worship **2** a synagogue **3** a place of worship for the Church of Jesus Christ of Latter-Day Saints **4** a meeting place for a fraternal order **5** an institution or building regarded as a guardian of, or place set aside for, a particular activity

tem·ple[2] /témp'l/ *n* **1** the part of each side of the head between the eye and the ear **2** either of the stem-shaped pieces on a pair of glasses that are connected to the frame and rest on the ears

tem·po /témpō/ (*pl* **-pi** /-pee/ *or* **-pos**) *n* **1** the speed of a piece of music **2** the pace or rate of an activity

tem·po·ral[1] /témprəl, -pərəl/ *adj* **1** of time **2** in the Christian church, of the laity rather than the clergy **3** of worldly life rather than spiritual life —**tem·po·ral·ly** *adv*

tem·po·ral[2] /témprəl, -pərəl/ *adj* of the temples of the head

tem·po·rar·y /témpə rèrree/ *adj* having a limited duration ■ *n* (*pl* **-ies**) a worker hired for a limited time —**tem·po·rar·i·ly** /témpə rérrəlee/ *adv*

SYNONYMS temporary, fleeting, passing, transitory, ephemeral, evanescent, short-lived CORE MEANING: lasting only a short time

---

tem·po·rize /témpə rìz/ (**-rized, -riz·ing**) *vi* maneuver, especially orally, so as to gain time ○ *temporized before answering the question* —**tem·po·ri·za·tion** /tèmpəri záysh'n/ *n*

~~temprature~~ incorrect spelling of **temperature**

tempt *vt* **1** incite desire in **2** incite to wrongdoing **3** invite or attract ○ *brochures tempted us to go* **4** risk the possible destructive powers of ○ *tempt fate* —**tempt·a·ble** *adj* —**tempt·ing** *adj* —**tempt·ing·ly** *adv*

temp·ta·tion /temp táysh'n/ *n* **1** a desire for something considered wrong **2** the incitement of desire in somebody **3** a person or thing that tempts somebody

temp·tress /témptriss/ n a woman regarded as sexually alluring (dated; sometimes offensive)

tem·pu·ra /tem poόra/ n a Japanese dish of vegetables or seafood coated in light batter and deep-fried

ten n the number 10 —**ten** adj, pron —**tenth** n, adj, adv

ten·a·ble /ténnab'l/ adj justifiable with reasoned arguments —**ten·a·bil·i·ty** /ténnə billətee/ n —**ten·a·bly** adv

te·na·cious /tə náyshəss/ adj 1 very determined or stubborn 2 difficult to loosen or shake off o a tenacious head cold 3 able to remember many things —**te·na·cious·ly** adv —**te·na·cious·ness** n —**te·nac·i·ty** /tə nássətee/ n

ten·an·cy /ténnansee/ (pl -cies) n 1 possession or occupancy of property or land owned by somebody else for a fixed period in return for rent 2 the period of somebody's tenancy

ten·ant /ténnənt/ n 1 a renter of property 2 the occupier of a place ■ vti occupy somebody else's property as a tenant —**ten·ant·ed** adj

ten·ant farm·er n somebody who rents and farms a piece of land

Ten Com·mand·ments npl the ten laws given by God to Moses, according to the Bible

tend[1] vi 1 be generally inclined or likely to do something, or be in the habit of doing something 2 move gradually or slightly in a particular direction

tend[2] vt 1 take care of 2 be in charge of o tend bar —**ten·dance** n

~~tendancy~~ incorrect spelling of **tendency**

ten·den·cy /téndənsee/ (pl -cies) n 1 a way that somebody or something typically behaves or is likely to behave 2 a gradual movement or development in a given direction

ten·den·tious /ten dénshəss/ adj promoting a specific cause or supporting a specific view

ten·der[1] /téndər/ adj 1 painful when touched or pressed 2 showing care, gentleness, and feeling 3 kind and sympathetic o a tender disposition 4 pleasantly soft for eating 5 young, vulnerable, or delicate o children at the tender age of five —**ten·der·ly** adv —**ten·der·ness** n

ten·der[2] /téndər/ v 1 vt offer something formally in writing o tendered her resignation 2 vi offer to undertake a job or supply goods o tender for a contract 3 vt offer something as payment ■ n 1 a formal offer to undertake a job or supply goods 2 money o legal tender —**ten·der·a·ble** adj

tend·er[3] /téndər/ n 1 a small boat used to go to and from a larger boat 2 the rear part of a steam locomotive that carries its coal and water 3 somebody who tends something or somebody

ten·der·foot /téndər foŏt/ (pl -feet /-feet/ or -foots) n 1 a beginner (infml) 2 also

Ten·der·foot a member of the lowest rank in the Boy Scouts

ten·der·heart·ed /téndər haártəd/ adj kindly and caring —**ten·der·heart·ed·ly** adv —**ten·der·heart·ed·ness** n

ten·der·ize /téndə rīz/ (-ized, -iz·ing) vt make meat tender —**ten·der·i·za·tion** /téndəri záysh'n/ n —**ten·der·iz·er** n

ten·der·loin /téndər lòyn/ n a prime cut of meat from the curve of the ribs at the backbone

ten·di·ni·tis /téndə nítiss/, **ten·do·ni·tis** n inflammation of a tendon

ten·don /téndən/ n a tough band of tissue connecting a muscle to a bone —**ten·di·nous** /-dənəss/ adj

ten·dril /téndril/ n a thin plant part that coils around and attaches the plant to a support

ten·e·ment /ténnəmənt/ n an urban, often rundown, apartment building

~~tenent~~ incorrect spelling of **tenant**

~~Tenessee~~ incorrect spelling of **Tennessee**

ten·et /ténnət/ n an established fundamental belief

ten·fold /tén fòld/ adj 1 multiplied by ten 2 made up of ten parts ■ adv ten times over

ten-gal·lon hat n a cowboy hat with a large round crown

ten·ge /téngày/ (pl same) n the main unit of Kazakh currency

Tenn. abbr Tennessee

ten·ner /ténnər/ n US, Can, ANZ ten dollars, or a ten-dollar bill (infml)

~~Tennesee~~ incorrect spelling of **Tennessee**

Ten·nes·see /ténnə seé/ 1 state in the east central United States. Cap. Nashville. Pop. 5,689,283 (2000). 2 river of the SE United States, rising in E Tennessee and flowing through N Alabama, W Tennessee, and W Kentucky to the Ohio River. Length 652 mi./1,050 km. —**Ten·nes·se·an** n, adj

ten·nis /ténniss/ n a racket game played by two or four players who hit a ball over a net across a rectangular court

ten·nis el·bow n painful inflammation of the tendon in the outer elbow caused by repetitive strain

ten·nis shoe n a sneaker for athletic activities

Ten·ny·son /ténniss'n/, **Alfred, 1st Baron Tennyson of Freshwater and Aldworth** (1809–92) British poet —**Ten·ny·so·ni·an** /ténni sōnee ən/ n, adj

ten·on /ténnən/ n a projection on a piece of wood for fitting into a mortise on another piece to make a joint

ten·or /ténnər/ n 1 the highest natural adult male singing voice, or a man with this voice 2 the way something is progressing (fml) 3 overall nature, pattern, or meaning (fml) o the positive tenor of the reply

ten·pin /tén pìn/ n a bottle-shaped bowling pin

ten·pins /ténn pinz/, **ten·pin bowl·ing** *n* a bowling game using ten pins and a large ball (+ *sing verb*)

tense¹ /tenss/ *adj* (**tens·er, tens·est**) **1** worried and nervous **2** causing anxiety or nervousness o *a tense wait* **3** stretched tight or held stiffly o *tense muscles* ■ *vti* (**tensed, tens·ing**) make or become tense —**tense·ly** *adv* —**tense·ness** *n*

tense² /tenss/ *n* the form of a verb that expresses the time at which action takes place in relation to the speaker or writer o *in the future tense*

ten·sile /téns'l, tén síl/ *adj* **1** of tension **2** capable of stretching or being stretched —**ten·sil·i·ty** /ten síllatee/ *n*

ten·sile strength *n* the maximum stretching force that a material can withstand

ten·sion /ténshən/ *n* **1** anxious feelings **2** an uneasy or hostile feeling in a relationship (often *pl*) **3** the buildup of suspense in a fictional work **4** the tautness of something **5** a pulling or stretching force **6** voltage or electromotive force (*often in combination*) o *high-tension wires* —**ten·sion·al** *adj*

ten·sor /ténsər, tén sàwr/ *n* a muscle that tenses or stretches a part of the body

tent *n* a collapsible movable fabric shelter held up by poles and kept in place by ropes and pegs

ten·ta·cle /téntək'l/ *n* a long flexible organ used by some animals for holding, feeling, or moving —**ten·ta·cled** *adj*—**ten·tac·u·lar** /ten tákyələr/ *adj*

ten·ta·tive /téntətiv/ *adj* **1** hesitant or uncertain **2** rough or provisional o *tentative plans* —**ten·ta·tive·ly** *adv* —**ten·ta·tive·ness** *n*

ten·ter·hook /téntər hóòk/ ◇ **on tenterhooks** anxious or in great suspense

ten·u·ous /ténnyoo əss/ *adj* weak and unconvincing —**te·nu·i·ty** /te noō ətee/ *n* —**ten·u·ous·ly** *adv*—**ten·u·ous·ness** *n*

ten·ure /ténnyər/ *n* **1** occupation of an official position, or the period of occupation (*fml*) **2** the rights of a tenant to hold property **3** possession of permanent status as a teacher at an institution of higher learning —**ten·ured** *adj*

Ten·zing Nor·kay /ténzing náwrkay/ (1914?–86) Nepalese mountaineer who was one of the first two climbers to reach the summit of Mount Everest (1953)

Ten·zin Gyat·so /ténzin gyát sò/ (b. 1935) 14th Dalai Lama (1940–)

te·pee /teé peé/, **tee·pee** *n* a Native North American conical tent dwelling

tep·id /téppid/ *adj* **1** lukewarm o *tepid water* **2** unenthusiastic o *tepid applause* —**te·pid·i·ty** /tə píddətee/ *n* —**tep·id·ly** *adv* —**tep·id·ness** *n*

te·qui·la /tə keélə/ *n* a Mexican alcoholic drink made from the agave plant

⚡ **ter·a·byte** /térrə bìt/ *n* in computing, an information unit of one trillion bytes

⚡ **ter·a·flop** /térrə flòp/ *n* a measure of computer speed that is one million million floating-point operations per second

ter·bi·um /túrbee əm/ *n* (*symbol* **Tb**) a silvery gray metallic chemical element. Use: lasers, X-rays, television tubes. —**ter·bic** *adj*

ter·cen·ten·a·ry /tùrs'n ténnəree, tùr séntə nèrree/ (*pl* **-ries**), **ter·cen·ten·ni·al** /-ténnee əl/ *n* a 300th anniversary —**ter·cen·ten·a·ry** *adj*

Mother Teresa

Te·re·sa (of Cal·cut·ta) /tə reéssə-/, **Mother** (1910–97) Albanian-born nun

Te·resh·ko·va /tə resh kôvə/, **Valentina** (b. 1937) Soviet cosmonaut and the first woman in space (1963)

~~terestrial~~ incorrect spelling of **terrestrial**

ter·i·ya·ki /térree yaákee/ *n* a Japanese dish of marinated and broiled shellfish or meat

term *n* **1** a specific name or word for something **2** the period of time something lasts, with a fixed beginning and end (*fml*) o *during her term of office* **3** a period of time that a political or legal body continues meeting **4** a division of an academic year **5** a specific time, especially for making a payment **6** the expected time for the birth of a child o *a pregnancy that came to term* **7** a mathematical expression forming part of a fraction, proportion, or series ■ **terms** *npl* **1** the way people get along together o *parted on good terms* **2** the conditions that make up an agreement or contract o *the terms of the lease* **3** the words used or chosen when speaking or writing o *overly technical terms* ■ *vt* describe with a specific word o *termed the situation precarious* ◇ **come to terms (with)** reach a state of acceptance about something ◇ **in terms of** in relation to

ter·ma·gant /túrməgənt/ *n* a woman regarded as quarrelsome and fault-finding (*insult*)

⚡ **ter·mi·nal** /túrmən'l/ *adj* **1** causing death o *a terminal illness* **2** dying of a fatal illness, or relating to patients so affected o *terminal care* **3** of or at the very end of something ■ *n* **1** a place at the end of a transportation route **2** a conductor attached to the point where electricity enters or leaves a circuit o *a battery terminal* **3** a remote input or output device linked to computer, or a combination of such devices —**ter·mi·nal·ly** *adv* ◇ See note at **deadly**

ter·mi·nate /túrmə nàyt/ (-nat·ed, -nat·ing) v 1 vti finish ○ *terminate a broadcast* 2 vt fire an employee —**ter·mi·na·tion** /tùrmə náysh'n/ n —**ter·mi·na·tor** n

ter·mi·nol·o·gy /tùrmə nóllǝjee/ (pl -gies) n 1 specialized vocabulary, or an example of this 2 the study of names and terms —**ter·mi·no·log·i·cal** /tùrminə lójjik'l/ adj —**ter·mi·nol·o·gist** n

ter·mi·nus /túrmǝnǝss/ (pl -ni /-nì/ or -nus·es) n 1 a station, town, or city where a transportation route ends 2 a point where something ends

ter·mite /túr mìt/ n an insect that lives in large colonies and destroys wood

term pa·per n a long paper written for a school class

tern (pl terns or same) n a black-and-white seabird related to the gull

ter·race /térrǝss/ n 1 a flat area beside a building used for sitting or eating outdoors 2 a balcony 3 a porch or walkway with pillars at the side 4 a rooftop patio 5 one of a series of flat strips of land constructed in steps on a hillside for growing crops 6 an artificially constructed bank of ground 7 a row of identical houses joined together at the sides 8 a street set on a hill ■ vt (-raced, -rac·ing) convert land into a terrace or terraces

ter·rac·ing /térrǝssing/ n the making of a terrace or terraces

ter·ra cot·ta /tèrrǝ kóttǝ/ n 1 a reddish brown pottery clay 2 something made of terra cotta

ter·ra fir·ma /tèrrǝ fúrmǝ/ n dry land

ter·rain /tǝ ráyn/ (pl -rains or same) n 1 a specific area of land ○ *surveyed the local terrain* 2 topography ○ *mountainous terrain*

ter·ra in·cog·ni·ta /-in kog néetǝ, -in kógnitǝ/ (pl ter·rae in·cog·ni·tae /tèrree in kog néetee, -in kógnitee/) n 1 an unexplored region 2 an unexplored subject

ter·ra·pin /térrǝpin/ (pl -pins or same) n 1 a moderate-sized turtle that lives in brackish water 2 a small freshwater turtle

ter·rar·i·um /tǝ ráiree ǝm/ (pl -ums or -a /-ree ǝ/) n an enclosure for keeping plants or small animals indoors in a simulated natural environment

~~terrestial~~ incorrect spelling of terrestrial

ter·res·tri·al /tǝ réstree ǝl/ adj 1 of the Earth 2 belonging to the land 3 living or growing on land 4 broadcast by a land-based transmitter ■ n in science fiction, a person or animal that lives on Earth

ter·res·tri·al link n a telecommunications connection running on or under the ground

ter·ri·ble /térrǝb'l/ adj 1 very serious or severe 2 very unpleasant 3 extremely low in quality ○ *a terrible movie* 4 very ill or unhappy 5 very troubling ○ *a terrible shock* —**ter·ri·bly** adv

ter·ri·er /térree ǝr/ n a breed of small dog originally bred for hunting animals in burrows

ter·ri·fic /tǝ ríffik/ adj 1 very good (infml) 2 very great in size, force, or degree ○ *a terrific snowstorm* —**ter·rif·i·cal·ly** adv

~~terrifiely~~ incorrect spelling of terrifically

ter·ri·fy /térrǝ fì/ (-fied, -fies) vt 1 make very frightened 2 coerce or intimidate —**ter·ri·fy·ing** adj —**ter·ri·fy·ing·ly** adv

ter·rine /te reén, tǝ-/ n 1 a small tight-lidded dish for cooking pâté 2 a coarse pâté cooked in a terrine

ter·ri·to·ri·al /tèrrǝ táwree ǝl/ adj 1 of land or water owned by a country 2 asserting ownership of an area and protecting it against intruders —**ter·ri·to·ri·al·ly** adv

ter·ri·to·ri·al wa·ters npl the area of sea around a country's coast recognized as being under that country's jurisdiction

ter·ri·to·ry /tèrrǝ táwree/ (pl -ries) n 1 land, or an area of land 2 a geographic area owned and controlled by a country 3 also **Ter·ri·to·ry** an area of a country that is not a state or province but has a separate government 4 a field of knowledge, inquiry, or experience 5 an area that an animal considers its own and defends against intruders 6 the district that a traveling salesperson covers ◇ **come or go with the or somebody's territory** be an inseparable part of or accompaniment to something else (infml) ○ *Danger goes with a firefighter's territory.*

ter·ror /térrǝr/ n 1 intense fear 2 terrorism 3 a cause or source of fear 4 a young person regarded as highly annoying (infml offensive)

ter·ror·ism /térrǝ rìzzǝm/ n the unlawful use or threat of violence to intimidate or coerce, usually for political or ideological reasons —**ter·ror·ist** n

ter·ror·ize /térrǝ rìz/ (-ized, -iz·ing) vt 1 intimidate or coerce with violence or the threat of violence 2 make very fearful over a period of time —**ter·ror·i·za·tion** /tèrrǝri záysh'n/ n

ter·ry /térree/, **ter·ry cloth** n a fabric with uncut loops of thread on both sides. Use: towels, bath mats, bathrobes.

terse (ters·er, ters·est) adj 1 brief and unfriendly ○ *a terse reply* 2 concise —**terse·ly** adv —**terse·ness** n

ter·ti·a·ry /túrshee èrree, -shǝree/ adj third (fml) ■ n **Ter·ti·a·ry** a period of geologic time 65–1.64 million years ago —**Ter·ti·a·ry** adj

TESL /téss'l/ abbr teaching (of) English as a second language

test n 1 a series of questions, problems, or tasks to gauge somebody's knowledge, ability, or experience 2 a trial use of a process or equipment to find out whether it works 3 a basis for the evaluation of somebody or something 4 a difficult situation or event that will provide information about somebody or something **5** a medical examination of a part of the body **6** a procedure to detect the presence or properties of a substance ■ *v* **1** *vt* use something on a trial basis in order to evaluate it **2** *vt* ask somebody questions or set somebody a task in order to gauge knowledge, ability, or experience **3** *vt* carry out a medical or scientific test on something **4** *vi* achieve a particular test result o *has tested positive for the virus* —**test·a·ble** *adj* —**test·ing** *adj*

ORIGIN Test came via French from a Latin word meaning "earthenware pot." The original English meaning was "pot in which metals were heated," and the use of this means in investigating the properties of metals gave rise in the late 16C to the sense "investigative or trial procedure."

tes·ta·ment /téstəmənt/ *n* **1** a proof of something **2** a will o *the decedent's last will and testament* **3** **Tes·ta·ment** each half of the Christian Bible **4** **Tes·ta·ment** a copy of the New Testament —**tes·ta·men·ta·ry** /tèstə méntəree, -méntree/ *adj*

test ban *n* an international agreement banning nuclear weapons testing

test case *n* **1** an important legal case that establishes a precedent **2** a case intended to test the constitutionality of a statute

test drive *n* a short drive to try out a car before buying it

test·er /téstər/ *n* **1** somebody who tests new products **2** a sample of a product, especially a cosmetic **3** a piece of equipment for checking the proper functioning of something

tes·tes plural of **testis**

tes·ti·cle /téstik'l/ *n* either of the male sperm-producing glands with their surrounding membranes —**tes·tic·u·lar** /te stíkyələr/ *adj*

tes·ti·fy /téstə fì/ (**-fied, -fies**) *vi* **1** make a declaration under oath in court **2** make a factual statement based on personal experience **3** be proof or evidence *(fml)* —**tes·ti·fi·er** *n*

tes·ti·mo·ni·al /tèstə mónee əl/ *n* **1** a statement backing up a claim **2** a favorable report on somebody or something **3** a tribute to somebody or something —**tes·ti·mo·ni·al** *adj*

tes·ti·mo·ny /téstə mònee/ (*pl* **-nies**) *n* **1** evidence given by a witness in court **2** proof of something

tes·tis /téstiss/ (*pl* **-tes** /-tèez/) *n* either of the male sperm-producing glands

tos·tos·ter·one /te stóstə ròn/ *n* a male hormone produced in the testicles and responsible for the development of secondary sex characteristics

test pat·tern *n* a pattern transmitted to help in tuning a television set

test pi·lot *n* a pilot who flies new aircraft to test their performance

test tube *n* a glass tube closed and rounded at one end and open at the other, used in a laboratory

test-tube *adj* made in a test tube or by other artificial means

test-tube ba·by *n* a baby conceived from an egg fertilized in a laboratory and then inserted into the womb *(infml)*

tes·ty /téstee/ (**-ti·er, -ti·est**) *adj* impatient or irritable —**tes·ti·ly** *adv* —**tes·ti·ness** *n*

tet·a·nus /tétt'nəss/ *n* an infectious disease causing severe muscular spasms —**tet·a·nal** *adj*

tête-à-tête /tàytə táyt/ *n* a private conversation between two people ■ *adj, adv* in private between two people

teth·er /téthər/ *n* a rope attached to an animal and fixed at the other end to restrict its movement ■ *vt* tie an animal with a tether

Te·ton[1] /tée tòn, teét'n/ (*pl same or* **-tons**), **Te·ton Da·ko·ta** *n* **1** a member of a group of Native North American peoples who now live mainly in North and South Dakota **2** the language of the Teton people —**Te·ton** *adj*

Te·ton[2] /tée tòn/ range of the Rocky Mountains in NW Wyoming and SW Idaho. Highest peak Grand Teton 13,770 ft./4,197 m.

tet·ra /téttrə/ (*pl* **-ras** *or same*) *n* a brightly colored freshwater fish popular as an aquarium fish

tetra- *prefix* four o *tetrahedron*

tet·ra·he·dron /tèttrə heédrən/ (*pl* **-drons** *or* **-dra** /-drə/) *n* a solid figure with four faces

Teu·ton·ic /too tónnik, tyoo-/ *adj* of German-speaking peoples

Te·vet /táy vàyss, te vét/, **Te·bet** *n* the 10th month of the year in the Jewish calendar

Tex. *abbr* Texas

Tex·as /téksəss/ state of the SW United States. Cap. Austin. Pop. 20,851,820 (2000). —**Tex·an** *n, adj*

Tex-Mex /téks mèks/ *adj* with a blend of Texan and Mexican cultures or cuisines

text *n* **1** written, typed, or printed words **2** the main body of text, e.g., in a book or article, as distinct from illustrations, headings, and other material **3** a textbook **4** a Bible passage used as the basis of a sermon ■ *vt* send a text message to somebody on their cellphone —**text·u·al** *adj*

text·book /tékst bòòk/ *n* a book containing essential information for a course of study ■ *adj* typical and thus a suitable example for study

⨏ **text ed·i·tor** *n* a computer program allowing the creation and editing of text

⨏ **text file** *n* a computer file of alphanumeric characters

tex·tile /tékstīl/ n a fabric

⚡ **text mes·sage** n a message sent in textual form, especially to a cellphone or pager —**text-mes·sag·ing** n

⚡ **text proc·ess·ing** n the use of computers to manipulate text

tex·ture /tékschər/ n 1 the feel of a surface 2 the structure of a substance or material ■ vt (-tured, -tur·ing) give a rough or grainy feel to —**tex·tur·al** adj —**tex·tured** adj

tex·tured veg·e·ta·ble pro·tein n full form of TVP

Th symbol thorium

Thack·er·ay /tháko ràу/, **William Makepeace** (1811–63) British novelist

Thad·dae·us /tháddee əss, thə deé əss/ n one of the 12 apostles of Jesus Christ

Thai /tī/ (pl **Thais** or same) n 1 somebody from Thailand 2 the official language of Thailand —**Thai** adj

Thai·land /tí lànd, -lənd/ country in Southeast Asia. Cap. Bangkok. Pop. 61,797,751 (2001).

Thai·land, Gulf of wide inlet of the South China Sea in S Thailand. Length 500 mi./800 km.

tha·lid·o·mide /thə líddə mīd/ n a synthetic drug formerly used as a sedative but found to damage fetuses

thal·li·um /thállee əm/ n (symbol **Tl**) a toxic metallic chemical element. Use: manufacture of low-melting glass, photocells, infrared detectors.

Thames /temz/ major river of S England, flowing through London and emptying into the North Sea. Length 210 mi./338 km.

than stressed /than/ unstressed /thən/ conj 1 introduces the second element of a comparison o We're older than he is. 2 when o Barely had she opened the door than the phone started to ring. ■ prep in contrast with or in preference to (infml) o I'm older than him ◊ See note at **then**

USAGE **than he or than him?** Because **than** is a preposition as well as a conjunction, either construction is possible, as is the fuller form than he is. The form than him is common in conversation and other spoken contexts (We're older than him) but is still frowned upon in formal writing where We're older than he is is preferred.

thane /thayn/ n 1 an Anglo-Saxon nobleman who held lands in return for military service to a lord 2 a feudal baron in Scotland —**thane·ship** n

thank vt 1 express gratitude to 2 blame or hold responsible for something

thank·ful /thángkfəl/ adj 1 feeling gratitude 2 glad about something —**thank·ful·ness** n

thank·ful·ly /thángkfəlee/ adv 1 with gratitude 2 expresses relief (infml) o Thankfully, they were all safe.

thank·less /thángkləss/ adj 1 unappreciated 2 ungrateful —**thank·less·ly** adv —**thank·less·ness** n

thanks npl 1 gratitude or appreciation 2 an expression of gratitude ■ interj expresses gratitude

thanks·giv·ing /thàngks gívving, thángks gĺvving/ n 1 a prayer of thanks 2 a giving of thanks 3 **Thanks·giv·ing, Thanks·giv·ing Day** a legal holiday in the United States. Date: 4th Thursday in November. 4 **Thanks·giv·ing, Thanks·giv·ing Day** a legal holiday in Canada. Date: 2nd Monday in October.

thank-you n an expression of gratitude ■ adj expressing gratitude

Thant /thaant, thant/, **U** (1909–74) Burmese politician and secretary-general of the United Nations (1961–71)

that /that/ adj, pron 1 indicates somebody or something already mentioned or identified, or something understood by both speaker and hearer o later that week o Do you remember that? 2 indicates distance from the speaker o that girl over there ■ pron introduces a clause identifying the noun it follows o The committee that deals with such matters. ■ conj 1 introduces a comment or fact o said that he would 2 introduces a result o so loud that I jumped 3 introduces a cause o felt hurt that she said so 4 introduces a purpose o gave his life that others could live ■ adv 1 to the indicated degree o came that close to crashing 2 so very (infml) o didn't think they'd be that annoyed ◊ **that is** in other words ◊ **that's that** that is finished

USAGE For centuries **that** has been used to refer to people as well as things. Though occasionally clumsy, this usage is correct: He's the one that did it.; Anything or anyone that helps me is my friend.

USAGE **that or which?** The relative pronoun **that** introduces a restrictive clause, i.e., a clause providing essential information: A car that has bald tires is not roadworthy. When the relative clause is nonrestrictive, i.e., it gives information that is additional rather than necessary for identifying the noun it follows, **which** is used and is preceded by a comma: The largest house, which stands on the corner, is up for sale.

thatch n 1 plant material such as straw or rushes used for a roof 2 a roof of thatch ■ vti roof a building with thatch —**thatched** adj —**thatch·er** n

British Information Services

Margaret Thatcher

Thatch·er /tháchər/, **Margaret, Baroness Thatcher of Kesteven** (*b.* 1925) first woman prime minister of Great Britain (1979–90)

thaw *v* **1** *vti* change from a solid to a liquid state **2** *vti* change from a frozen to an unfrozen state **3** *vi* become less cold or numb **4** *vi* be warm enough for snow or ice to melt ■ *n* **1** the process of thawing **2** a period of weather warm enough to melt snow and ice

the /thee/ (*unstressed before a consonant*) /thə/ *adj* indicates somebody or something already mentioned or identified, or something understood by both speaker and hearer ◦ *the state you're in* ◦ *the clock on the wall* ◦ *Put them in the small bag.* ◦ *the president of the United States* ■ indicates a generic class ◦ *the rich* ◦ *good for the heart* ■ *adv* **1** to that extent (*before comparatives*) ◦ *the worse for wear* **2** by how much or by that much (*before each of two comparative adjectives or adverbs*) ◦ *The more you exercise, the better you'll feel.*

the·a·ter /thée ətər/, **the·a·tre** *n* **1** a place where plays and other entertainments are performed **2** a place where movies are shown **3** a room with tiers of seats **4** plays and other dramatic literature **5** drama as an art or profession **6** a place of significant events ◦ *the theater of war*

the·at·ri·cal /thee áttrik'l/ *adj* **1** of the theater **2** marked by exaggerated or artificial emotion ■ *n* an actor ■ **the·at·ri·cals**, **the·at·rics** *npl* **1** the performance of plays **2** dramatic behavior —**the·at·ri·cal·i·ty** /thee àttri kállətee/ *n* —**the·at·ri·cal·ly** *adv*

Thebes /theebz/ **1** city of ancient Greece, northwest of present-day Athens **2** capital of ancient Egypt, south of present-day Cairo —**The·ban** *n, adj*

thee /thee/ *pron* the objective form of "thou" (*archaic*)

theft *n* the stealing of property

~~**theif**~~ incorrect spelling of **thief**

their /thair/ *adj* **1** belonging to or associated with them **2** △ belonging to or associated with him or her (*infml*) ◦ *Everyone should have their own copy* ◊ See note at **they**

USAGE **their, there,** or **they're?** **Their** is used before a noun: *Their* [not *They're* or *There*] *attitudes have changed.* **There** can be an adverb or a pronoun: *Look over there* [not *their* or *they're*]. *There* [not *They're* or *Their*]

are several unanswered questions. **They're** is a contraction of "they are," as in *They're* [not *There* or *Their*] *sitting in the front row.*

theirs /thairz/ *pron* **1** that or those belonging to them **2** that or those belonging to him or her (*infml*)

the·ism /thée ìzzəm/ *n* **1** belief in one God **2** belief in a god or gods —**the·ist** *n* —**the·is·tic** /thee ístik/ *adj* —**the·is·ti·cal** *adj*

them /them/ *pron* **1** the objective form of "they" **2** him or her (*infml*)

the·mat·ic /thə máttik/ *adj* of or being a theme —**the·mat·i·cal·ly** *adv*

theme *n* **1** a subject of something spoken or written **2** a distinct and unifying idea **3** a repeated melody in a piece of music **4** a piece of music identified with a movie or broadcast ◊ See note at **subject**

theme park *n* an amusement park designed around a particular subject or idea

theme song *n* a tune identifying somebody or something

~~**themometer**~~ incorrect spelling of **thermometer**

them·self /thəm sélf/ *pron* himself or herself (*nonstandard*) ◦ *as anybody can see for themself*

them·selves /thəm sélvz, them-/ *pron* **1** the reflexive form of "they" or "them" ◦ *hurt themselves* **2** their normal selves ◦ *not feeling themselves today* **3** the emphatic form of "they" or "them" ◦ *did it themselves* **4** himself or herself (*infml*) ◦ *Everyone should do it themselves.*

then /then/ *adv* **1** indicates a specific time in the past or future ◦ *We were much happier then.* **2** after that **3** therefore **4** in addition ■ *adj* being at that time ◦ *my then teacher*

SPELLCHECK Do not confuse the spelling of **then** and **than** (indicating a comparison), which sound similar.

thence /thenss/ *adv* from that place or time (*fml or literary*)

thence·forth /thenss fáwrth/ *adv* from then on (*fml or literary*)

thence·for·ward /thenss fáwrwərd/ *adv* from there or then on (*fml or literary*)

theo- *prefix* god ◦ *theology*

the·oc·ra·cy /thee ókrəssee/ (*pl* **-cies**) *n* **1** government by a god or by priests **2** a community governed by a god or by priests —**the·o·crat** /thée ə kràt/ *n* —**the·o·crat·ic** /thée ə kráttik/ *adj* —**the·o·crat·i·cal·ly** *adv*

the·od·o·lite /thee óddə lìt/ *n* a surveyor's instrument for measuring angles —**the·od·o·lit·ic** /thee òddə líttik/ *adj*

the·ol·o·gy /thee ólləjee/ (*pl* **-gies**) *n* **1** the study of religion, especially God's relation to the world **2** a religious theory or system of belief —**the·o·lo·gi·an** /thée ə lójən/ *n* —**the·o·log·i·cal** /thée ə lójjik'l/ *adj* —**the·o·lo·gist** *n*

the·o·rem /thée ərəm, theerəm/ *n* **1** a proposition or formula that is provable from a set of axioms and basic assumptions **2** an idea accepted as true —**the·o·re·mat·ic** /ˌthēə ərə máttik, thēərə máttik/ *adj*

the·o·ret·i·cal /thēə ə réttik'l/, **the·o·ret·ic** /-réttik/ *adj* **1** based on theory **2** dealing with theory rather than practical applications **3** hypothetical —**the·o·ret·i·cal·ly** *adv*

the·o·re·ti·cian /ˌthēə ərə tish'n, thēərə-/ *n* somebody skilled in theorizing

the·o·rist /thēə ə rist, thēərist/ *n* a holder or expounder of a theory

the·o·rize /thēə ə ríz, thēər íz/ *v* **1** *vi* speculate or form a theory about something **2** *vt* conceive of theoretically —**the·o·ri·za·tion** /ˌthēə əri záysh'n, thēəri-/ *n*

the·o·ry /thēə əree, thēəree/ (*pl* -**ries**) *n* **1** the body of rules, principles, and techniques used in a subject **2** abstract thought or speculation **3** an idea formed by speculation **4** a set of hypothetical circumstances **5** a scientific principle used to explain phenomena

~~theorys~~ incorrect spelling of **theories**

the·os·o·phy /thee óssəfee/ (*pl* -**phies**) *n* a religious system based on intuitive insight —**the·o·soph·ic** /thēə ə sóffik/ *adj* —**the·o·soph·i·cal** *adj*

ther·a·peu·tic /ˌthèrrə pyóotik/ *adj* of the treatment or prevention of disease —**ther·a·peu·ti·cal·ly** *adv*

ther·a·peu·tic clon·ing *n* the use of cloning to produce new body tissues

ther·a·py /thérrəpee/ (*pl* -**pies**) *n* **1** treatment that is meant to cure a physical or mental disorder (*often in combination*) **2** psychotherapy —**ther·a·pist** *n*

there /thair/ *unstressed* /thər/ *adv* **1** at or to that place or point ○ *stop there* ○ *go there* **2** on that matter ○ *I can agree with you there.* **3** identifies somebody or something ○ *that house there* ■ *pron* introduces a sentence stating that something or somebody exists ○ *There's a hole in it.* ○ *Once upon a time there was a prince.* ■ *interj* expresses strong feelings or reassurance ◊ **be there for** be ready to give your support or sympathy to ◊ **not all there** not fully conscious, rational, or aware ◊ See note at **their**

USAGE When **there** is followed by a verb like *be*, *appear*, or *seem*, the verb must agree with the grammatical subject coming *after* it: *There are* [not is] *beaches and motels nearby. There appear* [not appears] *to be mistakes in your essay.* There's stands for "there is" and should be used only with a singular grammatical subject: *There's a lot still to be done. There's a car in the garage.* Don't say: *There's three cars in the garage. There's a lot of children in the hall.*

there·a·bouts /ˌthàirə bówts/, **there·a·bout** *adv* near that place or number

there·af·ter /thair áftər/ *adv* after that time

there·by /thair bí/ *adv* **1** by means of or because of that **2** in connection with that

~~therefor~~ incorrect spelling of **therefore**

there·fore /tháir fàwr/ *adv* **1** and so, or because of that **2** accordingly, or to that purpose

there·from /thair fróm/ *adv* from there (*archaic or fml*)

there·in /thair ín/ *adv* in that matter or detail

there·in·af·ter /ˌthàir in áftər/ *adv* from then on (*fml*)

there·of /thair úv, -óv/ *adv* (*fml*) **1** of or about that **2** from that cause or for that reason

there·on /thair ón/ *adv* on that place or surface (*fml*)

there·to /thair tóo/ *adv* to that thing just mentioned (*fml*)

there·up·on /ˌthàirə pón/ *adv* **1** immediately after or in consequence of that **2** upon or concerning that point (*fml*)

there·with /thair wíth, -wíth/, **there·with·al** /-with áwl, -with-/ *adv* **1** with that, or as well as that (*fml*) **2** at that point, or immediately

~~therfore~~ incorrect spelling of **therefore**

therm *n* a unit of heat equal to 1.055×10^8 joules

ther·mal /thúrm'l/ *adj* **1** involving heat **2** hot or warm ○ *thermal baths* **3** describes clothing designed to retain body heat ■ *n* a current of warm air rising through cooler surrounding air —**ther·mal·ly** *adv*

ther·mal im·ag·ing *n* the use of a device that detects areas of different temperatures and displays them on a screen

⚡**ther·mal print·er** *n* a device that produces visible characters by moving heated wires over special paper

thermo- *prefix* heat ○ *thermometer*

ther·mo·bar·ic /ˌthùrmō baárrik, -bárrik/ *adj* describes a bomb containing explosive gas that is released and detonated

ther·mo·cou·ple /thúrmō kúpp'l/ *n* a temperature-measuring device in which two wires of different metals are joined

ther·mo·dy·nam·ics /ˌthùrmō dī námmiks/ *n* the branch of physics that deals with the conversions of forms of energy from one to another (+ *sing verb*) ■ *npl* the processes of thermodynamics (+ *pl verb*) —**ther·mo·dy·nam·ic** *adj* —**ther·mo·dy·nam·i·cist** *n*

ther·mom·e·ter /thər mómmətər/ *n* an instrument for measuring temperature

ther·mo·nu·cle·ar /ˌthùrmō nóoklee ər/ *adj* of nuclear fusion

ther·mo·plas·tic /ˌthùrmō plástik/ *n* a material that softens when heated, without a change in its intrinsic properties —**ther·mo·plas·tic** *adj* —**ther·mo·plas·tic·i·ty** /ˌthùrmō pla stíssətee/ *n*

Ther·mop·y·lae /thər móppəlee/ pass in ancient Greece, northwest of Athens, site of a major battle between the Greeks and Persians in 480 BC

Ther·mos /thúrməss/ *tdmk* a trademark for a vacuum bottle

ther·mo·sphere /thúrmə sfeer/ *n* an atmospheric region beginning about 53 mi./85 km above the Earth's surface

ther·mo·stat /thúrmə stàt/ *n* 1 a device that regulates temperature by means of a sensor 2 a device that activates something, e.g., a fire alarm, in response to a temperature change —**ther·mo·stat·ic** /thùrmə státtik/ *adj* —**ther·mo·stat·i·cal·ly** *adv*

~~thesarus~~ incorrect spelling of **thesaurus**

the·sau·rus /thə sáwrəss/ (*pl* -**ri** /-rì/ *or* -**rus·es**) *n* 1 a book listing groups of words related in meaning 2 a book of specialist vocabulary

ORIGIN **Thesaurus** was adopted from a Latin word meaning "storehouse, treasury" that is also the source of *treasure*.

these /theez/ *pron, adj* the plural of "this"

the·sis /théessiss/ (*pl* -**ses** /-séez/) *n* 1 a proposition advanced as an argument 2 a lengthy academic dissertation based on original research

thes·pi·an /théspee ən/ *n* an actor

ORIGIN **Thespians** are named for Thespis, a Greek poet of the 6C BC who was regarded as the founder of Greek tragedy.

Thes·sa·lo·ni·ans /thèssə lóhee ənz/ *n* either of two books of the Bible, originally letters written to the church in Thessaloníki by St. Paul. (+ *sing verb*)

Thes·sa·lo·ní·ki /thè saa law néekee/ city in NE Greece. Pop. 383,967 (1991).

Thes·sa·ly /théssəlee/ region of north central Greece —**Thes·sa·li·an** /thə sáylee ən/ *n, adj*

the·ta /tháytə, théetə/ *n* the 8th letter of the Greek alphabet

they /thay/ *pron* 1 the people or things already mentioned or identified, or understood by both the speaker and hearer 2 people in general 3 he or she *(infml)*

USAGE Because English does not have a gender-neutral third person singular pronoun that can be used to refer to people, **they**, together with associated words such as *their*, is often used in this role: *Everyone we approached gave their permission.* In more formal contexts it is necessary to use *he or she*, which can be cumbersome. Avoid the problem in writing by recasting the sentence: *All the people we approached gave their permission*, or *We got permission from everyone we approached.*

they'd /thayd/ *contr* 1 they had 2 they would

they'll /thayl/ *contr* 1 they shall 2 they will

they're /thair/ *contr* they are ◊ See note at **their**

they've /thayv/ *contr* they have

thi·a·mine /thí ə mèen, -əmin/, **thi·a·min** /-əmin/ *n* a B vitamin that plays a role in carbohydrate metabolism

thick *adj* 1 deep or broad 2 large in diameter 3 having a particular depth or breadth 4 densely filled or covered ◊ *thick with dust* 5 hard to see through 6 composed of many densely packed things ◊ *a thick forest* 7 having a liquid consistency that is not free-flowing 8 very pronounced or noticeable ◊ *a thick accent* 9 regarded as slow to learn or understand *(infml insult)* 10 made of a heavy material 11 on very friendly terms *(infml)* ■ *n* 1 the most active part ◊ *the thick of the battle* 2 the densest part —**thick·ly** *adv* ◊ **through thick and thin** in both good times and bad times

thick·en /thíkən/ *v* 1 *vti* make or become thick or thicker 2 *vi* become more complex ◊ *The plot thickens.* —**thick·en·er** *n* —**thick·en·ing** *n*

thick·et /thíkit/ *n* a thick growth of small trees or bushes

thick·ness /thíknəss/ *n* 1 the quality of being thick 2 a dimension between two surfaces of an object, especially the shortest dimension 3 a single layer

thick·set /thík sèt/ *adj* 1 with a stocky build 2 growing closely together

thick-skinned *adj* 1 unsympathetic to others' feelings 2 not easily offended by criticism

thief /theef/ (*pl* **thieves** /theevz/) *n* somebody who steals —**thiev·ish** /théevish/ *adj*

~~thier~~ incorrect spelling of **their**

thigh /thī/ *n* the top part of the leg between the knee and the hip

thim·ble /thímb'l/ *n* a cover for the finger to protect it when sewing —**thim·ble·ful** *n*

Thim·phu /thímfoo/, **Thim·bu** /-boo/ capital of Bhutan. Pop. 22,000 (1999).

thin *adj* (**thin·ner, thin·nest**) 1 shallow or narrow 2 having a small diameter ◊ *thin wire* 3 with little body fat 4 sparsely distributed ◊ *thin hair* 5 watery 6 made of lightweight material 7 easy to see through 8 lacking volume or resonance ◊ *a thin sound* ■ *vti* (**thinned, thin·ning**) make or become thin or thinner —**thin·ly** *adv* —**thin·ness** *n*

SYNONYMS **thin, lean, slim, slender, emaciated, scraggy, scrawny, skinny** CORE MEANING: without much flesh, the opposite of fat

thine /thīn/ *pron, adj* yours or your *(archaic; before vowels)*

thing *n* 1 an inanimate object 2 an unspecified item 3 an occurrence ◊ *The fire was a terrible thing.* 4 a word or thought ◊ *Don't say another thing.* 5 a detail or piece of information ◊ *forgot one important thing* 6 an aim or objective ◊ *The thing is to win.* 7 a responsibility or concern ◊ *several things to finish* 8 an act or deed ◊ *do great things* 9 a living being **10** a preferred activity *(infml)* ○ *not my thing* **11** a fashion *(infml)* ○ *the latest thing* ■ **things** *npl* **1** personal belongings **2** equipment for a particular purpose ○ *our camping things*

ORIGIN The long-lost ancestral meaning of **thing** is "time." Its prehistoric Germanic precursor evolved semantically via "appointed time" to "judicial or legislative assembly." This was the meaning it originally had in English, and it survives in other Germanic languages (the Icelandic parliament is known as the *Althing*, literally "general assembly"). In English, however, the word moved on through "subject for discussion in such an assembly" to "subject in general, affair, matter" and finally "entity, object."

thing·a·ma·jig /thíngəmə jìg/, **thing·um·a·jig, thing·a·ma·bob** /-bòb/, **thing·um·a·bob, thing·um·my** /thíngəmee/ *(pl -mies)*, **thing·y** /thíngee/ *(pl -ies)* n somebody or something whose name is temporarily forgotten or not known

think (thought /thawt/) v **1** *vti* use the mind to form thoughts, consider ideas, and make judgments **2** *vt* have as an opinion **3** *vti* imagine or understand something or the possibility of something ○ *I can't think of leaving without you.* **4** *vti* bring something to mind **5** *vt* view in a particular way ○ *thought her most generous* **6** *vti* intend or decide to do something ○ *He thought he'd stay after all.* **7** *vt* expect ○ *didn't think you'd be early* —**think·a·ble** *adj* —**think·er** *n* —**think·ing** *n, adj* ◊ **think better of** change your mind about ◊ **think nothing of** regard as easy or ordinary ◊ **think twice** reconsider very carefully

□ **think up** *vt* invent or devise

think·ing cap ◊ **put your thinking cap on** think carefully about something, especially to find a solution to a problem

think tank *n* a committee of experts who give advice, especially to a government

thin·ner /thínnər/ *n* a liquid that dilutes paint or varnish

thin-skinned *adj* **1** sensitive to criticism **2** with a thin peel

third *n* **1** one of three parts into which something is or could be divided **2** the one after the second in a series —**third** *adj, adv*

third base *n* in baseball, the third of four bases, which must be touched to score a run, or the player positioned close to it

third class *n* the category two below the best —**third-class** *adj, adv*

third-de·gree burn *n* the most severe class of burn, with serious damage to the skin and tissues beneath

third·ly /thúrdlee/ *adv* as a third point

third par·ty *n* **1** somebody involved in a legal matter but not as a principal party **2** a third major political party

third per·son *n* the form of a verb or pronoun that refers to somebody or something being spoken about

third-rate *adj* of a low or the lowest quality

Third Reich *n* the Nazi regime in Germany between 1933 and 1945

Third World, third world *n* the developing nations —**Third World·er** *n*

thirst *n* **1** the desire or need for liquid to drink **2** a craving ○ *a thirst for knowledge* —**thirst** *vi*

thirst·y /thúrstee/ *(-i·er, -i·est)* *adj* **1** wanting or needing liquid to drink **2** having a craving —**thirst·i·ly** *adv* —**thirst·i·ness** *n*

thir·teen /thər teén/ *n* the number 13 —**thir·teen** *adj, pron* —**thir·teenth** *n, adj, adv*

thir·ty /thúrtee/ *n (pl -ties)* the number 30 ■ **thir·ties** *npl* **1** the numbers 30 to 39, particularly as a range of temperatures **2** the years from 30 to 39 in a century or somebody's life —**thir·ty** *adj, pron* —**thir·ti·eth** *n, adj, adv*

this /thiss/ *adj, pron* **1** indicates somebody or something present or close by ○ *This book is brilliant.* ○ *Is this what you're looking for?* **2** indicates somebody or something just mentioned ○ *This vacation – how much is it going to cost?* ○ *Is this why you've been happy lately?* **3** indicates words to follow ○ *All I can say is this – I didn't know about it.* **4** indicates a particular time in the present or past ○ *I expected him back before this.* ■ *adv* emphasizes the degree of a feeling or quality ○ *was this close to leaving* ◊ **this and that** miscellaneous unimportant things

this·tle /thíss'l/ *n* a plant with prickly stems and leaves and rounded, usually purple, flowers

this·tle·down /thíss'l dòwn/ *n* **1** the fluffy mass of hairs attached to the seeds of a thistle **2** a fine silky substance

thith·er /thíthər/ *adv* in that direction *(archaic fml)*

~~thoght~~ incorrect spelling of **thought**

Thom·as, St. *(fl AD 1C)* one of the 12 apostles of Jesus Christ

Thom·as, Clarence *(b. 1948)* associate justice of the US Supreme Court (1991–)

Dylan Thomas

Thom·as, Dylan (1914–53) Welsh poet

Thomp·son /tómps'n/, **Benjamin, Count Rumford** (1753–1814) US-born British physicist and politician best known for his research into the nature of heat and friction

Thom·son /tóms'n/, **Virgil** (1896–1989) US composer and critic

thong n 1 a long thin piece of leather 2 a whip 3 a light sandal held on by a strip between the toes 4 a narrow strip of fabric with a waistband, used as underwear or beach-wear

Thor /thawr/ n in Norse mythology, the god of thunder

tho·rax /tháw ràks/ (pl -rax·es or -ra·ces /tha ráy seèz, tháwrə-/) n 1 the upper part of the body, enclosed by the ribs 2 the part between the head and abdomen of an insect, crustacean, or arachnid —**tho·rac·ic** /thə rássik/ adj

Library of Congress

Henry David Thoreau

Tho·reau /thə rố, tháw rố/, **Henry David** (1817–62) US essayist and philosopher

tho·ri·um /tháwree əm/ n (symbol **Th**) a soft radioactive element. Use: alloys, source of nuclear energy. —**tho·ric** adj

thorn /thawrn/ n 1 a sharp point on a plant stem 2 a plant with thorns —**thorned** adj

thorn·y /tháwrnee/ (-i·er, -i·est) adj 1 problematic 2 prickly with thorns —**thorn·i·ness** n

thor·ough /thúrrő/ adj 1 extremely careful and accurate 2 done fully —**thor·ough·ly** adv —**thor·ough·ness** n ◊ See note at **careful**

ORIGIN **Thorough** was originally a form of *through*, and used to be used as a preposition and adverb in the same way. The adjective sense that survives developed from "through so as to affect every part."

thor·ough·bred /thúrrə brèd/ n 1 a purebred animal 2 **Thor·ough·bred** a breed of racehorse descended from English mares and Arabian stallions —**thor·ough·bred** adj

thor·ough·fare /thúrrə fàir/ n 1 a public road 2 a route or passage from one place to another

thor·ough·go·ing /thùrrő gố ing, thùrrə-/ adj 1 thoroughly done 2 in every respect o a thoroughgoing pragmatist

Thorpe /thawrp/, **Jim** (1888–1953) US athlete

those /thőz/ pron, adj the plural of "that"

thou /thow/, **Thou** pron you (when addressing God)

though /thő/ conj although ■ adv 1 and yet 2 nevertheless ◊ See note at **although**

thought /thawt/ n 1 the process of thinking or considering 2 an idea produced by mental activity 3 a set of ideas o medieval religious thought 4 reasoning power 5 an intention, expectation, or hope o entertains no thoughts of failing 6 compassionate consideration o no thought for other people ■ past participle, past tense of **think**

thought·ful /tháwtfəl/ adj 1 considerate 2 appearing to be in deep thought —**thought·ful·ly** adv —**thought·ful·ness** n

thought·less /tháwtləss/ adj 1 inconsiderate 2 done without thought —**thought·less·ly** adv —**thought·less·ness** n

thought-out adj planned (usually in combination)

thought-pro·vok·ing adj making somebody reflect deeply

~~thourough~~ incorrect spelling of **thorough**

thou·sand /thówz'nd/ n (pl same or -sands) 1 the number 1,000 2 a large number (infml) ■ **thou·sands** npl very many —**thou·sandth** adj, adv, n

Thou·sand Is·lands group of more than 1,000 small islands in the St. Lawrence River, between SE Ontario, Canada, and N New York.

~~thousend~~ incorrect spelling of **thousand**

Thrace /thrayss/ region in SE Europe, including parts of present-day Greece, Bulgaria, and Turkey —**Thra·cian** adj, n

thrall /thrawl/ n the state of being dominated (literary) o in the thrall of greed —**thrall·dom** n

thrash v 1 vt beat a person or animal with a whip or stick 2 vt defeat an opponent or team decisively 3 vti toss the body and limbs about ■ n a beating with a whip or stick —**thrash·ing** n

⚡**thread** /thred/ n 1 fine twisted cord. Use: sewing, weaving. 2 a piece of thread 3 a very thin strand, trickle, or wisp 4 the helical or spiral ridge on a screw 5 something connecting elements of a story, discussion, or series of events 6 a set of related messages in an Internet discussion group ■ v 1 vt pass thread, tape, or film through something 2 vt string beads on a thread 3 vti make your way through something, following a winding route —**thread-like** adj

thread·bare /thréd bàir/ adj 1 worn away to reveal threads 2 overused so no longer convincing 3 meager o a threadbare existence

threat /thret/ n 1 a declaration of an intent to cause harm 2 an indication of something bad o a threat of rain 3 somebody or something likely to cause harm

threat·en /thrétt'n/ vti 1 express a threat against somebody 2 be a threat to the wellbeing of somebody or something 3 be a sign of something bad —**threat·en·ing** adj —**threat·en·ing·ly** adv

three n the number 3 —**three** adj, pron

three-D, 3-D n a three-dimensional effect

three·di·men·sion·al *adj* **1** having the dimensions of height, width, and depth **2** appearing to have depth behind a flat surface —**three-di·men·sion·al·i·ty** *n*

three·fold /thrē fōld/ *adj* **1** consisting of three **2** three times as many or much ■ *adv* by three times

three-leg·ged race *n* a race between pairs of runners who have their adjacent legs tied together

Three Mile Is·land island in the Susquehanna River in SE Pennsylvania, site of a major nuclear reactor accident in 1979

three-ply *adj* with three layers or strands

three-quar·ter *adj* being three-fourths of something measurable or countable ○ *a three-quarter coat*

three-ring cir·cus *n* **1** a circus with three rings **2** a hectic situation (*infml*)

three Rs /-aarz/, **3 Rs** *npl* reading, writing, and arithmetic

three·score /thrē skawr/ *adj, n* sixty (*archaic*)

three·some /thrēssəm/ *n* **1** a group of three **2** an activity for three

three-wheel·er *n* a vehicle with three wheels

Three Wise Men *n* in Christianity, the three Magi

thren·o·dy /thrénnədee/ (*pl* -dies) *n* a lament for the dead —**thre·nod·ic** /thrə nóddik/ *adj* —**thren·o·dist** *n*

thresh *v* **1** *vti* separate the seeds from harvested plants with a machine or flail **2** *vi* move about violently —**thresh** *n* —**thresh·er** *n*

~~threshhold~~ incorrect spelling of **threshold**

thresh·old /thré shōld/ *n* **1** a piece of wood or stone that forms the bottom of a doorway **2** an entrance **3** the point at which something starts

threw past tense of **throw**

thrice *adv* three times (*literary*)

thrift *n* **1** the prudent use of money and goods **2** a savings and loan association, savings bank, or credit union

thrift shop *n* a store that sells used goods for charity

thrift·y /thríftee/ (-i·er, -i·est) *adj* careful with money and resources —**thrift·i·ly** *adv* —**thrift·i·ness** *n*

thrill *vti* **1** make or be very excited or pleased **2** vibrate or cause to vibrate ■ *n* **1** a cause of great excitement **2** a feeling of great excitement —**thrill·ing** *adj* —**thrill·ing·ly** *adv*

thrill·er /thríllər/ *n* a book, play, or movie with an exciting plot

thrive /thrīv/ (**thrived** or **throve** /thrōv/, **thrived** or **thriv·en** /thrívv'n/, **thriv·ing**) *vi* **1** grow well **2** be successful

throat /thrōt/ *n* **1** the part of the digestive and breathing passage between the rear of the mouth and the esophagus **2** the front of the neck **3** a narrow part or passage

throat·y /thrōtee/ (-i·er, -i·est) *adj* deep or rough in sound or tone —**throat·i·ly** *adv* —**throat·i·ness** *n*

throb (**throbbed**, **throb·bing**) *vi* **1** beat or pulsate rapidly and forcefully **2** have a regular or rhythmic beat —**throb** *n* —**throb·bing·ly** *adv*

throe /thrō/ *n* a spasm of pain

throm·bo·sis /throm bóssiss/ (*pl* -ses /-bō seez/) *n* the formation or presence of blood clots in an artery —**throm·bot·ic** /throm bóttik/ *adj*

throne /thrōn/ *n* **1** a ceremonial chair for a monarch or bishop **2** the power of a monarch

throng *n* a large crowd ■ *v* **1** *vt* crowd into or around **2** *vi* move in a crowd

throt·tle /thrótt'l/ *n* **1** a valve controlling the flow of a fluid, especially fuel and air entering an engine **2** a control for a throttle ■ *vt* (-tled, -tling) **1** regulate fuel flow or engine speed using a throttle **2** kill a person or animal by choking **3** silence or suppress somebody or something

through /throo/ *prep, adv* **1** passing from one side or end of something to the other **2** traveling across or to various places in a town, country, or area **3** among or in the midst of people or things ○ *wandering through the crowds* **4** past the limitations or difficulties of a barrier or problem **5** to a successful conclusion ■ *prep* **1** by means of **2** happening or existing over the extent of **3** because of **4** up to and including ■ *adv* completely and in every part ■ *adj* going directly without stopping or requiring a change ○ *a through road* ◊ **be through with** have finished with, or have no further connections with (*infml*) ◊ **through and through** completely

through·out /throo ówt/ *prep, adv* through the whole of

✝ **through·put** /throo poot/ *n* the volume of data or material processed over a given period

through·way /throo wày/ *n* an expressway

throve past tense of **thrive**

throw /thrō/ *vt* (**threw** /throo/, **thrown** /thrōn/) **1** propel something from the hand and through the air **2** put or drop something carelessly **3** force somebody or something into a particular place or condition ○ *was thrown into confusion* **4** hurl somebody to the ground **5** project light, or cast a shadow by blocking light **6** cast doubt or suspicion **7** take somebody by surprise (*infml*) **8** move an operating switch or lever **9** show an extreme reaction ○ *throw a tantrum* **10** direct or deliver something such as a punch **11** make an object on a potter's wheel **12** host a party ■ *n* **1** an act or way of throwing **2** a distance or score thrown —**throw·er** *n*

SYNONYMS throw, chuck, fling, heave, hurl,

toss, cast CORE MEANING: send something through the air

□ **throw away** or **out** vt discard something
□ **throw up** vti vomit (infml)

throw·a·way /thró ə wày/ n 1 an advertising leaflet or handbill 2 an abandoned child or young person ■ adj 1 said or written in an offhand manner 2 designed to be thrown away after use 3 abandoned by parents or guardians 4 wasteful and tending to discard things too readily ◇ a throwaway society

throw·back /thró bàk/ n 1 an organism with the characteristics of an earlier type or ancestor 2 reversion to an earlier type 3 a contemporary person or thing that seems to belong to the past

throw pil·low n a small pillow for decoration

thru /throo/ prep, adv, adj through (infml)

thrum (thrummed, thrum·ming) v 1 vti strum on a stringed instrument 2 vi tap or beat steadily or monotonously —**thrum** n

~~thruogh~~ incorrect spelling of **through**

thrush[1] (pl **thrush·es** or same) n a songbird with a speckled breast

thrush[2] n a fungal infection of the mouth or vagina

thrust v (thrust) 1 vti push forcefully 2 vt force to go somewhere or do something ◇ was thrust into the limelight 3 vti stretch or extend ◇ spires thrusting into the sky ■ n 1 a forceful push 2 forward movement 3 a stabbing action 4 the reactive force of expelled gases generated by a rocket or jet engine 5 the propulsive force of a rotating propeller 6 the gist or main purpose ◇ the thrust of her argument 7 the force exerted by one structure on another —**thrust·ing** adj

thru·way /throo wày/ n a throughway (infml)

Thu·cyd·i·des /thoo síddi dèèz/ (460?–400? BC) Athenian historian

thud n a dull heavy sound or blow —**thud** vi

thug n a brutal and violent person, especially a criminal —**thug·ger·y** n —**thug·gish** adj

ORIGIN The original **thugs** were members of a group of robbers and murderers in India, worshipers of the goddess Kali, who usually strangled their victims. The first English references to them appear in the early 19C, and by the 1830s the name **thug** was being given to any violent robber.

thu·li·um /thóolee əm/ n (symbol **Tm**) a gray metallic chemical element. Use: X-ray source.

thumb /thum/ n 1 the shortest thickest digit on the human hand located next to the forefinger, or a corresponding digit on an animal's hand 2 a section of a glove or mitten for the thumb ■ v 1 vti hitch a ride by signaling with the thumb to passing drivers 2 vt make dirty by handling 3 vti flip through printed matter ◇ all thumbs

extremely awkward or clumsy ◇ **stick out like a sore thumb** be obvious, or conspicuously out of place ◇ **twiddle your thumbs** be idle ◇ **under somebody's thumb** under somebody's influence and control

thumb in·dex n a series of labeled indentations in the edge of a book, to help find a place —**thumb-in·dex** vt

⚡ **thumb·nail** /thúm nàyl/ n 1 a nail of a thumb 2 a miniature graphic image on a computer monitor ■ adj concise ◇ a thumbnail sketch

thumb·screw /thúm skròo/ n 1 an instrument of torture that crushes people's thumbs 2 a flat-headed screw to be turned with the thumb and forefinger

thumb·tack /thúm tàk/ n a tack for pinning up papers ■ vt pin up with a thumbtack

thump v 1 vti strike somebody or something heavily with the fist or an object 2 vi beat fast or loudly (refers to the heart) 3 vi make a dull heavy sound —**thump** n

thun·der /thúndər/ n 1 a loud rumbling noise following lightning 2 a noise resembling thunder ■ v 1 vi make a loud rumbling noise 2 vti shout something loudly and angrily ◇ **steal somebody's thunder** present somebody else's idea or expression as if it were your own

Thun·der Bay city in SW Ontario, Canada, on Thunder Bay, an arm of Lake Superior. Pop. 113,662 (1996).

thun·der·bolt /thúndər bòlt/ n 1 a flash of lightning accompanied by thunder 2 a sudden shocking occurrence

thun·der·clap /thúndər klàp/ n a crash of thunder

thun·der·cloud /thúndər klòwd/ n a dark cloud that produces thunder and lightning

thun·der·head /thúndər hèd/ n the upper rounded mass of a cloud associated with thunderstorms

thun·der·ous /thúndərəss, -drəss/ adj 1 very loud 2 angry and threatening —**thun·der·ous·ly** adv

thun·der·storm /thúndər stàwrm/ n a storm with thunder and lightning

thun·der·struck /thúndər strùk/ adj extremely surprised or incredulous

Thur·ber /thúrbər/, **James** (1894–1961) US writer and cartoonist

Thurs., Thur. abbr Thursday

Thurs·day /thúrz dày, -dee/ n the 4th day of the week

ORIGIN Thursday meant literally "day of thunder." It was a translation of Latin Jovi dies "day of Jove (Jupiter)."

thus /thuss/ adv (fml) 1 consequently 2 like this ◇ **thus far** up to this point

thwack vt hit hard with a flat object —**thwack** n

thwart /thwawrt/ vt prevent from being successful ■ n a crosswise seat in a boat

thy /thī/ *adj* your *(archaic)*

thyme /tīm, thīm/ *n* a small low-growing plant with aromatic leaves used in cooking ◊ See note at **time**

thy·mus /thī́məss/ *(pl* **-mus·es** *or* **-mi** /mī́/), **thy·mus gland** *n* an organ of the immune system, located at the base of the neck

thy·roid /thī́ royd/ *n* **1** the thyroid gland **2** a preparation obtained from an animal's thyroid gland. Use: treating conditions of the thyroid gland. ■ *adj also* **thy·roi·dal** /thī róyd'l/ of the thyroid gland

thy·roid gland *n* a ductless gland in the base of the neck that secretes hormones responsible for controlling metabolism and growth

thy·self /thī sélf/ *pron* yourself *(archaic)*

ti /tee/ *n* a syllable used in singing the 7th note of a scale

Ti *symbol* titanium

Tian Shan ◊ **Tien Shan**

ti·ar·a /tee aára, -érra/ *n* **1** a woman's jeweled head ornament **2** a crown consisting of three coronets with an orb on top, worn by popes

Ti·ber /tíbər/ river of central Italy, emptying into the Tyrrhenian Sea. Length 252 mi./406 km.

Ti·be·ri·us /tī beéree əss/ (42 BC–AD 37) Roman emperor (AD 14–37)

Ti·bet /tə bét/ former independent state and provincial-level administrative area of SW China. With an average elevation of more than 12,000 ft./4,000 m, it is the highest region in the world. Cap. Lhasa. Pop. 2,440,000 (1997). —**Ti·bet·an** *adj, n*

tib·i·a /tíbbee ə/ *(pl* **-ae** /-bee eè/ *or* **-as)** *n* the inner and larger bone of the lower leg —**tib·i·al** *adj*

tic /tik/ *n* **1** a sudden involuntary twitch of a muscle **2** a quirk of behavior

tick[1] *n* a recurring click, especially one made by a clock or watch —**tick** *vi*

tick[2] *n* a tiny bloodsucking parasitic insect

tick[3] *n* a cloth covering of a pillow or mattress

tick·er /tíkər/ *n* **1** somebody's heart *(slang)* **2** an electronic device that displays the prices of securities, formerly a telegraphic device that printed them on a paper strip

tick·er tape *n* paper tape from a ticker

tick·er-tape pa·rade *n* a parade honoring somebody who is showered with confetti, formerly ticker tape, thrown from buildings

tick·et /tíkit/ *n* **1** a printed piece of paper or cardboard entitling the holder to go somewhere or do something **2** a notification of a traffic offense **3** a label or tag showing the price of an article **4** a group of candidates running for office together ■ *vt* attach or issue a ticket to

tick·et scal·per *n* somebody who sells tickets at inflated prices

tick·ing /tíking/ *n* strong cotton fabric. Use: mattress and pillow covers.

tick·le[1] /tík'l/ **(-led, -ling)** *v* **1** *vt* make somebody laugh and twitch by lightly touching a sensitive part of the body **2** *vti* cause itchiness in a part of the body **3** *vt* please or amuse *(often passive)* —**tick·le** *n*

tick·le[2] /tík'l/ *Can* a strait or harbor entrance

tick·lish /tíklish/ *adj* **1** sensitive to tickling **2** problematic —**tick·lish·ly** *adv* —**tick·lish·ness** *n*

tick-tack-toe, tic-tac-toe *n* a game played with a grid to be marked with O's and X's

tid·al /tíd'l/ *adj* of or affected by tides

tid·al wave *n* **1** a huge ocean wave **2** an overwhelming surge ◊ *a tidal wave of emotion*

tid·bit /tíd bìt/ *n* a morsel of food

tid·dly·winks /tíddlee wìngks/, **tid·dle·dy·winks** /tídd'ldee-/ *n* a game in which players flip plastic disks into a cup (+ *sing verb*)

tide /tīd/ *n* **1** the cyclical rise and fall of the ocean and other open waters produced by the attraction of the Moon and Sun **2** an inflow or outflow of water as the ocean rises or falls **3** a general trend **4** a period of time *(archaic; usually in combination)* ◊ *harvest tide* —**tide·less** *adj* ◊ **turn the tide** reverse the course of events

---

ORIGIN Tide originally meant "time." The sense "rise and fall of the sea" arose in the 14C, probably under the influence of related Dutch and German words that had developed the meaning "fixed time." The original sense "time" has been longest preserved in compounds such as *eventide*, *Christmastide*, *noontide*, *Whitsuntide*, and *Yuletide*, all of which are now archaic or literary.

SPELLCHECK Do not confuse the spelling of **tide** and **tied** (past tense and past participle of *tie*), which sound similar.

☐ **tide over** *vt* help through a difficult time

tide-mark /tíd màark/ *n* **1** *also* **tide·line** a mark left by the highest or lowest point of a tide **2** a marker indicating the levels of tides

tid·ings /tídingz/ *npl* news *(literary)*

ti·dy /tídee/ *adj* **(-di·er, -di·est) 1** neat in appearance **2** methodical **3** considerable *(infml)* ◊ *a tidy sum* ■ *vti* **(-died, -dies)** make somebody or something neat —**ti·di·ly** *adv* —**ti·di·ness** *n*

tie /tī/ *v* **(tied** /tīd/, **ty·ing** /tī ing/) **1** *vt* fasten things together with rope, string, or something similar **2** *vt* fasten something with a knot or bow **3** *vt* make a knot or bow **4** *vt* connect or link people or things **5** *vt* restrict somebody to particular conditions **6** *vi* have an equal score in a game or competition ■ *n* **1** a strip of fabric worn around the neck under a shirt collar **2** a long thin piece of material for attaching or fastening something **3** a connection or link **4** an equal outcome in a game or competition **5** a restriction **6** a strengthening beam ◊ See note at **tide**

☐ **tie up** v **1** vt bind using rope, string, or cord **2** vti moor a boat or ship by securing lines **3** vt occupy or keep busy **4** vt use for one purpose that precludes others ○ *money tied up in a savings account*

tie·break·er /tíˈbràykər/, **tie·break** n a method of deciding the winner of a game or competition when there is a tie —**tie·break·ing** adj

tie clip, tie clasp n a clip for holding a necktie in place

tie-dye vt dye designs on cloth by tying portions of it with waxed thread so that only exposed areas take the dye —**tie·dye·ing** n

tie-in n **1** a link or relationship **2** a product that is sold or marketed through its connection with another

~~tieing~~ incorrect spelling of **tying**

Tien Shan /tyèn sháan/, **Tian Shan** mountain range in Central Asia, stretching from Kyrgyzstan through NW China to Mongolia. Highest peak Victory Peak 24,406 ft./7,439 m. Length 1,500 mi./2,400 km.

Ti·e·po·lo /tee éppə lò, tyéppò lò/, **Giovanni Battista** (1696–1770) Italian artist

tier /teer/ n **1** a row of seats in a rising series **2** a layer (*often in combination*) ▪ vt arrange in rising rows —**tiered** adj ◊ See note at **tear**

Ti·er·ra del Fue·go /tee èrrə del fwáygò/ archipelago off the tip of S South America, belonging partly to Argentina and partly to Chile

tie tack, tie tac, tie-pin /tíˈpìn/ n a decorative pin for a necktie

tie-up n **1** a connection **2** a delay or obstruction

tiff n **1** a minor quarrel **2** a brief period of bad temper —**tiff** vi

⚡ **TIFF** /tif/ abbr tagged image file format

Tif·fa·ny /tíffənee/, **Charles Lewis** (1812–1902) US jeweler and retailer

⚡ **TIFF file, TIF file** n a graphic file in a format often used for storing bit-mapped images

tif·fin /tíffin/ n S Asia **1** a light midday meal or snack **2** also **tif·fin car·ri·er** a carrier for prepared food consisting of several stacked metal containers

ti·ger /tígər/ (pl **-gers** or **same**) n **1** a large wild cat with a tawny coat and black stripes **2** a fierce person

ti·ger lil·y n a lily with dark-spotted red or orange flowers

tight /tit/ adj **1** fitting closely or too closely ○ *a tight sweater* **2** stretched so that there is no slack **3** firmly secured or held **4** sealed against leaks or exposure to air **5** strictly controlled ○ *tight security* **6** cramped and

preventing free movement **7** allowing no extra time or money **8** miserly **9** closely contested **10** drunk (*slang*) **11** personally close or intimate (*infml*) —**tight** adv —**tight·en** vti —**tight·ly** adv —**tight·ness** n

tight-fist·ed /tít fístəd/ adj disinclined to spend money —**tight·fist·ed·ness** n

tight-knit /tít nít/ adj **1** closely united by affection or loyalty **2** well-organized to function as a unit

tight-lipped adj **1** unwilling to talk **2** having the lips firmly pressed

tight·rope /tít ròp/ n a rope stretched taut above the ground for somebody to perform a balancing act on ◊ **walk a tightrope** have to deal cautiously with a precarious situation

tight-wad /tít wòd/ n somebody considered to dislike spending money (*insult*)

ti·gress /tígrəss/ n **1** a female tiger **2** a fierce woman

Tig·ris /tígriss/ river in SW Asia, rising in SE Turkey and flowing through Iraq to the Euphrates River. Length 1,180 mi./1,900 km.

Ti·jua·na /ti wáanə, -hwáanə/ city in NW Mexico, near the US border. Pop. 991,592 (1995).

tike n = **tyke**

tik·ka /tíkə/ adj a South Asian dish of pieces of meat that are marinated and then roasted

til·de /tíldə/ n a mark (~) placed over a letter to indicate a specific pronunciation

tile /til/ n **1** a thin piece of baked clay or synthetic material used with others as a covering for floors, roofs, or walls **2** a short pipe in a drain **3** a playing piece in some board games ▪ vt (**tiled, til·ing**) lay tiles on —**til·er** n —**til·ing** n

till[1], **'til, 'till** conj, prep until

> **USAGE till** or **until**? **Till** is an older form of **until**, not a shortening as the forms *'til* or *'till* would suggest. It is more likely to be heard in speech: *Just wait till we get home!* **Until** is more usual at the beginning of a sentence: *Until last week no decision had been taken.*

till[2] n **1** a container for money taken from customers **2** money

till[3] vt prepare land for crops —**till·er** n

till·age /tíllij/ n **1** the tilling of land **2** tilled land

til·ler /tíllər/ n a handle for steering a boat

tilt v **1** vti move so as to slope or slant **2** vi tend toward a particular view or side in a dispute **3** vti charge an opponent with a lance **4** vi joust ▪ n **1** an act of tilting **2** a slope or incline **3** a tendency toward a particular view or side in a dispute **4** a joust **5** **(at) full tilt** at full speed

tim·ber /tímbər/ n **1** growing trees **2** wooded land **3** wood or logs that can be used as a building material **4** a large piece of wood used as a support or as part of a framework —**tim·bered** adj

tim·ber·line /tímbər lìn/ n the altitude above which trees will not grow

tim·bre /támbər, taáNbrə/ n the distinctive quality of a sound other than its pitch or volume

Tim·buk·tu ◆ **Tombouctou**

time /tím/ n **1** (symbol t) a dimension that distinguishes events taking place at the same point in space **2** a period during which something exists or happens **3** a system for measuring intervals of time **4** the minute or hour as indicated on a clock **5** a moment or period when something occurs or is designated to occur **6** a suitable moment **7** a period with a particular quality (often pl) ○ rough times **8** a limited but unspecified period ○ stayed for a time **9** a period in history (often pl) ○ in Shakespeare's time **10** the present (often pl) ○ technology that is ahead of the times **11** a prison term (infml) ○ doing time **12** an instance ○ told you three times **13** the tempo or rhythm of music ■ vt (timed, tim·ing) **1** measure how long something takes **2** plan the moment or occasion for ○ time an entrance ◊ **at one time 1** at a time in the past **2** simultaneously ◊ **at the same time 1** simultaneously **2** nevertheless ◊ **at times** sometimes ◊ **for the time being** for a short time starting from now ◊ **from time to time** occasionally ◊ **have the time of your life** have a very enjoyable experience ◊ **in good time 1** early enough **2** quickly ◊ **in (less than) no time** in a very short period of time ◊ **in time 1** early enough **2** after some time has passed **3** in the correct rhythm ◊ **in your own time** at a speed or pace that feels comfortable ◊ **keep time 1** show the time accurately **2** do something in the correct rhythm, or in the same rhythm as somebody or something else ◊ **mark time 1** march in rhythm without moving forward **2** do nothing while waiting for something to happen ◊ **on time** at the scheduled time ◊ **pass the time of day (with)** engage in casual conversation with somebody ◊ **play for time** delay action or a decision in the hope that conditions will improve ◊ **take your time** take whatever time is necessary ◊ **time after time, time and (time) again** repeatedly

---

SPELLCHECK Do not confuse the spelling of **time** and **thyme** (the herb), which may sound similar.

---

time and mo·tion stud·y n an analysis of working practices aimed at increasing efficiency

time bomb n **1** a bomb that is set to explode at a fixed time **2** a future danger though not a current one

time cap·sule n a container with items representative of the present, buried for a future generation to find

time·card /tím kaàrd/ n an employee's record of working hours to be stamped by a time clock

time clock n a clock with a mechanism for stamping a card when an employee starts and finishes work

time-con·sum·ing adj taking up a great deal of time

time frame n a period during which something takes place or is planned to take place

time-hon·ored adj respected because of being traditional

time·keep·er /tím kèepər/ n **1** somebody recording the time, e.g., during a sports event **2** a watch or clock —**time·keep·ing** n

time lag n a delay between two connected events

time·less /tímləss/ adj **1** unchanged and unchanging **2** eternal —**time·less·ly** adv —**time·less·ness** n

time lim·it n a maximum time allowed

time line n a chronology of significant events shown pictorially

time·ly /tímlee/ (-li·er, -li·est) adj occurring at an appropriate time —**time·li·ness** n —**time·ly** adv

time ma·chine n a fictional or hypothetical machine for traveling through time

time-off n time not spent at work

time out n a short break

⚡**time-out** /tím òwt/ n **1** a time during which a game temporarily stops **2** an interruption in the operation of a computer when a command is not responded to in a predetermined time

time·piece /tím pèess/ n an instrument such as a watch or clock for indicating the time

tim·er /tímər/ n **1** a device that can be set to do something at a given time **2** somebody or something that records or measures time

times prep multiplied by

time-sav·ing /tím sàyving/ adj designed to reduce the time taken to do something

time·scale /tím skàyl/ n **1** a period of time scheduled for the completion of something **2** a measurement of time relative to the time in which a typical event occurs

time-serv·er /tím sùrvər/ n an opportunist whose opinions and behavior change to suit the times —**time·serv·ing** n, adj

time-share /tím shàir/ n **1** the joint ownership of property by people who use it at different times **2** a house or apartment owned and used in this way

⚡**time-shar·ing** n **1** the joint ownership of property by people who use it at different times **2** a technique for simultaneous use of central computer resources by remote terminals —**time-share** vti —**time-shar·er** n

time sheet n a record of the hours somebody has worked

time sig·na·ture n a symbol showing musical meter

time·ta·ble /tím tàyb'l/ n a schedule, especially a list of arrival and departure times for trains or buses —**time·ta·ble** vi

time tri·al n a race in which competitors compete individually against the clock

time warp n a hypothetical distortion in space-time

time·worn /tím wàwrn/ adj 1 having deteriorated through long use 2 overused and no longer effective

time zone n any of the areas of the world in which the same standard time is used

tim·id /tímmid/ adj lacking courage or assertiveness —**ti·mid·i·ty** /ti míddətee/ n —**tim·id·ly** adv

tim·ing /tíming/ n 1 the ability to choose, or the choice of, the best moment to do or say something 2 the recording of the time taken to do something

Ti·mor /teè mawr, tee máwr/ largest and easternmost of the Lesser Sunda Islands, in the Malay Archipelago. Pop. 3,900,000 (1990).

tim·or·ous /tímmərəss/ adj fearful and hesitant —**tim·or·ous·ly** adv —**tim·or·ous·ness** n

Ti·mor Sea arm of the Indian Ocean separating the island of Timor from N Australia

Tim·o·thy /tímməthee/ n either of two books of the Bible, originally letters from St. Paul to his disciple Timothy.

tim·pa·ni /tímpənee/, **tym·pa·ni** n a set of kettledrums used in an orchestra (+ sing or pl verb) —**tim·pa·nist** n

tin n 1 (symbol Sn) a silvery metallic chemical element. Use: alloys such as solder, bronze, and pewter, protective coating for steel. 2 a container with a lid, made of sheet metal ■ adj made of tin ■ vt (tinned, tin·ning) coat with tin

tin can n a container made of tin or aluminum

tinc·ture /tíngkchər/ n 1 a solution of a plant extract or chemical in alcohol 2 a tint or slight coloration 3 a tiny amount of something ■ vt (-tured, -tur·ing) 1 add a tint to 2 suffuse with a quality o praise tinctured with criticism

tin·der /tíndər/ n material such as dry sticks for starting a fire

tin·der·box /tíndər bòks/ n 1 a box containing tinder 2 somebody or something potentially violent

tine /tín/ n a prong of an implement or utensil such as a fork —**tined** adj

tin·foil /tín fòyl/ n aluminum or tin in a very thin sheet

ting n a light high-pitched ringing sound —**ting** vti

tinge /tinj/ (tinged, tinge·ing or ting·ing) vt 1 add a slight amount of color to 2 mix a slight amount of something with o a celebration tinged with sadness —**tinge** n

tin·gle /tíng g'l/ (-gled, -gling) vti feel or cause a stinging, prickling, or vibrating sensation —**tin·gle** n —**tin·gling·ly** adv —**tin·gly** adj

tin god n somebody self-important and overbearing

tin·ker /tíngkər/ n 1 an unskillful worker 2 an act of tinkering with something 3 a traveling mender of pots and pans and other household utensils ■ vi 1 fiddle or meddle with something in an attempt to repair or improve it 2 work as a tinker —**tin·ker·er** n

tin·kle /tíngk'l/ vti (-kled, -kling) make or cause to make light metallic ringing sounds ■ n a tinkling sound —**tin·kly** adj

tin·ni·tus /ti nítəss, tínnitəss/ n a persistent ringing or roaring noise in the ear

tin·ny /tínnee/ (-ni·er, -ni·est) adj 1 having a thin metallic sound 2 of tin 3 tasting of metal —**tin·ni·ness** n

tin plate n iron or steel in thin sheets coated with tin —**tin-plate** vt

tin·pot adj regarded as inferior (infml)

tin·sel /tínsəl/ n 1 glittering material in thin strips, used for decoration 2 something glamorous but worthless —**tin·sel** adj

Tin·sel·town /tínsəl tòwn/ n Hollywood (infml disapproving)

tint n 1 a shade of a color, especially a pale one 2 a trace of color 3 a hair dye —**tint** vti —**tint·er** n

tin·tin·nab·u·la·tion /tìntə nabyə láysh'n/ n a pealing of bells

Tin·to·ret·to /tìntə réttó/ (1518?–94) Italian painter

ti·ny /tínee/ (-ni·er, -ni·est) adj very small —**ti·ni·ness** n

-tion suffix an action or process, or the result of it o pollution

tip[1] n 1 a narrow or pointed end 2 a part fitted on an end ■ vt (tipped, tip·ping) 1 provide or be the end of 2 cover the end of ◊ **on the tip of somebody's tongue** nearly, but not quite, brought to mind ◊ **the tip of the iceberg** the small visible or obvious part of a largely unseen problem or difficulty

tip[2] v (tipped, tip·ping) 1 vti tilt or slant 2 vti knock or be knocked over 3 vt take off your hat as a greeting ■ n 1 an act of tipping 2 a tilt or slant

tip[3] n 1 a gift of money for a service 2 a piece of useful information or advice ■ vti (tipped, tip·ping) give somebody a tip

□ **tip off** vt give a warning or advance notice to

tip[4] n 1 a light glancing blow 2 in baseball, a hit that glances off the bat ■ v (tipped, tip·ping) 1 vt deflect a baseball off the bat 2 vi Southern US walk quietly on tiptoe

tipical incorrect spelling of **typical**

tip-off n (infml) 1 a warning or piece of advance information 2 a sign of something

tip·pet /típpit/ n a stole or cape with ends that hang in front

tip·ple /típp'l/ (**-pled, -pling**) *vi* drink alcohol habitually or repeatedly —**tip·pler** *n*

tip·ster /típstər/ *n* somebody who sells information to horserace bettors and speculators

tip·sy /típsee/ (**-si·er, -si·est**) *adj* slightly drunk —**tip·si·ly** *adv* —**tip·si·ness** *n*

tip·toe /típ tṓ/ (**-toed**) *vi* 1 walk on the toes and balls of the feet with the heels raised 2 move or proceed very cautiously —**tip·toe** *n, adj, adv*

tip·top /típ tòp/ *adj* of the highest quality (*infml*)

ti·rade /tī ráyd, tī ráyd/ *n* a long angry speech

ti·ra·mi·su /teèrə meè soò, teèrə mi soò/ *n* an Italian dessert made with layers of sponge cake soaked in espresso coffee, Marsala, mascarpone cheese, and chocolate

Ti·ra·na /ti raánə/ capital of Albania, in the central part of the country. Pop. 244,200 (1990).

tire[1] /tīr/ *n* a rubber or metal edging for a wheel

tire[2] /tīr/ (**tired, tir·ing**) *vti* 1 make or become tired 2 lose interest or cause to lose interest in something —**tir·ing** *adj*

tired /tīrd/ *adj* 1 needing rest 2 having lost patience or interest —**tired·ly** *adv* —**tired·ness** *n*

tire·less /tīrləss/ *adj* apparently immune to fatigue —**tire·less·ly** *adv* —**tire·less·ness** *n*

tire·some /tīrsəm/ *adj* causing annoyance or fatigue —**tire·some·ly** *adv* —**tire·some·ness** *n*

ti·ro *n* = tyro

Ti·rol /tə rṓl, tī rṓl/, **Ty·rol** province in W Austria. Cap. Innsbruck. Pop. 663,603 (1998). —**Ti·ro·le·an** /tīrrə leè ən/ *n, adj* —**Tir·o·lese** /tīrrə leèz/ *n, adj*

'tis /tiz/ *contr* it is (*literary*)

Tish·ri /tíshree/ (*pl* **-ris**) *n* the 7th month of the year in the Jewish calendar

tis·sue /tíshoo/ *n* 1 a piece of soft absorbent paper 2 a group of cells in an organism that are similar in form or function 3 an intricate series *o a tissue of lies*

tis·sue pa·per *n* thin soft paper. Use: wrapping and protecting delicate items.

tit[1] *n* a teat

tit[2] *n* a small songbird with a short bill

Ti·tan /tīt'n/ *n* 1 in Greek mythology, each of 12 rulers of the universe who were overthrown by Zeus 2 the largest moon of Saturn 3 **ti·tan** a powerful or impressive person

ti·tan·ic /tī tánnik/ *adj* enormous in size or power —**ti·tan·i·cal·ly** *adv*

ti·ta·ni·um /tī táynee əm/ *n* (*symbol* **Ti**) a silvery metallic chemical element. Use: alloys for aerospace industry.

tit for tat *n* the repaying of a wrong or injury by inflicting equivalent harm on the doer

tithe /tīth/ *n* 1 one tenth of somebody's income or produce given to support a church or its clergy 2 a voluntary contribution or tax ■ *v* (**tithed, tith·ing**) 1 *vti* give something as a tithe 2 *vt* collect a tithe from —**tith·er** *n*

Ti·tian /tíshən/ (1485?–1576) Italian painter

Ti·ti·ca·ca, Lake /títti kaakə/ largest lake in South America, extending from SE Peru to W Bolivia

tit·il·late /títt'l àyt/ (**-lat·ed, -lat·ing**) *vti* excite somebody pleasurably, usually in a slightly sexual way —**tit·il·lat·ing·ly** *adv* —**tit·il·la·tion** /títt'l áysh'n/ *n*

tit·i·vate /títti vàyt/ (**-vat·ed, -vat·ing**) *vti* spruce up —**tit·i·va·tion** /títti váysh'n/ *n*

ti·tle /tīt'l/ *n* 1 a name that identifies a literary, artistic, or musical work 2 a descriptive heading 3 a designation added to a name to indicate rank or status 4 a name describing a job position in an organization 5 the status of champion in a sport or competition 6 a legitimate right or proof of a right 7 a published work 8 the legal right to possession of property, or a document giving this right ■ **ti·tles** *npl* credits or subtitles on a screen —**ti·tled** *adj*

ti·tle deed *n* a document that is evidence of somebody's legal right to property

ti·tle·hold·er /tīt'l hòldər/ *n* 1 a holder of a championship title 2 somebody with a legal title to property —**ti·tle·hold·ing** *n*

ti·tle page *n* a page of a book showing the title and author

ti·tle role *n* a role in a play or film that gives the work its name

ti·tlist /tīt'list/ *n* a champion who holds a title

tit·mouse /tít mòwss/ (*pl* **-mice** /-mīss/) *n* a small insect-eating bird

ORIGIN Titmouse is a 16C alteration, under the influence of *mouse*, of the earlier form *titmose*. **Tit** formed compounds meaning "small," and probably came from a Scandinavian language. *Mose* represents an ancient Germanic root itself meaning "titmouse."

Tito

Ti·to /teètō/ (1892–1980) Yugoslav patriot and president of Yugoslavia (1942–77)

tit·ter /títtər/ *vi* laugh lightly and nervously —**tit·ter·ing·ly** *adv*

tit·tle-tat·tle /títt'l tàtt'l/ *n* gossip —**tit·tle-tat·tle** *vi*

tit·u·lar /títchəlar/ adj 1 in name only 2 holding a title of rank —**tit·u·lar·ly** adv —**tit·u·lar·y** n

Ti·tus /títəss/ n a book of the Bible, originally a letter traditionally believed to be from St. Paul to his disciple Titus.

tiz·zy /tízzee/ n a state of nervous agitation (infml)

Tl symbol thallium

TLA abbr three-letter acronym

TLC abbr tender loving care (infml)

Tlin·git /tling git, tlíngit/ (pl -gits or same) n 1 a member of a group of Native North American peoples who live mainly on coastal SE Alaska and in British Columbia 2 the language of the Tlingit people —**Tlin·git** adj

Tm symbol thulium

TM abbr 1 trademark 2 transcendental meditation

TN abbr Tennessee

TNT n a yellow flammable compound. Use: explosive. Full form **trinitrotoluene**

to (stressed) /too/ (unstressed) /tŏ, tə/ prep 1 indicates direction, destination, or position 2 forms the infinitive of verbs 3 indicates purpose o used to chop vegetables with 4 indicates a recipient (with a noun phrase to form the indirect object) o gave it to me 5 indicates who or what a feeling or action is directed toward o grateful to them 6 indicates attachment 7 until o from Tuesday to Saturday 8 indicates a range o everything from pollution to pesticides 9 indicates the result of a change o excitement turned to gloom 10 indicates equality o 12 inches to the foot 11 as compared with o 5 to 3 in our favor ■ adv /too/ 1 so as to be shut or almost shut o pushed the door to 2 so as to be conscious again o came to

SPELLCHECK Do not confuse the spelling of **to**, **too** ("as well"), or **two** ("number 2"), which sound similar.

toad n a terrestrial amphibian similar to a frog but with dry warty skin

toad·stool /tŏd stool/ n a poisonous fungus with a round flat cap on a stalk

toad·y /tŏdee/ (pl -ies) n a servile and ingratiating person —**toad·y** vi —**toad·y·ism** n

ORIGIN Toady is an early 19C shortening of toadeater, a name that originated in the dubious selling methods of itinerant doctors. They employed an assistant who pretended to eat a toad (toads were thought to be poisonous), so that the doctor could appear to effect a miraculous cure with his medicine.

to and fro /-frŏ/ adv 1 back and forth 2 here and there —**to-and-fro** adj, n —**to·ing and fro·ing** n

toast /tŏst/ n 1 bread browned with dry heat, or a piece of this 2 a call to honor somebody or something by raising a glass and drinking 3 a raising of glasses and drinking in

response to a toast ■ v 1 vti brown food with dry heat, or become browned 2 vt warm the body or part of the body near a source of heat 3 vti drink a toast in somebody's honor

toast·er /tŏstər/ n a small appliance for making toast

toast·mas·ter /tŏst màstər/ n somebody who proposes toasts and introduces speakers at a banquet or reception

toast·mis·tress /tŏst místrəss/ n a woman who proposes toasts and introduces speakers at a banquet or reception

toast·y /tŏstee/ (-i·er, -i·est) adj pleasantly warm

to·bac·co /tə bákō/ (pl -cos or same) n 1 dried leaves processed for smoking in cigarettes, cigars, and pipes 2 the plant that produces tobacco

to·bac·co·nist /tə bákənist/ n a seller of tobacco products and supplies

~~tobacco~~ incorrect spelling of **tobacco**

To·ba·go /tə báygō/ island in the Caribbean, part of Trinidad and Tobago. Pop. 50,282 (1990).

To·bit /tŏbit/ n a book of the Roman Catholic Bible and the Protestant Apocrypha, traditionally attributed to Tobit, an Israelite living in Nineveh

to·bog·gan /tə bóggən/ n a long narrow sled without runners ■ vi ride on a toboggan —**to·bog·gan·er** n —**to·bog·gan·ist** n

to·by jug /tŏbee-/ n a beer mug or jug in the shape of a rotund man

toc·ca·ta /tə kaátə/ (pl -tas) n a keyboard composition written in a free style that includes full chords and elaborate runs

Tocque·ville /tók vìll, -/ **Alexis de** (1805–59) French historian and political writer

toc·sin /tóksin/ n 1 an alarm sounded by means of a bell 2 a bell that sounds a tocsin

to·day /tə dáy/ n 1 this day, as distinct from yesterday or tomorrow 2 the present age or period in history —**to·day** adv

tod·dle /tódd'l/ (-dled, -dling) vi take short unsteady steps, as a child does when learning to walk —**tod·dle** n

tod·dler /tóddlər/ n a young child who is learning to walk

tod·dy /tóddee/ (pl -dies) n a drink of an alcoholic spirit mixed with hot water and sugar

to-do /tə doo/ (pl to-dos) n a commotion (infml)

toe n 1 each of the digits of the foot of human beings and some vertebrates 2 the part of something such as a shoe or sock that covers the toes ■ vt (toed) touch with the toes —**toed** adj ◊ **on your toes** alert and ready for action ◊ **step on somebody's toes** interfere with something considered to be that person's responsibility

toe·hold /tŏ hŏld/ n 1 a small recess in rock

that can support a climber's toe **2** a small advantage or gain

toe·nail /tố nàyl/ *n* a nail on a toe

toe-to-toe *adj* opposing ■ *adv* in direct opposition

tof·fee /táwfee, tóffee/ *n* a candy made by boiling brown sugar or molasses with butter

to·fu /tố foò/ *n* soybean curd pressed into a cake

togs *npl* clothes (*infml*)

to·ga /tốgə/ *n* a garment worn by citizens of ancient Rome, consisting of a piece of cloth draped around the body —**to·gaed** *adj*

to·geth·er /tə géthər/ *adv* **1** in company with others **2** interacting or in a relationship with one another **3** by joint effort **4** into contact, or into a unified whole o *sewn together* **5** collectively **6** in agreement **7** simultaneously **8** uninterruptedly o *raining four days together* ■ *adj* stable and self-confident (*infml*)

to·geth·er·ness /tə géthərnəss/ *n* a feeling of closeness with others

⚡**tog·gle** /tóggʻl/ *v* (**-gled, -gling**) **1** *vti* switch between two computer operations with one key **2** *vt* supply or fasten with toggles ■ *n* **1** a key for switching between two computer operations **2** a peg or rod inserted into a loop to hold or fasten something

⚡**tog·gle switch** *n* **1** a small spring-loaded switch for opening and closing an electrical circuit manually **2** a toggle for switching between computer operations

To·go /tốgō/ country in West Africa, on the Gulf of Guinea. Cap. Lomé. Pop. 5,153,088 (2001).

To·ho·no O'O·dham /tō hốnō ố ə daam/ (*pl same or* **To·ho·no O'O·dhams**) *n* a member of a Native North American people who now live mainly in N Mexico and S Arizona. Also called **Papago**

toil[1] *n* hard work ■ *vi* **1** work hard **2** progress slowly and with difficulty —**toil·er** *n*

toil[2] *n* a net, snare, or other trap (*literary; often pl*)

toi·let /tóylət/ *n* **1** a fixture with a waste drain and a flush for disposing of feces and urine **2** a room with a toilet **3** an outdoor toilet **4** *also* **toi·lette** /twaa lét/ washing, dressing, and attending to your personal appearance (*fml*)

toi·let pa·per *n* paper for cleaning the body after urinating or defecating

toi·let roll *n* a roll of toilet paper

toi·let train·ing *n* the process of teaching a young child to control bladder and bowel movements and to use a toilet

toi·let wa·ter *n* light perfume

To·jo Hi·de·ki /tōjō hee dek ĭ/ (1884–1948) Japanese general and prime minister (1941–44)

to·ken /tốkən/ *n* **1** something representing something else **2** a disk used like money **3** a keepsake ■ *adj* existing or done as a gesture only

to·ken·ism /tốkə nìzzəm/ *n* the making of only a symbolic or minimal effort to do something —**to·ken·is·tic** /tốkə nístik/ *adj*

To·ky·o /tốkee ō/ capital of Japan, on Tokyo Bay, on the coast of E Honshu Island. Pop. 7,919,771 (2000).

to·lar /tốlaar/ *n* the main unit of Slovenian currency

told past tense, past participle of **tell**

To·le·do /tə leédō/ **1** major river port in NW Ohio. Pop. 312,174 (1998). **2** historic city and administrative center of **Toledo Province**, central Spain. Pop. 63,561 (1991).

To·le·do, Alejandro (*b.* 1946) president of Peru (2001–)

tol·er·a·ble /tóllərəbʻl/ *adj* **1** capable of being tolerated **2** fairly good —**tol·er·a·bly** *adv*

tol·er·ance /tóllərənss/ *n* **1** the acceptance of the different views of others **2** the ability to endure hardship or annoyance **3** the loss of response to a drug after prolonged use or exposure **4** an allowance made for deviation from a standard, or the limit within which deviation is allowed

tol·er·ant /tóllərənt/ *adj* **1** accepting the different views of others **2** able to withstand harsh treatment or annoyance **3** no longer responding to a drug —**tol·er·ant·ly** *adv*

tol·er·ate /tóllə ràyt/ (**-at·ed, -at·ing**) *vt* **1** be willing to allow something to happen or exist **2** endure the unpleasant effect of something **3** accept the existence of different views —**tol·er·a·tion** /tóllə ráysh'n/ *n* —**tol·er·a·tion·ist** *n, adj*

Tol·kien /tốl keen, tól-/, **J. R. R.** (1892–1973) South African-born British scholar and writer

toll[1] /tōl/ *n* **1** a fee for using a road or crossing a bridge **2** deaths or damage sustained in an accident or disaster **3** a fee for a service **4** a charge for a long-distance telephone call

toll[2] /tōl/ *v* **1** *vti* ring a bell slowly and repeatedly **2** *vt* announce with the tolling of a bell —**toll** *n*

toll·booth /tốl bòoth/ *n* a booth on a road or bridge for collecting tolls

toll bridge *n* a bridge where a toll is payable

toll-free *adj* describes a telephone call charged to the person called —**toll-free** *adv*

toll·gate /tốl gàyt/ *n* a barrier where a toll must be paid to proceed

Count Leo Tolstoy

Tol·stoy /táwl stòy/, **Leo** (1828–1910) Russian writer

tom *n* the male of various animals, especially a domestic cat

Tom, Dick, and Harry /-hérree/ *n* anyone and everyone

tom·a·hawk /tómmə hàwk/ *n* a Native North American weapon in the form of a small ax —**tom·a·hawk** *vt*

to·ma·to /tə máytō, -maátō/ (*pl* **-toes**) *n* 1 a round red vegetable with pulpy flesh 2 a plant that produces tomatoes

tomb /toom/ *n* 1 a grave 2 a burial chamber

Tom·bouc·tou /tòN book toó/, **Tim·buk·tu** /tim buk-/ city in central Mali, on the southern edge of the Sahara Desert. Pop. 36,000 (1998).

tom·boy /tóm bòy/ *n* a girl who enjoys boys' activities —**tom·boy·ish** *adj*

tomb·stone /toòm stòn/ *n* an ornamental stone that marks a grave

tom·cat /tóm kàt/ *n* a male domestic cat

tome /tōm/ *n* a large or serious book (*fml or humorous*)

tom·fool·er·y /tom foŏlərèe/ *n* silliness (*infml*)

~~tommorrow~~ incorrect spelling of **tomorrow**

to·mog·ra·phy /tə móggrəfee/ *n* the use of ultrasound, gamma rays, or X-rays to produce a focused image of the structures across a specific depth within the body

to·mor·row /tə máwrō/ *n* 1 the day after today 2 the future ■ *adv* 1 on the day after today 2 in the future ◊ **like** *or* **as if there was** *or* **were no tomorrow** with great speed, intensity, or carelessness (*infml*)

tom-tom, tam-tam *n* 1 a drum hit with the hands 2 a deep-sided drum in a modern drum kit

ton /tun/ *n* 1 a US unit of weight equal to 2,000 lb 2 a UK unit of weight equal to 2,240 lb 3 a metric ton 4 a unit measuring a ship's displacement equal to 35 cubic feet/0.85 cubic meters of water 5 a large amount (*infml; often pl*) ■ *adv* **tons** a great deal

ton·al /tṓn'l/ *adj* 1 of tone 2 of harmonic music —**ton·al·ly** *adv*

to·nal·i·ty /tō nállətee/ *n* 1 the quality of tone of an instrument or voice 2 a system or arrangement of musical tones in relation to a tonic

tone /tōn/ *n* 1 a particular kind of sound 2 a way of saying something, or the general quality of something, that indicates an attitude ○ *the optimistic tone of the report* 3 the prevailing character or style of something ○ *Neon signs lower the tone of the place.* 4 a shade of a color 5 the natural firmness of somebody's muscles 6 the timbre of a voice or instrument 7 a musical note ■ *v* (**toned, ton·ing**) 1 *vi* blend in with something 2 make muscles firmer and stronger —**tone·less** *adj*

☐ **tone down** *vt* make less intense or extreme

☐ **tone up** *vt* make muscles firmer and stronger

tone-deaf *adj* unable to differentiate between musical notes —**tone-deaf·ness** *n*

tone lan·guage *n* a language in which the pitch of sounds affects meaning

tone po·em *n* an orchestral piece of music based on a literary or artistic theme

ton·er /tṓnər/ *n* 1 a cosmetic that firms the skin 2 ink for laser printers and photocopiers

Ton·ga /tóng gə/ independent island nation consisting of more than 150 islands in the S Pacific Ocean. Cap. Nukualofa. Pop. 104,227 (2001). —**Ton·gan** *n, adj*

tongs *npl* a utensil with two arms for grabbing and lifting things

tongue /tung/ *n* 1 a fleshy organ inside the mouth that is used for tasting and licking 2 an animal's tongue as food 3 a language 4 a way of speaking (*fml*) 5 the flap over the instep of a shoe ■ **tongues** *npl* speech in no known language that results from religious ecstasy ■ *vt* (**tongued, tongu·ing**) touch with the tongue —**tongued** *adj* ◊ **hold your tongue** keep silent ◊ See note at **language**

tongue-in-cheek *adj* joking

tongue-lash·ing *n* a severe scolding

tongue-tied *adj* speechless through nervousness

tongue twist·er *n* a word or phrase that is difficult to say

ton·ic /tónnik/ *n* 1 something that lifts the spirits 2 *also* **ton·ic wa·ter** a carbonated drink flavored with quinine 3 *regional* in Boston, a soft drink 4 the first note of a musical scale ■ *adj* 1 lifting the spirits 2 boosting energy 3 of muscle tone 4 of the first note of a musical scale —**ton·i·cal·ly** *adv*

ton·ic sol-fa *n* a musical scale system using syllables that are movable depending on the key of the piece

to·night /tə nít/ *n* the night of the present day —**to·night** *adv*

Ton·kin, Gulf of /tón kìn, tóng-/ arm of the South China Sea, on the coast of NE Vietnam and SE China

ton·nage /túnnij/ *n* 1 weight in tons 2 the size or capacity of a ship 3 the weight of the cargo of a ship 4 a duty charged on the cargo of a ship

tonne /tun/ n a metric ton

ton·sil /tónsəl/ n an oval mass of tissue, especially each of the two at the back of the mouth —**ton·sil·lar** adj

~~tonsilitis~~ incorrect spelling of **tonsillitis**

ton·sil·lec·to·my /tònsə léktəmee/ (pl **-mies**) n the surgical removal of inflamed tonsils

ton·sil·li·tis /tònsə lítiss/ n inflammation of the tonsils —**ton·sil·lit·ic** /-líttik/ adj

ton·so·ri·al /ton sáwree əl/ adj of barbers (fml or humorous)

ton·sure /tónshər/ n a partially shaved head —**ton·sure** vt

ton·y /tónee/ adj stylish (infml)

too /too/ adv 1 as well o caught the virus too 2 more than is desirable o too flamboyant for my taste 3 adds emphasis o too kind 4 very (in negative statements) o didn't look too happy 5 indeed o You did too! ◊ See note at **to**

took past tense of **take**

tool /tool/ n 1 a device for doing a particular kind of work 2 the cutting part of a machine 3 a bookbinder's implement for making a design on leather 4 a means to an end 5 something used for a job o Words are the poet's tool. ■ v 1 vt cut or shape using hand tools 2 vt provide with tools 3 vti drive a car in a particular way (slang)

⚡**tool·bar** /tool baàr/ n a row of icons on a computer screen that are clicked on to perform functions

tool·kit /tool kit/ n a set of tools

tool·shed /tool shèd/ n a shed for storing tools

toot n the sound of a vehicle's horn ■ vti make a short hooting sound

tooth /tooth/ n (pl **teeth** /teeth/) 1 a whitish bony object in the mouth that is used for biting and chewing 2 a part resembling a tooth 3 an indentation ■ **teeth** npl effective power o sanctions without teeth —**toothed** adj ◊ **get** or **sink your teeth into** start doing something that will be challenging ◊ **in the teeth of** against opposition or contradiction from ◊ **set somebody's teeth on edge** irritate somebody

tooth·ache /tooth àyk/ n pain in a tooth

tooth·brush /tooth brùsh/ n a brush for cleaning teeth

tooth fair·y n in children's folklore, a fairy that replaces a child's lost baby tooth with money

tooth·less /toothləss/ adj 1 lacking teeth 2 lacking power

tooth·paste /tooth pàyst/ n a paste for cleaning teeth

tooth·pick /tooth pìk/ n a stick used for removing food from between the teeth

tooth pow·der n a tooth-cleansing powder that is mixed with water

tooth·some /toothsəm/ adj delicious —**tooth·some·ly** adv —**tooth·some·ness** n

tooth·y /toothee/ (-i-er, -i-est) adj having many

or large teeth —**tooth·i·ly** adv —**tooth·i·ness** n

top[1] n 1 the highest part or point 2 an upper surface 3 a lid or cover 4 a garment for the upper body 5 the most important one 6 the best part 7 the most excellent or intense level o at the top of her voice 8 the beginning or earliest part o the top of the news ■ adj 1 uppermost or highest 2 leading or most successful 3 of the best quality 4 maximum ■ vt (**topped**, **top·ping**) 1 add a topping to food 2 cut the top off something 3 be at the head of a list or ranking 4 exceed somebody or something 5 reach the apex of something —**top·most** adj ◊ **blow your top** lose your temper (infml) ◊ **off the top of your head** without thinking deeply or planning

☐ **top out** vi add the final level to a building

top[2] n a spinning toy

to·paz /tó pàz/ n 1 a transparent brown gemstone. Use: gems. 2 a yellowish gemstone

top·coat /tóp kòt/ n 1 a final coat of paint 2 a lightweight outdoor coat

top dog n the most powerful person in a group or organization (infml)

top dol·lar n a very high price (infml)

top-down adj 1 controlled by the most senior people 2 working from the general to the specific

top-draw·er adj of the highest level of excellence

To·pe·ka /tə peèkə/ capital of Kansas. Pop. 118,977 (1998).

top-flight /tóp flìt/ adj outstanding

top hat n a man's formal tall hat

top-heav·y adj 1 unbalanced because of being too heavy at the top 2 describes an organization that has too many executives —**top-heav·i·ness** n

to·pi /tópee/ (pl **-pis** or same) n an antelope with curved horns

to·pi·ar·y /tópee èrree/ n 1 the art of trimming bushes into decorative shapes 2 decoratively shaped bushes —**to·pi·ar·ist** n

top·ic /tóppik/ n a subject that is written or spoken about ◊ See note at **subject**

top·i·cal /tóppik'l/ adj 1 of current interest 2 describes medication applied externally —**top·i·cal·i·ty** /tòppi kállətee/ n —**top·i·cal·ly** adv

top·knot /tóp nòt/ n a ribbon or an arrangement of hair worn on the top of the head

top·less /tópləss/ adj 1 with nothing covering the breasts 2 permitting women to show their breasts in public o topless beaches 3 with no top part —**top·less·ness** n

top-lev·el adj 1 involving important people 2 at the most senior level

⚡**top-lev·el do·main** n the part of an Internet address that comes after the dot

top·notch /tóp nòch, tóp nóch/ adj excellent (infml) —**top·notch·er** n

to·pog·ra·phy /tə póggrəfee/ n 1 the mapping of the surface features of the Earth 2 the physical features of an area —**to·pog·ra·pher** n —**top·o·graph·ic** /tòppə gráffik/ adj —**top·o·graph·i·cal** adj

top·per /tóppər/ n a person or machine that removes or adds tops

top·ping /tópping/ n a garnish for food

top·ple /tópp'l/ (-pled, -pling) vti 1 fall or make something fall over 2 overthrow somebody

top-rat·ed adj highly rated

top round n a cut of beef from the outer thigh

top-se·cret adj highly secret

top·side /tóp sìd/ n 1 an upper side 2 the part of a ship's hull above the water 3 the highest rank —**top·side** adj, adv —**top·sides** adv

top·soil /tóp sòyl/ n the top layer of soil

top·spin /tóp spìn/ n forward spin given to a ball

top·sy-tur·vy /tòpsee túrvee/ adj, adv 1 upside down 2 in or into confusion ■ n disorder or confusion —**top·sy-tur·vi·ly** adv —**top·sy-tur·vi·ness** n

To·rah /táwrə/ n 1 the first five books of the Hebrew Bible, or a scroll containing these 2 the body of teachings in the Hebrew Bible and the Talmud

torch n 1 a burning stick used as a light source 2 a device that emits a flame, used especially in welding ■ vt deliberately set on fire (slang)

torch·light /táwrch lìt/ n 1 the light of a torch 2 a burning torch

tore past tense of **tear**[1]

tor·e·a·dor /táwree ə dàwr/ n a bullfighter

tor·ment vt /tawr mént/ 1 inflict torture, pain, or anguish on 2 tease ■ n /táwr mènt/ 1 torture 2 a cause of annoyance or anguish —**tor·ment·ed** /tawr méntəd/ adj —**tor·ment·ed·ly** adv —**tor·men·tor** n

torn past participle of **tear**[1]

tor·na·do /tawr náydō/ (pl -dos or -does) n a destructive column of swirling wind —**tor·nad·ic** /-náydik, -náddik/ adj

ORIGIN **Tornado** looks like a genuine Spanish word, but in fact it was formed in English. It is probably an alteration of Spanish *tronada* "thunderstorm," associated with the verb *tornar* "turn." It was first used in the mid-16C for any violent thunderstorm in the tropical Atlantic, but by the early 17C had come to suggest swirling winds.

~~tornament~~ incorrect spelling of **tournament**

To·ron·to /tə róntō/ capital of Ontario Province, Canada. Pop. 653,734 (1996). —**To·ron·to·ni·an** /tə ròn tōnee ən, tàwrən-/ n, adj

tor·pe·do /tawr peedō/ n (pl -does) 1 a self-propelled underwater missile 2 a type of firework that explodes when it hits a surface ■ vt (-doed, -do·ing, -does) 1 hit

with an underwater torpedo 2 destroy (infml)

tor·pid /táwrpid/ adj 1 sluggish 2 dormant —**tor·pid·i·ty** /tawr píddətee/ n

tor·por /táwrpər/ n 1 lack of energy 2 dormancy —**tor·por·if·ic** /tàwrpə ríffik/ adj

torque /tawrk/ n 1 a force that causes a rotating or twisting movement 2 a measurement of the ability of a rotating mechanism to overcome resistance —**torque** vt

Tor·que·ma·da /tàwrkə máadə, tàwrkay máathaa/, **Tomás de** (1420–98) Spanish monk and grand inquisitor

tor·rent /táwrənt/ n 1 a fast and powerful rush of liquid 2 a forceful outpouring

tor·ren·tial /taw rénshəl, tə-/ adj flowing or falling fast and powerfully —**tor·ren·tial·ly** adv

tor·rid /táwrid/ adj full of passion —**tor·rid·i·ty** /taw ríddətee/ n —**tor·rid·ly** adv —**tor·rid·ness** n

tor·sion /táwrsh'n/ n 1 the twisting of an object by applying equal and opposite torques 2 mechanical stress on a twisted object —**tor·sion·al** adj

tor·so /táwrsō/ (pl -sos or -si /-see/) n 1 the upper part of the human body, excluding the head and arms 2 a sculpture of somebody's torso

tort n a civil wrongdoing for which damages can be sought

tor·til·la /tawr tée yə/ n a flat Mexican bread cooked on a hot griddle

tor·til·la chip n a corn chip

tor·toise /táwrtəss/ n 1 a slow-moving land-dwelling reptile with a shell 2 somebody or something that moves slowly

ORIGIN The word for the **tortoise** originally had a wide variety of forms, derived from French *tortue*, Spanish *tortuga*, and their source medieval Latin *tortuca*, a word whose ultimate origin is unknown. The modern form emerged in the mid-16C. The name for the reptile the *turtle* is thought to be an alteration of French *tortue* "tortoise."

tor·toise·shell /táwrtəss shèl/, **tor·toise shell** n 1 the outer part of the shell of a turtle. Use: combs, ornaments, jewelry. 2 a synthetic substance that resembles tortoiseshell 3 a cat with black and brown markings ■ adj mottled yellow and brown

Tor·tu·ga Is·land /tawr tòogə-/ island off N Haiti, in the Caribbean. Pop. 22,880 (1982).

tor·tu·ous /táwrchoo əss/ adj with many turns or bends —**tor·tu·ous·ly** adv —**tor·tu·ous·ness** n

tor·ture /táwrchər/ n 1 the deliberate inflicting of pain 2 a method of inflicting pain 3 anguish ■ vt (-tured, -tur·ing) 1 deliberately inflict pain on somebody 2 cause somebody anguish 3 distort something —**tor·tur·er** n —**tor·tur·ous** adj —**tor·tur·ous·ly** adv

To·ry /táwree/ (*pl* -ries) *n* 1 an American supporter of Britain during the American Revolution 2 a member or supporter of the Conservative Party in the United Kingdom or Canada —**To·ry** *adj* —**To·ry·ism** *n*

Tos·ca·ni·ni /tòskə neénee/, **Arturo** (1867-1957) Italian-born US conductor

toss *v* 1 *vt* lightly throw something 2 *vti* throw or be thrown up and down or to and fro 3 *vti* throw a coin to decide something 4 *vt* mix a salad with a dressing 5 *vt* jerk the head upward 6 *vi* move restlessly, especially in sleep ■ *n* 1 an act of lightly throwing something 2 a jerk of the head ◊ See note at **throw**

□ **toss off** *vt* do quickly

toss-up /tóss ùp/ *n* 1 a deciding throw of a coin 2 an even chance

tot *n* 1 a little child (*infml*) 2 a small amount

to·tal /tót'l/ *n* a sum of amounts added or considered together ■ *adj* 1 complete or utter 2 with all amounts or elements considered together ■ *vt* 1 add things together 2 amount to a particular total 3 kill somebody or destroy something (*slang*) ○ *totaled the car* —**to·tal·ly** *adv*

to·tal e·clipse *n* an eclipse of the entire surface of the Sun or another astronomical object

to·tal·i·tar·i·an /tō tàllə táiree ən/ *adj* of a centralized system of government in which a single party or leader exercises dictatorial control —**to·tal·i·tar·i·an** *n* —**to·tal·i·tar·i·an·ism** *n*

to·tal·i·ty /tō tállətee/ (*pl* -ties) *n* 1 completeness 2 a total amount

tote /tōt/ *vt* (**tot·ed, tot·ing**) carry something heavy (*infml*) ■ *n* also **tote bag** a large soft bag with handles

to·tem /tótəm/ *n* 1 an object, animal, plant, or other natural phenomenon revered as a symbol of a people 2 a carving or other representation of a totem —**to·tem·ic** /tō témmik/ *adj*

to·tem pole *n* a Native North American pole carved with totems

tot·ter /tóttər/ *vi* 1 walk unsteadily 2 wobble ■ *n* a wobbling gait —**tot·ter·ing, tot·ter·y** *adj*

tou·can /tóo kàn/ (*pl* -cans *or same*) *n* a tropical bird with a large curved beak

touch /tuch/ *v* 1 *vti* be, or put a part of the body, in contact with something so as to feel it 2 *vti* be, or put something, in contact with something else 3 *vt* disturb something by handling 4 *vt* affect somebody emotionally 5 *vt* consume even a small amount of food or drink (*usually in negatives*) ○ *never touches meat* 6 *vt* deal or become involved with something or somebody ○ *won't touch that issue* 7 *vt* match something or somebody in excellence ■ *n* 1 the sense by which objects are felt through contact with the body 2 the qualities of something as per-

ceived by feeling it 3 an instance of coming into contact with something 4 a light stroke 5 a small amount 6 a distinctive style ○ *a sure touch* 7 a detail 8 the fact of being in communication —**touch·a·ble** *adj* —**touch·er** *n* ◊ **a touch** somewhat ◊ **be touch and go** be highly uncertain or unpredictable

□ **touch down** *vi* land in an aircraft or spacecraft

□ **touch off** *vt* 1 make explode 2 initiate

□ **touch on** *or* **up·on** *vt* 1 mention briefly 2 verge on

□ **touch up** *vt* make small improvements or changes to ○ *touched up the photograph*

touch-and-go *adj* uncertain or risky

touch·down /túch dòwn/ *n* 1 in football, a score achieved by being in possession of the ball behind an opponent's goal line 2 in football, a scoring play 3 a landing made by an aircraft or spacecraft

tou·ché /too sháy/ *interj* 1 in fencing, acknowledges a scoring hit 2 acknowledges a telling remark

touched /tucht/ *adj* affected emotionally

touch foot·ball *n* an informal version of football

touch·ing /túching/ *adj* causing feelings of tenderness or pity —**touch·ing·ly** *adv* ◊ See note at **moving**

touch·line /túch lìn/ *n* a side boundary of a playing field

⚡ **touch pad** *n* 1 an electronic input device operated by touch 2 on a laptop computer, a surface that is touched to move the cursor

⚡ **touch screen** *n* a computer screen operated by touch

touch·stone /túch stòn/ *n* 1 an excellent example regarded as a standard 2 a hard black stone formerly used to test the quality of gold rubbed against it

touch-type *vi* type without looking at the keyboard —**touch-typ·ist** *n*

touch·y /túchee/ (-i·er, -i·est) *adj* easily upset —**touch·i·ly** *adv* —**touch·i·ness** *n*

tough /tuf/ *adj* 1 durable 2 hard to chew or cut 3 physically or mentally very strong 4 characterized by antisocial behavior 5 strong-minded 6 difficult to deal with 7 severe or strict ○ *tough on crime* 8 unfortunate or hard to endure (*infml*) ○ *a tough break* ■ *n* somebody who is aggressive or antisocial ■ *interj* expresses a lack of sympathy when something unfortunate happens —**tough·ly** *adv* —**tough·ness** *n* ◊ **tough it out** endure through a time of difficulty (*infml*) ◊ See note at **hard**

tough·en /túff'n/ *vti* 1 make or become tougher or more durable 2 make or become stronger

tough love *n* a caring but strict attitude

tough-mind·ed *adj* determined and realistic —**tough-mind·ed·ly** *adv* —**tough-mind·ed·ness** *n*

Tou·louse /too looz/ *n* city in SW France. Pop. 390,350 (1999).

Tou·louse-Lau·trec /too looz lō trék/, **Henri de** (1864–1901) French artist

tou·pee /too páy/ *n* a partial wig worn to cover a bald area

tour /toor/ *n* 1 a pleasure trip 2 a trip to several places to play or perform 3 a brief trip for the purpose of viewing something ■ *vti* take part in a tour of a place

tour de force /toor do fáwrss/ (*pl* **tours de force** /pronunc. same/) *n* a skillful feat

tour·ism /toor izzəm/ *n* 1 travel undertaken for pleasure 2 the travel business 3 travel to benefit from a service or activity, especially when it is unobtainable at home ○ *health tourism*

tour·ist /toorist/ *n* somebody who travels for pleasure —**tour·ist·y** *adj*

tour·ist class *n* the cheapest class of travel on an aircraft or ship

tour·ist trap *n* a place where prices are inflated to take advantage of its popularity with tourists

tour·ma·line /toormolin, -leen/ *n* a variously colored glassy mineral. Use: electronics, optics, gems.

tour·na·ment /toornəmənt, túrnəmənt/ *n* 1 an event made up of a series of games or contests 2 a medieval contest involving mock fighting

~~tournement~~ incorrect spelling of **tournament**

tour·ni·quet /túrnikət/ *n* a band tightened around an arm or leg to stop bleeding

tou·sle /tówz'l/ *vt* (**-sled, -sling**) ruffle or tangle hair ■ *n* a tangled mass —**tou·sled** *adj*

Tous·saint L'Ou·ver·ture /too sàN loo ver chōōər, -túr/, **François Dominique** (1743–1803) Haitian general and independence leader

tout /towt/ *v* 1 *vi* try aggressively to attract customers or support 2 *vt* advertise or offer for sale 3 *vt* praise ○ *being touted as the best novel in years* ■ *n* somebody who sells information about racehorses —**tout·er** *n*

tow[1] /tō/ *vt* pull something heavy by a rope or chain ■ *n* an act of towing something, or the state of being towed ◊ See note at **pull**

tow[2] /tō/ *n* fibers that are ready for spinning

to·ward /tawrd, tə wáwrd/, **to·wards** /tawrdz, tə wáwrdz/ *prep* 1 in a particular direction 2 shortly before ○ *toward midnight* 3 with a particular audience intended ○ *geared toward teenagers* 4 regarding

tow·a·way zone *n* an area of restricted parking

tow·bar /tō báar/ *n* a metal bar fitted to a vehicle to allow it to tow others

tow·el /tów əl/ *n* 1 an absorbent cloth used for drying the body 2 a cloth for drying dishes ■ *vt* (**-eled** *or* **-elled, -el·ing** *or* **-el·ling**) dry somebody with a towel ◊ **throw in the towel** admit defeat

tow·el·ette /tów ə lét/ *n* a moistened cloth for cleaning the face

tow·el·ing /tów əling/, **tow·el·ling** *n* an absorbent looped fabric. Use: towels, bathrobes.

⨍tow·er /tów ər/ *n* 1 a tall building or structure 2 a fortress 3 a tall shelf for storing CDs 4 a tall slim case for the CPU and drives of a computer ■ *vi* 1 be tall or much taller than somebody or something else 2 be much superior

tow·er·ing /tów əring/ *adj* 1 high or tall 2 outstanding —**tow·er·ing·ly** *adv*

tow·head /tō hèd/ *n* 1 somebody with light blond hair 2 a head of light blond hair —**tow·head·ed** *adj*

tow·line /tō lìn/ *n* a towrope

town /town/ *n* 1 a populated area that is larger than a village and smaller than a city 2 a large urban area 3 a unit of local government that is smaller than a county or city 4 the nearest town, or the town center ○ *going into town* 5 the population of a settled area ○ *The whole town's talking about it.* 6 the nonacademic population of a university town —**towns·man** *n* —**towns·wom·an** *n* ◊ **on the town** enjoying the entertainment available in a town or city (*infml*) ◊ See note at **city**

town-and-gown *adj* of students and local residents of a university town

town clerk *n* a town official who keeps records

town coun·cil *n* a group of people who govern a town

town cri·er *n* somebody who makes public announcements

town hall *n* the building that houses the offices of a local administration

town house *n* 1 *also* **town-house** /tówn hòwss/ a row house, especially in a fashionable area 2 a house in a town owned by somebody who also has a country house

town·ie /tównee/, **town·y** (*pl* **-ies**) *n* 1 a town dweller (*infml*) 2 a nonacademic resident of a university town

town meet·ing *n* 1 a public meeting of a town's inhabitants 2 a meeting of the voters of a town to make legislative decisions

town·scape /tówn skàyp/ *n* 1 the visible area of a town 2 a picture of a town

town·ship /tówn shìp/ *n* 1 a subdivision of a county 2 an area of surveyed land equal to 36 square miles

towns·peo·ple /tównz pèep'l/, **towns·folk** /-fōk/ *npl* the inhabitants of a town

tow·path /tō pàth/ (*pl* **-paths** /-pàthz, -pàths/) *n* a path beside a canal

tow·rope /tō ròp/ *n* a rope for towing

tow truck /tō-/ n a truck for towing away vehicles

tox·e·mi·a /tok seēmee ə/ n the presence of bacter al toxins in the blood —**tox·e·mic** adj

tox·ic /tóksik/ adj 1 poisonous, or involving something poisonous 2 deadly —**tox·i·cal·ly** adv —**tox·ic·i·ty** /tok síssətee/ n

tox·i·col·o·gy /tòksi kóllǝjee/ n the scientific study of poisons, their effects, and their antidotes —**tox·i·co·log·i·cal** /tòksikə lój,,k'l/ adj —**tox·i·co·log·i·cal·ly** adv —**tox·i·col·o·gist** n

tox·ic shock syn·drome n a serious circulatory failure caused by toxin-producing bacteria

tox·in /tóksin/ n 1 a poison produced by a living organism 2 any substance that accumulates in the body and causes it harm

toy n 1 a thing to play with 2 a replica 3 an animal belonging to a miniature breed
□ **toy with** vt 1 play or fiddle with 2 think about

Tpke. abbr turnpike (in place names)

tr. abbr 1 transitive 2 transpose 3 transposition

trace[1] /trayss/ n 1 an indication of the former presence of something 2 a tiny quantity 3 a footprint 4 a path made by people or animals regularly passing 5 a line made by a recording instrument 6 a drawing made using tracing paper ■ v (traced, trac·ing) 1 vt search and find somebody or something 2 vti follow something's course of development, or be able to be followed along a course 3 vti copy something using tracing paper 4 vt draw something carefully —**trace·a·ble** adj —**trace·less** adj

ORIGIN The Latin word tractus "drawing," from which trace is derived, passed into early French as trait "pulling, draft," hence "harness strap." English trait derives from this. The French plural trais was borrowed into English in the 14C as trace "harness strap." It also formed the basis of a Latin verb that evolved into French tracier, from which English in the 14C got the verb trace. A noun trace was also derived from tracier, and this too was acquired by English as trace, in the 13C. At first it denoted a "path" or "track"; the modern sense "indication of the former presence of something" did not develop until the 17C.

trace[2] /trayss/ n a strap or chain attached to a horse's harness by which it pulls something along (often pl)

trac·er /tráyssər/ n 1 also **trac·er bul·let** a chemically treated bullet that leaves behind a glowing trail 2 also **trac·er el·e·ment** a substance used in biological or medical experiments or tests so that its movements can be monitored from its color, radioactivity, or other property 3 an investigation or investigator 4 somebody or something that makes tracings

trac·er·y /tráyssəree/ (pl -ies) n an interlaced pattern —**trac·er·ied** adj

tra·che·a /tráykee ə/ (pl -ae /-kee eè/ or -as) n 1 the human windpipe (technical) 2 a breathing tube in insects and related air-breathing invertebrate animals —**tra·che·al** adj

tra·che·ot·o·my /tràykee óttəmee/ (pl -mies) n a cut through the trachea to assist breathing in medical emergencies

tra·cho·ma /trə kṓmə/ n a contagious bacterial eye disease —**tra·cho·ma·tous** adj

trac·ing /tráyssing/ n 1 a traced copy 2 a graphic record made by an instrument such as a seismograph

trac·ing pa·per n translucent paper for copying something showing through it

track n 1 a mark left by something that passes 2 a path or trail 3 the metal structure that trains run on 4 the course followed by somebody who is traveling 5 a line of action or thought 6 a course for running or racing 7 the sports that take place on a track and adjacent field 8 a separate item on or section of a recording or storage medium 9 the treads of a tank or bulldozer 10 a course of study tailored to students' abilities 11 a supporting rail for a curtain or something similar ■ v 1 vti follow a path or trail 2 vt follow the flight path of an aircraft or spacecraft 3 vt follow the progress of somebody or something 4 vt follow a moving object with a camera 5 vt carry something on the shoes and leave it on a surface ○ tracking in mud 6 vt assign a student to a track —**track·a·ble** adj ◊ **in your tracks** immediately (infml) ◊ **make tracks** leave (infml)
□ **track down** vt find by searching

track and field n athletic sports played on a running track and adjacent field —**track-and-field** adj

✦ **track·ball** /trák bàwl/ n a rotating ball in a socket used instead of a computer mouse

track·er /trákər/ n somebody who follows a trail

track e·vent n a competition on a running track

track·ing /tráking/ n 1 a mechanism in video recorders that finds the best picture 2 the grouping of students according to their abilities

track·ing sta·tion n a site for monitoring the movement of something such as a missile or space vehicle

track meet n an athletic competition consisting of track events

track rec·ord n 1 a record of past performance (infml) 2 a record for a particular sports arena

track·suit /trák sòot/ n a loose top and pants worn before and after exercise

tract[1] *n* **1** an area of land or water **2** a group of bodily organs that provide for the passage of something

tract[2] *n* a religious or moralistic pamphlet

trac·ta·ble /tráktəb'l/ *adj* **1** easy to persuade or control **2** easy to bend or shape —**trac·ta·bly** *adv*

tract house *n* one of many similar houses —**tract hous·ing** *n*

trac·tion /tráksh'n/ *n* **1** the application of a pulling force for medical purposes **2** adhesive friction between a moving object and a surface **3** the act or process of pulling **4** a means of moving vehicles —**trac·tion·al** *adj*

trac·tor /tráktər/ *n* **1** a farm vehicle used in fields **2** the front part of a two-part truck, used to pull a trailer

trac·tor-trail·er *n* a truck consisting of a tractor and trailer

Tra·cy /tráyssee/, **Spencer** (1900–67) US actor

trade *n* **1** an area of business or industry **2** a skilled occupation, usually one requiring manual labor **3** people in a particular industry *o a reception for the trade only* **4** the activity of buying and selling **5** work in commerce, not in a profession **6** customers or sales *o losing trade to the competition* **7** an exchange **8** a trade wind (*often pl*) ■ *v* (**trad·ed, trad·ing**) **1** vi buy and sell goods **2** vt exchange **3** vt deal in —**trad·a·ble** *adj* —**trade·less** *adj* —**trad·er** *n*

~~tradegy~~ incorrect spelling of **tragedy**

trade-in *n* **1** an item used in partial payment **2** the act of trading something in

trade·mark /tráyd maàrk/ *n* **1** a company's identifying name or symbol for a product, legally registered so that no other manufacturer can use it **2** a distinctive characteristic ■ *vt* **1** register a name or symbol as a trademark **2** label a product with a trademark

trade name *n* a product name

trade-off /tráyd àwf, -òf/ *n* an exchange involving compromise

trade route *n* a route used by traders

trade se·cret *n* a company secret concerning a product

trades·man /tráydzmən/ (*pl* -men /-mən/) *n* **1** a skilled worker **2** a storekeeper (*dated*)

trades·peo·ple /tráydz pèep'l/ *npl* **1** skilled workers **2** storekeepers (*dated*)

trade wind *n* a prevailing tropical wind blowing toward the equator

~~tradgedy~~ incorrect spelling of **tragedy**

trad·ing card *n* a card with a picture or information that is one of a set designed to be collected

trad·ing post *n* **1** a store in a remote area **2** a location in a stock exchange

tra·di·tion /trə dísh'n/ *n* **1** a long-established custom or belief **2** a body of long-established customs or beliefs that serve as

precedents **3** the handing down of customs and beliefs ◊ See note at **habit**

tra·di·tion·al /trə díshən'l, -dìshnəl/ *adj* **1** based on or done according to tradition **2** describes older styles of jazz —**tra·di·tion·al·ly** *adv*

tra·di·tion·al·ism /trə díshən'l ìzzəm, -dìshnə lìzzəm/ *n* respect for tradition —**tra·di·tion·al·ist** *n* —**tra·di·tion·al·is·tic** /trə dìshən'l ístik, -dìshnə lístik/ *adj*

tra·duce /trə dóoss/ (-**duced, -duc·ing**) *vt* disparage or defame —**tra·duce·ment** *n*

Tra·fal·gar, Cape /trə fálgər/ cape in SW Spain between Cádiz and the Strait of Gibraltar

traf·fic /tráffik/ *n* **1** the movement of vehicles on roads in a particular area **2** the movement of ships, trains, or aircraft, or the volume of people or goods transported by sea, rail, or air **3** the business of transporting goods or people **4** illegal trade **5** the flow or volume of communications ■ *vi* (-**ficked, -fick·ing**) **1** trade illegally **2** have dealings

traf·fic cir·cle *n* a road junction with a central island

traf·fic cone *n* a movable cone-shaped marker used on roads

traf·fic is·land *n* a pedestrian area in the middle of a road

traf·fic jam *n* a line of vehicles at a standstill

traf·fic light *n* a signal using red, green, and amber lights to control traffic

tra·ge·di·an /trə jéedee ən/ *n* **1** an actor in tragedies **2** somebody who writes tragedies

trag·e·dy /trájjədee/ (*pl* -**dies**) *n* **1** a very sad event **2** an event that causes great suffering **3** a tragic play or other piece of literature

---

ORIGIN Tragedy goes back through French to a Greek word meaning literally "goat's song." The name may derive from a type of ancient Greek drama in which the chorus, who commented on the action of the play, were dressed as satyrs, mythological woodland creatures who were half man, half goat.

---

trag·ic /trájjik/, **trag·i·cal** /-ik'l/ *adj* **1** very sad or upsetting, especially because of involving death or loss *o a tragic accident* **2** of dramatic or literary tragedy *o a tragic hero* —**trag·i·cal·ly** *adv*

trag·i·com·e·dy /tràjji kómmədee/ (*pl* -**dies**) *n* a work that combines tragedy and comedy —**trag·i·com·ic** *adj* —**trag·i·com·i·cal** *adj*

trail *v* **1** *vt* follow a person or animal by using marks or signs left behind **2** *vti* fall behind somebody in a competition **3** *vi* lag behind **4** *vti* drag something, or be dragged **5** *vi* hang or float loosely ■ *n* **1** a route through countryside **2** marks or a scent left where somebody or something moved **3** a path □ **trail away** *or* **off** *vi* grow fainter

trail bike *n* a motorcycle for off-road use

trail·blaz·er /tráyl blàyzər/, **trail·break·er** /-bràykər/ *n* 1 a pioneer or innovator in a specific field 2 somebody who makes a new route through wilderness —**trail·blaz·ing** *adj, n*

trail·er /tráylər/ *n* 1 a vehicle for towing behind another vehicle 2 the rear part of a two-part truck, used for hauling freight 3 a mobile home 4 an advertisement for a movie or television program, containing extracts from it 5 somebody or something that lags behind ■ *vi* 1 live in a trailer 2 go in a trailer

trail·er park *n* a place to park and live in a house trailer

trail·ing ar·bu·tus /-aar byóotəss/ *n* a trailing evergreen bush with leathery leaves and clusters of pink-and-white flowers

train *n* 1 a number of linked railroad cars 2 a trailing part of a gown 3 a long moving line 4 the people and vehicles supporting an army 5 a sequence of events, actions, or things 6 an entourage ■ *v* 1 *vti* learn or teach skills 2 *vt* domesticate an animal 3 *vti* prepare for a sporting competition 4 *vt* make a plant or hair grow as wanted 5 *vt* focus or aim a device ○ *trained her binoculars on the nest* —**train·ing** *n* ◊ See note at **teach**

train·ee /tray née/ *n* somebody who is undergoing training —**train·ee·ship** *n*

train·er /tráynər/ *n* somebody who trains animals or people

traipse /trayps/ (**traipsed**, **traips·ing**) *vi* wander without purpose

trait /trayt/ *n* 1 an individual characteristic 2 an inherited characteristic

trai·tor /tráytər/ *n* a disloyal person, especially one who commits treason —**trai·tor·ous** *adj*

Tra·jan /tráyjən/ (53?–117) Roman emperor (AD98–117)

tra·jec·to·ry /trə jéktəree/ (*pl* **-ries**) *n* the path of a flying object

Traj·kov·ski /trī káwfskee/, **Boris** (*b.* 1956) president of the Former Yugoslav Republic of Macedonia (1999–)

tram *n* 1 a cable car 2 a vehicle on rails used in a coal mine

~~tramatic~~ incorrect spelling of **traumatic**

tram·mel /trámm'l/ *n* 1 something that limits freedom 2 a shackle for a horse ■ *vt* 1 restrain or confine 2 ensnare

tramp *n* 1 a homeless person who moves from place to place 2 an offensive term for a woman regarded as sexually promiscuous 3 the sound of walking feet 4 a heavy step 5 a cargo ship without a regular route ■ *v* 1 *vi* tread heavily 2 *vi* walk a long way 3 *vt* cover a particular distance wearily on foot 4 *vt* crush something underfoot —**tramp·er** *n* —**tramp·ish** *adj*

tram·ple /trámp'l/ (**-pled**, **-pling**) *vti* 1 tread heavily on something 2 treat somebody arrogantly

tram·po·line /trámpə lèen/ *n* a stretched canvas for gymnastic tumbling and jumping —**tram·po·line** *vi* —**tram·po·lin·er** *n* —**tram·po·lin·ist** *n*

tram·way /trám wày/ *n* a system of cable cars with overhead cables

trance *n* 1 a dazed state 2 a hypnotic or cataleptic state 3 a rapturous state

tranche /traansh/ *n* a portion of an investment issue or loan

tran·quil /trángkwəl, tránkwəl/ *adj* 1 free from commotion 2 free from anxiety or agitation —**tran·quil·li·ty** /trang kwíllətee/ *n* —**tran·quil·ly** *adv*

tran·quil·ize /trángkwə līz, tránkwə-/ (**-ized**, **-iz·ing**), **tran·quil·lize** *vti* make or become calm, especially using medication —**tran·quil·i·za·tion** /tràngkwəli záysh'n, trànkwəli-/ *n*

tran·quil·iz·er /trángkwə līzər, tránkwə-/, **tran·quil·liz·er** *n* 1 a calming drug. Use: treatment of anxiety, neuroses, psychoses. 2 something that makes a person or animal calm

trans. *abbr* 1 transaction 2 transferred 3 transitive 4 translated 5 translation 6 transportation 7 transpose 8 transverse

trans- *prefix* 1 across, on the other side of, beyond ○ *transcontinental* 2 through ○ *transfusion* 3 indicating change, transfer, or conversion ○ *transliterate*

trans·act /tran zákt, -sákt/ *vt* conduct business

⚡ **trans·ac·tion** /tran zákshən, -sákshən/ *n* 1 a business deal 2 an interaction (*fml*) 3 the act of negotiating 4 an addition to a database —**trans·ac·tion·al** *adj*

trans·at·lan·tic /trànzət lántik, trànsət-/ *adj* 1 crossing the Atlantic 2 beyond the Atlantic

Trans·cau·ca·sia /trànss kaw káyzhə, -káyzee ə/ region of SE Europe, between the Black and Caspian seas. It consists of the republics of Georgia, Armenia, and Azerbaijan. —**Trans·cau·ca·sian** *adj, n*

⚡ **trans·ceiv·er** /trans séevər, tran-/ *n* 1 a combined radio transmitter and receiver 2 a data transmitter and receiver

trans·cend /tran sénd/ *vt* 1 go beyond a limit 2 surpass something in quality or achievement

trans·cen·dent /tran séndənt/ *adj* 1 superior in quality or achievement 2 beyond the limits of experience 3 beyond all known categories 4 independent of the material world —**tran·scen·dence** *n* —**tran·scen·dent** *n* —**tran·scen·dent·ness** *n*

tran·scen·den·tal /tràn sen dént'l/ *adj* 1 not experienced but knowable 2 mystical —**tran·scen·den·tal·ly** *adv*

tran·scen·den·tal med·i·ta·tion *n* a form of meditation in which a mantra is repeated

trans·con·ti·nen·tal /tràns kontə nént'l/ *adj*

1 extending across a continent **2** from or on the other side of a continent

tran·scribe /tran skríb/ (**-scribed, -scrib·ing**) *vt* **1** write a copy of something **2** write something out in full form from notes **3** write sounds phonetically **4** arrange a piece of music for a different instrument **5** record something for later broadcasting

tran·script /trán skrìpt/ *n* **1** a written record **2** a student's academic record

tran·scrip·tion /tran skrípshən/ *n* **1** the process of transcribing something **2** something transcribed —**tran·scrip·tion·al** *adj*

trans·duc·er /tranz dóossər, trans-/ *n* a device that transforms one type of energy into another

tran·sept /trán sèpt/ *n* **1** the crosswise part of a church **2** an arm of a transept

trans·fer *v* /trans fúr, tráns fùr/ (**-ferred, -fer·ring**) **1** *vti* start working or studying elsewhere, or send to do so **2** *vti* move from one place or thing to another **3** *vti* pass from one person to another **4** *vti* change vehicles or aircraft **5** *vt* give ownership of something to somebody **6** *vt* copy an image onto another surface ■ *n* /tráns fùr/ **1** a change of place **2** a ticket that allows a passenger to transfer during a journey **3** a player or worker who is transferred **4** the passing of property to a new owner **5** a design applied to a surface —**trans·fer·al** /trans fúr əl/ *n* —**trans·fer·a·ble** *adj*

~~transfered~~ incorrect spelling of **transferred**

trans·fer·ence /tránsfərənss, trans fúr ənss/ *n* **1** the act of transferring something from one place or person to another **2** the process of being transferred

trans·fig·ure /trans fíggyər/ (**-ured, -ur·ing**) *vt* change the appearance of to reveal great beauty or spirituality —**trans·fig·u·ra·tion** /trans fìggyə ráysh'n/ *n* —**trans·fig·ure·ment** *n*

trans·fix /trans fíks/ *vt* **1** make somebody immobile with shock **2** pierce somebody or something through with a weapon —**trans·fix·ion** /trans fíkshən/ *n*

trans·form /trans fáwrm/ *vti* change completely or dramatically —**trans·form·a·ble** *adj* —**trans·for·ma·tion** /trànsfər máysh'n/ *n* —**trans·for·ma·tion·al** *adj* —**trans·for·ma·tion·al·ly** *adv* —**trans·form·a·tive** *adj* ◊ See note at **change**

trans·form·er /trans fáwrmər/ *n* **1** a device that changes electrical voltage, current, phase, or impedance **2** somebody or something that transforms

trans·fuse /trans fyóoz/ (**-fused, -fus·ing**) *vt* **1** give a blood transfusion to **2** spread throughout something and affect every part of it

trans·fu·sion /trans fyóozh'n/ *n* the process of transferring blood or blood products into somebody's bloodstream

trans·gen·der /trans jéndər, tranz-/ *adj* of transgendered people

trans·gen·dered /trans géndərd, tranz-/ *adj* adopting the dress, behavior, or physiology of a member of the opposite sex

trans·gen·ic /tranz jénnik, trans-/ *adj* **1** with genes from a different species **2** involving the transfer of genetic material

trans·gress /tranz gréss/ *v* **1** *vi* do something wrong **2** *vt* break a law —**trans·gres·sion** *n* —**trans·gres·sive** *adj* —**trans·gres·sor** *n*

tran·sient /tránshənt, tránzhənt, tránzee ənt/ *adj* **1** short in duration **2** not permanently settled in a place ■ *n* somebody who stays in a place only briefly —**tran·sience** *n* —**tran·sient·ly** *adv*

tran·sis·tor /tran zístər/ *n* **1** a small solid-state electronic device used as an amplifier and rectifier **2** *also* **tran·sis·tor ra·di·o** a small portable radio

tran·sis·tor·ize /tran zístə rìz/ (**-ized, -iz·ing**) *vt* equip with transistors

tran·sit /tránzit/ *n* **1** the act of traveling across or through a place **2** a system of public transportation **3** a public transport system **4** the passage of a planet across the Sun ■ *vti* pass or cause to pass through a place

tran·si·tion /tran zísh'n/ *n* the process of change from one state, form, style, or activity to another —**tran·si·tion·al** *adj*

tran·si·tive /tránzitiv/ *adj* describes a verb that requires a direct object —**tran·si·tive·ly** *adv* —**tran·si·tiv·i·ty** /tránzi tívvətee/ *n*

tran·sit lounge *n* an airport waiting room for passengers who are making a connecting flight

tran·si·to·ry /tránzə tàwree/ *adj* not permanent or lasting —**tran·si·to·ri·ly** /tránzə táwrəlee/ *adv* —**tran·si·to·ri·ness** *n* ◊ See note at **temporary**

⨍ trans·late /trans láyt, tranz-/ (**-lat·ed, -lat·ing**) *v* **1** *vti* turn words into a different language **2** *vi* be capable of being translated **3** *vt* convert computer data to a different form **4** *vt* rephrase something in simpler terms **5** *vt* interpret the meaning of something **6** *vti* change the form of something, or undergo a change in form —**trans·lat·a·ble** *adj* —**trans·la·tor** *n*

trans·la·tion /trans láysh'n, tranz-/ *n* **1** a version of a word, phrase, or text in another language **2** the act of translating something into a different language —**trans·la·tion·al** *adj*

trans·lit·er·ate /trans líttə ràyt, tranz-/ (**-at·ed, -at·ing**) *vt* transcribe something into another alphabet —**trans·lit·er·a·tion** /trans líttə ráysh'n, tranz-/ *n*

trans·lu·cent /trans lóos'nt, tranz-/ *adj* letting only some light through —**trans·lu·cence** *n* —**trans·lu·cen·cy** *n*

trans·mi·gra·tion /tránz mī gráysh'n/ *n* **1** movement from or to another region or country **2** in some religions, the passing of the soul after death into another body

—**trans·mi·grate** *vi* —**trans·mi·gra·tion·al** *adj*

trans·mis·sion /tranz míshʻn/ *n* **1** the act of transmitting something **2** something that is transmitted **3** a radio or television broadcast **4** a mechanism in a motor vehicle that transfers power from the engine to the wheels **5** a set of gears in a vehicle

trans·mit /tranz mít/ (**-mit·ted**, **-mit·ting**) *v* **1** *vt* send something or pass something on to another place or person **2** *vt* communicate information **3** *vti* send a signal **4** *vti* broadcast a program —**trans·mis·si·ble**, **trans·mit·ta·ble** *adj* —**trans·mis·sive** —**trans·mit·tal** *n*

trans·mit·ter /tranz mítter/ *n* **1** an agent or means of transmission **2** a piece of broadcasting equipment that generates and sends out radio waves

trans·mog·ri·fy /tranz móggre fī/ (**-fied**, **-fies**) *vt* change the form or appearance of, especially grotesquely —**trans·mog·ri·fi·ca·tion** /-mòggrəfi káyshʻn/ *n*

trans·mute /tranz myóot/ (**-mut·ed**, **-mut·ing**) *vti* **1** change from one form, substance, or state to another **2** change from one chemical element to another, or undergo this change —**trans·mut·a·ble** *adj* —**trans·mu·ta·tion** /trànz myoo táyshʻn/ *n* ◊ See note at **change**

trans·na·tion·al /tranz náshən'l, -náshnəl/ *adj* including, extending over, or operating in several nations

tran·som /tránsəm/ *n* **1** a crosspiece above a window or door or in a window **2** a window above a door

trans·par·en·cy /trans pérrənsee/ (*pl* **-cies**) *n* **1** the state of being transparent **2** a positive photographic image on transparent material

trans·par·ent /trans pérrənt/ *adj* **1** easily seen through **2** fine enough to see through **3** obvious and easy to recognize —**trans·par·ent·ly** *adv*

tran·spire /tran spír/ (**-spired**, **-spir·ing**) *v* **1** *vt* come to light **2** *vi* happen **3** *vti* give off a vapor through the pores —**tran·spi·ra·tion** /tránspə ráysh'n/ *n*

trans·plant *vt* /trans plánt/ **1** relocate a plant **2** move somebody to another place **3** transfer a body organ from one place or body to another ■ *n* /tráns plànt/ **1** a surgical procedure in which an organ is transplanted **2** a transplanted organ or tissue **3** a resident from elsewhere (*infml*) —**trans·plan·ta·tion** /tràns plan táysh'n/ *n*

trans·po·lar /trans pólər/ *adj* crossing a polar region

tran·spond·er /tran spóndər/, **tran·spon·dor** *n* **1** a radio or radar transceiver **2** a satellite receiver and transmitter

trans·port *vt* /trans páwrt/ **1** carry or take something somewhere **2** make somebody imagine being elsewhere **3** affect somebody with strong emotion ■ *n* /tráns pàwrt/

1 a vehicle that carries people or goods **2** an experience or display of intense emotion (*often pl*) —**trans·port·a·bil·i·ty** /tráns pàwrtə bíllətee/ *n* —**trans·port·a·ble** *adj*

trans·por·ta·tion /tránspər táysh'n/ *n* **1** the transporting of people or goods from one place to another **2** a means of transporting people or goods

trans·port·er /trans páwrtər/ *n* **1** somebody or something that transports something **2** a large vehicle for heavy loads

trans·pose /trans pṓz/ (**-posed**, **-pos·ing**) *v* **1** *vt* reverse the order of things **2** *vt* change the setting of something ◊ *transposing the action from Shakespeare's time to the present* **3** *vti* change a piece of music to a different key —**trans·pos·al** *n* —**trans·po·si·tion** /tránspə zísh'n/ *n*

⚡ **trans·put·er** /trans pyóotər/ *n* a powerful microchip with the capability of a microprocessor

trans·sex·u·al /trans sékshoo əl/ *n* **1** somebody who has undergone treatment to change his or her anatomical sex **2** somebody who identifies himself or herself as a member of the opposite sex —**trans·sex·u·al** *adj* —**trans·sex·u·al·ism** *n*

tran·sub·stan·ti·a·tion /trànsəb stanshee áysh'n/ *n* **1** the doctrine of the Roman Catholic and Eastern Orthodox Christian churches that the bread and wine in Communion become the body and blood of Christ **2** the process in which one substance changes into another (*fml*)

Trans·vaal /tránz vàal/ former province of South Africa, in the northeast of the country

trans·verse /tranz vúrs/ *adj* going across something ■ *n* a crosswise part —**trans·verse·ly** *adv*

trans·ves·tite /tranz vés tìt/ *n* somebody who dresses like the opposite sex —**trans·ves·tism** *n*

Tran·syl·va·nia /trànssil váynyə/ historic region in E Europe that now forms the central and northwestern parts of Romania —**Tran·syl·va·ni·an** *adj, n*

Tran·syl·va·ni·an Alps mountain range in the Carpathian Mountains, extending through south central Romania. Highest peak Mt. Moldoveanu 8,395 ft./2,544 m.

trap *n* **1** a device designed to catch animals **2** a plan to trick somebody **3** a confining situation **4** a device such as a curved section of a drainpipe that prevents the passage of gas **5** a trapdoor **6** the mouth (*infml*) ■ *v* (**trapped**, **trap·ping**) **1** *vt* catch something in a trap **2** *vi* set traps for animals **3** *vt* hold something in a tight grip or narrow space **4** *vt* place somebody in a confining situation **5** *vt* take somebody by surprise **6** *vt* prevent air from escaping —**trap·per** *n*

trap·door /tráp dàwr/ *n* a movable panel in a floor or ceiling

tra·peze /trə peéz/ *n* a bar attached to suspended ropes, used by acrobats

> **ORIGIN Trapeze** came through French from the Latin word that was separately adopted as *trapezium* "four-sided figure." The reference was to the shape made by the trapeze's rope and crossbar and the roof or other supporting structure. **Trapeze** is first recorded in English in the mid-19C.

tra·pe·zi·um /trə peèzee əm/ (*pl* **-ums** *or* **-a** /-zee ə/) *n* a quadrilateral with no parallel sides —**tra·pe·zi·al** *adj*

trap·e·zoid /tráppə zòyd/ *n* a quadrilateral with two parallel sides —**tra·pe·zoid·al** /tràppə zóyd'l/ *adj*

trap·pings /tráppingz/ *npl* **1** accessories and outward signs **2** an ornamental harness for a horse

Trap·pist /tráppist/ *n* a member of a silent order of austere Christian monks

trap·shoot·ing /tráp shòoting/ *n* shooting at clay pigeons —**trap·shoot** *n* —**trap·shoot·er** *n*

trash *n* **1** discarded material **2** nonsense **3** poor quality literature or art **4** an offensive term for somebody regarded as socially or morally inferior ■ *vt* (*infml*) **1** destroy something **2** criticize somebody savagely

trash can *n* a garbage can (*infml*)

trash·y /tráshee/ (**-i·er**, **-i·est**) *adj* of little worth or merit —**trash·i·ly** *adv* —**trash·i·ness** *n*

trat·to·ri·a /tràətə reè ə/ (*pl* **-as** *or* **-e** /-reè è/) *n* a simple Italian restaurant

trau·ma /trówmə, tráwmə/ (*pl* **-mas** *or* **-ma·ta** /-mətə/) *n* **1** a deep emotional shock, often having long-lasting psychological effects **2** a physical injury —**trau·mat·ic** /trow máttik, traw-/ *adj* —**trau·ma·tize** *vt*

tra·vail /trə váyl, trá vàyl/ *n* **1** hard work **2** childbirth (*archaic*) —**tra·vail** *vi*

trav·el /tráv'l/ *v* **1** *vi* go on a journey **2** *vt* journey through an area **3** *vt* cover a particular distance **4** *vi* go at a particular speed **5** *vi* tolerate being transported ○ *Snakes do not travel well.* **6** *vi* be transmitted ○ *News travels fast.* **7** *vi* associate with a particular group **n** the activity of traveling — **trav·els** *npl* a series of journeys ■ *adj* for travelers

trav·el a·gen·cy *n* a business that arranges travel —**trav·el a·gent** *n*

trav·el·er /tráv'lər/ *n* **1** somebody on a journey **2** somebody who has traveled

trav·el·er's check *n* an internationally accepted check

trav·e·logue /trávvə lòg/, **trav·e·log** *n* a movie or lecture on travel

tra·verse *v* /trə vúrss/ (**-versed**, **-vers·ing**) **1** *vt* move across an area **2** *vti* move back and forth across something **3** *vt* extend across something **4** *vti* move at an angle across a rock face while ascending or descending **5** *vti* follow a zigzag course down a ski slope ■ *n* /trá vərss, trə vúrss/ **1** a journey or route across, over, or through something **2** a crosswise beam, barrier, or other element ■ *adj* /trá vərss, trə vúrss/ crosswise —**tra·vers·a·ble** *adj* —**tra·vers·al** *n*

trav·es·ty /trávvəstee/ (*pl* **-ties**) *n* **1** false representation **2** a grotesque imitation of something —**trav·es·ty** *vt*

> **ORIGIN Travesty** was taken in the mid-17C from French *travesti* "dressed in disguise."

trawl *n* a commercial fishing net dragged along the sea bottom ■ *vti* fish with a trawl

trawl·er /tráwlər/ *n* **1** a fishing boat used in trawling **2** somebody who trawls —**trawl·er·man** *n*

tray *n* **1** a flat carrier for small objects **2** the objects carried on a tray

treach·er·ous /tréchərəss/ *adj* **1** betraying trust or confidence **2** involving hidden dangers —**treach·er·ous·ly** *adv* —**treach·er·ous·ness** *n*

treach·er·y /tréchəree/ *n* betrayal

trea·cle /treék'l/ *n* something cloying —**trea·cly** *adj*

tread /tred/ *vti* (**trod** *or* **tread·ed**, **trod·den** /tródd'n/ *or* **trod**) walk or step on, across, or along something ■ *n* **1** a way or act of treading **2** the horizontal part of a step **3** the grooved outer surface of a tire —**tread·less** *adj*

tread·le /trédd'l/ *n* a foot-operated pedal ■ *vti* (**-led**, **-ling**) power a machine with a treadle

tread·mill /tréd mil/ *n* **1** a device that is turned by people or animals walking on it, providing power **2** an exercise machine on which you can walk or run

trea·son /treéz'n/ *n* betrayal of your country

trea·son·a·ble /treéz'nab'l/, **trea·son·ous** /treéz'nəss/ *adj* of treason, or punishable as treason

treas·ure /trézhər/ *n* **1** jewels and precious objects **2** somebody or something considered valuable ■ *vt* (**-ured**, **-ur·ing**) **1** regard as valuable **2** accumulate and store as something valuable

treas·ure hunt *n* a game in which players solve a series of clues leading to a hidden prize

treas·ur·er /trézhərər/ *n* a manager of the finances of an organization —**treas·ur·er·ship** *n*

treas·ure-trove *n* anything of value that is discovered

treas·ur·y /trézhəree/ (*pl* **-ies**) *n* **1** a store of money **2** a place for things of value **3** a collection of valuable things **4 Treas·ur·y** in many countries, the government department responsible for managing revenue

Treas·ur·y bill *n* a short-term US government obligation

treat /treet/ *v* 1 *vt* regard or deal with somebody or something in a particular way 2 *vt* give medical aid to cure an illness or patient 3 *vt* subject something to a process or agent 4 *vt* pay for somebody else's food, drink, or entertainment 5 *vt* provide somebody with something pleasurable 6 *vi* discuss a topic ■ *n* 1 an entertainment paid for by somebody else 2 the act of paying for somebody else 3 something enjoyable —**treat·a·ble** *adj*

trea·tise /tréetiss/ *n* a detailed written account of a subject

treat·ment /tréetmənt/ *n* 1 the provision of medical care 2 a particular remedy or medical procedure 3 a way of handling something 4 the presentation of a subject 5 an act of subjecting something to a physical, chemical, or biological process or agent

trea·ty /tréetee/ (*pl* **-ties**) *n* 1 an agreement between countries 2 a pact

treb·le /trébb'l/ *adj* 1 three times as many or as much 2 of the highest musical range ■ *n* 1 a high-pitched instrument, voice, or sound 2 the higher audio frequency range in sound reproduction 3 a control for high-frequency audio responses ■ *vti* (**-led, -ling**) make or become three times as many or as much —**treb·ly** *adv*

treb·le clef *n* a clef that puts G above middle C on the second line

~~trecherous~~ incorrect spelling of **treacherous**

tree *n* 1 a large perennial woody plant, usually with a single main stem 2 a large plant resembling a tree 3 something that is branched like a tree 4 a wooden support 5 a diagram of a branching hierarchical structure ■ *vt* (**treed**) force up a tree —**tree·less** *adj*

tree house *n* a platform or house in a tree

tree line *n* 1 the timberline 2 the edge of a forest

tree sur·geon *n* somebody who treats diseased or damaged trees —**tree sur·ger·y** *n*

tree·top /trée tòp/ *n* the top of a tree

tree·ware /trée wàir/ *n* books and other material printed on paper made from wood pulp

tre·foil /trée fòyl, tré-/ *n* 1 a plant with three-lobed leaves 2 an object or design with three lobes or connected parts

trek *vi* (**trekked, trek·king**) 1 make a long difficult journey 2 go slowly or laboriously ■ *n* a long difficult journey —**trek·ker** *n*

trel·lis /trélliss/ *n* 1 a lattice for supporting a plant 2 any latticework structure

trem·ble /trémb'l/ *vi* (**-bled, -bling**) 1 shake

slightly but uncontrollably 2 vibrate 3 be afraid —**trem·ble** — **trem·bling** *adj*

tre·men·dous /trə méndəss/ *adj* 1 very large, powerful, or great 2 very good, successful, or impressive —**tre·men·dous·ly** *adv*

trem·o·lo /trémmə lò/ (*pl* **-los**) *n* 1 a quavering sound in music produced by rapid repetition of a tone or rapid alternation between two tones 2 a device for producing a tremolo

trem·or /trémmər/ *n* 1 a minor earthquake 2 a trembling, e.g., from fear or illness —**trem·or·ous** *adj*

trem·u·lous /trémmyələss/ *adj* 1 trembling 2 fearful —**trem·u·lous·ly** *adv*

trench *n* 1 a deep ditch with steep sides 2 a long excavation, used as protection against enemy fire 3 a valley on the ocean floor —**trench** *vt*

trench·ant /trénchənt/ *adj* 1 direct and deliberately hurtful 2 effective and incisive —**trench·an·cy** *n*

trench coat *n* a long double-breasted raincoat with a belt

trench·er /trénchər/ *n* a wooden platter (*archaic*)

trench war·fare *n* 1 warfare between armies in trenches 2 long-standing and bitter conflict

trend *n* 1 a tendency 2 a prevailing style ■ *vi* tend or move

trend·set·ter /trénd sèttər/ *n* somebody or something starting a trend —**trend·set·ting** *adj*

trend·y /tréndee/ (**-i·er, -i·est**) *adj* adopting the latest fad (*infml*) —**trend·i·ly** *adv* —**trend·i·ness** *n*

Tren·ton /trént'n/ capital of New Jersey. Pop. 84,494 (1998).

trep·i·da·tion /tréppi dáysh'n/ *n* apprehension

tres·pass /tréspəss, -pàss/ *vi* 1 enter somebody else's land unlawfully 2 encroach on somebody's privacy or time 3 break a moral or social law (*archaic*) ■ *n* 1 unlawful entry onto somebody else's land 2 a sin (*archaic*) —**tres·pass·er** *n*

tress *n* a lock of hair

tres·tle /tréss'l/ *n* 1 a supporting framework consisting of a horizontal beam with a pair of splayed legs at each end 2 a tower for supporting a bridge

tres·tle ta·ble *n* a table with a top supported on trestles

tri- *prefix* three, third o *trilateral*

tri·ad /trí àd, -əd/ *n* 1 a set of three 2 a musical chord consisting of three notes —**tri·ad·ic** /trí áddik/ *adj*

tri·age /tree aàzh, trée aàzh/ *n* the process of prioritizing patients for medical treatment

tri·al /trí əl, trīl/ *n* 1 a formal legal process to determine an issue 2 a difficult test 3 a painful experience 4 a troublesome person or thing 5 an effort (*fml*) 6 a preliminary

competition ■ *adj* **1** experimental **2** of a court trial

tri·al bal·loon *n* a proposal put forward to test opinion

tri·al court *n* a court in which a case is first decided

tri·al run *n* a test of something new

tri·an·gle /trī àng g'l/ *n* **1** a three-sided geometric figure **2** an object with three sides **3** a drafting instrument for ruling lines **4** a percussion instrument consisting of a metal bar bent into a triangle shape —**tri·an·gu·lar** /trī àng gyələr/ *adj* —**tri·an·gu·lar·i·ty** /trī àng gyə lérrətee/ *n*

Tri·as·sic /trī ássik/ *n* a period of geologic time 248–206 million years ago —**Tri·as·sic** *adj*

tri·ath·lon /trī áthlən, -lòn/ *n* an athletic contest with three long-distance events —**tri·ath·lete** *n*

trib·al·ism /trīb'l ìzzəm/ *n* **1** the customs and social organization of a tribe **2** allegiance to a group —**trib·al·is·tic** /trīb'l ístik/ *adj*

tribe /trīb/ *n* **1** a society whose members have common ancestors, customs, and leadership **2** a group with something in common —**trib·al** *adj* —**trib·al·ly** *adv*

tribes·man /trībzmən/ (*pl* -**men** /-mən/) *n* a man tribe member

tribes·peo·ple /trībz peep'l/ *npl* members of a tribe

tribes·wom·an /trībz woommən/ (*pl* -**wom·en** /-wimmin/) *n* a woman tribe member

trib·u·la·tion /trìbbyə láysh'n/ *n* **1** great hardship or distress **2** a cause of suffering

tri·bu·nal /trī byoon'l, tri-/ *n* **1** a law court **2** a body appointed to make a judgment or carry out an inquiry

trib·une /trī byoon, tri byoon/ *n* **1** a representative elected by the Roman common people **2** a defender of public rights —**trib·une·ship** *n*

trib·u·tar·y /trìbbyə tèrree/ *n* (*pl* -**ies**) **1** a stream that feeds a larger body of water **2** somebody who pays a monetary tribute ■ *adj* **1** flowing into a larger body of water **2** paid as a tribute

trib·ute /tríbbyoot/ *n* **1** an expression of gratitude or praise **2** evidence of the value of something **3** payment made by one ruler to another

trice *n* a brief moment

tri·cen·ten·ni·al /trī ssen ténnee əl, trī ss'n-/ *adj* of a 300th anniversary

tri·ceps /trī sèps/ (*pl* -**ceps·es** or same) *n* a muscle attached at three points, especially the muscle at the back of the upper arm

tri·cer·a·tops /trī sérrə tòps/ (*pl* same or -**tops·es**) *n* a three-horned plant-eating dinosaur

trick *n* **1** a cunning deception **2** a prank **3** a special skill ○ *taught me the tricks of the trade* **4** a skillful act designed to entertain people **5** a deceptive effect of light **6** a peculiar habit **7** an unforeseen event ○ *a cruel trick of fate* **8** the cards won by a player in a round ■ *vt* cheat or deceive ■ *adj* **1** of tricks **2** made as an imitation so that it can be used to play a joke on somebody **3** displaying symptoms of injury from time to time (*infml*) ◊ **do the trick** be effective and do what is needed (*infml*) ◊ **not miss a trick** notice everything that is happening (*infml*)

trick·er·y /tríkəree/ (*pl* -**ies**) *n* the use of tricks or deception

trick·le /trík'l/ (-**led**, -**ling**) *v* **1** *vti* flow, or cause to flow, slowly in a thin stream **2** *vi* move slowly or gradually —**trick·le** *n*

trick·le-down the·o·ry *n* the economic theory that financial benefits received by big businesses and wealthy people will spread to the rest of society

trick or treat *n* a Halloween custom in which children playfully threaten to play tricks on neighbors unless they are given candy ■ *interj* a greeting used by children when trick-or-treating

trick-or-treat *vi* ask for candy on Halloween

trick·ster /tríkstər/ *n* somebody who plays tricks

trick·sy /tríksee/ *adj* mischievous —**trick·si·ness** *n*

trick·y /tríkee/ (-**i·er**, -**i·est**) *adj* **1** difficult to do or deal with **2** crafty or sly —**trick·i·ly** *adv* —**trick·i·ness** *n*

tri·col·or /trī kùllər/ *n* **1** a three-colored flag **2** *also* **Tri·col·or** the French national flag ■ *adj also* **tri·col·ored** three-colored

tri·cy·cle /tríssik'l/ *n* a three-wheeled vehicle, usually driven by pedals —**tri·cy·cle** *vi* —**tri·cy·clist** *n*

tri·dent /trīd'nt/ *n* **1** a three-pronged spear **2** in classical mythology, the three-pronged spear of Poseidon or Neptune

tried past tense, past participle of **try** ■ *adj* (*often in combination*) **1** proved to be good **2** subjected to stress or worry

tri·en·ni·al /trī énnee əl/ *adj* **1** happening every three years **2** lasting three years ■ *n* a 3rd anniversary —**tri·en·ni·al·ly** *adv*

Tri·este /tree ést/ seaport of Friuli-Venezia Region, NE Italy. Pop. 217,865 (1999).

Tri·este, Gulf of inlet of the N Adriatic Sea, bordered by Italy, Slovenia, and Croatia

tri·fec·ta /trī féktə/ *n* US, Can, Aus a bet on the first 3 winners in a race

tri·fle /trīf'l/ *n* **1** something trivial **2** a small quantity —**tri·fler** *n*

☐ **trifle with** *vt* treat thoughtlessly

tri·fling /trīfling/ *adj* **1** insignificant **2** frivolous —**tri·fling·ly** *adv*

trig·ger /tríggər/ *n* **1** a small lever that fires a gun **2** a lever that operates a mechanism **3** a stimulus for something ■ *vt* set something off, or make something happen

trig·o·nom·e·try /trigɡə nómmətree/ n the branch of mathematics that deals with functions of angles and arcs —**trig·o·no·met·ric** /triɡɡənə méttrik/ adj —**trig·o·no·met·ri·cal** adj

tri·lat·er·al /trī láttərəl, -láttrəl/ adj 1 three-sided 2 involving three countries or parties ■ n a three-sided geometric figure —**tri·lat·er·al·ly** adv

tri·lin·gual /trī líng gwəl/ adj 1 knowing three languages 2 written in three languages —**tri·lin·gual** —**tri·lin·gual·ism** n —**tri·lin·gual·ly** adv

trill n 1 a warbling sound 2 a melodic ornament consisting of a rapid alternation between two notes —**trill** vti

tril·lion /trílljən/ (pl same or **-lions**) n the number 1 followed by 12 zeros —**tril·lion** adj

tri·lo·bite /trílə bīt/ n an extinct ocean arthropod of the Paleozoic era with a flat oval body in three sections

tril·o·gy /trílləjee/ (pl **-gies**) n a set of three related artistic works

trim v (**trimmed**, **trim·ming**) 1 vt make something neat by cutting 2 vt cut something to the required size 3 vt remove an excess by cutting 4 vt decorate something 5 vti change the arrangement of sails on a boat 6 vt make adjustments to improve an aircraft's stability in flight ■ adj (**trim·mer**, **trim·mest**) 1 slim and fit-looking 2 neat and tidy ■ n 1 an act of cutting something, e.g., hair, to neaten it 2 a decoration 3 decorative parts of a motor vehicle 4 decorative additions to a building 5 the appearance of a vessel ready to sail —**trim** adv —**trim·ly** n —**trim·ness** n

tri·ma·ran /trímə ràn/ n a sailboat with three hulls

tri·mes·ter /trī méstər/ n 1 a period of three months 2 one of three college terms —**tri·mes·tral** adj

trim·mer /trímmər/ n 1 a device used for trimming 2 somebody who alters an opinion according to circumstances (disapproving)

Trin·i·dad /trínni dàd/ island in the Caribbean, part of Trinidad and Tobago. Pop. 1,065,245 (1998). —**Trin·i·dad·i·an** /trínni dáddee ən/ n, adj

Trin·i·dad and To·ba·go country in the Caribbean, comprising two islands off the NE coast of Venezuela. Cap. Port-of-Spain. Pop. 1,169,682 (2001).

trin·i·ty /trínnitee/ (pl **-ties**) n 1 a group of three 2 **Trin·i·ty** in Christianity, the union of the Father, Son, and Holy Spirit in a single God

trin·ket /tríngkit/ n 1 an ornament or piece of jewelry of little value 2 something trivial

tri·o /trée ō/ (pl **-os**) n 1 a group of three related people or things 2 a group of three musicians playing together 3 a musical composition for three players

trip n 1 a journey or outing 2 a fall or stumble 3 a light or nimble step 4 an error 5 a switch that activates a mechanism 6 a drug-induced hallucination (slang) ■ v (**tripped**, **trip·ping**) 1 vti stumble or fall, or cause to stumble or fall, by catching the foot 2 vti make or cause to make a mistake 3 vi move with rapid light steps 4 vt cause a device to operate 5 vi experience hallucinatory drug effects (slang)

tri·par·tite /trī paàr tīt/ adj 1 involving three parties or groups 2 having or divided into three parts

tripe /trīp/ n 1 the stomach lining of a cow or sheep as food 2 nonsense (infml)

tri·ple /trípp'l/ adj 1 having three parts 2 three times as much 3 done three times ■ v (**-pled**, **-pling**) 1 vti make or become three times as much 2 vi make a hit in baseball that allows the batter to reach third base ■ n 1 something three times greater than usual or another 2 a set of three 3 in baseball, a hit that gets the batter to third base —**tri·ply** adv

tri·ple·head·er n three sports games played in a row

tri·ple jump n an athletic event involving three jumps, landing on one foot, then the other, then both feet, in continuous motion

trip·let /trípplət/ n 1 a group of three related things 2 any of three offspring born together

trip·li·cate adj /trípplikət/ threefold ■ n /trípplikət/ the state of having three identical parts or copies o in triplicate ■ vt /trípplikàyt/ (**-cat·ed**, **-cat·ing**) make three copies of —**trip·li·ca·tion** /trippli káysh'n/ n

tri·pod /trī pòd/ n 1 a three-legged support, e.g., for a camera 2 a three-legged object, e.g., a cauldron or stool —**tri·po·dal** /tríppəd'l, trī pòdd'l/ adj

Trip·o·li /tríppəlee/ capital of Libya. Pop. 1,682,000 (1995).

trip·tych /tríptik/ n a work of art in three panels

trip·wire /tríp wīr/ n a wire that activates a trap, alarm, or other device

Tri·rat·na /tree rátnə, -rútnə/ n the three principal components of Buddhism, namely the Buddha or teacher, the teaching, and the priesthood

tri·sect /trī sèkt, trī sékt/ vt divide into three parts —**tri·sec·tion** n

tri·state /trī stàyt/ adj of three adjoining states

trite /trīt/ (**trit·er**, **trit·est**) adj overused and lacking originality —**trite·ly** adv —**trite·ness** n

trit·i·um /tríttee əm/ n (symbol T) a radioactive isotope of hydrogen

tri·umph /trī əmf/ n 1 a success or victory 2 great joy or pride about success or victory ■ vi 1 win or succeed 2 be exultant —**tri·um·phal** /trī úmfəl/ adj —**tri·um·phant** /trī úmfənt/ adj —**tri·um·phant·ly** adv

tri·um·vi·rate /trī úmvərət, -úmvə ràyt/ *n* 1 a group of three rulers of ancient Rome 2 a group of three people sharing authority 3 the term of office of a triumvirate —**tri·um·vir** *n* —**tri·um·vi·ral** *adj*

triv·et /trívvit/ *n* a three-legged stand or support, e.g., for a hot dish

triv·i·a /trívvee ə/ *n* unimportant things (+ *sing or pl verb*)

triv·i·al /trívvee əl/ *adj* 1 having little importance or value 2 commonplace —**triv·i·al·i·ty** /trívvee állətee/ *n* —**triv·i·al·ly** *adv*

ORIGIN Medieval teachers and scholars recognized seven liberal arts: the lower three, grammar, logic, and rhetoric, were known as the *trivium*, and the upper four, arithmetic, astronomy, geometry, and music, were known as the *quadrivium*. The notion of "less important subjects" led in the 16C to the use of the derived adjective **trivial** for "commonplace, of little importance."

triv·i·al·ize /trívvee ə līz/ (-ized, -iz·ing) *vt* treat something as less important or valuable than it really is —**triv·i·al·i·za·tion** /trívvee əli záysh'n/ *n*

tro·chee /trōkee/ *n* a metrical foot consisting of a stressed syllable followed by an unstressed syllable —**tro·cha·ic** /trō káy ik/ *adj*

trod past tense, past participle of **tread**

trod·den past participle of **tread**

trog·lo·dyte /trógglə dīt/ *n* 1 a cave dweller 2 somebody living in seclusion —**trog·lo·dyt·ic** /trógglə díttik/ *adj*

troi·ka /tróykə/ *n* a Russian carriage drawn by three horses harnessed abreast

Tro·jan /trójən/ *n* 1 a citizen of ancient Troy 2 a determined or courageous person —**Tro·jan** *adj*

⚡**Tro·jan horse** *n* 1 in Greek mythology, a hollow horse containing Greek soldiers, left at the gates of Troy 2 a treacherous or subversive element concealed within an organization 3 a destructive computer program

Tro·jan War *n* the ten-year siege of Troy by the Greeks to recover Helen, the abducted wife of King Menelaus

troll[1] /trōl/ *vti* fish by dragging a baited line through water behind a boat —**troll** *n* —**troll·er** *n*

troll[2] /trōl/ *n* in Scandinavian folklore, an imaginary being depicted as a giant or a dwarf that lives in caves or under bridges

trol·ley /tróllee/ (*pl* -leys) *n* 1 *also* **trol·ley car** a streetcar 2 a device that collects power from an overhead wire 3 a wheeled table for food and drink 4 a cart on rails or suspended from a rail 5 a wheeled cart, e.g., for luggage or shopping, pushed by hand 6 *also* **trol·ley bus** an electric bus powered by overhead wires

trol·lop /trólləp/ *n* an offensive term for a woman regarded as promiscuous or messy (*dated*)

Trol·lope /trólləp/, **Anthony** (1815–82) British novelist —**Trol·lop·i·an** /trə lóppee ən/ *adj*

trom·bone /trom bṓn, trəm bṓn, tróm bṓn/ *n* a brass musical instrument with a U-shaped sliding part —**trom·bon·ist** *n*

trompe l'oeil /tràwmp lóy/ (*pl* **trompe l'oeils** /*pronunc. same*/) *n* 1 a painting technique that creates an illusion of three-dimensionality 2 an artistic work that uses trompe l'oeil

Trond·heim /trón hàym/ city in central Norway, on **Trondheim Fjord**. Pop. 145,778 (1998).

troop /troop/ *n* 1 a large group 2 a unit of soldiers ■ **troops** *npl* soldiers ■ *vi* 1 go as a large orderly group 2 go as if marching

SPELLCHECK Do not confuse the spelling of **troop** and **troupe** ("group of traveling performers"), which sound similar.

troop·er /troopər/ *n* 1 a member of a cavalry unit 2 a cavalry horse 3 a mounted police officer 4 a state trooper

troop·ship /troop ship/ *n* a ship for transporting military personnel

trope /trōp/ *n* a word or expression used figuratively

tro·phy /trōfee/ (*pl* -phies) *n* 1 a token of victory, especially a cup or other award given to the winner of a sporting contest 2 a symbol of personal success

trop·ic /tróppik/ *n* each of the lines of latitude at 23° 26′ north and south of the equator ■ **trop·ics** *npl* the area between the two tropics —**trop·ic** *adj*

trop·i·cal /tróppik'l/ *adj* 1 of or typical of the tropics 2 hot and sultry —**trop·i·cal·ly** *adv*

tro·pism /trṓ pìzzəm/ *n* involuntary movement in response to a stimulus such as heat or light

tro·po·pause /trṓpə pàwz, tróppə-/ *n* the boundary between the troposphere and the stratosphere

tro·po·sphere /trṓpə sfèer, tróppə-/ *n* the lowest and most dense layer of the atmosphere —**tro·po·spher·ic** /trṓpə sfeèrik, tròppə-, -sférrik/ *adj*

trot /trot/ *vi* (**trot·ted, trot·ting**) 1 move at a pace between walking and cantering (*refers to horses*) 2 move at a jogging pace ■ *n* 1 a trotting pace 2 a ride on a trotting horse

troth /troth/ *n* a solemn vow, especially between an engaged or married couple (*fml*)

Trot·sky /trótskee/, **Leon** (1879–1940) Russian revolutionary leader —**Trots·ky·ite** *n, adj*

trou·ba·dour /troobə dàwr, -dòor/ *n* 1 a writer or singer of love poems or songs, especially in medieval Europe 2 a strolling singer, especially in a restaurant

trou·ble /trúbb'l/ *n* **1** a condition of distress, worry, difficulty, or danger **2** a cause of trouble **3** a failing or drawback **4** a problematic medical condition ○ *back trouble* **5** effort ○ *went to a lot of trouble* **6** disorder or unrest ■ *vt* (**-bled, -bling**) **1** worry or upset **2** cause pain to **3** disturb, inconvenience, or impose on —**trou·bled** *adj* —**trou·bling** *adj* ◊ See note at **bother**

trou·ble·mak·er /trúbb'l màykər/ *n* somebody who constantly causes trouble —**trou·ble·mak·ing** *n, adj*

trou·ble·shoot·er /trúbb'l shòotər/ *n* **1** somebody who finds and solves problems **2** a mediator —**trou·ble·shoot·ing** *n*

trou·ble·some /trúbb'lsəm/ *adj* causing or involving trouble

trou·ble spot *n* a place where trouble, especially political unrest, occurs

trough /trawf/ *n* **1** a long narrow open container, e.g., for animal food or water **2** a channel for liquid **3** an area of low atmospheric pressure **4** a sunken area **5** a low point, e.g., in an economic cycle

trounce /trownss/ (**trounced, trounc·ing**) *vt* defeat decisively ◊ See note at **defeat**

troupe /troop/ *n* a group of traveling performers ■ *vi* (**trouped, troup·ing**) travel or perform with a troupe ◊ See note at **troop**

troup·er /tróopər/ *n* **1** a member of a troupe **2** somebody reliable and dedicated

trou·sers /trówzərz/ *npl* a garment for the lower body with separate sections covering the legs —**trou·ser** *adj* —**trou·sered** *adj*

trous·seau /tróo sò, troo sồ/ (*pl* **-seaus** *or* **-seaux** /tróo sòz, troo sồz/) *n* a set of clothes and linen collected by a bride

trout /trowt/ (*pl* **trouts** *or same*) *n* **1** a freshwater fish related to the salmon **2** trout as food

trove /trõv/ *n* **1** a collection of valuables **2** a valuable discovery

trow·el /trów əl/ *n* **1** a flat-bladed hand tool used for spreading and smoothing **2** a short-handled digging tool with a curved blade —**trow·el** *vt*

troy *adj* in troy weight

Troy ancient Greek city in present-day NW Turkey, on the Aegean Sea

troy weight *n* a system of weights based on a 12-ounce pound

tru·ant /tróo ənt/ *n* **1** somebody absent from school without permission or good reason **2** a shirker (*dated*) —**tru·an·cy** *n* —**tru·ant** *adj, vi*

truce /trooss/ *n* **1** an agreed break in fighting or arguing **2** an agreement to stop fighting or arguing

truck[1] *n* **1** a large road vehicle for transporting goods **2** a wheeled unit used for moving heavy objects ■ *vti* transport goods by truck —**truck·er** *n* —**truck·ing** *n*

truck[2] *n* **1** dealings (*infml*) ○ *have no truck with that kind of behavior* **2** market produce ■ *vti* **1** exchange or barter something **2** have dealings with somebody

truck·le /trúk'l/ (**-led, -ling**) *vi* be submissive

truck stop *n* a service station and restaurant for truck drivers

truc·u·lent /trúkyələnt/ *adj* aggressively defiant or uncooperative —**truc·u·lence** *n*

Tru·deau /troo dồ/, **Pierre** (1919–2000) prime minister of Canada (1968–79 and 1980–84)

trudge /truj/ *vti* (**trudged, trudg·ing**) walk wearily ■ *n* a long walk

true /troo/ *adj* (**tru·er, tru·est**) **1** real, factual, or correct **2** genuine **3** personally faithful **4** committed, e.g., to a cause or belief **5** conforming to a standard or measure **6** rightful or legitimate **7** in relation to the Earth's poles rather than to points of magnetic attraction ○ *true north* **8** meeting criteria for inclusion in a category ○ *A shooting star is not a true star.* ■ *adv* **1** so as to correspond with reality or fact ○ *didn't ring true* **2** accurately **3** honestly ■ *vt* (**trued, tru·ing** *or* **true·ing**) make straight or level ■ *n* **1** correct alignment ○ *out of true* **2** absolute truth —**true·ness** *n*

~~truely~~ incorrect spelling of **truly**

Truf·faut /troo fồ/, **François** (1932–84) French movie director and critic

truf·fle /trúff'l/ *n* **1** a fleshy fungus eaten as a delicacy **2** a soft rich chocolate candy

tru·ism /tróo izzəm/ *n* an obvious statement —**tru·is·tic** /troo ístik/ *adj*

Tru·ji·llo /troo khée yō, -hée-/ city in NW Peru. Pop. 627,553 (1995).

~~truley~~ incorrect spelling of **truly**

tru·ly /tróolee/ *adv* **1** sincerely **2** adds emphasis ○ *truly remarkable* **3** completely ○ *Only she can truly appreciate my feelings.*

Harry S. Truman

Tru·man /tróomən/, **Harry S.** (1884–1972) 33rd president of the United States (1945–53)

trump, trump card *n* **1** in a card game, a card from a suit declared to be highest in value **2** a highly valuable resource or advantage ■ *vt* **1** defeat by playing a trump **2** outdo □ **trump up** *vt* invent in order to deceive or cheat ○ *a trumped-up charge*

trump·er·y /trúmpəree/ (*pl* **-ies**) *n* (*literary*) **1** something showy but worthless **2** nonsense

trum·pet /trúmpət/ *n* **1** a brass instrument with a flared bell **2** something shaped like a

trumpet ■ *vt* announce loudly or proudly —**trum·pet·er** *n*

trumps *n* the suit in a card game with the highest value (+ *sing* or *pl verb*)

trun·cate /trúng kàyt/ (**-ca·ted, -cat·ing**) *vt* shorten by removing a part —**trun·ca·ted** *adj* —**trun·ca·tion** /trung káysh'n/ *n*

trun·cheon /trúnchən/ *n* a police officer's short heavy stick —**trun·cheon** *vt*

trun·dle /trúnd'l/ *vti* (**-dled, -dling**) move slowly and heavily on wheels ■ *n* **trun·dle bed** a bed stored beneath another

trunk *n* 1 the main stem of a tree 2 a storage compartment in an automobile 3 a large traveling case 4 the body excluding the head and limbs 5 the long muscular flexible snout of an elephant 6 the main part of something that branches ■ **trunks** *npl* men's shorts worn as swimwear

truss *vt* 1 bind somebody or something tightly 2 tie meat for cooking 3 support a structure with a framework of beams 4 support a hernia ■ *n* 1 a support for a hernia 2 a supporting framework of beams

trust *n* 1 confidence in and reliance on good qualities 2 care *o children in the trust of a daycare center* 3 a position of obligation or responsibility 4 hope for the future 5 a responsibility that somebody has 6 the holding and managing of another's property, or a legal arrangement for this 7 a cartel ■ *v* 1 *vti* rely on somebody or something 2 *vt* place confidence in the decisions and behavior of 3 *vt* place in the care of somebody 4 *vt* hope or suppose *o I trust you know what you're doing.* —**trust·a·ble** *adj*

trus·tee /tru stée/ *n* 1 somebody holding and managing another's property 2 a member of a board of financial managers —**trus·tee·ship** *n*

trust·ful /trústfəl/ *adj* willing to trust people —**trust·ful·ly** *adv* —**trust·ful·ness** *n*

trust fund *n* a fund managed on behalf of another

trust·ing /trústing/ *adj* tending to trust people —**trust·ing·ly** *adv* —**trust·ing·ness** *n*

trust·wor·thy /trúst wùrthee/ *adj* honest or reliable —**trust·wor·thi·ness** *n*

trust·y /trústee/ *adj* (**-i·er, -i·est**) reliable ■ *n* (*pl* **-ies**) a trusted person, especially a prisoner —**trust·i·ly** *adv* —**trust·i·ness** *n*

truth /trooth/ *n* 1 correspondence to fact or reality 2 something that corresponds to fact or reality 3 a true statement 4 an obvious fact 5 something generally believed 6 honesty 7 descriptive accuracy

Truth /trooth/, **Sojourner** (1797?–1883) US abolitionist

truth·ful /tróothfəl/ *adj* 1 honest 2 accurate in description —**truth·ful·ly** *adv* —**truth·ful·ness** *n*

try *v* (**tried, tries**) 1 *vti* make an effort to do something 2 *vt* test or sample something for the purpose of assessment 3 *vt* strain or vex somebody or something *o trying my patience* 4 *vt* subject somebody to a legal trial 5 *vt* conduct a case in court ■ *n* (*pl* **tries**) an effort *o a good try*

□ **try out** *vt* test for suitability or skills

~~tryed~~ incorrect spelling of **tried**

try·ing /trí ing/ *adj* stressful —**try·ing·ly** *adv*

try·out /trí òwt/ *n* a test of an applicant's suitability or skills

tryst /trist/ *n* a secret meeting, especially between lovers —**tryst** *vi*

tsar /zaar, tsaar/, **czar, tzar** *n* 1 formerly, a Russian emperor 2 a person given authority in a particular area (*infml*) *o a drugs tsar* —**tsar·dom** *n* —**tsar·ist** *n, adj*

tsa·ri·na /zaa réenə, tsaa-/ *n* formerly, a Russian empress, or a tsar's wife or widow

tset·se fly /tsétsee-, sétsee-/ *n* a fly that transmits sleeping sickness

T-shirt, tee shirt *n* a collarless short-sleeved shirt without fastenings

tsp. *abbr* teaspoon

T-square *n* a T-shaped drawing-board ruler

tsu·na·mi /tsoo naámee, soo-/ (*pl* **-mis**) *n* a large ocean wave caused by movement of the Earth's surface —**tsu·na·mic** *adj*

tub *n* 1 a low round open container 2 a tub-shaped container with a lid for soft foods 3 a bathtub —**tub** *vti*

tu·ba /toobə/ *n* a low-pitched brass instrument played with the open end pointing upward

tub·by /túbbee/ *adj* (**-bi·er, -bi·est**) *adj* 1 overweight (*infml; sometimes offensive*) 2 tub-shaped —**tub·bi·ness** *n*

tube /toob, tyoob/ *n* 1 a long hollow cylinder for transporting liquids or gases 2 a collapsible tube-shaped container with a cap 3 London's subway system, or a train that runs on it (*infml*) 4 a cathode ray tube in a television 5 television (*infml*)

tu·ber /toobər, tyoo-/ *n* 1 a fleshy underground plant part from which new growth sprouts 2 a nodule on the body —**tu·ber·ous** *adj*

tu·ber·cle /toobərk'l, tyoo-/ *n* 1 a nodule 2 a small rounded swelling in the lungs characteristic of tuberculosis

tu·ber·cu·lin /tə búrkyəlin, too-/ *n* a liquid obtained from the tubercle-causing bacillus, used to test for tuberculosis

tu·ber·cu·lo·sis /tə bùrkyə lṓssiss, too-/ *n* an infectious disease in which small rounded swellings form in the lungs —**tu·ber·cu·lar** /tə búrkyələr, too-/ *adj* —**tu·ber·cu·lous** /tə búrkyəlass, too-/ *adj*

tube top *n* a stretchy strapless top for women

tub·ing /toobing, tyoobing/ *n* 1 a system of tubes 2 material used for tubes

Library of Congress/Corbis

Harriet Tubman

Tub·man /túbmən/, **Harriet** (1830–1913) US abolitionist

tu·bu·lar /toõbyələr, tyoõ-/ *adj* tube-shaped

tuck *v* 1 *vt* push or fold into position 2 *vti* draw or be drawn in 3 *vt* sew a fold in ■ *n* 1 a fold sewn into something to reduce its size or for decoration 2 in cosmetic surgery, a removal of loose skin

□ **tuck away** *vt* put somewhere safe or concealed

□ **tuck in** *or* **up** *vt* make comfortable in bed by securing the bedclothes

tuck·er /túkər/ *vt* tire out (*infml*)

Tuc·son /toõ sòn/ city in S Arizona. Pop. 460,466 (1998).

Tu·dor /toõdər/ *adj* of the English royal family that ruled between 1485 and 1603 —**Tu·dor** *n*

Tues·day /toõz dày, -dee, tyoõz-/ *n* the 2nd day of the week

> **ORIGIN Tuesday** is named for Tiu, a Germanic god of war identified with Mars (the Latin equivalent meant "Mars' day"). The Germanic first element is related to Latin *deus* "god."

tuft *n* a bunch of fibers, hair, feathers, or grass held or growing together —**tuft** *vti*—**tuft·ed** *adj*

tug *v* (**tugged, tug·ging**) 1 *vti* pull sharply 2 *vt* tow or haul with effort ■ *n* 1 a sharp or strong pull 2 a struggle between opposing forces 3 *also* **tug·boat** a small powerful boat used for towing ◊ See note at **pull**

tug of war *n* 1 a contest in which two teams pull at opposite ends of a rope 2 a struggle between evenly matched parties or influences

tu·grik /toõgrik/ (*pl* same *or* **tu·griks**) *n* the main unit of Mongolian currency

tu·i·tion /too ísh'n, tyoo-/ *n* 1 a fee for instruction 2 instruction given individually or in a small group —**tu·i·tion·al** *adj*

tu·la·re·mi·a /toõlə reèmee ə/ *n* a bacterial disease of rabbits and rodents that can spread to human beings —**tu·la·re·mic** *adj*

tu·lip /toõlip, tyoõlip/ *n* a spring-flowering plant with cup-shaped flowers

> **ORIGIN Tulip** is ultimately the same word as **turban**. Both came through Turkish from Persian *dulband* "turban." The immediate source of English **tulip** was French *tulipe*, where the final consonant of *tulipan* "turban,

tulip" had been lost. The name was given to the plant because of the shape of the expanded flower.

tulle /tool/ *n* a thin netted fabric. Use: evening or ballet dresses, veils.

Tul·sa /túlssə/ city in NE Oklahoma. Pop. 381,393 (1998).

tum·ble /túmb'l/ (**-bled, -bling**) *vi* 1 fall suddenly, often rolling over 2 roll around 3 perform gymnastic or acrobatic leaps or rolls 4 reduce steeply ○ *Prices have tumbled.* 5 cascade —**tum·ble** *n*

tum·ble·down /túmb'l dòwn/ *adj* dilapidated

tum·bler /túmblər/ *n* 1 a drinking glass with no stem or handle 2 an acrobat 3 the part of a lock that is engaged by a key

tum·ble·weed /túmb'l weèd/ (*pl* **-weeds** *or* same) *n* a plant of dry regions that withers and is blown around by the wind

tu·mes·cent /too méss'nt, tyoo-/ *adj* swollen or swelling —**tu·mes·cence** *n*

tum·my /túmmee/ (*pl* **-mies**) *n* the stomach (*infml*)

tu·mor /toõmər, tyoõmər/ *n* 1 an uncontrolled growth of tissue 2 a swelling in or on the body

tu·mult /toõ mùlt, tyoõ-/ *n* 1 noisy commotion 2 emotional upheaval

tu·mul·tu·ous /too múlchoo əss, tə-, tyoo-/ *adj* 1 noisy and unrestrained 2 confused and agitated —**tu·mul·tu·ous·ness** *n*

tu·mu·lus /toõmyələss/ (*pl* **-li** /-lì/) *n* an ancient burial mound

tun *n* a large beer or wine cask

tu·na /toõnə, tyoõnə/ (*pl* same *or* **-nas**) *n* 1 a large sea fish 2 *also* **tu·na fish** tuna as food

tun·dra /túndrə/ *n* the plain with permanently frozen subsoil that stretches across Arctic North America, Europe, and Asia

tune /toon, tyoon/ *n* 1 a simple melody 2 a song ■ *vt* (**tuned, tun·ing**) 1 adjust a musical instrument for pitch 2 adjust an engine to make it run better 3 adjust a radio or television to a station or channel —**tun·a·ble** *adj* —**tune·less** *adj* —**tune·less·ly** *adv* —**tune·less·ness** *n* ◊ **call the tune** be in charge ◊ **change your tune** change your attitude or opinion ◊ **in tune** 1 played or sung at the appropriate pitch 2 in accord or agreement 3 adjusted to the correct frequency ◊ **to the tune of** to the amount of ○ *in debt to the tune of $10,000*

tune·ful /toõnf'l, tyoõnf'l/ *adj* having a pleasant melody or sound —**tune·ful·ly** *adv* —**tune·ful·ness** *n*

tun·er /toõnər, tyoõnər/ *n* 1 somebody who tunes musical instruments 2 a device that receives signals, e.g., in a hi-fi system

tune-up *n* an act of tuning an engine

tung·sten /túngstən/ *n* (*symbol* **W**) a hard gray metallic chemical element. Use: high-temperature alloys, lamp filaments, high-speed cutting tools.

tu·nic /toŏnik, tyoŏnik/ *n* a loose garment that usually extends to the hip or knee

tun·ing fork *n* a two-pronged metal fork that produces a sound, used in tuning musical instruments

Tu·nis /toŏniss, tyoŏniss/ capital of Tunisia. Pop. 674,100 (1995).

Tu·ni·sia /too neĕzha, tyoo-/ country in North Africa. Cap. Tunis. Pop. 9,705,102 (2001). —**Tu·ni·sian** *n, adj*

tun·nel /túnn'l/ *n* 1 a passageway under or through an obstruction, such as road or mountain 2 an underground passage ■ *v* 1 *vti* make a tunnel through or under something 2 *vt* dig something resembling a tunnel

tun·nel vi·sion *n* 1 a condition in which peripheral vision is lost 2 narrow-minded thinking

tun·ny /túnnee/ (*pl* same *or* -nies) *n* a tuna

tuque /took/ *n Can* a close-fitting woolen cap

tur·ban /túrban/ *n* a headdress that consists of a long piece of fabric wrapped around the head —**tur·baned** *adj*

tur·bid /túrbid/ *adj* 1 opaque and muddy 2 dense and cloudy —**tur·bid·i·ty** /tur bíddatee/ *n* —**tur·bid·ly** *adv*

tur·bine /túr bĭn, -bin/ *n* a machine powered by rotating blades

tur·bo·charg·er /túrbō chaàrjar/ *n* a turbine that increases the power of an internal-combustion engine —**tur·bo·charged** *adj*

tur·bot /túrbat/ (*pl* same *or* -bots) *n* 1 a nearly circular flatfish 2 turbot as food

tur·bu·lent /túrbyalant/ *adj* 1 moving violently 2 marked by change and unrest o *a turbulent year in politics* 3 atmospherically unstable —**tur·bu·lence** *n* —**tur·bu·lent·ly** *adv*

tu·reen /ta reĕn, toŏ-/ *n* a large serving bowl for soups and stews

turf (*pl* **turfs** *or* **turves** /turvz/) *n* 1 grass and the dense layer of underlying soil and roots 2 artificial grass 3 a piece of soil with grass growing in it 4 peat for fuel 5 horseracing, or a horseracing track 6 somebody's territory (*infml*)

Ivan Turgenev

Popperfoto

Tur·ge·nev /toor gáynyaf/, **Ivan** (1818–83) Russian writer

tur·gid /túrjid/ *adj* 1 pompous and over-complicated 2 swollen or distended by a buildup of fluid —**tur·gid·i·ty** /tur jíddatee/ *n* —**tur·gid·ness** *n*

Tu·rin /toor rín, tyoor-/ capital of **Turin Province**, Piedmont Region, NW Italy. Pop. 909,717 (1999).

Tur·ing /tyoóring/, **Alan** (1912–54) British mathematician. He was a major figure in the theoretical development of the computer.

⚡ **Tur·ing ma·chine** *n* a mathematical model of a hypothetical computer

Turk /turk/ *n* 1 somebody from Turkey 2 a member of a Turkish-speaking ethnic group

tur·key /túrkee/ (*pl* -keys) *n* 1 a large bird with a bare wattled head 2 turkey as food 3 a failure (*slang*) 4 an offensive term for somebody regarded as unintelligent or incompetent (*slang*)

ORIGIN Although North American, the bird is indeed named for the country of Turkey. The Europeans who first encountered it saw a resemblance to the guinea fowl. *Turkeycock* and *turkeyhen* were 16C names for guinea fowl, which were imported through Turkish territory. Shortenings of these forms were adopted in the mid-16C for the **turkey** itself.

Tur·key /túrkee/ country in SE Europe and SW Asia. Cap. Ankara. Pop. 66,493,970 (2001).

Turk·ish /túrkish/ *adj* 1 of Turkey 2 of the Turkish language ■ *n* the official language of Turkey —**Turk·ish·ness** *n*

Turk·ish bath *n* a steam bath followed by a shower and massage

Turk·ish de·light *n* a soft candy made with flavored gelatin

Turk·men·i·stan /túrk meni stán, -staàn/ country in SW Central Asia, on the Caspian Sea. Cap. Ashgabat. Pop. 4,603,244 (2001). —**Turk·men** /túrk mèn/ *n, adj*

Turks and Cai·cos Is·lands /túrks and kày koss-, -kĩkŏss-/ British dependency consisting of two island groups in the Caribbean. Cap. Cockburn Town. Pop. 18,122 (2001).

tur·mer·ic /túrmarik/ *n* 1 a bright yellow spice. Use: cooking, yellow dye. 2 a plant with rhizomes that are dried to produce turmeric

tur·moil /túr mòyl/ *n* confused disturbance or commotion

turn *v* 1 *vti* move to face a different direction 2 *vti* move around an axis 3 *vt* move a control on a machine 4 *vti* go or cause to go in a different direction 5 *vt* go around a corner 6 *vt* move something to expose the other side o *turned the pages* 7 *vti* change into a different form o *turned into a butterfly* 8 *vti* change color 9 *vti* redirect, or be redirected o *Her thoughts turned to the past.* 10 *vi* appeal to somebody or something for help 11 *vti* upset or become upset o *violence that turned my stomach* 12 *vt* twist an ankle 13 *vt* pass a particular time or age 14 *vi* become sour (*refers to milk*) 15 *vti* change or cause to change allegiance ■ **n 1** a time when somebody may or must do something **2** a change of direction **3** a rotation **4** a winding of something such as wire around something else **5** a sudden fright **6** the end of a period o *at the turn of the century* —**turn·er** n ◊ **at every turn** everywhere ◊ **out of turn 1** not in a regular or correct order **2** in an inappropriate way, or at an inappropriate time

□ **turn down** vt **1** reject **2** reduce the volume or intensity of

□ **turn in** v **1** vt submit something **2** vt take somebody to the police **3** vi go to bed *(infml)* **4** vt produce a particular result o *turned in a creditable performance*

□ **turn off** v **1** vt operate a control to stop **2** vti make or become uninterested or unresponsive *(infml)*

□ **turn on** vt **1** operate a control to start **2** make excited or aroused *(infml)*

□ **turn out** v **1** vt switch off **2** vi come to an event **3** vi end up **4** vt create or produce o *turning out 400 cars a week*

□ **turn over** vt **1** think about **2** give to somebody else

□ **turn up** v **1** vt increase the volume or intensity of something **2** vi be found **3** vt find something by searching **4** vi arrive

turn·a·bout /túrnə bòwt/ n a complete shift in something such as policy or attitude

turn·a·round /túrnə ròwnd/ n **1** the time it takes to complete an order or task or to prepare an aircraft, ship, or vehicle between trips **2** a big improvement **3** a complete shift in policy or attitude

turn·coat /túrn kòt/ n a traitor

Tur·ner /túrnər/, **J. M. W.** (1775–1851) British painter and watercolorist

Tur·ner, Nat (1800–31) US leader of enslaved people

turn·ing point n an important moment of change

turn·ing ra·di·us n the smallest circle in which a vehicle can make a complete turn

tur·nip /túrnip/ n **1** a white rounded root eaten as a vegetable **2** a plant that produces turnips

turn·key /túrn kèe/ adj ready to use on delivery or installation ■ n *(pl* -**keys)** a keeper of keys, especially a jailer *(archaic)*

turn·off /túrn àwf, -òf/ n **1** something disgusting or off-putting *(infml)* **2** a road branching off a main road

turn of phrase n a particular way of expressing yourself

turn-on n somebody or something causing sexual arousal *(infml)*

turn·out /túrn òwt/ n **1** total attendance or participation **2** a widened part of a street

turn·o·ver /túrn òvər/ n **1** a filled pastry made by folding one half of a piece of dough over the other half **2** the amount of business transacted over a given period **3** the

number of employees who leave and are replaced **4** in basketball or football, a loss of possession of the ball

turn·pike /túrn pìk/ n a toll road, especially an expressway or highway

turn·stile /túrn stìl/ n a revolving barrier

turn·ta·ble /túrn tàyb'l/ n **1** a revolving platform on a phonograph **2** a rotating platform for turning a locomotive

tur·pen·tine /túrpən tìn/ n a substance obtained from pine trees, or an oil distilled from it. Use: paint solvent, in medicine. —**tur·pen·tine** vt

tur·pi·tude /túrpə tòòd/ n immorality *(fml)*

tur·quoise /túr kwòyz, -kòyz/ n **1** a semiprecious stone. Use: gems. **2** a greenish-blue color —**tur·quoise** adj

tur·ret /túrrət/ n **1** a dome or rotating structure containing a gun **2** a small tower projecting from a building

tur·tle /túrt'l/ n **1** a reptile with paddle-shaped limbs **2** turtle as food

tur·tle·dove /túrt'l dùv/ n a dove with a purring call

ORIGIN The *turtledove* was earlier simply the *turtle*. The name derives from Latin *turtur*, an imitation of the bird's cooing sound. It is unrelated to *turtle* the reptile, which is probably an alteration of French *tortue* "tortoise."

tur·tle·neck /túrt'l nèk/ n **1** a high turned-over collar **2** a top or sweater with a turtleneck

Tus·ca·ny /túskənee/ region in N Italy. Cap. Florence. Pop. 3,528,563 (1998).

tusk n an enlarged projecting tooth —**tusked** adj

tus·sle /túss'l/ (**-sled, -sling**) vi have a vigorous fight or struggle —**tus·sle** n

tus·sock /tússək/ n a small thick clump of grass

tut, tut-tut interj expresses disapproval ■ vi (**tut·ted, tut·ting; tut-tut·ted, tut-tut·ting**) make a clicking sound with the tongue to express disapproval

Tu·tan·kha·men /tòòt'n kaáamən/, **Tu·tan·kha·mun** /-kaa mòòn/ (1343–1325 BC) Egyptian pharaoh

tu·te·lage /tòòt'lij, tyòòt'lij/ n **1** instruction and guidance **2** supervision by a tutor or guardian **3** the state of being a tutor or guardian

tu·tor /tòòtər, tyòòtər/ n a teacher of an individual pupil or a small group —**tu·tor** vti —**tu·tor·age** n —**tu·tor·ship** n ◊ See note at **teach**

tu·to·ri·al /too táwree əl, tyoo-/ n **1** a lesson forming part of a manual or computer program **2** a lesson with a tutor ■ adj of a tutor

tut·ti-frut·ti /tòòtee fròòtee/ n *(pl* **tut·ti-frut·tis)** n ice cream containing mixed fruit

tu·tu /tòòtoo/ n a ballet dancer's short skirt that stands out from the body

Tu·tu /toŏtoō/, **Desmond** (b. 1931) South African archbishop and political activist

Tu·va·lu /too vaáloo, toŏva loó/ country consisting of coral islands in the W Pacific Ocean. Cap. Funafuti. Pop. 10,991 (2001). —**Tu·val·u·an** n, adj

tux /tuks/ n a tuxedo (infml)

tux·e·do /tuk seédō/ (pl -dos or -does) n 1 a man's formal jacket 2 a set of men's formal clothing

---

ORIGIN The **tuxedo** is named for the town of Tuxedo Park, New York, where the jacket was first worn at a country club in 1886. The first printed record of the name is from 1889.

TV n television (infml)

TV din·ner n a precooked meal that can be reheated and eaten from the tray it comes in

TVP n a soya food product that is flavored to taste like meat. Full form **textured vegetable protein**

twad·dle /twódd'l/ n nonsense (infml) —**twad·dle** vi —**twad·dler** n

twain /twayn/ n two (literary)

Library of Congress

Mark Twain

Twain /twayn/, **Mark** (1835–1910) US writer

twang n 1 the sound of a tight string vibrating 2 a nasal twang in various accents —**twang** vti —**twang·y** adj

tweak /tweek/ vt 1 pinch and twist sharply 2 adjust slightly (infml) —**tweak** n

tweed n a woolen cloth with a flecked appearance ■ **tweeds** npl clothes made of tweed

---

ORIGIN Tweed is an alteration of tweel, a Scottish form of twill, influenced by the name of the Tweed, a river in S Scotland and NE England. Early accounts date the coinage of **tweed** to 1831, and ascribe it to the London cloth merchant James Locke (although Locke himself in his book Tweed and Don (1860) does not make any such claim). The term was in general use by 1850, and it was registered as a trademark.

---

tweed·y /tweédee/ (-i·er, -i·est) adj 1 of or like tweed 2 casual and informal —**tweed·i·ness** n

tweet n a high-pitched sound made by a bird —**tweet** vi

tweet·er /tweétər/ n a high-frequency loudspeaker

tweez·er /tweézər/ n = tweezer npl ■ npl a tool with two narrow pivoted arms used for plucking or holding small things

~~twelth~~ incorrect spelling of **twelfth**

twelve n the number 12 —**twelfth** n, adj, adv —**twelve** adj, pron

twelve-month /twélv mùnth/ n a year (archaic)

~~twelveth~~ incorrect spelling of **twelfth**

twen·ty /twéntee/ n the number 20 ■ **twen·ties** npl 1 the numbers 20 to 29, particularly as a range of temperatures 2 the years from 20 to 29 in a century or somebody's life —**twen·ti·eth** n, adj, adv—**twen·ty** adj, pron

24/7 /twèntee fawr sévv'n/ adv, adj twenty four hours a day, seven days a week

twerp /twurp/ n an offensive term for somebody regarded as foolish (slang)

twice adv 1 two times 2 double

twid·dle /twídd'l/ (-dled, -dling) vti 1 turn a knob or dial back and forth 2 keep twisting or turning something in a bored or absentminded way —**twid·dler** n

twig n a small branch —**twig·let** n

twi·light /twí līt/ n 1 the time just after sunset or just before sunrise 2 the faint light of twilight 3 a closing or declining period o the twilight of the empire —**twi·lit** adj

twi·light war n a period of ominous inactivity that occurs in or before a war

twi·light zone n an uncertain area between two opposing conditions

twill n a strong fabric with diagonal ribs

twin n 1 each of two offspring born together 2 somebody or something similar or identical to another

twin bed n each of a pair of matching single beds

Twin Cit·ies npl Minneapolis and St. Paul.

twine /twīn/ n 1 strong string 2 something made by twisting strands ■ v (twined, twin·ing) 1 vti twist around or together 2 vi follow a winding course

twinge /twinj/ n 1 a brief pain 2 a brief uncomfortable emotion —**twinge** vti

twin·kle /twíngk'l/ v (-kled, -kling) 1 shine with flickering light 2 shine with amusement or mischief (refers to people's eyes) ■ n 1 a bright unsteady light 2 a brightness in somebody's eyes —**twink·ly** adj

twin·kling /twíngkling/ n a moment ■ adj flickering

twirl /twurl/ v 1 vti spin around quickly 2 vt fiddle with something by turning or twisting it 3 vi turn suddenly and face the other way ■ n 1 a quick spinning movement 2 a spiral —**twir·ly** adj

twist v 1 vti make the ends of something turn in opposite directions 2 vti distort the shape or position of something 3 vti wind around something or together 4 vt injure part of the body by moving awkwardly 5 vti rotate 6 vt distort the meaning of something 7 vi constantly change direction ■ n 1 a twisting movement **2** something shaped by being twisted **3** an unexpected development **4** a bend **5** a 1960s dance with rotation of the hips **6** a painful wrench —**twist·a·ble** *adj* —**twist·ed** *adj* —**twist·ing·ly** *adv* —**twist·y** *adj*

twist·er /twístər/ *n* a tornado *(infml)*

twit *n* an offensive term for somebody regarded as unthinking *(slang insult)* ■ *vt* (**twit·ted, twit·ting**) tease somebody playfully *(dated)* —**twit·ter** *n*

twitch *v* **1** *vi* jerk slightly **2** *vt* pull lightly and quickly ■ *n* **1** a jerky movement **2** a rapid involuntary muscle contraction

twitch·y /twíchee/ (**-i·er, -i·est**) *adj* **1** nervous **2** twitching —**twitch·i·ly** *adv* —**twitch·i·ness** *n*

twit·ter /twíttər/ *vi* **1** make a succession of chirping sounds *(refers to birds)* **2** chatter ■ *n* **1** a twittering sound **2** excitement or agitation —**twit·ter·y** *adj*

two /too/ (*pl* **twos**) *n* the number 2 —**two** *adj, pron* ◊ See note at **to**

two-bit *adj* cheap *(infml)*

two-di·men·sion·al *adj* **1** having the dimensions of length and width **2** lacking depth of character —**two-di·men·sion·al·i·ty** /too dì mènshə nálletee, too dī-/ *n* —**two-di·men·sion·al·ly** *adv*

two-edged *adj* **1** having two sharp edges **2** having two opposite effects

two-faced *adj* **1** hypocritical **2** having two surfaces —**two-fac·ed·ly** /tòo fáyssədli/ *adv* —**two-fac·ed·ness** /tòo fáyssədnəss/ *n*

two-fold /tòo fóld/ *adj* **1** having two parts or elements **2** double ■ *adv* doubly

two-hand·ed *adj* **1** using two hands **2** designed for two people —**two-hand·ed·ly** *adv*

two-hand·er *n* **1** a tennis shot made with the racket gripped in both hands **2** somebody who hits two-handers

two-piece *adj* having two parts or pieces

two-ply *adj* having two layers or strands

two-seat·er *n* **1** a vehicle with two seats **2** a seat for two people

two-sid·ed *adj* **1** having two surfaces **2** having two contesting sides

two·some /tóossəm/ *n* a pair of people

two-step *n* **1** a ballroom dance in 2/4 time **2** the music for a two-step —**two-step** *vi*

two-time (**two-timed, two-tim·ing**) *vt* be unfaithful to a romantic or sexual partner *(infml)* —**two-tim·er** *n* —**two-tim·ing** *adj*

two-tone *adj* having two colors or shades

two-way *adj* **1** moving in both directions **2** involving two participants **3** able to transmit and receive

TX *abbr* Texas

⨍ txt *abbr* a file extension indicating a basic text file

ty·coon /tī kóon/ *n* somebody powerful and wealthy in business

ORIGIN Tycoon was originally a title applied by non-Japanese people to the shogun of Japan who was in power between 1857 and 1868. The Japanese word from which it was adopted was formed from Chinese elements meaning "great" and "lord." In the US it was used as a nickname for Abraham Lincoln, and then extended to any powerful person, in particular (from the 1920s) one in business.

tyke /tīk/, **tike** *n* a small child

Ty·ler /tílər/, **John** (1790–1862) 10th president of the United States (1841–45)

Tyn·dale /tínd'l/, **Tin·dal, William** (1492?–1536) English religious reformer

type /tīp/ *n* **1** a kind or sort **2** a representative member of a category **3** a small block with a raised character on one side, used in printing **4** blocks of type collectively **5** printed letters on a page ■ *v* (**typed, typ·ing**) **1** *vti* produce words or characters using a typewriter or computer keyboard **2** *vt* classify

SYNONYMS type, kind, sort, category, class, species, genre CORE MEANING: a group having a common quality or qualities

type·cast /típ kàst/ (**-cast**) *vt* **1** cast repeatedly in similar acting roles **2** cast in a suitable role

type·face /típ fàyss/ *n* **1** a style of printed characters **2** the surface of a block of type

type·script /típ skrìpt/ *n* a typed document

type·set·ter /típ sèttər/ *n* a person or machine that prints text for printing —**type·set** *vt* —**type·set·ting** *n*

type·writ·er /típ rìtər/ *n* a machine with keys that are pressed to print words on paper —**type·write** *vt* —**type·writ·ten** *adj*

ty·phoid /tí fòyd/ *n* a serious bacterial disease of the digestive system ■ *adj* of typhoid or typhus —**ty·phoi·dal** /tí fóyd'l/ *adj*

ty·phoon /tī fóon/ *n* a violent tropical storm in the W Pacific and Indian oceans —**ty·phon·ic** /tī fónnik/ *adj*

ty·phus /tífəss/, **ty·phus fe·ver** *n* an infectious disease that causes fever —**ty·phous** *adj*

typ·i·cal /típpik'l/ *adj* **1** having the characteristics of a particular type **2** usual, or conforming to expectation —**typ·i·cal·i·ty** /tìppi kállətee/ *n* —**typ·i·cal·ly** *adv* —**typ·i·cal·ness** *n*

typ·i·fy /típpə fì/ (**-fied, -fies**) *vt* **1** be typical of **2** epitomize or embody —**typ·i·fi·ca·tion** /tìppəfi káysh'n/ *n*

typ·ist /típist/ *n* an operator of a typewriter or keyboard

ty·po /típō/ (*pl* **-pos**) *n* an error in typing or printing *(infml)*

ty·pog·ra·phy /tī póggrəfee/ *n* **1** the preparation of texts for printing **2** the appearance of printed matter —**ty·pog·ra·pher** n —**ty·po·graph·i·cal** /tīpə gráffik'l/ adj

ty·pol·o·gy /tī póllajee/ n the study or classification of types —**ty·po·log·i·cal** /tīpə lójjik'l/ adj —**ty·po·log·i·cal·ly** adv —**ty·pol·o·gist** n

ty·ran·ni·cal /ti ránnik'l/, **ty·ran·nic** /ti ránnik/ adj 1 ruling absolutely and oppressively 2 authoritarian —**ty·ran·ni·cal·ly** adv

tyr·an·nize /tírrə nīz/ (-nized, -niz·ing) vt 1 govern cruelly 2 treat harshly

ty·ran·no·saur /ti ránnə sàwr/, **ty·ran·no·saur·us** /ti ránnə sáwrəss/, **ty·ran·no·saur·us rex** /-réks/ n a large flesh-eating dinosaur that walked on powerful hind legs and had small forelegs

tyr·an·ny /tírrənee/ (pl -nies) n 1 cruelty and injustice in the use of power 2 oppressive government 3 a cruel act —**tyr·an·nous** adj

ty·rant /tírant/ n 1 an absolute and oppressive ruler 2 an authoritarian person

~~tyrany~~ incorrect spelling of **tyranny**

tyre n UK = tire[2]

Tyre /tīr/ town in S Lebanon. It was the most important city of ancient Phoenicia. Pop. 120,000 (1988). —**Tyr·i·an** /tírree ən/ adj

ty·ro /tírō/ (pl -ros), **ti·ro** n a beginner —**ty·ron·ic** /tī rónnik/ adj ◊ See note at **beginner**

Ty·rol = Tirol

~~tyrrany~~ incorrect spelling of **tyranny**

Tyr·rhe·ni·an Sea /ti réenee ən-/ arm of the Mediterranean Sea between W Italy and the islands of Corsica, Sardinia, and Sicily

tzar n = tsar

U

u (pl **u's**), **U** (pl **U's** or **Us**) n the 21st letter of the English alphabet

U[1] symbol uranium

U[2] abbr university

UAE abbr United Arab Emirates

UAW, U.A.W. abbr Automobile, Aerospace, and Agricultural Implement Workers of America

u·biq·ui·tous /yoo bíkwitəss/ adj present everywhere —**u·biq·ui·tous·ly** adv —**u·biq·ui·tous·ness** n —**u·biq·ui·ty** n

U-boat n a German submarine

ORIGIN **U-boat** is a partial translation of German U-Boot, a shortening of Unterseeboot, literally "under sea boat." A **U-boat** was first mentioned in English in 1916.

U·ca·ya·li /ōō kaa yaàlee/ river in E Peru. Length 1,200 mi. / 1,900 km.

UCLA abbr University of California at Los Angeles

ud·der /úddər/ n a bag-shaped milk-secreting organ of a cow, sheep, or goat

Ud·jung Pan·dang /ōojoong pan dáng/ capital of Sulawesi Selantan Province, on S Sulawesi, Indonesia. Pop. 944,372 (1990).

UFO /yoō ef ṑ, yoō fṑ/ (pl **UFOs**) n an unidentified flying object

U·gan·da /yoo gándə/ country in E Africa. Cap. Kampala. Pop. 23,985,712 (2001). —**U·gan·dan** n, adj

ug·ly /úgglee/ (-li·er, -li·est) adj 1 unattractive to look at 2 angry 3 threatening —**ug·li·ly** adv —**ug·li·ness** n ◊ See note at **unattractive**

ug·ly duck·ling n an unattractive or undervalued person or thing

---

ORIGIN The original **ugly duckling** appears in a children's story by Hans Christian Andersen, in which a cygnet raised by a duck is considered ugly until it grows into a beautiful swan.

UHF n a frequency range between 300 and 3000 megahertz. Full form **ultrahigh frequency**

ǂ**UI** abbr user interface

UK abbr United Kingdom

U·kraine /yoo kráyn/ country in E Europe. Cap. Kiev. Pop. 48,760,474 (2001).

U·krain·i·an /yoo kráynee ən/ n 1 somebody from Ukraine 2 the official language of Ukraine —**U·krain·i·an** adj

u·ku·le·le /yoōkə láylee/, **u·ke·le·le** n a small stringed instrument resembling a guitar

---

ORIGIN **Ukulele** was adopted in the late 19C from a Hawaiian word meaning literally "jumping flea." The reason for the name is not known for certain, but it may have been the Hawaiian nickname of Edward Purvis, a British army officer who popularized the instrument.

U·laan·baa·tar /ōō laan baá tàwr/ capital of the Republic of Mongolia. Pop. 600,900 (1992).

u·la·ma /ōolə maá/, **u·le·ma** npl a body of Islamic scholars who have jurisdiction over legal and social matters for the people of Islam

U·lan-U·de /oo laàn oo dáy/ port in S Siberian Russia. Pop. 410,359 (1995).

ul·cer /úlsər/ n 1 a sore on the skin or on a mucous membrane, especially the stomach lining 2 a corrupting or debilitating influence —**ul·cer·ous** adj

ul·cer·ate /úlsə ràyt/ (-at·ed, -at·ing) vti develop, or undergo the development of, an ulcer or ulcers —**ul·cer·a·tion** /úlsə ráysh'n/ n

ul·na /úlnə/ (pl **-nae** /-nee/ or **-nas**) n 1 the longer bone of the human forearm 2 a bone of the lower forelimb of an animal —**ul·nar** adj

ul·ster /úlstər/ n a man's long heavy double-breasted overcoat

Ul·ster /úlstər/ 1 historic province in the north of Ireland 2 Northern Ireland (infml) —**Ul·ster·man** n —**Ul·ster·wom·an** n

ul·te·ri·or /ul téeree ər/ adj 1 underlying or existing in addition ○ an ulterior motive 2 lying outside

ul·ti·mate /últimət/ adj 1 greatest (infml) 2 final 3 fundamental 4 farthest away —**ul·ti·mate** n —**ul·ti·mate·ly** adv

ul·ti·ma·tum /ùltə máytəm/ (pl -tums or -ta /-tə/) n a final demand accompanied by a threat

ul·tra /últrə/ adj 1 extreme 2 holding extremist views —**ul·tra** n

ultra- prefix 1 more than normal, excessively, completely ○ ultracautious 2 outside the range of ○ ultrasound

ul·tra·ma·rine /ùltrəmə reen/ n a deep blue pigment or color —**ul·tra·ma·rine** adj

ul·tra·son·ic /ùltrə sónnik/ adj of or having frequencies above the range of human hearing

ul·tra·sound /últrə sównd/ n 1 ultrasonic sound 2 an imaging technique that uses high-frequency sound for medical examinations

ul·tra·vi·o·let /ùltrə ví ələt/ adj of or producing light beyond the violet end of the visible spectrum —**ul·tra·vi·o·let** n

ul·u·late /yóolyə làyt, úll-/ (-lat·ed, -lat·ing) vi howl or wail, in grief or in jubilation —**ul·u·la·tion** /yòolyə láysh'n, ùllyə-/ n

U·lys·ses /yoo lísseez/ n the Roman name for Odysseus

um·ber /úmbər/ n 1 a brown pigment or dye made from soil 2 soil used for umber

um·bil·i·cal /um bíllik'l/ adj 1 of the umbilical cord 2 resembling a navel ■ n an umbilical cord

um·bil·i·cal cord n 1 the tube connecting a fetus to the placenta 2 a cable or pipe providing an essential link or supply of something

um·bil·i·cus /um bíllikəss, ùmbi líkəss/ (pl -ci /-sī/ or -cus·es) n a navel (technical)

um·bra /úmbrə/ (pl -bras or -brae /-bree/) n 1 a shadow caused by the complete blockage of all light 2 the darkest part of the shadow cast by an astronomical object during an eclipse —**um·bral** adj

um·brage /úmbrij/ n offense ○ take umbrage

um·brel·la /um bréllə/ n 1 a round collapsible canopy that protects somebody from rain or sun 2 something resembling an umbrella in shape or function ■ adj 1 co-ordinating or protecting member organizations 2 including a number of things ○ an umbrella term

um·laut /óom lòwt/ n 1 a change in a vowel sound under the influence of a vowel in the next syllable 2 two dots above a vowel indicating an umlaut —**um·laut** vti

um·pire /úm pìr/ n 1 an official who supervises and enforces the rules of a game 2 somebody who settles a dispute —**umpire** vti

ORIGIN "An umpire" was originally "a noumpere." The n was lost when this common combination of words was misinterpreted. Noumpere came from a French word meaning literally "not an equal."

ump·teen /úmp tèen, úm-/ adj very many (infml) —**ump·teenth** adj

UN, U.N. abbr United Nations

un- prefix 1 not ○ unavoidable 2 opposite of, lack of ○ unrest 3 do the opposite of, reverse ○ uninstall 4 deprive of, remove something from ○ unburden 5 release from ○ uncork 6 completely ○ unloose

un·a·bashed /ùnnə básht/ adj not ashamed or embarrassed —**un·a·bash·ed·ly** /-báshədlee/ adv

un·a·bat·ed /ùnnə báytəd/ adj just as forceful as before

un·a·ble /un áyb'l/ adj not able

un·ac·cept·a·ble /ùnnək séptəb'l/ adj 1 below the required standard 2 unable to be accepted —**un·ac·cept·a·bil·i·ty** /-septə bíllətee/ n —**un·ac·cept·a·bly** adv

un·ac·com·pa·nied /ùnnə kúmpəneed/ adj, adv 1 alone 2 without other musical instruments or voices

un·ac·count·a·ble /ùnnə kówntəb'l/ adj 1 inexplicable 2 not answerable to anyone —**un·ac·count·a·bil·i·ty** /-kòwntə bíllətee/ n —**un·ac·count·a·bly** adv

un·ac·cus·tomed /ùnnə kústəmd/ adj 1 not accustomed to something 2 unfamiliar —**un·ac·cus·tomed·ness** n

un·ac·quaint·ed /ùnnə kwáyntəd/ adj 1 unfamiliar with something 2 unknown to somebody —**un·ac·quaint·ed·ness** n

un·a·dul·ter·at·ed /ùnnə dúltə ràytəd/ adj 1 not mixed or diluted with anything else 2 absolute ○ unadulterated joy

un·ad·ven·tur·ous /ùnnəd vénchərəss/ adj 1 cautious 2 unexciting —**un·ad·ven·tur·ous·ly** adv

un·af·fect·ed /ùnnə féktəd/ adj 1 not affected by something 2 sincere, genuine, and natural —**un·af·fect·ed·ly** adv

un·a·fraid /ùnnə fráyd/ adj not afraid

un·aid·ed /un áydəd/ adj alone and without help

un·al·loyed /ùnnə lóyd/ adj 1 containing no impurities, and mixed with no other metals 2 absolute ○ unalloyed pleasure

un·al·ter·a·ble /un áwltərəb'l/ adj unable to be changed —**un·al·ter·a·ble·ness** n —**un·al·ter·a·bly** adv

un·am·big·u·ous /ùn am bíggyoo əss/ adj clear

and unable to be misunderstood —**un·am·big·u·ous·ly** adv

un·A·mer·i·can adj **1** at odds with US ways and traditions **2** not loyal to the United States

u·nan·i·mous /yoo nánnəməss/ adj **1** agreed on by everyone **2** in complete agreement —**u·na·nim·i·ty** /yòonə nímmətee/ n —**u·nan·i·mous·ly** adv

un·an·swer·a·ble /un ánsərəb'l/ adj **1** impossible to answer or solve **2** impossible to contradict or deny

un·ap·pe·tiz·ing /un áppə tīzing/ adj **1** not stimulating the appetite **2** not appealing —**un·ap·pe·tiz·ing·ly** adv

un·ap·proach·a·ble /ùnnə prṓchəb'l/ adj **1** too unfriendly to approach or contact **2** inaccessible —**un·ap·proach·a·bil·i·ty** /-prṓchə bíllətee/ n —**un·ap·proach·a·bly** adv

⚡ **un·ar·chive** /un aár kīv/ (**-chived, -chiv·ing**) vt retrieve a computer file from archive storage

un·ar·gu·a·ble /un árgyoo əb'l/ adj undeniably true or correct —**un·ar·gu·a·bly** adv

un·armed /un aármd/ adj **1** without weapons **2** with the firing mechanism disabled

un·a·shamed /ùnnə sháymd/ adj **1** not ashamed or apologetic **2** unrestrained —**un·a·sham·ed·ly** /-sháymədlee/ adv

un·asked /un áskt/ adj **1** not having been asked **2** coming to a gathering without being invited

un·as·sail·a·ble /ùnnə sáylab'l/ adj **1** impossible to challenge o an unassailable lead **2** impossible to attack —**un·as·sail·a·bly** adv

un·as·sist·ed /ùnnə sístəd/ adj **1** not given any help, or performed without help **2** performed or scored by a player without help from a teammate

un·as·sum·ing /ùnnə sṓoming/ adj modest —**un·as·sum·ing·ly** adv —**un·as·sum·ing·ness** n

un·at·tached /ùnnə tácht/ adj **1** without a spouse or partner **2** not attached to something

un·at·tend·ed /ùnnə téndəd/ adj **1** with no one present to listen, watch, or participate **2** not taken care of or dealt with **3** not escorted (fml)

un·at·trac·tive /ùnnə tráktiv/ adj **1** not having a pleasing appearance **2** not having obvious advantages or interesting aspects —**un·at·trac·tive·ly** adv —**un·at·trac·tive·ness** n

---

SYNONYMS unattractive, unsightly, ugly, hideous, homely, plain CORE MEANING: not pleasant to look at

---

un·at·trib·ut·ed /ùn ə tríbbyətəd/ adj not credited to any source or creator

unatural incorrect spelling of **unnatural**

un·a·vail·a·ble /ùnnə váylǝb'l/ adj **1** not obtainable or able to be used **2** unable to undertake something —**un·a·vail·a·bil·i·ty** /-vaylǝ bíllǝtee/ n

un·a·vail·ing /ùnnə váyling/ adj useless or futile —**un·a·vail·ing·ly** adv

un·a·void·a·ble /ùnnǝ vóydǝb'l/ adj impossible to avoid —**un·a·void·a·bly** adv

un·a·ware /ùnnǝ wáir/ adj **1** not aware **2** not knowledgeable ■ adv unawares —**un·a·ware·ness** n

un·a·wares /ùnnǝ wáirz/ adv **1** unexpectedly o caught me unawares **2** without intending to

un·bal·anced /un bállǝnst/ adj **1** lacking a balanced distribution of weight **2** psychologically unstable **3** done or provided from only one perspective

un·bear·a·ble /un báirǝb'l/ adj too unpleasant to tolerate —**un·bear·a·bly** adv

un·beat·a·ble /un béetǝb'l/ adj too good to surpass

un·beat·en /un béet'n/ adj **1** undefeated or not whipped or pounded o unbeaten eggs **2** not

un·be·com·ing /ùnbi kúmming/ adj **1** not making somebody look attractive **2** not right or proper —**un·be·com·ing·ly** adv

un·be·known /ùnbi nṓn/, **un·be·knownst** /-nṓnst/ adj **1** happening without somebody knowing **2** not known to somebody ■ adv without being noticed

un·be·lief /ùnbi léef/ n lack of religious or political belief —**un·be·liev·er** n —**un·be·liev·ing** adj

un·be·liev·a·ble /ùnbi léevǝb'l/ adj **1** impossible to believe **2** extraordinary —**un·be·liev·a·bly** adv

un·bend /un bénd/ (**-bent** /-bént/) vti **1** make or become more relaxed or informal **2** make or become straight —**un·bend·a·ble** adj

un·bend·ing /un bénding/ adj **1** inflexible in opinions or attitudes **2** strictly applied or observed —**un·bend·ing·ly** adv

un·bi·ased /un bī ǝst/, **un·bi·assed** adj fair, impartial, or objective

un·bid·den /un bídd'n/ adj, adv (literary) **1** spontaneous **2** unsolicited

un·blem·ished /un blémmisht/ adj **1** not marked with imperfections **2** not spoiled by errors

un·blink·ing /un blíngking/ adj **1** without hesitation **2** without blinking —**un·blink·ing·ly** adv

un·block /un blók/ vt remove a blockage from

un·born /un báwrn/ adj not yet born

un·bos·om /un bṓozzǝm/ vr say what is on your mind (literary) o unbosomed himself to us

un·bound·ed /un bṓwndǝd/ adj **1** not restrained **2** without restrictions

un·bowed /un bṓwd/ adj **1** not defeated or subdued **2** remaining erect, not bent

un·bridge·a·ble /un bríjǝb'l/ adj **1** impossible to span with a bridge **2** impossible to reduce o *an unbridgeable gulf between the two parties*

un·bri·dled /un brĭd'lld/ *adj* 1 openly expressed 2 without a bridle

un·bro·ken /un brōkən/ *adj* 1 without gaps or pauses 2 intact 3 undefeated 4 untamed 5 viable or in force

un·bur·den /un bûrd'n/ *vt* get something off your mind by telling somebody (*fml*)

un·but·ton /un bútt'n/ *vt* undo the buttons of

un·called-for /un káwld-/ *adj* unjustified

un·can·ny /un kánnee/ *adj* 1 very strange or eerie 2 unexpectedly accurate —**un·can·ni·ly** *adv* —**un·can·ni·ness** *n*

un·cared-for /ùn káird-/ *adj* neglected

un·car·ing /un káiring/ *adj* 1 unsympathetic 2 unconcerned o *uncaring of what others might think* —**un·car·ing·ly** *adv*

un·ceas·ing /un séessing/ *adj* never stopping —**un·ceas·ing·ly** *adv* —**un·ceas·ing·ness** *n*

un·cer·e·mo·ni·ous /un sèrrə mṓnee əss/ *adj* 1 abrupt and rude 2 informal —**un·cer·e·mo·ni·ous·ly** *adv*

un·cer·tain /un súrt'n/ *adj* 1 lacking clear knowledge or a definite opinion 2 not yet known or settled —**un·cer·tain·ly** *adv* —**un·cer·tain·ty** *n* ◊ See note at **doubtful**

un·char·ac·ter·is·tic /un kàrrəktə rístik/ *adj* not typical or usual —**un·char·ac·ter·is·ti·cal·ly** *adv*

un·char·i·ta·ble /un chérrətəb'l/ *adj* lacking in kindness or mercy —**un·char·i·ta·bly** *adv*

un·chart·ed /un chaártəd/ *adj* 1 not mapped 2 unknown

un·checked /un chékt/ *adj* 1 not limited or controlled 2 not verified or tested

un·civ·il /un sívv'l/ *adj* rude —**un·civ·il·ly** *adv*

un·civ·i·lized /un sívv'l ìzd/ *adj* 1 not culturally advanced 2 far from settled areas

un·clad /un klád/ *adj* naked

un·clas·si·fied /un klássə fīd/ *adj* 1 not arranged systematically 2 available for examination by anyone

un·cle /úngk'l/ *n* a parent's brother or brother-in-law

un·clean /un kleen/ *adj* 1 dirty 2 sinful, especially involving a sexual sin —**un·clean·ness** *n* ◊ See note at **dirty**

un·clear /un kleer/ *adj* 1 not obvious 2 not sure —**un·clear·ly** *adv*

Un·cle Sam *n* 1 a personification of the United States 2 the United States, its government, or its people

ORIGIN Uncle Sam was invented from *US*, an abbreviation for the United States. It is first recorded in 1813.

un·clothed /ùn klṓthd/ *adj* having no clothes or covering on

un·coil /un kóyl/ *vti* unwind, or release from being coiled

un·com·fort·a·ble /un kúmfərtəb'l, un kúmftərb'l/ *adj* 1 not physically comfortable 2 awkward or uneasy —**un·com·fort·a·bly** *adv*

un·com·mon /un kómmən/ *adj* 1 rare 2 very great —**un·com·mon·ly** *adv* —**un·com·mon·ness** *n*

un·com·mu·ni·ca·tive /ùnkə myoonə kàytiv, -kətiv/ *adj* not willing or tending to say much —**un·com·mu·ni·ca·tive·ness** *n* ◊ See note at **silent**

un·com·pre·hend·ing /un kòmprə hénding/ *adj* unable to understand —**un·com·pre·hend·ing·ly** *adv*

un·com·pro·mis·ing /un kómprə mīzing/ *adj* not willing to compromise or give in —**un·com·pro·mis·ing·ly** *adv*

un·con·cerned /ùnkən súrnd/ *adj* 1 not anxious 2 uninterested, or unwilling to become involved —**un·con·cern·ed·ly** /-súrnədlee/ *adv*

un·con·di·tion·al /ùnkən díshən'l, -díshnəl/ *adj* with no conditions or limitations —**un·con·di·tion·al·ly** *adv*

un·con·gen·ial /ùnkən jeènyəl/ *adj* 1 unfriendly 2 unsuitable or unappealing o *finds the job uncongenial* —**un·con·gen·ial·ly** *adv*

un·con·scion·a·ble /un kónshənəb'l/ *adj* 1 morally unacceptable 2 unreasonable —**un·con·scion·a·bly** *adv*

un·con·scious /un kónshəss/ *adj* 1 experiencing temporary loss of all senses 2 unaware ■ *n* the part of the mind containing things the person is unaware of —**un·con·scious·ly** *adv* —**un·con·scious·ness** *n*

~~unconscious~~ incorrect spelling of **unconscious**

un·con·sti·tu·tion·al /un kònstə toōshən'l, -toōshnəl/ *adj* contrary to a constitution —**un·con·sti·tu·tion·al·i·ty** /-toōsh'n állətee/ *n* —**un·con·sti·tu·tion·al·ly** *adv*

un·con·trol·la·ble /ùnkən trṓləb'l/ *adj* 1 too strongly felt to be suppressed 2 too unruly or wild to control —**un·con·trol·la·bly** *adv*

un·con·ven·tion·al /ùnkən vénshən'l/ *adj* different from what is usual or standard —**un·con·ven·tion·al·i·ty** /-vènshə nállətee/ *n* —**un·con·ven·tion·al·ly** *adv*

un·con·vinc·ing /ùnkən vínsing/ *adj* 1 not able to persuade people to believe or accept something as real 2 not impressive —**un·con·vinc·ing·ly** *adv*

un·cooked /un kookt/ *adj* not having been cooked

un·co·op·er·a·tive /ùn kō óppərətiv/ *adj* unwilling to cooperate —**un·co·op·er·a·tive·ly** *adv*

un·co·or·di·nat·ed /un kò áwrd'n àytəd/ *adj* 1 clumsy in movement or action 2 not organized

un·cork /un káwrk/ *vt* 1 remove the cork from a bottle 2 release something repressed

un·cou·ple /un kúpp'l/ (-pled, -pling) v 1 vti unfasten 2 vt release from restraint

un·couth /un kooth/ adj 1 ill-mannered 2 awkward —**un·couth·ly** adv —**un·couth·ness** n

un·cov·er /un kúvvər/ v 1 vti take the cover off something 2 vt expose or reveal something secret or previously hidden

un·crewed /un krood/ adj having no personnel, especially no pilot or crew

un·crit·i·cal /un kríttik'l/ adj not critical or discriminating —**un·crit·i·cal·ly** adv

un·cross /un kráwss, un króss/ vt straighten out from a crossed position

unc·tion /úngkshən/ n 1 the anointing of somebody with oil 2 an oil, ointment, or salve used in a rite or medical treatment 3 real or pretended earnestness 4 flattering efforts to charm

unc·tu·ous /úngkchoo əss/ adj 1 excessively ingratiating 2 oily, fatty, or greasy —**unc·tu·ous·ly** adv —**unc·tu·ous·ness** n

un·curl /un kúrl/ vti unwind from a curl, coil, or spiral

un·cut /un kút/ adj 1 not cut with a sharp implement 2 complete and unabridged 3 describes a gemstone before facets have been cut o uncut diamonds

un·daunt·ed /un dáwntəd/ adj not frightened or deterred —**un·daunt·ed·ly** adv —**un·daunt·ed·ness** n

un·de·cid·ed /úndi sídəd/ adj 1 not yet having made a choice or decision 2 not yet finalized —**un·de·cid·ed·ness** n

⚡**un·de·lete** /úndi leét/ (-let·ed, -let·ing) vt reinstate an electronic file or text that has been deleted

un·de·mon·stra·tive /úndi mónstrətiv/ adj tending not to show emotion openly —**un·de·mon·stra·tive·ness** n

un·de·ni·a·ble /úndi ní əb'l/ adj 1 unquestionably true or real 2 unable to be refused —**un·de·ni·a·bly** adv

un·der /úndər/ prep 1 below the top or base of 2 beneath a layer of 3 less than 4 subordinate to 5 subject to the control or authority of o under existing legislation 6 during the rule of 7 in view of o impossible under these conditions 8 undergoing o under scrutiny 9 using as a protective pretense or pretext o traveling under a false name 10 classified as or in o filed under "Miscellaneous" 11 powered by o under sail ■ adv 1 below a surface or point 2 fewer or less ■ adv, adj in a subservient position (infml) o keeping the masses under

under- prefix 1 too little, less than usual o underachiever o underpay 2 below, underneath o underpants o underscore 3 subordinate, of lower rank o undersecretary

un·der·a·chiev·er /úndər ə cheévər/ n somebody who does less well than expected —**un·der·a·chieve** vi

un·der·age /úndər áyj/ adj 1 below the legal or required age for something 2 done by underage people o underage driving

un·der·arm /úndər áarm/ adj on the underside of the arm, or used in the armpit ■ n 1 the underside of the arm on the body or a garment 2 the armpit —**un·der·arm** adv

un·der·bel·ly /úndər bèllee/ (pl -lies) n 1 the lowest part of an animal's belly 2 a weak or vulnerable point

un·der·bite /úndər bìt/ n a dental condition in which the lower incisor teeth overlap the upper

un·der·booked /úndər bóokt/ adj not having attracted enough bookings

un·der·brush /úndər brùsh/ n undergrowth

un·der·car·riage /úndər kèrrij/ n 1 the framework of struts and wheels supporting an aircraft on the ground 2 the supporting structure underneath a vehicle

un·der·charge vti /úndər cháarj/ (-charged, -charg·ing) not charge enough ■ n /úndər cháarj/ an excessively low price

un·der·class /úndər klàss/ n a social class so poor and deprived as to be outside mainstream society

un·der·clothes /úndər klòz, -klòthz/ npl underwear

un·der·coat /úndər kòt/ n 1 a coat of paint beneath the final coat 2 paint for use as an undercoat 3 a dense layer of short hair under an animal's outer coat ■ vt 1 paint with an undercoat 2 apply a protective coating to a vehicle's underside

un·der·cov·er /úndər kúvvər/ adj secretly gathering information —**un·der·cov·er** adv

un·der·cur·rent /úndər kúrrənt/ n 1 an underlying current of water or air 2 a hidden feeling or force o an undercurrent of resentment

un·der·cut /úndər kút/ (-cut, -cut·ting) v 1 vt charge a lower amount than 2 vt reduce the force of 3 vt cut the lower part of 4 vt hit a ball so as to give it backspin —**un·der·cut** /úndər kùt/ n

un·der·de·vel·oped /úndər di vélləpt/ adj 1 not grown to the full or usual extent 2 without the means for economic growth —**un·der·de·vel·op·ment** n

un·der·dog /úndər dàwg, -dòg/ n 1 the expected loser of a contest 2 somebody at a disadvantage

un·der·done /úndər dún/ adj inadequately cooked

un·der·em·ployed /úndər im plóyd/ adj not being used fully —**un·der·em·ploy·ment** n

un·der·es·ti·mate v /úndər éstə màyt/ (-mat·ed, -mat·ing) 1 vti make too low an estimate of something 2 vt make too low a judgment of the worth of ■ n /úndər éstəmət/ an estimate that is too low —**un·der·es·ti·ma·tion** /úndər èstə máysh'n/ n

un·der·fi·nanced /ùndər fī nànst, -fi nánst/ *adj* without sufficient money or funding

un·der·floor /ùndər flåwr/ *adj* beneath the flooring

un·der·foot /ùndər fŏŏt/ *adv* 1 beneath the feet 2 in the way

un·der·fund /ùndər fúnd/ *vt* not provide enough funding for

un·der·gar·ment /ùndər gàarmənt/ *n* a garment worn as underwear

un·der·go /ùndər gố/ (**-went** /-wént/, **-gone** /-gáwn, -gón/, **-go·ing**, **-goes**) *vt* experience or endure

un·der·grad·u·ate /ùndər grájjoo ət/ *n* a student studying for a first degree

un·der·ground *adj* /ùndər grównd/ 1 beneath the Earth's surface 2 covert 3 contrary to the prevailing culture ■ *n* /úndər grównd/ 1 a secret resistance movement 2 a movement contrary to the prevailing culture 3 *UK* a subway system ■ *adv* /úndər grównd/ 1 below ground 2 secretly

un·der·growth /úndər grŏwth/ *n* vegetation growing under the trees in a forest

un·der·hand /ùndər hánd/ *adj* 1 secret and dishonest 2 with the arm kept below shoulder height —**un·der·hand** *adv* —**un·der·hand·ed** *adj, adv* —**un·der·hand·ed·ly** *adv* —**un·der·hand·ed·ness** *n*

un·der·lay *vt* /ùndər láy/ (**-laid** /-láyd/) lay something underneath something else ■ *n* /úndər làу/ 1 a layer of cushioning under a carpet 2 a base, support, or foundation underneath something —**un·der·laid** *adj*

un·der·lie /ùndər lī/ (**-lay** /-láy/, **-lain** /-láyn/, **-ly·ing**) *vt* 1 lie or be put underneath 2 be the basis or cause of

un·der·line *vt* /ùndər lín, úndər lìn/ (**-lined**, **-lin·ing**) 1 draw or type a line below 2 emphasize ■ *n* /úndər lìn/ a line drawn or typed below something

un·der·ling /úndərling/ *n* a servant or subordinate, especially one regarded as of little importance

un·der·ly·ing /úndər lĭ ing/ *adj* 1 lying underneath 2 hidden and significant 3 basic or essential

un·der·mine /ùndər mín, úndər mìn/ (**-mined**, **-min·ing**) *vt* 1 weaken by removing material from below 2 weaken gradually or imperceptibly o *undermined her confidence*

un·der·neath /ùndər néeth/ *prep, adv* 1 below or beneath something, and perhaps covered by it 2 underlying something shown on the surface or openly expressed ■ *adv, adj* on the lower part or the part that faces the ground ■ *n* the lower part, or the part that faces the ground

un·der·nour·ished /ùndər núr isht/ *adj* not having had enough food or nutrients for health

un·der·pants /úndər pànts/ *npl* briefs or shorts used as underwear

un·der·parts /úndər paàrts/ *npl* the sides and belly of an animal

un·der·pass /úndər pàss/ *n* 1 a road under another road or a railroad 2 a tunnel for pedestrians under a road or railroad

un·der·pay /ùndər páy/ (**-paid** /-páyd/) *vt* not pay enough —**un·der·pay·ment** *n*

un·der·pin /ùndər pín/ (**-pinned**, **-pin·ning**) *vt* 1 support by propping from below 2 act as a support or foundation for o *the facts that underpin these assumptions*

un·der·pin·ning /ùndər pínning/ *n* 1 a support for a weakened structure 2 a foundation or basis (*usually pl*)

un·der·play /ùndər pláy/ *v* 1 *vti* act a role subtly or with restraint 2 *vt* present or deal with in a subtle or restrained way

un·der·pop·u·lat·ed /ùndər póppyə làytəd/ *adj* having a population smaller than desirable or expected —**un·der·pop·u·la·tion** /ùndər popyə láysh'n/ *n*

un·der·priv·i·leged /ùndər prívvəlijd/ *adj* denied social privileges and rights, usually as a result of poverty (*euphemistic*)

un·der·rate /ùndər ráyt/ (**-rat·ed**, **-rat·ing**) *vt* give or have too low an assessment of

un·der·run /ùndər rún/ *vt* (**-ran** /-rán/, **-run**, **-run·ning**) pass or move under ■ *n* /úndər rùn/ 1 a lower-than-estimated cost 2 a lower-than-required production run

un·der·score *vt* /ùndər skáwr/ (**-scored**, **-scor·ing**) 1 draw a line under 2 emphasize ■ *n* /úndər skàwr/ a line drawn under something

un·der·sea /ùndər sée/ *adj* of the area below the surface of the sea ■ *adv* also **un·der·seas** to the area below the surface of the sea

un·der·sec·re·tar·y /ùndər sékrə tèrree/ (*pl* **-ies**) *n* an assistant secretary in a government department —**un·der·sec·re·tar·i·at** /ùndər sekrə térree ət/ *n*

un·der·sell /ùndər sél/ (**-sold** /-sốld/) *vt* 1 sell something below the proper value 2 sell goods more cheaply than a competitor 3 present or advertise the merits of somebody or something with too little enthusiasm

un·der·shirt /úndər shùrt/ *n* an undergarment for the upper body

un·der·shorts /úndər shàwrts/ *npl* shorts worn as underpants

un·der·side /úndər sīd/ *n* 1 the lower side, or the side facing the ground 2 an undesirable, and usually hidden, aspect

un·der·signed /ùndər sínd/ *n* the person whose signature appears below (*fml*) —**un·der·signed** *adj*

un·der·sized /ùndər sízd/, **un·der·size** /-síz/ *adj* smaller than the usual or preferred size

un·der·skirt /úndər skùrt/ *n* a skirt worn underneath another one

un·der·sold past tense, past participle of **undersell**

un·der·spend /úndər spénd/ (**-spent** /-spént/) vi spend less than usual or expected

un·der·stand /úndər stánd/ (**-stood** /-stoód/) v 1 vti grasp the meaning of something 2 vti realize or be aware of something 3 vt know and be able to use ○ understands Spanish 4 vti know the character or situation of and sympathize with somebody 5 vt interpret in a particular way ○ understood it as a peaceful gesture 6 vt take as settled or agreed 7 vt gather or assume by learning or hearing ○ He is, I understand, expected later. —**un·der·stand·a·ble** adj —**un·der·stand·a·bly** adv

un·der·stand·ing /úndər stánding/ n 1 the ability to understand something or somebody 2 somebody's interpretation of something 3 a state of mutual comprehension or agreement ○ came to an understanding 4 knowledge of and sympathy with another's character or situation ■ adj sympathetically aware of another's character or situation —**un·der·stand·ing·ly** adv

un·der·state /úndər stáyt/ (**-stat·ed**, **-stat·ing**) vt 1 express with restraint 2 describe as being less than its true amount ○ understate the cost

un·der·stat·ed /úndər stáytəd/ adj subtly restrained

un·der·state·ment /úndər stáytmənt, úndər stàytmənt/ n 1 a deliberately restrained or muted statement or way of expressing yourself 2 a statement that reports something as less large or significant than it is

un·der·stood /úndər stoód/ past tense, past participle of **understand** ■ adj agreed, assumed, or implied

un·der·stud·y /úndər stùddee/ (pl -ies) n 1 an actor who learns the role of another actor so as to be able to act as a replacement 2 a trained substitute —**un·der·stud·y** vti

un·der·take /úndər táyk/ (**-took** /-toók/, **-tak·en** /-táykən/, **-tak·ing**) v 1 vti make a commitment to do something 2 vt set about doing

un·der·tak·er /úndər táykər/ n a funeral director

un·der·tak·ing /úndər táyking/ n 1 a task or project 2 a commitment to do something 3 the business of an undertaker

un·der·the·count·er adj sold secretly or illegally

un·der·tone /úndər tòn/ n 1 a low or quiet tone 2 something suggested or implied rather than stated openly

un·der·tow /úndər tò/ n 1 the pull of water away from a shore after a wave has broken 2 an underlying feeling or force that is opposite to the apparent one ○ an undertow of dissatisfaction

un·der·used /úndər yoózd/ adj insufficiently used —**un·der·use** /-yoóss/ n

un·der·val·ue /úndər vállyoo/ (**-ued**, **-u·ing**) vt 1 estimate or set at too low a value 2 hold in lower esteem than is deserved or appropriate —**un·der·val·u·a·tion** /úndər valyoo áysh'n/ n

un·der·wa·ter /úndər wáwtər/ adj below the surface of water —**un·der·wa·ter** adv

un·der way, **un·der·way** /úndər wáy/ adj in motion or progress

un·der·wear /úndər wàir/ n clothes worn underneath other clothes and usually not meant to be visible

un·der·weight /úndər wáyt, úndər wàyt/ adj not heavy enough

un·der·went past tense of **undergo**

un·der·whelm /úndər wélm, -hwélm/ vt fail to impress (humorous) —**un·der·whelm·ing** adj

un·der·wire /úndər wìr/ n a wire under each cup of a bra to provide support —**un·der·wired** adj

un·der·world /úndər wùrld/ n 1 criminal society ○ an underworld shooting 2 in Greek and Roman mythology, the abode of the dead

un·der·write /úndər rít, úndər rìt/ (**-wrote** /-rót, -ròt/, **-writ·ten** /-rítt'n, -rìtt'n/, **-writ·ing**) vti 1 issue insurance for somebody or something 2 agree to buy unsold securities at a fixed price and time 3 agree to cover the losses of somebody or something

un·der·writ·er /úndər rìtər/ n 1 somebody who underwrites 2 somebody whose job is to assess risks and fix insurance premiums

un·de·served /úndi zúrvd/ adj not deserved —**un·de·serv·ed·ly** /-zúrvədlee/ adv

un·de·sir·a·ble /úndi zírəb'l/ adj not wanted, liked, or approved of ■ n somebody regarded as undesirable —**un·de·sir·a·bíl·i·ty** /-zìrə bíllətee/ n —**un·de·sir·a·bly** adv

un·de·vel·oped /úndi vélləpt/ adj 1 not exploited or used in a productive way 2 without the means for economic growth (sometimes offensive) 3 not processed to produce a photographic negative or print 4 not grown to maturity

un·did past tense of **undo**

un·dies /úndeez/ npl underwear, especially for women and girls (infml)

un·dis·put·ed /ún di spyoótəd/ adj accepted as true, valid, or rightfully deserving the description

un·di·vid·ed /ún di vídəd/ adj 1 not separated or split 2 concentrated on one thing

un·do /un doó/ (**-did** /-díd/, **-done** /-dún/, **-do·ing**, **-does** /-dúz/) v 1 vti unfasten, untie, or unwrap, or become unfastened, untied, or unwrapped 2 vt cancel or reverse the effect of an action 3 vt bring somebody or something to ruin or disaster (literary)

un·do·ing /un doó ing/ n the act of bringing somebody or something to ruin or disaster, or the cause of this ○ Pride was our undoing.

un·done /un dún/ past participle of **undo** ■ adj 1 not yet done or completed 2 unfastened, untied, or unwrapped 3 brought to ruin or disaster (fml or humorous)

un·doubt·ed /un dówtəd/ adj not subject to doubt or dispute —**un·doubt·ed·ly** adv

~~**undoubtly**~~ incorrect spelling of **undoubtedly**

un·dreamed-of /un dreémd-/, **un·dreamt-of** /-drémt-/ adj impossible to imagine in advance

un·dress /un dréss/ vti remove the clothes from somebody's or your own body ■ n 1 the state of having no clothes on 2 informal clothing or an everyday uniform

un·dressed /un drést/ adj 1 naked, or scantily clothed 2 not processed or treated 3 without a sauce or salad dressing 4 without a bandage or sterile dressing ◊ See note at **naked**

un·due /un doó/ adj 1 excessive, inappropriate, or unjustified 2 not payable now

un·du·late /únjə làyt, úndyə-/ (-lat·ed, -lat·ing) v 1 vti have or give a movement or appearance resembling waves 2 vi go up and down gracefully —**un·du·la·tion** /ùnjə láysh'n, ùndyə-/ n

un·du·ly /un doólee/ adv excessively

un·dy·ing /un dí ing/ adj not diminishing over time

un·earned /un úrnd/ adj 1 not gained by work 2 undeserved

un·earth /un úrth/ vt 1 dig out of the ground 2 discover or disclose

un·earth·ly /un úrthlee/ adj 1 not being or seeming to be from this world 2 inappropriate or unreasonable (fml) —**un·earth·li·ness** n

un·eas·y /un eézee/ (-i·er, -i·est) adj 1 anxious or afraid 2 uncertain and not easing anxiety —**un·ease** n —**un·eas·i·ly** adv —**un·eas·i·ness** n ◊ See note at **worry**

~~**unecessary**~~ incorrect spelling of **unnecessary**

un·ec·o·nom·ic /un èkə nómmik, -eèkə-/ adj 1 not making a profit 2 also **un·ec·o·nom·i·cal** /-nómmik'l/ not efficient

un·ed·u·cat·ed /un éjjə kàytəd/ adj not educated, or not well educated

un·e·mo·tion·al /únni mṓshən'l, -mósh·nəl/ adj 1 showing little or no feeling 2 reasoned and objective —**un·e·mo·tion·al·ly** adv

un·em·ploy·a·ble /ùnnim plóyəb'l/ adj lacking the skills, education, or ability to get a job

un·em·ployed /ùnnim plóyd/ adj 1 without a paid job 2 not in use

un·em·ploy·ment /ùnnim plóymənt/ n 1 the condition of having no job 2 the number of unemployed people 3 also **un·em·ploy·ment com·pen·sa·tion** government payments to an unemployed person

un·end·ing /un énding/ adj continuing or seeming to continue forever

un·en·vi·a·ble /un énvee əb'l/ adj unpleasant or difficult ◊ had the unenviable task of breaking the bad news —**un·en·vi·a·bly** adv

un·e·qual /un eékwəl/ adj 1 not measurably the same 2 variable 3 not evenly balanced or matched 4 without the necessary ability to do something ◊ unequal to the task —**un·e·qual·ly** adv

un·e·qualed /un eékwəld/, **un·e·qualled** adj unparalleled or unprecedented

un·e·quiv·o·cal /ùnni kwívvək'l/ adj allowing for no doubt or misinterpretation —**un·e·quiv·o·cal·ly** adv

un·err·ing /un érring/ adj consistently accurate —**un·err·ing·ly** adv

UNESCO /yoō néskō/, **U·nes·co** n a UN agency that promotes international collaboration on culture, education, and science. Full form **United Nations Educational, Scientific, and Cultural Organization**

un·eth·i·cal /un éthik'l/ adj not conforming to agreed standards of moral conduct ◊ unethical business practices —**un·eth·i·cal·ly** adv

un·e·ven /un eévən/ adj 1 not level or flat 2 varying 3 not straight or parallel 4 not equal 5 not divisible by two —**un·e·ven·ly** adv —**un·e·ven·ness** n

un·e·vent·ful /ùnni véntfəl/ adj with nothing remarkable happening —**un·e·vent·ful·ly** adv —**un·e·vent·ful·ness** n

un·ex·cep·tion·a·ble /ùnnik sépshənəb'l/ adj providing no grounds for criticism

un·ex·cep·tion·al /ùnnik sépshən'l/ adj not special or unusual —**un·ex·cep·tion·al·ly** adv

un·ex·pect·ed /ùnnik spéktəd/ adj coming as a surprise —**un·ex·pect·ed·ly** adv —**un·ex·pect·ed·ness** n

un·fail·ing /un fáyling/ adj 1 always reliable or constant 2 always accurate or faultless —**un·fail·ing·ly** adv

un·fair /un fáir/ adj 1 not equal or just 2 not ethical in business dealings —**un·fair·ly** adv —**un·fair·ness** n

un·faith·ful /un fáythfəl/ adj 1 untrue to commitments or beliefs 2 not faithful to your spouse or partner —**un·faith·ful·ly** adv —**un·faith·ful·ness** n

un·fa·mil·iar /ùnfə mílleər/ adj 1 not previously known or experienced, or not recognized 2 with no previous knowledge or experience ◊ unfamiliar with the software —**un·fa·mil·iar·i·ty** /ùnfə mil yárreree/ n —**un·fa·mil·iar·ly** adv

un·fash·ion·a·ble /un fásh'nəb'l/ adj 1 not in the current style 2 not socially approved of —**un·fash·ion·a·bly** adv

un·fas·ten /un fáss'n/ vt separate the parts of something so as to release a fastening

un·fath·om·a·ble /un fáthəməb'l/ adj impossible to understand —**un·fath·om·a·bly** adv

un·fa·vor·a·ble /un fáyvərəb'l/ *adj* 1 expressing disapproval or opposition 2 unlikely to be beneficial —**un·fa·vor·a·bly** *adv*

un·feel·ing /un féeling/ *adj* 1 not sympathetic 2 numb —**un·feel·ing·ly** *adv*

un·fet·tered /un féttərd/ *adj* free of or freed from restrictions

un·fin·ished /un fínnisht/ *adj* 1 not completed 2 not finally treated with something such as dye, paint, or varnish

un·fit /un fít/ *adj* 1 unsuitable 2 unqualified 3 not fit and healthy —**un·fit·ly** *adv* —**un·fit·ness** *n*

un·flag·ging /un flágging/ *adj* remaining strong and unchanging —**un·flag·ging·ly** *adv*

un·flap·pa·ble /un fláppəb'l/ *adj* remaining composed under all circumstances —**un·flap·pa·bil·i·ty** *n*

un·flinch·ing /un flínching/ *adj* with no fear of hesitation —**un·flinch·ing·ly** *adv*

un·fold /un fóld/ *vti* 1 open and spread out 2 make or be understood by gradual exposure

un·fore·seen /únfər séen, -fawr-/ *adj* not expected beforehand

un·for·get·ta·ble /únfər géttəb'l/ *adj* remarkable and never to be forgotten —**un·for·get·ta·bly** *adv*

un·for·giv·a·ble /únfər gívvəb'l/ *adj* so bad that it can never be forgiven —**un·for·giv·a·bly** *adv*

un·for·giv·ing /únfər gívving/ *adj* 1 unwilling to forgive 2 providing no margin for mistakes

un·formed /un fáwrmd/ *adj* 1 with no real shape 2 not yet fully developed

un·for·tu·nate /un fáwrchənət/ *adj* 1 never experiencing good luck 2 accompanied by or bringing bad luck 3 inappropriate o *an unfortunate choice of words* ■ *n* somebody unlucky or lacking adequate resources —**un·for·tu·nate·ly** *adv*

un·found·ed /un fówndəd/ *adj* not supported by evidence

un·fre·quent·ed /un freekwəntəd, ùn free kwéntəd/ *adj* not often visited

un·friend·ly /un fréndlee/ *adj* 1 hostile or cold in manner 2 unfavorable —**un·friend·li·ness** *n*

un·furl /un fúrl/ *vti* unroll or spread out

un·fur·nished /un fúrnisht/ *adj* without furniture

Un·ga·va /óong gaávə, òong gáyvə/ region of NE Canada, east of Hudson Bay

Un·ga·va Bay inlet of Hudson Strait in NE Quebec, Canada

un·god·ly /un góddlee/ *adj* 1 not revering God 2 wicked 3 inappropriate or unreasonable (*infml*) —**un·god·li·ness** *n*

un·gov·ern·a·ble /un gúvvərnəb'l/ *adj* incapable of being controlled

un·gra·cious /un gráyshəss/ *adj* ill-mannered —**un·gra·cious·ly** *adv*

un·gram·mat·i·cal /úngrə máttik'l/ *adj* not using correct grammar —**un·gram·mat·i·cal·ly** *adv*

un·grate·ful /un gráytfəl/ *adj* not thankful or appreciative —**un·grate·ful·ly** *adv* —**un·grate·ful·ness** *n*

un·guard·ed /un gaárdəd/ *adj* 1 with no protection 2 not wary —**un·guard·ed·ly** *adv*

un·guent /úng gwənt/ *n* a healing or soothing ointment

un·hand /un hánd/ *vt* let go of somebody by releasing a grasp (*archaic or humorous*)

un·hap·py /un háppee/ (**-pi·er, -pi·est**) *adj* 1 not cheerful or joyful 2 unfortunate —**un·hap·pi·ly** *adv* —**un·hap·pi·ness** *n*

un·health·y /un hélthee/ (**-i·er, -i·est**) *adj* 1 affected by ill health 2 bad for the health 3 symptomatic of ill health 4 harmful to the character 5 morally corrupt —**un·health·i·ly** *adv* —**un·health·i·ness** *n*

un·heard /un húrd/ *adj* 1 not perceived by the ear 2 not given a hearing

un·heard-of *adj* 1 unknown 2 unprecedented

un·help·ful /un hélpfəl/ *adj* not providing or willing to provide help —**un·help·ful·ly** *adv*

un·hinge /un hínj/ (**-hinged, -hing·ing**) *vt* 1 remove something from its hinges 2 make somebody mentally unstable

un·ho·ly /un hólee/ (**-li·er, -li·est**) *adj* 1 not blessed or consecrated 2 defying religious laws 3 extremely bad

un·hook /un hóok/ *vt* 1 remove from a hook 2 undo the hooks of

un·hoped-for /un hópt-/ *adj* not expected but very welcome

un·hur·ried /un húrreed/ *adj* done in a relaxed and deliberate way —**un·hur·ried·ly** *adv*

un·hy·gi·en·ic /ùn hījee énnik, -jénnik, -jéenik/ *adj* not clean, sanitary, or healthy

uni- *prefix* one, single o *unicellular*

u·ni·cam·er·al /yoòni kámmərəl/ *adj* with one legislative chamber —**u·ni·cam·er·al·ism** *n*

⨍ u·ni·cast /yoóni kàst/ *n* a transmission from one computing terminal to one other

UNICEF, **U·ni·cef** /yoóni sèf/, *n* a UN agency that works for the protection and survival of children around the world. Full form **United Nations Children's Fund**

u·ni·cel·lu·lar /yoòni séllyələr/ *adj* single-celled

u·ni·corn /yoóni kàwrn/ *n* a mythical one-horned horse

u·ni·cy·cle /yoóni sìk'l/ *n* a pedal-powered vehicle with a single wheel and a seat on a frame above it —**u·ni·cy·clist** *n*

un·i·den·ti·fied /ùn ⊤ déntə fíd/ *adj* 1 unable

to be recognized or named **2** wanting to remain anonymous

U·ni·fi·ca·tion Church *n* a religious denomination founded in 1954 by Sun Myung Moon

u·ni·form /yóonə fáwrm/ *n* **1** a distinctive set of clothes indicating somebody's occupation or membership in a particular group **2 U·ni·form** a communications code word for the letter "U" ■ *adj* **1** unchanging or unvarying **2** conforming to one standard **3** like another or others —**u·ni·formed** *adj* —**u·ni·for·mi·ty** /yóonə fáwrmətee/ *n* —**u·ni·form·ly** *adv*

⨍ **U·ni·form Re·source Lo·ca·tor** *n* full form of URL

u·ni·fy /yóonə fī/ (-fied, -fies) *vt* make into a single unit or entity —**u·ni·fi·ca·tion** /yóonəfi káysh'n/ *n* —**u·ni·fied** *adj* —**u·ni·fy·ing** *adj*

u·ni·lat·er·al /yóonə láttərəl/ *adj* decided by, done by, or affecting one party only —**u·ni·lat·er·al·ly** *adv*

u·ni·lat·er·al·ism /yóonə láttərə lìzzəm/ *n* the exercise of a foreign policy that pays little or no regard to the views of allies

un·i·mag·i·na·ble /ùnni májjənəb'l/ *adj* beyond imagination —**un·i·mag·i·na·bly** *adv*

un·im·peach·a·ble /ùnnim peéchəb'l/ *adj* **1** impossible to discredit or challenge **2** faultless —**un·im·peach·a·bly** *adv*

un·im·por·tant /ùnnim páwrt'nt/ *adj* of little or no significance —**un·im·por·tance** *n*

un·in·cor·po·rat·ed /ùnnin káwrpə ràytəd/ *adj* not designated as belonging to a specific country or municipality

un·in·hab·it·a·ble /ùnnin hábbitəb'l/ *adj* not fit to be lived in

un·in·hab·it·ed /ùnnin hábbitəd/ *adj* with no one living there

un·in·hib·it·ed /ùnnin híbbitəd/ *adj* not subject to social or other constraints —**un·in·hib·it·ed·ly** *adv*

un·in·i·ti·at·ed /ùnni níshee àytəd/ *adj* without knowledge or experience of a subject or activity ■ *npl* uninitiated people

un·in·spired /ùnnin spírd/ *adj* lacking originality

un·in·spir·ing /ùnnin spíring/ *adj* not inspiring

⨍ **un·in·stall** /ùnnin stáwl/ *vt* remove software from a computer

un·in·tel·li·gi·ble /ùnnin téllijəb'l/ *adj* impossible to understand —**un·in·tel·li·gi·bly** *adv*

un·in·ten·tion·al /ùnnin ténshən'l/ *adj* not done on purpose —**un·in·ten·tion·al·ly** *adv*

un·in·ter·est·ed /un íntrəstəd/ *adj* lacking interest or concern —**un·in·ter·est·ed·ly** *adv* ◊ See note at **disinterested**

un·in·ter·est·ing /un íntrəsting/ *adj* without interesting qualities —**un·in·ter·est·ing·ly** *adv*

un·in·ter·rupt·ed /ùnnintə rúptəd/ *adj* **1** without interruption or break **2** without obstructions

un·ion /yóonyən/ *n* **1** the joining of people or things together, or the result of this **2** agreement **3** *also* **Un·ion** an organization or building providing recreational facilities for students **4** a marriage **5** sexual intercourse **6** a political alliance **7** a labor union **8 Un·ion** the North in the Civil War **9 Un·ion** the United States of America **10 Un·ion** the union of Great Britain and Northern Ireland

un·ion·ism /yóonyə nìzzəm/ *n* **1** the principles of labor unions **2** advocacy of labor unions **3 Un·ion·ism** support for the union of Great Britain with Northern Ireland —**un·ion·ist** *n*, *adj*

un·ion·ize /yóonyə nìz/ (-ized, -iz·ing) *vti* organize workers into or join a labor union —**un·ion·i·za·tion** /yóonyəni záysh'n/ *n*

Un·ion Jack, Un·ion flag *n* the flag of the United Kingdom

un·ion ter·ri·to·ry, Un·ion Ter·ri·to·ry *n* a territory in India ruled directly by the central government

~~unique~~ incorrect spelling of **unique**

u·nique /yoo néek/ *adj* **1** being the only one **2** very unusual and worthy of note **3** limited to somebody or something —**u·nique·ly** *adv* —**u·nique·ness** *n*

USAGE The use of **unique** in its sense "worthy of note" is common in marketing and advertising (*Don't miss this unique offer*), as well as in conversation. Many dictionaries and usage guides argue that **unique** is an absolute concept and so cannot be used with qualifying words such as *very* and *rather*, but this stricture seems pedantic. It is, however, best avoided in formal writing.

---

u·ni·sex /yóoni sèks/ *adj* **1** suitable for either sex **2** not distinctly male or female

u·ni·son /yóoniss'n, -z'n/ *n* **1** musical notes at the same pitch **2** the performance of musical parts at the same pitch or an octave apart

u·nit /yóonit/ *n* **1** one person, thing, or group **2** a discrete part **3** a group with a particular function **4** a component, or an assembly of components **5** *US, Can, Aus, NZ* one of a number of similar residences in a building or development **6** a standard measurement whose multiples are used in determining quantity **7** a number less than ten

---

ORIGIN The term **unit** was introduced in the 1570s by the English mathematician, astrologer, and magician John Dee. It is formed from Latin *unus* "one," probably on the model of *digit*.

U·ni·tar·i·an /yóoni táiree ən/ *n* a member of a Christian Church that rejects the doctrine of the Trinity and stresses individual conscience —**U·ni·tar·i·an** adj —**U·ni·tar·i·an·ism** n

u·ni·tar·y /yóoni tèrree/ adj 1 of a unit 2 characterized by unity 3 undivided and existing as a unit —**u·ni·tar·i·ly** adv

u·nite /yoo nít/ (**u·nit·ed, u·nit·ing**) vti 1 come or bring together to form a unit 2 join in marriage

u·nit·ed /yoo nítəd/ adj 1 combined into one 2 in agreement or harmony

U·nit·ed Ar·ab E·mir·ates federation of seven independent states on the E Arabian Peninsula, including Abu Dhabi and Dubai. Cap. Abu Dhabi. Pop. 2,407,460 (2001).

U·nit·ed King·dom country in NW Europe, comprising the historic kingdoms of England and Scotland, the principality of Wales, and the province of Northern Ireland. Cap. London. Pop. 59,647,790 (2001).

U·nit·ed Na·tions n an organization of nations formed in 1945 to promote peace, security, and international cooperation

U·nit·ed States, U·nit·ed States of A·mer·i·ca country in central North America, comprising 50 states. Cap. Washington, D.C. Pop. 278,058,880 (2001).

u·nit·ize /yoóni tìz/ (**-ized, -iz·ing**) vti make or become one

u·nit price n a price per item or measure

u·ni·ty /yoónətee/ (pl **-ties**) n 1 the state of being one 2 the combining of separate entities into one 3 a whole formed by combining separate entities 4 harmony of opinion, interests, or feeling 5 the arrangement of artistic elements to create an overall aesthetic impression 6 in mathematics, the number 1

u·ni·ver·sal /yóonə vúrs'l/ adj 1 of or affecting the whole world or everybody in it 2 of the universe or cosmos 3 of or affecting all those in a particular group or category 4 applicable to all situations or purposes ■ n a characteristic common to everybody or to all people or things in a particular group or category —**u·ni·ver·sal·i·ty** /-vur sállətee/ n —**u·ni·ver·sal·ly** adv ◊ See note at **widespread**

U·ni·ver·sal Prod·uct Code n a bar code

U·ni·ver·sal Time, U·ni·ver·sal Time Co·or·di·nat·ed n 1 the time in the zone that includes the prime meridian. Also called **Greenwich Mean Time** 2 an international time standard based on International Atomic Time

u·ni·verse /yoónəvərs/ n 1 the totality of all the matter and energy in space 2 the Earth and humanity

u·ni·ver·si·ty /yoónə vúrsətee/ (pl **-ties**) n an educational institution for undergraduates and postgraduates

⫶ UNIX /yoóniks/ tdmk a trademark for a widely used computer operating system that can support multitasking in a multiuser environment

un·just /un júst/ adj not just or fair —**un·just·ly** adv —**un·just·ness** n

un·jus·ti·fi·a·ble /un jústə fì ʼab'l, ùn justə fì əbʼl/ adj wrong and impossible to justify —**un·jus·ti·fi·a·bly** adv

un·kempt /un kémpt/ adj needing combing or grooming

ORIGIN Unkempt literally means "uncombed."

un·kind /un kínd/ adj 1 lacking kindness 2 severe, harsh, or inclement —**un·kind·ly** adv —**un·kind·ness** n

un·know·ing /un nó ing/ adj 1 unaware 2 unintentional —**un·know·ing·ly** adv

un·known /un nón/ adj 1 not known or identified ○ an unknown assailant 2 without somebody's knowledge ○ Unknown to her family, she left town. 3 not famous ■ n 1 somebody or something unknown 2 somebody or something not widely known

un·law·ful /un láwf'l/ adj not in accordance with or recognized by the law —**un·law·ful·ly** adv

SYNONYMS unlawful, illegal, illicit, wrongful CORE MEANING: not in accordance with laws or rules

un·lead·ed /un léddəd/ adj not containing lead or a compound of lead as an additive ■ n unleaded gasoline

un·learn /un lúrn/ (**-learned** /un lúrnd/ or **-learnt** /un lúrnt/) vt 1 rid the mind of 2 break the habit or end the practice of

un·leash /un leésh/ vt 1 free from a leash 2 allow to have its full effect

un·leav·ened /un lévvənd/ adj made without a raising agent

un·less /un léss/ conj except under the circumstances that

un·let·tered /un léttərd/ adj 1 not well educated 2 unable to read and write

un·like /un lík/ prep 1 dissimilar to or different from 2 in contrast with 3 untypical of —**un·like·ness** n

un·like·ly /un líklee/ (**-li·er, -li·est**) adj 1 improbable 2 not believable —**un·like·li·hood** n —**un·like·li·ness** n

un·lim·it·ed /un límmitəd/ adj 1 without restrictions or controls 2 lacking or appearing to lack a boundary or end

un·list·ed /un lístəd/ adj 1 US, Can, ANZ not included in a telephone directory available to the public 2 not on a list 3 not listed on a stock exchange and so not traded there

un·lit /un lít/, **un·light·ed** /-lítəd/ adj 1 not having lighting 2 not alight

un·load /un lód/ vti 1 remove a cargo or load from a carrier 2 discharge passengers or cargo **3** remove the charge from a gun **4** get relief from troubles by sharing them with somebody else **5** pass on or sell something unwanted **6** take the film out of a camera

un·lock /un lók/ *v* **1** *vti* open after being locked **2** *vt* give access to for the first time **3** *vt* release a pent-up emotion **4** *vt* reveal or explain

un·looked-for /un lóokt-/ *adj* unexpected

un·loose /un lōóss/ (-**loosed**, -**loos·ing**), **un·loos·en** /-lōóss'n/ *vt* **1** unfasten **2** set free by untying **3** release from restraint or confinement

un·love·ly /un lúvvlee/ (-**li·er**, -**li·est**) *adj* **1** not beautiful **2** not pleasurable —**un·love·li·ness** *n*

un·luck·y /un lúkee/ (-**i·er**, -**i·est**) *adj* **1** having bad luck **2** full of misfortune or failure **3** bringing misfortune —**un·luck·i·ness** *n*

un·made /un máyd/ *adj* not made neat and tidy after being slept in o *an unmade bed*

un·manned /un mánd/ *adj* uncrewed (*often offensive*)

un·man·ner·ly /un mánnərlee/ *adj* lacking good manners —**un·man·ner·li·ness** *n*

un·mask /un másk/ *v* **1** *vti* remove a mask from somebody's face **2** *vt* expose the true nature of

un·matched /un mácht/ *adj* **1** not belonging to a matching pair **2** having no equal or rival

un·men·tion·a·ble /un ménshənəb'l/ *adj* not to be mentioned, especially in polite conversation —**un·men·tion·a·ble** *n* —**un·men·tion·a·ble·ness** *n* —**un·men·tion·a·bly** *adv*

un·mis·tak·a·ble /únmi stáykəb'l/ *adj* easily recognized or understood —**un·mis·tak·a·bly** *adv*

~~unmistakeable~~ incorrect spelling of **unmistakable**

un·mit·i·gat·ed /un mítti gàytəd/ *adj* **1** not lessened or eased in any way **2** complete and utter —**un·mit·i·gat·ed·ly** *adv*

un·moved /un mōóvd/ *adj* not affected emotionally ◊ See note at **impassive**

un·named /un náymd/ *adj* **1** not mentioned by name **2** having no name

un·nat·u·ral /un nácherəl/ *adj* **1** contrary to the laws of nature **2** contrary to natural feelings or expected standards of behavior **3** artificial —**un·nat·u·ral·ly** *adv* —**un·nat·u·ral·ness** *n*

un·nec·es·sar·y /un néssə sèrree/ *adj* **1** not essential or required **2** unjustified and hurtful —**un·nec·es·sar·i·ly** *adv*

un·nerve /un núrv/ (-**nerved**, -**nerv·ing**) *vt* **1** deprive of resolve or courage **2** make nervous —**un·nerv·ing** *adj* —**un·nerv·ing·ly** *adv*

un·num·bered /un númbərd/ *adj* **1** too many to be counted **2** lacking an identifying number

un·ob·tru·sive /ùnnəb trōóssiv/ *adj* not conspicuous or assertive —**un·ob·tru·sive·ly** *adv*

un·of·fi·cial /ùnnə físh'l/ *adj* **1** not authorized or approved **2** not acting or done officially —**un·of·fi·cial·ly** *adv*

un·op·posed /ùnnə pózd/ *adj, adv* **1** meeting with no opposition **2** having no opponent

un·or·gan·ized /un áwrgə nìzd/ *adj* **1** not done or acting in an organized way **2** not unionized

un·pack /un pák/ *v* **1** *vti* remove the contents from something such as a box or luggage **2** *vt* remove from a container or packaging

un·paid /un páyd/ *adj* **1** awaiting payment **2** working or worked for no pay o *unpaid volunteers* o *unpaid overtime*

un·pal·at·a·ble /un pállətəb'l/ *adj* **1** having an unpleasant taste **2** hard or disagreeable to accept —**un·pal·at·a·bly** *adv*

un·par·al·leled /un pérrə lèld/ *adj* having no equal or parallel in kind or quality

un·par·lia·men·ta·ry /ùn paarlə méntəree/ *adj* not acceptable according to the practice of a parliament

un·per·son /ún pùrs'n/ *n* somebody whose existence is not acknowledged

ORIGIN Unperson was introduced by George Orwell in his novel *Nineteen Eighty-Four* (1949).

un·pick /un pík/ *vt* undo by pulling out the threads or stitches of

un·planned /un pland/ *adj* not happening according to a plan

un·pleas·ant /un plézz'nt/ *adj* **1** not pleasing **2** unfriendly or unkind —**un·pleas·ant·ly** *adv* —**un·pleas·ant·ness** *n*

un·plug /un plúg/ (-**plugged**, -**plug·ging**) *vt* **1** disconnect by pulling a plug out of a socket **2** disconnect from a supply of electricity

un·plugged /un plúgd/ *adv, adj* without amplified musical instruments

un·pop·u·lar /un póppyələr/ *adj* not liked —**un·pop·u·lar·i·ty** /ùn poppyə lárrətee/ *n* —**un·pop·u·lar·ly** *adv*

un·prac·ticed /un práktist/ *adj* **1** untrained or inexperienced **2** not done frequently

un·prec·e·dent·ed /un préssə dèntəd/ *adj* having no earlier parallel or equivalent

un·pre·dict·a·ble /ùnprə díktəb'l/ *adj* difficult to predict —**un·pre·dict·a·bly** *adv*

un·pre·pared /ùnprə páird/ *adj* **1** not ready for something or not expecting something to happen **2** not made ready as required or expected **3** improvised —**un·pre·par·ed·ly** /-páirdlee, -páirədlee/ *adv* —**un·pre·par·ed·ness** /-páirdnəss, -páirədnəss/ *n*

un·pre·pos·sess·ing /ùn preepə zéssing/ *adj* not producing a favorable impression —**un·pre·pos·sess·ing·ly** *adv*

un·pre·ten·tious /ùnprə ténshəss/ *adj* natural and modest —**un·pre·ten·tious·ly** *adv*

un·prin·ci·pled /un prínsəp'ld/ *adj* not moral or ethical

un·print·a·ble /un príntəb'l/ *adj* not fit for publication

un·pro·duc·tive /ùnprə dúktiv/ *adj* 1 fruitless 2 producing little —**un·pro·duc·tive·ly** *adv* —**un·pro·duc·tive·ness** *n*

un·pro·fes·sion·al /ùnprə féshən'l, -féshnəl/ *adj* 1 contrary to professional standards 2 amateurish —**un·pro·fes·sion·al·ism** *n* —**un·pro·fes·sion·al·ly** *adv*

un·prof·it·a·ble /un próffitəb'l/ *adj* 1 making no profit 2 not helpful or useful —**un·prof·it·a·bil·i·ty** /un pròffitə bíllətee/ *n* —**un·prof·it·a·bly** *adv*

un·prom·is·ing /un prómmissing/ *adj* 1 unlikely to succeed 2 unfavorable —**un·prom·is·ing·ly** *adv*

un·prompt·ed /un prómptəd/ *adj* spontaneous

un·pro·nounce·a·ble /ùnprə nównsəb'l/ *adj* difficult to pronounce

un·pro·tect·ed /ùnprə téktəd/ *adj* 1 having no protection from harm 2 lacking safety precautions

un·prov·en /un próovən/ *adj* 1 not tried and tested 2 not proved

un·qual·i·fied /un kwóllə fīd/ *adj* 1 lacking qualifications or the qualifications required 2 not limited by any condition or reservation 3 complete and absolute o *an unqualified success*

un·quench·a·ble /un kwénchəb'l/ *adj* 1 impossible to satisfy 2 inextinguishable

un·ques·tion·a·ble /un kwéschənəb'l/ *adj* 1 impossible to doubt 2 universally recognized and acknowledged —**un·ques·tion·a·bly** *adv*

un·ques·tioned /un kwéschənd/ *adj* 1 not asked questions 2 undisputed

un·ques·tion·ing /un kwéschəning/ *adj* not asking questions or expressing doubt —**un·ques·tion·ing·ly** *adv*

un·quote /un kwót/ *adv* indicates the end of a quotation

un·rav·el /un rávv'l/ *vti* 1 separate the strands of or undo the stitches of, or become unraveled 2 disentangle or become disentangled 3 make or become less complex and more understandable

un·read·a·ble /un réedəb'l/ *adj* 1 illegible 2 not enjoyable to read —**un·read·a·bly** *adv*

un·re·al /un rée əl/ *adj* 1 not real or existing 2 not true or genuine 3 excellent (*infml*) —**un·re·al·i·ty** /ùnree állətee/ *n* —**un·re·al·ly** *adv*

un·re·al·is·tic /ùn ree ə lístik/ *adj* not taking into account the way the world actually is and how events are likely to happen —**un·re·al·is·ti·cal·ly** *adv*

un·rea·son·a·ble /un réez'nəb'l/ *adj* 1

acting with or subject to reason 2 excessive —**un·rea·son·a·bly** *adv*

un·rea·son·ing /un réez'ning/ *adj* not having sound judgment or reasoning —**un·rea·son·ing·ly** *adv*

un·rec·og·niz·a·ble /un rékəg nīzəb'l/ *adj* not able to be recognized —**un·rec·og·niz·a·bly** *adv*

un·rec·og·nized /un rékəg nīzd/ *adj* not formally given legal or independent status

un·re·con·struct·ed /un rèekən strúktəd/ *adj* 1 clinging to outdated beliefs 2 not rebuilt

un·re·deemed /un ri déemd/ *adj* 1 not made acceptable 2 not paid off or cashed in

un·re·fined /ùnri fīnd/ *adj* 1 not processed 2 vulgar

un·re·gen·er·ate /ùnri jénnərət/ *adj* 1 not reformed spiritually and not repentant 2 clinging to outdated beliefs 3 stubborn —**un·re·gen·er·ate·ly** *adv*

un·re·lat·ed /ùn ri láytəd/ *adj* not connected by similarities, source, or family

un·re·lent·ing /ùnri lénting/ *adj* 1 determined and unyielding 2 not lessening or easing up —**un·re·lent·ing·ly** *adv*

un·re·li·a·ble /ùnri lí əb'l/ *adj* not able to be relied on or trusted —**un·re·li·a·bil·i·ty** /ùnri lī ə bíllətee/ *n* —**un·re·li·a·bly** *adv*

un·re·lieved /ùnrə leévd/ *adj* unvaried and monotonous

un·re·mark·a·ble /ùnri maárkəb'l/ *adj* not noteworthy —**un·re·mark·a·bly** *adv*

un·re·marked /ùnri maárkt/ *adj* unnoticed

un·re·mit·ting /ùnri mítting/ *adj* continuing without slackening or easing —**un·re·mit·ting·ly** *adv*

un·re·peat·a·ble /ùnri peétəb'l/ *adj* 1 not able to be repeated 2 too shocking to repeat

un·re·pent·ant /ùnri péntənt/, **un·re·pent·ing** /-ing/ *adj* feeling no regret for wrongdoing

un·re·quit·ed /ùnri kwítəd/ *adj* not reciprocated

un·re·served /ùnri zúrvd/ *adj* 1 not reserved for a particular use 2 given without qualification —**un·re·serv·ed·ly** /-zúrvədlee/ *adv*

un·rest /un rést/ *n* 1 social or political discontent that disrupts the established order 2 anxiety

un·re·strained /ùnri stráynd/ *adj* 1 not controlled or restricted 2 spontaneous —**un·re·strain·ed·ly** /ùnri stráynədlee/ *adv*

un·ri·valed /un rív'ld/, **un·ri·valled** *adj* without a rival or equal

un·roll /un ról/ *vti* 1 unwind or uncoil 2 disclose or become disclosed gradually

un·ruf·fled /un rúff'ld/ *adj* calm and poised, especially in a crisis

un·ru·ly /un róolee/ (**-li·er**, **-li·est**) *adj* difficult to control —**un·ru·li·ness** *n*

SYNONYMS unruly, intractable, recalcitrant, obstreperous, willful, wild,

wayward CORE MEANING: not submitting to control

un·safe /un sáyf/ (-saf·er, -saf·est) *adj* 1 dangerous 2 in danger

un·said /un séd/ *adj* not mentioned

un·sat·is·fac·to·ry /un sàtiss fáktəree/ *adj* not adequate, acceptable, or satisfying —**un·sat·is·fac·to·ri·ly** *adv*

un·sat·u·rat·ed /un sáchə ràytəd/ *adj* 1 describes a solution that is able to dissolve more of a substance 2 describes fats with a high proportion of fatty acid molecules with double bonds, regarded as healthy in the diet

un·sa·vor·y /un sáyvəree/ *adj* 1 distasteful 2 immoral 3 tasting or smelling unappetizing —**un·sa·vor·i·ness** *n*

un·scathed /un skáythd/ *adj* unhurt or undamaged

un·sci·en·tif·ic /ùn sī ən tíffik/ *adj* 1 not scientific in method or principle 2 not informed about science —**un·sci·en·tif·i·cal·ly** *adv*

un·scram·ble /un skrámb'l/ (-bled, -bling) *vt* 1 restore order to something jumbled or confused 2 make a message understandable by undoing the effects of scrambling —**un·scram·bler** *n*

un·screw /un skroó/ *vti* 1 remove or loosen the screws holding something, or have the screws removed 2 open something by removing a threaded lid or cap, or be opened in this way 3 remove or adjust something by rotating, or be removed or adjusted by rotating

un·scru·pu·lous /un skroópyələss/ *adj* not restrained by moral or ethical principles —**un·scru·pu·lous·ly** *adv* —**un·scru·pu·lous·ness** *n*

un·sea·son·a·ble /un seéz'nəb'l/ *adj* 1 unusual for the time of year 2 not timely —**un·sea·son·a·bly** *adv*

un·seat /un seét/ *vt* 1 eject from a saddle 2 remove from office

un·se·cured /ùnsə kyoórd/ *adj* 1 not made secure 2 not protected against financial loss

un·seed·ed /un seédəd/ *adj* in sports, not ranked as a seed

un·seem·ly /un seémlee/ *adj* contrary to good taste or appropriate behavior —**un·seem·li·ness** *n*

un·seen /un seén/ *adj* not seen or observed

un·sel·fish /un sélfish/ *adj* not selfish —**un·sel·fish·ly** *adv* —**un·sel·fish·ness** *n*

un·set·tle /un sétt'l/ (-tled, -tling) *vt* 1 disrupt 2 make upset or insecure —**un·set·tling** *adj*

un·set·tled /un sétt'ld/ *adj* 1 lacking order or stability 2 changeable ○ *unsettled weather* 3 not resolved or decided ○ *an unsettled issue* 4 not inhabited or colonized 5 unpaid ○ *unsettled debts* 6 not regular or fixed ○ *an unsettled lifestyle*

un·shak·a·ble /un sháykəb'l/, **un·shake·a·ble** *adj* firm and certain whatever happens —**un·shak·a·bly** *adv*

un·shak·en /un sháykən/ *adj* firm and certain in spite of something that has happened

⚡**un·shift** /un shíft/ *vi* release the depressed shift key on a computer keyboard or typewriter

un·sight·ly /un sítlee/ *adj* unappealing to look at —**un·sight·li·ness** *n* ◊ See note at **un·attractive**

un·skilled /un skíld/ *adj* 1 lacking skill or training 2 not requiring special skills

un·skill·ful /un skílfəl/ *adj* not skilled or skillful —**un·skill·ful·ly** *adv*

un·smil·ing /un smíling/ *adj* showing no signs of pleasure, amusement, or approval ○ *his grim unsmiling manner* —**un·smil·ing·ly** *adv*

un·so·cia·ble /un sóshəb'l/ *adj* 1 not liking or seeking the company of other people 2 not encouraging social interaction —**un·so·cia·bil·i·ty** /un sòshə bíllətee/ *n* —**un·so·cia·bly** *adv*

un·so·cial /un sósh'l/ *adj* not liking or seeking the company of other people

un·so·phis·ti·cat·ed /ùnsə fístə kàytəd/ *adj* 1 not worldly or sophisticated 2 simple and lacking in refinements

un·sound /un sównd/ *adj* 1 unhealthy 2 not solid or firm structurally 3 based on unreliable information or reasoning ○ *an unsound conclusion* 4 not safe or secure financially ○ *unsound investments* —**un·sound·ly** *adv* —**un·sound·ness** *n*

un·spar·ing /un spáiring/ *adj* 1 merciless 2 generous in giving —**un·spar·ing·ly** *adv*

un·speak·a·ble /un speékəb'l/ *adj* 1 not describable in words 2 extremely bad or awful —**un·speak·a·bly** *adv*

un·spec·i·fied /un spéssə fíd/ *adj* not stated explicitly

un·spoiled /un spóyld/ *adj* 1 unchanged by development 2 not damaged

un·spo·ken /un spókən/ *adj* not mentioned

un·sport·ing /un spáwrting/ *adj* not fair —**un·sport·ing·ly** *adv*

un·sta·ble /un stáyb'l/ *adj* 1 not firm, solid, or fixed 2 likely to fall or collapse 3 lacking mental stability 4 subject to change —**un·sta·ble·ness** *n* —**un·sta·bly** *adv*

un·stead·y /un stéddee/ *adj* 1 not firmly fixed 2 likely to fall 3 changeable —**un·stead·i·ly** *adv* —**un·stead·i·ness** *n* —**un·stead·y** *vt*

un·stick /un stík/ (-stuck) *vt* cause to stop sticking

un·stint·ing /un stínting/ *adj* given or giving generously —**un·stint·ing·ly** *adv*

un·stop /un stóp/ (-stopped, -stop·ping) *vt* 1 remove a stopper from 2 unblock

un·stop·pa·ble /un stóppəb'l/ *adj* impossible to stop —**un·stop·pa·bly** *adv*

⚡**un·sub·scribe** /ùn səb scríb/ *vi* end a subscription to something, especially an e-mail mailing list

un·suc·cess·ful /ùnsək sésfəl/ *adj* not resulting in or achieving success —**un·suc·cess·ful·ly** *adv*

un·suit·a·ble /un sóotəb'l/ *adj* not appropriate —**un·suit·a·bil·i·ty** /un sóotə bíllətee/ *n* —**un·suit·a·bly** *adv*

un·suit·ed /un sóotəd/ *adj* 1 lacking the right qualities 2 incompatible

un·sung /un súng/ *adj* not praised or honored

un·sure /un shóor/ *adj* 1 uncertain 2 not confident ◊ See note at doubtful

un·sus·pect·ing /ùnsə spékting/ *adj* not suspicious or aware —**un·sus·pect·ing·ly** *adv*

un·sus·tain·a·ble /ùnsə stáynəb'l/ *adj* 1 unable to be maintained 2 not maintaining the ecological balance of an area

un·swerv·ing /un swúrving/ *adj* steady and unchanging —**un·swerv·ing·ly** *adv*

un·sym·pa·thet·ic /un símpə théttik/ *adj* showing no sympathy or approval —**un·sym·pa·thet·i·cal·ly** *adv*

un·tan·gle /un táng g'l/ (**-gled, -gling**) *vt* 1 free from tangles 2 clarify or resolve the complexities of

un·tapped /un tápt/ *adj* 1 not yet in use, but available 2 not opened

un·ten·a·ble /un ténnəb'l/ *adj* impossible to defend in an argument —**un·ten·a·bly** *adv*

un·think·a·ble /un thíngkəb'l/ *adj* 1 too strange or extreme to be considered 2 impossible even to conceive of

un·think·ing /un thíngking/ *adj* done without thinking of the consequences —**un·think·ing·ly** *adv*

un·ti·dy /un tídee/ (**-di·er, -di·est**) *adj* 1 not neat or tidy 2 not properly organized or ordered —**un·ti·di·ly** *adv* —**un·ti·di·ness** *n* —**un·ti·dy** *vt*

un·tie /un tí/ (**-tied, -ty·ing**) *v* 1 *vti* undo a knot or similar fastening in something, or become undone 2 *vt* free somebody or something that is tied up

un·til /un tíl/ *conj, prep* 1 up to a time or event but not afterward ◦ *lived at home until she left school* ◦ *from 1999 until 2002* 2 before ◦ *agrees not to speak until the verdict is announced* ◦ *did not go until Monday* ◊ See note at till

~~until~~ incorrect spelling of until

un·time·ly /un tímlee/ *adj* 1 occurring at an inappropriate time 2 occurring prematurely —**un·time·li·ness** *n* —**un·time·ly** *adv*

un·tir·ing /un tíring/ *adj* 1 not becoming tired 2 continuing in spite of difficulties —**un·tir·ing·ly** *adv*

un·ti·tled /un tít'ld/ *adj* 1 unnamed 2 not belonging to the nobility

un·to /úntoo/ *prep* (*archaic*) 1 to ◦ *the elders of Gilead said unto Jephthah* ◦ *and they said unto God* 2 until ◦ *faithful unto death*

un·told /un tóld/ *adj* 1 not revealed or related 2 unable to be described or counted

un·touch·a·ble /un túchəb'l/ *adj* 1 not to be touched 2 out of reach 3 above criticism ■ *n also* **Un·touch·a·ble** an offensive term for a member of a hereditary Hindu class regarded as unclean by the four castes

un·touched /un túcht/ *adj* 1 not touched or handled 2 not eaten or drunk 3 not injured, damaged, or harmed 4 not changed or altered 5 emotionally unaffected

un·to·ward /un táwrd/ *adj* 1 causing misfortune ◦ *several untoward events* 2 inappropriate ◦ *untoward rudeness* 3 unexpected —**un·to·ward·ly** *adv*

un·trained /un tráynd/ *adj* lacking any training in a specific skill

un·tram·meled /un trámm'ld/ *adj* not restricted or restrained

un·treat·ed /un tréetəd/ *adj* 1 not subjected to a physical process 2 not given medical attention

un·tried /un tríd/ *adj* 1 not tested or proved 2 not tried in court

un·trou·bled /un trúbb'ld/ *adj* not anxious or disturbed

un·true /un tróo/ *adj* 1 wrong or false 2 unfaithful —**un·tru·ly** *adv*

un·truth /un tróoth/ *n* 1 something that is untrue 2 lack of truth ◊ See note at lie

un·truth·ful /un tróothfəl/ *adj* 1 untrue 2 not telling the truth —**un·truth·ful·ly** *adv* —**un·truth·ful·ness** *n*

un·tu·tored /un tóotərd/ *adj* 1 not formally taught 2 unsophisticated

un·typ·i·cal /un típpik'l/ *adj* lacking the characteristics shared by others of a particular type —**un·typ·i·cal·ly** *adv*

un·un·bi·um /ún un bée əm/ *n* (*symbol* **Uub**) an artificially produced, highly unstable radioactive chemical element with an atomic number of 112

un·un·hex·i·um /ún un héksee əm/ *n* (*symbol* **Uuh**) an artificially produced, highly unstable radioactive chemical element with an atomic number of 116

un·un·nil·i·um /ún un íllee əm/ *n* (*symbol* **Uun**) an artificially produced, highly unstable radioactive chemical element with an atomic number of 110

un·un·qua·di·um /ún un kwáydee əm/ *n* (*symbol* **Uuq**) an artificially produced, highly unstable radioactive chemical element with an atomic number of 114

un·un·un·i·um /ún un únnee əm/ *n* (*symbol* **Uuu**) an artificially produced, highly unstable radioactive chemical element with an atomic number of 111

un·used /un yóozd, -yóost/ *adj* 1 never having been used 2 not in use 3 not familiar with or accustomed to something

un·u·su·al /un yóozhoo əl/ *adj* 1 not common or familiar 2 remarkable or out of the ordinary —**un·u·su·al·ly** *adv* —**un·u·su·al·ness** *n*

un·ut·ter·a·ble /un úttərəb'l/ *adj* unable to be expressed or described because of emotional intensity —**un·ut·ter·a·bly** *adv*

un·var·nished /un vaárnisht/ *adj* 1 without a coat of varnish 2 presented with no attempt to disguise the truth ○ *the unvarnished facts*

un·veil /un váyl/ *vt* 1 remove a veil or covering from 2 reveal for the first time —**un·veil·ing** *n*

un·voiced /un vóyst/ *adj* 1 not spoken 2 pronounced without vibration of the vocal cords

un·want·ed /un wóntəd/ *adj* not welcome or needed

un·war·rant·ed /un wáwrəntəd/ *adj* not justified or deserved

un·war·y /un wáiree/ *adj* failing to be alert and cautious

un·wa·ver·ing /un wáyvəring/ *adj* steady and firm in purpose —**un·wa·ver·ing·ly** *adv*

un·well /un wél/ *adj* not in good health

un·whole·some /un hólsəm/ *adj* 1 harmful to health 2 regarded as harmful to the character or morals —**un·whole·some·ness** *n*

~~unwieldly~~ incorrect spelling of **unwieldy**

un·wield·y /un wéeldee/ *adj* not easy to handle because of being large, heavy, or awkward —**un·wield·i·ness** *n*

un·will·ing /un wílling/ *adj* 1 not willing to do something 2 given reluctantly or grudgingly —**un·will·ing·ly** *adv* —**un·will·ing·ness** *n*

SYNONYMS **unwilling, reluctant, disinclined, averse, hesitant, loath** CORE MEANING: lacking the desire to do something

---

un·wind /un wínd/ (-wound /-wównd/) *vti* 1 undo from being wound 2 relax after a time of stress or worry

un·wise /un wíz/ (-wis·er, -wis·est) *adj* lacking wisdom —**un·wise·ly** *adv*

un·wit·ting /un wítting/ *adj* 1 unaware of what is happening 2 said or done unintentionally —**un·wit·ting·ly** *adv*

un·wont·ed /un wáwntəd, -wónt-, -wúnt-/ *adj* unusual or unexpected (*literary*)

un·work·a·ble /un wúrkəb'l/ *adj* 1 too complicated or ambitious to be practical 2 not able to be cut, shaped, or otherwise worked —**un·work·a·bly** *adv*

un·world·ly /un wúrldlee/ *adj* 1 not materialistic 2 inexperienced —**un·world·li·ness** *n*

un·wor·thy /un wúrthee/ *adj* 1 not deserving a particular benefit, privilege, or compliment 2 beneath somebody's usual standards of behavior ○ *conduct unworthy of them* 3 without value or merit —**un·wor·thi·ly** *adv* —**un·wor·thi·ness** *n*

un·wound past tense, past participle of **unwind**

un·wrap /un ráp/ (-wrapped, -wrap·ping) *vt* remove the wrapping from

un·writ·ten /un rítt'n/ *adj* 1 not written down 2 generally accepted though not formally recorded ○ *an unwritten law*

un·yield·ing /un yéelding/ *adj* 1 stubborn 2 inflexible —**un·yield·ing·ly** *adv*

⚡**un·zip** /un zíp/ (-zipped, -zip·ping) *v* 1 *vti* undo the zipper of something such as clothing or luggage, or be opened by this means 2 *vt* decompress a computer file

up *prep, adv* 1 in, at, or to a higher level or position 2 along ○ *went up the road* ■ *adv* 1 thoroughly or completely ○ *tore up the photograph* 2 upright ○ *sitting up in bed* 3 so as to detach or remove something ○ *pulling up weeds* 4 into consideration ○ *The subject didn't come up.* 5 in or toward a northerly position ○ *up in Alaska* 6 to a higher value 7 to a greater intensity 8 so as to move near ○ *ran up to me* ■ *adj* 1 increased ○ *Her grades are up.* 2 out of bed 3 facing or raised upward 4 going higher or north 5 cheerful 6 over or finished 7 nominated or in the running ○ *up for promotion* 8 having knowledge ○ *well up on the subject* ■ *vt* (upped, up·ping) raise or increase ◇ **up against it** facing difficulty or danger ◇ **up to** 1 occupied with or involved in 2 able to undertake or endure 3 as many as, or as long as 4 until

up-and-com·ing *adj* already successful and becoming more so

up·beat /úp beet/ *n* an unaccented beat in music, especially one that ends a bar ■ *adj* optimistic (*infml*)

up·braid /up bráyd/ *vt* speak harshly and critically to

up·bring·ing /úp bringing/ *n* the manner and circumstances in which somebody is brought up

UPC *abbr* Universal Product Code

up·com·ing /úp kúmming/ *adj* forthcoming

up·coun·try /úp kúntree/ *adj* coming from or located in the interior of a country ■ *n* an inland region ■ *adv* toward the interior of a country

up·date *vt* /up dáyt/ (-dat·ed, -dat·ing) provide with the most recent information ■ *n* /úp dàyt/ a communication of the latest information —**up·dat·a·ble** *adj*

John Updike

Up·dike /úp dík/, **John** (*b.* 1932) US writer

up·draft /úp dràft/ *n* an air current moving upward

up·end /up énd/ *vti* place, stand, or turn on one end

up·front, up-front /up frúnt/ *adj (infml)* 1 frank or straightforward 2 in advance —**up front** *adv* —**up-front·ness** *n*

up·grade *v* /úp gràyd, up gráyd/ (**-grad·ed, -grad·ing**) 1 *vt* promote somebody or increase the status of somebody's job or position 2 *vti* improve the quality or performance of something 3 *vti* exchange something for another of better quality ■ *n* /úp gràyd/ 1 an improvement in the quality or performance of something 2 something that improves quality or performance 3 an upward slope ■ *adj* /úp gràyd/ sloping upward ■ *adv* /úp gràyd/ uphill —**up·grad·a·ble** *adj*

up·heav·al /up héev'l/ *n* 1 a sudden change in political or social conditions or personal circumstances 2 a sudden rising of part of the Earth's crust

up·hill *adv* /up híl/ 1 up a slope 2 against resistance or in spite of difficulty ■ *adj* /úp híl/ 1 going higher on a slope 2 on higher ground 3 requiring a lot of effort

up·hold /up hóld/ (**-held** /-héld/) *vt* maintain or support —**up·hold·er** *n*

up·hol·ster /up hólstər, ə pól-/ *vt* fit furniture with padding and coverings —**up·hol·ster·er** *n*

up·hol·ster·y /up hólstəree, ə pól-/ *n* 1 materials used for upholstering furniture 2 the work of upholstering

~~upholstry~~ incorrect spelling of **upholstery**

up·keep /úp kèep/ *n* 1 maintenance in proper condition or operation 2 the cost of providing maintenance

up·land /úplənd, úp lànd/ *n* high land —**up·land** *adj*

up·lift *vt* /up líft/ 1 physically lift 2 improve the spiritual level or living conditions of ■ *n* /úp lìft/ 1 something uplifting to the spirit 2 a lifting up —**up·lift·ing** *adj*

up·link /úp lìngk/ *n* a transmitter on the ground sending messages to aircraft or satellites ■ *vti* transmit a message via an uplink

⚡ **up·load** /úp lòd/ *vti* transfer data or programs, usually from a peripheral to a central computer

up·mar·ket *adj* /úp màarkət/ intended for wealthy consumers ■ *adv* /úp màarkət, ùp màarkət/ toward more expensive tastes

up·on /ə pón/ *prep* on *(fml)*

up·per /úppər/ *adj* 1 higher in position or rank ○ *the upper deck* ○ *upper management* 2 more distant or inland ○ *the upper reaches of the river* ■ *n* 1 the higher of two people or objects 2 the part of a boot or shoe covering the upper surface of the foot 3 a stimulant drug *(slang)*

up·per·case /ùppər káyss/ *n* capital letters —**up·per·case** *adj* —**up·per·case** *vt*

up·per class *n* 1 the highest social class, or its members *(often pl)* 2 the group of students in the junior or senior class —**up·per·class** *adj*

up·per-class·man /ùppər klássmən/ *(pl* **-men** /-mən/) *n* a student in the junior or senior class

up·per crust *n* the highest social class *(infml)*

up·per·cut /úppər kùt/ *n* a swinging upward blow to an opponent's chin —**up·per·cut** *v*

up·per hand *n* the dominant position

up·per house *n* the smaller and less representative house in a two-house legislature, e.g., the US Senate

up·per·most /úppər mòst/ *adj, adv* in the highest position or rank

Up·per Vol·ta /ùppər vólta, ùppər vôlta/ former name for **Burkina Faso**

up·pi·ty /úppitee/ *adj* presumptuous *(infml)* —**up·pi·ty·ness** *n*

up·right /úp rìt/ *adj* 1 standing vertically or erect 2 righteous or moral ■ *adv* vertically ■ *n* 1 a vertical support 2 *also* **upright pi·an·o** a piano with an upright rectangular case and strings mounted vertically —**up·right·ly** *adv* —**up·right·ness** *n*

up·ris·ing /úp rìzing/ *n* a rebellion

up·riv·er /úp rìvvər/ *adv, adj* toward or closer to the source of a river

up·roar /úp ràwr/ *n* 1 a noisy disturbance 2 an argument

ORIGIN Uproar is not etymologically connected to *roar*. It came from Dutch *oproer* (or a closely related early German form), literally "stirring up," formed from *roer* "motion." The original meaning in English (early 16C) was "tumult, popular uprising," but the word was early associated with *roar* and developed (mid-16C) into "noisy disturbance."

---

up·roar·i·ous /up ráwree əss/ *adj* 1 involving an uproar 2 hilarious —**up·roar·i·ous·ly** *adv* —**up·roar·i·ous·ness** *n*

up·root /up róot/ *vt* 1 pull up from soil by the roots 2 displace from a home or habitual environment —**up·root·ed·ness** *n*

up·rush /úp rùsh/ *n* an upward rush

up·sa·dai·sy *interj* = **upsy-daisy**

up·scale /úp skàyl/ *adj, adv* expensive

up·set *v* /up sét/ (**-set, -set·ting**) 1 *vti* turn or tip over accidentally, usually spilling the contents 2 *vt* disturb the usual order or course of 3 *vt* cause emotional distress to 4 *vt* defeat unexpectedly ■ *n* /úp sèt/ 1 an unexpected problem causing distress or a change of plans 2 an unexpected result or defeat 3 a mild illness of the stomach ■ *adj* /up sét/ 1 overturned or spilled 2 distressed or sad 3 affected by indigestion or nausea

up·shot /úp shòt/ *n* the result or outcome

up·side /úp sìd/ *n* the positive side or aspect of a situation or event

up·side down adv **1** so that the side that should be higher is lower **2** in complete confusion or disorder —**up·side-down** adj

up·si·lon /úpsi lòn, yoópsi lòn/ n the 20th letter of the Greek alphabet

up·stage /up stáyj/ vt (-staged, -stag·ing) **1** outdo and divert attention from somebody else **2** make another actor turn away from the audience by moving toward the back of the stage ■ adv, adj toward or at the back of the stage ■ n the back of the stage

up·stairs adv /up stáirz/ on, to, or toward an upper floor ■ n /úp stáirz/ an upper floor

up·stand·ing /up stánding, úp stànding/ adj honest and socially responsible —**up·stand·ing·ness** n

up·start /úp staàrt/ n somebody with newly acquired status who is regarded as arrogant

up·state /up stáyt, úp stàyt/ n the northern part of a state ■ adj, adv in, to, or from upstate —**up·stat·er** n

up·stream /up stréèm, úp stréèm/ adv **1** in or toward the source of a river or stream **2** in an early stage of an industrial or commercial operation

up·surge /úp sùrj/ n a sudden increase

up·swing /úp swìng/ n an increase or improvement

up·sy-dai·sy /úpsee dàyzee/, **up·sa·dai·sy** /úpsə-/ interj reassures a child being lifted or who has just fallen (baby talk)

up·take /úp tàyk/ n a vent for smoke or air

up·tem·po, up·tem·po /úp tèmpō/ n a fast tempo ■ adj fast-paced and exciting

up·tight /up tít/ adj tense and anxious (infml) —**up·tight·ness** n

⚡up·time /úp tìm/ n the time during which a computer or machine is in operation

up-to-date adj **1** familiar with or reflecting current knowledge or fashions **2** of the current time

up-to-the-min·ute adj familiar with or reflecting the most recent knowledge or fashions

up·town /úp tòwn/ n the upper or northern part of a city ■ adv toward the upper part of a city —**up·town·er** /úp tòwnər, úp tównər/ n

up·trend /úp trènd/ n an improving trend

up·turn v /úp tùrn, up túrn/ **1** vti turn over or upside down **2** vt turn upward ■ n /úp tùrn/ an improvement in the economy or business conditions

up·ward /úpwərd/ adv **1** toward a higher level **2** toward the interior or toward a source ■ adj going or directed toward a higher level —**up·ward·ly** adv

up·ward·ly mo·bile adj aspiring to a higher social class

up·wind adv /up wìnd/, adj /úp wìnd/ **1** against the wind **2** on the windward side

Ur /ur, oor/ ancient city of Mesopotamia, in present-day SE Iraq

U·ral /yoórəl/ river of S Russia and NW Kazakhstan, flowing southward into the Caspian Sea. Length 1,509 mi./2,428 km.

U·ral Moun·tains mountain system in W Russia, the traditional dividing line between Asia and Europe. Highest peak Mt. Narodnaya 6,214 ft./1,894 m. Length 1,490 mi./2,400 km.

u·ra·ni·um /yoo ráynee əm/ n (symbol **U**) a radioactive chemical element. Use: in one isotope, as fuel in nuclear reactors and weapons.

U·ra·nus /yoórənəss, yoo ráynəss/ n **1** in Greek mythology, the god ruling the heavens, husband of Gaia and father of the Titans **2** the 7th planet from the Sun

ur·ban /úrbən/ adj of a city

ur·bane /ur báyn/ (-ban·er, -ban·est) adj sophisticated, refined, or courteous —**ur·bane·ly** adv /ur bánnətee/ n

ur·ban·ite /úrbə nìt/ n a city dweller

ur·ban·ize /úrbə nìz/ (-ized, -iz·ing) vt **1** make into a town or city **2** cause to migrate to a town or city —**ur·ban·i·za·tion** /úrbəni záysh'n/ n

ur·ban leg·end, ur·ban myth n a bizarre and untrue story circulating in a society

ur·ban re·new·al n redevelopment of urban areas

ur·ban sprawl n expansion of an urban area into the surrounding countryside

ur·chin /úrchin/ n a mischievous child

Ur·du /óor doò, úr-/ n the official language of Pakistan, spoken also in Bangladesh and parts of India —**Ur·du** adj

u·re·a /yoo reé ə/ n a constituent of the urine of mammals. Use: fertilizers, animal feed, manufacture of resins. —**u·re·al** adj

u·re·mi·a /yoo reémee ə/ n a form of blood poisoning caused by the accumulation of products that are usually eliminated in urine

u·re·ter /yoo reétər, yoórətər/ n each of a pair of ducts that carry urine from the kidneys to the bladder

u·re·thra /yoo reéthrə/ n (pl -thras or -thrae /-three/) n a tube for discharging urine from the body —**u·re·thral** adj

urge /urj/ vt (urged, urg·ing) **1** advise or encourage strongly to do something **2** advocate earnestly ■ n a strong need or impulse

ur·gent /úrjənt/ adj **1** requiring immediate action **2** showing earnestness —**ur·gen·cy** n —**ur·gent·ly** adv

u·ri·nal /yoórən'l/ n **1** a receptacle attached to a wall for men to urinate into **2** a place with urinals

u·ri·nar·y /yoórə nèrree/ adj of urine or the organs that form and excrete urine

u·ri·nate /yoörə nàyt/ (-nat·ed, -nat·ing) *vi* expel urine —**u·ri·na·tion** /yoörə náysh'n/ *n*

u·rine /yoórin/ *n* a yellowish liquid containing waste products that is excreted by the kidneys and discharged through the urethra —**u·ri·nous** /u/ *adj*

⚡ **URL** *n* an address identifying the location of a file on the Internet. Full form **Uniform Resource Locator**

urn *n* **1** an ornamental vase with a pedestal **2** a vase for the ashes of somebody cremated **3** a large vessel with a spigot, for hot drinks

u·ro·gen·i·tal /yoörō jénnit'l/, **u·ri·no·gen·i·tal** /yoörə nō jénnit'l/ *adj* of the urinary and reproductive organs

u·rol·o·gy /yoò rólləjee/ *n* the branch of medicine that deals with the urinary and urogenital system —**ur·o·log·ic** /yoörə lójjik/ *adj* —**u·rol·o·gist** *n*

ur·sine /úr sīn, -sèen/ *adj* of or like bears

ur·ti·car·i·a /úrti káiree ə/ *n* a skin rash marked by itching and small pale or red swellings *(technical)*

U·ru·guay /yoörə gwī, -gwày/ **1** river in SE South America, rising in S Brazil and entering the Atlantic Ocean through the Río de la Plata. Length 990 mi./1,600 km. **2** country in SE South America. Cap. Montevideo. Pop. 3,360,105 (2001). —**U·ru·guay·an** /yoörə gwī ən/ *n, adj*

us /uss/ *pron* me and another person or other people *(after a verb or preposition)*

US, U.S. *abbr* United States

USA, U.S.A. *abbr* **1** United States Army **2** United States of America

⚡ **us·a·bil·i·ty en·gi·neer** *n* somebody employed to observe people learning to use new products prior to their release in the marketplace —**us·a·bil·i·ty en·gi·neer·ing** *n*

us·a·ble /yoözəb'l/, **use·a·ble** *adj* fit for use —**us·a·bil·i·ty** /yoözə bíllətee/ *n* —**us·a·bly** *adv*

USAF, U.S.A.F. *abbr* United States Air Force

us·age /yoóssij, yóoz-/ *n* **1** the using of something, or the way in which or degree to which something is used **2** an accepted practice or procedure **3** the way language is actually used

~~usally~~ incorrect spelling of **usually**

USCG, U.S.C.G. *abbr* United States Coast Guard

USDA *abbr* United States Department of Agriculture

use *v* /yooz/ (**used, us·ing**) **1** *vt* put into action or service for some purpose **2** *vt* expend or consume **3** *vt* manipulate or exploit ○ *the type who uses people* **4** *vti* consume drugs or alcohol regularly **5** *vt* behave in a particular way toward ○ *uses his employees poorly* ■ *n* /yooss/ **1** the using of something **2** the state of being used for something **3** a way of

using something **4** the right or ability to use something **5** the purpose for which something is used **6** usefulness **7** the occasion or need to use something —**us·er** *n* ◇ **make use of** use ◇ **use** *or* **used to** used as a modal verb to indicate habitual or customary past action ○ *Did you use to go?* ○ *We used to eat out more often.*

SYNONYMS use, employ, make use of, utilize CORE MEANING: put something to use

---

USAGE used to *or* **use to**? The spelling **used to**, with a *-d*, is a form indicating habitual or customary past actions, as in *On Saturdays we used* [not *use*] *to go to ballgames.* (People tend to drop the *-d* because it is inaudible in many oral contexts. This practice is unacceptable in writing.) When *did* precedes **use(d) to**, the correct form is *use to*, as in *Did you use to go to ballgames every Saturday? Didn't she use to live in this dorm?*

☐ **use up** *vt* expend or consume, often until none is left

~~useage~~ incorrect spelling of **usage**

used[1] /yoozd/ *adj* **1** previously owned **2** having been put to a purpose or expended

used[2] /yoost/ *adj* accustomed to or familiar with something ○ *We're not used to this weather.*

use·ful /yoósfəl/ *adj* **1** serving a purpose **2** having value or benefit —**use·ful·ly** *adv* —**use·ful·ness** *n*

~~usefull~~ incorrect spelling of **useful**

~~useing~~ incorrect spelling of **using**

use·less /yoósslass/ *adj* **1** not fit for use **2** unsuccessful, or unlikely to be worthwhile **3** not able to do something properly *(infml)* —**use·less·ly** *adv* —**use·less·ness** *n*

⚡ **Use·net** /yoóz nèt/ *n* a worldwide system for distributing newsgroup messages over the Internet or other networks

us·er-friend·ly *adj* easy to operate or understand ○ *user-friendly software* —**us·er-friend·li·ness** *n*

⚡ **us·er group** *n* a group of computer users who exchange and provide information about hardware or software

⚡ **us·er in·ter·face** *n* the part of the design of a computer, peripheral device, or program that accepts commands from and returns information to the user

~~usful~~ incorrect spelling of **useful**

ush·er /úshər/ *n* **1** somebody who shows people to their seats **2** a doorkeeper **3** an official who walks before somebody of rank in a procession ■ *vt* escort to or from a place or seat

☐ **usher in** *vt* herald or introduce

USMC *abbr* United States Marine Corps

USN *abbr* United States Navy

USO *abbr* United Service Organizations

USP¹ *abbr* United States Pharmacopoeia

USP² *n* a product's differentiating characteristic *(in advertisements and marketing)* Full form **unique selling proposition, unique selling point**

USPS *abbr* United States Postal Service

U.S.S. *abbr* United States Ship

U.S.S.R., USSR *abbr* Union of Soviet Socialist Republics

u·su·al /yŏozhoo əl/ *adj* customary or characteristic ■ *n* the ordinary way of things —**u·su·al·ly** *adv* —**u·su·al·ness** *n*

SYNONYMS usual, customary, habitual, routine, wonted CORE MEANING: often done, used, bought, or consumed

~~usualy~~ incorrect spelling of **usually**

u·surp /yoo súrp, -zúrp/ *vti* seize something without the right to do so —**u·sur·pa·tion** /yoòssər páysh'n, yoòzər-/ *n* —**u·surp·er** *n*

u·su·ry /yŏozhəree/ *n (pl* **-ries)** *n* the lending of money at an exorbitant rate of interest —**u·su·rer** *n* —**u·su·ri·ous** /yoo zhóoree əss/ *adj* —**u·su·ri·ous·ly** *adv*

UT *abbr* **1** Universal Time **2** Utah

Ut. *abbr* Utah

U·tah /yŏo taa, -taw/ state in the W United States. Cap. Salt Lake City. Pop. 2,233,169 (2000). —**U·ta·han** /yŏo tàa ən, -tàw ən/ *n, adj*

UTC *abbr* Universal Time Coordinated

Ute /yoot/ *(pl* same or **Utes)** *n* **1** a member of a Native North American people who mainly live in Colorado, Utah, and New Mexico **2** the Uto-Aztecan language of the Ute people. Native speakers: 2,500.

u·ten·sil /yoo ténss'l/ *n* a tool or container, especially one for use in a kitchen

u·ter·us /yŏotərəss/ *n (pl* **-us·es** or **-i** /-rī/) *n* a hollow organ in the pelvic cavity of female animals, in which the embryo develops *(technical)* —**u·ter·ine** /yŏotərin, -rīn/ *adj*

u·til·i·tar·i·an /yoo tíllə táiree ən/ *adj* **1** of or advocating utilitarianism **2** designed to be practical rather than beautiful ■ *n* a believer in utilitarianism

u·til·i·tar·i·an·ism /yoo tíllə táiree ə nìzzəm/ *n* **1** the ethical doctrine that the greatest happiness of the greatest number should be the criterion of the virtue of an action **2** the doctrine that value lies in usefulness

⚡**u·til·i·ty** /yoo tíllətee/ *n (pl* **-ties) 1** usefulness **2** something useful **3** a company that provides an essential public service such as gas or water, or a service so supplied **4** *also* **u·til·i·ty pro·gram** a computer program that performs routine tasks and supports operations ■ *adj* **1** designed for practical use **2** able to perform several functions

u·til·i·ty room *n* a room in a house containing large domestic appliances

u·til·ize /yŏot'l īz/ *(*-**ized,** -**iz·ing)** *vt* make use of —**u·til·iz·a·ble** *adj* —**u·til·i·za·tion** /yŏot'li záysh'n/ *n* —**u·til·iz·er** *n* ◊ See note at **use**

ut·most /út mòst/, **ut·ter·most** /úttər mòst/ *adj* **1** of the greatest degree **2** located at an extremity ■ *n* the greatest degree or amount

u·to·pi·a /yoo tṓpee ə/, **U·to·pi·a** *n* an ideal and perfect state —**u·to·pi·an** *adj, n*

ORIGIN The original **utopia** was the ideal state in *Utopia* (1516), a work written in Latin by Sir Thomas More. He coined the name from Greek *ou* "not" and *topos* "place," literally meaning "the land of nowhere."

U·trecht /yŏo trèkt, ṓo trèkht/ city in the central Netherlands. Pop. 234,323 (2000).

ut·ter¹ /úttər/ *vt* **1** say **2** emit as a vocal sound —**ut·ter·a·ble** *adj*

ut·ter² /úttər/ *adj* absolute or total

ut·ter·ance /úttərənss/ *n* **1** something said **2** a way of speaking **3** an act of speaking

ut·ter·ly /úttərlee/ *adv* to a complete or total extent

ut·ter·most *adj, n* = **utmost**

U-turn *n* **1** a turn made to face the opposite direction **2** a reversal of action or policy

UV *abbr* ultraviolet

u·vu·la /yŏovyələ/ *n (pl* -**las** or -**iae** /-lèe/) *n* a fleshy flap hanging at the back of the throat —**u·vu·lar** *adj*

Uz·bek·i·stan /ŏoz béki stàn, -staàn/ country in Central Asia. Cap. Tashkent. Pop. 25,155,064 (2001).

U·zi /ŏozee/ *n* a 9 mm compact submachine gun

ORIGIN The **Uzi** is unusual in being named for the given name of Uzi el-Gal, a 20C Israeli army officer and weapons designer, rather than his surname.

V

v¹ *(pl* **v's)**, **V** *(pl* **V's** or **Vs)** *n* the 22nd letter of the English alphabet

v² *abbr* **1** velocity **2** verb

V¹ *symbol* **1** electromotive force **2** potential **3** potential energy **4** vanadium **5** volt **6** volume

V² *abbr* **1** vector **2** verb **3** volt

v. *abbr* volume

VA, Va. *abbr* Virginia

va·can·cy /váykənsee/ *(pl* -**cies)** *n* **1** a vacant position or hotel room **2** the state of being vacant

va·cant /váykənt/ *adj* **1** having no occupant or contents **2** not filled by an incumbent or employee ○ *The post remains vacant.* **3** lacking any sign of mental activity or expression ○ *a vacant stare* —**va·cant·ly** *adv*

SYNONYMS vacant, empty, void CORE MEANING: lacking contents or occupants

va·cate /váy kàyt/ (-cat·ed, -cat·ing) *vt* **1** give up occupancy of **2** resign from **3** make legally invalid

va·ca·tion /vay káysh'n, və-/ *n* a period of time away from work or study for rest and relaxation ■ *vi* take a vacation —**va·ca·tion·er** *n*

vac·ci·nate /váksə nàyt/ (-nat·ed, -nat·ing) *vt* administer a vaccine to —**vac·ci·na·tion** /vàksə náysh'n/ *n*

⚡ **vac·cine** /vak seen, vák seèn/ *n* **1** a preparation administered to protect the body against a specific disease **2** a piece of software that protects a computer against viruses

ORIGIN Vaccine derives from a Latin adjective meaning "of a cow." It was used by the British physician Edward Jenner at the end of the 18C in the terms *vaccine disease*, meaning "cowpox," and hence *vaccine inoculation*, meaning the technique he developed for preventing smallpox by injecting people with cowpox virus. There is no evidence of the use of *vaccine* as a noun to denote the inoculated material until the 1840s.

~~vaccum, vacuum, vacum~~ incorrect spelling of **vacuum**

vac·il·late /vássə làyt/ (-lat·ed, -lat·ing) *vi* **1** be indecisive or irresolute **2** sway from side to side —**vac·il·la·tion** /vàssə láysh'n/ *n* ◊ See note at **hesitate**

va·cu·i·ty /va kyoo ətee/ (*pl* -ties) *n* a lack of intelligent or serious content

vac·u·ole /vákyoo òl/ *n* a membrane-bound compartment containing fluid in the cytoplasm of a cell —**vac·u·o·lar** /vàkyoo ólər, vákyoo əlàr/ *adj*

vac·u·ous /vákyoo əss/ *adj* **1** lacking or showing a lack of ideas or intelligence **2** empty *(archaic)* —**vac·u·ous·ly** *adv* —**vac·u·ous·ness** *n*

vac·u·um /vákyoo əm, vákyəm/ *n* (*pl* -ums *or* -a /-ə/) **1** a space that is completely empty of matter **2** a space from which all the gas has been removed **3** emptiness caused by the absence of something **4** *also* **vac·u·um clean·er** an electrical cleaning appliance that uses suction ■ *vti* clean something using a vacuum cleaner

vac·u·um bot·tle *n* a bottle with 2 walls enclosing a vacuum

vac·u·um-packed *adj* packed in a container from which most of the air has been removed

vac·u·um pump *n* a device for removing air

Va·do·da·ra /və dódə ràa/ city in W India. Pop. 1,031,346 (1991).

Va·duz /vaa doòts, faa-/ capital of Liechtenstein. Pop. 5,106 (1999).

vag·a·bond /vággə bònd/ *n* **1** a homeless wanderer **2** a beggar —**vag·a·bond** *adj*, *vi* —**vag·a·bond·age** *n*

va·gi·na /və jínə/ (*pl* -nas *or* -nae /-nee/) *n* the part of the female reproductive tract that connects the vulva to the cervix —**va·gi·nal** /vájjən'l/ *adj*

va·grant /váygrənt/ *n* **1** somebody who wanders from place to place **2** somebody who is illegally living on the streets ■ *adj* **1** homeless **2** wandering from place to place —**va·gran·cy** *n*

vague /vayg/ (vagu·er, vagu·est) *adj* **1** not explicit **2** not distinctly seen **3** not clearly perceived in the mind —**vague·ly** *adv* —**vague·ness** *n*

vain /vayn/ *adj* **1** excessively proud **2** unsuccessful ○ *a vain attempt to escape* **3** lacking substance or real meaning —**vain·ly** *adv* ◊ **in vain** fruitlessly, pointlessly, or unsuccessfully

SPELLCHECK Do not confuse the spelling of **vain**, **vane** ("a rotating blade"), and **vein** ("a blood vessel"), which sound similar.

SYNONYMS vain, empty, hollow, idle CORE MEANING: without substance or unlikely to be carried though

vain·glo·ri·ous /vayn gláwree əss/ *adj* excessively proud or ostentatious *(literary)* —**vain·glo·ry** /váyn glàwree/ *n*

Vais·a·kha /víss àakə/ *n* the 2nd month of the year in the Hindu calendar

Vaj·pa·yee /vàj páyee/, **Atal Bihari** (*b.* 1924) Indian prime minister (1996 and 1998–)

val. *abbr* value

val·ance /vállənss, váyl-/ *n* a cover for a curtain rod

vale /vayl/ *n* a valley *(often in place names)*

SPELLCHECK Do not confuse the spelling of **vale** and **veil** ("a face covering"), which sound similar.

val·e·dic·tion /vàllə díkshən/ *n* (*fml*) **1** the act of saying goodbye **2** a farewell speech

val·e·dic·to·ri·an /vàllə dik táwree ən/ *n* the best student in a graduating class

val·e·dic·to·ry /vàllə díktəree/ (*fml*) *n* (*pl* -ries) a farewell speech, especially one by the best student in a graduating class ■ *adj* saying goodbye

va·lence /váylənss/, **va·len·cy** /-see/ (*pl* -cies) *n* **1** the combining power of atoms measured by the number of electrons the atom or group will receive, give up, or share in forming a compound **2** a measure of an atom's combining power

Va·len·ci·a /və lénshee ə, -see ə/ **1** capital of the autonomous region of **Valencia** in E Spain. Pop. 739,412 (1998). **2** city in N Venezuela. Pop. 1,034,033 (1992 estimate).

val·en·tine /vállən tìn/ *n* **1** a Valentine's Day card **2** somebody who receives a valentine

Val·en·tine's Day *n* a day when romantic messages are traditionally sent. Date: February 14.

Val·en·ti·no /vállən teenō/, **Rudolph** (1895–1926) Italian-born US actor

val·et *n* /vállət, vá láy, va láy/ **1** somebody who performs a car parking service **2** a male employee who cleans the clothes of hotel guests **3** a personal male servant who looks after a man's clothes and prepares his meals —**val·et** *vti*

ORIGIN Valet is essentially the same word as *varlet*, and both go back through French to the Latin word from which *vassal* derives. The forms diverged in French. In early English use a **valet** was an attendant for a horseman or knight, and *varlet* was similarly used, but in the 16C it developed derogatory associations that **valet** avoided.

~~valey~~ incorrect spelling of **valley**

Val·hal·la /val hállə, vaal háalə/ *n* in Norse mythology, a hall where slain heroes live

val·iant /vállyənt/ *adj* courageous —**val·iant·ly** *adv*

val·id /vállid/ *adj* **1** able to be justified or believed **2** legally binding or effective —**va·lid·i·ty** /və líddətee/ *n* —**val·id·ly** *adv* —**va·lid·ness** *n*

SYNONYMS valid, cogent, convincing, reasonable, sound CORE MEANING: worthy of acceptance or credence

val·i·date /válli dàyt/ (**-dat·ed**, **-dat·ing**) *vt* **1** confirm the truthfulness of something **2** make something legal —**val·i·da·tion** /válli dáysh'n/ *n*

Val·kyr·ie /val keéree, válkəree/ *n* in Norse mythology, a woman attendant escorting the dead to Valhalla —**Val·kyr·i·an** /val keéree ən/ *adj*

Val·la·do·lid /vàalə do líd/ capital of **Valladolid Province**, N Spain. Pop. 319,946 (1998).

Val·let·ta /və léttə/ capital and chief port of Malta. Pop. 7,100 (1999).

val·ley /vállee/ *n* (*pl* **-leys**) **1** a low-lying area between mountains or hills **2** low-lying land around a river —**val·leyed** *adj*

Val·ley Forge village in SE Pennsylvania that served as the winter headquarters in 1777–78 for George Washington and the Continental Army during the American Revolution

val·or /vállər/ *n* courage —**val·or·ous** *adj*

Val·pa·rai·so /vàlpə ráyzō, -rízō/ capital of **Valparaíso Region** in central Chile. Pop. 293,800 (1998).

val·u·a·ble /vállyoo əb'l/ *adj* **1** worth a great deal of money **2** very important because of usefulness, scarcity, or personal attachment ■ *n* a valuable item (*often pl*) —**val·u·a·bly** *adv*

val·u·a·tion /vàllyoo áysh'n/ *n* **1** an appraisal of the monetary value of something **2** the price of something —**val·u·a·tion·al** *adj*

~~valuble~~ incorrect spelling of **valuable**

val·ue /vállyoo/ *n* **1** monetary worth **2** an adequate return on something o *value for money* **3** worth or importance **4** a numerical quantity assigned to a mathematical symbol **5** the length of a musical note **6** the lightness or darkness of a color ■ **val·ues** *npl* principles or standards ■ *vt* (**-ued**, **-u·ing**) **1** estimate the value of **2** regard highly

⚡**val·ue-add·ed net·work** *n* full form of **VAN**

val·ue-add·ed tax *n* full form of **VAT**

valve *n* **1** a device that controls the flow of a liquid **2** a part on a brass instrument that is pressed to make a note **3** a flap in a bodily organ, e.g., the heart **4** either of the hinged parts of a shell

va·moose /va moòss, və-/ (**-moosed**, **-moos·ing**) *vi* go away quickly (*slang*)

vamp[1] *n* a woman who is regarded as seductive (*sometimes offensive*) —**vamp** *vt* —**vamp·ish** *adj* —**vamp·y** *adj*

vamp[2] *n* **1** the upper part of a shoe **2** an improvised musical introduction ■ *v* **1** *vt* put a vamp on a shoe **2** *vti* improvise a musical introduction or accompaniment

vam·pire /vám pìr/ *n* **1** in folklore, a corpse that is believed to rise each night from the grave to suck blood from living people **2** also **vam·pire bat** a bat of tropical America that sucks blood —**vam·pir·ic** /vam pírrik/ *adj*

van[1] *n* an enclosed motor vehicle with rear or side doors

van[2] *n* the leading position (*infml*)

van[3], **Van** see also under surname

⚡**VAN** /van/ *n* a private computer network. Full form **value-added network**

va·na·di·um /və náydee əm/ *n* (*symbol* **V**) a silvery-white metallic chemical element. Use: catalyst, alloyed with steel.

ORIGIN Vanadium was named in 1830 for the Scandinavian goddess Vanadis (Freya) by a Swedish chemist who found some of the element in iron. It had earlier been discovered in Mexican lead ores in 1810 and called *erythronium*, but *vanadium* is the name that stood the test of time.

Van Al·len /van állən/, **James** (b. 1914) US physicist and discoverer of two radiation belts encircling Earth

Van Bu·ren /-byoórən/, **Martin** (1782–1862) 8th president of the United States (1837–41)

Van·cou·ver /van koōvər/ city in SW British Columbia, Canada. Pop. 514,008 (1996).

Van·cou·ver, Mt. peak of the St. Elias Range in SW Yukon Territory, Canada. Height 15,840 ft./4,828 m.

Van·cou·ver Is·land island of SW Canada, off SW British Columbia in the Pacific Ocean. Pop. 702,000.

van·dal /vánd'l/ n 1 somebody who illegally damages or destroys property 2 **Van·dal** a member of an ancient Germanic people who conquered much of the Mediterranean region between AD 300 and 500 —**Van·dal·ic** /van dállik/ adj —**van·dal·ism** n

ORIGIN The reputation of the **Vandals** for wanton destruction was the impetus for the English adaptation of their name in the 17C to describe a person who wantonly and willfully damages or destroys another person's property.

van·dal·ize /vánd'l īz/ (**-ized, -iz·ing**) vt illegally damage or destroy property —**van·dal·i·za·tion** /vànd'li záysh'n/ n

Van·der·bilt /vándər bilt/, **Cornelius** (1794–1877) US industrialist

vane /vayn/ n 1 a rotating blade, e.g., on a propeller 2 a weather vane 3 a stabilizer on a missile 4 a blade of a feather ◊ See note at **vain**

van Gogh /van gò, -gáwkh/, **Vincent** (1853–90) Dutch painter

van·guard /ván gaärd/ n 1 the leading position or people in any action or movement 2 the divisions of an army that lead an advance —**van·guard·ism** n

va·nil·la /və nílə/ n 1 a long pod of a tropical climbing orchid. Use: flavoring. 2 a substance extracted from vanilla. Use: flavoring, perfumes. ■ adj 1 flavored with vanilla 2 plain or dull

van·ish /vánnish/ vi 1 disappear suddenly 2 stop existing —**van·ish·ment** n

van·ish·ing point n 1 an apparent meeting point of parallel lines 2 a point where something disappears

van·i·ty /vánnətee/ (pl **-ties**) n 1 excessive pride 2 something that somebody is vain about 3 also **van·i·ty case** a small cosmetics case 4 a dressing table

van·i·ty pub·lish·ing n publishing of books at the author's expense

van·i·ty ta·ble n a dressing table

van·quish /vángkwish/ vt 1 defeat opponents in battle or competition 2 overcome an emotion —**van·quish·er** n —**van·quish·ment** n ◊ See note at **defeat**

van·tage point /vántij-/ n 1 a position that gives a good view 2 a personal standpoint

Van·u·a·tu /vaànoo aàtoo/ country in the SW Pacific Ocean, comprising approximately 80 islands. Cap. Port-Vila. Pop. 192,910 (2001).

Van·zet·ti /van zéttee/, **Bartolomeo** (1888–1927) Italian-born US anarchist

vap·id /váppid/ adj lacking interest or liveliness —**va·pid·i·ty** /və píddətee/ n —**vap·id·ly** adv

va·por /váypər/ n 1 moisture particles visible in the air as mist 2 the gaseous state of a liquid or solid at a temperature below its boiling point ■ **va·pors** npl low spirits or hysteria (literary or ironic) —**va·por·y** adj

va·por·ize /váypə rīz/ (**-ized, -iz·ing**) vti 1 change into, or cause something to change into, vapor 2 vanish or cause to vanish —**va·por·i·za·tion** /vàypəri záysh'n/ n

va·por lock n an obstructive pocket of vaporized gasoline in a motor vehicle's fuel line

va·por trail n a trail of condensed vapor left in the air by an aircraft

⌁ **va·por·ware** /váypər wàir/ n software that has been advertised but not developed

va·que·ro /vaa káirō/ (pl **-ros**) n Can, Southwest US a cowboy

Va·ra·na·si /və raánəssee/ city in N India, on the Ganges River. Pop. 929,270 (1991).

~~variety~~ incorrect spelling of **variety**

Mario Vargas Llosa

Var·gas Llo·sa /vaàrgəss yóssə/, **Mario** (b. 1936) Peruvian writer and critic ■

var·i·a·ble /váiree əb'l/ adj 1 likely to vary or change 2 capricious in nature 3 not having a fixed numeric value ■ n 1 something that can vary or change 2 a symbol that represents an unspecified or unknown mathematical quantity —**var·i·a·bil·i·ty** /vàiree ə bíllətee/ n —**var·i·a·ble·ness** n —**var·i·a·bly** adv

var·i·ance /váiree ənss/ n 1 a change in something 2 a difference between things 3 disagreement o a witness's testimony at variance with the facts 4 a dispensation to ignore a rule or law o a zoning variance

var·i·ant /váiree ənt/ adj 1 differing slightly 2 changeable ■ n a slightly different form

var·i·a·tion /vàiree áysh'n/ n 1 the act of varying 2 the state of being different 3 degree of difference 4 something that differs slightly from something else 5 an altered version of a musical theme —**var·i·a·tion·al** adj

~~variety~~ incorrect spelling of **variety**

var·i·col·ored /váiri kùllərd/ adj multicolored

var·ied /váireed/ *adj* 1 diverse 2 having been changed —**var·ied·ness** *n*

var·i·e·gate /váiree ə gàyt/ (**-gat·ed**, **-gat·ing**) *vt* 1 change the look of, especially by adding different colors 2 add variety to —**var·i·e·ga·tion** /vàiri ə gáysh'n, vàri gáysh'n/ *n*

var·i·e·gat·ed /váiree ə gàytəd/ *adj* 1 with patches of different colors 2 diverse

va·ri·e·ty /və ríʹətee/ (*pl* **-ties**) *n* 1 the quality of being varied 2 a specific type 3 a collection of varied things 4 entertainment made up of different acts

~~varigate~~ incorrect spelling of **variegate**

var·i·ous /váiree əss/ *adj* of different kinds —**var·i·ous·ly** *adv*

var·let /vaárlət/ *n* (*archaic*) 1 a rascal 2 a servant or page

var·mint /vaármint/ *n* a troublesome person or animal (*regional*)

var·nish /vaárnish/ *n* 1 a transparent resin solution that gives a surface a protective gloss 2 a smooth coating of varnish ■ *vt* 1 apply varnish to 2 make superficially attractive —**var·nish·er** *n*

var·si·ty /vaársətee/ (*pl* **-ties**) *n* the main sports team representing a university or school

var·y /váiree/ (**-ied**, **-ies**) *v* 1 *vti* undergo or cause to undergo change 2 *vi* be different 3 *vt* give variety to —**var·y·ing** *adj* —**var·y·ing·ly** *adv* ◊ See note at **change**

vas·cu·lar /váskyələr/ *adj* of fluid-carrying vessels in animals and plants

vase /vayss, vayz, vaaz/ *n* a container for cut flowers

va·sec·to·my /və séktəmee/ (*pl* **-mies**) *n* the surgical cutting of the sperm duct to make a male sterile

vas·sal /váss'l/ *n* 1 a dependent holder of land in a feudal society 2 a slave —**vas·sal** *adj*

vast *adj* very great in size or amount —**vast·ly** *adj* —**vast·ness** *n*

vat *n* a large container for liquid

VAT /vèe ay tèe, vat/, **V.A.T** *n* a tax added to the value of a product. Full form **value-added tax**

Vat·i·can Cit·y /váttikən-/ papal state, an enclave within Rome, Italy. Pop. 850 (1997).

va·tu /vaá toò/ (*pl* same) *n* a unit of currency in Vanuatu

vaude·ville /váwd vìl, váwdə-/ *n* popular theatrical entertainment featuring short comic plays and song and dance acts —**vaude·vil·lian** /vàwd víllee ən, vàwdə-/ *adj*, *n*

ORIGIN Vaudeville comes from a French word that was earlier *vau de vire* and in full *chanson du Vau dē Vire* "song of the Valley of Vire." In 15C France there was a fashion for songs from this valley, in the Calvados region of Normandy (particularly popular, apparently, were the satirical songs composed by a local man, Olivier Basselin). The geographic connection had been lost by the time English

acquired the word, and the element *-vire* had been replaced with *-ville* "town." The semantic transition from "popular song" to "theatrical entertainment" is not recorded until the early 19C.

vault¹ /vawlt/ *n* 1 a strengthened room for valuables 2 an arched ceiling 3 a room with an arched ceiling 4 a burial chamber 5 something that arches overhead (*literary*) ◊ *the great vault of the sky* ■ *v* 1 *vt* put an arched structure over 2 *vi* form a vault —**vault·ed** *adj*

vault² /vawlt/ *v* 1 *vti* spring over an object, often using the hands or a pole 2 *vi* rise suddenly to prominence —**vault** *n* —**vault·er** *n*

vaunt·ed /váwntəd/ *adj* boasted about (*disapproving*) ◊ *their vaunted home and car*

V-chip *n* an electronic chip in a television that enables parents to block programs with sexual or violent content

vCJD *n* a form of Creutzfeldt-Jakob disease with a shorter incubation period. Full form **variant Creutzfeldt-Jakob disease**

VCR *n* a tape recorder that can record and play videocassettes. Full form **videocassette recorder**

VD *abbr* venereal disease

VDR *abbr* 1 videodisk recorder 2 videodisk recording

✦**VDT** *abbr* video display terminal

've *contr* have

veal /veel/ *n* meat from a young calf

Veb·len /vébblən/, **Thorstein** (1857–1929) US economist

vec·tor /véktər/ *n* 1 a quantity with direction and magnitude 2 a disease-transmitting organism —**vec·to·ri·al** /vek táwree əl/ *adj*

✦**vec·tor graph·ics** *npl* COMPUT = **object-oriented graphics**

Ve·da /váydə, véedə/ *n* a Hindu sacred text —**Ve·da·ic** /vi dáy ik, vay-/ *adj*

vee·jay /vèe jày/ *n* a video jockey ■ *vi* work or act as a video jockey

veep *n* a vice president (*slang*)

veer *vti* change or cause to change direction, opinion, or purpose ■ *n* a change in direction

veg /vej/, **veg out** *vi* relax or loaf (*slang*)

ve·gan /véegən, véjjən/ *n* a person who never eats animal products —**ve·gan** *adj* —**ve·gan·ism** *n*

veg·e·ta·ble /véjjətəb'l/ *n* 1 an edible plant 2 any plant 3 an offensive term for somebody whose brain functions have been severely reduced by injury ■ *adj* consisting of vegetables

veg·e·tal /véjjət'l/ *adj* 1 relating to plants 2 involving growth rather than sexual reproduction

veg·e·tar·i·an /vèjjə táiree ən/ *n* somebody

who does not eat meat or fish —**veg·e·tar·i·an** adj —**veg·e·tar·i·an·ism** n

veg·e·tate /véjjə tàyt/ (-tat·ed, -tat·ing) vi 1 grow or sprout like a plant 2 live or behave in a dull or inactive way (sometimes disapproving)

veg·e·ta·tion /vèjjə táysh'n/ n 1 plants in general 2 the process of vegetating —**veg·e·ta·tion·al** adj

veg·e·ta·tive /véjjə tàytiv/ adj 1 of or typical of plants 2 involving growth rather than sexual reproduction 3 describes reproduction from the body cells of a parent rather than from specialized sex cells

~~vegetable~~ incorrect spelling of **vegetable**

ve·he·ment /vée əmənt/ adj 1 full of strong feeling or conviction 2 strong or energetic —**ve·he·mence** n —**ve·he·ment·ly** adv

~~vehical~~ incorrect spelling of **vehicle**

ve·hi·cle /vée ik'l, -hìk'l/ n 1 a means of transport for moving people or things 2 a medium for communicating or expressing something —**ve·nic·u·lar** /vee híkyələr/ adj

veil /vayl/ n 1 a covering of netting or fabric worn by women over their heads or faces 2 something that obscures like a curtain ■ vt 1 cover with a veil 2 hide or disguise —**veiled** adj ◊ See note at **vale**

vein /vayn/ n 1 a vessel that carries blood to the heart 2 a sap-conducting bundle of vessels visible on a leaf 3 a layer of mineral in the ground 4 a particular quality or mood 5 a streak of different color ■ vt 1 form veins in 2 streak o green marble veined with white —**veined** adj ◊ See note at **vain**

ve·la plural of **velum**

Ve·láz·quez /və laàss kèss/, Diego (1599–1660) Spanish painter

Vel·cro /vél krò/ tdmk a trademark for a fastener consisting of two strips, one with a dense layer of hooks and the other of loops that interlock with them

vel·lum /véllam/ n 1 high quality parchment made of animal skin 2 off-white heavy paper resembling vellum —**vel·lum** adj

vel·o·ci·rap·tor /və lóssə ràptər/ n a small two-legged carnivorous dinosaur

ve·loc·i·ty /və lóssətee/ (pl -ties) n 1 rate of speed 2 the rate of change over time in the position of an object as it moves in space

ve·lo·drome /véllə dròm/ n a stadium for bicycle races

ve·lour /və lóor/, **ve·lours** n a thick-piled fabric like velvet. Use: upholstery, clothing.

ve·lum /véeləm/ (pl -la /-lə/) n the soft palate —**ve·lar** adj

vel·vet /vélvət/ n 1 a fabric with a soft lustrous pile. Use: clothing, draperies, upholstery. 2 something smooth and soft like velvet ■ adj 1 made of velvet 2 like velvet —**vel·vet·y** adj

vel·vet·een /vèlvə teèn/ n a fabric resembling velvet. Use: clothing, draperies, upholstery.

ve·nal /veèn'l/ adj 1 open to bribery 2 corrupt —**ve·nal·i·ty** /vee nállətee/ n —**ve·nal·ly** adv

vend v 1 vt sell goods from a vending machine 2 vti sell goods on the street

ven·det·ta /ven détta/ n 1 a blood feud between families 2 any prolonged feud or hostile campaign

vend·ing ma·chine n a machine that dispenses goods when you insert money

ven·dor /véndər/, **vend·er** n a seller of goods

ve·neer /və neèr/ n 1 a thin layer of a superior material spread over the surface of something inferior 2 a deceptive appearance ■ vt spread a veneer over a surface

ven·er·a·ble /vénnərəb'l/ adj 1 worthy of respect because of age or status 2 revered because of religious associations —**ven·er·a·bly** adv

ven·er·ate /vénnə ràyt/ (-at·ed, -at·ing) vt respect or honor —**ven·er·a·tion** /vènnə ráysh'n/ n

ve·ne·re·al /və neèree əl/ adj associated with or passed on through sex

ve·ne·re·al dis·ease n a sexually transmitted infection (dated)

Ve·ne·tian /və neèsh'n/ adj of Venice —**Ve·ne·tian** n

Ve·ne·tian blind, ve·ne·tian blind n a blind made of thin slats

Ven·e·zue·la /vènnə zwáylə/ country in NE South America, on the Caribbean Sea and the Atlantic Ocean. Cap. Caracas. Pop. 23,916,810 (2001). —**Ven·e·zue·lan** n, adj

~~vengance, vengence~~ incorrect spelling of **vengeance**

ven·geance /vénjənss/ n revenge ◊ **with a vengeance** in an extreme or intense manner

venge·ful /vénjfəl/ adj 1 wanting revenge 2 done in order to get revenge —**venge·ful·ly** adv —**venge·ful·ness** n

ve·ni·al /veènee əl, veènyəl/ adj forgivable —**ve·ni·al·i·ty** /vèenee állətee/ n

Ven·ice /vénniss/ seaport in NE Italy, built on islands in a lagoon in the **Gulf of Venice**, an arm of the N Adriatic Sea. Pop. 291,531 (1999).

ven·i·son /vénniss'n, -z'n/ n meat from a deer

Venn di·a·gram n a representation of mathematical sets that uses overlapping circles

ORIGIN The diagram is named for the British specialist in logic John Venn (1834–1923).

ven·om /vénnəm/ n 1 a poisonous fluid injected by an animal 2 malice —**ven·om·ous** adj —**ven·om·ous·ly** adv

ve·nous /veènəss/ adj 1 of veins 2 having veins

vent[1] n an opening that allows air, gas, smoke, or steam to enter or escape ■ vti

1 release emotions ○ *She vented her frustration on her family.* ○ *He's just venting.* **2** let something out through a vent **3** make a vent in something ◊ **give vent to** express a strong feeling or emotion freely

vent² *n* a vertical slit in the seam of a jacket or other garment —**vent·ed** *adj*

ven·ti·late /vént'l àyt/ (**-lat·ed, -lat·ing**) *vt* **1** admit fresh air into a room **2** put a vent for air in something **3** expose something to moving fresh air **4** examine issues publicly **5** supply oxygen to the blood through the blood vessels of the lungs —**ven·ti·la·tion** /vèntə làysh'n/ *n*

ven·ti·la·tor /vént'l àytər/ *n* **1** a device for circulating fresh air **2** a machine that helps somebody to breathe

ven·tral /véntrəl/ *adj* **1** of the lower surface of an animal's body, or the front of the human body ○ *ventral fin* **2** of the abdomen —**ven·tral·ly** *adv*

ven·tri·cle /véntrik'l/ *n* a hollow in a body part, especially a chamber in the heart or a brain cavity

ven·tril·o·quism /ven tríllə kwìzzəm/, **ven·tril·o·quy** /-kwee/ *n* the art of producing vocal sounds that seem to come from something other than the speaker

ven·tril·o·quist /ven trílləkwist/ *n* somebody who throws his or her voice, especially a performer who makes a puppet appear to speak

ven·ture /vénchər/ *n* **1** a new business enterprise **2** a risky project ■ *v* (**-tured, -tur·ing**) **1** *vi* make a dangerous trip **2** *vt* express tentatively ○ *ventured a suggestion* **3** *vti* dare to do something **4** *vt* put at risk

ven·ture cap·i·tal *n* money for high-risk investment —**ven·ture cap·i·tal·ist** *n*

ven·ture·some /vénchərsəm/ *adj* (*fml*) **1** adventurous **2** involving risk —**ven·ture·some·ness** *n*

ven·ue /vén yòo/ *n* **1** the place where an event is held **2** the scene of a crime **3** the place in which a trial is held

Ve·nus /véenəss/ *n* **1** in Roman mythology, the goddess of love. Greek equivalent **Aphrodite 2** the planet that is 2nd from the Sun —**Ve·nu·sian** /və nóosh'n, vi nóoshee ən/ *adj, n*

Ve·nus fly·trap /-flí tràp/ *n* a plant that traps and consumes insects

ve·rac·i·ty /və rássətee/ *n* (*pl* -**ties**) **1** truth or accuracy **2** a true statement —**ve·ra·cious** /və ráyshəss/ *adj* —**ve·ra·cious·ness** *n*

Ve·ra·cruz /vèrrə króoz/ city in E Mexico, on the Gulf of Mexico. Pop. 425,140 (1995).

ve·ran·da /və rándə/, **ve·ran·dah** *n* a porch extending along an outside wall of a building —**ve·ran·daed** *adj*

verb *n* a word that indicates an action, existence, or possession

ver·bal /vúrb'l/ *adj* **1** using words rather than pictures or action **2** oral rather than written **3** involving skill with words **4** of or forming verbs ■ *n* a word formed from a verb —**ver·bal·ly** *adv*

SYNONYMS **verbal, spoken, oral** CORE MEANING: expressed in words

ver·bal·ize /vúrb'l ìz/ (**-ized, -iz·ing**) *vt* **1** express something in words **2** make a word into a verb —**ver·bal·i·za·tion** /vùrb'li záysh'n/ *n*

ver·bal noun *n* a noun ending in "-ing" that is formed from a verb, e.g., "hiking"

ver·ba·tim /vər báytim/ *adj, adv* using identical words

ver·bi·age /vúrbee ij/ *n* an excess of words

ver·bose /vər bṓss/ *adj* using too many words —**ver·bose·ly** *adv* —**ver·bose·ness** *n* —**ver·bos·i·ty** /vər bóssətee/ *n* ◊ See note at **wordy**

ver·bo·ten /vər bṓt'n, fər-/ *adj* not allowed

ver·dant /vúrd'nt/ *adj* **1** with lush green growth **2** green —**ver·dan·cy** *n*

Verde, Cape ♦ Cape Verde

Ver·di /váirdee/, **Giuseppe** (1813–1901) Italian composer

ver·dict /vúrdikt/ *n* **1** a jury's decision **2** any decision or opinion

ver·di·gris /vúrdi grèess, -griss, -grèe/ *n* **1** a green deposit on copper **2** a greenish powder formed by the action of acetic acid on copper. Use: paint pigment, fungicide.

ORIGIN **Verdigris** came from a French word meaning literally "green of Greece." The reason for the Greek association is not known.

Ver·dun /vur dún/ town in NE France, site of one of the longest and bloodiest battles of World War I. Pop. 19,624 (1999).

ver·dure /vúrjər/ *n* **1** the vivid green color of plants **2** vegetation

verge¹ *n* **1** the point beyond which something happens **2** a boundary or edge □ **verge on** *or* **upon** *vt* **1** border on an area **2** come close to a particular quality or condition

verge² (**verged, verg·ing**) *vi* move in a particular direction

ver·i·fy /vérrə fì/ (**-fied, -fies**) *vt* **1** prove something **2** check whether something is true —**ver·i·fi·a·ble** /vèrrə fí ab'l, vèrrə fí ab'l/ *adj* —**ver·i·fi·a·bly** *adv* —**ver·i·fi·ca·tion** /vèrrəfi káysh'n/ *n*

ver·i·ly /vérralee/ *adv* to be sure (*archaic*)

ver·i·si·mil·i·tude /vèrrə si millə tòod/ *n* (*fml*) **1** the appearance of being true **2** something that seems true but is not

ver·i·ta·ble /vérrətəb'l/ *adj* absolute —**ver·i·ta·bly** *adv*

ver·i·ty /vérrətee/ *n* (*pl* -**ties**) *n* (*fml*) **1** truth or reality **2** something that is true

Ver·laine /ver láyn, -lén/, **Paul** (1844–96) French poet

Ver·meer /vər meér, -máir/, **Jan** (1632–75) Dutch artist

ver·mi·cel·li /vùrmə séllee, -chéllee/ n pasta in long thin threads

ver·mic·u·lite /vər míkyə lìt/ n a compound of aluminum, magnesium, or iron. Use: insulation, lubricant, horticulture.

ver·mi·form /vúrmi fàwrm/ adj shaped like a worm

ver·mil·ion /vər míllyən/, **ver·mil·lion** n 1 a red pigment 2 a bright red color —**ver·mil·ion** adj

ver·min /vúrmin/ n harmful or destructive small animals or insects such as rats or cockroaches —**ver·min·ous** adj

Ver·mont /vər mónt/ state in the NE United States. Cap. Montpelier. Pop. 608,827 (2000). —**Ver·mon·ter** n

ver·mouth /vər móoth/ n wine flavored with herbs

ver·nac·u·lar /vər nákyələr/ n 1 the ordinary language spoken by a specific people 2 the language of a specific profession or class —**ver·nac·u·lar** adj

ver·nal /vúrn'l/ adj of the spring

Verne /vurn/, **Jules** (1828–1905) French writer

Ve·ro·na /və róna/ capital of **Verona Province**, Veneto Region, N Italy. Pop. 254,712 (1999). —**Ver·o·nese** /vèrrə neéz, -neéss/ n, adj

Ve·ro·ne·se /vèrrə náyzee/, **Paolo** (1528–88) Italian artist

Ver·raz·za·no /vèrrə zaànō, vè raa tsaà-/, **Ver·ra·za·no, Giovanni da** (1480?–1527?) Italian explorer

ver·ru·ca /və róoka/ (pl -**cae** /-kee/) n a wart on the foot

Ver·sailles /vər sí/ n a 17C palace near Paris

ver·sa·tile /vúrsət'l/ adj 1 having many uses 2 having many skills —**ver·sa·tile·ly** adv —**ver·sa·til·i·ty** /vùrsə tíllətee/ n

verse n 1 a section of a song or poem 2 a numbered division of a chapter of the Bible 3 poetry 4 a particular form of poetry o in blank verse

versed /vurst/ adj skilled or knowledgeable

ver·si·fy /vúrsə fì/ (-**fied**, -**fies**) v 1 vt change prose into poetry 2 vi write poetry —**ver·si·fi·ca·tion** /vùrsəfi káysh'n/ n

ver·sion /vúrzh'n/ n 1 an account of something 2 a specific form or variety of something o a later version of the text 3 an adaptation 4 a translation —**ver·sion·al** adj

ver·so /vúr sò/ (pl -**sos**) n 1 the back of a printed page 2 a left-hand page in a book

ver·sus /vúrsəss/ prep 1 against 2 as opposed to

ver·te·bra /vúrtəbrə/ (pl -**brae** /-bray, -brèe/ or -**bras**) n a bone in the spinal column —**ver·te·bral** adj

ver·te·brate /vúrtəbrət, -bràyt/ n an animal with a backbone —**ver·te·brate** adj

veterinarian incorrect spelling of veterinarian

ver·tex /vúr tèks/ (pl -**ti·ces** /-ti seéz/ or -**tex·es**) n 1 the highest point 2 the point of a geometric figure that is opposite the base 3 a point where the two sides of a figure or angle intersect

ver·ti·cal /vúrtik'l/ adj 1 at right angles to the horizon or to the base of something 2 directly overhead ■ n 1 something vertical 2 an upright position —**ver·ti·cal·ly** adv

ver·tig·i·nous /vur tíjjənəss/ adj 1 so high as to cause dizziness 2 suffering from vertigo 3 rotating around an axis —**ver·tig·i·nous·ly** adv

ver·ti·go /vúrti gò/ n a condition marked by a whirling sensation that causes a loss of balance

verve n 1 creative enthusiasm 2 vitality

ver·y /vérree/ adv quite o very cold ■ adj 1 absolute in the extreme o at the very back of the hall 2 right or suitable o the very person I wanted to see o the very thing I need 3 precisely as emphasized o shook the industry to its very foundation

ves·pers /véspərz/, **Ves·pers** n an evening church service (+ sing or pl verb)

Ves·puc·ci /ves póochee/, **Amerigo** (1454–1512) Italian explorer

ves·sel /véss'l/ n 1 a container 2 a ship or boat 3 a tubular structure that conducts fluid around the body or through a plant

vest n 1 a sleeveless garment, open or with buttons down the front 2 UK, NZ an undershirt ■ v 1 vt confer power or rights on somebody 2 vti dress in vestments

Ves·ta /vésta/ n in Roman mythology, the goddess of the hearth. Greek equivalent **Hestia**

ves·tal vir·gin /vést'l-/ n in ancient Rome, a celibate woman consecrated to the goddess Vesta

vest·ed in·ter·est n 1 a right to possess property in the future 2 a special interest in something for reasons of private gain

ves·ti·bule /vésti byòol/ n 1 an entrance hall 2 a cavity or space in the body that serves as the entrance to another cavity or canal

ves·tige /véstij/ n 1 a trace of something gone 2 the slightest amount

ves·tig·i·al /ve stíjjee əl/ adj remaining after the rest has disappeared or dwindled —**ves·tig·i·al·ly** adv

vest·ing /vésting/ n the granting of pension rights to an employee

vest·ment /véstmənt/ n 1 a robe worn to show rank 2 a ceremonial robe worn by members of the clergy

ves·try /véstree/ (pl -**tries**) n 1 a room in a church where vestments and sacred objects are stored 2 a meeting room in a church

Ve·su·vi·us, Mt. /və soovee əss/ active volcano overlooking the Bay of Naples, S Italy. An eruption in AD 79 destroyed the Roman cities of Pompeii and Herculaneum. Height 4,190 ft./1,277 m.

vet[1] *n* a veterinarian ■ *vt* (**vet·ted**, **vet·ting**) examine somebody or something in order to determine suitability

vet[2] *n* a veteran soldier *(infml)*

vetch *n* a climbing or twining plant with small flowers. Use: silage, fodder.

vet·er·an /véttərən/ *n* 1 somebody who was formerly in the armed forces 2 an experienced soldier 3 somebody with a lot of experience —**vet·er·an** *adj*

Vet·er·ans Day *n* a holiday honoring war veterans. Date: November 11.

vet·er·i·nar·i·an /véttərə náiree ən, vèttrə-/ *n* a practitioner of veterinary medicine

vet·er·i·nar·y /véttərə nèrree, véttrə-/ *adj* of animal diseases

~~vetinary~~ incorrect spelling of **veterinary**

ve·to /veétō/ *n* (*pl* **-toes**) 1 the right to reject something, especially a piece of legislation 2 an exercise of the right to reject something 3 a prohibition ■ *vt* (**-toed**, **-to·ing**, **-toes**) 1 reject 2 prohibit —**ve·to·er** *n*

vex *vt* annoy —**vex·ing·ly** *adv*

vex·a·tion /vek sáysh'n/ *n* 1 the state of being vexed 2 the act of vexing 3 something that vexes

vex·a·tious /vek sáyshəss/ *adj* troublesome or annoying —**vex·a·tious·ly** *adv*

vexed /vekst/ *adj* 1 irritated 2 much debated ○ *a vexed issue such as global warming* —**vex·ed·ly** /véksədlee/ *adv*

vg *abbr* very good

⚡**VGA** *n* a specification for computer screens. Full form **video graphics array**

VHF, vhf *abbr* very high frequency

VHS *tdmk* a trademark for a video recording system

vi·a /ví ə, vee ə/ *prep* 1 by way of 2 by means of

vi·a·ble /ví əb'l/ *adj* 1 practicable or worthwhile 2 able to survive, grow, or develop 3 describes a fetus that is able to survive outside the womb —**vi·a·bil·i·ty** /ví ə bíllətee/ *n* —**vi·a·bly** *adv*

vi·a·duct /ví ə dùkt/ *n* a bridge consisting of a series of arches that spans a valley

vi·al /ví əl/ *n* a small glass bottle for medicine

vi·and /ví ənd/ *(fml)* *n* an article of food ■ **vi·ands** *npl* food provisions

vibe /víb/ *n* an atmosphere or feeling *(slang; often pl)*

vi·brant /víbrənt/ *adj* 1 pulsating with energy 2 having a full rich sound that resonates 3 dazzlingly bright —**vi·bran·cy** *n* —**vi·brant·ly** *adv*

vi·bra·phone /víbrə fòn/ *n* a percussion instrument with metal bars —**vi·bra·phon·ist** *n*

vi·brate /ví bràyt/ (**-brat·ed**, **-brat·ing**) *v* 1 *vti* make or cause to make small movements back and forth rapidly 2 *vi* resonate —**vi·bra·tor** *n* —**vi·bra·to·ry** /víbrə tàwree/ *adj*

vi·bra·tion /ví bráysh'n/ *n* 1 the process or an instance of shaking or moving back and forth very rapidly 2 the atmosphere given off by a place or situation, or the feeling conveyed *(infml; often pl)* —**vi·bra·tion·al** *adj*

vi·bra·to /vi braátō/ *(pl* **-tos**) *n* a throbbing effect produced in playing a musical instrument or singing

vic·ar /víkər/ *n* 1 a cleric in the Episcopal Church who is in charge of a chapel 2 a member of the Anglican clergy 3 a Roman Catholic priest who represents or deputizes for a bishop —**vic·ar·age** /víkərij/ *n*

vi·car·i·ous /ví káiree əss, vi-/ *adj* 1 experienced through another person by sympathy or imagination 2 endured for somebody else —**vi·car·i·ous·ly** *adv* —**vi·car·i·ous·ness** *n*

vice /víss/ *n* 1 an immoral habit 2 immoral conduct 3 a mild character flaw

vice ad·mi·ral *n* a naval officer of a rank above rear admiral —**vice-ad·mi·ral·ty** *n*

vice pres·i·dent *n* a president's deputy —**vice-pres·i·den·cy** *n* —**vice-pres·i·den·tial** *adj*

vice·roy /víss ròy/ *n* a governor who represents a sovereign in a colony —**vice·roy·ship** *n*

vice squad *n* a police division enforcing laws relating to gambling, drug abuse, and prostitution

vi·ce ver·sa /víss vúrssə, vìssə-/ *adv* the other way around

Vi·chy /veéshee/ city in central France. It was the seat of a French government that collaborated with the Germans during World War II. Pop. 26,528 (1999).

vi·cin·i·ty /və sínnətee/ (*pl* **-ties**) *n* 1 the area surrounding or near a place 2 proximity 3 an approximate amount or number ○ *something in the vicinity of 1,000 miles*

vi·cious /víshəss/ *adj* 1 ferocious and violent 2 dangerous and aggressive 3 intended to cause harm —**vi·cious·ly** *adv* —**vi·cious·ness** *n*

vi·cious cir·cle, vi·cious cy·cle *n* a situation that is worsened by attempts to solve it

vi·cis·si·tude /vi síssi tòod/ *n* variability *(literary)* ■ **vi·cis·si·tudes** *npl* unexpected and often unwelcome changes

Vicks·burg /víks bùrg/ city in W Mississippi, site of a Union victory in 1863 during the Civil War. Pop. 27,221 (1998).

vic·tim /víktim/ *n* 1 somebody hurt or killed 2 somebody or something harmed or adversely affected **3** a living being used for a sacrifice —**vic·tim·hood** n

vic·tim·ize /víktə mìz/ (**-ized, -iz·ing**) vt **1** treat unfairly **2** make into a victim —**vic·tim·i·za·tion** /víktəmi záysh'n/ n

vic·tor /víktər/ n **1** a winner **2** **Vic·tor** a communications code word for the letter "V"

Vic·tor Em·man·u·el II /víktər i mánnyoo əl/ (1820–78) king of Sardinia (1849–61) and first king of Italy (1861–78)

Vic·to·ri·a /vik táwree ə/ **1** capital of British Columbia, Canada. Pop. 73,504 (1996). **2** capital of the Republic of Seychelles. Pop. 60,000 (1994).

Vic·to·ri·a (1819–1901) queen of the United Kingdom (1837–1901)

Vic·to·ri·a, Lake largest lake in Africa, with shorelines in Tanzania, Uganda, and Kenya

Vic·to·ri·a Falls falls in south central Africa on the Zambezi River, on the border between Zambia and Zimbabwe. Height 355 ft./108 m.

Vic·to·ri·a Is·land island in the Arctic Archipelago, N Canada, divided between Nunavut and the Northwest Territories

Vic·to·ri·a Land region of Antarctica, west of the Ross Sea

Vic·to·ri·an /vik táwree ən/ adj **1** of the time of Queen Victoria **2** conventional, hypocritical, or prudish ■ n somebody who lived in Queen Victoria's reign —**Vic·to·ri·an·ism** n

Vic·to·ri·a·na /vik tàwree ánnə, -aánə/ npl objects from the time of Queen Victoria

vic·to·ri·ous /vik táwree əss/ adj **1** having won **2** of victory —**vic·to·ri·ous·ly** adv —**vic·to·ri·ous·ness** n

vic·to·ry /víktəree/ (pl **-ries**) n **1** the defeat of an opponent or enemy **2** success in a difficult situation

vict·uals /vítt'lz/ npl food or other provisions (often humorous)

ORIGIN Victuals retains a pronunciation appropriate to the French word from which it was adopted, but the spelling has been altered to conform to the original source, Latin *victualia*. This was formed from *victus* "livelihood, food," a derivative of the verb *vivere* "live." **Victuals** are thus etymologically what you need to live on.

vi·cu·ña /vī kóonyə, vī kóonə, vi-/ n **1** a South American mammal related to the llama **2** a fine cloth made from vicuña wool

Vi·dal /vi daál/, **Gore** (b. 1925) US writer

vid·e·o /víddee ō/ n (pl **-os**) **1** the visual part of a television broadcast **2** a videocassette (infml) **3** something recorded onto videotape o *a video of my brother's wedding* ■ adj of television, especially the reproduction of images

⚡**vid·e·o a·dapt·er** n COMPUT = **graphics card**

⚡**vid·e·o ar·cade** n a place where people pay to play video games

vid·e·o cam·er·a n a camera that uses videotape

⚡**vid·e·o card** n a circuit board that enables a computer to display screen information

vid·e·o·cas·sette /víddee ō kə sèt/ n a cassette that contains videotape

vid·e·o·cas·sette re·cord·er n full form of **VCR**

vid·e·o·con·fer·enc·ing /víddee ō kònfərənsing/ n the holding of a meeting in which participants in different places communicate via video —**vid·e·o·con·fer·ence** n

⚡**vid·e·o·disk** /víddee ō dìsk/, **vid·e·o·disc** n a disk on which video and audio information is recorded digitally

⚡**vid·e·o dis·play ter·mi·nal** n the part of a computer that consists of the monitor, the keyboard, and the mouse, or simply of a touch-sensitive screen

⚡**vid·e·o game** n an electronic game played on a computer or television screen or on a hand-held device with a screen

vid·e·og·ra·phy /víddee ōggrəfee/ n the art of recording with a video camera —**vid·e·og·ra·pher** n

vid·e·o jock·ey n a presenter of music videos on television

⚡**vid·e·o·phone** /víddee ō fōn/ n a communication device that simultaneously transmits the speech and a video image of the caller

vid·e·o re·cord·er n MEDIA = **VCR**

vid·e·o·tape /víddee ō tàyp/ n magnetic tape on which pictures and sound can be recorded ■ vt (**-taped, -tap·ing**) record on videotape

vid·e·o·text /víddee ō tèkst/ n a video communications service that gives access to pages of information

~~vidio~~ incorrect spelling of **video**

vie /vī/ (**vied, vy·ing**) vi compete

~~viel~~ incorrect spelling of **veil**

Vi·en·na /vee énnə/ capital of Austria. Pop. 1,606,843 (1999). —**Vi·en·nese** /vèe ə néez, -néess/ n, adj

Vien·tiane /vyen tyaán/ capital of Laos. Pop. 528,109 (1995).

Vi·e·ques, Is·la de /vee áy kayss/ island off the coast of E Puerto Rico, used by the US navy for gunnery and bombing practice. Pop. 8,602 (1990).

Vi·et·cong /vee èt káwng, vyèt-/ (pl same or **Vi·et Cong**) n a Communist guerrilla in the Vietnam War

Vi·et·nam /vee èt naám/ country in Southeast Asia, on the South China Sea. Cap. Hanoi. Pop. 79,939,014 (2001). —**Vi·et·nam·ese** /vee ètnə méez, vyètnə-, -méess/ n, adj

Vi·et·nam War n a conflict in Vietnam (1954–75) that involved US forces

view /vyoo/ *n* **1** an act of looking at something **2** a range of vision **3** a scene **4** a pictorial representation **5** a perspective **6** an opinion ■ *vt* **1** observe or watch **2** inspect **3** consider or think of a range of things —**view·a·ble** *adj* —**view·er** *n* —**view·ing** *n* ◊ **in view of** because of or bearing in mind ◊ **on view** put somewhere so as to be seen ◊ **take a dim view of** disapprove of ◊ **with a view to** with the aim, intention, or hope of

view·find·er /vyoo fīndər/ *n* a device on a camera that shows what will appear in the picture

view·point /vyoo pòynt/ *n* **1** a point of view **2** a viewing location

vig·il /vijjəl/ *n* **1** a period of keeping watch during the night **2** the eve of a festival or holy day ■ **vig·ils** *npl* religious services at night

vig·i·lant /vijjələnt/ *adj* watchful, especially for danger —**vig·i·lance** *n* —**vig·i·lant·ly** *adv* ◊ See note at **cautious**

vig·i·lan·te /vijjə lántee/ *n* a citizen, especially a member of a volunteer group, who enforces the law without having the authority to do so

vi·gnette /vin yét/ *n* **1** a brief scene **2** a short essay **3** a picture without a border that gradually fades into the background at the edges **4** a small design printed on a book page —**vi·gnet·tist** *n*

vig·or /viggər/ *n* **1** great strength and energy **2** intensity **3** legal validity

vig·or·ous /viggərəss/ *adj* **1** very strong and healthy **2** energetic —**vig·or·ous·ly** *adv* —**vig·or·ous·ness** *n*

Vi·king /víking/ *n* a member of an ancient Scandinavian seafaring people

~~village~~ incorrect spelling of **village**

vile /vīl/ (**vil·er, vil·est**) *adj* **1** disgusting **2** wicked **3** very unpleasant —**vile·ly** *adv* —**vile·ness** *n* ◊ See note at **mean**

vil·i·fy /villə fī/ (**-fied, -fies**) *vt* make malicious and abusive statements about —**vil·i·fi·ca·tion** /villəfi káysh'n/ *n* —**vil·i·fi·er** *n* ◊ See note at **malign**

vil·la /villə/ *n* a large expensive country house

Vil·la /vee yə/, **Pancho** (1878–1923) Mexican revolutionary

vil·lage /villij/ *n* **1** a small rural community **2** the inhabitants of a village **3** a small incorporated community —**vil·lag·er** *n*

vil·lain /villən/ *n* **1** an evil character, e.g., in a movie **2** a person regarded as wicked or contemptible (*archaic or humorous*) **3** HIST = **villein**

vil·lain·ous /villənəss/ *adj* **1** wicked **2** unpleasant or undesirable —**vil·lain·ous·ly** *adv*

vil·lain·y /villənee/ *n* **1** evil conduct **2** the state of being evil

Vil·la-Lo·bos /vèelə lóboss, -lóboosh/, **Heitor** (1887–1959) Brazilian composer

~~villan~~ incorrect spelling of **villain**

~~villege~~ incorrect spelling of **village**

vil·lein /villən/, **vil·lain** *n* a feudal serf

Vil·ni·us /vilnee əss/ capital of Lithuania. Pop. 577,970 (2000).

vim *n* exuberant vitality and energy (*infml*)

~~vinagrette~~ incorrect spelling of **vinaigrette**

vin·ai·grette /vìnnə grét/ *n* a salad dressing with a base of vinegar and oil

vin·di·cate /víndi kàyt/ (**-cat·ed, -cat·ing**) *vt* **1** show to be blameless **2** justify or substantiate —**vin·di·ca·ble** *adj* —**vin·di·ca·tion** /vìndi káysh'n/ *n* —**vin·di·ca·tor** *n*

vin·dic·tive /vin díktiv/ *adj* **1** desiring revenge or done for revenge **2** spiteful

vine /vīn/ *n* **1** a climbing plant **2** the stem of a climbing plant **3** a grapevine —**vin·y** *adj*

vin·e·gar /vínnəgər/ *n* a sour-tasting liquid made by fermenting wine, cider, or beer —**vin·e·gar·y** *adj*

ORIGIN Vinegar came from French, and means literally "sour wine."

~~vinegarette~~ incorrect spelling of **vinaigrette**

vine·yard /vínnyərd/ *n* a place where grapes are grown

vingt-et-un /vàN tay úN/ *n* the card game blackjack

vin·i·cul·ture *n* = viticulture

Vin·land /vínnlənd/ coastal area of NE North America, now N Newfoundland, visited by Norse voyagers in about AD 986

Vin·son /vínss'n/, **Frederick M.** (1890–1953) chief justice of the US Supreme Court (1946–53)

Vin·son Mas·sif /-máss eef/ highest mountain in Antarctica, in the central Ellsworth Mountains. Height 16,066 ft./4,897 m.

vin·tage /víntij/ *n* **1** the year in which a wine was produced **2** a wine from a particular year or place **3** the harvesting of grapes **4** the period when something originated or flourished ■ *adj* **1** describes a high-quality wine from a single year **2** representing what is best or most typical **3** of high quality and lasting appeal

vin·tage car *n* an old car built between 1919 and 1930

vint·ner /víntnər/ *n* **1** a wine merchant **2** a maker of wines

vi·nyl /vín'l/ *n* a synthetic plastic or resin. Use: wallpaper, coverings. —**vi·nyl** *adj*

vi·ol /ví əl/ *n* a stringed instrument of the 16C and 17C

vi·o·la[1] /vee óla/ *n* a stringed instrument like a violin but slightly larger

ORIGIN The two English words **viola** are unrelated. The instrument name was adopted from Spanish and Italian, and probably derives from a word in the old language of

Provence that was related to *fiddle*. The flower name represents the Latin word for "violet."

vi·o·la² /ví ốlə, vee-, ví ələ/ *n* a small plant with flowers of various colors

~~violence~~ incorrect spelling of **violence**

vi·o·late /ví ə làyt/ (-lat·ed, -lat·ing) *vt* 1 act contrary to a law or rule 2 disturb something in a violent way 3 defile something sacred —**vi·o·la·ble** *adj* —**vi·o·la·tion** /ví ə láysh'n/ *n* —**vi·o·la·tive** *adj* —**vi·o·la·tor** *n*

vi·o·lence /ví ələnss/ *n* 1 physical force designed to cause injury or damage ○ *threats of violence* 2 the illegal use of unjustified force 3 extreme or destructive force ○ *the violence of the storm* 4 intensity of feeling or expression

vi·o·lent /ví ələnt/ *adj* 1 using or showing violence 2 intense ○ *a violent headache* ○ *violent passion* 3 caused by force —**vi·o·lent·ly** *adv*

vi·o·let /ví ələt/ *n* 1 a low-growing flowering plant with typically mauve or purple flowers 2 a purplish blue color —**vi·o·let** *adj*

vi·o·lin /ví ə lín/ *n* a stringed instrument held under the chin and played with a bow —**vi·o·lin·ist** *n*

VIP *abbr* very important person

vi·per /vípər/ *n* 1 any of a family of poisonous snakes 2 an adder 3 an offensive term for somebody regarded as treacherous (*offensive literary*) —**vi·per·ous** *adj*

ORIGIN *Viper* came via French from Latin *vipera* "snake." There was an ancient belief that the snake bore live young, and *vipera* was probably earlier *vivipera*, literally "live-bearing."

vi·ra·go /vi ráagō/ (*pl* -goes *or* -gos) *n* an offensive term for a woman regarded as overbearing and aggressive

⚡**vi·ral** /vírəl/ *adj* 1 caused by a virus 2 of or using unsolicited e-mails that are forwarded spontaneously from one user to another —**vi·ral** *n* —**vi·ral·ly** *adv*

Vir·gil /vúrjəl/, **Ver·gil** (70–19 BC) Roman poet —**Vir·gil·i·an** /vur jíllee ən/ *adj*

vir·gin /vúrjin/ *n* 1 somebody who has never had sex 2 a woman who has taken a religious vow of chastity 3 **Vir·gin, Vir·gin Mar·y** the mother of Jesus Christ ■ *adj* 1 of a virgin 2 pure or untouched ○ *virgin snow* 3 describes a natural area that has not been explored or exploited by human beings —**vir·gin·i·ty** /vər jínnətee/ *n*

vir·gin·al¹ /vúrjin'l/ *adj* 1 of a virgin 2 not corrupted or spoiled

vir·gin·al² /vúrjin'l/ *n* an old keyboard instrument like a small harpsichord —**vir·gin·al·ist** *n*

Vir·gin·ia /vər jínnyə/ state of the east central United States. Cap. Richmond. Pop. 7,078,515 (2000). —**Vir·gin·ian** *n, adj*

Vir·gin·ia Beach largest city in Virginia. Pop. 432,380 (1998).

Vir·gin·ia creep·er *n* a woody vine with bluish black berries

Vir·gin·ia reel *n* a country dance in which a caller instructs couples facing each other in long rows

Vir·gin Is·lands of the U·ni·ted States /vúrjin-/ unincorporated external territory of the United States in the Caribbean. Cap. Charlotte Amalie. Pop. 122,211 (2001).

Vir·go /vúrgō/ (*pl* -gos) *n* 1 a zodiacal constellation on the celestial equator 2 the 6th sign of the zodiac 3 somebody born under Virgo —**Vir·go** *adj* —**Vir·go·an** *n, adj*

vir·i·des·cent /veeri déss'nt/ *adj* greenish —**vir·i·des·cence** *n*

vir·id·i·an /və ríddee ən/ *n* 1 a green pigment 2 a bluish green color —**vir·id·i·an** *adj*

vir·ile /veerəl, ví ríl/ *adj* 1 having the characteristics of an adult male 2 forceful or energetic —**vi·ril·i·ty** /vi ríllitee/ *n*

vi·rol·o·gy /ví róllajee/ *n* the study of viruses —**vi·ro·log·ic** /vírə lójjik/ *adj* —**vi·ro·log·i·cal** *adj* —**vi·rol·o·gist** *n*

⚡**vir·tu·al** /vúrchoo əl/ *adj* 1 being something in effect, if not in reality or name 2 generated by computer —**vir·tu·al·ly** *adv*

⚡**vir·tu·al re·al·i·ty** *n* a computer simulation of three-dimensional space that the user can interact with

~~virtually~~ incorrect spelling of **virtually**

vir·tue /vúrchoo/ *n* 1 the quality of being morally good 2 a good or admirable quality 3 chastity ◇ **by virtue of** because of or through the power of

vir·tu·o·so /vùrchoo ốssố/ (*pl* -sos *or* -si /-óssee/) *n* 1 an exceptional performer 2 a highly talented person —**vir·tu·o·sic** /-óssik/ *adj* —**vir·tu·os·i·ty** /vùrchoo óssətee/ *n*

vir·tu·ous /vúrchoo əss/ *adj* 1 having or showing moral goodness 2 chaste —**vir·tu·ous·ly** *adv*

vir·u·lent /veeryəlant, veerə-/ *adj* 1 poisonous or damaging 2 malicious or bitter —**vir·u·lent·ly** *adv*

⚡**vi·rus** /vírəss/ *n* 1 a minute parasitic particle that multiplies in the cells of another organism 2 a disease caused by a virus 3 a contagious computer program. ◇ **Trojan horse, worm** ₆

vi·sa /veezə/ *n* a passport insertion that allows the bearer to enter or leave a specific country

~~visable~~ incorrect spelling of **visible**

vis·age /vízzij/ *n* the human face (*literary*)

vis-à-vis /veezə veé/ *prep* 1 regarding 2 opposite ■ *adv* face to face

vis·cer·a /víssərə/ *npl* the internal organs of the body

vis·cer·al /víssərəl/ *adj* 1 instinctual 2 emotional 3 of the viscera —**vis·cer·al·ly** *adv*

vis·cid /vissid/ *adj* thick and sticky —**vis·cid·i·ty** /vi siddətee/ *n* —**vis·cid·ly** *adv*

vis·cose /vis kòss/ *n* 1 soft rayon made from a thick cellulose solution 2 the cellulose used in making viscose

vis·cos·i·ty /vis kóssətee/ (*pl* -ties) *n* 1 a thick sticky quality 2 the property of a fluid that resists flowing

vis·count /ví kòwnt/ *n* 1 a British nobleman of a rank below baron 2 a European count's son or younger brother —**vis·count·cy** *n* —**vis·count·y** *n*

vis·count·ess /ví kòwntəss/ *n* 1 a woman with the rank of viscount 2 a viscount's wife or widow

vis·cous /vískəss/ *adj* 1 thick and sticky 2 describes a fluid that has a relatively high resistance to flow —**vis·cous·ly** *adv* —**vis·cous·ness** *n*

vise /víss/ *n* a tool with jaws for keeping an object immobile while it is worked on —**vise·like** *adj*

Vish·nu /vísh noo/ *n* the Hindu god called the Preserver

vis·i·bil·i·ty /vizzə bíllətee/ *n* 1 the ability to be seen 2 the distance within which it is possible to see things 3 a clear view

vis·i·ble /vízzəb'l/ *adj* 1 able to be seen 2 in sight 3 obvious or apparent 4 often in the public eye —**vis·i·bly** *adv*

vi·sion /vízh'n/ *n* 1 eyesight 2 a mental picture 3 something seen in a dream or trance 4 the ability to anticipate possible future developments 5 a beautiful person or thing —**vi·sion·al** *adj* —**vi·sion·less** *adj*

vi·sion·ar·y /vízh'n èrree/ *adj* 1 full of foresight 2 imaginary 3 idealistic and impracticable 4 given to dreaminess 5 of mystical visions ■ *n* (*pl* -ies) 1 somebody with great foresight 2 somebody who has visions

vis·it /vízzit/ *v* 1 *vti* go to see somebody or something 2 *vti* stay with somebody as a guest, or in a place as a tourist 3 *vt* go to inspect a place 4 *vt* inflict something on somebody *(archaic literary or fml)* ○ *an administration upon which many trials were visited* ■ *n* 1 a social or official call 2 a stay in a place 3 an official call paid for the purpose of inspection —**vis·it·a·ble** *adj*

vis·i·ta·tion /vízzi táysh'n/ *n* 1 a visit with a child granted to a divorced parent 2 an official visit 3 a divine punishment 4 a supposed appearance from the spirit world 5 **Vis·i·ta·tion** the Virgin Mary's visit to Elizabeth after the Annunciation 6 **Vis·i·ta·tion** the Christian festival that celebrates the Visitation. Date: July 2. —**vis·i·ta·tion·al** *adj*

vis·it·ing card *n* a calling card

vis·it·ing nurse *n* a registered nurse who provides medical care to sick people in their homes

vis·it·ing teach·er *n* a public-school teacher who provides in-home instruction to children with medical conditions preventing their school attendance

vis·i·tor /vízzitər/ *n* somebody who is visiting

vi·sor /vízər/, **vi·zor** *n* 1 a transparent front part of a helmet 2 a flap fitted over a windshield to shield the eyes from the sun's glare 3 a shade for the eyes 4 a cap brim 5 the front of a medieval helmet, with slits for the eyes —**vi·sored** *adj*

vis·ta /vístə/ *n* 1 a scenic view 2 a view through a narrow opening

VISTA *abbr* Volunteers in Service to America

Vis·tu·la /víschələ, víschóōlə/ longest river in Poland, emptying into the Baltic Sea at the Gulf of Gdansk. Length 675 mi./1,090 km.

vi·su·al /vízhoo əl/ *adj* 1 of vision 2 visible 3 done by sight only —**vi·su·al·ly** *adv*

vi·su·al·ize /vízhoo ə līz/ (-ized, -iz·ing) *vti* imagine —**vi·su·al·i·za·tion** /vízhoo əli záysh'n/ *n*

vi·su·al·ly im·paired *adj* having reduced vision or no vision

vi·ta /véétə/ (*pl* -tae /-tee/) *n* 1 HR = curriculum vitae 2 a short biography or autobiography

vi·tal /vít'l/ *adj* 1 crucial 2 of or needed for life ○ *vital bodily organs* 3 lively ○ *a vital neighborhood* —**vi·tal·ly** *adv* ◊ See note at **necessary**

vi·tal·i·ty /vī tállətee/ *n* 1 the quality of being lively 2 durability ○ *the vitality of cherished traditions*

vi·tals /vít'lz/ *npl* 1 the internal organs of the body that are essential to life 2 essentials

vi·tal sta·tis·tics *npl* data about the human populaton, including births and deaths

vi·ta·min /vítəmin/ *n* an organic substance essential to nutrition —**vi·ta·min·ic** /vítə mínnik/ *adj*

vi·ta·min A, **vi·ta·min A₁** *n* a fat-soluble vitamin found in some vegetables, fish, milk, and eggs, important for normal vision

vi·ta·min B *n* BIOCHEM = vitamin B complex

vi·ta·min B₁₂ *n* a water-soluble vitamin obtained only from animal products and fish, important for normal blood formation

vi·ta·min B₂ *n* riboflavin

vi·ta·min B com·plex *n* a group of water-soluble vitamins found in many foods

vi·ta·min C *n* a water-soluble vitamin found in fruits and leafy vegetables

vi·ta·min D *n* a fat-soluble vitamin that occurs in fish-liver oils and eggs, essential for the formation of bones and teeth

vi·ta·min E *n* a mixture of fat-soluble vitamins found in seed oils, essential for normal reproduction

vi·ta·min H *n* biotin

vi·ta·min K *n* a fat-soluble vitamin essential for blood clotting

vi·ti·ate /víshee àyt/ (-at·ed, -at·ing) *vt* (*fml*) 1 make ineffective 2 make defective 3 debase —**vi·ti·a·tion** /víshee áysh'n/ *n*

vit·i·cul·ture /vítti kúlchər, víti-/, **vin·i·cul·ture** /vínni-/ *n* the science or practice of growing grapes —**vit·i·cul·tur·al** /vítti kúlchərəl/ *adj* —**vit·i·cul·tur·ist** *n*

vit·re·ous /víttree əss/ *adj* 1 similar to glass 2 of glass —**vit·re·os·i·ty** /víttree óssətee/ *n*

vit·re·ous hu·mor *n* the fluid component of the gel that fills the main cavity of the eye

vit·ri·fy /vittrə fī/ (-fied, -fies) *vti* change into glass —**vit·ri·fi·ca·tion** /vittrəfi káysh'n/ *n*

vit·ri·ol /vittree ól/ *n* 1 bitterly expressed antipathy 2 sulfuric acid (*literary*)

vit·ri·ol·ic /vittree óllik/ *adj* expressing bitter hatred —**vit·ri·ol·i·cal·ly** *adv*

vit·tles /vítt'lz/ *npl* food (*infml*)

vi·tu·per·a·tion /vī tòopə ráysh'n, vi-/ *n* 1 an outburst of abuse 2 the use of violent abuse —**vi·tu·per·ate** /vī tòopə ràyt, vi-/ *vt* —**vi·tu·per·a·tive** /vī tòopərətiv, -ràytiv, vi-/ *adj*

vi·va /véevə/ *interj* long live

vi·va·ce /vi vaá chày, -vaáchee/ *adv* in a lively way (*musical direction*) —**vi·va·ce** *adj, n*

vi·va·cious /vi váyshəss/ *adj* lively and full of high spirits —**vi·va·cious·ly** *adv* —**vi·va·cious·ness** *n* —**vi·vac·i·ty** /vi vássətee/ *n*

Vi·val·di /vi vaáldee, -váwl-/, **Antonio** (1678–1741) Italian composer

vi·var·i·um /vī váiree əm/ (*pl* -a /-ə/ *or* -ums) *n* a place for keeping and watching small animals

vi·va vo·ce /vívə vóssee, véevə-/ *adv* orally

viv·id /vívvid/ *adj* 1 very bright 2 extremely clear or true to life 3 producing strong mental images 4 inventive *o a vivid imagination* —**viv·id·ly** *adv* —**viv·id·ness** *n*

vi·vip·a·rous /vī víppərəss, vi-/ *adj* bearing live young —**vi·vip·a·rous·ly** *adv*

viv·i·sect /vívvi sèkt/ *vti* operate on a live animal to gain knowledge of pathological or physiological processes —**viv·i·sec·tion** /vívvi séksh'n/ *n*

vix·en /víksən/ *n* 1 a female fox 2 an offensive term for a woman regarded as vindictive or bad-tempered —**vix·en·ish** *adj* —**vix·en·ly** *adj, adv*

viz. *adv* namely

vi·zier /vi zeér/ *n* a high-ranking diplomat in the former Turkish empire

vi·zor *n* = visor

VJ *abbr* video jockey

Vla·di·vos·tok /vlàddəvə stók, vlàddə vós tòk/ major port in SE Russia. Pop. 640,672 (1995).

⚡**VLSI** *adj* having thousands of components on a single microchip. Full form **very large-scale integration**

V-neck *n* a V-shaped neckline —**V-necked** *adj*

VOA *abbr* Voice of America

VOC *abbr* volatile organic compound

vo·cab·u·lar·y /vō kábbyə lèrree, və-/ (*pl* -ies) *n* 1 all the words known by a person or used in a language or profession 2 a list of words ◊ See note at **language**

vo·cal /vók'l/ *adj* 1 spoken 2 of the voice 3 having the power of speech 4 outspoken *o vocal objections* 5 of or for singing ■ *n* 1 the sung part of a song 2 a pop or jazz song —**vo·cal·i·ty** /vō kállətee/ *n* —**vo·cal·ly** *adv* —**vo·cal·ness** *n*

vo·cal cords *npl* membranes in the larynx that produce sounds by vibrating

vo·cal·ist /vók'list/ *n* a singer of pop songs

vo·cal·ize /vók'l īz/ (-ized, -iz·ing) *vti* 1 express something with the voice 2 transform a consonant into a vowel, or be transformed into a vowel —**vo·cal·i·za·tion** /vók'li záysh'n/ *n*

vo·ca·tion /vō káysh'n/ *n* 1 a profession 2 an urge to follow a specific career —**vo·ca·tion·al** *adj* —**vo·ca·tion·al·ly** *adv*

vo·ca·tion·al school *n* a school teaching a trade

voc·a·tive /vókətiv/ *adj* describes a word or grammatical case that indicates the person or thing addressed by the speaker —**voc·a·tive** *n*

vo·cif·er·ate /vō síffə ràyt/ (-at·ed, -at·ing) *vti* shout out —**vo·cif·er·a·tion** /-síffə ráysh'n/ *n*

vo·cif·er·ous /vō síffərəss/ *adj* 1 shouting noisily 2 full of noisy shouting —**vo·cif·er·ous·ly** *adv* —**vo·cif·er·ous·ness** *n*

⚡**vo·cod·er** /vó kòdər/ *n* a speech synthesizer

vod·ka /vódkə/ *n* a colorless distilled liquor made from a grain or from potatoes

vogue /vōg/ *n* 1 the prevailing fashion 2 popularity ■ *adj* fashionable

voice *n* 1 the sound made using the vocal organs 2 the sound of singing 3 the ability to use the voice for speaking or singing 4 a sound like the human voice 5 the right to state an opinion 6 an expressed opinion 7 a medium of communication or expression *o the voice of reason* 8 a singer or singing part 9 a form of a verb that indicates the relationship between subject and verb ■ *vt* (voiced, voic·ing) 1 express orally 2 pronounce with a vibration of the vocal cords —**voic·er** *n*

voice box *n* the larynx

voiced *adj* pronounced with a vibration of the vocal cords —**voic·ed·ness** /vóyssədnəss/ *n*

voice·less /vóysslass/ *adj* 1 saying nothing 2 unable to speak 3 pronounced without a vibration of the vocal cords —**voice·less·ly** *adv* —**voice·less·ness** *n*

voice mail *n* a computerized system for storing telephone messages

voice·o·ver /vóyss ōvər/ *n* the spoken words of an unseen commentator

voice·print /vóyss prínt/ *n* a representation of a voice in graph form

void /voyd/ *adj* 1 not legally valid 2 totally lacking in something (*fml*) 3 empty or vacant ■ *n* 1 a vacuum 2 a state of loss or a feeling of emptiness ■ *v* 1 *vt* make legally invalid 2 *vt* empty the contents of 3 *vti* empty the bowels or bladder —**void·a·ble** *adj* —**void·ness** *n* ◊ See note at **vacant**

voi·là /vwaa laá/ *interj* acknowledges or expresses satisfaction that something has been done

voile /voyl/ *n* a lightweight translucent fabric

⚡**VoIP** *n* a technology that enables voice messages to be sent via the Internet. Full form **voice over Internet protocol**

vol. *abbr* 1 volume 2 volunteer

vol·a·tile /vóllət'l/ *adj* 1 prone to sudden change 2 unstable and potentially dangerous 3 unpredictable or fickle 4 evaporating at a relatively low temperature 5 short-lived —**vol·a·til·i·ty** /vòllə tíllətee/ *n*

vol·can·ic /vol kánnik/ *adj* 1 of volcanoes 2 sudden and violent

vol·ca·no /vol káynō/ (*pl* -**noes** *or* -**nos**) *n* 1 an opening in the Earth's crust through which molten material is ejected 2 a mountain formed from the deposited material from a vent in the Earth's surface

ORIGIN **Volcanoes** are named for Vulcan, the Roman god of fire. The word was adopted from Italian in the early 17C.

vole /vōl/ (*pl* **voles** *or* same) *n* a small rodent like a mouse with a short tail

Vol·ga /vólgə, váwlgə/ longest river in Europe, in W Russia. It rises northwest of Moscow and flows southeast and south before emptying into the Caspian Sea. Length 2,300 mi./3,700 km.

Vol·go·grad /vólgə grád, vólgə-/ city in SW Russia. Pop. 1,260,171 (1995).

vo·li·tion /və lísh'n/ *n* 1 the exercise of the will 2 the ability to choose or decide —**vo·li·tion·al** *adj* —**vo·li·tion·al·ly** *adv*

vol·ley /vóllee/ *n* 1 a kick or hit of a ball before it bounces 2 a simultaneous firing of several weapons 3 a discharge of missiles fired simultaneously 4 a simultaneous expression of things, e.g., protests or questions ■ *vti* (-**leyed**, -**ley·ing**, -**leys**) 1 strike a

ball before it lands 2 fire weapons simultaneously —**vol·ley·er** *n*

vol·ley·ball /vóllee báwl/ *n* 1 a team sport in which the hands are used to hit a ball over a high net 2 the large inflated ball used in volleyball —**vol·ley·ball·er** *n*

volt¹ /vōlt/ *n* (*symbol* **V**) a unit of electric potential difference

ORIGIN The **volt** is named for Count Alessandro Volta (1745–1827), an Italian physicist who developed the first electric battery in 1800.

volt² /vōlt, vawlt/, **volte** *n* a circular motion by a horse in dressage

Vol·ta /vóltə, vóltə/ river in SE Ghana, emptying into the Atlantic Ocean. Length 930 mi./1,500 km.

volt·age /vóltij/ *n* electric potential expressed in volts

Vol·taire /vōl táir, vol-/ (1694–1778) French writer and philosopher

volte-face /váwlt faáss, vàwlt-/ *n* 1 a sudden reversal of opinion 2 a change in position to face the opposite direction

volt·me·ter /vólt meètər/ *n* an instrument that measures voltage

vol·u·ble /vóllyab'l/ *adj* talking a great deal —**vol·u·bil·i·ty** /vòllyə bíllətee/ *n* —**vol·u·bly** *adv*

vol·ume /vóllyəm, -yòòm/ *n* 1 loudness of sound 2 (*symbol* **V**) the three-dimensional space inside or occupied by an object 3 a sound control on something such as a television 4 a total amount 5 a book 6 one of a set of books 7 a set of consecutive magazine issues spanning one year ■ *adj* involving large quantities

vo·lu·mi·nous /və lóomənəss/ *adj* 1 having great size, capacity, or fullness 2 taking up many pages or books —**vo·lu·mi·nous·ly** *adv* —**vo·lu·mi·nous·ness** *n*

vol·un·tar·y /vóllən tèrree/ *adj* 1 acting or resulting from free will 2 done without pay or reward 3 controlled through conscious choices ■ *n* (*pl* -**ies**) 1 a short composition for a solo instrument 2 a short piece of church music —**vol·un·tar·i·ly** /vòllən térrəlee, vòllan tèrrəlee/ *adv*

vol·un·teer /vóllən teèr/ *n* 1 somebody who works without pay 2 somebody who does something voluntarily ■ *v* 1 *vi* offer to do military service 2 *vti* offer free help 3 *vti* do something by choice 4 *vt* give something such as information or an opinion without being asked

~~voluptious~~ incorrect spelling of **voluptuous**

vo·lup·tu·ar·y /və lúpchoo èrree/ (*pl* -**ies**) *n* somebody who enjoys the pleasures of the senses

vo·lup·tu·ous /və lúpchoo əss/ *adj* 1 sensual 2 devoted to a life of sensual pleasure —**vo·lup·tu·ous·ly** *adv* —**vo·lup·tu·ous·ness** *n*

vom·it /vómmit/ *vti* **1** expel stomach contents through the mouth **2** gush or cause to gush forth ■ *n* **1** expelled stomach contents **2** an act of vomiting

von, Von see also under surname

von Braun /von brówn/, **Wernher** (1912–77) German rocket engineer

von Neu·mann /von nóy maàn/, **John** (1903–57) Hungarian-born US mathematician. He developed game theory and quantum mechanics, and was a pioneer in computer theory and design.

von Stern·berg /von stúrn bùrg/, **Josef** (1894–1969) Austrian-born US movie director

von Stro·heim /von stró hìm/, **Erich** (1885–1957) Austrian-born US actor and movie director

voo·doo /vóō dòo/ *n* (*pl* **-doos**) **1** a Caribbean religion that involves supposed communication with ancestors **2** a practitioner of voodoo **3** a supposedly magic charm or spell used in voodoo ■ *vt* (**voo·dooed, voo·doo·ing, voo·doos**) cast a spell on

VOR *abbr* very-high-frequency omnidirectional radio range

vo·ra·cious /vaw ráyshəss, və-/ *adj* **1** very hungry **2** especially eager or insatiable —**vo·ra·cious·ly** *adv* —**vo·ra·cious·ness** *n* —**vo·rac·i·ty** /vaw rássətee, və-/ *n*

Vo·ro·nezh /və ráwnish/ city in W Russia. Pop. 1,084,734 (1995).

vor·tex /váwr tèks/ (*pl* **-tex·es** *or* **-ti·ces** /-tə sèez/) *n* **1** a whirling mass of water or air **2** a situation or feeling that engulfs everything else

Vosges /vózh/ mountain range in NE France. Length 120 mi./190 km. Highest peak Grand Ballon 4,672 ft./1,424 m.

vo·ta·ry /vótəree/ (*pl* **-ries**), **vo·ta·rist** /-rist/ *n* **1** a monk or nun **2** a devotee

vote *n* **1** a formal choice for or against, e.g., in an election or referendum **2** the act of casting a vote **3** the number of votes cast in an election **4** the right to cast a vote **5** the outcome of an election **6** the opinion expressed by a particular group ■ *v* (**vot·ed, vot·ing**) **1** *vti* indicate a formal preference **2** *vt* cast a vote for or against somebody ○ *was voted out of office* **3** *vt* make something available or create something by vote ○ *refused to vote additional funds for the new building* **4** *vt* indicate an opinion *(infml)* —**vot·er** *n*

vo·tive /vótiv/ *adj* **1** symbolizing a wish **2** fulfilling a vow —**vo·tive·ly** *adv*

vouch /vowch/ *vi* provide supporting evidence ○ *testimony that vouches for the defendant's credibility*

vouch·er /vówchər/ *n* **1** a substitute for money used for making purchases **2** a piece of documentary evidence **3** somebody or something that guarantees or provides proof

vouch·safe /vòwch sáyf, vówch sàyf/ (**-safed, -saf·ing**) *vt* (*fml*) **1** condescend to give some-

thing, e.g., a reply **2** promise, agree, or allow something

vow *n* a solemn pledge, e.g., one of the promises made by a bride and groom or by somebody joining a religious order ■ *v* **1** *vt* promise solemnly **2** *vti* dedicate somebody to something

vow·el /vów əl/ *n* a speech sound in which the air passes through the oral tract relatively unobstructed

⚡**vox·el** /vóksəl, vók sèl/ *n* a three-dimensional pixel

voy·age /vóy ij/ *n* a long journey, especially by sea or through space ■ *vti* (**-aged, -ag·ing**) go on a voyage —**voy·ag·er** *n*

voy·eur /voy yúr, vwaà yúr/ *n* **1** somebody who watches others for sexual pleasure **2** a fascinated observer of misery or scandal —**voy·eur·ism** *n* —**voy·eur·is·tic** /vòy yə rístik, vwaà yə-/ *adj*

VP, V.P. *abbr* vice president

⚡**VR** *abbr* virtual reality

⚡**VRML** *n* a computer-graphics programming language. Full form **Virtual Reality Modeling Language**

vs. *abbr* versus

V sign, V-sign *n* a victory sign made with the index and middle fingers in which the palm faces outward

V/STOL *abbr* vertical and short takeoff and landing

VT, Vt. *abbr* Vermont

VTOL /veé tàwl/ *n* full form **vertical takeoff and landing**

Vul·can /vúlkən/ *n* in Roman mythology, the god of fire. Greek equivalent **Hephaestus** —**Vul·ca·ni·an** /vul káynee ən/ *adj*

vul·gar /vúlgər/ *adj* **1** crude or indecent **2** tastelessly showy **3** lacking courtesy and manners **4** spoken by ordinary people —**vul·gar·ly** *adv*

vul·gar·i·an /vul gérree ən/ *n* a wealthy but tasteless or ostentatious person

vul·gar·ism /vúlgə rìzzəm/ *n* **1** a crude term **2** a term in ordinary people's language

vul·gar·i·ty /vul gárrətee/ (*pl* **-ties**) *n* **1** the quality of being vulgar **2** a crude or indecent remark or act

vul·gar·ize /vúlgə rìz/ (**-ized, -iz·ing**) *vt* **1** make less refined or of lower quality **2** present in a more accessible way —**vul·gar·i·za·tion** /vúlgəri záysh'n/ *n*

vul·gate /vúl gàyt, -gət/ *n* **1** ordinary speech **2 Vul·gate** a Latin version of the Bible authorized for use by Roman Catholics

vul·ner·a·ble /vúlnərəb'l/ *adj* **1** open to physical or emotional danger or harm **2** exposed to attack or damage **3** easily persuaded or tempted **4** physically or psychologically weak —**vul·ner·a·bil·i·ty** /vùlnərə bíllətee/ *n* —**vul·ner·a·bly** *adv*

vul·pine /vúl pìn/ *adj* **1** of or like a fox **2** having a trait attributed to foxes, especially cunning

vul·ture /vúlchər/ n 1 a large bird of prey that feeds on carrion 2 a person who waits to exploit somebody vulnerable

vul·va /vúlvə/ (pl **-vae** /-vee/ or **-vas**) n the external female genitals —**vul·val** adj —**vulvar** adj

vy·ing present participle of **vie**

W

w (pl **w's**), **W** (pl **W's** or **Ws**) n the 23rd letter of the English alphabet

W[1] symbol 1 tungsten 2 watt 3 weight 4 work

W[2] abbr 1 West 2 Western

w. abbr 1 week 2 width 3 with

w/ abbr with

⚡**W3** abbr World Wide Web

WA abbr Washington (State)

Wa·bash /wáw bàsh/ river in the north central United States, rising in W Ohio and emptying into the Ohio River in Indiana. Length 512 mi./824 km.

WAC[1] /wak/ (pl **WACs**) n a member of the WAC

WAC[2] abbr Women's Army Corps

wack·y /wákee/ (**-i-er, -i-est**), **whack·y** /wákee, hwákee/ adj 1 an offensive term meaning unconventional or unpredictable (slang) 2 entertainingly silly (infml) —**wack·i·ly** adv —**wack·i·ness** n

Wa·co /wáykō/ city in central Texas. Pop. 108,272 (1998).

wad /wod/ n 1 a small rounded mass of soft material used for packing or stuffing 2 a roll or small bundle of paper money 3 a rounded compressed lump of soft material, especially tobacco or gum 4 a plug or disk holding the powder or shot in a gun or cartridge ■ v (**wad·ded, wad·ding**) 1 vti compress or be compressed tightly 2 vt stuff or plug with wadding

wad·ding /wódding/ n 1 a soft protective material used in packaging 2 material for holding powder or shot in a gun or cartridge

wad·dle /wódd'l/ (**-dled, -dling**) vi walk with short steps and a side-to-side gait —**waddle** n —**wad·dly** adj

wade (**wad·ed, wad·ing**) v 1 vti walk in or through deep water or mud 2 vi get through something with difficulty o wading through the paperwork that had accumulated in her absence —**wad·a·ble** adj —**wade** n

□ **wade in** vti interrupt forcefully

wad·ers /wáydərz/ npl high waterproof boots or combined boots and trousers worn for fishing

wa·di /wáädee/ (pl **wa·dis** or **wa·dies**), **wa·dy** (pl **-dies**) n 1 a steep-sided watercourse through which water flows only after heavy rain 2 an oasis

wad·ing bird n a long-legged bird that stands in water to hunt for food

wad·ing pool n a shallow pool for children

⚡**wa·fer** /wáyfər/ n 1 a thin crisp cookie 2 a thin disk of unleavened bread used in the Christian Communion service 3 a slice of semiconducting material used as a base for an integrated circuit

wa·fer-thin adj extremely thin

waf·fle[1] /wóff'l/ n a thick light crisp pancake with a pattern of indentations on both sides

waf·fle[2] /wóff'l/ (**-fled, -fling**) vi be indecisive (infml) —**waf·fly** adj

waf·fle iron n an appliance for cooking waffles

waft /woft/ vti move gently through the air ■ n 1 something such as a scent carried on the air 2 a light breeze

wag[1] (**wagged, wag·ging**) vti move a body part rapidly to and fro, or be moved in this way —**wag** n

wag[2] n somebody witty (infml) —**wag·gish** adj

wage n a payment for work done on an hourly, daily, weekly, or piece-rate basis (often pl) ■ vt (**waged, wag·ing**) engage in a war or fight —**wage·less** adj

SYNONYMS wage, salary, pay, fee, remuneration, emolument, honorarium, stipend
CORE MEANING: money given for work done

wage earn·er n 1 somebody who supports a household by earning money 2 somebody who is paid wages

wage in·cen·tive n an additional amount of money paid for improved productivity

wa·ger /wáyjər/ n 1 a bet on an outcome in which the loser pays the winner a specific amount 2 an amount bet in a wager ■ vt bet money on an outcome

wag·gle /wágg'l/ (**-gled, -gling**) vti move rapidly back and forth —**wag·gle** n —**wag·gly** adj

Richard Wagner

Wag·ner /vaàgnər/, **Richard** (1813–83) German composer —**Wag·ner·i·an** /vaag neéree ən/ adj, n

wag·on /wággən/ n 1 a rectangular wheeled vehicle for carrying heavy loads, often pulled by an animal or tractor 2 a truck for selling or delivering goods 3 a police vehicle for transporting suspects or criminals **4** a child's four-wheeled cart with a long handle for pulling or steering —**wag·on·er** n ◇ **circle the wagons** take a defensive position *(infml)*

wag·on train n a line of covered wagons traveling cross-country

Wah·ha·bi /wɒ haàbee, waa-/ *(pl* -**bis**), **Wa·ha·bi** n a member of a very conservative Islamic group that rejects any innovation that occurred after the 3C of Islam —**Wah·ha·bism** n

wa·hi·ne /waa heénee, -nay/ n Hawaii, NZ a Hawaiian or Maori woman

waif /wayf/ n **1** somebody homeless or friendless, especially an abandoned child **2** a stray animal

Wai·ki·ki /wī kee keè/ beach resort on S Oahu Island, Hawaii

wail /wayl/ v **1** vti make a mournful cry, or utter something in this way **2** vi make a long high-pitched noise —**wail** n —**wail·er** n

> **SPELLCHECK** Do not confuse the spelling of **wail** and **whale** ("marine mammal"), which sound similar.

wain·scot /wáynskət, -skòt/ n a set of wooden panels lining the walls of a room ■ vt (-**scot·ed** or -**scot·ted**, -**scot·ing** or -**scot·ting**) cover a wall with paneling

waist /wayst/ n **1** the part of the body between the ribs and the hips **2** the part of a garment covering the waist **3** the middle part of something —**waist·ed** adj

> **SPELLCHECK** Do not confuse the spelling of **waist** and **waste** ("use carelessly"), which sound similar.

waist·band /wáyst bànd/ n a band of fabric circling the waist of a garment

waist·coat /wáyst kòt/ n UK, ANZ a vest for wearing over a shirt —**waist·coat·ed** adj

waist·line /wáyst lìn/ n **1** the measurement of somebody's waist **2** the point at which the bodice and skirt of a dress meet

wait /wayt/ vi **1** do nothing for a period of time, expecting something to happen **2** stop so that somebody can catch up **3** be postponed ○ *Fame would just have to wait.* **4** be ready or available for somebody ■ n a time spent waiting

> **SPELLCHECK** Do not confuse the spelling of **wait** and **weight** ("heaviness"), which sound similar.

□ **wait on** vt **1** serve somebody by bringing requested items **2** serve somebody with food and drink at a table

Waite /wayt/, **Morrison Remick** (1816–88) chief justice of the US Supreme Court (1874–88)

wait·er /wáytər/ n **1** somebody who brings food and drink to people at tables **2** a tray for carrying dishes or serving food

wait·ing game n a tactic whereby somebody waits for a situation to improve in his or her favor

wait·ing list n a list of people waiting for something that is not immediately available

wait·ing room n a room for people to wait in

wait·ress /wáytrəss/ n a woman who brings food and drink to people at tables

wait·staff /wáyt stàf/ n people serving in a restaurant

⨍ **wait state** n a period of time during which a CPU sits idle while a slower component functions

waive /wayv/ (**waived, waiv·ing**) vt **1** surrender a right or claim voluntarily **2** not enforce or apply something

> **SPELLCHECK** Do not confuse the spelling of **waive** and **wave** ("of the sea, of a hand"), which sound similar.

waiv·er /wáyvər/ n a formal statement relinquishing a right or claim

wake¹ v (**woke** or **waked, wok·en** /wókən/ or **waked, wak·ing**) **1** vti come or bring out of a state of sleep **2** vti become or make aware of something **3** vi hold a vigil over a corpse **4** vi be or stay awake ■ n **1** a watch kept over a corpse **2** a social gathering held after a funeral

wake² n **1** the track left in water by a vessel moving through it **2** the stream of turbulence in the air behind a moving aircraft or land vehicle **3** a position or the area behind somebody or something moving

wake·board·ing /wáyk bàwrding/ n a sport in which somebody standing on a board is pulled behind a boat to perform jumps in its wake —**wake·board** vi —**wake·board·er** n

wake·ful /wáykfəl/ adj **1** not sleeping **2** passed without sleep ○ *a wakeful night* —**wake·ful·ly** adv —**wake·ful·ness** n

Wake Is·land /wáyk-/ group of three islets constituting a coral atoll in the central Pacific Ocean, a territory of the United States. Pop. 126 (1997).

wak·en /wáykən/ vti rouse or be roused from sleep or inertia

wake-up call n **1** a telephone call to awaken a hotel guest **2** a frightening experience taken as a sign that a major change is needed

Wal·cott /wáwl kòt/, **Derek** (b. 1930) St. Lucian writer.

Wal·dorf sal·ad /wáwl dawrf-/ n a salad made with apples, celery, walnuts, and mayonnaise

Wales /waylz/ principality in Great Britain, part of the United Kingdom. Cap. Cardiff. Pop. 2,933,000 (1998).

walk /wawk/ v **1** vi move on foot at a moderate pace **2** vt travel along a path or through a place on foot **3** vt take an animal for exercise by walking **4** *vt* accompany somebody on foot to a particular place **5** *vt* help or force somebody to walk **6** *vti* in baseball, go or allow the batter to go to first base after four balls ■ *n* **1** a journey made on foot, especially for pleasure or exercise **2** the distance or time of a journey on foot **3** the slowest gait of a horse **4** a particular way of walking **5** a place or route for people walking **6** in baseball, reaching first base on four balls —**walk·a·ble** *adj* ◊ **walk all over 1** ignore the rights or feelings of **2** defeat easily

☐ **walk out** *vi* go on strike

walk·a·way /wáwkə wày/ *n* an easy victory *(slang)*

walk·er /wáwkər/ *n* **1** somebody who walks **2** a support for a baby learning to walk **3** a four-legged framework for somebody who cannot walk without support

Wal·ker /wáwkər/, **Alice** (*b.* 1944) US writer

walk·ie-talk·ie /wáwkee táwkee/, **walk·y-talk·y** (*pl* **walk·y-talk·ies**) *n* a hand-held radio transmitter and receiver

walk-in *adj* **1** large enough to enter ○ *a walk-in closet* **2** having direct access from the street ■ *n* **1** a cold storage room **2** an easy victory

walk·ing /wáwking/ *adj* **1** able to walk **2** used or designed for walking

walk·ing pa·pers *npl* formal notice of discharge *(infml)*

walk·ing stick *n* **1** a stick that assists in walking **2** a long brown or green insect resembling a twig

walk·ing wound·ed *npl* **1** casualties who can walk **2** people who continue to be affected by emotional trauma

walk-on *n* **1** a small nonspeaking part in a play or movie **2** somebody with a walk-on part

walk·out /wáwk òwt/ *n* **1** an organized strike in which workers leave the premises **2** a departure in protest or anger

walk·o·ver /wáwk òvər/ *n* an easy victory *(infml)*

walk-through *n* a rehearsal of a play without costumes or props, or of a television program without cameras

walk-up *n* **1** a building without an elevator *(infml)* **2** an apartment reached by stairs

walk·way /wáwk wày/ *n* a specially built path for pedestrians

wall /wawl/ *n* **1** a flat side of a building or room **2** a narrow upright structure, usually of stone or brick, that acts as a boundary or keeps something in or out **3** a physical or psychological obstacle **4** a lining or covering for something such as a body cavity, organ, or cell **5** in soccer, a line of defensive players trying to block a shot on goal ■ *vt* surround, separate, or close with a wall —**walled** *adj* ◊ **be climbing the wall** *or* **walls** be extremely bored or frustrated *(infml)* ◊ **drive somebody up the wall** annoy or irritate somebody to an extreme degree *(infml)* ◊ **hit a brick wall** encounter an insurmountable difficulty

wal·la·by /wólləbee/ (*pl* **-bies**) *n* an Australian marsupial like a small kangaroo

Wal·lace /wólliss/, **Alfred Russel** (1823–1913) British naturalist

Wal·lace, Henry A. (1888–1965) US agriculturalist and vice president (1941–45)

wall·board /wáwl bàwrd/ *n* plaster sandwiched between two layers of strong paper, used for covering interior walls

wall·chart /wáwl chàart/ *n* a chart designed to be displayed on a wall to provide information or help in teaching

ƒ **wal·let** /wóllət/ *n* **1** a small flat folding leather or plastic case for paper money and credit cards **2** a software program for making online purchases

wall·flow·er /wáwl flòwr/ *n* **1** a spring-flowering garden plant **2** somebody shy who remains unnoticed at a social event *(infml)*

wall hang·ing *n* a tapestry or other large flat object hung on a wall as a decoration

Wal·lis and Fu·tuna Is·lands /wólliss ənd foo tóonə-/ island group in the SW Pacific Ocean, an overseas territory of France. Cap. Mata Utu. Pop. 15,435 (2001).

Wal·loon /wo lóon, wə-/ *n* **1** a member of a French-speaking people of S Belgium **2** the French dialect of the Walloons

wal·lop /wólləp/ *(infml)* *vt* strike very hard ■ *n* a hard hit

wal·low /wólló/ *vi* **1** roll in mud or water **2** indulge yourself ■ *n* **1** an act of wallowing **2** a place where animals roll in mud or water

wall·pa·per /wáwl pàypər/ *n* decorative paper pasted on walls —**wall·pa·per** *vti*

Wall Street *n* the street in New York City where many major US financial institutions are located, or the US financial markets

wall-to-wall *adj* **1** completely covering a floor **2** completely filling, covering, or pervading something *(infml)*

wal·nut /wáwl nùt, -nət/ *n* **1** a wrinkled edible nut in a hard shell **2** a light ornamental wood. Use: cabinetmaking, paneling, veneers. **3** a tree that produces walnuts and walnut wood

---

ORIGIN Walnut means etymologically "foreign nut." The prehistoric Germanic peoples regarded the **walnut** as "foreign" because it did not originally grow in N Europe but was introduced from France and Italy.

---

wal·rus /wáwlrəss/ (*pl same or* **-rus·es**) *n* an Arctic sea mammal like a seal with large tusks and bristly whiskers

wal·rus mus·tache *n* a thick drooping mustache resembling a walrus's whiskers

Wal·ton /wáwltən/, **Izaak** (1593–1683) English writer

waltz /wawlts/ n (pl **waltz·es**) 1 a ballroom dance in triple time for couples 2 the music for a waltz ■ v (**waltz·es**) 1 vti dance or lead somebody in a waltz 2 vi move in a relaxed confident manner (infml)

Wam·pa·no·ag /wòmpə nố ag/ (pl same or -ags) n a member of an Algonquian people who lived in Rhode Island and Massachusetts —**Wam·pa·no·ag** adj

wam·pum /wómpəm/, **wam·pum·peag** /-pèeg/ n decorative beads formerly used as money by some Native North Americans

wan /won/ (**wan·ner, wan·nest**) adj 1 unhealthily pale 2 indicative of ill health or low spirits —**wan·ly** adv —**wan·ness** n

⚡**WAN** abbr wide-area network

wand /wond/ n 1 a thin rod with supposed magical powers 2 a thin staff carried as a symbol of office

wan·der /wóndər/ v 1 vti travel around without a purpose or destination 2 vi stray from a path or course 3 vi lose the ability to concentrate or pay attention ○ My mind was wandering. 4 vi follow a winding course 5 vi stroll somewhere 6 vi fail to think or speak coherently ■ n an aimless or leisurely act of moving from place to place —**wan·der·er** n —**wan·der·ing** adj —**wan·der·ing·ly** adv

---

SPELLCHECK Do not confuse the spelling of **wander** and **wonder** ("speculate about something," "be amazed by something"), which may sound similar.

---

wan·der·lust /wóndər lùst/ n a desire to travel

wane /wayn/ vi (**waned, wan·ing**) 1 show a decreasing illuminated surface (refers to the Moon or a planet) 2 decrease gradually in intensity or power ■ n 1 a gradual decrease in intensity or power 2 the time during which the Moon is waning

wan·gle /wáng g'l/ (infml) vt (-**gled, -gling**) 1 get something deviously 2 falsify accounts or records ■ n a devious method of getting something —**wan·gler** n

wan·na·be /wónnəbee/ n somebody emulating somebody else (infml disapproving)

want /wont/ vt 1 desire something ○ wants a new car 2 desire to do something or that something be done ○ wants his steak well done 3 wish to see or speak to somebody ○ You're wanted on the phone. 4 seek somebody as a suspect in a crime ○ want them for murder 5 need something (infml) ○ The closets want cleaning. ■ n 1 something desired or needed (usually pl) 2 a lack of something 3 poverty —**want·ed** adj

---

SYNONYMS want, desire, wish, long, yearn, covet, crave CORE MEANING: seek to have, do, or achieve

---

□ **want for** vt lack

want ad n a classified advertisement (infml)

want·ing /wónting/ adj lacking ■ prep missing something necessary ○ a chair wanting one leg ■ adj unsatisfactory ○ found their writing skills wanting

wan·ton /wóntən/ adj 1 sexually unrestrained 2 done without reason or provocation 3 done out of a desire to cause harm 4 excessive ■ n somebody without sexual restraint —**wan·ton·ly** adv —**wan·ton·ness** n

⚡**WAP** /wap/ n a standard protocol for data transmission between handheld wireless devices such as cellphones and the Internet or other networks. Full form **wireless application protocol**

wap·i·ti /wóppitee/ n (pl -**tis** or same) n a large deer with long antlers

war /wawr/ n 1 an armed conflict between countries or groups 2 a period of armed conflict 3 the techniques of armed conflict 4 a serious struggle, argument, or conflict 5 a sustained effort to end something harmful ○ the war on crime ■ vi (**warred, war·ring**) engage in war ◊ See note at **fight**

~~waranty~~ incorrect spelling of **warranty**

war·ble /wáwrb'l/ vti (-**bled, -bling**) sing a song or note with trills or modulations ■ n 1 the act of warbling 2 a warbling sound

war·bler /wáwrblər/ n 1 a brightly colored American songbird 2 a dull-colored songbird of Europe and Asia 3 somebody who warbles

war bride n a woman who marries a serviceman in wartime, especially one from another country

war chest n funds set aside for a war or campaign

war crime n a crime committed during a war in violation of international agreements on the conduct of warfare (often pl) —**war crim·i·nal** n

war cry n a battle cry

ward /wawrd/ n 1 an administrative or electoral division of an area 2 a room for patients in a hospital 3 a prison division 4 a child or young person under the care of a guardian or court 5 custody or protection —**ward·er** n

□ **ward off** vt 1 repel a blow or attack 2 avert something bad

-ward, -wards suffix 1 in a particular direction, or toward a particular place ○ homeward 2 lying or occurring in a particular direction ○ windward

war dance n a ceremonial dance performed before or after a battle

war·den /wáwrd'n/ n 1 a principal prison officer 2 an official responsible for enforcing regulations 3 a churchwarden —**war·den·ship** n

ward heel·er n a political lackey (infml)

ward·robe /wáwrd ròb/ n **1** a large closet or cupboard with a rail or shelves for clothes **2** all of somebody's clothes **3** a collection of clothes for a particular season or purpose

ward·robe mis·tress n a woman in charge of costumes in a theater or on a movie set

ward·room /wáwrd ròòm, -ròòm/ n a room on a warship used by all the officers except the captain

ware /wair/ n **1** similar things or things made of the same material ○ *flatware* **2** ceramics of a particular kind or made by a particular manufacturer ■ **wares** npl **1** things for sale **2** marketable skills

SPELLCHECK Do not confuse the spelling of **ware**, **wear** (clothing), and **where** ("in or to a place"), which sound similar.

ware·house n /wáir hòwss/ (pl **-hous·es** /-hówzəz/) a large building for storing goods or raw materials ■ vt /wáir hòwz, -hòwss/ (**-housed** /-hòwzd/, **-hous·ing** /-hòwzing/, **-hous·es** /-hòwzəz/) store in a warehouse —**ware·house·man** /-hòwssmən/ n —**ware·hous·er** n

ware·hous·ing /wáir hòwzing/ n the stock-piling of a security in order to force the price up as a result of the reduced supply

~~warf~~ incorrect spelling of **wharf**

war·fare /wáwr fàir/ n **1** the waging of a war **2** conflict or struggle

war·fa·rin /wáwrfərin/ n a colorless crystalline compound. Use: rat poison, anticoagulant in medicine.

war·fight·ing /wáwr fìting/ n the conducting of war —**war·fight·er** n

war game n **1** a military exercise **2** a game using model soldiers and equipment to re-enact a battle

war-game (**war-gamed**, **war-gam·ing**) v **1** vi be in a war game **2** vt test military strategy —**war-gam·er** n

war·head /wáwr hèd/ n the destructive material carried by a bomb, missile, rocket, or torpedo

AKG London

Andy Warhol

War·hol /wáwr hàwl, -hòl/, **Andy** (1928–87) US artist

war·horse /wáwr hàwrs/ n **1** a horse ridden in battle **2** a survivor of many conflicts (infml)

war·like /wáwr lìk/ adj **1** hostile **2** of war

war·lock /wáwr lòk/ n a male sorcerer

war·lord /wáwr làwrd/ n a powerful military leader not controlled by a government —**war·lord·ism** n

ORIGIN One of the first uses of **warlord** was by the poet Ralph Waldo Emerson in 1856. The term began to appear in the US and UK press with frequency during the late 1800s, referring to Kaiser Wilhelm II, emperor of Germany and king of Prussia (1888–1918). One of his many titles was the German word *Kriegsherr*, translated literally as "war man." English-speaking writers decided to translate this as "warlord," thereby causing it to become a household word.

warm /wawrm/ adj **1** moderately hot **2** providing heat or protection against cold **3** having or feeling too much heat **4** friendly **5** passionate **6** enthusiastic **7** describes a color suggesting warmth **8** describes a scent in hunting that is fresh and strong ■ v **1** vti make or become warm **2** vt make cheerful or happy **3** vi become enthusiastic ○ *warming to the idea* —**warm·ish** adj —**warm·ly** adv —**warm·ness** n

□ **warm up** vi prepare for strenuous exercise by performing gentle exercise

war ma·chine n the military resources with which a country can fight a war

warm-blood·ed adj with a constant body temperature independent of the environment —**warm-blood·ed·ness** n

⚡ **warm-boot** /wáwrm bòòt/ vt restart a computer without switching it off

warm-heart·ed adj having or showing a kind nature —**warm-heart·ed·ly** adv —**warm-heart·ed·ness** n

war·mon·ger /wáwr mùng gər, -mòng-/ n somebody eager for war —**war·mon·ger·ing** n

warmth /wawrmth/ n **1** a warm state, quality, or feeling **2** affection **3** a moderate amount of heat

warm-up n an act or period of warming up before strenuous exercise

warn /wawrn/ v **1** vti tell somebody about something that might cause injury or harm **2** vt tell somebody about something in advance **3** vt advise somebody against something potentially risky ○ *were warned against complacency*

SPELLCHECK Do not confuse the spelling of **warn** and **worn** (past participle of *wear*), which sound similar.

warn·ing /wáwrning/ n **1** a threat or a sign that something bad is going to happen **2** advice to be careful or stop doing something ■ adj meant to warn —**warn·ing·ly** adv

war of nerves n a psychological conflict

warp /wawrp/ vti **1** twist out of shape ○ *warped wood* **2** turn or be turned from a usual or correct course or condition ○ *warped judgment* ■ n **1** a distortion of the shape of something **2** a perversion of mind or character **3** the threads running lengthwise on a loom or a piece of fabric —**warp·age** n

war paint n paint for decorating warriors before a battle

war·path /wáwr pàth/ n formerly, a route taken by Native North Americans on the way to war ◊ **on the warpath** angry and in the mood for a confrontation (infml)

war·rant /wáwrənt/ n **1** an authorization **2** a certifying document **3** a document authorizing the police to do something **4** an option to buy stock at a later date and at a fixed price ■ vt **1** serve as a reason to do, believe, or think something **2** guarantee something such as the truth, accuracy, or dependability of something or somebody **3** authorize somebody —**war·rant·er** n

war·rant of·fi·cer n an officer in the US Army, Navy, Air Force, or Coast Guard of a rank above noncommissioned officer

war·ran·ty /wáwrəntee/ (pl **-ties**) n **1** a guarantee on purchased goods **2** a condition in an insurance contract in which the insured person guarantees that something is the case **3** a justification or authorization

war·ren /wáwrən/ n **1** a group of connected rabbit burrows **2** a building or area that is crowded or has a complicated layout

War·ren /wáwrən/, **Earl** (1891–1974) chief justice of the US Supreme Court (1953–69)

War·ren, Robert Penn (1905–89) US author and poet

~~warrent~~ incorrect spelling of **warrant**

war·ring /wáwring/ adj in conflict

war·ri·or /wáwree ər/ n somebody who fights or is experienced in warfare

War·saw /wáwr sàw/ capital of Poland. Pop. 1,632,500 (1997).

war·ship /wáwr ship/ n an armored ship for use in war

wart /wawrt/ n a small growth on the skin caused by a virus —**wart·y** adj ◊ **warts and all** including any flaws or disadvantages

wart hog n a wild hog with tusks and warty growths on its face

war·time /wáwr tìm/ n a period when a war is being fought

war-torn adj disrupted by war

War·wick /wáwr wik/ city in E Rhode Island on Narragansett Bay. Pop. 84,094 (1998).

war·y /wáiree/ (**-i·er, -i·est**) adj cautious —**war·i·ly** adv —**war·i·ness** n ◊ See note at **cautious**

was past tense of **be** (with I, he, she, it, and sing nouns)

wash /wosh/ v **1** vt clean something, e.g., clothes, with water and usually soap **2** vti remove or be removed by washing **3** vi clean yourself by washing **4** vi be washable **5** vt flow over something **6** vt move something along on water **7** vi be convincing (infml) ◊ That story won't wash. ■ n **1** an act of washing **2** a quantity of clothes washed or

to be washed **3** a lotion, antiseptic, or cosmetic applied to the skin **4** a flow of water against a surface **5** Southwest US a dry stream bed **6** a thin layer of color applied with a brush **7** a surge of disturbed water or air from an oar, propeller, or jet engine

□ **wash down** vt follow something drunk or eaten with another drink

□ **wash out** v **1** vt clean the inside of something **2** vti remove or be removed by washing

□ **wash up** vi wash the face and hands

Wash. abbr Washington

wash·a·ble /wóshəb'l/ adj capable of being washed without being damaged

wash·ba·sin /wósh bàyss'n/ n a basin for washing the face and hands or small articles

wash·board /wósh bàwrd/ n **1** a ridged board for rubbing clothes on when washing them **2** a ridged board used as a musical instrument to produce a scratching sound

wash·cloth /wósh klàwth/ n a cloth for washing the body

wash·day /wósh dày/ n a day for washing clothes

washed-out adj **1** faded **2** exhausted

washed-up adj not likely to be successful again (infml)

wash·er /wóshər/ n **1** a small ring for keeping a screw secure or preventing leakage at a joint **2** a washing machine or dishwasher **3** somebody who washes

wash·er·wom·an /wóshər wòommən/ (pl **-en** /-wìmmin/) n a woman paid to wash clothes

wash·ing /wóshing/ n **1** clothes that have been or are to be washed **2** the process of washing clothes

wash·ing ma·chine n a machine for washing clothes

wash·ing so·da n sodium carbonate crystals. Use: washing and cleaning.

Wash·ing·ton /wóshingtən/ **1** state of the NW United States. Cap. Olympia. Pop. 5,894,121 (2000). **2** also **Wash·ing·ton, D.C.** capital of the United States. The city of Washington has the same boundaries as the District of Columbia, a federal territory. Pop. 523,124 (1998). —**Wash·ing·to·ni·an** /wòshing tṓnee ən/ n, adj

Wash·ing·ton, Booker T. (1856–1915) US educator

George Washington

Wash·ing·ton, George (1732–99) 1st president of the United States (1789–97)

wash-out /wósh òwt/ n 1 a complete failure (infml) 2 erosion caused by running water

wash-room /wósh room, -rõom/ n 1 a room in a public place with a toilet and washing facilities 2 a public toilet (euphemistic)

wash-stand /wósh stand/ n a stand for a basin and pitcher for washing the face and hands

wash-tub /wósh tùb/ n a container for washing clothes

was-n't /wúzz'nt, wózz'nt/ contr was not

wasp /wosp/ n a black-and-yellow striped stinging winged insect

Wasp /wosp/, **WASP** n an offensive term for a white person from an Anglo-Saxon Protestant background (infml) —**Wasp-y** adj

wasp-ish /wóspish/, **wasp-y** /wóspee/ (-i-er, -i-est) adj 1 of wasps 2 easily irritated —**wasp-ish-ness** n

was-sail /wóss'l, wó sàyl/ (archaic) n 1 a salutation or toast made during festivities 2 a festive occasion at which people drink a great deal 3 mulled wine or ale drunk on a festive occasion ■ vi drink in celebration —**was-sail-er** n

wast-age /wáystij/ n 1 an amount wasted 2 loss caused through use, wear, decay, or leakage

waste /wayst/ v (**wast-ed, wast-ing**) 1 vt use carelessly or ineffectively 2 vt fail to make use of 3 vti become or make weaker or more ill 4 vt destroy ■ n 1 the careless or ineffective use of something 2 unwanted or unusable byproducts 3 liquid or solid matter excreted from the body after digestion 4 a wild area (often pl) 5 a destroyed area 6 garbage or trash ■ adj 1 useless or not needed 2 unproductive or uncultivated 3 excreted from the body after digestion —**wast-er** n ◊ See note at **waist**

waste-bas-ket /wáyst bàskət/, **waste-pa-per bas-ket** n a container for trash, especially paper

wast-ed /wáystəd/ adj 1 not used 2 useless 3 withered

waste-ful /wáystfəl/ adj 1 extravagant 2 causing waste or devastation —**waste-ful-ly** adv —**waste-ful-ness** n

waste-land /wáyst lànd/ n 1 a desolate area 2 an intellectually or spiritually barren place or time

waste-pa-per /wáyst pàypər/ n paper that is not needed and has been thrown away

waste pipe n a pipe carrying waste liquid from a sink or bath

wast-rel /wáystrəl/ n a person regarded as wasteful, extravagant, or lazy (insult)

watch /woch/ n 1 a small clock worn on the wrist or kept in a pocket 2 the act or a period of observing or guarding something 3 a fixed period of a day spent on duty on a ship 4 the members of a ship's crew on duty at one time ■ v 1 vti look carefully at

something 2 vi keep a lookout 3 vti monitor something or somebody —**watch-er** n

□ **watch over** vt look after or guard

watch-a-ble /wóchəb'l/ adj 1 observable 2 enjoyable to watch

watch-band /wóch bànd/ n US, Can, Aus a wristwatch strap

watch-dog /wóch dàwg/ n 1 a dog for guarding property or people 2 a person or organization guarding against undesirable practices ■ vti (**-dogged, -dog-ging**) be a watchdog over something

watch-ful /wóchfəl/ adj observing closely —**watch-ful-ly** adv —**watch-ful-ness** n

watch-mak-er /wóch màykər/ n somebody who makes or repairs watches

watch-man /wóchmən/ (pl **-men** /-mən/) n somebody employed to guard a building or area

watch-tow-er /wóch tòw ər/ n an observation tower for a guard to observe prisoners or for a lookout to watch for enemies or fires

watch-word /wóch wùrd/ n 1 a slogan 2 a password

wa-ter /wáwtər/ n 1 the liquid that falls as rain and forms lakes, rivers, and seas 2 an area of water 3 the surface of an area of water 4 a solution of a particular chemical or substance in water ◇ lavender water 5 a watery body fluid such as tears or urine 6 fluid surrounding a fetus (often pl) 7 a lustrous wavy pattern on a fabric such as silk ■ **wa-ters** npl 1 a particular area of sea 2 a naturally occurring water containing minerals ■ v 1 vt sprinkle or soak something with water 2 vt irrigate crops or land 3 vti give an animal water for drinking, or get water for drinking 4 vi fill with tears when irritated (refers to eyes) 5 vi produce saliva (refers to the mouth) 6 vt give a lustrous wavy pattern to a fabric such as silk —**wa-ter-less** adj ◇ **be dead in the water** have no chance of success or survival ◇ **be water under the bridge** be in the past and impossible to alter ◇ **hold water** be well-founded ◇ **in hot water** in trouble ◇ **muddy the waters** cause confusion ◇ **pour** or **throw cold water on** or **onto** discourage a plan or idea ◇ **tread water** maintain the status quo, but make no progress

□ **water down** vt 1 dilute 2 reduce the difficulty or offensiveness of —**wa-tered-down** adj

Wa-ter Bear-er n the zodiacal sign Aquarius

wa-ter bed n a bed with a water-filled mattress

wa-ter bird n a bird living near water

wa-ter bis-cuit n a thin plain cracker

wa-ter-borne /wáwtər bàwrn/ adj transported or transmitted by water

wa-ter buf-fa-lo n a large buffalo used for haulage and milk in Southeast Asia

wa·ter can·non n an apparatus producing a high-pressure jet of water, used for controlling crowds

Wa·ter Car·ri·er n the zodiacal sign Aquarius

wa·ter chest·nut n 1 a round white crunchy underground stem. Use: in Asian cooking. 2 a Chinese sedge plant that is the source of water chestnuts

wa·ter clos·et n a small room containing a toilet

wa·ter·col·or /wáwtər kùllər/ n 1 a painting made with pigments mixed with water 2 a pigment or pigments mixed with water (often pl) —**wa·ter·col·or·ist** n

wa·ter cool·er n a drinking-water dispenser

wa·ter·course /wáwtər kàwrss/ n 1 a natural or artificial channel for flowing water 2 the water flowing along a watercourse

wa·ter·craft /wáwtər kràft/ (pl same) n a boat or ship (fml)

wa·ter·cress /wáwtər krèss/ n a water plant with peppery leaves and stems. Use: salads, soups, garnish.

wa·ter·fall /wáwtər fàwl/ n a vertical flow of water falling over the edge of a steep place

wa·ter·fowl /wáwtər fòwl/ n (pl same or -fowls) any bird that swims on water ■ npl swimming game birds considered collectively

wa·ter·front /wáwtər frùnt/ n 1 the part of a town lying alongside a body of water 2 the land beside a body of water

wa·ter gate n 1 a floodgate 2 a gate leading into an area of water

Wa·ter·gate /wáwtər gàyt/ n 1 a 1972 US political scandal that led to President Nixon's resignation 2 a political scandal and attempted cover-up

ORIGIN The 1972 scandal began with a break-in at the US Democratic National Committee headquarters in the Watergate complex in Washington, D.C. **Watergate** has lent its second syllable *-gate* to the formation of numerous names for other subsequent scandals, domestic and foreign.

wa·ter hole n a water-filled hollow where animals drink

wa·ter hy·a·cinth n a water plant with glossy rounded leaves and blue flowers

wa·ter ice n a frozen dessert of sweet-flavored ice

wa·ter·ing can n a container with a handle and a spout for watering plants

wa·ter·ing hole n 1 a bar (infml) 2 also **wa·ter·ing place** a water hole

wa·ter lev·el n the height of the surface of a body of water

wa·ter lil·y n a water plant with floating leaves

wa·ter line n 1 a line on the hull of a ship indicating the level to which it can sink in the water 2 the line to which a body of water rises

wa·ter·logged /wáwtər làwgd/ adj saturated with water —**wa·ter·log** vt

Wa·ter·loo[1] /wáwtər lòò, wótər-/ town in central Belgium, site of Napoleon's defeat by British and Prussian forces on June 18, 1815. Pop. 28,111 (1995).

Wa·ter·loo[2] /wáwtər lòò, wàwtər lòò/ (pl -loos), **wa·ter·loo** n a defeat

wa·ter main n a large underground pipe bringing water

⚡ **wa·ter·mark** /wáwtər màark/ n 1 a hidden mark in paper visible when the paper is held up to the light 2 a line left by water 3 an embedded pattern of bits in a data file used in detecting unauthorized copies ■ vt put a watermark in paper

wa·ter·mel·on /wáwtər mèllən/ n 1 a large round green fruit with sweet juicy pink flesh and black seeds 2 a plant that produces watermelons

wa·ter me·ter n a device for recording the amount of water passing through pipes

wa·ter mill n a mill with water-powered machinery

wa·ter moc·ca·sin n a venomous snake with a brownish back and black bars that lives partly on land, partly in water

wa·ter pipe n 1 a pipe for conveying water 2 a pipe for smoking something such as marijuana in which the smoke is cooled by being drawn through water

wa·ter pis·tol n a squirt gun

wa·ter po·lo n a game played in a swimming pool by two teams trying to score points by sending a large ball into the opposing team's goal

wa·ter pow·er n electric power generated by the force of water

wa·ter·proof /wáwtər pròòf/ adj impervious to water —**wa·ter·proof** vt

Wa·ters /wáwtərz/, **Muddy** (1915–83) US blues guitarist and singer

wa·ter·shed /wáwtər shèd/ n 1 the region draining into a particular river, lake, or ocean 2 a long ridge separating watersheds 3 a major turning point

wa·ter·side /wáwtər sìd/ n the land beside an area of water ■ adj living, working, or located beside an area of water

wa·ter·ski /wáwtər skèe/ (-skied, -ski·ing, -skis) vi ski over water while being towed by a boat —**wa·ter ski** n —**wa·ter·ski·er** n —**wa·ter·ski·ing** n

wa·ter slide n a chute for sliding down into a swimming pool

wa·ter soft·en·er n an apparatus or a chemical for reducing the hardness of water

wa·ter·sol·u·ble adj dissolvable in water

wa·ter sports npl sports played on or in water

wa·ter ta·ble *n* the upper surface of ground water, below which pores in the rocks are filled with water

wa·ter·tight /wáwtər tìt/ *adj* 1 keeping water in or out 2 standing up to scrutiny ○ *a watertight argument* —**wa·ter·tight·ness** *n*

wa·ter tow·er *n* 1 a water storage tower 2 a firefighting apparatus for lifting hoses

wa·ter va·por *n* water in vapor form, but below boiling point

wa·ter·way /wáwtər wày/ *n* a river or canal used by boats

wa·ter wings *npl* inflatable arm supports for somebody learning to swim

wa·ter·works /wáwtər wùrks/ *n* 1 the system for supplying water to a community or area (+ *sing or pl verb*) 2 tears (*infml*; + *pl verb*)

wa·ter·y /wáwtəree/ *adj* 1 of or containing water 2 having excessive water 3 filled with tears 4 lacking force or intensity —**wa·ter·i·ness** *n*

Wat·son /wóts'n/, **James D.** (*b.* 1928) US biochemist. With Francis H. Crick and Maurice Wilkins he discovered the structure of DNA (1953).

Wat·son, Thomas J., Jr. (1914–93) US computer industry executive

watt /wot/ *n* (*symbol* **W**) the SI unit of electrical power equal to the power produced by a current of one ampere acting across a potential difference of one volt

Watt /wot/, **James** (1736–1819) British inventor

watt·age /wóttij/ *n* electrical power measured in watts

Wat·teau /wo tó, vaa-/, **Jean-Antoine** (1684–1721) French painter

wat·tle /wótt'l/ *n* 1 stakes interwoven with branches, used for walls, fences, and roofs 2 a loose fold of skin hanging from the throat or cheek of a bird or lizard —**wat·tled** *adj*

Waugh /waw/, **Evelyn** (1903–66) British novelist

⚡**wav** /wav/ *abbr* a file extension indicating a sound file

wave /wayv/ *v* (**waved, wav·ing**) 1 *vti* move the hand repeatedly from side to side or up and down as a greeting, farewell, or signal 2 *vti* move repeatedly in the air from side to side or up and down 3 *vt* direct somebody or something by waving 4 *vti* curl slightly ■ *n* 1 a moving ripple on a liquid or ocean 2 a waving of the hand 3 a line curving in alternating directions 4 an undulating motion 5 a sudden occurrence of repeated events ○ *a heat wave* 6 a sudden overwhelming feeling 7 an advancing or incoming group of people 8 a loose curve in the hair 9 an oscillation of energy traveling through a medium ○ *sound waves* ◊ **make waves** cause a disturbance or trouble ◊ See note at **waive**

wave·band /wáyv bànd/ *n* a range of radio transmission frequencies

⚡**wave file** *n* a computer file containing digitized sound waves

wave·form /wáyv fàwrm/ *n* a representation of the shape of a wave

wave·length /wáyv lèngth/ *n* 1 (*symbol* λ) in physics, the distance between two points on adjacent waves that have the same phase, e.g., the distance between two consecutive peaks or troughs 2 the wavelength of the radio wave used by a broadcasting station ◊ **be on the same wavelength** have the same opinions, attitudes, or tastes

wa·ver /wáyvər/ *vi* 1 fluctuate between possibilities or be indecisive 2 begin to change your opinion 3 move in one way and then another in an irregular pattern 4 tremble or flicker —**wa·ver** *n* —**wa·ver·ing·ly** *adv* ◊ See note at **hesitate**

wav·y /wáyvee/ (-i·er, -i·est) *adj* 1 forming a series of wave shapes 2 moving like a wave 3 describes hair with soft curves —**wav·i·ly** *adv* —**wav·i·ness** *n*

wax¹ *n* 1 a naturally occurring greasy substance 2 a wax preparation for polishing ■ *vt* 1 polish something with wax 2 remove unwanted hair from part of the body with wax —**wax·er** *n*

wax² *vi* 1 appear with a larger illuminated surface each night (*refers to the Moon or a planet*) 2 increase (*literary*) 3 talk about something in a particular way (*literary*) ○ *waxed lyrical*

wax bean *n* a yellow variety of string bean

wax·en /wáks'n/ *adj* 1 like wax 2 made of wax 3 pale and unhealthy-looking

wax·work /wáks wùrk/ *n* 1 a wax model of somebody 2 the art of using wax for modeling

wax·y /wáksee/ (-i·er, -i·est) *adj* 1 like wax 2 covered with or full of wax —**wax·i·ness** *n*

way /way/ *n* 1 a means, manner, or method of doing something ○ *I'll do it my way.* 2 a feature, aspect, or example ○ *In some ways, they're very similar.* 3 a particular state or condition ○ *He's in a bad way.* 4 something somebody wants to happen or to do ○ *always wants his own way* 5 a tradition, custom, or habit 6 a path or route from one place to another 7 a door or opening ○ *came in the front way* 8 a journey ○ *on my way home* 9 progress 10 a direction or position 11 space for action ○ *got out of the way* 12 a particular area or district (*infml*) ○ *out our way* 13 a distance away in space or time ○ *a long way off* 14 an extent or amount ■ *adv* 1 to a considerable degree or at a considerable distance (*infml*) ○ *way out of our price range* 2 very (*slang*) ◊ **by the way** incidentally ◊ **by way of** as a means of or for the purpose of ◊ **every which way** 1 in all directions 2 in every way possible (*infml*)

◇ **give way** become useless, break, or otherwise fail ◇ **go out of your way** do more than is usual or necessary ○ *went out of his way to welcome us* ◇ **have a way with** be good at dealing with ◇ **have it both ways** have the benefits of opposing situations or actions ◇ **in a big way** to a great degree or with great enthusiasm *(infml)* ◇ **in a way** from a certain point of view

SPELLCHECK Do not confuse the spelling of **way**, **weigh** ("find the weight of"), and **whey** ("watery part of milk"), which sound similar.

way·far·er /wáy fàirǝr/ *n* a traveler on foot *(literary)* —**way·far·ing** *n, adj*

way·lay /wáy lày/ (**-laid** /-làyd/) *vt* **1** lie in wait or ambush for **2** stop or accost

Wayne /wayn/, **Anthony** (1745–96) American soldier

John Wayne

Wayne, John (1907–79) US actor

-ways *suffix* in a particular direction or position ○ *sideways*

way·side /wáy sìd/ *n* the side of a road ■ *adj* situated at the side of a road ◇ **fall by the wayside** fail to continue or complete something

way sta·tion *n* **1** a small railroad station **2** a stopping place on a route

way·ward /wáywǝrd/ *adj* **1** willful or disobedient **2** erratic or unpredictable —**way·ward·ly** *adv* —**way·ward·ness** *n* ◇ See note at **unruly**

W.C. *n* a toilet. Full form **water closet**

we /wee/ *pron* **1** refers to the speaker or writer and one or more others *(1st person pl personal pronoun, used as the subject of a verb)* ○ *We're going on vacation.* **2** refers to all people or people in general ○ *We're getting closer to the election.* **3** used instead of "I" by a speaker or writer to include the listener or reader ○ *We will now consider the causes of the war.*

USAGE we or us? When **we** or **us** accompanies a noun, use **we** if the pronoun is the subject, **us** if the pronoun is the object of a verb or preposition: *We* [not *us*] *trainees have to stick together*; *For us* [not *we*] *trainees, there are many opportunities.*

weak /week/ *adj* **1** not physically or mentally strong **2** easily defeated or beaten **3** lacking strength of character **4** not powerful or intense **5** lacking particular skills or abilities ○ *weak*

in math **6** watery or tasteless ○ *weak tea* **7** unconvincing ○ *a weak argument* **8** describes a syllable or word that is not stressed or accented —**weak·en** *vti*

SPELLCHECK Do not confuse the spelling of **weak** and **week** ("a period of seven days"), which sound similar.

SYNONYMS weak, feeble, frail, infirm, debilitated, decrepit, enervated CORE MEANING: lacking physical strength or energy

weak·kneed *adj* easily persuaded or intimidated

weak·ling /weekling/ *n* a person regarded as weak

weak·ly /weeklee/ *adj* (**-li·er, -li·est**) sickly ■ *adv* without strength or force —**weak·li·ness** *n*

weak·mind·ed *adj* easily persuaded *(disapproving)* —**weak·mind·ed·ly** *adv* —**weak·mind·ed·ness** *n*

weak·ness /weeknǝss/ *n* **1** a lack of strength or determination **2** a weak point or flaw in something **3** a character flaw **4** a fondness for something

weak·willed *adj* lacking strong will

weal /weel/ *n* a raised reddened area on the skin

wealth /welth/ *n* **1** a large amount of money or possessions **2** the state of having wealth **3** an abundance of something

wealth·y /wélthee/ *adj* (**-i·er, -i·est**) *adj* **1** having a large amount of money or possessions **2** enjoying an abundance of something —**wealth·i·ly** *adv* —**wealth·i·ness** *n*

wean /ween/ *v* **1** *vti* start to give a baby or young animal food other than its mother's milk **2** *vt* stop somebody from having or doing something habitual or pleasurable

weap·on /wéppǝn/ *n* **1** a device designed to injure or kill somebody **2** something used to gain an advantage —**weap·oned** *adj*

weap·on·ize /wéppǝ nìz/ (**-ized, -iz·ing**) *vt* process chemical, nuclear, or biological material so that it can be deployed as a weapon —**weap·on·i·za·tion** /wèppǝni záysh'n/ *n*

weap·on of mass de·struc·tion *n* a weapon, typically nuclear, biological, or chemical, that causes overwhelming devastation and loss of life

weap·on·ry /wéppǝnree/ *n* weapons considered collectively

weap·ons-grade *adj* describes plutonium, uranium, or other material in a form suitable for manufacturing weapons

wear /wair/ *v* (**wore, worn**) **1** *vt* have something on the body, e.g., as clothing, decoration, or protection **2** *vt* display an expression on the face ○ *wearing a smile* **3** *vti* damage by using or rubbing, or be damaged in this way **4** *vt* produce a hole by using or rubbing **5** *vti* rub off or away **6** *vti* tire out **7** *vi* last in the same condition despite much use ○ *The* *carpet's wearing well.* **8** *vti* pass slowly ○ *as the evening wore on* ■ *n* **1** the act of wearing something **2** damage from being used or rubbed **3** the ability to last despite much use **4** clothing of a particular kind *(often in combination)* —**wear·er** *n* ◇ **the worse for wear** in a poor condition because of much use ◇ **wear thin** become unacceptable or implausible because of excessive use ○ *That excuse is beginning to wear a little thin.* ◇ See note at **ware**

☐ **wear down** *vti* overcome or be overcome gradually

☐ **wear off** *vi* lose effectiveness gradually

☐ **wear out** *v* **1** *vti* use something until it is no longer usable, or become useless through long use **2** *vt* exhaust somebody

⚡**wear·a·ble com·put·er** /wáirəb'l-/ *n* a small computer worn on the body

wear and tear /-táir/ *n* damage caused by use over a period of time

wear·ing /wáiring/ *adj* tiring —**wear·ing·ly** *adv*

wea·ri·some /weéreessəm/ *adj* tiring and tedious —**wea·ri·some·ly** *adv* —**wea·ri·some·ness** *n*

wea·ry /weéree/ *adj* (**-ri·er**, **-ri·est**) **1** tired **2** tiring ■ *vti* (**-ried**, **-ries**) become or make tired, bored, or impatient —**wea·ri·ly** *adv* —**wea·ri·ness** *n* —**wea·ry·ing** *adj*

wea·sel /weéz'l/ (*pl* **-sels** *or* same) *n* **1** a small brown furry mammal with a long body **2** somebody regarded as sly or underhanded (*infml insult*) —**wea·sel·ly** *adj*

weath·er /wéthər/ *n* **1** the state of the atmosphere with regard to conditions such as temperature, wind, or precipitation **2** bad weather ■ *adj* used in weather forecasting ■ *v* **1** *vt* come safely through a crisis **2** *vi* endure the damaging effects of the weather **3** *vti* expose or be exposed to the weather **4** *vti* change in color or texture because of exposure to the weather

> **SPELLCHECK** Do not confuse the spelling of **weather** and **whether** (indicating an alternative), which may sound similar.

weath·er·beat·en *adj* damaged or worn by exposure to the weather

weath·er·board /wéthər bàwrd/ *n* a clapboard or clapboards

weath·er·bound /wéthər bòwnd/ *adj* delayed or stopped by bad weather

weath·er bu·reau *n* an agency that collects meteorological information and provides weather forecasts

weath·er·cock /wéthər kòk/ *n* **1** a weather vane shaped like a rooster **2** somebody changeable or fickle

weath·er fore·cast *n* a broadcast announcing weather conditions —**weath·er fore·cast·er** *n* —**weath·er fore·cast·ing** *n*

weath·er·ize /wéthə rìz/ (**-ized**, **-iz·ing**) *vt* protect something against cold weather

weath·er·proof /wéthər pròof/ *adj* able to withstand bad weather —**weath·er·proof** *vt*

weath·er ship *n* a ship collecting meteorological data

weath·er sta·tion *n* a meteorological observation post

weath·er·strip /wéthər strìp/ (**-stripped**, **-strip·ping**) *vt* put weather stripping around a door or window

weath·er strip·ping *n* protective material around a door or window to keep out wind, rain, and cold

weath·er vane *n* a device mounted on a roof that turns to show the direction of the wind

weath·er·worn /wéthər wàwrn/ *adj* worn by exposure to the weather

weave[1] /weev/ *v* (**wove** /wōv/ *or* **weaved**, **wo·ven** /wōvən/ *or* **weaved**, **weav·ing**) **1** *vti* make cloth by interlacing vertical and horizontal threads **2** *vt* make something by interlacing strands **3** *vti* spin a web **4** *vt* construct a story by combining separate parts ■ *n* the way in which something is woven —**weav·er** *n*

weave[2] /weev/ (**weaved**, **weav·ing**) *vi* move forward in a zigzag course

⚡**web** *n* **1** a structure woven by a spider to catch its prey **2** a complex network ○ *a web of interconnecting wires* ○ *a web of deceit* **3** a membrane of skin between the toes of a bird or amphibian **4** a piece of woven fabric **5** *also* **Web** the World Wide Web (*infml*) —**webbed** *adj*

web·bing /wébbing/ *n* **1** a strong coarse fabric. Use: belts, harnesses, upholstery support. **2** the membrane of skin between a bird's or amphibian's toes

⚡**web brows·er** *n* a program for displaying and using pages on the World Wide Web

⚡**web bug** *n* a minute inclusion in a webpage or e-mail message designed to record information about the person reading it

⚡**web·cam** /wéb kàm/ *n* a video camera recording pictures that are broadcast live on the Internet

⚡**web·cast** /wéb kàst/ *n* a broadcast on the World Wide Web —**web·cast·ing** *n*

⚡**web crawl·er** *n* a program for searching through pages on the World Wide Web for documents containing a particular topic or set of words

⚡**web-en·a·ble** *vt* make a device such as a cellphone capable of accessing the Internet —**web·en·a·bled** *adj*

We·ber /váybər/, **Carl Maria von** (1786–1826) German composer

We·ber, Max (1864–1920) German economist and sociologist

Web·er /wébbər/, **Max** (1881–1961) Russianborn US artist

We·bern /váybərn/, **Anton Friedrich Wilhelm von** (1883–1945) Austrian composer

↯ **web·li·og·ra·phy** /wèbblee óggrəfee/ (*pl* **-phies**) *n* **1** a list of specific documents available on the World Wide Web **2** a list or catalog of all the web-based material relating to a specific subject

↯ **web·lish** /wébblish/ *n* the form of English used online

↯ **web·log** /wéb lòg/ *n* a frequently updated personal journal on a website, intended for public viewing

↯ **web·mas·ter** *n* a creator or maintainer of a website

↯ **web·page** /wéb pàyj/ *n* a computer file encoded in HTML and providing text and graphics, accessible through the World Wide Web

↯ **web·phone** /wéb fòn/ *n* a phone that uses the Internet to make connections and carry voice messages

↯ **web ring** *n* a series of interlinked websites visited one after the other until the first is reached again

↯ **web serv·er** *n* a program that provides webpages when requested by a client

↯ **web·site** /wéb sìt/ *n* a group of related webpages, or a program providing access to them

Web·ster /wébstər/, **Daniel** (1782–1852) US lawyer and secretary of state (1841–43 and 1850–52)

Web·ster, John (1578?–1632?) English playwright

Web·ster, Noah (1758–1843) US lexicographer

↯ **web·zine** /wéb zeèn/ *n* a website with magazine-style content and layout

wed /wed/ (**wed·ded** *or* **wed, wed·ding**) *v* **1** *vt* get married to somebody (*fml or literary*) ○ *wanted to wed a princess* **2** *vi* get married ○ *They wed in April.* **3** *vt* join a couple in marriage **4** *vt* unite two things

we'd /weed/ *contr* **1** we had **2** we would

Wed. *abbr* Wednesday

wed·ded /wéddəd/ *adj* **1** married **2** of marriage **3** committed to something ○ *wedded to the idea of reform*

wed·ding /wédding/ *n* **1** a marriage ceremony **2** the anniversary of a wedding (*in combination*)

wed·ding band, wed·ding ring *n* a band worn on the third finger of the left hand by somebody who is married

wed·ding dress *n* the dress worn by a bride at her wedding

wed·ding march *n* a piece of music played at a wedding when the bride enters

~~Wedensday~~ incorrect spelling of **Wednesday**

wedge *n* **1** a tapering solid block used to secure or separate two objects **2** a wedge-shaped object ○ *a wedge of cake* **3** something that acts like a wedge, e.g., by causing division ○ *drove a wedge between the two families* ■ *v* (**wedged, wedg·ing**) **1** *vt* force apart

with a wedge **2** *vt* secure with a wedge **3** *vti* squeeze into a small space —**wedg·y** *adj*

wed·lock /wéd lòk/ *n* the married state

ORIGIN Wedlock is not etymologically something people are "locked" into. The original form was *wedlac*, formed from *wed* "pledge" and a suffix meaning "action, proceedings."

Wednes·day /wénz dày, -deè/ *n* the 3rd day of the week

ORIGIN Wednesday is named for Woden (Odin), the chief Germanic god. The Latin equivalent meant "Mercury's day."

~~Wednsday~~ incorrect spelling of **Wednesday**

wee /wee/ *adj* small

weed[1] *n* **1** a wild plant growing where it is not wanted **2** a plant growing in water, especially seaweed **3** marijuana for smoking as a drug (*slang*) ■ *vti* remove weeds from the ground —**weed·er** *n*
□ **weed out** *vt* separate out undesirable elements

weed[2] *n* something worn as a sign of mourning ■ **weeds** *npl* a widow's black clothes (*literary*)

weed·kill·er /weéd kìllər/ *n* a chemical used to destroy weeds

weed·y /weèdee/ (**-i·er, -i·est**) *adj* **1** full of weeds **2** like a weed —**weed·i·ness** *n*

week /week/ *n* **1** a period of seven consecutive days **2** a calendar week of seven days beginning on a specific day, usually Sunday **3** the days of the week spent working ○ *goes to bed early during the week* ◊ See note at **weak**

week·day /weék dày/ *n* a day other than Saturday or Sunday

week·end /weék ènd/ *n* the period from Friday evening to Sunday evening ■ *vi* spend the weekend somewhere

week·end·er /weék èndər/ *n* **1** somebody spending a weekend somewhere **2** a small suitcase

week·long /weék làwng/ *adj* lasting a week

week·ly /weèklee/ *adj* **1** happening once a week **2** calculated by the week ○ *weekly pay* ■ *adv* **1** once a week **2** every week **3** by the week ■ *n* (*pl* **-lies**) a newspaper or magazine published once a week

week·night /weék nìt/ *n* the evening or night of a weekday

weep (**wept**) *v* **1** *vi* shed tears **2** *vti* leak fluid

weep·ie /weèpee/ *n* a sentimental movie, play, or book (*infml*)

weep·ing /weèping/ *adj* **1** with drooping branches ○ *a weeping birch* **2** shedding tears —**weep·ing·ly** *adv*

weep·ing wil·low *n* a willow tree with drooping branches

weep·y /weèpee/ (**-i·er, -i·est**) *adj* **1** inclined to weep (*infml*) **2** moving people to tears —**weep·i·ly** *adv*

wee·vil /wéev'l/ n 1 a destructive beetle with a snout 2 a beetle whose larvae live in the seeds of peas and beans —**wee·vi·ly** adj

weft n 1 the horizontal threads on a loom or piece of fabric 2 yarn used for the weft

weigh /way/ v 1 vt find out the weight of somebody or something 2 vi be a particular weight 3 vt measure or distribute something by weight 4 vt evaluate something o weighing my options 5 vi have importance o Her advice weighs heavily with him. 6 vi be burdensome o weighs on his mind 7 vti raise the anchor of a vessel ◊ See note at **way**

□ **weigh down** vt 1 oppress 2 burden or press down

□ **weigh in** vi 1 be weighed for a race or contest 2 have baggage weighed before a flight 3 contribute a comment (infml)

weigh-in n the weighing of a competitor before or after a race or contest

weight /wayt/ n 1 the heaviness of somebody or something 2 a system of standard measures for establishing the heaviness of somebody or something 3 (symbol W) the vertical force experienced by a mass because of gravity 4 a unit used as a measure of weight 5 a heavy object used to hold something down 6 a mental or moral burden 7 a heavy load to carry 8 importance or significance 9 the greater part of something 10 a heavy object used in weightlifting (often pl) 11 the thickness of cloth ■ vt add weight or weights to —**weight·ed** adj ◊ **pull your weight** do your fair share ◊ **throw your weight around** be domineering ◊ See note at **wait**

weight·less /wáytləss/ adj weighing nothing, especially because of being in a gravity-free environment —**weight·less·ly** adv —**weight·less·ness** n

weight·lift·ing /wáyt lìfting/ n the sport of lifting heavy objects such as dumbbells for exercise or in competition —**we'ght·lift·er** n

weight train·ing n physical training using weights to strengthen muscles

weight·y /wáytee/ (-i·er, -i·est) adj 1 heavy 2 important 3 influential —**weight·i·ly** adv —**weight·i·ness** n

~~weild~~ incorrect spelling of **wield**

weir /weer/ n 1 a dam across a river to regulate or change the flow of water 2 a barricade in a stream for catching fish

weird /weerd/ adj strange or unusual —**weird·ly** adv —**weird·ness** n

weird·o /wéerdō/ n an offensive term for a person regarded as strange or unconventional (slang)

Weiz·mann /víts màan, wítsmən/, **Chaim** (1874–1952) Russian-born chemist and first president of modern Israel (1949–52)

welch vi = **welsh**

Welch, Jack (b. 1936) US business executive

wel·come /wélkəm/ adj 1 received or accepted gladly o a welcome gift 2 freely invited or

permitted o You're welcome to stay for dinner. 3 having no obligation in return o You're welcome, it was no trouble. ■ n 1 a greeting or reception given to somebody on arrival 2 a particular reaction to something o received the proposal with a cautious welcome ■ vt (-comed, -com·ing) 1 greet or receive somebody in a polite or friendly way 2 accept something with pleasure ■ interj expresses a friendly or polite greeting to somebody on arrival —**wel·come·ly** adv —**wel·come·ness** n —**wel·com·er** n

wel·come mat n a doormat with the word "welcome" on it

✦ **wel·come page** n a website's opening page

wel·com·ing /wélkəming/ adj providing a warm and friendly greeting —**wel·com·ing·ly** adv

weld vti join pieces of metal or other material by heating, hammering, or pressure, or be joined in this way ■ n a joint formed by the fusion of pieces —**weld·er** n

wel·fare /wél fàir/ n 1 physical, social, or financial well-being 2 government financial aid and other benefits given to people in need ■ adj 1 aiding people in need 2 receiving government financial aid because of poverty or unemployment

wel·fare state n a political system or nation in which the government assumes responsibility for the welfare of citizens

well[1] n 1 a hole made in the ground to draw up water, petroleum, or natural gas 2 a spring of water 3 a source of a free and abundant supply of something 4 a container or sunken area for holding ink or another liquid 5 a vertical passage in a building, often used for stairs or elevators ■ v 1 vti rise or bring to the surface 2 vi surge from within o Fear welled up inside me. 3 vi become filled with liquid o My eyes welled with tears.

well[2] adv 1 efficiently, satisfactorily, or desirably o The presentation went very well. 2 ethically, properly, or courteously o treated us very well 3 skillfully or expertly o plays tennis really well 4 with justice and good reason o couldn't very well refuse 5 in ease and comfort o lives well 6 advantageously o married well 7 in a way that promotes good health and physical well-being o Mother and baby are doing well. 8 considerably o well past midnight 9 fully and thoroughly o stirring the mixture well 10 familiarly and intimately o knew him well ■ adj (bet·ter /béttər/, best) 1 mentally and physically healthy o I hope you're well. 2 proper or appropriate 3 satisfactory o Is everything well with you? o I had the impression that all was not well. ■ interj 1 expresses an emotion such as surprise, indignation, or approval o Well! Here you are at last! 2 introduces a comment or resumes a conversation o Well, it looks as if we'll be waiting a while. ◊ **as well** in addition ◊ **as well as** to an equal degree or extent ◊ **that's** *or* **it's (just) as well** it is fortunate

we'll /weel, wil/ *contr* 1 we shall 2 we will

well-ad·just·ed *adj* 1 successfully adapted to prevailing conditions 2 content with your own self and life and therefore emotionally stable

well-ad·vised *adj* acting prudently

Wel·land Ca·nal /wèllənd-/, **Wel·land Ship Ca·nal** canal system in Ontario, Canada, linking Lake Ontario and Lake Erie. It is part of the St. Lawrence Seaway. Length 28 mi./44 km.

well-ap·point·ed *adj* fully furnished or equipped

well-bal·anced *adj* 1 organized with all the parts in proportion 2 sensible and rational

well-be·haved *adj* behaving properly

well-be·ing *n* the state of being healthy, happy, and comfortable

well·born /wèl báwrn, wél bàwrn/ *adj* belonging to an aristocratic, respected, or wealthy family

well-bred *adj* 1 having or showing good manners 2 describes an animal with a desirable pedigree

well-built *adj* 1 physically big and strong 2 soundly constructed

well-cho·sen *adj* carefully selected

well-con·nect·ed *adj* with influential relatives or friends

well-de·fined *adj* 1 stated precisely and clearly 2 with a distinct outline or form

well-dis·posed *adj* sympathetic and likely to be helpful

well-done *adj* 1 performed correctly and well 2 cooked through

well-dressed *adj* wearing fashionable clothes

well-earned *adj* fully deserved as a result of hard work

Orson Welles

Welles /welz/, **Orson** (1915–85) US actor and director

well-es·tab·lished *adj* having been in existence long enough to become generally respected or successful

~~welfare~~ incorrect spelling of **welfare**

well-fed *adj* 1 with a good diet 2 overweight

well-found·ed *adj* supported by good reasons or solid evidence

well-groomed *adj* 1 taking care of your appearance 2 carefully cleaned, brushed, or tended

well-ground·ed *adj* familiar with all the essential details of a subject

well-heeled *adj* wealthy *(infml)*

well-in·formed *adj* having broad and detailed knowledge, especially of current affairs

Wel·ling·ton /wéllington/ capital of New Zealand, at the southern end of the North Island. Pop. 165,200 (1998).

Wel·ling·ton, Arthur Wellesley, 1st Duke of (1769–1852) British general and prime minister (1828–30)

well-in·ten·tioned *adj* intended or trying to help, but often producing a negative effect

well-kept *adj* 1 carefully tended 2 revealed to no one or to only a few people ◊ *a well-kept secret*

well-known *adj* 1 widely known 2 fully known or understood

well-man·nered *adj* polite and courteous

well-mean·ing *adj* intended or trying to help, but often producing a negative effect

well·ness /wélnəss/ *n* mental and physical health and well-being

well-nigh *adv* very nearly

well-off (**bet·ter-off, best-off**) *adj* fairly wealthy

well-oiled *adj* functioning smoothly

well-pre·served *adj* in good condition despite advanced age

well-read /-réd/ *adj* knowing much from reading widely

well-round·ed *adj* 1 with skills, experience, or achievements in many areas 2 comprehensive and varied

Wells, H. G. (1866–1946) British writer

Wells-Bar·nett /-baàrnət/, **Ida Bell** (1862–1931) US journalist and human rights campaigner

well-spo·ken *adj* 1 articulate and refined in speech 2 expressed appropriately

well·spring /wél spring/ *n* 1 the source of a spring or stream 2 a plentiful source of something

well-thought-of *adj* highly regarded

well-thought-out *adj* carefully planned

well-timed *adj* done at the right moment

well-to-do *adj* fairly wealthy

well-tried *adj* thoroughly tested and known to be reliable

well-turned *adj* 1 having a naturally graceful or attractive shape 2 skillfully expressed ◊ *a well-turned phrase*

well-wish·er *n* somebody expressing good wishes to somebody else —**well-wish·ing** *adj*, *n*

well-worn *adj* 1 showing signs of much wear 2 trite or hackneyed

welsh, welch *vi* an offensive term meaning fail to fulfill or honor an obligation —**welsh·er** *n*

Welsh *npl* the people of Wales ■ *n* a Celtic language spoken in Wales —**Welsh** *adj* —**Welsh·man** *n* —**Welsh·wom·an** *n*

Welsh rare·bit /-ráirbit/, **Welsh rab·bit** *n* a dish of melted cheese on toast

welt *n* 1 a ridge on the skin caused by a lash from a whip, scratch, or something similar 2 a strip sewn into a shoe between the upper and the sole to strengthen the seam 3 a reinforcement or decoration for a seam in a garment or pillow ■ *vt* beat somebody severely, especially with a whip

wel·ter /wéltər/ *n* 1 a confused mass of something 2 a confused condition ■ *vi* 1 wallow in something 2 lie soaked in liquid 3 be completely involved, absorbed, or entangled in something

wel·ter·weight /wéltər wàyt/ *n* 1 the weight category for boxers between lightweight and middleweight 2 a boxer who competes at welterweight

CORBIS/Philip Gould

Eudora Welty

Wel·ty /wéltee/, **Eudora** (1909–2001) US writer

wench *n* 1 a servant girl or young woman (*archaic*) 2 an offensive term for a young woman

wend *vti* travel or make one's way

went past tense of **go**[1]

wept past tense, past participle of **weep**

were past tense of **be**

we're /weer/ *contr* we are

were·n't /wurnt/ *contr* were not

were·wolf /wáir woolf, wúr-/ (*pl* **-wolves** /-woolvz/), **wer·wolf** (*pl* **-wolves**) *n* in folklore, a person who has been transformed into a wolf, or is capable of changing into a wolf

Wes·ley /wésslee, wéz-/, **John** (1703–91) British religious leader —**Wes·ley·an** *adj* —**Wes·ley·an·ism** *n*

Wes·sex /wéssiks/ ancient Anglo-Saxon kingdom in S England

west *n* 1 the direction in which the sun sets 2 the compass point opposite east 3 *also* **West** the part of an area or country that is in the west 4 *also* **West** the part of the United States west of the Mississippi River or west of the Allegheny Mountains 5 *also* **West** the countries of Europe and North and South America ■ *adj* 1 in the west 2 blowing from the west ■ *adv* toward the west —**west·bound** *adj*

West Af·ri·ca region in sub-Saharan W Africa, including Ghana and Nigeria

West Bank disputed territory in SW Asia, on the western bank of the Jordan River, bordered by Israel and Jordan. Pop. 2,090,713 (2001).

west·er·ly /wéstərlee/ *adj* 1 in the west 2 blowing from the west ■ *n* (*pl* **-lies**) a wind from the west —**west·er·ly** *adv*

west·ern /wéstərn/ *adj* 1 in the west 2 facing west 3 *also* **West·ern** of the west of a region or country 4 **West·ern** of or typical of Europe and the Americas, or their culture and society 5 **West·ern** characteristic of the US West in the early history of that nation ■ *n* **West·ern** a movie or novel set in the W United States, usually during the late 19C —**west·ern·most** *adj*

west·ern·er /wéstərnər/, **West·ern·er** *n* somebody from the west of a region or country

West·ern Front *n* a World War I battle line in W Europe

west·ern·ize /wéstər nìz/ (**-ized**, **-iz·ing**) *v* 1 *vti* adopt or cause to adopt Western customs 2 *vt* change to resemble Western practices —**west·ern·i·za·tion** /wèstərni záysh'n/ *n*

West·ern Sa·ha·ra disputed region in NW Africa

West·ern Sa·mo·a former name for **Samoa**

West Ger·ma·ny former republic of W Europe, now the western part of Germany —**West Ger·man** *n*, *adj*

West In·dies /-índeez/ former name for the islands of the Caribbean —**West In·di·an** *adj*, *n*

West·ing·house /wésting hòwss/, **George** (1846–1914) US engineer and industrialist

West·pha·lia /west fáylyə, -fáylee ə/ former province in NE Germany —**West·pha·lian** *n*, *adj*

West Point *n* the Military Academy at West Point, New York

West Vir·gin·ia state of the east central United States. Cap. Charleston. Pop. 1,808,344 (2000). —**West Vir·gin·ian** *n*, *adj*

west·ward /wéstwərd/ *adj* in the west ■ *n* a direction toward or point in the west ■ *adv* *also* **west·wards** toward the west —**west·ward·ly** *adv*, *adj*

wet *adj* 1 soaked or dampened with water or another liquid 2 not yet dry 3 not yet set o **wet** *concrete* 4 rainy, showery, misty, or foggy 5 allowing liquor sales (*infml*) ■ *n* 1 liquid or moisture 2 rainy or damp weather ■ *v* (**wet** *or* **wet·ted**, **wet·ting**) 1 *vti* make or become wet 2 *vt* make clothes or a bed wet by urinating accidentally —**wet·ly** *adv* —**wet·ness** *n* —**wet·tish** *adj*

wet blan·ket *n* a killjoy (*infml*)

wet·land /wét lànd/ *n* a swamp or marsh

wet look *n* a glossy sheen on material or the hair —**wet-look** *adj*

wet nurse *n* a woman who breast-feeds another person's baby

wet suit *n* a diver's tight-fitting rubber suit

we've *contr* we have

wf, w.f. *abbr* wrong font

whack /wak, hwak/ *vti* hit somebody or something with a loud sharp blow ■ *n* **1** a sharp blow **2** the sound of a sharp blow **3** an attempt *(slang)* ◊ **out of whack** not working properly *(infml)*

whacked /wakt, hwakt/ *adj* under the influence of drugs or alcohol *(slang)*

whack·y *adj* = **wacky**

whale¹ /wayl, hwayl/ *n* **1** a large ocean mammal with a blowhole on the top of its head, front flippers, and a flat horizontal tail **2** an impressive example *(infml)* ○ *a whale of a party* ■ *vi* (**whaled, whal·ing**) hunt whales —**whal·ing** *n* ◊ See note at **wail**

whale² /wayl, hwayl/ (**whaled, whal·ing**) *vt* **1** beat somebody physically **2** hit something forcefully

whale·bone /wáyl bṓn, hwáyl-/ *n* the bony plates in the mouths of some whales

whal·er /wáylər, hwáylər/ *n* **1** somebody who works in the whaling industry **2** a ship used to hunt or process whales

wham /wam, hwam/ *(infml)* *interj* represents the sound of a blow ■ *adv* suddenly and forcefully

wham·my /wámmee, hwámmee/ *(pl* -**mies**) *n* a jinx *(infml)*

whap *n, vt* = **whop**

wharf /wawrf, hwawrf/ *n* (*pl* **wharves** /wawrvz, hwawrvz/ *or* **wharfs**) a landing place for ships ■ *vt* unload or store cargo on a wharf

Edith Wharton

Whar·ton /wáwrt'n, hwáwrt'n/, **Edith** (1862–1937) US writer

what /wot, hwot/ *adj, pron* **1** requests information, e.g., about the identity or nature of something or somebody ○ *What time is it?* ○ *What are they doing?* **2** that which ○ *used what money they had* ○ *in what remains of the house* ■ *adj* adds emphasis ○ *What miserable weather!* ■ *adv* **1** in what respect or to what degree ○ *What does it matter?* **2** at a guess ○ *We've known each other for, what, ten years.* ■ *interj* expresses surprise, anger, or disappointment ◊ **what have you** other things similar to those just mentioned ◊ **what's**

what the true facts or actual situation *(infml)* ◊ **what with** because of

what-cha-ma-call-it /wòchəmə káwlit, hwòch-/ *n* something whose name has been forgotten or is not known *(infml)*

what-ev-er /wot évvər, hwot-/ *pron, adj* no matter what ■ *pron* an emphatic form of "what" ○ *Whatever is the matter now?* ■ *adj* of any kind

what-not /wót nòt, hwót-/ *n* **1** something of the same or a similar kind **2** a small lightweight set of shelves

what-so-ev-er /wòtsō évvər, hwòt-/ *adv* at all ○ *no water whatsoever* ■ *pron, adj* whatever *(fml)*

wheat /weet, hweet/ *n* **1** the edible seeds of a cereal plant, which are ground into flour **2** a cereal plant that produces wheat grains

wheat-en /wéet'n, hwéet'n/ *adj* made from wheat

wheat germ *n* the vitamin-rich center of a grain of wheat

Wheat-ley /wéetlee, hweét-/, **Phillis** (1753?–84) African-born US poet

whee-dle /wéed'l, hweéd'l/ (-**dled, -dling**) *v* **1** *vti* try to persuade somebody gently but persistently **2** *vt* obtain something by wheedling —**whee-dler** *n* —**whee-dling-ly** *adv*

wheel /weel, hweel/ *n* **1** a rotating round part or device *(often in combination)* **2** a round machine part that turns another **3** a steering wheel **4** a caster **5** something that resembles a wheel in shape or function **6** a turn or revolution **7** a movement in a circle ■ **wheels** *npl* **1** a car *(slang)* **2** the driving force or workings of something ■ *v* **1** *vti* move on wheels **2** *vt* transport somebody or something in a wheeled object **3** *vt* provide something with wheels **4** *vi* turn quickly **5** *vi* make a circular movement —**wheeled** *adj* ◊ **reinvent the wheel** waste time recreating something that already exists *(slang disapproving)* ◊ **wheel and deal** use complex and skillful, but sometimes slightly dishonest, negotiating techniques *(infml)*

wheel-bar-row /weél bàrrō, hweél-/ *n* a container with a wheel and handles that you push

wheel-base /weél bàyss, hweél-/ *n* the distance between the front and rear axles of a vehicle

wheel-chair /weél chàir, hweél-/ *n* a chair on wheels that somebody who cannot walk uses to move around

wheel-er-deal-er *n* a skilled but possibly dishonest operator *(infml)* —**wheel-er-deal-ing** *n*

wheel-house /weél hòwss, hweél-/ *(pl* -**hous-es** /-hòwzəz/) *n* the enclosure on a ship where the wheel or other steering device is housed

wheel-ie /weélee, hweélee/ *n* a bike rider's stunt on one wheel

wheel·wright /weel rìt, hweel-/ n somebody who makes or repairs wheels

wheeze /weez, hweez/ vi (**wheezed, wheez·ing**) breathe with a hoarse whistling sound ■ n 1 a noisy breathing sound 2 an often repeated joke (infml) —**wheez·i·ly** adv —**wheez·i·ness** n —**wheez·y** adj

whelk /welk, hwelk/ n (pl same or **whelks**) n a small ocean invertebrate animal with a conical shell

whelp /welp, hwelp/ n a young animal ■ vti bear young (refers to animals, especially carnivores)

when /wen, hwen/ conj 1 while ○ When we were in Los Angeles we enjoyed the fine weather. 2 as soon as ○ I'll do it when I can. 3 at a specific point ○ We got him when he was still a puppy. 4 each time ○ When I dial, I get a busy signal. 5 if ○ Why walk when you can ride? 6 although ○ They think I'm smart when I'm really not. ■ adv at or during which time ○ When did it happen? ■ n an unspecified time period (often pl) ○ We need to determine the whens and hows of this project.

whence /wenss, hwenss/ adv (literary) 1 from where ○ She returned whence she came. 2 from the place previously mentioned

when·ev·er /wen évvər, hwen-/ conj 1 at any time 2 at every time

when·so·ev·er /wènssō évvər, hwèn-/ adv, conj whenever (fml)

where /wair, hwair/ adv 1 in or to a place ○ Stay where you are. 2 asks about location, destination, origin, or purpose ○ Where will that attitude get you? ○ Where do they live? 3 in any situation in which ○ Where there's life, there's hope. ■ n an unknown place (usually pl) ○ The wheres of the proposed troop landings have yet to be decided. ◊ See note at **ware**

where·a·bouts /wáir ə bòwts, hwáir-/ adv in what place ■ n the location of somebody or something (+ sing or pl verb)

where·as /wair áz, hwair-/ conj 1 while on the other hand 2 because (fml) 3 connects a series of statements in legal documents (fml)

where·by /wair bí, hwair-/ adv by means of which

~~whereever~~ incorrect spelling of **wherever**

where·fore /wáir fàwr, hwáir-/ n a reason o the whys and wherefores of the issue ■ adv 1 therefore (fml) 2 for what reason (archaic)

where·in /wair ín, hwair-/ adv 1 in what specific way (fml) 2 where (archaic) o the land wherein they reside 3 during which (archaic)

where·of /wair óv, hwair-/ adv of what thing or person (fml)

where·so·ev·er /wàirssō évvər, hwàir-/ adv, conj wherever (fml)

where·to /wair tóo, hwair-/, **where·un·to** /-úntoo/ adv to which (fml)

where·up·on /wáirə pòn, hwàirə-/ conj at which point ○ The door opened, whereupon the guests entered the dining room.

wher·ev·er /wair évvər, hwair-/ conj 1 in, at, or to any place 2 every time or place that ■ adv 1 no matter where 2 at an unknown place 3 also **where ev·er** where indeed 4 also **where ev·er** an emphatic form of "where" ○ Wherever can it be?

where·with·al /wáirwith àwl, hwáir-/ n the money or resources required for a purpose

whet /wet, hwet/ vt 1 stimulate something, especially the appetite 2 sharpen a tool or weapon

wheth·er /wéthər, hwéthar/ conj 1 introduces alternatives 2 introduces an indirect question ○ I wonder whether it's worth the effort. ◊ **whether or no** whatever the circumstances might be ◊ See note at **weather**

whet·stone /wét stōn, hwét-/ n a stone for sharpening a tool or weapon

whey /way, hway/ n the watery part of curdled milk ◊ See note at **way**

which /wich, hwich/ det, pron, adj asks for something to be identified from a known group or range ○ Which hat should I wear? ■ pron 1 introduces a relative clause that provides additional information ○ We like the food, which is always delicious. 2 introduces a relative clause that provides identifying information o the money with which the project was funded 3 refers to a previous phrase or sentence ○ We had to leave early, which was a pity. ■ adj, pron 1 one from a known set ○ can't decide which activity would be best 2 indicates choice ○ Take which one you want. ◊ See note at **that**

SPELLCHECK Do not confuse the spelling of **which** and **witch** ("somebody with supposed magic powers"), which may sound similar.

---

which·ev·er /wich évvər, hwich-/ adj, pron no matter which

whiff /wif, hwif/ n 1 a slight or brief odor 2 a trace of something o a whiff of corruption 3 a gentle gust or puff 4 a sniff, smell, or brief inhalation of something ■ v 1 vti come or send in light gusts 2 vt smell, smell, or inhale

Whig /wig, hwig/ n 1 a supporter of the American Revolution 2 a member of a 19C US political party that supported loose interpretation of the Constitution and opposed the Democratic Party —**Whig·ger·y** n —**Whig·gish** adj —**Whig·gism** n

while /wil, hwil/ conj 1 at or during the same time 2 even though ○ While we support your tenacity, we cannot agree with your methods. 3 but on the other hand ■ n a fairly long period of time ○ This may take a while. ◊ **once in a while** very occasionally ◊ **worth (somebody's) while** deserving somebody's time, money, or support

---

SPELLCHECK Do not confuse the spelling of **while** and **wile** ("a cunning strategy"), which may sound similar.

☐ **while away** vt pass time idly

whim /wim, hwim/ n a passing impulse

~~whimp~~ incorrect spelling of **wimp**

whim·per /wímpər, hwím-/ vi 1 sob or whine softly 2 complain peevishly —**whim·per** n —**whim·per·ing·ly** adv

whim·si·cal /wímzik'l, hwím-/ adj 1 fanciful 2 odd in an endearing way 3 erratic or unpredictable —**whim·si·cal·i·ty** /wímzi kállətee, hwím-/ n —**whim·si·cal·ly** adv

whim·sy /wímzee, hwímzee/ (pl -sies) n 1 endearing quaintness or oddity 2 an impulsive notion

whine /wīn, hwīn/ v (**whined, whin·ing**) 1 vi make a long high-pitched plaintive sound 2 vi grumble peevishly 3 vt say something in an annoyingly plaintive voice ■ n 1 a whining cry or sound 2 a peevish complaint —**whin·er** n —**whin·ing·ly** adv —**whin·y** adj ◊ See note at **complain**

SPELLCHECK Do not confuse the spelling of **whine** and **wine** ("alcohol fermented from grapes"), which may sound similar.

---

whin·ny /wínnee, hwínnee/ (-nied, -nies) vi emit a soft neigh or a neighing sound —**whin·ny** n

whip /wip, hwip/ v (**whipped, whip·ping**) 1 vt hit a person or animal with a whip or something similar 2 vti strike against something sharply 3 vti flick rapidly to and fro with a lashing motion 4 vti move, remove, or produce rapidly 5 vt defeat somebody convincingly (infml) 6 vt beat a liquid such as cream until it is stiff or frothy 7 vt bind the end of a rope ■ n 1 a flexible rod, a strip of leather attached to a handle, or a similar instrument for inflicting pain 2 a lashing stroke or blow 3 something that resembles a whip in form, motion, or flexibility 4 **Whip** somebody in charge of discipline in a political party 5 a light creamy dessert —**whip·ping** n ◊ **crack the whip** enforce discipline

☐ **whip up** vt 1 provoke strong feelings in a group 2 prepare something rapidly, especially an impromptu meal (infml)

whip·cord /wíp kàwrd, hwíp-/ n strong fabric with a pattern of diagonal ribs

whip·lash /wíp làsh, hwíp-/ n 1 an injury to the neck caused by jerking 2 a lashing blow 3 the flexible part of a whip

whip·pet /wíppət, hwíppət/ n a fast slender dog bred for racing

whip·ping boy n somebody who is blamed for somebody else's faults

whip·ping cream n cream that stiffens when whipped

whip·saw /wíp sàw, hwíp-/ n a narrow crosscut saw ■ vt (-sawed or -sawn /-sàwn/) 1 cut with a whipsaw 2 cause to move or alternate back and forth sharply ○ was whipsawed by criticism from two sides 3 defeat in two ways simultaneously

whip·stitch /wíp stich, hwíp-/ n a small stitch passing over the edge of a piece of fabric —**whip·stitch** vt

whir /wur, hwur/ (**whirred, whir·ring**), **whirr** vti make a whirling or vibrating sound —**whir** n

whirl /wurl, hwurl/ v 1 vti turn or spin rapidly 2 vti move along while turning quickly 3 vi feel dizzy or confused 4 vti move very fast ■ n 1 a spinning motion 2 something that moves with a rapid circular or spiral motion 3 a sensation of spinning 4 a series of things that happen in quick succession —**whirl·y** adj ◊ **give something a whirl** try something (infml)

whirl·i·gig /wúrli gìg, hwúrli-/ n 1 a spinning toy 2 a merry-go-round

whirl·pool /wúrl pòol, hwúrl-/ n 1 a spiraling current of water 2 a pool or tub with water jets

whirl·wind /wúrl wìnd, hwúrl-/ n 1 a spinning column of air 2 something that happens or changes swiftly (often before nouns)

whisk /wisk, hwisk/ n 1 a kitchen utensil used with short quick movements to make soft substances thick and frothy 2 a brushing movement ■ v 1 vt beat with a whisk or something similar 2 vt brush away lightly 3 vti move quickly

whisk·er /wískər, hwískər/ n 1 a hair near an animal's mouth 2 a hair on somebody's face 3 a small margin ■ **whisk·ers** npl facial hair —**whisk·ered** adj —**whisk·er·y** adj

whis·key /wískee, hwískee/, **whis·ky** n 1 an alcoholic beverage made from fermented grain such as rye or barley 2 **Whis·key** a communications code word for the letter "W"

whis·per /wíspər, hwís-/ v 1 vti utter words voicelessly 2 vti speak or suggest something secretly, e.g., in conspiring or spreading gossip 3 vi rustle softly ■ n 1 a very low voice 2 something said quietly 3 a rumor 4 a rustling sound —**whis·per·er** n

whis·per·ing cam·paign n a deliberate attempt to defame somebody or something by circulating rumors

whist /wist, hwist/ n a card game for pairs of players

whis·tle /wíss'l, hwíss'l/ v (-tled, -tling) 1 vti make a shrill or musical sound through pursed lips 2 vi produce a shrill sound by forcing air or steam through a narrow opening 3 vi move at great speed with a shrill sound ■ n 1 a device that produces a shrill sound when air passes through it 2 a whistling sound —**whis·tling** adj ◊ **blow the whistle** report somebody for doing something wrong or illegal (infml)

whis·tle-blow·er n an informant, especially somebody who reports wrongdoing within an organization (infml) —**whis·tle-blow·ing** n

Whis·tler /wíssl∂r, hwíss-/, **James Abbott McNeill** (1834–1903) US artist

whis·tle-stop adj involving many rapid, frequent stops for the purpose of making public appearances —**whis·tle-stop** n, vi

whit /wit, hwit/ n the smallest amount

white /wit, hwit/ adj (**whit·er, whit·est**) **1** of the color of fresh snow **2** lacking color **3** also **White** belonging to a race of people with naturally pale skin **4** comparatively light in color **5** describes wine made from light-green grapes **6** lacking pigment **7** having a very pale complexion **8** having white parts or colorings **9** describes flour without bran or germ **10** made from white flour **11** describes hot beverages served with milk ■ n **1** the color of snow **2** white clothing (usually pl) **3** also **White** a pale-skinned person **4** the part of an egg that surrounds the yolk **5** the part of the eye that surrounds the eyeball **6** a light-colored game piece or player **7** a butterfly that is predominantly white —**white·ness** n —**whit·ish** adj

White /wit, hwit/, **Byron** (1917–2002) associate justice of the US Supreme Court (1962–93)

White, Edward Douglass (1845–1921) chief justice of the US Supreme Court (1910–21)

White, Stanford (1853–1906) US architect

white ant n a termite

white·bait /wit bàyt, hwit-/ (pl same) n a small young fish eaten whole, especially a herring

white blood cell n a blood cell that protects the body against infection

white·board /wit bàwrd, hwit-/ n a board with a white surface on which to write with erasable pens

white bread n bread made from white flour

white-bread adj regarded as characteristic of Caucasian and middle-class people (infml; sometimes offensive)

white-col·lar adj of office workers

white el·e·phant n **1** something very costly to maintain **2** a conspicuous failed venture **3** an unwanted object

white·fish /wit fish, hwit-/ (pl **-fish·es** or same) n **1** a freshwater fish with white or silvery skin **2** whitefish as food

white flag n a sign of truce or surrender

white flight n the departure of white people from areas where non-whites are settling

white goods npl household linen

⚡**white hat hack·er** n a benevolent computer hacker, especially one employed to counter malicious hacking

white heat n **1** a very high temperature **2** intense excitement

White·horse /wit hàwrss, hwit-/ capital of the Yukon Territory, Canada. Pop. 19,157 (1996).

white-hot adj **1** extremely hot **2** extremely excited

White House n **1** the official residence of the US President **2** the executive branch of the US government

white knight n **1** a rescuing hero **2** a financial savior

white lie n a harmless lie ◊ See note at **lie**

white mag·ic n magic supposedly practiced for good purposes

white meat n light-colored meat such as pork and chicken

White Moun·tains range of the Appalachian Mountains in N New Hampshire and SW Maine. Highest peak Mt. Washington 6,288 ft./1,917 m.

whit·en /wit'n, hwit'n/ vti make or become white

whit·en·er /wit'n∂r, hwit'n∂r/ n **1** a white coloring substance **2** a milk substitute added to hot beverages

White Nile section of the Nile River from near the Sudan-Uganda border to its junction with the Blue Nile at Khartoum. Length 1,295 mi./2,084 km.

white noise n low-volume electrical or radio interference

white·out /wit òwt, hwit-/ n loss of visibility due to heavy snow, or when low cloud merges with snow-covered land

white pag·es npl the section in a telephone book that lists personal phone numbers

white pa·per n **1** an official government report **2** an authoritative report

white pep·per n pepper made from husked peppercorns

White Plains city in SE New York. Pop. 49,944 (1998).

white sale n a sale of linens

white sauce n a thick milk-based sauce

white su·prem·a·cy n the discredited view that white people are genetically and culturally superior to people of all other races —**white su·prem·a·cist** n

white tie n **1** a white bow tie **2** a man's evening clothes, including a tailcoat and white bow tie

white-tie adj describes an event that requires formal evening clothes

white·wall /wit wàwl, hwit-/, **white·wall tire** n a car tire with a band of white around the side

white·wash /wit wòsh, hwit-/ n **1** a solution of lime in water used for painting walls **2** a cover-up (infml) ■ v **1** vt paint with whitewash **2** vti hide the truth about something —**white·wash·ing** n

white wa·ter n **1** fast-flowing foamy water **2** light-colored sea water visible in shallow water

white-wa·ter raft·ing /wit wawt∂r-, hwit-/ n rafting on a fast-flowing river

white whale n a small fish-eating whale

whith·er /wíthər, hwíthər/ *adv (literary)* **1** to what place **2** into what state

whit·ing /wíting, hwíting/ (*pl same*) *n* **1** a Pacific and Atlantic fish **2** whiting as food

Walt Whitman

Whit·man /wítmən, hwít-/, **Walt** (1819–92) US poet and essayist

Whit·ney, Mt. /wítnee, hwít-/ mountain in the Sierra Nevada, in E California. It is the highest point in the continental United States, excepting Alaska. Height 14,494 ft./4,418 m.

Whit·ney, Eli (1765–1825) US inventor of a cotton gin

Whit·tier /wíttee ər, hwíttee-/, **John Greenleaf** (1807–92) US poet and abolitionist

whit·tle /wítt'l, hwítt'l/ *vti* (**-tled, -tling**) carve with small cuts —**whit·tling** *n*

☐ **whittle away** *vt* use up gradually

☐ **whittle down** *vt* reduce gradually

whiz /wiz, hwiz/, **whizz** *vi* (**whizzed, whiz·zing, whiz·zes**) **1** move swiftly with a humming or buzzing noise **2** go or move quickly ■ *n* (*pl* **whiz·zes**) **1** a whizzing sound **2** *also* **wiz** an expert (*infml*) **3** a fast movement

whiz kid, whizz kid, wiz kid *n* somebody who is young and exceptionally talented (*infml*)

who /hoo/ *pron* **1** what person ○ *Who did that?* **2** introduces a relative clause ○ *The person who did that has left.*

USAGE who or whom? Whom as the form of **who** used as the object of a verb or preposition has fallen into disuse in many contexts. In speech, *Do you remember whom you saw?* may be expressed as *Do you remember who you saw?*, and *The man to whom I was talking* as *The man I was talking to.* In formal contexts, **whom** is still preferred by careful writers.

WHO *abbr* World Health Organization

whoa /wō, hwō/ *interj* expresses a command to stop

who'd /hood/ *contr* **1** who had **2** who would

who·dun·it /hoo dúnnit/, **who·dun·nit** *n* a novel, movie, or play that centers on the solving of a crime

who·ev·er /hoo évvər/ *pron* **1** an emphatic form of "who" ○ *Whoever could have dared to do that?* **2** any person who ○ *Whoever takes over will have to work hard.* ○ *You can bring whoever you like.*

whole /hōl/ *adj* **1** including all parts or aspects **2** not divided into parts **3** of full duration or extent ○ *the whole night* **4** unbroken or unimpaired **5** healed or healthy ■ *adv* **1** as a single piece ○ *swallowed the fish whole* **2** to a complete degree (*infml*) ○ *a whole new angle* ■ *n* **1** something complete **2** a single entity or unit —**whole·ness** *n* ◇ **on the whole 1** as a rule or in general **2** taking all relevant factors into account ◊ See note at **hole**

whole cloth *n* total fiction or fabrication

whole-grain /hōl gráyn/ *adj* containing or made with whole unprocessed cereal grains

whole-heart·ed /hōl haártəd/ *adj* enthusiastic and unreserved —**whole·heart·ed·ly** *adv* —**whole·heart·ed·ness** *n*

~~wholely~~ incorrect spelling of **wholly**

whole note *n* a long musical note

whole num·ber *n* a number that does not contain a fraction

whole·sale /hōl sáyl/ *n* the business of buying and selling goods in large quantities to businesses that sell them on ■ *adj* **1** of trade in large quantities **2** done on a large scale ■ *adv* **1** in bulk **2** in an indiscriminate manner ■ *vti* (**-saled, -sal·ing**) buy or sell goods wholesale —**whole·sal·er** *n*

whole·some /hōlssəm/ *adj* **1** beneficial to health **2** promoting moral well-being —**whole·some·ly** *adv* —**whole·some·ness** *n*

whole-wheat *adj* **1** not having had the bran removed **2** made with whole-wheat flour

who'll /hool/ *contr* **1** who shall **2** who will

whol·ly /hólee, hōl lee/ *adv* **1** completely and entirely **2** solely and exclusively

whom /hoom/ *pron* the form of "who" used as the object of a verb or preposition (*fml*) ○ *Whom did they choose?* ○ *the person to whom the letter is addressed* ◊ See note at **who**

whom·ev·er /hoom évvər/ *pron* a form of "whoever" used as the object of a verb or preposition

whomp /womp, hwomp/ *vti* strike hard and loudly ■ *n* a blow or the noise of a blow

whom·so·ev·er /hòom sō évvər/ *pron* whomever (*fml*)

whoop /hoop, whoop/ *v* **1** *vi* cry out in excitement or joy **2** *vt* exclaim loudly and excitedly **3** *vt* urge or drive forward with a whooping cry ■ *n* **1** a loud cry **2** the sharp shrill inhalation associated with whooping cough ◇ **whoop it up** have fun or celebrate in an extravagant or noisy way (*infml*)

whoop·ing cough /hóoping-, hwóoping-/ *n* an infectious bacterial disease accompanied by spasms of coughing followed by a sharp shrill inhalation

whoops /woops, hwoops/, **woops** *interj* indicates that a mistake has been made (*infml*)

whoosh /woosh, hwoosh/ *n* **1** a noise of rushing

air or water **2** a swift motion or rush ■ *vi* **1** make a rushing sound **2** move fast

whop /wop, hwop/, **whap** *vt* (**whopped, whop·ping; whapped, whap·ping**) (*infml*) **1** hit forcefully **2** defeat decisively ■ *n* a blow or the noise of a blow

whop·per /wóppər, hwóppər/ *n* (*infml*) **1** something very big of its kind **2** an outrageous lie

whop·ping /wópping, hwópping/ *adj* very big (*infml*)

whore /hawr/ *n* (*insult*) **1** an offensive term for a prostitute **2** an offensive term for somebody regarded as sexually indiscriminate —**whore·dom** *n*

whorl /wawrl, wurl, hwawrl, hwurl/ *n* **1** something spiral-shaped **2** a pattern of concentric ridges on a fingerprint **3** a circular arrangement of leaves or petals —**whorled** *adj*

who's /hooz/ *contr* **1** who has **2** who is ◊ See note at **whose**

whose /hooz/ *pron, adj* belonging to who or which ◊ *Whose boots are these?* ○ *a theater whose doors will always be open to talented performers*

> **USAGE** **whose or who's?** **Whose** means "of whom" or "of which" and denotes possession or association: *the children whose* [not *who's*] *father we met*, *a car whose* [not *who's*] *paint-work had been damaged*. (Some people dislike the use of **whose** to mean "of which," but it is a well-established use.) **Who's** is a contraction of *who is* or *who has*: *the friend who's* [not *whose*] *coming to dinner next week*; *Who's* [not *Whose*] *got my pen?*

who·so·ev·er /hóōssō évvər/ *pron* whoever (*fml*)

whup /wup, woŏp, hwup, hwoŏp/ *vt* (**whupped, whup·ping**) *vt* (*infml*) **1** beat or thrash somebody **2** defeat somebody

why /wī, hwī/ *adv* **1** for what reason ○ *Why didn't you call?* **2** because of what or which ○ *I don't know why he came.* ■ *interj* expresses surprise

WI *abbr* Wisconsin

W.I. *abbr* West Indies

Wich·i·ta[1] /wíchi tàw/ (*pl* same or **-tas**) *n* a member of a Native North American people who now live mainly in Oklahoma

Wich·i·ta[2] /wíchi tàw/ city in south central Kansas. Pop. 329,211 (1998).

wick *n* a string or strip of fabric that draws the fuel to the flame in candles and lamps ■ *vti* move liquid by capillary action

wick·ed /wíkid/ *adj* **1** very bad **2** playfully mischievous **3** tending to say unpleasant things —**wick·ed·ly** *adv* —**wick·ed·ness** *n*

wick·er /wíkər/, **wick·er·work** /wíkər wùrk/ *n* **1** woven twigs, canes, or reeds **2** things made of wicker

wick·et /wíkit/ *n* **1** a small door or gate **2** a small opening in a door or wall for communication **3** in croquet, a hoop **4** in cricket, the set of sticks defended by a batsman

wick·et·keep·er /wíkit kèepər/ *n* in cricket, a player who stands behind the wicket to catch the ball

wide *adj* (**wid·er, wid·est**) **1** having sides or edges far apart **2** having a particular distance between sides or edges **3** opened to a great extent **4** involving many types or choices **5** involving many people **6** large in scope **7** not hitting a target ■ *adv* (**wid·er, wid·est**) **1** to a great extent **2** over a large area **3** to the side of a target —**wide·ly** *adv* —**wid·en** *vti* —**wide·ness** *n* —**wid·ish** *adj*

-wide *suffix* effective throughout a particular place ○ *statewide*

⚡ **wide-ar·e·a net·work** *n* a network of computers connecting users over a wide area

wide-a·wake *adj* fully awake

wide-bod·y /wíd bòddee/ *n* a commercial jet aircraft with a fuselage wide enough to accommodate three rows of seats and two aisles

wide-eyed *adj* **1** with eyes wide open **2** easily fooled

wide-rang·ing *adj* affecting or dealing with many people or things

wide-screen *adj* **1** describes a movie or television program in which the image is much wider than standard **2** describes a television with a screen designed to accommodate wide-screen broadcasts —**wide screen** *n*

wide·spread /wíd sprèd/ *adj* **1** commonly seen or occurring **2** spread far apart

> **SYNONYMS** **widespread, prevalent, rife, epidemic, universal** CORE MEANING: occurring over a wide area

wid·get /wíjjit/ *n* any useful little device or mechanism, especially one whose name is unknown or forgotten (*humorous*)

wid·ow /wíddō/ *n* **1** a woman whose husband has died **2** a woman left behind by a partner who is frequently away (*only in combination*) ○ *a golf widow* **3** in printing, a short final line of a paragraph at the top or bottom of text ■ *vt* make somebody a widow or widower —**wid·ow·hood** *n*

wid·ow·er /wíddō ər/ *n* a man whose wife has died

width *n* **1** the distance across something **2** the state of being wide

width·wise /width wìz, wítth-/, **width·ways** /-wàyz/ *adv* across the width

~~wiegh~~ incorrect spelling of **weigh**

~~wieght~~ incorrect spelling of **weight**

wield /weeld/ *vt* **1** have and exercise something such as power **2** use or hold a weapon or tool —**wield·er** *n*

wie·ner /weénər/ *n* a frankfurter

~~wier~~ incorrect spelling of **weir**

~~wierd~~ incorrect spelling of **weird**

Wies·ba·den /veéss baàd'n, veéz-/ capital of Hesse State in west central Germany. Pop. 266,081 (1997).

Wie·sel /veéss'l/, **Elie** (*b.* 1928) Romanian-born US writer

wife (*pl* **wives** /wīvz/) *n* a woman to whom a man is married —**wife·hood** *n* —**wife·ly** *adj*

> **ORIGIN** A **wife** was originally a "woman" (as still dialectally in parts of the United Kingdom), but the specialization as "married woman" began as early as the written records.

wig *n* a covering of false hair worn on the head, e.g., to conceal baldness —**wigged** *adj*

wig·gle /wígg'l/ *vti* (**-gled, -gling**) make or cause to make small back-and-forth movements ■ *n* **1** an instance of wiggling **2** a wavy line —**wig·gly** *adj*

Wight, Isle of ◊ **Isle of Wight**

wig·wam /wíg wòm/ *n* a Native North American conical hut

Wil·ber·force /wílbər fàwrss/, **William** (1759–1833) British politician and political reformer

wild /wīld/ *adj* **1** not tame or domesticated **2** not cultivated **3** rough, desolate, and barren **4** enthusiastic or eager **5** an offensive term meaning supposedly culturally or socially inferior **6** overwhelmed by strong emotion ○ *wild with grief* **7** stormy ○ *wild winds and seas* **8** unruly or unrestrained **9** not carefully thought out ○ *What a wild idea!* **10** poorly aimed ■ *adv* in a wild state or manner ■ *n* **1** an undomesticated or uncultivated state **2** = **wilds** *npl* ■ **wilds** *npl* an uninhabited area —**wild·ly** *adv* —**wild·ness** *n* ◊ See note at **unruly**

wild boar *n* a wild pig with gray or black bristles and small tusks

⚡**wild card** *n* **1** an unpredictable person or thing (*slang*) **2** in card games, a card of no fixed value **3** a computer symbol that represents any character

wild·cat /wíld kàt/ *n* (*pl* **-cats** or **same**) **1** a wild European or Asian cat **2** a medium-sized wild feline animal such as a lynx or ocelot **3** a person regarded as quick-tempered (*sometimes offensive*) **4** an exploratory oil or gas well in a new area ■ *adj* not financially safe ■ *vti* (**-cat·ted, -cat·ting**) drill an exploratory well —**wild·cat·ting** *n, adj*

wild·cat strike *n* a sudden unofficial strike

wild·cat·ter /wíld kàttər/ *n* **1** an unethical businessperson **2** a participant in a wildcat strike

AKG London
Oscar Wilde

Wilde /wīld/, **Oscar** (1854–1900) Irish writer

wil·de·beest /wíldə beèst/ (*pl* **-beests** or **same**) *n* a gnu

Wil·der /wíldər/, **Billy** (1906–2002) Austrian-born US movie director

Wil·der, Thornton (1897–1975) US writer

wil·der·ness /wíldərnəss/ *n* **1** natural uncultivated land **2** a barren area **3** an uncomfortable or isolated situation

wild-eyed *adj* **1** having eyes wide with fear, anger, or other emotion **2** marked by extreme and impracticable ideas

wild·fire /wíld fīr/ *n* **1** a fire that spreads uncontrollably and rapidly **2** a phosphorescent light sometimes seen over marshy ground at night ◊ **like wildfire** very rapidly

wild·flow·er /wíld flòwr/ *n* an uncultivated flower

wild·fowl /wíld fòwl/ (*pl* **same**) *n* a bird hunted for sport —**wild·fowl·ing** *n*

wild-goose chase *n* a pointless search

wild·life /wíld līf/ *n* wild animals and other living things in their natural environment

wild oat *n* a weedy annual grass similar to cultivated oats

wild rice *n* **1** the dark edible grain of a grass that grows in water **2** a perennial North American grass that grows in water and produces wild rice grains

Wild West *n* the lawless W United States in the late 19C

wile /wīl/ *n* a trick or ruse ■ **wiles** *npl* trickery used to persuade somebody to do something ◊ See note at **while**

Wil·kins /wílkinz/, **Maurice** (*b.* 1916) New Zealand-born British biophysicist. With Francis H. Crick and James D. Watson he discovered the structure of DNA (1953).

Wil·kins, Roy (1901–81) US civil rights leader

will[1] *vi* **1** indicates future time ■ *modal v* **1** expresses polite offers or suggestions ○ *Will you join us?* **2** expresses requests or commands ○ *Will you please set the table?* **3** indicates customary behavior ○ *When they get together, they will talk all night.* **4** indicates willingness ○ *I will gladly join you.* **5** indicates ability or capacity ○ *This car will seat six.* **6** indicates expectation ○ *She will be married by now.*

will[2] *n* **1** the part of the mind that makes decisions **2** the power or process of making decisions **3** determination **4** a desire or an inclination **5** an attitude toward somebody else **6** a statement of the way a deceased person's property should be distributed ■ *vt* **1** try to cause something by thinking or wishing strongly **2** leave somebody something in a will ◊ **at will** when somebody wishes *(fml)*

Wil·lem·stad /vílləm stáat/ capital and port of the Netherlands Antilles, on S Curaçao. Pop. 125,000 (1985).

will·ful /wílfəl/, **wil·ful** *adj* **1** deliberate **2** stubborn —**will·ful·ly** *adv* —**will·ful·ness** *n*

Wil·liam I /wíllyəm/ (1028?–87) king of England (1066–87)

Wil·liam III (1650–1702) king of England, Scotland, and Ireland (1689–1702)

Wil·liam IV (1765–1837) king of the United Kingdom (1830–37)

Wil·liams /wíllyəmz/, **Roger** (1603–83) English-born American colonial cleric and founder of Rhode Island (1663)

Wil·liams, Ted (b. 1918) US baseball player

Wil·liams, Tennessee (1911–83) US playwright

Wil·liams, William Carlos (1883–1963) US writer

Wil·liams·burg /wíllyəmz bùrg/ city in SE Virginia, site of a restored colonial-era town. Pop. 11,971 (1998).

wil·lies /wílleez/ *npl* an anxious or fearful feeling *(infml)*

will·ing /wílling/ *adj* **1** ready to do something voluntarily **2** offered voluntarily —**will·ing·ly** *adv* —**will·ing·ness** *n*

will-o'-the-wisp /wíllə thə wísp/ *n* **1** a phosphorescent light sometimes seen at night above a marshy area **2** an elusive person or thing

wil·low /wílló/ *n* **1** a tree with long flexible branches **2** the wood from a willow tree. Use: furniture.

wil·low·y /wílló ee/ (**-i·er, -i·est**) *adj* tall, slim, and graceful

will·pow·er /wíl pòwr/ *n* determination and self-discipline

Wills, Helen Newington (1906–98) US tennis player

wil·ly-nil·ly /wíllee níllee/ *adv* **1** whether somebody wants it or not **2** haphazardly ■ *adj* **1** happening without choice **2** haphazard

Wil·ming·ton /wílmingtən/ **1** largest city in Delaware, in the north of the state. Pop. 71,678 (1998). **2** city in SE North Carolina. Pop. 55,530.

Wil·mut /wílmət/, **Ian** (b. 1944) Scottish embryologist, with Keith Campbell responsible for the first successful cloning of a mammal from adult cells

Wil·son /wílss'n/, **August** (b. 1945) US playwright

Woodrow Wilson

Wil·son, Woodrow (1856–1924) 28th president of the United States (1913–21) —**Wil·so·ni·an** /wil sónee ən/ *adj*

wilt *v* **1** *vti* droop or shrivel, or cause to droop or shrivel **2** *vi* become weak ■ *n* **1** the process of wilting **2** a plant disease that causes stems to droop and leaves to shrivel

wi·ly /wílee/ (**-li·er, -li·est**) *adj* cunningly crafty —**wil·i·ly** *adv* —**wil·i·ness** *n*

wimp *n* an offensive term for somebody regarded as timid, cowardly, or unassertive *(infml insult)* —**wimp·ish** *adj* —**wimp·y** *adj*

⚡**WIMP** /wimp/ *n* a computer user interface system. Full form **windows, icons, mice, and pull-down menus**

win *v* (**won** /wun/, **win·ning**) **1** *vti* achieve a victory in a competition, contest, or fight **2** *vt* get something for defeating others **3** *vt* cause somebody to win something ◊ *a shot that could win her the match* **4** *vt* gain something ◊ *has won the hearts of the voters* ◊ *an attitude that has won him few friends* ■ *n* **1** a victory **2** an amount of money won **3** a first place —**win·na·ble** *adj*

☐ **win over** *vt* persuade somebody to agree

wince (**winced, winc·ing**) *vi* **1** recoil involuntarily from pain or fear **2** make a pained expression —**wince** *n* ◊ See note at **recoil**

winch *n* **1** a lifting machine with a rotating cylinder **2** a crank or handle used for turning ■ *vt* move with a winch

wind[1] /wind/ *n* **1** air moving through the atmosphere **2** a current of air created artificially **3** breath or the power to breathe **4** news that hints at something **5** musical instruments that you blow through **6** a social or economic force *(literary)* ◊ *the winds of change* **7** air carrying a scent **8** stomach gas **9** idle talk ■ **winds** *npl* players of wind instruments ■ *v* **1** *vt* make somebody short of breath **2** *vt* let a horse rest **3** *vti* get a scent of somebody or something in the air —**wind·ed** *adj* ◊ **be in the wind** be about to happen ◊ **break wind** pass intestinal gas through the anus ◊ **get your** *or* **a second wind** recover your natural breathing pattern after a period of breathlessness and great effort ◊ **see which way** *or* **how the wind blows** find out the nature of a situation before making a decision ◊ **take the wind out of somebody's sails** make somebody feel deflated

wind² /wĭnd/ v (**wound** /wownd/) **1** vti go along a twisting or spiral course **2** vti coil around something **3** vti move by the operation of a turning mechanism ◇ *wound the window up* ◇ *wind the film back* **4** vt cause something to revolve **5** vt make the mechanism of a clockwork device work ■ n **1** a curve or bend **2** an act of winding something —**wind·er** n

☐ **wind up** v **1** vt finish an activity **2** vi end up (infml)

wind³ /wĭnd, wīnd/ (**wind·ed** or **wound** /wownd/) v **1** vti blow a horn or bugle **2** vt make a signal by blowing a horn or bugle

wind·bag /wĭnd bàg/ n a person regarded as a pompous, boring, incessant talker (infml insult)

wind·blown /wĭnd blōn/ adj **1** blown into disarray by the wind **2** growing in a shape caused by the wind

wind·break /wĭnd bràyk/ n an object or screen erected to lessen the force of the wind

wind·burn /wĭnd bùrn/ n a skin inflammation caused by exposure to harsh winds —**wind·burned** adj

wind·chill fac·tor /wĭnd chĭll-/, **wind·chill** n the cooling effect of wind on air temperature, or a measurement of this effect

wind·fall /wĭnd fàwl/ n **1** an amount of money obtained unexpectedly **2** a fruit blown down by the wind

wind farm /wĭnd-/ n an area on which a number of wind turbines are sited for electricity generation

Wind·hoek /wĭnd hŏŏk, wĭnt-, vĭnt-/ capital of Namibia. Pop. 169,000 (1997).

wind·ing /wīnding/ adj **1** twisting and curving **2** coiling or spiraling ■ n **1** a winding course **2** a wire coil that carries electricity

winding sheet n a sheet wrapped around a body for burial

wind in·stru·ment /wĭnd-/ n a musical instrument played by blowing

wind·jam·mer /wĭnd jàmmər/ n a large sailing ship

wind·lass /wĭndləss/ n a revolving lifting device —**wind·lass** vt

wind·mill /wĭnd mĭll/ n a building or device with revolving blades that harness wind power for grinding grain, pumping water, or generating electricity

⚡ **win·dow** /wĭndō/ n **1** a glass-covered opening designed to let light or air into a building or vehicle **2** a windowpane **3** a display in a store window **4** an opening above a counter where customers are dealt with **5** an opening similar to a window, e.g., in an envelope **6** a period of available time or opportunity **7** a rectangular section on a computer screen ◇ **be** or **go out the window** be lost for good (infml)

win·dow box n a box for plants on a window ledge

win·dow dress·ing n **1** the art of arranging a display in a store window **2** a deceptively appealing presentation

win·dow·pane /wĭndō pàyn/ n a sheet of glass in a window

win·dow seat n **1** an indoor seat under a window **2** a seat by a window, e.g., in a plane

win·dow-shop vi look at things in stores without buying anything —**win·dow-shop·per** n

win·dow·sill /wĭndō sĭll/ n a shelf along the bottom edge of a window

wind·pipe /wĭnd pīp/ n the tube in the body that takes air from the mouth into the lungs

wind scale /wĭnd-/ n a scale for measuring the force of wind

wind·screen /wĭnd skrēen/ n UK a screen protecting something from the wind

wind shear /wĭnd-/ n a sudden change in wind direction at different altitudes, causing dangerous downdrafts

wind·shield /wĭnd shēeld/ n **1** the front window of a vehicle, usually made of glass **2** UK = windscreen

wind·shield wip·er n a device for clearing a windshield

wind·sock /wĭnd sòk/ n a fabric tube that blows to show the wind direction

Wind·sor /wĭnzər/ **1** city in S Ontario, Canada. Pop. 197,694 (1996). **2** town in S England, on the Thames River, the site of **Windsor Castle**. Pop. 30,832 (1991).

wind·storm /wĭnd stàwrm/ n a storm with wind but no rain

Windsurfing

wind·surf /wĭnd sùrf/ vi ride and steer a sailboard on water —**wind·surf·er** n —**wind·surf·ing** n

wind·swept /wĭnd swèpt/ adj exposed to much wind

wind tun·nel /wĭnd-/ n a tunnel for testing aerodynamic properties

wind·up /wĭnd ùp/ adj operated by turning a handle ■ n **1** an ending **2** in baseball, a pitcher's preparation to throw

wind·ward /wĭndwərd/ adj facing the wind ■ adv into the wind ■ n the side of something that faces the wind

Wind·ward Is·lands group of islands in the E Caribbean Sea, including Martinique and the independent island states of Barbados,

Dominica, St. Lucia, Grenada, and St. Vincent and the Grenadines.

wind·y /wíndee/ (**-i·er, -i·est**) *adj* **1** with the wind blowing **2** a place where much wind blows **3** full of empty words (*infml*) —**wind·i·ly** *adv* —**wind·i·ness** *n*

wine /wīn/ *n* **1** alcohol fermented from grapes **2** alcohol fermented from a flower, another fruit, or a vegetable ○ *dandelion wine* **3** a dark purplish red color —**wine** *adj* ◊ See note at **whine**

wine cool·er *n* **1** a container for keeping wine chilled **2** a wine cocktail

wine·glass /wín glàss/ *n* a glass with a stem

win·er·y /wínəree/ (*pl* **-ies**) *n US, Can, ANZ* a place for making wine

Win·frey /wínfree/, **Oprah** (b. 1954) US talk show host and actor

wing *n* **1** a bird's, insect's, or bat's limb used for flying **2** a flat surface projecting from the side of an aircraft **3** any flat projecting part **4** the fact of being in flight ○ *birds on the wing* **5** a part of a building that projects from the middle **6** either of the longer sides of a sports field **7** in some team sports, an offensive player on the side of the field **8** a subsidiary group, especially a subdivision of a political group **9** an air force unit that is larger than a squadron but smaller than a group **10** one side of a military formation ■ **wings** *npl* **1** the sides of a theater stage that are not visible to the audience **2** a qualified pilot's badge ■ *v* **1** *vti* move swiftly **2** *vt* wound a bird by hitting its wing **3** *vt* wound somebody or damage something superficially —**winged** *adj* —**wing·less** *adj* ◊ **be (waiting) in the wings** be ready and prepared to do something ◊ **take under your wing** take care of somebody ◊ **wing it** improvise (*infml*)

wing chair *n* an armchair with high side panels

wing·er /wíngər/ *n* in soccer, a player who plays on a wing

wing nut *n* a nut with projections that allow it to be tightened by hand

wing·span /wíng spàn/, **wing·spread** /-sprèd/ *n* the distance between wingtips, e.g., of a bird

wing·tip /wíng tìp/ *n* the point of a wing that is farthest from the body

wink *vi* **1** gesture by closing one eye briefly **2** shine intermittently ■ *n* **1** a brief closing of one eye **2** a twinkling light **3** a short time ◊ **not sleep a wink, not get a wink of sleep** be unable to sleep

□ **wink at** *vt* pretend not to notice an offense (*infml*)

win·kle /wíngk'l/ *n* an edible shellfish of coastal waters

Win·ne·ba·go /wìnnə báygō/ (*pl* **same** *or* **-gos** *or* **-goes**) *n* **1** a member of a Native North American people who now live mainly in Wisconsin and Nebraska **2** the language of

the Winnebago people —**Win·ne·ba·go** *adj*

win·ner /wínnər/ *n* **1** somebody or something that wins a competition or contest **2** somebody or something successful

win·ning /wínning/ *adj* **1** victorious **2** charming ■ **win·nings** *npl* money won —**win·ning·ness** *n*

win·ning·est /wínningəst/ *adj* winning the most (*infml*)

Win·ni·peg /wínni pèg/ capital of Manitoba, Canada. Pop. 618,477 (1996).

Win·ni·peg, Lake freshwater lake in central Manitoba, Canada. Depth 60 ft./18m.

win·ni·tude /wínni tòod, -tyood/ *n* success or the fact of being successful

win·now /wínnō/ *v* **1** *vti* separate grain from chaff by tossing it in the air or blowing air through it **2** *vt* examine something to remove the bad parts —**win·now** *n*

win·o /wínō/ (*pl* **-os**) *n* an offensive term for a homeless person addicted to alcohol (*infml insult*)

win·some /wínssəm/ *adj* charming in manner —**win·some·ly** *adv* —**win·some·ness** *n*

win·ter /wíntər/ *n* the coldest season of the year ■ *v* **1** *vi* spend the winter somewhere **2** *vt* keep somewhere in winter

win·ter sport *n* a sport performed on snow or ice

win·ter squash *n* a hard-skinned squash

win·ter·time /wíntər tìm/ *n* the winter season

Win·throp /wínthrop/, **John** (1587–1649) and his son **John** (1605–76) English-born American colonial governors

win·try /wíntree/ (**-tri·er, -tri·est**), **win·ter·y** /wíntəree/ (**-ter·i·er, -ter·i·est**) *adj* **1** of or typical of winter **2** cheerless or unfriendly —**win·tri·ness** *n*

wipe *v* (**wiped, wip·ing**) **1** *vt* rub something with or on soft material to clean or dry it **2** *vti* remove or be removed by rubbing **3** *vt* remove a recording from a tape **4** *vt* remove something as if by wiping ■ *n* **1** a light rubbing stroke **2** a disposable cleaning cloth

□ **wipe out** *vt* destroy in large numbers (*infml*)

wip·er /wípər/ *n* a device for cleaning a windshield

wire *n* **1** a strand of metal **2** a metal strand encased in insulating material that carries an electric current **3** a cable that provides a telecommunications link **4** the finish line on a racetrack ■ *vt* (**wired, wir·ing**) **1** fasten something with wire **2** connect electrical equipment **3** fit somebody with a hidden listening device (*slang*) ◊ **have** *or* **get your wires crossed** have a misunderstanding

⚡ **wired** *adj* **1** equipped for accessing the Internet (*infml*) **2** nervy and overstimulated (*slang*)

wire·haired /wír hàird/ *adj* describes a dog with a rough coat

wire·less /wírləss/ *n* a radio *(dated)* ■ *adj* 1 not having or using wires 2 describes communications systems and devices that make use of cellphone technology ○ *wireless telephone technology* —**wire·less·ly** *adv*

⚡ **wire·less mark·up lan·guage** *n* a system for tagging computer text files that specifies the interfaces of narrowband wireless devices

wire ser·vice *n* a news agency

wire·tap /wír tàp/ *(-tapped, -tap·ping)* *vti* fit a secret connection to a telephone line to allow covert monitoring of conversations —**wire·tap** *n*

wir·ing /wíring/ *n* a system or layout of electrical wires

wir·y /wíree/ *(-i·er, -i·est)* *adj* 1 slim but strong 2 coarse in texture ○ *a dog with wiry hair* —**wir·i·ly** *adv* —**wir·i·ness** *n*

Wis. *abbr* Wisconsin

Wis·con·sin /wiss kónssin/ state of the north central United States. Cap. Madison. Pop. 5,363,675 (2000). —**Wis·con·sin·ite** *n*

wis·dom /wízdəm/ *n* 1 the good sense and judgment that come from experience 2 accumulated learning 3 a widely held opinion

Wis·dom of Sol·o·mon *n* a book of the Apocrypha expounding Jewish doctrines in the terminology of Greek philosophy

wis·dom tooth *n* one of the four backmost teeth

wise /wíz/ *(wis·er, wis·est)* *adj* 1 having acquired good sense and judgment from experience 2 sensible 3 having been well educated 4 shrewd 5 disrespectful *(infml)* —**wise·ly** *adv* ◇ **be** *or* **get wise (to)** be or become aware of *(infml)* ◇ **put wise (to)** inform somebody about something *(infml)*

-wise *suffix* 1 in a particular manner or direction ○ *clockwise* 2 with regard to *(infml)* ○ *salary-wise*

wise·a·cre /wíz àykər/ *n* an annoyingly authoritative or self-assured person *(infml)*

ORIGIN Wiseacre has no etymological connection with *acre*, the measurement of area. It came in the late 16C from early Dutch *wijsseggher* "soothsayer." The reason for the assimilation to *acre* is not known.

---

wise·crack /wíz kràk/ *(infml)* *n* a flippant remark ■ *vi* make wisecracks —**wise·crack·er** *n*

wise guy *n* an insolent person *(infml)*

wish /wish/ *v* 1 *vti* desire something 2 *vt* demand something 3 *vti* express a desire for ○ *wished us a safe journey* 4 *vt* want something to be otherwise 5 *vt* greet somebody in a particular way ○ *wished me good afternoon* ■ *n* 1 a yearning 2 an expression of a desire 3 something desired or demanded 4 a hope for somebody's welfare *(usually pl)* —**wish·er** *n* ◇ See note at **want**

wish·bone /wish bòn/ *n* a V-shaped bone in a bird's breast

wish·ful think·ing /wíshfəl-/ *n* the belief that wishes correspond with reality

wish list *n* a list of things you would like to have

wish·y-wash·y /wíshee wóshee/ *adj* *(infml)* 1 incapable of making firm decisions 2 lacking strength or color —**wish·y-wash·i·ness** *n*

wisp *n* 1 something thin and delicate, e.g., a piece of straw or a streak of smoke 2 a slender, delicate person 3 something insubstantial —**wisp·i·ness** *n* —**wisp·y** *adj*

wis·ter·i·a /wi steeree ə/ *(pl -as or same)* *n* a deciduous climbing flowering plant

wist·ful /wistfəl/ *adj* sadly pensive —**wist·ful·ly** *adv* —**wist·ful·ness** *n*

wit *n* 1 ingenious humor 2 witty speech or writing 3 a witty person ■ **wits** *npl* calm, shrewd commonsense ◇ **be at your wits' end** be in despair as to how to cope with something

witch /wich/ *n* 1 a woman deemed to have magic powers 2 a follower of a non-Christian religion based on nature 3 an offensive term for a woman regarded as unattractive or malicious *(insult)* ◇ See note at **which**

witch·craft /wích kràft/ *n* 1 the exercise of supposed magical powers 2 the effect of supposed magical powers

witch doc·tor *n* 1 a tribal healer or magician 2 in some African cultures, somebody who hunts witches

witch ha·zel *n* 1 a soothing lotion that contains extracts from specific bark and flowers. Use: astringent, relieving bruises and sprains. 2 a tree or bush from which witch hazel is obtained

witch-hunt *n* 1 an aggressive, persecuting campaign against dissenters or those suspected of wrongdoing 2 a persecution of witches —**witch-hunt·er** *n*

witch·ing hour /wíching-/ midnight

with /with, with/ *prep* 1 in the company of ○ *sit with the other children* 2 used or done together ○ *It doesn't go with roast beef.* 3 involving ○ *a meeting with department heads* 4 against ○ *competing with each other* 5 by means of ○ *treated with the drug* 6 carrying ○ *came in with a box of files* 7 having ○ *with English subtitles* 8 because of ○ *faint with anxiety* 9 on or in ○ *walls covered with photographs* 10 concerning ○ *not happy with the service* 11 in a particular way ○ *sitting with her hands on her lap* ○ *walking with a limp* 12 in view of ○ *with the problems in the economy* 13 in spite of ○ *With all his charm, I still wouldn't trust him.* 14 at the same time as or immediately after ○ *With that, he stormed out.* 15 following the direction of ○ *sail with the tide* 16 according to or in proportion to ○ *The risk increases with age.*

◊ **be with it 1** be fashionable (*infml dated*) **2** understand a situation (*infml*)

with·al /with áwl/ *adv* **1** moreover **2** nevertheless

with·draw /with dráw, with-/ (**-drew** /-dróo/, **-drawn** /-dráwn/) *v* **1** *vt* remove something or somebody from a group **2** *vt* retract an earlier statement **3** *vi* leave or retreat **4** *vt* take money from an account —**with·draw·able** *adj*

with·draw·al /with dráw əl, with-/ *n* **1** an instance of taking money from an account **2** a period of fighting an addiction, or the physical effects of fighting it **3** the act of withdrawing **4** the retreat of an army from an area

with·drawn /with dráwn, with-/ *past participle* of **withdraw** ■ *adj* **1** not sociable or outgoing **2** removed from the market

with·er /wíthər/ *v* **1** *vti* shrivel **2** *vi* fade away **3** *vti* make somebody feel embarrassed or foolish as the object of scorn —**with·ered** *adj* —**with·er·ing** *adj* —**with·er·ing·ly** *adv*

with·ers /wíthərz/ *npl* the ridge between the shoulder bones of a horse, or similar four-legged animal

with·hold /with hóld, with-/ (**-held** /-héld/) *vt* refuse to give something

with·hold·ing tax *n* the amount an employer withholds from wages to pay the employee's income tax

with·in /with ín/ *prep, adv* **1** inside a place **2** inside a group or organization **3** inside yourself ■ *prep* not beyond the limits, range, time, or extent of ◊ *trying to keep within our budget* ◊ *finish the job within a week* ■ *adv* indoors (*literary*)

~~withold~~ incorrect spelling of **withhold**

with·out /with ówt/ *prep* **1** not having ◊ *was left without food* **2** not accompanied by **3** not feeling ◊ *without remorse* **4** not happening ◊ *passed without objection* ■ *prep, adv* outside (*literary*) ◊ *without the city walls* ■ *conj* unless (*nonstandard*)

with·stand /with stánd, with-/ (**-stood** /-stood/) *vti* be resistant to something

wit·less /wítləss/ *adj* unintelligent ◊ *a witless comment* —**wit·less·ly** *adv* —**wit·less·ness** *n*

wit·ness /wítnəss/ *n* **1** somebody who sees a specific incident happen **2** somebody who countersigns a document **3** somebody who testifies to Christian beliefs ■ *vt* **1** see something happen **2** countersign a document **3** experience or be the time of important events or changes **4** be a sign or proof of —**wit·ness·a·ble** *adj*

wit·ness stand *n* a place in a courtroom where a witness gives evidence

Wit·ten·berg /vítt'n bùrg/ city in east central Germany where Martin Luther began his campaign for the reform of the Roman Catholic Church in 1517. Pop. 53,400 (1989).

Witt·gen·stein /vítgən shtīn, -stīn/, **Ludwig** (1889–1951) Austrian-born British philosopher

wit·ti·cism /wítti sìzzəm/ *n* a witty remark

wit·ty /wíttee/ (**-ti·er, -ti·est**) *adj* using words with ingenious humor —**wit·ti·ly** *adv* —**wit·ti·ness** *n*

Wit·wa·ters·rand /wit wáwtərz ránd/ rocky ridge in NE South Africa, the most productive gold-mining area in the world. Length 60 mi. / 100 km.

wives plural of **wife**

wiz (*pl* **wiz·zes**) *n* an expert (*infml*)

wiz·ard /wízzərd/ *n* **1** a man with supposed magic powers **2** somebody who excels at something (*infml*) —**wiz·ard·ly** *adj*

wiz·ard·ry /wízzərdree/ *n* **1** the art of wizards **2** impressive skill

wiz·ened /wízz'nd/ *adj* dried up or wrinkled

wiz kid *n* = **whiz kid** (*infml*)

wk. *abbr* **1** week **2** work

⚡**WML** *abbr* wireless markup language

woad *n* **1** a blue dye obtained from the leaves of a plant. Use: formerly, body paint. **2** the European plant whose leaves yield woad

wob·ble /wóbb'l/ (**-bled, -bling**) *v* **1** *vti* move from side to side **2** *vi* quaver —**wob·ble** *n* —**wob·bling·ly** *adv*

wob·bly /wóbblee/ (**-bli·er, -bli·est**) *adj* **1** unsteady or vacillating **2** feeling weak (*infml*) —**wob·bli·ness** *n*

Wode·house /wood hòwss/, **P. G.** (1881–1975) British writer

woe *n* **1** a serious misfortune **2** grief

woe·be·gone /wó bi gòn/ *adj* sorrowful

woe·ful /wófəl/ *adj* **1** unhappy **2** causing grief **3** pathetically bad —**woe·ful·ly** *adv* —**woe·ful·ness** *n*

wok *n* a large curved Chinese cooking pan

woke past tense of **wake**[1]

wok·en past participle of **wake**[1]

wold /wōld/ *n* upland

wolf /woolf/ *n* (*pl* **wolves** /woolvz/) **1** any of various carnivorous mammals, related to the dog, that hunt in packs **2** a greedy, cruel person **3** a sexually predatory man (*infml*) ■ *vt* eat quickly and greedily —**wolf·ish** *adj* —**wolf·ish·ly** *adv* ◊ **cry wolf** give a false alarm too many times, so that when help is really needed, no one will grow ◊ **throw to the wolves** abandon somebody so take blame or to be ruined

Wolfe /woolf/, **James** (1727–59) British general

Wolfe, Thomas (1900–38) US writer

Wolfe, Tom (*b.* 1930) US journalist and writer

wolf·hound /woolf hòwnd/ *n* a large breed of dog

wolf·ram /woolfrəm/ *n* tungsten (*archaic*)

wolf whis·tle *n* a whistle that signifies sexual interest —**wolf-whis·tle** *vti*

Woll·stone·craft /wóolstən kràft/, **Mary** (1759–97) British feminist

Wol·sey /wŏolzee/, **Thomas** (1475–1530) English cleric and politician

wol·ver·ine /wŏolvə reen/ (*pl* -ines or same) *n* a strong dark-furred carnivore of the weasel family

wom·an /wŏommən/ (*pl* -en /wímmin/) *n* **1** a female adult **2** women as a group **3** a wife or girlfriend (*infml; sometimes offensive*) —**wo·man·like** *adj*

wom·an·hood /wŏomman hŏod/ *n* **1** the condition of being a woman **2** women in general

wom·an·ize /wŏommə nīz/ (-ized, -iz·ing) *vi* be constantly seeking casual sex with women (*disapproving; refers to men*) —**wom·an·iz·er** *n*

wom·an·kind /wŏomman kind/, **wom·en·kind** /wímmin-/ *n* women as a group

wom·an·ly /wŏommənlee/ *adj* characteristic of mature women —**wom·an·li·ness** *n*

womb /woom/ *n* **1** a uterus **2** a place of origin

wom·bat /wóm bàt/ *n* a small Australian marsupial

wom·en plural of **woman**

wom·en·folk /wímmin fŏk/, **wom·en·folks** *npl* women collectively, or the women in a family or group (*dated*)

wom·en's lib *n* women's liberation (*infml*) —**wom·en's lib·ber** *n*

wom·en's lib·er·a·tion *n* a political movement to free women from social oppression

wom·en's move·ment *n* a movement to improve the position of women in society

wom·en's shel·ter *n* a safe place for battered women

wom·en's stud·ies *n* a course of study examining the roles and achievements of women (+ *sing or pl verb*)

won[1] /won/ (*pl* same) *n* the main unit of currency in North and South Korea

won[2] /wun/ past tense, past participle of **win**

won·der /wúndər/ *n* **1** amazed admiration **2** something marvelous ■ *adj* extraordinarily good ■ *v* **1** *vti* speculate about something **2** *vi* be amazed ◊ **no wonder** or **little wonder** it is not surprising ◊ See note at **wander**

won·der·ful /wúndərfəl/ *adj* **1** exciting admiration **2** very good or suitable —**won·der·ful·ly** *adv* —**won·der·ful·ness** *n*

won·der·land /wúndər lànd/ *n* a land of wonderful things

won·der·ment /wúndərmənt/ *n* **1** amazed admiration **2** puzzlement

won·drous /wúndrəss/ (*literary*) *adj* exciting wonder ■ *adv* to an amazing degree —**won·drous·ly** *adv* —**won·drous·ness** *n*

wonk *n* **1** a policy expert (*infml*) **2** a hardworking student (*infml disapproving*)

wont /wawnt, wont/ (*fml*) *adj* accustomed or likely to do something ◊ *He is wont to ask hard questions.* ■ *n* something that somebody often does ◊ *It is her wont to surf the Internet every night.* ◊ See note at **habit**

won't /wŏnt/ *contr* will not

wont·ed /wáwntəd, wŏntəd/ *adj* usual (*literary*) —**wont·ed·ly** *adv* ◊ See note at **usual**

woo (**wooed**, **woo·ing**, **woos**) *vti* **1** seek the love of a woman (*literary*) **2** try to please or attract somebody —**woo·ing·ly** *adv*

wood /wŏod/ *n* **1** the hard fibrous substance that trees are chiefly composed of **2** wood used as a fuel or building material **3** an area with trees ■ *adj* **1** made of wood **2** found or located among trees ■ *vt* cover an area with trees —**wood·ed** *adj* ◊ **out of the woods** out of danger or difficulty (*infml*)

ORIGIN The ancestral meaning of **wood** is probably "collection of trees, forest." The meanings "tree" (now obsolete) and "substance from which trees are made" are secondary developments. It has been suggested that **wood** may go back to an ancient source meaning "separate," in which case it would originally have denoted a "separated" or "remote" piece of territory. Since such remote, uninhabited areas were usually wooded, the word came to mean "forest."

SPELLCHECK Do not confuse the spelling of **wood** and **would** (indicating a conditional statement), which sound similar.

Wood /wŏod/, **Grant** (1892–1942) US artist

wood·block /wŏod blòk/ *n* a block of wood for making prints

wood·carv·ing /wŏod kàarving/ *n* **1** the art of carving wood **2** an object carved from wood

wood·chuck /wŏod chùk/ (*pl* -chucks or same) *n* a heavy-set North American rodent

wood·cock /wŏod kòk/ (*pl* -cocks or same) *n* a small stocky game bird with a long beak

wood·cut /wŏod kùt/ *n* **1** a block of wood for making prints **2** a print made with a woodcut

wood·cut·ter /wŏod kùttər/ *n* **1** a lumberjack **2** somebody who makes woodcut prints

wood·en /wŏbdd'n/ *adj* **1** made of wood **2** lacking flexibility or grace ◊ *a ballet dancer with wooden movements* **3** inexpressive —**wood·en·ly** *adv* —**wood·en·ness** *n*

Wood·hull /wŏod hùl/, **Victoria** (1838–1927) US feminist

wood·land /wŏoddlənd/ *n* an area of land that is covered with trees

wood·lot /wŏod lòt/ *n* a privately owned woodland

wood·peck·er /wŏod pèkər/ *n* a woodland bird that hammers trees with its beak to extract insects

wood·pile /wŏod pìl/ *n* a stack of firewood

Tiger Woods

Woods /wʊʊdz/, **Tiger** (b. 1975) US golfer

wood·shed /wʊʊd shĕd/ n a room or building for storing firewood

woods·y /wʊʊdzee/ (-i·er, -i·est) adj of the woods (infml)

wood tick n a tick that lives in or on wood and is a carrier of Rocky Mountain spotted fever

wood·wind /wʊʊd wĭnd/ n 1 the family of musical instruments that includes the flute and the clarinet (+ sing or pl verb) 2 an instrument of the woodwind family ■ **wood·winds** npl the players of woodwind instruments in an orchestra —**wood·wind** adj

wood·work /wʊʊd wùrk/ n items or parts made from wood —**wood·work·er** n ◊ **crawl** or **come out of the woodwork** appear suddenly and unexpectedly (slang)

wood·worm /wʊʊd wùrm/ n 1 damage to wood caused by wood-boring insects, especially larvae 2 a wood-boring larva

wood·y /wʊʊddee/ (-i·er, -i·est) adj 1 having many trees 2 made of wood 3 resembling wood

woo·er /wʊʊ ər/ n somebody trying to win affection

woof¹ /wʊʊf, woof/ n, interj the sound of a dog's bark —**woof** vi

woof² /wʊʊf/ n a woven fabric or its texture

woof·er /wʊʊffər/ n a loudspeaker for low frequencies

wool /wʊʊl/ n 1 yarn made from wool. Use: knitting, weaving. 2 the curly hair of sheep and some other mammals 3 material made of wool yarn 4 a mass of soft hairs that grows on some plants

wool·en /wʊʊllən/, **wool·len** adj 1 made of wool 2 producing wool items ■ n a wool garment

Virginia Woolf

Woolf /wʊʊlf/, **Virginia** (1882–1941) British novelist and critic

wool·gath·er·ing /wʊʊl gàthəring/ n the act of daydreaming —**wool·gath·er·er** n

wool·ly /wʊʊllee/ (-li·er, -li·est), **wool·y** (-i·er, -i·est) adj 1 made of wool 2 covered in furry hair 3 vague or lacking focus —**wool·li·ly** adv —**wool·li·ness** n

Wool·worth /wʊʊl wùrth/, **Frank W.** (1852–1919) US retailer

woops interj = whoops (infml)

wooz·y /wʊʊzee/ (-i·er, -i·est) adj 1 weak and dizzy 2 confused —**wooz·i·ly** adv —**wooz·i·ness** n

Worces·ter /wʊʊstər/ city in central Massachusetts. Pop. 166,535 (1998).

Worces·ter·shire sauce /wʊʊstər sheer-/ n a pungent dark brown flavoring sauce

⌁ **word** /wùrd/ n 1 a meaningful combination of sounds or letters that forms a unit of language 2 a brief comment or discussion ○ Could I have a word with you in my office, please? 3 information or news ○ Is there any word on your daughter? 4 a rumor ○ The word is that she's leaving the company. 5 a promise ○ I give you my word. 6 a command or verbal signal ○ He gave the word to attack. 7 a fixed number of bits processed by a computer as a unit 8 **Word**, **Word of God** holy Christian scriptures ■ **words** npl 1 an angry exchange 2 the text of a song ■ vt express in words —**word·ed** adj ◊ **be as good as your word** do as promised

word·ing /wùrding/ n the choice of words made by a writer or speaker

word·less /wùrdləss/ adj 1 not using words 2 unable to speak —**word·less·ly** adv —**word·less·ness** n

word of hon·or n a promise

word-per·fect adj absolutely correct and accurate

word·play /wùrd plày/ n clever use of words

⌁ **word proc·ess·ing** n the creation or manipulation of text using computers

⌁ **word proc·es·sor** n 1 a piece of equipment with a keyboard and screen for creating or manipulating text 2 a computer program for creating or manipulating text

Words·worth /wùrdz wùrth/, **William** (1770–1850) British poet —**Words·worth·i·an** /wùrdz wùrthee ən/ adj

⌁ **word wrap**, **word wrap·ping** n a word-processing feature that automatically takes a word over to the next line if it will not fit

word·y /wùrdee/ (-i·er, -i·est) adj using too many words —**word·i·ly** adv —**word·i·ness** n

---

SYNONYMS **wordy**, **verbose**, **long-winded**, **rambling**, **prolix**, **diffuse** CORE MEANING: too long or not concisely expressed

---

wore past tense of wear

work /wùrk/ n 1 a paid job or its duties 2 a place of employment 3 purposeful effort 4 something made or done ○ Your work is *satisfactory.* **5** an artistic or intellectual creation *(often pl)* **6** *(symbol* **W***)* the transfer of energy, measured as the product of the force applied to a body and the distance moved by that body in the direction of the force ■ *v* (**worked** *or* **wrought** *archaic* /rawt/) **1** *vi* have a job **2** *vti* make or cause to make a physical or mental effort **3** *vti* function or cause to function **4** *vi* be successful ○ *This relationship isn't working.* **5** *vti* shape a material, or be shaped **6** *vt* cultivate land **7** *vti* attain or cause to attain a particular condition ○ *The screw worked itself loose.* **8** *vti* move slowly and with effort ○ *worked his way through the crowd* **9** *vti* exercise a muscle or part of the body **10** *vt* provoke an emotional response in somebody **11** *vt* solve, e.g., a crossword puzzle ◇ **have your work cut out (for you)** be faced with a difficult task ◇ **in the works** being prepared or worked on ◇ See note at **wrought**

□ **work out** *v* **1** *vi* exercise your body **2** *vi* end satisfactorily **3** *vi* end in a particular way **4** *vt* resolve a difficulty **5** *vt* think something up **6** *vt* solve or calculate something

work·a·ble /wúrkəb'l/ *adj* **1** able to be done **2** able to be handled or shaped —**work·a·bly** *adv*

work·a·day /wúrkə dày/ *adj* **1** routine and commonplace **2** appropriate for work

work·a·hol·ic /wùrkə háwlik/ *n* a compulsively hard worker

⚡ **work·a·round** /wúrkə ròwnd/ *n* a technique that enables somebody to overcome a fault or defect in a computer program or system without actually correcting or eliminating it

work·bench /wúrk bènch/ *n* a carpenter's or mechanic's table

work·book /wúrk bòok/ *n* **1** a student's exercise book **2** an instruction book

work·day /wúrk dày/ *n* **1** a day for working **2** the hours in a day spent working ■ *adj* workaday

worked up *adj* in a state of heightened emotion, especially anger or nervousness *(infml)*

work·er /wúrkər/ *n* **1** a person who works **2** an employee **3** a member of the working class **4** an insect belonging to a group that does the work in a colony

work·ers' com·pen·sa·tion *n* money paid to workers injured on the job or affected with occupational diseases, or mandatory insurance paid into by employers to provide this

work eth·ic *n* a belief in the moral value of work

work·fare /wúrk fàir/ *n* a government program that obliges unemployed people to do community work in return for welfare payments

work force, work·force /wúrk fàwrss/ *n* **1** all the workers in a company **2** all the people in a specific place who are employed or employable

work·horse /wúrk hàwrss/ *n* **1** a hard-working person *(infml)* **2** a reliable tool or machine **3** a horse used for heavy work

work·house /wúrk hòwss/ *(pl* **-hous·es** /-hòwzəz/*)* *n* formerly, an institution in which poor people were given food and accommodation in return for unpaid work

work·ing /wúrking/ *adj* **1** functioning **2** worn at work **3** having a paid job **4** spent at work ○ *all his working life* **5** only adequate ○ *a working knowledge of Italian* **6** providing a basis for further work ○ *a working theory* ■ *n* **1** the process of shaping something **2** a jerking motion *(fml)* ■ **work·ings** *npl* **1** the way that something functions **2** the internal mechanism of a device

work·ing cap·i·tal *n* **1** the money that a company has available to use **2** the value of a company's current assets minus its liabilities

work·ing class *n* the part of society made up of people who do manual or unskilled work —**work·ing-class** *adj*

work·ing group *n* a group appointed to study something and report back on it

⚡ **work·ing stor·age** *n* temporary computer memory storage

work in pro·gress *n* an incomplete ongoing piece of work, especially an artistic work

work·load /wúrk lòd/ *n* **1** the amount of work that a machine does **2** the amount of work given to one person or group

work·man /wúrkmən/ *(pl* **-men** /-mən/*)* *n* **1** a man who does manual work **2** a man judged on his working ability

work·man·like /wúrkmən lìk/, **work·man·ly** /-lee/ *adj* thorough and satisfactory but not imaginative or original

work·man·ship /wúrkmən shìp/ *n* **1** the skill of a worker or artisan **2** the quality or result of somebody's skill

work·mate /wúrk màyt/ *n* a fellow worker

work of art *n* **1** a piece of fine art, e.g., a painting or sculpture **2** something made or done well

work·out /wúrk òwt/ *n* **1** a strenuous exercise session **2** a rigorous test

work·place /wúrk plàyss/ *n* a place of employment

work-re·lease *n* a program that allows prisoners to perform paid outside work

work·room /wúrk ròom, -ròòm/ *n* a room in which work, especially manual work, is done

works /wurks/ *n* *(pl same)* a place for industrial production ■ *npl* **1** everything *(infml)* **2** the interior driving mechanisms of a device **3** acts ◇ **in the works** being prepared or worked on

work·sheet /wúrk sheet/ n 1 a sheet of questions for students 2 a written record of work done or scheduled

work·shop /wúrk shòp/ n 1 a place where manual work is done 2 a group of people studying, discussing, or working on a creative project together

work·space /wúrk spàyss/ n an area in which to work

⚡**work·sta·tion** /wúrk stàysh'n/ n 1 an area of an office where a single person works 2 a single terminal of a computer network or mainframe 3 a powerful specialized computer

work sur·face n a flat area for working on

work·ta·ble /wúrk tàyb'l/ n a table at which work, e.g., writing or sewing, is done

work·top /wúrk tòp/ n a flat surface for food preparation

work·up /wúrk ùp/ n a complete diagnostic medical examination

work·week /wúrk weèk/, **work week** n the hours or days worked in a week

world /wurld/ n 1 the planet Earth 2 the Earth and everything on it 3 the human race or human society 4 a particular part of the Earth ○ the western world 5 an area of activity ○ the world of fashion 6 the universe 7 a realm or domain ○ the world of reptiles 8 an astronomical object supposedly inhabited ○ the alien worlds of science fiction 9 everything in somebody's life ○ Her entire world collapsed. 10 a great deal or amount ○ a world of difference ■ adj 1 of the entire world 2 exerting an influence globally ◇ **out of this world** extraordinarily good (infml) ◇ **think the world of** be extremely fond of somebody

World Bank n an agency of the United Nations that guarantees loans to member nations for reconstruction and development

world-beat·ing adj surpassing all others

world-class adj ranked among the best in the world

World Coun·cil of Church·es n an international church organization that promotes cooperation among churches

World Cup n a major international sports tournament

World Eng·lish n the English language in all its varieties

world-fa·mous adj internationally known

World Health Or·gan·i·za·tion n a United Nations medical organization that helps countries develop health services

World Her·i·tage Site n a globally significant site or structure given special protection

world·ly /wúrldlee/ adj 1 also **world·ly-wise** experienced in life 2 belonging to the physical world 3 materialistic —**world·li·ness** n

world mu·sic n music from countries outside the western world

world pow·er n an internationally powerful country

World Se·ries n a series of professional baseball games played each fall by the winners of the American league and the National League

world-shak·ing, **world-shat·ter·ing** adj with an extremely powerful effect or significance

World Trade Or·gan·i·za·tion n an organization that promotes international trade

world-view n a comprehensive interpretation or image of the universe and humanity

world war n a war involving many countries

World War I n a war fought in Europe from 1914 to 1918

World War II n a war fought in Europe, Africa, and Asia from 1939 to 1945

world-wea·ry adj bored with life —**world-wea·ri·ness** n

world-wide /wúrld wìd/ adj of the whole world ■ adv throughout the world

⚡**World Wide Web** n all the computer files located on computers that can be accessed via the Internet

⚡**worm** /wurm/ n 1 a long cylindrical invertebrate (often in combination) 2 an insect larva 3 something that resembles a worm in form or movement 4 an offensive term for somebody regarded as contemptible (insult) 5 an invasive computer program ■ v 1 vt proceed deviously ○ wormed her way out of trouble 2 vt obtain something deviously ○ They wormed his secret out of him. 3 vt treat a person or animal for parasitic worms 4 vi move like a worm

⚡**WORM** /wurm/ n a storage medium for computer data. Full form **write once read many (times)**

worm-eat·en adj 1 eaten into by worms 2 in a state of decay

worm·hole /wúrm hòl/ n 1 a hypothetical passage between widely separate parts of the universe 2 a hole made by a worm

worm·wood /wúrm wòod/ n a plant that yields a bitter-tasting extract. Use: flavoring for absinthe, formerly, medicine for intestinal worms.

worm·y /wúrmee/ adj 1 infested by worms 2 resembling a worm —**worm·i·ness** n

worn /wawrn/ past participle of **wear** ■ adj 1 showing the effects of wear 2 showing the effects of fatigue —**worn·ness** n ◇ See note at **warn**

worn-out adj 1 damaged or weakened by prolonged use 2 exhausted

wor·ri·some /wúrissəm/ adj 1 causing worry 2 tending to worry —**wor·ri·some·ly** adv

wor·ry /wúree/ v (-ried, -ries) 1 vti be or make anxious 2 vt bother or annoy somebody 3 vt try to bite an animal o *a dog suspected of worrying sheep* 4 vt tear at something with the teeth o *a dog worrying a bone* ■ n (pl -ries) 1 anxiety 2 a cause of anxiety —**wor·ried** adj —**wor·ried·ly** adv —**wor·ried·ness** n —**wor·ri·er** n —**wor·ry·ing** adj —**wor·ry·ing·ly** adv ◊ See note at **bother**

SYNONYMS worry, unease, care, anxiety, angst, stress CORE MEANING: a troubled mind

wor·ry beads npl beads to finger when feeling tense

wor·ry·wart /wúree wàwrt/ n somebody who worries excessively (infml)

worse /wurss/ comparative of **bad, badly, ill** ■ adj 1 less good 2 more severe o *Her fever is worse this morning.* 3 sicker o *The patient is worse today.* ■ adv to a worse degree ■ n something that is worse than something else —**wors·en** vti ◊ **be none the worse for** experience no harm or ill effects from ◊ **if (the) worse comes to (the) worst** if the situation reaches an intolerable state

wor·ship /wúrship/ v (-shiped or -shipped, -ship·ing or -ship·ping) 1 vti regard and show respect to somebody or something as a deity 2 vt love somebody or something deeply 3 vi take part in a religious service ■ n 1 religious adoration 2 religious services 3 great devotion 4 **Wor·ship** Can, UK a title of respect for a mayor, magistrate, or similar dignitary —**wor·ship·er** n

wor·ship·ful /wúrshipfəl/ adj showing worship —**wor·ship·ful·ly** adv

worst /wurst/ superlative of **bad, badly, ill** ■ adj least good or most unfavorable ■ adv least well or most unfavorably ■ n the worst thing ■ vt defeat somebody o *We were worsted by the visiting team.*

wor·sted /wúrstəd/ n 1 a smooth woven woolen cloth 2 the yarn from which worsted is made

worth /wurth/ n 1 the monetary value of something 2 the amount of something that can be bought for a particular sum of money 3 the goodness, usefulness, or importance of something or somebody 4 wealth o *her net worth* ■ adj 1 equal in value to a particular amount o *a painting worth thousands* 2 important or good enough to justify something o *His friendship is not worth having.*

worth·less /wúrthləss/ adj 1 having no value 2 lacking good, attractive, or admirable qualities —**worth·less·ly** adv —**worth·less·ness** n

worth·while /wùrth wíl, wúrth wíl, -hwíl/ adj sufficiently rewarding or beneficial to justify time or effort

wor·thy /wúrthee/ adj (-thi·er, -thi·est) 1 deserving o *worthy of respect* o *a worthy cause* 2 respectable o *a worthy person* ■ n (pl -thies) somebody regarded as good or moral (often ironic) o *colonial governors and other worthies* —**wor·thi·ly** adv —**wor·thi·ness** n

would /wŏŏd/ modal v 1 a form of "will" used in reported speech or to state what might happen o *You would know him if you saw him.* 2 expresses polite requests o *Would you mind closing the window?* 3 indicates habitual action in the past o *Every Sunday we would drive out to Coney Island.* ◊ See note at **wood**

USAGE **would have** or **would of?** Although the nonstandard form *would of* sounds similar to the contracted form *would've*, it is incorrect to use it for *would have*: *It would have/would've* [not *would of*] *been nice if you'd told me this before.* The same confusion arises with *could have* and *should have.*

would-be adj hoping to do or be o *a would-be poet*

would-n't /wŏŏd'nt/ contr would not

would've /wŏŏdəv/ contr would have (infml)

wound[1] /woond/ n 1 an injury to the body in which the skin or other tissue is cut or torn 2 an emotional injury ■ vti cause a wound to somebody or something o *was wounded in the leg* o *wounding her pride* —**wound·ed** adj —**wound·ing** adj

wound[2] 1 past participle, past tense of **wind**[2] 2 past participle, past tense of **wind**[3]

Wound·ed Knee /woondəd nee/ village in SW South Dakota, site of a massacre of mostly unarmed Native North Americans in 1890

wound up /wównd úp/ adj nervously agitated (infml)

wove past tense of **weave**[1]

wo·ven /wóvən/ past participle of **weave**[1] ■ adj created by weaving

wow[1] (infml) interj expresses surprise ■ vt impress greatly

wow[2] n a pitch fluctuation in recorded sound

⚡**WP** abbr 1 word processing 2 word processor

wpm, w.p.m. abbr words per minute

wrack /rak/ n 1 destruction 2 a remnant of something destroyed (literary)

wraith /rayth/ n 1 a ghost 2 a supposed apparition of somebody who is soon to die —**wraith-like** adj

Wran·gel Is·land /ráng g'l-/ island of NE Russia, in the Arctic Ocean

Wran·gell Moun·tains /ráng g'l-/ mountain range in SE Alaska. Highest peak Mt. Blackburn 16,390 ft./4,996 m.

wran·gle /ráng g'l/ v (-gled, -gling) 1 vi argue noisily 2 vt herd animals ■ n a long argument (infml)

wran·gler /ráng glər/ n somebody who takes care of horses

⚡**wrap** /rap/ v (wrapped, wrap·ping) 1 vt cover something by winding or folding paper, cloth, or a similar material around it 2 vti coil around something ○ *wrapped his arms around the pole* **3** *vt* give something an aura ○ *The whole affair was wrapped in secrecy.* **4** *vt* engross somebody ○ *wrapped in thought* **5** *vt* envelop something ○ *hilltops wrapped in mist* **6** *vti* take a word that is too long over to the next line, or be taken over for this reason ■ *n* **1** a shawl, cloak, or similar outer garment **2** material used for wrapping things **3** the completion of filming **4** a filled tortilla sandwich ○ *a ham and cheese wrap* ◊ **keep something under wraps** keep something secret

□ **wrap up** *vt* **1** complete *(infml)* **2** summarize

⚡ **wrap·a·round** /ráppə ròwnd/ *adj* curving around the sides of the thing it is attached to ■ *n* **1** a garment worn wrapped around the body **2** a computer function that automatically starts a new line

wrap·per /ráppər/ *n* **1** the paper, plastic, or other material wrapped around merchandise **2** a tobacco leaf that forms the outside of a cigar **3** a loose lounging garment

wrap·ping /rápping/ *n* the paper, plastic, or other material used to wrap things

wrap-up *n* a short final summary, e.g., at the end of a news bulletin

wrath /rath, raath/ *n* **1** great anger *(fml)* **2** divine retribution —**wrath·ful** *adj* —**wrath·ful·ly** *adv* ◊ See note at **anger**

wreak /reek/ *vt* **1** cause havoc or destruction **2** inflict revenge on somebody ◊ See note at **reek, wrought**

wreath /reeth/ *(pl* **wreaths** /reethz, reeths/*)* *n* **1** a circular arrangement of flowers or greenery **2** a hollow circular shape

wreathe /reeth/ *(* **wreathed, wreath·ing***)* *vt* **1** put a wreath on or around something **2** make things into a wreath by intertwining them ◊ **be wreathed in** be covered in or surrounded by ○ *was wreathed in smiles*

wreck /rek/ *vt* destroy, damage, or ruin something ■ *n* **1** a car crash **2** the remains of something wrecked, e.g., a sunken ship **3** destruction **4** somebody who looks or feels terrible

wreck·age /rékij/ *n* **1** the remains of something destroyed **2** the process of wrecking something *(fml)*

wreck·er /rékər/ *n* **1** a truck for towing vehicles **2** somebody who demolishes buildings or dismantles old cars and ships **3** somebody or something that destroys or ruins things

wren /ren/ *n* a small brown songbird

Wren /ren/, **Sir Christopher** (1632–1723) English architect, scientist, and mathematician

wrench /rench/ *v* **1** *vti* pull and twist something away **2** *vt* injure a part of your body by twisting it **3** *vi* move with a twisting movement ■ *n* **1** a tool used to grasp and turn objects such as nuts and bolts **2** a

sprain caused by twisting **3** a forceful twisting pull **4** a feeling of sadness and loss ○ *Leaving Chicago was a terrible wrench after having lived there for 20 years.*

wrest /rest/ *vt* **1** take control or power from somebody **2** pull something away forcibly **3** get something with effort ■ *n* a forceful pull

wres·tle /réss'l/ *(* **-tled, -tling***)* *v* **1** *vti* fight or participate in the sport of wrestling **2** *vti* have a struggling fight with somebody **3** *vi* struggle to do or deal with something ○ *spent the evening wrestling with his accounts* —**wres·tle** *n* —**wres·tler** *n*

wres·tling /réssling/ *n* a sport in which contestants fight by gripping and throwing

wretch /rech/ *n* **1** somebody who is pitied **2** an annoying person *(humorous)* ◊ See note at **retch**

wretch·ed /réchəd/ *adj* **1** unhappy or ill **2** appearing miserable or deprived **3** inadequate or of low quality **4** causing annoyance ○ *The wretched car won't start.* —**wretch·ed·ly** *adv* —**wretch·ed·ness** *n*

wrig·gle /rígg'l/ *(* **-gled, -gling***)* *v* **1** *vti* twist and turn **2** *vi* move while twisting and turning —**wrig·gle** *n* —**wrig·gly** *adj*

□ **wriggle out of** *vt* avoid doing or suffering the consequences of something

Wright /rīt/, **Frank Lloyd** (1867–1959) US architect

Wright, Richard (1908–60) US writer

Wilbur (right) and Orville Wright

Wright Broth·ers, Wilbur (1867–1912) and his brother **Orville** (1871–1948) US inventors and aviation pioneers who made the first successful flight of a powered aircraft (1903)

wring /ring/ *vt* (**wrung** /rung/*)* **1** twist and compress something in order to force liquid out **2** force liquid out of something by wringing it **3** extract something with difficulty ○ *finally managed to wring an answer out of him* **4** twist something forcibly and painfully ■ *n* an act of wringing something wet ◊ See note at **ring**

wring·er /ríngər/ *n* a machine that forces the water out of wet clothes ◊ **put through the wringer** subject to a very stressful experience *(infml)*

wrin·kle /ríngk'l/ *n* **1** a facial line caused by aging **2** a small fold in material **3** a problem **4** an ingenious new feature *(infml)* ○ *We've added a couple of new wrinkles to the policy.*

■ vti (-kled, -kling) make wrinkles in something, or develop wrinkles —**wrin·kled** adj —**wrin·kly** adj

wrist /rist/ n the joint that connects the hand to the arm

wrist·band /ríst bànd/ n 1 a band worn around the wrist, e.g., for identification or to absorb sweat 2 a watch strap 3 the part of a garment that fits around the wrist

⚡ **wrist sup·port, wrist rest** n a rest for a keyboarder's wrists

wrist·watch /ríst wòch/ n a watch worn on the wrist

writ /rit/ n a written court order

⚡ **write** /rīt/ (**wrote** /rōt/, **writ·ten** /rítt'n/, **writ·ing** /rīting/) v 1 vti put letters or numbers on a surface using a pen, pencil, or similar implement 2 vti create a book, poem, play, or piece of music, or other material for publication or performance 3 vt spell something ○ *two words that are written the same but mean different things* 4 vti compose and send a letter 5 vt fill in a check or other official form 6 vt say something in writing ○ *wrote that she would be back next week* 7 vi work as a writing tool ○ *This pen won't write.* 8 vt display a quality ○ *guilt written all over his face* 9 vt store computer data

ORIGIN The notion underlying **write** is of "cutting" or "scratching." The earliest form of writing involved cutting marks on hard materials such as stone and wood, and the same word was carried over when the technique of writing moved on to pen and ink.

☐ **write in** 1 vi write to an organization 2 vt add a name to a ballot 3 vt write details on a form

☐ **write off** vt 1 reduce the value of an asset for accounting purposes 2 remove a bad debt or valueless asset

☐ **write out** vt remove a character from a television or radio series

write-down n a reduction in the value of an asset for accounting purposes

write-in n 1 a vote adding a candidate to a ballot 2 a candidate added to a ballot

~~writeing~~ incorrect spelling of **writing**

~~writen~~ incorrect spelling of **written**

write-off n a reduction in the value of a business asset

⚡ **write-pro·tect·ed** adj describes a computer disk that cannot be altered or erased

writ·er /rítər/ n 1 somebody who writes books, articles, or similar material as a profession 2 the person who wrote a specific text or document 3 somebody with a particular style of handwriting or use of language

writ·er's block n a situation in which a writer lacks inspiration and cannot write

writ·er's cramp n a muscular spasm in the wrist

write-up n 1 a review of a performance, book, or recording 2 an overvaluation of business assets

writhe /rīth/ (**writhed, writh·ing**) vi 1 twist or squirm 2 experience a strong emotion such as embarrassment

writ·ing /ríting/ n 1 words or symbols that have been written down 2 written material such as books and poems 3 the activity or profession of a writer 4 handwriting ■ **writ·ings** npl somebody's written output ○ *Churchill's writings on the war* ◇ **the writing on the wall** an omen that signals an unpleasant outcome

writ·ing desk n a desk for writing at

writ·ing pa·per n paper for writing on

writ·ten past participle of **write**

~~writting~~ incorrect spelling of **writing**

Wroc·law /vráwt slàaf/ city in SW Poland. Pop. 639,400 (1997).

wrong /rong/ adj 1 incorrect ○ *the wrong answer* 2 holding a mistaken opinion ○ *I thought it would be fun, but I was wrong.* 3 not the intended or desired one ○ *sent to the wrong address* 4 not in a normal state ○ *What's wrong with you today?* 5 not conforming to accepted moral standards ○ *Stealing is wrong.* 6 unsuitable ○ *the wrong time of year to be planting seeds* 7 not functioning correctly ○ *Something's wrong with the TV.* ■ adv 1 incorrectly 2 in the wrong direction or a wrong manner ■ n 1 an action or situation that is not considered moral or just 2 unacceptable behavior ■ vt treat somebody unjustly ○ *felt he had been wronged* —**wrong·ly** adv —**wrong·ness** n

wrong·do·ing /ráwng dòo ing/ n behavior that is considered wrong —**wrong·do·er** n

wrong-foot vt catch an opponent off balance

wrong·ful /ráwngfəl/ adj 1 unlawful 2 unjust —**wrong·ful·ly** adv —**wrong·ful·ness** n ◇ See note at **unlawful**

wrong-head·ed adj 1 irrational ○ *a wrong-headed notion* 2 obstinately unreasonable —**wrong-head·ed·ly** adv —**wrong-head·ed·ness** n

wrote past tense of **write**

wrought /rawt/ past tense, past participle of **work** (archaic) ■ adj 1 made carefully or decoratively (often in combination) 2 describes decorative metalwork shaped by hammering

USAGE Wrought is a rare past tense and past participle not of **wreak** (for which the past tense is **wreaked**) but of **work**, though **worked** is the common, modern past tense of this verb. **Wrought** is seen only in specialized contexts such as *wrought iron*. *Wrought havoc* is not correct; it should be *wreaked havoc*.

wrought i·ron n a refined form of iron that is strong but easy to shape. Use: decorative metalwork. —**wrought-i·ron** adj

lution and of Cornwallis's surrender to George Washington on October 19, 1781

Yo·ru·ba /yáwrəbə/ (*pl* same or **-bas**) *n* 1 a member of a West African people 2 a West African language —**Yo·ru·ba** *adj* —**Yo·ru·ban** *adj*

Yo·sem·i·te Falls /yō sèmmotee-/ falls in the Yosemite National Park. Height 2,245 ft./739 m.

Yo·sem·i·te Na·tion·al Park national park in central California

you (*stressed*) /yoo/ (*unstressed*) /yə/ *pron* 1 the person or people being addressed 2 an unspecified person, or people in general ○ *then you mix them all together*

you-all, y'all /yawl/ *pron Southern US* all of you (*infml*)

you'd *contr* 1 you had 2 you would

you'll *contr* 1 you shall 2 you will

young /yung/ *adj* 1 not very old 2 of somebody's youth ○ *my younger days* 3 youthful ○ *very young for her age* 4 for young people ○ *young fashions* 5 recently begun ○ *The night is still young.* ■ *npl* 1 offspring ○ *watching her young* 2 young people ○ *a club for the young* —**young·ish** *adj*

Young /yung/, **Brigham** (1801–77) 2nd leader of the Church of Jesus Christ of Latter-Day Saints (1844–77)

young·ster /yúngstər/ *n* a child or young person ◊ See note at **youth**

Youngs·town /yúngz tòwn/ city in NE Ohio. Pop. 84,650 (1998).

your (*stressed*) /yawr, yoor/ (*unstressed*) /yər/ *adj* 1 belonging to the person or people spoken to ○ *What's your phone number?* 2 belonging or relating to an unspecified person ○ *the house on your left* 3 indicates somebody or something as an example or topic (*infml*) ○ *your typical neighborhood park*

USAGE your or **you're?** The word **your** is a pronominal adjective (*Your* [not *You're*] *e-mail password must be protected*), whereas **you're** is a contraction of "you are" (*You're* [not *Your*] *responsible for protecting your e-mail password*).

you're (*stressed*) /yoor, yawr/ (*unstressed*) /yər/ *contr* you are ◊ See note at **your**

yours /yawrz, yoorz/ *pron* 1 refers to something belonging to the person or people addressed ○ *This idea of yours is very interesting.* 2 *also* **Yours** a complimentary close to a letter ○ *Yours, Jane Doe*

your·self /yawr sélf, yoor-, yər-/ *pron* 1 refers to the person or people being addressed ○ *Don't hurt yourself.* 2 adds emphasis when addressing somebody or a group of people ○ *How would you yourself deal with that?* 3 your normal self ○ *You're just not yourself tonight.*

youth /yooth/ *n* 1 the time when somebody is

young 2 the state of being young 3 a young man ■ *npl* young people

SYNONYMS youth, child, kid, teenager, youngster CORE MEANING: somebody who is young

youth·ful /yóothfl/ *adj* 1 of or typical of young people 2 vigorous and energetic 3 not fully developed —**youth·ful·ly** *adv* —**youth·ful·ness** *n*

youth hos·tel *n* an establishment offering inexpensive lodging for young people

you've /yoov/ *contr* you have

yowl /yowl/ *vi* cry out mournfully or in pain —**yowl** *n*

yo-yo /yō yō/ *n* (*pl* **yo-yos**) a toy consisting of a spool that can be dropped and raised again using the string wound around it ■ *vi* (**yo-yoed, yo-yo-ing, yo-yos**) fluctuate

yo-yo di·et·ing *n* the repeated losing and regaining of weight

Y-pres /eeprə/ town in SW Belgium, site of several major battles of World War I. Pop. 35,409 (1995).

yr. *abbr* 1 year 2 younger 3 your

YT, Y.T. *abbr* Yukon Territory

yt·ter·bi·um /i túrbee əm/ *n* (*symbol* **Yb**) a rare metallic chemical element. Use: strengthening steel, in laser devices and portable X-ray machines. —**yt·ter·bic** *adj*

ORIGIN Ytterbium is named for Ytterby, a quarry in Sweden where *ytterbite*, a mineral containing the element, was found.

yt·tri·um /íttree əm/ *n* (*symbol* **Y**) a rare metallic chemical element. Use: superconductive alloys, permanent magnets. —**yt·tric** *adj*

yu·an /yoo áan/ (*pl* same) *n* the main unit of Chinese currency

Yu·ca·tán /yóokə tán, -taàn/ peninsula in E Central America, comprising three Mexican states, Belize, and part of N Guatemala

yuc·ca /yúkə/ *n* an evergreen flowering plant with sharp lance-shaped leaves

yuck, yuk *interj* expresses disgust (*slang*)

yuck·y /yúkee/ (**-i·er, -i·est**) *adj* unpleasant (*slang*) —**yuck·i·ness** *n*

Yu·go·sla·via /yòogō slaàvee ə/ country in SE Europe, consisting of Serbia and Montenegro. Cap. Belgrade. Pop. 11,206,039 (1998). —**Yu·go·slav** /yóogō slàav/ *n, adj* —**Yu·go·sla·vi·an** *adj, n*

Yu·kon /yóok on/ river in NW North America, rising in S Yukon Territory, Canada, and flowing through Alaska to the Bering Sea. Length 1,980 mi./3,190 km.

Yu·kon Ter·ri·to·ry territory in NW Canada. Cap. Whitehorse. Pop. 30,663 (2000).

Yu·kon Time *n* = Alaska Standard Time

Yule /yool/, **yule** *n* Christmas (*literary*)

yule log *n* a log traditionally burned on Christmas Eve

Yule·tide /yoôl tīd/ *n* the Christmas season

Yu·ma /yoôma/ *n* a member of a Native North American people of SW Arizona and neighboring areas —**Yu·ma** *adj*

yum·my /yúmmee/ (-mi·er, -mi·est) *adj* delicious (*infml*) —**yum·mi·ness** *n*

Yu·pik /yoô pik/ (*pl same or* -**piks**) *n* a member of an aboriginal people of W Alaska and parts of coastal Siberia —**Yu·pik** *adj*

yup·pie /yúppee/ *n* a young professional city-dweller regarded as materialistic and snobbish (*disapproving*)

> **ORIGIN Yuppie** was formed from the initial letters of "young urban professional," extended on the model of *hippie*. It first appeared in print in 1984 in the title of *The Yuppie Handbook.*

yup·pi·fy /yúppa fī/ (-**fied,** -**fies**) *vt* populate with yuppies (*disapproving*) —**yup·pi·fi·ca·tion** /yúppafi káysh'n/ *n*

yurt *n* a circular Asian tent made of animal skins, or any other structure so shaped

YWCA, Y.W.C.A. *abbr* Young Women's Christian Association

Z

z (*pl* z's), **Z** (*pl* Z's *or* Zs) *n* the 26th and final letter of the English alphabet

Z *symbol* impedance

Za·greb /záa greb/ capital of Croatia. Pop. 706,770 (1991).

Za·har·i·as /za hárree ass/, **Babe Didrikson** (1913–56) US athlete

zai·bat·su /zī baat soô/ (*pl same*) *n* a large Japanese industrial combine

Za·ire /zī eer, zaa-/ **1** former name for **Congo, Democratic Republic of the 2** former name for **Congo, Republic of the** —**Za·ir·e·an** /zī eéree ən, zaa-/ *adj*

za·kat /zakáat/ *n* an Islamic tax for charity

Zam·be·zi /zam beézee/ river in southern Africa, flowing through Zambia, Angola, Botswana, Zimbabwe, and Mozambique to the Indian Ocean. Length 1,650 mi./2,650 km.

Zam·bi·a /zámbee ə/ country in south central Africa. Cap. Lusaka. Pop. 9,770,199 (2001). —**Zam·bi·an** *n, adj*

za·ny /záynee/ *adj* (-**ni·er,** -**ni·est**) amusingly unconventional ■ *n* (*pl* -**nies**) a clown —**za·ni·ly** *adv* —**za·ni·ness** *n*

> **ORIGIN Zany** came via French from the name of a character in traditional Italian comedy who tried to imitate the antics of the clown.

It derives from a dialect form of the Italian man's name *Gianni*, a form of *Giovanni*. The earliest uses in English are as a noun, referring to a comic performer, a mimic, or a buffoon. An adjectival use is recorded from the early 17C, but the modern sense "amusingly unconventional" does not appear until the 19C.

Zan·zi·bar /zánzi baàr/ island of Tanzania, in the Indian Ocean. Pop. 456,934 (1995).

zap (**zapped, zap·ping**) *v* (*infml*) **1** *vt* destroy **2** *vi* change television channels using a remote control **3** *vt* cook in a microwave

Za·pa·ta /za paáta, saa paátaa/, **Emiliano** (1879–1919) Mexican revolutionary

Za·ra·go·za /zàrra góza/ capital of **Zaragoza** Province in the autonomous region of Aragon, NE Spain. Pop. 603,367 (1998).

Za·ra·thu·stra ♦ Zoroaster

zeal /zeel/ *n* enthusiasm, especially for a cause

zeal·ot /zéllat/ *n* a zealous follower, especially of a religious movement —**zeal·ot·ry** *n*

zeal·ous /zélloss/ *adj* full of zeal —**zeal·ous·ly** *adv* —**zeal·ous·ness** *n*

ze·bra /zeébra/ *n* a striped mammal that resembles a horse —**ze·brine** /zeé brīn, -brən/ *adj*

Zech·a·ri·ah /zèka rí əl *n* a book of the Bible, traditionally attributed to Zechariah, a Hebrew prophet

Zeit·geist /zīt gīst, tsīt-/ *n* the ideas and spirit of a specific time and place

Zen, Zen Bud·dhism *n* a form of Buddhism that developed in China

Zeng·er /zéng ər, zéng gər/, **John Peter** (1697–1746) German-born American newspaper publisher

ze·nith /zeénith/ *n* **1** the highest point reached by an astronomical object **2** the most successful or exciting point —**ze·nith·al** *adj*

Ze·no of Ci·ti·um /zeènō əv síttee əm/ (*fl* late 4C–early 3C BC) Greek philosopher

Ze·no of E·le·a /-eèlee ə/ (*fl* 5C BC) Greek mathematician and philosopher

Ze·pha·ni·ah /zèffa ní əl *n* a book of the Bible, traditionally attributed to Zephaniah, a Hebrew prophet

zeph·yr /zéffər/ *n* **1** a mild wind **2** a delicate fabric or garment

zep·pe·lin /zéppələn/ *n* a cylindrical airship

ze·ro /zeérō/ *n* (*pl* -**ros** *or* -**roes**) **1** the numerical symbol 0 **2** the number 0 **3** the starting point for values on a gauge **4** the temperature indicated by 0 **5** the lowest possible point ○ *Her spirits are at zero.* **6** somebody regarded as completely uninteresting and unimportant (*infml insult*) ■ *vt* (-**roed,** -**ro·ing**) set a gauge or other instrument to zero ■ *adj* **1** amounting to zero ○ *zero growth* **2** minimal (*infml*) ○ *had zero confidence*

□ **zero in** vi **1** locate a target and aim at it **2** identify something and concentrate on it

ze·ro-de·fect adj demanding, or having, no errors or defects

ze·ro hour n **1** the scheduled starting time of a military operation **2** the time when something important will occur

ze·ro op·tion n the offer to limit the number of nuclear weapons held if another nation makes the same offer

ze·ro tol·er·ance n the complete absence of leniency, especially in dealing with anti-social behavior

zest n **1** hearty enjoyment **2** an exciting element that adds to enjoyment **3** citrus peel used as a flavoring —**zest·ful** adj —**zest·ful·ly** adv —**zest·y** adj

ze·ta /záytə, zeétə/ n the 6th letter of the Greek alphabet

Zeus /zooss/ n in Greek mythology, the king of the gods

Zheng·zhou /jùng jó/ capital of Henan Province, E China, on the Huang He. Pop. 1,990,000 (1995).

Zhou En·lai /jò en lí/ (1898–1976) premier of the People's Republic of China (1949–75)

zig·zag /zíg zàg/ n **1** a line that takes alternating turns **2** something that repeatedly switches direction sharply ■ adv in sharply alternating directions ■ v (**-zagged**, **-zag·ging**) **1** vi proceed in a path with alternating sharp turns **2** vt make the pattern of a zigzag on

zilch pron nothing (infml) ○ took all the money and left us with zilch

ORIGIN The origin of **zilch** is not known. It first appeared as a generalized surname in the early 1930s ("Mr. Zilch," etc.). The earliest recorded use in the sense "nothing" dates from 1966.

zil·lion /zíllyən/ n a huge number of people or things (infml) —**zil·lion** adj

Zim·bab·we /zim baábwee, -way/ country in southern Africa. Cap. Harare. Pop. 11,365,366 (2001). —**Zim·bab·we·an** n, adj

zinc n (symbol **Zn**) a bluish metallic chemical element. Use: in alloys, protective corrosion-resistant metal coatings. —**zinc** vt

✦**zine** /zeen/ n a paper, Internet magazine, or other periodical for a specialist readership, published by the author (infml)

zing n **1** a short high-pitched humming sound **2** a lively and exciting quality (infml) ■ vi make a high-pitched humming noise (infml) —**zing·y** adj

zing·er /zíngər/ n a clever remark skillfully delivered (infml)

~~zink~~ incorrect spelling of **zinc**

Zi·on·ism /zí ə nìzzəm/ n the worldwide movement that seeks to maintain and further develop the Jewish state of Israel —**Zi·on·ist** adj, n

✦**zip**[1] n **1** a lively, exciting quality (infml) **2** a brief whizzing sound **3** also **zip·po** /zíppó/ zero or nothing at all (slang) ○ worked hard and got zip for my efforts ■ v (**zipped**, **zip·ping**) **1** vti fasten with a zipper **2** vti go or move very fast (infml) **3** vt compress a computer file

✦**zip**[2] abbr a file extension indicating a compressed file

ZIP Code tdmk a trademark for a mail delivery system using a set of numbers to identify a postal district

✦**zip file** n a compressed computer file

zip·per /zíppər/ n a clothes or luggage fastener with interlocking teeth

zip·py /zíppee/ (**-pi·er**, **-pi·est**) adj energetic (infml)

zir·con /zúr kòn/ n a hard mineral containing zirconium. Use: source of zirconium, gems.

zir·co·ni·um /zur kōnee əm/ n (symbol **Zr**) a grayish-white metallic chemical element. Use: coating nuclear reactor fuel rods. —**zir·con·ic** /-kónnik/ adj

zit n a pimple on the skin (slang) —**zit·ty** adj

zith·er /zíthər, zíthər/ n a flat box-shaped stringed instrument —**zith·er·ist** n

zlo·ty /zlóttee/ (pl **-ties** or same) n the main unit of currency in Poland

Zn symbol zinc

zo·di·ac /zṓdee àk/ n **1** an astrologically significant part of the sky, divided into 12 sections **2** an astrologer's chart linking the zodiac to 12 divisions of the year —**zo·di·a·cal** /zō dí ək'l/ adj

Zo·la /zṓlə, zṓ laà/, **Émile** (1840–1902) French novelist

zom·bie /zómbee/ n **1** an offensive term for somebody regarded as lacking energy or responsiveness (infml insult) **2** a corpse supposedly given life by voodoo **3** a voodoo spirit that supposedly revives a corpse **4** a snake god of voodoo —**zom·bi·fy** vt

zo·nal /zṓn'l/, **zo·na·ry** /zṓnəree/ adj **1** of zones **2** split into zones —**zo·nal·ly** adv

zone /zōn/ n **1** a separate area with a specific function **2** a subsection of an area **3** a horizontal climatic band around the Earth **4** an area distinguished from others, e.g., by its plants and animals or by a standard time ■ vti (**zoned**, **zon·ing**) **1** split something into zones **2** designate an area for a particular purpose —**zon·ing** n ◇ **in the zone** performing at your very best because you are so focused and well prepared (infml)

□ **zone out** vi lose your concentration or fall asleep (slang)

zonked /zongkt/, **zonked out** adj not conscious, alert, or energetic (slang)

zoo (pl **zoos**) n **1** also **zo·o·log·i·cal gar·den** a park that displays live animals in enclosures **2** a chaotic place (slang)

zoo·keep·er /zoó keepər/ n somebody who cares for zoo animals

zo·ol·o·gy /zō óllǝjee, zǝ wól-/ (*pl* **-gies**) *n* **1** the scientific study of animals **2** the animal life of a specific region —**zo·o·log·i·cal** /zō ǝ lójjik'l/ *adj* —**zo·ol·o·gist** *n*

zoom *v* **1** *vi* move speedily **2** *vi* increase suddenly **3** *vi* make a loud buzzing noise **4** *vti* climb steeply through the air, or make an aircraft climb steeply **5** *vi* simulate movement toward or away from an object with a camera lens that allows various focal lengths ■ *n* **1** *also* **zoom lens** a camera lens assembly that allows various focal lengths **2** a loud buzzing noise

Zo·ro·as·ter /záwrō àstǝr/, **Za·ra·thu·stra** /zàrrǝ thoóstrǝ/ (630?–550? BC) Persian prophet

Zo·ro·as·tri·an·ism /zàwrō ástree ǝ nìzzǝm/ *n* an ancient Persian religion centered on belief in a supreme deity and the struggle between good and evil —**Zo·ro·as·tri·an** *n*, *adj*

Zr *symbol* zirconium

zuc·chi·ni /zoo keénee/ (*pl same or* **-nis**) *n US*, *Can*, *Aus* **1** a small summer squash **2** the plant that produces zucchini

zuchini incorrect spelling of **zucchini**

Zu·lu /zoóloo/ (*pl same or* **-lus**) *n* **1** a member of a South African people **2** the Bantu language of the Zulu people **3** a communications code word for the letter "Z" —**Zu·lu** *adj*

Zu·ni /zoónee/ (*pl same or* **-is**), **Zu·ñi** /zoónyee, zoónee/ *n* **1** a member of a Pueblo people of W New Mexico **2** the language of the Zuni people —**Zu·ni** *adj*

Zu·rich /zoórik/ largest city in Switzerland, in the north of the country. Pop. 336,821 (1998).

zwie·back /sweé bàk/ *n* a sliced baked bread

zy·de·co /zíídǝ kò/ *n* popular music of S Louisiana, a mix of Caribbean tunes, French dance music, and blues

zy·gote /zí gòt/ *n* a fertilized ovum —**zy·got·ic** /zī góttik/ *adj*

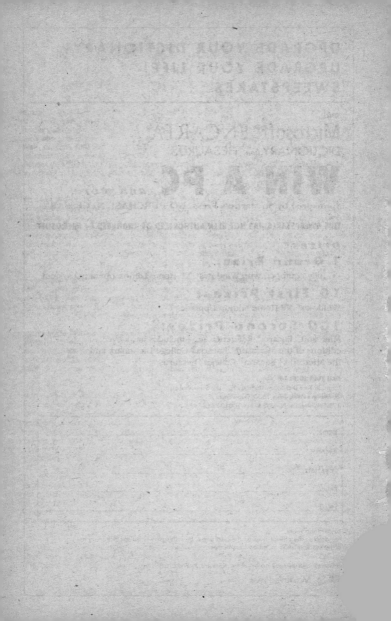

Upgrade Your Dictionary, Upgrade Your Life Sweepstakes
This Sweepstakes has not been authorized or endorsed by Dell Computers or Microsoft.

OFFICIAL RULES
NO PURCHASE NECESSARY TO ENTER OR WIN. PURCHASE WILL NOT INCREASE CHANCES OF WINNING.

1. To Enter: Complete Official Entry Form and mail to: Upgrade Your Dictionary, Upgrade Your Life Sweepstakes, c/o St. Martin's Press, 175 Fifth Avenue, Suite 1600, New York, NY 10010–7848, attention: JP, or enter online at www.collegedictionary.net. For a copy of the Official Entry Form, send a self-addressed, stamped envelope to: Entry Form, Upgrade Your Dictionary, Upgrade Your Life Sweepstakes, c/o St. Martin's Press, 175 Fifth Avenue, New York, NY 10010–7848, attention: JP. To be eligible, electronic entries must be received no later than 5:00pm EST on December 7, 2002. Mail-in entries must be postmarked by December 7, 2002, and received no later than December 14, 2002. Limit one entry per person, family, or household.

2. Random Drawing: Winners will be determined in a random drawing to be held on or about January 2, 2003, from all eligible entries received. Odds of winning depend on the number of eligible entries received. Potential winners will be notified by mail on or about January 22, 2003, and will be asked to execute and return an Affidavit of Eligibility, Liability/Publicity Release and prize acceptance form within fourteen (14) days of attempted notification. Non-compliance within time period may result in disqualification and selection of an alternate winner. Return of any prize or prize notification as undeliverable will result in disqualification and an alternate winner will be selected.

3. Prizes and Approximate Retail Values: One (1) grand prize: A Dell PC with Windows XP Home Edition Operating System and Monitor—approximate retail value $1,500. Ten (10) first prizes: A copy of Windows XP, Home Edition Upgrade—approximate retail value $99. One hundred (100) second prizes: A copy of the Microsoft® Encarta® College Dictionary and a copy of the Microsoft® Encarta® College Thesaurus—approximate retail value $46.90.

4. Eligibility: Open to legal U.S. and Canadian residents (excluding residents of the province of Quebec) who are 18 years of age or older at the time of entry. Employees of St. Martin's Press and its affiliates, and their directors, managers, officers and agents, and their immediate families or those living in the same household, are ineligible to enter. Potential Canadian winners will be required to correctly answer a time-limited arithmetic skill question by mail. Void in Puerto Rico and wherever else prohibited by law.

5. General Conditions: Winner responsible for all federal, state, and local taxes. No substitution or cash redemption of prizes permitted except by Sponsor due to unavailability. By accepting prize, all winners and, by entering, all Sweepstakes entrants release Sponsor and its affiliates from any and all liability for any loss, harm, damages, costs or expenses, including without limitation property damage, personal injury and/or death, arising out of participation in this sweepstakes, the acceptance, possession, use or misuse of any prize or any alleged defects in any prize. Without limiting the generality of the above, SPONSOR HEREBY DISCLAIMS ALL WARRANTIES, EXPRESS OR IMPLIED, WITH RESPECT TO THE PRIZES AWARDED, INCLUDING BUT NOT LIMITED TO THE WARRANTIES OF MERCHANTABILITY AND FITNESS FOR A PARTICULAR PURPOSE. By participating in this sweepstakes, entrants agree to be bound by these official rules, Sponsor's sweepstakes Policies (which are posted at www.collegedictionary.net) and the decisions of the Sponsor, which are final in all respects. For a copy of the Policies, send a stamped self-addressed envelope to Sweepstakes Policies, Upgrade Your Dictionary, Upgrade Your Life Sweepstakes, St. Martin's Press, 175 Fifth Avenue, Room 600, New York, New York 10010, attention: JP. All prizes will be awarded.

5. Winners List: For winners' names, available after March 1, 2003, send by May 1, 2003, a ~~st~~amped, self-addressed envelope to Winners List, Upgrade Your Dictionary, Upgrade Your ~~Lif~~e Sweepstakes, St. Martin's Press, 175 Fifth Avenue, Suite 1600, New York, NY ~~10~~010–7848, attention: JP.

~~S~~ponsor: St. Martin's Press, 175 Fifth Avenue, Suite 1600, New York, NY 10010–7848.